Play on words 2

P O W E R P A C K

Play on words 2

Interactive Bible stories

kevin mayhew

With special thanks to Peter and Chris Jackson who have written this collection of interactive Bible stories

First published in 2002 by
KEVIN MAYHEW LTD
Buxhall, Stowmarket, Suffolk IP14 3BW
E-mail: info@kevinmayhewltd.com

0 1 2 3 4 5 6 7 8 9

ISBN 1 84417 004 7
Catalogue No 1500560

Cover design by Jonathan Stroulger
Illustrated by Sally-Anne Norman
Edited and typeset by Elisabeth Bates
Printed and bound in Great Britain

CONTENTS

Introduction 7

Abraham and Isaac 9
Genesis 22

Blind Bartimaeus 11
Mark 10:46-52

Don't worry! 13
Matthew 6:25-34

Esau sells his birthright 15
Genesis 25:27-34

Esther 17
Esther 1-9

Isaac blesses Jacob 20
Genesis 27

Jesus enters Jerusalem as a king 22
Luke 19:28-40

Jesus in the Temple 24
Luke 2:41-52

John the Baptist's life 26
Matthew 3:1-6 and Mark 6:14-29

Joseph in Egypt 28
Genesis 39ff

Joseph the dreamer 31
Genesis 37

Moses and the golden calf 34
Exodus 32

Naboth's vineyard 36
1 Kings 21

Paul and Silas in prison 38
Acts 16:16-40

Pentecost 40
Acts 2:1-13

Samuel anoints David 42
1 Samuel 16:1-13

Simon the magician 44
Acts 8:4-25

The big party 46
Luke 14:15-24

The exodus 48
Exodus 7-12

The healing of Naaman 50
2 Kings 5

The resurrection of Jesus 52
John 20

The rich fool 54
Luke 12:13-21

The sower 56
Matthew 13:1-23

The visit of the wise men 58
Matthew 2:1-21

Water into wine 60
John 2:1-11

INTRODUCTION

This book contains a further 25 interactive dramas based on popular Bible stories. These have been used extensively in Powerpack meetings and have proved to be an enjoyable and successful way of reinforcing Bible stories. As the name suggests, everybody is involved in miming the actions to a given story. An important part of the appeal of the dramas is the humorous play on words. Although it is possible for one person to read the story and mime the actions at the same time, we have found it easier to have two people involved – one to read the story and one to do the actions.

The most obvious use of these dramas is to repeat and reinforce a Bible story which has already been told in some other way. However, they may also be used to reinforce a particular theme and for this purpose we have suggested some relevant teaching points at the beginning of each script. In such situations, the primary story for the meeting may not be that of the interactive drama, in which case we suggest you choose a drama based on a story the children know well or the play on words can leave them a little confused!

It should also be noted that very young children won't understand the play on words and, as this could lead to their misunderstanding the Bible story, some of the actions may need to be changed to give a more literal interpretation.

As well as using these dramas in children's meetings and school assemblies and the like, they can be very effective in an all-age context, since they are a good way of involving adults and children together. Adults seem to enjoy them as much as children! As with anything else, 'familiarity breeds contempt', so be careful not to overuse them.

When writing these scripts it hasn't always been easy to explain exactly the actions and expressions we have used, since sometimes it is better to complete the sense of a particular phrase and so combine the suggested actions into one longer movement. We would therefore encourage you always to prepare the dramas beforehand, deciding where to pause and which actions to join up, if any. You may also find that there are too many actions and you will need to cut some, or you may want to change some of the actions to suit your own situation or even add extra ones of your own.

In the scripts, *** following a word indicates an action, which is explained in the brackets. If the starred word appears later in the script, there is no explanation given but obviously repeat the same action. As you read the scripts you will see that we have used some standard actions and although you will soon become familiar with these, we felt it necessary to indicate them throughout so that each script can stand on its own. Occasionally the same word, which appears in several of the scripts, may be given a different action – that is to help counter predictability and to add variety.

We trust that you and your children will enjoy using these dramas. Have fun!

ABRAHAM AND ISAAC

Genesis 22

Teaching points
- *obedience*
- *trust in God*

There once lived a man called Abraham *** *(stroke beard)* and his wife Sarah *** *(mime 2 kisses)*. They had a son called Isaac *** *(ha! ha! ha! ha! ha!)*. (His name meant 'he laughs'.) He was only a boy *** *(indicate short height)*. They were a very happy *** *(hilarious silent laughter)* family. But one day God *** *(point upwards)* decided to test Abraham *** to see if he really did trust him.

So *** *(sew)* God *** said to Abraham *** 'Take your only son Isaac ***, whom you love *** *(hug self)* and go up *** *(aeroplane take off!)* to Mount Moriah *** *(indicate mountain)*. There you must sacrifice *** *(stab chest)* him and make a burnt offering *** *(indicate flames)* to me.'

Early the next morning *** *(stretch and yawn)* Abraham *** got up and saddled his donkey *** *(ee-aw!)*. He took with him two *** *(show 2 fingers)* servants *** *(bow head twice with hands together)* and his son Isaac ***. He took some wood *** *(knock on head)* for the burnt offering *** and set out for Mount Moriah *** on his donkey ***.

After travelling *** *(say 'clip-clop, clip-clop')* for three *** *(show 3 fingers)* days, Abraham *** said to his servants ***, 'You stay here with the donkey *** while I and the boy go over there *** *(point to one side)*. We will worship *** *(bowing down action)* and then we will come back *** *(touch back)* to you.'

So *** Abraham *** took the wood *** for *** *(show 4 fingers!)* the burnt offering *** and gave it to Isaac *** to carry, while he carried the fire *** *(indicate flames)* in a pot, and the knife. After a while Isaac *** said, 'Father? We have the wood *** and the fire *** but where is the sacrifice ***? Where is the lamb *** *(baa!)* for the burnt offering ***?'

Abraham answered, 'God *** will provide the lamb *** for the burnt offering ***, my son.'

After a while they reached the place for the sacrifice ***. Abraham *** built *** *(building action)* an altar and then he put the wood *** on it. He tied up *** *(mime being in a straitjacket)* Isaac *** and put him on top of the wood ***. Then Abraham *** took his knife and was just about to sacrifice *** his only son when God called out, 'Abraham ***, Abraham ***, do not harm the boy. Now I know that you would do anything for me. Now I know you will always obey me.'

Just then Abraham saw a ram *** *(baa!)* caught by its horns *** *(indicate horns)* in the bushes. So *** he sacrificed *** the ram *** as a burnt offering *** to God *** instead of his son. Abraham *** trusted God *** and obeyed him.

BLIND BARTIMAEUS

Mark 10:46-52

Teaching points
- *persistence in prayer*
- *Jesus is the healer*

There was once a blind *** *(cover eyes)* beggar *** *(mime begging or beg like a dog!)* called Bartimaeus *** *(left, right, march on the spot)*. Every day he would sit *** *(mime sitting position)* by the side *** *(touch your side)* of the road *** *(mime driving car)* begging *** for money *** *(rub palm)* and food *** *(rub tummy saying 'Yum, yum')*.

One day Jesus *** *(point upwards or use deaf signing, i.e. touch nail prints in palm of hand with opposite middle finger)* was in Jericho where blind *** Bartimaeus *** lived. Now Bartimaeus *** had heard *** *(cup hand around ear)* about all the amazing *** *(Look amazed and say 'Wow!')* things that Jesus *** had been doing – healing the sick *** *(pretend to vomit!)*, setting people free *** *(cross fists in front of you and then fling arms open wide!)* and even raising the dead *** *(mime being dead and coming alive)*. So, when blind *** Bartimaeus *** heard *** that Jesus *** was coming along the road *** where he was sat *** begging ***, he called out, 'Jesus, Son of David, have pity on me!' *** *(shout out 'Jesus, Son of David, have pity on me!')*

Many of the people who were following *** *(walk on the spot)* Jesus ***, shouted at him *** *(shout 'SHOUTED!')* and told him to be quiet *** *(say 'Ssh' loudly with finger on lips)*. But blind *** Bartimaeus *** shouted even louder, 'Jesus ***, Son of David, have pity on me!' *** *(shout 'Jesus, Son of David, have pity on me!' louder)*. Jesus *** heard *** the blind *** beggar *** shouting *** and so he stopped *** *(hand signal for stop)* and told the people to call him over *** *(arm over!)*.

So the people said to the blind *** man, 'Get to your feet *** *(hold nose, saying 'pooh!')*, Jesus *** is calling you.' With that, Bartimaeus *** jumped up *** *(jump)*, got to his feet ***, threw *** *(mime 'through' by passing finger through hole made by forefinger and thumb of other hand)* off his cloak and went to Jesus ***.

‘What do you want me to do for you?’ said Jesus ***.

‘Teacher *** *(mime writing on a board)*,’ said the blind *** beggar ***, ‘I want to see *** *(look through binoculars or mime ‘sea’)* again.’

‘Go *** *(point to one side)*,’ said Jesus ***, ‘your faith has made you well *** *(mime pulling water up from a well!)*.’ At once Bartimaeus ***, the blind *** beggar ***, was able to see *** again and he followed *** Jesus *** down the road ***.

DON'T WORRY!

Matthew 6:25-34

Teaching point

• *we need to trust God to look after us and not worry*

One day Jesus *** *(use deaf signing, i.e. touch nail prints in palm of hand with opposite middle finger)* was teaching *** *(mime writing on a board)* his followers *** *(walk on the spot)* and said,

'I tell you not *** *(tie a knot!)* to worry *** *(look worried, biting finger-nails)* about the food *** *(rub tummy, saying 'Yum, yum!)* you need to stay alive *** *(mime coming alive)* or about the clothes *** *(mime holding lapels)* you need for your body *** *(wiggle body!)*. Life *** *(mime coming alive)* is much more *** *(indicate large size)* important than food ***, and the body *** is much more important than clothes ***. Look at the birds *** *(flap wings and caw!)*, they don't sow *** *(sew!)* seeds or gather *** *(mime gathering)* a harvest. They don't have houses *** *(mime pointed roof)* or barns *** *(mime building)* in which to store their food *** – God *** *(point upwards)* feeds *** them.

'You are worth much more *** than birds ***. Can any of you live *** a bit longer *** *(say 'longer' slowly and stretch out arms)* by worrying *** about it? If you cannot do little *** *(indicate tiny length)* things, then why worry *** about the bigger *** *(indicate longer length)* things? Look at the wild *** *(act in a wild manner!)* flowers *** *(mime smelling a flower)*. See *** *(look through binoculars or mime 'sea')* how they grow *** *(mime growing up)*. They don't work *** *(mime being busy working)* or make clothes *** for themselves. But I tell you that even King Solomon *** *(indicate crown)*, the great *** *(thumbs up)* and rich *** *(rub palm)* king ***, was not dressed as beautifully *** *(kiss fingers, Italian-chef style!)* as one of these flowers ***.

'It is God *** who clothes *** the wild *** grass – grass that is here today *** *(point forward with both fingers)* and gone tomorrow *** *(point backwards with both thumbs)*, so *** *(sew)* how much more *** God *** will look after *** *(hand across eyes, leaning forward)* you. Don't always think about what you will eat *** *(mime eating food)* or drink *** *(mime drinking)*. Don't worry *** about it. All the people *** *(point round audience)* in the world *** *(mime world shape)* are worried *** about these things. Your Father *** knows that you need food *** and clothes ***, so *** don't worry *** but seek *** *(mime seeking with hand across eyes)* God's *** kingdom and all these things you need will be given to you *** *(show 2 fingers and point to audience)*.'

ESAU SELLS HIS BIRTHRIGHT

Genesis 25:27-34

Teaching points

- *commitment to God*
- *what's more important?*

There were once some twins *** *(show 2 fingers)*, called Jacob *** *(lightly stamp right foot)* and Esau *** *(lightly stamp left foot)*. They were the sons *** *(indicate short height on right side using right hand and then on left side using left hand)* of Isaac *** *(mime raising hat)* and Rebekah *** *(curtsey)*.

Esau *** was the older twin ***. He was first-born *** *(make a baby cry or suck thumb)*. The Bible *** *(open book)* tells us that he grew up *** *(mime growing up)* to be a strong man *** *(legs astride, flex muscles)* and his body was hairy *** *(ruffle hair)*. He was a very good *** *(thumbs up)* hunter *** *(mime shooting a bow and arrow)* and he loved being out in the fresh air *** *(take a deep breath)*. He became Isaac's *** favourite *** *(uh! oh!)* because Isaac *** loved to eat the animals that Esau *** had hunted *** and killed *** *(stab chest)*.

Jacob *** was the younger twin ***. He was a quiet man *** *(ssh!)* and liked to stay at home *** *(mime roof shape)*. He was Rebekah's *** favourite ***.

One day while Jacob *** was cooking *** *(mime stirring a saucepan)* some bean soup *** *(mime slurping soup)*, Esau *** came home *** from hunting ***. He was starving hungry *** *(hold stomach and screw face up)* and said to Jacob ***, 'I'm starving hungry ***. Give me some of that soup *** you are cooking ***.'

Jacob *** said, 'I will give it to you if you give me your rights *** *(mime 'writes')* as the first-born *** son ***.' This would mean that when Isaac *** died *** *(slump)*, Jacob *** would get twice as much of his father's property and money *** *(rub fingers and thumb together or rub palm)* as Esau ***. Jacob *** would get two shares *** *(mime sharing out)* and Esau *** would only get one share ***.

Esau *** hadn't eaten for a long *** *(stretch out arms)* time *** *(circle watch)* and was so hungry *** that he agreed *** *(nod head)*. Jacob *** made him promise *** *(cub or brownie promise)* to give up his rights *** and then he gave him some bread and soup ***.

Esau *** cared more about having some soup *** than keeping his rights *** as Isaac's *** first-born *** son ***.

ESTHER

Esther 1-9

Teaching points
- *stepping out for God*
- *obedience*

N.B. This is a particularly long story and you may need to cut some of the actions

Long *** *(stretch out arms slowly)* ago in the land of Persia, lived King Xerxes *** *(crown on head)* and his wife *** *(hug self)*, Queen Vashti *** *(wavy crown on head)*. One day King Xerxes *** decided to throw *** *(mime throwing a ball)* a big party *** *(party!)* and they invited many important *** *(hold lapels)* people. The party *** went on for days, and on the seventh *** *(show seven fingers)* day King Xerxes *** sent for his wife *** Queen Vashti ***.

Queen Vashti *** refused to come and King Xerxes *** was so angry *** *(look angry)* that he said he never wanted to see her again. So the search began for a new queen *** *(wavy crown on head)*. Beautiful *** *(wolf whistle or say 'Wow!')* girls were invited to go to the palace, have lots of beauty treatments *** *(mime rubbing cream into face, brushing hair, etc.)* and then after a year, King Xerxes *** would choose the one he wanted for his new queen ***.

Now living in that land was a man called Mordecai *** *(left, right on the spot)*. He was a Jew and he had a cousin called Esther *** *(curtsey)*. Esther *** was very beautiful *** *(WOW!)* and so Mordecai *** told her that perhaps she should go to the palace and see if she could become the next queen ***.

So that is what happened and King Xerxes *** loved Esther *** the most and made her his queen ***. Esther *** went to live in the palace and Mordecai *** told her not to tell King Xerxes *** that she was a Jew because Jews were not liked *** *(turn up nose, shake head)* very much.

Mordecai *** also had a job in the palace and so was able to keep in touch with Esther ***.

One day Mordecai *** heard *** *(cup hands behind ears)* two men plotting to kill *** *(stab chest)* King Xerxes *** and so he sent a message to Esther *** telling her to tell the king *** about it. As a result the two men were executed *** *(cut off head).*

Now the prime minister of the country was a man called Haman *** *(say 'Hey! Man!).* He was very wicked and evil *** *(wring hands while pulling an evil face)* and very proud *** *(look aloof and snooty)* and he decided that everyone should bow down *** *(bow low)* to him when he passed by.

Mordecai *** refused to do this and this made Haman *** very angry ***. So Haman *** went to King Xerxes *** and told him lies about the Jewish people and suggested that on the thirteenth *** *(show 13 fingers)* day of the thirteenth *** month, all the Jews should be executed ***. King Xerxes *** agreed and in that way Haman *** planned that Mordecai *** would also die *** *(die dramatically).*

Mordecai *** was very upset *** *(cry dramatically)* about this and sent a message to Queen *** Esther *** asking her to go to King Xerxes *** and beg *** *(beg like a dog)* him to change the law about executing *** all the Jews. Queen Esther *** knew that just going to see King Xerxes *** without being invited could mean her death ***, but she told Mordecai *** to get all the Jews in the city to pray *** *(praying hands)* and she would go to see the king ***.

King Xerxes *** was not cross *** *(make a cross sign)* with Esther *** but instead he told her to ask for up to half of his kingdom and it would be hers! What a surprise *** *(gasp)*! But Esther *** had a plan. She did not beg *** the king *** to change the law straight away but she invited him and Haman *** to a banquet *** *(mime eating food greedily).*

At the banquet *** King Xerxes *** asked Esther *** again what she wanted, but again she just asked them to come to another banquet *** the next day.

When Haman *** went home he passed Mordecai *** who would not bow down *** to him and again he was really angry ***. He told his wife *** and she suggested that he should build a gallows and then go and ask the king if he could hang *** *(strangle self)* Mordecai *** on it. So that's what he did.

That night King Xerxes *** couldn't sleep *** *(snore)* so he sent for his diaries and read about all the things that had happened in his kingdom. He read about how Mordecai *** had saved *** *(football save)* the king from a plot to kill *** him. He asked what reward Mordecai *** had received and his servants *** *(bow with hands together several times)* told him that nothing had been done.

Just then he saw Haman *** coming into the courtyard. He had come to ask the king *** if he could hang *** Mordecai ***. He called Haman and asked him what would be a good *** *(thumbs up)* thing to do to honour someone. Haman *** thought he was thinking of him, so he said that it would be good *** to dress him in royal robes *** *(give a twirl)*, put him on a royal horse *** *(neigh!)* and get one of his most important *** officials to lead him through the city square *** *(make square shape)*, saying 'See how the king *** rewards a man he wants to honour.'

Then the king *** said to Haman ***, 'I want you to do this for Mordecai ***!' Haman *** was furious *** *(jump up and down with anger)* but he had to obey the king ***.

Later that night, Queen Esther *** held the banquet *** for King Xerxes *** and Haman *** and when they had eaten she told them about Haman's *** wicked and evil *** plan to execute *** all the Jews and that she was one of them.

The king was furious *** with Haman *** and told his servants *** to take him out and hang *** *(strangle self)* him on the gallows he had built for Mordecai ***. Then King Xerxes *** appointed *** *(point several times)* Mordecai *** to be the new prime minister. Mordecai *** sent riders *** *(mime riding a horse)* on fast horses *** to all parts of the Persian Empire to say that the Jews were not to be executed ***.

So, because Queen *** Esther *** was brave *** *(native Indian call)* and risked her life by going to see King Xerxes ***, she saved *** her people.

ISAAC BLESSES JACOB

Genesis 27

Teaching point
• *being honest*

Isaac *** *(mime raising hat or stroke beard)* was now getting very old *** *(look old and shaky)*, and he was blind *** *(close or cover eyes)*. He knew it would not be very long *** *(stretch out arms)* before he would die*** *(slump)* and so it was time *** *(look at watch)* to bless *** *(lay hands on head)* his first-born *** *(suck thumb)* son *** *(indicate short height)*, Esau *** *(saw wood)*.

[This was a very special blessing *** *(hand on head)* and would mean that all the promises *** *(cub or brownie promise sign)* that God *** *(point upwards)* made to Isaac's *** father, Abraham, about being the father of a great nation, would be given to Esau ***. He would be successful and God *** would bless *** his whole life and he would be the head *** *(tap head)* of the family.]

So, Isaac *** sent for Esau *** and said to him, 'Take your bow *** *(mime playing the violin)* and arrows *** *(make a pointed shape with your hands)* and go hunting *** *(mime shooting a bow and arrow)*. Kill *** *(stab chest)* an animal and bring it back *** *(touch back)* and cook *** *(mime stirring a saucepan)* some of that really tasty *** *(kiss fingers, Italian-chef style)* food *** *(rub tummy – yum! yum!)* that I like. After I have eaten it, I will give you my blessing ***.'

Now Isaac's *** wife *** *(cuddle self)* Rebekah *** *(curtsey)* heard *** *(cup hand around ear)* Isaac *** speaking to Esau *** and was determined that it would be Jacob, the younger son ***, who would get the blessing ***. She had a plan *** *(look schemingly)*. She told Jacob to kill *** two *** *(show 2 fingers)* fat *** *(puff out cheeks)* goats *** *(head down, show horns)*. When he had killed *** the two *** fat *** goats ***, Rebekah made a really tasty *** meal for Isaac ***.

She told Jacob that he must pretend to be Esau *** and go and take the food *** to Isaac ***. Rebekah *** knew that Isaac *** wouldn't know it was Jacob because he was blind ***. But Jacob said, 'If my father touches me, he will know I'm not Esau ***, because Esau *** is a hairy *** *(ruffle hair)* man but I have smooth *** *(stroke arm slowly)* skin *** *(pinch skin)*.'

So Rebekah told Jacob to put on Esau's clothes *** *(mime putting on clothes)* and then she covered his arms *** *(stretch out both arms)* with goats' *** hair *** and sent *** *(sniff while squirting perfume)* Jacob in to see Isaac *** taking his favourite food ***.

Isaac *** was very old *** and was blind *** so he asked, 'Which of my sons *** are you?' 'I am Esau ***,' said Jacob. 'I have brought you your favourite food *** and am ready for you to give me your blessing ***.'

Isaac *** said, 'Are you really Esau ***? Please come closer so that I can touch you. Jacob came closer and Isaac *** touched him and felt his hairy *** arms *** and smelt his clothes *** and he thought it really was Esau ***. So he blessed *** Jacob instead of Esau ***. This meant that when Isaac *** died *** Jacob would be head *** of the family and not Esau ***.

As Jacob left his father, Esau *** came home from hunting ***. He made the tasty *** food *** which Isaac *** liked and took it to his father. He asked for his father's blessing ***. When Isaac realised that he had been tricked, he began to tremble *** *(mime trembling)* and shake *** *(mime shaking)* and was very upset *** *(cry dramatically)*.

Esau *** said, 'Father, give me your blessing *** too *** *(show two fingers)*.' But Isaac *** knew that he could not do that. He could only give one blessing ***.

Esau was very angry *** *(stamp foot, look angry)* and he promised *** that after his father had died ***, he would kill *** Jacob. So when Rebekah *** heard *** this, she sent *** Jacob away to stay with her family in another town.

JESUS ENTERS JERUSALEM AS A KING

Luke 19:28-40

Teaching point
- *Jesus is King – the story of Palm Sunday*

It was nearly the time *** *(look at watch)* for Jesus *** *(point upwards or use deaf signing action, i.e. touch nail prints on both palms with opposite middle fingers)* to be crucified *** *(mime arms outstretched as on a cross, drop head)* and as he came to a town near Jerusalem he said to two *** *(show 2 fingers)* of his followers *** *(walk on the spot)*, 'Go into the town and when you enter it, you will find a donkey *** *(ee-aw!)* tied up *** *(mime wrists being tied)*. No one has ever ridden *** *(mime riding a wild horse)* it before. Untie it *** *(mime freeing wrists)* and bring it to me. If anyone asks you why you are taking it, say that the Master *** *(point upwards)* needs it.'

So *** *(sew)* the two *** followers *** went into town and saw *** *(saw wood)* the donkey *** tied up *** just as Jesus *** had said. The followers *** untied it ***, but the owners of the donkey *** came out. 'Why are you untying *** the donkey ***?' they said. Jesus' *** followers *** answered, 'The Master *** needs it.' The owners seemed to understand and let them take the donkey *** to Jesus ***.

Then the followers *** threw *** *(mime 'through' – pass finger through hole made by forefinger and thumb of other hand)* their coats *** *(mime holding lapels)* onto the donkey's *** back *** *(touch back)* and helped Jesus *** onto it. As Jesus *** rode *** *(clip-clop, clip-clop)* towards Jerusalem, the followers *** spread *** *(mime spreading butter)* their coats *** on the road before him. They cut *** *(mime scissors cutting)* branches from the trees *(make tree shape)* and spread *** them on the ground.

The whole *** *(indicate 'hole')* crowd of followers *** were very happy *** *(hilarious silent laughter)* and began to shout *** *(shout 'SHOUT')* praises *** *(thumbs up and rotate hands vertically – as in deaf signing)* to God *** *(point upwards)*. They said, 'Hosanna! *** *(shout 'HOSANNA!')* Blessed is he who comes in the name of the Lord *** *(shout this last phrase)*. God bless the King. God bless the King ***.' *[Shout this last phrase while doing actions for 'God' (point upwards) and 'king' (indicate crown).]*

Some of the Pharisees *** *(Boo! Sss!)* said to Jesus ***, 'Teacher *** *(mime writing on board or pointing to someone)*, tell your followers *** not to say these things.' But Jesus *** answered, 'If my followers *** don't say these things, then these rocks *** *(mime rocking a baby)* will cry out *** *(cry 'out'!)*.

The next day, when Jesus *** was in the Temple *** *(make pointed shape)* children *** *(indicate differing heights)* began to praise *** him. The Pharisees *** complained but Jesus *** said, 'Haven't you read in the Scriptures *** *(open book)*? God *** wants children *** and even babies *** *(suck thumb)* to praise *** him.'

'Hallelujah! Praise you, Lord! *** *(shout this phrase)*'.

JESUS IN THE TEMPLE

Luke 2:41-52

Teaching point
- *seeking God as a priority*

Each year Mary *** *(lightly stamp right foot)* and Joseph *** *(lightly stamp left foot)* left Nazareth *** *(point to the right)* and went to Jerusalem *** *(point to the left)* to celebrate *** *(shout 'yippee!')* the feast *** *(mime eating food, rub tummy)* of the Passover *** *(look from one side to the other [pass] and then lifting head look back again [over]).*

When Jesus *** *(point upwards and shout 'hallelujah!')* was 12 *** *(show 12 fingers)* years old Mary *** and Joseph *** took him to Jerusalem *** too *** *(show 2 fingers)*. After celebrating *** the Passover ***, Mary *** and Joseph *** started on their way back *** *(touch back)* home *** *(mime flat roof shape)* to Nazareth ***, but Jesus *** stayed in Jerusalem ***.

Mary *** and Joseph *** did not know that Jesus *** was still in Jerusalem ***. They were travelling with a group of friends *** *(shake hands with self)* and relatives and so they thought that he was with them.

After they had travelled a whole *** *(make a hole with thumb and fore-finger)* day, they realised *** *(hand over mouth, draw in breath)* that he was missing. Where could he be? They asked all their friends *** and relatives but no one had seen him. So Mary *** and Joseph *** returned *** *(turn on the spot)* to Jerusalem *** to look *** *(look though binoculars)* for Jesus ***.

On the third day *** *(show three fingers)* they found Jesus *** in the Temple *** *(mime pointed roof shape)*. He was talking *** *(mime talking action with hand)* to the Jewish teachers, listening *** *(cup hand around ear)* to them and asking questions. Everyone around *** *(make circle shape)* him was amazed *** *(look surprised, say 'wow!')* at his under-standing.

Mary *** and Joseph *** were amazed *** too ***. Mary *** said to Jesus ***, 'My son, we have been really worried *** *(look worried, biting fingernails)* about you. Why did you do this to us?'

Jesus *** said, 'Don't you know that I have to be in my Father's *** *(point upwards)* house *** *(pointed roof shape)*.' Mary *** and Joseph *** did not understand *** *(look puzzled)* his answer. Jesus *** loved his Father *** in heaven. He wanted to talk about him and ask questions and learn as much as he could from the Jewish teachers.

Finally, Jesus *** returned *** home *** to Nazareth *** with Mary *** and Joseph ***. Mary *** thought a lot *** *(point to side of head)* about all that had happened in Jerusalem ***. She knew that Jesus *** was special, that he was God's *** Son and that in time he would have a very important job to do.

JOHN THE BAPTIST'S LIFE

Matthew 3:1-6 and Mark 6:14-29

Teaching point
- *sold out for God*

John *** *(salute)* the Baptist *** *(mime baptising)* grew up *** *(grow up)* to be strong *** *(flex muscles)* in spirit. He loved *** *(hug self)* God *** *(point upwards)* and always obeyed him. When he was old enough *** *(mime old person)* he went to live in the desert *** *(mime eating 'dessert' saying 'mm'! – leader says 'desert' not 'dessert'!).* He ate locusts *** *(ugh!)* and wild honey *** *(yummy!)* and he wore clothes made from camels' *** *(mime 2 humps)* hair *** *(pull hair)*. He spent time *** *(look at watch)* praying *** *(praying hands)* to God ***. He knew he had a very important *** *(look important holding lapels)* job to do for God ***.

One day the time *** came for John *** to go and preach *** *(mime preaching)* to the people of Israel. He told them that the Messiah, Jesus, *** *(use deaf signing action, i.e. touch nail prints in palms of each hand with opposite middle finger)* was coming soon and that they must be ready to meet him. The people were sorry *** *(cry dramatically)* for their sins. They repented *** *(turn full circle)* and were baptised *** in the River Jordan. Even Jesus *** himself was baptised *** by John ***, even though he had never done anything wrong *** *(draw X)*.

Now during the time *** when John *** was baptising *** in the River Jordan, King *** *(crown on head)* Herod *** *(boo!)* was king *** of Israel. Herod *** was a wicked *** *(wring hands while pulling an evil face)* king ***. He had done many wrong *** things. He had broken *** *(snapping action)* God's *** law *** *(wag finger or write)* and had married his own brother's wife *** *(cuddle self)* called Herodias *** *(ssss!)*.

So *** *(sew)* one day, John *** went to see King *** Herod *** to tell him that he was disobeying God's *** law ***. King *** Herod *** was very angry *** *(look angry)* – in fact he was livid *** *(look angry and* *jump up and down)*. He was so *** angry *** that he had John *** thrown into prison *** *(clunk! clink!)*. Herod *** wanted to kill John *** but he was afraid *** *(look fearful, biting nails)* of the people, because they thought John *** was a prophet – a man sent from God ***.

Not too *** *(show 2 fingers)* long *** *(say 'l - o - n - g' slowly stretching out arms)* after this, it was King *** Herod's *** birthday *** *(sing first line of 'Happy birthday to you')* and he threw a big party *** *(party!)*. During the party *** the daughter of Herodias *** danced *** *(dance)* and King *** Herod *** was so *** pleased *** *(cheesy grin)* that he said she could ask for anything at all, even up to half his kingdom, and he would give it to her. Herodias *** told her daughter to ask for the head *** *(tap top of head)* of John *** the Baptist ***.

King *** Herod *** was sad *** about this but he felt he had to keep his promise *** *(cubs'/brownies' salute)*. So *** he sent men to the prison *** and had John *** beheaded *** *(cut off head)*. They put John's *** head *** on a plate and took it to the girl who gave it to her mother, Herodias ***.

(Read without actions)

John's followers came and took his body and buried it. When Jesus heard what had happened to John, he left in a boat and went to a lonely place to be by himself. John had loved and served God but for him it meant that he was put to death. Jesus knew that one day it would be the same for him.

JOSEPH IN EGYPT

Genesis 39ff

Teaching point

- *God is with us in all circumstances*

NB This is a particularly long story and you may need to cut some of the actions

After Joseph *** *(hold lapels and look important)* had been sold *** *(show sole of shoe)* by his brothers *** *(indicate ascending heights)*, he was taken to Egypt and sold *** to Potiphar *** *(mime 'potty' – screwing action to side of head and then point far away)*, who was the captain *** *(salute)* of the palace guard *** *(stand to attention)*.

But the Lord *** *(point upwards)* was with Joseph *** and he made sure that Joseph was successful *** *(thumbs up)* in everything he did. Potiphar *** was very pleased *** *(cheesy grin)* with Joseph *** and allowed him to be his personal servant *** *(hands together, bowing head)*. He put Joseph *** in charge *** *(act and say 'charge'!)* of his whole *** *(indicate a 'hole'!)* household *** *(mime pointed roof and hold self!)* and of everything Potiphar *** owned.

Now Potiphar's *** wife *** *(cuddle self)* fell in love *** *(mime kiss, kiss, kiss!)* with Joseph ***. She tried to trick him into doing something very wrong *** *(tut, tut, tut!)* but Joseph *** would have none of it *** *(mime washing your hands of something)*. This made her angry *** *(grit teeth, look angry)* and she went to Potiphar *** and told him lies about Joseph *** – that he had done wrong *** to her. So Potiphar *** had Joseph *** thrown into prison *** *(close door, turn key saying clunk! clink!)*.

But the Lord *** was with Joseph *** and the prison *** guard *** was very kind to him and chose him to look after *** *(peer forward, hand across eyes)* the other prisoners. Among them were the king's *** *(indicate* *crown on head)* *** wine server *** *(mime drinking and say 'hic'!)* and baker *** *(knead dough)*.

One night they each had a dream *** *(rest head on hands and snore)* and neither of them could understand it *** *(scratch head)*. The wine server *** dreamt *** he saw a vine *** *(with hands together make a twisting, growing movement)* and on the vine *** there were three *** *(show 3 fingers)* branches *** *(make tree shape with arms as branches)*. Then the branches *** began to blossom *** *(wave branches)* and soon the grapes were ripe and he saw himself squeezing *** *(squeeze waist)* the juice into the king's *** cup. The baker *** dreamt *** that there were three *** bread baskets on his head *** *(hand flat on head)* and birds *** *(flying, swooping movement)* were eating the food out of the top basket.

They were worried *** *(look worried, biting fingernails)* and they told Joseph *** about their dreams ***. God *** told Joseph *** the meaning of the dreams ***.

The wine server's *** dream *** meant that in three *** days he would once again serve the king *** his wine ***. He was very pleased *** about that and promised that he would tell the king *** about Joseph *** when he got back to the palace. But sadly *** *(look sad, shaking head)* he forgot.

The baker's *** dream meant that in three *** days he would die *** *(die dramatically)*. The king *** would order his head to be cut off *** *(mime cutting off head)* and his body to be hung out *** *(go floppy)* and be eaten by the birds ***. Ugh! *** (ugh!).

So Joseph *** had to stay in the prison *** for a long time *** *(stretch out arms and circle watch)*. Had everyone forgotten about him? God *** hadn't! He had plans for Joseph ***.

Two *** *(show two fingers)* years after this, the king *** had a bad dream ***. He couldn't understand it ***. He dreamt *** he was standing on the banks of the River Nile *** *(mime flowing river)*. He saw seven *** *(show 7 fingers)* fat *** *(puff out cheeks and make a fat body shape)* and beautiful *** *(kiss fingers, Italian-chef style!)* cows *** *(moo! several times)* come up out of the river *** and eat grass *** *(munch, munch!)*. Then seven *** more cows *** came up out of the river *** but they were thin *** *(suck in cheeks and make a thin body shape)* and ugly *** *(pull an ugly face)*. Suddenly *** *(sudden, shocked reaction)*, the thin *** ugly

*** cows *** ate up the fat ***, beautiful *** cows ***. Then the king *** woke up.

The king *** then had another dream ***. He saw seven *** fat *** ears *** *(tug ear)* of corn and seven thin *** ears *** of corn and the fat *** ears *** ate up the thin *** ears ***! Then he woke up again.

He sent for all his magicians *** *(say '1-2-3 – open sesame!')* but none of them could understand *** the meaning of the dreams ***. Then the king's *** wine server *** remembered *** *(point to side head and open eyes wide)* Joseph *** and told the king *** about him. So the king *** sent for Joseph *** and God *** told him what the dreams *** meant.

Joseph *** told the king *** that both the dreams *** meant that there would be plenty of food *** *(rub tummy)* for seven *** years but then there would be a famine *** *(grip stomach, look in pain)* for the next seven *** years. He advised the king *** to build large barns to store the extra food *** and then it could be sold to feed the people when there was a famine ***.

The king *** knew that God *** was with Joseph ***, so he set him free from prison *** and put him in charge *** of the running *** *(run on the spot)* of his palace.

Now more than seven *** years later, ten of Joseph's *** brothers *** came to Egypt to buy food *** because of the famine ***. They didn't recognise Joseph *** at first and they had to bow down *** *(bow down)* before him because he was the most important person in Egypt apart from the king ***. So the dreams *** that Joseph *** had had years before came true – his brothers *** bowed down *** before him.

Joseph *** didn't tell them who he was at first, but sent them home and told them to bring their youngest *** *(indicate lowest height)* brother *** to him.

In time *** *(circle watch)* Joseph *** told them who he was. They were very afraid *** *(look afraid, biting fingernails)* but Joseph *** had already forgiven them. He gave them food *** and sent them home to fetch their father and come and live with him in Egypt.

JOSEPH THE DREAMER

Genesis 37

Teaching points

- *jealousy*
- *favouritism*
- *need to be wise*

There was once a young man called Joseph *** *(hold lapels and look important)*. Joseph was the son *** *(use deaf signing – i.e. pass back of hand under chin)* of Jacob *** *(stroke beard)*. Jacob *** had 12 *** *(show 12 fingers)* sons *** *(pass back of hand under chin several times)* and Joseph *** was his favourite *** *(uh! oh!)*. He loved him *** *(cuddle self)* more than any of his other sons *** and made him a long-sleeved robe *** *(mime long sleeves on both arms)*.

His brothers *** *(indicate ascending heights)* saw *** *(saw wood)* that Jacob *** loved *** Joseph *** more than them and that he was his favourite ***, and they began to hate *** *(mime looking full of hate)* him.

One night *** *(mime knight sword fighting)*, Joseph *** had a dream *** *(close eyes and snore or look dreamy)*. Next day he told his brothers *** about it. Perhaps that was a silly *** *(act in a silly way)* thing to do because it made his brothers *** hate *** him even more. Joseph *** said, 'Hey! Listen *** *(cup hand around ear)* to the dream *** I had. We were all working in the field, tying bundles *** *(mime tying bundles)* of corn. My bundle stood up and yours all bowed down *** *(bow down with a flourish as in Renaissance times)* to mine.'

The brothers *** knew that the dream *** was saying that one day Joseph *** would be a very important *** *(mime 'snooty' – finger under nose)* person and they may even have to bow down *** before him. That made them very angry *** *(grit teeth, look angry)*.

Another night *** Joseph *** had another dream ***. This time he saw *** the sun *** *(draw circle with hands)*, moon *** *(draw half-moon)* and stars *** *(indicate flashing lights with hands)* and they were all bowing down *** to him. Again, he told his brothers *** and they were even more angry *** and very jealous *** *(sneer)*.

One day Joseph's *** brothers *** left home and went to look after *** *(lean forward, peering into the distance)* their father's sheep *** *(baa!)* in another area. Jacob *** sent Joseph *** to go *** *(point to the side)* and see *** *(mime looking through binoculars)* if his brothers *** and the sheep *** were all right *** *(tick!)*.

When Joseph *** came near to where his brothers *** were looking after *** the sheep ***, they saw *** him coming and together they made a plan to kill him *** *(stab chest)*. They said, 'Here comes that dreamer *** *(look dreamy)*, our father's *** favourite ***. Let's kill him *** and throw his body into a well *** *(say 'Well!')*. We'll tell our father that a wild animal *** *(mime a roaring lion)* killed him ***. Then his dreams *** won't come true.'

Meanwhile, Reuben, Joseph's oldest brother *** *(indicate tallest height)*, who did not want to kill *** Joseph ***, suggested that they should just put him into a nearby dry well *** and leave him there. Secretly *** *(mime saying 'ssh' with finger on lips)* he planned to go and rescue Joseph *** when his brothers *** were not around *** *(turn around)* and send him back *** *(touch back)* home.

So when Joseph *** reached his brothers ***, they pulled off his long-sleeved robe *** and threw *** *(mime 'through' – pass forefinger through hole made by thumb and forefinger of opposite hand)* him into the deep well ***. Then they sat down to eat *** *(mime eating)*.

While they were eating *** a group of Ishmaelites came by. They were riding on camels *** *(mime 'spitting')*, going to Egypt. Now Judah, another of Joseph's *** brothers, *** had an idea. 'Why don't we sell Joseph *** to these men? Why kill him *** when we can get money *** *(rub palm)* for him.'

So that's what they did. They sold *** *(show sole of shoe)* Joseph *** to the Ishmaelites, who took him away to Egypt and sold *** him as a slave *** *(whiplash)*.

Meanwhile *** the brothers *** killed *** a goat and dipped Joseph's *** long-sleeved robe *** into its blood *** *(yuk!)*. Then they returned home and showed Jacob *** the long-sleeved robe *** which they said they had found. Jacob *** thought that a wild animal *** *(pounce/roar!)* had torn *** *(mime tearing)* Joseph *** to pieces. He was extremely sad

*** *(cry hysterically)* and tore his clothes *** *(mime tearing clothing)* to show just how sad *** he was and he said that he would always be sad *** until the day he died *** *(die!)*. But that wasn't the end of the story.

MOSES AND THE GOLDEN CALF

Exodus 32

Teaching points
- *worship only God*
- *only one true God*

This is a story *** *(open book)* about Moses *** *(left, right on the spot)*. Moses *** was the leader *** *(salute)* of all the people of Israel *** *(point to everyone)*. One day, God *** *(point upwards)* told Moses *** to go up *** *(aircraft take-off)* onto the mountain of Sinai *** *(indicate large mountain)* and there God *** would write his law *** *(write)*, the ten *** *(show 10 fingers)* commandments *** *(wag finger as in telling off)* on two *** *(show 2 fingers)* stone tablets *** *(swallow tablets/pills)*.

Moses *** was away for a lo . . . ng time *** *(say 'long' slowly, moving hands outward as in measuring, then look at watch)* and the people of Israel *** became discontented and bored *** *(look fed-up)*. They called Aaron *** *(shout AARON! or mime 'hair on'!)* and said 'We want a god we can see *** *(mime sea)* and touch *** *(touch shoulders)*. Let's build one *** *(building action)*.'

Now Aaron *** was afraid *** *(look terrified, biting nails)* of the people *** and although he knew that it was wrong *** *(make a cross)* he gave orders *** *(telling off action)* for all the people *** to bring their gold to melt it down *** *(pushing down action)* and make a golden calf *** *(show horns, head down and moo!)* that they could worship *** *(bow down)*.

Then the people of Israel *** were very happy *** *(hilarious silent laughter)*, they danced round *** *(dance around on the spot)* the golden calf *** and soon they became very wicked and evil *** *(wring hands while pulling an evil face)*.

Meanwhile Moses *** heard *** *(cup hand round ear)* the noise *** *(shout NOISE!)* and God *** told him to go down *** *(aircraft landing)* the mountain *** because the people *** were being very wicked and evil ***. Moses *** was very angry *** *(make angry expression)* when he saw *** *(saw wood)* the golden calf ***. He threw down *** *(smashing action)* the two *** stone tablets ***.

God *** too, was very angry *** with all the people *** and Moses *** prayed *** *(hands together)* for forty *** *(show 10 fingers four times)* days and nights. He did not eat *** *(eat)* or drink *** *(drink)* anything, but prayed *** that God *** would not destroy *** *(thump fist on open palm)* all the people ***. Then Moses *** threw *** *(mime 'through' – pass finger through hole made by thumb and forefinger of other hand)* the golden calf *** into the fire and destroyed it ***.

The people were very sorry *** *(rub eyes saying 'boo-hoo')* for being so wicked and evil *** and turned back *** *(turn back)* to God ***.

NABOTH'S VINEYARD

1 Kings 21

Teaching points
- *greed*
- *selfishness*

King Ahab *** *(indicate crown)* lived in the city of Jezreel *** *(fishing reel)*. Near the palace was a vineyard *** *(tread grapes – squelch! squelch!)* owned by a man called Naboth *** *(neigh!)*. One day King Ahab *** said to Naboth ***, 'Let me have your vineyard ***. It's close to my palace and I want to use it for growing vegetables. I will give you a better vineyard *** or pay you money *** *(stroke palm)* for it.'

'This vineyard *** belonged to my ancestors. I can't let you have it,' replied Naboth ***. King Ahab *** was angry *** *(pull angry face)* so *** *(sew)* he went home depressed *** *(look miserable)*. He lay down on his bed and sulked *** *(sulk, pout)*. He would not eat *** *(mime eating)*. His wife Jezebel *** *(boo!)* went to him and asked, 'Why are you depressed? *** Why won't you eat ***?'

'Because of Naboth ***,' said King Ahab ***, 'I offered to buy his vineyard ***, or give him another one but he said I couldn't have it.'

Jezebel *** said, 'Well are you the king *** or are you not *** *(mime tying a knot)*? Get out of bed! Cheer up *** *(give a cheer)* and eat ***. I will get you Naboth's *** vineyard ***.'

So *** Jezebel *** sent a message to the important *** *(hold lapels and look snooty)* leaders *** *(salute several times)* of Jezreel ***. 'Call all the people together *** *(link arms)* and invite Naboth ***. Get a couple of troublemakers *** *(wring hands and pull an evil face)* to accuse Naboth *** of cursing God *** *(point upwards)* and the king ***. Then take him out of the city and stone him to death *** *(cut throat, drop head)*.'

This is what the important *** leaders *** did and Naboth *** was stoned to death ***. Jezebel *** then told King Ahab *** to go and take possession of the vineyard ***. King Ahab *** went at once.

The Lord said to Elijah *** *(shout 'The Lord is God')*, 'Go to Jezreel ***, to King Ahab ***, and give him my message.' So *** Elijah *** went and gave him the Lord's *** message. 'Because of what you have done, the dogs ****(woof! woof!)* will lick *** *(mime licking)* up your blood *** *(ugh!)* in the same place they have licked *** up Naboth's *** blood ***. And the dogs *** will eat *** up the body of Jezebel *** in the city of Jezreel ***.'

When Elijah *** had finished speaking, King Ahab *** was very sorry *** *(cry dramatically)*. He tore his clothes *** *(mime tearing clothes)*, took them off and put on sackcloth. He would not eat ***, he slept *** *(head on hands and snore)* in sackcloth and went around sad ***.

The Lord *** said to Elijah ***, 'Because King Ahab *** is sorry *** and has humbled *** *(bow head)* himself, I will not bring disaster on him but I will on his family.' And it all happened just as the Lord *** had said.

N.B. Elijah's name means 'The Lord is God'.

PAUL AND SILAS IN PRISON

Acts 16:16-40

Teaching points
- *trust in God*
- *salvation*
- *God's power*

Once, while Paul *** *(lightly stamp right foot)* and Silas *** *(lightly stamp left foot)* were going to pray *** *(hands together)*, a servant girl *** *(curtsey)* met them. She had an evil spirit *** *(pull evil face)* in her. She could tell people's fortunes *** *(show four fingers and sing a tune)* and make a lot of money *** *(rub palm)* for her owners. The servant girl *** was following *** *(walk on the spot)* Paul *** and Silas *** and was shouting out *** *(shout 'out'!)*.

'These are servants *** *(hands together, bowing head)* of the Most High *** *(stretch up high)* God *** *(point upwards),'* she said. 'They are telling you how you can be saved *** *(mime football save)*.'

For several days she kept following them and shouting out ***, until one day Paul *** turned round *** *(turn round)* and said to the evil spirit ***, 'In the name of Jesus Christ *** *(use deaf signing action, i.e. touch nail prints in palm of each hand with the opposite middle finger)*, I command you to come out of her *** *(mime sending someone away)*.' Immediately the evil spirit *** came out ***.

The owners of the servant girl *** were furious *** *(stamp foot, mime being really angry)*. They knew that no longer *** *(outstretch arms)* would the servant girl *** be able to make a lot of money *** for them. So *** *(sew)* they grabbed *** *(grab by scruff of the neck)* Paul *** and Silas *** and dragged *** *(mime pulling someone along)* them before the Roman *** *(salute)* rulers *** *(mime the shape of a ruler!)* and told the Roman *** rulers *** that Paul *** and Silas *** were making trouble for the city *** *(sing football chant – 'City! City! City! City!')*. The Roman *** rulers *** tore *** *(mime tearing)* Paul's *** and Silas' *** clothes and had them beaten with rods *** *(mime beating)* again and again.

Then they were thrown into prison *** *(clunk! clink!)* and the jailer *** *(stand to attention)* was told to make sure he guarded them well. So *** he pinned down their feet *** *(hold nose and say 'pooh!')* between large blocks of wood *** *(knock on head!)*.

About midnight, Paul *** and Silas *** were praying *** *(hands together)* and singing songs *** *(use deaf signing – i.e. forefinger and middle finger together on both hands pointing upwards and making ascending circular motion)* to God ***, when suddenly *** *(look shocked and gasp)* there was a big earthquake *** *(mime circle with hands and then 'quake'!)*. It shook *** *(mime shaking someone)* the prison *** and all the doors broke open *** *(mime opening doors)* and all the chains *** *(clink! clink!)* fell off the prisoners.

The jailer woke up *** *(wake with a start!)* and saw *** *(saw wood)* that all the doors were open ***. He thought *** *(point to side of head)* that all the prisoners had escaped and so *** he took his sword *** *(mime taking out sword)* and was just about to kill *** *(mime stabbing stomach)* himself, when Paul *** shouted, 'Don't hurt yourself, we are all here *** *(shout this phrase)*!'

The jailer was very frightened *** *(look fearful, biting nails)* and he knew that this was a miracle *** *(wow!)* and that God *** had done this. He wanted to know what he needed to do to be saved ***. So, *** Paul *** and Silas *** told the jailer all about Jesus *** and that he must believe in him if he wanted to be saved ***. So there and then the jailer, and his wife *** *(cuddle self)*, his children *** *(indicate descending heights)* and all his household *** *(mime pointed roof and hold self!)* believed in Jesus *** and were baptised *** *(hold nose as if going under water)*. Then he took Paul *** and Silas *** back *** *(touch back)* to his house *** *(mime pointed roof)* and gave them food to eat *** *(mime eating food)*.

Next day, the Roman *** rulers *** sent a message to the jailer and told him to let Paul *** and Silas *** go free. Hooray *** *(shout 'Hooray!')*! God *** had answered their prayers ***.

PENTECOST

Acts 2:1-13

Teaching point

- *the coming of the Holy Spirit*

When the disciples were all gathered together *** *(mime gathering people to you)* Jesus *** *(use deaf signing action, i.e. touch nail prints in palm of each hand with opposite middle finger)* explained that when he returned to his Father *** *(point upwards)* they would be given the Holy Spirit *** *(hands make flame movements)*. Jesus *** said, 'When the Holy Spirit *** comes upon you *** *(point at others)*, you *** will receive power *** *(show muscles with one arm bent, fist towards face)*. You *** will be my witnesses in every part of the world *** *(make circle shape with arms)*.'

After Jesus *** had told the disciples this, he was lifted up *** *(crouch down small with arms extended and lift something up as well as body coming up)*. A cloud hid Jesus *** from their sight *** *(cover eyes)*.

The disciples then went back *** *(touch self on back)* to Jerusalem *** *(point to the right)* from the Mount *** *(make mountain shape with hands)* of Olives. When they entered the city they went to the upstairs *** *(mime climbing stairs)* room and prayed *** *(hands together)*.

On the day of Pentecost there was a huge *** *(stretch arms out wide)* meeting where they were gathered *** together in one *** *(show one finger)* place *** *(mime fish swimming with hand)*. Suddenly *** *(sudden, shocked reaction)* a noise like a strong *** *(show muscles with both arms)*, blowing *** *(blow)* wind came from heaven *** *(make shape of a rainbow above head and in front of you)* and filled the whole house *(pointed roof shape)*. They saw something like flames of fire *** *(cup hands together to make flame shape)* above each person's head *** *(mime flame of fire over head)*. Everyone *** *(point to everybody)* was filled with the Holy Spirit *** and began to speak *** *(say the word* *speak)* in different languages *** *(say gobbledy gook! gobbledy gook! fast)*.

Some religious Jews who were staying in Jerusalem *** heard *** *(cup hand around ear)* this noise *** *(shout 'noise'!)* and a crowd gathered together ***. They were all amazed *** *(WOW!)* to hear their own languages *** being spoken. 'Look *** *(make binoculars over eyes)* at those people speaking, aren't they all from Galilee?'

So, *** *(sew)* they all heard *** in their own language *** about the great *** *(thumbs up!)* things God *** *(point upwards)* had done. They were all amazed *** and confused *** *(point to side of head, frown and shake head)* asking each other, 'What does this mean?' But some others were making fun *** *(ha! ha! ha!)* of them, saying, 'They have had too much wine to drink *** *(sway about and say 'hic!')*.'

But after that, Peter, one of Jesus' *** followers *** *(walk on spot)* stood up in front of the crowd and told them all about Jesus *** – that although they had crucified *** *(stretch out arms as on a cross)* him and he had died ***, *(mime dying)* God *** had made him come alive *** *(come alive!)* again.

The people were amazed *** *(gasp!)* and cried out *** 'What should we do to be saved?' Peter told them to be really sorry *** *(cry dramatically)* for the wrong things they had done, believe in Jesus *** and be baptised *** *(hold nose and duck under water)* and then they would be saved.

That day 3000 people became Christians. Hallelujah! *** *(shout 'Hallelujah!')*.

SAMUEL ANOINTS DAVID

1 Samuel 16:1-13

Teaching points
- *God looks at the heart*
- *God's calling*

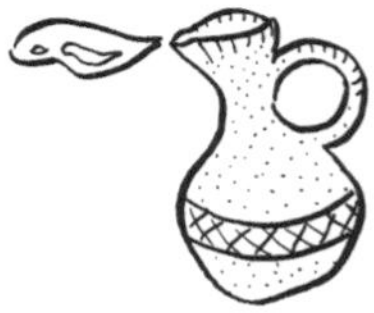

The Lord *** *(point upwards)* said to Samuel *** *(stroke beard)*, 'I am going to choose *** *(point to someone)* a new king *** *(indicate crown on head)*, because King *** Saul *** *(saw wood)* has done evil *** *(wring hands while pulling evil face)* in my sight *** *(point to eyes)*. I want you to go to a man called Jesse *** *(left, right on the spot)* who lives in the town of Bethlehem *** *(point to one side)*. I have chosen *** one of his sons *** *(use deaf signing – pass back of hand under chin – several times)* to be the next king *** of Israel. Take some olive oil *** *(say 'Oh, Popeye' in a whiny voice)* with you because you are going to anoint *** *(mime pouring oil on head)* him to be king ***.'

The Lord *** told Samuel *** to take a calf *** *(mime horns and say moo!)* with him and when he got to Bethlehem *** he was to call all the people together *** *(mime beckoning people)*, including Jesse *** and his sons *** and then make a sacrifice to the Lord ***. 'Then,' said the Lord ***, 'I will show you who the next king *** must be.'

So that's what Samuel *** did. At first the older leaders *** *(mime being elderly)* were worried *** *(look worried, biting fingernails)* and shook with fear *** *(tremble)*. They thought that they had done something wrong *** *(draw a cross)* and that Samuel *** had come to judge them *** *(wag finger with serious face)*. But Samuel *** told them not to be afraid *** *(tremble)* because he had come in peace *** *(finger on lips)*.

When Samuel *** had made the sacrifice and blessed all the people, he looked at Jesse's *** sons *** and listened to what the Lord *** would say. The oldest son *** *(indicate tallest height)* was Eliab. He was tall *** *(stretch up tall)* and handsome *** *(wolf whistle or pat face admiringly)*. Samuel *** thought that this must be the one the Lord *** would choose ***. But no *** *(say 'No?' questioningly)*, the Lord *** said, 'I do not see *** *(look through binoculars)* how you see ***. You look at the outside *** *(do a twirl)* of a person, but I look at the heart *** *(put hand on heart)*.'

So Samuel *** then looked at Abinadab, the next son *** *(indicate next tallest height)*, but again the Lord *** said 'No!' ***. Then Jesse *** told Shammah, the next eldest son *** to go before Samuel ***, but still *** *(freeze!)* the Lord *** said 'No!' ***

Soon Samuel *** had seen all the sons *** who were there but the Lord *** did not choose any of them. 'Jesse ***, do you have any more sons ***?' said Samuel ***. 'Well yes,' he said, 'there is still *** the youngest *** *(indicate lowest height)* – he is out in the fields, looking after *** *(hand across eyes, peer forward)* the sheep *** *(baa!)*.'

'I would like to see him,' said Samuel ***. So the youngest *** son *** was brought in from the fields. His name was David. David loved *** *(cuddle self)* God *** and his heart *** was true *** *(cross heart)*. As soon as Samuel *** saw David, the Lord *** told him that he was the one. So Samuel *** anointed *** him with olive oil *** to show that he was going to be the next king *** of Israel.

SIMON THE MAGICIAN

Acts 8:4-25

Teaching points
- *need for right motives*
- *God's gifts not for personal glory*

Now for some time *** *(look at watch)* a man *** *(indicate beard)* named Simon had practised magic *** *(mime silent explosion using fingers)* in the city and amazed *** *(look amazed, drop jaw)* all the people *** *(point round to audience)* of Samaria *** *(point to the right)*. He boasted *** *(hold lapels and nod head as if talking)* that he was someone great *** *(thumbs up)* and all the people *** gave him their attention *** *(stand to attention!)* and said, 'This man *** has got great *** power *** *(raise fist)*.'

They followed *** *(walk on the spot)* him because he had amazed *** them for a long *** *(say 'long' slowly and stretch out arms)* time *** with his magic ***. But when they believed Philip *** *(finger on lip or roll bottom lip with fingers)* as he preached about Jesus *** *(use deaf signing, i.e. touch nail prints in palm of each hand with opposite middle finger)*, all the people *** were baptised *** *(hold nose and duck down)*. Simon was also *** *(all sew)* baptised *** and he followed *** Philip *** everywhere, amazed *** by the great *** signs and miracles he saw *** *(saw wood)*.

When the apostles in Jerusalem *** *(point to the left)* heard *** *(cup hand round ear)* that Samaria *** had accepted the word of God *** *(point upwards)*, they sent Peter *** *(lightly stamp right foot on the spot)* and John *** *(lightly stamp left foot on the spot)* to them. When they arrived Peter *** and John *** prayed *** *(praying hands)* for them to receive the Holy Spirit *** *(make sound of wind and flame shapes)*, because the Holy Spirit *** had not yet come upon any of them. They had only been baptised *** into the name of Jesus ***. So *** *(sew)* Peter *** and John *** placed their hands *** *(hold out hands)* on them and they received the Holy Spirit ***.

When Simon the magician *** *(mime explosion using fingers)* saw *** that the Holy Spirit *** was given when Peter *** and John *** laid their hands *** on people, he offered them money *** *(stroke palm)*, and said, 'Give me also *** *(all sew)* this ability so *** that everyone on whom I lay my hands *** may receive the Holy Spirit ***.'

Peter *** told Simon that money *** could not buy the power *** *(flex biceps)* that came from the Holy Spirit ***, who was a gift from God. Peter *** was cross *** *(make a X)* with Simon and told him to repent *** *(turn round on the spot)* – to say sorry *** *(look down slowly)* to God *** and pray *** to God *** to forgive *** *(show 4 fingers and mime a giving action)* him because his heart *** *(hand on heart)* was not right *** *(hold out right hand)*. It was wicked *** *(wring hands pulling an evil face)* and selfish *** *(grabbing action, sneering, secretive)*.

Then Simon the magician *** said, 'Pray *** to the Lord *** *(point upwards)* for me so *** that nothing bad *** *(thumbs down)* will happen to me.'

The Bible *** *(open book)* doesn't tell us any more about Simon the magician ***. Did he really change and repent ***? We don't know, but we do learn from this Bible story *** *(open book as in charades)* that God's *** Holy Spirit *** is not given to us *** *(point to self)* so that other people *** will think we are great *** and powerful ***, but to help others *** *(point to audience)* and bring glory to God ***.

THE BIG PARTY

Luke 14:15-24

Teaching point
• *God's invitation of salvation is for all of us*

One day Jesus *** *(point upwards or use deaf signing action, i.e. touch nail prints in palm of each hand with opposite middle finger)* told the people this story *** *(open book as in charades)*:

'There was once a man *** *(left, right on the spot)* who prepared a large *** *(indicate large shape with arms, saying 'l - a - r - g - e' slowly)* feast *** *(rub tummy, say 'yum! yum!')*. The man *** invited *** *(mime beckoning people)* many people to come to his house *** *(mime pointed roof shape)*.

'As soon as the feast *** was ready, he sent *** *(mime putting on perfume)* his servant *** *(bow head with hands together)* to tell the people that it was time *** *(circle watch)* to come to the feast ***.

'But the people would not come to the feast ***. They all made excuses. One *** *(show 1 finger)* said, "I have just bought a field and I must go and look after it *** *(hand across eyes and lean forward)*." The second *** *(show 2 fingers)* said, "I have just bought five *** *(show 5 fingers)* pairs of oxen *** *(indicate horns, head down and moo 5 times)* and I must go and try them out." The third one said, "I've only just got married *** *(sing tune of 'Here comes the bride')*. I can't come now!"

'So the servant *** returned *** *(turn around on the spot)* to his master *** *(salute)* and told him everything that had happened. The man *** was furious *** *(stamp feet, be really angry)* and told his servant *** to go out into the streets and invite *** all the poor people *** *(show empty pockets)*, the crippled people *** *(scrunch up body)*, the blind people *** *(cover eyes)* and the lame people *** *(mime limping)* and tell them to come straight away *** *(stretch out arm quickly and pull it away!)*

'Some time *** later the servant *** returned *** and said to his master

***, "Master ***, I invited *** all the poor people ***, the crippled people ***, the blind people *** and the lame people ***, but there's still *** *(freeze!)* room for more."

'The master *** replied, "Go out to the roads and country lanes *** *(say 'Ooh arr!')* and tell all the people to come straight away ***. I want my house *** to be full *** *(breathe in, arms tightly by side)*! None of the people I first invited *** will ever eat *** *(mime knives and forks to mouth!)* with me in my house ***."'

THE EXODUS

Exodus 7-12

Teaching point
- *God is all-powerful*

The Lord *** *(use signing for 'Lord', i.e. make 'L' shapes with forefinger and thumb on each hand or point upwards)* said to Moses *** *(mow the lawn)*, 'I am the Lord ***. Now go *** *(point to side)* and tell *** *(wag finger in a 'telling-off' fashion)* Pharaoh *** *(row a boat)*, the king of Egypt *** *(indicate crown),* to let my people go *** *(shout, 'Let my people go!')*. I am going to make the king *** stubborn *** *(mime being stubborn, stamp foot, cross arms),'* said the Lord *** 'and then I will do many amazing miracles *** *(look amazed and say 'WOW!')*. But still *** *(freeze!)* Pharaoh *** will not listen *** *(cup hand round ear)*, so I am going to punish *** *(thump fist on open hand)* Egypt.

So *** *(sew)* Moses ***, who was 80 *** *(show 8 x 10 fingers)*, took his brother Aaron *** *(mime 'hair on')*, who was 83 *** *(show 8 x 10 + 3 fingers)*, and went to see Pharaoh ***, the king of Egypt ***. They told the king *** the message from God *** *(point upwards)* and said, 'Let my people go ***!' But Pharaoh *** said 'NO!' *** *(say 'NO!')* and so Aaron *** did what God *** had told him to do and threw down his staff *** *(mime throwing down staff)* and it became a snake *** *(ssssss!)*. The king *** called for his magicians *** *(say '1-2-3 – open sesame!')* and they threw down their staffs *** *(throw staff down several times)* and they changed into snakes *** *(several 'ssssss's!)* too *** *(show two fingers)*, but Aaron's *** snake *** swallowed up *** *(gulp!)* the other snakes ***.

But just as the Lord *** had said, Pharaoh *** said 'No! No! I will not let you go!' *** *(shout 'No! No! I will not let you go!')* and refused *** *(mime 'stop' sign)* to let the Israelites go. So *** the next day God *** told Moses *** and Aaron *** to go down to the river *** *(mime rippling)* and stretch out *** *(have a good stretch)* the staff over the river ***. And as they did that the river *** turned *** *(turn round)* into blood *** *(say YUK!)*. Again, the king *** called for his magicians *** and by using their evil power *** *(wring hands, while pulling an evil face)* they were able to change water into what looked like blood ***. But again Pharaoh *** said 'No! No! You cannot go!' *** and refused *** to let the Israelites go.

After this, God *** had to send many more really bad miracles *** or plagues on the people of Egypt before Pharaoh *** would let the Israelites go. He sent frogs *** *(croak)* to cover the land, he sent gnats and flies *** *(buzz)*, he sent a terrible disease which made all the horses *** *(neigh)*, donkeys *** *(ee-aw)*, camels *** *(pretend to spit)*, cattle *** *(moo)* and sheep *** *(baa)* that belonged to the Egyptians, really sick *** *(retch)*.

Still *** *(freeze!)* Pharaoh *** refused *** to let the people go. He said 'No! No! You cannot go ***!' Then God *** caused boils *** *(squeeze spot on face)* to break out *** *(mime 'break out')* on all the people of Egypt. After that, God *** sent huge hailstones *** *(mime 'hail' as in hailing a king and then make a huge stone shape)*, which killed animals and people. He sent thunder and lightning *** *(make explosive noise while indicating flashing lights)*.

Six times *** *(mime 6 multiplication signs)* during the plagues, Pharaoh *** gave in and said they could go but six times *** he changed his mind and said 'No! No! You cannot go ***!' Then God *** sent a huge number of locusts swooping over the land *** *(mime swooping down)*. They ate all the plants and the fruit on the trees *** *(make tree shapes)*. Then God made it go dark *** *(cover face)* all over the land.

At this point *** *(indicate point)* Pharaoh *** said 'Yes! Yes! Just go!' *** *(repeat phrase 'Yes! Yes! Just go!')*, but later he changed his mind again and said to Moses *** 'If I see you again, you will die *** *(stab chest and hang head)*.'

So finally, God *** told Moses *** that that night he would send the angel *** *(indicate halo)* of death *** *(pretend to die)* and all the first-born children *** *(indicate descending heights)* and animals, who lived in Egypt, would be struck down dead ***. So *** Moses *** told the people of Israel to do a special thing. They were to put blood *** *(yuk!)* on the doorposts *** *(mime shape of door frame)* of their houses *** *(make house shapes)* and when the angel *** of death *** came, he would pass over the houses *** which had blood *** on the doorposts ***.

After that terrible plague, Pharaoh let the people go. He said, 'Yes! Yes! Just go ***!' So the Israelites left Egypt and began their journey towards the Red Sea.

THE HEALING OF NAAMAN

2 Kings 5

Teaching points
- *God heals*
- *humility*

There was a man called Naaman *** *(stand to attention, stamp foot, arms by side)* who was commander *** *(salute)* of the army *** *(stroke arm)* of the king *** *(crown on head)* of Aram. Naaman *** was a mighty *** *(flex muscles)* and a brave *** *(place fist on brow or make native Indian call)* commander *** and the king *** liked him very much. Unfortunately Naaman had a skin disease *** *(pinch skin or say 'don't touch!')* which was catching *** *(catch a ball)* and that would mean *** *(pull a mean face)* that he would not be able to remain as commander *** of the king's *** army ***.

Now Naaman's *** wife *** *(cuddle self)* had a servant *** *(hands together, bowing low)*, a little girl *** *(indicate short height)* who had been taken captive from Israel. This little girl *** knew about a man called Elisha *** *(raise arms, look up)*. He was a prophet in Israel – a man who brought messages from God *** *(point upwards)* to the people *** *(hand out messages)*. Elisha *** had done many miracles *** *(wow!)* with God's *** power. So *** *(sew)* the little servant girl *** *(combine actions for girl and servant)* told Naaman's *** wife *** about Elisha *** and said that Naaman *** should meet him.

When Naaman's *** wife *** told him about this, he decided that he would go and find Elisha ***. Firstly, he went to the king *** and told him what the little servant girl *** had said. The king *** told him to go immediately, and gave him a letter *** *(mime writing)* to give to the king of Israel *** *(make different shaped crown)* telling him that Naaman *** was coming to him to be healed of his skin disease ***.

Naaman *** took with him silver and gold *** *(point to rings or jewellery)* and ten *** *(show 10 fingers)* sets of clothing *** *(hold lapels)* and presented himself to the king of Israel ***. The king was afraid *** *(look *afraid, biting fingernails)*. He knew that the skin disease *** was very catching ***. He said, 'I'm not God ***. I can't heal you.' He tore his clothes *** *(mime tearing clothes)* and was afraid *** that this was a trick and that the king of Aram was really going to attack *** *(mime fencing action – lunge)* his people again. When Elisha *** heard *** *(cup hand behind ear)* this he sent a message to the king of Israel *** and told him to send Naaman *** to him.

So *** Naaman *** went to Elisha's *** house *** *(pointed roof shape)*. Elisha *** sent out his servant *** to tell Naaman to go and wash *** *(mime washing)* in the river Jordan seven times *** *(show 7 fingers and a multiplication sign)* and then he would be healed.

Naaman *** was really angry *** *(mime being furious)* that Elisha *** hadn't even come to see him himself and that he had told him to wash *** in a dirty river *** *(yuk!)* and he refused to obey. His servants *** said to Naaman ***, 'If the prophet had told you to do a hard *** *(mime squeezing something hard)* thing you would have done it. So *** why not go and wash *** in the dirty river *** and then you will be healed from this terrible skin disease ***.

Naaman *** thought about it and decided to go down and wash *** in the dirty river ***. He dipped his head *** *(dip head)* under the water once, twice, three times, four times, five times, six times *** *(count these together)* but there was no change. But after the seventh time *** *(show 7 fingers and point to watch)* when he came up out of the dirty water *** the skin disease *** was completely gone. God *** had healed him.

Then Naaman *** and all his servants *** went to see Elisha ***. He said to Elisha ***, 'Look at me *** *(mime looking through binoculars)*, I'm completely healed. Now I know there is no God *** in all the earth *** *(mime circle with hands)* except your God ***. Please accept these gifts from me.' Naaman *** offered Elisha *** the silver and gold *** and the ten *** sets of clothes ***, but Elisha *** would not accept any of the gifts. He did not want to be paid for what God *** had done.

So Naaman *** returned to his own country and decided that from that day on he would only worship the one *** *(show 1 finger)* true *** *(cross heart)* God ***.

THE RESURRECTION OF JESUS

John 20

Teaching point
- *Jesus is alive!*

All the followers *** *(walk on the spot)* of Jesus *** *(use deaf signing, i.e. touch nail prints in palm of hand with opposite middle finger)* were very sad *** *(look really sad)*. The Roman soldiers *** *(stand to attention/ salute)* had crucified *** *(make cross with arms)* Jesus *** and now he was dead *** *(drop head)* and had been buried *** *(use both hands and make a downward movement)* in a tomb *** *(make a circle with arms)*.

The tomb *** was in a beautiful garden *** *(wow!)*. Early on the Sunday morning *** *(cock-a-doodle-doo!)*, while it was still dark *** *(cover face with hands)*, Mary Magdalene *** *(left, right march on the spot)* went to the tomb *** where Jesus *** had been buried ***. She saw *** *(saw wood!)* that the stone had been rolled away *** *(roll hands away from self)* from the tomb ***. Mary went running *** *(run on the spot)* to find Peter *** *(indicate right)* and John *** *(indicate left)* who were followers *** of Jesus ***. She told them that the guards *** *(salute)* must have taken Jesus *** out of the tomb ***. So *** *(sew)* immediately Peter *** and John *** went running *** to the tomb *** and found that Jesus *** was gone and only the linen wrappings *** *(mime wrapping a parcel)* were left *** *(point to the left)*. Immediately Peter *** and John *** went running *** back *** *(touch back)* to tell the other followers ***.

Mary *** stayed near the tomb *** and cried *** *(mime silent crying)*. Then she looked *** *(indicate binoculars)* into the tomb *** and saw *** two *** *(show 2 fingers)* angels *** *(indicate halo)* sitting *** *(mime sitting position)* where the body of Jesus *** had been. 'Why are you crying?' ***, they said. She answered, 'The guards *** have taken Jesus *** away and I don't know where they have put him!'

Just then Mary *** turned round *** *(turn round on the spot)* and Jesus *** was standing behind her *** *(use thumbs to point behind)*, but she did not know it was Jesus ***. She thought *** *(point to side of head)* it was the gardener *** *(mime digging soil)*.

'Why are you crying ***?' said Jesus ***. 'Who are you looking *** for?' *** *(show 4 fingers)*. Mary *** still thought *** it was the gardener *** and that perhaps he had taken the body of Jesus ***. But then Jesus *** said, 'Mary ***.' And suddenly *** *(shocked reaction)* she knew it was Jesus ***. She turned *** towards him but he said, 'Do not hold *** *(hug self)* me yet because I have got to go back *** to my Father *** *(point upwards)*, but go and tell my followers *** that I am alive *** *(mime coming alive)*.'

So *** Mary *** ran *** back *** to the place *** *(mime fish swimming)* where some of Jesus' *** followers *** were and told them everything she had seen. Jesus *** was dead *** but now he was alive ***. Hooray! *** *(shout 'hooray')*.

THE RICH FOOL

Luke 12:13-21

Teaching points
- *putting God first*
- *greed*
- *materialism*

One day, Jesus *** *(point upwards or use deaf signing action, i.e. touch nail prints in palm of each hand with opposite middle finger)* was teaching his followers *** *(walk on the spot)* about being greedy *** *(eat food greedily)* and about not worrying *** *(look worried, biting nails)* about getting loads of money *** *(stroke palm or rub thumb and fingers together)*. So *** *(sew)* he told this story *** *(open book as in charades)* to help his followers *** understand *** *(look puzzled, finger on lips)*:

'There was a rich man *** *(say 'Loads o' money!')* who owned some land *** *(aeroplane landing)* which grew a good crop of food *** *(yum! yum!)*. The rich man *** thought to himself *** *(look thoughtful, pointing to side of head)*, "What will I do? I have no place *** *(mime fish swimming)* to keep *** *(indicate castle keep)* all my crops." Then he said, "I know what I will do, I will tear *** *(mime tearing, making ripping noise)* down my barns *** *(make owl noise)* and build *** *(fist on fist)* bigger ones *** *(mime large shape)*. I will put *** *(mime shot put)* all my grain and other goods in my new barns ***."

'The rich man *** thought *** he was very clever *** *(breathe on knuckles and rub on chest)*. He would have enough food *** to last him for many years. Now he could rest *** *(relax, hands behind head, close eyes)*, eat *** *(mime eating with suitable sound effects)*, drink *** *(mime drinking with suitable sound effects)* and enjoy life *** *(party!)*.

'But God *** *(point upwards)* said to that rich man *** "You're a foolish man *** *(look foolish or silly)*. Tonight you will die *** *(die dramatically)*, and who will get those things you have saved *** *(football save!)* in your bigger *** barns ***?"'

Jesus *** told his followers *** that it was much more important *** *(look important, holding lapels)* to believe *** *(point to side of head)* in God *** and follow him than to save up *** *(high football save!)* loads of money *** for themselves *** *(point to self)* and forget about God ***.

THE SOWER

Matthew 13:1-23

Teaching point
• *responses to God's word*

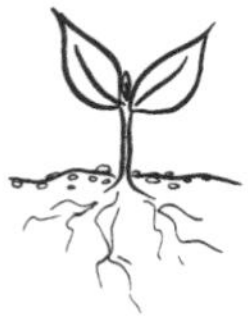

Jesus *** *(point upwards or use deaf signing action, i.e. touch nail prints on both palms with opposite middle fingers)* told many stories *** *(open book as in charades)* to teach the people *** *(point to audience)* many things. One day he said:

'A farmer *** *(ooh! arr!)* went out to plant his seed *** *(mime scattering seed)*. While he was planting ***, some seed fell *** *(trip over!)* along the roadside *** *(indicate bend in a road and touch side)*. The birds *** *(whistle or call like a bird)* came and ate up *** *(peck up)* all that seed.

'Some seed fell *** on rocky ground *** *(mime uneven surface)* where there wasn't enough soil. That seed grew very fast *** *(mime growing up fast)* because the soil was not deep *** *(say 'deep' in a deep voice)*. But when the sun *** *(mime sun shape)* rose *** *(sniff a rose)*, the plants *** *(make a suitable plant shape)* dried up *** *(shrivel up)*, because they did not have deep *** roots.

'Some of the farmer's *** seed fell *** among thorny weeds *** *(make a spiky plant shape saying 'Ouch!')*. The thorny weeds *** grew *** and choked *** *(strangling action)* the good plants ***.

'The rest of the seed fell *** on good ground *** *(thumbs up)* and strong *** *(flex muscles)* plants *** grew ***. Some plants *** gave 100 *** *(show 10 x 10 fingers)* times *** *(mime a 'times' sign)* more grain, some 60 *** *(show 6 x 10 fingers)* times *** and some 30 *** *(show 3 x 10 fingers)* times *** more grain.'

The people did not understand *** *(look puzzled)* the meaning of the story *** about the farmer ***, so *** *(sew)* Jesus *** had to tell them. He said:

'The seed *** that fell *** by the roadside *** is like the person who hears *** *(cup hand round ear)* the teaching about the kingdom *** *(indicate crown)* of God *** *(point upwards)* and does not understand it ***. The Evil One *** *(pull an evil face)* comes and snatches away *** *(snatching action)* the things that were sown in that person's heart *** *(mime heart shape or put hand over heart)*.

'The seed that fell *** on rocky ground *** is like a person who hears *** the teaching and quickly *** *(run quickly on the spot)* accepts it with joy *** *(shout 'Yippee!')*. But he does not let the teaching about the kingdom *** of God *** go deep *** into his life. He keeps it for only a short time *** *(indicate short person or length and point to watch)*. When persecution *** *(shield body action)* comes, he quickly *** gives up *** *(shrug shoulders)*.

'The seed that fell *** among thorny weeds *** is like the person who hears *** the teaching about the kingdom *** of God *** but lets worries *** *(look worried, biting nails)* about this life and love of money *** *(stroke palm of hand)* stop that teaching from growing ***. So *** the teaching does not produce fruit *** *(pick and eat apple)* in that person's life.

'The seed that fell *** on good ground *** is like a person who hears *** the teaching and understands it *** *(look enlightened and say 'Aah!')*. That person grows *** and produces fruit ***, sometimes 100 *** times *** more, sometimes 60 *** times *** more and sometimes 30 *** times *** more.'

So *** what sort of person are you? *** *(point to self)*.

THE VISIT OF THE WISE MEN

Matthew 2:1-21

Teaching point
- *wise men seek Jesus!*

One day a baby *** *(rock baby in arms)* called Jesus *** *(use deaf signing action, i.e. touch nail prints in palm of each hand with opposite middle finger)* was born *** *(baby cry)* in a town called Bethlehem *** *(point to the right)*. During this time *** *(look at watch)* a man called Herod *** *(boo!)* was king *** *(indicate crown)*. After Jesus *** had been born *** some wise men *** *(look thoughtful, outline face and stroke beard with hand slowly whilst saying 'hmm')* arrived in Jerusalem wanting to know where to find the baby *** that had been born *** to be king *** of the Jews. The wise men *** announced that they had seen his star *** *(clench fist and let go indicating flashing light/star)* and had come to worship *** *(kneel down)* him.

King *** Herod *** was very worried *** *(look worried, biting finger nails)* so *** *(sew)* he called a meeting of his advisers to find out where the Messiah was to be born ***. He was told it was to be in Bethlehem ***. So *** King *** Herod *** called a secret *** *(sshh!)* meeting with the wise men *** and told them to go and find out where the baby *** had been born ***. 'Come back,' he said, 'and tell me where he is so *** I can go to him.'

The wise men *** left King *** Herod *** and followed *** *(walk on spot)* the star *** until they found where Jesus *** was. They were so happy *** *(mime laughing)* and bowed down and worshipped *** him. They gave Jesus *** gifts of gold, frankincense and myrrh.

Whilst the wise men *** were sleeping *** *(put hands together and put to side of head)* after their long *** *(stretch out arms and say l - o - n - g)* journey, God *** *(point upwards)* told the wise men *** not to go back *** to King *** Herod ***. So *** they returned home a different way.

An angel *** *(indicate halo)* of the Lord *** *(point upwards)* spoke to

Joseph in a dream *** *(snore!)* and said, 'Quick, get up and take baby *** Jesus *** and Mary, his mother, and run *** *(run on spot)* away to Egypt *** *(point to the left)*. King *** Herod *** wants to kill *(stab self)* Jesus ***. Stay in Egypt *** until I tell you to return.'

Joseph listened to God *** and took Mary and Jesus *** and left Bethlehem *** quietly *** *(step on tiptoes twice)*. They travelled to Egypt ***. They stayed there until King *** Herod *** had died *** *(mime dying)*.

Meanwhile, King *** Herod *** was VERY angry *** *(shake fist)* that the wise men *** had not returned. He did not want anybody else to be king *** especially not a baby ***! So *** he declared that every baby *** boy of two *** *(show 2 fingers)* years or under *** *(duck down)*, in and around *** *(turn)* Bethlehem *** must be killed ***. However, Jesus *** was safe *** *(hug self)* because Joseph and Mary had listened to God *** and taken him to Egypt ***.

After King *** Herod *** had died ***, an angel *** of the Lord *** spoke to Joseph again in a dream ***. He said, 'It's now safe *** to go back to Israel because King *** Herod *** has died ***.'

Again Joseph obeyed God *** and they all travelled back *** *(touch back)* to Israel and settled in a town called Nazareth.

WATER INTO WINE

John 2:1-11

Teaching points
- *God gives the best*
- *life to the full*

There was once a wedding *** *(mime blowing a trumpet whilst humming 'Here comes the bride')* in the town of Cana *** *(pretend to be caning someone)* in Galilee. Jesus' *** *(point upwards or use deaf signing action, i.e. touch nail prints in palm of each hand with opposite middle finger)* mother was there. Jesus *** and his followers *** *(walk on spot)* had also been invited to the wedding ***. Everyone was having a great time *** *(look at watch)* partying *** *(dance on the spot)*. But then a disaster *** *(cover mouth and exclaim, 'oh, no!')* occurred. All the wine *** *(say wine in a whining voice)* had been drunk *** *(sway about, 'hic!')*. There was none *** *(hold hand up with clenched fist)* left, not even a drop.

Jesus' *** mother had a feeling that Jesus *** would be able to solve the problem so *** *(sew)* she went to look *** *(look through binoculars)* for him with the servants *** *(bow and offer goods)*. She found Jesus *** talking to his followers *** on the other side of the room. She said to him, 'They have no *** *(shake head in despair)* more wine ***. They have completely run *** *(run on spot)* out.'

Jesus *** asked, 'Why have you *** *(point at someone else)* come to tell me *** *(point at self)* this? My time *** has not yet come.' His mother turned *** *(turn around)*, looked *** *(look through binoculars)* at the servants *** and said, 'Do whatever Jesus *** tells you *** to do.'

Jesus *** told the servants *** to go and fill up six *** *(show 6 fingers)* stone water jars that the Jews used for their washing *** *(wash face)* ceremony. So *** the servants *** filled the six *** jars right up to the top *** *(place hand on head)*. Jesus *** then told the servants *** to take some out and to give it to the master of the wedding ***.

So *** the servants *** did as Jesus *** requested and took the water to the master of the wedding ***. When the master of the wedding *** tasted *** *(savour in mouth)* it, the water had become wine ***. Amazing! *** *(look amazed and say 'WOW!')*. The master of the wedding *** did not know where the wine *** had come from, it was a mystery to him, but the servants *** did.

The master of the wedding *** called the bridegroom and said, 'People usually serve their best wine *** first. Then when they serve the cheaper *** *(cheep! cheep!)* wine ***, they hope that people don't notice the difference. But you *** have saved *** *(mime football save)* the best wine *** until now. It's amazing ***.'

Everybody carried on partying *** at the wedding *** unaware of the great miracle that Jesus *** had performed.

So *** that is where Jesus *** performed his first miracle and his followers *** believed in him.

A-Z MERSE[illegible]

C000216150

CONTENTS

Key to Map Pages	2-3
Large Scale Liverpool City Centre	4-5
Map Pages	6-115
Postcode Map	116-117
Road Ma[illegible] (1:205,00[illegible]	[illegible]119
Index to S[illegible] and selected Places of Interest	120-198
Index to Hospitals etc.	199-200

REFERENCE

Motorway	M57
Primary Route	A59
Tunnel	
A Road	A580
B Road	B5202
Dual Carriageway	
One-way Street Traffic flow on A Roads is also indicated by a heavy line on the driver's left.	
Road Under Construction Opening dates are correct at the time of publication.	
Proposed Road	
Restricted Access	
Pedestrianized Road	
Track / Footpath	
Residential Walkway	
Railway	Level Crossing, Station, Tunnel
Built-up Area	ALDER ROAD
Local Authority Boundary	
Posttown Boundary	
Postcode Boundary (within Posttown)	
Map Continuation	60
Large Scale City Centre	4

Airport	
Car Park (Selected)	P
Church or Chapel	†
Cycleway (Selected)	
Fire Station	
Hospital	H
House Numbers (A & B Roads only)	21 65
Information Centre	i
National Grid Reference	445
Park & Ride	Esplanade P+R
Police Station	
Post Office	★
Safety Camera with Speed Limit Fixed cameras and long term road works cameras. Symbols do not indicate camera direction.	30
Toilet: without facilities for the Disabled with facilities for the Disabled Disabled use only	
Viewpoint	
Educational Establishment	
Hospital or Healthcare Building	
Industrial Building	
Leisure or Recreational Facility	
Place of Interest	
Public Building	
Shopping Centre or Market	
Other Selected Buildings	

SCALE

Map Pages 6-115

1:19,000 3⅓ inches (8.47cm) to 1 mile 5.26cm to 1km

0 ¼ ½ ¾ Mile

0 250 500 750 Metres 1 Kilometre

Map Pages 4-5

1:9,500 6⅔ inches (16.93cm) to 1 mile 10.52cm to 1km

0 ⅛ ¼ ⅜ Mile

0 100 200 300 400 500 Metres

Fairfield Road, Borough Green, Sevenoaks, Kent TN15 8PP
Telephone: 01732 781000 (Enquiries & Trade Sales)
01732 783422 (Retail Sales)
www.az.co.uk

Edition 4 2013

KEY TO MAP PAGES

LARGE SCALE
4 5
LIVERPOOL
CITY CENTRE

IRISH SEA

LIVERPOOL BAY

SOUTHPORT

FORMBY

CROSBY

BOOTLE

WALLASEY

LIVERPOOL

BIRKENHEAD

HOYLAKE

WEST KIRBY

HESWALL

BEBINGTON

NESTON

ELLESMERE PORT

ORMSKIRK

MAGHULL

KIRKBY

HUYTON

CONNAH'S QUAY

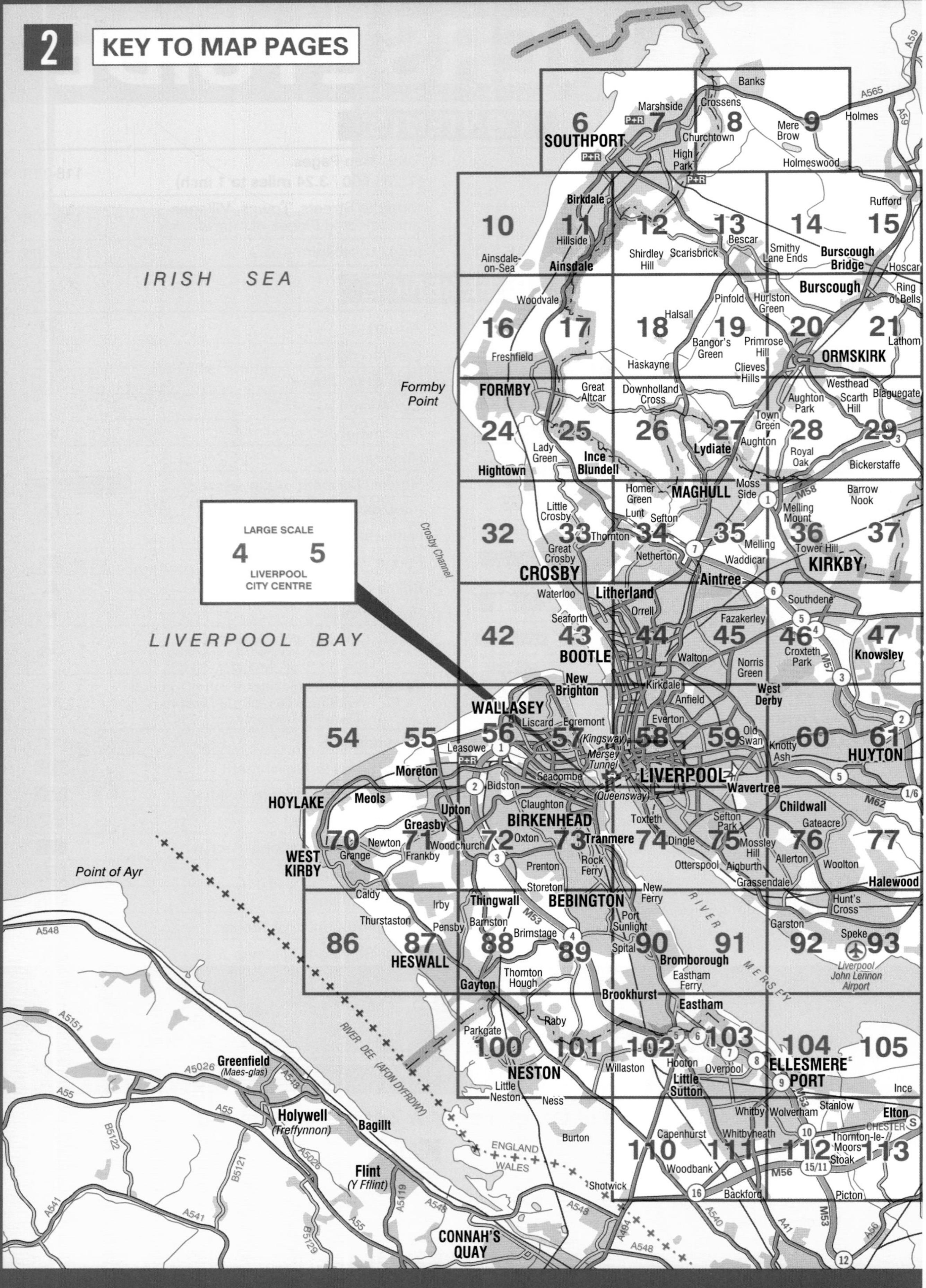

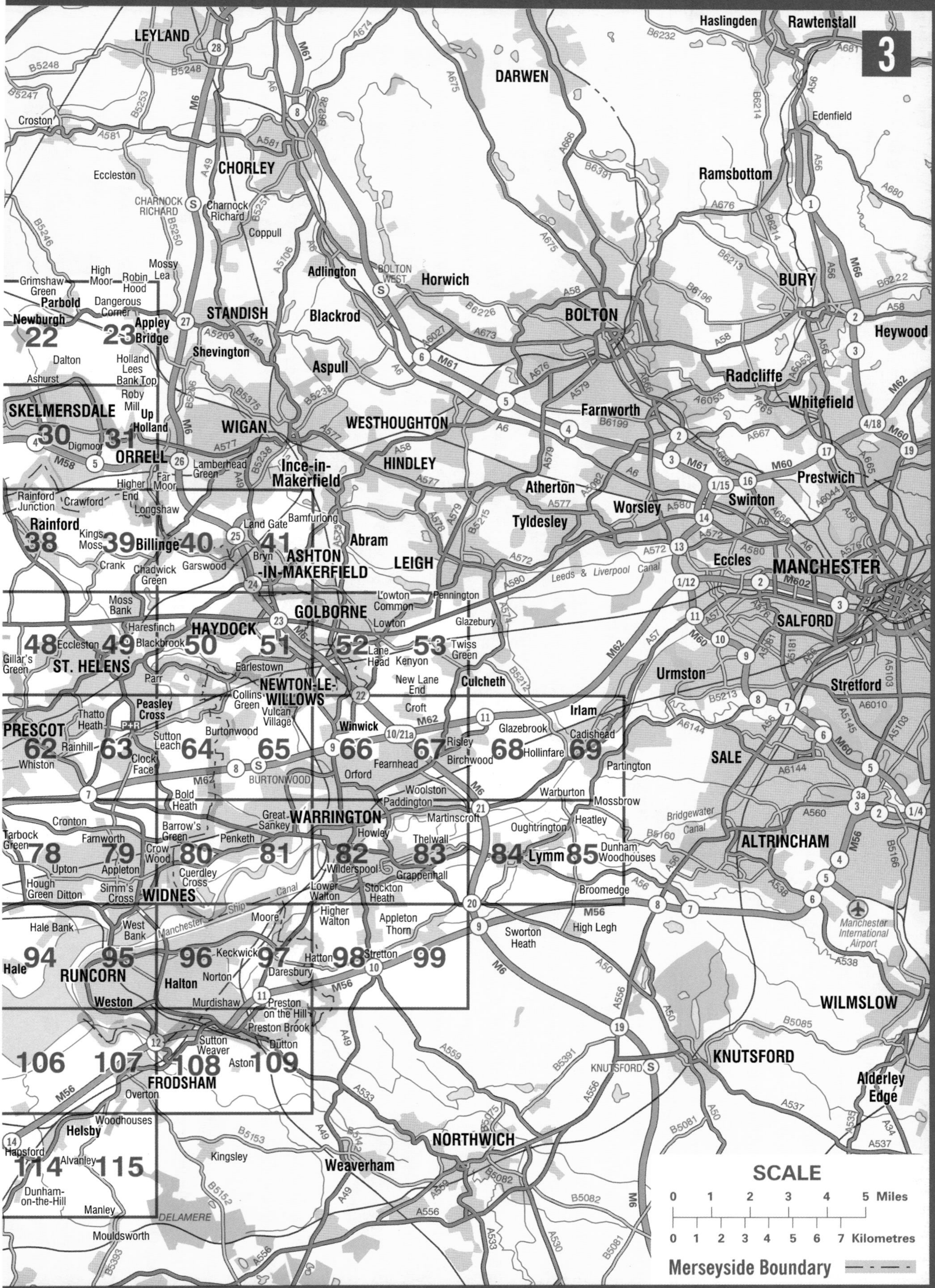
LEYLAND
DARWEN
Haslingden
Rawtenstall
Edenfield
Croston
Eccleston
CHORLEY
CHARNOCK RICHARD
Charnock Richard
Coppull
Ramsbottom
Grimshaw Green
High Moor
Robin Hood
Mossy Lea
Parbold
Dangerous Corner
Newburgh
Appley Bridge
STANDISH
Adlington
BOLTON WEST
Horwich
Blackrod
BOLTON
BURY
Heywood
Shevington
Aspull
Radcliffe
Whitefield
Dalton
Holland Lees
Bank Top
Ashurst
Roby Mill
Up Holland
SKELMERSDALE
WIGAN
WESTHOUGHTON
Farnworth
Digmoor
ORRELL
Lamberhead Green
Ince-in-Makerfield
HINDLEY
Prestwich
Higher End
Far Moor
Rainford Junction
Crawford
Longshaw
Atherton
Worsley
Swinton
Tyldesley
Rainford
Kings Moss
Billinge
Land Gate
Bamfurlong
Abram
Crank
Chadwick Green
Garswood
Bryn
ASHTON -IN-MAKERFIELD
LEIGH
Eccles
MANCHESTER
Leeds & Liverpool Canal
Moss Bank
Lowton Common
Pennington
GOLBORNE
Lowton
Glazebury
SALFORD
Haresfinch
HAYDOCK
Blackbrook
Eccleston
Gillar's Green
ST. HELENS
Lane Head
Kenyon
Twiss Green
Earlestown
Parr
NEWTON-LE-WILLOWS
New Lane End
Culcheth
Urmston
Stretford
Collins Green
Vulcan Village
Peasley Cross
Thatto Heath
PRESCOT
Rainhill
Whiston
Sutton Leach
Burtonwood
Clock Face
Winwick
Croft
Risley
Glazebrook
Irlam
Cadishead
Hollinfare
Birchwood
Fearnhead
Orford
BURTONWOOD
Partington
SALE
Bold Heath
Woolston
Paddington
Warburton
Mossbrow
Cronton
Barrow's Green
Great Sankey
WARRINGTON
Martinscroft
Oughtrington
Heatley
Tarbock Green
Farnworth
Penketh
Howley
Thelwall
Bridgewater Canal
ALTRINCHAM
Crow Wood
Upton
Appleton
Cuerdley Cross
Wilderspool
Grappenhall
Lymm
Dunham Woodhouses
Hough Green
Ditton
Simm's Cross
WIDNES
Lower Walton
Stockton Heath
Broomedge
Hale Bank
West Bank
Manchester Ship Canal
Moore
Higher Walton
Appleton Thorn
Sworton Heath
High Legh
Manchester International Airport
Hale
RUNCORN
Halton
Keckwick
Norton
Hatton
Daresbury
Stretton
Weston
Murdishaw
Preston on the Hill
Preston Brook
WILMSLOW
Sutton Weaver
Dutton
Aston
FRODSHAM
KNUTSFORD
Overton
Alderley Edge
Woodhouses
Helsby
NORTHWICH
Hapsford
Alvanley
Kingsley
Weaverham
Dunham-on-the-Hill
Manley
DELAMERE
Mouldsworth
22 23 30 31 38 39 40 41 48 49 50 51 52 53 62 63 64 65 66 67 68 69 78 79 80 81 82 83 84 85 94 95 96 97 98 99 106 107 108 109 114 115
M6 M61 M62 M60 M66 M58 M56 M602
SCALE
0 1 2 3 4 5 Miles
0 1 2 3 4 5 6 7 Kilometres
Merseyside Boundary

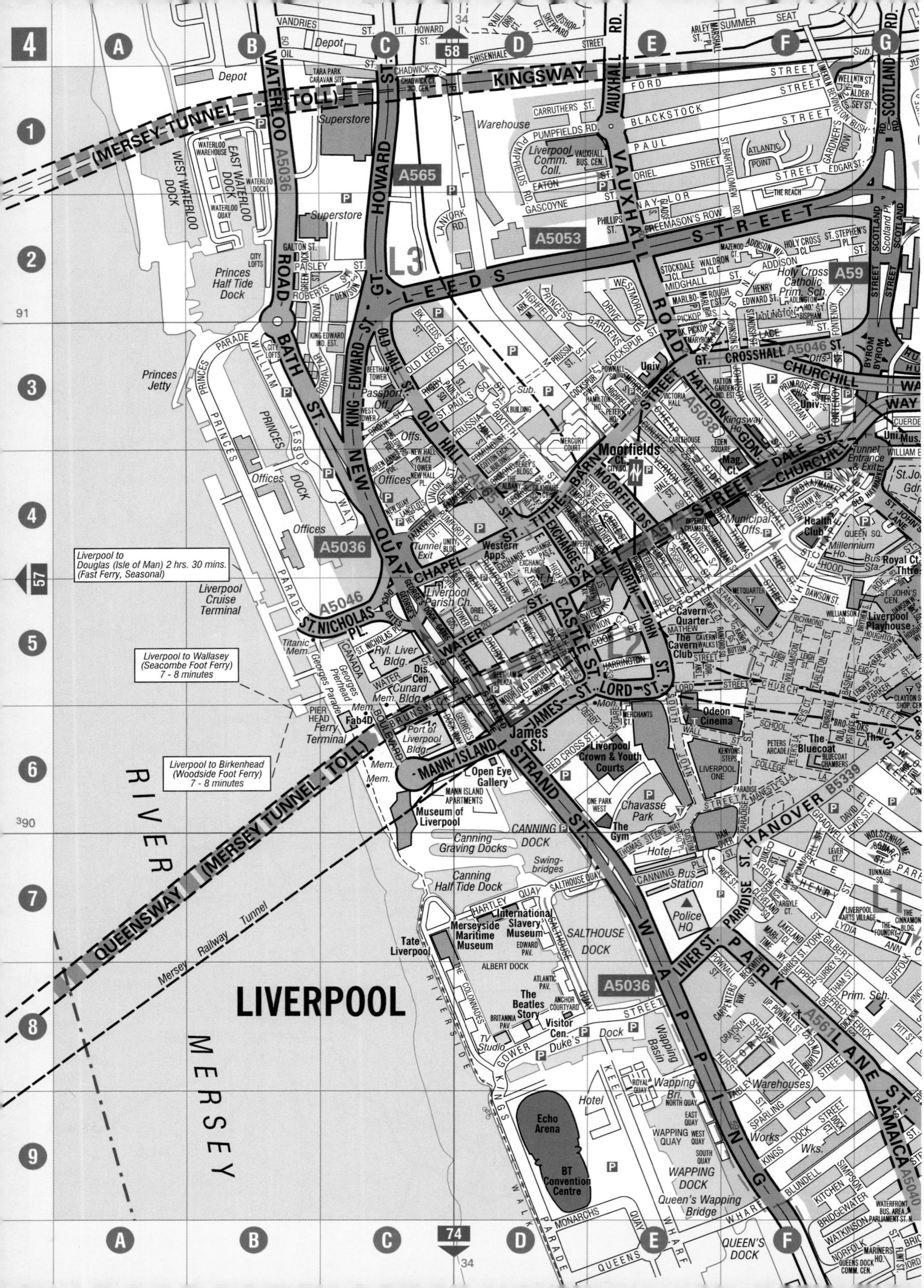
A
B
C
D
E
F
G
1
2
3
4
5
6
7
8
9
58
57
74
34
91
390
LIVERPOOL
RIVER
MERSEY
KINGSWAY
(MERSEY TUNNEL - TOLL)
QUEENSWAY (MERSEY TUNNEL - TOLL)
Mersey Railway Tunnel
Liverpool to Douglas (Isle of Man) 2 hrs. 30 mins. (Fast Ferry, Seasonal)
Liverpool to Wallasey (Seacombe Foot Ferry) 7 - 8 minutes
Liverpool to Birkenhead (Woodside Foot Ferry) 7 - 8 minutes
WATERLOO ROAD
A5036
A565
A5053
A59
A5046
A5038
A5040
A561
B5339
HOWARD ST.
LEEDS STREET
VAUXHALL RD.
SCOTLAND RD.
BATH ST.
NEW QUAY
KING EDWARD ST.
OLD HALL ST.
TITHEBARN ST.
DALE ST.
CHURCHILL WAY
CHAPEL ST.
WATER ST.
ST. NICHOLAS PL.
JAMES ST.
LORD ST.
CASTLE ST.
NORTH JOHN ST.
VICTORIA ST.
HANOVER ST.
PARADISE ST.
STRAND ST.
WAPPING
PARK LANE
JAMAICA ST.
MANN ISLAND
MOORFIELDS
Moorfields
Superstore
Warehouse
Depot
Liverpool Comm. Coll.
Princes Half Tide Dock
Princes Jetty
PRINCES DOCK
WEST WATERLOO DOCK
EAST WATERLOO DOCK
Liverpool Cruise Terminal
Offices
Tunnel Exit
Western Apps
Liverpool Parish Ch.
Ryl. Liver Bldg.
Cunard Mem. Bldg.
Port of Liverpool Bldg.
Dis. Cen.
Pier Head Ferry Terminal
Fab4D
Titanic Mem.
Georges Pierhead
Museum of Liverpool
Open Eye Gallery
MANN ISLAND APARTMENTS
Liverpool Crown & Youth Courts
Chavasse Park
The Gym
Hotel
CANNING DOCK
Canning Graving Docks
Canning Half Tide Dock
Swing-bridges
Merseyside Maritime Museum
International Slavery Museum
Tate Liverpool
ALBERT DOCK
SALTHOUSE DOCK
The Beatles Story
Visitor Cen.
TV Studio
Duke's Dock
Wapping Basin
Echo Arena
BT Convention Centre
WAPPING DOCK
Queen's Wapping Bridge
QUEEN'S DOCK
Police HQ
Canning Bus Station
Cavern Quarter
The Cavern Club
Odeon Cinema
The Bluecoat
LIVERPOOL ONE
Municipal Offs.
Health Club
Millennium Ho.
Royal Ct. Thtre.
Liverpool Playhouse
Tunnel Entrance & Exit
Holy Cross Catholic Prim. Sch.
Victoria Hall
Kingsway Ho.
Passport Off.
Warehouses
Works
Wks.
Prim. Sch.
L1
L2
L3
QUEENS DOCK COMM. CEN.
WATERFRONT BUS. AREA PARLIAMENT ST.

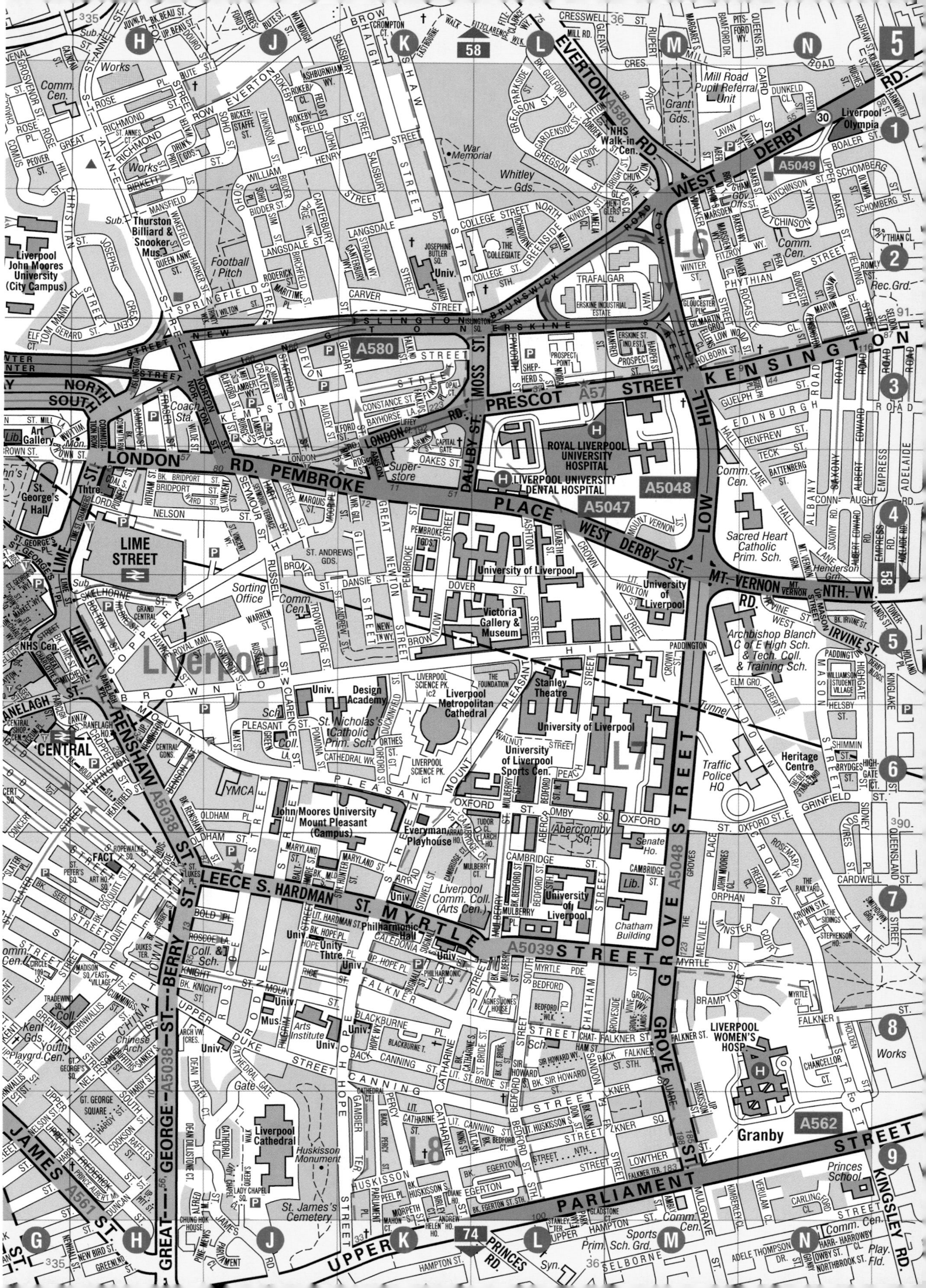

5
58
74
Liverpool
Liverpool Olympia
Mill Road Pupil Referral Unit
Grant Gds.
NHS Walk-in Cen.
War Memorial
Whitley Gds.
Thurston Billiard & Snooker Mus.
Football Pitch
Liverpool John Moores University (City Campus)
Comm. Cen.
Works
THE COLLEGIATE
ERSKINE INDUSTRIAL ESTATE
PROSPECT POINT
ROYAL LIVERPOOL UNIVERSITY HOSPITAL
LIVERPOOL UNIVERSITY DENTAL HOSPITAL
Super-store
Coach Sta.
Art Gallery
St. George's Hall
LIME STREET
Sorting Office
University of Liverpool
Victoria Gallery & Museum
Sacred Heart Catholic Prim. Sch.
Archbishop Blanch C of E High Sch. & Tech. Coll. & Training Sch.
Stanley Theatre
Design Academy
Liverpool Metropolitan Cathedral
St. Nicholas's Catholic Prim. Sch.
LIVERPOOL SCIENCE PK. ic1
LIVERPOOL SCIENCE PK. ic2
University of Liverpool Sports Cen.
Heritage Centre
Traffic Police HQ
CENTRAL
YMCA
John Moores University Mount Pleasant (Campus)
Everyman Playhouse
Abercromby Sq.
Senate Ho.
Liverpool Comm. Coll. (Arts Cen.)
Chatham Building
FACT
Philharmonic Hall
Unity Thtre.
Coll. & Sch.
Arts Institute
Chinese Arch
Youth Cen.
Kent Gds.
Liverpool Cathedral
Huskisson Monument
St. James's Cemetery
LIVERPOOL WOMEN'S HOSP.
Granby
Princes School
Sports Grd.
Tunnel
A580
A57
A5048
A5047
A5049
A5039
A5038
A562
A561
LONDON RD.
PEMBROKE PLACE
WEST DERBY ST.
PRESCOT STREET
KENSINGTON
ISLINGTON
MT. VERNON RD.
LOW HILL
GROVE STREET
MYRTLE STREET
LEECE ST.
HARDMAN ST.
RENSHAW ST.
BERRY ST.
GREAT GEORGE ST.
PARLIAMENT STREET
UPPER PARLIAMENT ST.
PRINCES RD.
UPPER DUKE STREET
HOPE STREET
RODNEY STREET
MOUNT PLEASANT
BROWNLOW HILL
OXFORD ST.
FALKNER ST.
CANNING STREET
CATHARINE STREET
BEDFORD ST. STH.
KINGSLEY RD.
EDINBURGH ROAD
IRVINE ST.
SMITHDOWN LANE
CROWN STREET
EVERTON RD.
WEST DERBY RD.

A B C D E F G
1 2 3 4 5 6 7 8 9
11

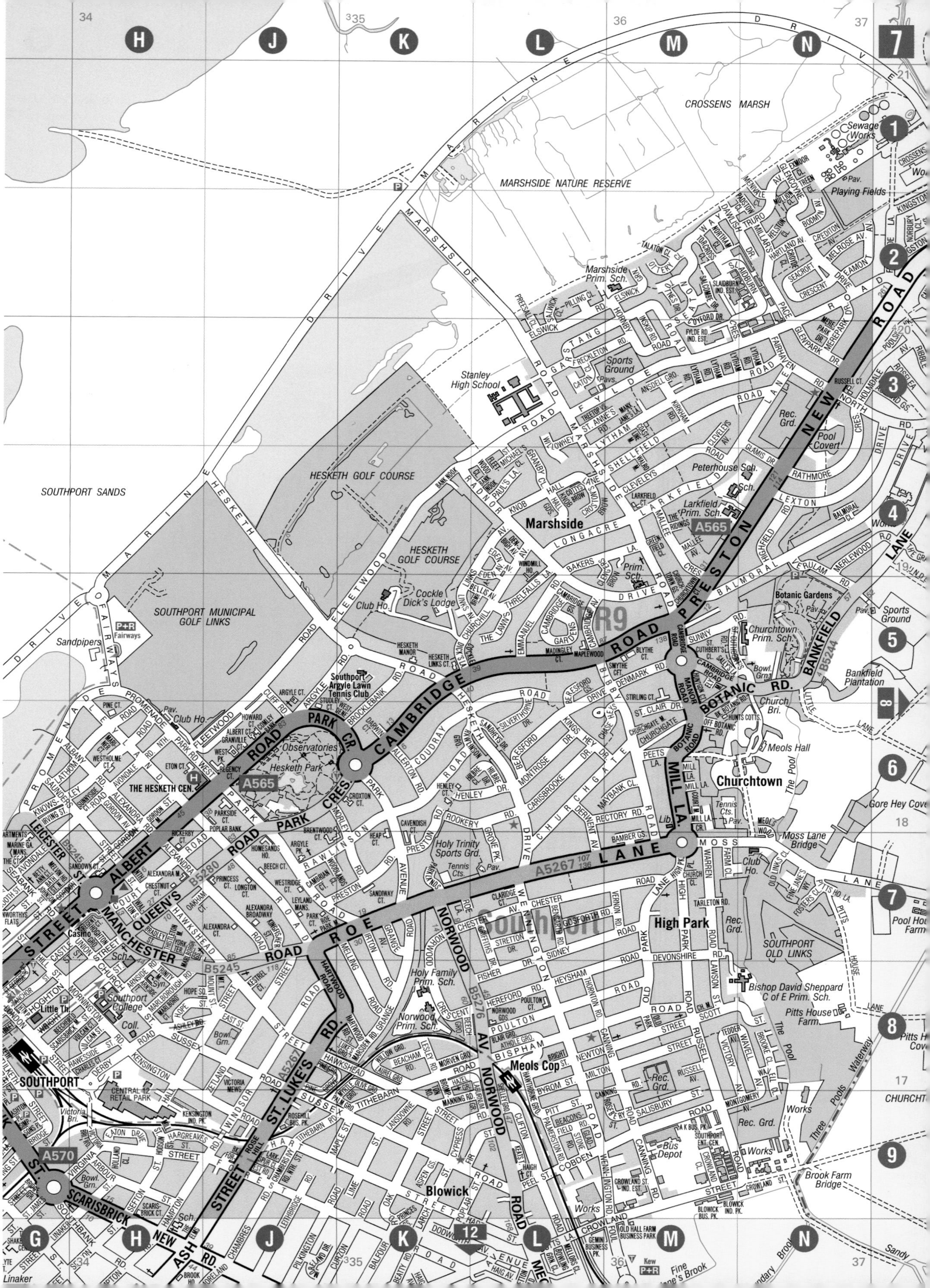
CROSSENS MARSH
MARSHSIDE NATURE RESERVE
Sewage Works
Playing Fields
MARINE DRIVE
MARSHSIDE ROAD
SOUTHPORT SANDS
HESKETH GOLF COURSE
HESKETH DRIVE
SOUTHPORT MUNICIPAL GOLF LINKS
Fairways
Sandpipers
Stanley High School
Sports Ground
Marshside Prim. Sch.
Marshside
Peterhouse Sch.
Larkfield Prim. Sch.
A565
PRESTON NEW ROAD
Pool Covert
Rec. Grd.
Botanic Gardens
Sports Ground
Bankfield Plantation
BANKFIELD LANE
B5244
Churchtown Prim. Sch.
Church Bri.
BOTANIC RD.
Meols Hall
Churchtown
MILL LA.
The Pool
Gore Hey Cove
Moss Lane Bridge
MOSS LANE
Club Ho.
Pool House Farm
PR9
FLEETWOOD ROAD
Club Ho.
Cockle Dick's Lodge
Southport Argyle Lawn Tennis Club
CAMBRIDGE ROAD
PARK CRES.
Observatories
Hesketh Park
A565
THE HESKETH CEN.
ALBERT ROAD
B5245
LEICESTER ST.
B5280
Holy Trinity Sports Grd.
Tennis Cts.
A5267
LANE
High Park
Rec. Grd.
SOUTHPORT OLD LINKS
Bishop David Sheppard C of E Prim. Sch.
Pitts House Farm
Southport
ROE LANE
Casino
MANCHESTER ROAD
QUEEN'S ROAD
HARTWOOD ROAD
Holy Family Prim. Sch.
Norwood Prim. Sch.
NORWOOD ROAD
B5276
NORWOOD AV.
Meols Cop
Southport College
Little Th.
SOUTHPORT
CENTRAL 12 RETAIL PARK
Victoria Bri.
A570
ST. LUKE'S RD.
Rec. Grd.
Bus Depot
Works
Rec. Grd.
Brook Farm Bridge
Three Pools Waterway
CHURCHTOWN
Blowick
ASH STREET
SCARISBRICK NEW RD.
Linaker
12
Fine Jane's Brook
Kew P+R
Sandy Brook
H J K L M N G
1 2 3 4 5 6 7 8 9
8
34 35 36 37
17 18 19 20 21

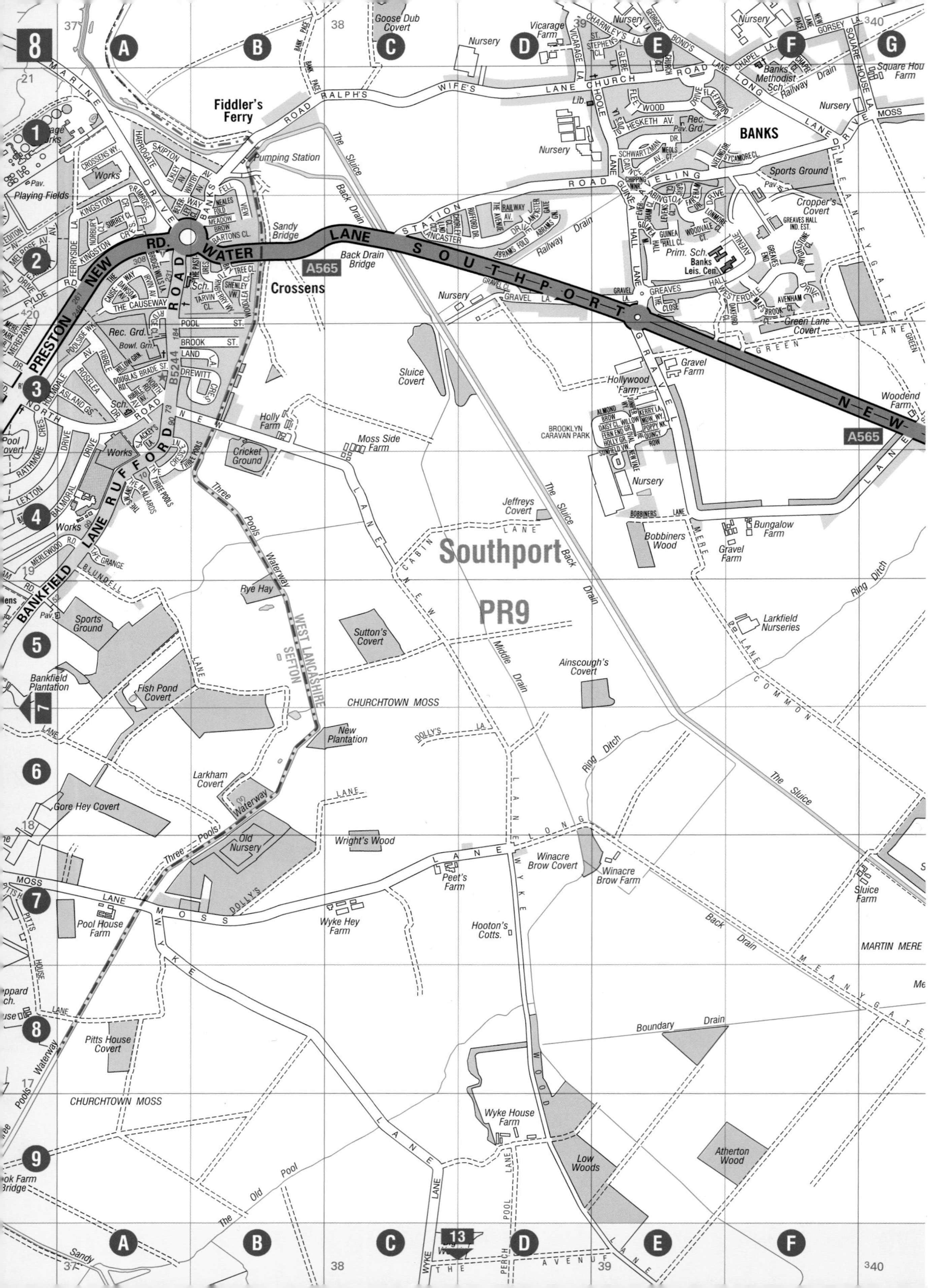
A
B
C
D
E
F
G
1
2
3
4
5
6
7
8
9
37
38
39
340
21
20
19
18
17
Goose Dub Covert
Vicarage Farm
Nursery
Square House Farm
Banks Methodist Sch.
Fiddler's Ferry
MARINE DRIVE
RALPH'S WIFE'S LANE
CHURCH ROAD
Lib.
HOOLE LA.
BANKS
Sports Ground
Pumping Station
The Sluice
Back Drain
Playing Fields
Works
Sandy Bridge
PRESTON NEW RD.
WATER LANE
SOUTHPORT NEW ROAD
A565
Back Drain Bridge
Crossens
Railway Drain
Prim. Sch.
Banks Leis. Cen.
GREAVES HALL IND. EST.
Cropper's Covert
Green Lane Covert
MEANYGATE
GREEN LANE
Rec. Grd.
Bowl. Grn.
B5244
ROAD
POOL ST.
BROOK ST.
Sch.
THE CAUSEWAY
FYLDE RD
NORTH ROAD
RUFFORD ROAD
BANKFIELD LANE
Sluice Covert
Hollywood Farm
Gravel Farm
BROOKLYN CARAVAN PARK
Woodend Farm
Holly Farm
Moss Side Farm
Cricket Ground
Three Pools Waterway
Jeffreys Covert
Nursery
BOBBINERS LANE
Bungalow Farm
Bobbiners Wood
Gravel Farm
Southport
PR9
CABIN LANE
Rye Hay
WEST LANCASHIRE
SEFTON
Sutton's Covert
Larkfield Nurseries
Ring Ditch
Sports Ground
Bankfield Plantation
Fish Pond Covert
Ainscough's Covert
CHURCHTOWN MOSS
COMMON LANE
New Plantation
DOLLY'S LA.
Middle Drain
7
Larkham Covert
Gore Hey Covert
Old Nursery
Wright's Wood
LONG LANE
Winacre Brow Covert
Winacre Brow Farm
Peet's Farm
DOLLY'S MOSS LANE
Pool House Farm
Wyke Hey Farm
Hooton's Cotts.
Sluice Farm
MARTIN MERE
WYKE LANE
Pitts House Covert
Boundary Drain
CHURCHTOWN MOSS
Wyke House Farm
WOOD LANE
Low Woods
Atherton Wood
The Old Pool
WYKE LANE
POOL LANE
13
THE PERCH AVENUE
Sandy

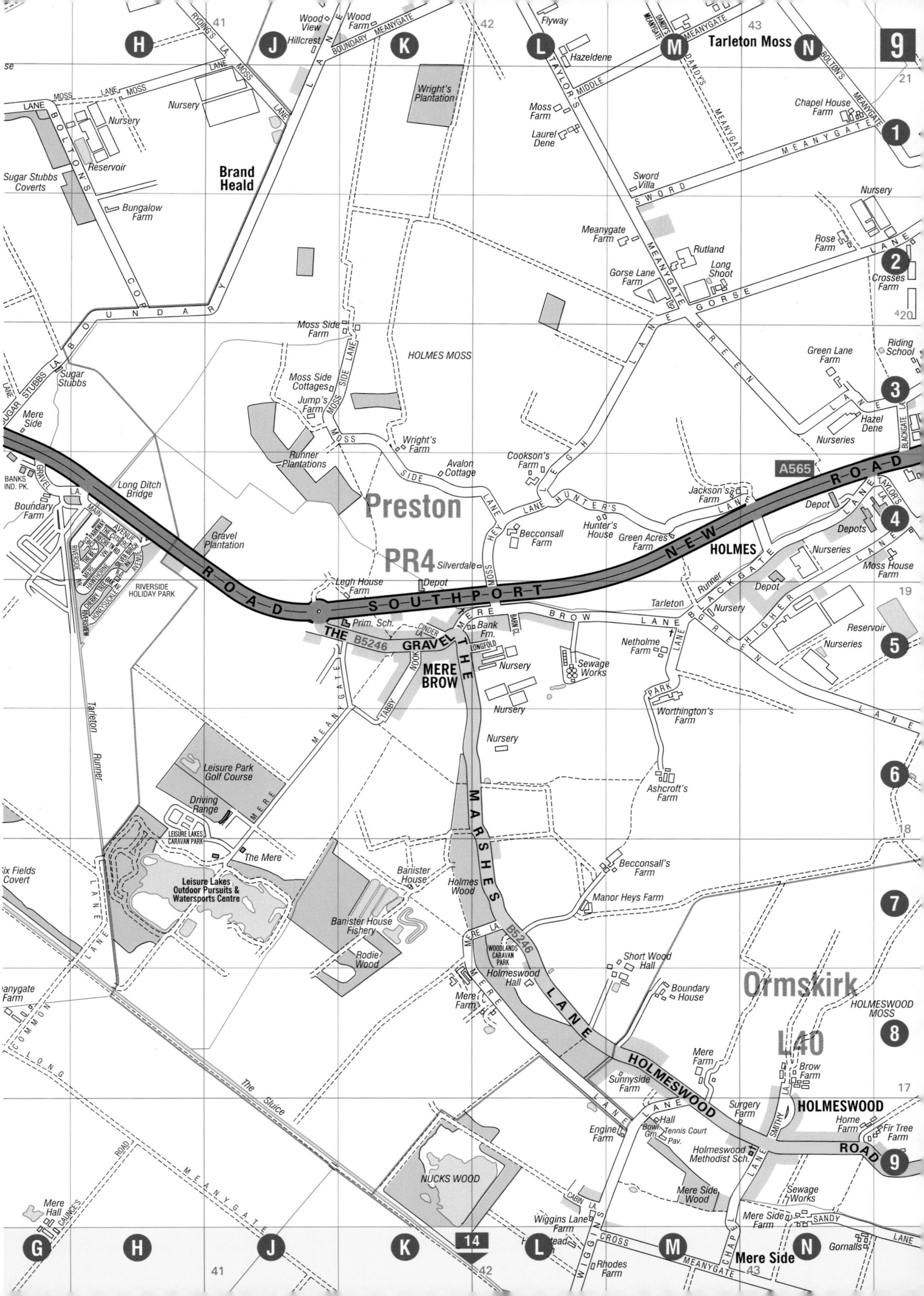
H
J
K
L
M
N
G
41
42
43
21
20
19
18
17
1
2
3
4
5
6
7
8
9
Tarleton Moss
Wood View
Wood Farm
Hillcrest
BOUNDARY MEANYGATE
RYDING'S LA.
Flyway
Hazeldene
DANDY'S MEANYGATE
MEANYGATE
BOLTON'S MEANYGATE
Chapel House Farm
Wright's Plantation
Nursery
Moss Farm
Laurel Dene
Brand Heald
Sugar Stubbs Coverts
Reservoir
Bungalow Farm
Sword Villa
SWORD
Meanygate Farm
Rutland
Long Shoot
Gorse Lane Farm
GORSE
GREEN LANE
Rose Farm
Crosses Farm
Moss Side Farm
HOLMES MOSS
Riding School
Green Lane Farm
Hazel Dene
Nurseries
Sugar Stubbs
Moss Side Cottages
Jump's Farm
MOSS SIDE LANE
Mere Side
Runner Plantations
Wright's Farm
Avalon Cottage
Cookson's Farm
LEIGH
BANKS IND. PK.
Long Ditch Bridge
Boundary Farm
Preston
A565
NEW ROAD
Jackson's Farm
Depot
Depots
HUNTER'S LANE
Hunter's House
Becconsall Farm
Green Acres Farm
HOLMES
Gravel Plantation
PR4
Silverdale
Legh House Farm
RIVERSIDE HOLIDAY PARK
SOUTHPORT ROAD
Tarleton
Runner
BLACKGATE
Nurseries
Moss House Farm
Nursery
Prim. Sch.
Bank Frm.
BROW LANE
Netholme Farm
HIGHER GREEN LANE
Reservoir
THE GRAVEL
B5246
MERE BROW
Nursery
Sewage Works
PARK
Worthington's Farm
MEANYGATE
Tarleton Runner
Nursery
Leisure Park Golf Course
Driving Range
Ashcroft's Farm
MARSHES
THE
LEISURE LAKES CARAVAN PARK
The Mere
Six Fields Covert
Leisure Lakes Outdoor Pursuits & Watersports Centre
Banister House
Holmes Wood
Becconsall's Farm
Manor Heys Farm
Banister House Fishery
Rodie Wood
WOODLANDS CARAVAN PARK
Holmeswood Hall
Short Wood Hall
Boundary House
Ormskirk
HOLMESWOOD MOSS
Meanygate Farm
COMMON LANE
Mere Farm
LANE
L40
Mere Farm
Brow Farm
Sunnyside Farm
HOLMESWOOD
The Sluice
Engine Farm
Hall
Bowl. Grn.
Tennis Court Pav.
Surgery Farm
Home Farm
Fir Tree Farm
HOLMESWOOD ROAD
Holmeswood Methodist Sch.
NUCKS WOOD
Mere Side Wood
Sewage Works
Mere Hall
CAUNCE'S
ROAD
LONG
MEANYGATE
Wiggins Lane Farm
CROSS MEANYGATE
Mere Side Farm
SANDY LANE
Gornalls
Mere Side
Rhodes Farm
CHAPEL LANE
WIGGINS

14

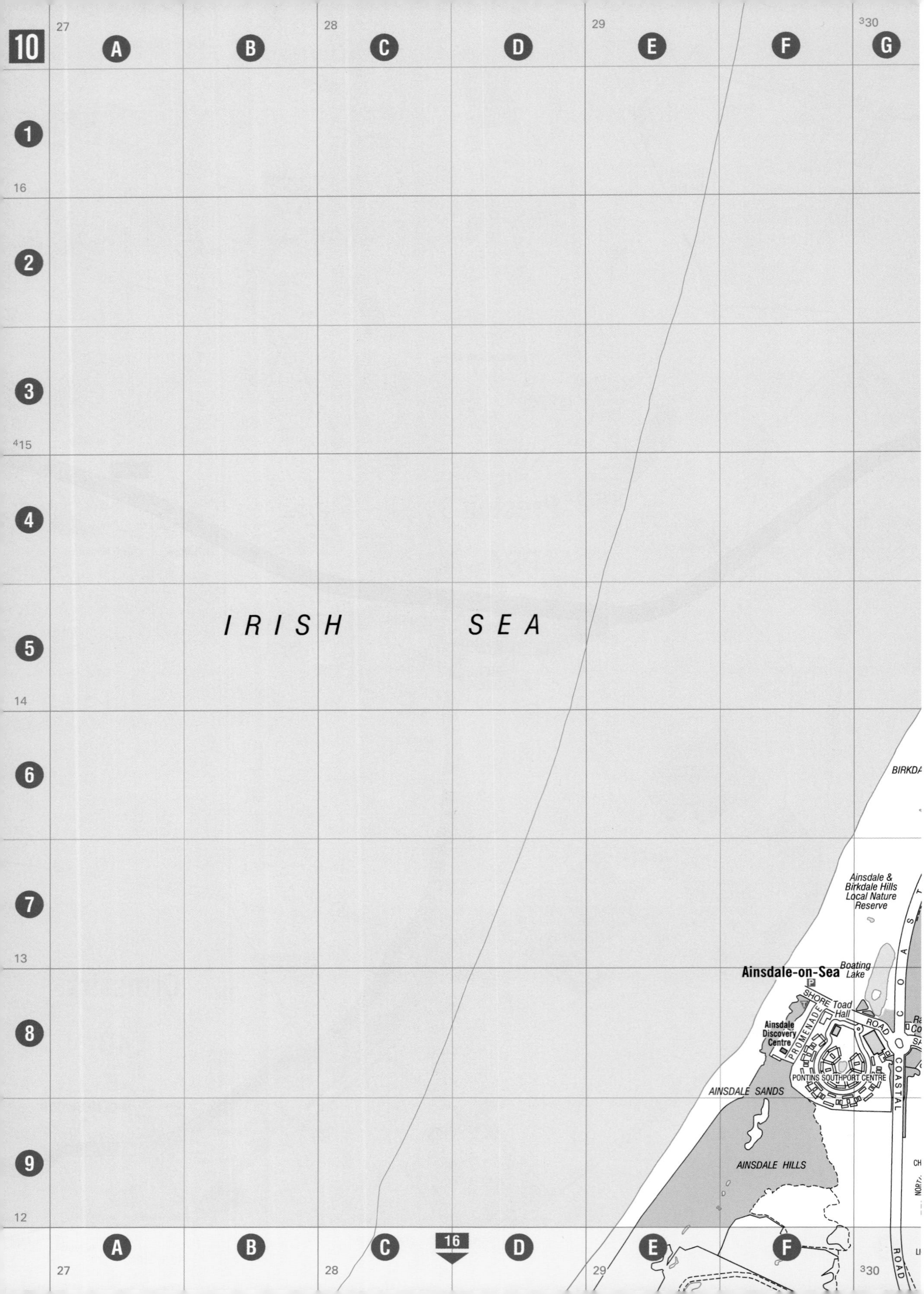
IRISH SEA
Ainsdale & Birkdale Hills Local Nature Reserve
Ainsdale-on-Sea
Boating Lake
SHORE ROAD
Toad Hall
Ainsdale Discovery Centre
PROMENADE
PONTINS SOUTHPORT CENTRE
COASTAL ROAD
AINSDALE SANDS
AINSDALE HILLS

16

Southport
PR8
BIRKDALE SANDS
BIRKDALE HILLS
ROYAL BIRKDALE GOLF COURSE
HILLSIDE GOLF COURSE
SOUTHPORT AND AINSDALE GOLF COURSE
AINSDALE HILLS
AINSDALE
Ainsdale
Birkdale
BIRKDALE
Hillside
COASTAL ROAD
WATERLOO ROAD
LULWORTH ROAD
LIVERPOOL ROAD
AUGHTON ROAD
EVERTON RD.
EASTBOURNE RD.
A565
A5267
B5208
B5243
Camping & Caravan Site
Miniature Railway
Playing Field
Croquet Lawn
Convent
Southport & Birkdale Sports Club
Greenbank High Sch.
Club House
Rugby Football Grd.
Rec. Grd.
Recreation Ground
Birkdale High Sch.
Cemetery
Hawes House
West House
Farnborough Rd. Jun. & Inf. Schs.
Prim. Sch.
Bedford Park
Gorsehill Farm
Anderson's Farm
White Otter Farm
Shoreside Prim. Sch.
SEFTON
WEST LANCASHIRE
HALSALL MOSS
Old Canal
Fine Jane's Brook
Sandy Brook
6
12
17

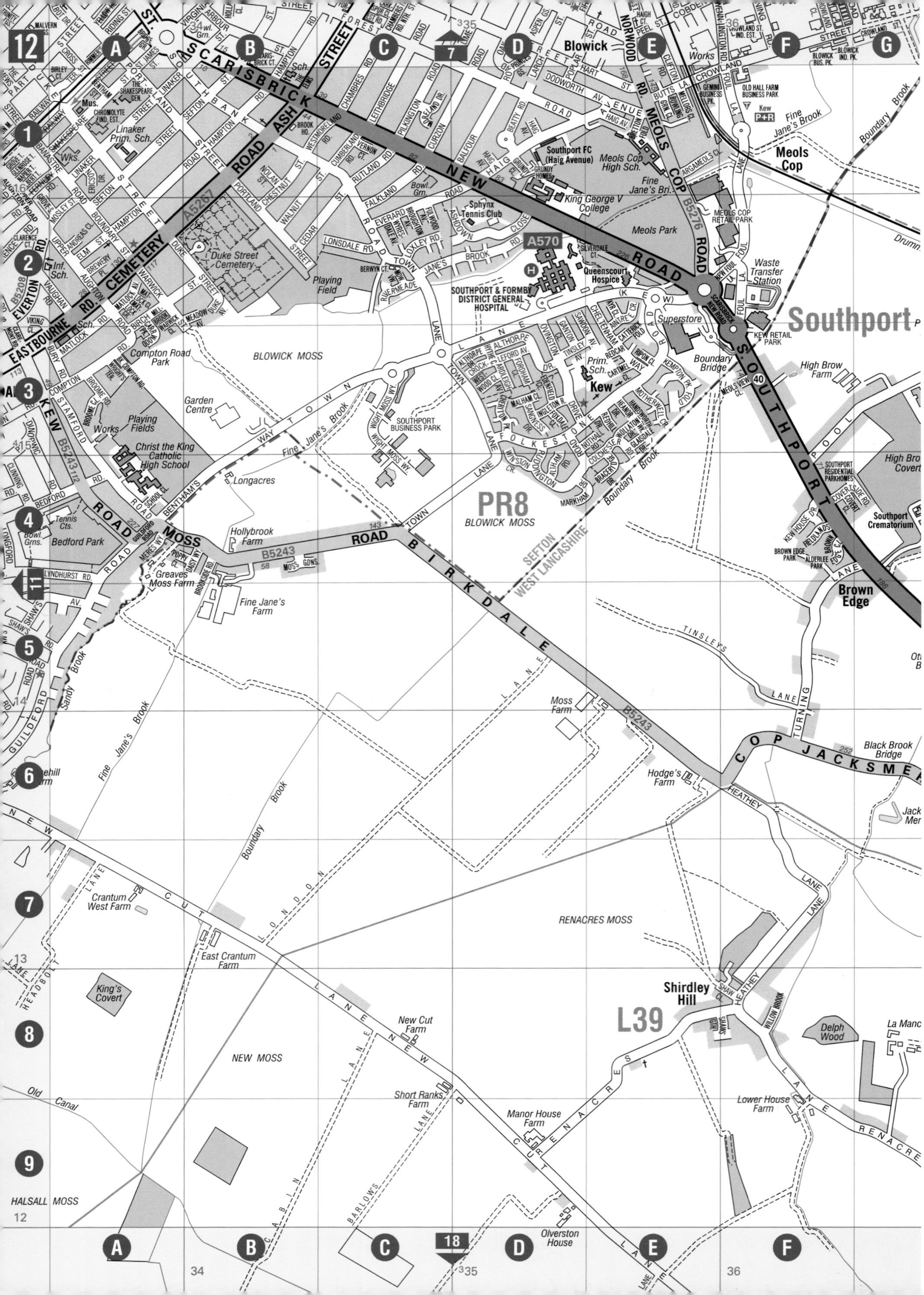

A
B
C
D
E
F
G
1
2
3
4
5
6
7
8
9
7
18
11
34
35
36
Blowick
Works
Mus.
Linaker Prim. Sch.
Wks.
Southport FC (Haig Avenue)
Meols Cop High Sch.
Meols Cop
Fine Jane's Brook
OLD HALL FARM BUSINESS PARK
GEMINI BUSINESS PK.
Kew P+R
King George V College
Sphynx Tennis Club
Bowl. Grn.
MEOLS COP RETAIL PARK
Meols Park
Waste Transfer Station
A570
A5267
B5276
B5208
B5243
Duke Street Cemetery
Playing Field
Queenscourt Hospice
SOUTHPORT & FORMBY DISTRICT GENERAL HOSPITAL
Superstore
Southport
KEW RETAIL PARK
Boundary Bridge
High Brow Farm
Compton Road Park
BLOWICK MOSS
Garden Centre
SOUTHPORT BUSINESS PARK
Prim. Sch.
Kew
Playing Fields
Works
Christ the King Catholic High School
Longacres
PR8
SEFTON
WEST LANCASHIRE
SOUTHPORT RESIDENTIAL PARKHOMES
High Brow Covert
Southport Crematorium
Tennis Cts.
Bowl. Grns.
Bedford Park
Hollybrook Farm
Greaves Moss Farm
Fine Jane's Farm
BROWN EDGE PARK
ALDERLEE PARK
Brown Edge
TINSLEYS LANE
TURNING LANE
Moss Farm
COP JACKSMERE
Black Brook Bridge
Hodge's Farm
HEATHEY LANE
Sandy Brook
Fine Jane's Brook
Boundary Brook
LONDON LANE
NEW CUT LANE
Crantum West Farm
East Crantum Farm
RENACRES MOSS
Shirdley Hill
L39
King's Covert
New Cut Farm
NEW MOSS
Delph Wood
Short Ranks Farm
Manor House Farm
RENACRES LANE
Lower House Farm
Old Canal
HALSALL MOSS
CABIN LANE
BARLOW'S LANE
Olverston House
SCARISBRICK NEW ROAD
ASH STREET
CEMETERY RD.
EASTBOURNE RD.
TOWN LANE
FOLKESTONE ROAD
BIRKDALE ROAD
MOSS ROAD
KEW ROAD
GUILDFORD ROAD
SOUTHPORT ROAD
MEOLS COP ROAD
NORWOOD RD.
CROWLAND ST.

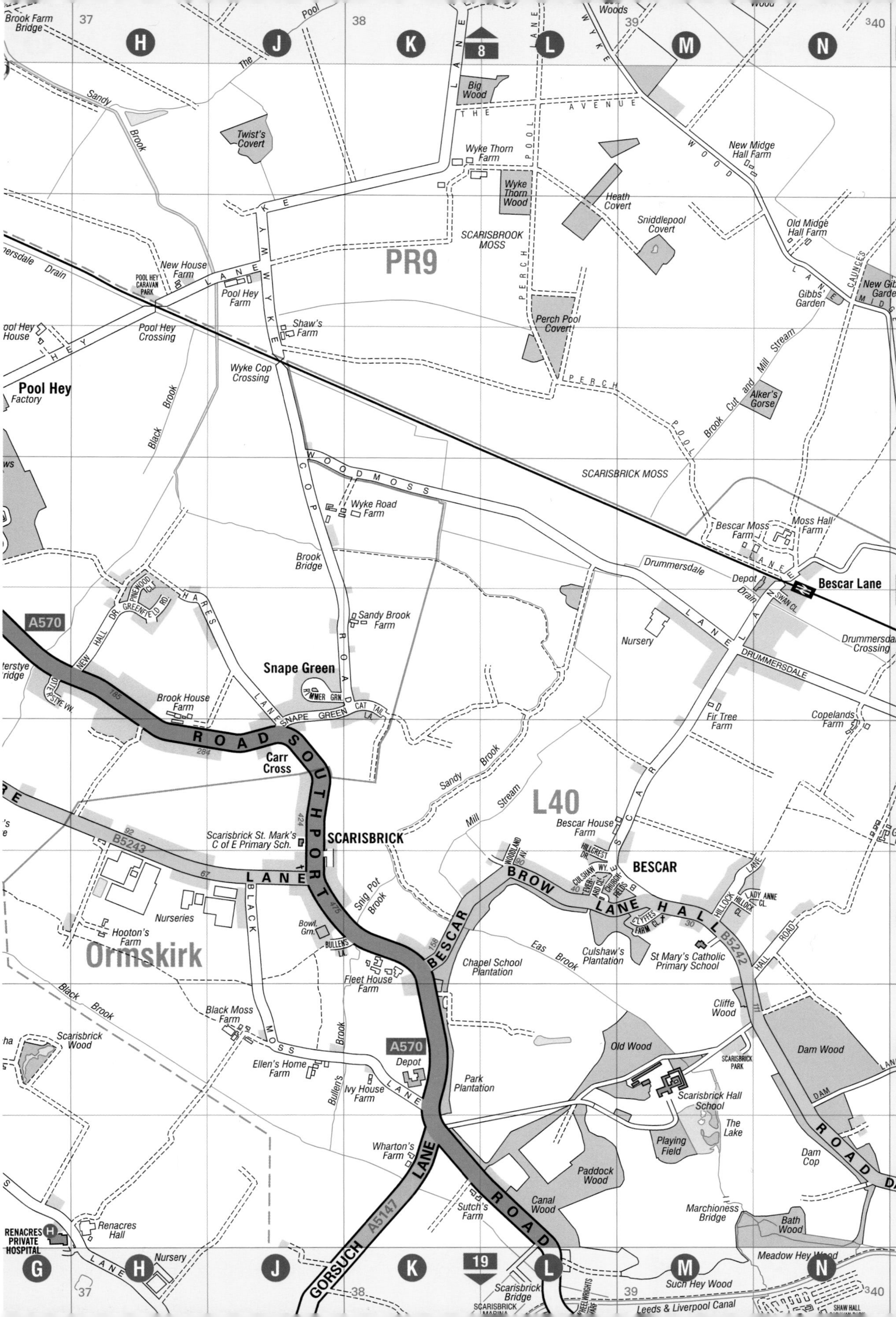

Brook Farm Bridge
Woods
H
J
K
8
L
M
N
The Pool
Big Wood
THE AVENUE
Sandy Brook
Twist's Covert
Wyke Thorn Farm
POOL
Wyke Thorn Wood
Heath Covert
Sniddlepool Covert
New Midge Hall Farm
WOOD
WYKE
LANE
Old Midge Hall Farm
ROAD
SCARISBROOK MOSS
PR9
PERCH
New House Farm
POOL HEY CARAVAN PARK
Pool Hey Farm
Drummersdale Drain
Pool Hey House
HEY
Pool Hey Crossing
Shaw's Farm
Perch Pool Covert
Gibbs' Garden
New Gibbs' Garden
CAUNCE'S
MIDGE
Brook Cut and Mill Stream
Alker's Gorse
Wyke Cop Crossing
Pool Hey
Factory
Black Brook
PERCH POOL
SCARISBRICK MOSS
WOODMOSS
COP
Wyke Road Farm
Bescar Moss Farm
Moss Hall Farm
Brook Bridge
Drummersdale
Depot
Bescar Lane
14
A570
PINEWOOD CL.
GREENFIELD RD.
NEW HALL DR.
HARES
Sandy Brook Farm
Nursery
SWAN CL.
Drummersdale Crossing
DRUMMERSDALE
Snape Green
RIMMER GRN.
Brook House Farm
SNAPE GREEN
CAT TAIL LA.
Fir Tree Farm
Copelands Farm
LANE
ROAD
SOUTHPORT
Carr Cross
Sandy Brook
Mill Stream
L40
SCAR
Bescar House Farm
Gill House Farm
B5243
LANE
Scarisbrick St. Mark's C of E Primary Sch.
SCARISBRICK
WOODLAND AV.
HILLCREST DR.
BESCAR
BROW
LANE
HALL
HILLOCK CL.
LADY ANNE CL.
BLACK
Snig Pot Brook
Nurseries
Hooton's Farm
Ormskirk
Bowl. Grn.
BULLENS LA.
BESCAR
Eas Brook
Chapel School Plantation
Culshaw's Plantation
St Mary's Catholic Primary School
B5242
HALL ROAD
Fleet House Farm
Black Brook
Black Moss Farm
Cliffe Wood
Scarisbrick Wood
MOSS
Brook
A570
Depot
Old Wood
Dam Wood
SCARISBRICK PARK
Ellen's Home Farm
Ivy House Farm
Bullen's
LANE
Park Plantation
Scarisbrick Hall School
DAM
The Lake
Playing Field
ROAD
Dam Cop
Wharton's Farm
LANE
Paddock Wood
A5147
Canal Wood
Sutch's Farm
Marchioness Bridge
Bath Wood
RENACRES PRIVATE HOSPITAL
Renacres Hall
GORSUCH
ROAD
G
H
Nursery
LANE
J
K
19
L
M
N
Meadow Hey Wood
Such Hey Wood
Scarisbrick Bridge
Leeds & Liverpool Canal
37
38
39
340
16
15
14
13
12
1
2
3
4
5
6
7
8
9

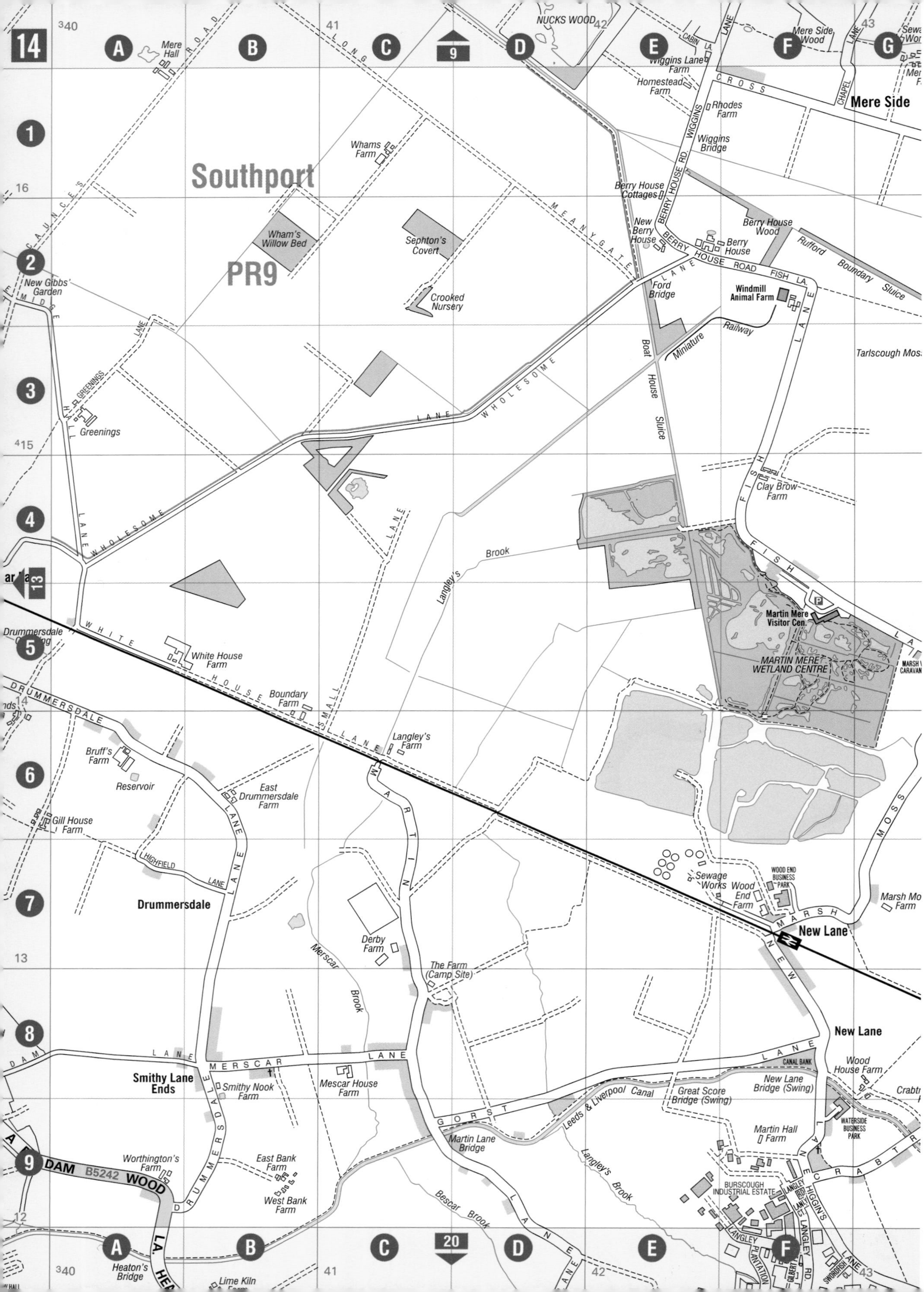

340
41
42
43
A
B
C
D
E
F
G
9
20
13
1
2
3
4
5
6
7
8
9
16
415
14
13
12
Mere Hall
NUCKS WOOD
Mere Side Wood
Mere Side
Wiggins Lane Farm
Homestead Farm
Rhodes Farm
Wiggins Bridge
CROSS
CHAPEL
CABIN LA.
LANE
WIGGINS
LONG
Southport
PR9
Whams Farm
Wham's Willow Bed
Sephton's Covert
Crooked Nursery
MEANYGATE
Berry House Cottages
BERRY HOUSE RD.
New Berry House
Berry House
Berry House Wood
BERRY HOUSE ROAD
FISH LA.
Rufford Boundary Sluice
Ford Bridge
Windmill Animal Farm
Miniature Railway
Boat House Sluice
Tarlscough Moss
New Gibbs' Garden
MIDGE
GREENINGS
HALL
Greenings
WHOLESOME LANE
CAUNCES
Clay Brow Farm
FISH LANE
Langley's Brook
Martin Mere Visitor Cen.
MARTIN MERE WETLAND CENTRE
MARSH CARAVAN
Drummersdale
WHITE HOUSE
White House Farm
Boundary Farm
SMALL LANE
Langley's Farm
DRUMMERSDALE
Bruff's Farm
Reservoir
East Drummersdale Farm
Gill House Farm
HIGHFIELD LANE
Drummersdale
MARTIN
Sewage Works
Wood End Farm
WOOD END BUSINESS PARK
MARSH
MOSS
Marsh Moss Farm
New Lane
NEW
Derby Farm
Mescar Brook
The Farm (Camp Site)
New Lane
DAM
LANE
MERSCAR LANE
Smithy Lane Ends
Smithy Nook Farm
Mescar House Farm
CANAL BANK
Wood House Farm
New Lane Bridge (Swing)
Great Score Bridge (Swing)
Leeds & Liverpool Canal
GORST
Martin Lane Bridge
Martin Hall Farm
WATERSIDE BUSINESS PARK
Crabtr
CRABTREE
Worthington's Farm
East Bank Farm
West Bank Farm
DAM WOOD
B5242
DRUMMERSDALE
Bescar Brook
Langley's Brook
BURSCOUGH INDUSTRIAL ESTATE
LANGLEY RD.
HIGGIN'S LANE
LANGLEY
PLANTATION
GILBERT
SWORDISH
Heaton's Bridge
Lime Kiln Farm
LA.

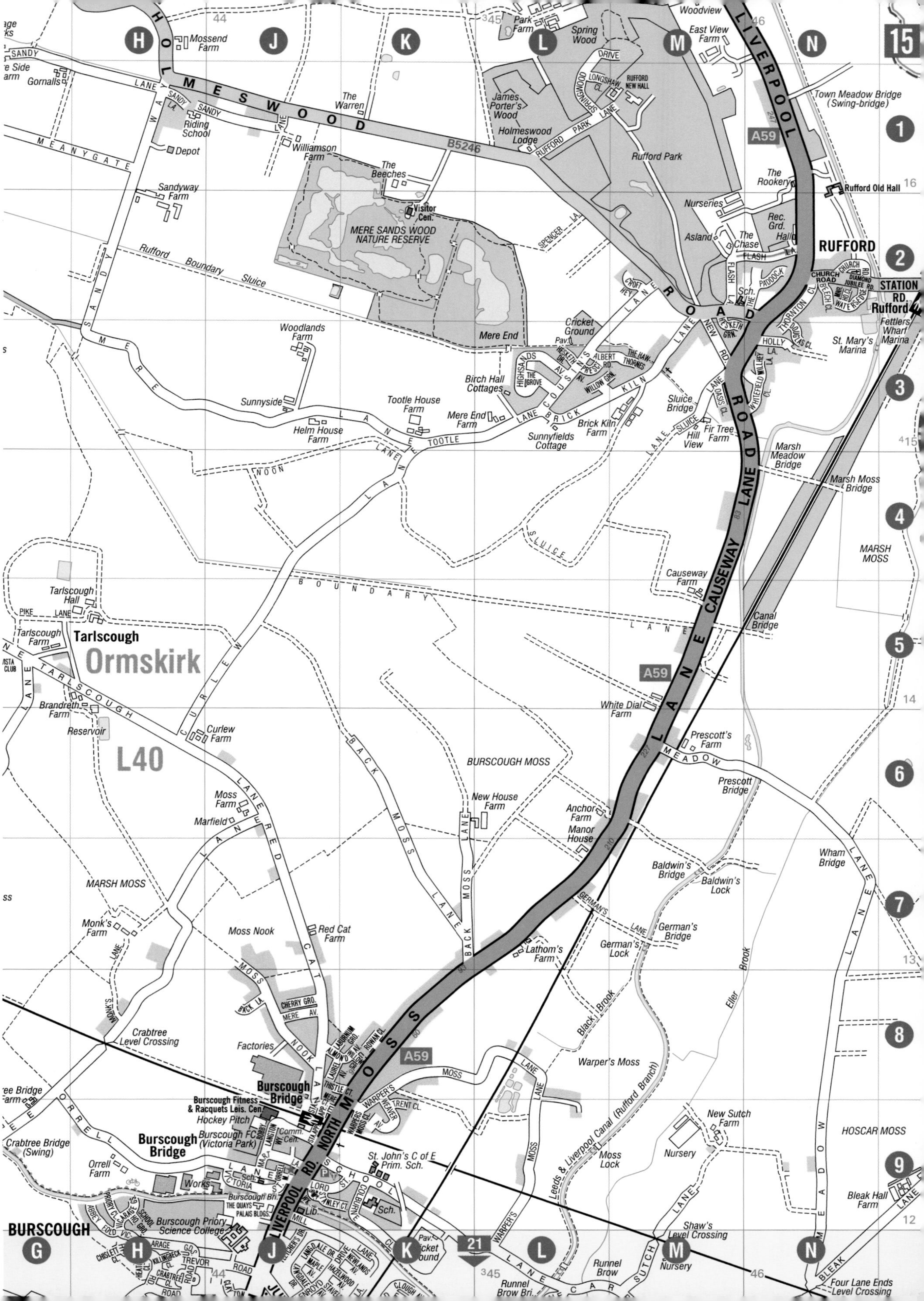
HOLMESWOOD
LIVERPOOL ROAD
B5246
A59
Mossend Farm
Park Farm
Spring Wood
East View Farm
Woodview
Gornalls
Sandy Lane
The Warren
James Porter's Wood
Rufford New Hall
Longshaw Cl.
Springwood Drive
Holmeswood Lodge
Rufford Park Lane
Rufford Park
Town Meadow Bridge (Swing-bridge)
Riding School
Depot
Williamson Farm
The Beeches
Meanygate
Sandyway Farm
Visitor Cen.
MERE SANDS WOOD NATURE RESERVE
The Rookery
Rufford Old Hall
Nurseries
Rec. Grd.
Hall
Asland
The Chase
Flash La.
RUFFORD
Rufford Boundary Sluice
Spencer La.
Sandy Lane
Woodlands Farm
Mere End
Cricket Ground
Pav.
Sch.
Church Road
Diamond Jubilee Rd.
Station Rd.
Rufford
Fettlers Wharf Marina
St. Mary's Marina
Holly La.
Thornton Cl.
Douglas Cl.
Hesketh Grn.
New Rd.
Croft Hey
Highsands
The Grove
Hesketh Dr.
Albert Rd.
The Hawthornes
Willow Grn.
Birch Hall Cottages
Mere Lane
Sunnyside
Tootle House Farm
Mere End Farm
Brick Kiln Lane
Brick Kiln Farm
Sunnyfields Cottage
Helm House Farm
Tootle Lane
Noon Lane
Sluice Bridge
Sluice Lane
Hill View
Fir Tree Farm
Oasis Cl.
Whitefield Cl.
Marsh Meadow Bridge
Marsh Moss Bridge
CAUSEWAY LANE
MARSH MOSS
Sluice
Causeway Farm
Boundary
Canal Bridge
Tarlscough Hall
Pike Lane
Tarlscough Farm
Tarlscough
Ormskirk
Vista Club
Tarlscough Lane
Brandreth Farm
Reservoir
L40
Curlew Lane
Curlew Farm
Back Moss Lane
BURSCOUGH MOSS
White Dial Farm
Prescott's Farm
Meadow Lane
Prescott Bridge
New House Farm
Moss Lane
Anchor Farm
Manor House
Moss Farm
Marfield
Red Cat Lane
Wham Bridge
Wham Lane
Baldwin's Bridge
Baldwin's Lock
MARSH MOSS
German's Lane
German's Bridge
German's Lock
Monk's Farm
Red Cat Farm
Moss Nook
Lathom's Farm
Eller Brook
Black Brook
Cherry Gro.
Mere Av.
Back La.
Monk's Lane
Crabtree Level Crossing
Factories
Moss Nook Lane
NORTH MOSS
Warper's Moss
Leeds & Liverpool Canal (Rufford Branch)
Burscough Bridge
Burscough Fitness & Racquets Leis. Cen.
Hockey Pitch
Burscough FC (Victoria Park)
Comm. Cen.
Warper's Moss Cl.
Trent Cl.
Crabtree Bridge (Swing)
Orrell Lane
Orrell Farm
Works
Victoria
Burscough Br.
The Quays
Palais Bldgs.
St. John's C of E Prim. Sch.
School Lane
Lib.
Sch.
New Sutch Farm
Nursery
Moss Lock
HOSCAR MOSS
Bleak Hall Farm
Shaw's Level Crossing
Burscough Priory Science College
BURSCOUGH
Trevor Road
Pav.
Cricket Ground
21
Warper's Lane
Car Sutch Lane
Runnel Brow
Runnel Brow Bri.
Nursery
Meadow Lane
Bleak Lane
Four Lane Ends Level Crossing
Liverpool Rd. North
G H J K L M N
1 2 3 4 5 6 7 8 9
44 345 46
16 415 14 13 12

IRISH SEA
MAD WHARF
MAD WHARF
AINSDALE SANDS
AINSDALE HILLS
AINSDALE SAND DUNES
NATIONAL NATURE RESERVE
West End Lodge
West End Plantation
COASTAL
FORMBY HILLS
Massam's Slack
Long Slack
AINSDALE SAND DUNES
NATIONAL NATURE RESERVE
WOODVALE AIRFIELD
Liverpool
L37
Cloven-le-Dale
Golf Cottage
Massam's Slack
FORMBY HILLS
FISHERMAN'S PATH
WOODLAND
Dale Slack Gutter
Riding Sch.
Wham Dyke
Freshfield Dune Heath
FORMBY GOLF COURSE
FORMBY HILLS
Freshfield
Club House
Freshfield
FRESHFIELD CARAVAN PARK
FORMBY NATURE RESERVE
Clarence High Sch.
Playing Field
BREWERY LA.
SIXTEEN ACRE
ST. ANNE'S RD.
STANLEY RD.
MASSAM'S LANE
ROAD
VICTORIA ROAD
SHIREBURN
HARINGTON
Cricket Grd.
Pavs.
RYEGROUND
CHURCH
PIERCEFIELD ROAD
DERBY RD.
OLD TOWN LANE
ST. GEORGE'S RD.
Formby High Sch.
Oakfield Unit
Formby Coll.
GRABURN
OLD MILL LA.
CABLE
FORMBY HILLS
Sandfield Farm
BLUNDELL AVENUE
DUNES AVENUE
LARKHILL LANE
WICKS
GREEN
WARREN
HOLMWOOD
COLLEGE AVENUE
FRESHFIELD ROAD
HALSALL LANE
LONSDALE
Formby Little Theatre
THE GALLERIES
THE CLOISTERS
FURNESS AV.
SCHOOL AV.
Lark Cotts.
Lark Hill
Nursing Home
HOLMWOOD CL.
B5424
Dobbs
Bowl. Grns.
St. Peters
CHURCH RD.
WHITEHOUSE
KENYONS
10
24
27
28
29
330
12
11
410
09
08
A
B
C
D
E
F
G
1
2
3
4
5
6
7
8
9

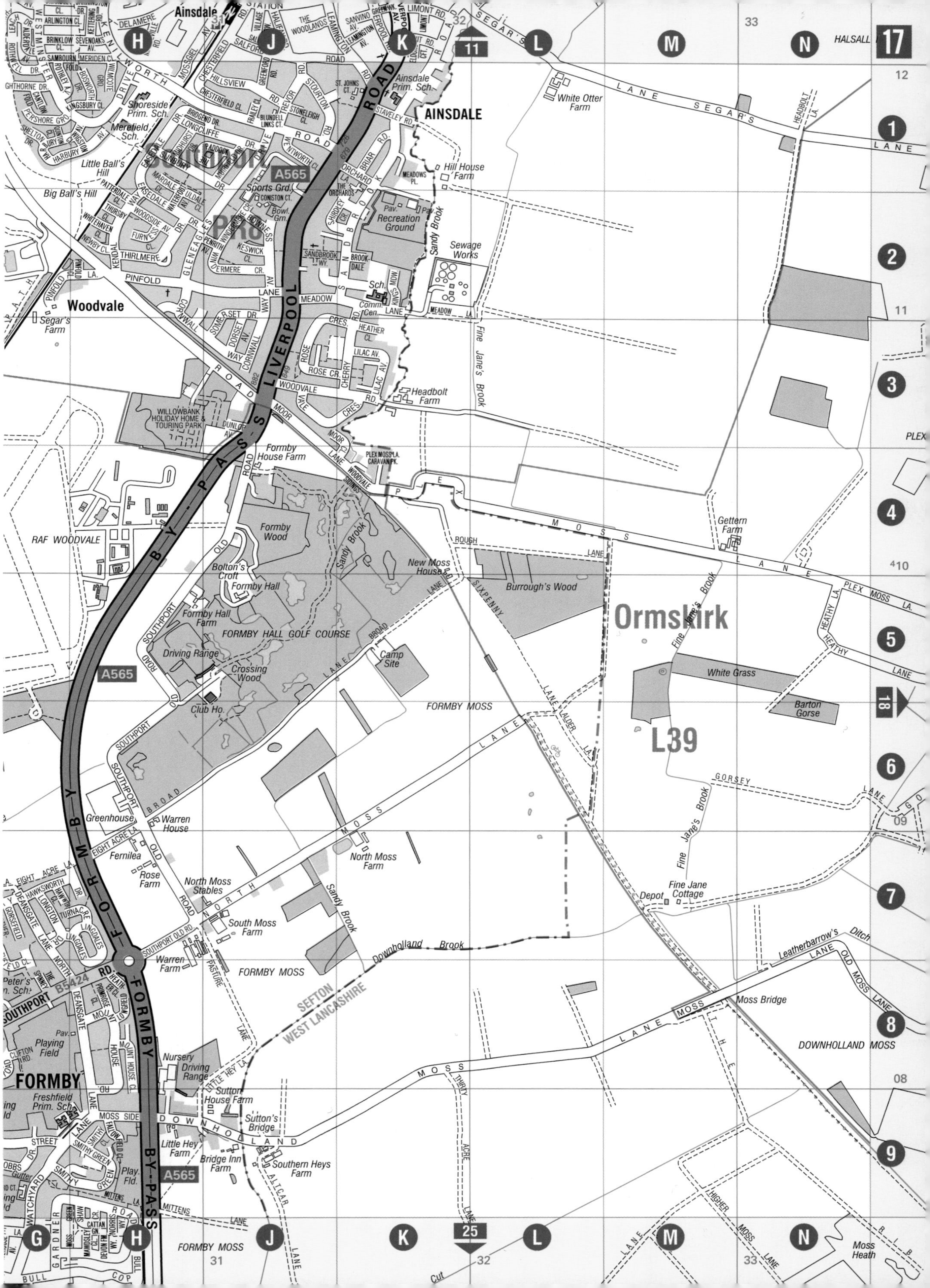

H
J
K
L
M
N
G
11
25
18
1
2
3
4
5
6
7
8
9
12
11
410
09
08
31
32
33
HALSALL
PLEX
Ainsdale
AINSDALE
Ainsdale Prim. Sch.
Shoreside Prim. Sch.
Merefield Sch.
Little Ball's Hill
Big Ball's Hill
Southport
PR8
Woodvale
Segar's Farm
Sports Grd.
Bowl. Grn.
Pav.
Recreation Ground
Sewage Works
Hill House Farm
White Otter Farm
Headbolt Farm
Sch.
Comm. Cen.
A565
LIVERPOOL ROAD
FORMBY BY-PASS
WILLOWBANK HOLIDAY HOME & TOURING PARK
PLEX MOSS LA. CARAVAN PK.
Formby House Farm
RAF WOODVALE
Formby Wood
Bolton's Croft
Formby Hall
Formby Hall Farm
FORMBY HALL GOLF COURSE
Driving Range
Crossing Wood
Club Ho.
Camp Site
New Moss House
Burrough's Wood
Ormskirk
Gettern Farm
White Grass
Barton Gorse
L39
FORMBY MOSS
Sandy Brook
Fine Jane's Brook
Greenhouse
Warren House
Fernilea
Rose Farm
North Moss Stables
North Moss Farm
South Moss Farm
Warren Farm
Downholland Brook
SEFTON
WEST LANCASHIRE
Fine Jane Cottage
Depot
Leatherbarrow's Ditch
Moss Bridge
DOWNHOLLAND MOSS
FORMBY
Playing Field
Freshfield Prim. Sch.
Nursery Driving Range
Sutton House Farm
Sutton's Bridge
Little Hey Farm
Bridge Inn Farm
Southern Heys Farm
Play. Fld.
B5424
Moss Heath
Cut
SEGAR'S LANE
PLEX MOSS LANE
HEATHY LANE
GORSEY LANE
BROAD LANE
NORTH MOSS LANE
MOSS LANE
DOWNHOLLAND
SOUTHPORT OLD RD.
OLD MOSS LANE
HIGHER MOSS LANE
MOOR LANE
WOODVALE RD.
MEADOW LANE
PINFOLD LA.

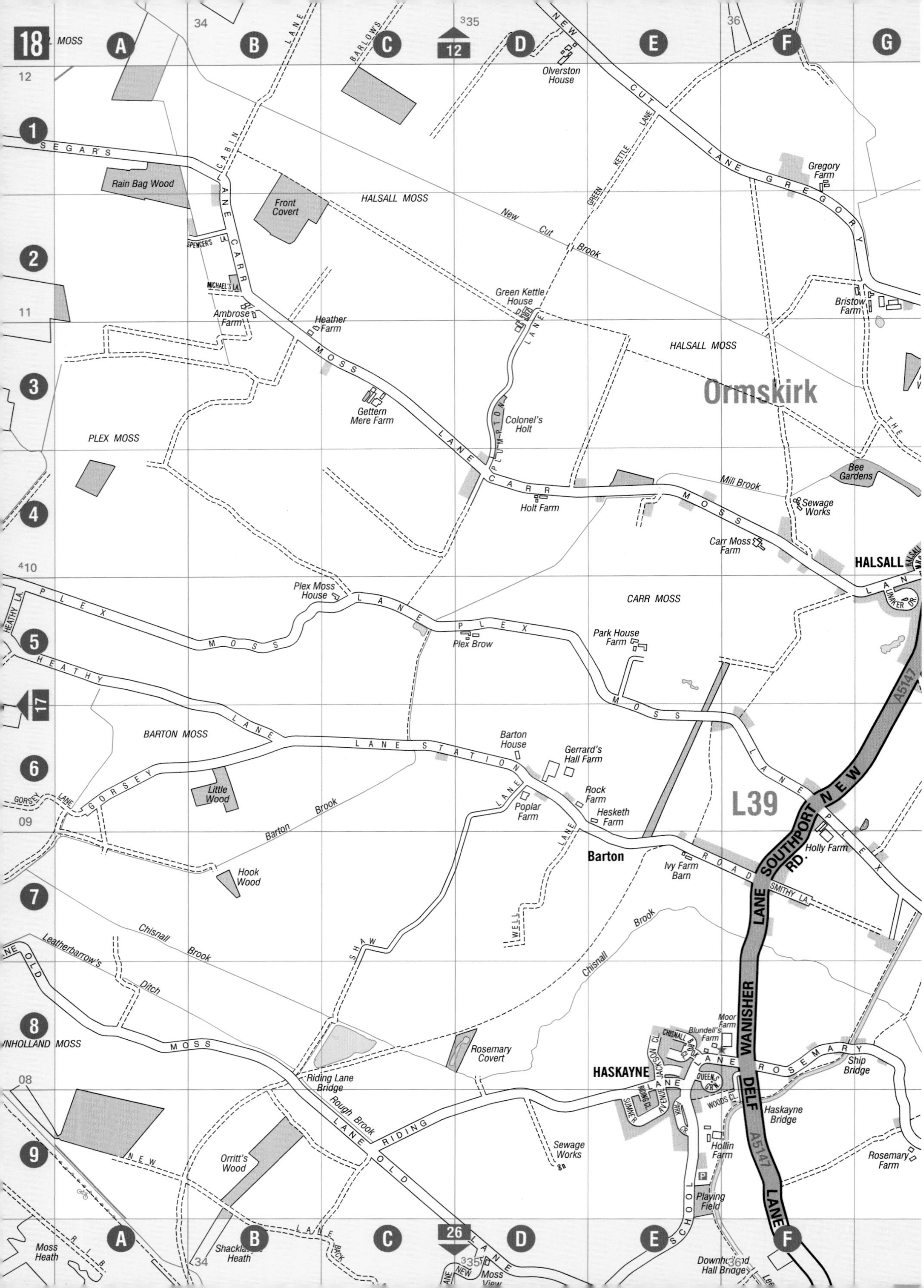
Ormskirk
L39
HALSALL
Barton
HASKAYNE
HALSALL MOSS
PLEX MOSS
CARR MOSS
BARTON MOSS
NHOLLAND MOSS
L MOSS
Rain Bag Wood
Front Covert
Olverston House
Gregory Farm
Bristow Farm
Green Kettle House
Ambrose Farm
Heather Farm
Gettern Mere Farm
Colonel's Holt
Holt Farm
Bee Gardens
Sewage Works
Carr Moss Farm
Plex Moss House
Plex Brow
Park House Farm
Barton House
Gerrard's Hall Farm
Rock Farm
Hesketh Farm
Poplar Farm
Little Wood
Hook Wood
Ivy Farm Barn
Holly Farm
Rosemary Covert
Riding Lane Bridge
Moor Farm
Blundell's Farm
Ship Bridge
Haskayne Bridge
Hollin Farm
Rosemary Farm
Sewage Works
Orritt's Wood
Playing Field
Shacklady's Heath
Moss Heath
Downholland Hall Bridge
Moss View
SEGAR'S LANE
CABIN LANE
CARR LANE
SPENCER'S LA.
MICHAEL'S LA.
MOSS LANE
CARR MOSS
NEW CUT LANE
GREGORY LANE
GREEN KETTLE LANE
PLUMPTON LANE
BARLOWS LANE
New Cut Brook
Mill Brook
PLEX MOSS LANE
HEATHY LA.
HEATHY LANE
MOSS LANE
LINAKER DR.
STATION LANE
GORSEY LANE
Barton Brook
WELL LANE
SHAW LANE
ROAD
SOUTHPORT NEW RD.
PLEX LANE
SMITHY LA.
A5147
Chisnall Brook
Leatherbarrow's Ditch
OLD MOSS LANE
Rough Brook
RIDING LANE
OLD LANE
NEW LANE
BACK LANE
RIB
WANISHER LANE
DELF LANE
ROSEMARY LANE
CHISNALL AVENUE
JACKSON CL.
QUEEN'S DR.
RIDING CL.
SUMNER
PARK CR.
WOODS CL.
SCHOOL LANE
12
26
17
A
B
C
D
E
F
G
1
2
3
4
5
6
7
8
9
34
335
36
12
11
410
09
08

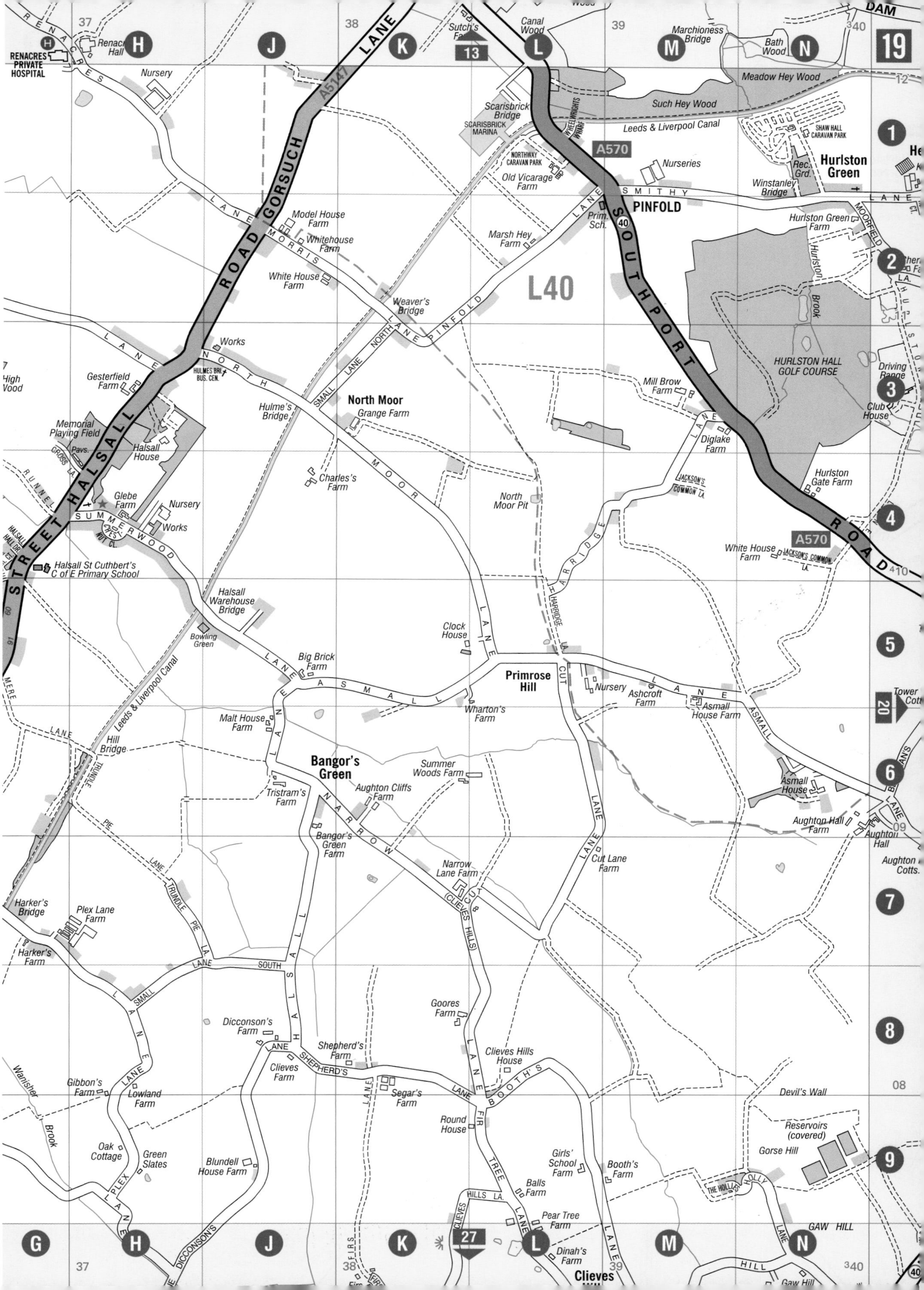
RENACRES PRIVATE HOSPITAL
Renacres Hall
Nursery
GORSUCH LANE
A5147
Sutch's Fm
13
Canal Wood
Marchioness Bridge
Bath Wood
DAM
Meadow Hey Wood
Such Hey Wood
Scarisbrick Bridge
SCARISBRICK MARINA
WHEELWRIGHTS WHARF
Leeds & Liverpool Canal
A570
SHAW HALL CARAVAN PARK
NORTHWAY CARAVAN PARK
Nurseries
Old Vicarage Farm
Hurlston Green
Rec. Grd.
Winstanley Bridge
SMITHY LANE
PINFOLD
Prim. Sch.
Model House Farm
Whitehouse Farm
MORRIS LANE
Marsh Hey Farm
Hurlston Green Farm
MOORFIELD
Hurlston Brook
White House Farm
L40
Weaver's Bridge
NORTH LANE
PINFOLD
Works
HULMES BRI. BUS. CEN.
NORTH MOOR LANE
SMALL LANE
Gesterfield Farm
High Wood
HURLSTON HALL GOLF COURSE
Driving Range
Club House
Mill Brow Farm
North Moor
Grange Farm
Hulme's Bridge
Memorial Playing Field
Pavs.
CROSS LA.
Halsall House
Diglake Farm
Charles's Farm
JACKSON'S COMMON LA.
Hurlston Gate Farm
RUNNEL
HALSALL
STREET
Glebe Farm
Nursery
SUMMERWOOD
Works
CHESNUT CL.
North Moor Pit
HALSALL HALL DR.
Halsall St Cuthbert's C of E Primary School
HARRIDGE LA.
White House Farm
A570
SOUTHPORT ROAD
Halsall Warehouse Bridge
Clock House
Bowling Green
Big Brick Farm
ASMALL LANE
Primrose Hill
CUT
Nursery
Ashcroft Farm
Asmall House Farm
Tower Cott.
20
MERE
Malt House Farm
Wharton's Farm
LANE
Hill Bridge
Leeds & Liverpool Canal
TRUNDLE
Bangor's Green
Summer Woods Farm
Tristram's Farm
Aughton Cliffs Farm
Asmall House
Aughton Hall Farm
Aughton Hall
Aughton Cotts.
PIE LANE
Bangor's Green Farm
NARROW
Narrow Lane Farm
Cut Lane Farm
CUT LANE
TRUNDLE PIE LA.
(CLIEVES HILLS)
Harker's Bridge
Plex Lane Farm
Harker's Farm
HALSALL
SOUTH LANE
SMALL LANE
Goores Farm
Dicconson's Farm
Shepherd's Farm
Clieves Hills House
SHEPHERD'S LANE
Clieves Farm
Segar's Farm
Wanisher Brook
Gibbon's Farm
Lowland Farm
BOOTH'S
Devil's Wall
Round House
FIR TREE LANE
Reservoirs (covered)
Oak Cottage
Green Slates
Gorse Hill
Girls' School Farm
Booth's Farm
Blundell House Farm
Balls Farm
HILLS LA.
CLIEVES
THE HOLLIES
HOLLY
PLEX LANE
Pear Tree Farm
GAW HILL LANE
27
DICCONSON'S
FIRS
Dinah's Farm
Clieves
HILL
Gaw Hill
G H J K L M N
1 2 3 4 5 6 7 8 9
37 38 39 340
12 410 09 08

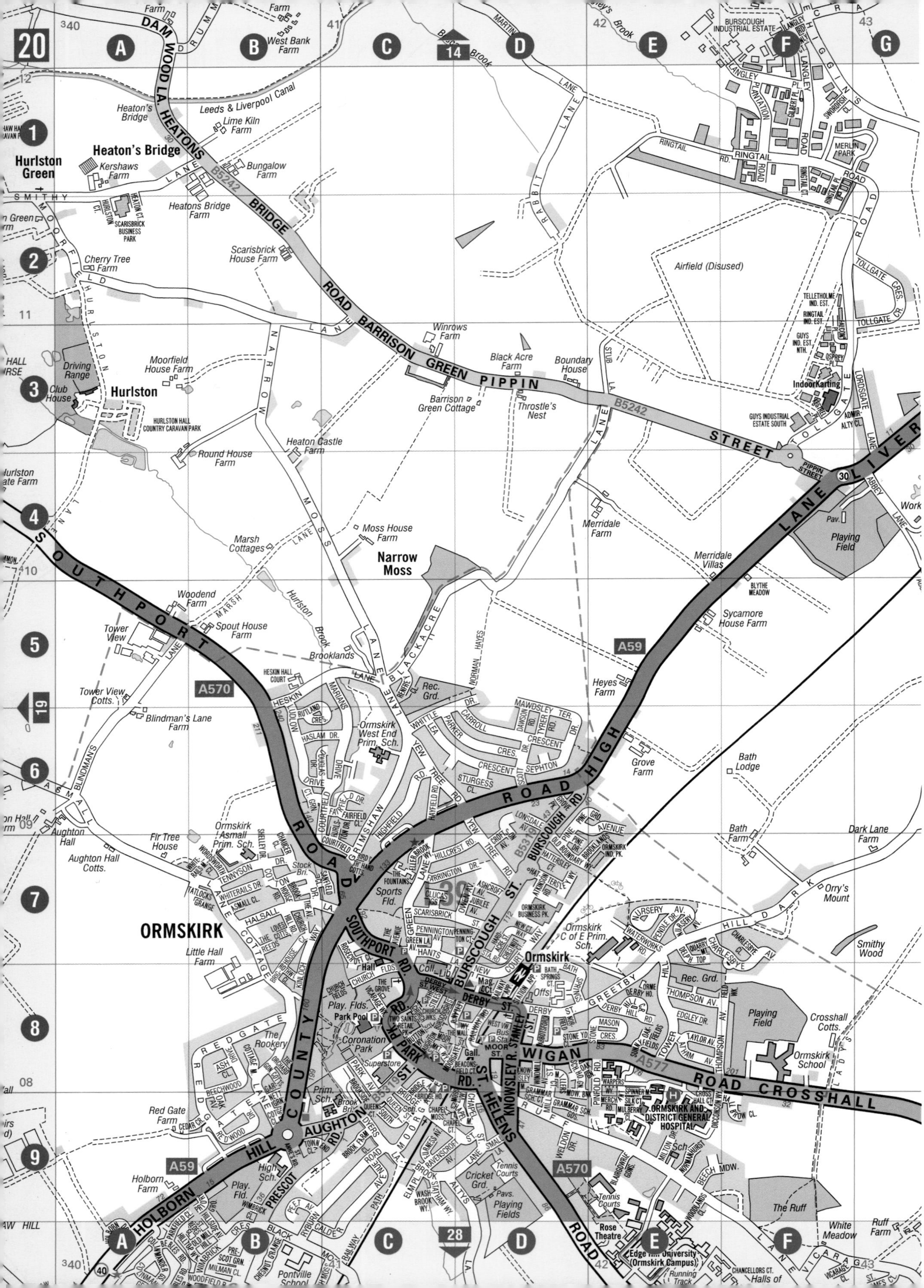

14
28
19
Heaton's Bridge
Hurlston Green
Hurlston
Narrow Moss
ORMSKIRK
Ormskirk
DAM WOOD LA.
HEATONS BRIDGE ROAD
BARRISON GREEN
PIPPIN STREET
B5242
Leeds & Liverpool Canal
West Bank Farm
Lime Kiln Farm
Kershaws Farm
Bungalow Farm
Heatons Bridge Farm
SCARISBRICK BUSINESS PARK
Cherry Tree Farm
Scarisbrick House Farm
Winrows Farm
Black Acre Farm
Boundary House
Barrison Green Cottage
Throstle's Nest
Moorfield House Farm
Driving Range
Club House
HURLSTON HALL COUNTRY CARAVAN PARK
Round House Farm
Heaton Castle Farm
Marsh Cottages
Moss House Farm
Merridale Farm
Merridale Villas
BLYTHE MEADOW
Sycamore House Farm
Woodend Farm
Spout House Farm
Tower View
Brooklands
Hurlston Brook
Tower View Cotts.
Blindman's Lane Farm
Heyes Farm
Grove Farm
Bath Lodge
Bath Farm
Dark Lane Farm
Orry's Mount
Smithy Wood
Crosshall Cotts.
Ormskirk School
Airfield (Disused)
BURSCOUGH INDUSTRIAL ESTATE
RINGTAIL RD.
MERLIN PARK
TOLLGATE CRES.
TOLLGATE CR.
Indoor Karting
GUYS INDUSTRIAL ESTATE SOUTH
PIPPIN STREET
Playing Field
Pav.
Work
A59
A570
A577
B5319
SOUTHPORT ROAD
LIVERPOOL LANE
HIGH LANE
ROAD
COUNTY ROAD
WIGAN ROAD
CROSSHALL
ST. HELENS ROAD
HOLBORN HILL
AUGHTON ST.
PRESCOT RD.
MOSS LANE
NARROW MOSS LANE
BLACKACRE LANE
NORMAN HAYES
HESKIN LANE
Ormskirk West End Prim. Sch.
Rec. Grd.
Ormskirk Asmall Prim. Sch.
Fir Tree House
Aughton Hall
Aughton Hall Cotts.
Little Hall Farm
The Rookery
Red Gate Farm
Holborn Farm
High Sch.
Play. Fld.
Coronation Park
Park Pool
Play. Flds.
Superstore
Prim. Sch.
Sports Fld.
Ormskirk C of E Prim. Sch.
Rec. Grd.
Playing Field
ORMSKIRK AND DISTRICT GENERAL HOSPITAL
Cricket Grd.
Tennis Courts
Playing Fields
Pavs.
Rose Theatre
Edge Hill University (Ormskirk Campus)
Running Track
Pontville School
The Ruff
White Meadow
Ruff Farm
Halls of

BURSCOUGH
Burscough Junction
Burscough Priory Science College
Richmond Park
Prim. Sch.
Pav. Cricket Ground
Runnel Brow
Runnel Brow Bri.
Brook Bridge
Shaw's Level Crossing
Nursery
Four Lane Ends Level Crossing
Bleak Hall Farm
Henry's Farm
Hoscar Hall Farm
Top Locks
Junction Bri.
Depot
Glovers Bridge (Swing)
Carr Lane Farm
Leeds & Liverpool Canal
Glovers Bridge
Briars Mill
Briars Hall Farm
Ring o' Bells
Pear Tree House
The Cottage
Moss Bridge
Duttons Farm
Taylor's Farm
Lowry Hill
Round Thorn Farm
St. John's Catholic Prim. Sch.
Platts Lane Lake
Burscough Hall Farm
L40
Wood Yard
Mill Dam Farm
Abbey Brook
Warm Row Farm
Speakman's Farm
Blythe Farm
Watkinson's Farm
Lower Park Farm
Ashfield House
LATHOM
Preston Lodges
Blythe Hall
Abbey Farm
Remains of Burscough Priory
ABBEY FARM CARAVAN PARK
Monastery Nurseries
Blythe Cottage
Hobb's Cross
Jump's Farm
Ayscoughs Farm
Bullen's Wood
Alice's Plantation
Blythe Ho.
Ormskirk
Abbey Bridge
Needless Inn Farm
Ormskirk Lathom Park C of E Prim. Sch.
Nelson's Cottages
THE ALMONRY
Beechlawn
Ellerbrook
Yew Trees Farm
Mains Wood
Gobbins Cottage
Robinsons Farm
Roscobel
Lathom Gardens
Lathom Park
LATHOM HOUSE
Sandiholme
Beech Trees
Club House
Jack Leg
Cranes Cotts.
Cranes Hall Farm
Cranes Hall
Home Farm
Black Plantation
Leas Farm
Lady's Walk Wood
Castlewood
ORMSKIRK GOLF COURSE
Coppy Wood
New Park Wood
New Park Brook
Research & Development Laboratories
Halsall's Lodge
Leveldale
Goose Island Pond
Postillion Cap
Lord's Cottage
Otterheads Farm
Stand Farm
Whitestones
Red Trees
Birchenholt
Mawdsley's Farm
HOLLAND BUSINESS PARK
Washway Farm
Moss View
WESTHEAD
Prim. Sch.
Playing Field
Dingle Heyes Farm
Dumbills
Wellfield
Sefton Brook Bridge
Sefton Brook
Castle Brook
A59
A5209
A577
B5240
B5421
LIVERPOOL ROAD SOUTH
SQUARE LANE
BRIARS LANE
LOWRY HILL LA.
COURSE LA.
HOBCROSS LANE
LADY LANE
BLYTHE LANE
ALLCES DRIVE
CRANES LANE
HALL LANE
SPA LANE
PLOUGH LANE
WIGAN ROAD
BROW
CASTLE LANE
SANDY LANE
LATHOM LANE
HOSCAR MOSS ROAD
HOLLOWFORD LANE
DAISY LANE
CARR LANE
MEADOW LANE
BLEAK LANE
SUTCH LANE
WARPER'S MOSS LA.
MOSS BRIDGE LANE
FIRSWOOD RD
DICK'S LANE
SCHOOL LANE
15
22
29
H J K L M N
G H J K L M N
1 2 3 4 5 6 7 8 9
44 345 46
12 11 410 09 08
30

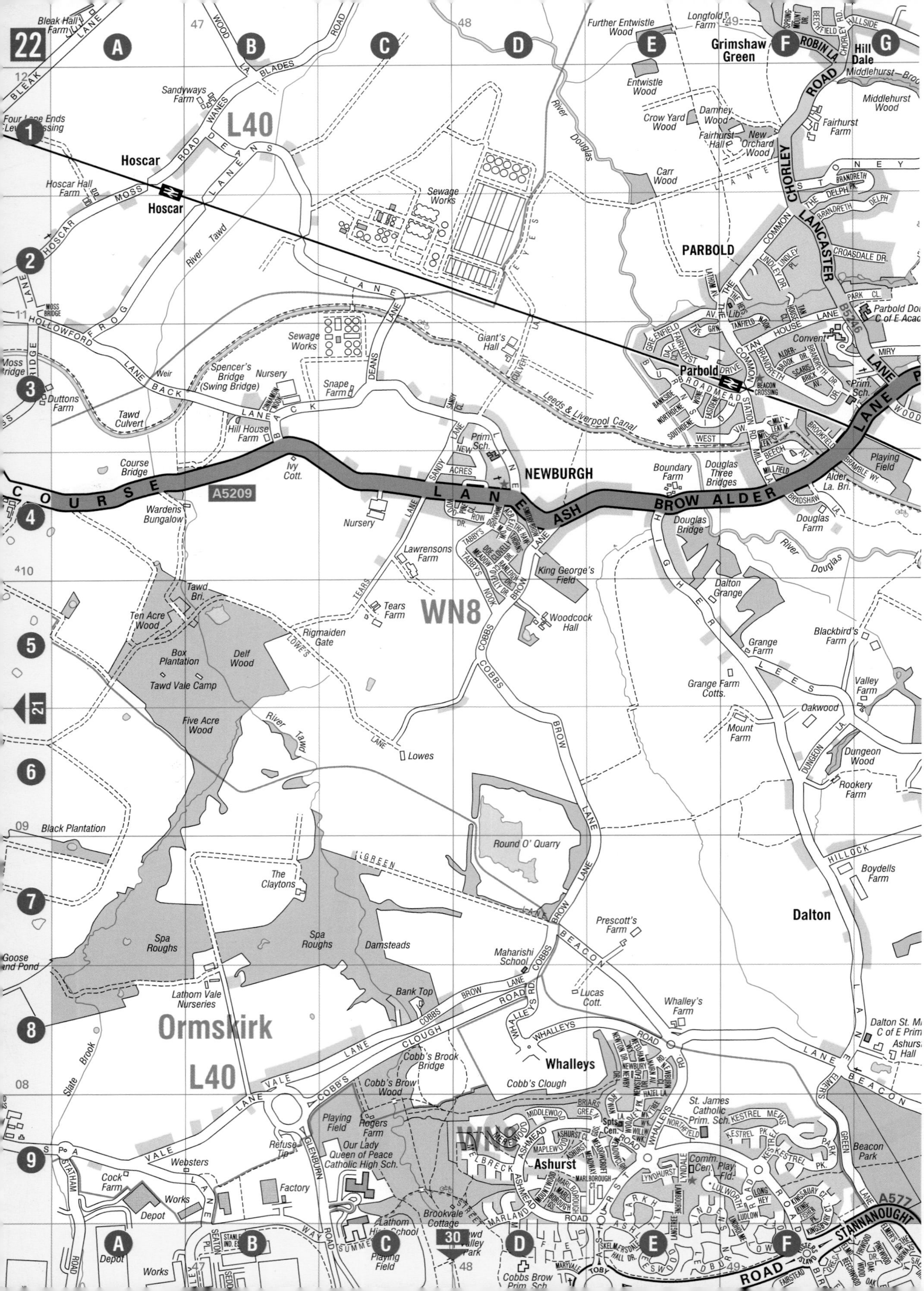
Bleak Hall Farm
BLEAK LANE
Four Lane Ends Level Crossing
Sandyways Farm
BLADES LA.
WOOD LA.
WANES
L40
DEANS LANE
Hoscar
Hoscar Hall Farm
MOSS ROAD
HOSCAR
Hoscar
River Tawd
Sewage Works
Further Entwistle Wood
Longfold Farm
Grimshaw Green
ROBIN LA.
BEECHFIELD RD.
HILLSIDE
Hill Dale
Middlehurst Wood
Entwistle Wood
Crow Yard Wood
Damney Wood
Fairhurst Hall
New Orchard Wood
Fairhurst Farm
River Douglas
Carr Wood
CHORLEY ROAD
STONEY LANE
BRANDRETH PK.
THE DELPH
DELPH
LANCASTER
COMMON
PARBOLD
CROASDALE DR.
LINDLEY DR.
LINDLEY PL.
LATHOM AV.
PARK CL.
Parbold Douglas C of E Academy
B5246
Convent
MIRY LANE
MOSS BRIDGE
HOLLOWFORD
FROG LANE
LANE
Sewage Works
Giant's Hall
Spencer's Bridge (Swing Bridge)
Nursery
Snape Farm
Moss Bridge
Duttons Farm
Weir
BACK LANE
Tawd Culvert
Hill House Farm
CINNAMON NOOK
SANDY CL.
Parbold
BROADMEAD
BEACON CROSSING
Leeds & Liverpool Canal
STATION RD.
WEST
MILL LANE
BEECH AV.
BROOKFIELD
Playing Field
BRAMBLE WY.
Prim. Sch.
WOOD
Course Bridge
Ivy Cott.
COURSE LANE
A5209
Prim. Sch.
NEW ACRES
SANDY LANE
NEWBURGH
Boundary Farm
Douglas Three Bridges
MILLFIELD
Alder La. Bri.
ASH BROW
ALDER LANE
BRADSHAW LA.
Wardens Bungalow
Nursery
Douglas Bridge
Douglas Farm
Lawrensons Farm
King George's Field
River Douglas
TEARS LANE
Tabby's Nook
BROW
Tawd Bri.
Ten Acre Wood
Tears Farm
WN8
Woodcock Hall
HIGHER LANE
Dalton Grange
Rigmaiden Gate
LOWE'S LANE
COBBS BROW
Box Plantation
Delf Wood
Tawd Vale Camp
Grange Farm
Blackbird's Farm
LEES LANE
Grange Farm Cotts.
Valley Farm
Oakwood
21
Five Acre Wood
River Tawd
Mount Farm
Lowes
DUNGEON LA.
Dungeon Wood
Rookery Farm
Black Plantation
Round O' Quarry
HILLOCK
Boydells Farm
GREEN LANE
The Claytons
Prescott's Farm
Dalton
Spa Roughs
Spa Roughs
Damsteads
BEACON LANE
Maharishi School
Goose and Pond
Lathom Vale Nurseries
Bank Top
Lucas Cott.
Whalley's Farm
Ormskirk
COBBS BROW ROAD
WHALLEYS RD.
WHALLEYS ROAD
Dalton St. Michael's C of E Prim.
Ashurst Hall
Cobb's Brook Bridge
CLOUGH LANE
Slate Brook
L40
Whalleys
Cobb's Clough
VALE LANE
Cobb's Brow Wood
ELMERS GREEN
BEACON LANE
Playing Field
Rogers Farm
St. James Catholic Prim. Sch.
KESTREL MEWS
KESTREL PK.
Beacon Park
Refuse Tip
Our Lady Queen of Peace Catholic High Sch.
Ashurst
MIDDLEWOOD
Spts Cen.
Comm. Cen.
Play Fld.
GLENBURN ROAD
SPA LANE
VALE LANE
Websters
STATHAM
Cock Farm
Works
Depot
Factory
Brookvale Cottage
Lathom High School
MARLAND
MARLBOROUGH
LULWORTH
LONG HEY
KINGSBURY CL.
A577
STANNANOUGHT ROAD
Depot
Works
STANLEY IND. EST.
Playing Field
30
Tawd Valley Park
Cobbs Brow Prim. Sch.
SKELMERSDALE HALL DR.
TOBY
FAIRSTEAD
47
48
49
08
09
410
11
12

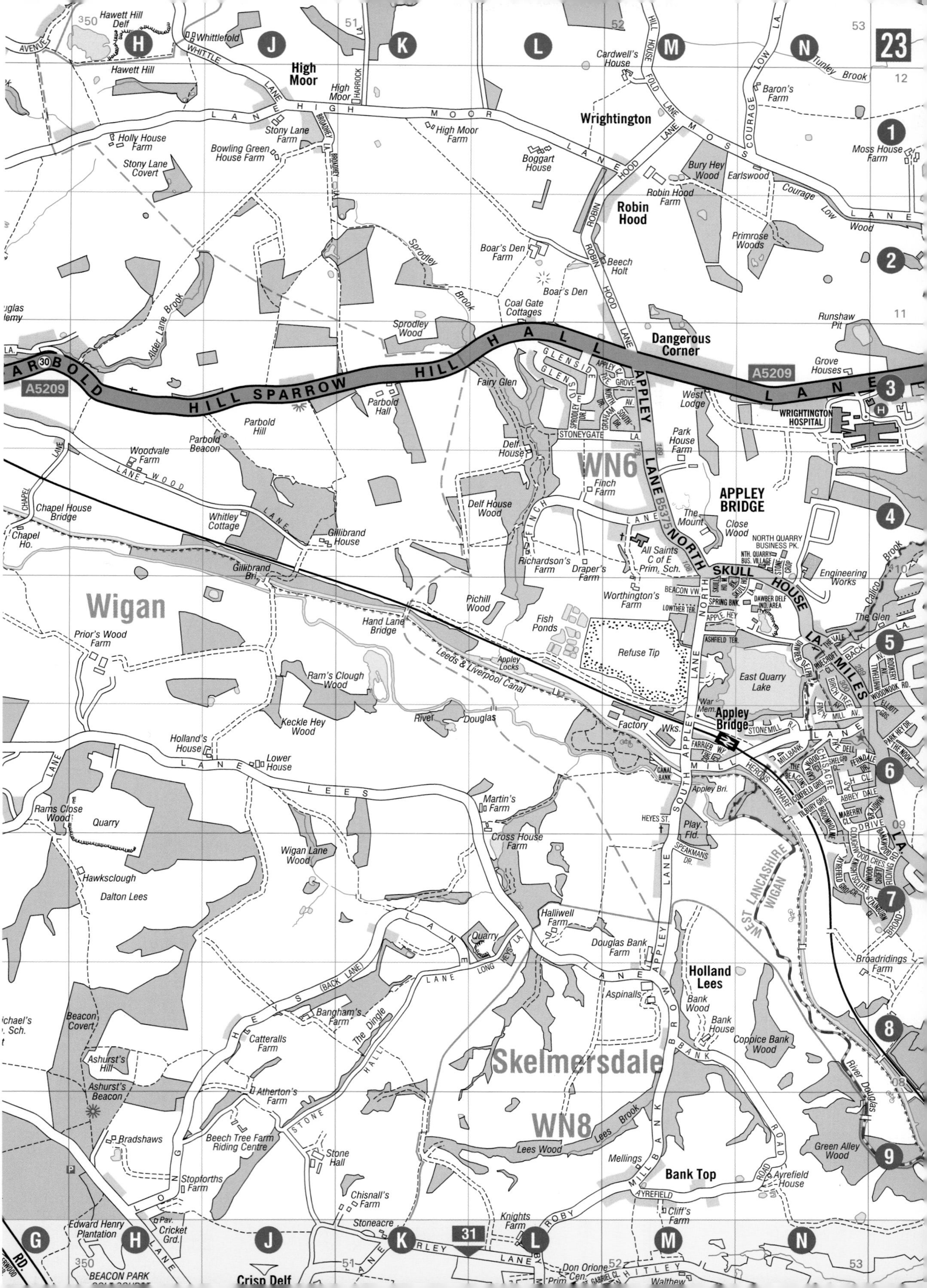

Hawett Hill Delf
Whittlefold
High Moor
High Moor
Hawett Hill
Cardwell's House
Baron's Farm
Tunley Brook
Wrightington
Stony Lane Farm
High Moor Farm
Holly House Farm
Bowling Green House Farm
Boggart House
Moss House Farm
Stony Lane Covert
Bury Hey Wood
Earlswood
Robin Hood Farm
Robin Hood
Courage Low Wood
Primrose Woods
Boar's Den Farm
Beech Holt
Sprodley Brook
Boar's Den
Coal Gate Cottages
Alder Lane Brook
Sprodley Wood
Dangerous Corner
Runshaw Pit
Grove Houses
A5209
HALL LANE
PARBOLD HILL SPARROW HILL
Fairy Glen
West Lodge
Wrightington Hospital
Parbold Hall
Parbold Hill
Parbold Beacon
Woodvale Farm
Delf House
Park House Farm
WN6
Finch Farm
Delf House Wood
APPLEY BRIDGE
Chapel House Bridge
Chapel Ho.
Whitley Cottage
Gillibrand House
The Mount
Close Wood
North Quarry Business Pk.
All Saints C of E Prim. Sch.
Richardson's Farm
Draper's Farm
Engineering Works
Gillibrand Bri.
Wigan
Worthington's Farm
Pichill Wood
Hand Lane Bridge
Fish Ponds
Refuse Tip
The Glen
Prior's Wood Farm
Appley Locks
Leeds & Liverpool Canal
East Quarry Lake
Ram's Clough Wood
River Douglas
Keckle Hey Wood
Factory
Wks.
Appley Bridge
Holland's House
Lower House
Appley Bri.
Rams Close Wood
Quarry
Martin's Farm
Play. Fld.
Cross House Farm
Wigan Lane Wood
Hawksclough
Dalton Lees
West Lancashire Wigan
Halliwell Farm
Quarry
Douglas Bank Farm
Broadridings Farm
Holland Lees
Aspinalls
Bangham's Farm
Beacon Covert
Bank Wood
The Dingle
Catteralls Farm
Bank House
Coppice Bank Wood
Ashurst's Hill
Skelmersdale
River Douglas
Ashurst's Beacon
Atherton's Farm
Bradshaws
Beech Tree Farm Riding Centre
WN8
Lees Brook
Lees Wood
Stone Hall
Green Alley Wood
Mellings
Stopforths Farm
Bank Top
Ayrefield House
Chisnall's Farm
Edward Henry Plantation
Cricket Grd.
Stoneacre
Knights Farm
Cliff's Farm
Beacon Park
Crisp Delf
Don Orione Cen.
Walthew

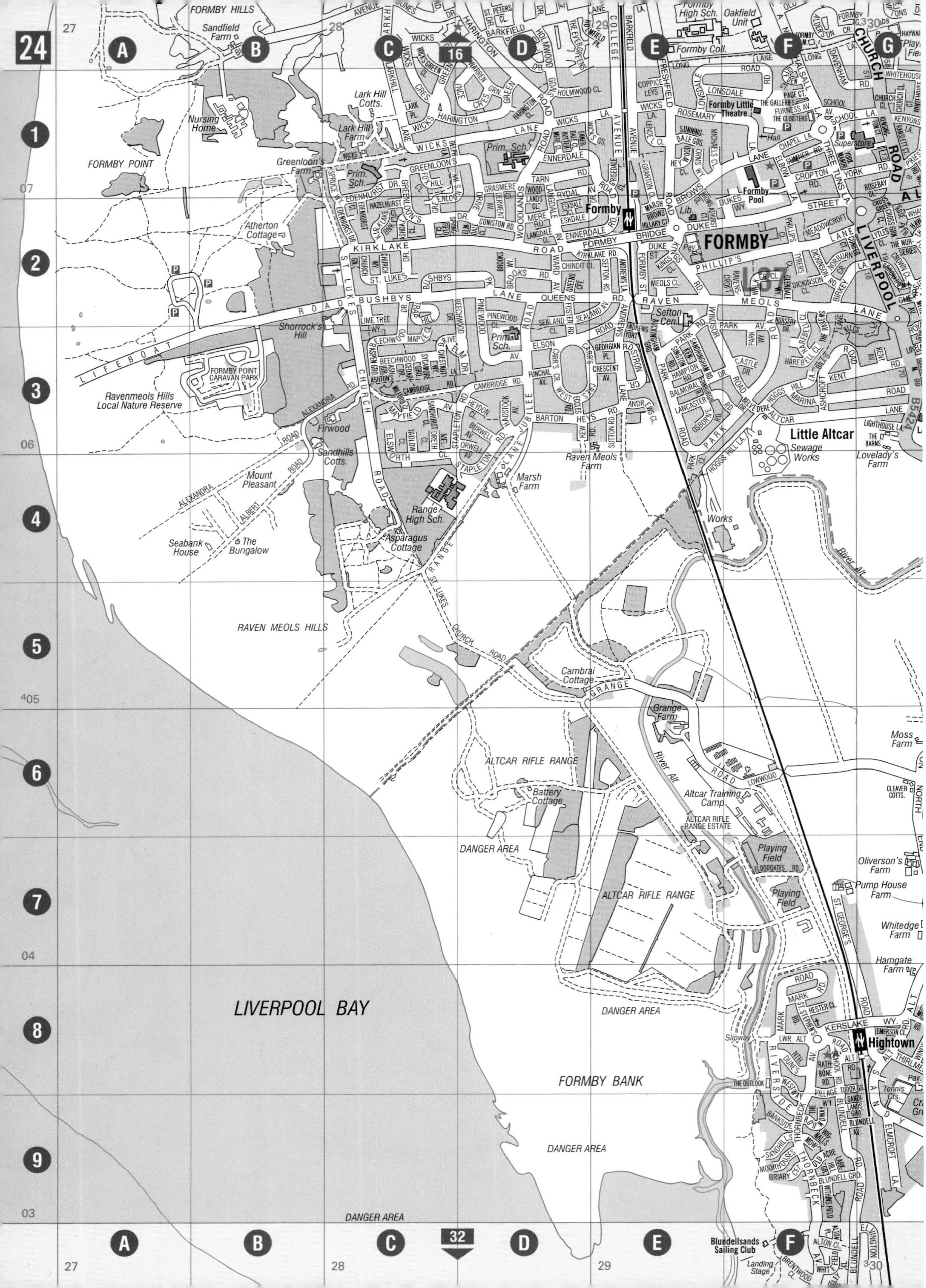
FORMBY HILLS
Sandfield Farm
Formby High Sch.
Oakfield Unit
Formby Coll.
16
Lark Hill Cotts.
Lark Hill Farm
Nursing Home
FORMBY POINT
Greenloon's Farm
Prim. Sch.
Formby Little Theatre
Superstore
Formby Pool
Formby
FORMBY
L37
Lib.
Pav.
Atherton Cottage
Shorrock's Hill
LIFEBOAT ROAD
FORMBY POINT CARAVAN PARK
Ravenmeols Hills Local Nature Reserve
Firwood
Sandhills Cotts.
Mount Pleasant
Seabank House
The Bungalow
Range High Sch.
Asparagus Cottage
Raven Meols Farm
Marsh Farm
Sefton Cen.
Little Altcar
Sewage Works
Lovelady's Farm
Works
River Alt
RAVEN MEOLS HILLS
Cambrai Cottage
Grange Farm
ALTCAR RIFLE RANGE
Battery Cottage
Altcar Training Camp
ALTCAR RIFLE RANGE ESTATE
DANGER AREA
Playing Field
Moss Farm
Oliverson's Farm
Pump House Farm
Whitedge Farm
Hamgate Farm
LIVERPOOL BAY
Hightown
FORMBY BANK
Slipway
THE OUTLOOK
Tennis Cts.
Blundellsands Sailing Club
Landing Stage
LIVERPOOL ROAD
B5424
A B C D E F G
1 2 3 4 5 6 7 8 9
27 28 29 330
07 06 05 04 03
32

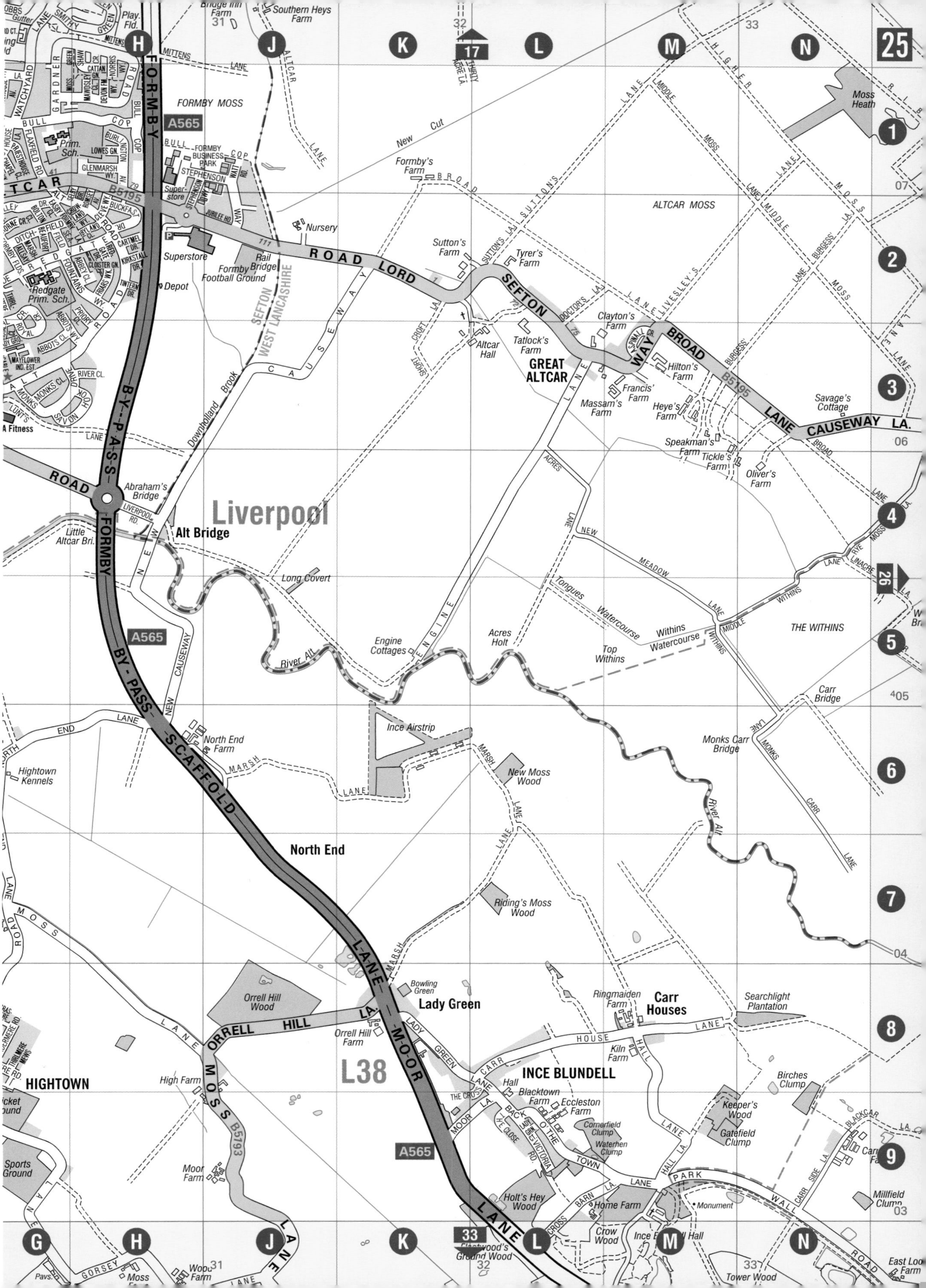

FORMBY MOSS
ALTCAR MOSS
Liverpool
GREAT ALTCAR
Alt Bridge
Abraham's Bridge
Little Altcar Bri.
Formby's Farm
Sutton's Farm
Tyrer's Farm
Altcar Hall
Tatlock's Farm
Clayton's Farm
Hilton's Farm
Francis' Farm
Massam's Farm
Heye's Farm
Speakman's Farm
Tickle's Farm
Oliver's Farm
Savage's Cottage
Moss Heath
Nursery
Superstore
Formby Football Ground
Rail Bridge
Depot
Redgate Prim. Sch.
Prim. Sch.
FORMBY BUSINESS PARK
SEFTON WEST LANCASHIRE
Downholland Brook
Long Covert
Engine Cottages
River Alt
Acres Holt
Top Withins
Withins Watercourse
Tongues Watercourse
THE WITHINS
Carr Bridge
Monks Carr Bridge
Ince Airstrip
North End Farm
Hightown Kennels
New Moss Wood
North End
Riding's Moss Wood
Orrell Hill Wood
Orrell Hill Farm
Lady Green
Bowling Green
Ringmaiden Farm
Carr Houses
Searchlight Plantation
Kiln Farm
INCE BLUNDELL
Hall
Blacktown Farm
Eccleston Farm
Cornerfield Clump
Waterhen Clump
Keeper's Wood
Gatefield Clump
Birches Clump
Millfield Clump
Holt's Hey Wood
Home Farm
Monument
Crow Wood
Fleetwood's Ground Wood
Tower Wood
East Lodge Farm
HIGHTOWN
High Farm
Moor Farm
Sports Ground
L38
A565
B5195
B5193
FORMBY BY-PASS
SCAFFOLD LANE
MOOR LANE
LORD SEFTON WAY
BROAD LANE
CAUSEWAY LA.
ORRELL HILL LA.
MOSS LANE

17
26
33

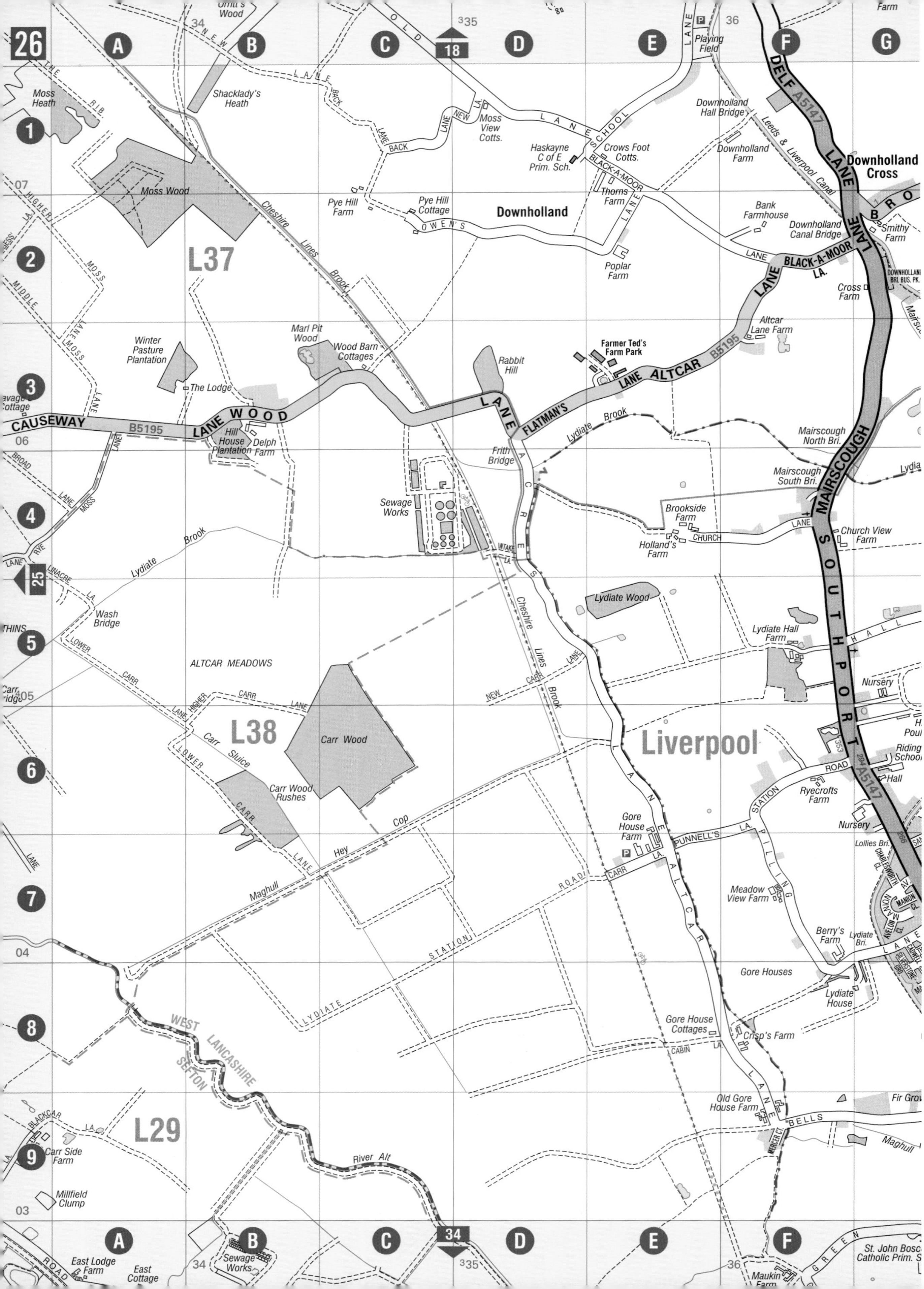

Moss Heath
Shacklady's Heath
Moss Wood
L37
Cheshire Lines Brook
Pye Hill Farm
Pye Hill Cottage
Moss View Cotts.
Haskayne C of E Prim. Sch.
Crows Foot Cotts.
Thorns Farm
Downholland
Poplar Farm
Playing Field
Downholland Hall Bridge
Downholland Farm
Leeds & Liverpool Canal
Downholland Cross
Bank Farmhouse
Downholland Canal Bridge
Smithy Farm
Cross Farm
DOWNHOLLAND BRI. BUS. PK.
Altcar Lane Farm
Farmer Ted's Farm Park
Rabbit Hill
Marl Pit Wood
Wood Barn Cottages
Winter Pasture Plantation
The Lodge
CAUSEWAY
B5195
LANE WOOD
Hill House Plantation
Delph Farm
ALTCAR LANE
FLATMAN'S
Lydiate Brook
Frith Bridge
Mairscough North Bri.
Mairscough South Bri.
MAIRSCOUGH LANE
Sewage Works
Brookside Farm
Holland's Farm
CHURCH LANE
Church View Farm
SOUTHPORT ROAD
A5147
Lydiate Wood
Lydiate Hall Farm
Nursery
Wash Bridge
ALTCAR MEADOWS
LOWER CARR LANE
HIGHER CARR LANE
L38
Carr Wood
Carr Sluice
Carr Wood Rushes
NEW CARR LANE
Liverpool
Riding School
Hall
STATION ROAD
Ryecrofts Farm
Gore House Farm
PUNNELL'S LA.
PILLING LANE
Meadow View Farm
Maghull Hey Cop
CARR LA.
Berry's Farm
Lydiate Bri.
Gore Houses
Lydiate House
STATION ROAD
LYDIATE
WEST LANCASHIRE
SEFTON
Gore House Cottages
Crisp's Farm
CABIN LA.
Old Gore House Farm
BELLS LANE
MERCER CT.
Fir Grove
Maghull
L29
BLACKCAR LA.
Carr Side Farm
River Alt
Millfield Clump
East Lodge Farm
East Cottage
Sewage Works
Maukin Farm
St. John Bosco Catholic Prim. S
GREEN
A B C D E F G
1 2 3 4 5 6 7 8 9
18
25
34

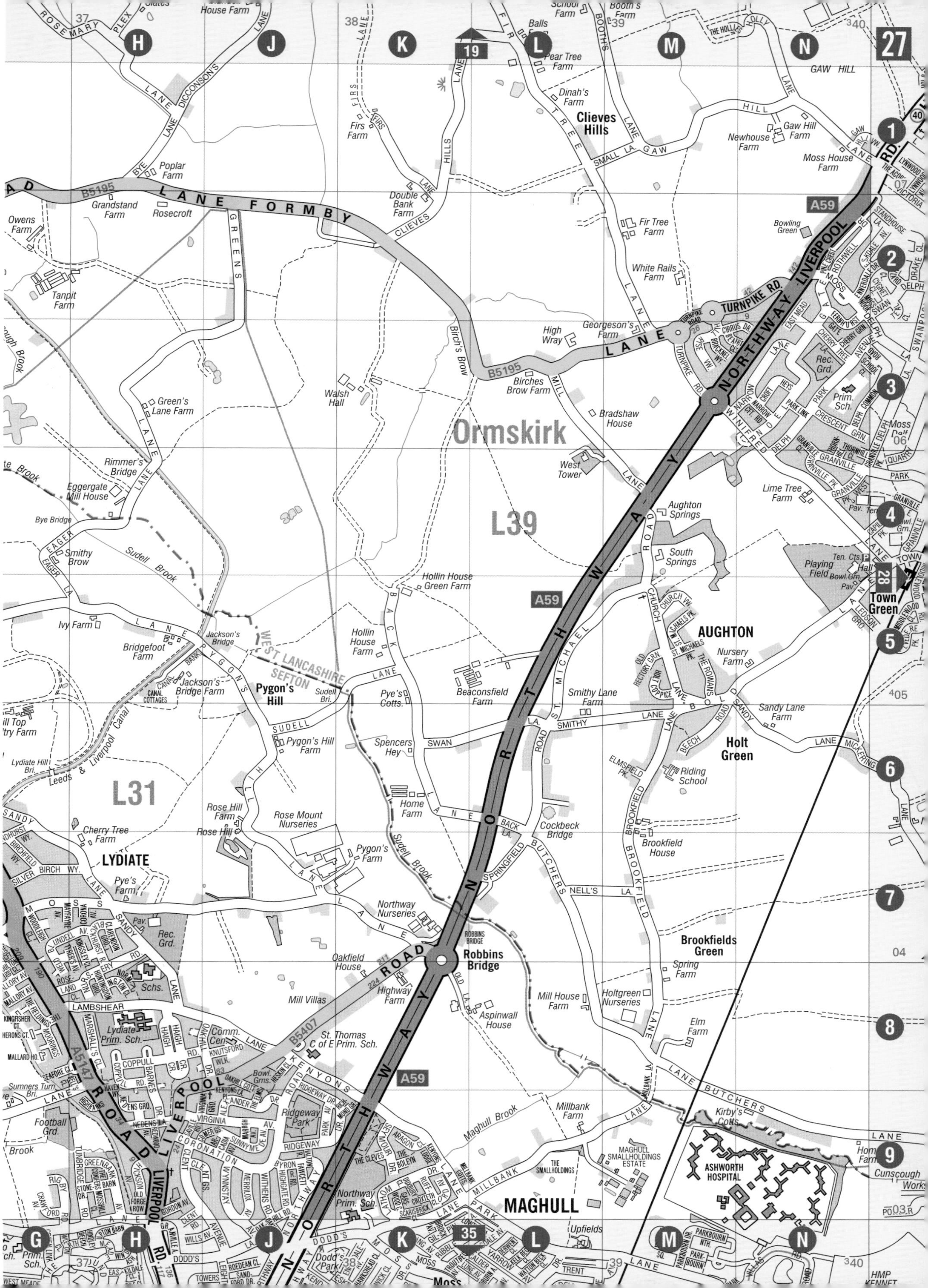

Clieves Hills
Ormskirk
L39
L31
AUGHTON
Holt Green
Pygon's Hill
LYDIATE
MAGHULL
Robbins Bridge
Brookfields Green
Town Green
GAW HILL
ASHWORTH HOSPITAL
MAGHULL SMALLHOLDINGS ESTATE
Pear Tree Farm
Dinah's Farm
Firs Farm
Double Bank Farm
Newhouse Farm
Gaw Hill Farm
Moss House Farm
Poplar Farm
Grandstand Farm
Rosecroft
Owens Farm
Tanpit Farm
Fir Tree Farm
White Rails Farm
Bowling Green
High Wray
Georgeson's Farm
Birches Brow Farm
Walsh Hall
Green's Lane Farm
Bradshaw House
West Tower
Rimmer's Bridge
Eggergate Mill House
Bye Bridge
Smithy Brow
Sudell Brook
Aughton Springs
South Springs
Lime Tree Farm
Playing Field
Hollin House Green Farm
Ivy Farm
Bridgefoot Farm
Jackson's Bridge
Hollin House Farm
WEST LANCASHIRE
SEFTON
Jackson's Bridge Farm
Canal Cottages
Beaconsfield Farm
Smithy Lane Farm
Nursery Farm
Sandy Lane Farm
Pye's Cotts.
Pygon's Hill Farm
Spencers Hey
Riding School
Lydiate Hill Bri.
Leeds & Liverpool Canal
Rose Hill Farm
Rose Mount Nurseries
Home Farm
Cockbeck Bridge
Cherry Tree Farm
Rose Hill
Pygon's Farm
Brookfield House
Pye's Farm
Northway Nurseries
Rec. Grd.
Oakfield House
Highway Farm
Mill Villas
Spring Farm
Mill House Farm
Holtgreen Nurseries
Aspinwall House
Elm Farm
Lydiate Prim. Sch.
St. Thomas C of E Prim. Sch.
Sumners Turn Bri.
Football Grd.
Ridgeway Park
Millbank Farm
Maghull Brook
Kirby's Cotts.
Cunscough Works
Northway Prim. Sch.
Upfields
The Smallholdings
LANE FORMBY
NORTHWAY
LIVERPOOL ROAD
TURNPIKE RD.
A59
B5195
B5407
A5147

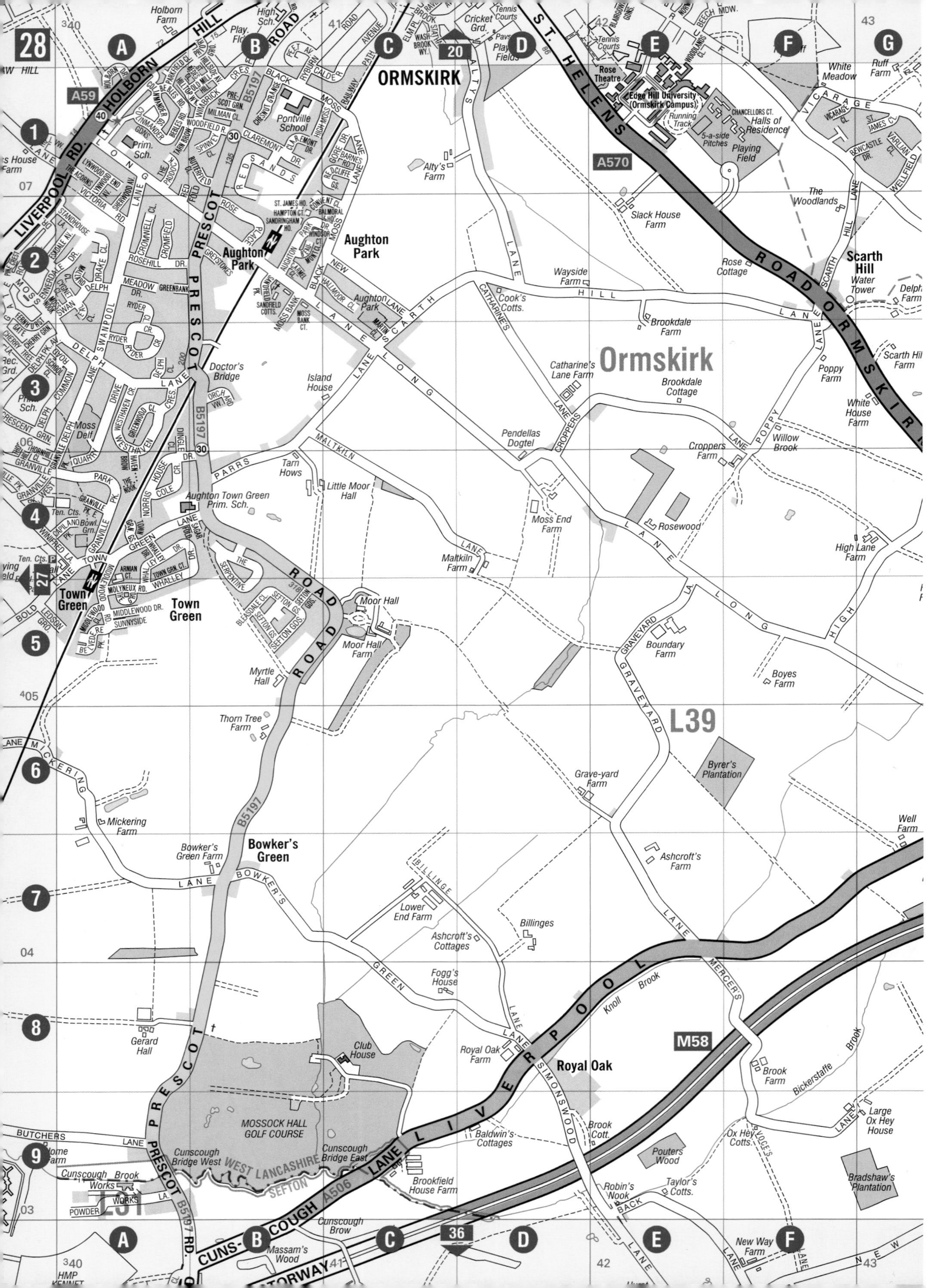
ORMSKIRK
Ormskirk
Aughton Park
Town Green
Bowker's Green
Royal Oak
Scarth Hill
L39
L31
A59
A570
A506
B5197
M58
20
27
36
HOLBORN HILL
LIVERPOOL RD.
PRESCOT ROAD
ST. HELENS ROAD
ORMSKIRK ROAD
LIVERPOOL ROAD
CUNSCOUGH LANE
LONG LANE
SCARTH HILL LANE
GRAVEYARD LANE
MERCER'S LANE
BOWKER'S GREEN LANE
MICKERING LANE
BUTCHERS LANE
SIMONSWOOD LANE
BILLINGE LANE
MALTKILN LANE
CROPPERS LANE
POPPY LANE
CATHARINE'S LANE
HIGH LANE
ALTYS LANE
Edge Hill University (Ormskirk Campus)
Halls of Residence
Rose Theatre
Pontville School
Holborn Farm
Alty's Farm
Slack House Farm
Wayside Farm
Brookdale Farm
Brookdale Cottage
Catharine's Lane Farm
Cook's Cotts.
Island House
Doctor's Bridge
Pendellas Dogtel
Croppers Farm
Willow Brook
Poppy Farm
White House Farm
Scarth Hill Farm
Rose Cottage
Water Tower
Delph Farm
Ruff Farm
White Meadow
The Woodlands
Tarn Hows
Little Moor Hall
Moss End Farm
Rosewood
High Lane Farm
Maltkiln Farm
Moor Hall
Moor Hall Farm
Boundary Farm
Boyes Farm
Myrtle Hall
Thorn Tree Farm
Byrer's Plantation
Grave-yard Farm
Well Farm
Mickering Farm
Bowker's Green Farm
Ashcroft's Farm
Lower End Farm
Billinges
Ashcroft's Cottages
Fogg's House
Gerard Hall
Club House
MOSSOCK HALL GOLF COURSE
Royal Oak Farm
Brook Farm
Large Ox Hey House
Ox Hey Cotts.
Brook Cott.
Pouters Wood
Baldwin's Cottages
Brookfield House Farm
Robin's Nook
Taylor's Cotts.
Bradshaw's Plantation
Cunscough Bridge West
Cunscough Bridge East
Cunscough Brook
Cunscough Brow
Massam's Wood
New Way Farm
WEST LANCASHIRE
SEFTON
Moss Delf
Aughton Town Green Prim. Sch.
Knoll Brook
Bickerstaffe Brook

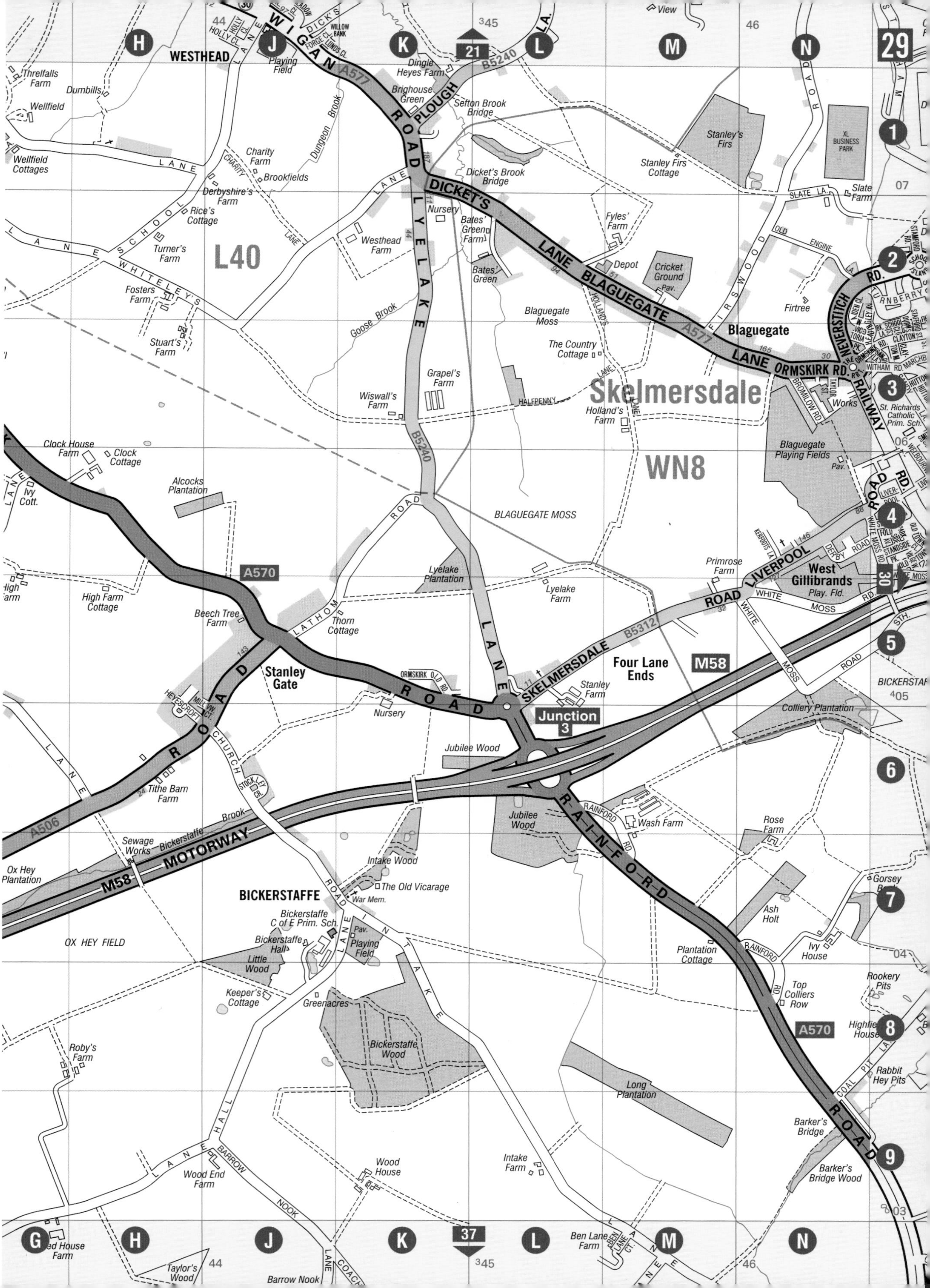
WESTHEAD
Threlfalls Farm
Dumbills
Wellfield
Wellfield Cottages
Playing Field
WIGAN
A577
Dingle Heyes Farm
Brighouse Green
PLOUGH
Sefton Brook Bridge
B5240
21
Dungeon Brook
Charity Farm
Brookfields
Derbyshire's Farm
Rice's Cottage
Turner's Farm
L40
SCHOOL
WHITELEY'S
Fosters Farm
Stuart's Farm
Goose Brook
Westhead Farm
Dicket's Brook Bridge
DICKET'S
LYELAKE
Nursery
Bates' Green Farm
Bates' Green
Stanley's Firs
Stanley Firs Cottage
XL BUSINESS PARK
Slate Farm
SLATE LA.
OLD ENGINE
Fyles' Farm
Depot
Cricket Ground
Pav.
BLAGUEGATE
LANE
HOLLAND'S
FIRSWOOD
Firtree
Blaguegate
Blaguegate Moss
The Country Cottage
Grapel's Farm
Wiswall's Farm
HALFPENNY
Skelmersdale
Holland's Farm
ORMSKIRK RD.
NEVERSTITCH RD.
RAILWAY
BROMILOW RD.
Works
St. Richards Catholic Prim. Sch.
WITHAM RD.
Blaguegate Playing Fields
WN8
Clock House Farm
Clock Cottage
Ivy Cott.
Alcocks Plantation
BLAGUEGATE MOSS
Lyelake Plantation
Lyelake Farm
Primrose Farm
LIVERPOOL
West Gillibrands
Play. Fld.
WHITE MOSS RD.
A570
High Farm
High Farm Cottage
Beech Tree Farm
LATHOM
Thorn Cottage
B5312
SKELMERSDALE
Four Lane Ends
M58
Stanley Gate
ORMSKIRK OLD RD.
ROAD
Nursery
Stanley Farm
Junction 3
BICKERSTAFFE
Colliery Plantation
Jubilee Wood
HEYESCROFT
MILL VW. CT.
CHURCH
STOCK LEY CR.
Tithe Barn Farm
RAINFORD RD.
Wash Farm
Rose Farm
A506
Sewage Works
Bickerstaffe Brook
MOTORWAY
Ox Hey Plantation
Intake Wood
The Old Vicarage
War Mem.
Bickerstaffe C of E Prim. Sch.
Playing Field
Bickerstaffe Hall
Little Wood
OX HEY FIELD
INTAKE
Ash Holt
Gorsey
Plantation Cottage
Ivy House
Keeper's Cottage
Greenacres
Top Colliers Row
Rookery Pits
Highfield House
Roby's Farm
Bickerstaffe Wood
COAL PIT LA.
Rabbit Hey Pits
Long Plantation
HALL
Barker's Bridge
Barker's Bridge Wood
BARROW NOOK
Wood End Farm
Wood House
Intake Farm
Ben Lane Farm
BEN LANE CT.
Red House Farm
Taylor's Wood
Barrow Nook
37
COACH
G
H
J
K
L
M
N
1
2
3
4
5
6
7
8
9
30
44
345
46
07
06
405
04
03

22
38
29
A
B
C
D
E
F
G
1
2
3
4
5
6
7
8
9
47
48
49
07
06
05
04
03
Webster's
Cock Farm
Works
Depot
Factory
Catholic High Sch.
Lathom High School
Brow Cottage
Tawd Valley Park
Ashurst
Playing Field
Cobbs Brow Prim. Sch.
Warehouse
Stanley Ind. Est.
Skelmersdale & Ormskirk College Stadium
HOUGHTON'S
ROAD
A577
HALFMILE ISLAND
TOBY ISLAND
STANLEY ISLAND
SCHOOL ISLAND
NEVERSTITCH
Slate Farm
Depots
Forsters Green
Birch Green
Prim. Sch.
Comm. Cen.
Skelmersdale Hall Clough
Westheads Clough
High School
Chapel House
Brookfield Park Prim. Sch.
Respite Cen.
Kiln Lane Play. Field
Trinity School
Prim. Sch.
GLENBURN A5068 RD.
Tawd Valley Park
SKELMERSDALE
Play. Fld.
Superstore
Bannatyne's Health Club
Skelmersdale
WN8
St. John's Catholic Prim. Sch.
Elmers Green Common
West Lancashire Coll. (Skelmersdale Campus)
Nye Bevan Pool
Bus Sta.
NHS
Lib.
Police HQ
Concourse Shopping Centre
Amphitheatre
Delf Clough
Elmer's Clough
Pennylands
St. Richards Catholic Prim. Sch.
RAILWAY
Works
Glenburn Sports College
Playing Field
HOPE ISLAND
Gym
Giggles
Offs.
WHITEHEY ISLAND
EXCHANGE ISLAND
B5312
ROAD
GRIMSHAW
40
Academy
Delph Side Prim. Sch.
Hillside Prim. Sch.
East Gillibrands
Works
Factory
Play. Fld.
Skelmersdale Sports Cen.
Tawd Bridge
St. Francis Assisi Prim. Sch.
West Lancs
Play. Fld.
WHITE MOSS RD.
MOSS ROAD
Peel Farm
White Moss
BICKERSTAFFE MOSS
Junction 4
M58
M58 MOTORWAY
A5068
Depot
Whitemoss Business Park
White Moss Farm
West Lancashire Investment Cen.
Warehouse
Little Digmoor Prim. Sch.
Digmoor
Bishop Martin C of E Prim. Sch.
Plantation
Midge Nook
Moss Lane Farm
Mole Hall
Nipe Bridge
Works
Gorsey Bank
BICKERSTAFFE MOSS
Moss Side Cottages
Higherend Farm
Hey's Crossing
Moss Farm
Moss Side Farm
Little Ferny Knoll
River Tawd
Pimbo Industrial Estate
Ormskirk
L39
UPHOLLAND MOSS
WEST LANCASHIRE
ST. HELENS
Rookery Pits
Coal Pit Lane Farm
Holly Lane Farm
Ferny Knoll
Highfield House
Brookdale
Holland Moss Business Park
Moor Side Farm
Factory
Rabbit Hey Pits
Big Ferny Knoll Farm
St. Helens
Barton Ho.
WA11
RAINFORD ROAD
A570
Holly Fold Place
Gate House
Holly Fold
Barker's Bridge Wood
Bawdy Brook Plantation
RAINFORD JUNCTION
Crawford

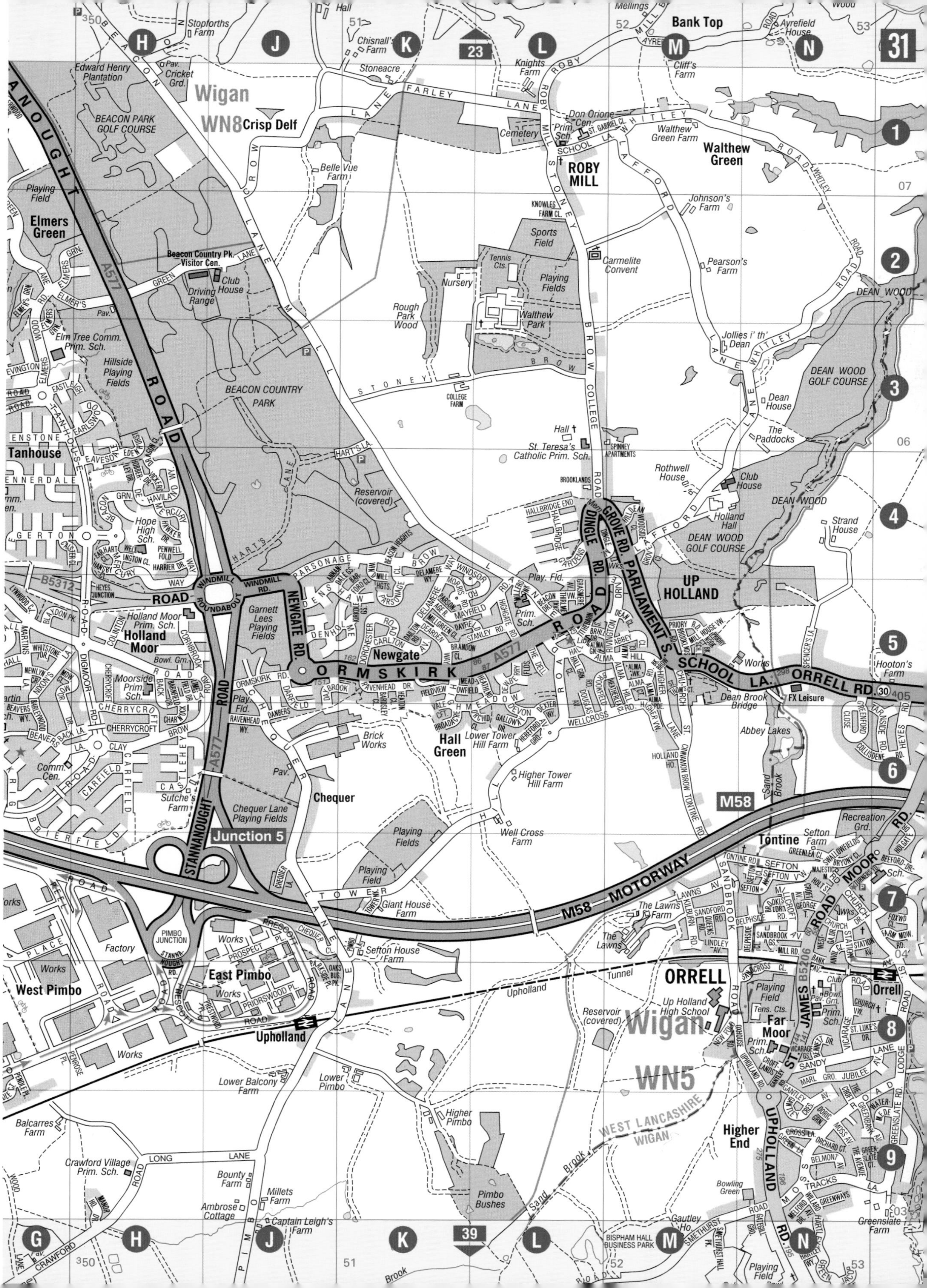
23
Wigan
WN8
Crisp Delf
Stopforths Farm
Chisnall's Farm
Stoneacre
Knights Farm
Bank Top
Cliff's Farm
Ayrefield House
Edward Henry Plantation
Cricket Grd.
BEACON PARK GOLF COURSE
FARLEY LANE
ROBY MILL
Don Orione Cen.
Prim. Sch.
Cemetery
ST. GABRIEL CL.
SCHOOL LA.
WHITLEY ROAD
Walthew Green Farm
Walthew Green
Playing Field
Elmers Green
Belle Vue Farm
CROW LANE
Johnson's Farm
KNOWLES FARM CL.
Sports Field
Beacon Country Pk. Visitor Cen.
Club House
Driving Range
Tennis Cts.
Playing Fields
Carmelite Convent
Pearson's Farm
Nursery
Rough Park Wood
Walthew Park
DEAN WOOD
Elm Tree Comm. Prim. Sch.
Hillside Playing Fields
BEACON COUNTRY PARK
STONEY BROW
COLLEGE FARM
Jollies i' th' Dean
DEAN WOOD GOLF COURSE
Dean House
The Paddocks
Tanhouse
Hall
St. Teresa's Catholic Prim. Sch.
SPINNEY APARTMENTS
HART'S LA.
Reservoir (covered)
BROOKLANDS
Rothwell House
Club House
Holland Hall
Hope High Sch.
HALLBRIDGE END
GROVE RD.
DINGLE RD.
PARLIAMENT ST.
DEAN WOOD GOLF COURSE
Strand House
B5312
WINDMILL ROUNDABOUT
WINDMILL RD.
HEYES JUNCTION
UP HOLLAND
Holland Moor Prim. Sch.
Holland Moor
Garnett Lees Playing Fields
NEWGATE RD.
Newgate
ORMSKIRK ROAD
A577
SCHOOL LA.
ORRELL RD.
Hooton's Farm
FX Leisure
Works
Moorside Prim. Sch.
Bowl. Grn.
CHERRYCROFT
Dean Brook Bridge
Abbey Lakes
Play. Fld.
Brick Works
Hall Green
Lower Tower Hill Farm
WELLCROSS RD.
Comm. Cen.
Higher Tower Hill Farm
Sutche's Farm
Chequer
Pav.
Chequer Lane Playing Fields
M58
Junction 5
STANNANOUGHT ROAD
Playing Fields
Well Cross Farm
Recreation Grd.
Tontine
Sefton Farm
M58 MOTORWAY
Playing Field
Giant House Farm
The Lawns Farm
The Lawns
TOWER HILL
PIMBO JUNCTION
Works
Factory
East Pimbo
Sefton House Farm
Tunnel
ORRELL
Orrell
West Pimbo
Upholland
Reservoir (covered)
Up Holland High School
Wigan
Playing Field
Far Moor
Prim. Sch.
WN5
Lower Balcony Farm
Lower Pimbo
Balcarres Farm
Higher Pimbo
WEST LANCASHIRE
WIGAN
Higher End
UPHOLLAND RD.
Crawford Village Prim. Sch.
LONG LANE
Bounty Farm
Millets Farm
Ambrose Cottage
Captain Leigh's Farm
Pimbo Bushes
Sand Brook
Bowling Green
Gautley Ho.
BISPHAM HALL BUSINESS PARK
Greenslate Farm
39
CRAWFORD
Brook
Playing Field
G H J K L M N
1 2 3 4 5 6 7 8 9

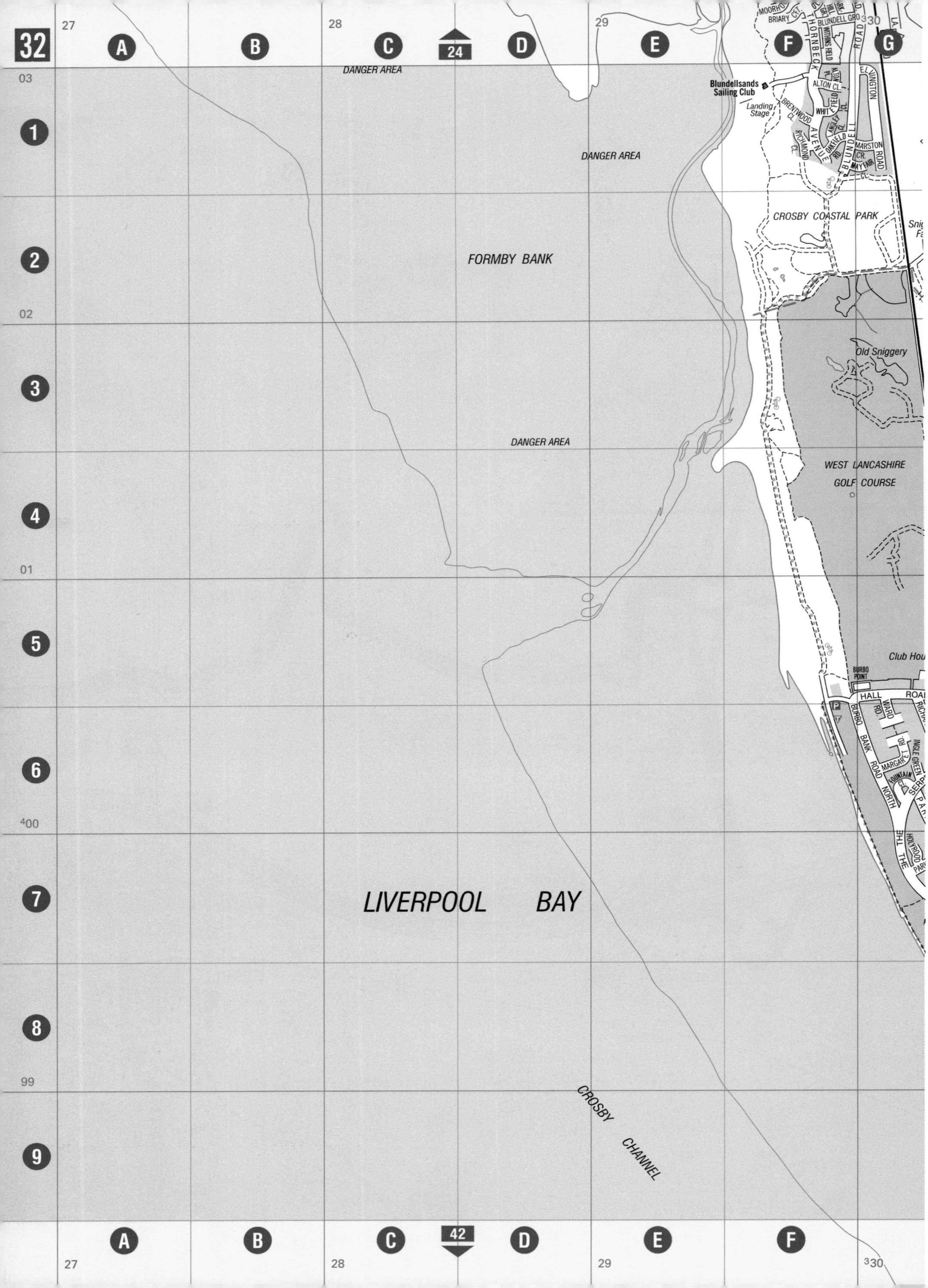
DANGER AREA
Blundellsands Sailing Club
Landing Stage
BRENTWOOD CL.
RICHMOND CL.
AVENUE
BLUNDELL ROAD
MARSTON CR.
ALTON CL.
ELLINGTON
BLUNDELL GRO.
HORNBECK
BRIARY
DANGER AREA
CROSBY COASTAL PARK
FORMBY BANK
Old Sniggery
DANGER AREA
WEST LANCASHIRE GOLF COURSE
BURBO POINT
HALL ROAD
WARD RD.
BURBO BANK ROAD NORTH
INGLE GREEN
LIVERPOOL BAY
CROSBY CHANNEL

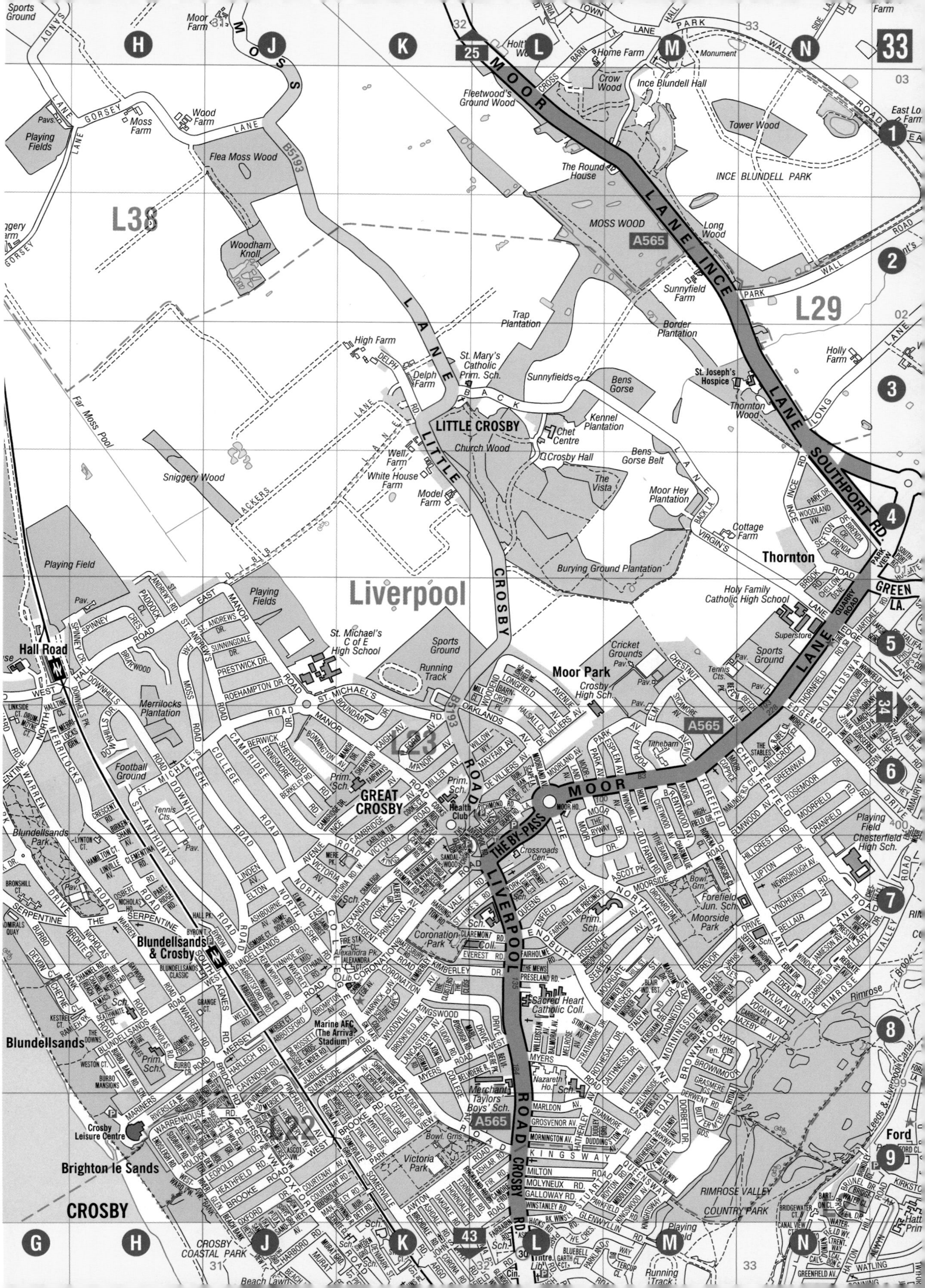

Liverpool
L38
L29
L23
L22
LITTLE CROSBY
GREAT CROSBY
CROSBY
Thornton
Moor Park
Blundellsands
Brighton le Sands
Hall Road
Blundellsands & Crosby
Ince Blundell Hall
INCE BLUNDELL PARK
Tower Wood
MOSS WOOD
Flea Moss Wood
Woodham Knoll
Sniggery Wood
Far Moss Pool
Fleetwood's Ground Wood
Trap Plantation
Border Plantation
Bens Gorse
Kennel Plantation
Church Wood
Crosby Hall
Bens Gorse Belt
The Vista
Moor Hey Plantation
Burying Ground Plantation
St. Joseph's Hospice
Thornton Wood
Holy Family Catholic High School
St. Michael's C of E High School
Crosby High Sch.
Sacred Heart Catholic Coll.
Merchant Taylors Boys' Sch.
Marine AFC (The Arriva Stadium)
Crosby Leisure Centre
Chesterfield High Sch.
Coronation Park
Victoria Park
Moorside Park
Merrilocks Plantation
RIMROSE VALLEY COUNTRY PARK
CROSBY COASTAL PARK
Leeds & Liverpool Canal
Ford
MOOR LANE
INCE LANE
SOUTHPORT RD.
LITTLE CROSBY LANE
CROSBY ROAD
LIVERPOOL ROAD
THE BY-PASS
A565
B5193
25
34
43

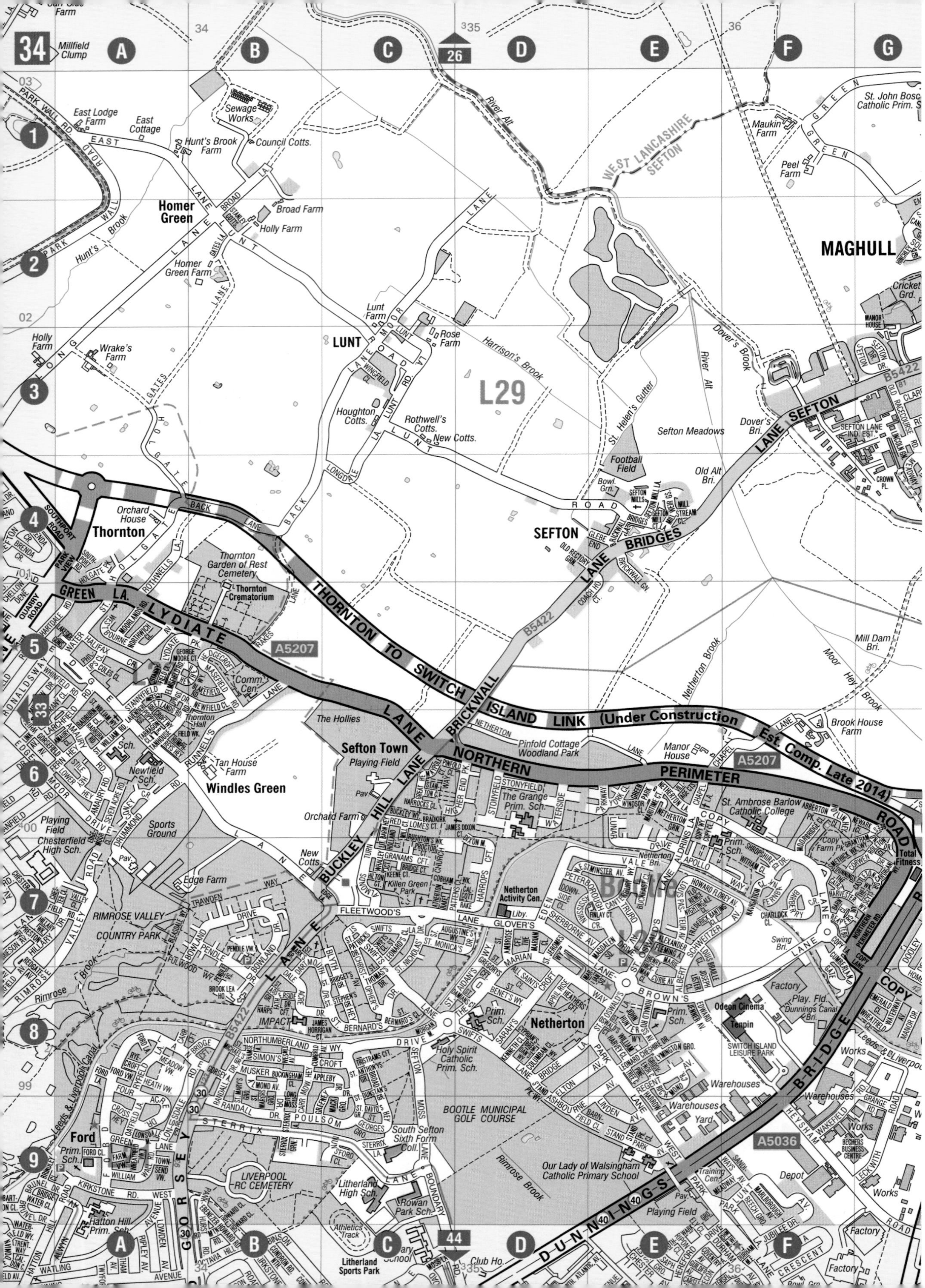

26
33
44
A
B
C
D
E
F
G
1
2
3
4
5
6
7
8
9
Millfield Clump
East Lodge Farm
East Cottage
Sewage Works
Hunt's Brook Farm
Council Cotts.
Homer Green
Broad Farm
Holly Farm
Homer Green Farm
Hunt's Brook
Holly Farm
Wrake's Farm
Lunt Farm
LUNT
Rose Farm
Harrison's Brook
L29
Houghton Cotts.
Rothwell's Cotts.
New Cotts.
River Alt
WEST LANCASHIRE
SEFTON
Maukin Farm
Peel Farm
St. John Bosco Catholic Prim. Sch.
MAGHULL
Cricket Grd.
Dover's Brook
St. Helen's Gutter
Sefton Meadows
Dover's Bri.
Sefton Lane Ind. Est.
Football Field
Bowl. Grn.
Old Alt Bri.
SEFTON
Orchard House
Thornton
Thornton Garden of Rest Cemetery
Thornton Crematorium
THORNTON TO SWITCH ISLAND LINK (Under Construction Est. Comp. Late 2014)
LYDIATE LANE
A5207
B5422
Comm. Cen.
Thornton Hall
Mill Dam Bri.
Moor Hey Brook
Netherton Brook
Brook House Farm
The Hollies
Sefton Town Playing Field
Tan House Farm
Newfield Sch.
Windles Green
Pinfold Cottage Woodland Park
Manor House
NORTHERN PERIMETER ROAD
The Grange Prim. Sch.
St. Ambrose Barlow Catholic College
Orchard Farm
Sports Ground
Playing Field
Chesterfield High Sch.
New Cotts.
Edge Farm
Killen Green Park
Netherton Activity Cen.
Liby.
Bootle
Total Fitness
RIMROSE VALLEY COUNTRY PARK
Rimrose Brook
Prim. Sch.
Swing Bri.
Factory
Play. Fld.
Dunnings Canal Bri.
Odeon Cinema
Tenpin
SWITCH ISLAND LEISURE PARK
IMPACT
Holy Spirit Catholic Prim. Sch.
Netherton
Warehouses
Works
Leeds & Liverpool Canal
BOOTLE MUNICIPAL GOLF COURSE
South Sefton Sixth Form Coll.
Our Lady of Walsingham Catholic Primary School
A5036
Ford
Prim. Sch.
LIVERPOOL RC CEMETERY
Litherland High Sch.
Rowan Park Sch.
Training Cen.
Depot
Playing Field
Hatton Hill Prim. Sch.
Athletics Track
Litherland Sports Park
Club Ho.
Factory
DUNNINGS BRIDGE ROAD
BECHERS BUSINESS CENTRE

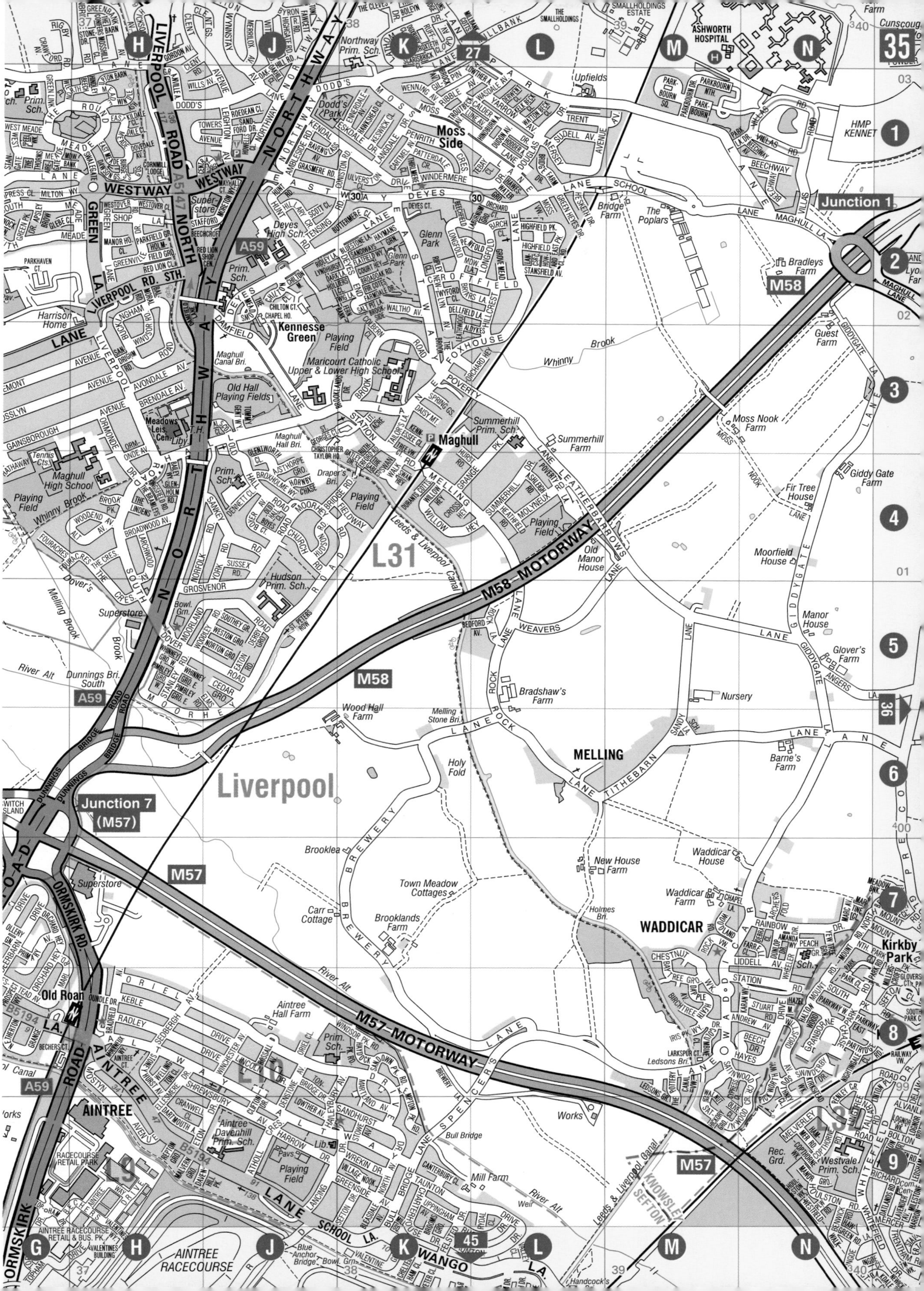
ASHWORTH HOSPITAL
HMP KENNET
Junction 1
Moss Side
WESTWAY
LIVERPOOL ROAD NORTH
NORTHWAY
A59
M58
M58-MOTORWAY
M57
M57-MOTORWAY
Junction 7 (M57)
Deyes High Sch.
Kennesse Green
Maricourt Catholic Upper & Lower High School
Maghull
Maghull High School
Old Hall Playing Fields
Meadows Leis. Cen.
Summerhill Prim. Sch.
Hudson Prim. Sch.
L31
Liverpool
MELLING
WADDICAR
Kirkby Park
Westvale Prim. Sch.
AINTREE
AINTREE RACECOURSE
RACECOURSE RETAIL PARK
Aintree Davenhill Prim. Sch.
L10
L9
Old Roan
Leeds & Liverpool Canal
River Alt
Whinny Brook
Melling Brook
Bradshaw's Farm
Wood Hall Farm
Brooklands Farm
Town Meadow Cottages
Waddicar House
New House Farm
Moorfield House
Manor House
Glover's Farm
Barne's Farm
Giddy Gate Farm
Moss Nook Farm
Guest Farm
Bradleys Farm
Mill Farm
KNOWSLEY
SEFTON
27
45
36
G H J K L M N
1 2 3 4 5 6 7 8 9

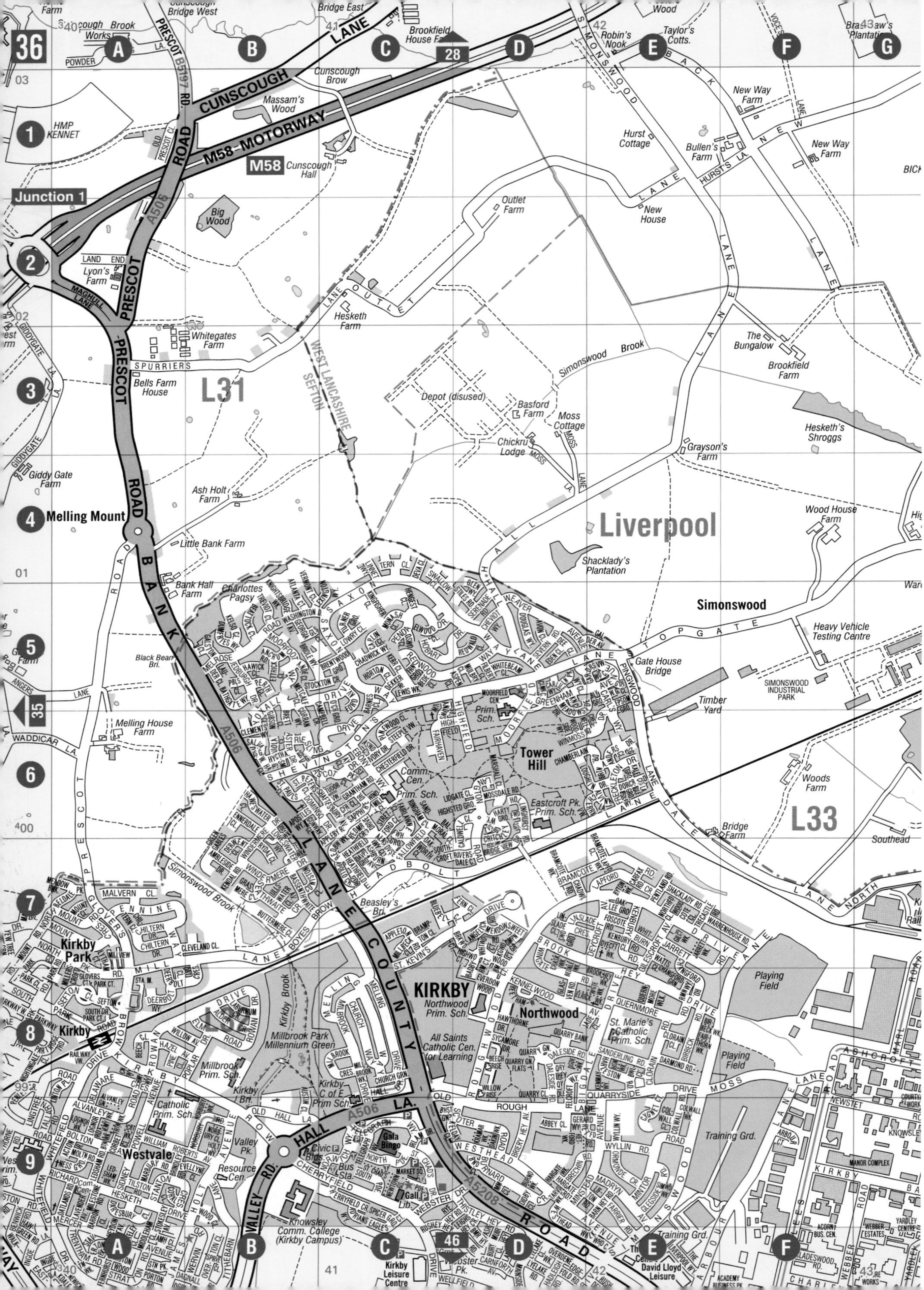
Cunscough Brook
Works
POWDER
Cunscough Bridge West
Bridge East
Brookfield House Farm
28
Robin's Nook
Taylor's Cotts.
Wood
A
B
C
D
E
F
G
03
CUNSCOUGH
LANE
Cunscough Brow
Massam's Wood
M58 MOTORWAY
M58
Cunscough Hall
PRESCOT B5197 RD.
PRESCOT ROAD
A506
OLD PRESCOT CL.
HMP KENNET
Junction 1
Big Wood
LAND END
Lyon's Farm
MAGHULL LANE
PRESCOT
SIMONSWOOD
BACK
LANE
New Way Farm
New Way Farm
Hurst Cottage
Bullen's Farm
HURST'S LA.
NEW
LANE
Outlet Farm
New House
Hesketh Farm
LANE OUTLET
02
Whitegates Farm
SPURRIERS
Bells Farm House
L31
GIDDYGATE LA.
WEST LANCASHIRE
SEFTON
Simonswood Brook
The Bungalow
Brookfield Farm
Depot (disused)
Basford Farm
Moss Cottage
MOSS LA.
Chickru Lodge
Hesketh's Shroggs
Grayson's Farm
Giddy Gate Farm
Ash Holt Farm
ROAD
Melling Mount
Little Bank Farm
Liverpool
Wood House Farm
Shacklady's Plantation
01
Bank Hall Farm
BANK
HALL
Simonswood
Heavy Vehicle Testing Centre
TOPGATE
Black Beam Bri.
ANGERS LANE
35
Melling House Farm
WADDICAR LA.
Gate House Bridge
Timber Yard
SIMONSWOOD INDUSTRIAL PARK
PINGWOOD
Tower Hill
Comm. Cen.
Prim. Sch.
Eastcroft Pk. Prim. Sch.
Woods Farm
L33
Bridge Farm
Southead
DALE
LANE
400
PRESCOT
ROAD
Simonswood Brook
HEADBOLT
LANE
Beasley's Bri.
LANE NORTH
MALVERN CL.
PENNINE
CHILTERN DR.
CLEVELAND CL.
Kirkby Park
BOYES BROW
COUNTY
LANE
KIRKBY
Northwood Prim. Sch.
Northwood
Playing Field
Kirkby
Kirkby Brook
Millbrook Park Millennium Green
All Saints Catholic Cen. for Learning
St. Marie's Catholic Prim. Sch.
Playing Field
Millbrook Prim. Sch.
KIRKBY ROW
Catholic Prim. Sch.
Westvale
Valley Pk.
Resource Cen.
Kirkby C of E Prim Sch.
OLD HALL LA.
A506
Civic Bldgs.
Gala Bingo
Bus Sta.
Lib.
Knowsley Comm. College (Kirkby Campus)
CHERRYFIELD
VALLEY RD.
HALL
ROUGH LANE
QUARRYSIDE DRIVE
MOSS
Training Grd.
Training Grd.
A5208
WESTHEAD
ROAD
MANOR COMPLEX
KIRKBY
KNOWSLEY
46
Kirkby Leisure Centre
Webster Pk.
David Lloyd Leisure
WEBBER
ESTATES
YARDLEY CENTRE
ACORN BUS. CEN.
ACADEMY BUSINESS PK.
99
340
41
42
43

H
J
K
L
M
N
G
29
47
38
WA11
L39
1
2
3
4
5
6
7
8
9
Ormskirk
Barrow Nook
St. Helens
Red House Farm
Taylor's Wood
Wood End Farm
Wood House
Intake Farm
Barker's Bridge Wood
Ben Lane Farm
Barrow Nook Farm
Bickerstaffe Delf Pond
Moss Side
Pimbley's Wood
Cropper's Wood
Ben Lane Cotts.
Lodge Farm
Brook Plantation
Bawdy Brook
New Lodge
Wheat Sheaf Plantation
Kenyon's Wood
Slack House
The Cottage
Moss House Farm
Birchall's Wood
Rigby's Wood
Works
Walkden House Farm
Voces Farm
Sewage Works
New Bridge
New Bridge Farm
NEWBRIDGE FARM CARAVAN PARK
Barrow Nook Hall
Moss Farm
Nursery Plantation
Abram's Farm
Siding Lane Cotts.
Tower Ho.
Mill
Timber Yard
Hall's Folly
Simonswood Brook
Camholes Wood
Coach Road Farm
Wild Goose Slack
Old House Farm
Moss Cottage
Woodward's Plantation
Freddy's Wood
Bullens Farm
Eccleston House
Spencer's House Farm
SIMONSWOOD MOSS
Acorn Venture
Works
NORTH MERSEY BUSINESS CEN.
Brown Birch Farm
Clare's Planta
Mossborough Hall
Bunker Hill Wood
Top House Farm
WEST LANCASHIRE
KNOWSLEY
ST. HELENS
Brown Birches
Moss Plantation
IMAGE BUSINESS PARK
CAPITOL TRADING PARK
LODGE WORKS
INDUSTRIAL PARK
Charnley Wood
Kirkby Moss
BICKERSTAFFE MOSS
BARROW NOOK LANE
COACH ROAD
INTAKE LANE
BEN LANE
MOSS LA.
LODGE LA.
SIDING LANE
SINEACRE LANE
DAIRY FARM ROAD
PERIMETER ROAD
WOODWARD ROAD
MOSS END WAY
BRADMAN ROAD
HAMMOND ROAD
BOUNDARY LANE
MOSSBOROUGH HALL LANE
NEW CUT LANE
DEPOT
344
345
46
400
99
01
02
03

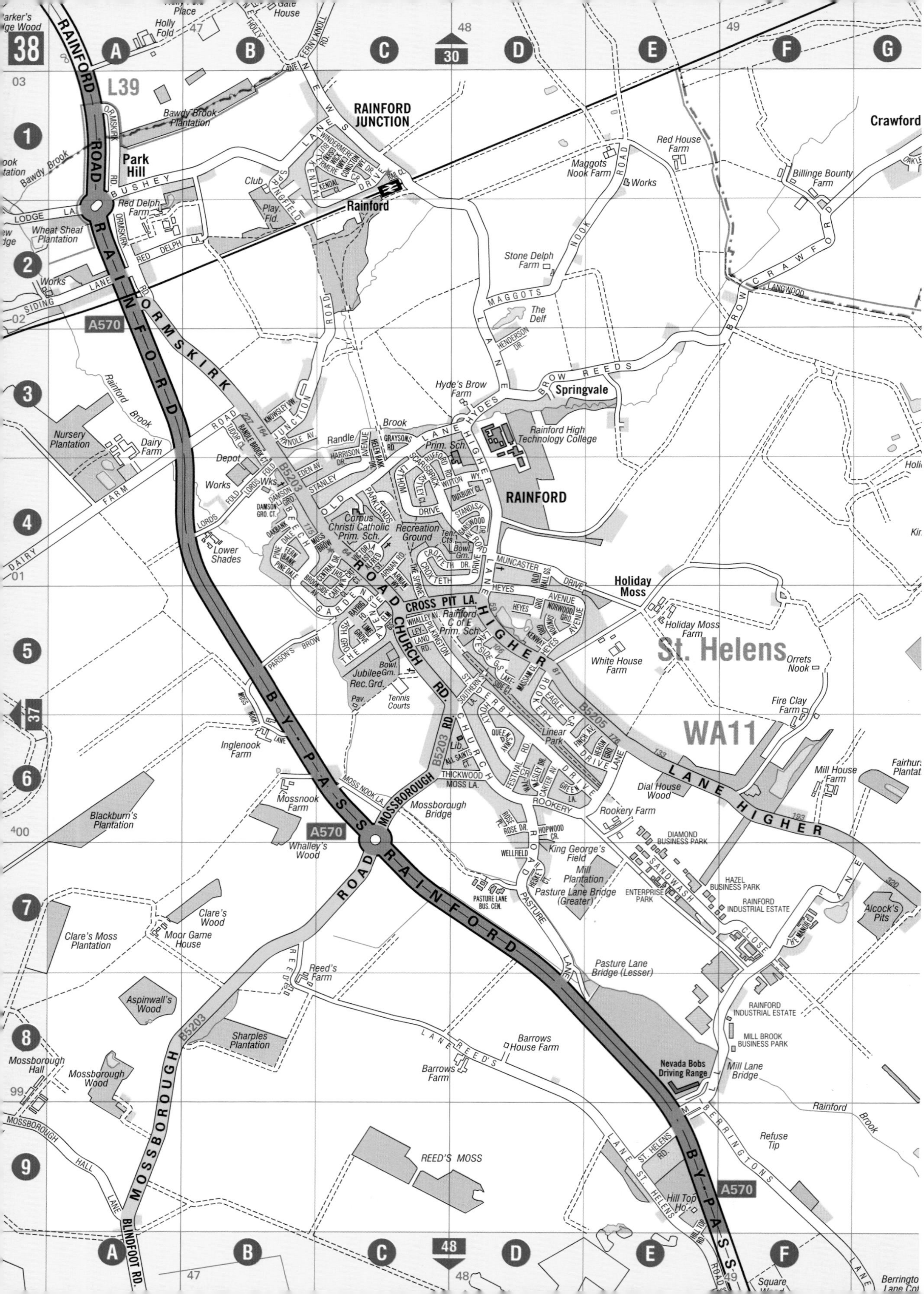
RAINFORD JUNCTION
Rainford
Park Hill
Crawford
Red House Farm
Maggots Nook Farm
Works
Billinge Bounty Farm
Bawdy Brook Plantation
Bawdy Brook
Red Delph Farm
Wheat Sheaf Plantation
Club
Play. Fld.
Stone Delph Farm
The Delf
Springvale
Hyde's Brow Farm
Rainford High Technology College
RAINFORD
Rainford Brook
Nursery Plantation
Dairy Farm
Depot
Works
Lower Shades
Corpus Christi Catholic Prim. Sch.
Recreation Ground
Prim. Sch.
Holiday Moss
Holiday Moss Farm
White House Farm
St. Helens
Orrets Nook
Fire Clay Farm
WA11
Rainford C of E Prim. Sch.
Jubilee Rec.Grd.
Tennis Courts
Inglenook Farm
Linear Park
Dial House Wood
Mill House Farm
Mossnook Farm
Mossborough Bridge
Rookery Farm
Blackburn's Plantation
Whalley's Wood
DIAMOND BUSINESS PARK
King George's Field
Mill Plantation
HAZEL BUSINESS PARK
Pasture Lane Bridge (Greater)
ENTERPRISE PARK
RAINFORD INDUSTRIAL ESTATE
Alcock's Pits
Clare's Wood
Moor Game House
Clare's Moss Plantation
Reed's Farm
Pasture Lane Bridge (Lesser)
Aspinwall's Wood
RAINFORD INDUSTRIAL ESTATE
MILL BROOK BUSINESS PARK
Sharples Plantation
Barrows House Farm
Mossborough Hall
Mossborough Wood
Barrows Farm
Nevada Bobs Driving Range
Mill Lane Bridge
Refuse Tip
REED'S MOSS
Hill Top Ho.
RAINFORD BY-PASS
A570
B5203
B5205
HIGHER LANE
CHURCH ROAD
MOSSBOROUGH ROAD
ORMSKIRK ROAD
CROSS PIT LA.
L39
37
30
48

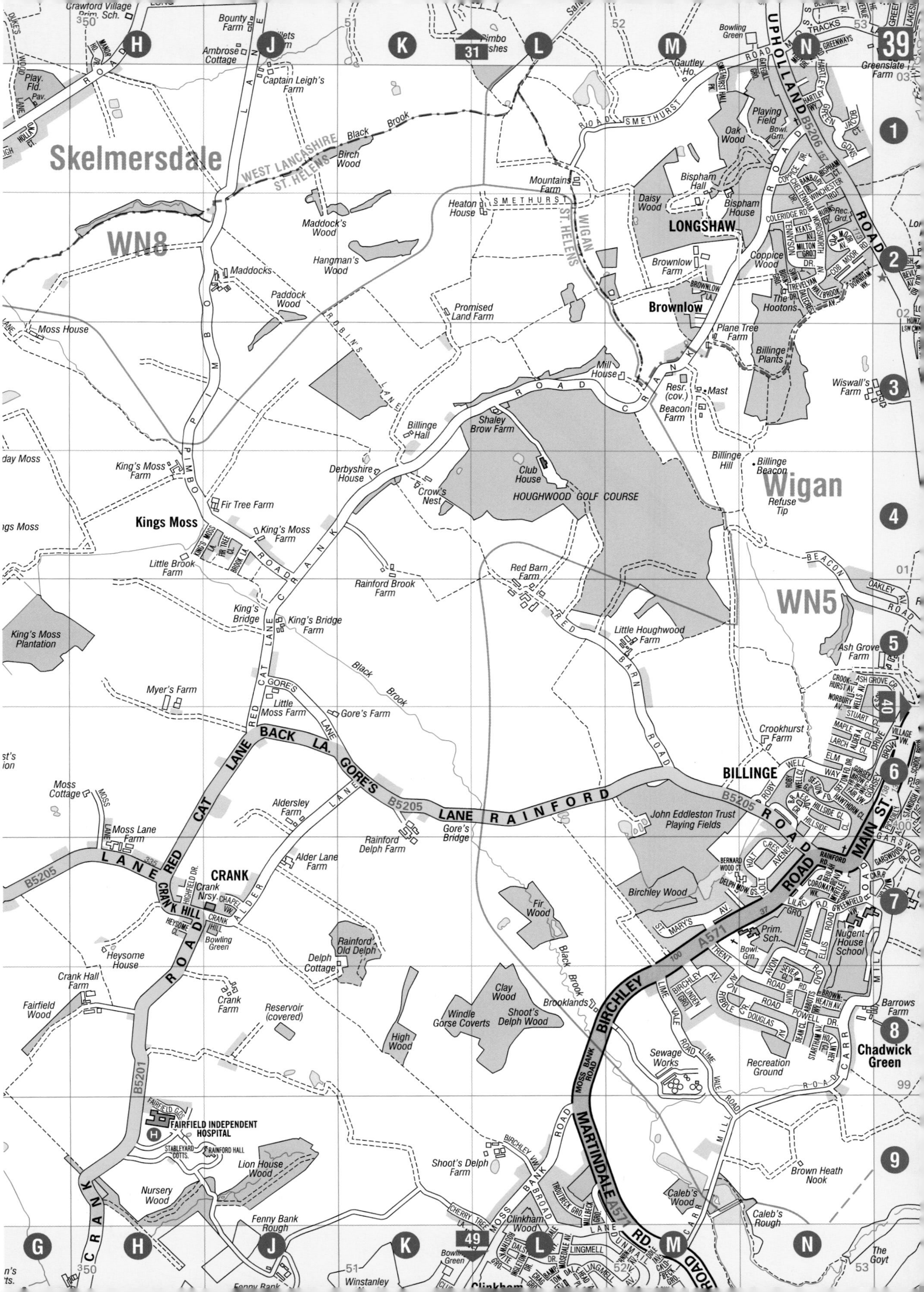
39
Skelmersdale
WN8
WN5
Wigan
LONGSHAW
Brownlow
BILLINGE
Kings Moss
CRANK
Chadwick Green
Crawford Village Prim. Sch.
Bounty Farm
Ambrose Cottage
Captain Leigh's Farm
Pimbo Lane
Play. Fld.
WEST LANCASHIRE
ST. HELENS
Black Brook
Birch Wood
Maddock's Wood
Hangman's Wood
Maddocks
Paddock Wood
Moss House
Gautley Ho.
Bowling Green
Greenslate Farm
Smethurst Road
Playing Field
Oak Wood
Mountains Farm
Heaton House
Bispham Hall
Bispham House
Daisy Wood
Brownlow Farm
Coppice Wood
The Hootons
Promised Land Farm
Robin's Lane
Plane Tree Farm
Billinge Plants
Wiswall's Farm
Mill House
Resr. (cov.)
Mast
Beacon Farm
Crank Road
Billinge Hall
Shaley Brow Farm
Club House
HOUGHWOOD GOLF COURSE
Billinge Hill
Billinge Beacon
Refuse Tip
King's Moss Farm
Derbyshire House
Crow's Nest
Fir Tree Farm
Kings Moss
Little Brook Farm
Rainford Brook Farm
Red Barn Farm
Beacon Road
Oakley Av.
King's Bridge
King's Bridge Farm
King's Moss Plantation
Little Houghwood Farm
Red Barn Road
Ash Grove Farm
Myer's Farm
Little Moss Farm
Gore's Farm
Red Cat Lane
Back La.
Gore's Lane
Crookhurst Farm
Moss Cottage
Aldersley Farm
B5205
Rainford Road
John Eddleston Trust Playing Fields
Moss Lane Farm
Gore's Bridge
Rainford Delph Farm
Alder Lane Farm
Crank Nrsy.
Crank Hill
Birchley Wood
Main St.
Fir Wood
Heysome House
Bowling Green
Rainford Old Delph
Delph Cottage
Prim. Sch.
A571
Nugent House School
Crank Hall Farm
Fairfield Wood
Crank Farm
Reservoir (covered)
Clay Wood
Windle Gorse Coverts
Shoot's Delph Wood
Brooklands
Birchley Road
Barrows Farm
High Wood
Sewage Works
Recreation Ground
B5201
FAIRFIELD INDEPENDENT HOSPITAL
Lion House Wood
Shoot's Delph Farm
Moss Bank Road
Martindale Rd.
Brown Heath Nook
Nursery Wood
Caleb's Wood
Caleb's Rough
Fenny Bank Rough
Clinkham Wood
Cherry Tree La.
49
31
Winstanley
Goyt
G H J K L M N
1 2 3 4 5 6 7 8 9
40

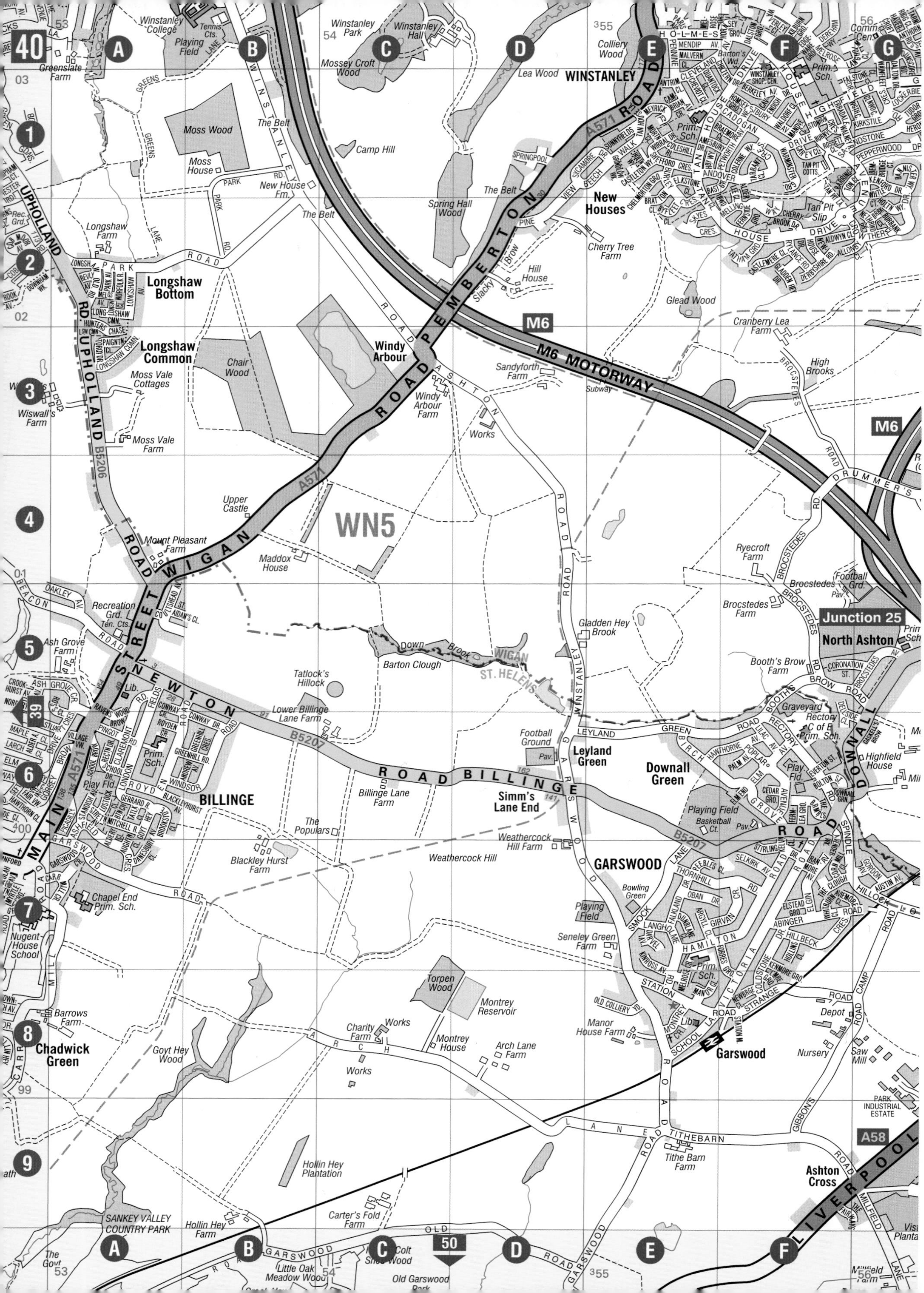

Winstanley College
Tennis Cts.
Playing Field
Winstanley Park
Winstanley Hall
Mossey Croft Wood
Colliery Wood
Lea Wood
WINSTANLEY
Greenslate Farm
Moss Wood
Moss House
The Belt
Camp Hill
New House Fm.
Spring Hall Wood
New Houses
Cherry Tree Farm
Tan Pit Slip
Longshaw Farm
Longshaw Bottom
Longshaw Common
Hill House
Glead Wood
Cranberry Lea Farm
Chair Wood
Windy Arbour
Windy Arbour Farm
Sandyforth Farm
Subway
M6
M6 MOTORWAY
High Brooks
Moss Vale Cottages
Wiswall's Farm
Moss Vale Farm
Works
Upper Castle
WN5
Mount Pleasant Farm
Maddox House
Ryecroft Farm
Brocstedes
Football Grd.
Brocstedes Farm
Junction 25
North Ashton
Recreation Grd.
Ten. Cts.
Gladden Hey Brook
Ash Grove Farm
Down Brook
Barton Clough
WIGAN
ST. HELENS
Booth's Brow Farm
Tatlock's Hillock
Graveyard
Rectory
C of E Prim. Sch.
Lower Billinge Lane Farm
Football Ground
Leyland Green
Downall Green
Highfield House
Billinge Lane Farm
Simm's Lane End
BILLINGE
Playing Field
Basketball Ct.
The Populars
Weathercock Hill Farm
Blackley Hurst Farm
Weathercock Hill
GARSWOOD
Chapel End Prim. Sch.
Bowling Green
Nugent House School
Seneley Green Farm
Torpen Wood
Montrey Reservoir
Manor House Farm
Barrows Farm
Charity Farm
Montrey House
Arch Lane Farm
Depot
Chadwick Green
Goyt Hey Wood
Garswood
Nursery
Saw Mill
PARK INDUSTRIAL ESTATE
A58
Tithe Barn Farm
Hollin Hey Plantation
Ashton Cross
SANKEY VALLEY COUNTRY PARK
Hollin Hey Farm
Carter's Fold Farm
Colt Shoo Wood
Little Oak Meadow Wood
Old Garswood Park
50
39
PEMBERTON ROAD
WIGAN ROAD
UPHOLLAND ROAD
STREET MAIN
NEWTON ROAD
BILLINGE ROAD
ASHTON ROAD
WINSTANLEY ROAD
GARSWOOD ROAD
DOWNALL ROAD
LIVERPOOL ROAD
TITHEBARN ROAD
ARCH LANE
OLD GARSWOOD ROAD
A571
B5206
B5207

Hawkley
Hawkley Hall High Sch.
WN3
Works
Total Fitness
Depot
Wheatlea Ind. Est.
Derbyshire Farm Business Park
Derbyshire House Farm
Rough Wood
Marus Bridge Retail Park
Hope Sch.
Hawkley Brook
Hawkley Brook Trading Est.
Warehouses
Ince Moss
Leeds & Liverpool Canal
Park House
WN2
Park Brook Farm
Park Brook Bri.
Bryn Hall
Bryn Hall Farm
Bamfurlong
Land Gate
Haslemere Industrial Estate
Landgate Industrial Estate
Link Farm
M6 Motorway
Park Lane Farm
Doe Ridings
Perry Brook Bri.
Landgate Fm.
Landgate Sch.
Edmund Collins Park
Drummersfield Farm
Wigan
Rose Hill
Bryn
Three Sisters Race Circuit
Boating Lake
Bryn Gates
Viridor Wood
Baldwins
Playing Field
Works
The Three Sisters Enterprise Park
Kingfisher Ct. Ind. Est.
South Lancashire Industrial Estate
Ashton Grange Ind. Est.
Warehouse
Depot
Lily Lane Farm
Lily Farm
Stubshaw Cross
Nicol Mere Prim. Sch.
Ashton Leisure Cen.
Potter's Farm
White Rushes Farm
Playing Fld.
WN4
Jubilee Parks
King George's Fld.
RL Hughes Prim. Sch.
Football Grd.
Prim. Sch.
Jameson's Farm
Charity Farm
Golborne Road Farm
Edge Green Farm
Sewage Farm
Town Green
Junction 24
Saw Mill
Garswood Park
Ashton-in-Makerfield Golf Course
Club Ho.
New Hall Wood
Long Covert
Ashton-in-Makerfield
Byrchall High Sch.
Ashton Heath
Ashton Heath Farm
Edge Green Common
Millingford Bri.
Paddock
Stables
Grandstands
51

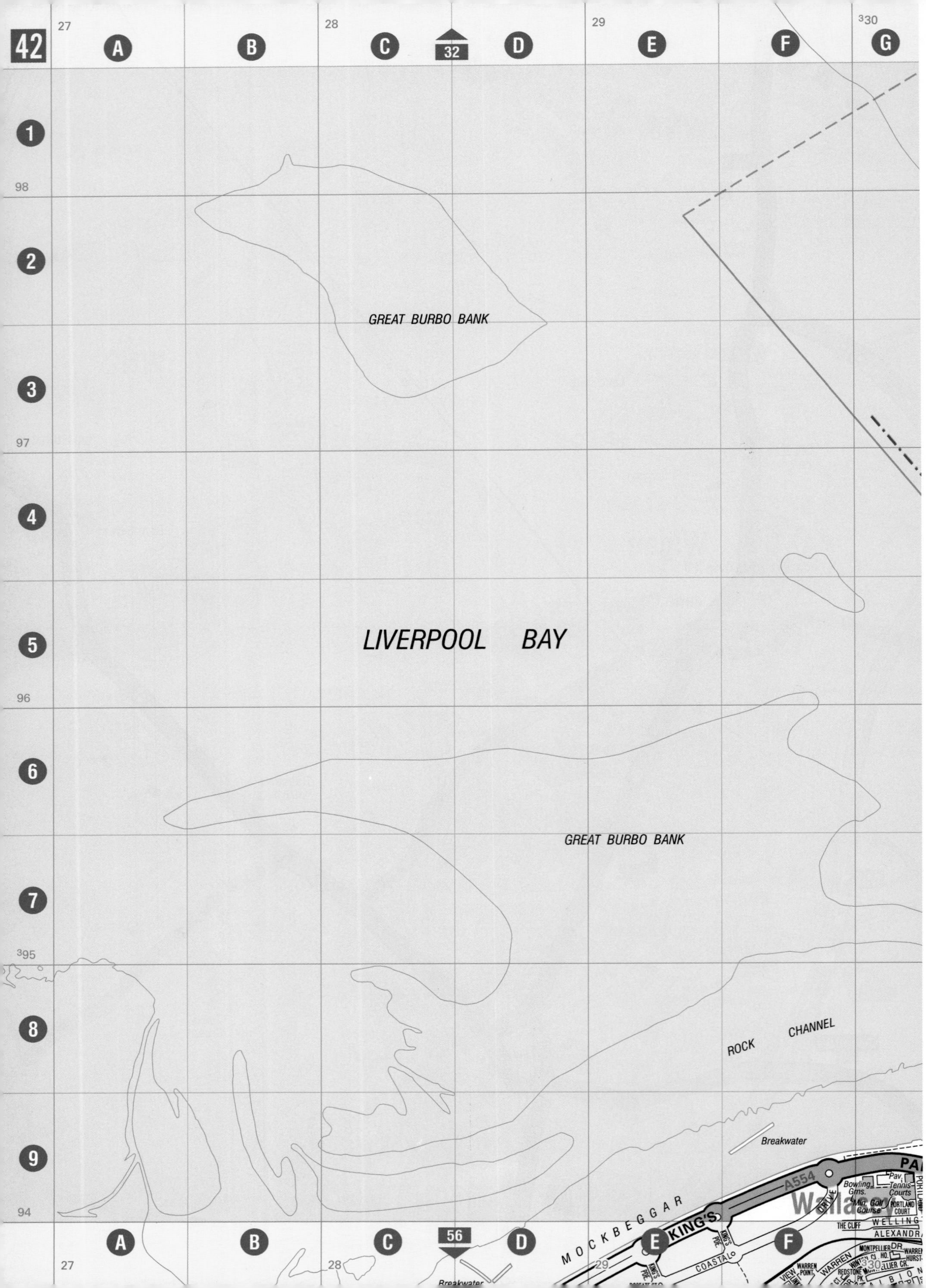
A
B
C
D
E
F
G
1
2
3
4
5
6
7
8
9
27
28
29
330
98
97
96
395
94
32
56
GREAT BURBO BANK
LIVERPOOL BAY
GREAT BURBO BANK
ROCK
CHANNEL
Breakwater
Breakwater
MOCKBEGGAR
KING'S
KING'S PDE.
COASTAL
DRIVE
A554
Wallasey
Bowling Grns.
Pav.
Tennis Courts
Min. Golf Course
PORTLAND COURT
THE CLIFF
WELLING
ALEXANDRA
MONTPELLIER DR.
WARREN
VIEW
WARREN POINT
REDSTONE PK.
ALBION

43
Brighton le Sands
CROSBY COASTAL PARK
Beach Lawn Garden
Adelaide Garden
Boating Lake
Waterloo
Crescent Garden
CROSBY
Paddling Pool
Marine Garden
MARINE LAKE
Crosby Lakeside Adventure Centre
Esplanade Cen.
Seaforth Nature Reserve
Radar Station
Wind Turbine
Warehouse
Works
Container Stacking Area
PORT OF LIVERPOOL EURO RAIL TERMINAL
L21
Travelling Crane
Timber Sheds
SEAFORTH CONTAINER PORT
ROYAL SEAFORTH DOCK
Grain Dock
Silos
P&O Irish Sea Ferries Terminal
Transit Shed
Branch Dock (No. 3)
Branch Dock (No. 2)
Branch Dock (No. 1)
GLADSTONE DOCK
Depot
Travelling Cranes
Coal Terminal
Hornby Dock
Lighthouse
Gladstone Lock
West Hornby Dock
Liverpool to Dublin 8 hours.
Bootle
L20
ALEXANDRA DOCK
LANGTON DOCK
Branch Dock
Brocklebank Dock
Canada Branch Dock (No. 3)
Canada Branch Dock (No. 2)
CANADA DOCK
CROSBY CHANNEL
SEFTON
WIRRAL
Rock Lighthouse
Fort Perch Rock Marine Radio Museum
Perch Rock
Breakwater
Marine Point Health & Fitness
The Light Cinema
Marine Lake
Amusement Park
Bowl. Alley
Theatre
MARINE PROMENADE
NEW BRIGHTON
CH45
Lifeboat Sta.
Seaforth
Liverpool
Warehouses
Trailer Park
No 1
Depot
Waterloo Park
Playing Field
Running Track
RIMROSE VALLEY COUNTRY PARK
Brookvale Local Nature Reserve
Rimrose Brook
LITHERLAND
Hatton Hill Park
NHS Walk-in Cen.
Seaforth & Litherland
RIMROSE BUS. PK.
LIVERPOOL INTERMODAL FREEPORT TERMINAL
ATLANTIC TERMINAL
CROSBY ROAD NORTH
CROSBY ROAD SOUTH
RIMROSE ROAD
PRINCESS WY.
KNOWSLEY RD.
MARSH LA.
DERBY RD.
REGENT RD.
A565
A5036
A566
A5098
B5421
33
57
44
G H J K L M N
1 2 3 4 5 6 7 8 9
31 32 33

LITHERLAND
Liverpool
Stanley Park
L30
L21
L20
BOOTLE
Bootle
Seaforth & Litherland
Orrell
Orrell Park
Victoria Park
Warbreck Park
Aintree
Walton
Rice La.
Kirkdale
Bankhall
WALTON
HMP LIVERPOOL
Rice Lane Recreation Ground
Derby Park
Bootle New Strand
Bootle Oriel Rd.
ANFIELD CEMETERY
Everton FC (Goodison Pk.)
Canada Branch Dock (No. 3)
Canada Branch Dock (No. 2)
LIVERPOOL RC CEMETERY
Litherland High Sch.
Litherland Sports Park
Savio Salesian Coll.
NETHERTON IND. ESTATE
BRIDLE ROAD IND. ESTATE
SENATE BUSINESS PARK
SEFTON BUSINESS PARK
Inland Container Depot
Aintree Curve
Walton Park Cemetery
Rice Lane City Farm
Hillside High Sch.
St. Monica's Cath. Prim. Sch.
St. Robert Bellarmine Cath. Prim. Sch.
The Hawthorne's Free School
Our Lady of Walsingham Catholic Primary School
A5036
A5038
A5090
A566
A567
A5098
A5057
A5058
A565
A59
A580
A5056
B5422
B5090
B5318
DUNNINGS BRIDGE ROAD
CHURCH ROAD
HAWTHORNE ROAD
STANLEY ROAD
LINACRE LANE
AINTREE ROAD
KNOWSLEY ROAD
MARSH LANE
DERBY ROAD
REGENT ROAD
RIMROSE ROAD
MERTON ROAD
BALLIOL ROAD
BREEZE HILL
QUEENS DRIVE
RICE LANE
ORMSKIRK ROAD
WARBRECK MOOR
WALTON VALE
MOSS LANE
HORNBY ROAD
SOUTHPORT ROAD
BAILEY DRIVE
NETHERTON WAY
COUNTY ROAD
WALTON LANE
HALE RD.
BREWSTER ST.
MELROSE RD.
GORSEY LA.
43
34
58

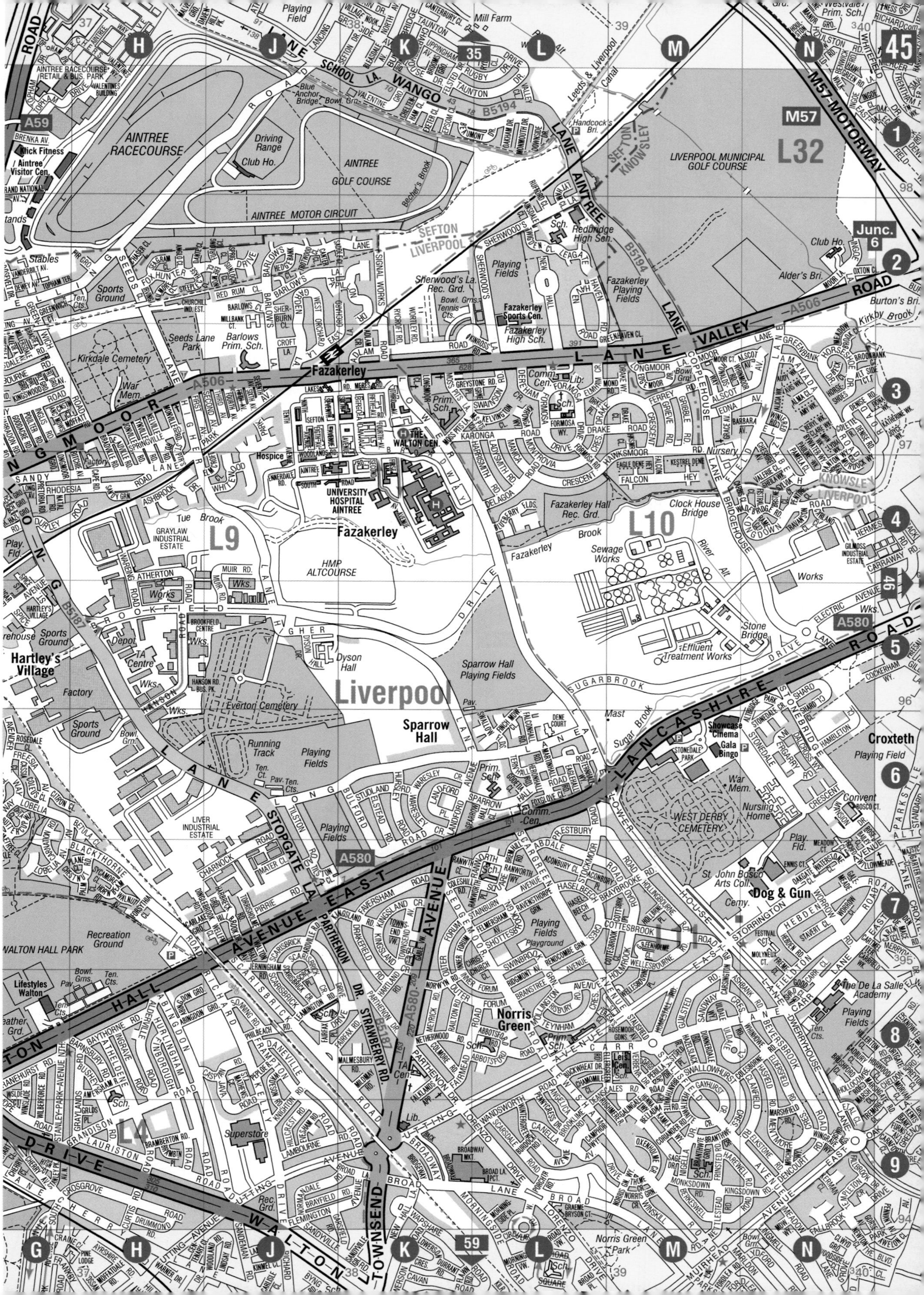

35
AINTREE RACECOURSE RETAIL & BUS. PARK
AINTREE RACECOURSE
Aintree Visitor Cen.
Klick Fitness
Driving Range
Club Ho.
AINTREE GOLF COURSE
AINTREE MOTOR CIRCUIT
Becher's Brook
SCHOOL LA.
WANGO
B5194
Mill Farm
Playing Field
Leeds & Liverpool Canal
Handcock's Bri.
SEFTON
KNOWSLEY
LIVERPOOL
LIVERPOOL MUNICIPAL GOLF COURSE
L32
M57
M57 MOTORWAY
Junc. 6
Club Ho.
Alder's Bri.
Burton's Bri.
Kirkby Brook
Redbridge High Sch.
Sherwood's La. Rec. Grd.
Playing Fields
Fazakerley Sports Cen.
Fazakerley High Sch.
Fazakerley Playing Fields
Stables
Sports Ground
Barlows Prim. Sch.
Seeds Lane Park
Kirkdale Cemetery
War Mem.
Fazakerley
A506
LONGMOOR LANE
VALLEY ROAD
THE WALTON CEN.
Hospice
UNIVERSITY HOSPITAL AINTREE
Fazakerley
HMP ALTCOURSE
GRAYLAW INDUSTRIAL ESTATE
L9
Tue Brook
Fazakerley Hall Rec. Grd.
Clock House Bridge
L10
Sewage Works
River Alt
Works
GILMOSS INDUSTRIAL ESTATE
46
ELECTRIC AVENUE
A580
Stone Bridge
Effluent Treatment Works
Nursery
KNOWSLEY
LIVERPOOL
BROOKFIELD
B5187
Hartley's Village
Sports Ground
Depot
TA Centre
Factory
Wks.
Dyson Hall
Sparrow Hall Playing Fields
Liverpool
Everton Cemetery
Running Track
Playing Fields
Sparrow Hall
SUGARBROOK
Mast
Sugar Brook
Showcase Cinema
Gala Bingo
EAST LANCASHIRE ROAD
Croxteth
Playing Field
Convent
LIVER INDUSTRIAL ESTATE
STOPGATE LA.
Playing Fields
WEST DERBY CEMETERY
War Mem.
Nursing Home
St. John Bosco Arts Coll.
Dog & Gun
Cemy.
Play Fld.
WALTON HALL PARK
Recreation Ground
WALTON HALL AVENUE EAST
PARTHENON DR.
AVENUE
Playing Fields
Playground
Lifestyles Walton
Norris Green
The De La Salle Academy
Playing Fields
STRAWBERRY RD.
A580
B5187
TA Cen.
Leis. Cen.
Superstore
L4
Lib.
BROADWAY MKT.
BROAD LANE
TOWNSEND
WALTON DRIVE
Norris Green Park
59
G
H
J
K
L
M
N
1
2
3
4
5
6
7
8
9

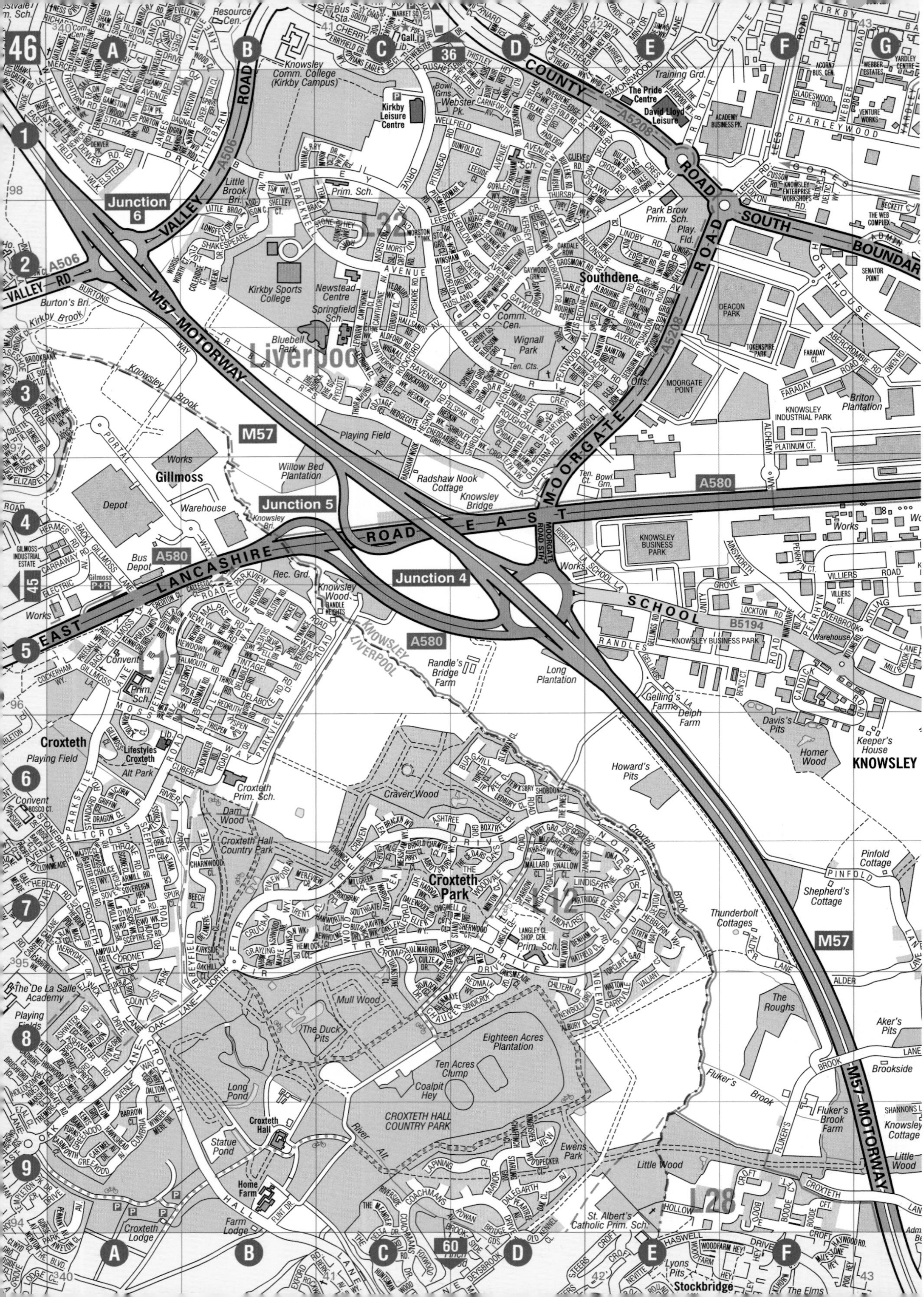
Knowsley Comm. College (Kirkby Campus)
Kirkby Leisure Centre
Webster Pk.
The Pride Centre
David Lloyd Leisure
Training Grd.
Academy Business Pk.
Acorn Bus. Cen.
Webber Estates
Yardley Centre
Venture Works
Charleywood
Knowsley Enterprise Workshops
The Web Complex
Senator Point
Deacon Park
Tokenspire Park
Faraday Ct.
Moorgate Point
Knowsley Industrial Park
Briton Plantation
Platinum Ct.
Junction 6
Valley Road
A506
Little Brook Bri.
Bewley Drive
Prim. Sch.
L32
Southdene
Park Brow Prim. Sch.
Play. Fld.
County Road
A5208
South Boundary Road
Kirkby Sports College
Newstead Centre
Springfield Sch.
Bluebell Park
Liverpool
Wignall Park
Comm. Cen.
Ten. Cts.
Burton's Bri.
Kirkby Brook
Knowsley Brook
M57 Motorway
M57
Playing Field
Willow Bed Plantation
Radshaw Nook Cottage
Knowsley Bridge
Moorgate Road
Portal Way
Works
Gillmoss
Depot
Warehouse
Junction 5
Knowsley Bri.
East Lancashire Road
A580
Gillmoss Industrial Estate
Bus Depot
Rec. Grd.
Knowsley Wood
Randle Heights
Junction 4
Knowsley Business Park
School Lane
B5194
Randles Road
Long Plantation
Randle's Bridge Farm
Knowsley / Liverpool
L11
Convent
Prim. Sch.
Lib.
Lifestyles Croxteth
Croxteth
Playing Field
Alt Park
Croxteth Prim. Sch.
Gelling's Farm
Delph Farm
Davis's Pits
Homer Wood
Keeper's House
KNOWSLEY
Howard's Pits
Craven Wood
Dam Wood
Croxteth Hall Country Park
Croxteth Park
L12
Langley Cl. Shop. Cen.
Prim. Sch.
Croxteth Brook
Pinfold Cottage
Shepherd's Cottage
Thunderbolt Cottages
Alder Lane
M57
The De La Salle Academy
Playing Fields
Mull Wood
The Duck Pits
Eighteen Acres Plantation
Ten Acres Clump
Coalpit Hey
Long Pond
The Roughs
Aker's Pits
Brook Lane
Brookside
Fluker's Brook
Fluker's Brook Farm
Knowsley Cottage
Croxteth Hall
Croxteth Hall Country Park
River Alt
Statue Pond
Ewens Park
Little Wood
Home Farm
Farm Lodge
Croxteth Lodge
Croxteth Hall Lane
St. Albert's Catholic Prim. Sch.
L28
Lyons Pits
Stockbridge
The Elms
45
60
36

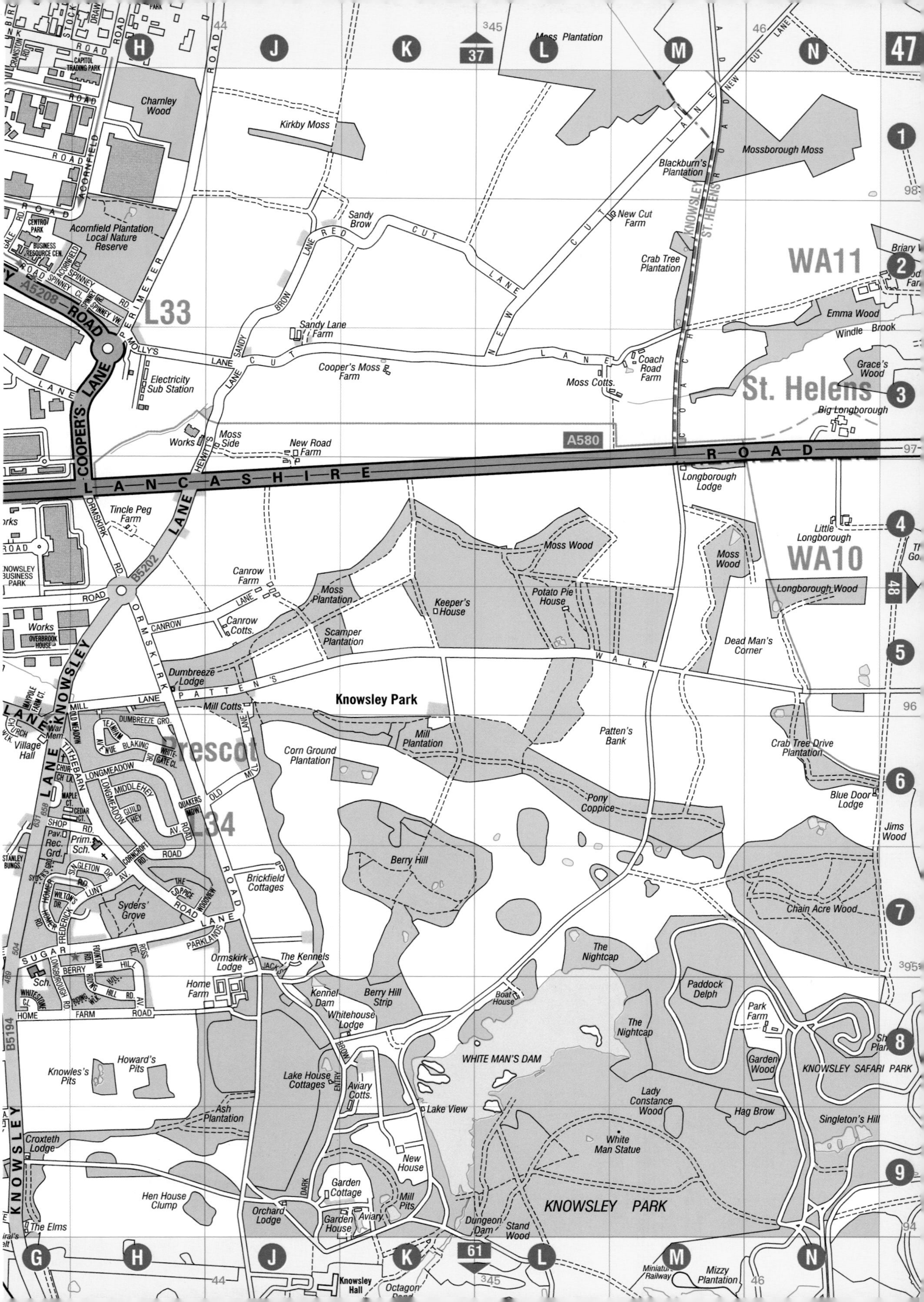
H
J
K
L
M
N
37
Moss Plantation
Charnley Wood
Kirkby Moss
Mossborough Moss
Blackburn's Plantation
KNOWSLEY ROAD
ST. HELENS ROAD
NEW CUT LANE
CAPITOL TRADING PARK
CENTRO PARK
BUSINESS RESOURCE CEN.
Acornfield Plantation Local Nature Reserve
ACORNFIELD ROAD
SPINNEY ROAD
A5208
PERIMETER RD.
L33
Sandy Brow
RED CUT LANE
SANDY BROW
New Cut Farm
Crab Tree Plantation
WA11
Emma Wood
Windle Brook
Sandy Lane Farm
Cooper's Moss Farm
MOLLY'S LANE
CUT LANE
SANDY LANE
Electricity Sub Station
COOPER'S LANE
Coach Road Farm
Moss Cotts.
Grace's Wood
St. Helens
Big Longborough
COACH ROAD
Works
Moss Side
New Road Farm
HEWITTS LANE
A580
LANCASHIRE ROAD
Longborough Lodge
Tincle Peg Farm
ORMSKIRK RD.
B5202
KNOWSLEY BUSINESS PARK
Canrow Farm
Moss Plantation
Moss Wood
Potato Pie House
Keeper's House
Moss Wood
Little Longborough
WA10
Longborough Wood
48
CANROW LANE
Canrow Cotts.
Works
OVERBROOK HOUSE
Scamper Plantation
Dead Man's Corner
Dumbreeze Lodge
PATTEN'S WALK
MILL LANE
Mill Cotts.
Knowsley Park
KNOWSLEY LANE
DUMBREEZE GRO.
BLAKING
Prescot
Mill Plantation
Patten's Bank
Crab Tree Drive Plantation
War Mem.
Village Hall
TITHEBARN
LONGMEADOW
MIDDLEHEY
GUILD HEY
Corn Ground Plantation
OLD MILL LANE
Pony Coppice
Blue Door Lodge
QUAKERS MDW.
L34
Jims Wood
Prim. Sch.
Rec. Grd.
STANLEY BUNGS.
CORNCROFT RD.
Berry Hill
ORMSKIRK ROAD
SYDER'S GRO.
SINGLETON DR.
Brickfield Cottages
LUNT
THE COPPICE
WOODVIEW
Syders' Grove
ROAD LANE
FREDERICK
Chain Acre Wood
HOMER
SUGAR LANE
FOUNTAIN RD.
BERRY HILL
ROSS CL.
PARKLANDS
Ormskirk Lodge
The Kennels
The Nightcap
Paddock Delph
Sch.
WHITESTONE CL.
LONGBOROUGH RD.
Home Farm
Kennel Dam
Berry Hill Strip
Boat House
Park Farm
HOME FARM ROAD
Whitehouse Lodge
The Nightcap
B5194
Howard's Pits
WHITE MAN'S DAM
Garden Wood
KNOWSLEY SAFARI PARK
Knowles's Pits
Lake House Cottages
Aviary Cotts.
Lady Constance Wood
Hag Brow
Ash Plantation
Lake View
Singleton's Hill
White Man Statue
Croxteth Lodge
KNOWSLEY
New House
Garden Cottage
Hen House Clump
Orchard Lodge
Mill Pits
KNOWSLEY PARK
Garden House
Aviary
Dungeon Dam
Stand Wood
The Elms
G
61
Knowsley Hall
Octagon
Miniature Railway
Mizzy Plantation
1
2
3
4
5
6
7
8
9
97
96
95
94
98
44
46
345

38
62
47
A570
A580
A58
B5203
B5201
Rainford By-Pass
Windle Moss
Moss Plantation
Square Wood
Pottery Farm
Berrington Lane Cot
Inglewood Farm
Long Wood
Blind Foot Farm
Harrison's Wood
Briary Wood
Woodside Farm
Grace's Wood
Watery Lane Farm
Moss Farm
Liverpool St Helens Rugby Football Club
Windle Brook Bridge
Brandreth House
Potter's House Farm
Potter's Wood
St. Helens Crematorium
Windle
Windle Farm
Catchdale Moss Farm
The Gorse
Orith Farm
Hilton's Farm
Recreation Ground
Bleak Hill Prim. Sch.
Higher Barrowfield Farm
Carmelite Convent
Catchdale Moss House
Park Side Farm
WA10
Smithy Heritage Cen.
Eccleston
Oasis Health & Fitness
Millbrook Rec. Grd.
Playing Field
De La Salle School
Howard's Farm
St. Julie's Catholic Prim. Sch.
Brook House Farm
Mill Brook
Jims Wood
Poplar Farm
Clay Lane Farm
Sports Ground
Mill Wood
Mill Dam
Pyke's Farm
Parkside Farm
Pilkington Sailing Club
Eccleston Top Dam
Eccleston Bottom Dam
Trap Wood
Burgesses Farm
Gillar's Green
Hall Farm
Old Joans Plantation
Eccleston Mere
Big Dam
St. Anns
Shaw's Plantation
Knowsley Safari Park
Grange Park Golf Course
Taylor Park
Little Dam
Mere View Farm
Mere Plantation
Burrow's Lane Farm
Prescot
Trapwood Cottage
Trap Lodge
Carmel College
Club Ho.
Broom Covert
Rugby Football Ground
Ivy House Farm
Roughley's Brow Farm
Sale's Wood
Gorse Plantation
L34
Pine Tree Farm
No. 4 Reservoir
No. 3 Reservoir
Prescot Cricket Ground
Broadway Badminton Centre
Grange Park
Catchdale Moss Lane
Gillar's Lane
Blindfoot Road
Moss Lane
Church Lane
Chapel La.
Millbrook Lane
Bleak Hill Road
Rainford Road
Knowsley Road
Millfields
Burrows Lane
Howards Lane
Houghtons Lane
Prescot Road
East Lancashire Road
Crank Road
Broadway

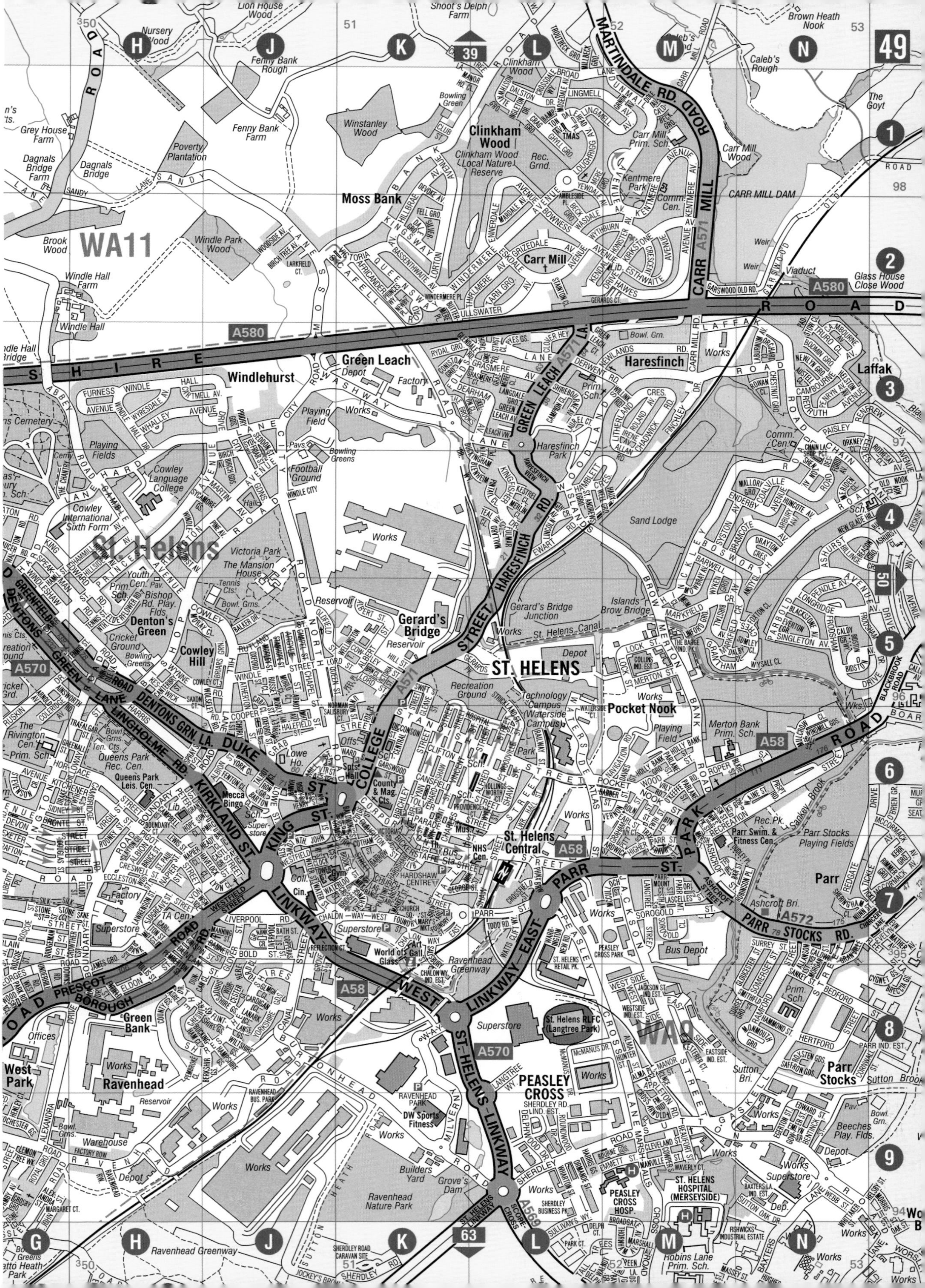
39
63
50
WA11
WA9
St. Helens
ST. HELENS
Moss Bank
Clinkham Wood
Clinkham Wood Local Nature Reserve
Carr Mill
CARR MILL DAM
Carr Mill Wood
Caleb's Rough
Brown Heath Nook
The Goyt
Glass House Close Wood
Windlehurst
Green Leach
Haresfinch
Laffak
Winstanley Wood
Fenny Bank Farm
Fenny Bank Rough
Poverty Plantation
Dagnals Bridge
Windle Hall
Windle Hall Farm
Windle Park Wood
Brook Wood
Grey House Farm
Nursery Wood
Lion House Wood
Shoot's Delph Farm
Cowley Language College
Cowley International Sixth Form
Victoria Park
The Mansion House
Gerard's Bridge
Gerard's Bridge Junction
Islands Brow Bridge
Sand Lodge
Haresfinch Park
Denton's Green
Cowley Hill
Queens Park Rec. Cen.
Queens Park Leis. Cen.
The Rivington Cen.
Recreation Ground
Technology Campus (Waterside Campus)
Pocket Nook
Merton Bank Prim. Sch.
St. Helens Canal
St. Helens Central
Hardshaw Centre
World of Glass
Ravenhead Greenway
St. Helens RLFC (Langtree Park)
Peasley Cross
Peasley Cross Hosp.
St. Helens Hospital (Merseyside)
Robins Lane Prim. Sch.
Parr
Parr Stocks
Parr Stocks Playing Fields
Parr Swim. & Fitness Cen.
Ashcroft Bri.
Sutton Bri.
Beeches Play. Flds.
Green Bank
West Park
Ravenhead
Ravenhead Nature Park
Ravenhead Park
Grove's Dam
DW Sports Fitness
Builders Yard
Sherdley Business Pk.
Fishwicks Industrial Estate
Sherdley Road Caravan Site
SHIRE ROAD
A580
A571
A570
A58
A572
A569
CARR MILL ROAD
MARTINDALE RD.
GREEN LEACH LA.
HARESFINCH RD.
HARESFINCH STREET
COLLEGE ST.
DUKE ST.
KING ST.
KIRKLAND ST.
LINKWAY
LINKWAY WEST
LINKWAY EAST
ST. HELENS LINKWAY
PARR ST.
PARK ROAD
PARR STOCKS RD.
PRESCOT ROAD
BOROUGH ROAD
DENTONS GRN. LA.
LINGHOLME RD.
WESTFIELD STREET
BASSENTHWAITE AV.
WINDERMERE AV.
ULLSWATER
BOSWORTH RD.
MERTON BANK ROAD
NORTH ROAD
CITY ROAD
WINDLE CITY
RAVENHEAD ROAD
BURTONHEAD ROAD
SUTTON ROAD
SHERDLEY RD.
GASKELL STREET
JACKSON STREET
WATERSIDE
G
H
J
K
L
M
N
1
2
3
4
5
6
7
8
9

Wigan WN4
WA11
St. Helens
Warrington
WA9
WA5
Pewfall
North Florida
Haydock
Blackbrook
Laffak
Broad Oak
Parr
Parr Stocks
Ashton's Green
Derbyshire Hill
MOSS NOOK
Worsley Brow
Collins Green
Ashton Cross
SANKEY VALLEY COUNTRY PARK
Old Garswood Park
Hollin Hey Plantation
Hollin Hey Farm
Carter's Farm
Higher Colt Shed Wood
Little Oak Meadow Wood
Crock Hey Wood
Deer House Farm
Old Garswood Hall Farm
Icehouse Plantation
Garswood Gates Farm
Glass House Close Wood
Florida Farm
Stanley Bank Farm
Stanley House Farm
St. Mary's Convent
Sankey Valley Visitor Centre
Haydock Sports Coll.
Haydock Sports Coll. Playing Field
Lyme House
Grange Valley Prim. Sch.
Callen's Farm
St. Helens Canal
St. Augustine of Canterbury Catholic High Sch.
Sewage Works
Depot
Cemetery
Sankey Brook
Fox Covert
Woodside Farm
Grange Farm
Rough Hey Wood
Hall House Farm
Woodhouse Farm
Pennington Lane Farm
Penkford Bri.
Gaskell Park
Broad Oak Prim. Sch.
Holy Spirit Prim. Sch.
Willow Green Youth Cen.
Lansbury Bridge School & Sports College
Lib. & Comm. Cen.
Playing Field
St. Cuthbert's Catholic College for Business and Enterprise
Recreation Ground
Moss House Farm
Collins Green Farm
Rose Villa
Moss Hall Farm
BURTONWOOD MOSS
Parr Moss
Sutton Oak C of E Prim. Sch.
Sutton Moss
White House Farm
Hillside
A58
A580
A599
A572
B5204
EAST LANCASHIRE ROAD
LIVERPOOL ROAD
BLACKBROOK ROAD
STANLEY BANK WAY
CLIPSLEY LANE
NEWTON ROAD
PENNINGTON ROAD
BROAD OAK RD
CHANCERY LA.
PARK RD.
FLEET LANE
BROAD LANE
PENKFORD LANE
PENNY LA.
GARSWOOD ROAD
OLD GARSWOOD ROAD
HAYDOCK LANE
40
49
64

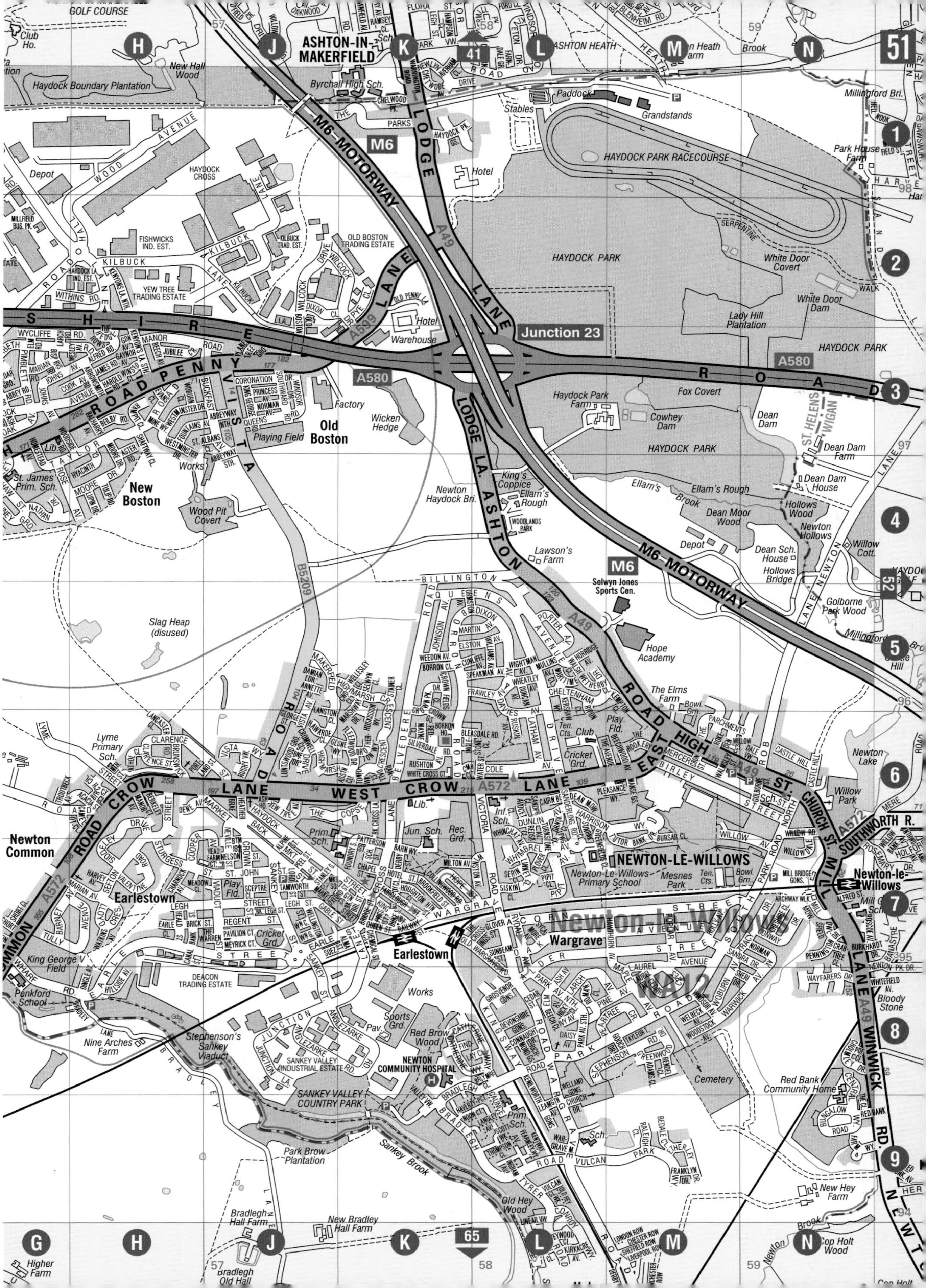
51
GOLF COURSE
Club Ho.
ASHTON-IN-MAKERFIELD
ASHTON HEATH
New Hall Wood
Haydock Boundary Plantation
Byrchall High Sch.
Millingford Bri.
Paddock
Grandstands
Stables
M6 MOTORWAY
M6
LODGE LANE
HAYDOCK PARK RACECOURSE
Park House Farm
Hotel
Depot
HAYDOCK CROSS
SERPENTINE
MILLFIELD BUS. PK.
FISHWICKS IND. EST.
KILBUCK TRAD. EST.
OLD BOSTON TRADING ESTATE
HAYDOCK PARK
White Door Covert
HAYDOCK LA. IND. EST.
YEW TREE TRADING ESTATE
White Door Dam
Lady Hill Plantation
Junction 23
Warehouse
A599
HAYDOCK PARK
SHIRE ROAD
A580
Haydock Park Farm
Fox Covert
ROAD PENNY
VISTA
Factory
Old Boston
Wicken Hedge
Cowhey Dam
Dean Dam
ST. HELENS WIGAN
Playing Field
HAYDOCK PARK
Dean Dam Farm
Lib.
St. James' Prim. Sch.
Works
New Boston
King's Coppice
Ellam's Rough
Newton Haydock Bri.
Ellam's Brook
Ellam's Rough
Dean Dam House
Hollows Wood
Wood Pit Covert
WOODLANDS PARK
Dean Moor Wood
Newton Hollows
Depot
Willow Cott.
Lawson's Farm
Dean Sch. House
Hollows Bridge
M6
Selwyn Jones Sports Cen.
52
B5209
BILLINGTON
Golborne Park Wood
A49
Slag Heap (disused)
Millingford
Hope Academy
The Elms Farm
Lyme Primary Sch.
Club
Cricket Grd.
Newton Lake
CROW LANE WEST CROW LANE
A572
Willow Park
Newton Common
Lib.
Prim. Sch.
Jun. Sch.
Rec. Grd.
Inf. Sch.
NEWTON-LE-WILLOWS
Newton-Le-Willows Primary School
Mesnes Park
Newton-le-Willows
Earlestown
Play. Fld.
Cricket Grd.
Newton-le-Willows
Wargrave
King George V Field
DEACON TRADING ESTATE
Earlestown
A49
Penkford School
Works
Sports Grd.
Pav.
Bloody Stone
Nine Arches Farm
Stephenson's Sankey Viaduct
Red Brow Wood
SANKEY VALLEY INDUSTRIAL ESTATE
NEWTON COMMUNITY HOSPITAL
Cemetery
Red Bank Community Home
SANKEY VALLEY COUNTRY PARK
Prim. Sch.
Park Brow Plantation
Sankey Brook
VULCAN PARK
WINWICK LANE
Old Hey Wood
New Hey Farm
Bradlegh Hall Farm
New Bradley Hall Farm
65
Brook
Cop Holt Wood
Higher Farm
Bradlegh Old Hall
G H J K L M N
1 2 3 4 5 6 7 8 9
57 58 59

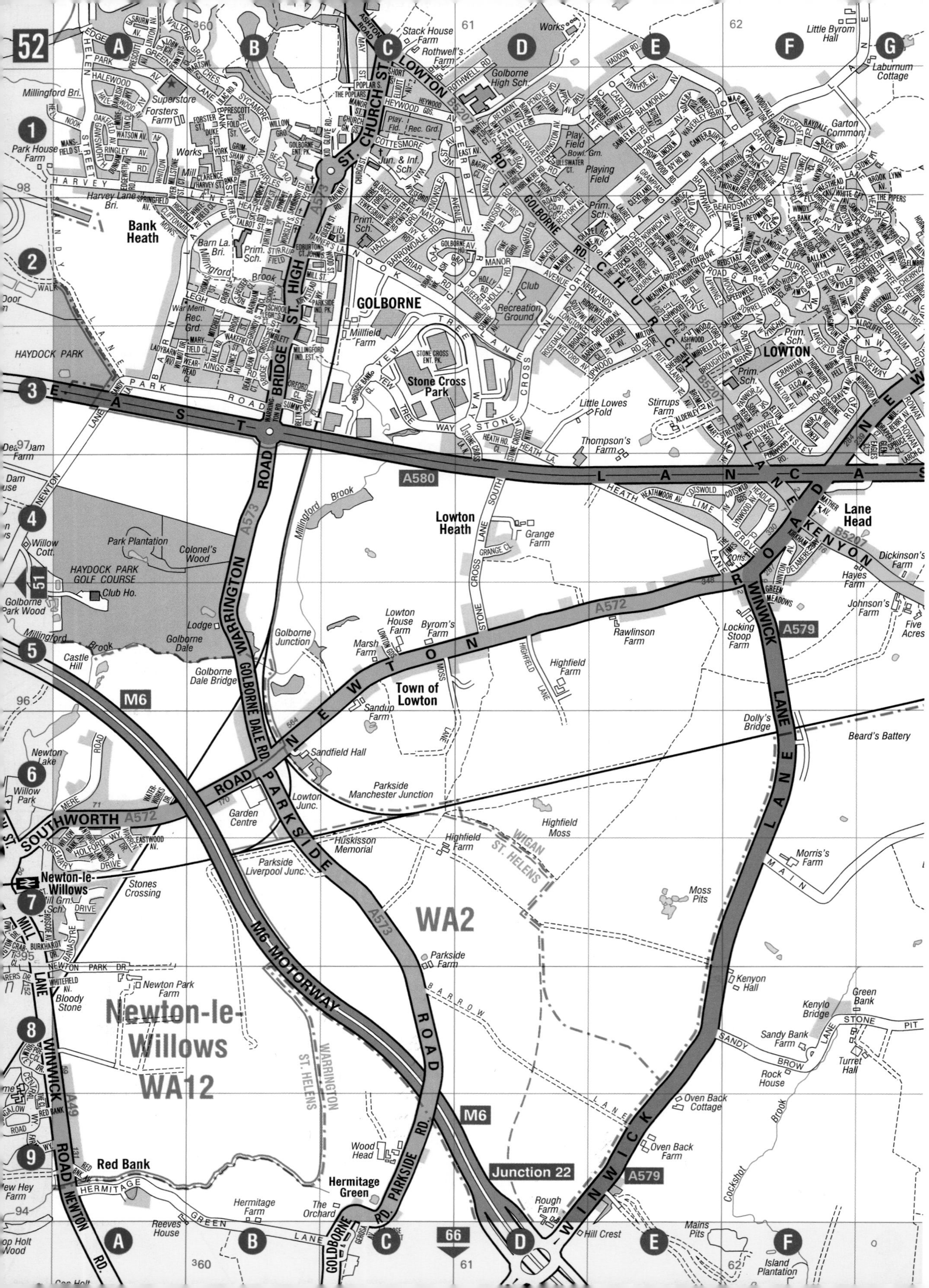
GOLBORNE
LOWTON
Lowton Heath
Town of Lowton
Lane Head
Bank Heath
Newton-le-Willows
WA12
WA2
Stone Cross Park
HAYDOCK PARK
HAYDOCK PARK GOLF COURSE
Park Plantation
Colonel's Wood
Golborne Dale
Golborne Dale Bridge
Castle Hill
Newton Lake
Willow Park
Red Bank
Hermitage Green
Highfield Moss
Moss Pits
Kenyon Hall
Kenylo Bridge
Green Bank
Sandy Bank Farm
Turret Hall
Rock House
Oven Back Cottage
Oven Back Farm
Rough Farm
Hill Crest
Mains Pits
Island Plantation
Wood Head
The Orchard
Hermitage Farm
Reeves House
Newton Park Farm
Bloody Stone
Stones Crossing
Parkside Liverpool Junc.
Huskisson Memorial
Parkside Farm
Parkside Manchester Junction
Lowton Junc.
Garden Centre
Sandfield Hall
Sandup Farm
Golborne Junction
Marsh Farm
Lowton House Farm
Byrom's Farm
Rawlinson Farm
Highfield Farm
Locking Stoop Farm
Dolly's Bridge
Beard's Battery
Morris's Farm
Johnson's Farm
Five Acres
Hayes Farm
Dickinson's Farm
Grange Farm
Little Lowes Fold
Stirrups Farm
Thompson's Farm
Millfield Farm
Recreation Ground
Playing Field
Golborne High Sch.
Stack House Farm
Rothwell's Farm
Little Byrom Hall
Laburnum Cottage
Garton Common
Millingford Bri.
Park House Farm
Forsters Farm
Superstore
Harvey Lane Bri.
Barn La. Bri.
War Mem. Rec. Grd.
Lodge
Club Ho.
Willow Cott.
Golborne Park Wood
M6
M6 MOTORWAY
A580
A572
A573
A579
A49
B5207
Junction 22
EAST LANCASHIRE ROAD
WARRINGTON ROAD
GOLBORNE DALE RD.
PARKSIDE ROAD
NEWTON ROAD
WINWICK LANE
WINWICK ROAD
NEWTON ROAD
SOUTHWORTH ROAD
CHURCH LANE
KENYON ROAD
HIGH ST.
BRIDGE ST.
ST. CHURCH ST.
LOWTON RD.
GOLBORNE RD.
HARVEY LANE
PARK ROAD
HEATH LANE
MOSS LANE
BARROW LANE
SANDY BROW
STONE PIT LANE
MAIN LANE
HERMITAGE GREEN LANE
WIGAN
ST. HELENS
WARRINGTON
51
66
A B C D E F G
1 2 3 4 5 6 7 8 9
360 61 62
98 97 96 95 94

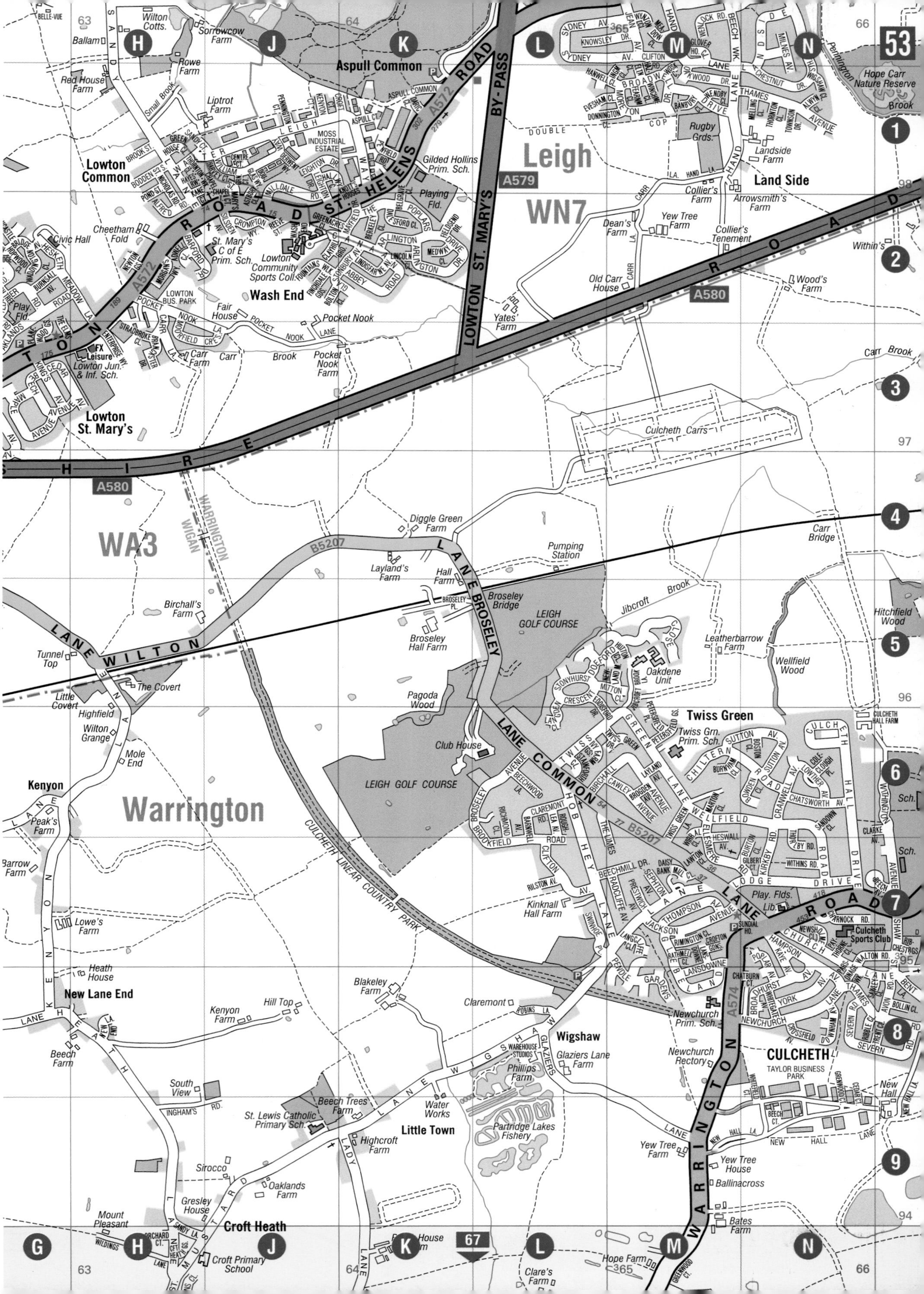
Aspull Common
Lowton Common
Leigh
WN7
Land Side
Wash End
Lowton St. Mary's
WA3
Warrington
Twiss Green
Kenyon
New Lane End
Wigshaw
CULCHETH
Little Town
Croft Heath
ST. HELENS ROAD
LOWTON ST. MARY'S BY-PASS
DOUBLE CARR ROAD
WARRINGTON ROAD
A572
A579
A580
A574
B5207
WILTON LANE
BROSELEY LANE
COMMON LANE
KENYON LANE
WIGSHAW LANE
STAR LANE
LEIGH GOLF COURSE
CULCHETH LINEAR COUNTRY PARK
Culcheth Carrs
Hope Carr Nature Reserve
Partridge Lakes Fishery
Moss Industrial Estate
Lowton Community Sports Coll.
St. Mary's C of E Prim. Sch.
Lowton Jun. & Inf. Sch.
Gilded Hollins Prim. Sch.
Twiss Grn. Prim. Sch.
Newchurch Prim. Sch.
St. Lewis Catholic Primary Sch.
Croft Primary School
Culcheth Sports Club
Taylor Business Park
Carr Brook
Pocket Nook Brook
Jibcroft Brook
Hitchfield Wood
Wellfield Wood
Pagoda Wood
Club House
Pumping Station
Broseley Bridge
Oakdene Unit
63
64
65
66
98
97
96
95
94

67

LIVERPOOL
EAST HOYLE BANK
Dove Point
Coastguard Station
SEABANK COTTAGE
NORTH WIRRAL
HOYLAKE
MEOLS
Meols
Great Meols
Great Meols Prim. Sch.
Meols Parade Gardens
Ten. Cts.
Promenade
Bowling Greens
Model Boating Pond
Comm. Cen.
Queens Park
Hoylake Cott.
Kingsmead School
Play. Flds.
Hoylake Lifeboat Mus.
Fornalls Bridge
MUMFORDS
NORTH SCHOOL
Rec.
Grd.
BIRKENHEAD ROAD
PARADE
PARKWAY
A553
CH47
70
Sch.

BAY
WALLASEY
EMBANKMENT
MOCKBEGGAR WHARF
Breakwater
WIRRAL COASTAL PARK
Leasowe Common
Moreton Common
Leasowe Lighthouse
Caravan Site
The Birket
Greenacres
Lingham Farm
Eve-a-lyn Farm
Arrowe Brook
Sewage Pumping Station
Refuse Tip
Parkfield House
PARK LANE HOLIDAY HOMES
WIRRAL BEACH CARAVAN PARK
Meols
Wirral
Sewage Works
Works
Clay Pit
Carr Hall Farm
Pasture Farm
Moreton Hills Golf Centre
Pasture Rd. Bri.
Moreton
MORETON
Ditton Lane Nature Area
Play Field
Play. Fld.
Bowl. Grn.
Leasowe
Reeds Bri.
Caravan Park
Club House
LEASOWE GOLF COURSE
Rugby Football Grounds
LEASOWE ROAD
PASTURE ROAD
A551
A553
Lingham Park
Lingham Prim. Sch.
Running Track
Bowling Greens
Eastway Prim. Sch.
Foxfield Sch.
Christ Church C of E Prim. Sch.
Recreation Ground
HOYLAKE ROAD
UPTON RD.
56
71
H
J
K
L
M
N
G
1
2
3
4
5
6
7
8
9
24
325
26
27
94
93
92
91
90

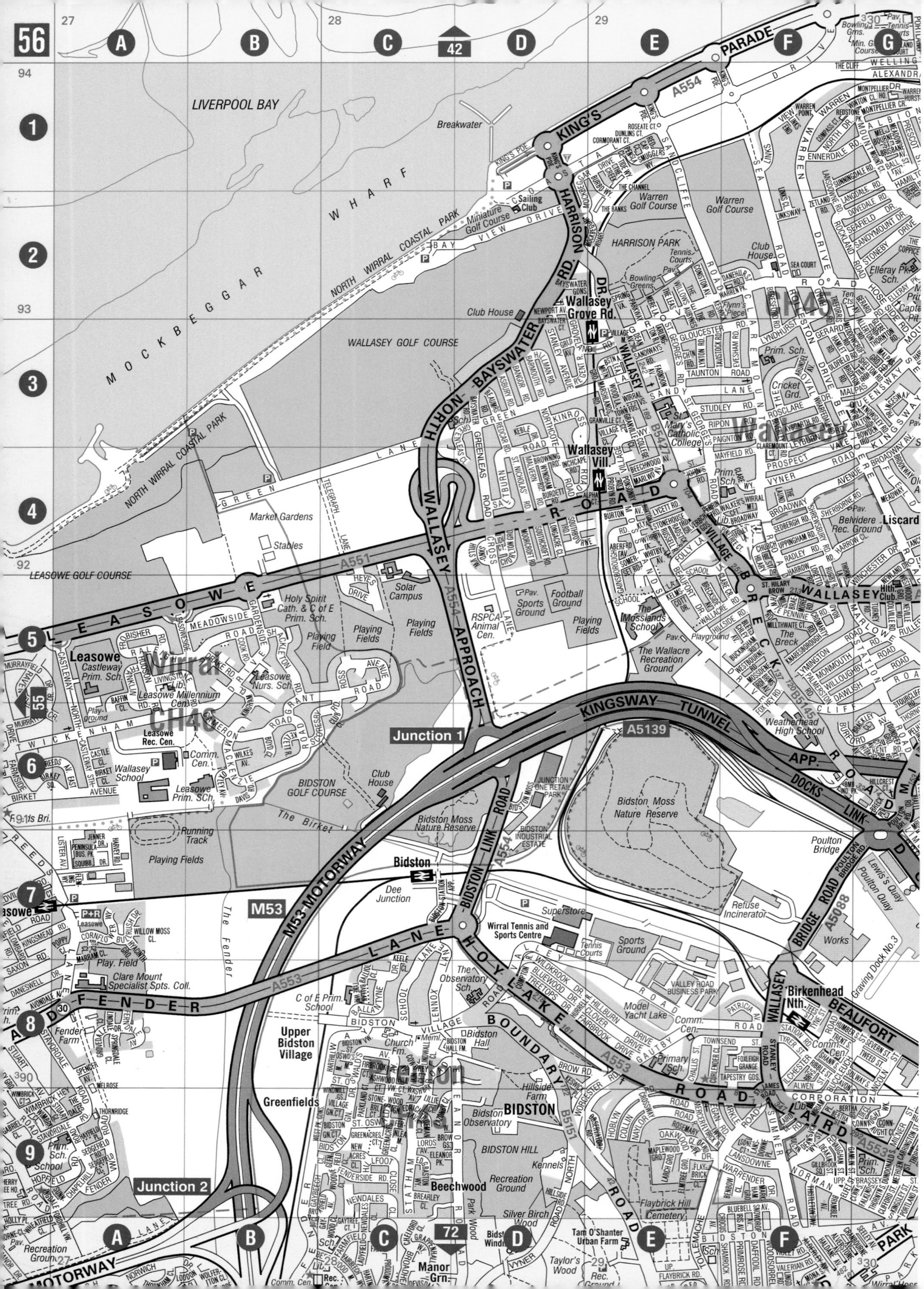

42
72
55
LIVERPOOL BAY
MOCKBEGGAR WHARF
Breakwater
NORTH WIRRAL COASTAL PARK
KING'S PARADE
A554
Sailing Club
Miniature Golf Course
BAY VIEW DRIVE
HARRISON DR.
HARRISON PARK
Warren Golf Course
Club House
WALLASEY GOLF COURSE
Wallasey Grove Rd.
BAYSWATER RD.
NORTH WALLASEY APPROACH
Wallasey
CH45
Wallasey Vill.
St. Mary's Catholic College
Cricket Grd.
Prim. Sch.
Liscard
Belvidere Rec. Ground
Market Gardens
Stables
LEASOWE GOLF COURSE
LEASOWE ROAD
A551
Holy Spirit Cath. & C of E Prim. Sch.
Solar Campus
Playing Fields
RSPCA Animal Cen.
Sports Ground
Football Ground
The Mosslands School
The Wallacre Recreation Ground
BRECK ROAD
WALLASEY VILLAGE
The Breck
Weatherhead High School
Leasowe
Castleway Prim. Sch.
Wirral
CH46
Leasowe Millennium Cen.
Leasowe Nurs. Sch.
Leasowe Rec. Cen.
Wallasey School
Leasowe Prim. Sch.
Junction 1
KINGSWAY TUNNEL APP.
A5139
DOCKS LINK
BIDSTON GOLF COURSE
Bidston Moss Nature Reserve
BIDSTON INDUSTRIAL ESTATE
The Birket
Running Track
Playing Fields
Poulton Bridge
Refuse Incinerator
Bidston
Dee Junction
M53
M53 MOTORWAY
BIDSTON LINK ROAD
Superstore
Wirral Tennis and Sports Centre
Sports Ground
HOYLAKE ROAD
A553
LANE
FENDER
Model Yacht Lake
VALLEY ROAD BUSINESS PARK
Birkenhead Nth.
BEAUFORT ROAD
A5088
BRIDGE ROAD
Works
Graving Dock No.3
Clare Mount Specialist Spts. Coll.
Fender Farm
C of E Prim. School
Upper Bidston Village
The Observatory Sch.
BOUNDARY ROAD
Bidston Hall
Bidston Observatory
BIDSTON
BIDSTON HILL
Recreation Ground
Kennels
Beechwood
Greenfields
Junction 2
Flaybrick Hill Cemetery
Silver Birch Wood
Tam O'Shanter Urban Farm
Taylor's Wood
Manor Grn.
LAIRD ST.
CORPORATION ROAD
MOTORWAY
Recreation Ground

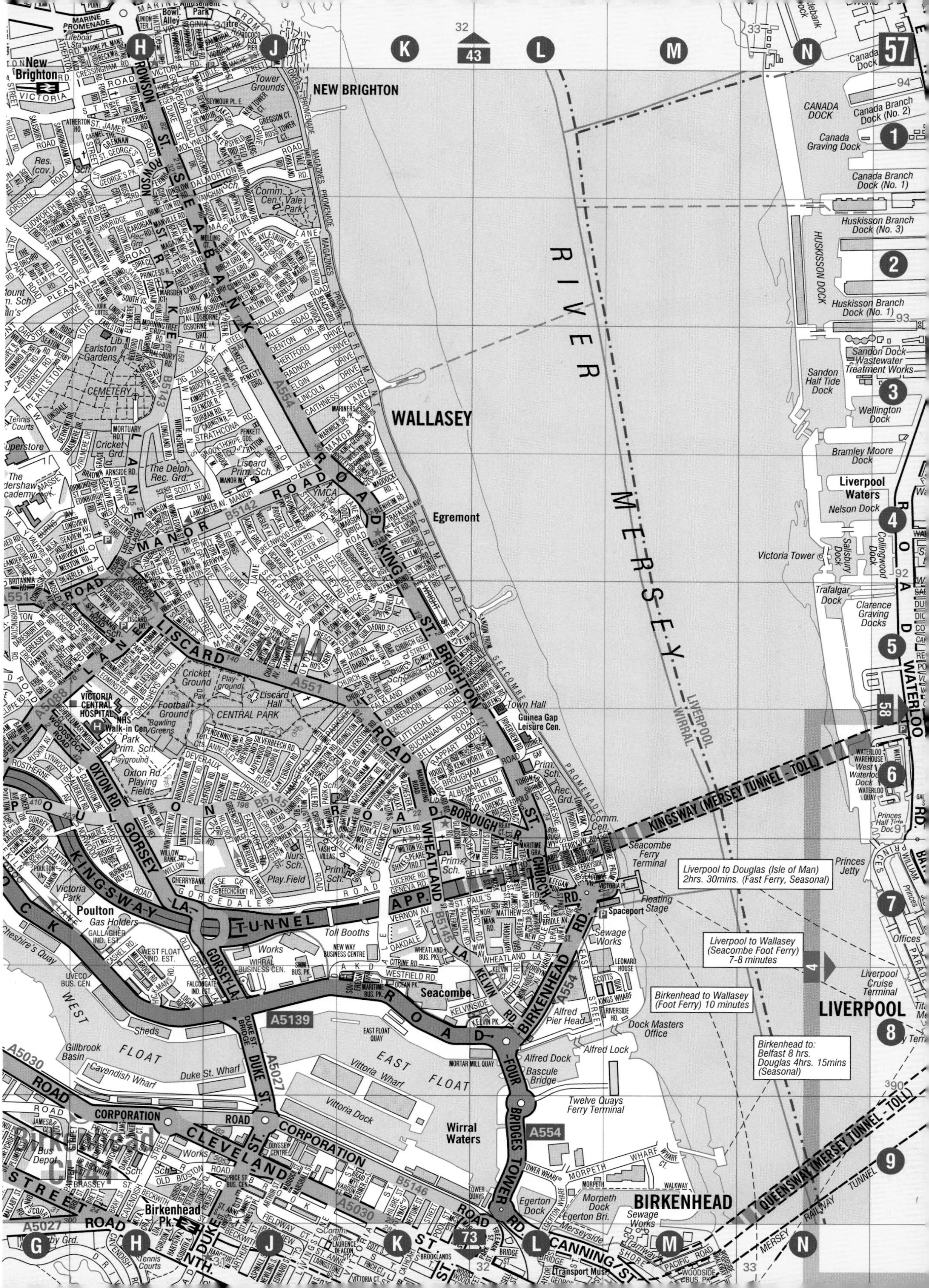
NEW BRIGHTON
New Brighton
WALLASEY
Egremont
RIVER MERSEY
LIVERPOOL
BIRKENHEAD
Seacombe
Poulton
Victoria Park
CENTRAL PARK
Liscard Hall
VICTORIA CENTRAL HOSPITAL
Guinea Gap Leisure Cen.
Town Hall
Seacombe Ferry Terminal
Spaceport
Floating Stage
Liverpool to Douglas (Isle of Man) 2hrs. 30mins. (Fast Ferry, Seasonal)
Liverpool to Wallasey (Seacombe Foot Ferry) 7-8 minutes
Birkenhead to Wallasey (Foot Ferry) 10 minutes
Birkenhead to: Belfast 8 hrs. Douglas 4hrs. 15mins (Seasonal)
KINGSWAY (MERSEY TUNNEL - TOLL)
QUEENSWAY (MERSEY TUNNEL - TOLL)
KINGSWAY TUNNEL APP.
Canada Dock
CANADA DOCK
Canada Branch Dock (No. 2)
Canada Graving Dock
Canada Branch Dock (No. 1)
Huskisson Branch Dock (No. 3)
HUSKISSON DOCK
Huskisson Branch Dock (No. 1)
Sandon Dock Wastewater Treatment Works
Sandon Half Tide Dock
Wellington Dock
Bramley Moore Dock
Liverpool Waters
Nelson Dock
Victoria Tower
Salisbury Dock
Collingwood Dock
Trafalgar Dock
Clarence Graving Docks
WATERLOO ROAD
Waterloo Warehouse
West Waterloo Dock
Princes Half Tide Dock
Princes Jetty
Liverpool Cruise Terminal
WEST FLOAT
EAST FLOAT
Gillbrook Basin
Cavendish Wharf
Duke St. Wharf
Vittoria Wharf
Vittoria Dock
Wirral Waters
Alfred Dock
Alfred Lock
Bascule Bridge
Twelve Quays Ferry Terminal
Egerton Dock
Morpeth Dock
Egerton Bri.
Sewage Works
Dock Masters Office
Alfred Pier Head
Toll Booths
WIRRAL BUSINESS CEN.
Birkenhead Pk.
CORPORATION ROAD
CLEVELAND STREET
DUKE ST.
FOUR BRIDGES
TOWER RD.
CANNING ST.
A554
A5139
A5027
A5030
A551
A5088
B5142
B5143
B5145
B5146
KING ST.
BRIGHTON ST.
SEABANK ROAD
RAKE LANE
LISCARD ROAD
MANOR ROAD
POULTON ROAD
BOROUGH ROAD
CHURCH ST.
BIRKENHEAD RD.
GORSEY LA.
WHEATLAND LA.
MAGAZINES PROMENADE
EGREMONT PROMENADE
SEACOMBE PROMENADE
Earlston Gardens
CEMETERY
Mersey Ferries
Transport Mus.
Woodside
Kings Wharf
Tower Quays
Oxton Rd. Playing Fields
H J K L M N G
32 33 43 58 73 4 1 2 3 5 6 7 8 9

A
B
C
D
E
F
G
1
2
3
4
5
6
7
8
9
44
57
74
4
5
Kirkdale
Bankhall
Canada Branch Dock (No. 3)
Canada Branch Dock (No. 2)
Canada Branch Dock (No. 1)
Huskisson Branch Dock (No. 3)
Huskisson Branch Dock (No. 1)
Sandon Dock Wastewater Treatment Works
Wellington Dock
Bramley Moore Dock
Liverpool Waters
Nelson Dock
Stanley Dock
Collingwood Dock
Stanley Warehouses
Salisbury Dock
Trafalgar Dock
Clarence Graving Docks
Waterloo Warehouse
Waterloo Dock
Princes Half Tide Dock
Princes Jetty
Liverpool Cruise Terminal
Liverpool to Wallasey (Seacombe Foot Ferry) 7-8 mins.
Titanic Mem.
Ferry Terminal
Museum of Liverpool
Canning Graving Docks
Canning Half Tide Dock
Tate Liverpool
Mersey Railway Tunnel
QUEENSWAY (MERSEY TUNNEL (TOLL))
LIVERPOOL
Albert Dock
The Beatles Story
Liverpool to Birkenhead (Woodside Foot Ferry) 7-8 minutes
Echo Arena
BT Convention Cen.
Wapping Basin
Duke's Dock
Everton FC (Goodison Pk.)
ANFIELD CEMETERY
Registrar's Office
Anfield Crematorium
STANLEY PARK
Anfield
L4
Abbey Lawns Nursing Home
Liverpool FC (Anfield)
L20
Sandhills
Sandhills Business Park
Lifestyles Everton
Everton
North Liverpool Academy
Rupert Lane Rec. Grd.
Faith Prim. Sch.
Vauxhall
Kingsway Park
L3
KINGSWAY (TOLL)
Liverpool John Moores Univ.
Moorfields
St George's Hall
LIME ST.
Sorting Office
Liverpool Uni. Dental Hosp.
Royal Liverpool Univ. Hosp.
University of Liverpool
Liverpool Metropolitan Cath.
John Moores University
Central
Kensington
Edge Hill
Granby
Liverpool Women's Hosp.
Huskisson Mon.
Liverpool Cathedral
A565
A5056
A5036
A5055
A5054
A5038
A567
A59
A5053
A5089
A5050
A580
A57
A5039
A5048
REGENT ROAD
DERBY ROAD
BANKHALL ST.
SANDHILLS LANE
BOUNDARY ST.
GREAT HOWARD STREET
WATERLOO RD.
LEEDS STREET
VAUXHALL ROAD
COMMERCIAL ROAD
STANLEY ROAD
MELROSE ROAD
KIRKDALE RD.
SCOTLAND RD.
WALTON RD.
EVERTON VALLEY
WALTON BRECK RD.
OAKFIELD RD.
ST. DOMINGO RD.
HEYWORTH ST.
ST. DOMINGO VALE
EVERTON BRECK
WEST DERBY ROAD
ISLINGTON
PRESCOT ST.
LONDON RD.
PEMBROKE PL.
BROWNLOW HILL
RENSHAW ST.
MYRTLE ST.
GROVE ST.
PARLIAMENT ST.
WAPPING
PARK LA.
STRAND ST.
JAMES ST.
NEW QUAY
BATH ST.
CASTLE ST.
DALE ST.
HANOVER ST.
BERRY ST.
HARDMAN ST.
OXFORD ST.
UPPER PARLIAMENT ST.
PRIORY RD.
COUNTY RD.
LANE

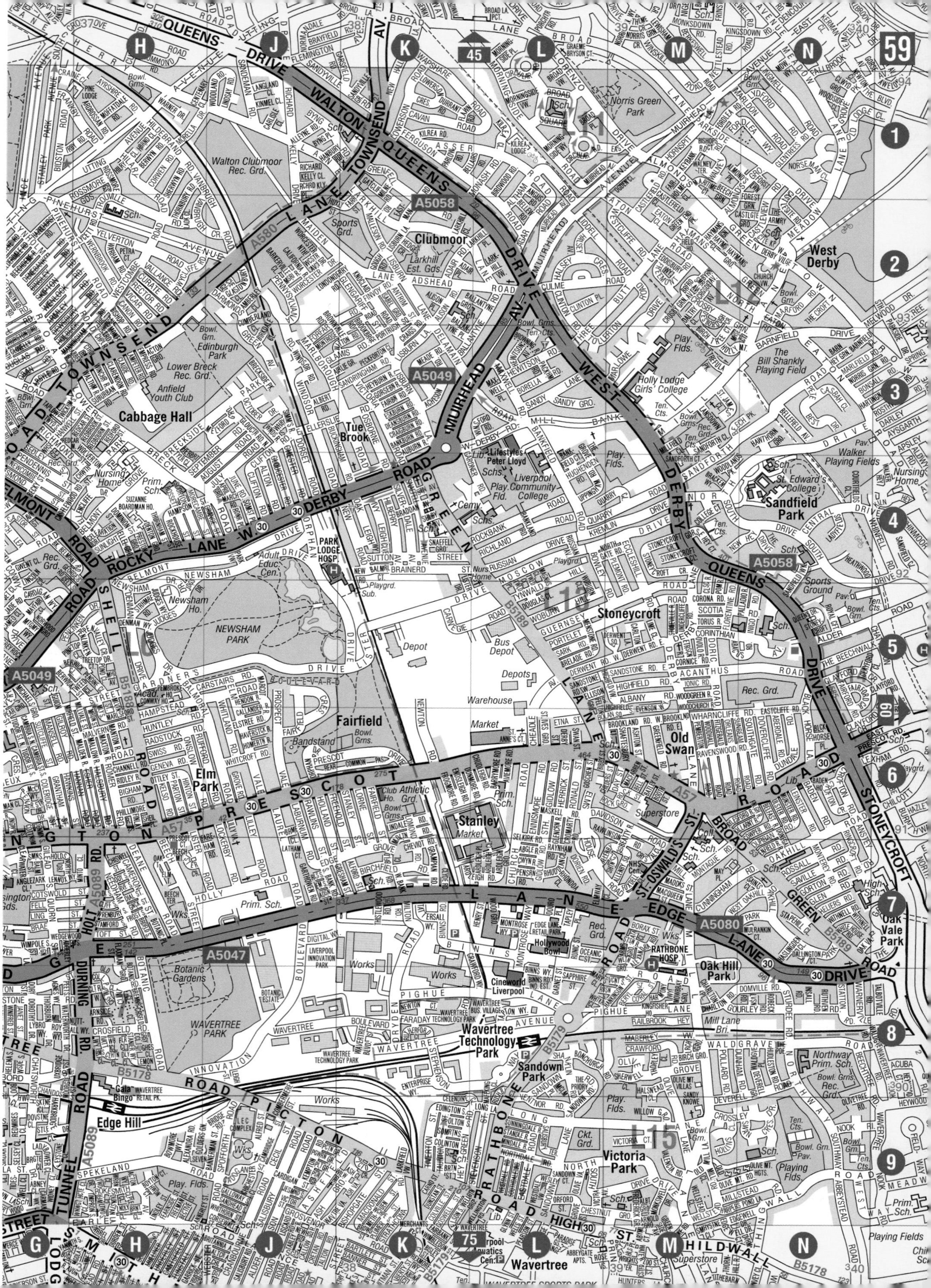

59
H
J
K
L
M
N
G
1
2
3
4
5
6
7
8
9
45
75
60
QUEENS DRIVE
WALTON
TOWNSEND LANE
TOWNSEND AV.
A5058
A580
A5049
A57
A5047
A5080
A5089
A5178
B5178
B5179
B5189
B5188
Walton Clubmoor Rec. Grd.
Clubmoor
Larkhill Est. Gds.
Norris Green Park
West Derby
The Bill Shankly Playing Field
Holly Lodge Girls' College
Walker Playing Fields
St. Edward's College
Sandfield Park
Edinburgh Park
Lower Breck Rec. Grd.
Anfield Youth Club
Cabbage Hall
Tue Brook
Lifestyles Peter Lloyd
Liverpool Community College
Newsham Ho.
NEWSHAM PARK
Park Lodge Hosp.
Depot
Bus Depot
Depots
Warehouse
Market
Stoneycroft
Fairfield
Old Swan
Elm Park
Stanley Market
Superstore
Oak Vale Park
Oak Hill Park
Rathbone Hosp.
Hollywood Bowl
Cineworld Liverpool
Botanic Gardens
WAVERTREE PARK
Liverpool Innovation Park
Wavertree Technology Park
Sandown Park
Mill Lane Bri.
Northway Prim. Sch.
Gala Bingo
Wavertree Retail Pk.
Edge Hill
Victoria Park
Liverpool Aquatics Cen.
Wavertree
Playing Fields
WEST DERBY RD.
DERBY LANE
MUIRHEAD AV.
ROCKY LANE
BELMONT ROAD
SHEIL ROAD
PRESCOT ROAD
EDGE LANE
EDGE LANE DRIVE
STONEYCROFT
BROAD GREEN ROAD
PICTON ROAD
RATHBONE ROAD
HIGH ST.
CHILDWALL
TUNNEL ROAD
SMITHDOWN
DURNING RD.

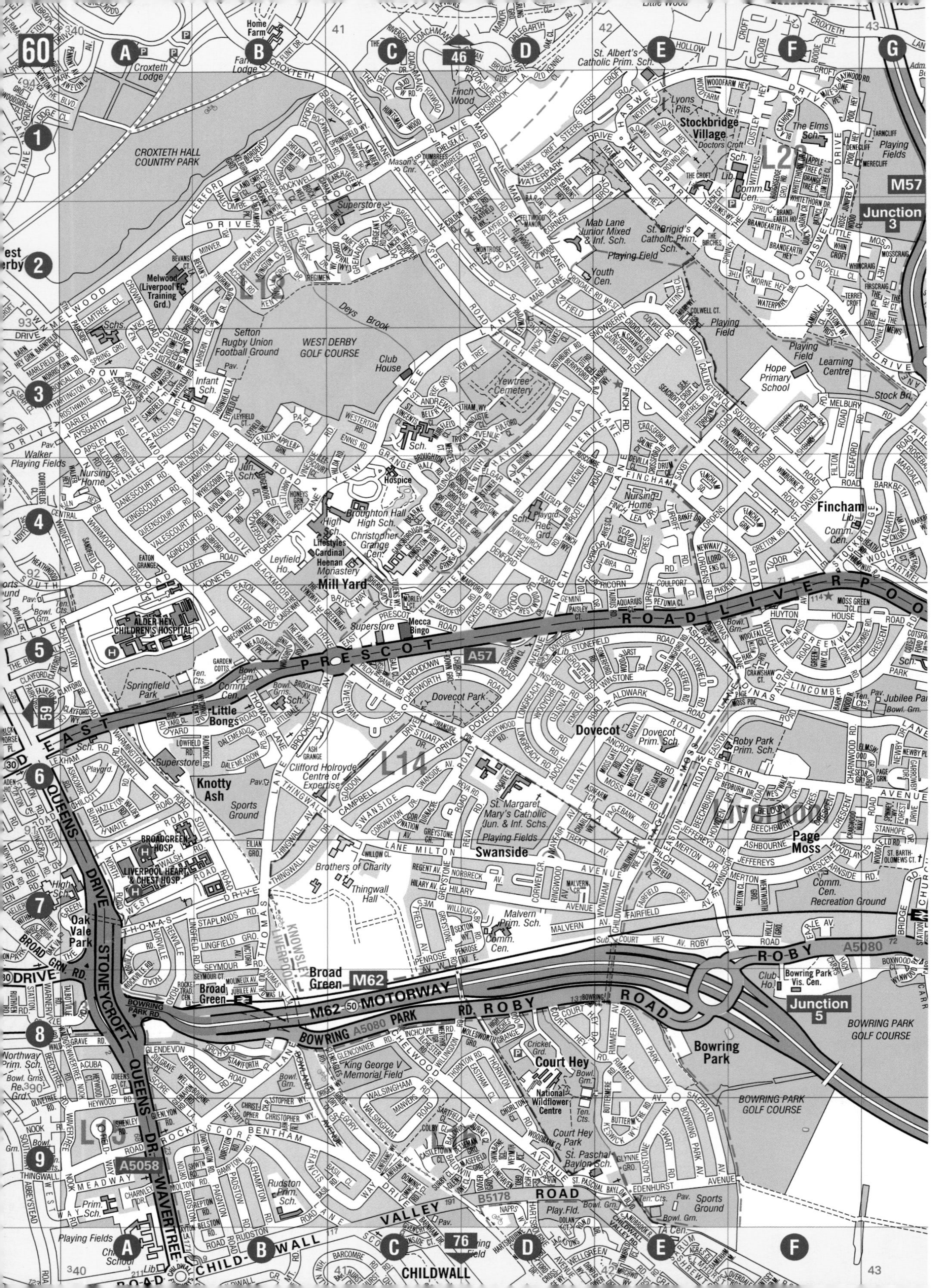

46
76
59
A
B
C
D
E
F
G
1
2
3
4
5
6
7
8
9
41
42
43
340
93
92
91
90
Croxteth Lodge
Home Farm
Farm Lodge
CROXTETH HALL COUNTRY PARK
Finch Wood
St. Albert's Catholic Prim. Sch.
Lyons Pits
Stockbridge Village
Doctors Croft
The Elms Sch.
Playing Fields
M57
Junction 3
L12
L28
L13
L14
L15
L16
Mason's Cnr.
Superstore
Mab Lane Junior Mixed & Inf. Sch.
St. Brigid's Catholic Prim. Sch.
Playing Field
Youth Cen.
West Derby
Melwood (Liverpool FC Training Grd.)
Sefton Rugby Union Football Ground
WEST DERBY GOLF COURSE
Deys Brook
Club House
Yewtree Cemetery
Hope Primary School
Learning Centre
Stock Bri.
Infant Sch.
Walker Playing Fields
Nursing Home
Jun. Sch.
Hospice
Broughton Hall High Sch.
Christopher Grange Cen.
Lifestyles
Cardinal Heenan
High Sch.
Leyfield Ho.
Monastery
Mill Yard
Rec. Grd.
Nursing Home
Fincham
Lib.
Comm. Cen.
ALDER HEY CHILDREN'S HOSPITAL
Superstore
Mecca Bingo
PRESCOT ROAD
LIVERPOOL ROAD
A57
EAST PRESCOT ROAD
Springfield Park
Little Bongs
Comm. Cen.
Dovecot Park
Dovecot
Dovecot Prim. Sch.
Roby Park Prim. Sch.
Jubilee Park
Knotty Ash
Sports Ground
Clifford Holroyde Centre of Expertise
St. Margaret Mary's Catholic Jun. & Inf. Schs.
Playing Fields
Page Moss
Swanside
BROADGREEN HOSP.
LIVERPOOL HEART & CHEST HOSP.
Brothers of Charity
Thingwall Hall
Malvern Prim. Sch.
Comm. Cen.
Recreation Ground
Oak Vale Park
QUEENS DRIVE
STONEYCROFT
KNOWSLEY
LIVERPOOL
Broad Green
M62
Junction 5
M62 MOTORWAY
ROBY ROAD
BOWRING PARK ROAD
A5080
Bowring Park Vis. Cen.
BOWRING PARK GOLF COURSE
Bowring Park
Northway Prim. Sch.
King George V Memorial Field
Court Hey
Cricket Grd.
National Wildflower Centre
Court Hey Park
St. Paschal Baylon Sch.
QUEENS DR. WAVERTREE
A5058
Rudston Prim. Sch.
Prim. Sch.
Playing Fields
Childwall School
B5178
VALLEY ROAD
Sports Ground
CHILDWALL
Play. Fld.

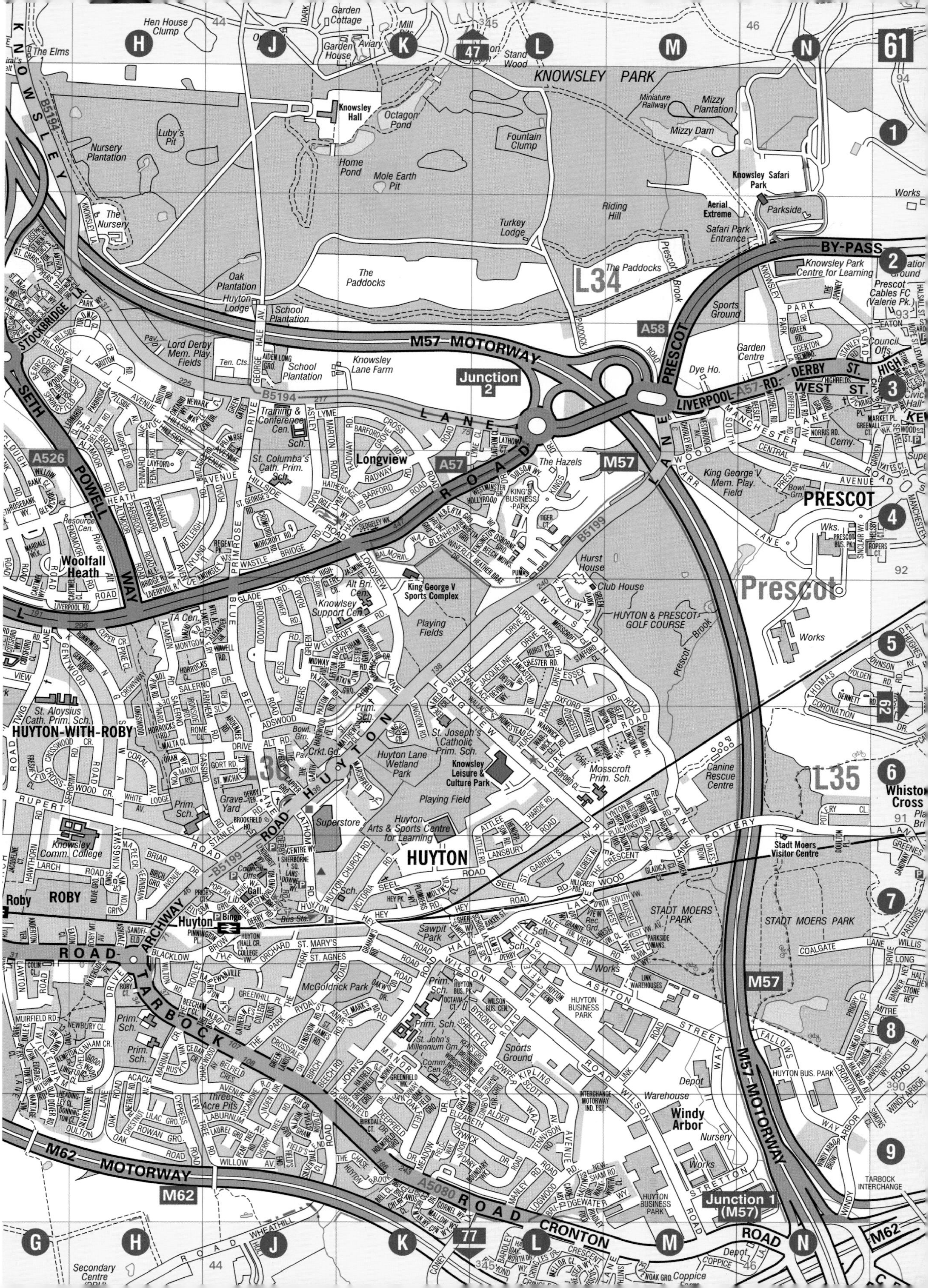
Hen House Clump
Garden Cottage
Garden House
Aviary
Mill Pit
47
Stand Wood
The Elms
KNOWSLEY PARK
Knowsley Hall
Octagon Pond
Home Pond
Mole Earth Pit
Luby's Pit
Nursery Plantation
Fountain Clump
Miniature Railway
Mizzy Plantation
Mizzy Dam
Knowsley Safari Park
Parkside
Works
Riding Hill
Aerial Extreme
Safari Park Entrance
Turkey Lodge
The Nursery
The Paddocks
Oak Plantation
Huyton Lodge
School Plantation
L34
Prescot Brook
BY-PASS
Knowsley Park Centre for Learning
Prescot Cables FC (Valerie Pk.)
Sports Ground
A58
PRESCOT
M57 MOTORWAY
Lord Derby Mem. Play. Fields
Ten. Cts.
School Plantation
Knowsley Lane Farm
Junction 2
Garden Centre
Dye Ho.
Council Offs.
DERBY ST.
WEST ST.
HIGH
LIVERPOOL A57 RD.
B5194
LANE
Training & Conference Cen.
Sch.
Longview
St. Columba's Cath. Prim. Sch.
A57
ROAD
The Hazels
M57
King's Business Park
King George V Mem. Play. Field
Cemy.
PRESCOT
A526
POWELL WAY
SETH
Resource Cen.
Woolfall Heath
River Alt
B5199
King George V Sports Complex
Alt Bri. Cen.
Knowlsey Support Cen.
Playing Fields
Hurst House
Club House
HUYTON & PRESCOT GOLF COURSE
Prescot
Works
TA Cen.
St. Aloysius Cath. Prim. Sch.
HUYTON-WITH-ROBY
Bowl. Grn.
Crkt. Gd.
Huyton Lane Wetland Park
St. Joseph's Catholic Prim. Sch.
Knowsley Leisure & Culture Park
Mosscroft Prim. Sch.
Canine Rescue Centre
L35
L36
Whiston Cross
Playing Field
Prim. Sch.
Grave Yard
Superstore
Huyton Arts & Sports Centre for Learning
Knowsley Comm. College
HUYTON
Stadt Moers Visitor Centre
ROBY
Roby
Council Offs.
Lib.
Huyton
Bingo
Bus Sta.
Sawpit Park
STADT MOERS PARK
ARCHWAY
ROAD
TARBOCK
McGoldrick Park
Prim. Sch.
Works
Link Warehouses
M57
Huyton Business Park
Sports Ground
St. John's Millennium Grn.
Comm. Cen.
Three Acre Pits
Depot
Warehouse
Interchange Motorway Ind. Est.
Windy Arbor
Nursery
Works
HUYTON BUS. PARK
M57 MOTORWAY
M62 MOTORWAY
M62
A5080 ROAD
CRONTON ROAD
Junction 1 (M57)
Huyton Business Park
Tarbock Interchange
77
62
Secondary Centre
Depot
Coppice
G H J K L M N
1 2 3 4 5 6 7 8 9
44 345 46
94 93 92 91 390

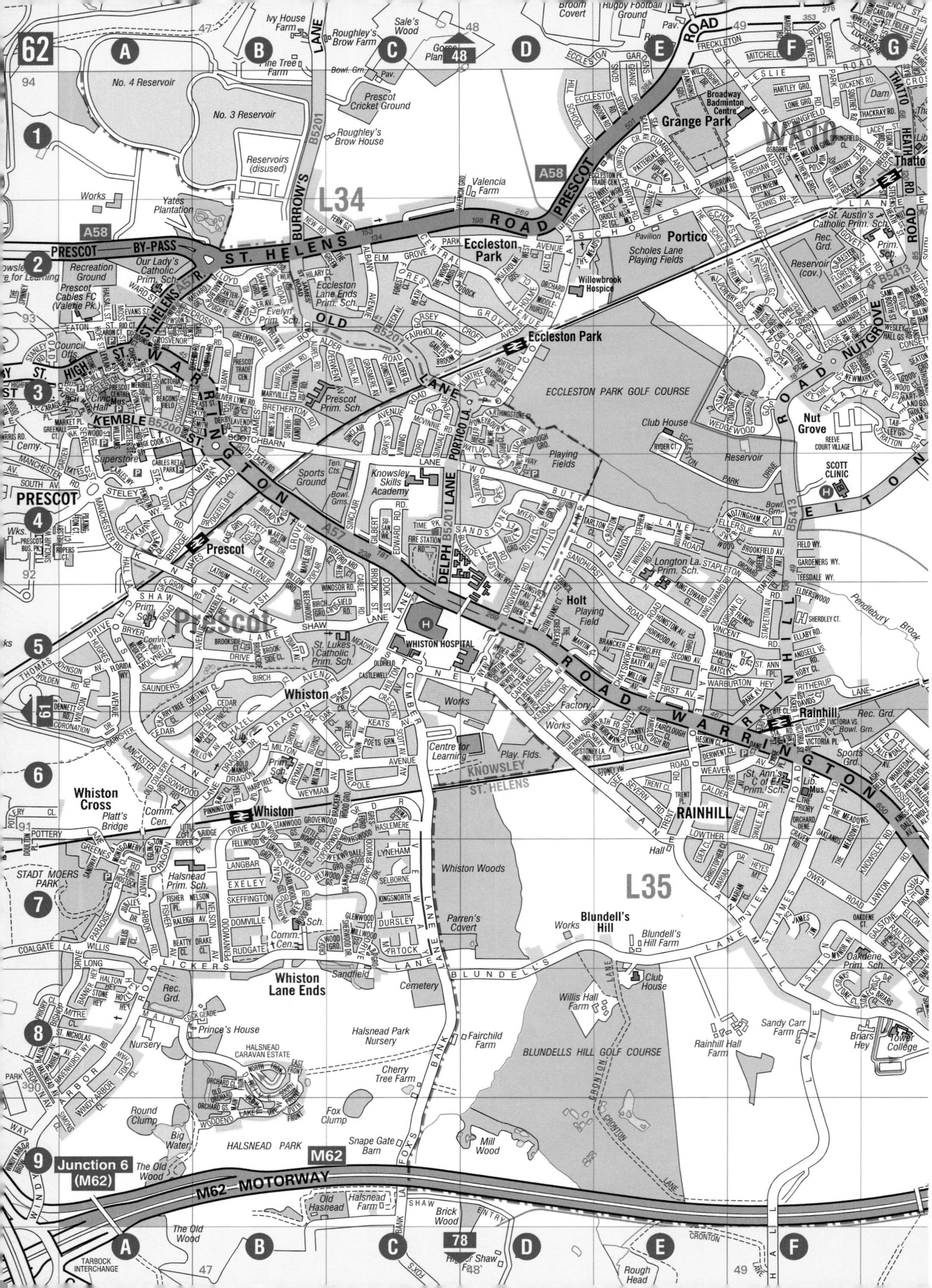

A
B
C
D
E
F
G
1
2
3
4
5
6
7
8
9
47
48
49
94
93
92
91
90
48
78
61
L34
L35
Ivy House Farm
Roughley's Brow Farm
Sale's Wood
Gorse Plan
Broom Covert
Rugby Football Ground
No. 4 Reservoir
No. 3 Reservoir
Pine Tree Farm
Prescot Cricket Ground
Roughley's Brow House
Reservoirs (disused)
Works
Yates Plantation
Valencia Farm
A58
PRESCOT BY-PASS
ST. HELENS ROAD
PRESCOT ROAD
BURROW'S LANE
B5201
Recreation Ground
Our Lady's Catholic Prim. Sch.
Prescot Cables FC (Valerie Pk.)
Eccleston Park
Eccleston Lane Ends Prim. Sch.
Evelyn Prim. Sch.
OLD LANE
B5207
Willowbrook Hospice
Portico
Scholes Lane Playing Fields
Pavilion
Grange Park
Broadway Badminton Centre
St. Austin's Catholic Prim. Sch.
Rec. Grd.
Reservoir (cov.)
Thatto Heath
B5413
NUTGROVE ROAD
Eccleston Park
ECCLESTON PARK GOLF COURSE
Club House
Reservoir
Nut Grove
Reeve Court Village
Scott Clinic
Council Offs.
HIGH ST.
WARRINGTON ROAD
A57
KEMBLE ST.
B5200
Prescot Prim. Sch.
Sports Ground
Knowsley Skills Academy
Playing Fields
Superstore
Cables Retail Park
Cemy.
PRESCOT
Prescot
Fire Station
DELPH LANE
Longton La. Prim. Sch.
Holt Playing Field
Pendlebury Brook
Prim. Sch.
Prescot
Comm. Cen.
St. Lukes Catholic Prim. Sch.
WHISTON HOSPITAL
Whiston
Works
Factory
Centre for Learning
Play. Flds.
KNOWSLEY
ST. HELENS
Rainhill
Rec. Grd.
Sports Grd.
St. Ann's C of E Prim. Sch.
Lib. Mus.
RAINHILL
Whiston Cross
Platt's Bridge
Comm. Cen.
Whiston
STADT MOERS PARK
Halsnead Prim. Sch.
Sch.
Comm. Cen.
Whiston Woods
Parren's Covert
Hall
Blundell's Hill
Works
Blundell's Hill Farm
Whiston Lane Ends
Sandfield
Rec. Grd.
Cemetery
Club House
Oakdene Prim. Sch.
Prince's House
Nursery
Halsnead Park Nursery
Fairchild Farm
Willis Hall Farm
BLUNDELLS HILL GOLF COURSE
Rainhill Hall Farm
Sandy Carr Farm
Briars Hey
Tower College
HALSNEAD CARAVAN ESTATE
Cherry Tree Farm
Round Clump
Fox Clump
Big Water
Mill Wood
HALSNEAD PARK
Snape Gate Barn
Junction 6 (M62)
M62
The Old Wood
M62 MOTORWAY
Old Hasnead
Halsnead Farm
Brick Wood
The Old Wood
TARBOCK INTERCHANGE
Higher Shaw Fa.
Rough Head
CRONTON

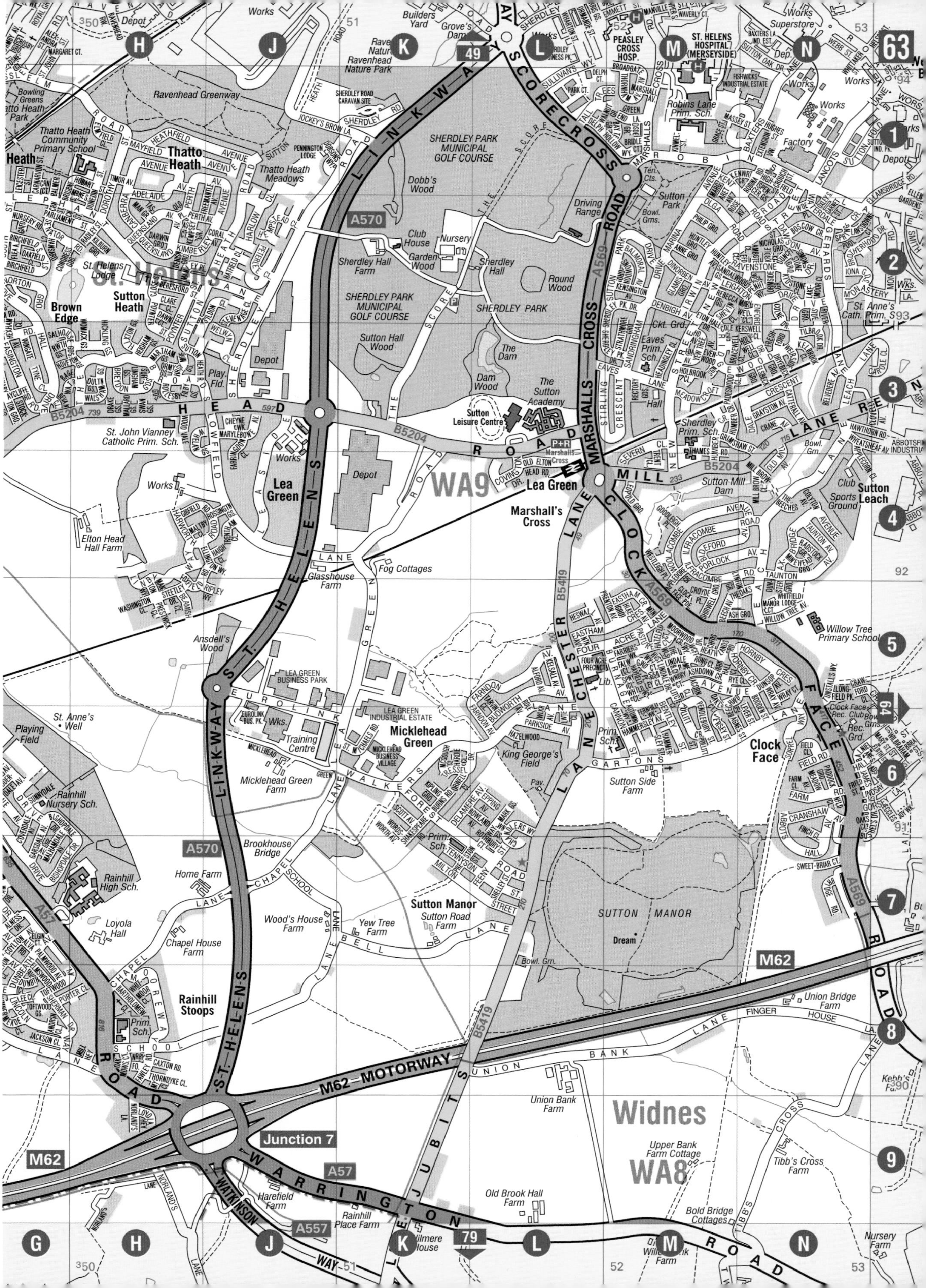
Thatto Heath
Thatto Heath Community Primary School
Ravenhead Greenway
Ravenhead Nature Park
Sherdley Road Caravan Site
Thatto Heath Meadows
Sherdley Park Municipal Golf Course
Dobb's Wood
Peasley Cross Hosp.
St. Helens Hospital (Merseyside)
Robins Lane Prim. Sch.
Fishwicks Industrial Estate
Superstore
Factory
Driving Range
Sutton Park
Club House
Nursery
Garden Wood
Sherdley Hall Farm
Sherdley Hall
Round Wood
Sherdley Park
St. Helens Lodge
St. Helens
Sutton Heath
Brown Edge
Sutton Hall Wood
Depot
The Dam
Dam Wood
The Sutton Academy
Sutton Leisure Centre
Eaves Prim. Sch.
Sherdley Prim. Sch.
St. Anne's Cath. Prim. Sch.
St. John Vianney Catholic Prim. Sch.
Lea Green
Marshall's Cross
WA9
Sutton Mill Dam
Club Sports Ground
Sutton Leach
Elton Head Hall Farm
Fog Cottages
Glasshouse Farm
Ansdell's Wood
Willow Tree Primary School
Lea Green Business Park
Lea Green Industrial Estate
Eurolink Bus. Pk.
Training Centre
Micklehead Green
Micklehead Business Village
Micklehead Green Farm
King George's Field
Sutton Side Farm
Clock Face
Clock Face Rec. Club
St. Anne's Well
Playing Field
Rainhill Nursery Sch.
Rainhill High Sch.
Home Farm
Brookhouse Bridge
Loyola Hall
Chapel House Farm
Wood's House Farm
Yew Tree Farm
Sutton Manor
Sutton Road Farm
Dream
Rainhill Stoops
Union Bridge Farm
Union Bank Farm
Widnes
WA8
Upper Bank Farm Cottage
Tibb's Cross Farm
Old Brook Hall Farm
Bold Bridge Cottages
Harefield Farm
Rainhill Place Farm
Nursery Farm
Junction 7
M62 Motorway
A570
A569
A57
A557
B5204
B5419
Linkway
St. Helens Linkway
Scorecross Road
Marshalls Cross Road
Clock Face Road
Warrington Road
Jubits Lane
Chester Lane
Mill Lane
Heath Road
49
64
79

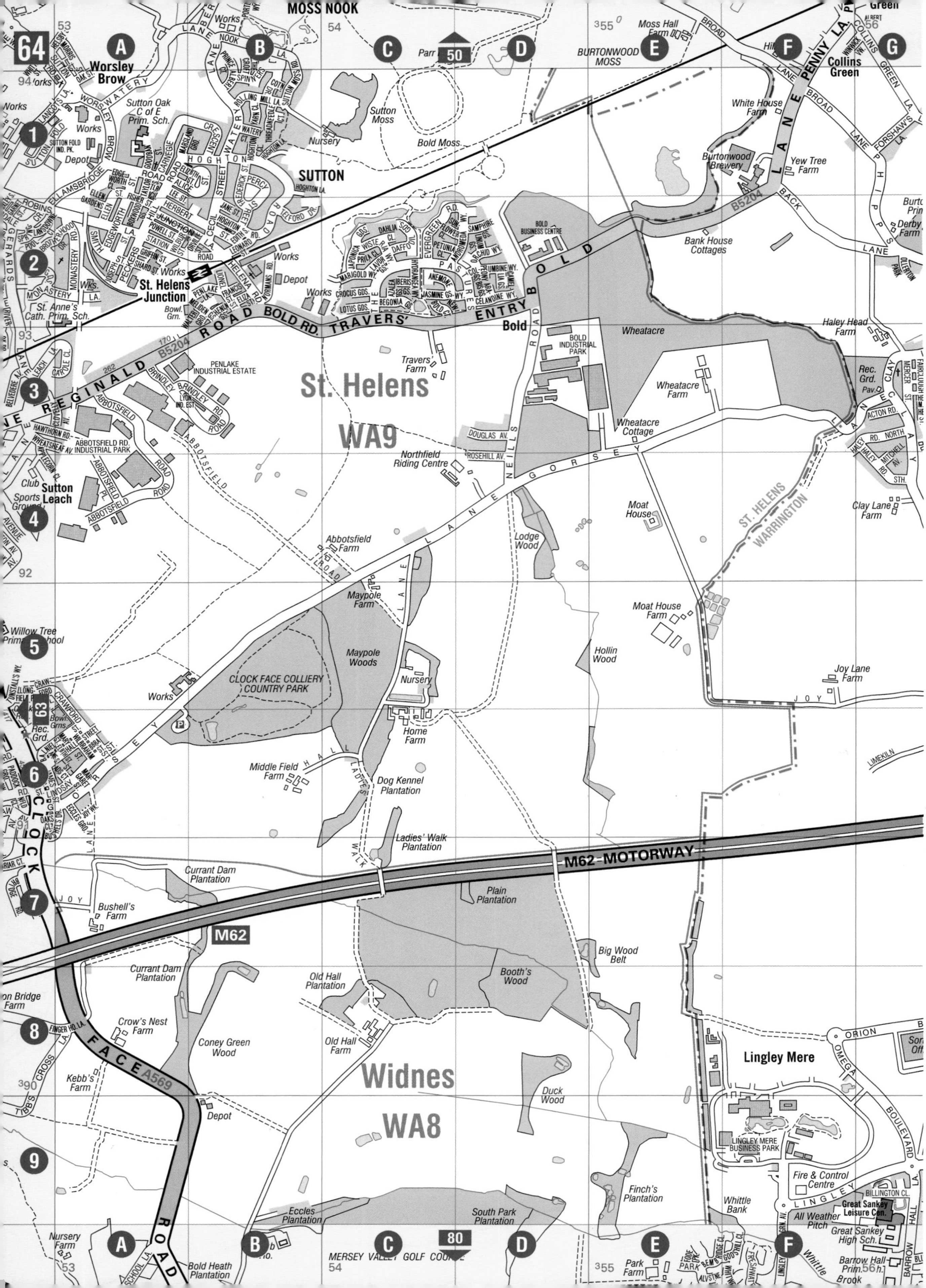
MOSS NOOK
50
Parr
Worsley Brow
Sutton Oak C of E Prim. Sch.
SUTTON FOLD IND. PK.
Depot
Works
Sutton Moss
Nursery
Bold Moss
SUTTON
Moss Hall Farm
BURTONWOOD MOSS
Collins Green
White House Farm
Burtonwood Brewery
Yew Tree Farm
Bank House Cottages
Derby Farm
BOLD BUSINESS CENTRE
St. Helens Junction
St. Anne's Cath. Prim. Sch.
Bowl. Grn.
Depot
Works
Bold
BOLD RD.
TRAVERS' ENTRY
REGINALD ROAD
B5204
PENLAKE INDUSTRIAL ESTATE
BRINDLEY LYON IND. EST.
ABBOTSFIELD RD. INDUSTRIAL PARK
Travers' Farm
BOLD INDUSTRIAL PARK
Wheatacre
Wheatacre Farm
Wheatacre Cottage
Haley Head Farm
Rec. Grd.
St. Helens
WA9
Northfield Riding Centre
Sutton Leach
Club
Sports Ground
GORSEY LANE
Moat House
Clay Lane Farm
ST. HELENS
WARRINGTON
Abbotsfield Farm
Lodge Wood
Maypole Farm
Willow Tree Primary School
Moat House Farm
Maypole Woods
Hollin Wood
CLOCK FACE COLLIERY COUNTRY PARK
Nursery
Works
Joy Lane Farm
JOY LANE
63
Rec. Grd.
Home Farm
Middle Field Farm
Dog Kennel Plantation
LIMEKILN
Ladies' Walk Plantation
M62 MOTORWAY
Currant Dam Plantation
Plain Plantation
Bushell's Farm
M62
Big Wood Belt
Currant Dam Plantation
Booth's Wood
Old Hall Plantation
Crow's Nest Farm
Coney Green Wood
Old Hall Farm
Lingley Mere
ORION
OMEGA
Kebb's Farm
Widnes
Duck Wood
CLOCK FACE ROAD
A569
Depot
WA8
LINGLEY MERE BUSINESS PARK
BOULEVARD
Fire & Control Centre
Finch's Plantation
Whittle Bank
All Weather Pitch
Great Sankey Leisure Cen.
Great Sankey High Sch.
Eccles Plantation
South Park Plantation
Nursery Farm
80
MERSEY VALLEY GOLF COURSE
Bold Heath Plantation
Park Farm
Barrow Hall Prim. Sch.
Whittle Brook

Newton-le-Willows
Vulcan Village
WA12
Sankey Canal
Sankey Brook
Bradley Hall Farm
New Bradley Hall Farm
Bradlegh Old Hall
Higher Farm
Hall Lane Farm
SANKEY VALLEY COUNTRY PARK
Winwick Junction
ALDER ROOT GOLF COURSE
Alder Root Wood
Cop Holt Wood
New Hey Farm
Newton Brook
WA2
Club Ho.
Red House Farm
Alder Root Farm
Play. Fld.
Boarded Barn Farm
Mill Farm Cottage
Vicarage
Stoneyard Cottages
Clayton's House Farm
Alder Lane Farm
Lower Alder Root Farm
Playing Field
Phipp's Bridge
BURTONWOOD IND. CEN.
Primrose Hill Farm
Comm. Cen.
BURTONWOOD
Ashton's Farm
Tan House Farm
Tan House Bridge
Lymedene
Brookside Cottage
Brook Head Farm
Pumping Station
Forest Farm
Old Lodge Farm
Phipp's Brook
Warrington
Causey Cottages
Causey West Bri.
Causey Bridge
Causeway Bridges Farm
HOLLINS PARK HOSPITAL
Coney Grove Woods
Jacklegs Plantation
Ivy Cottage
Highfield
Dial Post Farm
Finger Post
Burtonwood Service Area
WA5
M62 MOTORWAY
M62
Junction 8
Superstores
Superstore
ROYAL LONDON BUSINESS PARK
SANKEY VALLEY PARK
GEMINI BUSINESS PARK
Hotel
Wks.
Kingswood
Warehouses
INTERNATIONAL BUSINESS CEN.
Westbrook
Little Moss Wood
Callands
Comm. Cen.
Sch.
Dallam
Dallam Prim. Sch.
Prim. Sch.
Lib.
WESTBROOK CENTRE
Odeon Cin.
Mary Ann Meadows Plantation
Mary Ann Meadows
Cherry Tree Farm
Big Wood
Gulliver's Theme Park
Burtonwood Heritage Centre
Ladies Walk Wood
Bewsey New Hall
Old Hall
Bog Wood
Twig Wood
Twenty Acre Wood
Maze
Bewsey Old Hall
Bewsey Lock
Whittle Wood
Brow Farm
St. Rocco's Hospice
CROMWELL AVENUE
A574
BURTONWOOD ROAD
ALDER LANE
HOUSE LANE
FARMERS LANE
WESTBROOK WAY
CHARON WAY
EUROPA BOULEVARD

Red Bank
Reeves House
Cop Holt Wood
Cop Holt Farm
Hermitage Green
The Orchard
Rose Mount
Junction 22
A579
52
Rough Farm
Hill Crest
Mains Pits
Island Plantation
Southworth Hall
Cockshot Farm
M6 MOTORWAY
M6
Highfields
Asps Wood
Reservoir (cov.)
WINWICK
Winwick Green
The Lodge
Stone House Farm
Arbury Cotts.
Myddleton Hall
Myddleton Hall Farm
Arbury
HOLLINS PARK HOSPITAL
Winwick Leis. Cen.
Arbury Farm
Mainfield
Gorsey Brow
Spa Well House
Pumping Station
Warrington
Junction 10 (M62)
Coney Grove Woods
Garden of Remembrance
Delph Farm
Delph Farm Cottage
Superstore
Bowling Greens
Arbury Pits
Midhops Farm
M62
M62 MOTORWAY
Houghton Green
Junction 9
Warehouses
Peel Hall
Birch Tree Farm
Peel Cottage
Bowling Green Farm
Radley Plantation
Radley Farm
Radley Common
WA2
Hall Comm. Cen.
Peel Hall Park
SANKEY VALLEY PARK
GEMINI BUSINESS PARK
THE QUAY CENTRE
Depot
St. Andrew's C of E Prim. Sch.
Hulme
Winwick Quay
LA Bowl
Fordton Leis. Cen.
St. Stephen's Catholic Prim. Sch.
Houghton Hall
CROMWELL AVENUE
A574
Comm. Cen.
Works
Depot
ALBAN RETAIL PARK
Dallam
Dallam Prim. Sch.
Meadowside Prim. Sch.
Longford
Sports Grd.
Youth Cen.
Blackbrook
Orford
Brook Acre Prim. Sch.
WA5
LONG LANE
A50
WINSTANLEY IND. EST.
Warrington Collegiate
William Beamont High Sch.
WARRINGTON BUS. PARK
Football Pitches
ORFORD PARK
Sports Hall
Liby.
Sports Pitches
Playing Field
Longford Bridge
BIRCHWOOD
The Bennett Recreation Ground
SANKEY VALLEY PARK
Bewsey Lock
Sankey Brook
Works
A49
Total Fitness
KERFOOT BUS. PARK
GATEWAY TRADE PK.
Factory
Prim. Sch.
Cricket Grd.
Playing Field
Bewsey
Bewsey Pk.
HAWTHORNE BUS. PK.
82
Football Grd.
Prim. Sch.
Bruche
Bruche Park
St. Rocco's Hospice
KERFOOT BUSINESS PARK
St. Benedict's Catholic Prim.
65

Croft Heath
Croft Primary School
CROFT
Smithy Brow
WA3
Eaves Brow
Croft Golf Centre
M62 MOTORWAY
M62
Junction 21a (M6)
M6
HMP RISLEY
Risley
Birchwood Park
BIRCHWOOD GOLF COURSE
Locking Stumps
Locking Stumps Prim. Sch.
POULTON PARK GOLF COURSE
Cinnamon Brow
University of Chester (Warrington Campus)
BIRCHWOOD WAY
BIRCHWOOD
Birchwood High Sch.
Birchwood Leisure & Tennis Complex
BIRCHWOOD SHOPPING CENTRE
Birchwood
Oakwood
BIRCHWOOD FOREST PARK
Birchwood C of E Prim. Sch.
Birchwood Brook Park
Fearnhead
M6 MOTORWAY
WOOLSTON MOSS
Grange
GRANGE EMPLOYMENT CENTRE
Longbarn Prim. Sch.
Padgate
Padgate High Sch.
WOOLSTON PARK
WOOLSTON
WA1
Green Lane School
Bruche Prim. Sch.
Paddington
Woolston Prim. Sch.
Woolston Neighbourhood
Martinscroft
Moss Brow Cottages
New Moss Farm
53
83
68

Warrington
WA3
M62 MOTORWAY
Junction 11
M62
HOLCROFT LANE
B5212
Hole Mill Farm
Glaze Brook
Keeper's Cottage
Aikin Knowles's Bridge
Great Woolden Hall
GLAZEBROOK LANE
Nursery
HOLCROFT MOSS
GLAZEBROOK MOSS
Pestfurlong Moss
SILVER LANE
Pestfurlong Hill
BIRCHWOOD WAY
A574
Gorse Covert
Sch.
BIRCHWOOD FOREST PARK
RISLEY MOSS
Risley Moss Visitor Centre
Risley Moss Local Nature Reserve
ORDNANCE AVENUE
Oakwood
Hoyle's Moss Farm
SCHOOL LANE
New Hall Farm
Milverton Farm
Omrod Farm
Ivy Cottage
Bridge Farm
Townley Brow Farm
Hollingreave Farm
Rose Cottage
DAM HEAD
MOSS LANE
Moss Hall Farm
MOSS SIDE
Prospect Farm
PROSPECT LANE
Barn End Farm
Ash Tree Farm
Moss Side Farm No. 2
Moss Side Farm
Woodend Farm
Woodend Cottage
WOODEND LANE
The Bungalow
Top End Farm
Down's Covert
RIXTON MOSS
MOAT LANE
Works
RIXTON PARK HOMES
Cleveland's Farm
Rixton
Wks.
Rixton Claypits Local Nature Reserve
Brook Farm
Marsh Brook
Oaktree Cottage
MARTINCROFT MOSS
Moss Head
Rixton Firs
Lane End
Moss End Croft
Marshall's Farm
BROOK LANE
HOLLY BUSH LANE
Moss Farm
Green Alley Farm
Tomfield Wood
A57
Ramswood Nursery
Woodside Farm
Rixton New Hall
New Moss Farm
Nurseries
Lynbrook
Green Valley Farm
The Oaks
Moss Side Farm
M6 MOTORWAY
M6
Junction 21
MANCHESTER ROAD
84
Brookside Farm
Moss Side Farm
Swithen Hill Wood
Rixton Old Hall
67

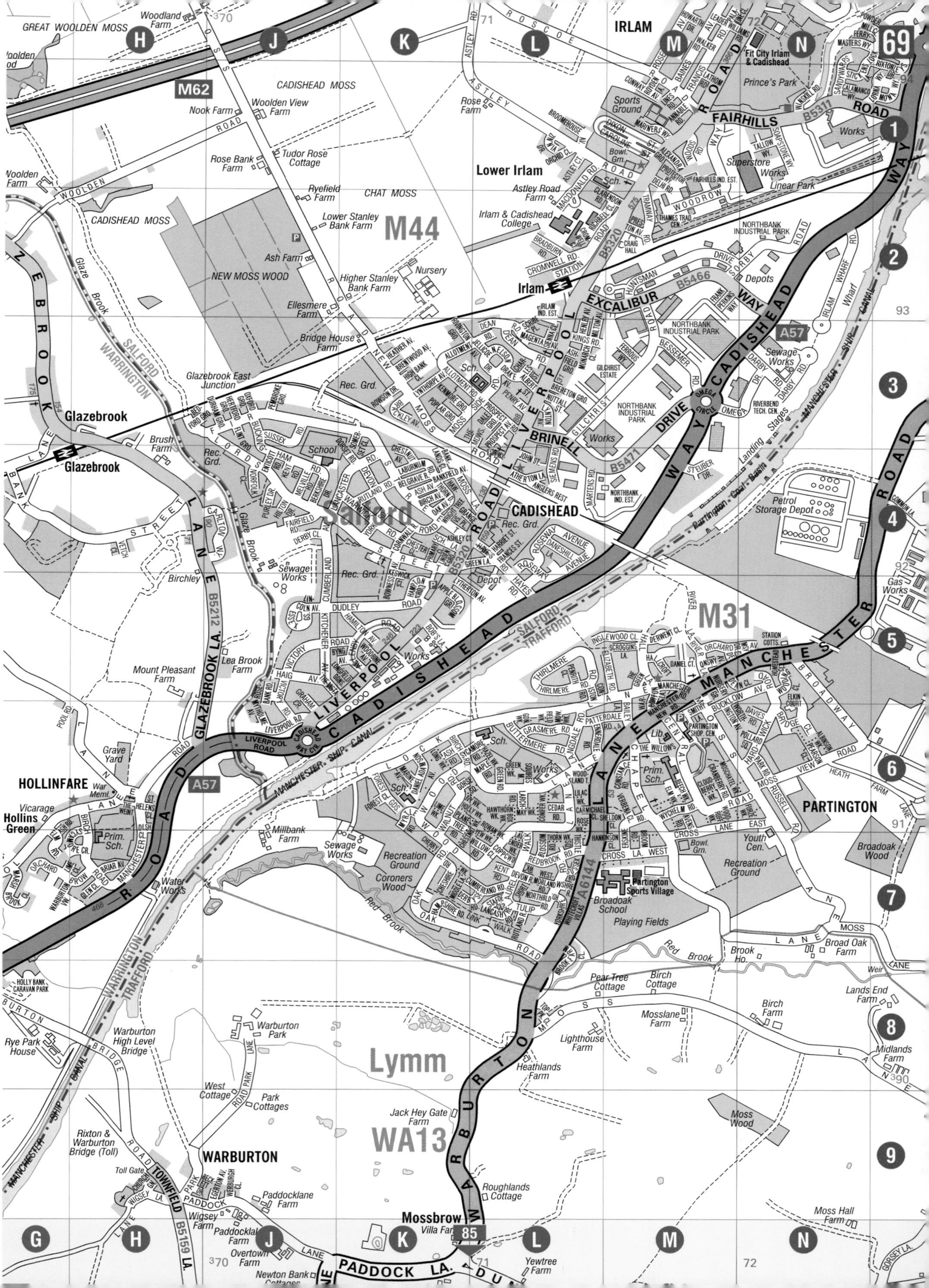

IRLAM
Lower Irlam
Irlam
CADISHEAD
PARTINGTON
Glazebrook
HOLLINFARE
Hollins Green
WARBURTON
Mossbrow
Lymm
M44
M31
WA13
M62
A57
B5320
B5311
B5466
B5471
B5212
B5159
A6144
GREAT WOOLDEN MOSS
CADISHEAD MOSS
CHAT MOSS
NEW MOSS WOOD
Woodland Farm
Woolden Farm
Nook Farm
Woolden View Farm
Rose Bank Farm
Tudor Rose Cottage
Ryefield Farm
Lower Stanley Bank Farm
Ash Farm
Higher Stanley Bank Farm
Ellesmere Farm
Bridge House Farm
Nursery
Glazebrook East Junction
Brush Farm
Birchley
Lea Brook Farm
Mount Pleasant Farm
Grave Yard
Vicarage
War Meml.
Prim. Sch.
Water Works
Millbank Farm
Sewage Works
Recreation Ground
Coroners Wood
Red Brook
HOLLY BANK CARAVAN PARK
Rye Park House
Warburton High Level Bridge
Warburton Park
West Cottage
Park Cottages
Rixton & Warburton Bridge (Toll)
Toll Gate
Paddocklane Farm
Wigsey Farm
Paddocklane Farm
Overtown Farm
Newton Bank Cottages
Jack Hey Gate Farm
Roughlands Cottage
Villa Farm
Yewtree Farm
Heathlands Farm
Lighthouse Farm
Mosslane Farm
Pear Tree Cottage
Birch Cottage
Brook Ho.
Broad Oak Farm
Lands End Farm
Birch Farm
Midlands Farm
Moss Wood
Moss Hall Farm
Weir
Broadoak Wood
Partington Sports Village
Broadoak School
Playing Fields
Youth Cen.
Recreation Ground
Bowl. Grn.
Lib.
PARTINGTON SHOP. CEN.
Petrol Storage Depot
Gas Works
Partington Coal Basin
Landing Stages
MANCHESTER SHIP CANAL
NORTHBANK INDUSTRIAL PARK
NORTHBANK IND. EST.
GILCHRIST ESTATE
RIVERBEND TECH. CEN.
OMEGA CIRCLE
Depots
Sewage Works
IRLAM IND. EST.
Works
Rec. Grd.
School
Salford
Irlam & Cadishead College
Astley Road Farm
Rose Farm
Sports Ground
Fit City Irlam & Cadishead
Prince's Park
Superstore
Linear Park
FAIRHILLS IND. EST.
THAMES TRAD. CEN.
Depot
SALFORD
WARRINGTON
TRAFFORD
CADISHEAD WAY
LIVERPOOL ROAD
MANCHESTER ROAD
GLAZEBROOK LA.
WARBURTON LANE
PADDOCK LA.
FAIRHILLS ROAD
EXCALIBUR WAY
BRINELL DRIVE
FLORDS CL.
Glaze Brook
H
J
K
L
M
N
G
1
2
3
4
5
6
7
8
9
370
71
72
390
93
92
91
94
85

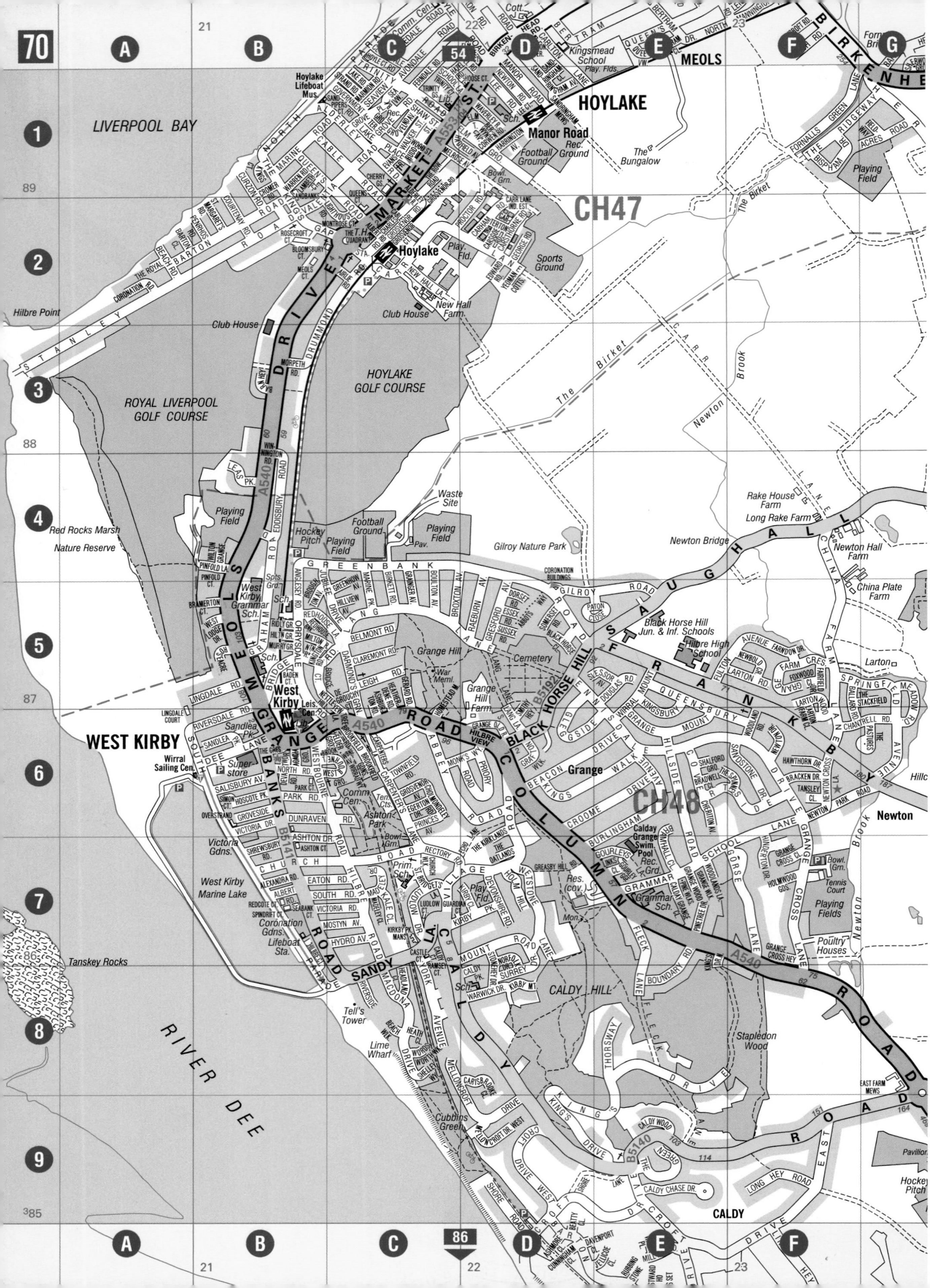
54
86
LIVERPOOL BAY
HOYLAKE
MEOLS
Manor Road
Hoylake
Hoylake Lifeboat Mus.
Kingsmead School
CH47
CH48
The Bungalow
The Birket
Newton Brook
Carr Lane
Hilbre Point
Club House
ROYAL LIVERPOOL GOLF COURSE
HOYLAKE GOLF COURSE
New Hall Farm
Sports Ground
Football Ground
Red Rocks Marsh Nature Reserve
Waste Site
Gilroy Nature Park
Newton Bridge
Rake House Farm
Long Rake Farm
Newton Hall Farm
China Plate Farm
SAUGHALL MASSIE ROAD
WEST KIRBY
West Kirby
Wirral Sailing Cen.
Grange Hill
Cemetery
Grange Hill Farm
Black Horse Hill Jun. & Inf. Schools
Hilbre High School
FRANKBY ROAD
Grange
Newton
Larton
COLUMBIA ROAD
GRANGE ROAD
MEOLS DRIVE
Victoria Gdns.
West Kirby Marine Lake
Coronation Gdns.
Lifeboat Sta.
Tanskey Rocks
RIVER DEE
Tell's Tower
Lime Wharf
Cubbins Green
CALDY HILL
Stapledon Wood
Calday Grange Swim. Pool
Calday Grange Gram. Sch.
Playing Fields
Poultry Houses
CALDY
Pavilion
Hockey Pitch
A540
A553
B5192
B5140
B5141
21
22
23
88
89
87
86
385

71
55
87
H
J
K
L
M
N
G
1
2
3
4
5
6
7
8
9
CH46
CH49
CH61
Wirral
HOYLAKE ROAD
A553
M53 MOTORWAY
M53
MORETON ROAD
UPTON ROAD
A551
ARROWE PARK ROAD
A5027
B5192
B5139
B5140
A540
MASSIE LANE
SAUGHALL MASSIE ROAD
GREASBY ROAD
ARROWE PARK
Saughall Massie
Three Lanes End
Three Lanes End Farm
Oldfield Manor Farm
Oldfield Court
The Heyes
Carr Farm
Carr Ho. Farm
Clay
Green Gates Farm
Diamond Farm
Prospect Farm
Barnacre
Nursery
Foxfield Sch.
UPTON
Upton Bridge
Superstore
GREASBY
Greasby Coronation Park
Brookdale Prim. Sch.
Bowling Greens
Ten. Cts.
Play Field
Comm. Cen.
Lib.
Day Cen.
Comm. Centre
Playground
Overchurch Jun. & Inf. Schools
Hayfield School
Recreation Ground
Warwick Hey Rec. Grd.
St. Joseph's Catholic Prim.
Upton Hall School
Cricket Ground
Arrowe Hill
Factories
ARROWE COMMERCIAL PARK
CHAMPIONS BUS. PARK
WIRRAL BUS. PK.
Playing Fields
Pavilion
Gorse Covert
ARROWE PARK HOSPITAL
NHS Walk in Centre
Fish Pond
Nicholson's Plantation
ARROWE COUNTRY PARK
ARROWE PARK GOLF COURSE
Tophouse Farm
Neilson's Plantation
Limbo Lane Plantation
Arrowe Brook
Arrowe Brook Farm
Arrowe Bridge
Greenhouse Farm
Greasby Copse
Greasby Brook
Arrow Brook
Larton Hey Farm
Nursery
Greasby Bri.
War Memorial
Football Ground
Manor Ho. Farm
Yew Tree Farm
Bay Tree Farm
Royden Hall
Bowling Green
FRANKBY
Croft Poultry Farm
Cemetery
Nurseries
Royden Manor
Birch House
Torpenhow
Greasby Inf. Sch.
Our Lady of Pity Catholic Prim. Sch.
Greasby Junior School
Green Gates
Redstones Farm
Quarry Farm
Hill Bark Farm House
Cricket Ground
Irby Hill
Irby Hill Farm
ROYDEN PARK
Frankby Mere
Model Railway Centre
Hill Bark
Roodee Mere
Thurstaston Common Local Nature Reserve
Paton Field (Sports Ground)
Playing Field
Thurstaston Hill
Thur's Stone
Benty Farm
Hillside Farm
Thurstaston Common Recreation Ground
Strowan
IRBY
Irby Prim. Sch.
Play Field
Playing Fields
MONTGOMERY HILL
TELEGRAPH ROAD
HILLBARK RD.
ARROWE BROOK ROAD
ARROWE BROOK LANE
MILL HILL
LIMBO LANE
THINGWALL ROAD
HEATHBANK
SANDY LANE
THORNS DRIVE
HILLVIEW ROAD
DINGWALL DRIVE
ARROWE AVENUE
FRANKBY STILES
LANE
WOODCHURCH ROAD
BIRCH AVENUE
ELM AVENUE
BEECH AVENUE
OLD GREASBY RD.
24
25
26
27
85
86
87
88
89

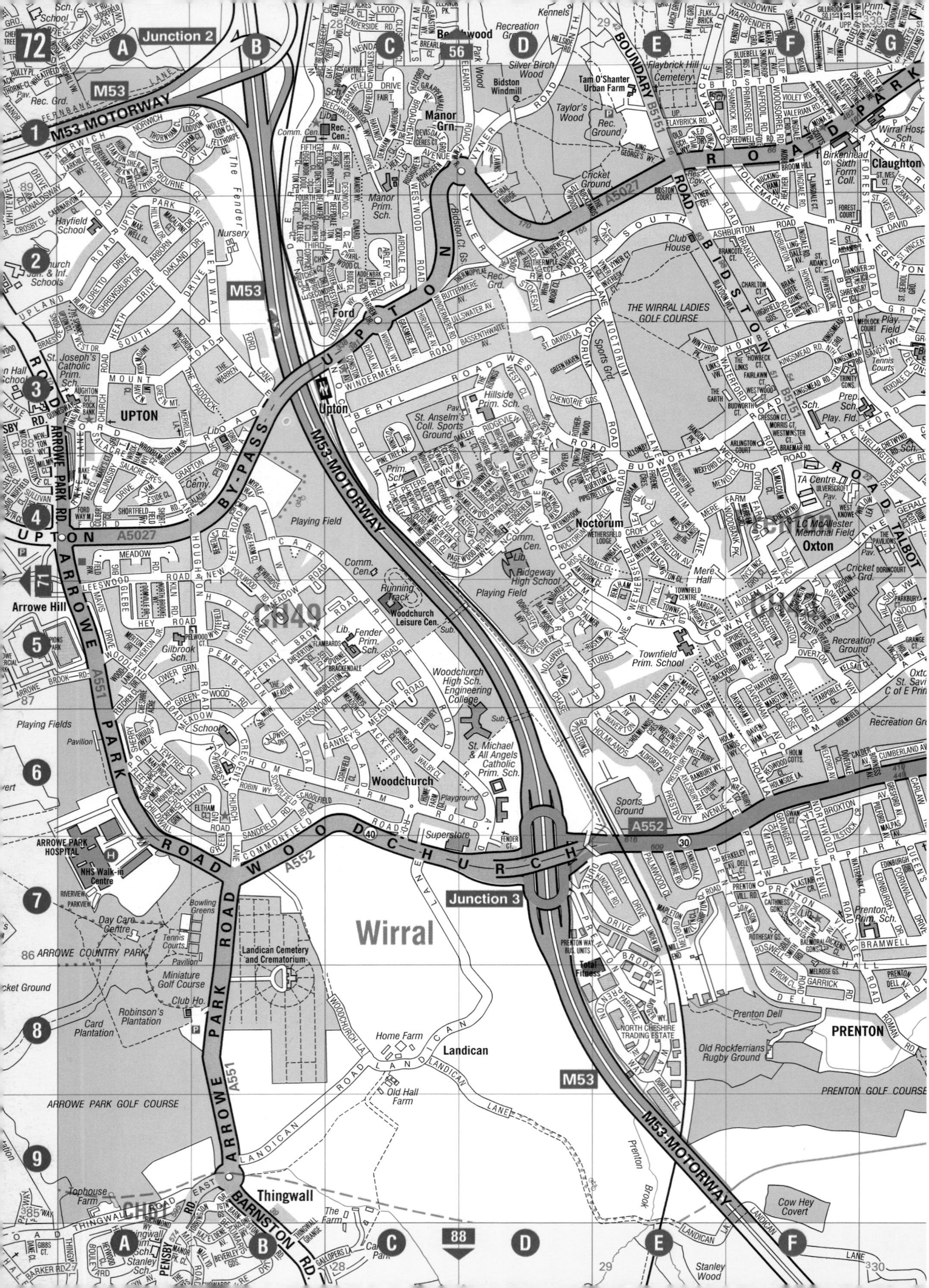

Junction 2
M53 MOTORWAY
Beechwood
56
Recreation Grd.
Silver Birch Wood
Bidston Windmill
Tam O'Shanter Urban Farm
Flaybrick Hill Cemetery
BOUNDARY
B5151
Taylor's Wood
Rec. Ground
Manor Grn.
Manor Prim. Sch.
Hayfield School
Church Jun. & Inf. Schools
Nursery
The Fender
M53
Cricket Ground
A5027
Birkenhead Sixth Form Coll.
Claughton
Wirral Hosp. Sch.
Club House
THE WIRRAL LADIES GOLF COURSE
Sports Grd.
St. Joseph's Catholic Prim. Sch.
UPTON
Upton
Ford
UPTON BY-PASS
M53 MOTORWAY
Hillside Prim. Sch.
St. Anselm's Coll. Sports Ground
Prim. Sch.
Cemy.
Playing Field
Noctorum
Comm. Cen.
Ridgeway High School
Playing Field
Mere Hall
Townfield Prim. School
LC McAllester Memorial Field
Oxton
TA Centre
Cricket Grd.
Recreation Ground
St. Saviour's C of E Prim.
Recreation Grd.
Arrowe Hill
71
UPTON
A5027
CH49
Running Track
Woodchurch Leisure Cen.
Lib.
Fender Prim. Sch.
Gilbrook Sch.
Woodchurch High Sch. Engineering College
St. Michael & All Angels Catholic Prim. Sch.
Woodchurch
Playground
Superstore
Playing Fields
Pavilion
School
ARROWE PARK
A551
ARROWE PARK HOSPITAL
NHS Walk-in Centre
WOODCHURCH ROAD
A552
40
30
Junction 3
Sports Ground
Wirral
Bowling Greens
Day Care Centre
Tennis Courts
Pavilion
ARROWE COUNTRY PARK
Landican Cemetery and Crematorium
Miniature Golf Course
Club Ho.
Robinson's Plantation
Card Plantation
Cricket Ground
Total Fitness
PRENTON WAY BUS. UNITS
NORTH CHESHIRE TRADING ESTATE
Prenton Dell
PRENTON
Old Rockferrians Rugby Ground
Prenton Prim. Sch.
PRENTON GOLF COURSE
Home Farm
Landican
Old Hall Farm
ARROWE PARK GOLF COURSE
ARROWE PARK ROAD
M53
M53 MOTORWAY
Prenton Brook
Cow Hey Covert
Tophouse Farm
Thingwall
BARNSTON RD.
The Farm
88
Stanley Wood
A B C D E F G
1 2 3 4 5 6 7 8 9

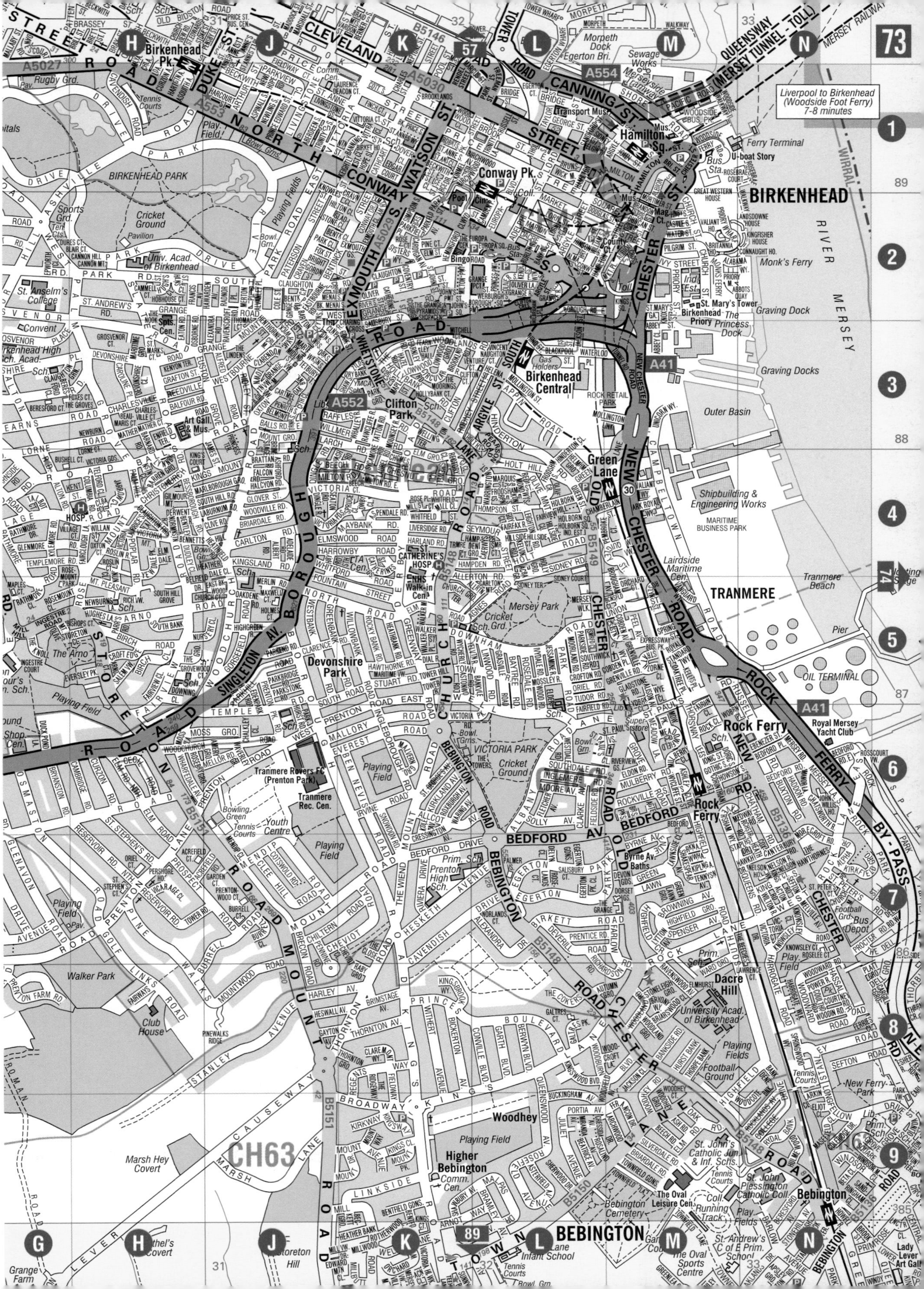
BIRKENHEAD
TRANMERE
Rock Ferry
Higher Bebington
Woodhey
Dacre Hill
BEBINGTON
Birkenhead Park
BIRKENHEAD PARK
Hamilton Sq.
Conway Pk.
Birkenhead Central
Green Lane
Rock Ferry
Bebington
RIVER MERSEY
Liverpool to Birkenhead (Woodside Foot Ferry) 7-8 minutes
Ferry Terminal
U-boat Story
Graving Dock
Graving Docks
Outer Basin
Shipbuilding & Engineering Works
MARITIME BUSINESS PARK
Lairdside Maritime Cen.
Tranmere Beach
OIL TERMINAL
Royal Mersey Yacht Club
Monk's Ferry
St. Mary's Tower
Birkenhead Priory
The Princess Dock
Morpeth Dock
Egerton Bri.
Sewage Works
Transport Mus.
Mersey Park
Devonshire Park
VICTORIA PARK
Tranmere Rovers FC (Prenton Park)
Tranmere Rec. Cen.
Walker Park
Club House
Marsh Hey Covert
University Acad. of Birkenhead
Univ. Acad. of Birkenhead
St. Anselm's College
Art Gall. & Mus.
Bebington Cemetery
The Oval Leisure Cen.
The Oval Sports Centre
St. John Plessington Catholic Coll.
St. John's Catholic Jun. & Inf. Schs.
New Ferry Park
Lady Lever Art Gall.
Grange Farm
Storeton Hill
QUEENSWAY (MERSEY TUNNEL - TOLL)
MERSEY RAILWAY
WIRRAL
A41
A552
A553
A554
A5027
A5029
A5030
B5136
B5148
B5149
B5150
B5151
B5146
CH63
BOROUGH ROAD
CONWAY STREET
NORTH ROAD
CHESTER STREET
NEW CHESTER ROAD
ROCK FERRY BY-PASS
BEDFORD AV
BEDFORD RD.
CHURCH ROAD
BEBINGTON ROAD
MOUNT ROAD
STORETON ROAD
SINGLETON AV.
KINGS LANE
STANLEY AVENUE
CAUSEWAY
57
74
89
G
H
J
K
L
M
N
1
2
3
4
5
6
7
8
9
31
32
33
85
86
87
88
89

A
B
C
D
E
F
G
58
4
5
73
90
89
88
87
86
1
2
3
4
5
6
7
8
9
Echo Arena
BT Convention Cen.
Queen's Wapping Bridge
Gala Leo Casino
Queen's Dock
Liverpool Watersports Cen.
Customs & Excise
Coburg Dock (Marina)
Brunswick Dock (Marina)
HMS Eaglet
Toxteth
Brunswick
Studio
Rec. Grd.
Greens Health & Fitness
Lifestyles Park Rd.
Liverpool Cathedral
Huskisson Mon.
LIVERPOOL WOMEN'S HOSP.
Granby
PARLIAMENT
UPPER PARLIAMENT ST.
WAPPING
CHALONER ST.
SEFTON ST.
JAMAICA ST.
ST. JAMES PL.
PARK PL.
PARK RD.
WARWICK
PRINCES RD.
KINGSLEY RD.
DEVONSHIRE RD.
BELVIDERE RD.
ULLET RD.
PRINCES PARK
Belvidere Academy
A562
A5036
A561
B5175
B5174
B5177
Dingle
St. Michael's
St. Michael's Hamlet
FESTIVAL GARDENS
University Academy Liverpool
RIVERSIDE DRIVE
Floating Stage
Rock Ferry Pier
Royal Mersey Yacht Club
RIVER MERSEY
LIVERPOOL
WIRRAL
ROCK FERRY BY-PASS
NEW FERRY BY-PASS
New Ferry Park
A41
B5136
NEW FERRY
Playing Field
Sewage Works
Lady Lever Art Gall.
BEBINGTON RD.
NEW CHESTER RD.
335
36
34

Wavertree
WAVERTREE SPORTS PARK
Wavertree Green
CHILDWALL
SMITHDOWN ROAD
Toxteth Park Cemetery
Princes Park
SEFTON PARK
Sefton Park
Sefton Park Palm House
Aigburth Vale
Liverpool
Mossley Hill
L18
QUEENS DRIVE
MOSSLEY HILL
MENLOVE AV.
Calderstones
Geoffrey Hughes Memorial Ground
Heron Eccles Playing Field
West Allerton
L17
AIGBURTH ROAD
Otterspool
Otterspool Park
Aigburth
Grassendale
L19
ST. MARY'S RD.
Cressington
Cressington Park
Sudley House
Holt Rec. Grd.
Liverpool Cricket Club
Alfred Holt Athletics Grd.
PROMENADE
A5089
A562
A5058
A561
B5175
B5179
B5178
B5180
59
91
76

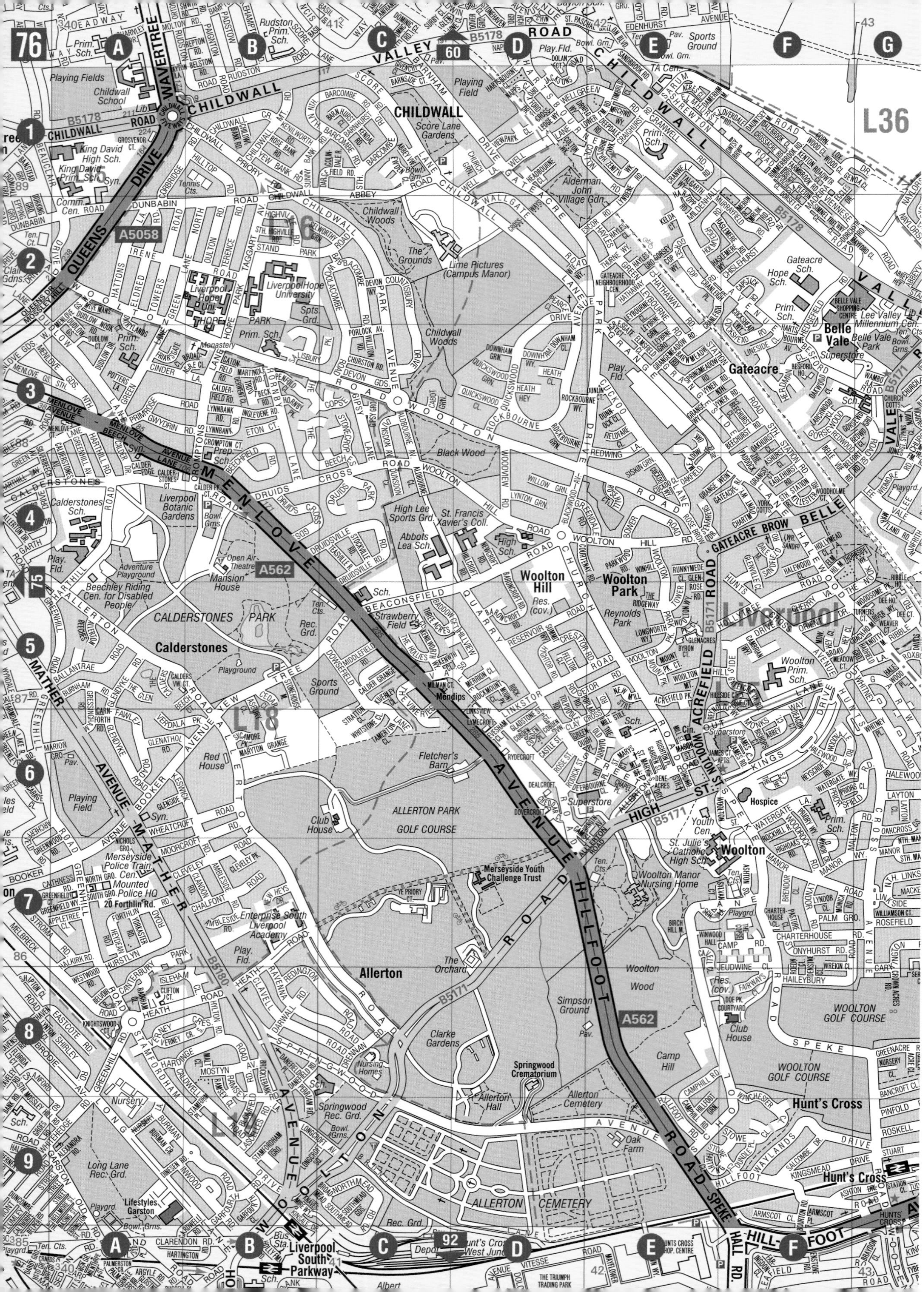

CHILDWALL
Childwall School
King David High Sch.
Score Lane Gardens
Childwall Woods
The Grounds
Lime Pictures (Campus Manor)
Alderman John Village Gdn.
Liverpool Hope University
Gateacre Sch.
Hope Sch.
Belle Vale
Belle Vale Park
Gateacre
Lee Valley Millennium Cen.
L36
L16
L18
L19
Black Wood
Calderstones Sch.
Liverpool Botanic Gardens
Calderstones
CALDERSTONES PARK
Mansion House
Beechley Riding Cen. for Disabled People
Strawberry Field
Sports Ground
St. Francis Xavier's Coll.
Abbots Lea Sch.
Woolton Hill
Woolton Park
Reynolds Park
Liverpool
Woolton Prim. Sch.
Mendips
Fletcher's Barn
ALLERTON PARK GOLF COURSE
Club House
Red House
Merseyside Police Train. Cen.
Mounted Police HQ
20 Forthlin Rd.
Enterprise South Liverpool Academy
Merseyside Youth Challenge Trust
Allerton
The Orchard
Clarke Gardens
Springwood Crematorium
Allerton Hall
Allerton Cemetery
ALLERTON CEMETERY
Oak Farm
Woolton Wood
Simpson Ground
Camp Hill
Woolton
St. Julie's Catholic High Sch.
Woolton Manor Nursing Home
Hospice
WOOLTON GOLF COURSE
Hunt's Cross
Long Lane Rec. Grd.
Lifestyles Garston
Springwood Rec. Grd.
Liverpool South Parkway
Hunt's Cross West Junc.
HUNTS CROSS SHOP. CENTRE
THE TRIUMPH TRADING PARK
MENLOVE AVENUE
QUEENS DRIVE
MATHER AVENUE
HILLFOOT ROAD
HILLFOOT AVENUE
SPEKE ROAD
WOOLTON ROAD
CHILDWALL VALLEY ROAD
CHILDWALL ROAD
ACREFIELD ROAD
HIGH ST.
ALLERTON ROAD
A5058
A562
B5178
B5171
B5180
60
75
92

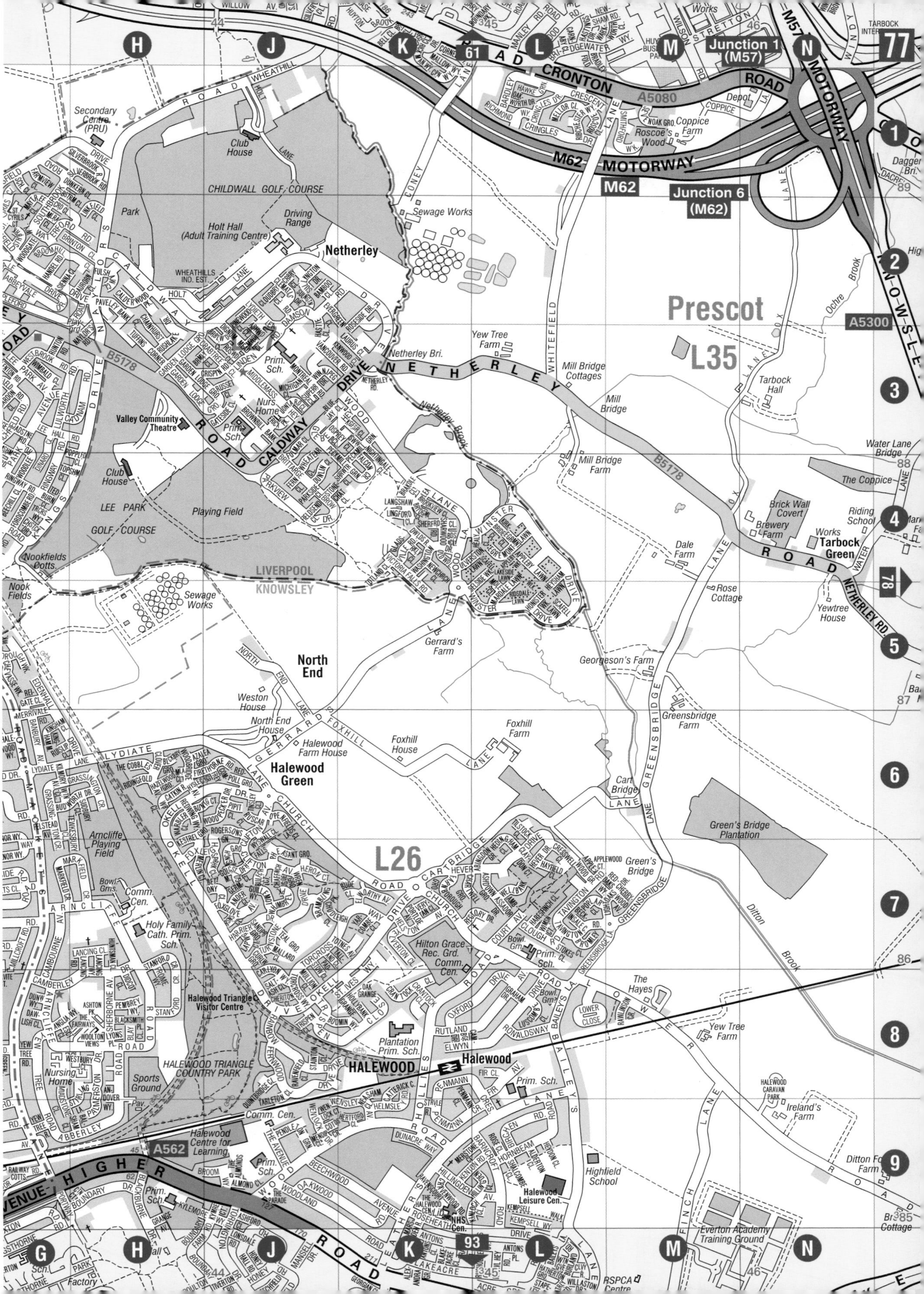

Junction 1 (M57)
M57 MOTORWAY
CRONTON ROAD
A5080
M62 MOTORWAY
M62
Junction 6 (M62)
Secondary Centre (PRU)
WHEATHILL ROAD
Club House
CHILDWALL GOLF COURSE
Park
Holt Hall (Adult Training Centre)
Driving Range
Sewage Works
Netherley
WHEATHILLS IND. EST.
CALDWAY DRIVE
Prescot
L35
A5300
Yew Tree Farm
Netherley Bri.
NETHERLEY ROAD
Mill Bridge Cottages
Mill Bridge
Tarbock Hall
B5178
Valley Community Theatre
Prim. Sch.
Nurs. Home
Netherley Brook
Mill Bridge Farm
Water Lane Bridge
The Coppice
Brick Wall Covert
Brewery Farm
Riding School
Works
Tarbock Green
Club House
LEE PARK
Playing Field
GOLF COURSE
Nookfields Cotts.
LIVERPOOL
KNOWSLEY
Dale Farm
Rose Cottage
Yewtree House
Nook Fields
Sewage Works
Gerrard's Farm
North End
Georgeson's Farm
Weston House
North End House
Halewood Farm House
Foxhill House
Foxhill Farm
Greensbridge Farm
Halewood Green
GERRARD LANE
CHURCH ROAD
Cart Bridge
Green's Bridge Plantation
L26
CARTBRIDGE ROAD
Green's Bridge
Arncliffe Playing Field
Comm. Cen.
Holy Family Cath. Prim. Sch.
Hilton Grace Rec. Grd. Comm. Cen.
Prim. Sch.
Ditton Brook
The Hayes
Halewood Triangle Visitor Centre
Nursing Home
HALEWOOD TRIANGLE COUNTRY PARK
Sports Ground
Plantation Prim. Sch.
HALEWOOD
Halewood
Yew Tree Farm
Prim. Sch.
HALEWOOD CARAVAN PARK
Ireland's Farm
Comm. Cen.
Halewood Centre for Learning
A562
HIGHER ROAD
Highfield School
Ditton Farm
Halewood Leisure Cen.
NHS Cen.
Everton Academy Training Ground
Factory
RSPCA Centre
G H J K L M N
1 2 3 4 5 6 7 8 9
61
78
93

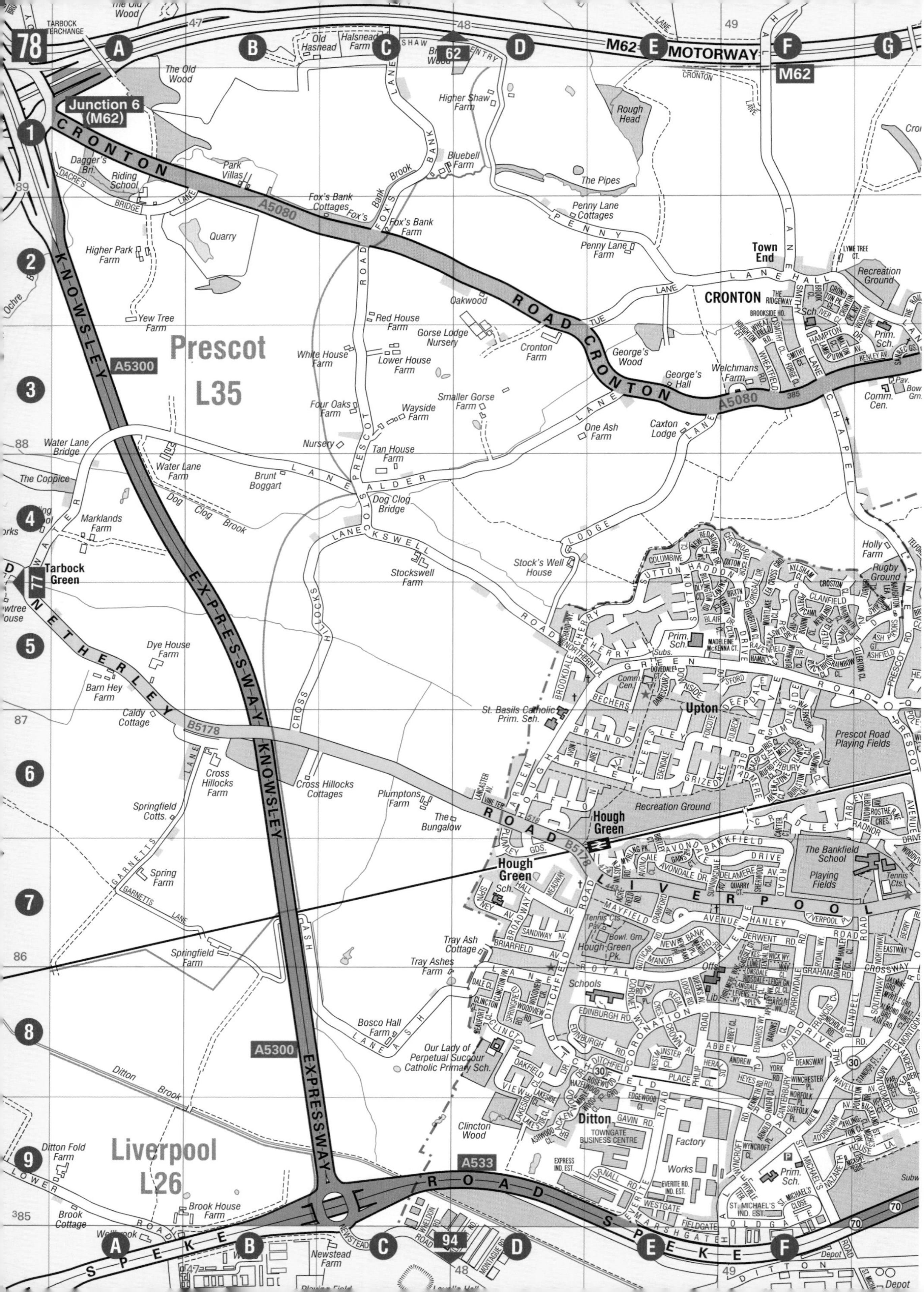

TARBOCK INTERCHANGE
The Old Wood
Old Hasnead
Halsnead Farm
M62 MOTORWAY
62
Junction 6 (M62)
CRONTON ROAD
A5080
Dagger's Bri.
Riding School
DACRE'S BRIDGE LANE
Park Villas
Fox's Bank Cottages
Fox's Bank Farm
Higher Shaw Farm
Bluebell Farm
Rough Head
The Pipes
Penny Lane Cottages
Penny Lane Farm
PENNY LANE
Quarry
Higher Park Farm
Yew Tree Farm
Town End
CRONTON
Recreation Ground
Oakwood
Red House Farm
Gorse Lodge Nursery
Cronton Farm
George's Wood
George's Hall
Welchmans Farm
Prescot L35
A5300
KNOWSLEY EXPRESSWAY
White House Farm
Lower House Farm
Four Oaks Farm
Wayside Farm
Smaller Gorse Farm
One Ash Farm
Caxton Lodge
Comm. Cen.
Prim. Sch.
Water Lane Bridge
Water Lane Farm
Brunt Boggart
Nursery
Tan House Farm
ALDER LANE
PRESCOT ROAD
The Coppice
Dog Clog Brook
Dog Clog Bridge
Marklands Farm
Tarbock Green
77
STOCKSWELL LANE
Stockswell Farm
Stock's Well House
LODGE LANE
HILLOCKS
NETHERLEY
Dye House Farm
Barn Hey Farm
Caldy Cottage
B5178
CROSS
Upton
St. Basils Catholic Prim. Sch.
Prescot Road Playing Fields
Cross Hillocks Farm
Cross Hillocks Cottages
Plumptons Farm
The Bungalow
Springfield Cotts.
Recreation Ground
Hough Green
The Bankfield School
Playing Fields
Spring Farm
GARNETTS LANE
LIVERPOOL ROAD
Springfield Farm
Tray Ash Cottage
Tray Ashes Farm
Hough Green Pk.
Schools
Bosco Hall Farm
ASH LANE
Our Lady of Perpetual Succour Catholic Primary Sch.
A5300
Ditton Brook
Clincton Wood
Ditton
TOWNGATE BUSINESS CENTRE
Factory
Works
EXPRESS IND. EST.
Ditton Fold Farm
Liverpool L26
A533
SPEKE ROAD
LOWER ROAD
Brook Cottage
Brook House Farm
Newstead Farm
94
ST. MICHAEL'S IND. EST.
70
Depot
DITTON
47
48
49
89
88
87
86
385

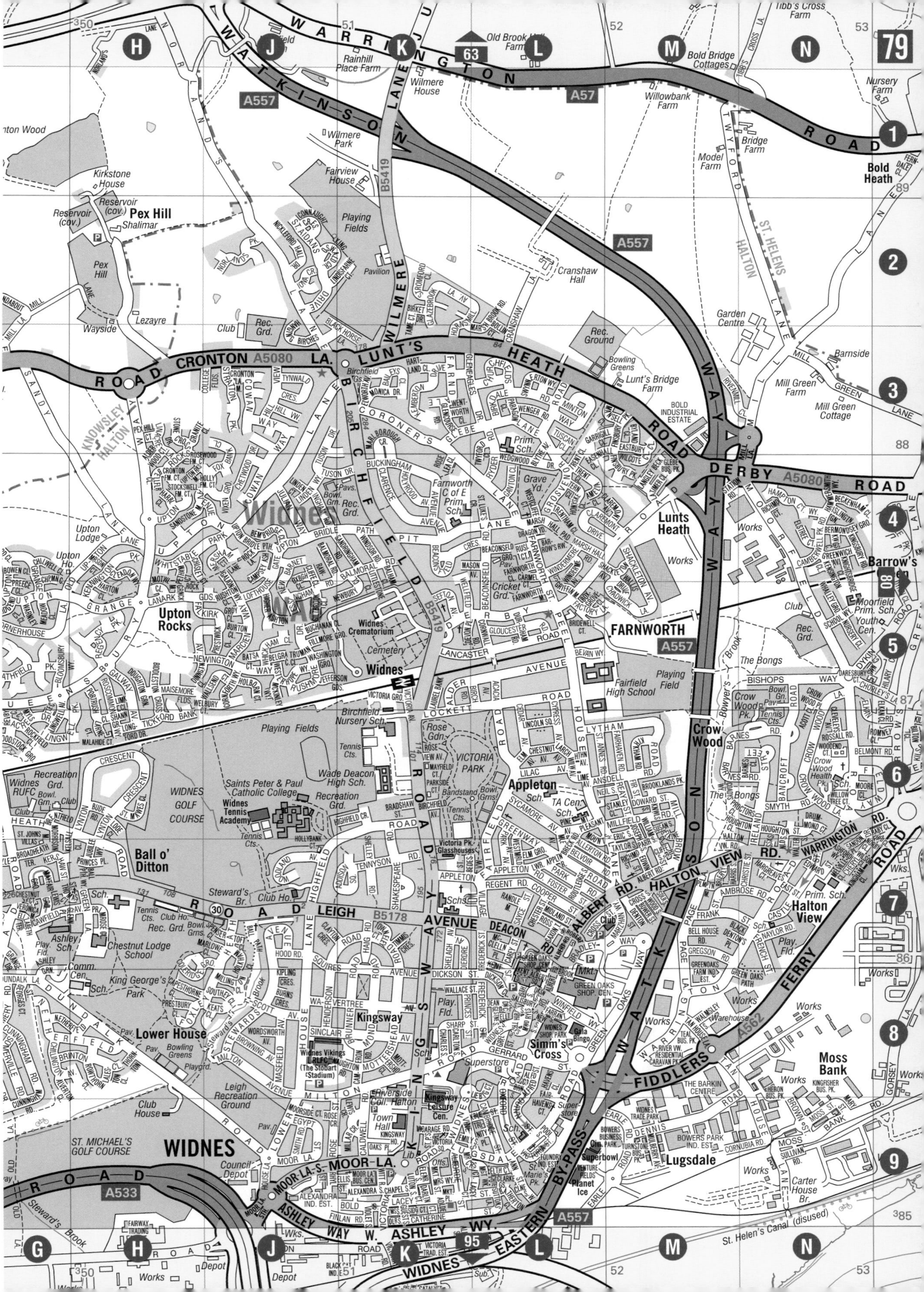
WARRINGTON ROAD
A57
63
WATKINSON WAY
A557
Rainhill Place Farm
Old Brook Hill Farm
Wilmere House
Bold Bridge Cottages
Willowbank Farm
Tibb's Cross Farm
Nursery Farm
Bridge Farm
Model Farm
Bold Heath
Wilmere Park
Fairview House
Kirkstone House
Reservoir (cov.)
Pex Hill
Shalimar
Playing Fields
Pavilion
WILMERE LANE
B5419
Cranshaw Hall
HALTON
ST. HELENS
Garden Centre
Barnside
Mill Green Farm
Mill Green Cottage
MILL GREEN LANE
Wayside
Lezayre
Rec. Grd.
Rec. Ground
Bowling Greens
Lunt's Bridge Farm
BOLD INDUSTRIAL ESTATE
CRONTON ROAD
A5080
LUNT'S HEATH ROAD
DERBY ROAD
KNOWSLEY
HALTON
BIRCHFIELD ROAD
Farnworth C of E Prim. Sch.
Grave Yd.
Widnes
Upton Lodge
Upton Ho.
Upton Rocks
Lunts Heath
Works
Barrow's Grn
80
Moorfield Prim. Sch.
Youth Cen.
Club
Rec. Grd.
Widnes Crematorium
Cemetery
Cricket Grd.
FARNWORTH
The Bongs
Widnes
Fairfield High School
Playing Field
Birchfield Nursery Sch.
Playing Fields
Tennis Cts.
Wade Deacon High Sch.
Saints Peter & Paul Catholic College
Recreation Grd.
Widnes Tennis Academy
VICTORIA PARK
Rose Gdn.
Bandstand
Victoria Pk. Glasshouses
Appleton
Crow Wood
Crow Wood Pk.
Crow Wood Health Cen.
Widnes RUFC
Recreation Grd.
WIDNES GOLF COURSE
Ball o' Ditton
Halton View
HALTON VIEW RD.
ALBERT RD.
WARRINGTON RD.
LEIGH AVENUE
B5178
DEACON RD
Steward's Br.
Club Ho.
Tennis Cts.
Club Ho.
Rec. Grd.
Chestnut Lodge School
Ashley Sch.
Comm. Cen.
King George's Park
Kingsway
GREEN OAKS SHOP. CEN.
Mkt.
Gala Bingo
Simm's Cross
Superstore
Lower House
Bowling Greens
Widnes Vikings LRFC (The Stobart Stadium)
Leigh Recreation Ground
Club House
Riverside Coll. Halton
Kingsway Leisure Cen.
Town Hall
ST. MICHAEL'S GOLF COURSE
WIDNES
Council Depot
MOOR LA.
FIDDLERS FERRY ROAD
A562
Moss Bank
Works
THE BARKIN CENTRE
WIDNES TRADE PARK
BOWERS BUSINESS PARK
Superbowl
Planet Ice
Lugsdale
Carter House Br.
St. Helen's Canal (disused)
EASTERN BY-PASS
ASHLEY WAY
A533
95
WIDNES
Steward's Brook
FAIRWAY TRADING
Depot
Works
G H J K L M N
1 2 3 4 5 6 7 8 9
350 51 52 353 385 86 87 88 89

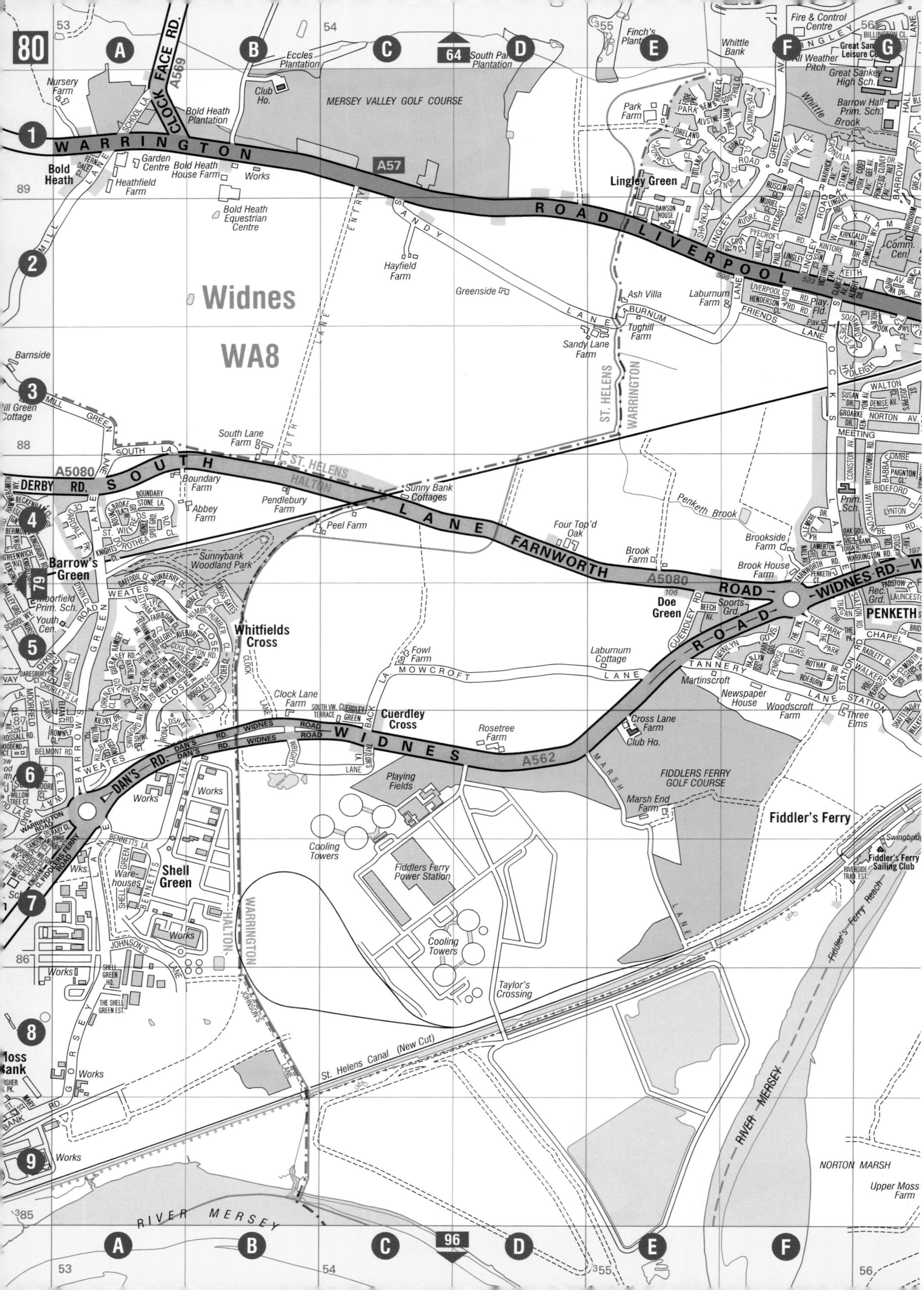

64
96
79
A
B
C
D
E
F
G
1
2
3
4
5
6
7
8
9
53
54
355
56
89
88
87
86
385
Nursery Farm
CLOCK FACE RD.
A569
SCHOOL LA.
Eccles Plantation
South Park Plantation
Finch's Plant.
Whittle Bank
Fire & Control Centre
Great Sankey Leisure Centre
All Weather Pitch
Great Sankey High Sch.
Barrow Hall Prim. Sch.
Whittle Brook
Club Ho.
MERSEY VALLEY GOLF COURSE
Bold Heath Plantation
Park Farm
WARRINGTON ROAD
LIVERPOOL ROAD
A57
Bold Heath
Garden Centre
Bold Heath House Farm
Works
Heathfield Farm
Bold Heath Equestrian Centre
Lingley Green
DAWSON HOUSE
MILL LANE
SANDY LANE
ENTRY LANE
Hayfield Farm
Greenside
Widnes
WA8
Ash Villa
Laburnum Farm
LABURNUM
Tughill Farm
Sandy Lane Farm
FRIENDS LANE
Play. Fld.
Barnside
ST. HELENS
WARRINGTON
Mill Green Cottage
MILL GREEN
South Lane Farm
SOUTH LA.
A5080
DERBY RD.
SOUTH LANE
FARNWORTH ROAD
ST. HELENS
HALTON
Boundary Farm
Abbey Farm
Pendlebury Farm
Sunny Bank Cottages
Peel Farm
Penketh Brook
Four Top'd Oak
Brook Farm
Brookside Farm
Brook House Farm
Prim. Sch.
Barrow's Green
Sunnybank Woodland Park
Moorfield Prim. Sch.
Youth Cen.
Whitfields Cross
Doe Green
Sports Grd.
WIDNES ROAD
WIDNES RD.
PENKETH
Rec. Grd.
Fowl Farm
MOWCROFT LANE
Laburnum Cottage
Martinscroft
Newspaper House
Woodscroft Farm
Three Elms
TANNERY LANE
STATION RD.
Clock Lane Farm
CLOCK LANE
Cuerdley Cross
Rosetree Farm
Cross Lane Farm
Club Ho.
WIDNES ROAD
A562
DAN'S RD.
WEATES
BARROWS GREEN LANE
Works
Playing Fields
FIDDLERS FERRY GOLF COURSE
Marsh End Farm
MARSH LANE
Fiddler's Ferry
Swingbridge
Fiddler's Ferry Sailing Club
RIVERSIDE TRAD. EST.
Cooling Towers
Fiddlers Ferry Power Station
Shell Green
Ware-houses
Wks.
BENNETTS LA.
JOHNSON'S LANE
Works
SHELL GREEN HO.
THE SHELL GREEN EST.
Taylor's Crossing
GORSEY LANE
Works
Moss Bank
St. Helens Canal (New Cut)
Works
Fiddler's Ferry Reach
RIVER MERSEY
NORTON MARSH
Upper Moss Farm
RIVER MERSEY

Whittle Wood
Brow Farm
Chapelford Urban Village
Great Sankey
Sankey (for Penketh)
WA5
Penketh High Sch.
Great Sankey Prim. Sch.
Heathside
WARRINGTON
Sankey Valley Park
St. Gregory's Catholic High School
The Peace Centre
Sacred Heart Catholic Prim. Sch.
David Lloyd Leisure
Sankey Bridges
Evelyn St. Prim. Sch.
Bank Quay
Warrington Hospital
St. Rocco's Hospice
Council Offs.
Bewsey Old Hall
Bewsey Lock
Twenty Acre Wood
Sports Ground
Penketh Business Pk.
Sankey Bridges Ind. Est.
Gatewarth Ind. Est.
Schools
Nursing Home
Penketh Hall
Swing Bridge
St. Helens Canal
Sankey Brook
Sewage Works
River Mersey
Penketh Reach
Richmond Bank
Penketh Bank
Bank Quay Reach
Tanks
Arpley Landfill Site
Runcorn & Latchford Canal
Moss Wood
Moss Side
WA4
Moore Bri.
Moore Nature Reserve
Birch Wood
Acton Grange Viaduct
Warehouses
Manchester Ship Canal
Moss Side Farm
Moore Lane Bridge (Swing)
Bellhouse Farm
Bell House
Mill Lane Cotts.
Grange Mill House
Higher Walton
Acton Grange Junction
Cockfight Cottages
Higher Walton Bridge
Moss Lane Farm
Football Grd.
The Big Riding School
Porch House
Bob's Bri.
Warrington
Halton
A57
A562
A547
Sankey Way
Penketh Road
Cromwell Avenue
Liverpool Road
Warrington Road
Runcorn Road
Chester Road
65
97
82

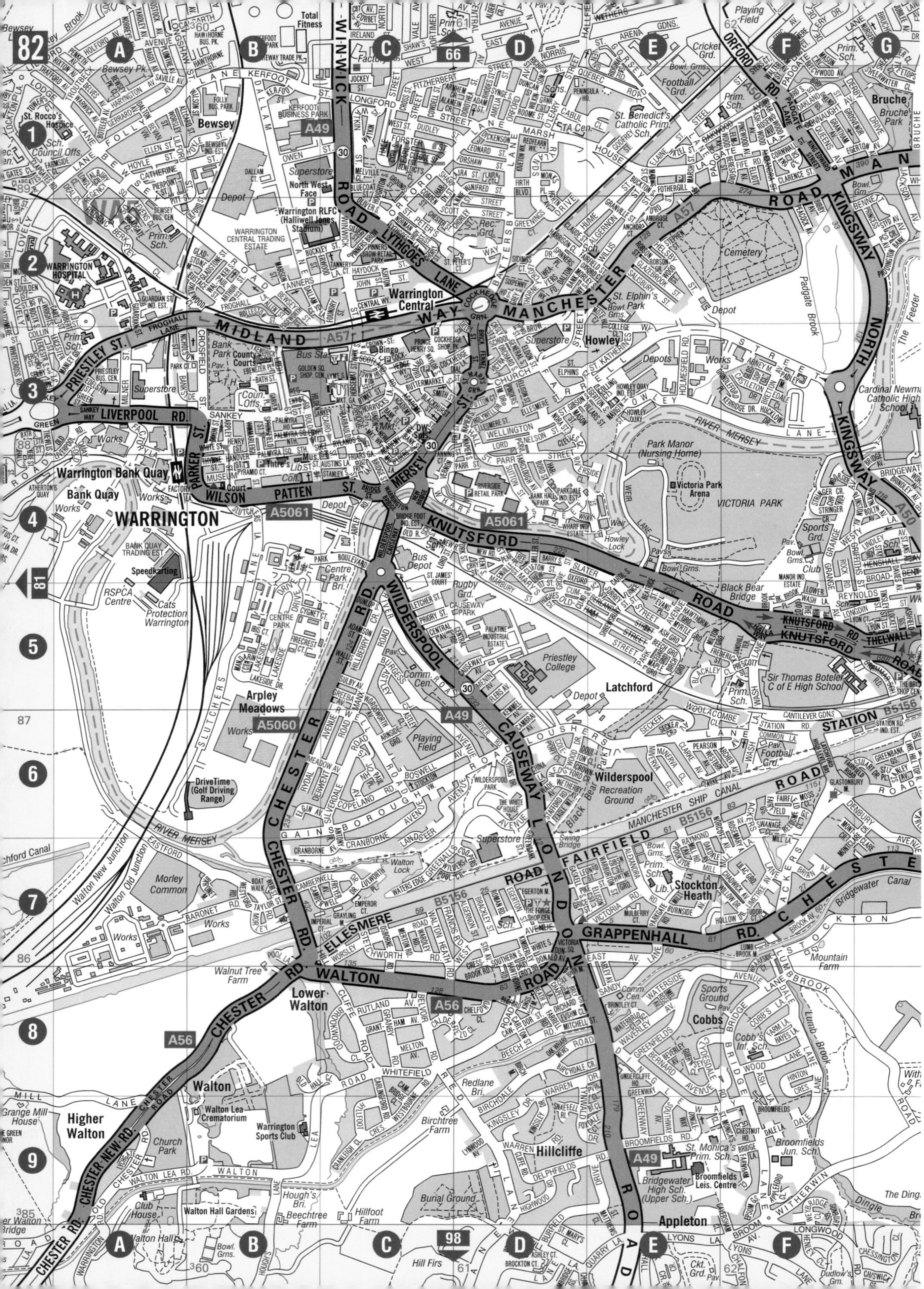
66
81
98
WARRINGTON
Bewsey
Bewsey Pk.
St. Rocco's Hospice
Council Offs.
Warrington Hospital
Warrington Central Trading Estate
Warrington RLFC (Halliwell Jones Stadium)
North West Face
Superstore
Kerfoot Business Park
Dallam
Warrington Central
Warrington Bank Quay
Bank Quay
County Courts
Bus Sta.
Golden Sq. Shop. Cen.
Cockhedge Shop. Pk.
Mkt.
Museum
Riverside Retail Park
Howley
St. Elphin's Park
St. Benedict's Catholic Prim. Sch.
Cemetery
Padgate Brook
Depot
Bruche
Bruche Park
Cardinal Newman Catholic High School
Park Manor (Nursing Home)
Victoria Park Arena
VICTORIA PARK
Black Bear Bridge
Howley Lock
Sir Thomas Boteler C of E High School
Priestley College
Latchford
Palatine Industrial Estate
Causeway Park
Rugby Grd.
Bus Depot
Centre Park
Centre Park Bri.
Bank Quay Trading Est.
Speedkarting
RSPCA Centre
Cats Protection Warrington
Arpley Meadows
DriveTime (Golf Driving Range)
Playing Field
Wilderspool Recreation Ground
Wilderspool
Black Bear Park
Swing Bridge
Superstore
Walton Lock
Morley Common
Walton New Junction
Walton Old Junction
River Mersey
Manchester Ship Canal
Bridgewater Canal
Stockton Heath
Lower Walton
Walnut Tree Farm
Walton
Higher Walton
Grange Mill House
Walton Lea Crematorium
Warrington Sports Club
Church Park
Club House
Walton Hall Gardens
Walton Hall
Hough's Bri.
Beechtree Farm
Hillfoot Farm
Burial Ground
Hill Firs
Redlane Bri.
Birchtree Farm
Hillcliffe
Cobbs
Sports Ground
Cobb's Inf. Sch.
Mountain Farm
Broomfields Jun. Sch.
St. Monica's Prim. Sch.
Bridgewater High Sch. (Upper Sch.)
Broomfields Leis. Centre
Appleton
Dingle
The Feeder
MIDLAND WAY
MANCHESTER ROAD
WINWICK ROAD
LITHGOES LANE
LIVERPOOL RD.
WILSON PATTEN ST.
KNUTSFORD ROAD
WILDERSPOOL CAUSEWAY
CHESTER RD.
LONDON ROAD
FAIRFIELD ROAD
GRAPPENHALL RD.
ELLESMERE ROAD
WALTON ROAD
CHESTER NEW RD.
KINGSWAY NORTH
A49
A50
A56
A57
A5060
A5061
B5156

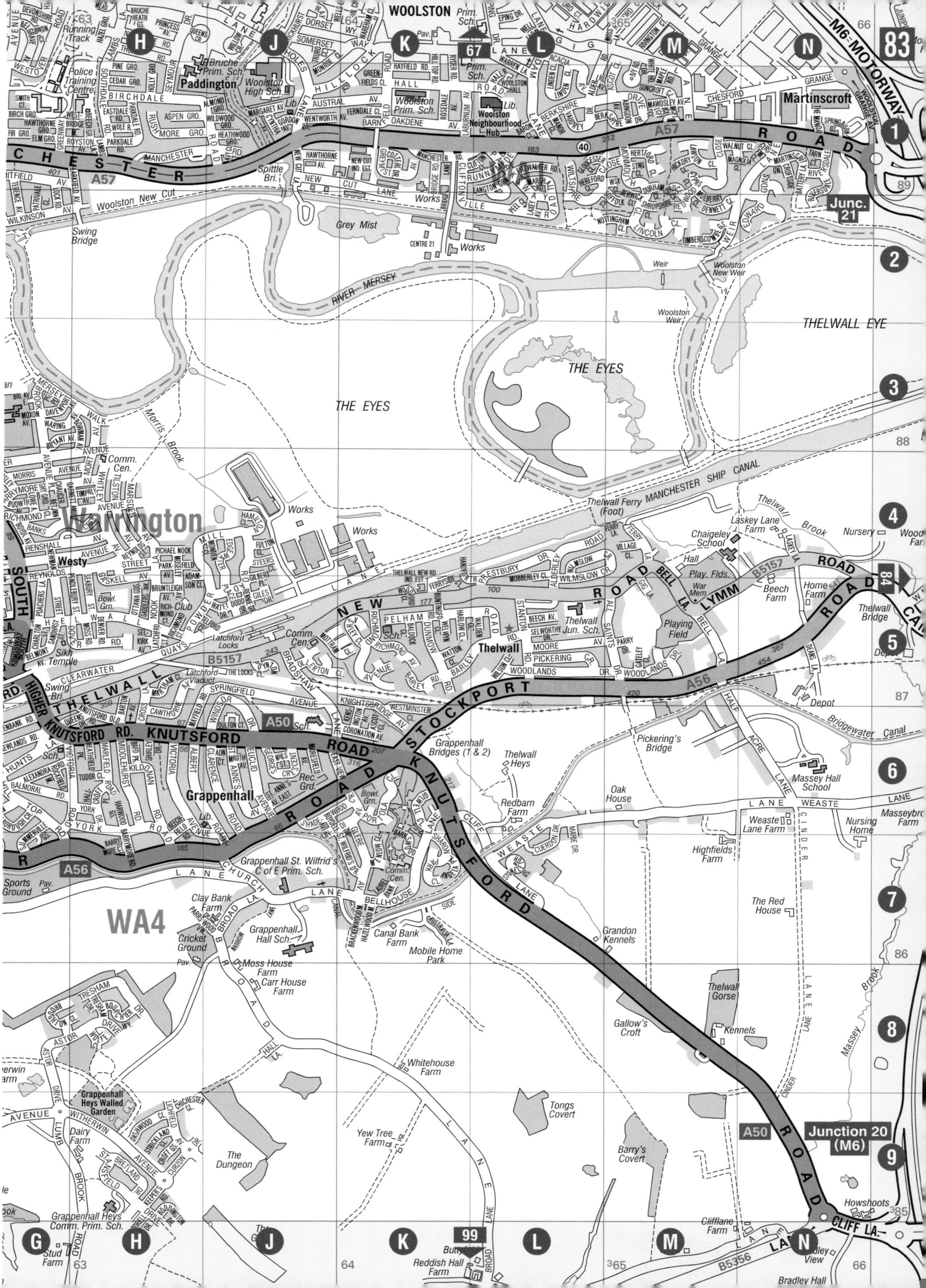
WOOLSTON
M6 MOTORWAY
Paddington
Martinscroft
Woolston High Sch.
Woolston Prim. Sch.
Woolston Neighbourhood Hub
Bruche Prim. Sch.
Police Training Centre
Running Track
CHESTER ROAD
A57
Woolston New Cut
Spittle Bri.
Grey Mist
Works
CENTRE 21
Swing Bridge
RIVER MERSEY
Weir
Woolston New Weir
Woolston Weir
THE EYES
THELWALL EYE
Junc. 21
Morris Brook
MANCHESTER SHIP CANAL
Thelwall Ferry (Foot)
Warrington
Westy
Laskey Lane Farm
Chaigeley School
Thelwall Brook
Nursery
Play. Flds.
War Mem.
Beech Farm
Home Farm
Thelwall Bridge
B5157
NEW ROAD
LYMM ROAD
Thelwall
Thelwall Jun. Sch.
Playing Field
Latchford Locks
Latchford Viaduct
Sikh Temple
THELWALL LANE
HIGHER KNUTSFORD RD.
KNUTSFORD ROAD
STOCKPORT ROAD
A56
A50
Depot
Bridgewater Canal
Pickering's Bridge
Grappenhall Bridges (1 & 2)
Thelwall Heys
Redbarn Farm
Oak House
Massey Hall School
WEASTE LANE
Weaste Lane Farm
Nursing Home
Masseybrook Farm
Highfields Farm
Grappenhall
Grappenhall St. Wilfrid's C of E Prim. Sch.
Sports Ground
WA4
Clay Bank Farm
Cricket Ground
Grappenhall Hall Sch.
Canal Bank Farm
Mobile Home Park
Moss House Farm
Carr House Farm
The Red House
Grandon Kennels
Thelwall Gorse
Gallow's Croft
Kennels
CINDER LANE
Massey Brook
Whitehouse Farm
Grappenhall Heys Walled Garden
Dairy Farm
Tongs Covert
Yew Tree Farm
The Dungeon
Barry's Covert
Junction 20 (M6)
Howshoots
Grappenhall Heys Comm. Prim. Sch.
Stud Farm
Clifflane Farm
CLIFF LA.
B5356
Reddish Hall Farm
Bradley Hall
84
67
99
1 2 3 4 5 6 7 8 9
G H J K L M N
63 64 365 66
85 86 87 88 89

Junction 21
MANCHESTER ROAD
A57
M6
Brookside Farm
Moss Side Farm
Swithen Hill Wood
Green Valley Farm
Woodside Farm
Lynbrook
The Oaks
Rixton Old Hall
Butchersfield Canal
RIVER MERSEY
BUTCHERSFIELD
Butchersfield Bight
Bollin Point
Rixton Junction
WARRINGTON TRAFFORD
WA3
Warrington
MANCHESTER SHIP CANAL
THELWALL EYE
THELWALL VIADUCT
River Bollin
Reddish Hall
Reddish
LYMM GOLF COURSE
Club House
Sow Brook
Playing Field
New Farm
Reddish Crossing
WA4
Statham Pools
Pool Farm
Playing Fld.
Whitbarrow Farm
Pump House
Nursery
Woodacre Farm
Statham Lodge
WHITBARROW ROAD
Statham Prim. Sch.
Statham
Statham Lodge Riding Centre
Thelwall Bridge
CAMSLEY LANE
A56
BOOTH'S HILL ROAD
EAGLE BROW
CHURCH RD.
HIGHER LANE
RUSHGREEN RD.
A6144
Bridgewater
Barsbank Aqueduct
Ridgway Grundy Meml. Park
LYMM
Depot
Ditchfield's Bri.
Camsley House Farm
Bridgewater Canal
Tennis Courts
Ravenbank Prim. Sch.
Play Fld.
Lymm Bri.
Lymm Dam
Works
Cherry Tree Prim. Sch.
Water Tower
Masseybrook Farm
Nursing Home
Booth's Hill Farm
Higher House Farm
Nursery
Ruloe
Res.
Cherrylane Farm
Rugby Ground
Reservoir
Crouchley Hall Farm
Tanners Pool
THE AVENUE
Crosfield Bridge
M6 MOTORWAY
B5158
Bradley Brook
Yewtree Farm
Crouchley Cottage
The Bongs
Cherry Hall Farm
Scholars Bri.
The Gorse
Kaylane
Mag Brook
Silent Valley Cottages
Willow Bed
Cornheys Cottage
Cornheys
Oxheys Farm
Knutsford WA16
Junc. 20
The Howlers
Redoak
Great Oak Farm
Long Shoots
M56
Poplar Park
Howshoots
Redbank Bridge
Big Wood
CLIFF LANE
A50
Broad Heyes Farm
Broad Heyes Cotts.
Poplar 2000
Hey Wood
CHERRY LANE
MAG LANE
CROUCHLEY LANE
LAKESIDE ROAD
BOOTH'S LANE
MASSEY BROOK LANE
WEASTE LANE
STOCKPORT ROAD
WARRINGTON ROAD
A B C D E F G
1 2 3 4 5 6 7 8 9
66 67 68 69
89 88 87 86
83
68

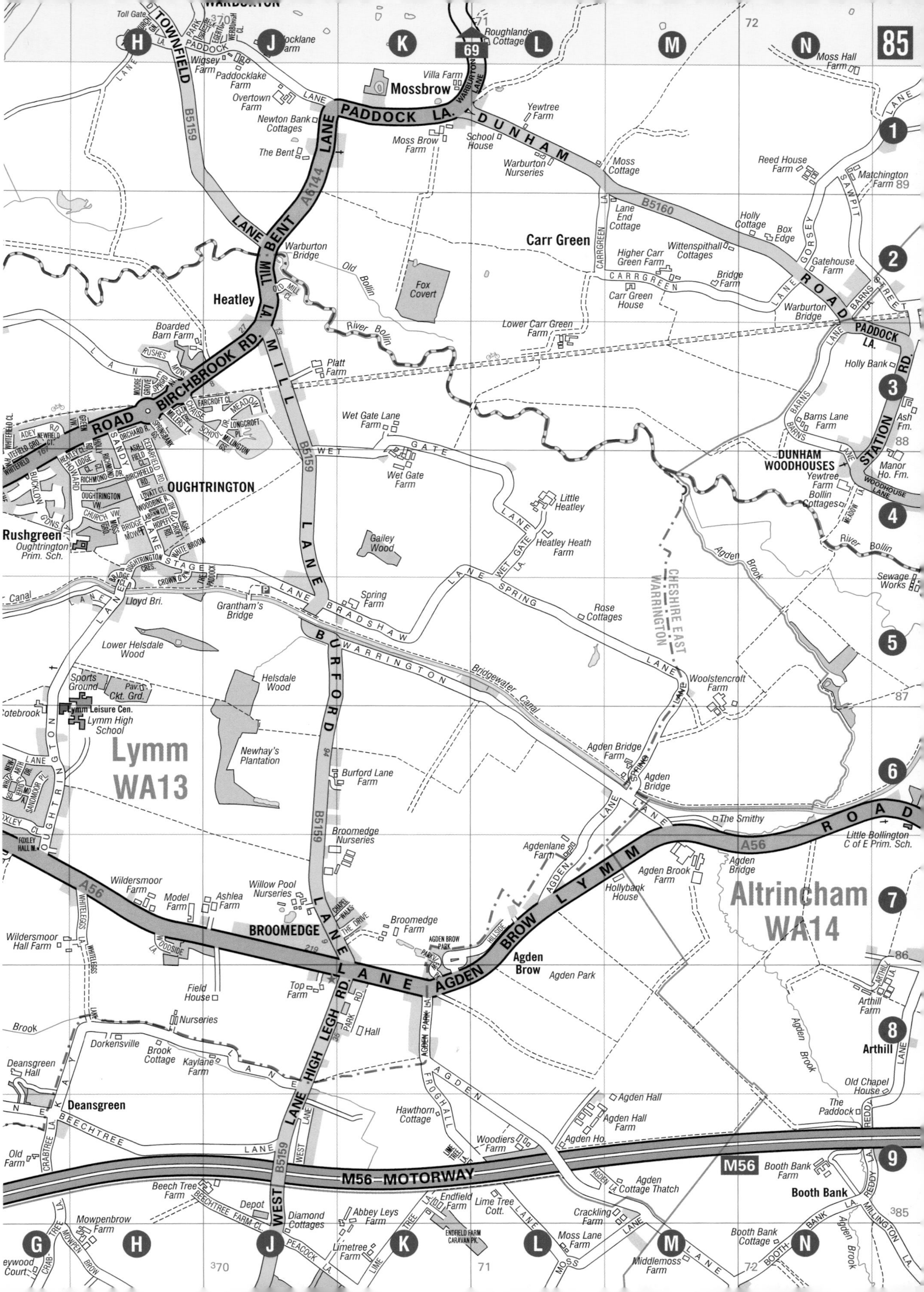

Mossbrow
Carr Green
Heatley
OUGHTRINGTON
Rushgreen
Oughtrington Prim. Sch.
Lymm
WA13
Altrincham
WA14
DUNHAM WOODHOUSES
BROOMEDGE
Agden Brow
Deansgreen
Arthill
Booth Bank
Toll Gate
Wigsey Farm
Paddocklake Farm
Overtown Farm
Newton Bank Cottages
The Bent
Villa Farm
Roughlands Cottage
Moss Brow Farm
School House
Yewtree Farm
Warburton Nurseries
Moss Cottage
Moss Hall Farm
Reed House Farm
Matchington Farm
Lane End Cottage
Holly Cottage
Box Edge
Higher Carr Green Farm
Wittenspithall Cottages
Bridge Farm
Carr Green House
Gatehouse Farm
Warburton Bridge
Warburton Bridge
Fox Covert
Old Bollin
River Bollin
Boarded Barn Farm
Platt Farm
Lower Carr Green Farm
Holly Bank
Ash Fm.
Barns Lane Farm
Manor Ho. Fm.
Yewtree Farm
Bollin Cottages
Wet Gate Lane Farm
Wet Gate Farm
Little Heatley
Gailey Wood
Heatley Heath Farm
Sewage Works
Spring Farm
Grantham's Bridge
Lloyd Bri.
Rose Cottages
CHESHIRE EAST
WARRINGTON
Agden Brook
Lower Helsdale Wood
Helsdale Wood
Sports Ground
Pav.
Ckt. Grd.
Lymm Leisure Cen.
Lymm High School
Bridgewater Canal
Woolstencroft Farm
Newhay's Plantation
Agden Bridge Farm
Agden Bridge
Burford Lane Farm
The Smithy
Broomedge Nurseries
Agdenlane Farm
Little Bollington C of E Prim. Sch.
Agden Bridge
Agden Brook Farm
Hollybank House
Wildersmoor Farm
Model Farm
Ashlea Farm
Willow Pool Nurseries
Broomedge Farm
Wildersmoor Hall Farm
Agden Park
Field House
Top Farm
Hall
Nurseries
Arthill Farm
Dorkensville
Brook Cottage
Kaylane Farm
Deansgreen Hall
Old Chapel House
The Paddock
Agden Hall
Agden Hall Farm
Agden Ho.
Hawthorn Cottage
Woodiers Farm
Old Farm
Booth Bank Farm
Agden Cottage Thatch
Beech Tree Farm
Depot
Diamond Cottages
Abbey Leys Farm
Endfield Farm
Lime Tree Cott.
ENDFIELD FARM CARAVAN PK.
Crackling Farm
Moss Lane Farm
Booth Bank Cottage
Mowpenbrow Farm
Limetree Farm
Middlemoss Farm
Heywood Court
PADDOCK LA.
DUNHAM ROAD
B5160
BENT LANE
A6144
B5159
TOWNFIELD
BIRCHBROOK RD.
MILL LANE
WET GATE LANE
SPRING LANE
BRADSHAW LANE
WARRINGTON LANE
BURFORD LANE
STATION RD.
A56
LYMM ROAD
AGDEN BROW
LANE
HIGH LEGH RD.
WEST LANE
KAY LANE
BEECHTREE LANE
M56 MOTORWAY
M56
69
H J K L M N G
1 2 3 4 5 6 7 8 9
370 71 72 385 89 88 87 86

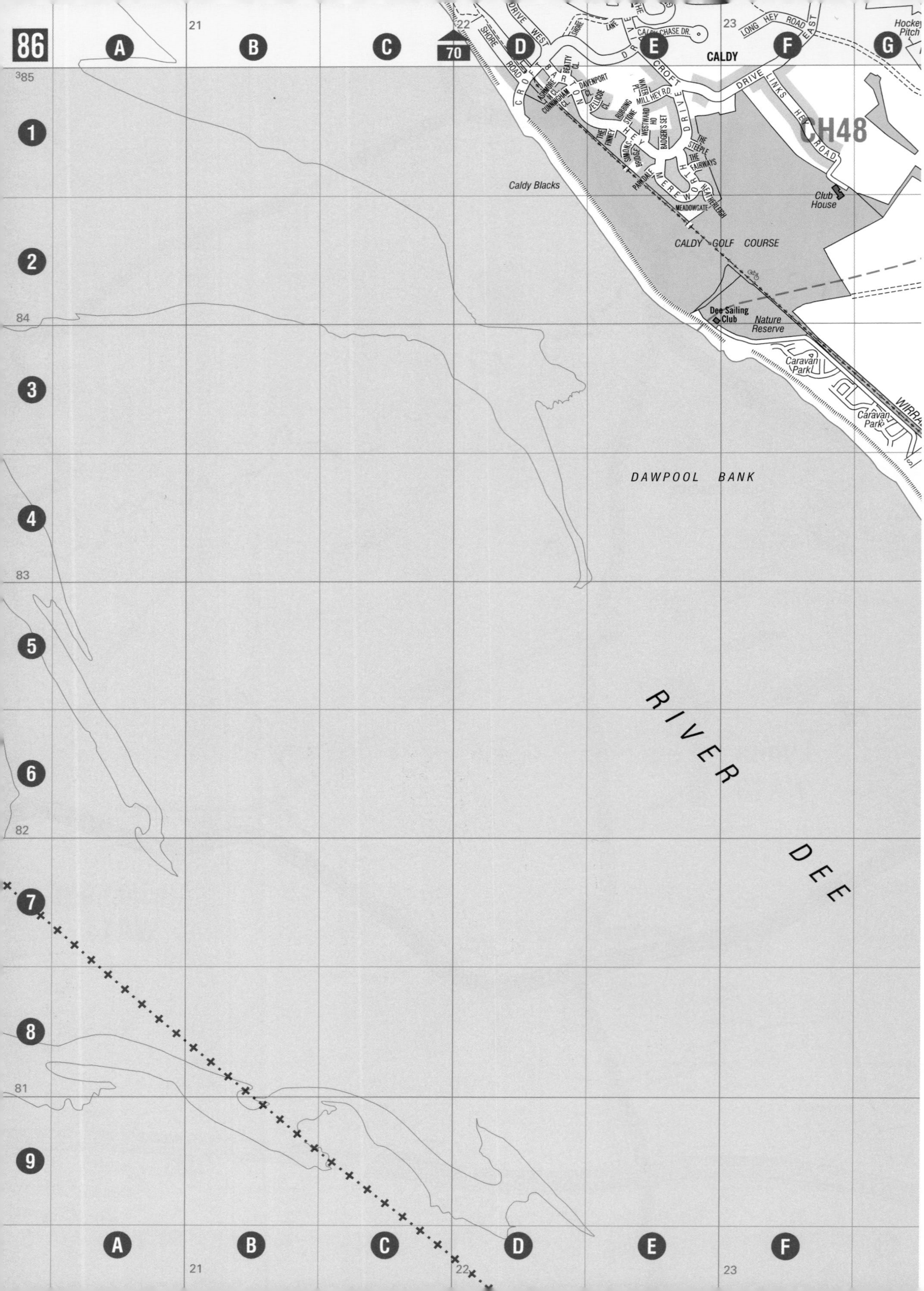
CALDY
CH48
DRIVE WEST
SHORE ROAD
SHORE LANE
CALDY CHASE DR.
LONG HEY ROAD
EAST
Hockey Pitch
CROFT DRIVE
BARTON
BEATTY CL.
ASHMORE CL.
CUNNINGHAM CL.
DAVENPORT CL.
JELLICOE CL.
WATER PL.
MILL HEY RD.
RUBBING STONE
WESTWARD HO
BADGER'S SET
THE FINNEY
SIMONS-BRIDGE
HEY
THE STEEPLE
THE FAIRWAYS
PARKDALE
MEREWORTH
HEATHERLEIGH
MEADOWGATE
LINKS HEY ROAD
Caldy Blacks
Club House
CALDY GOLF COURSE
Dee Sailing Club
Nature Reserve
Caravan Park
Caravan Park
WIRRA
DAWPOOL BANK
RIVER DEE
70
21
22
23
385
84
83
82
81
A
B
C
D
E
F
G
1
2
3
4
5
6
7
8
9

Playing Field
Thurstaston Hill
Thur's Stone
Benty Farm
Strowan
Thurstaston Common Recreation Ground
Hillside Farm
Dawpool C of E Prim. School
TELEGRAPH
THURSTASTON
Dawpool
Hill Farm
Rectory
Thurstaston Hall
Church Farm Organics
Camping Site
Hall Farm
Copperfields
Lee Farm
Wirral Country Park Visitor Centre
COUNTRY PARK
Dungeon Bridge
The Dungeon
Heswall Fields
White House
Sewage Works
Caravan Park
Slipway
Gayton Hole
GAYTON SANDS
Irby Heath
Irby Prim. Sch.
Play. Field
Playing Fields
Hall
Harrock Wood
Lib.
Irby Farm
IRBY
Irby Hall
CH61
A540
Pensby High School for Boys Specialist Sports College
Pensby High School for Girls
Cemetery
Wirral
Oldfield Farm
Cleaver Heath Nature Reserve
Dale Farm
Playing Field
Holiday Camp
Heswall Dales Local Nature Reserve
The Dales
The Cave
HESWALL
CH60
Dee Farm
Prim. Sch.
Park
Superstore
Bus Sta.
Adult Train. Cen.
Puddy Dale
Reservoir (covered)
Poll Hill
Sports Ground
Comm. Cen.
Pensby Wood
Day Cen.
Catholic Prim. Sch.
Pensby Primary Sch.
Pensby Hall
PENSBY
Club House

72
100
87
A
B
C
D
E
F
G
1
2
3
4
5
6
7
8
9
27
28
29
330
85
84
83
82
81
THINGWALL
PENSBY
BARNSTON
HESWALL
Gayton
Storeton Brickfields
CH61
CH60
CH64
Wirral
Neston
M53
M53 MOTORWAY
A551
A540
A5137
B5138
B5136
Tophouse Farm
The Farm
Caravan Park
Stanley Wood
Murrayfield Spire Hospital
Lower Heath Wood
Sewage Works
Football Ground
Cross Hill
Riding Centre
Gills Lane Farm
Youth Centre
New Hey Covert
New Hey Triangle
Ley Farm
Beech Farm
Bank Farm
Manor Farm
Carnsdale Farm
Greenheys Cottages
Pensby House Farm
Heswall Primary School
Whitfield Common
Tennis Courts
White House
Whitehouse Farm
Fairfield
Fairfield Lodge
The Brooklet
Melite Cottage
Westwood Hall
Cloverley
Dunster House
Lake Lodge
Heswall
Lane End Farm
Willow Bank House
Thornton Manor
Manor Wood
Hesketh Grange
Lodge Farm
New Hall Farm
New Hall Manor
Crows Nest
Bridges House Farm
Football Ground
Barnston Prim. Sch.
Play Field
The Beacons
Gayton Prim. Sch.
Gayton Hall
Thornton Hall
Widgeons Covert
Thingwall Prim. Sch.
Stanley Sch.
Thingwall Rec. Cen.
Res. (cov.)
Crosshill Reservoir (cov.)
Bowl Grn.
Ten. Cts.
Lib.
Bus Sta.
Putt. Grn.
Club
Prenton Brook
Landican Lane
Storeton Lane
Station Road
Gills Lane
Thingwall Road
Barnston Road
Whitehouse Lane
Brimstage Road
Telegraph Road
Chester Road
Whitfield Lane
Pensby Road
Mill Lane
Downham Road North
Gayton Road
Well Lane
Dawstone Road
Kingsway
Oaksway
Talbot Avenue
Manor Road
Station Road
Ridgewood Dr.
Rosemead Avenue
Ashlea Road
Greenbank Drive
Belmont Drive
Fender Wy.
Seven Acres Lane
Sparks Lane
The Leas
Regents Avenue
Barnsdale Avenue
Holmwood Drive
Woodlands Dr.
Beverley Dr.
Gayton Lane
Baskervyle Road
Hillside Road
Sandham Road
Broadmead
Eton Dr.
Oxford Drive
Neston Road

BEBINGTON
Bebington
Lower Bebington
Port Sunlight
Trafalgar
STORETON
BRIMSTAGE
THORNTON HOUGH
Raby Mere
Poulton
CH63
M53
M53-MOTORWAY
Junction 4
A5137
B5137
B5151
B5136
B5150
BRACKENWOOD GOLF COURSE
CLATTERBRIDGE HOSPITAL
CLATTERBRIDGE CENTRE FOR ONCOLOGY
St. John's Hospice
Claire Ho. Children's Hospice
Clatter Bridge
Wirral Grammar Sch. for Girls
Wirral Grammar Sch. for Boys
Bebington High Sports College
The Oval Sports Centre
Higher Bebington Recreation Ground
Bebington Cemetery
Town Lane Infant School
Storeton Hill
Brackenwood Park
Umberstone Covert
Lower Umberstone Covert
Brimstage Plantation
Rake Hey Covert
Ethel's Covert
Storeton Hall Farm
Storeton House Farm
Storeton Lodge
Brimstage Hall
Claremont House
Poulton Royd
Wirral Manor House
Rocklands Farm
New Rocklands
Thornton Grange
Rocklands Lodge
Rugby Football Grd.
Thornton Common
Rugby Football Ground
THORNTON COMMON ROAD
WILLASTON ROAD
CLATTERBRIDGE ROAD
MOUNT ROAD
BRIMSTAGE ROAD
SPITAL ROAD
CHURCH ROAD
HIGHER BEBINGTON ROAD
HEATH ROAD
STORETON LANE
RABY MERE ROAD
POULTON HALL ROAD
Raby Hall
Three Stacks
Four Lanes End Farm
Thornton Farm Cottages
Sewage Works
Graveyard
Club House
Lancelyn Farm
The Vineyard Farm
Poulton Hall
Council Offices
Research Centre
73
101
90
G H J K L M N
1 2 3 4 5 6 7 8 9
31 32 33
81 82 83 84 85

A
B
C
D
E
F
G
1
2
3
4
5
6
7
8
9
335
36
74
89
102
NEW FERRY
Sewage Works
Playing Field
Refuse Tip
Lady Lever Art Gall.
Port Sunlight Mus.
War Meml.
Mayer Park
Lower Bebington
Ormerod Gdns.
Port Sunlight
Gladstone Theatre
PORT SUNLIGHT
Works
Research Centre
Depot
Port Sunlight Golf Centre (Driving Range)
Bromborough Pool
Bromborough Pool Bridge
Cricket Ground
Sports Club
Sports Ground
Factory
HGV Test Centre
Warehouses
Factories
Bromborough Port
CH62
NEW CHESTER ROAD
NEW FERRY BY-PASS
A41
Spital
SPITAL ROAD
B5137
WIRRAL LEISURE PARK
CROFT RETAIL & LEISURE PARK
Odeon Cinema
Gala Bingo
Super-store
DW Fitness Club
RIVERVIEW BUSINESS PARK
Slack Wood
The Bowl
PLANTATION BUSINESS PARK
PLANTATION COURT
WIRRAL INTERNATIONAL BUSINESS PARK
Cowpasture Wood
Brotherton Park & Dibbinsdale Local Nature Reserve
Brotherton Park
Woods Lee Cottages
Woodslee Prim. Sch.
Poulton
Wirral
Job's Ferry
Oak Wood
Offices
Oil Storage Depots
Long Plantation
Poulton Lancelyn
Bromborough Rake
BROMBOROUGH
Rec. Ground
Civic Hall
Lib.
CH63
Rose Cott.
Poulton Hall
Poulton Bridge
Mendell Prim. Sch.
Professional Excellence Cen.
Playing Field
Tennis Courts
EASTHAM COUNTRY PARK
Eastham Ferry
The Warrens Farm
Eastham Woods
Leverhulme Sports Ground
Pavilion
Mayfields Remembrance Park
Wirral Metropolitan College
Bromborough
Raeburn Prim. Sch.
Plymyard Cemetery
EASTHAM LODGE GOLF COURSE
Tank Farm
Club House
Brookhurst Prim. Sch.
Nursery
EASTHAM
Clatter Brook
Club House
BROMBOROUGH GOLF COURSE
Brookhurst
Play. Field
Heygarth Prim. School
Torr Recreation Ground
Custom House
Queen
RABY HALL ROAD

37
38
39
340
H
J
K
L
M
N
G
1
2
3
4
5
6
7
8
9
83
82
81
85
84
75
92
103
RIVER
MERSEY
LIVERPOOL
WIRRAL
Alfred Holt Athletics Grd.
Pav.
Play Area
Nursing Home
Cressington
Cressington Park
Wood End Park
Liverpool
L19
A561
Garston Sands
Warehouses
Warehouse
Dock
Works
Jetty
Swing Bridge
Govt. Bldg.
WEAVER INDUSTRIAL ESTATE
ST. MARY'S RD.
GARSTON WY.
GRASSENDALE ESPLANADE
CRESSINGTON ESPLANADE
KNOWSLEY RD.
SALISBURY RD.
GROSVENOR RD.
WESTERN DR.
Eastham Locks
Elizabeth II Dock
MANCHESTER SHIP CANAL
Playing Field
Oil Storage Depot
ROAD

Long Lane Rec. Grd.
Lifestyles Garston
Bowl. Grns.
ISLAND
CLARENDON RD.
HARTINGTON
Ten. Cts.
Playgrd.
WOOLTON
HORROCKS AV.
B5171
Liverpool South Parkway
Bus Sta.
Sch.
HOLMAN RD.
HIGHBANK DR.
Enterprise South Liverpool Academy (Horrocks Avenue Campus)
Superstore
GARSTON
Play. Fields
NHS Treatment Cen.
GARSTON WAY
SPEKE ROAD
L19
A561
Depot
Gas Works
Holy Trinity Catholic Prim. Sch.
NHS Walk-in Cen.
Comm. Cen.
Sch.
Dock
Swing Bridge
Wks.
GARSTON INDUSTRIAL ESTATE
WEAVER INDUSTRIAL ESTATE
BLACKBURNE STREET
BRUNSWICK
Jetty
BANK'S ROAD
THE MATCHWORKS
MERSEY COTTS.
DAKOTA BUS. PK.
David Lloyd Racquet & Fitness Club
Hotel
Warehouse
Warehouse
DE HAVILLAND DRIVE
DAKOTA
LIVERPOOL INTERNATIONAL BUSINESS PARK
HURRICANE DR.
ESTUARY BOULEVARD
ESTUARY COMMERCE PARK
ESTUARY BANKS BUSINESS PARK
WINDWARD DR.
LEEWARD DRIVE
HERCULES DR.
NEW MERSEY SHOPPING PARK
NEW MERSEY RETAIL PARK
Bowl. Grn.
76
ALLERTON CEMETERY
Rec. Grd.
Pav.
Depot
Hunt's Cross West Junc.
Albert Junction
HUNTS CROSS SHOP. CENTRE
VITESSE ROAD
THE TRIUMPH TRADING PARK
TRIUMPH WAY
HERALD AVENUE
DOLOMITE AV.
SPITFIRE ROAD
STAG RD.
MAYFLOWER AV.
NORTH AV.
Works
Works
GOODLASS ROAD
PHOENIX PARK
A5275
Speke Junction
HILLFOOT ROAD
KINGSMEAD
STATION CL.
BARFORD ROAD
L25
Training Cen.
Factory
ADDENBROOKE DR.
EDWARD'S LANE
EDWARD'S LA. IND. EST.
ALDERMAN ROAD
SPEKE HALL ROAD
BRIDGE IND. EST.
OPCO COMPLEX
VENTURE POINT WEST
EVANS ROAD
OLD DISTILLERY RD.
SOUTHERN GATEWAY
All Weather Pitch
Bowl. Grn.
Works
Sports Grd.
Club
Factory
WINGS ENTERTAINMENT PARK
LONGMAN DR.
Works
SPEKE HALL AVENUE
CARTWRIGHTS FARM RD.
RAMSBURY
BANKS
SPINDUS
SPEKE HALL IND. EST.
SKY PARK INDUSTRIAL ESTATE
STIRLING RD.
OWEN DR.
DUNLOP RD.
SPEKE TOWN LA.
CHURCH RD.
SCHOOL HALL ROAD
GREYHOUND FARM RD.
ALL SAINTS
Bowl. Grns.
Club
Pav.
BAILEY'S LA.
SPEKE HALL WALK
Speke Dams
Stockton's Wood
BANK'S LANE
Speke Hall Garden & Estate
The Clough
Speke Home Farm
Liverpool Sailing Club
Yellow Submarine
Cargo & Service Cen.
Airport Terminal
RIVER MERSEY
91
104
A B C D E F G
1 2 3 4 5 6 7 8 9
340 41 42 43
85 84 83 82 81

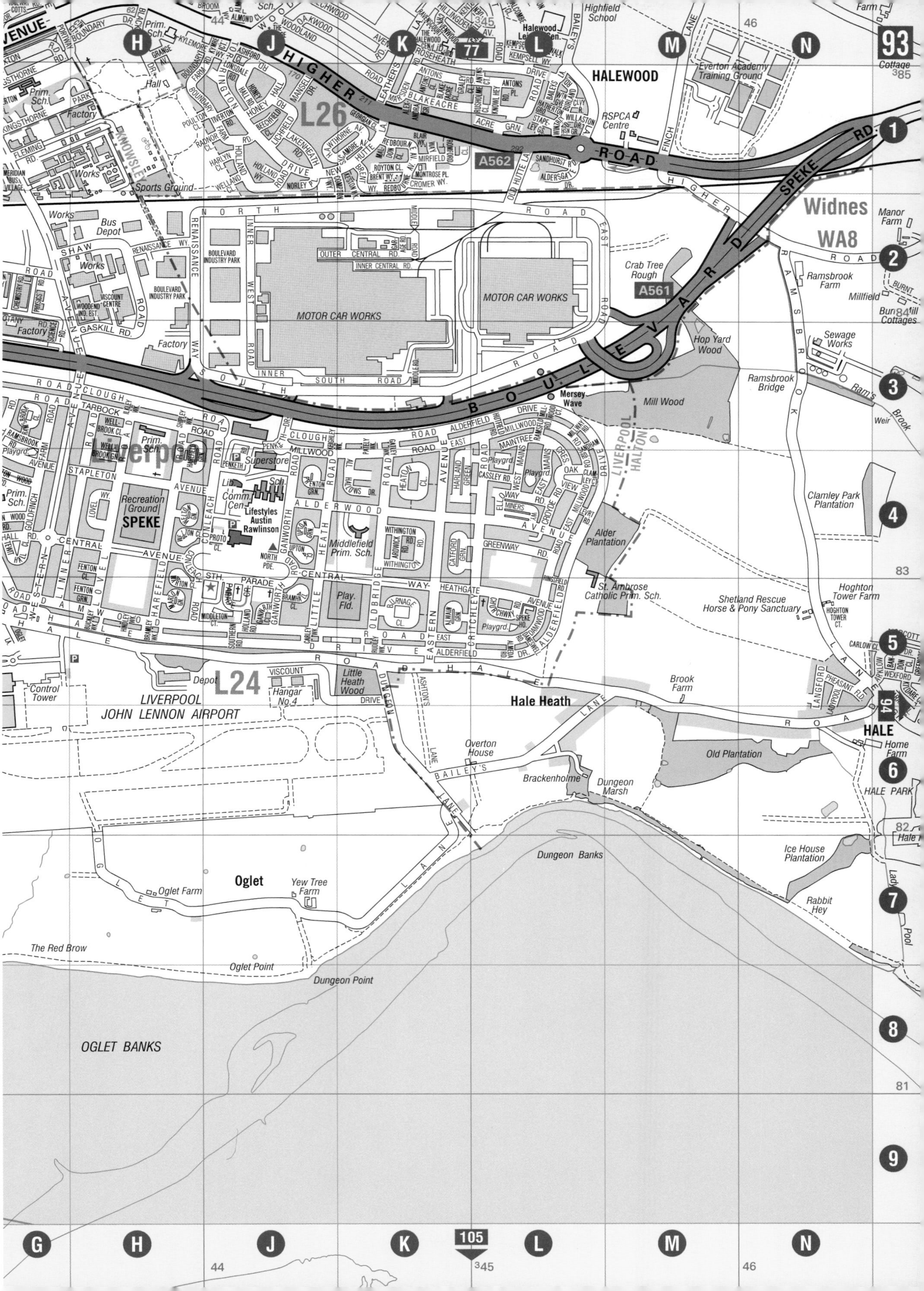
HALEWOOD
Highfield School
Halewood Leisure Cen.
Everton Academy Training Ground
HIGHER ROAD
L26
A562
RSPCA Centre
SPEKE RD.
Widnes
WA8
Manor Farm
Ramsbrook Farm
Millfield
Burnt Mill Cottages
NORTH ROAD
MOTOR CAR WORKS
BOULEVARD INDUSTRY PARK
OUTER CENTRAL RD.
INNER CENTRAL RD.
Crab Tree Rough
A561
Hop Yard Wood
Sewage Works
Ramsbrook Bridge
Mill Wood
Mersey Wave
BOULEVARD
LIVERPOOL
HALTON
Bus Depot
Works
Factory
Sports Ground
KNOWSLEY
Liverpool
SPEKE
Recreation Ground
Superstore
Lifestyles Austin Rawlinson
Middlefield Prim. Sch.
Clamley Park Plantation
Alder Plantation
St. Ambrose Catholic Prim. Sch.
Shetland Rescue Horse & Pony Sanctuary
Hoghton Tower Farm
Play. Fld.
L24
Depot
Hangar No.4
Little Heath Wood
Control Tower
LIVERPOOL JOHN LENNON AIRPORT
Hale Heath
Brook Farm
HALE
Home Farm
HALE PARK
Old Plantation
Overton House
Brackenholme
Dungeon Marsh
Dungeon Banks
Ice House Plantation
Rabbit Hey
Oglet
Oglet Farm
Yew Tree Farm
The Red Brow
Oglet Point
Dungeon Point
OGLET BANKS
G H J K L M N
1 2 3 4 5 6 7 8 9
77
94
105
44
345
46
81
82
83
84
85

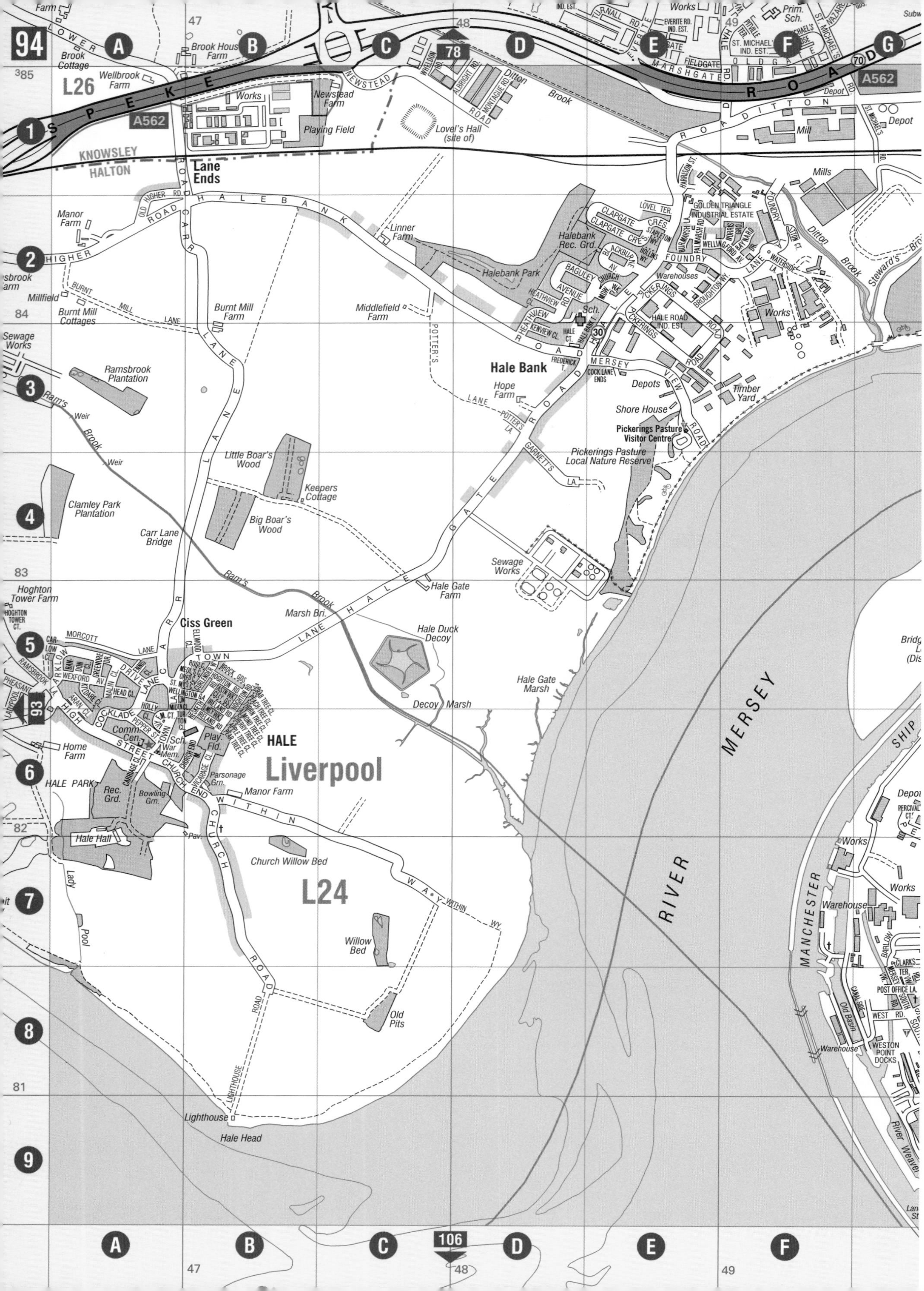
A
B
C
D
E
F
G
1
2
3
4
5
6
7
8
9
47
48
49
385
84
83
82
81
78
106
93
L26
L24
HALE
Liverpool
Hale Bank
Lane Ends
Ciss Green
KNOWSLEY
HALTON
RIVER MERSEY
SPEKE ROAD
A562
DITTON ROAD
MARSHGATE
FIELDGATE
OLD GATE
NEWSTEAD
WHELDON RD.
ALBRIGHT RD.
MONTAGUE RD.
EVERITE RD. IND. EST.
ST. MICHAEL'S IND. EST.
Prim. Sch.
Works
Depot
Mill
Mills
Brook Cottage
Brook House Farm
Wellbrook Farm
Newstead Farm
Playing Field
Lovel's Hall (site of)
Ditton Brook
Manor Farm
HIGHER ROAD
OLD HIGHER RD.
HALEBANK ROAD
CARR LANE
BURNT MILL LANE
Burnt Mill Cottages
Burnt Mill Farm
Millfield
Sewage Works
Ramsbrook Plantation
Rams Brook
Weir
Linner Farm
Halebank Park
Halebank Rec. Grd.
Middlefield Farm
POTTER'S LANE
Hope Farm
HALE GATE ROAD
GARNETT'S LA.
CLAPGATE CRES.
BAGULEY AVENUE
BLACKBURNE AV.
HEATHVIEW RD.
KENVIEW CL.
CHURCH
Sch.
30
FOUNDRY LANE
GOLDEN TRIANGLE INDUSTRIAL ESTATE
Warehouses
PICKERINGS ROAD
HALE ROAD IND. EST.
MERSEY VIEW ROAD
COCK LANE ENDS
FREDERICK T.
Depots
Timber Yard
Shore House
Pickerings Pasture Visitor Centre
Pickerings Pasture Local Nature Reserve
Waterside La.
Steward's Brook
Little Boar's Wood
Keepers Cottage
Big Boar's Wood
Clamley Park Plantation
Carr Lane Bridge
Hoghton Tower Farm
Hale Gate Farm
Marsh Bri.
HALE GATE LANE
Hale Duck Decoy
Decoy Marsh
Hale Gate Marsh
MORCOTT LANE
TOWN LANE
HIGH STREET
CHURCH END
HALE PARK
Home Farm
Rec. Grd.
Bowling Grn.
Hale Hall
Pav.
Parsonage Grn.
Manor Farm
Comm. Cen.
War Mem.
Play. Fld.
WITHIN WAY
CHURCH ROAD
Church Willow Bed
Willow Bed
Old Pits
Lady Pool
LIGHTHOUSE ROAD
Lighthouse
Hale Head
MANCHESTER SHIP CANAL
Warehouse
WESTON POINT DOCKS
Old Basin
WEST RD.
POST OFFICE LA.
River Weaver

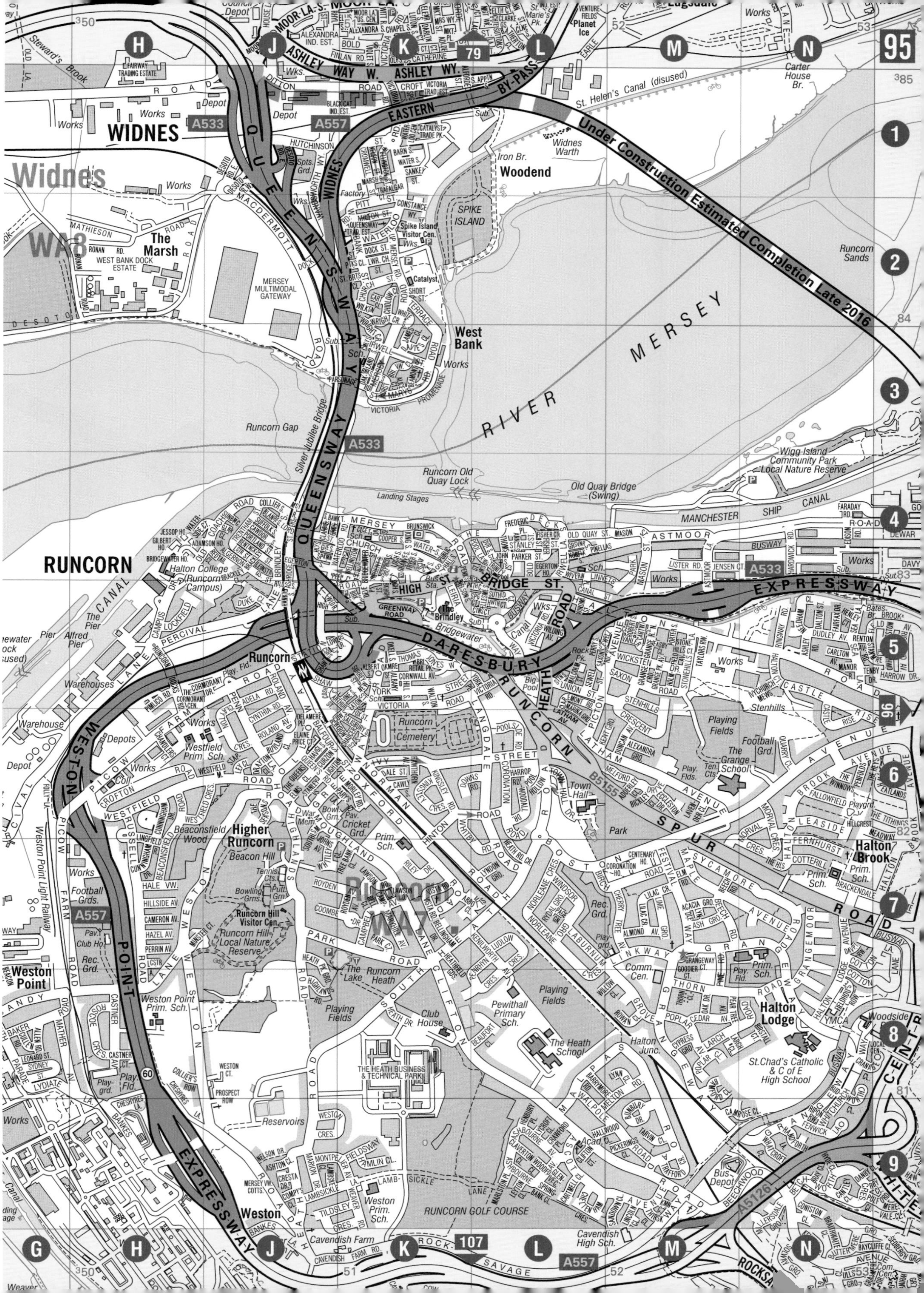
WIDNES
Widnes
WA8
The Marsh
WEST BANK DOCK ESTATE
MERSEY MULTIMODAL GATEWAY
FAIRWAY TRADING ESTATE
ASHLEY WAY W.
ASHLEY WY.
EASTERN BY-PASS
St. Helen's Canal (disused)
Under Construction Estimated Completion Late 2016
Widnes Warth
Woodend
SPIKE ISLAND
Spike Island Visitor Cen.
Catalyst
West Bank
Runcorn Sands
RIVER MERSEY
Runcorn Gap
Silver Jubilee Bridge
QUEENSWAY
A533
A557
Runcorn Old Quay Lock
Landing Stages
Old Quay Bridge (Swing)
Wigg Island Community Park Local Nature Reserve
MANCHESTER SHIP CANAL
RUNCORN
Halton College (Runcorn Campus)
The Pier
Alfred Pier
HIGH ST.
BRIDGE ST.
The Brindley
Bridgewater Canal
DARESBURY EXPRESSWAY
EXPRESSWAY
ASTMOOR
Runcorn
Warehouses
Warehouse
Depots
Westfield Prim. Sch.
Runcorn Cemetery
Stenhills
Playing Fields
The Grange School
Town Hall
Park
RUNCORN SPUR
Halton Brook
Beaconsfield Wood
Higher Runcorn
Beacon Hill
Cricket Grd.
Runcorn Hill Visitor Cen.
Runcorn Hill Local Nature Reserve
Runcorn WA7
WESTON POINT EXPRESSWAY
Weston Point Light Railway
Weston Point
Weston Point Prim. Sch.
The Lake
Runcorn Heath
Club House
Pewithall Primary Sch.
The Heath School
THE HEATH BUSINESS & TECHNICAL PARK
Reservoirs
Weston
Weston Prim. Sch.
RUNCORN GOLF COURSE
Cavendish Farm
Cavendish High Sch.
Halton Junc.
Halton Lodge
St.Chad's Catholic & C of E High School
Comm. Cen.
Bus Depot
A5126
ROCK SAVAGE
79
107
96
H J K L M N
G H J K L M N
1 2 3 4 5 6 7 8 9

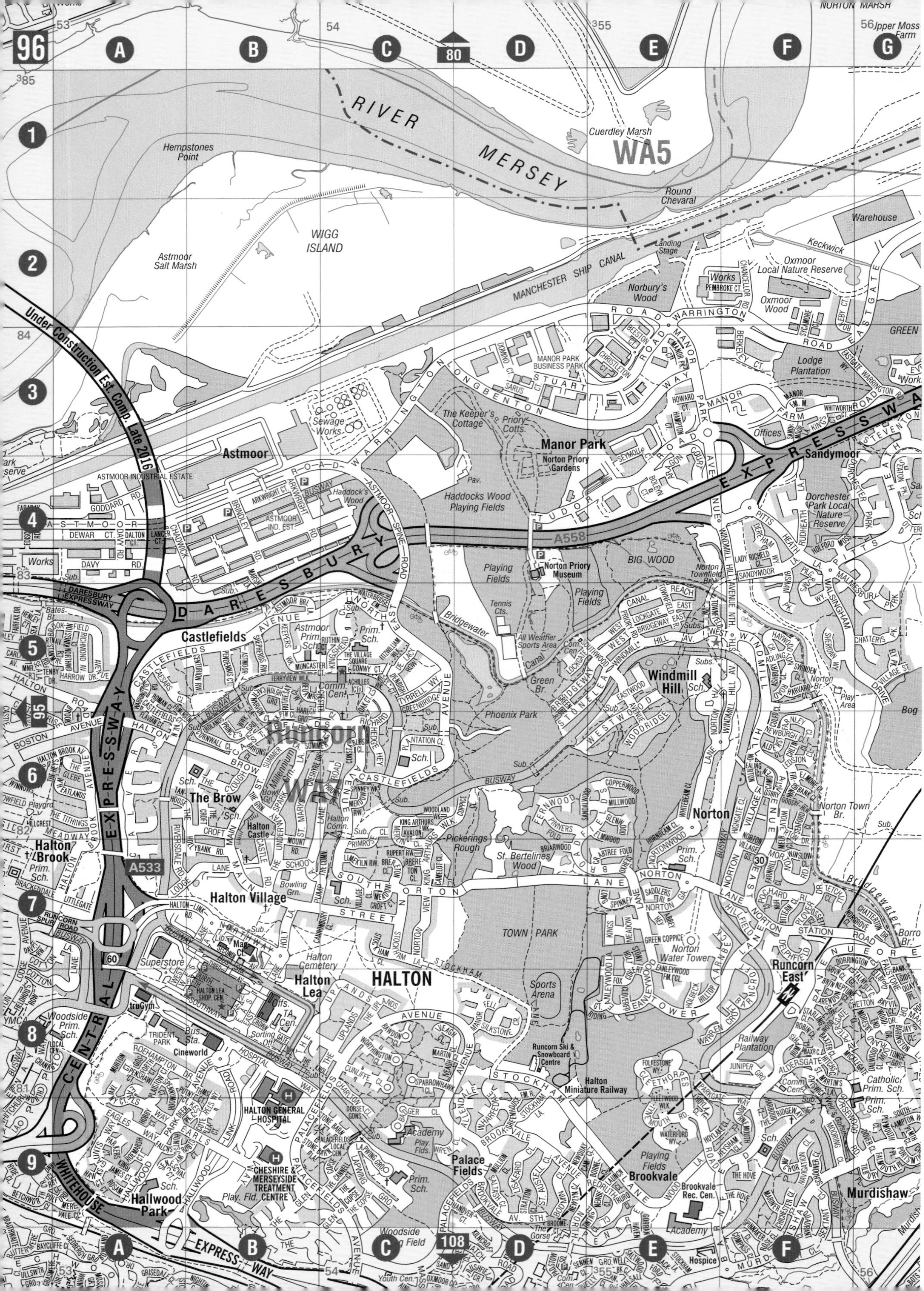

RIVER MERSEY
Cuerdley Marsh
WA5
Hempstones Point
Astmoor Salt Marsh
WIGG ISLAND
Round Chevaral
Warehouse
Keckwick
Oxmoor Local Nature Reserve
Oxmoor Wood
MANCHESTER SHIP CANAL
Landing Stage
Norbury's Wood
Works
PEMBROKE CT.
WARRINGTON ROAD
MANOR PARK BUSINESS PARK
Lodge Plantation
GREEN
Under Construction Est. Comp. Late 2016
Sewage Works
Astmoor
ASTMOOR INDUSTRIAL ESTATE
ASTMOOR IND. EST.
Haddock's Wood
The Keeper's Cottage
Priory Cotts.
Manor Park
Norton Priory Gardens
Haddocks Wood Playing Fields
Offices
Sandymoor
EXPRESSWAY
Dorchester Park Local Nature Reserve
DARESBURY EXPRESSWAY
A558
Playing Fields
Norton Priory Museum
BIG WOOD
Norton Townfield Br.
Castlefields
Bridgewater Canal
Tennis Cts.
All Weather Sports Area
Windmill Hill
Astmoor Prim. Sch.
Prim. Sch.
Comm. Cen.
Green Br.
Phoenix Park
Runcorn
WA7
Norton Br.
Bog
The Brow
Halton Castle
Pickerings Rough
St. Bertelines Wood
Norton
Norton Town Br.
Halton Brook
A533
Halton Village
SOUTH NORTON LANE
NORTON LANE
TOWN PARK
Bridgewater
Halton Cemetery
Halton Lea
HALTON
Superstore
HALTON LEA SHOP. CEN.
Sports Arena
Norton Water Tower
Runcorn East
Woodside Prim. Sch.
truGym
TRIDENT PARK
Bus Sta.
Cineworld
Railway Plantation
Runcorn Ski & Snowboard Centre
Halton Miniature Railway
CENTRAL EXPRESSWAY
HALTON GENERAL HOSPITAL
Academy
Catholic Prim. Sch.
CHESHIRE & MERSEYSIDE TREATMENT CENTRE
Palace Fields
Playing Fields
Brookvale
Brookvale Rec. Cen.
Murdishaw
Hallwood Park
Play. Fld.
Woodside Playing Field
Academy
Hospice
WHITEHOUSE EXPRESSWAY
80
108
95

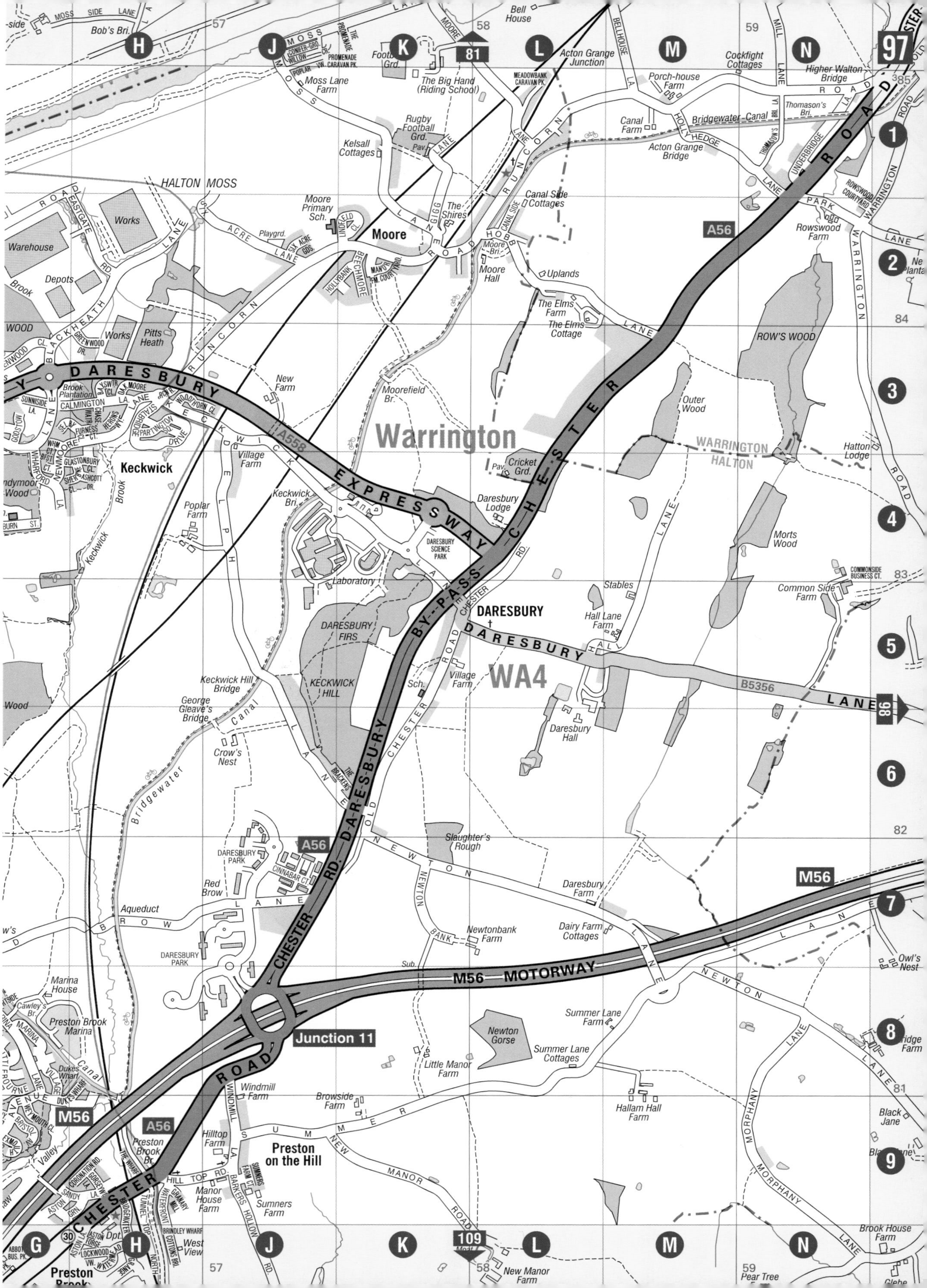
Moss Side Lane
Bob's Bri.
Bell House
Moss Lane Farm
The Big Hand (Riding School)
Acton Grange Junction
Meadowbank Caravan Pk.
Porch-house Farm
Cockfight Cottages
Higher Walton Bridge
Thomason's Bri.
Canal Farm
Bridgewater Canal
Acton Grange Bridge
Rugby Football Grd.
Kelsall Cottages
Halton Moss
Works
Warehouse
Depots
Moore Primary Sch.
Moore
Playgrd.
Canal Side Cottages
The Shires
Moore Bri.
Moore Hall
Uplands
Rowswood Farm
Warrington Road
The Elms Farm
The Elms Cottage
Pitts Heath
Row's Wood
Daresbury Expressway
A558
A56
New Farm
Moorefield Br.
Outer Wood
Warrington
Warrington
Halton
Hatton Lodge
Keckwick
Village Farm
Cricket Grd.
Poplar Farm
Keckwick Bri.
Daresbury Lodge
Daresbury Science Park
Morts Wood
Laboratory
Stables
Commonside Business Ct.
Common Side Farm
Daresbury
Hall Lane Farm
Daresbury Firs
Daresbury Lane
B5356
Keckwick Hill Bridge
Keckwick Hill
Village Farm
WA4
George Gleave's Bridge
Daresbury Hall
Crow's Nest
Chester Road
Daresbury By-Pass
Slaughter's Rough
Daresbury Park
Newton Lane
Red Brow
Daresbury Farm
M56
Aqueduct
Brow Lane
Newtonbank Farm
Dairy Farm Cottages
Owl's Nest
M56 Motorway
Marina House
Preston Brook Marina
Summer Lane Farm
Newton Gorse
Junction 11
Summer Lane Cottages
Little Manor Farm
Windmill Farm
Browside Farm
Hallam Hall Farm
Hilltop Farm
Preston on the Hill
Preston Brook Br.
Manor House Farm
Sumners Farm
Manor Road
Morphany Lane
Black Jane
Brook House Farm
West View
New Manor Farm
Preston Brook
Pear Tree
81
109
98

Warrington
WA4
Appleton
Dudlow's Green
Pewterspear
Stretton
Hatton
Lower Stretton
Norcott Brook
Appleton Park
Walton Hall Gardens
Walton Hall
Club House
Hough's Bri.
Beechtree Farm
Hillfoot Farm
Burial Ground
Bridgewater High Sch. (Sen. Sch.)
Broomfields Leis. Cen.
Bridgewater High Sch.
Play. Fld.
WALTON HALL GOLF COURSE
Hill Firs
Woodlands
The Cottage
The Kennels
New Plantation
Park House
Wood Cottage
Appleton Reservoir
Daintith's Farm
Bellfield Farm
Dennow Cottage
Dennow Farm
Dennow Wood
Bog Rough
Reservoir (cov.)
Obelisk
High Warren
Club House
WARRINGTON GOLF COURSE
The Hurst
Hillside Farm
Hatton Lodge
Old Gorse
Bluecoat Farm
Hatton Cottage
COMMONSIDE BUSINESS CT.
Great Shepcroft Farm
Shepcroft Cottages
Little Shepcroft Farm
Hatton Hall
Greenside Farm
Road Side Farm
Sports Ground
Pav.
Stretton St. Matthew's C of E Prim. Sch.
Mosswood Hall
The Barns
Dorothy Farm
Hotel
Oaktree Farm
CHESHIRE SPIRE HOSPITAL
New Farm
Hatton Lame Farm
Whitegate Farm
Fir Tree Farm
New House Farm
Junction 10
M56 MOTORWAY
M56
A56
A49
A559
B5356
Tanyard Farm
Mossways
Tanner's Row Cotts.
Keeper's Cottage
Owl's Nest Wood
Stretton Hall
Brookside Farm
Bradley Brook House
Lower Hall
Swallow Barns
Stretton House
Pillmoss Farm
Owl's Nest
Queastybirch Hall
Pillmoss Farm
Walnut Tree Farm
Stockley Rough
Penkridge Lake Farm
WARRINGTON HALTON
Cobbles
The Limes
Bradley Brook
Black Jane
Black Jane Farm
Newton House
Spring View Cottage
Greenbank
Greenbank Farm
The Woodlands
School Lane Cottage
Crowholt Farm
Brookfield House
Mill Pond
Brook House Farm
Crowholt Wood
Glebe Farm
Grimsditch Hall
Five Oaks Farm
Ashfield Farm
CHESTER RD.
WALTON LEA RD.
WARRINGTON RD.
HOUGH'S LANE
FIRS LANE
WINDMILL LANE
LONDON ROAD
LYONS LANE
DUDLOW GREEN
PEWTERSPEAR GREEN
LONGWOOD
HILLSIDE ROAD
ACTON AVENUE
SHEPCROFT LANE
STRETTON LANE
HATTON LANE
DARESBURY LA.
TARPORLEY RD.
NORTHWICH ROAD
WELL LANE
MOSS LANE
PILLMOSS LANE
SUMMER LANE
LIMES LANE
SCHOOL LANE
DARK LANE
GRIMSDITCH LANE
NEWTON LANE
HIGHER LANE
A B C D E F G
1 2 3 4 5 6 7 8 9
82
97
84
83
82
81
360
61
62

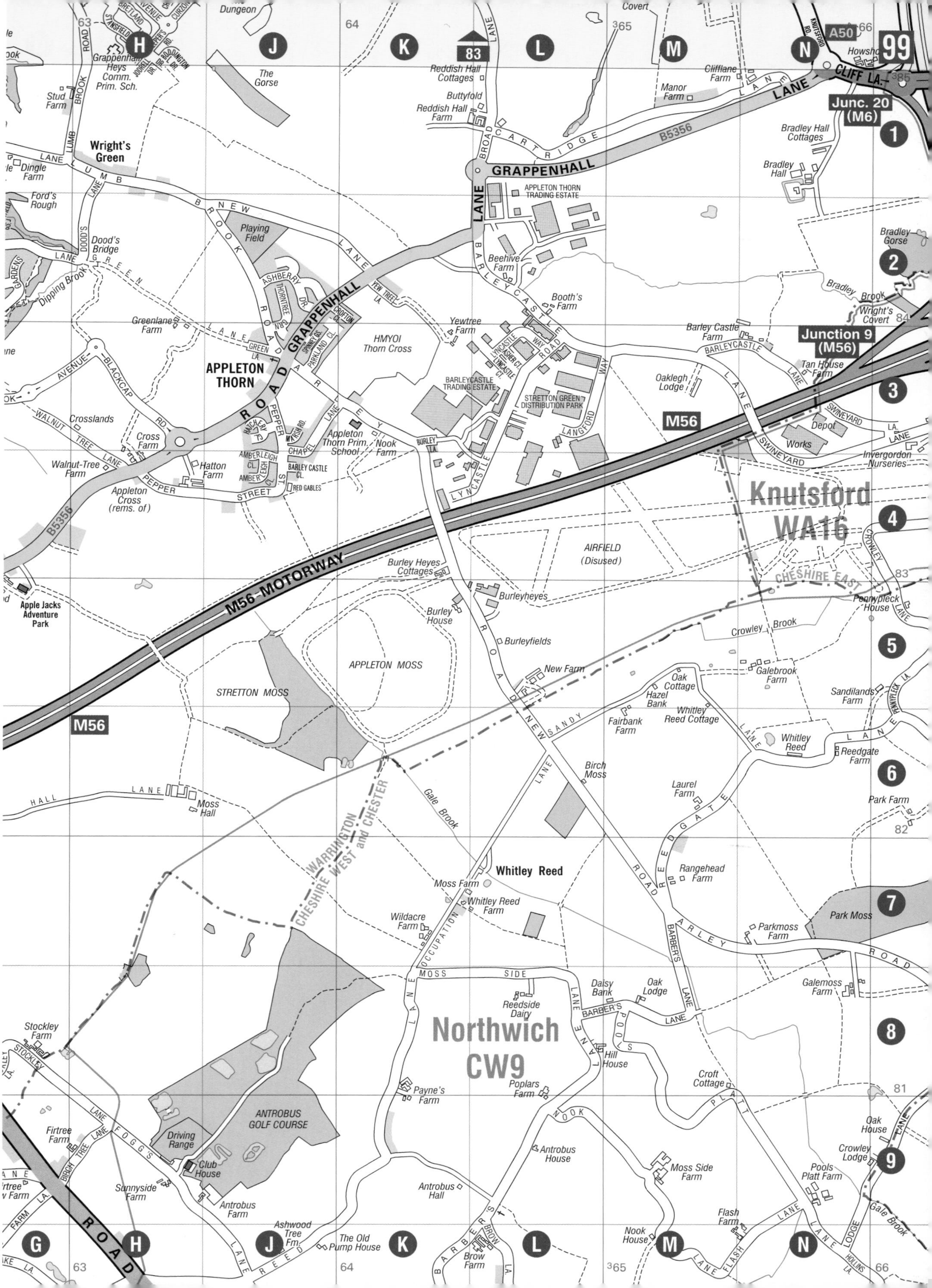
83
Junc. 20 (M6)
Junction 9 (M56)
M56
M56-MOTORWAY
B5356
A50
CLIFF LA.
Grappenhall Heys Comm. Prim. Sch.
Stud Farm
Wright's Green
Dingle Farm
Ford's Rough
Dood's Bridge
Dipping Brook
The Gorse
Dungeon
Playing Field
Greenlane Farm
APPLETON THORN
Crosslands
Cross Farm
Walnut-Tree Farm
Hatton Farm
Appleton Cross (rems. of)
Appleton Thorn Prim. School
Nook Farm
HMYOI Thorn Cross
Yewtree Farm
Reddish Hall Cottages
Buttyfold
Reddish Hall Farm
GRAPPENHALL
APPLETON THORN TRADING ESTATE
Beehive Farm
Booth's Farm
BARLEYCASTLE TRADING ESTATE
STRETTON GREEN DISTRIBUTION PARK
Covert
Manor Farm
Clifflane Farm
Howshaw
Bradley Hall Cottages
Bradley Hall
Bradley Gorse
Bradley Brook
Wright's Covert
Barley Castle Farm
Oakleigh Lodge
Tan House Farm
Depot
Works
Invergordon Nurseries
Knutsford WA16
AIRFIELD (Disused)
CHESHIRE EAST
Pennypleck House
Crowley Brook
Apple Jacks Adventure Park
Burley Heyes Cottages
Burleyheyes
Burley House
Burleyfields
APPLETON MOSS
STRETTON MOSS
New Farm
Galebrook Farm
Oak Cottage
Hazel Bank
Fairbank Farm
Whitley Reed Cottage
Sandilands Farm
Whitley Reed
Reedgate Farm
Birch Moss
Laurel Farm
Park Farm
Moss Hall
Gale Brook
WARRINGTON
CHESHIRE WEST and CHESTER
Whitley Reed
Rangehead Farm
Moss Farm
Whitley Reed Farm
Wildacre Farm
Parkmoss Farm
Park Moss
Galemoss Farm
Daisy Bank
Oak Lodge
Reedside Dairy
Northwich CW9
Hill House
Stockley Farm
Croft Cottage
Payne's Farm
Poplars Farm
ANTROBUS GOLF COURSE
Driving Range
Club House
Firtree Farm
Sunnyside Farm
Antrobus Farm
Antrobus House
Moss Side Farm
Antrobus Hall
Oak House
Crowley Lodge
Pools Platt Farm
Flash Farm
Nook House
Ashwood Tree Fm.
The Old Pump House
Brow Farm
ROAD
63
64
365
66
G
H
J
K
L
M
N
1
2
3
4
5
6
7
8
9
81
82
83
84
85

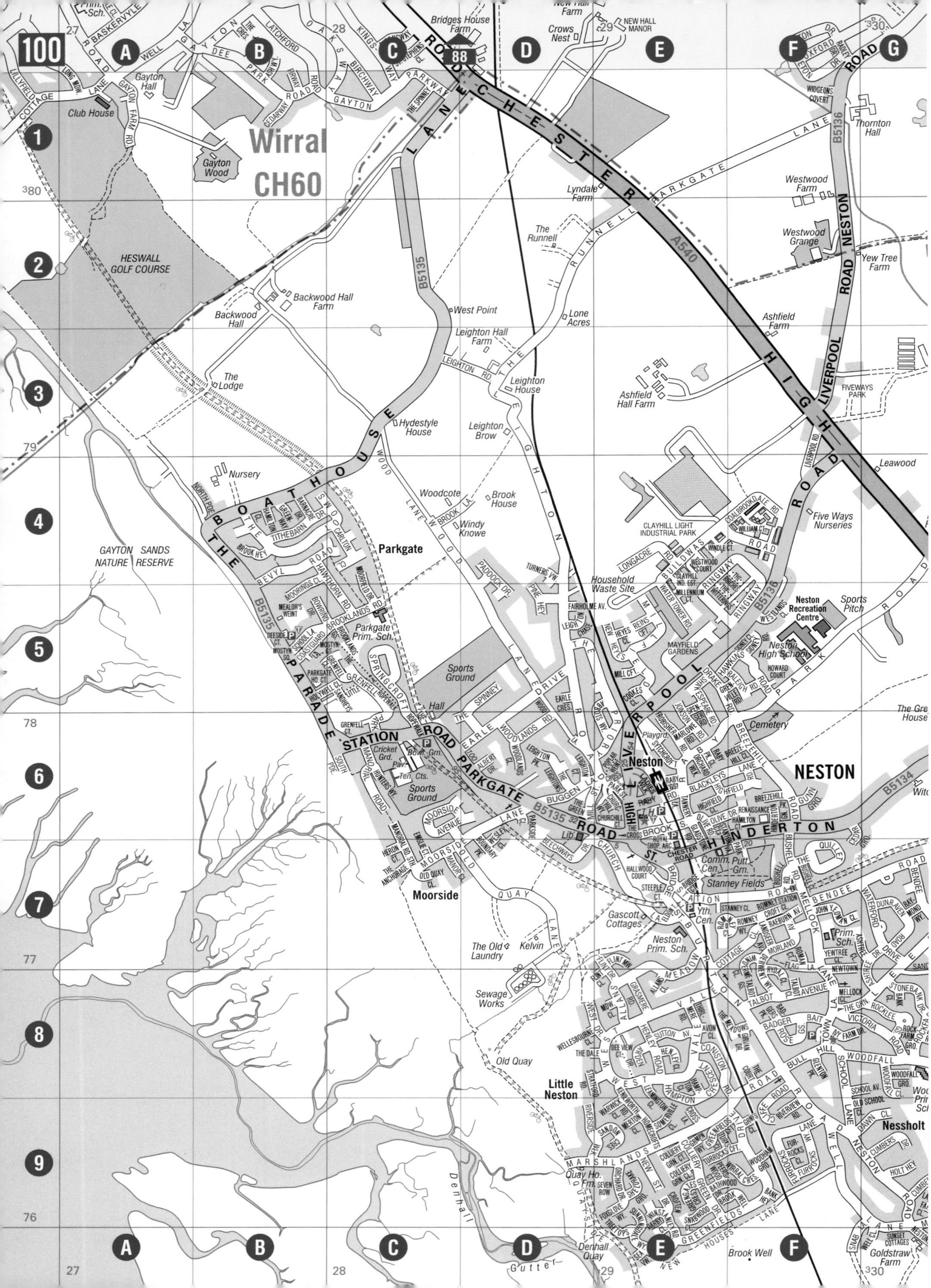
Wirral
CH60
HESWALL GOLF COURSE
GAYTON SANDS NATURE RESERVE
Gayton Hall
Gayton Wood
Club House
Bridges House Farm
88
Crows Nest
NEW HALL MANOR
Thornton Hall
Westwood Farm
Westwood Grange
Yew Tree Farm
Lyndale Farm
The Runnell
Backwood Hall Farm
Backwood Hall
West Point
Lone Acres
Leighton Hall Farm
Leighton House
Ashfield Farm
Ashfield Hall Farm
FIVEWAYS PARK
The Lodge
Hydestyle House
Leighton Brow
Leawood
Nursery
Woodcote
Brook House
Windy Knowe
Five Ways Nurseries
CLAYHILL LIGHT INDUSTRIAL PARK
Parkgate
Household Waste Site
Neston Recreation Centre
Sports Pitch
Neston High School
MAYFIELD GARDENS
Parkgate Prim. Sch.
Sports Ground
Hall
Cemetery
The Green House
Neston
NESTON
Cricket Grd.
Bowl. Grn.
Ten. Cts.
Sports Ground
Lib.
Comm. Putt. Cen.
Stanney Fields
Moorside
Gascott Cottages
Neston Prim. Sch.
The Old Laundry
Kelvin
Sewage Works
Old Quay
Little Neston
Nessholt
Quay Ho. Fm.
Denhall
Denhall Quay
Gutter
Brook Well
Goldstraw Farm
A540
B5135
B5136
B5134
CHESTER HIGH ROAD
LIVERPOOL ROAD
NESTON ROAD
BOATHOUSE LANE
THE PARADE
STATION ROAD
PARKGATE ROAD
HINDERTON ROAD
A
B
C
D
E
F
G
1
2
3
4
5
6
7
8
9
27
28
29
330
380
79
78
77
76

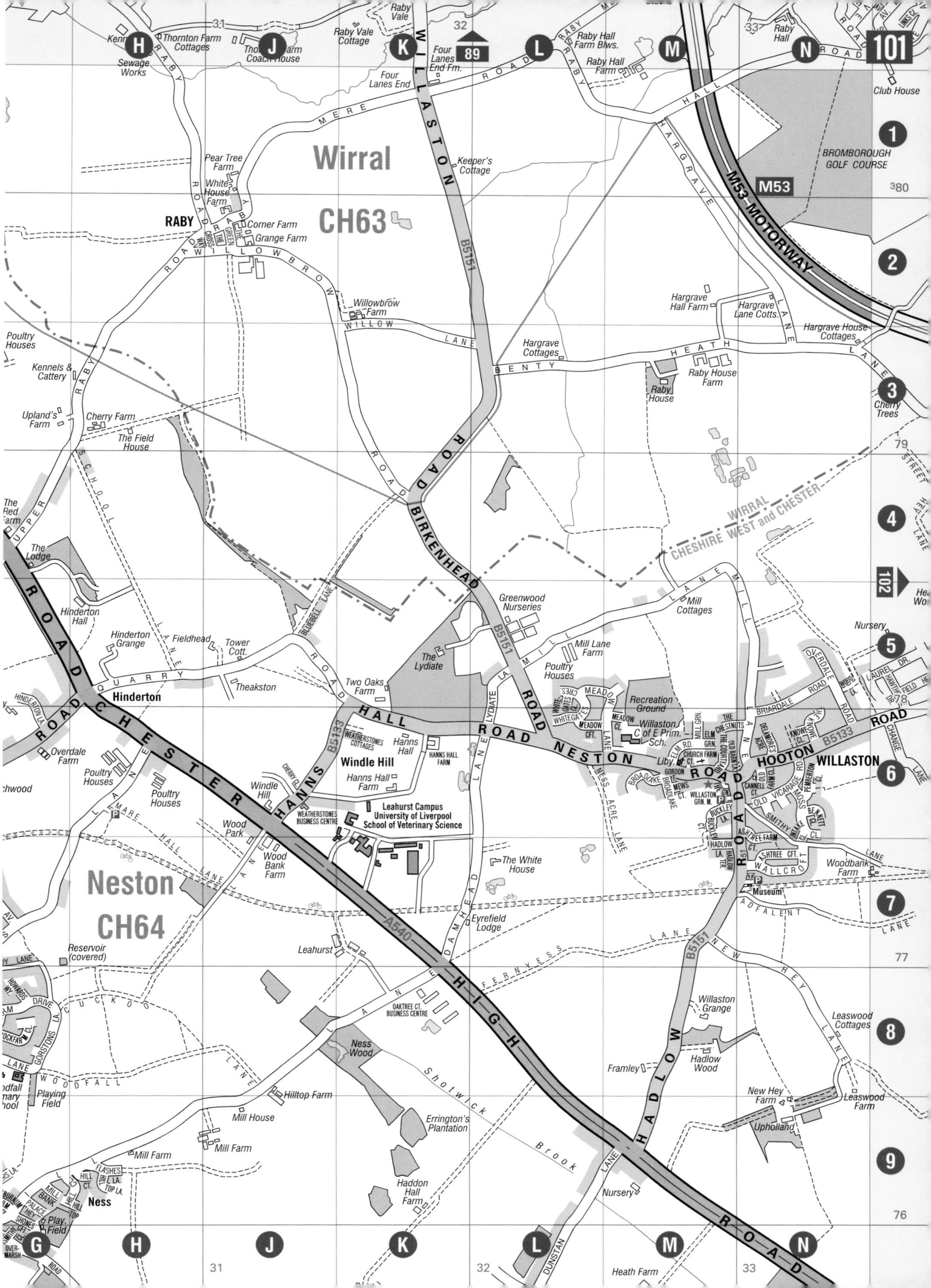
101
89
102
Wirral
CH63
Neston
CH64
RABY
Hinderton
Windle Hill
HOOTON
WILLASTON
Ness
Raby Vale
Thornton Farm Cottages
Sewage Works
Raby Vale Cottage
Four Lanes End Fm.
Four Lanes End
Raby Hall Farm Blws.
Raby Hall Farm
Raby Hall
Club House
BROMBOROUGH GOLF COURSE
M53 MOTORWAY
M53
Pear Tree Farm
White House Farm
Keeper's Cottage
Corner Farm
Grange Farm
Willowbrow Farm
Hargrave Hall Farm
Hargrave Lane Cotts.
Hargrave House Cottages
Hargrave Cottages
Raby House Farm
Raby House
Cherry Trees
Poultry Houses
Kennels & Cattery
Upland's Farm
Cherry Farm
The Field House
The Red Farm
The Lodge
Hinderton Hall
Hinderton Grange
Fieldhead
Tower Cott.
Theakston
Greenwood Nurseries
Mill Cottages
Mill Lane Farm
The Lydiate
Two Oaks Farm
Recreation Ground
Willaston C of E Prim. Sch.
WIRRAL
CHESHIRE WEST and CHESTER
Nursery
Overdale Farm
Hanns Hall
HANNS HALL FARM
Hanns Hall Farm
WEATHERSTONES COTTAGES
WEATHERSTONES BUSINESS CENTRE
Leahurst Campus University of Liverpool School of Veterinary Science
Wood Park
Wood Bank Farm
The White House
Eyrefield Lodge
Museum
Woodbank Farm
Reservoir (covered)
Leahurst
OAKTREE CT. BUSINESS CENTRE
Ness Wood
Willaston Grange
Leaswood Cottages
Hadlow Wood
Framley
Hilltop Farm
Mill House
Mill Farm
Errington's Plantation
Shotwick Brook
New Hey Farm
Leaswood Farm
Upholland
Haddon Hall Farm
Nursery
Playing Field
Play. Field
Heath Farm
WILLASTON ROAD
MERE ROAD
RABY ROAD
RABY HALL ROAD
HARGRAVE LANE
WILLOWBROW ROAD
WILLOW LANE
BENTY HEATH LANE
BIRKENHEAD ROAD
UPPER RAFY ROAD
SCHOOL LANE
BLUEBELL LANE
QUARRY ROAD
CHESTER ROAD
HINDERTON ROAD
HINDERTON LA.
HANNS HALL ROAD
NESTON ROAD
HOOTON ROAD
LYDIATE LANE
MILL LANE
NESS ACRE LANE
DAMHEAD LANE
HIGH ROAD
HADLOW ROAD
FERNYESS LANE
NEW HEY LANE
ADFALENT LANE
WALLCROFT
WOODFALL LANE
CUCKOO LANE
GORSTONS LA.
MARE HALL LANE
LEAHURST LANE
DUNSTAN LANE
OVERDALE ROAD
BRIARDALE ROAD
CHANGE LANE
LAUREL DR.
WOOD LA.
A540
B5151
B5133
31
32
33
380
79
78
77
76
1
2
3
4
5
6
7
8
9
G
H
J
K
L
M
N

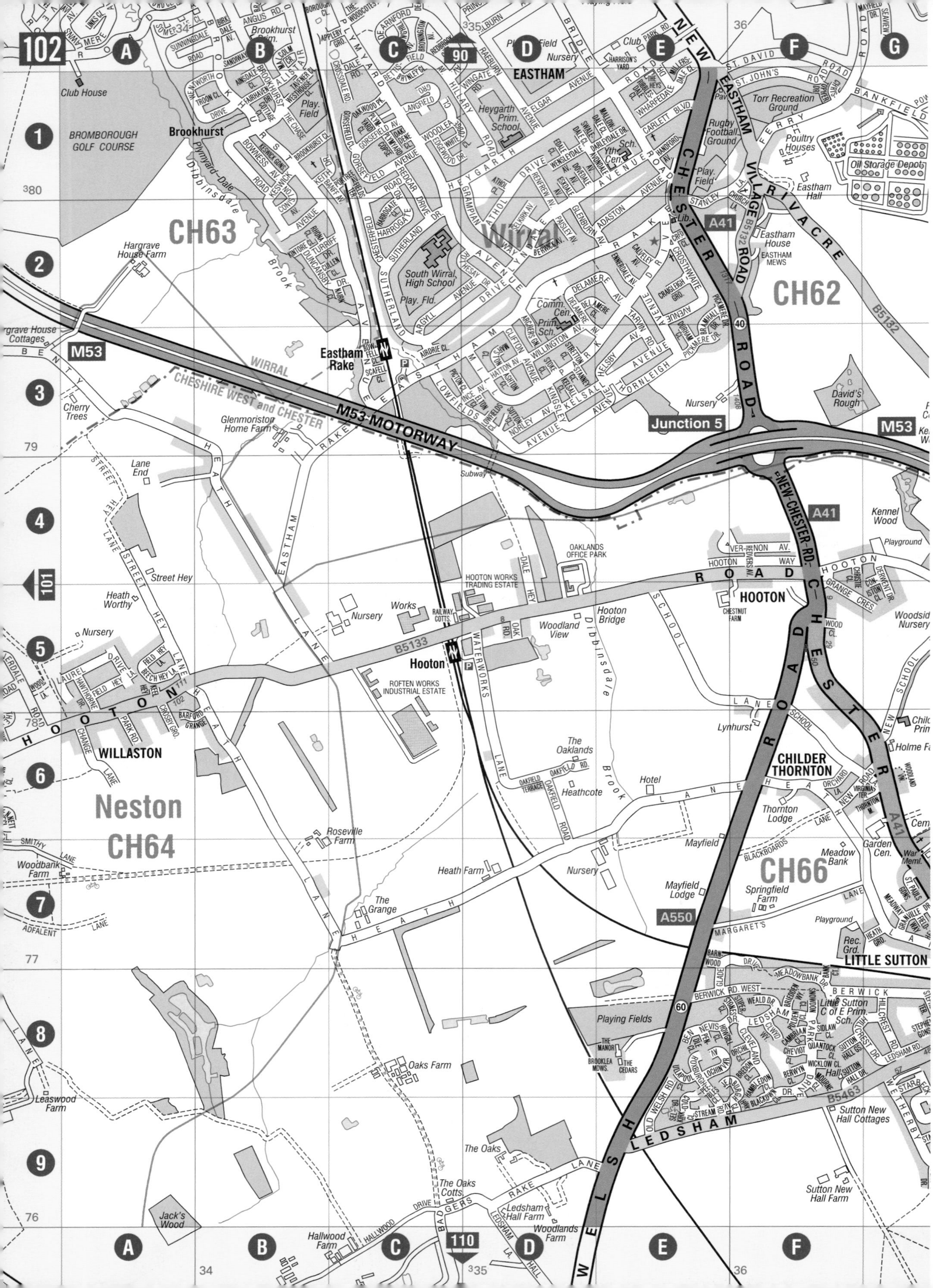
A
B
C
D
E
F
G
1
2
3
4
5
6
7
8
9
90
101
110
34
35
36
80
79
78
77
76
Club House
BROMBOROUGH GOLF COURSE
Brookhurst
Brookhurst Prim.
EASTHAM
Heygarth Prim. School
Play. Field
Nursery
Club
Torr Recreation Ground
Rugby Football Ground
Poultry Houses
Oil Storage Depot
Eastham Hall
Eastham House
EASTHAM MEWS
CH63
CH62
CH64
CH66
Wirral
Hargrave House Farm
South Wirral High School
Play. Fld.
Comm. Cen.
Prim. Sch.
Sch.
Ythc. Cen.
Lib.
Eastham Rake
M53
M53 MOTORWAY
Junction 5
WIRRAL
CHESHIRE WEST and CHESTER
A41
B5132
A550
B5133
B5463
NEW CHESTER ROAD
CHESTER ROAD
NEW CHESTER RD.
David's Rough
Nursery
Cherry Trees
Glenmoriston Home Farm
Lane End
Subway
Kennel Wood
Playground
OAKLANDS OFFICE PARK
HOOTON WORKS TRADING ESTATE
HOOTON ROAD
HOOTON
CHESTNUT FARM
Woodside Nursery
Street Hey
Heath Worthy
Works
Nursery
RAILWAY COTTS.
Woodland View
Hooton Bridge
Hooton
ROFTEN WORKS INDUSTRIAL ESTATE
Dibbinsdale Brook
Lynhurst
CHILDER THORNTON
Holme Farm
WILLASTON
The Oaklands
Heathcote
Hotel
Thornton Lodge
Neston
Roseville Farm
Mayfield
Meadow Bank
Garden Cen.
War Meml.
Woodbank Farm
Heath Farm
Nursery
Mayfield Lodge
Springfield Farm
The Grange
Playground
Rec. Grd.
LITTLE SUTTON
Playing Fields
Little Sutton C of E Prim. Sch.
Oaks Farm
THE MANOR
BROOKLEA MDWS.
THE CEDARS
Leaswood Farm
Sutton New Hall Cottages
The Oaks
The Oaks Cotts.
Sutton New Hall Farm
Jack's Wood
Ledsham Hall Farm
Woodlands Farm
Hallwood Farm
HEATH LANE
SMITHY LANE
ADFALENT LANE
STREET HEY LANE
EASTHAM RAKE
DALE HEY
SCHOOL LANE
WATERWORKS LANE
OAKFIELD ROAD
LEDSHAM ROAD
WELSH ROAD
OLD WELSH RD.
BERWICK RD. WEST
BADGERS RAKE
HALLWOOD DRIVE
LEDSHAM HALL LA.
BENTY HEATH LANE
VILLAGE ROAD
RIVACRE ROAD
ST. DAVID ROAD
ST. JOHN'S ROAD
FERRY ROAD
BANKFIELD ROAD
STANLEY LA.
HEYGARTH ROAD
SUTHERLAND AVENUE
MILL PARK DRIVE
KELSALL AVENUE
HORNLEIGH
CROSTHWAITE AVENUE
ELGAR AVENUE
CARLETT BLVD.
WHARFEDALE AV.
WINGATE RD.
HILLARY RD.
DALE RD.
VERNON AV.
CHRISTIE CL.
GRANGE CRES.
WOOD CL.
LAUREL DRIVE
FIELD HEY LA.
CROSBY GRO.
PARK RD.
BARFORD GRANGE
ORCHARD LA.
VIRGINIA TER.
BLACKBOARDS LANE
ST. MARGARET'S
BARNWOOD DRIVE
GLADE
MEADOWBANK DR.
BERWICK
HILLCREST RD.
LEDSHAM RD.
WETHERBY

91
104
111
Junc. 6
Junction 7
Junction 8
M53 MOTORWAY
M53
RIVER MERSEY
MANCHESTER SHIP CANAL
Oil Storage Depot
Oil Refinery
Tanks
Hooton Park Outdoor Karting Circuit
Hooton Park
Greenacres
Warehouse
HOOTON PARK AIRFIELD
Hangars
Kennelwood Cottages
Park Farm
Hooton Gardens
Vauxhall Motors FC (Rivacre Park)
Football Pitch
Playing Field
MOTOR CAR WORKS
Rivacre Wood
Well Wood
Booston Wood
Poole Hall Rocks
Mount Manisty
Poole Hall Sands
Works
Power Station
Manchester Ship Canal Railway
CH65
POOLE HALL INDUSTRIAL ESTATE
ROTHER DRIVE BUSINESS PARK
Comm. Cen.
Clayhill Wood
RIVACRE VALLEY COUNTRY PARK
Church Wood
HOOTON GOLF COURSE
Club Ho. Ellesmere Port Golf Centre
Rossmore Prim. Sch.
Ellesmere Port
Rivacre Valley Prim. Sch.
Cemetery
Overpool
ROSSMORE ROAD WEST
ROSSMORE ROAD EAST
Little Sutton
St. Mary of the Angels Catholic Prim. Sch.
Big Shallacres
ROSSMORE INDUSTRIAL ESTATE
JUNCTION EIGHT BUSINESS CENTRE
ELLESMERE PORT
Parklands Prim. Sch.
Tennis Courts
All Weather Sports Pitch
Playing Field
The Acorns Prim. & Nursery Sch.
West Cheshire College
Rec. Grd.
SUTTON WAY
Sports Academy Cen.
Playing Fields
Whitby
Civic Hall
Bingo
Bus Sta.
A41
A5032
B5132
B5463

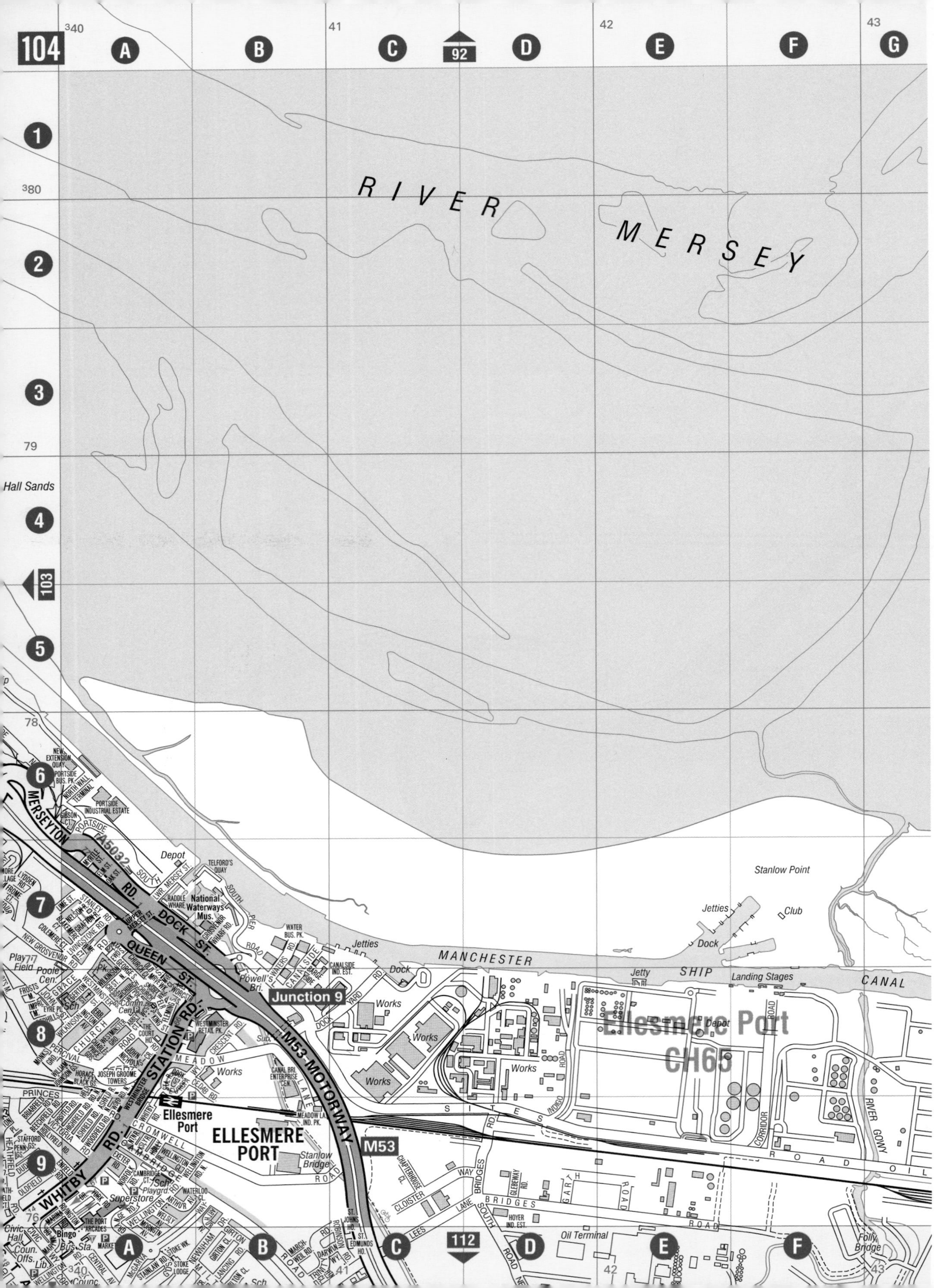

92
112
103
A
B
C
D
E
F
G
1
2
3
4
5
6
7
8
9
340
41
42
43
380
79
78
RIVER
MERSEY
Hall Sands
Stanlow Point
Jetties
Club
Dock
Jetties
MANCHESTER
SHIP
CANAL
Jetty
Landing Stages
Ellesmere Port
CH65
Depot
Works
Works
Works
Works
Works
Junction 9
M53 MOTORWAY
M53
ELLESMERE PORT
Ellesmere Port
Stanlow Bridge
National Waterways Mus.
Depot
PORTSIDE INDUSTRIAL ESTATE
NEW EXTENSION QUAY
PORTSIDE BUS. PK.
TELFORD'S QUAY
MERSEYTON
A5032
DOCK ST.
QUEEN ST.
STATION RD.
WHITBY RD.
CHURCH
CROMWELL
MEADOW
SITES
ROAD
OIL
RIVER GOWY
CORRIDOR
INDIGO
BRIDGES
SOUTH
Oil Terminal
Folly Bridge
Superstore
Bingo
Bus Sta.
Play Field
Poole Cen.
JOSEPH GROOME TOWERS
WESTMINSTER RETAIL PK.
CANAL BRI. ENTERPRISE CEN.
CANALSIDE IND. EST.
WATER BUS. PK.
HOYER IND. EST.
Powell's Bri.

H
J
K
L
M
N
G
44
345
46
93
106
113
380
79
78
77
76
INCE
BANKS
Frodsham
WA6
Chester
CH2
Works
Holme Farm
Sewage Works
Hall Farm
Wood Farm
KINSEY'S LANE
Yewtree Farm
MARSH LANE
Ince
GREENBANK
Lower Green Farm
STATION ROAD
POOL LANE
OIL REFINERY
Landing Stage
Landing Stage
SITES ROAD
Stanlow & Thornton
STANLOW
Bare Brick Ho.
Power Station
PERIMETER RD.
ORCHARDS
STATION RD
Ince & Elton
CHERRY

A
B
C
D
E
F
G
47
48
49
94
105
114
380
79
78
77
76
RIVER MERSEY
Frodsham Score
MANCHESTER SHIP CANAL
Frodsham Marsh Farm
Jetty
CROSS LANE
Works
Lordship Marsh
LORDSHIP LANE
ELTON LORDSHIP LANE
DRAKE LANE
Ince Marshes
MARSH
Works
Hill View Farm
Hope Farm
BLUE BRIDGE LANE
M56
M56 MOTORWAY
Helsby Marsh
Spring Farm
SMITHY
PERIMETER
ROAD
ELTON
HOOLPOOL LANE
LANE
LOWER
Meadow
CHESTER
Sch.
Hall

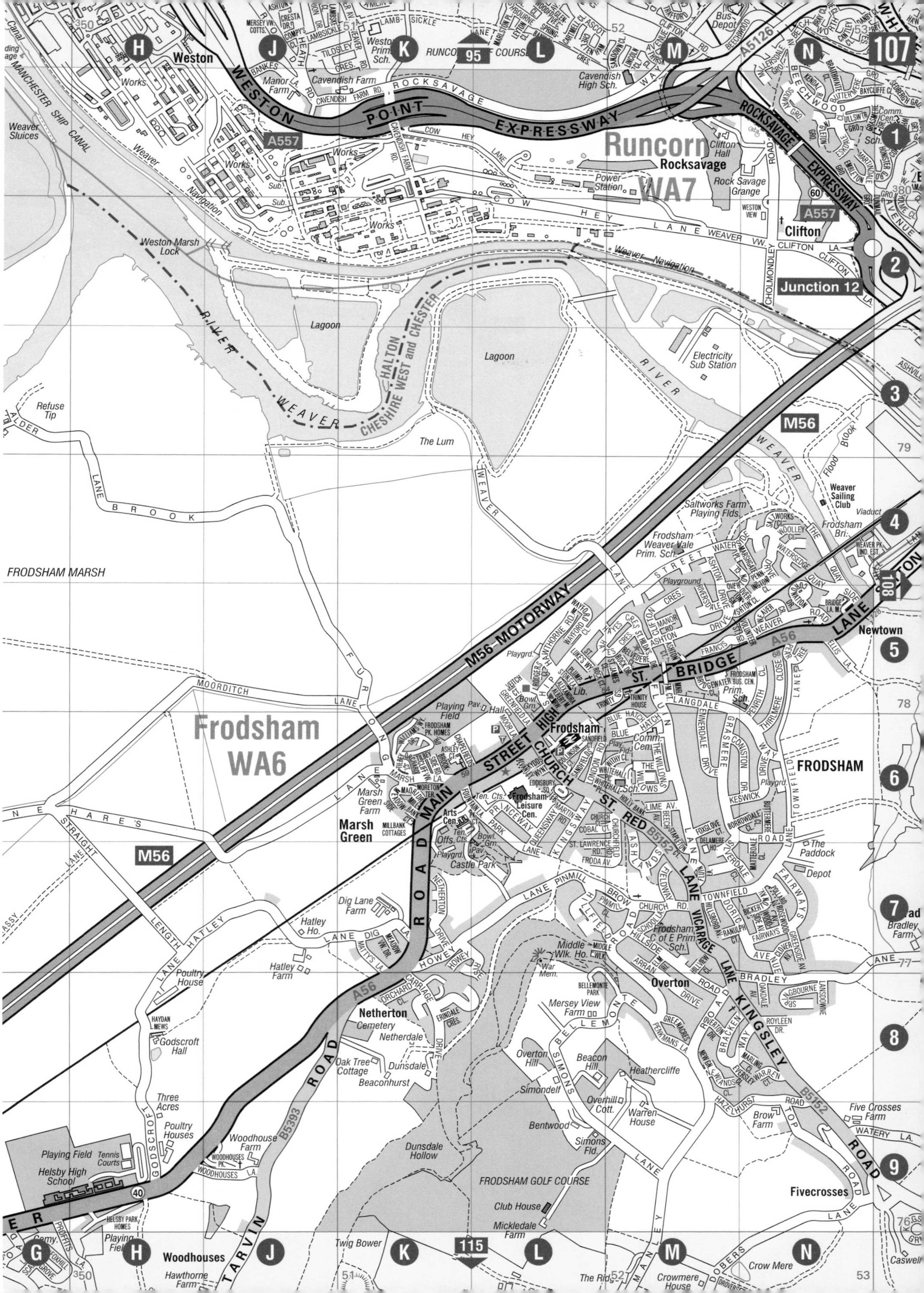

Weston
Runcorn
WA7
Rocksavage
Rocksavage Power Station
Rock Savage Grange
Clifton
Clifton Hall
Cavendish High Sch.
Cavendish Farm
Manor Farm
Weston Point Expressway
Rocksavage Expressway
Cow Hey Lane
Weaver Sluices
Manchester Ship Canal
Weaver Navigation
Weston Marsh Lock
River Weaver
Lagoon
Halton
Cheshire West and Chester
Electricity Sub Station
Junction 12
A557
A5126
M56
The Lum
Refuse Tip
Alder Lane
Brook Lane
Frodsham Marsh
M56 Motorway
Moorditch Lane
Furlong Lane
Frodsham
WA6
Marsh Lane
Marsh Green
Marsh Green Farm
Hares Lane
Straight Length
Weaver Sailing Club
Saltworks Farm Playing Flds.
Frodsham Weaver Vale Prim. Sch.
Frodsham Bri.
Viaduct
Newtown
Bridge Lane
Bridge St.
High Street
Main Street
Church St.
Red Lane
Main Road
Frodsham Leisure Cen.
Castle Park
Arts Cen.
FRODSHAM
The Paddock
Depot
Bradley Farm
Bradley Lane
Townfield
Vicarage Lane
Kingsley Road
Overton
Frodsham C of E Prim Sch.
Middle Wlk. Ho.
War Mem.
Bellemonte Park
Mersey View Farm
Overton Hill
Beacon Hill
Heathercliffe
Simondelf
Overhill Cott.
Warren House
Bentwood
Simons Fld.
Simons Lane
Dunsdale Hollow
Frodsham Golf Course
Club House
Mickledale Farm
Manley Lane
Netherton
Netherton Cemetery
Netherdale
Dunsdale
Oak Tree Cottage
Beaconhurst
Dig Lane Farm
Hatley Ho.
Hatley Farm
Hatley Lane
Poultry House
Haydan Mews
Godscroft Hall
Three Acres
Poultry Houses
Godscroft Lane
Woodhouse Farm
Woodhouses
Playing Field
Tennis Courts
Helsby High School
Helsby Park Homes
Tarvin Road
B5393
A56
B5152
Five Crosses Farm
Brow Farm
Watery La.
Fivecrosses
Crow Mere
Crowmere House
Twig Bower
Hawthorne Farm
Caswell
95
115
108

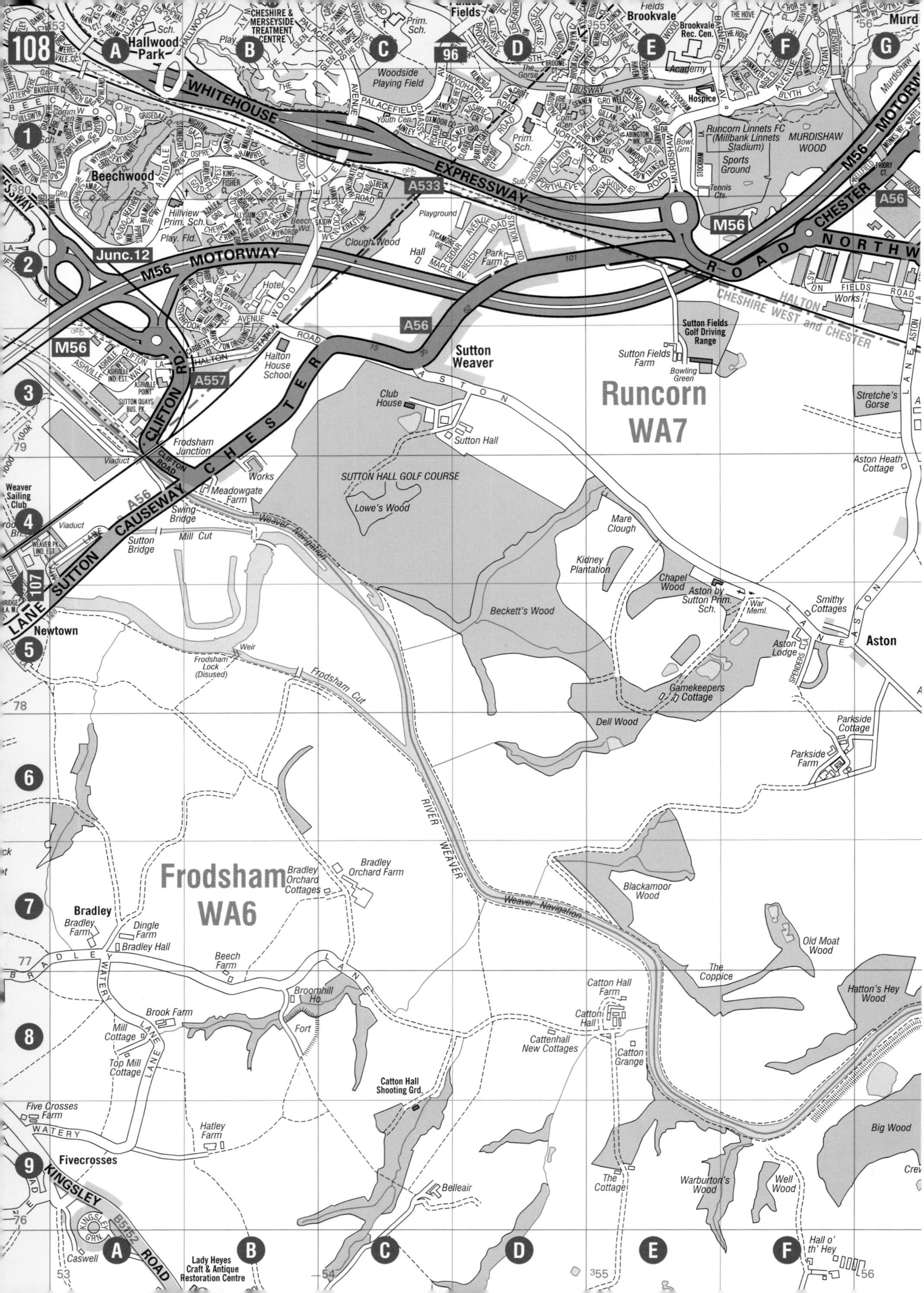
Hallwood Park
Cheshire & Merseyside Treatment Centre
Palace Fields
Brookvale
Brookvale Rec. Cen.
Academy
Murdishaw
Woodside Playing Field
Whitehouse
Expressway
Palacefields Avenue
Youth Cen.
Prim. Sch.
Hospice
Runcorn Linnets FC (Millbank Linnets Stadium)
Murdishaw Wood
Sports Ground
Tennis Cts.
Beechwood
Hillview Prim. Sch.
Play. Fld.
Clough Wood
Playground
Hall
Park Farm
A533
M56
A56
Junc.12
M56 Motorway
Chester Road
Northwich Road
Aston Fields Road
Works
Halton
Cheshire West and Chester
Sutton Fields Golf Driving Range
Sutton Fields Farm
Bowling Green
Hotel
Halton House School
Sutton Weaver
Aston Lane
A557
Clifton Rd.
Ashville Ind. Est.
Sutton Quays Bus. Pk.
Club House
Sutton Hall
Runcorn
WA7
Stretche's Gorse
Aston Heath Cottage
Frodsham Junction
Clifton Road
Viaduct
Works
Meadowgate Farm
Sutton Hall Golf Course
Lowe's Wood
Weaver Sailing Club
Swing Bridge
Sutton Bridge
Mill Cut
Sutton Causeway
Weaver Navigation
Mare Clough
Kidney Plantation
Chapel Wood
Aston by Sutton Prim. Sch.
War Meml.
Smithy Cottages
Beckett's Wood
Aston
Aston Lodge
Spenders La.
Newtown
Weir
Frodsham Lock (Disused)
Frodsham Cut
Gamekeepers Cottage
Dell Wood
Parkside Cottage
Parkside Farm
River Weaver
Frodsham
WA6
Bradley Orchard Cottages
Bradley Orchard Farm
Blackamoor Wood
Old Moat Wood
Bradley
Bradley Farm
Dingle Farm
Bradley Hall
Bradley Lane
Watery Lane
Beech Farm
Broomhill Ho.
The Coppice
Catton Hall Farm
Catton Hall
Hatton's Hey Wood
Brook Farm
Fort
Mill Cottage
Cattenhall New Cottages
Catton Grange
Top Mill Cottage
Catton Hall Shooting Grd.
Five Crosses Farm
Hatley Farm
Big Wood
Fivecrosses
Kingsley Road
B5152
The Cottage
Warburton's Wood
Well Wood
Belleair
Caswell
Kingsley Grn.
Lady Heyes Craft & Antique Restoration Centre
Hall o' th' Hey
96
107

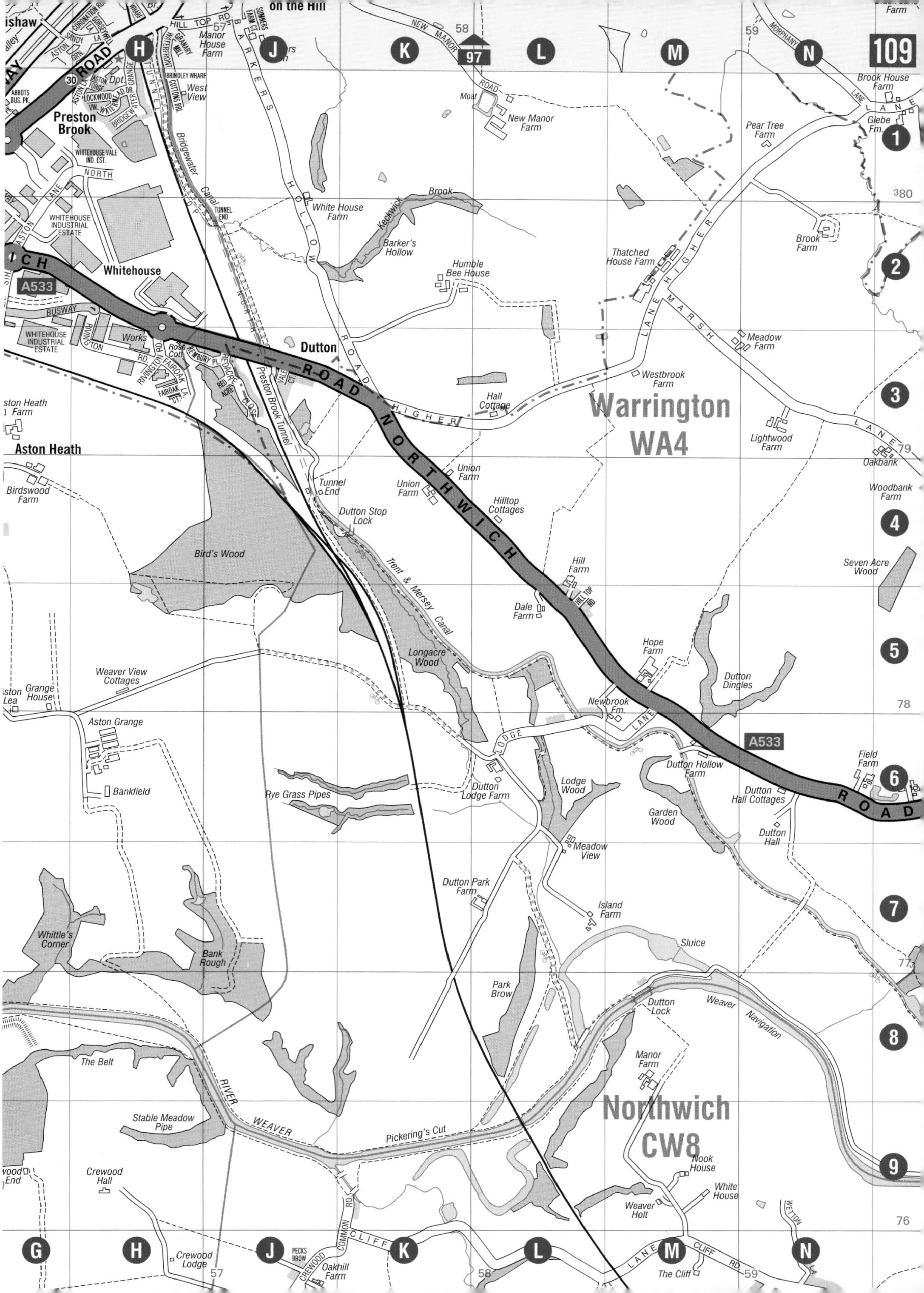

on the Hill
Preston Brook
Whitehouse
WHITEHOUSE VALE IND. EST.
WHITEHOUSE INDUSTRIAL ESTATE
ABBOTS BUS. PK.
Manor House Farm
Hill Top Rd.
West View
Bridgewater Canal
Tunnel End
BRINDLEY WHARF
White House Farm
Keckwick Brook
Barker's Hollow
Barkers Hollow
New Manor Road
New Manor Farm
Moat
97
Brook House Farm
Glebe Fm.
Pear Tree Farm
Brook Farm
Thatched House Farm
Higher Lane
Marsh Lane
Meadow Farm
Westbrook Farm
Humble Bee House
Dutton
Works
Rose Cott.
BUSWAY
A533
Northwich Road
Higher Lane
Hall Cottage
Warrington WA4
Lightwood Farm
Oakbank
Woodbank Farm
Seven Acre Wood
Aston Heath Farm
Aston Heath
Birdswood Farm
Preston Brook Tunnel
Tunnel End
Union Farm
Union Farm
Hilltop Cottages
Dutton Stop Lock
Bird's Wood
Trent & Mersey Canal
Hill Farm
Dale Farm
Longacre Wood
Hope Farm
Dutton Dingles
Weaver View Cottages
Aston Lea
Grange House
Aston Grange
Newbrook Fm.
Lodge Lane
Bankfield
Rye Grass Pipes
Dutton Lodge Farm
Lodge Wood
Dutton Hollow Farm
Field Farm
Dutton Hall Cottages
Garden Wood
Dutton Hall
Meadow View
Dutton Park Farm
Island Farm
Whittle's Corner
Bank Rough
Sluice
Park Brow
Dutton Lock
Weaver Navigation
The Belt
River Weaver
Manor Farm
Stable Meadow Pipe
Pickering's Cut
Northwich CW8
Nook House
White House
Crewood Hall
Weaver Holt
Crewood Lodge
Crewood Common Rd.
Cliff Lane
Cliff Rd.
The Cliff
Oakhill Farm
Pecks Brow
G
H
J
K
L
M
N
1
2
3
4
5
6
7
8
9
57
58
59
76
77
78
79
380

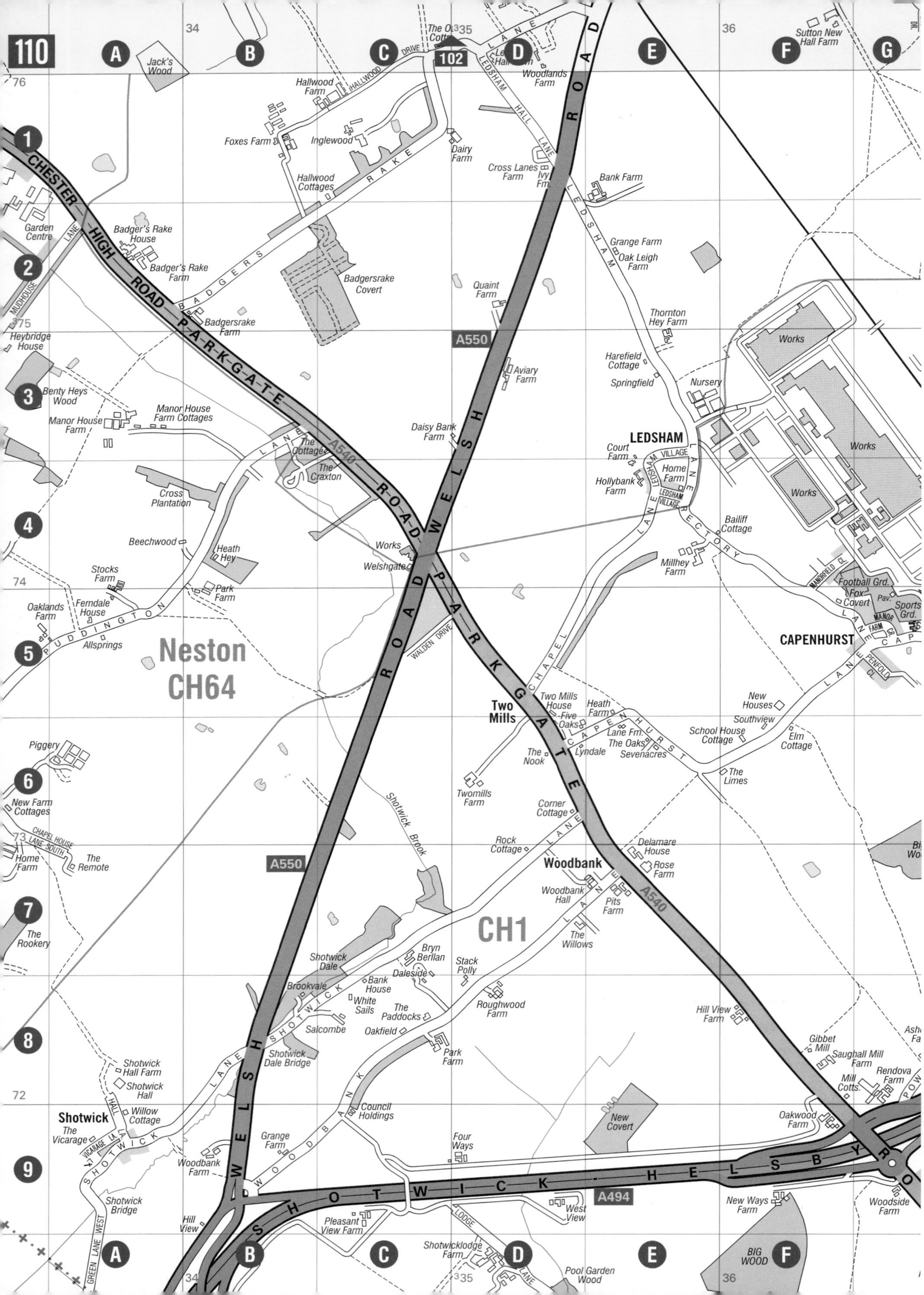
A
B
C
D
E
F
G
34
35
36
76
75
74
73
72
1
2
3
4
5
6
7
8
9
102
Jack's Wood
Sutton New Hall Farm
Hallwood Farm
HALLWOOD DRIVE
LEDSHAM HALL LANE
Woodlands Farm
Foxes Farm
Inglewood
RAKE
Dairy Farm
Cross Lanes Farm
Ivy Fm.
Bank Farm
Hallwood Cottages
Garden Centre
MUDHOUSE LANE
CHESTER HIGH ROAD
PARKGATE ROAD
Badger's Rake House
Badger's Rake Farm
BADGERS
Badgersrake Covert
Badgersrake Farm
Grange Farm
Oak Leigh Farm
LEDSHAM
Quaint Farm
Thornton Hey Farm
Heybridge House
A550
Harefield Cottage
Springfield
Works
Aviary Farm
Benty Heys Wood
Nursery
Manor House Farm Cottages
Manor House Farm
Daisy Bank Farm
LEDSHAM
Court Farm
LEDSHAM VILLAGE
Home Farm
Hollybank Farm
The Cottages
A540
The Craxton
Cross Plantation
WELSH ROAD
Works
Bailiff Cottage
RECTORY
Beechwood
Heath Hey
Welshgate
Millhey Farm
MANORFIELD CL.
Football Grd.
Fox Covert
Pav.
Sports Grd.
Stocks Farm
Park Farm
Oaklands Farm
Ferndale House
PUDDINGTON
Allsprings
WALDEN DRIVE
CHAPEL LANE
MANOR FARM CR.
CAPENHURST
PENFOLD CL.
Neston CH64
Two Mills
Two Mills House
Five Oaks
Heath Farm
Lane Fm.
The Oaks
Sevenacres
CAPENHURST
New Houses
Southview
School House Cottage
Elm Cottage
The Nook
Lyndale
The Limes
Piggery
Twomills Farm
New Farm Cottages
Shotwick Brook
Corner Cottage
CHAPEL HOUSE LANE SOUTH
Home Farm
The Remote
Rock Cottage
Delamare House
Rose Farm
Woodbank
A550
Woodbank Hall
Pits Farm
The Rookery
CH1
The Willows
Shotwick Dale
Bryn Berllan
Stack Polly
Daleside
Brookvale
Bank House
White Sails
The Paddocks
Roughwood Farm
Hill View Farm
Salcombe
Oakfield
Park Farm
Gibbet Mill
Saughall Mill Farm
Shotwick Dale Bridge
SHOTWICK LANE
Shotwick Hall Farm
Shotwick Hall
Mill Cotts.
Rendova Farm
Willow Cottage
Council Holdings
WOODBANK LANE
New Covert
Oakwood Farm
Shotwick
The Vicarage
VICARAGE LA.
HALL
Grange Farm
Four Ways
Woodbank Farm
SHOTWICK-HELSBY ROAD
A494
Shotwick Bridge
West View
New Ways Farm
Woodside Farm
Hill View
Pleasant View Farm
LODGE LANE
GREEN LANE WEST
Shotwicklodge Farm
BIG WOOD
Pool Garden Wood

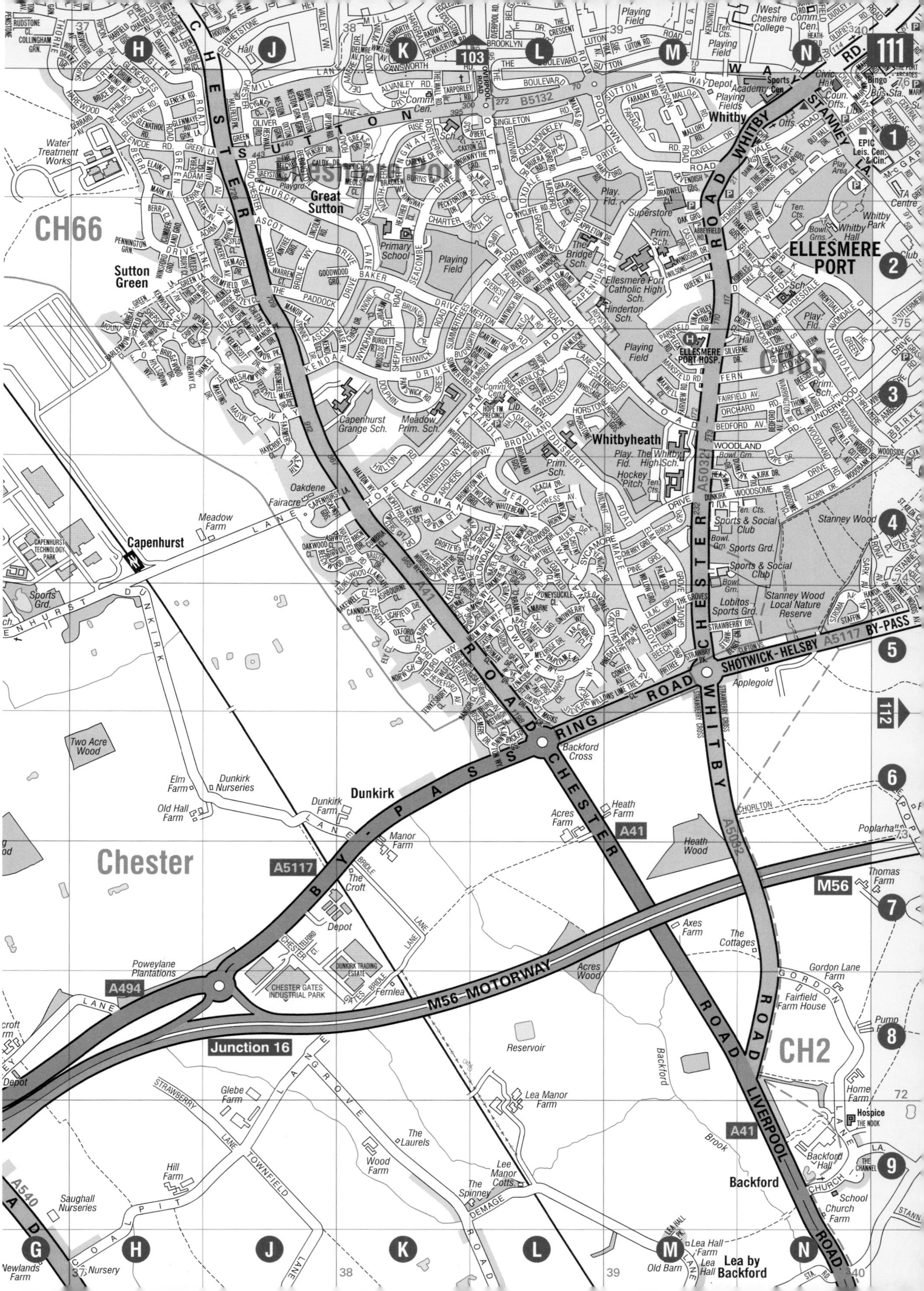
Ellesmere Port
ELLESMERE PORT
Great Sutton
Sutton Green
Whitby
Whitbyheath
Capenhurst
Chester
Dunkirk
Backford
Lea by Backford
CH66
CH65
CH2
M56 MOTORWAY
Junction 16
A41
A5117
A494
A5032
A540
M56
B5132
CHESTER ROAD
WHITBY ROAD
LIVERPOOL ROAD
SUTTON WAY
BY-PASS
RING ROAD
SHOTWICK-HELSBY BY-PASS
OVERPOOL ROAD
STANNEY LA.
WESTMINSTER BRIDGE
Capenhurst Grange Sch.
Meadow Prim. Sch.
Primary School
Playing Field
Ellesmere Port Catholic High Sch.
Hinderton Sch.
ELLESMERE PORT HOSP.
The Whitby High Sch.
The Bridge Sch.
Superstore
West Cheshire College
Civic Hall
EPIC Leis. Cen. & Cin.
Whitby Park
Whitby Hall
Stanney Wood
Stanney Wood Local Nature Reserve
Lobitos Sports Grd.
Sports & Social Club
Heath Wood
Acres Wood
Two Acre Wood
Water Treatment Works
CAPENHURST TECHNOLOGY PARK
Meadow Farm
Oakdene
Fairacre
Elm Farm
Dunkirk Nurseries
Old Hall Farm
Dunkirk Farm
Manor Farm
The Croft
Depot
CHESTER GATES INDUSTRIAL PARK
DUNKIRK TRADING ESTATE
Fernlea
Poweylane Plantations
Heath Farm
Acres Farm
Axes Farm
The Cottages
Thomas Farm
Poplarhall
Gordon Lane Farm
Fairfield Farm House
Reservoir
Glebe Farm
Lea Manor Farm
The Laurels
Wood Farm
Lee Manor Cotts.
The Spinney
Hill Farm
Saughall Nurseries
Newlands Farm
Nursery
Home Farm
Hospice
Backford Hall
School
Church Farm
Lea Hall Farm
Lea Hall
Old Barn
Backford Cross
Applegold
103
112
37
38
39
340
G
H
J
K
L
M
N
1
2
3
4
5
6
7
8
9
75
74
73
72
376

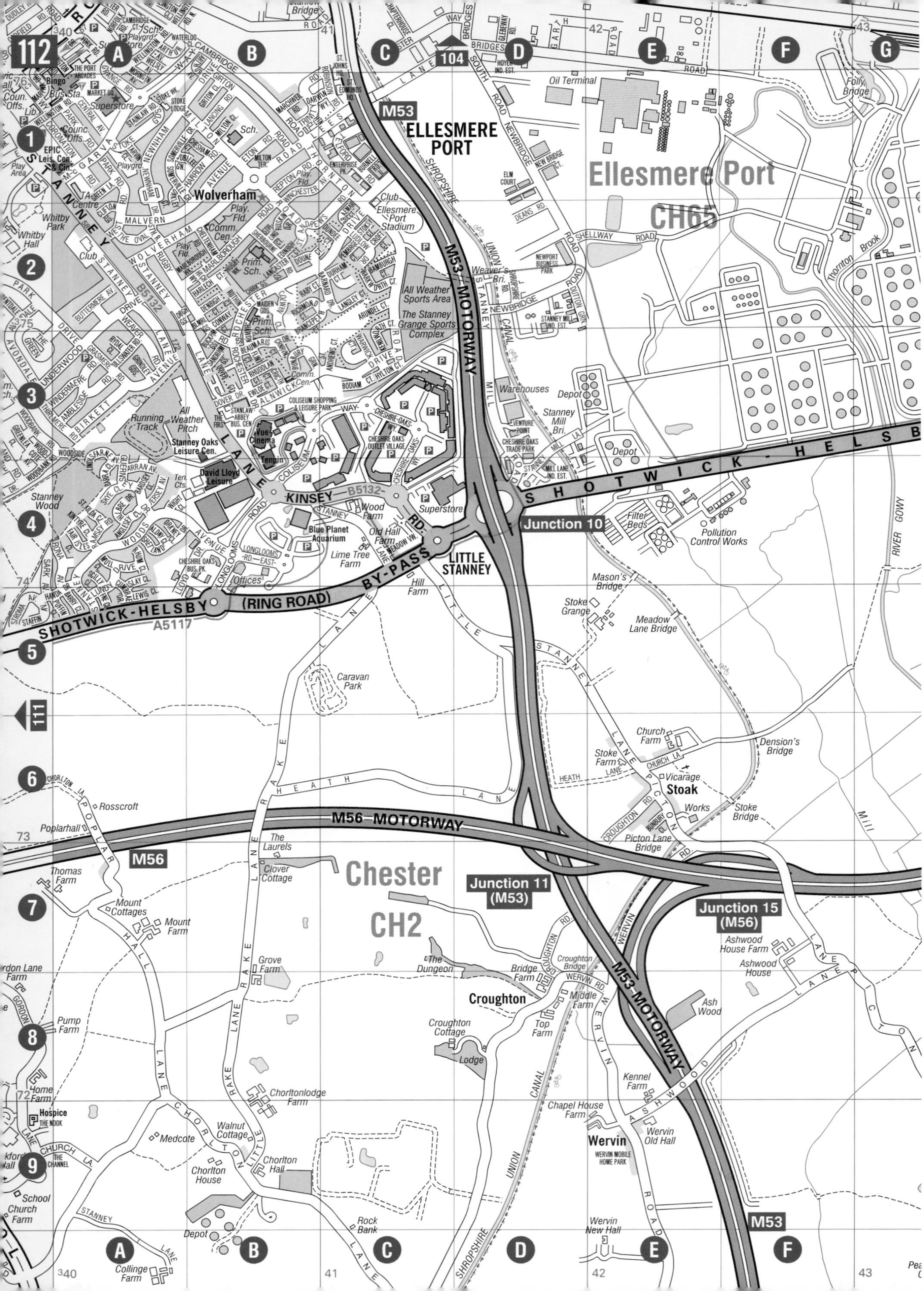
ELLESMERE PORT
Ellesmere Port
CH65
Wolverham
KINSEY
LITTLE STANNEY
M53
M53 MOTORWAY
M56
M56 MOTORWAY
Junction 10
Junction 11 (M53)
Junction 15 (M56)
SHOTWICK-HELSBY
BY-PASS
(RING ROAD)
A5117
B5132
STANNEY LANE
SHROPSHIRE UNION CANAL
Oil Terminal
Whitby Park
Whitby Hall
Stanney Wood
Running Track
All Weather Pitch
Stanney Oaks Leisure Cen.
David Lloyd Leisure
Vue Cinema
Tenpin
Blue Planet Aquarium
COLISEUM SHOPPING & LEISURE PARK
CHESHIRE OAKS OUTLET VILLAGE
Superstore
Ellesmere Port Stadium
All Weather Sports Area
The Stanney Grange Sports Complex
Warehouses
Depot
Stanney Mill Bri.
Filter Beds
Pollution Control Works
Mason's Bridge
Stoke Grange
Meadow Lane Bridge
Caravan Park
Church Farm
Stoke Farm
Dension's Bridge
Vicarage
Stoak
Works
Stoke Bridge
Picton Lane Bridge
Rosscroft
Poplarhall
Thomas Farm
Mount Cottages
Mount Farm
The Laurels
Clover Cottage
Chester
CH2
Grove Farm
The Dungeon
Bridge Farm
Croughton Bridge
Croughton
Middle Farm
Top Farm
Croughton Cottage
Lodge
Ashwood House Farm
Ashwood House
Ash Wood
Kennel Farm
Chapel House Farm
Wervin
WERVIN MOBILE HOME PARK
Wervin Old Hall
Wervin New Hall
Pump Farm
Home Farm
Hospice
Medcote
Walnut Cottage
Chorltonlodge Farm
Chorlton Hall
Chorlton House
Depot
Rock Bank
Collinge Farm
School
Church Farm
River Gowy
Thornton Brook
Folly Bridge
104
111

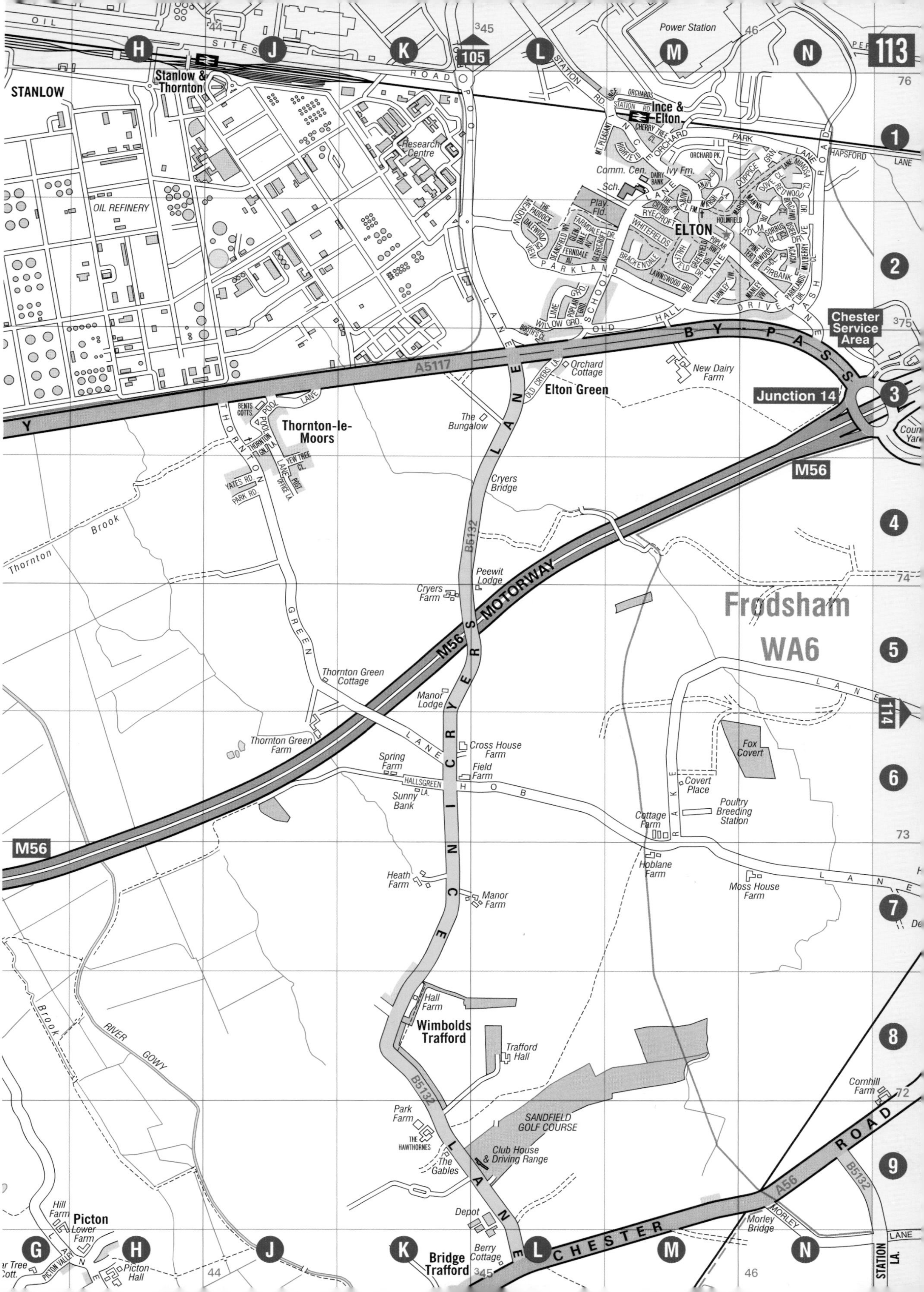
STANLOW
Stanlow & Thornton
OIL SITES ROAD
OIL REFINERY
Research Centre
Power Station
105
POOL LANE
STATION RD.
Ince & Elton
ORCHARDS
CHERRY TREE CL.
ORCHARD PARK LANE
MT. PLEASANT
HIGHFIELD
ORCHARD PK.
HAPSFORD LANE
Comm. Cen.
Ivy Fm.
Sch.
DAIRY BANK
Play. Fld.
ELTON
RYECROFT
WHITEFIELDS
BRACKENDALE
LAWNSWOOD GRO.
HOLMFIELD
COPPICE GRN.
MIMOSA CL.
DOVE CL.
REDWOOD DR.
SORBUS CL.
OSIER DR.
ACACIA AVE.
FIRBANK
MULBERRY
PARKLANDS DR.
ASH LANE
PARKLAND VIEW
MEADOW VIEW
THE PADDOCK
DALEWOOD CL.
DEANSFIELD WY.
GLEN DALE AV.
FARMDALE DR.
FERNDALE AV.
GLEBECROFT AV.
SCHOOL LA.
LIME
POPLAR GRO.
WILLOW GRO.
BOOTH'S CL.
OLD HALL DRIVE
BY-PASS
A5117
Chester Service Area
Junction 14
New Dairy Farm
Orchard Cottage
OLD CRYERS LA.
Elton Green
The Bungalow
BENTS COTTS
POOL LANE
Thornton-le-Moors
THORNTON GN. LA.
YEW TREE CL.
POST OFFICE LA.
YATES RD.
PARK RD.
THORNTON GREEN LANE
Cryers Bridge
M56
Thornton Brook
B5132
Peewit Lodge
Cryers Farm
M56 MOTORWAY
CRYERS LANE
Frodsham WA6
Thornton Green Cottage
Manor Lodge
Thornton Green Farm
Cross House Farm
Spring Farm
Field Farm
HALLSGREEN LA.
Sunny Bank
HOB LANE
RAKE LANE
Covert Place
Fox Covert
Poultry Breeding Station
Cottage Farm
Hoblane Farm
Moss House Farm
114
Heath Farm
Manor Farm
INCE LANE
Hall Farm
Wimbolds Trafford
Trafford Hall
Brook
RIVER GOWY
SANDFIELD GOLF COURSE
Park Farm
THE HAWTHORNES
The Gables
Club House & Driving Range
Cornhill Farm
A56
B5132
ROAD
Depot
Morley Bridge
MORLEY LANE
CHESTER ROAD
STATION LA.
Hill Farm
Picton
Lower Farm
PICTON VALLEY
Picton Hall
Tree Cott.
Berry Cottage
Bridge Trafford
H J K L M N G
1 2 3 4 5 6 7 8 9
44 345 46
76 375 74 73 72

114
106
113
Helsby Marsh
Spring Farm
Meadow Farm
Helsby Junction
Helsby
HELSBY
Helsby Hill
Fort
Harmers Lake Farm
Firs Farm
M56
M56 MOTORWAY
Chester Service Area
Junction 14
Council Yard
Lower Hapsford Hall
Sewage Works
Hapsford
A5117
A56
Green Acres
GREENACRES CARAVAN PARK
MERE'S EDGE BUSINESS PARK
Helsby Community Sports Club
Football Ground
Horn's Mill
Horns Mill Prim. Sch.
Horns Farm
Horn's Mill Bri.
Helsby Quarry Woodland Pk.
Ivy Dene
Birch Cottage
Rock Farm
Ashfield
Walnut Tree Farm
Poplar Tree Farm
Greenbank Farm
Alvanley Primary School
Hornsmill Brook
Woodhouse Poultry Farm
Greenwood
HELSBY GOLF COURSE
Club House
Wood Farm
Peckmill Brook
The Cedars
Peck Mill Farm
Green Gables
Abbot's Clough Farm
Hob Goblin Farm
Depot
Dunham Hall
Manor Farm
Dunham-on-the-Hill
Smithy Farm
Squarehouse Farm
Dunham House
Rock Farm
Town Farm
Willow Beds
Vicarage
CHESHIRE PARK HOMES
Cornhill Farm
The Grange
Barrow Lane Farm
Manley Mere Sail Sports & Adventure Trail
Dunham Heath
Lower Cottages
Homebank Farm
Lowerhall Farm
Rose Farm
New House Farm
Fox Cottage
Manley Ho. Farm
Bank Ho. Farm
Chester CH3
Barnhouse Fox Covert
CHESTER ROAD
MANLEY LANE
MORLEY LANE
STATION LA.
B5132
TOWERS LANE
PRIMROSE LANE

Helsby High School
ROAD
40
WOODHOUSES LA.
FRODSHAM GOLF COURSE
Club Ho
107
Fivecrosses
H
J
K
L
M
N
LANE
HELSBY HOMES
Playing Field
Cemy.
LANDSCAPE DENE
FOXHILL GROVE
PROFFITS
LANE
Woodhouses
Hawthorne Farm
CHESTNUT LANE
ROAD
Twig Bower
Mickledale Farm
The Ridge
Crowmere House
Crow Mere
Caswell
Firs View
Fort
Woodhouse Hill
Higher Mickledale Farm
DROVERS LANE
Crowmere Cottage
1
Chestnut Farm
The Cottage
Oak Mount Farm
Cromwell Court
Foxhill
Lodge
B5393
Shepherds Houses
DOBERS
NORTH
Spring Hill
Foxhill Wood
Snidley Moor
DOBERS
Foxhill Arboretum
Harrol Edge
2
Hilltop Equestrian Centre
Manor House Farm
Foxhill Farm
Teuthill Farm
Hillside Cottage
Newton
375
LANE
Alderhall
Foxhill
THE RIDGEWAY (COUNTRY HOLIDAY PK.)
The Royalty
MEETING HOUSE LA.
The Firs
3
HOLLY BANK
ALVANLEY PARK
WILLOW
HOLLOWS
TARVIN
Ridgeway Wood
BURROWS
COMMONSIDE
Queen Charlotte's Wood
RIDGEWAY
The Paddocks
RILEY BANK MEWS
WATERLOO
County Farmers Hatchery
Pav.
Cricket Grd.
Commonside Farm
Bowlingalley Farm
ROAD
NEWTON
4
Alvanley
Frodsham
WA6
Cliff Farm
Four Lane Ends
LANE
WATERLOO
74
ALVANLEY
NEW
BUSHELLS LANE
Cherry Tree Farm
Alvanley Hall
Birch Hill
Birchdale Farm
5
The Croft
Alvanley Hall Court
BIRCH HILL
LANE
LANE
Pye Corner Farm
Harcourt
Alvanley Cliff
Kingswood
Greengate Farm
Maiden's Cross
PALE
Austerson Old Hall
CROSSLEY PARK
Claim Farm
Kingswood Hall
ROWAN HO.
KINGSWOOD PARK
6
MANLEY
Crabtree Farm
73
Brook
Hillside Cottage
ROAD
Simmondshill Wood
Manley Old Hall
Manley Wood
New Pale Lodge
7
B5393
Manley Knoll
Black Wood
New Pale
The New Pale
Windmill Bank
Buckoak
SCHOOL LA.
Manley Village Sch.
Lodge
8
Sugar Lane Cottage
SUGAR
LANE
PINGOT LA.
Ravelstone
Manley Common
Overton Edge
Parkwood Farm
Meadow Bank
Stone House
QUARRY LA.
Highfields Farm
Tall Trees
PALE
72
Manor Farm
Timbers
Ravelstone Cottages
Kennel Wood
Manley Common Farm
QUARRY
MANLEY
Garden Wood
Garden Cottage
MANLEY
The Moss
Tigh Beag
Playing Field
NEW
DELAMERE FOREST PARK
ROAD
Craggon Cott.
Manley Hall
Moss Farm
FOUR LANE ENDS
9
Siddall's Hill
Acorn Cottage
LANE
DARK
Club
Rangeway Bank Farm
LANE
MOSS
MOSS DR.
Bowl Grn.
Tennis Courts
Fox Hollow
Rookery Wood
CHAPEL
TARVIN
ROAD
Boundary Cottage
ARK
Rookery Farm
LANE
Brook House
Ark Wood
LANE
G
H
J
K
L
M
N
ASHTON RD.
Rookery Cottage
WELL
LANE
STA. RD.
350
51
MOULDSWORTH
52
53

POSTCODE MAP

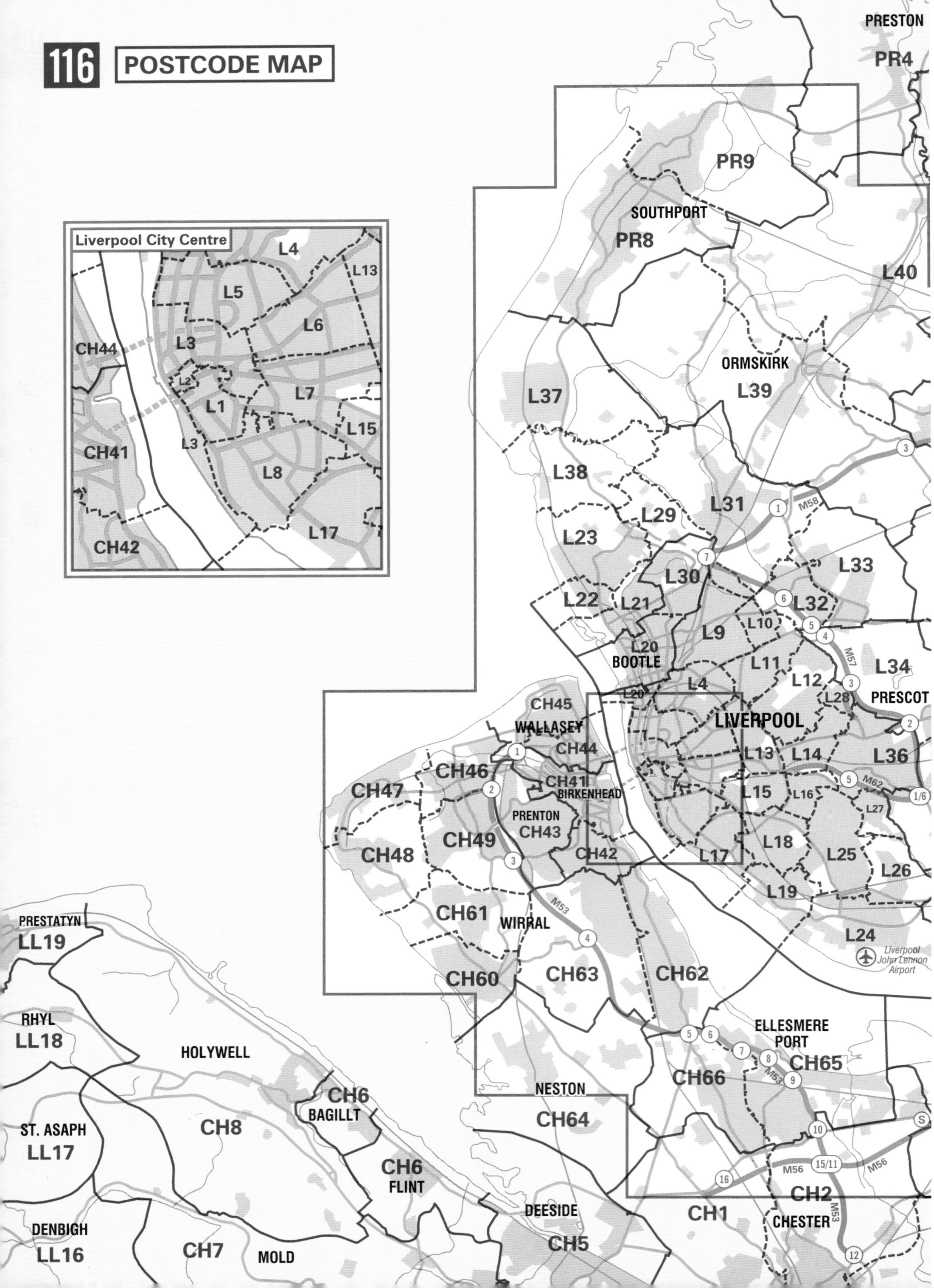

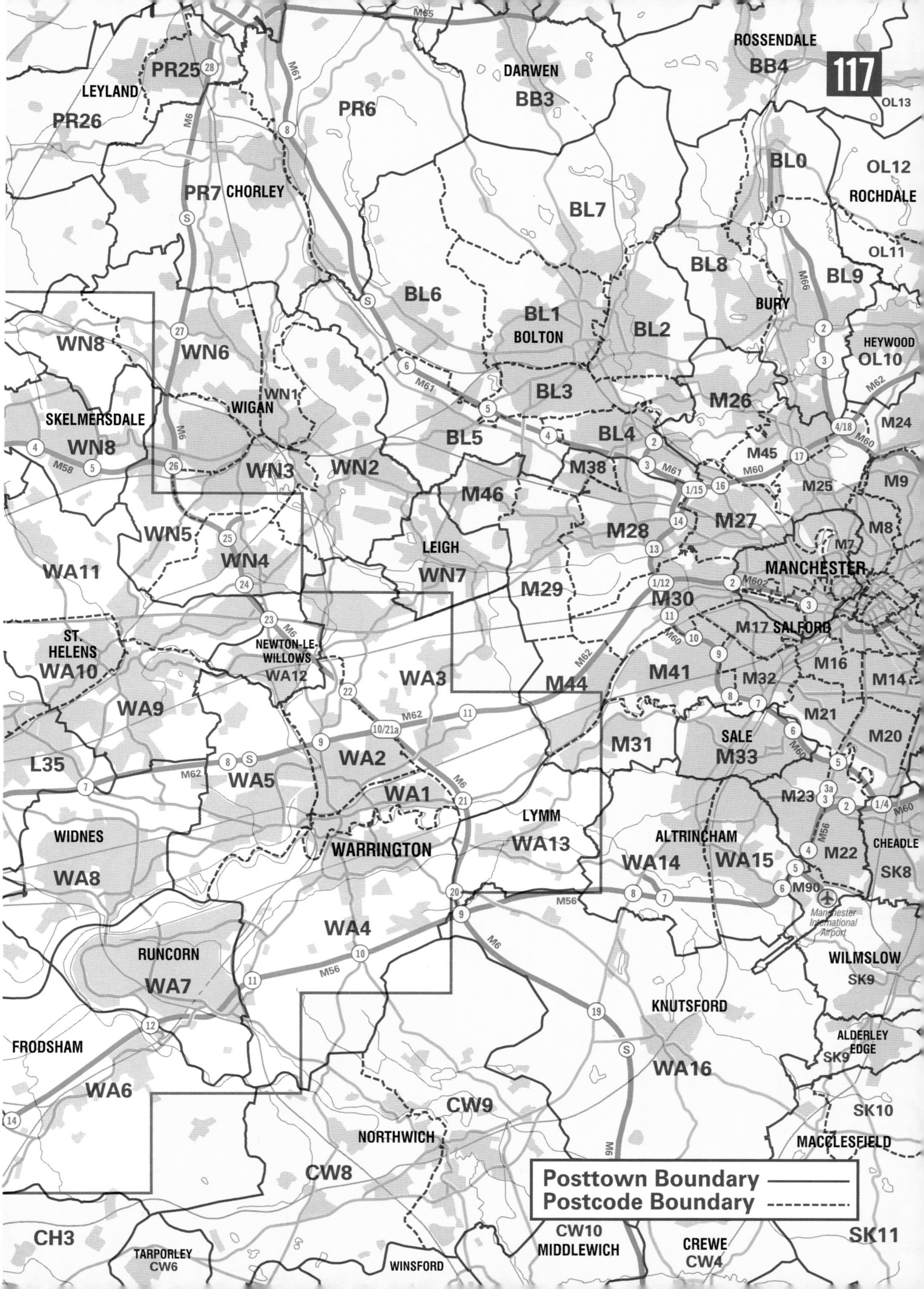

ROSSENDALE
BB4
OL13
DARWEN
BB3
LEYLAND
PR25
PR26
PR6
PR7 CHORLEY
BL0
OL12
ROCHDALE
BL7
OL11
BL8
BL9
BURY
BL6
BL1
BOLTON
BL2
HEYWOOD
OL10
WN8
WN6
WN1
WIGAN
SKELMERSDALE
WN8
BL3
M26
M24
BL5
BL4
M45
WN3
WN2
M38
M25
M9
M46
M27
M8
WN5
WN4
M28
LEIGH
WN7
M7
MANCHESTER
WA11
M29
M30
M602
ST. HELENS
WA10
NEWTON-LE-WILLOWS
WA12
M17 SALFORD
WA3
M41
M16
M44
M32
M14
WA9
M21
L35
WA2
WA5
M31
SALE
M33
M20
WA1
M23
LYMM
WA13
WIDNES
WARRINGTON
ALTRINCHAM
WA14
WA15
M22
CHEADLE
SK8
WA8
M90
Manchester International Airport
WA4
RUNCORN
WA7
WILMSLOW
SK9
KNUTSFORD
FRODSHAM
ALDERLEY EDGE
SK9
WA16
WA6
CW9
SK10
NORTHWICH
MACCLESFIELD
CW8
CH3
CW10
MIDDLEWICH
CREWE
CW4
SK11
TARPORLEY
CW6
WINSFORD
M65
M61
M6
M66
M62
M60
M58
M56
Posttown Boundary
Postcode Boundary

IRISH SEA
LIVERPOOL BAY
Liverpool to Dublin 8hrs.
Liverpool to: Douglas 2hrs. 30mins. (Fast Ferry, Seasonal)
Birkenhead to: Belfast 8hrs. Douglas 4hrs. 15mins. (Seasonal)
SOUTHPORT
Southport Sands
Banks
Tarleton
Marshside
Crossens
Churchtown
High Park
Birkdale
Hillside
Ainsdale
Ainsdale-on-Sea
Woodvale
Formby
Freshfield
FORMBY
Holmeswood
Mere Brow
Holmes
Scarisbrick
Burscough
Burscough Bridge
Halsall
Haskayne
ORMSKIRK
Aughton
Great Altcar
Lydiate
Ince Blundell
Hightown
MAGHULL
Little Crosby
Thornton
CROSBY
Great Crosby
LITHERLAND
Waterloo
Seaforth
Aintree
KIRKBY
Fazakerley
BOOTLE
Walton
Kirkdale
Anfield
Everton
West Derby
WALLASEY
New Brighton
Liscard
Egremont
Seacombe
Leasowe
Moreton
Meols
HOYLAKE
Hilbre Islands
West Kirby
Greasby
Upton
Bidston
BIRKENHEAD
Oxton
Tranmere
Prenton
BEBINGTON
Thingwall
Caldy
Thurstaston
Pensby
Barnston
Brimstage
HESWALL
Gayton
Parkgate
NESTON
Little Neston
Ness
Willaston
Burton
Puddington
Shotwick
Saughall
Sealand
Garden City
CONNAH'S QUAY
Flint (Y Fflint)
Bagillt
Holywell (Treffynnon)
Greenfield (Maes-glas)
Mostyn
Trelogan
Llanasa
Gwespyr
Gronant
Talacre
Point of Ayr
Whitford (Chwitffordd)
Halkyn (Helygain)
Bodfari
LIVERPOOL
Toxteth
Dingle
Aigburth
Garston
Childwall
Allerton
Woolton
HUYTON
Wavertree
Old Swan
Knotty Ash
Port Sunlight
Rock Ferry
New Ferry
Bromborough
Eastham
Hooton
ELLESMERE PORT
Stanlow
Little Sutton
Great Sutton
Ledsham
Capenhurst
Mollington
Backford
Upton
Mickle Trafford
RIVER DEE (AFON DYFRDWY)
RIVER MERSEY
DANGER AREA
A565
A570
A59
A5036
A580
A55
A548
A540
A41
A550
A494
M53
M57
M58
M62
SCALE 1: 205,000
0 1 2 3 Miles
0 1 2 3 4 5 Kilometres

Bretherton
Croston
Sollom
Eccleston
Mawdesley
Heskin Green
Charnock Richard
CHARNOCK RICHARD
Euxton
Buckshaw Village
Hartwood
Bolton Green
Charnock Green
Weld Bank
Cowling
Limbrick
CHORLEY
Wheelton
Brinscall
White Coppice
Anglezarke Resr.
Jubilee Tower
Whittlestone Head
Turton & Entwistle Resr.
Belmont
Belmont Resr.
Edgworth
RAMSBOTTOM
Stubbins
Shuttleworth
Holcombe
Chapeltown
Turton Bottoms
Hawkshaw
Nuttall
Dimple
Egerton
Dunscar
1498 Winter Hill
Rivington
Lever Park
Rivington Moor
Coppull
Coppull Moor
Adlington
BOLTON WEST
Grimeford Village
HORWICH
Holcombe Brook
Summerseat
Greenmount
Walmersley
Tottington
BURY
Walshaw
Elton
Chesham
Starling
Bradshaw
Harwood
Eagley
Bromley Cross
Toppings
Astley Bridge
Horrocks Fold
Barrow Bridge
Ainsworth
Breightmet
Redvales
Black Lane
RADCLIFFE
WHITEFIELD
Little Lever
FARNWORTH
Daubhill
Lostock Junction
Chew Moor
Hunger Hill
BOLTON
Wrightington Bar
High Moor
Robin Hood
Mossy Lea
Bispham Green
Hoscar
Grimshaw Green
Parbold
Dangerous Corner
Newburgh
Lathom
Appley Bridge
Shevington Vale
Shevington Moor
Shevington
STANDISH
Standish Lower Ground
Blackrod
Red Rock
Haigh
Scot Lane End
Aspull
Boar's Head
Marylebone
Crooke
Gathurst
Bank Top
Roby Mill
Holland Lees
Dalton
Ashurst
SKELMERSDALE
ORRELL
Up Holland
Digmoor
Pennylands
WIGAN
New Springs
WESTHOUGHTON
Wingates
Daisy Hill
Over Hulton
HINDLEY
Hindley Green
Scholes
Lamberhead Green
Ince-in-Makerfield
Platt Bridge
Kearsley
Park Lane
PRESTWICH
Clifton
Little Hulton
Walkden
ATHERTON
Tyldesley
Astley
WORSLEY
SWINTON
Pendlebury
ECCLES
Pendleton
SALFORD
Rainford Junction
Park Hill
Rainford
Crawford
Higher End
Far Moor
Longshaw
Billinge
Kings Moss
Crank
Bamfurlong
Bryn Gates
Land Gate
Bickershaw
Abram
Westleigh
Downall Green
Bryn
ASHTON-IN-MAKERFIELD
Simm's Lane End
Garswood
Chadwick Green
Moss Bank
LEIGH
Bedford
Blackmoor
Boothstown
Lowton
Pennington
GOLBORNE
Lowton Common
Glazebury
ST. HELENS
Haresfinch
Blackbrook
HAYDOCK
Eccleston
Gillar's Green
PRESCOT
Lane Head
Kenyon
New Lane End
Twiss Green
Fowley Common
Culcheth
Chat Moss
Davyhulme
Trafford Park
URMSTON
Flixton
Parr
Earlestown
Collins Green
NEWTON-LE-WILLOWS
Vulcan Village
Croft
Peasley Cross
Thatto Heath
Sutton Leach
Rainhill
Burtonwood
BURTONWOOD
Winwick
Glazebrook
Risley
Birchwood
Cadishead
Irlam
Ashton upon Mersey
Carrington
SALE
Whiston
Clock Face
Hollinfare
Partington
Woodhouses
Brooklands
Fearnhead
Orford
Woolston
Paddington
Martinscroft
WARRINGTON
Bold Heath
Great Sankey
Penketh
Barrow's Green
Town End
Cronton
Farnworth
Hough Green
Appleton
Tarbock Green
Warburton
Mossbrow
Broadheath
Timperley
Heatley
Oughtrington
Dunham Woodhouses
Dunham Town
ALTRINCHAM
Bowdon
Hale
Little Bollington
Lymm
Thelwall
Howley
Wilderspool
Cuerdley Cross
Ditton
Simm's Cross
WIDNES
Lower Walton
Grappenhall
POPLAR 2000
Broomedge
Halebarns
Ashley
Manchester Ship Canal
Moore
Higher Walton
Stockton Heath
Appleton Thorn
Hale Bank
West Bank
RUNCORN
Keckwick
Daresbury
Stretton
Swarton Heath
High Legh
Hoo Green
Bucklow Hill
Rostherne
Hatton
Norton
Halton
Weston
Murdishaw
Preston on the Hill
Preston Brook
Higher Whitley
Stockley Farm
Arley
Arley Hall
Bate Heath
Mere
Tatton Park
Mobberley
Frandley
Antrobus
Lower Whitley
Sutton Weaver
Dutton
Aston
Great Budworth
KNUTSFORD
Cross Town
Ollerton
Comberbach
Budworth Mere
Pickmere
Higher Wincham
Tabley
FRODSHAM
Bradley
Overton
Woodhouses
Helsby
CHESTER
Acton Bridge
Little Leigh
Barnton
Anderton
Marston
Wincham
Winnington
Plumley
Marthall
Over Peover
Peover Heath
Smithy Green
Lower Peover
Swan Green
Crowton
Kingsley
Commonside
NORTHWICH
Lostock Gralam
Lostock Green
Rudheath
Hapsford
Alvanley
Birch Hill
Weaverham
Dunham-on-the-Hill
Hatchmere
Norley
Cuddington
Leftwich
Hartford
Higher Shurlach
Lach Dennis
Blackden Heath
Jodrell Bank
Manley
Mouldsworth
Delamere Forest Park
Sandiway
Davenham
Mere Heath
Allostock
Goostrey
Withington Green
Bridge Trafford
Long Green
Little Barrow
Ashton Hayes
Delamere
Oakmere
Whitegate
Moulton
Bostock Green
Puddinglake
Byley
Cranage
Twemlow Green
Lower Withington
M6
M61
M62
M60
M66
M56
M602
A666
A56
A58
A673
A6027
A676
A6
A579
A577
A49
A580
A570
A572
A57
A5209
A50
A533
A556
A557
A562
A537
A538
A560
A5033
A54
A559

Including Streets, Places & Areas, Industrial Estates,
Selected Flats & Walkways, Service Areas, Stations and Selected Places of Interest.

HOW TO USE THIS INDEX

1. Each street name is followed by its Postcode District, then by its Locality abbreviation(s) and then by its map reference;
   e.g. **Abberley Rd.** L25: Hunts X . . . .9H **77** is in the L25 Postcode District and the Hunts Cross Locality and is to be found in square 9H on page **77**.
   The page number is shown in bold type.

2. A strict alphabetical order is followed in which Av., Rd., St., etc. (though abbreviated) are read in full and as part of the street name;
   e.g. **Apple Dell Av.** appears after **Appledale Dr.** but before **Appledore Ct.**

3. Streets and a selection of flats and walkways that cannot be shown on the mapping, appear in the index with the thoroughfare to which they are connected shown in brackets;
   e.g. **Abbotsford M.** *L39: Orm . . . .8D **20** (off Abbotsford)*

4. Addresses that are in more than one part are referred to as not continuous.

5. Places and areas are shown in the index in **BLUE TYPE** and the map reference is to the actual map square in which the town centre or area is located and not to the place name shown on the map; e.g. **AINTREE 8H 35**

6. An example of a selected place of interest is **British Lawnmower Mus. 1A 12**

7. An example of a station is **Aigburth Station (Rail) . . . .8K 75**, also included is **Park & Ride**.
   e.g. **Esplanade (Park & Ride) 8E 6**

8. Service Areas are shown in the index in **BOLD CAPITAL TYPE**; e.g. **BURTONWOOD SERVICE AREA 6K 65**

9. Map references for entries that appear on large scale pages **4** & **5** are shown first, with small scale map references shown in brackets; e.g. **Bath St.** L3: Liv 3B **4** (7A **58**)

GENERAL ABBREVIATIONS

All. : Alley
App. : Approach
Arc. : Arcade
Av. : Avenue
Bk. : Back
Blvd. : Boulevard
Bri. : Bridge
B'way. : Broadway
Bldg. : Building
Bldgs. : Buildings
Bungs. : Bungalows
Bus. : Business
C'way. : Causeway
Cen. : Centre
Chu. : Church
Circ. : Circle
Cl. : Close
Comn. : Common
Cnr. : Corner
Cott. : Cottage
Cotts. : Cottages
Ct. : Court
Cres. : Crescent
Cft. : Croft
Dr. : Drive
E. : East
Ent. : Enterprise
Est. : Estate
Fld. : Field
Flds. : Fields
Gdn. : Garden
Gdns. : Gardens
Gth. : Garth
Ga. : Gate
Gt. : Great
Grn. : Green
Gro. : Grove
Hgts. : Heights
Ho. : House
Ho's. : Houses
Ind. : Industrial
Info. : Information
Intl. : International
Junc. : Junction
La. : Lane
Lit. : Little
Lwr. : Lower
Mnr. : Manor
Mans. : Mansions
Mkt. : Market
Mdw. : Meadow
Mdws. : Meadows
M. : Mews
Mt. : Mount
Mus. : Museum
Nth. : North
Pde. : Parade
Pk. : Park
Pas. : Passage
Pav. : Pavilion
Pl. : Place
Pct. : Precinct
Prom. : Promenade
Ri. : Rise
Rd. : Road
Rdbt. : Roundabout
Shop. : Shopping
Sth. : South
Sq. : Square
Sta. : Station
St. : Street
Ter. : Terrace
Twr. : Tower
Trad. : Trading
Up. : Upper
Va. : Vale
Vw. : View
Vs. : Villas
Vis. : Visitors
Wlk. : Walk
W. : West
Yd. : Yard

LOCALITY ABBREVIATIONS

Act B : **Acton Bridge**
Aig : **Aigburth**
Ains : **Ainsdale**
Ain : **Aintree**
Aller : **Allerton**
Alv : **Alvanley**
Ant : **Antrobus**
App : **Appleton**
App T : **Appleton Thorn**
Appl B : **Appley Bridge**
Ash M : **Ashton-in-Makerfield**
Ast : **Astmoor**
Aston : **Aston**
Augh : **Aughton**
Back : **Backford**
Bam : **Bamfurlong**
Banks : **Banks**
Barn : **Barnston**
Bart : **Barton**
Beb : **Bebington**
Beech : **Beechwood**
Bic : **Bickerstaffe**
Bid : **Bidston**
Bil : **Billinge**
Birchw : **Birchwood**
Birkd : **Birkdale**
Birke : **Birkenhead**
Blun : **Blundellsands**
Bold : **Bold**
Bold H : **Bold Heath**
Boot : **Bootle**
Bri T : **Bridge Trafford**
Brim : **Brimstage**
Broad G : **Broad Green**
Brom : **Bromborough**
Brook : **Brookvale**
Burs : **Burscough**
Burt : **Burton**
Burtw : **Burtonwood**
Cad : **Cadishead**
Caldy : **Caldy**
Call : **Callands**
Cap : **Capenhurst**
Carr : **Carrington**
Cas : **Castlefields**
Chil T : **Childer Thornton**
Child : **Childwall**
Chor B : **Chorlton-by-Backford**
Clau : **Claughton**
Clftn : **Clifton**
Clock F : **Clock Face**
Coll G : **Collins Green**
Crank : **Crank**
Croft : **Croft**
Cron : **Cronton**
Crosb : **Crosby**
Crou : **Croughton**
Crow : **Crowton**
Crox : **Croxteth**
Cuerd : **Cuerdley**
Cul : **Culcheth**
Dalt : **Dalton**
Dares : **Daresbury**
Down : **Downholland**
Dun M : **Dunham Massey**
Dun H : **Dunham-on-the-Hill**
Dunk : **Dunkirk**
Dutt : **Dutton**
East : **Eastham**
Eccl : **Eccleston**
Eccl P : **Eccleston Park**
Ell P : **Ellesmere Port**
Elt : **Elton**
Faz : **Fazakerley**
Fearn : **Fearnhead**
Ford : **Ford**
Form : **Formby**
Frank : **Frankby**
Frod : **Frodsham**
Garst : **Garston**
Garsw : **Garswood**
Gate : **Gateacre**
Glaz : **Glazebrook**
G'bury : **Glazebury**
Golb : **Golborne**
Grap : **Grappenhall**
Gras : **Grassendale**
Grea : **Greasby**
Gt Alt : **Great Altcar**
Gt San : **Great Sankey**
Gt Sut : **Great Sutton**
Hale : **Hale**
Hale B : **Hale Bank**
Halew : **Halewood**
Hals : **Halsall**
Halt : **Halton**
Hap : **Hapsford**
Hatt : **Hatton**
Hay : **Haydock**
Hel : **Helsby**
Hesk B : **Hesketh Bank**
Hesw : **Heswall**
Hghr B : **Higher Bebington**
Hghr Wal : **Higher Walton**
Hghr Whi : **Higher Whitley**
High L : **High Legh**
Hight : **Hightown**
Holm : **Holmeswood**
Hoot : **Hooton**
Hoy : **Hoylake**
Hunts X : **Hunts Cross**
Huy : **Huyton**
Ince : **Ince**
Ince B : **Ince Blundell**
Irby : **Irby**
Irlam : **Irlam**
Kingsl : **Kingsley**
Kings M : **Kings Moss**
Kingsw : **Kingswood**
Kirkb : **Kirkby**
Kirkd : **Kirkdale**
Knott A : **Knotty Ash**
Know : **Knowsley**
Know I : **Knowsley Industrial Park**
Know P : **Knowsley Park**
Lath : **Lathom**
Lea B : **Lea-by-Backford**
Leas : **Leasowe**
Led : **Ledsham**
Leigh : **Leigh**
Lith : **Litherland**
Lit Ba : **Little Barrow**
Lit Bo : **Little Bollington**
Lit C : **Little Crosby**
Lit N : **Little Neston**
Lit Stan : **Little Stanney**
Lit Sut : **Little Sutton**
Liv : **Liverpool**
Lwr S : **Lower Stretton**
Lwr W : **Lower Whitley**
Low : **Lowton**
Lyd : **Lydiate**
Lymm : **Lymm**
Mag : **Maghull**
Manl : **Manley**
Manl C : **Manley Common**
Manor P : **Manor Park**
Mell : **Melling**
Meols : **Meols**
Mere B : **Mere Brow**
Mick T : **Mickle Trafford**
Mill : **Millington**
Moll : **Mollington**
Moore : **Moore**
More : **Moreton**
Moss H : **Mossley Hill**
Moul : **Mouldsworth**
Murd : **Murdishaw**
Ness : **Ness**
Nest : **Neston**
N'ley : **Netherley**
N'ton : **Netherton**
New B : **New Brighton**
Newb : **Newburgh**
New F : **New Ferry**
Newt : **Newton**
Newt W : **Newton-le-Willows**
Noct : **Noctorum**
Nor B : **Norcott Brook**
Nor : **Norley**
Norr G : **Norris Green**
Nort : **Norton**
Old H : **Old Hall**
Orm : **Ormskirk**
Orr : **Orrell**
Oxton : **Oxton**
Padd : **Paddington**
Padg : **Padgate**
Pal F : **Palace Fields**
Parb : **Parbold**
Park : **Parkgate**
Part : **Partington**
Penk : **Penketh**
Pens : **Pensby**
Pict : **Picton**
Platt B : **Platt Bridge**
Port S : **Port Sunlight**
Pren : **Prenton**
Presc : **Prescot**
Pres B : **Preston Brook**
Pres H : **Preston on the Hill**
Pudd : **Puddington**
Raby : **Raby**
Raby M : **Raby Mere**
Rainf : **Rainford**
Rainh : **Rainhill**
Ris : **Risley**
Rix : **Rixton**
Roby : **Roby**
Roby M : **Roby Mill**
Rock F : **Rock Ferry**
Ruf : **Rufford**
Run : **Runcorn**
St H : **St Helens**
Sau : **Saughall**
Scar : **Scarisbrick**
Sea : **Seaforth**
Seft : **Sefton**
Shev : **Shevington**
Shot : **Shotwick**
Sim : **Simonswood**
Skel : **Skelmersdale**

South : **Southport**
Speke : **Speke**
Spit : **Spital**
Stoak : **Stoak**
Stockb V : **Stockbridge Village**
Stockt H : **Stockton Heath**
Store : **Storeton**
Stret : **Stretton**
Sut L : **Sutton Leach**
Sut M : **Sutton Manor**
Sut W : **Sutton Weaver**
Tar G : **Tarbock Green**
Tarl : **Tarleton**
Thel : **Thelwall**
Thing : **Thingwall**
Thorn : **Thornton**
Thorn H : **Thornton Hough**
Thorn M : **Thornton-le-Moors**
Thurs : **Thurstaston**
Tran : **Tranmere**
Uph : **Upholland**
Upton : **Upton**
Wall : **Wallasey**
Walt : **Walton**
Warb : **Warburton**
Warr : **Warrington**
Water : **Waterloo**
Wav : **Wavertree**
Wer : **Wervin**
W Der : **West Derby**
W Kir : **West Kirby**
Westb : **Westbrook**
Westh : **Westhead**
West : **Weston**
West P : **Weston Point**
Westy : **Westy**
Whis : **Whiston**
Whit : **Whitby**
Wid : **Widnes**
Wigan : **Wigan**
Will : **Willaston**
Wim T : **Wimbolds Trafford**
Windle : **Windle**
Wind H : **Windmill Hill**
Wins : **Winstanley**
Win : **Winwick**
Woodb : **Woodbank**
Woodc : **Woodchurch**
Wools : **Woolston**
Woolt : **Woolton**
Wright : **Wrightington**

20 Forthlin Road (Childhood Home of Paul McCartney) 7A 76

A

Abacus Rd. L13: Liv 5M 59
Abberley Cl. WA10: St H 7J 49
Abberley Rd. L25: Hunts X 9H 77
Abberton Pk. L30: N'ton 6F 34
Abbey Cl. CH41: Birke 3M 73
L33: Kirkb 9D 36
L37: Form 2H 25
WA3: Croft 1H 67
WA8: Wid 8F 78
WN8: Uph 5M 31
Abbey Ct. CH65: Ell P 8A 104
L25: Woolt 6F 76
Abbey Dale WN6: Appl B 6N 23
Abbeydale L40: Burs 2K 21
Abbey Farm Caravan Pk. L40: Lath 5G 21
Abbeyfield Dr. L12: Crox 8B 46
Abbeyfield Ho. CH65: Whit 2M 111
Abbey Fold L40: Burs 9H 15
Abbey Gdns. PR8: Birkd 2N 11
Abbeygate Apartments L15: Wav 1L 75
Abbey Hey WA7: Nort 7E 96
Abbey La. L40: Burs, Lath 4G 20
Abbey La. Ind. Est. L40: Burs 4G 21
Abbey M. L8: Liv 3G 74
Abbeymill Ct. L15: Wav 1M 75
Abbey Rd. CH48: W Kir 6C 70
L6: Liv 3H 59
WA3: Low 2K 53
WA8: Wid 8E 78
WA10: St H 3G 49
WA11: Hay 3G 51
Abbeystead WN8: Skel 5E 30
Abbeystead Av. L30: N'ton 1F 44
Abbeystead Rd. L15: Wav 9N 59
Abbey St. CH41: Birke 3M 73
Abbeyvale Dr. L25: Gate 2G 76
Abbey Vw. L16: Child 1C 76
Abbeyway Nth. WA11: Hay 3J 51
Abbeyway Sth. WA11: Hay 4J 51
Abbeywood WN8: Skel 6F 30
Abbeywood Gro. L35: Whis 7C 62
Abbot Cl. CH43: Bid 2C 72
Abbotsbury Way L12: Crox 7C 46
Abbots Bus. Pk. WA7: Pres B 1G 109
Abbots Cl. L37: Form 3G 25
Abbots Dr. CH63: Beb 2M 89
Abbotsfield Cl. WA4: App 1F 98
Abbotsfield Rd. WA9: Bold, St H 3A 64
(not continuous)
Abbotsfield Rd. Ind. Est. WA9: St H 3A 64
Abbotsford L39: Orm 8D 20
Abbotsford Cl. WA3: Low 1E 52
Abbotsford Ct. L23: Blun 8J 33
Abbotsford Gdns. L23: Crosb 8J 33
Abbotsford M. *L39: Orm* 8D 20
(off Abbotsford)
Abbotsford Rd. L11: Norr G 8L 45
L23: Blun 8J 33
Abbotsford St. CH44: Wall 7L 57
Abbots Hall Av. WA9: Clock F 6N 63
Abbots M. CH65: Ell P 8N 103
Abbots Pk. WA7: Pres B 1G 108
Abbots Quay CH41: Birke 2N 73
Abbots Way CH48: W Kir 5D 70
CH64: Nest 5E 100
L37: Form 3G 25
WN5: Bil 8N 39
Abbott Dr. L20: Boot 5D 44
Abbotts Cl. L18: Moss H 5N 75
WA7: Run 7K 95
Abbottshey Av. L18: Moss H 5N 75
Abdale Rd. L11: Norr G 7L 45
Abercrombie Rd. L33: Know I 3F 46
Abercromby Sq. L7: Liv 6L 5 (9E 58)
Aberdale Rd. L13: Liv 6N 59
Aberdare Cl. WA5: Call 8N 65
Aberdeen St. CH41: Birke 1J 73
Aberford Av. CH45: Wall 4E 56
Abergele Rd. L13: Liv 7L 59
Aber St. L6: Liv 1M 5 (6F 58)
Abingdon Av. WA1: Wools 1M 83
Abingdon Gro. L4: Walt 8H 45
L26: Halew 7L 77
Abingdon Rd. CH49: Grea 5J 71
L4: Walt 8H 45
Abinger Rd. WN4: Garsw 7F 40
Abington Dr. PR9: Banks 2E 8
Abington Wlk. WA7: Brook 1E 108
Abney Cl. L7: Liv 9G 59
Abney M. WA1: Warr 3F 82
Aboyne Cl. L9: Walt 6F 44
Abrams Fold PR9: Banks 2D 8
Abrams Grn. PR9: Banks 2D 8
Abram St. L5: Liv 4D 58
Abstone Cl. WA1: Wools 1K 83
Abyssinia Cl. L15: Wav 1K 75
Acacia Av. L36: Huy 8H 61
WA1: Wools 9L 67
WA8: Wid 5L 79
Acacia Cl. CH2: Elt 2N 113
CH49: Grea 6K 71
Acacia Dr. CH66: Gt Sut 4L 111
Acacia Gro. CH44: Wall 7L 57
CH48: W Kir 6B 70
L9: Ain 4G 44
WA7: Run 7M 95
WA10: Eccl 6D 48
Acacia St. WA12: Newt W 6H 51
Academy, The *PR9: South* 7H 7
(off Manchester Rd.)
Academy Bus. Pk. L33: Know I 1F 46
Academy Pl. WA1: Warr 3C 82
Academy Sports Cen. 1N 111
Academy St. WA1: Warr 3C 82
Academy Way WA1: Warr 3C 82
Acanthus Rd. L13: Liv 5M 59
Access Rd. L12: W Der 2B 60
Acer Leigh L17: Aig 6J 75
Acheson Rd. L13: Liv 3K 59
Achilles Av. WA2: Warr 7C 66
Achilles Ct. WA7: Cas 5C 96
Ackerley Cl. WA2: Fearn 6G 67
Ackers Hall Av. L14: Knott A 5D 60
Ackers La. L23: Lit C 4J 33
WA4: Stockt H 6F 82
WA10: St H 6F 48
Ackers Rd. CH49: Woodc 6C 72
WA4: Stockt H 7F 82
Ackers St. L34: Presc 3A 62
Acland Rd. CH44: Wall 5H 57
Aconbury Cl. L11: Norr G 7L 45
Aconbury Pl. L11: Norr G 7L 45
Acorn Bus. Cen. L33: Know I 9F 36
Acorn Cl. CH63: Hghr B 1K 89
WA9: Clock F 5M 63
Acorn Ct. L8: Liv 2E 74
Acorn Dr. CH65: Whit 4N 111
Acornfield Cl. L33: Know I 2G 47
Acornfield Plantation Local Nature Reserve 2H 47
Acornfield Rd. L33: Know I 1H 47
Acorns, The L39: Augh 1A 28
Acorn St. WA12: Newt W 7L 51
Acorn Venture 7H 37
Acorn Way L20: Boot 5C 44
A Court WN4: Ash M 9K 41
Acrefield WN8: Newb 4D 22
Acrefield Ct. CH42: Tran 7H 73
Acrefield Pk. L25: Woolt 5E 76
Acrefield Rd. CH42: Tran 7H 73
L25: Woolt 5E 76
WA8: Wid 7E 78
Acregate WN8: Skel 5F 30
Acre Gro. L26: Halew 1L 93
Acre Gro. PR8: Birkd 2M 11
Acre La. CH60: Hesw 6C 88
CH62: Brom 7B 90
CH63: Brom 8B 90
Acre Rd. CH66: Gt Sut 9J 103
Acres Cl. L25: Gate 1E 76
Acresfield *L13: Liv* 7N 59
(off Broad Grn. Rd.)
Acresgate Ct. L25: Gate 3E 76
Acres La. L31: Lyd 4D 26
L37: Gt Alt 4L 25
L39: Down 4D 26
Acres Rd. CH47: Meols 1G 70
CH63: Beb 1M 89
Acreville Rd. CH63: Beb 2M 89
Acton Av. WA4: App 4E 98
Acton Cl. WA11: Hay 4E 50
Acton Gro. L6: Liv 3H 59
Acton La. CH46: More 1K 71
Acton Rake *L30: N'ton* 6C 34
(off Higher End Pk.)
Acton Rd. CH42: Rock F 7N 73
L32: Kirkb 9A 36
WA5: Burtw 3G 64
Acton Way L7: Liv 9H 59
Acuba Gro. CH42: Tran 4L 73
Acuba Rd. L15: Wav 8A 60
Adair Pl. L13: Liv 2K 59
Adair Rd. L13: Liv 2K 59
Adam Av. CH66: Gt Sut 1H 111
(not continuous)
Adam Cl. CH66: Gt Sut 1J 111
L19: Garst 2A 92
Adams Cl. WA12: Newt W 8M 51
Adamson Cl. WA4: Westy 5H 83
Adamson Ct. WA4: Grap 6J 83
Adamson Ho. WA7: Run 4H 95
Adamson St. L7: Liv 7J 59
WA4: Warr 5C 82
WN4: Ash M 8J 41
Adam St. L5: Liv 3E 58
WA2: Warr 1D 82
Adaston Av. CH62: East 2E 102
Adcote Cl. L14: Knott A 6D 60
Adcote Rd. L14: Knott A 6D 60
Addenbrook Cl. CH43: Bid 2C 72
Addenbrooke Dr. L24: Speke 1F 92
Adderley Cl. WA7: Run 6M 95
Adderley St. L7: Liv 7G 59
Addingham Av. WA8: Wid 9F 78
Addingham Rd. L18: Moss H 3N 75
Addington St. CH44: Wall 6K 57
Addison Cl. L32: Kirkb 2B 46
Addison Sq. WA8: Wid 7K 79
Addison St. L3: Liv 2F 4 (6C 58)
L20: Boot 5N 43
Addison Way L3: Liv 2F 4 (6C 58)
Adelaide Av. WA9: St H 2H 63
Adelaide Ct. WA8: Wid 9K 79
Adelaide Pl. L5: Liv 5D 58
Adelaide Rd. CH42: Tran 4J 73
L7: Liv 4N 5 (7G 58)
(not continuous)
L21: Sea 3M 43
Adelaide St. CH44: Wall 6H 57
Adelaide Ter. L22: Water 1J 43
Adela Rd. WA7: Run 5J 95
Adele Thompson Dr. L8: Liv 9N 5 (1F 74)
Adelphi St. CH41: Birke 2L 73
Adey Rd. WA13: Lymm 3G 85
Adfalent La. CH64: Will 7N 101
Adlam Cres. L9: Faz 3K 45
Adlam Rd. L9: Faz 3K 45
L10: Faz 3K 45
Adler Way L3: Liv 5E 74
Adlington Ct. WA3: Ris 3N 67
(not continuous)
Adlington Ho. L3: Liv 2F 4
Adlington Rd. WA7: Wind H 5F 96
Adlington St. L3: Liv 2F 4
Admin Rd. L33: Know I 2G 46
Admiral Gro. *L8: Liv* 3F 74
(off High Pk. St.)
Admirals Quay L23: Blun 7G 33
Admirals Rd. WA3: Birchw 5M 67
Admirals Sq. WA3: Birchw 6N 67
Admiral St. L8: Liv 3F 74
Admiralty Cl. L40: Burs 3F 20
Admiral Way L30: Boot 2D 44
Adrian's Way L32: Kirkb 9C 36
Adshead Rd. L13: Liv 2K 59
Adstone Rd. L25: Gate 3G 77
Adswood Rd. L36: Huy 6J 61
Adwell Cl. WA3: Low 2H 53
Aerial Extreme Knowsley 2M 61
Aerodrome, The L24: Speke 3C 92
Africander Rd. WA11: St H 2K 49
Afton WA8: Wid 6D 78
Agar Rd. L11: Norr G 2L 59
Agate St. L5: Liv 4F 58
AGDEN BROW 7L 85
Agden Brow WA13: Lymm 8K 85
Agden Brow Pk. WA13: Lymm 7K 85
Agden La. WA13: Lymm 8K 85 & 7L 85
WA14: Mill 8K 85
WA16: Lymm 8K 85
Agden Pk. La. WA13: Lymm 8K 85
Agincourt Rd. L12: W Der 4A 60
Agnes Gro. CH44: Wall 4J 57
Agnes Jones Ho. L8: Liv 8L 5 (9E 58)
Agnes Rd. CH42: Tran 5L 73
L23: Blun 8J 33
Agnes St. WA9: Clock F 6M 63
Agnes Way L7: Liv 8G 59
Agulnek Ct. L18: Moss H 5L 75
Aiden Long Gro. L34: Know P 3J 61
AIGBURTH 8K 75
Aigburth Dr. L17: Aig 3H 75
Aigburth Gro. CH46: More 9L 55
Aigburth Hall Av. L19: Aig 8L 75
Aigburth Hall Rd. L19: Aig 8M 75
Aigburth Ho. L17: Aig 5K 75
Aigburth Rd. L17: Aig 4G 74
L19: Aig, Gras 7K 75
Aigburth Station (Rail) 8K 75
Aigburth St. L7: Liv 9G 58
AIGBURTH VALE 5K 75
Aigburth Va. L17: Aig 6J 75
(not continuous)
L18: Moss H 5K 75
Ailsa Rd. CH45: Wall 4G 57
Aindow Ct. PR8: Birkd 3M 11
Ainley Cl. WA7: Brook 1C 108
Ainscough Rd. WA3: Birchw 6M 67
AINSDALE 9J 11
Ainsdale & Birkdale Hills Local Nature Reserve 7G 10
Ainsdale Cl. CH61: Thing 2A 88
CH63: Brom 1B 102
L10: Faz 2L 45
WA5: Penk 4H 81
Ainsdale Discovery Cen. 8F 10
AINSDALE-ON-SEA 8F 10
Ainsdale Rd. L20: Boot 5C 44
Ainsdale Sand Dunes National Nature Reserve 2E 16
Ainsdale Station (Rail) 9J 11
Ainsworth Av. CH46: More 1K 71
Ainsworth La. L34: Know 4F 46
Ainsworth Rd. WA10: St H 5G 49
Ainsworth St. L3: Liv 5J 5 (8D 58)
AINTREE 8H 35
Aintree Cl. CH46: Leas 6N 55
Aintree Ct. L10: Ain 8H 35
Aintree Cres. PR8: South 2E 12
Aintree Golf Course 1J 45
Aintree Gro. CH66: Gt Sut 2J 111
Aintree La. L10: Ain 8H 35
L10: Faz 1L 45
Aintree Motor Circuit 2J 45
Aintree Racecourse 1H 45
Aintree Racecourse Retail & Business Pk.
L9: Ain 1G 45
Aintree Rd. L9: Ain 4J 45
L20: Boot 6C 44
Aintree Station (Rail) 2G 44
Aintree Visitor Centre & Grand National Experience 1G 45
Aintree Way L9: Ain 9H 35
Airdale Cl. CH43: Bid 2C 72
Airdale Rd. L15: Wav 2L 75
Airdrie Cl. CH62: East 3C 102
Aire WA8: Wid 6E 78
Aire Cl. CH65: Ell P 7M 103
Airedale Cl. WA5: Gt San 1H 81
Airegate L31: Mag 1G 35
Airlie Gro. L13: Liv 3J 59
Airlie Rd. CH47: Hoy 2C 70
Aisthorpe Gro. L31: Mag 4J 35
Ajax Av. WA2: Warr 7C 66
Akbar, The CH60: Hesw 5K 87
A K Business Pk. PR9: South 9M 7
Akenside Ct. L20: Boot 4N 43
Akenside St. L20: Boot 4N 43
Alabama Way CH41: Birke 2M 73
Alamein Cres. WA2: Warr 1C 82
Alamein Rd. L36: Huy 5H 61
Alan's Way L33: Kirkb 6C 36
Alaska M. WA5: Gt San 1J 81
Alastair Cres. CH43: Pren 7F 72
Alban Retail Pk. WA2: Warr 7B 66
Alban Rd. L16: Child 9B 60
Albany, The L3: Liv 4D 4
Albany Av. L34: Eccl P 2C 62
Albany Cres. WA13: Lymm 4D 84
Albany Gdns. CH66: Lit Sut 7H 103
Albany Gro. WA13: Lymm 4C 84
Albany Rd. CH42: Rock F 6L 73
L7: Liv 4N 5 (7F 58)
L9: Ain 3G 44
L13: Liv 5M 59
L34: Presc 3B 62
PR9: South 6H 7
WA13: Lymm 5C 84
Albany Ter. WA7: Run 5K 95
Albemarle Rd. CH44: Wall 6K 57
Alberta Gro. L34: Presc 4K 61
Albert Ct. PR9: South 6J 7
WA8: Wid 7M 79
(off Albert Rd.)
Albert Dock L3: Liv 8D 4 (9B 58)
Albert Dock Vis. Cen. 8D 4 (9B 58)
Albert Dr. CH64: Nest 6D 100
L9: Walt 4E 44
WA5: Gt San 2F 80

Albert Edward Rd. L7: Liv 4N 5 (7F 58)
(not continuous)
Albert Gro. L15: Wav 9M 59
L23: Crosb 7K 33
Albert Pk. L17: Aig 3G 75
Albert Pl. PR9: South 7G 6
Albert Rd. CH42: Tran 4J 73
CH47: Hoy 2C 70
CH48: W Kir 7B 70
L13: Liv 3J 59
L22: Water 1K 43
L37: Form 4B 24
L40: Ruf 3L 15
PR9: South 7H 7
WA4: Grap 6H 83
WA8: Wid 8L 79
Albert Row WA6: Frod 5L 107
Albert Schweitzer Av. L30: N'ton 8E 34
Albert Sq. WA8: Wid 8L 79
Albert St. CH45: New B 9J 43
L7: Liv 5N 5 (8F 58)
M44: Cad 3L 69
WA7: Run 5K 95
WA10: St H 5K 49
WN4: Ash M 8K 41
Albert Ter. PR8: Birkd 1N 11
WA5: Coll G 9G 50
Albinson Wlk. M31: Part 6N 69
Albion Pl. CH45: New B 1H 57
Albion St. CH41: Birke 2M 73
(not continuous)
CH45: New B 1G 56
L5: Liv 3D 58
WA10: St H 7H 49
(not continuous)
Albourne Rd. L32: Kirkb 2E 46
Albright Rd. WA8: Wid 1D 94
Albury Cl. L12: Crox 8D 46
WA5: Warr 1A 82
WA11: Hay 3E 50
Albury Rd. L32: Kirkb 3D 46
Alcester Rd. L12: W Der 3A 60
Alchemy Way L33: Know I 3F 46
Alcock St. WA7: Run 4K 95
Alconbury Cl. WA5: Gt San 2L 81
Alcott Pl. WA2: Win 3B 66
Aldams Gro. L4: Kirkd 9D 44
Aldbourne Av. L25: Woolt 3C 76
Aldbourne Cl. L25: Woolt 4C 76
Aldcliffe WA3: Low 2G 52
Alder Av. L36: Huy 9L 61
WA8: Wid 5K 79
WN4: Ash M 6H 41
WN5: Bil 6N 39
Alderbank Rd. WA5: Gt San 2J 81
Alderbrook Dr. WN8: Parb 3F 22
Alder Cl. L34: Presc 3C 62
Alder Cres. L32: Kirkb 8B 36
WA2: Warr 9D 66
Alderdale Av. PR8: Ains 9G 11
Alder Dr. CH66: Gt Sut 4L 111
Alderfield Dr. L24: Speke 3K 93
Alder Gro. L22: Water 9K 33
Alder Hey Rd. WA10: St H 7F 48
Alder La. L34: Know 7F 46
(not continuous)
L39: Bart 6L 17
WA2: Warr 9C 66
WA5: Burtw 2J 65
WA6: Frod 3G 107
WA8: Cron 4C 78
WA11: Crank 7J 39
WN8: Parb 4F 22
Alder Lee Cl. WN3: Wins 1F 40
Alderlee Pk. PR8: South 4F 12
Alderley WN8: Skel 6F 30
Alderley Av. CH41: Birke 1F 72
WA3: Low 3E 52
Alderley Cl. WN5: Bil 6A 40
Alderley Rd. CH44: Wall 6H 57
CH47: Hoy 1C 70
WA4: Thel 5L 83
Alderman Rd. L24: Speke 1G 92
Alderney Cl. CH65: Ell P 4A 112
Alderney Rd. L5: Liv 4C 58
Alder Rd. CH63: Hghr B 3K 89
L12: W Der 5N 59
L34: Presc 3C 62
WA1: Wools 1L 83
WA3: Low 2G 53
Alder Root Golf Course 2M 65
Alder Root La. WA2: Win 2M 65
Aldersey Cl. WA7: Wind H 6F 96
Aldersey St. L3: Liv 1G 4 (6C 58)
Aldersgate CH42: Rock F 6M 73
Aldersgate Av. WA7: Murd 8F 96
Aldersgate Dr. L26: Halew 1L 93
Alderson Cres. L37: Form 9F 16
Alderson Rd. L15: Wav 1J 75
Alder St. WA12: Newt W 8L 51
Alderton Cl. L26: Halew 9L 77
Alderton Dr. WN4: Ash M 8H 41
Alderville Rd. L4: Walt 8H 45
Alderwood Av. L24: Speke 4J 93
Alderwood Ct. WA8: Wid 4H 79
Alderwood Lodge *L24: Speke 4L 93*
(off East Mains)
Aldewood Cl. WA3: Birchw 3B 68
Aldford Cl. CH43: Oxton 6E 72
CH63: Brom 9A 90
Aldford Rd. L32: Kirkb 3C 46
Aldgate CH65: Ell P 9M 103
Aldridge Cl. L12: Crox 7C 46
Aldridge Dr. WA5: Burtw 2H 65
Aldrins La. L30: N'ton 7E 34
Aldwark Rd. L14: Knott A 5E 60
Aldwych Rd. L12: W Der 3A 60
Aldwyn Cl. WN3: Wins 2F 40
Aldykes L31: Mag 3K 35
Alexander Cl. L40: Burs 2K 21
Alexander Dr. CH61: Pens 4M 87
L31: Lyd 9J 27
WA8: Wid 8G 78
Alexander Fleming Av. L30: N'ton 7E 34
Alexander Grn. L36: Huy 5J 61
Alexander Ho. L21: Sea 3M 43
L34: Presc 2A 62
(off Rio Ct.)
Alexander Wlk. *L4: Walt 1E 58*
(off Florence St.)
Alexander Way *L8: Liv 4E 74*
(off Park Hill Rd.)
Alexander Wharf *L31: Mag 2H 35*
(off Damfield La.)
Alexandra B'way. PR9: South 7J 7
Alexandra Cl. L6: Liv 6G 58
WN8: Skel 3B 30
Alexandra Ct. *CH45: New B 1G 56*
(off Alexandra Rd.)
L23: Crosb 7K 33
M31: Part 6M 69
(off Bailey La.)
PR9: South 7J 7
WA9: St H 1G 63
(off Carnarvon St.)
Alexandra Dr. CH42: Rock F 7L 73
L17: Aig 4G 75
L20: Boot 4D 44
WA10: St H 9G 49
(not continuous)
Alexandra Grn. L17: Aig 4G 75
Alexandra Gro. L26: Halew 1K 93
M44: Irlam 1M 69
WA7: Run 6M 95
Alexandra Ho. L17: Aig 4G 74
Alexandra Ind. Est. WA8: Wid 9J 79
Alexandra M. *L39: Orm 7C 20*
(off Courtfield)
PR9: South 7H 7
WA6: Frod 5L 107
Alexandra Mt. L21: Lith 2A 44
Alexandra Pk. L17: Aig 5G 75
Alexandra Rd. CH43: Oxton 3J 73
CH45: New B 1G 56
CH48: W Kir 7B 70
L7: Liv 9H 59
L13: Liv 7M 59
L19: Garst 9A 76
L22: Water 2L 43
L23: Crosb 7K 33
L37: Form 4A 24
L40: Burs 1H 21
PR9: South 6H 7
WA4: Grap 6G 83
WA4: Stockt H 7E 82
WN4: Ash M 7K 41
Alexandra St. CH65: Ell P 7A 104
WA1: Warr 1F 82
WA8: Wid 9K 79
WA10: St H 9G 49
Alexandra Ter. *L8: Liv 1E 74*
(off Princes Rd.)
Alexandra Vs. *L21: Lith 2A 44*
(off Alexandra Mt.)
Alex Cl. L8: Liv 2E 74
Alfonso Rd. L4: Kirkd 1C 58
Alford Av. WA9: Sut M 5L 63
Alforde St. WA8: Wid 9K 79
(not continuous)
Alford St. L7: Liv 7K 59
Alfred Cl. WA8: Wid 8L 79
Alfred M. L1: Liv 9H 5 (1D 74)
Alfred Rd. CH43: Oxton 3J 73
CH44: Wall 8L 57
WA3: Low 2H 53
WA11: Hay 3H 51
Alfred Stocks Ct. *L8: Liv 5F 74*
(off Turner Cl.)
Alfred St. L15: Wav 9J 59
M44: Cad 3L 69
(off Dean Rd.)
WA8: Wid 8L 79
WA10: St H 6L 49
WA11: Rainf 4C 38
WA12: Newt W 7N 51
Alfriston Rd. L12: W Der 3A 60
Algernon St. WA1: Warr 2E 82
WA4: Stockt H 7D 82
WA7: Run 4J 95
Alice Ct. WA8: Wid 3K 95
Alice St. WA9: St H 1A 64
Alicia Wlk. L10: Faz 3N 45
Alison Av. CH42: Rock F 5M 73
Alison Pl. L13: Liv 2K 59
Alison Rd. L13: Liv 2K 59
Alistair Dr. CH63: Brom 1B 102
Allangate Cl. CH49: Grea 6K 71
Allangate Rd. L19: Gras 8N 75
Allan Rd. WA11: St H 3M 49
Allans Cl. CH64: Nest 8E 100
Allans Mdw. CH64: Nest 8E 100
Allanson St. WA9: St H 7N 49
Allcard St. WA5: Warr 1A 82
Allcot Av. CH42: Tran 6K 73
Allenby Av. L23: Crosb 9M 33
Allenby Rd. M44: Cad 5K 69
Allenby Sq. L13: Liv 7M 59
Allendale WA7: Pal F 9D 96
Allendale Av. L9: Ain 3G 45
L35: Rainh 6G 62
Allengate L23: Crosb 6L 33
Allen Rd. WA7: West P 8G 95
Allen St. WA2: Warr 2B 82
Allerby Way WA3: Low 2F 52
Allerford Rd. L12: W Der 2A 60
ALLERTON 8B 76
Allerton Beeches L18: Moss H 5A 76
Allerton Dr. L18: Moss H 4N 75
Allerton Gro. CH42: Tran 5L 73
Allerton Park Golf Course 6C 76
Allerton Rd. CH42: Tran 5K 73
CH45: Wall 3G 56
L18: Aller, Moss H 3M 75
L25: Woolt 7D 76
PR9: South 6K 7
WA8: Wid 7L 79
Allesley Rd. L14: Knott A 4D 60
Alleyne Rd. L4: Walt 1J 59
All Hallows Dr. L24: Speke 4K 93
Allington St. L17: Aig 5G 74
Allinsons Ct. L21: Lith 2A 44
Allonby Cl. CH43: Noct 4E 72
WN3: Wins 2F 40
Allotment Rd. M44: Cad 3K 69
Allport La. CH62: Brom 7C 90
Allport La. Pct. CH62: Brom 6C 90
Allport Rd. CH62: Brom 9B 90
CH63: Brom 9B 90
Allports, The CH62: Brom 8C 90
All Saints Cl. L30: N'ton 8D 34
All Saints Ct. WA11: Rainf 6D 38
All Saints Dr. WA4: Thel 5M 83
All Saints Rd. L24: Speke 4G 92
Allscott Way WN4: Ash M 8L 41
Allysum Ct. WA7: Beech 2B 108
Alma Cl. L10: Faz 3N 45
WN8: Uph 5M 31
Alma Ct. PR8: Ains 7M 11
WN8: Uph 5M 31
Almacs Cl. L23: Blun 8H 33
Alma Grn. WN8: Uph 5L 31
Alma Gro. WN3: Wigan 1G 41
Alma Hill WN8: Uph 5L 31
Alman Ct. *L17: Aig 5G 75*
(off Bryanston Rd.)
Alma Pde. WN8: Uph 5M 31
Alma Pl. WA9: St H 8M 49
Alma Rd. L17: Aig 8K 75
PR8: Birkd 2N 11
WN8: Uph 5M 31
Alma St. CH41: Birke 2L 73
WA9: St H 8M 49
WA12: Newt W 7K 51
Alma Ter. *L15: Wav 9L 59*
(off Sandown La.)
Alma Wlk. WN8: Uph 5M 31
Almeda Rd. L24: Speke 5L 93
Almer Dr. WA5: Gt San 3L 81
Almond Av. L30: N'ton 8B 34
L40: Burs 8J 15
WA7: Run 7M 95
Almond Brow PR9: Banks 3E 8
Almond Cl. L26: Halew 9J 77
WA11: Hay 5B 50
Almond Ct. L19: Garst 2C 92
Almond Dr. WA5: Burtw 3H 65
Almond Gro. WA1: Padd 1J 83
WA8: Wid 8G 78
Almond Pl. CH46: More 9N 55
Almonds, The L26: Halew 9J 77
Almond's Grn. L12: W Der 1M 59
Almond's Gro. L12: W Der 2M 59
Almond's Pk. L12: W Der 1M 59
Almonds Turn L30: N'ton 7C 34
Almond Tree Cl. L24: Hale 6B 94
Almond Wlk. *M31: Part 6K 69*
(off Wood La.)
Almond Way CH49: Grea 6K 71
Almonry, The L40: Lath 6M 21
Alness Dr. L35: Rainh 7G 63
Alnwick Dr. CH46: More 9J 55
CH65: Ell P 3B 112
Aloeswood Cl. L6: Liv 4G 58
Alpass Av. WA5: Warr 9B 66
Alpass Rd. L17: Aig 5G 75
Alpha Ct. CH45: Wall 4E 56
Alpha Dr. CH42: Rock F 7N 73
Alpha St. L21: Lith 5A 44
Alpine Cl. WA10: St H 6F 48
Alpine St. WA12: Newt W 7J 51
Alresford Rd. L19: Aig 8L 75
Alroy Rd. L4: Walt 2F 58
Alscot Av. L10: Faz 3M 45
Alscot Cl. L31: Mag 3J 35
Alston Cl. CH62: Brom 6B 90
Alston Ct. PR8: Ains 8L 11
Alstonfield Rd. L14: Knott A 5E 60
Alston M. WA10: St H 2E 62
Alston Rd. L17: Aig 8K 75
Alt WA8: Wid 6E 78
Alt Av. L31: Mag 4H 35
ALT BRIDGE 4H 25
Altbridge Pk. L11: Crox 6N 45
(not continuous)
Altbridge Rd. L36: Huy 4H 61
Altcar Av. L15: Wav 1J 75
Altcar Dr. CH46: More 1L 71
Altcar La. L31: Lyd 7E 26
L37: Form 3F 24
(Belvedere Dr.)
L37: Form 9J 17
(Downholland Moss La.)
L39: Down 3E 26
Altcar Rifle Range Est. L38: Hight 6E 24
Altcar Rd. L20: Boot 5B 44
L37: Form, Gt Alt 2G 24
Altcross Rd. L11: Crox 6A 46
Altcross Way L11: Crox 6A 46
Altfield Rd. L14: Knott A 2D 60
Altfinch Cl. L14: Knott A 2E 60
Altham Rd. L11: Norr G 2L 59
PR8: South 4D 12
Althorpe Dr. PR8: South 3D 12
Althorp St. L8: Liv 5E 74
Altmoor Rd. L36: Huy 3H 61
Alton Av. L21: Lith 1N 43
Alton Cl. L38: Hight 1F 32
WN4: Ash M 7J 41
Alton Rd. CH43: Oxton 3G 73
L6: Liv 4J 59
Alt Rd. L20: Boot 5B 44
L36: Huy 6J 61
L37: Form 2G 25
L38: Hight 8F 24
(not continuous)
Alt Side Ct. L10: Faz 3N 45
Alt St. L8: Liv 1G 74
Altway L10: Ain 8H 35
Altway Ct. *L10: Ain 8H 35*
(off Altway)
Altys La. L39: Orm 9D 20
Alundale Ct. *L20: Boot 7B 44*
(off Clairville Cl.)
Alundale Rd. L12: W Der 4C 60
ALVANLEY 4G 115
Alvanley Dr. WA6: Hel 3F 114
Alvanley Grn. L32: Kirkb 9A 36
Alvanley Pk. WA6: Alv 3H 115
Alvanley Pl. CH43: Oxton 2J 73
Alvanley Rd. CH66: Gt Sut 1K 111
L12: W Der 4A 60
L32: Kirkb 9A 36
WA6: Hel 2F 114
Alvanley Ter. WA6: Frod 6L 107
Alvanley Vw. CH2: Elt 2M 113
Alvanley Way *CH66: Gt Sut 1K 111*
(off Gawsworth Rd.)
Alva Rd. L35: Rainh 7G 63
Alvega Cl. CH62: New F 9B 74
Alverstone Av. CH41: Birke 1F 72
Alverstone Cl. WA5: Gt San 1E 80
Alverstone Rd. CH44: Wall 6K 57
L18: Moss H 3L 75
Alverton Cl. WA8: Wid 8G 79
Alvina La. L4: Walt 2D 58
L33: Kirkb 6E 36
Alwain Grn. L24: Speke 5K 93
Alwen St. CH41: Birke 8F 56
Alwyn Av. L21: Lith 1A 44
Alwyn Cl. L17: Aig 5G 75
WN7: Leigh 1N 53
Alwyn Gdns. CH46: More 9N 55
Alwyn St. L17: Aig 5G 74
Amanda Rd. L10: Faz 3N 45
L35: Rainh 4E 62
Amanda Way L31: Mell 7N 35
Amaury Cl. L23: Thorn 6A 34
Amaury Rd. L23: Thorn 6A 34
Ambassador Dr. L26: Halew 7L 77
Ambergate WN8: Skel 5E 30
Ambergate Cl. WA9: St H 2N 63
Ambergate Rd. L19: Gras 9N 75
Amberleigh Cl. WA4: App T 4J 99
Amberley Av. CH46: More 1K 71
Amberley Cl. CH46: More 1K 71
L6: Liv 2J 59
Amberley St. L8: Liv 9M 5 (1F 74)
Amber Way L14: Knott A 2E 60
Ambleside Av. CH46: More 9L 55
Ambleside Cl. CH61: Thing 1A 88
CH62: Brom 8D 90
WA7: Beech 1A 108
Ambleside Cres. WA2: Warr 6D 66
Ambleside Dr. L33: Kirkb 7B 36
Ambleside Pl. WA11: St H 1L 49
Ambleside Rd. CH65: Ell P 3A 112
L18: Aller 7B 76
L31: Mag 1J 35
Ambrose Ct. WA1: Warr 2E 82
Amelia Cl. L6: Liv 2L 5 (6E 58)
WA8: Wid 4L 79
Amelia St. WA2: Warr 1D 82
Amersham WN8: Skel 5E 30
Amersham Rd. L4: Walt 8H 45
(not continuous)
Amery Gro. CH42: Tran 6J 73
Amesbury Dr. WN3: Wins 1E 40
Amethyst Cl. L6: Liv 5G 58
L21: Lith 2B 44
Amherst Rd. L17: Aig 6H 75

Amidian Ct. *CH44: Wall* 6H 57
(off Poulton Rd.)
Amis Gro. WA3: Low 2F 52
Amity St. L8: Liv 3E 74
Amos Av. L21: Lith 2B 44
Ampleforth Cl. L32: Kirkb 1A 46
Ampthill Rd. L17: Aig 6H 75
Ampulla Rd. L11: Crox 7A 46
Amy Wlk. L10: Faz 3N 45
Ancaster Rd. L17: Aig 6H 75
Ancholme Cl. L35: Whis 3D 62
Anchorage, The CH64: Park 7C 100
L3: Liv 2C 74
WA13: Lymm 5D 84
Anchorage La. L18: Moss H 5K 75
Anchor Cl. WA7: Murd 9F 96
Anchor Ct. PR8: Birkd 1M 11
WA1: Warr 2E 82
Anchor Courtyard L3: Liv 8D 4
Anchor St. PR9: South 8G 7
Ancient Mdws. L9: Ain 3G 45
Ancroft Rd. L14: Knott A 6E 60
Ancrum Rd. L33: Kirkb 5B 36
Anders Dr. L33: Kirkb 6E 36
Anderson Cl. CH61: Irby 1A 88
L35: Rainh 8G 63
WA2: Padg 7J 67
Anderson Ct. CH62: Brom 9C 90
Anderson Rd. L21: Lith 1C 44
Anderson St. L5: Liv 3D 58
(not continuous)
Anderson Trad. Est. *WA8: Wid* *1K 95*
(off Croft St.)
Anderson Way L21: Lith 1C 44
Anderton Ter. L36: Roby 7G 61
Andover Cl. WA2: Padg 8F 66
Andover Cres. WN3: Wins 1E 40
Andover Rd. WA11: Hay 2G 50
Andover Way L25: Hunts X 8H 77
Andreas Cl. PR8: Birkd 2A 12
Andrew Av. L31: Mell 8N 35
WN5: Bil 6B 40
Andrew Cl. WA8: Wid 8F 78
Andrew Ho. L8: Liv 9K 5
Andrews Cl. L37: Form 3E 24
Andrews La. L37: Form 2E 24
Andrew St. L4: Walt 9E 44
Andrew's Wlk. CH60: Hesw 7B 88
Andrews Yort L37: Form 3E 24
Andromeda Way WA9: Bold 2D 64
Anemone Way WA9: Bold 2C 64
ANFIELD 2F 58
Anfield 2F 58
Anfield Ct. L4: Walt 2F 58
Anfield Crematorium L4: Walt 1G 58
Anfield Rd. L4: Walt 2E 58
Angela St. L7: Liv 9G 58
Angelica Dr. L11: Norr G 8L 45
Angelica Rd. L32: Kirkb 7D 36
Angers La. L31: Mell 5N 35
Anglers Rest M44: Cad 4L 69
Anglesea Rd. L9: Walt 7F 44
Anglesea Way L8: Liv 4E 74
Anglesey Cl. CH65: Ell P 4A 112
Anglesey Rd. CH44: Wall 4H 57
CH48: W Kir 4B 70
Anglezark Cl. L7: Liv 7G 59
Anglezarke Rd. WA12: Newt W 8J 51
Anglia Way L25: Hunts X 8G 77
Anglican Ct. *L8: Liv* *1D 74*
(off Blair St.)
Anglo Cl. L9: Ain 2H 45
Angus Rd. CH63: Brom 9B 90
L11: Norr G 1L 59
Annable Rd. M44: Irlam 1M 69
Annandale Cl. L33: Kirkb 5B 36
Annandale Gdns. WN8: Uph 4J 31
Annan Gro. WN4: Ash M 6N 41
Ann Cl. CH66: Lit Sut 7J 103
Ann Conway Ho. *L15: Wav* *1K 75*
(off Garmoyle Cl.)
Anne Av. PR8: Ains 8L 11
Anne Gro. WA9: St H 2M 63
Annerley St. L7: Liv 9H 59
Annesley Rd. CH44: Wall 6J 57
L17: Aig 6H 75
Anne St. WA9: Clock F 6N 63
Annette Av. WA12: Newt W 5J 51
Annexe, The *PR9: South* *7H 7*
(off Hoghton Gro.)
Annie Rd. L20: Boot 4C 44
Annie St. WA2: Warr 2D 82
Ann St. WA7: Run 4L 95
WN8: Skel 4B 30
Ann St. W. WA8: Wid 9L 79
Anscot Av. CH63: Beb 1M 89
Ansdell Dr. WA10: Eccl 5E 48
Ansdell Gro. PR9: South 3M 7
Ansdell Rd. WA8: Wid 6L 79
Ansdell Vs. Rd. L35: Rainh 5F 62
Anson St. L3: Liv 4K 5 (7E 58)
Anstey Cl. CH46: More 8J 55
Anstey Rd. L13: Liv 6N 59
Ansty Cl. WA11: St H 5N 49
Anthony's Way CH60: Hesw 8A 88
Anthorn Cl. CH43: Noct 4D 72
Anthorn Rd. WN3: Wigan 1G 40
Antler Ct. WN4: Ash M 5K 41
Antonio St. L20: Boot 9C 44
Antons Cl. L26: Halew 1K 93
Antons Ct. L26: Halew 1L 93
Antons Rd. CH61: Pens 2A 88
L26: Halew 1K 93
Antony Rd. WA4: Warr 6C 82
Antrim Cl. WA11: Hay 4E 50
WN3: Wins 1E 40
Antrim Dr. CH66: Gt Sut 3L 111
Antrim Rd. WA2: Warr 7B 66
Antrim St. L13: Liv 2K 59
Antrobus Golf Course 9H 99
Anvil Cl. CH2: Elt 1M 113
L20: Boot .6A 44
WN5: Orr .7N 31
Anzacs, The CH62: Port S 1B 90
Anzio Rd. L36: Huy 5H 61
Apartments, The PR9: South 7G 6
Apex Ct. CH62: Brom 6D 90
Apollo Ct. *CH44: Wall* *4K 57*
(off Rudgrave Sq.)
Apollo Cres. L33: Kirkb 7C 36
Apollo Pk. WA5: Burtw 6K 65
Apollo Way L6: Liv 4G 58
L30: N'ton 7E 34
Apostles Way L33: Kirkb 6B 36
Appin Rd. CH41: Birke 3L 73
Apple Blossom Gro.
M44: Cad .5K 69
Appleby Cl. WA8: Wid 8F 78
Appleby Dr. L30: N'ton 8B 34
Appleby Grn. L12: W Der 3B 60
Appleby Gro. CH62: Brom 9C 90
Appleby Lawn L27: N'ley 4L 77
Appleby Rd. L33: Kirkb 7C 36
WA2: Warr 6D 66
Appleby Wlk. L27: N'ley 4L 77
WA8: Wid .8F 78
Applecorn Cl. WA9: Sut L 3N 63
Apple Ct. *L6: Liv* *6G 59*
(off Coleridge St.)
Applecross Cl. WA3: Birchw 3A 68
Appledale Dr. CH66: Whit 5M 111
Apple Dell Av. WA3: Golb 1D 52
Appledore Ct. L24: Speke 3F 92
Appledore Gro. WA9: Sut L 5M 63
Appleford Cl. WA4: App 9F 82
Applegarth CH46: More 2K 71
Apple Hey WN6: Appl B 5M 23
Apple Jacks Adventure Pk. 5G 99
APPLETON
WA4 . . . . .1F 98
WA8 . . . . .6L 79
Appleton Dr. CH49: Grea 5M 71
CH65: Whit 2L 111
Appleton Hall Gdns. WA4: App 2F 98
Appleton M. *WA13: Lymm* *4C 84*
(off Oldfield Rd.)
APPLETON PARK 3E 98
Appleton Rd. L4: Walt 9G 44
L21: Lith .1N 43
L32: Kirkb 7C 36
WA8: Wid .7L 79
WA9: St H 8M 49
WN8: Skel 2C 30
Appleton St. WA8: Wid 1L 95
APPLETON THORN 3J 99
Appleton Thorn Trad. Est.
WA4: App T 1L 99
Appleton Village WA8: Wid 7K 79
Apple Tree Cl. L24: Hale 6B 94
L28: Stockb V 1F 60
Appletree Cl. L18: Aller 7A 76
Apple Tree Gro. CH66: Gt Sut 5L 111
Appletree Gro. WA2: Fearn 7G 67
Applewood Ct. L26: Halew 7L 77
Applewood Gro. L26: Halew 7L 77
APPLEY BRIDGE 5M 23
Appley Bridge Station (Rail) 6M 23
Appley Cl. WN6: Appl B 3M 23
Appley La. Nth. WN6: Appl B 3M 23
Appley La. Sth. WN6: Appl B 7M 23
WN8: Roby M 7M 23
April Gro. L6: Liv 4J 59
April Ri. L30: N'ton 8D 34
Apsley Av. CH45: Wall 3H 57
Apsley Brow L31: Mag 2G 35
Apsley Gro. CH63: Beb 1N 89
Apsley Rd. CH62: New F 8A 74
L12: W Der 3A 60
Aquarius Cl. L14: Knott A 5E 60
Arabis Gdns. WA9: Bold 2D 64
Aragon Cl. L31: Mag 9K 27
Aragon Ct. WA7: Manor P 4E 96
Aran Cl. L24: Hale 5A 94
Arborn Dr. CH49: Upton 2A 72
Arbour Ct. L33: Know I 9F 36
Arbour La. L33: Know I 1E 46
Arbour St. PR8: South 9H 7
Arbour Wlk. WA6: Hel 3D 114
Arbury Av. WA11: St H 4N 49
Arbury Ct. WA2: Win 4C 66
Arbury La. WA2: Win 3D 66
Arcade, The CH65: Ell P 9M 103
Arcadia Av. L31: Lyd 9J 27
Archbishop Warlock Ct. L3: Liv 5B 58
Archbrook M. *L13: Liv* *4K 59*
(off Sutton St.)
Archer Av. WA4: Warr 6F 82
Archer Cl. L4: Kirkd 2D 58
Archerfield Rd. L18: Aller 6N 75
Archer Gro. WA9: St H 6A 50
Archers Ct. *CH49: Woodc* *6A 72*
(off Childwall Grn.)
Archers Cft. CH62: Brom 6C 90
Archers Fold L31: Mell 7N 35
Archers Grn. CH62: East 2D 102
Archers Grn. Rd. WA5: Westb 6J 65
Archer St. L4: Kirkd 2D 58
Archers Way CH49: Woodc 6A 72
CH66: Gt Sut 4K 111
Arch La. WN4: Garsw 8C 40
Arch Vw. Cres. L1: Liv 8H 5 (9D 58)
Archway Rd. L36: Huy 7H 61
Archway Wlk. WA12: Newt W 7N 51
Arctic Rd. L20: Boot 7N 43
Arden WA8: Wid 6D 78
Arden Cl. PR8: Ains 9G 11
WA3: Birchw 3B 68
Arden Dr. CH64: Nest 8E 100
Ardennes Rd. L36: Huy 6J 61
Arderne Cl. CH63: Spit 5A 90
Ardern Lea WA6: Alv 4G 115
Ardleigh Av. PR8: South 3D 12
Ardleigh Cl. L13: Liv 7L 59
Ardleigh Gro. L13: Liv 7L 59
Ardleigh Pl. L13: Liv 7L 59
Ardleigh Rd. L13: Liv 7K 59
Ardmore Rd. L18: Moss H 6M 75
Ardrossan Rd. L4: Walt 1H 59
Ardville Rd. L11: Norr G 7J 45
Ardwick Rd. L24: Speke 4K 93
Ardwick St. WA9: St H 7M 49
Arena Gdns. WA2: Warr 9E 66
Argameols Cl. PR8: South 1E 12
Argarmeols Gro. L37: Form 8E 16
Argarmeols Rd. L37: Form 7E 16
Argo Rd. L22: Water 1K 43
Argos Pl. L20: Kirkd 9C 44
Argos Rd. L20: Kirkd 9C 44
Argyle Ct. L1: Liv 7F 4
PR9: South 5J 7
Argyle Pk. PR9: South 7J 7
Argyle Rd. L4: Walt 3G 59
L19: Garst 1A 92
PR9: South 5J 7
Argyle St. CH41: Birke 2L 73
L1: Liv 7F 4 (9C 58)
WA10: St H 5J 49
Argyle St. Sth. CH41: Birke 3L 73
Argyll Av. CH62: East 2C 102
Argyll Cl. WN4: Garsw 7E 40
Ariel Wlk. WA3: Low 2G 52
Aries Cl. L14: Knott A 4E 60
Ariss Gro. L35: Whis 4D 62
Arizona Cres. WA5: Gt San 1K 81
Arkenshaw Rd. WA3: Croft 1H 67
Arkenstone Cl. WA8: Wid 6F 78
Arkle Rd. CH43: Bid 9F 56
Arkles La. L4: Walt 2F 58
Arkles Rd. L4: Walt 3F 58
Arklow Dr. L24: Hale 5A 94
Ark Royal Way CH41: Tran 4M 73
Arkwood Cl. CH62: Spit 4B 90
Arkwright Ct. WA7: Ast 4B 96
Arkwright Rd. WA7: Ast 4B 96
Arkwright St. L5: Liv 4D 58
Arlescourt Rd. L12: W Der 4A 60
Arley Av. WA4: Stockt H 8E 82
Arley Cl. CH43: Bid 2C 72
Arley Dr. WA8: Wid 6D 78
Arley Gro. WA13: Lymm 6G 84
Arley Rd. CW9: Ant 7M 99
WA4: App T 3J 99
Arley St. L3: Liv 1E 4 (5B 58)
Arlington Av. L18: Moss H 3L 75
Arlington Cl. PR8: Ains 9G 11
Arlington Ct. CH43: Oxton 3F 72
Arlington Dr. WA5: Penk 4G 81
WN7: Leigh 2K 53
Arlington Rd. CH45: Wall 3E 56
Armill Rd. L11: Crox 7A 46
Armitage Gdns. L18: Aller 7N 75
Armley Rd. L4: Walt 2G 59
Armour Av. WA2: Warr 7C 66
Armour Gro. L13: Liv 7M 59
Armoury, The L12: W Der 2N 59
Armoury Bank WN4: Ash M 8K 41
Armscot Cl. L25: Hunts X 9F 76
Armscot Pl. L25: Hunts X 9F 76
Armstrong Cl. WA3: Birchw 5L 67
Armstrong Quay L3: Liv 5E 74
Armthorpe Dr. CH66: Lit Sut 9G 103
Arncliffe Dr. WA5: Burtw 3H 65
Arncliffe Rd. L25: Hunts X, Woolt 7G 77
Arndale WA7: Beech 1A 108
Arnhem Cres. WA2: Warr 1D 82
Arnhem Rd. L36: Huy 5J 61
Arnian Ct. L39: Augh 4A 28
Arnian Rd. WA11: Rainf 4C 38
Arnian Way WA11: Rainf 4C 38
Arno Ct. CH43: Oxton 5H 73
Arnold Av. WA10: St H 5G 49
Arnold Cl. WA9: St H 9M 49
Arnold Cres. L8: Liv 2F 74
Arnold Gro. L15: Wav 9M 59
Arnold Pl. WA8: Wid 9F 78
Arnold St. CH45: Wall 4H 57
WA1: Warr *2E 82*
(off Manchester Rd.)
Arno Rd. CH43: Oxton 5H 73
Arnot Cl. WA10: St H 5J 49
Arnot St. L4: Walt 9E 44
Arnot Way CH63: Hghr B 1K 89
Arnside L21: Lith 2C 44
Arnside Av. L35: Rainh 5D 62
WA11: Hay 4D 50
Arnside Gro. WA4: Warr 6C 82
Arnside Rd. CH43: Oxton 4G 73
CH45: Wall 4H 57
L7: Liv 8H 59
L36: Huy .7F 60
PR9: South 8H 7
Arnside Ter. PR9: South 8H 7
Aron Ct. L34: Presc 3A 62
ARPLEY MEADOWS 5C 82
Arpley Rd. WA1: Warr 4C 82
Arpley St. WA1: Warr 3B 82
Arrad Ho. L7: Liv 6K 5
Arrad St. L7: Liv 7K 5 (9E 58)
Arran Av. CH65: Ell P 4A 112
Arran Cl. WA2: Fearn 7H 67
WA11: St H 4A 50
Arran Dr. WA6: Frod 7M 107
Arranmore Rd. L18: Moss H 6M 75
Arriva Stadium, The 8J 33
Arrivato Plaza *WA10: St H* *7L 49*
(off Hall St.)
Arrowe Av. CH46: More 1L 71
Arrowe Brook Ct. CH49: Grea 4M 71
Arrowe Brook La. CH49: Grea 7L 71
Arrowe Brook Rd. CH49: Woodc 6N 71
Arrowe Commercial Pk.
CH49: Upton 5N 71
Arrowe Country Pk. 7N 71
Arrowe Ct. *CH49: Woodc* *6A 72*
(off Childwall Grn.)
ARROWE HILL 5N 71
Arrowe Park Golf Course 8A 72
Arrowe Pk. Rd. CH49: Upton, Woodc . . .3A 72
Arrowe Rd. CH49: Grea 5L 71
Arrowe Side CH49: Grea 4M 71
Arrowsmith Rd. WA11: Hay 3H 51
ARTHILL 8N 85
Arthill La. WA14: Lit Bo 8N 85
Art Ho. Sq. L1: Liv 7H 5
Arthur Av. CH65: Ell P 9A 104
(not continuous)
Arthur St. CH41: Birke 1J 73
(not continuous)
L9: Walt 7E 44
L19: Garst 2B 92
WA2: Warr 2B 82
WA7: Run .5K 95
Arundel Av. CH45: Wall 3F 56
L8: Liv 2H 75
L17: Liv 2H 75
Arundel Cl. CH61: Pens 2M 87
L8: Liv 2F 74
Arundel Ct. CH65: Ell P 2C 112
Arundell Cl. WA5: Burtw 3H 65
Arundel Rd. PR8: Birkd 6M 11
Arundel St. L4: Walt 9D 44
Arvon St. L20: Boot 4C 44
Asbridge St. L8: Liv 2G 74
Asbury Cl. L18: Aller 5B 76
Asbury Rd. CH45: Wall 3D 56
Ascot Av. L21: Lith 2N 43
WA7: Run .9L 95
Ascot Cl. PR8: Birkd 1L 11
WA1: Wools 1M 83
WA4: Grap 6K 83
Ascot Dr. CH63: Beb 2M 89
CH66: Gt Sut 2J 111
L33: Kirkb 6C 36
Ascot Gro. CH63: Beb 2M 89
Ascot Pk. L23: Crosb 7M 33
Ascot Vw. L22: Water 9J 33
Ascroft Rd. L9: Ain 2G 44
Ash Av. M44: Cad 4K 69
WA12: Newt W 8L 51
Ashbank Rd. L11: Norr G 8M 45
Ashberry Dr. WA4: App T 2J 99
Ashbourne Av. L23: Blun 7J 33
L30: N'ton 9D 34
WA7: Run .9L 95
Ashbourne Cl. CH66: Gt Sut 5K 111
Ashbourne Cres. L36: Huy 7F 60
Ashbourne Rd. L17: Aig 6H 75
WA5: Gt San 3K 81
Ashbrook Av. WA7: Sut W 2A 108
Ashbrook Cres. WA2: Warr 9E 66
Ashbrook Dr. L9: Ain 4H 45
Ashbrook Ter. CH63: Beb 1N 89
Ash Brow WN8: Newb 4D 22
Ashburn Av. L33: Kirkb 7C 36
Ashburnham Way L3: Liv 1J 5 (6D 58)
Ashburton Av. CH43: Clau 2F 72
Ashburton Rd. CH43: Clau 2E 72
CH44: Wall 5H 57
CH48: W Kir 5C 70
Ashbury Cl. L14: Knott A 3F 60
WA7: Wind H 5F 96
Ashbury Dr. WA11: Hay 3E 50
Ashbury Rd. L14: Knott A 3F 60
Ashby Cl. CH46: More 8J 55
Ash Cl. CH66: Gt Sut 4L 111
L15: Wav .9K 59
L39: Orm .8B 20
WN6: Appl B 6N 23
Ashcombe Rd. L14: Knott A 6A 60
Ash Cres. L36: Huy 9J 61

Ashcroft Av. L39: Orm 7D **20**
Ashcroft Dr. CH61: Hesw 4N **87**
Ashcroft Rd. L33: Know I 8F **36**
L37: Form 3F **24**
WA13: Lymm 4H **85**
Ashcroft St. L20: Boot 7A **44**
WA9: St H 7M **49**
(not continuous)
Ashdale L36: Huy 7H **61**
Ashdale Cl. L37: Form 2C **24**
Ashdale Pk. CH49: Grea 5J **71**
Ashdale Rd. L9: Walt 6F **44**
L18: Moss H 3M **75**
L22: Water 9K **33**
WN3: Wigan 1J **41**
Ashdown Cl. PR8: South 2D **12**
Ashdown Cres. WA9: Clock F 5M **63**
Ashdown Dr. CH49: Grea 6K **71**
Ashdown Gro. L26: Halew 7L **77**
Ashdown La. WA3: Birchw 4A **68**
Asher Ct. WA4: App T 3L **99**
Ashfarm Ct. L14: Knott A 6D **60**
Ashfield L15: Wav 9J **59**
L35: Rainh 6G **62**
Ashfield Cl. WA13: Lymm 4H **85**
Ashfield Ct. *WA10: St H 7J 49*
(off Glover St.)
Ashfield Cres. CH62: Brom 7C **90**
WN5: Bil 6A **40**
Ashfield Gdns. WA4: Westy 5G **82**
Ashfield Gro. M44: Irlam 3L **69**
Ashfield Ho. *CH64: Nest 6E 100*
(off Churchill Way)
Ashfield Rd. CH62: Brom 7B **90**
CH65: Ell P 9A **104**
L17: Aig 6J **75**
Ashfield Rd. Nth. CH65: Ell P 9A **104**
Ashfield St. L5: Liv 4B **58**
Ashfield Ter. WN6: Appl B 5M **23**
Ashford Cl. L26: Halew 9J **77**
Ashford Dr. WA4: App 4F **98**
Ashford Rd. CH41: Birke 4J **73**
CH47: Meols 9D **54**
Ashford Way WA8: Wid 7N **79**
Ash Grange L14: Knott A 6B **60**
Ash Gro. CH45: New B 2J **57**
CH66: Lit Sut 8H **103**
L15: Wav 9J **59**
L21: Sea 4N **43**
L35: Presc 5B **62**
L37: Form 3C **24**
WA3: Golb 2C **52**
WA4: Warr 5E **82**
WA7: Run 7M **95**
WA8: Wid 8G **78**
WA9: Clock F 5M **63**
WA11: Rainf 5C **38**
WN8: Skel 3A **30**
Ash Gro. Cres. WN5: Bil 5N **39**
Ash Ho. WA12: Newt W 6J **51**
Ashland Av. WN4: Ash M 7J **41**
Ashlands WA6: Frod 7M **107**
Ash La. WA4: App 8F **82**
WA8: Wid 7B **78**
Ashlar Gro. L17: Aig 6K **75**
Ashlar Rd. L17: Aig 6K **75**
L22: Water 9L **33**
Ashlea Rd. CH61: Pens 4N **87**
Ashleigh Rd. L31: Mag 4L **35**
Ashley Av. CH47: Meols 8G **54**
Ashley Bus. Cen. *L34: Presc 3B 62*
(off East St.)
Ashley Cl. L33: Kirkb 6C **36**
L35: Rainh 7G **62**
WA4: Grap 5K **83**
Ashley Ct. M44: Cad 4K **69**
WA4: App 1D **98**
WA6: Frod 6K **107**
Ashley Grn. WA8: Wid 7G **79**
Ashley Rd. PR9: South 8H **7**
WA7: Run 5N **95**
WN8: Skel 1E **30**
Ashley St. CH42: Rock F 6M **73**
Ashley Way WA8: Wid 1K **95**
Ashley Way W. WA8: Wid 9J **79**
Ashmead Rd. WN8: Skel 9D **22**
Ashmore Cl. CH48: Caldy 1D **86**
WA3: Birchw 6A **68**
Ashmuir Hey L32: Kirkb 1D **46**
Ashover Av. L14: Knott A 5E **60**
Ash Priors WA8: Wid 5G **78**
Ashridge St. WA7: Run 4J **95**
Ash Rd. CH2: Elt 2N **113**
CH42: Tran 4K **73**
CH63: Hghr B 9M **73**
L21: Lith 3N **43**
M31: Part 6K **69**
WA2: Win 3C **66**
WA3: Rix 7G **69**
WA5: Penk 4H **81**
WA11: Hay 3G **51**
WA13: Lymm 5C **84**
Ash St. L20: Boot 6B **44**
PR8: South 1B **12**
Ashton Av. L35: Rainh 8F **62**
Ashton Cl. CH62: East 3D **102**
WA6: Frod 5N **107**
WA7: West 9J **95**
Ashton Ct. CH48: W Kir 7B **70**
WA6: Frod 5M **107**
ASHTON CROSS 9F **40**
Ashton Dr. CH48: W Kir 7B **70**
L25: Hunts X 9F **76**
WA6: Frod 4M **107**
Ashton Grange Ind. Est.
WN4: Ash M 5K **41**
Ashton Heath WN4: Ash M 9L **41**
ASHTON-IN-MAKERFIELD 8K **41**
Ashton-in-Makerfield Golf Course 9G **41**
Ashton Leisure Cen. 7J **41**
Ashton Pk. L25: Hunts X 8H **77**
Ashton Pl. PR8: South 9G **7**
Ashton Rd. PR8: Birkd 5M **11**
WA3: Golb 1C **52**
WA6: Nor 9N **115**
WA12: Newt W 4L **51**
WN5: Bil 3C **40**
ASHTON'S GREEN 7B **50**
Ashtons Grn. Dr. WA9: St H 8B **50**
Ashton's La. L24: Hale 5K **93**
L37: Form 3C **24**
Ashton Sq. L25: Woolt 7F **76**
Ashton St. L3: Liv 4L **5** (7E **58**)
L13: Liv 6M **59**
WA2: Warr 2C **82**
Ash Tree Apartments
CH44: Wall 6K **57**
Ashtree Cl. CH64: Lit N 7F **100**
Ashtree Cft. CH64: Will 7N **101**
Ashtree Dr. CH64: Lit N 8G **100**
Ashtree Farm Ct. CH64: Will 6N **101**
Ashtree Gro. L12: Crox 6C **46**
ASHURST 9E **22**
Ashurst Cl. L25: Gate 4F **76**
WA11: St H 4A **50**
WN8: Skel 9D **22**
Ashurst Ct. L37: Form 2E **24**
Ashurst Dr. WA11: St H 4N **49**
Ashurst Gdns. WN8: Skel 9D **22**
Ashurst Rd. WN8: Skel 1E **30**
Ash Va. L15: Wav 9K **59**
Ash Vs. CH44: Wall 7J **57**
Ashville Ind. Est. WA7: Sut W 3A **108**
Ashville Point WA7: Sut W 3A **108**
Ashville Rd. CH41: Birke 2G **73**
CH43: Clau 2G **73**
CH44: Wall 7K **57**
Ashville Way WA7: Sut W 3A **108**
Ashwall St. WN8: Skel 4A **30**
Ashwater Rd. L12: W Der 8A **46**
Ashway CH60: Hesw 9B **88**
Ashwell Av. WA3: Low 1E **52**
Ashwell St. L8: Liv 1D **74**
Ashwood *WN8: Skel 1F 30*
(off Forest Dr.)
Ashwood Av. WA1: Warr 1F **82**
WA3: Low 2E **52**
WN4: Ash M 9J **41**
Ashwood Cl. CH66: Gt Sut 4J **111**
L27: N'ley 3J **77**
L33: Kirkb 6C **36**
WA8: Wid 9D **78**
Ashwood Ct. CH43: Bid 8C **56**
WA3: Low 3E **52**
Ashwood Dr. L12: Crox 7B **46**
Ashwood La. CH2: Wer 9E **112**
Askern Rd. L32: Kirkb 2D **46**
Askett Cl. WA11: Hay 3F **50**
Askew Cl. CH44: Wall 5K **57**
Askew St. L4: Walt 9E **44**
Askham Cl. L8: Liv 1G **74**
Askrigg Av. CH66: Lit Sut 9G **103**
Asland Gdns. PR9: South 3A **8**
Asmall Cl. L39: Orm 7B **20**
Asmall La. L39: Hals 5K **19**
L39: Orm 6N **19**
L40: Scar 6N **19**
Aspen Cl. CH60: Hesw 7D **88**
CH66: Gt Sut 4K **111**
L33: Kirkb 5D **36**
Aspendale Rd. CH42: Tran 4K **73**
Aspen Gdns. PR8: South 9K **7**
WA9: St H 3F **62**
Aspen Gro. L8: Liv 2H **75**
L37: Form 3C **24**
WA1: Padd 1H **83**
Aspen Way WN8: Skel 2B **30**
Aspenwood WN4: Ash M 9J **41**
Aspes Rd. L12: W Der 2C **60**
Aspinall Cl. WA2: Fearn 6H **67**
Aspinall Cres. L37: Gt Alt 3M **25**
Aspinall St. CH41: Birke 1J **73**
L34: Presc 3A **62**
Aspley Ho. L22: Water 1L **43**
Aspull Cl. WA3: Birchw 5K **67**
ASPULL COMMON 1K **53**
Aspull Comn. WN7: Leigh 1K **53**
Aspull Ct. WN7: Leigh 1K **53**
Asquith Av. CH41: Birke 1H **73**
Asser Rd. L11: Norr G 1K **59**
Assheton Cl. WA12: Newt W 6K **51**
Assheton Wlk. L24: Hale 5B **94**
Assissian Cres. L30: N'ton 7D **34**
Astbury Cl. WA3: Low 2J **53**
Aster Cres. WA7: Beech 1B **108**
Aster Dr. L33: Kirkb 6B **36**
Asterfield Av. CH63: Hghr B 9L **73**
Aster Rd. WA11: Hay 3H **51**
Aster Wlk. *M31: Part 7M 69*
(off Cross La. W.)
Astley Cl. WA4: Warr 5C **82**
WA8: Wid 5F **78**
WA11: Rainf 4C **38**
Astley Ct. M44: Irlam 1L **69**
WN4: Ash M 6L **41**
Astley Rd. L36: Huy 3J **61**
M44: Irlam 1K **69**
ASTMOOR 4B **96**
Astmoor Bri. La. WA7: Cas 5B **96**
Astmoor Ind. Est. WA7: Ast 4B **96**
(Brindley Rd.)
WA7: Ast 4A **96**
(Goddard Rd.)
Astmoor La. WA7: Ast 4M **95**
WA7: Cas 5B **96**
Astmoor Rd. WA7: Ast 4M **95**
Astmoor Spine Rd. WA7: Ast 4C **96**
ASTON 5G **108**
Aston Av. WA3: Ris 5N **67**
Aston Cl. CH43: Oxton 5F **72**
Aston Ct. WA1: Wools 8K **67**
Aston Flds. Rd. WA7: Pres B 2F **108**
Aston Forge WA7: Pres B 1H **109**
Aston Grn. WA7: Pres B 9G **97**
ASTON HEATH 3G **109**
Aston La.
WA7: Aston, Sut W 3C **108**
WA7: Pres B 1H **109**
Aston La. Nth. WA7: Pres B 2G **109**
Aston La. Sth. WA7: Pres B 3G **108**
Aston St. L19: Garst 2B **92**
Astonwood Rd. CH42: Tran 5K **73**
Astor Dr. WA4: Grap 8G **83**
Astor St. L4: Walt 8E **44**
Atheldene Rd. L4: Walt 8H **45**
Athelstan Cl. CH62: Brom 6C **90**
Atherton Cl. L5: Liv 4D **58**
Atherton Ct. *CH45: New B 1G 57*
(off Alexandra Rd.)
Atherton Dr. CH49: Woodc 5A **72**
Atherton Ho. CH45: New B 1H **57**
Atherton La. M44: Cad 4L **69**
Atherton Rake L30: N'ton 7C **34**
Atherton Rd. CH65: Ell P 8L **103**
L9: Ain 4H **45**
Atherton's Quay WA5: Warr 4N **81**
Atherton St. CH45: New B 9G **43**
L34: Presc 3A **62**
WA10: St H 5J **49**
Athlone Rd. WA2: Warr 9B **66**
Athol Cl. CH62: East 1D **102**
WA12: Newt W 6H **51**
Athol Dr. CH62: East 2D **102**
Athole Gro. PR9: South 8L **7**
Atholl Cres. L10: Ain 9J **35**
Atholl Gro. WN3: Wigan 1J **41**
Athol St. CH41: Birke 1L **73**
L5: Liv 4B **58**
(Bangor St., not continuous)
L5: Liv 4A **58**
(Denbigh St., not continuous)
Atkinson, The 8G **6**
Atkinson Gro. L36: Huy 5K **61**
Atkinson Rd. L39: Orm 7D **20**
Atlanta Ct. L33: Kirkb 5B **36**
Atlantic Gdns. WA5: Gt San 9K **65**
Atlantic Pav. L3: Liv 8D **4** (9B **58**)
Atlantic Point L3: Liv 1F **4** (6C **58**)
Atlantic Rd. L20: Boot 7A **44**
Atlantic Terminal L20: Boot 7N **43**
Atlantic Way L3: Liv 3C **74**
L30: Boot 2D **44**
Atlas Bus. Complex L20: Boot 6N **43**
Atlas Rd. L20: Boot 6A **44**
Atlas St. WA9: St H 6L **49**
Atlas Way CH66: Ell P 7L **103**
Atterbury Cl. WA8: Wid 6F **78**
Atterbury St. L8: Liv 3D **74**
Attlee Rd. L36: Huy 6L **61**
Attwood St. L4: Walt 2E **58**
Atwell St. L6: Liv 5F **58**
Atworth Ter. *CH64: Will 6M 101*
(off Neston Rd.)
Aubourn Cl. WA8: Wid 5F **78**
Aubrey Ct. L6: Liv 5F **58**
Auburn Rd. CH45: Wall 2G **57**
L13: Liv 3K **59**
Aubynes, The CH45: Wall 2E **56**
Auckery Av. CH66: Gt Sut 2J **111**
Auckland Rd. L18: Moss H 3M **75**
Audlem Av. CH43: Oxton 5F **72**
Audlem Cl. WA7: Sut W 2B **108**
Audley St. L3: Liv 3J **5** (7D **58**)
Audre Cl. WA5: Gt San 2F **80**
Audrey Wlk. L10: Faz 3N **45**
AUGHTON 5M **27**
Aughton Cl. WN5: Bil 7A **40**
Aughton Ct. CH49: Upton 3A **72**
Aughton M. PR8: Birkd 1N **11**
AUGHTON PARK 2B **28**
Aughton Pk. Dr. L39: Augh 2B **28**
Aughton Park Station (Rail) 2B **28**
Aughton Rd. L20: Boot 5C **44**
PR8: Birkd 9E **6**
Aughton St. L39: Orm 9B **20**
(not continuous)
Augusta Cl. L13: Liv 7M **59**
Augusta Gro. WA5: Gt San 1J **81**
August Rd. L6: Liv 4J **59**
August St. L20: Boot 5B **44**
Aukland Gro. WA9: St H 3G **62**
Aurorean Cl. L27: N'ley 2H **77**
Austell Cl. WA11: St H 3N **49**
Austen Dr. WA2: Win 3B **66**
Austin Av. WA10: St H 1F **62**
WN4: Garsw 7G **40**
Austin Cl. L32: Kirkb 8B **36**
Austin St. CH44: Wall 7G **57**
Austral Av. WA1: Wools 1J **83**
Australia La. WA4: Grap 7K **83**
Autumn Gro.
CH42: Rock F 8L **73**
Autumn Way L20: Boot 5B **44**
WA9: Clock F 6M **63**
Avalon Ct. WA7: Cas 6C **96**
Avalon Ter. *L20: Boot 6A 44*
(off Tennyson St.)
Avebury Cl. WA3: Low 2F **52**
WA8: Wid 5A **80**
Aveley Cl. WA1: Padd 1J **83**
Aveling Dr. PR9: Banks 1E **8**
Avelon Cl. CH43: Noct 3D **72**
L31: Lyd 7G **26**
Avenham Cl. PR9: Banks 2F **8**
Avens Rd. M31: Part 6M **69**
Avenue, The CH62: Brom 7B **90**
L19: Garst 2C **92**
L26: Halew 9J **77**
L36: Huy 6J **61**
L39: Orm 7B **20**
(Church Hill Rd.)
L39: Orm 7C **20**
(Southport Rd.)
PR9: Banks 2D **8**
PR9: South 1K **13**
WA10: Eccl 7E **48**
WA11: Rainf 5C **38**
WA12: Newt W 6M **51**
WA13: Lymm 7C **84**
WN5: Bil 9N **31**
Averham Cl. WN4: Ash M 1K **51**
Avery Cl. WA2: Warr 7F **66**
Avery Cres. WA11: Hay 3E **50**
Avery Rd. WA11: Hay 3E **50**
Avery Sq. WA11: Hay 3E **50**
Aviary Ct. *L9: Walt 4E 44*
(off Dove Rd.)
Aviemore Cl. WN4: Garsw 7F **40**
Aviemore Dr. WA2: Fearn 6H **67**
Aviemore Rd. L13: Liv 6L **59**
Avington Cl. L12: W Der 2B **60**
Avis Wlk. L10: Faz 3N **45**
Avocet Cl. WA2: Warr 6E **66**
WA12: Newt W 6L **51**
Avolon Rd. L12: W Der 4B **60**
Avon WA8: Wid 6D **78**
Avon Av. WA5: Penk 4G **81**
Avon Cl. CH64: Nest 8E **100**
L4: Kirkd 1D **58**
L33: Kirkb 5D **36**
Avon Ct. L23: Crosb 6L **33**
Avondale CH65: Whit 2N **111**
Avondale Av. CH46: More 8N **55**
CH62: East 1E **102**
L31: Mag 3H **35**
Avondale Cl. WA8: Wid 7E **78**
Avondale Dr. WA8: Wid 7E **78**
Avondale Rd. CH47: Hoy 1C **70**
L15: Wav 2K **75**
PR9: South 7G **7**
WA11: Hay 3E **50**
Avondale Rd. Nth.
PR9: South 6H **7**
Avonmore Av. L18: Moss H 5M **75**
Avon Rd. WA3: Cul 8N **53**
WN4: Ash M 6N **41**
WN5: Bil 8M **39**
Avon St. CH41: Birke 8F **56**
L6: Liv 4G **59**
Awelon Cl. L12: W Der 1A **60**
Awesome Walls Climbing Cen. 4A **58**
Axbridge Av. WA9: Sut L 4N **63**
Axholme Cl. CH61: Thing 2B **88**
Axholme Rd. CH61: Thing 2A **88**
Ayala Cl. L9: Walt 3E **44**
Aycliffe Rd. WA9: St H 3G **63**
Aycliffe Wlk. WA8: Wid 8F **78**
Aylesbury Av. CH43: Oxton 6E **72**
Aylesbury Cl. CH66: Gt Sut 2H **111**
Aylesbury Rd. CH45: New B 2J **57**
Aylesford Rd. L13: Liv 6M **59**
Aylsham Cl. WA8: Wid 4F **78**
Aylsham Dr. CH49: Upton 1A **72**
Aylton Rd. L36: Huy 5F **60**
Aylward Pl. *L20: Boot 6A 44*
(off Glover Pl.)
Aynsley Ct. WA9: St H 3E **62**
Ayr Cl. PR8: South 2E **12**
Ayrefield Gro. WN6: Shev 7N **23**
Ayrefield Rd. WN8: Roby M 9M **23**
Ayres Ct. WA9: St H 2H **63**
Ayr Rd. L4: Walt 8F **44**
Ayrshire Gdns. WA10: St H 8H **49**
Ayrshire Rd. L4: Walt 1H **59**
Ayrton Ho. *L8: Liv 1G 75*
(off Commerce Way)
Aysgarth Av. L12: W Der 3A **60**
Aysgarth Rd. CH45: Wall 3F **56**
Ayton La. L16: Child 1A **76**
Azalea Gdns. WA9: Bold 2C **64**

Azalea Gro. L26: Halew 6H 77
WA7: Beech 2B 108

B

Babbacombe Rd. L16: Child 2C 76
WA5: Penk 4G 80
Bk. Barlow La. L4: Kirkd 1D 58
Bk. Bath St. PR9: South 7G 6
Bk. Beau St. L5: Liv 1H 5 (5D 58)
Bk. Bedford St. L7: Liv 7L 5
Bk. Belmont Rd. L6: Liv 4G 59
Bk. Berry St. L1: Liv 7H 5
Bk. Blackfield Ter. L4: Kirkd 2C 58
Bk. Bold St. L1: Liv 6H 5
Bk. Botanic Rd. PR9: South 6M 7
Bk. Boundary Cl. L5: Kirkd 3C 58
Bk. Bridge Rd. L23: Blun 8J 33
(off Riverslea Rd.)
Bk. Bridge St. WA12: Newt W 7K 51
Bk. Bridport St. L3: Liv 4H 5
Back Broadway L11: Norr G 9K 45
Bk. Brook Pl. WA4: Westy 5F 82
Back Brow WN8: Uph 5M 31
Bk. Canning St. L8: Liv 8K 5 (9E 58)
Bk. Catharine St. L8: Liv 8K 5
Bk. Chadwick Mt. L5: Liv 2D 58
Bk. Chatham Pl. L7: Liv 8G 58
(off Queensland St.)
Bk. Colquitt St. L1: Liv 7H 5 (9D 58)
Bk. Commutation Row L3: Liv 3H 5
Bk. Compton Rd. PR8: Birkd 3A 12
Bk. Crossland Ter. WA6: Hel 3E 114
Bk. Cross La. WA12: Newt W 6K 51
Bk. Dovecot Pl. L14: Knott A 5D 60
Bk. Egerton St. Nth. L8: Liv 9L 5
Bk. Egerton St. Sth. L8: Liv 9L 5
Bk. Falkner St. Sth. L8: Liv 8M 5 (9F 58)
BACKFORD 9N 111
Backford Cl. CH43: Oxton 5E 72
WA7: Brook 1E 108
Backford Gdns. CH1: Back 6L 111
Backford Rd. CH61: Irby 2L 87
Bk. Forest Rd. PR8: South 9J 7
(not continuous)
Bk. Forshaw St. WA2: Warr 1D 82
(off Forshaw St.)
Bk. Gillmoss La. L11: Crox 4A 46
Bk. Granton Rd. L5: Liv 3F 58
(off Salisbury Rd.)
Bk. Guilford St. L6: Liv 1L 5 (6E 58)
Bk. Hadfield Pl. L25: Woolt 6E 76
(off Church Rd.)
Bk. High St. L25: Woolt 6E 76
(off High St.)
WA7: Run 5K 95
Bk. Holland Pl. L7: Liv 8G 58
(off Wavertree Rd.)
Bk. Hope Pl. L1: Liv 7J 5
Bk. Huskisson St. L8: Liv 9K 5
Bk. Irvine St. L7: Liv 5N 5
Bk. Kelvin Gro. L8: Liv 2F 74
(off Kelvin Gro.)
Bk. Knight St. L1: Liv 8H 5
Back La. L23: Lit C 3L 33
L29: Seft, Thorn 4B 34
L39: Augh 5K 27
L39: Bic 9E 28
L39: Down 1C 26
L40: Burs 8J 15
WA5: Coll G 2F 64
WA5: Cuerd 6C 80
WA6: Alv 3F 114
WA11: Crank 6J 39
WN6: Appl B 5N 23
WN8: Dalt 8J 23
WN8: Newb 3A 22
WN8: Skel 5H 31
(Barnfield Dr.)
WN8: Skel 6G 31
(Beavers La.)
Bk. Langham St. L4: Walt 1E 58
Bk. Leeds St. L3: Liv 2C 4 (6A 58)
Bk. Legh St. WA12: Newt W 7J 51
Bk. Lime St. L1: Liv 5G 5
Bk. Little Canning St. L8: Liv 9L 5
Bk. Luton Gro. L4: Walt 1E 58
Bk. Market St. WA12: Newt W 6J 51
Bk. Maryland St. L1: Liv 7J 5
Bk. Menai St. CH41: Birke 2J 73
Bk. Mersey Vw. L22: Water 9J 33
Bk. Moss La. L40: Burs 7K 15
Bk. Mount St. L22: Water 1K 43
Bk. Mulberry St. L7: Liv 8L 5 (9E 58)
Bk. Oliver St. CH41: Birke 2L 73
(off Argyle St.)
Bk. Orford St. L15: Wav 9L 59
(off Sandown La.)
Back o' the Town La. L38: Ince B 9L 25
Bk. Percy St. L8: Liv 9K 5
Bk. Pickop St. L3: Liv 3E 4
Bk. Price St. CH41: Birke 1K 73
Bk. Renshaw St. L1: Liv 6H 5 (8D 58)
Bk. Rockfield Rd. L4: Walt 2E 58
(off Blessington Rd.)
Back St Bride St. L8: Liv 8L 5
Bk. Sandon St. L8: Liv 9L 5 (1E 74)
Bk. Sandown La. L15: Wav 9L 59
(off Sandown La.)
Bk. School La. WN8: Skel 3A 30
WN8: Uph 5M 31
Bk. Seaman Rd. L15: Wav 1K 75
(off Seaman Rd.)
Back Seaview CH47: Hoy 1C 70
Bk. Seel St. L1: Liv 7G 5
Bk. Sir Howard St. L8: Liv 8L 5
Bk. Skull Ho. La. WN6: Appl B 5N 23
Bk. South Rd. L22: Water 1L 43
Bk. Stanley Rd. L20: Boot 7B 44
Bk. Towerlands St. L7: Liv 8G 58
(off Church Mt.)
Bk. Virginia St. PR8: South 9G 7
Bk. Wellesley Rd. L8: Liv 4F 74
(off The Elms)
Bk. Westminster Rd.
L4: Kirkd 1D 58
Bk. Windsor Vw. L8: Liv 1G 75
(off Lodge La.)
Bk. Winstanley Rd.
L22: Water 9L 33
Bk. York Ter. L5: Liv 3D 58
Badbury Cl. WA11: Hay 3F 50
Badby Wood L33: Kirkb 7D 36
Baddow Cft. L25: Woolt 5C 76
Baden Ct. CH48: W Kir 5B 70
Baden Ho. L13: Liv 6N 59
Baden Rd. L13: Liv 6N 59
Bader Cl. CH61: Pens 4M 87
Badger Bait CH64: Lit N 8F 100
Badger Cl. WA7: Pal F 9C 96
Badgers Cl. CH66: Gt Sut 5L 111
Badgers Pk. CH64: Lit N 8F 100
Badgers Rake L37: Form 8C 16
Badgers Rake La.
CH66: Led, Lit Sut 2B 110
Badger's Set CH48: Caldy 1E 86
Badger Way CH43: Pren 8E 72
Badminton St. L8: Liv 5E 74
Baffin Cl. CH46: Leas 5A 56
Bagnall Cl. WA5: Gt San 3L 81
Bagnall St. L4: Walt 2F 58
Bagot Av. WA5: Warr 9A 66
Bagot St. L15: Wav 1J 75
Baguley Av. WA8: Hale B 2D 94
Bahama Cl. WA11: Hay 2F 50
Bahama Rd. WA11: Hay 2F 50
Baildon Grn. CH66: Lit Sut 9G 103
(off Dunmore Rd.)
Bailey Av. CH65: Ell P 8L 103
Bailey Ct. L20: Boot 3D 44
Bailey Dr. L20: Boot 4D 44
Bailey La. M31: Part 6M 69
Baileys Cl. WA8: Wid 3K 79
Bailey's La. L24: Hale 6K 93
L24: Speke 4E 92
L26: Halew 8L 77
Bailey St. L1: Liv 8H 5 (9D 58)
Bailey Way L31: Mag 4H 35
Bainbridge Av. WA3: Low 2G 52
Bainbridge Cres. WA5: Gt San 9G 65
Baines Av. M44: Irlam 1M 69
Bainton Cl. L32: Kirkb 3E 46
Bainton Rd. L32: Kirkb 3E 46
Baker Dr. CH66: Gt Sut 2K 111
Baker Rd. WA7: West P 8G 95
Bakersfield Dr. WA5: Gt San 1J 81
Bakers Grn. Rd. L36: Huy 5J 61
Bakers La. PR9: South 4L 7
Baker St. L6: Liv 1N 5 (6F 58)
L36: Huy 7L 61
WA9: St H 7M 49
Baker Way L6: Liv 2M 5 (6F 58)
Bakewell Cl. CH66: Gt Sut 5K 111
Bakewell Gro. L9: Ain 3G 45
Bakewell Rd. WA5: Burtw 2H 65
Bala Cl. WA5: Call 7N 65
Bala Gro. CH44: Wall 6G 56
Bala St. L4: Walt 3G 58
Balcarres Av. L18: Moss H 3L 75
Baldock Cl. WA4: Thel 5K 83
Baldwin Av. L16: Child 9C 60
Baldwin St. WA10: St H 6K 49
Bales, The L30: N'ton 7F 34
Balfe St. L21: Sea 4N 43
Balfour Av. L20: Boot 5A 44
Balfour Rd. CH43: Oxton 3H 73
CH44: Wall 7G 57
L20: Boot 5A 44
PR8: South 1D 12
Balfour St. L4: Walt 2E 58
WA7: Run 6J 95
WA10: St H 7G 48
Balham Cl. WA8: Wid 4K 79
Balharry Av. WA11: Hay 3H 51
Balker Dr. WA10: St H 5J 49
Ballantrae Rd. L18: Moss H 5A 76
Ballantyne Dr. CH43: Bid 8C 56
Ballantyne Gro. L13: Liv 2K 59
L20: Boot 4D 44
Ballantyne Pl. L13: Liv 2K 59
WA2: Win 3B 66
Ballantyne Rd. L13: Liv 3K 59
Ballantyne Wlk. CH43: Bid 8C 56
Ballantyne Way WA3: Low 2F 52
Ballard Rd. CH48: W Kir 5F 70
Ballater Dr. WA2: Warr 5F 66
Ball Av. CH45: New B 1G 56
Balliol Cl. CH43: Bid 8C 56
Balliol Gro. L23: Blun 9H 33
Balliol Ho. L20: Boot 8B 44
Balliol Rd. L20: Boot 8B 44
Balliol Way WN4: Ash M 7H 41
BALL O' DITTON 7H 79
Ball Path WA8: Wid 7J 79
Ball Path Way WA8: Wid 7H 79
Balls Pl. PR8: South 8G 6
Ball's Rd. CH43: Oxton 4H 73
Balls Rd. E. CH41: Birke 3J 73
Ball St. WA9: St H 6N 49
Balmer St. WA9: St H 1G 63
Balmoral Av. L23: Crosb 8L 33
WA3: Low 1E 52
WA9: St H 2M 63
Balmoral Cl. L33: Kirkb 6C 36
PR9: South 4N 7
Balmoral Ct. L13: Liv 4K 59
Balmoral Dr. L37: Form 3E 24
PR9: South 5M 7
WA6: Hel 1E 114
Balmoral Gdns. CH43: Pren 7F 72
CH65: Ell P 2B 112
Balmoral Gro. CH43: Noct 5D 72
Balmoral Ho. L39: Augh 2C 28
Balmoral Rd. CH45: New B 9J 43
L6: Liv 5H 59
L9: Walt 4F 44
L31: Mag 2H 35
WA4: Grap 6G 83
WA8: Wid 4J 79
WN4: Ash M 7J 41
Balmoral Way L34: Presc 4K 61
Balm St. L7: Liv 7G 59
Balniel St. WA9: Clock F 6N 63
Balsham Cl. L25: Hunts X 9H 77
Baltic Rd. L20: Boot 7A 44
Baltic St. L4: Walt 2F 58
Baltimore Gdns. WA5: Gt San 1L 81
Baltimore St. L1: Liv 7J 5 (9D 58)
Bamber Gdns. PR9: South 7M 7
Bamboo Cl. L27: N'ley 2J 77
Bamburgh Ct. CH65: Ell P 2C 112
Bamburgh Pl. WN4: Ash M 6J 41
Bamford Cl. WA7: Run 8M 95
Bamford Dr. L6: Liv 1M 5 (5F 58)
BAMFURLONG 4N 41
Bampton Av. WA11: St H 1L 49
Bampton Rd. L16: Child 9B 60
Banastre Dr. WA12: Newt W 7A 52
Banastre Rd. PR8: South 1N 11
Banbury Av. L25: Woolt 6G 77
Banbury Cl. WN7: Leigh 1M 53
Banbury Ct. L20: Boot 6C 44
(off Worcester Rd.)
Banbury Dr. WA5: Gt San 4L 81
Banbury Rd. WN5: Bil 1N 39
Banbury Way CH43: Oxton 6E 72
Bancroft Cl. L25: Hunts X 8G 76
Bancroft Rd. WA8: Wid 6N 79
Bandon Cl. L24: Hale 5A 94
Banff Av. CH63: East 1C 102
Bangor Cl. CH66: Gt Sut 6K 111
Bangor Rd. CH45: Wall 3D 56
BANGOR'S GREEN 6J 19
Bangor St. L5: Liv 4B 58
Banister House Fishery 7K 9
Bank Av. WN5: Orr 7N 31
Bank Brow WN8: Roby M 9M 23
Bankburn Rd. L13: Liv 3K 59
Bank Cl. CH64: Lit N 8G 100
Bank Dene CH42: Rock F 8N 73
Bankes La. WA7: West 1J 107
WA7: West P 9H 95
Bankfield WN8: Skel 5F 30
Bankfield Av. M44: Cad 4K 69
Bankfield Ct. CH62: Brom 4E 90
L13: Liv 4L 59
Bankfield La. PR9: South 5N 7
Bankfield Rd. L13: Liv 3L 59
WA8: Wid 7E 78
Bankfields Dr. CH62: East 1G 102
Bankfield St. L20: Kirkd 1A 58
Bank Gdns. WA5: Penk 4G 80
Bankhall La. L20: Kirkd 1B 58
Bank Hall Pk. WA1: Warr 4D 82
Bankhall Station (Rail) 1B 58
Bankhall St. L20: Kirkd 1B 58
BANK HEATH 2A 52
Bank Hey CH64: Lit N 9F 100
Bank Ho. La. WA6: Hel 1F 114
Bankland Rd. L13: Liv 4L 59
Banklands Cl. M44: Cad 4K 69
Bank La. L31: Mell 4A 36
L33: Kirkb 4A 36
Bank M. WA6: Hel 1F 114
Bank Nook PR9: South 4K 7
(not continuous)
Bank Pace PR9: Banks 1B 8
Bank Pas. PR8: South 8G 6
Bank Pl. WA3: Golb 1B 52
BANK QUAY 4N 81
Bank Quay Trad. Est.
WA1: Warr 4A 82
Bank Rd. L20: Boot 7A 44
WN8: Roby M 8M 23
BANKS 1E 8
Banks, The CH45: Wall 2E 56
Bank's Av. CH47: Meols 9E 54
Banksbarn WN8: Skel 5F 30
Banks Cres. WA4: Westy 4G 83
Bankside L38: Hight 9F 24
WA1: Warr 3A 82
WA7: Pres B 8G 96
WN8: Parb 3E 22
Bankside Av. WN4: Ash M 3J 41
Bankside Ct. L21: Lith 2N 43
Bankside Rd. CH42: Rock F 8M 73
Banks Ind. Pk. PR9: Banks 4G 9
Bank's La. L19: Garst 3B 92
L24: Speke 5D 92
Banks Leisure Cen. 2E 8
Bank Sq. PR9: South 7G 6
Banks Rd. CH48: W Kir 6B 70
CH60: Hesw 8K 87
L19: Garst 2A 92
PR9: South 2B 8
Bank St. CH41: Birke 2L 73
WA1: Warr 3C 82
WA3: Glaz 4G 69
WA3: Golb 1B 52
WA8: Wid 3K 95
WA10: St H 7H 49
WA12: Newt W 7H 51
Bank's Way L19: Garst 3B 92
BANK TOP 9M 23
Bankville Rd. CH42: Tran 5L 73
Bankwood WN6: Shev 7N 23
Bannatyne's Health Club
Skelmersdale 2E 30
Banner Hey L35: Whis 8A 62
Bannerman St. L7: Liv 9J 59
Banner St. L15: Wav 1K 75
WA10: St H 7J 49
Banner Wlk. WA10: St H 7J 49
(off Banner St.)
Banning Cl. CH41: Birke 1K 73
Bannister Way WN3: Wins 1G 40
Banstead Gro. L15: Wav 1N 75
Barbara Av. L10: Faz 3M 45
Barbara St. WA9: Clock F 6A 64
Barbauld St. WA1: Warr 3C 82
Barberry Cl. CH46: More 9J 55
Barberry Cres. L30: N'ton 7F 34
Barberry Wlk. M31: Part 6M 69
(off Wychelm Rd.)
Barber's La. CW9: Ant 7M 99
Barber St. WA9: St H 6M 49
Barbondale Cl. WA5: Gt San 1H 81
Barbour Dr. L20: Boot 4D 44
Barbrook Way L9: Walt 7G 44
Barchester Dr. L17: Aig 7H 75
Barclay St. L8: Liv 4E 74
Barcombe Rd. CH60: Hesw 6D 88
Bardale Gro. WN4: Ash M 8J 41
Bardley Cres. L35: Tar G 1L 77
Bardon Cl. L25: Gate 3G 77
Bardsay Rd. L4: Walt 9E 44
Bardsey Cl. CH65: Ell P 4A 112
Bardsley Av. WA5: Warr 7A 66
Bardsley Cl. WN8: Uph 5K 31
Barford Cl. CH43: Bid 2B 72
PR8: Ains 8G 11
WA5: Westb 8K 65
WN8: Uph 5K 31
Barford Dr. WA3: Low 2H 53
Barford Grange CH64: Will 6A 102
Barford Rd. L25: Hunts X 1F 92
L36: Huy 3K 61
Bargate Water WA9: St H 3G 63
Barge Ind. Park, The WA9: St H 5M 49
Barham Ct. WA3: Ris 5L 67
Barington Dr. WA7: Murd 8G 96
Barkbeth Rd. L36: Huy 4G 60
Barkbeth Wlk. L36: Huy 4G 60
Barkeley Dr. L21: Sea 4M 43
Barker Cl. L36: Huy 9K 61
Barker La. CH49: Grea 6K 71
(not continuous)
Barker Rd. CH61: Irby 1N 87
Barkers Hollow Rd.
WA4: Dutt, Pres H 9J 97
Barkerville Cl. L13: Liv 2J 59
Barker Way L6: Liv 4G 58
Barkfield Av. L37: Form 9E 16
Barkfield La. L37: Form 9D 16
Barkhill Rd. L17: Aig 7L 75
Barkin Centre, The WA8: Wid 8M 79
Barkis Cl. L8: Liv 3E 74
Bark Rd. L21: Lith 1B 44
Barley Castle Cl. WA4: App T 4J 99
Barleycastle La. WA4: App T 2L 99
Barleycastle Trad. Est. WA4: App T 3K 99
Barleyfield CH61: Pens 3M 87
Barley Mere Cl. WA12: Newt W 8L 51
Barleymow Cl. CH66: Gt Sut 3H 111
Barley Rd. WA4: Thel 5K 83
Barlow Av. CH63: Beb 1N 89
Barlow Gro. WA9: St H 8C 50
Barlow La. L4: Kirkd 1D 58
Barlows Cl. L9: Ain 2J 45
Barlow's La. L9: Ain 2J 45
L39: Hals 9C 12
Barlow St. L4: Kirkd 1D 58
Barlow Way WA7: West P 7G 94
Barmouth Cl. WA5: Call 7N 65
Barmouth Rd. CH45: Wall 3D 56
Barmouth Way L5: Liv 4B 58
Barnack Cl. WA1: Padg 9H 67
Barnacre Dr. CH64: Park 4B 100
Barnacre La. CH46: More 2J 71

Barnard Dr. CH65: Ell P 2C 112
Barnard Rd. CH43: Oxton 3H 73
Barnard St. WA5: Warr 5M 81
Barn Cl. L30: N'ton 7F 34
PR4: Mere B 5L 9
Barn Cft. WA6: Hel 1F 114
Barncroft CH61: Pens 4N 87
WA7: Nort 8F 96
Barncroft, The CH49: Grea 3L 71
Barncroft Pl. L23: Crosb 5L 33
Barncroft Rd. L26: Halew 9L 77
Barndale Rd. L18: Moss H 4L 75
Barnes Av. WA2: Fearn 7J 67
Barnes Cl. L33: Kirkb 5C 36
WA5: Gt San 3J 81
WA8: Wid 6N 79
Barnes Dr. L31: Lyd 8H 27
Barnes Grn. CH63: Spit 5N 89
Barnes Rd. L39: Augh 1C 28
WA8: Wid 6M 79
WN8: Skel 3B 30
Barnes St. L6: Liv 4F 58
Barneston Rd. WA8: Wid 5A 80
Barnet Cl. L7: Liv 9H 59
Barnett Av. WA12: Newt W 7G 51
Barnfield Av. WA7: Murd 9E 96
Barnfield Cl. CH47: Meols 8F 54
CH66: Gt Sut 3H 111
L12: W Der 3N 59
L30: N'ton 9D 34
Barnfield Dr. L12: W Der 3N 59
WN8: Skel 5H 31
Barnfield Rd. WA1: Wools 1K 83
Barnham Cl. L24: Speke 3F 92
WA3: Golb 2B 52
Barnham Dr. L16: Child 1C 76
Barn Hey CH47: Hoy 3B 70
Barn Hey Cres. CH47: Meols 9G 54
Barn Hey Grn. L12: W Der 3N 59
Barn Hey Rd. L33: Kirkb 9E 36
Barnhill Rd. L15: Wav 2M 75
Barnhouse La. CH3: Lit Ba 9D 114
Barnhurst Cl. L16: Child 1C 76
Barnhurst Rd. L16: Child 1C 76
Barn La. WA3: Golb 3A 52
WA5: Burtw 4H 65
Barnmeadow Rd. L25: Gate 3E 76
Barns, The L37: Form 3G 24
Barnsbury Rd. L4: Walt 8H 45
Barnsdale Av. CH61: Thing 2B 88
Barnside Ct. L16: Child 1C 76
Barns La. WA13: Warb 2N 85
WA14: Dun M, Warb 3N 85
Barnstaple Way WA5: Penk 4G 81
BARNSTON 4C 88
Barnston Av. CH65: Ell P 9L 103
Barnston La. CH46: More 8M 55
Barnston Rd. CH60: Hesw 8B 88
CH61: Barn, Thing 8B 88
L9: Ain 3G 44
Barnston Towers Cl.
CH60: Hesw 7C 88
Barnstream Cl. L27: N'ley 2G 77
Barn St. WA8: Wid 1K 95
Barnswood Cl. WA4: Grap 7K 83
Barnton Cl. L20: Boot 4B 44
WA3: Low 3E 52
Barn Way WA12: Newt W 7K 51
Barnwell Av. CH44: Wall 4H 57
WA3: Cul 6L 53
Barnwood CH66: Lit Sut 7E 102
Barnwood Rd. L36: Huy 5F 60
Baron Cl. WA1: Wools 1L 83
Baroncroft Rd. L25: Woolt 4D 76
Baronet M. WA4: Warr 7B 82
Baronet Rd. WA4: Warr 7B 82
Barons Cl. WA7: Cas 6B 96
WA8: Wid 8F 78
Barons Hey L28: Stockb V 1D 60
Barren Gro. CH43: Oxton 4H 73
Barrett Av. PR8: Birkd 4N 11
Barrett Rd. PR8: Birkd 4N 11
Barrington Cl. WN3: Wins 1F 40
Barrington Dr. PR8: Ains 9H 11
Barrington Rd. CH44: Wall 6J 57
L15: Wav 2K 75
Barrison Grn. L40: Scar 3C 20
Barrow Av. WA2: Warr 7F 66
Barrow Cl. L12: W Der 9A 46
Barrowdale Rd. WA3: Golb 2C 52
Barrowfield Rd. WA10: Eccl 5D 48
Barrow Hall La. WA5: Gt San 1G 80
Barrow La. WA2: Croft, Win 8C 52
WA3: Croft 8C 52
WA6: Dun H 8B 114
BARROW NOOK 1J 37
Barrow Nook La. L39: Bic 9J 29
Barrows Cotts. *L35: Whis 6B 62*
(off Cross La.)
BARROW'S GREEN 4N 79
Barrow's Grn. La.
WA8: Wid 6A 80
Barrow's Row WA8: Wid 4L 79
Barrow St. WA10: St H 7K 49
WN4: Ash M 6M 41
Barrule Cl. WA4: App 9E 82
Barry Cl. CH65: Ell P 5A 112
Barry Dr. L19: Garst 1N 91
Barrymore Av. WA4: Westy 4G 83
Barrymore Ct. WA4: Grap 7H 83
Barrymore Rd. L13: Liv 6L 59
WA4: Grap 7H 83
WA7: Run 8L 95
Barrymore Way CH63: Brom 9A 90
Barry St. WA4: Warr 4D 82
Barsbank Cl. WA13: Lymm 5C 84
Barsbank La. WA13: Lymm 5C 84
Barshaw Gdns. WA4: App 3F 98
Bartholomew Cl. L35: Rainh 8H 63
Bartlegate Cl. WA7: Brook 1D 108
Bartlett St. L15: Wav 1K 75
BARTON 7E 18
Barton Av. WA4: Grap 6H 83
Barton Cl. CH47: Hoy 2A 70
L21: Lith 9N 33
WA7: Murd 8F 96
WA10: St H 6J 49
Barton Clough WN5: Bil 6A 40
Barton Hey Dr. CH48: Caldy 1D 86
Barton Heys Rd. L37: Form 3D 24
Barton Rd. CH47: Hoy 2A 70
L9: Walt 6E 44
Bartons Cl. PR9: South 2B 8
Barton St. CH41: Birke 2J 73
(not continuous)
WA3: Golb 1B 52
Barwell Av. WA11: St H 4M 49
Barwell Cl. WA3: Golb 1D 52
Basil Cl. L16: Child 9C 60
Basildon Cl. WA9: St H 2J 63
Basil Grange Apartments
L12: W Der 4M 59
(off North Dr.)
Basil Rd. L16: Child 9B 60
Basing St. L19: Garst 9A 76
Baskervyle Cl. CH60: Hesw 9A 88
Baskervyle Rd. CH60: Hesw 9A 88
Basnett St. L1: Liv 5F 4 (8C 58)
Bassendale Rd. CH62: Brom 5D 90
Bassenthwaite Av. CH43: Noct 3D 72
L33: Kirkb 7B 36
WA11: St H 2K 49
Bassett Gro. WN3: Wins 1E 40
Bateman Cl. CH65: Ell P 8N 103
Bates Cres. WA10: St H 1G 62
Bates La. WA6: Hel 1G 114
Batey Av. L35: Rainh 5E 62
Batherton Cl. WA8: Wid 9L 79
Bathgate Way L33: Kirkb 5B 36
Bath Springs L39: Orm 8D 20
Bath Springs Ct. L39: Orm 8D 20
Bath St. CH62: Port S 2A 90
L3: Liv 3B 4 (7A 58)
L22: Water 2K 43
PR9: South 7G 6
WA1: Warr 3B 82
WA10: St H 7J 49
Bath St. Nth. PR9: South 7G 7
Bathurst Rd. L19: Gras 9N 75
Bathwood Dr. CH64: Lit N 9E 100
Batley St. L13: Liv 6M 59
Battenberg St. L7: Liv 4N 5 (7F 58)
Battersby La. WA2: Warr 2D 82
Battersea Ct. WA8: Wid 5J 79
Battery Cl. L17: Aig 6H 75
Battery La. WA1: Wools 1N 83
Battle Way *L37: Form 2H 25*
(off Buckfast Dr.)
Baucher Dr. L20: Boot 3D 44
Baumville Dr. CH63: Spit 5M 89
Bawtry Ct. WA2: Padg 8F 66
Baxter Cl. WA7: Murd 8F 96
(not continuous)
Baxters La. WA9: St H 1N 63
Baxters La. Ind. Est. WA9: St H 9N 49
Baxter St. WA5: Warr 3N 81
Baycliffe WA13: Lymm 6E 84
Baycliffe Cl. WA7: Beech 1N 107
Baycliff Rd. L12: W Der 1C 60
Bayfield Rd. L19: Gras 9M 75
Bayhorse La. L3: Liv 3K 5 (7E 58)
Baynard Dr. WA8: Hale B 2F 94
Baysdale Cl. L8: Liv 4F 74
Bayswater Cl. WA7: Nort 3H 97
Bayswater Ct. CH45: Wall 3D 56
Bayswater Gdns. CH45: Wall 2D 56
Bayswater Rd. CH45: Wall 3D 56
Baythorne Rd. L4: Walt 8H 45
Baytree Cl. CH66: Gt Sut 4L 111
PR9: South 2B 8
Bay Tree Gro. WA9: St H 1M 63
Baytree Gro. L31: Mell 8M 35
Baytree Rd. CH42: Tran 5L 73
CH48: Frank 6G 71
Bay Vw. Dr. CH45: Wall 2C 56
Bayvil Cl. WA7: Murd 8G 96
Beacham Rd. PR8: South 8K 7
Beach Bank L22: Water 9J 33
Beachcroft Rd. CH47: Meols 8F 54
Beach Gro. CH45: Wall 2J 57
Beach Lawn L22: Water 1J 43
Beach M. PR8: Birkd 9E 6
Beach Priory Gdns. PR8: South 9E 6
Beach Rd. CH47: Hoy 2A 70
L21: Lith 2N 43
PR8: Birkd 9E 6
Beach Wlk. CH48: W Kir 8C 70
Beacon Country Park 3J 31
Beacon Country Park Vis. Cen. 2H 31
Beacon Ct. CH60: Hesw 7A 88
Beacon Crossing WN8: Parb 3F 22
Beacon Dr. CH48: W Kir 6D 70
Beacon Grn. WN8: Skel 4H 31
Beacon Gro. WA11: St H 4N 49
Beacon Hgts. WN8: Uph 4K 31
Beacon Hill Vw. WA7: West P 8G 95
Beacon Ho. *L5: Liv 5D 58*
(off Portland Pl.)
Beacon La. CH60: Hesw 7A 88
L5: Liv 3E 58
WN8: Dalt 7D 22
Beacon Pde. CH60: Hesw 7A 88
Beacon Park Golf Course 2J 31
Beacon Rd. WN5: Bil 4N 39
Beacons, The CH60: Hesw 8A 88
L37: Form 1F 24
(off School La.)
WN6: Shev 6N 23
Beaconsfield L34: Presc 3A 62
Beaconsfield Cl. CH42: Tran 5M 73
Beaconsfield Ct. L39: Orm 8D 20
Beaconsfield Cres. WA8: Wid 4K 79
Beaconsfield Gro. WA8: Wid 4L 79
Beaconsfield Rd. CH62: New F 9A 74
L21: Sea 3M 43
L25: Woolt 5C 76
PR9: South 9L 7
WA7: Run 7H 95
WA8: Wid 5L 79
WA10: St H 5F 48
Beaconsfield St. L8: Liv 2F 74
Beaconsfield Ter. *L19: Garst 1N 91*
(off St Mary's Rd.)
Beacon Sports Hall, The 6K 49
Beacon Vw. WN6: Appl B 5M 23
Beacon Vw. Dr. WN8: Uph 5L 31
Beadnell Dr. WA5: Penk 5G 81
Beames Cl. L7: Liv 8H 59
Beamish Cl. WA4: App 4E 98
WA9: St H 5H 63
Beamont St. WA8: Wid 3K 95
Beardsmore Dr. WA3: Low 2F 52
Bearncroft WN8: Skel 6F 30
Beasley Cl. CH66: Gt Sut 2J 111
Beatles Story, The 8D 4 (9B 58)
Beatrice Av. CH63: Hghr B 9L 73
Beatrice St. L20: Boot 9C 44
WA4: Warr 5E 82
Beattock Cl. L33: Kirkb 5B 36
Beatty Av. WA2: Warr 8D 66
Beatty Cl. CH48: Caldy 1D 86
L35: Whis 7A 62
Beatty Rd. L13: Liv 6M 59
PR8: South 1D 12
Beauclair Dr. L15: Wav 1N 75
Beaufort L37: Form 2G 25
Beaufort Cl. L39: Augh 3M 27
WA5: Gt San 3J 81
WA7: Run 8L 95
WA8: Wid 8D 78
Beaufort Dr. CH44: Wall 4E 56
Beaufort Rd. CH41: Birke 8F 56
Beaufort St. L8: Liv 2D 74
(Hill St.)
L8: Liv 2D 74
(Mann St.)
L8: Liv 3D 74
(Northumberland St.)
WA5: Warr 4N 81
WA9: St H 9M 49
Beaumaris Ct. CH43: Oxton 3H 73
Beaumaris Dr. CH61: Thing 1B 88
CH65: Ell P 3B 112
Beaumaris Rd. CH45: Wall 3D 56
Beaumaris St. L20: Kirkd 1B 58
(not continuous)
Beaumaris Way WA7: Cas 5B 96
Beaumont Av. WA10: St H 6G 48
Beaumont Ct. *WA4: Warr 6D 82*
(off Elphins Dr.)
Beaumont Cres. L39: Augh 2B 28
Beaumont Dr. L10: Ain 1K 45
Beaumont St. L8: Liv 1G 74
Beau St. L3: Liv 5D 58
Beauworth Av. CH49: Grea 5K 71
Beaver Ct. WN4: Ash M 5L 41
Beaver Gro. L9: Ain 4F 44
Beavers La. WN8: Skel 6G 31
Beavers Way WN8: Skel 6G 31
BEBINGTON 1N 89
Bebington Rd. CH42: Rock F, Tran 6K 73
CH62: New F 9A 74
CH63: Beb 1N 89
CH66: Gt Sut 1J 111
Bebington Station (Rail) 9N 73
Bebles Rd. L39: Orm 1A 28
Bechers WA8: Wid 5E 78
Bechers Bus. Cen. L30: N'ton 9F 34
Bechers Ct. L30: N'ton 8G 35
Bechers Dr. L9: Ain 9H 35
Bechers Row L9: Walt 4E 44
Beck Cl. L10: Faz 3N 45
Beckenham Av. L18: Moss H 3L 75
Beckenham Cl. WA8: Wid 4N 79
Beckenham Rd. CH45: New B 9H 43
Becket St. L4: Kirkd 2C 58
(not continuous)
Beckett Cl. L33: Know I 2G 46
Beckett Dr. WA2: Win 4B 66
WA13: Warb 9J 69
Beckett Gro. CH63: Hghr B 9K 73
Beck Gro. WA11: St H 2L 49
Beckinsale Cl. L26: Halew 7L 77
Beck Rd. L20: Boot 5B 44
Beckwith Ct. *CH41: Birke 9J 57*
(off Beckwith St.)
Beckwith St. CH41: Birke 9H 57
L1: Liv 8F 4 (9C 58)
Beckwith St. E. CH41: Birke 1K 73
Becky St. L6: Liv 4G 59
Becontree Rd. L12: W Der 5B 60
Bective St. L7: Liv 9H 59
Bedale Cl. WA12: Newt W 9M 51
Bedale Wlk. L33: Kirkb 8D 36
Bedburn Dr. L36: Huy 6F 60
Bede Cl. L33: Kirkb 5C 36
Bedford Av. CH42: Rock F 7L 73
CH65: Whit 3M 111
L31: Mell 5L 35
Bedford Av. E. CH65: Whit 3N 111
Bedford Cl. L7: Liv 8L 5 (9E 58)
L36: Huy 6L 61
Bedford Ct. CH42: Rock F 6M 73
L7: Liv 9L 5
PR8: Birkd 4N 11
Bedford Dr. CH42: Rock F 7K 73
Bedford Gro. M44: Cad 3H 69
Bedford Pl. CH42: Rock F 6N 73
L20: Boot 9A 44
L21: Sea 3M 43
WN4: Ash M 6J 41
Bedford Rd. CH42: Rock F 6M 73
CH45: Wall 3H 57
L4: Walt 8C 44
L20: Boot 9B 44
PR8: Birkd 4N 11
Bedford Rd. E. CH42: Rock F 6N 73
Bedford St. WA4: Stockt H 8D 82
WA9: St H 8N 49
Bedford St. Nth. L7: Liv 6L 5 (8E 58)
Bedford St. Sth. L7: Liv 9L 5 (9E 58)
(not continuous)
Bedford Wlk. L7: Liv 8L 5
Beecham Cl. L36: Huy 8H 61
Beech Av. CH49: Upton 2L 71
CH61: Pens 3A 88
L17: Aig 6G 74
L23: Crosb 5N 33
L31: Mell 8N 35
L34: Eccl P 2C 62
WA3: Cul 7N 53
WA3: Low 3G 53
WA4: Thel 5L 83
WA5: Penk 5E 80
WA6: Frod 6M 107
WA9: Clock F 5M 63
WA11: Hay 3H 51
WN8: Parb 4F 22
Beechbank Rd. L18: Moss H 3K 75
Beechburn Cres. L36: Huy 6F 60
Beechburn Rd. L36: Huy 6E 60
Beech Cl. L12: Crox 7B 46
L32: Kirkb 8A 36
L40: Ruf 2N 15
M31: Part 6M 69
WA12: Newt W 8L 51
WN8: Skel 3B 30
Beech Cotts. WA4: Stret 5F 98
Beech Ct. CH42: Tran 4K 73
L18: Moss H 5A 76
PR9: South 7J 7
WA3: Ris 9N 53
Beechcroft L31: Mag 2H 35
Beechcroft Dr. CH65: Whit 2N 111
Beechcroft Rd. CH44: Wall 7J 57
Beechdale Rd. L18: Moss H 4M 75
Beechdene Rd. L4: Walt 2G 59
Beech Dr. L37: Form 9D 16
Beeches, The CH42: Rock F 7N 73
CH46: Leas 6M 55
CH66: Gt Sut 1J 111
L18: Moss H 3B 76
PR9: Banks 4H 9
WA6: Hel 1F 114
WA8: Wid 4N 79
(off Hampton Ct. Way)
WA9: Sut L 4N 63
Beechfield L31: Mag 2K 35
L36: Roby 7G 60
(off Church Rd.)
WN8: Parb 1F 22
Beechfield Cl. CH60: Hesw 8A 88
L26: Halew 1J 93
Beechfield Gdns. PR8: South 9E 6
Beechfield M. PR9: South 8G 7
Beechfield Rd. CH65: Ell P 9N 103
L18: Moss H 4B 76
WA4: Grap 6H 83
Beech Gdns. *WA7: Run 7M 95*
(off Beech Rd.)
WA11: Rainf 4B 38
Beech Grn. L12: W Der 1M 59
Beech Gro. CH66: Whit 5M 111
L9: Ain 4G 45
L21: Sea 4M 43
L30: N'ton 9F 34
PR9: South 8K 7
WA1: Padd 1H 83
WA4: Warr 5E 82
WA13: Lymm 6B 84

Beech Hey La. CH64: Will 5A 102
Beechill Cl. L25: Gate 4G 77
Beech La. L18: Moss H 3A 76
Beech Lawn L19: Gras 9L 75
Beech Mdw. L39: Orm 9E 20
Beech Mdws. L34: Presc 4L 61
Beechmill Dr. WA3: Cul 7M 53
Beechmore WA4: Moore 2K 97
Beech Mt. L7: Liv 7H 59
Beech Pk. L12: W Der 3M 59
L23: Crosb 5M 33
Beech Ri. L33: Kirkb 8D 36
Beech Rd. CH42: Tran 4J 73
CH60: Hesw 7C 88
CH63: Hghr B 9M 73
L4: Walt 8F 44
L36: Huy 8J 61
L39: Augh 6M 27
WA3: Golb 1B 52
WA4: Stockt H 8D 82
WA7: Run 7M 95
WA7: Sut W 2D 108
Beech St. L7: Liv 7H 59
L20: Boot 6B 44
WA10: St H 1G 62
WN4: Ash M 5J 41
Beech Ter. L7: Liv 7H 59
Beech Tree Av. WN6: Appl B 5N 23
Beech Tree Ct. *L19: Gras* *9L 75*
(off Beechwood Rd.)
Beechtree Farm Cl. WA16: High L 9H 85
Beech Tree Ho's. WN2: Bam 5N 41
Beechtree La. WA13: Lymm 9G 85
Beechtree Rd. L15: Wav 8N 59
Beechtrees WN8: Skel 5F 30
Beech Tree Wlk. WA6: Hel 1F 114
Beechurst Cl. L25: Gate 3F 76
Beechurst Rd. L25: Gate 3F 76
Beech Wlk. WN3: Wins 1E 40
WN7: Leigh 1M 53
Beechwalk, The L14: Knott A 5N 59
Beechway CH63: Beb 4M 89
L31: Mag 1N 35
Beechway Av. L31: Mag 1N 35
Beechways WA4: App 1E 98
Beechways Dr. CH64: Nest 7D 100
BEECHWOOD
CH43 9C 56
WA7 1A 108
Beechwood WN8: Skel 1F 30
Beechwood Av. CH45: Wall 4E 56
L26: Halew 9J 77
WA1: Padg 1F 82
WA5: Gt San 3H 81
WA7: Beech 9M 95
WA12: Newt W 6M 51
WN4: Ash M 9J 41
Beechwood Cl. L19: Gras 9M 75
WA9: Clock F 6M 63
Beechwood Ct. *CH49: Woodc* *7B 72*
(off Childwall Grn.)
L31: Mag *2L 35*
(off Deyes La.)
WN8: Skel 6G 30
Beechwood Dr. CH43: Bid 1C 72
CH66: Gt Sut 4J 111
L37: Form 3C 24
L39: Orm 8B 20
Beechwood Gdns. L19: Gras 9L 75
Beechwood Grn. L19: Gras 9M 75
Beechwood Gro. L35: Presc 5B 62
Beechwood La. WA3: Cul 6L 53
Beechwood Recreation Cen. 1C 72
Beechwood Rd. CH62: Brom 7B 90
L19: Gras 9L 75
L21: Lith 4A 44
Beechwood Rd. Sth. L19: Gras 1L 91
Beecroft Cl. WA5: Old H 8M 65
Beeford Dr. WN5: Orr 7N 31
Beesands Cl. L27: N'ley 4K 77
Beesley Rd. L34: Presc 3N 61
Beeston Cl. CH43: Bid 2C 72
WA3: Birchw 5K 67
Beeston Ct. WA7: Manor P 3E 96
Beeston Dr. CH61: Pens 3N 87
L30: N'ton 6G 34
Beeston Grn. CH66: Gt Sut 9K 103
Beeston Gro. L19: Gras 9M 75
Beeston St. L4: Kirkd 1D 58
Beetham Plaza L2: Liv 5D 4
Beetham Twr. L3: Liv 3C 4
Beetham Way L33: Kirkb 8D 36
Begonia Gdns. WA9: Bold 2C 64
Beilby Rd. WA11: Hay 3H 51
Beldale Pk. L32: Kirkb 7A 36
Beldon Cres. L36: Huy 6F 60
Belem Cl. L17: Aig 3H 75
Belem Twr. L17: Aig 3H 75
Belfast Rd. L13: Liv 6N 59
Belfield WN8: Skel 6G 30
Belfield Cres. L36: Huy 8J 61
Belfield Dr. CH43: Oxton 5H 73
Belford Dr. CH46: More 9K 55
Belfort Rd. L25: Gate 4F 76
Belfry Cl. CH46: More 8J 55
L12: W Der 3C 60
Belgrave Av. CH44: Wall 5J 57
WA1: Padg 9G 67
Belgrave Cl. WA8: Wid 5A 80
WN7: Leigh 2K 53
Belgrave Dr. CH65: Ell P 9L 103
Belgrave Pl. PR8: Birkd 3M 11
Belgrave Rd. L17: Aig 5G 74
L21: Sea 3M 43
M44: Cad 4K 69
PR8: Birkd 2M 11
Belgrave St. CH44: Wall 4H 57
Belgravia Ct. WA8: Wid 5J 79
Belhaven Rd. L18: Moss H 3L 75
Belladonna Rd. L11: Norr G 9M 45
Bellair Av. L23: Crosb 7N 33
Bellairs Rd. L11: Norr G 1K 59
Bellamy Rd. L4: Walt 8D 44
Bellcast Cl. WA4: App 2D 98
Bell Cl. L36: Huy 9K 61
Belldene Gro. CH61: Hesw 5N 87
Bellefield Av. L12: W Der 3N 59
Bellemonte Cotts. *WA6: Frod* *7N 107*
(off Rosewood Av.)
Bellemonte Pk. WA6: Frod 8L 107
Bellemonte Rd. WA6: Frod 8L 107
Bellerophon Way WA11: Hay 4G 50
BELLE VALE 3G 76
Belle Va. Rd. L25: Gate 4F 76
Belle Va. Shop. Cen.
L25: Gate 2F 76
Belle-Vue WA3: Low 1G 53
Belle Vue Rd. CH44: Wall 7L 57
L25: Gate 4F 76
Bellew Rd. L11: Norr G 2L 59
Bellfield Cres. CH45: New B 1G 57
Bellflower Cl. WA8: Wid 4H 79
Bellhouse La. WA4: Grap 7K 83
WA4: Hghr Wal 9M 81
Bell Ho. Rd. WA8: Wid 7M 79
Bellingham Dr. WA7: Run 7K 95
Bellini Cl. L21: Sea 4N 43
Bellis Av. PR9: South 5L 7
Bellis Gro. L33: Kirkb 6B 36
Bell La. L35: Rainh 7K 63
WA4: Thel 4M 83
WA9: Sut M 7K 63
Bellmore St. L19: Garst 9A 76
Bell Rd. CH44: Wall 6K 57
Bell's Cl. L31: Lyd 8H 27
Bellsfield Cl. WA13: Lymm 6F 84
Bells La. L31: Lyd 9F 26
Bell St. L13: Liv 6M 59
Belltower La. L7: Liv 7G 58
Bellward Cl. CH63: Spit 5M 89
Belmont CH41: Birke 3J 73
Belmont Av. CH62: Brom 6B 90
WA3: Golb 1D 52
WA4: Westy 5G 83
WN5: Bil 9N 31
Belmont Cl. L40: Burs 2J 21
Belmont Cres. WA5: Gt San 2H 81
Belmont Dr. CH61: Pens 3A 88
L6: Liv 4H 59
Belmont Gro. CH43: Oxton 3J 73
L6: Liv 4H 59
Belmont Pl. *L19: Garst* *1A 92*
(off Shrewsbury Rd.)
Belmont Rd. CH45: New B 9H 43
CH48: W Kir 5C 70
L6: Liv 4G 59
WA8: Wid 6N 79
Belmont St. PR8: South 9F 6
WA10: St H 7G 48
Belmont Vw. *L6: Liv* *4H 59*
(off W. Derby Rd.)
Beloe St. L8: Liv 4E 74
Belper St. L19: Garst 1N 91
Belsford Way L24: Speke 3F 92
Belston Rd. L16: Child 9B 60
Belton Cl. WA3: Golb 3B 52
Belton Rd. L36: Huy 3H 61
(not continuous)
Belvedere *WA7: Run* *4K 95*
(off Cooper St.)
Belvedere Av. WA9: Sut L 3N 63
Belvedere Cl. *L34: Presc* *2B 62*
(off Marlborough Rd.)
WA6: Frod 5M 107
Belvedere Dr. L37: Form 3F 24
WA5: Gt San 2K 81
Belvedere Pk. L39: Augh 5A 28
Belvedere Rd. PR8: Ains 9J 11
WA12: Newt W 6K 51
WN4: Ash M 8L 41
Belvidere Ct. *CH49: Woodc* *7A 72*
(off Childwall Grn.)
Belvidere Pk. L23: Crosb 8L 33
Belvidere Rd. CH45: Wall 3F 56
L8: Liv 3F 74
L23: Crosb 8K 33
Belvoir Rd. L18: Aller 8A 76
WA4: Walt 8C 82
WA8: Wid 7L 79
Bembridge Cl. WA5: Gt San 1E 80
WA8: Wid 4J 79
Bembridge Ct. WN3: Wins 1G 40
Bempton Rd. L17: Aig 6G 75
Benbow Cl. CH43: Bid 9F 56
Benbow St. L20: Boot 8A 44
Bendee Av. CH64: Lit N 7G 100
Bendee Rd. CH64: Lit N 7F 100
Benedict Cl. CH49: Woodc 4B 72
Benedict Ct. L20: Boot 9B 44
Benedict St. L20: Boot 9C 44
Benfleet Ho. *L19: Aig* *9L 75*
(off The Spinnakers)
Bengarth Rd. PR9: South 7L 7
Benjamin Fold WN4: Ash M 6K 41
Ben La. L39: Bic 2K 37
Ben La. Ct. L39: Bic 1M 37
Benledi St. L5: Liv 4C 58
Benmore Rd. L18: Moss H 6M 75
Bennet's La. CH47: Meols 7F 54
Bennett Av. WA1: Warr 2G 82
Bennett Cl. CH64: Will 6N 101
Bennett Dr. WN5: Orr 8N 31
Bennetts Hill CH43: Oxton 4H 73
Bennetts La. WA8: Wid 6A 80
Bennett St. L19: Garst 1A 92
WA1: Warr 3D 82
Bennett Wlk. CH61: Pens 4N 87
Ben Nevis Dr. CH66: Lit Sut 8E 102
Ben Nevis Rd. CH42: Tran 6K 73
Bennison Dr. L19: Gras 9M 75
Ben's Ct. L34: Know 5F 46
Benson Cl. CH49: Upton 4N 71
Benson Rd. WA3: Birchw 6L 67
Benson St. L1: Liv 6H 5 (8D 58)
Bentfield L17: Aig 8L 75
Bentfield Cl. CH63: Hghr B 9K 73
Bentfield Gdns.
CH63: Hghr B 9K 73
Bentham Av. WA2: Warr 6D 66
Bentham Cl. CH43: Noct 5E 72
Bentham Dr. L16: Child 9B 60
Bentham St. PR8: South 1A 12
Bentham's Way PR8: South 4A 12
Bentinck Cl. CH41: Birke 2J 73
Bentinck Pl. CH41: Birke 2J 73
Bentinck St. CH41: Birke 2J 73
(not continuous)
L5: Liv 4A 58
WA7: Run 4J 95
WA9: St H 9N 49
Bent La. WA3: Cul 8N 53
WA13: Warb 2J 85
Bentley Rd. CH43: Oxton 4H 73
CH61: Pens 2N 87
L8: Liv 2G 74
Bentley's Farm La. WA4: Hghr Whi 9G 98
Bentley St. WA9: Clock F 6M 63
Benton Cl. L5: Liv 3C 58
Bents Cotts. CH2: Thorn M 3J 113
Bent Way CH60: Hesw 6A 88
Benty Cl. CH63: Hghr B 3L 89
Benty Farm Gro. CH61: Pens 1A 88
Benty Heath La. CH64: Will 3L 101
CH66: Hoot 3L 101
Benwick Rd. L32: Kirkb 9N 35
Berbice Rd. L18: Moss H 3M 75
Beresford Av. CH63: Beb 9N 73
Beresford Cl. CH43: Oxton 3G 73
Beresford Ct. CH43: Oxton 3G 73
CH63: Beb *9N 73*
(off Beresford Av.)
Beresford Dr. PR9: South 6L 7
Beresford Gdns. PR9: South 5L 7
Beresford Rd. CH43: Oxton 3F 72
CH45: Wall 2F 56
L8: Liv 4E 74
Beresford St. L5: Liv 1J 5 (5D 58)
L20: Boot 9A 44
WA1: Warr 1F 82
WA9: St H 2H 63
Berey's Bldgs. L3: Liv 4D 4
Bergen Cl. L20: Boot 8D 44
Berkeley Av. CH43: Pren 7F 72
WN3: Wins 1F 40
Berkeley Cl. WA5: Warr 2A 82
WN7: Leigh 2K 53
Berkeley Ct. *CH49: Woodc* *6A 72*
(off Childwall Grn.)
WA7: Manor P 3F 96
WA12: Newt W 6H 51
Berkeley Dr. CH45: New B 2J 57
Berkeley Rd. L23: Crosb 6J 33
Berkeswell Rd. L11: Norr G 9M 45
Berkley Av. L12: W Der 1C 60
Berkley Cl. L8: Liv 2E 74
Berkley St. L8: Liv 1E 74
Berkshire Dr. M44: Cad 4J 69
WA1: Wools 1L 83
Berkshire Gdns. WA10: St H 8J 49
Bermondsey Gro. WA8: Wid 4N 79
Bermuda Rd. CH46: More 8K 55
Bernard Av. CH45: New B 2J 57
WA4: App 8E 82
Bernard Wood Ct. WN5: Bil 7M 39
Berner's Rd. L19: Gras 9N 75
Berner St. CH41: Birke 9K 57
Berrington Av. L25: Woolt 6E 76
Berrington Gro. WN4: Ash M 8J 41
Berringtons La. WA11: Rainf 9E 38
Berry Cl. CH66: Gt Sut 2H 111
WN8: Skel 2C 30
Berry Dr. CH66: Gt Sut 1H 111
Berryedge Cres. L36: Huy 3G 61
Berryford Rd. L14: Knott A 3D 60
Berry Hill Av. L34: Know 7H 47
Berry Ho. Rd. L40: Holm 2E 14
Berrylands Cl. CH46: More 8L 55
Berrylands Rd. CH46: More 8L 55
Berry Rd. WA8: Wid 7G 78
Berrys La. WA9: St H 9B 50
Berry St. L1: Liv 8H 5 (9D 58)
L20: Boot 8A 44
WN8: Skel 2C 30
Berry St. Ind. Est. *L20: Boot* *7A 44*
(off Berry St.)
Berrywood Dr. L35: Whis 7C 62
Bertha Gdns. CH41: Birke 9F 56
Bertha St. CH41: Birke 9F 56
Bertram Cl. CH47: Meols 9E 54
Bertram Dr. CH47: Meols 9D 54
Bertram Dr. Nth. CH47: Meols 9E 54
Bertram Rd. L17: Aig 4H 75
Bertram St. WA12: Newt W 7J 51
Berwick Av. CH62: East 2D 102
PR8: Ains 8K 11
Berwick Cl. CH46: More 9J 55
L6: Liv 5H 59
WA1: Wools 2M 83
Berwick Dr. L23: Crosb 6J 33
Berwick Gdns. CH66: Lit Sut 8G 103
Berwick Gro. CH66: Lit Sut 8G 103
Berwick Rd. CH66: Lit Sut 8F 102
Berwick Rd. W. CH66: Lit Sut 8E 102
Berwick St. L6: Liv 5G 59
Berwyn Av. CH47: Hoy 1D 70
CH61: Thing 1A 88
Berwyn Blvd. CH63: Hghr B 8L 73
Berwyn Cl. CH66: Lit Sut 8F 102
Berwyn Ct. PR8: South 2C 12
Berwyn Dr. CH61: Hesw 5N 87
Berwyn Gro. WA9: St H 7B 50
Berwyn Rd. CH44: Wall 4J 57
L4: Walt 1H 59
Beryl Rd. CH43: Noct 3C 72
Beryl St. L13: Liv 8M 59
Beryl Wlk. L10: Faz 3N 45
BESCAR 7M 13
Bescar Brow La. L40: Scar 7K 13
Bescar La. L40: Scar 7M 13
Bescar Lane Station (Rail) 4N 13
Besford Ho. L25: Gate 3F 76
Besford Rd. L25: Gate 3F 76
Bessborough Rd. CH43: Oxton 4H 73
Bessbrook Rd. L17: Aig 6K 75
Bessemer Rd. M44: Irlam 3M 69
Bessemer St. L8: Liv 4E 74
Beta Cl. CH62: New F 9N 73
Betchworth Cres. WA7: Beech 9N 95
Bethany Cl. WA11: Hay 3D 50
Bethany Ct. CH63: Spit 4N 89
Bethany Cres. CH63: Beb 2M 89
Bethel Gro. L17: Liv 2J 75
Betjeman Cl. WA4: Westy 4G 83
Betjeman Gro. L16: Child 9D 60
Betony Cl. L26: Halew 7J 77
Betsyfield Dr. WA3: Croft 2H 67
Bettisfield Av. CH62: Brom 1C 102
Betty Ann Ct. PR9: South 7G 7
Betula Bank PR8: Birkd 4N 11
Betula Cl. L9: Walt 6H 45
Beulah Av. WN5: Bil 7N 39
Bevan Cl. WA5: Gt San 2M 81
WA9: St H 3G 63
Bevan Ct. *WA4: Warr* *5C 82*
(off Dunlop St.)
Bevans Ct. L12: W Der 2A 60
Bevan's La. L12: W Der 2B 60
Bevan Vw. WA5: Warr 1A 82
Bevan Way WA8: Wid 5L 79
Beverley Av. WA4: App 8E 82
WN5: Bil 2A 40
Beverley Cl. PR9: South 2A 8
Beverley Dr. CH60: Hesw 9B 88
Beverley Gdns. CH61: Thing 1B 88
Beverley Rd. CH45: Wall 3F 56
CH62: New F 8A 74
L15: Wav 2M 75
WA5: Gt San 2L 81
Beverley Way CH66: Lit Sut 7H 103
Beversbrook Rd. L11: Norr G 8N 45
Bevington Bush L3: Liv 1F 4 (6C 58)
Bevington Hill L3: Liv 5C 58
Bevington St. L3: Liv 5C 58
WN4: Ash M 6H 41
Bevyl Rd. CH64: Park 4B 100
Bewcastle Dr. L40: Westh 1G 28
Bewey Cl. L8: Liv 4D 74
Bewley Dr. L32: Kirkb 1B 46
BEWSEY 1A 82
Bewsey Bus. Cen. WA5: Warr 2A 82
Bewsey Farm Cl.
WA5: Old H 9M 65
Bewsey Ind. Est. WA5: Warr 1B 82
Bewsey Pk. Cl. WA5: Warr 1A 82
Bewsey Rd. WA2: Warr 1A 82
WA5: Warr 1A 82
Bewsey St. WA2: Warr 2B 82
(not continuous)
WA10: St H 9G 48
Bexhill Av. WA2: Warr 5C 66
Bexhill Cl. L24: Speke 3F 92
Bexhill Gdns. WA9: St H 3F 62
Bianca St. L20: Boot 9B 44
Bibby Av. WA1: Warr 2F 82
Bibby Rd. PR9: South 5M 7
Bibbys La. L20: Boot 5N 43
Bibby St. L13: Liv 6L 59
BICKERSTAFFE 7K 29
Bickerstaffe St. L3: Liv 1J 5 (6D 58)
WA10: St H 7K 49

Bickerton Av. CH63: Hghr B 8K 73
WA6: Frod 7N 107
Bickerton Cl. WA3: Birchw 5L 67
Bickerton Rd. PR8: Birkd 2M 11
Bickerton St. L17: Aig 5H 75
Bickley Cl. WA2: Fearn 6G 67
WA7: Run 6M 95
Bicknell Cl. WA5: Gt San 9K 65
Bidder St. L3: Liv 1J 5 (6D 58)
Biddleston Cross WA8: Wid 5H 79
Bideford Av. WA9: Sut L 4M 63
Bideford Rd. WA5: Penk 4G 80
BIDSTON 9D 56
Bidston Av. CH41: Birke 1E 72
CH45: Wall 3E 56
WA11: St H 5N 49
Bidston Ct. CH43: Noct 1E 72
Bidston Golf Course 6C 56
Bidston Grn. CH66: Gt Sut 1J 111
Bidston Grn. Ct. CH43: Bid 9C 56
Bidston Grn. Dr. CH43: Bid 9C 56
Bidston Hall Farm CH43: Bid 8D 56
Bidston Ind. Est. CH44: Wall 6D 56
Bidston Link Rd. CH43: Bid 7D 56
CH44: Wall 7D 56
Bidston Moss CH44: Wall 6D 56
Bidston Moss Nature Reserve 6E 56
Bidston Rd. CH43: Clau, Oxton 2E 72
L4: Walt 1G 59
Bidston Station (Rail) 7C 56
Bidston Sta. App. CH43: Bid 7C 56
Bidston Vw. CH43: Bid 8C 56
Bidston Village Rd. CH43: Bid 8C 56
Bidston Way WA11: St H 5N 49
Bidston Windmill 1D 72
Bigdale Dr. L33: Kirkb 8D 36
Biggin Ct. WA2: Padg 8F 66
Bigham Rd. L6: Liv 6H 59
Biglands Dr. L36: Huy 9K 61
Big Meadow Rd. CH49: Woodc 4A 72
BILLINGE 6A 40
Billinge Cres. WA11: St H 4N 49
Billinge La. L39: Bic 7C 28
Billinge Rd. WN4: Garsw 6D 40
WN5: Bil 6D 40
Billingham Rd. WA9: St H 2G 62
Billings Cl. L5: Kirkd 3C 58
Billington Av. WA12: Newt W 4K 51
Billington Cl. WA5: Gt San 9G 64
Billington Rd. WA8: Wid 4E 78
Bill's La. L37: Form 3F 24
Bilston Rd. L17: Aig 8K 75
Bilton Cl. WA8: Wid 6A 80
Bingley Rd. L4: Walt 2G 59
Binns Rd. L7: Liv 7K 59
L13: Liv 7K 59
Binns Rd. Ind. Est. L13: Liv 8L 59
Binns Way L13: Liv 8L 59
Binsey Cl. CH49: Upton 3L 71
Birbeck Cl. WN3: Wins 2G 40
Birbeck Rd. L33: Kirkb 8E 36
Birbeck Wlk. L33: Kirkb 8E 36
Birchall Av. WA3: Cul 6L 53
Birchall St. L20: Kirkd 2B 58
WA3: Croft 2H 67
Birch Av. CH49: Upton 2L 71
L9: Ain 4G 44
L40: Burs 1J 21
M44: Cad 4K 69
WA2: Win 5B 66
WA10: St H 4J 49
Birchbrook Rd. WA13: Lymm 3H 85
Birch Cl. CH43: Oxton 5H 73
L31: Mag 2L 35
L35: Whis 5B 62
Birch Ct. *L8: Liv 4F 74*
(off Weller Way)
Birch Cres. WA12: Newt W 6H 51
Birchdale Cl. CH49: Grea 3L 71
Birchdale Cres. WA4: App 8D 82
Birchdale Rd. L9: Walt 6F 44
L22: Water 9K 33
WA1: Padd 1H 83
WA4: App 9D 82
Birchen Rd. L26: Halew 9L 77
Birches, The CH44: Wall 7L 57
CH64: Nest 4F 100
L28: Stockb V 2E 60
L37: Form 8E 16
Birches Cl. CH60: Hesw 7A 88
Birchfield CH46: More 1K 71
Birchfield Av. WA8: Wid 6K 79
Birchfield Cl. CH46: More 2K 71
L7: Liv 7K 59
Birchfield Rd. L4: Walt 8F 44
L7: Liv 7K 59
WA5: Gt San 3K 81
WA8: Wid 3K 79
WA13: Lymm 4H 85
Birchfield St. L3: Liv 2J 5 (6D 58)
WA9: St H 2G 63
Birchfield Way L31: Lyd 7G 27
Birch Gdns. WA10: St H 4J 49
BIRCH GREEN 2F 30
Birch Grn. L37: Form 8D 16
Birch Grn. Rd. WN8: Skel 1E 30
Birch Gro. CH45: New B 2J 57
CH66: Whit 4M 111
L15: Wav 8M 59
L35: Presc 5B 62
Birch Gro. L36: Huy 7H 61
WA1: Padd 1G 83
WA4: Warr 5E 82
WN4: Garsw 6E 40
Birch Heys CH48: Frank 7H 71
Birch Hill WA6: Kingsw 5M 115
Birch Hill M. L25: Woolt 7E 76
Birchill Rd. L33: Know I 9G 37
Birchley Av. WN5: Bil 8M 39
Birchley Rd. WN5: Bil 8M 39
Birchley St. WA10: St H 6K 49
Birchley Vw. WA11: St H 9L 39
Birchmere CH60: Hesw 5M 87
Birchmuir Hey L32: Kirkb 1D 46
Birchridge Cl. CH62: Spit 5B 90
Birch Rd. CH43: Oxton 5H 73
CH47: Meols 9F 54
CH63: Beb 3N 89
L36: Huy 8J 61
M31: Part 6K 69
WA3: Rix 6H 69
WA7: Run 7L 95
WA8: Wid 5L 79
WA11: Hay 3G 50
Birch St. L5: Liv 4A 58
PR8: South 2A 12
WN8: Skel 3B 30
Birch Tree Av. WA11: St H 2J 49
Birch Tree Ct. L12: W Der 3M 59
Birchtree Dr. L31: Mell 8M 35
Birch Tree La. WA4: Hghr Whi 9G 99
Birch Tree Rd. WA3: Low 2G 52
Birchtree Rd. L17: Aig 5K 75
Birchview Way CH43: Noct 3D 72
Birchway CH60: Hesw 9C 88
Birchways WA4: App 2F 98
BIRCHWOOD 7L 67
Birchwood Av. CH41: Birke 1L 73
Birchwood Blvd. WA3: Birchw 7L 67
Birchwood Cl. CH2: Elt 2N 113
CH41: Birke 1K 73
CH66: Gt Sut 4J 111
WN3: Wins 2F 40
Birchwood Corporate Ind. Est.
WA2: Birchw 7K 67
Birchwood Golf Course 3L 67
Birchwood La. WA4: Moore 8K 81
Birchwood Leisure & Tennis Complex
6L 67
Birchwood Office Pk. WA2: Fearn 6J 67
Birchwood One Bus. Pk.
WA3: Birchw 7M 67
BIRCHWOOD PARK 4M 67
Birchwood Pk. Av. WA3: Birchw, Ris 4L 67
Birchwood Point Bus. Pk.
WA3: Birchw 6L 67
Birchwood Science Pk. WA3: Ris 3M 67
Birchwood Shop. Cen. WA3: Birchw 6L 67
Birchwood Station (Rail) 7M 67
Birchwood Way L33: Kirkb 6E 36
WA2: Birchw 7K 67
WA2: Padg 9F 66
WA3: Birchw 6K 67
Bird i' th' Hand Cotts. L39: Orm 7C 20
Bird St. L7: Liv 1H 75
Birdwell Dr. WA5: Gt San 3J 81
Birdwood Rd. L11: Norr G 1L 59
BIRKDALE 2N 11
Birkdale Av. CH63: Brom 9B 90
Birkdale Cl. L6: Liv 3J 59
L36: Roby 8G 61
Birkdale Cop PR8: South 4C 12
Birkdale Ct. L36: Huy 9K 61
Birkdale Rd. WA5: Penk 4H 81
WA8: Wid 3L 79
Birkdale Station (Rail) 2M 11
Birkdale Trad. Est. PR8: Birkd 4M 11
BIRKENHEAD 2M 73
Birkenhead Central Station (Rail) 3L 73
Birkenhead North Station (Rail) 8F 56
Birkenhead Park Station (Rail) 9H 57
Birkenhead Priory 2M 73
Birkenhead Rd. CH44: Wall 8L 57
CH47: Hoy, Meols 9D 54
CH64: Will 4K 101
Birkenshaw Av. L23: Blun 6H 33
Birket Av. CH46: Leas 6N 55
Birket Cl. CH46: Leas 6A 56
Birket Dr. WA8: Wid 2K 79
Birket Ho. CH41: Birke 1K 73
Birket Sq. CH46: Leas 6N 55
Birkett Av. CH65: Ell P 3A 112
Birkett Rd. CH42: Rock F 7L 73
CH48: W Kir 4C 70
Birkett St. L3: Liv 1H 5 (6D 58)
Birkey La. L37: Form 2F 24
Birkin Cl. L32: Kirkb 2E 46
Birkin Rd. L32: Kirkb 2E 46
Birkin Wlk. L32: Kirkb 2E 46
Birkrig WN8: Skel 6G 30
Birkside Cl. WN3: Wigan 2J 41
Birley Ct. L8: Liv 9K 5
PR8: South 1A 12
Birley St. WA12: Newt W 6M 51
Birleywood WN8: Skel 6G 31
Birnam Dr. L35: Rainh 7G 62
Birnam Rd. CH44: Wall 6K 57
Birstall Av. WA11: St H 5M 49
Birstall Ct. WA7: Run 8N 95
Birstall Rd. L6: Liv 6G 58
Birt Cl. L8: Liv 1G 74
Birtles Rd. WA2: Warr 8D 66
Birtley Ct. WA8: Wid 7E 78
Bisham Pk. WA7: Nort 4F 96
Bishopdale Cl. WA5: Gt San 1H 81
Bishopdale Dr. L35: Rainh 6G 63
Bishop Dr. L35: Whis 8N 61
Bishopgate St. L15: Wav 9K 59
Bishop Reeves Rd. WA11: Hay 3G 51
Bishop Rd. CH44: Wall 7H 57
L6: Liv 2H 59
WA10: St H 5H 49
Bishops Ct. CH43: Oxton 5H 73
L12: W Der 1M 59
L25: Woolt 6F 76
WA2: Win 5A 66
Bishops Gdns. CH65: Ell P 9M 103
Bishop Sheppard Ct. L3: Liv 1D 4 (5B 58)
Bishops Way WA8: Wid 5N 79
Bisley St. CH45: Wall 4H 57
L15: Wav 1K 75
Bispham Ct. WN5: Bil 1N 39
Bispham Dr. CH47: Meols 1F 70
WN4: Ash M 6H 41
Bispham Ho. L3: Liv 2F 4
Bispham Rd. PR9: South 8L 7
WA5: Gt San 4K 81
Bittern Cl. WA2: Warr 6E 66
WA7: Nort 7F 96
Bixteth St. L3: Liv 3D 4 (7B 58)
Blackacre La. L39: Burs, Orm 5C 20
Black-A-Moor La. L39: Down 1E 26
Blackberry Gro. L26: Halew 6H 77
Blackboards La. CH66: Chil T 7F 102
BLACKBROOK
WA2 7G 66
WA11 4C 50
Blackbrook Av. WA2: Padg, Warr 5F 66
Blackbrook Cl. L9: Walt 7F 44
WA8: Wid 5F 78
Blackbrook Rd. WA11: St H 5A 50
Blackbrook Sq. WA2: Padg 7F 66
Blackburn Cl. WA3: Low 2F 52
Blackburne Av. WA8: Hale B 2E 94
Blackburne Cl. WA2: Padg 7K 67
Blackburne Dr. L25: Hunts X 9H 77
WA12: Newt W 6J 51
Blackburne Pl. L8: Liv 8K 5 (9E 58)
Blackburne St. L19: Garst 3A 92
Blackburne Ter. L8: Liv 8K 5
Blackcap Rd. WA4: App 3H 99
Blackcap Wlk. WA3: Birchw 6M 67
Blackcar La. L29: Thorn 9N 25
Black Cat Ind. Est. WA8: Wid 1J 95
Black Denton's Pl. WA8: Wid 7M 79
Blackdown Cl. CH66: Lit Sut 9F 102
Blackdown Gro. WA9: St H 8B 50
Blackeys La. CH64: Nest 6E 100
Blackfield St. L5: Kirkd 3C 58
Blackgate La. PR4: Tarl 5M 9
(not continuous)
Blackheath Dr. CH46: Leas 6N 55
Blackheath La. WA7: Manor P 3G 97
Black Horse Cl. CH48: W Kir 5D 70
Black Horse Hill CH48: W Kir 6D 70
Black Horse La. L13: Liv 5N 59
WA8: Wid 3K 79
Black Horse Pl. L13: Liv 6N 59
Blackhorse St. WA9: St H 6N 49
Blackhurst Rd. L31: Lyd 7H 27
Blackhurst St. WA1: Warr 3C 82
Blackledge Cl. WA2: Fearn 6H 67
Blackley Cl. WA4: Warr 5E 82
Blackley Gro. L33: Kirkb 5E 36
Blackleyhurst Av. WN5: Bil 6A 40
Black Lion La. CH66: Lit Sut 8G 103
Blacklock Hall Rd. L24: Speke 4G 92
Blacklow Brow L36: Huy 7H 61
Blackmoor Dr. L12: W Der 3A 60
Black Moss La. L39: Augh, Orm 1B 28
L40: Scar 7J 13
Blackpool St. CH41: Birke 3L 73
Blackrod Av. L24: Speke 3G 92
Blackshaw Dr. WA5: Gt San, Westb 8K 65
Blacksmith Pl. L25: Hunts X 8H 77
Blackstairs Rd. CH66: Ell P 7L 103
Blackstock Ct. *L30: N'ton 7C 34*
(off Granams Cft.)
Blackstock St. L3: Liv 1E 4 (6B 58)
Blackstone Av. WA11: St H 5N 49
Blackstone St. L5: Liv 3A 58
Blackthorn Cres. L28: Stockb V 1F 60
Blackthorne Av. CH66: Whit 5M 111
Blackthorne Cl. CH46: More 1N 71
Blackthorne Rd. L9: Walt 7H 45
Blackthorn Wlk. *M31: Part 7L 69*
(off Wood La.)
Blackwater Rd. L11: Crox 6B 46
Blackwood Av. L25: Woolt 4D 76
Blackwood Ct. *L16: Child 2A 76*
(off Woolton Rd.)
BLAGUEGATE 3M 29
Blaguegate La. WN8: Skel 2L 29
Blair Ct. CH43: Clau 2H 73
Blair Dr. WA8: Wid 5E 78
Blairgowrie Gdns. L39: Orm 9E 20
Blair Gro. PR9: South 8L 7
Blair Ind. Est. L23: Crosb 8M 33
Blair Pk. CH63: Spit 4A 90
Blair St. L8: Liv 1D 74
Blair Wlk. L26: Halew 1K 93
Blakeacre Cl. L26: Halew 1K 93
Blakeacre Rd. L26: Halew 1K 93
Blakefield Rd. L23: Thorn 5B 34
Blakehall WN8: Skel 5G 30
(not continuous)
Blakeley Brow CH63: Raby M 9N 89
Blakeley Ct. CH63: Raby M 9N 89
Blakeley Dell CH63: Raby M 9A 90
Blakeley Dene CH63: Raby M 8A 90
Blakeley Rd. CH63: Raby M 8N 89
Blakemere Ct. CH65: Ell P 7A 104
Blakeney Cl. CH49: Upton 1A 72
Blakenhall Way CH49: Upton 2L 71
Blakenhill Dr. WA5: Gt San 3K 81
Blaking Dr. L34: Know 6H 47
Blandford Cl. PR8: Birkd 1L 11
Blandford Rd. WA5: Gt San 3K 81
Blantyre Rd. L15: Wav 2K 75
Blantyre St. WA7: Run 4J 95
Blay Cl. L25: Hunts X 8H 77
Blaydon Cl. L30: N'ton 1F 44
Blaydon Gro. WA9: St H 2G 62
Blaydon Pk. WN8: Skel 5G 31
Blaydon Wlk. CH43: Clau 2E 72
Bleak Hill Cl. WA10: Windle 3F 48
Bleak Hill Rd. WA10: Eccl, Windle 5E 48
Bleak La. L40: Lath 1N 21
Bleaklow Cl. WN3: Wigan 1K 41
Bleasdale Av. L10: Ain 9K 35
Bleasdale Cl. CH49: Upton 2M 71
L39: Augh 5B 28
Bleasdale Rd. L18: Moss H 4N 75
WA12: Newt W 6K 51
Bleasdale Way L21: Ford 7A 34
Blenheim Av. L21: Lith 2B 44
Blenheim Cl. WA2: Padg 7F 66
Blenheim Dr. L34: Presc 4K 61
Blenheim Rd. CH44: Wall 4K 57
L18: Moss H 3L 75
PR8: Ains 8H 11
WN4: Ash M 9M 41
Blenheim St. L5: Liv 5B 58
Blenheim Way L24: Speke 4F 92
WA11: St H 4L 49
Blessington Rd. L4: Walt 2E 58
Bletchley Av. CH44: Wall 5F 56
Bligh St. L15: Wav 1K 75
Blindfoot Rd. WA11: Rainf 3A 48
Blindman's La. L39: Orm 6A 20
Blisworth St. L21: Lith 4A 44
Blithedale Ct. *CH42: Rock F 7N 73*
(off The Hawthornes)
Blomfield Rd. L19: Aller 9B 76
Bloomfield Grn. L17: Aig 4H 75
Bloomsbury Ct. CH47: Hoy 2B 70
Bloomsbury Way WA8: Wid 5G 79
Blossom Gro. L32: Kirkb 3D 46
Blossom Rd. M31: Part 7L 69
Blossom St. L20: Boot 5B 44
BLOWICK 9K 7
Blowick Bus. Pk. PR9: South 9M 7
Blowick Ind. Pk. PR9: South 9M 7
Blucher St. L22: Water 1J 43
Bluebell Av. CH41: Birke 9F 56
WA11: Hay 3G 50
Bluebell Cl. L22: Water 1L 43
L32: Kirkb 7C 36
Bluebell Ct. WA7: Beech 2B 108
Blue Bell La. L36: Huy 5J 61
Bluebell La. CH64: Nest 5J 101
Bluebell Rd. WA5: Warr 4N 81
Blueberry Flds. L10: Faz 4L 45
Blue Bri. La. WA6: Hel 9F 106
Bluecoat, The 6F 4 (8C 58)
Bluecoat Chambers L1: Liv 6F 4
Bluecoat St. WA2: Warr 1C 82
Bluefields St. L8: Liv 1E 74
Blue Hatch WA6: Frod 6M 107
Blue Jay Cl. L27: N'ley 3J 77
Blue Planet Aquarium 4B 112
Blue Ridge Cl. WA5: Gt San 1G 81
Bluestone La. L31: Mag 2K 35
Bluewood Dr. CH41: Birke 8D 56
Blundell Av. L37: Form 9B 16
L38: Hight 9G 24
PR8: Birkd 4M 11
Blundell Cres. PR8: Birkd 4M 11
Blundell Dr. PR8: Birkd 4M 11
Blundell Gro. L38: Hight 9F 24
Blundell La. PR9: South 4A 8
Blundell Links Ct. PR8: Ains 1J 17
Blundell Rd. L35: Whis 4D 62
L38: Hight 9F 24
WA8: Wid 8F 78
BLUNDELLSANDS 8H 33
Blundellsands Classic L23: Blun 8H 33
Blundellsands Ct. *L23: Blun 8H 33*
(off Blundellsands Rd. W.)
Blundellsands & Crosby Station (Rail)
7J 33
Blundellsands Rd. E. L23: Blun 7J 33
Blundellsands Rd. W. L23: Blun 8H 33
Blundellsands Sailing Club 1E 32
Blundells Dr. CH46: More 8M 55
BLUNDELL'S HILL 7E 62
Blundells Hill Golf Course 8E 62
Blundell's La. L35: Rainh 8D 62
Blundell St. L1: Liv 9F 4 (1C 74)
Blyth Cl. WA7: Murd 1F 108

Blythe Av. WA8: Wid 4L **79**
Blythe Ct. PR9: South 5M **7**
Blythe La. L40: Lath 5G **21**
Blythe Mdw. L40: Burs 5F **20**
Blythe M. PR8: Birkd 6N **11**
Blythewood WN8: Skel 5F **30**
Blyth Hey L30: N'ton 7C **34**
Blyth Rd. CH63: Brom 8B **90**
Blythswood St. L17: Aig 5G **74**
BMB Industrial Pk. CH44: Wall 6F **56**
Boaler St. L6: Liv 1N **5** (6F **58**)
Boaler St. Ind. Est. *L6: Liv 6G 58*
(off Boaler St.)
Boardmans La. WA9: St H 6A **50**
WA11: St H 6A **50**
Boathouse La. CH64: Park 4B **100**
Boat Stage WA13: Lymm 5E **84**
Boat Wlk. WA4: Warr 7B **82**
Bobbies La. WA10: Eccl 6D **48**
Bobbiners La. PR9: Banks 4E **8**
Bobby Langton Way L40: Burs 9J **15**
Bob Paisley Ct. *L5: Liv 3F 58*
(off Hartnup St.)
Bob's La. M44: Cad 5K **69**
Bodden St. WA3: Low 1H **53**
WA9: Clock F 5N **63**
Boddington Dr. WA4: Grap 9H **83**
Bodiam Ct. CH65: Ell P 3C **112**
Bodley St. L4: Walt 2E **58**
Bodmin Av. PR9: South 2N **7**
Bodmin Cl. WA7: Brook 9D **96**
Bodmin Gro. WA11: St H 3N **49**
Bodmin Rd. L4: Walt 9E **44**
Bodmin Way L26: Halew 8J **77**
Bognor Cl. L24: Speke 3F **92**
Bolan St. L13: Liv 6M **59**
BOLD 2D **64**
Bold Bus. Cen. WA9: Bold 2D **64**
Bolden Cl. L30: N'ton 1E **44**
Bolde Way CH63: Spit 6N **89**
BOLD HEATH 1A **80**
Bold Ind. Est. WA8: Wid 3M **79**
Bold Ind. Pk. WA9: Bold 3D **64**
Bold La. L39: Augh 5M **27**
WA5: Coll G 2D **64**
WA9: Bold 2D **64**
Bold Manor L35: Whis 6B **62**
Bold Pl. L1: Liv 7J **5** (9D **58**)
Bold Rd. WA9: St H 2B **64**
Bold St. L1: Liv 6G **5** (8C **58**)
PR9: South 7G **6**
WA1: Warr 3B **82**
WA7: Run .4L **95**
WA8: Wid .9K **79**
WA10: St H 7J **49**
Boleyn, The L31: Mag 9K **27**
Boleyn Ct. WA7: Manor P 4E **96**
Bolingbroke La. WA8: Wid 4A **80**
Bollin Cl. WA3: Cul 8N **53**
WA13: Lymm 4G **84**
Bollin Ct. WA8: Wid 3L **79**
Bollin Dr. WA13: Lymm 4G **84**
Bollington Cl. CH43: Oxton 5F **72**
Bolton Av. L32: Kirkb 9A **36**
WA4: Westy 4G **82**
Bolton Cl. L37: Form 2G **25**
WA3: Low .2J **53**
WA9: St H 6M **49**
Bolton Rd. CH62: Port S 2A **90**
PR8: Birkd 2N **11**
WN2: Bam 8K **41**
WN4: Ash M 8K **41**
Bolton Rd. E. CH62: Port S 1B **90**
Bolton's Cop PR9: Banks 1G **9**
Bolton's Meanygate PR4: Tarl 1N **9**
Bolton St. L3: Liv 5H **5** (8D **58**)
WA9: St H 6M **49**
(not continuous)
WN4: Garsw 6F **40**
Bolton Wlk. L32: Kirkb 9A **36**
Bonchurch Dr. L15: Wav 8L **59**
Bond Cl. WA5: Warr 4M **81**
Bond's La. PR9: Banks 1E **8**
Bond St. L3: Liv 5C **58**
L34: Presc 3A **62**
Bone Island WN8: Skel 4E **30**
Bonnington Av. L23: Crosb 6J **33**
Bonnington Cl. WA10: St H 7F **48**
Bonsall Rd. L12: W Der 3N **59**
Boode Cft. L28: Stockb V 9F **46**
Booker Av. L18: Moss H, Aller 7M **75**
BOOTH BANK 9N **85**
Boothbank La. WA14: Mill 9N **85**
Booth's Brow Rd. WN4: Ash M 5F **40**
Booth's Cl. CH2: Elt 3L **113**
Booths Hill Cl. WA13: Lymm 6C **84**
Booth's Hill Rd. WA13: Lymm 5C **84**
Booths La. L39: Augh 8L **19**
WA4: Hghr Whi 9F **98**
WA13: Lymm 6B **84**
Booth St. L13: Liv 6M **59**
PR9: South 7G **7**
WA5: Warr 4N **81**
WA9: St H 2G **62**
Boothwood Cl. L7: Liv 8G **59**
BOOTLE 7B **44**
Bootle Leisure Cen. 6B **44**
Bootle Municipal Golf Course 1D **44**
Bootle New Strand Station (Rail) 6B **44**
Bootle Oriel Road Station (Rail) 8A **44**
Borax St. L13: Liv 7M **59**
Bordehill Gdns. L12: W Der 1B **60**
Border Rd. CH60: Hesw 7B **88**
Border Way L5: Liv 3D **58**
Borella Rd. L13: Liv 3L **59**
Borough Pavement CH41: Birke 2L **73**
Borough Pl. *CH41: Birke 2L 73*
(off Grange Rd. E.)
Borough Rd. CH41: Birke 5J **73**
CH42: Rock F, Tran 5J **73**
CH44: Wall 6K **57**
WA10: St H 8H **49**
Borough Rd. E. CH41: Birke 2L **73**
CH44: Wall 7L **57**
Borough Way CH44: Wall 6L **57**
Borron Cl. WA12: Newt W 5K **51**
Borron Ho. WA12: Newt W 6K **51**
Borron Rd. WA12: Newt W 5K **51**
Borron Rd. Ind. Est. *WA12: Newt W 6K 51*
(off Borron Rd.)
Borrowdale L37: Form 8F **16**
Borrowdale Av. WA2: Warr 6D **66**
Borrowdale Cl. WA6: Frod 6M **107**
Borrowdale Rd. CH46: More 9L **55**
CH63: Beb 3L **89**
L15: Wav .2K **75**
WA8: Wid .8F **78**
WA10: St H 1E **62**
Bosco Ct. L11: Crox 6N **45**
Boscow Cres. WA9: St H 2N **63**
Bosnia St. L8: Liv 5F **74**
Bossom Ct. L22: Water 3K **43**
Bostock Grn. CH65: Ell P 8L **103**
Bostock St. L5: Liv 4C **58**
WA5: Warr 2N **81**
Boston Av. WA7: Run 7L **95**
Boston Blvd. WA5: Gt San 1J **81**
Boston Cl. WA3: Cul 6N **53**
Boswell Av. WA4: Warr 6C **82**
Boswell Rd. CH43: Pren 7F **72**
Boswell St. L8: Liv 1H **75**
L20: Boot 5N **43**
Bosworth Cl. CH63: Spit 5M **89**
Bosworth Dr. PR8: Ains 1H **17**
Bosworth Rd. WA11: St H 4M **49**
Botanic Est. L7: Liv 8J **59**
Botanic Gdns. 5N **7**
Botanic Gro. L7: Liv 8H **59**
Botanic Pl. L7: Liv 7H **59**
Botanic Rd. L7: Liv 8H **59**
PR9: South 6M **7**
Botany Rd. L24: Speke 2G **93**
Boteler Av. WA5: Warr 1A **82**
Boteler Ct. *WA4: Warr 6D 82*
(off Elphins Dr.)
Botley Cl. CH49: Upton 3L **71**
Boulevard L6: Liv 5J **59**
Boulevard, The CH65: Gt Sut 9L **103**
L8: Liv 2F **74**
L12: W Der 1N **59**
WA5: Burtw 6K **65**
Boulevard Bus. Pk. WA3: Birchw 7L **67**
Boulevard Industry Pk. L24: Halew 2H **93**
(not continuous)
Boulting Av. WA5: Warr 7A **66**
Boulton Av. CH48: W Kir 4C **70**
CH62: New F 8A **74**
Boundary Ct. WA10: St H 6H **49**
Boundary Dr. L23: Crosb 5K **33**
L25: Hunts X 9H **77**
Boundary Farm Rd. L26: Halew 1H **93**
Boundary La. CH60: Hesw 7A **88**
L6: Liv 5G **58**
L33: Kirkb 9J **37**
L40: Burs .1K **21**
L40: Burs, Ruf 5J **15**
PR4: Hesk B, Tarl 3H **9**
Boundary Meanygate PR4: Hesk B 1K **9**
Boundary Pk. CH64: Park 7D **100**
Boundary Rd. CH43: Bid, Noct 8D **56**
CH48: W Kir 8E **70**
CH62: Port S 9A **74**
L21: Lith .9C **34**
(not continuous)
L36: Huy .9K **61**
WA10: St H 7H **49**
Boundary Stone La. WA8: Wid 4A **80**
Boundary St. L5: Liv 3A **58**
PR8: South 2A **12**
WA1: Warr 1F **82**
Boundary St. E. L5: Liv 3D **58**
Boundary Wlk. L36: Huy 9L **61**
Bourchier Way WA4: Grap 8H **83**
Bourne Av. WA3: Low 2E **52**
Bourne Gdns. WA9: St H 9M **49**
Bournemouth Cl. WA7: Murd 9F **96**
Bourne St. L6: Liv 6G **58**
Bourton Rd. L25: Hunts X 9F **76**
Bousfield St. L4: Walt 2D **58**
Boverton Cl. WA5: Call 8N **65**
Bovey Ct. *WA1: Warr 4C 82*
(off St Austins La.)
Bowden Cl. L12: Crox 8C **46**
WA3: Cul .6N **53**
Bowden Rd. CH45: Wall 3G **56**
L19: Garst 1N **91**
Bowden St. L21: Lith 4A **44**
Bowdon Cl. WA1: Padg 9G **67**
WA10: Eccl 8E **48**
Bowen Cl. WA8: Wid 4G **79**
Bower Cres. WA4: Stret 5E **98**
Bower Gro. L21: Sea 3M **43**
Bower Ho. CH49: Upton 1N **71**
Bower Rd. CH60: Hesw 7C **88**
L25: Woolt 4E **76**
L36: Huy .5J **61**
Bowers Bus. Pk. WA8: Wid 9M **79**
Bowers Pk. Ind. Est. WA8: Wid 9M **79**
Bower St. WA8: Wid 7M **79**
Bowfell Cl. CH62: East 3C **102**
Bowfield Rd. L19: Gras 9N **75**
Bowgreen Cl. CH43: Bid 1C **72**
BOWKER'S GREEN 7B **28**
Bowker's Grn. La. L39: Augh, Bic 7B **28**
Bowl, The
Bromborough 5D **90**
Bowland Av. L16: Child 8B **60**
WA3: Golb 1D **52**
WA9: Sut M 6L **63**
WN4: Ash M 7K **41**
Bowland Cl. CH62: Brom 6C **90**
WA3: Birchw 4B **68**
WA7: Beech 1A **108**
Bowland Ct. *PR9: South 7H 7*
(off Gordon St.)
Bowland Dr. L21: Ford 7B **34**
Bowles St. L20: Boot 5N **43**
Bowley Rd. L13: Liv 4L **59**
Bowling Grn. Cl. PR8: South 1E **12**
Bowman Av. WA4: Westy 3H **83**
Bowmore Way L7: Liv 9H **59**
Bowness Av. CH43: Pren 6G **72**
CH63: Brom 1B **102**
M44: Cad .5K **69**
PR8: Ains .2J **17**
WA2: Warr 7D **66**
WA11: St H 2L **49**
Bowood Ct. WA2: Win 5B **66**
Bowood St. L8: Liv 5E **74**
Bowring Ct. L14: Broad G 8D **60**
Bowring Dr. CH64: Park 5B **100**
BOWRING PARK 8E **60**
Bowring Pk. Av. L16: Child 8E **60**
Bowring Park Golf Course 8F **60**
Bowring Pk. Rd. L14: Broad G 8A **60**
Bowring Park Vis. Cen. 8F **60**
Bowring St. L8: Liv 4F **74**
Bowscale Cl. CH49: Upton 3M **71**
Boxdale Ct. L18: Moss H 4M **75**
Boxdale Rd. L18: Moss H 4M **75**
Boxgrove Cl. WA8: Wid 5L **79**
Boxmoor Rd. L18: Moss H 6M **75**
Boxtree Cl. L12: Crox 6D **46**
Box Wlk. M31: Part 6L **69**
Boxwood Cl. L36: Roby 7G **60**
Boxwood Gdns. WA9: St H 2A **64**
Boycott St. L5: Liv 3F **58**
Boyd Cl. CH46: Leas 6B **56**
Boydell Av. WA4: Grap 6J **83**
WA4: Westy 4G **83**
Boydell Cl. L28: Stockb V 2F **60**
Boyer Av. L31: Mag 4J **35**
Boyes Brow L33: Kirkb 7B **36**
Boyes Ct. L31: Mag 4J **35**
Boyle Av. WA2: Warr 8F **66**
Boyton Ct. L7: Liv 9H **59**
Brabant Rd. L17: Aig 7K **75**
Braby Rd. L21: Lith 4B **44**
Bracebridge Dr. PR8: South 4E **12**
Bracewell Cl. WA9: St H 3M **63**
Bracken Cl. WA3: Birchw 4K **67**
Bracken Ct. WA9: Clock F 5M **63**
Brackendale CH2: Elt 2M **113**
CH49: Woodc 5C **72**
WA7: Run .7N **95**
Brackendale Av. L9: Ain 3G **45**
Bracken Dr. CH48: W Kir 6F **70**
Brackenhurst Dr. CH45: New B 2J **57**
Brackenhurst Grn. L33: Kirkb 9C **36**
Bracken La. CH63: Hghr B 2K **89**
Bracken Rd. CH66: Gt Sut 1K **111**
Brackens, The WA4: Dares 6K **97**
Brackenside CH60: Hesw 5N **87**
Bracken Wlk. *L32: Kirkb 1B 46*
(off Wervin Rd.)
Bracken Way L12: W Der 4M **59**
WA6: Frod 8M **107**
Brackenway L37: Form 7G **16**
Bracken Wood L12: Crox 6C **46**
Brackenwood Dr. WA8: Wid 9D **78**
Brackenwood Golf Course 2K **89**
Brackenwood Gro. L35: Whis 6C **62**
Brackenwood M. WA4: Grap 7K **83**
Brackenwood Rd. CH63: Hghr B 2K **89**
Brackley Av. M44: Cad 3K **69**
Brackley Cl. CH44: Wall 6G **56**
WA7: Run .4J **95**
Brackley St. WA4: Stockt H 7D **82**
WA7: Run .4J **95**
Bracknell Av. L32: Kirkb 1B **46**
Bracknell Cl. L32: Kirkb 2B **46**
Bracknel Way L39: Augh 3M **27**
Bradbourne Cl. L12: Crox 7C **46**
Bradburn Rd. M44: Irlam 2L **69**
Bradda Cl. CH49: Upton 1N **71**
Braddan Av. L13: Liv 4K **59**
Bradden Cl. CH63: Spit 5A **90**
Brade St. PR9: South 3A **8**
Bradewell Cl. L4: Kirkd 1D **58**
Bradewell St. L4: Kirkd 1D **58**
Bradfield Av. L10: Ain 8H **35**
Bradfield St. L7: Liv 7H **59**
Bradgate Cl. CH46: More 8J **55**
WA5: Warr 2A **82**
Bradkirk Ct. L30: N'ton 6C **34**
Bradlegh Rd. WA12: Newt W 8K **51**
BRADLEY 7A **108**
Bradley Fold L36: Huy 9L **61**
Bradley La. WA5: Burtw 8H **51**
WA6: Frod 8N **107**
WA12: Newt W 8H **51**
Bradley Pl. *PR8: South 8G 6*
(off Eastbank St.)
Bradley Rd. L21: Lith 1A **44**
Bradley St. PR9: South 7H **7**
Bradley Way WA8: Wid 7L **79**
Bradman Cl. CH45: Wall 4H **57**
Bradman Rd. CH46: More 8K **55**
L33: Know I 8G **37**
Bradmoor Rd. CH62: Brom 7C **90**
Bradshaw Cl. WA10: St H 6G **48**
Bradshaw La. WA4: Grap 5J **83**
WA13: Lymm 5K **85**
WN8: Parb 4F **22**
Bradshaw's La. PR8: Ains 8K **11**
Bradshaw St. WA8: Wid 6K **79**
Bradshaw Wlk. *L20: Boot 6A 44*
(off St James Dr.)
Bradstone Cl. L10: Faz 4N **45**
Bradville Rd. L9: Ain 3H **45**
Bradwall Cl. CH65: Whit 1M **111**
Bradwell Cl. CH48: W Kir 6E **70**
Bradwell Rd. WA3: Low 3F **52**
Braehaven Rd. CH45: New B 2J **57**
Braemar Av. PR9: South 5L **7**
(not continuous)
Braemar Cl. L35: Whis 6C **62**
WA2: Fearn 6H **67**
Braemar Ct. CH65: Ell P 2C **112**
Braemar Ho. CH43: Oxton 3F **72**
Braemar St. L20: Kirkd 9C **44**
Braemore Cl. WN3: Wins 1F **40**
Braemore Rd. CH44: Wall 5F **56**
Braeside Cl. CH66: Gt Sut 9H **103**
Braeside Cres. WN5: Bil 6N **39**
Braeside Gdns. CH49: Upton 3N **71**
Brae St. L7: Liv 7G **59**
Brahms Cl. L8: Liv 2G **74**
Braid Cres. L23: Crosb 8M **33**
Braidhaven WN6: Shev 6N **23**
Braid St. CH41: Birke 9K **57**
Braidwood Ct. *CH41: Birke 3J 73*
(off Mount Gro.)
Brainerd St. L13: Liv 4K **59**
Braithwaite Cl. L35: Rainh 6F **62**
WA7: Beech 9N **95**
Braithwaite Rd. WA3: Low 1E **52**
Brakedale Cl. L27: N'ley 4K **77**
Bramberton Pl. L4: Walt 9H **45**
Bramberton Rd. L4: Walt 9H **45**
Bramble Av. CH41: Birke 9F **56**
Bramble Cl. WA5: Penk 5G **81**
Brambles, The WA5: Burtw 2H **65**
WN4: Garsw 6F **40**
Bramble Way CH46: More 7L **55**
L40: Burs .1K **21**
WA7: Beech 2A **108**
WN8: Parb 4F **22**
Bramblewood Cl. CH43: Noct 4D **72**
L27: N'ley 3J **77**
Brambling Cl. WA7: Beech 1A **108**
Brambling Pk. L26: Halew 7J **77**
Brambling Way WA3: Low 3F **52**
Bramcote Av. WA11: St H 4M **49**
Bramcote Cl. L33: Kirkb 7E **36**
Bramcote Rd. L33: Kirkb 7D **36**
Bramcote Wlk. L33: Kirkb 7D **36**
Bramerton Ct. CH48: W Kir 5B **70**
Bramford Cl. CH49: Upton 3M **71**
Bramhall Cl. CH48: W Kir 6E **70**
L24: Speke 5J **93**
Bramhall Dr. CH62: East 3E **102**
Bramhall Rd. L22: Water 2L **43**
WN8: Skel 2C **30**
Bramhall St. WA5: Warr 3N **81**
(not continuous)
Bramhope Pk. L12: W Der 2B **60**
Bramley Av. CH63: Hghr B 9L **73**
Bramley Cl. CH66: Gt Sut 5L **111**
L27: N'ley 3H **77**
Bramley M. WA4: Stockt H 8D **82**
Bramleys, The L31: Mag 4H **35**
Bramley Wlk. L24: Speke 5H **93**
WA6: Hel 4D **114**
Bramley Way L32: Kirkb 8A **36**
Brampton Cl. L32: Kirkb 7C **36**
Brampton Ct. WA9: St H 7D **50**
Brampton Dr. L8: Liv 8M **5** (9F **58**)
Bramshill Cl. WA3: Birchw 3A **68**
Bramwell Av. CH43: Pren 7G **72**
Bramwell St. WA9: St H 6A **50**
Brancaster Dr. WA3: Low 3H **53**
Brancepeth Ct. CH65: Ell P 2B **112**
Branchway WA11: Hay 4F **50**
Brancker Av. L35: Rainh 5E **62**
Brancote Ct. CH43: Clau 2F **72**
Brancote Gdns. CH43: Clau 2F **72**
CH62: Brom 8C **90**
Brancote Mt. CH43: Clau 2F **72**
Brancote Rd. CH43: Clau 2F **72**

Brandearth Hey L28: Stockb V ... 2F **60**
Brandearth Ho. L28: Stockb V ... 2F **60**
BRAND HEALD ... 1J **9**
Brandon WA8: Wid ... 6E **78**
Brandon Cl. WN8: Uph ... 5K **31**
Brandon St. CH41: Birke ... 2M **73**
Brandreth Cl. L35: Rainh ... 6F **62**
Brandreth Delph WN8: Parb ... 2F **22**
Brandreth Dr. WN8: Parb ... 3F **22**
Brandreth Pk. WN8: Parb ... 1F **22**
Brandwood Av. WA2: Warr ... 7C **66**
Brandwood Ho. *WA1: Warr* ... *3D **82***
(off Hall St.)
Branfield Cl. L12: Crox ... 7C **46**
Bransdale Cl. WA5: Gt San ... 1H **81**
Bransdale Dr. WN4: Ash M ... 8M **41**
Bransfield Cl. WN3: Wigan ... 1J **41**
Bransford Cl. WN4: Ash M ... 9L **41**
Branstree Av. L11: Norr G ... 8L **45**
Brantfield Ct. WA2: Warr ... 7F **66**
Branthwaite Cres. L11: Norr G ... 8M **45**
Branthwaite Gro. L11: Norr G ... 9M **45**
Brasenose Rd.
L20: Boot, Kirkd ... 8A **44**
Brassey St. CH41: Birke ... 9H **57**
L8: Liv ... 2D **74**
Brathay Cl. WA2: Warr ... 6D **66**
Brattan Rd. CH41: Birke ... 4J **73**
Bratton Cl. WN3: Wins ... 2E **40**
Braunton Rd. CH45: Wall ... 3G **57**
L17: Aig ... 8K **75**
Bravery Ct. L19: Speke ... 3C **92**
Braybrooke Rd. L11: Norr G ... 7M **45**
Bray Cl. WA7: Beech ... 9N **95**
Braydon Cl. L25: Hunts X ... 1G **92**
Brayfield Rd. L4: Walt ... 9J **45**
Bray Rd. L24: Speke ... 3G **92**
Bray St. CH41: Birke ... 9H **57**
Brearley Cl. CH43: Bid ... 9C **56**
Breccia Gdns. WA9: St H ... 8A **50**
Brechin Rd. L33: Kirkb ... 9D **36**
Breck, The CH66: Ell P ... 7K **103**
Breckfield Pl. L5: Liv ... 4E **58**
Breckfield Rd. Nth. L5: Liv ... 3E **58**
Breckfield Rd. Sth. L6: Liv ... 4F **58**
Breck Pl. CH44: Wall ... 6G **56**
Breck Rd. CH44: Wall ... 5F **56**
L4: Walt ... 5E **58**
L5: Liv ... 5E **58**
WA8: Wid ... 7L **79**
Breckside Av. CH44: Wall ... 5E **56**
Breckside Pk. L6: Liv ... 3H **59**
Brecon Av. L30: N'ton ... 1E **44**
Brecon Ct. WA5: Call ... 7N **65**
Brecon Dr. CH66: Gt Sut ... 4K **111**
Brecon Rd. CH42: Tran ... 7J **73**
Brecon St. L6: Liv ... 6G **58**
Brecon Wlk. *L30: N'ton* ... *1F **44***
(off Durham Av.)
Bredon Cl. CH66: Lit Sut ... 8F **102**
Bredon Ct. L37: Form ... 9E **16**
Breeze Cl. L9: Walt ... 7E **44**
Breeze Hill L9: Walt ... 8E **44**
L20: Boot ... 7C **44**
Breezehill Cl. CH64: Nest ... 6F **100**
Breezehill Pk. CH64: Nest ... 6F **100**
Breezehill Rd. CH64: Nest ... 6F **100**
Breeze La. L9: Walt ... 7E **44**
Breeze Rd. PR8: Birkd ... 4L **11**
Brelade Rd. L13: Liv ... 5L **59**
Bremhill Rd. L11: Norr G ... 7L **45**
Bremner Cl. L7: Liv ... 8H **59**
Brenda Cres. L23: Thorn ... 4N **33**
Brendale Av. L31: Mag ... 3H **35**
Brendan's Way L30: N'ton ... 8D **34**
Brendon Av. L21: Lith ... 1N **43**
WA2: Warr ... 6B **66**
Brendon Gro. WA9: St H ... 6C **50**
Brendor Rd. L25: Woolt ... 7F **76**
Brenig St. CH41: Birke ... 8F **56**
Brenka Av. L9: Ain ... 1G **45**
Brentfield WA8: Wid ... 6G **79**
Brentnall Cl. WA5: Gt San ... 3L **81**
Brent Way L26: Halew ... 1K **93**
(not continuous)
Brentwood Av. L17: Aig ... 5H **75**
L23: Crosb ... 6M **33**
M44: Cad ... 3K **69**
Brentwood Cl. L38: Hight ... 1F **32**
WA10: Eccl ... 7E **48**
Brentwood Ct. *CH49: Woodc* ... *6A **72***
(off Childwall Grn.)
PR9: South ... 6J **7**
Brentwood Gro. L33: Kirkb ... 5C **36**
Brentwood St. CH44: Wall ... 6J **57**
Brereton Av. CH63: Beb ... 1N **89**
L15: Wav ... 2M **75**
Brereton Cl. WA7: Cas ... 7C **96**
(not continuous)
Brereton Gro. M44: Cad ... 3L **69**
Bretherton Ct. *L35: Rainh* ... *5F **62***
(off Ratcliffe Pl.)
L40: Burs ... 2K **21**
Bretherton Rd. L34: Presc ... 3B **62**
Bretland Dr. WA4: Grap ... 9H **83**
Bretlands Rd. L23: Thorn ... 5A **34**
Brett Cl. L33: Kirkb ... 6B **36**
Bretton Av. WA1: Warr ... 3F **82**
Bretton Fold PR8: South ... 1E **12**
Brett St. CH41: Birke ... 9H **57**
Brewery La. L31: Mell ... 7K **35**
(not continuous)
L37: Form ... 7F **16**
Brewery Pl. PR8: South ... 2A **12**
Brewster St. L4: Kirkd ... 9D **44**
L20: Boot ... 9D **44**
Breydon Gdns. WA9: St H ... 3H **63**
Brian Av. CH61: Irby ... 1N **87**
WA2: Warr ... 9E **66**
WA4: Stockt H ... 7F **82**
Brian Cummings Ct. L21: Lith ... 4A **44**
Briar Av. WA3: Rix ... 7H **69**
Briar Cl. WN4: Ash M ... 7J **41**
Briardale Gdns. CH66: Lit Sut ... 8H **103**
Briardale Rd. CH42: Tran ... 4J **73**
CH44: Wall ... 7L **57**
CH63: Hghr B ... 9M **73**
CH64: Will ... 6N **101**
CH66: Lit Sut ... 8H **103**
L18: Moss H ... 3L **75**
Briar Dr. CH60: Hesw ... 7A **88**
L36: Huy ... 7H **61**
Briarfield Av. WA8: Wid ... 7D **78**
Briarfield Rd. CH60: Hesw ... 7A **88**
CH65: Ell P ... 9N **103**
Briar Rd. PR8: Ains ... 1K **17**
WA3: Golb ... 2C **52**
Briars, The PR8: Birkd ... 5M **11**
Briars Brook L40: Lath ... 2L **21**
Briars Cl. L35: Rainh ... 8G **62**
Briars Grn. WA10: St H ... 5J **49**
WN8: Skel ... 9D **22**
Briars La. L31: Mag ... 2K **35**
L40: Lath ... 2L **21**
Briar St. L4: Kirkd ... 2C **58**
Briarswood Cl. CH42: Rock F ... 8M **73**
L35: Whis ... 6C **62**
Briar Wlk. WA3: Golb ... 2C **52**
Briarwood L23: Blun ... 5H **33**
WA7: Nort ... 7D **96**
Briarwood Av. WA1: Warr ... 1F **82**
Briarwood Rd. L17: Aig ... 5K **75**
Briary Cl. CH60: Hesw ... 6B **88**
Briary Cft. L38: Hight ... 9F **24**
Brickfields L36: Huy ... 8L **61**
Brickhurst Way WA1: Wools ... 9J **67**
Brick Kiln La. L40: Ruf ... 3L **15**
Brickmakers Arms Yd. *L39: Orm* ... *7B **20***
(off Whiterails Dr.)
Brick St. L1: Liv ... 9G **4** (1C **74**)
WA1: Warr ... 3D **82**
WA12: Newt W ... 7H **51**
Brickwall Grn. L29: Seft ... 4E **34**
Brickwall La. L29: Seft ... 6C **34**
Bride St. L4: Walt ... 8E **44**
Bridewell Ct. WA8: Wid ... 5L **79**
Bridge Av. L39: Orm ... 8C **20**
WA4: Westy ... 4G **82**
Bridge Av. E. WA4: Westy ... 3G **83**
Bridge Bank Cl. WA3: Golb ... 3C **52**
Bridge Cl. M31: Part ... 6N **69**
WA13: Lymm ... 5H **85**
Bridge Ct. CH48: W Kir ... 5B **70**
CH64: Nest ... 7E **100**
L30: N'ton ... 7C **34**
Bridge Cft. L21: Ford ... 8B **34**
Bridgecroft Rd. CH45: Wall ... 3H **57**
Bridge Farm Cl. CH49: Woodc ... 4B **72**
Bridge Farm Dr. L31: Mag ... 1L **35**
Bridgefield Cl. L25: Gate ... 1F **76**
Bridgefield Ct. L34: Presc ... 4B **62**
Bridge Foot Ind. Est. WA4: Warr ... 4C **82**
Bridgeford Av. L12: W Der ... 2M **59**
Bridge Gdns. L12: W Der ... 9D **46**
Bridge Gro. PR8: South ... 9G **7**
Bridgehall Dr. WN8: Uph ... 5L **31**
Bridge Ho. L39: Orm ... 9C **20**
Bridgehouse La. L10: Faz ... 4M **45**
Bridge Ind. Est. L24: Speke ... 2F **92**
Bridge La. L30: N'ton ... 8D **34**
WA1: Wools ... 2K **83**
WA4: App ... 8F **82**
WA6: Frod ... 5M **107**
Bridge La. M. WA6: Frod ... 5N **107**
Bridgeman St. WA5: Warr ... 4M **81**
WA10: St H ... 7G **49**
(not continuous)
Bridge Mdw. CH66: Gt Sut ... 3L **111**
WA13: Lymm ... 4H **85**
Bridgemere Cl. L7: Liv ... 6J **59**
Bridgemere Ho. L17: Aig ... 6J **75**
Bridgemill Cl. L27: N'ley ... 4K **77**
Bridgend Cl. WA8: Wid ... 5G **79**
Bridgend Dr. PR8: Ains ... 1H **17**
Bridgenorth Rd. CH61: Pens ... 3M **87**
Bridgeport M. WA5: Gt San ... 1J **81**
Bridge Retail Pk. WA7: Run ... 5K **95**
Bridge Rd. CH48: W Kir ... 5B **70**
L7: Liv ... 9J **59**
L18: Moss H ... 5M **75**
L21: Lith ... 3N **43**
(not continuous)
L23: Blun ... 8J **33**
L31: Mag ... 4J **35**
L34: Presc ... 4A **62**
L36: Roby ... 7G **60**
WA1: Wools ... 1K **83**
WA9: Clock F ... 7N **63**
Bridge Shop. Centre, The WA4: Warr ... 5G **82**
Bridgeside Dr. WA6: Hel ... 1E **114**
Bridges La. L29: Seft ... 4E **34**
Bridges Rd. CH65: Ell P ... 9D **104**
Bridge St. CH41: Birke ... 1L **73**
(not continuous)
CH62: Port S ... 2A **90**
(not continuous)
CH64: Nest ... 7E **100**
L20: Boot ... 8A **44**
L39: Orm ... 9C **20**
PR8: South ... 9G **7**
WA1: Warr ... 3C **82**
WA3: Golb ... 3B **52**
WA7: Run ... 5L **95**
WA10: St H ... 7K **49**
WA12: Newt W ... 7K **51**
BRIDGE TRAFFORD ... 9K **113**
Bridge Vw. Cl. WA8: Wid ... 3K **95**
Bridge Vw. Dr. L33: Kirkb ... 7D **36**
Bridge Wlk. *WA7: Pal F* ... *8B **96***
(within Halton Lea Shop. Cen.)
Bridgewater Av. WA4: Westy ... 4G **82**
Bridgewater Cl. L21: Lith ... 9N **33**
WA6: Frod ... 5M **107**
Bridgewater Ct. L21: Lith ... 9N **33**
Bridgewater Grange WA7: Pres B ... 1H **109**
Bridgewater Ho. WA7: Run ... 4H **95**
Bridgewater M. WA4: Stockt H ... 8D **82**
Bridgewater Pl. WA3: Ris ... 5M **67**
Bridgewater St. L1: Liv ... 9F **4** (1C **74**)
WA7: Run ... 4K **95**
WA13: Lymm ... 5E **84**
Bridgewater Way L36: Huy ... 9L **61**
Bridgeway L11: Norr G ... 9K **45**
Bridgeway E. WA7: Wind H ... 5E **96**
Bridgeway W. WA7: Wind H ... 5D **96**
Bridge Wills La. PR9: South ... 2A **8**
Bridgewood Dr. CH66: Gt Sut ... 3H **111**
Bridle Av. CH44: Wall ... 7L **57**
Bridle Cl. CH43: Bid ... 2B **72**
CH62: Brom ... 8D **90**
Bridle Ct. WA9: St H ... 1M **63**
Bridle La. CH1: Dunk, Lea B ... 7K **111**
Bridlemere Ct. WA1: Padg ... 9F **66**
Bridle Pk. CH62: Brom ... 8D **90**
Bridle Rd. CH44: Wall ... 7L **57**
CH62: Brom, East ... 8D **90**
L30: N'ton ... 2D **44**
Bridle Rd. Ind. Est. L30: N'ton ... 2E **44**
Bridle Way CH66: Gt Sut ... 2J **111**
L30: N'ton ... 2E **44**
L33: Kirkb ... 5B **36**
Bridport St. L3: Liv ... 4H **5** (7D **58**)
Briedden Way CH66: Lit Sut ... 8F **102**
Brierfield WN8: Skel ... 6G **31**
Brierfield Rd. L15: Wav ... 2L **75**
Brierley Cl. *L30: N'ton* ... *7G **34***
(off Beeston Dr.)
Brierley Ter. WA8: Wid ... 7M **79**
Briers Cl. WA2: Fearn ... 6G **67**
Briery Hey Av. L33: Kirkb ... 9D **36**
Brigadier Dr. L12: W Der ... 2C **60**
Brighouse Cl. L39: Orm ... 8B **20**
Brightgate Cl. L7: Liv ... 9G **59**
BRIGHTON LE SANDS ... 9H **33**
Brighton Rd. L22: Water ... 1K **43**
L36: Huy ... 6M **61**
PR8: Birkd ... 3N **11**
Brighton St. CH44: Wall ... 5K **57**
WA5: Warr ... 2N **81**
(not continuous)
Brighton Va. L22: Water ... 9J **33**
Brightstone Cl. PR9: Banks ... 2F **8**
Bright St. CH41: Birke ... 2J **73**
(not continuous)
L6: Liv ... 1M **5** (6F **58**)
PR9: South ... 8L **7**
Brightwell Cl. CH49: Upton ... 4N **71**
WA5: Gt San ... 3G **80**
Brignall Gro. WA3: Low ... 1E **52**
Brill St. CH41: Birke ... 9H **57**
Brimelow Cres. WA5: Penk ... 5G **81**
BRIMSTAGE ... 5H **89**
Brimstage Av. CH63: Hghr B ... 8K **73**
Brimstage Cl. CH60: Hesw ... 8C **88**
Brimstage Grn. CH60: Hesw ... 7D **88**
Brimstage Hall ... 5G **89**
Brimstage Hall Courtyard
CH63: Brim ... 5G **89**
Brimstage La. CH63: Brim, Store ... 5H **89**
Brimstage Rd. CH60: Hesw ... 8C **88**
CH63: Beb, Brim, Hghr B ... 8C **88**
L4: Walt ... 8D **44**
Brimstage St. CH41: Birke ... 3J **73**
Brindley, The ... 5K **95**
Brindley Av. WA4: Westy ... 4G **82**
Brindley Cl. L21: Lith ... 9N **33**
Brindley Ct. WA4: Stockt H ... 8E **82**
Brindley Rd. L32: Kirkb ... 9A **36**
WA7: Ast ... 4B **96**
WA9: St H ... 3A **64**
Brindley St. L8: Liv ... 2C **74**
WA7: Run ... 4J **95**
Brindley Wharf WA4: Pres H ... 1H **109**
Brinell Dr. M44: Irlam ... 3L **69**
Brinklow Cl. PR8: Ains ... 9G **11**
Brinley Cl. CH62: Brom ... 1C **102**
Brinton Cl. L27: N'ley ... 2G **77**
WA8: Wid ... 8G **79**
Brisbane Av. CH45: New B ... 1G **56**
Brisbane St. WA9: St H ... 2G **63**
Briscoe Av. CH46: More ... 1M **71**
Briscoe Dr. CH46: More ... 1M **71**
Bristol Av. CH44: Wall ... 5J **57**
WA7: Murd ... 9G **97**
Bristol Dr. CH66: Gt Sut ... 4K **111**
Bristol Rd. L15: Wav ... 2M **75**
Bristow Cl. WA5: Gt San ... 9K **65**
Britannia Av. L15: Wav ... 1J **75**
Britannia Cres. L8: Liv ... 5E **74**
Britannia Gdns. WA6: Hel ... 4E **114**
Britannia Ho. CH41: Birke ... 2M **73**
Britannia Pav. L3: Liv ... 8D **4** (9B **58**)
Britannia Rd. CH45: Wall ... 5G **57**
WA6: Hel ... 3E **114**
British Lawnmower Mus. ... 1A **12**
Britonside Av. L32: Kirkb ... 2E **46**
Brittarge Brow L27: N'ley ... 4J **77**
Britten Cl. L8: Liv ... 2G **75**
Broadacre WN8: Uph ... 6K **31**
Broadacre Cl. L18: Moss H ... 3B **76**
Broad Arpley La. *WA1: Warr* ... *4C **82***
(off Park Blvd.)
Broadbelt St. L4: Walt ... 8E **44**
Broadbent Av. WA4: Westy ... 4G **82**
Broad Birches CH65: Ell P ... 8M **103**
Broadfield Av. CH43: Bid ... 9C **56**
Broadfield Cl. CH43: Bid ... 1B **72**
Broadfields WA7: Nort ... 7E **96**
Broadgate Av. WA9: St H ... 9M **49**
BROAD GREEN ... 8B **60**
Broad Grn. Rd. L13: Liv ... 6M **59**
Broad Green Station (Rail) ... 8B **60**
Broadheath Av. CH43: Bid ... 1C **72**
Broadheath Ter. WA8: Wid ... 7G **79**
Broad Hey L30: N'ton ... 8C **34**
Broad Hey Cl. L25: Woolt ... 5F **76**
Broadhey La. WN6: Wright ... 1J **23**
Broadhurst Av. WA3: Cul ... 8N **53**
WA5: Warr ... 4M **81**
Broadhurst St. L17: Aig ... 5H **75**
Broadlake CH64: Will ... 6M **101**
Broadland Gdns. CH66: Gt Sut ... 3L **111**
Broadland Rd. CH66: Gt Sut ... 3L **111**
Broadlands L35: Presc ... 4B **62**
PR8: Birkd ... 3L **11**
Broad La. CH60: Hesw ... 6J **87**
L4: Walt ... 9K **45**
L11: Norr G ... 9K **45**
L29: Thorn ... 2B **34**
L32: Kirkb ... 2D **46**
L37: Form ... 6H **17**
L37: Gt Alt ... 1K **25**
L39: Down ... 2G **26**
WA4: Grap ... 7J **83**
WA5: Burtw, Coll G ... 9E **50**
WA11: St H ... 9L **39**
Broad La. Pct. L11: Norr G ... 9L **45**
Broadleaf Rd. L19: Gras ... 9L **75**
Broadley Av. WA3: Low ... 3D **52**
Broadmead CH60: Hesw ... 8C **88**
L19: Aller ... 9C **76**
WN8: Parb ... 3E **22**
BROAD OAK ... 6B **50**
Broad Oak Av. WA5: Penk ... 4G **81**
WA11: Hay ... 4C **50**
Broad Oak Rd. WA9: St H ... 7A **50**
Broadoak Rd. L14: Knott A ... 5D **60**
L31: Mag ... 2K **35**
Broadoaks CH49: Upton ... 2M **71**
Broad Pl. L11: Norr G ... 1L **59**
Broadriding Rd. WN6: Shev ... 7N **23**
Broads, The WA9: St H ... 3H **63**
Broad Sq. L11: Norr G ... 1L **59**
Broadstone Dr. CH63: Spit ... 5M **89**
Broad Vw. L11: Norr G ... 1L **59**
Broadway CH45: Wall ... 4F **56**
CH49: Grea ... 3M **71**
CH63: Hghr B ... 9K **73**
L9: Ain ... 3K **45**
L11: Norr G ... 9K **45**
M31: Part ... 5N **69**
WA8: Wid ... 7D **78**
WA10: Eccl ... 6D **48**
WA10: St H ... 1F **62**
Broadway Av. CH45: Wall ... 4F **56**
Broadway Badminton Cen. ... 1E **62**
Broadway Cl. PR8: Ains ... 9H **11**
Broadway Mkt. L11: Norr G ... 9K **45**
Broadwell Dr. WN7: Leigh ... 1M **53**
Broadwood Av. L31: Mag ... 4H **35**
Broadwood St. L15: Wav ... 1K **75**
Brock Av. L31: Mag ... 1K **35**
Brockenhurst Rd. L9: Walt ... 5F **44**
Brock Gdns. L24: Hale ... 5B **94**
Brock Hall Cl. WA9: Clock F ... 5M **63**
Brockhall Cl. L35: Whis ... 3D **62**
Brockholme Rd. L18: Moss H ... 7M **75**
Brocklebank La. L19: Aller ... 8B **76**
Brocklebank Rd. PR9: South ... 6K **7**
Brockley Av. CH45: New B ... 9H **43**
Brock Rd. WA3: Birchw ... 6L **67**
Brock St. L4: Kirkd ... 1D **58**
Brockton Ct. WA4: App ... 1D **98**
Brocstedes Av. WN4: Ash M ... 5G **40**
Brocstedes Rd. WN4: Ash M ... 3F **40**
(not continuous)
Brodie Av. L18: Moss H ... 5M **75**
L19: Aig, Aller ... 7N **75**
Brogden Av. WA3: Cul ... 6M **53**
BROMBOROUGH ... 6D **90**

Bromborough Golf Course ... 1A 102
BROMBOROUGH POOL ... 2C 90
BROMBOROUGH PORT ... 4D 90
Bromborough Rake Station (Rail) ... 7B 90
Bromborough Rd. CH63: Beb ... 2N 89
Bromborough Station (Rail) ... 8B 90
Bromborough Village Rd.
CH62: Brom ... 6D 90
Brome Way CH63: Spit ... 5A 90
Bromilow Rd. WA9: St H ... 8B 50
WN8: Skel ... 3N 29
Bromley Av. L18: Moss H ... 3L 75
WA3: Low ... 3E 52
Bromley Cl. CH60: Hesw ... 8M 87
L26: Halew ... 7L 77
WA2: Fearn ... 6G 67
Bromley Rd. CH45: New B ... 2G 57
Brompton Av. CH44: Wall ... 5J 57
L17: Liv ... 3H 75
L23: Crosb ... 8J 33
L33: Kirkb ... 6E 36
Brompton Ct. L17: Liv ... 3H 75
Brompton Gdns. WA5: Warr ... 1N 81
Brompton Ho. L17: Aig ... 3J 75
Brompton Rd. PR8: South ... 8K 7
Brompton Way CH66: Gt Sut ... 4K 111
Bromsgrove Rd.
CH49: Grea ... 4K 71
Bromyard Cl. L20: Boot ... 6A 44
Bronington Av. CH62: Brom ... 9C 90
Bronshill Ct. L23: Blun ... 7G 33
Bronte Cl. L23: Blun ... 7H 33
WA2: Win ... 3B 66
Bronte St. L3: Liv ... 4J 5 (8D 58)
WA10: St H ... 6G 49
Brook, The L31: Mag ... 3K 35
Brook Av. WA4: Stockt H ... 7F 82
WA4: Westy ... 3G 83
Brookbank Ct. L10: Faz ... 3N 45
Brookbridge Rd. L13: Liv ... 3K 59
Brook Cl. CH44: Wall ... 4J 57
WA8: Cron ... 2F 78
Brookdale PR8: Ains ... 2K 17
WA8: Wid ... 5D 78
Brookdale Av. Nth. CH49: Grea ... 4M 71
Brookdale Av. Sth. CH49: Grea ... 4M 71
Brookdale Cl. CH49: Grea ... 4M 71
Brookdale Rd. L15: Wav ... 2K 75
Brook Dr. WA5: Gt San ... 3J 81
Brooke Cl. PR9: South ... 8N 7
Brook End WA9: St H ... 9C 50
Brooke Rd. E. L22: Water ... 9K 33
Brooke Rd. W. L22: Water ... 9J 33
Brook Farm Cl. L39: Orm ... 9C 20
M31: Part ... 8L 69
Brookfield WN8: Parb ... 3F 22
Brookfield Av. L22: Water ... 2M 43
L23: Crosb ... 8K 33
L35: Rainh ... 4F 62
WA7: Run ... 5A 96
Brookfield Cen. L9: Ain ... 5H 45
Brookfield Cl. WA13: Lymm ... 5D 84
Brookfield Cotts. *WA13: Lymm ... 5D 84*
(off Elm Tree Rd.)
Brookfield Dr. L9: Ain, Faz ... 5H 45
Brookfield Gdns. CH48: W Kir ... 6C 70
Brookfield Ho. L36: Huy ... 6J 61
Brookfield La. L39: Augh ... 6M 27
Brookfield Pk. WA4: Grap ... 6H 83
Brookfield Rd. CH48: W Kir ... 6C 70
WA3: Cul ... 7L 53
WA13: Lymm ... 5D 84
WN8: Uph ... 5L 31
BROOKFIELDS GREEN ... 7M 27
Brookfield St. WA12: Newt W ... 7K 51
Brook Furlong WA6: Frod ... 4H 107
Brook Hey CH64: Park ... 4B 100
Brook Hey Dr. L33: Kirkb ... 7D 36
Brook Hey Wlk. L33: Kirkb ... 8E 36
Brookhill Cl. L20: Boot ... 7C 44
Brookhill Rd. L20: Boot ... 6C 44
Brook Ho. PR8: South ... 1B 12
Brook Ho. Ct. WA13: Lymm ... 6D 84
Brookhouse Gro. WA10: Eccl ... 7D 48
Brookhouse Rd. L39: Orm ... 7B 20
BROOKHURST ... 1B 102
Brookhurst Av. CH62: East ... 9B 90
CH63: Brom, East ... 9B 90
Brookhurst Cl. CH63: Brom ... 1B 102
Brookhurst Rd. CH63: Brom ... 9B 90
Brookland La. WA9: St H ... 8C 50
Brookland Rd. CH41: Birke ... 3K 73
Brookland Rd. E. L13: Liv ... 6M 59
Brookland Rd. W. L13: Liv ... 6M 59
Brooklands CH41: Birke ... 1K 73
L17: Aig ... 6J 75
L39: Orm ... 7E 20
WN8: Uph ... 4L 31
Brooklands, The L36: Huy ... 8J 61
Brooklands Av. L22: Water ... 2M 43
WN4: Ash M ... 9M 41
Brooklands Dr. L31: Mag ... 3J 35
WN5: Orr ... 7N 31
Brooklands Gdns. CH64: Park ... 5C 100
Brooklands Gro. L40: Lath ... 2K 21
Brooklands Pk. WA8: Wid ... 6M 79
Brooklands Rd. CH64: Park ... 5C 100
WA10: Eccl ... 6D 48
WN8: Uph ... 5M 31
Brookland St. WA1: Warr ... 1F 82
Brook La. CH64: Park ... 4C 100
L39: Orm ... 9C 20
WA3: Rix ... 8A 68
WA11: Kings M ... 4J 39
Brook Lea Ho. L21: Ford ... 8B 34
Brooklea Mdws. CH66: Lit Sut ... 8E 102
Brooklet Rd. CH60: Hesw ... 7C 88
Brooklime Rd. L11: Norr G ... 9L 45
Brooklyn Caravan Pk. PR9: Banks ... 3D 8
Brooklyn Dr. CH65: Gt Sut ... 9L 103
WA13: Lymm ... 4E 84
Brook Lynn Av. WA3: Low ... 1G 52
Brook Mdw. CH61: Irby ... 9M 71
Brook Pk. L31: Mag ... 4H 35
Brook Pl. WA4: Westy ... 5F 82
Brook Rd. CH66: Gt Sut ... 9J 103
L9: Walt ... 6F 44
L20: Boot ... 7A 44
L23: Thorn ... 5N 33
L31: Mag ... 3K 35
WA13: Lymm ... 4E 84
Brooks, The WA11: St H ... 3K 49
Brooks All. L1: Liv ... 6F 4 (8C 58)
Brookside L12: W Der ... 1D 60
L31: Mag ... 2K 35
L39: Orm ... 8C 20
Brookside Av. L14: Knott A ... 6B 60
L22: Water ... 2M 43
WA4: Stockt H ... 7E 82
WA5: Gt San ... 4J 81
WA10: Eccl ... 5E 48
WA11: Rainf ... 4B 38
WA13: Lymm ... 4C 84
WN4: Ash M ... 3H 41
Brookside Cl. L35: Presc ... 5B 62
WA11: Hay ... 3D 50
WN5: Bil ... 6A 40
Brookside Ct. L23: Crosb ... 7L 33
L35: Presc ... 5B 62
Brookside Cres. CH49: Upton ... 3L 71
Brookside Dr. CH49: Upton ... 3M 71
Brookside Rd. L35: Presc ... 5B 62
PR8: South ... 5B 12
WA6: Frod ... 6K 107
Brookside Vw. WA11: Hay ... 3D 50
Brookside Way WA11: Hay ... 3D 50
Brooks Rd. L37: Form ... 2D 24
Brook St. CH41: Birke ... 9J 57
CH62: Port S ... 1N 89
CH64: Nest ... 6E 100
L3: Liv ... 3C 4 (7A 58)
L35: Whis ... 4C 62
PR9: South ... 3B 8
WA3: Golb ... 2B 52
WA3: Low ... 1H 53
WA7: Run ... 5K 95
(not continuous)
WA8: Wid ... 8L 79
WA10: St H ... 7K 49
WN4: Ash M ... 9L 41
Brook St. E. CH41: Birke ... 1L 73
Brooks Way L37: Form ... 2D 24
Brook Ter. CH48: W Kir ... 6C 70
WA7: Run ... 6A 96
Brookthorpe Cl. CH45: Wall ... 3J 57
BROOKVALE ... 9E 96
Brook Va. L22: Water ... 2M 43
Brookvale Av. Nth. WA7: Brook ... 9D 96
Brookvale Av. Sth. WA7: Brook ... 9D 96
Brookvale Cl. WA5: Burtw ... 3H 65
Brookvale Local Nature Reserve ... 2M 43
Brookvale Recreation Cen. ... 9E 96
Brookview Cl. L27: N'ley ... 4K 77
Brook Wlk. CH61: Irby ... 9L 71
Brookward Ct. L32: Kirkb ... 7D 36
Brook Way WA5: Gt San ... 3J 81
Brookway CH43: Pren ... 7E 72
CH45: Wall ... 4G 56
CH49: Grea ... 3M 71
Brookway La. WA9: St H ... 9B 50
Brook Well CH64: Lit N ... 9E 100
Brookwood Cl. WA4: Walt ... 8C 82
Brookwood Rd. L36: Huy ... 5J 61
Broom Av. WA4: App ... 1F 98
Broom Cl. L34: Eccl P ... 3C 62
L40: Burs ... 1K 21
Broome Cl. PR8: Birkd ... 3A 12
Broome Ct. WA7: Brook ... 9D 96
BROOMEDGE ... 8J 85
Broomehouse Av. M44: Irlam ... 1L 69
Broome Rd. PR8: Birkd ... 3A 12
Broomfield Cl. CH60: Hesw ... 6K 87
Broomfield Gdns. L9: Walt ... 5E 44
Broomfield Rd. L9: Walt ... 5E 44
(not continuous)
Broomfields WA4: App ... 9F 82
Broomfields Leisure Cen. ... 9E 82
Broomfields Rd. WA4: App ... 9E 82
Broom Hill CH43: Clau ... 1F 72
Broomhill Cl. L27: N'ley ... 2G 77
Broomholme WN6: Shev ... 6N 23
Broomlands CH60: Hesw ... 7N 87
Broomleigh Cl. CH63: Hghr B ... 2K 89
Broom Rd. M31: Part ... 7M 69
WA10: St H ... 1E 62
Brooms Gro. L10: Ain ... 9K 35
Broom Way L26: Halew ... 9J 77
Broseley Av. CH62: Brom ... 6B 90
WA3: Cul ... 6L 53
Broseley La. WA3: Cul ... 5L 53
Broseley Pl. WA3: Cul ... 5K 53
Broster Av. CH46: More ... 9K 55
Broster Cl. CH46: More ... 9K 55
Brosters La. CH47: Meols ... 9E 54
Brotherhood Dr. WA9: St H ... 2N 63
Brotherton Cl. CH62: Brom ... 6B 90
Brotherton Park & Dibbinsdale
Local Nature Reserve ... 5B 90
Brotherton Way WA12: Newt W ... 6K 51
Brougham Av. CH41: Tran ... 5M 73
Brougham Rd. CH44: Wall ... 6K 57
Brougham Ter. L6: Liv ... 1M 5
Broughton Av. CH48: W Kir ... 5B 70
PR8: South ... 2C 12
WA3: Low ... 3E 52
Broughton Cl. WA4: Grap ... 8G 83
Broughton Dr. L19: Gras ... 9M 75
Broughton Hall Rd.
L12: W Der ... 4C 60
Broughton Rd. CH44: Wall ... 6H 57
Broughton Way WA8: Hale B ... 2E 94
BROW, THE ... 6B 96
Brow La. CH60: Hesw ... 8N 87
CW9: Ant ... 9L 99
Browmere Dr. WA3: Croft ... 2H 67
Brownbill Bank L27: N'ley ... 3J 77
BROWN EDGE
PR8 ... 4F 12
WA9 ... 2G 62
Brown Edge Cl. PR8: South ... 4F 12
Brownheath Av. WN5: Bil ... 8N 39
Brownhill Dr. WA1: Padg ... 9G 66
Browning Av. CH42: Rock F ... 7M 73
WA8: Wid ... 8J 79
Browning Cl. L36: Huy ... 8K 61
Browning Dr. CH65: Gt Sut ... 1L 111
WA2: Win ... 3B 66
Browning Grn. *CH65: Gt Sut ... 1L 111*
(off Browning Dr.)
Browning Rd. CH45: Wall ... 4D 56
L13: Liv ... 3L 59
L22: Water ... 9K 33
Browning St. L20: Boot ... 6N 43
BROWNLOW ... 2M 39
Brownlow Arc. WA10: St H ... 7K 49
Brownlow Hill L3: Liv ... 5H 5 (8D 58)
Brownlow La. WN5: Bil ... 2M 39
Brownlow Rd. CH62: New F ... 9A 74
Brownlow St. L3: Liv ... 5K 5 (8E 58)
Brownmoor Cl. L23: Crosb ... 7N 33
Brownmoor La. L23: Crosb ... 8M 33
Brownmoor Pk. L23: Crosb ... 8M 33
Brown's La. L30: N'ton ... 8E 34
Brown St. WA8: Wid ... 9N 79
Brownville Rd. L13: Liv ... 2J 59
Brow Rd. CH43: Bid ... 8D 56
Brows Cl. L37: Form ... 2E 24
Brow Side L5: Liv ... 5E 58
Brows La. L37: Form ... 2E 24
Broxholme Way L31: Mag ... 4J 35
Broxton Av. CH43: Pren ... 6F 72
CH48: W Kir ... 5C 70
Broxton Cl. WA8: Wid ... 5F 78
Broxton Rd. CH45: Wall ... 3F 56
CH66: Ell P ... 9K 103
Broxton St. L15: Wav ... 9K 59
Bruce Av. WA2: Warr ... 8E 66
Bruce Cres. CH63: Brom ... 9B 90
Bruce Dr. CH66: Gt Sut ... 1H 111
Bruce St. L8: Liv ... 4F 74
WA10: St H ... 7H 49
BRUCHE ... 1E 82
Bruche Av. WA1: Padd, Padg ... 1G 82
Bruche Dr. WA1: Padg ... 9G 66
Bruche Heath Gdns. WA1: Padg ... 9H 67
Bruera Rd. CH65: Gt Sut ... 1L 111
Brunel Dr. L21: Lith ... 9N 33
Brunel M. L6: Liv ... 4F 58
Brunel Rd. CH62: Brom ... 6E 90
Brunner Rd. WA8: Wid ... 8K 79
Brunsborough Cl. CH62: Brom ... 9B 90
Brunsfield Cl. CH46: More ... 1K 71
Brunstath Cl. CH60: Hesw ... 6C 88
Brunswick WA7: Run ... 4K 95
Brunswick Bus. Pk. L3: Liv ... 3C 74
(not continuous)
Brunswick Cl. L4: Kirkd ... 1D 58
WA5: Gt San ... 2J 81
Brunswick Ct. *CH41: Birke ... 1L 73*
(off Brunswick M.)
Brunswick Cres. CH66: Gt Sut ... 2K 111
Brunswick Ent. Cen. L3: Liv ... 3C 74
Brunswick M. CH41: Birke ... 1L 73
L22: Water ... 2L 43
Brunswick Pde. L22: Water ... 2K 43
Brunswick Pl. L20: Kirkd ... 1A 58
Brunswick Rd. L6: Liv ... 2L 5 (6E 58)
WA12: Newt W ... 6H 51
Brunswick Station (Rail) ... 4D 74
Brunswick St. L2: Liv ... 6C 4 (8B 58)
L3: Liv ... 6C 4 (8A 58)
L19: Garst ... 4A 92
(not continuous)
WA9: St H ... 7C 50
Brunswick Way L3: Liv ... 3C 74
Brunt La. L19: Aller ... 9C 76
Bruntleigh Av. WA4: Westy ... 5H 83
Brushford Cl. L12: W Der ... 8N 45
Bruton Rd. L36: Huy ... 3H 61
(not continuous)
Bryanston Rd. CH42: Tran ... 6G 73
L17: Aig ... 5G 74
Bryant Av. WA4: Westy ... 3G 83
Bryant Rd. L21: Lith ... 4A 44
Bryce Cl. CH62: Brom ... 4B 90
Bryce Dr. CH62: Brom ... 4B 90
Bryce Wlk. CH62: Brom ... 3B 90
Bryceway, The L12: Knott A ... 5B 60
Brydges St. L7: Liv ... 6N 5 (8F 58)
Bryer Rd. L35: Presc ... 5A 62
BRYN ... 5J 41
Bryn Bank CH44: Wall ... 5J 57
BRYN GATES ... 4N 41
Bryn Gates La. WN2: Bam ... 3L 41
Brynmor Rd. L18: Moss H ... 7M 75
Brynmoss Av. CH44: Wall ... 5F 56
Brynn St. WA8: Wid ... 8L 79
WA10: St H ... 6K 49
Bryn Rd. WN4: Ash M ... 5J 41
Bryn Rd. Sth. WN4: Ash M ... 7L 41
Bryn Station (Rail) ... 6J 41
Bryn St. WN2: Bam ... 4N 41
WN4: Ash M ... 8K 41
Bryn Vw. WN4: Ash M ... 5J 41
Bryony Cl. WN5: Orr ... 7N 31
Bryony Way CH42: Rock F ... 8M 73
Brythen St. L1: Liv ... 5G 4 (8C 58)
BT Convention Cen. ... 9D 4 (1B 74)
Buccleuch St. CH41: Birke ... 8F 56
Buchanan Cl. WA8: Wid ... 5J 79
Buchanan Rd. CH44: Wall ... 6K 57
L9: Walt ... 7E 44
Buchan Cl. WA5: Gt San ... 9K 65
Buckfast Av. WA11: Hay ... 3J 51
Buckfast Cl. L30: N'ton ... 7E 34
WA5: Penk ... 5G 81
Buckfast Ct. WA7: Nort ... 4G 97
Buckfast Dr. L37: Form ... 2H 25
Buckingham Av. CH43: Clau ... 1F 72
CH63: Hghr B ... 9L 73
L17: Liv ... 2J 75
WA8: Wid ... 4K 79
Buckingham Bingo
Bootle ... 7B 44
Buckingham Cl. L30: N'ton ... 8B 34
WA10: St H ... 8H 49
Buckingham Ct. L33: Kirkb ... 8D 36
L39: Augh ... 2C 28
(off Aughton Pk. Dr.)
Buckingham Dr. WA5: Gt San ... 4L 81
WA11: St H ... 3K 49
Buckingham Gdns. CH65: Ell P ... 3B 112
Buckingham Gro. L37: Form ... 3E 24
Buckingham Ho. L17: Aig ... 3J 75
Buckingham Rd. CH44: Wall ... 5F 56
L9: Walt ... 4F 44
L13: Liv ... 3J 59
L31: Mag ... 3H 35
M44: Cad ... 3J 69
Buckingham St. L5: Liv ... 4D 58
Buckland Cl. WA8: Wid ... 9G 78
Buckland Dr. CH63: Spit ... 5M 89
Buckland St. L17: Aig ... 5G 74
Buckley Ct. CH64: Will ... 6M 101
Buckley Hill La. L29: Seft ... 7C 34
Buckley La. CH64: Will ... 6M 101
Buckley St. WA2: Warr ... 2B 82
Buckley Wlk. L24: Speke ... 5H 93
Buckley Way L30: N'ton ... 6C 34
Bucklow Av. M31: Part ... 6M 69
Bucklow Gdns. WA13: Lymm ... 4G 85
BUCKOAK ... 8K 115
Buckthorn Cl. L28: Stockb V ... 2F 60
Buckthorn Gdns. WA9: St H ... 3F 62
Buckton St. WA1: Warr ... 1E 82
Buckwheat Dr. L11: Norr G ... 8L 45
Bude Cl. CH43: Bid ... 2C 72
Bude Ho. *CH43: Bid ... 2C 72*
(off Bude Cl.)
Bude Rd. WA8: Wid ... 6H 79
Budworth Av. WA4: Westy ... 4G 83
WA8: Wid ... 6G 78
WA9: Sut M ... 6L 63
Budworth Cl. CH43: Oxton ... 4E 72
WA7: Run ... 8N 95
Budworth Ct. CH43: Oxton ... 3F 72
Budworth Dr. L25: Woolt ... 6G 77
Budworth Rd. CH43: Noct, Oxton ... 4E 72
CH66: Gt Sut ... 3K 111
Buerton Cl. CH43: Noct ... 4E 72
Buffs La. CH60: Hesw ... 6B 88
Buggen La. CH64: Nest ... 6D 100
Buildwas Rd. CH64: Nest ... 4E 100
Bulford Rd. L9: Faz ... 6K 45
Bulkeley Rd. CH44: Wall ... 6K 57
Bull Bri. La. L10: Ain ... 9K 35
Bull Cop L37: Form ... 1G 25
(not continuous)
Bullens La. L40: Scar ... 7J 13
Bullens Rd. L4: Walt ... 1E 58
L32: Kirkb ... 1D 46
Bullfinch Ct. L26: Halew ... 7J 77
Bull Hill CH64: Lit N ... 8F 100
Bull La. L9: Ain ... 3G 44
L9: Walt ... 4E 44
Bullrush Dr. CH46: More ... 7A 56
Bulrushes, The L17: Aig ... 5E 74
Bulwer St. CH42: Rock F ... 6M 73
L5: Liv ... 4F 58
L20: Boot ... 5N 43

Bunbury Cl. CH2: Stoak 6E 112
Bunbury Dr. WA7: Run 9M 95
Bunbury Grn. CH65: Ell P 3B 112
Bundoran Rd. L17: Aig 6K 75
Bungalow Rd. WA12: Newt W 9N 51
Bungalows, The WN4: Ash M 4H 41
Bunter Rd. L32: Kirkb 3D 46
Bunting Cl. WA3: Low 2F 52
Bunting Ct. L26: Halew 6H 77
Buntingford Rd. WA4: Thel 5K 83
Burbank Cl. WN3: Wins 2G 40
Burbo Bank Rd. L23: Blun 7G 33
Burbo Bank Rd. Nth. L23: Blun 6F 32
Burbo Bank Rd. Sth. L23: Blun 8H 33
Burbo Cres. L23: Blun 8H 33
Burbo Mans. L23: Blun 8H 33
Burbo Point L23: Blun 5G 32
Burbo Way CH45: Wall 1E 56
Burden Rd. CH46: More 9K 55
Burdett Av. CH63: Spit 5M 89
Burdett Cl. CH63: Spit 5N 89
Burdett Rd. CH45: Wall 4D 56
CH66: Gt Sut 3K 111
L22: Water 9K 33
Burdett St. L17: Aig 5H 75
Burdock Rd. L11: Norr G 9L 45
Burfield Dr. WA4: App 1D 98
Burford Av. CH44: Wall 6F 56
Burford La. WA13: Lymm 5J 85
Burford Rd. L16: Child 8A 60
Burgess Av. WA4: Warr 5C 82
Burgess Gdns. L31: Mag 1H 35
Burgess' La. L37: Gt Alt 3M 25
Burgess St. L3: Liv 3J 5 (7D 58)
Burghill Rd. L12: Crox 6D 46
Burgundy Cl. L17: Aig 6H 75
Burkhardt Dr. WA12: Newt W 7N 51
Burland Cl. WA7: Run 6J 95
Burland Rd. L26: Halew 1L 93
Burleigh M. *L5: Liv 3E 58*
(off Burleigh Rd. Sth.)
Burleigh Rd. Nth. L5: Liv 3E 58
Burleigh Rd. Sth. L5: Liv 3E 58
Burley Av. WA3: Low 1E 52
Burley Cl. L32: Kirkb 1D 46
Burley Cres. WN3: Wins 1E 40
Burley La. WA4: App T 3K 99
Burlingham Av. CH48: W Kir 7E 70
Burlington Av. L37: Form 1H 25
Burlington Dr. WA5: Gt San 1J 81
Burlington Ho. L22: Water 1L 43
Burlington Rd. CH45: New B 9H 43
PR8: Birkd 3M 11
Burlington St. CH41: Birke 2L 73
L3: Liv 5B 58
Burman Cres. L19: Garst 9A 76
Burman Rd. L19: Garst 9A 76
Burmarsh La. WA8: Hale B 2E 94
Burnage Av. WA9: Clock F 5M 63
Burnage Cl. L24: Speke 5K 93
Burnand St. L4: Walt 2E 58
Burnard Cl. L33: Kirkb 9D 36
Burnard Cres. L33: Kirkb 9D 36
Burnard Wlk. L33: Kirkb 9D 36
Burnell Cl. WA10: St H 7J 49
Burnell Rd. CH65: Ell P 1C 112
Burnet Cl. WA2: Padg 7K 67
Burnet Rd. L5: Liv 3F 58
Burnfell WA3: Low 3F 52
Burnham Cl. WA3: Cul 6M 53
WA5: Penk 3H 81
WA8: Wid 5F 78
Burnham Rd. L18: Moss H 5A 76
Burnie Av. L20: Boot 5D 44
Burnley Av. CH46: More 9N 55
PR8: Ains 9K 11
Burnley Cl. L6: Liv 5F 58
Burnley Gro. CH46: More 8N 55
Burnley Rd. CH46: More 8N 55
PR8: Ains 9J 11
Burnsall Av. WA3: Low 2G 53
Burnsall Dr. WA8: Wid 5F 78
Burnsall St. L19: Garst 2C 92
Burns Av. CH45: Wall 4G 57
Burns Cl. CH66: Gt Sut 1K 111
L16: Child 9D 60
L35: Whis 6B 62
WN4: Ash M 5H 41
WN5: Bil 2N 39
Burns Cres. WA8: Wid 8J 79
Burns Gro. L36: Huy 8L 61
WA2: Warr 7D 66
Burnside WN8: Parb 3E 22
Burnside Av. CH44: Wall 7H 57
WA4: Stockt H 7E 82
Burnside Rd. CH44: Wall 7H 57
Burns Rd. WA9: Sut M 6K 63
Burns St. L20: Boot 5N 43
Burnt Ash Cl. L19: Gras 9L 75
Burnthwaite Rd. L14: Knott A 6A 60
Burnt Mill La. WA8: Hale B 2A 94
Burnvale WN3: Wins 1F 40
Burrell Cl. CH42: Tran 7J 73
Burrell Ct. CH42: Tran 7J 73
Burrell Dr. CH46: More 1L 71
Burrell Rd. CH42: Tran 7J 73
Burrell St. L4: Walt 1E 58
Burrough Cl. WA3: Birchw 6N 67
Burroughs Gdns. L3: Liv 5C 58
Burrow's Av. WA11: Hay 5B 50
Burrows Ct. L3: Liv 5B 58
WA9: St H 7A 50
(off Chancery La.)
Burrows La. L34: Eccl P 2B 62
WA6: Alv 4J 115
WA10: Eccl 2B 62
Burrows St. WA11: Hay 4C 50
Bursar Cl. WA12: Newt W 6M 51
BURSCOUGH 9J 15
BURSCOUGH BRIDGE 9H 15
Burscough Bridge Station (Rail) 9J 15
Burscough Fitness & Racquets Leisure Cen. 9J 15
Burscough Ind. Est. L40: Burs 9F 14
Burscough Junction Station (Rail) 1J 21
Burscough Rd. L39: Orm 7D 20
Burscough St. L39: Orm 8C 20
Burscough Wharf *L40: Burs 9J 15*
(off Liverpool Rd. Nth.)
Burton Av. CH45: Wall 4E 56
L35: Rainh 5D 62
Burton Cl. L1: Liv 8F 4 (9C 58)
L35: Rainh 5D 62
WA3: Cul 7N 53
WA8: Wid 5J 79
Burton Grn. CH66: Gt Sut 1J 111
Burtonhead Ct. *WA9: St H 9L 49*
(off Harris Gdns.)
Burtonhead Rd. WA9: St H 8J 49
WA10: St H 8J 49
Burton Rd. CH64: Lit N, Ness 7E 100
WA2: Warr 8E 66
Burton St. L5: Kirkd 3B 58
Burtons Way L32: Kirkb 2A 46
BURTONWOOD 3G 65
Burtonwood Cotts. WA9: St H 8E 50
Burtonwood Heritage Cen. 8M 65
Burtonwood Ind. Cen. WA5: Burtw 2H 65
Burtonwood Rd.
WA5: Burtw, Gt San, Westb 5H 65
BURTONWOOD SERVICE AREA 6K 65
Burtree Rd. L14: Knott A 3E 60
Burwain Ho. L19: Aig 9L 75
Burwell Av. L37: Form 3D 24
Burwell Cl. L33: Kirkb 8E 36
Burwen Dr. L9: Walt 4E 44
Bury Rd. PR8: Birkd 3A 12
Busby's Cotts. CH45: New B 1H 57
Bushbys La. L37: Form 2C 24
Bushbys Pk. L37: Form 2C 24
Bushell Cl. CH64: Nest 7F 100
Bushell Ct. CH43: Oxton 4G 73
Bushell Rd. CH64: Nest 7F 100
Bushells La. WA6: Kingsw 5L 115
Bushel's Dr. WA9: Clock F 6N 63
Bushey La. WA11: Rainf 1A 38
Bushey Rd. L4: Walt 8H 45
Bushley Cl. L20: Boot 6A 44
Bush Way CH60: Hesw 7L 87
Business Resource Cen.
L33: Know I 2G 47
Butchers La. L39: Augh 7L 27
WN4: Ash M 9K 41
Bute St. L5: Liv 1H 5 (6D 58)
(not continuous)
Butleigh Rd. L36: Huy 4H 61
Butler Cres. L6: Liv 6G 58
Butler St. L6: Liv 5G 58
Buttercup Cl. CH46: More 7A 56
L22: Water 1M 43
WA5: Warr 5N 81
Buttercup Way L9: Walt 6G 45
Butterfield Gdns. L39: Augh 1B 28
Butterfield St. L4: Walt 2E 58
Buttermarket St. WA1: Warr 3C 82
(not continuous)
Buttermere Av. CH43: Noct 2C 72
CH65: Ell P 2A 112
WA2: Warr 6D 66
WA11: St H 2K 49
WN4: Ash M 6K 41
Buttermere Cl. L31: Mag 2K 35
L33: Kirkb 7B 36
L37: Form 1D 24
WA6: Frod 6N 107
Buttermere Ct. *CH41: Birke 3J 73*
(off Penrith St.)
Buttermere Cres. *WA2: Warr 6D 66*
(off Buttermere Av.)
WA11: Rainf 1C 38
Buttermere Gdns. L23: Crosb 9M 33
Buttermere Gro. WA7: Beech 1N 107
Buttermere Rd. L16: Child 9E 60
M31: Part 6L 69
Buttermere St. L8: Liv 1G 75
Butterton Av. CH49: Upton 2L 71
Butterwick Dr. L12: Crox 7C 46
Button St. L2: Liv 5F 4 (8C 58)
Butts Grn. WA5: Westb 6J 65
Butts La. PR8: South 1E 12
Buxted Rd. L32: Kirkb 2E 46
Buxted Wlk. L32: Kirkb 2E 46
Buxton Cl. WA5: Gt San 9J 65
Buxton La. CH44: Wall 4E 56
Buxton Rd. CH42: Rock F 6N 73
Bye La. L39: Down 1H 27
Byerley St. CH44: Wall 6K 57
Byfleet Cl. WN3: Wins 2E 40
Byland Cl. L37: Form 2H 25
WA8: Wid 3M 79
Byles St. L8: Liv 4F 74
Byng Av. M44: Cad 5K 69
Byng Pl. L4: Walt 1J 59
Byng Rd. L4: Walt 1J 59
Byng St. L20: Boot 8A 44
By-Pass, The L23: Crosb 7L 33
Byrne Av. CH42: Rock F 7M 73
Byrne Avenue Baths 7M 73
Byrom St. L3: Liv 3G 4 (7C 58)
PR9: South 8L 7
Byron Av. L12: W Der 2M 59
L35: Whis 6C 62
Byron Cl. CH43: Pren 8F 72
L36: Huy 8L 61
L37: Form 9F 16
WA10: St H 5K 49
Byron Ct. L25: Woolt 5E 76
WA2: Warr 7D 66
Byron Rd. L23: Blun 7J 33
L31: Lyd 9J 27
Byron St. L20: Boot 5N 43
WA7: Run 6K 95
Byron Ter. L23: Blun 7H 33
Byton Wlk. L33: Kirkb 7E 36
Bywater Way L10: Faz 3N 45
Byway, The L23: Crosb 6L 33

C

CABBAGE HALL 3G 59
Cabes Cl. L14: Knott A 2E 60
Cabin La. L31: Lyd 8E 26
L39: Hals 1B 18
L40: Holm 9L 9
PR9: South 4C 8
Cablehouse L2: Liv 3E 4
Cable M. *PR9: South 8G 6*
(off Cable St.)
Cable Rd. CH47: Hoy 1B 70
L35: Presc 4C 62
Cables Retail Pk. L34: Presc 4A 62
Cable St. L37: Form 9G 16
PR9: South 8G 6
Cable Yard, The *L2: Liv 3E 4*
(off Cheapside)
Cabot Cl. WA5: Old H 8L 65
Cabot Grn. L25: Woolt 3C 76
Cabul Cl. WA2: Warr 1D 82
Cadbury Cl. L12: W Der 8N 45
Caddick Rd. L34: Know 5F 46
Cadet Way L12: W Der 2C 60
CADISHEAD 4L 69
Cadishead Way M44: Cad, Irlam 6K 69
Cadishead Way Circ. M44: Cad 6J 69
Cadnam Rd. L25: Gate 3H 77
Cadogan Dr. WN3: Wins 1F 40
Cadogan St. L15: Wav 9J 59
Cadshaw Cl. WA3: Birchw 4L 67
Cadwell Rd. L31: Lyd 7G 26
Caernarvon Cl. CH49: Upton 2A 72
WA7: Cas 5B 96
Caernarvon Ct. CH63: Beb 3M 89
CH65: Ell P 3B 112
Caerwys Gro. CH42: Tran 4L 73
Caesars Cl. WA7: Cas 5A 96
Cainfield Wlk. *L4: Kirkd 2C 58*
(off Upperbrook St.)
Cains Brewery 2D 74
Caird St. L6: Liv 1N 5 (6F 58)
Cairn Brae WA12: Newt W 6L 51
Cairn Ct. WA9: St H 1G 63
Cairnmore Rd. L18: Moss H 6M 75
Cairns St. L8: Liv 2F 74
Cairo St. L4: Kirkd 9D 44
WA1: Warr 3C 82
WA10: St H 9G 48
Caister Cl. WN8: Skel 4G 31
Caithness Ct. WA7: Run 5L 95
Caithness Dr. CH45: Wall 3J 57
L23: Crosb 8M 33
Caithness Gdns. CH43: Pren 7F 72
Caithness Rd. L18: Aller 7N 75
Calamanco Way M44: Irlam 1N 69
Calcott Rake L30: N'ton 7D 34
(not continuous)
Calday Grange Cl. CH48: W Kir 7E 70
Calday Grange Swimming Pool 6E 70
Calday Gro. WA11: Hay 2C 50
Caldbeck Av. WA2: Warr 7E 66
Caldbeck Cl. WN4: Ash M 7K 41
Caldbeck Gro. WA11: St H 1M 49
Caldbeck Rd. CH62: Brom 5C 90
Calder Av. CH43: Pren 6G 72
L39: Orm 1B 28
Calder Cl. L33: Kirkb 5E 36
WA8: Wid 5B 80
Calder Dr. L18: Moss H 3A 76
L31: Mag 1L 35
L35: Rainh 6E 62
Calder Edge L18: Moss H 4A 76
Calderfield Cl. WA4: Stockt H 8C 82
Calderfield Rd. L18: Moss H 3B 76
Calder Grange L18: Aller 5C 76
Calderhurst Dr. WA10: Windle 4E 48
Calder Pk. Ct. L18: Moss H 4B 76
Calder Rd. CH63: Hghr B 2K 89
L5: Liv 3E 58
Calders, The L18: Moss H 5A 76
CALDERSTONES 5A 76
Calderstones Av. L18: Moss H 3A 76
Calderstones Ct. L18: Moss H 4A 76
Calderstones Park 5A 76
Calderstones Rd.
L18: Moss H 4N 75
Calders Vw. Ct. L18: Moss H 5A 76
Calder Way CH66: Gt Sut 9H 103
Calderwood Pk. L27: N'ley 2H 77
Caldicott Av. CH62: Brom 8C 90
Caldon Cl. L21: Lith 1N 43
Caldway Dr. L27: N'ley 2H 77
Caldwell Av. WA5: Warr 7A 66
Caldwell Cl. L33: Kirkb 7D 36
Caldwell Dr. CH49: Woodc 6B 72
Caldwell Rd. L19: Aller 8A 76
WA8: Wid 9K 79
Caldwell St. WA9: St H 7N 49
CALDY 9E 70
Caldy Chase Dr. CH48: Caldy 9E 70
Caldy Ct. CH48: W Kir 7C 70
Caldy Dr. CH66: Gt Sut 1J 111
Caldy Golf Course 2F 86
Caldy Gro. WA11: St H 5N 49
Caldy Pk. CH48: W Kir 8D 70
Caldy Rd. CH45: Wall 4H 57
CH48: Caldy, W Kir 7C 70
L9: Ain 3F 44
Caldy Wood CH48: Caldy 9E 70
Caldywood Dr. L35: Whis 6B 62
Caledonian Cres. L21: Lith 1N 43
Caledonia St. L7: Liv 7K 5 (9E 58)
Calgarth Av. WA5: Warr 9B 66
Calgarth Rd. L36: Huy 4G 60
Calgary Way L36: Huy 4G 60
California Cl. WA5: Gt San 9L 65
California Rd. L13: Liv 2J 59
Callaghan Cl. L5: Liv 4C 58
Callander Rd. L6: Liv 6J 59
CALLANDS 7N 65
Callands Rd. WA5: Call 7L 65
Callard Cl. L27: N'ley 2G 77
Callender Gdns. WA6: Hel 3D 114
Callestock Cl. L11: Crox 5B 46
Callington Cl. L14: Knott A 3E 60
Callon Av. WA11: St H 5A 50
Callow Rd. L15: Wav 1J 75
Calmet Cl. L5: Liv 3D 58
Calmington La. WA7: Nort 3H 97
Calne Cl. CH61: Irby 9L 71
Calstock Cl. WA5: Penk 5G 80
Calthorpe St. L19: Garst 1N 91
Calthorpe Way CH43: Noct 2D 72
Calton Av. L18: Moss H 3M 75
Calvados Cl. L17: Aig 7H 75
Calveley Av. CH62: East 2E 102
Calveley Cl. CH43: Oxton 5E 72
Calveley Gro. L26: Halew 1L 93
Calverhall Way
WN4: Ash M 8J 41
Calverley Cl. WA7: Brook 1E 108
Calver Pk. Rd. WA2: Win 6A 66
Calver Rd. WA2: Win 5A 66
Calvers WA7: Halt 6A 96
Camberley Cl. PR8: Birkd 1L 11
Camberley Dr. L25: Hunts X 8G 77
Camberwell Dr. WA4: Warr 7B 82
Camberwell Pk. Rd.
WA8: Wid 4N 79
Camborne Av. L25: Woolt 7G 77
Camborne Cl. WA7: Brook 9E 96
Camborne Rd. WA5: Burtw 3H 65
Cambourne Av. WA11: St H 3N 49
Cambrai Av. WA4: Warr 6D 82
Cambrian Cl. *CH46: More 1J 71*
(off Cambrian Rd.)
CH66: Lit Sut 8F 102
Cambrian Ct. PR9: South 7J 7
Cambrian Cres. WN3: Wins 1E 40
Cambrian Rd. CH46: More 1K 71
Cambrian Way L25: Woolt 5F 76
Cambria St. Nth. L6: Liv 6G 59
Cambria St. Sth. L6: Liv 6G 59
Cambridge Arc. *PR8: South 8G 6*
(off Chapel St.)
Cambridge Av. L21: Lith 2A 44
L23: Crosb 7K 33
PR9: South 5L 7
Cambridge Cl. WA4: Stockt H 8C 82
Cambridge Ct. CH65: Ell P 9A 104
L7: Liv 6K 5 (9E 58)
PR9: South 5L 7
(off Cambridge Rd.)
Cambridge Dr. L23: Crosb 6J 33
L26: Halew 8K 77
Cambridge Gdns. PR9: South 5L 7
WA4: App 1D 98
WA6: Hel 1G 114
Cambridge Rd. CH42: Tran 6H 73
CH45: New B 2H 57
CH62: Brom 7D 90
CH65: Ell P 9A 104
L9: Ain 2G 44
L20: Boot 8C 44
L21: Sea 2M 43
L22: Water 3L 43
L23: Crosb 6J 33
L37: Form 3C 24
PR9: South 6K 7
WA10: St H 6H 49
WN8: Skel 3B 30

Cambridge St. L7: Liv 7L 5 (9E 58)
(not continuous)
L15: Wav 9J 59
(not continuous)
L34: Presc 3A 62
WA7: Run 5M 95
WA8: Wid 9L 79
Cambridge Walks *PR8: South 8G 6*
(off Eastbank St. Sq.)
Camdale Cl. L28: Stockb V 2F 60
Camden Cl. CH49: Woodc 4B 72
Camden Ct. WA7: Nort 6F 96
Camden Pl. CH41: Birke 2L 73
Camden Rd. CH65: Ell P 9M 103
Camden St. L3: Liv 3H 5 (7D 58)
Camelford Rd. L11: Crox 5B 46
Camellia Ct. L17: Aig 6F 74
Camellia Dr. WA5: Warr 4N 81
Camellia Gdns. WA9: Bold 2D 64
Camelot Cl. WA12: Newt W 6H 51
Camelot Ter. *L20: Boot 6A 44*
(off Tennyson St.)
Camelot Way WA7: Cas 7C 96
Cameo Cl. L6: Liv 5G 59
Cameron Av. WA7: Run 7H 95
Cameron Ct. WA2: Win 5B 66
Cameron Rd. CH46: Leas 6B 56
WA8: Wid 8K 79
Cameron St. L7: Liv 7H 59
Cammell Ct. CH43: Clau 2H 73
Camomile Wlk. *M31: Part 6M 69*
(off Wychelm Rd.)
Campbell Av. WA7: Run 7K 95
Campbell Cl. WA7: Run 7K 95
Campbell Cres. L33: Kirkb 5B 36
WA5: Gt San 2H 81
Campbell Dr. L14: Broad G 6C 60
Campbell Sq. L1: Liv 7F 4
Campbell St. L1: Liv 7F 4 (9C 58)
L20: Boot 7N 43
WA10: St H 6H 49
Campbeltown Rd. CH41: Tran 4M 73
Camperdown St. CH41: Birke 2M 73
Camphill Rd. L25: Woolt 8E 76
Camphor Way L11: Norr G 9L 45
Campion Cl. WA3: Birchw 5K 67
WA11: St H 3L 49
Campion Gro. L32: Kirkb 7D 36
WN4: Ash M 7H 41
Campion Way L36: Huy 1K 77
Camp Rd. L25: Woolt 7F 76
WA5: Old H 8M 65
WN4: Garsw 8G 40
Campsey Ash WA8: Wid 4J 79
Campus Dr. WA7: Run 5H 95
Camrose Cl. WA7: Run 9M 95
Camsley La. WA13: Lymm 5A 84
Cam St. L25: Woolt 6D 76
Canaan WA3: Low 2K 53
WN7: Low 2K 53
Canada Blvd. L3: Liv 5C 4 (8A 58)
Canada Cl. WA2: Fearn 7H 67
Canal Bank L31: Lyd 5H 27
L40: Burs 8F 14
L40: Lath 3N 21
WA13: Lymm 5C 84
(Statham Av.)
WA13: Lymm 5F 84
(Thirlmere Dr.)
WN6: Appl B 6M 23
Canal Bri. Ent. Cen. CH65: Ell P 8B 104
Canal Cotts. L31: Lyd 5H 27
Canal Reach WA7: Wind H 5E 96
Canal Side WA4: Grap 7J 83
WA4: Moore 2L 97
WA7: West P 8G 94
Canalside CH65: Ell P 8B 104
Canalside Gro. L5: Liv 4B 58
Canalside Ind. Est. CH65: Ell P 7C 104
Canal St. L20: Boot 8A 44
WA7: Run 5L 95
WA10: St H 8J 49
WA12: Newt W 7H 51
Canal Vw. L31: Mell 8M 35
WA13: Lymm 5D 84
Canal Vw. Ct. L21: Lith 1N 43
Canberra Av. *WA2: Warr 6E 66*
(off Canberra Sq.)
WA9: St H 2H 63
Canberra Sq. WA2: Warr 7E 66
Candia Towers *L5: Liv 3D 58*
(off Jason St.)
Candleston Cl. WA5: Call 8N 65
Canella Av. L11: Norr G 9L 45
Canford Cl. WA5: Gt San 2L 81
Cannell Ct. CH64: Will 6N 101
WA7: Pal F 9C 96
Cannell St. WA5: Warr 4M 81
Canning Pl. L1: Liv 7E 4 (9B 58)
Canning Rd. PR9: South 8M 7
Canning St. CH41: Birke 1L 73
L8: Liv 8K 5 (9E 58)
L22: Water 1K 43
Canniswood Rd. WA11: Hay 4C 50
Cann La. Nth. WA4: App 2F 98
Cann La. Sth. WA4: App 3F 98
Cannock Cl. CH66: Gt Sut 5K 111
Cannock Grn. L31: Mag 2G 34
Cannonbury Cl. WA7: Halt 7C 96
Cannon Hill CH43: Clau 2H 73
Cannon Mt. CH43: Clau 2H 73
Cannon St. CH65: Ell P 9M 103
WA9: Clock F 6M 63
Canon Rd. L6: Liv 2H 59
Canons Rd. WA5: Gt San 2M 81
Canon St. WA7: Run 4K 95
Canon Wilson Cl. WA11: Hay 4F 50
Canova Cl. *L27: N'ley 4K 77*
(off Victoria Falls Rd.)
Canrow La. L34: Know 5H 47
Cansfield Gro. WN4: Ash M 7J 41
Cansfield St. WA10: St H 6K 49
Canterbury Av. WA3: Low 8K 33
Canterbury Av. L22: Water 8K 33
WA3: Low 1E 52
Canterbury Cl. CH66: Gt Sut 5K 111
L10: Ain 9K 35
L34: Presc 2B 62
L37: Form 8F 16
PR8: Birkd 2M 11
Canterbury Pk. L18: Aller 8A 76
Canterbury Rd. CH42: Rock F 7N 73
CH44: Wall 6J 57
WA8: Wid 9F 78
Canterbury St. L3: Liv 2J 5 (6D 58)
L19: Garst 3A 92
WA4: Warr 4D 82
WA10: St H 5H 49
Canterbury Way L3: Liv 2K 5 (6E 58)
L30: N'ton 7E 34
Canter Cl. L9: Ain 2J 45
Cantilever Gdns. WA4: Warr 6F 82
Cantley Cl. WA7: Beech 9N 95
Cantlow Fold PR8: Ains 1G 17
Cantsfield St. L7: Liv 1H 75
Canvey Cl. L15: Wav 1N 75
Capella Cl. L17: Aig 9K 75
CAPENHURST 5G 110
Capenhurst Av. WA2: Fearn 7H 67
Capenhurst Gdns. CH66: Gt Sut 4J 111
Capenhurst La. CH1: Cap 6D 110
CH65: Whit 2L 111
CH66: Gt Sut 4J 111
Capenhurst Station (Rail) 4H 111
Capenhurst Technology Pk.
CH1: Cap 4G 111
Cape Rd. L9: Ain 4H 45
Capesthorne Cl. WA8: Wid 8H 79
Capesthorne Rd. WA2: Warr 8E 66
Capilano Pk. L39: Augh 4A 28
Capital Gate L3: Liv 3K 5 (7E 58)
Capitol Trad. Pk. L33: Know I 9H 37
Caplin Cl. L33: Kirkb 5C 36
Capper Gro. L36: Huy 6J 61
Capricorn Cres. L14: Knott A 4D 60
Capricorn Way L20: Boot 6A 44
Capstick Cres. L25: Gate 2F 76
Captain Charles Jones Wlk.
CH44: Wall 3K 57
(off Webster Av.)
Captains Cl. L30: Boot 2C 44
Captain's La. L30: Boot 2D 44
WN4: Ash M 8L 41
Caradoc Rd. L21: Sea 4N 43
Caraway Cl. *L23: Thorn 6A 34*
(off Tanhouse Rd.)
Caraway Gro. WA10: St H 6G 48
Carawood Cl. WN6: Shev 6N 23
Carbis Cl. L10: Faz 4M 45
Carden Cl. L4: Kirkd 2D 58
WA3: Birchw 5L 67
Cardeston Cl. WA7: Sut W 3B 108
Cardiff Cl. CH66: Gt Sut 5K 111
Cardiff St. WN8: Skel 3A 30
Cardiff Way L19: Garst 1N 91
Cardigan Av. CH41: Birke 2K 73
Cardigan Cl. WA5: Call 7M 65
WA10: St H 8J 49
Cardigan Rd. CH45: New B 2H 57
PR8: Birkd 5M 11
Cardigan St. L15: Wav 9J 59
Cardigan Way L6: Liv 5G 59
L30: N'ton 7G 34
Cardus Cl. CH46: More 9J 55
Cardwell Rd. L19: Garst 1B 92
Cardwell St. L7: Liv 7N 5 (9F 58)
Carey Av. CH63: Hghr B 1K 89
Carey Cl. WN3: Wins 1F 40
Carey St. WA8: Wid 7L 79
Carfax Rd. L33: Kirkb 7E 36
Carfield WN8: Skel 6H 31
Cargill Gro. CH42: Rock F 8A 74
Carham Rd. CH47: Hoy 2D 70
Carillion Cl. L11: Crox 7A 46
Carina Ct. L17: Aig 9L 75
Carina Pk. WA5: Westb 7K 65
Carisbrooke Cl. CH48: Caldy 8D 70
Carisbrooke Dr. PR9: South 6L 7
Carisbrooke Pl. L4: Kirkd 9E 44
Carisbrooke Rd. L4: Kirkd, Walt 8D 44
L20: Boot 8D 44
Carkington Rd. L25: Woolt 7G 76
Carlake Gro. L9: Ain 7H 45
Carland Cl. L10: Faz 4N 45
Carlaw Rd. CH42: Tran 6G 72
Carleen Cl. L17: Aig 6G 75
Carlett Blvd. CH62: East 1E 102
Carlett Pk. CH62: East 9E 90
Carlett Vw. L19: Garst 1A 92
Carley Wlk. L24: Speke 5J 93
Carlile Way L33: Kirkb 5D 36
Carlingford Cl. L8: Liv 9N 5 (1F 74)
Carlingford Rd. WA4: Stockt H 8C 82
Carlisle Av. L30: N'ton 1E 44
Carlisle Cl. L4: Walt 1J 59
Carlisle M. CH43: Oxton 3J 73
Carlisle Rd. PR8: Birkd 4N 11
Carlisle St. WA4: Stockt H 8D 82
Carlis Rd. L32: Kirkb 2D 46
Carlow Cl. L24: Hale 5N 93
Carlow St. WA10: St H 9G 48
Carlsruhe Ct. L8: Liv 3F 74
Carl's Way L33: Kirkb 5E 36
Carlton Av. WA7: Run 5N 95
WN8: Uph 5K 31
Carlton Bingo Club 4E 44
Carlton Cl. CH64: Park 4C 100
WN4: Ash M 7J 41
Carlton Cres. CH66: Ell P 6L 103
Carlton La. CH47: Meols 9D 54
L13: Liv 5M 59
Carlton Little Theatre 3J 73
Carlton Mt. CH42: Tran 5L 73
Carlton Rd. CH42: Tran 4J 73
CH45: New B 1H 57
CH63: Beb 3A 90
PR8: Ains 8J 11
WA3: Low 1E 52
WA13: Lymm 3H 85
(not continuous)
Carlton St. L3: Liv 5A 58
L34: Presc 3A 62
WA4: Stockt H 8D 82
WA8: Wid 8K 79
WA10: St H 7H 49
Carlton Ter. CH47: Meols 9D 54
L23: Crosb 7K 33
Carlton Way WA3: Glaz 4J 69
Carlyle Cres. CH66: Gt Sut 1K 111
Carlyon Way L26: Halew 8J 77
Carman Wlk. L7: Liv 9G 59
Carmarthen Cl. WA5: Call 7M 65
Carmarthen Cres. L8: Liv 2C 74
Carmel Cl. CH45: New B 1H 57
L39: Augh 2B 28
WA5: Call 7N 65
Carmel Ct. WA8: Wid 4L 79
Carmelite Cres. WA10: Eccl 5D 48
Carmichael Av. CH49: Grea 6L 71
Carmichael Cl. M31: Part 6L 69
Carnaby Cl. L36: Huy 9L 61
Carnaby Pl. WA5: Gt San 2K 81
Carnarvon Ct. L9: Walt 7E 44
Carnarvon Rd. L9: Walt 7E 44
PR8: Birkd 5M 11
Carnarvon St. WA9: St H 1G 63
Carnatic Cl. L18: Moss H 5L 75
Carnatic Ct. L18: Moss H 5K 75
Carnatic Rd. L18: Moss H 5K 75
Carnation Rd. L9: Walt 7G 45
Carneghie Ct. PR8: Birkd 2M 11
Carnegie Av. L23: Crosb 8K 33
Carnegie Cres. WA9: St H 1A 64
Carnegie Dr. WN4: Ash M 6J 41
Carnegie Rd. L13: Liv 5K 59
Carnforth Av. L32: Kirkb 1D 46
Carnforth Cl. CH41: Birke 3J 73
L12: W Der 9A 46
Carnforth Rd. L18: Moss H 6A 76
Carno St. L15: Wav 9K 59
Carnoustie Cl. CH46: More 8J 55
L12: W Der 3D 60
PR8: Birkd 2M 11
Carnoustie Gro. WA11: Hay 5C 50
Carnsdale Rd. CH46: More 9N 55
Carol Dr. CH60: Hesw 7C 88
Carole Cl. WA9: Sut L 3A 64
Carolina Rd. WA5: Gt San 1K 81
Carolina St. L20: Boot 7A 44
Caroline Pl. CH43: Oxton 3H 73
Caroline St. M44: Irlam 1M 69
WA8: Wid 9L 79
Carol St. WA4: Warr 4E 82
Caronia St. L19: Garst 2A 92
Carpathia St. L19: Garst 3A 92
Carpenter Gro. WA2: Padg 8H 67
Carpenter's La. CH48: W Kir 6C 70
Carpenters Row L1: Liv 8F 4 (9C 58)
Carraway Rd. L11: Crox 4A 46
Carr Bri. Rd. CH49: Woodc 4B 72
Carr Cl. L11: Norr G 8N 45
Carr Cft. L21: Ford 8A 34
CARR CROSS 6J 13
Carrfield Av. L23: Crosb 8N 33
Carrfield Wlk. L11: Norr G 7N 45
Carr Gate CH46: More 1J 71
CARR GREEN 2L 85
Carrgreen La. WA13: Warb 2L 85
Carr Hey CH46: More 1J 71
Carr Hey CH49: Woodc 6C 72
Carr Ho. La. CH46: More 9J 55
L38: Ince B 8L 25
CARR HOUSES 8M 25
Carriage Cl. L24: Hale 6A 94
Carriage Dr. WA6: Frod 8K 107
Carriage Gro. L20: Boot 7C 44
Carrick Ct. L23: Crosb 8N 33
Carrick Dr. CH65: Whit 3N 111
Carrickmore Av. L18: Moss H 6M 75
Carrington Cl. WA3: Birchw 5K 67
Carrington Rd. CH45: Wall 3J 57
Carrington St. CH41: Birke 9G 56
Carr La. CH46: More 8H 55
CH47: Hoy 2C 70
CH47: Meols 8G 55
CH48: W Kir 3E 70
L11: Norr G 8L 45
L24: Hale 5A 94
L31: Lyd 7E 26
L34: Presc 4M 61
L36: Roby 8G 60
L40: Lath 1L 21
PR8: Ains, Birkd 7M 11
(not continuous)
WA3: Low 3H 53
WA8: Hale B 2B 94
WN3: Wigan 1K 41
WN7: Leigh 2M 53
Carr La. E. L11: Norr G 8N 45
Carr La. Ind. Est. CH47: Hoy 2D 70
Carr Mdw. Hey L30: N'ton 9B 34
CARR MILL 2L 49
Carr Mill Cres. WN5: Bil 7A 40
Carr Mill Rd. WA11: St H 3M 49
WN5: Bil 8N 39
Carr Moss La. L39: Hals 2B 18
Carrock Rd. CH62: Brom 5D 90
Carroll Cres. L39: Orm 6D 20
Carrow Cl. CH46: More 1J 71
Carr Rd. L20: Boot 3C 44
Carr's Cres. L37: Form 3D 24
Carr's Cres. W. L37: Form 3D 24
Carr Side La. L29: Thorn 9N 25
Carrs Ter. L35: Whis 6A 62
Carr St. WA10: St H 5G 49
Carruthers St. L3: Liv 1D 4 (6B 58)
Carrville Way L12: Crox 8E 46
Carrwood Cl. WA11: Hay 4C 50
Carrwood Pk. PR8: South 3A 12
Carsdale Rd. L18: Moss H 3M 75
Carsgoe Rd. CH47: Hoy 2D 70
Carsington Rd. L11: Norr G 8M 45
Carstairs Rd. L6: Liv 5J 59
Carsthorne Rd. CH47: Hoy 2D 70
Cartbridge La. L26: Halew 7K 77
Carter Av. WA11: Rainf 6D 38
Carters, The CH49: Grea 4K 71
L30: N'ton 7F 34
Carter St. L8: Liv 1E 74
Carterton Rd. CH47: Hoy 2D 70
Cartier Cl. WA5: Old H 9L 65
Cartmel Av. L31: Mag 1K 35
WA2: Warr 6D 66
Cartmel Cl. CH41: Birke 3J 73
L36: Huy 5H 61
PR8: South 3E 12
Cartmel Dr. CH46: More 1M 71
CH66: Gt Sut 3L 111
L12: W Der 9A 46
L35: Rainh 5D 62
L37: Form 2H 25
Cartmell Av. WA10: St H 3H 49
Cartmell Cl. WA7: Run 9L 95
Cartmel Rd. L36: Huy 4G 60
Cartmel Ter. L11: Norr G 7N 45
Cartmel Way L36: Huy 5G 61
Cartridge La. WA4: Grap 1L 99
Cartwright Cl. WA11: Rainf 5C 38
Cartwright Ct. WA11: Rainf 4C 38
Cartwrights Farm Rd. L24: Speke 3E 92
Cartwright St. WA5: Warr 2N 81
WA7: Run 5M 95
Carvel Way L40: Burs 2K 21
Carver St. L3: Liv 2K 5 (6E 58)
Caryl Gro. L8: Liv 4D 74
Caryl St. L8: Liv 3D 74
(Atterbury St.)
L8: Liv 3D 74
(Park St.)
L8: Liv 2C 74
(Stanhope St.)
Casbah Cl. L12: W Der 3N 59
Cascade Rd. L24: Speke 1G 92
Case Gro. L35: Presc 4B 62
Case Rd. WA11: Hay 4F 50
Cases St. L1: Liv 5G 5 (8C 58)
Cashel Rd. CH41: Birke 7H 57
Caspian Pl. L20: Boot 7B 44
Caspian Rd. L4: Walt 8J 45
Cassia Cl. L9: Walt 6G 45
Cassino Rd. L36: Huy 6J 61
Cassio St. L20: Boot 8D 44
Cassley Rd. L24: Speke 4L 93
Cassville Rd. L18: Moss H 2M 75
Castell Gro. WA10: St H 7J 49
Castle Av. WA9: St H 7A 50
Castlebridge Ct. *CH42: Rock F 7M 73*
(off Old Chester Rd.)
Castle Cl. CH46: Leas 6A 56
Castle Ct. CH48: W Kir 7C 70
Castle Dr. CH60: Hesw 7N 87
CH65: Whit 2M 111
L37: Form 3F 24
Castlefield Cl. L12: W Der 2M 59
Castlefield Rd. L12: W Der 2M 59
CASTLEFIELDS 5C 96
Castlefields CH46: Leas 5N 55
Castlefields Av. E. WA7: Cas 6C 96
Castlefields Av. Nth. WA7: Cas 5A 96
Castlefields Av. Sth. WA7: Cas 6B 96
Castleford Ri. CH46: Leas 6M 55

Castleford St. L15: Wav 1M 75
Castlegate Gro. L12: W Der 2N 59
Castlegrange Cl. CH46: Leas 5M 55
Castle Grn. WA5: Westb 7K 65
Castleheath Cl. CH46: Leas 6M 55
Castlehey WN8: Skel 6H 31
Castle Hill L2: Liv 5D 4
WA12: Newt W 6N 51
Castle Keep L12: W Der 2N 59
Castle La. L40: Lath, Westh 7H 21
Castlemere Cl. WN3: Wins 2F 40
Castle Mt. *CH60: Hesw 7N 87*
(off The Mount)
Castle Park 7K 107
Castle Park Arts Cen. 6K 107
Castle Ri. WA7: Run 5N 95
Castle Rd. CH45: Wall 3G 57
WA7: Halt 7B 96
Castlesite Rd. L12: W Der 1N 59
Castle St. CH41: Birke 2M 73
L2: Liv 5D 4 (8B 58)
L25: Woolt 6D 76
PR9: South 7G 7
WA8: Wid 7N 79
Castleton Dr. L30: N'ton 7G 34
WA1: Warr 3F 82
Castleton Way WN3: Wins 1E 40
Castletown Cl. L16: Child 9C 60
Castleview Rd. L12: W Der 2N 59
Castle Wlk. PR8: South 9F 6
Castleway Nth. CH46: Leas 5A 56
Castleway Sth. CH46: Leas 6A 56
Castlewell L35: Whis 5C 62
Castlewood Rd. L6: Liv 4G 59
Castner Av. WA7: West P 8H 95
Castner Ct. WA7: West P 8H 95
Castor St. L6: Liv 4G 59
Catalyst Science Discovery Cen. 2K 95
Catalyst Trade Pk. WA8: Wid 1K 95
Catchdale Moss La. WA10: Eccl 4B 48
Catford Cl. WA8: Wid 6F 78
Catford Grn. L24: Speke 4K 93
Catfoss Cl. WA2: Padg 8F 66
Catharine's La. L39: Bic 2D 28
Catharine St. L8: Liv 8K 5 (9E 58)
Cathcart St. CH41: Birke 1K 73
Cathedral Cl. L1: Liv 9J 5 (1D 74)
Cathedral Ct. L1: Liv 8K 5
Cathedral Ga. L1: Liv 8J 5 (9D 58)
Cathedral Rd. L6: Liv 3H 59
Cathedral Wlk. L3: Liv 6J 5 (8E 58)
Catherine Ct. L21: Lith 4A 44
Catherine St. CH41: Birke 2K 73
L21: Lith 4A 44
WA5: Warr 1A 82
(not continuous)
WA8: Wid 9K 79
Catherine Way WA11: Hay 4B 50
WA12: Newt W 8K 51
Catkin Rd. L26: Halew 6H 77
Caton Cl. PR9: South 3L 7
Catonfield Rd. L18: Moss H 3B 76
Cat Tail La. PR8: South 5K 13
Cattan Grn. L37: Form 2H 25
Catterall Av. WA2: Warr 7E 66
WA9: Sut L 3N 63
Catterick Cl. L26: Halew 8K 77
Catterick Fold PR8: South 3E 12
Catton Hall Shooting Ground 8C 108
Caulfield Dr. CH49: Grea 5M 71
Caunce Av. PR9: Banks 1E 8
WA3: Golb 3B 52
WA11: Hay 4D 50
WA12: Newt W 9L 51
Caunce's Rd. PR9: South 2N 13
Causeway, The CH62: Port S 2A 90
L12: W Der 5B 60
PR9: South 2A 8
Causeway Av. WA4: Warr 5D 82
Causeway Cl. CH62: Port S 1A 90
Causeway Ho. CH46: Leas 5M 55
Causeway La. L37: Gt Alt 3N 25
L40: Ruf 5M 15
Causeway Pk. WA4: Warr 5D 82
Cavalier Cl. L23: Crosb 8M 33
Cavalier Dr. L19: Garst 2B 92
Cavalry Cl. L12: W Der 2C 60
Cavan Dr. WA11: Hay 3F 50
Cavan Rd. L11: Norr G 1K 59
Cavell Cl. L25: Woolt 7E 76
Cavell Dr. CH65: Whit 1M 111
Cavendish Av. WA3: Ris 4M 67
Cavendish Cl. WA5: Old H 1M 81
Cavendish Ct. PR9: South 6K 7
Cavendish Dr. CH42: Rock F 7K 73
L9: Walt 7F 44
WN3: Wins 1F 40
Cavendish Farm Rd. WA7: West 1J 107
(not continuous)
Cavendish Gdns. CH65: Whit 1M 111
L8: Liv 3F 74
Cavendish Pl. WA3: Ris 4N 67
Cavendish Rd. CH41: Birke 1H 73
CH45: New B 9H 43
L23: Blun 8J 33
PR8: Birkd 3M 11
Cavendish St. CH41: Birke 9H 57
WA7: Run 5J 95
(not continuous)
Cavern Club, The 5E 4
Cavern Ct. *L6: Liv 6G 59*
(off Coleridge St.)
Cavern Quarter 5E 4
Cavern Walks L2: Liv 5E 4
Caversham Cl. WA4: App 9F 82
Cawdor St. L8: Liv 2F 74
WA4: Stockt H 8D 82
WA7: Run 4J 95
Cawfield Av. WA8: Wid 7G 79
Cawley Av. WA3: Cul 6M 53
Cawley St. WA7: Run 6K 95
Cawood Cl. CH66: Lit Sut 9G 103
Cawthorne Av. L32: Kirkb 2C 46
WA4: Grap 6H 83
Cawthorne Cl. L32: Kirkb 2C 46
Cawthorne Wlk. L32: Kirkb 3C 46
Caxton Cl. CH43: Bid 2C 72
CH66: Gt Sut 1K 111
WA8: Wid 5F 78
WN3: Wigan 1H 41
Caxton Rd. L35: Rainh 8H 63
Cazneau St. L3: Liv 1G 5 (6C 58)
C Court WN4: Ash M 9K 41
Cearns Rd. CH43: Oxton 3G 73
Cecil Dr. WA10: Eccl 5D 48
Cecil Rd. CH42: Tran 6H 73
CH45: Wall 5G 57
CH62: New F 8A 74
L21: Sea 4M 43
Cecil St. L15: Wav 9J 59
WA9: St H 2B 64
Cedab Rd. CH65: Ell P 8B 104
Cedar Av. CH63: Hghr B 3L 89
CH66: Lit Sut 8H 103
WA3: Low 3G 53
WA7: Run 8M 95
WA7: Sut W 2D 108
WA8: Wid 6L 79
Cedar Cl. L18: Aller 5B 76
L35: Whis 5B 62
Cedar Ct. L34: Know 6H 47
WA3: Ris 8N 53
Cedar Cres. L36: Huy 8H 61
L39: Orm 9A 20
WA12: Newt W 8M 51
Cedardale Dr. CH66: Whit 5L 111
Cedardale Pk. WA8: Wid 4A 80
Cedardale Rd. L9: Walt 6F 44
Cedar Dr. L37: Form 3C 24
Cedarfield Rd. WA13: Lymm 3H 85
Cedar Gro. CH64: Nest 6F 100
L8: Liv 2H 75
L22: Water 9K 33
L31: Mag 5J 35
WA1: Padd 1H 83
WA4: Warr 5E 82
WA11: Hay 3G 51
WN4: Garsw 6F 40
WN8: Skel 3B 30
Cedar Rd. L9: Ain 4G 44
L35: Whis 6A 62
M31: Part 6L 69
WA5: Gt San 2H 81
Cedars, The CH46: More 1K 71
CH66: Lit Sut 8E 102
L12: Crox 7D 46
Cedar St. CH41: Birke 3K 73
L20: Boot 6B 44
PR8: South 2B 12
WA10: St H 8G 48
WA12: Newt W 8L 51
Cedar Ter. *L8: Liv 2H 75*
(off Cedar Gro.)
Cedarway CH60: Hesw 1B 100
Cedarways WA4: App 2E 98
Cedarwood Cl. CH49: Grea 4J 71
Cedarwood Ct. L36: Huy 9J 61
Celandine Way WA9: Bold 2D 64
Celebration Dr. L6: Liv 4H 59
Celendine Cl. L15: Wav 9K 59
Celia St. L20: Kirkd 9C 44
Celtic Rd. CH47: Meols 8F 54
Celtic St. L8: Liv 2F 74
Celt St. L6: Liv 5G 59
Cemeas Cl. L5: Liv 4B 58
Cemetery Rd. PR8: South 2A 12
Centenary Cl. L4: Walt 1H 59
Centenary Ho. WA7: Run 7M 95
Central 12 Retail Pk.
PR9: South 9H 7
Central Av. CH62: Brom 6B 90
CH65: Ell P 1A 112
L24: Speke 4H 93
L34: Eccl P 2C 62
L34: Presc 3N 61
PR8: Birkd 6M 11
WA2: Warr 9D 66
WA4: Warr 5C 82
Central Bldgs. *L23: Crosb 7L 33*
(off Church Rd.)
Central Dr. L12: W Der 4N 59
WA11: Hay 4D 50
WA11: Rainf 4C 38
Central Expressway WA7: Run 8A 96
Central Gdns. L1: Liv 6H 5
Central Pk. Av. CH44: Wall 5J 57
Central Rd. CH62: Port S 1A 90
(Osborne Ct.)
CH62: Port S 2A 90
(Wood St.)
Central Rd. M31: Part 6M 69
WA4: Warr 5D 82
Central Shop. Cen. L1: Liv 6G 5 (8C 58)
Central Sq. L31: Mag 1H 35
Central Station (Rail) 6G 5 (8C 58)
Central St. WA10: St H 6K 49
Central Way L24: Speke 4J 93
WA2: Warr 2C 82
WA12: Newt W 8N 51
Centre, The WA3: Ris 4M 67
Centre 21 WA1: Wools 2K 83
Centre Ct. WN7: Leigh 1J 53
Centre Pk. WA1: Warr 5B 82
Centre Pk. Sq. WA1: Warr 4B 82
Centreville Rd. L18: Moss H 2M 75
Centre Way L36: Huy 7J 61
Centro Pk. L33: Know I 2G 47
Centurion Cl. CH47: Meols 8F 54
WA3: Ris 4L 67
Centurion Dr. CH47: Meols 8F 54
Centurion Row WA7: Cas 5B 96
Century Bldgs. L3: Liv 4C 74
Century Rd. L23: Crosb 7K 33
Ceres Ct. CH43: Bid 1C 72
Ceres St. L20: Kirkd 9B 44
Cestrian Dr. CH61: Thing 2A 88
Chadlow Rd. L32: Kirkb 3D 46
Chadwell Rd. L33: Kirkb 7D 36
Chadwick Av. WA3: Croft 2J 67
WA4: Stockt H 7F 82
Chadwick Ct. Ind. Cen.
L3: Liv 1C 4 (6A 58)
CHADWICK GREEN 8N 39
Chadwick La. WA8: Wid 5M 79
Chadwick Pl. WA3: Ris 4M 67
Chadwick Rd. WA7: Ast 4A 96
WA11: St H 3M 49
Chadwick St. CH46: More 9M 55
L3: Liv 1C 4 (5A 58)
Chadwick Way L33: Kirkb 5C 36
Chaffinch Cl. L12: W Der 9D 46
WA3: Birchw 6N 67
Chaffinch Glade L26: Halew 7J 77
Chainhurst Cl. L27: N'ley 2H 77
Chain La. WA11: St H 3N 49
Chain La. Shop. Pct. WA11: St H 3N 49
Chain Wlk. WA10: St H 7F 48
Chaise Mdw. WA13: Lymm 3H 85
Chalfield Av. CH66: Gt Sut 9H 103
Chalfield Cl. CH66: Gt Sut 9H 103
Chalfont Cl. WA4: App 1F 98
Chalfont Rd. L18: Aller 7B 76
Chalfont Way L28: Stockb V 2F 60
Chalgrave Cl. WA8: Wid 5B 80
Chalice Way L11: Crox 7A 46
Chalkley Cl. CH42: Tran 6J 73
Chalkwell Dr. CH60: Hesw 8C 88
Challis St. CH41: Birke 8E 56
Challoner Cl. L36: Huy 9K 61
Chaloner Gro. L19: Gras 1L 91
Chaloner St. L3: Liv 1C 74
Chalon Way E. WA10: St H 7K 49
Chalon Way Ind. Est. WA10: St H 8K 49
Chalon Way W. WA10: St H 7J 49
Chamberlain Dr. L33: Kirkb 6D 36
Chamberlain St. CH41: Tran 4L 73
CH44: Wall 7G 57
WA10: St H 7G 48
Chambres Rd. PR8: South 1C 12
Chambres Rd. Nth. PR8: South 9J 7
Chamomile Cl. L11: Norr G 8L 45
Champions Bus. Pk. CH49: Upton 5N 71
Chancellor Ct. L8: Liv 8N 5 (9F 58)
Chancellor Rd. WA7: Manor P 2F 96
Chancellors Ct. L39: Orm 1F 28
Chancel St. L4: Kirkd 2C 58
Chancery La. WA9: St H 7A 50
Chandlers Ct. WA7: Run 6H 95
Chandlers Edge *CH65: Ell P 7B 104*
(off Grosvenor Wharf Rd.)
Chandlers Way WA9: Sut M 6L 63
Chandler Way WA3: Low 2F 52
Chandley Cl. PR8: Ains 9G 11
Chandos St. L7: Liv 8G 59
Change La. CH64: Will 6A 102
Changford Grn. L33: Kirkb 8E 36
Changford Rd. L33: Kirkb 7E 36
Channel, The CH2: Back 9N 111
CH45: Wall 1E 56
Channell Rd. L6: Liv 6H 59
Channel Reach L23: Blun 8H 33
Channel Rd. L23: Blun 8H 33
Chantler Av. WA4: Westy 4F 82
Chantrell Rd. CH48: W Kir 6F 70
Chantry, The WA10: St H 4G 49
Chantry Cl. CH43: Bid 2B 72
Chantry Wlk. CH60: Hesw 9A 88
WN4: Ash M 6H 41
Chapel Av. L9: Walt 4F 44
Chapel Cl. *CH65: Ell P 7A 104*
(off Grace Rd.)
PR9: Banks 1F 8
Chapel Ct. L39: Orm 9C 20
Chapelcroft Ct. L12: W Der 3A 60
Chapel Cross Rd. WA2: Fearn 7H 67
Chapelfields WA6: Frod 6K 107
CHAPELFORD URBAN VILLAGE 1K 81
Chapel Gallery, The 8D 20
Chapel Gdns. L5: Liv 4C 58
Chapelhill Rd. CH46: More 9N 55
CHAPEL HOUSE 3A 30
Chapel Ho. L22: Water 2K 43
L31: Mag 2J 35
Chapel Ho. La. Sth. CH64: Pudd 6A 110
Chapel Ho. M. WA3: Low 2D 52
Chapel Ho. Wlk. L37: Form 1G 25
Chapel La. CH1: Cap, Woodb 5D 110
CH3: Moul 9J 115
CH66: Led 5D 110
L30: N'ton 6E 34
L31: Mell 7M 35
L35: Rainh 8H 63
L37: Form 1F 24
L40: Burs 3J 21
L40: Holm 1F 14
M31: Part 6M 69
PR9: Banks 1F 8
WA3: Rix 8F 68
WA4: App T 4J 99
WA4: Stockt H 8D 82
WA5: Burtw 3G 65
WA6: Manl 9J 115
WA8: Cron, Wid 3F 78
WA10: Eccl 6E 48
WA13: Warb 6M 69
WN8: Parb 4G 23
Chapel M. *CH2: Elt 2M 113*
(off Marsh La.)
CH65: Whit 1N 111
L39: Orm 9D 20
Chapel Moss L39: Orm 9C 20
Chapel Pl. L19: Garst 1A 92
L25: Woolt 6E 76
WN4: Ash M 8K 41
Chapel Rd. CH47: Hoy 9D 54
L6: Liv 3H 59
L19: Garst 1A 92
(not continuous)
WA5: Penk 5G 80
Chapelside Cl. WA5: Gt San 2H 81
Chapel St. L3: Liv 4C 4 (7A 58)
L34: Presc 3A 62
L39: Orm 9D 20
PR8: South 8G 6
WA8: Wid 9K 79
WA10: St H 5J 49
WA11: Hay 4F 50
(not continuous)
WA12: Newt W 7K 51
WN4: Ash M 8K 41
Chapel Ter. L20: Boot 7A 44
WA3: Low 1J 53
Chapel Vw. CH62: East 9F 90
WA6: Hel 3E 114
WA11: Crank 7J 39
Chapel Wlk. WA3: Low 1J 53
Chapel Walks WA13: Lymm 7K 85
Chapel Yd. *L15: Wav 1M 75*
(off Waterloo St.)
WA2: Warr 2B 82
Chapman Cl. L8: Liv 3D 74
WA8: Wid 4G 79
Chapman Gro. L34: Presc 2B 62
Chapterhouse Cl. CH65: Ell P 9C 104
Chardstock Dr. L25: Gate 4G 77
Charing Cross CH41: Birke 3K 73
Charity La. L40: Westh 1J 29
Charlcombe St. CH42: Tran 4K 73
Charlecote St. L8: Liv 5E 74
Charles Av. PR8: Ains 8L 11
WA5: Gt San 2H 81
Charles Berrington Rd. L15: Wav 2M 75
Charles Best Grn. *L30: N'ton 7E 34*
(off Alexander Fleming Av.)
Charlesbye Av. L39: Orm 7E 20
Charlesbye Cl. L39: Orm 7F 20
Charles Ct. PR9: South 8H 7
Charles Forbes Ct. *WA1: Warr 3C 82*
(off Mersey St.)
Charles Price Gdns. CH65: Ell P 8A 104
Charles Rd. CH47: Hoy 2C 70
Charles St. CH41: Birke 1K 73
M44: Cad 3L 69
WA3: Golb 1B 52
WA8: Wid 8K 79
WA10: St H 6K 49
Charleston Cl. CH66: Gt Sut 2J 111
Charleston Gro. WA5: Gt San 2K 81
Charleston Rd. L8: Liv 4E 74
Charlesville CH43: Oxton 3H 73
Charlesville Ct. CH43: Oxton 3H 73
Charles Wlk. L14: Broad G 6D 60
Charlesworth Cl. L31: Lyd 7G 27
Charleywood Rd. L33: Know I 1F 46
Charlock Cl. L30: N'ton 7F 34
Charlock Wlk. *M31: Part 6M 69*
(off Central Rd.)
Charlotte Gro. WA5: Gt San 1L 81
Charlotte Rd. CH44: Wall 4K 57
Charlotte's Mdw. CH63: Beb 3N 89
Charlotte Wlk. WA8: Wid 9L 79
Charlotte Way L1: Liv 5G 5
Charlton Cl. WA7: Pal F 8C 96
Charlton Ct. CH43: Clau 2F 72
L25: Hunts X 9H 77
Charlton Pl. L13: Liv 8M 59
Charlton Rd. L13: Liv 8M 59
Charlton St. WA4: Westy 5G 83
Charlwood Av. L36: Huy 8J 61
Charlwood Cl. CH43: Bid 2C 72

Charmalue Av. L23: Crosb 7M 33
Charminster Cl. WA5: Gt San 3K 81
Charmouth Cl. L12: Crox 7C 46
WA12: Newt W 6K 51
Charnley Dr. L15: Wav 9A 60
Charnley's La. PR9: Banks 1E 8
Charnock WN8: Skel 6H 31
Charnock Av. WA12: Newt W 7H 51
Charnock Rd. L9: Ain 7J 45
WA3: Cul 7N 53
Charnwood Cl. L12: Crox 7B 46
WA3: Birchw 4B 68
Charnwood Rd. L36: Huy 6F 60
Charnwood St. WA9: St H 6A 50
Charon Way WA5: Westb 6J 65
Charter Av. WA5: Warr 9B 66
Charter Cres. CH66: Gt Sut 2K 111
Charter Ho. *CH44: Wall* 5K 57
(off Church St.)
Charterhouse Cl. L25: Woolt 7F 76
Charterhouse Dr. L10: Ain 9K 35
Charterhouse Rd. L25: Woolt 7F 76
Chartmount Way L25: Gate 4F 76
Chartwell Gdns. WA4: App 2G 98
Chartwell Gro. L26: Halew 7K 77
Chartwell Rd. PR8: Ains 8H 11
Chase, The CH60: Hesw 7A 88
CH63: Brom 1B 102
L36: Huy 9K 61
Chase Cl. PR8: Birkd 2M 11
Chase Dr. CH66: Gt Sut 3K 111
Chase Heys PR9: South 6M 7
Chaser Cl. L9: Ain 2H 45
Chasewater WA7: Nort 3H 97
Chase Way CH66: Gt Sut 3K 111
L5: Liv 5D 58
Chatbrook Cl. L17: Aig 9L 75
Chatburn Av. WA3: Golb 1D 52
Chatburn Ct. WA3: Cul 8N 53
Chater Cl. *L35: Whis* 3D 62
(off Watling Way)
Chatfield Dr. WA3: Birchw 6M 67
Chatham Cl. L21: Sea 3M 43
Chatham Ct. L22: Water 2L 43
Chatham Pl. L7: Liv 8G 58
Chatham Rd. CH42: Rock F 6N 73
Chatham St. L7: Liv 8L 5 (9E 58)
L8: Liv 8L 5 (9E 58)
Chatsworth Av. CH44: Wall 5J 57
L9: Walt 5E 44
WA3: Cul 6N 53
Chatsworth Cl. CH66: Gt Sut 9J 103
WN4: Ash M 7H 41
Chatsworth Dr. L7: Liv 8G 59
WA8: Wid 5F 78
Chatsworth Rd. CH42: Rock F 6N 73
CH61: Pens 2N 87
L35: Rainh 5E 62
PR8: Ains 8G 11
Chatteris Ct. *WA10: St H* 9G 48
(off Bewsey St.)
Chatteris Pk. WA7: Nort 5G 96
Chatterton Dr. WA7: Murd 7G 96
Chatterton Rd. L14: Knott A 5A 60
Chaucer Dr. L12: Crox 8C 46
Chaucer Pl. WA4: Westy 4G 83
Chaucer Rd. WA10: St H 4G 48
Chaucer St. L3: Liv 1G 5 (6C 58)
L20: Boot 6N 43
WA7: Run 6K 95
Cheadle Av. L13: Liv 6L 59
Cheapside L2: Liv 3E 4 (7B 58)
L37: Form 2G 24
Cheapside All. L2: Liv 4E 4
Cheddar Cl. L25: Woolt 6D 76
Cheddar Gro. L32: Kirkb 3C 46
WA5: Burtw 2H 65
Cheddon Way CH61: Pens 3M 87
Chedworth Dr. WA8: Wid 4F 78
Chedworth Rd. L14: Knott A 5C 60
Cheldon Rd. L12: W Der 8A 46
Chelford Av. WA3: Low 3E 52
Chelford Cl. CH43: Bid 1C 72
WA4: Stockt H 8D 82
WN3: Wigan 1H 41
Chelford Rd. WA10: Eccl 7E 48
Chellow Dene L23: Thorn 5N 33
Chelmarsh Av. WN4: Ash M 8L 41
Chelmorton Gro. WN3: Wins 2E 40
Chelmsford Cl. *L4: Kirkd* 2C 58
(off Harcourt St.)
Chelsea Ct. L12: W Der 1C 60
Chelsea Gdns. WA5: Gt San 4L 81
Chelsea Lea L9: Walt 4E 44
Chelsea Rd. L9: Walt 4F 44
L21: Lith 4A 44
Cheltenham Av. L17: Liv 2J 75
Cheltenham Cl. L10: Ain 1K 45
WA5: Gt San 9J 65
Cheltenham Cres. CH46: Leas 6M 55
L36: Roby 8H 61
WA7: Run 9L 95
Cheltenham Dr. WA12: Newt W 5L 51
WN5: Bil 1N 39
Cheltenham Rd. CH45: Wall 3E 56
CH65: Ell P 2B 112
Cheltenham Way PR8: South 2E 12
Chelwood Av. L16: Child 8C 60
Chelwood Pk. WN4: Ash M 1K 51
Chemical St. WA12: Newt W 7K 51
Chemistry Rd. L24: Speke 2G 93
Chenotrie Gdns. CH43: Noct 3D 72
Chepstow Av. CH44: Wall 5J 57
Chepstow Cl. WA5: Call 6N 65
Chepstow St. L4: Walt 9D 44
CHEQUER 6J 31
Chequer Cl. WN8: Uph 7J 31
Chequer La. WN8: Uph 6J 31
Chequers Gdns. L19: Aig 8L 75
Cheriton Av. CH48: W Kir 6E 70
Cheriton Cl. L26: Halew 8J 77
Cheriton Pk. PR8: South 3D 12
Chermside Rd. L17: Aig 7K 75
Cherry Av. L4: Walt 9G 45
Cherrybank CH44: Wall 7H 57
Cherry Blossom Rd. WA7: Beech 2B 108
Cherrybrook Dr. WN3: Wins 2F 40
Cherry Brow Ter. *CH64: Will* 6M 101
(off Hadlow Rd.)
Cherry Cl. CH64: Nest 6J 101
L4: Walt 9G 45
WA12: Newt W 6H 51
Cherry Cnr. WA13: Lymm 9A 84
Cherry Ct. *WA1: Warr* 3D 82
(off Orchard St.)
Cherrycroft WN8: Skel 5H 31
Cherrydale Rd. L18: Moss H 4M 75
Cherryfield Cres. L32: Kirkb 9C 36
Cherryfield Dr. L32: Kirkb 9B 36
Cherry Gdns. CH47: Hoy 1C 70
L32: Kirkb 3D 46
Cherry Grn. L39: Augh 3N 27
Cherry Gro. CH66: Whit 4M 111
L40: Burs 8J 15
Cherry La. L4: Walt 9G 44
WA13: Lymm 9B 84
Cherry Rd. PR8: Ains 3K 17
Cherry Sq. CH44: Wall 5H 57
Cherry Sutton WA8: Wid 5D 78
Cherry Tree Av. WA5: Penk 4H 81
WA7: Run 7M 95
WA13: Lymm 6D 84
Cherry Tree Cl. CH2: Elt 1M 113
L24: Hale 6B 94
L35: Whis 6A 62
WA11: Hay 5C 50
Cherry Tree Dr. WA9: St H 8C 50
Cherry Tree Ho. CH46: More 9N 55
Cherry Tree La. L39: Augh 3N 27
WA11: St H 9K 39
Cherry Tree M. CH60: Hesw 7A 88
Cherry Tree Rd. CH46: More 9N 55
L36: Huy 9J 61
PR9: Banks 5H 9
WA3: Low 2G 52
Cherry Va. L25: Woolt 5F 76
Cherry Vw. L33: Kirkb 6E 36
Cherry Wlk. M31: Part 7K 69
Cherrywood Av. L26: Halew 7M 77
Cherwell Cl. WA2: Warr 7E 66
Cheryl Dr. WA8: Wid 7N 79
Chesford Grange WA1: Wools 1M 83
Chesham Ct. CH65: Ell P 1B 112
Cheshire Acre CH49: Woodc 5A 72
Cheshire Av. L10: Faz 3N 45
Cheshire Cl. WA12: Newt W 7N 51
Cheshire Gdns. WA10: St H 8H 49
Cheshire Gro. CH46: More 1M 71
Cheshire Oaks Bus. Pk. CH65: Ell P 4B 112
Cheshire Oaks Outlet Village
CH65: Ell P 3C 112
Cheshire Oaks Trade Pk.
CH2: Lit Stan 3D 112
Cheshire Oaks Way CH65: Ell P 3C 112
Cheshire Pk. Homes WA6: Dun H 8A 114
Cheshire Rd. M31: Part 7K 69
Cheshire Way CH61: Pens 4N 87
Cheshyre Dr. WA7: Halt 6B 96
Cheshyres La. *WA1: Warr* 3C 82
(off Horsemarket St.)
WA7: West, West P 9H 95
(not continuous)
Chesnell Gro. L33: Kirkb 6E 36
Chesney Cl. L8: Liv 2D 74
Chesnut Gro. CH42: Tran 4K 73
L20: Boot 5A 44
(not continuous)
Chesnut Rd. L21: Sea 3M 43
Chessington Cl. WA4: App 1G 98
Chester Av. L30: N'ton 1E 44
PR9: South 7K 7
WA3: Low 2E 52
Chester Cl. L23: Crosb 7A 34
M44: Cad 4K 69
WA7: Cas 5C 96
Chester Ct. CH63: Beb 3M 89
Chester Dr. WN4: Ash M 9M 41
Chesterfield Cl. PR8: Ains 1J 17
Chesterfield Dr. L33: Kirkb 6C 36
Chesterfield Rd. CH62: East 2C 102
L23: Crosb 6N 33
PR8: Ains 1H 17
Chesterfield St. L8: Liv 1D 74
Chester Gates CH1: Dunk 7J 111
Chester Gates Ind. Pk. CH1: Dunk 8J 111
Chester High Rd.
CH64: Burt, Nest 1D 100 & 1A 110
CH66: Led 1A 110
Chester La. WA9: Sut M, St H 5L 63
Chester New Rd. WA4: Hghr Wal 9A 82
Chester Rd. CH1: Back 6L 111
CH2: Bri T 9L 113
CH60: Hesw 8B 88
CH64: Nest 7E 100
CH65: Whit 5M 111
CH66: Chil T, Gt Sut, Hoot, Lit Sut
5F 102
CH66: Whit 5M 111
L6: Liv 4J 59
L36: Huy 5L 61
PR9: South 7L 7
WA4: Dares, Hghr Wal 5K 97
(not continuous)
WA4: Dares, Pres H 7J 97
WA4: Grap, Stockt H 7F 82
WA4: Hghr Wal, Walt, Warr 6B 82
WA6: Dun H, Frod, Hel 4D 114
WA7: Sut W, Pres B 4B 108
Chester Row WA12: Newt W 1M 65
CHESTER SERVICE AREA 3A 114
Chester St. CH41: Birke 2M 73
CH44: Wall 6G 57
L8: Liv 1D 74
L34: Presc 3A 62
WA2: Warr 2C 82
WA8: Wid 7L 79
Chesterton Dr. WA2: Win 4B 66
Chesterton St. L19: Garst 3A 92
Chester Wlk. *L36: Huy* 5L 61
(off Chester Rd.)
Chestnut Av. CH66: Gt Sut 4L 111
L23: Crosb 5M 33
L36: Huy 9H 61
M44: Cad 4K 69
PR9: Banks 4H 9
(off Main Av.)
WA5: Gt San 2H 81
WA8: Wid 6L 79
WA11: Hay 5B 50
Chestnut Cl. CH49: Grea 7K 71
L35: Whis 5B 62
L39: Hals 4H 19
Chestnut Ct. L20: Boot 6A 44
L39: Orm 7D 20
PR9: South 7H 7
WA8: Wid 7G 79
Chestnut Dr. Sth. WN7: Leigh 1N 53
Chestnut Farm CH66: Hoot 5F 102
Chestnut Grange L39: Orm 1B 28
Chestnut Gro. CH62: Brom 7B 90
L15: Wav 9L 59
WA3: Low 2G 52
WA11: St H 3N 49
WN4: Ash M 7M 41
Chestnut Ho. *L20: Boot* 6A 44
(off St James Dr.)
WA4: App 9F 82
Chestnut La. WA6: Frod 1H 115
Chestnut Rd. L9: Walt 7G 45
Chestnuts, The CH64: Will 6M 101
Chestnut St. PR8: South 2B 12
Chestnut Wlk. L31: Mell 7M 35
M31: Part 7K 69
Chestnut Way L37: Form 3C 24
Cheswood Cl. L35: Whis 7B 62
Cheswood Ct. *CH49: Woodc* 6A 72
(off Childwall Grn.)
Chetham Ct. WA2: Win 6B 66
Chetton Dr. WA7: Murd 8G 96
Chetwode Av. WN4: Ash M 1K 51
Chetwood Av. L23: Crosb 6M 33
Chetwood Cl. WA12: Newt W 5K 51
Chetwood Dr. WA8: Wid 4J 79
Chetwynd Cl. CH43: Oxton 4F 72
Chetwynd Rd. CH43: Oxton 3G 72
Chetwynd St. L17: Aig 5G 75
Chevasse Wlk. L25: Woolt 5G 77
Cheverton Cl. CH49: Woodc 5B 72
Chevin Rd. L9: Walt 5F 44
Cheviot Av. WA2: Warr 6B 66
WA9: St H 7B 50
Cheviot Cl. CH42: Tran 7K 73
CH66: Lit Sut 8F 102
WN3: Wins 1E 40
Cheviot Rd. CH42: Tran 7J 73
L7: Liv 7K 59
Cheviot Way L33: Kirkb 5D 36
Cheyne Cl. L23: Blun 8G 33
Cheyne Gdns. L19: Aig 8L 75
Cheyne Wlk. WA9: St H 3J 63
Chicago Pl. WA5: Gt San 2K 81
Chichester Cl. L15: Wav 9J 59
WA4: Grap 9H 83
WA7: Murd 9F 96
Chidden Cl. CH49: Grea 5K 71
Chidlow Cl. WA8: Wid 2K 95
Chigwell Cl. L12: Crox 7C 46
Chilcott Rd. L14: Knott A 6A 60
Childer Cres. CH66: Lit Sut 7G 103
Childer Gdns. CH66: Lit Sut 7G 103
Childers St. L13: Liv 6M 59
CHILDER THORNTON 6F 102
CHILDWALL 1C 76
Childwall Abbey Rd. L16: Child 2B 76
Childwall Av. CH46: More 1L 71
L15: Wav 1J 75
Childwall Bank Rd. L16: Child 1B 76
Childwall Cl. CH46: More 1L 71
Childwall Ct. CH66: Ell P 6L 103
Childwall Cres. L16: Child 1B 76
Childwall Fiveways L15: Wav 1A 76
Childwall Gdns. CH66: Ell P 6L 103
Childwall Golf Course 1J 77
Childwall Grn. CH49: Woodc 6A 72
Childwall La. L14: Broad G 7E 60
L16: Child 2D 76
L25: Child 2D 76
Childwall Mt. Rd. L16: Child 1B 76
Childwall Pde. L14: Broad G 7E 60
Childwall Pk. Av. L16: Child 2B 76
Childwall Priory Rd. L16: Child 1B 76
Childwall Rd. CH66: Ell P 6L 103
L15: Wav 1M 75
Childwall Valley Rd. L16: Child 1B 76
L25: Gate 9E 60
L27: N'ley 9E 60
Chilhem Cl. L8: Liv 4E 74
Chilington Av. WA8: Wid 8G 79
Chillerton Rd. L12: W Der 1B 60
Chillingham St. L8: Liv 5F 74
Chilmark Rd. L5: Liv 3F 58
Chiltern Cl. L12: Crox 8D 46
L32: Kirkb 7A 36
WN4: Ash M 9L 41
Chiltern Cres. WA2: Warr 6B 66
Chiltern Dr. L32: Kirkb 7A 36
WN3: Wins 1F 40
Chiltern Pl. *WA2: Warr* 6B 66
(off Chiltern Rd.)
Chiltern Rd. CH42: Tran 7J 73
PR8: Ains 8G 11
WA2: Warr 6B 66
WA3: Cul 6M 53
WA9: St H 7B 50
Chilton Cl. L31: Mag 2J 35
Chilton Ct. L31: Mag 2J 35
Chilton Dr. CH66: Gt Sut 3K 111
Chilton M. L31: Mag 2J 35
Chilwell Cl. WA8: Wid 4G 79
Chimes Rd. WN4: Ash M 5H 41
China Farm La. CH48: W Kir 4F 70
China La. WA4: Warr 6D 82
Chindit Cl. L37: Form 2D 24
Chippenham Av. CH49: Grea 4K 71
Chippindall Cl. WA5: Gt San 3L 81
Chipping Av. PR8: Ains 9G 11
Chipping Mnr. PR9: Banks 1E 8
Chirkdale St. L4: Kirkd 9D 44
(not continuous)
Chirk Gdns. CH65: Ell P 2B 112
Chirk Way CH46: More 1N 71
Chirton Cl. WA11: Hay 3F 50
Chisacre Dr. WN6: Shev 6N 23
Chisenhale St. L3: Liv 1D 4 (5B 58)
Chisledon Cl. WA11: Hay 3F 50
Chislehurst Av. L25: Gate 2F 76
Chislet Ct. WA8: Wid 4H 79
Chislett Cl. L40: Burs 1H 21
Chisnall Av. WA10: St H 6F 48
Chisnall Brook Cl. L39: Down 8E 18
Chiswell St. L7: Liv 7H 59
Chiswick Cl. WA7: Murd 8F 96
Chiswick Gdns. WA4: App 1G 98
Cholmley Dr. WA12: Newt W 8N 51
Cholmondeley Rd. CH48: W Kir 6C 70
CH65: Gt Sut 1L 111
WA7: Clftn 2N 107
Cholmondeley St. WA8: Wid 3K 95
Cholsey Cl. CH49: Upton 4N 71
Chorley Cl. PR9: Banks 2C 8
Chorley Rd. L34: Presc 3M 61
WN8: Parb 1F 22
Chorley's La. WA8: Wid 5N 79
Chorley St. WA2: Warr 2C 82
(not continuous)
WA10: St H 6J 49
Chorley Way CH63: Spit 6N 89
Chorlton Cl. L16: Child 9D 60
WA7: Wind H 6F 96
Chorlton Gro. CH45: Wall 4D 56
Chorlton La. CH2: Chor B 6N 111
(not continuous)
Christchurch Cl. L11: Norr G 7L 45
Christchurch Rd. CH43: Oxton 4H 73
Christian St. L3: Liv 2G 5 (6D 58)
Christie Cl. CH66: Hoot 4F 102
Christie St. WA8: Wid 7N 79
Christines Cres. L40: Burs 1H 21
Christleton Cl. CH43: Oxton 6D 72
Christleton Ct. WA7: Manor P 3E 96
Christleton Dr. CH66: Ell P 8K 103
Christmas St. L20: Kirkd 9C 44
Christopher Cl. L16: Child 9B 60
L35: Rainh 7E 62
Christopher Dr. CH62: East 1F 102
Christophers Cl. CH61: Pens 3A 88
Christopher St. L4: Walt 1E 58
Christopher Taylor Ho.
L31: Mag 3J 35
Christopher Way L16: Child 9B 60
Christowe Wlk. *L11: Crox* 5A 46
(off Kennford Rd.)
Chris Ward Cl. L7: Liv 8H 59
Chromolyte Ind. Est.
PR8: South 1A 12
Chudleigh Cl. L26: Halew 7J 77
Chudleigh Rd. L13: Liv 6L 59
Chung Hok Ho. L1: Liv 9H 5
Church All. L1: Liv 6F 4 (8C 58)
Church Av. L9: Ain 3G 44

Church Cl. CH44: Wall 5K **57**
L37: Form 1G **24**
PR9: Banks 1E **8**
PR9: South 7M **7**
WA6: Frod 6L **107**
Church Cl. Ct. L37: Form 1G **24**
Church Cotts. L25: Gate 3G **76**
Church Cres. CH44: Wall 7L **57**
Churchdown Cl. L14: Knott A 5D **60**
Churchdown Gro. L14: Knott A 5C **60**
Churchdown Rd. L14: Knott A 5C **60**
Church Dr. CH62: Port S 1A **90**
WA2: Padg 8H **67**
WA12: Newt W 9L **51**
WN5: Orr 7N **31**
Church End L24: Hale 6A **94**
Church End M. L24: Hale 6B **94**
Church Farm CH63: Beb 2N **89**
Church Farm Ct. CH60: Hesw 8N **87**
CH64: Will 6M **101**
Church Farm Organics 2J **87**
Churchfield Ct. *L25: Gate 4G 77*
(off Jones Farm Rd.)
Churchfield Rd. L25: Gate 3G **76**
WA6: Frod 6M **107**
Church Flds. L39: Orm 8C **20**
Churchfields L40: Scar 7L **13**
PR8: Birkd 3M **11**
WA3: Croft 2J **67**
WA6: Hel 1F **114**
WA8: Wid 3L **79**
WA9: Clock F 5M **63**
Church Flats L4: Walt 8E **44**
Church Gdns. CH44: Wall 5K **57**
L20: Boot 7A **44**
Churchgate PR9: South 6L **7**
(not continuous)
Churchgate M. PR9: South 6M **7**
Church Grn. L16: Child 1D **76**
L32: Kirkb 8C **36**
L37: Form 2C **24**
WA13: Warb 9H **69**
WN8: Skel 3C **30**
Church Grn. Gdns WA3: Golb 1C **52**
Church Gro. L21: Sea 4M **43**
Church Hill CH45: Wall 4F **56**
Church Hill Rd. L39: Orm 7B **20**
Churchill Av. CH41: Birke 1H **73**
PR9: South 5K **7**
Churchill Ct. CH64: Nest 6E **100**
Churchill Gdns. WA9: St H 3F **62**
Churchill Gro. CH44: Wall 4J **57**
Churchill Ho. L21: Sea 3M **43**
Churchill Ind. Est. L9: Ain 2H **45**
Churchill Mans. *WA7: Run 4K 95*
(off Cooper St.)
Churchill Way CH64: Nest 6E **100**
Churchill Way Nth. L3: Liv 3F **4** (7C **58**)
Churchill Way Sth. L3: Liv 4F **4** (7C **58**)
Churchlands *CH44: Wall 7L 57*
(off Bridle Rd.)
Church La. CH2: Back 9N **111**
CH2: Stoak 6E **112**
CH44: Wall 5K **57**
(not continuous)
CH49: Woodc 6B **72**
CH61: Thurs 2J **87**
CH62: Brom 6C **90**
CH62: East 2F **102**
CH64: Nest 7E **100**
CH66: Gt Sut 1J **111**
L4: Walt 8E **44**
L17: Aig 7K **75**
L31: Lyd 4E **26**
L34: Know 6G **47**
L39: Augh 5M **27**
WA3: Cul 7N **53**
WA3: Low 2E **52**
WA4: Grap 7J **83**
WA10: Eccl 7D **48**
Churchmeadow Cl. CH44: Wall 5K **57**
Church Mdw. La. CH60: Hesw 8M **87**
Church Mdw. Wlk. WA8: Hale B 2E **94**
Church M. CH42: Rock F 7N **73**
PR9: South 8M **7**
Church Mt. L7: Liv 8G **58**
Church Pde. CH65: Ell P 8A **104**
Church Path L37: Form 8F **16**
Church Rd. CH42: Tran 5K **73**
CH44: Wall 7L **57**
CH48: W Kir 7B **70**
CH49: Upton 3A **72**
CH63: Beb 4N **89**
CH63: Thorn H 9H **89**
L4: Walt 8F **44**
L13: Liv 7L **59**
L15: Wav 2M **75**
L19: Garst 2A **92**
L20: Boot 4C **44**
L21: Lith 3A **44**
(not continuous)
L21: Sea 4M **43**
L22: Water 2K **43**
L23: Crosb 7K **33**
L24: Hale 6B **94**
L25: Woolt 4D **76**
L26: Halew 6J **77**
L31: Mag 4J **35**
L36: Roby 7G **60**
L37: Form 9G **16**
Church Rd. L39: Bic 6J **29**
L40: Ruf 2N **15**
PR9: Banks 1E **8**
WA6: Frod 7M **107**
WA11: Hay 4G **50**
WA11: Rainf 5C **38**
WA13: Lymm 5D **84**
WN8: Skel 3C **30**
Church Rd. Nth. L15: Wav 1M **75**
Church Rd. Sth. L25: Woolt 6E **76**
Church Rd. W. L4: Walt 8E **44**
Church Sq. CH62: Brom 6C **90**
WA10: St H 7K **49**
Church St. CH41: Birke 2M **73**
(not continuous)
CH44: Wall 5K **57**
CH65: Ell P 8A **104**
L1: Liv 5F **4** (8C **58**)
L20: Boot 7N **43**
L34: Presc 3A **62**
L39: Orm 8C **20**
PR9: South 8H **7**
WA1: Warr 3D **82**
WA3: Golb 1C **52**
WA6: Frod 6L **107**
WA7: Run 4K **95**
WA8: Wid 2K **95**
WA10: St H 7K **49**
WA12: Newt W 6N **51**
WN5: Orr 7N **31**
WN8: Uph 5M **31**
Church Ter. CH42: Tran 5K **73**
WN4: Ash M 9K **41**
CHURCHTOWN 6M **7**
Churchtown Ct. PR9: South 5M **7**
Churchtown Gdns. PR9: South 5M **7**
Church Vw. L12: W Der 2N **59**
L20: Boot 7A **44**
L39: Augh 5M **27**
WA13: Lymm 4H **85**
Church Vw. Ct. *L39: Orm 8C 20*
(off Burscough St.)
Churchview Rd. CH41: Birke 9H **57**
Church Wlk. CH48: W Kir 7C **70**
CH65: Ell P 8A **104**
L20: Boot 7A **44**
L34: Know 6G **47**
WA2: Win 3B **66**
WA10: Eccl 6D **48**
Church Walks L39: Orm 8C **20**
Churchward Ct. *L25: Woolt 6E 76*
(off Garden St.)
Church Way L30: N'ton 7C **34**
L32: Kirkb 8C **36**
L37: Form 2C **24**
WA6: Alv 4G **114**
Churchway Rd. L24: Speke 5L **93**
Churchwood Cl. CH62: Brom 6C **90**
Churchwood Ct. *CH49: Woodc 7B 72*
(off Childwall Grn.)
Churchwood Vw.
WA13: Lymm 5F **84**
Churnet St. L4: Kirkd 1D **58**
Churn Way CH49: Grea 4L **71**
Churston Rd. L16: Child 3C **76**
Churton Av. CH43: Oxton 5F **72**
Churton Ct. L6: Liv 1M **5** (6F **58**)
Ciaran Cl. L12: W Der 1B **60**
Cicely St. L7: Liv 8G **58**
Cinder La. L18: Moss H 3A **76**
L20: Boot 3C **44**
PR4: Mere B 5K **9**
WA4: Thel 6N **83**
Cineworld Cinema
Halton Lea 8A **96**
Liverpool 8L **59**
St Helens 7J **49**
Cinnabar Ct. WA4: Dares 7J **97**
CINNAMON BROW 6G **66**
Cinnamon Brow WN8: Uph 6M **31**
Cinnamon Building, The L1: Liv 7G **4**
Cinnamon La. WA2: Fearn 6G **67**
Cinnamon La. Nth.
WA2: Fearn 5G **66**
Cinnamon Nook WN8: Newb 3B **22**
Cinnamon Pk. WA2: Fearn 6J **67**
Circle 109 L1: Liv 8G **5**
Circular Dr. CH49: Grea 5L **71**
CH60: Hesw 6N **87**
CH62: Port S 9A **74**
Circular Rd. CH41: Birke 3K **73**
Circular Rd. E. L11: Norr G 1L **59**
Circular Rd. W. L11: Norr G 1L **59**
Cirencester Av. CH49: Grea 4K **71**
Cirrus Dr. L39: Augh 3M **27**
CISS GREEN 5A **94**
Citadel, The
St Helens 7K 49
(off Waterloo St.)
Citrine Rd. CH44: Wall 7K **57**
Citron Cl. L9: Walt 6G **45**
City Gdns. WA10: St H 3J **49**
City Lofts L3: Liv 2B **4**
(Waterloo Rd.)
L3: Liv 3B **4**
(William Jessop Way)
City Rd. L4: Walt 9E **44**
WA10: St H 3J **49**
City Sq. L2: Liv 4E **4**
Civic Cl. CH63: Beb 2N **89**
Civic Way CH63: Beb 2N **89**
CH65: Ell P 1N **111**
L36: Huy 7J **61**
Civil & Family Court
Liverpool 4E **4** (7B **58**)
Clairville PR8: Birkd 1M **11**
Clairville Cl. L20: Boot 7B **44**
Clairville Ct. *L20: Boot 7B 44*
(off Clairville Cl.)
Clairville Way L13: Liv 4K **59**
Clamley Ct. L24: Speke 4L **93**
Clamley Gdns. L24: Hale 5B **94**
Clanbrook Av. WA13: Lymm 6G **84**
Clandon Rd. L18: Aller 7B **76**
Clanfield Av. WA8: Wid 5F **78**
Clanfield Rd. L11: Norr G 8N **45**
Clanwood Cl. WN3: Wins 1G **40**
Clapgate Cres. WA8: Hale B 2E **94**
Clap Ga. La. WN3: Wigan 1G **41**
Clapgates Cres. WA5: Warr 1N **81**
Clapgates Rd. WA5: Warr 1N **81**
Clapham Rd. L4: Walt 3G **58**
Clare Cl. WA9: St H 2H **63**
Clare Cres. CH44: Wall 5F **56**
Clare Dr. CH65: Whit 3N **111**
Claremont Av. L31: Mag 3G **34**
PR8: Birkd 2N **11**
WA8: Wid 4M **79**
Claremont Cl. L21: Sea 3M **43**
Claremont Ct. CH45: Wall 3F **56**
Claremont Dr. L39: Augh 1B **28**
WA8: Wid 4L **79**
Claremont Gdns. PR8: Birkd 2N **11**
Claremont Rd. CH48: W Kir 5C **70**
L15: Wav 2K **75**
L21: Sea 3M **43**
L23: Crosb 7L **33**
PR8: Birkd 2N **11**
WA3: Cul 6L **53**
WA7: Run 5L **95**
WN5: Bil 6A **40**
Claremont Way CH63: Hghr B 8K **73**
Claremount Dr. CH63: Beb 3M **89**
Claremount Rd. CH44: Wall 2F **56**
CH45: Wall 2F **56**
Clarence Av. WA5: Gt San 2F **80**
WA8: Wid 4K **79**
Clarence Cl. WA9: St H 8M **49**
Clarence Ct. PR8: Birkd 2N **11**
Clarence Rd. CH42: Tran 5J **73**
CH44: Wall 7K **57**
PR8: Birkd 2N **11**
WA4: Grap 6J **83**
Clarence St. L3: Liv 5J **5** (8D **58**)
WA1: Warr 1F **82**
WA3: Golb 1B **52**
WA7: Run 4J **95**
WA12: Newt W 6H **51**
WN4: Ash M 6H **41**
Clarence Ter. WA7: Run 4K **95**
Clarendon Cl. CH43: Oxton 3J **73**
WA7: Murd 8F **96**
Clarendon Ct. WA2: Win 5A **66**
Clarendon Gro. L31: Lyd 7H **27**
Clarendon Rd. CH44: Wall 6K **57**
L6: Liv 3H **59**
L19: Garst 1A **92**
L21: Sea 4M **43**
M44: Irlam 2L **69**
Clare Rd. L20: Boot 8C **44**
Clares Farm Cl. WA1: Wools 1N **83**
Claret Cl. L17: Aig 7H **75**
Clare Wlk. L10: Faz 3N **45**
Clare Way CH45: Wall 4F **56**
Claribel St. L8: Liv 2F **74**
Claridge Ct. PR9: South 7L **7**
Clarke Av. CH42: Rock F 6L **73**
WA3: Cul 6N **53**
WA4: Warr 6E **82**
Clarke Gdns. WA8: Wid 9L **79**
Clarke's Cres. WA10: Eccl 6E **48**
Clarkfield Cl. L40: Burs 2K **21**
Clarks Ter. WA7: West P 7G **94**
Classic Rd. L13: Liv 5M **59**
Clatterbridge Rd. CH63: Spit 8K **89**
Claude Rd. L6: Liv 3H **59**
Claude St. WA1: Warr 2D **82**
CLAUGHTON 1F **72**
Claughton Cl. L7: Liv 8H **59**
Claughton Dr. CH44: Wall 6H **57**
Claughton Firs CH43: Oxton 4H **73**
Claughton Grn. CH43: Oxton 3G **73**
Claughton Pl. CH41: Birke 2J **73**
Claughton Rd. CH41: Birke 2J **73**
Claughton St. WA10: St H 6K **49**
Clavell Rd. L19: Aller 8B **76**
Claverton Cl. WA7: Run 9L **95**
Clay Brow Rd. WN8: Skel 6H **31**
Clay Cross Rd. L25: Woolt 6D **76**
Claydon Ct. L26: Halew 7L **77**
Claydon Gdns. WA3: Rix 8F **68**
Clayfield Cl. L20: Boot 8C **44**
Clayford Cres. L14: Knott A 5N **59**
Clayford Pl. L14: Knott A 5N **59**
Clayford Rd. L14: Knott A 5A **60**
Clayford Way L14: Knott A 5A **60**
Clayhill Grn. CH66: Lit Sut 7H **103**
Clayhill Gro. WA3: Low 2J **53**
Clayhill Ind. Est. CH64: Nest 4E **100**
Clayhill Light Ind. Pk. CH64: Nest 4E **100**
Clay La. WA5: Burtw 3G **64**
WA10: Eccl 7B **48**
Claypole Cl. L7: Liv 9H **59**
Clay St. L3: Liv 5A **58**
Clayton Av. WA3: Low 2F **52**
Clayton Cl. WA10: St H 7H **49**
Clayton Cres. WA7: Run 6J **95**
WA8: Wid 7J **79**
Clayton Gdns. L40: Burs 1J **21**
Clayton La. CH44: Wall 7G **57**
Clayton M. WN8: Skel 3A **30**
Clayton Pl. CH41: Birke 3J **73**
Clayton Rd. WA3: Ris 3N **67**
Clayton Sq. L1: Liv 5G **5**
Clayton Sq. Shop. Cen.
L1: Liv 5G **4** (8C **58**)
Clayton St. CH41: Birke 3J **73**
WN8: Skel 3A **30**
Cleadon Cl. L32: Kirkb 3E **46**
Cleadon Rd. L32: Kirkb 3E **46**
Cleadon Way WA8: Wid 4H **79**
Clearwater Cl. L7: Liv 7G **59**
Clearwater Quays WA4: Westy 5H **83**
Cleary St. L20: Boot 6A **44**
Cleaver Cotts. L38: Hight 6G **24**
Cleaver Heath Nature Reserve 5L **87**
Clee Hill Rd. CH42: Tran 7J **73**
Cleethorpes Rd. WA7: Murd 8E **96**
Cleeves Cl. WA1: Warr 3D **82**
Clegge St. WA2: Warr 1C **82**
Clegg St. L5: Liv 5D **58**
WN8: Skel 3A **30**
Clelland St. WA4: Warr 5D **82**
Clematis Rd. L27: N'ley 2J **77**
Clement Gdns. L3: Liv 5B **58**
Clementina Rd. L23: Blun 7H **33**
Clements Way L33: Kirkb 6B **36**
Clemmey Dr. L20: Boot 4D **44**
Clengers Brow PR9: South 5L **7**
Clent Av. L31: Lyd, Mag 9H **27**
Clent Gdns. L31: Lyd 9H **27**
Clent Rd. L31: Mag 9H **27**
Cleopas St. L8: Liv 4E **74**
Cleveland Av. WN3: Wins 1E **40**
Cleveland Cl. L32: Kirkb 7B **36**
Cleveland Dr. CH66: Lit Sut 8F **102**
WA3: Low 2E **52**
WN4: Ash M 7L **41**
Cleveland Gdns. WN4: Ash M 7L **41**
Cleveland Rd. WA2: Warr 6C **66**
Cleveland Sq. L1: Liv 7F **4** (9C **58**)
Cleveland St. CH41: Birke 9H **57**
WA9: St H 9M **49**
Cleveley Pk. L18: Aller 7B **76**
Cleveley Rd. CH47: Meols 9F **54**
L18: Aller 7A **76**
Cleveleys Av. PR9: South 3M **7**
WA8: Wid 6N **79**
Cleveleys Rd. PR9: South 4M **7**
WA5: Gt San 4K **81**
Cleves, The L31: Mag 9K **27**
Cleve Way L37: Form 2H **25**
CLIEVES HILLS 1L **27**
Clieves Hills L39: Hals 7K **19**
Clieves Hills La. L39: Augh 2K **27**
Clieves Rd. L32: Kirkb 1D **46**
Clifden Ct. L37: Form 1F **24**
Cliff, The CH45: New B 1F **56**
Cliff Dr. CH44: Wall 4K **57**
Cliffe Rd. CH64: Lit N 9F **100**
WA4: App 9D **82**
Cliffe St. WA8: Wid 7M **79**
Cliff La. CW8: Act B, Crow 9K **109**
WA4: Grap 1N **99**
(Grappenhall La.)
WA4: Grap 6L **83**
(Knutsford Rd.)
WA13: Lymm 9B **84**
Clifford Rd. CH44: Wall 6J **57**
PR8: Birkd 4N **11**
WA5: Penk 4J **81**
Clifford St. CH41: Birke 9G **56**
L3: Liv 3J **5** (7D **58**)
Cliff Rd. CH44: Wall 6F **56**
CW8: Act B 9M **109**
PR9: South 5J **7**
Cliff St. L7: Liv 7H **59**
Cliff Vw. WA6: Frod 6K **107**
CLIFTON 2N **107**
Clifton Av. CH62: East 3D **102**
L23: Crosb 6L 33
(off Liverpool Rd.)
L26: Halew 6J **77**
WA3: Cul 7L **53**
Clifton Cl. WA1: Wools 1L **83**
Clifton Ct. CH41: Birke 3K **73**
L19: Aller 8A **76**
WA7: Run 9L **95**
Clifton Cres. CH41: Birke 2L **73**
WA6: Frod 5M **107**
Clifton Dr. L10: Ain 9J **35**
Clifton Gdns. CH65: Ell P 2A **112**
Clifton Ga. *CH41: Birke 3L 73*
(off Clifton Rd.)
Clifton Gro. CH44: Wall 5K **57**
L5: Liv 5D **58**
Clifton La. WA7: Clftn 2N **107**
WA7: Sut W 3A **108**
Cliftonmill Mdws. WA3: Golb 2A **52**
CLIFTON PARK 3K **73**

Clifton Rd. CH41: Birke 3K 73
L6: Liv 4J 59
L37: Form 8G 17
PR8: South 9L 7
WA7: Run 8K 95
WA7: Sut W 3A 108
WN4: Ash M 5H 41
WN5: Bil 7N 39
WN7: Leigh 1M 53
Clifton Rd. E. L6: Liv 4J 59
Clifton St. L19: Garst 1A 92
WA4: Warr 4D 82
WA10: St H 6K 49
Clifton Vs. CH1: Back 5N 111
Cliftonville Rd. L34: Presc 3B 62
WA1: Wools 1K 83
Clincton Cl. WA8: Wid 8D 78
Clincton Vw. WA8: Wid 8D 78
CLINKHAM WOOD 1L 49
Clinkham Wood Local Nature Reserve 1K 49
Clinning Rd. PR8: Birkd 4N 11
Clinton Pl. L12: W Der 2L 59
Clinton Rd. L12: W Der 2L 59
Clint Rd. L7: Liv 8H 59
Clint Rd. W. L7: Liv 8H 59
Clint Way *L7: Liv* *8H 59* (off Clint Rd.)
Clipper Vw. CH62: New F 8B 74
Clipsley Brook Vw. WA11: Hay 4B 50
Clipsley Cres. WA11: Hay 3C 50
Clipsley La. WA11: Hay 4D 50
Clive Av. WA2: Warr 8D 66
Clive Lodge PR8: Birkd 4M 11
Clive Rd. CH43: Oxton 4J 73
PR8: Birkd 4M 11
CLOCK FACE 6N 63
Clock Face Colliery Country Pk. 5B 64
Clock Face Pde. WA9: Sut L 5M 63
Clock Face Rd.
WA8: Bold H, Clock F 4M 63
WA9: Clock F 4M 63
Clock La. WA5: Cuerd 5B 80
Clocktower, The *WA4: Warr* *6D 82* (off Elphins Dr.)
Clocktower Dr. L9: Walt 7E 44
Clock Twr. St. WA10: St H 7J 49
Cloister Grn. L37: Form 2H 25
Cloisters, The L23: Crosb 8K 33
L37: Form 1F 24
PR9: Banks 4H 9
PR9: South *7H 7* (off Hoghton Gro.)
WA10: Eccl 6E 48
Cloister Way CH65: Ell P 9C 104
Clorain Cl. L33: Kirkb 8E 36
Clorain Rd. L33: Kirkb 8E 36
Close, The CH49: Grea 6L 71
CH61: Irby 1L 87
CH63: Hghr B 7K 73
L9: Walt 6E 44
L23: Crosb 8K 33
L28: Stockb V 2G 60
L38: Ince B 9L 25
PR9: Banks 2E 8
WA10: Eccl 5D 48
WA11: Hay 5B 50
WA12: Newt W 9N 51
Closeburn Av. CH60: Hesw 9M 87
Close St. WA9: St H 2H 63
Cloudberry Cl. L27: N'ley 2J 77
Cloudberry Wlk. M31: Part 6M 69
Clough, The WA7: Halt 6B 96
WN4: Garsw 7F 40
Clough Av. L40: Burs 1K 21
WA2: Warr 7C 66
Clough Gro. WN4: Ash M 6H 41
Clough Rd. L24: Speke 3H 93 (not continuous)
L26: Halew 7L 77
Cloughwood Cres. WN6: Shev 7N 23
Clovelly Av. WA5: Gt San 1G 80
WA9: St H 3A 64
Clovelly Ct. CH49: Grea 5L 71
Clovelly Dr. PR8: Birkd 6L 11
WN8: Newb 4D 22
Clovelly Gro. WA7: Brook 1D 108
Clovelly Rd. L4: Walt 3G 59
Clover Av. L26: Halew 6H 77
WA6: Frod 7N 107
Clover Birches CH65: Ell P 7N 103
Clover Ct. WA7: Brook 1D 108
Cloverdale Dr. WN4: Ash M 9L 41
Cloverdale Rd. L25: Gate 1F 76
Clover Dr. CH41: Birke 8E 56
Cloverfield WA7: Nort 8E 96
WA13: Lymm 4F 84
Cloverfield Gdns. CH66: Lit Sut 7J 103
Clover Hey WA11: St H 3L 49
Club 3000 Bingo
Huyton 7J 61
CLUBMOOR 2K 59
Club St. WA11: St H 1K 49
Clucas Gdns. L39: Orm 7C 20
Clwyd Gro. L12: W Der 1N 59
Clwyd St. CH41: Birke 2K 73
CH45: New B 2G 57
Clwyd Way CH66: Lit Sut 8F 102
Clyde Rd. L7: Liv 7K 59
Clydesdale CH65: Whit 2N 111
Clydesdale Rd. CH44: Wall 4K 57
CH47: Hoy 9C 54
WA4: App 8E 82
Clyde St. CH42: Rock F 6M 73
L20: Kirkd 1B 58
Clyffes Farm Cl. L40: Scar 7M 13
Coach Ho. Ct. L29: Seft 5D 34
L40: Burs 2J 21
Coach Ho. M. L22: Water 1K 43
L25: Woolt 5G 76
Coachmans Dr. L12: W Der 9C 46
Coach Rd. L39: Bic 1K 37
WA11: Rainf, Kirkb 6M 37
Coadys Way WA8: Wid 6M 79
Coalbrookdale Rd. CH64: Nest 4F 100
Coalgate La. L35: Whis 7N 61
Coal Pit La. L39: Bic 8N 29
Coalpit La. CH1: Dunk, Lea B, Moll 9H 111
Coalport Wlk. WA9: St H 3F 62
Coal St. L3: Liv 4H 5 (7D 58)
Coalville Rd. WA11: St H 4N 49
Coastal Dr. CH45: Wall 2D 56
Coastal Point *CH46: Leas* *5M 55* (off Leasowe Rd.)
Coastal Rd. PR8: Ains, Birkd 8G 10
Coastguard La. CH64: Park 5B 100
Coastline M. PR9: South 3M 7
Cobal Ct. WA6: Frod 6L 107
Cobb Av. L21: Lith 4A 44
Cobbles, The L26: Halew 6H 77
Cobblestone Cnr. L19: Gras 9M 75
COBBS 8F 82
Cobbs Brow La. L40: Lath 8C 22
WN8: Newb 5D 22
Cobb's Clough Rd. L40: Lath 8C 22
Cobbs La. WA4: App 8F 82
Cobden Av. CH42: Tran 5M 73
Cobden Ct. CH42: Tran 5M 73
Cobden Pl. CH42: Tran 5M 73
L25: Woolt 6D 76
Cobden Rd. PR9: South 9L 7
Cobden St. L6: Liv 1L 5 (6E 58)
L25: Woolt 6D 76 (not continuous)
WA2: Warr 1C 82
WA12: Newt W 6M 51
Cobden Vw. L25: Woolt 6D 76
Cob Hall La. WA6: Manl 8G 114
Cobham Av. L9: Walt 4E 44
Cobham Rd. CH46: More 9L 55
Cobham Wlk. L30: N'ton 7C 34
Cob Moor Av. WN5: Bil 2N 39
Cob Moor Rd. WN5: Bil 2N 39
Coburg St. CH41: Birke 2K 73
Coburg Wharf L3: Liv 2B 74
Cochrane St. L5: Liv 4E 58
Cockburn St. L8: Liv 4E 74
Cockerell Cl. L4: Walt 2E 58
Cockerham Way L11: Crox 5N 45
Cock Glade L35: Whis 8A 62
Cockhedge Grn. WA1: Warr 2D 82
WA2: Warr 2D 82
Cockhedge La. WA1: Warr 3C 82
Cockhedge Shop. Pk. WA1: Warr 3C 82
Cockhedge Way WA1: Warr 3C 82
Cocklade La. L24: Hale 6A 94
Cock La. Ends WA8: Hale B 3E 94
Cockle Dick's La. PR9: South 5K 7
Cockshead Rd. L25: Gate 3F 76
Cockshead Way L25: Gate 2F 76
Cockspur St. L3: Liv 3E 4 (7B 58)
Cockspur St. W. L3: Liv 3D 4 (7B 58)
Coerton Rd. L9: Ain 3G 44
Coffin La. WN2: Bam 5M 41
Cokers, The CH42: Rock F 8L 73
Colbern Cl. L31: Mag 3K 35
Colbert Cl. CH49: Upton 4A 72
Colburn Cl. WN3: Wigan 1J 41
Colburne Cl. L40: Burs 9K 15
Colby Cl. L16: Child 9C 60
Colby Rd. WN3: Wigan 1K 41
Colchester Rd. PR8: South 4E 12
Colden Cl. L12: W Der 2C 60
Coldstone Dr. WN4: Garsw 8F 40
Coldstream Cl. WA2: Warr 5F 66
Coldstream Dr. CH66: Lit Sut 9E 102
Cole Av. WA12: Newt W 6L 51
Colebrooke Cl. WA3: Birchw 5A 68
Colebrooke Rd. L17: Aig 5G 74
Coleclough Pl. WA3: Cul 6N 53
Cole Cres. L39: Augh 4A 28
Coleman Dr. CH49: Grea 5J 71
Colemere Cl. WA1: Padg 8H 67
Colemere Ct. CH65: Ell P 7N 103
Colemere Dr. CH61: Thing 1B 88
Coleport Cl. WA4: Warr 6D 82
Coleridge Av. WA10: St H 6G 49
Coleridge Ct. L32: Kirkb 2B 46
Coleridge Dr. CH62: New F 9N 73
Coleridge Gro. WA8: Wid 7H 79
Coleridge Rd. WN5: Bil 2N 39
Coleridge St. L6: Liv 6G 59
L20: Boot 6N 43
Colerne Way WN3: Wins 1F 40
Colesborne Rd. L11: Norr G 8N 45
Coles Cres. L23: Thorn 5A 34
Coleshill Ri. WN3: Wins 1E 40
Coleshill Rd. L11: Norr G 7K 45
Cole St. CH43: Oxton 2J 73
Colette Rd. L10: Faz 3N 45
Coleus Cl. L9: Walt 6G 45
Colin Cl. L36: Roby 8G 61
Colindale Rd. L16: Child 1C 76
Colin Dr. L3: Liv 4B 58
Colinmander Gdns. L39: Orm 1A 28
Colinton WN8: Skel 5H 31
Colinton St. L15: Wav 9K 59
Coliseum Shopping & Leisure Pk.
CH65: Ell P 3B 112
Coliseum Way CH65: Ell P 4B 112
College Av. L23: Crosb 8K 33
L37: Form 8E 16
College Cl. CH43: Bid 2B 72
CH45: Wall 3E 56
L37: Form 9D 16
PR8: Birkd 3N 11
WA1: Warr 3E 82
WA2: Fearn 6J 67
College Ct. L12: W Der 4M 59
College Dr. CH63: Beb 9N 73
College Farm WN8: Roby M 3K 31
College Flds. L36: Huy 8J 61
WA8: Wid 3J 79
College Grn. Flats L23: Crosb 8K 33
College Island WN8: Skel 2E 30
College La. L1: Liv 6F 4 (8C 58)
College Path L37: Form 8D 16
College Pl. WA2: Padg 7K 67
College Rd. L23: Crosb 7J 33
WN8: Uph 3L 31
College Rd. Nth. L23: Blun 6J 33
College St. WA10: St H 6K 49 (not continuous)
College St. Nth. L6: Liv 2K 5 (6E 58)
College St. Sth. L6: Liv 2L 5 (6E 58)
College Vw. L36: Huy 7J 61
College Way WN8: Skel 2D 30
Collegiate, The L6: Liv 2L 5
Collegiate Rd. WA2: Warr 8C 66
Collier's Row WA7: West 8H 95
Collier St. WA7: Run 4J 95
Colliery Grn. Cl. CH64: Lit N 9E 100
Colliery Grn. Ct. CH64: Lit N 9E 100
Colliery Grn. Dr. CH64: Lit N 9E 100
Colliford Way L6: Liv 5F 58
Colling Ct. WA1: Warr 3E 82
Collingham Grn. CH66: Lit Sut 9G 103
Collingwood Cl. L4: Kirkd 1C 58
Collingwood Rd. CH63: Beb 3A 90
WA12: Newt W 7K 51
Collin Rd. CH43: Bid 9E 56
Collins Cl. L20: Boot 5N 43
COLLINS GREEN 9F 50
Collins Grn. La. WA5: Coll G 9G 50
Collins Ind. Est. WA9: St H 5M 49
Collinson Ct. WA6: Frod 6L 107
Collin St. WA5: Warr 3N 81
Collisdene Rd. WN5: Orr 6N 31
Colmoor Cl. L33: Kirkb 5D 36
Colmore Av. CH63: Spit 6M 89
Colmore Rd. L11: Norr G 8K 45
Colne Dr. WA9: St H 2N 63
Colne Rd. WA5: Burtw 3H 65
Colonel Dr. L12: W Der 2B 60
Colonnades, The L3: Liv 8D 4 (9A 58)
Colorado Cl. WA5: Gt San 1L 81
Colquitt St. L1: Liv 7H 5 (9D 58)
Coltart Rd. L8: Liv 2G 74
Colton Rd. L25: Gate 1E 76
Colton Wlk. L25: Gate 1D 76
Columban Cl. L30: N'ton 8D 34
Columbia Hall *WA8: Wid* *7L 79* (off Frederick St.)
Columbia La. CH43: Oxton 4H 73
Columbia Rd. CH43: Oxton 4H 73
L4: Walt 8F 44
L34: Presc 3B 62
Columbine Cl. L31: Mell 8M 35
WA8: Wid 4E 78
Columbine Wlk. *M31: Part* *6M 69* (off Central Rd.)
Columbine Way WA9: Bold 2D 64
Columbus Dr. CH61: Pens 4M 87
Columbus Pl. WA5: Gt San 1K 81
Columbus Quay L3: Liv 5D 74
Columbus St. WN4: Ash M 6H 41
Columbus Way *L21: Lith* *3A 44* (off Bridge Rd.)
Column Rd. CH48: Caldy, W Kir 6D 70
Colville Ct. WA2: Win 6B 66
Colville Rd. CH44: Wall 5G 56
Colville St. L15: Wav 9K 59
Colwall Cl. L33: Kirkb 9E 36
Colwall Rd. L33: Kirkb 9E 36
Colwall Wlk. L33: Kirkb 9E 36
Colwell Cl. L14: Knott A 2E 60
Colwell Ct. L14: Knott A 2E 60
Colwell Rd. L14: Knott A 3E 60
Colworth Rd. L24: Speke 3F 92
Colwyn Cl. CH65: Ell P 2B 112
WA5: Call 7N 65
Colwyn Rd. L13: Liv 7L 59
Colwyn St. CH41: Birke 9G 56
Colyton Av. WA9: Sut L 4N 63
Combermere St. L8: Liv 2E 74
L15: Wav 9J 59
Comely Av. CH44: Wall 5J 57
Comely Bank Rd. CH44: Wall 5K 57
Comer Gdns. L31: Lyd 9J 27
Comfrey Gro. L26: Halew 6J 77
Comley Bank PR9: South 6J 7
Commerce Way L8: Liv 1G 74
Commercial Rd. CH62: Brom 4D 90
L5: Kirkd 3B 58
Common, The WA7: Halt 7C 96
WN8: Parb 2F 22
Commonfield Rd. CH49: Woodc 7B 72
Common La. M31: Carr 4N 69
PR9: Banks, South 5F 8
WA3: Cul 6L 53
WA4: Lwr S 7F 98
WA4: Warr 6F 82
WA6: Hap 4A 114
Common Rd. WA12: Newt W 7G 51
Commonside WA6: Alv 3G 115
Commonside Bus. Pk. WA4: Hatt 4N 97
Common St. WA9: St H 2G 63
WA12: Newt W 7G 50
Commutation Row L3: Liv 3H 5 (7D 58)
Company's Cl. WA7: West 9J 95
Compass Cl. WA7: Murd 1F 108
Compass Ct. CH45: Wall 1F 56
Compton Cl. WA11: Hay 3E 50
Compton Pl. CH65: Ell P 9N 103
Compton Rd. CH41: Birke 8D 56
L6: Liv 5F 58
PR8: Birkd 3A 12
Compton Wlk. L20: Boot 6A 44
Compton Way L26: Halew 1K 93
Comus St. L3: Liv 1G 5 (6C 58)
Concert Sq. L1: Liv 6G 5
Concert St. L1: Liv 6G 5 (8C 58)
Concorde Av. WN3: Wigan 1K 41
Concorde Pl. WA2: Warr 7E 66
Concordia Av. CH49: Upton 3A 72
Concourse Shop. Cen. WN8: Skel 3E 30
Concourse Way WA9: St H 8B 50
Condor Cl. L19: Garst 1B 92
Condron Rd. Nth. L21: Lith 1B 44
Condron Rd. Sth. L21: Lith 1B 44
Conery Cl. WA6: Hel 1F 114
Coney Cres. L23: Thorn 6A 34
Coney Gro. WA7: Brook 1D 108
Coney La. L35: Tar G 1K 77
L36: Huy 1K 77
Coney Wlk. CH49: Upton 2L 71
Congress Gdns. WA9: St H 2G 63
Conifer Cl. CH66: Whit 5M 111
L9: Walt 7G 44
L33: Kirkb 6C 36
Conifer Ct. L37: Form 2F 24
Conifer Gro. WA4: Moore 9J 81
WA5: Gt San 1H 81
Conifers, The L31: Mag 9H 27
Conifer Wlk. M31: Part 6L 69
Coningsby Dr. CH45: Wall 5G 57
Coningsby Gdns. WA3: Low 2F 52
Coningsby Rd. L4: Walt 2F 58
Coniston Av. CH43: Noct 3C 72
CH45: Wall 2E 56
CH63: East 2B 102
L34: Presc 3C 62
WA5: Penk 4F 80
WN4: Ash M 7K 41
Coniston Cl. CH66: Hoot 5G 102
L9: Ain 3G 45
L33: Kirkb 7B 36
WA7: Beech 9N 95
Coniston Ct. PR8: Ains 2J 17
Coniston Dr. WA6: Frod 6N 107
Coniston Gro. WA11: St H 3K 49
Coniston Ho. L17: Aig 6K 75
Coniston Rd. CH61: Irby 1L 87
CH64: Nest 8E 100
L31: Mag 1K 35
L37: Form 2D 24
M31: Part 5L 69
Coniston St. L5: Liv 3F 58
Coniston Way WA11: Rainf 1C 38
Conleach Rd. L24: Speke 4J 93
Connaught Av. WA1: Warr 1F 82
Connaught Cl. CH41: Birke 9G 56
Connaught Cres. WA8: Wid 2J 79
Connaught Dr. WA12: Newt W 8L 51
Connaught Ho. CH41: Birke 2N 73
Connaught Rd. L7: Liv 4N 5 (7F 58) (not continuous)
Connaught Way CH41: Birke 9G 56
Connect Bus. Village L5: Kirkd 2B 58
Connolly Av. L20: Boot 5D 44
Connolly Ho. L20: Boot 8C 44
Conroy Way WA12: Newt W 9L 51
Consett Rd. WA9: St H 3G 62
Constables Cl. WA7: Cas 6C 96
Constance Rd. M31: Part 6M 69
Constance St. L3: Liv 3K 5 (7E 58)
WA10: St H 8G 48
Constance Way WA8: Wid 2K 95
Constantine Av. CH60: Hesw 6A 88
Convent Cl. CH42: Tran 4K 73
L19: Gras 9M 75
L39: Augh 2B 28
Conville Blvd. CH63: Hghr B 8L 73
Conway Av. M44: Irlam 1M 69
WA5: Warr 7A 66
Conway Cl. CH63: Hghr B 2K 89
L33: Kirkb 6B 36
WA5: Gt San 2H 81
Conway Ct. CH63: Beb 3M 89
CH65: Ell P 2B 112

Conway Cres. WN5: Bil 5A 40
Conway Dr. CH41: Birke 2K 73
WA12: Newt W 7N 51
WN5: Bil 6B 40
Conway Ho. L6: Liv 5H 59
Conway Lodge L5: Liv 4D 58
Conway Park Station (Rail) 1L 73
Conway Rd. WN4: Ash M 6N 41
Conway St. CH41: Birke 1K 73
(not continuous)
L5: Liv 4D 58
WA10: St H 8G 48
Conwy Ct. WA7: Cas 5C 96
Conwy Dr. L6: Liv 4G 59
Conyers Av. PR8: Birkd 3M 11
Coogee Av. WA5: Gt San 1G 80
Cook Av. WA11: Hay 3G 51
Cookes Cl. CH64: Nest 5E 100
Cooke St. WN4: Ash M 5H 41
Cook Rd. CH46: Leas 5B 56
Cooks Ct. L23: Crosb 6K 33
Cookson Rd. L21: Sea 4N 43
Cookson St. L1: Liv 9H 5 (1D 74)
Cooks Rd. L23: Crosb 6K 33
Cook St. CH41: Birke 3K 73
CH65: Ell P 8A 104
L2: Liv 5E 4 (8B 58)
L34: Presc 3A 62
L35: Whis 5C 62
Coombe Dr. WA7: Run 7J 95
Coombe Pk. CH66: Lit Sut 8H 103
Coombe Pk. Ct. CH66: Lit Sut 8H 103
Coombe Rd. CH61: Irby 9M 71
Cooperage Cl. L8: Liv 4D 74
Cooper Av. WA2: Warr 7C 66
WA12: Newt W 7H 51
Cooper Av. Nth. L18: Moss H 7M 75
Cooper Av. Sth. L19: Aig 7M 75
Cooper Cl. L19: Aig 8M 75
Cooper La. WA11: Hay 6D 50
Cooper's La. L33: Know I 4H 47
Coopers Pl. WA4: Warr 7D 82
Coopers Row *L22: Water* *2L 43*
(off Brunswick Pde.)
Cooper St. WA7: Run 4K 95
WA8: Wid 7L 79
WA10: St H 6J 49
Copeland Cl. CH61: Pens 3M 87
Copeland Gro. WA7: Beech 1A 108
Copeland Rd. WA4: Warr 6C 82
Copperas Hill L3: Liv 5H 5 (8D 58)
Copperas St. WA10: St H 7J 49
Copperfield Cl. L8: Liv 3E 74
WA3: Birchw 4K 67
Copperwood WA7: Nort 6E 96
Copperwood Dr. L35: Whis 7B 62
Coppice, The CH45: Wall 2G 56
L4: Walt 3H 59
L34: Know 7H 47
Coppice Cl. CH43: Bid 2B 72
WA7: Cas 6D 96
Coppice Cres. L36: Huy 5K 61
Coppice Dr. WN3: Wigan 1H 41
WN5: Bil 1N 39
Coppice Grange CH46: More 1K 71
Coppice Grn. CH2: Elt 1N 113
WA5: Westb 8J 65
Coppice Gro. CH49: Grea 6K 71
Coppice La. L35: Tar G 1M 77
Coppice Leys L37: Form 1E 24
Coppicewood Cl. M31: Part 7L 69
Coppins, The WA2: Warr 7D 66
Coppins Cl. WA6: Hel 1E 114
Copplehouse Ct. *L10: Faz* *3M 45*
(off Copplehouse La.)
Copplehouse La. L10: Faz 3M 45
Coppull Rd. L31: Lyd 8H 27
Copse, The L18: Moss H 3B 76
L25: Woolt 7F 76
L37: Form 9E 16
WA7: Pal F 9C 96
(not continuous)
WA12: Newt W 6J 51
Copse Gro. CH61: Irby 9M 71
Copsmead CH46: More 9N 55
Copthorne Rd. L32: Kirkb 9N 35
Copthorne Wlk. L32: Kirkb 9N 35
Copy Cl. L30: N'ton 6E 34
Copy La. L30: N'ton 6E 34
Copy Way L30: N'ton 6E 34
Coral Av. L36: Huy 6H 61
WA9: St H 2J 63
Coral Cl. L32: Kirkb 9A 36
Coral Dr. L20: Boot 7B 44
Coralin Way WN4: Ash M 4H 41
Coral Ridge CH43: Bid 1D 72
Coral St. L13: Liv 8M 59
Corbet Av. WA2: Warr 9C 66
Corbet Cl. L32: Kirkb 9A 36
Corbet St. WA2: Warr 9C 66
Corbet Wlk. L32: Kirkb 9A 36
Corbridge Rd. L16: Child 1A 76
Corbyn St. CH44: Wall 8L 57
Corfu St. CH41: Birke 2J 73
Coriander Rd. L11: Norr G 9M 45
Corinthian Av. L13: Liv 5M 59
Corinthian St. CH42: Rock F 6M 73
L21: Sea 3M 43
Corinth Twr. *L5: Liv* *3D 58*
(off Anderson St.)
Corinto St. L8: Liv 1E 74
Corkdale Rd. L9: Walt 5G 44
Cormorant Centre, The WA7: Run 5H 95
Cormorant Ct. CH45: Wall 1E 56
Cormorant Dr. WA7: Run 5H 95
Cornbrook WN8: Skel 5H 31
Corncroft Rd. L34: Know 7H 47
Corndale Rd. L18: Moss H 4M 75
Cornelian Gro. WN4: Ash M 6H 41
Cornelius Dr. CH61: Pens 2N 87
Cornel Way L36: Huy 9K 61
Corner Brook L28: Stockb V 2D 60
Cornerhouse La. WA8: Wid 5G 79
Cornett Rd. L9: Ain 3G 44
Corney St. L7: Liv 1H 75
Cornfield Cl. CH49: Woodc 6C 72
CH66: Gt Sut 4L 111
Cornfields Cl. L19: Garst 1N 91
Cornflower Way CH46: More 7A 56
Cornforth Way WA8: Wid 5J 79
Cornhill L1: Liv 8F 4 (9C 58)
Cornice Rd. L13: Liv 5M 59
Corniche Rd. CH62: Port S 1A 90
Corn Mill Cl. WN4: Garsw 7F 40
Cornmill Ct. WA3: Croft 1H 67
Cornmill Lodge L31: Mag 1H 35
Corn St. L8: Liv 3D 74
Cornubia Rd. WA8: Wid 9M 79
Cornwall Av. WA7: Run 5K 95
Cornwall Cl. WA7: Cas 6B 96
Cornwall Ct. CH63: Beb 3M 89
Cornwall Dr. CH43: Pren 7G 72
Cornwallis St. L1: Liv 9G 4 (9C 58)
(not continuous)
Cornwall Rd. L20: Boot 6C 44
M44: Cad 4K 69
WA8: Wid 5L 79
Cornwall St. WA1: Warr 1F 82
WA9: St H 8N 49
Cornwall Way PR8: Ains 2H 17
Cornwell Cl. CH62: New F 8A 74
Cornwood Cl. L25: Gate 1F 76
Corona Av. L31: Lyd 7H 27
Corona Rd. CH62: Port S 1B 90
L13: Liv 5M 59
L22: Water 1K 43
Coronation Av. CH45: New B 2H 57
L14: Broad G 6C 60
L37: Form 2G 24
WA4: Grap 6K 83
Coronation Bldgs. *CH45: Wall* *4H 57*
(off Wallasey Rd.)
CH48: W Kir 4D 70
Coronation Dr. CH62: Brom 4C 90
L14: Broad G 6C 60
L23: Crosb 8K 33
L35: Presc 5N 61
WA5: Penk 4H 81
WA6: Frod 5N 107
WA8: Wid 8E 78
WA11: Hay 3J 51
Coronation Ho. WA7: Run 7M 95
Coronation Rd. CH47: Hoy 2A 70
CH65: Ell P 1A 112
(not continuous)
L23: Crosb 8K 33
L31: Lyd 9H 27
WA7: Pres B 9H 97
WA7: Run 6L 95
WA10: Windle 5F 48
Coronation St. WN4: Ash M 5F 40
Coronation Wlk. PR8: South 8F 6
WN5: Bil 7N 39
Coroner's La. WA8: Wid 3K 79
Coronet Cl. WN6: Appl B 6M 23
Coronet Rd. L11: Crox 7A 46
Coronet Way WA8: Wid 8E 78
Corporal Way L12: W Der 2C 60
Corporation Rd. CH41: Birke 9F 56
Corporation St. PR8: South 8G 6
WA9: St H 6K 49
WA10: St H 6K 49
(not continuous)
Corporation Wharf L20: Boot 6C 44
Corridor Rd. CH65: Ell P 9F 104
Corrie Dr. CH63: Beb 3M 89
Corsewall St. L7: Liv 9J 59
Corsican Gdns. WA9: St H 2F 62
Cortsway CH49: Grea 3M 71
Cortsway W. CH49: Grea 3L 71
Corwen Cl. CH43: Bid 2B 72
CH46: More 1N 71
WA5: Call 8N 65
Corwen Cres. L14: Broad G 7D 60
Corwen Dr. L30: N'ton 7G 34
Corwen Rd. CH47: Hoy 1D 70
L4: Walt 1H 59
Cosgrove Cl. L6: Liv 2J 59
Coslett Dr. WA10: St H 7F 48
Cossack Av. WA2: Warr 8D 66
Costain St. L20: Kirkd 2B 58
Cote Lea Ct. WA7: Pal F 9B 96
Cotham St. WA10: St H 7K 49
Coton Way L32: Kirkb 8A 36
Cotsford Cl. L36: Huy 5G 61
Cotsford Pl. L36: Huy 5G 60
Cotsford Rd. L36: Huy 5G 60
Cotsford Way L36: Huy 5G 61
Cotswold Av. WA3: Low 4E 52
Cotswold Gdns. WA3: Low 4F 52
Cotswold Gro. WA9: St H 7C 50
Cotswold Pl. WA2: Warr 5C 66
Cotswold Rd. CH42: Tran 7J 73
WA2: Warr 6C 66
Cotswolds Cres. L26: Halew 9J 77
Cotswold St. L7: Liv 7G 59
Cottage Cl. CH63: Brom 1B 102
CH64: Lit N 7E 100
L32: Kirkb 3C 46
L39: Orm 9B 20
Cottage La. CH60: Hesw 9N 87
L39: Orm 7B 20
Cottage M. L39: Orm 8B 20
Cottage Pl. WA9: Clock F 5M 63
Cottage St. CH41: Birke 1K 73
Cottenham St. L6: Liv 6G 59
Cotterdale Cl. WA5: Gt San 1H 81
WA9: St H 3M 63
Cotterill WA7: Run 7N 95
Cotterill Dr. WA1: Wools 1K 83
Cottesbrook Cl. L11: Norr G 7M 45
Cottesbrook Pl. L11: Norr G 7M 45
Cottesbrook Rd. L11: Norr G 7M 45
Cottesmore Dr. CH60: Hesw 7D 88
Cottesmore Way WA3: Golb 1C 52
Cottham Dr. WA2: Fearn 6H 67
Cotton Dr. L39: Orm 7B 20
Cotton Exchange Bldg. L3: Liv 4D 4
Cotton La. WA7: Run 7N 95
Cottons Bri. WA4: Pres H 1H 109
Cotton St. L3: Liv 5A 58
Cotton Ter. WA9: St H 1B 64
Cottonwood L17: Aig 6F 74
Cottrell Cl. L19: Garst 3A 92
Cottys Brow PR9: South 4L 7
Coudray Rd. PR9: South 6K 7
Coulport Cl. L14: Knott A 5E 60
Coulsdon Pl. L8: Liv 4F 74
Coulthard Rd. CH42: Rock F 8N 73
Coulton Rd. WA8: Wid 5A 80
Coultshead Av. WN5: Bil 5A 40
Council Av. WN4: Ash M 8K 41
Council St. L35: Rainh 5D 62
Countess Pk. L11: Crox 8A 46
Countisbury Dr. L16: Child 2C 76
County Court
Birkenhead 2M 73
Runcorn 3B 82
St Helens 6K 49
Warrington 3B 82
County Dr. WA10: St H 8H 49
County Rd. L4: Walt 9E 44
L32: Kirkb 7C 36
L39: Orm 9B 20
Courage Low La. WN6: Wright 1N 23
Course La. WN8: Newb 4N 21
Court, The CH63: Beb 3N 89
CH64: Lit N 8F 100
L28: Stockb V 2G 60
PR9: South 7G 7
Court Av. L26: Halew 7L 77
Courtenay Av. L22: Water 9J 33
Courtenay Rd. CH47: Hoy 2B 70
L22: Water 9J 33
L25: Woolt 4D 76
Courtfield L39: Orm 6C 20
Courtfields Cl. L12: W Der 4N 59
Court Grn. L39: Orm 6B 20
COURT HEY 8D 60
Court Hey L31: Mag 2K 35
Court Hey Av. L36: Roby 7E 60
Court Hey Dr. L16: Child 8D 60
Court Hey Pk. 9D 60
Court Hey Rd. L16: Child 8D 60
Courthope Rd. L4: Walt 8G 44
Court House, The CH65: Ell P 8A 104
Courtier Cl. L5: Liv 5D 58
Courtland Rd. L18: Moss H 3N 75
Court M. PR9: South 6M 7
Courtney Av. CH44: Wall 6G 56
Courtney Rd. CH42: Rock F 8N 73
Court Rd. PR9: South 7H 7
Courtyard, The CH2: Elt 2M 113
CH64: Will 6M 101
L18: Moss H 5L 75
PR8: South *8G 6*
(off Lord St.)
WA12: Newt W *6N 51*
(off Golborne St.)
Courtyard Works L33: Know I 8G 36
Cousin's La. L40: Ruf 3L 15
Covent Gdn. L2: Liv 4D 4 (8B 58)
Coventry Av. CH66: Gt Sut 5K 111
L30: N'ton 1E 44
Coventry Rd. L15: Wav 2M 75
Coventry St. CH41: Birke 2K 73
Coverdale Av. L35: Rainh 6G 63
Coverdale Cl. WA5: Gt San 1H 81
Covert Cl. PR8: South 4F 12
Covertside CH48: W Kir 6E 70
Covertside Rd. PR8: South 4F 12
Covington Dr. WA9: St H 4L 63
Cowan Dr. L6: Liv 5F 58
Cowan Way WA8: Wid 3J 79
Cowdell St. WA2: Warr 1C 82
Cowdrey Av. CH43: Bid 8C 56
Cow Hey La. WA7: Clftn 1K 107
(not continuous)
Cow La. CH66: Lit Sut 8H 103
Cowley Cl. CH49: Upton 3L 71
Cowley Ct. WA10: St H 5H 49
COWLEY HILL 5J 49
Cowley Hill La. WA10: St H 5J 49
Cowley Rd. L4: Walt 9E 44
Cowley St. WA10: St H 5K 49
Cowper Rd. L13: Liv 6N 59
Cowper St. L20: Boot 5N 43
WA9: St H 9M 49
Cowper Way L36: Huy 8L 61
Coxfield Gro. WN6: Shev 6N 23
Coxheath CH42: Rock F 7N 73
Coyford Dr. PR9: South 3M 7
Coylton Av. L35: Rainh 7G 63
Crab La. WA2: Fearn 6H 67
Crab St. WA10: St H 6J 49
Crab Tree Cl. L24: Hale 5B 94
Crabtree Cl. L27: N'ley 3J 77
L40: Burs 1H 21
WA12: Newt W 7N 51
Crabtree Fold WA7: Nort 7E 96
Crabtree La. L40: Burs 9F 14
WA13: Lymm 9G 85
WA16: High L 9G 85
Cradley WA8: Wid 6F 78
Crag Gro. WA11: St H 1L 49
Craigburn Rd. L13: Liv 3K 59
Craig Gdns. CH66: Ell P 7K 103
Craig Hall M44: Irlam 2M 69
Craighurst Rd. L25: Gate 1E 76
Craigleigh Gro. CH62: East 2E 102
Craigmore Rd. L18: Moss H 7M 75
Craigside Av. L12: W Der 2M 59
Craigs Rd. L13: Liv 3K 59
Craigwood Way L36: Huy 6F 60
Craine Cl. L4: Walt 1G 59
Cramond Av. L18: Moss H 3L 75
Cranage Cl. WA7: Run 8N 95
Cranberry Cl. L27: N'ley 2J 77
WA10: St H 5J 49
Cranberry Ct. WN4: Ash M 3H 41
Cranberry Rd. M31: Part 6M 69
Cranborne Av. WA4: Warr 7B 82
Cranborne Rd. L15: Wav 1J 75
Cranbourne Av. CH41: Birke 1G 72
CH46: More 1L 71
CH47: Meols 8F 54
Cranbrook Av. WN4: Ash M 7J 41
Crane Av. WA9: Sut L 3N 63
Cranehurst Rd. L4: Walt 8G 45
Cranes La. L40: Lath 6H 21
Cranfield Rd. L23: Crosb 6N 33
WN3: Wigan 1J 41
Cranford Cl. CH62: East 2E 102
Cranford Ct. WA1: Wools 9M 67
Cranford Rd. L19: Gras 8N 75
Cranford St. CH44: Wall 7J 57
Cranham Av. WA3: Low 3F 52
CRANK 7H 39
Crank Hill WA11: Crank 7H 39
Crank Rd. WA11: Crank, St H 3F 48
WA11: Kings M 5J 39
WN5: Bil 3M 39
Cranleigh Cl. WA4: Stockt H 9C 82
Cranleigh Gdns. L23: Crosb 7K 33
Cranleigh Pl. L25: Gate 2E 76
Cranleigh Rd. L25: Gate 2E 76
Cranmer St. L5: Liv 4B 58
(not continuous)
Cranmore Av. L23: Crosb 9L 33
Cranshaw Av. WA9: Clock F 6N 63
Cranshaw La. WA8: Wid 3L 79
Cranston Cl. WA10: St H 5F 48
Cranston Rd. L33: Know I 9G 37
Cranswick Grn. CH66: Lit Sut 9H 103
Crantock Cl. L11: Crox 6A 46
L26: Halew 8K 77
Crantock Gro. WA10: Windle 3F 48
Cranwell Av. WA3: Cul 6N 53
Cranwell Cl. L10: Ain 9H 35
Cranwell Rd. CH49: Grea 5J 71
L25: Gate 1E 76
Cranwell Wlk. *L25: Gate* *1E 76*
(off Cranwell Rd.)
Crask Wlk. L33: Kirkb 7D 36
Craven Av. WA3: Low 3F 52
Craven Cl. CH41: Birke 2K 73
Craven Ct. WA2: Win 5A 66
Craven Lea L12: Crox 7C 46
Craven Rd. L12: W Der 2A 60
L35: Rainh 6F 62
Craven St. CH41: Birke 2J 73
L3: Liv 3J 5 (7D 58)
Cravenwood Rd. L26: Halew 9K 77
CRAWFORD 1G 38
Crawford Av. L18: Moss H 3L 75
L31: Mag 9G 27
WA8: Wid 7E 78
Crawford Cl. L12: W Der 2B 60
WA9: Clock F 5N 63
Crawford Dr. L15: Wav 8M 59
Crawford Pk. L18: Moss H 5L 75
Crawford Pl. WA7: Run 9L 95
Crawford Rd. WN8: Skel 2F 38
Crawford St. WA9: Clock F 5A 64
Crawford Way L7: Liv 7L 59
Crawley Av. WA2: Warr 6B 66
Crawshaw Ct. L36: Huy 5F 60
Crediton Av. PR9: South 2N 7
Crediton Cl. L11: Crox 5A 46
Creek, The CH45: Wall 1E 56

Cremona Cnr. L22: Water . . . 1L 43
(off South Rd.)
Cremorne Hey L28: Stockb V . . . 2F 60
Crescent, The CH48: W Kir . . . 6B 70
CH49: Grea . . . 5L 71
CH60: Hesw . . . 9B 88
CH61: Pens . . . 1N 87
CH63: Hghr B . . . 2L 89
CH65: Gt Sut . . . 9L 103
L20: Boot . . . 4D 44
L22: Water . . . 1L 43
L23: Thorn . . . 5N 33
L24: Speke . . . 3G 92
L31: Mag . . . 4H 35
L35: Whis . . . 5C 62
L36: Huy . . . 7L 61
PR9: South . . . 4A 8
WA13: Lymm . . . 6F 84
Crescent Av. L37: Form . . . 3E 24
WN4: Ash M . . . 7J 41
Crescent Ct. L21: Sea . . . 4N 43
Crescent Dr. WA6: Hel . . . 2E 114
Crescent Grn. L39: Augh . . . 3N 27
Crescent Rd. CH44: Wall . . . 5J 57
CH65: Ell P . . . 8B 104
L9: Walt . . . 6G 44
L21: Sea . . . 4N 43
L23: Blun . . . 6H 33
PR8: Birkd . . . 3M 11
Crescent Row WA7: Run . . . 5J 95
(off Hankey St.)
Crescents, The L35: Rainh . . . 5D 62
Cressbrook Rd. WA4: Stockt H . . . 7D 82
Cressida Av. CH63: Hghr B . . . 9L 73
Cressingham Rd. CH45: New B . . . 1H 57
Cressington Av. CH42: Tran . . . 7K 73
Cressington Esplanade L19: Gras . . . 1M 91
Cressington Gdns. CH65: Ell P . . . 8A 104
CRESSINGTON PARK . . . 9M 75
Cressington Station (Rail) . . . 9M 75
Cresson Ct. CH43: Oxton . . . 3F 72
Cresswell Cl. L26: Halew . . . 7L 77
WA5: Call . . . 7M 65
Cresswell St. L6: Liv . . . 1L 5 (5E 58)
(not continuous)
Cresta Dr. WA7: West . . . 9J 95
Cresttor Rd. L25: Woolt . . . 5D 76
Crestwood Av. WN3: Wigan . . . 1G 41
Creswell St. WA10: St H . . . 7H 49
Cretan Rd. L15: Wav . . . 1J 75
Crete Towers L5: Kirkd . . . 3D 58
Crewe Grn. CH49: Woodc . . . 6A 72
Crewood Comn. Rd. CW8: Kingsl . . . 9J 109
Criccieth Ct. CH65: Ell P . . . 3B 112
Cricket Cl. L19: Garst . . . 3B 92
Cricket Path L37: Form . . . 8F 16
PR8: Birkd . . . 3M 11
Cricklade Cl. L20: Boot . . . 6A 44
Criftin Cl. CH66: Gt Sut . . . 3H 111
Cringles Dr. L35: Tar G . . . 1L 77
CRISP DELF . . . 1J 31
Crispin Rd. L27: N'ley . . . 3J 77
Crispin St. WA10: St H . . . 7H 49
Critchley Rd. L24: Speke . . . 5L 93
Critchley Way L33: Kirkb . . . 7D 36
Croasdale Dr. WA7: Beech . . . 1A 108
WN8: Parb . . . 2F 22
Crockett's Wlk. WA10: Eccl . . . 5E 48
Crockleford Av. PR8: South . . . 3D 12
Crocus Av. CH41: Birke . . . 1F 72
Crocus Gdns. WA9: Bold . . . 2C 64
Crocus St. L5: Kirkd . . . 2C 58
Croesmere Dr. CH66: Gt Sut . . . 3J 111
CROFT . . . 2H 67
Croft, The CH49: Grea . . . 6L 71
L12: W Der . . . 2N 59
L28: Stockb V . . . 1E 60
L31: Lyd . . . 7G 27
L32: Kirkb . . . 3D 46
WA7: Halt . . . 6B 96
WA9: St H . . . 9B 50
WN5: Bil . . . 8N 31
Croft Av. CH62: Brom . . . 6B 90
L40: Burs . . . 2K 21
WN5: Orr . . . 7N 31
Croft Av. E. CH62: Brom . . . 5C 90
Croft Bus. Cen. CH62: Brom . . . 5D 90
Croft Bus. Pk. CH62: Brom . . . 5D 90
Croft Cl. CH43: Noct . . . 4E 72
CH62: Brom . . . 6C 90
Croft Cotts. CH66: Chil T . . . 6F 102
(off School La.)
Croft Ct. CH65: Ell P . . . 2C 112
WN7: Leigh . . . 1K 53
Croft Dr. CH46: More . . . 1M 71
CH48: Caldy . . . 1D 86
Croft Dr. E. CH48: Caldy . . . 9E 70
Croft Dr. W. CH48: Caldy . . . 9D 70
Croft Edge CH43: Oxton . . . 5H 73
Croft End WA9: St H . . . 9B 50
Croften Dr. CH64: Lit N . . . 9E 100
Crofters, The CH49: Grea . . . 4L 71
Crofters Cl. CH66: Gt Sut . . . 4K 111
Crofters Heath CH66: Gt Sut . . . 4K 111
Crofters La. L33: Kirkb . . . 6E 36
Croftfield L31: Mag . . . 2K 35
Croft Gdns. WA4: Grap . . . 9H 83
Croft Golf Cen. . . . 3K 67
Croft Grn. CH62: Brom . . . 4C 90
CROFT HEATH . . . 1H 67
Croft Heath Gdns. WA3: Croft . . . 1H 67
Croft Hey L40: Ruf . . . 2M 15
Croft Heys L39: Augh . . . 3N 27
Croft Ho. WA3: Croft . . . 2H 67
Croftlands WN5: Orr . . . 8N 31
Croft La. CH62: Brom . . . 6C 90
L9: Ain . . . 3J 45
Crofton Cl. WA4: App T . . . 2K 99
Crofton Cres. L13: Liv . . . 6N 59
Crofton Gdns. WA3: Cul . . . 7M 53
Crofton Rd. CH42: Tran . . . 5L 73
L13: Liv . . . 6N 59
WA7: Run . . . 6H 95
Croft Retail & Leisure Pk.
CH62: Brom . . . 4C 90
Croftside WA1: Wools . . . 1N 83
Croftson Av. L39: Orm . . . 7D 20
Croft St. WA3: Golb . . . 2B 52
WA8: Wid . . . 1K 95
Croftsway CH60: Hesw . . . 7L 87
Croft Technology Pk. CH62: Brom . . . 6E 90
Croft Trade Pk. CH62: Brom . . . 5D 90
Croft Way L23: Thorn . . . 6A 34
Croftwood Gro. L35: Whis . . . 7B 62
Cromarty Rd. CH44: Wall . . . 5F 56
L13: Liv . . . 6L 59
Cromdale Gro. WA9: St H . . . 8A 50
Cromdale Way WA5: Gt San . . . 2G 80
Cromer Dr. CH45: Wall . . . 4G 57
Cromer Rd. CH47: Hoy . . . 1B 70
L17: Aig . . . 7K 75
PR8: Birkd . . . 4L 11
Cromer Way L26: Halew . . . 1K 93
Cromfield L39: Augh . . . 2A 28
Cromford Rd. L36: Huy . . . 4J 61
Crompton Ct. L3: Liv . . . 1K 5
L18: Moss H . . . 3B 76
WN4: Ash M . . . 9K 41
Crompton Dr. L12: Crox . . . 7C 46
WA2: Win . . . 3B 66
Cromptons La. L18: Moss H . . . 4B 76
Crompton St. L5: Liv . . . 4C 58
Crompton Way WA3: Low . . . 2J 53
Cromwell Av. WA2: Warr . . . 7L 65
WA5: Gt San, Old H, Westb . . . 7L 65
Cromwell Av. Sth. WA5: Gt San . . . 4L 81
Cromwell Cl. L39: Augh . . . 2A 28
WA12: Newt W . . . 6J 51
Cromwell Ct. M44: Irlam . . . 2L 69
WA1: Warr . . . 3B 82
(off Dixon St.)
Cromwell Rd. CH65: Ell P . . . 9A 104
L4: Walt . . . 8E 44
M44: Irlam . . . 2L 69
Cromwell St. WA8: Wid . . . 1K 95
Crondall Gro. L15: Wav . . . 1N 75
CRONTON . . . 3F 78
Cronton Av. CH46: Leas . . . 6N 55
L35: Whis . . . 8N 61
Cronton Farm Ct. WA8: Wid . . . 4H 79
Cronton La. L35: Rainh . . . 8E 62
WA8: Cron . . . 1E 78
WA8: Wid . . . 3H 79
Cronton La. M. WA8: Wid . . . 3J 79
Cronton Pk. Av. WA8: Cron . . . 2F 78
Cronton Pk. Cl. WA8: Cron . . . 2F 78
Cronton Rd. L15: Wav . . . 3M 75
L35: Tar G . . . 1L 77
WA8: Cron, Wid . . . 3E 78
Cronulla Dr. WA5: Gt San . . . 1F 80
Crookall St. WN4: Ash M . . . 7L 41
Crookhurst Av. WN5: Bil . . . 5N 39
Croome Dr. CH48: W Kir . . . 6D 70
Croppers Hill Ct. WA10: St H . . . 8H 49
(off Prescot Rd.)
Croppers La. L39: Bic . . . 3D 28
Croppers Rd. WA2: Fearn . . . 6G 67
Cropper St. L1: Liv . . . 6H 5 (8D 58)
Cropton Rd. L37: Form . . . 1F 24
CROSBY . . . 2L 43
Crosby Av. WA5: Warr . . . 9A 66
Crosby Civic Hall (Theatre) . . . 1L 43
Crosby Cl. CH49: Upton . . . 2N 71
Crosby Coastal Pk. . . . 2F 32 & 1J 43
Crosby Grn. L12: W Der . . . 2M 59
Crosby Gro. CH64: Will . . . 5A 102
WA10: St H . . . 9G 49
Crosby Lakeside Adventure Cen. . . . 2K 43
Crosby Leisure Cen. . . . 9H 33
Crosby Rd. PR8: Birkd . . . 3M 11
Crosby Rd. Nth. L22: Water . . . 9L 33
Crosby Rd. Sth. L21: Sea . . . 2L 43
L22: Water . . . 2L 43
Crosender Rd. L23: Crosb . . . 8J 33
Crosfield Cl. L7: Liv . . . 8H 59
Crosfield Rd. CH44: Wall . . . 6J 57
L7: Liv . . . 8H 59
L35: Presc . . . 5C 62
Crosfield St. WA1: Warr . . . 3B 82
Crosfield Wlk. L7: Liv . . . 8H 59
(off Crosfield Cl.)
Crosgrove Rd. L4: Walt . . . 9H 45
Crosland Dr. WA6: Hel . . . 3D 114
Crosland Rd. L32: Kirkb . . . 1E 46
Cross, The CH62: Brom . . . 6D 90
CH64: Nest . . . 6E 100
L38: Ince B . . . 9K 25
WA13: Lymm . . . 5E 84
Crossacre Rd. L25: Gate . . . 1F 76
Cross Barn La. L38: Ince B . . . 1L 33
Crossdale Rd. CH62: Brom . . . 9C 90
L23: Crosb . . . 8J 33
Crossdale Way WA11: St H . . . 1L 49
CROSSENS . . . 3A 8
Crossens Way PR9: South . . . 1A 8
Cross Farm Rd. WA9: St H . . . 9M 49
Crossfield Av. WA3: Cul . . . 8N 53
WA13: Lymm . . . 5F 84
Crossfield Rd. WN8: Skel . . . 4F 30
Crossfield St. WA9: St H . . . 7L 49
Crossford Rd. L14: Knott A . . . 3E 60
Cross Gates WA8: Wid . . . 5B 80
Cross Grn. L37: Form . . . 2G 24
Cross Grn. Cl. L37: Form . . . 2G 24
Crosshall Brow L39: Orm . . . 8F 20
L40: Westh . . . 8F 20
Cross Hall Ct. L39: Orm . . . 9E 20
Crosshall St. L1: Liv . . . 4F 4 (7C 58)
Cross Hey L21: Ford . . . 9A 34
L31: Mag . . . 4K 35
Cross Hey Av. CH43: Noct . . . 3D 72
Cross Hillocks La. WA8: Wid . . . 6B 78
Crossings, The WA12: Newt W . . . 7L 51
Crossland M. WA13: Lymm . . . 4B 84
Crossland Ter. WA6: Hel . . . 3E 114
Cross La. CH45: Wall . . . 4D 56
CH63: Beb . . . 3M 89
CH64: Lit N . . . 9E 100
L35: Presc, Whis . . . 5A 62
L39: Hals . . . 4G 19
WA3: Croft . . . 2K 67
WA4: Grap . . . 6H 83
WA6: Frod . . . 6E 106
WA12: Newt W . . . 7K 51
WN5: Bil . . . 9N 31
Cross La. E. M31: Part . . . 7M 69
Cross La. Sth. WA3: Ris . . . 3M 67
Cross La. W. M31: Part . . . 7M 69
Crossledge Way L25: Gate . . . 1D 76
Crossley Av. CH66: Ell P . . . 8K 103
Crossley Dr. CH60: Hesw . . . 7L 87
L15: Wav . . . 9M 59
Crossley Pk. WA6: Kingsw . . . 6M 115
Crossley Rd. WA10: St H . . . 1G 62
Crossley St. WA1: Warr . . . 3D 82
Cross Mdw. Ct. WA9: St H . . . 8M 49
(off Appleton Rd.)
Cross Meanygate L40: Holm . . . 1F 14
Cross Pit La. WA11: Rainf . . . 5C 38
Cross St. CH41: Birke . . . 2M 73
CH62: Port S . . . 2A 90
CH64: Nest . . . 6E 100
L22: Water . . . 1K 43
L34: Presc . . . 2B 62
PR8: South . . . 9G 6
WA2: Warr . . . 1C 82
WA3: Golb . . . 3B 52
WA7: Run . . . 4K 95
WA8: Wid . . . 7L 79
(not continuous)
WA10: St H . . . 7K 49
Crossvale Rd. L36: Huy . . . 8J 61
Crossway CH43: Bid . . . 9E 56
WA8: Wid . . . 8G 78
Crossway, The CH63: Raby . . . 2J 101
Crossway Cl. WN4: Ash M . . . 6N 41
Crossways CH62: Brom . . . 4C 90
L25: Gate . . . 2D 76
Crosswood Cres. L36: Huy . . . 6G 61
Crosthwaite Av. CH62: East . . . 2E 102
Croston Av. L35: Rainh . . . 4E 62
Croston Cl. WA8: Wid . . . 5F 78
Croston's Brow PR9: South . . . 4L 7
Crouchley Hall M. WA13: Lymm . . . 7F 84
Crouchley La. WA13: Lymm . . . 6E 84
Crouch St. L5: Liv . . . 3F 58
WA9: St H . . . 1N 63
CROUGHTON . . . 8D 112
Croughton Ct. CH66: Ell P . . . 6L 103
Croughton Rd. CH2: Crou, Stoak . . . 7D 112
(not continuous)
CH66: Ell P . . . 6L 103
Crowe Av. WA2: Warr . . . 7C 66
Crowland Cl. PR9: South . . . 9M 7
Crowland St. PR9: South . . . 1E 12
Crowland St. Ind. Est. PR9: South . . . 9M 7
Crowland Way L37: Form . . . 2H 25
Crow La. WN8: Dalt . . . 1J 31
Crow La. E. WA12: Newt W . . . 6K 51
Crow La. W. WA12: Newt W . . . 6H 51
Crowley La. CW9: Ant . . . 4N 99
WA16: High L . . . 4N 99
Crowmarsh Cl. CH49: Upton . . . 4N 71
Crown Acres Rd. L25: Woolt . . . 8G 76
Crown Av. WA8: Wid . . . 8E 78
Crown Cl. L37: Form . . . 2G 24
Crown Court
Liverpool . . . 6E 4 (8B 58)
Crown Flds. Cl. WA12: Newt W . . . 5K 51
Crownford Cres. WA4: Warr . . . 6D 82
Crown Gdns. WA12: Newt W . . . 6K 51
Crown Ga. WA7: Pal F . . . 8B 96
Crown Grn. WA13: Lymm . . . 5H 85
Crown Pk. Dr. WA12: Newt W . . . 5K 51
Crown Rd. L12: W Der . . . 2A 60
Crown Sta. Pl. L7: Liv . . . 7N 5 (9F 58)
Crown St. L7: Liv . . . 4L 5 (7E 58)
(Elizabeth St.)
L7: Liv . . . 7N 5 (9F 58)
(Rosemary Cl.)
Crown St. L8: Liv . . . 7N 5 (9F 58)
WA1: Warr . . . 3C 82
WA9: St H . . . 2G 63
WA12: Newt W . . . 7J 51
Crownway L36: Huy . . . 5H 61
Crown Wood Ct. WN2: Bam . . . 4N 41
(off Fourth St.)
Crow St. L8: Liv . . . 2C 74
Crowther Dr. WN3: Wins . . . 2G 40
Crowther St. WA10: St H . . . 7H 49
CROW WOOD . . . 6N 79
Crow Wood La. WA8: Wid . . . 6N 79
Crow Wood Pl. WA8: Wid . . . 5N 79
Crow Wood Rd. WA3: Low . . . 1E 52
Croxdale Rd. L14: Knott A . . . 2E 60
Croxdale Rd. W. L14: Knott A . . . 2D 60
CROXTETH . . . 6A 46
Croxteth Av. CH44: Wall . . . 5H 57
L21: Lith . . . 3N 43
Croxteth Cl. L31: Mag . . . 9K 27
Croxteth Ct. L8: Liv . . . 2G 75
Croxteth Dr. L17: Aig . . . 3H 75
WA11: Rainf . . . 4C 38
Croxteth Ga. L17: Aig . . . 3H 75
Croxteth Gro. L8: Liv . . . 2H 75
Croxteth Hall . . . 9B 46
Croxteth Hall Country Pk. . . . 9C 46
Croxteth Hall La. L11: Crox . . . 7A 46
L12: Crox, W Der . . . 8A 46
Croxteth La. L34: Know . . . 9F 46
CROXTETH PARK . . . 7D 46
Croxteth Rd. L8: Liv . . . 2G 74
L20: Boot . . . 5A 44
Croxteth Vw. L32: Kirkb . . . 3D 46
Croxton Ct. PR9: South . . . 6K 7
Croyde Cl. PR9: South . . . 2N 7
Croyde Pl. WA9: Sut L . . . 5M 63
Croyde Rd. L24: Speke . . . 4L 93
Croydon Av. L18: Moss H . . . 3L 75
Croylands St. L4: Kirkd . . . 1D 58
Crucian Way L12: Crox . . . 7B 46
Crump St. L1: Liv . . . 1D 74
Crutchley Av. CH41: Birke . . . 9H 57
Cryers La. CH2: Thorn M . . . 6K 113
Crystal Cl. L13: Liv . . . 7M 59
Cubbin Cres. L5: Kirkd . . . 3C 58
Cubert Rd. L11: Crox . . . 6A 46
Cuckoo Cl. L25: Gate . . . 4E 76
Cuckoo La. CH64: Lit N, Nest . . . 8H 101
L25: Gate . . . 3E 76
Cuckoo Way L25: Gate . . . 4E 76
Cuerden St. L3: Liv . . . 3G 4 (7C 58)
CUERDLEY CROSS . . . 6C 80
Cuerdley Grn. WA5: Cuerd . . . 5C 80
Cuerdley Rd. WA5: Penk . . . 5E 80
Cuerdon Dr. WA4: Thel . . . 7L 83
Culbin Cl. WA3: Birchw . . . 3A 68
CULCHETH . . . 7N 53
Culcheth Hall Dr. WA3: Cul . . . 6N 53
Culcheth Hall Farm WA3: Cul . . . 6N 53
Culcheth Linear Country Pk. . . . 6J 53
Culcheth Sports Club . . . 7N 53
Culford Cl. WA7: Wind H . . . 6F 96
Cullen Av. L20: Boot . . . 5C 44
Cullen Cl. CH63: East . . . 2C 102
Cullen Dr. L21: Lith . . . 3N 43
Cullen Rd. WA7: West P . . . 8G 95
Cullen St. L8: Liv . . . 1H 75
Culme Rd. L12: W Der . . . 2L 59
Culshaw Way L40: Scar . . . 7L 13
Culvert La. WN8: Newb . . . 3D 22
Culzean Cl. L12: Crox . . . 7C 46
Cumberland Av. CH43: Pren . . . 6G 72
L17: Liv . . . 2J 75
L30: N'ton . . . 8B 34
M44: Cad . . . 5J 69
WA10: St H . . . 1E 62
Cumberland Cl. L6: Liv . . . 2J 59
Cumberland Cres. WA11: Hay . . . 4C 50
Cumberland Ga. L30: N'ton . . . 7F 34
Cumberland Gro. CH66: Gt Sut . . . 2H 111
Cumberland Rd. CH45: New B . . . 2J 57
M31: Part . . . 7L 69
PR8: South . . . 1C 12
Cumberland St. L1: Liv . . . 4E 4 (7B 58)
WA4: Warr . . . 5D 82
Cumber La. L35: Whis . . . 5C 62
Cumbers Dr. CH64: Ness . . . 9G 100
Cumbers La. CH64: Ness . . . 9G 100
Cumbrae Dr. CH65: Ell P . . . 5A 112
Cumbria Cl. CH66: Gt Sut . . . 4K 111
Cumbria Way L12: W Der . . . 9A 46
Cummings St. L1: Liv . . . 8H 5 (9D 58)
Cummins Av. L37: Form . . . 8E 16
Cumpsty Rd. L21: Lith . . . 1B 44
Cunard Av. CH44: Wall . . . 4K 57
Cunard Cl. CH43: Bid . . . 2C 72
Cunard Rd. L21: Lith . . . 3A 44
Cunliffe Av. WA12: Newt W . . . 5K 51
Cunliffe Cl. WA7: Pal F . . . 8C 96
Cunliffe St. L2: Liv . . . 3E 4 (7B 58)
Cunningham Cl. CH48: Caldy . . . 1D 86
WA5: Gt San . . . 3H 81
Cunningham Ct. WA10: St H . . . 7F 48
Cunningham Dr. CH63: Brom . . . 8B 90
WA7: Run . . . 7H 95
(not continuous)
Cunningham Rd. L13: Liv . . . 7M 59
WA8: Wid . . . 8G 79
Cunscough La. L31: Mag . . . 1B 36

Cuper Cres. L36: Huy 5H 61
Curate Rd. L6: Liv 2H 59
Curlender Cl. CH41: Birke 8E 56
Curlender Way L24: Hale 5B 94
Curlew Av. CH49: Upton 2L 71
Curlew Cl. CH49: Upton 2L 71
WA3: Low 2E 52
Curlew Ct. CH46: More 8K 55
Curlew Gro. L26: Halew 7J 77
WA3: Birchw 6M 67
Curlew La. L40: Burs, Ruf 6H 15
Curlew Way CH46: More 8K 55
Currans Rd. WA2: Warr 7C 66
Curran Way L33: Kirkb 6B 36
Curtana Cres. L11: Crox 7A 46
Curtis Rd. L4: Walt 9H 45
Curwell Cl. CH63: Spit 4A 90
Curzon Av. CH41: Birke 1H 73
CH45: New B 1H 57
Curzon Dr. WA4: Grap 9H 83
Curzon Pl. *WA12: Newt W* *7K 51*
(off King St.)
Curzon Rd. CH42: Tran 6H 73
CH47: Hoy 1B 70
L22: Water 1L 43
PR8: South 1C 12
Curzon St. WA7: Run 6J 95
Cusson Rd. L33: Know I 1F 46
Custley Hey L28: Stockb V 1F 60
Custom Ho. Pl. L1: Liv 7E 4 (9B 58)
Cut La. L33: Kirkb 3J 47
L39: Hals 5L 19
Cygnet Cl. CH66: Gt Sut 1J 111
L39: Augh 2A 28
Cygnet Ct. L33: Kirkb 9E 36
WA1: Warr 5B 82
Cygnet Gdns. WA9: St H 8A 50
Cynthia Av. WA1: Wools 1J 83
Cynthia Rd. WA7: Run 6J 95
Cypress Av. CH66: Gt Sut 4L 111
WA8: Wid 5L 79
Cypress Cl. L31: Mell 8M 35
WA1: Wools 1M 83
Cypress Cft. CH63: Spit 4A 90
Cypress Gdns. WA9: St H 2F 62
Cypress Gro. WA7: Run 8M 95
Cypress Rd. L36: Huy 9H 61
PR8: South 9K 7
Cyprian's Way L30: N'ton 8D 34
Cyprus Gro. L8: Liv 4F 74
Cyprus St. L34: Presc 3A 62
Cyprus Ter. CH45: New B 2H 57
Cyril Bell Cl. WA13: Lymm 5F 84
Cyril Gro. L17: Aig 6K 75
Cyril St. WA2: Warr 1C 82

D

DACRE HILL 8M 73
Dacre's Bri. La. L35: Tar G 1A 78
Dacre St. CH41: Birke 2L 73
L20: Boot 9A 44
Dacy Rd. L5: Liv 4F 58
Daffodil Cl. WA8: Wid 4A 80
Daffodil Gdns. WA9: Bold 2C 64
Daffodil Rd. CH41: Birke 1F 72
L15: Wav 2N 75
Dagnall Av. WA5: Warr 7A 66
Dagnall Rd. L32: Kirkb 1A 46
Dahlia Cl. L9: Walt 6G 45
WA9: Bold 2C 64
Dailton Rd. WN8: Uph 5K 31
Dairy Bank CH2: Elt 1M 113
Dairy Farm Cl. WA13: Lymm 5F 84
Dairy Farm Rd. WA11: Rainf 5M 37
Dairylands Cl. L16: Moss H 2A 76
Daisy Av. WA12: Newt W 8L 51
Daisy Bank Mill Cl. WA3: Cul 7M 53
Daisy Bank Rd. WA5: Penk 4H 81
WA13: Lymm 5C 84
Daisy Cl. PR9: Banks 3E 8
Daisy Gro. *L7: Liv* *8G 59*
(off Dorothy Dr.)
Daisy La. L40: Lath 1M 21
Daisy M. L21: Lith 4A 44
Daisy Mt. L31: Mag 3K 35
Daisy St. L5: Kirkd 2C 58
Daisy Wlk. CH44: Wall 6H 57
PR8: South *8K 7*
(off Beacham Rd.)
Daisy Way PR8: South 4B 12
Dakin Wlk. L33: Kirkb 9D 36
Dakota Bus. Pk. L19: Speke 3C 92
Dakota Dr. L24: Speke 4B 92
WA5: Gt San 1L 81
Dalby Cl. WA3: Birchw 4B 68
WA11: St H 5M 49
Dalcross Way L11: Crox 6N 45
Dale, The CH64: Nest 8D 100
WA5: Gt San, Penk 3H 81
Dale Acre Dr. L30: N'ton 8B 34
Dale Av. CH60: Hesw 6N 87
CH62: Brom 7C 90
CH66: Lit Sut 8H 103
Dalebrook Cl. L25: Gate 1F 76
Dale Cl. L31: Mag 1H 35
WA5: Warr 4N 81
WA8: Wid 8D 78
WN8: Parb 3E 22
Dale Ct. CH60: Hesw 7N 87
Dale Cres. WA9: Sut L 3N 63
Dalecrest WN5: Bil 2N 39
Dale Cft. WA6: Hap 4B 114
Dale Dr. CH65: Gt Sut 9L 103
Dale End Rd. CH61: Barn 3C 88
Dale Gdns. CH60: Hesw 6L 87
CH65: Whit 2N 111
Dalegarth Av. L12: W Der 9D 46
Dale Gro. M44: Cad 3L 69
Dale Hall L18: Moss H 6L 75
Dalehead Pl. WA11: St H 1L 49
Dale Hey CH44: Wall 6H 57
CH66: Hoot 4D 102
Dalehurst Cl. CH44: Wall 5K 57
Dale La. L33: Kirkb 6E 36
WA4: App 8F 82
(not continuous)
Dalemeadow Rd. L14: Knott A 6B 60
Dale M. L25: Gate 4F 76
Dale Rd. CH62: Brom 9C 90
WA3: Golb 3B 52
DALES, THE 7M 87
Dales, The CH46: More 9A 56
Dalesford Cl. WN7: Leigh 2K 53
Daleside Av. WN4: Ash M 3J 41
Daleside Cl. CH61: Irby 1N 87
Daleside Rd. L33: Kirkb 8D 36
Daleside Wlk. L33: Kirkb 8D 36
Dales Row L36: Huy 7M 61
Dale St. L2: Liv 4E 4 (7B 58)
L19: Garst 2A 92
WA7: Run 6K 95
Dales Wlk. L37: Form 7G 16
Dalesway CH60: Hesw 7M 87
Dale Vw. WA12: Newt W 6N 51
Dale Vw. Cl. CH61: Pens 2A 88
Dalewood L12: Crox 7C 46
Dalewood Cl. WA2: Warr 2B 82
Dalewood Cres. CH2: Elt 2L 113
Dalewood Gdns. L35: Whis 7C 62
Daley Pl. L20: Boot 3D 44
Daley Rd. L21: Lith 1B 44
DALLAM 7A 66
Dallam Ct. WA2: Warr 1B 82
Dallam La. WA2: Warr 1B 82
Dallas Dr. WA5: Gt San 1J 81
Dallas Gro. L9: Ain 4F 44
Dallington Ct. L13: Liv 7N 59
Dalmeny St. L17: Aig 5G 75
Dalmorton Rd. CH45: New B 1H 57
Dalry Cres. L32: Kirkb 3D 46
Dalrymple St. L5: Liv 4C 58
Dalry Wlk. L32: Kirkb 3D 46
Dalston Dr. WA11: St H 1L 49
Dalston Gro. WN3: Wins 1F 40
DALTON 7F 22
Dalton Av. WA3: Ris 3M 67
WA5: Warr 1A 82
Dalton Bank WA1: Warr 2D 82
Dalton Cl. L12: W Der 8A 46
Dalton Ct. WA7: Ast 4A 96
Dalton Dr. WN3: Wins 1G 40
Dalton Gro. WN4: Ash M 7J 41
Dalton Rd. CH45: New B 2J 57
Dalton St. WA3: Ris 4M 67
WA7: Run 5N 95
Daltry Cl. L12: W Der 2M 59
Dalwood Cl. WA7: Murd 8G 96
Damerham M. L25: Gate 1E 76
Damfield La. L31: Mag 2H 35
Dam Head La. WA3: Glaz, Rix 5F 68
Damhead La. CH64: Will 7K 101
Damian Dr. WA12: Newt W 5J 51
Dam La. L40: Scar 8N 13
WA1: Wools 1L 83
WA3: Croft 2G 66
WA3: Rix 4E 68
Damson Gro. WA11: Rainf 4B 38
Damson Gro. Ct. WA11: Rainf 4B 38
Damson Rd. L27: N'ley 2J 77
Damson Wlk. *M31: Part* *6K 69*
(off Wood La.)
Dam Wood La. L40: Scar 9A 14
Damwood Rd. L24: Speke 5G 93
Danbers WN8: Uph 6J 31
Danby Cl. L5: Liv 4E 58
WA5: Warr 1N 81
WA7: Beech 9N 95
Danby Fold L35: Rainh 6E 62
Dandy's Meanygate PR4: Tarl 1M 9
Dane Av. M31: Part 5M 69
Dane Bank Rd. WA13: Lymm 5E 84
Dane Bank Rd. E. WA13: Lymm 4E 84
Dane Cl. CH61: Irby 1N 87
Dane Ct. L35: Rainh 6F 62
Danefield Pl. L19: Aller 8B 76
Danefield Rd. CH49: Grea 6K 71
L19: Aller 8B 76
Danefield Ter. *L19: Aller* *9B 76*
(off Mather Av.)
Danehurst Rd. CH45: Wall 2F 56
L9: Ain 3G 44
Danesbury Cl. WN5: Bil 7A 40
Danescourt Rd. CH41: Birke 9G 57
L12: W Der 4A 60
Danescroft WA8: Wid 5E 78
Daneshill Cl. L17: Aig 9L 75
Daneshill La. M44: Cad 4L 69
Dane St. L4: Walt 9E 44
Daneswell Dr. CH46: More 8N 55
Daneswell Rd. L24: Speke 5L 93
Daneville Rd. L4: Walt 8J 45
Daneway PR8: Ains 8H 11
Danger La. CH46: More 7N 55
DANGEROUS CORNER 3M 23
Daniel Adamson Av.
M31: Part 6K 69
Daniel Cl. L20: Boot 4N 43
WA3: Birchw 5A 68
Daniel Ct. M31: Part 5M 69
Daniel Davies Dr. L8: Liv 1F 74
Daniel Ho. L20: Boot 8B 44
Daniels La. WN8: Skel 5F 30
Dannette Hey L28: Stockb V 3G 60
Dansie St. L3: Liv 5K 5 (8E 58)
Dan's Rd. WA8: Wid 6A 80
Dante Cl. L9: Ain 2H 45
Danube St. L8: Liv 1H 75
Dapple Heath Av. L31: Mell 8M 35
Darby Cl. CH64: Lit N 9E 100
Darby Gro. L19: Garst 1N 91
Darby Rd. L19: Gras 8M 75
M44: Irlam 3N 69
Darent Rd. WA11: Hay 3D 50
DARESBURY 5L 97
Daresbury Av. PR8: Ains 9G 11
Daresbury By-Pass WA4: Dares 6K 97
Daresbury Cl. L32: Kirkb 9A 36
Daresbury Ct. WA8: Wid 5N 79
Daresbury Expressway
WA4: Moore, Dares 3H 97
WA7: Run, Ast, Wind H, Nort 5K 95
Daresbury La. WA4: Dares, Hatt 5L 97
Daresbury Pk. WA4: Dares 7J 97
(not continuous)
Daresbury Rd. CH44: Wall 5G 57
WA10: Eccl 6E 48
Daresbury Science Pk. WA4: Dares 4K 97
Darfield WN8: Uph 5J 31
Daric Cl. WN7: Leigh 1K 53
Dark Ark La. WA6: Manl 9L 115
Dark Entry L34: Know P 9J 47
Dark La. L31: Mag 2J 35
L40: Lath 7F 20
WA4: Hghr Whi 9E 98
Darkstar Laser
St Helens *6K 49*
(off Central St.)
Darley Av. WA2: Warr 6F 66
Darley Cl. WA8: Wid 5E 78
Darleydale Dr. CH62: East 1E 102
Darley Dr. L12: W Der 3A 60
Darley Rd. WN3: Wigan 1K 41
Darlington Cl. CH44: Wall 5K 57
Darlington Ct. WA8: Wid 9K 79
Darlington St. CH44: Wall 5K 57
Darmond Rd. L33: Kirkb 8E 36
Darmond's Grn. CH48: W Kir 5C 70
Darmonds Grn. Av. L6: Liv 2J 59
Darnaway Cl. WA3: Birchw 3B 68
Darnley St. L8: Liv 3D 74
Darran Av. WN3: Wigan 1H 41
Darrel Dr. L7: Liv 1H 75
Darsefield Rd. L16: Child 1C 76
Dartford Cl. L14: Knott A 3D 60
Dartington Rd. L16: Child 9B 60
Dartmouth Av. L10: Ain 9H 35
Dartmouth Dr. L30: N'ton 7B 34
WA10: Windle 4F 48
Darvel Av. WN4: Garsw 7E 40
Darwall Rd. L19: Aller 8B 76
Darwen Gdns. WA2: Warr 8F 66
Darwen St. L5: Liv 4B 58
Darwick Dr. L36: Huy 9K 61
Darwin Ct. PR9: South 6K 7
Darwin Gro. WA9: St H 2H 63
Darwin Way CH65: Ell P 1B 112
Daryl Rd. CH60: Hesw 6A 88
Dashwood Cl. WA4: Grap 9H 83
Daten Av. WA3: Ris 3M 67
Daten Pk. WA3: Ris 3N 67
Daulby St. L3: Liv 4K 5 (7E 58)
Dauntsey Brow L25: Gate 1F 76
Dauntsey M. L25: Gate 1F 76
Davenham Av. CH43: Oxton 5F 72
WA1: Padg 9F 66
Davenham Cl. CH43: Oxton 6F 72
Davenham Ct. L15: Wav 1N 75
Davenham Rd. L37: Form 9F 16
Davenhill Pk. L10: Ain 9H 35
Davenport Av. WA4: Westy 3G 83
Davenport Cl. CH48: Caldy 1D 86
Davenport Gro. L33: Kirkb 7C 36
Davenport Rd. CH60: Hesw 8M 87
Davenport Row WA7: Run 7N 95
Daventree Rd. CH45: Wall 4H 57
Daventry Rd. L17: Aig 6K 75
David Lewis St. L1: Liv 6F 4 (8C 58)
David Lloyd Leisure
Ellesmere Port 4B 112
Liverpool 1E 46
Warrington 3L 81
David Lloyd Racquet & Fitness Club
Speke 3C 92
David Rd. WA13: Lymm 5C 84
David's Av. WA5: Gt San 3K 81
Davidson Rd. L13: Liv 6L 59
David St. L8: Liv 4E 74
Davids Wlk. L25: Woolt 5G 76
Davies Av. WA4: Westy 4G 82
WA12: Newt W 5L 51
Davies Cl. WA8: Wid 3K 95
Davies Rd. M31: Part 6N 69
Davies St. L1: Liv 4E 4 (7B 58)
L20: Boot 6C 44
WA9: St H 6M 49
Davies Way WA13: Lymm 5E 84
Davis Rd. CH46: Leas 6B 56
Davy Av. WA3: Ris 4N 67
Davy Cl. WA10: Eccl 5E 48
Davy Rd. WA7: Ast 4A 96
Davy St. L5: Liv 3F 58
Dawber Cl. L6: Liv 5F 58
Dawber Delf Ind. Area WN6: Appl B 5N 23
Dawber Delph WN6: Appl B 5N 23
Dawber St. WN4: Ash M 7M 41
Dawley Cl. WN4: Ash M 8J 41
Dawlish Cl. L25: Hunts X 8G 77
WA3: Rix 6H 69
Dawlish Dr. PR9: South 2M 7
Dawlish Rd. CH44: Wall 5F 56
CH61: Irby 2K 87
Dawlish Way WA3: Golb 1A 52
Dawn Cl. CH64: Ness 9G 100
WA9: St H 2H 63
Dawn Gdns. CH65: Whit 1N 111
Dawn Wlk. *L10: Faz* *4N 45*
(off Panton Way)
Dawpool Cotts. CH48: Caldy 1H 87
Dawpool Dr. CH46: More 9M 55
CH62: Brom 8B 90
Dawpool Farm CH61: Thurs 2J 87
Dawson Av. CH41: Birke 9H 57
PR9: South 2A 8
WA9: St H 2N 63
Dawson Gdns. L31: Mag 1H 35
Dawson Ho. WA5: Gt San 2E 80
Dawson Rd. L39: Orm 6D 20
Dawson St. L1: Liv 5F 4 (8C 58)
Dawson Way L1: Liv 5G 4
Dawstone Ri. CH60: Hesw 8N 87
Dawstone Rd. CH60: Hesw 8N 87
Daybrook WN8: Uph 5J 31
Dayfield WN8: Uph 5K 31
Days Mdw. CH49: Grea 5K 71
Day St. L13: Liv 6M 59
Deacon Cl. L22: Water 2K 43
Deacon Ct. L22: Water 2K 43
L25: Woolt 6F 76
Deacon Pk. L33: Know I 2F 46
Deacon Rd. WA8: Wid 7L 79
Deacons Cl. WA3: Croft 1H 67
Deacon Trad. Est. WA12: Newt W 8H 51
Deakin St. CH41: Birke 9F 56
Deal Cl. WA5: Warr 1A 82
Dealcroft L25: Woolt 6D 76
Dean Av. CH45: Wall 3E 56
Dean Cl. M31: Part 5M 69
WA8: Wid 8L 79
WN5: Bil 8N 39
WN8: Uph 5M 31
Dean Ct. WA3: Golb 3B 52
Dean Cres. WA2: Warr 7C 66
Dean Dillistone Ct. L1: Liv 9H 5
Deane Rd. L7: Liv 7H 59
Dean Ho. L22: Water 2L 43
Deanland Dr. L24: Speke 3F 92
Dean Mdw. WA12: Newt W 6L 51
Dean Patey Ct. L1: Liv 8H 5 (9D 58)
Dean Rd. M44: Cad 3L 69
WA3: Golb 3B 52
Deansburn Rd. L13: Liv 3K 59
Deanscales Rd. L11: Norr G 8L 45
Deans Ct. L37: Form 8F 16
Deansfield Way CH2: Elt 2L 113
Deansgate CH65: Ell P 9M 103
Deansgate La. L37: Form 8H 17
Deansgate La. Nth. L37: Form 7G 17
DEANSGREEN 9N 85
Deans La. L40: Lath 1B 22
WA4: Thel 5N 83
WN8: Newb 3C 22
Deans Rd. CH65: Ell P 2D 112
Dean St. L22: Water 2K 43
WA8: Wid 8L 79
Deans Way CH41: Birke 9F 56
Deansway WA8: Wid 8F 78
Deanwater Cl. WA3: Birchw 5L 67
Deanwood Cl. L35: Whis 7C 62
Dean Wood Golf Course 4M 31
Dearden Way WN8: Uph 5K 31
Dearham Av. WA11: St H 3K 49
Dearne Cl. L12: W Der 4C 60
Dearnford Av. CH62: Brom 9C 90
Dearnford Cl. CH62: Brom 9C 90
Dearnley Av. WA11: St H 5A 50
Deauville Rd. L9: Ain 3H 45
Debra Cl. CH66: Gt Sut 1H 111
L31: Mell 7N 35
Debra Rd. CH66: Gt Sut 2H 111
Decks, The WA7: Run 4K 95
Dee Cl. L33: Kirkb 5D 36
Dee Ct. L25: Gate 5G 76
Dee Ho. L25: Gate 5G 76
Dee La. CH48: W Kir 6B 70
Deeley Cl. L7: Liv 8H 59
Dee Pk. Cl. CH60: Hesw 9B 88
Dee Pk. Rd. CH60: Hesw 9B 88
Deepdale WA8: Wid 5F 78

Deepdale Av. L20: Boot 5N 43
WA11: St H 1M 49
Deepdale Cl. CH43: Bid 2C 72
WA5: Gt San 2H 81
Deepdale Dr. L35: Rainh 6G 62
Deepdale Rd. L25: Gate 1E 76
Deepfield Dr. L36: Huy 9K 61
Deepfield Rd. L15: Wav 2L 75
Deepwood Gro. L35: Whis 7B 62
Deerbarn Dr. L30: N'ton 7G 35
Deerbolt Cl. L32: Kirkb 8A 36
Deerbolt Cres. L32: Kirkb 8A 36
Deerbolt Way L32: Kirkb 8A 36
Deerbourne Cl. L25: Woolt 6D 76
Deerfield Cl. WA9: St H 6A 50
Dee Rd. L35: Rainh 6E 62
Deer Pk. Ct. WA7: Pal F 9A 96
Deerwood Cl. CH66: Lit Sut 7J 103
Deerwood Cres. CH66: Lit Sut 7J 103
Dee Sailing Club 2E 86
Deeside CH60: Hesw 7K 87
CH65: Whit 2N 111
Deeside Cl. CH43: Bid 2B 72
CH65: Whit 3N 111
Deeside Ct. CH64: Park 5B 100
Dee Vw. Ct. CH64: Nest 8E 100
Dee Vw. Rd. CH60: Hesw 7N 87
De Grouchy St. CH48: W Kir 5C 70
De-Haviland Way WN8: Skel 4H 31
De Havilland Dr. L24: Speke 3C 92
Deirdre Av. WA8: Wid 7K 79
Dekker Rd. L33: Kirkb 5C 36
Delabole Rd. L11: Crox 5B 46
De Lacy Row WA7: Cas 5C 96
Delafield Cl. WA2: Fearn 6G 66
Delagoa Rd. L10: Faz 4L 45
Delamain Rd. L13: Liv 3K 59
Delamere Av. CH62: East 2D 102
CH66: Gt Sut 9K 103
WA3: Low 4F 52
WA8: Wid 7F 78
WA9: Sut M 6K 63
Delamere Cl. CH43: Bid 2B 72
CH62: East 2D 102
L12: Crox 7B 46
Delamere Dr. CH66: Gt Sut 1K 111
Delamere Forest Pk. 9N 115
Delamere Grn. *CH66: Gt Sut* *1K 111*
(off Delamere Dr.)
Delamere Gro. *CH44: Wall* *7L 57*
(off Tudor Av.)
Delamere Ho. WA6: Frod 6M 107
Delamere Pl. WA7: Run 6J 95
Delamere Rd. PR8: Ains 9H 11
WN8: Skel 2C 30
Delamere St. WA5: Warr 3N 81
Delamere Way WN8: Uph 5K 31
Delamore Pl. L4: Kirkd 9D 44
Delamore's Acre CH64: Will 6N 101
Delamore St. L4: Kirkd 9D 44
Delavor Cl. CH60: Hesw 7M 87
Delavor Rd. CH60: Hesw 7L 87
Delaware Cres. L32: Kirkb 8A 36
Delaware Rd. L20: Boot 6B 44
Delenty Dr. WA3: Ris 5L 67
Delery Dr. WA1: Padg 9F 66
Delfby Cres. L32: Kirkb 1E 46
Delf Ho. WN8: Skel 3F 30
Delf La. L4: Walt 8F 44
L24: Speke 2F 92
L39: Down 8F 18
Delhi Rd. M44: Irlam 1M 69
Dell, The CH42: Rock F 7A 74
L12: W Der 1C 60
WN6: Appl B 6N 23
WN8: Uph 5L 31
Della Robbia Ho. *CH41: Birke* *3K 73*
(off Clifton Rd.)
Dell Cl. CH63: Brom 9A 90
Dell Ct. CH43: Pren 7F 72
Dell Dr. WA2: Fearn 7H 67
Dellfield La. L31: Mag 2K 35
Dell Gro. CH42: Rock F 8A 74
Dell La. CH60: Hesw 8B 88
Dellside Cl. WN4: Ash M 5F 40
Dellside Gro. WA9: St H 1M 63
Dell St. L7: Liv 7H 59
Delph, The WN8: Parb 2F 22
Delph Cl. L39: Augh 3A 28
Delph Comn. Rd. L39: Augh 3N 27
Delph Ct. L21: Lith 2N 43
WA9: St H 1L 63
Delph Dr. L40: Burs 1K 21
Delphfield WA7: Nort 7F 96
Delphfields Rd. WA4: App 9D 82
Delph Hollow Way WA9: St H 1L 63
Delph La. L35: Whis 4C 62
L37: Form 1C 24
L39: Augh 3A 28
WA2: Warr 3E 66
WA2: Win 5A 66
WA4: Dares 4J 97
Delph Mdw. Gdns. WN5: Bil 7M 39
Delph Pk. Av. L39: Augh 3N 27
Delph Rd. L23: Lit C 3K 33
Delphside Cl. WN5: Orr 7N 31
Delphside Rd. WN5: Orr 7N 31
Delph Top L39: Orm 7E 20
Delphwood Dr. WA9: St H 9L 49
Delta Cres. WA5: Westb 7L 65
Delta Dr. L12: W Der 1C 60
Delta Rd. L21: Lith 3A 44
WA9: St H 6B 50
Delta Rd. E. CH42: Rock F 7A 74
Delta Rd. W. CH42: Rock F 7A 74
Deltic Pl. L33: Know I 1F 46
Deltic Way L30: N'ton 2F 44
L33: Know I 2F 46
Delves Av. CH63: Spit 4M 89
WA5: Warr 1A 82
Delyn Cl. CH42: Rock F 7L 73
Demage Dr. CH66: Gt Sut 2J 111
Demage La. CH1: Lea B 9L 111
Demesne St. CH44: Wall 6L 57
Denbigh Av. PR9: South 4L 7
WA9: St H 2M 63
Denbigh Cl. WA6: Hel 4D 114
Denbigh Ct. CH65: Ell P 2B 112
WA7: Cas 5C 96
Denbigh Gdns. CH65: Ell P 2A 112
Denbigh Rd. CH44: Wall 6K 57
L9: Walt 7E 44
Denbigh St. L5: Liv 4A 58
Denbury Av. WA4: Stockt H 6G 82
Dencourt Rd. L11: Norr G 9N 45
Deneacres L25: Woolt 6E 76
Dene Av. WA12: Newt W 6H 51
Denebank Rd. L4: Walt 2G 59
Denecliff L28: Stockb V 1F 60
Dene Ct. L9: Faz 6L 45
Denefield Ho. PR8: South 9G 6
Denehurst Cl. WA5: Penk 4H 81
Deneshey Rd. CH47: Meols 9D 54
Denes Way L28: Stockb V 2E 60
Denford Cl. WN3: Wigan 1H 41
Denford Rd. L14: Knott A 4D 60
Denham Av. WA5: Gt San 3K 81
Denham Cl. CH43: Bid 1C 72
L12: Crox 7D 46
Denham Dr. WN3: Wigan 1J 41
Denholme WN8: Uph 5J 31
Denise Av. WA5: Penk 3G 80
Denise Rd. L10: Faz 3N 45
Denison Gro. WA9: St H 2H 63
Denison St. L3: Liv 2C 4 (6A 58)
Denman Dr. L6: Liv 5H 59
Denman Gro. *CH44: Wall* *7L 57*
(off Tudor Av.)
Denman St. L6: Liv 6G 59
Denman Way L6: Liv 5H 59
Denmark Rd. PR9: South 5M 7
Denmark St. L22: Water 1K 43
Dennett Cl. L31: Mag 4J 35
WA1: Wools 2M 83
Dennett Rd. L35: Presc 5N 61
Denning Dr. CH61: Irby 9L 71
Dennis Av. WA10: St H 2F 62
Dennis Rd. WA8: Wid 9M 79
Denny Cl. CH49: Upton 4N 71
Densham Av. WA2: Warr 8C 66
Denshaw WN8: Uph 5J 31
Denston Cl. CH43: Bid 1B 72
Denstone Av. L10: Ain 9J 35
Denstone Cl. L25: Woolt 8F 76
Dentdale Dr. L5: Liv 5D 58
Denton Dr. CH45: Wall 3J 57
Denton Gro. L6: Liv 4H 59
DENTON'S GREEN 5H 49
Dentons Grn. La.
WA10: St H 5G 49
Denton St. L8: Liv 4E 74
WA8: Wid 7M 79
Dentwood St. L8: Liv 4F 74
Denver Dr. WA5: Gt San 1K 81
Denver Pk. L32: Kirkb 1A 46
Denver Rd. L32: Kirkb 1A 46
WA4: Westy 5H 83
Denwall Ho. *CH64: Nest* *6E 100*
(off Churchill Way)
Depot Rd. L33: Know I 7H 37
Derby Bldgs. L7: Liv 5N 5
Derby Cl. M44: Cad 4J 69
WA12: Newt W 7K 51
Derby Ct. L37: Form 9E 16
Derby Dr. WA1: Warr 1F 82
WA11: Rainf 5D 38
Derby Gro. L31: Mag 5J 35
Derby Hall L17: Aig 4K 75
Derby Hill Cres. L39: Orm 8E 20
Derby Hill Rd. L39: Orm 8E 20
Derby Ho. *L39: Orm* *8D 20*
(off Derby St.)
Derby La. L13: Liv 5M 59
Derby Rd. CH42: Tran 5K 73
CH45: Wall 3G 57
L5: Kirkd 3A 58
L20: Boot, Kirkd 7A 44
L36: Huy 7J 61
(not continuous)
L37: Form 8E 16
PR9: South 8H 7
WA3: Golb 1D 52
WA4: Stockt H 7D 82
WA8: Wid 5K 79
WN8: Skel 4N 29
Derby Row WA12: Newt W 1M 65
Derbyshire Farm Bus. Pk.
WN3: Wigan 2J 41
DERBYSHIRE HILL 8C 50
Derbyshire Hill Rd. WA9: St H 7C 50
Derbyshire Rd. M31: Part 7K 69
WN3: Wins 2F 40
Derby Sq. L2: Liv 6E 4 (8B 58)
L34: Presc 3B 62
Derby St. L13: Liv 6L 59
L19: Garst 3A 92
L34: Presc 3N 61
L36: Huy 7L 61
L39: Orm 8D 20
WA12: Newt W 7K 51
Derby St. W. L39: Orm 8C 20
Derby Ter. L36: Huy 6J 61
Dereham Av. CH49: Upton 1A 72
Dereham Cres. L10: Faz 3L 45
Dereham Way WA7: Nort 4F 96
WN3: Wins 1F 40
Derek Av. WA2: Warr 7E 66
Derna Rd. L36: Huy 5H 61
Derringstone Cl. WA10: St H 9G 49
Derwent Av. L34: Presc 3C 62
L37: Form 2D 24
PR9: South 6L 7
WA3: Golb 1D 52
Derwent Cl. CH63: Hghr B 2K 89
L31: Mag 1L 35
L33: Kirkb 7B 36
L35: Rainh 6E 62
M31: Part 5M 69
Derwent Ct. L18: Moss H 3B 76
Derwent Dr. CH45: Wall 3G 57
CH61: Pens 3N 87
CH66: Hoot 4G 102
L21: Lith 2C 44
Derwent Rd. CH43: Oxton 4H 73
CH47: Meols 9F 54
CH63: Hghr B 2K 89
L23: Crosb 9M 33
WA4: Warr 6B 82
WA8: Wid 7F 78
WA11: St H 3L 49
WN4: Ash M 6N 41
Derwent Rd. E. L13: Liv 5M 59
Derwent Rd. W. L13: Liv 5L 59
Derwent Sq. L13: Liv 5M 59
Derwent Way CH64: Lit N 7F 100
WN7: Leigh 1J 53
Desborough Cres. L12: W Der 2M 59
Desford Av. WA11: St H 4N 49
Desford Cl. CH46: More 8J 55
Desford Rd. L19: Aig 8K 75
De Silva St. L36: Huy 7L 61
Desmond Cl. CH43: Bid 1C 72
Desmond Gro. L23: Crosb 8M 33
Desoto Rd. WA8: Wid 3G 95
Desoto Rd. E. WA8: Wid 1J 95
(not continuous)
Desoto Rd. W. WA8: Wid 1J 95
Detroit Cl. WA5: Gt San 2K 81
Deva Cl. L33: Kirkb 4C 36
Deva Rd. CH48: W Kir 6B 70
Deveraux Dr. CH44: Wall 6H 57
Deverell Gro. L15: Wav 8N 59
Deverell Rd. L15: Wav 9M 59
Deverill Rd. CH42: Rock F 7L 73
Devilla Cl. L14: Knott A 4E 60
De Villiers Av. L23: Crosb 6L 33
Devisdale Gro. CH43: Bid 1C 72
Devizes Cl. L25: Gate 1F 76
Devizes Dr. CH61: Irby 9L 71
Devoke Av. WA11: St H 1K 49
Devon Av. CH45: Wall 4J 57
WN8: Uph 6L 31
Devon Cl. L23: Blun 7G 33
Devon Ct. *L5: Liv* *4F 58*
(off Tynemouth Cl.)
Devondale Rd. L18: Moss H 3M 75
Devon Dr. CH61: Pens 3M 87
Devon Farm Way L37: Form 1H 25
Devonfield Rd. L9: Walt 5E 44
Devon Gdns. CH42: Rock F 7M 73
L16: Child 3C 76
Devon Pl. WA8: Wid 5K 79
Devonport St. L8: Liv 3E 74
Devon Rd. M31: Part 7L 69
M44: Cad 4K 69
Devonshire Cl. CH43: Oxton 3H 73
L33: Kirkb 7C 36
Devonshire Gdns. WA12: Newt W 8L 51
Devonshire M. *L8: Liv* *3G 74*
(off Devonshire Rd.)
DEVONSHIRE PARK 5J 73
Devonshire Pl. CH43: Oxton 3G 72
L5: Liv 3D 58
(not continuous)
WA7: Run 5K 95
Devonshire Rd. CH43: Oxton 3H 73
CH44: Wall 5H 57
(not continuous)
CH48: W Kir 7D 70
CH49: Upton 3M 71
CH61: Pens 3M 87
L8: Liv 3F 74
L22: Water 9J 33
PR9: South 7M 7
WA1: Padg 9G 67
WA10: St H 5G 48
Devonshire Rd. W. L8: Liv 3F 74
Devon St. L3: Liv 3J 5 (7D 58)
WA10: St H 6G 49
Devonwall Gdns. L8: Liv 3G 74
Devon Way L16: Child 2C 76
L36: Huy 5L 61
(not continuous)
Dewar Ct. WA7: Ast 4A 96
Dewar St. WA3: Ris 4M 67
Dewberry Cl. CH42: Tran 4K 73
Dewberry Flds. WN8: Uph 5L 31
Dewey Av. L9: Ain 2G 45
Dewhurst Rd. WA3: Birchw 6L 67
Dewlands Rd. L21: Sea 2M 43
Dewsbury Rd. L4: Walt 3G 59
Dexter St. L8: Liv 2D 74
Dexter Way WN8: Uph 6L 31
Deycroft Av. L33: Kirkb 7E 36
Deycroft Wlk. L33: Kirkb 7E 36
Deyes Ct. L31: Mag 2K 35
Deyes End L31: Mag 2K 35
Deyes La. L31: Mag 2J 35
(not continuous)
Deysbrook La. L12: W Der 3A 60
Deysbrook Side L12: W Der 3A 60
Deysbrook Way L12: W Der 1B 60
Dial Rd. CH42: Tran 5K 73
Dial St. L7: Liv 7H 59
WA1: Warr 3D 82
Diamond Bus. Pk. WA11: Rainf 6E 38
Diamond Jubilee Rd. L40: Ruf 2N 15
Diamond St. L5: Liv 5C 58
Diana Rd. L20: Boot 3C 44
Diana St. L4: Walt 1F 58
Diane Ho. L8: Liv 9K 5
Diane Rd. WN4: Ash M 6M 41
Dibbinsdale Rd. CH63: Brom 7A 90
Dibbins Grn. CH63: Brom 9A 90
Dibbins Hey CH63: Spit 5N 89
Dibbinview Gro. CH63: Spit 5A 90
Dibb La. L23: Lit C 4J 33
Dicconson's La. L39: Hals 1H 27
Dicconson St. WA10: St H 6K 49
Dicconson Way L39: Orm 9E 20
Dickens Av. CH43: Pren 7F 72
Dickens Cl. CH43: Pren 7F 72
L32: Kirkb 2B 46
Dickenson St. L1: Liv 8F 4 (9C 58)
WA2: Warr 1D 82
Dickens Rd. WA10: St H 1F 62
Dickens St. L8: Liv 2E 74
Dicket's La. WN8: Skel 1K 29
Dickinson Cl. L37: Form 2F 24
WA11: Hay 4C 50
Dickinson Ct. PR8: Birkd 4N 11
Dickinson Rd. L37: Form 2F 24
Dick's La. L40: Westh 9J 21
Dickson Cl. WA8: Wid 8L 79
Dickson St. L3: Liv 5A 58
WA8: Wid 8K 79
(not continuous)
Didcot Cl. L25: Hunts X 8H 77
Didsbury Cl. L33: Kirkb 9D 36
Digg La. CH46: More 8L 55
Digital Way L7: Liv 7J 59
Dig La. WA2: Fearn 5J 67
WA6: Frod 7K 107
DIGMOOR 6G 31
Digmoor Dr. WN8: Skel 5E 30
Digmoor Rd. L32: Kirkb 3D 46
WN8: Skel 5F 30
Digmoor Wlk. L32: Kirkb 3D 46
Dignum Mead L27: N'ley 3J 77
Dilloway St. WA10: St H 6H 49
Dinaro Cl. L25: Gate 4G 77
Dinas La. L36: Huy 5E 60
Dinas La. Pde. L14: Huy 5E 60
Dinesen Rd. L19: Garst 9A 76
DINGLE 5E 74
Dingle, The WA13: Lymm 5E 84
Dingle Av. WA12: Newt W 8H 51
WN8: Uph 4L 31
Dingle Bank Cl. WA13: Lymm 5E 84
Dinglebrook Rd. L9: Ain 7H 45
Dingle Brow L8: Liv 5F 74
Dingle Cl. L39: Augh 3A 28
Dingle Grange *L8: Liv* *5F 74*
(off Dingle Brow)
Dingle Gro. L8: Liv 4F 74
Dingle La. L8: Liv 5F 74
WA4: App 1G 98
Dingle Mt. L8: Liv 5F 74
Dingle Rd. CH42: Tran 4J 73
L8: Liv 5E 74
WN8: Uph 4L 31
Dingle Va. L8: Liv 5F 74
Dingleway WA4: App 8E 82
Dingley Av. L9: Walt 4E 44
Dingwall Dr. CH49: Grea 5L 71
Dinmore Rd. CH44: Wall 5H 57
Dinnington Ct. WA8: Wid 5H 79
Dinorben Av. WA9: St H 2M 63
Dinorwic Rd. L4: Walt 3F 58
PR8: Birkd 3N 11
Dinsdale Rd. CH62: Brom 5D 90
Dipping Brook Av. WA4: App 3F 98
Discovery Rd. L19: Garst 3B 92
Ditchfield L37: Form 2G 25
Ditchfield Pl. WA8: Wid 8E 78
Ditchfield Rd. WA5: Penk 5G 81
WA8: Wid 8D 78
DITTON 9E 78
Ditton Ct. WA8: Hale B 2F 94
Ditton La. CH46: Leas 6L 55

Ditton Rd. WA8: Wid 1F 94
Dixon Av. WA12: Newt W 5L 51
Dixon Cl. WA11: Hay 2J 51
Dixon M. L30: N'ton 7D 34
Dixon Rd. L33: Know I 1F 46
Dixon St. M44: Irlam 1M 69
WA1: Warr 3B 82
Dobbs Dr. L37: Form 9G 17
Dobers La. WA6: Frod, Newt 2M 115
Dobson St. L6: Liv 5F 58
Dobsons Way WA9: St H 1J 63
Dock Rd. CH41: Birke 7G 57
L19: Garst 2N 91
WA8: Wid 2J 95
(not continuous)
Dock Rd. Nth. CH62: Port S 1B 90
Dock Rd. Sth. CH62: Brom 3C 90
Docks Link CH44: Wall 6F 56
Dock St. CH65: Ell P 7A 104
WA8: Wid 2K 95
Dock Yd. Rd. CH65: Ell P 8B 104
Doctor's La. L37: Gt Alt 2L 25
Dodd Av. CH49: Grea 5L 71
WA10: St H 6F 48
Dodd Dr. WA4: Westy 5J 83
Doddridge Rd. L8: Liv 3D 74
Dodd's La. L31: Mag 1H 35
Dodleston Cl. CH43: Noct 4D 72
Dodman Rd. L11: Crox 5B 46
Dodson Cl. WN4: Ash M 8L 41
Dodworth Av. PR8: South 1D 12
Doeford Cl. WA3: Cul 5L 53
DOE GREEN 5F 80
Doe Mdw. WN8: Newb 4D 22
(not continuous)
Doe Pk. Courtyard L25: Woolt 8F 76
Doe's Mdw. Rd. CH63: Brom 8A 90
DOG & GUN 7N 45
Dolan Ct. L25: Gate 9D 60
Dolly's La. PR9: South 7B 8
(not continuous)
Dolmans La. *WA1: Warr* *3C 82*
(off Bridge St.)
Dolomite Av. L24: Speke 1D 92
Dolphin Cres. CH66: Gt Sut 3K 111
Domar Cl. L32: Kirkb 1D 46
Dombey Pl. *L8: Liv* *2E 74*
(off Dombey St.)
Dombey St. L8: Liv 2E 74
Domingo Dr. L33: Kirkb 6B 36
Dominic Cl. L16: Child 9C 60
Dominic Rd. L16: Child 9C 60
Dominion St. L6: Liv 4H 59
Domino Ct. WA7: Manor P 3D 96
Domville L35: Whis 7B 62
Domville Cl. WA13: Lymm 5E 84
Domville Dr. CH49: Woodc 5A 72
Domville Rd. L13: Liv 8N 59
Donaldson Ct. L5: Liv 3F 58
Donaldson St. L5: Liv 3F 58
Donalds Way L17: Aig 7K 75
Doncaster Dr. CH49: Upton 2N 71
Donegal Rd. L13: Liv 6N 59
Donne Av. CH63: Spit 4M 89
Donne Cl. CH63: Spit 4N 89
Donnington Cl. L36: Roby 9H 61
WN7: Leigh 1L 53
Donnington Lodge PR8: South 9E 6
Donsby Rd. L9: Ain 4G 44
Don Wlk. CH65: Ell P 7M 103
Dood's La. WA4: App 2H 99
Dooley Dr. L30: N'ton 7G 34
Doon Cl. L4: Kirkd 1D 58
Dorans La. L2: Liv 5E 4 (8B 58)
Dorbett Dr. L23: Crosb 9M 33
Dorchester Cl. CH49: Upton 4N 71
Dorchester Dr. L33: Kirkb 6E 36
Dorchester Pk. CH43: Noct 5D 72
WA7: Nort 4F 96
Dorchester Park Local Nature Reserve 4F 96
Dorchester Rd. L25: Gate 2F 76
WA5: Gt San 3K 81
WN8: Uph 5K 31
Dorchester Way CH43: Noct 5D 72
WA5: Burtw 3H 65
Doreen Av. CH46: More 9L 55
Dorgan Cl. L35: Rainh 5E 62
Doric Av. WA6: Frod 7M 107
Doric Grn. WN5: Bil 9N 31
Doric Rd. L13: Liv 5M 59
Doric St. CH42: Rock F 6M 73
L21: Sea 3M 43
Dorien Rd. L13: Liv 7L 59
Dorincourt CH43: Oxton 4G 72
Dorking Gro. L15: Wav 2N 75
Dorney Cl. WA4: App 1F 98
Dorney Ct. L12: W Der 1B 60
Dorothea Cl. WA8: Wid 4A 80
Dorothea St. WA2: Warr 1D 82
Dorothy Dr. L7: Liv 8G 59
Dorothy St. L7: Liv 8G 59
WA9: St H 2H 63
Dorringo Dr. L11: Norr G 8M 45
Dorrington Cl. WA7: Murd 7F 96
Dorrington Wlk. *L5: Liv* *5D 58*
(off Roscommon St.)
Dorrit St. L8: Liv 2E 74
Dorset Av. L15: Wav 1J 75
PR8: Ains 3J 17
Dorset Cl. L20: Boot 7C 44
Dorset Ct. L25: Gate 2F 76
Dorset Dr. CH61: Pens 3M 87
Dorset Gdns. CH42: Rock F 7M 73
WA7: Pal F 9C 96
Dorset Rd. CH45: New B 2G 57
CH48: W Kir 5D 70
L6: Liv 3J 59
L36: Huy 6L 61
M44: Cad 4K 69
WA10: St H 9G 48
Dorset Way WA1: Wools 9J 67
Double Cop WN7: Leigh 1L 53
Dougals Way WN7: Leigh 1J 53
Doughton Grn. WA8: Wid 5H 79
Douglas Av. WA9: Bold 3D 64
WN5: Bil 8N 39
WN8: Uph 5L 31
Douglas Cl. L13: Liv 5L 59
L40: Ruf 3N 15
WA8: Wid 5B 80
Douglas Dr. CH46: More 9L 55
L31: Mag 1L 35
L39: Orm 6B 20
Douglas Pl. L20: Boot 8A 44
Douglas Rd. CH48: W Kir 5E 70
L4: Walt 3G 59
PR9: South 3A 8
Douglas St. CH41: Birke 2L 73
WA10: St H 7G 49
Douglas Way L33: Kirkb 5D 36
Doulton Cl. CH43: Bid 1B 72
WA4: Warr 6D 82
Doulton Pl. L35: Whis 7N 61
Doulton St. WA10: St H 7G 48
Doune Ct. CH65: Ell P 2B 112
Dounrey Cl. WA2: Fearn 7H 67
Douro Pl. L13: Liv 7L 59
Douro St. L5: Liv 1H 5 (5D 58)
Dove Cl. CH2: Elt 1N 113
CH66: Ell P 7M 103
WA3: Birchw 5N 67
WA6: Hel 9F 106
DOVECOT 5D 60
Dovecot Av. L14: Knott A 6D 60
Dovecote Dr. WA11: Hay 3E 50
Dovecote Grn. WA5: Westb 8J 65
Dovecot Pl. *L14: Knott A* *5D 60*
(off Dovecot Av.)
Dove Ct. L25: Woolt 5F 76
Dovedale Av. CH62: East 1D 102
L31: Mag 1H 35
Dovedale Cl. CH43: Pren 6F 72
WA2: Warr 6F 66
Dovedale Ct. WA8: Wid 5E 78
Dovedale Cres. WN4: Ash M 3J 41
Dovedale Rd. CH45: Wall 2G 56
CH47: Hoy 9C 54
L18: Moss H 3L 75
WN4: Ash M 4J 41
Dovepoint Rd. CH47: Meols 8F 54
Dovercliffe Rd. L13: Liv 6N 59
Dover Cl. CH41: Birke 1K 73
WA7: Murd 9G 96
Dover Ct. CH65: Ell P 3B 112
Dovercroft L25: Woolt 6D 76
Dover Dr. CH65: Ell P 3B 112
Dover Gro. L16: Child 9D 60
Dove Rd. L9: Walt 4E 44
Dover Rd. L31: Mag 5H 35
PR8: Birkd 4L 11
WA4: Westy 5H 83
Dover St. L3: Liv 5K 5 (8E 58)
WA7: Run 4L 95
Dovesmead Rd. CH60: Hesw 8C 88
Dovestone Cl. L7: Liv 9G 59
Dove St. L8: Liv 1G 74
Dovey St. L8: Liv 3F 74
Doward St. WA8: Wid 6M 79
Dowhills Dr. L23: Blun 6H 33
Dowhills Pk. L23: Blun 5H 33
Dowhills Rd. L23: Blun 5H 33
DOWNALL GREEN 7F 40
Downall Grn. WN4: Garsw 6F 40
Downall Grn. Rd. WN4: Ash M 6G 40
Downbrook Way *WN4: Ash M* *6M 41*
(off North St.)
Downes Grn. CH63: Spit 6N 89
Downgreen Cl. L32: Kirkb 1A 46
Downham Av. WA3: Cul 8N 53
Downham Cl. L25: Woolt 3D 76
Downham Dr. CH60: Hesw 7A 88
Downham Grn. L25: Woolt 3D 76
Downham Rd. CH42: Tran 5K 73
Downham Rd. Nth. CH61: Hesw 5A 88
Downham Rd. Sth. CH60: Hesw 7A 88
Downham Wlk. WN5: Bil 2N 39
Downham Way L25: Woolt 3D 76
DOWNHOLLAND 2D 26
Downholland Bri. Bus. Pk.
L39: Down 2G 26
DOWNHOLLAND CROSS 2G 26
Downholland Moss La. L37: Form 9H 17
Downing Cl. CH43: Oxton 5H 73
Downing Rd. L20: Boot 8C 44
Downing St. L5: Liv 4F 58
Downlands Rd. L27: N'ley 4K 77
Downland Way WA9: St H 9B 50
Downs, The L23: Blun 8H 33
Downside WA8: Wid 5E 78
Downside Cl. L30: N'ton 7D 34
Downside Dr. L10: Ain 1L 45
Downs Rd. WA7: Run 6K 95
Downway La. WA9: St H 8G 49
Dowsefield La. L18: Aller 5C 76
Dragon Cl. L11: Crox 6A 46
WN8: Skel 4H 31
Dragon Cres. L35: Whis 5C 62
Dragon Dr. L35: Whis 6B 62
Dragon La. L35: Whis 7A 62
Dragon Wlk. *L11: Crox* *6A 46*
(off Dragon Cl.)
Dragon Yd. WA8: Wid 4L 79
Drake Av. M44: Cad 3L 69
Drake Cl. L10: Faz 3M 45
L35: Whis 7B 62
L39: Augh 2A 28
WA5: Old H 8M 65
Drake Cres. L10: Faz 3L 45
Drakefield Rd. L11: Norr G 7K 45
Drake Gdns. WA9: St H 3H 63
Drake Pl. L10: Faz 3L 45
Drake Rd. CH46: Leas 5B 56
CH64: Nest 5E 100
L10: Faz 3L 45
Drake St. L20: Boot 9A 44
WA10: St H 6G 49
Drake Way L10: Faz 3M 45
Drapers Ct. WA3: Low 3G 52
Draw Well Rd. L33: Know I 9H 37
Draycott St. L8: Liv 5E 74
Drayton Cl. CH61: Irby 2L 87
WA5: Gt San 2K 81
WA7: Run 6J 95
Drayton Cres. WA11: St H 4N 49
Drayton Rd. CH44: Wall 6K 57
L4: Walt 8F 44
Dream 7M 63
Drennan Rd. L19: Aller 8C 76
Drewell Rd. L18: Moss H 5L 75
Drewitt Cres. PR9: South 3B 8
Driffield Rd. L34: Presc 3N 61
Drinkwater Gdns. L3: Liv 1H 5 (6D 58)
Drive, The L12: W Der 4N 59
WA13: Lymm 7K 85
DriveTime (Golf Driving Range) 6B 82
Driveway L35: Whis 6C 62
Droitwich Av. CH49: Grea 4K 71
Dromore Av. L18: Moss H 5M 75
Dronfield Way L25: Gate 1D 76
(not continuous)
Drovers La. WA6: Frod 1M 115
Droxford Dr. L25: Gate 1D 76
Druids Cross Gdns. L18: Moss H 4B 76
Druids Cross Rd. L18: Moss H 4B 76
Druids Pk. L18: Moss H 4C 76
Druid St. WN4: Ash M 9L 41
Druidsville Rd. L18: Moss H 4C 76
Druids Way CH49: Woodc 6A 72
Drum Cl. L14: Knott A 4E 60
DRUMMERSDALE 7A 14
Drummersdale La. L40: Scar 5M 13
Drummer's La. WN4: Ash M 4F 40
Drummond Av. CH66: Gt Sut 1H 111
Drummond Ct. WA8: Wid 6N 79
Drummond Rd. CH47: Hoy 3B 70
L4: Walt 9H 45
L23: Thorn 6A 34
Drummoyne Ct. L23: Blun 6G 33
Druridge Dr. WA5: Penk 4H 81
Drury La. L2: Liv 5D 4 (8B 58)
Drybeck Gro. WA9: St H 3N 63
Dryburgh Way *L4: Kirkd* *1D 58*
(off Bradwell St.)
Dryden Av. WN4: Ash M 4H 41
Dryden Cl. CH43: Bid 1C 72
L35: Whis 6B 62
Dryden Gro. L36: Huy 8K 61
Dryden Pl. WA2: Warr 7D 66
Dryden Rd. L7: Liv 8K 59
Dryden St. L5: Liv 5C 58
L20: Boot 5N 43
Dryfield Cl. CH49: Grea 4L 71
Dublin Cft. CH66: Gt Sut 4K 111
Dublin St. L3: Liv 5A 58
Ducie St. L8: Liv 2G 74
Duckinfield St. L3: Liv 6K 5 (8E 58)
Duck Pond La. CH42: Tran 6G 73
Duckworth Gro. WA2: Padg 8H 67
Duddingston Av. L18: Moss H 3M 75
L23: Crosb 9L 33
Duddon Av. L31: Mag 1L 35
Duddon Cl. CH43: Oxton 5F 72
Dudleston Rd. CH66: Lit Sut 8G 103
Dudley Av. WA7: Run 5N 95
Dudley Cl. CH43: Oxton 4H 73
Dudley Cres. CH65: Hoot 3G 103
Dudley Gro. L23: Crosb 9L 33
Dudley Pl. WA9: St H 7N 49
Dudley Rd. CH45: New B 1G 57
CH65: Ell P 9N 103
L18: Moss H 3L 75
M44: Cad 5K 69
Dudley St. WA2: Warr 1C 82
WN4: Ash M 6J 41
Dudlow Ct. L18: Moss H 3A 76
Dudlow Dr. L18: Moss H 3A 76
Dudlow Gdns. L18: Moss H 3A 76
Dudlow Grn. Rd. WA4: App 2E 98
Dudlow La. L18: Moss H 2N 75
Dudlow Nook Rd. L18: Moss H 2A 76
DUDLOW'S GREEN 2F 98
Dugdale Cl. L19: Gras 9M 75
Duke Av. PR8: South 2B 12
Duke Cl. WA7: Run 5J 95
Duke of York Cotts. CH62: Port S 1N 89
Dukesbridge Ct. *WA13: Lymm* *5E 84*
(off New Rd.)
Dukes Rd. L5: Liv 3D 58
Dukes Ter. L1: Liv 7H 5 (9D 58)
Duke St. CH41: Birke 8J 57
CH45: New B 1H 57
L1: Liv 7F 4 (9C 58)
L19: Garst 1A 92
L22: Water 2K 43
L34: Presc 3A 62
L37: Form 2E 24
(not continuous)
PR8: South 9F 6
WA3: Golb 1B 52
WA10: St H 6J 49
WA12: Newt W 7K 51
WN4: Ash M 8L 41
Duke St. Bri. CH41: Birke 8J 57
Duke St. La. L1: Liv 7F 4 (9C 58)
Dukes Way L37: Form 2F 24
Dukes Wharf WA7: Pres B 9G 97
Duke's Wood La. WN8: Skel 9G 30
Dulas Grn. L32: Kirkb 1E 46
Dulas Rd. L15: Wav 2N 75
L32: Kirkb 1E 46
Dulson Way L34: Presc 4L 61
Dulverton Rd. L17: Aig 8K 75
Dumbarton St. L4: Walt 9D 44
Dumbrees Gdns. L12: W Der 1C 60
Dumbrees Rd. L12: W Der 1C 60
Dumbreeze Gro. L34: Know 6H 47
Dumfries Way L33: Kirkb 5B 36
Dunacre Way L26: Halew 9K 77
Dunbabin Rd. L15: Wav 2N 75
L16: Child 2A 76
Dunbar Cl. CH66: Lit Sut 9H 103
Dunbar Ct. CH66: Lit Sut 9H 103
Dunbar Cres. PR8: Birkd 6M 11
Dunbar Rd. PR8: Birkd 4L 11
Dunbar St. L4: Walt 8E 44
Dunbeath Av. L35: Rainh 8G 63
Dunbeath Cl. L35: Rainh 8G 63
Dunblane Cl. WN4: Garsw 7E 40
Duncan Av. WA7: Run 6M 95
WA12: Newt W 5L 51
Duncan Cl. WA10: St H 8H 49
Duncan Dr. CH49: Grea 4L 71
Duncansby Cres. WA5: Gt San 2G 80
Duncansby Dr. CH63: East 2B 102
Duncan St. CH41: Birke 2M 73
L1: Liv 9H 5 (1D 74)
WA2: Warr 1D 82
WA10: St H 7H 49
Dunchurch Rd. L14: Knott A 4D 60
Duncombe Rd. Nth. L19: Gras 9N 75
Duncombe Rd. Sth. L19: Garst 9N 75
Duncote Cl. CH43: Oxton 4G 72
L35: Whis 4D 62
Dundale Rd. L13: Liv 6N 59
Dundalk La. WA8: Wid 8G 79
Dundalk Rd. WA8: Wid 8G 79
Dundas St. L20: Boot 9A 44
Dundee Cl. WA2: Fearn 5F 66
Dundee Ct. CH65: Ell P 2C 112
Dundee Gro. CH44: Wall 6G 56
Dundonald Av. WA4: Stockt H 7D 82
Dundonald Rd. L17: Aig 7K 75
Dundonald St. CH41: Birke 9G 56
Dunedin St. WA9: St H 2H 63
Dunes Dr. L37: Form 9C 16
Dunes Splash World 8E 6
Dunes Way L5: Kirkd 3B 58
Dunfold Cl. L32: Kirkb 1D 46
Dungeon La. L24: Hale 5K 93
WN8: Dalt 6F 22
Dunham Av. WA3: Golb 1A 52
Dunham Cl. CH62: East 3E 102
Dunham Ct. WA6: Dun H 7B 114
DUNHAM HEATH 8D 114
DUNHAM-ON-THE-HILL 7B 114
Dunham Rd. L15: Wav 8N 59
WA13: Warb 1L 85
DUNHAM WOODHOUSES 4N 85
Dunkeld Cl. L6: Liv 1N 5 (6F 58)
Dunkerron Cl. L27: N'ley 1H 77
DUNKIRK 6K 111
Dunkirk Cres. CH65: Whit 4M 111
Dunkirk Dr. CH65: Whit 4N 111
Dunkirk La. CH1: Dunk 5H 111
CH65: Whit 4M 111
Dunkirk Rd. PR8: Birkd 4M 11
Dunkirk Trad. Est. CH1: Dunk 7K 111
Dunley Cl. *WA3: Birchw* *3A 68*
(off Rossendale Dr.)
Dunlin Av. WA12: Newt W 6L 51
Dunlin Cl. L27: N'ley 4J 77
WA2: Warr 6F 66
WA7: Beech 1B 108
Dunlin Ct. L25: Gate 3E 76
Dunlins Ct. CH45: Wall 1E 56
Dunlop Av. PR8: Ains 3J 17
Dunlop Dr. L31: Mell 7N 35
Dunlop Rd. L24: Speke 5G 92

Dunlop St. WA4: Warr 5C 82
Dunluce St. L4: Walt 9D 44
Dunmail Av. WA11: St H 1M 49
Dunmail Gro. WA7: Beech 2A 108
Dunmore Cres. CH66: Lit Sut 8G 103
Dunmore Rd. CH66: Lit Sut 8G 103
L13: Liv 6K 59
Dunmow Rd. WA4: Thel 5K 83
Dunmow Way L25: Hunts X 8G 77
Dunnerdale Rd. L11: Norr G 8M 45
Dunnett St. L20: Kirkd 9A 44
Dunning Cl. CH49: Upton 3M 71
Dunnings Bri. Rd. L30: N'ton 1D 44
Dunnings Wlk. L30: N'ton 7F 34
Dunnock Cl. L25: Gate 3E 76
WA2: Warr 6F 66
Dunnock Gro. WA3: Birchw 5M 67
Dunraven Rd. CH48: W Kir 6B 70
CH64: Lit N 7G 100
Dunriding La. WA10: St H 7G 48
Dunscar Cl. WA3: Birchw 4L 67
Dunscore Rd. WN3: Wins 1G 40
Dunscroft WA9: St H 2N 63
Dunsdale Dr. WN4: Ash M 8L 41
Dunsdon Cl. L25: Woolt 4C 76
Dunsdon Rd. L25: Woolt 3C 76
Dunsford WA8: Wid 5F 78
Dunsmore Cl. WA11: Hay 3E 50
Dunsop Av. WA9: Clock F 5N 63
Dunstall Cl. CH46: Leas 6M 55
Dunstan La. CH64: Burt 9L 101
L7: Liv 9H 59
Dunstan St. L15: Wav 9K 59
Dunster Gro. CH60: Hesw 8B 88
WA9: Sut L 5N 63
Dunster Rd. PR8: Birkd 6L 11
Durants Cotts. L31: Mag 4K 35
Durban Av. L23: Crosb 6L 33
Durban Rd. CH45: Wall 3H 57
L13: Liv 7N 59
Durden St. L7: Liv 1H 75
Dures Ct. CH43: Clau 2G 73
Durham Av. L30: N'ton 1E 44
Durham Cl. WA1: Wools 1M 83
Durham Ct. CH65: Ell P 2C 112
Durham Gro. M44: Cad 3J 69
Durham Mews E. L30: N'ton 1F 44
Durham Mews W.
L30: N'ton 1F 44
Durham Rd. L21: Sea 3M 43
WA8: Wid 5L 79
Durham St. L19: Garst 3B 92
WN8: Skel 2A 30
Durham Way L30: N'ton 1F 44
L36: Huy 6L 61
Durley Dr. CH43: Pren 7E 72
Durley Pk. Cl. CH43: Pren 8E 72
Durley Rd. L9: Ain 4G 45
Durlston Cl. WA8: Wid 6F 78
Durning Rd. L7: Liv 8H 59
Durrant Rd. L11: Norr G 1K 59
Durrell Way WA3: Low 2F 52
Dursley L35: Whis 7C 62
Dursley Dr. WN4: Ash M 7M 41
Durston Rd. L16: Child 9B 60
DUTTON 3J 109
Dutton Ct. WA1: Warr 3D 82
Dutton Dr. CH63: Spit 5M 89
Dutton Grn. CH2: Lit Stan 2D 112
Duxbury Cl. L31: Mag 9K 27
WA11: Rainf 4D 38
Duxford Ct. WA2: Padg 8F 66
Dwerryhouse La. L11: Norr G 8N 45
DW Fitness
Bromborough 5D 90
Halton 7M 79
St Helens 9K 49
Southport 7E 6
Warrington 3C 82
Dyers Cl. WA13: Lymm 4G 84
Dyers La. L39: Orm 9C 20
WA13: Lymm 4G 84
Dyer St. WA3: Golb 1A 52
Dyke St. L6: Liv 5F 58
Dykin Cl. WA8: Wid 5A 80
Dykin Rd. WA8: Wid 5N 79
Dylan Cl. L4: Walt 2E 58
Dymchurch Rd. L24: Speke 3F 92
Dymoke Rd. L11: Crox 7A 46
Dymoke Wlk. *L11: Crox* *7A 46*
(off Dymoke Rd.)
Dyson Hall Dr. L9: Faz 5J 45
Dyson St. L4: Walt 9E 44

E

Eager La. L31: Lyd 4G 27
Eagle Brow WA13: Lymm 5D 84
Eagle Cres. WA11: Rainf 5D 38
Eagle Dene L10: Faz 4M 45
Eaglehall Rd. L9: Faz 6L 45
Eaglehurst Rd. L25: Gate 4F 76
Eagle La. CH66: Lit Sut 7J 103
Eagle Mt. WA4: Warr 6D 82
Eagle Pk. Dr. WA2: Warr 8B 66
Eagles Ct. L32: Kirkb 9C 36
Eaglesfield Cl. WA9: St H 2N 63
Eagles Way WA7: Pal F 9A 96
Ealing Cl. WA7: Nort 6F 96
Ealing Rd. L9: Ain 3G 44
WA5: Gt San 3J 81
Eamont Av. PR9: South 2N 7
Eanleywood Farm Cl.
WA7: Nort 8E 96
Eanleywood La. WA7: Nort 8E 96
Eardisley Rd. L18: Moss H 2M 75
Earhart Cl. WN8: Skel 4H 31
Earle Av. L36: Roby 7F 60
Earle Cl. WA12: Newt W 7H 51
Earle Cres. CH64: Nest 5D 100
Earle Dr. CH64: Park 6D 100
Earle Rd. L7: Liv 9H 59
WA8: Wid 9M 79
EARLESTOWN 7K 51
Earlestown Station (Rail) 7K 51
Earle St. L3: Liv 3D 4 (7B 58)
WA12: Newt W 8H 51
(not continuous)
Earl Rd. L20: Boot 6C 44
Earl's Cl. L23: Crosb 8K 33
Earlsfield Rd. L15: Wav 2L 75
Earls Gdns. CH65: Ell P 9N 103
Earlston Rd. CH45: Wall 3G 57
Earl St. CH62: New F 8A 74
WA2: Warr 1C 82
WA9: St H 6M 49
Earls Way WA7: Pal F 8A 96
Earlswood WN8: Skel 3H 31
Earlswood Cl. CH46: More 9J 55
Earlwood Gdns. L35: Whis 7B 62
Earp St. L19: Garst 1A 92
Easby Cl. L37: Form 2G 25
WA7: Run 5M 95
Easby Rd. L4: Kirkd 2D 58
L5: Kirkd 2C 58
Easedale Dr. PR8: Ains 1H 17
Easedale Wlk. L33: Kirkb 6B 36
Easenhall Cl. WA8: Wid 4L 79
Easington Rd. WA9: St H 3G 63
E. Albert Rd. L17: Aig 4G 75
East Av. WA2: Warr 9D 66
WA3: Golb 1D 52
WA4: Stockt H 7E 82
WA5: Gt San 4J 81
East Bank CH42: Tran 5J 73
Eastbank Ho. *PR8: South* *9G 6*
(off Eastbank St.)
Eastbank St. PR8: South 8G 6
Eastbank St. Sq. PR8: South 8G 6
Eastbourne M. *L9: Ain* *3G 44*
(off Eastbourne Rd.)
Eastbourne Rd. CH41: Birke 2J 73
L9: Ain 3G 44
L22: Water 9H 33
PR8: Birkd 3N 11
Eastbourne Wlk. L6: Liv 1K 5 (5E 58)
Eastbury Cl. WA8: Wid 3M 79
Eastcliffe Rd. L13: Liv 6N 59
East Cl. L34: Eccl P 2D 62
Eastcote Rd. L19: Aller 8A 76
Eastcott Cl. CH49: Grea 5K 71
Eastcroft Rd. CH44: Wall 6J 57
Eastdale Rd. L15: Wav 9L 59
WA1: Padd 1H 83
E. Damwood Rd. L24: Speke 5K 93
Eastdene WN8: Parb 3E 22
Easter Ct. WA5: Westb 7K 65
Eastern Av. CH62: Brom 3C 90
L24: Speke 5K 93
Eastern Dr. L19: Gras 9M 75
E. Farm M. CH48: Caldy 8G 70
Eastfield Dr. L17: Aig 5H 75
Eastfield Wlk. L32: Kirkb 1N 45
E. Float Quay CH41: Birke 8K 57
Eastford Rd. WA4: Warr 7A 82
East Front L35: Whis 8B 62
Eastgate Rd. WA7: Manor P 2G 96
Eastgate Way WA7: Manor P 3F 96
EAST GILLIBRANDS 4D 30
EASTHAM 1D 102
Eastham Cl. L16: Child 8D 60
Eastham Country Pk. 7F 90
Eastham Cres. WA9: Clock F 5L 63
EASTHAM FERRY 7F 90
Eastham Lodge Golf Course 9F 90
Eastham M. CH62: East 2F 102
Eastham Rake CH62: East 4B 102
Eastham Rake Station (Rail) 3C 102
Eastham Village Rd. CH62: East 1F 102
Eastlake Av. L5: Liv 4E 58
E. Lancashire Rd. L11: Crox, Norr G 7K 45
L33: Know I 4D 46
L34: Know 4D 46
WA3: Golb, Low 3A 52
WA10: Eccl, St H, Windle 3A 48
WA11: Hay, St H 3A 48
WA12: Newt W 3A 48
WN7: Leigh 3A 52
East La. L29: Thorn 1A 34
WA7: Pal F 8B 96
Eastleigh WN8: Skel 3G 31
Eastleigh Dr. CH61: Irby 9L 71
East Mains L24: Speke 4L 93
Eastman Rd. L13: Liv 2K 59
East Mead L39: Augh 2N 27
East Meade L31: Mag 1H 35
E. Millwood Rd. L24: Speke 3K 93
East O' Hills Cl. CH60: Hesw 6A 88
Easton Cl. WN3: Wigan 1J 41
Easton Rd. CH62: New F 8A 74
L36: Huy 7E 60
E. Orchard La. L9: Ain 3J 45
EAST PIMBO 8J 31
E. Prescot Rd. L14: Knott A 6A 60
East Quay L3: Liv 9E 4 (1B 74)
East Rd. L14: Broad G 7A 60
L24: Halew 2L 93
L31: Mag 2L 35
East Side WA9: St H 8M 49
Eastside Ind. Est. WA9: St H 8M 49
East St. CH41: Birke 7L 57
L3: Liv 3D 4 (7B 58)
L22: Water 1K 43
L34: Presc 3B 62
PR9: South 8J 7
WA8: Wid 7N 79
WN4: Ash M 7M 41
East Vw. WA4: Grap 6J 83
Eastview Cl. CH43: Noct 4D 72
East Village L1: Liv 8H 5
Eastway CH46: More 8M 55
CH49: Grea 4M 71
CH66: Lit Sut 7J 103
L31: Mag 1J 35
(not continuous)
WA7: Pal F 8B 96
WA8: Wid 7G 78
Eastwell Rd. WN4: Ash M 8J 41
Eastwood L17: Aig 5F 74
WA7: Wind H 5E 96
Eastwood Av. WA12: Newt W 7A 52
Eastwood Rd. WA5: Burtw 2H 65
Eaton Av. CH44: Wall 5J 57
L20: Boot *5C 44*
(off Aughton Rd.)
L21: Lith 3A 44
Eaton Cl. L12: W Der 2M 59
L36: Roby 7H 61
Eaton Dr. PR8: South 9H 7
Eaton Gdns. L12: W Der 5B 60
Eaton Grange L12: W Der 4A 60
Eaton Rd. CH43: Oxton 3H 73
CH48: W Kir 7B 70
L12: W Der 2N 59
(not continuous)
L19: Gras 1M 91
L31: Mag 5J 35
WA10: St H 4G 49
Eaton Rd. Nth. L12: W Der 2M 59
Eaton St. CH44: Wall 4H 57
L3: Liv 1D 4 (6B 58)
L34: Presc 2A 62
WA7: Run 5K 95
EAVES BROW 2J 67
Eaves Brow Rd. WA3: Croft 2J 67
Eavesdale WN8: Skel 4H 31
Eaves La. WA9: St H 3N 63
Ebenezer Howard Rd. L21: Ford 9B 34
Ebenezer Pl. WA1: Warr 3B 82
Ebenezer St. CH42: Rock F 6N 73
WA11: Hay 4B 50
Eberle St. L2: Liv 4E 4 (7B 58)
Ebony Cl. CH46: More 9J 55
Ebony Way L33: Kirkb 6C 36
Ebor La. L5: Liv 5D 58
Ebrington St. L19: Garst 1A 92
Ecclesall Av. L21: Lith 2C 44
Eccles Dr. L25: Gate 1F 76
Ecclesfield Rd. WA10: Eccl 5D 48
Eccles Gro. WA9: Clock F 6A 64
Eccleshall Rd. CH62: Port S 1B 90
Eccleshill Rd. L13: Liv 4M 59
Eccles Rd. L37: Form 3D 24
ECCLESTON 5F 48
Eccleston Av. CH62: Brom 6B 90
CH66: Ell P 9K 103
Eccleston Cl. CH43: Oxton 5F 72
WA3: Birchw 4K 67
Eccleston Dr. WA7: Run 6M 95
Eccleston Gdns. WA10: St H 9D 48
ECCLESTON PARK 2D 62
Eccleston Pk. Dr. L35: Rainh 3E 62
Eccleston Park Golf Course 3E 62
Eccleston Park Station (Rail) 3D 62
Eccleston Pk. Trade Cen. WA10: St H 1E 62
Eccleston Rd. L9: Walt 4E 44
Eccleston St. L34: Presc 3A 62
WA10: St H 7H 49
Echo Arena 9D 4 (1B 74)
Echo La. CH48: W Kir 7D 70
Edale Cl. CH62: East 1D 102
WA1: Warr 3F 82
Edale Rd. L18: Moss H 4N 75
Edburton Ct. WA3: Golb 2B 52
Eddisbury Rd. CH44: Wall 4J 57
CH47: Hoy 4B 70
CH48: W Kir 4B 70
CH66: Whit 3L 111
Eddisbury Sq. WA6: Frod 6L 107
Eddisbury Way L12: W Der 2M 59
Eddisford Dr. WA3: Cul 5L 53
Eddleston St. WN4: Ash M 5H 41
Edelsten St. WA5: Warr 3A 82
Eden Av. PR9: South 4L 7
WA11: Rainf 4B 38
Edenbridge Gdns. WA4: App 4F 98
Eden Cl. CH66: Gt Sut 9H 103
L33: Kirkb 5D 36
L35: Rainh 7E 62
Edendale WA8: Wid 6E 78
Eden Dr. Nth. L23: Crosb 8N 33
Eden Dr. Sth. L23: Crosb 8N 33
Edenfield Cl. PR8: South 3D 12
Edenfield Cres. L36: Huy 6K 61
Edenfield Rd. L15: Wav 2L 75
Edenhall Dr. L25: Woolt 5G 77
Edenhurst WN8: Skel 4H 31
Edenhurst Av. CH44: Wall 4J 57
L16: Child 9E 60
Edenhurst Cl. L37: Form 2C 24
Edenhurst Ct. *L36: Huy* *5F 60*
(off Harrington Rd.)
Edenhurst Dr. L37: Form 2C 24
Edenpark Rd. CH42: Tran 5J 73
Eden Sq. L2: Liv 3E 4
Eden St. L8: Liv 1G 75
Eden Va. L30: N'ton 7D 34
Edgar Ct. CH41: Birke 1K 73
L21: Lith 1A 44
Edgars Dr. WA2: Fearn 8H 67
Edgar St. L3: Liv 1F 4 (6C 58)
Edgbaston Cl. L36: Roby 8G 61
Edgbaston Way CH43: Bid 9C 56
Edgefield Cl. CH43: Noct 4D 72
Edgefold Rd. L32: Kirkb 1D 46
Edge Grn. La. WA3: Golb 9N 41 & 1A 52
Edge Grn. St. WN4: Ash M 7M 41
Edge Gro. L7: Liv 7J 59
EDGE HILL 9G 58
Edgehill Rd. CH46: More 9K 55
Edge Hill Station (Rail) 9H 59
Edge Hill University
Ormskirk Campus 1E 28
Edge La. L7: Liv 8G 58
L13: Liv 8G 58
L23: Thorn 5N 33
Edge La. Dr. L13: Liv 7M 59
Edge La. Retail Pk. L13: Liv 7L 59
Edgeley Gdns. L9: Walt 4E 44
Edgemoor Cl. CH43: Bid 1B 72
L12: W Der 4B 60
L23: Thorn 6A 34
Edgemoor Dr. CH61: Irby 9K 71
L10: Faz 3M 45
L23: Thorn 6N 33
Edgemoor Rd. L12: W Der 4B 60
Edgerley Pl. WN4: Ash M 8J 41
Edgerton Rd. WA3: Low 2G 52
Edge St. WA9: St H 3F 62
Edgeware Gro. WN3: Wins 1F 40
Edgewater Pl. WA4: Westy 4J 83
Edgeway Rd. WN3: Wigan 2J 41
Edgewell Dr. L15: Wav 9N 59
Edgewood Cl. WA8: Wid 8E 78
Edgewood Dr. CH62: Brom 1C 102
Edgewood Rd. CH47: Meols 8E 54
CH49: Upton 2N 71
Edgeworth Cl. WA9: St H 1A 64
Edgeworth Rd. WA3: Golb 1A 52
Edgeworth St. WA2: Warr 2B 82
WA9: St H 2A 64
Edgley Dr. L39: Orm 8E 20
Edgworth Rd. L4: Walt 3G 58
Edinburgh Cl. L30: N'ton 2F 44
Edinburgh Ct. CH65: Ell P 2B 112
Edinburgh Dr. CH43: Pren 7G 72
L36: Huy 9L 61
Edinburgh Rd. CH45: Wall 4H 57
L7: Liv 3N 5 (7F 58)
(not continuous)
L37: Form 3E 24
WA8: Wid 8E 78
Edington St. L15: Wav 9K 59
Edison Rd. WA7: Ast 4N 95
Edith Rd. CH44: Wall 6L 57
L4: Walt 3F 58
L20: Boot 4C 44
Edith St. WA7: Run 4J 95
WA9: St H 2B 64
Edmondson St. WA9: St H 7B 50
Edmonton Cl. L5: Kirkd 3C 58
Edmund Ct. CH62: Brom 4C 90
Edmund St. L3: Liv 4D 4 (7B 58)
Edna Av. L10: Faz 3M 45
Edrich Av. CH43: Bid 9C 56
Edward Dr. WN4: Ash M 7K 41
Edward Gdns. WA1: Wools 2N 83
Edward Jenner Av. L30: N'ton 8E 34
Edward Manton Cl. CH63: Hghr B 1J 89
Edward Pav. L3: Liv 7D 4 (9B 58)
Edward Rd. CH47: Hoy 2D 70
L35: Whis 4C 62
WA5: Gt San 2F 80
Edward's La. L24: Speke 1F 92
Edward's La. Ind. Est.
L24: Speke 2F 92
Edward St. CH65: Ell P 7A 104
WA8: Wid 7N 79
WA9: St H 9N 49
WA11: Hay 4C 50
Edwards Way WA8: Wid 8F 78
Edwin St. WA8: Wid 7M 79
Effingham St. L20: Boot 9A 44
Egan Ct. *CH41: Birke* *1L 73*
(off Lord St.)
Egan Rd. CH43: Bid 9E 56
Egbert Rd. CH47: Meols 9D 54
Egdon Cl. WA8: Wid 6A 80
Egerton WN8: Skel 4G 31

Egerton Av. WA1: Warr 1F 82
(not continuous)
WA13: Warb 9J 69
Egerton Ct. CH41: Birke 1L 73
Egerton Dr. CH48: W Kir 6C 70
Egerton Gdns. CH42: Rock F 7L 73
Egerton Gro. CH45: Wall 4H 57
Egerton Ho. WA7: Run 4L 95
Egerton M. WA4: Stockt H 7D 82
Egerton Pk. CH42: Rock F 7L 73
Egerton Pk. Cl. CH42: Rock F 7L 73
Egerton Rd. CH43: Clau 2G 72
CH62: New F 9A 74
L15: Wav 1J 75
L34: Presc 3N 61
WA13: Lymm 6C 84
Egerton St. CH45: New B 1H 57
CH65: Ell P 8A 104
L8: Liv 9L 5 (1E 74)
WA1: Warr 3E 82
WA4: Stockt H 7D 82
WA7: Run 4J 95
WA9: St H 9N 49
Egerton Wharf CH41: Birke 9L 57
Eglington Av. L35: Whis 7A 62
EGREMONT 4K 57
Egremont Cl. L27: N'ley 4L 77
Egremont Lawn L27: N'ley 4L 77
Egremont Prom. CH44: Wall 3K 57
CH45: Wall 3K 57
Egypt St. WA1: Warr 3B 82
WA8: Wid 9J 79
Eight Acre La. L37: Form 7G 17
(not continuous)
Eighth Av. L9: Ain 3J 45
Eilian Gro. L14: Knott A 7B 60
Elaine Cl. CH66: Gt Sut 1H 111
WA8: Wid 6M 79
WN4: Ash M 6M 41
Elaine Norris Sports Cen. 5B 58
Elaine Price Ct. WA7: Run 6J 95
Elaine St. L8: Liv 2E 74
WA1: Warr 1E 82
Elbow La. L37: Form 1F 24
Elbrus Dr. CH66: Ell P 7L 103
Elcombe Av. WA3: Low 3F 52
Elder Av. L40: Burs 2K 21
Elderberry Cl. L11: Crox 8A 46
Elderberry Wlk. *M31: Part* *6L 69*
(off Wood La.)
Elderdale Rd. L4: Walt 2G 59
Elderflower Rd. WA10: St H 5H 49
Elder Gdns. L19: Gras 8N 75
Elder Gro. CH48: W Kir 6C 70
Eldersfield Rd. L11: Norr G 8N 45
Elderswood L35: Rainh 5F 62
Elderwood Rd. CH42: Tran 5L 73
Eldon Cl. *WA10: St H* *8H 49*
(off Eldon St.)
Eldon Gdns. WN4: Ash M 5J 41
Eldon Gro. *L3: Liv* *5C 58*
(off Limekiln La.)
Eldonian Way L3: Liv 5B 58
Eldon Pl. L3: Liv 5B 58
Eldon Rd. CH42: Rock F 6M 73
CH44: Wall 5H 57
Eldons Cft. PR8: Ains 9K 11
Eldon St. L3: Liv 5B 58
WA1: Warr 3D 82
WA10: St H 8H 49
Eldon Ter. CH64: Nest 7E 100
Eldred Rd. L16: Child 2A 76
Eleanor Pk. CH43: Bid 9C 56
Eleanor Rd. CH43: Bid 8D 56
CH46: More 8K 55
L20: Boot 4C 44
Eleanor St. CH65: Ell P 8A 104
L20: Kirkd 9A 44
WA8: Wid 9K 79
Electric Av. L10: Faz 5N 45
L11: Crox 5A 46
Elephant La. WA9: St H 2G 63
Elfet St. CH41: Birke 9F 56
Elgar Av. CH62: East 1D 102
Elgar Cl. CH65: Gt Sut 2L 111
Elgar Rd. L14: Knott A 4D 60
Elgin Av. WA4: Warr 6B 82
WN4: Garsw 7F 40
Elgin Ct. L35: Rainh 7G 63
Elgin Dr. CH45: Wall 3J 57
Elgin Way CH41: Birke 1L 73
Eliot Cl. CH62: New F 9N 73
Eliot St. L20: Boot 5A 44
Elizabeth Av. PR8: Ains 8L 11
Elizabeth Ct. WA8: Wid 9L 79
Elizabeth Dr. WA1: Padg 9H 67
Elizabeth Rd. L10: Faz 3N 45
L20: Boot 4C 44
L36: Huy 9K 61
M31: Part 5M 69
WA11: Hay 3G 50
Elizabeth St. L3: Liv 4L 5 (7E 58)
WA9: Clock F 6A 64
WA9: St H 1A 64
Elizabeth Ter. WA8: Wid 7G 79
Eliza St. WA9: St H 2B 64
Elkan Cl. WA8: Wid 5A 80
Elkan Rd. WA8: Wid 5N 79
Elkin Ct. M31: Part 5N 69
Elkstone Cl. WN3: Wins 1E 40
Elkstone Rd. L11: Norr G 9N 45
Ellaby Rd. L35: Rainh 5F 62
Ellamsbridge Rd. WA9: St H 1A 64
Elland Dr. CH66: Lit Sut 9H 103
Ellel Gro. L6: Liv 4H 59
Ellencliffe Dr. L6: Liv 4H 59
Ellen Gdns. WA9: St H 1A 64
Ellens Cl. L6: Liv 3M 5 (7F 58)
Ellen's La. CH63: Beb 2A 90
Ellen St. WA5: Warr 1A 82
WA9: St H 2A 64
Elleray Dr. L8: Liv 4E 74
Elleray Pk. Rd. CH45: Wall 2G 56
Ellerbrook Dr. L40: Burs 2K 21
Ellerbrook Way L39: Orm 7C 20
Ellerby Cl. WA7: Murd 8G 96
Ellergreen Rd. L11: Norr G 8L 45
Ellerman Rd. L3: Liv 5D 74
(not continuous)
Ellerslie Av. L35: Rainh 4E 62
Ellerslie Rd. L13: Liv 3J 59
Ellerton Av. CH66: Lit Sut 9H 103
Ellerton Cl. WA8: Wid 5G 78
Ellerton Way L12: Crox 7C 46
Ellesmere Dr. L10: Ain 9H 35
Ellesmere Gro. CH45: Wall 3H 57
ELLESMERE PORT 9A 104
Ellesmere Port Golf Cen. 7G 103
Ellesmere Port Station (Rail) 9A 104
Ellesmere Rd. WA3: Cul 6M 53
WA4: Stockt H, Walt 7C 82
WN4: Ash M 6H 41
Ellesmere St. WA1: Warr 3D 82
(not continuous)
WA7: Run 5L 95
Ellesworth Cl. WA5: Old H 9L 65
Ellington Dr. WA5: Gt San 3K 81
Ellington Way WA9: St H 4J 63
Elliot Dr. L32: Kirkb 2B 46
Elliot St. L1: Liv 5G 5 (8C 58)
WA8: Wid 8L 79
WA10: St H 7H 49
Elliott Av. WA1: Warr 1F 82
WA3: Golb 1C 52
Elliott Gdns. WN6: Appl B 6N 23
Ellis Ashton St. L36: Huy 7L 61
Ellis La. WA6: Frod 5N 107
Ellison Dr. WA10: St H 6F 48
Ellison Gro. L36: Huy 7H 61
Ellison St. L13: Liv 5L 59
WA1: Warr 3D 82
WA4: Stockt H 7E 82
Ellis Pl. L8: Liv 3E 74
Ellis Rd. WN5: Bil 7N 39
Ellis St. WA8: Wid 9K 79
Ellon Av. L35: Rainh 7G 62
Elloway Rd. L24: Speke 4L 93
Ellwood Cl. L24: Hale 5B 94
Elmar Rd. L17: Aig 6K 75
(not continuous)
Elm Av. CH49: Upton 2L 71
L23: Crosb 6M 33
WA3: Golb 1B 52
WA8: Wid 6L 79
WA12: Newt W 8L 51
WN4: Garsw 6F 40
Elm Bank *L4: Walt* *2E 58*
(off Walton Breck Rd.)
Elmbank Rd. CH62: New F 1A 90
L18: Moss H 3K 75
Elmbank St. CH44: Wall 6J 57
Elmbridge Ct. WA3: Low 2G 52
Elm Cl. CH61: Pens 3A 88
L12: Crox 7D 46
M31: Part 6M 69
Elm Ct. CH63: Hghr B 1K 89
CH65: Ell P 1D 112
L23: Blun 7J 33
WN8: Skel 3B 30
Elmcroft Cl. L9: Ain 4J 45
Elmcroft La. L38: Hight 9G 24
Elmdale Cl. L37: Form 2D 24
Elmdale Rd. L9: Walt 6F 44
Elmdene Ct. CH49: Grea 6K 71
Elm Dr. CH49: Grea 5K 71
L21: Sea 4M 43
L37: Form 3D 24
WN5: Bil 6N 39
ELMERS GREEN 2G 31
Elmers Grn. WN8: Skel 2G 31
(not continuous)
Elmer's Grn. La. WN8: Dalt, Skel 8F 22
(not continuous)
Elmers Wood Rd. WN8: Skel 3G 31
Elmfield Cl. WA9: St H 1H 63
Elmfield Rd. L9: Walt 5F 44
Elm Gdns. *L21: Sea* *4N 43*
(off Elm Rd.)
WA11: Rainf 5C 38
Elm Grn. CH64: Will 6M 101
Elm Gro. CH42: Tran 4K 73
CH47: Hoy 1D 70
CH66: Whit 4M 111
L7: Liv 5N 5 (8F 58)
L34: Eccl P 2C 62
WA1: Padd 1G 83
WA8: Wid 7L 79
WN8: Skel 3B 30
Elm Hall Dr. L18: Moss H 3M 75
Elmham Cres. L10: Faz 3L 45
Elm Ho. *L22: Water* *1L 43*
(off Lorne Rd.)
L34: Presc 3N 61
Elm Ho. M. L25: Gate 4F 76
Elmhow Gro. WN3: Wigan 1J 41
Elmhurst CH42: Rock F 8M 73
Elmhurst Rd. L25: Gate 1E 76
Elmore Cl. L5: Liv 4E 58
WA7: Wind H 6F 96
ELM PARK 6H 59
Elm Pk. Dr. PR8: Ains 9L 11
Elm Pk. Rd. CH45: Wall 2G 57
Elm Pl. L39: Orm 9C 20
Elmridge WN8: Skel 3G 30
Elm Ri. WA6: Frod 7M 107
Elm Rd. CH42: Tran 6H 73
(Elm Rd. Nth.)
CH42: Tran 5K 73
(Walker M.)
CH61: Irby 1N 87
CH63: Hghr B 9M 73
CH64: Will 6M 101
L4: Walt 8F 44
L21: Sea 4M 43
L32: Kirkb 8B 36
L40: Burs 2J 21
PR8: South 2A 12
WA2: Win 5B 66
WA3: Rix 7G 69
WA5: Penk 4H 81
WA7: Run 7M 95
WA9: St H 1G 63
WA10: St H 1G 63
WA11: Hay 3G 51
Elm Rd. Nth. CH42: Tran 6H 73
Elms, The L8: Liv 4F 74
L31: Lyd 9J 27
PR8: South 1B 12
(Ash St.)
PR8: South 9E 6
(Beach Priory Gdns.)
WA3: Low 3G 53
WA7: Run 6J 95
Elmsbury St. WN4: Ash M 6H 41
Elmsdale Rd. L18: Moss H 3M 75
Elmsett Cl. WA5: Gt San 3G 80
Elmsfield Cl. L25: Gate 3E 76
Elmsfield Pk. L39: Augh 6M 27
Elmsfield Rd. L23: Thorn 5A 34
Elms Ho. Rd. L13: Liv 6L 59
Elmsley Ct. L18: Moss H 5M 75
Elmsley Rd. L18: Moss H 4L 75
Elms Pk. CH61: Thing 2A 88
Elms Rd. L31: Mag 5J 35
Elmstead WN8: Skel 4G 30
Elm St. CH41: Birke 2K 73
CH65: Ell P 7A 104
L36: Huy 7L 61
Elmswood Av. L35: Rainh 8G 63
Elmswood Ct. L18: Moss H 5L 75
Elmswood Gro. L36: Huy 6G 60
Elmswood Rd. CH42: Tran 4J 73
CH44: Wall 5K 57
L17: Aig 6J 75
L18: Moss H 6K 75
Elm Ter. CH47: Hoy 1D 70
L7: Liv 7H 59
Elm Tree Av. WA1: Padg 9G 67
WA13: Lymm 6D 84
Elmtree Cl. L12: W Der 2A 60
Elm Tree Ct. CH47: Hoy 9D 54
Elmtree Gro. CH43: Bid 9E 56
Elm Tree Rd. WA3: Low 2G 52
WA13: Lymm 6D 84
Elmure Av. CH63: Hghr B 2K 89
Elm Va. L6: Liv 5J 59
Elmway Cl. L13: Liv 7L 59
Elmwood WA7: Nort 6E 96
WN8: Skel 1F 30
Elmwood Av. L23: Crosb 6N 33
WA1: Warr 1F 82
WN4: Ash M 9J 41
Elmwood Dr. CH61: Hesw 5N 87
Elphin Gro. L4: Walt 9F 44
Elphins Dr. WA4: Warr 6D 82
Elric Wlk. L33: Kirkb 8D 36
Elsbeck Gro. WA9: St H 3N 63
Elsie Rd. L4: Walt 3G 58
Elsmere Av. L17: Aig 5H 75
Elson Rd. L37: Form 3D 24
Elstead Gro. WN4: Garsw 7F 40
Elstead Rd. L9: Faz 6K 45
L32: Kirkb 1A 46
Elston Av. WA12: Newt W 5K 51
Elstow St. L5: Kirkd 2C 58
Elstree Ct. WA8: Wid 4N 79
Elstree Rd. L6: Liv 6J 59
Elswick WN8: Skel 4F 30
Elswick Grn. PR9: South 2M 7
Elswick Rd. PR9: South 3L 7
Elswick St. L8: Liv 5E 74
Elsworth Cl. L37: Form 3C 24
Eltham Av. L21: Lith 1A 44
Eltham Cl. CH49: Woodc 6B 72
WA8: Wid 5A 80
WN4: Ash M 8M 41
Eltham Grn. CH49: Woodc 6B 72
Eltham St. L7: Liv 7J 59
Eltham Wlk. WA8: Wid 5A 80
ELTON 2M 113
Elton Av. L23: Blun 7J 33
L30: N'ton 8D 34
Elton Cl. CH62: East 3D 102
WA3: Birchw 5K 67
WA3: Low 3F 52
Elton Dr. CH63: Spit 5N 89
ELTON GREEN 3L 113
Elton Head Rd. WA9: St H 4F 62
Elton La. WA6: Hel 1A 114
Elton Lordship La. WA6: Frod 8D 106
Elton St. L4: Walt 8E 44
Elvington Cl. WA7: Sut W 3B 108
Elvington Rd. L38: Hight 1G 32
Elway Rd. WN4: Ash M 7L 41
Elwick Dr. L11: Crox 8A 46
Elwood Cl. L33: Kirkb 5C 36
Elworth Av. WA8: Wid 3K 79
Elworthy Av. L26: Halew 7K 77
Elwyn Dr. L26: Halew 8K 77
Elwyn Rd. CH47: Meols 8F 54
Elwy St. L8: Liv 3F 74
Ely Av. CH46: More 9K 55
Ely Cl. CH66: Gt Sut 5K 111
L30: N'ton 1E 44
Ely M. PR9: South 5M 7
Ely Pk. WA7: Nort 5G 96
Ember Cres. L6: Liv 5E 58
Embledon St. L8: Liv 1G 74
Embleton Gro. WA7: Beech 1N 107
Emerald Cl. L30: N'ton 8G 34
Emerald St. L8: Liv 5F 74
Emerson Cl. L38: Hight 8G 24
Emerson St. L8: Liv 1E 74
Emery St. L4: Walt 9E 44
Emily St. WA8: Wid 9K 79
WA9: St H 2F 62
Emlyn St. WA9: St H 9N 49
Emmanuel Rd. PR9: South 5L 7
Emmett St. WA9: St H 9M 49
Emperor Ct. WA4: Warr 7C 82
Empire Rd. L21: Lith 4A 44
Empress Cl. L31: Mag 2G 35
Empress Rd. CH44: Wall 5J 57
L6: Liv 3H 59
L7: Liv 4N 5 (7G 58)
(not continuous)
Emslie Ct. CH64: Park 7C 100
Emstrey Wlk. L32: Kirkb 9A 36
Endborne Rd. L9: Walt 4F 44
Endbutt La. L23: Crosb 7L 33
Enderby Av. WA11: St H 4N 49
Endfield Farm Caravan Pk.
WA16: High L 9K 85
Endfield Pk. L19: Gras 8N 75
Endmoor Rd. L36: Huy 4H 61
Endsleigh Rd. L13: Liv 6K 59
L22: Water 9H 33
Enerby Cl. CH43: Bid 1C 72
Enfield Av. L23: Crosb 7L 33
Enfield Pk. Rd. WA2: Fearn 5G 66
Enfield Rd. CH65: Ell P 9N 103
L13: Liv 7N 59
Enfield St. WA10: St H 8H 49
Enfield Ter. CH43: Oxton 3H 73
Enford Dr. WA9: St H 2N 63
Engine La. L37: Gt Alt 5K 25
Enid St. L8: Liv 2E 74
Ennerdale WN8: Skel 4G 31
Ennerdale Av. CH62: East 2E 102
L31: Mag 1K 35
WA2: Warr 6C 66
WA11: St H 2L 49
WN4: Ash M 6K 41
Ennerdale Cl. L33: Kirkb 6B 36
L37: Form 1D 24
Ennerdale Dr. L21: Lith 2C 44
L39: Augh 2N 27
WA6: Frod 6M 107
Ennerdale Rd. CH43: Pren 7E 72
CH45: Wall 1F 56
L9: Ain 4J 45
L37: Form 1D 24
M31: Part 6L 69
Ennerdale St. L3: Liv 5C 58
Ennis Cl. L24: Hale 5A 94
Ennis Ct. L11: Norr G 7N 45
Ennisdale Dr. CH48: W Kir 5D 70
Ennismore Rd. L13: Liv 6L 59
L23: Crosb 6J 33
Ennis Rd. L12: W Der 3C 60
Ensor St. L20: Boot 9A 44
Enstone WN8: Skel 3G 31
Enstone Av. L21: Lith 1N 43
Enstone Rd. L25: Hunts X 1F 92
Ensworth Rd. L18: Moss H 3N 75
Enterprise Pk. CH65: Ell P 1C 112
WA11: Rainf 7E 38
Enterprise Way L13: Wav 8K 59
WA3: Low 3H 53
Enticott Rd. M44: Cad 4J 69
Enville St. WA4: Warr 4D 82
EPIC Leisure Centre & Cinema 1N 111
Epping Av. WA9: Sut M 6L 63
Epping Cl. L35: Rainh 7G 62
Epping Ct. CH60: Hesw 6A 88
Epping Dr. WA1: Wools 9L 67
Epping Gro. L15: Wav 2N 75
Epsom Cl. L10: Ain 1K 45
Epsom Gdns. WA4: App 9F 82
Epsom Gro. L33: Kirkb 5E 36

Epsom Rd. CH46: Leas 6N **55**
Epsom St. WA9: St H 6B **50**
Epsom Way L5: Liv 4C **58**
Epstein Ct. *L6: Liv 6G 59*
(off Coleridge St.)
Epstein Theatre, The 6G **4** (8C **58**)
Epworth Cl. CH43: Clau 2G **73**
WA5: Burtw 3H **65**
Epworth Grange *CH43: Clau 2G 73*
(off Epworth Cl.)
Epworth St. L6: Liv 3L **5** (7E **58**)
Eremon Cl. L9: Ain 2J **45**
Erfurt Av. CH63: Beb 3N **89**
Erica Ct. CH60: Hesw 5M **87**
Erica Pk. L27: N'ley 3J **77**
Eric Av. WA1: Padg 9F **66**
Eric Fountain Rd. CH65: Ell P 3J **103**
Eric Gro. CH44: Wall 5G **57**
Eric Rd. CH44: Wall 5G **57**
Ericson Dr. PR8: South 1A **12**
Eric St. WA8: Wid 6M **79**
Eridge St. L8: Liv 4F **74**
Erin Cl. L8: Liv 2D **74**
Erindale Cres. WA6: Frod 8K **107**
Erl St. L9: Ain 4F **44**
Ermine Cres. L5: Liv 4E **58**
Erradale Cres. WN3: Wins 1F **40**
Errington Av. CH65: Ell P 8A **104**
Errington Ct. L17: Aig 8K **75**
Errington St. L5: Kirkd 3B **58**
Errol St. L17: Aig 5G **74**
Erskine Cl. WA11: St H 4A **50**
Erskine Ind. Est. L6: Liv 2L **5** (6F **58**)
Erskine Rd. CH44: Wall 6J **57**
M31: Part 7M **69**
Erskine St. L6: Liv 3L **5** (7E **58**)
Erskine St. Ind. Est. L6: Liv 3M **5**
Erwood St. WA2: Warr 2C **82**
Erylmore Rd. L18: Moss H 7M **75**
Escolme Dr. CH49: Grea 5L **71**
Escor Rd. L25: Gate 2E **76**
Escort Cl. L25: Hunts X 8G **77**
Eshelby Cl. L22: Water 1L **43**
Esher Cl. CH43: Bid 1C **72**
CH62: New F 8A **74**
Eshe Rd. L23: Blun 7J **33**
Eshe Rd. Nth. L23: Blun 6H **33**
Esher Rd. CH62: New F 8A **74**
L6: Liv 6H **59**
Eskbank WN8: Skel 4F **30**
Eskbrook WN8: Skel 3F **30**
Eskburn Rd. L13: Liv 3K **59**
Eskdale CH65: Whit 2N **111**
WN8: Skel 4E **30**
Eskdale Av. CH46: More 8K **55**
CH62: East 1D **102**
L39: Augh 2N **27**
WA2: Warr 6D 66
(off Bentham Av.)
WA11: St H 2L **49**
Eskdale Cl. L37: Form 2D **24**
WA7: Beech 1N **107**
Eskdale Dr. L31: Mag 1K **35**
L37: Form 2D **24**
Eskdale Rd. L9: Walt 5F **44**
WN4: Ash M 6K **41**
Esk St. L20: Kirkd 1A **58**
Eslington St. L19: Gras 9M **75**
Esmond St. L6: Liv 4G **59**
Esonwood Rd. L35: Whis 6A **62**
Espin St. L4: Walt 9E **44**
Esplanade CH42: Rock F 6A **74**
PR8: South 9D **6**
Esplanade, The CH62: New F 7A **74**
L20: Boot 7B 44
(off Strand Shop. Cen.)
L22: Water 2K **43**
Esplanade (Park & Ride) 8E **6**
Esplen Av. L23: Crosb 6M **33**
Essex Gdns. M44: Cad 5J **69**
Essex Rd. CH48: W Kir 5D **70**
L36: Huy 5L **61**
PR8: Birkd 6N **11**
Essex Way L20: Boot 6C **44**
Esthwaite Av. WA11: St H 2M **49**
Estuary Banks L24: Speke 3D **92**
Estuary Banks Bus. Pk. L24: Speke 3D **92**
Estuary Blvd. L24: Speke 4D **92**
Estuary Commerce Pk. L24: Speke 3D **92**
(not continuous)
Etal Cl. L11: Norr G 9N **45**
Ethelbert La. CH47: Meols 9D **54**
Ethelbert Rd. CH47: Meols 9D **54**
Ethel Rd. CH44: Wall 6K **57**
Etherley Dr. WA12: Newt W 9M **51**
Etna St. L13: Liv 6L **59**
Eton Ct. L18: Moss H 3B **76**
PR9: South 6H **7**
Eton Dr. CH63: Thorn H 9F **88**
L10: Ain 9H **35**
Eton Hall Dr. WA9: St H 2M **63**
Eton Rd. CH65: Ell P 1B **112**
Eton St. L4: Walt 9E **44**
Etruscan Rd. L13: Liv 5M **59**
Ettington Dr. PR8: Ains 9G **11**
Ettington Rd. L4: Walt 2G **59**
Ettrick Cl. L33: Kirkb 5B **36**
Euclid Av. WA4: Grap 6J **83**
(not continuous)
Eurolink WA9: St H 5J **63**
Eurolink Bus. Pk. WA9: St H 6J **63**
Europa Blvd. CH41: Birke 2L **73**
WA5: Westb 7L **65**
Europa Centre, The CH41: Birke 2K **73**
Europa Pools 2K **73**
Europa Sq. CH41: Birke 2L **73**
Europa Way CH65: Ell P 8A **104**
Eustace St. WA2: Warr 2B **82**
Euston Gro. CH43: Oxton 3H **73**
Euston St. L4: Walt 8E **44**
Evans Bus. Pk. CH65: Ell P 5L **103**
Evans Cl. WA11: Hay 3H **51**
Evans Pl. WA4: Warr 5E **82**
Evans Rd. CH47: Hoy 1C **70**
L24: Speke 2F **92**
Evans St. L34: Presc 2A **62**
Evellynne Cl. L32: Kirkb 9B **36**
Evelyn Av. L34: Presc 3B **62**
WA9: St H 7A **50**
Evelyn Rd. CH44: Wall 6J **57**
Evelyn St. L5: Kirkd 3C **58**
WA5: Warr 4M **81**
WA9: St H 7A **50**
Evenson Way L13: Liv 5M **59**
Evenwood WA9: St H 3M **63**
WN8: Skel 3G **30**
Evenwood Cl. WA7: Manor P 3G **97**
Evenwood Ct. WN8: Skel 3F **30**
Everard Cl. L40: Scar 7L **13**
Everard Rd. PR8: South 2C **12**
Everdon Wood L33: Kirkb 8D **36**
Evered Av. L9: Walt 6F **44**
Everest Cl. CH66: Gt Sut 2L **111**
Everest Rd. CH42: Tran 6K **73**
L23: Crosb 7L **33**
Evergreen Cl. CH49: Upton 2M **71**
L27: N'ley 2J **77**
Evergreens, The L37: Form 9D **16**
Evergreen Way WA9: Bold 2C **64**
Everite Rd. WA8: Wid 9E **78**
Everite Rd. Ind. Est. WA8: Wid 9E **78**
Everleigh Cl. CH43: Bid 1B **72**
Eversham Cl. PR9: Banks 2E **8**
Eversleigh Dr. CH63: Beb 3N **89**
Eversley WA8: Wid 6E **78**
WN8: Skel 3G **30**
Eversley Cl. WA4: App 2F **98**
WA6: Frod 8N **107**
Eversley Pk. CH43: Oxton 5H **73**
Eversley St. L8: Liv 2F **74**
(not continuous)
EVERTON 4D **58**
Everton Brow L3: Liv 1J **5** (6D **58**)
Everton FC 9E **44**
Everton Gro. WA11: St H 5N **49**
Everton Rd. L6: Liv 1L **5** (5E **58**)
PR8: Birkd 2N **11**
Everton St. WN4: Garsw 6F **40**
Everton Valley L4: Walt 2D **58**
Everton Vw. L20: Boot 8A **44**
Everyman Liverpool Playhouse 6K **5** (8E **58**)
Every St. L6: Liv 5G **59**
Evesham Cl. L25: Woolt 6D **76**
WA4: Stockt H 8D **82**
WN7: Leigh 1L **53**
Evesham Rd. CH45: Wall 3F **56**
L4: Walt 9J **45**
Evington WN8: Skel 3G **31**
Ewanville L36: Huy 8J **61**
Ewart Rd. L16: Child 9E **60**
L21: Sea 3N **43**
WA11: St H 4L **49**
Ewden Cl. L16: Child 1C **76**
Ewloe Ct. CH65: Ell P 3B **112**
Excalibur Way M44: Irlam 2L **69**
Exchange Flags L2: Liv 4D **4**
Exchange Island WN8: Skel 4C **30**
Exchange Pas. E. L2: Liv 4D **4** (7B **58**)
Exchange Pas. W. L2: Liv 4D **4** (7B **58**)
Exchange Pl. L35: Rainh 6F **62**
Exchange St. WA10: St H 7K **49**
Exchange St. E. L2: Liv 4D **4** (7B **58**)
Exchange St. W. L2: Liv 5D **4** (8B **58**)
Exeley L35: Whis 7B **62**
Exeter Cl. L10: Ain 1K **45**
Exeter Rd. CH44: Wall 4J **57**
CH65: Ell P 9A **104**
L20: Boot 8B **44**
Exeter St. WA10: St H 7G **49**
Exford Rd. L12: W Der 1B **60**
Exmoor Cl. CH61: Pens 2N **87**
PR9: South 1N **7**
Exmouth Cl. CH41: Birke 2K **73**
Exmouth Cres. WA7: Murd 9G **97**
Exmouth Gdns. CH41: Birke 2K **73**
Exmouth St. CH41: Birke 2K **73**
Exmouth Way CH41: Birke 2K **73**
WA5: Burtw 3H **65**
Express Ind. Est. WA8: Wid 9D **78**
Expressway Bus. Pk. CH42: Tran 5M **73**
Extension Vw. WA9: St H 1N **63**
Eyes La. WN8: Parb 2D **22**
Eyre Pl. CH65: Ell P 8N **103**

F

Fab4D 6C **4** (8A **58**)
FACT 7H **5** (9D **58**)
Factory La. WA1: Warr 4A **82**
WA5: Warr 3A **82**
WA8: Wid 5L **79**
Factory Row WA10: St H 9H **49**
Fairacre Rd. L19: Gras 9M **75**
Fairacres Rd. CH63: Beb 3N **89**
Fairbairn Rd. L22: Water 1L **43**
Fairbank St. L15: Wav 1K **75**
Fairbeech M. CH43: Bid 1C **72**
Fairbourne Cl. WA5: Call 6N **65**
Fairbrook Dr. CH41: Birke 8E **56**
Fairbrother Cres. WA2: Warr 7E **66**
Fairburn WN8: Skel 1E **30**
Fairburn Cl. WA8: Wid 5A **80**
Fairburn Rd. L13: Liv 3K **59**
Fairclough Av. WA1: Warr 4D **82**
Fairclough Cl. L35: Rainh 6E **62**
Fairclough Cres. WA11: Hay 4C **50**
Fairclough La. CH43: Oxton 4H **73**
Fairclough Rd. L35: Rainh 6E **62**
L36: Huy 3G **60**
WA10: St H 6F **48**
Fairclough St. L1: Liv 6G **5** (8C **58**)
WA5: Burtw 3G **64**
WA12: Newt W 7K **51**
Fairfax Dr. WA7: Run 5N **95**
Fairfax Pl. L11: Norr G 8J **45**
Fairfax Rd. CH41: Tran 4L **73**
L11: Norr G 8K **45**
FAIRFIELD 6J **59**
Fairfield L23: Crosb 7L **33**
Fairfield Av. CH65: Whit 3M **111**
L36: Huy 7E **60**
Fairfield Cl. L36: Huy 7E **60**
L39: Orm 6C **20**
Fairfield Cres. CH46: More 9L **55**
L6: Liv 6J **59**
L36: Huy 7E **60**
Fairfield Dr. CH48: W Kir 5F **70**
L39: Orm 6C **20**
Fairfield Gdns. WA4: Stockt H 6F **82**
WA11: Crank 9H **39**
Fairfield Rd. CH42: Tran 6L **73**
M44: Cad 4J **69**
PR8: Ains 9J **11**
WA4: Stockt H 7D **82**
WA8: Wid 7L **79**
WA10: St H 5F **48**
WA13: Lymm 5F **84**
Fairfield St. L7: Liv 6K **59**
WA1: Warr 2D **82**
Fairford Cl. WA5: Gt San 2K **81**
Fairford Cres. L14: Knott A 5N **59**
Fairford Rd. L14: Knott A 5N **59**
Fairhaven L33: Kirkb 6C **36**
WN8: Skel 1F **30**
Fairhaven Cl. CH42: Rock F 6M **73**
WA5: Gt San 4K **81**
Fairhaven Dr. CH63: Brom 1B **102**
Fairhaven Ho. *L19: Aig 9L 75*
(off The Spinnakers)
Fairhaven Rd. PR9: South 3N **7**
WA8: Wid 6M **79**
Fairhavens Ct. WA8: Wid 8L **79**
Fairhills Ind. Est. M44: Irlam 1M **69**
Fairhills Rd. M44: Irlam 1M **69**
Fairholme Av. CH64: Nest 5D **100**
L34: Eccl P 3C **62**
WN4: Ash M 7K **41**
Fairholme Cl. L12: W Der 1M **59**
Fairholme M. *L23: Crosb 7L 33*
(off Fairholme Rd.)
Fairholme Rd. L23: Crosb 7L **33**
Fairhurst Dr. WN8: Parb 3E **22**
Fairhurst Ter. *L34: Presc 3B 62*
(off Scotchbarn La.)
Fair Isles Cl. CH65: Ell P 4A **112**
Fairlawn Cl. CH63: Raby M 9N **89**
Fairlawn Ct. CH43: Oxton 3F **72**
Fairlawne Cl. L33: Kirkb 6C **36**
Fairlie WN8: Skel 1F **30**
Fairlie Cres. L20: Boot 3C **44**
Fairlie Dr. L35: Rainh 7G **62**
Fairmead Rd. CH46: More 8M **55**
L11: Norr G 8K **45**
Fairmont Dr. WA5: Gt San 1J **81**
Fair Oak Ct. WA7: Pres B 3H **109**
Fairoak La. WA7: Pres B 3H **109**
Fairstead WN8: Skel 1F **30**
Fairthorn Wlk. L33: Kirkb 8E **36**
Fair Vw. WN5: Bil 6N **39**
Fairview CH41: Tran 4L **73**
Fair Vw. Av. WN5: Bil 6N **39**
Fairview Av. CH45: Wall 4G **57**
Fairview Cl. CH43: Oxton 5H **73**
WN4: Ash M 7K **41**
Fairview Pl. L8: Liv 3F **74**
Fairview Rd. CH43: Oxton 6H **73**
CH65: Whit 3M **111**
Fairview Way CH61: Pens 4N **87**
Fairway L36: Huy 5L **61**
WA10: Windle 5F **48**
Fairway, The L12: Knott A 5B **60**
Fairway Cres. CH62: Brom 3C **90**
Fairway Nth. CH62: Brom 3C **90**
Fairways CH42: Tran 8H **73**
L23: Crosb 6K **33**
PR9: South 5H **7**
WA4: App 2E **98**
WA6: Frod 7N **107**
Fairways, The CH48: Caldy 1E **86**
L25: Hunts X 8H **77**
WN4: Ash M 9G **40**
WN8: Skel 1G **30**
Fairways (Park & Ride) 5H **7**
Fairways Cl. L25: Woolt 8F **76**
Fairways Ct. L37: Form 8C **16**
Fairways Dr. CH66: Lit Sut 6J **103**
Fairway Sth. CH62: Brom 4C **90**
Fairway Trad. Est. WA8: Wid 9H **79**
Falcon Cres. L27: N'ley 4K **77**
Falcondale Rd. WA2: Win 3C **66**
Falconers Grn. WA5: Westb 7K **65**
Falconer St. L20: Boot 4N **43**
Falcongate Ind. Est. CH44: Wall 8J **57**
Falconhall Rd. L9: Faz 6L **45**
Falcon Hey L10: Faz 4M **45**
Falcon Pl. L40: Burs 3F **20**
Falcon Rd. CH41: Birke 4J **73**
CH66: Gt Sut 2L **111**
Falcons Way WA7: Pal F 9A **96**
Falkirk Av. WA8: Wid 5H **79**
Falkland WN8: Skel 1F **30**
Falkland Dr. WN4: Garsw 7E **40**
Falkland Rd. CH44: Wall 5K **57**
PR8: South 2C **12**
Falklands App. L11: Norr G 8K **45**
Falkland St. CH41: Birke 9G **56**
L3: Liv 3K **5** (7E **58**)
(not continuous)
Falkner Sq. L7: Liv 9F **58**
L8: Liv 9L **5** (1E **74**)
Falkner St. L7: Liv 8N **5** (9F **58**)
L8: Liv 8K **5** (9E **58**)
(not continuous)
Falkner Ter. L8: Liv 9M **5**
Fallbrook Dr. L12: W Der 9N **45**
Fallow Cl. WA9: Clock F 5M **63**
Fallowfield L33: Kirkb 7C **36**
WA7: Run 6N **95**
Fallowfield Cl. L37: Form 9H **17**
Fallowfield Gro. WA2: Padg 8J **67**
Fallowfield Rd. L15: Wav 2L **75**
Fallows Way L35: Whis 8N **61**
Falls La. L26: Halew 7J **77**
Falmouth Dr. WA5: Penk 5G **80**
Falmouth Pl. WA7: Murd 9G **96**
Falmouth Rd. L11: Crox 5B **46**
Falstaff St. L20: Kirkd 1B **58**
Falstone Cl. WA3: Birchw 3B **68**
WN3: Wins 1F **40**
Falstone Dr. WA7: Murd 7G **96**
Faraday Rd. CH65: Whit 1M **111**
L13: Wav 8K **59**
L33: Know I 3F **46**
WA7: Ast 4N **95**
Faraday St. L5: Liv 4F **58**
WA3: Ris 3M **67**
Farcroft Cl. WA13: Lymm 3J **85**
Fardon Cl. WN3: Wigan 1H **41**
Fareham Cl. CH49: Upton 2M **71**
Fareham Dr. PR9: Banks 2E **8**
Fareham Rd. L7: Liv 7J **59**
Faringdon Cl. L25: Hunts X 1F **92**
Farley Av. CH62: Brom 6B **90**
Farley La. WN8: Roby M 1K **31**
Farlow Rd. CH42: Rock F 7M **73**
Farmbrook Rd. L25: Gate 1F **76**
Farm Cl. CH49: Grea 4K **71**
PR9: South 7M **7**
WA9: Clock F 6N **63**
Farmdale Cl. L18: Moss H 6N **75**
Farmdale Dr. CH2: Elt 2L **113**
L31: Mag 2K **35**
Far Mdw. La. CH61: Irby 1K **87**
Farmer Pl. L20: Boot 3D **44**
Farmers Heath CH66: Gt Sut 3J **111**
Farmers La. WA5: Burtw 3J **65**
Farmer Ted's Farm Pk. 3E **26**
Farmfield Dr. CH43: Bid 1C **72**
Farm La. WA4: App 8F **82**
Farmleigh Gdns. WA5: Gt San 2L **81**
Farm Mdw. Rd. WN5: Orr 7N **31**
FAR MOOR 8N **31**
Far Moss Rd. L23: Blun 5H **33**
Farm Rd. WA9: Clock F 6N **63**
Farmside CH46: Leas 6N **55**
Farmside Cl. WA5: Warr 1N **81**
Farmstead Way CH66: Gt Sut 4K **111**
Farm Vw. L21: Ford 9A **34**
Farmview Cl. L27: N'ley 1G **77**
Farm Way WA12: Newt W 9N **51**
Farnborough Gro. L26: Halew 7K **77**
Farnborough Rd. PR8: Birkd 6M **11**
Farndale WA8: Wid 3K **79**
Farndale Cl. WA5: Gt San 1H **81**
Farndale Gro. WN4: Ash M 9L **41**
Farndon Av. CH45: Wall 3E **56**
WA9: Sut M 5L **63**
Farndon Dr. CH48: W Kir 5F **70**
Farndon Rd. CH66: Ell P 8K **103**
Farndon Way CH43: Oxton 4F **72**
Farne Cl. CH65: Ell P 5A **112**
Farnham Cl. L32: Kirkb 1D **46**
WA4: App 9F **82**
Farnhill Cl. WA7: Nort 7F **96**
Farnley Cl. WA7: Wind H 6F **96**
Farnside Ct. L17: Aig 9K **75**
FARNWORTH 5L **79**
Farnworth Av. CH46: Leas 6M **55**

Farnworth Cl. WA8: Wid 4L **79**
Farnworth Gro. L33: Kirkb 6C **36**
Farnworth M. WA8: Wid 5L **79**
Farnworth Rd. WA5: Penk 4D **80**
Farnworth St. L6: Liv 1N **5** (6G **58**)
WA8: Wid 4L **79**
WA9: St H 6M **49**
Farrant St. WA8: Wid 8L **79**
Farrar St. L13: Liv 2K **59**
Farrell Cl. L31: Mell 7N **35**
Farrell Rd. WA4: Stockt H 8D **82**
Farrell St. WA1: Warr 3D **82**
Farr Hall Dr. CH60: Hesw 8M **87**
Farr Hall Rd. CH60: Hesw 7M **87**
Farrier Rd. L33: Kirkb 9E **36**
Farriers Wlk. WA9: Clock F 5M **63**
Farriers Way CH48: Frank 6J **71**
L30: N'ton 2E **44**
Farrier Way WN6: Appl B 6M **23**
Farringdon Cl. WA9: St H 4J **63**
Farringdon Rd. WA2: Win 3C **66**
Farrington Dr. L39: Orm 7C **20**
Farthing Cl. L25: Hunts X 9E **76**
Farthings, The WA13: Lymm 4D **84**
Farthingstone Cl. L35: Whis 3D **62**
Fatherside Dr. L30: N'ton 8B **34**
Faulkner Cl. PR8: Ains 9J **11**
Faulkner Gdns. PR8: Ains 8J **11**
Faversham Rd. L11: Norr G 7K **45**
Faversham Way CH42: Rock F 6M **73**
Fawcett WN8: Skel 1E **30**
Fawcett Rd. L31: Lyd 9J **27**
Fawley Rd. L18: Moss H 6A **76**
L35: Rainh 8H **63**
FAZAKERLEY 3L **45**
Fazakerley Cl. L9: Walt 6F **44**
Fazakerley Rd. L9: Walt 6F **44**
L35: Presc 5B **62**
Fazakerley Sports Cen. 2L **45**
Fazakerley Station (Rail) 3J **45**
Fazakerley St.
L3: Liv 4C **4** (7A **58**)
Fearnham Cl. WN7: Leigh 1M **53**
FEARNHEAD 7H **67**
Fearnhead Cross
WA2: Fearn 7G **67**
Fearnhead La. WA2: Fearn 7H **67**
Fearnley Hall CH41: Birke 3K **73**
Fearnley Rd. CH41: Birke 3K **73**
Fearnley Way WA12: Newt W 9L **51**
Fearnside St. L7: Liv 9H **59**
Feather La. CH60: Hesw 7N **87**
Feathers, The WA10: St H 7G **48**
Feeny St. WA9: Sut M 7L **63**
Feilden Rd. CH63: Beb 3N **89**
Felcroft Way L33: Kirkb 9D **36**
Felicity Gro. CH46: More 8L **55**
Fell Gro. WA11: St H 2K **49**
Fell St. CH44: Wall 7L **57**
L7: Liv 7G **59**
Felltor Cl. L25: Woolt 5D **76**
Fell Vw. PR9: South 1B **8**
Fellwood Gro. L35: Whis 7B **62**
Felmersham Av.
L11: Norr G 7L **45**
Felspar Rd. L32: Kirkb 3D **46**
Felstead WN8: Skel 2E **30**
Felstead Av. L25: Woolt 6G **77**
Felsted Dr. L10: Ain 1K **45**
Felthorpe Cl. CH49: Upton 1B **72**
Felton Cl. CH46: More 9K **55**
Felton Ct. *L17: Aig 5H 75*
(off Lark La.)
Felton Gro. L13: Liv 5L **59**
Feltons WN8: Skel 2E **30**
Feltwell Rd. L4: Walt 3G **58**
Feltwood Cl. L12: W Der 2D **60**
Feltwood Mnr. L12: W Der 2D **60**
Feltwood Rd. L12: W Der 1D **60**
Feltwood Wlk. L12: W Der 2D **60**
Fendale Av. CH46: More 8A **56**
Fender Ct. CH49: Woodc 7D **72**
Fender La. CH43: Bid 8A **56**
CH46: More 8A **56**
Fenderside Rd. CH43: Bid 9C **56**
Fender Vw. Rd. CH46: More 9A **56**
Fender Way CH43: Bid 2B **72**
CH61: Pens 3A **88**
Fenham Dr. WA5: Penk 4G **81**
Fennel St. WA1: Warr 3D **82**
Fenney Ct. WN8: Skel 3F **30**
Fenton Cl. L24: Speke 4H **93**
L30: N'ton 2G **44**
WA8: Wid 5F **78**
WA10: St H 6J **49**
Fenton Grn. L24: Speke 5H **93**
Fenwick La. WA7: Run 9N **95**
Fenwick Rd. CH66: Gt Sut 3K **111**
Fenwick St. L2: Liv 5D **4** (8B **58**)
Ferguson Av. CH49: Grea 5L **71**
CH66: Ell P 8K **103**
Ferguson Dr. WA2: Warr 8E **66**
Ferguson Rd. L11: Norr G 1K **59**
L21: Lith 1B **44**
Fern Bank L31: Mag 2K **35**
WA11: Rainf 4B **38**
Fernbank Av. L36: Huy 7H **61**
Fernbank Cl. WA3: Ris 5M **67**
Fernbank Dr. L30: N'ton 7F **34**
Fernbank La. CH49: Upton 1N **71**
Fern Cl. L27: N'ley 4J **77**
L32: Kirkb 7D **36**
WA3: Birchw 5L **67**
WN8: Skel 3B **30**
Ferndale WN8: Skel 2E **30**
Ferndale Av. CH2: Elt 2L **113**
CH44: Wall 5J **57**
CH48: Frank 7J **71**
Ferndale Cl. L9: Walt 3F **44**
WA1: Wools 1K **83**
WA8: Bold H 1A **80**
Ferndale Dr. WN6: Appl B 6N **23**
Ferndale Rd. CH47: Hoy 1C **70**
L15: Wav 2K **75**
L22: Water 9K **33**
Fern End PR9: Banks 3E **8**
Fern Gdns. L34: Eccl P 2C **62**
Fern Gro. CH43: Noct 4D **72**
L8: Liv 2H **75**
L20: Boot 6B **44**
Fern Hey L23: Thorn 6A **34**
Fernhill CH45: New B 1H **57**
Fernhill Av. L20: Boot 7D **44**
Fernhill Cl. L20: Boot 7D **44**
(not continuous)
Fernhill Dr. L8: Liv 2F **74**
Fernhill Gdns. L20: Boot 7D **44**
Fernhill Mews E. *L20: Boot 7D 44*
(off Fernhill Rd.)
Fernhill Mews W. L20: Boot 7D **44**
Fernhill Rd. L20: Boot 4C **44**
Fernhill Wlk. WA9: Clock F 6M **63**
Fernhill Way L20: Boot 7D **44**
Fernhurst WA7: Run 7N **95**
Fernhurst Ga. L39: Augh 2N **27**
Fernhurst Rd. L32: Kirkb 1A **46**
Fernie Cres. L8: Liv 3E **74**
Fernlea Av. WA9: St H 2G **63**
Fernlea Gro. WN4: Garsw 6F **40**
Fernlea M. CH43: Bid 9C **56**
Fernlea Rd. CH60: Hesw 7A **88**
Fernleigh Rd. L13: Liv 6N **59**
Fernley Rd. PR8: South 1N **11**
Fern Lodge L8: Liv 2H **75**
Fern Rd. CH65: Whit 3M **111**
Ferns Cl. CH60: Hesw 6K **87**
Fernside Gro. WN3: Wins 2F **40**
Ferns Rd. CH63: Hghr B 2K **89**
Fernwood WA7: Nort 6D **96**
Fernwood Dr. L26: Halew 8J **77**
Fernwood Rd. L17: Aig 6K **75**
Ferny Brow Rd. CH49: Woodc 5B **72**
Fernyess La. CH64: Will 8L **101**
Ferny Knoll Rd. WA11: Rainf 9B **30**
Ferrer St. WN4: Ash M 5H **41**
Ferrey Rd. L10: Faz 3M **45**
Ferries Cl. CH42: Rock F 8N **73**
Ferrous Way M44: Irlam 3M **69**
Ferry La. WA4: Thel 4M **83**
Ferrymasters Way M44: Irlam 1N **69**
Ferry Rd. CH62: East 1F **102**
Ferryside CH44: Wall 7L **57**
WA7: Run 5K **83**
Ferryside La. PR9: South 2A **8**
Ferry Vw. Rd. CH44: Wall 7L **57**
Ferryview Wlk. WA7: Cas 5B **96**
Festival Av. WA2: Warr 7E **66**
Festival Ct. L11: Norr G 7N **45**
Festival Cres. WA2: Warr 7E **66**
Festival Gdns. 6F **74**
Festival Rd. CH65: Ell P 9L **103**
WA11: Rainf 6D **38**
Festival Ter. *WA7: Run 7M 95*
(off Festival Way)
Festival Way WA7: Run 7M **95**
Ffrancon Dr. CH63: Hghr B 9M **73**
FIDDLER'S FERRY
PR9 1A **8**
WA5 7F **80**
Fiddlers Ferry Golf Course 6E **80**
Fiddlers Ferry Rd. WA8: Wid 8M **79**
Fiddler's Ferry Sailing Club 7G **80**
Fidler St. WA10: St H 9G **48**
Field Av. L21: Lith 2N **43**
Field Cl. CH62: New F 8A **74**
L40: Burs 2K **21**
WA9: Clock F 6N **63**
Fieldfare Cl. L25: Gate 3E **76**
WA3: Birchw 5N **67**
WA3: Low 2E **52**
Fieldgate WA8: Wid 9E **78**
Field Hey La. CH64: Will 5A **102**
(not continuous)
Field Ho. L12: W Der 2M **59**
Fieldhouse Row WA7: Run 8N **95**
Fieldings, The L31: Lyd 8G **27**
Fielding St. L6: Liv 2N **5** (6F **58**)
Fieldlands PR8: South 4F **12**
Field La. L10: Faz 4M **45**
L21: Lith 1N **43**
WA4: App 1D **98**
Field Rd. CH45: New B 2H **57**
WA9: Clock F 6N **63**
Field's End L36: Huy 9J **61**
Fieldsend Cl. L27: N'ley 4J **77**
Fieldsend Dr. WN7: Leigh 2K **53**
Fieldside Rd. CH42: Rock F 6L **73**
Field St. L3: Liv 1J **5** (6D **58**)
(not continuous)
WN8: Skel 2A **30**
Fieldsway WA7: West 9K **95**
Fieldton Rd. L11: Norr G 8N **45**
Field Vw. L21: Lith 2N **43**
Fieldview WN8: Uph 5K **31**
Fieldview Dr. WA2: Warr 8D **66**
Field Wlk. L23: Thorn 6A **34**
L39: Orm 8F **20**
M31: Part 6L **69**
Field Way L35: Rainh 4F **62**
Fieldway CH45: Wall 4G **56**
CH47: Meols 1G **70**
CH60: Hesw 6C **88**
CH63: Hghr B 8K **73**
CH66: Lit Sut 7G **102**
L15: Wav 9A **60**
L31: Mag 4K **35**
L36: Huy 9K **61**
WA6: Frod 7M **107**
WA8: Wid 6A **80**
Fieldway Ct. CH41: Birke 9J **57**
Fife Rd. WA1: Warr 1F **82**
Fifth Av. CH43: Bid 1B **72**
L9: Ain 3K **45**
(Broadway)
L9: Ain 3J **45**
(Sixth Av.)
WA7: Pal F 8B **96**
Filbert Cl. L33: Kirkb 5D **36**
Filby Gdns. WA9: St H 3H **63**
Fildes Cl. WA5: Gt San 3L **81**
Fillmore Gro. WA8: Wid 5J **79**
Filton Rd. L14: Knott A 4F **60**
Finborough Rd. L4: Walt 8H **45**
FINCHAM 4F **60**
Fincham Grn. L14: Knott A 4F **60**
Fincham Rd. L14: Knott A 4E **60**
Fincham Sq. L14: Knott A 4E **60**
Finch Av. WA11: Rainf 6D **38**
Finch Cl. WA9: Clock F 6N **63**
Finch Ct. CH41: Birke 1K **73**
Finchdale Gdns. WA3: Low 2J **53**
Finchdean Cl. CH49: Grea 4K **71**
Finch Dene L14: Knott A 3D **60**
Finch La. L14: Knott A 3D **60**
L26: Halew 1M **93**
WN6: Appl B 4L **23**
Finch Lea Dr. L14: Knott A 4E **60**
Finchley Dr. WA11: St H 3M **49**
Finchley Rd. L4: Walt 2G **58**
Finch Mdw. Cl. L9: Faz 6L **45**
Finch Mill Av. WN6: Appl B 6N **23**
Finch Pl. L3: Liv 3K **5** (7E **58**)
Finch Rd. L14: Knott A 3E **60**
Finch Way L14: Knott A 4D **60**
Findlay Cl. WA12: Newt W 8K **51**
(not continuous)
Findley Dr. CH46: Leas 6N **55**
Findon WN8: Skel 3E **30**
Findon Rd. L32: Kirkb 2D **46**
Fine Jane's Way PR9: South 7N **7**
Fingall Rd. L15: Wav 2N **75**
Finger Ho. La. WA8: Bold H 8N **63**
Fingland Rd. L15: Wav 1K **75**
Finlan Rd. WA8: Wid 9J **79**
Finlay Av. WA5: Penk 5G **81**
Finlay Ct. L30: N'ton 7E **34**
Finlay St. L6: Liv 6H **59**
Finney, The CH48: Caldy 1E **86**
Finney Gro. WA11: Hay 4G **50**
Finningley Ct. WA2: Padg 8F **66**
Finsbury Cl. WA5: Gt San 4L **81**
Finsbury Pk. WA8: Wid 3M **79**
Finstall Rd. CH63: Spit 5M **89**
Finvoy Rd. L13: Liv 2K **59**
Fiona Wlk. L10: Faz 3N **45**
Fir Av. L26: Halew 8L **77**
Firbank CH2: Elt 2N **113**
Firbank Cl. WA7: Wind H 6F **96**
Firbeck WN8: Skel 3E **30**
Firbrook Ct. CH43: Bid 8C **56**
Fir Cl. L26: Halew 8L **77**
Fir Cotes L31: Mag 2K **35**
Firdale Rd. L9: Walt 6F **44**
Firdene Cres. CH43: Noct 4E **72**
Firecrest Ct. WA1: Warr 5B **82**
Firenza Av. CH65: Ell P 8M **103**
Fire Station Cl. L23: Crosb 7K **33**
Fire Station Rd. L35: Whis 4C **62**
Firethorne Rd. L26: Halew 6H **77**
Fir Gro. L9: Ain 2H **45**
WA1: Padd 1G **83**
Fir La. L15: Wav 1M **75**
Firman Cl. WA5: Gt San 9K **65**
Fir Rd. L22: Water 9L **33**
Firs, The CH65: Ell P 3B **112**
Firs Av. CH63: Beb 4M **89**
Firs Cl. L37: Form 8D **16**
Firscraig L28: Stockb V 2G **60**
Firs Cres. L37: Form 8D **16**
Firshaw Rd. CH47: Meols 8D **54**
Firs La. L39: Augh, Hals 1K **27**
WA4: App 2C **98**
Firs Link L37: Form 9D **16**
First Av. CH43: Bid 2C **72**
L9: Ain 3H **45**
(Higher La.)
L9: Ain 4K **45**
(Second Av.)
L23: Crosb 7K **33**
L35: Rainh 5E **62**
Firstone Gro. L32: Kirkb 2C **46**
Fir St. M44: Cad 3J **69**
PR8: South 9K **7**
WA8: Wid 6M **79**
WA10: St H 1G **62**
First St. WN2: Bam 4N **41**
Firswood Rd. WN8: Skel 2M **29**
Firth Blvd. WA2: Warr 1D **82**
Firthland Way WA9: St H 8B **50**
Fir Tree Av. WA3: Low 2G **52**
Firtree Av. WA1: Padg 9H **67**
Fir Tree Cl. WA4: Stret 6E **98**
WA11: Kings M 4J **39**
WN8: Skel 5G **30**
Fir Tree Dr. Nth. L12: Crox 7B **46**
Fir Tree Dr. Sth. L12: Crox 7B **46**
Firtree Gro. CH66: Whit 5M **111**
Fir Tree La. L39: Augh, Hals 9L **19**
WA5: Burtw 3J **65**
Fir Tree Wlk. WA3: Low 2G **52**
Firway CH60: Hesw 1B **100**
Firwood WN8: Skel 1G **30**
Firwood Gro. WN4: Ash M 9J **41**
Fisher Av. L35: Whis 7A **62**
WA2: Warr 8C **66**
Fisher Ct. WA7: Run 4L **95**
Fisher Dr. PR9: South 8L **7**
Fisherfield Dr. WA3: Birchw 3A **68**
Fishermans Cl. L37: Form 7E **16**
Fisherman's Path L37: Form 5C **16**
Fisher Pl. L35: Whis 7A **62**
Fishers La. CH61: Pens 3M **87**
Fisher St. L8: Liv 2C **74**
WA7: Run 4L **95**
WA9: St H 1A **64**
Fishguard Cl. L6: Liv 5E **58**
Fish La. L40: Burs, Holm 2F **14**
Fishwicks Ind. Est. WA9: St H 1M **63**
WA11: Hay 2H **51**
Fistral Cl. L10: Faz 4N **45**
Fistral Dr. WA10: Windle 4E **48**
Fit City
Irlam & Cadishead 1N **69**
Fitzclarence Wlk. L6: Liv 1L **5**
Fitzclarence Way L6: Liv 1L **5** (5E **58**)
Fitzgerald Rd. L13: Liv 6M **59**
Fitzherbert St. WA2: Warr 1C **82**
Fitzpatrick Ct. L3: Liv 5B **58**
Fitzroy Way L6: Liv 2M **5** (6F **58**)
Fitzwalter Rd. WA1: Wools 1L **83**
Fitzwilliam Wlk. WA7: Cas 5C **96**
FIVECROSSES 9N **107**
Fiveways WA10: Eccl 6D **48**
Fiveways Pk. CH64: Nest 3F **100**
Flag La. CH64: Lit N 7F **100**
Flail Cl. CH49: Grea 4K **71**
Flambards CH49: Woodc 5B **72**
Flamstead WN8: Skel 3F **30**
Flander Cl. WA8: Wid 6F **78**
Flashes La. CH64: Ness 9H **101**
Flash La. CW9: Ant 9M **99**
L40: Ruf 2N **15**
Flatfield Way L31: Mag 2K **35**
Flatman's La. L39: Down 3D **26**
Flatt La. CH43: Oxton 5F **72**
CH65: Ell P 9N **103**
Flavian Ct. WA7: Cas 6A **96**
Flawn Rd. L11: Norr G 1K **59**
Flaxfield Rd. L37: Form 1G **25**
Flaxfields L40: Lath 2K **21**
Flaxhill CH46: More 8L **55**
Flax La. L40: Lath 2K **21**
Flaxley Cl. WA3: Birchw 4A **68**
Flaxman Ct. *L7: Liv 7H 59*
(off Botanic Gro.)
Flaxman St. L7: Liv 7H **59**
Flaxton WN8: Skel 3F **30**
Flaybrick Cl. CH43: Bid 9E **56**
Fleck La. CH48: Caldy, W Kir 7E **70**
Fleetcroft Rd. CH49: Woodc 6A **72**
Fleet La. WA9: St H 7A **50**
Fleet La. Ind. Est. WA9: St H 8A **50**
Fleet St. CH65: Ell P 9M **103**
L1: Liv 6G **4** (8C **58**)
Fleetwood Cl. PR9: South 4L **7**
WA5: Gt San 4K **81**
Fleetwood Ct. *PR9: South 6J 7*
(off Park Rd.)
Fleetwood Cres. PR9: Banks 1E **8**
Fleetwood Dr. PR9: Banks 1E **8**
WA12: Newt W 6K **51**
Fleetwood Gdns. L33: Kirkb 6D **36**
(not continuous)
Fleetwood Pl. *L25: Woolt 6D 76*
(off Castle St.)
Fleetwood Rd. PR9: South 6H **7**
(not continuous)
Fleetwoods La. L30: N'ton 7C **34**
Fleetwood Wlk. WA7: Murd 8E **96**
Fleming Ct. L3: Liv 5B **58**
Fleming Dr. WA2: Win 3B **66**
WN4: Ash M 7M **41**
Fleming Rd. L24: Speke 1G **93**
Fleming St. CH65: Ell P 8A **104**
Flemington Av. L4: Walt 9J **45**
Fleming Way CH46: Leas 7A **56**
Flers Av. WA4: Warr 5D **82**
Fletcher Av. CH42: Rock F 6L **73**
L34: Presc 2B **62**
Fletcher Cl. CH49: Woodc 5A **72**

Fletcher Dr. L19: Gras . . . 9M **75**
Fletcher's Dr. L40: Burs . . . 1J **21**
Fletchers La. WA13: Lymm . . . 4F **84**
Fletchers Row *WA7: Halt* . . . *6B* **96**
(off Spark La.)
Fletcher St. WA4: Warr . . . 5C **82**
Flimby WN8: Skel . . . 3G **30**
Flint Cl. CH64: Nest . . . 8E **100**
Flint Ct. CH65: Ell P . . . 3B **112**
Flint Dr. CH64: Nest . . . 7E **100**
L12: Crox . . . 9B **46**
Flint Gro. M44: Cad . . . 3J **69**
Flint Mdw. CH64: Nest . . . 7E **100**
Flintshire Gdns. WA10: St H . . . 8J **49**
Flint St. L1: Liv . . . 9G **4** (1C **74**)
Flixton Gdns. WA9: St H . . . 3H **63**
Floodgates Rd. L38: Hight . . . 7F **24**
Floral Pavilion Theatre . . . 9J **43**
Floral Wood L17: Aig . . . 6E **74**
Flora St. WN4: Ash M . . . 9K **41**
Flordon WN8: Skel . . . 2G **30**
Florence Av. CH60: Hesw . . . 6N **87**
Florence Cl. L9: Walt . . . 7E **44**
Florence Ct. *L9: Walt* . . . *7E* **44**
(off Buchanan Rd.)
Florence Nightingale Cl. L30: N'ton . . . 7E **34**
Florence Rd. CH44: Wall . . . 6L **57**
Florence St. CH41: Birke . . . 2K **73**
L4: Walt . . . 1E **58**
WA4: Warr . . . 5E **82**
WA9: St H . . . 2F **62**
Florentine Rd. L13: Liv . . . 5M **59**
Florida Cl. WA5: Gt San . . . 1L **81**
Florida Ct. L19: Gras . . . 8N **75**
Florida Way L35: Presc . . . 5A **62**
Flowermead Cl. CH47: Meols . . . 8G **54**
Floyd Dr. WA2: Warr . . . 8C **66**
Fluin La. WA6: Frod . . . 5M **107**
Fluker's Brook La. L34: Know . . . 9F **46**
(not continuous)
Focus Building, The *L3: Liv* . . . *3F* **4**
(off Crosshall St.)
Fogg's La. CW9: Ant . . . 9H **99**
Foinavon Cl. L9: Walt . . . 3E **44**
Folds, The CH63: Thorn H . . . 9G **89**
Folds La. WA11: St H . . . 3K **49**
Folds Rd. WA11: Hay . . . 5B **50**
Fold St. WA3: Golb . . . 1B **52**
Foley Cl. L4: Kirkd . . . 2D **58**
Foley St. L4: Kirkd . . . 2D **58**
Folkestone Rd. PR8: South . . . 3D **12**
Folkestone Way WA7: Murd . . . 8E **96**
Folly La. CH44: Wall . . . 4E **56**
(not continuous)
WA5: Warr . . . 1A **82**
WA7: Run . . . 6G **95**
Fontenoy St. L3: Liv . . . 3F **4** (7C **58**)
Fonthill Cl. L4: Kirkd . . . 2C **58**
Fonthill Rd. L4: Kirkd . . . 1C **58**
Forbes Cl. WA3: Birchw . . . 5M **67**
FORD
CH43 . . . 2C **72**
L21 . . . 9A **34**
Ford Av. L33: Kirkb . . . 5C **36**
Ford Cl. CH49: Upton . . . 4B **72**
L20: Boot . . . 3D **44**
L21: Ford . . . 9A **34**
Fordcombe Rd. L25: Gate . . . 4G **77**
Ford Dr. CH49: Upton . . . 3B **72**
Fordham Cl. PR8: South . . . 3D **12**
Fordham St. L4: Kirkd . . . 1D **58**
Fordhill Vw. CH46: More . . . 1A **72**
Fordington Rd. WA5: Gt San . . . 3K **81**
Fordland Cl. WA3: Low . . . 1F **52**
Ford La. CH49: Upton . . . 3B **72**
L21: Ford . . . 9A **34**
Fordlea Rd. L12: W Der . . . 1M **59**
Fordlea Way L12: W Der . . . 1M **59**
Ford Rd. CH49: Upton . . . 3A **72**
L35: Presc . . . 3C **62**
Ford St. L3: Liv . . . 1E **4** (6B **58**)
WA1: Warr . . . 2E **82**
Fordton Leisure Cen. . . . 6B **66**
Ford Vw. L21: Ford . . . 8A **34**
Ford Way CH49: Upton . . . 4A **72**
Ford Way M. CH49: Upton . . . 4A **72**
Forefield La. L23: Crosb . . . 6M **33**
Foreland Cl. WA5: Gt San . . . 1E **80**
Forest Cl. CH47: Meols . . . 8E **54**
L34: Eccl P . . . 2C **62**
Forest Ct. CH43: Clau . . . 2F **72**
Forest Dr. L36: Huy . . . 6G **60**
WN8: Skel . . . 1F **30**
Forest Gdns. M31: Part . . . 6K **69**
Forest Grn. L12: W Der . . . 1N **59**
Forest Gro. L34: Eccl P . . . 2C **62**
Forest Lawn L12: W Der . . . 1N **59**
Forest Mead WA10: Eccl . . . 7D **48**
Forest Rd. CH43: Clau . . . 1G **72**
CH47: Meols . . . 8E **54**
CH60: Hesw . . . 6A **88**
CH66: Ell P . . . 7K **103**
PR8: South . . . 9J **7**
WA9: Sut M . . . 6K **63**
Forest Wlk. *WA7: Pal F* . . . *8B* **96**
(within Halton Lea Shop. Cen.)
Forfar Rd. L13: Liv . . . 3J **59**
Forge Cl. L40: Westh . . . 9J **21**
WA8: Cron . . . 3F **78**
Forge Cotts. L17: Aig . . . 4H **75**
Forge Rd. CH66: Lit Sut . . . 8H **103**
WA5: Gt San . . . 3H **81**
Forge Shop. Centre, The
WA4: Stockt H . . . 7D **82**
Forge St. L20: Kirkd . . . 1B **58**
FORMBY . . . 1F **24**
Formby Av. WA10: St H . . . 9G **49**
Formby Bri. L37: Form . . . 2E **24**
Formby Bus. Pk. L37: Form . . . 1H **25**
Formby By-Pass L37: Ains, Form . . . 7H **17**
L38: Ince B . . . 4H **25**
Formby Cl. WA5: Penk . . . 4H **81**
Formby Flds. L37: Form . . . 2G **25**
Formby Gdns. L37: Form . . . 9F **16**
Formby Golf Course . . . 8D **16**
Formby Hall Golf Course . . . 5J **17**
Formby La. L37: Form . . . 2G **25**
L39: Augh . . . 2J **27**
Formby Little Theatre . . . 1F **24**
Formby M. L37: Form . . . 9F **16**
Formby Nature Reserve . . . 8B **16**
Formby Point Caravan Pk. L37: Form . . . 3B **24**
Formby Pool . . . 1F **24**
Formby Station (Rail) . . . 2E **24**
Formby St. L37: Form . . . 2E **24**
Formosa Dr. L10: Faz . . . 3L **45**
Formosa Rd. L10: Faz . . . 3L **45**
Formosa Way L10: Faz . . . 3L **45**
Fornalls Grn. La. CH47: Meols . . . 1F **70**
Forres Gro. WN4: Garsw . . . 7F **40**
Forrester Av. WA9: St H . . . 2F **62**
Forrest St. L1: Liv . . . 8F **4** (9C **58**)
Forrest Way WA4: Warr . . . 5M **81**
WA5: Warr . . . 5M **81**
Forshaw Av. WA10: St H . . . 1F **62**
Forshaw's La. WA5: Burtw . . . 1G **64**
Forshaw St. WA2: Warr . . . 1D **82**
FORSTERS GREEN . . . 1G **30**
Forsters Grn. Rd. WN8: Skel . . . 1G **30**
Forster St. WA2: Warr . . . 1C **82**
WA3: Golb . . . 1B **52**
Forsythia Cl. L9: Walt . . . 7H **45**
Forsythia Wlk. *M31: Part* . . . *7L* **69**
(off Blossom Rd.)
Forthlin Rd. L18: Aller . . . 7A **76**
(not continuous)
Forth St. L20: Kirkd . . . 9B **44**
Forton Lodge Flats *L23: Blun* . . . *7J* **33**
(off Blundellsands Rd. E.)
Forton Rd. WN3: Wigan . . . 1H **41**
Fort Perch Rock Marine Radio Mus. . . . 8H **43**
Fort St. CH45: New B . . . 2J **57**
Forum Ct. PR8: South . . . 8F **6**
Forwood Rd. CH62: Brom . . . 7C **90**
Foscote Rd. L33: Kirkb . . . 7E **36**
Foster Cl. L35: Whis . . . 4D **62**
Foster Rd. L37: Form . . . 2D **24**
Fosters Cl. PR9: South . . . 7N **7**
Fosters Gro. WA11: Hay . . . 4B **50**
Fosters Island WN8: Skel . . . 1F **30**
Fosters Rd. WA11: Hay . . . 4B **50**
Foster St. L20: Kirkd . . . 2B **58**
WA8: Wid . . . 7L **79**
Fotherby Pl. WN3: Wigan . . . 1J **41**
Fothergill St. WA1: Warr . . . 1E **82**
Fotheringay Ct. *CH65: Ell P* . . . *3B* **112**
(off Rochester Dr.)
Foul La. PR8: South . . . 2F **12**
(not continuous)
PR9: South . . . 1F **12**
Foundation, The L3: Liv . . . 5L **5** (8E **58**)
Foundry, The L1: Liv . . . 7G **4**
Foundry Ind. Est. WA8: Wid . . . 9L **79**
Foundry La. WA8: Hale B . . . 2E **94**
Foundry St. WA2: Warr . . . 2C **82**
WA10: St H . . . 7K **49**
(not continuous)
WA12: Newt W . . . 7K **51**
Fountain Ct. L23: Blun . . . 6G **32**
Fountain La. WA6: Frod . . . 6K **107**
Fountain Rd. CH45: New B . . . 2H **57**
L34: Know . . . 7H **47**
Fountains, The L39: Orm . . . 7C **20**
Fountains Av. WA11: Hay . . . 3H **51**
Fountains Cl. L4: Walt . . . 2E **58**
WA7: Brook . . . 1E **108**
Fountains Ct. *L4: Kirkd* . . . *2C* **58**
(off Stanley Cl.)
Fountains Rd. L4: Kirkd, Walt . . . 2C **58**
(not continuous)
Fountain St. CH42: Tran . . . 5J **73**
WA9: St H . . . 3F **62**
Fountains Wlk. WA3: Low . . . 2J **53**
Fountains Way L37: Form . . . 2G **25**
Four Acre Dr. L21: Ford . . . 8A **34**
Four Acre La. WA9: Clock F . . . 5L **63**
Four Acre Pct. WA9: Clock F . . . 5L **63**
Fouracres L31: Mag . . . 4G **35**
Four Bridges CH41: Birke . . . 8L **57**
FOUR LANE ENDS . . . 5L **29**
Four La. Ends WA6: Manl . . . 9L **115**
Fourth Av. CH43: Bid . . . 2B **72**
L9: Ain . . . 3K **45**
(Broadway)
L9: Ain . . . 3J **45**
(Fifth Av.)
WA7: Pal F . . . 8B **96**
Fourth St. WN2: Bam . . . 4N **41**
Fowell Rd. CH45: New B . . . 1H **57**
Fowler Cl. L7: Liv . . . 8H **59**
Foxall Way CH66: Gt Sut . . . 3H **111**
Fox Bank Cl. WA8: Wid . . . 4J **79**
Foxcote WA8: Wid . . . 6E **78**
Foxcover Rd. CH60: Hesw . . . 8C **88**
Foxcovers Rd. CH63: Beb . . . 4N **89**
Fox Covert WA7: Nort . . . 8E **96**
Foxdale Cl. CH43: Oxton . . . 3G **72**
PR8: South . . . 3D **12**
Foxdale Ct. WA4: App . . . 9E **82**
Foxdale Rd. L15: Wav . . . 2L **75**
Foxdell Cl. L13: Liv . . . 7M **59**
Foxdene CH66: Lit Sut . . . 9H **103**
Foxdene Gro. WN3: Wins . . . 1G **41**
Foxes, The CH61: Thing . . . 1A **88**
Foxes Ct. CH43: Oxton . . . 3H **73**
Foxfield Cl. WA2: Warr . . . 6F **66**
Foxfield Rd. CH47: Meols . . . 9E **54**
WA9: St H . . . 5H **63**
Foxfold WN8: Skel . . . 1F **30**
Fox Gdns. WA13: Lymm . . . 4C **84**
Foxglove Av. L26: Halew . . . 7J **77**
L40: Burs . . . 1K **21**
Foxglove Cl. L9: Faz . . . 6L **45**
WA3: Low . . . 2E **52**
Foxglove Ct. WA6: Frod . . . 6M **107**
Foxglove Dell WA6: Alv . . . 3G **115**
Foxglove Rd. CH41: Birke . . . 1F **72**
Foxglove Wlk. *M31: Part* . . . *7M* **69**
(off Cross La. W.)
Foxglove Way CH64: Lit N . . . 9E **100**
Fox Hey Rd. CH44: Wall . . . 6F **56**
Foxhill Cl. L8: Liv . . . 2F **74**
L37: Form . . . 1C **24**
Foxhill Gro. WA6: Hel . . . 1G **115**
Foxhill La. L26: Halew . . . 6J **77**
Foxhills Cl. WA4: App . . . 4E **98**
Foxhouse La. L31: Mag . . . 3K **35**
Foxhunter Dr. L9: Ain . . . 2H **45**
Foxleigh L26: Halew . . . 7H **77**
Foxleigh Grange CH41: Birke . . . 8F **56**
Foxley Cl. WA13: Lymm . . . 6G **85**
Foxley Hall M. WA13: Lymm . . . 7G **85**
Foxley Heath WA8: Wid . . . 8H **79**
Fox Pl. WA10: St H . . . 6K **49**
Fox's Bank La. L35: Whis . . . 2C **78**
(not continuous)
Foxshaw Cl. L35: Whis . . . 8A **62**
Fox St. CH41: Birke . . . 2J **73**
L3: Liv . . . 1H **5** (5D **58**)
WA5: Warr . . . 3N **81**
WA7: Run . . . 6K **95**
Foxton Cl. CH46: More . . . 8J **55**
WA11: St H . . . 5N **49**
Foxwood L12: W Der . . . 1C **60**
WA9: St H . . . 2F **62**
Foxwood Cl. CH48: W Kir . . . 5F **70**
WN5: Orr . . . 7N **31**
Foy St. WN4: Ash M . . . 8K **41**
Frailey Cl. PR8: Ains . . . 1J **17**
Framlington Ct. WA7: Cas . . . 5A **96**
Frampton Rd. L4: Walt . . . 8J **45**
Francine Cl. L3: Liv . . . 4B **58**
Francis Av. CH43: Clau . . . 2H **73**
CH46: More . . . 9L **55**
Francis Cl. L35: Rainh . . . 5F **62**
WA8: Wid . . . 8F **78**
Francis Rd. M44: Irlam . . . 1M **69**
WA4: Stockt H . . . 7C **82**
WA6: Frod . . . 5M **107**
Francis St. M44: Cad . . . 4L **69**
WA9: St H . . . 2B **64**
Francis Way L16: Child . . . 9B **60**
FRANKBY . . . 6J **71**
Frankby Av. CH44: Wall . . . 5G **57**
Frankby Cl. CH49: Grea . . . 5J **71**
Frankby Grn. CH48: Frank . . . 6H **71**
Frankby Gro. CH49: Upton . . . 3N **71**
Frankby Rd. CH47: Meols . . . 9E **54**
CH48: Frank, W Kir . . . 5E **70**
CH49: Grea . . . 5E **70**
L4: Walt . . . 1G **59**
Frankby Stiles CH48: Frank . . . 5G **71**
Franklin Cl. WA5: Old H . . . 9L **65**
Franklin Gro. L33: Kirkb . . . 5C **36**
Franklin Pl. L6: Liv . . . 4G **58**
Franklin Rd. CH46: Leas . . . 5A **56**
Franklyn Dr. WA12: Newt W . . . 9M **51**
Frank Perkins Way M44: Irlam . . . 2M **69**
Frank St. WA8: Wid . . . 7M **79**
Franton Wlk. L32: Kirkb . . . 9A **36**
Fraser Rd. WA5: Gt San . . . 2F **80**
Fraser St. L3: Liv . . . 3H **5** (7D **58**)
Frawley Av. WA12: Newt W . . . 5L **51**
Freckleton Cl. WA5: Gt San . . . 4K **81**
Freckleton Dr. L33: Kirkb . . . 6E **36**
Freckleton Rd. PR9: South . . . 3L **7**
WA10: St H . . . 9E **48**
Freda Av. WA9: St H . . . 3M **63**
Frederick Banting Cl. L30: N'ton . . . 7E **34**
Frederick Gro. L15: Wav . . . 9M **59**
Frederick Lunt Av. L34: Know . . . 7G **47**
Frederick St. WA4: Warr . . . 5E **82**
WA8: Wid . . . 7L **79**
(not continuous)
WA9: St H . . . 1B **64**
WN4: Ash M . . . 6J **41**
Frederick Ter. WA8: Hale B . . . 3D **94**
Frederic Pl. WA7: Run . . . 4L **95**
Freedom Cl. L7: Liv . . . 7N **5** (9F **58**)
Freehold St. L7: Liv . . . 6J **59**
Freeland St. L4: Kirkd . . . 2D **58**
Freeman St. CH41: Birke . . . 1L **73**
L7: Liv . . . 9H **59**
Freemantle Av. WA9: St H . . . 2H **63**
Freemason's Row L3: Liv . . . 2E **4** (6B **58**)
Freemont Rd. L12: W Der . . . 2M **59**
Freeport Gro. L9: Ain . . . 3G **45**
Freesia Av. L9: Walt . . . 6G **45**
Freme Cl. L11: Norr G . . . 7N **45**
Fremont Pl. WA5: Gt San . . . 1K **81**
Frenchfield St. WA9: Clock F . . . 6N **63**
French St. WA8: Wid . . . 7N **79**
WA10: St H . . . 9G **48**
Frensham Cl. CH63: Spit . . . 5M **89**
FRESHFIELD . . . 8E **16**
Freshfield Caravan Pk. L37: Form . . . 7B **16**
Freshfield Cl. L36: Huy . . . 6G **61**
Freshfield Ct. L37: Form . . . 9E **16**
Freshfield Rd. L15: Wav . . . 2L **75**
L37: Form . . . 8E **16**
Freshfields Dr. WA2: Padg . . . 8J **67**
Freshfield Station (Rail) . . . 8E **16**
Freshford WA9: St H . . . 3N **63**
Freshmeadow La. WA6: Hel . . . 3D **114**
Freshwater Cl. WA5: Gt San . . . 1F **80**
Freyer Av. WA4: Warr . . . 7C **82**
Friars Av. WA5: Gt San . . . 3G **81**
Friars Cl. CH63: Beb . . . 2M **89**
Friars Ga. WA1: Warr . . . 4C **82**
Friarsgate Cl. L18: Moss H . . . 3A **76**
Friars La. WA1: Warr . . . 4C **82**
Friar St. L5: Liv . . . 4E **58**
WA10: St H . . . 4J **49**
Friars Wlk. L37: Form . . . 2H **25**
Friends La. WA5: Gt San . . . 2F **80**
Frinsted Rd. L11: Norr G . . . 9M **45**
Frith Ct. *L35: Rainh* . . . *5F* **62**
(off Ratcliffe Pl.)
Frobisher Ct. WA5: Old H . . . 9M **65**
Frobisher Rd. CH46: Leas . . . 5A **56**
CH64: Nest . . . 6E **100**
Froda Av. WA6: Frod . . . 7L **107**
FRODSHAM . . . 6L **107**
Frodsham Bus. Cen. WA6: Frod . . . 5M **107**
Frodsham Dr. WA11: St H . . . 5N **49**
Frodsham Golf Course . . . 9L **107**
Frodsham Leisure Cen. . . . 6L **107**
Frodsham Pk. Homes WA6: Frod . . . 6K **107**
Frodsham Rd. WA6: Alv . . . 4G **114**
Frodsham Station (Rail) . . . 6L **107**
Frodsham St. CH41: Tran . . . 4L **73**
(not continuous)
L4: Walt . . . 9E **44**
Froghall La. WA1: Warr . . . 2A **82**
WA2: Warr . . . 2B **82**
WA13: Lymm . . . 8K **85**
(not continuous)
WA16: High L . . . 8K **85**
Frog La. L40: Lath . . . 3A **22**
Frogmore Rd. L13: Liv . . . 6K **59**
Frome Cl. CH61: Irby . . . 9L **71**
Frome Ct. CH65: Ell P . . . 7N **103**
Frome Way L25: Hunts X . . . 8H **77**
Frontfield Ct. *WA9: St H* . . . *8M* **49**
(off Appleton Rd.)
Frost Dr. CH61: Irby . . . 1K **87**
Frosts M. CH65: Ell P . . . 8N **103**
Frost St. L7: Liv . . . 7H **59**
Fryer St. WA7: Run . . . 4K **95**
Fry St. WA9: St H . . . 7A **50**
(not continuous)
Fuchsia Cl. CH66: Gt Sut . . . 4L **111**
Fuchsia Wlk. CH49: Grea . . . 6K **71**
Fulbeck WA8: Wid . . . 6F **78**
Fulbeck Av. WN3: Wigan . . . 1H **41**
Fulbrook Cl. CH63: Spit . . . 5M **89**
Fulbrook Rd. CH63: Spit . . . 5M **89**
Fulford Cl. L12: W Der . . . 3D **60**
Fulford Pk. CH46: More . . . 9M **55**
Fullerton Gro. L36: Huy . . . 5J **61**
Fulmar Cl. L27: N'ley . . . 3J **77**
WA11: St H . . . 4L **49**
Fulmar Gro. L12: Crox . . . 7C **46**
Fulshaw Cl. L27: N'ley . . . 2H **77**
Fulton Av. CH48: W Kir . . . 5E **70**
Fulton Cl. WA4: Westy . . . 4J **83**
Fulton St. L5: Liv . . . 4A **58**
Fulwood Av. PR8: South . . . 2C **12**
Fulwood Cl. L17: Aig . . . 6J **75**
Fulwood Dr. L17: Aig . . . 6H **75**
Fulwood Gdns. CH66: Lit Sut . . . 8H **103**
Fulwood M. CH66: Lit Sut . . . 8H **103**
Fulwood Pk. L17: Aig . . . 7H **75**
Fulwood Rd. CH66: Lit Sut . . . 8H **103**
L17: Aig . . . 6H **75**
WA3: Low . . . 3F **52**
Fulwood Way L21: Ford . . . 7A **34**
Funchal Av. L37: Form . . . 3D **24**
Furlong Cl. L9: Ain . . . 2J **45**
Furness Av. L12: W Der . . . 9A **46**
L37: Form . . . 1F **24**
L39: Orm . . . 9C **20**
WA10: St H . . . 3H **49**
Furness Cl. CH49: Upton . . . 2M **71**
PR8: Ains . . . 2H **17**
Furness Ct. WA7: Nort . . . 3H **97**
Furness St. L4: Walt . . . 2D **58**
Furnival Dr. L40: Burs . . . 1H **21**
Furrocks Cl. CH64: Ness . . . 9F **100**
Furrocks La. CH64: Ness . . . 9F **100**

Furrocks Way CH64: Ness .9F 100
Furrows, The CH66: Gt Sut .5K 111
Furze Wlk. M31: Part .6N 69
Furze Way CH46: More .8M 55
FX Leisure
Lowton .3H 53
Orrell .5N 31
Fylde Rd. PR9: South .3L 7
Fylde Rd. Ind. Est. PR9: South .3M 7

G

Gable Ct. L11: Norr G .7K 45
Gable M. L37: Form .3G 24
Gables, The L31: Mag .4K 35
L34: Eccl P .3C 62
Gables Cl. WA2: Fearn .6G 66
Gable St. WA12: Newt W .7J 51
Gable Vw. L11: Norr G .7K 45
Gabriel Cl. CH46: More .9N 55
Gainford Cl. WA8: Wid .5F 78
Gainford Rd. L14: Knott A .3E 60
Gainsborough Av. L31: Mag .3G 35
Gainsborough Cl. L12: W Der .4C 60
Gainsborough Ct. WA8: Wid .7E 78
Gainsborough Rd. CH45: Wall .5E 56
CH49: Upton .2M 71
L15: Wav .2K 75
PR8: Birkd .3L 11
WA4: Warr .6B 82
Gairloch Cl. WA2: Fearn .5G 67
Gaisgill Ct. WA8: Wid .7F 78
Gala Bingo
Bromborough .4D 90
Kirkby .9C 36
Liverpool, E. Lancashire Rd. .6M 45
Liverpool, Wavertree Rd. .8H 59
Warrington .3C 82
Widnes .8L 79
Gala Cl. L14: Knott A .5C 60
Gala Leo Casino .1C 74
Galbraith Cl. L17: Aig .6H 75
Gale Av. WA5: Warr .8A 66
Galemeade L11: Norr G .7N 45
Gale Rd. L21: Lith .1B 44
L33: Know I .2G 47
Galingale Rd. L11: Norr G .9M 45
Galion Way WA8: Wid .4J 79
Gallagher Ind. Est. CH44: Wall .7H 57
Galleries, The L37: Form .1F 24
Gallopers La. CH61: Thing .1B 88
Galloway Dr. WN8: Uph .6L 31
Galloway Rd. L22: Water .9L 33
Galloway St. L7: Liv .9J 59
Galston Av. L35: Rainh .7G 62
Galston Cl. L33: Kirkb .5B 36
Galsworthy Av. L30: Boot .2C 44
Galsworthy Pl. L30: Boot .2D 44
Galsworthy Wlk. L30: Boot .3D 44
Galton St. L3: Liv .2B 4 (6A 58)
Galtres Ct. CH63: Hghr B .8L 73
Galtres Pk. CH63: Hghr B .8L 73
Galway Av. WA8: Wid .5H 79
Galway Cres. WA11: Hay .3F 50
Gambier Ter. L1: Liv .9K 5 (1E 74)
Gamble Av. WA10: St H .4H 49
Gamlin St. CH41: Birke .9F 56
Gamston Wood L32: Kirkb .1A 46
Ganneys Mdw. Cl. CH49: Woodc .5C 72
Ganney's Mdw. Rd. CH49: Woodc .6C 72
Gannock St. L7: Liv .7H 59
Gantley Av. WN5: Bil .8N 31
Gantley Cres. WN5: Bil .9N 31
Gantley Rd. WN5: Bil .8N 31
Ganton Cl. PR8: South .3D 12
WA8: Wid .4L 79
Ganworth Cl. L24: Speke .5J 93
Ganworth Rd. L24: Speke .5J 93
Garage Rd. L24: Halew .2K 93
Garden Apartments L18: Moss H .5L 75
Garden Cotts. L12: W Der .5B 60
L39: Orm .8B 20
Garden Ct. CH42: Tran .7J 73
Gardeners Vw. L33: Kirkb .5E 36
Gardeners Way L35: Rainh .4F 62
Garden Hey Rd. CH46: More .1J 71
CH47: Meols .9D 54
Gardenia Gro. L17: Aig .6F 74
Garden La. CH46: More .8M 55
L5: Liv .5E 58
L9: Ain .2J 45
Garden Lodge Gro. L27: N'ley .3H 77
Gardenside CH46: Leas .5B 56
Gardenside St. L6: Liv .1L 5 (6E 58)
Gardens Rd. CH63: Beb .2A 90
Garden St. L25: Woolt .6E 76
Garden Wlk. L34: Presc .4A 62
M31: Part .6L 69
Gardiner Av. WA11: Hay .4E 50
Gardiners Pl. WN8: Skel .4B 30
Gardner Av. L20: Boot .3C 44
Gardner Rd. L13: Liv .4K 59
L37: Form .1G 25
Gardner's Dr. L6: Liv .5H 59
Gardner's Row L3: Liv .1F 4 (6C 58)
Gareth Av. WA11: St H .4L 49
Garfield Ter. CH49: Upton .3A 72
Garfourth Cl. L19: Garst .9B 76
Garfourth Rd. L19: Garst .9B 76
Garmoyle Cl. L15: Wav .1K 75
Garmoyle Rd. L15: Wav .1K 75
Garner St. WA2: Warr .1D 82
Garnet St. L13: Liv .8L 59
WA9: St H .2N 63
Garnett Av. L4: Kirkd .1D 58
WA4: Westy .4H 83
Garnett Grn. L39: Orm .8B 20
Garnett Pl. WN8: Skel .5D 30
Garnetts La. L35: Tar G .7A 78
WA8: Hale B .3D 94
Garrett Fld. WA3: Ris .4L 67
Garrick Av. CH46: More .9K 55
Garrick Pde. PR8: South .9F 6
Garrick Rd. CH43: Pren .8F 72
Garrick St. L7: Liv .1H 75
Garrigill Cl. WA8: Wid .3L 79
Garrison Cl. L8: Liv .2G 74
Garrowby Dr. L36: Huy .6G 60
Garsdale Av. L35: Rainh .7G 63
Garsdale Cl. WA5: Gt San .1H 81
Garsfield Rd. L4: Walt .9J 45
Garside Av. WA3: Low .3E 52
Garside Gro. WN3: Wigan .1G 41
Garstang Rd. PR9: South .3L 7
GARSTON .1A 92
Garston Ind. Est. L19: Garst .3A 92
Garston Old Rd. L19: Garst, Gras .9N 75
Garston Way L19: Garst .1N 91
GARSWOOD .8E 40
Garswood Av. WA11: Rainf .4D 38
Garswood Cl. CH46: Leas .5M 55
L31: Mag .9K 27
Garswood Cres. WN5: Bil .7A 40
Garswood Old Rd. WA11: St H .2M 49
WN4: Garsw .1B 50
Garswood Rd. WA11: Hay .1D 50
WN4: Garsw .6D 40
WN5: Bil .7A 40
Garswood Station (Rail) .8E 40
Garswood St. L8: Liv .5E 74
WA10: St H .6K 49
WN4: Ash M .8K 41
Garter Cl. L11: Crox .7A 46
Garth, The CH43: Oxton .3E 72
L36: Huy .6J 61
Garth Blvd. CH63: Hghr B .8L 73
Garth Ct. L22: Water .1L 43
Garthdale Rd. L18: Moss H .4M 75
Garth Dr. L18: Moss H .4N 75
Garthowen Rd. L7: Liv .7J 59
Garth Rd. CH65: Ell P .9D 104
L32: Kirkb .2E 46
Garth Wlk. L32: Kirkb .2E 46
Garton Dr. WA3: Low .1F 52
Gartons La. WA9: Clock F, Sut M .6M 63
Garven Pl. WA1: Warr .3B 82
Garway L25: Woolt .5G 76
Garwood Cl. WA5: Westb .8L 65
Gascoyne St. L3: Liv .2D 4 (6B 58)
Gaskell Av. WA4: Westy .5H 83
Gaskell Ct. WA9: St H .7B 50
Gaskell Rake *L30: N'ton* .*6C 34*
(off Higher End Pk.)
Gaskell's Brow WN4: Ash M .6G 40
Gaskell St. WA4: Stockt H .7D 82
WA9: St H .9N 49
Gaskill Rd. L24: Speke .3H 93
Gatclif Rd. L13: Liv .1K 59
GATEACRE .3F 76
Gateacre Brow L25: Gate .4F 76
Gateacre Ct. CH66: Ell P .6L 103
L25: Gate .*1D 76*
(off Headbourne Cl.)
Gateacre Neighbourhood Cen.
L25: Gate .2E 76
Gateacre Pk. Dr. L25: Gate .1D 76
Gateacre Ri. L25: Gate .4F 76
Gateacre Va. Rd. L25: Woolt .5F 76
Gategill Gro. WN5: Bil .9N 31
Gateley Cl. WA4: Thel .5M 83
Gateside Ct. L27: N'ley .3J 77
Gates La. L29: Thorn .3A 34
Gatewarth Ind. Est. WA5: Warr .5M 81
Gatewarth St. WA5: Warr .5M 81
Gateway, The CH62: Brom .6D 90
Gateway Trade Pk. WA2: Warr .9B 66
Gathurst Ct. WA8: Wid .8G 78
Gatley Dr. L31: Mag .4K 35
Gatley Wlk. L24: Speke .3K 93
Gaunts Way WA7: Pal F .9A 96
Gautby Rd. CH41: Birke .8E 56
Gavin Rd. WA8: Wid .9E 78
Gaw Hill La. L39: Augh .1M 27
Gaw Hill Vw. L39: Augh .1N 27
Gawsworth Cl. CH43: Oxton .5F 72
WA10: Eccl .7E 48
Gawsworth Ct. WA3: Ris .4N 67
Gawsworth Rd. CH66: Gt Sut .9K 103
WA3: Golb .1A 52
Gaybeech Cl. CH43: Bid .9B 56
Gayhurst Av. WA2: Fearn .7G 67
Gayhurst Cres. L11: Norr G .8M 45
Gaynor Av. WA11: Hay .3H 51
GAYTON .8B 88
Gayton Av. CH45: New B .1H 57
CH63: Hghr B .8J 73
Gayton Farm Rd. CH60: Hesw .1A 100
Gayton La. CH60: Hesw .9B 88
Gayton Mill Cl. CH60: Hesw .8B 88
Gayton Parkway CH60: Hesw .1C 100
Gayton Rd. CH60: Hesw .9N 87
Gayton Sands Nature Reserve .4A 100
Gaytree Ct. CH43: Bid .1C 72
Gaywood Av. L32: Kirkb .2D 46
Gaywood Cl. CH43: Bid .1C 72
L32: Kirkb .2D 46
Gaywood Ct. L23: Blun .8H 33
Gaywood Grn. L32: Kirkb .2D 46
Gellings La. L34: Know .5E 46
Gellings Rd. L34: Know .5E 46
Gelling St. L8: Liv .3E 74
Gemini Bus. Pk. PR9: South .1E 12
WA5: Westb .6L 65
(not continuous)
Gemini Cl. L20: Boot .6A 44
Gemini Dr. L14: Knott A .5D 60
Gemini Pk. WA5: Westb .6M 65
Gem St. L5: Liv .4B 58
General Dr. L12: W Der .2B 60
General St. WA1: Warr .3D 82
Genesis Centre, The WA3: Ris .4M 67
Geneva Cl. *L36: Huy* .*5J 61*
(off Salerno Dr.)
Geneva Rd. CH44: Wall .7K 57
L6: Liv .6H 59
Genista Cl. L9: Walt .7F 44
Genoa Cl. L25: Gate .1F 76
Gentwood Pde. L36: Huy .5H 61
Gentwood Rd. L36: Huy .5G 61
George Cl. WA6: Hel .3D 114
George Dr. PR8: Ains .9L 11
George Hale Av. L34: Know P .3J 61
George Harrison Cl. L6: Liv .6G 58
George Moore Ct. L23: Thorn .5A 34
George Rd. CH47: Hoy .2D 70
WA5: Gt San .4L 81
Georges Cres. WA4: Grap .6J 83
George's Dock Gates L3: Liv .5C 4 (8A 58)
Georges Dock Way L3: Liv .6D 4 (8A 58)
George's La. PR9: Banks .1E 8
George's Rd. L6: Liv .4G 59
George St. CH41: Birke .5H 57
CH65: Ell P .7A 104
L3: Liv .4D 4 (7B 58)
WA10: St H .7K 49
WA12: Newt W .6J 51
WN4: Ash M .7L 41
George Ter. WN5: Orr .7N 31
Georgia Av. CH62: Brom .4D 90
L33: Kirkb .5B 36
Georgia Cl. L20: Boot .7B 44
Georgian Cl. L26: Halew .1K 93
L35: Eccl P .3D 62
Georgian Pl. L37: Form .3E 24
Georgia Pl. WA5: Gt San .1L 81
Geraint St. L8: Liv .2E 74
Gerald Rd. CH43: Oxton .4G 72
Gerard Av. CH45: Wall .2G 56
Gerard Centre, The WN4: Ash M .8K 41
Gerard Rd. CH45: Wall .3F 56
CH48: W Kir .5C 70
GERARD'S BRIDGE .5K 49
Gerards Ct. WA11: St H .2L 49
Gerards La. WA9: St H, Sut L .2N 63
Gerards Pk. WA10: St H .5L 49
Gerard St. L3: Liv .3G 5 (7D 58)
WN4: Ash M .8K 41
Gerard Way L33: Kirkb .9D 36
Germander Cl. L26: Halew .7J 77
German's La. L40: Burs .7L 15
Gerneth Cl. L24: Speke .3G 92
Gerneth Rd. L24: Speke .4F 92
Gerosa Av. WA2: Win .1C 66
Gerrard Av. CH66: Gt Sut .1H 111
WA5: Warr .1A 82
Gerrard Pl. WN8: Skel .4C 30
Gerrard Rd. WA3: Croft .2H 67
WN5: Bil .6A 40
Gerrard's La. L26: Halew .6J 77
Gerrard St. WA8: Wid .8L 79
Gertrude Rd. L4: Walt .3G 58
Gertrude St. CH41: Birke .2M 73
WA9: St H .2F 62
Geves Gdns. L22: Water .1L 43
Ghyll Gro. WA11: St H .1L 49
Gibbons Av. WA10: St H .7F 48
Gibbon's Rd. WN4: Garsw .9F 40
Gibbs Ct. CH61: Irby .1N 87
Gibfield Rd. WA9: St H .4H 63
Gibraltar Row L3: Liv .3C 4 (7A 58)
Gibson Cl. CH61: Pens .4N 87
L33: Kirkb .6B 36
Gibson Ct. CH65: Ell P .6A 104
Gibson Rd. L8: Liv .1E 74
Gibson Sq. *WA3: Golb* .*2B 52*
(off Turton St.)
Gibson St. WA1: Warr .3D 82
WA4: Stockt H .7E 82
Gibson Ter. *CH44: Wall* .*4K 57*
(off Royden Av.)
Giddygate La. L31: Mag, Mell .3N 35
Gidlow Rd. L13: Liv .6L 59
Gidlow Rd. Sth. L13: Liv .7L 59
Gigg La. WA4: Moore .2K 97
Giggles Fun Cen. .4A 30
Gig La. WA1: Wools .9L 67
WA4: Thel .5M 83
Gilbert Cl. CH63: Spit .5M 89
Gilbert Ct. WA3: Cul .7N 53
Gilbert Ho. WA7: Run .4H 95
Gilbert Pl. L40: Burs .1F 20
WA4: Westy .5J 83
Gilbert Rd. L35: Whis .4C 62
Gilbert St. L1: Liv .7F 4 (9C 58)
Gilchrist Rd. M44: Irlam .3L 69
Gildarts Gdns. L3: Liv .5B 58
Gildart St. L3: Liv .3K 5 (7E 58)
Gilderdale Cl. WA3: Birchw .4B 68
Gilead St. L7: Liv .7G 59
Gilescroft Av. L33: Kirkb .7E 36
Gilescroft Wlk. L33: Kirkb .7E 36
Giles Dr. WA4: Westy .5J 83
Gillan Cl. WA7: Brook .1E 108
GILLAR'S GREEN .8B 48
Gillars Grn. Dr. WA10: Eccl .7C 48
Gillar's La. WA10: Eccl .7B 48
Gillbrook Sq. CH41: Birke .9F 56
Gilleney Gro. L35: Whis .4D 62
Gillibrands Rd. WN8: Skel .4C 30
GILLMOSS .5B 46
Gillmoss Cl. L11: Crox .6A 46
Gillmoss Ind. Est. L10: Faz .4N 45
Gillmoss La. L11: Crox .5A 46
Gills La. CH61: Barn, Pens .3A 88
Gill St. L3: Liv .4K 5 (7E 58)
Gilman St. L4: Walt .2F 58
Gilmartin Gro. L6: Liv .3M 5 (6F 58)
Gilmoss (Park & Ride) .4A 46
Gilmour Mt. CH43: Oxton .4H 73
Gilpin Av. L31: Mag .1K 35
Gilroy Nature Pk. .4D 70
Gilroy Rd. CH48: W Kir .5D 70
L6: Liv .6G 59
Giltbrook Cl. WA8: Wid .5J 79
Gilwell Av. CH46: More .1M 71
Gilwell Cl. CH46: More .1M 71
WA4: Grap .6K 83
Ginnel, The CH62: Port S .2A 90
Gipsy Gro. L18: Moss H .3C 76
Gipsy La. L18: Moss H .3C 76
Girton Av. L20: Boot .8D 44
WN4: Ash M .7H 41
Girton Cl. CH65: Ell P .1B 112
Girton Rd. CH65: Ell P .1B 112
Girtrell Cl. CH49: Upton .3L 71
Girtrell Rd. CH49: Upton .3L 71
Girvan Cres. WN4: Garsw .7F 40
Girvan Dr. CH64: Lit N .8F 100
Gisburn Av. WA3: Golb .1A 52
Givenchy Cl. L16: Child .9C 60
Glacier Bldg. L3: Liv .4D 74
Gladden Hey Dr. WN3: Wins .2F 40
Gladden Pl. WN8: Skel .4B 30
Glade, The CH47: Meols .8E 54
Glade Dr. CH66: Lit Sut .8E 102
Glade Pk. Ct. L8: Liv .4G 74
Glade Rd. L36: Huy .5J 61
Gladeswood Rd. L33: Know I .1F 46
Gladeville Rd. L17: Aig .6K 75
Gladica Cl. L36: Huy .7M 61
Gladstone Av. L16: Child .9E 60
L21: Sea .*3N 43*
(off Gladstone Rd.)
Gladstone Cl. CH41: Birke .2K 73
Gladstone Ct. L8: Liv .9L 5
Gladstone Hall Rd. CH62: Port S .2A 90
Gladstone M. WA2: Warr .2B 82
Gladstone Rd. CH42: Rock F .5M 73
CH44: Wall .6K 57
CH64: Nest .6E 100
L7: Liv .8G 58
L9: Walt .7F 44
L19: Garst .1A 92
L21: Sea .3M 43
PR9: South .9L 7
Gladstone St. L3: Liv .2E 4 (6B 58)
L25: Woolt .6D 76
WA2: Warr .2B 82
WA8: Wid .8L 79
WA10: St H .7G 48
Gladstone Ter. *CH64: Will* .*6M 101*
(off Neston Rd.)
Gladstone Theatre .3A 90
Gladstone Way WA12: Newt W .6J 51
Gladsville Rd. L27: N'ley .4K 77
Glaisdale Cl. WN4: Ash M .8L 41
Glaisdale Dr. PR8: South .3E 12
Glaisher St. L5: Liv .3F 58
Glamis Cl. CH43: Noct .5D 72
Glamis Dr. PR9: South .4N 7
Glamis Gro. WA9: St H .2M 63
Glamis Rd. L13: Liv .3J 59
Glamorgan Cl. WA10: St H .8J 49
Glan Aber Pk. L12: W Der .1C 60
Glasier Rd. CH46: More .8K 55
Glaslyn Way L9: Walt .7F 44
Glastonbury Av. WA3: Low .2K 53
Glastonbury Cl. L6: Liv .2J 59
WA7: Nort .4H 97
Glastonbury M. WA4: Stockt H .6F 82
Glasven Rd. L33: Kirkb .8D 36
GLAZEBROOK .3G 69
Glazebrook La. WA3: Glaz .2G 68
WA8: Wid .2K 79
Glazebrook Station (Rail) .4G 69
Glazebrook St. WA1: Warr .2E 82
Glaziers La. WA3: Cul .8L 53
Gleadmere WA8: Wid .6F 78
Gleaner Cl. WA7: Run .4J 95

Gleaston Cl. CH62: Brom 6C 90
Gleave Cl. WA5: Burtw 3H 65
Gleave Cres. L6: Liv 1L 5 (5F 58)
Gleave St. WA10: St H 6K 49
Glebe, The WA7: Run 6A 96
Glebe Av. WA4: Grap 7K 83
WN4: Ash M 9L 41
Glebe Bus. Pk. WA8: Wid 4M 79
Glebe Cl. L31: Mag 2G 35
Glebecroft Av. CH2: Elt 2L 113
Glebe End L29: Seft 4E 34
Glebe Hey L27: N'ley 3J 77
Glebe Hey Rd. CH49: Woodc 5A 72
Glebeland WA3: Cul 7M 53
Glebelands Rd. CH46: More 9M 55
Glebe La. PR9: Banks 1E 8
WA8: Wid 3K 79
Glebe Pl. PR9: South 8G 6
Glebe Rd. CH45: Wall 3G 56
WN8: Skel 4D 30
Glebeway Way CH65: Ell P 9D 104
Gleggside CH48: W Kir 6D 70
Glegg St. L3: Liv 5A 58
Glegside Rd. L33: Kirkb 9E 36
Glen, The CH63: Spit 4B 90
L18: Moss H 5A 76
WA7: Pal F 9B 96
Glenacres L25: Woolt 5E 76
Glenalmond Rd. CH44: Wall 5K 57
Glenathol Rd. CH66: Gt Sut 1H 111
L18: Moss H 6A 76
Glenavon Rd. CH43: Pren 7G 73
L16: Child 9A 60
Glen Bank L22: Water 9J 33
Glenbank Cl. L9: Walt 5F 44
Glenburn Av. CH62: East 2D 102
Glenburn Rd. CH44: Wall 6K 57
WN8: Skel 9B 22
Glenby Av. L23: Crosb 9M 33
Glencairn Rd. L13: Liv 6L 59
Glen Cl. WA3: Rix 7H 69
Glencoe Rd. CH45: Wall 3H 57
CH66: Gt Sut 1H 111
Glenconner Rd. L16: Child 8C 60
Glencourse Rd. WA8: Wid 3K 79
Glencoyne Dr. PR9: South 1N 7
Glencroft Cl. L36: Huy 4G 61
Glendale Av. CH2: Elt 2L 113
WN4: Ash M 7L 41
Glendale Cl. L8: Liv 5E 74
Glendale Gro. CH63: Spit 5A 90
L33: Kirkb 6E 36
Glendale Rd. WA11: St H 3K 49
Glendale Wlk. WA5: Gt San 9J 65
Glendale Way L37: Form 2F 24
Glendevon Rd. L16: Child 8A 60
L36: Huy 8J 61
Glendower Rd. L22: Water 1L 43
Glendower St. L20: Boot 9B 44
Glendyke Rd. CH66: Gt Sut 1H 111
L18: Moss H 6A 76
Gleneagles Cl. CH61: Pens 3N 87
L33: Kirkb 5B 36
WA3: Low 3G 52
Gleneagles Dr. PR8: Ains 2H 17
WA8: Wid 3K 79
WA11: Hay 5C 50
Gleneagles Rd. CH66: Gt Sut 9H 103
L16: Child 8C 60
Glenesk Rd. CH66: Gt Sut 1H 111
Glenfield Cl. CH43: Bid 9C 56
CH46: More 8J 55
Glenfield Rd. L15: Wav 2M 75
Glengariff St. L13: Liv 2K 59
Glengarth Cl. CH47: Meols 9F 54
Glenhead Rd. L19: Aller 8N 75
Glenholm Rd. L31: Mag 4H 35
Glenluce Rd. L19: Aig 8N 75
Glenlyon Rd. L16: Child 9A 60
Glenmarsh Cl. CH63: Hghr B 2K 89
L12: W Der 3A 60
Glenmarsh Way L37: Form 1H 25
Glenmaye Cl. L12: Crox 8C 46
Glenmaye Rd. CH66: Gt Sut 1H 111
Glenmore Av. L18: Moss H 5M 75
Glenmore Rd. CH43: Oxton 4G 73
Glenn Pl. WA8: Wid 7H 79
Glenpark Dr. PR9: South 3N 7
Glen Pk. Rd. CH45: Wall 2G 57
Glen Rd. CH66: Gt Sut 9H 103
L13: Liv 7N 59
Glen Ronald Dr. CH49: Grea 3L 71
Glenrose Rd. L25: Woolt 4E 76
Glenrose Ter. PR8: Birkd 1N 11
Glenroyd Dr. L40: Burs 1J 21
Glenside L18: Aller 6A 76
WN6: Appl B 3L 23
Glenton Pk. CH64: Lit N 8F 100
Glentree Cl. CH49: Grea 3L 71
Glentrees Rd. L12: W Der 1N 59
Glentworth Cl. L31: Mag 4J 35
Glenville Cl. L25: Woolt 4F 76
WA7: Run 9L 95
Glenvine Cl. L16: Child 9C 60
Glen Way L33: Kirkb 5D 36
Glenway Cl. L12: Crox 6D 46
Glenwood WA7: Nort 6E 96
Glenwood Cl. CH66: Lit Sut 8H 103
L35: Whis 7C 62
Glenwood Dr. CH61: Irby 9M 71
Glenwood Gdns.
CH66: Lit Sut 8H 103
Glenwood Rd. CH66: Lit Sut 8H 103
Glenwyllin Rd. L22: Water 9L 33
Globe Rd. L20: Boot 6A 44
Globe St. L4: Walt 2D 58
Glossop Cl. WA1: Warr 3F 82
Gloucester Av. WA3: Golb 1C 52
Gloucester Cl. CH66: Gt Sut 5K 111
WA1: Wools 1L 83
Gloucester Ct. L6: Liv 2N 5 (6F 58)
Gloucester Pl. L6: Liv 2M 5
Gloucester Rd. CH45: Wall 3E 56
L6: Liv 4J 59
L20: Boot 6C 44
L36: Huy 6L 61
PR8: Birkd 1M 11
WA8: Wid 5L 79
Gloucester Rd. Nth. L6: Liv 3J 59
Gloucester St. WA9: St H 8N 49
Glover Ho. Cl. WN7: Leigh 1M 53
Glover Pl. L20: Boot 6A 44
Glover Rd. WA3: Birchw 5K 67
GLOVERS BRIDGE 2K 21
Glover's Brow L32: Kirkb 7A 36
Glovers Ct. L32: Kirkb 8A 36
Glover's La. L30: N'ton 7D 34
Glover St. CH42: Tran 4J 73
WA10: St H 8J 49
WA12: Newt W 7L 51
Glyn Av. CH62: Brom 8D 90
Glynne Gro. L16: Child 9E 60
Glynn St. L15: Wav 1L 75
Glyn Rd. CH44: Wall 4H 57
Goddard Rd. WA7: Ast 4A 96
Godetia Cl. L9: Faz 6L 45
Godfrey Pilkington Art Gallery 7K 49
Godfrey St. WA2: Warr 1E 82
Godscroft La. WA6: Frod 9H 107
Godshill Cl. WA5: Gt San 1F 80
Godstow WA7: Nort 3G 97
Go Karting 7E 6
GOLBORNE 2B 52
Golborne Dale Rd. WA12: Newt W 5B 52
Golborne Ent. Pk. WA3: Golb 1B 52
Golborne Ho. WA3: Golb 2C 52
Golborne Rd. WA2: Win 3B 66
WA3: Low 2D 52
WN4: Ash M 7M 41
Golborne St. WA12: Newt W 6N 51
Goldcliff Cl. WA5: Call 7M 65
Goldcrest Cl. L12: Crox 6D 46
WA7: Beech 1B 108
Goldcrest M. L26: Halew 7J 77
Goldendale Wlk. WA5: Gt San 1L 81
Golden Gro. L4: Walt 9F 44
Golden Sq. Shop. Cen. WA1: Warr 3B 82
Golden Triangle Ind. Est.
WA8: Hale B 2E 94
Golders Grn. L7: Liv 9H 59
Goldfinch Cl. L26: Halew 7J 77
Goldfinch Farm Rd. L24: Speke 4G 93
Goldfinch La. WA3: Birchw 5M 67
Goldie St. L4: Walt 2E 58
Goldsmith Rd. CH43: Pren 7F 72
Goldsmith St. L6: Liv 6G 58
L20: Boot 6N 43
Goldsmith Way CH43: Pren 7F 72
Goldsworth Fold L35: Rainh 6D 62
Golf Links Rd. CH42: Tran 7H 73
Golf Rd. L37: Form 8E 16
Gondover Av. L9: Walt 4E 44
Gonville Rd. L20: Boot 8C 44
Gooch Dr. WA12: Newt W 8M 51
Goodacre Rd. L9: Ain 3G 45
Goodakers Ct. CH49: Woodc 6A 72
(off Childwall Grn.)
Goodakers Mdw. CH49: Woodc 6A 72
Goodall Pl. L4: Kirkd 1D 58
Goodall St. L4: Kirkd 9D 44
Goodban St. WA9: St H 1A 64
Goodier Ct. WA7: Run 7M 95
Goodison Av. L4: Walt 1E 58
Goodison Park 1E 58
Goodison Pl. L4: Walt 9E 44
Goodison Rd. L4: Walt 9E 44
Goodlass Rd. L24: Speke 1E 92
Goodleigh Pl. WA9: Sut L 4M 63
Good Shepherd Cl. L11: Norr G 8N 45
Goodwood Cl. L36: Roby 8H 61
Goodwood Ct. WA9: St H 3G 62
Goodwood Dr. CH46: Leas 6N 55
Goodwood Gro. CH66: Gt Sut 2J 111
Goodwood St. L5: Liv 4C 58
Gooseberry Hollow WA7: Wind H 6F 96
Gooseberry La. WA7: Nort 6F 96
Goose Green, The CH47: Meols 8E 54
Goose La. WA4: Hatt 5A 98
Goostrey Cl. CH63: Spit 6A 90
Gordale Cl. L8: Liv 4F 74
WA5: Gt San 1H 81
Gordon Av. CH49: Grea 5M 71
CH62: Brom 8D 90
L22: Water 9J 33
L31: Mag 9H 27
PR9: South 6H 7
WA1: Wools 1J 83
WA11: Hay 3H 51
WN4: Garsw 7G 40
Gordon Ct. CH49: Grea 5M 71
Gordon Dr. L14: Broad G 6C 60
L19: Gras 9M 75
Gordon La. CH2: Back 8N 111
Gordon M. PR9: South 6H 7
Gordon Pl. L18: Moss H 5M 75
Gordon Rd. CH45: New B 2J 57
L21: Sea 3M 43
Gordon St. CH41: Birke 2J 73
L15: Wav 1K 75
PR9: South 7G 7
Gordon Ter. CH64: Will 6M 101
Gordon Way PR9: South 7H 7
(off Gordon St.)
Gore Dr. L39: Augh 1C 28
Goree L2: Liv 5C 4 (8B 58)
Goree Piazza L2: Liv 5D 4
(off The Strand)
Gores La. L37: Form 8E 16
WA11: Crank 5J 39
Gores Rd. L33: Know I 1F 46
Gore St. L8: Liv 2D 74
Gorleston M. L32: Kirkb 1D 46
Gorleston Way L32: Kirkb 1D 46
Gorran Haven WA7: Brook 9E 96
Gorse Av. L12: W Der 9N 45
Gorsebank Rd. L18: Moss H 3K 75
Gorsebank St. CH44: Wall 6J 57
Gorseburn Rd. L13: Liv 3K 59
GORSE COVERT 3B 68
Gorse Covert Rd. WA3: Birchw 4A 68
Gorse Cres. CH44: Wall 7J 57
Gorsedale Pk. CH44: Wall 7K 57
Gorsedale Rd. CH44: Wall 7H 57
L18: Moss H 4M 75
Gorsefield L37: Form 7G 17
WA9: St H 2G 63
Gorsefield Av. CH62: Brom 1C 102
L23: Thorn 6N 33
Gorsefield Cl. CH62: Brom 1C 102
Gorsefield Rd. CH42: Tran 5J 73
Gorse Hey Ct. L13: W Der 4M 59
Gorsehill Rd. CH45: New B 2G 57
CH60: Hesw 6A 88
Gorselands Ct. L17: Aig 6J 75
Gorse La. CH48: W Kir 7F 70
PR4: Tarl 2M 9
Gorse Rd. CH47: Meols 9E 54
Gorse Sq. M31: Part 6K 69
Gorse Way L37: Form 9C 16
Gorsewood Cl. L25: Gate 3G 76
(off Gorsewood Rd.)
Gorsewood Gro. L25: Gate 3F 76
Gorsewood Rd. L25: Gate 3F 76
WA7: Murd 9F 96
Gorsey Av. L30: N'ton 8B 34
Gorsey Brow WN5: Bil 6N 39
Gorsey Brow Cl. WN5: Bil 6N 39
Gorsey Cop Rd. L25: Gate 2E 76
Gorsey Cop Way L25: Gate 2E 76
Gorsey Cft. L34: Eccl P 2C 62
Gorsey La. CH44: Wall 7H 57
L21: Ford 1A 44
L30: N'ton 1A 44
L38: Hight 2G 33
L39: Bart 6M 17
PR9: Banks 1F 8
WA1: Warr 9E 66
WA2: Warr 9E 66
WA5: Burtw 4D 64
WA8: Wid 8A 80
WA9: Bold, Clock F 6A 64
WA13: Warb 2N 85
Gorsey Pl. WN8: Skel 5D 30
Gorseyville Cres. CH63: Hghr B 2L 89
Gorseyville Rd. CH63: Hghr B 2L 89
Gorseywell La. WA7: Pres B 9H 97
Gorst La. L40: Burs 9D 14
Gorstons La. CH64: Lit N 8G 101
Gorst St. L4: Walt 2E 58
Gorsuch La. L40: Scar 2J 19
Gorton Rd. L13: Liv 7N 59
Gort Rd. L36: Huy 6J 61
Goschen St. L5: Liv 2E 58
L13: Liv 6L 59
Gosford St. L8: Liv 4E 74
Gosforth Ct. WA7: Pal F 8A 96
Gosforth Rd. PR9: South 7L 7
Gosling Cl. WA4: Hatt 5B 98
Gosling Rd. WA3: Croft 2J 67
Gosport Cl. WA2: Padg 8F 66
Goswell St. L15: Wav 9K 59
Gotham Rd. CH63: Spit 5N 89
Gothic St. CH42: Rock F 6M 73
Gough Av. WA2: Warr 7B 66
Gough Rd. L13: Liv 2K 59
Goulden St. WA5: Warr 2N 81
Goulders Ct. WA7: Brook 1D 108
Gourley Grange CH48: W Kir 7E 70
Gourley Rd. L13: Liv 8N 59
Gourleys La. CH48: W Kir 7E 70
Government Rd. CH47: Hoy 1C 70
Govett Rd. WA9: St H 2F 62
Gower Gdns. L40: Burs 2K 21
Gower St. L3: Liv 8D 4 (9B 58)
L20: Boot 5A 44
WA9: St H 9N 49
Gowery, The L37: Form 1G 24
(off Church Rd.)
Gowrie Gro. L21: Lith 3A 44
Gowy Ct. CH66: Ell P 6K 103
Goyt Hey Av. WN5: Bil 6A 40
Graburn Rd. L37: Form 9F 16
Grace Av. L10: Faz 3M 45
WA2: Warr 9C 66
Grace Cl. CH45: Wall 4H 57
Grace Rd. CH65: Ell P 8N 103
L9: Walt 4F 44
Grace St. L8: Liv 4E 74
WA9: St H 1M 63
Gradwell St. L1: Liv 6F 4 (8C 58)
Graeme Bryson Ct. L11: Norr G 9L 45
Grafton Cres. L8: Liv 2D 74
Grafton Dr. CH49: Upton 4A 72
PR8: Ains 9G 11
Grafton Gro. L8: Liv 4D 74
Grafton Rd. CH45: New B 2H 57
CH65: Ell P 7A 104
Grafton St. CH43: Oxton 3H 73
L8: Liv 5E 74
(Beresford Rd.)
L8: Liv 2C 74
(Stanhope St., not continuous)
WA5: Warr 2N 81
WA10: St H 7G 49
WA12: Newt W 7K 51
Grafton Wlk. CH48: W Kir 6D 70
Graham Av. CH66: Gt Sut 9J 103
WN6: Appl B 3M 23
Graham Cl. WA8: Wid 7F 78
Graham Cres. M44: Cad 5J 69
Graham Dr. L26: Halew 8L 77
Graham Rd. CH48: W Kir 5B 70
WA8: Wid 8F 78
Graham's Rd. L36: Huy 7K 61
Graham St. WA9: St H 6M 49
Grainger Av. CH43: Pren 6F 72
CH48: W Kir 4C 70
L20: Boot 5D 44
Grain Ind. Est. L8: Liv 4D 74
Graley Cl. L26: Halew 1K 93
Grammar School Ct. L39: Orm 8D 20
WA4: Warr 5G 82
(off Grammar School Rd.)
Grammar School Gdns. L39: Orm 9D 20
Grammar School La. CH48: W Kir 7E 70
Grammar School Rd. WA4: Warr 5G 82
WA13: Lymm 6F 84
Grampian Av. CH46: More 9N 55
Grampian Rd. L7: Liv 7K 59
Grampian Way CH46: More 9M 55
CH62: East 2D 102
CH64: Lit N 9E 100
WA3: Low 1E 52
Granams Cft. L30: N'ton 7C 34
Granard Rd. L15: Wav 2M 75
Granary Mill WA4: Pres H 9H 97
Granary Way L3: Liv 2C 74
Granborne Chase L32: Kirkb 8N 35
GRANBY 9N 5 (1F 74)
Granby Cl. PR9: South 4L 7
WA7: Brook 1E 108
Granby Cres. CH63: Spit 5N 89
Granby Rd. WA4: Walt 8C 82
Granby St. L8: Liv 9N 5 (1F 74)
Grand Central L3: Liv 5H 5
Grandison Rd. L4: Walt 9H 45
Grand National Av. L9: Ain 1G 45
GRANGE
CH48 6D 70
WA1 8L 67
Grange, The CH42: Rock F 7M 73
CH44: Wall 5J 57
L20: Boot 4B 44
PR9: South 4A 8
Grange & Pyramids Shop. Centre, The
CH41: Birke 2K 73
Grange Av. CH45: Wall 3H 57
L12: W Der 4C 60
L25: Hunts X 9H 77
PR9: South 7K 7
WA4: Westy 4F 82
Grange Av. Nth. L12: W Der 4C 60
Grange Cl. WA3: Low 4D 52
Grange Ct. CH43: Oxton 5G 72
L15: Wav 1L 75
(off Grange Ter.)
L23: Blun 8J 33
Grange Cres. CH66: Hoot 5F 102
Grange Cross Cl. CH48: W Kir 7F 70
Grange Cross Hey CH48: W Kir 7F 70
Grange Cross La. CH48: W Kir 7F 70
Grange Dr. CH60: Hesw 5N 87
CH63: Thorn H 8G 89
WA5: Penk 4J 81
WA8: Wid 7G 79
WA10: St H 1E 62
Grange Employment Cen.
WA1: Wools 8M 67
Grange Farm Cl. WA5: Gt San 2M 81
Grange Farm Cres. CH48: W Kir 5F 70
Grange Grn. Mnr. WA4: Hghr Wal 9N 81
Grangehurst Ct. L25: Gate 4F 76
Grange La. L25: Gate 3E 76
L37: Form 8E 16
Grangemeadow Rd. L25: Gate 3E 76
Grangemoor WA7: Run 7N 95
Grange Mt. CH43: Oxton 3J 73
CH48: W Kir 6E 70
CH60: Hesw 6N 87
Grange Old Rd. CH48: W Kir 6D 70

GRANGE PARK 1E 62
Grange Pk. L31: Mag 4K 35
Grange Pk. Av. WA7: Run 5M 95
Grange Park Golf Course 9F 48
Grange Pk. Rd. WA10: St H 9F 48
Grange Pl. CH41: Birke 2J 73
M44: Cad 4K 69
Grange Pct. CH41: Birke 2L 73
Grange Rd. CH41: Birke 2K 73
(not continuous)
CH48: W Kir 6B 70
CH60: Hesw 5N 87
CH65: Ell P 9A 104
L30: N'ton 9G 34
L38: Hight 5E 24
PR9: South 8K 7
WA7: Run 5M 95
WA11: Hay, Newt W 5F 50
WN4: Ash M 5H 41
Grange Rd. E. CH41: Birke 2L 73
Grange Rd. Nth. WA7: Run 5M 95
Grange Rd. W. CH41: Birke 2H 73
CH43: Oxton 2H 73
Grange Road West Sports Cen. 3H 73
Grangeside L25: Gate 3E 76
Grange St. L6: Liv 4J 59
Grange Ter. L15: Wav 1L 75
Grange Valley WA11: Hay 4F 50
Grange Vw. CH43: Oxton 3J 73
Grange Wlk. CH48: W Kir 7E 70
Grange Way L25: Gate 3E 76
Grangeway WA7: Run 7M 95
Grangeway Ct. WA7: Run 7M 95
Grange Weint L25: Gate 4E 76
Grange Wood CH48: W Kir 7E 70
Grangewood L16: Child 8D 60
Granite Ter. L36: Huy 7L 61
Granston Cl. WA5: Call 7N 65
Grant Av. L15: Wav 2L 75
Grant Cl. L14: Knott A 6E 60
WA5: Old H 8M 65
WA10: St H 6H 49
Grant Ct. *L20: Boot 7B 44*
(off Clairville Cl.)
Grantham Av. WA1: Warr 1F 82
WA4: Walt 8C 82
Grantham Cl. CH61: Pens 3M 87
PR8: Birkd 5N 11
Grantham Cres. WA11: St H 5M 49
Grantham Rd. L33: Kirkb 6C 36
PR8: Birkd 5N 11
Grantham St. L6: Liv 6G 59
Grantham Way L30: N'ton 7G 34
Grantley Rd. L15: Wav 2N 75
Grantley St. WN4: Ash M 6J 41
Granton Cl. L37: Form 1E 24
Granton Rd. L5: Liv 3F 58
Grant Rd. CH46: Leas 6B 56
L14: Knott A 6D 60
Grantwood WN4: Ash M 6J 41
Granville Av. L31: Mag 1H 35
Granville Cl. CH45: Wall 3E 56
L39: Augh 3N 27
Granville Ct. CH45: Wall 3E 56
PR9: South 6J 7
Granville Dr. CH66: Lit Sut 7G 102
Granville Pk. L39: Augh 4N 27
Granville Pk. W. L39: Augh 4N 27
Granville Rd. L15: Wav 1J 75
L19: Garst 1A 92
PR8: Birkd 3K 11
Granville St. WA1: Warr 2E 82
WA7: Run 4K 95
WA9: St H 7N 49
GRAPPENHALL 6H 83
Grappenhall Heys Walled Garden 9H 83
Grappenhall La. WA4: App T, Grap 3J 99
Grappenhall Rd. CH65: Gt Sut 1L 111
WA4: Stockt H 7E 82
Grappenhall Way CH43: Bid 1C 72
Grasmere Av. CH43: Noct 3C 72
L34: Presc 3C 62
WA2: Warr 6E 66
WA11: St H 3L 49
WN8: Uph 5L 31
Grasmere Cl. L33: Kirkb 7B 36
WA11: St H 3L 49
Grasmere Ct. *CH41: Birke 3J 73*
(off Penrith St.)
WA11: St H 3L 49
Grasmere Dr. CH45: Wall 3H 57
L21: Lith 1D 44
WA7: Beech 1N 107
WN4: Ash M 6K 41
Grasmere Fold WA11: St H 3L 49
Grasmere Gdns. L23: Crosb 8M 33
Grasmere Ho. *L17: Aig 6J 75*
(off Mossley Hill Dr.)
Grasmere Rd. CH64: Nest 8E 100
CH65: Ell P 3A 112
L31: Mag 1J 35
L37: Form 1D 24
L38: Hight 8G 24
M31: Part 6L 69
WA6: Frod 6M 107
WA13: Lymm 4F 84
Grasmere St. L5: Liv 4G 58
GRASSENDALE 8M 75
Grassendale Ct. *L19: Gras 9M 75*
(off Grassendale Rd.)
Grassendale Esplanade
L19: Gras 1L 91
Grassendale La. L19: Gras 9M 75
Grassendale Rd. L19: Gras 9M 75
Grassington Cres. L25: Woolt 6G 77
Grassmoor Cl. CH62: Brom 7D 90
Grasswood Rd. CH49: Woodc 6B 72
Grassy La. WA6: Frod 7G 107
Grasville Rd. CH42: Tran 5L 73
Gratrix Rd. CH62: Brom 7C 90
Gratton Pl. WN8: Skel 4D 30
Gravel, The PR4: Mere B 5J 9
Gravel Cl. PR9: Banks 2D 8
Gravel La. PR9: Banks 2D 8
(not continuous)
Graveyard La. L39: Bic 5E 28
Gray Av. WA11: Hay 4F 50
Gray Gro. L36: Huy 9K 61
Graylag Cl. WA7: Beech 1B 108
Graylands Pl. L4: Walt 9H 45
Graylands Rd. CH62: Port S 1B 90
L4: Walt 9H 45
Graylaw Ind. Est. L9: Ain 4H 45
Grayling Dr. L12: Crox 7B 46
Grayling M. WA4: Warr 7C 82
Gray's Av. L35: Presc 3C 62
Grayson M. *CH41: Birke 1M 73*
(off John St.)
Graysons Rd. WA11: Rainf 3C 38
Grayson St. L1: Liv 8F 4 (9C 58)
Grayston Av. WA9: Sut L 3N 63
Gray St. L20: Boot 5N 43
GREASBY 5L 71
Greasby Dr. CH66: Gt Sut 1K 111
Greasby Hill Rd. CH48: W Kir 7D 70
Greasby Rd. CH44: Wall 5G 57
CH49: Grea 5K 71
GREAT ALTCAR 3L 25
Great Ashfield WA8: Wid 5G 78
Gt. Charlotte St. L1: Liv 5G 5 (8C 58)
(Elliot St.)
L1: Liv 5G 4 (8C 58)
(Roe St.)
GREAT CROSBY 6L 33
Gt. Crosshall St. L3: Liv 3E 4 (7C 58)
Great Delph WA11: Hay 3F 50
Gt. George Pl. L1: Liv 1D 74
Gt. George Sq. L1: Liv 9H 5 (9D 58)
Gt. George's Rd. L22: Water 2K 43
Gt. George's Sq. L1: Liv 8H 5
Gt. George St. L1: Liv 9H 5 (9D 58)
Gt. Heath Rd. L4: Kirkd 2C 58
Great Hey L30: N'ton 6C 34
Gt. Homer St. L5: Liv 3D 58
Gt. Homer St. Shop. Cen. L5: Liv 4D 58
Gt. Howard St. L3: Liv 2C 4 (6A 58)
L5: Liv 3A 58
GREAT MEOLS 8F 54
Gt. Mersey St. L5: Kirkd 3C 58
(not continuous)
Gt. Nelson St. L3: Liv 5C 58
Gt. Newton St. L3: Liv 4K 5 (7E 58)
Gt. Orford St. L3: Liv 6K 5 (8E 58)
Gt. Richmond St. L3: Liv 1G 5 (6D 58)
Great Riding WA7: Nort 8E 96
GREAT SANKEY 2H 81
Great Sankey Leisure Cen. 9F 64
GREAT SUTTON 1J 111
Gt. Western Ho. CH41: Birke 1M 73
Greaves Cl. PR9: Banks 1E 8
Greaves Hall Av. PR9: Banks 2E 8
Greaves Hall Ind. Est. PR9: Banks 2F 8
Greaves St. L8: Liv 3E 74
Grebe Av. WA10: St H 1D 62
Grecian St. L21: Sea 2M 43
Grecian Ter. L5: Liv 4E 58
Gredington St. L8: Liv 4F 74
Greeba Av. WA4: Warr 5C 82
Greek St. L3: Liv 4J 5 (7D 58)
WA7: Run 4J 95
Green, The CH48: Caldy 9E 70
CH62: Brom 2C 90
CH63: Raby 2J 101
CH64: Lit N 8F 100
CH64: Nest 6D 100
CH64: Will 6M 101
CH65: Whit 3N 111
L13: Liv 7A 60
L23: Crosb 7K 33
L34: Eccl P 2C 62
M31: Part 5M 69
WA7: Halt 6B 96
WN8: Parb 3E 22
Greenacre L40: Westh 9J 21
Greenacre Cl. L25: Hunts X 8G 76
Greenacre Dr. CH63: Brom 8B 90
Greenacre Rd. L25: Hunts X 8G 76
Greenacres WA6: Frod 8M 107
Greenacres, The WA13: Lymm 4G 84
Greenacres Caravan Pk. WA6: Hap 4A 114
Greenacres Cl. CH43: Bid 9C 56
WN7: Leigh 2J 53
Greenacres Ct. CH43: Bid 9C 56
Greenall Av. WA5: Penk 4F 80
Greenall Ct. L34: Presc 3N 61
Greenalls Av. WA4: Warr 7C 82
Greenall St. WA10: St H 6H 49
WN4: Ash M 6K 41
GREEN BANK 8H 49
Green Bank CH63: Brim 5G 89
Greenbank CH2: Ince 9L 105
L22: Water 2L 43
L39: Augh 2A 28
Greenbank Av. CH45: New B 2H 57
CH66: Lit Sut 7H 103
L31: Mag 9H 27
WN5: Bil 9N 31
Greenbank Ct. L17: Aig 3K 75
Greenbank Cres. WA10: St H 7J 49
Greenbank Dr. CH61: Pens 4N 87
L10: Faz 3N 45
L17: Aig 4K 75
PR8: Birkd 4L 11
Greenbank Gdns. WA4: Stockt H 6G 82
Greenbank La. L17: Aig 4K 75
Greenbank Rd. CH42: Tran 5J 73
CH48: W Kir 4C 70
L18: Moss H 3K 75
WA4: Stockt H 6G 82
Greenbank Sports Academy 4K 75
Greenbank St. WA4: Warr 7D 82
Greenbridge Cl. WA7: Cas 5C 96
Greenbridge Rd. WA7: Wind H 5D 96
Greenburn Av. WA11: St H 1M 49
Green Coppice WA7: Nort 7E 96
Green Ct. WN7: Leigh 1J 53
Greencroft Hey CH63: Spit 5A 90
Greencroft Rd. CH44: Wall 6J 57
Greendale Rd. CH62: Port S 1N 89
L25: Woolt 4D 76
Green End La. WA9: St H 1M 63
Green End Pk. L12: W Der 2M 59
Greenes Rd. L35: Whis 7A 62
Greenfield Av. WN8: Parb 3E 22
Greenfield Cl. PR9: South 4M 7
Greenfield Ct. L18: Aller 7A 76
Greenfield Dr. L36: Huy 9K 61
Greenfield Gdns. CH2: Elt 2M 113
Greenfield Gro. L36: Huy 8K 61
Greenfield La. CH60: Hesw 5K 87
L21: Lith 1N 43
WA6: Frod 5L 107
Greenfield Rd. CH66: Lit Sut 7G 103
L13: Liv 6M 59
PR8: South 5H 13
WA10: St H 5G 49
GREENFIELDS 9C 56
Greenfields Av. CH62: Brom 8B 90
WA4: App 8E 82
Greenfields Cl. CH64: Lit N 9F 100
WA1: Wools 1K 83
WA12: Newt W 6L 51
Greenfields Cres. CH62: Brom 8B 90
WN4: Ash M 7L 41
Greenfields Cft. CH64: Lit N 9E 100
Greenfields Dr. CH64: Lit N 9E 100
Greenfield Vw. WN5: Bil 7N 39
Greenfield Wlk. L36: Huy 8K 61
Greenfield Way CH44: Wall 5H 57
L18: Aller 7A 76
Greenfinch Cl. L12: Crox 7D 46
Greenfinch Gro. L26: Halew 7J 77
Greenford Cl. WN5: Orr 6N 31
Greenford Rd. PR8: Ains 1J 17
Green Gables L33: Kirkb 7B 36
Greengables Cl. L8: Liv 3F 74
Green Gates L36: Huy 3J 61
Greengates Cres. CH64: Lit N 9E 100
Greenham Av. L33: Kirkb 5D 36
Green Haven CH43: Noct 3D 72
Greenhaven *WN8: Uph 5L 31*
(off Tower Hill Rd.)
Greenhaven Cl. L10: Faz 3M 45
Greenheath Way CH46: Leas 6N 55
Greenhey Dr. L30: N'ton 9B 34
Greenhey Pl. WN8: Skel 4C 30
Greenhey Pl. Bus. Pk. WN8: Skel 4C 30
Green Heys Dr. L31: Mag 2L 35
Greenheys Gdns. L8: Liv 2H 75
Greenheys Rd. CH44: Wall 6H 57
CH61: Irby 2K 87
L8: Liv 2G 74
Greenhill Av. L18: Moss H 3A 76
Greenhill Cl. L18: Moss H 6N 75
Greenhill Cres. WN5: Bil 6B 40
Greenhill La. WA4: Lwr W 9C 98
Greenhill Pl. L36: Huy 8J 61
Greenhill Rd. L18: Aller, Moss H 5N 75
L19: Aller 8A 76
WN5: Bil 6B 40
Greenholme Cl. L11: Norr G 7M 45
Green Ho. Cl. WA3: Low 1H 53
Greenhouse Farm Rd.
WA7: Pal F 9D 96
Greenhow Av. CH48: W Kir 5C 70
Greenings Ct. WA2: Warr 2D 82
Greenings La. PR9: South 3A 14
Green Jones Brow WA5: Burtw 3H 65
Green Kettle La. L39: Hals 2E 18
Greenlake Rd. L18: Moss H 6N 75
Greenlands L36: Huy 8J 61
Greenland St. L1: Liv 9H 5 (1C 74)
Green La. CH41: Tran 4L 73
CH45: Wall 3D 56
(Redcar Rd.)
CH45: Wall 4B 56
(Telegraph La.)
CH62: East 7E 90
CH63: Beb 2M 89
CH65: Ell P 1A 112
Green La. CH66: Gt Sut 1H 111
(not continuous)
L3: Liv 6J 5 (8D 58)
L13: Liv 4K 59
L18: Moss H 4N 75
(not continuous)
L21: Ford 9A 34
L21: Sea 3N 43
(not continuous)
L22: Water 9J 33
L23: Thorn 5A 34
L31: Mag 1F 34
(not continuous)
L37: Form 8F 16
L39: Orm 7C 20
L40: Lath 7C 22
M44: Cad 4L 69
PR4: Tarl 5M 9
(Blackgate La.)
PR4: Tarl 3M 9
(Gorse La.)
PR9: Banks 3F 8
WA1: Padg 9H 67
WA2: Win 2B 66
WA4: App, App T 2G 98
WA5: Burtw 2G 65
WA8: Wid 7H 79
WA10: Eccl 4B 48
WA11: Rainf 6D 38
WN5: Bil 9N 31
Green Lane, The L40: Burs 1K 21
Green La. Av. L39: Orm 7C 20
Green La. Cl. WA2: Win 2B 66
Green La. Nth. L16: Child 2A 76
Green Lane Station (Rail) 4M 73
Green La. W. CH1: Shot 9A 110
Green Lawn CH42: Rock F 7M 73
L36: Huy 5L 61
Green Lawn Gro. CH42: Rock F 7M 73
Green Lawns Dr. CH66: Gt Sut 5L 111
GREEN LEACH 3K 49
Green Leach Av. WA11: St H 3L 49
Green Leach Ct. WA11: St H 3L 49
Green Leach La. WA11: St H 3L 49
Greenlea Cl. CH63: Beb 1M 89
CH65: Whit 3N 111
WN5: Orr 7N 31
Greenleaf St. L8: Liv 1H 75
Greenleas Cl. CH45: Wall 3D 56
Greenleas Rd. CH45: Wall 3D 56
Greenleigh Rd. L18: Moss H 6N 75
Green Link L31: Mag 1G 35
Greenloon's Dr. L37: Form 1C 24
Greenloon's Wlk. L37: Form 2C 24
Green Mdws. WA3: Low 5F 52
Green Mt. CH49: Upton 3A 72
Greenoaks Farm Ind. Est. WA8: Wid 7M 79
Green Oaks Path WA8: Wid 8N 79
Green Oaks Shop. Cen. WA8: Wid 7L 79
(Deacon Rd.)
WA8: Wid 8L 79
(Green Oaks Way)
Green Oaks Way WA8: Wid 8L 79
Greenock M. WA8: Wid 5H 79
Greenock St. L3: Liv 2B 4 (6A 58)
Greenodd Av. L12: W Der 9A 46
Greenore Dr. L24: Hale 5A 94
Greenough Av. L35: Rainh 4F 62
Greenough St. L25: Woolt 6D 76
Green Pk. L30: N'ton 6E 34
Green Pk. Dr. L31: Mag 2G 35
Green Rd. L34: Presc 3N 61
M31: Part 6L 69
Greensbridge La. L26: Halew, Tar G 7L 77
L35: Tar G 6M 77
Greenshank Cl. WA12: Newt W 6L 51
Greens Health & Fitness
Liverpool 5E 74
Greenside L6: Liv 2L 5 (6E 58)
Greenside Av. L10: Ain 9K 35
L15: Wav 9M 59
WA6: Frod 7N 107
Greenside Cl. L33: Kirkb 5E 36
Greens La. L31: Lyd 2J 27
WN5: Bil 1A 40
Greenslate Ct. WN5: Bil 9N 31
Greenslate Rd. WN5: Bil 9N 31
Green St. L5: Liv 5B 58
WA5: Warr 3N 81
(not continuous)
Greens Wlk. *L17: Aig 5K 75*
(off Aigburth Va.)
Green Vw. WA13: Lymm 3H 85
Greenville Cl. CH63: Beb 2M 89
Greenville Dr. L31: Mag 2H 35
Greenville Rd. CH63: Beb 2M 89
Green Wlk. M31: Part 6L 69
PR8: Ains 9K 11
Greenway CH49: Grea 4M 71
CH61: Pens 3M 87
CH62: Brom 4C 90
CH64: Park 4B 100
L23: Crosb 6N 33
L36: Huy 5F 60
WA1: Padd 1G 83
WA4: App 8E 82
WA5: Gt San 1G 80
WN4: Ash M 7J 41
Greenway, The L12: Knott A 5C 60
Greenway Av. WN8: Skel 5E 30

Greenway Cl. L36: Huy 5F **60**
WA6: Hel 2E **114**
WN8: Skel 2B **30**
Greenway Rd. CH42: Tran 5K **73**
L24: Speke 4L **93**
WA7: Run 5K **95**
WA8: Wid 6L **79**
Greenways WN5: Bil 9N **31**
Greenways Ct. CH62: Brom 9B **90**
Greenwell Rd. WA11: Hay 4E **50**
Greenwich Av. WA8: Wid 4N **79**
Greenwich Ct. L9: Ain 2G **45**
Greenwich Rd. L9: Ain 2G **45**
Greenwood Cl. L34: Presc 3B **62**
L39: Augh 3A **28**
Greenwood Ct. WA3: Ris 8N **53**
(Cedar Ct.)
WA3: Ris 1M **67**
(Warrington Rd.)
WA9: Clock F 5M **63**
Greenwood Cres. WA2: Warr 7E **66**
Greenwood Dr. WA7: Manor P 3H **97**
WA12: Newt W 8M **51**
Greenwood Gdns. PR8: Birkd 1N **11**
Greenwood La. CH44: Wall 4J **57**
Greenwood Rd. CH47: Meols 9F **54**
CH49: Woodc 5A **72**
L18: Aller 7N **75**
WA13: Lymm 6E **84**
Greetby Hill L39: Orm 8E **20**
Greetby Pl. WN8: Skel 4D **30**
Greetham St. L1: Liv 8F **4** (9C **58**)
Gregory Cl. L16: Child 9C **60**
WA5: Old H 1L **81**
Gregory La. L39: Hals 1F **18**
Gregory Row *WA3: Low* *1H **53***
(off Sandy La.)
Gregory Way L16: Child 9C **60**
Gregson Ct. CH45: New B 1J **57**
Gregson Rd. L35: Presc 5A **62**
WA8: Wid 7M **79**
Gregsons Av. L37: Form 8E **16**
Gregson St. L6: Liv 1L **5** (6E **58**)
Grenadier Dr. L12: W Der 2C **60**
Grenfell Cl. CH64: Park 5C **100**
Grenfell Ct. CH64: Park 6C **100**
Grenfell Pk. CH64: Park 5C **100**
Grenfell Rd. L13: Liv 1K **59**
Grenfell St. WA8: Wid 8L **79**
Grennan, The CH45: New B 1H **57**
Grennan Ct. *CH45: New B* *1H **57***
(off The Grennan)
Grenville Cres. CH63: Brom 8B **90**
Grenville Dr. CH61: Pens 4M **87**
Grenville Rd. CH42: Tran 5M **73**
CH64: Nest 5E **100**
Grenville St. Sth. L1: Liv 8G **5** (9C **58**)
Grenville Way CH42: Tran 5M **73**
Gresford Av. CH43: Pren 6G **72**
CH48: W Kir 5D **70**
L17: Liv 2K **75**
Gresford Cl. L35: Whis 6C **62**
WA5: Call 7N **65**
Gresham St. L7: Liv 7K **59**
Gresley Cl. L7: Liv 8H **59**
Gressingham Rd. L18: Moss H 5A **76**
Gretton Rd. L14: Knott A 4F **60**
Greyfriars WN4: Ash M 7H **41**
Greyfriars Cl. WA2: Fearn 7H **67**
Greyfriars Rd. PR8: Ains 8H **11**
Greyhound Farm Rd. L24: Speke 4G **92**
Greymist Av. WA1: Wools 1K **83**
Grey Rd. L9: Walt 6E **44**
WN4: Ash M 7J **41**
Greys Ct. WA1: Wools 8K **67**
Greystoke Cl. CH49: Upton 4N **71**
Greystokes L39: Augh 2B **28**
Greystone Cres. L14: Broad G 6C **60**
Greystone Pl. L10: Faz 3L **45**
Greystone Rd. L10: Faz 3K **45**
L14: Broad G 7C **60**
WA5: Penk 4H **81**
Greystones CH66: Gt Sut 1J **111**
Grey St. L8: Liv 2E **74**
WA1: Warr 2D **82**
Gribble Rd. L10: Faz 3M **45**
Grice St. WA4: Stockt H 7D **82**
Gridleford Pl. WA1: Warr 3F **82**
Grierson St. L8: Liv 1G **75**
Grieve Rd. L10: Faz 3M **45**
Griffin Av. CH46: More 9M **55**
Griffin Cl. L11: Crox 6A **46**
WA10: Eccl 6C **48**
Griffin M. WA8: Wid 5L **79**
Griffin St. WA9: St H 2A **64**
Griffiths Av. WA3: Ris 4M **67**
Griffiths Cl. CH49: Grea 5K **71**
Griffiths Dr. PR9: South 7L **7**
Griffiths Rd. L36: Huy 7J **61**
Griffiths St. L1: Liv 8H **5** (9D **58**)
WA4: Westy 4G **82**
Griffon Ho. *PR9: South* *5L **7***
(off Cambridge Rd.)
Grimrod Pl. WN8: Skel 5D **30**
Grimsby Ct. L19: Garst 1N **91**
Grimsditch La. WA4: Lwr W, Nor B 9B **98**
Grimshaw Ct. WA3: Golb 1B **52**
GRIMSHAW GREEN 1F **22**
Grimshaw La. L39: Orm 7C **20**
Grimshaw Rd. WN8: Skel 4D **30**
Grimshaw St. L20: Boot 8A **44**
WA3: Golb 1B **52**
WA9: Sut L 3M **63**
Grindley Gdns. CH65: Ell P 3A **112**
Grindlow Wlk. WN3: Wins 1E **40**
Grinfield St. L7: Liv 6N **5** (8F **58**)
Grinshill Cl. L8: Liv 2F **74**
Grinstead Cl. PR8: Birkd 5M **11**
Grinton Cres. L36: Roby 7H **61**
Grisedale Av. WA2: Warr 6C **66**
Grisedale Cl. L37: Form 1E **24**
WA7: Beech 1A **108**
Grisedale Rd. CH62: Brom 7E **90**
Grizedale WA8: Wid 6E **78**
Grizedale Av. WA11: St H 2L **49**
Groarke Dr. WA5: Penk 3F **80**
Groes Rd. L19: Gras 9N **75**
Grogan Sq. L20: Boot 4C **44**
Gronow Pl. *L20: Boot* *4D **44***
(off Hughes Dr.)
Grosmont Rd. L32: Kirkb 2D **46**
Grosmont Way WA8: Wid 4A **80**
Grosvenor Av. CH48: W Kir 6C **70**
L23: Crosb 9L **33**
WA1: Warr 1F **82**
WA3: Low 2E **52**
Grosvenor Cl. L30: N'ton 8E **34**
PR8: Birkd 3L **11**
WA5: Gt San 3L **81**
Grosvenor Ct. CH43: Oxton 3H **73**
CH47: Hoy 2C **70**
L15: Wav 1A **76**
L18: Moss H 5K **75**
L34: Presc *3A **62***
(off Grosvenor Rd.)
Grosvenor Dr. CH45: New B 1H **57**
Grosvenor Gdns. PR8: Birkd 3M **11**
WA12: Newt W 8L **51**
Grosvenor Grange WA1: Wools 8J **67**
Grosvenor Pl. CH43: Oxton 3G **73**
PR8: Birkd 3M **11**
Grosvenor Rd. CH43: Oxton 2G **72**
CH45: New B 1H **57**
CH47: Hoy 2C **70**
L4: Walt 8E **44**
L15: Wav 9J **59**
L19: Gras 1M **91**
L31: Mag 5H **35**
L34: Presc 3A **62**
PR8: Birkd 2K **11**
WA8: Wid 4L **79**
WA10: St H 8G **48**
WA11: Hay 3D **50**
Grosvenor St. CH44: Wall 4H **57**
L3: Liv 1G **5** (6C **58**)
WA7: Run 4L **95**
Grosvenor Ter. *L8: Liv* *4G **74***
(off Wellesley Rd.)
Grosvenor Wharf Rd. CH65: Ell P 7B **104**
Grounds St. WA2: Warr 1C **82**
Grove, The CH43: Oxton 5H **73**
CH44: Wall 6J **57**
CH63: Beb 2N **89**
L13: Liv 3L **59**
L28: Stockb V 2G **60**
L39: Augh 5A **28**
L39: Orm 8C **20**
L40: Ruf 3L **15**
WA3: Low 1E **52**
WA5: Penk 4H **81**
WA10: Windle 5F **48**
WA13: Lymm 5E **84**
WN6: Appl B 3M **23**
Grove Av. CH60: Hesw 6N **87**
WA13: Lymm 5C **84**
Grove Bank WA6: Hel 1F **114**
Grove Cl. WN8: Uph 4M **31**
Grovedale Dr. CH46: More 8A **56**
Grovedale Rd. L18: Moss H 3L **75**
Grovehurst Av. L14: Knott A 5D **60**
Groveland Av. CH45: Wall 3D **56**
CH47: Hoy 1C **70**
Groveland Rd. CH45: Wall 3D **56**
Grovelands L7: Liv 8M **5**
Grove Mead L31: Mag 2L **35**
Grove Pk. L8: Liv 2H **75**
L39: Orm 6D **20**
PR9: South 7L **7**
Grove Pk. Av. L12: W Der 1N **59**
Grove Pl. CH47: Hoy 1C **70**
Grove Ri. WA13: Lymm 5E **84**
Grove Rd. CH1: Moll 8J **111**
CH42: Rock F 6M **73**
CH45: Wall 3E **56**
CH47: Hoy 1C **70**
L6: Liv 6J **59**
WN8: Uph 4M **31**
Groves, The CH43: Oxton 3H **73**
CH66: Whit 5M **111**
L7: Liv 7M **5**
L32: Kirkb 3C **46**
Groveside CH48: W Kir 6B **70**
L7: Liv 8M **5** (9F **58**)
Grove Sq. CH62: New F 9N **73**
Grove St. CH62: New F 9A **74**
L7: Liv 8M **5** (9F **58**)
L15: Wav 9L **59**
L20: Boot 6N **43**
PR8: South 2N **11**
WA4: Warr 5D **82**
Grove St. WA7: Run 4J **95**
WA10: St H 7J **49**
WN4: Ash M 7J **41**
Grove Ter. CH47: Hoy 1C **70**
PR8: Birkd 1N **11**
WA6: Hel 1F **114**
Grove Way L7: Liv 8M **5** (9F **58**)
Grovewood PR8: Birkd 1L **11**
Grovewood Ct. CH43: Oxton 5H **73**
Grovewood Gdns. L35: Whis 6B **62**
Grundy Cl. PR8: South 1D **12**
WA8: Wid 5J **79**
Grundy Homes PR8: South 1D **12**
Grundy St. L5: Kirkd 3A **58**
WA3: Golb 3B **52**
Guardian Ct. CH48: W Kir 7C **70**
PR8: Birkd 1M **11**
Guardian St. WA5: Warr 2A **82**
Guardian St. Ind. Est. WA5: Warr 2A **82**
Guelph Pl. L7: Liv 3N **5**
Guelph St. L7: Liv 3M **5** (7F **58**)
Guernsey Cl. WA4: App 8E **82**
Guernsey Dr. CH65: Ell P 4A **112**
Guernsey Rd. L13: Liv 5L **59**
WA8: Wid 5A **80**
Guest St. WA8: Wid 9K **79**
Guffitts Cl. CH47: Meols 8F **54**
Guffitt's Rake CH47: Meols 8F **54**
Guildford Av. L30: N'ton 1E **44**
Guildford Cl. WA2: Padg 8H **67**
Guildford Rd. PR8: Birkd 7M **11**
Guildford St. CH44: Wall 5K **57**
Guildhall Rd. L9: Ain 4F **44**
Guild Hey L34: Know 6H **47**
Guillemot Way L26: Halew 7J **77**
Guilsted Rd. L11: Norr G 8M **45**
Guinea Gap CH44: Wall 6L **57**
Guinea Gap Leisure Cen. 6L **57**
Guinea Hall Cl. PR9: Banks 2E **8**
Guinea Hall La. PR9: Banks 1E **8**
Guinea Hall M. PR9: Banks 2E **8**
Guion Rd. L21: Lith 3A **44**
Guion St. L6: Liv 5G **59**
Gulliver's Theme Pk. 8N **65**
Gulls Way CH60: Hesw 7L **87**
Gunn Gro. CH64: Nest 6F **100**
Gunning Av. WA10: Eccl 5E **48**
Gunning Cl. WA10: Eccl 5E **48**
Gurnall St. L4: Walt 2E **58**
Gutticar Rd. WA8: Wid 7E **78**
Guy Cl. CH41: Tran 4L **73**
Guys Ind. Est. Nth. L40: Burs 3F **20**
Guys Ind. Est. Sth. L40: Burs 3F **20**
Gwendoline Cl. CH61: Thing 2A **88**
Gwendoline St. L8: Liv 2E **74**
Gwenfron Rd. L6: Liv 6G **58**
Gwent Cl. L6: Liv 4G **59**
Gwent St. L8: Liv 2F **74**
Gwladys St. L4: Walt 9E **44**
Gwydir St. L8: Liv 3F **74**
Gwydrin Rd. L18: Moss H 3A **76**
Gym, The
Liverpool 6E **4**
Gym Health & Fitness, The
St Helens 7J **49**

H

Hackett Av. L20: Boot 4C **44**
Hackett Pl. L20: Boot 4C **44**
Hackins Hey L2: Liv 4D **4** (7B **58**)
Hackthorpe St. L5: Liv 2D **58**
Hadassah Gro. L17: Aig 4H **75**
Hadden Cl. L35: Rainh 5D **62**
Haddock St. L20: Kirkd 9A **44**
Haddon Av. L9: Walt 4E **44**
Haddon Dr. CH61: Pens 3N **87**
WA8: Wid 4E **78**
Haddon Ho. *CH64: Nest* *6E **100***
(off Churchill Way)
Haddon Rd. CH42: Rock F 6N **73**
WA3: Low 1E **52**
WN3: Wigan 1G **41**
Haddon St. WN4: Ash M 6H **41**
Haddon Wlk. L12: Crox 7C **46**
Hadfield Av. CH47: Hoy 1D **70**
Hadfield Cl. WA8: Wid 7A **80**
Hadfield Gro. L25: Woolt 5G **76**
Hadington Rd. L23: Crosb 8M **33**
Hadleigh Cl. WA5: Gt San 3F **80**
Hadleigh Gro. WA7: Cas 5B **96**
Hadleigh Rd. L32: Kirkb 1D **46**
Hadley Av. CH62: Brom 6B **90**
Hadlow La. CH64: Will 7M **101**
Hadlow Rd. CH64: Will 9M **101**
Hadlow Road Station Mus. 7N **101**
Hadlow Ter. CH64: Will 7M **101**
Hadstock Av. L37: Form 3D **24**
Haggerston Rd. L4: Walt 8F **44**
Hague Bush Cl. WA3: Low 1F **52**
Hahnemann Rd. L4: Walt 8D **44**
Haig Avenue 1D **12**
Haig Av. CH46: More 9N **55**
M44: Cad 5J **69**
PR8: South 1D **12**
WA5: Gt San 4J **81**
Haigh Cl. WA9: St H 4J **63**
Haigh Ct. PR8: South 9L **7**
Haigh Cres. L31: Lyd 8H **27**
Haigh Rd. L22: Water 1L **43**
Haigh St. L3: Liv 1K **5** (5E **58**)
(not continuous)
Haig Rd. WA8: Wid 7K **79**
Haileybury Av. L10: Ain 9J **35**
Haileybury Rd. L25: Woolt 8F **76**
Hailsham Rd. L19: Aig 8L **75**
Halby Rd. L9: Ain 4G **44**
Halcombe Rd. L12: W Der 1B **60**
Halcyon Rd. CH41: Birke 4J **73**
Haldane Av. CH41: Birke 1F **72**
Haldane Rd. L4: Walt 8F **44**
HALE 6A **94**
HALE BANK 2E **94**
Halebank Rd. WA8: Hale B 2B **94**
Hale Bank Ter. WA8: Hale B 3D **94**
Hale Ct. WA8: Hale B 3D **94**
Hale Dr. L24: Hale, Speke 5H **93**
Halefield St. WA10: St H 6J **49**
(not continuous)
Hale Ga. Rd. WA8: Hale B 5C **94**
Hale Gro. WA5: Gt San 2J **81**
WN4: Ash M 6H **41**
HALE HEATH 5L **93**
Hale M. WA8: Wid 9F **78**
Hale Rd. CH45: Wall 3J **57**
L4: Walt 9D **44**
L24: Speke 4F **92**
(not continuous)
WA8: Hale B, Wid 3E **94**
Hale Rd. Ind. Est. WA8: Hale B 2E **94**
Hale St. L2: Liv 4E **4** (7B **58**)
WA2: Warr 1C **82**
Hale Vw. WA7: Run 7H **95**
Hale Vw. Rd. L36: Huy 7L **61**
WA6: Hel 1F **114**
HALEWOOD 9K **77**
Halewood Av. WA3: Golb 1A **52**
Halewood Caravan Pk. L26: Halew 8N **77**
Halewood Centre, The L26: Halew 9K **77**
Halewood Cl. L25: Gate 4F **76**
Halewood Dr. L25: Woolt 6F **76**
(Kings Dr.)
L25: Woolt 6G **76**
(Layton Rd.)
HALEWOOD GREEN 6J **77**
Halewood Leisure Cen. 9L **77**
Halewood Pl. L25: Woolt 5G **76**
Halewood Rd. L25: Gate, Woolt 4F **76**
Halewood Station (Rail) 8K **77**
Halewood Triangle Country Pk. 8H **77**
Halewood Triangle Vis. Cen. 8H **77**
Halewood Way L25: Woolt 6G **77**
Haley Rd. Nth. WA5: Burtw 3G **64**
Haley Rd. Sth. WA5: Burtw 4G **64**
Half Acre La. WA4: Thel 5M **83**
Half Crown St. L5: Kirkd 3B **58**
Halfmile Island WN8: Skel 1C **30**
Halfpenny Cl. L19: Gras 9N **75**
Halfpenny La. WN8: Skel 3L **29**
Half-Tide Wharf L3: Liv 1B **74**
Halidon Ct. L20: Boot 6N **43**
Halifax Cl. WA2: Warr 7E **66**
Halifax Cres. L23: Thorn 5A **34**
Halifax Rd. PR8: Ains 9J **11**
Halkirk Rd. L18: Aller 7A **76**
Halkyn Av. L17: Liv 2J **75**
Halkyn Dr. L5: Liv 4F **58**
Hallam Wlk. *L7: Liv* *8H **59***
(off Crosfield Rd.)
Hallastone Rd. WA6: Hel 1E **114**
Hall Av. WA8: Wid 7D **78**
Halla Way WA4: Warr 5F **82**
Hallbridge Gdns. WN8: Uph 4L **31**
Hall Brow Cl. L39: Orm 9F **20**
Hallcroft M31: Part 5M **69**
WN8: Skel 2F **30**
Hallcroft Pl. WA4: Grap 6H **83**
Hall Dr. CH49: Grea 5K **71**
L32: Kirkb 8C **36**
WA4: App 1E **98**
Hallfield Dr. CH2: Elt 2M **113**
Hallfield Pk. CH66: Gt Sut 1J **111**
Hallfields Rd. WA2: Warr 9E **66**
HALL GREEN 5K **31**
Hall Grn. WN8: Uph 5L **31**
Hall Grn. Cl. WN8: Uph 5L **31**
Halliday Cl. WA3: Birchw 6N **67**
Halliwell Jones Stadium 2B **82**
Hall La. CH1: Shot 9A **110**
L7: Liv 3M **5** (7F **58**)
L9: Ain 3G **44**
L31: Lyd 5G **26**
L31: Mag 4H **35**
L32: Kirkb 9B **36**
L33: Sim, Kirkb 4D **36**
L34: Presc 4A **62**
L35: Cron, Rainh 1F **78**
L36: Huy 7K **61**
L38: Ince B 8M **25**
L39: Bic 9J **29**
L40: Lath 8L **21**
M31: Part 5M **69**
WA4: Dares 5L **97**
WA4: Grap 8J **83**
WA4: Lwr S, Stret 7E **98**
WA5: Burtw 2J **65**
WA8: Cron 1F **78**
WA9: Bold 6B **64**
WN6: Appl B 3L **23**

Hallmoor Cl. L39: Augh .2C 28
Hall Nook WA5: Penk .4H 81
Hallows Av. WA2: Warr .8E 66
Hall Pk. L23: Blun .7H 33
Hall Rd. L40: Scar .7M 13
WA1: Wools .1K 83
WA11: Hay .3G 50
Hall Rd. E. L23: Blun .5H 33
Hall Road Station (Rail) .5G 33
Hall Rd. W. L23: Blun .5G 32
Hallsands Rd. L32: Kirkb .2C 46
Hallsgreen La. CH2: Wim T .6K 113
Hallside Cl. L19: Aig .8M 75
Hall St. PR9: South .9H 7
WA1: Warr .3D 82
WA9: Clock F .6N 63
WA10: St H .7K 49
WN2: Bam .4N 41
Hall Ter. WA5: Gt San .1G 81
Halltine Cl. L23: Blun .6G 33
Hallville Rd. CH44: Wall .6J 57
L18: Moss H .3M 75
Hall Wood Av. WA11: Hay .2H 51
Hallwood Cl. WA7: Run .9L 95
Hallwood Ct. CH64: Nest .7E 100
Hallwood Dr. CH66: Led .1C 110
Hallwood Link Rd. WA7: Pal F .9B 96
HALLWOOD PARK .9A 96
Hallwood Pk. Av. WA7: Pal F .9A 96
Hallwood Wlk. CH65: Ell P .7N 103
Hallworthy Cl. WN7: Leigh .1J 53
HALSALL .4H 19
Halsall Av. WA2: Warr .9E 66
Halsall Bldgs. *PR9: South .7J 7*
(off Manchester Rd.)
Halsall Cl. L23: Crosb .6L 33
WA7: Brook .1E 108
Halsall Ct. *L39: Orm .7B 20*
(off Halsall La.)
Halsall Grn. CH63: Spit .6A 90
Halsall Hall Dr. L39: Hals .4G 19
Halsall La. L37: Form .1F 24
L39: Hals .8J 19
L39: Orm .7B 20
Halsall Mnr. Ct. L39: Hals .4G 18
Halsall Rd. L20: Boot .4B 44
L39: Hals .4H 19
PR8: Birkd .6M 11
Halsall St. L34: Presc .2A 62
Halsbury Rd. CH45: Wall .3H 57
L6: Liv .6H 59
Halsey Av. L12: W Der .2L 59
Halsey Cres. L12: W Der .2L 59
Halsnead Av. L35: Whis .8N 61
Halsnead Caravan Est. L35: Whis .8B 62
Halsnead Cl. L15: Wav .8M 59
Halstead Rd. CH44: Wall .6J 57
L9: Walt .4E 44
Halstead Wlk. *L32: Kirkb .1A 46*
(off Downgreen Cl.)
HALTON .8B 96
HALTON BROOK .7A 96
Halton Brook Av. WA7: Run .7N 95
Halton Brow WA7: Halt .6A 96
Halton Castle .6B 96
Halton Chase L40: Westh .9J 21
Halton Ct. WA7: Run .5N 95
Halton Cres. CH49: Grea .5J 71
CH66: Gt Sut .3L 111
Halton Hey L35: Whis .8A 62
HALTON LEA .8B 96
Halton Lea Shop. Cen.
WA7: Pal F .8B 96
Halton Link Rd. WA7: Pal F .7A 96
HALTON LODGE .7M 95
Halton Lodge Av. WA7: Run .8N 95
Halton Miniature Railway .8E 96
Halton Rd. CH45: Wall .3G 56
CH66: Gt Sut .4K 111
L31: Lyd .9J 27
WA5: Gt San .2H 81
WA7: Run .5L 95
Halton Sta. Rd. WA7: Sut W .3B 108
Halton St. WA11: Hay .4G 50
HALTON VIEW .7N 79
Halton Vw. Rd. WA8: Wid .7M 79
HALTON VILLAGE .7B 96
Halton Wlk. *L25: Gate .2E 76*
(off Hartsbourne Av.)
Halton Way CH66: Gt Sut .4K 111
Halton Wood L32: Kirkb .8N 35
Hambledon Cl. CH66: Lit Sut .8F 102
Hambledon Dr. CH49: Grea .4K 71
Hamble Dr. WA5: Penk .5H 81
Hambleton Cl. L11: Crox .6N 45
WA8: Wid .5F 78
Hamblett Cres. WA11: St H .4L 49
Hamer St. WA10: St H .6J 49
Hamer St. Sth. *WA10: St H .7J 49*
(off Nth. John St.)
Hamil Cl. CH47: Meols .8F 54
Hamilton Av. M44: Cad .5K 69
Hamilton Cl. CH64: Park .4B 100
WA4: Westy .4J 83
Hamilton Ct. CH64: Nest .6F 100
L23: Blun .7H 33
Hamilton Ho. L3: Liv .3E 4
Hamilton La. CH41: Birke .1L 73
Hamilton Plaza *CH41: Birke .2M 73*
(off Duncan St.)
Hamilton Rd. CH45: New B .1G 56
L5: Liv .4E 58
WA10: Windle .4F 48
WN4: Garsw .7E 40
Hamilton Sq. CH41: Birke .1M 73
Hamilton Square Station (Rail) .1M 73
Hamilton St. CH41: Birke .2L 73
(not continuous)
Hamlet Ct. L17: Aig .5H 75
Hamlet Rd. CH45: Wall .3F 56
Hamlin Cl. WA7: West .9K 95
Hamlin Rd. L19: Garst .1B 92
Hammersley Av. WA9: Clock F .6M 63
Hammersley St. WA9: Clock F .6M 63
Hammersmith Way WA8: Wid .4N 79
Hammill Av. WA10: St H .4H 49
Hammill St. WA10: St H .5G 49
Hammond Rd. L33: Know I .8G 37
Hammond St. WA9: St H .8N 49
Hamnett Ct. WA3: Birchw .6M 67
Hamnett Rd. L34: Presc .2B 62
Hampden Gro. CH42: Tran .4L 73
Hampden Rd. CH42: Tran .4K 73
Hampden St. L4: Walt .8E 44
Hampshire Av. L30: N'ton .8B 34
Hampshire Gdns. WA10: St H .8J 49
Hampshire Rd. M31: Part .7K 69
Hampson Av. WA3: Cul .7N 53
Hampson Cl. WN4: Ash M .9K 41
Hampson St. L6: Liv .4H 59
Hampstead Rd. CH44: Wall .6J 57
L6: Liv .6H 59
Hampton Chase CH43: Noct .5D 72
Hampton Cl. CH64: Nest .8E 100
WA8: Wid .5A 80
Hampton Ct. L39: Augh .2B 28
WA7: Manor P .3E 96
Hampton Ct. Rd. L12: W Der .4B 60
Hampton Ct. Way WA8: Wid .4N 79
Hampton Cres. CH64: Nest .8E 100
Hampton Dr. WA5: Gt San .4L 81
WA8: Cron .3F 78
Hampton Gdns. CH65: Ell P .9M 103
Hampton Pl. WA11: St H .4L 49
Hampton Rd. L37: Form .3E 24
M44: Cad .5K 69
PR8: South .2A 12
Hamptons, The L37: Form .9G 16
Hampton St. L8: Liv .9K 5 (1E 74)
Hamsterley Cl. WA3: Birchw .3B 68
Hanbury Rd. L4: Walt .1J 59
Hancock Ct. *WA4: Warr .4D 82*
(off Barry St.)
Handa Dr. CH65: Ell P .5N 111
Handel Ct. L8: Liv .2G 75
Handel Rd. L27: N'ley .2G 77
Handfield Pl. L5: Liv .4F 58
Handfield Rd. L22: Water .1K 43
Handfield St. L5: Liv .4F 58
Handford Av. CH62: East .1E 102
Handforth Cl. WA4: Thel .4K 83
Handforth La. WA7: Run .9N 95
Hand La. WN7: Leigh .1M 53
Handley Ct. L19: Aig .8L 75
Handley Dr. WA2: Padg .8F 66
Handley St. WA7: Run .4J 95
Hands St. L21: Lith .4A 44
Handsworth Wlk. PR8: South .3E 12
Hanford Av. L9: Walt .4E 44
Hanging Birches WA8: Wid .3J 79
Hankey Dr. L20: Boot .5D 44
Hankey St. WA7: Run .5J 95
Hankinson Cl. M31: Part .7M 69
Hankinson St. L13: Liv .8M 59
Hankin St. L5: Liv .4C 58
Hanley Cl. WA8: Wid .7F 78
Hanley Rd. WA8: Wid .7F 78
Hanlon Av. *L20: Boot .4C 44*
(off Ainsdale Rd.)
Hanmer Rd. L32: Kirkb .9N 35
Hannah Cl. CH61: Pens .4M 87
Hannan Rd. L6: Liv .6H 59
Hanns Hall Farm CH64: Will .6K 101
Hanns Hall Rd.
CH64: Nest, Will .6J 101
Hanover Cl. CH43: Clau .2F 72
Hanover Ct. WA7: Brook .9D 96
Hanover St. L1: Liv .7F 4 (8C 58)
WA1: Warr .4B 82
Hansard Ct. WA9: St H .2G 63
Hansby Cl. WN8: Skel .4H 31
Hansby Dr. L24: Speke .2F 92
Hanson Pk. CH43: Oxton .3E 72
Hanson Rd. L9: Ain .5H 45
Hanson Rd. Bus. Pk. L9: Ain .5H 45
Hans Rd. L4: Walt .9F 44
Hants La. L39: Orm .7C 20
Hanwell Cl. WN7: Leigh .1L 53
Hanwell St. L6: Liv .3G 59
Hanworth Cl. L12: Crox .7C 46
HAPSFORD .4B 114
Hapsford Cl. WA3: Birchw .6K 67
Hapsford La. WA6: Hel .1N 113
(Ash Rd.)
WA6: Hel .4B 114
(Moor La.)
Hapsford Rd. L21: Lith .4A 44
Hapton St. L5: Liv .3D 58
Harbern Cl. L12: W Der .3B 60
Harbord Rd. L22: Water .1J 43
Harbord St. L7: Liv .8G 58
WA1: Warr .4D 82
Harbord Ter. L22: Water .1J 43
Harborne Dr. CH63: Spit .5M 89
Harbour Cl. WA7: Murd .9F 96
Harbour Dr. L19: Garst .3A 92
Harbreck Gro. L9: Ain .7J 45
Harbury Av. PR8: Ains .1G 17
Harcourt Av. CH44: Wall .6L 57
Harcourt Cl. WA3: Birchw .6M 67
Harcourt St. CH41: Birke .1J 73
L4: Kirkd .2C 58
Hardacre St. L39: Orm .7D 20
Hardie Av. CH46: More .8K 55
Hardie Cl. WA9: Sut M .6K 63
Hardie Rd. L36: Huy .6L 61
Harding Av. CH63: Beb .3M 89
WA2: Warr .8F 66
Harding Cl. L5: Liv .4F 58
Hardinge Rd. L19: Aller .8A 76
Harding Rd. L40: Burs .1H 21
Hardknott Rd. CH62: Brom .6D 90
Hard La. WA10: St H .4G 49
Hardman St. L1: Liv .7J 5 (9D 58)
Hardrow Cl. WN3: Wigan .1K 41
Hardshaw Cen. WA10: St H .7K 49
Hardshaw St. WA10: St H .7K 49
Hardwick Grange WA1: Wools .8L 67
Hardwick Rd. M31: Part .6N 69
WA7: Ast .4N 95
WN4: Ash M .6J 41
Hardy Cl. CH66: Gt Sut .2L 111
Hardy Rd. WA13: Lymm .6C 84
Hardy St. L1: Liv .9G 5 (1D 74)
L19: Garst .3B 92
WA2: Warr .2C 82
(not continuous)
Harebell Cl. L37: Form .3F 24
WA8: Wid .4H 79
Harebell St. L5: Kirkd .2C 58
Hare Cft. L28: Stockb V .1D 60
Harefield Grn. L24: Speke .4H 93
Harefield Rd. L24: Speke .5H 93
HARESFINCH .3L 49
Haresfinch Cl. L26: Halew .7L 77
Haresfinch Rd. WA11: St H .4L 49
Haresfinch Vw. WA11: St H .4L 49
Hares La. PR8: South .5H 13
WA6: Frod .6H 107
Harewell Rd. L11: Norr G .9M 45
Harewood Av. CH66: Gt Sut .1G 111
PR8: Ains .8J 11
Harewood Cl. L36: Huy .6J 61
Harewood Rd. CH45: New B .2G 57
Harewood St. L6: Liv .5F 58
Harfield Gdns. CH66: Lit Sut .9H 103
Harford Cl. WA5: Penk .4H 81
Hargate Rd. L33: Kirkb .9D 36
Hargate Wlk. L33: Kirkb .9D 36
Hargrave Av. CH43: Oxton .5E 72
Hargrave Cl. CH43: Oxton .5E 72
Hargrave Dr. CH66: Gt Sut .9K 103
Hargrave La. CH64: Will .1M 101
Hargreaves Ct. WA8: Wid .7N 79
Hargreaves Ho. *WA8: Wid .7N 79*
(off Hargreaves Ct.)
Hargreaves Rd. L17: Aig .5H 75
Hargreaves St. PR8: South .9H 7
WA9: St H .6A 50
Harington Cl. L37: Form .1D 24
Harington Grn. L37: Form .1C 24
Harington Rd. L37: Form .8C 16
Harkbridge Dr. L7: Liv .9G 59
Harker St. L3: Liv .2H 5 (6D 58)
Harland Dr. WN4: Ash M .8L 41
Harland Grn. L24: Speke .4K 93
Harland Rd. CH42: Tran .4K 73
Harlech Cl. WA5: Call .7N 65
Harlech Ct. CH63: Beb .3M 89
CH65: Ell P .2B 112
Harlech Gro. WA7: Cas .5B 96
Harlech Rd. L23: Blun .8J 33
Harlech St. CH44: Wall .7L 57
L4: Kirkd, Walt .9D 44
WN4: Ash M .6H 41
Harlech Way CH65: Ell P .2B 112
Harleston Rd. L33: Kirkb .8E 36
Harleston Wlk. L33: Kirkb .8E 36
Harley Av. CH63: Hghr B .8J 73
Harley St. L9: Walt .4F 44
Harlian Av. CH46: More .1L 71
Harlow Cl. WA4: Thel .5K 83
WA9: St H .2J 63
Harlow St. L8: Liv .4D 74
Harlyn Cl. L26: Halew .1J 93
Harlyn Gdns. WA5: Penk .5F 80
Harmony Way L13: Liv .8M 59
Harn, The CH66: Gt Sut .2H 111
Harold Av. WN4: Ash M .6J 41
Haroldene Gro. L34: Presc .4K 61
Harold Newgrass Dr. L19: Garst .2N 91
Harold Rd. WA11: Hay .3H 51
Harper Rd. L9: Walt .6F 44
Harpers Pond La. L15: Wav .9M 59
Harpers Rd. WA2: Padg .8H 67
Harper St. L6: Liv .3M 5 (7F 58)
Harps Cft. L30: N'ton .8B 34
Harptree Cl. L35: Whis .6B 62
Harpur Cl. CH66: Gt Sut .1J 111
Harradon Rd. L9: Ain .3G 45
Harridge La. L40: Scar .5L 19
Harrier Dr. L26: Halew .7J 77
WN8: Skel .4H 31
Harrier Rd. WA2: Padg .7G 66
Harriet St. M44: Cad .4L 69
Harringay Av. L18: Moss H .3L 75
Harrington Av. CH47: Hoy .1D 70
Harrington Rd. L3: Liv .4D 74
L21: Lith .1C 44
L23: Crosb .7K 33
L36: Huy .5F 60
Harrington St. L2: Liv .5E 4 (8B 58)
Harrington Vw. *CH44: Wall .4K 57*
(off Greenwood La.)
Harris Cl. CH63: Spit .5N 89
Harris Dr. L20: Boot .4B 44
L30: Boot .3C 44
Harris Gdns. WA9: St H .9L 49
Harrismith Rd. L10: Faz .3L 45
Harrison Cl. WA1: Warr .2D 82
Harrison Dr. CH45: Wall .2D 56
L20: Boot .7D 44
WA11: Hay .4C 50
WA11: Rainf .3C 38
Harrison Hey L36: Huy .8J 61
Harrison Sq. WA5: Warr .8A 66
Harrisons Ter. CH66: Lit Sut .8H 103
Harrison St. WA8: Hale B .1E 94
Harrison's Yd. CH62: East .9E 90
Harrison Way L3: Liv .4D 74
WA12: Newt W .6L 51
Harris St. WA8: Wid .7M 79
WA10: St H .6H 49
Harrock La. WN6: Wright .1K 23
Harrocks Cl. L30: N'ton .6C 34
Harrock Wood Cl. CH61: Irby .1M 87
Harrod Dr. PR8: Birkd .3L 11
Harrogate Cl. CH62: East .2C 102
WA5: Gt San .8J 65
Harrogate Dr. L5: Liv .4E 58
Harrogate Rd. CH42: Rock F .8N 73
CH62: East .2C 102
Harrogate Wlk. CH42: Rock F .8N 73
Harrogate Way PR9: South .1A 8
Harron Cl. L32: Kirkb .9A 36
Harrop Rd. WA7: Run .6L 95
Harrops Cft. L30: N'ton .7D 34
Harrowby Cl. L8: Liv .9N 5 (1F 74)
Harrowby Rd. CH42: Tran .4J 73
CH44: Wall .5L 57
L21: Sea .3M 43
Harrowby Rd. Sth. CH42: Tran .4J 73
Harrowby St. L8: Liv .9N 5 (1F 74)
(Granby St.)
L8: Liv .1F 74
(Park Way)
Harrow Cl. CH44: Wall .4F 56
L30: N'ton .9E 34
WA4: App .1F 98
Harrow Dr. L10: Ain .9J 35
WA7: Run .5A 96
Harrow Gro. CH62: Brom .7D 90
Harrow Rd. CH44: Wall .4F 56
CH65: Ell P .1B 112
L4: Walt .3G 58
Harsnips WN8: Skel .2F 30
Hartdale Rd. L18: Moss H .4M 75
L23: Thorn .5N 33
Hartford Cl. CH43: Oxton .5F 72
Hartford Dr. CH65: Whit .1L 111
Harthill Av. L18: Moss H .4N 75
Harthill M. CH43: Bid .8C 56
Harthill Rd. L18: Moss H .3A 76
Hartington Av. CH41: Birke .1H 73
Hartington Rd. CH44: Wall .5H 57
L8: Liv .2H 75
L12: W Der .3N 59
L19: Garst .1A 92
WA10: St H .5F 48
Hartington Ter. *L19: Garst .1N 91*
(off St Mary's Rd.)
Hartismere Rd. CH44: Wall .6K 57
Hartland WN8: Skel .2F 30
Hartland Av. PR9: South .2N 7
Hartland Cl. WA8: Wid .3K 79
Hartland Gdns. WA9: St H .3G 62
Hartland Rd. L11: Norr G .8K 45
Hartley Av. L9: Ain .5G 44
Hartley Cl. L4: Walt .2E 58
WA13: Lymm .5F 84
Hartley Cres. PR8: Birkd .4M 11
Hartley Grn. Gdns. WN5: Bil .1N 39
Hartley Gro. L33: Kirkb .6D 36
WA10: St H .1F 62
Hartley Quay L3: Liv .7D 4 (9B 58)
Hartley Rd. PR8: Birkd .4M 11
HARTLEY'S VILLAGE .5G 45
Hartley's Village L9: Ain .5G 45
Hartley Way WN5: Bil .1N 39
Hartnup St. L5: Liv .3F 58
(Glaisher St.)
L5: Liv .3E 58
(Mycroft Cl.)
Hartnup Way CH43: Bid .1C 72
Harton Cl. WA8: Wid .5H 79
Hartopp Rd. L25: Gate .2E 76
Hartopp Wlk. *L25: Gate .1E 76*
(off Hartopp Rd.)
Hartor Cl. L5: Liv .3D 58
(not continuous)

Hartsbourne Av. L25: Gate 9D 60
(not continuous)
Hartsbourne Cl. L25: Gate 1D 76
Hartsbourne Wlk. L25: Gate 1E 76
Hartshead WN8: Skel 2F 30
Hart's La. WN8: Uph 4J 31
Hart St. L3: Liv 4J 5 (7D 58)
PR8: South 9J 7
Hart St. Bri. *PR8: South* *9J 7*
(off Hart St.)
Hartswell Cl. WA3: Golb 1B 52
Hartswood Cl. WA4: App 4F 98
Hartwell St. L21: Lith 4A 44
Hartwood Cl. L32: Kirkb 3D 46
Hartwood Rd. L32: Kirkb 3D 46
PR9: South 8J 7
Hartwood Sq. L32: Kirkb 3D 46
Harty Rd. WA11: Hay 5C 50
Harvard Cl. WA7: Wind H 5F 96
Harvard Ct. WA2: Win 6B 66
Harvard Gro. L34: Presc 2B 62
Harvest Ct. CH46: More 8M 55
Harvester Way CH49: Grea 4K 71
L30: N'ton 7F 34
Harvest La. CH46: More 8L 55
Harvest Way WA9: Clock F 5M 63
Harvey Av. CH49: Grea 5L 71
WA12: Newt W 7H 51
Harvey Ct. WA2: Warr 6C 66
WA3: Golb 1B 52
WN7: Leigh 1J 53
Harvey La. WA3: Golb 1A 52
Harvey Rd. CH45: Wall 3G 56
CH46: Leas 7A 56
Harvington Dr. PR8: Ains 9G 11
Harwich Gro. L16: Child 9D 60
Harwood Gdns. WA4: Grap 6H 83
Harwood Rd. L19: Garst 1B 92
Harworth Rd. WA9: St H 4H 63
Haryngton Av. WA5: Warr 1A 82
Haselbeech Cl. L11: Norr G 7L 45
Haselbeech Cres. L11: Norr G 7L 45
Haseldine St. WN4: Ash M 5H 41
Hasfield Rd. L11: Norr G 8N 45
HASKAYNE 8E 18
Haslam Dr. L39: Orm 6B 20
Haslemere L35: Whis 6C 62
Haslemere Dr. WA5: Penk 4F 80
Haslemere Ind. Est.
WN4: Ash M 3J 41
Haslemere Rd. L25: Gate 2F 76
Haslemere Way L25: Gate 2E 76
Haslingden Cl. L13: Liv 7N 59
Haslington Gro. L26: Halew 1L 93
Hassal Rd. CH42: Rock F 8N 73
Hassness Cl. WN3: Wigan 1K 41
Hastie Cl. L27: N'ley 3J 77
Hastings Av. WA2: Warr 5C 66
Hastings Dr. L36: Huy 9L 61
Hastings Rd. L22: Water 9H 33
PR8: Birkd 4L 11
Haswell Dr. L28: Stockb V 1E 60
Hatchery Cl. WA4: App T 3J 99
Hatchings, The WA13: Lymm 6E 84
Hatchmere Cl. CH43: Oxton 5F 72
WA5: Warr 2N 81
Hatfield Cl. L12: Crox 7D 46
WA9: St H 2J 63
Hatfield Gdns. L36: Huy 8K 61
WA4: App 3F 98
Hatfield Rd. L20: Boot 7D 44
PR8: Ains 8J 11
Hathaway L31: Mag 4G 35
Hathaway Cl. L25: Gate 2E 76
Hathaway Rd. L25: Gate 2E 76
Hatherley Av. L23: Crosb 9L 33
Hatherley Cl. L8: Liv 1F 74
(not continuous)
Hatherley St. CH44: Wall 7L 57
L8: Liv 1F 74
Hathersage Rd. L36: Huy 4J 61
Hatherton Gro. L26: Halew 1L 93
Hatley La. WA6: Frod 7H 107
Hattersley Ct. L39: Orm 7D 20
Hattersley Way L39: Orm 7D 20
Hatters Row *WA1: Warr* *3C 82*
(off Horsemarket St.)
HATTON 6A 98
Hatton Av. CH62: East 3D 102
Hatton Cl. CH60: Hesw 6L 87
Hatton Gdn. L3: Liv 3E 4 (7B 58)
Hatton Gdn. Ind. Est. L3: Liv 3F 4
Hatton Hill Rd. L21: Lith 1N 43
Hatton La. WA4: Hatt, Stret 6B 98
Hattons La. L16: Child 2A 76
Hauxwell Gro. WA11: St H 4M 49
Havannah La. WA9: St H 7D 50
Havelock Cl. WA10: St H 7J 49
Havelock Rd. L20: Boot 4B 44
Haven Brow L39: Augh 4A 28
Haven Rd. L10: Faz 2L 45
Haven Wlk. L31: Lyd 8H 27
Havercroft Cl. WN3: Wigan 1G 40
Havergal St. WA7: Run 6J 95
Haverstock Rd. L6: Liv 6J 59
Haverton Wlk. L12: Crox 7C 46
(not continuous)
Haverty Pct. WA12: Newt W 9K 51
Havisham Cl. WA3: Birchw 4L 67
Hawarde Cl. WA12: Newt W 6J 51
Hawarden Av. CH43: Oxton 2J 73
CH44: Wall 5J 57
L17: Liv 2K 75
Hawarden Ct. CH63: Beb 3M 89
Hawarden Gdns. CH65: Ell P 3B 112
Hawarden Gro. L21: Sea 4N 43
Hawdon Ct. L7: Liv 9H 59
Hawes Av. WA11: St H 2M 49
Hawes Cres. WN4: Ash M 6K 41
Hawesside St. PR9: South 8H 7
Haweswater Av. WA11: Hay 4C 50
Haweswater Cl. L33: Kirkb 6B 36
WA7: Beech 1C 108
Haweswater Gro. L31: Mag 1L 35
Hawgreen Rd. L32: Kirkb 9N 35
Hawick Cl. CH66: Lit Sut 9F 102
L33: Kirkb 5B 36
Hawke Grn. L35: Tar G 1L 77
Hawker Dr. WN8: Skel 4H 31
Hawke St. L3: Liv 5H 5 (8D 58)
Hawkesworth St. L4: Walt 3F 58
Hawkhurst Cl. L8: Liv 4E 74
Hawkhurst Dr. CH42: Rock F 7N 73
Hawkins Rd. CH64: Nest 5E 100
Hawkins St. L6: Liv 6G 59
HAWKLEY 1K 41
Hawkley Av. WN3: Wigan 1H 41
Hawkley Brook Ct. WN3: Wigan 1H 41
Hawksclough WN8: Skel 2G 30
Hawks Ct. WA7: Pal F 9A 96
Hawkshaw Cl. WA3: Birchw 5K 67
Hawkshead Av. L12: W Der 9A 46
Hawkshead Cl. L31: Mag 1K 35
WA7: Beech 1C 108
Hawkshead Dr. L21: Lith 2C 44
Hawkshead Rd. CH62: Brom 6D 90
WA5: Burtw 3G 65
Hawkshead St. PR8: South 8J 7
PR9: South 7H 7
Hawksmoor Cl. L10: Faz 3M 45
Hawksmoor Rd. L10: Faz 4M 45
Hawksmore Cl. CH49: Upton 2L 71
Hawkstone Gro. WA6: Hel 1F 114
Hawkstone St. L8: Liv 3F 74
(not continuous)
Hawkstone Wlk. *L8: Liv* *4F 74*
(off Hawkstone St.)
Hawks Way CH60: Hesw 7M 87
Hawksworth Cl. L37: Form 7G 17
Hawksworth Dr. L37: Form 7G 17
Hawley Brook Trad. Est.
WN3: Wigan 1G 41
Hawleys Cl. WA5: Warr 8A 66
Hawleys La. WA2: Warr 8A 66
WA5: Warr 8A 66
Haworth Dr. L20: Boot 3C 44
Hawthorn Av. L40: Burs 1K 21
WA7: Run 6K 95
WA8: Wid 6L 79
WA12: Newt W 7M 51
WN4: Garsw 6E 40
Hawthorn Cl. WA11: Hay 5C 50
WN5: Bil 6N 39
Hawthorn Cres. WN8: Skel 3B 30
Hawthorn Dr. CH48: W Kir 6F 70
CH61: Hesw 4N 87
M44: Cad 4K 69
WA10: Eccl 6E 48
Hawthorne Av. L26: Halew 1J 93
WA1: Wools 1J 83
WA5: Gt San 2H 81
Hawthorne Bus. Pk. WA5: Warr 9B 66
Hawthorne Ct. *L21: Lith* *2A 44*
(off Sefton Rd.)
Hawthorne Cres. L37: Form 2G 24
Hawthorne Dr. CH64: Will 5A 102
L33: Kirkb 8D 36
PR9: Banks 5H 9
Hawthorne Gro. CH44: Wall 7L 57
PR9: South 8L 7
WA1: Padd 1G 83
WA4: Stockt H 7E 82
Hawthorne Rd. CH42: Tran 5K 73
L20: Boot 5C 44
L21: Lith 2A 44
WA4: Stockt H 8D 82
WA6: Frod 5L 107
Hawthornes, The CH2: Wim T 9K 113
CH42: Rock F 7N 73
L40: Ruf 3M 15
Hawthorne St. WA5: Warr 9B 66
Hawthorn Gro. L12: W Der 3N 59
WA4: Warr 5E 82
Hawthorn La. CH62: Brom 7C 90
Hawthorn Rd. CH64: Park 4B 100
CH66: Lit Sut 8H 103
L34: Presc 3B 62
L36: Roby 7G 61
WA9: Sut L 3N 63
WA13: Lymm 5D 84
Hawthorns, The CH66: Ell P 7L 103
WN8: Newb 4D 22
Hawthorn Wlk. M31: Part 6L 69
Haxted Gdns. L19: Garst 1B 92
Haycroft Cl. CH66: Gt Sut 3J 111
Haydan M. WA6: Frod 8H 107
Haydn Rd. L14: Knott A 3D 60
HAYDOCK 4E 50
Haydock Cross WA11: Hay 1H 51
Haydock Ind. Est. WA11: Hay 2G 50
Haydock La. WA11: Hay 4E 50
(not continuous)
Haydock La. Ind. Est. WA11: Hay 2H 51
Haydock Leisure Cen. 4D 50
Haydock Pk. Gdns. WA12: Newt W 1K 51
Haydock Park Golf Course 5A 52
Haydock Park Racecourse 1M 51
Haydock Pk. Rd. L10: Ain 8K 35
Haydock Rd. CH45: Wall 2J 57
Haydock St. WA2: Warr 2C 82
WA10: St H 7K 49
WA12: Newt W 6J 51
WN4: Ash M 9K 41
Hayes Av. L35: Presc 4B 62
Hayes Cres. WA6: Frod 5M 107
Hayes Dr. L31: Mell 8N 35
Hayes La. WA4: App 8F 82
Haye's Rd. M44: Cad 4L 69
(not continuous)
Hayes Row WA3: Low 1H 53
Hayes St. WA10: St H 1F 62
Hayfell Rd. WN3: Wigan 2J 41
Hayfield Cl. L26: Halew 7L 77
Hayfield Pl. CH46: More 9A 56
Hayfield Rd. L39: Orm 6C 20
WA1: Wools 1K 83
Hayfield St. L4: Walt 2E 58
Hayfield Way WA9: Clock F 5M 63
Haylemere Ct. PR8: Birkd 1L 11
Hayles Cl. L25: Gate 2E 76
Hayles Grn. L25: Gate 2E 76
Hayles Gro. L25: Gate 2E 76
Hayling Ho. L19: Aig 9L 75
Haylock Cl. L8: Liv 4E 74
Haymans Cl. L12: W Der 2M 59
Haymans Grn. L12: W Der 2M 59
L31: Mag 2K 35
Haymans Gro. L12: W Der 2M 59
Hayscastle Cl. WA5: Call 8N 65
Hayward Ct. L37: Form 9G 16
Haywood Cl. WA3: Low 1F 52
Haywood Cres. WA7: Wind H 5F 96
Haywood Gdns. WA10: St H 8G 48
Haywood Rd. L28: Stockb V 1F 60
Hazel Av. L32: Kirkb 8A 36
L35: Whis 6B 62
WA7: Run 7H 95
Hazelbank Gdns. L37: Form 8E 16
Hazelborough Cl. WA3: Birchw 4B 68
Hazel Bus. Pk. WA11: Rainf 7F 38
Hazel Cl. CH66: Gt Sut 4L 111
Hazel Ct. *L8: Liv* *4F 74*
(off Byles St.)
L20: Boot 8B 44
Hazeldale Rd. L9: Walt 6F 44
Hazeldene Av. CH45: Wall 4G 57
CH61: Thing 1B 88
Hazeldene Way CH61: Thing 1B 88
Hazel Dr. WA13: Lymm 6F 84
Hazelfield Ct. WA9: Clock F 5M 63
Hazel Gro. CH61: Irby 9L 71
CH63: Hghr B 3L 89
L9: Ain 4G 45
L23: Crosb 8M 33
L32: Kirkb 2D 46
PR8: South 8K 7
WA1: Padd 9H 67
WA3: Golb 2C 52
WA10: St H 7F 48
Hazelhurst Cl. L37: Form 2C 24
Hazelhurst Gro. WN4: Ash M 7L 41
Hazelhurst Rd. L4: Walt 2G 59
Hazel La. WN8: Skel 9E 22
Hazelmere Ho. *L17: Aig* *6J 75*
(off Mossley Hill Dr.)
Hazel M. L31: Mell 8N 35
Hazel Rd. CH41: Birke 3K 73
CH47: Hoy 1D 70
L36: Huy 4K 61
Hazelslack Rd. L11: Norr G 8M 45
Hazel St. WA1: Warr 1E 82
Hazelton Cl. WN7: Leigh 1M 53
Hazel Wlk. M31: Part 6L 69
Hazelwood CH49: Grea 3L 71
Hazelwood Av. L40: Burs 1J 21
Hazelwood Cl. WA8: Wid 8D 78
WA9: Sut M 6L 63
Hazelwood Gro. L26: Halew 6H 77
Hazelwood M. WA4: Grap 7K 83
Hazlehurst Rd. WA6: Frod 9M 107
Hazleton Rd. L14: Knott A 6A 60
Headbolt La. L33: Kirkb 7C 36
PR8: Ains 1N 17
PR8: Birkd 8N 11
Headbourne Cl. L25: Gate 1D 76
Headbourne Ct. *L25: Gate* *1D 76*
(off Headbourne Cl.)
Head Farm Ct. WA12: Newt W 7J 51
Headingley Cl. L36: Roby 9G 61
WA9: St H 3M 63
Headingly Av. WN8: Skel 3N 29
Headington Rd. CH49: Upton 3L 71
Headland Cl. CH48: W Kir 8C 70
WA3: Low 4F 52
Headley Cl. WA10: St H 7J 49
Head St. L8: Liv 2D 74
Heald St. L19: Garst 1A 92
WA12: Newt W 7H 51
Healy Cl. L27: N'ley 4L 77
Heanor Dr. PR8: South 3E 12
Heap Ct. PR9: South 7K 7
Hearne Rd. WA10: St H 6G 48
Hearts Health Club
Great Crosby 6K 33
Hearts Ladies Health Club
Wallasey 5G 56
Heartwood Cl. L9: Walt 3F 44
Heath Av. CH65: Whit 4M 111
Heathbank Av. CH44: Wall 6G 56
CH61: Irby 9K 71
Heathbank Rd. CH42: Tran 5K 73
Heath Business & Technical Park, The
WA7: West 8K 95
Heath Cl. CH48: W Kir 8C 70
L25: Woolt 3D 76
L34: Eccl P 2C 62
Heathcote Cl. L7: Liv 9H 59
Heathcote Gdns. CH63: Beb 2M 89
Heathcote Rd. L4: Walt 8E 44
Heath Ct. CH66: Lit Sut 7G 103
Heathdale CH63: Beb 4M 89
Heath Dr. CH49: Upton 3A 72
CH60: Hesw 6N 87
WA7: West 8K 95
Heather Av. M44: Cad 3K 69
Heather Bank CH63: Hghr B 1K 89
Heather Brae L34: Presc 4L 61
WA12: Newt W 6J 51
Heather Brow CH43: Clau 1F 72
Heather Cl. CH46: More 8K 55
CH66: Gt Sut 2K 111
L4: Walt 1E 58
L33: Kirkb *7C 36*
(off Heathfield Dr.)
L37: Form 8H 17
L40: Burs 1J 21
PR8: Ains 3K 17
WA3: Birchw 4L 67
WA7: Beech 2A 108
Heather Ct. *L4: Walt* *1E 58*
(off Tetlow St.)
Heatherdale Cl. CH42: Tran 4J 73
Heatherdale Rd. L18: Moss H 4M 75
Heather Dene CH62: Brom 4C 90
Heatherdene Rd. CH48: W Kir 5C 70
Heatherfield Ct. *CH42: Tran* *4J 73*
(off Victoria Flds.)
Heathergreen Ct. L4: Walt 9G 45
Heather Gro. WN4: Ash M 7N 41
Heatherlea Cl. WN8: Uph 5M 31
Heatherleigh CH48: Caldy 1E 86
WA9: St H 3F 62
Heatherleigh Cl. L9: Walt 3F 44
Heather Rd. CH60: Hesw 6A 88
CH63: Hghr B 3K 89
Heathers Cft. L30: N'ton 8D 34
Heather Wlk. *M31: Part* *6L 69*
(off Gorse Sq.)
Heather Way L23: Thorn 5A 34
Heatherways L37: Form 7G 16
Heathey La. L39: Hals, South 6F 12
Heath Farm La. M31: Part 6N 69
Heathfield CH62: Brom 5C 90
L40: Burs 1K 21
Heathfield Av. WA9: St H 1H 63
Heathfield Cl. L21: Lith 4B 44
L37: Form 7G 16
Heathfield Ct. CH65: Ell P 9N 103
Heathfield Dr. L20: Boot 4B 44
L33: Kirkb 7C 36
Heathfield Gdns. WA7: Run 7K 95
Heathfield Ho. CH61: Thing 1A 88
Heathfield Pk. WA4: Grap 6H 83
WA8: Wid 5G 79
Heathfield Rd. CH43: Oxton 4J 73
CH63: Beb 2M 89
CH65: Ell P 9N 103
L15: Wav 2M 75
L22: Water 9J 33
L31: Mag 4L 35
PR8: Ains 8L 11
Heathfield St. L1: Liv 6H 5 (8D 58)
(not continuous)
Heathgate WN8: Skel 2F 30
Heathgate Av. L24: Speke 5K 93
Heath Gro. CH66: Lit Sut 7G 102
Heath Hey L25: Woolt 3D 76
Heath Ho. Cl. WA3: Low 3D 52
Heathland WN8: Uph 5L 31
Heathland Rd. WA9: Clock F 5M 63
Heathlands, The CH46: Leas 5M 55
Heathlands Rd. CH66: Lit Sut 8G 103
Heath La. CH2: Lit Stan, Stoak 6B 112
(not continuous)
CH64: Will 5B 102
CH66: Chil T, Lit Sut 7C 102
WA3: Croft 8H 53
WA3: Low 3D 52
(not continuous)
Heathmoor Av. WA3: Low 4E 52
Heathmoor Rd. CH46: More 8L 55
Heath Pk. Gro. WA7: Run 7J 95
Heath Rd. CH63: Beb, Hghr B 2L 89
L19: Aller 8A 76
L36: Huy 4G 60
WA5: Penk 3H 81
WA7: Run 7K 95
WA8: Wid 6G 79
WN4: Ash M 9K 41
Heath Rd. Cres. WA7: Run 7L 95

Heath Rd. Sth. WA7: Run, West 1J 107
Heathside CH60: Hesw 6K 87
Heath St. WA3: Golb 2B 52
WA4: Stockt H 8D 82
WA9: St H 2G 62
WN4: Ash M 9L 41
Heath Vw. L21: Ford 8A 34
Heathview Cl. WA8: Hale B 2D 94
Heathview Rd. WA8: Hale B 3D 94
Heathwaite Cres. L11: Norr G 9M 45
Heathway CH60: Hesw 8B 88
Heathwood L12: W Der 4N 59
Heathwood Gro. WA1: Padd 1J 83
Heathy La. L39: Bart 5N 17
HEATLEY 2J 85
Heatley Cl. CH43: Bid 1C 72
WA13: Lymm 4G 85
Heaton Cl. L24: Speke 4K 93
L40: Burs 1H 21
WN8: Uph 5K 31
Heaton Ct. L40: Scar 2A 20
WA3: Ris 3N 67
HEATON'S BRIDGE 1A 20
Heatons Bri. Rd. L40: Scar 1A 20
Hebburn Way L12: Crox 7E 46
Hebden Pde. L11: Norr G 7A 46
Hebden Rd. L11: Norr G 7N 45
Hebdon Cl. WN4: Ash M 6J 41
Hedgebank Cl. L9: Ain 2J 45
Hedgecote L32: Kirkb 3C 46
Hedgecroft L23: Thorn 5B 34
Hedgefield Rd. L25: Gate 3F 76
Hedge Hey WA7: Cas 6C 96
Hedgerows, The WA11: Hay 3H 51
Hedges Cres. L13: Liv 2K 59
Hedingham Cl. L26: Halew 7L 77
Hedworth Gdns. WA9: St H 3G 62
Heigham Gdns. WA9: St H 3H 63
Heights, The WA6: Hel 1F 114
Helena Rd. WA9: St H 2B 64
Helena St. CH41: Birke 3L 73
L7: Liv 8G 59
L9: Walt 7E 44
Helen Bank Dr. WA11: Rainf 3C 38
Helen Ho. L8: Liv 9K 5
Helen St. WA3: Golb 9N 41
WN4: Ash M 7J 41
Helford Cl. L35: Whis 3D 62
Helford Rd. L11: Crox 5B 46
Heliers Rd. L13: Liv 7N 59
Hell Nook WA3: Golb 1N 51
Helmingham Gro. CH41: Tran 4L 73
Helmsdale WN8: Skel 2F 30
Helmsdale La. WA5: Gt San 2L 81
Helmsley Cl. WA5: Warr 1N 81
Helmsley Rd. L26: Halew 9K 77
HELSBY 2E 114
Helsby Av. CH62: East 3E 102
Helsby Community Sports Club 3D 114
Helsby Ct. L34: Presc 4A 62
Helsby Golf Course 5E 114
HELSBY MARSH 9D 106
Helsby Pk. Homes WA6: Frod 9H 107
Helsby Rd. L9: Ain 3G 44
WA6: Alv 3F 114
Helsby Station (Rail) 1E 114
Helsby St. L7: Liv 6N 5 (8F 58)
WA1: Warr 2E 82
WA9: St H 9A 50
Helsby Way WN3: Wins 1E 40
Helston Av. L26: Halew 7K 77
WA11: St H 3N 49
Helston Cl. PR9: South 2N 7
WA5: Penk 3G 81
WA7: Brook 1D 108
Helston Grn. L36: Huy 6M 61
Helston Rd. L11: Crox 5B 46
Helton Cl. CH43: Noct 5E 72
Hemans St. L20: Boot 6N 43
Hemer Ter. L20: Boot 5N 43
Hemingford Cl. CH66: Gt Sut 2J 111
Hemingford St. CH41: Birke 2K 73
Hemlegh Va. WA6: Hel 3E 114
Hemlock Cl. L12: Crox 7B 46
Hemmingsway L35: Rainh 6D 62
Hempstead Cl. WA9: St H 2J 63
Hemsworth Av. CH66: Lit Sut 9H 103
Henbury Gdns. WA4: App 4F 98
Henbury Pl. WA7: Run 9L 95
Henderson Cl. CH49: Upton 2L 71
WA5: Gt San 2F 80
Henderson Dr. WA11: Rainf 3D 38
Henderson Rd. L36: Huy 6L 61
WA8: Wid 8J 79
Hendon Rd. L6: Liv 5J 59
Hendon Wlk. CH49: Grea 5K 71
Hengest Cl. L33: Kirkb 5C 36
Henglers Cl. L6: Liv 2M 5 (6F 58)
Henley Av. L21: Lith 2N 43
M44: Irlam 3L 69
Henley Cl. CH63: Spit 5N 89
CH64: Nest 8E 100
WA4: App 1F 98
Henley Ct. PR9: South 6K 7
WA7: Run 5N 95
WA10: St H 9G 49
Henley Dr. PR9: South 6K 7
Henley Ho. L19: Aig 9L 75
Henley Rd. CH64: Nest 8E 100
L18: Moss H 3N 75
Henllan Gdns. WA9: St H 2B 64
Henlow Av. L32: Kirkb 2D 46
Henna Way L11: Norr G 9M 45
Hennawood Cl. L6: Liv 4G 58
Henrietta Gro. L34: Presc 4K 61
Henry Edward St. L3: Liv 2F 4 (6C 58)
Henry Hickman Cl. L30: N'ton 7E 34
Henry St. CH41: Birke 2L 73
L1: Liv 7F 4 (9C 58)
L13: Liv 7L 59
WA1: Warr 3B 82
WA8: Wid 7M 79
WA10: St H 6J 49
WA13: Lymm 5E 84
Henshall Av. WA4: Westy 4G 82
Henthorne Rd. CH62: New F 8A 74
Henthorne St. CH43: Oxton 3J 73
Hepherd St. WA5: Warr 4M 81
Herald Av. L24: Speke 1D 92
Herald Cl. L11: Crox 7A 46
Heralds Cl. WA8: Wid 8E 78
Heralds Grn. WA5: Westb 7J 65
Herbarth Cl. L9: Walt 7E 44
Herberts La. CH60: Hesw 7N 87
Herbert St. WA5: Burtw 3G 65
WA9: St H 2A 64
Herbert Taylor Cl. L6: Liv 4H 59
Herbie Higgins Cl. L8: Liv 2F 74
Herculaneum Ct. L8: Liv 5E 74
Herculaneum Rd. L8: Liv 4D 74
Hercules Dr. L24: Speke 4D 92
Herdman Cl. L25: Gate 3F 76
Hereford Av. CH49: Upton 2M 71
CH66: Gt Sut 5K 111
WA3: Golb 1C 52
Hereford Cl. WA1: Wools 1L 83
WA10: St H 8J 49
WN4: Ash M 9M 41
Hereford Dr. L30: N'ton 1E 44
Hereford Gro. WN8: Uph 6L 31
Hereford Rd. L15: Wav 2M 75
L21: Sea 3L 43
PR9: South 8L 7
Heriot St. L5: Kirkd 3C 58
(not continuous)
Hermes Cl. *L30: Boot 2D 44*
(off Atlantic Way)
Hermes Rd. L11: Crox 4N 45
Hermitage, The *CH60: Hesw 8N 87*
(off School Hill)
HERMITAGE GREEN 1C 66
Hermitage Grn. La. WA2: Win 9A 52
Hermitage Gro. L20: Boot 3C 44
Herm Rd. L5: Liv 4B 58
Heron Bus. Pk. WA8: Wid 8N 79
Heron Cl. WA7: Nort 7F 96
Heron Ct. CH64: Park 7C 100
L26: Halew 7J 77
Herondale Rd. L18: Moss H 4M 75
Heron Dr. WN3: Wins 1G 40
Heron Gro. WA11: Rainf 6E 38
Heronhall Rd. L9: Faz 6L 45
Heronpark Way CH63: Spit 5A 90
Heron Rd. CH47: Meols 1G 70
CH48: W Kir 1G 70
Herons Ct. L31: Lyd 8G 27
Herons Way WA7: Nort 3H 97
Herons Wharf WN6: Appl B 6N 23
Hero St. L20: Boot 8C 44
Herrick St. L13: Liv 6L 59
Hertford Cl. L26: Halew 9K 77
WA1: Wools 1M 83
Hertford Dr. CH45: Wall 3J 57
Hertford Gro. M44: Cad 3J 69
Hertford Rd. L20: Boot 8B 44
Hertford St. WA9: St H 8N 49
Hesketh Av. CH42: Rock F 7K 73
PR9: Banks 1E 8
Hesketh Cl. WA5: Penk 4H 81
Hesketh Ct. WA11: Rainf 7D 38
Hesketh Dr. CH60: Hesw 6A 88
L31: Mag 2L 35
L40: Ruf 3L 15
PR9: South 5K 7
Hesketh Golf Course 5K 7
Hesketh Grn. L40: Ruf 3M 15
Hesketh Links Ct. PR9: South 5K 7
Hesketh Mnr. PR9: South 5K 7
Hesketh Mdw. La. WA3: Low 2G 53
Hesketh Rd. L24: Hale 6B 94
L40: Burs 1H 21
PR9: South 4J 7
Hesketh St. L17: Aig 4H 75
WA5: Warr 4M 81
Hesketh St. Nth. WA5: Warr 4M 81
Hesketh Vw. *PR9: South 6K 7*
(off Park Cres.)
Hesketh Wlk. CH62: Brom 4B 90
Hesketh Way CH62: Brom 4B 90
Heskin Cl. L31: Lyd 8J 27
L32: Kirkb 3C 46
L35: Rainh 6E 62
Heskin Hall Ct. L39: Orm 5B 20
Heskin La. L39: Orm 5B 20
L40: Scar 5B 20
Heskin Rd. L32: Kirkb 3C 46
Heskin Wlk. L32: Kirkb 3C 46
Hessle Dr. CH60: Hesw 8N 87
Hesslewell Ct. CH60: Hesw 6A 88
Hester Cl. L38: Hight 8F 24
HESWALL 7A 88
Heswall Av. CH63: Hghr B 8J 73
WA3: Cul 7M 53
WA9: Clock F 5L 63
Heswall Dales Local Nature Reserve 6M 87
Heswall Golf Course 1A 100
Heswall Mt. CH61: Thing 2A 88
Heswall Point CH60: Hesw 7A 88
Heswall Rd. CH66: Gt Sut 1J 111
L9: Ain 3G 44
Heswall Station (Rail) 7D 88
Hever Dr. L26: Halew 7K 77
Heversham WN8: Skel 2F 30
Heward Av. WA9: St H 3M 63
Hewitson Av. L13: Liv 3L 59
Hewitson Rd. L13: Liv 3L 59
Hewitt Av. WA10: St H 6F 48
Hewitt's La. L33: Kirkb 4H 47
L34: Know 4H 47
Hewitts Pl. *L2: Liv 4E 4*
(off Vernon St.)
Hewitt St. WA4: Warr 4D 82
Hexagon, The *L20: Boot 7B 44*
(off Strand Shop. Cen.)
Hexham Cl. L30: N'ton 1F 44
WA9: St H 3G 63
Heyburn Rd. L13: Liv 3K 59
Heydale Rd. L18: Moss H 4M 75
Heydean Rd. L18: Aller 7A 76
Heydean Wlk. *L18: Aller 7A 76*
(off Heydean Rd.)
Heydon Av. L32: Kirkb 1A 46
Heydon Cl. L26: Halew 9L 77
L37: Form 3D 24
Heyes, The L25: Woolt 6F 76
Heyes Av. WA11: Hay 5F 50
WA11: Rainf 5D 38
Heyescroft L39: Bic 5H 29
Heyes Dr. CH45: Wall 5C 56
WA13: Lymm 6C 84
Heyes Gro. WA11: Rainf 5D 38
Heyes Junc. WN8: Skel 5H 31
Heyesmere Ct. L17: Aig 9L 75
Heyes Mt. L35: Rainh 7F 62
Heyes Rd. WA8: Wid 8F 78
WN5: Orr 6N 31
Heyes St. L5: Liv 4F 58
WN6: Appl B 6M 23
Heyeswood WA11: Hay 4F 50
Heyfield Pk. Rd. CH66: Lit Sut 7G 103
Heygarth Dr. CH49: Grea 4L 71
Heygarth Rd. CH62: East 1D 102
Hey Grn. Rd. L15: Wav 9K 59
Hey Lock Cl. WA12: Newt W 1L 65
Hey Pk. L36: Huy 7K 61
Hey Rd. L36: Huy 7K 61
Heys, The CH62: East 1E 102
PR8: Birkd 2K 11
WA7: Run 6A 96
WN8: Parb 2F 22
Heys Av. CH62: Brom 7C 90
Heyscroft Rd. L25: Woolt 6F 76
Heysham Cl. WA7: Murd 9F 96
Heysham Lawn L27: N'ley 5L 77
Heysham Rd. L30: N'ton 9F 34
PR9: South 8L 7
Heysmoor Hgts. L8: Liv 2G 75
Heysome Cl. WA11: Crank 7H 39
Heythrop Dr. CH60: Hesw 7C 88
Heyville Rd. CH63: Hghr B 1L 89
Heywood Av. WA3: Golb 1C 52
Heywood Blvd. CH61: Thing 1A 88
Heywood Cl. CH61: Thing 1A 88
L37: Form 1E 24
WA12: Newt W 1L 65
Heywood Ct. L15: Wav 8A 60
Heywood Gdns. L35: Whis 7B 62
WA3: Golb 1C 52
Heywood Rd. CH66: Gt Sut 9H 103
L15: Wav 9A 60
Heyworth St. L5: Liv 4E 58
Hibbert St. WA8: Wid 8L 79
Hickling Gdns. WA9: St H 3H 63
Hickmans Rd. CH41: Birke 8H 57
Hickory Cl. WA1: Wools 1M 83
WA12: Newt W 8L 51
Hickory Gro. L31: Mell 9M 35
Hickson Av. L31: Mag 9H 27
Hicks Rd. L21: Sea 3N 43
L22: Water 9L 33
Higgins La. L40: Burs 9F 14
Highacre Rd. CH45: New B 2G 57
Higham Av. WA5: Warr 8A 66
WA10: Eccl 7C 48
Higham Sq. L5: Liv 5D 58
High Bank Cl. CH43: Noct 3D 72
M44: Cad 3K 69
Highbank Dr. L19: Garst 1B 92
Highbanks L31: Lyd 9H 27
High Beeches L16: Child 8D 60
High Beeches Cres. WN4: Ash M 5J 41
High Carrs L36: Roby 7F 60
Highclere Cres. L36: Huy 4J 61
Highcroft, The CH63: Beb 2N 89
Highcroft Av. CH63: Beb 2N 89
Highcroft Grn. CH63: Beb 2N 89
Highcross *WA11: Rainf 4C 38*
(off Victoria St.)
Higher Ashton WA8: Wid 5J 79
HIGHER BEBINGTON 9K 73
Higher Bebington Rd. CH63: Hghr B 1K 89
Higher Carr La. L38: Gt Alt 6B 26
HIGHER END 9N 31
Higher End Pk. L30: N'ton 6C 34
Higher Knutsford Rd. WA4: Stockt H 5G 83
Higher La. L9: Ain, Faz 3H 45
(not continuous)
PR4: Tarl 5N 9
WA4: Dutt, Lwr W 3K 109
WA11: Crank, Rainf 3D 38
WA13: Lymm 6E 84
WN8: Dalt 4E 22
WN8: Uph 5M 31
Higher Moss La. L37: Gt Alt 9M 17
Higher Parr St. WA9: St H 7M 49
Higher Rd. L25: Hunts X 9H 77
L26: Halew 1M 93
WA8: Hale B 1M 93
HIGHER RUNCORN 6J 95
Higher Vw. WN8: Uph 6M 31
HIGHER WALTON 9A 82
Highfield CH2: Elt 1M 113
L33: Kirkb 6C 36
Highfield Av. WA3: Golb 2A 52
WA4: App 3E 98
WA5: Gt San 3J 81
Highfield Cl. CH44: Wall 6G 57
CH64: Nest 6E 100
Highfield Cres. CH42: Rock F 7M 73
WA8: Wid 6K 79
Highfield Dr. CH49: Grea 4L 71
WA11: Crank 7H 39
WA13: Lymm 6C 84
Highfield Gdns. CH43: Clau 2F 72
Highfield Grange Av.
WN3: Wigan, Wins 1F 40
Highfield Gro. CH42: Rock F 7M 73
L23: Crosb 6M 33
Highfield La. L40: Scar 7A 14
WA2: Win 1D 66
WA3: Low 5D 52
Highfield Pk. L31: Mag 2L 35
Highfield Rd. CH42: Rock F 6M 73
CH64: Nest 6E 100
CH65: Ell P 9A 104
CH66: Lit Sut 8G 103
L9: Walt 6E 44
L13: Liv 5M 59
L21: Lith 2N 43
L36: Huy 3H 61
L39: Orm 6C 20
PR9: South 4N 7
WA8: Wid 7J 79
WA13: Lymm 5C 84
Highfield Rd. Nth. CH65: Ell P 8A 104
Highfields CH60: Hesw 6N 87
L34: Presc 3N 61
Highfield Sth. CH42: Rock F 9M 73
Highfield Sq. L13: Liv 5M 59
Highfield St. L3: Liv 2D 4 (6B 58)
(not continuous)
WA9: St H 1N 63
Highfield Vw. L13: Liv 5M 59
Highgate Cl. CH60: Hesw 5N 87
WA7: Nort 6F 96
Highgate Ct. L7: Liv 6N 5
Highgate Rd. L31: Lyd 9J 27
WN8: Uph 5L 31
High Gates Cl. WA5: Warr 1N 81
High Gates Lodge WA5: Warr 1N 81
Highgate St. L7: Liv 5N 5 (7F 58)
Highgreen Rd. CH42: Tran 5J 73
Highgrove Pk. L19: Gras 8M 75
Highlands Rd. WA7: Run 6J 95
High La. L39: Bic 5F 28
L40: Burs 6E 20
High Legh WA10: Eccl 7E 48
High Legh Rd. WA13: Lymm 8J 85
Highmarsh Cres. WA12: Newt W 5K 51
Highmeadow WN8: Uph 5K 31
HIGH MOOR 1J 23
High Moor La. WN6: Wright 1J 23
High Moss L39: Orm 1B 28
High Mt. CH60: Hesw 7N 87
Highoaks Rd. L25: Woolt 7F 76
HIGH PARK 7M 7
High Pk. Pl. PR9: South 7M 7
High Pk. Rd. PR9: South 7M 7
Highpark Rd. CH42: Tran 5J 73
High Pk. St. L8: Liv 3E 74
Highsands Av. L40: Ruf 3L 15
Highsted Gro. L33: Kirkb 6C 36
High St. CH62: Brom 6D 90
CH64: Nest 6E 100
L2: Liv 4D 4 (7B 58)
L15: Wav 9L 59
L24: Hale 6A 94
L25: Woolt 6E 76
L34: Presc 3A 62
WA3: Golb 2B 52
WA6: Frod 6L 107
WA7: Run 5J 95
WA12: Newt W 6M 51
WN8: Skel 4A 30
Hightor Rd. L25: Woolt 5D 76
HIGHTOWN 8F 24
Hightown Station (Rail) 8G 24
High Vw. WA6: Hel 1F 114
Highville Rd. L16: Child 2B 76

High Warren Cl. WA4: App 2C **98**
Highwood Ct. L33: Kirkb 7D **36**
Highwood Rd. WA4: App 9D **82**
Highwoods Cl. WN4: Ash M 6J **41**
Hignett Av. WA9: St H 8C **50**
Higson Ct. L8: Liv 5F **74**
Hilary Av. L14: Broad G 7C **60**
WA3: Low 1E **52**
Hilary Cl. L4: Walt 1H **59**
L34: Eccl P 2B **62**
WA5: Gt San 2F **80**
WA8: Wid 5A **80**
Hilary Dr. CH49: Upton 2A **72**
Hilary Mans. *CH44: Wall 5G* ***56***
(off Colville Rd.)
Hilary Rd. L4: Walt 1H **59**
Hilberry Av. L13: Liv 4K **59**
Hilbre Av. CH44: Wall 5G **57**
CH60: Hesw 9M **87**
Hilbre Cl. PR9: South 6L **7**
Hilbre Ct. CH48: W Kir 7B **70**
Hilbre Dr. CH65: Ell P 4A **112**
PR9: South 6L **7**
Hilbre Rd. CH48: W Kir 7C **70**
Hilbre St. CH41: Birke 9K **57**
L3: Liv 5H **5** (8D **58**)
Hilbre Vw. CH48: W Kir 6D **70**
Hilda Rd. L12: W Der 4C **60**
Hildebrand Cl. L4: Walt 1H **59**
Hildebrand Rd. L4: Walt 1H **59**
Hilden Pl. WA2: Warr 8E **66**
Hilden Rd. WA2: Padg 8F **66**
Hilden Sq. WA1: Warr 3B **82**
Hillaby Cl. L8: Liv 2F **74**
Hillam Rd. CH45: Wall 3D **56**
Hillary Ct. L37: Form 2E **24**
Hillary Cres. L31: Mag 2J **35**
Hillary Dr. L23: Crosb 7N **33**
Hillary Rd. CH62: East 1C **102**
Hillary Wlk. L23: Crosb 7N **33**
Hillbark Rd. CH48: Frank 6H **71**
Hillbeck Cres. WN4: Garsw 7F **40**
Hillberry Cres. WA4: Warr 5C **82**
Hillbrae Av. WA11: St H 2K **49**
Hillbrook Dr. L9: Ain 7J **45**
Hillburn Dr. CH41: Birke 8E **56**
HILLCLIFFE 9D **82**
Hill Cliffe Rd. WA4: Walt 7C **82**
Hill Cl. CH64: Ness 9H **101**
Hill Ct. CH64: Ness 9H **101**
Hill Crest L20: Boot 8D **44**
Hillcrest L31: Mag 2L **35**
WA7: Run 6N **95**
WN8: Skel 5E **30**
Hillcrest Av. L36: Huy 7L **61**
Hillcrest Ct. CH44: Wall 6G **56**
Hillcrest Dr. CH49: Grea 5K **71**
CH66: Lit Sut 8F **102**
L40: Scar 6L **13**
Hillcrest Pde. L36: Huy 7L **61**
Hillcrest Rd. CH66: Lit Sut 8G **102**
L4: Walt 9J **45**
L23: Crosb 7N **33**
L39: Orm 7C **20**
Hillcroft Rd. CH44: Wall 6J **57**
L25: Woolt 4D **76**
HILL DALE 1G **22**
Hilldean WN8: Uph 4M **31**
Hillerton Cl. L12: W Der 8N **45**
Hillfield WA6: Frod 7L **107**
WA7: Nort 7F **96**
Hillfield Dr. CH61: Hesw, Pens 5N **87**
Hillfield Rd. CH66: Lit Sut 7J **103**
Hillfoot Av. L25: Hunts X 1F **92**
Hillfoot Cl. CH43: Bid 9C **56**
Hillfoot Cres. WA4: Stockt H 9C **82**
Hillfoot Grn. L25: Woolt 9E **76**
Hillfoot Rd. L25: Hunts X, Woolt 7D **76**
Hill Gro. CH46: More 1M **71**
Hillhead Rd. L20: Boot 8D **44**
Hill Ho. Fold La. WN6: Wright 1M **23**
Hillingden Av. L26: Halew 9K **77**
Hillingden Cl. L26: Halew 9L **77**
Hillingdon Av. CH61: Hesw 5N **87**
Hillingdon Rd. L15: Wav 2N **75**
Hillock Cl. L40: Scar 7M **13**
Hillock La. L40: Scar 7M **13**
WA1: Wools 1J **83**
WN8: Dalt 7F **22**
Hill Ridge CH43: Noct 3D **72**
Hill Rise Vw. L39: Augh 3M **27**
Hill Rd. CH43: Clau 1E **72**
Hill Rd. Nth. WA6: Hel 2F **114**
Hill Rd. Sth. WA6: Hel 2F **114**
Hillsboro Av. WA6: Frod 7M **107**
Hill School Rd. WA10: St H 1D **62**
Hillsdown Way CH66: Gt Sut 3H **111**
HILLSIDE 5L **11**
Hillside WA13: Lymm 7L **85**
Hillside Av. L36: Huy 3G **61**
L39: Orm 9B **20**
WA7: Run 7H **95**
WA10: St H 4H **49**
WA12: Newt W 8H **51**
WN4: Ash M 3H **41**
WN8: Parb 1G **22**
Hillside Cl. CH41: Tran 4L **73**
L20: Boot 8D **44**
WA6: Hel 1G **114**
WN5: Bil 6N **39**
Hillside Ct. CH41: Tran 4L **73**
L25: Woolt 5E **76**
Hillside Cres. L36: Huy 3G **61**
Hillside Dr. CH66: Ell P 6K **103**
L25: Woolt 5F **76**
Hillside Golf Links 5L **11**
Hillside Gro. WA5: Penk 4H **81**
Hillside Rd. CH41: Tran 4L **73**
CH43: Bid 9D **56**
CH44: Wall 5E **56**
CH48: W Kir 6E **70**
CH60: Hesw 8A **88**
L18: Moss H 3N **75**
L36: Huy 4J **61**
PR8: Birkd 5L **11**
WA4: App 4D **98**
WA6: Frod 7M **107**
Hillside Station (Rail) 5L **11**
Hillside St. L6: Liv 1L **5** (6E **58**)
Hillside Vw. CH43: Oxton 5G **72**
Hillsmore Way L5: Liv 3E **58**
Hills Pl. L15: Wav 1M **75**
Hill St. L8: Liv 2C **74**
(not continuous)
L23: Crosb 8M **33**
L34: Presc 3A **62**
PR9: South 8G **7**
WA1: Warr 3C **82**
WA7: Run 5K **95**
WA10: St H 5K **49**
Hill St. Bus. Cen. *L8: Liv 2C* ***74***
(off Hill St.)
Hillsview Rd. PR8: Ains 1J **17**
Hilltop WA7: Nort 8E **96**
Hill Top La. CH64: Ness 9H **101**
Hilltop La. CH60: Hesw 7B **88**
Hill Top Rd. WA1: Wools 9K **67**
WA4: Dutt 5L **109**
WA4: Pres H 9H **97**
WA4: Stockt H 6G **83**
WA11: Rainf 9E **38**
WA13: Lymm 6C **84**
Hilltop Rd. L16: Child 1B **76**
Hilltop Wlk. L39: Orm 1A **28**
Hill Vw. WA8: Wid 3J **79**
Hillview L17: Aig 6K **75**
Hill Vw. Av. WA6: Hel 4D **114**
Hillview Av. CH48: W Kir 5C **70**
Hillview Cl. WA6: Frod 7M **107**
Hillview Ct. CH43: Bid 8C **56**
Hill Vw. Dr. CH49: Upton 2A **72**
Hillview Gdns. L25: Woolt 5D **76**
Hillview Rd. CH61: Irby 9K **71**
Hillwood Cl. CH63: Spit 6N **89**
Hilton Av. WA5: Gt San 3K **81**
Hilton Cl. CH41: Birke 2J **73**
Hilton Ct. L30: N'ton 7C **34**
Hilton Dr. M44: Cad 4J **69**
Hilton Gro. CH48: W Kir 5B **70**
Hilton St. WN4: Ash M 8L **41**
Himalayan Birch Cl. CH66: Ell P 8K **103**
Hinchley Grn. L31: Mag 2G **34**
Hinckley Rd. WA11: St H 5M **49**
Hindburn Av. L31: Mag 1L **35**
HINDERTON 5H **101**
Hinderton Cl. CH41: Birke 4L **73**
Hinderton Dr. CH48: W Kir 7F **70**
CH60: Hesw 9N **87**
Hinderton Grn. CH64: Nest 6F **100**
Hinderton La. CH64: Nest 5G **101**
Hinderton Rd. CH41: Birke 3L **73**
CH64: Nest 6F **100**
Hindle Av. WA5: Warr 8A **66**
Hindley Beech L31: Mag 1H **35**
Hindley Wlk. L24: Speke 5H **93**
Hindlip St. L8: Liv 5F **74**
Hind St. CH41: Birke 3L **73**
Hinson St. CH41: Birke 2L **73**
Hinton Cres. WA4: App 8F **82**
Hinton Rd. WA7: Run 7K **95**
Hinton St. L6: Liv 6H **59**
L21: Lith 4A **44**
Hitchens Cl. WA7: Murd 8F **96**
HMP Altcourse L9: Faz 4J **45**
HMP Kennet L31: Mag 1A **36**
HMP Liverpool L9: Walt 5E **44**
HMP Risley WA3: Ris 1M **67**
HMYOI Thorn Cross WA4: App T 3K **99**
Hobart Dr. L33: Kirkb 5C **36**
Hobart St. WA9: St H 1H **63**
Hobberley Dr. WN8: Skel 4H **31**
Hobb La. WA4: Dares, Moore 2L **97**
Hobby Ct. WA7: Pal F 9A **96**
Hobcross La. L40: Lath 4L **21**
Hob Hey La. WA3: Cul 6L **53**
Hobhouse Ct. CH43: Clau 2H **73**
Hob La. CH2: Wim T 6L **113**
WA6: Dun H 6L **113**
Hoblyn Rd. CH43: Bid 9E **56**
Hockenhall All. L2: Liv 4E **4** (7B **58**)
Hockenhull Cl. CH63: Spit 5N **89**
Hodder Av. L31: Mag 1L **35**
Hodder Cl. WA11: St H 3L **49**
Hodder Rd. L5: Liv 3E **58**
Hodder St. L5: Liv 3E **58**
Hodge St. PR8: South 8G **6**
Hodgkinson Av. WA5: Warr 8A **66**
Hodnet Dr. WN4: Ash M 8L **41**
Hodson Pl. L6: Liv 5F **58**
Hodson St. PR8: South 9H **7**
Hogarth Dr. CH43: Noct 5D **72**
Hogarth St. *L21: Sea 4N* ***43***
(off Seaforth Va. Nth.)
Hogarth Wlk. L4: Kirkd 1C **58**
Hoggs Hill La. L37: Form 4E **24**
Hoghton Cl. WA9: St H 1B **64**
Hoghton Gro. PR9: South 7H **7**
Hoghton La. WA9: St H 1B **64**
(not continuous)
Hoghton Pl. PR9: South 8G **7**
Hoghton Rd. L24: Hale 5B **94**
WA9: St H 1B **64**
Hoghton St. PR9: South 8G **7**
Hoghton Twr. Ct. L24: Hale 5N **93**
Holbeck WA7: Nort 8E **96**
Holbeck St. L4: Walt 3G **59**
Holborn Ct. WA8: Wid 5J **79**
Holborn Dr. L39: Orm 1A **28**
Holborn Hill CH41: Tran 4L **73**
L39: Orm 1A **28**
Holborn Sq. CH41: Tran 4L **73**
Holborn Sq. Ind. Est. CH41: Tran 4L **73**
Holborn St. L6: Liv 3M **5** (7F **58**)
Holbrook Cl. WA5: Gt San 2G **80**
WA9: St H 3M **63**
Holcombe Av. WA3: Golb 2D **52**
Holcombe Cl. CH49: Grea 4L **71**
Holcroft La. WA3: Cul 1E **68**
Holden Gro. L22: Water 9J **33**
Holden Rd. L22: Water 9H **33**
L35: Presc 5N **61**
Holden Rd. E. L22: Water 9J **33**
Holden St. L8: Liv 8N **5** (9G **58**)
Holden Ter. L22: Water 9J **33**
Holdsworth Dr. L7: Liv 7G **59**
Holes La. WA1: Wools 9J **67**
Holford Av. WA5: Warr 9A **66**
Holford Moss WA7: Nort 4F **96**
Holford Way WA12: Newt W 7A **52**
Holgate L23: Thorn 3A **34**
Holgate Dr. WN5: Orr 7N **31**
Holgate Pk. L23: Thorn 4A **34**
HOLIDAY MOSS 5E **38**
Holingsworth Ct. WA10: St H 6L **49**
Holkham Cl. WA8: Wid 7J **79**
Holkham Gdns. WA9: St H 3G **62**
Holland Bus. Pk. L40: Lath 9N **21**
Holland Cl. PR8: South 9H **7**
Holland Ct. L30: N'ton 7C **34**
WN8: Skel 1G **39**
Holland Gro. CH60: Hesw 6N **87**
Holland Ho. WN8: Uph 6M **31**
HOLLAND LEES 8M **23**
HOLLAND MOOR 5H **31**
Holland Moss WN8: Skel 7D **30**
Holland Moss Bus. Pk. WN8: Skel 8G **30**
Holland Pl. L7: Liv 5N **5** (8G **58**)
Holland Rd. CH45: Wall 2J **57**
L24: Speke 5J **93**
L26: Halew 1J **93**
Holland's La. WN8: Skel 2L **29**
Holland St. L7: Liv 6J **59**
Holland Way L26: Halew 1J **93**
Holley Ct. *L35: Rainh 6F* ***62***
(off Rainhill Rd.)
Holliers Cl. L31: Mag 2J **35**
Hollies, The L25: Woolt 5C **76**
L39: Augh 9M **19**
PR8: South 9E ***6***
(off Beechfield Gdns.)
WA7: Run 7N **95**
Hollies Rd. L26: Halew 9K **77**
HOLLINFARE 6H **69**
Hollingbourne Pl. L11: Norr G 7M **45**
Hollingbourne Rd. L11: Norr G 7M **45**
Hollinghurst Rd. L33: Kirkb 6D **36**
Hollington Way WN3: Wins 1E **40**
Hollingwood Cl. WN4: Ash M 8J **41**
Hollingworth Cl. L9: Walt 7F **44**
Hollin Hey Cl. WN5: Bil 8N **39**
Hollinhey Cl. L30: N'ton 6F **34**
Hollins Cl. L15: Wav 9M **59**
WN4: Garsw 7F **40**
Hollins Dr. WA2: Win 3B **66**
HOLLINS GREEN 7G **69**
Hollins La. CW9: Ant 9N **99**
WA2: Win 3N **65**
Hollins Way WA8: Hale B 2E **94**
Hollocombe Rd. L12: W Der 8N **45**
Holloway WA7: Run 6J **95**
Hollow Cft. L28: Stockb V 9E **46**
Hollow Dr. WA4: Stockt H 7F **82**
Hollowford La. L40: Lath 2N **21**
Holly Av. CH63: Beb 4M **89**
WA12: Newt W 7M **51**
Holly Bank WA6: Alv 3G **115**
WA6: Frod 6M **107**
WA13: Lymm 6D **84**
Hollybank WA4: Moore 2J **97**
Holly Bank Caravan Pk. WA3: Rix 8G **69**
Holly Bank Cotts. *M31: Part 5M* ***69***
(off Manchester Rd.)
Hollybank Ct. CH41: Birke 3K **73**
WA8: Wid 6J **79**
Hollybank Grange L26: Halew 8K **77**
Holly Bank Gro. WA9: St H 6M **49**
Hollybank Rd. CH41: Birke 3K **73**
L18: Moss H 3K **75**
WA7: Halt 7B **96**
Holly Bank St. WA9: St H 6M **49**
Hollybrook Rd. PR8: South 1N **11**
Holly Bush La. WA3: Rix 9C **68**
Holly Bush Sq. WA3: Low 1F **52**
Holly Cl. L24: Hale 5A **94**
L40: Westh 9J **21**
WA10: Eccl 6E **48**
WN8: Skel 3B **30**
Holly Ct. L20: Boot 5A **44**
WA6: Hel 9F **106**
Holly Cres. WA11: Rainf 5D **38**
Hollydale Rd. L18: Moss H 3M **75**
Holly Farm Ct. WA8: Wid 4J **79**
Holly Farm Rd. L19: Garst 1B **92**
Hollyfield Rd. CH65: Ell P 9N **103**
L9: Walt 5E **44**
Holly Fold La. L39: Bic 9B **30**
WA11: Bic 9B **30**
Holly Gro. CH42: Tran 4L **73**
L21: Sea 4M **43**
L36: Roby 7F **60**
PR9: Banks 3E **8**
WA1: Padd 1H **83**
Hollyhedge La. WA4: Hghr Wal 1M **97**
Holly Hey L35: Whis 8A **62**
Hollyhurst Cl. L8: Liv 3F **74**
Holly La. L39: Augh 9N **19**
L39: Bic 8A **30**
L40: Ruf 3N **15**
Hollymead Cl. L25: Gate 4F **76**
Holly M. L23: Crosb 6M **33**
Holly Mt. L12: W Der 3M **59**
WA10: St H 8G **48**
Holly Pl. CH46: More 1N **71**
Holly Rd. CH65: Ell P 9A **104**
L7: Liv 7J **59**
WA3: Golb 2D **52**
WA5: Penk 3G **81**
WA11: Hay 5B **50**
WA13: Lymm 3H **85**
Hollyrood L34: Presc 4L **61**
Holly St. L20: Boot 6B **44**
Holly Ter. WA5: Penk 4H **81**
Hollytree Rd. L25: Woolt 5F **76**
Holly Wlk. M31: Part 6K **69**
Hollywood Bowl
Liverpool 7L **59**
Hollywood Rd. L17: Aig 5K **75**
Holman Rd. L19: Garst 1B **92**
Holm Cotts. CH43: Oxton 6F **72**
Holmdale Av. PR9: South 3N **7**
Holm Dr. CH2: Elt 2N **113**
Holme Cl. L34: Eccl P 2D **62**
Holmefield Av. L19: Aig 7M **75**
Holmefield Rd. L19: Aig 8L **75**
Holme Rd. WA10: St H 8E **48**
HOLMES 4M **9**
Holmes Ct. CH42: Tran 5J **73**
WA3: Birchw 5K **67**
Holmesfield Rd. WA1: Warr 3E **82**
Holmes Ho. Av. WN3: Wins 1E **40**
Holmes La. *L21: Lith 3N* ***43***
(off Bridge Rd.)
Holmes St. L8: Liv 1H **75**
Holme St. L5: Kirkd 3B **58**
Holmesway CH61: Pens 3N **87**
HOLMESWOOD 9N **9**
Holmeswood Rd.
L40: Holm, Ruf 8M **9** & 1H **15**
Holmfield CH2: Elt 2M **113**
CH43: Oxton 6F **72**
Holmfield Av. WA7: Run 5M **95**
Holmfield Dr. CH66: Gt Sut 2J **111**
Holmfield Gro. L31: Mag 2H **35**
L36: Huy 9K **61**
Holmfield Pk. L37: Form 9E **16**
Holm Hey Rd. CH43: Pren 6F **72**
Holm Hill CH48: W Kir 7D **70**
Holmlands Cres. CH43: Oxton 6E **72**
Holmlands Dr. CH43: Oxton 6E **72**
Holmlands Way CH43: Oxton 6F **72**
Holm La. CH43: Oxton 6F **72**
Holmleigh Rd. L25: Gate 2E **76**
Holm Oak Way CH66: Gt Sut 5L **111**
Holmrook Rd. L11: Norr G 8M **45**
Holmside Cl. CH46: More 9N **55**
Holmside La. CH43: Oxton 6F **72**
Holm Vw. Cl. CH43: Oxton 5G **72**
Holmville Rd. CH63: Hghr B 2L **89**
Holmway CH63: Hghr B 2M **89**
Holmwood Av. CH61: Thing 2C **88**
Holmwood Cl. L37: Form 1D **24**
WN4: Ash M 6J **41**
Holmwood Dr. CH61: Thing 2C **88**
CH65: Whit 2N **111**
L37: Form 9D **16**
Holmwood Gdns. CH48: W Kir 7F **70**
L37: Form 9D **16**
HOLT 5D **62**
Holt Av. CH46: More 9M **55**
WN5: Bil 7N **39**
Holt Coppice L39: Augh 5M **27**
Holt Cres. WN5: Bil 7N **39**
HOLT GREEN 6M **27**
Holt Hey CH64: Ness 9G **100**
Holt Hill CH41: Birke 4L **73**
Holt Hill Ter. CH42: Tran 3L **73**
Holt La. L27: N'ley 1J **77**
(not continuous)
L35: Rainh 5D **62**
WA7: Halt 7B **96**

Holton Way WN3: Wins 2G 40
Holt Rd. CH41: Tran 4L 73
L7: Liv 7H 59
Holt St. WN5: Orr 7N 31
Holtswell Cl. WA3: Low 1F 52
Holt Way L32: Kirkb 9B 36
Holy Cross Cl. L3: Liv 2F 4 (6C 58)
Holyhead Cl. WA5: Call 6M 65
Holyrood L23: Blun 7G 32
Holyrood Av. WA8: Wid 4K 79
Holywell Cl. CH64: Park 5B 100
WA9: St H 3N 63
Holywell Dr. WA1: Warr 3D 82
Homechase Ho. *PR8: Birkd 2M 11*
(off Chase Cl.)
Homecrofts CH64: Lit N 9E 100
Homedove Ho. L23: Blun 7J 33
Home Farm 9B 46
Home Farm Cl. CH49: Woodc 6C 72
Home Farm Rd. CH49: Woodc 6B 72
L34: Know 8G 47
Homeport Ho. *PR9: South 7H 7*
(off Hoghton St.)
HOMER GREEN 2B 34
Homer Rd. L34: Know 7G 47
Homerton Cl. CH65: Ell P 1B 112
Homerton Rd. L6: Liv 6J 59
Homesands Ho. PR9: South 7J 7
Homestall Rd. L11: Norr G 8M 45
Homestead Av. L30: N'ton 8G 34
WA11: Hay 3G 51
Homestead Cl. L36: Huy 6L 61
M31: Part 5N 69
Homestead M. CH48: W Kir 6C 70
Homeway WA6: Hel 3E 114
Honeybourne Dr. L35: Whis 3D 62
Honey Hall Rd. L26: Halew 1J 93
Honeys Grn. Cl. L12: W Der 4B 60
Honeys Grn. La. L12: W Der 4B 60
Honeys Grn. Pct. L12: W Der 4B 60
Honey Spot Gro. WA8: Wid 4A 80
Honey St. WA9: St H 2F 62
Honeysuckle Av. PR9: Banks 5H 9
WA5: Warr 4N 81
Honeysuckle Cl. CH66: Gt Sut 5L 111
L26: Halew 6H 77
WA8: Wid 4L 79
Honeysuckle Dr. L9: Walt 7G 44
Honister Av. WA2: Warr 7D 66
WA11: St H 2M 49
Honister Gro. WA7: Beech 1A 108
Honister Wlk. L27: N'ley 5L 77
Honiston Av. L35: Rainh 5E 62
Honiton Rd. L17: Aig 7K 75
Honiton Way WA5: Penk 4G 81
Hood La. WA5: Gt San 3L 81
Hood La. Nth. WA5: Gt San 2L 81
Hood Mnr. Cen. WA5: Gt San 2L 81
Hood Rd. WA8: Wid 7J 79
Hood St. CH44: Wall 6K 57
L1: Liv 4F 4 (7C 58)
L20: Boot 5N 43
Hookstone Dr. CH66: Lit Sut 8H 103
Hoole La. PR9: Banks 1E 8
Hoole Rd. CH49: Woodc 5B 72
Hoolpool La. WA6: Hel 9C 106
Hoose Ct. CH47: Hoy 1D 70
HOOTON 5F 102
Hooton Golf Course 7G 103
Hooton Grn. CH66: Hoot 4F 102
Hooton Hey CH66: Gt Sut 9J 103
Hooton La. CH66: Hoot 5G 103
Hooton Pk. Airfield CH65: Hoot 3H 103
Hooton Pk. La. CH65: Hoot 4H 103
Hooton Park Outdoor Karting Circuit
2H 103
Hooton Rd. CH64: Will 6N 101
CH66: Hoot 6N 101
L9: Ain 3G 44
Hooton Station (Rail) 5C 102
Hooton Way CH66: Hoot 4E 102
Hooton Works Trad. Est.
CH66: Hoot 4D 102
Hope Carr Nature Reserve 1N 53
Hope Cl. WA10: St H 6H 49
Hope Cotts. *CH66: Chil T 6F 102*
(off New Rd.)
Hope Cft. CH66: Gt Sut 3L 111
Hope Farm Pct. CH66: Gt Sut 3L 111
Hope Farm Rd. CH66: Gt Sut 4K 111
Hopefield Rd. WA13: Lymm 4H 85
Hope Island WN8: Skel 4D 30
Hope Pk. L16: Child 3B 76
Hope Pl. L1: Liv 7J 5 (9D 58)
Hope Sq. PR9: South 8H 7
Hope St. CH41: Birke 1K 73
CH45: New B 1H 57
L1: Liv 8K 5 (9E 58)
L34: Presc 3A 62
PR9: South 8H 7
WA12: Newt W 7K 51
WN4: Ash M 6M 41
Hope Way L8: Liv 8K 5 (9E 58)
Hopfield Rd. CH46: More 9N 55
Hopkins Cl. WA10: St H 6G 48
Hopwood Cl. WA3: Low 2G 53
Hopwood Cres. WA11: Rainf 6D 38
Hopwood St. L5: Liv 4C 58
WA1: Warr 2D 82
(not continuous)
Horace Black Gdns. CH65: Ell P 8A 104
Horace St. WA10: St H 6G 49
Horatio St. CH41: Birke 2K 73
Horbury Gdns. CH66: Lit Sut 9H 103
Hornbeam Av. CH66: Gt Sut 4L 111
Hornbeam Cl. CH46: More 9J 55
WA7: Wind H 6E 96
WA11: Hay 5B 50
Hornbeam Cres. WN4: Ash M 8K 41
Hornbeam Rd. L9: Walt 7H 45
L26: Halew 9L 77
Hornby Av. CH62: Brom 6B 90
L20: Boot 5A 44
Hornby Blvd. L20: Boot 4A 44
L21: Lith 4A 44
Hornby Chase L31: Mag 4J 35
Hornby Cl. L9: Walt 6E 44
Hornby Ct. CH62: Brom 6C 90
L9: Walt 5F 44
Hornby Cres. WA9: Clock F 5N 63
Hornby Flats *L21: Lith 4A 44*
(off Linacre Rd.)
Hornby La. L18: Moss H 3B 76
WA2: Win 3B 66
Hornby Pk. L18: Moss H 3B 76
Hornby Pl. L9: Walt 5F 44
Hornby Rd. CH62: Brom 6B 90
L9: Walt 6E 44
L20: Boot 5A 44
(Hornby Av.)
L20: Boot 6B 44
(Roby St.)
PR9: South 2M 7
Hornby St. CH41: Birke 2M 73
L21: Sea 4N 43
L23: Crosb 7L 33
Hornby Wlk. L5: Liv 5B 58
Horncastle Cl. WA3: Low 2G 52
Hornchurch Dr. WA5: Gt San 2K 81
Horne St. L6: Liv 5G 58
Hornet Cl. L6: Liv 4F 58
Hornhouse La. L33: Know I 2F 46
Hornsey Gro. WN3: Wins 1F 40
Hornsey Rd. L4: Walt 3G 58
Hornsmill Av. WA8: Wid 3K 79
Hornsmill Way WA6: Hel 2D 114
Hornspit La. L12: W Der 1M 59
Horridge Av. WA12: Newt W 5L 51
Horringford Rd. L19: Aig 8L 75
Horrocks Av. L19: Garst 1B 92
Horrocks Cl. L36: Huy 5H 61
Horrocks La. WA1: Warr 3C 82
Horrocks Rd. L36: Huy 6H 61
Horseman Pl. CH44: Wall 7L 57
Horsemarket St. WA1: Warr 3C 82
Horseshoe Cl. WA9: St H 7C 50
Horseshoe Cres. WA2: Warr 6F 66
Horseshoe Dr. L10: Faz 3N 45
Horsey Mere Gdns. WA9: St H 3H 63
Horsfall Gro. L8: Liv 4D 74
Horsfall St. L8: Liv 4D 74
Horstone Cres. CH66: Gt Sut 3L 111
Horstone Gdns. CH66: Gt Sut 3M 111
Horstone Rd. CH66: Gt Sut 3L 111
Horton Cl. L33: Kirkb 5C 36
Horwood Av. L35: Rainh 5E 62
Horwood Cl. L12: W Der 8A 46
HOSCAR 1A 22
Hoscar Ct. WA8: Wid 9G 78
Hoscar Moss Rd. L40: Lath 2N 21
Hoscar Station (Rail) 1A 22
Hoscote Pk. CH48: W Kir 6B 70
Hose Side Rd. CH45: Wall 2G 56
Hospital St. WA10: St H 6L 49
Hospital Way WA7: Pal F 8B 96
Hosta Cl. L33: Kirkb 6B 36
Hostock Cl. L35: Whis 7A 62
Hotel St. WA12: Newt W 7K 51
Hotham St. L3: Liv 4H 5 (7D 58)
Hothfield Rd. CH44: Wall 6K 57
Hotspur St. L20: Boot 1B 58
HOUGH GREEN 7D 78
Hough Grn. Rd. WA8: Wid 6D 78
Hough Green Station (Rail) 7E 78
Hough's La. WA4: Hghr Wal 2B 98
Houghton Av. WA2: Warr 2D 82
Houghton Cl. WA8: Wid 6M 79
WA12: Newt W 7K 51
Houghton Cft. WA8: Cron 3F 78
HOUGHTON GREEN 5F 66
Houghton La. L1: Liv 5G 4 (8C 58)
Houghton Rd. CH49: Woodc 4B 72
L24: Hale 5B 94
Houghton's La. WA10: Eccl 4C 48
WN8: Skel 3F 30
(not continuous)
Houghton's Rd. WN8: Skel 1C 30
Houghton St. L1: Liv 5G 4 (8C 58)
L34: Presc 3A 62
L35: Rainh 6F 62
WA2: Warr 1C 82
WA8: Wid 6N 79
WA12: Newt W 7K 51
Houghton Way L1: Liv 5G 4
Houghwood Golf Course 4L 39
Houghwood Grange WN4: Ash M 8H 41
Hougoumont Av. L22: Water 1L 43
Hougoumont Gro. L22: Water 1L 43
Houlding St. L4: Walt 3F 58
Houlgrave Rd. L5: Liv 4B 58
Houlston Rd. L32: Kirkb 9N 35
Houlston Wlk. L32: Kirkb 9N 35
Hourd Way CH66: Gt Sut 5K 111
House La. WA8: Wid 9J 79
Houston Gdns. WA5: Gt San 9J 65
Hove, The WA7: Murd 9F 96
(not continuous)
Hoveton Gdns. WA9: St H 3G 63
Howard Av. CH62: Brom 7D 90
WA13: Lymm 4H 85
Howard Cl. L21: Ford 9B 34
(not continuous)
L31: Mag 2L 35
Howard Ct. CH64: Nest 5F 100
PR9: South 6J 7
WA7: Manor P 3E 96
Howard Dr. L19: Gras 9M 75
Howard Florey Av.
L30: N'ton 7E 34
Howard's La. WA10: Eccl 6B 48
Howards Rd. CH61: Thing 1B 88
Howard St. WA10: St H 1G 62
Howards Way CH64: Lit N 8G 101
Howarth Ct. WA7: Run 5L 95
Howarth Dr. M44: Irlam 1M 69
Howbeck Cl. CH43: Clau 2F 72
Howbeck Ct. CH43: Oxton 3F 72
Howbeck Dr. CH43: Clau 2F 72
Howbeck Rd. CH43: Oxton 3F 72
Howden Dr. L36: Huy 6E 60
Howell Dr. CH49: Grea 6L 71
Howell Rd. CH62: New F 9N 73
Howells Av. CH66: Gt Sut 2H 111
Howells Cl. L31: Mag 1J 35
Howe St. L20: Boot 9A 44
Howey La. WA6: Frod 7K 107
Howey Ri. WA6: Frod 7K 107
Howgill Cl. CH66: Lit Sut 8E 102
HOWLEY 3D 82
Howley La. WA1: Warr 3E 82
Howley Quay WA1: Warr 3E 82
Howley Quay Ind. Est. WA1: Warr 3E 82
Howson Rd. WA2: Warr 7D 66
Howson St. CH42: Rock F 6M 73
Hoyer Ind. Est. CH65: Ell P 9D 104
HOYLAKE 2C 70
Hoylake Cl. WA7: Murd 9E 96
(not continuous)
Hoylake Golf Course 2C 70
Hoylake Gro. WA9: Clock F 5M 63
Hoylake Lifeboat Mus. 1B 70
Hoylake Rd. CH41: Birke 7D 56
CH46: More 1J 71
Hoylake Station (Rail) 2C 70
Hoyle Ct. Rd. CH47: Hoy 9C 54
Hoyle Rd. CH47: Hoy 9C 54
Hoyle St. WA5: Warr 1A 82
Hucklow Dr. WA1: Warr 3F 82
Huddleston Cl. CH49: Woodc 5B 72
Hudleston Rd. L15: Wav 8N 59
Hudson Cl. WA5: Old H 9M 65
Hudson Gro. WA3: Low 2F 52
Hudson Pl. CH49: Upton 2M 71
Hudson Rd. CH46: Leas 5A 56
L31: Mag 4J 35
WA2: Padg 7F 66
Hudswell Cl. L30: N'ton 1G 44
Hughenden Rd. L13: Liv 4L 59
Hughes Av. L35: Presc 5A 62
WA2: Warr 7E 66
Hughes Cl. L7: Liv 8H 59
Hughes Dr. L20: Boot 4D 44
Hughes La. CH43: Oxton 5H 73
Hughes Pl. WA2: Warr 7E 66
Hughes St. L6: Liv 1N 5 (5F 58)
(not continuous)
L19: Garst 2A 92
WA4: Warr 5D 82
WA9: St H 1N 63
Hughestead Gro. L19: Garst 1N 91
Hughson St. L8: Liv 3D 74
Hull Cl. L19: Garst 1N 91
HULME 6C 66
Hulme Cl. CH62: Brom 3B 90
Hulmes Bri. Bus. Cen. L39: Hals 3H 19
Hulme St. PR8: South 8F 6
Hulme Wlk. CH62: Brom 3B 90
Hulmewood CH63: Beb 9N 73
Hulton Av. L35: Whis 5C 62
Humber Cl. L4: Kirkd 1D 58
WA8: Wid 5B 80
Humber Cres. WA9: Sut L 3M 63
Humber Rd. CH66: Gt Sut 3L 111
WA2: Warr 7F 66
Humber St. CH41: Birke 8F 56
Hume Ct. CH47: Meols 9D 54
Hume St. WA1: Warr 2E 82
Humphrey's Cl. WA7: Murd 8F 96
Humphreys Hey L23: Thorn 6A 34
Huncote Av. WA11: St H 4N 49
Hunslet Rd. L9: Ain 4G 44
Hunstanton Cl. CH49: Upton 1A 72
Hunt Cl. WA5: Gt San 9K 65
Hunter Av. WA2: Warr 6C 66
Hunter Cl. L34: Presc 3B 62
Hunters Chase WN5: Bil 2A 40
Hunters Ct. WA6: Hel 1G 114
WA7: Pal F 9A 96
Hunters La. L15: Wav 1M 75
PR4: Tarl 4L 9
Hunter St. L3: Liv 3G 4 (7C 58)
WA9: St H 8M 49
Hunters Way CH64: Park 6C 100
Huntingdon Ct. PR9: South 5M 7
Huntingdon Gro. L31: Lyd 8H 27
Huntington Cl. CH46: More 9J 55
Huntley Av. WA9: St H 2M 63
Huntley Gro. WA9: St H 2M 63
Huntley Rd. L6: Liv 6H 59
Huntley St. WA5: Gt San 4L 81
Hunt Rd. L31: Mag 1J 35
WA11: Hay 4G 50
Hunts Cotts. PR9: South 6M 7
HUNTS CROSS 9F 76
Hunts Cross L25: Hunts X 9G 76
Hunts Cross Av. L25: Woolt 5F 76
(not continuous)
Hunts Cross Shop. Pk. L24: Hunts X 1E 92
Hunt's Cross Station (Rail) 9G 76
Hunts Fld. Cl. WA13: Lymm 6D 84
Hunts La. WA4: Stockt H 6G 83
Huntsman Cl. L25: Hunts X 7H 77
Huntsman Dr. M44: Irlam 2M 69
Huntsman Wood L12: W Der 1C 60
Hurford Av. CH65: Gt Sut 1L 111
Hurley Cl. WA5: Gt San 3L 81
Hurlingham Rd. L4: Walt 8H 45
HURLSTON 3A 20
Hurlston Av. WN8: Skel 4F 30
Hurlston Ct. L40: Scar 2A 20
Hurlston Dr. L39: Orm 6C 20
HURLSTON GREEN 1N 19
Hurlston Hall Country Caravan Pk.
L40: Scar 3A 20
Hurlston Hall Golf Course 3A 20
Hurlston La. L40: Scar 2A 20
Hurrell Rd. CH41: Birke 8D 56
Hurricane Dr. L24: Speke 4D 92
Hursley Rd. L9: Faz 6K 45
Hurst Bank CH42: Rock F 8M 73
Hurstlyn Rd. L18: Aller 7A 76
Hurst Pk. Cl. L36: Huy 5L 61
Hurst Pk. Dr. L36: Huy 5L 61
Hurst Rd. L31: Mag 4K 35
Hurst's La. L39: Bic 1E 36
Hurst St. L1: Liv 8F 4 (9C 58)
WA8: Wid 3K 95
Hurstwood L37: Form 8E 16
Huskisson St. L8: Liv 9K 5 (1E 74)
Huskisson Way WA12: Newt W 6K 51
Hutchinson Cl. CH43: Bid 2B 72
Hutchinson St. L6: Liv 2N 5 (6F 58)
WA8: Wid 1J 95
Hutchinson Wlk. L6: Liv 2N 5 (6F 58)
Hutfield Rd. L24: Speke 3L 93
Hutton Cl. WA3: Cul 5M 53
Hutton Ct. WN8: Skel 3A 30
Hutton Rd. WN8: Skel 3A 30
Hutton Way L39: Orm 8C 20
Huxley Cl. CH46: More 9J 55
Huxley Ct. CH66: Ell P 6L 103
Huxley St. L13: Liv 2J 59
HUYTON 7J 61
Huyton & Prescot Golf Course 5L 61
Huyton Av. WA10: St H 4H 49
Huyton Brook L36: Huy 9K 61
Huyton Bus. Pk. L35: Whis 8N 61
L36: Huy 8L 61
(Brickfields)
L36: Huy 8K 61
(Octavia Ct.)
L36: Huy 9M 61
(Stretton Way)
Huyton Chu. Rd. L36: Huy 7J 61
Huyton Gallery 7J 61
Huyton Hall Cres. L36: Huy 7J 61
Huyton Hey Rd. L36: Huy 7J 61
Huyton Ho. Rd. L36: Huy 5F 60
Huyton La. L34: Presc 6J 61
L36: Huy 6J 61
Huyton Lane Wetland Pk. 6K 61
Huyton Station (Rail) 7J 61
HUYTON-WITH-ROBY 6G 61
Hyacinth Av. L33: Kirkb 6B 36
Hyacinth Cl. WA11: Hay 4H 51
Hyacinth Gro. CH46: More 7A 56
Hyacinth Wlk. *M31: Part 7L 69*
(off Redbrook Rd.)
Hyde Cl. CH65: Gt Sut 1L 111
WA7: Beech 9N 95
Hyde Rd. L22: Water 1K 43
Hyde's Brow WA11: Rainf 3D 38
Hydrangea Way WA9: Bold 2C 64
Hydro Av. CH48: W Kir 7C 70
Hygeia St. L6: Liv 5F 58
Hylton Av. CH44: Wall 5G 57
Hylton Ct. CH65: Ell P 3C 112
Hylton Rd. L19: Aller 8B 76
Hyslop St. L8: Liv 2D 74
Hythe Av. L21: Lith 2B 44
Hythe Cl. PR8: South 3D 12
Hythedale Cl. L17: Aig 6H 75

I

Ibbotson's La. L17: Aig 4K 75
Iberis Gdns. WA9: Bold 2C 64
Ibis Ct. WA1: Warr 5B 82
Ibstock Rd. L20: Boot 5A 44

Idaho Wlk. *WA5: Gt San* .2L *81*
(off Washington Dr.)
Iffley Cl. CH49: Upton .3L **71**
Ikin Cl. CH43: Bid .8C **56**
Ilchester Rd. CH41: Birke .8F **56**
CH44: Wall .6K **57**
L16: Child .8C **60**
Ilex Av. WA2: Win .3C **66**
Ilford Av. CH44: Wall .7H **57**
L23: Crosb .6K **33**
Ilford St. L3: Liv .3K **5** (7E **58**)
Ilfracombe Rd. WA9: Sut L .4M **63**
Iliad St. L5: Liv .5D **58**
Ilkley Av. PR9: South .1A **8**
Ilkley Wlk. L24: Speke .3H **93**
Ilsley Cl. CH49: Upton .4N **71**
Image Bus. Pk. L33: Know I .9H **37**
Imber Rd. L32: Kirkb .2D **46**
Imison St. L9: Walt .7E **44**
Imison Way L9: Walt .7D **44**
Immingham Dr. L19: Garst .1N **91**
Imperial Av. CH45: Wall .3J **57**
Imperial Chambers L1: Liv .4E **4**
Imperial Ct. L2: Liv .4D **4**
WA4: Warr .7B **82**
Imperial M. CH65: Ell P .8N **103**
Imrie St. L4: Walt .8E **44**
INCE .8L **105**
Ince Av. CH62: East .3D **102**
L4: Walt .1G **59**
L21: Lith .3A **44**
L23: Crosb .6J **33**
INCE BLUNDELL .9L **25**
Ince Cl. CH43: Oxton .4F **72**
Ince Cres. L37: Form .1D **24**
Ince & Elton Station (Rail) .1M **113**
Ince Gro. CH43: Oxton .4F **72**
Ince La. CH2: Elt .1M **113**
CH2: Wim T .6K **113**
L23: Thorn .2M **33**
Incemore Rd. L18: Moss H .7N **75**
Ince Orchards CH2: Elt .1M **113**
Ince Rd. L23: Thorn .4N **33**
Inchcape Rd. CH45: Wall .4D **56**
L16: Child .8C **60**
Inchfield WN8: Skel .2E **30**
Index St. L4: Walt .9E **44**
Indiana Gro. WA5: Gt San .1J **81**
Indigo Rd. CH65: Ell P .9D **104**
Indoor Karting
Burscough .3F **20**
Ingestre Ct. CH43: Oxton .5G **73**
Ingestre Rd. CH43: Oxton .5G **73**
Ingham Av. WA12: Newt W .9L **51**
Ingham Rd. WA8: Wid .4J **79**
Ingham's Rd. WA3: Croft .9H **53**
Ingleborough Rd. CH42: Tran .6K **73**
Ingleby Rd. CH44: Wall .6G **57**
CH62: New F .8A **74**
Ingledene Rd. L18: Moss H .3B **76**
Inglefield Ct. *CH42: Rock F* .7N *73*
(off The Hawthornes)
Ingle Grn. L23: Blun .6G **32**
Inglegreen CH60: Hesw .7B **88**
Ingleholme Gdns. L34: Eccl P .2D **62**
Ingleholme Rd. L19: Aig .7M **75**
Inglemere Rd. CH42: Rock F .6L **73**
Inglemoss Dr. WA11: Rainf .1E **48**
Inglenook Rd. WA5: Penk .4H **81**
Inglesham Cl. WN7: Leigh .1M **53**
Ingleside Ct. L23: Blun .8J **33**
Inglestone Cl. WA12: Newt W .6K **51**
Ingleton Cl. CH49: Grea .4L **71**
Ingleton Dr. WA11: St H .1L **49**
Ingleton Grn. L32: Kirkb .2D **46**
Ingleton Gro. WA7: Beech .1N **107**
Ingleton Rd. L18: Moss H .3L **75**
L32: Kirkb .2D **46**
PR8: South .3D **12**
Inglewhite WN8: Skel .2D **30**
Inglewhite Island WN8: Skel .2E **30**
Inglewood L12: Crox .8E **46**
Inglewood Av. CH46: More .1L **71**
Inglewood Cl. M31: Part .5L **69**
WA3: Birchw .3B **68**
Inglewood Rd. WA11: Rainf .1F **48**
Inglis Rd. L9: Ain .3G **45**
Ingoe Cl. L32: Kirkb .1N **45**
Ingoe La. L32: Kirkb .1N **45**
(not continuous)
Ingram WN8: Skel .3E **30**
Ingrave Rd. L4: Walt .8H **45**
Ingrow Rd. L6: Liv .6G **59**
Inigo Rd. L13: Liv .5N **59**
Inley Cl. CH63: Spit .5N **89**
Inley Rd. CH63: Spit .5M **89**
Inman Av. WA9: St H .8D **50**
Inman Rd. CH49: Upton .2M **71**
L21: Lith .3A **44**
Inner Central Rd. L24: Halew .2K **93**
Inner Forum L11: Norr G .7K **45**
Inner Gosling Cl. WA4: Hatt .6A **98**
Inner South Rd. L24: Halew .3J **93**
Inner West Rd. L24: Halew .2J **93**
Innisfree Cl. CH66: Gt Sut .9H **103**
Innovation Blvd. L7: Liv .8J **59**
Insall Rd. L13: Liv .8N **59**
WA2: Padg .7G **66**
Inskip WN8: Skel .2D **30**
Inskip Ct. WN8: Skel .2E **30**
Inskip Rd. PR9: South .3M **7**
Intake Cl. CH64: Will .6N **101**
Intake La. L37: Down .4D **26**
L39: Bic .7K **29**
Interchange Motorway Ind. Est.
L36: Huy .8L **61**
International Bus. Cen. WA5: Westb .7L **65**
International Slavery Mus. .7D **4** (9B **58**)
Inveresk Ct. CH43: Noct .2E **72**
Invergarry Rd. L11: Crox .6N **45**
Invincible Cl. L30: Boot .2D **44**
Inward Way CH65: Ell P .7N **103**
Inwood Rd. L19: Garst .9B **76**
Iona Cl. L12: Crox .7E **46**
Iona Cres. WA8: Wid .2J **79**
Iona Gdns. WA9: St H .2N **63**
Ionic Rd. L13: Liv .5M **59**
Ionic St. CH42: Rock F .6M **73**
L21: Sea .3M **43**
Ipswich Cl. L19: Garst .1N **91**
IRBY .1L **87**
Irby Av. CH44: Wall .5G **57**
Irby Cl. CH66: Gt Sut .1K **111**
IRBY HEATH .1K **87**
IRBY HILL .8K **71**
Irby Rd. CH61: Hesw, Irby, Pens .2L **87**
L4: Walt .1G **59**
Irbyside Rd. CH48: Frank .7J **71**
Ireland Rd. L24: Hale .5B **94**
(not continuous)
WA11: Hay .4E **50**
Ireland St. WA2: Warr .9C **66**
WA8: Wid .7N **79**
Irene Av. WA11: St H .3M **49**
Irene Rd. L16: Child .2A **76**
Ireton St. L4: Walt .8E **44**
Iris Av. CH41: Birke .1F **72**
Iris Cl. WA8: Wid .6F **78**
Iris Gro. L33: Kirkb .6B **36**
Iris Pk. Wlk. L31: Mell .8M **35**
Iris Wlk. *M31: Part* .7M *69*
(off Cross La. W.)
IRLAM .1N **69**
Irlam Dr. L32: Kirkb .9C **36**
Irlam Ho. L20: Boot .7A **44**
Irlam Ind. Est. M44: Irlam .2L **69**
Irlam Pl. L20: Boot .6A **44**
Irlam Rd. L20: Boot .6A **44**
Irlam Station (Rail) .2L **69**
Irlam Wharf Rd. M44: Irlam .2N **69**
Ironbridge Vw. L8: Liv .4E **74**
Ironside Rd. L36: Huy .5H **61**
Irton Rd. PR9: South .7K **7**
Irvin Av. PR9: South .2A **8**
Irvine Rd. CH42: Tran .6K **73**
Irvine St. L7: Liv .5N **5** (8F **58**)
Irvine St. W. L7: Liv .5N **5** (8F **58**)
Irvine Ter. CH62: New F .8B **74**
Irving Cl. L9: Ain .2H **45**
Irving St. PR9: South .6G **7**
Irwell WN8: Skel .1D **30**
Irwell Chambers L3: Liv .4D **4**
Irwell Cl. L17: Aig .5K **75**
Irwell Ho. L17: Aig .5K **75**
Irwell La. L17: Aig .5K **75**
WA7: Run .4L **95**
Irwell Rd. WA4: Warr .6C **82**
Irwell St. WA8: Wid .3K **95**
Irwin Rd. WA9: St H .2M **63**
Isaac St. L8: Liv .4E **74**
Isabel Gro. L13: Liv .2K **59**
Isherwood Cl. WA2: Fearn .6G **67**
Island Pl. L19: Garst .1A **92**
Island Rd. L19: Garst .1A **92**
L21: Lith .3N **43**
Island Rd. Sth. L19: Garst .1B **92**
Islands Brow WA11: St H .4L **49**
Isla Sq. L5: Liv .3E **58**
Islay Cl. CH65: Ell P .4A **112**
Isleham Cl. L19: Aller .8A **76**
Islington L3: Liv .3H **5** (7D **58**)
L23: Crosb .7K **33**
Islington Grn. WA8: Wid .4N **79**
Islington Sq. L3: Liv .3L **5** (6E **58**)
Islip Cl. CH61: Irby .9L **71**
Ismay Dr. CH44: Wall .4K **57**
Ismay Rd. L21: Lith .3A **44**
Ismay St. L4: Walt .9E **44**
Ivanhoe Av. WA3: Low .1E **52**
Ivanhoe Rd. L17: Aig .4H **75**
L23: Blun .7J **33**
Ivatt Way L7: Liv .8H **59**
Iveagh Cl. WA7: Pal F .8C **96**
Iver Cl. WA8: Cron .2F **78**
Ivernia Rd. L4: Walt .8G **44**
Ivor Rd. CH44: Wall .4J **57**
Ivory Dr. L33: Kirkb .6C **36**
Ivy Av. CH63: Hghr B .2L **89**
L19: Gras .9N **75**
L35: Whis .5D **62**
WA12: Newt W .8L **51**
Ivybridge WN8: Skel .2E **30**
Ivychurch M. WA7: Run .5N **95**
Ivy Cl. L40: Burs .2L **21**
Ivy Ct. WA9: St H .6M **49**
Ivydale WN8: Skel .2E **30**
Ivydale Rd. CH42: Tran .5L **73**
L9: Walt .6G **44**
L18: Moss H .4M **75**
Ivy Farm Ct. L24: Hale .6A **94**
Ivy Farm Dr. CH64: Lit N .8F **100**
Ivy Farm Gdns. WA3: Cul .6L **53**
Ivy Farm Rd. L35: Rainh .5E **62**
Ivy Ho. Rd. WA3: Low .1E **52**
Ivyhurst Cl. L19: Aig .8L **75**
Ivy La. CH46: More .7M **55**
Ivy Leigh L13: Liv .4K **59**
Ivy Rd. WA1: Wools .1M **83**
WA3: Golb .2C **52**
Ivy St. CH41: Birke .2M **73**
PR8: South .9J **7**
WA7: Run .6K **95**
WN4: Ash M .8K **41**
Ivy Wlk. M31: Part .6K **69**

J

Jackies La. WA13: Lymm .4F **84**
Jack McBane Ct. L3: Liv .5B **58**
Jack's Brow L34: Know P .7J **47**
Jacksfield Way L19: Gras .9L **75**
Jacksmere La. L40: Scar .6F **12**
PR8: South .6F **12**
Jackson Av. WA1: Padd .1G **82**
WA3: Cul .7M **53**
Jackson Cl. CH63: Hghr B .8M **73**
L35: Rainh .8G **63**
L39: Down .8E **18**
Jackson's Comn. La. L40: Scar .4M **19**
(not continuous)
Jacksons Pond Dr. L25: Gate .1D **76**
Jackson St. CH41: Birke .3L **73**
L19: Garst .1A **92**
WA5: Burtw .3G **65**
WA9: St H .7M **49**
WA11: Hay .3C **50**
Jackson St. Ind. Est. WA9: St H .8M **49**
Jacks Wood Av. CH65: Ell P .7N **103**
Jacks Wood Grn. CH65: Ell P .8N **103**
Jacob Ct. WN5: Bil .1N **39**
Jacobs Cl. L21: Lith .4A **44**
Jacob St. L8: Liv .4E **74**
Jacqueline Ct. L36: Roby .7G **61**
Jacqueline Dr. L36: Huy .5L **61**
Jade Cl. L33: Kirkb .8E **36**
Jade Rd. L6: Liv .5G **59**
Jamaica St. L1: Liv .9G **4** (1C **74**)
James Av. CH66: Gt Sut .2H **111**
Jamesbrook Cl. CH41: Birke .9G **57**
James Clarke St. L5: Liv .5B **58**
James Cl. WA8: Wid .3K **95**
James Ct. L25: Woolt .6F **76**
James Ct. Apartments L25: Woolt .6E **76**
James Dixon Ct. L30: N'ton .6C **34**
James Dunne Av. L5: Liv .4B **58**
James Gro. WA10: St H .8H **49**
James Holt Av. L32: Kirkb .1A **46**
James Hopkins Way L4: Kirkd .2C **58**
James Horrigan Ct. L30: N'ton .8B **34**
James Larkin Way L4: Kirkd .2C **58**
James Rd. L25: Woolt .6F **76**
WA11: Hay .3H **51**
James Simpson Way *L30: N'ton* .7E *34*
(off Alexander Fleming Av.)
James St. CH43: Oxton .4J **73**
CH44: Wall .7L **57**
L2: Liv .6D **4** (8B **58**)
L19: Garst .1A **92**
WA1: Warr .3C *82*
(off Buttermarket St.)
WA9: Clock F .6N **63**
WN2: Bam .4N **41**
James Street Station (Rail) .6D **4** (8B **58**)
Jamestown Av. WA5: Gt San .1J **81**
Jamieson Av. L23: Crosb .7N **33**
Jamieson Rd. L15: Wav .1K **75**
Jane's Brook Rd. PR8: South .2C **12**
Jane St. WA9: St H .2B **64**
Janet St. L7: Liv .8G **59**
Japonica Gdns. WA9: Bold .2C **64**
Jardin M. *L17: Aig* .4G *75*
(off Parkfield M.)
Jarrett Rd. L33: Kirkb .7E **36**
Jarrett Wlk. L33: Kirkb .7E **36**
Jarrow Cl. CH43: Oxton .4H **73**
Jasmine Cl. CH49: Upton .1L **71**
L5: Liv .5E **58**
Jasmine Ct. L36: Huy .4K **61**
Jasmine Gdns. WA5: Warr .4N **81**
WA9: Bold .2C **64**
Jasmine Gro. WA8: Wid .8G **78**
Jasmine M. L17: Aig .5F **74**
Jasmine Wlk. *M31: Part* .7M *69*
(off Erskine Wlk.)
Jason St. L5: Liv .3D **58**
Jason Wlk. L5: Liv .3D **58**
Java Rd. L4: Walt .8J **45**
Jay Cl. WA3: Birchw .5N **67**
Jay's Cl. WA7: Murd .8G **96**
Jean Av. WN7: Leigh .1M **53**
Jean Wlk. L10: Faz .4N **45**
Jedburgh Av. CH66: Lit Sut .8E **102**
Jedburgh Dr. L33: Kirkb .5B **36**
Jefferey Cres. L36: Huy .7F **60**
Jeffereys Dr. L36: Huy .6E **60**
Jefferson Dr. WA5: Gt San .1J **81**
Jefferson Gdns. WA8: Wid .5J **79**
Jeffreys Dr. CH49: Grea .3L **71**
Jellicoe Av. M44: Cad .3L **69**
Jellicoe Cl. CH48: Caldy .1E **86**
Jenkinson St. L3: Liv .1J **5** (6D **58**)
Jenner Dr. CH46: Leas .7A **56**
Jennet Hey WN4: Ash M .5H **41**
Jensen Ct. WA7: Ast .4M **95**
Jericho Cl. L17: Aig .6J **75**
Jericho Ct. L17: Aig .6J **75**
Jericho Farm Cl. L17: Aig .7J **75**
Jericho Farm Wlk. L17: Aig .7J **75**
Jericho La. L17: Aig .7J **75**
Jermyn St. L8: Liv .2F **74**
Jerningham Rd. L11: Norr G .7J **45**
Jersey Av. CH65: Ell P .4A **112**
L21: Lith .1A **44**
Jersey Cl. L20: Boot .7B **44**
Jersey St. L20: Boot .7B **44**
WA9: Clock F .6M **63**
Jervis Cl. WA2: Fearn .6H **67**
Jesmond St. L15: Wav .9J **59**
Jessamine Rd. CH42: Tran .5L **73**
Jessop Ct. *CH66: Lit Sut* .8H *103*
(off Black Lion La.)
Jessop Ho. WA7: Run .4H **95**
Jet Cl. L6: Liv .5G **59**
Jeudwine Cl. L25: Woolt .7F **76**
Jibcroft Brook La. WA3: Cul .5M **53**
Joan Av. CH46: More .9L **55**
CH49: Grea .4M **71**
Joan Bartlett Cl. CH65: Ell P .8L **103**
Jocelyn Cl. CH63: Spit .4N **89**
Jockey's Brow La. WA9: St H .1J **63**
Jockey St. WA2: Warr .1C **82**
Jodrell Dr. WA4: Grap .1H **99**
John Bagot Cl. L5: Liv .4D **58**
John Hunter Way L30: N'ton .8E **34**
John Lennon Dr. L6: Liv .6G **59**
John Lennon Statue .5E **4**
(off Mathew St., above The Cavern Club)
John Lloyd Ct. *M44: Irlam* .1M *69*
(off Alexandra Gro.)
John Middleton Cl. L24: Hale .5A **94**
John Moores Cl. L7: Liv .7M **5** (9F **58**)
John Moores University
Hope Pl. .9E **58**
John Morris Ho. *WA1: Warr* .3D *82*
(off Mersey St.)
John Nicholas Cres. CH65: Ell P .8A **104**
John Rd. WA13: Lymm .5C **84**
Johns Av. WA7: Run .7J **95**
WA11: Hay .3G **51**
Johnson Av. L35: Presc .5A **62**
WA12: Newt W .5K **51**
Johnson Gro. L12: W Der .4C **60**
Johnson Rd. CH43: Pren .7F **72**
Johnson's La. WA8: Wid .7A **80**
Johnson St. L3: Liv .3F **4** (7C **58**)
PR9: South .7G **7**
WA9: St H .6M **49**
Johnson Wlk. *L7: Liv* .8H *59*
(off Claughton Cl.)
Johnston Av. L20: Boot .4D **44**
John St. CH41: Birke .1M **73**
CH65: Ell P .8N **103**
L3: Liv .1J **5** (6D **58**)
M44: Cad .4L **69**
WA2: Warr .2C **82**
WA3: Golb .2B **52**
WN4: Ash M .6M **41**
John Willis Ho. CH42: Rock F .6N **73**
John Yeoman Cl. CH64: Lit N .7F **100**
Jones Farm Rd. L25: Gate .3G **76**
Jonson Rd. CH64: Nest .5E **100**
Jonville Rd. L9: Ain .3H **45**
Jordan St. L1: Liv .9G **4** (1C **74**)
Joseph Gardner Way L20: Boot .5A **44**
Joseph Groome Towers CH65: Ell P .8A **104**
Josephine Butler Sq. L6: Liv .2K **5**
Joseph Lister Cl. L30: N'ton .8E **34**
Joseph St. WA8: Wid .6M **79**
WA9: St H .2A **64**
Joshua Cl. L5: Liv .3D **58**
Joyce Wlk. L10: Faz .3A **46**
Joy La. WA5: Burtw .5F **64**
WA8: Clock F .7A **64**
WA9: Clock F .7A **64**
Joy Wlk. WA9: Clock F .6A **64**
Jubilee Av. L14: Broad G .8B **60**
L39: Orm .7D **20**
WA1: Padg .9G **66**
WA5: Penk .4G **81**
WN5: Orr .8N **31**
Jubilee Ct. *PR9: South* .7M *7*
(off Church Cl.)
WA3: Golb .1B *52*
(off Grimshaw St.)
WA11: Hay .3D **50**
Jubilee Cres. CH62: Port S .2A **90**
WA11: Hay .3H **51**
Jubilee Dr. CH48: W Kir .4B **70**
L7: Liv .7G **58**
L30: N'ton .1F **44**
L35: Whis .7A **62**
WN8: Skel .4B **30**
Jubilee Grn. CH65: Ell P .1A **112**
Jubilee Gro. WA13: Lymm .4C **84**
Jubilee Ho. L37: Form .2J **25**
Jubilee Rd. L21: Lith .3A **44**
L23: Crosb .8J **33**
L37: Form .3D **24**
Jubilee Sports Bank .7G **58**

Jubilee Way WA2: Warr 9C 66
WA8: Wid 7H 79
Jubits La. WA8: Bold H 9K 63
WA9: Sut M 9K 63
Juddfield St. WA11: Hay 4C 50
Judges Dr. L6: Liv 5H 59
Judges Way L6: Liv 5H 59
Jugglers Yd. L3: Liv 2E 4
(off Midghall St.)
Julian Way WA8: Wid 4J 79
Julie Gro. L12: W Der 4D 60
Juliet Av. CH63: Hghr B 9L 73
July Rd. L6: Liv 4J 59
July St. L20: Boot 5B 44
Junction Eight Bus. Cen.
CH65: Ell P 8M 103
Junction La. L40: Burs 1J 21
WA9: St H 2A 64
WA12: Newt W 8J 51
Junction One Retail Pk.
CH44: Wall 6D 56
Junction Rd. WA11: Rainf 3B 38
June Av. CH62: Brom 7D 90
June Rd. L6: Liv 4J 59
June St. L20: Boot 6B 44
Juniper Cl. CH49: Grea 6K 71
L28: Stockb V 2F 60
WA10: St H 6G 48
Juniper Dr. CH66: Gt Sut 4K 111
Juniper Gdns. L23: Thorn 5A 34
Juniper Gro. CH66: Gt Sut 4L 111
WA7: Murd 8F 96
Juniper La. WA3: Wools 9A 68
Juniper St. L20: Kirkd 1B 58
Juniper Way PR9: Banks 3E 8
Jupiter Gro. WN3: Wigan 1G 41
Jurby Ct. WA2: Padg 8G 66
Justan Way L35: Rainh 4E 62
Juvenal Pl. L3: Liv 1H 5 (5D 58)
Juvenal St. L3: Liv 1G 5 (6C 58)

K

Kaber Ct. L8: Liv 4D 74
Kaigh Av. L23: Crosb 6K 33
Kale Cl. CH48: W Kir 7C 70
Kale Gro. L33: Kirkb 6E 36
Kamala Way L11: Norr G 9M 45
Kane Ct. WA3: Low 2H 53
Kansas Pl. WA5: Gt San 1K 81
Kara Cl. L20: Boot 7B 44
Karan Way L31: Mell 8N 35
Karen Cl. WA5: Burtw 3H 65
Karen Way CH66: Gt Sut 2J 111
Karonga Rd. L10: Faz 3K 45
Karonga Way L10: Faz 3L 45
Karslake Rd. CH44: Wall 6K 57
L18: Moss H 3L 75
Katherine Wlk. L10: Faz 3A 46
Kaye Av. WA3: Cul 7N 53
Kay La. WA13: Lymm 8G 85
Kearsley Cl. L4: Walt 2D 58
Kearsley St. L4: Walt 2D 58
Keats Av. L35: Whis 6C 62
WN5: Bil 2N 39
Keats Cl. CH66: Gt Sut 5K 111
WA8: Wid 8J 79
Keats Gro. L36: Huy 8K 61
WA2: Warr 7D 66
Keats St. L20: Boot 5A 44
Keats Ter. PR8: South 9L 7
Keble Dr. CH45: Wall 3D 56
L10: Ain 8H 35
Keble Rd. L20: Boot 9B 44
Keble St. L6: Liv 2N 5 (6F 58)
WA8: Wid 9L 79
KECKWICK 3H 97
Keckwick La. WA4: Dares 3H 97
Kedleston St. L8: Liv 4F 74
Keegan Dr. CH44: Wall 7L 57
Keele Cl. CH43: Bid 7C 56
Keel Hey CH64: Will 5A 102
Keel Wharf L3: Liv 8E 4 (1B 74)
Keenan Dr. L20: Boot 5D 44
Keene Ct. L30: N'ton 7C 34
Keepers La. CH63: Store 2H 89
Keeper's Rd. WA4: Grap 9H 83
Keepers Wlk. WA7: Cas 5B 96
Keighley Av. CH45: Wall 4E 56
Keightley St. CH41: Birke 1K 73
Keir Hardie Av. L20: Boot 5D 44
Keith Av. L4: Walt 9E 44
WA5: Gt San 2F 80
Keith Dr. CH63: East 1B 102
Keithley Wlk. L24: Speke 3J 93
Kelbrook Cl. WA9: St H 3N 63
Kelburn Ct. WA3: Ris 3N 67
Kelburn Gro. L12: W Der 1B 60
Kelby Cl. L8: Liv 4F 74
Kelda Ct. L25: Gate 2E 76
Kelday Cl. L33: Kirkb 9C 36
Kelk Beck Cl. L31: Mag 1L 35
Kellet's Pl. CH42: Rock F 5M 73
Kellett Rd. CH46: Leas 6B 56
Kellitt Rd. L15: Wav 1K 75
Kelly Dr. L20: Boot 5D 44
Kelly St. L34: Presc 3B 62
Kelmscott Cl. CH66: Gt Sut 3J 111
Kelmscott Dr. CH44: Wall 5E 56
Kelsall Av. CH62: East 3D 102
WA9: Sut M 5L 63
Kelsall Cl. CH43: Oxton 5F 72
CH62: East 3D 102
WA3: Birchw 6K 67
WA8: Wid 7G 79
Kelsey Cl. WA10: St H 6G 48
Kelso Cl. L33: Kirkb 5B 36
Kelso Rd. L6: Liv 6H 59
Kelton Gro. L17: Aig 6K 75
Kelvin Cl. WA3: Birchw 3L 67
WN4: Garsw 7F 40
Kelvin Ct. CH44: Wall 8L 57
Kelvin Gro. L8: Liv 2F 74
WN3: Wigan 1G 41
(not continuous)
Kelvington Cl. L10: Faz 3L 45
Kelvin Pk. CH41: Birke 8L 57
Kelvin Rd. CH41: Tran 4L 73
CH44: Wall 8L 57
Kelvinside CH44: Wall 8K 57
L23: Crosb 9M 33
Kelvin St. WA3: Ris 3M 67
Kemberton Dr. WA8: Wid 3K 79
Kemble St. L6: Liv 6G 58
L34: Presc 3A 62
Kemlyn Rd. L4: Walt 2F 58
Kemmel Av. WA4: Warr 6D 82
Kemp Av. L5: Liv 3E 58
Kempsell Wlk. L26: Halew 9L 77
Kempsell Way L26: Halew 9L 77
Kempsey Gro. WA9: St H 2H 63
Kempson Ter. CH63: Beb 3M 89
Kempston St. L3: Liv 3J 5 (7D 58)
Kempton Cl. L36: Roby 8G 61
WA7: Run 9M 95
WA12: Newt W 5M 51
Kempton Pk. Fold PR8: South 3E 12
Kempton Pk. Rd. L10: Ain 8K 35
Kempton Rd. CH62: New F 8A 74
L15: Wav 9J 59
Kemsley Rd. L14: Knott A 6D 60
Kenbury Cl. L33: Kirkb 7E 36
Kenbury Rd. L33: Kirkb 7E 36
Kendal Av. WA2: Warr 7D 66
Kendal Cl. CH63: Beb 1M 89
CH66: Gt Sut 3J 111
WA11: Rainf 1C 38
Kendal Dr. CH66: Gt Sut 3J 111
L31: Mag 1J 35
L35: Rainh 6D 62
WA11: Rainf 1B 38
WA11: St H 2L 49
Kendal Gro. WN4: Ash M 7K 41
Kendal M. L33: Kirkb 7B 36
(off Windermere Dr.)
Kendal Pk. L12: W Der 3B 60
Kendal Ri. WA7: Beech 1N 107
Kendal Rd. CH44: Wall 7G 57
L16: Child 1C 76
L33: Kirkb 7B 36
WA8: Wid 7F 78
Kendal St. CH41: Birke 2L 73
Kendal Way PR8: Ains 2H 17
Kendricks Fold L35: Rainh 6E 62
Kendrick St. WA1: Warr 3B 82
Kenford Dr. WN3: Wins 1G 40
Kenilworth Av. WA7: Run 7L 95
Kenilworth Cl. L25: Woolt 5C 76
Kenilworth Ct. CH65: Ell P 3C 112
Kenilworth Dr. CH61: Pens 2M 87
WA1: Padg 9G 67
Kenilworth Gdns.
CH49: Upton 2M 71
WA12: Newt W 8L 51
Kenilworth Rd. CH44: Wall 6K 57
CH64: Nest 8E 100
L16: Child 1B 76
L23: Blun 7J 33
PR8: Ains 9H 11
WA3: Low 3F 52
Kenilworth St. L20: Boot 7A 44
Kenilworth Way L25: Woolt 5C 76
Kenley Av. WA8: Cron 3G 78
Kenmare Rd. L15: Wav 2K 75
Kenmay Wlk. L33: Kirkb 8E 36
Ken M. L20: Boot 4B 44
Kenmore Gro. M44: Cad 3K 69
WN4: Garsw 7F 40
Kenmore Rd. CH43: Pren 7E 72
Kennelwood Av. L33: Kirkb 8D 36
Kennessee Cl. L31: Mag 3K 35
KENNESSE GREEN 3J 35
Kenneth Cl. L30: N'ton 8D 34
L34: Presc 4A 62
Kenneth Rd. WA8: Wid 9F 78
Kennet Rd. CH63: Hghr B 2K 89
WA11: Hay 4E 50
Kennford Rd. L11: Crox 5A 46
Kennington Pk. WA8: Wid 5H 79
KENSINGTON 7G 59
Kensington L7: Liv 3N 5 (7F 58)
Kensington Av. WA4: Grap 6K 83
WA9: St H 2M 63
Kensington Cl. WA8: Wid 4N 79
Kensington Ct. L37: Form 1G 24
Kensington Dr. L34: Presc 4L 61
Kensington Gdns. CH46: More 9M 55
Kensington Ind. Est.
PR9: South 9H 7
Kensington Rd. CH65: Ell P 9M 103
L37: Form 3E 24
PR9: South 8H 7
Kensington St. L6: Liv 3N 5 (7F 58)
Kent Av. L21: Lith 2B 44
L37: Form 3G 24
Kent Cl. CH63: Brom 7A 90
L20: Boot 6C 44
(off Brookhill Rd.)
Kent Gro. WA7: Run 6L 95
Kentmere Av. WA11: St H 2M 49
Kentmere Dr. CH61: Pens 4N 87
Kentmere Pl. WA2: Warr 6B 66
Kent M. CH43: Oxton 4H 73
(off Kent St.)
Kenton Cl. L25: Gate 1F 76
L37: Form 7F 16
Kenton Rd. L26: Halew 9K 77
Kentridge Dr. CH66: Gt Sut 2J 111
Kent Rd. CH44: Wall 6G 56
L37: Form 3F 24
M31: Part 7L 69
M44: Cad 4J 69
PR8: Birkd 2N 11
WA5: Gt San 4L 81
WA9: St H 1M 63
Kents Bank L12: W Der 9A 46
Kent St. CH43: Oxton 4H 73
L1: Liv 8G 5 (9C 58)
WA4: Warr 4D 82
WA8: Wid 7L 79
Kentucky Cl. WA5: Gt San 1K 81
Kentway WA12: Newt W 9L 51
Kentwell Gro. L12: W Der 2B 60
Kenview Cl. WA8: Hale B 3D 94
Kenway WA11: Rainf 5D 38
Kenwick Cl. CH66: Gt Sut 2H 111
Kenwood Cl. L27: N'ley 3K 77
Kenworthys Flats PR9: South 7G 7
Kenwright Cres. WA9: St H 1M 63
Kenwyn Rd. CH45: Wall 4H 57
KENYON 6G 53
Kenyon Av. WA5: Penk 3G 80
Kenyon Cl. L33: Kirkb 5D 36
Kenyon Ct. L8: Liv 2E 74
(off Park Rd.)
WN7: Leigh 1J 53
Kenyon La. WA3: Croft 8G 53
WA3: Cul, Low 4F 52
Kenyon Rd. L15: Wav 3M 75
Kenyons La. L31: Lyd, Mag 8J 27
L37: Form 1G 24
Kenyons La. Nth. WA11: Hay 2H 51
Kenyons La. Sth. WA11: Hay 3H 51
Kenyons Lodge L31: Mag 9K 27
Kenyons Pl. L31: Lyd 9J 27
Kenyons Steps L1: Liv 6F 4
Kenyon Ter. CH43: Oxton 3H 73
Kepler St. L21: Sea 4N 43
Keppel St. L20: Boot 9A 44
Kerfoot Bus. Pk. WA2: Warr 9B 66
(not continuous)
Kerfoots La. WN8: Skel 4N 29
Kerfoot St. WA2: Warr 1B 82
Kerman Cl. L12: W Der 9N 45
Kerr Cl. L33: Kirkb 5C 36
Kerr Gro. WA9: St H 7A 50
Kerridge Dr. WA1: Warr 3F 82
Kerris Cl. L17: Aig 6H 75
Kerry Cft. CH66: Gt Sut 4K 111
Kerry La. PR9: Banks 3E 8
Kerrysdale Cl. WA9: St H 2N 63
Kersey Rd. L32: Kirkb 2D 46
Kersey Wlk. L32: Kirkb 2D 46
Kershaw Av. L23: Crosb 8M 33
Kershaw St. WA8: Wid 7G 79
Kershaw Way WA12: Newt W 5L 51
Kerslake Way L38: Hight 8F 24
Kerswell Cl. WA9: St H 3N 63
Kerton Row PR8: Birkd 2M 11
Keston Wlk. L26: Halew 1K 93
Kestrel Av. CH49: Upton 2L 71
Kestrel Cl. CH49: Upton 2L 71
WA11: St H 4L 49
Kestrel Ct. L23: Blun 8G 33
PR9: South 8J 7
Kestrel Dene L10: Faz 4M 45
Kestrel Dr. WN4: Ash M 5L 41
Kestrel Gro. L26: Halew 7H 77
Kestrel La. WA3: Birchw 5M 67
Kestrel M. WN8: Skel 9F 22
Kestrel Pk. WN8: Skel 9F 22
Kestrel Pl. L40: Burs 3F 20
Kestrel Rd. CH46: More 8K 55
CH60: Hesw 8C 88
Kestrels Way WA7: Pal F 9B 96
Keswick Av. CH63: East 1B 102
WA2: Warr 7D 66
Keswick Cl. L31: Mag 1K 35
M44: Cad 5K 69
PR8: Ains 2J 17
WA8: Wid 7F 78
Keswick Cres. WA2: Warr 7D 66
Keswick Dr. L21: Lith 2C 44
WA6: Frod 6M 107
Keswick Gdns. CH63: Brom 1B 102
Keswick Pl. CH43: Bid 8D 56
Keswick Rd. CH45: Wall 2E 56
L18: Aller 6A 76
WA10: St H 5H 49
Keswick Vs. L16: Child 9E 60
(off Buttermere Rd.)
Keswick Way L16: Child 9E 60
WA11: Rainf 1C 38
Ketterer Ct. WA9: St H 8M 49
Kettering Rd. PR8: Ains 9H 11
Kevelioc Cl. CH63: Spit 4M 89
KEW 3D 12
Kew (Park & Ride) 1F 12
Kew Gdns. Cl. WA8: Wid 4N 79
Kew Ho. Dr. PR8: South 4F 12
Kew Retail Pk. PR8: South 3F 12
Kew Rd. L37: Form 3D 24
PR8: Birkd 3N 11
Kew St. L5: Liv 4C 58
Keybank Rd. L12: W Der 1M 59
Keyes Cl. WA3: Birchw 5N 67
Keyes Gdn. WA3: Birchw 5N 67
Keys Ct. L1: Liv 6F 4 (8C 58)
Keystone Cl. L7: Liv 9G 59
Kiddman St. L9: Walt 7E 44
Kid Glove Rd. WA3: Golb 1C 52
Kidstone Cl. WA9: St H 2N 63
Kielder Cl. WN4: Ash M 4H 41
Kilbuck La. WA11: Hay 2H 51
Kilburn Av. CH62: East 9D 90
WN4: Ash M 7M 41
Kilburn Gro. WA9: St H 2H 63
WN3: Wins 1F 40
Kilburn Rd. WN5: Orr 7M 31
Kilburn St. L21: Lith 4A 44
Kildale Cl. L31: Mag 1H 35
Kildare Cl. L24: Hale 5A 94
Kildonan Rd. L17: Aig 6J 75
WA4: Grap 6H 83
Kilford Cl. WA5: Call 7N 65
Kilgraston Gdns. L17: Aig 7L 75
Killarney Gro. CH44: Wall 6G 56
Killarney Rd. L13: Liv 6N 59
Killester Rd. L25: Gate 4F 76
Killingbeck Cl. L40: Burs 1H 21
Killington Cl. WN3: Wigan 1K 41
Killington Way L4: Kirkd 1D 58
Killingworth La. WA3: Birchw 4A 68
Kilmalcolm Cl. CH43: Oxton 4F 72
Kilmore Cl. L9: Ain 2H 45
Kilmory Av. L25: Woolt 6G 77
Kiln Cl. WA10: Eccl 5F 48
Kilncroft WA7: Brook 1D 108
(not continuous)
Kiln Hey L12: W Der 4A 60
Kiln La. WA10: Eccl, St H 5E 48
WN8: Skel 2B 30
Kiln Rd. CH49: Woodc 5A 72
Kilnyard Rd. L23: Crosb 7K 33
Kilrea Cl. L11: Norr G 1L 59
Kilrea Lodge L11: Norr G 1L 59
Kilrea Rd. L11: Norr G 1K 59
Kilsail Rd. L32: Kirkb 3E 46
Kilsby Dr. WA8: Wid 6A 80
Kilshaw Rd. WA5: Burtw 3H 65
Kilshaw St. L6: Liv 1N 5 (5F 58)
(not continuous)
Kilsyth Cl. WA2: Fearn 5G 67
Kimberley Av. L23: Crosb 8K 33
WA9: St H 2H 63
Kimberley Cl. L8: Liv 9M 5 (1F 74)
Kimberley Dr. L23: Crosb 8K 33
WA4: Stockt H 7D 82
Kimberley Pl. WN4: Ash M 8L 41
Kimberley Rd. CH45: Wall 3H 57
Kimberley St. WA5: Warr 3N 81
Kindale Rd. CH43: Pren 7E 72
Kinder Gro. WN4: Ash M 5H 41
Kinder St. L6: Liv 2L 5 (6E 58)
King Arthurs Wlk. WA7: Cas 6C 96
King Av. L20: Boot 4D 44
King Edward Cl. L35: Rainh 5E 62
King Edward Dr. CH62: Port S 1A 90
King Edward Ind. Est. L3: Liv 3B 4
King Edward Pde. L3: Liv 3C 4
King Edward Rd. L35: Rainh 5E 62
WA10: St H 4G 49
King Edward St. L3: Liv 3C 4 (7A 58)
WA1: Warr 1F 82
Kingfield Rd. L9: Walt 5E 44
Kingfisher Bus. Pk. L20: Boot 3B 44
WA8: Wid 8N 79
Kingfisher Cl. L27: N'ley 3K 77
L33: Kirkb 5C 36
WA3: Birchw 5N 67
WA7: Beech 1B 108
Kingfisher Ct. L31: Lyd 8G 27
PR9: South 7J 7
WN4: Ash M 5K 41
Kingfisher Ct. Ind. Est.
WN4: Ash M 5K 41
Kingfisher Dr. WA11: St H 4L 49
Kingfisher Gro. L12: W Der 9D 46
Kingfisher Ho. CH41: Birke 2N 73
L13: Liv 8M 59
Kingfisher Pk. WN8: Skel 9F 22
Kingfisher Way CH49: Upton 2L 71
King George V Sports Complex 5K 61
King George Cl. WN4: Ash M 8K 41
King George Cres. WA1: Warr 1F 82
King George Dr. CH44: Wall 3K 57
King George Rd. WA11: Hay 3J 51
King George's Dr. CH62: Port S 1A 90
King George's Way CH43: Bid 1E 72

Kingham Cl. CH46: Leas 6B 56
L25: Woolt 6G 77
WA8: Wid 7N 79
Kingham M. L25: Woolt 6G 77
King James Ct. WA7: Pal F 9A 96
Kinglake Rd. CH44: Wall 5K 57
Kinglake St. L7: Liv 5N 5 (8G 58)
Kinglass Rd. CH63: Spit 4A 90
King Oswald Cres. WA8: Wid 2J 79
King's Av. CH47: Meols 9E 54
WA3: Low 3G 53
Kingsbrook Way CH63: Hghr B 8K 73
King's Brow CH63: Hghr B 1K 89
Kingsbury CH48: W Kir 5E 70
Kingsbury Cl. PR8: Ains 1H 17
WA4: App 4E 98
Kingsbury Ct. WN8: Skel 9F 22
Kingsbury Rd. WA8: Wid 4N 79
King's Bus. Pk. L34: Presc 4L 61
Kings Cl. CH63: Hghr B 9K 73
L17: Aig 6H 75
L37: Form 2E 24
Kings Ct. CH43: Oxton 4H 73
CH47: Hoy 1B 70
CH63: Hghr B 9K 73
L21: Sea 3M 43
WA7: Manor P 3F 96
Kingscourt Rd. L12: W Der 4A 60
Kingsdale Av. CH42: Tran 6K 73
L35: Rainh 6G 62
Kingsdale Rd. L18: Moss H 3M 75
WA5: Gt San 9H 65
Kings Dock St. L1: Liv 9F 4 (1C 74)
Kingsdown Rd. L11: Norr G 9M 45
Kingsdown St. CH41: Tran 4L 73
Kings Dr. CH48: Caldy 9D 70
CH61: Pens 2N 87
L25: Gate 4G 77
L25: Woolt 6F 76
L34: Presc 4L 61
WA6: Hel 2E 114
King's Dr. Nth. CH48: W Kir 7E 70
Kingsfield Rd. L31: Mag 4H 35
King's Gap, The CH47: Hoy 1B 70
Kingshead Cl. WA7: Cas 5C 96
Kingsheath Av. L14: Knott A 5C 60
Kings Hey Dr. PR9: South 6L 7
Kingsland Cres. L11: Norr G 7K 45
Kingsland Grange WA1: Wools 8K 67
Kingsland Rd. CH42: Tran 4J 73
L11: Norr G 7K 45
King's La. CH63: Hghr B 9K 73
Kingsley Av. CH62: East 3D 102
Kingsley Cl. CH61: Pens 4A 88
L31: Lyd 7H 27
Kingsley Cres. WA7: Run 6K 95
Kingsley Dr. WA4: App 9D 82
Kingsley Grn. WA6: Frod 9A 108
Kingsley Rd. CH44: Wall 6H 57
CH65: Ell P 9A 104
L8: Liv 9N 5 (1G 74)
WA6: Frod, Newt 8N 107
WA7: Run 6K 95
WA10: St H 4G 48
Kingsley St. CH41: Birke 9G 56
Kings Lynn Dr. L19: Garst 1N 91
Kingsmead Ct. WA3: Croft 1H 67
Kingsmead Dr. L25: Hunts X 9F 76
Kingsmead Gro. CH43: Oxton 3F 72
Kings Mdw. PR8: Ains 2K 17
WA7: Nort 7E 96
Kingsmead Rd. CH43: Oxton 3F 72
CH46: More 7N 55
Kingsmead Rd. Nth. CH43: Oxton 3F 72
Kingsmead Rd. Sth. CH43: Oxton 3F 72
Kings M. CH66: Lit Sut 7H 103
WA4: Stockt H 8D 82
KINGS MOSS 4J 39
Kings Moss La. WA11: Kings M 4H 39
Kings Mt. CH43: Oxton 4H 73
Kingsnorth L35: Whis 7C 62
Kings Pde. CH45: New B 9G 43
CH45: Wall, New B 1D 56
L3: Liv 8D 4 (1B 74)
Kings Pk. L21: Sea 3M 43
Kings Rd. CH63: Hghr B 8K 73
CH66: Lit Sut 7H 103
L20: Boot 8B 44
L23: Crosb 7K 33
L37: Form 2E 24
M44: Irlam 3L 69
WA2: Fearn 7H 67
WA3: Golb 3B 52
WA10: St H 8F 48
WN4: Ash M 6J 41
Kings Sq. CH41: Birke 2M 73
Kings Ter. L20: Boot 9B 44
Kingsthorne Pk. L25: Hunts X 1G 93
Kingsthorne Rd. L25: Hunts X 1G 92
Kingston Av. WA5: Gt San 2G 81
Kingston Cl. CH46: More 9M 55
L12: W Der 4C 60
WA7: Run 5A 96
WN3: Wigan 1K 41
Kingston Cres. PR9: South 2A 8
King St. CH42: Rock F 7N 73
CH44: Wall 4K 57
CH65: Ell P 8A 104
L19: Garst 3A 92
L22: Water 1K 43
King St. PR8: South 9F 6
WA7: Run 4K 95
WA10: St H 7J 49
WA12: Newt W 7K 51
Kingsville Rd. CH63: Hghr B 2L 89
Kings Wlk. CH42: Rock F 7N 73
CH48: W Kir 6D 70
KINGSWAY 8K 79
Kingsway CH45: Wall 3G 56
CH60: Hesw 9C 88
CH63: Hghr B 9K 73
L3: Liv 1D 4 (6B 58)
L22: Water 9L 33
L35: Presc 4A 62
L36: Huy, Roby 5H 61
PR8: South 8F 6
WA6: Frod 6L 107
WA8: Wid 9K 79
WA11: St H 2K 49
WA12: Newt W 8L 51
Kingsway Ct. L3: Liv 5C 58
Kingsway Ho. *WA4: Westy* *4G 82*
(off Kingsway Sth.)
WA8: Wid 9K 79
Kingsway Leisure Cen. 8K 79
Kingsway Nth. WA1: Warr 2F 82
Kingsway Pde. *L36: Huy* *5G 61*
(off Kingsway)
Kingsway Pk. L3: Liv 5C 58
Kingsway Sth. WA4: Westy 3F 82
Kingsway Tunnel App. CH44: Wall 6E 56
Kingswell Cl. L7: Liv 9G 58
Kings Wharf CH41: Birke 8M 57
KINGSWOOD
WA5 7J 65
WA6 5M 115
Kingswood L36: Huy 6H 61
Kingswood Av. L9: Ain 3G 45
L22: Water 9M 33
Kingswood Blvd. CH63: Hghr B 8L 73
Kingswood Ct. L33: Kirkb 7D 36
Kingswood Dr. L23: Crosb 8K 33
Kingswood Ho. PR8: Birkd 1M 11
Kingswood Pk. PR8: Birkd 1M 11
WA6: Kingsw 6N 115
Kingswood Pk. M. PR8: Birkd 9E 6
Kingswood Rd. CH44: Wall 4J 57
WA5: Westb 7J 65
Kington Rd. CH48: W Kir 5B 70
Kinley Gdns. *L20: Boot* *5D 44*
(off Wheatley Av.)
Kinloch Cl. L26: Halew 9L 77
Kinloch Way L39: Orm 8B 20
Kinloss Rd. CH49: Grea 5K 71
Kinmel Cl. CH41: Birke 1K 73
L4: Walt 1J 59
Kinmel St. L8: Liv 3F 74
WA9: St H 1M 63
Kinnaird Rd. CH45: Wall 3G 57
Kinnaird St. L8: Liv 5F 74
Kinnerley Rd. CH65: Whit 2M 111
Kinnerton Cl. CH46: More 9J 55
Kinnington Way CH1: Back 6L 111
Kinniside Rd. WN3: Wigan 1J 41
Kinnock Pk. WA5: Burtw 3G 65
Kinross Av. WN4: Garsw 7E 40
Kinross Cl. WA2: Fearn 5G 66
Kinross Rd. CH45: Wall 3D 56
L10: Faz 3L 45
L22: Water 2L 43
Kinsale Dr. L19: Aller 9B 76
WA3: Birchw 5K 67
Kinsey Rd. CH65: Ell P 4B 112
Kinsey's La. CH2: Ince 8K 105
Kinsman Ho. L19: Gras 9N 75
Kintore Cl. CH63: East 2B 102
Kintore Dr. WA5: Gt San 2F 80
Kintore Rd. L19: Gras 9N 75
Kintyre Cl. CH65: Ell P 4A 112
Kipling Av. CH42: Rock F 7M 73
L36: Huy 8L 61
WA2: Warr 8D 66
Kipling Cres. WA8: Wid 8J 79
Kipling Gro. WA9: Sut M 6K 63
Kipling St. L20: Boot 5N 43
Kirby Cl. CH48: W Kir 7D 70
Kirby Mt. CH48: W Kir 8D 70
Kirby Pk. CH48: W Kir 7D 70
Kirby Pk. Mans. CH48: W Kir 7C 70
Kirby Rd. L20: Boot 4C 44
Kirkacre Av. WA12: Newt W 1L 65
Kirkbride Cl. L27: N'ley 4L 77
Kirkbride Lawn *L27: N'ley* *4L 77*
(off Kirkbride Cl.)
Kirkbride Wlk. *L27: N'ley* *4L 77*
(off Kirkbride Cl.)
Kirkburn Cl. L8: Liv 4E 74
KIRKBY 9C 36
Kirkby Bank Rd. L33: Know I 9F 36
Kirkby Gallery 9C 36
Kirkby Leisure Cen. 1C 46
KIRKBY PARK 8A 36
Kirkby Rd. WA3: Cul 7N 53
Kirkby Row L32: Kirkb 8A 36
Kirkby Station (Rail) 8A 36
Kirkcaldy Av. WA5: Gt San 2F 80
Kirk Cotts. CH45: Wall 2H 57
KIRKDALE 1D 58
Kirkdale Gdns. WN8: Uph 5K 31
Kirkdale Rd. L5: Kirkd 3C 58
Kirkdale Station (Rail) 9C 44
Kirkdale Va. L4: Walt 2D 58
Kirket Cl. CH63: Beb 3N 89
Kirket La. CH63: Beb 3M 89
Kirkfield Gro. CH42: Rock F 7N 73
Kirkham Av. WA3: Low 4F 52
Kirkham Cl. WA5: Gt San 4K 81
Kirkham Rd. PR9: South 3M 7
WA8: Wid 6M 79
Kirklake Bank L37: Form 2C 24
Kirklake Rd. L37: Form 2C 24
Kirkland Av. CH42: Tran 6K 73
Kirkland Cl. L9: Walt 3E 44
Kirkland Rd. CH45: New B 1J 57
Kirklands, The CH48: W Kir 7D 70
Kirkland St. WA10: St H 6J 49
Kirklees Rd. PR8: Birkd 5M 11
Kirkmaiden Rd. L19: Aller 8N 75
Kirkman Fold L35: Rainh 6E 62
Kirkmore Rd. L18: Moss H 6M 75
Kirkmount CH49: Upton 3A 72
Kirk Rd. L21: Lith 4B 44
Kirkside Cl. L12: Crox 7B 46
Kirkstall Dr. L37: Form 2H 25
Kirkstall Rd. PR8: Birkd 4M 11
Kirkstead Wlk. L31: Mell 8N 35
Kirkstead Way WA3: Golb 2B 52
Kirkstile Cres. WN3: Wins 1G 40
Kirkstone Av. WA2: Warr 7D 66
WA11: St H 2M 49
Kirkstone Cres. WA7: Beech 2C 108
Kirkstone Rd. Nth. L21: Lith 1B 44
Kirkstone Rd. Sth. L21: Lith 2C 44
Kirkstone Rd. W. L21: Ford, Lith 9A 34
Kirk St. L5: Liv 3D 58
Kirkwall Dr. WA5: Penk 5J 81
Kirkway CH45: Wall 2H 57
CH49: Grea 4M 71
CH49: Upton 3N 71
CH63: Hghr B 9K 73
Kitchener Av. M44: Cad 5J 69
Kitchener Dr. L9: Walt 4E 44
Kitchener St. WA10: St H 6G 49
Kitchen St. L1: Liv 9F 4 (1C 74)
Kitling Rd. L34: Know 5F 46
Kiverley Cl. L18: Aller 5C 76
Kiveton Dr. WN4: Ash M 9L 41
Kiveton Wlk. WA2: Warr 1D 82
Klick Fitness
Aintree 1G 45
Knap, The CH60: Hesw 9A 88
Knaresborough Rd. CH44: Wall 5F 56
Knavesmire Way L19: Aller 9B 76
Knebworth Cl. L12: W Der 2B 60
Knighton Rd. L4: Walt 9J 45
Knight Rd. WA5: Burtw 3H 65
Knightsbridge Av. WA4: Grap 5K 83
Knightsbridge Cl. WA8: Wid 4N 79
Knightsbridge Ct. CH43: Noct 5D 72
WA1: Warr *3B 82*
(off Palmyra Sq. Nth.)
Knightsbridge Wlk. L33: Kirkb 5B 36
Knightscliffe Cres. WN6: Shev 7N 23
Knights Cl. WA8: Wid 4A 80
Knights Grange WA9: St H 6M 49
Knight St. L1: Liv 8H 5 (9D 58)
Knightsway L22: Water 9M 33
Knightswood Ct. L18: Aller 8A 76
Knob Hall Gdns. PR9: South 4L 7
Knob Hall La. PR9: South 4L 7
Knoclaid Rd. L13: Liv 2K 59
Knoll, The CH43: Oxton 5G 73
WA7: Pal F 8B 96
Knottingley Dr. CH66: Gt Sut 9H 103
Knott's Ho's. WN7: Leigh 1K 53
KNOTTY ASH 6A 60
Knotty M. L25: Woolt 5G 76
Knowe, The CH64: Will 6N 101
Knowle Av. PR8: Ains 8J 11
Knowle Cl. CH66: Gt Sut 2K 111
L12: W Der 8A 46
Knowles, The L23: Blun 8H 33
Knowles Farm Cl. WN8: Roby M 2L 31
Knowles Ho. Av. WA10: Eccl 7C 48
Knowles St. CH41: Birke 1J 73
WA8: Wid 6M 79
Knowl Hey Rd. L26: Halew 1L 93
KNOWSLEY 6H 47
Knowsley Av. WA3: Golb 2C 52
Knowsley Bus. Pk. L34: Know 4E 46
(School La., not continuous)
L34: Know 4G 47
(Villiers Rd.)
Knowsley Cl. CH42: Rock F 7N 73
Knowsley Ct. CH42: Rock F 7N 73
Knowsley Dr. WN7: Leigh 1L 53
Knowsley Ent. Workshops
L33: Know I 1F 46
Knowsley Expressway L35: Tar G 2A 78
WA8: Wid 6B 78
Knowsley Hall 1K 61
Knowsley Hgts. L36: Huy 4J 61
Knowsley Ind. Pk. L33: Know I 3F 46
(Faraday Rd.)
L33: Know I 9G 36
(Manor Complex)
Knowsley La. L34: Know, Know P 9G 47
L36: Huy 9G 47
Knowsley Leisure & Culture Pk. 6K 61
Knowsley M. L39: Orm 8D 20
KNOWSLEY PARK 5K 47
Knowsley Pk. La. L34: Presc 2N 61
Knowsley Rd. CH42: Rock F 7N 73
CH45: Wall 3G 56
L19: Gras 1M 91
L20: Boot 5N 43
L35: Rainh 7G 62
L39: Orm 9D 20
PR9: South 6G 7
WA10: St H 7F 48
Knowsley Safari Pk. 1N 61
Knowsley St. L4: Walt 8E 44
Knowsley Vw. WA11: Rainf 3B 38
Knox Cl. CH62: Port S 1A 90
Knox St. CH41: Birke 2M 73
Knutsford Cl. WA10: Eccl 8E 48
Knutsford Grn. CH46: More 8M 55
Knutsford Old Rd. WA4: Grap 6H 83
Knutsford Rd. CH46: More 8M 55
WA4: Grap 6H 83
WA4: Warr 4C 82
Knutsford Wlk. L31: Lyd 8J 27
Kramar Wlk. L33: Kirkb 9D 36
Kremlin Dr. L13: Liv 4L 59
Kronsbec Av. CH66: Lit Sut 8J 103
Kydds Wynt WA6: Frod 6L 107
Kylemore Av. L18: Moss H 5L 75
Kylemore Cl. CH61: Pens 4M 87
Kylemore Ct. L26: Halew 9J 77
Kylemore Dr. CH61: Pens 4M 87
Kylemore Rd. CH43: Oxton 4G 73
Kylemore Way CH61: Pens 4M 87
(not continuous)
L26: Halew 9H 77
Kynance Rd. L11: Crox 5B 46

L

LA Bowl
Warrington 6B 66
Laburnam St. WN4: Ash M 9K 41
Laburnum Av. L36: Huy 9J 61
WA1: Wools 1K 83
WA11: St H 3N 49
Laburnum Ct. *L8: Liv* *4F 74*
(off Weller Way)
WA13: Lymm 4H 85
Laburnum Cres. L32: Kirkb 8B 36
Laburnum Dr. WN8: Skel 3A 30
Laburnum Farm Cl. CH64: Ness 9G 101
Laburnum Gro. CH61: Irby 1L 87
CH66: Whit 5M 111
L15: Wav *9M 59*
(off Chestnut Gro.)
L31: Mag 2L 35
L40: Burs 8K 15
PR8: South 8L 7
WA7: Run 7L 95
Laburnum La. WA5: Gt San 2E 80
Laburnum Pl. L20: Boot 7C 44
Laburnum Rd. CH43: Oxton 4J 73
CH45: New B 2H 57
L7: Liv 6J 59
M44: Cad 4K 69
WA3: Low 3G 52
Laburnum Ter. *L19: Garst* *1A 92*
(off Chapel Rd.)
Lace St. L3: Liv 3F 4 (7C 58)
Lacey Ct. WA8: Wid 9L 79
Lacey Rd. L34: Presc 4B 62
Lacey St. WA8: Wid 9K 79
WA10: St H 1G 62
Laddock Cl. L4: Walt 2H 59
Ladies Wlk. CH64: Nest 6E 100
WA2: Win 3A 66
WA9: Bold 6C 64
Lady Acre Cl. WA13: Lymm 6D 84
Lady Alice's Dr. L40: Lath 5H 21
Lady Anne Cl. L40: Scar 7N 13
Ladybarn Av. WA3: Golb 3A 52
Ladybower Cl. CH49: Upton 2M 71
L7: Liv 9G 59
Lady Chapel Cl. L1: Liv 9J 5 (1D 74)
Lady Chapel Sq. L1: Liv 9J 5
Ladycroft Cl. WA1: Wools 1M 83
Ladyewood Rd. CH44: Wall 6J 57
Ladyfield CH43: Bid 1C 72
Ladyfields L12: W Der 4N 59
LADY GREEN 8K 25
Lady Grn. Ct. L38: Ince B 9L 25
Lady Grn. La. L38: Ince B 8K 25
Lady Heyes Craft & Antique Restoration Cen. 9B 108
Lady La. WA3: Croft 9K 53
Lady Lever Art Gallery 1A 90
Lady Mountford Ho. L18: Moss H 5L 75
Ladypool L24: Hale 6N 93
Lady Richeld Cl. WA7: Nort 4F 96
Ladysmith Av. WN4: Ash M 8L 41
Ladysmith Rd. L10: Faz 3L 45
Lady's Wlk. L40: Lath, Westh 8F 20
Ladywood Rd. WA5: Old H 8L 65
LAFFAK 3N 49
Laffak Rd. WA11: St H 3M 49
Lafford La. WN8: Roby M, Uph 1M 31
LA Fitness
Formby 3G 25
Mossley Hill 5M 75
Lagan Ho. CH46: Leas 5M 55

Laggan St. L7: Liv 7G 59
Lagrange Arc. WA10: St H 7K 49
Laira Ct. WA2: Warr 1D 82
Laira St. WA2: Warr 1D 82
Laird Cl. CH41: Birke 9F 56
Lairds Pl. L3: Liv 5C 58
Laird St. CH41: Birke 9F 56
Laithwaite Cl. WA9: Sut M 6L 63
Lake Ent. Pk. CH62: Brom 5D 90
Lakeland Av. WN4: Ash M 7L 41
Lakeland Cl. L1: Liv 7F 4 (9C 58)
Lake La. WA4: Hghr Whi 9G 99
Lakemoor Cl. WA9: St H 2N 63
Lakenheath Rd. L26: Halew 1J 93
Lake Pl. CH47: Hoy 1C 70
Lake Rd. CH47: Hoy 1C 70
L15: Wav 1M 75
Lakeside Cl. WA8: Wid 9D 78
Lakeside Ct. CH45: New B 1J 57
WA11: Rainf 5D 38
Lakeside Dr. WA1: Warr 5B 82
Lakeside Gdns. L23: Thorn 5A 34
WA11: Rainf 5D 38
Lakeside Lawn L27: N'ley 4L 77
Lakeside Miniature Railway 8E 6
Lakeside Rd. WA13: Lymm 7D 84
Lakeside Vw. L22: Water 2K 43
Lakes Rd. L9: Ain 3J 45
Lake St. L4: Walt 2F 58
Lake Vw. L35: Whis 9B 62
Lake Vw. Ct. L4: Walt 8F 44
Lakeview Ct. PR9: South 7G 6
(off Promenade)
Laleston Cl. WA8: Wid 8H 79
Lambert St. L3: Liv 3J 5 (7D 58)
(Kempston St.)
L3: Liv 3J 5
(Lambert Way)
Lambert Way L3: Liv 3J 5 (7D 58)
Lambeth Ct. CH47: Hoy 1B 70
Lambeth Rd. L4: Kirkd 2C 58
L5: Kirkd 2C 58
Lambourn Av. WA8: Cron 3F 78
Lambourne WN8: Skel 9E 22
Lambourne Cl. CH66: Gt Sut 5L 111
Lambourne Gro. WA9: St H 7C 50
Lambourne Rd. L4: Walt 9J 45
Lambrigg Row L5: Liv 2E 58
Lambshear La. L31: Lyd 8H 27
Lambsickle Cl. WA7: West 9J 95
Lambsickle La. WA7: Run, West 9J 95
Lambs La. WA1: Padd 1H 83
WA1: Padd, Padg 9H 67
Lambton Rd. L17: Aig 5G 74
Lamerton Cl. WA5: Penk 4F 80
Lammermoor Rd. L18: Moss H 6M 75
Lampeter Cl. WA5: Call 7N 65
Lampeter Rd. L6: Liv 3H 59
Lamport Cl. WA8: Wid 5A 80
Lamport St. L8: Liv 2D 74
Lanark Cl. WA10: St H 8J 49
Lanark Gdns. WA8: Wid 5H 79
Lancashire Gdns. WA10: St H 8J 49
Lancashire Rd. M31: Part 7L 69
Lancaster Av. CH45: Wall 4H 57
L17: Liv 2J 75
L23: Crosb 8K 33
L35: Whis 6A 62
WA3: Golb 2D 52
WA7: Run 7H 95
WA8: Wid 6D 78
Lancaster Cl. CH62: Port S 1A 90
L5: Kirkd 3C 58
L31: Mag 2L 35
PR8: Birkd 2L 11
WA2: Padg 7G 66
WA12: Newt W 6H 51
Lancaster Ct. WA4: Stockt H 7F 82
(off Lime Tree Av.)
Lancaster Cres. WN8: Skel 3B 30
Lancaster Dr. PR9: Banks 2C 8
Lancaster Gdns. CH65: Ell P 2B 112
PR8: Birkd 2L 11
Lancaster Ga. PR9: Banks 2D 8
Lancaster La. WN8: Parb 2F 22
Lancaster Rd. L36: Huy 5L 61
L37: Form 3E 24
M44: Cad 4J 69
PR8: Birkd 3K 11
WA8: Wid 5K 79
Lancaster St. L5: Kirkd 3C 58
L9: Walt 7E 44
WA5: Warr 3N 81
Lancaster Wlk. L36: Huy 5L 61
(off Lancaster Rd.)
Lance Cl. L5: Liv 4E 58
Lancefield Rd. L9: Walt 5E 44
Lance Gro. L15: Wav 1M 75
Lance La. L15: Wav 1M 75
Lancelots Hey L3: Liv 4C 4
Lancelyn Ct. CH63: Spit 4N 89
Lancelyn Pct. CH63: Spit 4N 89
(off Spital Rd.)
Lancelyn Ter. CH63: Beb 3M 89
Lancer Ct. WA7: Ast 4A 96
Lancers Cft. CH66: Gt Sut 4K 111
Lancer Way L12: W Der 2C 60
Lancing Av. WA2: Warr 5B 66
Lancing Cl. L25: Hunts X 7H 77
Lancing Dr. L10: Ain 9J 35
Lancing Rd. CH65: Ell P 1B 112
L25: Hunts X 7H 77
Lancing Way L25: Hunts X 7H 77
Lancots La. WA9: St H 1N 63
Landcut La. WA3: Birchw 6L 67
Land End L31: Mag 2A 36
Lander Cl. WA5: Old H 1M 81
Lander Rd. L21: Lith 4A 44
Landford Av. L9: Faz 6K 45
Landford Pl. L9: Faz 6K 45
LAND GATE 3J 41
Landgate Ind. Est. WN4: Ash M 3J 41
Landgate La. WN4: Ash M 4H 41
LANDICAN 8C 72
Landican Cemetery & Crematorium
CH49: Woodc 7B 72
Landican La. CH49: Woodc 8C 72
CH63: Store 1E 88
Landican Rd. CH49: Woodc 9B 72
Land La. PR9: South 3B 8
Landor Cl. L5: Liv 4B 58
WA3: Low 2F 52
Landscape Dene WA6: Hel 1G 115
Landsdowne Ho. CH41: Birke 2N 73
Landseer Av. CH64: Lit N 7F 100
WA4: Warr 7C 82
Landseer Rd. L5: Liv 4E 58
LAND SIDE 1N 53
Landside WN7: Leigh 1N 53
LANE ENDS 1B 94
LANE HEAD 4F 52
Lane Head Av. WA3: Low 1F 52
Lanfranc Cl. L16: Child 9C 60
Lanfranc Way L16: Child 9C 60
Langbar L35: Whis 7B 62
Langcliffe Cl. WA3: Cul 7M 53
Langdale Av. CH61: Pens 3N 87
L37: Form 1D 24
WA3: Golb 1D 52
WA13: Lymm 4F 84
Langdale Cl. L32: Kirkb 1D 46
L37: Form 2D 24
WA2: Warr 6F 66
WA8: Wid 8F 78
Langdale Ct. CH41: Birke 9H 57
Langdale Dr. L31: Mag 1K 35
L40: Burs 1J 21
Langdale Gdns. PR8: Birkd 5M 11
Langdale Gro. WA11: St H 3L 49
Langdale Rd. CH45: Wall 2F 56
CH63: Beb 3L 89
L15: Wav 2K 75
M31: Part 6L 69
WA7: Run 6L 95
Langdale St. L20: Boot 7C 44
Langdale Way WA6: Frod 5M 107
Langden Cl. WA3: Cul 6L 53
Langfield WA3: Low 3F 52
Langfield Gro. CH62: Brom 1C 102
Langford L24: Hale 5N 93
Langford Rd. L19: Aig 8L 75
Langford Way WA4: App T 3L 99
Langham Av. L17: Aig 5H 75
Langham Ct. L4: Walt 1E 58
Langham St. L4: Walt 1E 58
Langham St. Ind. Est. L4: Walt 1E 58
(off Langham St.)
Langholm Cl. WN3: Wins 1G 40
Langholm Rd. WN4: Garsw 7E 40
Langland Cl. L4: Walt 1J 59
WA5: Call 7N 65
Lang La. CH48: W Kir 5C 70
Lang La. Sth. CH48: W Kir 6D 70
Langley Av. WA12: Newt W 9L 51
Langley Beck WA8: Wid 4M 79
Langley Cl. CH63: Spit 5N 89
L12: Crox 7D 46
L38: Hight 1F 32
WA3: Golb 1D 52
Langley Cl. Shop. Cen. L12: Crox 7D 46
Langley Ct. CH65: Ell P 2C 112
L40: Burs 9F 14
Langley Pl. L40: Burs 1F 20
Langley Rd. CH63: Spit 5N 89
L40: Burs 9F 14
Langley St. L8: Liv 2D 74
Langrove St. L5: Liv 4D 58
Langsdale St. L3: Liv 2J 5 (6D 58)
(not continuous)
Langshaw Lea L27: N'ley 4K 77
Langstone Av. CH49: Grea 5K 71
Langton Cl. WA8: Wid 5E 78
WA12: Newt W 6J 51
Langton Grn. WA1: Wools 1L 83
Langton Rd. L15: Wav 1J 75
L33: Kirkb 6D 36
Langtree WN8: Skel 1E 30
Langtree Park 8L 49
Langtree St. WA9: St H 7M 49
Langtree Way WA9: St H 8L 49
Langtry Cl. L4: Kirkd 1C 58
Langtry Rd. L4: Kirkd 1C 58
Langwell Cl. WA3: Birchw 4A 68
Langwood La. WA11: Rainf 2F 38
Lansbury Av. WA9: St H 8A 50
Lansbury Rd. L36: Huy 7L 61
Lansdown L12: W Der 3M 59
Lansdowne WA3: Cul 8M 53
WA6: Frod 8N 107
Lansdowne Cl. CH41: Birke 9G 56
Lansdowne Ct. CH43: Bid 9F 56
WA9: St H 2N 63
Lansdowne Pl. CH43: Bid 9F 56
L5: Liv 3E 58
Lansdowne Rd. CH41: Birke 9F 56
CH43: Bid 9F 56
CH45: Wall 1F 56
PR8: South 9K 7
Lansdowne Way L36: Huy 7J 61
Lanville Rd. L19: Aig 7N 75
Lanyork Rd. L3: Liv 2C 4 (6A 58)
Lapford Cres. L33: Kirkb 7E 36
Lapford Wlk. L33: Kirkb 7E 36
Lapwing Cl. L12: W Der 9C 46
WA3: Low 2E 52
WA12: Newt W 6L 51
Lapwing Ct. L26: Halew 7J 77
Lapwing Gro. WA7: Pal F 9C 96
Lapwing La. WA4: Moore 9H 81
Lapwing Ri. CH60: Hesw 9N 87
Lapworth Cl. CH46: More 9J 55
Lapworth St. L5: Kirkd 3C 58
Larch Av. WA5: Penk 3G 81
WA8: Wid 6L 79
WA12: Newt W 8L 51
Larch Cl. L19: Gras 9L 75
WA3: Low 4G 52
WA7: Run 8M 95
WN5: Bil 6N 39
WN8: Skel 3B 30
Larch Ct. L8: Liv 4F 74
(off Weller Way)
Larchdale Cl. CH66: Whit 5L 111
Larchdale Gro. L9: Walt 6G 44
Larchfield Rd. L23: Thorn 6N 33
Larch Gro. CH43: Bid 9E 56
L15: Wav 8M 59
Larch Ho. L7: Liv 7L 5
Larch Lea L6: Liv 4G 58
(not continuous)
Larch Rd. CH42: Tran 3J 73
L36: Roby 7G 61
M31: Part 6L 69
WA7: Run 8M 95
WA11: Hay 3G 51
Larch St. PR8: South 1D 12
Larchtree M. L12: W Der 1C 60
Larch Way L37: Form 9D 16
Larchways WA4: App 2E 98
Larchwood Av. L31: Mag 4H 35
Larchwood Cl. CH61: Pens 4N 87
L25: Gate 3F 76
Larchwood Dr.
CH63: Hghr B 9M 73
Larcombe Av. CH49: Upton 3N 71
Larkfield Av. WA1: Padd 1H 83
Larkfield Cl. L17: Aig 6H 75
Larkfield Ct. PR9: South 4M 7
WA11: St H 2J 49
Larkfield Gro. L17: Aig 6H 75
Larkfield La. PR9: South 4M 7
Larkfield Rd. L17: Aig 6H 75
Larkfield Vw. L15: Wav 9K 59
Larkhill WN8: Skel 9E 22
Larkhill Av. CH49: Upton 1A 72
Larkhill Cl. L13: Liv 2K 59
Larkhill Gro. L38: Hight 9F 24
Larkhill La. L13: Liv 2K 59
L37: Form 9C 16
Larkhill Pl. L13: Liv 2L 59
Larkhill Vw. L13: Liv 2L 59
Larkhill Way CH49: Upton 1A 72
Larkin Cl. CH62: New F 9N 73
Lark La. L17: Aig 5H 75
Larkspur Cl. PR8: South 9J 7
WA7: Beech 2B 108
Larkspur Ct. L31: Mell 8M 35
Larkspur Gro. WA5: Warr 5M 81
Larkstoke Cl. WA4: App 1F 98
Larksway CH60: Hesw 7B 88
Lark Way L17: Aig 5H 75
Larne Ct. WA8: Wid 6H 79
Larton Farm Cl. CH48: W Kir 6F 70
Larton Rd. CH48: W Kir 5F 70
Lartonwood CH48: W Kir 5F 70
Lascelles Rd. L19: Aller 9B 76
Lascelles St. WA9: St H 7M 49
Laskey La. WA4: Thel 4N 83
LATCHFORD 5E 82
Latchford High Level Bri.
WA4: Warr 6F 82
Latchford Rd. CH60: Hesw 9B 88
Latchford St. WA4: Westy 5H 83
Late Moffatt Rd. W. L9: Ain 3G 45
(off Moffatt Rd.)
Latham Av. L39: Orm 8E 20
WA6: Hel 4E 114
WA7: Run 6L 95
WA12: Newt W 6L 51
Latham Ct. L7: Liv 7J 59
Latham St. L5: Kirkd 3C 58
(not continuous)
Latham Way CH63: Spit 5A 90
Lathbury La. L17: Aig 3K 75
LATHOM 5M 21
Lathom Av. CH44: Wall 5H 57
L21: Sea 4M 43
(off Chatham Cl.)
WA2: Warr 9C 66
WN8: Parb 2E 22
Lathom Cl. L21: Sea 4M 43
(off Chatham Cl.)
L36: Huy 3L 61
L40: Burs 1J 21
Lathom Ct. L36: Huy 3L 61
Lathom Dr. L31: Mag 9K 27
WA11: Rainf 4C 38
Lathom Ho. L40: Lath 6M 21
Lathom La. L40: Lath 6G 21
LATHOM PARK 6N 21
Lathom Rd. L20: Boot 5B 44
L36: Huy 6J 61
L39: Bic 5J 29
M44: Irlam 1M 69
PR9: South 6G 7
Lathum Cl. L35: Presc 4B 62
Latimer Cl. WA8: Wid 4M 79
Latimer St. L5: Liv 3C 58
Latrigg Rd. L17: Aig 6K 75
Lauder Cl. L33: Kirkb 5B 36
Launceston Cl. WA7: Brook 9E 96
Launceston Dr. WA5: Penk 5G 80
Laund, The CH45: Wall 4F 56
Laurel Av. CH60: Hesw 6N 87
CH63: Hghr B 3L 89
L40: Burs 8J 15
WA1: Wools 1L 83
WA12: Newt W 8M 51
Laurel Bank WA4: Grap 7K 83
WA8: Wid 5K 79
Laurelbanks CH60: Hesw 6M 87
Laurel Ct. L7: Liv 6J 59
(off Laurel Rd.)
WA11: St H 3L 49
Laurel Dr. CH64: Will 5A 102
CH65: Whit 3N 111
WA10: Eccl 6C 48
WN8: Skel 2B 30
Laurel Farm Ct. CH2: Elt 1M 113
Laurel Gro. L8: Liv 2H 75
L22: Water 9K 33
L36: Huy 9J 61
PR8: South 8K 7
WA3: Low 2E 52
WN4: Ash M 7K 41
Laurelhurst Av. CH61: Pens 3A 88
Laurel Rd. CH42: Tran 4K 73
L7: Liv 6J 59
L34: Presc 3B 62
WA10: St H 8G 48
WA11: Hay 5B 50
Laurels, The CH46: Leas 6M 55
Laurel Wlk. M31: Part 7L 69
Laurel Way WA10: St H 8G 48
Laurelwood Dr. CH66: Gt Sut 5K 111
Laurence Deacon Ct. CH41: Birke 1K 73
Lauren Cl. L36: Huy 7M 61
Lauriston Rd. L4: Walt 9H 45
Laurus Cl. L27: N'ley 3K 77
Lavan Cl. L6: Liv 1M 5 (6F 58)
Lavan St. L6: Liv 1N 5 (6F 58)
Lavender Av. L32: Kirkb 9A 36
Lavender Cl. WA7: Run 6M 95
Lavender Cres. L34: Presc 3B 62
Lavender Gdns. L23: Thorn 6A 34
WA5: Warr 4N 81
WA9: Bold 2C 64
Lavender Wlk. M31: Part 7L 69
WN4: Garsw 6F 40
Lavender Way L9: Walt 6G 45
Lavrock Bank L8: Liv 4D 74
Lawford Dr. CH60: Hesw 7C 88
Lawler Gro. L34: Presc 2B 62
Lawler St. L21: Lith 4A 44
Lawn Av. WA1: Padg 9G 66
Lawnhurst Gro. L17: Aig 8K 75
Lawns, The CH43: Bid 1D 72
PR9: South 5L 7
Lawns Av. CH63: Raby M 9A 90
WN5: Orr 7M 31
Lawnside Cl. CH42: Rock F 7M 73
Lawnswood Gro. CH2: Elt 2M 113
Lawrence Cl. L19: Gras 9M 75
Lawrence Ct. CH42: Rock F 8N 73
Lawrence Gro. L15: Wav 1K 75
Lawrence Rd. L15: Wav 1J 75
WA10: Windle 4F 48
Lawrenson St. WA10: St H 7H 49
Lawson Cl. WA1: Wools 1M 83
Lawson Ho. WA7: Run 7K 95
Lawson Rd. WA7: Run 7K 95
Lawson St. PR9: South 8M 7
Lawson Wlk. L12: Crox 7B 46
Lawswood L37: Form 8E 16
Lawton Av. L20: Boot 5D 44
Lawton Cl. WA3: Cul 7M 53
Lawton Rd. L22: Water 9K 33
L35: Rainh 7G 62
L36: Roby 8G 61
Lawton St. L1: Liv 6H 5 (8D 58)
Laxey Av. WA1: Wools 2L 83
Laxey St. L8: Liv 2D 74
Laxton Cl. CH66: Gt Sut 5L 111
Laxton Rd. L25: Hunts X 9G 77
Layford Rd. L36: Huy 4H 61
Layland Av. WA3: Cul 6M 53
Layton Av. CH43: Pren 6F 72
Layton Cl. L25: Woolt 6G 76
WA3: Birchw 6M 67
Layton Rd. L25: Woolt 6G 76

Layton Way L34: Presc 4A 62
Lazenby Cres. WN4: Ash M 8H 41
Lazonby Cl. CH43: Bid 9C 56
LEA BY BACKFORD 9M 111
Leach Cft. L28: Stockb V 2E 60
Leach La. WA9: Sut L 5N 63
Leach St. WA10: St H 6J 49
Leach Vw. WA11: St H 3L 49
Leach Way CH61: Irby 1K 87
Lea Cl. CH43: Noct 4E 72
Lea Cres. L39: Orm 6C 20
Leacroft WN4: Ash M 5H 41
Leacroft Rd. WA3: Ris 3N 67
Lea Cross Gro. WA8: Wid 5F 78
Leadenhall Cl. L5: Liv 3E 58
Leader Williams Rd.
M44: Irlam 1M 69
Leafield Cl. CH61: Irby 1N 87
Leafield Rd. L25: Hunts X 1F 92
Leagate L10: Faz 2L 45
Leagate Cl. WN3: Wigan 1G 41
LEA GREEN 4J 63
Lea Grn. Bus. Pk. WA9: St H 5J 63
Lea Grn. Ind. Est. WA9: St H 6K 63
Lea Grn. Rd. WA9: St H 6J 63
Lea Green Station (Rail) 4L 63
Lea Hall Pk. CH1: Lea B 9M 111
Leamington Av. PR8: Ains 9K 11
WA12: Newt W 9L 51
Leamington Cl. CH64: Nest 8E 100
WA5: Gt San 9J 65
Leamington Rd. L11: Norr G 8J 45
PR8: Ains 9J 11
Leamoore Cl. L12: Knott A 3D 60
Leander Rd. CH45: Wall 4G 57
Lea Rd. CH44: Wall 4J 57
Leas, The CH45: Wall 2E 56
CH61: Thing 1B 88
Leas Cl. CH66: Gt Sut 9H 103
Leaside WA7: Run 6N 95
WA9: St H 4J 63
LEASOWE 5B 56
Leasowe (Park & Ride) 7A 56
Leasowe Av. CH45: Wall 3E 56
Leasowe Gdns. CH46: Leas 6M 55
Leasowe Golf Course 5N 55
Leasowe Lighthouse 6K 55
Leasowe Recreation Cen. 6A 56
Leasowe Rd. CH44: Wall 6L 55
CH45: Wall 6L 55
CH46: Leas 6L 55
L9: Ain 3G 44
Leasoweside CH46: Leas 5A 56
Leasowe Station (Rail) 7N 55
Leas Pk. CH47: Hoy 4B 70
Leatham Cl. WA3: Birchw 6M 67
Leatherbarrows La. L31: Mag, Mell 4L 35
Leather La. L2: Liv 4E 4
Leather's La. L26: Halew 1K 93
Leathwood L31: Mag 3K 35
Leaway CH49: Grea 4L 71
Leawood Gro. CH46: More 9N 55
L E C Complex L15: Wav 9J 59
Leckwith Rd. L30: N'ton 9G 34
Leda Gro. *L17: Aig* *4H 75*
(off Hesketh St.)
Ledburn WN8: Skel 1E 30
Ledbury Cl. CH43: Oxton 6E 72
L12: Crox 6D 46
WA10: Eccl 7E 48
Ledger Rd. WA11: Hay 5C 50
Ledmore Gro. WN4: Garsw 8F 40
LEDSHAM 4E 110
Ledsham Cl. CH43: Noct 4E 72
WA3: Birchw 6K 67
Ledsham Ct. CH66: Lit Sut 8H 103
Ledsham Hall La. CH66: Led 9D 102
Ledsham La. CH66: Led 1D 110
Ledsham Pk. Dr. CH66: Lit Sut 8F 102
Ledsham Rd. CH66: Lit Sut 9E 102
L32: Kirkb 9A 36
Ledsham Village CH66: Led 4E 110
Ledsham Wlk. L32: Kirkb 9A 36
Ledson Gro. L39: Augh 5N 27
Ledson Pk. L33: Kirkb 5D 36
Ledsons Gro. L31: Mell 8M 35
Ledston Cl. WA7: Wind H 6F 96
Ledyard Cl. WA5: Old H 1M 81
Leece St. L1: Liv 7J 5 (9D 58)
Lee Cl. L35: Rainh 8G 63
Lee Ct. CH47: Hoy 1D 70
WA2: Warr 7D 66
Leecourt Cl. L12: W Der 4B 60
Leeds St. L3: Liv 2C 4 (6A 58)
Lee Hall Rd. L25: Gate 3G 77
Leeming Gro. L19: Garst 2A 92
Lee Pk. Av. L25: Gate 3G 77
Lee Park Golf Course 4H 77
Lee Rd. CH47: Hoy 1D 70
Lees, The WA5: Gt San 9J 65
(not continuous)
Lees Av. CH42: Rock F 6M 73
Leeside Av. L32: Kirkb 2C 46
Leeside Cl. L32: Kirkb 1D 46
Lees La. CH64: Lit N, Nest 8G 100
CH65: Ell P 1C 112
L12: W Der 2B 60
WN8: Dalt, Roby M 5F 22
Lees Rd. L33: Know I 1F 46
Lee St. WA9: St H 1A 64
Leeswood L22: Water 1L 43
WN8: Skel 1E 30
Leeswood Rd. CH49: Woodc 5A 72
Lee Vale Rd. L25: Gate 4G 76
Lee Valley Millennium Cen. 2G 76
Leeward Dr. L24: Speke 3E 92
Legh Ct. WA3: Golb 2B 52
Legh La. PR4: Tarl 4L 9
Legh Rd. CH62: New F 9A 74
WA11: Hay 4C 50
Legh St. WA1: Warr 3B 82
WA3: Golb 2B 52
WA12: Newt W 7H 51
(not continuous)
WA13: Lymm *2B 84*
(off Bridgewater St.)
WN4: Ash M 9K 41
Legion La. CH62: Brom 6C 90
Legion Rd. WA10: St H 1G 62
Leicester Av. L22: Water 9K 33
Leicester Rd. L20: Boot 6C 44
Leicester St. PR9: South 6G 7
WA5: Warr 3N 81
(not continuous)
WA9: St H 1G 63
Leigh Av. WA8: Wid 7J 79
Leigh Bri. Way *L5: Liv* *4B 58*
(off New Hedley Gro.)
Leigh Golf Course 6K 53
Leigh Grn. Cl. WA8: Wid 8F 78
Leigh Pl. L1: Liv 5G 4
Leigh Rd. CH48: W Kir 5C 70
Leighs Hey Cres. L32: Kirkb 9D 36
Leigh St. L1: Liv 5F 4 (8C 58)
(not continuous)
L7: Liv 8J 59
Leighton Av. CH47: Meols 9F 54
L31: Mag 1J 35
Leighton Chase CH64: Nest 5D 100
Leighton Ct. CH64: Nest 6D 100
Leighton Dr. WA9: St H 2M 63
WN7: Leigh 1J 53
Leighton Pk. CH64: Nest 6D 100
Leighton Rd. CH41: Tran 4L 73
CH64: Nest 3C 100
Leightons, The CH64: Nest 6D 100
Leighton St. L4: Kirkd 9D 44
Leinster Gdns. WA7: Run 4J 95
Leinster Rd. L13: Liv 6N 59
Leinster St. WA7: Run 4J 95
Leiria Way WA7: Run 5K 95
Leison St. L4: Kirkd 2C 58
L5: Kirkd 3C 58
Leiston Cl. CH61: Irby 9M 71
Leisure Lakes Caravan Pk.
PR4: Mere B 6H 9
Leisure Lakes Outdoor Pursuits & Watersports Cen. 7H 9
Lemon Cl. L7: Liv 8H 59
Lemon Gro. L8: Liv 2H 75
Lemon St. L5: Kirkd 3C 58
Lemon Tree Wlk. WA10: St H 9G 49
Lendel Cl. L37: Form 1E 24
Lenfield Dr. WA11: Hay 4B 50
Lenham Way L24: Speke 3F 92
Lennox Av. CH45: New B 2H 57
Lennox La. CH43: Bid 8C 56
Lennox Way L7: Liv 7G 59
Lenthall St. L4: Walt 8E 44
Lenton Av. L37: Form 9D 16
Lenton Rd. L25: Gate 3G 77
Lentworth Ct. L17: Aig 9L 75
Leo Cl. L14: Knott A 5D 60
Leominster Rd. CH44: Wall 5H 57
Leonard Cheshire Dr.
L30: N'ton 8E 34
Leonard Ho. CH41: Birke 7M 57
Leonards Cl. L36: Huy 3H 61
Leonard St. WA2: Warr 1D 82
WA4: Stockt H 7E 82
WA7: West P 8G 95
WA9: St H 2B 64
Leon Cl. WA5: Gt San 1F 80
Leonora St. L8: Liv 4F 74
Leopold Gro. WA9: Sut L 4M 63
Leopold Rd. L7: Liv 7G 58
(not continuous)
L22: Water 9J 33
Leopold St. CH44: Wall 6L 57
Lesley Rd. PR8: South 8K 7
Leslie Av. CH49: Grea 5L 71
Leslie Rd. WA10: St H 1F 62
Lesseps Rd. L8: Liv 1H 75
Lessingham Rd. WA8: Wid 5J 79
Lester Cl. L4: Kirkd 2D 58
Lester Dr. CH61: Irby 9K 71
WA10: Eccl 5D 48
Lester Gro. L36: Huy 5K 61
Lestock St. L8: Liv 1D 74
Leta St. L4: Walt 9E 44
(not continuous)
Letchworth St. L6: Liv 4H 59
Lethbridge Cl. L5: Kirkd 3B 58
Lethbridge Rd. PR8: South 1C 12
Letitia St. L8: Liv 3E 74
Levens Cl. PR9: Banks 2E 8
WA5: Warr 2A 82
Levens Hey CH46: More 9L 55
Leven St. L4: Kirkd 1D 58
Levens Way WA8: Wid 8F 78
Leven Wlk. CH66: Ell P 6M 103
Lever Av. CH44: Wall 7L 57
Lever C'way.
CH63: Hghr B, Store 2G 89
Lever Ct. L1: Liv 7F 4 (9C 58)
Leveret Rd. L24: Speke 4L 93
Leverhulme Ct. CH63: Beb 3N 89
Lever St. WA9: Clock F 6N 63
Lever Ter. *CH42: Tran* *5L 73*
(off Summerford Cl.)
Leveson Rd. L13: Liv 8N 59
Levisham Gdns. WA5: Warr 1N 81
Lewis Av. WA5: Warr 7A 66
Lewis Cl. CH65: Ell P 5A 112
Lewis Cres. WA8: Wid 9K 79
Lewis Gro. WA8: Wid 7G 79
Lewisham Rd. CH62: Port S 1B 90
L11: Norr G 8L 45
Lewis St. WA10: St H 7H 49
Lewis Wlk. L33: Kirkb 5C 36
Lexden St. WA5: Warr 2N 81
Lexham Rd. L14: Knott A 6A 60
Lexington Wlk. *WA5: Gt San* *1L 81*
(off Boston Blvd.)
Lexington Way L33: Kirkb 5C 36
Lexton Dr. PR9: South 4N 7
Leybourne Av. PR8: Ains 7M 11
Leybourne Cl. L25: Gate 2E 76
Leybourne Grn. L25: Gate 3E 76
Leybourne Gro. L25: Gate 3E 76
Leybourne Rd. L25: Gate 2E 76
Leyburn Cl. L32: Kirkb 3C 46
(not continuous)
Leyburn Rd. CH45: Wall 3F 56
Ley Cl. WA9: Clock F 5M 63
Leyfield Cl. L12: W Der 3B 60
Leyfield Ct. L12: W Der 3B 60
Leyfield Rd. L12: W Der 3A 60
Leyfield Wlk. L12: W Der 3B 60
Leyland Cl. PR9: Banks 2C 8
LEYLAND GREEN 6D 40
Leyland Grn. Rd.
WN4: Garsw 6E 40
Leyland Gro. WA11: Hay 4D 50
Leyland Mans. PR9: South 7J 7
Leyland Rd. PR9: South 6H 7
WA11: Rainf 5C 38
Leyland St. L34: Presc 3A 62
Leyland Way L39: Orm 8D 20
Leyton Cl. WA7: Run 9L 95
Liberton Ct. *L5: Liv* *3F 58*
(off St Domingo Va.)
Liberty Cl. WA5: Gt San 1L 81
Liberty Pl. WA10: St H 7G 49
Liberty St. L15: Wav 1K 75
Libra Cl. L14: Knott A 4E 60
Library St. WA10: St H 7K 49
Librex Cl. L20: Boot 4B 44
Libson Cl. WA2: Fearn 6H 67
Lichfield Av. L22: Water 8K 33
WA3: Low 2E 52
WA4: Grap 9H 83
Lichfield Cl. L30: N'ton 1F 44
Lichfield Dr. CH66: Gt Sut 5K 111
Lichfield Gro. WN4: Ash M 9L 41
Lichfield Rd. L15: Wav 2M 75
L26: Halew 1J 93
Lichfield St. CH45: New B 2J 57
Lickers La. L35: Whis 7A 62
Liddell Av. L31: Mell 7N 35
Liddell Ct. CH45: Wall 4D 56
Liddell Rd. L12: W Der 2L 59
Lidderdale Ct. *L15: Wav* *2K 75*
(off Lidderdale Rd.)
Lidderdale Rd. L15: Wav 2K 75
Lidgate Cl. L33: Kirkb 6C 36
Liebig Ct. WA8: Wid 8L 79
Liege Ho. *CH49: Upton* *2N 71*
(off Manorside Cl.)
Lifeboat Rd. L37: Form 3A 24
Lifestyles
Alsop 8E 44
Croxteth 6A 46
Everton 3D 58
Garston 9A 76
Liverpool - Millennium 4F 4
Liverpool - Peter Lloyd 3L 59
Mill Yard - Cardinal Heenan 4B 60
Norris Green - Ellergreen 8M 45
Speke - Austin Rawlinson 4J 93
Toxteth - Park Road 3E 74
Toxteth Sports Cen. 2E 74
Walton 8G 45
Wavertree - Tennis Cen. 1L 75
Liffey Ct. L3: Liv 3K 5
Liffey St. L8: Liv 1G 74
Lifton Rd. L33: Kirkb 9E 36
Lightbody St. L5: Liv 4A 58
Lightburn St. WA7: Run 6J 95
Light Cinema, The 9H 43
Lightfoot Cl. CH60: Hesw 8B 88
Lightfoot La. CH60: Hesw 8B 88
Lighthorne Dr. PR8: Ains 1G 17
Lighthouse La. L37: Form 3G 24
Lighthouse Rd. CH47: Hoy 2C 70
L24: Hale 9B 94
Lightoaks Dr. L26: Halew 7M 77
Lightstream Dr. L24: Speke 1F 92
Lightwood Dr. L7: Liv 9H 59
Lightwood St. L7: Liv 9H 59
Lilac Av. PR8: Ains 3K 17
WA5: Gt San 3J 81
WA8: Wid 6L 79
WN4: Garsw 6F 40
Lilac Cres. WA7: Run 7M 95
Lilac Gro. CH66: Whit 5M 111
L36: Huy 9H 61
WA4: Stockt H 7F 82
WA11: Hay 5B 50
WN5: Bil 7N 39
WN8: Skel 3B 30
Lilac Rd. WA3: Golb 1B 52
Lilac Wlk. M31: Part 6L 69
Lilford Av. L9: Walt 4E 44
WA5: Warr 9N 65
Lilford Dr. WA5: Gt San 2H 81
Lilford St. WA5: Warr 1A 82
(not continuous)
Lilley Rd. L7: Liv 6J 59
Lillian Rd. L4: Walt 3G 58
Lillie Cl. CH43: Bid 9C 56
Lillyfield CH60: Hesw 9N 87
Lilly Grn. *L4: Walt* *9G 44*
(off Lilly Gro.)
Lilly Gro. L4: Walt 9G 44
(not continuous)
Lilly Va. L7: Liv 6J 59
Lily Gro *L7: Liv* *8G 59*
(off Dorothy Dr.)
Lily La. WN2: Bam, Platt B 4N 41
Lily Pl. WN4: Ash M 9L 41
Lily Rd. L21: Lith 4A 44
Lily St. WN4: Ash M 6N 41
Limbo La. CH61: Irby 8L 71
Lime Av. CH63: Hghr B 3K 89
WA6: Frod 6M 107
WA8: Wid 6L 79
Lime Cl. L13: Liv 5M 59
WA3: Rix 7G 69
Lime Ct. WN8: Skel 3B 30
Limedale Rd. L18: Moss H 3M 75
Limefield Av. WA13: Lymm 6F 84
Limefield Dr. WN8: Skel 5H 31
Lime Gro. CH2: Elt 2L 113
L8: Liv 2H 75
L21: Sea 4N 43
WA3: Low 4E 52
WA7: Run 7M 95
WA11: Rainf 5C 38
WN8: Skel 3B 30
Limehurst Gro. CH62: Brom 9C 90
Limekiln La. CH44: Wall 7G 56
L3: Liv 1F 4 (5C 58)
(not continuous)
L5: Liv 4C 58
WA5: Burtw 6G 64
Limekiln Row WA7: Cas 7C 96
Limerick Cl. WA8: Wid 5H 79
Limes, The CH49: Upton 3N 71
WA3: Cul 6L 53
WA3: Low 4F 52
WA13: Lymm 5D 84
Limes La. WA4: Hghr Whi 8D 98
Lime St. CH65: Ell P 7N 103
L1: Liv 4G 5 (7C 58)
PR8: South 9K 7
Lime St. Chambers L1: Liv 4H 5
Lime Street Station (Rail) 4H 5 (8D 58)
Limetree Av. WA1: Padg 9H 67
WA4: Stockt H 7F 82
Lime Tree Cl. CH66: Whit 5M 111
Limetree Cl. L9: Walt 7G 45
Lime Tree Gro. CH60: Hesw 7C 88
Lime Tree La.
WA16: High L 9K 85
WA13: Lymm 9K 85
Lime Tree Way L37: Form 2C 24
Lime Va. Rd. WN5: Bil 8M 39
Lime Wlk. M31: Part 6K 69
Limeways WA4: App 2F 98
Limont Rd. PR8: Ains 9K 11
Linacre Ho. L20: Boot 8B 44
Linacre La. L20: Boot 5B 44
L38: Gt Alt 4N 25
WA8: Wid 3H 79
Linacre Rd. L21: Lith 3A 44
Linaker Dr. L39: Hals 5G 18
Linaker St. PR8: South 1A 12
Linbeck Gro. WA3: Low 1F 52
Linby Way WA9: St H 5H 63
Lincoln Av. M44: Cad 5J 69
WA3: Low 1E 52
Lincoln Cl. L6: Liv 5G 59
L36: Huy 6M 61
WA1: Wools 2M 83
WA7: Run 9M 95
WN7: Leigh 2K 53
Lincoln Ct. WA6: Hel 2E 114
Lincoln Cres. L20: Boot 8B 44
WA11: St H 4L 49
Lincoln Dr. CH45: Wall 3J 57
L10: Ain 8J 35
WN4: Ash M 9L 41
Lincoln Grn. L31: Mag 3G 34
Lincoln Rd. CH66: Gt Sut 2J 111
PR8: Birkd 5N 11
WA10: St H 8G 48
Lincoln Sq. WA8: Wid 6L 79
Lincoln St. CH41: Birke 8G 56
L19: Garst 3A 92

Lincoln Way L35: Rainh 8G **63**
L36: Huy 6M 61
(off Lincoln Cl.)
Lincombe Rd. L36: Huy 5F **60**
Lindale Cl. CH46: More 8A **56**
Lindale Dr. WA9: Clock F 5M **63**
Lindale Rd. L7: Liv 6K **59**
Lindby Cl. L32: Kirkb 2E **46**
Lindby Rd. L32: Kirkb 2E **46**
Linden Av. L23: Blun 7J **33**
L30: N'ton 9E **34**
WN4: Ash M .6H **41**
Linden Cl. CH66: Gt Sut 5L **111**
WA1: Wools .1L **83**
WA13: Lymm .4G **84**
Linden Ct. WA8: Wid 4J **79**
Linden Dr. CH43: Pren 7E **72**
L36: Huy 9J **61**
WA6: Hel 4E **114**
Linden Gro. CH45: Wall 2H **57**
M44: Cad 4K **69**
WN5: Bil 8M **39**
Linden Rd. L27: N'ley 3J **77**
Lindens WN8: Skel 9E **22**
Lindens, The CH43: Oxton 3J **73**
L31: Mag 4H **35**
Linden Way WA8: Wid 4J **79**
WA10: Eccl .6E **48**
Lindenwood L32: Kirkb 2D **46**
Lindeth Av. CH44: Wall 7H **57**
Lindfield Cl. L8: Liv 4E **74**
WA4: Moore .2K **97**
Lindholme WN8: Skel 1F **30**
Lindi Av. WA4: Grap 7J **83**
Lindisfarne Av. CH65: Ell P 4A **112**
WA3: Low 2K **53**
Lindisfarne Ct. WA8: Wid 2J **79**
Lindisfarne Dr. L12: Crox 7D **46**
Lindley Av. WA4: Westy 4G **82**
WN5: Orr 7M **31**
Lindley Cl. L7: Liv 9H **59**
Lindley Dr. WN8: Parb 2F **22**
Lindley St. L7: Liv 9H **59**
Lindrick Cl. L35: Rainh 5D **62**
Lindsay Rd. L4: Walt 1J **59**
Lindsay St. WA9: Clock F 6N **63**
Lind St. L4: Walt 9E **44**
Lindsworth Cl. WA5: Gt San 2L **81**
Lindwall Cl. CH43: Bid 8C **56**
Linear Pk. CH46: More 8K **55**
Linear Vw. WA12: Newt W 9L **51**
Lineside Cl. L25: Gate 3F **76**
Lines Rd. M44: Irlam 1M **69**
Linford Gro. WA11: St H 5M **49**
Lingdale Av. CH43: Clau 2F **72**
Lingdale Ct. CH43: Clau 1F **72**
CH48: W Kir .6A **70**
Lingdale Rd. CH43: Clau 1F **72**
CH48: W Kir .5B **70**
Lingdale Rd. Nth. CH41: Birke 1F **72**
Lingdales L37: Form 7H **17**
Lingfield Cl. L30: N'ton 1F **44**
L36: Roby 8G **61**
Lingfield Gro. L14: Broad G 7B **60**
Lingfield Rd. L14: Broad G 7A **60**
WA7: Run 6H **95**
Lingford Cl. L27: N'ley 4K **77**
Lingham Cl. CH46: More 7L **55**
Lingham La. CH46: More 6K **55**
(not continuous)
Lingholme Rd. WA10: St H 6H **49**
Lingley Ct. WA5: Gt San 2F **80**
LINGLEY GREEN 1F **80**
Lingley Grn. Av. WA5: Gt San 2E **80**
LINGLEY MERE 8F **64**
Lingley Mere Bus. Pk. WA5: Gt San 9F **64**
Lingley Rd. WA5: Gt San 2F **80**
Lingmell Av. WA11: St H 1L **49**
Lingmell Rd. L12: W Der 1N **59**
Lingmoor Cl. WN3: Wigan 2J **41**
Ling St. L7: Liv 7G **59**
Lingtree Rd. L32: Kirkb 9N **35**
Lingwell Av. WA8: Wid 6G **79**
Lingwell Pk. WA8: Wid 6G **79**
Lingwood Rd. WA5: Gt San 2H **81**
Linhope Way L17: Aig 5H **75**
Link Av. L23: Thorn 6N **33**
WA11: St H .4A **50**
Linkfield Cl. L27: N'ley 2H **77**
Link Rd. L36: Huy 8M **61**
Links, The CH43: Oxton 3F **72**
WA3: Birchw 3L **67**
Links Av. CH66: Lit Sut 7H **103**
PR9: South 5K **7**
Links Cl. CH45: Wall 2F **56**
CH48: W Kir .7E **70**
CH63: Raby M 9A **90**
Links Hey Rd. CH48: Caldy 1F **86**
Linkside CH63: Hghr B 9K **73**
Linkside Av. WA2: Win 3C **66**
Linkside Ct. L23: Blun 6G **33**
Linkside Rd. L25: Woolt 7G **76**
Linkside Way CH66: Gt Sut 5L **111**
Links Rd. L32: Kirkb 2E **46**
Linkstor Rd. L25: Woolt 6D **76**
Links Vw. CH43: Oxton 3E **72**
CH45: Wall 1F **56**
CH66: Lit Sut .7H **103**
Linksview L25: Woolt 6D **76**
Linksway CH45: Wall 2F **56**
Link Wlk. M31: Part 7L **69**
Link Warehouses L36: Huy 8M **61**
Linkway WA7: Run 7M **95**
WA10: Windle 4E **48**
Linkway Av. WN4: Ash M 6N **41**
Linkway E. WA9: St H 8L **49**
Linkway W. WA9: St H 7J **49**
WA10: St H .7J **49**
Linner Rd. L24: Speke 5G **93**
Linnet Cl. L17: Aig 3H **75**
WA2: Warr 6E **66**
WA12: Newt W 7L **51**
Linnet Ct. L17: Aig 4H **75**
Linnet Gro. WA3: Birchw 6M **67**
Linnet Ho. L17: Aig 3H **75**
Linnet La. L17: Aig 3G **75**
Linnets Pk. WA7: Run 4L **95**
Linnets Way CH60: Hesw 7M **87**
Linnet Way L33: Kirkb 4C **36**
Linslade Cl. L33: Kirkb 7D **36**
Linslade Cres. L33: Kirkb 7D **36**
Linton Av. WA3: Golb 1A **52**
Linton Pl. L32: Kirkb 8A **36**
Linton St. L4: Walt 9E **44**
Linum Gdns. WA9: Bold 2D **64**
Linville Av. L23: Blun 7H **33**
Linwood Cl. WA7: Brook 1E **108**
Linwood Gro. L35: Whis 7B **62**
Linwood Rd. CH42: Tran 5L **73**
Lionel St. WA9: St H 2B **64**
Lions Cl. CH43: Clau 2F **72**
Lipton Cl. L20: Boot 8B **44**
Lisburn La. L13: Liv 2K **59**
Lisburn Rd. L17: Aig 6K **75**
LISCARD 4H **57**
Liscard Cres. CH44: Wall 5H **57**
Liscard Gro. CH44: Wall 5G **57**
Liscard Ho. CH44: Wall 5H **57**
Liscard Rd. CH44: Wall 5H **57**
(not continuous)
L15: Wav 1J **75**
Liscard Village CH45: Wall 4H **57**
Liscard Way CH44: Wall 5H **57**
Liskeard Cl. WA7: Brook 9D **96**
Lisleholme Cl. L12: W Der 3A **60**
Lisleholme Cres. L12: W Der 3A **60**
Lisleholme Rd. L12: W Der 3A **60**
Lismore Ct. L23: Blun 7J **33**
Lismore Pk. PR8: Birkd 2M **11**
Lismore Rd. L18: Moss H 6M **75**
Lister Av. CH46: Leas 7A **56**
Lister Cres. L7: Liv 7H **59**
Lister Dr. L6: Liv 5K **59**
L13: Liv 5K **59**
Lister Rd. L7: Liv 6H **59**
WA7: Ast 4M **95**
Liston St. L4: Walt 8E **44**
Litcham Cl. CH49: Upton 1A **72**
Litchborough Gro. L35: Whis 3D **62**
LITHERLAND 1A **44**
Litherland Av. CH46: More 8L **55**
Litherland Cres. WA11: St H 3M **49**
Litherland Ho. L20: Boot 6C **44**
Litherland Pk. L21: Lith 2A **44**
Litherland Rd. L20: Boot 4B **44**
Litherland Sports Pk. 1C **44**
Lithou Cl. L5: Liv 4C **58**
Little Acre L31: Mag 3K **35**
LITTLE ALTCAR 3G **25**
Lit. Barn Hey L30: N'ton 7C **34**
Little Birches CH65: Ell P 8M **103**
LITTLE BONGS 5B **60**
Littlebourne WA7: Murd 8G **97**
Lit. Brewery La. L37: Form 7F **16**
Lit. Brook La. L32: Kirkb 2B **46**
Lit. Canning St. L8: Liv 9K **5** (1E **74**)
Lit. Catharine St. L8: Liv 9K **5** (1E **74**)
Littlecote Cl. WA9: Clock F 5M **63**
Littlecote Gdns. WA4: App 4E **98**
Little Ct. L3: Liv 5B **58**
Little Cft. L35: Whis 6A **62**
LITTLE CROSBY 3K **33**
Lit. Crosby Rd. L23: Crosb, Lit C 3K **33**
Littledale L14: Knott A 6B **60**
Littledale Rd. CH44: Wall 6K **57**
WA5: Gt San .1H **81**
Little Delph WA11: Hay 3E **50**
Littlegate WA7: Run 7A **96**
Little Green CH66: Gt Sut 2J **111**
Lit. Hardman St. L1: Liv 7J **5** (9D **58**)
Lit. Heath Rd. L24: Speke 5J **93**
Lit. Heyes St. L5: Liv 3F **58**
Lit. Hey La. L37: Form 8J **17**
Lit. Howard St. L3: Liv 1C **4** (5A **58**)
Lit. Huskisson St. L8: Liv 9L **5** (1E **74**)
Little La. CH64: Park 5C **100**
PR9: South 5N **7**
Littlemore Cl. CH49: Upton 3L **71**
Lit. Moss Hey L28: Stockb V 2F **60**
LITTLE NESTON 9E **100**
Lit. Parkfield Rd. L17: Aig 4G **75**
Lit. Rake La. CH2: Chor B, Lit Stan . . .9B **112**
Littler Rd. WA11: Hay 5C **50**
Little St Bride St. L8: Liv 8K **5** (9E **58**)
LITTLE STANNEY 4C **112**
Lit. Stanney La.
CH2: Lit Stan, Stoak 5C **112**
Littlestone Cl. WA8: Wid 4K **79**
Lit. Storeton La. CH63: Store 1G **89**
Little St. WA9: St H 9A **50**
LITTLE SUTTON 8H **103**
Little Sutton Station (Rail) 8H **103**
Littleton Cl. CH43: Noct 4E **72**
WA5: Gt San .4M **81**
LITTLE TOWN 9K **53**
Little Whissage CH66: Gt Sut 3L **111**
Littlewood Cl. L35: Whis 6B **62**
Lit. Woolton St. L7: Liv 5M **5** (8F **58**)
Littondale Av. L35: Rainh 7G **63**
Liver Ind. Est. L9: Ain 6H **45**
Livermore Ct. L8: Liv 2H **75**
LIVERPOOL 6E **4** (8B **58**)
Liverpool Aquatics Cen. 1L **75**
Liverpool Arts Village L1: Liv 7F **4**
Liverpool Av. PR8: Ains 9K **11**
Liverpool Cathedral Church of Christ
. . . . .9J **5** (1D **74**)
Liverpool Cruise Terminal 5B **4** (8A **58**)
Liverpool Empire Theatre 4H **5** (7D **58**)
Liverpool FC 2F **58**
Liverpool Innovation Pk.
L7: Liv 7J **59**
Liverpool Intermodal Freeport Terminal
L20: Boot 6N **43**
Liverpool International Bus. Pk.
L24: Speke .4D **92**
LIVERPOOL JOHN LENNON AIRPORT
. . . . .6G **92**
Liverpool John Moores University
City Campus -
Scotland Rd. 2G **5** (6C **58**)
William Brown St. 3G **4** (7C **58**)
IM Marsh Campus 7L **75**
Mount Pleasant Campus 6J **5** (8D **58**)
Myrtle St. 7K **5** (9E **58**)
The Henry Cotton Campus 3F **4**
Tithebarn St. 3E **4** (7B **58**)
Liverpool Metropolitan Cathedral of
Christ the King (RC) 5K **5** (8E **58**)
Liverpool Municipal Golf Course 2N **45**
Liverpool Olympia 1N **5** (6F **58**)
Liverpool One L1: Liv 6E **4** (8B **58**)
Liverpool Parish Church 5C **4**
Liverpool Pl. WA8: Wid 7F **78**
Liverpool Playhouse 5G **4** (8C **58**)
Liverpool Rd. CH1: Back 9N **111**
CH64: Nest .6E **100**
(not continuous)
L14: Huy 5F **60**
L23: Crosb 6L **33**
L31: Lyd 9H **27**
L34: Presc 3M **61**
L36: Huy 5F **60**
(not continuous)
L37: Form 2G **24**
L39: Augh 2N **27**
L39: Bic 9C **28**
L40: Ruf 1N **15**
M44: Cad, Irlam 6J **69**
PR8: Birkd, Ains 2N **11**
WA5: Gt San .2E **80**
WA5: Warr 3A **82**
WA8: Wid 7E **78**
WA10: St H .7J **49**
WA11: Hay 3C **50**
(not continuous)
WN4: Ash M, Garsw 9F **40**
WN8: Skel 4N **29**
(not continuous)
Liverpool Rd. Nth. L31: Mag 9H **27**
L40: Burs 1J **21**
Liverpool Rd. Sth. L31: Mag 2H **35**
L40: Burs 4G **20**
Liverpool Row WA12: Newt W 1M **65**
Liverpool Sailing Club 5C **92**
Liverpool Science Pk. ic1
L3: Liv 6K **5** (8E **58**)
Liverpool Science Pk. ic2 L3: Liv 5K **5**
Liverpool South Parkway Station (Rail)
. . . . .1B **92**
Liverpool St. WA10: St H 7J **49**
LIVERPOOL WATERS 4A **58**
Liverpool Watersports Cen. 2C **74**
Liverpool Way, The L33: Kirkb 1E **46**
Liversidge Rd. CH42: Tran 4K **73**
Liver St. L1: Liv 8E **4** (9B **58**)
Livesley's La. L37: Gt Alt 2M **25**
Livingston Av. L17: Aig 4H **75**
Livingston Ct. L17: Aig 4H **75**
(not continuous)
Livingston Dr. L17: Aig 5H **75**
Livingston Dr. Nth. L17: Aig 5H **75**
Livingston Dr. Sth. L17: Aig 5H **75**
Livingstone Cl. WA5: Old H 1M **81**
Livingstone Gdns. CH41: Birke 1J **73**
Livingstone Rd. CH46: Leas 5A **56**
CH65: Ell P 7A **104**
Livingstone St. CH41: Birke 1J **73**
WN4: Ash M .6J **41**
Llandaff Cl. CH66: Gt Sut 4K **111**
Llanrwst Cl. L8: Liv 3D **74**
Lloyd Av. CH41: Birke 1H **73**
Lloyd Cl. L6: Liv 5E **58**
Lloyd Cres. WA12: Newt W 7H **51**
Lloyd Dr. CH49: Grea 5K **71**
CH65: Ell P 5A **112**
Lloyd Rd. L34: Presc 2B **62**
Lloyd St. WA11: Hay 4B **50**
Lobelia Av. L9: Walt 6G **45**
Lobelia Gro. WA7: Beech 1B **108**
Lobelia Wlk. M31: Part 7L 69
(off Redbrook Rd.)
Local Cen. WA7: Run 8A **96**
Lochinvar St. L9: Walt 7E **44**
Lochinver Av. CH66: Lit Sut 8E **102**
Lochmore Rd. L18: Moss H 7N **75**
Lochryan Rd. L19: Aller 8N **75**
Loch St. WA7: Run 4K **95**
(not continuous)
Locker Av. WA2: Warr 7C **66**
Lockerbie Cl. WA2: Warr 6F **66**
Lockerbie Pl. WN3: Wins 1G **40**
Lockerby Rd. L7: Liv 6J **59**
Locker Pk. CH49: Grea 4K **71**
Locke St. L19: Garst 3A **92**
Lockett Rd. WA8: Wid 6K **79**
WN4: Ash M .5K **41**
Lockett St. WA4: Warr 5G **82**
Lockfield WA7: Run 5H **95**
Lockfields Vw. L3: Liv 4B **58**
Lockgate E. WA7: Wind H 5E **96**
Lockgate W. WA7: Wind H 5D **96**
LOCKING STUMPS 4K **67**
Locking Stumps Cen. WA3: Birchw 5K **67**
Locking Stumps La.
WA3: Birchw, Fearn 6J **67**
Lockington Cl. L8: Liv 4F **74**
Lock La. M31: Part 6K **69**
Lock Rd. CH62: East 7F **90**
WA1: Padd 2G **83**
Locks, The WA4: Grap 5J **83**
Lock St. WA9: St H 5M **49**
Lockton La. WA5: Warr 1N **81**
Lockton Rd. L34: Know 5F **46**
Lockwood Vw. WA7: Pres B 1H **109**
Loddon Cl. CH49: Upton 1B **72**
Lodge, The CH43: Noct 2D **72**
Lodge Cl. WA13: Lymm 4H **85**
Lodge Dr. WA3: Cul 7N **53**
Lodge Hollow WA6: Hel 1E **114**
Lodge La. CH1: Sau 9D **110**
CH62: Port S 1A **90**
CW9: Ant 9N **99**
L8: Liv 1G **75**
L39: Bic 2N **37**
WA4: Dutt 6L **109**
WA5: Warr 1N **81**
WA7: Halt 7A **96**
WA8: Cron 4D **78**
WA12: Newt W 1K **51**
(not continuous)
Lodge Rd. WA8: Wid 8E **78**
WN5: Orr 8N **31**
Lodge Works L33: Know I 8G **37**
Lodwick St. L20: Kirkd 9A **44**
Lofthouse Ga. WA8: Wid 5J **79**
Logan Rd. CH41: Birke 8H **57**
Logfield Dr. L19: Garst 2B **92**
Lognor Rd. L32: Kirkb 9A **36**
Lognor Wlk. L32: Kirkb 9A **36**
Logwood Rd. L36: Huy 9L **61**
Lois Ct. CH45: Wall 3J **57**
Lombard Rd. CH46: More 7N **55**
Lombardy Av. CH49: Grea 6J **71**
Lomond Gro. CH46: More 9N **55**
CH66: Gt Sut 2L **111**
Lomond Rd. L7: Liv 6K **59**
Londonderry Rd. L13: Liv 2J **59**
London Flds. WN5: Bil 6A **40**
London La. PR8: South 7B **12**
London Rd. L3: Liv 4H **5** (7D **58**)
WA4: App, Stockt H, Stret 7D **82**
WA6: Frod 6L **107**
London Row WA12: Newt W 1M **65**
London Sq. PR9: South 8G **6**
London St. PR9: South 8G **7**
Longacre PR9: South 4L **7**
Longacre Cl. CH45: Wall 4D **56**
Longacre Rd. CH64: Nest 4E **100**
Long Acres CH49: Grea 3L **71**
Long Av. L9: Ain 4G **45**
Longbarn Blvd. WA2: Birchw 7K **67**
Long Barn La. WA2: Fearn 7J **67**
Longbarn La. WA1: Wools 8L **67**
WA2: Padg 7K **67**
Longbenton Way WA7: Manor P 3D **96**
Longborough Rd. L34: Know 7G **47**
Longbutt La. WA13: Lymm 5F **84**
(not continuous)
Longcliffe Dr. PR8: Ains 1H **17**
Longcroft Av. L19: Aller 9B **76**
Longcroft Pl. WA13: Lymm 3J **85**
Longcroft Sq. L19: Aller 9B **76**
Longdale La. L29: Seft 4C **34**
Longden Rd. WN4: Ash M 8J **41**
Longdin St. WA4: Westy 5F **82**
Longdown Rd. L10: Faz 4N **45**
Longfellow Cl. L32: Kirkb 2B **46**
Longfellow Dr. CH62: New F 9N **73**
Longfellow St. L8: Liv 1H **75**
(not continuous)
L20: Boot 5N **43**
Longfield L37: Form 8H **17**
Longfield Av. L23: Crosb 5L **33**
Longfield Cl. CH49: Grea 4L **71**
Longfield Gdns. M44: Cad 5K **69**
WA2: Warr 8D **66**
Longfield Pk. WA9: Clock F 5N **63**
Longfield Rd. L21: Lith 4A **44**
WA2: Warr 8D **66**

Longfield Wlk. L23: Crosb 5L 33
Longfold L31: Mag 2K 35
PR4: Mere B 5L 9
LONGFORD 8C 66
Longford Dr. WA8: Wid 6H 79
Longford Rd. PR8: Birkd 4N 11
Longford St. L8: Liv 5F 74
WA2: Warr 1C 82
Long Hey L35: Whis 7A 62
WN8: Skel 9F 22
Long Hey Rd. CH48: Caldy 9F 70
Long Heys La. WN8: Dalt 9H 23
Longland Rd. CH45: Wall 3H 57
Long La. L9: Ain, Faz 4G 45
L15: Wav 9L 59
L19: Garst 9A 76
L29: Thorn 3N 33
L37: Form 9E 16
L39: Augh, Bic 1A 28
PR9: Banks 1F 8
WA2: Warr 8C 66
WN8: Uph 9H 31
Longleat Cl. WA5: Warr 1A 82
Longlooms Rd. CH65: Ell P 4B 112
Longlooms Rd. E. CH65: Ell P 4B 112
Longman Dr. L24: Speke 3F 92
Longmead Av. WN4: Ash M 7L 41
Long Meadow CH60: Hesw 9N 87
WA10: Eccl 6E 48
Longmeadow Rd. L34: Know 6H 47
Long Meanygate PR9: South 6D 8
Longmoor Cl. L10: Faz 3K 45
Longmoor Gro. L9: Ain 4G 45
Longmoor La. L9: Ain 4G 44
L10: Faz 3M 45
Long Moss L30: N'ton 8B 34
Longreach Rd. L14: Knott A 5D 60
Longridge Av. CH49: Upton 2M 71
WA11: St H 5N 49
Longridge Wlk. L4: Kirkd 1D 58
LONGSHAW 2N 39
Longshaw Av. WN5: Bil 2A 40
LONGSHAW BOTTOM 2A 40
Longshaw Cl. L40: Ruf 1L 15
WN5: Bil 2A 40
LONGSHAW COMMON 3A 40
Longshaw Comn. WN5: Bil 2A 40
(not continuous)
Longshaw Old Rd. WN5: Bil 2A 40
Longshaw St. WA5: Warr 7A 66
Long Spinney WA7: Nort 7E 96
Longster Cl. WA6: Hel 3E 114
Longstone Wlk. L7: Liv 9G 58
Longton Av. WA3: Low 2D 52
Longton Ct. PR9: South 7J 7
Longton Dr. L37: Form 7G 17
Longton La. L35: Rainh 4E 62
LONGVIEW 4K 61
Longview Av. CH45: Wall 4G 57
L35: Rainh 5D 62
Longview Cres. L36: Huy 6K 61
Longview Dr. L36: Huy 5K 61
Longview La. L36: Huy 4K 61
Longview Rd. L35: Rainh 5D 62
L36: Huy 6K 61
Longville St. L8: Liv 3D 74
Long Wlk. M31: Part 6K 69
Longwood Cl. WA11: Rainf 1F 48
Longwood Rd. WA4: App 1F 98
Longworth Way L25: Woolt 5E 76
Lonie Gro. WA10: St H 1F 62
Lonmore Cl. PR9: Banks 2E 8
Lonsboro Rd. CH44: Wall 6J 57
Lonsdale Av. CH45: Wall 3G 57
L39: Orm 6D 20
WA10: St H 2E 62
Lonsdale Cl. L21: Ford 9A 34
WA5: Gt San 9G 65
WA8: Wid 8F 78
Lonsdale M. L21: Ford 9A 34
Lonsdale Rd. L21: Ford 9A 34
L26: Halew 1J 93
L37: Form 1E 24
PR8: South 2C 12
Lonsdale Vs. CH45: Wall 3G 57
(off Seaview Rd.)
Looe Cl. WA8: Wid 6H 79
Looe Rd. L11: Crox 5B 46
Looms, The CH64: Park 4B 100
Loomsway CH61: Irby 1K 87
Lopwell Dr. L6: Liv 5F 58
Loraine St. L5: Liv 4E 58
Lordens Cl. L14: Knott A 4E 60
Lordens Rd. L14: Knott A 4E 60
(not continuous)
Lord Nelson St. L1: Liv 4H 5 (7D 58)
L3: Liv 4H 5 (7D 58)
WA1: Warr 3D 82
Lords Av. CH43: Bid 9C 56
Lord Sefton Way L37: Gt Alt 2K 25
Lords Fold WA11: Rainf 4B 38
Lordsgate Dr. L40: Burs 2J 21
Lordsgate La. L40: Burs 3G 20
Lordship La. WA6: Frod 8C 106
Lords La. WA3: Birchw 5K 67
Lords St. M44: Cad 4J 69
Lord St. CH41: Birke 1L 73
L2: Liv 5E 4 (8B 58)
L19: Garst 3B 92
L40: Burs 9J 15
Lord St. PR8: South 9F 6
PR9: South 9F 6
WA3: Croft 1H 67
WA4: Warr 4C 82
WA7: Run 4J 95
WA10: St H 5J 49
(not continuous)
WA12: Newt W 7J 51
WN4: Ash M 7M 41
Lord St. W. PR8: South 9F 6
Loreburn Rd. L15: Wav 2M 75
Lorenzo Dr. L11: Norr G 9K 45
Loretto Dr. CH49: Upton 2A 72
Loretto Rd. CH44: Wall 4F 56
Lorna Way M44: Irlam 1N 69
Lorn Ct. CH41: Birke 2L 73
Lorne Ct. CH43: Oxton 4H 73
Lorne Rd. CH43: Oxton 4G 73
L22: Water 1K 43
Lorne St. L7: Liv 6K 59
Lorn St. CH41: Birke 2L 73
Lorton Av. WA11: St H 2K 49
Lorton St. L8: Liv 1G 75
Lostock Av. WA5: Warr 9A 66
Lostock Cl. WN5: Bil 6A 40
Lothair Rd. L4: Walt 2F 58
Lothian St. L8: Liv 2F 74
Lotus Ct. WA5: Warr 4N 81
Lotus Gdns. WA9: Bold 2C 64
Loudon Gro. L8: Liv 2F 74
Lough Grn. CH63: Spit 5N 89
Loughlin Dr. L33: Kirkb 6D 36
Loughrigg Av. WA11: St H 1L 49
Louis Braille Cl. L30: N'ton 7E 34
Louisiana Dr. WA5: Gt San 2K 81
Louis Pasteur Av. L30: N'ton 7E 34
Loushers La. WA4: Warr 6D 82
Lovage Cl. WA2: Padg 7K 67
Lovatt Ct. WA13: Lymm 4H 85
Lovelace Rd. L19: Gras 9N 75
Lovelady Gro. L37: Form 3G 24
Love La. CH44: Wall 6G 57
L3: Liv 5B 58
Lovel Rd. L24: Speke 5H 93
Lovel Ter. WA8: Hale B 2E 94
Lovel Way L24: Speke 4H 93
Lovely La. WA5: Warr 2N 81
Loves Cotts. L39: Orm 7B 20
Lovett Dr. L35: Presc 4B 62
Low Bank Rd. WN4: Ash M 7G 40
Lowbridge Ct. L19: Garst 1B 92
Lowcroft WN8: Skel 1F 30
Lowden Av. L21: Lith 1A 44
Lowe Av. WA5: Westy 4G 83
Lowell St. L4: Walt 9E 44
Lwr. Alt Rd. L38: Hight 8F 24
Lwr. Appleton Rd. WA8: Wid 7L 79
Lwr. Bank Vw. L20: Kirkd 9A 44
LOWER BEBINGTON 2N 89
Lwr. Breck Rd. L6: Liv 3H 59
Lowerbrook Way L4: Kirkd 2C 58
Lwr. Carr La. L38: Gt Alt 5A 26
Lwr. Castle St. L2: Liv 5D 4 (8B 58)
Lwr. Church St. WA8: Wid 2K 95
Lower Cl. L26: Halew 8L 77
Lwr. Farm Rd. L25: Gate 1E 76
Lowerfield Gdns. WA3: Golb 1D 52
Lwr. Flaybrick Rd. CH43: Bid 9E 56
Lwr. Gill St. L3: Liv 4K 5 (7E 58)
Lower Grn. CH49: Woodc 5A 72
Lwr. Hall St. WA10: St H 6L 49
Lower Hey L23: Thorn 6A 34
Lwr. Hill Top Rd. WA4: Stockt H 6G 82
LOWER HOUSE 8H 79
Lower Ho. La. L11: Norr G 6M 45
WA8: Wid 9J 79
LOWER IRLAM 1M 69
Lower La. L9: Faz 3K 45
Lwr. Mersey St. CH65: Ell P 7A 104
Lwr. Mersey Vw. L20: Kirkd 9A 44
Lwr. New Hall Pl. L3: Liv 4C 4
Lower Promenade
PR8: South 8F 6
PR9: South 7G 6
Lwr. Rake La. WA6: Hel 1E 114
Lower Rd. CH62: Port S 1A 90
L26: Halew 8M 77
WA8: Hale B 8M 77
Lwr. Robin Hood La. WA6: Hel 2E 114
Lower Sandfield L25: Gate 4F 76
Lowerson Cres. L11: Norr G 1K 59
Lowerson Rd. L11: Norr G 1K 59
LOWER STRETTON 7F 98
Lwr. Thingwall La.
CH61: Thing 1C 88
LOWER WALTON 8C 82
Lwr. Wash La. WA4: Westy 5F 82
Lowes Grn. L37: Form 1H 25
Lowe's La. WN8: Newb 5B 22
Lowestoft Dr. L19: Garst 1N 91
Lowe St. WA3: Golb 2B 52
WA10: St H 6J 49
Lowe St. Sth. WA10: St H 7J 49
Loweswater Cl. WA2: Warr 6C 66
Loweswater Cres. WA11: Hay 4C 50
Loweswater Way L33: Kirkb 6B 36
Lowfield La. WA9: St H 3J 63
Lowfield Rd. L14: Knott A 6A 60
Lowfields Av. CH62: East 3C 102
Lowfields Cl. CH62: East 3D 102
Low Hill L6: Liv 2M 5 (6F 58)
L7: Liv 4M 5 (7F 58)
WA6: Dun H 8A 114
Lowlands Rd. WA7: Run 5J 95
Lowndes Rd. L6: Liv 3J 59
Lowry Bank CH44: Wall 6L 57
Lowry Cl. L33: Kirkb 5C 36
WA5: Gt San 2M 81
Lowry Hill La. L40: Lath 3M 21
Lowther Av. L10: Ain 9J 35
L31: Mag 1K 35
WA3: Cul 6N 53
Lowther Cres. WA10: St H 1E 62
Lowther Dr. L35: Rainh 6E 62
Lowther St. L8: Liv 9M 5 (1F 74)
Lowther Ter. WN6: Appl B 5M 23
LOWTON 3G 53
Lowton Bus. Pk. WA3: Low 2H 53
LOWTON COMMON 1H 53
Lowton Gdns. WA3: Low 5C 52
LOWTON HEATH 4D 52
Lowton Rd. WA3: Golb 1C 52
LOWTON ST MARY'S 3H 53
Lowton St Mary's By-Pass
WN7: Leigh 3K 53
Low Wood L38: Hight 6F 24
Low Wood Gro. CH61: Barn 3C 88
Lowwood Gro. CH41: Birke 3K 73
Lowwood Rd. CH41: Birke 3K 73
Low Wood St.
L6: Liv 3M 5 (6F 58)
Loxdale Cl. L8: Liv 4F 74
Loxdale Dr. CH65: Gt Sut 2L 111
Loxley Cl. WA5: Gt San 9J 65
Loxley Rd. PR8: South 2C 12
Loxton Cres. WN3: Wigan 1K 41
Loxwood Cl. L25: Gate 1F 76
Loyola Hey L35: Rainh 9H 63
Lucan Rd. L17: Aig 6K 75
Lucas Ct. L35: Rainh 5F 62
(off Ratcliffe Pl.)
Lucerne Rd. CH44: Wall 7K 57
Lucerne St. L17: Aig 5H 75
Lucius Cl. L9: Walt 3E 44
Lucknow St. L17: Aig 4H 75
Ludlow WN8: Skel 9F 22
Ludlow Cl. WA1: Padg 8J 67
Ludlow Ct. CH48: W Kir 7C 70
Ludlow Cres. WA7: Run 7L 95
Ludlow Dr. CH48: W Kir 7C 70
CH65: Ell P 2C 112
L39: Orm 6B 20
Ludlow Gro. CH62: Brom 6C 90
Ludlow St. L4: Kirkd 9E 44
Ludwig Rd. L4: Walt 3G 58
Lugard Rd. L17: Aig 6K 75
LUGSDALE 9M 79
Lugsdale Rd. WA8: Wid 9K 79
Lugsmore La. WA10: St H 9G 48
Luke St. CH44: Wall 7L 57
L8: Liv 2E 74
WN4: Ash M 6M 41
Lulworth WN8: Skel 9E 22
Lulworth Av. L22: Water 9J 33
Lulworth Lodge PR8: Birkd 1M 11
Lulworth Pl. WA4: Warr 7C 82
Lulworth Rd. L25: Gate 3G 77
PR8: Birkd 2M 11
Lulworth Vw. PR8: Birkd 2L 11
Lumb Brook M. WA4: Stockt H 7F 82
Lumb Brook Rd. WA4: App, App T 9G 83
Lumbbrook Rd. WA4: App 7F 82
Lumber La. WA5: Burtw 1G 65
Lumina CH62: Brom 5D 90
Lumley Rd. CH44: Wall 6K 57
Lumley St. L19: Garst 9N 75
Lumley Wlk. L24: Hale 6B 94
Lunar Dr. L30: N'ton 6E 34
Lunar Rd. L9: Ain 4G 44
Lunds Cl. L40: Westh 9J 21
Lundy Dr. CH65: Ell P 5A 112
Lune Av. L31: Mag 1K 35
Lunehurst WA3: Low 2F 52
Lunesdale Av. L9: Ain 3G 44
Lune St. L23: Crosb 7L 33
Lune Way WA8: Wid 7F 78
Lunsford Rd. L14: Knott A 5D 60
LUNT 3C 34
Lunt Av. L30: N'ton 9F 34
L35: Whis 6B 62
Lunt La. L29: Seft 3C 34
Lunt Rd. L20: Boot 4B 44
L29: Seft, Thorn 2B 34
LUNTS HEATH 4L 79
Lunt's Heath Rd. WA8: Wid 3K 79
Lunt's La. L37: Form 3G 25
Luntswood Gro. WA12: Newt W 6J 51
Lupin Dr. WA11: Hay 4H 51
Lupton Dr. L23: Crosb 7N 33
Lupus Way CH66: Gt Sut 2L 111
Luscombe Cl. L26: Halew 8L 77
Lusitania Rd. L4: Walt 8F 44
Luther Gro. WA9: St H 8D 50
Luton Gro. L4: Walt 1E 58
Luton Rd. CH65: Ell P 9L 103
Luton St. L5: Kirkd 3A 58
WA8: Wid 9K 79
Lutyens Cl. L4: Walt 1E 58
Luxmore Rd. L4: Walt 9F 44
Lybro Way L7: Liv 8G 59
Lycett Rd. CH44: Wall 4E 56
L4: Walt 2H 59
Lyceum Pl. L1: Liv 6G 5
Lychgate WA4: Hghr Wal 9A 82
Lycroft Cl. WA7: Run 9L 95
Lydbrook Cl. CH42: Rock F 5M 73
Lydbury Cl. WA5: Call 7M 65
Lydbury Cres. L32: Kirkb 2D 46
Lydden Rd. CH65: Ell P 7N 103
Lydford Rd. L12: W Der 1N 59
Lydia Ann St. L1: Liv 7F 4 (9C 58)
LYDIATE 7G 27
Lydiate, The CH60: Hesw 8N 87
Lydiate La. CH64: Will 6L 101
L23: Seft, Thorn 5A 34
L25: Woolt 6G 77
L26: Halew 6H 77
L29: Thorn 5A 34
WA7: West P 8G 95
Lydiate Pk. L23: Thorn 5A 34
Lydiate Rd. L20: Boot 5B 44
Lydiate Sta. Rd. L31: Lyd 8B 26
Lydia Wlk. L10: Faz 3N 45
Lydieth Lea L27: N'ley 2J 77
Lydney Rd. L36: Huy 5F 60
Lydstep Ct. WA5: Call 7N 65
Lyelake Cl. L32: Kirkb 1D 46
Lyelake Gdns. L32: Kirkb 1D 46
(off Lyelake Rd.)
Lyelake La. L39: Bic 2K 29
L40: Westh 2K 29
Lyelake Rd. L32: Kirkb 1D 46
Lyle St. L5: Liv 4C 58
Lyme Cl. L36: Huy 3L 61
Lymecroft L25: Woolt 6D 76
Lyme Cross Rd. L36: Huy 3J 61
Lyme Gro. L36: Huy 4J 61
WA13: Lymm 6C 84
Lyme St. WA1: Warr 3C 82
WA11: Hay 4G 50
WA12: Newt W 6G 51
Lyme Tree Ct. WA8: Cron 2F 78
Lymewood Ct. WA11: Hay 3G 50
Lymington Gro. L30: N'ton 8E 34
Lymington Rd. CH44: Wall 5F 56
LYMM 5E 84
Lymm Bri. WA13: Lymm 5E 84
Lymm Golf Course 3D 84
Lymm Hall WA13: Lymm 5E 84
Lymmhay La. WA13: Lymm 4E 84
Lymmington Av.
WA13: Lymm 5C 84
Lymm Leisure Cen. 6H 85
Lymm Quay WA13: Lymm 5E 84
Lymm Rd. CH43: Bid 1D 72
WA4: Thel 5M 83
WA13: Lymm 7L 85
WA14: Lit Bo 7L 85
Lynas Gdns. L19: Gras 8N 75
Lynas St. CH41: Birke 9K 57
Lyncastle Rd. WA4: App T 4K 99
Lyncastle Way WA4: App T 3L 99
Lyncot Rd. L9: Ain 2G 44
Lyncroft Rd. CH44: Wall 7J 57
Lyndale WA7: Run 7M 95
WN8: Skel 9E 22
Lyndale Av. CH62: East 2D 102
WA2: Fearn 7G 67
WA2: Warr 9E 66
Lyndene Rd. L25: Gate 2E 76
Lyndhurst L31: Mag 2J 35
WN8: Skel 9E 22
Lyndhurst Av. CH61: Pens 4A 88
L18: Moss H 5L 75
Lyndhurst Cl. CH61: Thing 2A 88
Lyndhurst Rd. CH45: Wall 3F 56
CH47: Meols 8F 54
CH61: Irby 2K 87
L18: Moss H 4L 75
L23: Crosb 7N 33
PR8: Birkd 4N 11
Lyndhurst Way L36: Huy 7J 61
Lyndon Dr. L18: Moss H 4N 75
Lyndon Gro. WA7: Run 7L 95
Lyndor Cl. L25: Woolt 7F 76
Lyndor Rd. L25: Woolt 7F 76
Lyneal Av. CH66: Gt Sut 2H 111
Lyneham L35: Whis 7C 62
Lynham Av. WA5: Gt San 3K 81
Lynholme Rd. L4: Walt 2G 59
Lynmouth Rd. L17: Aig 8K 75
Lynnbank CH43: Oxton 4H 73
Lynnbank Rd. L18: Moss H 3B 76
Lynn Cl. WA7: Run 8M 95
WA10: St H 6F 48
Lynndene CH66: Lit Sut 7J 103
Lynscott Pl. L16: Child 9B 60
Lynsted Rd. L14: Knott A 5D 60
Lynthorpe Av. M44: Cad 3K 69
Lynton Av. M44: Cad 3L 69
Lynton Cl. CH60: Hesw 9B 88
L19: Aller 8N 75
WA5: Penk 4G 80
Lynton Ct. L23: Blun 7H 33
Lynton Cres. WA8: Wid 6H 79
Lynton Dr. CH63: Beb 4N 89
PR8: Birkd 5L 11
Lynton Gdns. WA4: App 3E 98
Lynton Grn. L25: Woolt 4D 76
Lynton Gro. WA9: Sut L 4M 63

Lynton Rd. CH45: Wall . . . 3E 56
L36: Huy . . . 6M 61
PR8: Birkd . . . 6L 11
Lynton Way WA10: Windle . . . 4E 48
Lynwood Av. CH44: Wall . . . 6G 57
L39: Augh . . . 1A 28
WA3: Low . . . 4F 52
WA4: App . . . 9D 82
Lynwood Cl. WN8: Skel . . . 5G 31
Lynwood Dr. CH61: Irby . . . 1M 87
Lynwood End L39: Augh . . . 1A 28
Lynwood Gdns. L9: Walt . . . 5E 44
Lynwood Rd. L9: Walt . . . 5E 44
Lynxway, The L12: Knott A . . . 5B 60
Lyon Cl. WA10: St H . . . 7J 49
Lyon Ct. WA4: Warr . . . 5G 82
Lyon Ind. Est. WA9: St H . . . 3A 64
Lyon Rd. L4: Walt . . . 3G 58
Lyons Cl. CH46: More . . . 8M 55
Lyons La. WA4: App . . . 1E 98
(not continuous)
Lyons Pl. L25: Hunts X . . . 8H 77
Lyons Rd. CH46: More . . . 8M 55
PR8: Birkd . . . 1N 11
WA5: Penk . . . 4H 81
Lyon St. L19: Garst . . . 3A 92
WA4: Warr . . . 5G 82
WA10: St H . . . 7H 49
WN4: Ash M . . . 4H 41
Lyra Rd. L22: Water . . . 1K 43
Lysander Cl. L6: Liv . . . 5F 58
Lysander Dr. WA2: Padg . . . 7F 66
Lyster Cl. WA3: Birchw . . . 6N 67
Lyster Rd. L20: Boot . . . 7N 43
Lytham Cl. L10: Faz . . . 1L 45
WA5: Gt San . . . 5J 81
Lytham Ct. L32: Kirkb . . . 7A 36
Lytham Rd. PR9: South . . . 3M 7
WA8: Wid . . . 6L 79
WN4: Ash M . . . 6H 41
Lytham Way L12: W Der . . . 3D 60
Lytherton Av. M44: Cad . . . 5K 69
Lythgoes La. WA2: Warr . . . 2C 82
(not continuous)
Lytles Cl. L37: Form . . . 2G 24
Lyttelton Rd. L17: Aig . . . 6K 75
Lytton Av. CH42: Rock F . . . 7M 73
Lytton Gro. *L21: Sea* . . . *4N 43*
(off Ash Gro.)
Lytton St. L6: Liv . . . 1L 5 (6E 58)

M

Maberley Vw. L15: Wav . . . 8M 59
Maberry Cl. WN6: Shev . . . 6N 23
Mab La. L12: W Der . . . 1D 60
McAllester Lodge *CH43: Oxton* . . . *4F 72*
(off Bidston Rd.)
Macalpine Cl. CH49: Upton . . . 2A 72
Macbeth St. L20: Kirkd . . . 9B 44
McBride St. L19: Garst . . . 1A 92
McCarthy Cl. WA3: Birchw . . . 6A 68
McClellan Pl. WA8: Wid . . . 7L 79
McCormack Av. WA9: St H . . . 6A 50
McCulloch St. WA9: St H . . . 7M 49
Macdermott Rd. WA8: Wid . . . 2J 95
Macdona Dr. CH48: W Kir . . . 8C 70
Macdonald Av. WA11: St H . . . 5A 50
Macdonald Dr. CH49: Grea . . . 5L 71
Macdonald Rd. CH46: More . . . 9K 55
M44: Irlam . . . 2L 69
Macdonald St. L15: Wav . . . 9K 59
Mace Rd. L11: Crox . . . 7A 46
McFarlane Av. WA10: St H . . . 6F 48
Macfarren St. L13: Liv . . . 6M 59
McGarva Way CH65: Ell P . . . 1A 112
McGill Ct. *CH41: Birke* . . . *1K 73*
(off Cathcart St.)
McGough Cl. WA9: Sut M . . . 6K 63
McKeagney Gdns. WA8: Wid . . . 9G 78
McKee Av. WA2: Warr . . . 7C 66
Mackenzie Rd. CH46: Leas . . . 6B 56
McKeown Cl. L5: Liv . . . 4C 58
Mackets Cl. L25: Woolt . . . 7G 76
Macket's La.
L25: Woolt, Hunts X . . . 6G 77
Mack Gro. L30: N'ton . . . 9C 34
McKinley St. WA5: Gt San . . . 1J 81
McKinley Way WA8: Wid . . . 5J 79
McManus Dr. WA9: St H . . . 8L 49
McMinnis Av. WA9: St H . . . 8C 50
McNair Hall L18: Moss H . . . 5L 75
Macqueen St. L13: Liv . . . 7M 59
McVinnie Rd. L35: Presc . . . 3C 62
Maddock Rd. CH44: Wall . . . 4K 57
Maddocks St. L13: Liv . . . 7M 59
Maddock St. CH41: Birke . . . 9J 57
Maddrell St. L3: Liv . . . 5A 58
Madeira Dr. L25: Gate . . . 2F 76
Madelaine St. L8: Liv . . . 2F 74
Madeleine McKenna Ct. WA8: Wid . . . 5E 78
Madeley Cl. CH48: W Kir . . . 7C 70
WN3: Wigan . . . 1G 41
Madeley Dr. CH48: W Kir . . . 7C 70
Madeley St. L6: Liv . . . 6H 59
Madingley Ct. PR9: South . . . 5L 7
Madison Sq. L1: Liv . . . 8H 5 (9D 58)
Madryn Av. L33: Kirkb . . . 9E 36
Madryn St. L8: Liv . . . 3F 74
Maelor Cl. CH63: Brom . . . 9B 90
Maesbrook Cl. PR9: Banks . . . 2F 8
Mafeking Cl. L15: Wav . . . 8L 59
Mafeking Pl. WN4: Ash M . . . 8L 41
Magazine Av. CH45: New B . . . 2H 57
Magazine Brow CH45: New B . . . 2J 57
Magazine La. CH45: New B . . . 2H 57
Magazine Rd. CH62: Brom . . . 4C 90
Magazines Prom.
CH45: New B . . . 1J 57
Magazine Wlk. CH62: Brom . . . 4C 90
Magdala St. L8: Liv . . . 1H 75
Magdalen Dr. WN4: Ash M . . . 7H 41
Magdalene Wlk. *CH65: Ell P* . . . *1C 112*
(off Robinson Rd.)
Magdalen Ho. L20: Boot . . . 8B 44
Magdalen Sq. L30: N'ton . . . 7E 34
Magenta Av. M44: Irlam . . . 3L 69
Maggots Nook Rd.
WA11: Rainf . . . 2D 38
MAGHULL . . . 1J 35
Maghull La. L31: Mag . . . 2N 35
Maghull Smallholdings Est.
L31: Mag . . . 9M 27
Maghull Station (Rail) . . . 4K 35
Magistrates' Court
Liverpool . . . *4F 4*
(off Victoria St.)
Liverpool & Knowsley . . . 4F 4
Ormskirk . . . 8D 20
Runcorn (Halton) . . . 7B 96
St Helens . . . 6K 49
South Sefton . . . 7B 44
Warrington . . . 4B 82
Wirral . . . 2M 73
Mag La. WA13: Lymm . . . 9F 84
WA16: High L . . . 9F 84
Magnolia Cl. CH66: Gt Sut . . . 4L 111
L26: Halew . . . 6H 77
M31: Part . . . *7L 69*
(off Redbrook Rd.)
WA1: Wools . . . 1M 83
WA11: Hay . . . 5B 50
Magnolia Dr. WA7: Beech . . . 2B 108
Magnolia Wlk. CH49: Grea . . . 6K 71
Magnus Cl. L13: Liv . . . 4L 59
Maguire Av. L20: Boot . . . 6D 44
Mahon Av. L20: Boot . . . 4C 44
Mahon Ct. L8: Liv . . . 9K 5
Maiden Cl. WN8: Skel . . . 2N 29
Maiden Gdns. CH65: Ell P . . . 2B 112
Maiden La. L13: Liv . . . 2J 59
Maidford Rd. L14: Knott A . . . 4D 60
Maidstone Cl. L25: Hunts X . . . 8G 77
Maidstone Dr. L12: W Der . . . 4D 60
Main Av. PR9: Banks . . . 4H 9
WA10: St H . . . 1F 62
Main Cl. WA11: Hay . . . 4C 50
Main Dr. L35: Whis . . . 8A 62
Maine Gdns. WA5: Gt San . . . 1J 81
Main Front L35: Whis . . . 9B 62
Main La. WA3: Croft . . . 7F 52
Main Rd. CH62: Port S . . . 3A 90
Mainsail Cl. L3: Liv . . . 5B 58
Mainside Rd. L32: Kirkb . . . 1D 46
Main St. WA6: Frod . . . 6K 107
WA7: Halt . . . 6B 96
WN5: Bil . . . 7N 39
Maintree Cres. L24: Speke . . . 3L 93
Mainwaring Rd. CH44: Wall . . . 6K 57
CH62: Brom . . . 7C 90
Mairesfield Av. WA4: Grap . . . 6J 83
Mairscough La. L31: Lyd . . . 4F 26
L39: Down . . . 4F 26
Maisemore Flds. WA8: Wid . . . 5H 79
Maitland Cl. L8: Liv . . . 1G 75
Maitland Rd. CH45: New B . . . 1J 57
Maitland St. L8: Liv . . . 1G 75
Majestic Cl. L11: Crox . . . 7A 46
Majestic M. WN5: Orr . . . 7N 31
Major Cross St. WA8: Wid . . . 9K 79
Major St. L5: Kirkd . . . 3C 58
Makepeace Wlk. *L8: Liv* . . . *2E 74*
(off Thackeray Cl.)
Makerfield Dr. WA12: Newt W . . . 5J 51
Makin St. L4: Walt . . . 8E 44
Malahide Ct. WA8: Wid . . . 6H 79
Malcolm Av. WA2: Warr . . . 8E 66
Malcolm Cres. CH63: Brom . . . 9B 90
Malcolm Gro. L20: Kirkd . . . 9C 44
Malcolm Pl. L15: Wav . . . 8L 59
Malcolm St. WA7: Run . . . 5L 95
Malden Rd. L6: Liv . . . 6H 59
Maldon Cl. L26: Halew . . . 1K 93
Maldwyn Rd. CH44: Wall . . . 4H 57
Maley Cl. L8: Liv . . . 4F 74
Malham Av. WN3: Wigan . . . 1J 41
Malham Cl. PR8: South . . . 3D 12
WA5: Gt San . . . 9G 65
Malhamdale Av. L35: Rainh . . . 7G 63
Malika Pl. WN4: Ash M . . . 5G 41
Malin Cl. L24: Hale . . . 5A 94
Maliston Rd. WA5: Gt San . . . 3K 81
Mall, The L5: Liv . . . 4F 58
L39: Orm . . . 8C 20
WA1: Warr . . . *3C 82*
(within Golden Sq. Shop. Cen.)
Mallaby Ct. *CH41: Birke* . . . *9G 57*
(off Mallaby St.)
Mallaby St. CH41: Birke . . . 9G 57
Mallard Cl. L12: Crox . . . 7D 46
L26: Halew . . . 7J 77
L39: Augh . . . 2A 28
WA2: Warr . . . 6E 66
WA7: Beech . . . 1B 108
Mallard Gdns. WA9: St H . . . 3H 63
Mallard Ho. L31: Lyd . . . 8G 27
Mallard La. WA3: Birchw . . . 6N 67
Mallards, The PR9: South . . . 4A 8
Mallard Way CH46: More . . . 8K 55
WA11: St H . . . 4L 49
Mallee Av. PR9: South . . . 4M 7
Mallee Cres. PR9: South . . . 4M 7
Malleson Rd. L13: Liv . . . 2K 59
Mallins Cl. L8: Liv . . . 4F 74
Mallory Av. L31: Lyd . . . 8G 27
Mallory Gro. WA11: St H . . . 4N 49
Mallory Rd. CH42: Tran . . . 6K 73
CH65: Whit . . . 1M 111
Mallowdale Cl. CH62: East . . . 1E 102
Mallow Rd. L6: Liv . . . 6H 59
Mallow Wlk. *M31: Part* . . . *7M 69*
(off Broom Rd.)
Mallow Way L36: Huy . . . 9K 61
Malmesbury Cl. CH49: Grea . . . 4K 71
Malmesbury Pk. WA7: Nort . . . 4F 96
Malmesbury Rd. L11: Norr G . . . 8K 45
Malpas Av. CH43: Pren . . . 6G 72
Malpas Dr. CH63: Hghr B . . . 9L 73
WA5: Gt San . . . 3L 81
Malpas Gro. CH45: Wall . . . 3G 56
Malpas Rd. CH45: Wall . . . 3F 56
CH65: Gt Sut . . . 1L 111
L11: Crox . . . 5B 46
WA7: Run . . . 8L 95
Malpas Way WA5: Gt San . . . 4L 81
Malta Cl. L36: Huy . . . 6H 61
Malta St. L8: Liv . . . 3E 74
Malta Wlk. L8: Liv . . . 3E 74
Maltby Cl. WA9: St H . . . 4H 63
Malt Ho. Ct. WA10: Windle . . . 4F 48
Maltkiln La. L39: Augh . . . 3B 28
Maltmans Rd. WA13: Lymm . . . 5D 84
Malton Av. WA3: Low . . . 3F 52
Malton Cl. WA8: Cron . . . 3F 78
Malton Rd. L25: Woolt . . . 7F 76
Malt St. L7: Liv . . . 9G 58
Malvern Av. CH65: Ell P . . . 2A 112
L14: Broad G . . . 7D 60
Malvern Cl. L32: Kirkb . . . 7A 36
WA5: Gt San . . . 9J 65
WN3: Wins . . . 1E 40
WN4: Ash M . . . 7K 41
Malvern Ct. PR8: South . . . 9F 6
Malvern Cres. L14: Broad G . . . 7D 60
Malvern Gdns. PR8: South . . . 9F 6
Malvern Gro. CH42: Tran . . . 6K 73
L10: Ain . . . 9H 35
Malvern Rd. CH45: Wall . . . 4D 56
L6: Liv . . . 6H 59
L20: Boot . . . 5B 44
WA9: St H . . . 7B 50
Malwood St. L8: Liv . . . 4E 74
Manchester New Rd. M31: Part . . . 6M 69
Manchester Rd. L34: Presc . . . 3M 61
M31: Carr, Part . . . 5M 69
PR9: South . . . 7H 7
WA1: Padd, Warr, Wools . . . 2D 82
WA3: Rix, Wools . . . 1A 84
Manchester Row WA12: Newt W . . . 1M 65
Mancroft Cl. WA1: Wools . . . 1M 83
Mandarin Ct. WA1: Warr . . . 5B 82
Mandela Ct. L8: Liv . . . 3G 74
Manderston Dr. L12: W Der . . . 2B 60
Manderville Cl. WN3: Wins . . . 1F 40
Mandeville Rd. PR8: Ains . . . 9H 11
Mandeville St. L4: Walt . . . 8E 44
Manesty's La. L1: Liv . . . 6F 4 (8C 58)
Manfield WN8: Skel . . . 1D 30
Manfred St. L6: Liv . . . 3M 5 (7F 58)
Manhattan Gdns.
WA5: Gt San . . . 9K 65
Manica Cres. L10: Faz . . . 3L 45
Manion Av. L31: Lyd . . . 7G 26
Manion Cl. L31: Lyd . . . 7G 26
MANLEY . . . 9J 115
Manley Cl. CH43: Oxton . . . 5F 72
MANLEY COMMON . . . 8M 115
Manley Gdns. WA5: Warr . . . 3A 82
Manley La. WA6: Dun H, Manl . . . 8B 114
(not continuous)
Manley Mere Sail Sports & Adventure Trail
. . . 8D 114
Manley Pl. WA9: St H . . . 2H 63
Manley Quarry WA6: Manl . . . 8G 115
Manley Rd. L22: Water . . . 9J 33
L36: Huy . . . 9L 61
WA6: Alv, Frod . . . 6K 115
WA6: Alv, Manl . . . 5G 115
Manley Vw. CH2: Elt . . . 2N 113
Manna Dr. CH2: Elt . . . 2N 113
Mannering Ct. *L17: Aig* . . . *4H 75*
(off Mannering Rd.)
Mannering Rd. L17: Aig . . . 4G 75
Manners La. CH60: Hesw . . . 9M 87
Manningham Rd. L4: Walt . . . 3G 59
Manning Rd. PR8: South . . . 9K 7
Manning St. WA10: St H . . . 7J 49
Mannington Cl. CH47: Meols . . . 9F 54
Mann Island L3: Liv . . . 6C 4 (8B 58)
Mann Island Apartments
L3: Liv . . . 6D 4 (8A 58)
Mann St. L8: Liv . . . 2D 74
Manor, The CH66: Lit Sut . . . 8E 102
WA1: Wools . . . 1N 83
WA11: Rainf . . . 7F 38
Manor Av. L23: Crosb . . . 6K 33
L35: Rainh . . . 7F 62
L40: Burs . . . 3H 21
WA3: Golb . . . 2D 52
WA12: Newt W . . . 6H 51
Manorbier Cres. L9: Walt . . . 7F 44
Manor Cl. CH64: Park . . . 7C 100
L20: Boot . . . 8D 44
WA1: Wools . . . 1L 83
WA13: Lymm . . . 6E 84
WN4: Garsw . . . 8E 40
Manor Complex L33: Know I . . . 9G 36
Manor Ct. *CH48: W Kir* . . . *5B 70*
(off Bridge Rd.)
CH49: Grea . . . 5K 71
CH61: Irby . . . 1L 87
WA3: Golb . . . 2D 52
WA9: Sut L . . . 5N 63
Manor Cres. L25: Woolt . . . 7F 76
L40: Burs . . . 3H 21
Manor Dr. CH49: Upton . . . 1N 71
L23: Crosb . . . 6K 33
L30: N'ton . . . 8G 34
L40: Burs . . . 3H 21
Mnr. Farm Ct. WA6: Frod . . . 5M 107
Mnr. Farm Courtyard WA4: Moore . . . 2K 97
Mnr. Farm Cres. CH1: Cap . . . 5G 110
Mnr. Farm M. WA7: Manor P . . . 3F 96
Mnr. Farm Rd. L36: Huy . . . 8K 61
WA7: Manor P . . . 3E 96
Manor Fell WA7: Pal F . . . 8D 96
Manorfield Cl. CH1: Cap . . . 4F 110
Manor Gdns. L40: Burs . . . 3H 21
MANOR GREEN . . . 1C 72
Manor Gro. L32: Kirkb . . . 9N 35
WN8: Skel . . . 3C 30
Manor Hill CH43: Clau, Oxton . . . 2G 72
Manor Ho. CH62: Brom . . . 7C 90
CH66: Gt Sut . . . *3J 111*
(off Kelmscott Cl.)
L17: Aig . . . 5G 75
L31: Mag . . . 2G 34
Manor House, The CH49: Upton . . . 1N 71
Manor Ho. Cl. L31: Mag . . . 2H 35
L40: Ruf . . . 2N 15
WA11: St H . . . 1K 49
Manor Ho. Dr. WN8: Skel . . . 9H 31
Manorial Rd. CH64: Park . . . 6C 100
Manorial Rd. Sth. CH64: Park . . . 6C 100
Manor Ind. Est. WA4: Westy . . . 4F 82
Manor La. CH42: Rock F . . . 6N 73
CH45: Wall . . . 4J 57
CH66: Gt Sut . . . 2J 111
Manor Lodge L37: Form . . . 9E 16
Manor M. CH45: Wall . . . 4J 57
MANOR PARK . . . 3E 96
Manor Pk. Av. WA7: Manor P . . . 3E 96
Manor Pk. Bus. Pk. WA7: Manor P . . . 3D 96
Manor Pk. Cl. CH61: Thing . . . 1A 88
Manor Pk. Ct. WA7: Manor P . . . 3E 96
Manor Pk. Dr. CH66: Gt Sut . . . 3J 111
Manor Pl. CH62: Brom . . . 2C 90
WA8: Wid . . . 7E 78
Manor Rd. CH44: Wall . . . 4H 57
CH45: Wall . . . 4H 57
CH47: Hoy . . . 9D 54
CH61: Irby . . . 1L 87
CH62: East . . . 9C 90
CH63: Brim, Thorn H . . . 6F 88
L23: Blun, Crosb . . . 5J 33
L25: Woolt . . . 7F 76
L40: Burs . . . 3H 21
PR9: South . . . 5M 7
WA6: Frod . . . 5M 107
WA7: Run . . . 5N 95
WA8: Wid . . . 7E 78
WA11: Hay . . . 3H 51
WA13: Lymm . . . 6E 84
(not continuous)
Manor Road Station (Rail) . . . 1D 70
Manorside Cl. CH49: Upton . . . 2N 71
Manor St. WA3: Golb . . . 1C 52
WA9: St H . . . 8M 49
Manor Vw. L12: W Der . . . 9D 46
Manor Way CH43: Bid . . . 1C 72
L25: Woolt . . . 7F 76
(not continuous)
Manorwood Dr. L35: Whis . . . 7B 62
Mansart Cl. WN4: Ash M . . . 8M 41
Manse Gdns. WA12: Newt W . . . 6M 51
Mansell Cl. WA8: Wid . . . 3M 79
Mansell Dr. L26: Halew . . . 1J 93
Mansell Rd. L6: Liv . . . 6G 59
Mansfield Cl. WA3: Birchw . . . 5A 68
Mansfield Rd. CH65: Whit . . . 3M 111
L20: Boot . . . 8B 44
Mansfield St. L3: Liv . . . 2H 5 (6D 58)
WA3: Golb . . . 1A 52
Mansion Dr. L11: Crox . . . 6N 45
Manston Rd. WA5: Penk . . . 5H 81
Manton Rd. L6: Liv . . . 6H 59
Manton Way WA9: St H . . . 5H 63
Manvers Rd. L16: Child . . . 9C 60
Manville Rd. CH45: New B . . . 2H 57

Manville St. WA9: St H 9M 49
Manx Jane's La. PR9: South 3M 7
Manx Rd. WA4: Warr 5C 82
Maori Dr. WA6: Frod 6K 107
Maple Av. CH66: Lit Sut 8H 103
L40: Burs 1J 21
WA3: Low 3G 53
WA7: Run 7M 95
WA7: Sut W 2C 108
WA8: Wid 7L 79
WA11: Hay 3D 50
WA12: Newt W 8M 51
Maple Cl. L12: Crox 7B 46
L21: Sea 4N 43
L35: Whis 6B 62
L37: Form 3C 24
WN5: Bil 6N 39
Maple Ct. L21: Lith 2A 44
L34: Know 6G 47
WN8: Skel 6C 30
Maple Cres. L36: Roby 7H 61
WA5: Penk 4H 81
Mapledale Rd. L18: Moss H 3N 75
Maple Gro. CH62: Brom 7B 90
CH66: Whit 4M 111
L8: Liv 2H 75
L35: Presc 4B 62
WA4: Warr 5E 82
WA10: St H 7F 48
Maple Leaf Dr. L36: Huy 3H 61
Maple Rd. M31: Part 6L 69
WA1: Wools 1M 83
WA2: Win 3C 66
Maples Ct. CH43: Oxton 5G 73
Maple St. CH41: Birke 3K 73
PR8: South 9J 7
WN4: Ash M 5J 41
Mapleton Cl. CH43: Pren 7E 72
Mapleton Dr. WA7: Sut W 3B 108
Maple Tree Gro. CH60: Hesw 7C 88
Maple Vw. WN8: Skel 6C 30
Maplewood L32: Kirkb 2D 46
PR9: South 5L 7
WN8: Skel 9D 22
Maplewood Cl. L27: N'ley 3J 77
WA8: Wid 9D 78
Maplewood Gro. CH43: Bid 9E 56
Mapplewell Cres. WA5: Gt San 2J 81
Marathon Cl. L6: Liv 5E 58
Marble Pl. Shop. Cen.
PR8: South 8G 6
Marbury Gdns. CH65: Ell P 8L 103
Marbury Rd. L32: Kirkb 9A 36
Marbury St. WA4: Warr 5D 82
Marc Av. L31: Mell 7N 35
Marcham Way L11: Norr G 9N 45
Marchbank Rd. WN8: Skel 3A 30
Marchfield Rd. L9: Walt 5E 44
Marchmount Dr. L23: Crosb 8M 33
March Rd. L6: Liv 4J 59
Marchweil Rd. CH65: Ell P 1B 112
Marchwood Way L25: Gate 1E 76
Marcien Way WA8: Wid 5J 79
Marcot Rd. L6: Liv 5J 59
Marcross Cl. WA5: Call 8N 65
Marcus Ct. *L36: Huy 5L 61*
(off Mosscroft Cl.)
Marcus St. CH41: Birke 9K 57
(not continuous)
Mardale Av. WA2: Warr 6C 66
WA11: St H 2L 49
Mardale Cl. L27: N'ley 5L 77
PR8: Ains 1H 17
Mardale Cres. WA13: Lymm 5F 84
Mardale Lawn L27: N'ley 5L 77
Mardale Rd. L36: Huy 4G 60
Mardale Wlk. *L27: N'ley 5L 77*
(off Mardale Cl.)
L36: Huy 4G 61
Mare Hall La. CH64: Nest 6H 101
Mareth Cl. L18: Moss H 6M 75
Marford Rd. L12: W Der 2N 59
Marfords Av. CH63: Brom 8B 90
Margaret Av. L20: Boot 4B 44
WA1: Wools 1J 83
WA9: St H 1M 63
Margaret Ct. WA8: Wid 9L 79
WA10: St H 9G 49
Margaret Rd. L4: Walt 8D 44
L23: Blun 6G 32
Margaret's La. CH66: Chil T 7E 102
Margaret St. L6: Liv 1M 5 (5F 58)
WA9: Clock F 6A 64
Margery Rd. WA10: St H 9F 48
Margreen Rd. L4: Kirkd 2C 58
Marian Av. WA12: Newt W 7H 51
Marian Cl. L35: Rainh 7F 62
Marian Close, The L30: N'ton 7D 34
Marian Dr. CH46: More 9M 55
L35: Rainh 7E 62
Marian Rd. WA11: Hay 3G 51
Marians Dr. L39: Orm 5C 20
Marian Sq. L30: N'ton 8E 34
Marian Way, The L30: N'ton 8D 34
Maria Rd. L9: Walt 7E 44
Marie Curie Av. L30: N'ton 7E 34
(not continuous)
Marie Dr. WA4: Thel 7L 83
Marigold Pl. WA5: Warr 5N 81
Marigold Way WA9: Bold 2C 64
Marina Av. L21: Lith 3A 44
WA5: Gt San 4K 81
WA9: St H 2M 63
Marina Cres. L30: N'ton 1F 44
L36: Huy 8H 61
Marina Dr. CH65: Ell P 1N 111
WA2: Warr 8D 66
Marina Gro. WA7: Run 5L 95
Marina La. WA7: Murd 8G 96
Marina Rd. L37: Form 3F 24
Marina Village WA7: Pres B 8G 97
Marina Wlk. *CH65: Ell P 1A 112*
(within The Port Arcades)
Marine AFC 8J 33
Marine Av. M31: Part 6K 69
Marine Cres. L22: Water 1K 43
Marine Dr. CH60: Hesw 8L 87
PR8: South 8E 6
PR9: South 4H 7
Marine Ga. Mans. PR9: South 7G 7
Marine Lake 8F 6
Marine Pde. PR8: South 7F 6
Marine Pk. CH48: W Kir 4C 70
Marine Pk. Mans. CH45: New B 9H 43
Marine Point CH45: New B 9H 43
Marine Point Health & Fitness 9G 43
Marine Prom. CH45: New B 9H 43
Mariner Cl. WA7: Murd 9F 96
Mariner Ct. PR9: South 6H 7
Marine Rd. CH47: Hoy 1B 70
PR8: South 9D 6
Mariners Ho. L1: Liv 9G 4
Mariners Pk. CH45: Wall 3K 57
Mariners Rd. CH45: New B 2J 57
L23: Blun 9H 33
Mariners Way *L20: Boot 7B 44*
(off Strand Shop. Cen.)
M44: Irlam 1M 69
Mariners Wharf *CH65: Ell P 7B 104*
(off Grosvenor Wharf Rd.)
L3: Liv 2B 74
Marine Ter. CH45: Wall 2J 57
L22: Water 2K 43
Marion Dr. WA7: West 9J 95
Marion Gro. L18: Moss H 6A 76
Marion Rd. L20: Boot 4C 44
Marion St. CH41: Birke 2L 73
Maritime Bus. Pk. CH41: Birke 8K 57
CH41: Tran 4M 73
Maritime Cen. L21: Sea 3L 43
Maritime Cl. WA12: Newt W 5L 51
Maritime Ct. *CH49: Woodc 7B 72*
(off Childwall Grn.)
L12: W Der 1M 59
L30: N'ton 6E 34
PR8: South 8F 6
Maritime Ent. Pk. L20: Boot 7A 44
Maritime Grange CH44: Wall 7L 57
Maritime Gro. CH43: Oxton 3H 73
Maritime Lodge *L5: Liv 3E 58*
(off Towson St.)
Maritime Pk. CH43: Oxton 3J 73
Maritime Pl. L3: Liv 2J 5 (6D 58)
Maritime Vw. CH42: Tran 5K 73
Maritime Way L1: Liv 7F 4 (9C 58)
Marius Cl. L4: Walt 1E 58
Mark Av. CH66: Gt Sut 1H 111
Markden M. L8: Liv 1E 74
Market App. WN4: Ash M 8K 41
Market Ga. WA1: Warr 3C 82
Market Hall PR8: South 8G 6
Market Pl. L34: Presc 3A 62
WA8: Wid 9K 79
WA12: Newt W 7J 51
Market Pl. Sth. CH41: Birke 2M 73
Market Sq. CH65: Ell P 1A 112
L1: Liv 5G 4
L32: Kirkb 9C 36
Market St. CH41: Birke 2L 73
CH47: Hoy 2C 70
PR8: South 8F 6
WA8: Wid 9K 79
WA10: St H 7K 49
WA12: Newt W 6J 51
Market Way L1: Liv 5G 5
L39: Orm 8C 20
Markfield Cres. L25: Woolt 7G 77
WA11: St H 5M 49
Markfield Rd. L20: Boot 5A 44
Markham Dr. PR8: South 4D 12
Markham Gro. CH43: Bid 9F 56
Mark Rake CH62: Brom 6C 90
Mark Rd. L38: Hight 8F 24
Mark St. CH44: Wall 7L 57
L5: Liv 2D 58
Marksway CH61: Pens 3A 88
Marland WN8: Skel 9D 22
Marlborough WN8: Skel 9D 22
Marlborough Av. L30: N'ton 9F 34
L31: Lyd 9J 27
Marlborough Ct. *L17: Aig 6K 75*
(off Aigburth Va.)
PR9: South 8H 7
WN8: Skel 9D 22
Marlborough Cres. WA4: Stockt H 6G 83
WA8: Wid 3K 79
Marlborough Dr. WA6: Hel 3E 114
Marlborough Gdns. PR9: South 7H 7
WN8: Skel 9D 22
Marlborough Gro. CH43: Oxton 4J 73
Marlborough Pl. L3: Liv 2E 4 (6B 58)
Marlborough Rd. CH45: New B 2J 57
CH65: Ell P 2B 112
L13: Liv 3J 59
L22: Water 2L 43
L23: Crosb 8K 33
L34: Presc 2B 62
PR9: South 8H 7
Marlborough St. L3: Liv 2E 4 (6B 58)
Marlborough Ter. *PR9: South 8H 7*
(off Marlborough Rd.)
Marlborough Wlk. CH65: Ell P 2B 112
Marlborough Way WA11: Hay 2G 50
Marlbrook Rd. L25: Gate 2F 76
Marlcroft Dr. L17: Aig 8K 75
Marldon Av. L23: Crosb 9L 33
Marldon Rd. L12: W Der 1M 59
Marled Hey L28: Stockb V 1E 60
Marley Cl. L35: Rainh 8H 63
Marlfield Av. WA13: Lymm 6G 85
Marlfield La. CH61: Pens 3A 88
Marlfield Rd. L12: W Der 3N 59
WA4: Grap 6H 83
Marl Gro. WN5: Orr 8N 31
Marline Av. CH63: Brom 9B 90
Marling Cl. WA6: Frod 8N 107
Marling Pk. WA8: Wid 7E 78
Marlow Cl. WA3: Birchw 4K 67
Marlowe Cl. WA8: Wid 7J 79
Marlowe Dr. L12: W Der 3M 59
Marlowe Rd. CH44: Wall 5G 56
CH64: Nest 6E 100
Marl Rd. L30: N'ton 8G 35
L33: Know I 8G 36
Marlsford St. L6: Liv 6H 59
Marlston Av. CH61: Irby 1N 87
Marlston Pl. WA7: Run 9L 95
Marlwood Av. CH45: Wall 4E 56
Marmaduke St. L7: Liv 8G 58
Marmion Av. L20: Boot 3D 44
Marmion Cl. WA3: Low 1F 52
Marmion Rd. CH47: Hoy 1C 70
L17: Aig 4H 75
Marmonde St. L4: Walt 1D 58
Marnell Cl. L5: Liv 4B 58
Marnwood Rd. L32: Kirkb 1B 46
Marnwood Wlk. L32: Kirkb 1A 46
Marple Cl. CH43: Oxton 5E 72
Marquis St. CH41: Tran 4L 73
CH62: New F 9A 74
L3: Liv 4J 5 (7D 58)
Marram Cl. CH46: More 7A 56
Marrick Cl. WN3: Wigan 1J 41
Marron Av. WA2: Warr 7C 66
Marryat Cl. WA2: Win 3B 66
Marsden Av. WA4: Westy 4H 83
WA10: St H 6G 48
Marsden Cl. CH44: Wall 4K 57
Marsden Ct. CH45: New B 2H 57
WA8: Wid 4H 79
Marsden Rd. L26: Halew 1K 93
PR9: South 8K 7
Marsden St. L6: Liv 2M 5 (6F 58)
Marsden Way L6: Liv 2M 5 (6F 58)
MARSH, THE 2H 95
Marshall Av. WA5: Warr 7A 66
WA9: St H 1M 63
Marshall Cl. L33: Kirkb 6D 36
Marshall Pl. L3: Liv 1E 4 (5B 58)
Marshall Rd. WA1: Wools 1L 83
Marshallsay L37: Form 2G 25
Marshall's Cl. L31: Lyd 8H 27
MARSHALL'S CROSS 4L 63
Marshalls Cross (Park & Ride) 3L 63
Marshalls Cross Rd. WA9: St H 3L 63
Marshall St. CH41: Birke 9J 57
Marsham Cl. CH49: Upton 1A 72
Marsham Rd. L25: Gate 3G 77
Marsh Av. L20: Boot 4D 44
Marsh Brook Cl. WA3: Rix 7G 69
Marsh Brook Rd. WA8: Wid 3L 79
Marsh Brows L37: Form 2E 24
Marshes Lane, The PR4: Mere B 5K 9
Marshfield Cl. L36: Huy 6K 61
Marshfield Ct. CH46: Leas 6M 55
Marshfield Rd. L11: Norr G 9N 45
(not continuous)
Marshgate WA8: Wid 9E 78
Marshgate Pl. WA6: Frod 4N 107
Marshgate Rd. L12: W Der 8N 45
MARSH GREEN 6K 107
Marsh Hall Pad WA8: Wid 4L 79
Marsh Hall Rd. WA8: Wid 4L 79
Marsh Ho. La. WA1: Warr 1D 82
WA2: Warr 1D 82
Marshlands Rd. CH45: Wall 3E 56
CH64: Lit N 9D 100
Marsh La. CH2: Elt 1M 113
(not continuous)
CH2: Ince 8K 105
CH63: Hghr B 9J 73
L20: Boot 6N 43
L38: Ince B 6J 25
L40: Scar 5B 20
WA4: Dutt, Lwr W 2M 109
WA5: Cuerd 6E 80
WA6: Frod 6K 107
WA6: Hel 8K 105
WA7: Ast 4B 96
Marsh Moss La. L40: Burs 7F 14
Marsh Rd. WA4: App T 3J 99
MARSHSIDE 4M 7
Marshside Cl. L8: Liv 3E 74
Marshside Nature Reserve 1L 7
Marshside Rd. PR9: South 2K 7
Marsh St. L20: Kirkd 9C 44
WA1: Warr 1E 82
WA8: Wid 1K 95
WA9: St H 7M 49
Marsh Vista Caravan Club L40: Burs 5G 14
Marshway Dr. WA12: Newt W 6K 51
Marsland Gro. WA9: St H 1A 64
Marson St. WA2: Warr 2B 82
Marston Cl. CH43: Oxton 5F 72
CH62: East 3D 102
Marston Cres. L38: Hight 1G 32
Marston Gdns. CH65: Ell P 8L 103
Marsworth Dr. L6: Liv 5E 58
Marten Av. CH63: Brom 8B 90
Martensen St. L7: Liv 8G 58
Martens Rd. M44: Irlam 4L 69
Martham Cl. WA4: Grap 5H 83
Martham Gdns. WA9: St H 3H 63
Martial Arts Studio, The *6K 49*
(off Tolver St.)
Martin Av. WA2: Warr 8F 66
WA10: St H 4J 49
WA12: Newt W 5K 51
Martin Cl. CH61: Irby 1K 87
L18: Moss H 7M 75
L35: Rainh 5D 62
L39: Augh 3C 28
WA7: Pal F 8C 96
Martindale Gro. WA7: Beech 1N 107
Martindale Rd. CH62: Brom 6D 90
L18: Moss H 3B 76
WA11: St H 9L 39
Martine Cl. L31: Mell 7N 35
Martin Gro. L35: Presc 4B 62
Martinhall Rd. L9: Faz 6L 45
Martin La. L40: Burs 6C 14
Martin Mere Vis. Cen. 5F 14
Martin Mere Wetland Cen. 5F 14
Martin Rd. L18: Moss H 7M 75
WA6: Frod 6L 107
MARTINSCROFT 1M 83
Martinscroft Grn. WA1: Wools 1N 83
Martins La. CH44: Wall 5J 57
WN8: Skel 5G 31
Martland Av. L10: Ain 8K 35
WA3: Low 3E 52
Martland Rd. L25: Gate 4G 76
Mart La. L40: Burs 9J 15
Martlesham Cres. CH49: Grea 5J 71
Martlett Rd. L12: W Der 4B 60
Martock L35: Whis 7C 62
Marton Cl. L24: Speke 5H 93
WA3: Cul 6M 53
Marton Grn. L24: Speke 5H 93
Marton Rd. L36: Huy 3J 61
Marus Av. WN3: Wigan 1H 41
Marus Bri. Retail Pk.
WN3: Wigan 1H 41
Marus Bri. Rdbt. WN3: Wigan 1H 41
Marvin St. L6: Liv 2N 5 (6F 58)
Marwood Towers *L5: Liv 3D 58*
(off Boundary St. E.)
Mary Av. PR8: Ains 8L 11
Marybone L3: Liv 3E 4 (7C 58)
Marybone Apartments *L3: Liv 2F 4*
(off Marybone)
Marybone Student Village
L3: Liv 3F 4
(off Marybone)
Maryfield Cl. WA3: Golb 3B 52
Maryhill Rd. WA7: Run 7K 95
Maryland Cl. WA5: Gt San 1L 81
Maryland Ho. *L20: Boot 7B 44*
(off Georgia Cl.)
Maryland La. CH46: More 8L 55
Maryland St. L1: Liv 7J 5 (9D 58)
Marylebone Av. WA9: St H 3J 63
Marymount Cl. CH44: Wall 6H 57
Maryport Cl. L5: Liv 3E 58
Mary Rd. L20: Boot 4C 44
Mary Stockton Ct. *L21: Sea 4N 43*
(off Seaforth Va. W.)
Mary St. WA8: Wid 9N 79
WA9: Clock F 6A 64
Maryton Grange L18: Aller 6B 76
Maryvale WN8: Skel 1D 30
Maryville Cl. CH65: Ell P 8A 104
Maryville Rd. L34: Presc 3B 62
Maryville Wlk. CH65: Ell P 8A 104
Marywell Cl. WA9: St H 2N 63
Marzhan Way WA8: Wid 7M 79
Masefield Av. WA8: Wid 8J 79
Masefield Cl. CH62: New F 9N 73
Masefield Cres. L30: Boot 2C 44
Masefield Dr. WA2: Win 4B 66
Masefield Gro. L16: Child 9D 60
WA10: St H 5G 48
Masefield Pl. L30: Boot 2D 44
Masefield Rd. L23: Thorn 5B 34
Maskell Rd. L13: Liv 6L 59
Maslin Dr. L5: Liv 3F 58
Mason Av. WA1: Padg 9F 66
WA8: Wid 4L 79
Mason Cl. CH66: Gt Sut 3J 111
WN4: Ash M 7M 41

Mason St. CH45: New B 1H 57
L7: Liv 5N 5 (8F 58)
L22: Water 1K 43
L25: Woolt 6E 76
WA1: Warr 3D 82
WA7: Run 4M 95
Massam Cl. WA11: Rainf 5D 38
Massam's La. L37: Form 7E 16
Massey Av. WA5: Warr 7A 66
WA13: Lymm 6A 84
Massey Brook La. WA13: Lymm 6A 84
Masseyfield Rd. WA7: Brook 1C 108
Massey Pk. CH45: Wall 4G 57
Massey St. CH41: Birke 9K 57
WA9: St H 1M 63
Master's Way L19: Garst 3B 92
Matchwood Cl. L19: Garst 2B 92
Matchworks, The L19: Garst 2C 92
Mater Cl. L9: Ain 7J 45
Mather Av. L18: Aller, Moss H 4N 75
L19: Aller 7A 76
WA3: Low 4F 52
WA7: West P 8G 95
WA9: St H 7A 50
Mather Ct. CH43: Oxton 3H 73
Mather Rd. CH43: Oxton 3H 73
Mathers Cl. WA2: Fearn 5H 67
Mathew St. L2: Liv 5E 4 (8B 58)
Mathieson Rd. WA8: Wid 2H 95
Matlock Av. L9: Walt 4F 44
PR8: Birkd 2A 12
Matlock Cl. PR8: Birkd 2A 12
WA5: Gt San 8J 65
Matlock Cres. PR8: Birkd 2A 12
Matlock Rd. PR8: Birkd 3A 12
Matterdale Cl. WA6: Frod 7N 107
Matterhorn Rd. CH66: Ell P 7L 103
Matthew Cl. CH44: Wall 7L 57
Matthews St. WA1: Warr 1E 82
Matthew St. CH44: Wall 7L 57
Matty's La. WA6: Frod 7K 107
Maud Roberts Ct. L21: Lith 2N 43
Maud St. L8: Liv 2F 74
Maunders Ct. L23: Crosb 6M 33
Maureen Wlk. L10: Faz 3N 45
Mauretania Rd. L4: Walt 8F 44
Maurice Jones Ct. CH46: More 8M 55
Mavis Dr. CH49: Woodc 5A 72
Mawdsley Av. WA1: Wools 1M 83
Mawdsley Cl. L37: Form 1H 25
Mawdsley Ter. L39: Orm 5D 20
Mawson Cl. WA5: Old H 9M 65
Max Rd. L14: Knott A 4D 60
Maxton Rd. L6: Liv 6H 59
Maxwell Cl. CH49: Upton 2A 72
CH65: Whit 3M 111
Maxwell Ct. CH42: Tran 5J 73
Maxwell Pl. L13: Liv 3L 59
Maxwell Rd. L13: Liv 3L 59
Maxwell St. WA3: Ris 3M 67
WA10: St H 7H 49
May Av. CH44: Wall 7K 57
Maybank Cl. PR9: South 6M 7
Maybank Gro. L17: Aig 7L 75
Maybank Rd. CH42: Tran 4K 73
Mayberry Gro. WA2: Padg 8H 67
Maybrook Pl. *WA4: Warr 5G 82*
(off Knutsford Rd.)
Maybury Way L17: Aig 6H 75
May Cl. L21: Lith 4A 44
Mayer Av. CH63: Beb 3M 89
Mayew Rd. CH61: Irby 1N 87
Mayfair Av. L14: Broad G 7D 60
L23: Crosb 6L 33
Mayfair Cl. L6: Liv 5G 59
L38: Hight 1G 32
WA5: Gt San 1F 80
Mayfair Ct. *CH43: Oxton 5H 73*
(off The Grove)
Mayfair Dr. WN3: Wigan 1H 41
Mayfair Gro. WA8: Wid 7G 79
Mayfayre Av. L31: Lyd 7G 27
Mayfield Av. L37: Form 3C 24
WA8: Wid 7E 78
WA9: St H 1H 63
Mayfield Cl. L12: W Der 3A 60
Mayfield Ct. L37: Form 8E 16
WA8: Wid 6K 79
Mayfield Dr. CH62: East 9G 90
WN7: Leigh 2K 53
Mayfield Gdns. CH64: Nest 5E 100
L19: Gras 9M 75
Mayfield Rd. CH45: Wall 4F 56
CH63: Beb 4N 89
L19: Gras 9M 75
WA4: Grap 6H 83
WN8: Uph 5K 31
Mayfields CH66: Ell P 7L 103
L4: Kirkd 1D 58
Mayfields Ho. *CH62: New F 9A 74*
(off Mayfields Nth.)
Mayfields Nth. CH62: New F 9A 74
Mayfields Sth. CH62: New F 9A 74
Mayfield St. WN4: Ash M 8J 41
Mayfield Vw. WA13: Lymm 6E 84
Mayflower Av. L24: Speke 1E 92
Mayflower Ind. Est. L37: Form 3G 25
Mayford Cl. L25: Gate 2G 76
Mayhall Ct. L31: Mag 1J 35
May Pl. L13: Liv 7M 59
Maypole Ct. L30: N'ton 6C 34
Maypole Farm Ct. L34: Know 5G 47
May Rd. CH60: Hesw 7A 88
May St. L3: Liv 6J 5 (8D 58)
L20: Boot 5B 44
WA3: Golb 1C 52
Maythorn Av. WA3: Croft 2H 67
Maytree Cl. L27: N'ley 2G 77
Maytree Wlk. WN8: Skel 9E 22
Mayville Rd. L18: Moss H 3N 75
May Wlk. M31: Part 6L 69
Mazenod Ct. L3: Liv 2F 4
Mazzini Cl. L5: Liv 4D 58
Mead Av. L21: Lith 2B 44
Meade Cl. L35: Rainh 8G 63
Meade Rd. L13: Liv 3K 59
Meadfoot Rd. CH46: More 8L 55
Meadow, The CH49: Woodc 5B 72
(not continuous)
Meadow Av. PR8: South 2B 12
WA4: Warr 6B 82
WA9: Clock F 6N 63
Meadow Bank L31: Mag 1G 35
L32: Kirkb 7A 36
L39: Orm 9D 20
Meadowbank Caravan Pk.
WA4: Moore 1L 97
Meadowbank Cl. L12: W Der 4C 60
Meadowbank Dr. CH66: Lit Sut 8F 102
Meadowbarn Cl. L32: Kirkb 1C 46
Meadowbridge Cl. L40: Westh 9J 21
Meadowbrook L40: Burs 2H 21
Meadow Brook Cl. L10: Faz 3N 45
Meadowbrook Rd. CH46: More 1L 71
Meadow Brow PR9: South 2B 8
Meadow Cl. CH64: Nest 8E 100
CH64: Will 6M 101
L40: Westh 9J 21
WA6: Hel 2E 114
WA8: Wid 5G 79
WA12: Newt W 7H 51
WN7: Leigh 1M 53
WN8: Skel 5G 31
Meadowclough WN8: Skel 9E 22
Meadow Ct. L11: Norr G 7N 45
L25: Woolt 5F 76
Meadow Cres. CH49: Woodc 6A 72
Meadow Cft. CH64: Will 6L 101
Meadowcroft CH60: Hesw 6C 88
L37: Form 2F 24
WA9: St H 3M 63
WN4: Ash M 5H 41
WN8: Skel 9E 22
Meadowcroft Ct. WA7: Cas 7C 96
Meadowcroft Pk. L12: W Der 5B 60
Meadowcroft Rd. CH47: Meols 8F 54
Meadow Dr. L36: Huy 9K 61
L39: Augh 2A 28
Meadowfield WN8: Uph 5K 31
Meadowfield Cl. CH42: Rock F 6M 73
L9: Walt 3F 44
Meadowgate CH48: Caldy 2E 86
Meadow Hey L20: Boot 5N 43
Meadow Hey Cl. L25: Woolt 5F 76
Meadow La. CH42: Rock F 6M 73
CH64: Will 5L 101
CH65: Ell P 8A 104
L12: W Der 9N 45
L31: Mag 2K 35
L40: Burs, Lath 6M 15
PR8: Ains 2J 17
WA2: Fearn 7H 67
WA9: St H 8B 50
WA14: Dun M 4N 85
Meadow La. Ind. Pk. CH65: Ell P 9B 104
Meadow Oak Dr. L25: Gate 4E 76
Meadow Pk. CH42: Rock F 6M 73
Meadow Rd. CH48: W Kir 5G 70
Meadow Row WA7: Cas 6C 96
Meadows, The *CH41: Birke 1K 73*
(off Conway St.)
CH62: Brom 8C 90
CH64: Lit N 8F 100
L31: Mag 2J 35
L35: Rainh 6F 62
M44: Cad 3K 69
Meadowside CH46: Leas 5B 56
WA6: Frod 6K 107
Meadowside Av. WN4: Ash M 3J 41
Meadowside Dr. L33: Kirkb 5D 36
Meadowside Rd. CH62: Brom 8C 90
Meadows Leisure Cen. 3H 35
Meadow St. CH45: New B 1G 56
Meadowsweet Rd. L32: Kirkb 7D 36
Meadow Vw. CH2: Elt 2L 113
CH65: Ell P 4C 112
L21: Ford 8A 34
PR8: South 2C 12
WA13: Lymm 4D 84
Meadow Vw. Dr. WA6: Frod 7K 107
Meadow Wlk. CH61: Pens 4M 87
M31: Part 6L 69
WA7: Pal F 8B 96
(within Halton Lea Shop. Cen.)
Meadow Way L12: W Der 9N 45
PR9: Banks 3E 8
Mead Rd. WA1: Padg 9H 67
Meads, The L34: Eccl P 2D 62
Meadway CH45: Wall 4G 56
CH49: Upton 2B 72
Meadway CH60: Hesw 9N 87
CH62: Spit 5B 90
CH66: Lit Sut 7G 102
L15: Wav 9A 60
L30: N'ton 9F 34
L31: Mag 4G 34
L35: Whis 5C 62
WA3: Low 2E 52
WA7: Run 6A 96
WA8: Wid 7D 78
WN8: Skel 9E 22
Mealor's Weint CH64: Park 5B 100
Meander, The L12: W Der 9C 46
Meanygate PR9: Banks 1F 8
Measham Cl. WA11: St H 5M 49
Measham Way L12: Crox 7C 46
Mecca Bingo
Birkenhead 2K 73
Ellesmere Port 1N 111
Liverpool 5C 60
St Helens 6J 49
Southport 8F 6
Medbourne Ct. L32: Kirkb 2D 46
Medbourne Cres. L32: Kirkb 2D 46
Meddowcroft Rd. CH45: Wall 3F 56
Medea Cl. L5: Liv 3D 58
Medlar Way WN4: Ash M 6H 41
Medlock Ct. CH43: Oxton 3G 72
Medlock St. L4: Kirkd 1D 58
Medway *L20: Boot 7B 44*
(off Strand Shop. Cen.)
Medway Cl. WA2: Warr 7F 66
WN4: Ash M 5H 41
WN7: Leigh 2K 53
Medway Ct. WA9: St H 7B 50
Medway Rd. CH42: Rock F 6N 73
Meerbrook Gro. *L33: Kirkb 6D 36*
(off Langton Rd.)
Meeting Ho. La. WA6: Frod, Newt 3N 115
Meeting La. WA5: Penk 3F 80
Melbourne Cl. L24: Speke 3F 92
Melbourne St. CH45: New B 1G 56
WA9: St H 2H 63
Melbreck WN8: Skel 9D 22
Melbreck Rd. L18: Aller 7N 75
Melbury Ct. WA3: Ris 3N 67
Melbury Rd. L14: Knott A 3F 60
Melda Cl. L6: Liv 2L 5 (6E 58)
Meldon Cl. L12: W Der 8A 46
Meldreth Cl. L37: Form 3C 24
Meldrum Rd. L15: Wav 2N 75
Melford Ct. WA1: Wools 9L 67
Melford Dr. CH43: Pren 7E 72
WA7: Run 6M 95
WN4: Ash M 7J 41
WN5: Bil 9N 31
Melford Gro. L6: Liv 3J 59
Meliden Gdns. WA9: St H 2B 64
Meliden Gro. WA6: Hel 4E 114
Melksham Dr. CH61: Irby 9L 71
MELLING 6L 35
Melling Av. L9: Ain 3G 44
Melling Cl. WN7: Leigh 1N 53
Melling Ct. CH45: New B 2J 57
Melling Dr. L32: Kirkb 8C 36
Melling La. L31: Mag 4K 35
MELLING MOUNT 4A 36
Melling Rd. CH45: New B 2J 57
L9: Ain 2G 45
L10: Ain 2G 45
L20: Boot 5B 44
PR9: South 7K 7
Mellings Av. WN5: Bil 2A 40
Melling Way L32: Kirkb 8C 36
WN3: Wins 2F 40
Mellock Cl. CH64: Lit N 8F 100
Mellock La. CH64: Lit N 7F 100
Melloncroft Dr. CH48: Caldy 8C 70
Melloncroft Dr. W. CH48: Caldy 9D 70
Mellor Cl. L35: Tar G 1L 77
WA7: Wind H 7F 96
Mellor Rd. CH42: Tran 6J 73
Mellors Cl. PR8: South 1E 12
Melly Rd. L17: Aig 5G 75
Melmerby Cl. WN4: Ash M 8H 41
Melrose CH46: More 8A 56
Melrose Av. CH47: Hoy 1C 70
L23: Crosb 8L 33
PR9: South 2N 7
WA4: App 8E 82
WA5: Burtw 2H 65
WA10: Eccl 5E 48
Melrose Cres. WN4: Garsw 8E 40
Melrose Dr. CH66: Gt Sut 5L 111
WN3: Wins 1E 40 & 1F 40
Melrose Gdns. CH43: Pren 8F 72
Melrose Pk. *L22: Water 2L 43*
(off Melrose Rd.)
Melrose Rd. L4: Kirkd 1C 58
L22: Water 2L 43
L33: Kirkb 5B 36
Melton Av. WA4: Walt 8C 82
Melton Cl. CH49: Upton 3M 71
Melton Rd. WA7: Run 9M 95
Melverley Rd. L32: Kirkb 9N 35
Melville CH62: New F 7A 74
Melville Av. CH42: Rock F 7N 73
Melville Cl. WA2: Warr 1C 82
WA8: Wid 7N 79
WA10: St H 6G 48
Melville Pl. L7: Liv 7M 5 (9F 58)
Melville Rd. CH63: Hghr B 2L 89
L20: Boot 3B 44
M44: Cad 4J 69
Melville St. L8: Liv 3F 74
Melvin Ho. PR9: South 7G 7
Melwood Dr. L12: W Der 2A 60
Melwood (Liverpool FC Training Ground) 2A 60
Menai M. *L34: Presc 3B 62*
(off St James' Rd.)
Menai Rd. L20: Boot 4C 44
Menai St. CH41: Birke 2J 73
Mendell Cl. CH62: Brom 7D 90
Mendell Ct. CH62: Brom 7D 90
Mendip Av. WA2: Warr 6C 66
WN3: Wins 1E 40
Mendip Cl. CH42: Tran 7J 73
CH66: Gt Sut 2K 111
L26: Halew 9J 77
Mendip Gro. WA9: St H 7B 50
Mendip Rd. CH42: Tran 7J 73
L15: Wav 2M 75
Mendips (Childhood Home of John Lennon) 5C 76
Menin Av. WA4: Warr 5D 82
Menivale Cl. PR9: South 1N 7
Menlo Av. CH61: Irby 1N 87
Menlo Cl. CH43: Oxton 4E 72
Menlove Av. L18: Aller, Moss H 3N 75
L25: Woolt 4B 76
Menlove Ct. L18: Moss H 3A 76
Menlove Gdns. Nth. L18: Moss H 3N 75
Menlove Gdns. Sth. L18: Moss H 3N 75
Menlove Gdns. W. L18: Moss H 3N 75
Menlove Mans. L18: Moss H 2A 76
Menlow Cl. WA4: Grap 7K 83
Menstone Rd. L13: Liv 5L 59
Mentmore Cres. L11: Norr G 9N 45
Mentmore Gdns. WA4: App 2G 98
Mentmore Rd. L18: Moss H 6M 75
MEOLS 9F 54
Meols Cl. CH66: Gt Sut 1K 111
L24: Hale 5B 94
L37: Form 2E 24
MEOLS COP 1E 12
Meols Cop Retail Pk. PR8: South 2F 12
Meols Cop Rd. PR8: South 1E 12
Meols Cop Station (Rail) 8L 7
Meols Ct. CH47: Hoy 2B 70
PR9: Banks 1E 8
Meols Dr. CH47: Hoy 5B 70
CH48: W Kir 5B 70
Meols Pde. CH47: Meols 9C 54
Meols Station (Rail) 9F 54
Meols Vw. Cl. PR8: South 3F 12
Meols Wood PR9: South 6N 7
Mercer Av. L32: Kirkb 9A 36
Mercer Ct. L12: W Der 3C 60
L20: Boot 7B 44
(off Clairville Cl.)
L31: Lyd 9F 26
Mercer Dr. L4: Kirkd 2D 58
Mercer Rd. CH43: Bid 9E 56
WA11: Hay 4F 50
Mercer's La. L39: Bic 8E 28
Mercer St. L19: Garst 2A 92
WA5: Burtw 3G 64
WA12: Newt W 6M 51
Mercer Wlk. *CH65: Ell P 1A 112*
(within The Port Arcades)
Merchant Cl. L30: N'ton 2G 44
Merchant Rd. L39: Orm 9E 20
Merchants Ct. L2: Liv 6E 4
L15: Wav 9K 59
Merchants Cres. WA3: Low 1F 52
Mercury Ct. L2: Liv 3D 4 (7B 58)
Mercury Way WN8: Skel 4H 31
Mere Av. CH63: Raby M 9A 90
L40: Burs 8J 15
Mere Bank L17: Aig 4K 75
Merebank CH43: Oxton 4E 72
MERE BROW 5K 9
Mere Brow La. PR4: Mere B 5K 9
Merecliff L28: Stockb V 1G 60
Mere Cl. CH66: Gt Sut 3J 111
WN8: Skel 2C 30
Mere Ct. L40: Burs 8J 15
Merecroft Av. CH44: Wall 7J 57
Meredale Rd. L18: Moss H 4M 75
Meredith Av. WA4: Grap 6J 83
Meredith St. L19: Garst 2C 92
Mere Farm Gro. CH43: Oxton 4F 72
Mere Farm Rd. CH43: Oxton 4E 72
Mere Grn. L4: Walt 9F 44
Mere Gro. WA11: St H 1L 49
Mereheath CH46: Leas 6M 55
Mereheath Gdns. *CH46: Leas 6M 55*
(off Mereheath)
Mere Hey WA10: Eccl 7D 48
Mereland Way WA9: St H 8B 50
Mere La. CH45: Wall 2E 56
CH60: Hesw 5M 87
L5: Liv 4E 58
L39: Hals 5G 19
L40: Ruf 3H 15
PR4: Mere B 7K 9
PR9: Banks 4E 8
Mere Meanygate PR4: Mere B 6J 9
Mere Pk. L23: Blun 7J 33

Merepark Dr. PR9: South . . . 3N 7
Mere Pk. Rd. CH49: Grea . . . 5K 71
Mere Rd. L37: Form . . . 2D 24
WA2: Fearn . . . 7H 67
WA12: Newt W . . . 6A 52
WN4: Ash M . . . 7L 41
Mere Sands Wood Nature Reserve . . . 2K 15
Mere Sands Wood Nature Reserve Vis. Cen. . . . 2K 15
Mere's Edge Bus. Pk.
WA6: Hel . . . 3D 114
MERE SIDE . . . 1G 14
Meres Rd. L9: Ain . . . 3K 45
Meres Way PR8: South . . . 4A 12
Merevale Cl. WA7: Beech . . . 9A 96
Mere Vw. PR9: Banks . . . 4H 9
WA6: Hel . . . 3D 114
Mereview Cres. L12: Crox . . . 7B 46
Mere Vw. Gdns. WA4: App . . . 2F 98
Merewood L32: Kirkb . . . 2D 46
WN8: Skel . . . 9D 22
Merewood Cl. WA2: Warr . . . 6E 66
Mereworth CH48: Caldy . . . 1E 86
Meribel Cl. L23: Crosb . . . 6N 33
Meribel Sq. L34: Presc . . . 3A 62
Meriden Av. CH63: Spit . . . 6N 89
Meriden Cl. PR8: Ains . . . 9H 11
WA11: St H . . . 4N 49
Meriden Rd. L25: Gate . . . 2F 76
Meridian Bus. Village
L24: Speke . . . 1G 93
Merlewood Av. PR9: South . . . 4N 7
Merlin Av. CH49: Upton . . . 2L 71
Merlin Cl. CH49: Upton . . . 2L 71
WA7: Cas . . . 6C 96
WA11: St H . . . 4L 49
Merlin Ct. L26: Halew . . . 7H 77
Merlin Pk. L40: Burs . . . 1F 20
Merlin Rd. CH42: Tran . . . 5J 73
Merlin St. L8: Liv . . . 2E 74
Merrick Cl. WA2: Warr . . . 6F 66
Merrills La. CH49: Upton . . . 3A 72
Merrilocks Grn. L23: Blun . . . 6G 33
Merrilocks Rd. L23: Blun . . . 6G 33
Merrilox Av. L31: Lyd . . . 9J 27
Merrion Cl. L25: Woolt . . . 5D 76
Merritt Av. CH41: Birke . . . 9H 57
Merrivale Rd. L25: Woolt . . . 6G 77
Merrydale Dr. L11: Crox . . . 7A 46
Merscar La. L40: Scar . . . 8B 14
Mersey Av. L19: Aig . . . 8L 75
L31: Mag . . . 1L 35
L37: Form . . . 7E 16
Merseybank Ho. CH62: New F . . . 8A 74
(off New Ferry Rd.)
Merseybank Rd. CH62: New F . . . 8A 74
Mersey Cotts. L19: Garst . . . 2B 92
Mersey Ct. CH44: Wall . . . 7L 57
(off Borough Rd. E.)
L23: Crosb . . . 8J 33
Mersey Dr. M31: Part . . . 5N 69
Mersey Ho. L20: Boot . . . 6A 44
Mersey La. Sth. CH42: Rock F . . . 6N 73
Mersey Multimodal Gateway
WA8: Wid . . . 2J 95
Mersey Rd. CH42: Rock F . . . 6N 73
L17: Aig . . . 9K 75
L23: Blun, Crosb . . . 8J 33
WA7: Run . . . 4J 95
(not continuous)
WA8: Wid . . . 3K 95
Merseyside Maritime Mus. . . . 7D 4 (9B 58)
Merseyside Tramway . . . 1L 73
Merseyside Youth Challenge Trust . . . 7D 76
Mersey St. CH44: Wall . . . 7L 57
WA1: Warr . . . 4C 82
WA9: St H . . . 7C 50
Mersey Ter. CH65: Ell P . . . 7A 104
(off Lwr. Mersey St.)
Merseyton Rd. CH65: Ell P . . . 6N 103
Merseyton Rd. Workshops
CH65: Ell P . . . 7A 104
(off Merseyton Rd.)
Mersey Tunnel - Toll
L3: Liv . . . 1A 4 (6M 57)
(not continuous)
Mersey Valley Golf Course . . . 1B 80
Mersey Vw. CH41: Tran . . . 4L 73
(off Marquis St.)
CH63: Hghr B . . . 1K 89
L22: Water . . . 9J 33
WA7: West P . . . 8G 94
Mersey Vw. Cotts. WA7: West . . . 9J 95
Mersey Vw. Rd. WA8: Hale B . . . 3E 94
Mersey Wlk. CH42: Tran . . . 5L 73
WA4: Westy . . . 3G 83
Mersey Wave . . . 3L 93
Mersham Ct. WA8: Wid . . . 4J 79
Merstone Ct. L26: Halew . . . 9K 77
Merthyr Gro. L16: Child . . . 8C 60
Merton Bank Rd. WA9: St H . . . 5M 49
Merton Cl. CH64: Nest . . . 9E 100
L36: Huy . . . 7F 60
Merton Cres. L36: Huy . . . 7F 60
Merton Dr. CH49: Woodc . . . 5A 72
L36: Huy . . . 7E 60
Merton Gro. L20: Boot . . . 7B 44
L23: Blun . . . 8J 33
Merton Ho. L20: Boot . . . 7B 44
Merton Pl. CH43: Oxton . . . 2J 73
Merton Rd. CH45: Wall . . . 4G 57
CH65: Hoot . . . 3G 103
CH66: Gt Sut . . . 2L 111
L20: Boot . . . 7B 44
Merton St. WA9: St H . . . 5M 49
Merton Towers L20: Boot . . . 7C 44
Mertoun Rd. WA4: Walt . . . 7C 82
Mesham Cl. CH49: Upton . . . 3M 71
Metcalf Cl. L33: Kirkb . . . 5B 36
Meteor Cres. WA2: Warr . . . 6E 66
Methuen St. CH41: Birke . . . 9G 56
L15: Wav . . . 9K 59
Metquarter L1: Liv . . . 5F 4 (8C 58)
Mevagissey Rd. WA7: Brook . . . 1E 108
Mews, The L17: Aig . . . 7L 75
L23: Crosb . . . 8L 33
L28: Stockb V . . . 2G 60
PR8: South . . . 1N 11
WA5: Burtw . . . 3G 64
Mews Ct. CH64: Will . . . 6M 101
Meyrick Cl. WN3: Wins . . . 1E 40
Meyrick Ct. WA12: Newt W . . . 7J 51
Meyrick Rd. L11: Norr G . . . 8K 45
Miami Cl. WA5: Gt San . . . 1K 81
Micawber Cl. L8: Liv . . . 3E 74
Michael Dragonette Ct. L3: Liv . . . 5B 58
Michaels Cl. L37: Form . . . 1E 24
Michael's La. L39: Hals . . . 2B 18
Michigan Cl. L27: N'ley . . . 3J 77
Michigan Pl. WA5: Gt San . . . 1L 81
Mickering La. L39: Augh . . . 6N 27
Micklefield Rd. L15: Wav . . . 2L 75
Micklegate WA7: Murd . . . 8F 96
Micklehead Bus. Village WA9: St H . . . 6K 63
MICKLEHEAD GREEN . . . 6K 63
Micklehead Grn. WA9: St H . . . 6J 63
Mickleton Dr. PR8: Ains . . . 9G 11
Middlefield Rd. L18: Aller . . . 5C 76
Middleham Cl. L32: Kirkb . . . 1A 46
Middlehey Av. L34: Know . . . 6H 47
Middlehurst Av. WA10: St H . . . 6J 49
Middlehurst Cl. L34: Eccl P . . . 2D 62
Middlehurst Rd. WA4: Grap . . . 6H 83
Middle La. M31: Part . . . 7K 69
Middlemass Hey L27: N'ley . . . 3J 77
Middle Meanygate PR4: Tarl . . . 1L 9
Middle Moss La. L37: Gt Alt . . . 1M 25
Middle Rd. L24: Halew . . . 2K 93
(not continuous)
Middlesex Rd. L20: Boot . . . 6C 44
Middleton Ct. L24: Speke . . . 5J 93
Middleton Rd. L7: Liv . . . 7K 59
L22: Water . . . 9M 33
Middle Wlk. WA6: Frod . . . 7L 107
Middle Way L11: Crox . . . 6B 46
Middle Withins La. L38: Gt Alt . . . 5M 25
Middlewood L32: Kirkb . . . 2D 46
WA3: Low . . . 2F 52
WN8: Skel . . . 9D 22
Middlewood Cl. L39: Augh . . . 5A 28
Middlewood Dr. L39: Augh . . . 5A 28
Middlewood Rd. L39: Augh . . . 4A 28
Midge Hall La. PR9: South . . . 2N 13
Midghall St. L3: Liv . . . 2E 4 (6B 58)
Midhurst Dr. PR8: Ains . . . 1H 17
Midhurst Rd. L12: Crox . . . 7D 46
Midland St. CH43: Oxton . . . 3J 73
WA8: Wid . . . 7L 79
Midland Ter. L22: Water . . . 1K 43
Midland Way WA1: Warr . . . 3B 82
WA2: Warr . . . 3B 82
Midlothian Dr. L23: Blun . . . 8J 33
Midway Rd. L36: Huy . . . 5J 61
Midwood St. WA8: Wid . . . 8L 79
Milbrook Cres. L32: Kirkb . . . 8C 36
Milbrook Dr. L32: Kirkb . . . 8C 36
Milbrook Wlk. L32: Kirkb . . . 8C 36
Mildenhall Cl. WA5: Gt San . . . 2K 81
Mildenhall Rd. L25: Gate . . . 2E 76
Mildenhall Way L25: Gate . . . 2F 76
(off Mildenhall Rd.)
Mildmay Rd. L11: Norr G . . . 8K 45
L20: Boot . . . 5A 44
Mile End L5: Liv . . . 5C 58
Miles Cl. CH49: Grea . . . 5K 71
WA3: Birchw . . . 6N 67
Miles La. CH49: Grea . . . 6K 71
WN6: Appl B, Shev . . . 5N 23
(not continuous)
Miles St. L8: Liv . . . 4F 74
Milestone Hey L28: Stockb V . . . 1F 60
Milestone Rd. L32: Kirkb . . . 9A 36
Milford Cl. L37: Form . . . 3C 24
Milford Dr. L12: Crox . . . 7C 46
Milford Gdns. WA4: App . . . 3E 98
Milford St. L5: Kirkd . . . 3B 58
Milk St. WA10: St H . . . 7K 49
Millachip Ct. L6: Liv . . . 5G 58
(off White Rock St.)
Milland Cl. L11: Crox . . . 7A 46
Millar Cres. WA8: Wid . . . 9K 79
Millar's Pace PR9: South . . . 2N 7
Mill Av. WA5: Gt San . . . 1G 80
Mill Bank CH64: Ness . . . 9G 101
L13: Liv . . . 3L 59
Millbank WA13: Lymm . . . 5E 84
WN6: Appl B . . . 6N 23
Millbank Brow L40: Burs . . . 2K 21
Millbank Cotts. L31: Mag . . . 9K 27
WA6: Frod . . . 6K 107
Millbank Ct. L9: Ain . . . 2J 45
WA6: Frod . . . 6K 107
Millbank La. L31: Augh, Mag . . . 9L 27
L39: Augh . . . 9M 27
Mill Bank Rd. CH44: Wall . . . 6G 57
Millbeck Cl. L32: Kirkb . . . 7C 36
Millbeck Gro. WA11: St H . . . 9L 39
Mill Bri. Gdns. WA12: Newt W . . . 7N 51
Millbrook PR8: South . . . 2A 12
Mill Brook Bus. Pk. WA11: Rainf . . . 8F 38
Millbrook Cl. WN8: Skel . . . 2B 30
Millbrook Ct. L34: Know . . . 5G 46
Millbrook La. WA10: Eccl . . . 6E 48
Millbrook Rd. CH41: Birke . . . 7H 57
Mill Brow CH63: Hghr B . . . 1K 89
WA8: Wid . . . 6M 79
WA9: Sut L . . . 4N 63
WA10: Eccl . . . 6E 48
Mill Brow Cl. WA9: Sut L . . . 4N 63
Millbutt Cl. CH63: Hghr B . . . 1K 89
Mill Cl. CH42: Tran . . . 4K 73
L23: Crosb . . . 5L 33
WA2: Fearn . . . 6F 66
Mill Ct. CH65: Ell P . . . 8L 103
L30: N'ton . . . 6C 34
Mill Cft. CH64: Nest . . . 5E 100
Millcroft L23: Crosb . . . 6N 33
Millcroft Av. WN5: Orr . . . 7N 31
Millcroft Pk. CH49: Grea . . . 5J 71
Millcroft Rd. L25: Woolt . . . 7G 77
Milldale Rd. WN7: Leigh . . . 1J 53
Mill Dam Cl. L40: Burs . . . 3H 21
Mill Dam La. L40: Burs, Lath . . . 3G 21
Millennium Bus. Pk. WA3: Birchw . . . 7L 67
Millennium Ct. CH64: Nest . . . 5E 100
Millennium Rd. L8: Liv . . . 2F 74
Millennium Wlk. WA5: Gt San . . . 1K 81
(off Arizona Cres.)
Miller Av. L23: Crosb . . . 6K 33
Miller Cl. WN8: Skel . . . 6F 30
Millers Bri. L20: Boot . . . 8A 44
Millers Bri. Ind. Est. L20: Boot . . . 8A 44
Millers Cl. CH46: More . . . 1J 71
Millers Ct. L39: Orm . . . 8D 20
Millerscroft L32: Kirkb . . . 8A 36
Millersdale WA9: Clock F . . . 5M 63
Millersdale Av. L9: Ain . . . 3G 45
Millersdale Cl. CH62: East . . . 1E 102
Millersdale Gro. WA7: Beech . . . 9N 95
Millersdale Rd. L18: Moss H . . . 4M 75
Millers Fold WA10: Eccl . . . 6E 48
Millers La. WA13: Lymm . . . 3H 85
Millers Nook WN8: Uph . . . 5L 31
Miller St. WA4: Warr . . . 4D 82
Millers Way CH46: More . . . 9K 55
Mill Farm Cl. WA2: Warr . . . 6F 66
Millfield CH64: Nest . . . 5E 100
WN8: Parb . . . 4F 22
Millfield Bus. Pk. WA11: Hay . . . 2G 51
Millfield Cl. CH63: Hghr B . . . 2K 89
L13: W Der . . . 3M 59
Millfield La. WA11: Hay . . . 9G 40
WN4: Ash M . . . 9G 40
Millfield Rd. WA8: Wid . . . 6M 79
Millfields WA10: Eccl . . . 7D 48
Millfield Ter. CH66: Lit Sut . . . 7H 103
Mill Grn. CH64: Will . . . 6M 101
Millgreen Cl. L12: Crox . . . 7C 46
WN8: Uph . . . 5K 31
Mill Grn. La. WA8: Wid . . . 3N 79
Mill Gro. L21: Lith . . . 2A 44
Mill Hey L35: Rainh . . . 8H 63
Mill Hey La. L40: Ruf . . . 3N 15
Mill Hey Rd. CH48: Caldy . . . 1E 86
Mill Hill CH43: Oxton . . . 5G 73
Mill Hill Rd. CH61: Irby . . . 8K 71
Mill Ho. Av. WA4: Stockt H . . . 7E 82
Millhouse Cl. CH46: More . . . 8J 55
Millhouse Ct. L12: W Der . . . 3M 59
Mill Ho. La. WA3: Birchw, Croft . . . 3H 67
Millhouse La. CH46: More . . . 8J 55
Mill Ho. Lodge PR8: Ains . . . 9K 11
Mill Ho. Vw. WN8: Uph . . . 5M 31
Millingford Gro. WN4: Ash M . . . 8K 41
Millingford Ind. Est. WA3: Golb . . . 3B 52
Millington Cl. CH43: Pren . . . 7E 72
WA7: Sut W . . . 2B 108
WA8: Wid . . . 8J 79
Millington Gdns. WA13: Lymm . . . 3J 85
Millington La. WA14: Mill . . . 9N 85
Mill La. CH44: Wall . . . 6G 56
CH49: Grea . . . 5K 71
CH60: Hesw . . . 7B 88
CH64: Ness . . . 9G 101
CH64: Will . . . 5L 101
CH66: Ell P, Gt Sut . . . 1J 111
(not continuous)
L3: Liv . . . 3G 5 (7C 58)
L12: W Der . . . 3M 59
L13: Liv . . . 7M 59
L15: Wav . . . 7M 59
L20: Boot . . . 7C 44
L32: Kirkb . . . 7A 36
L34: Know . . . 5H 47
L35: Rainh . . . 7F 62
L39: Augh . . . 3L 27
L40: Burs . . . 9J 15
(not continuous)
PR9: South . . . 6M 7
WA2: Warr . . . 5F 66
Mill La. WA2: Win . . . 4N 65
WA4: Hghr Wal . . . 9N 81
WA4: Stockt H . . . 7E 82
(not continuous)
WA5: Warr . . . 3N 81
WA6: Frod . . . 4A 108
WA8: Cron . . . 3G 79
WA8: Wid, Bold H . . . 3N 79
WA9: Sut L . . . 4M 63
WA11: Rainf . . . 8E 38
WA12: Newt W . . . 7N 51
WA13: Lymm . . . 2J 85
WN6: Appl B . . . 6M 23
WN8: Dalt, Uph . . . 2J 31
WN8: Parb . . . 4F 22
WN8: Skel . . . 2C 30
(not continuous)
Mill La. Cres. PR9: South . . . 6M 7
Mill La. Ind. Est. CH2: Lit Stan . . . 4D 112
Mill Leat Cl. WN8: Parb . . . 3F 22
Mill Leat M. WN8: Parb . . . 3F 22
Mill Mdw. WA12: Newt W . . . 7N 51
Millom Av. L35: Rainh . . . 5E 62
Millom Gro. L12: W Der . . . 9A 46
WA10: St H . . . 1F 62
Mill Pk. Dr. CH62: East . . . 3D 102
Millport Cl. WA2: Fearn . . . 7H 67
Mill Ri. WA6: Hel . . . 1F 114
Mill Rd. CH61: Thing . . . 1A 88
CH62: Brom . . . 4C 90
CH63: Hghr B . . . 9K 73
L6: Liv . . . 1L 5 (5E 58)
(not continuous)
PR8: Ains . . . 9K 11
WN5: Orr . . . 7N 31
Millrose Cl. WN8: Skel . . . 2C 30
Mill Spring Ct. L20: Boot . . . 7C 44
Mill Sq. L10: Ain . . . 9K 35
Millstead Rd. L15: Wav . . . 9M 59
Millstead Wlk. L15: Wav . . . 9M 59
(off Millstead Rd.)
Mill Stile L25: Woolt . . . 6E 76
Millstone Ct. WA3: Golb . . . 1A 52
Mill Stream Cl. L29: Seft . . . 4E 34
Millstream Way L4: Kirkd . . . 2C 58
Mill St. CH42: Tran . . . 4K 73
CH64: Nest . . . 6D 100
L8: Liv . . . 2D 74
L25: Woolt . . . 6E 76
L34: Presc . . . 3A 62
L39: Orm . . . 9D 20
PR8: South . . . 9H 7
WA3: Golb . . . 2B 52
WA10: St H . . . 6J 49
WN4: Ash M . . . 9L 41
Mill Ter. CH63: Hghr B . . . 2K 89
Millthwaite Ct. CH44: Wall . . . 5F 56
Millthwaite Rd. CH44: Wall . . . 5F 56
Millvale St. L6: Liv . . . 6H 59
Mill Vw. L8: Liv . . . 3D 74
Millview L32: Kirkb . . . 7A 36
Mill Vw. Ct. L39: Bic . . . 5H 29
Mill Vw. Dr. CH63: Hghr B . . . 1J 89
Millway Rd. L24: Speke . . . 3L 93
Mill Weir Gdns. L29: Seft . . . 4E 34
Millwood CH63: Hghr B . . . 1K 89
WA7: Nort . . . 6E 96
Millwood Av. WA10: Eccl . . . 7C 48
Millwood Cl. WN4: Ash M . . . 6J 41
Millwood Ct. L24: Speke . . . 3L 93
Millwood Gdns. L35: Whis . . . 7C 62
Millwood Rd. L24: Speke . . . 4J 93
MILL YARD . . . 5B 60
Mill Yd. CH61: Thing . . . 1B 88
Milman Cl. CH49: Upton . . . 4N 71
L39: Orm . . . 1B 28
Milman Ct. L25: Woolt . . . 5C 76
Milman Rd. L4: Walt . . . 9E 44
Milner Cop CH60: Hesw . . . 7A 88
Milne Rd. L13: Liv . . . 1K 59
Milner Rd. CH60: Hesw . . . 7A 88
L17: Aig . . . 7K 75
Milner St. CH41: Birke . . . 9G 56
WA5: Warr . . . 3A 82
Milnes Av. WN7: Leigh . . . 1N 53
Milnthorpe Cl. L4: Kirkd . . . 1D 58
Milnthorpe Rd. WA5: Burtw . . . 3G 65
Milnthorpe St. L19: Garst . . . 1A 92
Milroy Way L7: Liv . . . 8G 59
Milton Av. L14: Broad G . . . 7C 60
L35: Whis . . . 6B 62
M44: Irlam . . . 3L 69
WA8: Wid . . . 8J 79
WA12: Newt W . . . 7K 51
Milton Cl. CH65: Ell P . . . 1B 112
L35: Whis . . . 6B 62
Milton Cres. CH60: Hesw . . . 6A 88
Milton Dr. L39: Orm . . . 9E 20
Milton Grn. CH61: Thing . . . 1B 88
Milton Gro. WA4: Warr . . . 5E 82
WA6: Hel . . . 4D 114
WN5: Bil . . . 2N 39
Milton Pavement CH41: Birke . . . 2K 73
Milton Rd. CH42: Tran . . . 4J 73
CH44: Wall . . . 7K 57
CH48: W Kir . . . 5B 70
CH65: Ell P . . . 1B 112
L4: Walt . . . 8D 44
L7: Liv . . . 7K 59
L22: Water . . . 9L 33

Milton Rd. WA3: Low 3E 52
WA8: Wid 8J 79
Milton Rd. E. CH42: Tran 4K 73
Milton St. L20: Boot 6A 44
PR9: South 8L 7
WA8: Wid 2K 95
WA9: Sut M 7K 63
Milton Ter. CH65: Ell P 1B 112
Milton Way L31: Mag 2G 35
Milvain Dr. WA2: Warr 8D 66
Milverny Way WA9: St H 9K 49
Milverton St. L6: Liv 5H 59
Mimosa Cl. CH2: Elt 1N 113
Mimosa Rd. L15: Wav 1N 75
Mindale Rd. L15: Wav 9L 59
Minehead Gro. WA9: Sut L 4N 63
Minehead Rd. L17: Aig 7K 75
Miners Way L24: Speke 4L 93
WA8: Wid 9K 79
Minerva Cl. WA4: Warr 6E 82
Mines Av. L17: Aig 9L 75
L34: Presc 3B 62
Mine Way WA11: Hay 3H 51
Minnesota Dr. WA5: Gt San 2J 81
Minstead Av. L33: Kirkb 9D 36
Minster Ct. L7: Liv 7M 5 (9F 58)
WA7: Run 7H 95
Mint Casino
Stockport 7H 7
Minto Cl. L7: Liv 7H 59
Minton Cl. L12: Crox 7D 46
Minton Way WA8: Wid 3L 79
Mintor Rd. L33: Kirkb 9E 36
Minver Rd. L12: W Der 2B 60
Miranda Av. CH63: Hghr B 9L 73
Miranda Pl. L20: Kirkd 9C 44
Miranda Rd. L20: Boot 9C 44
Miranda Rd. Sth. L20: Kirkd 9C 44
Mirfield Cl. L26: Halew 1K 93
WA3: Low 3E 52
Mirfield St. L6: Liv 6G 59
Miriam Pl. CH41: Birke 9F 56
Miriam Rd. L4: Walt 3F 58
Miry La. WN8: Parb 3G 22
Miskelly St. L20: Kirkd 1B 58
Missouri Dr. WA5: Gt San 1J 81
Missouri Rd. L13: Liv 2J 59
Mistle Thrush Way L12: Crox 7D 46
Miston St. L20: Kirkd 1B 58
Misty Cl. WA8: Wid 6F 78
Mitchell Av. WA5: Burtw 4G 64
Mitchell Ct. CH41: Birke 3K 73
Mitchell Cres. L21: Lith 2A 44
Mitchell Pl. L1: Liv 5H 5 (8C 58)
Mitchell Rd. L34: Presc 3N 61
WA10: St H 9F 48
WN5: Bil 6A 40
Mitchell St. WA3: Golb 3B 52
WA4: Stockt H 8D 82
WN4: Ash M 9L 41
Mithril Cl. WA8: Wid 5A 80
Mitre Cl. L35: Whis 8A 62
Mittens La. L37: Form 9H 17
Mitton Cl. WA3: Cul 5M 53
Mitylene St. L5: Liv 3D 58
Moat La. WA3: Rix 7E 68
Mobberley Cl. WA4: Thel 5L 83
Mobberley Ct. CH63: Spit 4N 89
Mobberley Way CH63: Spit 4N 89
Mockbeggar Dr. CH45: Wall 2D 56
Mockbeggar Wharf CH45: Wall 2E 56
Modred St. L8: Liv 3E 74
Moel Famau Vw. L17: Aig 6G 75
Moelwyn Dr. CH66: Ell P 7L 103
Moffatdale Rd. L4: Walt 1H 59
Moffatt Rd. L9: Ain 3H 45
Moira Sephton Ct. CH43: Noct 4D 72
(off Sandalwood Dr.)
Moira St. L6: Liv 3L 5 (7E 58)
Molesworth Gro. L16: Child 8D 60
Molineux Av. L14: Broad G 8B 60
Molland Cl. L12: W Der 1B 60
Mollington Av. L11: Norr G 8L 45
Mollington Link CH41: Birke 3L 73
Mollington Rd. CH44: Wall 6J 57
L32: Kirkb 9A 36
Mollington St. CH41: Birke 3L 73
Molly's La. L33: Kirkb 3H 47
Molton Rd. L16: Child 9A 60
Molyneux Av. WA5: Warr 9A 66
Molyneux Cl. CH49: Upton 3N 71
L35: Presc 5A 62
L36: Huy 7K 61
Molyneux Ct. L11: Norr G 7N 45
L14: Broad G 8B 60
(off Molineux Av.)
Molyneux Dr. CH45: New B 1H 57
L35: Presc 5A 62
Molyneux Rd. L6: Liv 6G 58
L18: Moss H 4L 75
L22: Water 9L 33
L31: Mag 4L 35
L39: Augh 5A 28
Molyneux Way L10: Ain 8H 35
Monaghan Cl. L9: Walt 3F 44
Monarch Cl. M44: Irlam 3L 69
Monarchs Quay L3: Liv 9D 4 (1B 74)
Monash Cl. L33: Kirkb 5C 36
Monash Rd. L11: Norr G 1L 59
Monastery La. WA9: St H 2N 63
Monastery Rd. L6: Liv 3H 59
WA9: St H 2A 64
Mona St. CH41: Birke 1F 72
L20: Boot 4C 44
WA10: St H 8G 48
Mona Way M44: Irlam 1N 69
Mond Rd. L10: Faz 3M 45
WA8: Wid 8K 79
Monfa Rd. L20: Boot 4B 44
Monica Dr. WA8: Wid 3K 79
Monica Rd. L25: Woolt 7F 76
Monica Ter. WN4: Ash M 9K 41
Moniven Cl. WA4: Westy 4J 83
Monkfield Way L19: Garst 3B 92
Monk Rd. CH44: Wall 5H 57
Monks Carr La. L38: Gt Alt 6N 25
Monks Cl. L37: Form 3G 25
Monksdown Rd. L11: Norr G 9M 45
Monks Dr. L37: Form 3G 25
Monks Ferry CH41: Birke 2M 73
Monksferry Wlk. L19: Gras 9L 75
Monks Gro. CH65: Ell P 8N 103
Monk's La. L40: Burs 8H 15
Monks Pl. WA2: Warr 1D 82
Monks St. WA5: Warr 2N 81
Monk St. *CH41: Birke 2M 73*
(off Cross St.)
L5: Liv 3E 58
Monks Way CH48: W Kir 6C 70
CH63: Beb 3M 89
L25: Woolt 6F 76
WA7: Pres B 1G 108
Monkswell Dr. L15: Wav 9M 59
Monkswell St. L8: Liv 5F 74
Monkswood Cl. WA5: Call 7N 65
Monmouth Cl. WA1: Wools 1M 83
Monmouth Cres. WN4: Ash M 9L 41
Monmouth Dr. L10: Ain 1L 45
Monmouth Gro. WA9: St H 8N 49
Monmouth Rd. CH44: Wall 5F 56
Monro Cl. L8: Liv 4E 74
Monroe Cl. WA1: Wools 1J 83
Monro St. L8: Liv 4E 74
Mons Sq. *L20: Boot 7B 44*
(off Strand Shop. Cen.)
Montague Rd. L13: Liv 7M 59
WA8: Wid 1D 94
Montagu M. L37: Form 8E 16
Montagu Rd. L37: Form 7E 16
Montana Cl. WA5: Gt San 1L 81
Montclair Dr. L18: Moss H 2N 75
Montclare Cres. WA4: Stockt H 7F 82
Montcliffe Cl. WA3: Birchw 4K 67
Monterey Cl. WA5: Gt San 2K 81
Monterey Rd. L13: Liv 7N 59
Montfort Dr. L19: Gras 9M 75
Montgomery Av. PR9: South 9M 7
Montgomery Cl. L35: Whis 7A 62
WA5: Gt San 9J 65
Montgomery Hill CH48: Caldy, Frank 8G 71
Montgomery Rd. L9: Walt 4F 44
L36: Huy 5H 61
WA8: Wid 8G 78
Montgomery Way L6: Liv 5G 59
Montpelier Av. WA7: West 9J 95
Montpelier Dr. L8: Liv 4E 74
Montpellier Ct. *CH45: New B 1G 56*
(off Montpellier Cres.)
Montpellier Cres. CH45: New B 1G 56
Montpellier Ho. CH45: New B 1G 56
Montreal Rd. L27: N'ley 3J 77
Montrey Cres. WN4: Garsw 8E 40
Montrose Av. CH44: Wall 8L 57
Montrose Bus. Pk. *L7: Liv 7K 59*
(off Tattersall Way)
Montrose Cl. WA2: Fearn 5G 66
Montrose Ct. CH47: Hoy 2C 70
L12: W Der 2D 60
Montrose Dr. PR9: South 6L 7
Montrose Pl. L26: Halew 1K 93
Montrose Rd. L13: Liv 3J 59
Montrose Way L13: Liv 7L 59
Montrovia Cres. L10: Faz 3L 45
Monument Pl. L3: Liv 4K 5 (7E 58)
Monville Rd. L9: Ain 3H 45
Moorbridge Cl. L30: N'ton 7F 34
Moor Cl. L23: Crosb 6M 33
PR8: Ains 3J 17
Moor Coppice L23: Crosb 6M 33
Moor Ct. L10: Faz 3M 45
Moorcroft Rd. CH45: Wall 4D 56
L18: Aller 7A 76
Moorditch La. WA6: Frod 5J 107
Moor Dr. L23: Crosb 6L 33
WN8: Skel 5G 31
MOORE 2K 97
Moore Av. CH42: Rock F 6L 73
WA4: Thel 5L 83
WA9: St H 7D 50
Moore Cl. WA8: Wid 6N 79
Moore Dr. WA11: Hay 3H 51
Moore Gro. WA13: Lymm 3H 85
Moore La. WA4: Moore 9K 81
Moore Nature Reserve 8K 81
Moore's Ho. L4: Walt 8E 44
Moore St. L20: Boot 5A 44
Mooreway L35: Rainh 8H 63
Moorfield L33: Kirkb 6D 36
Moorfield Cen. L33: Kirkb 6D 36
Moorfield Cres. WA3: Low 3H 53
Moorfield Dr. CH64: Park 4C 100
Moorfield La. L40: Scar 2N 19
Moorfield Rd. L23: Crosb 6N 33
WA8: Wid 4N 79
WA10: St H 5F 48
Moorfields L2: Liv 4E 4 (7B 58)
Moorfields Av. CH43: Noct 4D 72
Moorfields Station (Rail) 4E 4 (7B 58)
Moorfoot Rd. WA9: St H 7B 50
Moorfoot Rd. Ind. Est. WA9: St H 6B 50
Moorfoot Way L33: Kirkb 5B 36
Moorgate L39: Orm 9C 20
Moorgate Av. L23: Crosb 8M 33
Moorgate La. L32: Kirkb 2E 46
Moorgate Point L33: Know I 3E 46
Moorgate Rd. L33: Kirkb 4D 46
Moorgate Rd. Sth. L34: Know 4D 46
Moorgate St. L7: Liv 8G 59
Moorhead Cl. L21: Lith 3N 43
Moorhey Rd. L31: Mag 4J 35
Moor Ho. L23: Crosb 6L 33
Moorhouses L38: Hight 9F 24
Mooring Cl. WA7: Murd 9F 96
Moorings, The CH41: Birke 3K 73
CH60: Hesw 7K 87
L31: Lyd 8G 27
Moorings Cl. CH64: Park 5B 100
Moorland Av. L23: Crosb 6L 33
Moorland Cl. CH60: Hesw 8A 88
Moorland Dr. WA7: Murd 8G 96
Moorland Pk. CH60: Hesw 8A 88
Moorland Rd. CH42: Tran 5L 73
CH66: Ell P 6K 103
L31: Mag 1B 35
WN4: Ash M 7N 41
Moorlands Rd. L23: Thorn 5A 34
Moor La. CH60: Hesw 7N 87
L4: Walt 7F 44
L10: Faz 3M 45
L23: Crosb 6L 33
L23: Crosb, Thorn 6L 33
L29: Seft 3C 34
L32: Kirkb 2N 45
L38: Ince B 8K 25
PR8: Ains 3J 17
WA6: Frod 6L 107
WA6: Hap 3B 114
WA8: Wid 9J 79
(not continuous)
Moor La. Bus. Cen. WA8: Wid 9K 79
Moor La. Sth. WA8: Wid 9J 79
MOOR PARK 5L 33
Moor Pl. L3: Liv 4J 5 (7D 58)
Moor Rd. WN5: Orr 7N 31
MOORSIDE 7C 100
Moorside WA4: Westy 4F 82
Moorside Av. CH64: Park 6C 100
Moorside Cl. L23: Crosb 7M 33
Moorside Ct. WA8: Wid 9J 79
Moorside La. CH64: Park 7C 100
Moorside Rd. L23: Crosb 7M 33
Moor St. L2: Liv 5D 4 (8B 58)
L39: Orm 8C 20
(not continuous)
Moorway CH60: Hesw 7B 88
Moorwood Cres. WA9: Clock F 5M 63
Moran Dr. WA5: Gt San 2J 81
Moray Cl. WA10: St H 5H 49
Morcott La. L24: Hale 5A 94
Morcroft Rd. L36: Huy 4J 61
Morden Av. WN4: Ash M 7J 41
Morden St. L6: Liv 6H 59
Morecambe St. L6: Liv 4H 59
Morecroft Rd. CH42: Rock F 7N 73
Moreland Dr. PR8: South 1C 12
Morella Rd. L4: Walt 1H 59
Morello Cl. WA10: St H 5J 49
Morello Dr. CH63: Spit 5A 90
Moresby Cl. WA7: Murd 8G 96
Moret Cl. L23: Crosb 6N 33
MORETON 9M 55
Moreton Av. WA9: Clock F 5M 63
Moreton Cl. WA3: Golb 1A 52
WN3: Wins 1E 40
MORETON COMMON 5L 55
Moreton Dr. WN7: Leigh 1M 53
Moreton Gro. CH45: Wall 3E 56
Moreton Hills Golf Cen. 7L 55
Moreton Rd. CH49: Upton 1N 71
Moreton Station (Rail) 7M 55
Moreton Ter. WA6: Frod 6K 107
Morgan Av. WA2: Warr 7D 66
Morgan M. L30: N'ton 8C 34
Morgan St. WA9: St H 8N 49
Morgans Way WA3: Low 2H 53
Morland Av. CH62: Brom 9C 90
CH64: Lit N 7F 100
Morley Av. CH41: Birke 9H 57
Morley Ct. L14: Knott A 5C 60
Morley La. CH3: Lit Ba 9N 113
WA6: Lit Ba 9N 113
Morley Rd. CH44: Wall 6G 56
PR9: South 6K 7
WA4: Warr 7B 82
WA7: Run 6K 95
Morley St. L4: Walt 2D 58
WA1: Warr 2D 82
WA10: St H 5J 49
(not continuous)
Morley Way WA10: St H 6J 49
Morningside L23: Crosb 8M 33
Morningside Pl. L11: Norr G 9L 45
Morningside Rd. L11: Norr G 9L 45
Morningside Vw. L11: Norr G 1L 59
Morningside Way L11: Norr G 1L 59
Mornington Av. CH65: Ell P 9A 104
L23: Crosb 9L 33
Mornington Rd. CH45: New B 3H 57
PR9: South 8H 7
Mornington St. L8: Liv 3D 74
Morpeth Cl. CH46: More 9J 55
Morpeth Rd. CH47: Hoy 3B 70
Morpeth St. L8: Liv 9K 5 (1E 74)
Morpeth Walkway CH41: Birke 9L 57
Morpeth Wharf CH41: Birke 9L 57
Morphany La. WA4: Dares 9N 97
Morris Av. WA4: Westy 4G 83
Morris Cl. WA11: Hay 5C 50
Morris Ct. CH43: Oxton 3F 72
Morris La. L39: Hals 2J 19
Morrison Cl. WA5: Gt San 3J 81
Morrison M. WA8: Wid 6G 79
Morris Rd. WN8: Uph 5K 31
Morrissey Cl. WA10: St H 6G 48
Morris St. WA9: St H 9A 50
Morston Av. L32: Kirkb 2C 46
Morston Cres. L32: Kirkb 2C 46
Morston Wlk. L32: Kirkb 2C 46
Mortar Mill Quay CH41: Birke 8K 57
Mort Av. WA4: Westy 4H 83
Mortimer Av. WA2: Warr 9C 66
Mortimer St. CH41: Birke 2M 73
Mortlake Cl. WA8: Wid 5F 78
Morton Av. WA6: Hel 4E 114
Morton Cl. WA5: Old H 9L 65
Morton Ho. L18: Moss H 5L 75
Morton Rd. WA7: Nort 7F 96
Morton St. L8: Liv 3E 74
(not continuous)
Mortuary Rd. CH45: Wall 3H 57
Morvah Cl. L12: W Der 8A 46
Morval Cres. L4: Walt 8D 44
WA7: Run 6N 95
Morven Cl. WA2: Warr 6F 66
Morven Gro. PR8: South 8K 7
Moschatel Wlk. M31: Part 6M 69
Moscow Dr. L13: Liv 4L 59
Mosedale Av. WA11: St H 1L 49
Mosedale Gro. WA7: Beech 1A 108
Mosedale Rd. CH62: Brom 5D 90
L9: Walt 5F 44
Moseley Av. CH45: Wall 5G 57
WA4: Westy 4H 83
Moseley Rd. CH63: Spit 6N 89
Moses St. L8: Liv 4E 74
Mosley St. PR8: South 2A 12
Moss Av. WN5: Bil 9N 31
MOSS BANK
WA8 9N 79
WA11 2K 49
Moss Bank L39: Augh 2B 28
Moss Bank Ct. L39: Augh 2B 28
Moss Bank Pk. L21: Lith 2N 43
Moss Bank Rd. WA8: Wid 9N 79
WA11: St H 2J 49
Mossborough Hall La. WA11: Rainf 9M 37
Mossborough Rd. WA11: Rainf 9A 38
Moss Bri. L40: Lath 2A 22
Moss Bri. La. L40: Lath 3N 21
MOSSBROW 1K 85
Moss Brow WA11: Rainf 4C 38
Mossbrow Rd. L36: Huy 5J 61
Moss Cl. CH64: Will 6N 101
WA4: Stockt H 6F 82
Mosscraig L28: Stockb V 2G 60
Mosscroft Cl. L36: Huy 5L 61
Mossdale Cl. WA5: Gt San 1J 81
Mossdale Dr. L35: Rainh 6G 62
Mossdale Rd. L33: Kirkb 6D 36
WN4: Ash M 3J 41
Moss Delph La. L39: Augh 2N 27
Mossdene Rd. CH44: Wall 5F 56
Moss Dr. WA6: Manl 9J 115
Moss End Way L33: Know I 8H 37
Mossfield Rd. L9: Walt 4E 44
Moss Gdns. PR8: South 4B 12
Moss Ga. WA3: Birchw 3A 68
Moss Ga. Gro. L14: Knott A 6E 60
Moss Ga. Rd. L14: Knott A 6E 60
Mossgiel Av. PR8: Ains 1H 17
Moss Grn. L37: Form 1G 25
Moss Grn. Cl. L36: Huy 5F 60
Moss Grn. Way WA9: St H 9C 50
Moss Gro. CH42: Tran 6H 73
L8: Liv 2H 75
WA13: Lymm 4H 85
Moss Hall La. WA4: Lwr S 6G 98
Mosshey Ct. CH63: Spit 4N 89
Moss Hey La. PR4: Mere B 4L 9
Mosshill Cl. L31: Mag 9H 27
Moss Ind. Est. WN7: Leigh 1J 53
Mosslake Way L4: Kirkd 2C 58
Mosslands WA10: Eccl 6D 48
Mosslands Cl. CH66: Gt Sut 3K 111
Mosslands Dr. CH44: Wall 4E 56
CH45: Wall 4E 56
Moss La. CH42: Tran 6H 73
L9: Walt 4E 44
L20: Boot 4D 44
L21: Lith 2A 44

Moss La. L23: Lit C .9J **25**
L31: Lyd .7G **27**
L31: Mag .1K **35**
(not continuous)
L33: Kirkb .8F **36**
L33: Sim .3D **36**
L38: Hight .7G **25**
L39: Bic .1K **37**
L39: Down .8M **17**
L40: Burs .8K **15**
M31: Part, Warb .6M **69**
M44: Cad .4K **69**
PR9: Banks .1G **8**
PR9: South .7M **7**
WA1: Wools .9M **67**
WA3: Low .5C **52**
WA3: Rix .4E **68**
WA4: Moore .9J **81**
WA6: Manl .9J **115**
WA9: St H .8C **50**
WA11: Crank .6H **39**
WA11: Windle .3C **48**
WA13: Warb .8L **69**
WA16: High L .9L **85**
WN6: Wright .1M **23**
WN8: Skel .6C **30**
Moss La. Vw. WN8: Skel .6C **30**
Mosslawn Rd. L32: Kirkb .1E **46**
Mosslea Pk. L18: Moss H .4L **75**
Mossley Av. CH62: Brom .7C **90**
L18: Moss H .3L **75**
Mossley Ct. L18: Moss H .5M **75**
MOSSLEY HILL .5L **75**
Mossley Hill Dr. L17: Aig .3J **75**
(not continuous)
Mossley Hill Rd. L18: Moss H .6L **75**
L19: Aig .6L **75**
Mossley Hill Station (Rail) .5M **75**
Mossley Rd. CH42: Tran .5L **73**
MOSS NOOK .9B **50**
Moss Nook L39: Augh .2N **27**
L40: Burs .8J **15**
Moss Nook La. L31: Mag, Mell .3M **35**
WA11: Rainf .5B **38**
(not continuous)
Mossock Hall Golf Course .8C **28**
Moss Pits Cl. L10: Faz .3L **45**
Moss Pits La. L10: Faz .3K **45**
L15: Wav .2N **75**
Moss Rd. M44: Cad .1J **69**
PR8: South .4A **12**
WA4: Westy .5H **83**
WN5: Bil .9N **31**
MOSS SIDE
L31 .1K **35**
WA4 .9H **81**
Moss Side L14: Knott A .6E **60**
L37: Form .9H **17**
Moss Side La. CW9: Ant .8K **99**
PR4: Mere B .3J **9**
WA3: Rix .6E **68**
WA4: Moore .9G **81**
Moss Side Rd. M44: Cad .3K **69**
Moss St. L6: Liv .3L **5** (7E **58**)
L19: Garst .1A **92**
L34: Presc .2A **62**
WA8: Wid .9N **79**
Mossvale CH66: Lit Sut .6J **103**
Moss Vw. L21: Lith .2B **44**
L31: Mag .2L **35**
L39: Orm .9D **20**
Moss Vw. Rd. M31: Part .6N **69**
Mossville Cl. L18: Moss H .6M **75**
Mossville Rd. L18: Moss H .6N **75**
Moss Way L11: Crox .5A **46**
Mossy Bank Rd. CH44: Wall .5K **57**
Moston Gro. WA13: Lymm .5D **84**
Moston Way CH66: Gt Sut .2L **111**
Mostyn Av. CH48: W Kir .7C **70**
CH60: Hesw .7K **87**
L10: Ain .8H **35**
L19: Aller .8B **76**
Mostyn Cl. L4: Kirkd .2D **58**
Mostyn Gdns. CH64: Park .5B **100**
Mostyn Sq. CH64: Park .5B **100**
Mostyn St. CH44: Wall .6H **57**
Mote Hill Ct. WA1: Warr .2E **82**
Motherwell Cl. WA8: Wid .5H **79**
Motherwell Cres. PR8: South .3E **12**
Mottershead Cl. WA8: Wid .8K **79**
Mottershead Rd. WA8: Wid .8K **79**
Mottram Cl. L33: Kirkb .9D **36**
WA4: Grap .5J **83**
Moughland La. WA7: Run .6J **95**
Moulders La. WA1: Warr .4C **82**
Mould St. L5: Liv .3C **58**
MOULDSWORTH .9K **115**
Moulton Cl. WA7: Sut W .2B **108**
Mounsey Rd. CH42: Tran .3K **73**
Mount, The CH44: Wall .5J **57**
CH60: Hesw .7N **87**
WN8: Skel .4E **30**
Mountain Vw. WA6: Hel .2E **114**
Mount Av. CH60: Hesw .7N **87**
CH63: Hghr B .9K **73**
L20: Boot .3C **44**
Mount Cl. L32: Kirkb .7A **36**
Mount Ct. CH45: Wall .1G **56**
CH60: Hesw .7N **87**
Mount Cres. L32: Kirkb .7A **36**
Mount Dr. CH63: Hghr B .9K **73**
Mt. Farm Way CH66: Gt Sut .3H **111**
Mount Gro. CH41: Birke .3J **73**
Mount Gro. Pl. *CH41: Birke* .*3J* ***73***
(off Mount Gro.)
Mt. Haven Cl. CH49: Upton .3A **72**
Mount Ho. Cl. L37: Form .8H **17**
Mount Ho. Rd. L37: Form .8H **17**
Mount Olive CH43: Oxton .5G **73**
Mount Pk. CH63: Hghr B .9K **73**
L25: Woolt .5E **76**
Mount Pk. Ct. L25: Woolt .5E **76**
Mt. Pleasant CH2: Elt .1L **113**
CH43: Oxton .5H **73**
L3: Liv .6H **5** (8D **58**)
L22: Water .1K **43**
WA8: Wid .6L **79**
Mt. Pleasant Av. WA9: St H .7C **50**
Mt. Pleasant Cl. CH45: New B .2H **57**
Mt. Pleasant Rd.
CH45: New B, Wall .3G **56**
Mount Rd. CH42: Tran .7J **73**
CH45: Wall .1G **56**
CH48: W Kir .7D **70**
CH49: Upton .3A **72**
CH63: Hghr B, Spit .5L **89**
L32: Kirkb .8N **35**
(not continuous)
WA7: Halt .7B **96**
Mount St. L1: Liv .8J **5** (9D **58**)
L22: Water .1K **43**
L25: Woolt .6E **76**
PR9: South .8J **7**
WA8: Wid .6L **79**
Mount Ter. PR9: South .8J **7**
Mount Vernon L7: Liv .5N **5** (8F **58**)
Mt. Vernon Grn. L7: Liv .4N **5** (7F **58**)
Mt. Vernon Rd. L7: Liv .4M **5** (7F **58**)
Mt. Vernon St. L7: Liv .4M **5** (7F **58**)
Mountview Cl. L8: Liv .3F **74**
Mount Way CH63: Hghr B .9K **73**
Mountwood WN8: Skel .9D **22**
Mountwood Lodge
PR8: Ains .9J **11**
Mountwood Rd. CH42: Tran .8J **73**
Mourne Cl. CH66: Lit Sut .8F **102**
Mowbray Av. WA11: St H .5M **49**
Mowbray Ct. L20: Kirkd .9B **44**
Mowbray Gro. L13: Liv .8M **59**
Mowcroft La. WA5: Cuerd .5C **80**
Mowpen Brow WA16: High L .9H **85**
Moxon Av. WA4: Westy .3G **83**
Moxon St. WA10: St H .8F **48**
Moxon Way WN4: Ash M .7M **41**
Moyles Cl. WA8: Wid .6G **79**
Mozart Cl. L8: Liv .2G **74**
Mr Hardman's Photographic Studio
.8J **5** (9D **58**)
Mudhouse La. CH64: Burt .2A **110**
Muirfield Cl. L12: W Der .3C **60**
WA2: Fearn .6H **67**
Muirfield Dr. PR8: Ains .1J **17**
Muirfield Rd. L36: Roby .8G **61**
Muirhead Av. L6: Liv .5H **59**
L13: Liv, W Der .3K **59**
Muirhead Av. E. L11: Norr G .1M **59**
Muir Rd. L9: Ain .4J **45**
Mulberry Av. WA3: Low .3G **52**
WA8: Wid .9M **79**
WA10: St H .7F **48**
Mulberry Cl. CH2: Elt .2N **113**
CH42: Rock F .6M **73**
L33: Kirkb .5D **36**
L39: Orm .9E **20**
WA1: Wools .2M **83**
Mulberry Ct. L7: Liv .7L **5**
WA4: Stockt H .7E **82**
Mulberry Gro. CH44: Wall .6K **57**
Mulberry Pl. L7: Liv .7L **5** (9E **58**)
Mulberry Rd. CH42: Rock F .6M **73**
Mulberry St. L7: Liv .7L **5** (9E **58**)
Mulcrow Cl. WA9: St H .6N **49**
Mulgrave St. L8: Liv .9M **5** (1F **74**)
Mull Cl. CH65: Ell P .4A **112**
Mullein Cl. WA3: Low .2E **52**
Mullen Cl. WA5: Warr .8A **66**
Mulliner St. L7: Liv .1H **75**
Mullins Av. WA12: Newt W .5L **51**
Mullion Cl. L26: Halew .8J **77**
PR9: South .2N **7**
WA7: Brook .9D **96**
Mullion Gro. WA2: Padg .8H **67**
Mullion Rd. L11: Crox .5A **46**
Mullion Wlk. L11: Crox .5A **46**
Mullrea Cl. L27: N'ley .2G **77**
Mullwood Cl. L12: Crox .7D **46**
Mulrankin Ct. L13: Liv .7N **59**
Mulveton Rd. CH63: Spit .4M **89**
Mumfords Gro. CH47: Meols .8F **54**
Mumfords La. CH47: Meols .8E **54**
(not continuous)
Muncaster Cl. CH62: Brom .6C **90**
Muncaster Ct. WA7: Cas .5B **96**
Muncaster Dr. WA11: Rainf .4D **38**
Munster Rd. L13: Liv .6N **59**
Murat Gro. L22: Water .1J **43**
Murat St. L22: Water .1J **43**
Murcote Rd. L14: Knott A .4D **60**
MURDISHAW .9F **96**
Murdishaw Av. WA7: Brook, Murd .1E **108**
Murdock Way L10: Faz .4N **45**
Muriel Cl. WA5: Gt San .2F **80**
Muriel St. L4: Walt .1F **58**
Murphy Gro. WA9: St H .6A **50**
Murrayfield Dr. CH46: Leas .5N **55**
Murrayfield Rd. L25: Gate .2F **76**
Murrayfield Wlk. *L25: Gate* .*1F* ***76***
(off Murrayfield Rd.)
Murray Gro. CH48: W Kir .5B **70**
Museum of Liverpool .6C **4** (8A **58**)
Museum St. WA1: Warr .4B **82**
Musker Dr. L30: N'ton .8B **34**
Musker Gdns. L23: Crosb .8M **33**
Musker St. L23: Crosb .8M **33**
Muspratt Rd. L21: Sea .5N **43**
Mustard La. WA3: Croft .1H **67**
Muttocks Rake *L30: N'ton* .*6C* ***34***
(off Great Hey)
Mycroft Cl. L5: Liv .3E **58**
Myddleton La. WA2: Win .3C **66**
Myers Av. L35: Whis .4D **62**
Myerscough Av. L20: Boot .5D **44**
Myers Ct. L23: Crosb .9M **33**
Myers Rd. E. L23: Crosb .8L **33**
Myers Rd. W. L23: Crosb .8K **33**
Mylia Cl. L14: Knott A .6E **60**
Mynsule Rd. CH63: Spit .4M **89**
Myrtle Av. WA11: Hay .3D **50**
WN4: Ash M .5H **41**
Myrtle Ct. L7: Liv .9F **58**
L8: Liv .8N **5** (9F **58**)
Myrtle Gro. CH44: Wall .6L **57**
L22: Water .9K **33**
PR8: South .9K **7**
WA4: Warr .5E **82**
WA8: Wid .8G **78**
WN5: Bil .7N **39**
Myrtle Pde. L7: Liv .8L **5** (9E **58**)
Myrtle Rd. M31: Part .6K **69**
Myrtle St. CH65: Ell P .7A **104**
L7: Liv .7K **5** (9E **58**)
Myrtle Way CH49: Woodc .4B **72**
Mystery Cl. L15: Wav .1K **75**
Mystic M. *L39: Orm* .*8C* ***20***
(off Burscough St.)
Mytholme Av. M44: Cad .6J **69**

N

Naburn Gro. CH46: More .1M **71**
Nairn Av. WN8: Skel .8E **22**
Nairn Cl. CH63: East .2C **102**
WA2: Fearn .6J **67**
Nansen Cl. WA5: Old H .1M **81**
Nansen Gro. L4: Walt .9F **44**
Nant Pk. Ct. CH45: New B .1J **57**
Nantwich Cl. CH49: Woodc .6A **72**
Nantwich Rd. CH66: Gt Sut .2L **111**
Napier Cl. WA10: St H .7H **49**
Napier Dr. CH46: More .9N **55**
Napier Rd. CH62: New F .8A **74**
Napier St. L20: Boot .9A **44**
WA1: Warr .3D **82**
(not continuous)
WA10: St H .7H **49**
Napier Ter. PR8: Birkd .1N **11**
Naples Rd. CH44: Wall .6K **57**
Napps Cl. L25: Gate .1D **76**
Napps Wlk. *L25: Gate* .*1D* ***76***
(off Napps Cl.)
Napps Way CH61: Hesw .5A **88**
L25: Gate .9D **60**
Nares Cl. WA5: Old H .8L **65**
Narrow Cft. Rd. L39: Augh .3N **27**
Narrow La. L39: Augh .3N **27**
L39: Hals .6K **19**
WA4: Grap .7J **83**
NARROW MOSS .4C **20**
Narrow Moss La. L40: Scar .3B **20**
Naseby Cl. CH43: Noct .4C **72**
Naseby St. L4: Walt .8E **44**
Nashville Dr. WA5: Gt San .1K **81**
Natal Rd. L9: Ain .4G **45**
Nathan Dr. WA11: Hay .4G **51**
Nathan Gro. L33: Kirkb .7D **36**
National Waterways Mus. .7B **104**
National Wildflower Cen. .8D **60**
Naughton Lea WA8: Wid .5G **78**
Naughton Rd. WA8: Wid .8K **79**
Navenby Rd. WN3: Wigan .1J **41**
Navigation Cl. L30: N'ton .7F **34**
WA7: Murd .9F **96**
Navigation Rd. WA9: St H .6M **49**
Navigation St. WA1: Warr .3E **82**
Navigation Wharf L3: Liv .2C **74**
Naylor Av. WA3: Golb .2C **52**
Naylor Cl. CH66: Ell P .6L **103**
Naylor Ct. CH66: Ell P .8K **103**
Naylor Cres. CH66: Ell P .6L **103**
Naylor Grn. CH66: Ell P .6L **103**
Naylor Pl. CH66: Ell P .6L **103**
Naylor Rd. CH43: Bid .9E **56**
CH66: Ell P .7L **103**
WA8: Wid .7N **79**
Naylorsfield Dr. L27: N'ley .2G **76**
Naylor's Rd. L25: Gate .3H **77**
L27: N'ley .2H **77**
Naylor St. L3: Liv .2E **4** (6B **58**)
WA1: Warr .3C **82**
Naylor Wlk. CH66: Ell P .7L **103**
Nazareth Ho. La. WA8: Wid .9F **78**
Nazeby Av. L23: Crosb .8N **33**
Neale Dr. CH49: Grea .5M **71**
Neales Fold PR9: South .2B **8**
Neasham Cl. L26: Halew .8K **77**
Nedens Gro. L31: Lyd .9H **27**
Nedens La. L31: Lyd .9H **27**
Needham Cl. WA7: Run .5N **95**
Needham Cres. CH43: Noct .4D **72**
Needham Rd. L7: Liv .7H **59**
Needham Way WN8: Skel .8E **22**
Needwood Dr. CH63: Beb .4M **89**
Neills Rd. WA9: Bold .4D **64**
Neilson Rd. L17: Aig .5G **75**
Neilson St. L17: Aig .5G **75**
Neil St. WA8: Wid .6M **79**
Nell's La. L39: Augh .7L **27**
Nelson Av. L35: Whis .7B **62**
Nelson Ct. CH42: Rock F .7N **73**
CH45: New B .9H **43**
PR8: Birkd .2M **11**
Nelson Dr. CH61: Pens .3M **87**
M44: Cad .3L **69**
WA7: West .9J **95**
Nelson Ho. CH42: Rock F .7N **73**
Nelson Memorial .*4D 4*
(off Exchange Pas. E.)
Nelson Pl. L35: Whis .7B **62**
Nelson Rd. CH42: Rock F .7N **73**
CH65: Ell P .7A **104**
L7: Liv .8G **58**
L21: Lith .*3A* ***44***
(off Bridge Rd.)
WA3: Ris .5L **67**
Nelson's Cft. CH63: Beb .4N **89**
Nelson St. CH45: New B .2J **57**
L1: Liv .9G **5** (1C **74**)
(not continuous)
L15: Wav .9K **59**
L20: Boot .8A **44**
PR8: South .9F **6**
WA7: Run .5K **95**
WA8: Wid .1K **95**
WA12: Newt W .7J **51**
(not continuous)
Nelville Rd. L9: Ain .3H **45**
Nemos Cl. WA6: Hel .3F **114**
Neptune Cl. WA7: Murd .8F **96**
Neptune St. CH41: Birke .9K **57**
NESS .9G **101**
Ness Acre La. CH64: Will .6L **101**
Nesse Ho. *CH64: Nest* .*6E* ***100***
(off Churchill Way)
Ness Gro. L32: Kirkb .9A **36**
NESSHOLT .9F **100**
NESTON .6E **100**
Neston Av. WA9: Clock F .5L **63**
Neston Cl. WA6: Hel .3D **114**
Neston Gdns. *CH41: Birke* .*9H* ***57***
(off Churchview Rd.)
Neston Grn. CH66: Gt Sut .1J **111**
(not continuous)
Neston Recreation Cen. .5F **100**
Neston Rd. CH63: Thorn H .2F **100**
CH64: Burt, Ness .9F **100**
CH64: Nest .2F **100**
CH64: Will .6L **101**
Neston Station (Rail) .6E **100**
Neston St. L4: Walt .9E **44**
Netherby St. L8: Liv .5E **74**
Netherfield WA8: Wid .8G **79**
Netherfield Cl. CH43: Noct .4C **72**
Netherfield Rd. Nth. L5: Liv .3D **58**
Netherfield Rd. Sth. L5: Liv .5D **58**
NETHERLEY .3J **77**
Netherley Rd. L27: N'ley .3K **77**
L35: Tar G .3K **77**
WA8: Wid .5N **77**
Netherpool Rd. CH66: Ell P .7L **103**
NETHERTON
L30 .8E **34**
WA6 .7K **107**
Netherton Activity Cen. .7D **34**
Netherton Dr. WA6: Frod .7K **107**
Netherton Grange L30: N'ton .8G **35**
Netherton Grn. L30: N'ton .6E **34**
Netherton Ind. Est. L30: N'ton .2E **44**
Netherton La. L30: N'ton .6D **34**
(not continuous)
Netherton Pk. Rd. L21: Lith .2C **44**
Netherton Rd. CH46: More .9M **55**
L18: Moss H .7M **75**
L20: Boot .4C **44**
Netherton Way *L30: Boot* .*2D* ***44***
(off Captain's La.)
L30: N'ton .1D **44**
Netherwood Gro. WN3: Wins .2G **40**
Netherwood Rd. L11: Norr G .8K **45**
Netley St. L4: Kirkd .1D **58**
Nettle Hill CH48: W Kir .5B **70**
Nettlestead Rd. L11: Norr G .1M **59**
Neva Av. CH46: More .9L **55**
Nevada Bobs Driving Range .8E **38**
Nevada Cl. WA5: Gt San .9L **65**
Neverstitch Cl. WN8: Skel .2C **30**
Neverstitch Rd. WN8: Skel .3N **29**
Neville Av. WA2: Warr .8E **66**
WA9: St H .8D **50**
Neville Cl. CH43: Noct .4C **72**

Neville Cres. WA5: Penk .5J 81
Neville Rd. CH44: Wall .5G 56
CH62: Brom .8D 90
L22: Water .1L 43
Neville St. WA12: Newt W .6J 51
Nevill St. PR9: South .7G 6
Nevin St. L6: Liv .2M 5 (6F 58)
Nevison St. L7: Liv .8G 58
Nevitte Cl. L28: Stockb V .1E 60
New Acres WN8: Newb .3D 22
New Acres Cl. CH43: Bid .9C 56
New Albert Ter. WA7: Run .4L 95
(off Frederic Pl.)
Newark Cl. CH43: Noct .4C 72
L30: N'ton .6G 34
L36: Huy .3H 61
Newark Dr. WA5: Gt San .2J 81
Newark St. L4: Walt .9E 44
Newarth Dr. WA13: Lymm .6G 85
New Bank Pl. WA8: Wid .7E 78
New Bank Rd. WA8: Wid .7E 78
New Barn Av. WN4: Ash M .8L 41
New Barnet WA8: Wid .5J 79
New Bird St. L1: Liv .9H 5 (1C 74)
New Bold Ct. WA9: Bold .2C 64
Newbold Cres. CH48: W Kir .5F 70
Newbold Gro. L12: Crox .8D 46
Newborough Av. L18: Moss H .3L 75
L23: Crosb .7N 33
Newborough Cl. WA5: Call .7M 65
NEW BOSTON .4G 51
New Bridge WA1: Warr .4C 82
WA4: Warr .4C 82
Newbridge Cl. CH49: Woodc .4B 72
WA5: Call .7L 65
WA7: Brook .9E 96
WN4: Garsw .8F 40
New Bridge Ct. CH65: Ell P .1D 112
Newbridge Farm Caravan Pk.
L33: Sim .4J 37
Newbridge Rd. CH2: Lit Stan .2D 112
CH65: Ell P .1D 112
NEW BRIGHTON .9H 43
New Brighton Station (Rail) .1G 57
NEWBURGH .4D 22
Newburgh Cl. WA7: Wind H .6F 96
Newburn CH43: Oxton .3H 73
Newburn Cl. WN8: Skel .8E 22
Newburns La. CH43: Oxton .5H 73
Newburn St. L4: Walt .8E 44
Newbury Cl. L36: Roby .8H 61
WA8: Wid .5K 79
Newbury Rd. WN8: Skel .8E 22
Newbury Way CH46: Leas .6N 55
L12: W Der .4C 60
Newby Av. L35: Rainh .5D 62
Newby Cl. PR8: Ains .2H 17
Newby Dr. L36: Huy .6G 60
WN8: Skel .8E 22
Newby Gro. L12: W Der .8A 46
Newby Pl. WA11: St H .2K 49
Newby St. L4: Walt .1E 58
New Carr La. L31: Gt Alt .5D 26
Newcastle Rd. L15: Wav .2M 75
New Causeway L37: Gt Alt .4H 25
L38: Ince B .6H 25
New Chester Rd. CH41: Birke, Tran .3M 73
CH42: Rock F, Tran .6N 73
CH62: Brom, East, New F, Port S .1B 90
CH66: Hoot .4F 102
Newchurch Cl. L27: N'ley .4K 77
Newchurch La. WA3: Cul .8N 53
Newcombe Av. WA2: Warr .9F 66
Newcombe St. L6: Liv .4G 59
New Ct. Way L39: Orm .8D 20
Newcroft Rd. L25: Woolt .4D 76
New Cross St. L34: Presc .2A 62
WA10: St H .6J 49
(Henry St.)
WA10: St H .7J 49
(Westfield St.)
New Cross St. Sth. WA10: St H .7J 49
(off Nth. John St.)
New Cut Cl. PR8: Birkd .6N 11
New Cut Ind. Est. WA1: Wools .1K 83
New Cut La. L33: Kirkb, Rainf .3L 47
L39: Hals .8C 12
PR8: Birkd .6N 11
WA1: Wools .1J 83
WA11: Rainf .1M 47
Newdales Cl. CH43: Bid .9C 56
Newdown Rd. L11: Crox .5B 46
Newdown Wlk. L11: Crox .5B 46
Newell Rd. CH44: Wall .4H 57
Newenham Cres. L14: Knott A .5C 60
New Extension Quay CH65: Ell P .6N 103
NEW FERRY .9A 74
New Ferry By-Pass
CH62: New F, Port S .8A 74
New Ferry Rd. CH62: New F .9A 74
Newfield Cl. L23: Thorn .5B 34
Newfield Ct. WA13: Lymm .3G 85
Newfield Rd. WA13: Lymm .5D 84
Newfields WA10: St H .6F 48
Newfield Ter. WA6: Hel .3E 114
New Fold WN5: Orr .8M 31
New Fort Way L20: Boot .4N 43
New Foul La. PR8: South .2F 12
NEWGATE .5K 31
Newgate Rd. WN8: Uph .5J 31
New Glade Hill WA11: St H .4N 49
New Grey Rock Cl. L6: Liv .5G 58
New Grosvenor Rd. CH65: Ell P .7N 103
New Hall L10: Faz .2L 45
New Hall Dr. PR8: South .5H 13
New Hall La. CH47: Hoy .2C 70
L11: Norr G .1K 59
WA3: Cul, Ris .9M 53
(not continuous)
New Hall Mnr. CH64: Nest .9E 88
New Hall Pl. L3: Liv .4C 4 (7A 58)
Newhall St. L1: Liv .9H 5 (1C 74)
New Hampshire Cl. WA5: Gt San .1K 81
Newhaven Rd. CH45: New B .2J 57
WA2: Warr .5C 66
New Hawthorne Gdns. L18: Moss H .5L 75
New Hedley Gro. L5: Liv .4B 58
New Henderson St. L8: Liv .2D 74
New Hey L12: W Der .4M 59
New Heyes CH64: Nest .5E 100
New Hey La. CH64: Will .7M 101
New Hey Rd. CH49: Woodc .4B 72
New Heys Dr. L18: Aller .7B 76
Newholme Cl. L12: Crox .7C 46
Newhope Rd. CH41: Birke .1J 73
Newhouse Dr. WN3: Wins .2F 40
Newhouse Rd. L15: Wav .1J 75
NEW HOUSES .1E 40
New Houses La. CH64: Lit N .9E 100
New Hutte La. L26: Halew .1J 93
Newick Pk. L32: Kirkb .1A 46
Newick Rd. L32: Kirkb .1A 46
Newington L1: Liv .6H 5 (8D 58)
Newington Way WA8: Wid .5J 79
New Islington L3: Liv .3H 5 (7D 58)
Newland Cl. WA8: Wid .5F 78
Newland Ct. L17: Aig .5H 75
Newland Dr. CH44: Wall .5G 56
Newland M. WA3: Cul .5M 53
Newlands Av. L40: Burs .1K 21
Newlands Cl. WA6: Frod .8M 107
Newlands Dr. WA3: Low .2E 52
Newlands Rd. CH63: Beb .3A 90
WA4: Stockt H .6G 83
WA11: St H .3M 49
NEW LANE .8F 14
New La. L39: Augh .2C 28
L39: Down .1D 26
(Back La.)
L39: Down .9A 18
(Old Moss La.)
L40: Burs .7F 14
PR9: South .3B 8
WA3: Croft .2H 67
WA4: App T .2J 99
NEW LANE END .8H 53
New La. End WA3: Croft .8H 53
New La. Pace PR9: Banks .1F 8
New Lane Station (Rail) .7F 14
Newling St. CH41: Birke .1J 73
Newlove Av. WA10: St H .7F 48
Newlyn Av. L21: Lith .1N 43
L31: Mag .2K 35
Newlyn Cl. CH47: Meols .8F 54
WA7: Brook .9D 96
Newlyn Dr. WN4: Ash M .9K 41
WN8: Skel .5G 31
Newlyn Gdns. WA5: Penk .5F 80
Newlyn Gro. WA11: St H .3N 49
Newlyn Rd. CH47: Meols .8F 54
L11: Crox .5B 46
Newlyn Wlk. L11: Crox .5B 46
New Mnr. Rd. WA4: Pres H .9K 97
Newman St. L4: Kirkd .2C 58
WA4: Westy .4G 83
New Mkt. Cl. L21: Lith .3A 44
Newmarket Gdns. WA9: St H .3F 62
New Mkt. Hall WA7: Run .4K 95
(off Granville St.)
New Mkt. Wlk. WA1: Warr .3C 82
New Meadow La. L37: Gt Alt .4L 25
New Mersey Retail Pk. L24: Speke .2D 92
New Mersey Shop. Pk. L24: Speke .2D 92
New Mill Stile L25: Woolt .5E 76
Newmoore La. WA7: Nort .4G 97
Newmorn Ct. L17: Aig .6H 75
New Moss Rd. M44: Cad .3K 69
Newnham Dr. CH65: Ell P .1A 112
New Palace Amusement Pk. .9H 43
NEW PALE .8M 115
New Pale Rd. WA6: Kingsw, Manl C .4L 115
Newport Av. CH45: Wall .2D 56
Newport Bus. Pk. CH65: Ell P .2D 112
Newport Cl. CH43: Noct .4C 72
Newport Ct. L5: Liv .4B 58
New Quay L3: Liv .4C 4 (7A 58)
Newquay Cl. WA7: Brook .9D 96
New Quay Ter. L3: Liv .4C 4
New Red Rock Vw. L6: Liv .5G 58
New Rd. CH66: Chil T .6F 102
CW9: Ant .6L 99
L13: Liv .4K 59
L34: Eccl P .2B 62
L37: Form .8G 16
L40: Ruf .3M 15
WA4: Warr .4C 82
(not continuous)
WA13: Lymm .5E 84
New Rd. Ct. L13: Liv .4K 59
(off Oak Leigh)
New School La. CH66: Chil T .6G 102
Newsham Cl. WA8: Wid .4E 78
Newsham Dr. L6: Liv .5H 59
(not continuous)
Newsham Rd. L36: Huy .9L 61
Newsham St. L5: Liv .4C 58
Newsholme Cl. WA3: Cul .7N 53
News La. WA11: Rainf .1C 38
Newstead Av. L23: Blun .8H 33
Newstead Dr. WN8: Skel .8E 22
Newstead Rd. L8: Liv .1H 75
WA8: Wid .1C 94
Newstet Rd. L33: Know I .9F 36
New St. CH44: Wall .7L 57
CH64: Lit N .9E 100
L39: Hals .6F 18
WA7: Run .5K 95
WA8: Wid .8L 79
WA9: St H, Sut L .4M 63
WN4: Ash M .7L 41
NEWTON
CH48 .6F 70
WA6 .3N 115
Newton Av. WA3: Ris .4M 67
Newton Bank WA4: Dares .7K 97
Newton Cl. L12: W Der .1N 59
NEWTON COMMON .7G 51
Newton Ct. CH42: Rock F .7N 73
(off New Chester Rd.)
L13: Wav .8K 59
Newton Cross La. CH48: W Kir .6F 70
Newton Dr. CH48: W Kir .6F 70
WN8: Skel .8E 22
Newton Gdns. WA3: Low .2H 53
Newton Gro. WA2: Fearn .6G 66
Newton Hollows WA6: Frod .4M 115
Newton La. WA4: Dares, Lwr W .7K 97
(not continuous)
WA12: Newt W .4N 51
NEWTON-LE-WILLOWS .6M 51
Newton-le-Willows Station (Rail) .7N 51
Newton Pk. Dr. WA12: Newt W .7A 52
Newton Pk. Rd. CH48: W Kir .6F 70
Newton Rd. CH44: Wall .5G 57
CH47: Hoy .1D 70
CH65: Ell P .9A 104
L13: Liv .5K 59
WA2: Win .9A 52
WA3: Low .6B 52
WA9: St H .7C 50
WN5: Bil .5A 40
Newton St. CH41: Birke .1K 73
PR9: South .8L 7
Newton Wlk. L20: Boot .6A 44
(off Capricorn Way)
Newton Way CH49: Upton .3N 71
L3: Liv .5K 5 (8E 58)
New Tower Ct. CH45: New B .1J 57
NEWTOWN .5N 107
Newtown CH64: Lit N .8F 100
Newtown Gdns. L32: Kirkb .9C 36
New Vale PR9: Banks .4E 8
New Way L39: Bic .1F 36
Newway L14: Knott A .4E 60
New Way Bus. Cen. CH44: Wall .7K 57
New William Cl. M31: Part .5M 69
(off Moss La.)
Nicander Rd. L18: Moss H .3L 75
Nicholas Ho. L23: Blun .7H 33
Nicholas Rd. L23: Blun .7H 33
WA8: Wid .8F 78
Nicholas St. L3: Liv .1F 4 (6C 58)
Nicholl Rd. WA10: Eccl .4D 48
Nicholls Dr. CH61: Pens .3N 87
Nicholls St. WA4: Grap .6J 83
Nichols Gro. L18: Aller .7A 76
Nicholson St. WA1: Warr .3A 82
WA9: St H .6A 50
Nickleby Cl. L8: Liv .3E 74
Nickleford Hall Dr. WA8: Wid .2J 79
Nicola Ct. CH45: Wall .3J 57
Nicol Av. WA3: Wools .9N 67
Nicol Mere Dr. WN4: Ash M .5J 41
Nicol Rd. WN4: Ash M .6J 41
Nidderdale Av. L35: Rainh .6G 62
Nigella Dr. L11: Norr G .9M 45
Nigel Rd. CH60: Hesw .7C 88
Nigel Wlk. WA7: Cas .5C 96
Nightingale Cl. L27: N'ley .3K 77
L32: Kirkb .8N 35
WA3: Birchw .5N 67
WA7: Beech .1B 108
Nightingale Rd. L12: Crox .7D 46
Nimrod St. L4: Walt .9E 44
Ninth Av. L9: Ain .3J 45
Nipe La. WN8: Skel .7D 30
Nithsdale Rd. L15: Wav .2K 75
Nixons La. PR8: Ains .7L 11
WN8: Skel .5G 31
Nixon St. L4: Walt .8E 44
Noble Cl. WA3: Birchw .6M 67
NOCTORUM .4D 72
Noctorum Av. CH43: Noct .3C 72
Noctorum Dell CH43: Noct .4D 72
Noctorum La. CH43: Noct, Oxton .2D 72
Noctorum Rd. CH43: Noct .3D 72
Noctorum Way CH43: Noct .4D 72
Noel Ga. L39: Augh .3N 27
Noel St. L8: Liv .1H 75
Nolan St. PR8: South .1B 12
Nook, The CH2: Back .9N 111
CH43: Oxton .2H 73
CH48: Frank .6J 71
L25: Gate .5F 76
L39: Augh .4A 28
WA10: Windle .4E 48
WN6: Appl B .6N 23
Nook La. CW9: Ant .9L 99
WA2: Fearn .7J 67
WA3: Golb .2C 52
WA4: Westy .5H 83
WA9: St H .9B 50
Nook Ri. L15: Wav .9N 59
Noonan Cl. L9: Walt .6E 44
Noon Ct. WA12: Newt W .9K 51
Noon La. L40: Ruf .4J 15
Nora St. WA1: Warr .3D 82
Norbreck Av. L14: Broad G .7D 60
Norbreck Cl. WA5: Gt San .4J 81
Norburn Cres. L37: Form .2F 24
Norbury Av. CH63: Hghr B .2L 89
L18: Moss H .3L 75
WA2: Warr .9E 66
WN5: Bil .5N 39
Norbury Cl. CH63: Hghr B .2M 89
L32: Kirkb .9B 36
PR9: South .2A 8
WA8: Wid .7N 79
Norbury Fold L35: Rainh .8H 63
Norbury Rd. L32: Kirkb .9B 36
Norbury Wlk. L32: Kirkb .9B 36
Norcliffe Rd. L35: Rainh .5E 62
Norcott Av. WA4: Stockt H .6E 82
NORCOTT BROOK .9D 98
Norcott Dr. WA5: Burtw .3H 65
Norden Cl. WA3: Birchw .4K 67
Norfield L39: Orm .8D 20
Norfolk Cl. CH43: Noct .4C 72
L20: Boot .6C 44
(off Brookhill Rd.)
M44: Cad .4J 69
Norfolk Dr. CH48: W Kir .7D 70
WA5: Gt San .2G 81
Norfolk Gro. PR8: Birkd .5M 11
Norfolk Pl. L21: Sea .3N 43
WA8: Wid .8F 78
Norfolk Rd. CH65: Ell P .9A 104
L31: Mag .4H 35
PR8: Birkd .5M 11
WA10: St H .9G 48
WN5: Bil .2A 40
Norfolk St. L1: Liv .9F 4 (1C 74)
WA7: Run .4L 95
Norgate St. L4: Walt .2E 58
Norgrove Cl. WA7: Murd .7F 96
Norlands Ct. CH42: Rock F .7L 73
Norland's La. L35: Rainh .9H 63
WA8: Cron, Wid .9H 63
Norlands Pk. WA8: Wid .2J 79
Norland St. WA8: Wid .7N 79
Norleane Cres. WA7: Run .7L 95
Norley Av. CH62: East .3D 102
CH65: Ell P .8L 103
Norley Cl. WA5: Warr .2N 81
Norley Dr. WA10: Eccl .7D 48
Norley Pl. L26: Halew .1J 93
Norman Av. WA11: Hay .3J 51
WA12: Newt W .7N 51
Normanby Cl. WA5: Warr .1N 81
Norman Cl. CH66: Gt Sut .5L 111
Normandale Rd. L4: Walt .9J 45
Normandy Rd. L36: Huy .6H 61
Norman Hayes L39: Orm .5D 20
Normanhurst L39: Orm .9E 20
Norman Rd. CH44: Wall .7L 57
L20: Boot .3B 44
L23: Crosb .8K 33
WA7: Run .6K 95
Norman Salisbury Ct. WA10: St H .5K 49
Normans Rd. WA9: St H .2B 64
Normanston Cl. CH43: Oxton .4H 73
Normanston Rd. CH43: Oxton .4H 73
Norman St. CH41: Birke .9F 56
L3: Liv .3K 5
WA2: Warr .2C 82
Normanton Av. L17: Aig .5H 75
Norma Rd. L22: Water .1L 43
Normington Cl. L31: Lyd .8H 27
Norreys Av. WA5: Warr .9A 66
Norris Cl. CH43: Noct .4C 72
NORRIS GREEN .8L 45
Norris Grn. Cres. L11: Norr G .9M 45
Norris Grn. Rd. L12: W Der .3N 59
Norris Grn. Way L11: Norr G .9M 45
Norris Gro. WA8: Hale B .2F 94
Norris Ho. Dr. L39: Augh .4A 28
Norris Rd. L34: Presc .3N 61
Norris St. WA2: Warr .9D 66
Norris Way L37: Form .1H 25
Norseman Cl. L12: W Der .1N 59
Northam Cl. PR9: South .2M 7
NORTH ASHTON .5F 40
Nth. Atlantic Av. L30: N'ton .1D 44
Nth. Atlantic Cl. L36: Huy .5J 61
North Av. L10: Ain .9K 35
L24: Speke .1E 92
WA2: Warr .9C 66
Northbank Ind. Est. M44: Irlam .4M 69
Northbank Ind. Pk. M44: Irlam .2N 69
(not continuous)

Nth. Barcombe Rd. L16: Child 1B 76
Northbrook Cl. L8: Liv 1F 74
Nth. Brooke Way CH49: Woodc 5A 72
Northbrook Rd. CH44: Wall 6K 57
Northbrook St. L8: Liv 9N 5 (1F 74)
(Granby St.)
L8: Liv 1F 74
(Rosebery St.)
Northbury Rd. CH66: Gt Sut 4K 111
Nth. Cantril Av. L12: W Der 1C 60
Nth. Cheshire Trad. Est.
CH43: Pren 8E 72
North Cl. CH62: Brom 5B 90
Northcote Cl. L5: Liv 5E 58
Northcote Rd. CH45: Wall 3D 56
L9: Walt 7E 44
Northdale Rd. L15: Wav 9L 59
WA1: Padd 9H 67
Northdene WN8: Parb 3E 22
North Dingle L4: Kirkd 1C 58
(not continuous)
North Dr. CH45: Wall 1F 56
CH60: Hesw 8A 88
L12: W Der 4M 59
L15: Wav 9L 59
WN6: Appl B 3M 23
North Dunes L38: Hight 8F 24
NORTH END
L26 5J 77
L38 7J 25
North End La. L26: Halew 5J 77
L38: Hight 6G 25
Northern La. WA8: Wid 5D 78
Northern Perimeter Rd.
L30: N'ton 6D 34
Northern Ri. CH66: Gt Sut 2K 111
Northern Road, The
L23: Crosb 6L 33
Northfield WN8: Skel 9E 22
Northfield Cl. L33: Kirkb 7E 36
WA9: Clock F 6N 63
Northfield Ct. WA3: Golb 1D 52
Northfield Rd. L9: Walt 4D 44
L20: Boot 4D 44
NORTH FLORIDA 2F 50
Nth. Florida Rd. WA11: Hay 2F 50
North Front L35: Whis 8B 62
Northgate Rd. L13: Liv 4M 59
North Gro. L18: Aller 7A 76
North Hill St. L8: Liv 3E 74
Nth. John St. L2: Liv 4E 4 (8B 58)
WA10: St H 7J 49
(not continuous)
Northleach Dr. PR8: Ains 9G 11
Nth. Linkside Rd. L25: Woolt 7G 76
Nth. Manor Way L25: Woolt 7G 76
North Meade L31: Mag 1H 35
Northmead Rd. L19: Aller 9C 76
Nth. Mersey Bus. Cen.
L33: Know I 7G 37
NORTH MOOR 3K 19
Nth. Moor La. L39: Hals 3J 19
Nth. Moss La. L37: Form 7J 17
Nth. Mossley Hill Rd.
L18: Moss H 4L 75
Nth. Mount Rd. L32: Kirkb 7N 35
Northolt Ct. WA2: Padg 8F 66
Northop Rd. CH45: Wall 3F 56
North Pde. CH47: Hoy 1B 70
CH64: Park 4B 100
L24: Speke 4J 93
L32: Kirkb 9C 36
North Pk. Brook Rd. WA5: Call 7N 65
North Pk. Ct. *CH44: Wall* *6L 57*
(off Demesne St.)
North Pk. Rd. L32: Kirkb 7N 35
Nth. Parkside Wlk. *L12: W Der* *1M 59*
(off Parkside Dr.)
Nth. Perimeter Rd. L33: Know I 7F 36
Nth. Quarry Bus. Pk.
WN6: Appl B 4N 23
Nth. Quarry Bus. Village
WN6: Appl B 4N 23
North Quay L3: Liv 9E 4 (1B 74)
Northridge Rd. CH61: Pens 2A 88
North Rd. CH42: Tran 5J 73
CH48: W Kir 6B 70
CH65: Ell P 2H 103
(not continuous)
L14: Broad G 7A 60
L19: Gras 1L 91
L24: Halew 2J 93
PR9: South 3N 7
WA10: St H 5J 49
North St. L3: Liv 3F 4 (7C 58)
PR9: South 7H 7
WA11: Hay 4G 50
WA12: Newt W 6H 51
WN4: Ash M 7M 41
Nth. Sudley Rd. L17: Aig 6K 75
North Ter. CH47: Meols 8E 54
Northumberland Gro. L8: Liv 3C 74
Northumberland Rd. M31: Part 7L 69
Northumberland St. L8: Liv 3D 74
Northumberland Ter. L5: Liv 3D 58
Northumberland Way
L30: N'ton 8B 34
North Vw. *CH66: Lit Sut* *8H 103*
(off Station Rd.)
L7: Liv 5N 5 (8F 58)
North Vw. L36: Huy 7L 61
WA5: Gt San 1G 81
Nth. Wallasey App. CH45: Wall 3C 56
Nth. Wall Terminal
CH65: Ell P 6A 104
Northway CH60: Hesw 6D 88
L15: Wav 8N 59
L31: Augh, Lyd, Mag 4H 35
(not continuous)
L39: Augh 6L 27
WA2: Warr 8C 66
WA7: Pal F 7B 96
WA8: Wid 7G 78
WA13: Lymm 4D 84
WN8: Skel 1E 30
Northway Caravan Pk. L40: Scar 1L 19
Northways CH62: Brom 4C 90
North West Face Indoor Climbing Cen.
1B 82
North West Museum of Road Transport
6K 49
Northwich Cl. L23: Thorn 5A 34
Northwich Rd.
WA4: Dutt, Lwr W 3K 109
WA4: Hghr Whi, Lwr S 7F 98
WA7: Brook 1D 108
WA7: Dutt, Pres B 2F 108
Nth. William St. CH44: Wall 7L 57
North Wirral Coastal Pk. 7G 54
NORTHWOOD 9D 36
Northwood Av. WA12: Newt W 6A 52
Northwood Rd. CH43: Pren 6F 72
L36: Huy 5K 61
WA7: Run 5A 96
NORTON 7F 96
Norton Av. WA5: Penk 3G 80
Norton Ct. *CH44: Wall* *6L 57*
(off Borough Rd.)
Norton Dr. CH61: Irby 9K 71
Norton Ga. WA7: Nort 7E 96
Norton Gro. L31: Mag 5J 35
WA9: St H 2G 63
Norton Hill WA7: Wind H 6E 96
Norton La. WA7: Halt, Nort 7C 96
(not continuous)
WA7: Nort 6F 96
Norton Priory Gdns. 4D 96
Norton Priory Mus. 4D 96
Norton Rd. CH48: W Kir 5B 70
Norton's La. WA6: Lit Ba 9D 114
Norton Sta. Rd. WA7: Murd, Nort 7F 96
Norton St. L3: Liv 3H 5 (7D 58)
L20: Boot 5A 44
Norton Vw. WA7: Halt 7C 96
Norton Village WA7: Nort 7F 96
Norton Village Gdns. WA7: Nort 7F 96
Nortonwood La. WA7: Wind H 7E 96
Norville CH66: Lit Sut 7J 103
Norville Rd. L14: Broad G 7A 60
Norwich Av. WA3: Low 2E 52
WN4: Ash M 9M 41
Norwich Dr. CH49: Upton 1A 72
CH66: Gt Sut 5K 111
Norwich Rd. L15: Wav 2M 75
Norwich Way L32: Kirkb 9C 36
Norwood Av. L21: Lith 1A 44
PR9: South 7K 7
WA3: Low 3G 52
WN4: Ash M 5H 41
Norwood Ct. CH49: Grea 5L 71
Norwood Cres. PR9: South 7K 7
Norwood Gdns. PR9: South 8L 7
Norwood Gro. L6: Liv 5G 59
WA11: Rainf 5D 38
Norwood Rd. CH44: Wall 7H 57
CH49: Grea 4L 71
PR8: South 8L 7
Norwyn Rd. L11: Norr G 8K 45
Nostell Rd. WN4: Ash M 6J 41
Nottingham Cl. L35: Rainh 4F 62
WA1: Wools 2L 83
Nottingham Rd. L36: Roby 8G 61
Nowshera Av. CH61: Pens 2N 87
Nuffield Cl. CH49: Upton 4N 71
Nuffield Rd. L20: Boot 8B 44
Nun Cl. CH43: Oxton 5H 73
Nunn St. WA9: St H 7N 49
Nunsford Cl. L21: Lith 9C 34
Nunthorpe Av. L34: Know 5F 46
Nurseries, The L37: Form 2G 24
Nurse Rd. CH61: Thing 1B 88
Nursery Av. L39: Orm 7C 20
Nursery Cl. CH43: Oxton 5H 73
L25: Hunts X 8G 76
WA8: Wid 5N 79
Nursery Dr. L37: Form 2F 24
Nursery Gro. M31: Part 5M 69
Nursery La. L19: Garst 9A 76
Nursery Rd. L31: Lyd 8H 27
WA1: Padg 9G 66
WA9: St H 2G 63
NUT GROVE 3F 62
Nutgrove Av. WA9: St H 2G 62
Nutgrove Hall Dr. WA9: St H 2G 62
Nutgrove Rd. WA9: St H 3F 62
Nuthall Rd. PR8: South 3E 12
Nut St. WA9: St H 2G 62
Nuttall Ct. WA3: Birchw 5K 67
Nuttall St. M44: Cad 3L 69
Nuttall Way L7: Liv 8H 59
Nye Bevan Pool 3E 30
Nyland Rd. L36: Huy 4H 61

O

Oak Av. CH49: Upton 2L 71
L9: Ain 4G 44
L39: Orm 9B 20
M44: Cad 4K 69
PR9: Banks 5H 9
WA3: Golb 2C 52
WA11: Hay 3G 51
WA12: Newt W 7L 51
Oak Bank CH41: Birke 3J 73
Oakbank Rd. L18: Moss H 3K 75
Oakbank St. CH44: Wall 6J 57
Oakbourne Cl. L17: Aig 6H 75
Oak Cl. CH46: More 1L 71
L12: W Der 9D 46
L35: Whis 6B 62
Oak Ct. *L8: Liv* *4F 74*
(off Weller Way)
WA7: Cas 5C 96
Oak Cres. WN8: Skel 3A 30
Oakcross Gdns. L25: Woolt 6G 76
Oakdale Av. CH44: Wall 7K 57
WA4: Stockt H 7E 82
WA6: Frod 8N 107
Oakdale Cl. L32: Kirkb 1A 46
Oakdale Dr. CH49: Grea 6K 71
Oakdale Rd. CH44: Wall 7K 57
L18: Moss H 3M 75
L22: Water 9K 33
Oakdale Row L32: Kirkb 2D 46
Oakdene Av. CH66: Gt Sut 9H 103
WA1: Wools 1K 83
Oakdene Cl. CH62: Brom 1C 102
Oakdene Ct. L35: Rainh 7G 62
Oakdene Rd. CH42: Tran 5J 73
L4: Walt 2G 58
Oak Dr. L40: Burs 2K 21
WA7: Run 8M 95
Oakenden Cl. WN4: Ash M 5J 41
Oakenholt Rd. CH46: More 8M 55
Oakes St. L3: Liv 4K 5 (7E 58)
Oakfield L4: Walt 3G 58
Oakfield Av. L25: Gate 4E 76
WA3: Golb 1A 52
Oakfield Cl. WA9: St H 2G 63
Oakfield Dr. L36: Huy 9K 61
L37: Form 9D 16
WA8: Wid 8D 78
Oakfield Gro. L36: Huy 9K 61
Oakfield Rd. CH62: Brom 7B 90
CH66: Chil T 6D 102
L4: Walt 3F 58
L38: Hight 1F 32
Oakfields L39: Orm 8E 20
Oakfield Ter. CH66: Chil T 6D 102
Oakford Cl. PR9: Banks 2F 8
Oak Gdns. WA5: Penk 4F 80
Oakgate Cl. L11: Norr G 7N 45
Oak Grange L26: Halew 8K 77
Oak Grn. L39: Orm 8D 20
Oak Gro. CH65: Whit 2M 111
Oakham Ct. PR9: South 7H 7
Oakham Dr. CH46: More 8J 55
L10: Ain 1L 45
Oakham St. L8: Liv 2C 74
Oakhill Cl. L12: Crox 7B 46
L31: Mag 1J 35
Oakhill Cott. La. L31: Lyd 8J 27
Oakhill Dr. L31: Lyd 8J 27
OAK HILL PARK 7N 59
Oakhill Pk. L13: Liv 7N 59
Oakhill Rd. L13: Liv 7N 59
L31: Mag 1J 35
Oakhouse Pk. L9: Walt 7E 44
Oakhurst Cl. L25: Gate 3F 76
Oakland Cl. L21: Lith 4B 44
Oakland Dr. CH49: Upton 2A 72
Oakland Gdns. WA1: Warr 1F 82
Oakland Rd. L19: Aig 8L 75
Oaklands CH62: Brom 9C 90
L35: Rainh 6F 62
Oaklands Av. L23: Crosb 6L 33
Oaklands Ct. WA9: Clock F 5M 63
Oaklands Dr. CH61: Hesw 6A 88
CH63: Beb 1N 89
WA13: Lymm 6D 84
Oaklands Office Pk.
CH66: Hoot 4D 102
Oaklands Rd. WA3: Low 3G 53
Oaklands Ter. CH61: Hesw 5A 88
Oakland St. WA1: Warr 1F 82
WA8: Wid 3K 95
Oakland Va. CH45: New B 1J 57
Oak La. L12: W Der 9A 46
Oak La. Nth. L12: Crox 8A 46
Oakleaf M. CH43: Noct 3D 72
Oaklea Rd. CH61: Irby 1N 87
Oaklee Gro. L33: Kirkb 7E 36
Oak Leigh L13: Liv 4K 59
Oakleigh WN8: Skel 1G 38
Oakleigh Gro. CH63: Beb 1M 89
Oakley Av. WN5: Bil 5A 40
Oakley Cl. L12: Crox 7C 46
Oakley Ct. CH65: Ell P 1A 112
Oak Mdws. Ct. L35: Rainh 8H 63
Oakmere Cl. CH46: Leas 5M 55
L9: Walt 3F 44
Oakmere Dr. CH49: Grea 4K 71
CH66: Gt Sut 4L 111
WA5: Penk 5H 81
Oakmere St. WA7: Run 5K 95
Oakmoore WA7: Nort 3H 97
Oakridge Cl. CH62: Spit 5B 90
Oakridge Rd. CH62: Spit 5B 90
Oak Rd. CH63: Hghr B 9M 73
CH66: Hoot 5D 102
L35: Whis 6B 62
L36: Huy 9H 61
M31: Part 7K 69
WA5: Penk 5H 81
WA13: Lymm 5C 84
Oaks, The CH62: Brom 7B 90
L12: Crox 7D 46
WA8: Wid *4N 79*
(off Hampton Ct. Way)
WA9: Sut L 5N 63
Oaks Bus. Pk. WN8: Uph 8J 31
Oaks Cl. WA9: Clock F 6N 63
Oaks La. CH61: Pens 3A 88
Oaksmeade Cl. L12: Crox 8D 46
Oaks Pl. WA8: Wid 9K 79
Oakston Av. L35: Rainh 7G 62
Oak St. CH65: Ell P 7A 104
L20: Boot *6B 44*
(off Holly St.)
PR8: South 9K 7
WA3: Croft 2H 67
WA9: St H 1A 64
WN4: Ash M 5J 41
Oaksway CH60: Hesw 9B 88
Oak Ter. L7: Liv 7H 59
Oakthorn Gro. WA11: Hay 4E 50
Oak Tree Ct. WN8: Skel 1G 30
Oaktree Ct. Bus. Cen. CH64: Ness 8K 101
Oaktree Gdns. *L9: Faz* *6L 45*
(off Ternhall Way)
Oaktree Pl. CH42: Rock F 5M 73
Oak Tree Rd. WA10: Eccl 5D 48
Oak Vale L13: Liv 7N 59
OAK VALE PARK 7N 59
Oak Vw. L24: Speke 4L 93
Oakways WA4: App 2E 98
Oak Wharf M. WA4: App 8D 82
OAKWOOD 6N 67
Oakwood WN8: Skel 1G 30
Oakwood Av. PR8: Ains 8L 11
WA1: Warr 1E 82
WN4: Ash M 9J 41
Oakwood Cl. CH66: Gt Sut 4J 111
L25: Gate 3F 76
Oakwood Dr. CH43: Bid 9E 56
L36: Huy 8K 61
PR8: Ains 9L 11
WN7: Leigh 1M 53
Oakwood Ga. WA3: Birchw 5L 67
Oakwood Pk. CH43: Bid 9E 56
CH62: Brom 1C 102
Oakwood Rd. L26: Halew 9J 77
Oakworth Cl. L33: Kirkb 7C 36
Oakworth Dr. CH62: New F 9B 74
L35: Tar G 1L 77
Oarside Dr. CH45: Wall 3G 57
Oasis Cl. L40: Ruf 3M 15
Oasis Health & Fitness
Eccleston 5G 48
Oatfield La. L21: Ford 9A 34
Oatlands, The CH48: W Kir 7D 70
Oatlands Rd. L32: Kirkb 9A 36
Oban Dr. CH60: Hesw 7A 88
WN4: Garsw 7E 40
Oban Gro. WA2: Fearn 6H 67
Oban Rd. L4: Walt 3G 59
Oberon St. L20: Boot 9B 44
O'Brien Gro. WA9: St H 6A 50
Observatory Rd. CH43: Bid 9E 56
Occupation La. CW9: Ant 7K 99
Oceanic Rd. L13: Liv 7L 59
Ocean Pk. CH41: Wall 8K 57
Ocean Plaza PR8: South 7F 6
(not continuous)
Ocean Rd. L21: Lith 3A 44
O'Connell Cl. WA11: Hay 4E 50
O'Connell Rd. L3: Liv 5C 58
O'Connor Gro. L33: Kirkb 5C 36
Octavia Ct. L36: Huy 8K 61
Octavia Hill Rd. L21: Ford 1B 44
October Dr. L6: Liv 3J 59
Oddfellows Arms Yd. *L25: Woolt* *6E 76*
(off Allerton Rd.)
Odeon Cinema
Bootle 8F 34
Bromborough 4D 90
Liverpool 6E 4 (8B 58)
Warrington 8K 65
Odessa Wlk. WA5: Gt San 2K 81
Odsey St. L7: Liv 7H 59
Odyssey Cen. CH41: Birke 9J 57
Off Botanic Rd. PR9: South 6M 7
Off Lyons La. WA4: App 2F 98
Ogden Cl. L13: W Der 1M 59
Ogle Cl. L35: Presc 4B 62
OGLET 7J 93
Oglet La. L24: Hale 7H 93
L24: Speke 5G 93
Ogle Way L36: Huy 4J 61

Ohio Gro. WA5: Gt San 2L 81
Oil Sites Rd. CH65: Ell P 7B 104
Oil St. L3: Liv 1B 4 (5A 58)
O'Keeffe Rd. WA9: St H 6M 49
Okehampton Rd. L16: Child 9B 60
Okell Dr. L26: Halew 6H 77
Okell St. WA7: Run 5K 95
Oklahoma Blvd. WA5: Gt San 2J 81
Old Acre L38: Hight 9F 24
Old Albert Ter. *WA7: Run 4L 95*
(off Thomas St.)
Old Alder La. WA5: Burtw 3M 65
Old Barn La. CH64: Will 6M 101
Old Barn Rd. CH44: Wall 6G 57
L4: Walt 3G 58
Old Bidston Rd. CH41: Birke 9H 57
OLD BOSTON 3H 51
Old Boston WA11: Hay 2J 51
Old Boston Trad. Est.
WA11: Hay .2K 51
Old Boundary Way L39: Orm 7D 20
Oldbridge Rd. L24: Speke 5K 93
Old Cherry La. WA13: Lymm 9A 84
Old Chester Rd. CH41: Tran 4L 73
CH42: Rock F, Tran 7M 73
CH63: Beb, Hghr B 7M 73
CH66: Gt Sut 9J 103
WA4: Dares 6K 97
WA4: Hghr Wal 9A 82
WA6: Hel .2E 114
Old Church Cl. CH65: Ell P 7A 104
L9: Ain 3G 44
Old Churchyard L2: Liv 5D 4 (8A 58)
Old Clatterbridge Rd. CH63: Spit 5L 89
Old Coach Rd. WA7: Run 4J 95
Old College Pl. L7: Liv 8H 59
Old Colliery Rd. L35: Whis 6A 62
Old Colliery Yd. WN4: Garsw 8E 40
Old Court Ho. Rd. CH62: Brom 2C 90
Old Cryers La. CH2: Elt 3L 113
Old Distillery Rd. L24: Speke 2G 92
Old Dover Rd. L36: Roby 9G 61
Old Eccleston La. WA10: St H 7F 48
Old Elton Head Rd. WA9: St H 4L 63
Old Engine La. WN8: Skel 2N 29
Old Farm Cl. CH64: Will 6N 101
Old Farm Rd. L23: Crosb 7M 33
L32: Kirkb .4D 46
Oldfield L35: Whis 5C 62
Oldfield Cl. CH60: Hesw 5M 87
Oldfield Dr. CH60: Hesw 5L 87
Oldfield Gdns. CH60: Hesw 6L 87
Oldfield La. CH48: W Kir 4H 71
Oldfield Rd. CH45: Wall 3F 56
CH60: Hesw 5L 87
CH65: Ell P 9N 103
L19: Aig 8M 75
WA13: Lymm 4B 84
Oldfield St. WA10: St H 5J 49
Oldfield Way CH60: Hesw 5L 87
Old Forge Row L31: Mag 9H 27
Oldgate WA8: Wid 9F 78
Old Gorsey La. CH44: Wall 7H 57
Old Greasby Rd. CH49: Upton 3N 71
OLD HALL 9M 65
Old Hall L35: Whis 9B 62
Old Hall Cl. L31: Mag 4J 35
WA4: Hghr Wal 8B 82
Old Hall Dr. CH65: Whit 1N 111
WN4: Ash M 9J 41
Old Hall Farm Bus. Pk.
PR9: South .1F 12
Old Hall Gdns. WA11: Rainf 4D 38
Old Hall La. CH2: Elt 3L 113
L32: Kirkb .9B 36
Old Hall Rd. CH62: Brom 6D 90
L31: Mag 3J 35
WA5: Old H 9M 65
Old Hall St. L3: Liv 3C 4 (7A 58)
Oldham Pl. L1: Liv 6J 5 (8D 58)
Oldham St. L1: Liv 7H 5 (9D 58)
WA4: Warr .5D 82
Old Haymarket L1: Liv 4F 4 (7C 58)
(not continuous)
Old Hey Wlk. WA12: Newt W 9L 51
Old Higher Rd. WA8: Hale B 2A 94
Old Hutte La. L24: Halew 2L 93
L26: Halew .2L 93
Old Kennel Cl. L12: W Der 1D 60
Old La. CH60: Hesw 7D 88
L31: Lyd 8K 27
L34: Eccl P 2C 62
L35: Eccl P 2C 62
L35: Rainh .6E 62
L37: Form .7F 16
L39: Down .9C 18
WA8: Wid .9G 79
WA11: Rainf 4C 38
Old Leeds St. L3: Liv 3C 4 (7A 58)
Old Links Cl. PR9: South 7N 7
Old Liverpool Rd. WA5: Warr 4M 81
Old Lodge Cl. L12: W Der 1N 59
Old Market Pl. *WA1: Warr 3C 82*
(off Lyme St.)
Old Maryland La. CH46: More 8M 55
Old Meadow L34: Know 6H 47
Old Meadow Rd. CH61: Pens 3M 87
Old Mill, The *CH66: Lit Sut 7H 103*
(off Station Rd.)
Old Mill Av. WA9: Sut L 4N 63
Old Mill Cl. CH60: Hesw 8B 88
L15: Wav 9M 59
WA13: Lymm 2J 85
Old Mill Hill L39: Orm 1B 28
Old Mill La. L15: Wav 9M 59
L34: Know .6J 47
L37: Form .9F 16
Old Moss La. L39: Down 7N 17
Old Nook La. WA11: St H 4A 50
Old Orchard L35: Whis 8B 62
Old Park La. PR9: South 8M 7
Old Penny La. WA11: Hay 2K 51
Old Pewterspear La. WA4: App 4E 98
Old Post Office Pl. L1: Liv 6F 4
Old Prescot Cl. L31: Mag 1A 36
Old Pump La. CH49: Grea 5K 71
Old Quarry, The L25: Woolt 6E 76
Old Quay Cl. CH64: Park 7C 100
Old Quay La. CH64: Park 7D 100
Old Quays, The WA4: Westy 5F 82
Old Quay St. WA7: Run 4L 95
Old Racecourse Rd. L31: Mag 3G 34
Old Rectory Grn. L29: Seft 4D 34
L39: Augh .5M 27
Old Riding L14: Knott A 4D 60
Old Rd. WA4: Warr 4C 82
WN4: Ash M 7J 41
Old Roan Station (Rail) 8H 35
Old Ropery L2: Liv 5D 4
Old Rough La. L33: Kirkb 8C 36
Old School Cl. CH64: Lit N 9F 100
Old School House, The *CH43: Oxton . . .3G 72*
(off Beresford Rd.)
Old School Ho. La. WA2: Win 2B 66
Old School Pl. WN4: Ash M 9J 41
Old School Way CH41: Birke 1E 72
Old Smithy La. WA13: Lymm 6C 84
Old Stableyard, The L7: Liv 6N 5 (8F 58)
OLD SWAN .6M 59
Old Thomas La. L14: Broad G 8B 60
Old Town Cl. WN8: Skel 4A 30
Old Town Ct. L37: Form 9E 16
Old Town La. L37: Form 9E 16
Old Town Way WN8: Skel 4A 30
Old Upton La. WA8: Wid 4H 79
Old Vicarage Rd. CH64: Will 6N 101
Old Wargrave Rd. WA12: Newt W 7K 51
Old Welsh Rd. CH66: Lit Sut 9E 102
Old Whint Rd. WA11: Hay 4C 50
(Edward St.)
WA11: Hay .6C 50
(Harty Rd.)
Old Wood La. L27: N'ley 4K 77
Old Wood Rd. CH61: Pens 3N 87
Oleander Dr. WA10: St H 6F 48
O'Leary St. WA2: Warr 1D 82
Olga Rd. WA9: St H 2M 63
Olinda St. CH62: New F 9A 74
Olive Cl. L31: Mell 9M 35
Olive Cres. CH41: Tran 4L 73
Olivedale Rd. L18: Moss H 3L 75
Olive Dr. CH64: Nest 6E 100
Olive Gro. L15: Wav 8M 59
L30: N'ton .1F 44
L36: Roby .7H 61
PR8: South .8K 7
WN8: Skel .3B 30
Olive La. L15: Wav 8M 59
Olive Mt. CH41: Tran 4L 73
Olive Mt. Hgts. L15: Wav 9N 59
Olive Mt. Rd. L15: Wav 9M 59
Olive Mt. Vs. L15: Wav 8M 59
Olive Mt. Wlk. *L15: Wav 9N 59*
(off Olive Mt. Rd.)
Oliver Ho. *CH66: Gt Sut 1J 111*
(off Oliver La.)
Oliver La. CH41: Birke 2L 73
CH66: Gt Sut 1J 111
Oliver Lyme Ho. *L34: Presc 3B 62*
(off Lavender Cres.)
Oliver Lyme Rd. L34: Presc 3B 62
Olive Rd. CH64: Nest 6E 100
L22: Water .2L 43
Oliver Rd. WA10: St H 9F 48
Oliver St. CH41: Birke 2K 73
WA2: Warr .2C 82
Oliver St. E. CH41: Birke 2L 73
Olivetree Rd. L15: Wav 9N 59
Olive Va. L15: Wav 9L 59
Olivia Cl. CH43: Noct 4C 72
Olivia M. CH43: Noct 4C 72
Olivia St. L20: Boot 9C 44
Olivia Way L36: Huy 7M 61
Ollerton Cl. CH43: Noct 4C 72
WA4: Grap .5J 83
Ollerton Pk. WA5: Burtw 2G 64
Ollery Grn. L30: N'ton 7G 35
Ollier St. WA8: Wid 9K 79
Olney St. L4: Walt 8E 44
Olton St. L15: Wav 9K 59
Olympia Pl. WA5: Gt San 1K 81
Olympia St. L6: Liv 1N 5 (6F 58)
Olympic Way L30: N'ton 2G 44
WA2: Birchw 7K 67
Omega Blvd. WA5: Gt San 8F 64
Omega Circ. M44: Irlam 3M 69
Omega Dr. M44: Irlam 3M 69
O'Neill St. L20: Boot 6A 44
One Park W. L1: Liv 6E 4 (8B 58)
Onslow Cres. PR8: Birkd 4N 11
Onslow Rd. CH45: New B 1H 57
CH62: New F 8A 74
L6: Liv 6H 59
Ontario Cl. L27: N'ley 3J 77
Ontario Way L36: Huy 3H 61
Opal Cl. L6: Liv 5G 58
L21: Lith 2B 44
Opal Ct. L3: Liv 3K 5
Opco Complex L24: Speke 2F 92
Open Eye Gallery 6D 4 (8B 58)
Openfields Cl. L26: Halew 6J 77
Openshaw La. *M44: Cad 3L 69*
(off Prospect Av.)
Oppenheim Av. WA10: St H 1F 62
Orange Gro. L8: Liv 2H 75
WA2: Warr .7F 66
Orange Tree Cl. L28: Stockb V 1F 60
Oran Way L36: Huy 6H 61
Orb Cl. L11: Crox 7A 46
Orb Wlk. *L11: Crox 7A 46*
(off Sceptre Rd.)
Orchard, The CH45: Wall 2G 57
L17: Aig 7L 75
L35: Rainh .4F 62
L36: Huy 7J 61
L39: Orm 8B 20
WA6: Hel .3E 114
WN8: Skel .4A 30
Orchard Av. L14: Broad G 8B 60
M31: Part .5M 69
WA13: Lymm 5F 84
Orchard Brow WA3: Rix 7G 69
Orchard Cl. CH66: Gt Sut 4L 111
L34: Eccl P 2D 62
L35: Whis .8B 62
WA6: Frod 8K 107
WA11: St H 3N 49
Orchard Ct. CH41: Tran 5M 73
L31: Mag 2L 35
WA3: Croft 1H 67
WA6: Frod 6K 107
WN5: Bil 9N 31
Orchard Dale L23: Crosb 7M 33
Orchard Dene L35: Rainh 6F 62
Orchard Dr. CH64: Lit N 9E 100
Orchard Gdns. L35: Whis 9B 62
Orchard Grange CH46: More 1K 71
Orchard Haven CH66: Gt Sut 4K 111
Orchard Hey L30: N'ton 7G 35
L31: Mag 3L 35
WA10: Eccl 7D 48
Orchard La. CH66: Chil T 6F 102
PR8: Ains .1K 17
Orchard Pk. CH2: Elt 1M 113
Orchard Pk. La. CH2: Elt 1M 113
Orchard Pl. CH62: Spit 5A 90
WA6: Hel .1F 114
Orchard Rd. CH46: More 8M 55
CH65: Whit 3M 111
WA13: Lymm 3H 85
Orchards, The PR8: Ains 1K 17
Orchard St. WA1: Warr 3D 82
WA2: Fearn 7H 67
WA4: Stockt H 8D 82
WN4: Ash M 8L 41
Orchard Vw. L39: Augh 3B 28
Orchard Wlk. CH64: Nest 6E 100
WA7: Pal F 8B 96
(within Halton Lea Shop. Cen.)
Orchard Way CH63: Hghr B 1K 89
WA8: Wid .5D 78
Orchid Cl. M44: Irlam 1L 69
WN8: Uph .6L 31
Orchid Gro. L17: Aig 5E 74
Orchid Way WA9: Bold 2D 64
Orchil Cl. CH66: Lit Sut 8F 102
Ordnance Av. WA3: Birchw 5M 67
O'Reilly Ct. L3: Liv 5B 58
ORFORD 7E 66
Orford Av. WA2: Warr 1D 82
Orford Cl. L24: Hale 5B 94
WA3: Golb 3B 52
Orford Grn. WA2: Warr 8E 66
Orford La. WA2: Warr 2C 82
Orford Pk. WA2: Warr 8C 66
Orford Rd. WA1: Warr 9E 66
WA2: Warr .9E 66
Orford St. L15: Wav 9L 59
WA1: Warr .3C 82
Oriel Cl. L2: Liv 5D 4
L10: Ain 8J 35
Oriel Ct. CH42: Tran 7H 73
Oriel Cres. L20: Kirkd 9B 44
Oriel Dr. L10: Ain 8H 35
Oriel Lodge L20: Boot 8B 44
Oriel Rd. CH42: Tran 5L 73
L20: Boot .7A 44
L20: Kirkd .9B 44
WN4: Ash M 7H 41
Oriel St. L3: Liv 1E 4 (6B 58)
Orient Dr. L25: Woolt 5F 76
Origen Rd. L16: Child 8B 60
Oriole Cl. WA10: St H 2E 62
Orion Blvd. WA5: Gt San 8G 64
Orith Av. WA10: Eccl 7C 48
Orkney Cl. CH65: Ell P 4A 112
WA8: Wid .5A 80
WA11: St H 3N 49
Orlando Cl. CH43: Noct 4C 72
Orlando Dr. WA5: Gt San 1L 81
Orlando St. L20: Boot 9B 44
Orleans Ct. *WA5: Gt San 2K 81*
(off Louisiana Dr.)
Orleans Rd. L13: Liv 6M 59
Ormande St. WA9: St H 9L 49
Orme Ho. L39: Orm 8E 20
Ormerod Ct. CH63: Beb 2N 89
Ormesby Gdns. WA9: St H 3H 63
Ormesby Gro. CH63: Raby M 9A 90
Ormiston Rd. CH45: New B 2H 57
Ormond Av. L40: Westh 9J 21
Ormond Cl. WA8: Wid 6F 78
Ormonde Av. L31: Mag 4H 35
Ormonde Cres. L33: Kirkb 9E 36
Ormonde Dr. L31: Mag 3H 35
Ormond M. CH43: Noct 4C 72
Ormond St. CH45: Wall 4H 57
L3: Liv 4D 4 (7B 58)
Ormond Way CH43: Noct 4C 72
Ormsby St. L15: Wav 1K 75
Ormside Gro. WA9: St H 2N 63
ORMSKIRK 8C 20
Ormskirk Bus. Pk. L39: Orm 7D 20
Ormskirk Civic Hall 8C 20
Ormskirk Golf Course 6J 21
Ormskirk Ind. Pk. L39: Orm 7E 20
Ormskirk Old Rd. L39: Bic 5K 29
Ormskirk Rd. L9: Ain 2G 44
L10: Ain 7G 35
L34: Know .4H 47
L39: Bic 3F 28
WA11: Bic, Rainf 1A 38
(not continuous)
WA11: Rainf 2A 38
WN8: Skel .3N 29
(Bromilow Rd.)
WN8: Skel .4E 30
(Spencers La.)
WN8: Uph .5J 31
Ormskirk Station (Rail) 8D 20
Ormskirk St. WA10: St H 6K 49
Orms Way L37: Form 1E 24
Orphan Dr. L6: Liv 4J 59
(not continuous)
Orphan St. L7: Liv 7M 5 (9F 58)
ORRELL
L20 . . . . .3C 44
WN5 . . . . .7N 31
Orrell Cl. WA5: Gt San 2J 81
Orrell Hey L20: Boot 3C 44
Orrell Hill La. L38: Ince B 8J 25
Orrell La. L9: Walt 4F 44
L20: Boot .3D 44
L40: Burs .9H 15
Orrell Lodge L20: Boot 4D 44
Orrell M. L40: Burs 9J 15
Orrell Mt. L20: Boot 3B 44
Orrell Mt. Ind. Est. L20: Boot 3B 44
ORRELL PARK 4E 44
Orrell Park Station (Rail) 4F 44
Orrell Rd. CH45: New B 2J 57
L20: Boot .2B 44
L21: Lith 2B 44
WN5: Orr .5N 31
Orrell Station (Rail) 8N 31
Orrell St. WA9: St H 7M 49
Orret's Mdw. Rd. CH49: Woodc 5B 72
Orrysdale Rd. CH48: W Kir 5B 70
Orry St. L5: Liv 4C 58
Orsett Rd. L32: Kirkb 2D 46
Orston Cres. CH63: Spit 5N 89
Ortega Cl. CH62: New F 9B 74
Orthes St. L3: Liv 6K 5 (8E 58)
Orton Rd. L16: Child 9A 60
Orton Way WN4: Ash M 8H 41
Orville St. WA9: St H 2B 64
Orwell Cl. L37: Form 3D 24
WA9: Sut M 6K 63
Orwell Rd. L4: Kirkd 1C 58
Osbert Rd. L23: Blun 7H 33
Osborne Av. CH45: New B 2H 57
WA2: Warr .8E 66
Osborne Ct. *CH43: Oxton 2H 73*
(off Osborne Rd.)
CH62: Port S 1A 90
WA10: St H 1F 62
Osborne Gro. CH45: New B 3H 57
L34: Presc .4L 61
Osborne Rd. CH43: Oxton 3H 73
CH45: New B 2J 57
L13: Liv 3K 59
L21: Lith 1B 44
(not continuous)
L37: Form .3E 24
PR8: Ains .9H 11
WA3: Low .3F 52
WA4: Walt .7C 82
WA10: Eccl 5D 48
WN4: Ash M 7J 41
Osborne Va. CH45: New B 2H 57
Osborne Wood L17: Aig 7J 75
Osbourne Cl. CH62: Brom 8D 90
Osier Cl. CH2: Elt 2N 113
Osmaston Rd. CH42: Tran 6G 73
Osprey Cl. L27: N'ley 3J 77
WA2: Warr .6F 66
WA7: Beech 1B 108
Osprey Pl. L40: Burs 3F 20
Ossett Cl. CH43: Noct 4C 72
WA7: Nort .7F 96

Osterley Gdns. L9: Walt 4E 44
O'Sullivan Cres. WA11: St H 5A 50
Oswald Cl. L33: Kirkb 5C 36
Oteley Av. CH62: Brom 7C 90
Othello Cl. L20: Kirkd 9B 44
Ottawa Gdns. WA4: Westy 5H 83
Otterburn Cl. CH46: More 9J 55
Otterburn St. WA7: Nort 4G 96
OTTERSPOOL 7H 75
Otterspool Dr. L17: Aig 8J 75
Otterspool Rd. L17: Aig 7J 75
Otterstye Vw. PR8: South 5G 13
Otterton Rd. L11: Crox 5A 46
Ottery Cl. PR9: South 2M 7
Ottley St. L6: Liv 6H 59
Otway St. L19: Garst 2A 92
OUGHTRINGTON 4H 85
Oughtrington Cres.
WA13: Lymm 4H 85
Oughtrington La. WA13: Lymm 6G 85
Oughtrington Vw.
WA13: Lymm 4H 85
Oulton Cl. CH43: Oxton 5E 72
L31: Lyd 8G 27
Oulton Ct. WA4: Grap 6J 83
Oulton Gdns. WA9: St H 3H 63
Oulton La. L36: Roby 9H 61
Oulton Rd. L16: Child 2B 76
Oulton Way CH43: Oxton 6E 72
Oundle Dr. L10: Ain 8H 35
Oundle Pl. L25: Hunts X 9F 76
Oundle Rd. CH46: More 8M 55
Outer Central Rd. L24: Halew 2J 93
Outer Forum L11: Norr G 7K 45
Out La. L25: Woolt 6E 76
Outlet La. L31: Mell 2C 36
L39: Bic 2C 36
Outlook, The L38: Hight 8F 24
Oval, The CH45: Wall 3F 56
CH65: Ell P 2A 112
PR9: Banks 3E 8
Oval Leisure Centre, The 9M 73
Overbrook Ho. L34: Know 5G 47
Overbrook La. L34: Know 5F 46
Overbury St. L7: Liv 8G 58
Overchurch Rd. CH49: Upton 2M 71
Overdale Av. CH61: Barn 2D 88
Overdale Rd. CH64: Will 5N 101
Overdene Wlk. L32: Kirkb 1D 46
Overgreen Gro. CH46: More 8L 55
Overmarsh CH64: Ness 9G 101
OVERPOOL 8K 103
Overpool Gdns. CH66: Gt Sut 2L 111
Overpool Rd.
CH66: Ell P, Gt Sut, Whit 8L 103
(not continuous)
Overpool Station (Rail) 8K 103
Overstrand CH48: W Kir 6B 70
OVERTON 8M 107
Overton Av. L21: Lith 1A 44
Overton Cl. CH43: Oxton 5F 72
L32: Kirkb 1B 46
WA6: Frod 5M 107
Overton Dr. WA6: Frod 8M 107
Overton Grn. WA6: Frod 5N 107
Overton Rd. CH44: Wall 5H 57
Overton St. L7: Liv 8G 58
Overton Way CH43: Oxton 5F 72
Ovington Cl. WA7: Sut W 3B 108
Ovington Dr. PR8: South 3D 12
Ovolo Rd. L13: Liv 5M 59
Owen Av. L39: Orm 7D 20
Owen Cl. WA10: St H 9G 48
Owen Dr. L24: Speke 4F 92
Owen Rd. L4: Kirkd 1C 58
L33: Know I 3G 46
L35: Rainh 7F 62
Owens Cnr. WA4: App 4E 98
Owen's La. L39: Down 2C 26
Owen St. WA2: Warr 1B 82
WA10: St H 9G 48
Owlsfield WA12: Newt W 7N 51
Oxborough Cl. WA8: Wid 4J 79
Oxbow Rd. L12: W Der 1C 60
Oxendale Cl. L8: Liv 1G 74
Oxenham Rd. WA2: Warr 6C 66
Oxenholme Cres.
L11: Norr G 9M 45
Oxford Av. L20: Boot 7D 44
L21: Lith 2A 44
Oxford Cl. CH66: Gt Sut 5K 111
L17: Aig 6H 75
Oxford Ct. L22: Water 9J 33
PR8: Birkd 2M 11
WA1: Warr 2E 82
Oxford Dr. CH63: Thorn H 9F 88
L22: Water 9J 33
L26: Halew 8K 77
Oxford Gdns. PR8: Birkd 2L 11
Oxford Gro. M44: Cad 3J 69
Oxford Ho. *L20: Boot 7D 44*
(off Fernhill Rd.)
Oxford Rd. CH44: Wall 5J 57
L9: Ain 2G 44
L20: Boot 7C 44
L22: Water 9J 33
L36: Huy 5L 61
PR8: Birkd 1L 11
WA7: Run 6K 95
WN8: Skel 3B 30
Oxford St. *CH65: Ell P 8A 104*
(off Worcester St.)
L7: Liv 6K 5 (8E 58)
(not continuous)
WA4: Warr 4D 82
WA8: Wid 8L 79
WA10: St H 6J 49
(Cooper St.)
WA10: St H 5J 49
(Rutland St.)
WA12: Newt W 7J 51
Oxford St. E. L7: Liv 6N 5 (8F 58)
Oxheys WA7: Nort 7E 96
Oxhouse Rd. WN5: Orr 8N 31
Ox La. L35: Tar G 4M 77
Oxley Av. CH46: Leas 6B 56
Oxley St. WA9: St H 2N 63
Oxmead Cl. WA2: Padg 8J 67
Oxmoor Cl. WA7: Brook 1C 108
Oxmoor Local Nature Reserve 2F 96
OXTON 4F 72
Oxton Cl. L17: Aig 6H 75
L32: Kirkb 2N 45
WA8: Wid 4F 78
Oxton Ct. CH43: Oxton 4H 73
Oxton Grn. CH66: Gt Sut 1J 111
Oxton Rd. CH41: Birke 3J 73
CH44: Wall 6H 57
Oxton St. L4: Walt 1E 58

P

Pacific Rd. CH41: Birke 1M 73
L20: Boot 7A 44
(Atlantic Rd.)
L20: Boot 6A 44
(Globe Rd.)
Packenham Rd. L13: Liv 3L 59
Padbury St. L8: Liv 3F 74
PADDINGTON 9G 67
Paddington L7: Liv 5M 5 (8F 58)
(not continuous)
Paddington Bank WA1: Warr 2G 82
Paddock, The CH2: Elt 2L 113
CH46: More 1K 71
CH49: Upton 3B 72
CH60: Hesw 7C 88
CH66: Gt Sut 2J 111
L25: Gate 4F 76
L32: Kirkb 3B 46
L34: Eccl P 2D 62
L37: Form 8G 16
L39: Augh 1A 28
L40: Ruf 2N 15
PR8: Ains 1H 17
WA6: Hel 3F 114
WA13: Lymm 5J 85
WN4: Ash M 5H 41
Paddock Cl. L23: Blun 5H 33
Paddock Dr. CH64: Park 4D 100
Paddock Gro. WA9: Clock F 6N 63
Paddock La. WA13: Warb 9H 69
WA14: Dun M 3N 85
Paddock Ri. WA7: Beech 2A 108
Paddock Rd. L34: Presc 3L 61
WN8: Skel 7F 30
Padeswood Cl. WA9: St H 3M 63
PADGATE 8G 67
Padgate Bus. Pk. WA1: Padg 9J 67
Padgate La. WA1: Padg, Warr 1E 82
(not continuous)
Padgate Station (Rail) 8H 67
Padley M. WA1: Warr 3F 82
Padstow Cl. L26: Halew 7J 77
PR9: South 2N 7
WA5: Penk 5G 80
Padstow Dr. WA10: Windle 4E 48
Padstow Rd. CH49: Grea 5K 71
L16: Child 9B 60
Padstow Sq. WA7: Brook 1D 108
Pagebank Rd. L14: Knott A 6E 60
Page Ct. L37: Form 1F 24
Pagefield Rd. L15: Wav 2M 75
Page Grn. L36: Huy 6G 60
Page La. WA8: Wid 7M 79
PAGE MOSS 6F 60
Page Moss Av. L36: Huy 5F 60
Page Moss La. L14: Knott A 6E 60
Page Moss Pde. L36: Huy 5F 60
Page Wlk. L3: Liv 2J 5 (6D 58)
(not continuous)
Pagewood Cl. CH43: Noct 4C 72
Paignton Cl. L36: Huy 6M 61
WA5: Penk 4G 80
WN5: Bil 3A 40
Paignton Rd. CH45: Wall 3F 56
L16: Child 9B 60
Painswick Rd. CH66: Gt Sut 3K 111
Paisley Av. CH62: East 2D 102
WA11: St H 3N 49
Paisley Ct. L14: Knott A 5D 60
Paisley St. L3: Liv 2B 4 (6A 58)
Palace Arc. *WN4: Ash M 8K 41*
(off Foy St.)
PALACE FIELDS 9C 96
Palacefields Av. WA7: Pal F 9B 96
Palacefields Local Cen.
WA7: Pal F 9C 96
Palace Hey CH64: Ness 9G 101
Palace Rd. L9: Ain 4F 44
PR8: Birkd 1L 11
Palais Bldgs. L40: Burs 9J 15
Palatine, The L20: Boot 7B 44
Palatine Arc. WA10: St H 7K 49
Palatine Cl. M44: Irlam 1M 69
Palatine Ind. Est. WA4: Warr 5D 82
Palatine Rd. CH44: Wall 7K 57
CH62: Brom 6B 90
PR8: Birkd 1M 11
Palermo Cl. CH44: Wall 7K 57
Paley Cl. L4: Walt 2E 58
Palin Dr. WA5: Gt San 2H 81
Palladio Rd. L13: Liv 5N 59
Palliser Cl. WA3: Birchw 6A 68
Pall Mall L3: Liv 1D 4 (6B 58)
Palmarsh Rd. WA8: Hale B 2E 94
Palm Av. WN4: Garsw 6F 40
Palm Cl. L9: Walt 7H 45
Palm Ct. *L8: Liv 4F 74*
(off Weller Way)
WN8: Skel 2B 30
Palmer Cl. CH43: Noct 5D 72
WA10: St H 6J 49
Palmer Cres. WA5: Old H 9M 65
Palmerston Av. L21: Lith 3N 43
Palmerston Cl. L18: Moss H 5L 75
Palmerston Ct. L18: Moss H 5M 75
Palmerston Cres. L19: Garst 1A 92
Palmerston Dr. L21: Lith 3A 44
L25: Hunts X 9H 77
Palmerston Rd. CH44: Wall 5F 56
L18: Moss H 5L 75
L19: Garst 1A 92
PR9: South 9L 7
Palmerston St. CH42: Rock F 6M 73
Palmer Vs. CH42: Rock F 7L 73
Palm Gro. CH43: Oxton 2H 73
CH66: Whit 4M 111
L25: Woolt 7F 76
PR8: South 9K 7
Palm Hill CH43: Oxton 4H 73
Palmwood Av. L35: Rainh 7G 63
Palmwood Cl. CH43: Pren 7E 72
Palmyra Ho. WA1: Warr 3B 82
Palmyra Sq. Nth. WA1: Warr 3B 82
Palmyra Sq. Sth. WA1: Warr 3B 82
Palomar Cl. L8: Liv 1G 74
Paltridge Way CH61: Pens 3N 87
Pamela Cl. L10: Faz 4N 45
Pampas Gro. L9: Walt 6G 44
Panama Av. L30: N'ton 1E 44
Pangbourne Cl. WA4: App 1F 98
Pankhurst Rd. L21: Ford 9B 34
Pansy St. L5: Kirkd 2C 58
Panton Way L10: Faz 4N 45
Papillon Dr. L9: Ain 2J 45
Parade, The CH64: Park 4B 100
L15: Wav 8N 59
L26: Halew 9J 77
Parade Cres. L24: Speke 5J 93
Parade St. WA10: St H 6K 49
Paradise Gdns. L15: Wav 1L 75
Paradise Island Bingo 9D 44
Paradise La. L35: Whis 7A 62
L37: Form 7F 16
Paradise Pl. L1: Liv 6F 4
Paradise St. L1: Liv 7F 4 (9C 58)
Paragon Cl. WA8: Wid 3L 79
PARBOLD 3F 22
Parbold Av. WA11: St H 5N 49
Parbold Cl. L40: Burs 2J 21
Parbold Ct. WA8: Wid 8G 78
Parbold Hill WN8: Parb 3G 23
Parbold Station (Rail) 3F 22
Parbrook Cl. L36: Huy 3H 61
Parbrook Rd. L36: Huy 3H 61
Parchments, The WA12: Newt W 6M 51
Pardoe Ct. L40: Burs 2K 21
Paris Av. WN3: Wins 1E 40
Parish M. L14: Knott A 5C 60
Park, The L36: Huy 8J 61
WA5: Penk 5F 80
(not continuous)
Park & Ride
Esplanade 8E 6
Fairways 5H 7
Gilmoss 4A 46
Kew 1F 12
Leasowe 7A 56
Marshalls Cross 3L 63
Park Av. CH44: Wall 6K 57
L9: Ain 3J 45
L18: Moss H 5K 75
L23: Crosb 6L 33
L31: Lyd 9J 27
L34: Eccl P 2C 62
L35: Rainh 5F 62
L37: Form 3F 24
L39: Orm 8C 20
PR9: South 6K 7
WA3: Golb 1A 52
WA4: Warr 5E 82
WA8: Wid 6L 79
WA11: Hay 4C 50
WN5: Bil 2A 40
Park Av. Nth. WA12: Newt W 8L 51
Park Av. Sth. WA12: Newt W 8L 51
Park Blvd. WA1: Warr 4C 82
Parkbourn L31: Mag 1M 35
Parkbourn Dr. L31: Mag 1M 35
Parkbourn Nth. L31: Mag 1M 35
Parkbourn Sq. L31: Mag 1M 35
Parkbridge Rd. CH42: Tran 5J 73
Park Brow Dr. L32: Kirkb 2D 46
Parkbury Ct. CH43: Oxton 5G 72
Park Cl. CH41: Birke 2J 73
L32: Kirkb 7N 35
L37: Form 4E 24
WN8: Parb 2G 22
Park Ct. CH48: W Kir 6B 70
L22: Water 2L 43
L32: Kirkb 8A 36
PR9: South 7J 7
WA1: Warr 3A 82
WA6: Frod 6L 107
WA7: Run 7K 95
WA9: St H 1L 63
Park Cres. L39: Down 9E 18
PR9: South 6J 7
WA4: App 1E 98
Park Cres. Ct. *PR9: South 6K 7*
(off Park Cres.)
Parkdale CH48: Caldy 1E 86
Parkdale Av. L9: Walt 3F 44
Parkdale Ind. Est. WA1: Warr 4D 82
Parkdale Rd. WA1: Padd 1H 83
Park Dr. CH41: Birke 1G 72
(not continuous)
CH43: Clau 1G 72
CH65: Whit 2N 111
L23: Blun 6G 32
L23: Thorn 4N 33
Parkend Rd. CH42: Tran 5J 73
Parker Av. L21: Sea 3M 43
Parker Cl. L30: N'ton 1G 44
Parker Cres. L39: Orm 6C 20
Parkers Ct. WA7: Pal F 9A 96
Parker St. L1: Liv 5G 4 (8C 58)
WA1: Warr 4B 82
WA7: Run 4L 95
Parkfield Av. CH41: Birke 2K 73
L30: N'ton 2F 44
WA4: Westy 4H 83
Parkfield Cl. L39: Orm 1A 28
Parkfield Dr. CH44: Wall 5H 57
CH65: Whit 3M 111
WA6: Hel 2E 114
Parkfield Gro. L31: Mag 2H 35
Parkfield M. L17: Aig 4G 75
Parkfield Pl. CH41: Birke 2K 73
Parkfield Rd. CH63: Beb 4N 89
L17: Aig 4G 75
L22: Water 9L 33
Parkfields La. WA2: Fearn 7G 67
PARKGATE 5B 100
Parkgate Cl. L17: Aig 7K 75
Parkgate Ho. *CH64: Park 4B 100*
(off Greenway)
Parkgate Ho. Ct. CH64: Park 5B 100
Parkgate La. CH64: Nest 1E 100
Parkgate Rd.
CH1: Woodb, Moll, Sau 5D 110
CH64: Nest 6D 100
CH66: Led 3B 110
WA4: Stockt H 7E 82
Parkgate Way WA7: Murd 8E 96
Park Gro. CH41: Birke 3K 73
Parkhaven Ct. L31: Mag 2G 35
Park Hey Dr. WN6: Appl B 6N 23
PARK HILL 1A 38
Parkhill Ct. *L8: Liv 4E 74*
(off Park Hill Rd.)
Park Hill Rd. L8: Liv 4E 74
Parkhill Rd. CH42: Tran 5J 73
Parkholme L22: Water 1L 43
Parkhurst Rd. CH42: Tran 6J 73
Park Ind. Est. WN4: Ash M 9G 40
Parkinson Rd. L9: Walt 6F 44
Parkland Cl. L8: Liv 3F 74
WA4: App T 3J 99
Parkland Ct. CH43: Bid 9C 56
CH49: Woodc 6A 72
(off Childwall Grn.)
Parkland Dr. CH2: Elt 2L 113
Parklands CH66: Lit Sut 9H 103
L34: Know 7H 47
PR9: South 7K 7
WA8: Wid 5F 78
WA11: Rainf 4C 38
WN8: Skel 2G 30
Parklands Dr. CH2: Elt 2N 113
CH60: Hesw 9B 88
Parklands Gdns. CH66: Lit Sut 8J 103
Parklands Vw. CH66: Lit Sut 8J 103
Parklands Way L22: Water 1L 43
Park La. CH47: Meols 8G 55
L1: Liv 7F 4 (9C 58)
L20: Boot 3C 44
L30: N'ton 9E 34
L31: Mag 9L 27
PR4: Tarl 5M 9
WA4: App, Hghr Wal 2N 97
WA6: Frod 6L 107
WA13: Warb 8J 69
Park La. Dr. L31: Mag 1M 35
Park Lane Holiday Homes
CH47: Meols 7H 55
Park La. W. L30: N'ton 8E 34
Parklea CH66: Lit Sut 8J 103

Park Link L39: Augh 3N 27
Park Pl. L8: Liv 2D 74
L20: Boot 7B 44
Park Pool 8C 20
Park Rd. CH2: Thorn M 4J 113
CH42: Tran 5L 73
CH44: Wall 6J 57
CH47: Meols 8F 54
CH48: W Kir 6B 70
CH60: Hesw 6B 88
CH62: East 9E 90
CH62: Port S 2A 90
CH64: Will 6A 102
CH65: Ell P 1A 112
(not continuous)
L8: Liv 2E 74
L22: Water 1L 43
L32: Kirkb 8N 35
(not continuous)
L34: Presc 2N 61
L37: Form 3E 24
L39: Orm 8C 20
M31: Part 6N 69
PR9: South 6J 7
WA2: Warr 8E 66
WA3: Golb 3A 52
WA5: Gt San 1E 80
WA7: Run 7J 95
WA8: Wid 7L 79
WA9: St H 7M 49
WA11: St H 7M 49
WA13: Lymm 8K 85
WA13: Warb 9H 69
WN5: Bil 2A 40
(not continuous)
Park Rd. E. CH41: Birke 2J 73
Park Rd. Nth. CH41: Birke 1G 72
WA12: Newt W 7N 51
Park Rd. Sth. CH43: Clau 2H 73
WA12: Newt W 8L 51
Park Rd. W. CH43: Clau 1G 72
PR9: South 6H 7
Parks, The WA12: Newt W 1K 51
Parkside CH44: Wall 6J 57
L20: Boot 6B 44
(off Strand Shop. Cen.)
Parkside Av. WA9: Sut M 6L 63
WN4: Ash M 3H 41
WN8: Skel 4A 30
Parkside Cl. CH63: Beb 1N 89
CH64: Park 6D 100
L27: N'ley 4J 77
Parkside Ct. PR9: South 6J 7
WA8: Wid 6K 79
Parkside Dr. L12: W Der 1M 59
Parkside Ind. Pk. WA3: Golb 2B 52
Parkside Mans. L36: Huy 7M 61
Parkside Pl. WN8: Uph 8J 31
Parkside Rd. CH42: Tran 5L 73
CH63: Beb 1N 89
WA2: Win 9C 52
WA3: Win 6B 52
Parkside St. L6: Liv 1L 5 (6E 58)
Parkstile La. L11: Crox 6A 46
Parkstone Rd. CH42: Tran 5J 73
Park St. CH41: Birke 2K 73
(not continuous)
CH44: Wall 5J 57
CH64: Nest 6E 100
L8: Liv 3D 74
(not continuous)
L20: Boot 7B 44
(not continuous)
WA9: St H 6M 49
WA11: Hay 4B 50
Parksway WA1: Wools 1L 83
Park Ter. L22: Water 2L 43
Park Va. CH64: Nest 7F 100
Parkvale Av. CH43: Pren 8E 72
Park Va. Rd. L9: Walt 4F 44
Park Vw. CH62: Brom 7B 90
CH62: New F 8A 74
L6: Liv 4J 59
L9: Walt 6F 44
(off Brook Rd.)
L17: Aig 3K 75
L22: Water 9K 33
L23: Thorn 4A 34
L36: Huy 5G 60
WA2: Warr 6F 66
WN4: Ash M 9K 41
Parkview CH49: Woodc 7A 72
Parkview Cl. CH41: Birke 1J 73
Parkview Ct. CH60: Hesw 7N 87
Parkview Dr. L27: N'ley 4J 77
Park Vw. Flats L21: Lith 2N 43
Parkview Pk. WA13: Lymm 7K 85
Parkview Rd. L11: Crox 4B 46
Park Wall Rd. L29: Ince B, Thorn 9M 25
Park Way L8: Liv 9L 5 (1E 74)
(not continuous)
L36: Huy 2H 61
L37: Form 3F 24
Parkway CH45: Wall 2E 56
CH47: Meols 9F 54
CH61: Irby 9N 71
L23: Crosb 9M 33
L30: N'ton 6E 34
PR9: Banks 4H 9
Parkway Cl. CH61: Irby 9N 71
Parkway East L32: Kirkb 8N 35
Parkway West L32: Kirkb 8N 35
Park West CH60: Hesw 8L 87
Parkwood Cl. CH62: Brom 6D 90
WA13: Lymm 6D 84
Parkwood Rd. L25: Woolt 4E 76
L35: Whis 7B 62
Parlane St. WA9: St H 6M 49
(not continuous)
Parle Ct. L6: Liv 4G 58
Parliament Bus. Pk. *L8: Liv 1G 75*
(off Commerce Way)
Parliament Cl. L1: Liv 9J 5 (1D 74)
Parliament Pl. L8: Liv 9K 5 (1E 74)
Parliament St. L8: Liv 1C 74
WA9: St H 2G 63
WN8: Uph 5M 31
Parliament Way CH66: Gt Sut 5L 111
Parlington Cl. WA8: Wid 9F 78
Parlow Rd. L11: Norr G 1K 59
Parnell Rd. CH63: Spit 5N 89
PARR 7A 50
Parren Av. L35: Whis 8N 61
Parr Gro. CH49: Grea 4K 71
WA11: Hay 4C 50
Parr Hall 4B 82
Parr Ind. Est. WA9: St H 8N 49
Parr Mt. Ct. WA9: St H 7M 49
Parr Mt. St. WA9: St H 7M 49
Parrs Corner Trad. Est. *L20: Boot 6B 44*
(off Stanley Rd.)
Parrs La. L39: Augh 4B 28
Parr's Rd. CH43: Oxton 5H 73
PARR STOCKS 8N 49
Parr Stocks Rd. WA9: St H 7N 49
Parr St. L1: Liv 7G 4 (9C 58)
WA1: Warr 4D 82
(not continuous)
WA8: Wid 7M 79
WA9: St H 7L 49
Parr Swimming & Fitness Cen. 6N 49
Parrs Wood Vw. WA4: Grap 7H 83
Parry Dr. WA4: Thel 5M 83
Parry's La. WA7: Run 6K 95
Parry St. CH44: Wall 7K 57
Parsonage Brow WN8: Uph 4J 31
Parsonage Cl. WN8: Uph 5K 31
Parsonage Rd. WA8: Wid 3J 95
WN8: Uph 5K 31
Parsonage Wlk. WA3: Cul 8N 53
Parsonage Way WA5: Gt San 3J 81
Parson's Brow WA11: Rainf 5B 38
Parthenon Dr. L11: Norr G 7J 45
PARTINGTON 6M 69
Partington Av. L20: Boot 6D 44
Partington Shop. Cen. M31: Part 6M 69
Partington Sports Village 7M 69
Partington Sq. WA7: Nort 3H 97
Parton St. L6: Liv 6H 59
Partridge Cl. L12: Crox 7D 46
WA3: Birchw 5M 67
Partridge Lakes Fishery 9L 53
Partridge Rd. L23: Blun 7H 33
L32: Kirkb 8N 35
Part St. PR8: South 1N 11
Pasadena Av. WA5: Gt San 1J 81
Pass Way *WA11: St H 2M 49*
(off Honister Av.)
Pasture Av. CH46: More 7M 55
Pasture Cl. L25: Woolt 7F 76
WA9: Clock F 5M 63
WN4: Ash M 5G 41
Pasture Cres. CH46: More 8M 55
Pasture Dr. WA3: Croft 2H 67
Pasture La. L37: Form 8J 17
WA2: Padg 8J 67
WA11: Rainf 7D 38
Pasture La. Bus. Cen. WA11: Rainf 7D 38
Pasture Rd. CH46: More 6L 55
Pastures, The CH48: W Kir 6G 70
PR9: South 2B 8
WA9: Bold 2C 64
Pateley Cl. L32: Kirkb 1A 46
Pately Wlk. L24: Speke 3K 93
Paterson St. CH41: Birke 2J 73
Patmos Cl. L5: Liv 3D 58
Paton Cl. CH48: W Kir 5E 70
Patricia Av. CH41: Birke 8F 56
Patricia Ct. *WA10: St H 6J 49*
(off Albion St.)
Patricia Gro. L20: Boot 4C 44
Patrick Av. L20: Boot 3C 44
Patrivale Cl. WA1: Padd 2G 83
Patten La. *WA1: Warr 3C 82*
(off Barbauld St.)
Pattens Cl. L30: N'ton 7C 34
Patten St. CH41: Birke 9H 57
Patten's Wlk. L34: Know P 5H 47
Patterdale Av. WA2: Warr 7D 66
Patterdale Cl. PR8: Ains 1H 17
Patterdale Cres. L31: Mag 1K 35
Patterdale Dr. WA10: St H 1E 62
Patterdale Rd. CH63: Beb 4M 89
L15: Wav 2L 75
M31: Part 6L 69
WN4: Ash M 3J 41
Patterson Cl. WA3: Birchw 6M 67
Patterson St. WA12: Newt W 7K 51
Patton Dr. WA5: Gt San 2K 81
Paul Cl. WA5: Gt San 2K 81
Pauldings La. L21: Lith 2N 43
Pauline Wlk. L10: Faz 3N 45
Paul McCartney Way L6: Liv 6G 59
Paul Orr Ct. L3: Liv 1D 4 (5B 58)
Paulsfield Dr. CH46: More 1M 71
Paul's La. PR9: South 4L 7
Paul St. L3: Liv 1E 4 (6B 58)
WA2: Warr 2B 82
Paulton Cl. L8: Liv 4E 74
Paveley Bank L27: N'ley 2H 77
Pavilion Bingo Club 1G 75
(off Lodge La.)
Pavilion Cl. L8: Liv 1G 74
Pavilion Ct. WA12: Newt W 7J 51
Pavilions, The CH43: Oxton 4G 72
Paxton Pl. WN8: Skel 8F 30
Paxton Rd. L36: Huy 5J 61
Payne Cl. WA5: Gt San 2M 81
Paythorne Cl. WA3: Cul 7N 53
Peace Dr. WA5: Gt San 3M 81
Peacehaven WN8: Skel 3B 30
Peacehaven Cl. L16: Child 9D 60
Peach Gro. L31: Mell 7N 35
WA11: Hay 3G 50
Peach St. L7: Liv 6L 5 (8E 58)
Peach Tree Cl. L24: Hale 5B 94
Peacock Av. WA1: Warr 2F 82
Peacock La. WA16: High L 9J 85
Pearce Cl. L25: Woolt 7E 76
Pear Gro. L6: Liv 6G 59
Pearl Way L6: Liv 5G 58
Pearson Av. WA4: Warr 6E 82
Pearson Cl. M31: Part 6N 69
Pearson Ct. L15: Wav 2M 75
Pearson Dr. L20: Boot 3D 44
Pearson Rd. CH42: Tran 3L 73
Pearson St. L15: Wav 1L 75
Pear Tree Av. WA7: Run 8M 95
Peartree Av. L12: W Der 9D 46
Pear Tree Cl. CH60: Hesw 6C 88
L24: Hale 6B 94
WA6: Frod 5N 107
Peartree Cres. WA12: Newt W 8L 51
Pear Tree Pl. WA4: Warr 4D 82
Pear Tree Rd. L36: Huy 9J 61
Peartree Way CH66: Gt Sut 4K 111
Peasefield Rd. L14: Knott A 5E 60
Peasley Cl. WA2: Padg 8J 67
PEASLEY CROSS 9M 49
Peasley Cross La. WA9: St H 7L 49
Peatwood Av. L32: Kirkb 3D 46
Peckers Hill Rd. WA9: St H 2A 64
Peckfield Cl. WA7: Brook 1C 108
Peckforton Cl. L13: Liv 3K 59
Peckforton Dr. CH66: Gt Sut 2K 111
WA7: Sut W 2B 108
Peckmill Grn. L27: N'ley 4K 77
Peck Mill La. WA6: Hel 6D 114
Pecks Brow CW8: Kingsl 9J 109
Pecksniff Cl. L8: Liv 3E 74
Peebles Av. WA11: St H 3N 49
Peebles Cl. CH66: Lit Sut 8E 102
L33: Kirkb 5B 36
WN4: Garsw 7E 40
Peel Av. CH42: Tran 5M 73
Peel Cl. L35: Whis 6B 62
WA1: Wools 2L 83
Peel Ho. L21: Sea 4N 43
Peel Ho. La. WA8: Wid 5L 79
Peel Pl. L8: Liv 9K 5 (1E 74)
WA10: St H 5K 49
Peel Rd. L20: Boot 5N 43
WN8: Skel 7G 31
Peel St. L8: Liv 4F 74
PR8: South 9L 7
WA7: Run 4J 95
WA12: Newt W 7J 51
Peel Wlk. L31: Mag 1G 35
Peerswood Ct. CH64: Lit N 9E 100
Peet Av. L39: Orm 9B 20
WA10: St H 6F 48
Peets La. PR9: South 6M 7
Peet St. L7: Liv 8G 59
Pelham Dr. L30: N'ton 2D 44
Pelham Gro. L17: Aig 4H 75
Pelham Rd. CH44: Wall 6G 56
WA4: Thel 5K 83
Pelwood Ct. CH49: Woodc 5B 72
Pemberton Cl. CH64: Will 6N 101
Pemberton Rd. CH49: Woodc 5B 72
L13: Liv 6M 59
WN3: Wins 3C 40
WN5: Wins 3C 40
Pembertons Ct. *L34: Presc 3B 62*
(off Scotchbarn La.)
Pemberton St. WA10: St H 7H 49
Pembrey Way L25: Hunts X 8H 77
Pembridge Ct. CH65: Ell P 2C 112
Pembridge Gdns. *CH65: Ell P 2C 112*
(off Rochester Dr.)
Pembroke Av. CH46: More 1M 71
Pembroke Cl. WA10: St H 8H 49
Pembroke Ct. CH41: Tran 4M 73
WA7: Manor P 2E 96
Pembroke Dr. CH65: Whit 2M 111
Pembroke Gdns. L3: Liv 4K 5 (7E 58)
WA4: App 3E 98
Pembroke Gro. M44: Cad 3J 69
Pembroke Ho. L6: Liv 5H 59
Pembroke Pl. L3: Liv 4J 5 (7D 58)
Pembroke Rd. L20: Boot 7B 44
Pembroke St. L3: Liv 4K 5 (7E 58)
Pembury Cl. L12: Crox 7C 46
Penare WA7: Brook 1E 108
Penarth Cl. L7: Liv 9G 58
Pencombe Rd. L36: Huy 5F 60
Penda Dr. L33: Kirkb 5C 36
Pendennis Ct. WA7: Cas 5B 96
Pendennis Rd. CH44: Wall 6J 57
Pendennis St. L6: Liv 4G 59
Pendine Cl. L6: Liv 5H 59
WA5: Call 7L 65
Pendle Av. WA11: St H 5N 49
Pendlebury St. WA4: Westy 5H 83
WA9: Clock F 6M 63
Pendle Cl. CH49: Upton 2M 71
CH66: Lit Sut 8E 102
Pendle Ct. WN8: Skel 9G 30
Pendle Dr. L21: Ford 7B 34
L39: Orm 7E 20
Pendle Gdns. WA3: Cul 8M 53
Pendle Pl. WN8: Skel 8G 31
Pendle Rd. WA3: Golb 1D 52
Pendleton Ct. L34: Presc 4A 62
Pendleton Grn. L26: Halew 9J 77
Pendleton Rd. L4: Walt 8F 44
Pendle Vw. L21: Ford 7B 34
Pendle Vs. L21: Ford 8B 34
Penfield Rd. WN7: Leigh 1K 53
Penfold L31: Mag 2K 35
Penfold Cl. CH1: Cap 5G 110
L18: Moss H 3B 76
Penfolds WA7: Run 6N 95
Pengwern Gro. L15: Wav 9J 59
Pengwern St. L8: Liv 3F 74
Pengwern Ter. *CH45: Wall 2J 57*
(off Holland Rd.)
Penhale Cl. L17: Aig 6G 75
Penhurst Way WA9: St H 2N 63
Peninsula Bus. Pk. CH46: Leas 7A 56
Peninsula Cl. CH45: Wall 1E 56
Peninsula Ho. WA2: Warr 1D 82
Penistone Dr. CH66: Lit Sut 9G 103
PENKETH 4H 81
Penketh Av. WA5: Warr 9A 66
Penketh Bus. Pk. WA5: Gt San 4K 81
Penketh Ct. WA5: Penk 4F 80
WA7: Run 5L 95
Penketh Dr. L24: Speke 3J 93
Penketh Parish Swimming Pool 4G 81
Penketh Pl. WN8: Skel 7F 30
Penketh Rd. L24: Speke 4J 93
WA5: Gt San 4J 81
Penketh's La. WA7: Run 4K 95
Penkett Ct. CH45: Wall 3J 57
Penkett Gdns. CH45: Wall 3J 57
Penkett Gro. CH45: Wall 3J 57
Penkett Rd. CH45: Wall 3H 57
Penkford La. WA5: Coll G 9F 50
Penkford St. WA12: Newt W 7G 50
Penkmans La. WA6: Frod 8M 107
Penlake La. WA9: St H 2B 64
Penley Cres. L32: Kirkb 9N 35
Penlinken Dr. L6: Liv 5G 59
Penmann Cl. L26: Halew 8K 77
Penmann Cres. L26: Halew 8K 77
Penmark Cl. WA5: Call 2N 65
Penmon Dr. CH61: Pens 4N 87
Pennant Av. L12: W Der 9A 46
Pennant Cl. WA3: Birchw 6A 68
Pennard Av. L36: Huy 4H 61
(not continuous)
Penn Gdns. CH65: Ell P 9N 103
Pennine Av. WN3: Wins 1E 40
Pennine Cl. WA9: St H 7A 50
Pennine Dr. WA9: St H 7B 50
Pennine La. WA3: Golb 1D 52
Pennine Pl. WN8: Skel 6E 30
Pennine Rd. CH42: Tran 7J 73
CH44: Wall 5F 56
WA2: Warr 7F 66
Pennine Wlk. CH66: Lit Sut 8G 103
Pennine Way L32: Kirkb 7A 36
Pennington Av. L20: Boot 3D 44
L39: Orm 7C 20
Pennington Cl. WA6: Frod 4N 107
Pennington Ct. L39: Orm 7D 20
WN7: Leigh 1J 53
Pennington Dr. WA12: Newt W 7N 51
Pennington Gdns. *L34: Presc 3A 62*
(off Houghton St.)
Pennington Grn. CH66: Gt Sut 2H 111
Pennington La. WA9: Coll G, St H 7E 50
Pennington Lodge WA9: St H 1J 63
Pennington Rd. L21: Lith 4B 44
Pennington St. L4: Walt 8E 44
Penn La. WA7: Run 5J 95
Pennsylvania Rd. L13: Liv 2J 59
Pennybutts Cl. WA3: Golb 1A 52
Pennycress Dr. L11: Norr G 8L 45
Pennyford Dr. L18: Moss H 5K 75
PENNYLANDS 3A 30
Penny La. L18: Moss H 4L 75
WA5: Coll G 1F 64
WA8: Cron 2D 78
WA11: Hay 3H 51
Penny La. Neighbourhood Cen.
L15: Wav 2M 75
Pennypleck La. CW9: Ant 5N 99
Pennystone Cl. CH49: Upton 2L 71

Pennywood Dr. L35: Whis 7B 62
Penpoll Cl. L20: Boot 4B 44
Penrhos Rd. CH47: Hoy 2B 70
Penrhyd Rd. CH61: Irby 2L 87
Penrhyn Av. CH61: Thing 1A 88
L21: Lith .3A 44
Penrhyn Ct. L34: Know 4F 46
Penrhyn Cres. WA7: Run 8L 95
Penrhyn Rd. L34: Know 5F 46
Penrhyn St. L5: Liv 4C 58
Penrith Av. PR8: Ains 2J 17
WA2: Warr 7D 66
Penrith Cl. M31: Part 5L 69
WA6: Frod 5N 107
Penrith Cres. L31: Mag 1K 35
WN4: Ash M 7K 41
Penrith Rd. WA10: St H 1E 62
Penrith St. CH41: Birke 3J 73
Penrose Av. E. L14: Broad G 7D 60
Penrose Av. W. L14: Broad G 7C 60
Penrose Gdns. WA5: Penk 5F 80
Penrose Pl. WN8: Skel 8H 31
Penrose St. L5: Liv 3E 58
Penry Av. M44: Cad 3L 69
Penryn Av. WA11: St H 3N 49
Penryn Cl. WA5: Penk 5G 81
Pensall Dr. CH61: Hesw 5N 87
Pensarn Gdns. WA5: Call 7M 65
Pensarn Rd. L13: Liv 7L 59
PENSBY 3A 88
Pensby Cl. CH61: Thing 2A 88
Pensby Dr. CH66: Gt Sut 1J 111
Pensby Hall La. CH61: Hesw 5N 87
Pensby Rd. CH60: Hesw 7N 87
CH61: Hesw, Irby, Pens 7N 87
Pensby St. CH41: Birke 9J 57
Penshaw Cl. L14: Knott A 3E 60
Penshaw Ct. WA7: Pal F 8A 96
Pentire Av. WA10: Windle 4E 48
Pentire Cl. L10: Faz 4N 45
Pentland Av. L4: Walt 9F 44
WA2: Warr 6C 66
WA9: St H 7B 50
Pentland Pl. WA2: Warr 6C 66
Pentland Rd. L33: Kirkb 7E 36
Penty Pl. PR8: South 9G 6
Penuel Rd. L4: Walt 8E 44
Penvalley Cres. L6: Liv 5H 59
Penwell Fold WN8: Skel 4H 31
Peony Gdns. WA9: Bold 2D 64
Peover St. L3: Liv 1G 5 (6C 58)
Peploe Rd. L4: Walt 8J 45
Peplow Rd. L32: Kirkb 9N 35
Peppers, The WA13: Lymm 5F 84
Pepper St. L24: Hale 6A 94
WA4: App T 4H 99
WA13: Lymm 5E 84
Pepperwood Dr. WN3: Wins 1G 40
Pera Cl. L6: Liv 2N 5 (6F 58)
Perch Pool La. L40: Scar 3L 13
PR9: South 2L 13
Percival Ct. PR8: South 9F 6
(off Lord St.)
WA7: Run .6G 94
Percival La. WA7: Run 6G 94
Percival Rd. CH65: Ell P 8N 103
Percival St. WA1: Warr 3D 82
Percival Way WA10: St H 5F 48
Percy Rd. CH44: Wall 7L 57
Percy St. L8: Liv 9K 5 (1E 74)
L20: Boot .5A 44
WA5: Warr 3N 81
(not continuous)
WA9: St H 1B 64
Percy Vs. L9: Walt 6F 44
(off Cedardale Rd.)
Perilla Dr. L11: Norr G 8M 45
Perimeter Rd. L33: Know I 2H 47
WA6: Hel 9N 105
Perriam Rd. L19: Aller 8B 76
Perrin Av. WA7: Run 7H 95
Perrin Rd. CH45: Wall 4E 56
Perrins Rd. WA5: Burtw 3H 65
Perrybrook Wlk. WN4: Ash M 7M 41
(off North St.)
Perrygate Cl. L7: Liv 9G 58
Perry St. L8: Liv 2C 74
WA7: Run .5L 95
Pershore Gro. PR8: Ains 1G 17
Pershore Ho. CH42: Tran 7H 73
Pershore Rd. L32: Kirkb 2C 46
Perth Av. WA9: St H 2H 63
Perth Cl. L33: Kirkb 5B 36
WA2: Fearn 5G 67
Perth St. L6: Liv 1N 5 (6F 58)
Pete Best Dr. L12: W Der 3N 59
Peterborough Cl. CH66: Gt Sut 6L 111
Peterborough Dr. L30: N'ton 7D 34
Peterborough Rd. L15: Wav 2M 75
Peter Ho. L2: Liv 3E 4
Peterhouse M. L20: Boot 7C 44
Peterhouse Wlk. WN4: Ash M 7H 41
Peter Kane Sq. WA3: Golb 2B 52
(off Heath St.)
Peterlee Cl. WA9: St H 2J 63
Peterlee Way L30: N'ton 1F 44
Peter Mahon Way L20: Boot 6A 44
Peter Price's La. CH63: Hghr B 3L 89
Peter Rd. L4: Walt 8D 44
(not continuous)
Peters Arc. L1: Liv 6F 4
Peters Av. L40: Burs 1J 21
Petersfield Cl. L30: N'ton 1E 44
Petersfield Gdns. WA3: Cul 6M 53
Petersgate WA7: Murd 8F 96
Petersham Dr. WA4: App 2F 98
Peter's La. L1: Liv 6F 4 (8C 58)
Peterstone Cl. WA5: Call 6M 65
Peter St. CH44: Wall 7L 57
L1: Liv 4F 4 (7C 58)
WA3: Golb 2B 52
WA10: St H 6H 49
WN4: Ash M 8L 41
Peterwood CH42: Rock F 7N 73
Petham Ct. WA8: Wid 4H 79
Petherick Rd. L11: Crox 5A 46
Petra Ct. L4: Walt 2H 59
Petunia Cl. L14: Knott A 5E 60
WA9: Bold 2C 64
Petworth Av. WA2: Warr 6C 66
WN3: Wins 1F 40
Petworth Cl. L24: Speke 3F 92
Petworth Rd. PR8: Ains 8H 11
Peveril Cl. WA4: App 8E 82
Peveril St. L9: Walt 7E 44
PEWFALL 1E 50
PEWTERSPEAR 3G 98
Pewterspear Grn. Rd. WA4: App 4E 98
Pewterspear La. WA4: App 3E 98
PEX HILL 2H 79
Pex Hill Ct. WA8: Wid 3H 79
Pharmacy Rd. L24: Speke 3G 92
Pheasant Cl. WA3: Birchw 5N 67
Pheasant Fld. L24: Hale 5N 93
Pheasant Gro. L26: Halew 7J 77
Philbeach Rd. L4: Walt 8J 45
L11: Norr G 8J 45
Philharmonic Ct. L8: Liv 8K 5
Philip Dr. PR8: Ains 8M 11
Philip Gro. WA9: St H 2M 63
Philip Leverhulme Lodge
CH62: Port S 1A 90
Philip Rd. WA8: Wid 8E 78
Philips La. CH66: Gt Sut 1H 111
Phillimore Rd. L6: Liv 6H 59
Phillip Gro. L12: W Der 4D 60
Phillips Cl. L23: Thorn 5A 34
L37: Form 2F 24
Phillips Dr. WA5: Gt San 2G 81
Phillip's La. L37: Form 2E 24
Phillips St. L3: Liv 2E 4 (6B 58)
Phillips Way CH60: Hesw 7M 87
Phipps La. WA5: Burtw 1G 64
Phoenix Av. WA5: Warr 7A 66
Phoenix Brow WA9: St H 7L 49
Phoenix Dr. L14: Knott A 5E 60
Phoenix Pk. L24: Speke 2E 92
Phoenix Pl. WA5: Gt San 1J 81
Physics Rd. L24: Speke 2G 93
Phythian Cl. L6: Liv 2N 5 (6G 58)
Phythian Cres. WA5: Penk 4H 81
Phythian St. L6: Liv 2M 5 (6F 58)
WA11: Hay 4B 50
Picadilly WN5: Bil 6A 40
Pichael Nook WA4: Westy 4H 83
Pickerill Rd. CH49: Grea 5L 71
Pickering Cres. WA4: Thel 5L 83
Pickering Rake L30: N'ton 6C 34
(off Red Lomes)
Pickering Rd. CH45: New B 1H 57
Pickerings Cl. WA7: Run 9M 95
Pickerings Pasture Local Nature Reserve
. . . . .3D 94
Pickerings Pasture Vis. Cen. 3E 94
Pickerings Rd. WA8: Hale B 2E 94
Pickering St. L6: Liv 4F 58
Pickles Dr. L40: Burs 1H 21
Pickmere Dr. CH62: East 3E 102
(not continuous)
WA7: Brook 1E 108
Pickmere St. WA5: Warr 3N 81
Pickop St. L3: Liv 2E 4 (7B 58)
Pickwick St. L8: Liv 2E 74
Pickworth Way L31: Mell 9N 35
Picow Farm Rd. WA7: Run, West P 6H 95
Picow St. WA7: Run 6J 95
PICTON 9H 113
Picton Av. WA7: Run 6L 95
Picton Cl. CH43: Oxton 4F 72
CH62: East 3C 102
WA3: Birchw 5K 67
Picton Cres. L15: Wav 9K 59
Picton Gro. L15: Wav 9J 59
Picton La.
CH2: Mick T, Pict, Stoak, Wer 6E 112
Picton Rd. L15: Wav 9J 59
L22: Water 1K 43
Picton Valley CH2: Pict 9G 113
Piele Rd. WA11: Hay 3F 50
Piercefield Ct. L37: Form 8F 16
Piercefield Rd. L37: Form 9F 16
Pier Head L3: Liv 6B 4 (8A 58)
Pier Ho. CH45: New B 9J 43
Pierpoint St. WA5: Warr 1A 82
Pighue La. L7: Liv 8K 59
L13: Liv .8M 59
Pigot Pl. WA4: Westy 3G 83
Pigot St. WA10: St H 7H 49
Pigott's Rake L30: N'ton 6C 34
(off Higher End Pk.)
Pike Ho. Rd. WA10: Eccl 5D 48
Pike La. L40: Burs 5G 15
Pikelaw Pl. WN8: Skel 7F 30
Pike Pl. WA10: Eccl 6E 48
Pikes Bri. Fold WA10: Eccl 6D 48
Pikes Hey Rd. CH48: Caldy 9G 71
Pike St. WA4: Stockt H 7D 82
Pilch Bank Rd. L14: Knott A 5C 60
Pilch La. L14: Knott A 5C 60
Pilch La. E. L36: Huy, Roby 7E 60
Pilgrim Cl. WA2: Win 3B 66
Pilgrim St. CH41: Birke 2M 73
L1: Liv 8J 5 (9D 58)
Pilgrims Way WA7: Nort 4F 96
Pilkington Ct. L34: Presc 4A 62
Pilkington Rd. PR8: South 1C 12
Pilkington Sailing Club 7D 48
Pilkington St. WA11: Rainf 5C 38
Pilling Cl. PR9: South 2L 7
Pilling La. L31: Lyd 7F 26
Pilling Pl. WN8: Skel 7F 30
Pillmoss La. WA4: Hatt, Lwr W 6B 98
Pilot Gro. L15: Wav 9J 59
Pimblett Rd. WA11: Hay 3G 51
Pimblett St. WA3: Golb 3B 52
Pimbley Gro. E. L31: Mag 5H 35
Pimbley Gro. W. L31: Mag 5H 35
Pimbo Ind. Est. WN8: Skel 7F 30
(not continuous)
Pimbo Junc. WN8: Skel 7H 31
Pimbo La. WN8: Uph 3J 39
Pimbo Rd. WA11: Kings M 4H 39
WN8: Skel 6F 30
Pimhill Cl. L8: Liv 2F 74
Pimlico Rd. WA7: Run 5H 95
Pincroft Way L4: Kirkd 2C 58
(off Fountains Rd.)
Pinders Farm Dr. WA1: Warr 3D 82
Pine Av. CH63: Beb 4M 89
L39: Orm .7D 20
WA8: Wid .6L 79
WA10: St H 4J 49
WA12: Newt W 8L 51
Pine Cl. L32: Kirkb 8A 36
L35: Whis 6B 62
L36: Huy .5H 61
WA11: Hay 4E 50
WN8: Newb 4D 22
WN8: Skel 3C 30
Pine Ct. CH41: Birke 2K 73
L8: Liv 4F 74
(off Byles St.)
PR9: South 6H 7
Pine Crest L39: Augh 2N 27
Pine Dale WA11: Rainf 4B 38
Pinedale Cl. CH43: Noct 4D 72
CH66: Whit 5M 111
Pine Dr. L39: Orm 7D 20
Pinefield Cl. L5: Liv 3E 58
Pine Gro. CH66: Whit 4M 111
L20: Boot 6C 44
L22: Water 9K 33
L39: Orm .6D 20
PR9: South 8J 7
WA1: Padd 1H 83
WA3: Golb 2D 52
Pine Hey CH64: Nest 5D 100
Pinehurst Av. L4: Walt 2G 59
L22: Water 8J 33
Pinehurst Rd. L4: Walt 2G 59
Pinehurst Wlk. WA5: Gt San 1J 81
Pinellas WA7: Run 4L 95
Pine Lodge L4: Walt 1H 59
Pine M. L1: Liv 9H 5 (1D 74)
Pinemore Rd. L18: Moss H 6M 75
Pineridge Cl. CH62: Spit 4B 90
Pine Rd. CH60: Hesw 6C 88
WA7: Run .8M 95
Pines, The CH63: Spit 4A 90
L12: Crox 6D 46
WA8: Wid .4N 79
(off Hampton Ct. Way)
Pinetop Cl. L6: Liv 5G 59
Pine Tree Av. CH43: Noct 4C 72
Pinetree Cl. CH46: More 9N 55
L30: N'ton 8E 34
Pinetree Ct. CH44: Wall 4F 56
Pinetree Dr. CH48: W Kir 7E 70
Pinetree Gro. CH46: More 9N 55
Pinetree Rd. L36: Huy 9H 61
Pine Vw. WN3: Wins 2D 40
Pine Vw. Dr. CH61: Hesw 5N 87
Pine Wlk. M31: Part 6L 69
(off Wood La.)
Pine Walks CH42: Tran 7H 73
CH48: W Kir 7E 70
Pinewalks Ridge CH42: Tran 8J 73
Pine Way CH60: Hesw 5M 87
Pineways WA4: App 2E 98
Pinewood WN4: Ash M 9J 41
WN8: Skel 1G 30
Pinewood Av. L12: Crox 7B 46
L37: Form 2D 24
WA1: Warr 1F 82
Pinewood Cl. CH2: Elt 2N 113
L27: N'ley 2J 77
L37: Form 2D 24
PR8: South 5H 13
Pinewood Dr. CH60: Hesw 7B 88
Pinewood Gdns. L33: Kirkb 6C 36
Pinewood Rd. WA5: Burtw 2H 65
PINFOLD 2M 19
Pinfold Cl. L30: N'ton 6C 34
PR8: Ains 2H 17
Pinfold Cottage Woodland Pk. 6D 34
Pinfold Ct. CH48: W Kir 4B 70
L23: Crosb 6K 33
Pinfold Cres. L32: Kirkb 2E 46
Pinfold Dr. WA10: Eccl 7D 48
Pinfold La. CH48: W Kir 4B 70
L34: Know 7F 46
L40: Scar 3K 19
PR8: Ains 2G 17
(not continuous)
Pinfold Pl. WN8: Skel 8G 30
Pinfold Rd. L25: Hunts X 9G 76
L39: Orm .9E 20
Pingot La. WA6: Manl 8K 115
Pingot Rd. WN5: Bil 6A 40
Pingwood La. L33: Kirkb 5E 36
Pinmill Brow WA6: Frod 7L 107
Pinmill Cl. WA6: Frod 7M 107
Pinners Brow WA2: Warr 2C 82
Pinners Brow Retail Pk. WA2: Warr 2C 82
Pinners Fold WA7: Nort 6D 96
Pinnington Pl. L36: Huy 7H 61
Pinnington Rd. L35: Whis 6B 62
Pintail Cl. WA11: St H 4L 49
Pioneer Pk. CH65: Ell P 6L 103
Pipers, The CH60: Hesw 6L 87
WA3: Low 2G 52
Piper's Cl. CH60: Hesw 7L 87
Piper's End CH60: Hesw 7L 87
Pipers La. CH60: Hesw 5K 87
Pipistrelle Ri. CH43: Noct 4D 72
Pipit Av. WA12: Newt W 7L 51
Pipit Cl. L26: Halew 6J 77
Pipit La. WA3: Birchw 6M 67
Pippin St. L40: Burs 3D 20
Pippits Row WA7: Beech 2A 108
Pirrie Rd. L9: Ain 7J 45
Pitch Cl. CH49: Grea 4L 71
Pit Hey Pl. WN8: Skel 7F 30
Pit La. WA8: Wid 4K 79
Pit Pl. L25: Woolt 6E 76
Pitsford Way L6: Liv 1M 5 (5F 58)
Pitsmead Rd. L32: Kirkb 1C 46
Pittsburgh Ct. WA5: Gt San 2M 81
Pitts Heath La. WA7: Nort 4F 96
Pitts Ho. La. PR9: South 7N 7
Pitt St. L1: Liv 8G 4 (9C 58)
PR9: South 9L 7
WA5: Warr 2A 82
WA8: Wid .2K 95
WA9: St H 7M 49
Pitville Av. L18: Moss H 5M 75
Pitville Cl. L18: Moss H 6M 75
Pitville Gro. L18: Moss H 5N 75
Pitville Rd. L18: Moss H 5M 75
Pitville Ter. WA8: Wid 9F 78
Plaistow Ct. WA7: Pal F 8A 96
Plane Cl. L9: Walt 7H 45
Planet Ice
Widnes 9L 79
Plane Tree Gro. WA11: Hay 3J 51
Plane Tree Rd. CH63: Hghr B 3L 89
Planetree Rd. L12: W Der 2D 60
M31: Part 6K 69
Planewood Gdns. WA3: Low 3G 53
Plantation Bus. Pk. CH62: Brom 5E 90
Plantation Cl. WA7: Cas 6C 96
Plantation Ct. CH62: Brom 5E 90
Plantation Dr. CH66: Ell P 7K 103
Plantation Rd. CH62: Brom 6E 90
L40: Burs 1F 20
Planters, The CH49: Grea 4K 71
L30: N'ton 7F 34
(off Harvester Way)
Platinum Ct. L33: Know I 3F 46
Platt Gro. CH42: Rock F 8N 73
Platts La. L40: Burs 3H 21
Platts La. Ind. Est. L40: Burs 3H 21
Platts St. WA11: Hay 4C 50
Plattsville Rd. L18: Moss H 3M 75
Playfield Rd. L12: W Der 2D 60
Playfield Wlk. L12: W Der 2D 60
Plaza Blvd. L8: Liv 2C 74
Plaza Cinema
Waterloo 1L 43
Pleasance Way WA12: Newt W 6L 51
Pleasant Hill St. L8: Liv 2C 74
Pleasant St. CH45: New B 2H 57
L3: Liv 6J 5 (8D 58)
L20: Boot 8A 44
Pleasant Vw. L20: Boot 8A 44
Pleasington Cl. CH43: Noct 4E 72
Pleasington Dr. CH43: Noct 4E 72
Pleck Rd. CH65: Whit 3M 111
Plemont Rd. L13: Liv 4M 59
Plemston Ct. CH66: Ell P 6L 103
Plex La. L39: Hals 6F 18
Plex Moss La. L39: Hals 4K 17
Plex Moss La. Caravan Pk.
PR8: Ains 4K 17
Plinston Av. WA4: Westy 4G 82
Plough La. L40: Lath 1K 29
Ploughmans Cl. CH66: Gt Sut 5K 111
Ploughmans Way CH66: Gt Sut 5K 111
Plover Cl. WA12: Newt W 7L 51
Plover Dr. WA7: Nort 7F 96

Plovers La. WA6: Hel 9F 106
Plover Way WA3: Low 2F 52
Pluckington Rd. L36: Huy 6M 61
Plumbers Way L36: Huy 7K 61
Plumer St. CH41: Birke 9G 57
L15: Wav 1K 75
Plumley Gdns. WA8: Wid 6D 78
Plumpstons La. WA6: Frod 5L 107
Plumpton La. L39: Hals 4D 18
Plumpton M. WA8: Wid 7M 79
Plumpton St. L6: Liv 5E 58
Plumtre Av. WA5: Warr 9A 66
Plum Tree Cl. L28: Stockb V 1F 60
Plumtree Cl. L35: Eccl P 3D 62
Plymouth Cl. L19: Garst 2N 91
WA7: Murd 9G 96
(not continuous)
Plymyard Av. CH62: Brom, East 9C 90
Plymyard Cl. CH62: Brom 1C 102
Plymyard Copse CH62: Brom 1C 102
Plymyard Ct. *CH62: Brom* *9B 90*
(off Plymyard Av.)
Poachers La. WA4: Westy 5G 83
Pochard Ri. WA7: Nort 7F 96
POCKET NOOK 7M 49
Pocket Nook La. WA3: Low 2H 53
Pocket Nook St. WA9: St H 6M 49
Pocklington Ct. WA2: Padg 8G 66
Podium Rd. L13: Liv 5M 59
Poets Cnr. CH62: Port S 2A 90
Poets Grn. L35: Whis 6C 62
(not continuous)
Polden Cl. CH66: Lit Sut 8F 102
Poleacre Dr. WA8: Wid 6G 78
Polinda Gdns. WA10: St H 1F 62
Pollard Av. WA6: Frod 7N 107
Pollard Rd. L15: Wav 8M 59
Pollard Sq. M31: Part 6N 69
POLL HILL 5N 87
Poll Hill Rd. CH60: Hesw 6N 87
Pollitt Cres. WA9: Clock F 6M 63
Pollitt Sq. CH62: New F 8B 74
Pollitt St. WA9: Clock F 6M 63
Polperro Cl. L11: Crox 5B 46
WA5: Penk 5G 80
Pomfret St. L8: Liv 2E 74
Pomona St. L3: Liv 6J **5** (8D **58**)
Pond Cl. L6: Liv 5H 59
Pond Grn. Way WA9: St H 9B 50
Pond St. WA3: Low 2H 53
Pond Vw. Cl. CH60: Hesw 7C 88
Pond Wlk. WA9: St H 9C 50
Pondwater Cl. L32: Kirkb 1C 46
Ponsonby Rd. CH45: Wall 4E 56
Pontins Southport Cen. PR8: Ains 8F 10
Pool Bank CH62: Port S 9A 74
Poolbank Rd. CH62: New F 9A 74
Poole Av. WA2: Warr 7C 66
Poole Cres. WA2: Warr 7C 66
Poole Hall Ind. Est. CH66: Ell P 6L 103
Poole Hall La. CH66: Ell P 6K 103
Poole Hall Rd. CH65: Ell P 6L 103
Pool End WA9: St H 8B 50
Poole Rd. CH44: Wall 4K 57
POOL HEY 3G 13
Pool Hey L28: Stockb V 1F 60
(not continuous)
Pool Hey Caravan Pk. PR9: South 2H 13
Pool Hey La. PR8: South 3F 12
PR9: South 3F 12
Pool Hollow WA7: Run 6L 95
Pool La. CH2: Elt, Ince 9K 105
CH2: Thorn M 3J 113
CH49: Woodc 6A 72
CH62: Brom 2B 90
WA4: Walt 7B 82
WA7: Run 4L 95
WA13: Lymm 4B 84
Pool Rd. WA3: Rix 6G 69
Poolside Rd. WA7: Run 6L 95
Poolside Wlk. PR9: South 3A 8
Pools Platt La. CW9: Ant 8M 99
Poolstock La. WN3: Wigan 1H 41
Pool St. CH41: Birke 1K 73
PR9: South 2A 8
WA8: Wid 9L 79
Pooltown Rd. CH65: Ell P, Whit 8L 103
Poolwood Rd. CH49: Woodc 4B 72
Pope St. L20: Boot 5A 44
POPLAR 2000 SERVICE AREA 9A 84
Poplar Av. CH49: Upton 3N 71
L23: Crosb 6M 33
WA3: Cul 7N 53
WA5: Penk 4G 81
WA7: Run 8M 95
WA10: Eccl 6D 48
WA12: Newt W 7M 51
WN4: Garsw 6F 40
Poplar Bank L36: Huy 7J 61
PR9: South 6J 7
Poplar Cl. CH65: Whit 1N 111
L26: Halew 7L 77
WA7: Run 8M 95
Poplar Ct. *L8: Liv* *4F 74*
(off Byles St.)
WN8: Skel 6C 30
Poplar Dr. CH63: Beb 3A 90
L5: Liv 4F 58
L32: Kirkb 8B 36
WN8: Skel 3C 30
Poplar Farm Cl. CH46: More 2K 71
Poplar Gro. CH2: Elt 2L 113
CH42: Tran *4K 73*
(off Ash Rd.)
L21: Sea 4M 43
L35: Presc 4B 62
M44: Cad 3K 69
WA10: St H 7F 48
WA11: Hay 4E 50
Poplar Hall La. CH2: Chor B 6A 112
Poplar Rd. CH43: Oxton 4H 73
L25: Woolt 5E 76
WA11: Hay 4E 50
Poplar Row CH2: Elt 2M 113
Poplars, The L40: Burs 3J 21
WA3: Golb 1C 52
WA13: Lymm 4D 84
WN7: Leigh 2K 53
Poplars Av. WA2: Warr 5B 66
(not continuous)
Poplars Pl. *WA2: Warr* *7E 66*
(off Hughes Av.)
Poplar St. PR8: South 1D 12
WA3: Golb 1C 52
Poplar Ter. CH45: New B 2H 57
Poplar Vw. WA4: Moore 1J 97
Poplar Wlk. *M31: Part* *6K 69*
(off Long Wlk.)
Poplar Way L4: Kirkd 1C 58
Poplar Weint CH64: Nest 6E 100
Poppleford Cl. L25: Gate 4H 77
Poppy Cl. CH46: More 7A 56
PR8: South 4A 12
Poppyfields WA5: Warr 5M 81
Poppy La. L39: Bic 3F 28
Poppy Nook PR9: Banks 3E 8
Poppy Pl. L22: Water 1L 43
Poppy Rd. L23: Thorn 6A 34
Porchester Rd. L11: Norr G 9L 45
Porchfield Cl. L11: Norr G 7N 45
Porlock Av. L16: Child 3C 76
WA9: Sut L 4M 63
Porlock Cl. CH60: Hesw 9B 88
WA5: Penk 4G 81
Portal M. CH61: Pens 4N 87
Portal Rd. CH61: Pens 4N 87
Portal Way L11: Crox 3A 46
Port Arcades, The CH65: Ell P 9A 104
Portbury Cl. CH62: Port S 1B 90
Portbury Wlk. CH62: Port S 1A 90
Portbury Way CH62: Port S 1B 90
Port C'way. CH62: Brom 3B 90
Portelet Rd. L13: Liv 5L 59
Porter Av. WA12: Newt W 5L 51
Porter Cl. L35: Rainh 8G 63
Porter St. L3: Liv 5A 58
WA7: Run 5M 95
Portgate Cl. L12: W Der 8A 46
Porthcawl Cl. WA8: Wid 5F 78
Porthleven Rd. WA7: Brook 1D 108
Portia Av. CH63: Hghr B 9L 73
Portia St. L20: Kirkd 9B 44
PORTICO 2E 62
Portico Av. L35: Eccl P 3D 62
Portico Ct. *L35: Eccl P* *3D 62*
(off Portico La.)
Portico La. L34: Eccl P 3D 62
L35: Eccl P 3D 62
L35: Presc, Eccl P 3C 62
Portland Av. L22: Water 9J 33
Portland Ct. CH45: New B 9G 42
Portland Gdns. *L5: Liv* *5B 58*
(off Green St.)
Portland Gate *CH62: Port S* *1B 90*
(off Portbury Cl.)
Portland Pl. L5: Liv 5D 58
WA6: Hel 1F 114
Portland Rd. WA5: Gt San 1J 81
Portland St. CH41: Birke 9G 56
CH45: New B 9G 42
L5: Liv 5B 58
PR8: South 9F 6
WA7: Run 4J 95
WA12: Newt W 6H 51
Portland Way WA9: St H 9B 50
Portlemouth Rd. L11: Crox 5A 46
Portloe Av. L26: Halew 7K 77
Portman Rd. L15: Wav 1J 75
Porto Hey Rd. CH61: Irby 2L 87
Portola Cl. WA4: Grap 6K 83
Porton Rd. L32: Kirkb 1A 46
Portreath Way WA10: Windle 4E 48
Portree Av. CH63: East 1C 102
Portree Cl. L9: Walt 6E 44
Portrush Cl. WA8: Wid 5H 79
Portrush St. L13: Liv 3K 59
Portside WA7: Pres B 8G 97
Portside Bus. Pk. CH65: Ell P 6N 103
Portside Ind. Est. CH65: Ell P 6A 104
Portside Nth. CH65: Ell P 6N 103
Portside Sth. CH65: Ell P 6A 104
Portsmouth Pl. WA7: Murd 9G 96
PORT SUNLIGHT 1A 90
Port Sunlight Golf Centre (Driving Range) 2B 90
Port Sunlight Mus. 1A 90
Port Sunlight Station (Rail) 2A 90
Port Talbot Cl. L19: Garst 1N 91
Portway L25: Hunts X 9G 77
Portwood Cl. L7: Liv 9G 59
Post Office Av. *PR9: South* *8G 7*
(off Anchor St.)
Post Office La. CH2: Thorn M 4J 113
WA7: West P 8G 94
Potter Cl. WN8: Skel 6F 30
Potter Pl. WN8: Skel 7G 30
Potters La. L18: Moss H 3A 76
WA8: Hale B 3C 94
Pottery, The L31: Mell 9M 35
Pottery Cl. L35: Whis 6N 61
Pottery Flds. L34: Presc 3A 62
Pottery La. L35: Whis 6M 61
L36: Huy 6M 61
Poulevara Ho. *L13: Liv* *7N 59*
(off W. Oakhill Pk.)
Poulsom Dr. L30: N'ton 9B 34
Poulter Rd. L9: Ain 3G 45
POULTON
CH44 .... 7G 57
CH63 .... 5N 89
Poulton Bri. Rd. CH41: Birke 7F 56
CH44: Wall 6G 56
Poulton Cl. L26: Halew 1H 93
Poulton Ct. PR9: South 8L 7
Poulton Cres. WA1: Wools 9K 67
Poulton Dr. WA8: Wid 9G 78
WN4: Ash M 6H 41
Poulton Grn. Cl. CH63: Spit 6M 89
Poulton Hall Rd. CH44: Wall 6G 57
CH63: Raby M 8N 89
Poulton Park Golf Course 5H 67
Poulton Rd. CH44: Wall 6G 57
CH63: Spit 4N 89
PR9: South 8L 7
Poulton Royd Dr. CH63: Spit 5M 89
Poulton Vale CH44: Wall 7G 57
Pound Rd. CH66: Lit Sut 7H 103
Poverty La. L31: Mag 3K 35
(not continuous)
Povey Rd. WA2: Warr 8D 66
Powder Mill Cl. M44: Irlam 1N 69
Powder Mill Rd. WA4: Westy 5H 83
Powder Works La. L31: Mag 9A 28
Powell Av. WA3: Ris 5M 67
Powell Dr. WN5: Bil 8N 39
Powell St. WA4: Warr 5G 82
WA9: St H 2A 64
Powerhouse *L8: Liv* *1G 75*
(off Commerce Way)
Power House Rd. CH62: East 1G 102
Powerleague
Liverpool 2D 58
Power Rd. CH42: Rock F 8N 73
CH62: Brom 6E 90
Powey La. CH1: Moll 8G 110
Powis St. L8: Liv 3F 74
Pownall Sq. L3: Liv 3E **4** (7B **58**)
Pownall St. L1: Liv 7E **4** (9B **58**)
Powys St. *WA5: Warr* *3A 82*
(off Old Liverpool Rd.)
Poynter St. WA9: St H 2H 63
Poynton Cl. WA4: Grap 5J 83
Pratt Rd. L34: Presc 3N 61
Precincts, The L23: Crosb 7L 33
Preece Cl. WA8: Wid 5G 79
Preesall Cl. PR9: South 2L 7
Preesall Way L11: Crox 5A 46
(not continuous)
Premier Bowl 7E 6
Premier St. L5: Liv 4E 58
(not continuous)
Prentice Rd. CH42: Rock F 7L 73
PRENTON 7F 72
Prenton Av. WA9: Clock F 5M 63
Prenton Dell Av. CH43: Pren 8G 72
Prenton Dell Rd. CH43: Pren 7E 72
Prenton Farm Rd. CH43: Pren 8G 73
Prenton Golf Course 8H 73
Prenton Grn. L24: Speke 4J 93
Prenton Hall Rd. CH43: Pren 7F 72
Prenton La. CH42: Tran 7H 73
Prenton Park 6J 73
Prenton Pk. Rd. CH42: Tran 5J 73
Prenton Rd. E. CH42: Tran 6J 73
Prenton Rd. W. CH42: Tran 6J 73
Prenton Village Rd. CH43: Pren 7F 72
Prenton Way CH43: Pren 7D 72
Prenton Way Bus. Units CH43: Pren 7D 72
Prentonwood Ct. CH42: Tran 7J 73
PRESCOT 3A 62
Prescot Bus. Pk. L34: Presc 4N 61
Prescot By-Pass L34: Presc 3M 61
Prescot Cen. L34: Presc 3A 62
Prescot Ct. L7: Liv 7H 59
Prescot Dr. L6: Liv 6J 59
Prescot Grn. L39: Orm 1B 28
Prescot Mus. 3A 62
Prescot Rd. L7: Liv 6J 59
L13: Liv 6J 59
L31: Mag, Mell 2A 36
L39: Augh, Orm 2B 28
WA8: Cron 4C 78
WA8: Wid 5G 78
WA10: St H 1D 62
Prescot Station (Rail) 4B 62
Prescot St. CH45: New B 1G 56
L7: Liv 3L **5** (7E **58**)
Prescott Av. L40: Ruf 3L 15
WA3: Golb 1A 52
Prescot Trade Cen. L34: Presc 3B 62
Prescott Rd. WN8: Skel 7J 31
Prescott St. WA3: Golb 1B 52
WA4: Warr 5F 82
Preseland Rd. L23: Crosb 8L 33
Prestbury Av. CH43: Oxton 6E 72
PR8: Ains 9H 11
WN3: Wigan 1G 41
Prestbury Cl. CH43: Oxton 6E 72
WA8: Wid 8H 79
Prestbury Dr. WA4: Thel 4L 83
WA10: Eccl 8E 48
Prestbury Rd. L11: Norr G 6L 45
Preston Av. L34: Presc 4N 61
M44: Irlam 2M 69
PRESTON BROOK 9H 97
Preston Gro. L6: Liv 4H 59
Preston New Rd. PR9: South 5M 7
PRESTON ON THE HILL 9J 97
Preston Rd. PR9: South 7K 7
Preston St. L1: Liv 4F **4** (7C **58**)
WA9: Sut M 7K 63
Preston Way L23: Crosb 7N 33
Prestwich Av. WA3: Cul 7M 53
Prestwick Cl. WA8: Wid 5J 79
WA9: St H 5H 63
Prestwick Dr. L23: Blun 5J 33
Prestwood Ct. WA3: Ris 2A 68
Prestwood Cres. L14: Knott A 5D 60
Prestwood Pl. WN8: Skel 8J 31
Prestwood Rd. L14: Knott A 5D 60
Pretoria Rd. L9: Ain 4G 45
WN4: Ash M 7K 41
Price Gro. WA9: St H 8C 50
Price's La. CH43: Oxton 4H 73
Price St. CH41: Birke 9H 57
L1: Liv 7F **4** (9B **58**)
Price St. Bus. Cen. CH41: Birke 9J 57
Pride Centre, The 1E 46
Pride Cl. WA12: Newt W 8N 51
Priestfield Rd. CH65: Ell P 9N 103
Priesthouse Cl. L37: Form 1G 25
Priesthouse La. L37: Form 1G 24
Priestley Bus. Cen. WA5: Warr 3A 82
Priestley Ct. *WA4: Warr* *6D 82*
(off Elphins Dr.)
Priestley St. WA5: Warr 3A 82
Priestner Dr. WA6: Hel 1E 114
Primary Av. L30: N'ton 7G 35
Primary Cl. M44: Cad 4K 69
Primrose Cl. L37: Form 8H 17
PR9: South 1A 8
WA2: Warr 7E 66
WA7: Cas 7C 96
WA8: Wid 7H 79
Primrose Ct. *CH45: New B* *1H 57*
(off Egerton St.)
L36: Huy 3J 61
Primrose Dr. L36: Huy 4J 61
Primrose Gro. CH44: Wall 7L 57
WA11: Hay 3G 50
PRIMROSE HILL 5L 19
Primrose Hill CH62: Port S 1N 89
L3: Liv 3F **4** (7C **58**)
Primrose La. WA6: Alv, Hel 4D 114
Primrose M. WA6: Alv 4G 114
Primrose Pl. *WN4: Ash M* *9K 41*
(off Haydock St.)
Primrose Rd. CH41: Birke 1F 72
L18: Moss H 3A 76
Primrose St. L4: Kirkd 2C 58
Primrose Vw. WN4: Ash M 9K 41
Primula Cl. WA9: Bold 2C 64
Primula Dr. L9: Walt 6G 44
WA3: Low 2E 52
Prince Albert Ct. WA9: St H 9B 50
Prince Albert M. L1: Liv 9H 5
Prince Alfred Rd. L15: Wav 1M 75
Prince Andrew's Gro. WA10: Windle 4F 48
Prince Charles Gdns. PR8: Birkd 1M 11
Prince Edward St. CH41: Birke 1J 73
Prince Edwin St. L5: Liv 5D 58
Prince Henry Sq. WA1: Warr 3C 82
Prince Rupert's Tower 5E 58
Princes Av. CH48: W Kir 6C 70
CH62: East 9D 90
L8: Liv 1E 74
L23: Crosb 7K 33
Princes Blvd. CH63: Hghr B 8K 73
Prince's Cl. WA7: Cas 6B 96
Princes Ct. L8: Liv 2G 74
Princes Gdns. L3: Liv 2D **4** (6B **58**)
PR8: South 9K 7
Princes Ga. E. L8: Liv 2G 74
Princes Ga. Ho. *L8: Liv* *2G 74*
(off Kingsley Rd.)
Princes Ga. W. L8: Liv 2G 74
Princes Pde. L3: Liv 3B **4** (7A **58**)
PRINCES PARK 2G 74
Princes Pk. Mans. L8: Liv 3G 75
Princes Pavement CH41: Birke 2L 73
Princes Pl. WA8: Wid 7H 79
Princes Rd. CH65: Ell P 8L 103
L8: Liv 9L **5** (1E **74**)
WA10: St H 9F 48
Princess Av. WA1: Padg 9H 67
WA1: Warr 2G 82
WA5: Gt San 1G 80
WA10: St H 5H 49
WA11: Hay 3J 51
WN4: Ash M 8L 41

Princess Ct. PR9: South .7J 7
Princess Cres. WA1: Warr .2G 82
Princess Dr. L12: W Der .1C 60
L14: Knott A .1C 60
Princess Rd. CH45: New B .2H 57
WA13: Lymm .5C 84
WN4: Ash M .8K 41
Princess St. WA5: Warr .4M 81
WA7: Run .4K 95
Princess Ter. CH43: Oxton .3J 73
Princes St. L2: Liv .4E 4 (7B 58)
L20: Boot .9A 44
PR8: South .9F 6
WA8: Wid .8K 79
WA12: Newt W .7K 51
Princess Way L21: Lith, Sea .4M 43
Prince St. L22: Water .2L 43
WN4: Ash M .6J 41
Princes Way WA11: St H .2K 49
Princesway CH45: Wall .3G 56
Princeton Ct. WA5: Gt San .2M 81
Princeway WA6: Frod .6L 107
Prince William St. L8: Liv .2D 74
Priors Cl. L25: Woolt .6F 76
Priorsfield CH46: More .9M 55
Priorsfield Rd. L25: Woolt .6F 76
Prior St. L20: Boot .4N 43
Priorswood Pl. WN8: Skel .8J 31
Priory, The CH64: Nest .5D 100
L15: Wav .8L 59
L35: Rainh .6F 62
WA2: Win .2B 66
Priory Cl. CH63: Beb .4N 89
L17: Aig .6G 74
L35: Whis .8N 61
L37: Form .2H 25
L40: Burs .9H 15
WA7: Halt .6C 96
Priory Ct. L36: Huy .7H 61
PR8: South .9E 6
WA7: Pres B .1G 108
Priory Farm Cl. L19: Gras .9M 75
Priory Gdns. PR8: Birkd .2M 11
WA10: St H .3J 49
Priory Grange PR8: Birkd .2N 11
Priory Gro. L39: Orm .9B 20
Priory M. CH41: Birke .2M 73
PR8: South .9E 6
Priory Nook WN8: Uph .5M 31
Priory Rd. CH44: Wall .6L 57
CH48: W Kir .6D 70
L4: Walt .1F 58
WA7: Wind H .5E 96
WN4: Ash M .6H 41
WN8: Uph .5M 31
Priory St. CH41: Birke .2M 73
L19: Garst .3B 92
WA4: Warr .5C 82
Priory Way L25: Woolt .6F 76
Priory Wharf CH41: Birke .2M 73
Pritchard Av. L21: Sea .3M 43
Pritt St. L3: Liv .1H 5 (6D 58)
Private Dr. CH61: Barn .2D 88
Prizett Rd. L19: Gras .9N 75
Probyn Rd. CH45: Wall .4E 56
Procter Rd. CH42: Rock F .7N 73
Proctor Ct. L30: N'ton .7C 34
Proctor Rd. CH47: Hoy .2D 70
L37: Form .9C 16
Proctors Cl. WA8: Wid .6M 79
Proffits La. WA6: Hel .9G 107
Progress Pl. L1: Liv .4E 4
Promenade PR8: Ains .8F 10
PR8: South .8F 6
PR9: South .6G 7
Promenade, The L17: Aig .7G 74
L19: Aig .9J 75
WA4: Moore .9K 81
Promenade Caravan Pk. WA4: Moore .9J 81
Promenade Gdns. L17: Aig .5E 74
Prophet Wlk. L8: Liv .3E 74
Prospect Av. M44: Cad .3L 69
Prospect Ct. *L6: Liv .6J 59*
(off Prospect Va.)
Prospect La. WA3: Rix .6C 68
Prospect Pl. WN8: Skel .7J 31
Prospect Point L6: Liv .3L 5 (7E 58)
Prospect Rd. CH42: Tran .7H 73
M44: Cad .3L 69
WA9: St H .6N 49
Prospect Row WA7: West .8J 95
Prospect St. L6: Liv .3M 5 (7F 58)
Prospect Va. CH45: Wall .4F 56
L6: Liv .5J 59
Prospect Way L30: N'ton .8G 35
Protector Way M44: Irlam .1M 69
Proto Cl. L24: Speke .4J 93
Proudman Dr. CH43: Bid .1C 72
Providence Ct. WA10: St H .6K 49
Providence Cres. L8: Liv .2D 74
Provident St. WA9: St H .7C 50
Province Pl. L20: Boot .4C 44
Province Rd. L20: Boot .4C 44
Prussia St. L3: Liv .3D 4 (7B 58)
(not continuous)
Public Hall St. WA7: Run .4K 95
Puddington La. CH64: Burt, Pudd .5A 110
Pudsey St. L1: Liv .4H 5 (7D 58)
Puffin Cl. CH65: Ell P .5A 112
Pugin St. L4: Walt .2D 58
Pulford Av. CH43: Pren .6G 72
Pulford Cl. WA7: Beech .9A 96
Pulford Rd. CH63: Beb .2M 89
CH65: Gt Sut .1L 111
Pulford St. L4: Walt .2E 58
Pullman Cl. CH60: Hesw .7D 88
Puma Ct. L34: Presc .4L 61
Pumpfields Rd. L3: Liv .1D 4 (6B 58)
Pump La. CH49: Grea .3J 71
WA7: Halt .7B 96
Punnell's La. L31: Lyd .7E 26
Purbeck Dr. CH61: Irby .9L 71
Purdy Cl. WA5: Old H .8M 65
Purley Dr. M44: Cad .4J 69
Purley Gro. L18: Moss H .6M 75
Purley Rd. L22: Water .9J 33
Purser Gro. L15: Wav .9J 59
Putney Ct. WA7: Pal F .8A 96
Pye Cl. WA11: Hay .2K 51
Pyecroft Cl. WA5: Gt San .2F 80
Pyecroft Rd. WA5: Gt San .2F 80
Pye Rd. CH60: Hesw .7N 87
Pyes Gdns. WA11: St H .3L 49
Pyes La. L36: Huy .2G 61
Pye St. L15: Wav .1M 75
PYGON'S HILL .5J 27
Pygon's Hill La. L31: Lyd .5J 27
Pym St. L4: Walt .8E 44
Pyramid Arts Cen. .4B 82
Pyramid Ct. WA1: Warr .4B 82
Pyrus Gro. WA6: Hel .9F 106

Q

Quadrangle, The L18: Moss H .4N 75
Quadrant, The CH47: Hoy .2C 70
WA3: Ris .3M 67
(off Faraday St.)
Quadrant Cl. WA7: Murd .9F 96
Quail Cl. WA2: Warr .6E 66
Quaker La. CH60: Hesw .6M 87
Quakers All. L2: Liv .4E 4
Quakers Mdw. L34: Know .6H 47
Quantock Cl. CH66: Lit Sut .8F 102
WN3: Wins .1E 40
Quarry Av. CH63: Beb .3M 89
Quarry Bank CH41: Birke .3K 73
L33: Kirkb .8D 36
Quarry Bank Flats *CH41: Birke .3K 73*
(off Quarry Bank)
Quarrybank St. CH41: Birke .3J 73
Quarrybank Workshops *CH41: Birke .3J 73*
(off Quarrybank St.)
Quarry Cl. CH61: Hesw .5N 87
L13: Liv .4M 59
L33: Kirkb .8D 36
WA7: Run .6N 95
Quarry Ct. WA8: Wid .7F 78
Quarry Dale L33: Kirkb .8D 36
Quarry Dr. L39: Augh .4A 28
Quarry Grn. L33: Kirkb .8D 36
Quarry Grn. Flats L33: Kirkb .8D 36
Quarry Hey L33: Kirkb .8D 36
Quarry Junc. WN8: Skel .4F 30
Quarry La. CH61: Thing .1A 88
WA4: App .1E 98
WA6: Manl .8G 115
Quarry Mt. L39: Orm .7E 20
Quarry Pk. *L35: Rainh .8G 63*
(off Lincoln Way)
Quarry Pl. *L25: Woolt .6D 76*
(off Quarry St.)
Quarry Rd. CH64: Nest .5H 101
L13: Liv .4L 59
L20: Boot .8C 44
L23: Thorn .5N 33
Quarry Rd. E. CH60: Hesw .6M 87
CH61: Hesw .6M 87
CH63: Beb .3N 89
Quarry Rd. W. CH60: Hesw .6M 87
Quarryside Dr. L33: Kirkb .8E 36
Quarry St. L25: Woolt .5D 76
Quarry St. Sth. L25: Woolt .6E 76
Quarry Way L36: Huy .7L 61
Quartz Way L21: Lith .2B 44
Quay, The WA6: Frod .4N 107
Quay Bus. Cen. WA2: Win .5A 66
Quay Centre, The WA2: Win .5A 66
Quay Fold WA5: Warr .3A 82
Quayle Cl. WA11: Hay .4E 50
Quay Pl. WA7: Pres B .8G 96
Quays, The L40: Burs .9J 15
Quay Side WA6: Frod .4N 107
Quayside CH64: Lit N .9D 100
CH65: Ell P .7B 104
(off Grosvenor Wharf Rd.)
Quayside M. WA13: Lymm .5F 84
Queastybirch La. WA4: Hatt .6B 98
Quebec Quay L3: Liv .2B 74
Quebec Rd. WA2: Warr .1E 82
Queen Anne Pde. L3: Liv .4C 4
Queen Anne St. L3: Liv .2H 5 (6D 58)
PR8: South .8G 6
(off Market St.)
Queen Av. L2: Liv .5E 4
Queen Charlotte Vs. *PR8: Ains .9J 11*
(off Station Rd.)
Queen Elizabeth Ct. L21: Lith .2N 43
Queen Mary's Dr. CH62: Port S .1A 90
Queens Av. CH47: Meols .9E 54
CH65: Whit .2M 111
L37: Form .8E 16
WA1: Warr .1F 82
WA8: Wid .8E 78
WN4: Ash M .8K 41
Queensberry St. L8: Liv .3E 74
Queensbury CH48: W Kir .5E 70
Queensbury Av. CH62: Brom .6D 90
Queensbury Way WA8: Wid .5G 79
Queens Cl. L19: Garst .1A 92
WA7: Run .6J 95
Queens Ct. CH47: Hoy .1C 70
L6: Liv .4F 58
L15: Wav .8A 60
L39: Orm .9C 20
Queenscourt Rd. L12: W Der .4A 60
Queens Cres. WA1: Padg .9H 67
Queens Cft. L37: Form .2D 24
Queensdale Rd. L18: Moss H .3M 75
Queens Dock Commercial Cen.
L1: Liv .9F 4 (1C 74)
Queens Dr. CH43: Pren .7G 72
CH60: Hesw .7M 87
L12: W Der .5N 59
WA3: Golb .2D 52
WA4: Grap .6H 83
WA6: Hel .2E 114
WA10: Windle .4F 48
WA12: Newt W .5K 51
Queens Dr. Mossley Hill
L18: Moss H .4K 75
Queens Dr. Stoneycroft L13: Liv .4M 59
L15: Wav .4M 59
Queens Dr. Walton L4: Walt .8F 44
Queens Dr. Wavertree L15: Wav .8A 60
Queens Dr. W. Derby L13: W Der .1K 59
Queens Gdns. CH65: Ell P .9N 103
Queens Grn. L39: Down .8E 18
Queen's Hotel Ct. *PR9: South .7G 6*
(off Promenade)
Queensland Av. WA9: St H .2H 63
Queensland Pl. WA9: St H .2H 63
Queensland St. L7: Liv .7N 5 (8G 58)
Queens M. L6: Liv .5F 58
Queens Park Leisure Cen. .6H 49
Queen Sq. L1: Liv .4G 4 (7C 58)
Queens Rd. CH42: Rock F .7N 73
CH44: Wall .5L 57
CH47: Hoy .1B 70
CH66: Lit Sut .7H 103
L6: Liv .1N 5 (4F 58)
L20: Boot .8B 44
L23: Crosb .7L 33
L34: Presc .3B 62
L37: Form .2D 24
PR9: South .7H 7
WA7: Run .6J 95
WA10: St H .9F 48
WA11: Hay .3J 51
WN4: Ash M .7K 41
WN5: Orr .7M 31
Queen St. CH41: Tran .4L 73
CH45: Wall .4H 57
CH65: Ell P .7A 104
L19: Garst .2A 92
L22: Water .2K 43
L39: Orm .9C 20
WA3: Golb .2C 52
WA7: Run .4K 95
WA10: St H .5J 49
WA12: Newt W .7K 51
Queen's Wlk. L1: Liv .9J 5
Queensway CH41: Birke .7A 4 (9N 57)
CH45: Wall .3G 56
CH60: Hesw .9C 88
L22: Water .9M 33
M31: Part .5M 69
WA6: Frod .6L 107
WA7: Run .4J 95
WA8: Wid .1J 95
WA11: Rainf .6D 38
WA11: St H .2K 49
Queensway Trad. Est. WA8: Wid .2K 95
Queens Wharf L3: Liv .9E 4 (1B 74)
Queenswood Av. CH63: Hghr B .8L 73
Quernmore Rd. L33: Kirkb .8E 36
Quernmore Wlk. L33: Kirkb .8E 36
Quickswood Cl. L25: Woolt .3D 76
Quickswood Dr. L25: Woolt .3D 76
Quickswood Grn. L25: Woolt .3D 76
Quickthorn Cres. L28: Stockb V .2F 60
Quigley Av. L30: N'ton .1F 44
Quigley St. CH41: Tran .4M 73
Quill Ct. *M44: Irlam .3L 69*
(off Magenta Av.)
Quillet, The CH64: Nest .7F 100
Quincey Row PR9: Banks .3E 8
Quinesway CH49: Upton .3N 71
Quinn St. WA8: Wid .9L 79
Quintbridge Cl. L26: Halew .9J 77
Quinton Cl. PR8: Ains .1G 17
Quorn St. L7: Liv .7G 59

R

Rabbit La. L40: Burs .2D 20
RABY .2J 101
Raby Av. CH63: Raby M .9A 90
Raby Cl. CH60: Hesw .8N 87
CH63: Raby M .8N 89
WA8: Wid .6A 80
Raby Ct. CH65: Ell P .2B 112
Raby Dell CH63: Raby M .9A 90
Raby Dr. CH46: More .1L 71
CH63: Raby M .8N 89
Raby Gdns. CH64: Nest .6E 100
Raby Gro. CH63: Hghr B .8K 73
Raby Hall Rd. CH63: Brom, Raby M .1L 101
RABY MERE .8N 89
Raby Mere Rd. CH63: Raby, Raby M .2J 101
(not continuous)
Raby Pk. Cl. CH64: Nest .6E 100
Raby Pk. Rd. CH64: Nest .6E 100
Raby Rd. CH63: Raby, Thorn H .9H 89
CH64: Nest .6E 100
Racecourse Retail Pk. L9: Ain .9G 35
Racefield Cl. WA13: Lymm .5F 84
Rachel St. L5: Liv .5C 58
Radburn Cl. L23: Thorn .6A 34
Radburn Rd. L23: Thorn .6A 34
Radcliffe Av. WA3: Cul .7M 53
Raddel La. WA4: Hghr Whi .9D 98
Raddle Wharf CH65: Ell P .7A 104
Raddon Pl. WA4: Westy .5F 82
Radford Av. CH63: Spit .5A 90
Radford Cl. WA8: Wid .9F 78
Radlett Cl. WA5: Penk .5G 80
Radley Ct. PR8: South .8F 6
Radley Dr. CH63: Thorn H .9F 88
L10: Ain .8H 35
Radley La. WA2: Warr .5E 66
Radley Rd. CH44: Wall .4F 56
Radleys Ct. *L8: Liv .2E 74*
(off Up. Warwick St.)
Radley St. WA9: St H .2H 63
Radmore Rd. L14: Knott A .6B 60
Radnor Av. CH60: Hesw .6N 87
Radnor Cl. L26: Halew .1J 93
Radnor Dr. CH45: Wall .3J 57
L20: Boot .7D 44
PR9: South .4L 7
WA8: Wid .6G 78
Radnor Pl. CH43: Oxton .2J 73
L6: Liv .4J 59
Radnor St. WA5: Warr .2N 81
Radshaw Nook L32: Kirkb .4C 46
Radstock Gro. WA9: Sut L .4N 63
Radstock Rd. CH44: Wall .4E 56
L6: Liv .6H 59
Radstock Wlk. *L26: Halew .1K 93*
(off Romford Way)
Radway Grn. CH66: Gt Sut .9K 103
Radway Rd. L36: Huy .4K 61
Raeburn Av. CH48: W Kir .5D 70
CH62: East .9C 90
CH64: Lit N .7F 100
Raffles Rd. CH42: Tran .3J 73
Raffles St. L1: Liv .9H 5 (1D 74)
Rafter Av. L20: Boot .4D 44
(not continuous)
Raglan Cl. L19: Garst .2A 92
Raglan Ct. WA3: Ris .3N 67
Raikes Cl. WA5: Gt San .2L 81
Railbrook Hey L13: Liv .8M 59
Rail Cl. WA11: Rainf .1C 38
Railside Ct. L5: Liv .4B 58
Railton Av. L35: Rainh .7G 62
Railton Cl. L35: Rainh .8G 62
Railton Rd. L11: Norr G .8K 45
Railway App. L39: Orm .8D 20
Railway Av. PR9: Banks .2D 8
Railway Cotts. CH66: Hoot .5C 102
L25: Hunts X .9G 77
Railway Island WN8: Skel .4A 30
Railway Path L39: Orm .1C 28
Railway Rd. L39: Orm .8D 20
WA3: Golb .1C 52
WN8: Skel .3N 29
Railway St. L19: Garst .2A 92
PR8: South .1N 11
WA10: St H .6L 49
WA12: Newt W .7K 51
Railway Ter. PR8: South .1N 11
Railway Vw. L32: Kirkb .8A 36
Railyard, The L7: Liv .7N 5 (9F 58)
Rainbow Cl. WA8: Wid .5F 78
Rainbow Dr. L26: Halew .8J 77
L31: Mell .7N 35
Raines Cl. CH49: Grea .4M 71
RAINFORD .4D 38
Rainford Av. L20: Boot .5D 44
Rainford By-Pass
WA11: Rainf, Windle .2A 38
Rainford Gdns. L2: Liv .5F 4
Rainford Hall Cotts. WA11: Crank .9J 39
Rainford Ind. Est. WA11: Rainf .7F 38
(not continuous)
RAINFORD JUNCTION .1C 38
Rainford Rd. L39: Bic .6L 29
WA10: St H, Windle .3F 48
WA11: Rainf .6L 29
WA11: Windle .3F 48
(not continuous)
WN5: Bil .6L 39
Rainford Sq. L2: Liv .5E 4 (8B 58)
Rainford Station (Rail) .1C 38
Rainham Cl. L19: Aller .8A 76
RAINHILL .6F 62

Rainhill Rd. L35: Rainh ... 5F 62
WA9: St H ... 5F 62
Rainhill Station (Rail) ... 6F 62
RAINHILL STOOPS ... 8H 63
Rainhill Trials Exhibition ... 6F 62
Raithby Dr. WN3: Wigan ... 1J 41
Rake, The CH62: Brom ... 7B 90
Rake Cl. CH49: Upton ... 4A 72
Rake Hey CH46: More ... 9J 55
Rake Hey Cl. CH46: More ... 9K 55
Rake La. CH2: Chor B, Lit Stan ... 7B 112
CH45: New B, Wall ... 2H 57
CH49: Upton ... 4A 72
WA6: Dun H ... 6M 113
WA6: Hel ... 1F 114
(Hawkstone Gro.)
WA6: Hel ... 8C 106
(Lordship La.)
Rake M. CH49: Upton ... 4A 72
Rakersfield Ct. CH45: New B ... 1J 57
Rakersfield Rd. CH45: New B ... 1J 57
Rakes La. L29: Seft ... 5B 34
Raleigh Av. L35: Whis ... 7A 62
Raleigh Cl. WA5: Old H ... 8M 65
WA12: Newt W ... 9M 51
Raleigh Rd. CH46: Leas ... 5A 56
CH64: Nest ... 5F 100
Raleigh St. L20: Boot ... 9A 44
Ralph's Wife's La. PR9: Banks ... 1C 8
Rambaldi Sq. *WA8: Wid* ... *7L 79*
(off Cross St.)
Rame Cl. L10: Faz ... 4N 45
Ramford St. WA9: St H ... 8N 49
Ramilies Rd. L18: Moss H ... 3L 75
Ramleh Pk. L23: Blun ... 8G 33
Rampit Cl. WA11: Hay ... 3H 51
Ramsay Cl. WA3: Birchw ... 6M 67
Ramsbrook Cl. L24: Speke ... 3G 93
Ramsbrook La. L24: Hale ... 2N 93
WA8: Hale B ... 2N 93
Ramsbrook Rd. L24: Speke ... 3G 93
Ramsbury Dr. L24: Speke ... 3F 92
Ramsey Cl. L19: Aller ... 8B 76
L35: Whis ... 6B 62
WA8: Wid ... 5A 80
WN4: Ash M ... 9K 41
Ramsey Ct. CH48: W Kir ... 8C 70
Ramsey Rd. CH65: Ell P ... 4A 112
L19: Aller ... 8B 76
Ramsfield Rd. L24: Speke ... 3L 93
Ramsons Cl. L26: Halew ... 7J 77
Randall Cl. WA12: Newt W ... 6K 51
Randall Dr. L30: N'ton ... 9B 34
Randle Av. WA11: Rainf ... 3B 38
Randle Brook Ct. WA11: Rainf ... 3B 38
Randle Cl. CH63: Spit ... 5N 89
Randle Hgts. L11: Crox ... 5C 46
Randle Mdw. CH66: Gt Sut ... 3L 111
Randle Mdw. Ct. *CH66: Gt Sut* ... *3L 111*
(off Randle Mdw.)
Randle M. WA8: Wid ... 7L 79
Randles Rd. L34: Know ... 5E 46
Randolph St. L4: Walt ... 2E 58
Randon Gro. WA10: St H ... 6J 49
Ranelagh Av. L21: Lith ... 2N 43
Ranelagh Dr. PR8: Ains ... 7M 11
Ranelagh Dr. Nth. L19: Gras ... 8M 75
Ranelagh Dr. Sth. L19: Gras ... 8M 75
Ranelagh Ho. L1: Liv ... 6H 5
Ranelagh Pl. L3: Liv ... 5H 5 (8D 58)
Ranelagh St. L1: Liv ... 6G 5 (8C 58)
Ranfurly Rd. L19: Gras ... 9N 75
Range La. L37: Form ... 4C 24
Rangemoor Cl. WA3: Birchw ... 3A 68
Rangemore Rd. L18: Moss H ... 7M 75
Rankin Hall L18: Moss H ... 6K 75
Rankin St. CH44: Wall ... 7G 57
Rankin Way CH62: Brom ... 6D 90
Ranleigh Dr. WN8: Newb ... 4D 22
Ranmore Av. WN4: Garsw ... 7F 40
Rannoch Cl. CH66: Gt Sut ... 2L 111
Ranslett Ct. L37: Form ... 1G 24
Ranulph Ct. WA6: Frod ... 7M 107
Ranworth Cl. L11: Norr G ... 7K 45
Ranworth Dr. WA3: Low ... 3F 52
Ranworth Gdns. WA9: St H ... 3G 63
Ranworth Pl. L11: Norr G ... 7K 45
Ranworth Rd. WA5: Gt San ... 2G 81
Ranworth Sq. L11: Norr G ... 7L 45
Ranworth Way L11: Norr G ... 7L 45
Rappart Rd. CH44: Wall ... 6K 57
Rashid Mufti Ct. L8: Liv ... 2F 74
Ratcliffe Pl. L35: Rainh ... 5E 62
Rathbone Hall L17: Aig ... 4K 75
Rathbone Rd. L13: Liv, Wav ... 9L 59
L15: Wav ... 9L 59
L38: Hight ... 8F 24
Rathlin Cl. WA8: Wid ... 5A 80
Rathmell Cl. WA3: Cul ... 7M 53
Rathmore Av. L18: Moss H ... 5M 75
Rathmore Cl. CH43: Oxton ... 5G 73
Rathmore Cres. PR9: South ... 4N 7
Rathmore Dr. CH43: Oxton ... 4G 73
Rathmore Rd. CH43: Oxton ... 4G 73
Raven Cl. L6: Liv ... 2N 5 (6F 58)
Ravendale Cl. CH43: Noct ... 4D 72
Ravenfield Cl. L26: Halew ... 8J 77
Ravenfield Dr. WA8: Wid ... 5F 78
Ravenglass Av. L31: Mag ... 1J 35
RAVENHEAD ... 8H 49
Ravenhead Av. L32: Kirkb ... 3C 46
Ravenhead Bus. Pk. WA10: St H ... 8J 49
Ravenhead Dr. WN8: Uph ... 5K 31
Ravenhead Pk. WA9: St H ... 9K 49
Ravenhead Rd. WA10: St H ... 9H 49
Ravenhead Row WA10: St H ... 9H 49
Ravenhead Way WN8: Uph ... 6J 31
Ravenhill Cres. CH46: Leas ... 5N 55
Ravenhurst Ct. WA3: Ris ... 4N 67
Ravenhurst Way L35: Whis ... 8A 62
Ravenmeols Hills Local Nature Reserve ... 3A 24
Raven Meols La. L37: Form ... 2E 24
Ravenna Rd. L19: Aller ... 8B 76
Ravens, The L37: Form ... 3F 24
Ravens Ct. L26: Halew ... 9K 77
Ravenscourt *WA13: Lymm* ... *5F 84*
(off Pepper St.)
Ravenscroft L37: Form ... 2F 24
Ravenscroft Av. L39: Orm ... 9C 20
Ravenscroft Rd. CH43: Oxton ... 3J 73
Ravensdale Cl. WA2: Warr ... 6E 66
Ravensthorpe Grn. L11: Norr G ... 7L 45
Ravenstone Cl. CH49: Upton ... 1N 71
Ravenstone Dr. WA9: St H ... 2N 63
Ravenstone Rd. L19: Aller ... 8N 75
Ravenswood Av. CH42: Rock F ... 8M 73
Ravens Wood Brow WN5: Bil ... 6A 40
Ravenswood Rd. CH61: Hesw ... 5A 88
L13: Liv ... 6M 59
Raven Way *L20: Boot* ... *7B 44*
(off Strand Shop. Cen.)
Rawcliffe Cl. WA8: Wid ... 4J 79
Rawcliffe Rd. CH42: Tran ... 3K 73
L9: Walt ... 6E 44
Rawdon Cl. WA7: Pal F ... 8C 96
Rawlings Cl. WA3: Birchw ... 6N 67
Rawlinson Ct. *PR9: South* ... *7J 7*
(off Rawlinson Rd.)
Rawlinson Cres. L26: Halew ... 8M 77
Rawlinson Gro. PR9: South ... 6K 7
Rawlinson Rd. L13: Liv ... 6L 59
PR9: South ... 7J 7
Rawlins St. L7: Liv ... 6J 59
Rawson Cl. L21: Sea ... 3M 43
Rawson Rd. L21: Sea ... 2M 43
Raydale Cl. L9: Walt ... 7F 44
WA3: Low ... 1F 52
Raymond Av. L30: N'ton ... 1F 44
WA4: Stockt H ... 7E 82
Raymond Pl. L5: Liv ... 5C 58
Raymond Rd. CH44: Wall ... 6J 57
Raymond Way CH64: Lit N ... 7G 100
Raynham Rd. L13: Liv ... 7L 59
Rayrig Fold WA11: Rainf ... 5C 38
Reach, The L3: Liv ... 2F 4 (6C 58)
Reade Cl. CH63: Spit ... 6N 89
Reading Cl. L5: Kirkd ... 2C 58
Reading St. L5: Kirkd ... 2C 58
Reads Ct. L9: Walt ... 4E 44
Reaper Cl. WA5: Gt San ... 2M 81
Reapers Way L30: N'ton ... 7F 34
Rear Comn. Pas. L6: Liv ... 6J 59
Reay Ct. CH44: Wall ... 6L 57
Reay St. WA8: Wid ... 6M 79
Rebecca Gdns. WA9: St H ... 2M 63
Recreation Av. WN4: Ash M ... 7M 41
Recreation Dr. WN5: Bil ... 6A 40
Recreation Rd. PR9: Banks ... 4H 9
Recreation St. WA9: St H ... 6M 49
Rector Rd. L6: Liv ... 2H 59
Rectory Av. WA3: Low ... 2D 52
Rectory Cl. CH42: Tran ... 4K 73
CH60: Hesw ... 8N 87
WA2: Win ... 3C 66
Rectory Dr. L26: Halew ... 7K 77
Rectory Gdns. WA9: St H ... 3M 63
WA13: Lymm ... 5E 84
Rectory La. CH1: Cap ... 4E 110
CH60: Hesw ... 8M 87
WA2: Win ... 3B 66
WA13: Lymm ... 6E 84
Rectory Rd. CH48: W Kir ... 7C 70
PR9: South ... 6M 7
WN4: Garsw ... 6F 40
Redacre Cl. WA4: Dutt ... 3J 109
RED BANK ... 9N 51
Red Bank WA12: Newt W ... 9N 51
Red Bank Av. WA12: Newt W ... 9A 52
Red Barnes L37: Form ... 8F 16
Red Barn Rd. WN5: Bil ... 5L 39
Redbourne Av. L26: Halew ... 1K 93
Redbourne Dr. WA8: Wid ... 4E 78
Redbourn St. L6: Liv ... 3H 59
Redbrook Cl. CH62: Brom ... 9C 90
Redbrook Rd. M31: Part ... 7L 69
Redbrook St. L6: Liv ... 3H 59
Red Brow La. WA4: Dares ... 7G 96
WA7: Murd ... 7G 96
Redbrow Way L33: Kirkb ... 7C 36
Redburn Cl. L8: Liv ... 4F 74
Redcap Cl. CH45: Wall ... 1E 56
Redcar Cl. PR8: South ... 3E 12
Redcar Dr. CH62: East ... 1C 102
Redcar M. L6: Liv ... 3G 59
Redcar Rd. CH45: Wall ... 3D 56
Redcar St. L6: Liv ... 3H 59
Red Cat La. L40: Burs ... 6J 15
WA11: Crank ... 7H 39
Redcliffe Gdns. L39: Augh ... 1C 28
Redcote Ct. CH48: W Kir ... 7B 70
Redcroft CH49: Grea ... 5K 71
Red Cross St. L2: Liv ... 6D 4 (8B 58)
Red Cut La. L33: Kirkb ... 2J 47
Red Delph La. WA11: Rainf ... 2A 38
REDDISH ... 3G 84
Reddish Cres. WA13: Lymm ... 4F 84
Reddish La. WA13: Lymm ... 4E 84
(not continuous)
Redditch Cl. CH49: Grea ... 4K 71
Reddy La. WA14: Lit Bo, Mill ... 9N 85
(not continuous)
Redesdale Cl. WA2: Warr ... 7F 66
Redfearn Wlk. WA2: Warr ... 1D 82
Redfern St. L20: Kirkd ... 1B 58
Redfield Cl. CH44: Wall ... 5K 57
Red Fold L39: Augh ... 1A 28
Redford Cl. CH49: Grea ... 4K 71
Redford St. L6: Liv ... 3H 59
Red Gables WA4: App T ... 4J 99
Redgate L37: Form ... 2G 25
L39: Orm ... 8B 20
Redgate Av. L23: Crosb ... 7N 33
Redgate Dr. L37: Form ... 2H 25
WA9: St H ... 7N 49
Redgate Rd. WN4: Ash M ... 5K 41
Redgrave Ct. L20: Boot ... 8B 44
Redgrave St. L7: Liv ... 7H 59
Redhill Av. L32: Kirkb ... 2D 46
Redhill Cl. WA5: Gt San ... 2K 81
Redhill Dr. PR8: South ... 3E 12
Red Hill Rd. CH63: Store ... 2H 89
Redhills M. CH65: Ell P ... 8N 103
Redhillswood Cl. CH65: Ell P ... 7N 103
Redhouse Bank CH48: W Kir ... 5B 70
Redhouse La. CH48: W Kir ... 5B 70
Redington Rd. L19: Aller ... 8B 76
Redland Cl. WN2: Bam ... 4N 41
Redland Rd. *L9: Ain* ... *2G 44*
(off Lyncot Rd.)
Red La. WA4: App ... 8C 82
WA6: Frod ... 6M 107
Red Lion Cl. L31: Mag ... 2H 35
Red Lion La. CH66: Lit Sut ... 7H 103
Red Lion Shop. Cen. L31: Mag ... 2H 35
Red Lomes L30: N'ton ... 6C 34
Redmain Gro. WA3: Low ... 2F 52
Redmain Way L12: Crox ... 8D 46
Redmayne Cl. WA12: Newt W ... 6K 51
Redmere Dr. CH60: Hesw ... 7D 88
Redmires Cl. L7: Liv ... 9G 59
Redmont St. CH41: Tran ... 4L 73
Redmoor Cres. L33: Kirkb ... 6C 36
Redoaks Way L26: Halew ... 7M 77
Red Pike CH66: Lit Sut ... 6J 103
Redpoll Gro. L26: Halew ... 6J 77
Redpoll La. WA3: Birchw ... 5M 67
Red Rocks Marsh Nature Reserve ... 4A 70
Red Rock St. L6: Liv ... 5G 58
Red Rum Cl. L9: Ain ... 2J 45
Redruth Av. WA11: St H ... 3N 49
Redruth Cl. WA7: Brook ... 9E 96
Redruth Rd. L11: Crox ... 5B 46
Redsands L39: Augh ... 1B 28
Redshank Cl. WA12: Newt W ... 6L 51
Redshank La. WA3: Birchw ... 5N 67
Redstart Cl. WA3: Low ... 2F 52
Redstone Cl. CH47: Meols ... 9E 54
Redstone Dr. CH60: Hesw ... 6K 87
Red Stone Hill WA6: Hel ... 1F 114
Redstone M. CH47: Meols ... 9E 54
Redstone Pk. CH45: Wall ... 1F 56
Redstone Ri. CH43: Noct ... 2D 72
Redstone Way L35: Whis ... 4D 62
Redtail Cl. WA7: Run ... 4J 95
Redvales Ct. WA3: Birchw ... 5K 67
Redvers Av. CH66: Hoot ... 4F 102
Redvers Dr. L9: Walt ... 4E 44
Redwald Cl. L33: Kirkb ... 5D 36
Redwing La. L25: Gate ... 4E 76
Redwing Way L26: Halew ... 6H 77
Redwood Av. L31: Lyd ... 9H 27
Redwood Cl. CH43: Oxton ... 6F 72
L25: Gate ... 3G 76
WA1: Wools ... 2M 83
Redwood Ct. *L8: Liv* ... *4F 74*
(off Byles St.)
Redwood Dr. CH2: Elt ... 1N 113
CH66: Gt Sut ... 4L 111
L39: Orm ... 9B 20
WA11: Hay ... 5B 50
Redwood Gro. *L20: Boot* ... *6B 44*
(off Strand Rd.)
Redwood Rd. L25: Gate ... 3F 76
Redwood Way L33: Kirkb ... 5C 36
Reedale Cl. L18: Moss H ... 4M 75
Reedale Rd. L18: Moss H ... 4M 75
Reedgate La. CW9: Ant ... 7M 99
Reed La. CW9: Ant ... 9J 99
Reedmace Rd. L5: Liv ... 3E 58
Reeds, The L39: Orm ... 7B 20
Reeds Av. E. CH46: Leas ... 6N 55
Reeds Av. W. CH46: Leas ... 6N 55
Reeds Brow WA11: Rainf ... 3E 38
Reeds La. CH46: Leas, More ... 5N 55
WA11: Rainf ... 7B 38
Reedsmere Cl. WA4: Stockt H ... 6F 82
Reeds Rd. L36: Huy ... 5J 61
Reedville CH43: Oxton ... 3H 73
Reedville Gro. CH46: Leas ... 7N 55
Reedville Rd. CH63: Beb ... 2M 89
Reel Cinema
Widnes ... 9L 79
Rees Pk. L40: Burs ... 1K 21
Reeve Ct. Village WA9: St H ... 3F 62
Reeves Av. L20: Boot ... 5D 44
Reeves St. WA9: St H ... 7A 50
Reeve St. WA3: Low ... 2J 53
Reflection Ct. WA10: St H ... 7J 49
Regal Cl. CH66: Gt Sut ... 2K 111
Regal Ct. PR8: Ains ... 9K 11
Regal Cres. WA8: Wid ... 8E 78
Regal Dr. WA10: Windle ... 5F 48
Regal Rd. L11: Crox ... 7A 46
Regal Wlk. L4: Walt ... 2E 58
Regency Ct. *CH42: Rock F* ... *7N 73*
(off Rock La. W.)
PR9: South ... 6J 7
Regency Gdns. PR8: Birkd ... 2L 11
Regency Pk. WA8: Wid ... 5H 79
Regency Sq. WA5: Warr ... 1A 82
Regent Av. L14: Broad G ... 7C 60
L30: N'ton ... 8E 34
WA1: Padg ... 9H 67
WA11: Hay ... 3D 50
WN4: Ash M ... 6H 41
Regent Cl. PR8: Birkd ... 2M 11
Regent Ct. PR9: South ... 7H 7
Regent M. PR8: Birkd ... 2M 11
Regent Pk. L36: Huy ... 4J 61
Regent Rd. CH45: Wall ... 3D 56
L3: Liv ... 5M 43
L5: Kirkd, Liv ... 5M 43
L20: Boot, Kirkd ... 5M 43
L23: Crosb ... 7K 33
PR8: Birkd ... 2L 11
WA8: Wid ... 7L 79
Regents Cl. CH61: Thing ... 1B 88
Regents Fld. L37: Form ... 8D 16
Regents Rd. WA10: St H ... 8F 48
Regent St. CH65: Ell P ... 9L 103
L3: Liv ... 5A 58
WA1: Warr ... 3B 82
WA7: Run ... 4K 95
WA12: Newt W ... 7J 51
Regents Way CH63: Hghr B ... 8K 73
Regiment Way L12: W Der ... 2B 60
Regina Av. L22: Water ... 9J 33
Reginald Rd. WA9: St H ... 3A 64
Regina Rd. L9: Walt ... 4F 44
Reid Av. WA5: Warr ... 9A 66
Reid Ct. CH66: Lit Sut ... 7H 103
Reigate Cl. L25: Woolt ... 5G 77
Reins Cft. CH64: Nest ... 5E 100
Rembury Pl. WA4: Dutt ... 3H 109
Renacres La. L39: Hals ... 9D 12
Renaissance CH64: Nest ... 6F 100
Renaissance Way L24: Halew ... 2H 93
Rendal Cl. L5: Liv ... 4F 58
Rendcombe Grn. L11: Norr G ... 7L 45
Rendel Cl. WA12: Newt W ... 8M 51
Rendelsham Cl. CH49: Upton ... 3M 71
Rendel St. CH41: Birke ... 1K 73
Rendlesham Cl. WA3: Birchw ... 3B 68
Renfrew Av. CH62: East ... 1D 102
WA11: St H ... 3N 49
Renfrew Cl. WN3: Wigan ... 1J 41
Renfrew St. L7: Liv ... 3N 5 (7F 58)
Renfrey Cl. L39: Orm ... 5C 20
Renlake Ind. Est. WA9: St H ... 3B 64
Rennell Rd. L14: Knott A ... 6A 60
Rennie Av. WA10: St H ... 6F 48
Rennie Dr. WA4: Westy ... 5J 83
Renown Cl. WA3: Ris ... 5L 67
Renown Way L24: Speke ... 1E 92
Renshaw St. L1: Liv ... 6H 5 (8D 58)
Renton Av. WA7: Run ... 5N 95
Renville Rd. L14: Broad G ... 7A 60
Renwick Av. L35: Rainh ... 5D 62
Renwick Rd. L9: Walt ... 5F 44
Renwick Sq. WN4: Ash M ... 8H 41
Repton Gro. L10: Ain ... 9H 35
Repton Rd. CH65: Ell P ... 1B 112
L16: Child ... 9B 60
Reservoir Rd. CH42: Tran ... 7H 73
L25: Woolt ... 5D 76
Reservoir Rd. Nth. CH42: Tran ... 6H 73
Reservoir St. L6: Liv ... 5F 58
WA9: St H ... 2F 62
Rest Hill Rd. CH63: Store ... 2H 89
Retford Rd. L33: Kirkb ... 9D 36
Retford Wlk. L33: Kirkb ... 9D 36
Reva Rd. L14: Broad G ... 6D 60
Revesby Cl. WA8: Wid ... 6G 79
Rex Cohen Ct. L17: Aig ... 3K 75
Rexmore Rd. L18: Moss H ... 6M 75
Rexmore Way L15: Wav ... 1K 75
Reynolds Av. WA3: Ris ... 4M 67
WA9: St H ... 8D 50
Reynolds Cl. L6: Liv ... 5F 58
Reynolds St. WA4: Westy ... 5F 82
Reynolds Way L25: Woolt ... 6E 76
Rhiwlas St. L8: Liv ... 3F 74
Rhodesia Rd. L9: Ain ... 4G 45
Rhodes St. WA2: Warr ... 1D 82
Rhodesway CH60: Hesw ... 8B 88
Rhona Cl. CH63: East ... 2B 102
Rhona Dr. WA5: Gt San ... 2G 80
Rhosesmor Cl. L32: Kirkb ... 3D 46
Rhosesmor Rd. L32: Kirkb ... 4D 46

Rhuddlan Cl. L13: Liv . . . 7L **59**
Rhuddlan Ct. CH65: Ell P . . . 3B **112**
Rhum Cl. CH65: Ell P . . . 4A **112**
Rhyl St. L8: Liv . . . 3E **74**
WA8: Wid . . . 9J **79**
Rialto Cl. L8: Liv . . . 1E **74**
Rib, The L37: Form, Gt Alt . . . 8M **17**
Ribble Av. L31: Mag . . . 1K **35**
L35: Rainh . . . 6F **62**
PR9: South . . . 3A **8**
Ribble Cl. WA3: Cul . . . 8N **53**
WA8: Wid . . . 5B **80**
Ribble Cres. WN5: Bil . . . 8M **39**
Ribbledale Rd. L18: Moss H . . . 4M **75**
Ribble Ho. L25: Gate . . . 4G **76**
Ribble Rd. L25: Gate . . . 5G **76**
Ribblers La. L32: Kirkb . . . 3B **46**
L34: Know . . . 4D **46**
Ribblesdale CH65: Whit . . . 2N **111**
Ribblesdale Av. L9: Ain . . . 3G **44**
Ribblesdale Cl. CH62: East . . . 1E **102**
Ribble St. CH41: Birke . . . 8F **56**
Ribchester Gdns. WA3: Cul . . . 7N **53**
Ribchester Way L35: Tar G . . . 1L **77**
Rice Hey Rd. CH44: Wall . . . 4J **57**
Rice La. CH44: Wall . . . 4J **57**
(not continuous)
L9: Walt . . . 7E **44**
Rice Lane City Farm . . . 6E **44**
Rice Lane Station (Rail) . . . 5F **44**
Rice St. L1: Liv . . . 8J **5** (9D **58**)
Richard Allen Way *L5: Liv* . . . *5E 58*
(off Netherfield Rd. Sth.)
Richard Chubb Dr. CH44: Wall . . . 3K **57**
Richard Cl. WA7: Cas . . . 6C **96**
Richard Gro. L12: W Der . . . 4C **60**
Richard Hesketh Dr.
L32: Kirkb . . . 9A **36**
Richard Kelly Cl. L4: Walt . . . 1J **59**
Richard Kelly Dr. L4: Walt . . . 8J **45**
Richard Kelly Pl. L4: Walt . . . 1J **59**
Richard Martin Rd. L21: Ford . . . 1B **44**
Richard Reynolds Ct. *M44: Cad* . . . *3L 69*
(off Dean Rd.)
Richard Rd. L23: Blun . . . 6G **32**
Richards Gro. WA9: St H . . . 6A **50**
Richardson Rd. CH42: Rock F . . . 7L **73**
Richardson St. L7: Liv . . . 1H **75**
WA2: Warr . . . 9D **66**
Richbell Cl. M44: Irlam . . . 2L **69**
Richland Rd. L13: Liv . . . 4L **59**
Richmond Av. L21: Lith . . . 2N **43**
L40: Burs . . . 2J **21**
WA4: Grap . . . 5K **83**
WA4: Westy . . . 4G **83**
WA7: Run . . . 5A **96**
WA11: Hay . . . 3D **50**
Richmond Cl. CH63: Beb . . . 1N **89**
L38: Hight . . . 1F **32**
WA3: Cul . . . 6L **53**
WA10: Eccl . . . 6D **48**
WA13: Lymm . . . 4H **85**
Richmond Ct. CH65: Ell P . . . 2B **112**
L6: Liv . . . *4F 58*
(off Richmond Ter.)
L21: Lith . . . *3A 44*
(off Delta Rd.)
L40: Burs . . . 2J **21**
WA4: Westy . . . 5H **83**
WA8: Wid . . . 4N **79**
Richmond Cres. L30: N'ton . . . 8E **34**
Richmond Dr. WA13: Lymm . . . 4H **85**
Richmond Gdns. WA12: Newt W . . . 8L **51**
Richmond Gro. L31: Lyd . . . 9K **27**
Richmond M. L40: Burs . . . 2K **21**
Richmond Pk. L6: Liv . . . 3G **59**
Richmond Rd. CH63: Beb . . . 1M **89**
L23: Crosb . . . 6L **33**
PR8: Birkd . . . 4M **11**
WN4: Ash M . . . 6H **41**
Richmond Row L3: Liv . . . 1H **5** (6D **58**)
Richmond St. CH45: New B . . . 9H **43**
L1: Liv . . . 5F **4** (8C **58**)
WA4: Westy . . . 5H **83**
WA8: Wid . . . 7M **79**
Richmond Ter. L6: Liv . . . 4G **58**
Richmond Way CH61: Hesw . . . 5N **87**
CH61: Thing . . . 9A **72**
L35: Tar G . . . 1L **77**
Rich Vw. CH43: Oxton . . . 5H **73**
Rickaby Cl. CH63: Brom . . . 7B **90**
Rickerby Ct. PR9: South . . . 7H **7**
Rickman St. L4: Kirkd . . . 2C **58**
Rickman Way L36: Huy . . . 9K **61**
Ridding La. WA7: Brook . . . 1D **108**
Riddings, The CH65: Whit . . . 1N **111**
Riddock Rd. L21: Lith . . . 5A **44**
Rides, The WA11: Hay . . . 4F **50**
Ridge, The CH60: Hesw . . . 5L **87**
Ridgebourne Cl. WA5: Call . . . 7M **65**
Ridge Cl. PR9: South . . . 2A **8**
Ridgefield Rd. CH61: Pens . . . 2N **87**
Ridgemere Rd. CH61: Pens . . . 2N **87**
Ridgetor Rd. L25: Woolt . . . 5D **76**
Ridgeview Rd. CH43: Noct . . . 3D **72**
Ridgeway WA3: Low . . . 3G **52**
Ridgeway, The CH47: Meols . . . 1F **70**
CH60: Hesw . . . 8B **88**
CH63: Hghr B . . . 8K **73**
L25: Woolt . . . 5E **76**
Ridgeway, The WA6: Frod . . . 2H **115**
WA7: Murd . . . 9F **96**
WA8: Cron . . . 2F **78**
Ridgeway Cl. CH66: Gt Sut . . . 3H **111**
Ridgeway, The (Country Holiday Pk.)
WA6: Frod . . . 3K **115**
Ridgeway Dr. L31: Lyd . . . 8J **27**
Ridgewell Av. WA3: Low . . . 2D **52**
Ridgewell Cl. L21: Lith . . . 3N **43**
Ridgewood Dr. CH61: Pens . . . 3M **87**
WA9: St H . . . 3M **63**
Ridgewood Way L9: Walt . . . 3F **44**
Ridgmont Av. L11: Norr G . . . 8L **45**
Ridgway Gdns. WA13: Lymm . . . 5D **84**
Ridgway St. WA2: Warr . . . 1E **82**
Riding Cl. L39: Down . . . 9E **18**
WA9: Clock F . . . 5M **63**
Ridingfold L26: Halew . . . 6H **77**
Riding Hill Rd. L34: Know . . . 8H **47**
Riding Hill Wlk. L34: Know . . . 8H **47**
Riding La. L39: Down . . . 9C **18**
WN4: Ash M . . . 5N **41**
Ridings, The CH43: Noct . . . 3D **72**
PR9: South . . . 4M **7**
Ridings Hey CH43: Noct . . . 4D **72**
Riding St. L3: Liv . . . 4K **5** (7E **58**)
PR8: South . . . 9G **6**
Ridley Dr. WA5: Gt San . . . 4L **81**
Ridley Gro. CH48: W Kir . . . 5B **70**
Ridley La. L31: Mag . . . 2J **35**
Ridley Rd. L6: Liv . . . 6H **59**
Ridley St. CH43: Oxton . . . 3J **73**
Ridsdale WA8: Wid . . . 8F **78**
Ridsdale Lawn L27: N'ley . . . 5L **77**
Riesling Dr. L33: Kirkb . . . 6B **36**
Rigby Dr. CH49: Grea . . . 6L **71**
Rigby Rd. L31: Mag . . . 9G **27**
Rigbys La. WN4: Ash M . . . 8M **41**
(not continuous)
Rigby St. L3: Liv . . . 3C **4** (7A **58**)
WA3: Golb . . . 2B **52**
WA10: St H . . . 7J **49**
(Clock Twr. St.)
WA10: St H . . . 6J **49**
(Henry St.)
WN4: Ash M . . . 8J **41**
Rigby St. Sth. *WA10: St H* . . . *7J 49*
(off Nth. John St.)
Riley Av. L20: Boot . . . 5C **44**
Riley Bank M. WA6: Frod . . . 4L **115**
Riley Dr. WA7: Run . . . 7K **95**
Rilston Av. WA3: Cul . . . 7L **53**
Rimington Av. WA3: Golb . . . 1D **52**
Rimington Cl. WA3: Cul . . . 7M **53**
Rimmer Av. L16: Child . . . 8E **60**
Rimmerbrook Rd. L25: Gate . . . 1F **76**
Rimmer Cl. L21: Lith . . . 3A **44**
Rimmer Grn. PR8: South . . . 5J **13**
Rimmer Gro. WA9: St H . . . 7A **50**
Rimmer's Av. L37: Form . . . 7E **16**
PR8: South . . . 9G **6**
Rimmer St. L3: Liv . . . 3J **5** (7D **58**)
Rimmington Rd. L17: Aig . . . 6K **75**
Rimrose Bus. Pk. L20: Boot . . . 6N **43**
Rimrose Rd. L20: Boot . . . 5N **43**
Rimrose Valley Country Pk. . . . 7A **34**
Rimrose Valley Rd. L23: Crosb . . . 8N **33**
Rimsdale Cl. L17: Aig . . . 9K **75**
Ringcroft Rd. L13: Liv . . . 6N **59**
Ringley Av. WA3: Golb . . . 1A **52**
RING O' BELLS . . . 3M **21**
Ring O'Bells La. L40: Lath . . . 3M **21**
Ringo Starr Dr. L6: Liv . . . 6G **59**
Ring Rd. CH1: Back . . . 6L **111**
CH2: Lit Stan . . . 5B **112**
CH66: Back . . . 6L **111**
Ringsfield Rd. L24: Speke . . . 5L **93**
Ringtail Ct. L40: Burs . . . 1F **20**
Ringtail Ind. Est. L40: Burs . . . 2F **20**
Ringtail Pl. L40: Burs . . . 2F **20**
Ringtail Rd. L40: Burs . . . 1E **20**
Ringway CH64: Nest . . . 4E **100**
CH66: Gt Sut . . . 1K **111**
Ringway Rd. L25: Gate . . . 4G **77**
WA7: Run . . . 5N **95**
Ringways CH62: Brom . . . 4C **90**
Ringwood CH43: Oxton . . . 5G **72**
Ringwood Av. L14: Broad G . . . 7D **60**
Ringwood Cl. WA3: Birchw . . . 4B **68**
Rio Ct. L34: Presc . . . 2A **62**
Ripley Av. L21: Lith . . . 1A **44**
Ripley Cl. L31: Mag . . . 2K **35**
Ripley St. WA5: Warr . . . 1N **81**
Ripley Way WA9: St H . . . 5J **63**
Ripon Av. CH66: Lit Sut . . . 9H **103**
WA3: Low . . . 2E **52**
Ripon Cl. L30: N'ton . . . 1E **44**
L36: Huy . . . 6L **61**
PR8: South . . . 3E **12**
WA12: Newt W . . . 6L **51**
Ripon Dr. WN4: Ash M . . . 9M **41**
Ripon Rd. CH45: Wall . . . 3E **56**
Ripon Row WA7: Run . . . 9N **95**
Ripon St. CH41: Tran . . . 4L **73**
L4: Walt . . . 9E **44**
Risbury Rd. L11: Norr G . . . 8L **45**
Rishton Cl. L5: Liv . . . 4F **58**
Rishton St. *L5: Liv* . . . *4F 58*
(off Tynemouth Cl.)
RISLEY . . . 3M **67**
Risley Employment Area WA3: Ris . . . 2N **67**
Risley Moss Local Nature Reserve . . . 5B **68**
Risley Moss Vis. Cen. . . . 4A **68**
Risley Rd. WA3: Ris . . . 4N **67**
Ritchie Av. L9: Ain . . . 4H **45**
Ritherup La. L35: Rainh . . . 5F **62**
Ritson St. L8: Liv . . . 2G **74**
Rivacre Brow CH66: Ell P . . . 7K **103**
Rivacre Bus. Cen. CH66: Ell P . . . 9K **103**
Rivacre Park . . . 5H **103**
Rivacre Rd. CH62: East . . . 1F **102**
CH65: Hoot . . . 4H **103**
CH66: Ell P, Hoot . . . 4H **103**
Rivacre Valley Country Pk. . . . 6J **103**
Riva La. CH60: Hesw . . . 5M **87**
Rivenhall Sq. L24: Speke . . . 3F **92**
Rivenmill Cl. WA8: Wid . . . 3M **79**
River Avon St. L8: Liv . . . 1H **75**
(not continuous)
Riverbank Cl. CH60: Hesw . . . 9N **87**
Riverbank Rd. CH60: Hesw . . . 9M **87**
CH62: Brom . . . 3D **90**
L19: Gras . . . 9M **75**
Riverbend Technology Cen.
M44: Irlam . . . 3N **69**
River Cl. L37: Form . . . 3H **25**
River Gro. CH62: New F . . . 8A **74**
River La. M31: Part . . . 5M **69**
Rivermeade PR8: South . . . 2C **12**
Riverpark Gdns. *L8: Liv* . . . *2D 74*
(off Hyslop St.)
River Rd. WA4: Warr . . . 5C **82**
(not continuous)
Riversdale WA1: Wools . . . 1N **83**
WA6: Frod . . . 5M **107**
Riversdale Cl. L33: Kirkb . . . 7D **36**
Riversdale Ct. L19: Aig . . . 8L **75**
Riversdale M. L19: Aig . . . 8L **75**
Riversdale Rd. CH44: Wall . . . 5K **57**
CH48: W Kir . . . 6B **70**
L19: Aig . . . 9L **75**
L21: Sea . . . 3M **43**
WA7: Halt . . . 6A **96**
Riverside CH48: W Kir . . . 8C **70**
CH62: Port S . . . 2A **90**
L12: W Der . . . 9C **46**
L38: Hight . . . 8F **24**
Riverside Bowl . . . 9H **43**
Riverside Cl. L20: Boot . . . 5N **43**
WA1: Warr . . . 4D **82**
Riverside Ct. CH62: New F . . . 7A **74**
Riverside Dr. L3: Liv . . . 5D **74**
L17: Aig . . . 6F **74**
Riverside Gro. WA9: St H . . . 2N **63**
Riverside Holiday Pk. PR9: Banks . . . 5H **9**
Riverside Ho. CH41: Birke . . . 8M **57**
Riverside M. L36: Huy . . . 3G **61**
Riverside Retail Pk. WA1: Warr . . . 4D **82**
Riverside Trad. Est. WA5: Penk . . . 7F **80**
Riverside Vw. L17: Aig . . . 7H **75**
Riverside Wlk. CH64: Lit N . . . 9D **100**
L3: Liv . . . 3C **74**
(Atlantic Way)
L3: Liv . . . 8C **4** (9A **58**)
(The Colonnades)
PR9: Banks . . . 4H **9**
Riverslea Rd. L23: Blun . . . 9H **33**
River St. CH41: Birke . . . 2K **73**
Riversview PR9: Banks . . . 5H **9**
River Vw. *CH41: Tran* . . . *4L 73*
(off Marquis St.)
CH62: New F . . . 8B **74**
L22: Water . . . 9J **33**
Riverview CH49: Woodc . . . 7A **72**
Riverview Bus. Pk. CH62: Brom . . . 5E **90**
Riverview Gdns. CH42: Rock F . . . 6M **73**
River Vw. Residential Caravan Pk.
WA8: Wid . . . 8M **79**
Riverview Rd. CH44: Wall . . . 6L **57**
CH62: Brom . . . 4E **90**
CH64: Lit N . . . 9F **100**
Riverview Wlk. *L8: Liv* . . . *4E 74*
(off Cockburn St.)
River Wlk. *WA7: Pal F* . . . *8B 96*
(within Halton Lea Shop. Cen.)
River Way L25: Gate . . . 5G **76**
Riverwood Rd. CH62: Brom . . . 6E **90**
Riviera Dr. CH42: Rock F . . . 7K **73**
L11: Crox . . . 6A **46**
Rivington Av. CH43: Noct . . . 4E **72**
WA3: Golb . . . 1D **52**
WA10: St H . . . 4H **49**
Rivington Cl. PR8: Birkd . . . 3N **11**
Rivington Ct. WA1: Wools . . . 9M **67**
Rivington Dr. L40: Burs . . . 2J **21**
WN8: Uph . . . 5M **31**
Rivington Gro. M44: Cad . . . 3K **69**
Rivington Rd. CH44: Wall . . . 6K **57**
CH65: Ell P . . . 9A **104**
WA7: Pres B . . . 3H **109**
WA10: St H . . . 7G **49**
Rivington St. WA10: St H . . . 8G **48**
RIXTON . . . 7G **68**
Rixton Av. WA5: Warr . . . 9A **66**
Rixton Claypits Local Nature Reserve
. . . 7F **68**
Rixtonleys Dr. M44: Irlam . . . 1N **69**
Rixton Pk. Homes WA3: Rix . . . 7F **68**
Roadside Ct. WA3: Low . . . 2D **52**
Roadwater Cl. L25: Gate . . . 1F **76**
Robarts Rd. L4: Walt . . . 3G **58**
ROBBINS BRIDGE . . . 7K **27**
Robbins Bri. L31: Lyd . . . 7K **27**
Robeck Rd. L13: Liv . . . 8N **59**
Robert Dr. CH49: Grea . . . 5M **71**
Robert Gro. L12: W Der . . . 4C **60**
Roberts Av. WA11: Hay . . . 5C **50**
Roberts Ct. WA7: Pal F . . . 9B **96**
Roberts Dr. L20: Boot . . . 3D **44**
Roberts Fold WA3: Birchw . . . 5L **67**
Robertson St. L8: Liv . . . 3D **74**
Roberts St. L3: Liv . . . 2B **4** (6A **58**)
Robert St. CH41: Birke . . . 1K **73**
WA5: Warr . . . 2A **82**
WA7: Run . . . 5M **95**
WA8: Wid . . . 7L **79**
Robina Rd. WA9: St H . . . 1N **63**
Robin Cl. WA7: Murd . . . 8F **96**
ROBIN HOOD . . . 2L **23**
Robin Hood La. WA6: Hel . . . 4E **114**
WN6: Wright . . . 2L **23**
Robin La. WN8: Parb . . . 1F **22**
Robins Cft. CH66: Gt Sut . . . 3L **111**
Robins La. WA3: Cul . . . 8L **53**
WA9: St H . . . 1M **63**
WA11: Kings M . . . 3K **39**
Robinson Pl. WA9: St H . . . 7N **49**
Robinson Rd. CH65: Ell P . . . 1C **112**
L21: Lith . . . 1B **44**
Robin Way CH49: Woodc . . . 6B **72**
Rob La. WA12: Newt W . . . 6N **51**
Robsart St. L5: Liv . . . 4D **58**
Robson Gro. WA1: Warr . . . 2E **82**
Robson St. L5: Liv . . . 2E **58**
L13: Liv . . . 8M **59**
WA1: Warr . . . 2E **82**
Robson Way WA3: Low . . . 2G **52**
ROBY . . . 7G **61**
Roby Cl. L35: Rainh . . . 5F **62**
Roby Ct. L36: Roby . . . 8H **61**
Roby Gro. WA5: Gt San . . . 2J **81**
ROBY MILL . . . 1L **31**
Roby Mill WN8: Roby M . . . 9L **23**
Roby Mt. Av. L36: Roby . . . 7H **61**
Roby Rd. L14: Broad G . . . 8D **60**
L36: Roby . . . 7E **60**
(not continuous)
Roby Station (Rail) . . . 7G **60**
Roby St. L15: Wav . . . 1K **75**
L20: Boot . . . 6B **44**
WA10: St H . . . 9G **48**
Roby Well Way WN5: Bil . . . 6N **39**
Rocastle Cl. L6: Liv . . . 2N **5** (6F **58**)
Rochester Av. L30: N'ton . . . 1E **44**
Rochester Cl. WA3: Golb . . . 2B **52**
WA5: Gt San . . . 3L **81**
Rochester Dr. CH65: Ell P . . . 2B **112**
Rochester Gdns. WA10: St H . . . 9G **49**
Rochester Rd. CH42: Rock F . . . 6N **73**
Rock, The WA6: Hel . . . 3E **114**
Rock Av. CH60: Hesw . . . 6N **87**
Rock Bank CH49: Upton . . . 3A **72**
Rockbank Rd. L13: Liv . . . 4L **59**
Rockbourne Av. L25: Woolt . . . 3D **76**
Rockbourne Grn. L25: Woolt . . . 3D **76**
Rockbourne Way L25: Woolt . . . 3D **76**
Rock Cl. CH42: Rock F . . . 6M **73**
Rock Ct. WA6: Frod . . . 5L **107**
Rock Dr. WA6: Frod . . . 5M **107**
Rocket Trad. Cen. L14: Broad G . . . 8A **60**
Rockfarm Cl. CH64: Lit N . . . 8G **101**
Rockfarm Dr. CH64: Lit N . . . 8G **100**
Rockfarm Gro. CH64: Lit N . . . 8G **100**
ROCK FERRY . . . 7N **73**
Rock Ferry By-Pass CH42: Rock F . . . 5N **73**
Rock Ferry Station (Rail) . . . 6M **73**
Rockfield Cl. WA8: Wid . . . 6G **79**
Rockfield Dr. WA6: Hel . . . 3F **114**
Rockfield Gdns. *L31: Mag* . . . *1H 35*
(off East Meade)
Rockfield M. WA4: Grap . . . 6G **83**
Rockfield Rd. L4: Walt . . . 2E **58**
Rockford Av. L32: Kirkb . . . 3C **46**
Rockford Cl. L32: Kirkb . . . 3C **46**
Rockford Gdns. WA5: Gt San . . . 9J **65**
Rockford Wlk. L32: Kirkb . . . 3C **46**
Rock Gro. L13: Liv . . . 6M **59**
Rockhill Rd. L25: Woolt . . . 6F **76**
Rockhouse St. L6: Liv . . . 4H **59**
Rockingham Cl. WA3: Birchw . . . 3C **68**
Rockingham Ct. L33: Kirkb . . . 7D **36**
Rockland Rd. CH45: Wall . . . 2F **56**
L22: Water . . . 9L **33**
Rocklands, The CH43: Noct . . . 2D **72**
Rocklands Av. CH63: Beb . . . 9N **73**
Rocklands La. CH63: Thorn H . . . 7J **89**
Rock La. L31: Mell . . . 5L **35**
WA8: Wid . . . 5H **79**
Rock La. E. CH42: Rock F . . . 7N **73**
Rock La. W. CH42: Rock F . . . 7M **73**
Rocklee Gdns. CH64: Lit N . . . 8G **100**
Rockley St. L4: Kirkd, Walt . . . 1D **58**
(not continuous)
Rocklis Grange *CH64: Nest* . . . *6E 100*
(off Tannery La.)
Rockmount Cl. L25: Woolt . . . 5D **76**
Rockmount Pk. L25: Woolt . . . 5D **76**
Rockmount Rd. L17: Aig . . . 7L **75**
Rock Pk. CH42: Rock F . . . 6N **73**
(not continuous)

Rock Pk. Rd. CH42: Rock F 7A 74
Rockpoint Av. CH45: New B 2J 57
Rock Retail Pk. CH41: Birke 3L 73
Rock Rd. WA4: Westy 4F 82
ROCKSAVAGE 1M 107
Rocksavage Expressway
WA7: Clftn 1N 107
Rocksavage Way WA7: Run 1K 107
Rockside Rd. L18: Moss H 7M 75
Rock St. L13: Liv 6M 59
WA10: St H 1F 62
Rock Vw. L31: Mell 7M 35
Rockville Rd. L14: Broad G 8A 60
Rockville St. CH42: Rock F 6M 73
Rockwell Cl. L12: W Der 1B 60
Rockwell Rd. L12: W Der 1B 60
Rocky Bank Rd. CH42: Tran 5K 73
Rocky La. CH60: Hesw 7N 87
L6: Liv 4H 59
L16: Child 9A 60
Rocky La. Sth. CH60: Hesw 7A 88
Rococo Sq. CH45: New B 9J 43
Roderick Rd. L4: Walt 8F 44
Roderick St. L3: Liv 2J 5 (6D 58)
Rodgers Cl. WA6: Frod 5L 107
Rodick St. L25: Woolt 6D 76
Rodmell Rd. L9: Ain 4G 44
Rodney St. CH41: Birke 3K 73
L1: Liv 8J 5 (9D 58)
WA10: St H 7H 49
Roe All. L1: Liv 6G 4
Roeburn Way WA5: Penk 5F 80
Roedean Cl. L25: Woolt 7F 76
L31: Mag 1J 35
Roehampton Dr. L23: Blun 5J 33
WA7: Pal F 8A 96
Roe La. PR9: South 7K 7
Roemarsh Cl. L12: W Der 8N 45
Roemarsh Ct. WA7: Pal F 9A 96
Roe Pk. M. PR9: South 7J 7
Roe St. L1: Liv 5G 4 (8C 58)
Roften Works Ind. Est. CH66: Hoot 5C 102
Roger Arden Ct. L20: Boot 6C 44
Rogers Av. L20: Boot 5D 44
Rogersons Grn. L26: Halew 6J 77
Rokeby Av. WA3: Low 1E 52
Rokeby Cl. L3: Liv 1J 5 (6D 58)
L20: Boot 3D 44
Rokeby Ct. WA7: Manor P 2F 96
Rokeby St. L3: Liv 1J 5 (6D 58)
Rokeden WA12: Newt W 6M 51
Roker Av. CH44: Wall 6G 57
Rokesmith Av. L7: Liv 9H 59
Roklis Bldg. *CH44: Wall 5K 57*
(off Liscard Rd.)
Roklis Ct. *CH49: Upton 4A 72*
(off Rake La.)
Roland Av. CH63: Hghr B 1K 89
WA7: Run 5J 95
WA11: St H 3M 49
Rolands Wlk. WA7: Cas 6B 96
Roleton Cl. L30: N'ton 7G 34
Rollesby Gdns. WA9: St H 3H 63
Rolleston Dr. CH45: Wall 2F 56
CH63: Beb 3N 89
Rolleston St. WA2: Warr 2B 82
Rolling Mill La. WA9: St H 1B 64
Roman Cl. WA7: Cas 5A 96
WA12: Newt W 8L 51
Roman Ct. CH64: Lit N 7F 100
Roman Rd. CH43: Pren 8G 72
CH47: Meols 8E 54
CH63: Store 8G 73
WA4: Stockt H 7D 82
WN4: Ash M 6J 41
Roman Way L33: Kirkb 8E 36
Rome Cl. L36: Huy 6H 61
Romer Rd. L6: Liv 6H 59
Romford Way L26: Halew 1K 93
(not continuous)
Romiley Dr. WN8: Skel 2C 30
Romiley Rd. CH66: Ell P 8K 103
Romilly St. L6: Liv 2N 5 (6G 58)
Romley St. L4: Walt 9E 44
Romney Cl. CH64: Lit N 7E 100
WA8: Wid 6A 80
Romney Cft. CH64: Lit N 7F 100
Romney Way CH64: Lit N 7F 100
Romsey Av. L37: Form 2H 25
Romsey Gro. WN3: Wins 1F 40
Romulus St. L7: Liv 7J 59
Rona Av. CH65: Ell P 4A 112
Ronald Cl. L22: Water 1M 43
Ronald Dr. WA2: Fearn 7J 67
Ronald Rd. L22: Water 1M 43
Ronald Ross Av. L30: N'ton 8E 34
Ronaldshay WA8: Wid 6A 80
Ronald St. L13: Liv 6L 59
Ronaldsway CH49: Upton 2N 71
CH60: Hesw 9N 87
L10: Faz 3M 45
L23: Thorn 5N 33
L26: Halew 8L 77
Ronan Cl. L20: Boot 6N 43
Ronan Rd. WA8: Wid 2H 95
(not continuous)
Rone Cl. CH46: More 9L 55
Rookery, The WA12: Newt W 6M 51
Rookery Av. WN4: Ash M 9K 41
WN6: Appl B 5N 23
Rookery Dr. L19: Aig 8L 75
WA11: Rainf 5D 38
Rookery La. WA11: Rainf 6D 38
Rookery Rd. PR9: South 6K 7
Rookley Cl. L27: N'ley 4K 77
Rooks Way CH60: Hesw 7M 87
Rooley, The L36: Huy 8H 61
Roome St. WA2: Warr 1D 82
Roosevelt Dr. L9: Ain 2G 45
Roper's Bri. Cl. L35: Whis 7A 62
Ropers Ct. L34: Presc 4A 62
Roper St. L8: Liv 3E 74
WA9: St H 6M 49
Ropewalk, The CH64: Park 5C 100
Ropewalks Sq. L1: Liv 7H 5
Ropeworks Cl. L20: Boot 5C 44
Rosalind Av. CH63: Hghr B 9L 73
Rosalind Way L20: Kirkd 9C 44
Rosam Ct. WA7: Pal F 9A 96
Rosclare Dr. CH45: Wall 3F 56
Roscoe & Gladstone Hall L17: Aig 4K 75
Roscoe Av. WA2: Warr 9E 66
WA12: Newt W 7N 51
Roscoe Cl. L35: Tar G 1L 77
Roscoe Cres. WA7: West P 8H 95
Roscoe La. L1: Liv 7H 5 (9D 58)
Roscoe Pl. L1: Liv 7H 5 (9D 58)
Roscoe Rd. M44: Irlam 1L 69
Roscoe St. L1: Liv 8J 5 (9D 58)
WA10: St H 7G 49
Roscommon St. L5: Liv 5D 58
Roscommon Way WA8: Wid 5H 79
Roscote, The CH60: Hesw 8N 87
Roscote Cl. CH60: Hesw 8N 87
Roseacre CH48: W Kir 5B 70
Roseate Ct. CH45: Wall 1E 56
Rose Av. L20: Boot 3B 44
M44: Irlam 1M 69
WA9: St H 2M 63
WA11: Hay 4G 51
Rose Bailey Cl. L11: Norr G 6N 45
Rose Bank WA13: Lymm 5E 84
Rose Bank Rd. L16: Child 1B 76
Rosebank Rd. L36: Huy 4G 60
M44: Cad 5J 69
Rosebank Way L36: Huy 4G 61
Rosebay Cl. L37: Form 1G 24
Roseberry Rd. WN4: Ash M 6J 41
Rosebery Av. CH44: Wall 5J 57
L22: Water 9J 33
Rosebery Gro. CH42: Tran 6H 73
Rosebery Rd. WA10: St H 5G 48
Rosebery St. L8: Liv 1F 74
PR9: South 9M 7
Rosebourne Cl. L17: Aig 6H 75
Rose Brae L18: Moss H 4N 75
Rosebrae Ct. CH41: Birke 1M 73
CH60: Hesw 6A 88
Rosebrae Walkway CH41: Birke 1N 73
Rose Brow L25: Woolt 4E 76
Rose Cl. L26: Halew 9L 77
WA7: Murd 1F 108
Rose Ct. CH41: Birke 2K 73
L15: Wav 1K 75
Rose Cres. PR8: Ains 3J 17
WA8: Wid 9J 79
WN8: Skel 3B 30
Rosecroft CH62: Brom 9B 90
Rosecroft Cl. L39: Orm 7C 20
Rosecroft Ct. CH47: Hoy 2B 70
Rosedale Av. L23: Crosb 7L 33
WA1: Wools 1K 83
WA3: Low 3D 52
Rosedale Cl. L9: Walt 6G 45
Rosedale Rd. CH42: Tran 5L 73
L18: Moss H 4N 75
Rose Dr. WA11: Rainf 6D 38
Rosefield Av. CH63: Hghr B 9L 73
Rosefield Rd. L25: Woolt 7G 76
Rose Gdns. CH64: Lit N 8F 100
Rosegarth Grn. *L13: Liv 5N 59*
(off Black Horse La.)
Roseheath Dr. L26: Halew 9K 77
ROSE HILL 4H 41
Rose Hill L3: Liv 1G 5 (6C 58)
PR9: South 9J 7
Rosehill Av. WA9: Bold 4D 64
Rosehill Bus. Pk. PR9: South 9J 7
Rosehill Ct. L25: Woolt 4E 76
Rosehill Dr. L39: Augh 2A 28
Rosehill Vw. WN4: Ash M 4H 41
Roseland Cl. L31: Lyd 8G 27
Roselands Ct. CH42: Rock F 7L 73
Rose La. L18: Moss H 5L 75
Rose Lea Cl. WA8: Wid 4K 79
Roselea Dr. PR9: South 3A 8
Roselee Ct. CH42: Rock F 7N 73
Rosemary Av. WA4: Stockt H 6F 82
WA7: Beech 2B 108
Rosemary Cl. CH43: Bid 9E 56
L7: Liv 7N 5 (9F 58)
WA5: Gt San 2L 81
Rosemary Dr. WA12: Newt W 7N 51
Rosemary La. L37: Form 1E 24
L39: Down 8F 18
Rosemary Wlk. *M31: Part 7M 69*
(off Broom Rd.)
Rosemead Av. CH61: Pens 3N 87
Rosemere Dr. CH1: Back 6L 111
Rosemont Rd. L17: Aig 6L 75
Rosemoor Dr. L23: Crosb 6N 33
Rosemoor Gdns. L11: Norr G 8M 45
WA4: App 2G 98
Rose Mt. CH43: Oxton 5H 73
WA2: Win 1C 66
Rosemount Cl. CH43: Oxton 5G 73
Rose Mt. Dr. CH45: Wall 3G 57
Rosemount Pk. CH43: Oxton 4G 73
Rose Path L37: Form 2G 24
Rose Pl. CH42: Tran 4K 73
L3: Liv 1G 5 (6C 58)
(not continuous)
L39: Augh 2B 28
WA11: Rainf 6D 38
Roseside Dr. L27: N'ley 2K 77
Rose St. L1: Liv 4G 5 (8C 58)
L25: Woolt 6D 76
WA8: Wid 9J 79
Rose Ter. L18: Moss H 4M 75
Rose Theatre 1E 28
Rose Va. L5: Liv 5D 58
(not continuous)
Rose Vw. Av. WA8: Wid 6K 79
Rose Vs. L15: Wav 1L 75
Rose Wlk. M31: Part 6L 69
Rosewarne Cl. L17: Aig 6G 75
Roseway Av. M44: Cad 4L 69
Rosewood *PR9: South 5L 7*
(off Cambridge Rd.)
Rosewood Av. WA1: Warr 1F 82
WA6: Frod 7N 107
Rosewood Cl. L27: N'ley 3J 77
L28: Stockb V 2F 60
Rosewood Dr. CH46: More 9J 55
Rosewood Farm Ct. WA8: Wid 4H 79
Rosewood Gdns. L11: Norr G 9N 45
Rosewood Gro. WA8: Wid 8E 78
Roseworth Av. L9: Walt 3F 44
Rosina Cl. WN4: Ash M 5H 41
Roskell Rd. L25: Hunts X 9G 76
Roslin Ct. CH43: Oxton 4H 73
Roslin Rd. CH43: Oxton 4H 73
CH61: Irby 1L 87
Roslyn St. CH41: Tran 5M 73
CH42: Tran 5M 73
Rossall Av. L10: Ain 8J 35
Rossall Cl. L24: Hale 5B 94
Rossall Ct. CH46: Leas 7N 55
Rossall Gro. CH66: Lit Sut 8J 103
Rossall Rd. CH46: More 8N 55
L13: Liv 7N 59
WA5: Gt San 4K 81
WA8: Wid 6N 79
Ross Av. CH46: Leas 5C 56
Rossbank Rd. CH65: Ell P 7M 103
Rosscliffe Rd. CH65: Ell P 7M 103
Ross Cl. L34: Know 7H 47
WA5: Old H 1M 81
WN5: Bil 5A 40
Rosscourt Vw. CH42: Rock F 6N 73
Ross Dr. CH66: Gt Sut 9H 103
Rossendale Cl. CH43: Noct 4D 72
Rossendale Dr. WA3: Birchw 3A 68
Rosset Cl. WN3: Wins 1F 40
Rossett Av. L17: Liv 2K 75
Rossett Cl. WA5: Call 7N 65
Rossett Rd. L23: Crosb 8J 33
Rossett St. L6: Liv 4H 59
Rossfield Rd. CH65: Ell P 7M 103
Rossington Gdns. WA9: St H 4J 63
Rossini St. L21: Sea 4N 43
Rossiter Dr. CH43: Bid 2C 72
Rosslyn Av. L31: Mag 3G 35
Rosslyn Cres. CH46: More 9M 55
Rosslyn Dr. CH46: More 9M 55
Rosslyn Pk. CH46: More 1M 71
Rosslyn St. L17: Aig 5G 74
Rossmore Bus. Pk. CH65: Ell P 7N 103
Rossmore Bus. Village CH65: Ell P 7N 103
Rossmore Ct. CH66: Ell P 8K 103
Rossmore Gdns. CH66: Lit Sut 8J 103
L4: Walt 1H 59
Rossmore Ind. Est. CH65: Ell P 7M 103
(not continuous)
Rossmore Rd. E. CH65: Ell P 7L 103
Rossmore Rd. W.
CH66: Ell P, Lit Sut 7J 103
Rossmore Trad. Est. CH65: Ell P 8M 103
Rossmount Rd. CH65: Ell P 8M 103
Ross Rd. CH65: Ell P 8M 103
Ross St. WA8: Wid 7L 79
Ross Twr. Ct. CH45: New B 1J 57
Rosswood Rd. CH65: Ell P 8M 103
Rostherne Av. CH44: Wall 6G 57
CH66: Gt Sut 1K 111
WA3: Low 2E 52
Rostherne Cl. WA5: Warr 4M 81
Rostherne Cres. WA8: Wid 6G 78
Rosthwaite Cl. WN3: Wigan 1J 41
Rosthwaite Gro. WA11: St H 1L 49
Rosthwaite Rd. L12: W Der 3A 60
Rostron Cres. L37: Form 3E 24
Roswell Ct. L28: Stockb V 3F 60
Rosyth Cl. WA2: Fearn 6G 67
Rothay Dr. WA5: Penk 5F 80
Rothbury Cl. CH46: More 9K 55
WA7: Beech 9A 96
Rothbury Ct. WA9: Sut M 7L 63
Rothbury Rd. L14: Knott A 3D 60
Rother Dr. CH65: Ell P 7M 103
Rother Dr. Bus. Pk. CH65: Ell P 7M 103
Rotherham Cl. L36: Huy 5K 61
Rotherwood CH43: Noct 3D 72
Rotherwood Cl. CH63: Hghr B 1K 89
Rothesay Cl. WA7: Cas 5B 96
WA11: St H 3A 50
Rothesay Ct. CH63: Beb 3M 89
Rothesay Dr. CH62: East 2D 102
L23: Crosb 8L 33
Rothesay Gdns. CH43: Pren 7F 72
Rothley Av. PR8: Ains 1G 17
Rothsay Cl. L5: Liv 5E 58
Rothwell Cl. L39: Orm 8B 20
Rothwell Dr. L39: Augh 2N 27
PR8: Ains 9G 11
Rothwell Rd. WA3: Golb 1D 52
Rothwells La. L23: Thorn 5A 34
Rothwell St. L6: Liv 5F 58
Rotten Row PR8: South 1L 11
Rotunda St. L5: Liv 4C 58
Roughdale Av. L32: Kirkb 3D 46
WA9: Sut M 5L 63
Roughdale Cl. L32: Kirkb 3D 46
Rough La. L39: Bart 4K 17
Roughlea Av. WA3: Cul 6L 53
Roughley Av. WA5: Warr 4M 81
Roughley Ho. *CH41: Birke 1M 73*
(off Bridge St.)
Roughsedge Ho. L28: Stockb V 1F 60
Roughwood Dr. L33: Kirkb 8D 36
Roundabout, The WA8: Cron 2G 78
WN8: Skel 3N 29
Round Hey L28: Stockb V 1E 60
Round Meade, The L31: Mag 1G 35
Round Thorn WA3: Croft 1H 67
Roundway, The L38: Hight 9F 24
Roundwood Dr. WA9: St H 9L 49
Routledge St. WA8: Wid 7L 79
Row, The CH47: Hoy 1C 70
Rowan Av. L12: W Der 9D 46
WA3: Low 3G 52
Rowan Cl. L40: Burs 8K 15
WA5: Gt San 2H 81
WA7: Run 8M 95
WA11: Hay 5B 50
WA11: St H 3N 49
Rowan Ct. CH49: Grea 6J 71
CH63: Hghr B 1K 89
Rowan Dr. L32: Kirkb 8A 36
Rowan Gro. CH63: Hghr B 3L 89
L36: Huy 9H 61
Rowan Ho. WA6: Kingsw 6N 115
Rowan La. WN8: Skel 9E 22
Rowans, The L39: Augh 5M 27
WA8: Wid 4N 79
(off Hampton Ct. Way)
Rowan Tree Cl. CH49: Grea 5J 71
Rowan Wlk. M31: Part 6L 69
Rowena Cl. L23: Crosb 7M 33
Rowen Ct. L17: Aig 6K 75
Rowland Cl. WA2: Fearn 6H 67
Rowlings Way *L32: Kirkb 2D 46*
(off Park Brow Dr.)
Rowsley Gro. L9: Ain 3G 45
Rowson Ct. *CH45: New B 1H 57*
(off Pickering Rd.)
Rowson Dr. M44: Cad 3K 69
Rowson St. CH45: New B 9H 43
L34: Presc 2A 62
Rowswood Courtyard WA4: Hghr Wal 1N 97
Rowthorn Cl. WA8: Wid 8H 79
Rowton Cl. CH43: Oxton 5F 72
Roxborough Cl. WA5: Burtw 3J 65
Roxborough Wlk. L25: Woolt 5G 76
Roxburgh Av. CH42: Tran 6K 73
L17: Aig 5H 75
Roxburgh Rd. CH66: Lit Sut 8E 102
Roxburgh St. L4: Kirkd 8D 44
L20: Boot 8D 44
Royal, The CH47: Hoy 2A 70
Royal Av. WA8: Wid 8E 78
Royal Birkdale Golf Course 5K 11
Royal Cl. L37: Form 3G 24
Royal Ct. *CH42: Rock F 7N 73*
(off Rock La. W.)
Royal Court Theatre 4G 4 (8C 58)
Royal Cres. L37: Form 3G 24
Royal Cft. L12: W Der 5N 59
Royal Gro. WA10: St H 9G 49
Royal Liverpool Golf Course 3B 70
Royal Liverpool Philharmonic Hall
7K 5 (9E 58)
Royal London Bus. Pk. WA5: Westb 6N 65
Royal Mail St. L3: Liv 5H 5 (8D 58)
Royal Mersey Yacht Club 6N 73
ROYAL OAK 8D 28
Royal Pk. PR8: Birkd 2L 11
Royal Pl. WA8: Wid 8E 78
Royal Quay L3: Liv 8E 4 (9B 58)
Royal Shop. Arc. CH64: Nest 7E 100
Royal Standard Way CH42: Tran 5M 73
Royal St. L4: Walt 2D 58
Royal Ter. PR8: South 8F 6
Royden Av. CH44: Wall 4K 57
M44: Irlam 1M 69
WA7: Run 7J 95
WN3: Wigan 1J 41
Royden Cres. WN5: Bil 6A 40
Royden Rd. CH49: Upton 2M 71
WN5: Bil 6A 40

Royden Way L3: Liv .5D 74
Royleen Dr. WA6: Frod .8N 107
Roysten Gdns. WA9: St H .8N 49
Royston Av. WA1: Padd .1H 83
Royston Cl. CH66: Gt Sut .2L 111
WA3: Low .2F 52
Royston St. L7: Liv .8G 58
Royton Cl. L26: Halew .1K 93
Royton Rd. L22: Water .9M 33
Rozel Cres. WA5: Gt San .4K 81
Rubbing Stone CH48: Caldy .1E 86
Ruby Cl. L21: Lith .2B 44
Ruby St. L8: Liv .5E 74
(not continuous)
Rudd Av. WA9: St H .8D 50
Ruddington Rd. PR8: South .4D 12
Rudd St. CH47: Hoy .1C 70
Rudgate L35: Whis .7B 62
Rudgrave M. CH44: Wall .4K 57
Rudgrave Pl. CH44: Wall .4K 57
Rudgrave Sq. CH44: Wall .4K 57
Rudheath La. WA7: Nort .4F 96
Rudley Wlk. L24: Speke .5K 93
Rudloe Ct. WA2: Padg .8G 66
Rudstone Cl. CH66: Lit Sut .9G 103
Rudston Rd. L16: Child .9A 60
Rudyard Cl. L14: Knott A .6A 60
Rudyard Rd. L14: Knott A .6A 60
Ruecroft Cl. WN6: Appl B .5N 23
Ruff La. L39: Orm .9D 20
L40: Westh .9D 20
RUFFORD .2N 15
Rufford Av. L31: Mag .9K 27
Rufford Cl. L10: Faz .1L 45
L35: Presc .4C 62
WA8: Wid .6F 78
Rufford Ct. WA1: Wools .9M 67
Rufford Dr. PR9: Banks .2D 8
Rufford New Hall L40: Ruf .1M 15
Rufford Old Hall .1N 15
Rufford Pk. La. L40: Ruf .1L 15
Rufford Rd. CH44: Wall .6J 57
L6: Liv .6H 59
L20: Boot .5B 44
PR9: South .4A 8
WA11: Rainf .4C 38
Rufford Station (Rail) .2N 15
Rufford St. WN4: Ash M .6H 41
Rufford Wlk. WA11: St H .4A 50
Rugby Dr. L10: Ain .1K 45
Rugby Rd. CH44: Wall .5F 56
CH65: Ell P .2A 112
L9: Ain .2G 44
Rugby Wlk. CH65: Ell P .2B 112
Ruislip Cl. L25: Woolt .6G 77
Ruislip Ct. WA2: Padg .8G 66
Rullerton Rd. CH44: Wall .5G 56
Rumford Pl. L3: Liv .4C 4 (7B 58)
Rumford St. L2: Liv .4D 4 (7B 58)
Rumney Pl. L4: Kirkd .1D 58
(not continuous)
Rumney Rd. L4: Kirkd .1D 58
Rumney Rd. W. L4: Kirkd .1C 58
RUNCORN .4K 95
Runcorn Docks Rd. WA7: Run .5H 95
Runcorn East Station (Rail) .8F 96
Runcorn Golf Course .8K 95
Runcorn Hill Local Nature Reserve .7J 95
Runcorn Hill Vis. Cen. .7J 95
Runcorn Rd.
WA4: Hghr Wal, Moore .3H 97
Runcorn Ski & Snowboard Cen. .8D 96
Runcorn Spur Rd. WA7: Run .5L 95
Runcorn Station (Rail) .5J 95
Runcorn Swimming Pool .4L 95
Rundle Rd. L17: Aig .6K 75
Rundle St. CH41: Birke .9G 57
Runic St. L13: Liv .7L 59
Runnel, The L39: Hals .3G 18
Runnell, The CH64: Nest .3D 100
Runnell's La. L23: Thorn .6B 34
Runnymede L36: Huy .5H 61
WA1: Wools .1L 83
Runnymede Cl. L25: Woolt .4E 76
Runnymede Ct. *WA8: Wid* .7M 79
(off William St.)
Runnymede Dr. WA11: Hay .4C 50
Runnymede Gdns. *WA8: Wid* .7M 79
(off Cliffe St.)
Runnymede Wlk. *WA8: Wid* .6M 79
(off William St.)
Runton Rd. L25: Gate .3G 77
Rupert Dr. L6: Liv .1M 5 (5F 58)
Rupert Rd. L36: Huy .6G 61
Rupert Row WA7: Cas .7C 96
Ruscar Cl. L26: Halew .6J 77
Ruscolm Cl. WA5: Gt San .1F 80
Ruscombe Rd. L14: Knott A .4D 60
Rushbury Ct. L15: Wav .9L 59
Rushden Rd. L32: Kirkb .1E 46
Rushes Mdw. WA13: Lymm .3H 85
Rushey Hey Rd. L32: Kirkb .9C 36
Rushfield Cres. WA7: Brook .1D 108
Rush Gdns. WA13: Lymm .4G 84
RUSHGREEN .4G 84
Rushgreen Cl. CH43: Bid .1C 72
Rushgreen Rd. WA13: Lymm .4F 84
Rushlake Dr. L27: N'ley .3H 77
Rushmere Rd. L11: Norr G .9M 45
Rushmoor Av. WN4: Ash M .7N 41
Rushmore Dr. WA8: Wid .5J 79
Rushmore Gro. WA1: Padd .1H 83
Rusholme Cl. L26: Halew .1L 93
Rushton Av. WA12: Newt W .6K 51
Rushton Cl. WA5: Burtw .2H 65
WA8: Wid .5J 79
Rushton Pl. L25: Woolt .6E 76
Rushtons, The CH66: Lit Sut .7H 103
Rushton's Wlk. L30: N'ton .6C 34
Rushy Vw. WA12: Newt W .6J 51
Ruskin Av. CH42: Rock F .7M 73
CH44: Wall .6G 57
WA2: Warr .7D 66
WA12: Newt W .6L 51
Ruskin Cl. L20: Boot .7B 44
Ruskin Dr. CH65: Ell P .2B 112
WA10: St H .6G 49
Ruskin St. L4: Kirkd .9D 44
Ruskin Way CH43: Noct .5E 72
L36: Huy .8H 61
Rusland Av. CH61: Pens .3N 87
Rusland Rd. L32: Kirkb .2D 46
Russeldene Rd.
WN3: Wigan .1G 40
Russell Av. PR9: South .8M 7
Russell Ct. PR9: South .3N 7
WA8: Wid .4L 79
Russell Pl. L19: Garst .1A 92
Russell Rd. CH42: Rock F .5M 73
(not continuous)
CH44: Wall .4E 56
L18: Moss H .3L 75
L19: Garst .1A 92
L36: Huy .7M 61
M31: Part .6N 69
PR9: South .8M 7
WA7: Run .6H 95
Russell St. CH41: Birke .1L 73
L3: Liv .4J 5 (8D 58)
Russet Cl. L27: N'ley .3J 77
WA10: St H .5J 49
Russian Av. L13: Liv .4L 59
Russian Dr. L13: Liv .4L 59
Rutherford Cl. L13: Wav .8K 59
Rutherford Rd. L18: Moss H .2N 75
L31: Mag .4K 35
WA10: Windle .4F 48
Rutherglen Av. L23: Crosb .9M 33
Ruth Evans Ct. L35: Rainh .5D 62
Ruthin Cl. WA5: Call .6N 65
Ruthin Ct. CH65: Ell P .2B 112
WA7: Cas .5C 96
Ruthin Wlk. WA6: Hel .4D 114
Ruthven Ct. L21: Lith .3N 43
Ruthven Rd. L13: Liv .8N 59
L21: Lith .3N 43
Rutland Av. L17: Liv .2J 75
L26: Halew .8K 77
WA3: Low .3E 52
WA4: Walt .8C 82
Rutland Cl. L5: Liv .4F 58
Rutland Cres. L39: Orm .6B 20
Rutland Dr. WN4: Ash M .7L 41
Rutland Ho. L17: Aig .3J 75
L23: Blun .8H 33
Rutland Rd. M31: Part .7L 69
M44: Cad .4K 69
PR8: South .1C 12
Rutland St. L20: Boot .6C 44
WA7: Run .5J 95
WA10: St H .5J 49
Rutland Way L36: Huy .6M 61
Rutter Av. WA5: Warr .7A 66
Rutter St. L8: Liv .3D 74
Ryburn Rd. L39: Orm .1B 28
Rycot Rd. L24: Speke .3F 92
Rycroft Rd. CH44: Wall .6J 57
CH47: Meols .9F 54
L10: Faz .2K 45
Rydal Av. CH43: Noct .3C 72
L23: Crosb .9M 33
L34: Presc .3C 62
L37: Form .1D 24
WA4: Warr .6B 82
Rydal Bank CH44: Wall .5J 57
CH63: Beb .9N 73
Rydal Cl. CH61: Pens .3N 87
CH64: Lit N .8F 100
CH65: Ell P .3A 112
L10: Ain .9L 35
L33: Kirkb .7B 36
WN4: Ash M .7L 41
Rydal Gro. WA6: Hel .4E 114
WA7: Run .7L 95
WA11: St H .3K 49
Rydal Rd. L36: Huy .8J 61
Rydal St. L5: Liv .3F 58
WA12: Newt W .7L 51
Rydal Way WA8: Wid .7F 78
Rydecroft L25: Woolt .6D 76
Ryder Cl. L35: Rainh .5D 62
L39: Augh .2A 28
Ryder Ct. L35: Rainh .3E 62
Ryder Cres. L39: Augh .3A 28
PR8: Birkd .6L 11
Ryder Rd. WA1: Wools .9K 67
WA8: Wid .4L 79
Rydinge, The L37: Form .7G 16
Ryding's La. PR9: Banks .1H 9
Rye Cl. WA9: Clock F .5M 63
Ryecote L32: Kirkb .3C 46
Ryecroft CH2: Elt .2M 113
L21: Ford .8A 34
Ryecroft Av. WA3: Low .1F 52
Ryecroft Rd. CH60: Hesw .8C 88
Ryedale Cl. L8: Liv .1G 74
Ryefield La. L21: Ford .8A 34
Ryegate Rd. L19: Gras .8N 75
Ryeground La. L37: Form .8G 16
Rye Gro. L12: W Der .3C 60
Rye Hey Rd. L32: Kirkb .9C 36
Rye Moss La. L37: Gt Alt .4N 25
Ryfields Village
WA2: Warr .9E 66
Rylance Rd. WN3: Wins .2F 40
Ryland Pk. CH61: Thing .2A 88
Rylands Dr. WA2: Warr .1D 82
Rylands Hey CH49: Grea .4L 71
Rylands St. WA1: Warr .3C 82
WA8: Wid .8L 79
Ryleys Gdns. L2: Liv .4E 4
Rymer Gro. L4: Walt .9F 44
Rymers Grn. L37: Form .9E 16

S

Sabre Cl. WA7: Murd .8F 96
Sackville Rd. WA10: Windle .4F 48
Saddle Cl. L9: Ain .2J 45
Saddlers Ri. WA7: Nort .7E 96
Saddlers Wlk. WA4: Westy .5H 83
Saddlestone Gro. L8: Liv .3D 74
Sadler's La. WA11: Windle .3B 48
Sadler St. WA8: Wid .7M 79
Saffron Cl. WA2: Padg .8J 67
WA3: Low .2F 52
Saffron Gdns. WA9: St H .8N 49
Saffron M. L23: Thorn .5A 34
Saffron Wlk. *M31: Part* .7M 69
(off Cross La. W.)
Sagar Fold L39: Augh .4B 28
Sage Cl. WA2: Padg .7K 67
Sage Dr. L11: Norr G .9M 45
St Agnes Rd. L4: Kirkd .1C 58
L36: Huy .7J 61
St Aidan's Cl. WN5: Bil .5A 40
St Aidans Ct. CH43: Clau .2F 72
WA9: Clock F .6A 64
St Aidans Dr. WA8: Wid .2J 79
St Aidan's Gro. L36: Huy .2G 61
St Aidan's Ter. CH43: Clau .2F 72
St Aidan's Way L30: N'ton .8C 34
St Alban Rd. WA5: Penk .3G 81
St Albans L6: Liv .4G 58
St Albans Cl. WA11: Hay .3H 51
St Albans Ct. L5: Liv .4B 58
St Albans Rd. CH43: Clau .1G 72
CH44: Wall .5H 57
L20: Boot .7B 44
St Alban's Sq. L20: Boot .8B 44
St Alexander Cl. L20: Kirkd .9C 44
St Ambrose Ct. *WA4: Warr* .6C 82
(off Boswell Av.)
St Ambrose Cft. L30: N'ton .7D 34
St Ambrose Gro. L4: Walt .3G 59
St Ambrose Rd. WA8: Wid .7M 79
St Ambrose Way *L3: Liv* .5D 58
(off Everton Brow)
St Andrew Rd. L4: Walt .3G 58
St Andrews Av. L12: W Der .3C 60
St Andrews Cl. WA2: Fearn .5H 67
St Andrews Ct. CH43: Noct .2D 72
CH65: Ell P .3C 112
L22: Water .2L 43
PR8: South .9G 6
St Andrews Dr. L23: Blun .5J 33
L36: Huy .2G 61
St Andrews Gdns. L3: Liv .4J 5 (7D 58)
St Andrews Gro. L30: N'ton .8B 34
WA11: St H .4L 49
St Andrews Pl. *L17: Aig* .5H 75
(off Normanton Av.)
PR8: South .9G 6
St Andrews Rd. CH43: Oxton .2H 73
CH63: Beb .3N 89
CH65: Ell P .2B 112
L20: Boot .4B 44
L23: Blun .5H 33
St Andrew St. L3: Liv .5K 5 (8E 58)
St Andrews Vw. L33: Kirkb .5C 36
St Anne's Av. WA4: Grap .6J 83
St Anne's Av. E. WA4: Grap .6J 83
St Annes Cl. CH41: Birke .1K 73
L37: Form .7F 16
St Anne's Cotts. *L14: Knott A* .6A 60
(off Rudyard Cl.)
St Annes Ct. L3: Liv .1H 5
L13: Liv .6L 59
L17: Aig .7K 75
St Annes Gdns. L17: Aig .7L 75
St Annes Gro. CH41: Birke .9J 57
L17: Aig .7K 75
St Anne's Ho. *L20: Boot* .8C 44
(off University Rd.)
St Anne's Path L37: Form .7F 16
St Anne's Pl. CH41: Birke .9J 57
St Annes Rd. L17: Aig .7L 75
L36: Huy .8J 61
L37: Form .7F 16
St Annes Rd. L39: Orm .9B 20
PR9: South .3L 7
WA8: Wid .6L 79
St Annes Ter. CH41: Birke .9J 57
St Anne St. CH41: Birke .1J 73
(Livingstone Gdns.)
CH41: Birke .1K 73
(Robert St.)
CH41: Birke .9J 57
(St Anne's Pl.)
L3: Liv .1H 5 (5D 58)
St Annes Way CH41: Birke .1K 73
St Ann Pl. L35: Rainh .5F 62
ST ANNS .8G 48
St Ann's Rd. WA10: St H .7F 48
St Anthony Pl. WA2: Win .3C 66
St Anthony's Cl. L36: Huy .2G 61
St Anthony's Gro. L30: N'ton .8C 34
St Anthony's Rd. L23: Blun .6H 33
St Anthonys Shop. Cen. L5: Liv .4D 58
St Asaph Dr. WA5: Call .6M 65
St Asaph Gro. L30: N'ton .1E 44
St Asaph Rd. CH66: Gt Sut .5K 111
St Augustine's Av. WA4: Westy .4G 82
St Augustine St. L5: Liv .4C 58
St Augustine's Way L30: N'ton .7C 34
St Austell Cl. CH46: More .8J 55
WA5: Penk .5G 81
WA7: Brook .9D 96
St Austells Rd. L4: Walt .8D 44
St Austins La. WA1: Warr .4C 82
St Barnabas Pl. WA5: Warr .2N 81
St Bartholomew Rd. L3: Liv .1F 4 (6C 58)
St Bartholomews Ct. L36: Huy .7G 60
St Bedes Cl. L39: Orm .1B 28
St Bedes Vw. WA8: Wid .7K 79
St Benedict's Cl. WA2: Warr .1C 82
St Benedict's Gro. L36: Huy .2G 61
St Benet's Way L30: N'ton .8D 34
St Bernards Cl. L8: Liv .1G 74
L30: N'ton .8C 34
St Bernard's Dr. L30: N'ton .8C 34
St Brendan's Cl. L36: Huy .2G 61
St Brides Cl. WA5: Penk .5G 80
St Bride's Rd. CH44: Wall .4K 57
St Bride St. L8: Liv .8L 5 (9E 58)
St Bridgets Cl. WA2: Fearn .6G 66
WA8: Wid .2K 95
St Bridget's Gro. L30: N'ton .8C 34
St Bridget's La. CH48: W Kir .7C 70
St Brigid's Cres. *L5: Liv* .4B 58
(off Silvester St.)
St Catherine's Cl. L36: Huy .8J 61
St Catherines Gdns. CH42: Tran .4K 73
St Catherine's Rd. L20: Boot .7B 44
St Chad's Dr. L32: Kirkb .9C 36
St Chads Pde. L32: Kirkb .9C 36
St Christopers Dr. L36: Huy .2G 61
St Christopher's Av. L30: N'ton .7C 34
St Clair Dr. PR9: South .6M 7
St Columba's Cl. CH44: Wall .4K 57
St Cuthberts Cl. L12: Crox .7C 46
PR9: South .5M 7
St Cuthbert's Rd. PR9: South .5M 7
St Cyrils Cl. L27: N'ley .2G 77
St Cyril's Ct. L27: N'ley .2G 77
St Damian's Cft. L30: N'ton .8D 34
St David Rd. CH43: Clau .2G 72
CH62: East .9F 90
St David's Cl. L35: Rainh .5F 62
St Davids Dr. CH66: Gt Sut .5L 111
WA5: Call .7N 65
St David's Gro. L30: N'ton .9C 34
St Davids La. CH43: Noct .3D 72
St Davids Rd. L4: Walt .3G 58
L14: Knott A .4F 60
St Domingo Gro. L5: Liv .3F 58
St Domingo Rd. L5: Liv .2D 58
St Domingo Va. L5: Liv .3E 58
St Dunstan's Gro. L30: N'ton .8C 34
St Edmond's Rd. L20: Boot .8B 44
St Edmunds Ho. CH65: Ell P .1C 112
St Edmund's Rd. CH63: Beb .2M 89
St Edwards Cl. CH41: Birke .9H 57
St Edwards M. *CH41: Birke* .9H 57
(off Old Bidston Rd.)
St Elizabeth Av. L20: Boot .4B 44
St Elmo Rd. CH44: Wall .4K 57
St Elphins Cl. WA1: Warr .3D 82
St Gabriel Cl. WN8: Roby M .1L 31
St Gabriel's Av. L36: Huy .7L 61
St Georges Av. CH42: Tran .6K 73
CH66: Gt Sut .5L 111
WA10: Windle .5F 48
St Georges Cl. WA4: App .4F 98
St Georges Ct. L31: Mag .3J 35
WA8: Wid .8G 79
St George's Gro. CH46: More .9L 55
L30: N'ton .9C 34
St George's Hall .4G 5 (7C 58)
St George's Hill L5: Liv .4E 58
St George's Mt. CH45: New B .1H 57
St George's Pk. CH45: New B .1H 57
St George's Pl. L1: Liv .4G 5 (7C 58)
PR9: South .8G 7
St Georges Rd. CH45: Wall .3E 56
L36: Huy .4J 61
L37: Form .9E 16
L38: Hight .7F 24
WA10: St H .8G 48

St George's Way CH63: Thorn H 8G 89
L1: Liv 5G 5
St Gerard Cl. L5: Liv 3C 58
St Gregory's Cft. L30: N'ton 7D 34
ST HELENS 7K 49
St Helens Central Station (Rail) 7L 49
St Helens Cl. CH43: Clau 2H 73
WA3: Rix 6H 69
St Helens Crematorium
WA10: Windle 3F 48
St Helens Junction Station (Rail) 2B 64
St Helens Linkway L35: Rainh 8J 63
WA9: Rainh, St H 8K 49
St Helens Retail Pk. WA9: St H 7L 49
St Helens RLFC 8L 49
St Helens Rd. L34: Presc, Eccl P 2A 62
L39: Orm 8D 20
WA11: Rainf 9E 38
WN7: Leigh 2J 53
St Helens Theatre Royal 7K 49
St Hilary Brow CH44: Wall 5F 56
St Hilary Dr. CH45: Wall 4F 56
St Hilda's Dr. WA6: Frod 5M 107
St Hilda St. L4: Walt 1D 58
St Hugh's Cl. CH43: Clau 2H 73
St Hugh's Ho. L20: Boot 8B 44
St Ives Ct. CH43: Clau 1G 72
St Ives Gro. L13: Liv 6L 59
St Ives Rd. CH43: Clau 2G 72
St Ives Way L26: Halew 8K 77
St James Cen. *CH41: Birke 9F 56*
(off Laird St.)
St James Cl. CH49: Grea 4L 71
L12: W Der 3M 59
L40: Westh 1G 28
WA6: Frod 5M 107
St James Ct. *CH45: New B 1H 57*
(off Victoria Rd.)
WA4: Warr 4C 82
St James Dr. L20: Boot 6A 44
St James Ho. L39: Augh 2B 28
St James M. L20: Boot 6A 44
St James Mt. L35: Rainh 7F 62
St James Pl. L8: Liv 1D 74
St James Rd. CH41: Birke 9F 56
CH45: New B 1H 57
L1: Liv 9J 5 (1D 74)
L34: Eccl P, Presc 2B 62
L35: Rainh 7F 62
L36: Huy 8J 61
WN5: Orr 8N 31
St James St. L1: Liv 9G 4 (1C 74)
PR8: South 9G 7
St James Way *L30: N'ton 7C 34*
(off St Nicholas' Dr.)
St Jerome's Way L30: N'ton 7D 34
St John Av. WA4: Warr 6C 82
St Johns Av. L9: Walt 5F 44
St Johns Brow WA7: Run 4L 95
St John's Cen. L1: Liv 5G 4 (8C 58)
St John's Cl. CH47: Meols 9E 54
St Johns Ct. L22: Water 1K 43
PR8: Ains 1K 17
WA1: Warr 1G 82
(off Grantham Av.)
St Johns Ho. CH65: Ell P 9C 104
L20: Boot 7C 44
St John's La. L1: Liv 4G 4 (7C 58)
St John's Pavement
CH41: Birke 2K 73
St John's Pl. L22: Water 1K 43
St John's Rd. CH45: Wall 4E 56
CH62: East 1F 102
L20: Boot 8A 44
L22: Water 1K 43
L36: Huy 8K 61
PR8: Birkd 5M 11
St John's Sq. CH41: Birke 2K 73
L1: Liv 5G 5
St John's Ter. *L20: Boot 9A 44*
(off St John's Rd.)
St John St. CH41: Birke 2K 73
WA7: Run 4L 95
WA10: St H 1G 63
WA12: Newt W 7J 51
St Johns Vs. WA8: Wid 6G 79
St John's Way L1: Liv 5G 5
St Josephs Cl. L36: Huy 2G 61
WA5: Penk 3G 80
WA9: St H 9M 49
(off Cleveland St.)
St Josephs Cres. L3: Liv 2H 5 (6D 58)
St Jude's Cl. L36: Huy 2G 61
St Katherines Way WA1: Warr 3E 82
St Kevin's Dr. L32: Kirkb 7C 36
St Kilda Cl. CH65: Ell P 4A 112
St Kilda's Rd. CH46: More 1M 71
St Laurence Cl. CH41: Birke 1K 73
St Laurence Dr. CH41: Birke 1K 73
St Laurence Gro. L32: Kirkb 2D 46
St Lawrence Cl. L8: Liv 4F 74
St Lawrence Rd. WA6: Frod 7L 107
St Leonard's Cl. L30: N'ton 7C 34
St Lucia Rd. CH44: Wall 4K 57
St Luke's Av. WA3: Low 2E 52
St Lukes Chu. Rd. L37: Form 2C 24
(not continuous)
St Lukes Cl. L14: Knott A 3D 60
St Luke's Ct. L4: Walt 8F 44
St Luke's Cres. WA8: Wid 4L 79
St Lukes Dr. L37: Form 2C 24
WN5: Orr 8N 31
St Luke's Gro. *L30: N'ton 7C 34*
(off Dartmouth Dr.)
PR9: South 8K 7
St Lukes Ho. WN4: Ash M 7L 41
St Lukes Pl. L1: Liv 7H 5 (9D 58)
St Luke's Rd. L23: Crosb 7K 33
PR9: South 9J 7
WA10: St H 7G 48
St Luke's Way L36: Huy 2G 61
WA6: Frod 5L 107
St Margaret's Av. WA2: Warr 8E 66
St Margaret's Gro. L30: N'ton 9B 34
St Margaret's Rd. CH47: Hoy 2B 70
St Marks Ct. CH43: Oxton 3H 73
St Marks Cres. CH66: Gt Sut 5L 111
St Mark's Gro. L30: N'ton 7B 34
St Mark's Rd. L36: Huy 8K 61
St Mark's St. WA11: Hay 4C 50
St Martins Dr. CH66: Gt Sut 3J 111
St Martins Gro. L32: Kirkb 3D 46
St Martin's Ho. L20: Boot 7B 44
St Martin's La. WA7: Murd 8F 96
St Martins M. L5: Liv 5D 58
St Mary's Arc. *WA10: St H 7K 49*
(within St Mary's Mkt.)
St Mary's Av. CH44: Wall 5H 57
L4: Walt 8F 44
WN5: Bil 7M 39
St Mary's Cl. L13: Liv 8L 59
L20: Boot 7A 44
L24: Hale 5A 94
WA4: App 1D 98
St Marys Ct. CH49: Upton 4A 72
L25: Woolt 6E 76
WA3: Low 1J 53
WA4: Warr 4D 82
(off St Mary's St.)
St Marys Gdns. PR8: Ains 7M 11
St Mary's Ga. CH41: Birke 2M 73
St Mary's Grn. WA1: Warr 3D 82
St Mary's Gro. L4: Walt 8F 44
L30: N'ton 8B 34
St Mary's La. L4: Walt 8F 44
St Mary's Mkt. WA10: St H 7K 49
St Mary's Pl. L4: Walt 8F 44
St Marys Rd. L19: Garst, Gras 9N 75
L22: Water 1M 43
L36: Huy 7J 61
WA5: Gt San, Penk 3H 81
WA7: Halt 6B 96
WA8: Wid 3K 95
St Mary's St. CH44: Wall 5H 57
L25: Woolt 6E 76
WA4: Warr 4D 82
St Mary's Tower 2M 73
St Mathews Cl. L4: Walt 8J 45
L36: Huy 6K 61
St Matthew's Av. L21: Lith 2B 44
St Matthews Cl. WA4: App 9E 82
St Matthews Gro. WA10: St H 1F 62
St Mawes Cl. WA8: Wid 6H 79
St Mawes Way WA10: Windle 4E 48
St Mawgan Ct. WA2: Padg 7G 66
St Michael Rd. L39: Augh 6L 27
St Michael's Chu. Rd. L17: Aig 5G 75
St Michaels Cl. L17: Aig 6H 75
PR9: South 4L 7
WA8: Wid 9F 78
St Michaels Ct. L36: Huy 6J 61
St Michael's Golf Course 9H 79
St Michaels Gro. CH46: More 9L 55
L6: Liv 5G 59
L30: N'ton 8B 34
St Michael's Hall L17: Aig 6G 75
ST MICHAEL'S HAMLET 6G 74
St Michael's Ind. Est. WA8: Wid 9F 78
St Michaels Pk. CH62: Port S 1A 90
L39: Augh 5M 27
St Michaels Rd. L17: Aig 6G 75
L23: Blun, Crosb 6H 33
WA8: Wid 9F 78
WA9: St H 6K 63
St Michael's Station (Rail) 6G 74
St Michael's Vw. WA8: Wid 9G 78
St Monica's Cl. WA4: App 9F 82
St Monica's Dr. L30: N'ton 7C 34
St Nicholas' Dr. L30: N'ton 7C 34
St Nicholas Gro. WA9: St H 2N 63
St Nicholas Pl. L3: Liv 5B 4 (8A 58)
(not continuous)
St Nicholas Rd. CH45: Wall 4D 56
L35: Whis 8A 62
WA3: Low 1H 53
St Oswald's Av. CH43: Bid 8C 56
St Oswalds Cl. WA2: Win 3C 66
St Oswald's Ct. L30: N'ton 8E 34
St Oswald's La. L30: N'ton 8E 34
St Oswald's M. CH43: Bid 8C 56
St Oswald's Rd. WN4: Ash M 9J 41
St Oswald's St. L13: Liv 7M 59
St Paschal Baylon Blvd.
L16: Child 9D 60
St Patricks Cl. L33: Kirkb 6C 36
WA8: Wid 2K 95
St Patrick's Dr. L30: N'ton 7C 34
St Paul's Av. CH44: Wall 7L 57
St Pauls Cl. CH42: Rock F 6L 73
L33: Kirkb 6B 36
St Pauls Gdns. CH66: Lit Sut 7G 102
St Pauls Mansion PR8: South 9F 6
St Paul's Pas. *PR8: South 9F 6*
(off St Paul's St.)
St Pauls Pl. L20: Boot 8C 44
St Paul's Rd. CH42: Rock F 6M 73
CH44: Wall 7K 57
WA8: Wid 9K 79
St Paul's Sq. L3: Liv 3C 4 (7A 58)
(not continuous)
PR8: South 9F 6
St Paul's St. PR8: South 9F 6
St Paul St. WA10: St H 7H 49
St Paul's Vs. CH42: Rock F 6M 73
St Peter's Av. L37: Form 9D 16
St Peters Cl. CH60: Hesw 8N 87
L33: Kirkb 6B 36
L37: Form 9D 16
WA13: Lymm 4G 84
St Peter's Ct. CH42: Rock F 7N 73
L17: Aig 4G 75
WA2: Warr 2C 82
St Peter's Ho. L20: Boot 8C 44
St Peter's M. CH42: Rock F 7A 74
St Peter's Rd. CH42: Rock F 7N 73
L9: Ain 3H 45
PR8: Birkd 3N 11
St Peters Row L31: Mag 5J 35
St Peter's Sq. L1: Liv 7H 5
St Peter's Way CH43: Noct 4C 72
WA2: Warr 2C 82
St Philip's Av. L21: Lith 2B 44
St Richards Cl. L20: Kirkd 9C 44
Saints Cl. L13: Liv 7N 59
St Seiriol Gro. CH43: Clau 2G 72
St Stephen Rd. WA5: Gt San, Penk 3H 81
St Stephen's Av. WA2: Warr 6C 66
St Stephens Cl. CH60: Hesw 9C 88
L25: Gate 3G 76
PR9: Banks 1E 8
St Stephen's Ct. CH42: Tran 7H 73
St Stephens Gro. L30: N'ton 8C 34
St Stephen's Pl. L3: Liv 2F 4 (6C 58)
St Stephen's Rd. CH42: Tran 6H 73
L38: Hight 8F 24
St Teresa's Cl. L11: Norr G 8L 45
St Teresa's Rd. WA10: St H 6G 48
St Thomas Cl. WA10: St H 4G 48
St Thomas Ct. WA8: Wid 7G 79
St Thomas's Ct. WN8: Uph 5M 31
St Thomas's Dr. L30: N'ton 8C 34
St Thomas' Vw. CH65: Whit 1N 111
St Vincent Rd. CH43: Clau 2G 72
CH44: Wall 4K 57
WA5: Penk 3H 81
St Vincents Cl. L12: W Der 3C 60
St Vincent St. L3: Liv 4J 5 (7D 58)
St Vincent's Way PR8: Birkd 2N 11
St Vincent Way L3: Liv 4J 5
St Werburgh's Sq. CH41: Birke 2L 73
St Wilfreds Rd. WA8: Wid 4A 80
St Wilfrid's Dr. WA4: Grap 7K 83
St William Rd. L23: Thorn 6A 34
St William Way L23: Thorn 5A 34
St Winifred Rd. CH45: New B 2H 57
L35: Rainh 4E 62
St Wyburn Ct. *PR8: Birkd 1M 11*
(off Westcliffe Rd.)
Saker St. L4: Walt 2E 58
Salacre Cl. CH49: Upton 4B 72
Salacre Cres. CH49: Upton 4A 72
Salacre La. CH49: Upton 3A 72
Salacre Ter. *CH49: Upton 3A 72*
(off Salacre La.)
Salcombe Dr. L25: Hunts X 9F 76
PR9: South 2M 7
Salem Vw. CH43: Oxton 5H 73
Salerno Dr. L36: Huy 5H 61
Salesbury Way WN3: Wigan 1J 41
Saleswood Av. WA10: Eccl 7D 48
Salford Ct. PR8: Ains 9J 11
Salford Rd. PR8: Ains 9J 11
Salhouse Gdns. WA9: St H 3G 63
Saline Cl. L14: Knott A 3E 60
Salisbury Av. CH48: W Kir 6B 70
L30: N'ton 1F 44
Salisbury Cl. CH66: Gt Sut 5L 111
Salisbury Ct. CH42: Rock F 7L 73
Salisbury Dr. CH62: New F 9A 74
Salisbury Hall L18: Moss H 6L 75
Salisbury Ho. L20: Boot 6A 44
Salisbury Pk. L16: Child 3B 76
Salisbury Rd. CH45: New B 1G 57
L5: Liv 3F 58
L15: Wav 1J 75
L19: Gras 1M 91
L20: Boot 6A 44
WA11: Hay 2G 50
WN4: Ash M 6J 41
Salisbury St. CH41: Birke 3K 73
L3: Liv 1J 5 (5E 58)
L34: Presc 3A 62
PR9: South 9M 7
WA1: Warr 2E 82
WA3: Golb 2B 52
WA7: Run 6K 95
WA8: Wid 8L 79
WA10: St H 7K 49
Salisbury Ter. L15: Wav 9L 59
Salkeld Av. WN4: Ash M 8H 41
Sallowfields WN5: Orr 7N 31
Sally's La. PR9: South 5M 7
Salop St. L4: Walt 1E 58
Saltash Cl. L26: Halew 8J 77
WA7: Brook 9D 96
Saltburn Rd. CH45: Wall 4D 56
Saltergate Rd. L8: Liv 4F 74
Saltersgate CH66: Gt Sut 3L 111
Salthouse Quay L3: Liv 7D 4 (9B 58)
Saltney St. L3: Liv 5A 58
Salton Gdns. WA5: Warr 1N 81
Saltpit La. L31: Mag 2K 35
Saltwood Dr. WA7: Brook 1E 108
Saltworks Cl. WA6: Frod 4N 107
Salvia Way L33: Kirkb 6B 36
Salvin Cl. WN4: Ash M 8M 41
Salwick Cl. PR9: South 2L 7
Samaria Av. CH62: New F 9B 74
Sambourn Fold PR8: Ains 9G 11
Samphire Gdns. WA9: Bold 2D 64
Samuel St. WA5: Warr 4N 81
WA9: St H 2G 62
Samwoods Ho. *WN4: Ash M 6J 41*
(off Whitledge Grn.)
Sanbec Gdns. WA8: Cron 3G 78
Sandalwood L23: Crosb 7K 33
WA7: Nort 6D 96
Sandalwood Cl. L6: Liv 4G 58
WA2: Warr 7E 66
Sandalwood Dr. CH43: Noct 4D 72
Sandalwood Gdns. WA9: St H 2M 63
Sandbanks CH47: Hoy 1B 70
Sandbeck St. L8: Liv 5E 74
Sandbrook Ct. CH46: More 9M 55
Sandbrook Gdns. WN5: Orr 7N 31
Sandbrook La. CH46: More 9M 55
Sandbrook Rd. L25: Gate 9E 60
PR8: Ains 2K 17
WN5: Orr 7M 31
Sandbrook Way PR8: Ains 2J 17
Sandcliffe Rd. CH45: Wall 1E 56
Sandcross Cl. WN5: Orr 8N 31
Sandeman Rd. L4: Walt 1J 59
Sanderling Rd. L33: Kirkb 8E 36
WA12: Newt W 6L 51
Sanders Hey Cl. WA7: Brook 1C 108
Sanderson Cl. WA5: Gt San 2F 80
Sandfield L36: Huy 7H 61
Sandfield Av. CH47: Meols 8E 54
Sandfield Cl. CH63: Hghr B 1K 89
L12: W Der 4A 60
WA3: Low 2F 52
Sandfield Cotts. L39: Augh 2B 28
Sandfield Ct. WA6: Frod 6L 107
Sandfield Cres. L35: Whis 4D 62
WA10: St H 7J 49
(off Liverpool Rd.)
Sandfield Golf Course 9L 113
Sandfield Hey *L12: W Der 3A 60*
(off Sandfield Pk. E.)
SANDFIELD PARK 4N 59
Sandfield Pk. CH60: Hesw 7L 87
L39: Augh 2B 28
Sandfield Pk. E. L12: W Der 3A 60
Sandfield Pl. L20: Boot 6A 44
Sandfield Rd. CH45: New B 2H 57
CH49: Woodc 6B 72
CH63: Hghr B 1K 89
L20: Boot 8C 44
L25: Gate 4F 76
WA10: Eccl 5D 48
Sandfields WA6: Frod 6L 107
Sandfield Ter. CH45: New B 2H 57
Sandfield Wlk. L13: W Der 5N 59
Sandford Dr. L31: Mag 1J 35
Sandford Rd. WN5: Orr 7M 31
Sandford St. CH41: Birke 1L 73
Sandforth Cl. L12: W Der 3M 59
Sandforth Ct. L13: W Der 4M 59
Sandforth Rd. L12: W Der 4M 59
Sandgate Cl. L24: Speke 3F 92
Sandham Gro. CH60: Hesw 7C 88
Sandham Rd. L24: Speke 3L 93
Sandhead St. L7: Liv 9J 59
Sandhey Rd. CH47: Meols 9D 54
Sandheys CH64: Park 5C 100
Sandheys Av. L22: Water 1J 43
Sandheys Cl. L4: Walt 2D 58
Sandheys Dr. PR9: South 6L 7
Sandheys Gro. L22: Water 9J 33
Sandheys Rd. CH45: New B 2H 57
Sandheys Ter. L22: Water 1J 43
Sandhills L38: Hight 9F 24
Sandhills, The CH46: Leas 6M 55
Sandhills Bus. Est. L5: Kirkd 3B 58
Sandhills Bus. Pk. L5: Kirkd 2B 58
Sandhills La. L5: Kirkd 2A 58
Sandhills Station (Rail) 3B 58
Sandhills Vw. CH45: Wall 4D 56
Sandhill Ter. WA4: Warr 5F 82
Sandhurst L23: Blun 7J 33
Sandhurst Cl. L21: Sea 3M 43
L37: Form 3C 24
Sandhurst Dr. L10: Ain 9K 35
Sandhurst Rd. L26: Halew 1L 93
L35: Rainh 4D 62
Sandhurst St. L17: Aig 5G 74
WA4: Westy 5G 83
Sandhurst Way L31: Lyd 7G 27
Sandicroft Cl. WA3: Birchw 4K 67

Sandicroft Rd. L12: Crox 8D 46
San Diego Dr. WA5: Gt San 2K 81
Sandilands Gro. L38: Hight 9F 24
Sandino St. L8: Liv 2E 74
Sandiway CH47: Meols 8E 54
CH63: Brom 9B 90
L35: Whis 7A 62
L36: Huy 8K 61
Sandiway Av. WA8: Wid 7D 78
Sandiway Ct. PR9: South 7K 7
Sandiways L31: Mag 2K 35
Sandiways Av. L30: N'ton 9F 34
Sandiways Rd. CH45: Wall 3E 56
Sandlea Pk. CH48: W Kir 6B 70
Sandlewood Gro. L33: Kirkb 7D 36
Sandmoor Pl. WA13: Lymm 6G 85
Sandon Cl. L35: Rainh 5E 62
Sandon Ct. *L22: Water* *1K 43*
(off Sandon St.)
Sandon Cres. CH64: Lit N 9E 100
Sandon Gro. WA11: Rainf 5D 38
Sandon Ind. Est. L5: Kirkd 3A 58
Sandon Lodge *L21: Sea* *4N 43*
(off Seaforth Rd.)
Sandon Pl. WA8: Wid 7N 79
Sandon Prom. CH44: Wall 5L 57
Sandon Rd. CH44: Wall 5L 57
PR8: Birkd 5M 11
Sandon St. L8: Liv 8L 5 (9E 58)
L22: Water 1K 43
Sandon Way L5: Kirkd 3A 58
Sandown Cl. WA3: Cul 6N 53
WA7: Run 9M 95
Sandown Ct. L15: Wav 9L 59
PR9: South 7H 7
Sandown La. L15: Wav 9L 59
SANDOWN PARK 8L 59
Sandown Pk. Rd. L10: Ain 8K 35
Sandown Rd. L15: Wav 8L 59
L21: Sea 3M 43
Sandpiper Cl. CH49: Upton 2L 71
WA12: Newt W 6L 51
Sandpiper Gro. L26: Halew 7J 77
Sandpipers Ct. CH47: Hoy 1C 70
L22: Water *9J 33*
(off Bridge Rd.)
Sandra Dr. WA12: Newt W 7M 51
Sandridge Rd. CH45: New B 2H 57
CH61: Pens 2N 87
Sandringham Av. CH47: Meols 9D 54
L22: Water 2L 43
WA6: Hel 2E 114
Sandringham Cl. CH47: Meols 1D 70
CH62: New F 9N 73
L33: Kirkb 6C 36
Sandringham Ct. *PR9: South* *7G 7*
(off Gordon St.)
WA3: Low *3F 52*
(off Thurlow)
Sandringham Dr. CH45: New B 1G 57
L17: Aig 4G 74
WA5: Gt San 4L 81
WA9: St H 3M 63
Sandringham Gdns. CH65: Ell P 3B 112
Sandringham Ho. L39: Augh 2B 28
Sandringham M. CH47: Meols 1D 70
Sandringham Rd. L13: Liv 3K 59
L22: Water 2L 43
L31: Mag 3H 35
L37: Form 3E 24
PR8: Ains 9J 11
PR8: Birkd 3L 11
WA8: Wid 4K 79
Sandrock Cl. CH45: New B 2H 57
Sandrock Rd. CH45: New B 2H 57
Sands Rd. L18: Moss H 4L 75
Sandstone CH45: Wall 4J 57
Sandstone Cl. L35: Rainh 8F 62
Sandstone Dr. CH48: W Kir 6F 70
L35: Whis 4D 62
Sandstone M. WA8: Wid 4H 79
Sandstone Rd. WN3: Wins 1G 40
Sandstone Rd. E. L13: Liv 5M 59
Sandstone Rd. W. L13: Liv 5L 59
Sandstone Wlk. CH60: Hesw 8A 88
Sandwash Cl. WA11: Rainf 7E 38
Sandway Cres. L11: Norr G 8M 45
Sandwith Cl. WN3: Wigan 1K 41
Sandy Brow La. L33: Kirkb 3J 47
WA3: Croft 8F 52
Sandy Cl. WN8: Newb 3C 22
Sandy Ct. WN7: Leigh 1H 53
Sandy Grn. L9: Ain 4H 45
Sandy Gro. L13: Liv 3L 59
Sandy Ho. L21: Sea 3M 43
Sandy Knowe L15: Wav 8M 59
Sandy La. CH45: Wall 3E 56
CH48: W Kir 8C 70
CH60: Hesw 6A 88
CH61: Irby 9K 71
CH64: Lit N 7G 100
CW9: Ant 6L 99
L9: Ain 4G 45
L13: Liv 3L 59
L21: Sea 3N 43
(not continuous)
L31: Lyd 6G 27
L31: Mell 6M 35
L38: Hight 8G 24
L39: Augh 6N 27
Sandy La. L40: Holm 1G 15
(not continuous)
L40: Lath 6G 21
WA2: Warr 6C 66
(not continuous)
WA3: Croft 1H 67
WA3: Golb 2A 52
WA3: Low 1H 53
WA4: Stockt H 8E 82
WA5: Penk 4J 81
WA6: Hel 3E 114
WA7: Pres B 9H 97
WA7: Run, West P 8G 95
WA8: Cron, Wid 3G 79
WA8: Wid 2C 80
WA11: St H 1H 49
WA13: Lymm 3H 85
WN5: Orr 8N 31
WN8: Newb 4C 22
WN8: Skel 3A 30
(not continuous)
Sandy La. Cen. WN8: Skel 3A 30
Sandy La. Nth. CH61: Irby 9K 71
Sandy La. W. WA2: Warr 6B 66
SANDYMOOR 4F 96
Sandymoor La. WA7: Nort 3F 96
(Kings Ct.)
WA7: Nort 4F 96
(Lady Richeld Cl.)
Sandymount Dr. CH45: Wall 2G 56
CH63: Beb 3M 89
Sandy Rd. L21: Sea 2M 43
Sandyville Gro. L4: Walt 1K 59
Sandyville Rd. L4: Walt 1J 59
Sandywarps M44: Irlam 1N 69
Sandy Way CH43: Oxton 3G 72
L40: Holm 2H 15
Sanfield Cl. L39: Orm 7C 20
Sangness Dr. PR8: South 3D 12
SANKEY BRIDGES 4M 81
Sankey Bridges Ind. Est.
WA5: Gt San 4L 81
Sankey (for Penketh) Station (Rail) 2H 81
Sankey Grn. WA5: Warr 3N 81
Sankey La. WA4: Hatt 6A 98
Sankey Mnr. WA5: Gt San 2H 81
Sankey Rd. L31: Mag 4J 35
WA11: Hay 5B 50
Sankey St. L1: Liv 8H 5 (9D 58)
WA1: Warr 3B 82
WA3: Golb 2B 52
WA8: Wid 1K 95
WA9: St H 8N 49
WA12: Newt W 7J 51
Sankey Valley Country Pk. 6C 50
Sankey Valley Country Pk. Vis. Cen. 4A 50
Sankey Valley Ind. Est.
WA12: Newt W 8J 51
Sankey Valley Pk. 2N 81
Sankey Way WA5: Gt San, Warr 3J 81
Santa Rose Blvd. WA5: Gt San 1J 81
Santon Av. L13: Liv 4K 59
Santon Dr. WA3: Low 2F 52
Sanvino Av. PR8: Ains 9K 11
Sapphire Dr. L33: Kirkb 6C 36
Sapphire St. L13: Liv 8L 59
Sarah's Cft. L30: N'ton 8D 34
Sark Av. CH65: Ell P 4N 111
Sark Rd. L13: Liv 5L 59
Sarsfield Av. WA3: Low 2E 52
Sartfield Cl. L16: Child 9C 60
Sarum Rd. L25: Gate 1E 76
Sarus Ct. WA7: Manor P 3D 96
Satinwood Cl. WN4: Ash M 8H 41
Satinwood Cres. L31: Mell 8M 35
SAUGHALL MASSIE 2K 71
Saughall Massie La. CH49: Upton 3M 71
Saughall Massie Rd. CH48: W Kir 5E 70
CH49: Grea, Upton 5E 70
Saughall Rd. CH46: More 1K 71
CH49: Upton 1K 71
Saunby Cl. L19: Garst 2A 92
Saunders Av. L35: Presc 5A 62
Saundersfoot Cl. WA5: Call 7N 65
Saunders St. PR9: South 6G 7
Saunderton Cl. WA11: Hay 3E 50
Savannah Pl. WA5: Gt San 1L 81
Saville Av. WA5: Warr 1A 82
Saville Rd. L13: Liv 7N 59
L31: Lyd 9H 27
Savon Hook L37: Form 3G 25
Savoylands Cl. L17: Aig 6H 75
Sawdon Av. PR8: South 2D 12
Sawley Av. WA3: Low 1E 52
Sawley Cl. WA3: Cul 8N 53
WA7: Murd 8G 96
Sawpit La. L36: Huy 7K 61
Sawpit St. WA13: Warb 1N 85
WA14: Dun M 1N 85
Sawyer Dr. WN4: Ash M 8M 41
Saxby Rd. L14: Knott A 4E 60
Saxenholme PR8: Birkd 1M 11
Saxon Cl. L6: Liv 5G 58
WA4: App 2C 98
Saxon Ct. WA10: St H 5H 49
Saxonia Rd. L4: Walt 8G 44
Saxon Lodge PR8: Birkd 1M 11
Saxon Rd. CH46: More 8N 55
CH47: Meols 9D 54
L23: Crosb 8K 33
Saxon Rd. PR8: Birkd 1M 11
WA7: Run 5L 95
Saxon Ter. WA8: Wid 7L 79
Saxon Way CH66: Gt Sut 5L 111
L33: Kirkb 5C 36
Saxony Rd. L7: Liv 4N 5 (7F 58)
(not continuous)
Sayce St. WA8: Wid 7L 79
Scafell Av. WA2: Warr 6D 66
Scafell Cl. CH62: East 3C 102
CH66: Ell P 7L 103
Scafell Lawn L27: N'ley 5L 77
Scafell Rd. WA11: St H 2J 49
Scafell Wlk. L27: N'ley 4L 77
(not continuous)
Scaffold La. L38: Ince B 6H 25
Scape La. L23: Crosb 6L 33
Scargreen Av. L11: Norr G 7L 45
SCARISBRICK 7J 13
Scarisbrick Av. L21: Lith 3A 44
PR8: South 8F 6
WN8: Parb 3F 22
Scarisbrick Bus. Pk. L40: Scar 2A 20
Scarisbrick Cl. L31: Mag 9K 27
Scarisbrick Ct. PR8: South 9H 7
Scarisbrick Cres. L11: Norr G 7J 45
Scarisbrick Dr. L11: Norr G 7J 45
Scarisbrick Ho. *L39: Orm* *8D 20*
(off Abbotsford)
Scarisbrick Marina L40: Scar 1L 19
Scarisbrick New Rd.
PR8: South 9H 7
Scarisbrick Pk. L40: Scar 8M 13
Scarisbrick Pl. L11: Norr G 8J 45
Scarisbrick Rd. L11: Norr G 8J 45
WA11: Rainf 4C 38
Scarisbrick St. L39: Orm 7C 20
PR9: South 8G 7
Scarsdale Rd. L11: Norr G 9L 45
SCARTH HILL 2F 28
Scarth Hill La. L39: Augh, Orm 3C 28
L40: Westh 2F 28
Scarth Pk. WN8: Skel 5F 30
Sceptre Cl. WA12: Newt W 7J 51
Sceptre Rd. L11: Crox 6A 46
Sceptre Wlk. L11: Crox 7A 46
Scholars' Ct. *CH64: Nest* *6E 100*
(off Cross St.)
Scholars Grn. La. WA13: Lymm 5F 84
Scholar St. L7: Liv 1H 75
Scholes, The WA10: St H 2E 62
Scholes La. WA9: St H 2E 62
WA10: St H 2E 62
Scholes Pk. WA10: St H 2E 62
Schomberg St. L6: Liv 1N 5 (6F 58)
School Av. CH64: Lit N 8F 100
L37: Form 1F 24
School Brow WA1: Warr 3D 82
WN5: Bil 6A 40
School Cl. CH46: More 8N 55
L27: N'ley 1G 77
L39: Augh 3N 27
PR8: Birkd 4A 12
School Dr. WA13: Lymm 3J 85
WN5: Bil 6A 40
Schoolfield Cl. CH49: Woodc 6B 72
Schoolfield Rd. CH49: Woodc 6B 72
School Hill CH60: Hesw 8N 87
School Ho. Grn. L39: Orm 8D 20
School Ho. Gro. L40: Burs 9H 15
School Island WN8: Skel 2A 30
School La. CH2: Elt 2L 113
CH43: Bid 8C 56
CH44: Wall 4E 56
CH45: Wall 5E 56
CH47: Hoy 1C 70
(not continuous)
CH47: Meols 8E 54
CH61: Thurs 1J 87
CH62: New F 9A 74
CH63: Hghr B 1K 89
CH64: Lit N 8F 100
CH64: Nest 4H 101
CH64: Park 5B 100
CH66: Chil T 5E 102
L1: Liv 6F 4 (8C 58)
L10: Ain 9J 35
L21: Lith 2A 44
L21: Sea 3N 43
L25: Woolt 9E 76
L31: Mag 1M 35
L31: Mell 6M 35
L34: Know 4E 46
L35: Rainh 8H 63
(not continuous)
L36: Huy 7L 61
L37: Form 1F 24
L39: Down 1E 26
L40: Burs, Lath 9J 15
L40: Westh 2H 29
M44: Cad 4K 69
WA3: Ris 4C 68
WA3: Rix 7G 68
WA4: Hghr Whi 9E 98
WA6: Frod 7M 107
WA6: Manl 8K 115
WA7: Halt 7B 96
WA8: Bold H 1A 80
WN4: Garsw 8E 40
WN8: Roby M 1L 31
School La. WN8: Skel 2A 30
WN8: Uph 5M 31
School Rd. CH65: Ell P 9N 103
L38: Hight 8F 24
WA2: Warr 8D 66
School St. WA3: Golb 2B 52
WA4: Warr 4C 82
WA11: Hay 4B 50
WA12: Newt W 7K 51
WN4: Ash M 6M 41
School Ter. WA3: Golb 2B 52
School Way L24: Speke 4F 92
WA8: Wid 5N 79
Schooner Cl. WA7: Murd 9F 96
Schubert Cl. CH66: Gt Sut 1K 111
Schwartzman Dr. PR9: Banks 1E 8
Science Pk. Nth. WA3: Birchw 3L 67
Science Pk. Sth. WA3: Ris 4L 67
Science Rd. L24: Speke 3G 93
Scilly Cl. CH65: Ell P 4A 112
Scone Cl. L11: Crox 7A 46
Score, The WA9: St H 3K 63
(not continuous)
Scorecross WA9: St H 9L 49
Score La. L16: Child 8A 60
Scoresby Rd. CH46: Leas 6B 56
Scorpio Cl. L14: Knott A 4E 60
Scorton St. L6: Liv 4H 59
Scotchbarn La. L34: Presc 3B 62
L35: Presc 3B 62
Scoter Rd. L33: Kirkb 9D 36
Scotia Av. CH62: New F 9B 74
L30: N'ton 1D 44
Scotia Rd. L13: Liv 5M 59
Scotia Wlk. WA3: Low 2G 52
Scotland Rd. L3: Liv 2G 4 (6C 58)
L5: Liv 5C 58
WA1: Warr 3C 82
Scott Av. L35: Whis 6C 62
L36: Huy 8L 61
WA8: Wid 8J 79
WA9: Sut M 6K 63
Scott Cl. L4: Walt 2E 58
L31: Mag 2J 35
Scott Dr. L39: Orm 6D 20
Scotton Av. CH66: Lit Sut 9G 103
Scott Rd. WA3: Low 1E 52
Scotts Pl. CH41: Birke 1F 72
Scotts Quays CH41: Birke 8L 57
Scott St. CH45: Wall 4H 57
L20: Boot 5A 44
PR9: South 8M 7
WA2: Warr 2C 82
Scott Wlk. WA12: Newt W 9L 51
Scribe Pl. M44: Irlam 3L 69
Scroggins La. M31: Part 5M 69
Sculthorpe Cl. WA10: St H 7F 48
Scythes, The CH49: Grea 4K 71
L30: N'ton 7G 34
Scythia Cl. CH62: New F 8B 74
Seabank Av. CH44: Wall 4J 57
Seabank Cott. CH47: Meols 7F 54
Seabank Ct. CH48: W Kir 7B 70
Seabank Rd. CH44: Wall 1H 57
CH45: New B, Wall 1H 57
CH60: Hesw 9M 87
PR9: South 7G 7
Seabury St. WA4: Westy 5H 83
Seacole Cl. L8: Liv 2G 75
SEACOMBE 8K 57
Seacombe Dr. CH66: Gt Sut 2K 111
Seacombe Prom. CH44: Wall 5L 57
(not continuous)
Seacombe Vw. CH44: Wall 7L 57
Sea Ct. CH45: Wall 2F 56
Seacroft Cl. L14: Knott A 3E 60
Seacroft Cres. PR9: South 2N 7
Seacroft Rd. L14: Knott A 3E 60
Seafarers Dr. L25: Gate 4E 76
Seafield L37: Form 2G 25
Seafield Av. CH60: Hesw 9M 87
L23: Crosb 8L 33
Seafield Dr. CH45: Wall 2G 56
Seafield Rd. CH62: New F 8A 74
L9: Walt 5E 44
L20: Boot *6A 44*
(off Cleary St.)
PR8: Ains 8J 11
Seaford Cl. WA7: Wind H 6F 96
Seaford Pl. WA2: Warr 5B 66
Seafore Cl. L31: Lyd 8G 27
SEAFORTH 3M 43
Seaforth Dr. CH46: More 1M 71
Seaforth & Litherland Station (Rail) 3N 43
Seaforth Nature Reserve 3J 43
Seaforth Rd. L21: Sea 5N 43
Seaforth Va. Nth. L21: Sea 4N 43
Seaforth Va. W. L21: Sea 4N 43
Seagram Cl. L9: Ain 2H 45
Sealand Av. L37: Form 2D 24
Sealand Cl. L37: Form 2D 24
WA2: Padg 9F 66
Sea La. WA7: Run 5N 95
Sealy Cl. CH63: Spit 6N 89
Seaman Rd. L15: Wav 1K 75
Seaport St. L8: Liv 2G 74
Sea Rd. CH45: Wall 1F 56
Seascale Av. WA10: St H 1E 62
Seasons, The WA7: Run 6J 95
Seath Av. WA9: St H 6A 50

Seathwaite Cl. L23: Blun 8H **33**
WA7: Beech 1A **108**
Seathwaite Cres. L33: Kirkb 7B **36**
Seaton Cl. L12: Crox 7E **46**
Seaton Gro. WA9: St H 3G **62**
Seaton Pk. WA7: Nort 4G **96**
Seaton Pl. WN8: Skel 1B **30**
Seaton Rd. CH42: Tran 4J **73**
CH45: Wall 3G **57**
Seaton Way PR9: South 2M **7**
Seattle Cl. WA5: Gt San 1K **81**
Sea Vw. CH64: Lit N 9E **100**
Seaview CH47: Hoy 1C **70**
Seaview Av. CH45: Wall 4G **57**
CH61: Irby 1L **87**
CH62: East 9G **90**
Seaview La. CH61: Irby 1L **87**
Sea Vw. Rd. L20: Boot 6N **43**
Seaview Rd. CH45: Wall 3G **56**
Seaview Ter. L22: Water 1J **43**
Seawood Gro. CH46: More 1L **71**
Secker Av. WA4: Warr 6E **82**
Secker Cres. WA4: Warr 6E **82**
Second Av. CH43: Bid 2B **72**
L9: Ain 4K **45**
(First Av.)
L9: Ain 3J **45**
(Third Av.)
L23: Crosb 7K **33**
L35: Rainh 5E **62**
WA7: Pal F 7B **96**
Sedbergh Av. L10: Ain 8H **35**
Sedbergh Gro. WA7: Beech 1A **108**
Sedbergh Rd. CH44: Wall 4F **56**
Sedburgh Gro. L36: Huy 6G **60**
Sedburn Rd. L32: Kirkb 3E **46**
Seddon Cl. WA10: Eccl 7C **48**
Seddon Pl. WN8: Skel 1B **30**
Seddon Rd. L19: Garst 1A **92**
WA10: St H 1E **62**
Seddons Ct. L34: Presc 3A **62**
Seddon St. L1: Liv 7F **4** (9C **58**)
WA10: St H 3J **49**
Sedgefield Cl. CH46: More 9A **56**
Sedgefield Rd. CH46: More 9A **56**
Sedgeley Wlk. L36: Huy 4K **61**
Sedgemoor Rd. L11: Norr G 7K **45**
Sedgewick Cres. WA5: Burtw 3G **65**
Sedley St. L6: Liv 3G **59**
Sedum Gro. L33: Kirkb 6B **36**
Seeds La. L9: Ain 2H **45**
Seeley Av. CH41: Birke 1G **72**
Seel Rd. L36: Huy 7K **61**
Seel St. L1: Liv 6G **4** (8C **58**)
SEFTON 4E **34**
Sefton Av. L21: Lith 3A **44**
WA8: Wid 5K **79**
WN5: Orr 7N **31**
Sefton Bus. Pk. L30: N'ton 2F **44**
(not continuous)
Sefton Cl. L32: Kirkb 8A **36**
WN5: Orr 7N **31**
Sefton Dr. L8: Liv 3H **75**
L10: Ain 9K **35**
L23: Thorn 4N **33**
L31: Mag 3G **34**
L32: Kirkb 8A **36**
Sefton Fold Dr. WN5: Bil 6N **39**
Sefton Fold Gdns. WN5: Bil 6N **39**
Sefton Gdns. L39: Augh 5B **28**
Sefton Gro. L17: Aig 4H **75**
Sefton Ho. L9: Ain 3G **44**
L40: Burs 2K **21**
Sefton La. L31: Mag 3F **34**
Sefton La. Ind. Est. L31: Mag 3F **34**
Sefton Mill Ct. L29: Seft 4E **34**
Sefton Mill La. L29: Seft 4E **34**
Sefton Mills L29: Seft 4E **34**
Sefton Moss La. L30: N'ton 8C **34**
Sefton Moss Vs. L21: Lith 2A **44**
SEFTON PARK 4K **75**
Sefton Pk. Ct. *L17: Aig 6K 75*
(off Aigburth Va.)
Sefton Park Palm House 4J **75**
Sefton Pk. Rd. L8: Liv 2G **75**
Sefton Rd. CH42: Rock F 7N **73**
CH45: New B 2H **57**
CH62: New F 8N **73**
L9: Ain 3J **45**
L9: Walt 6F **44**
L20: Boot 5C **44**
L21: Lith 2A **44**
L37: Form 2E **24**
WN4: Ash M 5H **41**
WN5: Orr 7N **31**
Sefton St. L3: Liv 2C **74**
L8: Liv 2C **74**
L21: Lith 2A **44**
(not continuous)
PR8: South 2A **12**
WA12: Newt W 7H **51**
SEFTON TOWN 7C **34**
Sefton Vw. L21: Lith 2A **44**
L23: Crosb 7N **33**
WN5: Orr 7N **31**
Segar's La. L39: Hals 1M **17**
PR8: Ains 9K **11**
Seiont Ho. L8: Liv 3E **74**
Selborne L35: Whis 7C **62**
Selborne Cl. L8: Liv 1F **74**
Selborne St. L8: Liv 9M **5** (1E **74**)
Selbourne Cl. CH49: Woodc 5C **72**
Selby Cl. WA7: Nort 3G **97**
WA10: St H 8G **49**
Selby Dr. L37: Form 2H **25**
Selby Grn. CH66: Lit Sut 9G **103**
Selby Gro. L36: Huy 6M **61**
Selby Pl. WN8: Skel 1A **30**
Selby Rd. L9: Walt 4F **44**
Selby St. CH45: Wall 4H **57**
WA5: Warr 3N **81**
(not continuous)
Seldon St. L6: Liv 2N **5** (6G **58**)
Selina Rd. L4: Walt 8E **44**
Selkirk Av. CH62: East 2D **102**
WA4: Westy 5H **83**
WN4: Garsw 7F **40**
Selkirk Cl. CH66: Lit Sut 9E **102**
Selkirk Dr. WA10: Eccl 5E **48**
Selkirk Rd. L13: Liv 6L **59**
Sellar St. L4: Kirkd 2D **58**
Selsdon Rd. L22: Water 9J **33**
Selsey Cl. L7: Liv 9G **59**
Selside WN3: Wigan 1K **41**
Selside Lawn *L27: N'ley 4L 77*
(off Selside Wlk.)
Selside Wlk. L27: N'ley 5L **77**
Selston Cl. CH63: Spit 5N **89**
Selworthy Dr. WA4: Thel 5L **83**
Selworthy Grn. L16: Child 2B **76**
Selworthy Rd. PR8: Birkd 3K **11**
(not continuous)
Selwyn Cl. WA8: Wid 5A **80**
WA12: Newt W 5K **51**
Selwyn Jones Sports Cen. 4L **51**
Selwyn St. L4: Kirkd 9D **44**
Senate Bus. Pk. L30: N'ton 2E **44**
Senator Point L33: Know I 2G **46**
Senator Rd. WA9: St H 2G **63**
Seneschal Ct. WA7: Pal F 9A **96**
Sennen Cl. WA7: Brook 1D **108**
Sennen Rd. L32: Kirkb 2D **46**
Sentinel Way L30: N'ton 2F **44**
Sephton Av. WA3: Cul 7M **53**
Sephton Dr. L39: Orm 6D **20**
September Rd. L6: Liv 4H **59**
Serenade Rd. L33: Kirkb 5D **36**
Sergeant Rd. L12: W Der 2C **60**
Sergrim Rd. L36: Huy 6G **61**
Serin Cl. WA12: Newt W 7L **51**
Serpentine, The L19: Gras 8M **75**
L23: Blun 7G **32**
L39: Augh 4B **28**
Serpentine North, The L23: Blun 6G **32**
Serpentine Rd. CH44: Wall 4J **57**
Serpentine South, The L23: Blun 7H **33**
Serpentine Wlk. WA12: Newt W 2M **51**
Servia Rd. L21: Lith 3A **44**
Servite Cl. L22: Water 9J **33**
Servite Ct. L25: Woolt 8G **76**
Servite Ho. L17: Aig 4G **74**
Sessions Rd. L4: Kirkd 1D **58**
Seth Powell Way L36: Huy 3G **61**
Seven Acre Rd. L23: Thorn 6A **34**
Seven Acres La. CH61: Thing 1A **88**
Sevenoak Gro. L35: Tar G 1M **77**
Sevenoaks Av. PR8: Ains 9H **11**
Sevenoaks Cl. L5: Liv 4D **58**
Seven Row CH64: Lit N 9E **100**
Seventh Av. L9: Ain 3J **45**
(Lakes Rd.)
L9: Ain 3J **45**
(Sixth Av.)
Severn Cl. WA2: Warr 7F **66**
WA8: Wid 5B **80**
WA9: Sut L 4M **63**
WN5: Bil 8N **39**
Severn Rd. L33: Kirkb 5D **36**
L35: Rainh 6E **62**
WA3: Cul 8N **53**
WN4: Ash M 6N **41**
Severn St. CH41: Birke 8G **56**
L5: Liv 3E **58**
Severnvale CH65: Whit 2N **111**
Severs St. L6: Liv 5G **58**
Sewell St. L34: Presc 3A **62**
WA7: Run 5L **95**
(Perry St.)
WA7: Run 5L **95**
(Union St.)
Sextant Cl. WA7: Murd 9F **96**
Sexton Av. WA9: St H 8D **50**
Sexton Way L14: Broad G 7D **60**
Seymour Ct. CH42: Tran 4L **73**
L14: Broad G 8B **60**
WA7: Manor P 4E **96**
Seymour Dr. CH66: Ell P 8K **103**
L31: Mag 9K **27**
WA1: Padd, Padg 1H **83**
Seymour Pl. E. CH45: New B 1J **57**
Seymour Pl. W. CH45: New B 1H **57**
Seymour Rd. L14: Broad G 7B **60**
L21: Lith 3A 44
(off Bridge Rd.)
Seymour St. CH42: Tran 4L **73**
CH45: New B 1H **57**
L3: Liv 4J **5** (7D **58**)
L20: Boot 8A **44**
Seymour Ter. L3: Liv 4J **5**
Shacklady Rd. L33: Kirkb 7E **36**
Shackleton Av. WA8: Wid 4M **79**
Shackleton Cl. WA5: Old H 9L **65**
Shackleton Rd. CH46: Leas 5B **56**
Shadewood Cres. WA4: Grap 6J **83**
Shadowbrook Dr. L24: Speke 1G **92**
Shadwell St. L5: Liv 4A **58**
Shaftesbury Av. L33: Kirkb 6C **36**
PR8: Birkd 6N **11**
WA5: Penk 6G **80**
Shaftesbury Gro. PR8: Birkd 5N **11**
Shaftesbury Rd. L23: Crosb 7K **33**
PR8: Birkd 6N **11**
Shaftesbury St. L8: Liv 2D **74**
Shaftesbury Ter. L13: Liv 6M **59**
Shaftesbury Way WA5: Burtw 2H **65**
Shaftway Cl. WA11: Hay 3H **51**
Shakespeare Av. CH42: Rock F 7M **73**
L32: Kirkb 2B **46**
Shakespeare Centre, The
PR8: South 1A **12**
Shakespeare Cl. L6: Liv 5F **58**
Shakespeare Gro. WA2: Warr 7D **66**
(not continuous)
Shakespeare Rd. CH44: Wall 7K **57**
CH64: Nest 5E **100**
WA8: Wid 7K **79**
WA9: Sut M 6K **63**
Shakespeare St. L20: Boot 5N **43**
PR8: South 1A **12**
Shalcombe Cl. L26: Halew 9L **77**
Shaldon Cl. L32: Kirkb 2E **46**
Shaldon Gro. L32: Kirkb 2E **46**
Shaldon Rd. L32: Kirkb 3E **46**
Shaldon Wlk. L32: Kirkb 2E **46**
Shalem Ct. CH63: Hghr B 1K **89**
Shalford Gro. CH48: W Kir 6E **70**
Shallcross Ct. *L6: Liv 5F 58*
(off Shallcross Pl.)
Shallcross Pl. L6: Liv 5F **58**
Shallmarsh Cl. CH63: Hghr B 2K **89**
Shallmarsh Rd. CH63: Hghr B 2K **89**
Shalom Ct. L17: Aig 2K **75**
Shamrock Rd. CH41: Birke 1F **72**
Shand St. L19: Garst 3A **92**
Shanklin Cl. WA5: Gt San 2E **80**
Shanklin Rd. L15: Wav 8L **59**
Shannon Gro. WA8: Wid 6H **79**
Shannon Ho. CH46: Leas 5M **55**
Shannons La. L34: Know 9G **46**
Shannon St. CH41: Birke 8F **56**
Shard Cl. L11: Crox 5N **45**
Shard St. WA9: St H 2A **64**
Sharon Pk. Cl. WA4: Grap 7K **83**
Sharpeville Cl. L4: Kirkd 2C **58**
Sharples Cres. L23: Crosb 7M **33**
Sharp St. WA2: Warr 1C **82**
WA8: Wid 8K **79**
Sharrock St. PR8: South 8G **6**
Sharwood Rd. L27: N'ley 4K **77**
Shavington Av. CH43: Oxton 5F **72**
Shawbury Av. CH63: Hghr B 9K **73**
Shawbury Gro. WA1: Padg 9H **67**
Shaw Cl. CH66: Gt Sut 1L **111**
L39: Hals 8F **12**
Shaw Cres. L37: Form 9H **17**
Shawell Ct. WA8: Wid 6A **80**
Shaw Entry L35: Whis 9C **62**
Shaw Hall Caravan Pk. L40: Scar 1N **19**
Shaw Hill St. L1: Liv 4F **4** (7C **58**)
Shaw La. CH49: Grea 6K **71**
L35: Presc, Whis 5A **62**
L39: Bart 7C **18**
Shaw Rd. L24: Speke 2G **93**
Shaws All. L1: Liv 8F **4** (9C **58**)
Shaw's Av. PR8: Birkd 5N **11**
WA2: Warr 9C **66**
Shaws Dr. CH47: Meols 9E **54**
Shaws Gth. L39: Hals 8F **12**
Shaw's Rd. PR8: Birkd 5N **11**
Shaw St. CH41: Birke 3K **73**
CH47: Hoy 1C **70**
L6: Liv 1K **5** (5E **58**)
WA3: Cul 7N **53**
WA7: Run 5J **95**
(not continuous)
WA10: St H 7L **49**
WA11: Hay 4G **51**
WN4: Ash M 6K **41**
Shawton Rd. L16: Child 9B **60**
Shearman Cl. CH61: Pens 3A **88**
Shearman Rd. CH61: Pens 3A **88**
Shearwater Cl. L27: N'ley 4K **77**
Sheen Rd. CH45: New B 2J **57**
Sheepfield Cl. CH66: Lit Sut 7H **103**
Sheerwater Cl. WA1: Padg 1G **82**
Sheffield Cl. WA5: Gt San 3L **81**
Sheffield Row WA12: Newt W 1M **65**
Shefford Cres. WN3: Wins 1E **40**
Sheila Wlk. L10: Faz 4N **45**
Sheilings, The WA3: Low 2G **52**
Sheil Pl. L6: Liv 6H **59**
Sheil Rd. L6: Liv 5H **59**
Shelagh Av. WA8: Wid 7K **79**
Sheldon Cl. CH63: Spit 6N **89**
M31: Part 6M **69**
Sheldon Rd. L12: W Der 1B **60**
Sheldrake Gro. CH64: Lit N 9E **100**
Shelley Cl. L36: Huy 8K **61**
Shelley Ct. L32: Kirkb 2B **46**
Shelley Dr. L39: Orm 7B **20**
Shelley Gro. PR8: South 9L **7**
WA4: Westy 4G **83**
Shelley Pl. L35: Whis 6C **62**
Shelley Rd. WA8: Wid 7K **79**
Shelley St. L20: Boot 6A **44**
(not continuous)
WA9: Sut M 7L **63**
Shelley Way CH48: W Kir 8C **70**
Shellfield Rd. PR9: South 4M **7**
SHELL GREEN 7A **80**
Shell Grn. WA8: Wid 7A **80**
Shell Grn. Estate, The WA8: Wid 8A **80**
Shell Grn. Ho. WA8: Wid 8A **80**
Shellingford Cl. WN6: Shev 6N **23**
Shellingford Rd. L14: Knott A 5E **60**
Shellway Rd. CH65: Ell P 2D **112**
Shelmore Dr. L8: Liv 4E **74**
Shelton Cl. L13: Liv 7M **59**
WA8: Wid 5B **80**
Shelton Dr. PR8: Ains 1G **17**
Shelton Rd. CH45: Wall 3G **56**
Shenley Cl. CH63: Beb 1M **89**
Shenley Rd. L15: Wav 9A **60**
Shenley Way PR9: South 2B **8**
Shenstone St. L7: Liv 8G **58**
Shenton Av. WA11: St H 4N **49**
Shepcroft La. WA4: Stret 5D **98**
Shepherd Cl. CH49: Grea 4K **71**
Shepherds Fold Cl. L8: Liv 2F **74**
Shepherd's La. L39: Hals 8J **19**
Shepherds Row WA7: Cas 5B **96**
Shepherd St. L6: Liv 3L **5** (7E **58**)
Sheppard Av. L16: Child 9E **60**
Shepperton Cl. WA4: App 1F **98**
Shepsides Cl. CH66: Gt Sut 2H **111**
Shepston Av. L4: Walt 9F **44**
Shepton Rd. CH66: Gt Sut 3K **111**
Sherborne Av. L25: Hunts X 8H **77**
L30: N'ton 7D **34**
Sherborne Cl. WA7: Nort 4H **97**
Sherborne Rd. CH44: Wall 4F **56**
Sherborne Sq. L36: Huy 7J **61**
Sherbourne Rd. CH65: Ell P 2B **112**
Sherbourne Way WA5: Burtw 3H **65**
Sherbrooke Cl. L14: Knott A 5C **60**
Sherburn Cl. L9: Ain 2J **45**
Sherdley Bus. Pk. WA9: St H 9L **49**
Sherdley Ct. L35: Rainh 5F **62**
Sherdley Park 2L **63**
Sherdley Pk. Dr. WA9: St H 2M **63**
Sherdley Park Municipal Golf Course 2K **63**
Sherdley Rd. WA9: St H 9L **49**
(Delphwood Dr.)
WA9: St H 3J **63**
(Welwyn Cl., not continuous)
Sherdley Rd. Caravan Site
WA9: St H 1K **63**
Sherdley Rd. Ind. Est. WA9: St H 9L **49**
Sherford Cl. L27: N'ley 4K **77**
Sheridan Av. WA3: Low 3E **52**
Sheridan Pl. WA2: Win 4B **66**
Sheridan Way WA7: Nort 5F **96**
Sheri Dr. WA12: Newt W 8M **51**
Sheriff Cl. L5: Liv 5D **58**
Sheringham Cl. CH49: Upton 1A **72**
WA9: St H 7N **49**
Sheringham Rd. WA5: Gt San 2G **81**
Sherlock Av. WA11: Hay 3G **50**
Sherlock La. CH44: Wall 7G **57**
(not continuous)
Sherman Dr. L35: Rainh 8G **63**
Sherrat St. WN8: Skel 3A **30**
Sherringham Rd. PR8: Birkd 4L **11**
Sherry Ct. L17: Aig 3K **75**
Sherry La. CH49: Woodc 6A **72**
Sherwell Cl. L15: Wav 8M **59**
Sherwood Av. CH61: Irby 9K **71**
L23: Crosb 6K **33**
L39: Augh 2A **28**
WN4: Ash M 7L **41**
Sherwood Cl. L35: Rainh 4E **62**
WA8: Wid 7F **78**
Sherwood Ct. L12: Crox 7D **46**
L36: Huy 7K **61**
Sherwood Cres. WA5: Burtw 3G **65**
Sherwood Dr. CH63: Hghr B 9L **73**
L35: Whis 7C **62**
WN8: Skel 1G **30**
Sherwood Gro. CH47: Meols 9G **54**
WA6: Hel 2D **114**
Sherwood Ho. PR8: Ains 9J **11**
Sherwood Lodge PR8: Birkd 1M **11**
Sherwood Rd. CH44: Wall 6J **57**
CH47: Meols 9G **55**
L23: Crosb 6J **33**
Sherwood Row *L26: Halew 1J 93*
(off Honey Hall Rd.)
Sherwood's La. L10: Faz 2L **45**
Sherwood St. L3: Liv 5A **58**
Sherwyn Rd. L4: Walt 1H **59**
Shetland Cl. WA2: Fearn 5F **66**
WA8: Wid 5A **80**
Shetland Dr. CH62: Brom 7D **90**
CH65: Ell P 4A **112**
Shevington Cl. WA8: Wid 5A **80**
WA9: St H 2M **63**
Shevington's La. L33: Kirkb 6B **36**
Shevington Wlk. WA8: Wid 5A **80**
Shewell Cl. CH42: Tran 4K **73**

Shiel Rd. CH45: New B 2H 57
Shiggins Cl. WA5: Gt San 2M 81
Shillingford Cl. WA4: App 2F 98
Shimmin St. L7: Liv 6N 5 (8F 58)
Shipley Wlk. L24: Speke 3H 93
Ship St. WA6: Frod 5L 107
Shipton Cl. CH43: Pren 7E 72
L19: Aller 8N 75
WA5: Gt San 9K 65
WA8: Wid 5G 78
Shirdley Av. L32: Kirkb 3D 46
Shirdley Cres. PR8: Ains 2J 17
SHIRDLEY HILL 8F 12
Shirdley Wlk. L32: Kirkb 3D 46
Shirebourne Av. WA11: St H 3L 49
Shireburn Rd. L37: Form 8C 16
Shiregreen WA9: St H 3M 63
Shires, The WA10: St H 8H 49
Shirley Dr. WA4: Grap 6H 83
Shirley Rd. L19: Aller 8A 76
Shirley St. CH44: Wall 6L 57
Shirwell Gro. WA9: Sut L 5M 63
Shobdon Cl. L12: Crox 6D 46
Shones Cft. CH64: Ness 9G 101
Shop La. L31: Mag 2H 35
Shop Rd. L34: Know 6G 47
Shore Bank CH62: New F 8B 74
Shore Dr. CH62: Port S 1B 90
Shorefields CH62: New F 8B 74
Shorefields Ho. CH62: New F 9B 74
Shorefields Village L8: Liv 5E 74
Shoreham Dr. WA5: Penk 5J 81
Shore La. CH48: Caldy 9D 70
Shore Rd. CH41: Birke 1M 73
CH48: Caldy 9D 70
L20: Boot 5M 43
PR8: Ains 8F 10
Shore Road Pumping Station 1M 73
Short Cl. WA12: Newt W 7G 51
Short Cft. La. L37: Gt Alt 3K 25
Shortfield Rd. CH49: Upton 4A 72
Shortfield Way CH49: Upton 4A 72
Short St. WA3: Golb 1C 52
WA8: Wid 2K 95
WA11: Hay 4G 50
WA12: Newt W 7G 51
Short Wlk. M31: Part 7L 69
Shortwood Rd. L14: Knott A 6D 60
Shorwell Cl. WA5: Gt San 1E 80
Shottesbrook Grn. L11: Norr G 7L 45
SHOTWICK 9A 110
Shotwick Helsby By-Pass
CH1: Back 5N 111
CH1: Back, Dunk, Moll, Shot 9B 110
CH2: Elt, Lit Stan, Thorn M 4E 112
CH65: Ell P 5N 111
CH66: Back 9B 110
Shotwick La. CH1: Shot, Woodb 9A 110
Showcase Cinema
Liverpool 6M 45
Shrewsbury Av. L10: Ain 8H 35
L22: Water 8K 33
Shrewsbury Cl. CH43: Clau 2F 72
Shrewsbury Dr. CH49: Upton 2A 72
Shrewsbury Pl. *L19: Garst 1A 92*
(off Shrewsbury Rd.)
Shrewsbury Rd. CH43: Clau, Oxton 1F 72
CH44: Wall 4F 56
CH48: W Kir 7B 70
CH60: Hesw 6A 88
CH65: Ell P 9A 104
(off Norfolk Rd.)
L19: Garst 1A 92
Shrewsbury St. WA4: Warr 5E 82
Shrewton Rd. L25: Gate 1E 76
Shropshire Cl. L30: N'ton 7F 34
WA1: Wools 2M 83
Shropshire Gdns. WA10: St H 8J 49
Shropshire Rd. CH2: Lit Stan 2D 112
Sibford Rd. L12: W Der 4B 60
Sibley Av. WN4: Ash M 7M 41
Siddeley Dr. WA12: Newt W 7H 51
Siddeley St. L17: Aig 5H 75
Sidgreave St. WA10: St H 7H 49
Siding Ct. WA8: Wid 9K 79
Siding La. L33: Sim 5G 37
WA11: Rainf 2N 37
Sidings, The L7: Liv 7N 5
Sidings Ct. WA1: Warr 2D 82
Sidlaw Av. WA9: St H 7B 50
Sidlaw Cl. CH66: Lit Sut 8F 102
Sidmouth Cl. WA5: Penk 4G 81
WA10: Windle 4F 48
Sidmouth Gro. WN3: Wigan 1G 41
Sidney Av. CH45: New B 1G 57
Sidney Cl. CH64: Nest 5F 100
Sidney Ct. CH42: Tran 5L 73
Sidney Pl. L7: Liv 6N 5 (8F 58)
Sidney Powell Av. L32: Kirkb 9A 36
Sidney Rd. CH42: Tran 4L 73
CH64: Nest 5F 100
L20: Boot 8C 44
PR9: South 7L 7
Sidney St. CH41: Birke 1L 73
WA10: St H 6G 49
Sidney Ter. CH42: Tran 5L 73
Sidwell St. L19: Garst 1A 92
Siemens Rd. M44: Irlam 4L 69
Sienna Cl. L27: N'ley 2G 77
M44: Irlam 3L 69
Signal Works Rd. L9: Ain, Faz 2K 45
Silcock's Funland 7F 6
Silcock St. WA3: Golb 2B 52
Silcroft Rd. L32: Kirkb 2C 46
Silk Ct. L39: Orm 9E 20
Silkhouse Ct. L2: Liv 4D 4
Silkhouse La. L3: Liv 4D 4
Silkstone Cl. L7: Liv 9G 59
WA10: St H 7G 49
Silkstone Cres. WA7: Pal F 8D 96
Silkstone St. WA10: St H 7G 49
(not continuous)
Silsden Av. WA3: Low 2J 53
Silver Av. WA11: Hay 5C 50
Silverbeech Av. L18: Moss H 4N 75
Silverbeech Rd. CH44: Wall 6J 57
Silver Birch Av. PR9: Banks 4H 9
Silverbirch Gdns. CH44: Wall 4E 56
Silver Birch Gro. WN4: Ash M 6J 41
Silver Birch Way L31: Lyd 7G 27
Silverbirch Way CH66: Whit 5L 111
Silverbrook Rd. L27: N'ley 1H 77
Silverburn Av. CH46: More 8M 55
Silverdale Av. L13: Liv 4K 59
Silverdale Cl. L36: Huy 9J 61
WA6: Frod 7M 107
Silverdale Ct. PR8: Birkd 2L 11
PR8: South 2E 12
Silverdale Dr. L21: Lith 2C 44
Silverdale Gro. WA11: St H 2K 49
Silverdale Rd. CH43: Oxton 4G 72
CH63: Hghr B 9M 73
WA4: Warr 6C 82
WA12: Newt W 6K 51
Silverlake Cl. L4: Walt 7F 44
Silver La. WA3: Ris 2M 67
(not continuous)
Silverlea Av. CH45: Wall 4H 57
Silver Leigh L17: Aig 7J 75
Silverlime Gdns. WA9: St H 2F 62
Silverne Dr. CH65: Whit 3M 111
Silverstone Dr. L36: Roby 9H 61
Silverstone Gro. L31: Lyd 7G 26
Silver St. WA2: Warr 2C 82
Silverthorne Dr. PR9: South 6L 7
Silverton Rd. L17: Aig 8K 75
Silverwell Rd. L11: Crox 5B 46
Silverwell Wlk. L11: Crox 5B 46
Silverwing Ho. L19: Aig 9L 75
Silvester St. L5: Liv 4B 58
Simkin Av. WA4: Westy 4G 82
Simms Av. WA9: St H 7A 50
SIMM'S CROSS 8L 79
SIMM'S LANE END 6D 40
Simm's Rd. L6: Liv 3J 59
Simnel Cl. L25: Gate 2F 76
Simon Ct. CH48: W Kir 6B 70
Simonsbridge CH48: Caldy 1E 86
Simons Cl. L35: Whis 9A 62
Simon's Cft. L30: N'ton 8B 34
Simonside WA8: Wid 6F 78
Simons La. WA6: Frod 8L 107
Simonstone Gro. WA9: St H 2N 63
SIMONSWOOD 5E 36
Simonswood Ind. Pk. L33: Sim 5F 36
Simonswood La. L33: Kirkb 1E 46
L39: Bic 8D 28
Simonswood Wlk. L33: Kirkb 9E 36
Simpson's Pl. PR8: South 9G 7
Simpson St. CH41: Birke 2K 73
L1: Liv 9F 4 (1C 74)
Sim St. L3: Liv 2J 5 (6D 58)
Sinclair Av. L35: Presc 4C 62
WA2: Warr 7C 66
WA8: Wid 8J 79
Sinclair Cl. L35: Presc 3C 62
Sinclair Dr. L18: Moss H 2N 75
Sinclair St. L19: Garst 2A 92
Sinclair Way L34: Presc 4N 61
Sineacre La. L33: Sim 3J 37
L39: Bic 3J 37
Singleton Av. CH42: Tran 5J 73
WA11: St H 5N 49
Singleton Dr. L34: Know 7H 47
Singleton Rd. CH65: Gt Sut 1L 111
Sirdar Cl. L7: Liv 9G 59
Sir Howard St. L8: Liv 8L 5 (9E 58)
Sir Howard Way L8: Liv 8L 5
Sir Thomas St. L1: Liv 4E 4 (7C 58)
Siskin Cl. WA12: Newt W 7L 51
Siskin Grn. L25: Gate 4E 76
Sisters Way CH41: Birke 2K 73
Six Acre Gdns. WA4: Moore 2J 97
Six Acre La. WA4: Moore 2H 97
Sixpenny La. L39: Bart 5L 17
Sixpenny Wlk. WA1: Warr 2D 82
Sixteen Acre La. L37: Form 7G 16
Sixth Av. L9: Ain 3K 45
(Broadway)
L9: Ain 3J 45
(Seventh Av.)
Skeffington L35: Whis 7B 62
Skelhorne St. L3: Liv 5H 5 (8D 58)
SKELMERSDALE 3E 30
Skelmersdale Hall Dr. WN8: Skel 1E 30
(not continuous)
Skelmersdale Rd. L39: Bic 5L 29
WN8: Skel 5L 29
Skelmersdale Sports Cen. 5F 30
Skelton Cl. WA11: St H 3L 49
Skelton St. WN4: Ash M 5H 41
Skerries Rd. L4: Walt 3F 58
Skiddaw Cl. WA7: Beech 2C 108
Skiddaw Rd. CH62: Brom 5D 90
Skipton Av. PR9: South 1A 8
Skipton Cl. WA7: Cas 6B 96
Skipton Dr. CH66: Lit Sut 1H 111
Skipton Rd. L4: Walt 2G 59
L36: Huy 6M 61
Skirving Pl. L5: Liv 3C 58
Skirving St. L5: Liv 3D 58
Skitters Gro. WN4: Ash M 7G 41
Skull Ho. La. WN6: Appl B 4M 23
Skull Ho. M. WN6: Appl B 5M 23
Skye Cl. CH65: Ell P 4A 112
WA8: Wid 5A 80
Skyes Cres. WN3: Wins 2E 40
Skyhawk Av. L19: Speke 3C 92
Sky Lark Ri. WA9: St H 7C 50
Sky Park Ind. Est. L24: Speke 4F 92
Slackey's La. PR9: South 3A 8
Slackswood Cl. CH65: Ell P 7N 103
Slade La. CH63: Thorn H 8H 89
Slag La. WA3: Low 2E 52
WA11: Hay 2D 50
(not continuous)
Slaidburn Cl. WN3: Wigan 1J 41
Slaidburn Cres. PR9: South 2M 7
WA3: Golb 1A 52
Slaidburn Ind. Est. PR9: South 2M 7
Slate La. WN8: Skel 1N 29
Slater Pl. L1: Liv 7G 5 (9C 58)
Slater St. L1: Liv 7G 5 (9C 58)
WA4: Warr 4D 82
Slatey Rd. CH43: Oxton 2H 73
Sleaford Rd. L14: Knott A 4F 60
Sleepers Hill L4: Walt 2E 58
Slessor Av. CH48: W Kir 5E 70
Slim Rd. L36: Huy 6J 61
Slingsby Dr. CH49: Upton 4A 72
Sluice La. L40: Ruf 4L 15
Slutchers La. WA1: Warr 4B 82
Smallacres CH65: Ell P 7L 103
Small Av. WA2: Warr 7D 66
Small Cres. WA2: Warr 7D 66
Smallholdings, The L31: Mag 9L 27
Small La. L39: Augh 1M 27
L39: Orm 9D 20
L40: Scar 6C 14
Small La. Nth. L39: Hals 3J 19
Small La. Sth. L39: Hals 8H 19
Smallridge Cl. CH61: Pens 3M 87
Smallshaw Cl. WN4: Ash M 9J 41
Smallwood M. CH60: Hesw 5M 87
Smeaton St. L4: Kirkd 9D 44
(not continuous)
Smethick Wlk. L30: N'ton 7F 34
Smethurst Hall Pk. WN5: Bil 1M 39
Smethurst Rd. WA11: Kings M 2L 39
WN5: Bil 1M 39
Smilie Av. CH46: More 8K 55
Smith Av. CH41: Birke 9H 57
Smith Ct. WA1: Padd 1G 83
Smith Cres. WA2: Warr 9E 66
Smithdown Gro. L7: Liv 7N 5 (9F 58)
Smithdown La. L7: Liv 5M 5 (8F 58)
(Elm Gro.)
L7: Liv 9G 58
(Malt St.)
Smithdown Pl. L15: Wav 3M 75
Smithdown Rd. L7: Liv 1H 75
L15: Wav 1H 75
Smith Dr. L20: Boot 5D 44
WA2: Warr 9E 66
Smithfield St. L3: Liv 3E 4 (7B 58)
WA9: St H 8N 49
Smithford Wlk. L35: Tar G 1M 77
Smithills Cl. WA3: Birchw 4L 67
Smith Pl. L5: Kirkd 3C 58
Smith Rd. WA8: Wid 9J 79
Smith St. L5: Kirkd 2D 58
L34: Presc 3B 62
WA1: Warr 3C 82
WA9: St H 2A 64
WN8: Skel 3A 30
SMITHY BROW 2G 66
Smithy Brow WA3: Croft 2G 66
WN8: Newb 4D 22
Smithy Cl. CH64: Ness 9G 101
L37: Form 9H 17
WA8: Cron 3F 78
Smithy Ct. CH66: Lit Sut 8H 103
Smithy Grn. L37: Form 9H 17
Smithy Heritage Cen. 5E 48
Smithy Hey CH48: W Kir 6D 70
Smithy Hill CH63: Thorn H 9G 89
Smithy La. CH64: Will 6N 101
CH66: Lit Sut 8H 103
L39: Augh 6L 27
L39: Bart 7F 18
L40: Holm 9N 9
L40: Scar 1M 19
M31: Part 6M 69
WA3: Croft 1H 67
WA6: Hel 9F 106
WA8: Cron 2F 78
SMITHY LANE ENDS 8A 14
Smithystone Cl. L15: Wav 1M 75
Smithy Wlk. L40: Burs 9J 15
SMM Business Pk. CH41: Birke 7J 57
Smock La. WN4: Garsw 7E 40
Smollett St. L6: Liv 6G 58
L20: Boot 4A 44
Smugglers Way CH45: Wall 1E 56
Smythe Cft. PR9: South 5M 7
Smyth Rd. WA8: Wid 6N 79
Snab La. CH64: Ness 9F 100
Snabwood Cl. CH64: Lit N 9E 100
Snaefell Av. L13: Liv 4K 59
Snaefell Gro. L13: Liv 4K 59
Snaefell Ri. WA4: App 9D 82
SNAPE GREEN 5J 13
Snape Grn. PR8: South 6J 13
Snave Cl. L21: Lith 5A 44
Snowberry Cl. WA8: Wid 4A 80
Snowberry Cres. WA5: Warr 5M 81
Snowberry Rd. L14: Knott A 3E 60
Snowberry Wlk. *M31: Part 6L 69*
(off Wood La.)
Snowberry Way CH66: Whit 5L 111
Snowden Rd. CH46: More 9K 55
Snowdon Cl. CH66: Lit Sut 8F 102
WA5: Gt San 2G 81
Snowdon Gro. WA9: St H 2M 63
Snowdon La. L5: Liv 4B 58
Snowdon Rd. CH42: Tran 6K 73
Snowdrop Av. CH41: Birke 9F 56
Snowdrop Cl. WA7: Beech 2B 108
Snowdrop M. L21: Lith 4A 44
Snowdrop St. L5: Kirkd 2C 58
Soane Cl. WN4: Ash M 8M 41
Soapstone Way M44: Irlam 1N 69
Soho Pl. L3: Liv 2J 5 (6D 58)
Soho St. L3: Liv 1J 5 (6D 58)
(not continuous)
Solar Rd. L9: Ain 4G 44
Solly Av. CH42: Rock F 6L 73
Solomon St. L7: Liv 7G 59
Solway Cl. WA2: Fearn 5G 67
WN4: Ash M 7J 41
Solway Gro. WA7: Beech 1N 107
Solway St. CH41: Birke 8G 56
Solway St. E. L8: Liv 1G 75
Solway St. W. L8: Liv 1G 74
Soma Av. L21: Lith 2B 44
Somerford Ho. L23: Blun 8H 33
Somerford Rd. L14: Knott A 5E 60
Somerford Wlk. WA8: Wid 5A 80
Somerley Cl. L12: W Der 1B 60
Somerset Cl. M44: Cad 3K 69
Somerset Dr. PR8: Ains 3J 17
Somerset Pl. L6: Liv 4J 59
Somerset Rd. CH45: Wall 4E 56
CH48: W Kir 5D 70
CH61: Pens 3M 87
L20: Boot 6C 44
L22: Water 9J 33
Somerset St. WA9: St H 8N 49
Somerset Way WA1: Wools 9J 67
Somerton St. L15: Wav 9K 59
Somerville Cl. CH63: Brom 9A 90
CH64: Lit N 9E 100
Somerville Cres. CH65: Ell P 1A 112
Somerville Gro. L22: Water 9K 33
Somerville Rd. L22: Water 9K 33
WA8: Wid 8G 79
Somerville Wlk. *WA5: Gt San 1L 81*
(off Boston Blvd.)
Sommer Av. L12: W Der 2M 59
Sonning Av. L21: Lith 1N 43
Sonning Rd. L4: Walt 8J 45
Sorany Cl. L23: Thorn 5N 33
Sorbus Cl. CH2: Elt 2N 113
Sorby Rd. M44: Irlam 2M 69
Sorogold Cl. WA9: St H 7M 49
Sorogold St. WA9: St H 7M 49
Sorrel Cl. CH43: Noct 3D 72
WA2: Padg 7K 67
Sorrel Way WA9: Clock F 6N 63
Sougher's La. WN4: Ash M 5G 41
Sth. Albert Rd. L17: Aig 4G 75
Southampton Dr. L19: Garst 1N 91
Southampton Way WA7: Murd 9G 96
Sth. Atlantic Av. L30: N'ton 1E 44
South Av. L34: Presc 3M 61
WA2: Warr 9C 66
WA4: Stockt H 7D 82
South Bank CH43: Oxton 5H 73
Sth. Bank Rd. L7: Liv 7J 59
L19: Gras 9N 75
Southbank Rd. PR8: South 9G 7
Sth. Bank Ter. WA7: Run 4J 95
Sth. Barcombe Rd. L16: Child 1C 76
Sth. Boundary Rd. L33: Know I 2F 46
Southbourne Rd. CH45: Wall 4D 56
Southbrook Rd. L27: N'ley 2G 77
Southbrook Way L27: N'ley 2G 77
Sth. Cantril Av. L12: W Der 2D 60
Sth. Chester St. L8: Liv 2E 74
Southcroft L33: Kirkb 7C 36
Southcroft Rd. CH45: Wall 4D 56
South Dale WA5: Penk 3H 81
Southdale Rd. CH42: Rock F 6L 73
L15: Wav 9L 59
WA1: Padd 1H 83
Southdean Rd. L14: Knott A 3F 60
SOUTHDENE 2D 46
Southdene WN8: Parb 3E 22
South Dr. CH49: Upton 3A 72
CH60: Hesw 8A 88

South Dr. CH61: Irby 2K 87
L12: W Der 4M 59
L15: Wav 9L 59
WN6: Appl B 3M 23
Southern Cres. L8: Liv 3D 74
Southern Gateway L24: Speke 2G 92
Southern Rd. L24: Speke 5J 93
PR8: South 9F 6
Southern's La. WA11: Rainf 5D 38
Southern St. WA4: Stockt H 7D 82
Southey Cl. WA8: Wid 8J 79
Southey Gro. L31: Mag 5J 35
Southey Rd. WA10: St H 1F 62
Southey St. L15: Wav 1K 75
L20: Boot 6A 44
(not continuous)
Sth. Ferry Quay L3: Liv 2C 74
Southfield Rd. CH66: Lit Sut 8H 103
L9: Walt 4E 44
Southfields Av. WA5: Gt San 3H 81
South Front L35: Whis 8B 62
Southgate Cl. L12: Crox 7C 46
Southgate Rd. L13: Liv 6N 59
South Gro. L8: Liv 4F 74
L18: Aller 7A 76
South Hey Rd. CH61: Irby 2L 87
Sth. Highville Rd. L16: Child 2B 76
South Hill PR8: South 9F 6
South Hill Gro. CH43: Oxton 5H 73
L8: Liv 4F 74
South Hill Rd. CH43: Oxton 4J 73
L8: Liv 5E 74
Sth. Hunter St. L1: Liv 7K 5 (9E 58)
Sth. John St. L1: Liv 6E 4 (8B 58)
WA9: St H 7M 49
Sth. Lancashire Ind. Est.
WN4: Ash M 5K 41
Southlands Av. WA5: Penk 5H 81
Southlands Ct. *WA7: Run* 7J 95
(off Southlands M.)
Southlands M. WA7: Run 7J 95
South La. WA8: Wid 4A 80
South La. Entry WA8: Wid 4B 80
South Mnr. Way L25: Woolt 7G 76
South Meade L31: Mag 2G 35
Southmead Gdns. L19: Aller 9C 76
Southmead Rd. L19: Aller 9C 76
Sth. Mossley Hill Rd. L19: Aig, Gras 7M 75
Southney Cl. L31: Mell 8N 35
South Pde. CH48: W Kir 6B 70
CH64: Park 6C 100
L23: Crosb 8M 33
L24: Speke 4J 93
L32: Kirkb 9C 36
WA7: West P 8G 94
South Pk. Ct. *CH44: Wall* 6L 57
(off Demesne St.)
L32: Kirkb 8A 36
South Pk. Rd. L32: Kirkb 8N 35
Sth. Parkside Dr. L12: W Der 2A 60
Sth. Parkside Wlk. *L12: W Der* 1N 59
(off Parkside Dr.)
South Pk. Way L20: Boot 8C 44
Sth. Pier Rd. CH65: Ell P 7B 104
SOUTHPORT 8G 7
Southport & Ainsdale Golf Course 8K 11
Southport & Birkdale Sports Club 3L 11
Southport Argyle Lawn Tennis Club 5K 7
Southport Bus. Cen. *PR9: South* 8G 7
(off Lord St.)
Southport Bus. Pk. PR8: South 3C 12
Southport Crematorium PR8: South 4G 12
Southport Eco Vis. Cen. 8D 6
Southport Ent. Cen. PR9: South 9M 7
Southport FC 1D 12
Southport Little Theatre 8G 7
Southport Model Railway Village 8F 6
Southport Municipal Golf Links 6H 7
Southport New Pleasureland 8E 6
Southport New Rd. PR4: Mere B, Tarl 5K 9
PR9: Banks 2C 8
Southport Old Links 7N 7
Southport Old Rd. L37: Form 6H 17
Southport Pier 6E 6
Southport Pier Tram 7E 6
Southport Residential Parkhomes
PR8: South 4F 12
Southport Rd. L20: Boot 4D 44
L23: Thorn 4N 33
L31: Lyd 4F 26
L37: Form 8G 17
L39: Bart 7F 18
L39: Orm 7C 20
L40: Scar 2M 19
PR8: South 3F 12
Southport Sailing Club 6G 6
Southport Station (Rail) 8G 7
Southport St. WA9: St H 7C 50
Southport Theatre & Convention Cen. 7F 6
Southport Watersports Cen. 7G 6
South Quay L3: Liv 9E 4 (1B 74)
Southridge Rd. CH61: Pens 2A 88
South Rd. CH42: Tran 5J 73
CH48: W Kir 7B 70
CH65: Ell P 9D 104
(Bridges Rd.)
CH65: Ell P 2A 112
(Malvern Av.)
CH65: Hoot 3H 103
L9: Ain 4J 45
South Rd. L14: Broad G 6B 60
L19: Gras 1M 91
L22: Water 2K 43
L24: Halew 3J 93
WA7: West P 8G 94
Sth. Sefton Bus. Cen. L20: Boot 7A 44
South Sta. Rd. L25: Gate 3F 76
South St. L8: Liv 3F 74
WA8: Wid 8L 79
WA9: St H 2G 62
Sth. Sudley Rd. L19: Aig 7M 75
South Ter. L39: Orm 9C 20
South Vw. CH62: Brom 2C 90
L8: Liv 4F 74
(off Dentwood St.)
L22: Water 2L 43
L36: Huy 7M 61
South Vw. Ct. L22: Water 2L 43
South Vw. Ter. WA5: Cuerd 5C 80
South Vs. CH45: New B 2H 57
Southward Rd. WA11: Hay 3J 51
Southwark Gro. L30: N'ton 1E 44
Southway L15: Wav 9N 59
WA7: Pal F 8B 96
(not continuous)
WA8: Wid 8G 78
WN8: Skel 4E 30
(not continuous)
Southway Av. WA4: App 9E 82
Southwell Cl. WA3: Low 2D 52
Southwell Pl. L8: Liv 3D 74
Southwell St. L8: Liv 3D 74
Southwick Rd. CH42: Tran 5L 73
Southwold Cres. WA5: Gt San 2F 80
Southwood Av. WA7: Wind H 5E 96
Southwood Cl. L32: Kirkb 2E 46
Southwood Rd. CH62: Brom 6E 90
L17: Aig 6G 74
Southworth Av. WA5: Warr 9A 66
Southworth La. WA2: Win 2E 66
WA3: Croft 2E 66
Southworth Rd. WA12: Newt W 7N 51
Sovereign Cl. WA3: Low 3F 52
WA7: Murd 8F 96
Sovereign Ct. WA3: Birchw 5K 67
Sovereign Hey L11: Crox 7A 46
Sovereign Rd. L11: Crox 7A 46
Sovereign Way CH41: Birke 8K 57
L11: Crox 7A 46
Spaceport 7M 57
Spa Fold L40: Lath 9L 21
Spa La. L40: Lath 9L 21
Spark Hall Cl. WA4: Stret 5F 98
Spark La. WA7: Halt 6B 96
Sparks Cft. CH62: Port S 1B 90
Sparks La. CH61: Thing 1A 88
Sparling St. L1: Liv 9F 4 (1C 74)
(not continuous)
SPARROW HALL 6L 45
Sparrow Hall Cl. L9: Faz 6K 45
Sparrow Hall Rd. L9: Faz 6L 45
Sparrowhawk Cl. L26: Halew 7J 77
WA7: Pal F 8C 96
Sparrow Hill WN8: Parb 3J 23
Spawell Cl. WA3: Low 1F 52
Speakman Av. WA12: Newt W 5L 51
Speakman Rd. WA10: St H 4G 49
Speakmans Dr. WN6: Appl B 7M 23
Speakman St. WA7: Run 4J 95
Speakman Way L34: Presc 4A 62
Speedkarting 4A 82
Speedwell Cl. CH60: Hesw 7C 88
WA3: Low 2F 52
Speedwell Dr. CH60: Hesw 7C 88
Speedwell Rd. CH41: Birke 1F 72
SPEKE 5J 93
Speke Blvd. L24: Speke 3F 92
Speke Chu. Rd. L24: Speke 4F 92
Speke Hall Av. L24: Speke 4E 92
Speke Hall Garden & Estate 5D 92
Speke Hall Ind. Est.
L24: Speke 4E 92
Speke Hall Rd. L24: Speke 2E 92
L25: Hunts X 2E 92
Speke Ho. L24: Speke 5L 93
Spekeland Rd. L7: Liv 9H 59
Speke Rd. L19: Garst 2A 92
L24: Speke 2B 92
L25: Hunts X, Woolt 6F 76
L26: Halew 1N 93
WA8: Wid 1N 93
Speke Town La. L24: Speke 3F 92
Spellow La. L4: Walt 1E 58
Spellow Pl. L3: Liv 4C 4
Spence Av. L20: Boot 5C 44
Spencer Av. CH46: More 8A 56
Spencer Cl. L36: Huy 9K 61
Spencer Gdns. WA9: St H 1N 63
Spencer La. L40: Ruf 2L 15
Spencer Pl. L20: Boot 3C 44
Spencers La. L31: Mell 9K 35
L39: Hals 2B 18
WN5: Orr 5N 31
WN8: Skel 4E 30
Spencer St. L6: Liv 5E 58
Spenders La. WA7: Aston 5F 108
Spennymoor Ct. WA7: Pal F 8A 96
Spenser Av. CH42: Rock F 7M 73
Spenser Cl. WA8: Wid 7J 79
Spenser Rd. CH64: Nest 5E 100
Spenser St. L20: Boot 6A 44
Sphynx Tennis Club 2D 12
Spicer Gro. L32: Kirkb 9C 36
Spice St. L9: Ain 4G 45
Spike Island Vis. Cen. 2K 95
Spilsby Sq. WN3: Wigan 1J 41
Spindle Cl. L6: Liv 5E 58
Spindle Hillock WN4: Garsw 6F 40
Spindrift Ct. CH48: W Kir 7B 70
Spindus Rd. L24: Speke 4E 92
Spinnaker Cl. WA7: Murd 9F 96
Spinnakers, The L19: Aig 9L 75
Spinner M. L39: Orm 8E 20
Spinners Dr. WA9: St H 1B 64
Spinners Pl. WA1: Warr 2D 82
Spinney, The CH48: W Kir 6F 70
CH49: Upton 2A 72
CH60: Hesw 1C 100
CH63: Spit 4A 90
CH64: Park 5D 100
L28: Stockb V 2F 60
L34: Presc 2N 61
L37: Form 8G 17
WA11: Rainf 4C 38
Spinney Apartments WN8: Uph 3M 31
Spinney Av. WA8: Wid 7D 78
Spinney Cl. L33: Know I 2G 47
L39: Orm 1B 28
WA9: Clock F 5M 63
Spinney Cres. L23: Blun 5H 33
Spinney Dr. CH66: Gt Sut 3J 111
Spinney Gdns. WA4: App T 3J 99
Spinney Grn. WA10: Eccl 7D 48
Spinney Rd. L33: Know I 2H 47
Spinney Vw. L33: Know I 2H 47
Spinney Wlk. WA7: Cas 6C 96
Spinney Way L36: Huy 6G 60
Spion Kop WN4: Ash M 8J 41
Spire Grn. L9: Walt 4F 44
Spires, The WA10: Eccl 6D 48
Spires Gdns. WA2: Win 2B 66
SPITAL 4A 90
Spital Heyes CH63: Spit 4A 90
Spital Rd. CH62: Brom, Spit 4N 89
CH63: Spit 4N 89
Spital Station (Rail) 4A 90
Spitfire Rd. L24: Speke 1D 92
Spofforth Rd. L7: Liv 9J 59
Spooner Av. L21: Lith 3B 44
Sprainger St. L3: Liv 5A 58
Sprakeling Pl. L20: Boot 3D 44
Spray St. WA10: St H 6H 49
Spreyton Cl. L12: W Der 8A 46
Sprig Cl. L9: Ain 2J 45
Spring Av. CH66: Lit Sut 8H 103
Spring Bank WN6: Appl B 5M 23
Springbank Cl. WA7: Run 9L 95
Springbank Gdns. WA13: Lymm 3H 85
Springbank Rd. L4: Walt 4G 58
Springbourne WA6: Frod 8N 107
Springbourne Rd. L17: Aig 6G 75
Springbrook Cl. WA10: Eccl 6D 48
Springburn Gdns. WA1: Wools 1N 83
Spring Cl. L33: Kirkb 6E 36
PR8: Birkd 1N 11
Spring Ct. WA7: Run 5L 95
Springcroft CH64: Park 5C 100
Springdale Cl. CH46: More 8A 56
L12: W Der 2A 60
Springfield L3: Liv 2H 5 (6D 58)
(not continuous)
WA11: Rainf 1B 38
Springfield Av. CH48: W Kir 5F 70
L21: Lith 2B 44
WA1: Padg 9G 67
WA3: Golb 2A 52
WA4: Grap 5J 83
WA6: Hel 2E 114
WA13: Lymm 3H 85
Springfield Cl. CH49: Woodc 6C 72
L37: Form 2C 24
L40: Burs 2H 21
WA10: St H 1F 62
Springfield Cres. L36: Huy 3G 61
Springfield La. WA10: Eccl 5D 48
Springfield Pk. WA11: Hay 3E 50
Springfield Pl. CH44: Wall 5K 57
Springfield Rd. L39: Augh 7L 27
WA8: Wid 8D 78
WA10: St H 1F 62
Springfields WA6: Hel 2E 114
Springfield Sq. L4: Walt 1E 58
Springfield St. WA1: Warr 3B 82
Springfield Way L12: W Der 1C 60
Spring Gdns. CH66: Lit Sut 8H 103
L31: Mag 3K 35
Spring Gro. L12: W Der 3A 60
Springhill Av. CH62: Brom 9C 90
Springhill Ct. L15: Wav 2M 75
Springholm Dr. WA4: App 4E 98
Spring La. WA3: Croft 3J 67
WA13: Lymm 5L 85
Springmeadow Rd. L25: Gate 3E 76
Springmount WA3: Low 2F 52
Springmount Dr. WN8: Parb 1F 22
Springpool WA9: St H 2N 63
WN3: Wins 1D 40
Springs Cl. *L20: Boot* 6C 44
(off Davies St.)
Springside Cl. L36: Huy 3G 61
Spring St. CH42: Tran 5M 73
WA8: Wid 1K 95
SPRINGVALE 3D 38
Spring Vale CH45: Wall 2E 56
Springvale Cl. L32: Kirkb 1B 46
Springville Rd. L9: Ain 3H 45
Springwell Rd. L20: Boot 3B 44
Springwood Av. L19: Aller 8B 76
L25: Woolt 8B 76
Springwood Ct. *L19: Aller* 9B 76
(off Brocklebank La.)
Springwood Crematorium L25: Aller 8D 76
Springwood Dr. L40: Ruf 1L 15
Springwood Gro. L32: Kirkb 3D 46
Springwood Way CH62: New F 8N 73
Sprodley Dr. WN6: Appl B 3L 23
Spruce Cl. CH42: Tran 4K 73
WA1: Wools 1M 83
WA3: Low 3G 52
Spruce Gro. L28: Stockb V 2F 60
Spruce Way L37: Form 1C 24
Sprucewood Cl. L6: Liv 4G 58
Spunhill Av. CH66: Gt Sut 2H 111
Spur, The L23: Crosb 8K 33
Spur Cl. L11: Crox 7A 46
Spurgeon Cl. L5: Liv 4E 58
Spurling Rd. WA5: Burtw 3H 65
Spurriers La. L31: Mell 3A 36
Spurstow Cl. CH43: Oxton 5F 72
Spymers Cft. L37: Form 7G 16
Square, The CH2: Ince 9L 105
WA13: Lymm 5E 84
Square Ho. La. PR9: Banks 1F 8
Square La. L40: Burs 2J 21
Squibb Dr. CH46: Leas 7A 56
Squires Av. WA8: Wid 7J 79
Squires Cl. WA11: Hay 4D 50
Squires M. M31: Part 6L 69
Squires St. L7: Liv 6N 5 (8F 58)
Squirrel Grn. L37: Form 8C 16
Stable Cl. CH49: Grea 4L 71
Stables, The L23: Crosb 6N 33
Stables Bus. Centre, The *L13: Liv* 2K 59
(off Larkhill La.)
Stables Ct. *WA9: St H* 8M 49
(off Appleton Rd.)
Stableyard Cotts. WA11: Crank 9H 39
Stackfield, The CH48: W Kir 5G 70
Stadium Ct. CH62: Brom 5E 90
Stadium Rd. CH62: Brom 4D 90
Stadt Moers Pk. 7M 61
Stadt Moers Vis. Cen. 7N 61
Staffin Av. CH65: Ell P 5N 111
Stafford Cl. L36: Huy 5L 61
Stafford Gdns. CH65: Ell P 9N 103
Stafford Moreton Way
L31: Mag 2H 35
Stafford Rd. PR8: Birkd 5N 11
WA4: Warr 6D 82
WA10: St H 9G 48
Staffordshire Cl. L5: Liv 3D 58
M31: Part 7L 69
Stafford St. L3: Liv 3J 5 (7D 58)
WN8: Skel 2A 30
Stage La. WA13: Lymm 4H 85
Stag Rd. L24: Speke 1C 92
Stainburn Av. L11: Norr G 7L 45
Stainburn Cl. WN6: Shev 7N 23
Stainer Cl. L14: Knott A 4D 60
WA12: Newt W 5K 51
Staines Cl. WA4: App 2F 98
Stainforth Cl. WA3: Cul 6L 53
Stainmore Cl. WA3: Birchw 3B 68
Stainton Cl. L26: Halew 8J 77
WA11: St H 2L 49
Stairhaven Rd. L19: Aller 7N 75
Stakes, The CH46: Leas 6M 55
Stalbridge Av. L18: Moss H 3L 75
Stalbridge Dr. WA7: Nort 3H 97
Staley Av. L23: Crosb 8M 33
Stalisfield Av. L11: Norr G 8M 45
Stalisfield Pl. L11: Norr G 8M 45
Stalmine Rd. L9: Walt 6F 44
Stamford Ct. L20: Boot 7C 44
Stamfordham Dr. L19: Aller 8A 76
Stamfordham Gro. L19: Aller 9B 76
Stamfordham Pl. L19: Aller 9B 76
Stamford Rd. PR8: Birkd 3A 12
WN8: Skel 2A 30
Stamford St. CH65: Ell P 9M 103
L7: Liv 7H 59
Stanbridge Cl. WA5: Gt San 2K 81
Stanbury Av. CH63: Beb 1N 89
Standale Rd. L15: Wav 9L 59
Standard Rd. L11: Crox 6A 46
Standedge Way L14: Knott A 3E 60
Standen Cl. WA10: St H 6H 49
Stand Farm Rd. L12: Crox 7D 46
Standhouse La. L39: Augh 2A 28
Standingwood Rd. CH65: Ell P 7N 103
Standish Av. WN5: Bil 6A 40
Standish Ct. WA8: Wid 8G 78
Standish Dr. WA11: Rainf 4D 38
Standish St. L3: Liv 2F 4 (7C 58)
WA10: St H 6K 49
Stand Pk. Av. L30: N'ton 9E 34
Stand Pk. Cl. L30: N'ton 9E 34
Stand Pk. Rd. L16: Child 2B 76
Stand Pk. Way L30: N'ton 8D 34
Standring Gdns. WA10: St H 1E 62

Standside Pk. WN8: Skel 4A 30
Stanedge Gro. WN3: Wigan 1K 41
Stanfield Av. L5: Liv 4E 58
Stanfield Dr. CH63: Beb 4M 89
Stanford Av. CH45: New B 2H 57
Stanford Cres. L25: Hunts X 7H 77
Stangate L31: Mag 1G 35
Stanhope Dr. CH62: Brom 6C 90
L36: Huy 6G 60
Stanhope St. L8: Liv 2C 74
(not continuous)
WA10: St H 5J 49
Stanier Way L7: Liv 8H 59
Staniforth Pl. L16: Child 8B 60
Stanlaw Abbey Bus. Cen.
CH65: Ell P 3B 112
Stanlawe Rd. L37: Form 7E 16
Stanlaw Rd. CH65: Ell P 1A 112
STANLEY 7K 59
Stanley Av. CH45: Wall 3D 56
CH63: Hghr B 8H 73
PR8: Birkd 3M 11
WA4: Stockt H 6G 82
WA5: Gt San 1F 80
WA11: Rainf 4B 38
Stanley Bank Rd. WA11: Hay 3C 50
Stanley Bank Way WA11: Hay 4B 50
Stanley Bungs. L34: Know 7G 47
Stanley Cl. CH44: Wall 7L 57
L4: Kirkd 2C 58
WA8: Wid 6M 79
Stanley Cotts. L29: Thorn 2B 34
Stanley Ct. CH42: Tran 5M 73
L40: Burs 9J 15
Stanley Cres. L34: Presc 3N 61
Stanley Gdns. L9: Walt 5E 44
STANLEY GATE 5J 29
Stanley Ho. L20: Boot 6A 44
Stanley Ind. Est. WN8: Skel 1B 30
Stanley Island WN8: Skel 2B 30
Stanley La. CH62: East 2E 102
STANLEY PARK 1B 44
Stanley Park 1F 58
Stanley Pk. L21: Lith 1N 43
Stanley Pk. Av. Nth. L4: Walt 9G 45
(not continuous)
Stanley Pk. Av. Sth. L4: Walt 1G 59
Stanley Pl. WA4: Stockt H 6G 82
Stanley Pct. L20: Boot 7B 44
Stanley Rd. CH41: Birke 8F 56
CH47: Hoy 3A 70
CH62: New F 8N 73
CH65: Ell P 7A 104
L5: Kirkd, Liv 1C 58
L20: Boot, Kirkd 5B 44
L20: Kirkd 9C 44
L22: Water 2L 43
L31: Mag 5H 35
L36: Huy 7J 61
L37: Form 7E 16
WN8: Uph 5L 31
Stanley St. CH44: Wall 7L 57
L1: Liv 4E 4 (7B 58)
L7: Liv 6K 59
L19: Garst 3B 92
L39: Orm 8D 20
PR9: South 8G 6
WA1: Warr 4C 82
WA7: Run 4L 95
WA12: Newt W 7J 51
Stanley Ter. CH45: New B 2H 57
L8: Liv 9L 5
L18: Moss H 5M 75
Stanley Theatre 5L 5 (8E 58)
Stanley Vs. WA7: Run 6J 95
Stanley Way WN8: Skel 1B 30
STANLOW 1G 113
Stanlowe Vw. L19: Gras 1L 91
Stanlow & Thornton Station (Rail) . . . 9J 105
Stanmore Pk. CH49: Grea 5J 71
Stanmore Rd. L15: Wav 2N 75
WA7: Run 5N 95
Stannanought Rd. WN8: Skel 1F 30
(not continuous)
Stanner Cl. WA5: Call 7M 65
Stanney Cl. CH62: East 3D 102
CH64: Nest 7E 100
Stanney La. CH2: Back 9A 112
CH2: Lit Stan 4C 112
CH65: Ell P 1N 111
(not continuous)
Stanney Mill Ind. Est. CH2: Lit Stan . . . 2D 112
Stanney Mill La. CH2: Lit Stan 4D 112
Stanney Mill Rd. CH2: Lit Stan 2D 112
Stanney Oaks Leisure Cen. 3A 112
Stanney Wood Local Nature Reserve
. . . . 5N 111
Stanney Woods Av. CH65: Ell P 5A 112
Stannyfield Cl. L23: Thorn 5A 34
Stannyfield Dr. L23: Thorn 5A 34
Stansfield Av. L31: Mag 2L 35
WA1: Warr 2G 82
Stansfield Dr. WA4: Grap 9H 83
Stanstead Av. WA5: Penk 5H 81
Stanton Av. L21: Lith 1N 43
Stanton Cl. L30: N'ton 6C 34
WA11: Hay 4E 50
WN3: Wigan 1K 41
Stanton Ct. CH64: Nest 6E 100
Stanton Cres. L32: Kirkb 9A 36
Stanton Rd. CH63: Beb 4L 89
L18: Moss H 3L 75
WA4: Thel 5L 83
Stanwood Cl. WA10: Eccl 7C 48
Stanwood Gdns. L35: Whis 6B 62
Stanza Ct. L5: Liv 4D 58
Stapehill Cl. L13: Liv 7N 59
Stapeley Gdns. L26: Halew 1L 93
Staplands Rd. L14: Broad G 7B 60
Stapleford Ct. CH66: Ell P 6L 103
Stapleford Rd. L25: Gate 2G 76
Staplehurst Cl. L12: Crox 7C 46
Staplehurst Dr. CH42: Rock F 7N 73
Stapleton Av. CH49: Grea 4L 71
L24: Speke 4H 93
L35: Rainh 5F 62
WA2: Warr 9E 66
Stapleton Cl. L25: Gate 1F 76
L35: Rainh 5F 62
Stapleton Ct. WA6: Frod 6M 107
Stapleton Rd. L35: Rainh 4E 62
L37: Form 3D 24
Stapleton Way WA8: Hale B 2E 94
Stapley Cl. WA7: Run 6J 95
Starbeck Dr. CH66: Lit Sut 8G 102
Starkey Gro. WA4: Westy 4G 82
Star La. WA13: Lymm 4C 84
Starling Cl. WA7: Murd 8F 96
Starling Gro. L12: W Der 9D 46
Starling Way L30: Boot 2C 44
Star St. L8: Liv 2D 74
Startham Av. WN5: Bil 8N 39
Starworth Dr. CH62: New F 9B 74
STATHAM 4D 84
Statham Av. WA2: Warr 7D 66
WA13: Lymm 5C 84
Statham Cl. WA13: Lymm 5D 84
Statham Dr. WA13: Lymm 5D 84
Statham La. WA3: Rix 1B 84
WA13: Lymm 3B 84
Statham Rd. CH43: Bid 9C 56
WN8: Skel 9A 22
Statham Way L39: Orm 9C 20
Station App. CH46: More 7M 55
CH47: Meols 9F 54
L39: Orm 8D 20
L40: Burs 9J 15
(not continuous)
Station Av. CH66: Lit Sut 7H 103
WA6: Hel 1E 114
WN5: Orr 7N 31
Station Cl. CH64: Nest 7F 100
L25: Hunts X 9G 76
Station Cotts. M31: Part 5N 69
Station Ct. CH66: Lit Sut 7H 103
Station Grn. CH66: Lit Sut 7H 103
Station La. CH3: Lit Ba 9A 114
Station M. L32: Kirkb 8A 36
WN4: Garsw 8F 40
Station Pas. *L9: Walt* *6F 44*
(off Walton Pk.)
Station Rd. CH1: Lea B 9N 111
CH2: Elt 1M 113
CH2: Ince 9L 105
CH3: Moul 9K 115
CH41: Birke 8F 56
CH44: Wall 5G 56
CH47: Hoy 2C 70
CH60: Hesw 9N 87
CH61: Barn 2D 88
CH61: Thurs 3G 87
CH63: Store 2D 88
CH64: Nest 7E 100
(not continuous)
CH64: Park 6C 100
CH65: Ell P 8A 104
(not continuous)
CH66: Lit Sut 8H 103
L25: Gate 3E 76
L31: Lyd 6F 26
L31: Mag 3K 35
L31: Mell 8N 35
L34: Presc 3A 62
(not continuous)
L35: Rainh 6F 62
L36: Roby 7G 60
L39: Bart 6C 18
L39: Orm 7D 20
L40: Ruf 2N 15
M44: Irlam 2L 69
PR8: Ains 9J 11
PR9: Banks 2C 8
WA2: Padg 8H 67
WA4: Warr 6F 82
WA5: Gt San 3H 81
WA5: Penk 5F 80
WA7: Run 5J 95
WA7: Sut W 2D 108
WA8: Wid 4M 79
WA9: St H 2A 64
WA11: Hay 4E 50
WA14: Dun M 3N 85
WN4: Garsw 8E 40
WN8: Parb 3F 22
Station Rd. Ind. Est. WA4: Warr 6G 82
Station Rd. Nth. WA2: Fearn 7H 67
Station Rd. Sth. WA2: Padg 8H 67
Station St. L35: Rainh 6F 62
Statton Rd. L13: Liv 8N 59
Staveley Av. L40: Burs 1J 21
Staveley Rd. L19: Gras 8N 75
PR8: Ains 1K 17
WN8: Skel 1B 30
Stavert Cl. L11: Norr G 7N 45
Staverton Pk. L32: Kirkb 1A 46
Stavordale Rd. CH46: More 8N 55
Steble St. L8: Liv 3E 74
Steel Av. CH45: Wall 3J 57
Steel Ct. L5: Liv 4B 58
Steel St. WA1: Warr 1E 82
Steeple, The CH48: Caldy 1E 86
Steeplechase Cl. L9: Ain 2H 45
Steeple Ct. CH64: Nest 7E 100
Steeple Vw. L33: Kirkb 6C 36
Steers Cl. WA4: Westy 4J 83
Steers Cft. L28: Stockb V 1D 60
Steetley Dr. WA9: St H 5H 63
Stein Av. WA3: Low 2F 52
Steinberg Ct. L3: Liv 5B 58
Steley Way L34: Presc 4A 62
Stella Nova L20: Boot 7B 44
Stella Pct. L21: Sea 4N 43
Stenhills Cres. WA7: Run 5M 95
Stephens Gdns. CH66: Lit Sut 8G 102
Stephen's Gro. WA6: Hel 3E 114
Stephens La. L2: Liv 4E 4
Stephenson Ct. *L7: Liv* *8H 59*
(off Crosfield Rd.)
Stephenson Ho. L7: Liv 7N 5 (9F 58)
Stephenson Rd. L13: Liv 7M 59
WA12: Newt W 8L 51
Stephenson's Sankey Viaduct 8H 51
Stephenson Way L13: Wav 8K 59
L37: Form 1H 25
Stephens Ter. CH66: Lit Sut 8G 102
Stephen St. WA1: Warr 2E 82
Stephen Way L35: Rainh 4E 62
Stepney Gro. L4: Walt 9F 44
Sterling Way L5: Kirkd 3C 58
Sterndale Cl. L7: Liv 9G 59
Sterrix Av. L30: N'ton 9B 34
Sterrix Grn. L21: Lith 9B 34
Sterrix La. L21: Lith 9B 34
L30: N'ton 9B 34
Stetchworth Rd. WA4: Walt 7C 82
Steuber Dr. M44: Irlam 4M 69
Steve Biko Cl. L8: Liv 1G 75
Stevenage Cl. WA9: St H 2J 63
Stevenson Cres. WA10: St H 6G 49
Stevenson Dr. CH63: Spit 4M 89
Stevenson St. L15: Wav 9L 59
Stevens Rd. CH60: Hesw 8C 88
Stevens St. WA9: St H 1G 62
Steventon WA7: Nort 3G 96
Steward Ct. L35: Presc 4C 62
Stewards Av. WA8: Wid 8J 79
Stewart Av. L20: Boot 6D 44
Stewart Cl. CH61: Pens 4N 87
Stickens Lock La. M44: Irlam 1N 69
Stile Hey L23: Thorn 6A 34
Stiles, The L39: Orm 8C 20
Stiles Rd. L33: Kirkb 5D 36
Stillington Rd. L8: Liv 4F 74
Stiperstones Cl. CH66: Lit Sut 8F 102
Stirling Av. L23: Crosb 8L 33
Stirling Cl. WA1: Wools 1M 83
Stirling Ct. CH65: Ell P 2B 112
PR9: South 5M 7
Stirling Cres. WA9: St H 3L 63
Stirling Dr. WN4: Garsw 7F 40
Stirling La. L25: Hunts X 9H 77
Stirling Rd. L24: Speke 4F 92
Stirling St. CH44: Wall 7H 57
Stirrup Cl. WA2: Fearn 6H 67
Stirrup Fld. WA3: Golb 2B 52
STOAK 6E 112
Stoak Lodge CH65: Ell P 1A 112
Stobart Stadium, The 8J 79
Stockbridge La. L36: Huy 4F 60
(not continuous)
Stockbridge Pl. L5: Liv 4F 58
Stockbridge St. L5: Liv 4F 58
STOCKBRIDGE VILLAGE 1E 60
Stockdale Cl. L3: Liv 2E 4 (6B 58)
Stockdale Ct. WA5: Gt San 1G 81
Stockdale Dr. WA5: Gt San 1G 81
Stockham Cl. WA7: Halt 7C 96
Stockham La.
WA7: Brook, Halt, Murd, Pal F 7C 96
(not continuous)
Stockley Cres. L39: Bic 6J 29
Stockley La. WA4: Hghr Whi, Lwr S 8G 98
Stockmoor Rd. L11: Norr G 7L 45
Stockpit Rd. L33: Know I 9G 37
Stockport Rd. WA4: Grap, Thel 6K 83
Stocks Av. WA9: St H 7A 50
Stocks Court, The WA3: Low 2E 52
Stocks La. WA5: Gt San, Penk 3F 80
Stockswell Farm Ct. WA8: Wid 4H 79
Stockswell Rd. WA8: Wid 4C 78
Stockton Cres. L33: Kirkb 5B 36
Stockton Gro. WA9: St H 3G 63
STOCKTON HEATH 7E 82
Stockton La. WA4: Grap 7F 82
Stockton Vw. WA4: Warr 6C 82
Stockton Wood Rd. L24: Speke 4G 92
Stockville Rd. L18: Moss H 4C 76
Stoddart Rd. L4: Walt 8F 44
Stoke Cl. CH62: East 3D 102
Stoke Gdns. CH65: Ell P 1A 112
Stoker Way L9: Walt 5F 44
Stokesay CH43: Noct 2D 72
Stokesay Ct. CH65: Ell P 2C 112
Stokes Cl. L26: Halew 7L 77
Stokesley Av. L32: Kirkb 9A 36
Stokes St. WA3: Ris 4M 67
Stoke St. CH41: Birke 9H 57
Stoke Wlk. CH65: Ell P 1A 112
Stoneacre Gdns. WA4: App 3F 98
Stonebank Dr. CH64: Lit N 8G 100
Stonebarn Dr. L31: Mag 9H 27
Stone Barn La. WA7: Pal F 9C 96
Stonebridge La. L11: Crox 5N 45
Stoneby Dr. CH45: Wall 2G 56
Stonechat Cl. L27: N'ley 4J 77
WA3: Low 2F 52
WA7: Beech 1A 108
Stone Ct. WA11: Hay 4D 50
Stonecrop L18: Moss H 3C 76
WN6: Appl B 4N 23
Stonecrop Cl. WA3: Birchw 5K 67
WA7: Beech 2B 108
Stone Cross Dr. WA8: Wid 3H 79
Stonecross Dr. L35: Rainh 8G 62
Stone Cross La. Nth. WA3: Low 3D 52
Stone Cross La. Sth. WA3: Low 5D 52
STONE CROSS PARK 3C 52
Stonedale Cres. L11: Crox 6N 45
Stonedale Pk. L11: Crox 6M 45
Stonefield Rd. L14: Knott A 5D 60
Stonefont Cl. L9: Walt 7F 44
Stonegate Dr. L8: Liv 4E 74
Stone Hall La. WN8: Dalt 9J 23
Stonehaven WN3: Wins 1F 40
Stonehaven Cl. L16: Child 9D 60
Stonehaven Dr. WA2: Fearn 6H 67
Stone Hey L35: Whis 8A 62
Stonehey Dr. CH48: W Kir 7D 70
Stonehey Rd. L32: Kirkb 2C 46
Stonehey Wlk. L32: Kirkb 2C 46
Stonehill Av. CH63: Beb 1N 89
L4: Walt *3G 58*
(off Stonehill St.)
Stonehill Cl. WA4: App 3E 98
Stonehills Ct. WA7: Run 5M 95
Stonehills La. WA7: Run 5M 95
Stonehill St. L4: Walt 3G 58
Stonehouse M. L18: Aller 5B 76
Stonehouse Rd. CH44: Wall 4E 56
Stonelea WA7: Wind H 6D 96
Stoneleigh Cl. PR8: Ains 1J 17
Stoneleigh Ct. *WA4: Grap* *7L 83*
(off Cliff La.)
Stoneleigh Gdns. WA4: Grap 7L 83
Stoneleigh Gro. CH42: Rock F 8M 73
Stone Mason Cres. L39: Orm 8E 20
Stonemasons Ct. *L25: Woolt* *5E 76*
(off Clay Cross Rd.)
Stonemill Ri. WN6: Appl B 6N 23
Stone Pit Cl. WA3: Low 1G 52
Stone Pit La. WA3: Croft 8G 52
Stoneridge Ct. CH43: Bid 9C 56
Stone Sq. L20: Boot 5D 44
Stone St. L3: Liv 5A 58
L34: Presc 3A 62
Stonethwaite Cl. WN3: Wigan 1J 41
Stoneville Rd. L13: Liv 5M 59
Stoneway Ct. CH60: Hesw 6N 87
Stone Yd. Cl. L39: Orm 8D 20
Stoney Brow WN8: Roby M 1L 31
STONEYCROFT 5M 59
Stoneycroft L12: W Der 5N 59
Stoneycroft Cl. L13: Liv 4M 59
Stoneycroft Cres. L13: Liv 4M 59
Stoneygate La. WN6: Appl B 3L 23
Stoney Hey Rd. CH45: New B 2G 57
Stoneyhurst Av. L10: Ain 8H 35
Stoney La. L35: Rainh, Whis 5C 62
WN6: Wright 1F 22
WN8: Parb 1F 22
Stoney La. Ind. Est. L35: Rainh 6D 62
Stoney Vw. L35: Rainh 6E 62
Stonham Cl. CH49: Upton 3M 71
Stonyfield L30: N'ton 6D 34
Stony Holt WA7: Nort 7E 96
Stonyhurst Cl. WA11: St H 3L 49
Stonyhurst Cres. WA3: Cul 5L 53
Stonyhurst Rd. L25: Woolt 7F 76
Stopford St. L8: Liv 4E 74
Stopgate La. L9: Ain, Faz 6J 45
L33: Sim 5E 36
Store St. L20: Kirkd 9C 44
STORETON 2H 89
STORETON BRICKFIELDS 2E 88
Storeton Cl. CH43: Oxton 5H 73
Storeton La. CH61: Barn 4C 88
Storeton Rd. CH42: Tran 5H 73
CH43: Oxton 5H 73
Stormont Rd. L19: Garst 9N 75
Storrington Av. L11: Norr G 7N 45
Storrsdale Rd. L18: Moss H 5N 75
Stour Av. L35: Rainh 6F 62
Stourcliffe Rd. CH44: Wall 5G 56
Stour Ct. CH65: Ell P 7N 103
Stourport Cl. CH49: Grea 4K 71
Stourton Rd. L32: Kirkb 2C 46
PR8: Ains 1J 17
Stourton St. CH44: Wall 7J 57
Stourvale Rd. L26: Halew 9K 77
Stowe Av. L10: Ain 9K 35

Stowe Cl. L25: Hunts X 9E 76
Stowell St. L7: Liv 7K 5 (9E 58)
Stowford Cl. L12: W Der 8A 46
Strada Way L3: Liv 2K 5 (6E 58)
Stradbroke Cl. WA3: Low 3H 53
Strafford Dr. L20: Boot 6D 44
Straight Length WA6: Frod 6G 107
Straker Av. CH65: Ell P 8L 103
Strand, The L2: Liv 5D 4 (8B 58)
WN4: Ash M 7K 41
Strand Av. WN4: Ash M 7K 41
Strand Rd. CH47: Hoy 1C 70
L20: Boot 7N 43
(not continuous)
Strand Shop. Cen. L20: Boot 7B 44
Strand St. L1: Liv 6D 4 (8B 58)
L2: Liv 6D 4 (8B 58)
Strand Vw. L20: Boot 7N 43
Strange Rd. WN4: Garsw 8F 40
Stratford Cl. PR8: Ains 8G 11
Stratford Rd. CH64: Nest 8D 100
L19: Aig 8L 75
Strathallan Cl. CH60: Hesw 5M 87
Strathcona Rd. CH45: Wall 3J 57
L15: Wav 1K 75
Strathearn Rd. CH60: Hesw 9N 87
Strathlorne Cl. CH42: Tran 5M 73
Strathmore Av. WN4: Ash M 6J 41
Strathmore Dr. L23: Crosb 8L 33
Strathmore Gro. WA9: St H 3M 63
Strathmore Rd. L6: Liv 5H 59
Stratton Cl. CH45: Wall 3J 57
L18: Aller 6C 76
WA7: Brook 9D 96
Stratton Dr. WA9: St H 3G 62
Stratton Pk. WA8: Wid 3J 79
Stratton Rd. L32: Kirkb 1A 46
WA5: Gt San 3K 81
Stratton Wlk. L32: Kirkb 1A 46
Strauss Cl. L8: Liv 2G 75
Strawberry Cl. WA3: Birchw 5K 67
Strawberry Cross CH1: Back 5M 111
Strawberry Dr. CH66: Whit 5M 111
Strawberry Field 5C 76
Strawberry Grn. CH66: Whit 5M 111
Strawberry La. CH1: Moll 8H 111
Strawberry Pk. CH66: Whit 5M 111
Strawberry Rd. L11: Norr G 8K 45
Streatham Av. L18: Moss H 3L 75
Street Hey La. CH64: Will 4A 102
Stretford Cl. L33: Kirkb 6C 36
STRETTON 5E 98
Stretton Av. CH44: Wall 5G 57
WA3: Low 3F 52
WA9: St H 7B 50
WN5: Bil 6A 40
Stretton Cl. CH43: Oxton 5E 72
CH62: East 3D 102
L12: Crox 7E 46
Stretton Dr. PR9: South 7L 7
Stretton Grn. Distribution Pk.
WA4: App T 3L 99
Stretton Rd. WA4: App T, Stret 5E 98
Stretton Way L36: Huy 9M 61
Strickland Cl. WA4: Grap 9H 83
Strickland St. WA10: St H 5L 49
Stringer Cres. WA4: Westy 4F 82
Stringhey Rd. CH44: Wall 4J 57
Stroma Av. CH65: Ell P 5N 111
Stroma Rd. L18: Aller 7N 75
Stromford Cl. WA8: Wid 2K 79
Stromness Cl. WA2: Fearn 6J 67
Stroud Cl. CH49: Grea 5K 71
Stuart Av. CH46: More 8N 55
L25: Hunts X 9G 76
Stuart Cl. CH46: More 9A 56
Stuart Cres. WN5: Bil 6N 39
Stuart Dr. L14: Broad G 6C 60
WA4: Stockt H 6G 82
Stuart Gro. L20: Kirkd 9C 44
Stuart Rd. CH42: Tran 5K 73
L4: Walt 8D 44
L22: Water 9L 33
L23: Crosb 9L 33
L31: Mell 8N 35
WA7: Manor P 3D 96
WA10: Windle 4F 48
Stuart Rd. Nth. L20: Boot 7D 44
Stubbs La. CH43: Noct 5E 72
Stub La. L40: Burs 3E 20
STUBSHAW CROSS 6M 41
Studholme St. L20: Kirkd 2B 58
Studland Rd. L9: Faz 6K 45
Studley Ct. PR9: South 5J 7
Studley Rd. CH45: Wall 3E 56
Sturdee Rd. L13: Liv 8N 59
Sturgess Cl. L39: Orm 6D 20
Sturgess St. WA12: Newt W 7H 51
Sturton Av. WN3: Wigan 1G 41
Suburban Rd. L6: Liv 3H 59
Sudbrook Cl. WA3: Low 2F 52
Sudbury Cl. L25: Woolt 6H 77
WN3: Wigan 1K 41
Sudbury Gdns. WA9: St H 3F 62
Sudbury Rd. L22: Water 9H 33
Sudell Av. L31: Mag 1L 35
Sudell La. L31: Lyd 6J 27
L39: Augh 6J 27
Sudley Grange L17: Aig 7K 75
Sudley House 6L 75
Sudworth Rd. CH45: New B 2G 57
Suez St. WA1: Warr 3C 82
WA12: Newt W 7J 51
Suffield Rd. L4: Kirkd 1C 58
Suffolk Av. CH65: Ell P 9M 103
Suffolk Cl. WA1: Wools 2M 83
Suffolk Pl. WA8: Wid 9F 78
Suffolk Rd. PR8: Birkd 6N 11
Suffolk St. L1: Liv 8G 4 (9C 58)
L20: Boot 6C 44
WA7: Run 4J 95
Suffton Pk. L32: Kirkb 1A 46
Sugarbrook La. L10: Faz 5L 45
Sugar La. L34: Know 7G 47
WA6: Manl 8G 115
Sugar St. L9: Ain 5G 44
Sugar Stubbs La. PR9: Banks 3G 9
Sugnall St. L7: Liv 8K 5 (9E 58)
(not continuous)
Sulby Av. L13: Liv 4K 59
WA4: Warr 5C 82
Sulby Cl. PR8: Birkd 3M 11
Sulgrave Cl. L16: Child 8A 60
Sullington Dr. L27: N'ley 2J 77
(not continuous)
Sullivan Av. CH49: Upton 4N 71
Sullivan Rd. WA8: Wid 9N 79
Sullivans Way WA9: St H 1L 63
Sumley Cl. WA11: St H 5N 49
Summer Cl. WA7: Halt 6B 96
Summercroft Cl. WA3: Golb 3B 52
Summerfield CH62: Brom 5C 90
Summerfield Av. WA5: Warr 7A 66
WA10: Eccl 7C 48
Summerford Cl. CH42: Tran 5L 73
Summerhill Dr. L31: Mag 4L 35
Summer La.
WA4: Dares, Hatt, Pres H 9J 97
WA7: Halt 6B 96
Summer Rd. L20: Boot 5B 44
Summers Av. L20: Boot 6D 44
Summer Seat L3: Liv 1F 4 (5C 58)
L20: Boot 7N 43
Summers Rd. L3: Liv 3C 74
Summer St. WN8: Skel 1C 30
Summertrees Av. CH49: Grea 4L 71
Summertrees Cl. CH49: Grea 4L 71
Summertrees Rd. CH66: Gt Sut 3K 111
Summerville Gdns. WA4: Stockt H 7G 83
Summerwood CH61: Irby 9L 71
Summerwood Cl. L39: Hals 4H 19
Summit, The CH44: Wall 4J 57
Summit Cl. WA4: Lwr S 6F 98
Summit Way L25: Woolt 5D 76
Sumner Av. L39: Down 9E 18
Sumner Cl. L5: Liv 4B 58
L35: Rainh 8G 62
Sumner Gro. *L33: Kirkb 6D 36*
(off Mossdale Rd.)
Sumner Rd. CH43: Bid 9F 56
L37: Form 1F 24
Sumners Farm Ct. WA4: Pres H 9J 97
Sumner St. WA11: Hay 4C 50
Sunbeam Cl. WA7: Run 4J 95
Sunbeam Rd. L13: Liv 6M 59
Sunbeam St. WA12: Newt W 7L 51
Sunbourne Rd. L17: Aig 6G 75
Sunbury Dr. PR8: Ains 1H 17
Sunbury Gdns. WA4: App 9F 82
Sunbury Rd. CH44: Wall 6J 57
L4: Walt 2G 58
Sunbury St. WA10: St H 1F 62
Suncourt PR8: Birkd 9E 6
Suncroft Cl. WA1: Wools 1M 83
Suncroft Rd. CH60: Hesw 8C 88
Sundale Av. L35: Presc 3C 62
Sundene Lodge L22: Water 3L 43
Sundew Cl. L9: Walt 3E 44
Sundial Ho. WA3: Cul 7N 53
Sundridge St. L8: Liv 4F 74
Sunfield Cl. CH66: Gt Sut 2J 111
Sunfield Rd. CH46: More 7N 55
Sunfield Vw. PR9: Banks 4E 8
Sunflower Cl. WA9: Bold 2C 64
Sunflower Dr. WA5: Warr 5M 81
Sunlight St. L6: Liv 4H 59
Sunloch Cl. L9: Ain 2J 45
Sunningdale CH46: More 9A 56
Sunningdale Av. WA8: Wid 7E 78
Sunningdale Cl. L36: Roby 8G 61
WA5: Burtw 2H 65
Sunningdale Dr. CH61: Thing 2A 88
CH63: Brom 9A 90
L23: Blun 5J 33
Sunningdale Gdns. L37: Form 1E 24
Sunningdale Rd. CH45: Wall 1F 56
L15: Wav 9L 59
Sunningdale Way CH64: Lit N 9E 100
Sunniside La. WA7: Nort 3G 97
Sunny Bank CH63: Hghr B 1K 89
Sunnybank CH49: Upton 2N 71
Sunnybank Av. CH43: Noct 4D 72
Sunnybank Cl. WA12: Newt W 6L 51
Sunny Bank Rd. L16: Child 1B 76
Sunnydale L35: Rainh 6G 63
Sunnyfields L39: Orm 8E 20
WN3: Wins 1E 40
Sunnygate Rd. L19: Gras 8M 75
Sunnymede Dr. L31: Lyd 9J 27
Sunny Rd. PR9: South 5M 7
Sunnyside CH46: More 7L 55
CH65: Ell P 8A 104
L8: Liv 3G 74
L39: Augh 5A 28
PR8: Birkd 3M 11
WA5: Gt San 2G 81
Sunnyside Ct. PR9: South 6H 7
Sunnyside Rd. L23: Crosb 8J 33
WN4: Ash M 5H 41
Sunrise Cl. L19: Gras 9N 75
Sunsdale Rd. L18: Moss H 3M 75
Sunset Blvd. WA5: Gt San 2K 81
Sunset Cl. *L33: Kirkb 6E 36*
(off Freckleton Dr.)
Sunset Cotts. CH64: Ness 9G 100
Superbowl
Widnes 9L 79
Superior Cl. L27: N'ley 3J 77
Surby Cl. L16: Child 9C 60
Surlingham Gdns.
WA9: St H 3H 63
Surrey Av. CH49: Upton 3M 71
Surrey Cl. PR9: South 2A 8
Surrey Dr. CH48: W Kir 8D 70
Surrey St. CH44: Wall 6G 57
L1: Liv 8F 4 (9C 58)
L20: Boot 6C 44
WA4: Warr 5E 82
WA7: Run 5K 95
WA9: St H 7N 49
Susan Dr. WA5: Penk 3F 80
Susan Gro. CH46: More 9L 55
Susan St. WA8: Wid 6M 79
Susan Wlk. L35: Whis 4C 62
Sussex Cl. CH61: Pens 3M 87
L20: Boot 6C 44
Sussex Gro. WA9: St H 8N 49
Sussex Rd. CH48: W Kir 5D 70
L31: Mag 4J 35
M31: Part 7L 69
M44: Cad 3J 69
PR8: South 9J 7
PR9: South 8H 7
Sussex St. L20: Boot 6C 44
L22: Water 9J 33
WA8: Wid 7N 79
Sutch La. L40: Lath 1M 21
WA13: Lymm 5G 84
Sutcliffe St. L6: Liv 6G 59
Sutherland Ct. WA7: Run 5L 95
Sutherland Dr. CH62: East 2C 102
Sutherland Rd. L34: Presc 3B 62
SUTTON 1B 64
Sutton Av. CH64: Nest 8E 100
WA3: Cul 6M 53
Sutton C'way. WA6: Frod 4A 108
Sutton Cl. CH62: East 3D 102
Sutton Fields Golf Driving Range 2E 108
Sutton Fold WA9: St H 1N 63
Sutton Fold Ind. Pk.
WA9: St H 1A 64
SUTTON GREEN 2H 111
Sutton Hall Dr. CH66: Lit Sut 8F 102
Sutton Hall Gdns.
CH66: Lit Sut 8F 102
Sutton Hall Golf Course 3C 108
SUTTON HEATH 2J 63
Sutton Heath Rd. WA9: St H 3H 63
SUTTON LEACH 4N 63
Sutton Leisure Cen. 3L 63
SUTTON MANOR 7L 63
Sutton Manor 7M 63
Sutton Moss Rd. WA9: St H 1B 64
Sutton Oak Dr. WA9: St H 9N 49
Sutton Pk. Dr. WA9: St H 2M 63
Sutton Quays Bus. Pk.
WA7: Sut W 3A 108
Sutton Rd. CH45: New B 2H 57
L37: Form 3E 24
WA9: St H 9M 49
Suttons La. L37: Gt Alt 2L 25
WA8: Wid 9L 79
Sutton St. L13: Liv 4K 59
WA1: Warr 4D 82
WA7: Run 5L 95
Suttons Way *L26: Halew 7J 77*
(off Betony Cl.)
Sutton Way CH65: Gt Sut, Whit 9L 103
CH66: Gt Sut 1J 111
SUTTON WEAVER 3D 108
Sutton Wood Rd. L24: Speke 4G 92
Suzanne Boardman Ho. L6: Liv 4H 59
Swainson Rd. L10: Faz 3L 45
Swale Av. L35: Rainh 6F 62
Swaledale Av. L35: Rainh 6G 62
Swaledale Cl. CH62: East 1D 102
WA5: Gt San 1H 81
Swalegate L31: Mag 1H 35
Swale Rd. CH65: Ell P 7M 103
Swallow Cl. L12: Crox 7D 46
L27: N'ley 3K 77
L33: Kirkb 4C 36
WA3: Birchw 5N 67
Swallow Ct. WA10: St H 7G 48
Swallowfield Gdns. WA4: App 2G 98
Swallow Flds. L9: Faz 6L 45
Swallowhurst Cres. L11: Norr G 8M 45
Swanage Cl. WA4: Stockt H 6F 82
Swan All. *L39: Orm 8C 20*
(off Burscough St.)
Swan Av. WA9: St H 8C 50
Swan Cl. CH66: Gt Sut 3J 111
L40: Scar 5N 13
Swan Ct. CH43: Pren 6F 72
Swan Cres. L15: Wav 9N 59
Swan Delph L39: Augh 2A 28
Swanfield Wlk. *WA3: Golb 1A 52*
(off Walters Grn. Cres.)
Swan Gdns. WA9: St H 3H 63
Swan Hey L31: Mag 4K 35
Swan La. L39: Augh 6K 27
Swanpool La. L39: Augh 3A 28
Swan Rd. WA12: Newt W 6F 50
Swansea Cl. L19: Garst 1N 91
SWANSIDE 6C 60
Swanside Av. L14: Broad G 6C 60
Swanside Pde. L14: Knott A 6C 60
Swanside Rd. L14: Broad G 6C 60
Swanston Av. L4: Walt 9F 44
Swan St. L13: Liv 6L 59
Swan Wlk. L31: Mag 4K 35
Sweden Gro. L22: Water 1K 43
Sweet Briar Cl. WA9: Clock F 7N 63
Sweetfield Gdns. CH66: Lit Sut 7J 103
Sweetfield Rd.
CH66: Lit Sut 7J 103
Sweeting St. L2: Liv 5E 4 (8B 58)
Swift Cl. WA2: Warr 6F 66
Swift Gro. L12: Crox 6D 46
Swift's Cl. L30: N'ton 7C 34
Swifts Fold WN8: Skel 4A 30
Swifts La. L30: N'ton 7C 34
Swift St. WA10: St H 5K 49
Swift's Weint *CH64: Park 5B 100*
(off Coastguard La.)
Swinbrook Grn. L11: Norr G 7L 45
Swinburne Cl. L16: Child 9D 60
Swinburne Rd. WA10: St H 5G 48
Swinburn Gro. WN5: Bil 2N 39
Swindale Av. WA2: Warr 6C 66
Swindale Cl. L8: Liv 1G 74
Swinden Cl. WA7: Wind H 5F 96
Swinderby Dr. L31: Mell 8N 35
Swindon Cl. CH49: Grea 4K 71
L5: Kirkd 2C 58
Swindon St. L5: Kirkd 2C 58
Swineyard La.
WA16: High L 3N 99
Swinford Av. WA8: Wid 6A 80
Swinhoe Pl. WA3: Cul 7L 53
Swireford Rd. WA6: Hel 3E 114
Swisspine Gdns. WA9: St H 2F 62
Swiss Rd. L6: Liv 6H 59
Switch Island L30: N'ton 6G 35
Switch Island Leisure Pk.
L30: N'ton 8F 34
Sword Cl. L11: Crox 7A 46
Swordfish Cl. L40: Burs 1F 20
Sword Meanygate PR4: Tarl 2M 9
Sword Wlk. L11: Crox 7A 46
Swynnerton Way WA8: Wid 3L 79
Sybil Rd. L4: Walt 2F 58
Sycamore Av. CH49: Upton 1L 71
L23: Crosb 5M 33
L26: Halew 1K 93
WA3: Golb 1B 52
WA8: Wid 6L 79
WA11: Hay 5C 50
WA12: Newt W 7L 51
Sycamore Cl. CH49: Upton 1L 71
L9: Walt 7H 45
PR9: Banks 1F 8
WA10: Eccl 6E 48
Sycamore Ct. *L8: Liv 4F 74*
(off Weller Way)
WA7: Manor P 3F 96
Sycamore Cres. WA3: Rix 7H 69
(not continuous)
Sycamore Dr. CH66: Whit 4L 111
L33: Kirkb 8D 36
WA7: Sut W 2C 108
WA13: Lymm 4D 84
WN3: Wins 1D 40
WN8: Skel 2B 30
Sycamore Gdns. WA10: St H 4H 49
Sycamore Gro. L37: Form 3C 24
Sycamore La. WA5: Gt San 2K 81
(not continuous)
Sycamore Pk. L18: Aller 6B 76
Sycamore Ri. CH49: Grea 6K 71
Sycamore Rd. CH42: Tran 4K 73
L22: Water 9L 33
L36: Huy 9J 61
M31: Part 6K 69
WA7: Run 7M 95
Syddall St. WA10: St H 3J 49
Sydenham Av. L17: Liv 3H 75
Sydenham Ho. L17: Aig 3J 75
Syder's Gro. L34: Know 7G 47
Sydney Av. WN7: Leigh 1L 53
Sydney St. L9: Ain 4F 44
WA7: West P 8G 95
Syers Ct. WA1: Warr 1F 82
Sylvan Ct. L25: Woolt 7F 76
Sylvandale Gro. CH62: Brom 5C 90
Sylvania Rd. L4: Walt 8F 44
Sylvia Cl. L10: Faz 4N 45
Sylvia Cres. WA2: Warr 8E 66
Synge St. WA2: Warr 1D 82
Syren St. L20: Kirkd 1B 58

Syston Av. WA11: St H 4M 49
Sytchcroft CH64: Nest 6E 100

T

Tabby Nook PR4: Mere B 6K 9
Tabby's Nook WN8: Newb 4D 22
Tabley Av. WA8: Wid 6F 78
Tabley Cl. CH43: Oxton 6F 72
Tabley Gdns. WA9: St H 3G 62
Tabley Rd. L15: Wav 1J 75
Tabley St. L1: Liv 9F 4 (9C 58)
Tace Cl. L8: Liv 1E 74
Tadlow Cl. L37: Form 3C 24
Taggart Av. L16: Child 2B 76
Tagus Cl. L8: Liv 2G 75
Tagus St. L8: Liv 2G 75
Tailor's La. L31: Mag 3K 35
Talaton Cl. PR9: South 2M 7
Talbot Av. CH63: Brim 6G 88
CH64: Lit N 8F 100
Talbot Cl. CH64: Lit N 8F 100
WA3: Birchw 6M 67
WA10: St H 6J 49
Talbot Ct. CH43: Oxton 4G 73
L36: Huy 8J 61
Talbot Dr. PR8: South 9G 6
Talbot Gdns. CH64: Lit N 8F 100
Talbot Rd. CH43: Oxton 4G 72
CH66: Gt Sut 2L 111
WA6: Dun H 6B 114
Talbot St. PR8: South 1N 11
WA3: Golb 2B 52
Talbotville Rd. L13: Liv 8A 60
Talgarth Way L25: Gate 1E 76
Taliesin St. L5: Liv 4C 58
Talisman Cl. WA7: Murd 8G 96
Talisman Way L20: Boot 6N 43
Talland Cl. L26: Halew 7J 77
Tallarn Rd. L32: Kirkb 9N 35
Tallow Way M44: Irlam 1N 69
Tall Trees WA9: St H 1L 63
Talman Gro. WN4: Ash M 8M 41
Talton Rd. L15: Wav 1J 75
Tamar Cl. L6: Liv 5F 58
Tamar Gro. CH46: More 9L 55
Tamarisk Gdns. WA9: St H 2F 62
Tamar Rd. WA11: Hay 4E 50
Tame Ct. WA8: Wid 3K 79
Tamerton Cl. L18: Aller 6C 76
Tamneys, The WN8: Skel 3C 30
Tam O'Shanter Urban Farm 1E 72
Tamworth St. L8: Liv 3D 74
WA10: St H 6H 49
WA12: Newt W 7J 51
Tanar Cl. CH63: Spit 4A 90
Tanat Dr. L18: Moss H 4N 75
Tancaster WN8: Skel 3B 30
Tancred Rd. CH45: Wall 4G 56
L4: Walt 2F 58
Tanfield Nook WN8: Parb 3F 22
Tanfields WN8: Skel 3C 30
TANHOUSE 3G 30
Tanhouse WA7: Halt 6A 96
Tan Ho. Cl. WN8: Parb 2F 22
Tan Ho. Dr. WN3: Wins 1E 40
Tan Ho. La. WA5: Burtw 5H 65
WA8: Wid 8M 79
WN3: Wins 1E 40
WN8: Parb 3F 22
Tanhouse Rd. L23: Thorn 6A 34
WN8: Skel 4F 30
Tankersley Gro. WA5: Gt San 3J 81
Tanners La. WA2: Warr 2B 82
WA3: Golb 2B 52
Tannery Ct. WA2: Warr 2C 82
Tannery La. CH64: Nest 6E 100
WA5: Penk 5E 80
Tanning Ct. WA1: Warr 4C 82
Tan Pit Cotts. WN3: Wins 1F 40
Tan Pit La. WN3: Wins 1F 40
Tansley Cl. CH48: W Kir 6F 70
Tanworth Gro. CH46: More 8J 55
Tapestry Gdns. CH41: Birke 8F 56
Tapley Pl. L13: Liv 7L 59
Taplow Cl. WA4: App 1F 98
Taplow St. L6: Liv 3G 59
Tapton Way L13: Wav 8L 59
Tara Pk. Caravan Site L3: Liv . . . 1C 4 (6A 58)
TARBOCK GREEN 4N 77
Tarbock Interchange L35: Whis 9N 61
Tarbock Rd. L24: Speke 3H 93
L36: Huy 8H 61
Tarbot Hey CH46: More 9K 55
Tarbrock Ct. *L30: N'ton 6C 34*
(off Great Hey)
Target Rd. CH60: Hesw 7J 87
Tariff St. L5: Liv 4C 58
Tarleton Cl. L26: Halew 9J 77
TARLETON MOSS 1M 9
Tarleton Rd. PR9: South 7M 7
Tarleton St. L1: Liv 5F 4 (8C 58)
TARLSCOUGH 5G 15
Tarlscough La. L40: Burs 5G 15
Tarlswood WN8: Skel 3C 30
Tarlton Cl. L35: Rainh 4D 62
Tarnbeck WA7: Nort 8E 96
Tarn Brow L39: Orm 1A 28
Tarncliff L28: Stockb V 1G 60
Tarn Cl. WN4: Ash M 6K 41
Tarn Ct. WA1: Wools 1N 83
Tarn Gro. WA11: St H 2L 49
Tarnmere Cl. L4: Walt 7F 44
Tarnrigg Cl. WN3: Wigan 1G 40
Tarn Rd. L37: Form 1D 24
Tarnside Rd. WN5: Orr 6N 31
Tarnway WA3: Low 3G 52
Tarporley Cl. CH43: Oxton 5F 72
WA10: Eccl 7E 48
Tarporley Rd. CH66: Gt Sut 1K 111
WA4: Stret, Lwr W, Nor B 5E 98
(not continuous)
Tarragon Cl. L23: Thorn 6A 34
Tarran Dr. CH46: More 7L 55
Tarran Rd. CH46: More 7L 55
Tarrant Cl. WN3: Wins 1F 40
Tarran Way E. CH46: More 7L 55
Tarran Way Nth. CH46: More 7L 55
Tarran Way Sth. CH46: More 7L 55
Tarran Way W. CH46: More 6L 55
Tarves Wlk. L33: Kirkb 9D 36
Tarvin Cl. CH65: Ell P 1A 112
PR9: South 2B 8
WA3: Low 3F 52
WA7: Run 9M 95
WA9: Sut M 5L 63
Tarvin Rd. CH62: East 2E 102
WA6: Alv, Frod 3G 115
WA6: Manl 9K 115
Tasker Ter. L35: Rainh 5F 62
Tasman Cl. WA5: Old H 9L 65
Tasman Gro. WA9: St H 2H 63
Tate Cl. WA8: Wid 6G 79
Tate Liverpool 7C 4 (9A 58)
Tate St. L4: Walt 1E 58
Tatham Gro. WN3: Wins 2F 40
Tatlock Cl. WN5: Bil 6A 40
Tatlocks Grange L39: Orm 7B 20
Tatlock St. L5: Liv 5B 58
Tattersall Pl. L20: Boot 8A 44
Tattersall Rd. L21: Lith 3N 43
Tattersall Way L7: Liv 7K 59
Tatton Ct. WA1: Wools 9L 67
Tatton Dr. WN4: Ash M 6H 41
Tatton Rd. CH42: Tran 3K 73
L9: Walt 4F 44
Taunton Av. WA9: Sut L 4N 63
Taunton Dr. L10: Ain 9K 35
Taunton Rd. CH45: Wall 3E 56
L36: Huy 7M 61
Taunton St. L15: Wav 9K 59
Taurus Pk. WA5: Westb 5M 65
Taurus Rd. L14: Knott A 5E 60
Tavener Cl. CH63: Brom 1B 102
Tavington Rd. L26: Halew 7L 77
Tavistock Dr. PR8: Ains 8H 11
Tavistock Rd. CH45: Wall 3E 56
WA5: Penk 4G 80
Tavlin Av. WA5: Warr 8A 66
Tavy Rd. L6: Liv 5F 58
TAWD BRIDGE 5F 30
Tawd Rd. WN8: Skel 4F 30
Tawd St. L4: Kirkd 1D 58
Tawny Ct. WA7: Pal F 8A 96
Tayleur Ter. WA12: Newt W 8M 51
Taylforth Cl. L9: Walt 5F 44
Taylor Av. L39: Orm 8E 20
Taylor Bus. Pk. WA3: Ris 8N 53
Taylor Cl. WA9: St H 1A 64
Taylor Rd. WA11: Hay 4G 51
Taylors Cl. L9: Walt 7D 44
Taylors La. L9: Walt 7D 44
PR4: Tarl 4N 9
WA5: Cuerd 6C 80
Taylor's Meanygate PR4: Hesk B, Tarl 1L 9
Taylors Row WA7: Run 5M 95
Taylor St. CH41: Birke 1L 73
L5: Liv 4C 58
WA3: Golb 1D 52
(off Lowton Rd.)
WA4: Warr 7B 82
WA8: Wid 7M 79
WA9: St H 1A 64
WN8: Skel 3N 29
Taylor St. Ind. Est. L5: Liv 4D 58
Teakwood Cl. L6: Liv 4G 58
Teal Bus. Pk. WA8: Wid 8M 79
Teal Cl. L39: Augh 2A 28
WA2: Warr 6F 66
WA11: St H 4L 49
Teal Gro. L26: Halew 7J 77
WA3: Birchw 6N 67
Teals Way CH60: Hesw 7L 87
Tears La. WN8: Newb 5C 22
Teasville Rd. L18: Moss H 4C 76
Tebay Cl. L31: Mag 1L 35
Tebay Rd. CH62: East 7D 90
Teck St. L7: Liv 4N 5 (7F 58)
Tedburn Cl. L25: Gate 4G 77
Tedbury Cl. L32: Kirkb 2C 46
Tedbury Wlk. L32: Kirkb 2C 46
Tedder Av. PR9: South 8M 7
Tedder Sq. WA8: Wid 8G 78
Teddington Cl. WA4: App 2F 98
Teehey Cl. CH63: Hghr B 1K 89
Teehey Gdns. CH63: Hghr B 1K 89
Teehey La. CH63: Hghr B 1K 89
Tees Cl. L4: Kirkd 9D 44
Tees Ct. CH65: Ell P 7M 103
Teesdale Cl. WA5: Gt San 1H 81
Teesdale Rd. CH63: Beb 3L 89
WA11: Hay 3E 50
Teesdale Way L35: Rainh 4F 62
Tees Pl. L4: Kirkd 9D 44
Tees St. CH41: Birke 8F 56
L4: Kirkd 9C 44
Teign Cl. L6: Liv 5F 58
Teignmouth Cl. L19: Garst 1N 91
Teilo St. L8: Liv 3F 74
Telary Cl. L5: Liv 4B 58
Telegraph Ho. L23: Crosb 6L 33
Telegraph La. CH45: Wall 4C 56
Telegraph Rd. CH48: Caldy 9G 71
CH60: Hesw 9G 71
CH61: Thurs 9G 71
Telegraph Way L32: Kirkb 9C 36
Telford Cl. CH43: Oxton 4H 73
WA4: Westy 5J 83
WA8: Wid 4G 78
Telford Ct. CH1: Dunk 7J 111
L7: Liv 8G 58
Telford Dr. WA9: St H 2B 64
Telford Rd. CH65: Ell P 1C 112
Telford's Quay CH65: Ell P 7B 104
Telletholme Ind. Est. L40: Burs 2F 20
Tempest Hey L2: Liv 4D 4 (7B 58)
Temple Ct. L2: Liv 5E 4 (8B 58)
WA3: Ris 3M 67
Temple La. L2: Liv 4E 4 (7B 58)
Templemartin *WN8: Skel 2C 30*
(off Thorpe)
Templemore Av. L18: Moss H 5M 75
Templemore Rd. CH43: Oxton 4G 73
Temple Rd. CH42: Tran 6J 73
Temple St. L2: Liv 4E 4 (7B 58)
Templeton Cres. L12: W Der 9N 45
Templeton Dr. WA2: Fearn 6H 67
Tenbury Cl. WA5: Gt San 9J 65
Tenbury Dr. WN4: Ash M 7H 41
Tenby WN8: Skel 2B 30
Tenby Av. L21: Lith 1N 43
Tenby Cl. WA5: Call 7A 66
Tenby Dr. CH46: More 9N 55
WA7: Run 5N 95
Tennis St. WA10: St H 5H 49
Tennis St. Nth. WA10: St H 5H 49
Tennyson Av. CH42: Rock F 7M 73
Tennyson Dr. L39: Orm 7B 20
WA2: Warr 7D 66
WN5: Bil 2N 39
Tennyson Rd. CH65: Whit 1M 111
L36: Huy 9L 61
WA8: Wid 7K 79
Tennyson St. L20: Boot 5A 44
WA9: Sut M 7K 63
Tennyson Way L32: Kirkb 1B 46
Tenpin
Bootle 8F 34
Ellesmere Port 4B 112
Tensing Cl. WA5: Gt San 9K 65
Tensing Rd. L31: Mag 2J 35
Tenterden St. L5: Liv 5C 58
Tenth Av. L9: Ain 3J 45
Terence Av. WA1: Padd 2G 83
Terence Rd. L16: Child 2B 76
Terminus Rd. CH62: Brom 4C 90
L36: Huy 4F 60
Tern Cl. L33: Kirkb 4C 36
WA8: Wid 4L 79
Ternhall Rd. L9: Faz 6L 45
Ternhall Way L9: Faz 6L 45
Tern Way CH46: More 8J 55
WA10: St H 2D 62
Terrace Rd. WA8: Wid 2K 95
Terret Cft. L28: Stockb V 2F 60
Tetbury St. CH41: Birke 3J 73
Tetchill Cl. CH66: Gt Sut 3J 111
WA7: Nort 7F 96
Tetlow St. L4: Walt 1E 58
Tetlow Way L4: Walt 1E 58
Teulon Cl. L4: Walt 1E 58
Teversham WN8: Skel 2C 30
Teviot WN8: Skel 2B 30
Tewit Hall Cl. L24: Speke 4G 93
Tewit Hall Rd. L24: Speke 4G 92
Tewkesbury *WN8: Skel 2B 30*
(off Tenby)
Tewkesbury Cl. CH66: Gt Sut 5K 111
L12: Crox 6D 46
L25: Woolt 6H 77
Tewkesbury Rd. WA3: Golb 2C 52
Teynham Av. L34: Know 6H 47
Teynham Cres. L11: Norr G 8L 45
Thackeray Cl. L8: Liv 2E 74
Thackeray Ct. *L8: Liv 2E 74*
(off Pomfret St.)
Thackeray Gdns. L30: Boot 2C 44
Thackray Rd. WA10: St H 1G 62
Thames Av. WN7: Leigh 1N 53
Thames Cl. WA2: Warr 7E 66
Thamesdale CH65: Whit 2N 111
Thames Gdns. CH65: Whit 2M 111
Thames Rd. WA3: Cul 8N 53
WA9: Sut L 3M 63
Thames Side CH65: Whit 2N 111
Thames St. L8: Liv 2G 74
Thames Trad. Cen. M44: Irlam 2M 69
Thanet WN8: Skel 2C 30
Thatchers Mt. WA5: Coll G 9F 50
THATTO HEATH 1H 63
Thatto Heath Rd. WA9: St H 1G 62
WA10: St H 1G 62
Thatto Heath Station (Rail) 1G 62
The . . . . . .
Names prefixed with 'The' for example 'The Academy' are indexed under the main name such as 'Academy, The'
Thealby Cl. WN8: Skel 2B 30
THELWALL 5L 83
Thelwall La. WA4: Warr, Westy 5G 82
Thelwall New Rd. WA4: Grap, Thel 5H 83
Thelwall New Rd. Ind. Est.
WA4: Thel 4K 83
Thelwall Rd. CH66: Gt Sut 1K 111
Thermal Rd. CH62: Brom 3C 90
Thermopylae Ct. CH43: Noct 2D 72
Thermopylae Pas. CH43: Noct 2D 72
Thetford Rd. WA5: Gt San 2G 81
Thewlis St. WA5: Warr 3N 81
Thickwood Moss La. WA11: Rainf 6C 38
THINGWALL 1A 88
Thingwall Av. L14: Knott A 7B 60
Thingwall Dr. CH61: Irby 1A 88
Thingwall Grange CH61: Thing 1B 88
Thingwall Hall Dr. L14: Broad G 7B 60
Thingwall La. L14: Knott A, Broad G 6B 60
Thingwall Recreation Cen. 1B 88
Thingwall Rd. CH61: Irby 1L 87
L15: Wav 1N 75
Thingwall Rd. E. CH61: Thing 1A 88
Third Av. CH43: Bid 2B 72
L9: Ain 3J 45
(Fourth Av.)
L9: Ain 3K 45
(Meres Rd.)
L23: Crosb 7K 33
WA7: Pal F 7B 96
Third St. WN2: Bam 4N 41
Thirlmere Av. CH43: Noct 2C 72
L21: Lith 2C 44
L37: Form 2G 25
WA2: Warr 6D 66
WA11: St H 2K 49
WN4: Ash M 7L 41
WN8: Uph 5L 31
Thirlmere Cl. L31: Mag 1K 35
WA6: Frod 6N 107
Thirlmere Ct. *L5: Liv 4F 58*
(off Harding Cl.)
Thirlmere Dr. CH45: Wall 4H 57
L21: Lith 2C 44
PR8: Ains 2H 17
WA13: Lymm 5F 84
Thirlmere Grn. L5: Liv 4F 58
Thirlmere M. L38: Hight 8G 25
Thirlmere Rd. CH64: Nest 8E 100
CH65: Whit 3N 111
L5: Liv 4F 58
L38: Hight 8G 24
M31: Part 5L 69
WA3: Golb 1D 52
Thirlmere Wlk. L33: Kirkb 7B 36
Thirlmere Way WA8: Wid 8F 78
Thirlstane St. L17: Aig 5G 75
Thirsk WN8: Skel 2C 30
Thirsk Cl. WA7: Run 9M 95
Thirty Acre La. L37: Form 8K 17
Thistle Ct. L40: Burs 8J 15
Thistledown Cl. L17: Aig 5F 74
Thistle Sq. M31: Part 7L 69
Thistleton Av. CH41: Birke 9F 56
Thistleton Cl. WA9: St H 6A 50
Thistleton M. PR9: South 7H 7
Thistle Wlk. *M31: Part 7L 69*
(off Thistle Sq.)
Thistlewood Rd. L7: Liv 7K 59
Thistley Hey Rd. L32: Kirkb 9D 36
Thomas Cl. CH65: Whit 3N 111
L19: Garst 2A 92
Thomas Ct. CH43: Oxton 3J 73
WA7: Pal F 8B 96
Thomas Dr. L14: Broad G 7A 60
L35: Presc 5N 61
Thomas Jones Way WA7: Run 5K 95
Thomas La. L14: Broad G, Knott A 5B 60
Thomas More Dr. PR8: Ains 8L 11
Thomason's Bri. La. WA4: Hghr Wal 1N 97
Thomas Steers Way L1: Liv 7E 4 (8B 58)
Thomas St. CH41: Birke 3L 73
WA3: Golb 2B 52
WA7: Run 4L 95
WA8: Wid 9K 79
Thomaston St. L5: Liv 3D 58
(not continuous)
Thomas Winder Ct. *L5: Kirkd 3C 58*
(off Sterling Way)
Thompson Av. L39: Orm 8E 20
WA3: Cul 7M 53
Thompson Cl. WA12: Newt W 9L 51
Thompson St. CH41: Tran 4L 73
WA3: Ris 4M 67
WA10: St H 9G 48
WN4: Ash M 7M 41
Thomson Rd. L21: Sea 3M 43
(not continuous)
Thomson St. L6: Liv 5G 58
Thorburn Cl. CH62: New F 8A 74
Thorburn Ct. CH62: New F 7A 74
Thorburn Cres. CH62: New F 8A 74

Thorburn Dr. L7: Liv .8G 59
Thorburn Lodge CH62: New F .7A 74
Thorburn Rd. CH62: New F .8A 74
Thoresby Cl. WN3: Wigan .1G 41
Thorlby Rd. WA3: Cul .7N 53
Thorley Cl. L15: Wav .8M 59
Thornaby Gro. WA9: St H .3G 62
Thornbeck Av. L38: Hight .9F 24
Thornbeck Cl. L12: Crox .7D 46
Thornbridge Av. L21: Lith .2C 44
L40: Burs .2J 21
Thornbrook Cl. L12: W Der .2B 60
Thornbury WN8: Skel .2C 30
Thornbury Av. WA3: Low .3F 52
Thornbury Rd. L4: Walt .2H 59
Thornbush Cl. WA3: Low .1F 52
Thornby WN8: Skel .2C 30
Thorncliffe Rd. CH44: Wall .6G 56
Thorn Cl. WA5: Penk .5H 81
WA7: Run .8M 95
Thorncroft Dr. CH61: Barn .3B 88
Thorndale WN8: Skel .2C 30
Thorndale Rd. L22: Water .9K 33
Thorndyke Cl. L35: Rainh .8H 63
Thorne Dr. CH66: Lit Sut .9G 103
Thorne La. CH44: Wall .4F 56
Thornes Rd. L6: Liv .6G 58
Thorness Cl. CH49: Grea .6K 71
Thorneycroft Dr. WA1: Warr .2D 82
Thorneycroft St. CH41: Birke .9G 56
Thornfield Cl. WA3: Golb .2D 52
Thornfield Hey CH63: Spit .5N 89
Thornfield Rd. L9: Walt .5E 44
L23: Thorn .5N 33
Thornham Av. WA9: St H .1M 63
Thornham Cl. CH49: Upton .1A 72
Thornhead La. L12: W Der .3B 60
Thornhill WN8: Skel .2C 30
Thornhill Cl. L39: Augh .4N 27
Thornhill Rd. L15: Wav .1M 75
WN4: Garsw .7E 40
Thornholme Cres. L11: Norr G .9M 45
Thornhurst L32: Kirkb .3C 46
Thornleigh Av. CH62: East .3E 102
Thornleigh Dr. CH66: Ell P .8K 103
Thornley Cl. WA13: Lymm .5C 84
Thornley Rd. CH46: More .1K 71
WA13: Lymm .5C 84
Thornridge CH46: More .9A 56
Thorn Rd. WA1: Padd .9H 67
WA7: Run .8M 95
WA10: St H .7F 48
Thorns, The L31: Mag .1G 35
Thorns Dr. CH49: Grea .6K 71
Thornside Wlk. L25: Gate .4F 76
THORNTON .5N 33
Thornton WA8: Wid .8H 79
WN8: Skel .2C 30
Thornton Av. CH63: Hghr B .8K 73
L20: Boot .3C 44
Thornton Cl. L40: Ruf .2N 15
WA3: Low .1H 53
WN4: Ash M .7H 41
WN7: Leigh .1N 53
Thornton Comn. Rd.
CH63: Raby M, Thorn H .8H 89
Thornton Crematorium L23: Thorn .5B 34
Thornton Cres. CH60: Hesw .9B 88
Thorntondale Dr. WA5: Gt San .1G 81
Thornton Grn. La. CH2: Thorn M .3J 113
Thornton Gro. CH63: Hghr B .8K 73
THORNTON HOUGH .9H 89
THORNTON-LE-MOORS .3J 113
Thornton M. CH66: Chil T .6G 102
Thornton Rd. CH45: Wall .3G 56
CH63: Hghr B .8K 73
CH65: Ell P .1B 112
L16: Child .8C 60
L20: Boot .5B 44
(not continuous)
PR9: South .8L 7
WA5: Gt San .4K 81
Thornton St. CH41: Birke .9G 56
L21: Lith .4A 44
Thorn Tree Cl. L24: Hale .6B 94
Thorntree Cl. L17: Aig .5F 74
Thorntree Grn. WA4: App T .2J 99
Thorn Wlk. M31: Part .7L 69
Thornwood WN8: Skel .2C 30
Thornwood Cl. L6: Liv .4G 58
Thornwythe Gro. CH66: Gt Sut .1K 111
Thornycroft Rd. L15: Wav .1J 75
Thoroughgood Cl. L40: Burs .3H 21
Thorpe WN8: Skel .2C 30
Thorpe Bank CH42: Rock F .8M 73
Thorstone Dr. CH61: Irby .9K 71
Thorsway CH42: Rock F .6M 73
CH48: Caldy .8E 70
Threadneedle Ct. WA9: St H .1B 64
Three Acres Cl. L25: Woolt .5C 76
Three Butt La. L12: W Der .3L 59
THREE LANES END .3J 71
Three Oaks Cl. L40: Lath .3M 21
Three Pools PR9: South .4A 8
(not continuous)
Three Sisters Enterprise Park, The
WN4: Ash M .5K 41
Three Sisters Race Circuit .4L 41
Three Sisters Rd. WN4: Ash M .5K 41
Three Tuns La. L37: Form .1F 24
Threlfalls La. PR9: South .5L 7
Threlfall St. L8: Liv .4F 74
Thresher Av. CH49: Grea .4K 71
Threshers, The L30: N'ton .7G 34
(off Reapers Way)
Throne Rd. L11: Crox .7A 46
Throne Wlk. L11: Crox .6A 46
(off Throne Rd.)
Thurcroft Dr. WN8: Skel .2B 30
Thurlby Cl. WN4: Ash M .7M 41
Thurlow WA3: Low .3F 52
Thurne Way L25: Gate .2E 76
Thurnham St. L6: Liv .4H 59
Thursby Cl. L32: Kirkb .2D 46
PR8: Ains .2H 17
Thursby Cres. L32: Kirkb .1D 46
Thursby Dr. L32: Kirkb .1D 46
Thursby Rd. CH62: Brom .5D 90
Thursby Wlk. L32: Kirkb .2D 46
THURSTASTON .2J 87
Thurstaston Common Local Nature Reserve
.8H 71
Thurstaston Rd. CH60: Hesw .6M 87
CH61: Irby, Thurs .2J 87
Thurston WN8: Skel .2B 30
(not continuous)
Thurston Av. WN3: Wigan .1K 41
Thurston Billiard & Snooker Mus.
.2H 5 (6D 58)
Thurston Cl. WA5: Gt San .2M 81
Thurston Rd. L4: Walt .3G 59
Thynne St. WA1: Warr .4B 82
Tibb's Cross La. WA8: Bold H .9N 63
Tiber St. L8: Liv .2G 75
Tichbourne Way L6: Liv .2L 5 (6E 58)
Tickford Bank WA8: Wid .6H 79
Tickle Av. WA9: St H .7N 49
Tidal La. WA1: Padg .9G 67
Tideswell Cl. L7: Liv .9G 59
Tide Way CH45: Wall .1E 56
Tiger Ct. L34: Presc .4L 61
Tilbey Dr. WA6: Frod .6K 107
Tilbrook Dr. WA9: St H .3N 63
Tilbury Gro. WN6: Shev .6N 23
Tilbury Pl. WA7: Murd .9G 96
Tilcroft WN8: Skel .2B 30
Tildsley Cres. WA7: West .9J 95
Tilia Rd. L5: Liv .3F 58
Tilley St. WA1: Warr .3D 82
Tillotson Cl. L8: Liv .3D 74
Tilman Cl. WA5: Gt San .9J 65
Tilney St. L9: Walt .4F 44
Tilstock Av. CH62: New F .8A 74
Tilstock Cl. L26: Halew .6L 77
Tilstock Cres. CH43: Pren .7F 72
Tilston Av. WA4: Westy .4H 83
Tilston Cl. L9: Faz .7J 45
Tilston Rd. CH45: Wall .3G 56
L9: Faz .6J 45
L32: Kirkb .9A 36
Timberland Cl. L25: Gate .1E 76
Timberscombe Gdns. WA1: Wools .2M 83
Time Pk. L35: Whis .4C 62
Timmis Cl. WA2: Fearn .6H 67
Timmis Cres. WA8: Wid .7K 79
Timms Cl. L37: Form .8F 16
Timms La. L37: Form .8F 16
Timon Av. L20: Boot .6D 44
Timor Av. WA9: St H .1H 63
Timperley Av. WA4: Westy .4H 83
Timperley Ct. WA8: Wid .8L 79
(off Alfred St.)
Timpron St. L7: Liv .9H 59
Timway Dr. L12: W Der .1C 60
Tinas Way CH49: Upton .3A 72
Tinling Cl. L34: Presc .3B 62
Tinsley Av. PR8: South .3D 12
Tinsley Cl. L26: Halew .6J 77
Tinsley's La. PR8: South .5E 12
Tinsley St. L4: Walt .2F 58
WA4: Westy .5G 82
Tintagel WN8: Skel .2A 30
Tintagel Cl. WA7: Brook .9E 96
Tintagel Rd. L11: Crox .5B 46
Tintern Av. WN4: Ash M .8M 41
Tintern Cl. WA5: Call .7N 65
Tintern Dr. CH46: More .9M 55
L37: Form .2H 25
Tiptree Cl. L12: Crox .6D 46
Titchfield St. L3: Liv .5B 58
L5: Liv .5B 58
Tithebarn Cl. CH60: Hesw .8N 87
Tithebarn Dr. CH64: Park .4B 100
Tithebarn Gro. L15: Wav .1M 75
Tithebarn La. L31: Mell .6M 35
L32: Kirkb .1B 46
Tithebarn Rd. L23: Crosb .7M 33
L34: Know .6G 47
PR8: South .9J 7
WN4: Garsw .9E 40
Tithebarn St. L2: Liv .4D 4 (7B 58)
WN8: Uph .5L 31
Titherington Way L15: Wav .2J 75
Tithings, The WA7: Run .6A 96
Tiverton Av. CH44: Wall .5G 57
WN8: Skel .2B 30
Tiverton Cl. L36: Huy .6M 61
WA8: Wid .5F 78
Tiverton Rd. L26: Halew .1J 93
Tiverton Sq. WA5: Penk .4G 81
Tiverton St. L15: Wav .9K 59
TMAS Health & Fitness .1L 49
Tobermory Cl. WA11: Hay .5C 50
Tobin Cl. L5: Liv .5B 58
Tobin St. CH44: Wall .5K 57
Tobruk Rd. L36: Huy .5H 61
Toby Island WN8: Skel .1E 30
Todd Rd. WA9: St H .7L 49
Todd's La. PR9: Banks .1E 8
Toft Cl. WA8: Wid .7J 79
Toft St. L7: Liv .7H 59
Toftwood Av. L35: Rainh .8G 63
Toftwood Gdns. L35: Rainh .8G 63
Tokenspire Pk. L33: Know I .3F 46
Toleman Av. CH63: Beb .2N 89
Toll Bar Pl. WA2: Warr .5B 66
(off Poplars Av.)
Toll Bar Rd. WA2: Warr .6B 66
Tollemache Rd. CH41: Birke .1F 72
CH43: Bid .1F 72
CH43: Clau .1F 72
Tollemache St. CH45: New B .1J 57
Tollerton Rd. L12: W Der .3L 59
Tollgate Cres. L40: Burs .2G 20
Tollgate Rd. L40: Burs .3F 20
Tolpuddle Rd. L25: Woolt .5D 76
Tolpuddle Way L4: Kirkd .1C 58
Tolver Ho. WA10: St H .6K 49
(off Tolver St.)
Tolver Rd. WN4: Ash M .5J 41
Tolver St. WA10: St H .6K 49
Tomlinson Av. WA2: Warr .9E 66
Tom Mann Cl. L3: Liv .3G 5 (7C 58)
Tommy Gent Way L31: Mag .3J 35
Tonbridge Cl. L24: Speke .3F 92
Tonbridge Dr. L10: Ain .8J 35
Tongbarn WN8: Skel .2B 30
TONTINE .7N 31
Tontine Rd. WN5: Orr .7M 31
WN8: Uph .6M 31
Toothill Cl. WN4: Ash M .6K 41
Tootle La. L40: Ruf .3K 15
Top Acre Rd. WN8: Skel .5F 30
Topaz Cl. L4: Walt .8D 44
Topcliffe Gro. L12: Crox .7E 46
Topgate Cl. CH60: Hesw .7B 88
Topham Dr. L9: Ain .9G 35
Topham Ter. L9: Ain .2G 45
Top Pk. Cl. WA13: Warb .8L 69
Topping Ct. WA3: Birchw .5K 67
Top Rd. WA6: Frod .9N 107
Top Sandy La. WA2: Warr .6C 66
Topsham Cl. L25: Gate .4G 77
Torcross Cl. PR9: South .2M 7
Torcross Way L25: Gate .4G 77
L26: Halew .7J 77
Tordelow Cl. L6: Liv .5F 58
Toronto Cl. L36: Huy .2H 61
Toronto St. CH44: Wall .6L 57
Torpoint Cl. L14: Knott A .3E 60
Torquay Dr. WN5: Bil .3A 40
Torr Dr. CH62: East .8F 90
Torridon Gro. CH66: Gt Sut .2L 111
Torrington Dr. CH61: Thing .1B 88
L26: Halew .9J 77
Torrington Gdns. CH61: Thing .9B 72
Torrington Rd. CH44: Wall .5G 57
L19: Gras .9N 75
Torrisholme Rd. L9: Ain .7J 45
Torus Rd. L13: Liv .5M 59
Torver Cl. WN3: Wigan .1J 41
Tor Vw. L15: Wav .2M 75
Torwood CH43: Noct .1D 72
Total Fitness
Bootle .7G 34
Prenton .8D 72
Warrington .9B 66
Wigan .1H 41
Totland Cl. L27: N'ley .4K 77
WA5: Gt San .1E 80
Totnes Av. L26: Halew .7K 77
Totnes Dr. PR9: South .2M 7
Totnes Rd. L11: Crox .5A 46
Tourist Info. Cen.
Liverpool John Lennon Airport .5G 92
Runcorn .4K 95
St Helens .7K 49
Southport .8G 6
Warrington .3C 82
Tourney Grn. WA5: Westb .7J 65
Towcester St. L21: Lith .4A 44
Tower Bldgs. PR9: South .7H 7
(off Gordon St.)
Tower End L37: Form .8C 16
Tower Gdns. L3: Liv .5D 4 (8B 58)
TOWER HILL .5D 36
Tower Hill CH42: Tran .5K 73
L39: Orm .8E 20
Tower Hill Rd. WN8: Uph .7J 31
Towerlands St. L7: Liv .5N 5 (8G 58)
Tower La. WA7: Nort .8E 96
WA13: Lymm .6F 84
Tower Nook WN8: Uph .7K 31
Tower Prom. CH45: New B .9J 43
Tower Quays CH41: Birke .9L 57
Tower Rd. CH41: Birke .9L 57
CH42: Tran .7H 73
(Reservoir Rd.)
CH42: Tran .5K 73
(Tower Hill)
Tower Rd. Nth. CH60: Hesw .5M 87
Tower Rd. Sth. CH60: Hesw .6N 87
Towers, The CH42: Tran .6L 73
Towers Av. L31: Mag .1J 35
Towers Ct. WA5: Warr .1N 81
Towers La. WA6: Alv, Hel .5D 114
Towers Rd. L16: Child .2A 76
Tower St. L3: Liv .3C 74
Tower Way L25: Woolt .5E 76
Tower Wharf CH41: Birke .9L 57
Towneley Ct. WA8: Wid .7K 79
TOWN END .2F 78
Town End Cl. L39: Orm .9B 20
Townfield Av. WN4: Ash M .9K 41
Townfield Cen. CH43: Oxton .5E 72
Townfield Cl. CH43: Oxton .5E 72
Townfield Gdns. CH63: Hghr B .9M 73
Townfield La. CH1: Moll .9J 111
CH43: Oxton .5E 72
CH63: Beb .9M 73
CH63: Beb, Hghr B .9M 73
WA2: Win .4B 66
WA6: Frod .7M 107
WA13: Warb .9H 69
Townfield Rd. CH48: W Kir .6C 70
WA7: Wind H .5E 96
Town Flds. CH45: Wall .3E 56
Townfields WN4: Ash M .8J 41
Townfield Vw. WA7: Wind H .5E 96
Townfield Wlk. WA12: Newt W .6K 51
Townfield Way CH44: Wall .5H 57
Towngate Bus. Cen. WA8: Wid .9E 78
TOWN GREEN
L39 .4A 28
WN4 .8M 41
Town Grn. Ct. L39: Augh .4A 28
Town Grn. Gdns. L39: Augh .4A 28
Town Grn. La. L39: Augh .4A 28
Town Green Station (Rail) .5A 28
Town Hall Dr. WA7: Run .6L 95
Town Hill WA1: Warr .3C 82
Town La. CH63: Hghr B .1K 89
CH64: Lit N .8F 100
L24: Hale .6A 94
PR8: South .2C 12
Town La. (Kew) PR8: South .3B 12
Townley Ct. CH47: Hoy .1C 70
(off Seaview)
Town Mdw. La. CH46: More .9J 55
TOWN OF LOWTON .5C 52
Town Rd. CH42: Tran .5K 73
Town Row L12: W Der .2N 59
Townsend Av. L11: Norr G .1K 59
L13: Liv .1K 59
Townsend La. L4: Walt .3G 59
L6: Liv .3G 59
L13: Liv .3G 59
Townsend St. CH41: Birke .8E 56
L5: Kirkd .3B 58
Townsend Vw. L11: Norr G .7K 45
L21: Ford .9A 34
Townshend Av. CH61: Irby .2L 87
Townson Dr. WN7: Leigh .1N 53
Town Sq. WA7: Pal F .8B 96
(within Halton Lea Shop. Cen.)
Town Vw. CH43: Oxton .3J 73
Town Vw. M. CH43: Oxton .3J 73
Town Wlk. WA7: Pal F .8B 96
(within Halton Lea Shop. Cen.)
Towson St. L5: Liv .3E 58
(Adam St.)
L5: Liv .3F 58
(Hartnup St.)
TOXTETH .4E 74
Toxteth Gro. L8: Liv .4F 74
Toxteth St. L8: Liv .3E 74
(not continuous)
Tracks La. WN5: Bil .9N 31
Tracy Dr. WA12: Newt W .7N 51
Tradewind Sq. L1: Liv .8G 5
TRAFALGAR .3N 89
Trafalgar Av. CH44: Wall .4K 57
Trafalgar Ct. PR8: Birkd .3M 11
WA8: Wid .1K 95
Trafalgar Dr. CH63: Beb .3N 89
Trafalgar Rd. CH44: Wall .4J 57
PR8: Birkd .4L 11
Trafalgar St. WA10: St H .6H 49
Trafalgar Way L6: Liv .2L 5 (6E 58)
Trafford Av. WA5: Warr .1N 81
Trafford Cres. WA7: Run .9M 95
Tragan Dr. WA5: Penk .5F 80
Tramway Rd. L17: Aig .5H 75
M44: Irlam .2M 69
TRANMERE .5M 73
Tranmere Ct. CH42: Tran .4K 73
Tranmere Recreation Cen. .6J 73
Tranmere Rovers FC .6J 73
Trap Hill L37: Form .2C 24
Trapwood Cl. WA10: Eccl .7E 48
Travanson Cl. L10: Faz .4N 45
Travers' Entry WA9: Bold .2C 64
Traverse St. WA9: St H .7M 49
Travis Dr. L33: Kirkb .6D 36
Travis St. WA8: Wid .8L 79
Trawden Way L21: Ford .7B 34
Traynor Ct. CH43: Oxton .3G 73
(off Beresford Rd.)
Treborth St. L8: Liv .3F 74
Trecastle Rd. L33: Kirkb .7E 36

Tree Bank Cl. WA7: Run 7K 95
Treen Cl. PR9: South 1N 7
Treesdale Cl. PR8: Birkd 2M 11
Treetop Ct. L6: Liv 5H 59
Treetops CH64: Lit N 9E 100
Treetops Cl. WA1: Padg 1G 82
Treetops Dr. CH41: Birke 8D 56
Treetop Vs. PR9: South 3L 7
Tree Vw. Ct. L31: Mag 3K 35
Trefoil Cl. L8: Liv 2E 74
WA3: Birchw 4K 67
Treforris Rd. CH45: Wall 2F 56
Trefula Pk. L12: W Der 3M 59
Trelawney Cl. L25: Gate 2F 76
Tremore Cl. L12: W Der 9N 45
Trenance Cl. WA7: Brook 1E 108
Trendeal Rd. L11: Crox 5B 46
Trent Av. L14: Broad G 6D 60
L31: Mag 1L 35
Trent Cl. L12: Crox 7B 46
L35: Rainh 6E 62
L40: Burs 9K 15
WA3: Cul 8N 53
WA8: Wid 4L 79
WA9: Sut L 4M 63
Trentdale CH65: Whit 2N 111
Trentham Av. L18: Moss H 3L 75
Trentham Cl. WA8: Wid 4L 79
WA9: St H 4J 63
Trentham Rd. CH44: Wall 6J 57
L32: Kirkb 1A 46
Trentham St. WA7: Run 4J 95
Trentham Wlk. L32: Kirkb 1A 46
Trent Pl. L35: Rainh 6E 62
Trent Rd. L35: Rainh 6E 62
WN4: Ash M 6N 41
WN5: Bil 7M 39
Trent St. CH41: Birke 8F 56
L5: Kirkd 3B 58
Trent Way CH60: Hesw 9B 88
L21: Lith 1N 43
Tresham Dr. WA4: Grap 8H 83
Tressel Dr. WA9: Sut M 6K 63
Tressell St. L9: Walt 7E 44
Trevelyan Dr. WN5: Bil 2N 39
Trevelyan St. L9: Walt 7E 44
Treviot Cl. L33: Kirkb 5B 36
Trevor Dr. L23: Crosb 8M 33
Trevor Rd. L9: Walt 4F 44
L40: Burs 1H 21
PR8: Ains 1J 17
Triad, The L20: Boot 6B 44
Trident Bus. Pk. WA3: Ris 3M 67
Trident Pk. WA7: Pal F 8A 96
Trimley Cl. CH49: Upton 3M 71
Tring Cl. CH49: Upton 1A 72
Trinity Ct. CH47: Hoy 1C 70
WA3: Ris 4N 67
Trinity Gdns. CH43: Oxton 3F 72
CH47: Hoy 1C 70
PR8: South 9F 6
WA6: Frod 5M 107
WN4: Ash M 7H 41
Trinity Gro. L23: Blun 8H 33
Trinity Ho. WA6: Frod 5M 107
Trinity La. CH41: Birke 1L 73
Trinity M. PR9: South 8H 7
Trinity Pl. L20: Boot 7C 44
WA8: Wid 9L 79
Trinity Rd. CH44: Wall 4H 57
CH47: Hoy 1C 70
CH65: Ell P 1B 112
L20: Boot 8B 44
Trinity St. CH41: Birke 1J 73
WA7: Run 4L 95
WA9: St H 6M 49
Trinity Wlk. L3: Liv 2J 5
Trispen Cl. L26: Halew 8J 77
Trispen Rd. L11: Crox 6B 46
Trispen Wlk. *L11: Crox 6B 46*
(off Trispen Rd.)
Tristram's Cft. L30: N'ton 8C 34
Triumph Trading Park, The
L24: Speke 1D 92
Triumph Way L24: Hunts X, Speke 1D 92
Troon Cl. CH63: Brom 1B 102
L12: W Der 3C 60
WA11: Hay 5C 50
Trooper Cl. L12: W Der 2C 60
Trossach Cl. WA2: Warr 7F 66
Trotwood Cl. L9: Ain 2J 45
Troutbeck Av. L31: Mag 1K 35
WA5: Warr 1A 82
WA12: Newt W 6G 51
Troutbeck Cl. CH49: Woodc 6A 72
WA7: Beech 1C 108
Troutbeck Gro. WA11: St H 9L 39
Troutbeck Rd. L18: Moss H 3B 76
WN4: Ash M 6L 41
Trouville Rd. L4: Walt 2H 59
Trowbridge St. L3: Liv 5J 5 (8D 58)
Trueman Cl. CH43: Bid 9C 56
Trueman St. L3: Liv 3F 4 (7C 58)
truGym
Halton Lea 8A 96
Truman Cl. WA8: Wid 5J 79
Trumans La. CH66: Lit Sut 7H 103
Trundle Pie La. L39: Hals 6H 19
Truro Av. L30: N'ton 7E 34
PR9: South 2N 7
Truro Cl. CH66: Gt Sut 5L 111
WA1: Wools 9J 67
WA7: Brook 9E 96
WA11: St H 3N 49
Truro Rd. L15: Wav 2M 75
Truscott Rd. L40: Burs 1H 21
Tryfan Cl. CH66: Ell P 7L 103
Tudor Av. CH44: Wall 7L 57
CH63: Beb 4N 89
L14: Knott A 4F 60
Tudor Cl. CH66: Gt Sut 5L 111
L7: Liv 6L 5 (8E 58)
WA4: Grap 6H 83
WA11: Rainf 3B 38
Tudor Ct. *L19: Gras 9M 75*
(off Dugdale Cl.)
WA4: Stockt H 7F 82
Tudor Gdns. L38: Hight 8F 24
Tudor Grange CH49: Grea 5L 71
Tudor Gro. WN3: Wins 1G 40
Tudor Mans. PR8: South 9E 6
Tudor Rd. CH42: Tran 5L 73
L23: Crosb 8K 33
L25: Hunts X 9G 76
PR8: Ains 8H 11
WA7: Manor P 4D 96
Tudor St. Nth. L6: Liv 6G 59
Tudor St. Sth. L6: Liv 6G 59
Tudor Vw. L33: Kirkb 6C 36
(not continuous)
Tudorville Rd. CH63: Beb 2M 89
Tudor Way CH60: Hesw 7B 88
TUE BROOK 3K 59
Tue La. WA8: Cron 2E 78
Tuffins Cnr. L27: N'ley 3H 77
Tulip Av. CH41: Birke 1F 72
Tulip Gro. WA5: Warr 5N 81
Tulip Rd. L15: Wav 1N 75
M31: Part 7L 69
WA11: Hay 4H 51
Tulketh St. PR8: South 8G 7
Tullimore Rd. L18: Moss H 7M 75
Tullis St. WA10: St H 8H 49
Tulloch St. L6: Liv 6G 58
Tully Av. WA12: Newt W 7G 51
Tulsa Gdns. WA5: Gt San 1J 81
Tumilty Av. L20: Boot 6D 44
Tunbridge Cl. WA5: Gt San 9J 65
Tundra Cl. L4: Walt 8F 44
Tunnage Sq. L1: Liv 7G 4
Tunnel End WA4: Dutt 2J 109
Tunnel Rd. CH41: Birke 3M 73
L7: Liv 9G 59
Tunnel Top Nth. WA4: Dutt 9H 97
WA7: Pres B 9H 97
Tunstall Cl. CH49: Upton 3M 71
Tunstall St. L7: Liv 1H 75
Tunstalls Way WA9: Clock F 5N 63
Tupelo Cl. L12: Crox 6D 46
Tupman St. L8: Liv 3E 74
Turmar Av. CH61: Thing 1B 88
Turnacre L14: Broad G 6C 60
L37: Form 7G 17
Turnall Rd. WA8: Wid 9E 78
Turnberry WN8: Skel 2A 30
Turnberry Cl. CH46: More 8J 55
L12: W Der 3D 60
L36: Roby 8G 61
WA13: Lymm 4C 84
Turnberry Way PR9: South 2B 8
Turnbridge Rd. L31: Mag 9H 27
Turner Av. L20: Boot 3D 44
Turner Cl. L8: Liv 5F 74
WA8: Wid 5G 78
Turner Gro. L33: Kirkb 5C 36
Turner Home, The L8: Liv 4G 74
Turners Ct. L25: Gate 5G 76
Turner St. CH41: Birke 3J 73
Turners Vw. CH64: Nest 4D 100
Turners Yd. WN5: Orr 7N 31
Turney Rd. CH44: Wall 5G 56
Turnill Dr. WN4: Ash M 9K 41
Turning La. PR8: South 6F 12
Turnpike Rd. L39: Augh 2M 27
Turnstone Av. WA12: Newt W 6L 51
Turnstone Bus. Pk.
WA8: Wid 9M 79
Turnstone Cl. L12: Crox 7C 46
Turnstone Dr. L26: Halew 7J 77
Turret Hall Dr. WA3: Low 2F 52
Turret Rd. CH45: Wall 3G 57
Turriff Dr. CH63: East 2B 102
Turriff Rd. L14: Knott A 4E 60
Turrocks Cl. CH64: Lit N 9E 100
Turrocks Cft. CH64: Lit N 9E 100
Turton Cl. L24: Hale 6A 94
WA3: Birchw 4K 67
Turton St. L5: Kirkd 3C 58
WA3: Golb 2B 52
Tuscan Cl. WA8: Wid 3L 79
Tuson Dr. WA8: Wid 4J 79
Tutor Bank Dr.
WA12: Newt W 7M 51
Tweed Cl. L6: Liv 5H 59
Tweedsmuir Cl. WA2: Fearn 5H 67
Tweed St. CH41: Birke 8G 56
Twenty Acre Rd. WA5: Old H 9L 65
Twickenham Dr. CH46: Leas 6N 55
L36: Roby 8G 61
Twickenham St. L6: Liv 3G 59
Twigden Cl. L10: Faz 2L 45
Twig La. L31: Mag 2K 35
L36: Huy 6G 61
TWISS GREEN 6M 53
Twiss Grn. Dr. WA3: Cul 6M 53
Twiss Grn. La. WA3: Cul 6L 53
Twist Av. WA3: Golb 2D 52
Twistfield Cl. PR8: Birkd 1M 11
Two Acre Gro. CH66: Gt Sut 4L 111
Two Butt La.
L35: Whis, Rainh 4D 62
Twomey Cl. L5: Liv 5B 58
TWO MILLS 5D 110
Two Saints Retail Pk.
L39: Orm 8C 20
Twyford Av. L21: Lith 1A 44
Twyford Cl. L31: Mag 2K 35
WA8: Wid 4L 79
Twyford La. WA8: Wid 1M 79
Twyford Pl. WA9: St H 7M 49
Twyford St. L6: Liv 3G 59
Tyberton Pl. L25: Hunts X 1G 92
Tyburn Cl. CH63: Spit 5M 89
Tyburn Rd. CH63: Spit 5M 89
Tyle St. L20: Kirkd 2A 58
Tyndall Av. L22: Water 2M 43
Tyne Cl. L4: Kirkd 1D 58
WA2: Warr 7F 66
WA9: St H 3G 63
Tynemouth Cl. L5: Liv 4F 58
Tynemouth Rd. WA7: Murd 9E 96
Tynesdale CH65: Whit 2N 111
Tyne St. CH41: Birke 8F 56
Tynron Gro. CH43: Noct 4D 72
Tynville Rd. L9: Ain 3H 45
Tynwald Cl. L13: Liv 4L 59
Tynwald Cres. WA8: Wid 3J 79
Tynwald Dr. WA4: App 8D 82
Tynwald Hill L13: Liv 5L 59
Tynwald Pl. L13: Liv 5L 59
Tynwald Rd. CH48: W Kir 6B 70
Tyrer Gro. L34: Presc 2B 62
Tyrer Rd. L39: Orm 6D 20
WA12: Newt W 9L 51
Tyrers Av. L31: Lyd 7G 27
Tyrers Cl. L37: Form 2F 24
Tyrer St. CH41: Birke 8F 56
L1: Liv 5G 4 (8C 58)
Tyrer Wlk. WA3: Low 2G 52
Tyrrell Way WA7: Cas 5C 96

U

U-boat Story 1N 73
Uldale Cl. L11: Norr G 8M 45
PR8: Ains 2H 17
Uldale Way L11: Norr G 8M 45
Ullapool Cl. CH66: Lit Sut 8E 102
Ullet Rd. L8: Liv 4G 74
L17: Aig 4G 74
Ullet Wlk. L17: Aig 3J 75
Ullswater Av. CH43: Noct 2D 72
WA2: Warr 6D 66
WA11: St H 2K 49
WN4: Ash M 7K 41
Ullswater Cl. L33: Kirkb 7B 36
Ullswater Gro. WA7: Beech 1N 107
Ullswater Ho. L17: Aig 6J 75
WA3: Golb 1D 52
Ullswater Rd. CH65: Ell P 3A 112
WA3: Golb 1D 52
Ullswater St. L5: Liv 3F 58
Ulster Rd. L13: Liv 6N 59
Ulverscroft CH43: Oxton 4F 72
Ulverston Av. WA2: Warr 6C 66
Ulverston Cl. L31: Mag 1K 35
WA11: Hay 4C 50
Ulverston Lawn L27: N'ley 4K 77
Underbridge La.
WA4: Hghr Wal 1N 97
Undercliffe Ho. WA4: App 8E 82
Undercliffe Rd. L13: Liv 5M 59
Underhill Rd. WA10: St H 8G 49
Underley St. L7: Liv 1H 75
Underley Ter. CH62: New F 9A 74
Underwater Street Discovery Cen.
5C 4 (8A 58)
Underway, The WA7: Halt 7B 96
Underwood Dr.
CH65: Ell P, Whit 3N 111
Unicorn Rd. L11: Crox 6A 46
Unicorn Way CH41: Tran 3M 73
Union Bank La. WA8: Bold H 8L 63
Union Ct. L2: Liv 5E 4 (8B 58)
Union Sq. WA5: Gt San 9J 65
Union St. CH42: Tran 5M 73
CH44: Wall 5K 57
L3: Liv 4C 4 (7A 58)
PR9: South 7H 7
WA1: Warr 3C 82
WA7: Run 5L 95
WA10: St H 5K 49
Union Ter. CH45: New B 9H 43
Unit Rd. PR8: Ains 9K 11
Unity Bldg. L3: Liv 4C 4
Unity Gro. L34: Know 5E 46
Unity Theatre 7J 5
University of Chester
Warrington Campus 6J 67
University of Liverpool
Cambridge St. 7L 5 (9E 58)
Central Campus 6L 5 (8E 58)
North Campus 4L 5 (8E 58)
Peach St. 6L 5 (8F 58)
School of Veterinary Science,
Leahurst Campus 6K 101
University of Liverpool Library 7M 5
University of Liverpool Sports Cen.
6L 5 (8E 58)
University Rd. L20: Boot 8C 44
Unsworth Av. WA3: Low 1F 52
Unsworth Ct. WA2: Padg 8G 66
Upavon Av. CH49: Grea 5J 71
Upchurch Cl. L8: Liv 4E 74
UP HOLLAND 5L 31
Upholland Rd. WN5: Bil 8N 31
Upholland Station (Rail) 8J 31
Upland Cl. WA10: St H 1E 62
Upland Dr. WN4: Ash M 7M 41
Upland Rd. CH49: Upton 2N 71
WA10: St H 1E 62
Uplands, The CH43: Oxton 4E 72
WA7: Pal F 8B 96
Uplands Rd. CH62: Brom 6B 90
Up. Aughton Rd. PR8: Birkd 1N 11
Up. Baker St. L6: Liv 1N 5 (6F 58)
Up. Beau St. L5: Liv 1H 5 (5D 58)
Up. Beckwith St. CH41: Birke 9H 57
UPPER BIDSTON VILLAGE 8C 56
Up. Brassey St. CH41: Birke 9F 56
Upperbrook Way L4: Kirkd 2C 58
Up. Bute St. L5: Liv 5D 58
Up. Duke St. L1: Liv 8H 5 (9D 58)
Up. Essex St. L8: Liv 3E 74
Up. Flaybrick Rd. CH41: Birke 1E 72
Up. Frederick St.
L1: Liv 8F 4 (9C 58)
(not continuous)
Up. Hampton St. L8: Liv 9L 5 (1E 74)
Up. Harrington St. L8: Liv 2D 74
Up. Hill St. L8: Liv 2D 74
(not continuous)
Up. Hope Pl. L7: Liv 7K 5 (9E 58)
Up. Huskisson St. L8: Liv 9M 5 (1F 74)
Up. Mann St. L8: Liv 2D 74
(not continuous)
Up. Mason St. L7: Liv 5N 5 (8F 58)
Up. Mersey Rd. WA8: Wid 2K 95
Up. Mersey St. CH65: Ell P 7A 104
Upper Newington L1: Liv 6H 5 (8D 58)
Up. Park St. L8: Liv 3E 74
Up. Parliament St. L8: Liv 9K 5 (1D 74)
Up. Pitt St. L1: Liv 8G 5 (9C 58)
(not continuous)
Up. Pownall St. L1: Liv 8F 4 (9C 58)
Up. Raby Rd. CH63: Raby 4G 101
CH64: Nest 4G 101
Up. Rice La. CH44: Wall 4J 57
Up. Stanhope St. L8: Liv 1D 74
(not continuous)
Up. Warwick St. L8: Liv 2E 74
Up. William St. L3: Liv 5A 58
Uppingham WN8: Skel 3A 30
Uppingham Av. L10: Ain 9K 35
Uppingham Rd. CH44: Wall 4F 56
L13: Liv 4L 59
UPTON
CH49 3A 72
WA8 5E 78
Upton Av. PR8: Ains 8H 11
Upton Barn L31: Mag 1H 35
Upton Bridle Path WA8: Wid 4J 79
Upton By-Pass CH49: Upton 2M 71
Upton Cl. CH49: Upton 3N 71
L24: Speke 4J 93
WA3: Low 2E 52
Upton Ct. CH49: Upton 2A 72
Upton Dr. WA5: Penk 3H 81
Upton Grange WA8: Wid 5G 79
Upton Grn. L24: Speke 4J 93
Upton La. WA8: Wid 4H 79
Upton Mdw. CH49: Upton 4N 71
Upton Pk. Dr. CH49: Upton 2A 72
Upton Rd. CH41: Birke 3C 72
CH43: Bid, Noct 3C 72
CH46: More 9M 55
CH66: Gt Sut 1J 111
UPTON ROCKS 5J 79
Upton Rocks Av. WA8: Wid 4H 79
Upton Rocks M. WA8: Wid 4H 79
Upton Station (Rail) 3C 72
Upwood Rd. WA3: Low 3E 52
Ure Ct. CH65: Ell P 7M 103
Urmson Rd. CH45: Wall 4H 57
Urmston Av. WA12: Newt W 5K 51
Ursula St. L20: Boot 9C 44
Utkinton Cl. CH43: Oxton 5F 72
Utting Av. L4: Walt 2G 58
Utting Av. E. L11: Norr G 9K 45
UVECO Bus. Cen. CH41: Birke 8H 57
Uxbridge St. L7: Liv 8G 59
(not continuous)

V

Vahler Ter. WA7: Run 5M 95
Vale, The WN6: Appl B 5N 23
Vale Av. WA2: Warr 9C 66

Vale Ct. L21: Sea . . . 4N 43
(off Seaforth Va. Nth.)
WA4: Dutt . . . 3J 109
Vale Cres. PR8: Ains . . . 3J 17
Vale Cft. WN8: Uph . . . 6K 31
Vale Dr. CH45: New B . . . 2J 57
Vale Gdns. CH65: Whit . . . 1N 111
WA6: Hel . . . 1E 114
Vale Gro. L32: Kirkb . . . 1E 46
Vale La. L40: Lath . . . 9A 22
(not continuous)
Vale Lodge L9: Walt . . . 6E 44
Valencia Gro. L34: Eccl P . . . 2D 62
Valencia Rd. L15: Wav . . . 9M 59
Valentia Rd. CH47: Hoy . . . 2B 70
Valentine Gro. L10: Ain . . . 1K 45
Valentine Rd. WA12: Newt W . . . 7H 51
Valentines Bldg. L9: Ain . . . 1H 45
Valentines Way L9: Ain . . . 9H 35
Vale Owen Rd. WA2: Warr . . . 8E 66
Valerian Rd. CH41: Birke . . . 1F 72
Valerie Cl. L10: Faz . . . 4N 45
Vale Rd. CH65: Whit . . . 1N 111
L23: Crosb . . . 7K 33
L25: Woolt . . . 5C 76
Valescourt Rd. L12: W Der . . . 4A 60
Valiant Cl. L12: Crox . . . 8E 46
WA2: Padg . . . 7G 66
Valiant Ho. CH41: Birke . . . 2M 73
Valiant Way CH41: Tran . . . 4M 73
Valkyrie Rd. CH45: Wall . . . 4G 57
Vallance Rd. L4: Walt . . . 2H 59
Valleybrook Gro. CH63: Spit . . . 5A 90
Valley Cl. L10: Ain . . . 1L 45
L23: Crosb . . . 7A 34
Valley Community Theatre . . . 3H 77
Valley Ct. WA2: Padg . . . 8G 66
Valley Dr. CH66: Gt Sut . . . 9J 103
Valley Rd. CH41: Birke . . . 7D 56
CH62: Brom . . . 7C 90
L4: Walt . . . 3F 58
L32: Faz, Kirkb . . . 3M 45
Valley Rd. Bus. Pk.
CH41: Birke . . . 8E 56
Valley Vw. CH66: Gt Sut . . . 9J 103
WA12: Newt W . . . 8K 51
Vanbrugh Cres. L4: Walt . . . 2H 59
Vanbrugh Rd. L4: Walt . . . 1H 59
Vancouver Rd. L27: N'ley . . . 3J 77
Vanderbilt Av. L9: Ain . . . 2G 45
Vanderbyl Av. CH62: Spit . . . 5B 90
Vandries St. L3: Liv . . . 1B 4 (5A 58)
Vandyke St. L8: Liv . . . 1H 75
Vanguard Ct. WA3: Ris . . . 5L 67
(off Renown Cl.)
Vanguard St. L5: Liv . . . 3E 58
Vanguard Way CH41: Tran . . . 5M 73
Vardon St. CH41: Birke . . . 9K 57
Varley Rd. L19: Aig . . . 7M 75
WA9: St H . . . 6M 49
Varlian Cl. L40: Westh . . . 1G 28
Varthen St. L5: Liv . . . 3F 58
Vaudrey Dr. WA1: Wools . . . 1L 83
Vaughan Cl. L37: Form . . . 9D 16
Vaughan Rd. CH45: New B . . . 1J 57
PR8: Birkd . . . 2A 12
Vaughan St. CH41: Birke . . . 9F 56
Vaux Cres. L20: Boot . . . 5C 44
VAUXHALL . . . 5B 58
Vauxhall Bus. Cen. L3: Liv . . . 1D 4
Vauxhall Cl. WA5: Penk . . . 4H 81
Vauxhall Motors FC . . . 5H 103
Vauxhall Rd. L3: Liv . . . 1E 4 (6B 58)
L5: Liv . . . 5B 58
Vaux Pl. L20: Boot . . . 5C 44
Venables Cl. CH63: Spit . . . 6A 90
Venables Dr. CH63: Spit . . . 5N 89
Venables Way CH65: Ell P . . . 8N 103
Venice St. L5: Liv . . . 3E 58
Venmore St. L5: Liv . . . 3E 58
(not continuous)
Venns Rd. WA2: Warr . . . 9E 66
Ventnor Cl. WA5: Gt San . . . 1E 80
Ventnor Rd. L15: Wav . . . 9L 59
Ventura Dr. WA5: Gt San . . . 1K 81
Venture Ct. CH41: Birke . . . 3L 73
Venture Flds. WA8: Wid . . . 9L 79
Venture Point CH2: Lit Stan . . . 3D 112
Venture Point W. L24: Speke . . . 2F 92
Venture Works L33: Know I . . . 1G 46
Verbena Cl. M31: Part . . . 6M 69
WA7: Beech . . . 2B 108
Verbena Dr. L11: Norr G . . . 8M 45
Verdala Pk. L18: Moss H . . . 6A 76
Verdi Av. L21: Sea . . . 4N 43
Verdi St. L21: Sea . . . 4M 43
Verdi Ter. L21: Sea . . . 5M 43
Vere St. L8: Liv . . . 3D 74
Vermont Av. L23: Crosb . . . 7K 33
Vermont Cl. L33: Kirkb . . . 4B 36
WA5: Gt San . . . 1L 81
Vermont Rd. L23: Crosb . . . 7K 33
Vermont Way L20: Boot . . . 6B 44
Verne Wlk. WN4: Ash M . . . 8M 41
Verney Cres. L19: Aller . . . 8A 76
Verney Cres. Sth. L19: Aller . . . 8A 76
Vernon Av. CH44: Wall . . . 7K 57
CH66: Hoot . . . 4F 102
Vernon Ct. PR8: South . . . 1C 12
Vernon Rd. PR9: South . . . 7M 7
Vernon St. L2: Liv . . . 4E 4 (7B 58)
WA1: Warr . . . 4C 82
WA9: St H . . . 6M 49
Verona St. L5: Liv . . . 3E 58
Veronica Cl. L12: Crox . . . 7C 46
Veronica M. WA8: Wid . . . 7G 79
Veronica Way CH66: Lit Sut . . . 7J 103
Verulam Cl. L8: Liv . . . 9N 5 (1F 74)
Verulam Rd. PR9: South . . . 4N 7
Verwood Cl. CH61: Irby . . . 9L 71
Verwood Dr. L12: Crox . . . 7E 46
Veryan Cl. L26: Halew . . . 7K 77
Vescock St. L5: Liv . . . 5C 58
Vesta Rd. L19: Garst . . . 3B 92
Vesty Bus. Pk. L30: N'ton . . . 2F 44
Vesty Rd. L30: N'ton . . . 2F 44
Vesuvian Dr. L19: Garst . . . 3B 92
Vesuvius Pl. L5: Kirkd . . . 3C 58
Vesuvius St. L5: Kirkd . . . 3C 58
Vetch Cl. WA3: Glaz . . . 4H 69
Viaduct St. WA12: Newt W . . . 7J 51
Vicarage Cl. CH42: Tran . . . 7H 73
L18: Moss H . . . 6N 75
L24: Hale . . . 6B 94
L37: Form . . . 9D 16
L40: Westh . . . 1F 28
Vicarage Dr. WA11: Hay . . . 3C 50
Vicarage Gdns. L40: Burs . . . 9H 15
WN5: Orr . . . 8N 31
Vicarage Gro. CH44: Wall . . . 4J 57
Vicarage Hill WA6: Hel . . . 1F 114
Vicarage La. CH1: Shot . . . 9A 110
L40: Westh . . . 1F 28
PR9: Banks . . . 1D 8
WA6: Frod . . . 7M 107
WA6: Hel . . . 1F 114
Vicarage Lawn L25: Gate . . . 3G 76
Vicarage Pl. L34: Presc . . . 3N 61
Vicarage Rd. L37: Form . . . 9D 16
WA8: Wid . . . 9K 79
WA11: Hay . . . 3C 50
WN4: Ash M . . . 9J 41
WN5: Orr . . . 8N 31
Vicarage Wlk. L39: Orm . . . 8C 20
WA4: Stockt H . . . 8D 82
(off Southern St.)
Vicar Rd. L6: Liv . . . 2H 59
Viceroy Ct. PR8: South . . . 9F 6
Viceroy St. L5: Liv . . . 3E 58
Vickers Dr. WN8: Skel . . . 4H 31
Victoria Av. CH60: Hesw . . . 9N 87
L14: Broad G . . . 7B 60
L15: Wav . . . 9L 59
L23: Blun . . . 7J 33
WA4: Grap . . . 6H 83
WA5: Gt San . . . 2F 80
WA8: Wid . . . 5K 79
WA11: St H . . . 2K 49
Victoria Bri. Rd. PR8: South . . . 9H 7
Victoria Bldgs. L37: Form . . . 8E 16
Victoria Cl. L17: Aig . . . 5K 75
Victoria Ct. CH42: Rock F . . . 7N 73
L15: Wav . . . 9M 59
L17: Aig . . . 4G 75
(off Lit. Parkfield Rd.)
PR8: Birkd . . . 2M 11
(not continuous)
WN8: Skel . . . 3A 30
(off Ormskirk Rd.)
Victoria Dr. CH42: Rock F . . . 7N 73
CH48: W Kir . . . 6B 70
L9: Walt . . . 4E 44
Victoria Falls Rd. L27: N'ley . . . 4K 77
Victoria Flds. CH42: Tran . . . 4J 73
Victoria Gallery & Museum . . . 5L 5 (8E 58)
Victoria Gdns. CH43: Oxton . . . 4H 73
WA4: Westy . . . 5G 83
(off Kingsway Sth.)
Victoria Gro. WA8: Wid . . . 5K 79
Victoria Hall L2: Liv . . . 3E 4
Victoria Hall Wlk. CH63: Hghr B . . . 1K 89
Victoria Ho. L34: Presc . . . 3A 62
Victoria La. CH43: Oxton . . . 4H 73
Victoria Leisure & Fitness
Southport . . . 7G 6
(off Promenade)
Victoria M. CH65: Ell P . . . 9N 103
(off Victoria Rd.)
PR9: South . . . 8J 7
Victoria Mt. CH43: Oxton . . . 4H 73
Victoria Pde. CH45: New B . . . 9J 43
VICTORIA PARK
L15 . . . 9M 59
L20 . . . 3D 44
Victoria Park
City Rd. . . . 4J 49
Knutsford Rd. . . . 4F 82
Victoria Pk. WN8: Skel . . . 3N 29
Victoria Park Arena . . . 4E 82
Victoria Park Glasshouses . . . 7K 79
Victoria Pk. Rd. CH42: Tran . . . 6K 73
Victoria Pl. CH44: Wall . . . 7M 57
L35: Rainh . . . 6F 62
WA4: Stockt H . . . 7D 82
(off Victoria Sq.)
Victoria Prom. WA8: Wid . . . 3K 95
Victoria Rd. CH42: Tran . . . 4J 73
CH45: New B . . . 1G 57
CH48: W Kir . . . 7B 70
CH63: Hghr B . . . 1K 89
Victoria Rd. CH64: Lit N . . . 8F 100
CH65: Ell P . . . 9N 103
L13: Liv . . . 3K 59
L17: Aig . . . 5K 75
L22: Water . . . 2L 43
L23: Crosb . . . 7K 33
L36: Huy . . . 7K 61
L37: Form . . . 8B 16
L38: Ince B . . . 9L 25
L39: Augh . . . 1A 28
WA4: Grap . . . 6G 83
WA4: Stockt H . . . 7E 82
WA5: Gt San . . . 4K 81
WA5: Penk . . . 4F 80
WA7: Run . . . 5K 95
(not continuous)
WA8: Wid . . . 9K 79
WA12: Newt W . . . 6L 51
WN4: Garsw . . . 8F 40
Victoria Rd. W. L23: Blun . . . 7J 33
Victoria Sq. WA4: Stockt H . . . 7D 82
WA8: Wid . . . 9K 79
WA10: St H . . . 6K 49
Victoria St. CH62: Port S . . . 2A 90
L1: Liv . . . 5E 4 (8B 58)
L2: Liv . . . 5E 4 (8B 58)
L35: Rainh . . . 6F 62
L40: Burs . . . 9J 15
PR9: South . . . 7G 6
WA1: Warr . . . 3D 82
WA8: Wid . . . 9L 79
WA10: St H . . . 5K 49
WA11: Rainf . . . 4C 38
Victoria Ter. L15: Wav . . . 2M 75
(off Prince Alfred Rd.)
L35: Rainh . . . 6F 62
Victoria Trad. Est. L35: Rainh . . . 6F 62
(off Victoria St.)
WA8: Wid . . . 1K 95
Victoria Vs. L35: Rainh . . . 6F 62
Victoria Way L37: Form . . . 8D 16
PR8: South . . . 8E 6
Victor St. L15: Wav . . . 9J 59
Victory Av. PR9: South . . . 8M 7
Victory Cl. L30: Boot . . . 2D 44
Victory Rd. M44: Cad . . . 5J 69
Vienna St. L5: Liv . . . 3E 58
Viennese Rd. L25: Gate . . . 2F 76
View 146 L5: Liv . . . 4D 58
Viewpark Cl. L16: Child . . . 1D 76
View Rd. L35: Rainh . . . 7F 62
Viking Cl. L21: Lith . . . 3N 43
PR8: Birkd . . . 2N 11
Viking Ct. WA8: Wid . . . 9K 79
(off Vine St.)
Village, The CH63: Beb . . . 1N 89
Village Cl. CH45: Wall . . . 3E 56
WA4: Thel . . . 4M 83
WA7: Cas . . . 7C 96
WN8: Skel . . . 4A 30
Village Ct. CH43: Oxton . . . 4G 73
CH61: Irby . . . 1L 87
L17: Aig . . . 6H 75
Village Courts L30: N'ton . . . 6E 34
Village Grn. Ct. CH43: Bid . . . 9C 56
Village M. CH45: Wall . . . 3E 56
CH63: Hghr B . . . 1K 89
Village Nook L10: Ain . . . 9K 35
Village Rd. CH43: Oxton . . . 4G 72
CH48: W Kir . . . 7C 70
CH60: Hesw . . . 8N 87
CH63: Hghr B . . . 1K 89
WA6: Dun H . . . 8B 114
Village Row PR8: Ains . . . 9J 11
Village Sq. CH64: Will . . . 6M 101
(off Buckley La.)
Village Square, The WA7: Cas . . . 5C 96
Village St. L6: Liv . . . 5E 58
WA7: Nort . . . 5G 96
Village Vw. WN5: Bil . . . 6A 40
Village Way CH45: Wall . . . 4E 56
L38: Hight . . . 8F 24
WN8: Skel . . . 4A 30
Villa Gloria Cl. L19: Aig . . . 8M 75
Villars St. WA1: Warr . . . 3E 82
Villas Rd. L31: Mag . . . 1N 35
Villiers Ct. L34: Know . . . 5F 46
Villiers Cres. WA10: Eccl . . . 5C 48
Villiers Rd. L34: Know . . . 4F 46
Vincent Cl. WA5: Old H . . . 9K 65
Vincent Ct. L1: Liv . . . 8G 4 (9C 58)
Vincent Naughton Ct. CH41: Birke . . . 3L 73
Vincent Rd. L21: Lith . . . 1B 44
L35: Rainh . . . 5E 62
Vincent St. CH41: Birke . . . 2K 73
L13: Liv . . . 8M 59
WA10: St H . . . 6K 49
Vine Cres. WA5: Gt San . . . 2H 81
Vine Ho. L21: Sea . . . 4N 43
Vineries, The L25: Woolt . . . 5C 76
Vine Rd. CH66: Gt Sut . . . 4L 111
Vineside Rd. L12: W Der . . . 4B 60
Vine St. L7: Liv . . . 8M 5 (9F 58)
WA7: Run . . . 5K 95
WA8: Wid . . . 9K 79
Vine Ter. WA8: Wid . . . 6D 78
Vineyard St. L19: Garst . . . 2C 92
Vining Rd. L35: Presc . . . 3C 62
Vining St. L8: Liv . . . 2E 74
Viola Cl. L33: Kirkb . . . 6B 36
Viola St. L20: Boot . . . 9B 44
Violet Cl. WA3: Birchw . . . 5K 67
Violet Cft. CH63: Beb . . . 3M 89
Violet Rd. CH41: Birke . . . 1F 72
L21: Lith . . . 4A 44
Violet St. WA8: Wid . . . 9K 79
WN4: Ash M . . . 9K 41
Virgil St. L5: Liv . . . 5D 58
WA10: St H . . . 6H 49
Virginia Av. L31: Lyd . . . 9J 27
Virginia Gdns. WA5: Gt San . . . 9K 65
Virginia Gro. L31: Lyd . . . 9H 27
Virginia Rd. CH45: New B . . . 9H 43
Virginia St. PR8: South . . . 9H 7
Virginia Ter. CH66: Chil T . . . 6F 102
Virgin's La. L23: Thorn . . . 4M 33
Viscount Cen. L24: Speke . . . 2H 93
Viscount Dr. L24: Hale . . . 5J 93
Viscount Rd. WA2: Padg . . . 7F 66
Vista, The M44: Cad . . . 5J 69
Vista Av. WA12: Newt W . . . 6J 51
Vista Rd. WA7: Run . . . 7K 95
WA11: Hay . . . 3J 51
WA12: Newt W . . . 3J 51
Vista Way WA12: Newt W . . . 6J 51
Vitesse Rd. L24: Speke . . . 1D 92
Vittoria Cl. CH41: Birke . . . 1K 73
Vittoria Ct. CH41: Birke . . . 1K 73
Vittoria St. CH41: Birke . . . 1J 73
Viva Way CH65: Ell P . . . 8M 103
Vivian Av. CH44: Wall . . . 7L 57
Vivian Dr. PR8: Birkd . . . 4N 11
Vixen Gro. WA8: Wid . . . 4J 79
Voce's La. L39: Bic . . . 9F 28
Voelas St. L8: Liv . . . 2F 74
Vogan Av. L23: Crosb . . . 8N 33
Volunteer St. WA6: Frod . . . 5N 107
WA10: St H . . . 6J 49
Vose Cl. WA5: Gt San . . . 2M 81
Vronhill Cl. L8: Liv . . . 2F 74
Vue Cinema
Birkenhead . . . 2L 73
Ellesmere Port . . . 3B 112
Southport . . . 7E 6
Vulcan Cl. CH41: Birke . . . 9F 56
L19: Garst . . . 3A 92
WA2: Padg . . . 7G 66
WA12: Newt W . . . 9L 51
Vulcan Ct. PR9: South . . . 8H 7
Vulcan Pk. Way WA12: Newt W . . . 9L 51
Vulcan St. CH41: Birke . . . 9F 56
L3: Liv . . . 5A 58
L20: Boot . . . 6N 43
PR9: South . . . 8H 7
VULCAN VILLAGE . . . 1L 65
Vyner Cl. CH43: Noct . . . 2E 72
Vyner Ct. CH43: Noct . . . 2E 72
Vyner Cft. CH43: Clau . . . 2E 72
Vyner Pk. CH43: Noct . . . 2E 72
Vyner Rd. CH45: Wall . . . 4F 56
Vyner Rd. Nth. CH43: Bid . . . 1D 72
L25: Gate . . . 3E 76
Vyner Rd. Sth. CH43: Bid, Noct . . . 2D 72
L25: Gate . . . 3F 76
Vyrnwy St. L5: Liv . . . 3F 58

W

WADDICAR . . . 7M 35
Waddicar La. L31: Mell . . . 8M 35
Waddington Cl. WA2: Padg . . . 8G 66
WA3: Low . . . 2G 53
Wade Av. WA4: Warr . . . 6D 82
Wadebridge Rd. L10: Faz . . . 4N 45
Wadeson Rd. L4: Walt . . . 8J 45
Wadeson Way WA3: Croft . . . 2J 67
Wadham Pk. L20: Boot . . . 8C 44
Wadham Rd. L20: Boot . . . 9B 44
Wagon La. WA11: Hay . . . 6D 50
Waine Gro. L35: Whis . . . 4D 62
Waine St. WA9: St H . . . 6N 49
WA11: Hay . . . 4B 50
Wainfleet Cl. WN3: Wins . . . 1G 40
Wainwright Cl. L7: Liv . . . 9H 59
Wainwright Ct. WA2: Warr . . . 7D 66
Wainwright Gro. L19: Garst . . . 1A 92
Wakefield Dr. CH46: Leas . . . 5N 55
Wakefield Rd. CH66: Gt Sut . . . 4K 111
L30: N'ton . . . 9F 34
Wakefield St. L3: Liv . . . 2H 5 (6D 58)
WA3: Golb . . . 3B 52
Walby Cl. CH49: Woodc . . . 6C 72
Walcot Pl. WN3: Wigan . . . 1H 41
Walden Cl. WA4: Thel . . . 5L 83
Walden Dr. CH1: Woodb . . . 5C 110
Walden Rd. L14: Knott A . . . 6A 60
Waldgrave Pl. L15: Wav . . . 8N 59
Waldgrave Rd. L15: Wav . . . 8M 59
Waldorf Cl. WN3: Wins . . . 1F 40
Waldron WN8: Skel . . . 4A 30
Waldron Cl. L3: Liv . . . 2E 4 (6B 58)
Walford Cl. CH63: Spit . . . 5M 89
Walford Rd. WN4: Ash M . . . 8L 41
Walk, The L24: Speke . . . 5D 92
L28: Stockb V . . . 2G 60
(off Dannette Hey)
PR8: Birkd . . . 2N 11
Walkden Ho. WN4: Ash M . . . 6H 41
Walker Art Gallery . . . 3G 5 (7C 58)

Walker Av. WA9: Sut M . . . 6L 63
Walker Cl. L37: Form . . . 2F 24
Walker Dr. L20: Boot . . . 3B 44
Walker Hgts. CH42: Tran . . . 5K 73
(off Walker St.)
Walker M. CH42: Tran . . . 5K 73
Walker Pl. CH42: Tran . . . 5K 73
Walker Rd. L21: Lith . . . 3N 43
M44: Irlam . . . 1M 69
Walker's Cft. CH45: Wall . . . 4F 56
Walkers La. CH66: Lit Sut . . . 8H 103
WA5: Penk . . . 5G 80
WA9: Sut M . . . 6K 63
Walker St. CH42: Tran . . . 5K 73
CH47: Hoy . . . 1C 70
CH62: Port S . . . 1A 90
L6: Liv . . . 2M 5 (6F 58)
WA2: Warr . . . 2B 82
Walker Way L9: Walt . . . 4E 44
Wallace Av. L36: Huy . . . 5L 61
Wallace Dr. L36: Huy . . . 5K 61
Wallace St. L9: Ain . . . 4F 44
WA8: Wid . . . 8K 79
Wallacre Rd. CH44: Wall . . . 5E 56
WALLASEY . . . 4E 56
Wallasey Bri. Rd. CH41: Birke . . . 8F 56
Wallasey Golf Course . . . 2D 56
Wallasey Grove Road Station (Rail) . . . 3E 56
Wallasey Rd. CH44: Wall . . . 5F 56
CH45: Wall . . . 5F 56
Wallasey Village CH44: Wall . . . 3E 56
CH45: Wall . . . 3E 56
Wallasey Village Station (Rail) . . . 4E 56
Wallbrook Av. WN5: Bil . . . 2N 39
Wallcroft CH64: Will . . . 7N 101
Wallcroft St. WN8: Skel . . . 4B 30
Waller Cl. L4: Kirkd . . . 2D 58
Waller St. L20: Boot . . . 4A 44
Wallgarth Cl. WN3: Wins . . . 1G 40
Wallgate Rd. L25: Gate . . . 2D 76
Wallgate Way L25: Gate . . . 2D 76
Wallingford Rd. CH49: Upton . . . 4N 71
Wallis Dr. WA8: Wid . . . 5M 79
Wallis St. WA4: Warr . . . 5C 82
Wallrake CH60: Hesw . . . 8N 87
Wallsend Ct. WA8: Wid . . . 5J 79
Wall St. L1: Liv . . . 6E 4 (8B 58)
Walmer Ct. PR8: Birkd . . . 2M 11
Walmer Rd. L22: Water . . . 2L 43
PR8: Birkd . . . 3N 11
Walmesley Rd. WA10: Eccl . . . 5D 48
Walmsley Dr. WA11: Rainf . . . 6D 38
Walmsley St. CH44: Wall . . . 4J 57
L5: Liv . . . 4B 58
WA8: Wid . . . 8M 79
WA12: Newt W . . . 6M 51
Walney Rd. L12: W Der . . . 1M 59
WN3: Wins . . . 1F 40
Walney Ter. L12: W Der . . . 1M 59
Walnut Av. L9: Walt . . . 7H 45
Walnut Cl. WA1: Wools . . . 1M 83
Walnut Gro. CH66: Whit . . . 4L 111
L31: Mell . . . 8M 35
WA9: St H . . . 1L 63
Walnut Rd. M31: Part . . . 6K 69
Walnut St. L7: Liv . . . 6L 5
PR8: South . . . 2B 12
Walnut Tree La. WA4: App . . . 3G 99
Walpole Av. L35: Whis . . . 6C 62
Walpole Gro. WA2: Warr . . . 7D 66
Walpole Rd. WA7: Run . . . 9L 95
Walro M. PR9: South . . . 4M 7
Walsham Gdns. WA9: St H . . . 3H 63
Walsh Cl. L5: Liv . . . 5B 58
WA12: Newt W . . . 5L 51
Walsh Rd. L14: Broad G . . . 7A 60
Walsingham Ct. CH44: Wall . . . 6K 57
(off Liscard Rd.)
Walsingham Dr. WA7: Nort . . . 5F 96
Walsingham Rd. CH44: Wall . . . 6K 57
L16: Child . . . 8C 60
WA5: Penk . . . 3H 81
Walter Beilin Ct. L17: Aig . . . 3K 75
Walter Gro. WA9: St H . . . 2B 64
Walter Leigh Way WA3: Low . . . 1H 53
WN7: Leigh . . . 1H 53
Walters Grn. Cres. WA3: Golb . . . 1A 52
Walter St. L5: Liv . . . 4A 58
WA1: Warr . . . 1F 82
WA8: Wid . . . 7N 79
WN4: Ash M . . . 6M 41
Waltham Ct. WA7: Nort . . . 3G 97
Waltham Rd. L6: Liv . . . 3H 59
WALTHEW GREEN . . . 1M 31
Waltho Av. L31: Mag . . . 2K 35
WALTON
L4 . . . 8G 45
WA4 . . . 8B 82
Walton Av. WA5: Penk . . . 3G 80
Walton Breck Rd. L4: Walt . . . 2E 58
Walton Hall Av. L4: Walt . . . 8F 44
L11: Norr G . . . 7J 45
Walton Hall Gdns. . . . 9B 82
Walton Hall Golf Course . . . 9A 82
Walton Hall Rd. L4: Walt . . . 8G 44
Walton Heath Rd. WA4: Walt . . . 7C 82
Walton La. L4: Walt . . . 2E 58
WA3: Ris . . . 4M 67
Walton Lea Crematorium
WA4: Hghr Wal . . . 9B 82
Walton Lea Rd. WA4: Hghr Wal . . . 9A 82
(not continuous)
Walton Pk. L9: Walt . . . 6F 44
Walton Rd. L4: Walt . . . 2D 58
WA3: Cul . . . 7N 53
WA4: Stockt H, Walt . . . 8C 82
WA10: St H . . . 4G 49
Walton Station (Rail) . . . 6E 44
Walton St. CH41: Birke . . . 2L 73
PR9: South . . . 7H 7
WA7: Run . . . 5K 95
Walton Va. L9: Walt, Ain . . . 4F 44
Walton Village L4: Walt . . . 8E 44
(not continuous)
Wambo La. L25: Gate . . . 3G 76
Wandsworth Rd. L11: Norr G . . . 9L 45
Wandsworth Way WA8: Wid . . . 2J 95
Wanes Blades Rd. L40: Lath . . . 1B 22
Wango La. L10: Ain . . . 1K 45
Wanisher La. L39: Down . . . 8F 18
Wansfell Pl. WA2: Warr . . . 6B 66
Wantage Vw. L36: Roby . . . 9G 61
Wapping L1: Liv . . . 8E 4 (9B 58)
Wapping Quay L3: Liv . . . 9E 4 (1B 74)
Wapshare Rd. L11: Norr G . . . 9K 45
Warbler Cl. L26: Halew . . . 6H 77
Warbreck Av. L9: Walt, Ain . . . 3F 44
Warbreck Moor L9: Ain . . . 4G 44
WARBRECK PARK . . . 3F 44
Warbreck Rd. L9: Walt . . . 4F 44
WARBURTON . . . 9H 69
Warburton Bri. Rd. WA3: Rix . . . 8G 68
Warburton Bri Rd. WA13: Warb . . . 8G 68
Warburton Cl. WA13: Lymm . . . 4G 84
Warburton Hey L35: Rainh . . . 5E 62
Warburton La. M31: Part . . . 5M 69
M31: Part, Warb . . . 1K 85
WA13: Warb . . . 1K 85
Warburton St. WA4: Stockt H . . . 7E 82
Warburton Vw. WA3: Rix . . . 7G 69
Ward Av. L37: Form . . . 2D 24
Ward Cl. WA5: Gt San . . . 8K 65
Warden St. L4: Walt . . . 1D 58
Wardgate Av. L12: Crox . . . 7C 46
Ward Gro. CH42: Rock F . . . 8M 73
Wardley Rd. WA4: Walt . . . 7C 82
Wardour St. WA5: Warr . . . 2N 81
Ward Rake L30: N'ton . . . 7C 34
(off Granams Cft.)
Ward Rd. L23: Blun . . . 6G 32
Ward St. L3: Liv . . . 4H 5 (7D 58)
L34: Presc . . . 2A 62
WA10: St H . . . 6K 49
Ware Cl. WN4: Ash M . . . 7M 41
Wareham Cl. WA1: Wools . . . 9K 67
WA11: Hay . . . 3E 50
Warehouse Studios WA3: Cul . . . 8L 53
Wareing Rd. L9: Ain . . . 4H 45
Waresley Cres. L9: Faz . . . 6K 45
WARGRAVE . . . 7L 51
Wargrave M. WA12: Newt W . . . 9L 51
Wargrave Rd. WA12: Newt W . . . 7K 51
Warham Rd. L4: Walt . . . 2H 59
Waring Av. CH42: Tran . . . 6K 73
WA4: Westy . . . 3G 83
WA9: St H . . . 8D 50
Warkworth Cl. L36: Huy . . . 9L 61
WA8: Wid . . . 5F 78
Warkworth Ct. CH65: Ell P . . . 2C 112
Warmington Rd. L14: Knott A . . . 6A 60
Warminster Gro. WN3: Wins . . . 1F 40
Warmwell Cl. L24: Speke . . . 4F 92
(off Cartwrights Farm Rd.)
Warner Dr. L4: Walt . . . 1H 59
Warnerville Rd. L13: Liv . . . 8N 59
Warnley Cl. WA8: Wid . . . 5G 79
Warper's Moss Cl. L40: Burs . . . 9K 15
Warper's Moss La. L40: Burs . . . 9K 15
Warpers Way L39: Orm . . . 8E 20
Warren, The CH49: Upton . . . 3B 72
WA12: Newt W . . . 7J 51
Warren Ct. CH66: Gt Sut . . . 2J 111
PR8: Birkd . . . 1L 11
WA6: Frod . . . 8N 107
Warren Cft. WA7: Nort . . . 8E 96
Warrender Dr. CH43: Bid . . . 9F 56
Warren Dr. CH43: Bid . . . 2C 72
CH45: Wall, New B . . . 1F 56
CH66: Ell P . . . 7K 103
WA4: App . . . 8D 82
WA12: Newt W . . . 6A 52
Warren Golf Course . . . 2F 56
Warren Grn. L37: Form . . . 9D 16
Warren Hey CH63: Spit . . . 6N 89
Warrenhouse Rd. L22: Water . . . 9H 33
L33: Kirkb . . . 7E 36
Warren Hurst CH45: New B . . . 1G 56
Warren La. CH62: Brom, East . . . 6E 90
(not continuous)
WA1: Wools . . . 9L 67
Warren Pk. CH45: Wall . . . 2F 56
Warren Point CH45: Wall . . . 1F 56
Warren Rd. CH47: Hoy . . . 1B 70
L23: Blun . . . 6G 33
PR9: South . . . 7M 7
WA2: Warr . . . 8E 66
WA4: App . . . 9D 82
Warren St. L3: Liv . . . 5J 5 (8D 58)
Warren Way CH60: Hesw . . . 6L 87
WARRINGTON . . . 3C 82
Warrington Av. CH65: Whit . . . 3N 111
Warrington Bank Quay Station (Rail) . . . 4A 82
Warrington Bri. WA1: Warr . . . 4C 82
Warrington Bus. Pk. WA2: Warr . . . 8D 66
Warrington Central Station (Rail) . . . 2C 82
Warrington Central Trad. Est.
WA2: Warr . . . 2B 82
Warrington Golf Course . . . 2E 98
Warrington La. WA13: Lymm . . . 5K 85
WA14: Lit Bo . . . 5K 85
Warrington Museum & Art Gallery . . . 4B 82
Warrington New Rd. WA9: St H . . . 7L 49
Warrington Rd. L34: Presc . . . 3A 62
L35: Presc, Rainh, Whis . . . 3A 62
WA3: Birchw, Cul, G'bury, Ris . . . 6K 67
(not continuous)
WA3: Golb . . . 3B 52
WA4: Hatt, Hghr Wal . . . 2N 97
WA5: Penk . . . 4G 80
WA7: Cas . . . 5A 96
WA7: Manor P . . . 3C 96
(not continuous)
WA8: Bold H . . . 9J 63
WA8: Wid . . . 8M 79
WA12: Newt W . . . 5B 52
WA13: Lymm . . . 5A 84
WN3: Wigan . . . 2H 41
WN4: Ash M . . . 9K 41
Warrington Sports Club . . . 9B 82
Warrington St. CH41: Tran . . . 4L 73
Warrington Wolves RLFC . . . 2B 82
Warton Cl. L25: Woolt . . . 6G 77
WA5: Penk . . . 5J 81
Warton St. L20: Boot . . . 4A 44
Warton Ter. L20: Boot . . . 4A 44
Warwick Av. L23: Crosb . . . 8K 33
WA5: Gt San . . . 1F 80
WA5: Warr . . . 1A 82
WA12: Newt W . . . 8M 51
WN4: Ash M . . . 9M 41
Warwick Cl. CH43: Oxton . . . 3J 73
CH64: Nest . . . 9E 100
L36: Huy . . . 6L 61
PR8: South . . . 2A 12
Warwick Ct. CH65: Ell P . . . 3C 112
L8: Liv . . . 2F 74
(off Gwent St.)
Warwick Dr. CH45: Wall . . . 3J 57
CH48: W Kir . . . 8D 70
Warwick Gro. WA7: Cas . . . 6B 96
Warwick Rd. CH49: Upton . . . 3M 71
L20: Boot . . . 6C 44
L36: Huy . . . 6L 61
M44: Cad . . . 4K 69
Warwick St. L8: Liv . . . 2D 74
PR8: South . . . 2A 12
WA10: St H . . . 7G 48
Wasdale Av. L31: Mag . . . 1L 35
WA11: St H . . . 2L 49
Wasdale Rd. L9: Walt . . . 5F 44
Washbrook Av. CH43: Bid . . . 9C 56
Washbrook Cl. WA10: Eccl . . . 6E 48
Washbrook Way L39: Orm . . . 9C 20
WASH END . . . 2J 53
Wash End WA3: Low . . . 2J 53
Washington Cl. WA8: Wid . . . 5J 79
WA9: St H . . . 5H 63
Washington Dr. L33: Kirkb . . . 5B 36
WA5: Gt San . . . 1L 81
Washington Pde. L20: Boot . . . 6B 44
Washington Rd. L27: N'ley . . . 4K 77
Wash La. WA4: Warr . . . 6F 82
Washway La. WA10: St H . . . 3J 49
WA11: St H . . . 3J 49
Wasley Cl. WA2: Fearn . . . 6H 67
Wastdale Ct. CH46: More . . . 8K 55
Wastdale Dr. CH46: More . . . 8K 55
Wastdale M. CH46: More . . . 8K 55
Wastdale Rd. WN4: Ash M . . . 3J 41
Wastle Bri. Rd. L36: Huy . . . 4J 61
Watchfield Cl. L24: Speke . . . 4F 92
(off Cartwrights Farm Rd.)
Watchyard La. L37: Form . . . 1G 25
Waterbridge Ct. WA4: App . . . 8E 82
WA13: Lymm . . . 5B 84
Waterbridge M. WA7: Cas . . . 5C 96
Water Bus. Pk. CH65: Ell P . . . 7B 104
Waterdale Cres. WA9: St H . . . 2N 63
Waterdale Pl. WA9: St H . . . 2N 63
Waterfall Dr. L4: Walt . . . 7F 44
Waterfield Cl. CH63: Hghr B . . . 2K 89
Waterfield Way L21: Lith . . . 1N 43
Waterfoot Av. PR8: Ains . . . 2H 17
Waterford Dr. CH64: Lit N . . . 7G 100
Waterford Rd. CH43: Oxton . . . 3F 72
L27: N'ley . . . 2G 77
Waterford Way WA7: Murd . . . 9E 96
Waterfront WA4: Pres H . . . 9H 97
Waterfront, The PR9: South . . . 7F 6
Waterfront Business Area L8: Liv . . . 1D 74
Waterfront Business Area Parliament St. Nth.
L1: Liv . . . 1D 74
(off New Bird St.)
L1: Liv . . . 9G 4
(Simpson St.)
Waterfront Business Area Parliament St. Sth.
L8: Liv . . . 2D 74
(off Stanhope St.)
Waterfront Dr. WA4: Westy . . . 5J 83
Watergate La. L25: Woolt . . . 6F 76
Watergate Way L25: Woolt . . . 6F 76
Waterhouse Cl. L6: Liv . . . 3G 59
Waterland La. WA9: St H . . . 8B 50
Water La. L35: Tar G . . . 4N 77
PR9: South . . . 2B 8
WATERLOO . . . 1L 43
Waterloo Cen. WA8: Wid . . . 1K 95
Waterloo Cl. CH65: Ell P . . . 9A 104
L22: Water . . . 2K 43
Waterloo Ct. CH63: Beb . . . 1N 89
L22: Water . . . 2L 43
Waterloo Dock L3: Liv . . . 1B 4 (6A 58)
Waterloo La. WA6: Frod, Kingsw . . . 4M 115
WATERLOO PARK . . . 1M 43
Waterloo Pl. CH41: Birke . . . 3L 73
Waterloo Quay L3: Liv . . . 2B 4 (6A 58)
Waterloo Rd. CH45: New B . . . 9H 43
L3: Liv . . . 1B 4 (5A 58)
L21: Sea . . . 4L 43
L22: Water . . . 2L 43
PR8: Birkd . . . 4L 11
WA7: Run . . . 4J 95
(not continuous)
WA8: Wid . . . 2K 95
Waterloo Station (Rail) . . . 1L 43
Waterloo St. L15: Wav . . . 1M 75
WA10: St H . . . 7J 49
Waterloo Warehouse L3: Liv . . . 1B 4 (6A 58)
Watermead Dr. WA7: Pres B . . . 1H 109
Watermede WN5: Bil . . . 9N 31
Waterpark Cl. CH43: Pren . . . 7F 72
Waterpark Dr. L28: Stockb V . . . 1D 60
Waterpark Ho. CH42: Tran . . . 6H 73
(off Storeton Rd.)
Waterpark Rd. CH42: Tran . . . 7F 72
CH43: Pren . . . 7F 72
Watersedge WA4: Warr . . . 7C 82
Watersedge WA6: Frod . . . 4N 107
Watersedge Apartments
CH45: New B . . . 9J 43
(off Egerton St.)
Watersedge Dr. L40: Ruf . . . 2N 15
Waterside L30: N'ton . . . 6D 34
WA4: App . . . 8E 82
WA9: St H . . . 6L 49
Waterside Bus. Pk. L40: Burs . . . 9F 14
Waterside Ct. WA7: Run . . . 4H 95
WA9: St H . . . 6L 49
Waterside Dr. WA6: Frod . . . 4M 107
Waterside La. WA8: Hale B . . . 2F 94
Waterside Pk. L36: Roby . . . 8H 61
Waters Rd. CH65: Ell P . . . 7B 104
Waterstone Cl. L11: Norr G . . . 7N 45
Water St. CH41: Birke . . . 2M 73
CH44: Wall . . . 5K 57
CH62: Port S . . . 2B 90
L2: Liv . . . 5D 4 (8B 58)
L3: Liv . . . 5C 4 (8A 58)
L22: Water . . . 2L 43
(off Brunswick Pde.)
L23: Thorn . . . 5A 34
WA7: Run . . . 4K 95
WA8: Wid . . . 1K 95
WA10: St H . . . 7J 49
WA12: Newt W . . . 6L 51
Water Twr. Rd. CH64: Nest . . . 5E 100
Waterway Av. L30: N'ton . . . 8G 34
Waterways WA5: Gt San . . . 2M 81
Waterworks Dr. WA12: Newt W . . . 6A 52
Waterworks La. CH66: Hoot . . . 5D 102
WA2: Win . . . 3C 66
Waterworks Rd. L39: Orm . . . 7E 20
Waterworks St. L20: Boot . . . 7C 44
Waterworth Dr. L7: Liv . . . 8G 59
Watery Ct. WA9: St H . . . 1B 64
Watery La. WA2: Win . . . 3N 65
WA6: Frod . . . 8A 108
WA9: St H . . . 1A 64
WA10: Windle . . . 3D 48
WA11: Windle . . . 3C 48
Watford Rd. L4: Walt . . . 2G 58
Watkin Cl. L30: N'ton . . . 1G 44
Watkins Av. WA12: Newt W . . . 7H 51
Watkinson St. L1: Liv . . . 9F 4 (1C 74)
Watkinson Way WA8: Wid . . . 9J 63
Watkin St. WA2: Warr . . . 1C 82
Watling Av. L21: Lith . . . 1N 43
Watling Way L35: Whis . . . 3D 62
Watmough St. L5: Liv . . . 1J 5 (5D 58)
Watson Av. WA3: Golb . . . 1A 52
WN4: Ash M . . . 8L 41
Watson Ct. CH41: Birke . . . 1M 73
(off Argyle St.)
Watson St. CH41: Birke . . . 1K 73
Watton Beck Cl. L31: Mag . . . 1L 35
Watton Cl. L12: Crox . . . 8E 46
WA4: Thel . . . 5K 83
Watts Clift Way WA9: St H . . . 7L 49
Watts Cl. L33: Kirkb . . . 7E 36
Watts La. L20: Boot . . . 3C 44
Wauchope St. L15: Wav . . . 9K 59
Wavell Av. PR9: South . . . 8N 7
WA8: Wid . . . 8F 78
Wavell Cl. PR9: South . . . 8N 7
Wavell Rd. L36: Huy . . . 5J 61
Waverley WN8: Skel . . . 3A 30
Waverley Av. WA4: App . . . 8E 82
Waverley Ct. WN3: Wins . . . 1F 40
Waverley Dr. L34: Presc . . . 4K 61

Waverley Gro. CH42: Tran 6J 73
Waverley Ho. L19: Aig 9L 75
Waverley Rd. CH47: Hoy 1D 70
L17: Aig 4H 75
L23: Blun 8J 33
WA3: Low 1E 52
Waverley St. L20: Boot 7A 44
PR8: South 8F 6
Waverly Ct. WA9: St H 9M 49
Waverton Av. CH43: Oxton 6E 72
Waverton Rd. CH66: Gt Sut 9K 103
WAVERTREE 9L 59
Wavertree Athletics Cen. 1L 75
Wavertree Av. L13: Wav 8K 59
WA8: Wid 8J 79
Wavertree Blvd. L7: Liv 8J 59
Wavertree Blvd. Sth. L7: Liv 8K 59
Wavertree Bus. Pk. L15: Wav 1L 75
Wavertree Bus. Village L13: Wav 8L 59
Wavertree Ct. CH66: Ell P 7L 103
Wavertree Gdns. L15: Wav 1L 75 (off Prince Alfred Rd.)
WAVERTREE GREEN 1N 75
Wavertree Grn. L15: Wav 1M 75
Wavertree Ho. L13: Liv 8M 59 (off Binns Rd.)
Wavertree Nook Rd. L15: Wav 8A 60
Wavertree Retail Pk. L7: Liv 8H 59
Wavertree Rd. L7: Liv 8G 58
Wavertree Sports Pk. 1L 75
Wavertree Technology Pk. L7: Liv 8J 59
L13: Wav 8K 59
Wavertree Technology Park Station (Rail) 8L 59
Wavertree Va. L15: Wav 9J 59
Wayfarers Arc. PR8: South 8G 6
Wayfarers Dr. WA12: Newt W 8N 51
Wayford Cl. WA6: Frod 5L 107
Wayford M. WA6: Frod 5L 107
Waylands Dr. L25: Hunts X 9F 76
Waymark Gdns. WA9: Sut M 6L 63
Wayside Cl. WA13: Lymm 6D 84
Wayville Cl. L18: Moss H 6N 75
Waywell Cl. WA2: Fearn 6G 67
Weald Dr. CH66: Lit Sut 8F 102
Weardale Rd. L15: Wav 2K 75
Wearhead Cl. WA3: Golb 3B 52
Weaste La. WA4: Thel 7L 83
Weates Cl. WA8: Wid 5A 80
Weatherstones Bus. Cen. CH64: Nest 6J 101
Weatherstones Cotts. CH64: Nest 6K 101
Weaver Av. L33: Kirkb 5D 36
L35: Rainh 6E 62
L40: Burs 9K 15
Weaver Ct. L25: Gate 5G 76
Weaver Cres. WA6: Frod 5N 107
Weaver Gro. WA9: St H 7C 50
Weaver Ho. L25: Gate 5G 76 (off Ribble Rd.)
Weaver Ind. Est. L19: Garst 3A 92
Weaver La. WA6: Frod 4L 107
Weavermill Pk. WN4: Ash M 9L 41
Weaver Pk. Ind. Est. WA6: Frod 4N 107
Weaver Rd. CH65: Ell P 2A 112
WA6: Frod 5N 107
WA7: West 9K 95
Weaver Sailing Club 4N 107
Weavers Fold WA1: Warr 2D 82
Weaverside Av. WA7: Sut W 2B 108
Weavers La. L31: Mag 5L 35
Weaver St. L9: Walt 7E 44
Weaver Vw. WA7: Clftn 2M 107
Webb Cl. L7: Liv 8H 59
Webb Dr. WA5: Burtw 3H 65
Webber Estates L33: Know I 9G 36
Webber Rd. L33: Know I 1F 46
Webb St. L7: Liv 1H 75
WA9: St H 9N 49
Web Complex, The L33: Know I 2G 46
Webster Av. CH45: Wall 4K 57
L20: Boot 6D 44
Webster Ct. WA5: Westb 7K 65
Webster Dr. L32: Kirkb 9C 36
Webster Rd. L7: Liv 1J 75
Websters Holt CH49: Upton 2N 71
Websters La. CH66: Gt Sut 3L 111
Webster St. L3: Liv 3F 4 (7C 58)
L21: Lith 4A 44
Weddell Cl. WA5: Old H 1M 81
Wedge Av. WA11: Hay 5C 50
Wedgewood Dr. WA4: Warr 6D 82
Wedgewood Gdns. WA9: St H 3E 62
Wedgewood St. L7: Liv 7G 59
Wedgwood Dr. WA8: Wid 4L 79
Wednesbury Dr. WA5: Gt San 2H 81
Weedon Av. WA12: Newt W 5K 51
Weightman Gro. L9: Ain 4F 44
Weint, The WA3: Rix 6H 69
Weir La. WA1: Wools 2M 83
WA4: Warr 4E 82
Weirside WA9: St H 3N 63
Weir St. WA4: Warr 7B 82
Welbeck Av. L18: Moss H 3L 75
WA12: Newt W 8M 51
Welbeck Ct. L22: Water 1K 43 (off Mt. Pleasant)
Welbeck Rd. PR8: Birkd 2M 11
WN4: Ash M 6L 41
Welbeck Ter. PR8: Birkd 2N 11
Welbourne WN8: Skel 4A 30
Welbourne Rd. L16: Child 8A 60
Weldale Ho. PR8: Birkd 2M 11
Weld Blundell Av. L31: Lyd 8G 27
Weld Dr. L37: Form 9D 16
Weldon Dr. L39: Orm 9D 20
Weldon St. L4: Walt 8E 44
Weld Pde. PR8: Birkd 2M 11
Weld Rd. L23: Blun 8J 33
PR8: Birkd 1L 11
Welford Av. CH43: Pren 6F 72
WA3: Low 3D 52
Welford Cl. WA9: St H 2N 63
Welland Cl. L26: Halew 1J 93
Welland Gdns. WA12: Newt W 8L 51
Welland Rd. CH63: Hghr B 2K 89
WN4: Ash M 6N 41
Wellbank Dr. L26: Halew 7L 77
Wellbrae Cl. CH49: Upton 3L 71
Wellbrook Cl. L24: Speke 3H 93
WA7: Brook 1E 108
Wellbrooke Cl. WN4: Ash M 8L 41
Wellbrook Grn. L24: Speke 4H 93
Wellbrow Rd. L4: Walt 8F 44
Well Cl. CH64: Ness 9G 100
Wellcroft Gdns. WA13: Lymm 6G 84
Wellcroft Rd. L36: Huy 5J 61
Wellcross Rd. WN8: Uph 6L 31
Wellens Wlk. WA10: St H 7F 48
Weller St. L8: Liv 3E 74
Weller Way L8: Liv 4F 74
Wellesbourne Cl. CH64: Nest 8D 100
Wellesbourne Pl. L11: Norr G 8M 45
Wellesbourne Rd. L11: Norr G 7M 45
Wellesley Av. CH65: Ell P 9A 104
Wellesley Cl. WA12: Newt W 5K 51
Wellesley Gro. CH63: Beb 1N 89
Wellesley Rd. CH44: Wall 5H 57 (not continuous)
L8: Liv 4F 74
Wellesley Ter. L8: Liv 4F 74
Wellesley Wlk. CH65: Ell P 9A 104 (off Wellesley Av.)
Well Farm Cl. WA1: Wools 9L 67
Wellfarm Cl. L9: Ain 7J 45
Wellfield WA7: Pres B 1G 108
WA8: Wid 5K 79
WA11: Rainf 7D 38
Wellfield Av. L32: Kirkb 1C 46
Wellfield La. L40: Westh 1G 28
Wellfield Pl. L8: Liv 4F 74
Wellfield Rd. L9: Walt 6F 44
WA3: Cul 6M 53
Wellfield St. WA5: Warr 2N 81 (not continuous)
Wellgreen Rd. L25: Gate 1D 76
Wellgreen Wlk. L25: Gate 1E 76 (off Wellgreen Rd.)
Wellingford Av. WA8: Hale B 2E 94
Wellington Av. L15: Wav 2J 75
Wellington Cl. CH63: Beb 1N 89
CH65: Ell P 9A 104
L10: Ain 8H 35
WA2: Padg 7G 66
WA12: Newt W 7J 51
WN8: Skel 4H 31
Wellington Ct. CH65: Ell P 9A 104 (off Arthur Av.)
Wellington Employment Pk. Sth. L5: Kirkd 3B 58
Wellington Flds. L15: Wav 2J 75
Wellington Gdns. L22: Water 1K 43 (off Mason St.)
WA12: Newt W 7J 51
Wellington Ga. L24: Hale 5A 94
Wellington Gro. L15: Wav 9K 59
Wellington Mans. CH45: New B 9G 43 (off Atherton St.)
Wellington Rd. CH43: Oxton 3G 72
CH45: New B 1G 56
CH63: Beb 1N 89
CH65: Ell P 1N 111 (not continuous)
L8: Liv 4E 74
L15: Wav 1K 75
L21: Lith 3N 43
Wellington Rd. Nth. CH65: Ell P 9A 104
Wellington St. L3: Liv 1F 4 (6C 58)
L19: Garst 1A 92
L22: Water 1K 43
PR8: South 9F 6
WA1: Warr 3D 82
WA7: Run 4K 95
WA8: Wid 1K 95
WA12: Newt W 7J 51
Wellington St. Ind. Est. WA8: Wid 1K 95 (off Wellington St.)
Wellington St. Workshops WA1: Warr 3D 82 (off Wellington St.)
Wellington Ter. CH41: Birke 3K 73
L8: Liv 3F 74
WA10: St H 5K 49
Well La. CH42: Rock F, Tran 5K 73
CH49: Grea 5K 71
CH60: Hesw 9A 88
CH63: Hghr B 1K 89
CH64: Ness 9F 100
L16: Child 1D 76
L20: Boot 7C 44
Well La. L25: Gate 1D 76
L39: Bart 7D 18
WA4: Lwr S 7F 98
WA5: Penk 5G 81 (not continuous)
WA6: Manl 9J 115
Well La. Gdns. L20: Boot 7C 44
Wells Av. WN5: Bil 5N 39
Wells Cl. CH66: Gt Sut 5K 111
WA1: Wools 9J 67
Wells St. L15: Wav 1L 75
Wellstead Cl. L15: Wav 9M 59
Wellstead Rd. L15: Wav 9M 59
Wellstead Wlk. L15: Wav 9M 59 (off Wellstead Rd.)
Wellswood Rd. CH66: Ell P 7K 103
Wellwood Cl. CH65: Ell P 7N 103
Welsby Cl. WA2: Fearn 6G 66
Welshampton Cl. CH66: Gt Sut 3J 111
Welshpool Cl. WA5: Call 6M 65
Welsh Rd. CH1: Woodb 9B 110
CH66: Chil T, Led, Lit Sut 4C 110
Welton Av. CH49: Upton 3N 71
Welton Cl. L24: Speke 4H 93
Welton Grn. L24: Speke 4H 93
Welton Rd. CH62: Brom 5C 90
Welwyn Av. PR8: Ains 8L 11
Welwyn Cl. WA4: Thel 5K 83
WA9: St H 3J 63
Wembley Gdns. L9: Walt 4E 44
Wembley Rd. L18: Moss H 4N 75
L23: Crosb 8M 33
Wendell St. L8: Liv 1H 75
Wendlebury Cl. WN7: Leigh 1M 53
Wendover Av. L17: Aig 5H 75
Wendover Cl. CH43: Noct 4D 72
WA11: Hay 3F 50
Wendron Rd. L11: Crox 5B 46
Wenger Rd. WA8: Wid 3L 79
Wenlock Cl. WA1: Padg 9H 67
Wenlock Ct. L26: Halew 9J 77
Wenlock Dr. L26: Halew 9J 77
Wenlock Gdns. CH66: Gt Sut 3L 111
Wenlock La. CH66: Gt Sut 3L 111
Wenlock Rd. L4: Walt 2G 59
WA7: Beech 2C 108
WN7: Leigh 1M 53
Wenning Av. L31: Mag 1K 35
Wennington Rd. PR9: South 7L 7 (not continuous)
Wensley Av. L26: Halew 9K 77
Wensleydale L9: Walt 3F 44
Wensleydale Av. CH62: East 1D 102
L35: Rainh 6G 62
Wensleydale Cl. L31: Mag 1G 35
WA5: Gt San 9H 65
Wensley Rd. L9: Walt 3F 44
WA3: Low 3F 52
Wentworth Av. CH45: New B 2H 57
WA1: Wools 1J 83
Wentworth Cl. CH43: Noct 4D 72
PR8: Ains 1J 17
WA8: Wid 3K 79
Wentworth Dr. CH63: Brom 1B 102
L5: Liv 5E 58
Wentworth Gro. L36: Huy 7F 60
Wentworth Rd. WN4: Ash M 6J 41
Werburgh Cl. WA13: Warb 9J 69
Wernbrook Cl. CH43: Noct 4D 72
Wernbrook Rd. L4: Walt 2H 59
WERVIN 9E 112
Wervin Cl. CH43: Oxton 6E 72
Wervin Mobile Home Pk. CH2: Wer 9E 112
Wervin Rd. CH2: Crou, Stoak, Upton, Wer 8E 112
CH43: Oxton 6E 72
L32: Kirkb 1B 46
Wesley Av. CH44: Wall 4J 57
WA11: Hay 3H 51
Wesley Cl. CH64: Park 6D 100
Wesley Gro. CH44: Wall 6L 57
Wesley Hall Gdns. WA9: St H 3G 62
Wesley Pl. L15: Wav 9L 59
Wesley St. L22: Water 2K 43
PR8: South 8G 6
Wessex Cl. WA1: Wools 1M 83
W. Albert Rd. L17: Aig 4G 75
W. Alfred Ct. CH43: Oxton 3J 73 (off Alfred Rd.)
West Allerton Station (Rail) 7N 75
West Av. WA2: Warr 9C 66
WA3: Golb 1C 52
WA4: Stockt H 7D 82
WEST BANK 3K 95
Westbank Av. CH45: New B 2J 57
W. Bank Dock Est. WA8: Wid 2H 95
W. Bank Rd. L7: Liv 7K 59
Westbank Rd. CH42: Tran 5J 73
W. Bank St. WA8: Wid 2K 95
Westbourne Av. CH48: W Kir 6C 70
L23: Thorn 5A 34
Westbourne Gdns. PR8: Birkd 2K 11
Westbourne Gro. CH48: W Kir 6C 70
Westbourne Rd. CH41: Birke 3J 73
CH43: Oxton 3J 73
CH44: Wall 5F 56
CH48: W Kir 6B 70
PR8: Birkd 2K 11
WA4: Stockt H 9C 82
Westbridge M. WA1: Padd 1G 83
WESTBROOK 7K 65
Westbrook Av. L34: Presc 3M 61
WA4: Warr 6E 82
Westbrook Cen. WA5: Westb 8K 65 (not continuous)
Westbrook Cres. WA5: Gt San, Westb 8K 65 (not continuous)
Westbrook Rd. CH46: More 1K 71
L25: Gate 3G 77
Westbrook Way WA5: Westb 8J 65
W. Brow Gdns. CH43: Bid 9C 56
Westbury Av. WN3: Wins 1F 40
Westbury Cl. L17: Aig 7H 75
L25: Hunts X 8H 77
WA1: Padg 9H 67
Westbury St. CH41: Tran 4L 73
West Cheshire Sailing Club 2D 56
Westcliffe Ct. PR8: Birkd 1M 11
WA8: Wid 4L 79
Westcliffe Rd. L12: W Der 2M 59
PR8: Birkd 1L 11
Westcliff Gdns. WA4: App 4F 98
West Cl. CH43: Noct 3D 72
L34: Eccl P 2D 62
Westcombe Rd. L4: Walt 2H 59
Westcott Rd. L4: Walt 3G 58
Westcott Way CH43: Noct 4D 72
Westdale Rd. CH42: Rock F 6L 73
L15: Wav 9L 59
WA1: Padd 1H 83
Westdale Vw. L15: Wav 9L 59
Westdene PR9: South 6K 7
WN8: Parb 3E 22
WEST DERBY 2N 59
West Derby Golf Course 3C 60
W. Derby Rd. L6: Liv 1M 5 (6F 58) (Low Hill)
L6: Liv 4J 59 (Orphan Dr.)
L13: Liv 3L 59
W. Derby St. L7: Liv 4L 5 (7F 58)
W. Derby Village L12: W Der 2N 59
West Dr. CH49: Upton 3A 72
CH60: Hesw 8A 88
CH64: Nest 8D 100
WA5: Gt San 4K 81
West End Gro. WA11: Hay 4B 50
West End Rd. WA11: Hay 4B 50
West End Ter. PR8: South 8F 6 (off West St.)
Westenra Av. CH65: Ell P 8L 103
Westerdale Dr. PR9: Banks 2F 8
Westerhope Way WA8: Wid 5J 79
Western Approaches Mus. (Underground Wartime Mus.) 4D 4 (7B 58)
Western Av. CH62: Brom 4C 90
L24: Speke 5G 93
L36: Huy 6E 60
Western Dr. L19: Gras 9M 75
Westerton Rd. L12: W Der 3C 60
Westfield Av. L14: Broad G 7C 60
WN4: Ash M 7J 41
Westfield Cres. WA7: Run 6H 95
Westfield Dr. L12: Crox 8C 46
Westfield M. WA7: Run 6J 95
Westfield Rd. CH44: Wall 8K 57
L9: Walt 4D 44
WA7: Run 6H 95
Westfields Dr. L20: Boot 3E 44
Westfield St. WA10: St H 7J 49 (not continuous)
Westfield Wlk. L32: Kirkb 9N 35
W. Float Ind. Est. CH41: Birke 7H 57
Westford Rd. WA4: Warr 7B 82
Westgate WA8: Wid 9E 78
WN8: Skel 3A 30
Westgate Dr. WN5: Orr 7N 31
Westgate Health & Fitness 4A 30
Westgate Ind. Est. WN8: Skel 4A 30
Westgate M. WN8: Skel 3A 30 (off Westgate)
Westgate Rd. CH62: Port S 3A 90
L15: Wav 3M 75
WEST GILLIBRANDS 4N 29
West Gro. CH60: Hesw 7N 87
Westhaven Cres. L39: Augh 3A 28
Westhay Cres. WA3: Birchw 4A 68
WESTHEAD 9J 21
Westhead Av. L33: Kirkb 9D 36
WA3: Low 1F 52
Westhead Cl. L33: Kirkb 1E 46
Westhead Wlk. L33: Kirkb 9D 36
W. Heath Gro. WA13: Lymm 4C 84
West Hill PR8: South 9F 6
Westholme Ct. PR9: South 6H 7
Westhouse Cl. CH63: Brom 1B 102
West Hyde WA13: Lymm 5C 84
WEST KIRBY 6B 70
West Kirby Concourse (Leisure Cen.) 5B 70
W. Kirby Rd. CH46: More 2K 71
West Kirby Station (Rail) 6B 70
West Knowe CH43: Oxton 4F 72
West Lancashire Golf Course 5G 33
W. Lancashire Investment Cen. WN8: Skel 6C 30
West Lancashire Yacht Club 6F 6
Westland Dr. WA2: Padg 8F 66

Westlands Cl. CH64: Nest 5F 100
West La. L37: Form 7F 16
WA7: Pal F 8A 96
WA13: Lymm 9J 85
WA16: High L 9J 85
Westleigh Pl. WA9: Sut L 4M 63
W. Lodge Dr. CH48: W Kir 5B 70
West Mains L24: Speke 4L 93
West Meade L31: Mag 1G 35
Westminster Av. L30: N'ton 7D 34
Westminster Bri. CH65: Ell P 9A 104
Westminster Chambers L1: Liv 4F 4
(off Crosshall St.)
Westminster Cl. L4: Kirkd 1D 58
WA4: Grap 6K 83
WA8: Wid 8E 78
Westminster Ct. CH43: Oxton 3F 72
Westminster Dr. CH62: Brom 8C 90
PR8: Ains 9G 11
WA11: Hay 3H 51
Westminster Gro. CH65: Ell P 8A 104
L34: Presc 4L 61
Westminster Ind. Pk. CH65: Ell P 8L 103
Westminster Pl. WA1: Warr 3C 82
(off Winwick St.)
Westminster Retail Pk. CH65: Ell P 8B 104
Westminster Rd. CH44: Wall 5H 57
CH65: Ell P 8A 104
L4: Kirkd 9C 44
Westmoreland Rd. CH45: New B 2J 57
PR8: South 1B 12
Westmorland Av. L30: N'ton 8B 34
WA8: Wid 7L 79
Westmorland Dr. L3: Liv 2E 4 (6B 58)
Westmorland Pl. L5: Liv 4C 58
Westmorland Rd. L36: Huy 7J 61
M31: Part 7L 69
W. Oakhill Pk. L13: Liv 7M 59
WESTON 9J 95
Westonby Ct. WN4: Ash M 8M 41
Weston Ct. L23: Blun 8H 33
WA7: West 8J 95
Weston Cres. WA7: West 9J 95
Weston Gro. L26: Halew 1L 93
L31: Mag 5J 35
WESTON POINT 8G 95
Weston Point Docks WA7: West P 8G 94
Weston Point Expressway
WA7: Run, West 6H 95
Weston Rd. WA7: Run, West 7H 95
Weston Vw. WA7: Clftn 2N 107
W. Orchard La. L9: Ain 2J 45
Westover Cl. L31: Mag 2H 35
Westover Rd. L31: Mag 2H 35
WA1: Padg 1G 83
WEST PARK 8G 49
West Pk. PR9: South 6J 7
West Pk. Cl. WN8: Skel 4A 30
West Pk. Dr. CH66: Gt Sut 5L 111
West Pk. Gdns. CH43: Bid 9C 56
West Pk. Rd. WA10: St H 8G 49
WEST PIMBO 8G 31
Westport Bus. Pk. L20: Kirkd 2B 58
West Quay L3: Liv 9E 4 (1B 74)
West Quay Rd. WA2: Win 6A 66
Westridge Ct. PR9: South 7J 7
West Rd. CH43: Noct 3D 72
CH65: Ell P 2A 112
CH65: Ell P, Hoot 3H 103
L14: Broad G 7A 60
WA7: West P 8G 94
Westry Cl. CH46: More 9J 55
West Side WA9: St H 8M 49
West Side Av. WA11: Hay 4C 50
Westside Ind. Est. WA9: St H 8M 49
West St. CH45: Wall 4H 57
L34: Presc 3N 61
PR8: South 8F 6
WA2: Warr 1C 82
WA10: St H 9G 48
West Twr. L3: Liv 3C 4
WESTVALE 9A 36
West Vale CH64: Nest 8E 100
West Vw. CH41: Tran 4M 73
CH66: Chil T 6F 102
(off Orchard La.)
L36: Huy 7M 61
L39: Orm 8D 20
WA2: Padg 8H 67
WN8: Parb 3E 22
West Vw. Av. L36: Huy 7M 61
West Vw. Cl. L36: Huy 7M 61
Westview Cl. CH43: Noct 4D 72
Westward Ho CH48: Caldy 1E 86
Westward Vw. L17: Aig 5F 74
L22: Water 9H 33
Westway CH43: Noct 4D 72
CH46: More 8M 55
CH49: Grea 4L 71
CH60: Hesw 9N 87
L15: Wav 9N 59
L31: Mag 1H 35
L38: Hight 8F 24
WA7: Pal F 8A 96
Westway Sq. CH46: More 8M 55
Westwick Pl. L36: Huy 6F 60
Westwood WA7: Wind H 6E 96
Westwood Cl. PR8: South 3D 12
Westwood Ct. CH43: Oxton 3F 72
CH64: Nest 4E 100
Westwood Gro. CH44: Wall 5G 56
Westwood Rd. CH43: Bid 2C 72
L18: Aller 8A 76
WESTY 4G 82
Westy La. WA4: Westy 4F 82
Wet Ga. La. WA13: Lymm 4J 85
Wetherby Av. CH45: Wall 4E 56
WA4: Warr 6D 82
Wetherby Cl. WA12: Newt W 5L 51
Wetherby Ct. L36: Huy 4G 60
Wetherby Way CH66: Lit Sut 8G 102
Wethersfield Lodge CH43: Noct 4E 72
Wethersfield Rd. CH43: Noct 5E 72
Wetstone La. CH48: W Kir 7D 70
Wetton La. CW8: Act B 9N 109
Wexford Av. L24: Hale 5A 94
Wexford Cl. CH43: Oxton 4E 72
WA11: Hay 3F 50
Wexford Rd. CH43: Oxton 4F 72
Wexwood Gro. L35: Whis 7C 62
Weybourne Cl. CH49: Upton 1A 72
Weybridge Cl. WA4: App 9F 82
Weyman Av. L35: Whis 6B 62
Weymoor Cl. CH63: Spit 5M 89
Weymouth Av. WA9: St H 9B 50
Weymouth Cl. L16: Child 9D 60
WA7: Murd 9G 97
Weymouth Rd. WA5: Burtw 3H 65
Whaley La. CH61: Irby 1N 87
Whalley Av. WA10: St H 3H 49
WA11: Rainf 5C 38
Whalley Cl. WN3: Wigan 1J 41
Whalley Ct. L30: N'ton 7C 34
Whalley Dr. L37: Form 2G 24
L39: Augh 4A 28
Whalley Gro. WA8: Wid 5N 79
Whalley Rd. CH42: Tran 3K 73
WHALLEYS 8E 22
Whalleys Rd. WN8: Skel 8D 22
Whalley St. L8: Liv 4E 74
WA1: Warr 2D 82
Wharf, The WA7: Pres B 9H 97
Wharfdale Cl. WA5: Gt San 1J 81
Wharfedale WA7: Pal F 9D 96
Wharfedale Av. CH42: Tran 6H 73
Wharfedale Dr. CH62: East 1E 102
L35: Rainh 6G 62
Wharfedale Rd. CH45: Wall 3F 56
Wharfedale St. L19: Garst 2C 92
Wharfe La. CH65: Ell P 7M 103
Wharf Ind. Est. WA1: Warr 4D 82
Wharford La. WA7: Nort 4G 97
Wharf Rd. WA12: Newt W 8G 51
Wharfside Ct. WA4: App 7F 82
Wharf St. CH62: Port S 2B 90
WA1: Warr 4C 82
Wharmby Rd. WA11: Hay 4G 50
Wharncliffe Rd. L13: Liv 6M 59
Wharton Cl. CH49: Upton 2L 71
Wharton St. WA9: St H 9L 49
Whatcroft Cl. WA7: Run 9N 95
Wheatacre WN8: Skel 4B 30
Wheatcroft Cl. WA5: Gt San 2L 81
Wheatcroft Rd. L18: Aller 6A 76
Wheatear Cl. L27: N'ley 4J 77
Wheatfield Cl. CH46: More 1N 71
CH66: Gt Sut 2H 111
L30: N'ton 8G 34
Wheatfield Rd. WA8: Cron 3F 78
Wheatfield Vw. L21: Ford 9A 34
Wheat Hill Rd. L36: Huy 1J 77
Wheathills Ind. Est. L27: N'ley 2H 77
Wheatland Bus. Pk. CH44: Wall 7K 57
Wheatland Cl. WA9: Clock F 5M 63
Wheatland La. CH44: Wall 6K 57
Wheatland Rd. CH60: Hesw 8C 88
Wheatlands WA7: Run 6A 96
Wheat La. L40: Lath 2L 21
Wheatlea Ind. Est. WN3: Wigan 2H 41
Wheatlea Rd. WN3: Wigan 1H 41
Wheatley Av. L20: Boot 5D 44
WA12: Newt W 5L 51
Wheatsheaf Av. WA9: Sut L 3N 63
Wheatsheaf Wlk. L39: Orm 8C 20
(off Burscough St.)
Wheeler Dr. L31: Mell 8N 35
Wheelwrights Wharf L40: Scar 1L 19
Whelan Gdns. WA9: St H 3H 63
Wheldon Rd. WA8: Wid 1C 94
Wheldrake Cl. CH66: Lit Sut 9G 103
Whelmar Ho. WN8: Skel 3F 30
Whernside WA8: Wid 6F 78
Whetstone Ct. CH41: Birke 3K 73
(off Whetstone La.)
Whetstone Hey CH66: Gt Sut 9J 103
Whetstone La. CH41: Birke 3K 73
Whickham Cl. WA8: Wid 5J 79
Whimbrel Av. WA12: Newt W 7L 51
Whimbrel Cl. WA7: Beech 1B 108
Whimbrel Pk. L26: Halew 7J 77
Whinberry Dr. L32: Kirkb 1B 46
Whinbury Ct. WA9: Clock F 5M 63
Whinchat Av. WA12: Newt W 6L 51
Whinchat Cl. WA3: Low 3F 52
Whinchat Dr. WA3: Birchw 6N 67
Whincraig L28: Stockb V 2F 60
Whinfell Gro. WA7: Beech 1A 108
Whinfell Rd. L12: W Der 4A 60
Whinfield Rd. L9: Walt 4E 44
L23: Thorn 5N 33
Whinhowe Rd. L11: Norr G 8N 45
Whinmoor Cl. CH43: Noct 2D 72
Whinmoor Rd. L10: Faz 3M 45
L12: W Der 4A 60
Whinney Gro. E. L31: Mag 5H 35
Whinney Gro. W. L31: Mag 5H 35
WHISTON 6B 62
WHISTON CROSS 6A 62
Whiston La. L36: Huy 5L 61
WHISTON LANE ENDS 7B 62
Whiston Station (Rail) 6B 62
Whitbarrow Rd. WA13: Lymm 4C 84
Whitburn WN8: Skel 3A 30
Whitburn Cl. WN4: Garsw 7F 40
Whitburn Rd. L33: Kirkb 7E 36
WHITBY 1M 111
Whitby Av. CH45: Wall 4E 56
PR9: South 1B 8
WA2: Warr 7E 66
WHITBYHEATH 3L 111
Whitby Rd. CH1: Back 5M 111
CH65: Ell P, Whit 1N 111
(not continuous)
WA7: Run 6K 95
Whitby St. L6: Liv 3J 59
Whitchurch Cl. WA1: Padg 9H 67
Whitchurch Way WA7: Run 9N 95
Whitcroft Rd. L6: Liv 6J 59
Whitebeam Av. CH66: Gt Sut 4L 111
Whitebeam Cl. L33: Kirkb 5D 36
WA7: Wind H 6E 96
Whitebeam Dr. L12: Crox 7B 46
Whitebeam Gdns. WA9: St H 3F 62
Whitebeam Wlk. CH49: Grea 6J 71
White Broom WA13: Lymm 4H 85
Whitechapel L1: Liv 5F 4 (8C 58)
White Clover Sq. WA13: Lymm 6G 85
Whitecroft Av. WA3: Low 1F 52
Whitecroft Rd. CH66: Gt Sut 3K 111
WN3: Wigan 1J 41
Whitecroft Vs. M31: Part 7L 69
White Cross Ct. WA12: Newt W 6K 51
Whitecross Rd. WA5: Warr 3N 81
Whitefield WA13: Lymm 4G 85
Whitefield Av. L4: Kirkd 1D 58
WA12: Newt W 8A 52
Whitefield Cl. CH49: Woodc 5B 72
L38: Hight 1F 32
L40: Ruf 3N 15
WA3: Golb 2B 52
WA13: Lymm 3G 85
Whitefield Ct. WA3: Ris 8N 53
Whitefield Dr. L32: Kirkb 9N 35
Whitefield Gro. WA13: Lymm 4G 85
Whitefield La. L35: Tar G 3L 77
Whitefield Rd. L6: Liv 5G 58
WA4: Stockt H 8C 82
WA10: St H 5G 48
Whitefields CH2: Elt 2M 113
WHITEFIELDS CROSS 5B 80
Whitefield Way L6: Liv 5F 58
White Friars WA10: Eccl 6D 48
Whitegate Av. WA3: Cul 8N 53
Whitegate Cl. L34: Know 6H 47
Whitegates Cl. CH64: Will 5L 101
Whitegates Cres. CH64: Will 6L 101
Whitehall Av. WN6: Appl B 5N 23
Whitehall Cl. L4: Kirkd 9D 44
Whitehall Pl. WA6: Frod 6M 107
(not continuous)
Whitehart Cl. L4: Walt 9G 44
Whitehaven Cl. PR8: Ains 2H 17
Whitehaven Rd. L5: Liv 3E 58
Whiteheath Way CH46: Leas 6N 55
Whitehedge Rd. L19: Garst 9N 75
Whitehey WN8: Skel 4B 30
Whitehey Island WN8: Skel 4B 30
Whitehey Rd. WN8: Skel 4B 30
WHITEHOUSE 2H 109
White House, The WA4: Warr 6D 82
Whitehouse Av. L37: Form 1G 24
White Ho. Cl. WA11: Hay 4D 50
White Ho. Dr. WA1: Wools 1M 83
Whitehouse Expressway
WA7: Brook, Pal F 9A 96
Whitehouse Ind. Est. WA7: Pres B 2G 109
(not continuous)
White Ho. La. L40: Scar 5A 14
Whitehouse La. CH60: Hesw 6C 88
CH63: Brim 6C 88
L37: Form 1G 24
Whitehouse Rd. L13: Liv 7N 59
Whitehouse Va. Ind. Est.
WA7: Pres B 1H 109
Whitelands Mdw. CH49: Upton 3M 71
Whiteledge Rd. WN8: Skel 5E 30
Whiteleggs La. WA13: Lymm 7H 85
Whiteley's La. L40: Westh 2H 29
White Lodge Av. L36: Huy 6H 61
White Lodge Cl. CH62: Brom 1C 102
White Lodge Dr. WN4: Ash M 7M 41
Whitely Gro. L33: Kirkb 5E 36
White Mdw. Dr. L23: Thorn 6N 33
Whitemere Ct. CH65: Ell P 7A 104
WHITE MOSS 5B 30
Whitemoss Bus. Pk. WN8: Skel 6B 30
White Moss Rd. WN8: Skel 5N 29
White Moss Rd. Sth. WN8: Skel 5N 29
White Oak Lodge L19: Gras 9L 75
(off Beechwood Rd.)
Whiterails Dr. L39: Orm 7B 20
Whiterails M. L39: Orm 7B 20
White Rock St. L6: Liv 5G 58
Whitesands Rd. WA13: Lymm 4C 84
Whiteside Av. WA11: St H 5A 50
Whiteside Cl. CH49: Upton 4A 72
L5: Liv 4C 58
Whiteside Rd. WA11: Hay 4D 50
Whitestocks WN8: Skel 4B 30
Whitestone Cl. L34: Know 8G 47
White St. WA1: Warr 3B 82
WA4: Stockt H 7D 82
WA8: Wid 2K 95
Whitethorn Av. WA5: Gt San 3H 81
Whitethorn Dr. L28: Stockb V 1F 60
Whitethroat Wlk. WA3: Birchw 6N 67
Whitewell Dr. CH49: Upton 2N 71
Whitewood Cl. WN4: Ash M 5J 41
Whitewood Pk. L9: Ain 4J 45
Whitfield Av. WA1: Padd 1G 83
Whitfield Ct. CH42: Tran 4K 73
Whitfield Gro. WA11: Hay 4C 50
Whitfield La. CH60: Hesw 5A 88
Whitfield Lodge WA9: Sut L 5N 63
Whitfield Rd. L9: Walt 5F 44
WHITFIELDS CROSS 5A 80
Whitfield St. CH42: Tran 4K 73
Whitford Rd. CH42: Tran 4J 73
Whitham Av. L23: Crosb 8M 33
Whithill Wlk. WN4: Ash M 6J 41
Whithorn St. L7: Liv 9J 59
Whitland Rd. L6: Liv 6J 59
Whitledge Grn. WN4: Ash M 6J 41
Whitledge Rd. WN4: Ash M 6J 41
Whitley Av. WA4: Westy 4H 83
Whitley Cl. WA7: Run 7J 95
Whitley Dr. CH44: Wall 4K 57
WHITLEY REED 7L 99
Whitley Rd. WN8: Roby M, Uph 1M 31
Whitley St. L3: Liv 5A 58
Whitlow Av. WA3: Golb 1A 52
Whitlow Rd. L5: Liv 3F 58
Whitman St. L15: Wav 1K 75
Whitmoor Cl. L35: Rainh 8H 63
Whitney Pl. L25: Woolt 6G 76
Whitney Rd. L25: Woolt 5G 76
Whitstable Pk. WA8: Wid 4H 79
Whitstone Cl. L18: Aller 6C 76
Whitstone Dr. WN8: Skel 5G 31
Whittaker Av. WA2: Warr 7E 66
Whittaker Cl. L13: Liv 8L 59
Whittaker St. WA9: St H 9N 49
Whittier St. L8: Liv 1H 75
Whittington Ho. L21: Lith 3N 43
(off Beach Rd.)
Whittle Av. WA5: Gt San 9H 65
WA11: Hay 5C 50
Whittle Cl. L5: Kirkd 3D 58
Whittle Ct. WN3: Wins 1G 40
Whittle Dr. L39: Orm 6C 20
Whittle Hall La. WA5: Gt San 2H 81
Whittle La. WN6: Wright 1H 23
Whittle St. L5: Kirkd 3D 58
WA10: St H 9G 48
Whittlewood Cl. WA3: Birchw 4A 68
Whittlewood Ct. L33: Kirkb 7D 36
Whitwell Cl. WA5: Gt San 1F 80
Whitworth Cl. WA3: Birchw 6M 67
Whitworth Ct. WA7: Manor P 3F 96
Wholesome La. L40: Scar, Burs 4A 14
Wicket Cl. L11: Crox 5B 46
Wickham Cl. CH44: Wall 7K 57
Wicklow Cl. CH66: Lit Sut 8F 102
Wicks Cres. L37: Form 9C 16
Wicks Gdns. L37: Form 1E 24
Wicks Grn. L37: Form 1C 24
Wicks Grn. Cl. L37: Form 9C 16
Wicks La. L37: Form 1C 24
(not continuous)
Wicksten Dr. WA7: Run 5M 95
Widdale Av. L35: Rainh 6G 62
Widdale Cl. WA5: Gt San 1H 81
Widgeons Covert CH63: Thorn H 1F 100
Widmore Rd. L25: Gate 4G 76
WIDNES 8L 79
Widnes Crematorium WA8: Wid 5K 79
Widnes Eastern By-Pass WA8: Wid 1J 95
Widnes Golf Course 7J 79
Widnes Rd. WA5: Cuerd, Penk 6B 80
WA8: Wid 9K 79
(not continuous)
Widnes Shopping Pk. WA8: Wid 8L 79
Widnes Station (Rail) 5K 79
Widnes Tennis Academy 6J 79
Widnes Trade Pk. WA8: Wid 9M 79
Widnes Vikings RLFC 8J 79
Widney Cl. L7: Liv 9G 59
Wiend, The CH42: Rock F 7K 73
CH63: Beb 2N 89
Wigan Rd. L39: Orm 8D 20
L40: Westh 9J 21
WN4: Ash M 3H 41
WN5: Bil 4B 40
WN8: Skel 3C 30
Wiggins La. L40: Holm 1E 14
Wigg Island Community Pk.
Local Nature Reserve 3N 95
Wight Cl. CH65: Ell P 4A 112
Wightman Av. WA12: Newt W 5L 51
Wightman St. L6: Liv 6G 58

Wight Moss Way PR8: South 3C 12
Wigmore Cl. WA3: Birchw 3A 68
Wignall Cl. L32: Kirkb 3C 46
Wignalls Mdw. L38: Hight 9F 24
Wigsey La. WA13: Warb 1G 84
WIGSHAW 8L 53
Wigshaw Cl. WN7: Leigh 1N 53
Wigshaw La. WA3: Cul 8K 53
Wigston Cl. PR8: Ains 1H 17
Wilberforce Rd. L4: Walt 9G 45
Wilbraham Pl. L5: Liv 4C 58
Wilbraham St. CH41: Birke 2L 73
L5: Liv 4C 58
WA9: Clock F 6A 64
Wilburn St. L4: Walt 9E 44
Wilbur St. WA9: St H 2A 64
Wilcock Cl. L5: Liv 4C 58
Wilcock Rd. WA11: Hay 2J 51
Wilcote Cl. WA8: Wid 4M 79
Wilcove WN8: Skel 3C 30
Wild Arum Cl. WA3: Low 2F 52
Wildbrook Dr. CH41: Birke 8D 56
Wildcherry Gdns. WA9: St H 2E 62
WILDERSPOOL 6D 82
Wilderspool C'way. WA4: Warr 4C 82
Wilderspool Cres. WA4: Warr 7C 82
Wilderspool Pk. WA4: Warr 6D 82
Wilde St. L3: Liv 3H 5 (7D 58)
Wilding Av. WA7: Run 5L 95
Wildings Old La. WA3: Croft 1H 67
Wild Pl. L20: Boot 3D 44
Wildwood Gro. WA1: Padd 1J 83
Wilfer Cl. L7: Liv 9H 59
Wilfred Owen Dr. CH41: Birke 1E 72
Wilkes Av. CH46: Leas 6B 56
Wilkie St. L15: Wav 1K 75
Wilkinson Av. WA1: Padd 2G 83
Wilkinson Cl. WA8: Wid 2K 95
Wilkinson Ct. *L15: Wav* *9J 59*
(off Willow Rd.)
Wilkinson St. CH41: Birke 3J 73
CH65: Ell P 8N 103
WA2: Warr 1D 82
Wilkinson St. M. *CH65: Ell P* *8A 104*
(off Wilkinson St. Nth.)
Wilkinson St. Nth. CH65: Ell P 8A 104
Wilkin St. L4: Kirkd 2D 58
Willan St. CH43: Oxton 4H 73
Willard Av. WN5: Bil 9N 31
Willard Dr. L20: Boot 4B 44
WILLASTON 6M 101
Willaston Dr. L26: Halew 1L 93
Willaston Grn. M. CH64: Will 6M 101
Willaston Rd. CH46: More 8L 55
CH63: Raby, Thorn H 9K 89
L4: Walt 9G 44
Willedstan Av. L23: Crosb 8L 33
William Beamont Way *WA1: Warr* *3B 82*
(off Ebenezer Pl.)
William Brown St. L3: Liv 4G 4 (7C 58)
(not continuous)
William Ct. CH64: Nest 4F 100
William Harvey Cl. L30: N'ton 8E 34
William Henry St. L3: Liv 1J 5 (6D 58)
L20: Boot .8A 44
William Jessop Way L3: Liv 3B 4 (7A 58)
William Johnson Gdns. CH65: Ell P 8N 103
William Morris Av. L20: Boot 5D 44
William Moult St. L5: Liv 4C 58
William Penn Cl. WA5: Penk 3G 81
William Rd. WA11: Hay 5B 50
William Roberts Av. L32: Kirkb 9A 36
Williams Av. L20: Boot 5D 44
WA12: Newt W 5L 51
Williamson Art Gallery & Museum 3H 73
Williamson Ct. L25: Woolt 7G 76
L26: Halew .7L 77
Williamson Sq. L1: Liv 5F 4 (8C 58)
Williamson St. L1: Liv 5F 4 (8C 58)
WA9: St H .6M 49
Williamson Student Village
L7: Liv 5N 5
Williamson Tunnels Heritage Cen. 6N 5
Williams St. L34: Presc 3A 62
William St. CH41: Birke 2L 73
CH44: Wall .7L 57
WA8: Wid 6M 79
WA10: St H 6K 49
Williams Way WA6: Frod 6K 107
William Wall Rd. L21: Ford 9A 34
William Way WN7: Leigh 1J 53
Willingdon Rd. L16: Child 8C 60
Willington Av. CH62: East 3D 102
Willink Rd. WA11: St H 3M 49
Willis Cl. L35: Whis 7A 62
Willis La. L35: Whis 7A 62
Willis St. WA1: Warr 2E 82
Williton Rd. L16: Child 3C 76
Willmer Rd. CH42: Tran 3J 73
L4: Walt 2G 58
Willoughby Cl. WA5: Old H 8L 65
Willoughby Dr. WA10: St H 1E 62
Willoughby Rd. CH44: Wall 5F 56
L14: Broad G 7C 60
L22: Water 1L 43
Willow Av. L32: Kirkb 8A 36
L35: Whis .6B 62
L36: Huy 9J 61
WA8: Wid 6L 79
WA12: Newt W 6M 51
Willow Bank CH44: Wall 7H 57
L40: Westh 9J 21
PR9: Banks *4H 9*
(off Main Av.)
WA6: Alv .3G 115
WA12: Newt W 7A 52
Willowbank Cl. L36: Huy 4G 61
Willowbank Holiday Home & Touring Pk.
PR8: Ains .3H 17
Willowbank Rd. CH42: Tran 5K 73
CH62: New F 1A 90
Willow Brook L39: Hals 8F 12
Willowbrow Rd. CH63: Raby 2J 101
Willow Cl. CH44: Wall 7H 57
L14: Broad G 7C 60
WA7: Run .8L 95
WA13: Lymm 4E 84
Willow Ct. CH63: Hghr B 1K 89
WA2: Win .6A 66
WA9: Clock F *5N 63*
(off Clock Face Rd.)
WA12: Newt W 6M 51
Willow Cres. L40: Burs 8K 15
WA1: Padg 9J 67
WA4: Moore 9J 81
Willowcroft Rd. CH44: Wall 7J 57
Willowdale WA12: Newt W 7N 51
Willowdale Rd. L9: Walt 6F 44
L18: Moss H 3L 75
Willowdale Way CH66: Gt Sut, Whit . . .4L 111
Willow Dr. WA4: Stockt H 7F 82
WN8: Skel .3B 30
Willow End L40: Burs 1K 21
Willowfield Gro. WN4: Ash M 9J 41
Willow Grn. L25: Woolt 4D 76
L39: Orm *8D 20*
(off School Ho. Grn.)
L40: Ruf 3L 15
PR9: South 3A 8
Willow Gro. CH2: Elt 2L 113
CH46: More 1L 71
CH66: Whit 4M 111
L15: Wav 9M 59
L35: Presc .4B 62
L37: Form .9F 16
PR8: South .8K 7
PR9: Banks .3E 8
WA3: Golb .1B 52
WN4: Ash M 6N 41
Willowherb Cl. L26: Halew 6H 77
Willow Hey L31: Mag 4K 35
WN8: Skel .3C 30
Willowhey PR9: South 3L 7
Willow Ho. L21: Sea 4N 43
Willow La. CH63: Raby 3K 101
WA4: App .3E 98
Willow Lea CH43: Oxton 4G 72
Willowmeade L11: Norr G 7N 45
Willow Moss Cl. CH46: More 7A 56
Willow Pk. CH49: Grea 4K 71
PR8: South 1N 11
Willow Ri. L33: Kirkb 8D 36
Willow Rd. L15: Wav 9K 59
M31: Part .7L 69
WA10: St H 7F 48
WA11: Hay 3G 50
WA12: Newt W 6N 51
Willows, The CH45: Wall 2E 56
M31: Part .6M 69
PR8: South *9E 6*
(off Beechfield Gdns.)
WA5: Gt San 3H 81
WA6: Frod 6M 107
WA9: Clock F 5M 63
Willow Tree Av. WA9: Sut L 5N 63
Willow Tree Ct. WA8: Wid 6N 79
Willow Wlk. WN8: Skel 9E 22
Willow Way L11: Crox 5B 46
L23: Crosb 6L 33
Wills Av. L31: Mag 1H 35
Willsford Av. L31: Mell 8N 35
Wilmcote Gro. PR8: Ains 1H 17
Wilmere La. WA8: Wid 3K 79
Wilmot Av. WA5: Gt San 2H 81
Wilmot Dr. WA3: Golb 3A 52
Wilmslow Av. CH66: Gt Sut 9K 103
Wilmslow Cres. WA4: Thel 4L 83
Wilmslow Dr. CH66: Gt Sut 9K 103
Wilne Rd. CH45: Wall 3G 57
Wilsden Rd. WA8: Wid 7E 78
Wilsford Cl. WA3: Golb 1C 52
Wilson Av. CH44: Wall 5L 57
Wilson Bus. Cen. L36: Huy 8L 61
Wilson Cl. WA4: Thel 5L 83
WA8: Wid 7N 79
WA10: St H 7H 49
Wilson Gro. L19: Garst 1A 92
Wilson La. WA3: Ris 4M 67
Wilson Patten St. WA1: Warr 4B 82
Wilson Rd. CH44: Wall 5L 57
L35: Presc .6A 62
L36: Huy 7K 61
Wilsons La. CH65: Whit 2M 111
L21: Lith .2A 44
Wilson St. WA5: Warr 1B 82
Wilstan Av. CH63: Hghr B 2K 89
Wilstone Cl. L6: Liv 5E 58
Wilton Grange CH48: W Kir 4B 70
Wilton Gro. L13: Liv 7M 59
Wilton La. WA3: Cul 5H 53
Wilton Rd. CH42: Rock F 7N 73
L36: Huy 8H 61
Wilton's Dr. L34: Know 7G 47
Wilton St. CH44: Wall 5H 57
L3: Liv 2J 5
WN4: Ash M 5J 41
Wiltshire Cl. WA1: Wools 1L 83
Wiltshire Dr. *L30: N'ton* *8C 34*
(off Simon's Cft.)
Wiltshire Gdns. WA10: St H 8J 49
Wiltshire Rd. M31: Part 7L 69
Wimbald Cl. L25: Gate 3G 77
Wimbledon St. CH45: Wall 4H 57
L15: Wav 1K 75
WIMBOLDS TRAFFORD 8K 113
Wimborne Av. CH61: Thing 2A 88
Wimborne Cl. L14: Knott A 3F 60
Wimborne Pl. L14: Knott A 4F 60
Wimborne Rd. L14: Knott A 3E 60
Wimborne Way CH61: Irby 9L 71
Wimbrick Cl. CH46: More 9N 55
L39: Orm 9B 20
Wimbrick Ct. CH46: More 9N 55
Wimbrick Cres. L39: Orm 1B 28
Wimbrick Hey CH46: More 9N 55
Wimpole St. L7: Liv 7G 59
Winchcombe Cl.
WN7: Leigh 1M 53
Winchester Av. CH65: Ell P 1B 112
L10: Ain 8J 35
L22: Water .9J 33
WA5: Gt San 3L 81
WN4: Ash M 8J 41
Winchester Cl. L25: Woolt 9F 76
Winchester Dr. CH44: Wall 5G 56
Winchester Pl. WA8: Wid 8F 78
Winchester Rd. L6: Liv 3H 59
WA11: Hay 1G 50
WN5: Bil 1N 39
Winchfield Rd. L15: Wav 2L 75
Windbourne Rd. L17: Aig 6G 75
Windermere Av. WA2: Warr 6D 66
WA8: Wid 4L 79
WA11: St H 2K 49
Windermere Cl. CH64: Lit N 7F 100
Windermere Ct. *CH41: Birke* *3J 73*
(off Penrith St.)
Windermere Cres. PR8: Ains 2J 17
Windermere Dr. L12: W Der 9A 46
L31: Mag 1K 35
L33: Kirkb .7B 36
WA11: Rainf 1C 38
Windermere Ho. L17: Aig 6J 75
Windermere Pl. WA11: St H 2K 49
Windermere Rd. CH43: Noct 2C 72
CH65: Ell P 3A 112
L38: Hight .8G 24
WA11: Hay 4D 50
Windermere St. L5: Liv 3F 58
WA8: Wid 4L 79
Windermere Ter. L8: Liv 3G 75
Windfield Cl. L33: Kirkb 5E 36
Windfield Gdns. CH66: Lit Sut 7J 103
Windfield Grn. L19: Garst 4B 92
Windfield Rd. L19: Garst 3B 92
Windgate WN8: Skel 4C 30
WINDLE 4E 48
Windle Ash L31: Mag 1H 35
Windle Av. L23: Crosb 7N 33
Windlebrook Cres. WA10: Windle 4E 48
Windle City WA10: St H 4J 49
Windle Ct. CH64: Nest 4E 100
WA3: Birchw 5K 67
Windle Gro. WA10: Windle 4F 48
Windle Hall Dr. WA10: St H 3H 49
WINDLE HILL 6J 101
WINDLEHURST 4J 49
Windlehurst Av. WA10: St H 4H 49
WINDLES GREEN 6A 34
Windleshaw Rd. WA10: St H 4G 49
Windle St. WA10: St H 5J 49
Windle Va. WA10: St H 5H 49
Windmill Animal Farm 2F 14
Windmill Av. L23: Crosb 6M 33
L39: Orm 8D 20
Windmill Cl. L33: Kirkb 6C 36
WA4: App .1D 98
Windmill Gdns. CH43: Bid 9C 56
WA9: St H .6N 49
Windmill Hgts. WN8: Uph 4K 31
WINDMILL HILL 5E 96
Windmill Hill Av. E.
WA7: Nort, Wind H 5F 96
Windmill Hill Av. Nth.
WA7: Wind H 4F 96
Windmill Hill Av. Sth.
WA7: Wind H 6F 96
Windmill Hill Av. W. WA7: Wind H 5E 96
Windmill Ho. PR9: South 4L 7
Windmill La. WA4: App 1D 98
WA4: Pres H 8J 97
WA5: Penk .3G 81
Windmill Rd. WN8: Uph 5J 31
Windmill Rdbt. WN8: Skel 5J 31
Windmill St. WA7: Run 5L 95
Window La. L19: Garst 3A 92
Windrows WN8: Skel 3C 30
Windscale Rd. WA2: Fearn 7H 67
Windsor Av. L21: Lith 2N 43
WA12: Newt W 8M 51
Windsor Cl. CH49: Grea 5L 71
CH62: New F 9N 73
L30: N'ton .6E 34
L40: Burs 2J 21
Windsor Ct. *L8: Liv* *2E 74*
(off Northumberland St.)
L20: Boot *5D 44*
(off Windsor Rd.)
L39: Augh .2B 28
PR8: Birkd 2L 11
Windsor Dr. CH65: Whit 2M 111
WA4: Grap .6J 83
WA6: Hel 3E 114
WA11: Hay 3J 51
Windsor Gro. WA7: Run 7L 95
Windsor M. CH62: New F 9N 73
Windsor Pk. Cl. L10: Ain 8K 35
Windsor Rd. L9: Walt 4F 44
L13: Liv 3J 59
L20: Boot .5D 44
L23: Crosb 6K 33
L31: Mag .3H 35
L35: Presc 5C 62
L36: Huy .7E 60
L37: Form .2E 24
PR9: South 9J 7
WA3: Golb 2D 52
WA8: Wid .4K 79
WA10: St H 7G 48
WN4: Ash M 9K 41
WN5: Bil 6A 40
WN8: Uph .4K 31
Windsor St. CH41: Birke 3J 73
CH45: New B 9H 43
L8: Liv 1E 74
WA5: Warr 2N 81
Windsor Vw. L8: Liv 1G 75
Windus St. WA10: St H 7H 49
Windward Dr. L24: Speke 3D 92
Windways CH66: Lit Sut 7J 103
WINDY ARBOR 9M 61
Windy Arbor Brow L35: Whis 9N 61
Windy Arbor Cl. L35: Whis 9A 62
Windy Arbor Rd. L35: Whis 7A 62
WINDY ARBOUR 3C 40
Windy Bank CH62: Port S 1A 90
(not continuous)
Windy Bank Av. WA3: Low 2F 52
Windy Harbour Rd. PR8: Birkd 7L 11
Wineva Gdns. L23: Crosb 8M 33
Winfield Way WA8: Wid 8L 79
Winford St. CH44: Wall 6K 57
Winfrith Cl. CH63: Spit 5M 89
Winfrith Dr. CH63: Spit 5M 89
Winfrith Rd. L25: Gate 4G 76
WA2: Fearn 7H 67
Wingate Av. WA9: St H 3G 63
Wingate Cl. CH43: Noct 4E 72
Wingate Rd. CH62: East 1D 102
L17: Aig 6K 75
L33: Kirkb .7D 36
Wingate Wlk. L33: Kirkb 8E 36
Wingfield Cl. L29: Seft 3C 34
Wingrave Way L11: Norr G 9N 45
Wings Entertainment Pk. L24: Speke . . .3F 92
Winhill L25: Woolt 4E 76
Winifred La. L39: Augh 3M 27
Winifred Rd. L10: Faz 3N 45
Winifred St. L7: Liv 8G 59
WA2: Warr 1D 82
Winkle St. L8: Liv 3E 74
Winmarleigh St. WA1: Warr 3B 82
Winmoss Dr. L33: Kirkb 6D 36
Winnbourne Gdns. WA9: Sut M 6L 63
Winnington Rd. CH47: Hoy 3B 70
Winnipeg Dr. L27: N'ley 3J 77
Winnows, The WA7: Run 6N 95
Winsford Cl. WA11: Hay 3H 51
Winsford Dr. WA5: Burtw 2G 65
Winsford Gro. CH66: Gt Sut 2H 111
Winsford Rd. L13: Liv 3L 59
Winsham Cl. L32: Kirkb 2D 46
Winsham Rd. L32: Kirkb 2C 46
Winskill Rd. L11: Norr G 9M 45
M44: Irlam 1N 69
Winslade Ct. L4: Walt 8G 45
Winslade Rd. L4: Walt 9G 45
Winslow Cl. WA7: Nort 7F 96
Winslow St. L4: Walt 9E 44
WINSTANLEY 1F 40
Winstanley Cl. WA5: Gt San 3L 81
Winstanley Ho. *CH62: New F* *9A 74*
(off Winstanley Rd.)
Winstanley Ind. Est. WA2: Warr 8C 66
Winstanley Rd. CH62: New F 9A 74
CH64: Lit N 9E 100
L22: Water 9L 33
WN4: Ash M 5D 40
WN5: Bil 1B 40
WN8: Skel .4C 30
Winstanley Shop. Cen. WN3: Wins 1F 40
Winster Dr. L27: N'ley 4L 77
Winster M. WA10: St H 1E 62
Winsters, The WN8: Skel 3C 30
Winston Av. WA9: St H 8D 50
WA12: Newt W 7L 51
Winston Cres. PR8: South 4D 12
Winston Dr. CH43: Noct 3C 72
Winstone Rd. L14: Knott A 5E 60
Winston Gro. CH46: More 9M 55

Winterburn Cres. L12: W Der 2B 60
Wintergreen Av. L11: Norr G 9L 45
Wintergreen Wlk. M31: Part 6M 69
(off Wychelm Rd.)
Winter Gro. WA9: St H 7D 50
Winterhey Av. CH44: Wall 7H 57
Winterley Dr. L26: Halew 1L 93
Winter St. L6: Liv 2M 5 (6F 58)
Winthrop Pk. CH43: Oxton 3E 72
Winton Cl. CH45: New B 1G 56
Winton Gro. WA7: Wind H 6F 96
Winton Rd. WA3: Low 4F 52
WINWICK 3B 66
WINWICK GREEN 3B 66
Winwick La. WA3: Croft, Low 5F 52
Winwick Link Rd. WA2: Win 3C 66
Winwick Pk. Av. WA2: Win 4B 66
WINWICK QUAY 6B 66
Winwick Quay WA2: Win 6A 66
Winwick Rd. WA2: Warr 5B 66
(not continuous)
WA12: Newt W 8N 51
Winwick St. WA1: Warr 3C 82
WA2: Warr 2C 82
Winwick Vw. WA5: Coll G 9F 50
Winwood Hall L25: Woolt 7E 76
Wirral Beach Caravan Pk.
CH47: Meols 7G 55
Wirral Bus. Cen. CH41: Birke 7J 57
Wirral Bus. Pk. CH49: Upton 5N 71
Wirral Cl. CH63: Beb 4M 89
WA3: Cul 7M 53
Wirral Country Park 3G 86
Wirral Country Park Vis. Cen. 4G 87
Wirral Cres. CH64: Lit N 9F 100
Wirral Dr. WN3: Wins 1E 40
Wirral Gdns. CH63: Beb 4M 89
Wirral Intl. Bus. Pk. CH62: Brom 6E 90
Wirral Ladies Golf Course, The 2E 72
Wirral Leisure Pk. CH62: Brom 4D 90
Wirral Mt. CH45: Wall 4F 56
CH48: W Kir 6E 70
Wirral Mus. 2M 73
Wirral Sailing Cen. 6A 70
Wirral Tennis & Sports Cen. 7D 56
Wirral Transport Mus. 1L 73
Wirral Vw. L19: Gras 1L 91
Wirral Vs. CH45: Wall 3E 56
WIRRAL WATERS 9K 57
Wirral Way CH43: Noct 3C 72
CH48: W Kir 6C 70
Wisenholme Cl. WA7: Beech 1A 108
Wisteria Way WA9: Bold 2C 64
Witham Cl. L30: N'ton 7F 34
Witham Rd. WN8: Skel 3A 30
Withburn Cl. CH49: Upton 2M 71
Withens, The L28: Stockb V 2F 60
Withensfield CH45: Wall 3H 57
Withens La. CH44: Wall 3H 57
CH45: Wall 3H 57
Withens Rd. L31: Lyd 9J 27
Withers Av. WA2: Warr 9E 66
Withert Av. CH63: Hghr B 8K 73
Witherwin Av. WA4: App, Grap 9F 82
Withington Av. WA3: Cul 6N 53
Withington Rd. CH44: Wall 6J 57
L24: Speke 4K 93
Withins Fld. L38: Hight 9F 24
Withins La. L38: Gt Alt 5M 25
Withins Rd. WA3: Cul 7N 53
WA11: Hay 2G 51
Within Way L24: Hale 6B 94
Withnell Cl. L13: Liv 7N 59
Withnell Rd. L13: Liv 7N 59
Withy Cl. WA6: Frod 6M 107
Withycombe Rd. WA5: Penk 4G 80
Witley Av. CH46: More 8M 55
Witley Cl. CH46: More 8M 55
Witney Cl. CH49: Grea 5K 71
Witney Gdns. WA4: App 1G 98
Witsun Dr. L4: Kirkd 2D 58
Wittenham Cl. CH49: Upton 4N 71
Wittering La. CH60: Hesw 7L 87
Witterings, The CH64: Nest 5E 100
Witton Rd. L13: Liv 3J 59
Witton Way WA11: Rainf 4C 38
Witt Rd. WA8: Wid 9K 79
Wivenhoe Ho. L19: Aig 9L 75
(off The Spinnakers)
Wivern Pl. WA7: Run 4L 95
Woburn Av. WA12: Newt W 8M 51
Woburn Cl. L13: Liv 5L 59
WA11: Hay 3H 51
Woburn Dr. WA8: Cron 2G 78
Woburn Grn. L13: Liv 5L 59
(off Woburn Hill)
Woburn Hill L13: Liv 5L 59
Woburn Pl. CH42: Rock F 6M 73
Woburn Rd. CH45: Wall 3H 57
WA2: Win 5B 66
Wokefield Way WA10: St H 6F 48
Wokingham Gro. L36: Huy 9J 61
Wolfe Cl. WA4: Grap 8H 83
Wolfenden Av. L20: Boot 5D 44
Wolfe Rd. WA9: St H 8A 50
Wolferton Cl. CH49: Upton 1B 72
Wolfe St. L8: Liv 3D 74
Wolfrick Dr. CH63: Spit 6A 90
Wolfson Sq. WN4: Ash M 7H 41
Wollaton Dr. PR8: South 3E 12
Wolmer St. WN4: Ash M 7J 41
Wolseley Rd. WA10: St H 5J 49
Wolsey Cl. WN4: Ash M 6J 41
Wolsey St. L20: Kirkd 9B 44
Wolstenholme Sq. L1: Liv 7G 4 (9C 58)
WOLVERHAM 1B 112
Wolverham Rd. CH65: Ell P 2A 112
Wolverton WN8: Skel 4C 30
Wolverton Dr. WA7: Wind H 6F 96
Wolverton St. L6: Liv 4H 59
Womack Gdns. WA9: St H 3H 63
Woodacre Gro. CH66: Ell P 6L 103
Woodacre Rd. CH66: Ell P 6K 103
Woodale Cl. WA5: Gt San 1G 81
Woodall Dr. WA7: Run 6L 95
Wood Av. L20: Boot 5D 44
WOODBANK 7D 110
Woodbank Cl. L16: Child 9D 60
Woodbank La. CH1: Woodb 9B 110
Woodbank Pk. CH43: Oxton 4F 72
Woodbank Rd. CH65: Whit 3N 111
WA5: Penk 4J 81
Woodberry Cl. CH43: Noct 4D 72
L33: Kirkb 5D 36
Woodbine Av. M44: Cad 5K 69
Woodbine Rd. WA13: Lymm 4H 85
Woodbine St. L5: Kirkd 2C 58
Woodbourne Rd. L14: Knott A 5B 60
Woodbridge Av. L26: Halew 6H 77
Woodbridge Cl. WA4: App 3F 98
Woodbrook Av. L9: Walt 3E 44
Woodburn Blvd. CH63: Hghr B 8L 73
Woodburn Dr. CH60: Hesw 9N 87
WOODCHURCH 6B 72
Woodchurch Ct. CH42: Tran 5J 73
Woodchurch La. CH42: Tran 6H 73
CH49: Woodc 8C 72
CH66: Ell P 8K 103
Woodchurch Leisure Cen. 5C 72
Woodchurch Rd. CH41: Birke 5J 73
CH42: Tran 7B 72
CH43: Pren 7B 72
CH49: Woodc 7B 72
L13: Liv 5M 59
Wood Cl. CH41: Birke 1K 73
CH66: Hoot 5F 102
L32: Kirkb 9B 36
Woodcote Av. CH65: Whit 3N 111
Woodcote Bank CH42: Rock F 9N 73
Woodcote Cl. L33: Kirkb 7E 36
WA2: Warr 8E 66
Woodcotes, The CH62: Brom 9C 90
Woodcot La. CH60: Hesw 6M 87
Woodcroft WN6: Shev 7N 23
WN8: Skel 4C 30
Woodcroft Dr. CH61: Hesw 5N 87
Woodcroft Gdns. WA4: App 1F 98
Woodcroft La. CH63: Hghr B 8M 73
Woodcroft Rd. L15: Wav 1J 75
Woodcroft Way WA9: Clock F 5M 63
Woodedge WN4: Ash M 8H 41
WOODEND 1L 95
Woodend CH61: Pens 2N 87
L35: Whis 9B 62
WA7: Murd 8G 96
Woodend Av. L23: Crosb 5L 33
L24: Speke 1G 92
L25: Hunts X 1G 92
L31: Mag 4H 35
Wood End Bus. Pk. L40: Burs 7F 14
Woodend Ct. WA8: Wid 6N 79
Woodend Ind. Est. L24: Speke 2H 93
Woodend La. L24: Speke 3G 92
WA3: Rix 7C 68
WOOD END PARK 9L 75
Woodend Rd. CH65: Ell P 8L 103
Woodene Cl. L32: Kirkb 3E 46
Woodfall Cl. CH64: Lit N 8G 100
Woodfall Gro. CH64: Lit N 8G 100
Woodfall La. CH64: Lit N 8F 100
Woodfarm Hey L28: Stockb V 1E 60
Woodfield Av. CH63: Hghr B 9L 73
Woodfield Cres. WN4: Ash M 9J 41
Woodfield Rd. CH61: Pens 3M 87
CH63: Beb 4N 89
CH65: Ell P 9A 104
L9: Walt 5E 44
L36: Huy 7G 60
L39: Orm 1B 28
Woodfield Rd. Nth. CH65: Ell P 9A 104
Woodford Av. WA3: Low 3E 52
Woodford Cl. WA4: Thel 5K 83
WA6: Hel 3E 114
WA7: Run 9L 95
Woodford Rd. CH62: New F 8A 74
L14: Knott A 5C 60
WA10: Windle 4F 48
Woodgate L27: N'ley 2G 77
Woodger St. L19: Garst 2A 92
Wood Grn. CH43: Bid 9C 56
L34: Presc 3N 61
Woodgreen Rd. L13: Liv 5M 59
Wood Gro. L13: Liv 7L 59
Woodhall Cl. WA5: Gt San 9J 65
Woodhall Rd. L13: Liv 6M 59
Woodham Gro. CH64: Lit N 9F 100
Woodhatch Rd. WA7: Brook 1D 108
Woodhead Gro. WN3: Wigan 1K 41
Woodhead Rd. CH62: Port S 1B 90
Woodhead Row CH62: Port S 2B 90
Woodhead St. CH62: New F 9A 74
Wood Heath Way CH62: East 8F 90
WOODHEY 9L 73
Woodhey Ct. CH63: Hghr B 8M 73
Woodhey Gro. CH63: Hghr B 9M 73
Woodhey Rd. CH63: Hghr B 9M 73
L19: Gras 8M 75
Woodholme Ct. L25: Gate 4F 76
Woodhouse Cl. L4: Walt 2D 58
WA3: Birchw 6M 67
Woodhouse La.
WA14: Dun M 4N 85
WOODHOUSES 9J 107
Woodhouses La. WA6: Frod 9J 107
Woodhouses Pk. WA6: Frod 9J 107
Woodhurst Cl. L36: Huy 3G 61
Woodhurst Cres. L14: Knott A 5E 60
Wooding Cl. M31: Part 5N 69
Woodin Rd. CH42: Rock F 8N 73
Woodkind Hey CH63: Spit 5N 89
Woodland Av. CH47: Meols 8E 54
L40: Scar 7L 13
WA8: Wid 7J 79
WA12: Newt W 7A 52
WA13: Lymm 6G 84
Woodland Dr. CH45: New B 2J 57
CH49: Woodc 5A 72
WA13: Lymm 6F 84
WN4: Ash M 6K 41
Woodland Gro. CH42: Rock F 8M 73
Woodland Path L37: Ains, Form 4F 16
PR8: Ains 4F 16
Woodland Rd. CH42: Rock F 8M 73
CH48: W Kir 6F 70
CH49: Woodc 5A 72
CH65: Whit 3M 111
L4: Walt 1J 59
L21: Sea 3M 43
L26: Halew 9J 77
L31: Mell 7M 35
L36: Huy 3G 61
Woodlands, The CH41: Birke 3K 73
CH49: Upton 2N 71
L34: Eccl P 2C 62
L40: Burs 2L 21
PR8: Ains 9J 11
Woodlands Caravan Pk.
PR4: Mere B 7L 9
Woodlands Cl. CH64: Park 6D 100
L37: Form 1D 24
L39: Orm 9E 20
PR9: South 7J 7
Woodlands Dr. CH61: Barn 3C 88
WA4: Thel 5L 83
Woodlands La. CH48: W Kir 7E 70
Woodlands Pk. L12: W Der 4M 59
WA12: Newt W 4L 51
Woodlands Rd. CH61: Irby 2L 87
CH64: Park 6D 100
L9: Ain 4J 45
L17: Aig 6K 75
L36: Huy 7F 60
L37: Form 2D 24
WA11: St H 4L 49
Woodlands Sq. L27: N'ley 4L 77
(off Wood La.)
Woodland Ter. M31: Part 6L 69
Woodland Vw. CH66: Chil T 6G 102
L23: Thorn 4N 33
Woodland Wlk. CH62: Brom 6B 90
WA7: Cas 6C 96
Wood La. CH45: Wall 3E 56
CH49: Grea 3L 71
CH64: Park 4C 100
CH64: Will 5N 101
L27: N'ley 3K 77
L34: Presc 4M 61
L36: Huy 7M 61
L37: Down, Gt Alt 3B 26
L40: Lath 1B 22
M31: Part 6K 69
WA4: App 8F 82
WA7: Beech, Sut W 1B 108
WA7: Murd 9E 96
WN8: Parb 3G 22
Wood Lea L12: Crox 7C 46
Woodlea Cl. CH62: Brom 1C 102
PR9: South 2B 8
Woodlee Rd. L25: Gate 4G 77
Woodleigh Cl. L31: Lyd 7G 27
Woodley Fold WA5: Penk 5H 81
Woodley Park Centre 9E 22
Woodley Pk. Rd. WN8: Skel 9E 22
Woodley Rd. L31: Mag 5H 35
Woodmoss La. L40: Scar 4J 13
Woodnook Rd. WN6: Appl B 5N 23
Woodpecker Cl. CH49: Upton 3L 71
L12: W Der 9D 46
WA3: Birchw 5N 67
Woodpecker Dr. L26: Halew 6J 77
Woodridge WA7: Wind H 6E 96
Wood Rd. L26: Halew 9J 77
Woodrock Rd. L25: Woolt 6F 76
Woodrow WN8: Skel 4B 30
Woodrow Dr. WN8: Newb 4C 22
Woodrow Way M44: Irlam 2M 69
Woodruff St. L8: Liv 4E 74
Woodruff Wlk. M31: Part 6M 69
Woods Cl. L39: Down 9E 18
Woodside CH65: Whit 3A 112
Woodside Av. CH46: More 1L 71
PR8: Ains 2H 17
WA6: Frod 7N 107
WA11: St H 2J 49
WN4: Ash M 3J 41
Woodside Bus. Pk. CH41: Birke 1M 73
Woodside Cl. L12: W Der 1N 59
WN8: Uph 4M 31
Woodside Ferry App.
CH41: Birke 1M 73
Woodside Gdns. M31: Part 5M 69
(off Lock La.)
Woodside La. WA13: Lymm 7H 85
Woodside Rd. CH61: Irby 1M 87
WA5: Gt San 1H 81
WA11: Hay 3G 51
Woodside St. L7: Liv 8G 59
Woodside Walkway CH41: Birke 1M 73
Woodside Way L33: Kirkb 6D 36
Woods La. WN4: Ash M 6L 41
Woodsome Cl. CH65: Whit 4N 111
Woodsome Dr. CH65: Whit 4N 111
Woodsome Pk. L25: Gate 5G 76
Woodsorrel Rd. CH41: Birke 1F 72
L15: Wav 1N 75
Wood Sorrel Way WA3: Low 2F 52
Woods Rd. M44: Irlam 1M 69
Woodstock Av. WA12: Newt W 8M 51
Woodstock Cl. WN7: Leigh 1M 53
Woodstock Dr. PR8: Birkd 6M 11
Woodstock Gdns. WA4: App 1G 98
Woodstock Gro. WA8: Wid 6G 79
Woodstock Rd. CH44: Wall 6G 57
Woodstock St. L5: Liv 4C 58
Wood St. CH41: Birke 1K 73
CH47: Hoy 1C 70
CH62: Port S 2A 90
L1: Liv 6G 4 (8C 58)
L19: Garst 1A 92
L21: Lith 3A 44
L34: Presc 3A 62
WA1: Warr 2E 82
WA3: Golb 2C 52
WA8: Wid 7M 79
WA9: St H 6M 49
Woodthorn Cl. WA4: Dares 3H 97
WOODVALE 2J 17
Wood Va. WA9: St H 3H 63
Woodvale Cl. CH43: Bid 9C 56
WA2: Padg 8F 66
Woodvale Ct. CH49: Woodc 7A 72
(off Childwall Grn.)
PR9: Banks 2E 8
Woodvale Dr. WA3: Low 1F 52
Woodvale Rd. CH66: Lit Sut 8J 103
L12: Crox 7D 46
L25: Woolt 6F 76
PR8: Ains 3J 17
Woodvale Sidings PR8: Ains 4K 17
Woodview L34: Know 7H 47
Woodview Av. CH44: Wall 7L 57
Woodview Cres. WA8: Wid 8D 78
Woodview Rd. L25: Woolt 4D 76
WA8: Wid 8D 78
Woodville Av. L23: Crosb 8K 33
Woodville Pl. WA8: Wid 7G 78
Woodville Rd. CH42: Tran 4J 73
Woodville St. WA10: St H 6L 49
(not continuous)
Woodville Ter. L6: Liv 4G 58
Woodward Rd. CH42: Rock F 8N 73
L33: Know I 7G 37
Woodway CH49: Grea 4L 71
Woodway Ct. CH62: Brom 5D 90
Woodyear Rd. CH62: Brom 8D 90
Woolacombe Av. WA9: Sut L 4M 63
Woolacombe Cl. WA4: Warr 6E 82
Woolacombe Rd. L16: Child 2C 76
Woolden Rd. M44: Cad 2G 69
Wooler Cl. CH46: More 9K 55
Woolfall Cl. L36: Huy 5F 60
Woolfall Cres. L36: Huy 5F 60
WOOLFALL HEATH 4H 61
Woolfall Heath Av. L36: Huy 4G 60
Woolfall Ter. L21: Sea 4N 43
Woolhope Rd. L4: Walt 8G 44
Woollam Dr. CH66: Lit Sut 7J 103
Woolley Cl. WA6: Frod 4N 107
Woolmer Cl. WA3: Birchw 3B 68
Woolmoore Rd. L24: Speke 1G 92
WOOLSTON 1J 83
Woolston Grange Av.
WA1: Wools 7K 67
WA2: Padg 7K 67
Woolston Hall WA1: Wools 1L 83
Woolston Neighbourhood Hub 1L 83
Woolston Rd. WA11: Hay 3E 50
WOOLTON 6F 76
Woolton Cinema, The 6E 76
Woolton Cl. WN4: Ash M 6H 41
Woolton Ct. CH66: Ell P 6L 103
Woolton Golf Course 8F 76
WOOLTON HILL 5C 76
Woolton Hill Rd. L25: Woolt 4C 76
Woolton M. L25: Woolt 6E 76
(off Quarry St.)
Woolton Mt. L25: Woolt 5E 76
WOOLTON PARK 4E 76
Woolton Pk. L25: Woolt 4E 76
Woolton Pk. Cl. L25: Woolt 5E 76

Woolton Rd. L15: Wav 1M **75**
L16: Child 2A **76**
L19: Aller, Garst 1A **92**
L25: Aller 9B **76**
L25: Woolt .3C **76**
Woolton St. L25: Woolt 6E **76**
(not continuous)
Woolton Views L25: Hunts X 8H **77**
Worcester Av. L13: Liv 2J **59**
L22: Water .9K **33**
WA3: Golb .2C **52**
Worcester Cl. WA5: Gt San 3L **81**
WA10: St H 8J **49**
Worcester Ct. L20: Boot 7C **44**
Worcester Dr. L13: Liv 2J **59**
Worcester Dr. Nth. L13: Liv 2J **59**
Worcester Rd. CH43: Bid 9D **56**
L20: Boot 6C **44**
Worcester St. CH65: Ell P 8A **104**
Worcester Wlk. CH65: Ell P 8A **104**
Wordsworth Av. CH42: Rock F 7M **73**
WA4: Warr .5C **82**
WA8: Wid 8J **79**
WA9: Sut M 6K **63**
WN5: Bil 2N **39**
Wordsworth Cl. L39: Orm 7B **20**
Wordsworth Ct. L32: Kirkb 2A **46**
Wordsworth St. L8: Liv 1H **75**
L20: Boot 5N **43**
Wordsworth Wlk. CH48: W Kir 8C **70**
Wordsworth Way
CH66: Gt Sut 4K **111**
L36: Huy 8K **61**
World Museum Liverpool 3G **4** (7C **58**)
World of Glass, The 7K **49**
Worrow Cl. L11: Norr G 7N **45**
Worrow Rd. L11: Norr G 7N **45**
Worsborough Av. WA5: Gt San 3K **81**
Worsley Av. WA4: Westy 4G **82**
WORSLEY BROW 1A **64**
Worsley Brow WA9: St H 1A **64**
Worsley Rd. WA4: Walt 7C **82**
Worsley St. WA3: Golb 2B **52**
WA5: Warr .1A **82**
WA11: Hay .4B **50**
Worthing Cl. PR8: Birkd 3M **11**
Worthing St. L22: Water 9J **33**
Worthington Av. M31: Part 6M **69**
Worthington Cl. WA7: Pal F 8C **96**
Worthington Way
WN3: Wigan 1G **41**
Wortley Rd. L10: Faz 2K **45**
Wotton Dr. WN4: Ash M 8M **41**
Wray Av. WA9: Clock F 5N **63**
Wrayburn Cl. L7: Liv 9H **59**
Wray Ct. WA9: Clock F 5N **63**
Wrekin Cl. L25: Woolt 7F **76**
Wrekin Dr. L10: Ain 9K **35**
Wrenbury Cl. CH43: Oxton 6F **72**
WA7: Sut W 2B **108**
Wrenbury St. L7: Liv 7H **59**
Wren Cl. WA3: Birchw 5N **67**
WA7: Pal F .9C **96**
Wrenfield Gro. L17: Aig 6H **75**
Wren Gro. L26: Halew 7J **77**
Wrexham Cl. WA5: Call 7N **65**
Wright Cres. WA8: Wid 2K **95**
WRIGHTINGTON 1M **23**
WRIGHT'S GREEN 1H **99**
Wrights La. WA5: Burtw 5G **65**
WA5: Cuerd 6B **80**
Wrights Ter. L15: Wav 1M **75**
PR8: Birkd .3A **12**
Wright St. CH44: Wall 5K **57**
L5: Liv 4C **58**
PR9: South .8G **7**
WN4: Ash M 5H **41**
Wright Tree Vs. M44: Cad 4K **69**
Wrigley Rd. WA11: Hay 4G **50**
Wrigleys Cl. L37: Form 8F **16**
Wrigleys La. L37: Form 8F **16**
Wroxham Cl. CH49: Upton 3A **72**
WA6: Hel .1E **114**
Wroxham Ct. *CH49: Upton* *3A 72*
(off Wroxham Cl.)
Wroxham Dr. CH49: Upton 4A **72**
Wroxham Rd. WA5: Gt San 2F **80**
Wroxham Way CH49: Upton 3A **72**
Wryneck Cl. WA10: St H 1E **62**
Wrynose Rd. CH62: Brom 7D **90**
Wulstan St. L4: Kirkd 2C **58**
Wyatt Gro. WN4: Ash M 8M **41**
Wychelm Rd. M31: Part 6M **69**
Wycherley Rd. CH42: Tran 5K **73**
Wycherley St. L34: Presc 3A **62**
Wychwood CH49: Upton 3N **71**
Wychwood Av. WA13: Lymm 5C **84**
Wychwood Cl. L14: Knott A 5B **60**
Wycliffe Rd. CH65: Gt Sut 2L **111**
L4: Walt 2H **59**
WA11: Hay .3G **51**
Wycliffe St. CH42: Rock F 6M **73**
Wye Cl. CH42: Rock F 5M **73**
Wyedale CH65: Whit 2N **111**
Wyedale Rd. WA11: Hay 3E **50**
Wye St. L5: Liv 3E **58**
Wyke Cop Rd. PR8: South 2J **13**
PR9: South .2J **13**
Wykeham St. L4: Kirkd 2C **58**
Wyke La. PR9: South 7A **8**
Wyken Gro. WA11: St H 5M **49**
Wyke Rd. L35: Presc 4B **62**
Wyke Wood La. PR9: South 7D **8**
Wyllin Rd. L33: Kirkb 9E **36**
Wylva Av. L23: Crosb 8N **33**
Wylva Rd. L4: Walt 3F **58**
Wyncroft Cl. CH65: Whit 2N **111**
WA8: Wid 9F **78**
Wyncroft Rd. WA8: Wid 9F **78**
Wyncroft St. L8: Liv 4F **74**
Wyndale Cl. L18: Moss H 5N **75**
Wyndcote Rd. L18: Moss H 3N **75**
Wyndham Av. L14: Broad G 7E **60**
Wyndham Cres.
CH66: Gt Sut 3K **111**
Wyndham Rd. CH45: Wall 4D **56**
Wyndham St. L4: Walt 8E **44**
Wynne Rd. WA10: St H 5H **49**
Wynnstay Av. L31: Lyd 9J **27**
Wynnstay St. L8: Liv 2F **74**
Wynstay Rd. CH47: Meols 9D **54**
Wynton Cl. WN7: Leigh 1M **53**
Wynwood Pk. L36: Roby 8G **60**
Wyoming Cl. WA5: Gt San 2L **81**
Wyre Rd. L5: Liv 2E **58**
Wyrescourt Rd. L12: W Der 4B **60**
Wyresdale Av. PR8: South 2C **12**
WA10: St H 3H **49**
Wyresdale Rd. L9: Ain 3G **44**
Wyrevale Gro. WN4: Ash M 8L **41**
Wysall Cl. WA11: St H 5N **49**
Wyswall Cl. L26: Halew 7J **77**
Wythburn Cres. WA11: St H 2L **49**
Wythburn Gro. WA7: Beech 1A **108**
Wyvern Rd. CH46: More 9M **55**

X

X Building L3: Liv 3D **4** (7B **58**)
XL Business Pk. WN8: Skel 1N **29**

Y

Yanwath St. L8: Liv 1G **75**
Yarcombe Cl. L26: Halew 7K **77**
Yardley Av. WA5: Warr 9A **66**
Yardley Cen. L33: Know I 9G **36**
Yardley Dr. CH63: Spit 6N **89**
Yardley Rd. L33: Know I 1G **46**
Yarmouth Rd. WA5: Gt San 2G **81**
Yarn Cl. WA9: St H 1B **64**
Yarrow Av. L31: Mag 1L **35**
Yates Cl. WA5: Gt San 3L **81**
Yates Ct. L34: Presc 4A **62**
Yates Rd. CH2: Thorn M 4J **113**
Yates St. L8: Liv 3D **74**
Yeadon Wlk. L24: Speke 4G **92**
Yeald Brow WA13: Lymm 5B **84**
Yellow Ho. La. PR8: South 9G **6**
Yellow Submarine 5G **92**
Yelverton Cl. L26: Halew 7K **77**
Yelverton Rd. CH42: Tran 5L **73**
L4: Walt 2H **59**
Yeoman Cotts. CH47: Hoy 2D **70**
Yeoman Way CH66: Gt Sut 4K **111**
Yeovil Cl. WA1: Wools 9K **67**
Ye Priory Ct. L25: Aller 7C **76**
Yew Bank Rd. L16: Child 1B **76**
Yewdale WN8: Skel 3D **30**
Yewdale Av. WA11: St H 1L **49**
Yewdale Dr. CH66: Whit 4L **111**
Yewdale Pk. CH43: Oxton 4H **73**
Yewdale Rd. L9: Walt 6G **44**
WN4: Ash M .4J **41**
Yew Tree Av. WA9: St H 3M **63**
WA12: Newt W 6J **51**
Yew Tree Cl. CH2: Thorn M 4J **113**
CH49: Woodc 6A **72**
L12: W Der .3D **60**
WA13: Lymm 4E **84**
Yewtree Cl. CH64: Lit N 7F **100**
Yew Tree Ct. CH60: Hesw 7A **88**
Yew Tree Grn. L31: Mell 7N **35**
Yew Tree La. CH48: W Kir 6C **70**
L12: W Der .4C **60**
WA4: App T .2K **99**
Yew Tree Rd. CH46: More 7N **55**
CH63: Hghr B 3L **89**
L9: Walt 6E **44**
L18: Aller 5B **76**
L25: Hunts X 8G **77**
L36: Huy 9H **61**
L39: Orm 6C **20**
Yew Tree Trad. Est.
WA11: Hay .2H **51**
Yew Tree Way WA3: Golb 3C **52**
Yew Wlk. M31: Part 7L **69**
Yew Way CH46: More 8N **55**
Yorkaster Rd. L18: Aller 7A **76**
York Av. CH44: Wall 6K **57**
CH48: W Kir 8C **70**
L17: Liv 2J **75**
L23: Crosb .7K **33**
PR8: South .1N **11**
WA3: Cul 8N **53**
WA5: Gt San 1G **80**
York Cl. L30: N'ton 6E **34**
L37: Form 7F **16**
WA10: St H .6J **49**
York Cotts. L25: Gate 4F **76**
York Dr. WA4: Grap 6H **83**
York Gdns. PR8: Birkd 1N **11**
York Ho. L17: Aig 3J **75**
York Mnr. L37: Form 1F **24**
PR8: Birkd .1N **11**
York Pl. WA7: Run 5L **95**
York Rd. CH44: Wall 7K **57**
CH65: Ell P 9A **104**
L23: Crosb .7L **33**
L31: Mag 4J **35**
L36: Huy 6L **61**
L37: Form 1F **24**
M44: Cad 4K **69**
PR8: Birkd .2M **11**
WA4: Grap .6H **83**
WA8: Wid 8F **78**
WN4: Ash M 8K **41**
York Rd. Sth. WN4: Ash M 9L **41**
Yorkshire Gdns. WA10: St H 8J **49**
Yorkshire Rd. M31: Part 7L **69**
York St. CH62: Brom 2C **90**
L1: Liv 7F **4** (9C **58**)
L9: Walt 7E **44**
L19: Garst .3A **92**
L22: Water .2K **43**
WA3: Golb .1B **52**
WA4: Warr .4D **82**
WA7: Run 5K **95**
York Ter. L5: Liv 3D **58**
PR9: South .7H **7**
York Way L19: Garst 3B **92**
L36: Huy 6L **61**
Youatt Av. L35: Presc 5B **62**
Youens Way L14: Knott A 5C **60**
Youth Court
Liverpool .6E **4**
Yoxall Dr. L33: Kirkb 6B **36**
Yvonne Cl. WN4: Ash M 6M **41**

Z

Zander Gro. L12: Crox 7E **46**
Zante Cl. L5: Liv 3D **58**
Zara Ct. WA11: Hay 3E **50**
Zenith Wlk. L25: Gate 1E **76**
Zetland Rd. CH45: Wall 2F **56**
L18: Moss H 3L **75**
Zetland St. CH41: Birke 3K **73**
PR9: South .8J **7**
Zig Zag Rd. CH45: Wall 3H **57**
L12: W Der .4B **60**
Zinnia Dr. M44: Irlam 1L **69**
Zircon Cl. L21: Lith 2B **44**

HOSPITALS, HOSPICES and selected HEALTHCARE FACILITIES covered by this atlas.

N.B. Where it is not possible to name these facilities on the map, the reference given is for the road in which they are situated.

ALDER HEY CHILDREN'S HOSPITAL 5A **60**
Eaton Road
West Derby
LIVERPOOL
L12 2AP
Tel: 0151 2284811

ARROWE PARK HOSPITAL 7A **72**
Arrowe Park Road
WIRRAL
CH49 5PE
Tel: 0151 6785111

ASHTON HOUSE HOSPITAL 4H **73**
26 Village Road
Oxton
PRENTON
CH43 5SR
Tel: 0151 6539660

ASHWORTH HOSPITAL 9M **27**
Parkbourn
LIVERPOOL
L31 1HW
Tel: 0151 473 0303

BMI SEFTON HOSPITAL 4K **45**
University Hospital Aintree
Lower Lane
LIVERPOOL
L9 7AL
Tel: 0151 3306551

BROADGREEN HOSPITAL 7A **60**
Thomas Drive
LIVERPOOL
L14 3LB
Tel: 0151 7062000

CHESHIRE & MERSEYSIDE NHS TREATMENT CENTRE
. . . . .9B **96**
Earls Way
RUNCORN
WA7 2HH
Tel: 01928 574001

CHESHIRE SPIRE HOSPITAL 6E **98**
Fir Tree Close
Stretton
WARRINGTON
WA4 4LU
Tel: 0845 6022500

CLAIRE HOUSE CHILDREN'S HOSPICE 6K **89**
Clatterbridge Road
WIRRAL
CH63 4JD
Tel: 0151 3344626

CLATTERBRIDGE CENTRE FOR ONCOLOGY 6K **89**
Clatterbridge Road
WIRRAL
CH63 4JY
Tel: 0151 3341155

CLATTERBRIDGE HOSPITAL 6K **89**
Clatterbridge Road
Bebington
WIRRAL
CH63 4JY
Tel: 0151 3344000

ELLESMERE PORT HOSPITAL 3M **111**
114 Chester Rd.
Whitby
ELLESMERE PORT
CH65 6SG
Tel: 01244 362986

FAIRFIELD INDEPENDENT HOSPITAL 9H **39**
Crank Road
Crank
ST. HELENS
WA11 7RS
Tel: 01744 739311

HALTON GENERAL HOSPITAL 9B **96**
Hospital Way
RUNCORN
WA7 2DA
Tel: 01928 714567

HALTON HAVEN HOSPICE 1E **108**
Barnfield Avenue.
Murdishaw
RUNCORN
WA7 6EP
Tel: 01928 712728

HESKETH CENTRE 6H **7**
51-55 Albert Road
SOUTHPORT
PR9 0LT
Tel: 01704 383110

HOLLINS PARK HOSPITAL 3A **66**
Hollins Lane
WARRINGTON
WA2 8WA
Tel: 01925 664000

HOSPICE OF THE GOOD SHEPHERD 9N **111**
Gordon Lane
Backford
CHESTER
CH2 4DG
Tel: 01244 851091

LIVERPOOL HEART & CHEST HOSPITAL 7A **60**
Thomas Drive
LIVERPOOL
L14 3PE
Tel: 0151 2281616

LIVERPOOL SPIRE HOSPITAL 3L **75**
57 Greenbank Road
LIVERPOOL
L18 1HQ
Tel: 0151 7337123

LIVERPOOL UNIVERSITY DENTAL HOSPITAL 4L **5** (7E **58**)
Pembroke Place
LIVERPOOL
L3 5PS
Tel: 0151 7062000

LIVERPOOL WOMEN'S HOSPITAL 8N **5** (9F **58**)
Crown Street
LIVERPOOL
L8 7SS
Tel: 0151 7089988

MARIE CURIE CENTRE, LIVERPOOL 6F **76**
Speke Road
Woolton
LIVERPOOL
L25 8QA
Tel: 0151 8011400

MOSSLEY HILL HOSPITAL 5K **75**
Park Avenue
Mossley Hill
LIVERPOOL
L18 8BU
Tel: 0151 2503000

MURRAYFIELD SPIRE HOSPITAL 2D **88**
Holmwood Drive
Heswall
WIRRAL
CH61 1AU
Tel: 0845 6002110

NEWTON COMMUNITY HOSPITAL 8K **51**
Bradlegh Road
NEWTON-LE-WILLOWS
WA12 8RB
Tel: 01925 222731

NHS CHILDREN'S WALK-IN CENTRE (SMITHDOWN) 2J **75**
Smithdown Road
LIVERPOOL
L15 2LF
Tel: 0151 2854820

NHS WALK-IN CENTRE (BIRKENHEAD) 5K **73**
Derby Road
BIRKENHEAD
CH42 0LQ

NHS WALK-IN CENTRE (GARSTON) 3B **92**
70 Banks Road
LIVERPOOL
L19 8JZ

NHS WALK-IN CENTRE (KNOWSLEY HALEWOOD) 9K **77**
Halewood Centre
Roseheath Drive
LIVERPOOL
L26 9UH
Tel: 0151 244 3532

NHS WALK-IN CENTRE (KNOWSLEY - HUYTON) 7J **61**
Nutgrove Villa
Westmorland Road
Huyton
LIVERPOOL
L36 6GA
Tel: 0151 244 3150

NHS WALK-IN CENTRE (KNOWSLEY - KIRKBY) 9C **36**
St Chad's Clinic
57 St Chad's Drive
LIVERPOOL
L32 8RE
Tel: 0151 244 3180

NHS WALK-IN CENTRE (LITHERLAND TOWN HALL) 2A **44**
Hatton Hill Road
LIVERPOOL
L21 9JN
Tel: 0151 475 4840

NHS WALK-IN CENTRE (LIVERPOOL CITY CENTRE)
. . . . .5G **5** (8C **58**)
Unit 4
Charlotte Row
53 Great Charlotte Street
LIVERPOOL
L1 1HU
Tel: 0151 285 3535

NHS WALK-IN CENTRE (LIVERPOOL - OLD SWAN) 7M **59**
Old Swan Health Centre
St. Oswalds Street
LIVERPOOL
L13 2BY
Tel: 0151 285 3565

NHS WALK-IN CENTRE (MERSEY VIEW) 1M **5**
45 Everton Road
LIVERPOOL
L6 2EH

NHS WALK-IN CENTRE (ST HELENS) 7L **49**
Millennium Building
Bickerstaffe Street
ST. HELENS
WA10 1DH
Tel: 01744 627 400

NHS WALK-IN CENTRE (SKELMERSDALE) 3E **30**
116-118 The Concourse Shopping Centre
SKELMERSDALE
WN8 6LJ
Tel: 01695 588640

NHS WALK-IN CENTRE (WIRRAL) 6H **57**
Victoria Central Hospital
Mill Lane
WALLASEY
CH44 5UF
Tel: 0151 678 5111

NHS WALK-IN CENTRE (WIRRAL ARROWE PARK) 7A **72**
Arrowe Park Hospital
Arrowe Park Road
WIRRAL
CH49 5PE
Tel: 0151 6788496

ORMSKIRK AND DISTRICT GENERAL HOSPITAL 9E **20**
Wigan Road
ORMSKIRK
L39 2AZ
Tel: 01695 577111

PARK LODGE HOSPITAL 4J **59**
Orphan Drive
LIVERPOOL
L6 7UN
Tel: 0151 3308901

PEASLEY CROSS HOSPITAL 9M **49**
Marshalls Cross Road
ST. HELENS
WA9 3DE
Tel: 01744 458 459

PRIMARY CARE TREATMENT CENTRE 1A **92**
Church Road
Garston
LIVERPOOL
L19 2LP
Tel: 0151 330 8301

QUEENSCOURT HOSPICE 2E **12**
Town Lane
SOUTHPORT
PR8 6RE
Tel: 01704 544645

RATHBONE HOSPITAL 7M **59**
Mill Lane
Old Swan
LIVERPOOL
L13 4AW
Tel: 0151 4717810

RENACRES PRIVATE HOSPITAL 9G **13**
Renacres Lane
Halsall
ORMSKIRK
L39 8SE
Tel: 01704 841133

ROYAL LIVERPOOL UNIVERSITY HOSPITAL 3L **5** (7F **58**)
Prescot Street
LIVERPOOL
L7 8XP
Tel: 0151 7062000

ST CATHERINE'S HOSPITAL (BIRKENHEAD) 4K **73**
Church Road
BIRKENHEAD
CH42 0LQ
Tel: 0151 6787272

ST HELENS HOSPITAL (MERSEYSIDE) 9M **49**
Marshalls Cross Road
ST. HELENS
WA9 3DA
Tel: 01744 646461

ST JOHN'S HOSPICE IN WIRRAL 6L **89**
Mount Road
Higher Bebington
WIRRAL
CH63 6JE
Tel: 0151 3342778

ST JOSEPH'S HOSPICE 3M **33**
Ince Road
LIVERPOOL
L23 4UE
Tel: 0151 924 3812

ST ROCCO'S HOSPICE 1N **81**
Lockton Lane
WARRINGTON
WA5 0BW
Tel: 01925 575780

SCOTT CLINIC 4F **62**
Rainhill Road
ST. HELENS
WA9 5BD
Tel: 0151 430 6300

SMITHDOWN HEALTH PARK 2J **75**
Smithdown Road
LIVERPOOL
L15 2HE
Tel: 0151 33080

SOUTHPORT AND FORMBY DISTRICT GENERAL HOSPITAL 2D **12**
Town Lane
SOUTHPORT
PR8 6PN
Tel: 01704 547471

UNIVERSITY HOSPITAL AINTREE 4K **45**
Longmoor Lane
LIVERPOOL
L9 7AL
Tel: 0151 5255980

VICTORIA CENTRAL HOSPITAL 6H **57**
Mill Lane
WALLASEY
CH44 5UF
Tel: 0151 6787272

WALTON CENTRE FOR NEUROLOGY AND NEUROSURGERY 3K **45**
Lower Lane
LIVERPOOL
L9 7LJ
Tel: 0151 5253611

WARRINGTON HOSPITAL 2A **82**
Lovely Lane
WARRINGTON
WA5 1QG
Tel: 01925 635911

WHISTON HOSPITAL 5C **62**
Warrington Road
PRESCOT
L35 5DR
Tel: 0151 426 1600

WILLOWBROOK HOSPICE 2D **62**
Portico Lane
Eccleston Park
PRESCOT
L34 2QT
Tel: 0151 430 8736

WOODLANDS HOSPICE 4J **45**
Longmoor Lane
LIVERPOOL
L9 7LA
Tel: 0151 5292299

WRIGHTINGTON HOSPITAL 3N **23**
Hall Lane
Appley Bridge
WIGAN
WN6 9EP
Tel: 01942 244000

ZOE'S PLACE - BABY HOSPICE 4C **60**
Yew Tree Lane
LIVERPOOL
L12 9HH
Tel: 0151 2280353

MIX
Paper from responsible sources
FSC® C006021
FSC www.fsc.org

The representation on the maps of a road, track or footpath is no evidence of the existence of a right of way.

The Grid on this map is the National Grid taken from Ordnance Survey® mapping with the permission of the Controller of Her Majesty's Stationery Office.

SAFETY CAMERA INFORMATION

PocketGPSWorld.com's CamerAlert is a self-contained speed and red light camera warning system for SatNavs and Android or Apple iOS smartphones/tablets. Visit www.cameralert.co.uk to download.

Safety camera locations are publicised by the Safer Roads Partnership which operates them in order to encourage drivers to comply with speed limits at these sites. It is the driver's absolute responsibility to be aware of and to adhere to speed limits at all times.

By showing this safety camera information it is the intention of Geographers' A-Z Map Company Ltd., to encourage safe driving and greater awareness of speed limits and vehicle speed. Data accurate at time of printing.

Printed and bound in the United Kingdom by Polestar Wheatons Ltd., Exeter.

Robert Harding/Alamy

PHILIP'S ROA

2017 ESSENTIAL BRITAIN & IRELAND

II **Key to map symbols**

III **Motorway service areas**

IV **Restricted motorway junctions**

VI **Mobile Layby Cafés** – gourmet or gruesome?

VIII **Route planning maps**

XVIII **Road map of Ireland**

XX **Distances and journey times**

1 **Key to road map pages**

2 **Road maps of Britain**

161 **Urban approach maps**

- 161 Glasgow *approaches*
- 162 Birmingham *approaches*
- 164 London *approaches*
- 168 Manchester *approaches*

169 **Town plans**

- 169 Aberdeen, Birmingham
- 170 Bath, Bradford, Bristol
- 171 Cambridge, Cardiff, Coventry, Derby
- 172 Edinburgh, Glasgow
- 173 Gloucester, Hull, Leeds
- 174 London
- 176 Liverpool, Manchester
- 177 Leicester, Middlesbrough, Newcastle upon Tyne, Norwich
- 178 Nottingham, Oxford, Plymouth, Portsmouth
- 179 Reading, Sheffield, Southampton
- 180 Stoke-on-Trent (Hanley), Swansea, Worcester, York

181 **Index to road maps of Britain**

www.philips-maps.co.uk

Published by Philip's
a division of Octopus Publishing Group Ltd
www.octopusbooks.co.uk
Carmelite House, 50 Victoria Embankment
London EC4Y 0DZ
An Hachette UK Company
www.hachette.co.uk

Third edition 2016
First impression 2016

ISBN 978-1-84907-414-8

Cartography by Philip's

Information for National Parks, Areas of Outstanding Natural Beauty, National Trails and Country Parks in Wales supplied by the Countryside Council for Wales.

Information for National Parks, Areas of Outstanding Natural Beauty, National Trails and Country Parks in England supplied by Natural England. Data for Regional Parks, Long Distance Footpaths and Country Parks in Scotland provided by Scottish Natural Heritage.

Gaelic name forms used in the Western Isles provided by Comhairle nan Eilean.

Data for the National Nature Reserves in England provided by Natural England. Data for the National Nature Reserves in Wales provided by Countryside Council for Wales. Darparwyd data'n ymwneud â Gwarchodfeydd Natur Cenedlaethol Cymru gan Gyngor Cefn Gwlad Cymru.

Information on the location of National Nature Reserves in Scotland was provided by Scottish Natural Heritage.

Data for National Scenic Areas in Scotland provided by the Scottish Executive Office. Crown copyright material is reproduced with the permission of the Controller of HMSO and the Queen's Printer for Scotland. Licence number C02W0003960.

Printed in China.

*Data from Nielsen Total Consumer Market 2015 Weeks 1–48

Road map symbols

- M6 **Motorway, toll motorway**
- **Motorway junction** – full, restricted access
- **Motorway service area** – full, restricted access
- **Motorway under construction**
- A453 **Primary route** – dual, single carriageway
- **Service area, roundabout, multi-level junction**
- **Numbered junction** – full, restricted access
- **Primary route under construction**
- **Narrow primary route**
- Derby **Primary destination**
- A34 **A road** – dual, single carriageway
- **A road under construction, narrow A road**
- B2135 **B road** – dual, single carriageway
- **B road under construction, narrow B road**
- **Minor road** – over 4 metres, under 4 metres wide
- **Minor road with restricted access**
- **Distance in miles**
- **Scenic route**
- TOLL **Toll, steep gradient** – arrow points downhill
- **Tunnel**
- **National trail** – England and Wales
- **Long distance footpath** – Scotland
- **Railway with station**
- **Level crossing, tunnel**
- **Preserved railway with station**
- **National boundary**
- **County / unitary authority boundary**
- **Car ferry, catamaran**
- **Passenger ferry, catamaran**
- **Hovercraft**
- CALAIS **Ferry destination**
- Ferry **Car ferry** – river crossing
- **Principal airport, other airport**
- **National park**
- **Area of Outstanding Natural Beauty** – England and Wales **National Scenic Area** – Scotland **forest park / regional park / national forest**
- **Woodland**
- **Beach**
- **Linear antiquity**
- **Roman road**
- 1066 **Hillfort, battlefield** – with date
- 795 **Viewpoint, nature reserve, spot height** – in metres
- **Golf course, youth hostel, sporting venue**
- **Camp site, caravan site, camping and caravan site**
- P&R **Shopping village, park and ride**
- 29 **Adjoining page number** – road maps

Approach map symbols

- M6 **Motorway**
- **Toll motorway**
- **Motorway junction** – full, restricted access
- **Service area**
- **Under construction**
- A6 **Primary route** – dual, single carriageway
- **Service area**
- **Multi-level junction**
- **roundabout**
- **Under construction**
- A195 **A road** – dual, single carriageway
- B1288 **B road** – dual, single carriageway
- **Minor road** – dual, single carriageway
- **Ring road**
- **Distance in miles**
- **Congestion charge area**
- COSELEY **Railway with station**
- LOXDALE **Tramway with station**
- **Underground or metro station**

Town plan symbols

- **Motorway**
- **Primary route** – dual, single carriageway
- **A road** – dual, single carriageway
- **B road** – dual, single carriageway
- **Minor through road**
- **One-way street**
- **Pedestrian roads**
- **Shopping streets**
- **Railway with station**
- City Hall **Tramway with station**
- **Bus or railway station building**
- **Shopping precinct or retail park**
- **Park**
- **Building of public interest**
- **Theatre, cinema**
- **Parking, shopmobility**
- Bank **Underground station**
- West St **Metro station**
- **Hospital, Police station**
- PO **Post office**

Tourist information

- **Abbey, cathedral or priory**
- **Ancient monument**
- **Aquarium**
- **Art gallery**
- **Bird collection or aviary**
- **Castle**
- **Church**
- **Country park** England and Wales, Scotland
- **Farm park**
- **Garden**
- **Historic ship**
- **House**
- **House and garden**
- **Motor racing circuit**
- **Museum**
- **Picnic area**
- **Preserved railway**
- **Race course**
- **Roman antiquity**
- **Safari park**
- **Theme park**
- **Tourist information centre** open all year, open seasonally
- **Zoo**
- **Other place of interest**

Relief

Feet	metres
3000	914
2600	792
2200	671
1800	549
1400	427
1000	305
0	0

Road map scales

3·15 miles to 1 inch • 1:200 000

Parts of Scotland

4.18 miles to 1 inch • 1:265 000

Scottish Highlands and Islands

5.24 miles to 1 inch • 1:332 000

Orkney and Shetland Islands 1:400 000, 6.31 miles to 1 inch

Motorway service areas

Restricted motorway junctions

M1 Junction 34

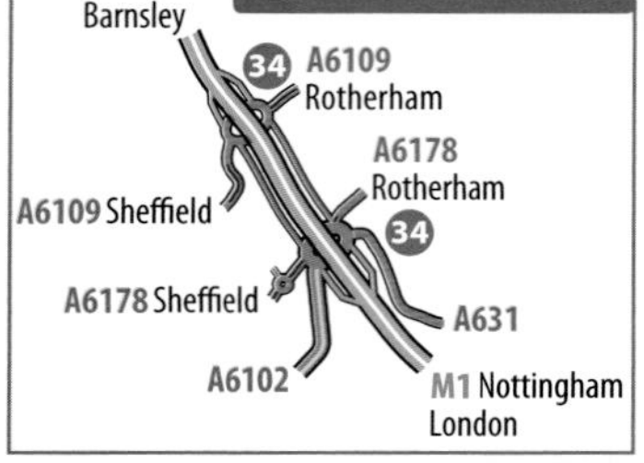

M1 Junctions 6, 6A
M25 Junctions 21, 21A

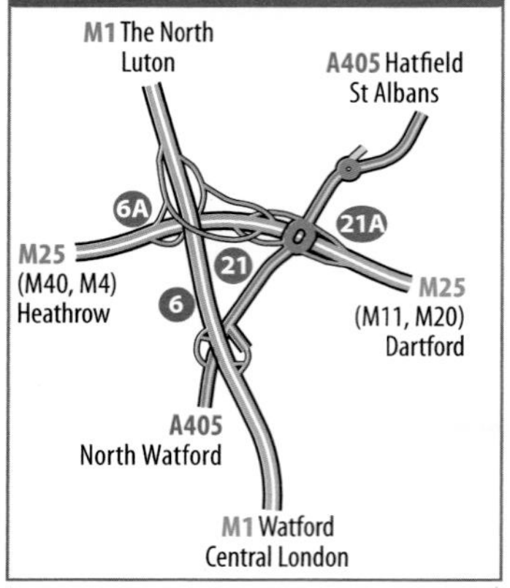

M4 Junctions 25, 25A, 26

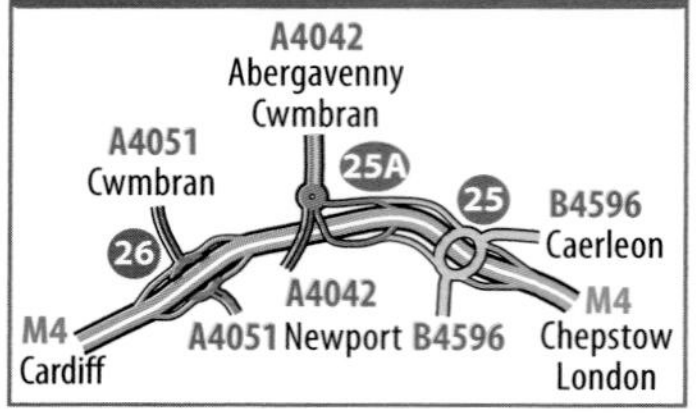

M5 Junction 11A

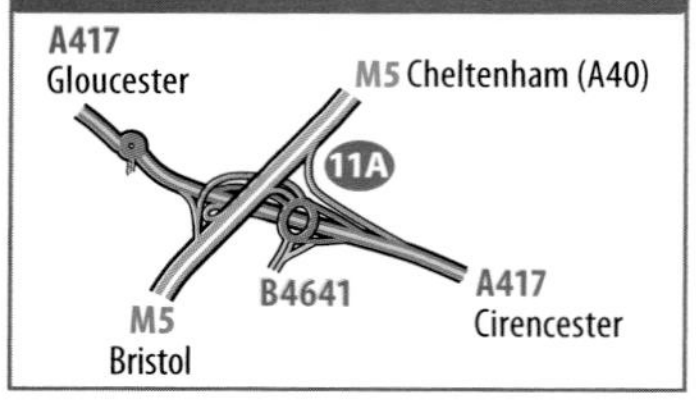

M8 Junctions 8, 9 · M73 Junctions 1, 2
M74 Junctions 2A, 3, 3A, 4

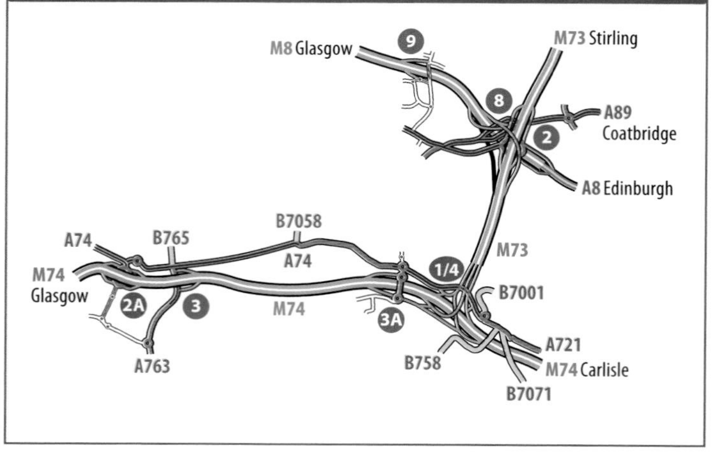

M1	Northbound	Southbound
2	No exit	No access
4	No exit	No access
6A	No exit. Access from M25 only	No access. Exit to M25 only
7	No exit. Access from A414 only	No access. Exit to A414 only
17	No access. Exit to M45 only	No exit. Access from M45 only
19	No exit to A14	No access from A14
21A	No access	No exit
23A		Exit to A42 only
24A	No exit	No access
35A	No access	No exit
43	No access. Exit to M621 only	No exit. Access from M621 only
48	No exit to A1(M) southbound	

M3	Eastbound	Westbound
8	No exit	No access
10	No access	No exit
13	No access to M27 eastbound	
14	No exit	No access

M4	Eastbound	Westbound
1	Exit to A4 eastbound only	Access from A4 westbound only
2	Access from A4 eastbound only	Access to A4 westbound only
21	No exit	No access
23	No access	No exit
25	No exit	No access
25A	No exit	No access
29	No exit	No access
38		No access
39	No exit or access	No exit
41	No access	No exit
41A	No exit	No access
42	Access from A483 only	Exit to A483 only

M5	Northbound	Southbound
10	No exit	No access
11A	No access from A417 eastbound	No exit to A417 westbound

M6	Northbound	Southbound
3A	No access. Exit to M42 northbound only	No exit. Access from M6 eastbound only
4A	No exit. Access from M42 southbound only	No access. Exit to M42 only
5	No access	No exit
10A	No access. Exit to M54 only	No exit. Access from M54 only
11A	No exit. Access from M6 Toll only	No access. Exit to M6 Toll only
20	No exit to M56 eastbound	No access from M56 westbound
24	No exit	No access
25	No access	No exit
30	No exit. Access from M61 northbound only	No access. Exit to M61 southbound only
31A	No access	No exit
45	No access	No exit

M6 Toll	Northbound	Southbound
T1		No exit
T2	No exit, no access	No access
T5	No exit	No access
T7	No access	No exit
T8	No access	No exit

M8	Eastbound	Westbound
8	No exit to M73 northbound	No access from M73 southbound
9	No access	No exit
13	No exit southbound	Access from M73 southbound only
14	No access	No exit
16	No exit	No access
17	No exit	No access
18		No exit
19	No exit to A814 eastbound	No access from A814 westbound
20	No exit	No access
21	No access from M74	No exit
22	No exit. Access from M77 only	No access. Exit to M77 only
23	No exit	No access
25	Exit to A739 northbound only. Access from A739 southbound only	Access from A739 southbound only
25A	No exit	No access
28	No exit	No access
28A	No exit	No access

M9	Eastbound	Westbound
1A	No exit	No access
2	No access	No exit
3	No exit	No access
6	No access	No exit
8	No exit	No access

M11	Northbound	Southbound
4	No exit. Access from A406 only	No access. Exit to A406 only
5	No access	No exit
9	No access	No exit
13	No access	No exit
14	No exit to A428 westbound	No exit. Access from A14 westbound only

M20	Eastbound	Westbound
2	No access	No exit
3	No exit Access from M26 eastbound only	No access Exit to M26 westbound only
11A	No access	No exit

M23	Northbound	Southbound
7	No exit to A23 southbound	No access from A23 northbound
10A	No exit	No access

M25	Clockwise	Anticlockwise
5	No exit to M26 eastbound	No access from M26 westbound
19	No access	No exit
21	No exit to M1 southbound. Access from M1 southbound only	No exit to M1 southbound. Access from M1. southbound only
31	No exit	No access

M27	Eastbound	Westbound
10	No exit	No access
12	No access	No exit

M40	Eastbound	Westbound
3	No exit	No access
7	No exit	No access
8	No exit	No access
13	No exit	No access
14	No access	No exit
16	No access	No exit

M42	Northbound	Southbound
1	No exit	No access
7	No access Exit to M6 northbound only	No exit Access from M6 northbound only
7A	No access. Exit to M6 southbound only	No exit
8	No exit. Access from M6 southbound only	Exit to M6 northbound only. Access from M6 southbound only

M45	Eastbound	Westbound
M1 J17	Access to M1 southbound only	No access from M1 southbound
With A45	No access	No exit

M48	Eastbound	Westbound
M4 J21	No exit to M4 westbound	No access from M4 eastbound
M4 J23	No access from M4 westbound	No exit to M4 eastbound

M49	Southbound	Northbound
18A	No exit to M5 northbound	No access from M5 southbound

M53	Northbound	Southbound
11	Exit to M56 eastbound only. Access from M56 westbound only	Exit to M56 eastbnd only. Access from M56 westbound only

M56	Eastbound	Westbound
2	No exit	No access
3	No access	No exit
4	No exit	No access
7		No access
8	No exit or access	No exit
9	No access from M6 northbound	No access to M6 southbound
15	No exit to M53	No access from M53 northbound

M57	Northbound	Southbound
3	No exit	No access
5	No exit	No access

M58	Eastbound	Westbound
1	No exit	No access

M60	Clockwise	Anticlockwise
2	No exit	No access
3	No exit to A34 northbound	No exit to A34 northbound
4	No access from M56	No exit to M56
5	No exit to A5103 southbound	No exit to A5103 northbound
14	No exit	No access
16	No exit	No access
20	No access	No exit
22		No access
25	No access	
26		No exit or access
27	No exit	No access

M61	Northbound	Southbound
2	No access from A580 eastbound	No exit to A580 westbound
3	No access from A580 eastbound. No access from A666 southbound	No exit to A580 westbound
M6 J30	No exit to M6 southbound	No access from M6 northbound

M62	Eastbound	Westbound
23	No access	No exit

M65	Eastbound	Westbound
9	No access	No exit
11	No exit	No access

M66	Northbound	Southbound
1	No access	No exit

M67	Eastbound	Westbound
1A	No access	No exit
2	No exit	No access

M69	Northbound	Southbound
2	No exit	No access

M73	Northbound	Southbound
2	No access from M8 or A89 eastbound. No exit to A89	No exit to M8 or A89 westbound. No access from A89

M74	Northbound	Southbound
3	No access	No exit
3A	No exit	No access
7	No exit	No access
9	No exit or access	No access
10		No exit
11	No exit	No access
12	No access	No exit

M77	Northbound	Southbound
4	No exit	No access
6	No exit	No access
7	No exit or access	
8	No access	No access

M80	Northbound	Southbound
4A	No access	No exit
6A	No exit	
8	Exit to M876 northbound only. No access	Access from M876 southbound only. No exit

M90	Northbound	Southbound
2A	No access	No exit
7	No exit	No access
8	No access	No exit
10	No access from A912	No exit to A912

M180	Eastbound	Westbound
1	No access	No exit

M621	Eastbound	Westbound
2A	No exit	No access
4	No exit	
5	No exit	No access
6	No access	No exit

M876	Northbound	Southbound
2	No access	No exit

A1(M)	Northbound	Southbound
2	No access	No exit
3		No access
5	No exit	No access
14	No exit	No access
40	No access	No exit
43	No exit. Access from M1 only	No access. Exit to M1 only
57	No access	No exit
65	No access	No exit

A3(M)	Northbound	Southbound
1	No exit	No access
4	No access	No exit

M3 Junctions 13, 14
M27 Junction 4

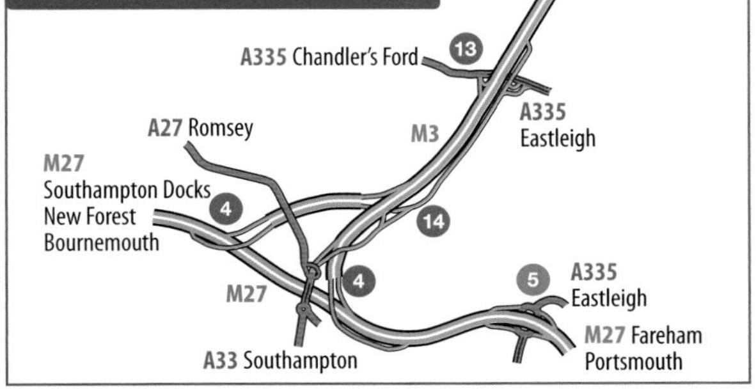

A38(M)	Northbound	Southbound
With Victoria Rd, (Park Circus) Birmingham	No exit	No access

A48(M)	Northbound	Southbound
M4 Junc 29	Exit to M4 eastbound only	Access from M4 westbound only
29A	Access from A48 eastbound only	Exit to A48 westbound only

A57(M)	Eastbound	Westbound
With A5103	No access	No exit
With A34	No access	No exit

A58(M)	Southbound
With Park Lane and Westgate, Leeds	No access

A64(M)	Eastbound	Westbound
With A58 Clay Pit Lane, Leeds	No access	No exit
With Regent Street, Leeds	No access	No access

A74(M)	Northbound	Southbound
18	No access	No exit
22		No exit

A194(M)	Northbound	Southbound
A1(M) J65 Gateshead Western Bypass	Access from A1(M) northbound only	Exit to A1(M) southbound only

M6 Junctions 3A, 4A · M42 Junctions 7, 7A, 8, 9
M6 Toll Junctions T1, T2

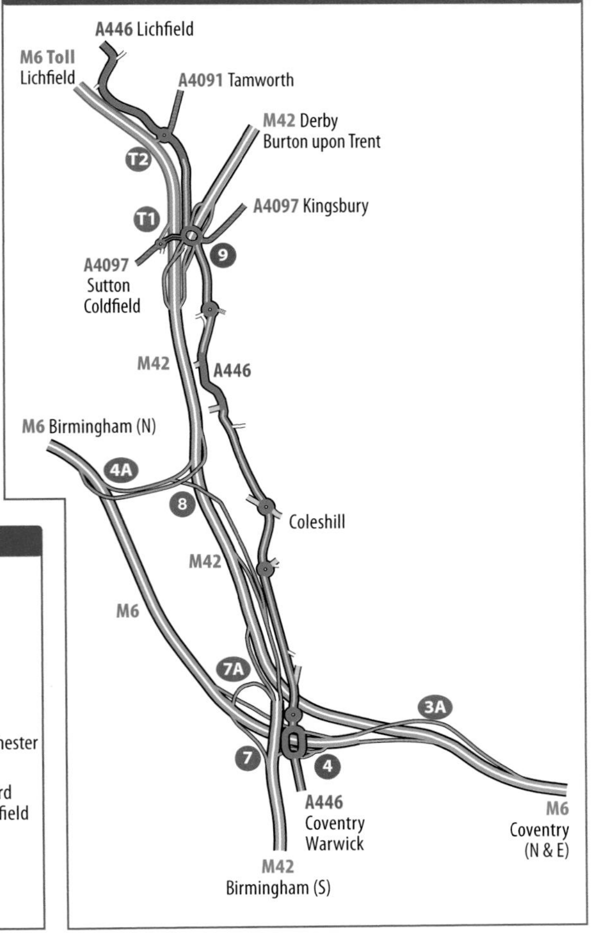

M62 Junctions 32A, 33 · A1(M) Junctions 40, 41

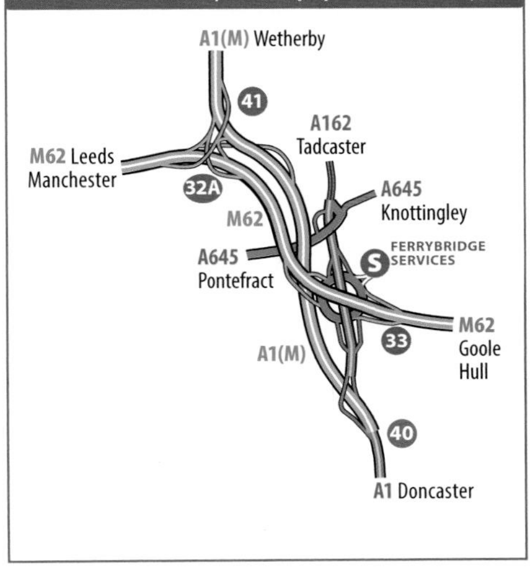

M6 Junction 20 · M56 Junction 4

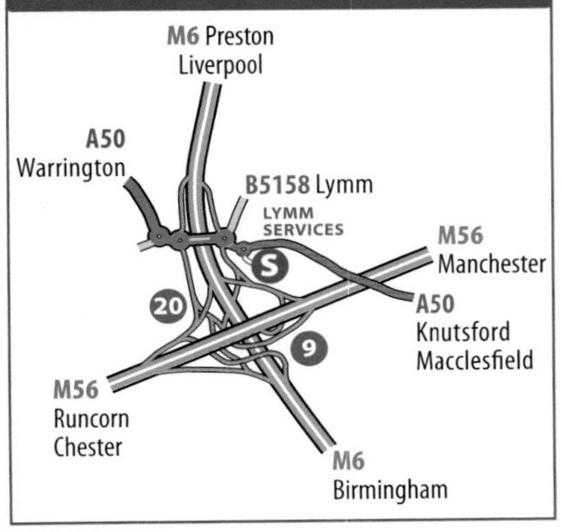

Mobile Layby Cafés – gourmet or gruesome?

Do you drive on by?

▲ A roadside snack van sign in Herefordshire *Jeff Morgan / Alamy*

Stephen Mesquita,
Philip's On the Road Correspondent

Have you ever done this? You're driving along on one of Britain's A-Roads. It's sometime between 6am and 2pm. You're feeling a bit peckish. You see a layby coming up. There's a notice by the road. Something about hot food. There's a van flying a Union Jack. There are a couple of truck drivers there, queueing up. You might even catch a tempting whiff of something frying.

And you drive straight past. Not really for you? You've never eaten in a layby so you'll wait for a place you know and recognise. Or buy a sandwich at the next petrol station.

Well, that's what I've always done.
Up until yesterday. That's when I set out, with my trusty accomplice (and Philip's Sales Supremo) Stuart, to see if my lifelong prejudices were justified.

▲ The first bacon butty of the day in a layby alongside the A43

Butty Vans

A quick word about terminology first.
We're going to drop the 'Mobile Layby Cafés' and go with 'Butty Vans'. Stuart and I were out to beat The Breakfast Buns from Butty Vans in One Morning Record.

And so it was with some trepidation that we set off from Northampton and headed for our first Butty Van. Here's confession number one: as soon as we'd photographed the bacon roll that we'd ordered, we polished it off.

This was a good start – and in stark contrast to our Motorway Service Area research, where the fare was so unappetising that we tried only a tiny portion of each item and left the rest.

And as the day started, so it went on. Of the eight buns, only one really disappointed. The other seven were tasty, hot, great value and came with friendly chat. Stuart and I polished almost all of them off – and two especially good ones were down the gullets of Philip's intrepid breakfast critics before you could say 'another bacon roll please'.

▼ Roadside snack van, Perthshire *Mar Photographics / Alamy*

Eight in a Day

Would I recommend eight in a day? As a gastronomic experience, no. It's too much salt intake (my car was littered with empty bottles of water by the end of the day). And I did long for a freshly made flat white by the end of the day.

But a Butty Van breakfast or snack every now and again? Absolutely. Now I've done it once, I'll be very happy to do it again. In fact, I'm rather ashamed I hadn't managed to overcome my prejudices before now.

So to answer my question. Gourmet: no. Gruesome: certainly not. A tasty roadside snack, piping hot, cooked to order and served with a smile – definitely.
I'll have one of those.

Butty Vans – what you need to know

- **Layby cafes are licensed by the local authority**, normally annually, to do business in a particular layby.
- **Food Hygiene is an important part of their credibility** – most of them display their certificates prominently.
- **You can't go there for dinner.** Most open early (often around 6am) and shut up around 2pm (sometimes 3pm).
- **They aren't just found in laybys on A Roads.** Some are on industrial estates and business parks.
- **The good ones are there come rain or shine** (bad weather can be good for business) most days of the year.
- **Most of them have a name:** we sampled the fare at Dom's Doorsteps, Taste Buds Snacks, Sizzlers, Delicias and Smell the Bacon.
- **It's a competitive business** – and their regulars (mostly truck drivers and white van men on A Roads) are discerning customers who expect tasty food at reasonable prices. We heard one van driver say he draws the line at paying £1 for a cup of tea.
- **We were made very welcome**, even though it was obvious we weren't their usual clientele.

Our thanks to all the proprietors who answered our questions about their businesses so openly.

Butty Vans vs. Motorway Service Areas– how they compare

If you're expecting Butty Vans to serve up the fare you get at your local deli, you probably don't need to read on. The buns are not made of artisanal sourdough ciabatta. The butter isn't Danish unsalted. The bacon didn't cost £15 a kilo. The eggs probably aren't fresh from the farm that morning. Butty Vans aren't posh.

But the point is this – all the Butty Vans we ate at were owned by people who took great pride in what they did. We met one real foody proprietor who told us he'd been to a burger fair the weekend before and always offered specials ('Codfinger'; 'Blue Burger Special'). All of them were aware that, to compete against the big brands, they had to offer good food at good prices.

The ingredients were perfectly decent. The bacon was almost universally of a better quality than we tasted last year in our Full English Breakfast campaign in Motorway Service Areas. And it was all cooked to order in front of you, which gave it one spectacular advantage over the Motorway Service Areas. It was hot.

And it was a fraction of the price.

The only disappointment was the tea and coffee.
But at £0.70–£0.80 a cup, you should know what you're getting and you get what you pay for – although at one Butty Van, the teabags were Yorkshire Tea.

You can compare further in our
Butty Van vs. Motorway Service Area checklist:

	Butty Vans	Motorway Services
Good Value for Money	✔	✗
Proud of what they do	✔	✗
Cooked to Order	✔	rarely
Meal Hot	✔	✗
Quality of ingredients	See above	See above
Quality of hot drinks	✗	✗
Friendly Service	✔	✗
Parking	✔	✔
Easy to find	✗	✔

Eight Meals in a Bun between 9am and 2pm – how was it for me?

Meal in a Bun One

Location	A43 West of Northampton
Meal	Bacon roll plus tea
Price	£2.50 plus £0.60

Verdict Generous helping of tasty bacon, cooked in front of us and piping hot. The tea was wet and warm.

Meal in a Bun Two

Location	A43 Brackley
Meal	Sausage and Bacon roll plus tea
Price	£3.20 plus £0.50

Verdict A breakfast on its own served with a smile and lots of chat.
The ingredients were nothing special but all tasty.

Meal in a Bun Three

Location	A422 between Buckingham and Milton Keynes
Meal	Bacon and Egg roll plus coffee
Price	£3.00 plus £0.80

Verdict Another very decent breakfast in a bun, with the egg cooked to order. Yorkshire Tea teabags spurned for instant coffee. Should have had the tea.

Meal in a Bun Four

Location	Harding Road, Milton Keynes
Meal:	Sausage and Egg roll plus tea
Price:	£2.25 plus £0.50

Verdict Sausage and egg: not expensive ingredients but properly cooked, nice and hot and at a nugatory price.

Meal in a Bun Five

Location	Yardley Road Industrial Estate, Olney
Meal	Double egg roll
Price	£2.50

Verdict I was stupid. I had a double egg sandwich (which was tasty) but I was rightly berated by Mr Sizzler for not being more adventurous and having one of his speciality burgers or chicken dishes. The things I sacrifice to make these surveys fair.

Meal in a Bun Six

Location	A505 West of Royston
Meal	Bacon Roll
Price	£2.00

Verdict The best bread (slightly toasted) and loads of decent bacon for £2.00. I rest my case. I should have added: cooked by Italians. They know how to cook, the Italians. Even good old English Bacon butties. Buonissimo!

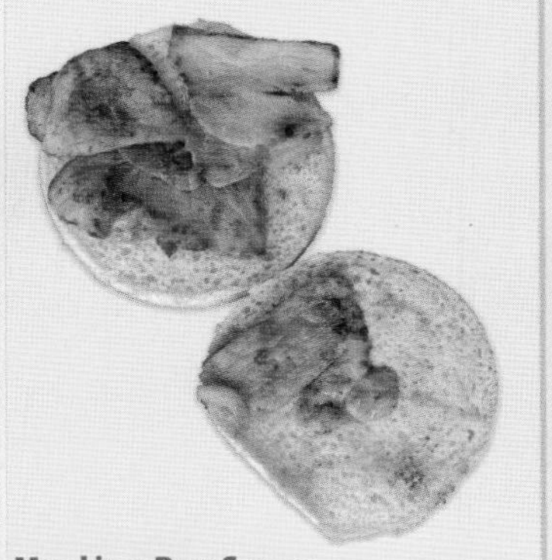

Meal in a Bun Seven

Location	A505 West of Royston
Meal	Bacon Roll
Price	£2.50

Verdict A bit disappointing. Bread tough, bacon tough. Our only below par experience of the day.

Meal in a Bun Eight

Location:	A505 East of Royston
Meal:	Sausage roll
Price:	£3.00

Verdict This café was called *Smell the Bacon* but the sausages were from *Musks* of Newmarket. They were delicious! They seemed to disappear remarkably quickly, Stuart.

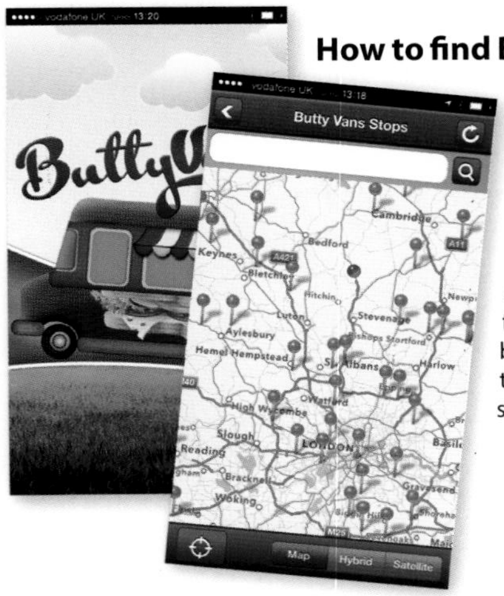

How to find Butty Vans

Most Butty Vans are either an 'impulse buy' (you see them as you pass by) or have their regular customers who know where they are. But say you are planning a journey and you want to know for sure there's a Butty Van at a point on your route. Then you need the free app from Butty Van Finder (go to buttyvan.com). We don't even need to describe it: these screen grabs say it all.

Enter the Butty Van Competition

Send us your personal recommendations for *Breakfast On the Move* (Butty Vans or anywhere else) by email, with pictures if possible, and tell us why you recommend them – or any amusing stories you have.

Send them by 31st December 2017.

The 25 best entries in our opinion will each receive a free copy of the *Philip's Royal Geographical Society Essential World Atlas* (worth £25).

Email your entries to buttyvan@octopusbooks.co.uk

For terms and conditions, visit www.octopusbooks.co.uk/assets/OctopusPublishingGroup/Downloads/PhilipsNavigatorCompetitionTandCs.pdf

Matt Botwood / Alamy

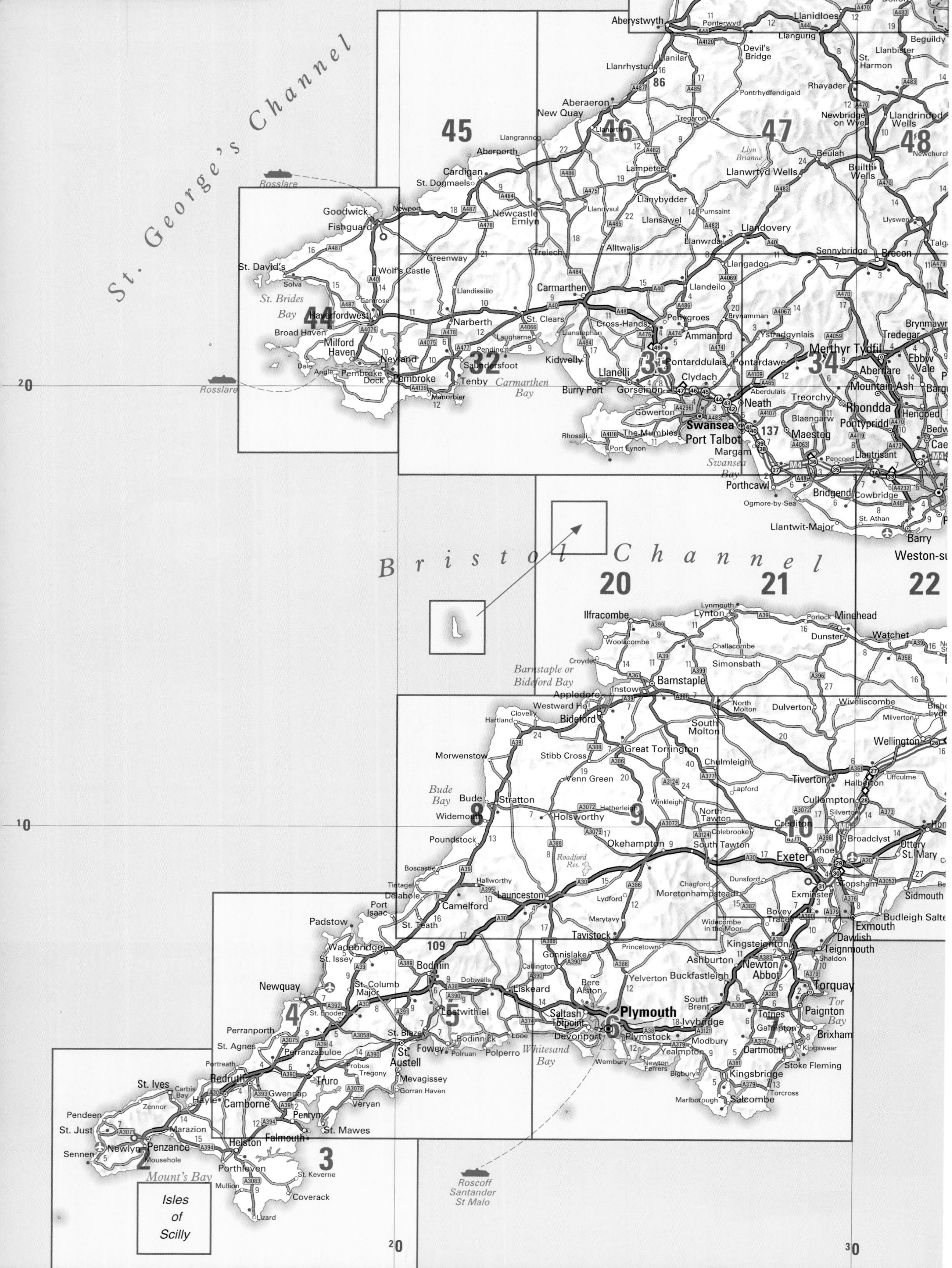
St. George's Channel
Bristol Channel
Rosslare
Aberdyfi
Borth
Talybont
Aberystwyth
Ponterwyd
Llanidloes
Llangurig
Newtown
Dolfor
Caersws
Beguildy
Llanbister
Devil's Bridge
St. Harmon
Llanrhystud
Llanilar
Rhayader
Pontrhydfendigaid
Aberaeron
New Quay
Tregaron
Newbridge on Wye
Llandrindod Wells
Llangrannog
Aberporth
Llyn Brianne
Beulah
Builth Wells
Newchurch
Cardigan
St. Dogmaels
Lampeter
Llanwrtyd Wells
Goodwick
Newport
Newcastle Emlyn
Llanybydder
Llandysul
Pumsaint
Llyswen
Fishguard
Llansawel
Llandovery
Alltwalis
Llanwrda
Sennybridge
Brecon
Talgarth
St. David's
Solva
Wolf's Castle
Greenway
Trelech
Llangadog
Carmarthen
Llandeilo
Llandissilio
St. Brides Bay
Camrose
Haverfordwest
Narberth
St. Clears
Cross-Hands
Penygroes
Brynamman
Ystradgynlais
Tredegar
Brynmawr
Broad Haven
Laugharne
Llanstephan
Ammanford
Merthyr Tydfil
Ebbw Vale
Milford Haven
Neyland
Pendine
Kidwelly
Pontarddulais
Pontardawe
Aberdare
Dale
Angle
Pembroke Dock
Pembroke
Saundersfoot
Tenby
Carmarthen Bay
Llanelli
Burry Port
Gorseinon
Clydach
Neath
Aberdulais
Mountain Ash
Treorchy
Rhondda
Manorbier
Gowerton
Swansea
Blaengarw
Hengoed
Rhossili
The Mumbles
Port Talbot
Maesteg
Pontypridd
Port Eynon
Margam
Swansea Bay
Llantrisant
Pencoed
Porthcawl
Bridgend
Cowbridge
Ogmore-by-Sea
St. Athan
Llantwit-Major
Barry
Weston-super-Mare
Ilfracombe
Lynmouth
Lynton
Porlock
Minehead
Dunster
Watchet
Woolacombe
Challacombe
Simonsbath
Croyde
Barnstaple or Bideford Bay
Barnstaple
Instow
Appledore
Westward Ho!
North Molton
South Molton
Dulverton
Wiveliscombe
Milverton
Wellington
Hartland
Clovelly
Bideford
Morwenstow
Stibb Cross
Great Torrington
Chulmleigh
Tiverton
Halberton
Uffculme
Venn Green
Lapford
Bude Bay
Bude
Stratton
Widemouth
Holsworthy
Hatherleigh
Winkleigh
North Tawton
Cullompton
Silverton
Crediton
Colebrooke
Broadclyst
Ottery St. Mary
Poundstock
Okehampton
South Tawton
Exeter
Pinhoe
Roadford Res.
Boscastle
Hallworthy
Chagford
Dunsford
Topsham
Sidmouth
Tintagel
Delabole
Launceston
Lydford
Moretonhampstead
Exminster
Port Isaac
Camelford
Marytavy
Bovey Tracey
Budleigh Salterton
Exmouth
Padstow
St. Teath
Tavistock
Widecombe in the Moor
Dawlish
Teignmouth
Shaldon
Wadebridge
St. Issey
Gunnislake
Princetown
Kingsteignton
Bodmin
Callington
Ashburton
Newton Abbot
Newquay
St. Columb Major
Dobwalls
Liskeard
Bere Alston
Yelverton
Buckfastleigh
Torquay
St. Enoder
Lostwithiel
Saltash
Torpoint
Plymouth
South Brent
Ivybridge
Totnes
Paignton
Tor Bay
Perranporth
St. Blazey
Bodinnick
Looe
Devonport
Plymstock
Galmpton
Brixham
St. Agnes
Perranzabuloe
St. Austell
Fowey
Polruan
Polperro
Whitesand Bay
Yealmpton
Modbury
Dartmouth
Kingswear
Portreath
Probus
Tregony
Wembury
Newton Ferrers
Stoke Fleming
St. Ives
Carbis Bay
Redruth
Truro
Mevagissey
Bigbury
Kingsbridge
Hayle
Camborne
Gwennap
Gorran Haven
Veryan
Torcross
Zennor
Marlborough
Salcombe
Pendeen
Penryn
St. Just
Marazion
St. Mawes
Falmouth
Sennen
Newlyn
Penzance
Mousehole
Helston
Porthleven
St. Keverne
Mount's Bay
Mullion
Coverack
Lizard
Isles of Scilly
Roscoff Santander St Malo

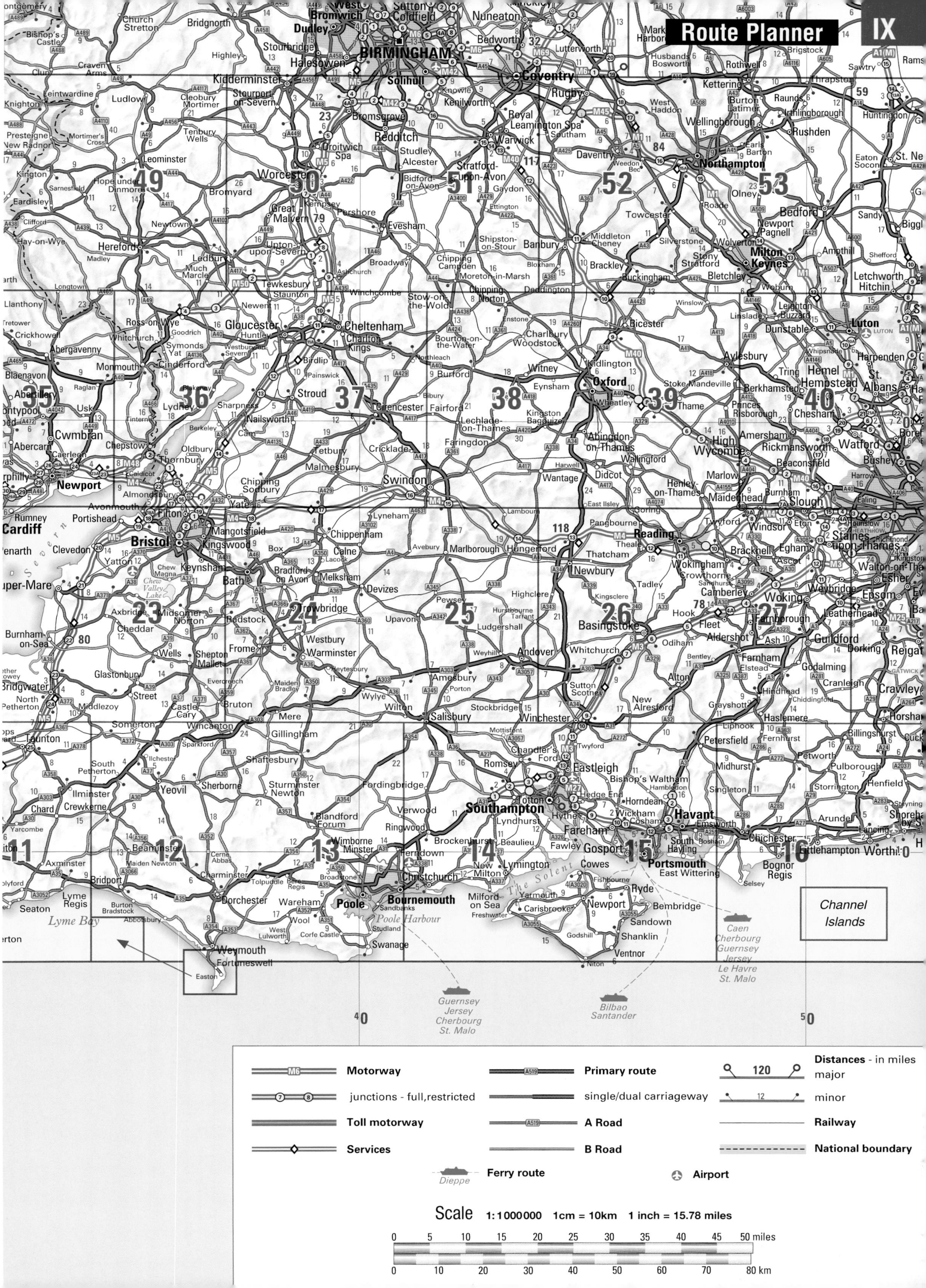
Channel Islands
Motorway
junctions - full,restricted
Toll motorway
Services
Ferry route
Dieppe
Primary route
single/dual carriageway
A Road
B Road
Airport
Distances - in miles
major
minor
Railway
National boundary
Scale 1:1000000 1cm = 10km 1 inch = 15.78 miles
0 5 10 15 20 25 30 35 40 45 50 miles
0 10 20 30 40 50 60 70 80 km

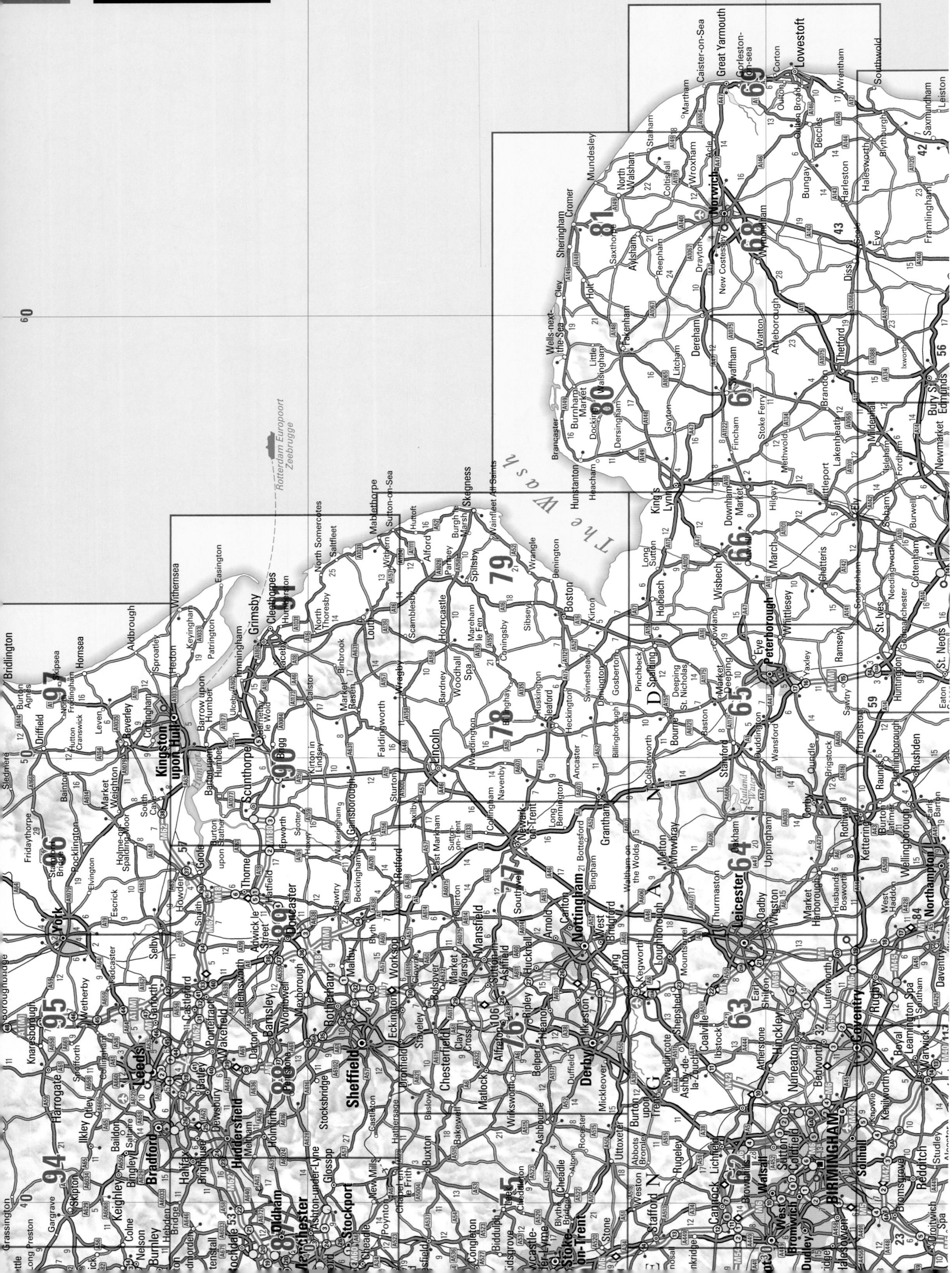
The Wash
Rotterdam Europoort
Zeebrugge
York
Leeds
Bradford
Sheffield
Nottingham
Derby
Leicester
Lincoln
Norwich
Peterborough
Kingston upon Hull
Doncaster
Coventry
BIRMINGHAM
Northampton
Great Yarmouth
Lowestoft
Cromer
Skegness
Boston
Grimsby
Cleethorpes
King's Lynn

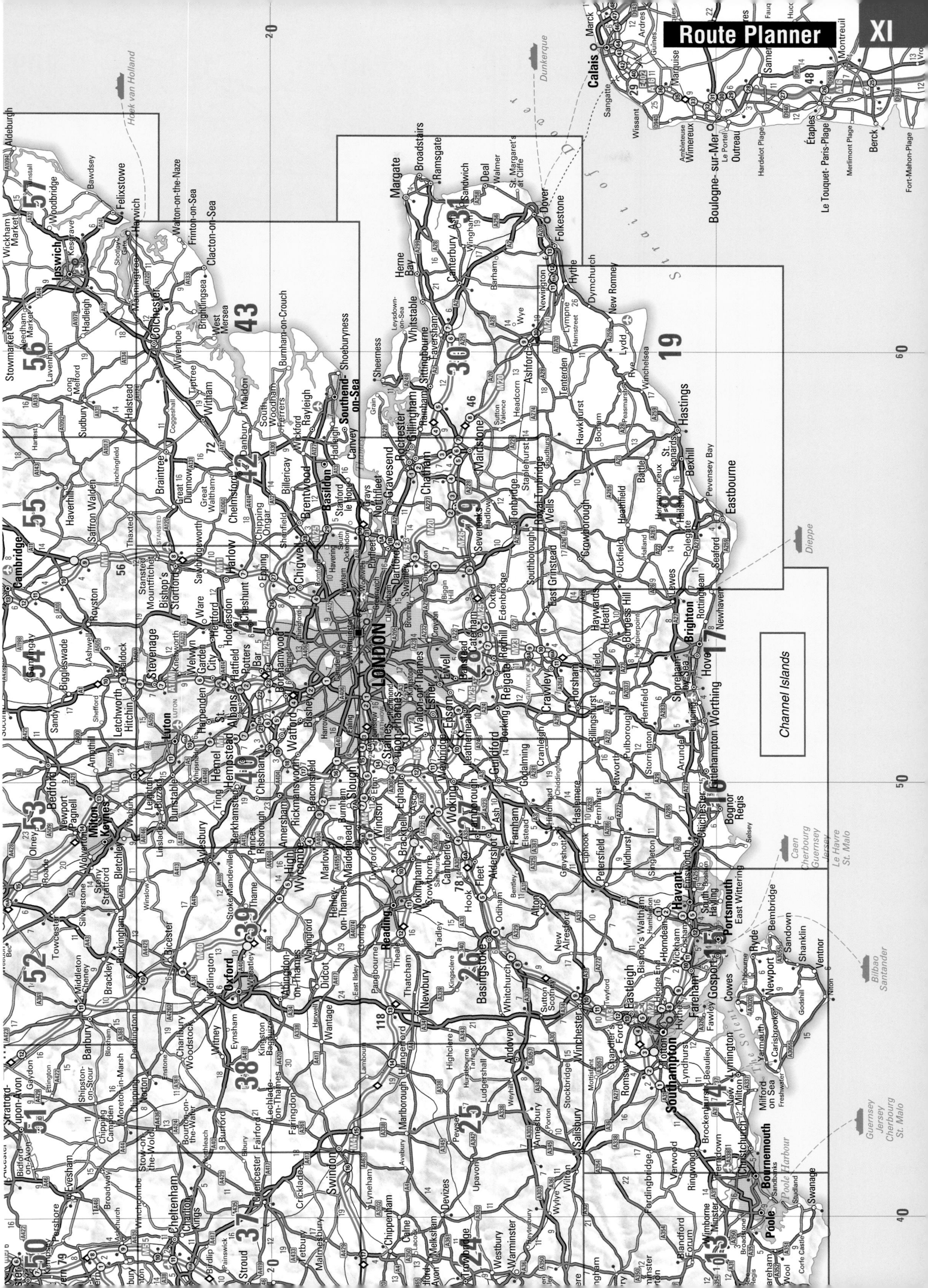
LONDON
Cambridge
Bedford
Milton Keynes
Luton
Oxford
Reading
Swindon
Chelmsford
Colchester
Ipswich
Felixstowe
Harwich
Southend-on-Sea
Basildon
Maidstone
Canterbury
Dover
Folkestone
Ashford
Margate
Ramsgate
Hastings
Eastbourne
Brighton
Worthing
Crawley
Guildford
Basingstoke
Winchester
Southampton
Portsmouth
Bournemouth
Poole
Salisbury
Newbury
Cheltenham
Calais
Boulogne-sur-Mer
Dunkerque
Dieppe
Hoek van Holland
Channel Islands
Strait of Dover

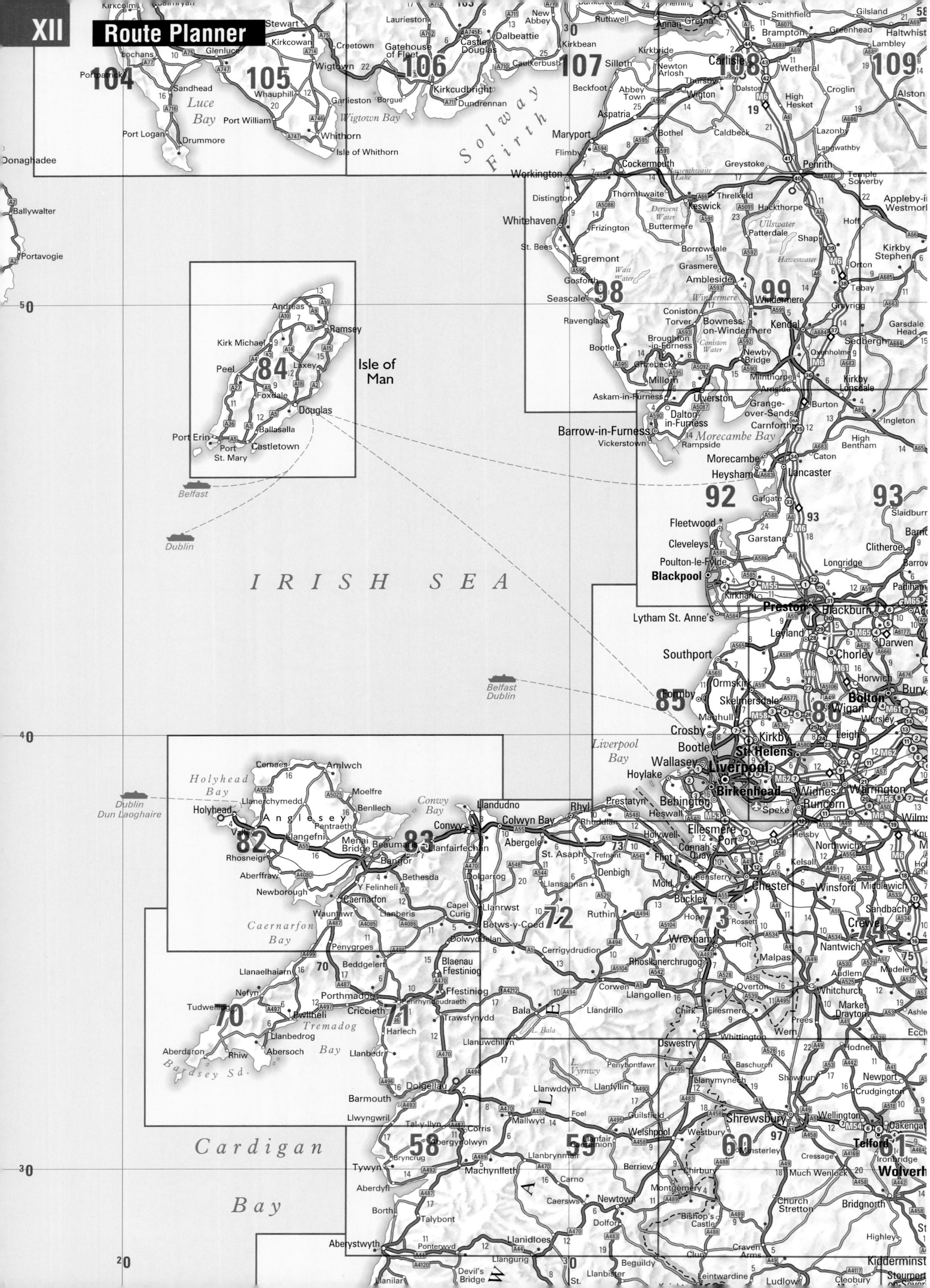
104
105
106
107
108
109
Stewart
Kirkcowan
Glenluce
Portpatrick
Sandhead
Luce
Bay
Port William
Port Logan
Drummore
Whauphill
Wigtown
Creetown
Gatehouse of Fleet
Garlieston
Wigtown Bay
Whithorn
Isle of Whithorn
Lauriestone
Castle Douglas
Dalbeattie
New Abbey
Kirkcudbright
Dundrennan
Kirkbean
Solway Firth
Ruthwell
Annan
Gretna
Silloth
Carlisle
Brampton
Haltwhistle
Gilsland
Smithfield
Greenhead
Lambley
Wetheral
Newton Arlosh
Kirkbride
Abbey Town
Beckfoot
Thursby
Wigton
Dalston
High Hesket
Croglin
Alston
Aspatria
Maryport
Flimby
Bothel
Caldbeck
Lazonby
Langwathby
Cockermouth
Bassenthwaite Lake
Greystoke
Penrith
Workington
Temple Sowerby
Appleby-in-Westmorland
Distington
Thornthwaite
Threlkeld
Keswick
Hackthorpe
Whitehaven
Frizington
Derwent Water
Buttermere
Ullswater
Patterdale
Shap
Hoff
Kirkby Stephen
St. Bees
Egremont
Borrowdale
Grasmere
Haweswater
Orton
Tebay
Wast Water
Ambleside
Gosforth
Seascale
98
99
Windermere
Grayrigg
Ravenglass
Coniston
Torver
Bowness-on-Windermere
Kendal
Sedbergh
Garsdale Head
Broughton-in-Furness
Coniston Water
Newby Bridge
Oxenholme
Bootle
Grizebeck
Millom
Milnthorpe
Arnside
Kirkby Lonsdale
Askam-in-Furness
Ulverston
Grange-over-Sands
Burton
Dalton-in-Furness
Carnforth
Ingleton
Barrow-in-Furness
Vickerstown
Rampside
Morecambe Bay
High Bentham
Morecambe
Caton
Heysham
Lancaster
92
93
Galgate
Slaidburn
Fleetwood
Garstang
Cleveleys
Clitheroe
Poulton-le-Fylde
Longridge
Blackpool
Kirkham
Preston
Blackburn
Padiham
Lytham St. Anne's
Leyland
Darwen
Southport
Chorley
Ormskirk
Horwich
Formby
85
86
Skelmersdale
Bolton
Bury
Wigan
Maghull
Worsley
Crosby
Kirkby
Leigh
Bootle
St. Helens
Liverpool Bay
Wallasey
Liverpool
Hoylake
Birkenhead
Widnes
Warrington
Bebington
Runcorn
Heswall
Speke
Prestatyn
Rhyl
Rhuddlan
Holywell
Ellesmere Port
Connah's Quay
Helsby
Northwich
Knutsford
Flint
Kelsall
Queensferry
Chester
Winsford
Middlewich
Mold
Buckley
Sandbach
Hope
73
74
75
Crewe
Wrexham
Holt
Nantwich
Malpas
Rhosllanerchrugog
Audlem
Madeley
Whitchurch
Overton
Corwen
Llangollen
Ellesmere
Chirk
Market Drayton
Prees
Wem
Whittington
Oswestry
Hodnet
Baschurch
Shawbury
Newport
Crudgington
Llanymynech
Shrewsbury
Wellington
Oakengates
Telford
Guilsfield
Welshpool
Westbury
60
61
Minsterley
Cressage
Ironbridge
Wolverhampton
Berriew
Chirbury
Much Wenlock
Montgomery
Church Stretton
Bridgnorth
Newtown
Bishop's Castle
Highley
Dolfor
Kidderminster
Clun
Craven Arms
Beguildy
Leintwardine
Llanbister
Ludlow
Cleobury
Stourport
84
Andreas
Ramsey
Kirk Michael
Peel
Laxey
Isle of Man
Foxdale
Douglas
Ballasalla
Port Erin
Port St. Mary
Castletown
Belfast
Dublin
IRISH SEA
Belfast
Dublin
Donaghadee
Ballywalter
Portavogie
Holyhead Bay
Cemaes
Amlwch
Moelfre
Benllech
Llanerchymedd
Holyhead
Anglesey
Valley
Pentraeth
82
83
Llangefni
Menai Bridge
Beaumaris
Rhosneigr
Bangor
Dublin
Dun Laoghaire
Conwy Bay
Llandudno
Conwy
Colwyn Bay
Llanfairfechan
Abergele
St. Asaph
Trefnant
Denbigh
Aberffraw
Bethesda
Dolgarrog
Llansannan
Newborough
Y Felinheli
Caernarfon
Llanberis
Capel Curig
Llanrwst
Ruthin
72
Waunfawr
Betws-y-Coed
Caernarfon Bay
Penygroes
Dolwyddelan
Cerrigydrudion
Blaenau Ffestiniog
Llanaelhaearn
Beddgelert
70
71
Ffestiniog
Porthmadog
Nefyn
Penrhyndeudraeth
Tudweiliog
Pwllheli
Criccieth
Trawsfynydd
Bala
Llandrillo
Llanbedrog
Tremadog Bay
Harlech
L. Bala
Aberdaron
Rhiw
Abersoch
Llanbedr
Llanuwchllyn
Bardsey Sd.
L. Vyrnwy
Penybontfawr
Dolgellau
Llanwddyn
Llanfyllin
Barmouth
Llwyngwril
Tal-y-llyn
Corris
Mallwyd
Foel
58
59
Aberangell
Abergynolwyn
Llanfair Caereinion
Cardigan
Bryncrug
Tywyn
Llanbrynmair
Machynlleth
Aberdyfi
Carno
Bay
Caersws
Borth
Talybont
Aberystwyth
Llanidloes
Ponterwyd
Llangurig
Devil's Bridge
Llanilar
WALES
50
40
30
20

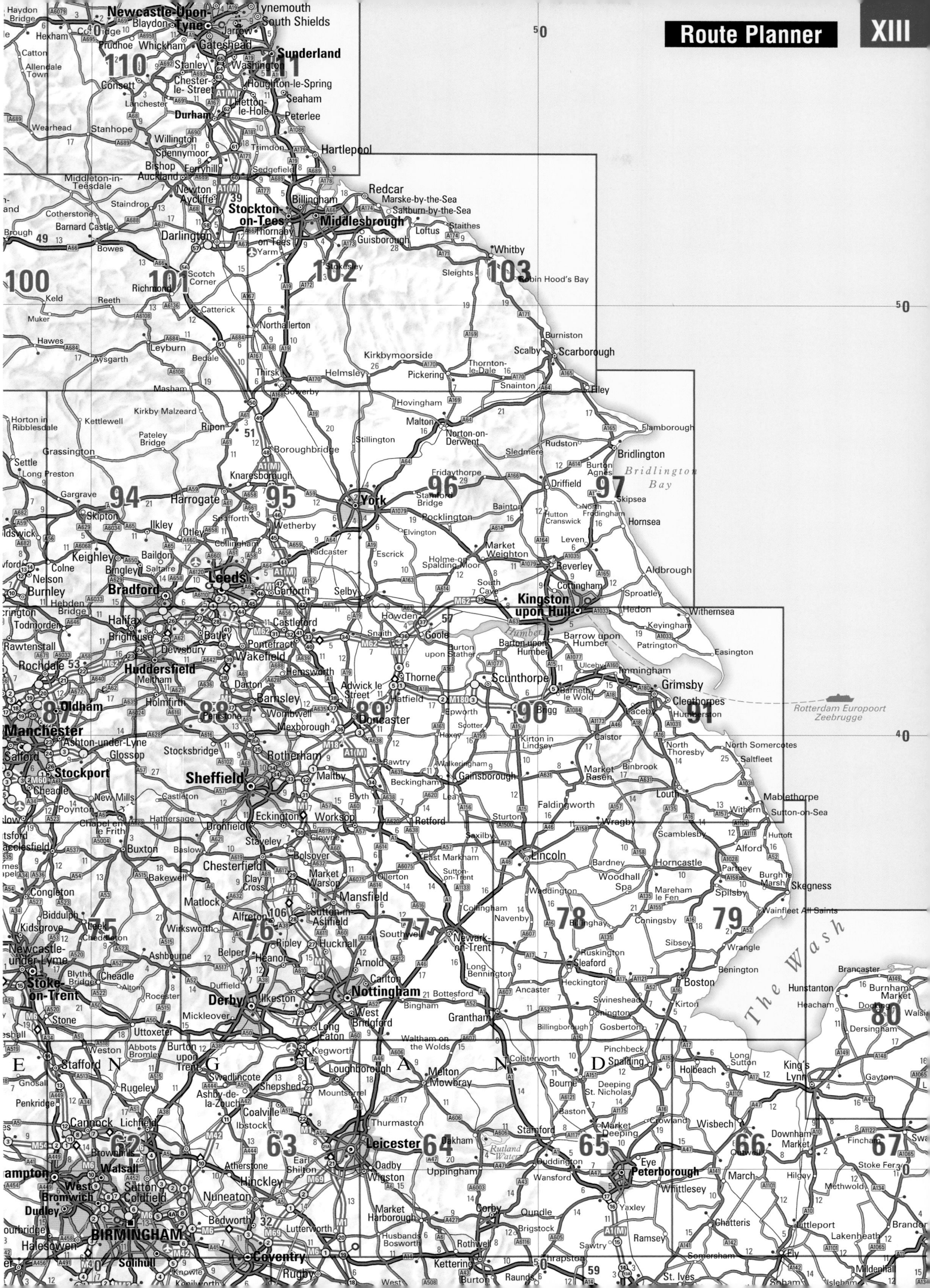
Newcastle-Upon-Tyne
Tynemouth
South Shields
Gateshead
Sunderland
Durham
Hartlepool
Redcar
Middlesbrough
Stockton-on-Tees
Darlington
Whitby
Scarborough
Filey
Bridlington
Bridlington Bay
Northallerton
Thirsk
Ripon
Harrogate
York
Leeds
Bradford
Halifax
Huddersfield
Wakefield
Kingston upon Hull
Humber
Grimsby
Cleethorpes
Scunthorpe
Doncaster
Barnsley
Rotherham
Sheffield
Manchester
Oldham
Stockport
Chesterfield
Mansfield
Lincoln
Skegness
Boston
The Wash
Nottingham
Derby
Stoke-on-Trent
Leicester
Peterborough
King's Lynn
Coventry
BIRMINGHAM
Walsall
Wolverhampton
Rotterdam Europoort
Zeebrugge
E N G L A N D

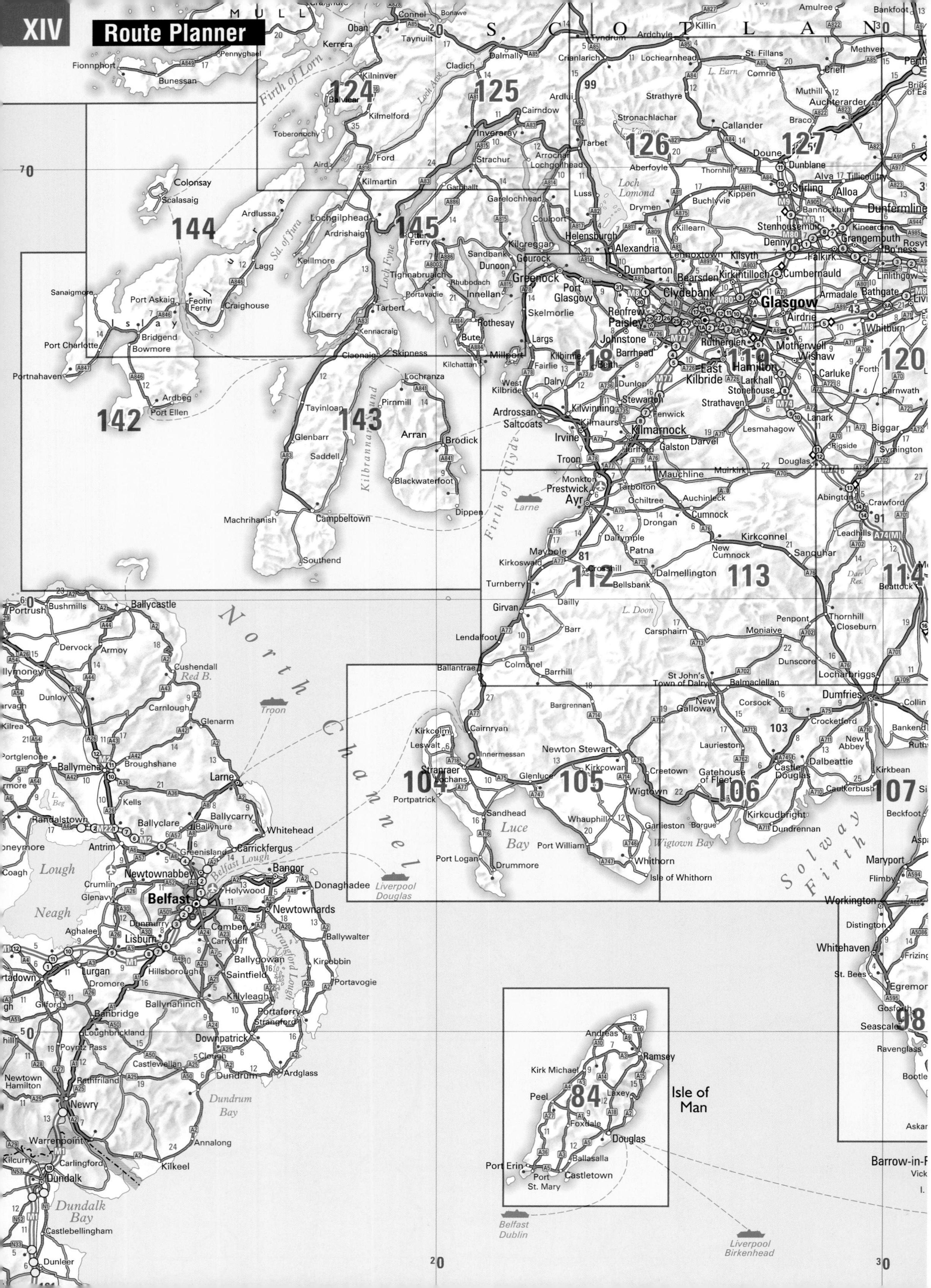
SCOTLAND
MULL
Oban
Kerrera
Taynuilt
Connel
Bonawe
Dalmally
Killin
Tyndrum
Crianlarich
Lochearnhead
St. Fillans
Comrie
Crieff
Methven
Perth
Amulree
Bankfoot
Fionnphort
Bunessan
Pennyghael
Firth of Lorn
Kilninver
Cladich
Loch Awe
124
125
126
127
99
Kilmelford
Cairndow
Inveraray
Strachur
Arrochar
Lochgoilhead
Tarbet
Luss
Strathyre
Stronachlachar
Callander
Doune
Dunblane
Muthill
Auchterarder
Braco
Toberonochy
Ford
Aird
Kilmartin
Colonsay
Scalasaig
Jura
Ardlussa
Sd. of Jura
Lochgilphead
Ardrishaig
Garelochhead
Coulport
Helensburgh
Alexandria
Loch Lomond
Aberfoyle
Drymen
Buchlyvie
Kippen
Stirling
Alloa
Dunfermline
Alva
Tillicoultry
Bannockburn
Stenhousemuir
Denny
Falkirk
Grangemouth
Bo'ness
Kincardine
Rosyth
144
145
Otter Ferry
Kilgreggan
Gourock
Greenock
Port Glasgow
Dumbarton
Clydebank
Bearsden
Kirkintilloch
Kilsyth
Lennoxtown
Cumbernauld
Linlithgow
Bathgate
Armadale
Whitburn
Glasgow
Airdrie
Coatbridge
Renfrew
Paisley
Johnstone
Rutherglen
Motherwell
Wishaw
Hamilton
East Kilbride
Larkhall
Stonehouse
Carluke
Forth
Carnwath
Lanark
Biggar
Symington
Strathaven
Lesmahagow
Douglas
Abington
Crawford
Keillmore
Lagg
Port Askaig
Feolin Ferry
Craighouse
Islay
Sanaigmore
Port Charlotte
Bridgend
Bowmore
Portnahaven
Ardbeg
Port Ellen
142
Tighnabruaich
Portavadie
Rhubodach
Sandbank
Dunoon
Innellan
Rothesay
Bute
Millport
Kilchattan
Skelmorlie
Largs
Kilbirnie
Beith
Fairlie
Dalry
West Kilbride
Barrhead
Dunlop
Stewarton
Kilwinning
Kilmaurs
Fenwick
Kilmarnock
Hurlford
Galston
Darvel
Ardrossan
Saltcoats
Irvine
Troon
118
119
120
Tarbert
Kennacraig
Claonaig
Skipness
Kilberry
Loch Fyne
Lochranza
Pirnmill
Arran
Brodick
Blackwaterfoot
Dippen
Kilbrannan Sound
Tayinloan
Glenbarr
Saddell
143
Machrihanish
Campbeltown
Southend
Firth of Clyde
Monkton
Prestwick
Ayr
Tarbolton
Mauchline
Muirkirk
Ochiltree
Auchinleck
Cumnock
Drongan
Dalrymple
Patna
New Cumnock
Kirkconnel
Sanquhar
Leadhills
Maybole
Kirkoswald
Crosshill
Dalmellington
Bellsbank
Turnberry
Girvan
Dailly
Barr
L. Doon
Carsphairn
Moniaive
Penpont
Thornhill
Closeburn
Beattock
Dunscore
Lendalfoot
Colmonel
Barrhill
Ballantrae
St John's Town of Dalry
Balmaclellan
Lochaerbriggs
Dumfries
Collin
112
113
114
81
91
Larne
Troon
North Channel
Ballycastle
Portrush
Bushmills
Dervock
Armoy
Cushendall
Red B.
Dunloy
Carnlough
Glenarm
Ballymena
Broughshane
Kells
Larne
Ballyclare
Ballynure
Ballycarry
Whitehead
Randalstown
Antrim
Greenisland
Carrickfergus
Belfast Lough
Newtownabbey
Bangor
Donaghadee
Holywood
Belfast
Crumlin
Glenavy
Lough Neagh
Dunmurry
Lisburn
Comber
Newtownards
Carryduff
Ballywalter
Ballygowan
Kircubbin
Hillsborough
Saintfield
Strangford Lough
Portavogie
Lurgan
Dromore
Killyleagh
Portaferry
Strangford
Gilford
Banbridge
Ballynahinch
Loughbrickland
Downpatrick
Poyntz Pass
Clough
Castlewellan
Dundrum
Ardglass
Rathfriland
Newry
Dundrum Bay
Annalong
Warrenpoint
Kilkeel
Carlingford
Dundalk
Dundalk Bay
Castlebellingham
Dunleer
Newtown Hamilton
Portglenone
Kirkcolm
Leswalt
Stranraer
Lochans
Portpatrick
Cairnryan
Innermessan
104
105
106
107
103
Glenluce
Newton Stewart
Kirkcowan
Creetown
Wigtown
Gatehouse of Fleet
Kirkcudbright
Dundrennan
Castle Douglas
Dalbeattie
Crocketford
Corsock
New Galloway
Laurieston
Bargrennan
New Abbey
Kirkbean
Caulkerbush
Sandhead
Luce Bay
Port William
Whauphill
Garlieston
Borgue
Wigtown Bay
Whithorn
Isle of Whithorn
Port Logan
Drummore
Liverpool Douglas
Solway Firth
Maryport
Flimby
Workington
Distington
Whitehaven
St. Bees
Egremont
Gosforth
Seascale
98
Ravenglass
Bootle
Askam
Barrow-in-F
Isle of Man
84
Andreas
Ramsey
Kirk Michael
Peel
Laxey
Foxdale
Douglas
Port Erin
Port St. Mary
Ballasalla
Castletown
Belfast Dublin
Liverpool Birkenhead
20
30
70
60
50

NORTH SEA
Amsterdam
Firth of Forth
Firth of Tay
Kielder Water
Morecambe Bay
Dundee
Carnoustie
Monifieth
Invergowrie
Tayport
Newport-on-Tay
Leuchars
Wormit
Scone
Balbeggie
Newburgh
St. Andrews
Cupar
Auchtermuchty
Ladybank
Ceres
Crail
Anstruther
St. Monance
Falkland
Leslie
Kinross
Markinch
Glenrothes
Leven
Elie
I. of May
Buckhaven
Lochgelly
Kirkcaldy
Cowdenbeath
Burntisland
Inverkeithing
North Berwick
Gullane
Dunbar
Queensferry
Edinburgh
Prestonpans
East Linton
Musselburgh
Tranent
Haddington
Cockburnspath
Dalkeith
Gifford
Currie
Loanhead
Bonnyrigg
St. Abb's
Coldingham
Eyemouth
Grantshouse
Penicuik
Gorebridge
Ayton
Preston
Chirnside
Duns
Berwick-upon-Tweed
Leadburn
West Linton
Westruther
Lauder
Fountainhall
Greenlaw
Swinton
Scremerston
Blyth Bridge
Stow
Peebles
Leitholm
Gordon
Coldstream
Lowick
Earlston
Innerleithen
Galashiels
Broughton
Kelso
Flodden
Belford
Bamburgh
Seahouses
Melrose
Maxwellheugh
Selkirk
Doddington
Yarrow
Ancrum
Town Yetholm
Wooler
Chatton
Beadnell
North Charlton
Morebattle
Embleton
Jedburgh
Wooperton
Longhoughton
Roberton
Denholm
Alnwick
Lesbury
Alnmouth
Ramseycleuch
Hawick
Moffat
Alwinton
Warkworth
Teviothead
Catcleugh
Rothbury
Amble
Longframlington
Eskdalemuir
Rochester
Widdrington
Otterburn
Longhorsley
Kielder
Boreland
West Woodburn
Ashington
Newbiggin-by-the-Sea
Hartburn
Pegswood
Morpeth
Newcastleton
Langholm
Lockerbie
Kirkwhelpington
Bedlington
Blyth
Bellingham
Whalton
Cramlington
Eaglesfield
Wark
Colwell
Belsay
Ecclefechan
Canonbie
Ponteland
Whitley Bay
Kirkpatrick-Fleming
Humshaugh
Longbenton
Longtown
Haydon Bridge
Newcastle-Upon-Tyne
Tynemouth
Smithfield
Gilsland
Blaydon
South Shields
Annan
Gretna
Jarrow
Greenhead
Haltwhistle
Hexham
Corbridge
Brampton
Gateshead
Sunderland
Lambley
Prudhoe
Whickham
Kirkbride
Carlisle
Catton
Newton Arlosh
Wetheral
Allendale Town
Washington
Stanley
Houghton-le-Spring
Consett
Chester-le-Street
Thursby
Dalston
Abbey Town
Wigton
High Hesket
Croglin
Alston
Seaham
Hetton-le-Hole
Lanchester
Durham
Peterlee
Bothel
Caldbeck
Lazonby
Wearhead
Stanhope
Willington
Langwathby
Trimdon
Hartlepool
Spennymoor
Cockermouth
Greystoke
Penrith
Bishop Auckland
Ferryhill
Sedgefield
Temple Sowerby
Middleton-in-Teesdale
Redcar
Thornthwaite
Threlkeld
Newton Aycliffe
Billingham
Marske-by-the-Sea
Keswick
Appleby-in-Westmorland
Staindrop
Stockton-on-Tees
Saltburn-by-the-Sea
Hackthorpe
Cotherstone
Middlesbrough
Derwent Water
Ullswater
Hoff
Barnard Castle
Thornaby on Tees
Loftus
Staithes
Buttermere
Patterdale
Brough
Darlington
Guisborough
Shap
Yarm
Borrowdale
Kirkby Stephen
Bowes
Whitby
Haweswater
Grasmere
Orton
Stokesley
Wast Water
Ambleside
Scotch Corner
Sleights
Robin Hood's Bay
Tebay
Richmond
Windermere
Keld
Reeth
Catterick
Coniston
Grayrigg
Torver
Bowness-on-Windermere
Kendal
Garsdale Head
Muker
Northallerton
Burniston
Broughton-in-Furness
Coniston Water
Sedbergh
Hawes
Leyburn
Scalby
Scarborough
Grizebeck
Newby Bridge
Oxenholme
Aysgarth
Bedale
Kirkbymoorside
Thornton-le-Dale
Millom
Milnthorpe
Kirkby Lonsdale
Thirsk
Helmsley
Pickering
Arnside
Masham
Sowerby
Snainton
Filey
Ulverston
Grange-over-Sands
Burton
Hovingham
Dalton-in-Furness
Kirkby Malzeard
Carnforth
Ingleton
Horton in Ribblesdale
Kettlewell
Malton
Norton-on-Derwent
Ripon
Pateley Bridge
Rampside
High Bentham
Boroughbridge
Stillington
Rudston
Isle of Walney
Morecambe
Caton
Grassington
Sledmere
Settle
Heysham
Lancaster
Long Preston
Knaresborough
Fridaythorpe
Burton Agnes
Driffield
Gargrave
Galgate
Harrogate
York
Stamford Bridge
Slaidburn
Skipton
Spofforth
Bainton
North Frodingham
Hutton Cranswick
Fleetwood
Wetherby
Pocklington
Ilkley
Otley
Elvington
Barnoldswick
Garstang
Collingham
Cleveleys
Clitheroe
Keighley
Baildon
Tadcaster
Escrick
Market Weighton
Leven

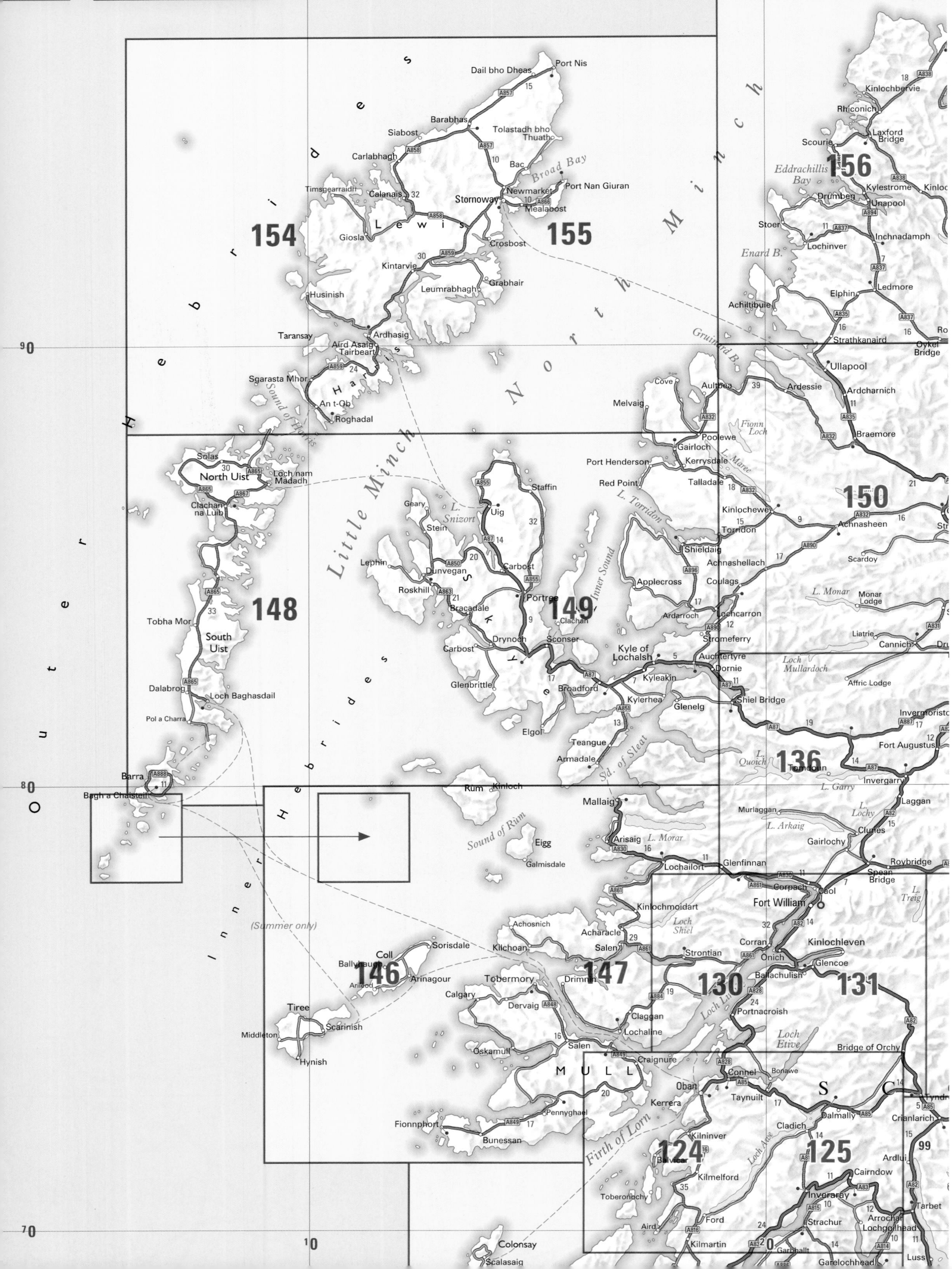
154
155
156
150
148
149
136
147
146
130
131
124
125
99
Outer Hebrides
Inner Hebrides
North Minch
Little Minch
Lewis
Harris
North Uist
South Uist
Skye
MULL
Port Nis
Dail bho Dheas
Barabhas
Siabost
Tolastadh bho Thuath
Carlabhagh
Bac
Broad Bay
Port Nan Giuran
Timsgearraidh
Calanais
Stornoway
Newmarket
Mealabost
Giosla
Crosbost
Kintarvie
Leumrabhagh
Grabhair
Husinish
Taransay
Ardhasig
Aird Asaig
Tairbeart
Sgarasta Mhor
Sound of Harris
An t-Ob
Roghadal
Solas
Loch nam Madadh
Clachan na Luib
Tobha Mor
Dalabrog
Loch Baghasdail
Pol a Charra
Barra
Bagh a Chaisteil
Geary
L. Snizort
Uig
Staffin
Stein
Lephin
Dunvegan
Roskhill
Bracadale
Carbost
Portree
Inner Sound
Clachan
Drynoch
Sconser
Glenbrittle
Broadford
Elgol
Kyle of Lochalsh
Kyleakin
Kylerhea
Glenelg
Teangue
Armadale
Sd. of Sleat
Rùm
Kinloch
Sound of Rùm
Eigg
Galmisdale
Mallaig
Arisaig
L. Morar
Lochailort
Glenfinnan
(Summer only)
Coll
Sorisdale
Ballyhaugh
Arileod
Arinagour
Tiree
Scarinish
Middleton
Hynish
Achosnich
Kilchoan
Acharacle
Salen
Kinlochmoidart
Loch Shiel
Tobermory
Calgary
Dervaig
Drimnin
Claggan
Lochaline
Oskamull
Salen
Craignure
Fionnphort
Pennyghael
Bunessan
Oban
Kerrera
Firth of Lorn
Kilninver
Balvicar
Kilmelford
Toberonochy
Ford
Aird
Kilmartin
Colonsay
Scalasaig
Cove
Aultbea
Melvaig
Gruinard B.
Poolewe
Fionn Loch
Gairloch
Kerrysdale
L. Maree
Port Henderson
Red Point
Talladale
L. Torridon
Kinlochewe
Torridon
Shieldaig
Achnashellach
Applecross
Coulags
Ardarroch
Lochcarron
Stromeferry
Auchtertyre
Dornie
Shiel Bridge
Kinlochbervie
Rhiconich
Laxford Bridge
Scourie
Eddrachillis Bay
Kylestrome
Drumbeg
Unapool
Stoer
Lochinver
Inchnadamph
Enard B.
Achiltibuie
Elphin
Ledmore
Strathkanaird
Oykel Bridge
Ullapool
Ardessie
Ardcharnich
Braemore
Achnasheen
Scardoy
L. Monar
Monar Lodge
Liatrie
Cannich
Loch Mullardoch
Affric Lodge
Invermoriston
Fort Augustus
L. Quoich
Tomdoun
L. Garry
Invergarry
Laggan
Murlaggan
L. Arkaig
L. Lochy
Clunes
Gairlochy
Roybridge
Spean Bridge
L. Treig
Corpach
Caol
Fort William
Corran
Strontian
Kinlochleven
Onich
Ballachulish
Glencoe
Loch Linnhe
Portnacroish
Loch Etive
Bridge of Orchy
Connel
Bonawe
Taynuilt
Dalmally
Cladich
Loch Awe
Tyndrum
Crianlarich
Ardlui
Cairndow
Inveraray
Strachur
Arrochar
Lochgoilhead
Tarbet
Luss
Garelochhead

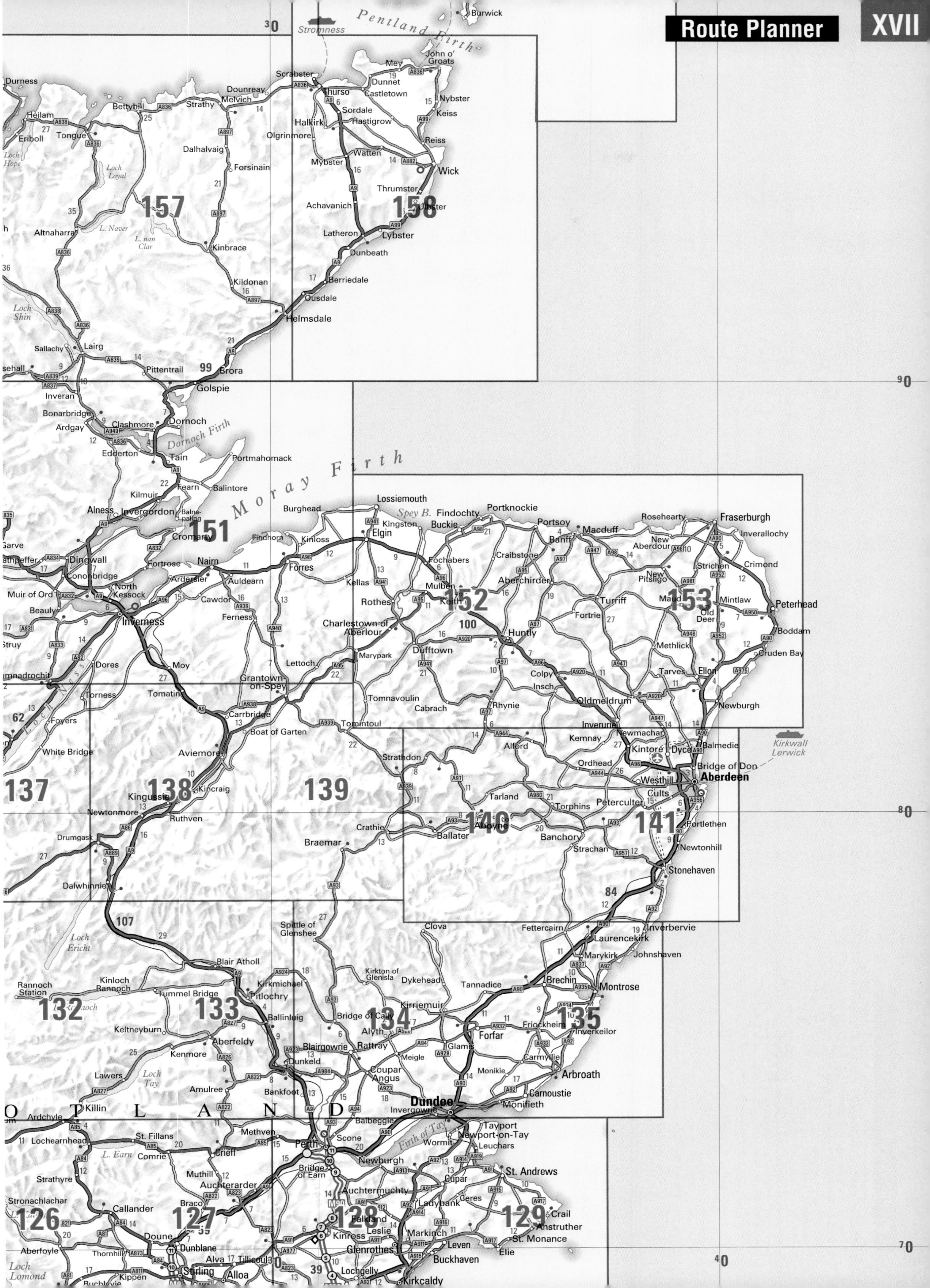
Pentland Firth
Stromness
Burwick
John o' Groats
Mey
Dunnet
Castletown
Scrabster
Thurso
Dounreay
Melvich
Strathy
Bettyhill
Durness
Heilam
Eriboll
Tongue
Loch Hope
Loch Loyal
Dalhalvaig
Forsinain
Halkirk
Sordale
Hastigrow
Olgrinmore
Nybster
Keiss
Reiss
Watten
Mybster
Wick
Thrumster
Ulbster
Achavanich
Latheron
Lybster
Dunbeath
Berriedale
Ousdale
Helmsdale
Kildonan
Kinbrace
L. nan Clar
L. Naver
Altnaharra
Loch Shin
Lairg
Sallachy
Pittentrail
Brora
Golspie
Inveran
Bonarbridge
Ardgay
Clashmore
Dornoch
Dornoch Firth
Edderton
Tain
Portmahomack
Fearn
Balintore
Kilmuir
Alness
Invergordon
Balnapaling
Cromarty
Moray Firth
Burghead
Lossiemouth
Findhorn
Kinloss
Elgin
Spey B.
Kingston
Findochty
Portknockie
Buckie
Portsoy
Banff
Macduff
Rosehearty
Fraserburgh
Inverallochy
New Aberdour
Crimond
Strichen
New Pitsligo
Maud
Mintlaw
Old Deer
Peterhead
Boddam
Cruden Bay
Craibstone
Aberchirder
Turriff
Fortrie
Fochabers
Mulben
Keith
Rothes
Charlestown-of-Aberlour
Huntly
Dufftown
Methlick
Tarves
Ellon
Newburgh
Colpy
Insch
Oldmeldrum
Rhynie
Cabrach
Tomnavoulin
Marypark
Garve
Dingwall
Cononbridge
Fortrose
Muir of Ord
North Kessock
Ardersier
Nairn
Auldearn
Forres
Kellas
Cawdor
Ferness
Beauly
Inverness
Struy
Dores
Moy
Lettoch
Grantown-on-Spey
Tomatin
Torness
Foyers
Carrbridge
Boat of Garten
Tomintoul
White Bridge
Aviemore
Kincraig
Kingussie
Newtonmore
Ruthven
Drumgask
Dalwhinnie
Loch Ness
Loch Ericht
Strathdon
Inverurie
Newmachar
Kemnay
Alford
Kintore
Dyce
Balmedie
Kirkwall
Lerwick
Ordhead
Westhill
Bridge of Don
Aberdeen
Cults
Peterculter
Tarland
Torphins
Aboyne
Ballater
Banchory
Crathie
Braemar
Strachan
Portlethen
Newtonhill
Stonehaven
Clova
Fettercairn
Inverbervie
Laurencekirk
Marykirk
Johnshaven
Montrose
Brechin
Spittle of Glenshee
Kirkton of Glenisla
Dykehead
Tannadice
Kirriemuir
Blair Atholl
Kinloch Rannoch
Rannoch Station
Tummel Bridge
Kirkmichael
Pitlochry
Ballinluig
Bridge of Cally
Alyth
Keltneyburn
Aberfeldy
Kenmore
Blairgowrie
Rattray
Dunkeld
Meigle
Glamis
Forfar
Friockheim
Inverkeilor
Carmyllie
Arbroath
Monikie
Carnoustie
Monifieth
Lawers
Loch Tay
Amulree
Bankfoot
Coupar Angus
Dundee
Invergowrie
Killin
Ardchyle
Balbeggie
Tayport
Newport-on-Tay
Firth of Tay
Wormit
Leuchars
Lochearnhead
St. Fillans
L. Earn
Comrie
Crieff
Methven
Perth
Scone
Newburgh
Bridge of Earn
Muthill
Auchterarder
Strathyre
Auchtermuchty
Cupar
St. Andrews
Ceres
Ladybank
Crail
Anstruther
St. Monance
Elie
Stronachlachar
Callander
Braco
Falkland
Kinross
Leslie
Markinch
Glenrothes
Leven
Buckhaven
Doune
Dunblane
Aberfoyle
Thornhill
Loch Lomond
Kippen
Stirling
Alva
Tillicoultry
Alloa
Lochgelly
Kirkcaldy
Buchlyvie
SCOTLAND
157
158
151
152
153
137
138
139
140
141
132
133
134
135
126
127
128
129
62
99
100
107
84
30
40
90
80
70

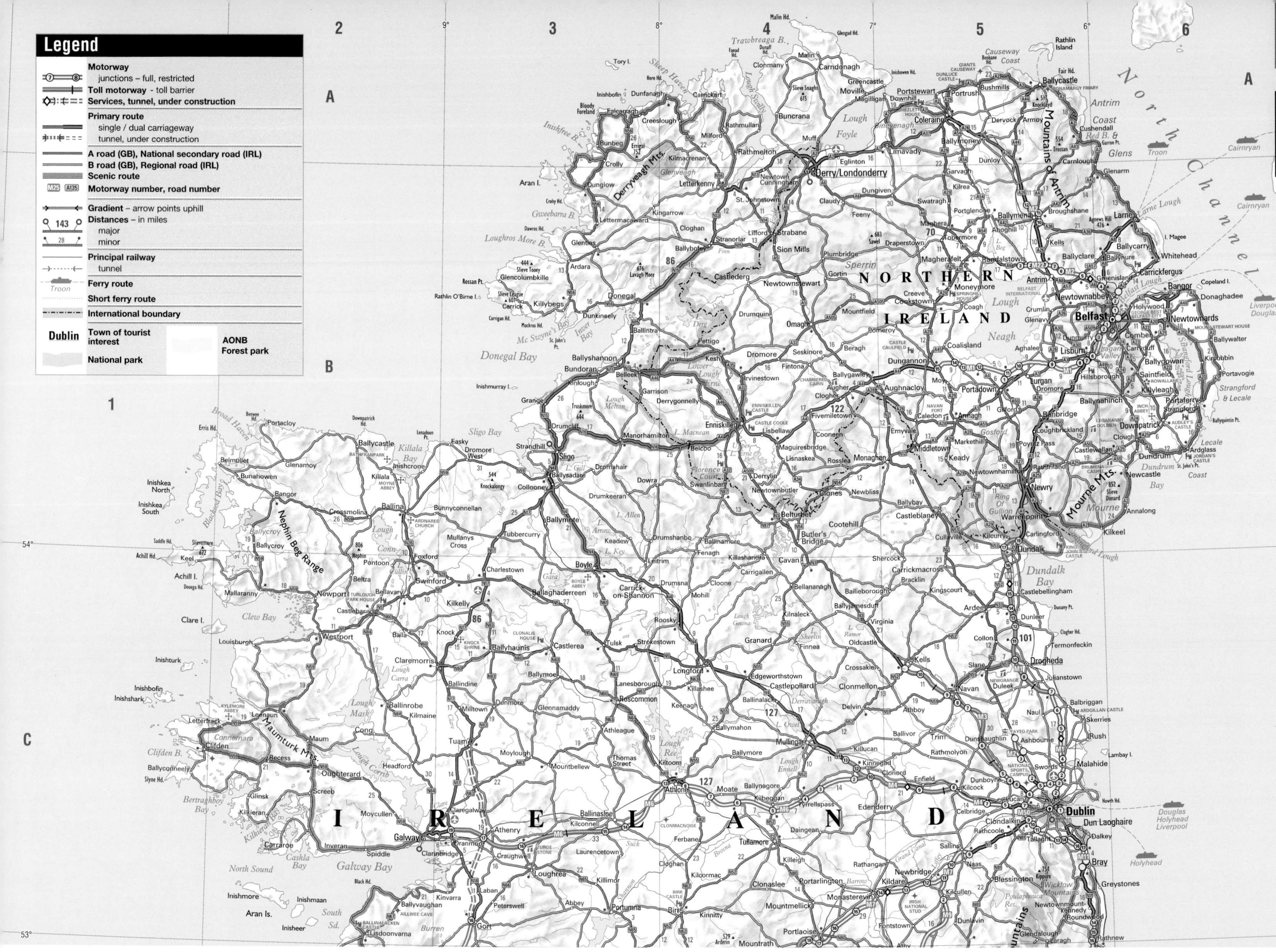
Legend
Motorway
junctions – full, restricted
Toll motorway – toll barrier
Services, tunnel, under construction
Primary route
single / dual carriageway
tunnel, under construction
A road (GB), National secondary road (IRL)
B road (GB), Regional road (IRL)
Scenic route
Motorway number, road number
Gradient – arrow points uphill
Distances – in miles
major
minor
Principal railway
tunnel
Ferry route
Short ferry route
International boundary
Dublin
Town of tourist interest
National park
AONB
Forest park
North Channel
NORTHERN IRELAND
IRELAND
Mountains of Antrim
Mourne Mts.
Derryveagh Mts.
Nephin Beg Range
Maumturk Mts.
Belfast
Dublin
Derry/Londonderry
Galway
Sligo
Donegal Bay
Galway Bay
Dundalk Bay
Clew Bay
Aran Is.

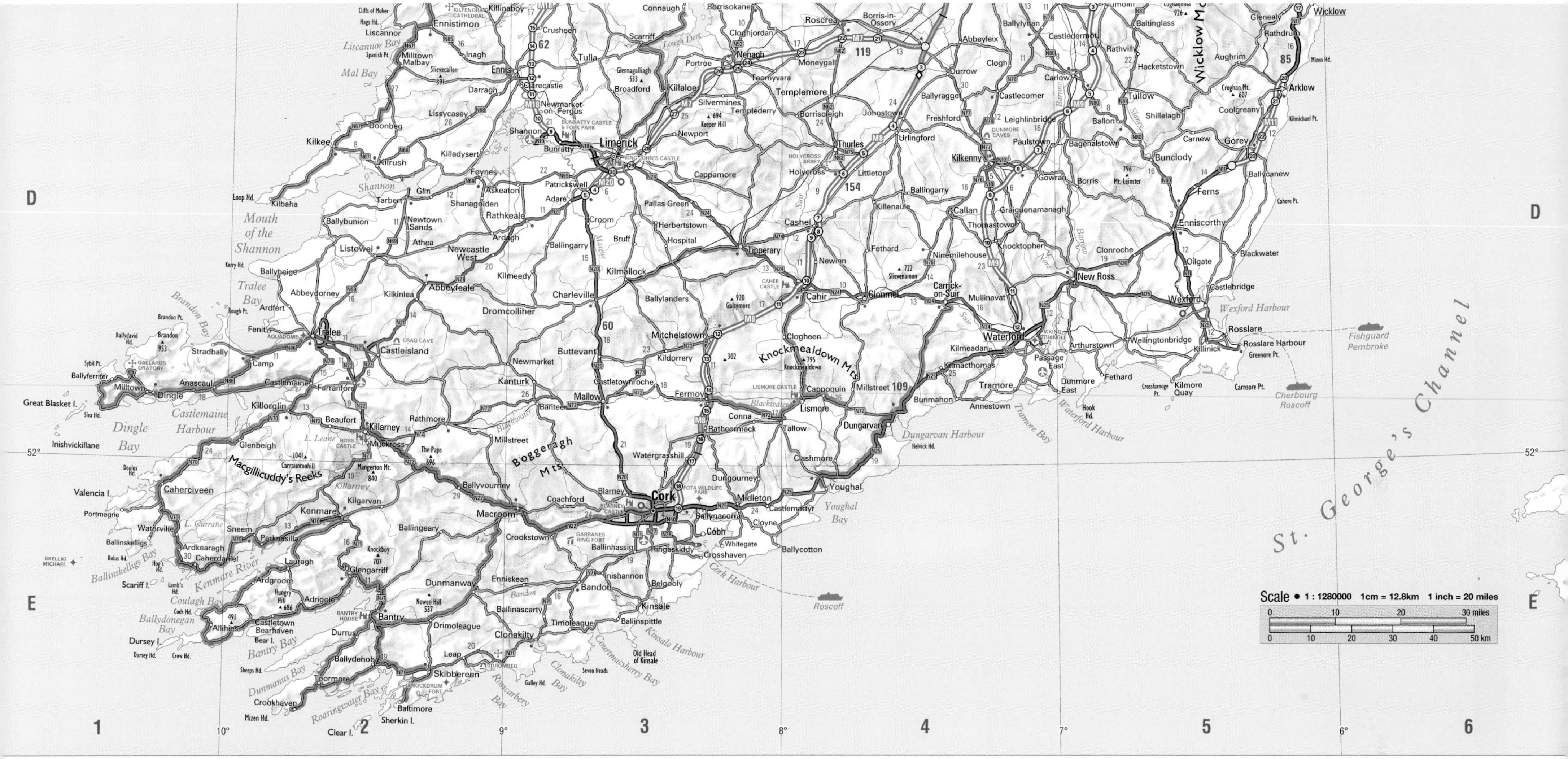

Index to Ireland

A

Abbey C3
Abbeydorney D2
Abbeyfeale D2
Abbeyleix D4
Adare D3
Adrigole E2
Aghalee B5
Ahoghill B5
Allihies E1
Anascaul D1
Annalong B6
Annestown D4
Antrim B5
Ardagh D2
Ardara B3
Ardee C5
Ardfert D2
Ardglass B6
Ardgroom E2
Ardkearagh E1
Arklow D5
Armagh B5
Armoy A5
Arthurstown D5
Ashbourne C5
Askeaton D3
Athboy C5
Athea D2
Athenry C3
Athleague C3
Athlone C4
Athy D5
Augher B4
Aughnacloy B5
Aughrim D5

B

Bailieborough C5
Balbriggan C5
Balla C2
Ballaghaderreen C3
Ballina B2
Ballinalack C4
Ballinamore B4
Ballinascarty E3
Ballinasloe C3
Ballindine C3
Ballingarry, *Limerick* D3
Ballingarry, *Tipperary* D4
Ballingeary E2
Ballinhassig E3
Ballinrobe C2
Ballinskellings E1
Ballinspittle E3
Ballintra B3
Ballivor C5
Ballon D5
Ballybay B5
Ballybofey B4
Ballybunion D2
Ballycanew D5
Ballycarry B6
Ballycastle, *Antrim* A5
Ballycastle, *Mayo* B2
Ballyclare B6
Ballyconneely C1
Ballycotton E3
Ballycroy B2
Ballydehob E2
Ballyferriter D1
Ballygawley B4
Ballygowan B6
Ballyhaunis C3
Ballyheige D2
Ballyjamesduff C4
Ballylanders D3
Ballylynan D4
Ballymahon C4
Ballymena B5
Ballymoe C3
Ballymoney A5
Ballymore C4
Ballymote B3
Ballynacorra E3
Ballynagore C4
Ballynahinch B6
Ballynure B6
Ballyragget D4
Ballysadare B3
Ballyshannon B3
Ballyvaughan C2
Ballyvourney E2
Ballywalter B6
Baltimore E2
Baltinglass D5
Banbridge B5
Bandon E3
Bangor, *Down* B6
Bangor, *Mayo* B2
Banteer D3
Bantry E2
Beaufort D2
Belcoo B4
Belfast B6
Belgooly E3
Bellananagh C4
Bellavary C2
Belleek B3
Belmullet B2
Beltra C2
Belturbet B4
Beragh B4
Birr C4
Blackwater D5
Blarney E3
Blessington C5
Borris D5
Borris-in-Ossory D4
Borrisokane D3
Borrisoleigh D4
Boyle C3
Bracklin C5
Bray C5
Broadford D3
Broughshane B5
Bruff D3
Bunahowen B2
Bunbeg A3
Bunclody D5
Buncrana A4
Bundoran B3
Bunmahon D4
Bunnyconnellan B2
Bunratty D3
Bushmills A5
Butler's Bridge B4
Buttevant D3

C

Caher D4
Caherciveen E1
Caherdaniel E1
Caledon B5
Callan D4
Camp D2
Cappamore D3
Cappoquin D4
Carlingford B5
Carlow D5
Carndonagh A4
Carnew D5
Carnlough B6
Carraroe C2
Carrick B3
Carrick-on-Shannon C3
Carrick-on-Suir D4
Carrickart A4
Carrickfergus B6
Carrickmacross C5
Carrigallen C4
Carryduff B6
Cashel D4
Castlebar C2
Castlebellingham C5
Castleblaney B5
Castlebridge D5
Castlecomer D4
Castlederg B4
Castledermot D5
Castleisland D2
Castlemaine D2
Castlemartyr E3
Castlepollard C4
Castlerea C3
Castletown Bearhaven E2
Castletownroche D3
Castlewellan B6
Cavan C4
Celbridge C5
Charlestown C3
Charleville D3
Clarecastle D3
Claregalway C3
Claremorris C2
Clarinbridge C3
Clashmore D4
Claudy B4
Clifden C1
Clogh D4
Cloghan, *Donegal* B4
Cloghan, *Offaly* C4
Clogheen D4
Clogher B4
Cloghjordan D3
Clonakilty E3
Clonaslee C4
Clondalkin C5
Clones B4
Clonmany A4
Clonmel D4
Clonmellon C4
Clonord C4
Clonroche D5
Cloone C4
Clough B6
Cloyne E3
Coachford E3
Coagh B5
Coalisland B5
Cóbh E3
Coleraine A5
Collon C5
Collooney B3
Comber B6
Cong C2
Conna D3
Connaugh D3
Cookstown B5
Coolgreany D5
Cooneen B4
Cootehill B4
Cork E3
Craughwell C3
Creeslough A4
Creeve B5
Crolly A3
Crookhaven E2
Crookstown E3
Croom D3
Crossakiel C4
Crosshaven E3
Crossmolina B2
Crumlin B5
Crusheen D3
Cullaville B5
Cushendall A5

D

Daingean C4
Darragh D2
Delvin C4
Derry/Londonderry B4
Derrygonnelly B4
Derrylin B4
Dervock A5
Dingle D1
Donaghadee B6
Donegal B3
Doonbeg D2
Downhill A5
Downpatrick B6
Dowra B3
Draperstown B5
Drimoleague E2
Drogheda C5
Dromahair B3
Dromcolliher D3
Dromore, *Down* B5
Dromore, *Tyrone* B4
Dromore West B3
Drumcliff B3
Drumkeeran B3
Drumquin B4
Drumshanbo B3
Drumsna C4
Dublin C5
Duleek C5
Dun Laoghaire C5
Dunboyne C5
Dundalk B5
Dundrum B6
Dunfanaghy A4
Dungannon B5
Dungarvan D4
Dungiven B5
Dunglow B3
Dungourney E3
Dunkineely B3
Dunlavin C5
Dunleer C5
Dunloy A5
Dunmanway E2
Dunmore C3
Dunmore East D5
Dunmurry B5
Dunshaughlin C5
Durrow D4
Durrus E2

E

Easky B3
Edenderry C4
Edgeworthstown C4
Eglinton A4
Emyvale B5
Enfield C5
Ennis D3
Enniscorthy D5
Enniskean E3
Enniskillen B4
Ennistimon D2

F

Falcarragh A3
Farranfore D2
Feeny B4
Fenagh B4
Fenit D2
Ferbane C4
Fermoy D3
Ferns D5
Fethard, *Tipperary* D4
Fethard, *Wexford* D5
Finnea C4
Fintona B4
Fivemiletown B4
Fontstown C5
Foxford C2
Foynes D2
Freshford D4

G

Galway C2
Garrison B3
Garvagh B5
Gilford B5
Glenamoy B2
Glenarm B6
Glenavy B5
Glenbeigh D2
Glencolumbkille B3
Glendalough C5
Glenealy D5
Glengarriff E2
Glennamaddy C3
Glenties B3
Glin D2
Glinsk C2
Gorey D5
Gort C3
Gortin B4
Gowran D4
Graiguenamanagh D5
Granard C4
Grange B3
Greencastle A5
Greenisland B6
Greystones C5

H

Hacketstown D5
Headford C2
Herbertstown D3
Hillsborough B5
Holycross D4
Holywood B6
Hospital D3

I

Inagh D2
Inishannon E3
Inishcrone B2
Inveran C2
Irvinestown B4

J

Johnstown D4
Julianstown C5

K

Kanturk D3
Keadew B3
Keady B5
Keel C1
Keenagh C4
Kells, *Antrim* B5
Kells, *Meath* C5
Kenmare E2
Kesh B4
Kilbaha D2
Kilbeggan C4
Kilcock C5
Kilconnell C3
Kilcormac C4
Kilcullen C5
Kilcurry B5
Kildare C5
Kildorrery D3
Kilgarvan E2
Kilkee D2
Kilkeel B6
Kilkelly C3
Kilkenny D4
Kilkieran C2
Kilkinlea D2
Kill D4
Killadysert D2
Killala B2
Killaloe D3
Killarney D2
Killashandra B4
Killashee C4
Killeigh C4
Killenaule D4
Killimor C3
Killinaboy D2
Killinick D5
Killorglin D2
Killucan C4
Killybegs B3
Killyleagh B6
Kilmacrenan A4
Kilmacthomas D4
Kilmaine C2
Kilmallock D3
Kilmeadan D4
Kilmeedy D3
Kilmore Quay D5
Kilnaleck C4
Kilrea B5
Kilrush D2
Kiltoom C3
Kingarrow B3
Kingscourt C5
Kinlough B3
Kinnegad C4
Kinnitty C4
Kinsale E3
Kinvarra C3
Kircubbin B6
Knock C3
Knocktopher D4

L

Laban C3
Lanesborough C4
Laragh C5
Larne B6
Lauragh E2
Laurencetown C3
Leap E2
Leenaun C2
Leighlinbridge D5
Leitrim C3
Letterfrack C2
Letterkenny B4
Lettermacaward B3
Lifford B4
Limavady A5
Limerick D3
Lisbellaw B4
Lisburn B5
Liscannor D2
Lisdoonvarna C2
Lismore D4
Lisnaskea B4
Lissycasey D2
Listowel D2
Littleton D4
Longford C4
Loughbrickland B5
Loughrea C3
Louisburgh C2
Lucan C5
Lurgan B5

M

Macroom E3
Maghera B5
Magherafelt B5
Magilligan A5
Maguiresbridge B4
Malahide C5
Malin A4
Mallaranny C2
Mallow D3
Manorhamilton B3
Markethill B5
Maum C2
Middletown B5
Midleton E3
Milford A4
Millstreet, *Cork* D2
Millstreet, *Waterford* D4
Milltown, *Galway* C3
Milltown, *Kerry* D1
Milltown Malbay D2
Mitchelstown D3
Moate C4
Mohill C4
Monaghan B5
Monasterevin C4
Moneygall D4
Moneymore B5
Mountbellew C3
Mountfield B4
Mountmellick C4
Mountrath D4
Moville A4
Moy B5
Moycullen C2
Moylough C3
Muckross D2
Muff A4
Muine Bheag D5
Mullanys Cross B3
Mullinavat D4
Mullingar C4

N

Naas C5
Naul C5
Navan C5
Nenagh D3
New Ross D5
Newbliss B4
Newbridge C5
Newcastle B6
Newcastle West D2
Newinn D4
Newmarket D3
Newmarket-on-Fergus D3
Newport, *Mayo* C2
Newport, *Tipperary* D3
Newry B5
Newtown Cunningham B4
Newtown Sands D2
Newtownabbey B6
Newtownards B6
Newtownbutler B4
Newtownhamilton B5
Newtown-mountkennedy C5
Newtownshandrum D3
Newtownstewart B4
Ninemilehouse D4

O

Oilgate D5
Oldcastle C4
Omagh B4
Oranmore C3
Oughterard C2

P

Pallas Green D3
Parknasilla E2
Passage East D5
Passage West E3
Patrickswell D3
Paulstown D4
Peterswell C3
Pettigo B4
Plumbridge B4
Pomeroy B5
Pontoon C2
Portacloy B2
Portadown B5
Portaferry B6
Portarlington C4
Portavogie B6
Portglenone B5
Portlaoise C4
Portmagne E1
Portroe D3
Portrush A5
Portstewart A5
Portumna C3
Poyntz Pass B5

R

Randalstown B5
Rathangan C5
Rathcoole C5
Rathcormack D3
Rathdrum D5
Rathfriland B5
Rathkeale D3
Rathmelton A4
Rathmolyon C5
Rathmore D2
Rathmullan A4
Rathnew D5
Rathvilly D5
Ratoath C5
Recess C2
Ringaskiddy E3
Roosky C4
Roscommon C3
Roscrea D4
Rosmult D4
Rosslare D5
Rosslare Harbour D5
Rosslea B4
Roundwood C5
Rush C5

S

Saint Johnstown B4
Saintfield B6
Sallins C5
Scarriff D3
Screeb C2
Seskinore B4
Shanagolden D2
Shercock C5
Shillelagh D5
Silvermines D3
Sion Mills B4
Skerries C5
Skibbereen E2
Slane C5
Sligo B3
Sneem E2
Spiddle C2
Strabane B4
Stradbally D1
Strandhill B3
Strangford B6
Stranorlar B4
Strokestown C3
Swanlinbar B4
Swatragh B5
Swinford C3
Swords C5

T

Tallaght C5
Tallow D4
Tarbert D2
Templederry D3
Templemore D4
Termonfeckin C5
Thomas Street C3
Thomastown D4
Thurles D4
Timoleague E3
Timolin D5
Tipperary D3
Tobermore B5
Toomyvara D3
Toormore E2
Tralee D2
Tramore D4
Trim C5
Tuam C3
Tubbercory B3
Tulla D3
Tullamore C4
Tullow D5
Tulsk C3
Tyrrellspass C4

U

Urlingford D4

V

Virginia C4

W

Warrenpoint B5
Waterford D4
Watergrasshill D3
Waterville E1
Wellingtonbridge D5
Westport C2
Wexford D5
Whitegate E3
Whitehead B6
Wicklow D5

Y

Youghal E4

Distance table

How to use this table

Distances are shown in miles and kilometres with estimated journey times in hours and minutes.

For example: the distance between Dover and Fishguard is 331 miles or 533 kilometres with an estimated journey time of 6 hours, 20 minutes.

Estimated driving times are based on an average speed of 60mph on Motorways and 40mph on other roads. Drivers should allow extra time when driving at peak periods or through areas likely to be congested.

	Fishguard	Exeter	Edinburgh	Dundee	Dover
Dover					
Dundee					523 / 842 / 9:10
Edinburgh				56 / 90 / 1:30	462 / 744 / 8:10
Exeter			450 / 724 / 8:00	518 / 834 / 9:10	248 / 399 / 4:40
Fishguard		230 / 370 / 4:30	399 / 642 / 7:30	460 / 740 / 8:30	331 / 533 / 6:20
Fort William	486 / 782 / 9:30	560 / 901 / 10:20	144 / 232 / 3:30	127 / 204 / 3:10	596 / 959 / 11:00

	Swansea	Stranraer	Southampton	Shrewsbury	Sheffield	Portsmouth	Plymouth	Oxford	Oban	Nottingham	Norwich	Newcastle upon Tyne	Manchester	Liverpool	Lincoln	Leicester	Leeds	Land's End	Kyle of Lochalsh	Kingston upon Hull	John o' Groats	Inverness	Holyhead	Harwich	Great Yarmouth	Gloucester	Glasgow	Fort William	Fishguard	Exeter	Edinburgh	Dundee	Dover	Doncaster	Carlisle	Cardiff	Cambridge	Bristol	Brighton	Braemar	Bournemouth	Blackpool	Birmingham	Berwick-upon-Tweed	Ayr	Aberystwyth	Aberdeen	London
London																																																
Aberdeen																																																517 / 832 / 11:20
Aberystwyth																																															445 / 716 / 8:40	211 / 340 / 4:40
Ayr																																														317 / 510 / 6:10	183 / 295 / 4:20	394 / 634 / 7:20
Berwick-upon-Tweed																																													134 / 216 / 3:00	311 / 501 / 6:20	182 / 293 / 4:40	352 / 567 / 7:30
Birmingham																																												274 / 441 / 5:30	289 / 465 / 5:30	114 / 183 / 2:50	420 / 676 / 8:30	117 / 188 / 2:50
Blackpool																																											123 / 198 / 2:40	181 / 291 / 3:50	180 / 290 / 3:30	153 / 246 / 3:20	308 / 496 / 6:20	226 / 364 / 4:30
Bournemouth																																										270 / 435 / 5:00	147 / 237 / 3:10	412 / 663 / 7:50	436 / 702 / 8:00	207 / 333 / 4:30	564 / 908 / 10:20	107 / 172 / 2:40
Braemar																																									524 / 843 / 9:30	281 / 452 / 5:20	385 / 620 / 7:10	148 / 238 / 3:20	143 / 230 / 3:00	405 / 652 / 7:50	59 / 95 / 1:30	482 / 776 / 10:30
Brighton																																								534 / 859 / 9:40	92 / 148 / 2:10	286 / 460 / 5:20	163 / 262 / 3:20	409 / 658 / 7:40	446 / 718 / 8:00	253 / 407 / 5:10	573 / 922 / 10:30	52 / 84 / 1:50
Bristol																																							147 / 237 / 4:10	477 / 768 / 8:40	82 / 132 / 2:30	204 / 328 / 3:50	81 / 130 / 2:00	362 / 583 / 6:50	370 / 595 / 6:40	125 / 201 / 3:00	493 / 793 / 9:10	122 / 196 / 2:50
Cambridge																																						169 / 272 / 3:10	116 / 187 / 2:20	438 / 705 / 7:50	154 / 248 / 3:00	208 / 335 / 3:50	100 / 161 / 2:10	306 / 493 / 5:40	357 / 575 / 6:20	214 / 344 / 4:20	471 / 758 / 10:00	54 / 87 / 1:30
Cardiff																																					190 / 306 / 3:30	45 / 72 / 1:20	182 / 293 / 3:40	483 / 778 / 8:40	117 / 188 / 3:00	209 / 336 / 4:00	103 / 166 / 2:20	368 / 592 / 7:00	382 / 615 / 7:00	105 / 169 / 2:40	505 / 813 / 9:20	157 / 253 / 3:20
Carlisle																																				289 / 465 / 5:20	264 / 425 / 4:40	277 / 446 / 5:00	370 / 596 / 6:40	196 / 316 / 3:50	343 / 552 / 6:20	87 / 140 / 1:50	196 / 315 / 3:50	87 / 140 / 2:10	93 / 150 / 2:00	224 / 360 / 4:30	221 / 356 / 4:30	301 / 484 / 5:40
Doncaster																																			142 / 229 / 3:00	209 / 336 / 4:00	116 / 187 / 2:10	175 / 282 / 3:20	236 / 380 / 4:30	310 / 499 / 5:40	235 / 378 / 4:20	94 / 151 / 1:50	94 / 151 / 2:00	184 / 296 / 3:50	235 / 378 / 4:20	176 / 283 / 3:40	344 / 554 / 6:50	171 / 275 / 3:30
Dover																																		242 / 390 / 4:30	389 / 626 / 7:00	238 / 383 / 4:30	125 / 201 / 2:30	202 / 325 / 3:50	82 / 132 / 2:20	553 / 890 / 9:50	174 / 280 / 4:30	312 / 502 / 5:40	194 / 312 / 3:50	424 / 683 / 7:50	478 / 769 / 8:30	297 / 478 / 5:50	588 / 947 / 10:40	71 / 114 / 2:00
Dundee																																	523 / 842 / 9:10	275 / 443 / 5:00	152 / 245 / 3:00	441 / 710 / 8:00	406 / 654 / 7:10	430 / 692 / 7:40	517 / 832 / 9:10	52 / 84 / 1:20	495 / 797 / 8:50	239 / 385 / 4:30	349 / 562 / 6:20	113 / 182 / 2:40	117 / 188 / 2:30	376 / 605 / 7:10	67 / 108 / 1:50	448 / 721 / 8:40
Edinburgh																																56 / 90 / 1:30	462 / 744 / 8:10	219 / 352 / 4:00	96 / 154 / 2:00	385 / 620 / 7:00	345 / 555 / 6:10	373 / 600 / 6:50	456 / 734 / 8:20	91 / 146 / 2:10	439 / 707 / 8:00	183 / 295 / 3:30	292 / 470 / 5:30	57 / 92 / 1:40	73 / 117 / 1:50	320 / 515 / 6:20	125 / 201 / 3:10	390 / 628 / 7:20
Exeter																															450 / 724 / 8:00	518 / 834 / 9:10	248 / 399 / 4:40	251 / 404 / 4:30	353 / 568 / 6:20	121 / 195 / 2:30	249 / 401 / 4:30	76 / 122 / 1:40	184 / 296 / 5:00	550 / 885 / 9:40	82 / 132 / 2:20	282 / 454 / 5:10	157 / 253 / 3:10	428 / 689 / 7:50	446 / 718 / 7:50	201 / 323 / 4:10	569 / 916 / 10:20	181 / 291 / 3:40
Fishguard																														230 / 370 / 4:30	399 / 642 / 7:30	460 / 740 / 8:30	331 / 533 / 6:20	247 / 398 / 4:50	297 / 478 / 5:40	112 / 180 / 2:40	270 / 435 / 5:10	154 / 248 / 3:20	291 / 468 / 5:40	493 / 794 / 9:10	222 / 357 / 4:40	209 / 336 / 4:10	170 / 274 / 3:40	371 / 597 / 7:20	373 / 600 / 7:00	56 / 90 / 1:30	504 / 811 / 10:10	260 / 418 / 5:20
Fort William																													486 / 782 / 9:30	560 / 901 / 10:20	144 / 232 / 3:30	127 / 204 / 3:10	596 / 959 / 11:00	357 / 575 / 7:00	206 / 332 / 4:30	485 / 781 / 9:10	479 / 771 / 9:00	486 / 782 / 9:10	575 / 926 / 10:50	125 / 201 / 3:10	539 / 867 / 10:10	296 / 476 / 6:00	392 / 631 / 7:40	190 / 306 / 4:40	133 / 214 / 3:20	430 / 692 / 8:40	149 / 240 / 3:50	510 / 821 / 9:50
Glasgow																												101 / 163 / 2:50	376 / 605 / 7:10	449 / 723 / 8:00	44 / 71 / 1:20	83 / 134 / 2:00	488 / 786 / 8:40	249 / 401 / 4:40	96 / 154 / 2:10	385 / 620 / 7:00	372 / 599 / 6:40	373 / 600 / 6:50	468 / 753 / 8:30	110 / 177 / 2:30	439 / 707 / 8:00	183 / 295 / 3:40	292 / 470 / 5:30	101 / 163 / 2:40	33 / 53 / 1:10	320 / 515 / 6:20	145 / 233 / 3:30	397 / 639 / 7:30
Gloucester																											346 / 557 / 6:10	454 / 731 / 8:30	153 / 246 / 3:10	111 / 179 / 2:10	349 / 562 / 6:10	410 / 660 / 7:10	191 / 307 / 3:30	150 / 241 / 2:50	247 / 398 / 4:20	56 / 90 / 1:20	123 / 198 / 2:20	35 / 56 / 1:00	159 / 256 / 3:10	443 / 713 / 8:00	99 / 159 / 2:40	174 / 280 / 3:10	56 / 90 / 1:20	318 / 512 / 6:00	330 / 531 / 5:50	102 / 164 / 2:30	468 / 753 / 8:30	109 / 175 / 2:30
Great Yarmouth																										225 / 362 / 4:40	419 / 674 / 8:00	527 / 848 / 10:20	366 / 589 / 7:20	335 / 539 / 6:30	386 / 621 / 7:30	484 / 779 / 9:00	185 / 298 / 4:00	167 / 269 / 3:40	320 / 515 / 6:20	284 / 457 / 5:50	82 / 132 / 2:10	275 / 443 / 5:40	180 / 290 / 4:10	477 / 768 / 9:10	240 / 386 / 5:00	252 / 406 / 5:10	180 / 290 / 4:10	345 / 555 / 7:00	402 / 647 / 7:40	294 / 473 / 6:20	517 / 832 / 10:50	128 / 206 / 3:40
Harwich																									82 / 132 / 2:10	196 / 316 / 4:00	432 / 695 / 8:10	543 / 874 / 10:30	337 / 542 / 6:40	279 / 449 / 5:20	413 / 665 / 7:40	469 / 755 / 8:40	125 / 201 / 2:50	194 / 312 / 4:00	336 / 541 / 6:20	246 / 396 / 5:00	67 / 108 / 1:50	217 / 349 / 4:30	128 / 206 / 3:00	504 / 811 / 9:20	187 / 301 / 4:00	275 / 443 / 5:20	167 / 269 / 3:40	372 / 599 / 7:20	425 / 684 / 8:00	281 / 452 / 5:50	535 / 861 / 11:20	76 / 122 / 2:20
Holyhead																								349 / 562 / 7:10	334 / 538 / 7:00	191 / 307 / 4:00	330 / 531 / 6:40	438 / 705 / 8:50	167 / 269 / 4:00	282 / 454 / 5:40	333 / 536 / 6:40	394 / 634 / 7:30	360 / 580 / 7:00	181 / 291 / 3:50	231 / 372 / 4:50	216 / 348 / 5:40	270 / 435 / 5:20	206 / 332 / 4:30	334 / 538 / 6:40	426 / 686 / 8:20	288 / 463 / 5:50	141 / 227 / 3:20	148 / 238 / 3:30	311 / 501 / 6:30	305 / 491 / 6:10	111 / 179 / 2:50	439 / 707 / 8:40	269 / 433 / 5:40
Inverness																							474 / 763 / 9:40	569 / 916 / 11:00	553 / 890 / 11:00	504 / 811 / 9:30	166 / 267 / 4:00	66 / 106 / 1:40	542 / 872 / 10:30	618 / 995 / 11:30	158 / 254 / 3:50	132 / 212 / 3:20	622 / 1001 / 11:30	383 / 617 / 7:30	262 / 422 / 5:30	549 / 884 / 10:20	505 / 813 / 9:30	539 / 867 / 10:10	617 / 993 / 11:30	75 / 121 / 2:00	597 / 961 / 11:20	348 / 560 / 7:00	458 / 737 / 9:00	215 / 346 / 5:10	199 / 320 / 4:30	486 / 782 / 9:40	105 / 169 / 2:50	550 / 885 / 10:40
John o' Groats																						129 / 208 / 3:20	603 / 970 / 12:40	693 / 1116 / 14:00	677 / 1090 / 14:00	628 / 1011 / 12:30	295 / 475 / 7:10	195 / 314 / 5:00	671 / 1080 / 13:40	744 / 1197 / 14:30	285 / 459 / 7:00	259 / 417 / 6:30	746 / 1201 / 14:40	507 / 816 / 10:30	391 / 629 / 8:40	680 / 1094 / 13:30	630 / 1014 / 12:30	668 / 1075 / 13:20	741 / 1193 / 14:40	202 / 325 / 5:00	724 / 1165 / 14:20	478 / 769 / 10:00	574 / 924 / 11:50	342 / 550 / 8:10	328 / 528 / 7:40	601 / 967 / 12:40	232 / 373 / 5:50	663 / 1067 / 13:30
Kingston upon Hull																					518 / 834 / 10:50	394 / 634 / 7:50	231 / 372 / 4:50	196 / 316 / 4:10	207 / 333 / 5:20	169 / 272 / 3:10	254 / 409 / 4:50	369 / 594 / 7:20	280 / 451 / 5:30	309 / 497 / 5:40	234 / 377 / 4:30	295 / 475 / 5:30	256 / 412 / 4:50	47 / 76 / 1:10	158 / 254 / 3:00	244 / 393 / 4:40	139 / 224 / 3:10	233 / 375 / 4:20	245 / 394 / 4:40	327 / 526 / 6:10	264 / 425 / 5:00	127 / 204 / 2:30	134 / 216 / 2:50	185 / 298 / 3:50	251 / 404 / 4:40	223 / 359 / 4:40	364 / 586 / 7:20	184 / 296 / 3:50
Kyle of Lochalsh																				445 / 716 / 9:00	189 / 304 / 4:40	84 / 135 / 2:10	514 / 827 / 10:40	611 / 983 / 12:10	602 / 969 / 12:10	528 / 850 / 10:20	179 / 288 / 4:40	79 / 127 / 2:00	567 / 913 / 11:20	628 / 1011 / 12:00	216 / 348 / 5:20	186 / 299 / 4:40	671 / 1080 / 12:50	432 / 695 / 8:40	275 / 443 / 6:10	564 / 908 / 11:10	555 / 893 / 10:50	552 / 888 / 10:50	651 / 1048 / 12:40	159 / 256 / 4:00	618 / 995 / 12:10	372 / 599 / 7:50	471 / 758 / 9:40	263 / 423 / 6:20	212 / 341 / 5:10	499 / 803 / 10:20	189 / 304 / 4:50	586 / 943 / 11:40
Land's End																			763 / 1228 / 15:10	421 / 678 / 8:20	868 / 1397 / 17:20	741 / 1193 / 14:20	405 / 652 / 8:30	390 / 628 / 8:00	446 / 718 / 9:10	235 / 378 / 5:00	573 / 922 / 10:50	686 / 1104 / 13:20	353 / 568 / 7:20	123 / 198 / 3:20	574 / 924 / 10:50	642 / 1033 / 12:00	381 / 613 / 7:40	374 / 602 / 7:20	477 / 768 / 9:10	245 / 394 / 5:20	374 / 602 / 7:20	200 / 322 / 4:40	308 / 496 / 7:50	665 / 1070 / 12:30	205 / 330 / 5:20	405 / 652 / 8:00	281 / 452 / 6:00	552 / 888 / 10:40	570 / 917 / 10:50	313 / 504 / 6:50	692 / 1114 / 13:10	297 / 478 / 6:30
Leeds																		405 / 652 / 8:00	394 / 634 / 8:20	55 / 89 / 1:30	487 / 784 / 10:20	360 / 579 / 7:10	176 / 283 / 4:00	223 / 359 / 4:30	196 / 315 / 4:20	174 / 280 / 3:20	215 / 346 / 4:10	329 / 530 / 6:40	237 / 381 / 4:40	270 / 435 / 5:00	202 / 325 / 4:00	258 / 415 / 4:50	260 / 418 / 4:50	29 / 47 / 0:50	119 / 192 / 2:30	232 / 373 / 4:20	145 / 233 / 2:50	194 / 312 / 3:50	260 / 419 / 5:00	293 / 472 / 5:30	255 / 410 / 4:50	72 / 116 / 1:40	113 / 182 / 2:30	156 / 251 / 3:20	212 / 341 / 4:00	169 / 272 / 3:40	327 / 526 / 6:50	189 / 304 / 3:50
Leicester																	95 / 153 / 2:00	320 / 515 / 6:30	500 / 805 / 9:50	102 / 164 / 2:10	588 / 947 / 11:50	461 / 742 / 8:50	190 / 306 / 4:00	147 / 237 / 3:10	140 / 225 / 3:20	85 / 137 / 1:40	314 / 505 / 5:40	422 / 679 / 8:00	209 / 336 / 4:10	196 / 315 / 3:40	296 / 476 / 5:20	349 / 562 / 6:20	185 / 298 / 3:30	74 / 119 / 1:30	206 / 332 / 3:50	154 / 248 / 3:00	68 / 109 / 1:20	120 / 193 / 2:30	166 / 267 / 3:20	389 / 626 / 7:00	158 / 254 / 3:10	140 / 225 / 2:40	39 / 63 / 1:10	252 / 406 / 5:00	299 / 481 / 5:20	153 / 246 / 3:20	414 / 666 / 7:40	97 / 156 / 2:20
Lincoln																51 / 82 / 1:20	68 / 109 / 1:50	371 / 597 / 7:30	476 / 766 / 9:40	44 / 71 / 1:20	554 / 892 / 11:30	427 / 687 / 8:30	216 / 348 / 4:40	155 / 249 / 3:30	128 / 206 / 3:20	159 / 256 / 3:10	291 / 468 / 5:30	399 / 642 / 7:50	272 / 438 / 5:30	247 / 398 / 4:40	258 / 415 / 5:00	314 / 505 / 5:50	202 / 325 / 4:00	39 / 63 / 1:10	191 / 307 / 3:40	208 / 335 / 4:10	85 / 137 / 2:20	183 / 295 / 3:40	197 / 317 / 4:00	357 / 575 / 6:40	209 / 336 / 4:10	128 / 206 / 2:40	90 / 145 / 2:10	224 / 360 / 4:40	274 / 441 / 5:10	199 / 320 / 4:20	383 / 616 / 7:20	131 / 211 / 3:10
Liverpool															129 / 208 / 2:50	130 / 209 / 2:40	75 / 121 / 1:50	361 / 581 / 7:20	407 / 655 / 8:30	130 / 209 / 2:40	511 / 822 / 10:40	382 / 615 / 7:40	102 / 164 / 2:40	265 / 427 / 5:20	240 / 386 / 5:00	140 / 225 / 2:40	216 / 348 / 4:10	329 / 530 / 6:40	160 / 257 / 3:30	237 / 381 / 4:30	216 / 348 / 4:10	286 / 460 / 5:20	299 / 481 / 5:30	86 / 138 / 1:50	120 / 193 / 2:30	169 / 272 / 3:20	194 / 312 / 3:40	161 / 259 / 3:10	272 / 438 / 5:10	318 / 512 / 6:00	234 / 377 / 4:30	49 / 79 / 1:20	93 / 150 / 2:10	219 / 352 / 4:30	213 / 343 / 4:10	104 / 167 / 2:40	341 / 549 / 6:40	202 / 325 / 4:10
Manchester														35 / 56 / 1:10	84 / 135 / 2:00	92 / 148 / 2:00	40 / 64 / 1:10	361 / 581 / 7:20	406 / 654 / 8:30	95 / 153 / 2:10	500 / 805 / 10:30	373 / 600 / 7:30	124 / 200 / 3:00	228 / 367 / 4:40	212 / 341 / 4:30	126 / 203 / 2:30	215 / 346 / 4:10	329 / 530 / 6:40	197 / 317 / 4:00	236 / 380 / 4:20	215 / 346 / 4:10	285 / 459 / 5:20	276 / 444 / 5:10	61 / 98 / 1:30	119 / 192 / 2:30	183 / 295 / 3:40	165 / 266 / 3:10	161 / 259 / 3:10	257 / 414 / 4:50	318 / 512 / 6:00	227 / 365 / 4:20	48 / 77 / 1:20	80 / 129 / 2:00	196 / 315 / 4:00	212 / 341 / 4:00	129 / 208 / 3:00	340 / 547 / 6:30	185 / 298 / 3:50
Newcastle upon Tyne													132 / 212 / 2:50	168 / 270 / 3:20	159 / 256 / 3:20	187 / 301 / 3:40	92 / 148 / 2:10	498 / 802 / 9:40	318 / 512 / 7:00	132 / 212 / 2:50	395 / 636 / 8:50	268 / 431 / 5:40	272 / 438 / 5:40	308 / 496 / 6:00	281 / 452 / 5:40	266 / 428 / 4:50	148 / 238 / 3:10	253 / 407 / 5:20	329 / 529 / 6:20	364 / 586 / 6:30	110 / 177 / 2:20	166 / 267 / 3:20	358 / 576 / 6:30	114 / 183 / 2:20	57 / 92 / 1:50	325 / 523 / 6:00	241 / 388 / 4:20	299 / 481 / 5:30	352 / 567 / 6:30	201 / 323 / 4:00	347 / 558 / 6:30	129 / 208 / 2:40	207 / 333 / 4:10	64 / 103 / 1:50	149 / 240 / 3:00	257 / 414 / 5:20	235 / 378 / 4:50	286 / 460 / 5:40
Norwich												264 / 425 / 5:20	185 / 298 / 4:30	220 / 354 / 4:40	105 / 169 / 2:50	119 / 192 / 3:20	176 / 283 / 3:50	421 / 678 / 8:40	582 / 937 / 11:50	149 / 240 / 4:00	654 / 1053 / 13:30	529 / 852 / 10:30	311 / 501 / 6:40	73 / 117 / 2:00	20 / 32 / 0:40	204 / 328 / 4:10	385 / 620 / 9:00	504 / 811 / 10:00	343 / 552 / 7:00	308 / 496 / 6:00	366 / 589 / 7:00	422 / 679 / 8:00	174 / 280 / 3:50	147 / 237 / 3:20	289 / 465 / 5:40	262 / 422 / 5:20	62 / 100 / 1:50	252 / 406 / 5:10	175 / 282 / 4:00	457 / 735 / 8:40	214 / 344 / 4:40	232 / 373 / 4:50	166 / 267 / 3:50	328 / 528 / 6:40	382 / 615 / 7:20	276 / 444 / 6:00	496 / 798 / 9:40	114 / 183 / 3:30
Nottingham											130 / 209 / 3:40	157 / 253 / 3:10	73 / 118 / 1:40	98 / 158 / 2:10	35 / 56 / 1:10	25 / 40 / 0:50	70 / 113 / 1:40	345 / 555 / 7:00	479 / 771 / 9:40	90 / 145 / 2:00	557 / 896 / 11:30	430 / 692 / 8:20	185 / 298 / 4:00	150 / 241 / 3:20	153 / 246 / 3:30	110 / 177 / 2:10	293 / 472 / 5:30	401 / 646 / 7:50	220 / 354 / 4:30	221 / 356 / 4:10	262 / 422 / 4:50	328 / 528 / 6:00	205 / 330 / 3:50	43 / 69 / 1:10	194 / 312 / 3:40	172 / 277 / 3:20	83 / 134 / 1:40	145 / 233 / 3:00	193 / 311 / 3:50	353 / 568 / 6:30	183 / 295 / 3:40	111 / 179 / 2:20	50 / 80 / 1:20	221 / 356 / 4:30	274 / 441 / 5:10	164 / 264 / 3:40	393 / 633 / 7:30	122 / 196 / 2:40
Oban										390 / 628 / 7:30	492 / 792 / 9:40	233 / 375 / 4:50	307 / 494 / 6:00	308 / 496 / 6:10	387 / 623 / 7:30	419 / 674 / 7:50	307 / 494 / 6:00	665 / 1070 / 12:50	128 / 206 / 3:10	346 / 557 / 6:40	244 / 393 / 6:10	117 / 188 / 3:00	427 / 687 / 8:30	524 / 843 / 10:00	515 / 829 / 10:00	441 / 710 / 8:10	92 / 148 / 2:30	49 / 79 / 1:20	481 / 774 / 9:10	549 / 884 / 10:00	123 / 198 / 3:00	117 / 188 / 2:50	585 / 942 / 10:40	346 / 557 / 6:40	188 / 303 / 4:00	477 / 768 / 9:00	468 / 753 / 8:40	465 / 748 / 8:40	565 / 910 / 10:30	141 / 227 / 3:30	530 / 853 / 9:50	285 / 459 / 5:40	384 / 618 / 7:30	180 / 290 / 4:20	94 / 151 / 2:20	412 / 663 / 8:10	178 / 286 / 4:20	499 / 803 / 9:30
Oxford									462 / 744 / 8:30	109 / 175 / 2:10	145 / 233 / 3:50	260 / 418 / 4:50	144 / 232 / 2:50	172 / 277 / 3:20	137 / 221 / 2:50	73 / 117 / 1:30	168 / 270 / 3:10	274 / 441 / 5:40	550 / 885 / 10:40	192 / 309 / 3:40	656 / 1056 / 13:00	532 / 856 / 10:00	238 / 383 / 4:50	145 / 233 / 3:10	200 / 322 / 4:20	52 / 84 / 1:30	356 / 573 / 6:30	472 / 760 / 9:00	205 / 330 / 4:10	156 / 251 / 3:00	372 / 599 / 6:40	433 / 697 / 7:40	141 / 227 / 2:50	145 / 233 / 2:40	260 / 418 / 4:40	108 / 174 / 2:20	83 / 134 / 1:40	74 / 119 / 1:40	108 / 174 / 2:20	465 / 749 / 8:20	90 / 145 / 2:00	187 / 301 / 3:30	64 / 103 / 1:30	324 / 521 / 6:10	353 / 568 / 6:20	154 / 248 / 3:20	483 / 777 / 8:50	57 / 92 / 1:40
Plymouth								199 / 320 / 4:00	587 / 945 / 11:00	267 / 430 / 5:10	343 / 552 / 7:00	410 / 660 / 7:40	283 / 455 / 5:30	283 / 455 / 5:30	293 / 472 / 5:50	242 / 389 / 4:40	316 / 509 / 6:00	89 / 143 / 2:20	674 / 1085 / 13:10	355 / 571 / 6:40	790 / 1271 / 15:40	664 / 1069 / 12:30	328 / 528 / 6:40	309 / 497 / 6:10	365 / 588 / 7:20	157 / 253 / 3:20	495 / 797 / 9:10	595 / 958 / 11:20	264 / 425 / 5:30	46 / 74 / 1:30	496 / 798 / 9:00	552 / 888 / 10:00	300 / 483 / 5:50	297 / 478 / 5:40	399 / 642 / 7:20	167 / 269 / 3:40	293 / 472 / 5:30	122 / 196 / 2:50	224 / 361 / 6:00	587 / 945 / 10:40	128 / 206 / 3:30	328 / 528 / 6:10	203 / 327 / 4:20	474 / 763 / 9:00	492 / 792 / 9:00	237 / 382 / 5:10	615 / 990 / 11:20	218 / 351 / 4:40
Portsmouth							176 / 283 / 4:50	77 / 124 / 1:40	545 / 877 / 10:00	191 / 307 / 3:40	207 / 333 / 4:20	337 / 542 / 6:10	236 / 380 / 4:30	254 / 409 / 4:50	201 / 323 / 4:00	162 / 261 / 3:10	257 / 414 / 4:50	259 / 417 / 5:40	633 / 1019 / 12:10	269 / 433 / 5:00	737 / 1186 / 14:30	613 / 987 / 11:30	311 / 501 / 6:10	166 / 267 / 3:40	221 / 356 / 4:40	119 / 192 / 3:00	448 / 721 / 8:10	555 / 893 / 10:20	251 / 404 / 5:00	135 / 217 / 2:40	453 / 729 / 8:10	514 / 827 / 9:00	130 / 209 / 2:50	234 / 377 / 4:20	348 / 560 / 6:10	142 / 229 / 3:00	144 / 232 / 2:50	97 / 156 / 2:10	48 / 77 / 1:40	547 / 881 / 9:50	52 / 84 / 1:30	264 / 425 / 4:50	141 / 227 / 3:00	401 / 645 / 7:30	430 / 692 / 7:40	222 / 357 / 4:40	560 / 901 / 10:10	70 / 113 / 2:00
Sheffield						230 / 370 / 4:20	283 / 455 / 5:30	135 / 217 / 2:40	339 / 546 / 6:30	37 / 60 / 1:00	146 / 235 / 3:20	125 / 201 / 2:40	38 / 61 / 1:00	72 / 116 / 1:40	46 / 74 / 1:20	62 / 100 / 1:20	33 / 53 / 1:00	361 / 581 / 7:10	427 / 687 / 8:40	65 / 105 / 1:30	520 / 837 / 10:50	393 / 632 / 7:40	168 / 270 / 3:40	187 / 301 / 3:50	166 / 267 / 3:40	126 / 203 / 2:20	248 / 399 / 4:40	348 / 560 / 6:50	215 / 346 / 4:20	237 / 381 / 4:20	235 / 378 / 4:20	291 / 468 / 5:20	245 / 394 / 4:30	18 / 29 / 0:40	152 / 245 / 3:00	194 / 312 / 3:40	120 / 193 / 2:20	161 / 259 / 3:10	226 / 364 / 4:20	320 / 515 / 6:00	216 / 348 / 4:10	86 / 138 / 1:50	76 / 122 / 1:50	190 / 306 / 4:00	245 / 394 / 4:30	159 / 256 / 3:30	360 / 579 / 6:50	159 / 256 / 3:20
Shrewsbury					82 / 132 / 2:10	207 / 333 / 3:50	225 / 362 / 4:40	106 / 171 / 2:10	364 / 586 / 7:00	93 / 150 / 2:00	205 / 330 / 4:20	201 / 323 / 3:50	69 / 111 / 1:40	58 / 93 / 1:50	133 / 214 / 2:50	84 / 135 / 1:40	109 / 175 / 2:20	303 / 488 / 6:10	451 / 726 / 9:00	169 / 272 / 3:10	567 / 912 / 11:30	438 / 705 / 8:20	113 / 182 / 2:50	240 / 386 / 4:40	225 / 362 / 4:40	77 / 124 / 1:30	272 / 438 / 5:00	382 / 615 / 7:20	145 / 233 / 3:10	179 / 288 / 3:20	274 / 441 / 5:00	330 / 531 / 6:00	251 / 404 / 4:30	109 / 175 / 2:10	176 / 283 / 3:20	111 / 179 / 2:20	159 / 256 / 3:00	103 / 166 / 2:50	226 / 364 / 4:20	371 / 597 / 6:50	185 / 298 / 3:40	98 / 158 / 2:00	45 / 72 / 1:20	265 / 426 / 5:10	269 / 433 / 5:00	77 / 124 / 2:10	399 / 642 / 7:30	160 / 258 / 3:20
Southampton				185 / 298 / 4:10	199 / 320 / 3:40	21 / 34 / 0:50	151 / 243 / 4:10	64 / 103 / 1:30	530 / 853 / 9:40	176 / 283 / 3:20	206 / 332 / 4:20	324 / 521 / 5:50	221 / 356 / 4:10	239 / 385 / 4:30	204 / 328 / 4:00	137 / 220 / 2:40	232 / 373 / 4:20	228 / 367 / 5:00	618 / 995 / 12:00	256 / 412 / 4:40	723 / 1164 / 14:10	598 / 963 / 11:10	293 / 472 / 5:50	164 / 264 / 3:30	220 / 354 / 4:40	105 / 169 / 2:40	433 / 697 / 7:40	541 / 871 / 10:00	233 / 375 / 4:40	105 / 169 / 3:00	438 / 705 / 7:50	500 / 805 / 8:50	143 / 230 / 2:50	209 / 336 / 3:50	324 / 521 / 5:50	121 / 195 / 2:30	148 / 238 / 2:50	76 / 122 / 2:20	61 / 98 / 1:50	532 / 856 / 9:30	31 / 50 / 1:00	251 / 404 / 4:40	128 / 206 / 2:40	388 / 624 / 7:10	417 / 671 / 7:30	201 / 323 / 4:10	547 / 880 / 10:00	77 / 124 / 2:00
Stranraer			445 / 716 / 8:20	277 / 446 / 5:30	263 / 423 / 5:20	461 / 742 / 8:40	500 / 805 / 9:40	379 / 610 / 7:10	148 / 238 / 3:40	290 / 467 / 5:50	403 / 649 / 8:10	158 / 254 / 3:40	220 / 354 / 4:40	221 / 356 / 4:40	298 / 480 / 6:00	330 / 531 / 6:20	220 / 354 / 4:40	585 / 942 / 11:30	263 / 423 / 6:30	259 / 417 / 5:20	379 / 610 / 9:00	262 / 422 / 6:00	338 / 544 / 7:00	410 / 660 / 8:10	426 / 686 / 8:40	343 / 552 / 6:30	84 / 135 / 2:30	195 / 314 / 4:50	392 / 631 / 7:50	454 / 731 / 8:30	124 / 200 / 3:00	167 / 269 / 3:40	496 / 798 / 9:10	257 / 414 / 5:10	101 / 163 / 2:40	390 / 628 / 7:30	379 / 610 / 7:10	378 / 608 / 7:20	475 / 765 / 9:00	194 / 312 / 4:20	444 / 715 / 8:30	188 / 303 / 4:00	297 / 478 / 6:00	170 / 274 / 4:10	51 / 82 / 1:20	325 / 523 / 6:50	228 / 367 / 5:10	402 / 647 / 7:50
Swansea		417 / 671 / 7:50	161 / 259 / 3:00	118 / 190 / 2:20	217 / 349 / 4:00	182 / 293 / 3:30	206 / 332 / 4:10	141 / 227 / 2:40	506 / 815 / 9:20	192 / 309 / 3:40	301 / 485 / 6:00	347 / 559 / 6:20	187 / 301 / 3:30	195 / 314 / 3:40	233 / 375 / 4:30	177 / 285 / 3:20	248 / 399 / 4:40	285 / 459 / 6:00	594 / 956 / 11:30	264 / 425 / 4:50	696 / 1120 / 13:40	572 / 921 / 10:40	184 / 296 / 4:50	267 / 430 / 5:10	329 / 530 / 6:30	89 / 143 / 1:50	409 / 658 / 7:20	496 / 798 / 9:20	67 / 108 / 1:50	161 / 259 / 3:00	412 / 663 / 7:20	473 / 761 / 8:20	274 / 441 / 5:00	232 / 373 / 4:10	309 / 497 / 5:30	41 / 66 / 1:10	227 / 365 / 4:10	85 / 137 / 1:50	222 / 357 / 4:20	505 / 813 / 9:00	167 / 269 / 3:20	216 / 348 / 4:00	119 / 192 / 2:30	383 / 616 / 7:10	379 / 610 / 6:50	73 / 117 / 2:00	507 / 816 / 9:20	194 / 312 / 4:00
York	272 / 438 / 5:10	222 / 357 / 4:40	258 / 415 / 5:10	133 / 214 / 2:40	52 / 84 / 1:20	278 / 448 / 5:10	333 / 536 / 6:20	181 / 291 / 3:20	309 / 497 / 6:00	77 / 124 / 1:40	181 / 291 / 4:20	84 / 135 / 2:20	64 / 103 / 1:30	99 / 159 / 2:10	75 / 121 / 1:50	108 / 174 / 2:10	24 / 39 / 0:50	411 / 661 / 8:00	407 / 655 / 8:20	37 / 60 / 1:10	479 / 771 / 10:10	352 / 566 / 7:00	204 / 328 / 4:20	228 / 367 / 4:40	201 / 323 / 4:20	189 / 304 / 3:30	217 / 349 / 4:10	330 / 531 / 6:30	261 / 420 / 5:10	287 / 462 / 5:10	194 / 312 / 3:40	250 / 402 / 4:40	282 / 454 / 5:10	34 / 55 / 1:00	121 / 195 / 2:30	244 / 393 / 4:40	165 / 266 / 3:10	222 / 357 / 4:10	275 / 443 / 5:10	285 / 459 / 5:20	269 / 433 / 5:00	96 / 154 / 2:00	130 / 209 / 2:40	148 / 238 / 3:10	214 / 344 / 4:00	195 / 314 / 4:10	319 / 513 / 6:10	207 / 333 / 4:10

Supporting

THINK!

Travel safe – Don't drive tired

Key to road map pages

123	**Road map pages at 1:200 000** 3.15 miles to 1 inch
145	**Road map pages at 1:265 000** approximately 4 miles to 1 inch
157	**Map pages at 1:332 000** approximately 5 miles to 1 inch
	(Orkney and Shetland Islands at 1:400 000, approximately 6.25 miles to 1 inch)

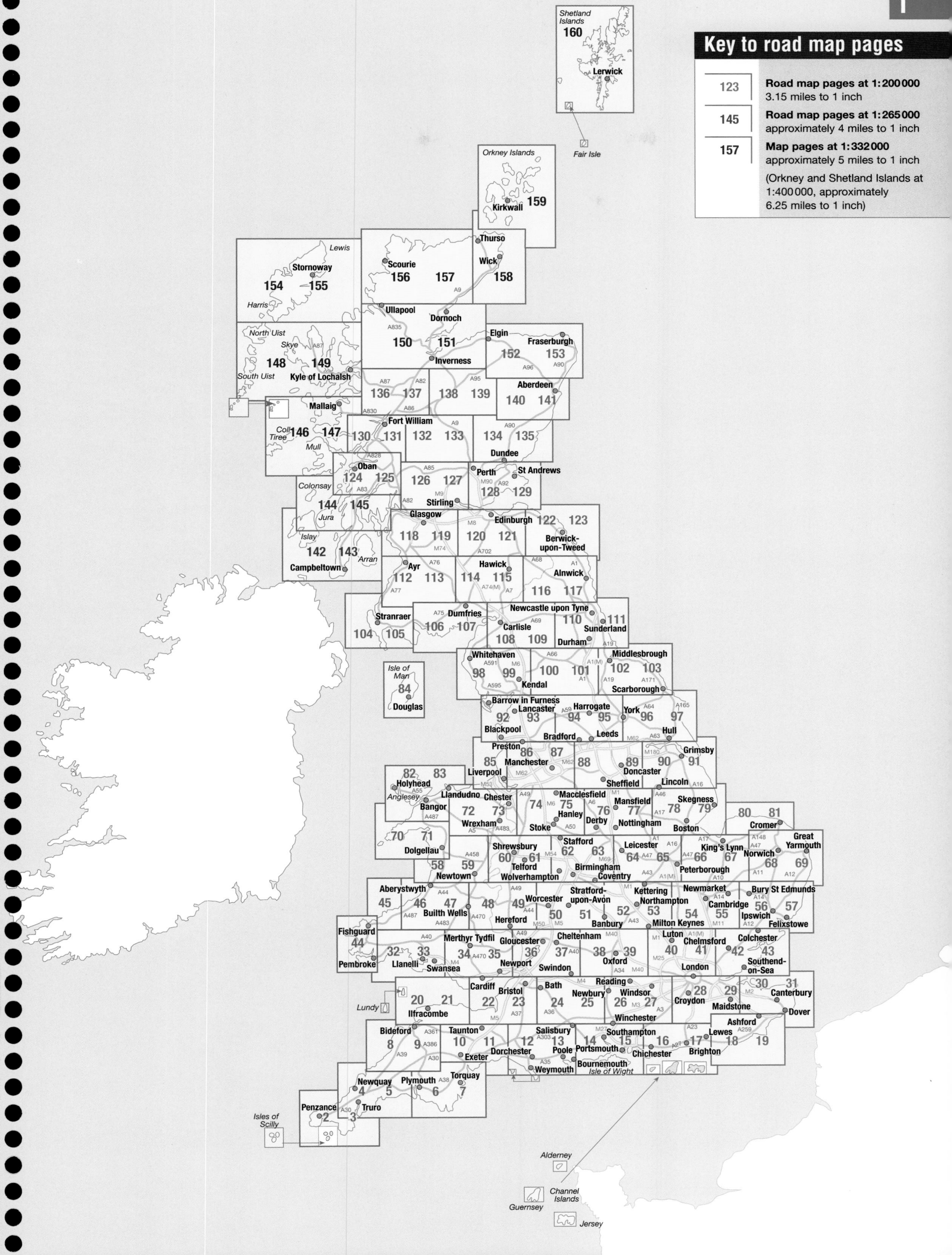

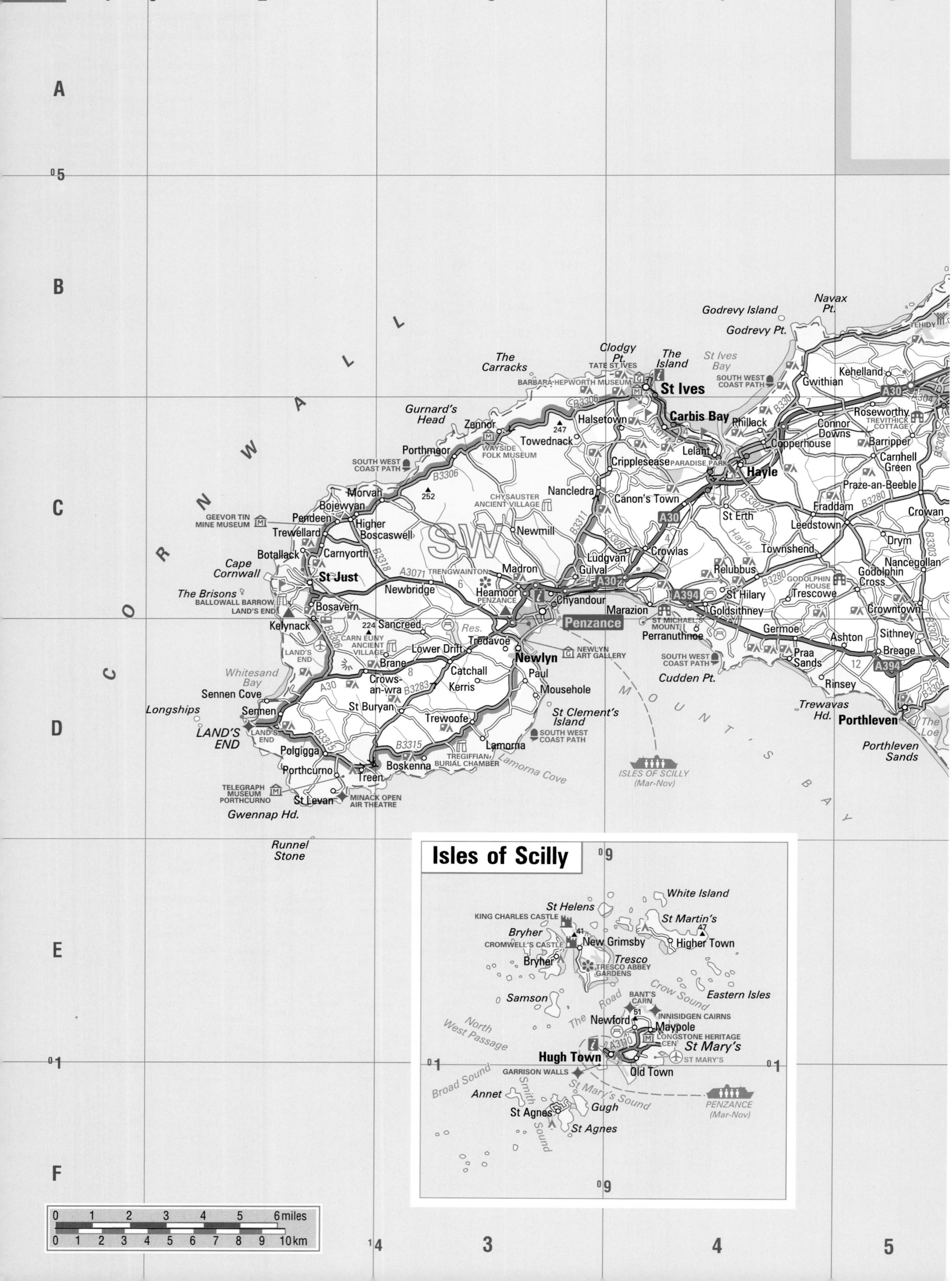
CORNWALL
SW
St Ives
Carbis Bay
Hayle
St Just
Penzance
Newlyn
Porthleven
Clodgy Pt.
The Island
St Ives Bay
TATE ST IVES
BARBARA HEPWORTH MUSEUM
The Carracks
Gurnard's Head
Zennor
WAYSIDE FOLK MUSEUM
Towednack
Halsetown
Porthmeor
SOUTH WEST COAST PATH
Morvah
Bojewyan
Pendeen
Higher Boscaswell
GEEVOR TIN MINE MUSEUM
Trewellard
Botallack
Carnyorth
Cape Cornwall
The Brisons
BALLOWALL BARROW
LAND'S END
Bosavern
Kelynack
Newbridge
TRENGWAINTON
Madron
Heamoor
Gulval
Ludgvan
Crowlas
Chyandour
Marazion
ST MICHAEL'S MOUNT
Perranuthnoe
Newmill
CHYSAUSTER ANCIENT VILLAGE
Nancledra
Canon's Town
Cripplesease
Lelant
PARADISE PARK
Godrevy Island
Godrevy Pt.
Navax Pt.
TEHIDY
Gwithian
Kehelland
Phillack
Connor Downs
Copperhouse
Roseworthy
TREVITHICK COTTAGE
Barripper
Carnhell Green
Praze-an-Beeble
Fraddam
Crowan
St Erth
Leedstown
Drym
Townshend
Nancegollan
Godolphin Cross
GODOLPHIN HOUSE
Relubbus
St Hilary
Trescowe
Goldsithney
Crowntown
Germoe
Ashton
Sithney
Breage
Praa Sands
Rinsey
Cudden Pt.
Trewavas Hd.
The Loe
Porthleven Sands
MOUNT'S BAY
Sancreed
CARN EUNY ANCIENT VILLAGE
Res.
Tredavoe
Lower Drift
Brane
Catchall
Crows-an-wra
Kerris
Paul
Mousehole
NEWLYN ART GALLERY
St Clement's Island
St Buryan
Trewoofe
Lamorna
Lamorna Cove
TREGIFFIAN BURIAL CHAMBER
Boskenna
Treen
Whitesand Bay
Sennen Cove
Sennen
Longships
LAND'S END
Polgigga
Porthcurno
TELEGRAPH MUSEUM PORTHCURNO
St Levan
MINACK OPEN AIR THEATRE
Gwennap Hd.
Runnel Stone
ISLES OF SCILLY (Mar-Nov)
A30
A3071
A394
B3306
B3318
B3315
B3283
B3311
B3309
B3301
B3302
B3280
B3303
B3304
252
247
224
Isles of Scilly
White Island
St Helens
St Martin's
KING CHARLES CASTLE
Bryher
CROMWELL'S CASTLE
New Grimsby
Higher Town
Tresco
TRESCO ABBEY GARDENS
Eastern Isles
Samson
Crow Sound
The Road
BANT'S CARN
INNISIDGEN CAIRNS
Newford
Maypole
North West Passage
LONGSTONE HERITAGE CEN
St Mary's
Hugh Town
ST MARY'S
GARRISON WALLS
Old Town
Broad Sound
Smith Sound
St Mary's Sound
Annet
St Agnes
Gugh
PENZANCE (Mar-Nov)
0 1 2 3 4 5 6 miles
0 1 2 3 4 5 6 7 8 9 10 km

5
6
7
8
9
A
B
C
D
E
F
Penhale Pt.
Holywell
Holywell Bay Fun Park
Carines
Kestle Mill
Dairy Land Farm World
St Columb Road
Fraddon
Indian Queens
Trezaise
Bugle
Penhale
St Dennis
Hensbarrow
Whitemoor
Downs
China Clay
Stenalees
Penwithick
Ligger or Perran Bay
Cubert
Penhale Sands
Mount
Rejerrah
St Newlyn East
Trerice
Gummow's Shop
St Enoder
Retew
Treviscoe
Nanpean
Carthew
Trethurgy
St Blazey
South West Coast Path
Rose
Perran Round
Lappa Valley Steam Railway
Summercourt
Brighton
Trethosa
Foxhole
Wheal Martyn China Clay Heritage Centre
Eden Project
Perranporth
Newlyn Downs
Mitchell
Carclaze
Boscoppa
Goonhavern
Bolingey
Carland Cross
Trelassick
High Street
St Austell
Perranzabuloe
Zelah
St Stephen
Trewoon
Holmbush
Shipwreck Heritage Centre
St Agnes Hd.
Trevellas
New Mills
Coombe
St Mewan
Charlestown
St Agnes
Mithian
St Allen
Callestick
Cornish Cyder Farm
St Erme
Trispen
Ladock
Grampound Road
Sticker
Polgooth
St Austell Brewery
Porthpean
Goonbell
Marazanvose
Hewas Water
Allet
Trenarren
Porthtowan
Mount Hawke
Shortlanesend
Probus
Grampound
Trewithen
Black Hd.
Three Burrows
Blackwater
P&R
Tresillian
Creed
The Lost Gardens of Heligan
St Ewe
Pentewan
Mevagissey Bay
Portreath
Mawla
Truro
Kenwyn
Tresawle
Polmassick
Kestle
World of Model Railway
Tolgus Mill
Cornish Gold
Scorrier
Chacewater
Threemilestone
Royal Cornwall Mus
Cathedral
Merther
Tregony
Mevagissey
Portreath
Illogan
Portmellon
Cornish Mines & Engines
St Day
Baldhu
Kea
St Clement
Trevarrick
Chapel Pt.
Roscroggan
Redruth
Twelve Heads
Ruan Lanihorne
Gorran Churchtown
St Michael Caerhays
Pool
Tuckingmill
Cambrea
Carharrack
Bissoe
Malpas
Playing Place
St Michael Penkevil
Lamorran
Gorran Haven
Carnkie
Gwennap Pit
Gwennap
Carnon Downs
Old Kea
Portholland
Boswinger
Camborne
Lanner
Treworga
Philleigh
Trelissick
Penare
Shire Horse Farm
Four Lanes
Perranarworthal
Penpol
Veryan
Portloe
Veryan Bay
Troon
Devoran
Feock
Trelissick
Treworlas
South West Coast Path
Dodman Pt.
Ponsanooth
Penhalvaen
Stithians
Burnthouse
Mylor Bridge
Trewithian
Carne
Gerrans Bay
Nare Hd.
Stithians Res.
St Just in Roseland
Carrick Roads
Penmarth
Burras
Penryn
Flushing
Gerrans
Portscatho
Carnkie
Rame
Longdowns
Mabe Burnthouse
Falmouth
St Mawes
Greeb Pt.
Releath
Porkellis
Art Gallery
National Maritime
Bohortha
Poldark Mine
Budock Water
Pendennis Castle
Wendron
Seworgan
Treverva
Pendennis Pt.
Zone Pt.
Penjerrick
Falmouth Bay
Helston Railway
Constantine
Mawnan Smith
South West Coast Path
Trewennack
Porth Navas
Glendurgan
Rosemullion Hd.
Helston
Helford Passage
Trebah
Mawnan
Helford River
Gweek
National Seal Sanctuary
Flambards Experience
Helford
St Anthony-in-Meneage
Nare Pt.
SW
Mawgan
Manaccan
Garras
St Martin
Halliggye Fogou
Trelowarren
Newtown
Tregidden
Porthallow
Berepper
Gunwalloe
Porthoustock
Cury
Cross Lanes
St Keverne
Manacle Pt.
Traboe
The Manacles
Lowland Pt.
Goonhilly Downs
Mullion
Penhale
The Lizard
Trelan
Coverack
Mullion Cove
Gwenter
Chynhalls Pt.
Mullion Cove
Mullion Island
Kuggar
Black Hd.
Predannack Wollas
St Ruan
Ruan Minor
Vellan Hd.
Grade
Cadgwith
South West Coast Path
Kynance Cove
Lizard
Hot Pt.
Lizard Point
C O R N W A L L
A30
A39
A390
A394
A3083
A3078
B3285
B3284
B3277
B3298
B3297
B3280
B3289
B3291
B3293
B3294
B3296
B3275
B3279
B3287
B3273
B3274
A3058
A3075
A3076
A3047
B3301

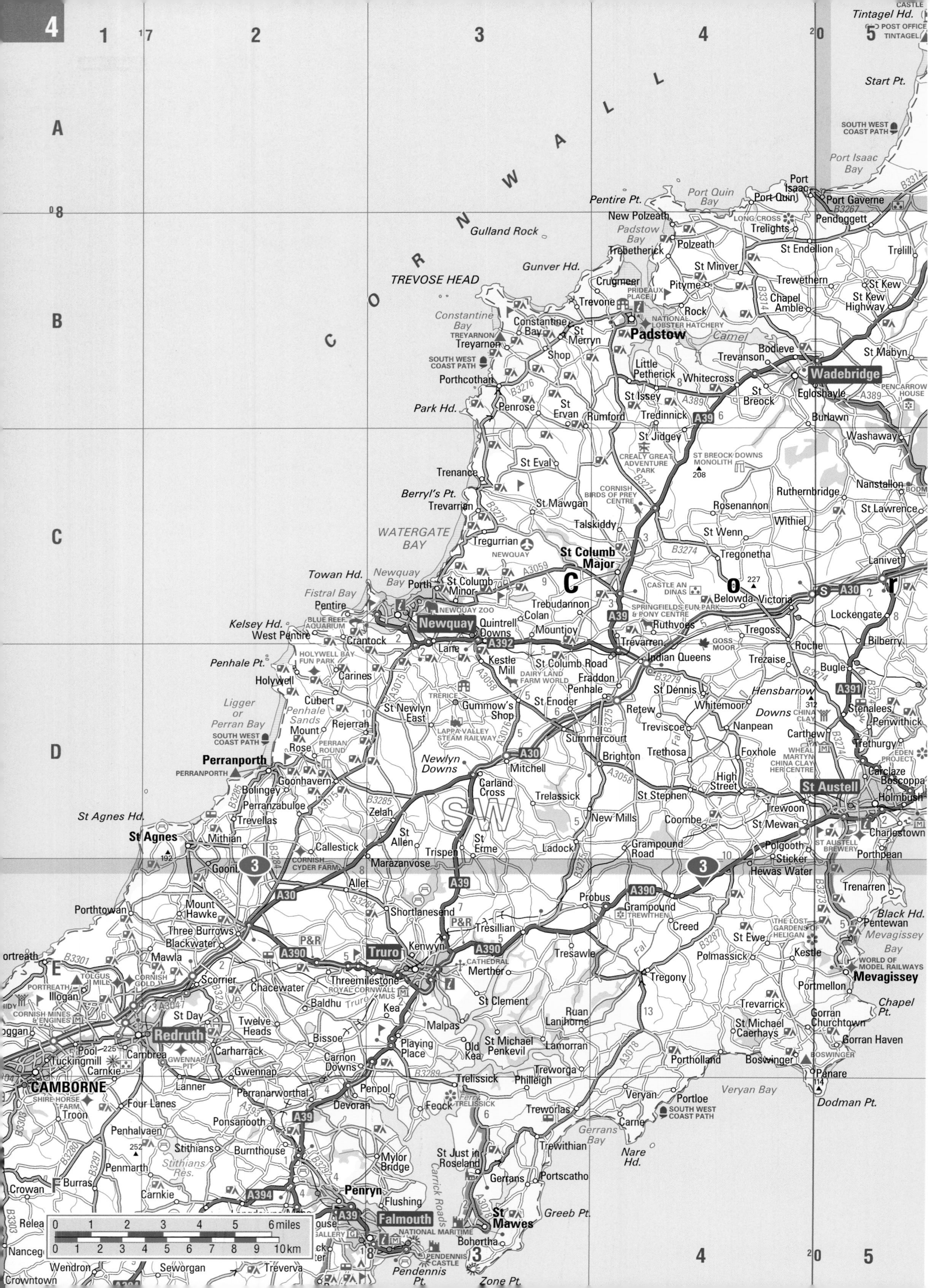
CORNWALL
Tintagel Hd.
TINTAGEL
Start Pt.
SOUTH WEST COAST PATH
Port Isaac Bay
Port Isaac
Port Gaverne
Port Quin
Port Quin Bay
Pentire Pt.
New Polzeath
Padstow Bay
Polzeath
Gulland Rock
Trebetherick
LONG CROSS
Trelights
Pendoggett
St Endellion
Trelill
St Minver
Trewethern
St Kew
St Kew Highway
Chapel Amble
Gunver Hd.
TREVOSE HEAD
Crugmeer
Pityme
Trevone
PRIDEAUX PLACE
Rock
NATIONAL LOBSTER HATCHERY
Constantine Bay
Constantine
TREYARNON
Treyarnon
St Merryn
Padstow
Camel
Shop
Trevanson
Bodieve
St Mabyn
SOUTH WEST COAST PATH
Porthcothan
Little Petherick
Whitecross
Wadebridge
PENCARROW HOUSE
St Issey
St Breock
Egloshayle
Park Hd.
Penrose
St Ervan
Rumford
Tredinnick
Burlawn
St Jidgey
Washaway
CREALY GREAT ADVENTURE PARK
ST BREOCK DOWNS MONOLITH
208
Trenance
St Eval
Nanstallon
Berryl's Pt.
Trevarrian
St Mawgan
CORNISH BIRDS OF PREY CENTRE
Ruthernbridge
Rosenannon
St Lawrence
Talskiddy
Withiel
WATERGATE BAY
Tregurrian
NEWQUAY
St Wenn
St Columb Major
Tregonetha
Lanivet
Towan Hd.
Newquay Bay
Porth
St Columb Minor
CASTLE AN DINAS
227
Fistral Bay
Pentire
Belowda
Victoria
NEWQUAY ZOO
Trebudannon
Colan
SPRINGFIELDS FUN PARK & PONY CENTRE
Lockengate
Kelsey Hd.
BLUE REEF AQUARIUM
Newquay
Quintrell Downs
Mountjoy
Ruthvoes
Tregoss
West Pentire
Crantock
Lane
Trevarren
GOSS MOOR
Roche
Bilberry
Penhale Pt.
HOLYWELL BAY FUN PARK
Kestle Mill
St Columb Road
Indian Queens
Trezaise
Bugle
Holywell
Carines
DAIRY LAND FARM WORLD
Fraddon
Penhale
St Dennis
Hensbarrow Downs
312
TRERICE
Ligger or Perran Bay
Cubert
Penhale Sands
St Newlyn East
Gummow's Shop
St Enoder
Retew
Whitemoor
CHINA CLAY
Stenalees
Penwithick
Mount
Rejerrah
LAPPA VALLEY STEAM RAILWAY
Treviscoe
Nanpean
Carthew
SOUTH WEST COAST PATH
Rose
PERRAN ROUND
Summercourt
WHEAL MARTYN CHINA CLAY HERITAGE CENTRE
Trethurgy
EDEN PROJECT
Perranporth
PERRANPORTH
Goonhavern
Newlyn Downs
Mitchell
Brighton
Trethosa
Foxhole
Carclaze
Boscoppa
Bolingey
Carland Cross
High Street
St Austell
Holmbush
Perranzabuloe
Trelassick
St Stephen
St Agnes Hd.
Zelah
SW
Trewoon
Trevellas
New Mills
Coombe
St Mewan
Charlestown
St Agnes
Mithian
St Allen
Trispen
St Erme
Ladock
Grampound Road
Polgooth
ST AUSTELL BREWERY
Porthpean
192
Callestick
Sticker
CORNISH CYDER FARM
Marazanvose
Goonhavern
Hewas Water
Allet
Trenarren
Porthtowan
Mount Hawke
Shortlanesend
Probus
Grampound
TREWITHEN
Black Hd.
Pentewan
Three Burrows
Blackwater
Tresillian
Creed
THE LOST GARDENS OF HELIGAN
Mevagissey Bay
St Ewe
Mawla
Truro
Kenwyn
CATHEDRAL
Tresawle
Polmassick
Kestle
Portreath
TOLGUS MILL
CORNISH GOLD
Scorrier
Chacewater
Threemilestone
ROYAL CORNWALL MUS
Merther
Tregony
WORLD OF MODEL RAILWAYS
Mevagissey
PORTREATH
Illogan
Portmellon
CORNISH MINES & ENGINES
Baldhu
Kea
St Clement
Trevarrick
Chapel Pt.
St Day
Twelve Heads
Malpas
Ruan Lanihorne
Gorran Churchtown
Redruth
Bissoe
Playing Place
St Michael Penkevil
Lamorran
St Michael Caerhays
Gorran Haven
Pool
Tuckingmill
Cambrea
Carnkie
GWENNAP PIT
Carharrack
Carnon Downs
Old Kea
Treworga
Portholland
Boswinger
BOSWINGER
Gwennap
Penare
CAMBORNE
Lanner
Trelissick
Philleigh
114
SHIRE HORSE FARM
Perranarworthal
Penpol
Veryan
Portloe
Veryan Bay
Four Lanes
Devoran
Feock
TRELISSICK
Dodman Pt.
Troon
Ponsanooth
Treworlas
SOUTH WEST COAST PATH
Carne
Penhalvaen
Gerrans Bay
Stithians
Burnthouse
Trewithian
252
Stithians Res.
Mylor Bridge
St Just in Roseland
Nare Hd.
Penmarth
Carrick Roads
Gerrans
Portscatho
Crowan
Burras
Carnkie
Penryn
Flushing
Greeb Pt.
Falmouth
St Mawes
NATIONAL MARITIME
Bohortha
PENDENNIS CASTLE
Pendennis Pt.
Zone Pt.
Wendron
Seworgan
Treverva
Crowntown
Nanceg
Relea
A30
A39
A390
A392
A3059
A3058
A3075
A3076
A394
A393
A3047
A389
A391
A3078
B3314
B3267
B3276
B3274
B3275
B3279
B3285
B3284
B3277
B3298
B3301
B3303
B3280
B3297
B3289
B3287
B3273
P&R
0 1 2 3 4 5 6 miles
0 1 2 3 4 5 6 7 8 9 10 km
1 2 3 4 5
A B C D E F

5
Boscastle
Tintagel
Treknow
Trewarmett
Trebarwith
Treligga
Delabole
Valley Truckle
Camelford
Helstone
St Teath
Treveighan
Michaelstow
St Tudy
St Breward
Row
Wenfordbridge
Bradford
Blisland
Helland
Camel
Bodmin Forest
Bodmin
BODMIN AND WENFORD RAILWAY
LANHYDROCK HOUSE
Trebyan
Sweethouse
Redmoor
Lostwithiel
RESTORMEL CASTLE
Lanlivery
Luxulyan
Milltown
Penpillick
St Blazey
Par
Tywardreath
Golant
Polkerris
Menabilly
SHIPWRECK & HERITAGE CENTRE
Fowey
Polruan
Bodinnick
ST CATHERINE'S CASTLE
ST. AUSTELL BAY
Gribbin Hd.
Pencarrow Hd.
SOUTH WEST COAST PATH
Davidstow
Trewassa
Tremail
Hallworthy
Davidstow Moor
THE ARTHURIAN CENTRE
CORNWALL AT WAR
Crowdy Res.
High Moor
420 BROWN WILLY
331 GARROW TOR
MUSEUM OF SMUGGLING
Bolventor
Codda
Temple
Dozmary Pool
Colliford Lake
BODMIN MOOR
Millpool
Maidenwell
Cardinham
Warleggan
Mount
St Neot
Ley
CARNGLAZE SLATE CAVERNS
West Taphouse
East Taphouse
Doublebois
Dobwalls
Braddock
Couch's Mill
Bocaddon
Lerryn
Lanreath
St Veep
Penpoll
Lanteglos Highway
Trenewan
Lansallos
Herodsfoot
Muchlarnick
Pelynt
Polperro
HERITAGE MUSEUM
Talland Bay
Porthallow
Looe
West Looe
East Looe
OLD GUILDHALL
Looe Bay
St George's or Looe I.
Tremaine
Treneglos
Tresmeer
Cold Northcott
Tregeare
St Clether
Laneast
Altarnun
Trewint
Trewen
Polyphant
Lewannick
Congdon's Shop
Trebartha
North Hill
396 KILMAR TOR
Henwood
Rilla Mill
Upton Cross
THE HURLERS STONE CIRCLES
Minions
Siblyback Lake
369 CARADON HILL
Commonmoor
GOLITHA FALLS
KING DONIERT'S STONE
TRETHEVY QUOIT
Darite
St Cleer
Tremar
Merrymeet
Liskeard
St Pinnock
St Keyne
Trewidland
Duloe
Sandplace
Morval
St Martin
MONKEY SANCTUARY
North Petherwin
Bridgetown
Werrington
Yeolmbridge
Egloskerry
Langore
St Stephen's
Launceston
LAUNCESTON STEAM RAILWAY
HIDDEN VALLEY DISCOVERY PARK
Piper's Pool
TRETHORNE LEISURE FARM
Tregadillett
Daw's House
South Petherwin
Lawhitton
Dutson
Broadwoodwidger
Cross Green
DINGLE'S FAIRGROUND HERITAGE CENTRE
Stowford
Liftondown
Lifton
Tinhay
Portgate
Kelly
Chillaton
Bradstone
Lezant
Trekenner
Trebullett
Treburley
Rezare
Coad's Green
Milton Abbot
Dunterton
Sydenham Damerel
Bray Shop
Stoke Climsland
Horsebridge
Bathpool
Linkinhorne
South Hill
Downgate
Luckett
Latchley
Chilsworthy
Gunnislake
Gulworthy
Golberdon
Kelly Bray
KIT HILL
St Ann's Chapel
Drakewalls
Albaston
Pensilva
Trevigro
Haye
Callington
Harrowbarrow
DUPATH WELL HOUSE
COTEHELE
Calstock
St Dominick
TAMAR VALLEY
Bere Alston
Gang
St Ive
Newbridge
Pengover Green
Quethiock
St Mellion
Weir Quay
Pillaton
Menheniot
Blunts
Cargreen
Hatt
Landulph
Botusfleming
Tideford Cross
Landrake
SALTASH SERVICES
Tideford
Trematon
Saltash
Trerulefoot
Widegates
Hessenford
St Erney
St Stephens
MARY NEWMAN'S COTTAGE
St Germans
Polbathic
ANTONY HOUSE
Seaton
Downderry
Sheviock
Crafthole
Antony
Torpoint
Devonport
Portwrinkle
St John
Cremyll
Millbrook
SOUTH WEST COAST PATH
Freathy
Whitsand Bay
Kingsand
Cawsand
Rame
Rame Hd.
Penlee Pt.
ROSCOFF SANTANDER (Mar-Nov) ST MALO (Nov-Mar)
Cornwall
SX
A30
A39
A38
A390
A395
A388
A387
A374
B3254
B3257
B3247
B3253
B3359
B3269
B3268
B3266
B3262
B3263
B3314
TOLL
A B C D E F
5 6 7 8 9

DARTMOOR
DARTMOOR
NATIONAL PARK
FOREST
Dev
SX
TAMAR VALLEY
SOUTH
Plymouth
Tavistock
Saltash
Torpoint
Devonport
Plymstock
Plympton
Ivybridge
Yelverton
Horrabridge
Buckfastleigh
Kingsbridge
Salcombe
Modbury
Callington
Broadwoodwidger
Cross Green
Bridestowe
Thrushelton
Stowford
Lewdown
Lewtrenchard
Portgate
Lifton
Liftondown
Tinhay
Dutson
Lydford
Shortacombe
Coryton
Lawhitton
Kelly
Bradstone
Chillaton
North Brentor
Black Down
Willsworthy
Milton Abbot
Dunterton
Mary Tavy
Horndon
Cudliptown
Peter Tavy
Lamerton
Wilminstone
Sydenham Damerel
Horsebridge
Stoke Climsland
Luckett
Latchley
Downgate
Chilsworthy
Gunnislake
Gulworthy
St Ann's Chapel
Drakewalls
Albaston
Calstock
St Dominick
Bere Alston
Weir Quay
Bere Ferrers
Whitchurch
Grenofen
Higher Walreddon
Buckland Monachorum
Crapstone
Milton Combe
Lopwell
Walkhampton
Dousland
Sheepstor
Meavy
Clearbrook
Shaugh Prior
Bickleigh
Roborough
Tamerton Foliot
Wotter
Lee Moor
Merrivale
Rundlestone
Two Bridges
Princetown
Sampford Spiney
Whiteworks
Hexworthy
Dartmeet
Poundsgate
Buckland in the Moor
Holne
Buckfast
Dean
Dean Prior
Didworthy
Rattery
South Brent
Gidleigh
Murchington
Easton
Chagford
Teigncombe
Frenchbeer
Lettaford
North Bovey
Postbridge
Bellever
Widecombe in the Moor
Bonehill
Ponsworthy
Newbridge
St Mellion
Pillaton
Cargreen
Hatt
Botusfleming
Landulph
Landrake
Tideford
Trematon
St Erney
St Stephens
St Germans
St Budeaux
Crownhill
Eggbuckland
Sheviock
Crafthole
Antony
Portwrinkle
St John
Millbrook
Cremyll
Freathy
Kingsand
Cawsand
Rame
Rame Hd.
Penlee Pt.
Whitsand Bay
Drake's I.
The Sound
Hooe
Staddiscombe
Down Thomas
Bovisand Bay
Heybrook Bay
Wembury
Wembury Bay
Great Mew Stone
Knighton
Elburton
Brixton
Yealmpton
Newton Ferrers
Noss Mayo
Worswell
Stoke Pt.
Battisborough Cross
Mothecombe
Holbeton
Luson
Ermington
Westlake
Kingston
Ringmore
Bigbury
Bigbury on Sea
Burgh I.
Bantham
Thurlestone
Bigbury Bay
St Ann's Chapel
Drakeland Corner
Lutton
Cornwood
Harford
Sparkwell
Lee Mill
Bittaford
Cheston
Ugborough
Avonwick
Lincombe
Diptford
North Huish
Curtisknowle
Brownston
Loddiswell
Woodleigh
Aveton Gifford
Churchstow
West Alvington
Buckland
South Milton
Woolston
Galmpton
Hope
Bolt Tail
Bolberry
Malborough
Soar
East Portlemouth
Bolt Hd.
Ugborough Moor
Burrator Res.
Plym Forest
HIGH WILLHAYS
OKEMENT HILL
HANGINGSTONE HILL
CUT HILL
SITTAFORD TOR
ROUGH TOR
GT. MIS TOR
HAMELDOWN TOR
RYDER'S HILL
SHELL TOP
UPPER PLYM VALLEY
DENDLES WOOD
WISTMAN'S WOOD
DARTMOOR ZOOLOGICAL PARK
PLYM VALLEY RAILWAY
SALTRAM
ROYAL CITADEL
MOUNT EDGCUMBE
ANTONY HOUSE
MARY NEWMAN'S COTTAGE
MERCHANT'S HOUSE
BUCKLAND ABBEY
THE GARDEN HOUSE
COTEHELE
KIT HILL
DUPATH WELL HOUSE
LYDFORD GORGE
OVERBECKS MUSEUM AND GARDEN
SOUTH WEST COAST PATH
ROSCOFF
SANTANDER (Mar-Nov)
ST MALO (Nov-Mar)
A30
A386
A388
A390
A38
A374
A379
A3121
A381
B3212
B3357
B3362
B3257
B3251
B3373
B3413
B3432
B3417
B3271
B3249
B3247
B3186
B3392
B3213
B3196
B3387
B3206
0 1 2 3 4 5 6 miles
0 1 2 3 4 5 6 7 8 9 10 km

Dunsford
Shillingford St George
Alphington
P&R
Exeter
Topsham
Clyst St George
Woodbury Salterton
Newton Poppleford
Cotmaton
Sidmouth
Doccombe
Moretonhampstead
Bridford
Bridfordmills
Doddiscombsleigh
Exminster
Kennford
Ebford
Woodbury
Colaton Raleigh
Exton
Bicton Park
Black Hill
Yettington
Otterton
Ladram Bay
Christow
Higher Ashton
Lower Ashton
Kenn
Powderham
Powderham Castle
River Exe
Lympstone
A La Ronde
East Budleigh
Otterton Mill
South West Coast Path
Canonteign Falls
Trusham
Kenton
Withycombe Raleigh
Knowle
Budleigh Salterton
Danger Pt.
Lustleigh
Manaton
Water
Hennock
Starcross
Littleham
Fairlynch Arts Centre and Museum
Cockwood
Exmouth
World of Country Life
Dawlish Warren
Exmouth Model Railway
Straight Pt.
East Dartmoor Woods & Heaths
Bovey Tracey
Chudleigh
Ashcombe
Haytor Information Centre
Chudleigh Knighton
Craft Centre
Ugbrooke House
Brimley
Haytor Vale
Ilsington
Heathfield
Ideford
Luton
Dawlish
Little Haldon
Liverton
Coldeast
Stover
Trago Mills
Preston
Holcombe
Sigford
Teigngrace
Bishopsteignton
Teignmouth
Kingsteignton
Teign
Bickington
Highweek
Newton Abbot
Shaldon
Shaldon Wildlife Trust
Combeinteignhead
South West Coast Path
Bradley
West Ogwell
Netherton
Stokeinteignhead
Ashburton
East Ogwell
Decoy
Wolborough
Plant World
Babbacombe Bay
Prickly Ball Farm
Woodland
Denbury
Abbotskerswell
Coffinswell
Maidencombe
Forder Grn.
Kingskerswell
Torbryan
Ipplepen
North Whilborough
Barton
Watcombe
Landscove
Buckfast Butterflies & Dartmoor Otter Sanctuary
Broadhempston
Model Village
SX
SY
Babbacombe
Shiphay
Compton
Compton Castle
Torquay
Torre
Torre Abbey
Kent's Cavern Prehistoric Caves
Staverton
Cockington
Wellswood
Hope's Nose
Dartington
Littlehempston
Dartington Hall
Living Coasts
Dartington Cider Press Centre
Shinner's Bridge
Marldon
Berry Pomeroy Castle
Hollicombe
South Devon Railway
Berry Pomeroy
Blagdon
Torbay
Cott
Castle
Totnes
Kirkham
Paignton
Tigley
Collaton St Mary
Dartmouth Steam Railway
Belsford
Zoo
TORBAY
Tor Bay
Dart
Harberton
Goodrington
Golden Hind
Ashprington
Stoke Gabriel
Brixham
Berry Head
Harbertonford
Churston Ferrers
Galmpton
Greenway
Tuckenhay
Cornworthy
St Mary's Bay
Crabadon
Washbourne
Dittisham
River Dart
Sharkham Pt.
Halwell
Allaleigh
Capton
Hillhead
Moreleigh
Woodlands Leisure Park
Dartmouth
Ferry
Newcomen Engine House
Woodford
Blackawton
Kingswear
Scabbacombe Hd.
Millcombe
Bayards Cove Fort
Warfleet
Coleton Fishacre
Bowden
Dartmouth Castle
Mew Stone
East Allington
Stoke Fleming
Blackpool
Strete
Goveton
Harleston
Slapton
Sherford
Frittiscombe
Slapton Ley
Slapton Sands
Start Bay
Frogmore
Stokenham
Charleton
Chillington
Torcross
Kernborough
Beeson
South Pool
Beesands
Kellaton
Hallsands
South Allington
Start Point
East Prawle
Lannacombe Bay
Prawle Pt.
DEVON
A B C D E F
5 6 7 8 9

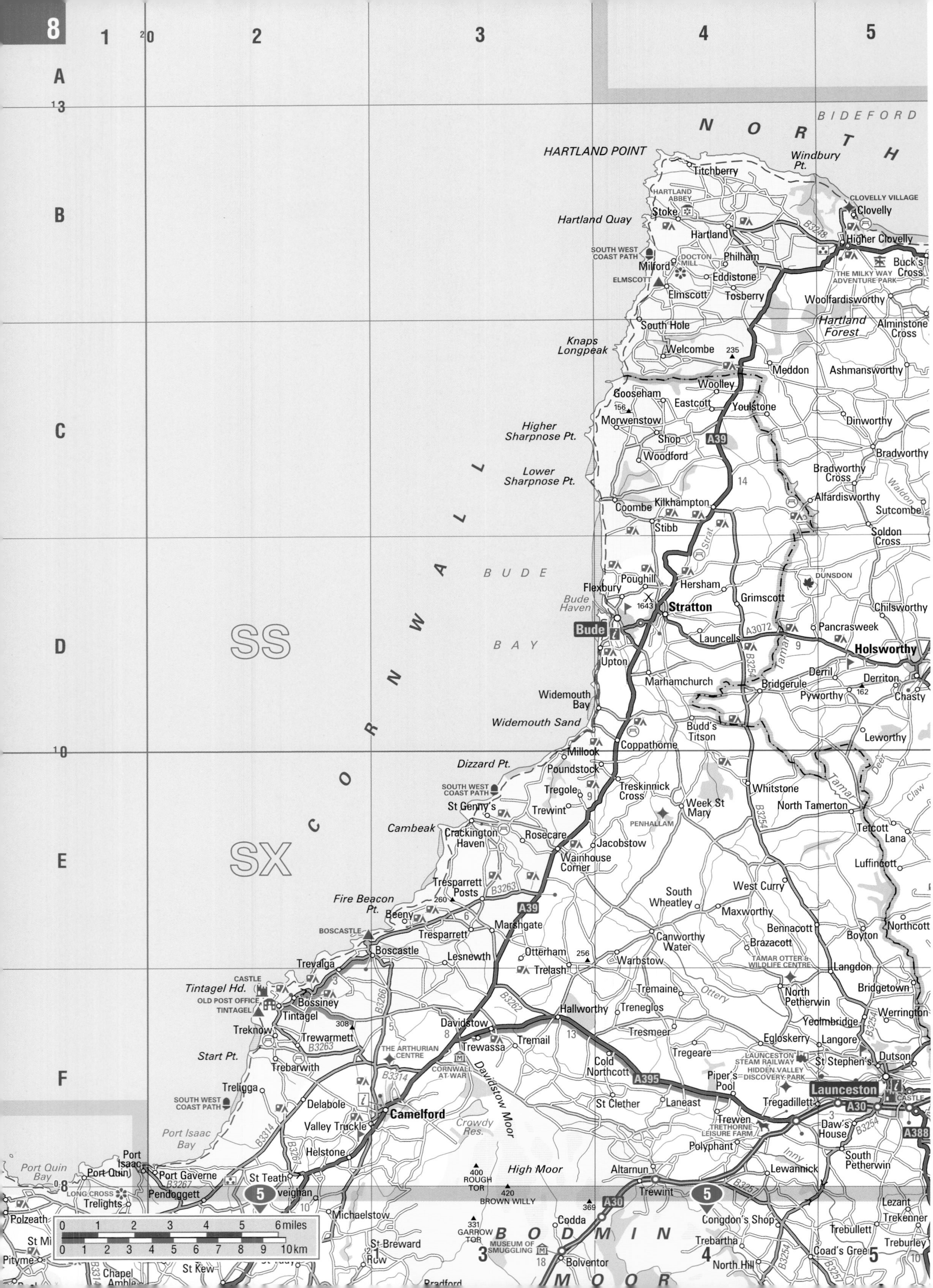
1
2
3
4
5
A
B
C
D
E
F
SS
SX
NORTH
BIDEFORD
HARTLAND POINT
Windbury Pt.
Titchberry
HARTLAND ABBEY
Stoke
Hartland Quay
Hartland
CLOVELLY VILLAGE
Clovelly
Higher Clovelly
B3248
SOUTH WEST COAST PATH
DOCTON MILL
Philham
Milford
Buck's Cross
ELMSCOTT
Eddistone
THE MILKY WAY ADVENTURE PARK
Elmscott
Tosberry
Woolfardisworthy
South Hole
Hartland Forest
Alminstone Cross
Knaps Longpeak
Welcombe
235
Meddon
Ashmansworthy
Woolley
Gooseham
156
Eastcott
Youlstone
Morwenstow
Dinworthy
Higher Sharpnose Pt.
Shop
A39
Woodford
Bradworthy
Lower Sharpnose Pt.
Bradworthy Cross
14
Waldon
Alfardisworthy
Coombe
Kilkhampton
Sutcombe
Stibb
Soldon Cross
CORNWALL
BUDE
Strat
DUNSDON
Poughill
Hersham
Flexbury
Grimscott
Bude Haven
1643
Stratton
Chilsworthy
Bude
A3072
Pancrasweek
BAY
Launcells
9
Holsworthy
Upton
B3254
Tamar
Derril
Derriton
Marhamchurch
Bridgerule
162
Pyworthy
Chasty
Widemouth Bay
Budd's Titson
Widemouth Sand
Lewworthy
Millook
Coppathorne
Dizzard Pt.
Poundstock
Deer
Treskinnick Cross
Whitstone
Tregole
9
Claw
St Gennys
Trewint
Week St Mary
North Tamerton
PENHALLAM
Cambeak
Crackington Haven
Rosecare
Tetcott
Lana
Jacobstow
Wainhouse Corner
Luffincott
Tresparrett Posts
B3263
Fire Beacon Pt.
260
South Wheatley
West Curry
Beeny
6
Maxworthy
Marshgate
Bennacott
BOSCASTLE
Tresparrett
Canworthy Water
Northcott
Boyton
Brazacott
Boscastle
Lesnewth
Otterham
256
TAMAR OTTER & WILDLIFE CENTRE
Warbstow
Langdon
Trevalga
Trelash
CASTLE
Tintagel Hd.
3
Tremaine
Ottery
North Petherwin
Bridgetown
OLD POST OFFICE
Bossiney
B3266
B3262
Treneglos
TINTAGEL
Hallworthy
Werrington
Tintagel
308
Yeolmbridge
Treknow
Davidstow
Tresmeer
Trewarmett
8
Tremail
13
Egloskerry
Langore
B3263
Trewassa
THE ARTHURIAN CENTRE
Dutson
Start Pt.
Tregeare
LAUNCESTON STEAM RAILWAY
St Stephen's
Trebarwith
Cold Northcott
HIDDEN VALLEY DISCOVERY PARK
B3314
CORNWALL AT WAR
Davidstow Moor
A395
Piper's Pool
Treligga
Launceston
SOUTH WEST COAST PATH
Delabole
St Clether
Laneast
Tregadillett
A30
CASTLE
Camelford
Crowdy Res.
Trewen
Daw's House
Valley Truckle
TRETHORNE LEISURE FARM
A388
Port Isaac Bay
B3254
Helstone
Polyphant
Inny
South Petherwin
Port Isaac
Port Quin Bay
B3267
High Moor
400 ROUGH TOR
Altarnun
Lewannick
Port Quin
Port Gaverne
St Teath
Trewint
B3257
LONG CROSS
Trelights
Pendoggett
5
veighan
10
420 BROWN WILLY
A30
5
Lezant
Trekenner
Polzeath
369
Michaelstow
Codda
Congdon's Shop
331 GARROW TOR
BODMIN MOOR
Trebullett
St Mi
Treburley
0 1 2 3 4 5 6 miles
0 1 2 3 4 5 6 7 8 9 10 km
St Breward
MUSEUM OF SMUGGLING
Trebartha
Pityme
Row
18
B3254
Coad's Green
Chapel Amble
St Kew
Bolventor
North Hill
Bradford

LUNDY (Mar-Oct)
Braunton Burrows
Chivenor
Taw
Barnstaple
Goodleigh
Brayford
High Bray
North Heasley
Pilt
MUSEUM OF BARNSTAPLE & NORTH DEVON
Gunn
Charles
Heasley Mill
South Radworthy
Fremington
Westacott
Yelland
Bickington
P&R
Bickleton
Newport
West Buckland
East Buckland
NORTH DEVON MARITIME MUSEUM
Instow
Bishops Tawton
Landkey
Swimbridge Newland
Swimbridge
NORTHAM BURROWS
Appledore
Westward Ho!
TAPELEY PARK GDNS
Tawstock
Torridge
Westleigh
Northam
North Molton
BAY
DEVON
Filleigh
Orchard Hill
Horwood
Newton Tracey
Ensis
Herner
Cobbaton
THE BIG SHEEP
Eastleigh
Mole
Bideford
QUINCE HONEY FARM
Abbotsham
BURTON ART GALL & MUS
East-the-Water
Hiscott
Chapelton
East Stowford
COBBATON COMBAT COLLECTION
Woodtown
Handy Cross
Alverdiscott
Fishleigh Barton
Chittlehampton
South Molton
Bish Mill
Yeo
Fairy Cross
ATLANTIC VILLAGE
Landcross
Buck's Mills
Horns Cross
Ford
Woodtown
Umberleigh
Clapworthy
Bishops Nympton
Yarnscombe
Atherington
Littleham
Goldworthy
Warkleigh
George Nympton
Alswear
Satterleigh
Langridge Ford
Marians
Weare Giffard
Parkham
Buckland Brewer
Monkleigh
Sherwood Green
High Bickington
Chittlehamholt
Parkham Ash
High Bullen
DARTINGTON CRYSTAL
Romansleigh
St Giles in the Wood
Frithelstock
Great Torrington
King's Nympton
Frithelstock Stone
Taddiport
Tythecott
Kingscott
Roborough
R.H.S. GARDEN ROSEMOOR
West Putford
East Putford
Little Torrington
Burrington
Cadbury Barton
Week
Elstone
GNOME RESERVE & GARDEN
Langtree
Beaford
Bulkworthy
Stibb Cross
Riddlecombe
Chulmleigh
West Worlington
Cheldon
Peters Marland
Ashreigney
Abbots Bickington
Newton St Petrock
Woollaton
Winswell
Chawleigh
Merton
Dolton
SS
Huish
Ashley
Venn Green
Milton Damerel
Hollocombe
Filleigh
Buckland Filleigh
Dowland
Wembworthy
Eastington
Holsworthy Beacon
Petrockstow
Shebbear
Meeth
Iddesleigh
Winkleigh
Lapford
Thornbury
Coldridge
Nymet Rowland
Bradford
Brushford
Woodacott
Devon
Sheepwash
Broadwood Kelly
Black Torrington
Cookbury
Holemoor
Monkokehampton
West Leigh
Bondleigh
East Leigh
Highampton
Hatherleigh
Zeal Monachorum
Down St Mary
Brandis Corner
Whimble
Hollacombe
Honeychurch
Graddon Moor
Chilla
WINSFORD WALLED GARDEN
Exbourne
Lew
Jacobstowe
North Tawton
Bow
Halwill Junction
Sampford Courtenay
Nymet Tracey
Colebrook
Halwill
Beaworthy
Inwardleigh
Clawton
Northlew
Itton
Oak Cross
Hillerton
Ashbury
Patchacott
DARTMOOR RAILWAY
Quoditch
Folly Gate
Taw Green
BROADBURY
Spreyton
Okehampton
Ashwater
Eworthy
Sticklepath
Ettisleigh
Henford
South Tawton
Carey
Germansweek
Boasley Cross
FINCH FOUNDRY
South Zeal
Chapmans Well
Thorndon Cross
Belstone
Whiddon Down
Cheriton Bishop
Virginstow
OKEHAMPTON (Dartmoor)
East Panson
Roadford Res.
CASTLE
Okehampton Camp
SOURTON CROSS SERVICES
Meldon
BRACKEN TOR
Crockernwell
Gridley Corner
Bratton Clovelly
Okehampton Common
Drewsteignton
Grinacombe Moor
COSDON HILL
St Giles on the Hth.
Throwleigh
CASTLE DROGO
Sourton
YES TOR
Sandypark
Wonson
Broadwoodwidger
Thrushel
Bridestowe
BLACK-A-TOR COPSE
HIGH WILLHAYS
Easton
Teign
Gidleigh
Murchington
Cross Green
Bridestowe and Sourton Common
SX
Chagford
Thrushelton
DINGLE'S FAIRGROUND HERITAGE CENTRE
Stowford
Lewdown
Shortacombe
OKEMENT HILL
Teigncombe
DARTMOOR
Liftondown
Portgate
Lewtrenchard
HANGINGSTONE HILL
Frenchbeer
Lifton
Tinhay
Lydford
LYDFORD
Lettaford
THE MINIATURE PONY CENTRE
North Bovey
Coryton
LYDFORD GORGE
NATIONAL
Lawhitton
CUT HILL
SITTAFORD TOR
Kelly
Chillaton
North Brentor
Black Down
Willsworthy
Manaton
Tamar
GRIMSPOUND
Bradstone
DARTMOOR
PARK
HAMELDOWN TOR
Milton Abbot
Horndon
POSTBRIDGE INFORMATION CENTRE
ROUGH TOR
Postbridge
Dunterton
Mary Tavy
Cudliptown
HOUND TOR
Rezare
Peter Tavy
Bellever
FOREST
Bonehill
Widecombe in the Moor
Haytor Vale
Sydenham Damerel
Lamerton
Wilminstone
GT. MIS TOR
WISTMAN'S WOOD
LLEVER (Dartmoor)
PREHISTORIC
Merrivale
A39
A361
A377
A386
A388
A3072
A3079
A3124
A30
A382
B3233
B3232
B3227
B3217
B3226
B3096
B3042
B3220
B3215
B3206
B3212
B3362
B3387

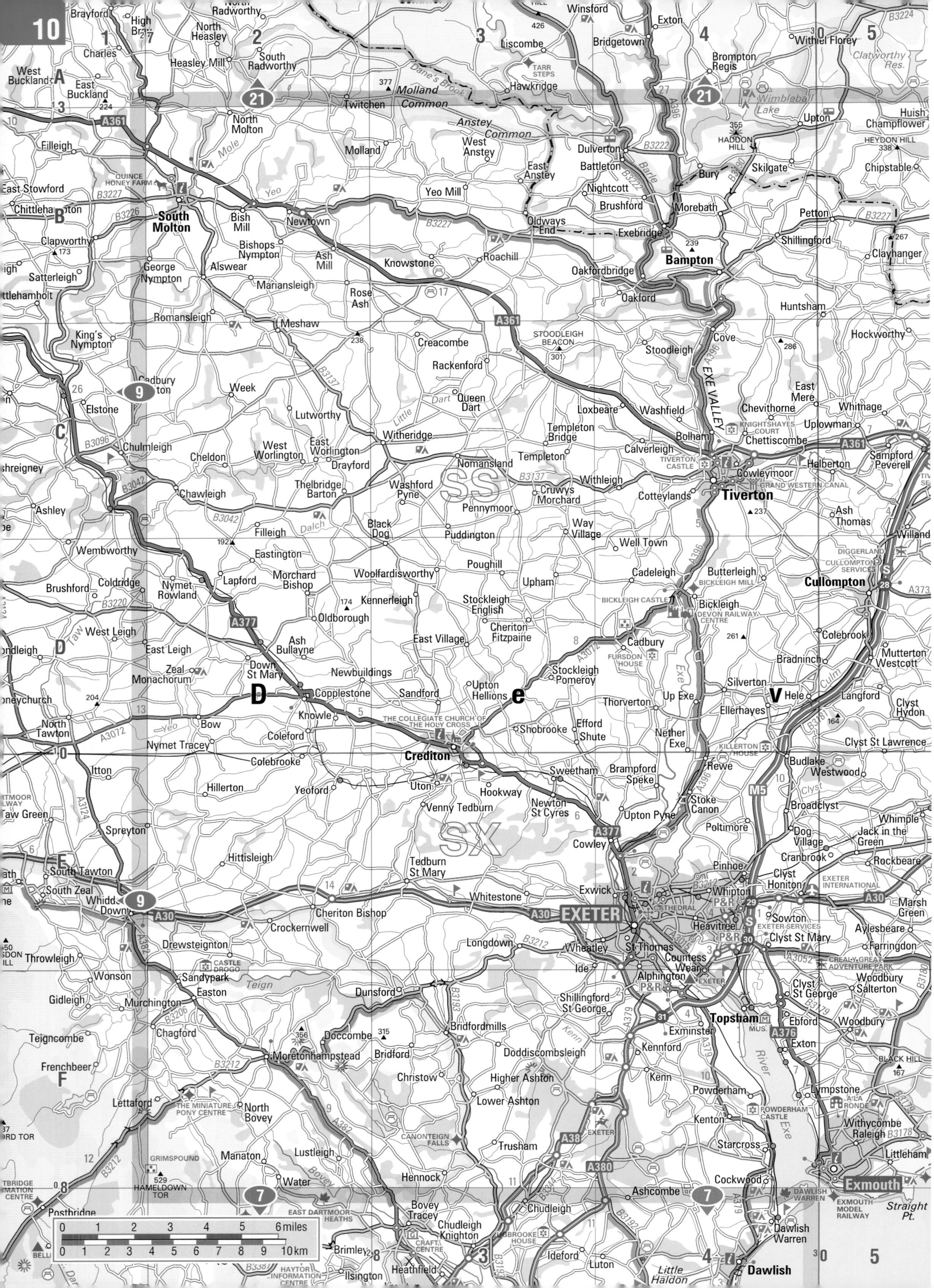

Brayford
High Bray
North Radworthy
North Heasley
Heasley Mill
South Radworthy
Winsford
Exton
Bridgetown
Liscombe
Withiel Florey
Clatworthy Res.
Charles
West Buckland
East Buckland
Twitchen
Molland Common
TARR STEPS
Hawkridge
Dane's Brook
Brompton Regis
Wimbleball Lake
Huish Champflower
Upton
North Molton
Anstey Common
West Anstey
Molland
HADDON HILL
HEYDON HILL
Filleigh
Dulverton
Battleton
East Anstey
Skilgate
Chipstable
QUINCE HONEY FARM
East Stowford
Chittlehampton
South Molton
Bish Mill
Newtown
Yeo Mill
Nightcott
Brushford
Morebath
Bury
Petton
Clapworthy
Satterleigh
Bishops Nympton
Ash Mill
Oldways End
Exebridge
Bampton
Shillingford
Clayhanger
George Nympton
Alswear
Mariansleigh
Knowstone
Roachill
Oakfordbridge
Oakford
Rose Ash
Romansleigh
Meshaw
Huntsham
King's Nympton
Creacombe
STOODLEIGH BEACON
Stoodleigh
Cove
Hockworthy
Rackenford
EXE VALLEY
Cadbury Barton
Week
Queen Dart
Loxbeare
Washfield
East Mere
Chevithorne
Whitnage
Elstone
Lutworthy
Little Dart
Templeton Bridge
KNIGHTSHAYES COURT
Uplowman
Chulmleigh
West Worlington
East Worlington
Witheridge
Templeton
Calverleigh
Bolham
Chettiscombe
Sampford Peverell
Cheldon
Drayford
Nomansland
TIVERTON CASTLE
Cowleymoor
Halberton
Chawleigh
Thelbridge Barton
Washford Pyne
Cruwys Morchard
Withleigh
Cotteylands
Tiverton
GRAND WESTERN CANAL
Ashley
Pennymoor
Ash Thomas
Filleigh
Black Dog
Dalch
Puddington
Way Village
Willand
Wembworthy
Eastington
Well Town
DIGGERLAND
CULLOMPTON SERVICES
Brushford
Coldridge
Nymet Rowland
Lapford
Morchard Bishop
Woolfardisworthy
Poughill
Upham
Cadeleigh
Butterleigh
BICKLEIGH MILL
Cullompton
BICKLEIGH CASTLE
Bickleigh
DEVON RAILWAY CENTRE
Kennerleigh
Stockleigh English
Oldborough
Cheriton Fitzpaine
West Leigh
East Village
Cadbury
FURSDON HOUSE
Colebrook
Mutterton
Westcott
Bradninch
East Leigh
Ash Bullayne
Zeal Monachorum
Down St Mary
Newbuildings
Stockleigh Pomeroy
Silverton
Hele
Langford
Copplestone
Sandford
Upton Hellions
Thorverton
Up Exe
Ellerhayes
Clyst Hydon
North Tawton
Knowle
Bow
Coleford
THE COLLEGIATE CHURCH OF THE HOLY CROSS
Shobrooke
Efford
Shute
Nether Exe
KILLERTON HOUSE
Clyst St Lawrence
Nymet Tracey
Colebrooke
Crediton
Budlake
Westwood
Itton
Hillerton
Yeoford
Uton
Sweetham
Brampford Speke
Rewe
Hookway
Venny Tedburn
Newton St Cyres
Upton Pyne
Stoke Canon
Broadclyst
Taw Green
Spreyton
Poltimore
Whimple
Dog Village
Jack in the Green
Cowley
Cranbrook
Rockbeare
Hittisleigh
Tedburn St Mary
Pinhoe
South Tawton
South Zeal
Clyst Honiton
EXETER INTERNATIONAL
Whiddon Down
Cheriton Bishop
Whitestone
Exwick
Whipton
Marsh Green
EXETER
CATHEDRAL
Crockernwell
Heavitree
Sowton
EXETER SERVICES
Aylesbeare
Drewsteignton
Longdown
Wheatley
St Thomas
Clyst St Mary
Farringdon
Throwleigh
CASTLE DROGO
Ide
Countess Wear
CREALY GREAT ADVENTURE PARK
Wonson
Sandypark
Teign
Alphington
Woodbury Salterton
Easton
Dunsford
Shillingford St George
Clyst St George
Gidleigh
Murchington
Topsham
Ebford
Woodbury
Chagford
Bridfordmills
Exminster
Teigncombe
Doccombe
Kennford
Exton
Moretonhampstead
Bridford
Doddiscombsleigh
BLACK HILL
Frenchbeer
Christow
Higher Ashton
Kenn
Lympstone
Powderham
Lettaford
THE MINIATURE PONY CENTRE
North Bovey
Lower Ashton
POWDERHAM CASTLE
A LA RONDE
Kenton
Withycombe Raleigh
CANONTEIGN FALLS
Trusham
Starcross
Littleham
Manaton
Lustleigh
GRIMSPOUND
HAMELDOWN TOR
Water
Hennock
Cockwood
Exmouth
Ashcombe
DAWLISH WARREN
EXMOUTH MODEL RAILWAY
Straight Pt.
Postbridge
EAST DARTMOOR HEATHS
Bovey Tracey
Chudleigh
Chudleigh Knighton
UGBROOKE HOUSE
Dawlish Warren
CRAFT CENTRE
Brimley
Ideford
Heathfield
HAYTOR INFORMATION CENTRE
Ilsington
Luton
Little Haldon
Dawlish
SS
SX
6 miles
10 km

West Bagborough
Courtway
Goathurst
North Petherton
Huntworth
Westonzoyland Pumping Station
King's Sedge Moor
Willett
Lydeard St Lawrence
Temple of Harmony
Fyne Court
Broomfield
Northmoor Green or Moorland
Middlezoy
Tolland
East Combe
Cothelstone
Brompton Ralph
Combe Florey
Cushuish
North Newton
Othery
Pathe
High Ham
Henley
Clatworthy
Tarr
Thurloxton
Bridgwater & Taunton Canal
Maunsel Locks
Burrow-bridge
Stembridge Tower
Langley Marsh
Priors
Bishops Lydeard
Fulford
Pickney
Kingston St Mary
Hestercombe Gardens
Hedging
Lyng
Stathe
Aller
Low Ham
Maundown
Wiveliscombe
Fitzhead
Nailsbourne
West Monkton
West Lyng
Athelney
Parrett
Pitney
Halse
Cheddon Fitzpaine
Monkton Heathfield
Durston
Creech Heathfield
Tone
Stoke St Gregory
Langport
Vale of Taunton Deane
Preston Bowyer
Heathfield
Staplegrove
Bathpool
North End
Meare Green
Willows & Wetlands Visitor Centre
West Sedge Moor
Huish Episcopi
Milverton
Hillcommon
Norton Fitzwarren
Creech St Michael
Knapp
Curry Rivel
Langport & River Parrett Visitor Centre
Waterrow
Oake
Bishop's Hull
Somerset Cricket Museum
Ruishton
North Curry
Muchelney
Abbey
Bathealton
Hillfarance
Taunton
Thornfalcon
Drayton
East Nynehead
Bradford-on-Tone
Henlade
Langford Budville
Nynehead
Sheppy's Cider
Fivehead
Isle
Kittisford
Runnington
Trull
Stoke St Mary
Wrantage
Appley
Cothay
Wellington
Staplehay
Taunton Deane Services
Orchard Portman
West Hatch
Hatch Beauchamp
Curry Mallet
Isle Brewers
Isle Abbotts
Kingsbury Episcopi
Ashbrittle
Thorne St Margaret
Rockwell Green
West Buckland
Thurlbear
Hambridge
Holywell Lake
Beercrocombe
Pitminster
Corfe
Hatch Green
Westport
West Lambrook
East Lambrook
East Lambrook Manor
Martock
Holcombe Rogus
Sampford Arundel
Angersleigh
Blagdon Hill
Staple Fitzpaine
Puckington
Barrington Court
Barrington
South Petherton
Bower Hinton
Wrangway
Ford Street
Bickenhall
Ilton
Westleigh
Blackdown Hills
Staple Hill
Curland
Barrington Hill
Ashill
Stocklinch
Shepton Beauchamp
Burlescombe
Nicholashayne
Windmill Hill
Broadway
Ashwell
Norton sub Hamdon
Clayhidon
Horton
Ilminster
Seavington St Michael
Stratton
Appledore
Rosemary Lane
Churchstanton
Fyfett
Buckland St Mary
Seavington St Mary
Chiselborough
Culm Valley
Culmstock
Blackdown
Donyatt
Perry's Cider
Lopen
Uffculme
Hemyock
Stapley
Crock Street
Kingstone
Dinnington
West Chinnock
Coldharbour Mill
Hackpen Hill
Churchinford
Bishopswood
Combe St Nicholas
Dowlish Wake
Hinton St George
Merriott
Craddock
Bolham Water
Cricket Malherbie
Smithincott
Ashill
Marsh
Whitestaunton
Hornsbury Mill
Chillington
Abbey
Smeatharpe
Wadeford
Cudworth
Chaffcombe
Crewkerne
Blackborough
Newcott
Howley
Cricket St Thomas
Hewish
Yarcombe
Wambrook
Chard
Misterton
Kentisbeare
Sheldon
Dunkeswell
Upottery
Forton
Whatley
Wayford
Winsham
Clapton
Seaborough
Black Down
Luppitt
Rawridge
Tatworth
Dulford
Kerswell
Hills
Beacon
Stockland
Furley
South Chard
Forde Abbey and Gardens
Drimpton
Norman's Green
Broadhembury
Millhayes
Chardstock
Tytherleigh
Thorncombe
Burstock
Wick
Membury
Alston
Broadwindsor
Monkton
Holditch
Plymtree
Combe Raleigh
Heathstock
Payhembury
Cotleigh
Smallridge
Birdsmoorgate
The Craft and Design Centre
Tale
Awliscombe
Ham
Colestocks
Buckerell
Dalwood
Hawkchurch
Marshalsea
Bettiscombe
Wilmington
Honiton
Weycroft
Netherbury
Talaton
Feniton
Offwell
Burrow Farm
Axminster
Marshwood
Pilsdon
Fenny Bridges
Escot Park
Gittisham
Alfington
Shute
Kilmington
Shute Barton
Broad Oak
Fairmile
Ottery St Mary
Church Green
Wootton Fitzpaine
Whitchurch Canonicorum
Northleigh
Whitford
Farway
East Devon
Musbury
Ryall
West Hill
Broad Down
Southleigh
Colyton
Morcombelake
Char
Symondsbury
Bridport
Wiggaton
Uplyme
Charmouth
Charmouth Heritage Coast Centre
Tipton St John
Sidbury
Colyford
Combpyne
Lyme Regis
Chideock
Blackbury Camp
Axmouth
Rousdon
Aquarium
Dinosaurland
Seatown
Eype
Venn Ottery
Harcombe
Seaton Tramway
South West Coast Path
Harpford
Bowd
Sidford
Beer Quarry Caves
Axmouth to Lyme Regis Undercliffs
West Bay
Newton Poppleford
Weston
Vicarage
Beer
Seaton
Charlton Bay
Hawkerland
Marine House
Seaton Bay
Lyme Bay
Sid
Salcombe Regis
Branscombe
Colaton Raleigh
Cotmaton
Dorset & East Devon Coast World Heritage Site
Beer Hd.
Bicton Park
Sidmouth
Yettington
Ladram Bay
Otterton
Otterton Mill
East Budleigh
Otter
South West Coast Path
Knowle
Budleigh Salterton
Danger Pt.
Fairlynch Arts Centre and Museum
World of Country Life
ST
SY
M5
A30
A35
A38
A303
A358
A361
A372
A378
A3052
A373
A375
B3170
B3168
B3162
B3165
B3178
B3174
B3180
B3227
B3224
B3188
B3187
B3391
B3440
B3177
B3176
B3172
B3261
B3167
B3164
B3165
B3259
12
22
5
6
7
8
9
A
B
C
D
E
F
G

King's Sedge Moor
SOMERSET LEVELS
Middlezoy
Othery
Pathe
Moorland
Burrow-bridge
Stathe
Athelney
Stoke St Gregory
West Sedge Moor
Curry Rivel
Henley
High Ham
Low Ham
Aller
Langport
Huish Episcopi
LANGPORT & R PARRETT VISITOR CENTRE
Muchelney
Drayton
Fivehead
Isle Brewers
Isle Abbotts
Hambridge
Puckington
Ilton
Stocklinch
Shepton Beauchamp
Barrington
BARRINGTON COURT
Ashwell
Ilminster
Donyatt
PERRYS CIDER
Kingstone
Dowlish Wake
Cricket Malherbie
HORNSBURY MILL
Cudworth
Chaffcombe
Cricket St Thomas
Chillington
Hinton St George
Dinnington
Seavington St Mary
Seavington St Michael
Lopen
Over Stratton
South Petherton
West Lambrook
East Lambrook
E. LAMBROOK MANOR
Westport
Kingsbury Episcopi
Stapleton
Long Load
Long Sutton
Pitney
Somerton
Dundon
Compton Dundon
Littleton
Street
Butleigh
Baltonsborough
Barton St David
Kingweston
Keinton Mandeville
Charlton Adam
Charlton Mackerell
LYTES CARY MANOR
Kingsdon
Cary Fitzpaine
West Lydford
East Lydford
Lydford-on-Fosse
Southwood
Hornblotton Green
Sutton
Alford
Lovington
Ansford
Castle Cary
Pitcombe
Cole
Redlynch
Stoney Stoke
Shepton Montague
Hardway
ALFRED'S TOWER
Charlton Musgrove
Leigh Common
HADSPEN GARDEN
Bratton Seymour
Wincanton
Bayford
Stoke Trister
Yarlington
North Cadbury
Galhampton
Babcary
North Barrow
South Barrow
HAYNES MOTOR MUS
Sparkford
Holton
Maperton
South Cadbury
Compton Pauncefoot
Blackford
Lattiford
North Cheriton
South Cheriton
Horsington
Abbas Combe
Templecombe
Charlton Horethorne
Corton Denham
Sutton Montis
Queen Camel
West Camel
Podimore
Northover
Ilchester
Yeovilton
FLEET AIR ARM MUS
Bridgehampton
Limington
Chilton Cantelo
Marston Magna
SANDFORD ORCAS MANOR HOUSE
Rimpton
Sandford Orcas
Adber
Ashington
Tintinhull
TINTINHULL GARDEN
Chilthorne Domer
Ash
Coat
Martock
Hurst
Bower Hinton
TREASURER'S HO
Stoke sub Hamdon
STOKE-SUB-HAMDON PRIORY
MONTACUTE HOUSE
Montacute
HAM HILL
Norton sub Hamdon
Odcombe
Brympton
Chiselborough
West Chinnock
Preston Plucknett
Yeovil
YEOVIL
Yeovil Marsh
Mudford
Trent
Nether Compton
Over Compton
Poyntington
Oborne
Sherborne
SHERBORNE CASTLE
SHERBORNE OLD CASTLE
Goathill
Milborne Port
Milborne Wick
Stowell
Yenston
Henstridge Ash
Henstridge Marsh
Henstridge
Stalbridge
Purse Caundle
Stalbridge Weston
Haydon
North Wootton
Stourton Caundle
Bishop's Caundle
Alweston
Lydlinch
Folke
Longburton
Holwell
Woodbridge
King's Stag
Crouch Hill
BLACKMOOR VALE
West Coker
North Coker
East Coker
Barwick
Stoford
Bradford Abbas
Thornford
Lillington
East Chinnock
HARDINGTON MOOR
Hardington Mandeville
Ryme Intrinseca
Beer Hackett
Yetminster
Closworth
Pendomer
Merriott
Haselbury Plucknett
North Perrott
Hardington Marsh
Crewkerne
Hewish
Misterton
South Perrott
Halstock
Melbury Osmond
Chetnole
Leigh
Holnest
Glanvilles Wootton
Pulham
Hazelbury Bryan
Hermitage
Middlemarsh
Westfields
Mappowder
Dultish
Whatley
Winsham
Wayford
Clapton
Seaborough
Mosterton
Chedington
Corscombe
West Chelborough
Melbury Sampford
Melbury Bubb
Evershot
Hilfield
Lyon's Gate
Buckland Newton
Minterne Magna
MINTERNE HOUSE & GARDENS
Batcombe
Holywell
Frome St Quintin
Up Cerne
Alton Pancras
Plush
Chard
FORDE ABBEY AND GARDENS
Thorncombe
Drimpton
Holditch
Burstock
Broadwindsor
THE CRAFT AND DESIGN CENTRE
Birdsmoorgate
Hawkchurch
Marshalsea
Bettiscombe
Beaminster
Rampisham
Stoke Abbott
Netherbury
Marshwood
Pilsdon
Mapperton
MAPPERTON
Hooke
Wraxall
Cattistock
Up Sydling
Cerne Abbas
CERNE ABBAS GIANT
Sydling St Nicholas
Piddletrenthide
White Lackington
Piddlehinton
Chilfrome
Toller Porcorum
Maiden Newton
Nether Cerne
Godmanstone
Melplash
North Poorton
Toller Fratrum
HOG CLIFF
Forston
Charlton Down
Broad Oak
Salwayash
West Milton
Powerstock
Nettlecombe
Wynford Eagle
Frampton
Grimstone
Wootton Fitzpaine
Whitchurch Canonicorum
Ryall
Dottery
Bradpole
Loders
Eggardon Down
Uploders
West Compton
Muckleford
Stratton
Charminster
Bradford Peverell
Morcombelake
Charmouth
Symondsbury
Bridport
Chideock
Eype
Seatown
Walditch
Bothenhampton
Shipton Gorge
Askerswell
Chilcombe
Kingston Russell
Compton Valence
Winterbourne Abbas
Dorchester
THE TUTANKHAMUN EXHIBITION
Stinsford
Kingston Maurward
HARDY'S COTTAGE GARDEN
Lyme Regis
CHARMOUTH HERITAGE COAST CENTRE
AQUARIUM
DINOSAURLAND
SOUTH WEST COAST PATH
West Bay
Litton Cheney
Long Bredy
LITTON CHENEY
POOR LOT BARROWS
NINE STONES
Winterbourne Steepleton
MILITARY MUSEUM
THE DINOSAUR MUSEUM
Martinstown
MAIDEN CASTLE
Winterborne Monkton
West Stafford
Whitcombe
Winterborne Herringston
West Knighton
Broadmayne
Burton Bradstock
Puncknowle
Littlebredy
VALLEY OF STONES
KINGSTON RUSSELL STONE CIRCLE
Black Down
HARDY MONUMENT
Swyre
West Bexington
Portesham
SOUTH WEST COAST PATH
DORSET & EAST DEVON COAST WORLD HERITAGE SITE
Abbotsbury
ABBOTSBURY CHILDREN'S FARM
SUB TROPICAL GARDENS
ST CATHERINES CHAPEL
SWANNERY
Rodden
Upwey
Bincombe
WHITE HORSE
Poxwell
Broadwey
Littlemoor
Preston
Upton
Osmington
Osmington Mills
Langton Herring
Nottington
Overcombe
JORDAN HILL ROMAN TEMPLE
Radipole
CHESIL BEACH
Chickerell
BENNETTS WATER GARDENS
SEA LIFE
Melcombe Regis
Westham
Weymouth
WEYMOUTH
Charlestown
NOTHE FORT
BREWER'S QUAY AND TIMEWALK
Rodwell
Wyke Regis
Portland Harbour
Weymouth
BREWER'S QUAY AND TIMEWALK
Rodwell
Wyke Regis
Portland Harbour
WEYMOUTH & PORTLAND NATIONAL SAILING ACADEMY
PORTLAND
PORTLAND CASTLE
Fortuneswell
West Bay
Grove
Easton
Weston
PORTLAND
MUSEUM
Southwell
Bill of Portland
Dorset
DORSET
ST
SY
0 1 2 3 4 5 6 miles
0 1 2 3 4 5 6 7 8 9 10 km

Stourton
White Sheet Hill
Down
Berwick St Leonard
Fonthill Bishop
Vale of Wardour
Grovely Wood
Newton
Mere
West Knoyle
Hindon
Chilmark
Teffont Magna
Dinton
Baverstock
Ditchampton
Stratford Sub Castle
Old Sarum
New Sarum
Zeals
Penselwood
Bourton
Queen Oak
The Green
Fonthill Gifford
Ridge
Teffont Evias
Chicksgrove
Barford St Martin
Wilton
Burcombe
Quidhampton
Wilton House
Bemerton
Netherhampton
Huntingford
East Knoyle
Tisbury
Compton Chamberlayne
West Harnham
East Harnham
Milton on Stour
Sedgehill
Newtown
Hatch
Sutton Mandeville
Fovant
Cucklington
Gillingham
Elm Hill
Swallowcliffe
Cranborne
Stratford Tony
Coombe Bissett
Salisbury
Wyke
Ham Common
Semley
Old Wardour Castle
Ansty
Prescombe Down
Broad Chalke
Bishopstone
Odstock
Buckhorn Weston
Motcombe
Donhead St Andrew
White Sheet Hill
West End
Fifield Bavant
Stoke Farthing
Croucheston
Homington
Nunton
Kington Magna
Knap Corner
Donhead St Mary
Milkwell
Mount Sorrel
Ebbesbourne Wake
West Stour
Ivy Cross
Berwick St John
Alvediston
Bowerchalke
East Stour
Shaftesbury
Ludwell
Charlton
Woodminton
Chase and
Rockbourne Down
Wick Down
Fifehead Magdalen
Stour Provost
Stour Row
Cann
Cann Common
Win Green
Martin Drove End
Guy's Marsh
Todber
Melbury Abbas
Melbury Down
Woodyates
Martin
Martin Down
Tidpit
Whitsbury
Breamore House & Museum
Upper Street
Pillwell
Marnhull
Margaret Marsh
Bedchester
Compton Abbas
Ashmore
Tollard Royal
Chase
Deanland
Sixpenny Handley
Pentridge
Pentridge Hill
Rockbourne
Outwick
Roman Villa
Burgate
Hinton St Mary
East Orchard
West Orchard
Fontmell Magna
Larmer Tree Gardens
Woodcutts
West
Damerham
Sturminster Newton
Manston
Sutton Waldron
Dean
Sandleheath
Ashford
Fiddleford Manor
Fiddleford
Hammoon
Iwerne Courtney or Shroton
Iwerne Minster
Farnham
Monkton Up Wimborne
Alderholt Mill
Fordingbridge
Newton
Broad Oak
Child Okeford
Hambledon Hill
Stubhampton
Chettle House
Chettle
Cashmoor
Cranborne
Manor Garden
Alderholt
Bickton
Fifehead Neville
Tarrant Gunville
Wiltshire
Gussage St Michael
Wimborne St Giles
Cripplestyle
Edmondsham Ho
Edmondsham
Charing Cross
Shillingstone
Tarrant Hinton
Knowlton Church
Gussage All Saints
Heavy Horse Centre
Okeford Fitzpaine
Long Crichel
Knowlton
Verwood
Ibsley
Kingston
Stourpaine
Pimperne
Tarrant Launceston
Moor Crichel
Downs
Woodlands
Ringwood
Durweston
Tarrant Monkton
Ringwood Forest
Ibberton
Turnworth
Royal Signals Museum
Manswood
Horton
Blashford
Woolland
Bryanston
Blandford Forum
Tarrant Rawston
Witchampton
Chalbury
Chalbury Common
Stoke Wake
Tarrant Rushton
Hinton Martell
Mannington
Three Legged Cross
Moors Valley
Ashley
Higher Ansty
Blandford St Mary
Tarrant Keyneston
Gaunt's Common
Stanbridge
Holt
Holt Heath
Ashley Heath
St Ives
St Leonards Services
Winterborne Houghton
Winterborne Stickland
Charlton Marshall
Tarrant Crawford
Allen
Broom Hill
West Moors
Hilton
Winterborne Clenston
Thorncombe
Honeybrook Farm
Avon Heath
Melcombe Bingham
Milton Abbey
Whatcombe
Spetisbury
Clapgate
Canford Bottom
St Leonards
Kings
Milton Abbas
Charlton Down
Shapwick
Kingston Lacy
Hillbutts
Colehill
Walford Mill
Trickett's Cross
Matchams
Dorset
Winterborne Whitechurch
Sturminster Marshall
Pamphill
Wimborne Minster
Stapehill
Ferndown
Cheselbourne
Almer
Knoll Gdns
Hampreston
Longham
Avon
Dewlish
Winterborne Kingston
Winterborne Zelston
Corfe Mullen
East End
Oakley
Canford Magna
Merley
West Parley
Parley Cross
Bournemouth
Hurn
Adventure Wonderland
Milborne St Andrew
Anderson
Bearwood
Bear Cross
Kinson
Ensbury
Holdenhurst
Jumpers Green
Martyrs Museum
Morden
Hill View
Broadstone
Canford Heath
Puddletown
Tolpuddle
Bere Regis
Bloxworth
East Morden
Lytchett Matravers
Moordown
Athelhampton
Burleston
Affpuddle
Turners Puddle
Slepe
Lytchett Minster
Waterloo
Newtown
Talbot Village
Winton
Red House Mus.
Briants Puddle
Farmer Palmer's Farm Park
Upton
Poole
Branksome
Pokesdown
Wick
Tincleton
Wareham Forest
Lane End
Morden Bog
Holton Heath
Hamworthy
Parkstone
Westbourne
Boscombe
Southbourne
Art Gall and Mus
Woodsford
Cloud's Hill
Lilliput
Branksome Park
Scaplen's Court Museum
Canford Cliffs
Oceanarium
Moreton
Bovington Camp
Trigon Hill
Sandford
Compton Acres
Poole Harbour
Crossways
Monkey World
Tank Museum
Northport
Arne
Brownsea I.
Brownsea Island
Stokeford
Wareham
Poole Bay
Sandbanks
Mill House Cider Museum
East Burton
Wool
Stoborough
Ridge
Ferry
Toll
Warmwell
East Stoke
West Holme
Stoborough Green
Stoborough Heath
Hartland Moor
Studland Beach and Nature Reserve
Studland
Owermoigne
East Knighton
Middlebere Heath
Wytch Heath
Newton Heath
Winfrith Newburgh
Coombe Keynes
Grange Heath
The Blue Pool
Norden Heath
Studland Bay
Cherbourg
Holworth
Chaldon Herring or East Chaldon
Lulworth Castle
East Creech
Isle of
Studland and Godlingston Heath
Chaldon Down
South West Coast Path
West Lulworth
Dorset
East Lulworth
Purbeck Hills
Church Knowle
Corfe Castle
Model Village & Gardens
Nine Barrow Down
The Foreland
South West Coast Path
Jersey
Guernsey (April-Oct)
St. Malo (May-Sept)
Ringstead Bay
Durdle Door
Lulworth Cove
Heritage Centre
Steeple
Purbeck
Ulwell
New Swanage
Tyneham
Kingston
Harman's Cross
Swanage Bay
Swanage
Swanage Railway
Bay
Worbarrow Bay
Kimmeridge
Kimmeridge Bay
Langton Matravers Mus
Langton Matravers
Peveril Pt.
Acton
Durlston Head
Worth Matravers
Durlston
Tilly Whim Caves
SU
SZ

Newton
Woodford
Winterbourne Earls
Firsdown
East Winterslow
Middle Winterslow
The Common
WHITESHOOT HILL
Broughton
Little Somborne
Up Somborne
Houghton
Stratford
Sub Castle
OLD SARUM
New Sarum
West Winterslow
ALL SAINTS CHURCH
FLOWERDOWN BARROWS
Ditchampton
Wilton
Laverstock
Pitton
King's Somborne
Ashley
Sparsholt
Barford St Martin
Burcombe
Quidhampton
Bemerton
Salisbury
25
Horsebridge
FARLEY MOUNT
WILTON HOUSE
Netherhampton
Milford
Farley
West Tytherley
East Tytherley
West Harnham
East Harnham
Britford
East Grimstead
West Dean
Brook
SALISBURY
Coombe Bissett
MOMPESSON HOUSE
Alderbury
MOTTISFONT ABBEY
Lockerley
Butt's Green
Stratford Tony
Whaddon
West Grimstead
East Dean
Mottisfont
Michelmersh
Standon
Bishopstone
Odstock
Bodenham
PEPPERBOX HILL
Braishfield
Stoke Farthing
Croucheston
Homington
Nunton
Carter's Clay
Kent's Oak
Timsbury
Pucknall
Hursley
A354
Charlton-All-Saints
Whiteparish
Newtown
Awbridge
HILLIER GARDENS
Abbotswood
Ampfield
Upper Ratley
Wick Down
Wick
Newton
NEWHOUSE
Sherfield English
Cupernham
Romsey
Whitenap
Chandler's Ford
Rockbourne Down
Morgan's Vale
Redlynch
LANGLEY WOOD
Landford Manor
Martin Drove End
Downton
Woodfalls
Lover
East Wellow
North Baddesley
BREAMORE HOUSE & MUSEUM
Plaitford
West Wellow
BROADLANDS
Martin
MARTIN DOWN
Tidpit
Whitsbury
Upper Street
North Charford
Hale
Landford
Canada
Ridge
Chilworth
Toothill
Breamore
Nomansland
Lee
Upton
Entridge
Rockbourne
Outwick
ROMAN VILLA
Burgate
OWER SERVICES
Ower
Wigley
ROWNHAMS SERVICES
Rownhams
13
Damerham
Woodgreen
PAULTONS PARK
M27
Nursling
Bassett
SU
Bramshaw
Newbridge
Calmore
Coxford
Swaythling
Sandleheath
Ashford
Godshill
Brook Hill
Brook
Testwood
M271
Southampton
ALDERHOLT MILL
Fordingbridge
Blissford
Fritham
Cadnam
Copythorne
Winsor
Totton
Wimpson
Portswood
Shirley
Cranborne
Alderholt
Stuckton
Millbrook
Bitterne
MANOR GARDEN
Cripplestyle
Charing Cross
Bickton
Hyde
FURZEY GDNS
Bartley
Netley Marsh
TOLL
ELING TIDE MILL
Eling
CITY ART GALL
Northam
EDMONDSHAM HO
Edmondsham
Hungerford
Stoney Cross
Woodlands
SOUTHAMPTON
Itchen
North Gorley
Broomy Lodge
Minstead
HEAVY HORSE CENTRE
South Gorley
Newtown
Ashurst
LONGDOWN FARM
SEA CITY MUS
Pooksgreen
Marchwood
Woolston
Verwood
Ibsley
Mockbeggar
Linwood
Hampshire
NEW FOREST WILDLIFE PARK
NETLEY ABBEY
Woodlands
Ringwood Forest
Moyles Court
A338
A31
Emery Down
Lyndhurst
NEW FOREST CENTRE
Hythe
Dibden
Rockford
Blashford
REPTILIARY
Clayhill
Dibden Purlieu
Mannington
Linford
Three Legged Cross
MOORS VALLEY
Picket Post
Burley Lodge
Bank
Denny Lodge
Buttsash
New Forest National Park
Ashley
Ringwood
Beaulieu Heath
Hardley
HOLT HEATH
Ashley Heath
Moortown
Burley Street
Holbury
West Moors
St Ives
ST LEONARDS SERVICES
RAPTOR AND REPTILE CENTRE
BURLEY
Bisterne Close
Burley
New Park
Balmerlawn
Hill Top
NATIONAL MOTOR MUS
Blackfield
Broom Hill
AVON HEATH
St. Leonards
Kingston
KINGSTON GREAT COMMON
Brockenhurst
PALACE HO
Beaulieu
ABBEY
MATCHAMS
Trickett's Cross
Hatchet Gate
Langley
Stapehill
Ferndown
Setley
East Boldre
KNOLL GDNS
Beaulieu Heath
EXBURY
Exbury
Bucklers Hard
MARITIME MUSEUM
Battramsley
Longham
West Parley
Thorney Hill
Avon
Ripley
Wootton
Sway
Bull Hill
Lepe
BOURNEMOUTH
A338
Bransgore
Boldre
Pilley
Norleywood
Needs Ore Pt.
Parley Cross
Hurn
Sopley
Bashley
SPINNERS
Portmore
East End
HAMPSHIRE
A348
Kinson
Bear Cross
Ensbury
ADVENTURE WONDERLAND
Neacroft
Beckley
Mount Pleasant
Golden Hill
Hordle
Buckland
Walhampton
Holdenhurst
Winkton
Godwinscroft
New Milton
Bournemouth
Jumpers Green
Hinton
SAMMY MILLER'S MOTORCYCLE MUS
Ashley
LYMINGTON
Pennington
SOUTH
Waterford
THE
Moordown
Burton
Walkford
Everton
Woodside
Thorness Bay
Newtown
Talbot Village
Highcliffe
Old Milton
BRAXTON
RED HOUSE MUS
Somerford
HIGHCLIFFE CASTLE
Barton on Sea
Downton
Lymore
Lower Pennington
Newtown Bay
Branksome
Purewell
NEWTOWN HARBOUR
Pokesdown
Wick
CHRISTCHURCH
KEYHAVEN & PENNINGTON MARSHES
Hamstead
Westbourne
PRIORY CHURCH
Mudeford
Milford on Sea
Keyhaven
Porchfield
Boscombe
Christchurch Bay
OLD TOWN HALL
Lilliput
Branksome Park
ART GALL AND MUS
Southbourne
Sconce Pt.
Cranmore
Newtown
Canford Cliffs
Bournemouth
Hengistbury Head
HURST CASTLE
FORT VICTORIA
Shalfleet
COMPTON ACRES
OCEANARIUM
VISITOR CENTRE
ISLAND PLANETARIUM
Norton
Yarmouth
Thorley Street
Ningwood
Colwell Bay
Sandbanks
POOLE BAY
SZ
Totland
Norton Green
Wellow
Newbridge
CALBOURNE WATER MILL
Totland Bay
TOTLAND BAY
Pound Green
Freshwater
CHESSELL POTTERY BARNS
Calbourne
STUDLAND BEACH AND NATURE RESERVE
Alum Bay
Freshwater Bay
Afton
ISLE
Studland Bay
The Needles
THE NEEDLES PARK
THE NEEDLES OLD BATTERY
Freshwater Bay
Shalcombe
Brighstone Forest
Hulverstone
Brook
Mottistone
WIGHT
The Foreland
SOUTH WEST COAST PATH
GUERNSEY (April-Oct)
JERSEY
ST. MALO (May-Sept)
CHERBOURG
The Undercliff
Moortown
Brighstone
BRIGHSTONE
Limerstone
Yafford
Thorncross
Brighstone Bay
Swanage Bay
Atherfield Pt.
0 1 2 3 4 5 6 miles
0 1 2 3 4 5 6 7 8 9 10 km
1
2
3
4
5
A
B
C
D
E
F

SOUTH DOWNS NATIONAL PARK
SU
SZ
Winchester
Kings Worthy
New Alresford
Four Marks
Selborne
Liphook
Petersfield
EASTLEIGH
Bishopstoke
Fair Oak
Bishop's Waltham
Twyford
West End
Hedge End
Wickham
Waterlooville
Horndean
HAVANT
Emsworth
Chichester
Fareham
Portchester
Portsmouth
PORTSMOUTH
GOSPORT
Southsea
Lee-on-the-Solent
Hill Head
Fawley
Calshot
SOLENT
SPITHEAD
HAYLING ISLAND
South Hayling
East Wittering
Selsey
SELSEY BILL
CHICHESTER HARBOUR
Cowes
East Cowes
RYDE
Isle of Wight
NEWPORT
Bembridge
Sandown
Shanklin
Ventnor
Niton
CAEN
LE HAVRE
ST. MALO
BILBAO
SANTANDER
CHERBOURG (April-Sept)
GUERNSEY
JERSEY

Haslemere
Liphook
Grayswood
Shottermill
Hammer
Camelsdale
Linchmere
Kingsley Green
Standford
Whitehill
Bramshott
Conford
Greatham
Empshott
Longmoor Camp
Liss Forest
West Liss
East Liss
Liss
Langley
Rake
Hill Brow
Steep Marsh
Sheet
Petersfield
Rogate
Milland
Borden
Fernhurst
Henley
Lickfold
Lurgashall
Northchapel
Fisherstreet
Ramsnest Common
Plaistow
Alfold
Alfold Bars
Loxwood
Ifold
Tisman's Common
Rowhook
Rudgwick
Bucks Green
Park Street
Slinfold
Broadbridge Heath
Strood Green
The Haven
Itchingfield
Five Oaks
Barns Green
Roundstreet Common
Newpound Common
Wisborough Green
Kirdford
Mackerel's Common
Balls Cross
Strood Green
Billingshurst
Parbrook
Brooks Green
Coneyhurst
Adversane
SOUTH DOWNS NATIONAL PARK
HOLLYCOMBE STEAM COLLECTION
BLACK DOWN
EBERNOE COMMON
FISHERS FARM PARK
ASHFORD HANGERS
Chithurst
Iping
Woolbeding
Easebourne
Halfway Bridge
Lodsworth
Upperton
PETWORTH HO
Petworth
Bedham
Byworth
Tillington
Selham
South Ambersham
Midhurst
Stedham
Trotton
Minsted
Dumpford
Nyewood
Nursted
Buriton
East Harting
South Harting
Elsted
Didling
Bepton
Treyford
LINCH DOWN
West Lavington
Heyshott
Cocking
Graffham
Duncton
East Lavington
Codmore Hill
Stopham
Fittleworth
Pulborough
Coates
Coldwaltham
Nutbourne
Marehill
Hardham
Wiggonholt
Greatham
Broadford Bridge
North Heath
Gay Street
West Chiltington
West Chiltington Common
Coolham
COOLHAM AIRFIELD D-DAY MEMORIAL
Shipley
Whitehall
Broomer's Corner
Goose Green
Spear Hill
Thakeham
Ashington
West Sussex
Barlavington
Sutton
Bignor
ROMAN VILLA
Waterfield
Rackham
Amberley
Cootham
PARHAM
Storrington
Wiston
Rock
Sullington
Washington
KITHURST HILL
AMBERLEY MUS
Bury
West Burton
Houghton
Upwaltham
North Marden
Compton
Up Marden
West Marden
East Marden
Chilgrove
UPPARK
Finchdean
Forestside
Stoughton
KINGSLEY VALE
Singleton
Charlton
East Dean
West Dean
WEST DEAN GARDENS
WEALD AND DOWNLAND OPEN AIR MUSEUM
GOODWOOD
ST. ROCHE'S HILL
BOW HILL
STANSTED PARK
Walderton
STANE STREET
Madehurst
Eartham
North Stoke
South Stoke
Arundel Park
Offham
Burpham
HARROW HILL
North End
Findon
THE WILDFOWL AND WETLANDS CENTRE
ARUNDEL
Arundel
Crossbush
Patching
High Salvington
Clapham
Salvington
Durrington
Woodend
West Stoke
Mid Lavant
East Lavant
GOODWOOD HOUSE
Halnaker
Westbourne
Funtington
Woodmancote
East Ashling
West Ashling
Summersdale
Strettington
Boxgrove
Westerton
Slindon
Fontwell
Walberton
Hermitage
Hambrook
Nutbourne
Southbourne
Broadbridge
Fishbourne
Chichester
CATH.
Westhampnett
Tangmere
AVIATION MUS
DENMANS
Norton
FONTWELL PARK
Eastergate
Aldingbourne
Nyton
Oving
Woodgate
Westergate
Barnham
MUSEUM AND HERITAGE CENTRE
Tortington
Ford
Lyminster
Wick
Poling
Angmering
Hammerpot
Hangleton
Chidham
Bosham
BOSHAM WALK
FISHBOURNE PALACE
Apuldram
PALLANT HOUSE
Colworth
Yapton
Climping
Bilsham
Rustington
East Preston
Ferring
Goring-by-Sea
West Worthing
Kingston Gorse
Thorney
West Thorney
CHICHESTER HARBOUR
Chichester Harbour
West Itchenor
Donnington
Hunston
North Mundham
Runcton
Merston
North Bersted
Shripney
Flansham
LITTLEHAMPTON
SUSSEX FALCONRY CENTRE
South Mundham
South Bersted
Shipton Green
Birdham
Street End
Nyetimber
Rose Green
Aldwick
Felpham
SOUTHCOAST WORLD
Middleton-on-Sea
HARBOUR PARK
Bognor Regis
Acre Street
West Wittering
Somerley
Highleigh
EARNLEY BUTTERFLIES AND GARDENS
Sidlesham
Pagham
East Wittering
Earnley
Bracklesham
Norton
Church Norton
Selsey
SELSEY BILL
SU
SZ
Alderney
3½ miles to 1 inch
DIELETTE ST. PETER PORT (Apr-Sept)
Quesnard Pt.
Braye
Longis Bay
Brehou
Clonque Bay
St Anne
ALDERNEY
Telegraph Bay
Guernsey
3½ miles to 1 inch
POOLE (April-Oct)
PORTSMOUTH
L'Ancresse Bay
Le Plomb
Grand Havre
La Fontenelle
GUERNSEY
SARK
L'Islet
St Sampson
Cobo Bay
Vazon Bay
Belle Greve Bay
SHELL BEACH
Herm
Lihou I.
Le Villocq
BEAU SEJOUR CENTRE
MUSEUM & ART GALL
Mont Saint
St Peter Port
Jethou
Res.
HUGO'S HOUSE
VICTOR
CASTLE CORNET
Rocquaine Bay
THE LITTLE CHAPEL
Carmel
Fort George
Pleinmont Pt.
GUERNSEY
Moulpied
ST. HELIER
Le Planel
La Planque
St Martin's Pt.
ST. HELIER ST. MALO
Pointe de la Moye
Icart Pt.
Moulin Huet Bay
DIELETTE CARTERET ALDERNEY GRANVILLE (Apr-Sept)
0 1 2 3 4 5 6 miles
0 1 2 3 4 5 6 7 8 9 10 km

Horsham
Roffey
Colgate
St Leonard's Forest
Pease Pottage
Tilgate
Tilgate Forest Row
Balcombe
Balcombe Lane
Selsfield Common
West Hoathly
Sharpthorne
Wakehurst Place
Priest House
Highbrook
Handcross
Nymans Garden
Staplefield
Ardingly
Horsted Keynes
Chelwood Gate
Chelwood Common
Coleman's Hatch
Wych Cross
Ashdown Forest
Upper Hartfield
Lye Green
Friar's Gate
Boarshead
Crowborough
Poundfield
Jarvis Brook
Danehill
Nutley
Duddleswell
Fairwarp
High Hurstwood
Butcher's Cross
Ashfold Crossways
Mannings Heath
Monk's Gate
Slaugham
Lower Beeding
Nuthurst
Southwater Street
Southwater
Copsale
Warninglid
Crabtree
Maplehurst
Brook Street
Borde Hill Garden
Slough Green
Whitemans Green
Cuckfield
Lindfield
Haywards Heath
Heaven Farm
Sheffield Green
Splayne's Green
Sheffield Park
Fletching
Bluebell Railway
Cackle Street
Maresfield
Pound Green
Buxted
Ringles Cross
Hadlow Down
Cross in Hand
Bolney
Ansty
Scayne's Hill
Cowfold
West Grinstead
Kent Street
Wineham
Hickstead
Twineham
All England Jumping Course
Sayers Common
Burgess Hill
Wivelsfield
Wivelsfield Green
North Chailey
Chailey
South Street
Newick
Grisling Common
Uckfield
Framfield
Blackboys
Ridgewood
Little Horsted
E. Sussex National
Isfield
Lavender Line Steam Railway
Halland
East Hoathly
Waldron
Foxhunt Green
Dial Post
Partridge Green
West End
Henfield
Blackstone
Albourne
Washbrooks Farm Centre
Hurstpierpoint
Hurst Wickham
Ditchling Common
Plumpton Green
Plumpton
Chiltington
East Chiltington
Spithurst
Barcombe Cross
Barcombe
Rose Hill
Shortgate
Chiddingly
Whitesmith
Laughton
Golden Cross
Ashurst
Woodmancote
Hassocks
Keymer
Ditchling
Streat
Westmeston
Mus of Art & Craft
Clayton
Pyecombe
Ditchling Beacon
Offham
Hamsey
Cooksbridge
Boyle Side
Ringmer
Mt. Harry
Small Dole
Poynings
Fulking
Edburton
Saddlescombe
Devil's Dyke
Truleigh Hill
Steyning
Bramber
Upper Beeding
St Mary's House
Botolphs
Coombes
Stanmer Park
Stanmer
Wallands Park
Lewes
South Malling
Cliffe Hill
Anne of Cleves Ho
Lewes Downs (Mount Caburn)
Glynde
Glynde Place
Glyndebourne
Mark Cross
Lower Dicker
Ripe
Chalvington
Patcham
Coldean
Falmer
Kingston near Lewes
Brighton and Hove
Mile Oak
Westdene
Withdean
Portslade
West Blatchington
Preston Manor
Preston
Moulsecoomb
Bevendean
Castle Hill
Iford
Rodmell
Monks Ho
Beddingham
Firle Pl
West Firle
Charleston Farmhouse
Alciston
Firle Beacon
Selmeston
Arlington
Berwick
Drusillas Park
Wilmington
Alfriston
The Long Man of Wilmington
Lullington Heath
Litlington
Charleston Manor
Westdean
Clergy House
North Lancing
Sompting
Broadwater
Lancing
South Lancing
East Worthing
Worthing
Shoreham
Shoreham-by-Sea
Kingston by Sea
Southwick
Portslade-by-Sea
Hove
Brighton
Royal Pavilion
Brighton i360 Tower
Brighton Sea Life
Marlipins Museum
Kemp Town
Ovingdean
Woodingdean
Rottingdean
Brighton Marina
Volk's Electric Railway
Telscombe
Saltdean
Telscombe Cliffs
Peacehaven
Southease
Piddinghoe
Newhaven
Tarring Neville
South Heighton
Denton
Paradise Park
Norton
Bishopstone
Newhaven Fort
Seaford
East Blatchington
Seven Sisters
Friston
South Downs Way
Birling Gap
Dieppe
South Downs
TQ
TV
Jersey
3½ miles to 1 inch
Grosnez Pt.
Plémont Pt.
Sorel Pt.
Ronez Pt.
St John's Bay
Belle Hougue Pt.
North Coast Visitor Centre
St John's
Bouley Bay
Tour de Rozel
Rozel
La Coupe Pt.
Carteret Sark
St Mary's
Trinity
Durrell Wildlife Conservation Trust (Zoo)
JERSEY
St Ouens
Kempt Tower Visitor Centre
St Ouen's Bay
Carrefour Selous
St Peter's
St Martin's
St Catherine's Bay
La Hougue Bie
Mont Orgueil Castle
Gorey
Five Oaks
Red Houses
St Aubin
St Helier
Jersey Museum
Grouville
Royal Bay of Grouville
Corbière Pt.
St Brelade
St Brelades Bay
St Aubin's Bay
St Clements
Sark (Apr-Sept)
Elizabeth Castle
Fort Regent Leisure Centre
La Rocque Pt.
St. Peter Port Poole
Noirmont Pt.
Le Nez Pt.
St Clements Bay
St. Peter Port Portsmouth
St. Malo
Granville St. Peter Port Carteret (Apr-Sept)
A
B
C
D
E
F
G
5
6
7
8
9
18
28

Paddock Wood
Claygate
Marden
Hawkenbury
Headcorn
Staplehurst
Penshurst
Bidborough
Southborough
High Brooms
Matfield
Pembury
Brenchley
Castle Hill
Marden Beech
Marden Thorn
Sinkhurst Green
Knox Bridge
Frittenden
Lashenden
Chiddingstone Hoath
Speldhurst
Petteridge
Horsmonden
Cowden
Blackham
Fordcombe
Rusthall
ROYAL TUNBRIDGE WELLS
Hazel Street
Collier's Green
Cranbrook Common
Three Chimneys
Sissinghurst Castle
Ashurst
Langton Green
Hawkenbury
Lamberhurst Quarter
Goudhurst
Iden Green
Wilsley Pound
Sissinghurst
Groombridge
Spa Valley Railway
Bells Yew Green
Bayham Abbey
Lamberhurst
Finchcocks
Cranbrook Museum
Union Mill
Cranbrook
East End
Hartfield
Forest Way
Eridge Green
Frant
Scotney Castle
Kilndown
Withyham
Upper Hartfield
Hook Green
Hartley
Lye Green
Wood's Green
Cousley Wood
Bedgebury Pinetum
Bedgebury Forest
Benenden
Friar's Gate
Boarshead
Mark Cross
Durgates
Wadhurst
Bewl Water
Three Leg Cross
Gill's Green
Iden Green
Rolvenden
Flimwell
High Street
Hawkhurst
Dingleden
Ashdown Forest Llama Park
ASHDOWN FOREST
Crowborough
Poundfield
Bestbeech Hill
Riseden
Town Row
Shover's Green
Wallcrouch
Union Street
Ticehurst
Four Throws
Horns Corner
The Moor
Sandhurst
Linkhill
Jarvis Brook
Rotherfield
Tidebrook
Pashley Manor Gardens
Stonegate
Swiftsden
Hurst Green
Sandhurst Cross
Newenden
Nutley
Duddleswell
Coggins Mill
Mayfield
TQ
Witherenden Hill
Etchingham
Bodiam
Great Dixter
Fairwarp
Hurstwood
Butcher's Cross
Rother
Northbridge Street
Northiam
Maresfield
Hadlow Down
Five Ashes
Burwash Common
Burwash
Salehurst
Ewhurst Green
Clayhill
Pound Green
Bateman's
Robertsbridge
Rother Valley Rly
Buxted
Ringles Cross
Cross in Hand
Broad Oak
Burwash Weald
Oxley's Green
Staple Cross
Millcorner
Horns Cross
Grisling Common
Uckfield
Blackboys
Cade Street
Punnett's Town
John's Cross
Cripp's Corner
Framfield
Heathfield
Brightling
Vinehall Street
Broadland Row
Ridgewood
Little London
Old Heathfield
Three Cups Corner
Darwell Hole
Mountfield
Broad Oak
Waldron
Maynard's Green
Rushlake Green
Dallington
Whatlington
Sedlescombe
Little Horsted
Foxhunt Green
Warbleton
Netherfield
Sedlescombe Street
Brede
Canadia
Horam
Vine's Cross
East Hoathly
Penhurst
Battle
Guestling Thorn
Halland
Burlow
Foul Mile
Rose Hill
Ponts Green
Three Oaks
Shortgate
1066 Abbey
Telham
Kent Street
Westfield
Chiddingly
Gun Hill
Bodle Street Green
Catsfield
Broyle Side
Laughton
Whitesmith
Chiddingly Parish Church
Cowbeech
Baldslow
Golden Cross
Henley's Down
Ringmer
Lower Horsebridge
Hellingly
Herstmonceux
Windmill Hill
Ninfield
Crowhurst
St Helen's
Mark Cross
Hollington
Glyndebourne
Lower Dicker
Herstmonceux Castle
Boreham Street
Ore
Ripe
Upper Horsebridge
Magham Down
International Study Centre
Observatory Science Centre
Lunsford's Cross
Silverhill
Lewes Downs (Mount Caburn)
Upper Dicker
Hooe Common
Queens Univ Canada
Glynde
Chalvington
Hailsham
St Leonards
Glynde Place
Hooe
Wartling
Sidley
Michelham Priory
Little Common
Hastings
Bulverhythe
West Marina
Selmeston
Arlington
Pevensey
Firle Pl
West Firle
Cooden
Levels
BEXHILL
Charleston Farmhouse
Alciston
Old Mint House
Hankham
Pevensey Services
Norman's Bay
Firle Beacon
Polegate
Berwick
Drusillas Park
Pevensey
Tarring Neville
Wilmington
Folkington
Stone Cross
Westham
Pevensey Bay
South Heighton
Alfriston
Friday Street
The Long Man of Wilmington
Denton
Hampden Park
Norton
Lullington Heath
Willingdon
Langney
Bishopstone
Litlington
Jevington
South Downs Way
St Anthony's Hill
Newhaven
Charleston Manor
East Blatchington
Westdean
Willingdon Hill
Roselands
Towner Gallery
Seaford
Seven Sisters
Eastbourne
How We Lived Then' Mus
Friston
East Dean
Dieppe
South Downs Way
Seven Sisters Sheep Centre
Holywell
Birling Gap
Beachy Head
TV
East Sussex
WEALD
0 1 2 3 4 5 6 miles
0 1 2 3 4 5 6 7 8 9 10 km

Headcorn
Smarden Bell
Maltman's Hill
Godinton House
Great Chart
Ashford
Kennington
Brook
Hastingleigh
Hinxhill
Lymbridge Green
Rhodes Minnis
Elham
Swingfield Minnis
Smarden
Haffenden Quarter
Wissenden
Willesborough
Willesborough Lees
Brabourne
North Downs Way
Stowting
Ottinge
Kent Battle of Britain Museum
Densole
Drellingore
Bether
Sevington
Brabourne Lees
Lyminge
Paddlesworth
Hawkinge
West Hougham
Standen
Stubbs Cross
Kingsnorth
Mersham
Smeeth
Stop 24 Services
Postling
Etchinghill
Channel Tunnel
Capel le Ferne
Biddenden
Tanden
Shadoxhurst
Cheeseman's Green
Sellindge
Sellindge Lees
Beachborough
Stanford
Newington
A262
Bromley Green
Aldington Frith
Clap Hill
E. Stour
M20
High Halden
Biddenden Vineyard
Henghurst
Aldington
Bonnington
Newingreen
Pedlinge
Elham Valley Rly Mus
Cheriton
Folkestone
Kent & East Sussex Railway
St Michael's
Shirkoak
Orlestone
Ham Street Woods
Court-at-Street
Port Lympne Wild Animal Park and Gardens
Lympne
Saltwood
Rotunda
Parkgate
Tenterden
Woodchurch
South of England Rare Breeds Cen
Ruckinge
Bilsington
Military Canal
Brockhill
Sandgate
Cliff Lift
Hythe
West Hythe
Leigh Green
Brook Street
Kenardington
Hamstreet
Royal
Palmarsh
Colonel Stephens Railway Museum
Warehorne
B2067
B2080
Burmarsh
Newchurch
A259
Romney, Hythe and Dymchurch Railway
Small Hythe
Reading Street
Appledore Heath
A2070
Horne's Place Chapel
Snave
Rolvenden Layne
Smallhythe Place
Isle of Oxney
Appledore
Romney Marsh
Dymchurch
Peening Quarter
Stone
Snargate
St Mary in the Marsh
Martello Tower
Wittersham
Brenzett
Ivychurch
Romney Warren
St Mary's Bay
Rother
Ham Green
The Stocks
Aeronautical Museum
TR
Rother Levels
Farm World
Brookland
Old Romney
Littlestone on Sea
Four Oaks
Beckley
Iden
Houghton Green
Walland Marsh
New Romney
Romney Sands
Peasmarsh
Rye Foreign
Playden
East Guldeford
Greatstone on Sea
Tillingham
Rye
Lydd
Lydd (London Ashford)
Lydd on Sea
Rye Heritage Centre
Denge Marsh
Udimore
Camber
Lydd International Raceway
Rye Harbour
Dungeness
Brede
Camber Castle
Denge Beach
Winchelsea
Rye Bay
Dungeness Power Station & Information Centre
The Old Lighthouse
Winchelsea Court Hall Museum
Winchelsea Beach
Icklesham
Pett
Guestling Green
Cliff End
Fairlight
Fairlight Cove
Hastings 's Caves
Water World
English Channel
A B C D E F G
5 6 7 8 9

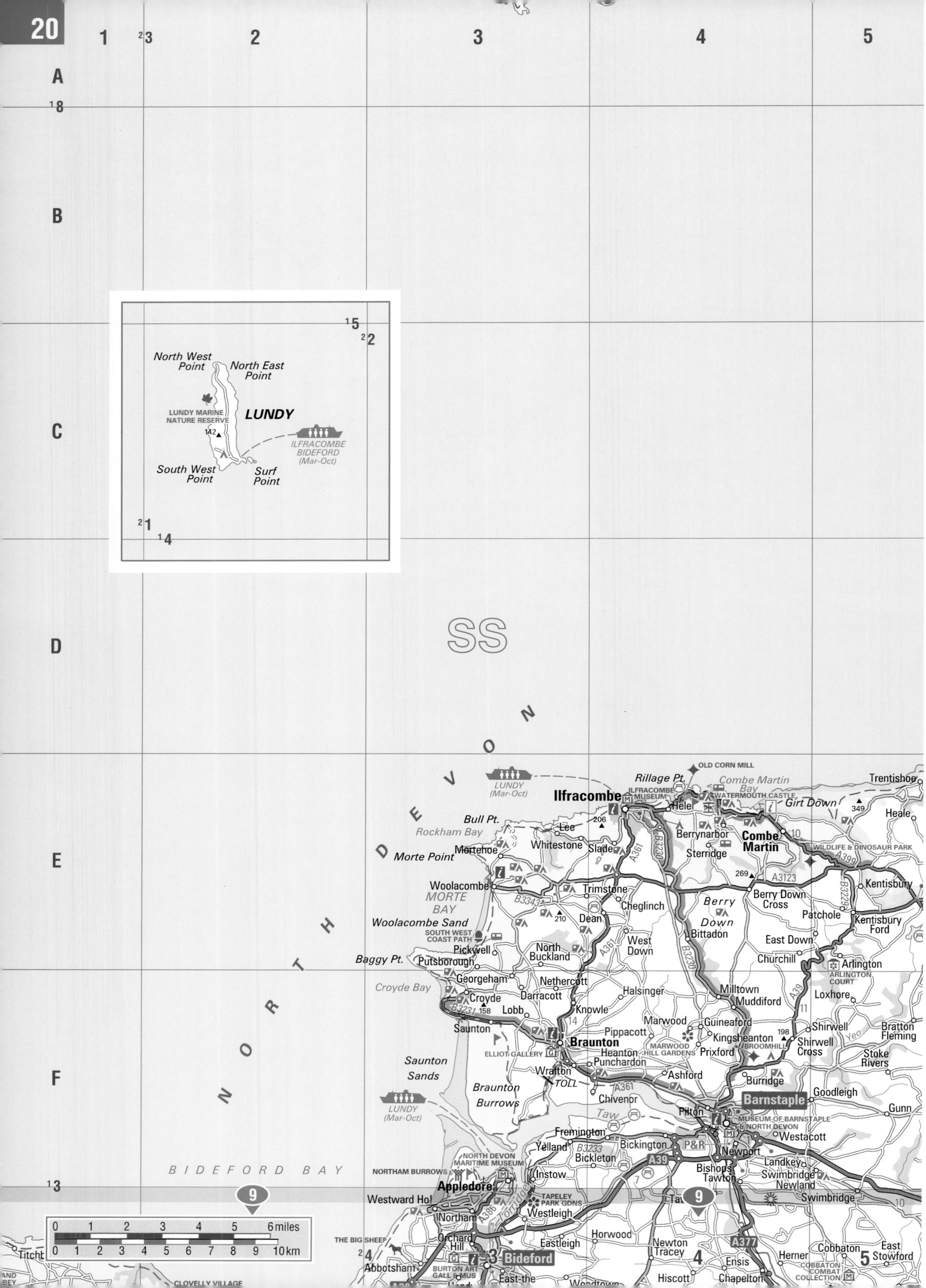
1
2
3
4
5
A
B
C
D
E
F
North West Point
North East Point
LUNDY
LUNDY MARINE NATURE RESERVE
142
ILFRACOMBE BIDEFORD (Mar-Oct)
South West Point
Surf Point
SS
NORTH DEVON
LUNDY (Mar-Oct)
Rillage Pt.
OLD CORN MILL
Combe Martin Bay
Trentishoe
Ilfracombe
ILFRACOMBE MUSEUM
WATERMOUTH CASTLE
Hele
Girt Down
349
Heale
Bull Pt.
Lee
206
Rockham Bay
Berrynarbor
Combe Martin
Mortehoe
Whitestone
Slade
Sterridge
WILDLIFE & DINOSAUR PARK
Morte Point
269
A3123
A399
Woolacombe
Trimstone
Berry Down Cross
Kentisbury
MORTE BAY
Cheglinch
Berry Down
Patchole
B3343
210
Dean
Kentisbury Ford
Woolacombe Sand
SOUTH WEST COAST PATH
Bittadon
West Down
East Down
Pickwell
North Buckland
Baggy Pt.
Putsborough
Churchill
Arlington
ARLINGTON COURT
Georgeham
Croyde Bay
Nethercott
Milltown
Loxhore
Croyde
Darracott
Halsinger
Muddiford
B3231
158
Lobb
Knowle
Marwood
Guineaford
Shirwell
Bratton Fleming
Saunton
Pippacott
Kingsheanton
198
Braunton
MARWOOD HILL GARDENS
BROOMHILL
Shirwell Cross
ELLIOT GALLERY
Heanton Punchardon
Prixford
Stoke Rivers
Saunton Sands
Wrafton
TOLL
Ashford
Burridge
Braunton Burrows
A361
Chivenor
Goodleigh
Barnstaple
LUNDY (Mar-Oct)
Taw
Pilton
Gunn
MUSEUM OF BARNSTAPLE & NORTH DEVON
Fremington
Westacott
Yelland
B3233
Bickington
P&R
Newport
NORTH DEVON MARITIME MUSEUM
Bickleton
A39
Landkey
BIDEFORD BAY
NORTHAM BURROWS
Instow
Bishops Tawton
Swimbridge
Newland
Appledore
9
Westward Ho!
TAPELEY PARK GDNS
Swimbridge
Northam
Westleigh
A386
Torridge
THE BIG SHEEP
Orchard Hill
Horwood
Newton Tracey
A377
Eastleigh
Cobbaton
East Stowford
Herner
Abbotsham
Bideford
BURTON ART GALL & MUS
Ensis
COBBATON COMBAT COLLECTION
East-the-Water
Hiscott
Chapelton
CLOVELLY VILLAGE
0 1 2 3 4 5 6 miles
0 1 2 3 4 5 6 7 8 9 10 km

Bryncethin
Aberkenfig
Kenfig Hill
Cefn Cross
Sarn
Pyle (Y Pil)
North Cornelly
Cefn Cribbwr
Kenfig Burrows
South Cornelly
KENFIG POOL AND DUNES
Pencoed
Coity
Bridgend (Pen-y-bont ar Ogwr)
Brynna
Llanharan
Brynsadler
Llanharry
Pontyclun
Laleston
Coychurch
Tythegston
St Mary Hill
Treoes
Craig Penllyn
Nottage
Newton
Hutchwns
Clevis
Merthyr Mawr
OGMORE CASTLE
MERTHYR MAWR WARREN
Porthcawl
CONEY BEACH
Ewenny
Corntown
Llangan
Llansannor
Ogmore
Ogmore-by-Sea
St Brides Major
Penllyn
Maendy
Aberthin
Ystradowen
Vale of Glamorgan (Bro Morgannwg)
Welsh St Donats
Tusker Rock
Colwinston
Pentre Meyrick
Cowbridge (Y Bont-Faen)
Llanblethian
Penuchadre
Llysworney
Llandow
Llandough
St Hilary
Southerndown
GLENMORGAN HERITAGE COAST CENTRE
WALES COAST PATH
Wick
Llanmihangel
St Mary Church
OLD BEAUPRE CASTLE
Broughton
Sigingstone
Monknash
Flemingston
Llanmaes
Eglwys-Brewis
Llanbethery
Marcross
Llantwit Major (Llanilltud Fawr)
Boverton
St Athan
St Donat's
Nash Pt. Trwyn yr As
East Aberthaw
Rhoose (Y Rhws)
Breaksea Pt. Trwyn Breaksea
MÔR HAFREN
BRISTOL CHANNEL
SS
Foreland Pt.
Highveer Pt.
Lynmouth Bay
Woody Bay
Lynmouth
Countisbury
Lynton
Martinhoe
WATERSMEET HOUSE
Brendon
Malmsmead
CULBONE HILL
Porlock Bay
Porlock Weir
Hurlstone Pt.
Bossington
SELWORTHY BEACON
Allerford
Selworthy
Woodcombe
Minehead
WEST SOMERSET RAILWAY
Alcombe
Barbrook
Oare
East Ilkerton
Cheriton
Porlock
West Luccombe
Luccombe
Periton
Marsh Street
Martinhoe Cross
Furzehill
Shallowford
EXMOOR
Brendon Common
HAWKCOMBE WOODS
Holnicote Estate
Parracombe
Blue Anchor Bay
Dunster
Blackmoor Gate
EXMOOR FOREST
Wootton Courtenay
Challacombe Common
DUNKERY BEACON
Cowbridge
Timberscombe
Carhampton
Blue Anchor
Old Cleeve
Pinkworthy Pond
Exe Plain
Challacombe
EXMOOR ZOO
NATIONAL PARK
Withycombe
Bilbrook
BRENDON FOREST
Rodhuish
Knightacott
Shoulsbarrow Common
Simonsbath
Edgcott
Exford
Luckwell Bridge
Cutcombe
Wheddon Cross
Luxborough
Roadwater
Leworthy
LYPE HILL
Kingsbridge
Benton
Lydcott
HORSEN HILL
Withypool Common
Withypool
BRENDON HILLS
Treborough
Brayford
High Bray
North Radworthy
WINSFORD HILL
Winsford
Exton
North Heasley
Withiel Florey
Clatworthy Res.
Charles
Heasley Mill
South Radworthy
Liscombe
Bridgetown
Brompton Regis
West Buckland
East Buckland
TARR STEPS
Hawkridge
Molland Common
Twitchen
Wimbleball Lake
Anstey Common
Upton
Huish Champflower
Filleigh
Molland
West Anstey
HADDON HILL
Dulverton
East Anstey
Battleton
Bury
Skilgate
Chipstable
QUINCE HONEY FARM
South Molton
Yeo Mill
Nightcott
Waterrow
M4
A39
A361
A396
B3223
B3224

Cardiff
(Caerdydd)
CARDIFF
(CAERDYDD)
Vale of Glamorgan
(Bro Morgannwg)
PENARTH
BARRY
(Y BARRI)
Barry Island
Cowbridge
(Y Bont-Faen)
Llantwit Major
(Llanilltud Fawr)
Rhoose
(Y Rhws)
Llantrisant
Pencoed
Whitchurch
Rumney
Penarth
Sully Island
Ynys Sili
Lavernock Pt.
Trwyn Larnog
Flat Holm
Steep Holm
Breaksea Pt.
Trwyn Breaksea
ABER HAFREN
MOUTH OF THE SEVERN
MÔR HAFREN
BRISTOL CHANNEL
ST
BRIDGWATER BAY
Weston-super-Mare
Weston Bay
Sand Pt.
Sand Bay
Kewstoke
Milton
Brean Down
Uphill
Hutton
Bleadon
Brean
BERROW FLATS
Lympsham
Eastertown
Gore Sands
Berrow
Brent Knoll
East Brent
Burnham-on-Sea
Edithmead
Highbridge
Watchfield
STERT FLATS
Stolford
Steart
Huntspill
Bason Bridge
East Huntspill
Minehead
Woodcombe
Alcombe
Marsh Street
Dunster
Blue Anchor Bay
Watchet
Williton
Washford
Carhampton
Timberscombe
BRENDON FOREST
BRENDON HILLS
Luxborough
Roadwater
Monksilver
Stogumber
Elworthy
Withiel Florey
Clatworthy Res.
Brompton Regis
Wimbleball Lake
Upton
Wiveliscombe
Somerset
QUANTOCK FOREST
QUANTOCK HILLS
Kilve
Holford
Nether Stowey
Over Stowey
Stogursey
Cannington
Combwich
Pawlett
Puriton
Dunball
Woolavington
Bawdrip
Chilton Trinity
Wembdon
Bridgwater
Chedzoy
Durleigh
Enmore
Goathurst
North Petherton
Huntworth
Spaxton
Cothelstone
Broomfield
Bishops Lydeard
Kingston St Mary
West Monkton
Monkton Heathfield
Creech Heathfield
North Newton
Thurloxton
Lyng
Durston
TAUNTON DEANE
Staplegrove
Bathpool
Milverton
Hillcommon
Norton
0 1 2 3 4 5 6 miles
0 1 2 3 4 5 6 7 8 9 10 km

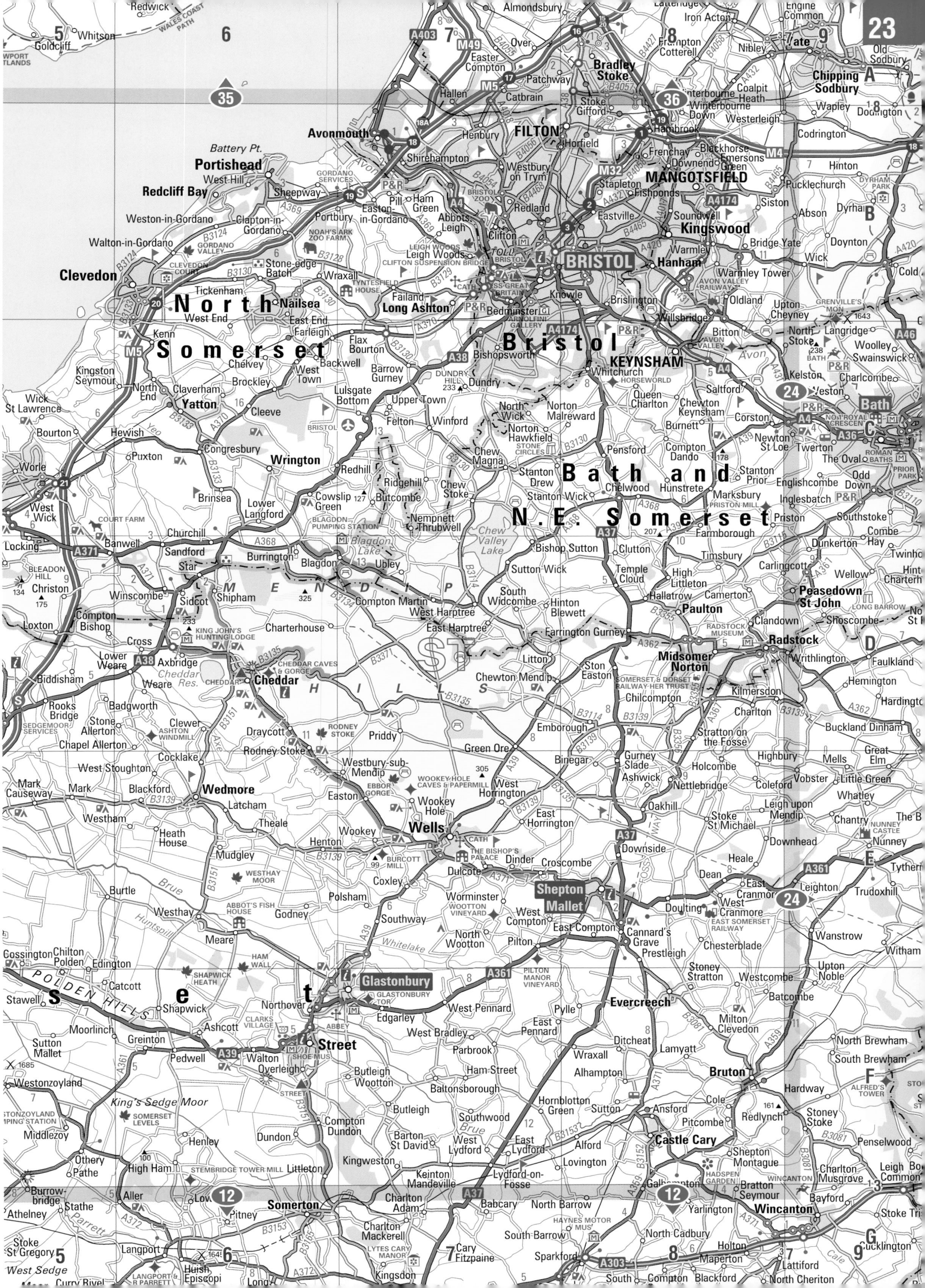
Avonmouth
Portishead
Redcliff Bay
Clevedon
FILTON
Bradley Stoke
MANGOTSFIELD
Kingswood
BRISTOL
Hanham
North Somerset
Nailsea
Long Ashton
Bristol
KEYNSHAM
Bath
Yatton
Wrington
Bath and N.E. Somerset
Cheddar
Wedmore
Wells
Shepton Mallet
Glastonbury
Street
Evercreech
Bruton
Castle Cary
Wincanton
Somerton
Midsomer Norton
Radstock
Paulton
Peasedown St John
Chipping Sodbury
MENDIP HILLS
POLDEN HILLS
King's Sedge Moor
Chew Valley Lake
M5
M4
M32
M49
A37
A38
A39
A361
A303
35
36
24
12

Yate
Chipping Sodbury
Little Sodbury
Old Sodbury
Badminton
Little Badminton
Luckington
Alderton
Norton
Hullavington
Corston
Rodbourne
Startley
Great Somerford
Dauntsey
Brinkworth
Callow Hill
Grittenham
Lower Stanton St Quintin
Stanton St Quintin
Lower Seagry
Upper Seagry
Tockenham Wick
Tockenham
Lyneham
Church End
Bradenstoke
Winterbourne
Coalpit Heath
Westerleigh
Wapley
Dodington
Acton Turville
Tormarton
Littleton Drew
Grittleton
Leigh Delamere
Burton
Sutton Benger
Christian Malford
Hambrook
Frenchay
Codrington
Emersons Green
Downend
Nettleton
Castle Combe
Kington St Michael
Kington Langley
Foxham
Preston
Goatacre
West Kington
Yatton Keynell
West End
Spirthill
MANGOTSFIELD
Pucklechurch
Hinton
Dyrham
Abson
Siston
Kingswood
West Littleton
North Wraxall
Ford
Hardenhuish
Langley Burrell
East Tytherton
West Tytherton
Hilmarton
Highway
Bridge Yate
Doynton
Marshfield
Slaughterford
Biddestone
Chippenham
Bremhill
Compton Bassett
Hanham
Warmley
Warmley Tower
Wick
Cold Ashton
Thickwood
Colerne
Corsham
Studley
Calne
Cherhill
Oldland
Upton Cheyney
St Catherine
Alcombe
Easton
Notton
Derry Hill
Willsbridge
Bitton
North Stoke
Langridge
Woolley
Swainswick
Northend
Batheaston
Box
Hawthorn
Gastard
Lacock
Sandy Lane
Mile Elm
Quemerford
Blackland
Calstone Wellington
KEYNSHAM
Kelston
Weston
Charlcombe
Bathford
Neston
Whitley
Bowden Hill
Stockley
Saltford
Chewton Keynsham
Corston
Bath
Bathampton
Monkton Farleigh
Atworth
Shaw
Beanacre
Chittoe
Bromham
Heddington
Burnett
Compton Dando
Newton St Loe
Twerton
Claverton
South Wraxall
Norrington Common
Broughton Common
Sandridge
St Edith's
Bishops Cannings
Stanton Prior
The Oval
Combe Down
Odd Down
Bradford Leigh
Broughton Gifford
Melksham
Roundway
Hunstrete
Englishcombe
Monkton Combe
Bradford-on-Avon
Holt
Bowerhill
Sells Green
Rowde
Coate
Devizes
Marksbury
Inglesbatch
Priston
Southstoke
Seend Cleeve
Seend
Etchilhampton
Farmborough
Combe Hay
Dunkerton
Limpley Stoke
Winsley
Turleigh
Staverton
Semington
Poulshot
Hilperton
Timsbury
Twinhoe
Freshford
Westwood
Trowle Common
Great Hinton
Stert
High Littleton
Carlingcott
Wellow
Hinton Charterhouse
Farleigh Hungerford
Ashton Common
Keevil
Bulkington
Potterne
Worton
Hallatrow
Camerton
Peasedown St John
Trowbridge
Steeple Ashton
Marston
Potterne Wick
Urchfont
Paulton
Clandown
Shoscombe
Norton St Philip
Tellisford
Wingfield
Southwick
West Ashton
Radstock
Midsomer Norton
Writhlington
Faulkland
North Bradley
Yarnbrook
Heywood
Coulston
Great Cheverell
Littleton Pannell
Eastcott
Easterton
Market Lavington
West Lavington
Kilmersdon
Hemington
Woolverton
Rode
Hawkeridge
Erlestoke
Little Cheverell
Edington
Bratton
Charlton
Hardington
Laverton
Beckington
Lullington
Rudge
Buckland Dinham
Stratton on the Fosse
Westbury
Westbury Leigh
Littleton Down
Gore Cross
Oldford
Holcombe
Highbury
Mells
Great Elm
Berkley
Dilton Marsh
Upton Scudamore
Summer Down
West Lavington Down
Tilshead
Nettlebridge
Coleford
Vobster
Little Green
Clink
Frome
Chapmanslade
Corsley
Whatley
Oakhill
Leigh upon Mendip
Stoke St Michael
Chantry
Nunney
The Butts
Warminster
Downhead
Corsley Heath
Tytherington
Heale
Dean
West Woodlands
Bugley
Boreham
Chitterne
Doulting
Leighton
Trudoxhill
Crockerton
Bishopstrow
Norton Bavant
Heytesbury
West Cranmore
Wanstrow
Horningsham
Shear Cross
Sutton Veny
Knook
Upton Lovell
Prestleigh
Chesterblade
Witham Friary
Longbridge Deverill
Tytherington
Corton
Codford St Peter
Codford St Mary
Stoney Stratton
Westcombe
Upton Noble
Bruton Forest
Gare Hill
Maiden Bradley
Boyton
Sherrington
Evercreech
Batcombe
Monkton Deverill
Brixton Deverill
Stockton
Deptford
Steeple Langford
Wylye
Milton Clevedon
Kilmington
North Brewham
South Brewham
Kingston Deverill
CRANBORNE
Great Ridge
Hanging Langford
Little Langford
Lamyatt
Norton Ferris
Pertwood
Bruton
Hardway
Keysley Down
Chicklade
Cole
Stourton
Berwick St Leonard
Fonthill Bishop
Grovely
Ansford
Pitcombe
Redlynch
Stoney Stoke
Mere
West Knoyle
Hindon
Chilmark
Teffont Magna
Baverstock
Dinton
Castle Cary
Shepton Montague
Penselwood
Zeals
Queen Oak
The Green
Fonthill Gifford
Ridge
Teffont Evias
CHASE
Chicksgrove
Charlton Musgrove
Leigh Common
Bourton
Barrow Street
East Knoyle
Tisbury
Bratton Seymour
Bayford
Huntingford
Galhampton
Yarlington
Milton on Stour
Sedgehill
Newtown
Hatch
Sutton Mandeville
Fovant
Compton Chamberlayne
Swallowcliffe
North Cadbury
Gillingham
Ham Common
Semley
Ansty
Broad Chalke
Lattiford
Compton
Blackford
North Cheriton
Wyke
Fifield
Wilts
SALISBURY PLAIN
VALE OF WARDOUR
0 1 2 3 4 5 6 miles
0 1 2 3 4 5 6 7 8 9 10 km

Swindon
Royal Wootton Bassett
The Marsh
Hinton Parva
Idstone
Bishopstone
Kingston Warren
Bassett
LAMBOURN DOWNS
Wanborough
Coate
COATE WATER
North Wroughton
Wroughton
Liddington
Elcombe
Badbury
Upper Lambourn
Fawley
Farnborough
South Fawley
Broadtown Lane
Chiseldon
Lambourn
Lilley
Bushton
Broad Town
Baydon
Brightwalton
CLYFFE PYPARD
Uffcott
BARBURY CASTLE
Upper Upham
Leckhampstead Thicket
Clyffe Pypard
Broad Hinton
Eastbury
East Garston
Chaddleworth
Woodsend
Aldbourne
MEMBURY SERVICES
Woodlands St Mary
Leckhampstead
Clevancy
MARLBOROUGH DOWNS
Winterbourne Bassett
Great Shefford
HACKPEN HILL
Southend
Ogbourne St George
Preston
Shefford Woodlands
Berwick Bassett
Ogbourne St Andrew
Weston
Welford
Winterbourne
WINDMILL HILL
Winterbourne Monkton
Rockley
Whittonditch
Ramsbury
Hungerford Newtown
Wickham
Westbrook
Yatesbury
THE RIDGEWAY
FYFIELD DOWN
Ogbourne Maizey
Boxford
AVEBURY MANOR
Avebury
Chilton Foliat
SNELSMORE COMMON
STONE CIRCLE
Mildenhall
Axford
Bagnor
W KENNETT AVENUE
Fyfield
Marlborough
Kennet
Hungerford
SILBURY HILL
Halfway
Stockcross
Donnington
Beckhampton
Manton
Froxfield
West Kennett
Savernake Forest
Avington
Speen
LONG BARROW
East Kennett
West Overton
Lockeridge
THE SANCTUARY
CHISBURY CHAPEL
Kintbury
Newbury
Clench Common
Cadley
Chisbury
Little Bedwyn
Laylands Green
Enborne
TAN HILL
Hamstead Marshall
MILK HILL
Bagshot
Great Bedwyn
Horton
Allington
PEWSEY DOWNS
Huish
Durley
Inkpen
Upper Green
Stanton St Bernard
West Stowell
Wootton Rivers
Oare
Shalbourne
Ball Hill
Crofton
Ham
West Woodhay
All Cannings
CROFTON BEAM ENGINES
North End
Alton Priors
Stibb Green
Woolton Hill
Broad Laying
New Mill
Eastcourt
WALBURY HILL
WILTON WINDMILL
Honey Street
Wilton
Rivar
Buttermere
East Woodhay
Wilcot
Burbage
Combe
East End
VALE OF PEWSEY
Pewsey
Easton Royal
Woodborough
Milton Lilbourne
West Grafton
East Grafton
Marten
Highclere
Beechingstoke
Bottlesford
Southcott
Wexcombe
Oxenwood
Patney
Manningford Bruce
HENGE
Hilcott
Wedhampton
Linkenholt
Faccombe
HIGHCLERE CASTLE
Chirton
Marden
Tidcombe
Fosbury
Vernham Street
Netherton
North Newnton
Manningford Bohune
Wilsford
Ashmansworth
HAYDOWN HILL
Pewsey Down
Brunton
Vernham Dean
Crux Easton
Charlton
Aughton
Rushall
Upavon
Collingbourne Kingston
Upton
Woodcott
Lower Everleigh
Sunton
Upper Chute
Chute Standen
Ibthorpe
Cadley
Dunley
Everleigh
Collingbourne Ducis
Hurstbourne Tarrant
West Chisenbury
East Chisenbury
Lower Chute
Binley
Tangley
Compton
Collingbourne Forest
WILTSHIRE
Doles Wood
Stoke
Black Heath
Compton Down
Enford
Wildhern
Fifield
Haxton Down
Coombe
Ludgershall
St Mary Bourne
West Down
Enford Down
Fittleton
Hatherden
Little London
Clanville
Enham Alamein
Smannell
Tidworth
North Tidworth
Orcheston Down
Netheravon
DOVECOTE
Appleshaw
Penton Mewsey
Picket Piece
Whitchurch
Figheldean
South Tidworth
Charlton
Kimpton
Fyfield
Hurstbourne Priors
SALISBURY
Ablington
Weyhill
FINKLEY DOWN FARM PARK
Thruxton
Knighton Down
Shipton Bellinger
Andover Down
Orcheston
Milston
THRUXTON
WEYHILL SERVICES
Andover
THE HAWK CONSERVANCY TRUST
Elston
Durrington
Middleton
Longparish
Larkhill
Bulford Camp
Monxton
Shrewton
VISITOR CENTRE
Quarley
Amport
Anna Valley
Upper Clatford
Forton
WOODHENGE
Bulford
BEACON HILL
Abbotts Ann
Harewood Forest
TIDBURY RING
Countess
Cholderton
STONEHENGE
CHOLDERTON CHARLIE'S FARM
Goodworth Clatford
Grateley
Bullington
West Amesbury
Amesbury
Palestine
Wherwell
Newton Stacey
Winterbourne Stoke
Barton Stacey
Berwick St James
Wilsford
Newton Tony
Chilbolton
SUTTON SCOTNEY SERVICES
Boscombe
Allington
Fullerton
Lake
Great Durnford
MUSEUM OF ARMY FLYING
Stapleford
Upper Woodford
Over Wallop
Middle Wallop
Longstock
Little Wishford
Idmiston
Porton
Nether Wallop
Leckford
Middle Woodford
Gomeldon
Great Wishford
Stoford
Winterbourne Dauntsey
Winterbourne Gunner
Lopcombe Corner
Crawley
Worthy Down
South Newton
Stockbridge
Wood
Lower Woodford
East Winterslow
Winterbourne Earls
Chilhampton
Firsdown
Little Somborne
Middle Winterslow
The Common
WHITESHOOT HILL
Broughton
Up Somborne
Littleton
Barford St Martin
WILTON
Ditchampton
Stratford sub Castle
OLD SARUM
New Sarum
ALL SAINTS CHURCH
Houghton
West Winterslow
FLOWERDOWN BARROWS
Wilton
Quidhampton
Laverstock
Pitton
King's Somborne
Ashley
Sparsholt
Burcombe
WILTON HOUSE
Salisbury
Horsebridge
West Tytherley
FARLEY MOUNT
Bemerton
Farley
Netherhampton
Milford
West Harnham
East Tytherley
East Harnham
Brook
FARLEY MOUNT
Stanmore
Coombe Bissett
Britford
East Grimstead
West Dean
MOTTISFONT ABBEY
Stratford Tony
MOMPESSON HOUSE
Alderbury
West Grimstead
Lockerley
Butt's Green
Standon
Olivers Battery
Odstock
Whaddon
East Dean
Mottisfont
Michelmersh
Bishopstone
Homington
Nunton
Bodenham
PEPPERBOX HILL
Braishfield

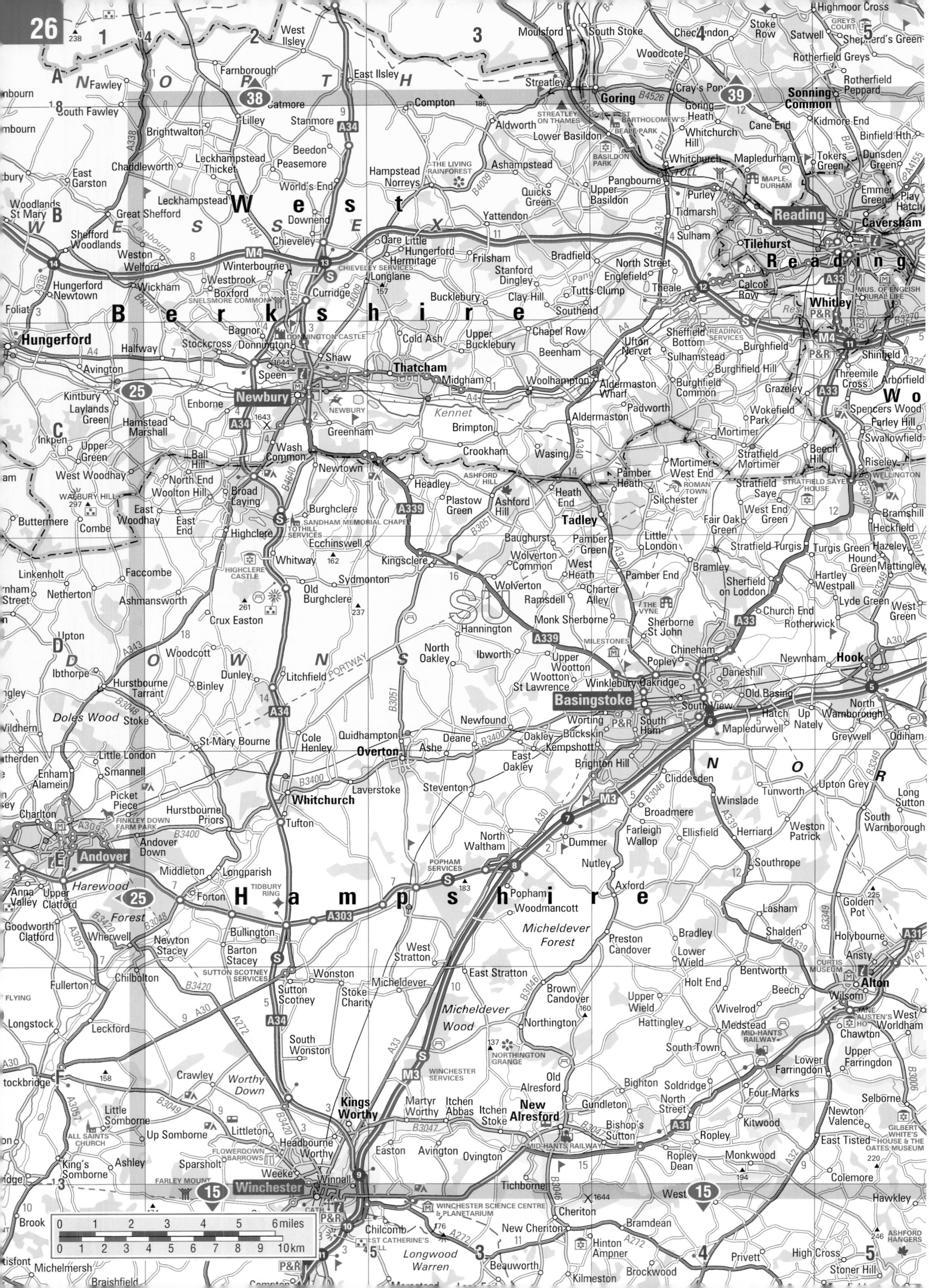
West Berkshire
Berkshire
Hampshire
Reading
Newbury
Basingstoke
Andover
Winchester
Hungerford
Thatcham
Tadley
Whitchurch
Overton
Kings Worthy
New Alresford
Alton
Hook
Goring
Caversham
Tilehurst
Theale
Whitley
Sonning Common
Streatley
Moulsford
South Stoke
Checkendon
Stoke Row
Highmoor Cross
Satwell
Shepherd's Green
Rotherfield Greys
Rotherfield Peppard
Woodcote
Cray's Pond
Goring Heath
Whitchurch Hill
Cane End
Kidmore End
Binfield Hth.
Mapledurham
Tokers Green
Dunsden Green
Emmer Green
Play Hatch
Purley
Tidmarsh
Sulham
Pangbourne
Upper Basildon
Lower Basildon
Aldworth
Compton
East Ilsley
West Ilsley
Farnborough
Catmore
Lilley
Stanmore
Beedon
Peasemore
Fawley
South Fawley
Brightwalton
Chaddleworth
Leckhampstead Thicket
Leckhampstead
East Garston
Woodlands St Mary
Great Shefford
Shefford Woodlands
Weston
Welford
Wickham
Hungerford Newtown
Winterbourne
Westbrook
Boxford
Chieveley
Downend
World's End
Hampstead Norreys
Ashampstead
Quicks Green
Yattendon
Hermitage
Frilsham
Bradfield
Stanford Dingley
Clay Hill
Tutts Clump
Englefield
North Street
Southend
Bucklebury
Upper Bucklebury
Cold Ash
Chapel Row
Beenham
Curridge
Longlane
Bagnor
Donnington
Stockcross
Halfway
Speen
Shaw
Avington
Kintbury
Laylands Green
Enborne
Hamstead Marshall
Inkpen
Upper Green
West Woodhay
Ball Hill
North End
Woolton Hill
Broad Laying
East Woodhay
East End
Buttermere
Combe
Highclere
Burghclere
Newtown
Wash Common
Greenham
Brimpton
Crookham
Midgham
Woolhampton
Aldermaston Wharf
Aldermaston
Padworth
Wasing
Headley
Plastow Green
Ashford Hill
Heath End
Pamber Heath
Silchester
Mortimer
Mortimer West End
Stratfield Mortimer
Beech Hill
Riseley
Stratfield Saye
West End Green
Fair Oak Green
Bramshill
Heckfield
Ufton Nervet
Sheffield Bottom
Sulhamstead
Burghfield
Burghfield Hill
Burghfield Common
Grazeley
Wokefield Park
Three Mile Cross
Shinfield
Arborfield
Spencers Wood
Farley Hill
Swallowfield
Calcot Row
Ecchinswell
Whitway
Kingsclere
Sydmonton
Old Burghclere
Baughurst
Wolverton Common
Wolverton
West Heath
Pamber Green
Little London
Ramsdell
Charter Alley
Pamber End
Bramley
Sherfield on Loddon
Stratfield Turgis
Turgis Green
Hazeley
Hound Green
Mattingley
Hartley Westpall
Lyde Green
West Green
Church End
Rotherwick
Monk Sherborne
Sherborne St John
Chineham
Popley
Daneshill
Newnham
Old Basing
North Warnborough
Up Nately
Hatch
Mapledurwell
Greywell
Odiham
Linkenholt
Faccombe
Netherton
Ashmansworth
Crux Easton
Upton
Woodcott
Ibthorpe
Hurstbourne Tarrant
Binley
Dunley
Litchfield
Hannington
North Oakley
Ibworth
Upper Wootton
Wootton St Lawrence
Winklebury
Oakridge
South View
South Ham
Worting
Buckskin
Kempshott
Brighton Hill
Oakley
East Oakley
Deane
Newfound
Ashe
Quidhampton
Cole Henley
St Mary Bourne
Stoke
Doles Wood
Little London
Smannell
Enham Alamein
Picket Piece
Charlton
Hurstbourne Priors
Andover Down
Laverstoke
Steventon
Tufton
Cliddesden
Winslade
Tunworth
Upton Grey
Long Sutton
South Warnborough
Weston Patrick
Herriard
Ellisfield
Farleigh Wallop
Broadmere
Dummer
Nutley
North Waltham
Southrope
Axford
Popham
Woodmancott
Middleton
Longparish
Forton
Harewood Forest
Anna Valley
Upper Clatford
Goodworth Clatford
Wherwell
Bullington
Newton Stacey
Barton Stacey
West Stratton
East Stratton
Micheldever
Micheldever Forest
Micheldever Wood
Preston Candover
Brown Candover
Lower Wield
Upper Wield
Bradley
Lasham
Shalden
Golden Pot
Holybourne
Ansty
Bentworth
Holt End
Beech
Wilsom
Wivelrod
Medstead
Hattingley
Chawton
West Worldham
Upper Farringdon
Lower Farringdon
South Town
Four Marks
Northington
Old Alresford
Bighton
Soldridge
North Street
Gundleton
Bishop's Sutton
Ropley
Ropley Dean
Kitwood
Newton Valence
Selborne
East Tisted
Monkwood
Colemore
Hawkley
Chilbolton
Fullerton
Wonston
Sutton Scotney
Stoke Charity
South Wonston
Longstock
Leckford
Stockbridge
Crawley
Worthy Down
Little Somborne
Up Somborne
Littleton
King's Somborne
Ashley
Sparsholt
Headbourne Worthy
Weeke
Winnall
Martyr Worthy
Itchen Abbas
Itchen Stoke
Easton
Avington
Ovington
Tichborne
Cheriton
New Cheriton
Bramdean
Hinton Ampner
Brockwood
Kilmeston
Beauworth
Chilcomb
Longwood Warren
West Meon (West)
Privett
High Cross
Stoner Hill
Brook
Michelmersh
Braishfield
M4
M3
A34
A339
A33
A303
A4
A30
A31
A32
A272
A338
A343
A3057
B3400
B3047
B3046
B3051
B3349
B3420
B3048
B4000
B4494
B4009
B4526
B471
B3030
B3006
A340
38
39
25
15
Highclere Castle
Basildon Park
Beale Park
The Living Rainforest
Maple-Durham
Mus. of English Rural Life
Stratfield Saye House
Wellington
The Vyne
Milestones
Sandham Memorial Chapel
Tothill Services
Chieveley Services
Reading Services
Popham Services
Winchester Services
Sutton Scotney Services
Finkley Down Farm Park
Tidbury Ring
Northington Grange
Mid-Hants Railway
Jane Austen's House
Curtis Museum
Gilbert White's House & The Oates Museum
Ashford Hangers
Winchester Science Centre & Planetarium
St Catherine's Hill
Flowerdown Barrows
Farley Mount
All Saints Church
Donnington Castle
Snelsmore Common
Walbury Hill
Roman Town
Ashford Hill
Portway
Kennet
0 1 2 3 4 5 6 miles
0 1 2 3 4 5 6 7 8 9 10 km

Henley-on-Thames
Remenham
Hurley
Windsor
Burnham
Farnham Royal
Wexham Street
Stoke Green
Iver Heath
Uxbridge
Hillingdon
Yeading
Cowley
Maidenhead
Taplow
Bray
Slough
SLOUGH
Yiewsley
Hayes
Southall
Cox Grn.
Knowl Hill
Littlewick Green
Wargrave
Shiplake
Dorney
Eton Wick
Langley
Richings Park
West Drayton
Harmondsworth
Harlington
Sipson
Cranford
Heston
Brentford
Maidenhead
Waltham St Lawrence
White Waltham
Woodlands Park
Holyport
Fifield
Eton
Datchet
Colnbrook
Longford
HEATHROW AIRPORT
Isleworth
Twyford
Ruscombe
Paley Street
Touchen End
Oakley Green
WINDSOR
Horton
Stanwell Moor
Stanwell
HOUNSLOW
Woodley
Shurlock Row
Whistley Green
Jealott's Hill
Hawthorn Hill
Maiden's Green
Cranbourne
Old Windsor
Wraysbury
West Bedfont
East Bedfont
Hurst
Moss End
Warfield
Winkfield
GREAT PARK
Englefield Green
Hythe End
EGHAM
Feltham
Earley
Winnersh
Binfield
Newell Grn.
Winkfield Row
Woodside
Staines-upon-Thames
Ashford
Hanworth
Teddington
Emmbrook
Popeswood
Burleigh
Bullbrook
Hampton
Sindlesham
WOKINGHAM
Bracknell
Ascot
Sunninghill
Virginia Water
Thorpe
Laleham
Littleton
Sunbury-on-Thames
Arborfield Cross
Eastheath
Easthampstead
South Ascot
Sunningdale
West Molesey
East Molesey
Barkham
Bracknell Forest
Broomhall
Lyne
CHERTSEY
Shepperton
Walton-on-Thames
Arborfield Garrison
The Throat
Addlestone
WEYBRIDGE
Esher
Wick Hill
Crowthorne
Windlesham
Ottershaw
Hersham
Finchampstead
Little Sandhurst
Bagshot
Burrowhill
New Haw
Claygate
Eversley
Sandhurst
Lightwater
Chobham
Woodham
Byfleet
Whiteley Village
Eversley Cross
Yateley
CAMBERLEY
West End
Castle Green
West Byfleet
Cobham
Oxshott
Frogmore
York Town
Donkey Town
Bisley
Knaphill
Cheapside
Wisley
Stoke D'Abernon
Bramshill Forest
Blackwater
Hawley
Frimley
Chobham Ridges
Horsell
WOKING
Pyrford
Downside
Hartfordbridge
Fox Lane
Farnborough Green
Deepcut
Brookwood
St John's
Old Woking
Ripley
Martyr's Green
Leatherhead Common
Hartley Wintney
Phoenix Green
Cove
Frimley Green
Mayford
Send Marsh
Send
Ockham
Fetcham
West Heath
Mytchett
Pirbright
Fox Corner
Burntcommon
Little Bookham
Winchfield
Fleet
Pondtail
FARNBOROUGH
Sutton Green
Effingham
East Horsley
Great Bookham
Dogmersfield
Worplesdon
West Horsley
Crookham Village
Ash Vale
Willey Green
Pitch Place
Slyfield
Burpham
West Clandon
East Clandon
Westhumble
Church Crookham
Long Valley
ALDERSHOT
Wyke
Normandy
Stoughton
Wood Street
Merrow
Ranmore Common
Mill Lane
Ewshot
Heath End
Ash
Flexford
Wanborough
Guildford
Newland's Corner
Crondall
Hog Hatch
Badshot Lea
Upper Hale
Tongham
Hogs Back
Onslow Village
Gomshall
Abinger Hammer
Westcott
Farnham
Runfold
Seale
Puttenham
Littleton
Compton
Shalford
Chilworth
Albury
Shere
Wotton
Well
Dippenhall
The Sands
Shackleford
Hurtmore
Blackheath
Brook
Sutton
Abinger Common
Wrecclesham
Norney
Farncombe
Bramley
Wonersh
Farley Green
Holmbury St Mary
South Holmwood
Lower Froyle
The Bourne
Peper Harow
Eashing
Godalming
Shamley Green
Peaslake
Coldharbour
Bentley
Rowledge
Elstead
Milford
Hurt Wood
Froyle
Tilford
Thorncombe Street
Blacknest
Spreakley
Millbridge
Bucks Horn Oak
Frensham
Rushmoor
Tuesley
Grafham
Rowly
Forest Green
Binsted
Wheatley
Wheelerstreet
Hydestile
Ewhurst
Hascombe
Ewhurst Green
Ockley
Wyck
Thursley
Witley
Kingsley
East Worldham
Churt
Bowlhead Green
Wormley
Hambledon
Cranleigh
Walliswood
Sleaford
Beacon Hill
Brook
Sandhills
Loxhill
Oakwoodhill
Oakhanger
Arford
Lindford
Bordon Camp
Headley
Hindhead
Combe Common
Dunsford
Ellen's Green
Kingsfold
Bordon
Grayshott
Chiddingfold
Alfold Crossways
Rowhook
Whitehill
Standford
Grayswood
Rudgwick
Warnham
Blackmoor
Bramshott
Shottermill
Alfold
Conford
Haslemere
Alfold Bars
Tisman's Common
Bucks Green
Strood Green
Broadbridge Heath
Hammer
Ramsnest Common
Park Street
Greatham
Liphook
Camelsdale
Fisherstreet
Loxwood
Slinfold
Empshott
Longmoor Camp
Linchmere
Kingsley Green
Plaistow
Ifold
The Haven
Liss Forest
Langley
Northchapel
Mackerel's Common
Roundstreet Common
Itchingfield
West Liss
Fernhurst
Five Oaks
East Liss
Rake
Newpound Common
Southwater Street
Liss
Milland
Balls Cross
Barns Green
Steep Marsh
Hill Brow
Lurgashall
Kirdford
Wisborough Green
Southwater
Henley
Billingshurst

Uxbridge
Willesden
Camden
Islington
Barking
EALING
Acton
Paddington
City
Woolwich
Hayes
Southall
Kensington
Westminster
Southwark
Bermondsey
Blackwall Tunnel
Hammersmith
Chelsea
LAMBETH
Deptford
Greenwich
Brentford
Fulham
Battersea
Lewisham
HEATHROW AIRPORT
HOUNSLOW
Richmond
Wandsworth
Catford
Feltham
Twickenham
Streatham
Staines upon-Thames
Ashford
Teddington
Wimbledon
Merton
BROMLEY
Sunbury-on-Thames
Kingston upon Thames
Mitcham
Beckenham
Surbiton
New Malden
Morden
CHERTSEY
Walton-on-Thames
Croydon
WEYBRIDGE
Esher
Carshalton
Cheam
Sutton
Wallington
Byfleet
Ewell
Purley
Cobham
Oxshott
EPSOM
BANSTEAD
Coulsdon
Warlingham
Biggin Hill
Leatherhead
Ashtead
Tadworth
Kingswood
CATERHAM
Great Bookham
Merstham
Limpsfield
Oxted
Westerham
Dorking
Redhill
Reigate
Westcott
Salfords
Edenbridge
Horley
Lingfield
GATWICK AIRPORT
Cranleigh
Three Bridges
East Grinstead
Crawley
Horsham
Balcombe
Wych Cross
St Leonard's Forest
Hurt Wood
0 1 2 3 4 5 6 miles
0 1 2 3 4 5 6 7 8 9 10 km

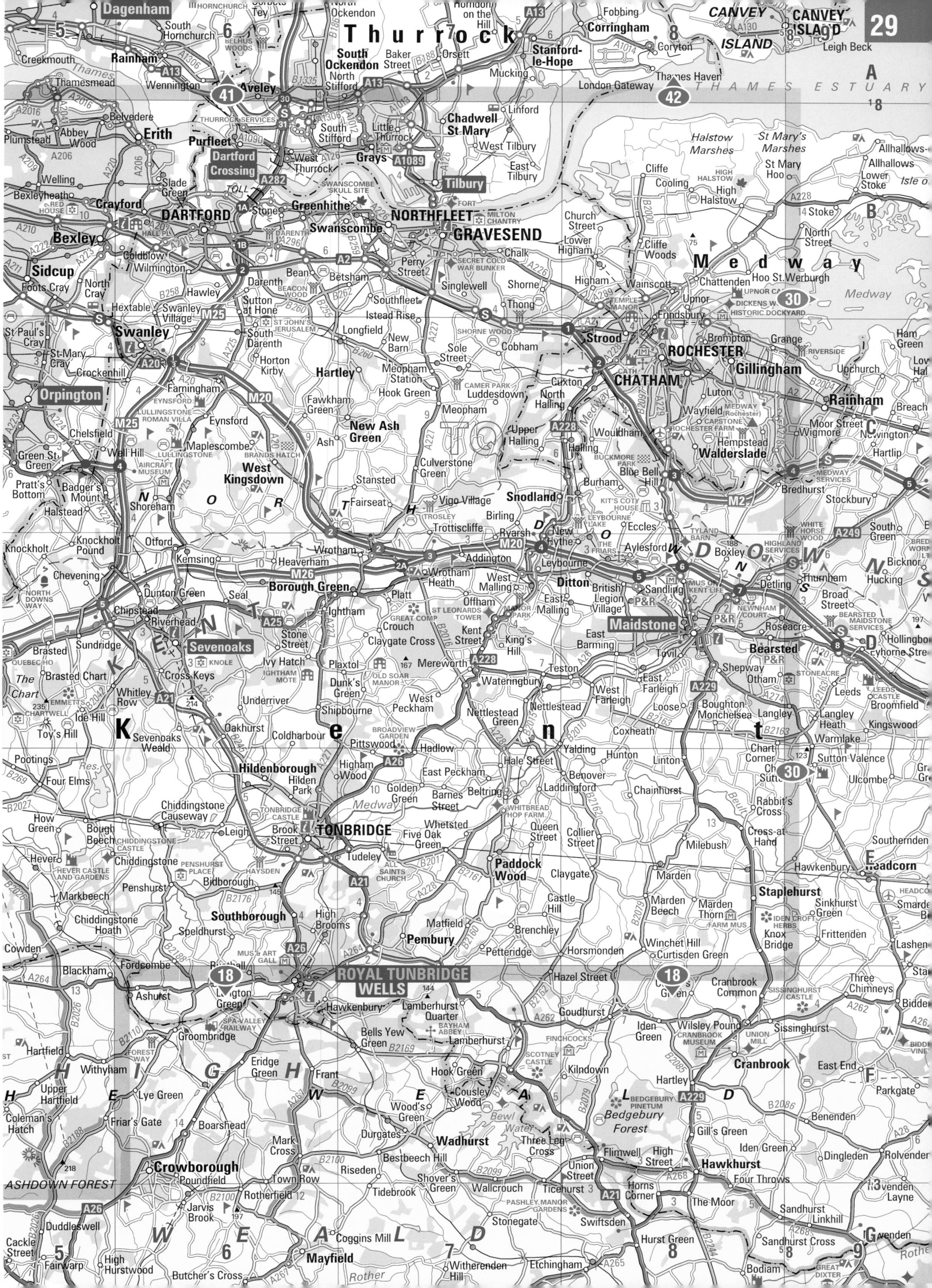

Dagenham
Thurrock
South Ockendon
Rainham
Aveley
Purfleet
Grays
Tilbury
Chadwell St Mary
Stanford-le-Hope
Corringham
CANVEY ISLAND
THAMES ESTUARY
Erith
Dartford Crossing
Bexley
Sidcup
DARTFORD
Greenhithe
Swanscombe
NORTHFLEET
GRAVESEND
Swanley
Orpington
Strood
ROCHESTER
Gillingham
CHATHAM
Rainham
Medway
Walderslade
Snodland
West Kingsdown
New Ash Green
Hartley
Meopham
Borough Green
Wrotham
Maidstone
Ditton
Aylesford
West Malling
Sevenoaks
Bearsted
Kent
KENT
NORTH DOWNS
TQ
Hildenborough
TONBRIDGE
Paddock Wood
Staplehurst
Headcorn
Marden
Southborough
Pembury
ROYAL TUNBRIDGE WELLS
Crowborough
Wadhurst
Cranbrook
Hawkhurst
Bedgebury Forest
Mayfield
ASHDOWN FOREST
HIGH WEALD
Goudhurst
Lamberhurst
Edenbridge
Groombridge
Frant
Rotherfield
Ticehurst
Stonegate
Hurst Green
Bodiam

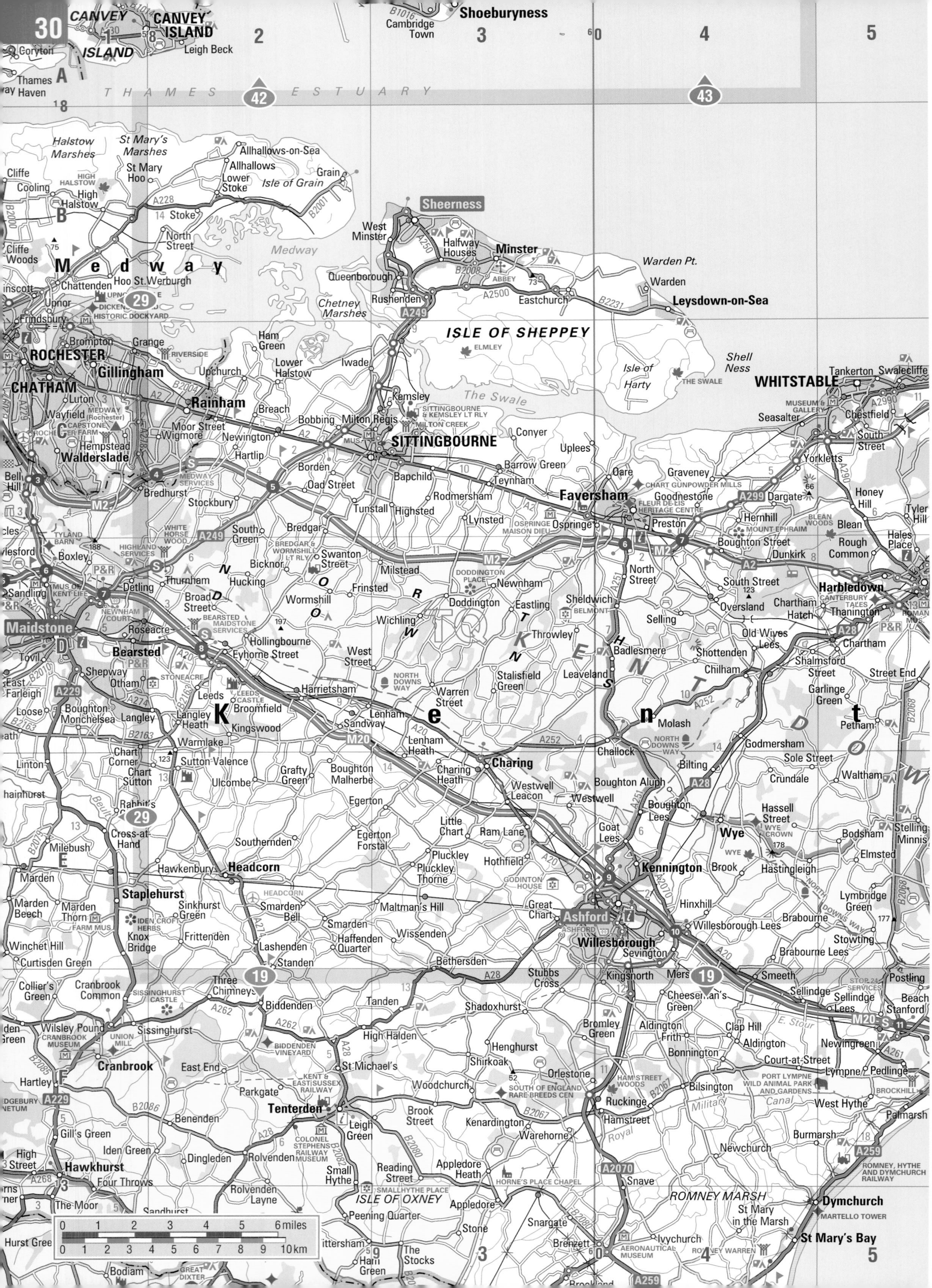
CANVEY ISLAND
CANVEY ISLAND
Leigh Beck
Shoeburyness
Cambridge Town
Corytori
Thames Haven
THAMES ESTUARY
42
43
Halstow Marshes
St Mary's Marshes
Allhallows-on-Sea
Allhallows
Grain
Cliffe
Cooling
High Halstow
St Mary Hoo
Lower Stoke
Isle of Grain
Stoke
North Street
Sheerness
West Minster
Halfway Houses
Minster
Warden Pt.
Warden
Leysdown-on-Sea
Eastchurch
Queenborough
Rushenden
Cliffe Woods
Medway
Chattenden
Hoo St.Werburgh
Upnor
Frindsbury
HISTORIC DOCKYARD
Chetney Marshes
ISLE OF SHEPPEY
ELMLEY
Brompton
ROCHESTER
Grange
Gillingham
RIVERSIDE
Ham Green
Lower Halstow
Iwade
Upchurch
CHATHAM
Rainham
Breach
Isle of Harty
THE SWALE
Shell Ness
WHITSTABLE
Tankerton
Swalecliffe
The Swale
Kemsley
SITTINGBOURNE & KEMSLEY LT RLY
MILTON CREEK
Luton
Wayfield
Moor Street
Wigmore
Bobbing
Milton Regis
SITTINGBOURNE
Conyer
Seasalter
Chestfield
South Street
Hempstead
Walderslade
Newington
Hartlip
Uplees
Yorkletts
Bell Hill
MEDWAY SERVICES
Bredhurst
Borden
Oad Street
Bapchild
Barrow Green
Teynham
Oare
Graveney
CHART GUNPOWDER MILLS
Faversham
Goodnestone
FLEUR DE LIS HERITAGE CENTRE
Dargate
Honey Hill
Stockbury
Rodmersham
Tunstall
Highsted
Lynsted
OSPRINGE MAISON DIEU
Ospringe
Preston
Hernhill
BLEAN WOODS
Blean
Tyler Hill
MOUNT EPHRAIM
South Green
Bredgar
BREDGAR & WORMSHILL LT RLY
Swanton Street
Boughton Street
Rough Common
Hales Place
Boxley
Dunkirk
Milstead
DODDINGTON PLACE
Newnham
North Street
South Street
Harbledown
Sandling
Detling
Thurnham
Hucking
Fristed
Doddington
Eastling
Sheldwich
BELMONT
Overland
CANTERBURY TALES
Chartham Hatch
Thanington
MUS OF KENT LIFE
Broad Street
Wormshill
Selling
Old Wives Lees
Chartham
NEWNHAM COURT
BEARSTED MAIDSTONE SERVICES
Maidstone
Roseacre
Wichling
Throwley
Bearsted
Hollingbourne
Eyhorne Street
West Street
Badlesmere
Shottenden
Shalmsford Street
Tovil
Shepway
Otham
STONEACRE
Chilham
Leaveland
Street End
East Farleigh
Leeds
LEEDS CASTLE
Stalisfield Green
NORTH DOWNS WAY
Harrietsham
Warren Street
Garlinge Green
Loose
Boughton Monchelsea
Langley
Langley Heath
Broomfield
Lenham
Molash
Petham
Kingswood
Sandway
Kent
Lenham Heath
Godmersham
Warmlake
Challock
Charing
Sole Street
Chart Corner
Sutton Valence
Grafty Green
Boughton Malherbe
Charing Heath
Bilting
Linton
Chart Sutton
Ulcombe
Westwell Leacon
Westwell
Boughton Aluph
Crundale
Waltham
Egerton
Boughton Lees
Hassell Street
WYE CROWN
Stelling Minnis
Rabbit's Cross
Cross-at-Hand
Little Chart
Ram Lane
Goat Lees
Wye
Bodsham
Southernden
Egerton Forstal
Milebush
Pluckley
Hothfield
WYE
Brook
Elmsted
Hastingleigh
Marden
Hawkenbury
Headcorn
Pluckley Thorne
GODINTON HOUSE
Kennington
Staplehurst
HEADCORN
Sinkhurst Green
Smarden Bell
Maltman's Hill
Great Chart
Ashford
Hinxhill
Lymbridge Green
Marden Beech
Marden Thorn
FARM MUS
IDEN CROFT HERBS
Knox Bridge
Frittenden
Smarden
Haffenden Quarter
Wissenden
Willesborough
Sevington
Willesborough Lees
Brabourne
Stowting
Winchet Hill
Curtisden Green
Lashenden
Standen
Bethersden
Brabourne Lees
Collier's Green
Cranbrook Common
SISSINGHURST CASTLE
Three Chimneys
Biddenden
Tanden
Stubbs Cross
Kingsnorth
Mersham
Smeeth
Sellindge
Postling
Shadoxhurst
Cheeseman's Green
Sellindge Lees
Stanford
Wilsley Pound
CRANBROOK MUSEUM
Sissinghurst
UNION MILL
BIDDENDEN VINEYARD
High Halden
Bromley Green
Aldington Frith
Clap Hill
Aldington
Newingreen
Cranbrook
East End
St Michael's
Henghurst
Shirkoak
Bonnington
Court-at-Street
Lympne
Pedlinge
KENT & EAST SUSSEX RAILWAY
Orlestone
HAM STREET WOODS
Bilsington
PORT LYMPNE WILD ANIMAL PARK AND GARDENS
BROCKHILL
Hartley
Parkgate
Woodchurch
SOUTH OF ENGLAND RARE BREEDS CEN
Ruckinge
Military Canal
West Hythe
Tenterden
Brook Street
Hamstreet
Palmarsh
Benenden
Leigh Green
Kenardington
Warehorne
Royal
Burmarsh
Gill's Green
COLONEL STEPHENS RAILWAY MUSEUM
Newchurch
High Street
Iden Green
Dingleden
Rolvenden
ROMNEY, HYTHE AND DYMCHURCH RAILWAY
Hawkhurst
Small Hythe
Reading Street
Appledore Heath
SMALLHYTHE PLACE
HORNE'S PLACE CHAPEL
Snave
Four Throws
Rolvenden Layne
ISLE OF OXNEY
ROMNEY MARSH
Dymchurch
The Moor
Sandhurst
Appledore
St Mary in the Marsh
MARTELLO TOWER
Peening Quarter
Snargate
Stone
Brenzett
Ivychurch
Hurst Green
Wittersham
AERONAUTICAL MUSEUM
ROMNEY WARREN
St Mary's Bay
The Stocks
Ham Green
Bodiam
GREAT DIXTER
Brookland
0 1 2 3 4 5 6 miles
0 1 2 3 4 5 6 7 8 9 10 km
19
29
M2
M20
A2
A20
A28
A249
A229
A252
A251
A2070
A259
A262
A274
A228
A2500
B2231
A299
A290
A2990
A261

5
6
7
8
9
A
B
C
D
E
F
G
TURNER CONTEMPORARY
THE SHELL GROTTO
Margate
Cliftonville
Foreness Pt.
Westgate on Sea
MARGATE
DREAMLAND
B2052
Kingsgate
NORTH FORELAND
LIGHTHOUSE
Northdown
St Peter's
BROADSTAIRS
BLEAK HOUSE
DICKENS HOUSE MUSEUM
Dumpton
RECULVER
RECULVER TOWERS AND ROMAN FORT
Minnis Bay
HERNE BAY
Reculver
Birchington
Hillborough
QUEX HOUSE
Isle of Thanet
SPITFIRE AND HURRICANE MEM
Northwood
A255
Beltinge
A299
A28
Acol
Greenhill
Herne
Broomfield
St Nicholas at Wade
A299
WINDMILL
A253
B2190
B2050
A256
Newington
Boyden Gate
Sarre
Manston
A299
Ramsgate
MARITIME MUSEUM
Hoath
Chislet
Monkton
Minster
Way
Cliffsend
Pegwell
Calcott
Upstreet
Stour
PEGWELL BAY
SANDWICH & PEGWELL BAY
Pegwell Bay
West Stourmouth
ST. AUGUSTINE'S CROSS
A291
Hersden
A28
East Stourmouth
A256
Broadoak
Grove
STODMARSH
Westmarsh
Preston
RICHBOROUGH CASTLE
Ware
Sturry
Westbere
Fordwich
Stodmarsh
Elmstone
Hoaden
AMPHITHEATRE
Great Stonar
P&R
Canterbury
Wickhambreux
WINGHAM WILDLIFE PARK
A257
Sandwich Bay
A257
Ickham
Sandwich
ST. AUGUSTINE'S ABBEY
Littlebourne
Wingham
Guilton
Ash
TOLL
ROYAL ST. GEORGE'S
CANTERBURY
HOWLETTS WILD ANIMAL PARK
Marshborough
A2050
Bramling
Staple
Woodnesborough
Stone Cross
TR
P&R
Bekesbourne
A2
Gore
Worth
Nackington
Patrixbourne
Goodnestone
Ham
A258
Adisham
GOODNESTONE PARK
Eastry
Bridge
NORTH DOWNS WAY
Finglesham
Lower Hardres
Chillenden
Knowlton
Sholden
MARITIME AND LOCAL HISTORY MUSEUM
Aylesham
Betteshanger
DEAL
THE DOWNS
Bishopsbourne
Easole Street
Nonington
DEAL CASTLE
Kingston
B2046
Northbourne
Upper Hardres Court
Snowdown
Tilmanstone
Great Mongeham
Elvington
Walmer
Barham
Womenswold
WALMER CASTLE AND GARDENS
Derringstone
Barfrestone
EAST KENT RLY
Ripple
Bossingham
Woolage Green
Eythorne
East Studdal
Sutton
ELHAM VALLEY VINEYARD
A2
West Langdon
Ringwould
Kingsdown
Shepherdswell
Coxhill
A256
East Langdon
Martin
A258
Denton
LYDDEN
Coldred
Martin Mill
Wingmore
Wootton
A260
Whitfield
Lyminge Forest
Selsted
Lydden
Guston
St Margaret's at Cliffe
ST JOHN'S COMMANDERY
LYDDEN TEMPLE EWELL
Elham
Temple Ewell
West Cliffe
THE BAY MUSEUM
Ewell Minnis
Swingfield Street
Rhodes Minnis
BUTTERFLY CENTRE
CRABBLE CORN MILL
St Margaret's Bay
THE PINES GARDEN
Swingfield Minnis
A2
Buckland
SOUTH FORELAND
A256
Ottinge
Alkham
ROMAN PAINTED HOUSE
WHITE CLIFFS
Densole
Maxton
CASTLE & HELLFIRE CORNER
CALAIS DUNKERQUE
KENT BATTLE OF BRITAIN MUSEUM
Drellingore
Lyminge
West Hougham
Farthingloe
DOVER
Paddlesworth
Hawkinge
Etchinghill
B2011
A20
Aycliff
DE BRADELEI WHARF
CHANNEL TUNNEL
Capel le Ferne
SAMPHIRE HOE
borough
EAST CLIFF & WARREN
Newington
A20
East Wear Bay
ELHAM VALLEY RLY MUS
Cheriton
Folkestone
Saltwood
ROTUNDA
Sandgate
CLIFF LIFT
Hythe
19
CHANNEL
TUNNEL

MYNYDD PRESELI
Pontfaen
Crymych
Tegryn
Cwmorgan
Tanglwst
Pentre-galar
Mynachlog-ddu
Hermon
Llanfyrnach
Hen-feddau fawr
Dinas
Trelech
Bryn-Iwan
Cwmduad
New Inn
Rosebush
Puncheston
Castlebythe
Tufton
Henry's Moat
Maenclochog
Llangolman
Glandy Cross
Glandwr
Hebron
Blaen-waun
Pen-y-bont
Blaen-y-coed
Cynwyl Elfed
Woodstock
Wallis
New Moat
Efailwen
Pant-y-Caws
Llanglydwen
Cefn-y-pant
Cwmbach
Llanwinio
Talog
Bwlchnewydd
LLYS-Y-FRAN RESERVOIR
Llys-y-frân
Walton East
Llanycefn
Pen-ffordd
Maesgwynne
Cross-hands
Login
Llanboidy
Cwmfelin Mynach
Gellywen
Ty-hen
Abernant
Newchurch
Dyffryn
SN
Llandissilio
Hiraeth
Henllan Amgoed
Meidrim
Merthyr
Tre-vaughan
Carmarthen (Caerfyrddin)
Clarbeston
Clarbeston Road
Bletherston
Llanfallteg
Llangynin
Sarnau
Llanllwch
CORS GOCH, LLANLLWCH
Gelli
Clunderwen
Cwmfelin Boeth
Bancyfelin
Wiston
LLAWHADEN CASTLE
Bethesda
Llawhaden
Robeston Wathen
Whitland
Pwll-trap
Llangynog
Llangain
Llanddewi Velfrey
Trevaughan
Backe
St Clears (Sanclêr)
The Rhos
Narberth (Arberth)
WILSON MUSEUM
Blackpool
Crinow
Lampeter Velfrey
Llwyn-y-brain
Llanddowror
Afon Tâf
Afon Cywyn
Morfa Bach
Afon Tywi
PICTON CASTLE & GARDENS
BLUE LAGOON
Minwear
Cross Hands
OAKWOOD
Landshipping
Templeton
Cold Blow
Princes Gate
Tavernspite
Halfpenny Furze
Llanybri
Red Roses
Llandawke
DYLAN THOMAS BOATHOUSE
Llansteffan
CASTLE
Laugharne
Landshipping Quay
Martletwy
Ludchurch
Longstone
Llanteg
Llansadurnen
Broadway
Ferryside
Brook
FOLLY FARM
Black Tar
Yerbeston
Reynalton
Marros
MUSEUM OF SPEED
Broadlay
Loveston
Thomas Chapel
Stepaside
COLBY WOODLAND GARDEN
Pendine
East Marsh
Llansaint
Cresswell Quay
Begelly
Kilgetty
Amroth
Lawrenny
Jeffreyston
Cresselly
Pendine Sands
Traeth Pentywyn
West Williamston
Broadmoor
Carew Newton
CAREW CASTLE
East Williamston
Saundersfoot
PEMBROKESHIRE COAST
ARFORDIR PENFRO
Cosheston
Redberth
Carew
Milton
Sageston
Broadfield
Pembrey Forest
Pembroke (Penfro)
Carew Cheriton
TENBY DINOSAUR PARK
New Hedges
TUDOR MERCHANT'S HOUSE
LAMPHEY BISHOP'S PALACE
MANOR HOUSE WILDLIFE PARK
Lamphey
St Florence
Gumfreston
Tenby (Dinbych-y-Pysgod)
CARMARTHEN BAY
BAE CAERFYRDDIN
PEMBREY
Hodgeston
Jameston
Penally
Freshwater East
Lydstep
Giltar Pt.
Caldey Sound
Cheriton or Stackpole Elidor
MANORBIER CASTLE
Manorbier
Trewent Pt.
Trwyn Trewent
Old Castle Hd.
Caldey Island
Ynys Bŷr
Chapel Pt.
Trwyn Capel
Stackpole Hd.
Pen Stackpole
SS
Burry Holms
Rhossili Bay
Bae Rhossili
Worms Head
Penrhyn-Gŵyr
A40
A477
A478
A4075
A4066
A484
B4313
B4329
B4299
B4298
B4312
B4314
B4316
B4318
B4328
B4586
B4584
B4585
B4139
B4333
45
46
44
0 1 2 3 4 5 6 miles
0 1 2 3 4 5 6 7 8 9 10 km

Carmarthenshire
(Sir Gaerfyrddin)
Swansea
(Abertawe)
Brechfa Forest
Llandovery
Gwernogle
Abergorlech
Afon Cothi
Talley
Cwmdwr
Myrtle Hill
Nant-y-ffin
Pen-y-garn
Cynros
Cwm-byr
Waunclunda
Llansadwrn
Llanwrda
Alltwalis
Mynydd Rhos-Wen
Cwmdu
Halfway
Felindre
Cilgwyn
Myddfai
Llanpumsaint
Llanllawddog
Brechfa
Soar
Ashfield
Llangadog
Usk Reservoir
Pontarsais
Horeb
Llanfynydd
Hermon
Pant-glas
Capel Isaac
Salem
Manordeilo
Cwmifor
Gwili Railway
Rhydargaeau
Pant-teg
Felingwm uchaf
Pantgwyn
Dyffryn Ceidrych
Talsarn
Llanddeusant
Twynllanan
Bethlehem
Bronwydd Arms
Peniel
Felingwm isaf
Llanfihangel-uwch-Gwili
Pen-y-banc
Rhosmaen
Pontbren Araeth
Pont-ar-llechau
Ffynnon ddrain
Capel Gwyn
Broad Oak
Pentrefelin
Court Henry
Dinefwr Park
Vale of Tywi
Dyffryn Tywi
Trichrug
Capel Gwynfe
Pont Aber
White Mill
Pont-ar-gothi
Llangathen
Aberglasney
Cilsan
Llandeilo
Neuadd
Abergwili
Carmarthen
Nantgaredig
Llanegwad
Felindre
Dryslwyn
Ffairfach
Black Mountain
Y Mynydd Du
Tanerdy
Llangunnor
Capel Dewi
Llanarthne
Afon Tywi
Gelli Aur
Golden Grove
Trapp
Carreg Cennen Castle & Farm
Foel Fraith
Pensarn
Johnstown
Nantycaws
The National Botanic Garden of Wales
Penrhiwgoch
Temple Bar
Milo
Llandyfan
Cwmffrwd
Llanddarog
Maesybont
Carmel
Croesyceiliog
Idole
Bancycapel
Cwmisfael
Porthyrhyd
Gwendraeth Fach
Llyn Llech Owain
Foel-gastell
Pentre-Gwenlais
Llandybie
Dre-fach
Twynmynydd
Brynamman
Rhosaman
Llangendeirne
Cefneithin
Gorslas
Caer-bryn
Glanaman
Afon Aman
Crwbin
Drefach
Cwm-y-glo
Pen-y-groes
Tir-y-dail
Cwmllynfell
Ystradowen
Pontantwn
Bancffosfelen
Cwm-mawr
Cross Hands
Morfa
Saron
Pontamman
Garnant
Gwaun-Leision
Tairgwaith
Llandyfaelog
Pontyberem
Tumble
Penybanc
Ammanford
(Rhydaman)
Betws
Gwaun-Cae-Gurwen
Upper Cwm-twrch
Cwmgiedd
Meinciau
Pentre
Cwmgwili
Capel Hendre
Pantyffynnon
Tycroes
Cwmgors
Lower Cwm-twrch
Ystradgynlais
Kidwelly Industrial Museum
Four Roads
Pont-Henri
Greynor
Garnswllt
Gurnos
Ystalyfera
Mynyddygarreg
Pontyates
Llannon
Mynydd y Gwair
Kidwelly
(Cydweli)
Cynheidre
Llwyn-têg
Pont Abraham Services
Sylen
Godre'r-graig
Swansea Valley
Cwm Abertawe
Carway
Ffos Las
Five Roads
Llanedi
Sardis
Graig Fawr
Climaen gwyn
Ynys-meudwy
Trimsaran
Horeb
Lliedi Resrs.
Fforest
Pentrebach
Rhyd-y-fro
Cilybebyll
Crynant
Mynydd March-Hywel
Pontardawe
Glantawe Riverside Park
Pembrey
Pinged
Waun-y-clyn
Hendy
Pontarddulais
Cwm-Dulais
Rhyd-y-gwin
Craig-cefn-parc
Trebanos
Gellinudd
Rhôs
Cefn Coed Colliery Mus
Cwmbach
Felinfoel
Allt
Felindre
Rhyd-y-pandy
Alltwen
Achddu
Pwll
Furnace
Llangennech
Waungron
Faerdre
Clydach
Cilfrew
Aberdulais
Falls
Tonna
Burry Port
(Porth Tywyn)
Sandy
Dafen
Bryn
Grovesend
Pontlliw
Swansea Services
Ynystawe
Pant-lasau
Glais
Bryn-coch
Rhydding
Neath Abbey
Cadoxton-Juxta-Neath
Neath Museum
Millennium Coastal Park Discovery Centre
Llanelli
Llwyn-hendy
Bynea
Yspitty
Penllergaer
Gorseinon
Llangyfelach
Heol-las
Birchgrove
Morriston
Skewen
Neath
(Castell-Nedd)
Machynys
Morfa
Wildfowl and Wetlands Trust
Loughor
Cadle
Llansamlet
Pentre-dwr
Cimla
Whiteford Pt.
Trwyn Whiteford
Llanrhidian Sands
Traeth Llanrhidian
Pen-clawdd
Gowerton
Fforest-fach
Landore
Pentre-chwyth
Cwm
Bon-y-maen
Llandarcy
Briton Ferry
Pontrhydyfen
Crofty
Blue Anchor
Waunarlwydd
Cwmdu
Foxhole
Swansea
(Abertawe)
Crymlyn Bog and Pant-y-Sais
Wernffrwd
Llanmorlais
Three Crosses
Dunvant
Plantasia
Port Tennant
Pwll-y-glaw
Cheriton
Landimore
Weobley Castle
Killay
Sketty
Brynbryddan
Baglan
Llanmadoc
Burry Green
Llethrid
Upper Killay
Clyne Valley
Brynmill
Swansea Museum
Mynydd Dinas
Cwmafan
Llangennith
Llanrhidian
Gower
Swansea
Ilston
Mayals
National Waterfront Museum
Aberavon
Burry
Reynoldston
Black Pill
The Beacon
Lunnon
West Cross
Swansea Bay
Port Talbot
Goytre
Llanddewi
Gower Heritage Centre
Kittle
Bishopston
Mansfield
Lovespoon Gallery
Oystermouth Castle
Taibach
Rhossili
Knelston
Parkmill
Pennard
Oldway
Newton
The Mumbles
(Y Mwmbwls)
Bae Abertawe
Margam
Middleton
Scurlage
Penrice
Nicholaston
Penmaen
Oxwich
Southgate
Groes
Gower Coast
Pilton Green
Oxwich Bay
Bae Oxwich
Mumbles Hd.
Trwyn yr Mwmbwls
Horton
Oxwich Castle
Pwlldu Hd.
Pen Pwlldu
Overton
Port-Eynon
Port Eynon
Port Eynon Bay
Bae Port Eynon
Port Eynon Pt.
Trwyn Port Eynon
SN
SS
Kenfig
Mawdlam
Kenfig Pool and Dunes
Kenfig Burrows
Royal Porthcawl
Hutchwn
Porthca

Llandovery
Halfway
Myrtle Hill
Llanwrda
Cilgwyn
Myddfai
Llywel
Trecastle
Usk Reservoir
Llangadog
Cwmwysg
Pont ar Hydfer
Sennybridge
(Pont Senni)
Defynnog
Pentre'r-felin
Trallong
Aberyscir
Penpont
Llanspyddid
Llanfaes
Brecon
(Aberhonddu)
Llandefaelog Fach
Llanddew
Garthbrengy
Felinfach
Talachddu
Pont-faen
Pwllgloyw
Sarnau
Nant Bran
Pentre-bach
Llanywern
Llechfaen
Llanhamlach
Llanfrynach
Pencelli
Libanus
Tai'r-Bull
Mynydd Illtyd
Glas Fynydd Forest
Crai
Felin-Crai
Heol Senni
Talsarn
Twynllanan
Llanddeusant
Pont-ar-llechau
Capel Gwynfe
Pont Aber
Neuadd
Dyffryn Ceidrych
SN
BLACK MOUNTAIN
Y MYNYDD DU
FAN BRYCHEINIOG
Cray Res.
FAN GIHIRYCH
FFOREST FAWR
BRECON BEACONS
PEN Y FAN
FAN FAWR
Beacons Res.
Ystradfellte Res.
Cantref Res.
Neuadd Reservoirs
Talybont Res.
Abercynafon
Pontsticill Reservoir
Pontsticill
Vaynor
Nant-ddu
Llwyn-on Res.
Glyn Tarell
LLWYN Y CELYN
CRAIG CERRIG GLEISIAD A FAN FRYNYCH
THE NATIONAL SHOWCAVES FOR WALES
DAN-YR-OGOF
Glyntawe
Craig-y-nos
Penwyllt
OGOF FFYNNON DDU
Pen-y-cae
Abercraf
Caehopkin
Coelbren
WALES APE & MONKEY SANCTUARY
Brynamman
Rhosaman
Cwmllynfell
Ystradowen
Gwaun-Leision
Tairgwaith
Upper Cwm-twrch
Cwmgiedd
Penrhos
Lower Cwm-twrch
Gurnos
Ystradgynlais
Ystalyfera
Cwmgors
Onllwyn
Dyffryn Cellwen
Seven Sisters
Nant-y-cafn
Pontneddfechan
Glyn-neath
(Glynedd)
Morfa Glas
Penderyn
Pontbren Llwyd
Ystradfellte
Cefn-coed-y-cymmer
Dowlais
Gellideg
Pen-yr-Heolgerrig
Merthyr Tydfil
(Merthyr Tudful)
Pentrebach
Abercanaid
Troedyrhiw
Hirwaun
Rhigos
Cwm-hwnt
Tre-Gibbon
Penywaun
Trecynon
Llwydcoed
Cwmdare
ABERDARE
(ABERDÂR)
Aber-nant
Cwmbach
Aberaman
Cwmaman
MOUNTAIN ASH
(ABERPENNAR)
Penrhiwceiber
Aberfan
Bedlinog
Cwmfelin
Merthyr Vale
Treharris
Godre'r-graig
Climaen gwyn
Ynys-meudwy
SWANSEA VALLEY
CWM ABERTAWE
Rhyd-y-fro
Pontardawe
Cilybebyll
Gellinudd
Rhôs
Alltwen
Trebanos
Clydach
Crynant
Rheola Forest
VALE OF NEATH
CWM NEDD
Blaengwrach
Cwmgwrach
Resolven
Melincourt
Clyne
Cilfrew
Aberdulais
Glais
Bryn-coch
Rhydding
Birchgrove
Neath Abbey
Tonna
Cadoxton-Juxta-Neath
Skewen
Neath
(Castell-Nedd)
Cimla
Briton Ferry
Neath Port Talbot
(Castell-Nedd Port Talbot)
Rhondda Cynon Taf
Glyncorrwg
Blaenrhondda
Tynewydd
Treherbert
Blaen-gwynfi
Aber-gwynfi
Cymer
Croeserw
Duffryn
Caerau
Spelter
Dyffryn
Pontrhydyfen
Baglan
Pwll-y-glaw
Brynbryddan
Bryn
Cwmafan
Aberavon
Port Talbot
Goytre
Taibach
Margam
Groes
Maerdy
Treorchy
(Treorci)
Pentre
Ferndale
St Gwynno Forest
Cwm-parc
RHONDDA
Ystrad
Ton-Pentre
Gelli
Llwynypia
Clydach Vale
Tonypandy
Penygraig
Trealaw
Tylorstown
Pont-y-gwaith
Wattstown
Ynyshir
Porth
Trebanog
Trehafod
PONTYPRIDD
Ynysboeth
Abercynon
Ynysybwl
Glyncoch
Glyntaff
Treforest
Pen-y-coedcae
Rhydyfelin
Tonyrefail
Blaengarw
Nant-y-moel
Price Town
Wyndham
Nantyffyllon
MAESTEG
Pontycymer
Garth
Cwmfelin
Llangynwyd
Pont Rhyd-y-cyff
Ogmore Vale
Ogmore Forest
Evanstown
Gilfach Goch
Lewistown
Bryn Golau
Hendreforgan
Pant-yr-awel
Glynogwr
Blackmill
Llangeinor
Bettws
Bridgend
(Pen-y-bont ar Ogwr)
Brynmenyn
Bryncethin
Heol-y-Cyw
Coytrahen
Tondu
Aberkenfig
Sarn
Kenfig Hill
Cefn Cross
Cefn Cribbwr
Pyle
(Y Pil)
North Cornelly
Kenfig
Mawdlam
Kenfig Burrows
South Cornelly
Pen-y-fai
Pendre
Coity
Pencoed
Brynna
Llanharan
Talbot Green
Llantrisant
Bryncae
Dolau
Llanilid
Llanharry
Brynsadler
Pontyclun
Cross Inn
Creigiau
Miskin
Groes-faen
Capel Llanilltern
Talygarn
Beddau
Castellau
Coedely
Upper Church Village
Llantwit Fardre
Church Village
Efail Isaf
Hawthorn
Laleston
Coychurch
St Mary Hill
Treoes
Corntown
Llangan
Llansannor
Craig-Penllyn
Tythegston
Merthyr Mawr
Newton
Clevis
Porthcawl
Ewenny
Ogmore
Penllyn
Maendy
Aberthin
Ystradowen
Welsh St Donats
Pendoylan
Peterston super-Ely
St Brides super Ely
St George's
SWANSEA BAY
BAE ABERTAWE
SS
MAERDY
M4
0 1 2 3 4 5 6 miles
0 1 2 3 4 5 6 7 8 9 10 km

BLACK MOUNTAINS
Y MYNYDDOEDD DUON
Talgarth
Llanfilo
Trefecca
Tredomen
Llandefaelog-tre'r-graig
Llanfihangel Tal-y-llyn
Talyllyn
Llangors
Llangorse Lake
Llangasty Talyllyn
Cathedine
Scethrog
Cross Oak
Llansantffraed
Talybont-on-Usk
Aber-Village
Bwlch
Cwmdu
Cwmrhos
Gaer
Tretower
TRETOWER CASTLE & COURT
PEN CERIG-CALCH
Coed-yr-ynys
Llangynidr
Llanbedr
Crickhowell
Llangenny
Ffawyddog
Llangattock
Cwrt-y-gollen
Glangrwyney
GARN CAWS
Mynydd Llangynidr
Mynydd Llangattock
Mynydd Troed
Pengenffordd
Llanelieu
THE TUMPA
Llanveynoe
Michaelchurch Escley
Middle Maes-coed
St Margaret's
Newton
Bacton
Lower Maes-coed
Abbey Dore
Longtown
Llanthony
Clodock
Ewyas Harold
Pontrilas
Rowlestone
Monmouth Cap
Llangua
Walterstone
Oldcastle
HATTERRALL HILL
Cwmyoy
Tre-wyn
Pandy
Stanton
Llanfihangel-Crucorney
LLANFIHANGEL COURT
Bettws
Llantilio Pertholey
Mardy
Llwyn-du
Abergavenny (Y Fenni)
Gilwern
Llanelly
Clydach
Govilon
Llanfoist
Blackrock
Brynmawr
Beaufort
Garnlydan
Rassau
Trefil
Tafarnau-bach
Dukestown
Sirhowy
Princetown
Tredegar
EBBW VALE (GLYN EBWY)
Nantyglo
Coalbrookvale
Blaina
Blaenavon
Forge Side
BLAENAVON IRONWORKS
BIG PIT MINING MUSEUM
Garn-yr-erw
Llanelly Hill
BLORENGE
Llanellen
Llanover
Rhymney (Rhymni)
Georgetown
Llechryd
Pontlottyn
Abertysswg
New Tredegar (Tredegar Newydd)
Fochriw
Tirphil
Deri
Waunlwyd
Cwm
Abertillery (Abertyleri)
Cwmtillery
East Bank
Varteg
Cwmavon
Garndiffaith
Abersychan
Talywain
Torfaen (Tor-faen)
Aberbeeg
St Illtyd
Brynithel
Llanhilleth (Llanhiledd)
Cwm Ffrwd-oer
Trevethin
Pontypool (Pont-y-pŵl)
Griffithstown
Swffryd
Crumlin (Crymlyn)
Newbridge
Oakdale
Blackwood (Coed Duon)
Argoed
Markham
Hollybush
Manmoel
Trinant
Bargoed (Bargod)
Gilfach
Pengam
Trelewis
Gelligaer
Pontllanfraith
Nelson
Hengoed
Ystrad-mynach
Maesycwmmer
Wyllie
Ynysddu
Cwmfelinfach
Cwmcarn
Abercarn
Lanfach
Pontywaun
Crosskeys
Risca (Rhisga)
Caerphilly (Caerffili)
CAERPHILLY (CAERFFILI)
Senghenydd
Abertridwr
Llanbradach
Bedwas
Machen
Lower Machen
Rogerstone
Penyrheol
Trecenydd
Rudry
Nantgarw
Thornhill
Taff's Well
Tongwynlais
Llanishen
Rhiwbina
Whitchurch
Cardiff (Caerdydd)
CARDIFF
Pentyrch
Radyr
Llandaff
Canton
St Fagans
Ely
Cathays
Roath
Heath
Birchgrove
Cyncoed
Lisvane
Llanedeyrn
St Mellons
Llanrumney
Rumney
Michaelston-super-Ely
Newton
Peterstone Wentlooge
St Brides Wentlooge
Marshfield
Castleton
Coedkernew
Michaelston-y-Fedw
Blaenpennal
Pentrepoeth
Bassaleg
Duffryn
Rhiwderin
Bettws
Malpas
Newport (Casnewydd)
Maindee
Christchurch
Caerleon (Caerllion)
Lliswerry
Pye Corner
Nash
Goldcliff
Whitson
Redwick
Caldicot Level
Summerleaze
Langstone
Llanmartin
Llanwern
Bishton
Wilcrick
Llandevenny
Magor
Rogiet
Undy
Llanfihangel Rogiet
Caldicot
Penhow
Llanbeder
Cat's Ash
Parc-Seymour
Llanvaches
Llanhennock
Ponthir
Llanfrechfa
Llantarnam
Croes-y-mwyalch
Cwmbran (Cwmbrân)
Pontnewydd
Oakfield
Henllys
Castell-y-bwch
Upper Cwmbran
Lowlands
Croesyceiliog
Llandegveth
Tredunnock
Newbridge-on-Usk
Llangybi
Llantrisant
Llanllowell
Coed-y-paen
New Inn
Glascoed
Usk (Brynbuga)
Llanbadoc
Monkswood
Little Mill
Penperlleni
Goetre
Kemeys Commander
Llancayo
Llangwm
Gwernesney
Llandenny
Gwehelog
Bettws Newydd
Twyn-y-Sheriff
Kingcoed
Llangovan
Monmouthshire (Sir Fynwy)
Raglan
Llanfair Kilgheddin
Nant-y-derry
Pen-groes-oped
Rhyd-y-meirch
Llanvihangel Gobion
Llangattock nigh Usk
Bryngwyn
Llanarth
Coed Morgan
Llanddewi Rhydderch
Llanvapley
Llantilio Crossenny
Llanvetherine
Bryn-y-gwenin
Llanfaenor
Wayne Green
Upper Green
Bont
Llangattock Lingoed
Cross Ash
Newcastle
Llanvihangel-Ystern-Llewern
Wernyrheolydd
Penrhôs
Tregare
Dingestow
Pen-yr-heol
Llangattock-Vibon-Avel
Onen
Monmouth (Trefynwy)
Wonastow
Mitcheltroy Common
Pen-y-clawdd
Cwmcarvan
Llanishen
Llansoy
Trelleck Grange
Devauden
Wolvesnewton
Kilgwrrwg Common
Newchurch
Gaerllwyd
Earlswood
Llanvair Discoed
Shirenewton
Chepstow Pk. Wood
Itton Common
Highmoor Hill
St Bride's Netherwent
Caerwent
Crick
Grosmont
White Rocks
Kentchurch
Garway
Garway Hill
Hoaldalbert
Broad Oak
Skenfrith
Norton
Crossway
St Maughans
Llanrothal
Welsh Newton
Maypole
Buckholt
Kilpeck
Wormbridge
Howton
Orcop Hill
Orcop
Bagwy Llydiart
Llanwarne
Dewsall Court
Kivernoll
Didley
St Devereux
Much Dewchurch
Wormelow Tump
Winnal
Cockyard
Thruxton
St Mary's Gate
Portishead
Battery Pt.
Redcliff Bay
West Hill
Sheepway
Avonmouth
SECOND SEVERN CROSSING
Newton

Monmouthshire
(Sir Fynwy)
Gloucestershire
South
Gloucestershire
SO
ST
FOREST OF DEAN
Monmouth
(Trefynwy)
Ross-on-Wye
Chepstow
(Cas-gwent)
Cinderford
Coleford
Lydney
Newent
Dursley
Thornbury
Yate
Chipping Sodbury
Bradley Stoke
FILTON
MANGOTSFIELD
Caldicot
Wotton-under-Edge
Frampton on Severn
Redcliff Bay
River Severn
The Noose
Wye
Monnow (Mynwy)
Tidenham Chase
Chepstow Pk. Wood
Wormbridge
Kilpeck
Much Dewchurch
Wormelow Tump
Pontrilas
Kentchurch
Grosmont
Skenfrith
Garway
Broad Oak
Llangarron
Llancloudy
St Weonards
St Owens Cross
Peterstow
Bridstow
Goodrich
Kerne Bridge
Walford
Welsh Bicknor
English Bicknor
Symonds Yat
Whitchurch
Ganarew
Dixton
Wyesham
Penallt
Mitchel Troy
Redbrook
Newland
Clearwell
St Briavels
Trellech
Llandogo
Tintern Parva
Brockweir
St Arvans
Tutshill
Sedbury
Beachley
Raglan
Llanishen
Devauden
Shirenewton
Mathern
Caerwent
Portskewett
Sudbrook
Rogiet
Magor
Undy
Redwick
Summerleaze
Pilning
Severn Beach
Aust
Olveston
Almondsbury
Patchway
Henbury
Hallen
Easter Compton
Frenchay
Winterbourne
Iron Acton
Frampton Cotterell
Pucklechurch
Hinton
Tormarton
Dodington
Codrington
Wickwar
Hillesley
Hawkesbury
Horton
Little Sodbury
Old Sodbury
Charfield
Kingswood
Cromhall
Tortworth
Falfield
Rockhampton
Oldbury-on-Severn
Berkeley
Sharpness
Slimbridge
Cambridge
Cam
Uley
North Nibley
Blakeney
Awre
Newnham
Westbury-on-Severn
Mitcheldean
Longhope
Huntley
Highnam
Churcham
Minsterworth
Elmore
Tibberton
Taynton
Lea
Linton
Gorsley
Kilcot
Dymock
Much Marcle
Donnington
Bromsberrow Hth.
Fownhope
Sollers Hope
Brockhampton
Ballingham
How Caple
Hoarwithy
Harewood End
Sellack
Kings Caple
Upton Bishop
Weston under Penyard
Coughton
Pontshill
Ruardean
Drybrook
Nailbridge
Brierley
Bream
Parkend
Yorkley
Whitecroft
Aylburton
Alvington
Woolaston
Tidenham
Chapel Hill
Llangovan
Llandenny
Wonastow
Dingestow
Rockfield
Llanvihangel-Ystern-Llewern
Onen
Llangattock-Vibon-Avel
Welsh Newton
St Maughans
Llanrothal
Newcastle
Cross Ash
Crossway
M4
M5
M48
M49
M50
M32
A40
A48
A49
A38
A46
A403
A449
A4137
TOLL
SECOND SEVERN CROSSING
SEVERN ROAD BRIDGE PONT HAFREN
0 1 2 3 4 5 6 miles
0 1 2 3 4 5 6 7 8 9 10 km

Bushley
Long Green
Forthampton
Newtown
Tewkesbury
Ashchurch
Aston Cross
Teddington
Washbourne
Alderton
Toddington
Stanton
Snowshill
Snowshill Lavender
Gloucestershire Warwickshire Steam Railway
Stanway
Stanway House
Arboretum
Bourton on the Hill
Eldersfield
Walton Cardiff
Fiddington
Oxenton
Alstone
Dixton
Didbrook
Hailes Abbey
Sezincote
Corse Lawn
Chaceley
Odda's Chapel
Deerhurst
Tredington
Gotherington
Gretton
Greet
Hailes
Winchcombe Pottery
Farmcote
Ford
Longborough
Condicote
Donnington
Tirley
Apperley
Stoke Orchard
Bishop's Cleeve
Langley Hill
Winchcombe
Sudeley Castle and Gardens
Temple Guiting
Hasfield
Coombe Hill
Hardwicke
Elmstone Hardwicke
Woodmancote
Cleeve Hill
Railway Mus
Cotswold Farm Park
Upper Swell
Stow-on-the-Wold
Ashleworth
Leigh
Kineton
Lower Swell
Belas Knap Long Barrow
Severn
Norton
Boddington
Swindon
Southam
Cheltenham
The Cotswold Way
Charlton Abbots
Barton
Guiting Power
Uckington
Stow-on-the-Wold
Sandhurst
Down Hatherley
Staverton
Staverton Bridge
Arle
Golden Valley
Gallery & Museum
Prestbury
Battledown
Hawling
Naunton
Upper Slaughter
Nature in Art
Maisemore
Twigworth
Sandfields
Cheltenham
Brockhampton
Lower Slaughter
The Old Mill
Wyck Rissington
Over Bridge
Longford
Parton
Gloucestershire
Lansdown
Charlton Kings
Whittington
Sevenhampton
Up Hatherley
Holst's Birthplace
Syreford
Notgrove Long Barrow
Notgrove
Salperton
Bourton-on-the-Water
Model Village
Birdland Park & Gardens
Docks
Cath
Gloucester Waterways Museum
Churchdown
Longlevens
Badgeworth
Leckhampton
Dowdeswell
Andoversford
Cold Aston
Little Rissington
Clapton-on-the-Hill
Gloucester
Barnwood
Hucclecote
Shurdington
Crickley Hill
Ullenwood
Shipton Solers
Shipton
Hazleton
Turkdean
Windrush
Great Rissington
Hempsted
Matson
Brockworth
Great Witcombe
Bentham
Coberley
Compton Abdale
Hampnett
Farmington
Tuffley
Upton St Leonard's
Cowley
Withington
Cassey Compton
Yanworth
Northleach
Sherborne
Quedgeley
Whaddon
Robinswood Hill
Prinknash Abbey & Bird Park
Villa
Cotswold
Birdlip
Cranham
Colesbourne
Chedworth Roman Villa
Eastington
Lodge Park
Gloucester Services
Brookthorpe
Brimpsfield
Elkstone
Cotswold Commons and Beechwoods
Chedworth
Fossebridge
Coln St Dennis
Rococo Gardens
Sheepscombe
Syde
Whiteway
Haresfield
Harescombe
Painswick
The Camp
Winstone
Rendcomb
Foss Cross
Coln Rogers
Winson
Aldsworth
Miserden Park
Miserden
Woodmancote
Calmsden
Pitchcombe
Whiteshill
Slad
Sudgrove
Duntisbourne Abbots
Duntisbourne Leer
North Cerney
Ablington
Randwick
Arlington
Bibury
Arlington Row
Stonehouse
Ebley
Stroud
Bisley
Edgeworth
Duntisbourne Rouse
Bagendon
Coln St Aldwyn's
Eastleach Turville
Eastcombe
Bournes Green
Daglingworth
Barnsley
Hatherop
King's Stanley
Rodborough
Oakley Wood
Baunton
Quenington
Fyfield
Leonard Stanley
Woodchester
Thrupp
Chalford
Oakridge
Sapperton
Stratton
Ampney Crucis
Ampney St Mary
Southrop
Brownshill
Brimscombe
Frampton Mansell
Cirencester
Littleworth
Woodchester Park
Nympsfield Long Barrow
Amberley
Hyde
Cirencester Lock Up
Coates
Chesterton
Roman Amphitheatre
Preston
Ampney St Peter
Poulton
Milton End
Fairford
Windsoredge
Minchinhampton
Harnhill
Driffield
Meysey Hampton
Horcott
Lechlade-on-Thames
Nailsworth
Box
Tarlton
Source of the Thames
Siddington
Whiteway
Cherington
Whelford
Horsley
Avening
Rodmarton
Ewen
South Cerney
Marston Meysey
Dunfield
Inglesham
Trull House Gardens
Kemble
Kingscote
Tetbury Upton
Culkerton
Poole Keynes
Keynes
Neigh Bridge
Shorncote
Cotswold Water Park
Cerney Wick
Down Ampney
Latton
Kempsford
Chavenage House
Ashley
Somerford Keynes
Ashton Keynes
North Meadow
The Thames Path
Castle Eaton
Hannington Wick
Beverston
Chelworth
Oaksey
Cricklade
Tetbury
Chedglow
Crudwell
Eastcourt
Swill Brook
Leigh
Hannington
Long Newnton
Chelworth Green
Highworth
Leighterton
Doughton
Hankerton
Upper Minety
Minety
Purton Stoke
Swindon and Cricklade Railway
Blunsdon St Andrew
Broad Blunsdon
Stanton Fitzwarren
Sevenhampton
Westonbirt Arboretum
Shipton Moyne
Brokenborough
Perry Green
Stanton Park
Oldbury on the Hill
Westonbirt
Filands
Charlton
Haydon Wick
Penhill
South Marston
Easton Grey
Garsdon
Purton
Widham
Upper Stratton
Didmarton
Sopworth
Malmesbury
Queen Street
Dogridge
Stratton St Margaret
Pinehurst
Gorse Hill
Sherston
Foxley
Lea
Lydiard Green
Lydiard Millicent
Rodbourne Cheney
Cleverton
The Common
Lydiard Park
Steam
Walcot
Swindon
Luckington
Norton
Corston
Little Somerford
Callow Hill
Hook
Rodbourne
Little Badminton
Badminton
Brinkworth
The Marsh
Alderton
Rodbourne
Dauntsey
Royal Wootton Bassett
Coate
Coate Water
Hullavington
Startley
Great Somerford
Grittenham
North Wroughton
Acton Turville
Littleton Drew
Grittleton
Stanton St Quintin
Lower Stanton St Quintin
Lower Seagry
Upper Seagry
Tockenham Wick
Wroughton
Elcombe
Badbury
Burton
Leigh Delamere
Tockenham
Bradenstoke
Lyneham
Church End
Chiseldon
Leigh Delamere Services
Sutton Benger
Christian Malford
Kington St Michael
Broad Town
West Kington
Nettleton
Castle Combe
Yatton Keynell
Kington Langley
West End
Foxham
Preston
Goatacre
Bushton
Clyffe Pypard
Uffcott
Barbury Castle
Castle Combe
North Wraxall
Ford
Langley Burrell
Spirthill
Broad Hinton
Clevancy
Cotswolds
Gloucester
SP
SU
M5
M4
A40
A417
A419
A429
A436
A46
A38
A433
A350
A3102
A4019
A4198
A346
A44
A424
A361
B4077
B4632
B4425
B4040
B4042
B4696
B4005
B4069
B4122
50
51
38
24
25

Batsford
Bourton on the Hill
Moreton-in-Marsh
Lemington
Great Wolford
Whichford
Hook Norton
Wigginton
South Newington
Barford St John
Barford St Michael
Clifton
Deddington
Hempton
Worton
Great Rollright
Swerford
Long Compton
Barton on the Heath
Little Compton
Sezincote
Cutsdean
Longborough
Condicote
Donnington
Evenlode
Chastleton
Salford
Over Norton
Chipping Norton
Little Tew
Great Tew
Over Worton
Duns Tew
North Aston
Somerton
Middle Aston
Upper Heyford
Lower Heyford
Steeple Aston
Steeple Barton
Middle Barton
Westcott Barton
Sandford St Martin
Ledwell
Heythrop
Church Enstone
Enstone
Lidstone
Gagingwell
Cleveley
Kiddington
Over Kiddington
Glympton
Rousham House
Temple Guiting
Kineton
Upper Swell
Lower Swell
Stow-on-the-Wold
Broadwell
Adlestrop
Cornwell
Daylesford
Oddington
Maugersbury
Naunton
Upper Slaughter
Lower Slaughter
Wyck Rissington
Icomb
Kingham
Churchill
Bledington
Sarsden
Chadlington
Spelsbury
Taston
Bourton-on-the-Water
Notgrove
Cold Aston
Little Rissington
Upper Rissington
Westcote
Bruern Abbey
Lyneham
Idbury
Fifield
Clapton-on-the-Hill
Great Rissington
Milton under Wychwood
Shipton-under-Wychwood
Ascott-under-Wychwood
Chilson
Charlbury
Wychwood Forest
Stonesfield
Fawler
Finstock
Woodstock
Blenheim Palace
Combe
Tackley
Wootton
Bunkers Hill
Shipton on Cherwell
Thrupp
Kidlington
Bladon
Begbroke
Yarnton
Turkdean
Farmington
Sherborne
Northleach
Great Barrington
Taynton
Fulbrook
Burford
Little Barrington
Windrush
Eastington
Lodge Park
Leafield
Ramsden
Fordwells
Asthall Leigh
Swinbrook
Asthall
Minster Lovell
Whiteoak Green
Hailey
Crawley
East End
North Leigh
New Yatt
Freeland
Long Hanborough
Church Hanborough
Barnard Gate
Cassington
Witney
Coln St Dennis
Coln Rogers
Winson
Aldsworth
Westwell
Signet
Holwell
Shilton
Bradwell Grove
Cotswold Wildlife Park
Charterville Allotments
Curbridge
Brize Norton
Carterton
Cogges
High Cogges
South Leigh
Eynsham
Swinford
Wytham
Wolvercote
Farmoor
Farmoor Reservoir
Botley
Ducklington
Ablington
Arlington
Bibury
Eastleach Turville
Eastleach Martin
Coln St Aldwyn's
Hatherop
Quenington
Fyfield
Filkins
Broughton Poggs
Southrop
Alvescot
Kencot
Broadwell
Black Bourton
Lew
Hardwick
Sutton
Stanton Harcourt
West End
Cumnor
North Hinksey
Chawley
Yelford
Aston
Brighthampton
Cote
Bampton
Standlake
Northmoor
Eaton
Boars Hill
Wootton
Bessels Leigh
Appleton
Little Faringdon
Langford
Clanfield
Weald
Shifford
Lamborough Hill
Foxcombe Hill
Sunningwell
Poulton
Milton End
Fairford
Horcott
Meysey Hampton
Lechlade-on-Thames
Grafton
Radcot
Kelmscot
Kelmscott Manor
Eaton Hastings
Chimney
Duxford
Carswell Marsh
Hinton Waldrist
Longworth
Netherton
Fyfield
Tubney
Cothill
Shippon
Whelford
Inglesham
Marston Meysey
Dunfield
Down Ampney
Kempsford
Latton
Buscot
Buscot Park
Upper Inglesham
Littleworth
Buckland
Southmoor
Kingston Bagpuize
Pusey
Frilford
Garford
Marcham
Caldecott
Castle Eaton
Hannington Wick
Hannington
Faringdon
Badbury Hill
Coleshill
Great Coxwell
Shellingford
Little Coxwell
Hatford
Charney Bassett
Stanford in the Vale
Lyford
Cricklade
Highworth
Fernham
Baulking
Goosey
West Hanney
East Hanney
Denchworth
Drayton
Milton
Steventon
Broad Blunsdon
Blunsdon St Andrew
Stanton Fitzwarren
Sevenhampton
Watchfield
Longcot
Shrivenham
Uffington
Vale of White Horse
Grove
Milton Hill
Harwell
Rowstock
Widham
Haydon Wick
Penhill
Upper Stratton
Stratton St Margaret
Purton
South Marston
Woolstone
Kingston Lisle
Sparsholt
West Challow
East Challow
Childrey
Wantage
West Hendred
East Hendred
Ardington
Lockinge
East Ginge
West Ginge
Lydiard Millicent
Pinehurst
Gorse Hill
Rodbourne Cheney
Rodbourne
Walcot
Swindon
Bourton
Compton Beauchamp
Uffington Castle
Whitehorse Hill
Wayland's Smithy
Letcombe Regis
Letcombe Bassett
The Ridgeway
Chilton
Coate
Wanborough
Ashbury
Idstone
Bishopstone
Hinton Parva
Kingston Warren
West Ilsley
East Ilsley
North Wroughton
Wroughton
Liddington
Lambourn Downs
Ashdown Park
Farnborough
Fawley
Chiseldon
Badbury
Upper Lambourn
South Fawley
Catmore
Lilley
Stanmore
Elcombe
Broadtown Lane
Lambourn
Brightwalton
Baydon
Chaddleworth
Leckhampstead Thicket
Beedon
Peasemore
Eastbury
East Garston
Woodsend
Aldbourne
World's End
Hinton

0 1 2 3 4 5 6 miles
0 1 2 3 4 5 6 7 8 9 10 km

Buckingham
Bletchley
Winslow
Bicester
Aylesbury
Thame
Oxford
Headington
Cowley
Wheatley
Wendover
Princes Risborough
Chinnor
Haddenham
High Wycombe
Marlow
Henley-on-Thames
Wallingford
Didcot
Goring
Maidenhead
Twyford
Abingdon-on-Thames
Sonning Common
Prestwood
Great Missenden
Weston Turville
Aston Clinton
Kidlington
Tingewick
Gawcott
Steeple Claydon
Middle Claydon
East Claydon
Quainton
Waddesdon
Brill
Boarstall
Long Crendon
Chearsley
Cuddington
Stone
Watlington
Benson
Dorchester
Cholsey
Nettlebed
Nuffield
Stokenchurch
West Wycombe
Bourne End
Cookham
Hambleden
Medmenham
Woodcote
Pangbourne
Whitchurch
Streatley
Blewbury
B u c k i n g h a m
Windsor and Maidenhead
SP
SU
52
53
40
26
27
M40
A41
A40
A34
A418
A4010
A413
A421
A404
A4130
A4074
A329
Oxford Services
Cherwell Valley Services
Bicester Village
Waddesdon Manor
Claydon House
Boarstall Tower
Brill Windmill
Buckinghamshire Railway Centre
Rycote Chapel
Stonor
Greys Court
Maharajah's Well
Didcot Railway Centre
Chinnor & Princes Risborough Railway
Hughenden Manor
West Wycombe Caves
Wycombe Air Park
River & Rowing Museum
Mapledurham
Basildon Park
Beale Park
The Living Rainforest

Bletchley
Fenny Stratford
Far Bletchley
Tattenhoe
Woburn
Woburn Safari Park
Eversholt
Church End
Woburn Abbey
Tingrith
Westoning
Pulloxhill
Higham Gobion
Apsley End
Pirton
Ickleford
Little Horwood
Newton Longville
Little Brickhill
Great Brickhill
Central
Milton Bryan
Harlington
Sharpenhoe
Barton-le-Clay
Pegsdon
Knocking Hoe
HITCHIN
Drayton Parslow
Mursley
Stoke Hammond
Potsgrove
Battlesden
Kings Wood
Stockgrove Park
Toddington
Toddington Services
Sundon Hills
Streatley
Barton Hills
Upper Sundon
Charlton
Swanbourne
North End
Soulbury
Heath and Reach
Bedfordshire
Hockliffe
Tebworth
Lower Sundon
Galley Hill
Lilley
Great Offley
Gosmore
St Ippollytts
Stewkley
South End
Leighton Buzzard
Eggington
Wingfield
Chalton
Sundon Park
Limbury
Preston
Dunton
Linslade
Tilsworth
Burcott
Leighton Buzzard Railway
Stanbridge
Houghton Regis
Luton
Stopsley
Cockernhoe Green
King's Walden
St Paul's Walden
Creslow
Wing
Ascott
Billington
Mead Open Farm
Lower End
Totternhoe
Dunstable
Leagrave
Biscot
Hart Hill
Breachwood Green
Cublington
Ledburn
Eaton Green
Church End
The Guided Busway
Priory Church of St Peter
Whitchurch
Slapton
Eaton Bray
Farley Hill
London Luton
Whitwell
Aston Abbotts
Edlesborough
Dunstable Downs
Kensworth
Caddington
Stockwood Craft Mus
Peter's Green
Kimpton
Hardwick
Mentmore
Wingrave
Horton
Whipsnade
Slip End
Ayot St Lawrence
Weedon
Rowsham
Ivinghoe Aston
Kensworth Common
East Hyde
Blackmore End
Hulcott
Cheddington
Ivinghoe
Whipsnade Wild Animal Park
Woodside Farm and Wildfowl Park
Kinsbourne Green
Batford
Shaw's Corner
Long Marston
Dagnall
Studham
Markyate
Bierton
Aylesbury
Puttenham
Marsworth
Pitstone Green
Pitstone
Ringshall
Jockey End
Flamstead
Marshall's Heath
HARPENDEN
Wheathampstead
Wilstone
Tring Wharf
Little Gaddesden
Trowley Bottom
Hatching Green
Buckland
Drayton Beauchamp
New Mill
Ashridge Park
Redbourn
Southcourt
Weston Turville
Aston Clinton
Tring
Aldbury
Great Gaddesden
Water End
Childwick Green
Sandridge
Stoke Mandeville
Bishopstone
Halton
Wigginton
Nettleden
Jersey Farm
Ridgeway Path
Hastoe
Northchurch
Potten End
Piccotts End
Old Gorhambury House
Townsend
Marshalswick
Kimble Wick
North Lee
Terrick
Nash Lee
Butler's Cross
Wendover
Berkhamsted
Berkhamsted Castle
Gadebridge
St Albans
Roman Theatre of Verulamium
Fleetville
Little Kimble
Ellesborough
St Leonard's
Cholesbury
Buckland Common
Bourne End
Boxmoor
The Camp
Meadle
Great Kimble
Ashley Green
Hemel Hempstead
St.Stephens
Sopwell
Askett
Bellingdon
Dunsmore
The Lee
Lee Clump
Chartridge
Whelpley Hill
Felden
Gdns of the Rose
Chiswell Green
Bedmond
London Colney
Monks Risborough
Lye Green
Bovingdon
Primrosehill
Princes Risborough
Little Hampden
Ballinger Common
Kings Langley
De Havilland Aircraft Heritage Cen
Botley
Bovingdon Green
Great Hampden
South Heath
Leyhill
Chesham
Chipperfield
Abbots Langley
Bricket Wood
Colney Street
Shenleybury
Shenley
Loosley Row
Prestwood
Great Missenden
Hyde Heath
Flaunden
Radlett
Lacey Green
Speen
Little Kingshill
Chesham Bois
Latimer
Sarratt
Green Street
Walters Ash
Upper North Dean
Great Kingshill
Little Missenden
Chenies
Chenies Manor Ho
Aldenham
Letchmore Heath
Bledlow Ridge
Cryers Hill
Holmer Green
Amersham
Little Chalfont
Chorleywood
Watford
BOREHAMWOOD
Bradenham
Widmer End
Naphill
Hughenden Valley
Hughenden Manor
Penn Street
Coleshill
Croxley Green
Aldenham
Elstree
West Wycombe
West Wycombe Caves
Downley
Hazlemere
Winchmore Hill
Chalfont St Giles
Chiltern Open Air Mus
RICKMANSWORTH
Oxhey
Bushey
Bushey Heath
High Wycombe
Tylers Green
Penn
Knotty Green
Milton's Cottage
Seer Green
South Oxhey
Stanmore
Rickmansworth Aquadrome
Maple Cross
Eastbury
Batchworth Heath
Booker
Wycombe Marsh
Forty Green
Bekonscot Model Village
Jordans
Chalfont Common
Lane End
Loudwater
Beaconsfield
Chalfont St Peter
Bishop's Wood
Northwood
Hatch End
Harrow Weald
Edgware
Wycombe Air Park
Frieth
Flackwell Heath
Harefield
Bayhurst Wood
Ruislip Woods
Pinner
Wealdstone
HARROW
Greenhill
Marlow Bottom
Little Marlow
Wooburn Green
Beaconsfield Services
Odds Farm Park
Hedgerley
Gerrards Cross
Denham
Denham Green
Ruislip Common
Eastcote
Rayners Lane
Lower Woodend
Bovingdon Green
Well End
Wooburn
Hedsor
Tatling End
Ruislip
Harrow on the Hill
Hambleden
Marlow
Bourne End
Cores End
Stanley Spencer Gallery
Burnham Beeches
Fulmer
Ickenham
Wembley
Mill End
Bisham
Cookham Dean
Cookham
Farnham Common
Stoke Poges
Northolt
Medmenham
Cliveden
Cookham Rise
Black Park
Iver Heath
Uxbridge
Sudbury
Alperton
Hurley
Windsor
Park Corner
Wexham Street
Farnham Royal
Burnham
Stoke Green
Hillingdon
Perivale
Pinkneys Grn.
Furze Platt
Langley Park
London Motorcycle Mus
Yeading
Burchett's Green
Taplow
Cowley
Greenford
Maidenhead
Slough
SLOUGH
George Green
Iver
Yiewsley
Hayes
Southall
EALING
Warren Row
and
Cox Grn.
West Drayton
Hanwell
Knowl Hill
Bray
Dorney
Eton Wick
Langley
Richings Park
Heston Services
Osterley Park Ho
Littlewick Green
Upton
Harmondsworth
Harlington
Cranford
Brentford
Wargrave
Eton
Windsor Castle
Datchet
Colnbrook
Sipson
Heston
Kew
Syon Ho
Kew Gdns
St Lawrence
Touchen End
Oakley Green
Poyle
Longford
London Heathrow
Isleworth
Twyford
WINDSOR
HEATHROW
0 1 2 3 4 5 6 miles
0 1 2 3 4 5 6 7 8 9 10 km

LETCHWORTH
Baldock
Wallington
Roe Green
Mill End
Buckland
Chipping
Wyddial
Langley
Lower Green
Upper Green
Newport
Howlett End
Debden
Wicken Bonhunt
Rickling
Widdington
Debden Cross
Anstey
Meesden
Clavering
Brent Pelham
Starlings Green
Berden
Hamperden End
Cutlers Green
Willian
Walsworth
Clothall
Rushden
Weston
Throcking
Hare Street
Great Hormead
Great Wymondley
Little Wymondley
Hall's Green
Cromer
Cottered
Buntingford
Stocking Pelham
Ugley
Henham
Graveley
Ardeley
Aspenden
Westmill
Hay Street
Furneaux Pelham
East End
Manuden
Ugley Green
Elsenham
Broxted
Duton Hill
Walkern
Wood End
Gravesend
Farnham Green
Molehill Green
Brick End
Stevenage
Benington
Nasty
Braughing
Clapgate
Farnham
Stansted Mountfitchet
STANSTED AIRPORT
Aston End
Shephall
Great Munden
Albury
Albury End
Little Hadham
Birchanger
Bambers Green
Langley
Hautwick
Levens Green
Puckeridge
Wellpond Green
Takeley
Broadwater
Aston
Standon
Hadham Ford
BISHOP'S STORTFORD
Bragbury End
Dane End
Bury Green
Takeley Street
Smith's Green
Old Knebworth
Knebworth
Whempstead
Collier's End
Latchford
Hope End Green
Datchworth
Watton at Stone
Much Hadham
Thorley Street
Gt. Hallingbury
Codicote
Sacombe
Barwick
High Cross
Hadham Cross
Thorley
Datchworth Green
Woolmer Green
Bull's Green
Wadesmill
Perry Green
Spellbrook
Lit. Hallingbury
Great Canfield
Oaklands
Burnham Green
Stapleford
Tonwell
Baker's End
Allens Green
High
Welwyn
Ayot St Peter
Harmer Green
Bramfield
Chapmore End
Thundridge
Wareside
Widford
Sawbridgeworth
Hatfield Heath
Hatfield Broad Oak
WELWYN GARDEN CITY
Digswell Park
Tewin
Waterford
Hertford
Ware
Hunsdon
High Wych
Aythorpe Roding
Sheering
Leaden Roding
Panshanger
Great Amwell
Stanstead Abbotts
Eastwick
Gilston
White Roding
Margaret Roding
Woodhall
Hertingfordbury
St Margarets
Matching
Matching Tye
Abbess Roding
Stanborough
Hall Grove
Cole Green
Hertford Heath
Hailey
Churchgate Street
Matching Green
Hatfield Hyde
Letty Green
Harlow
Netteswell
Beauchamp Roding
Hatfield Garden Village
The Ryde
Essendon
HODDESDON
Rye Park
Roydon
Gt. Parndon
Tye Green
Potter Street
High Laver
Little Laver
Hatfield
Bayford
Brickendon
Foster Street
Magdalen Laver
South Hatfield
Little Berkhamsted
Wildhill
Roydon Hamlet
Latton Bush
Hastingwood
Fyfield
Willingale
Woodside
Epping Green
Wormley West End
Broxbourne
Nazeing
Lower Nazeing
Broadley Common
Moreton
Colney Heath
Bell Bar
Newgate Street
Wormley
Thornwood Common
Bovinger
Bobbingworth
Norton Mandeville
Welham Green
Hammond Street
Bumble's Green
Epping Green
Shelley
Water End
Brookmans Park
Flamstead End
Turnford
Epping Upland
North Weald Bassett
Toot Hill
Greensted
High Ongar
South Mimms
Goff's Oak
Northaw
Cuffley
CHESHUNT
Coopersale Common
Epping
Chipping Ongar
Nine Ashes
POTTERS BAR
Waltham Cross
WALTHAM ABBEY
Upshire
Ivy Chimneys
Fiddlers Hamlet
Stanford Rivers
Stondon Massey
Botany Bay
Forty Hill
Theydon Bois
Little End
Stapleford Tawney
Doddinghurst
Enfield Chase
Enfield Wash
High Beach
Debden
Kelvedon Hatch
Monken Hadley
Sewardstone
Navestock Heath
Arkley
BARNET
Cockfosters
ENFIELD
Sewardstonebury
Ponders End
Loughton
Epping Forest
Abridge
Navestock Side
Pilgrims Hatch
Totteridge
East Barnet
Winchmore Hill
Stapleford Abbotts
Lambourne End
South Weald
Friern Barnet
Southgate
Edmonton
Chingford
Buckhurst Hill
Chigwell
Chigwell Row
Havering-atte-Bower
Noak Hill
BRENTWOOD
Mill Hill
Finchley
Wood Green
Grange Hill
Hainault
Harold Hill
Woodford Bridge
Woodford
Great Warley
Tottenham
Collier Row
Hornsey
Barkingside
Gidea Park
Harold Wood
Kingsbury
Hendon
Walthamstow
Romford
Newbury Park
Cranham
Golders Green
Highgate
Wanstead
Seven Kings
Hornchurch
Hampstead
Stoke Newington
Leytonstone
Leyton
Cricklewood
Forest Gate
Manor Park
Ilford
Becontree
Rush Green
Elm Park
Upminster
Willesden
Hackney
East Ham
Barking
Dagenham
Hacton
Corbets Tey
North Ockendon
Harlesden
Camden
Islington
Bethnal Green
Stratford
South Hornchurch
Kilburn
Shoreditch
West Ham
Creekmouth
Rainham
South Ockendon
Finsbury
Holborn
City
Poplar
Beckton
Thamesmead
Wennington
Aveley
North Stifford
Acton
Paddington
Hyde Park
Kensington
Westminster
Southwark
Bermondsey
Blackwall Tunnel
North Woolwich
Woolwich Ferry
Chiswick
Woolwich
Plumstead
Abbey Wood
Erith
Purfleet
South Stifford
Hammersmith
Chelsea
LAMBETH
Deptford
Greenwich
Charlton
Dartford Crossing
West Thurrock
Grays
Kew Br.
Fulham
Battersea
Peckham
Camberwell
New Cross
Kidbrooke
Welling
Slade Green
Putney
Bexleyheath
London
Greater
Thames
M25
M11
A1(M)
M1
A10
A120
A414
A602
A12
A13
A406
A127
A1400

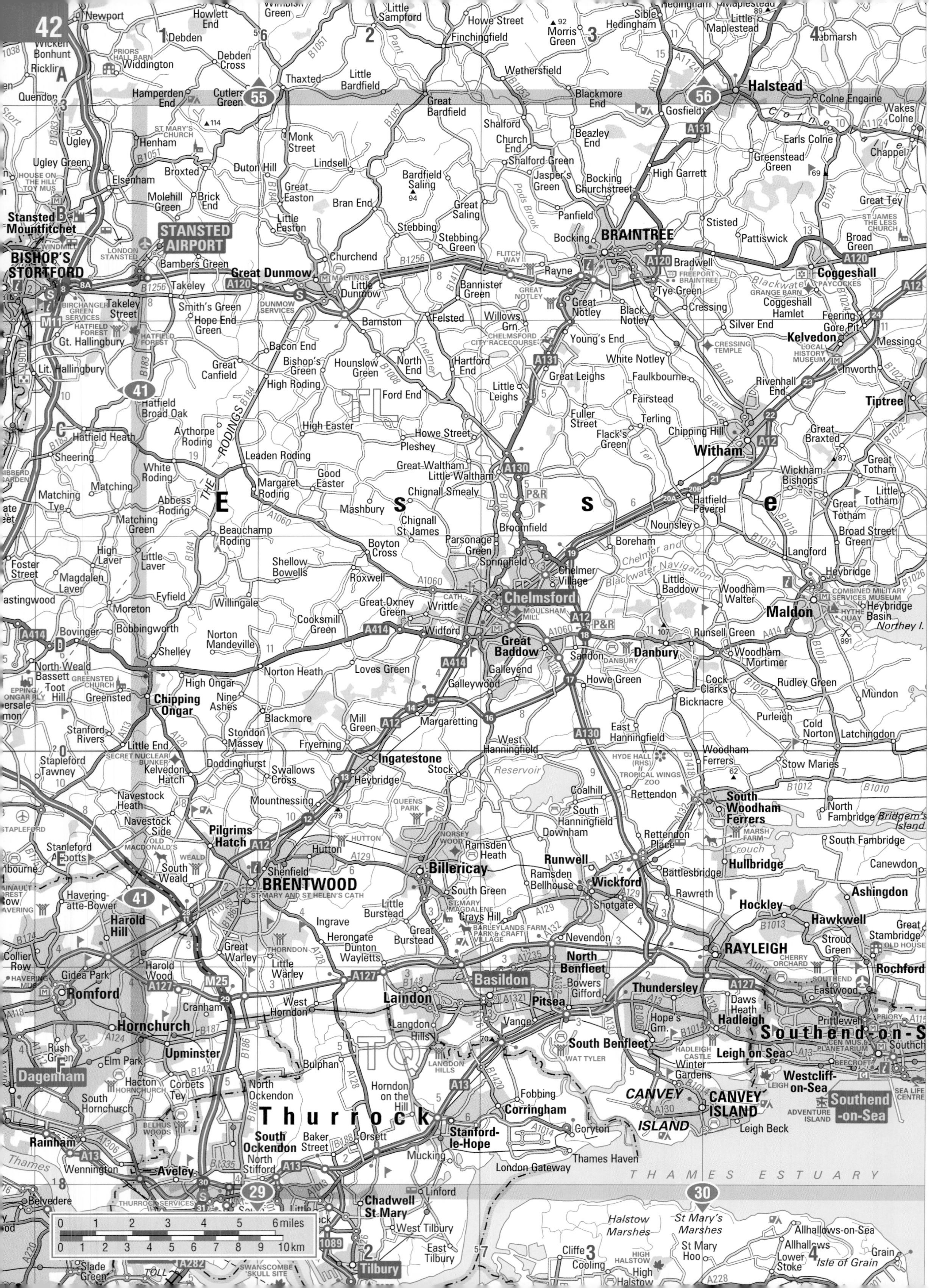
Newport
Howlett End
Little Sampford
Howe Street
Morris Green
Sible Hedingham
Little Maplestead
Debden
Debden Cross
Widdington
Wicken Bonhunt
Rickling
Quendon
Thaxted
Little Bardfield
Finchingfield
Wethersfield
Hamperden End
Cutlers Green
Great Bardfield
Shalford
Blackmore End
Halstead
Colne Engaine
Wakes Colne
Gosfield
Earls Colne
Chappel
Ugley
Ugley Green
Henham
Monk Street
Lindsell
Church End
Beazley End
Shalford Green
Jasper's Green
Bocking Churchstreet
Greenstead Green
High Garrett
Elsenham
Broxted
Duton Hill
Great Easton
Bardfield Saling
Bran End
Great Saling
Panfield
Stansted Mountfitchet
Molehill Green
Brick End
Little Easton
Stebbing
Stebbing Green
Stisted
Pattiswick
Great Tey
Broad Green
STANSTED AIRPORT
BISHOP'S STORTFORD
Churchend
Bocking
BRAINTREE
Bradwell
Coggeshall
Bambers Green
Great Dunmow
Takeley
Little Dunmow
Rayne
Tye Green
Coggeshall Hamlet
Smith's Green
Hope End Green
Barnston
Bannister Green
Felsted
Great Notley
Black Notley
Cressing
Silver End
Feering
Kelvedon
Gore Pit
Messing
Gt. Hallingbury
Lit. Hallingbury
Bacon End
Bishop's Green
Hounslow Green
North End
Willows Grn.
Hartford End
Young's End
White Notley
Inworth
Great Canfield
High Roding
Ford End
Little Leighs
Great Leighs
Faulkbourne
Rivenhall End
Tiptree
Hatfield Broad Oak
Fairstead
Fuller Street
Terling
Flack's Green
Chipping Hill
Witham
Great Braxted
Hatfield Heath
Aythorpe Roding
High Easter
Howe Street
Pleshey
Sheering
Leaden Roding
White Roding
Matching
Great Waltham
Little Waltham
Good Easter
Margaret Roding
Wickham Bishops
Great Totham
Little Totham
Matching Tye
Abbess Roding
Chignall Smealy
Mashbury
Chignall St James
Hatfield Peverel
Nounsley
Matching Green
Beauchamp Roding
Broomfield
Boreham
Broad Street Green
Parsonage Green
Boyton Cross
High Laver
Little Laver
Foster Street
Shellow Bowells
Springfield
Chelmer Village
Langford
Heybridge
Magdalen Laver
Roxwell
Little Baddow
Woodham Walter
Fyfield
Willingale
Chelmsford
Moreton
Great Oxney Green
Writtle
Heybridge Basin
Maldon
Northey I.
Cooksmill Green
Bovinger
Bobbingworth
Norton Mandeville
Widford
Great Baddow
Danbury
Russell Green
Woodham Mortimer
Sandon
Shelley
North Weald Bassett
Toot Hill
Greensted
High Ongar
Norton Heath
Loves Green
Galleyend
Galleywood
Howe Green
Cock Clarks
Rudley Green
Bicknacre
Mundon
Chipping Ongar
Nine Ashes
Blackmore
Mill Green
Margaretting
Purleigh
Cold Norton
Latchingdon
Stanford Rivers
Stondon Massey
Fryerning
West Hanningfield
East Hanningfield
Little End
Ingatestone
Stock
Woodham Ferrers
Stow Maries
Stapleford Tawney
Doddinghurst
Kelvedon Hatch
Swallows Cross
Heybridge
Coalhill
Rettendon
South Woodham Ferrers
North Fambridge
Navestock Heath
Mountnessing
South Hanningfield
Navestock Side
Downham
Pilgrims Hatch
Ramsden Heath
Rettendon Place
South Fambridge
Stapleford Abbotts
Hutton
Billericay
Runwell
Ramsden Bellhouse
Wickford
Battlesbridge
Hullbridge
Canewdon
South Weald
Shenfield
BRENTWOOD
South Green
Shotgate
Rawreth
Ashingdon
Havering-atte-Bower
Little Burstead
Crays Hill
Hockley
Hawkwell
Harold Hill
Ingrave
Herongate
Great Burstead
Nevendon
RAYLEIGH
Great Stambridge
Great Warley
Dunton Wayletts
North Benfleet
Stroud Green
Collier Row
Harold Wood
Little Warley
Basildon
Rochford
Gidea Park
Romford
Bowers Gifford
Thundersley
Eastwood
Cranham
West Horndon
Laindon
Pitsea
Daws Heath
Hornchurch
Vange
Hope's Grn.
Hadleigh
Prittlewell
Langdon Hills
South Benfleet
Southend-on-Sea
Rush Green
Elm Park
Upminster
Leigh on Sea
Bulphan
Dagenham
Hacton
Corbets Tey
North Ockendon
Horndon on the Hill
Fobbing
Corringham
Westcliff-on-Sea
South Hornchurch
CANVEY ISLAND
Thurrock
South Ockendon
Baker Street
Orsett
Stanford-le-Hope
Coryton
Leigh Beck
Southend-on-Sea
Rainham
Wennington
Aveley
North Stifford
Mucking
Thames Haven
London Gateway
THAMES ESTUARY
Belvedere
Chadwell St Mary
Linford
Halstow Marshes
St Mary's Marshes
Allhallows-on-Sea
West Tilbury
East Tilbury
Cliffe
Cooling
St Mary Hoo
Allhallows
Lower Stoke
Isle of Grain
Grain
High Halstow
Tilbury
Slade Green
0 1 2 3 4 5 6 miles
0 1 2 3 4 5 6 7 8 9 10 km

HARWICH
Dovercourt
Upper Dovercourt
Parkeston
Harwich Redoubt Fort
Hoek van Holland
Shotley Gate
Shop Corner
Harkstead
Upper Street
Holbrook Bay
Stour
Brantham
Stour Valley
Cattawade
Mistley Towers
Mistley
Bradfield
Wrabness
Manningtree
Lawford
Dedham
Bridge Cottage
Sir Alfred Munnings Art Museum
Dedham Heath
St Mary
Nayland
Bures
Mount Bures
Wormingford
Little Horkesley
Boxted
Boxted Heath
Boxted Cross
Langham
Great Horkes
Weston Homes Community Stad.
East Anglian Railway Museum
Fordham
West Bergholt
Horkesley Heath
Colchester North
Mile End
Ardleigh
Little Bromley
Horsley Cross
Horsleycross Street
Bradfield Heath
Wix
Little Oakley
Great Oakley
Parson's Heath
Highwoods
Eight Ash Green
Fordstreet
Aldham
St Botolph's Priory
Colchester
Fox Street
Crockleford Heath
Great Bromley
Elmstead Market
Tendring Green
Little Bentley
Stone's Green
Beaumont
Horsey Island
The Naze
Marks Tey
Stanway
Lexden
Beacon End
Earthworks
Abbey Field
Shrub End
Old Heath
Wivenhoe Cross
Hare Green
Balls Green
Beth Chatto Gdns
Tendring
Thorpe Green
Hamford Water
Thorpe-le-Soken
Kirby-le-Soken
Maritime Museum
Copford Green
Maypole Green
Bourne Mill
Blackheath
Wivenhoe
Frating Green
Great Bentley
Weeley
Weeley Heath
Colchester Zoo
Easthorpe
Heckfordbridge
Layer de la Haye
Rowhedge
Alresford
Aingers Green
Kirby Cross
Walton-on-the-Naze
Frinton-on-Sea
Hardy's Green
Birch
Smythe's Green
Birch Green
Malting Green
Fingringhoe
Thorrington
Row Heath
Little Clacton
Clacton Village
Great Holland
Abberton
Abberton Reservoir
Langenhoe
Layer Marney
Layer Breton
Layer Marney Tower
River Colne
Brightlingsea
St Osyth Heath
Holland Haven
Peldon
St Osyth Priory
St Osyth
Great Clacton
Holland-on-Sea
Clacton-on-Sea
Mersea Island
East Mersea
Cudmore Grove
Point Clear
Oxley Green
Paternoster Heath
Great Wigborough
Copt Hall Marshes
Blue Row
Colne Estuary
Salcott
Jaywick
Tolleshunt D'Arcy
Blackwater Estuary
West Mersea
Mersea Island Museum
Colne Pt.
Tolleshunt Major
The Nass
Virley Channel
Tollesbury
Goldhanger
Sales Pt.
St Peters on the Wall
Bradwell Waterside
Blackwater
Osea I.
Bradwell on Sea
TM
Ramsey Island
St Lawrence
Tillingham
Dengie
Steeple
Asheldham
Mayland
Southminster
Althorne
Ray Sand
Stoneyhills
Mangapps Railway Mus
Montsale
Deal Hall
Ostend
Burnham-on-Crouch
Creaksea
Foulness Sand
Foulness Pt.
Crouch
TR
Paglesham Churchend
Wallasea Wetlands
Courtsend
Paglesham Eastend
Churchend
Ballards Gore
Potton Island
FOULNESS ISLAND
Maplin Sands
Barling
Havengore Island
Little Wakering
Great Wakering
Bournes Green
North Shoebury
Shoeburyness
Thorpe Bay
Cambridge Town
Shoeburyness
A12
A120
A133
A137
A134
B1352
B1035
B1414
B1033
B1029
B1027
B1028
B1025
B1026
B1022
B1023
B1032
B1336
B1021
B1018
B1010
B1017
B1016
A13
56
57
30
A
B
C
D
E
F
G
5
6
7
8

ROSSLARE
Strumble Head
Pen Caer
Dinas Head
Tresinwen
Llanwnda
Fishguard Bay
Bae Abergwaun
Brynhenllan
PWLL DERI
Goodwick
(Wdig)
Lower Town
Dinas Cross
A487
Trefasser
Penbwchdy
Dyffryn
Fishguard
(Abergwaun)
45
Manorowen
St Nicholas
PEMBROKESHIRE COAST PATH
LLWYBR ARFORDIR PENFRO
TREGWYNT WOOLLEN MILL
A40
Llanychaer
Scleddau
Pontfaen
Ynysduellyn
Abercastle
Granston
Penclegyr
Porthgain
Trefin
Trecwn
B4313
Mathry
Newbridge
CORSYDD LLANGLOFFAN
Abereiddy
Llanrhian
Penparc
Castlemorris
B4331
Croes-goch
B4330
Little Newcastle
Puncheston
ST. DAVID'S HEAD
PENMAEN DEWI
Tretio
Treleddyd-fawr
Treffynnon
Treglemais
Treddiog
Letterston
Castlebythe
Tufton
Carnhedryn
Llanreithan
Welsh Hook
St Dogwells
Whitesand Bay
Porth-mawr
ST DAVID'S
Rhodiad
Caerfarchell
Llandeloy
Wolf's Castle
B4329
BISHOP'S PALACE
B4583
A487
Pont-yr-hafod
Ambleston
Woodstock
Rhosson
Whitchurch
Middle Mill
Trefgarn Owen
Hayscastle
Rinaston
Wallis
Ramsey Island
Ynys Dewi
RAMSEY ISLAND
Ramsey Sound
CATHEDRAL
St David's
(Tyddewi)
Nine Wells
Solva
Hayscastle Cross
Brimaston
LLYS-Y-FRAN RESERVOIR
Mountain Water
Treffgarne
Triffleton
Penycwm
DUDWELL MT.
Leweston
Spittal
Walton East
SCOLTON MANOR
Newgale
Pembrokeshire
(Sir Benfro)
Wolfsdale
Roch Gate
Roch
Camrose
A40
Rudbaxton
Clarbeston Road
Keeston
Nolton Haven
Simpson Cross
Tangiers
Leechpool
SM
ST. BRIDES BAY
BAE SAIN FFRAID
Pelcomb Cross
Crundale
Wiston
Nolton
Lambston
B4330
Haverfordwest
(Hwlffordd)
Druidston
Pelcomb Bridge
Slade
Portfield Gate
CASTLE MUSEUM AND ART GALLERY
BROAD HAVEN
Haroldston West
B4341
Dreenhill
Uzmaston
The Rhos
Broad Haven
B4327
Merlin's Bridge
Millin Cross
PICTON CASTLE & GARDENS
Little Haven
Broadway
Pope Hill
Minwear
Walton West
Boulston
Talbenny
Landshipping
Tower Point
Trwyn Twr
North Johnston
Freystrop
Martletwy
St Bride's
Walwyn's Castle
Hook
Wooltack Point
Trwyn Wooltack
Tiers Cross
Landshipping Quay
NATIONAL NATURE RESERVE
Skomer Island
Ynys Skomer
SKOMER ISLAND
Marloes
B4327
Hasguard
Robeston Cross
Johnston
A4076
Llangwm
Black Tar
MARLOES SANDS
Rosemarket
Broad Sound
Thornton
Steynton
Hill Mountain
Port Lion
Houghton
St Ishmael's
Sandy Haven
Herbrandston
A477
Gateholm Island
Ynys Gateholm
Milford Haven
(Aberdaugleddau)
Honeyborough
Lawrenny
Dale
B4325
Burton
West Williamston
Hakin
Waterston
Neyland
MILFORD HAVEN
ABERDAUGLEDDYF
Llanstadwell
UPTON CASTLE GARDENS
Skokholm Island
Ynys Skokholm
TOLL
Pembroke Dock
(Doc Penfro)
Cosheston
CAREW CASTLE
Angle
Angle Bay
Bae Angle
PEMBROKE DOCK SUNDERLAND TRUST
32
Milton
Pwllcrochan
Pennar
B4322
St Ann's Hd.
Pentir St. Ann
Rhoscrowther
Pembroke
(Penfro)
LAMPHEY BISHOP'S PALACE
ROSSLARE
Sheep Island
Ynys y Defaid
B4320
Monkton
Hundleton
B4320
Lamphey
Freshwater West
Maiden Wells
B4584
Hodgeston
B4319
St Twynnells
B4319
Freshwater East
Castlemartin
Warren
St Petrox
Cheriton or Stackpole Elidor
Trewent Pt.
Trwyn Trewent
Linney Hd.
Pentir Linney
Merrion
Stackpole
ELEGUG STACKS
Bosherston
STACKPOLE
The Wash
Stackpole Hd.
Pen Stackpole
PEMBROKESHIRE COAST PATH
LLWYBR ARFORDIR PENFRO
St Govan's Hd.
Pen St Gofan
PEMBROKESHIRE COAST
ARFORDIR PENFRO
SR
0 1 2 3 4 5 6 miles
0 1 2 3 4 5 6 7 8 9 10 km

CARDIGAN BAY
BAE CEREDIGION
SN
46
Cwmtudu Cwmtydu
Ynys-Lochtyn
Llangrannog
Blaencelyn
Pontgarreg
Penbryn
Parcllyn
Tresaith
Aberporth
Penmorfa
Brynhoffnant
Sarnau
Cardigan I. Ynys Aberteifi
Cemaes Head Pen Cemaes
Gwbert
Felinwynt
Blaenannerch
Aberporth West Wales Airport
Tan-y-groes
Glynarthen
Y Ferwig
Tremain
Blaenporth
Rhydlewis
Poppit Sands
Cippyn
Cardigan (Aberteifi)
Penparc
Bettws Ifan
Hawen
Beulah
PEMBROKESHIRE COAST
ARFORDIR PENFRO
St Dogmaels
Abbey
Bridgend
Castle
Llangoedmor
Pantgwyn
Ponthirwaun
Bryngwyn
Brongest
Troedyraur
Moylgrove
Pembrokeshire Coast Path
Llwybr Arfordir Penfro
Monington
Coedmor
Llechryd
Llandygwydd
Capel Tygwydd
Croft
Pen-y-bryn
Cilgerran Castle
Cilgerran
Newport Bay
Dinas Head
Bae Trefdraeth
Glanrhyd
Bridell
Carreg-wen
Cwm-cou
Llandyfriog
Aber-banc
Fishguard Bay
Bae Abergwaun
Berry Hill
Nevern
Pontgareg
Llantood
Coracle Centre & Flour Mill
Cenarth
Newcastle Emlyn (Castell Newydd Emlyn)
Pentrecagal
Brynhenllan
Parrog
Newport (Trefdraeth)
Felindre Farchog
Pengelli Forest
A487
Rhos-hill
Abercych
Newchapel
Clynfyw
Aber-Arad
National Wool Museum
Lower Town
Dinas Cross
Castell Henllys Fort
Eglwyswrw
Boncath
Cilwendeg
Penrherber
Felindre
Fishguard (Abergwaun)
Carningli
Ty Canol
Dyfed Shires & Leisure Farm
Bro Meigan Gardens
Llanfair-Nant-Gwyn
Blaenffos
Cheese Farm
Cwmhiraeth
Cilgwyn
Crosswell
Afon Nevern
Bwlchygroes
Cwmcych
Capel Iwan
Llanychaer
Brynberian
Pontyglasier
Eglwyswen
Penygroes
Star
Clydey
Moelfre
Cwmorgan
Tanglwst
Pontfaen
Crymych
Tegryn
Trecwn
MYNYDD PRESELI
Pentre-galar
Hermon
Llanfyrnach
Hen-feddau fawr
Bryn-Iwan
Foel-Cwmcerwyn
Mynachlog-ddu
Dinas
Trelech
Little Newcastle
Puncheston
New Inn
Rosebush
Castlebythe
32
44
Glandwr
Hebron
Blaen-waun
Pen-y-bont
Glandy Cross
Llanglydwen
Cwmbach
Llanwinio
Ambleston
Woodstock
New Moat
Pant-y-Caws
Cefn-y-pant
Talog
0 1 2 3 4 5 6 miles
0 1 2 3 4 5 6 7 8 9 10 km

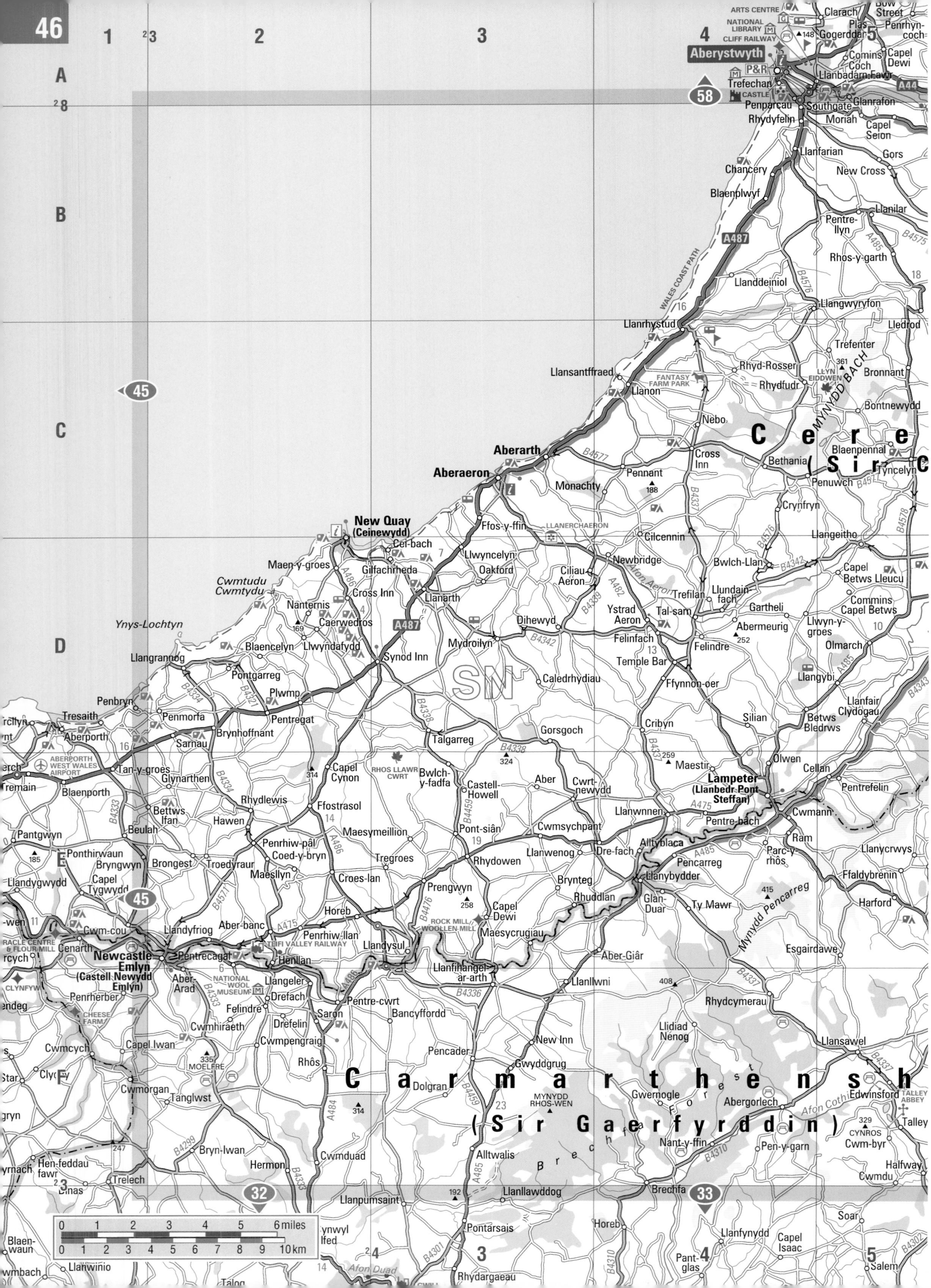
1
2
3
4
5
A
B
C
D
E
F
Aberystwyth
ARTS CENTRE
NATIONAL LIBRARY
CLIFF RAILWAY
Clarach
Bow Street
Plas Gogerddan
Penrhyn-coch
Comins Coch
Capel Dewi
Llanbadarn Fawr
Trefechan
CASTLE
P&R
58
A44
Penparcau
Southgate
Glanrafon
Rhydyfelin
Moriah
Capel Seion
Llanfarian
Gors
Chancery
New Cross
Blaenplwyf
Llanilar
Pentre-llyn
A487
A485
B4575
Rhos-y-garth
WALES COAST PATH
Llanddeiniol
B4576
Llangwyryfon
Llanrhystud
Lledrod
Trefenter
Llansantffraed
Rhyd-Rosser
LLYN EIDDWEN
361
Bronnant
FANTASY FARM PARK
Llanon
Rhydfudr
MYNYDD BACH
Bontnewydd
45
Nebo
Ceredigion (Sir C
Aberarth
B4577
Cross Inn
Blaenpennal
Bethania
Tyncelyn
Aberaeron
Pennant
188
Monachty
Penuwch
B4337
Crynfryn
New Quay (Ceinewydd)
Ffos-y-ffin
LLANERCHAERON
Cilcennin
Llangeitho
B4578
Cei-bach
Maen-y-groes
Gilfachrheda
Llwyncelyn
Newbridge
Bwlch-Llan
B4342
Capel Betws Lleucu
Cwmtudu Cwmtydu
A486
Oakford
Ciliau Aeron
A482
Afon Aeron
Trefilan
Llundain-fach
Commins Capel Betws
Cross Inn
Llanarth
B4339
Nanternis
Caerwedros
169
Dihewyd
Ystrad Aeron
Tal-sarn
Gartheli
Llwyn-y-groes
Abermeurig
Ynys-Lochtyn
Blaencelyn
Llwyndafydd
Mydroilyn
B4342
Felinfach
252
Olmarch
Felindre
Llangrannog
Synod Inn
Temple Bar
Pontgarreg
SN
Caledrhydiau
Ffynnon-oer
Llangybi
B4334
B4321
Plwmp
Llanfair Clydogau
Penbryn
Tresaith
Penmorfa
Pentregat
Silian
Betws Bledrws
Aberporth
Brynhoffnant
B4338
Cribyn
Sarnau
Talgarreg
Gorsgoch
ABERPORTH WEST WALES AIRPORT
Tan-y-groes
324
259
Maestir
Olwen
Glynarthen
314
Capel Cynon
RHOS LLAWR CWRT
Bwlch-y-fadfa
Castell-Howell
Aber
Cwrt-newydd
Lampeter (Llanbedr Pont Steffan)
Cellan
Pentrefelin
Tremain
Blaenporth
Rhydlewis
Ffostrasol
B4459
Llanwnnen
A475
Cwmann
Bettws Ifan
Hawen
Pentre-bach
A4333
Beulah
Maesymeillion
Pont-siân
Cwmsychpant
Pantgwyn
Penrhiw-pâl
Coed-y-bryn
Alltyblaca
Ram
Ponthirwaun
Bryngwyn
185
Brongest
Troedyraur
Tregroes
Rhydowen
Llanwenog
Dre-fach
A485
Pencarreg
Parc-y-rhôs
Llanycrwys
Capel Tygwydd
Maesllyn
Croes-lan
Brynteg
Llanybydder
Ffaldybrenin
Llandygwydd
Prengwyn
415
Mynydd Pencarreg
Rhuddlan
Glan-Duar
Ty Mawr
Harford
B4571
Horeb
258
Capel Dewi
Cwm-cou
Llandyfriog
Aber-banc
A475
ROCK MILL WOOLLEN MILL
Penrhiw-llan
Maesycrugiau
Esgairdawe
Cenarth
TEIFI VALLEY RAILWAY
Llandysul
Newcastle Emlyn (Castell Newydd Emlyn)
Pentrecagal
Henllan
Llanfihangel-ar-arth
Aber-Giâr
Aber-Arad
NATIONAL WOOL MUSEUM
Llangeler
B4336
Llanllwni
408
CLYNFYW
Drefach
Penrherber
B4333
Felindre
Pentre-cwrt
Rhydcymerau
CHEESE FARM
Bancyffordd
Cwmhiraeth
Drefelin
Saron
Llidiad Nenog
Capel Iwan
Cwmpengraig
New Inn
Llansawel
Cwmcych
335
MOELFRE
Pencader
Gwyddgrug
Rhôs
Carmarthenshire
Clydey
Cwmorgan
Dolgran
(Sir Gaerfyrddin)
B4459
Gwernogle
Forest
Abergorlech
Afon Cothi
Edwinsford
TALLEY ABBEY
Tanglwst
314
23
MYNYDD RHOS-WEN
Brechfa
329
CYNROS
Talley
A484
Cwm-byr
B4299
Bryn-Iwan
247
Alltwalis
Nant-y-ffin
B4310
Pen-y-garn
A485
Hermon
B4333
Cwmduad
Halfway
Cwmdu
Hen-feddau fawr
Trelech
32
33
Dinas
Llanpumsaint
192
Llanllawddog
Brechfa
Soar
0 1 2 3 4 5 6 miles
0 1 2 3 4 5 6 7 8 9 10 km
Blaen-waun
Pontarsais
Horeb
Llanfynydd
Capel Isaac
B4301
Pant-glas
B4310
B4302
Llanwinio
Afon Duad
Rhydargaeau
Salem
Talog

Hafren Forest
Llanidloes
Pen-bont Rhydybeddau
Dyffryn Castell
Pant Mawr
Glynbrochan
Newchapel
Capel Bangor
Dollwen
Goginan
SILVER MOUNTAIN EXPERIENCE
Llanifyny
Cwmbelan
GLYNDWR'S WAY
A44
Cwmbrwyno
58
Llangurig
59
564
584
Llaith
VALE OF RHEIDOL RAILWAY
Afon Rheidol
RHEIDOL HYDRO ELECTRIC STATION
Ystumtuen
Aberffrwd
Ysbytycynfyn
COED RHEIDOL
David's Well
A4120
Pisgah
Llanfihangel-y-Creuddyn
Mynydd Bach
Devil's Bridge
610 PEN Y GARN
B4518
Nantgwyn
493 RED LION
Trisant
B4343
Cnwch-coch
Blaenycwm
Pant-y-dwr
A470
B4340
Abermagwr
New Row
B4574
Cwmystwyth
Bwlch-y-sarnau
Crosswood
HAFOD ESTATE
498
St Harmon
Llanafan
Pont-rhyd-y-groes
571 GEIFAS
Wye (Gwy)
Wenallt
Mynydd Bach
371
Ysbyty Ystwyth
505 MOEL HYWEL
Tynygraig
Tanyrhydiau
572 TRAWSALLT
Craig-goch Res.
B4340
Ystradmeurig
CLAERWEN
WELSH ROYAL CRYSTAL
Rhayader
(Rhaeadr Gwy)
Gaufron
Ffair-Rhos
Penygarreg Res.
Swydd-ffynnon
Pontrhydfendigaid
Llansantffraed Cwmdeuddwr
A44
48
Nantmel
Glan Teifi
STRATA FLORIDA ABBEY
Elan Village
THE GIGRIN FARM RED KITE FEEDING CENTRE
Garreg-ddu Res.
B4518
Gwyst
530 DIBYN DU
Claerwen Reservoir
Nant-glas
CORS CARON
Llanwrthwl
digion
eredigion)
Afon Claerwen
Caban-coch Res.
Argoed
249
Ty'n-yr-eithin
Llandrindod Wells
Llanyre
(Llandrindod)
B4343
A470
A4081
WELSH GOLD CENTRE
Tywi Forest
Powys
537 DRUM-DDU
Ithon
Tregaron
508 Y DRUM
B4358
NATIONAL COLLEC
Newbridge on Wye
Howe
645 DRYGARN FAWR
Disserth
532 BRYN CRWN
Cross
DOLGOCH
SN
A483
Llanafan-fawr
Llanddewi-Brefi
484 ESGAIR CERRIG
Pentre-rhew
CORS Y LLYN
TYNCORNEL
500
NANT IRFON
B4358
Pentre-llwyn-llwyd
Cwmbach
Builth Road
463
Soar-y-Mynydd
Llyn Brianne Res.
Troed-rhiwdalar
484 BRYN BRAWD
Abergwesyn
Llanelw
456
Beulah
Cilmery
Oaklands
Llanfechan
A483
487
Builth Wells
Cwm Irfon
Garth
Tyn-y-graig
(Llanfair-ym-Muallt)
Mynydd Trawsnant
CAMBRIAN WOOLLEN MILL
441
ALLT RHYD Y GROES
Irfon
Llanddewi'r Cwm
Llanwrtyd
Maesmynis
440
Ystradffin
Llanwrtyd Wells
Llangammarch Wells
Alltm
(Llanwrtud)
459
B4519
Ffarmers
Afon Cothi
Mynydd Mallaen
Nant-y-Bai
Cefn-gorwydd
474 DRUM-DDU
B4520
Mynydd Epynt
Cwrt-y-cadno
Rhandirmwyn
Pentre Dolau-Honddu
48
Gwenddw
Llandre
434 ESGAIR FERCHON
Crychan Forest
463 BRYN DU
Pumsaint
Caeo Forest
DOLAUCOTHI GOLD MINES
Cynghordy
Tirabad
Upper Chapel
Cilycwm
433
Caio
341
Llanfair-ar-y-bryn
Llaneglwys
Divlyn
16
Porthyrhyd
Siloh
456
Crugybar
Blaendyryn
Merthyr Cynog
Honddu
A482
B4302
Pentre-ty-gwyn
Mynydd Bwlch-y-groes
423
Lower Chapel
Babel
442
Llandovery
A483
Llandeilo'r Fan
Llanfihangel Nant Bran
Pont-faen
Pwllgloyw
Garthb
ire
(Llanymddyfri)
Cwmdwr
Halfway
Pentre-bach
Nant Bran
Sarnau
Llandefaelog Fach
Waunclunda
Llansadwrn
Llanwrda
Myrtle Hill
A40
Llanddew
A40
A4069
Llywel
Pentre'r-felin
Battle
Felindre
Cilgwyn
33
Myddfai
440
Usk
34
Trallong
Aberyscir
BRECON GAER ROMAN FORT
CATHEDRAL
Brecon
Ashfield
(Wysg)
(Aberhonddu)
Usk Reservoir
Trecastle
Sennybridge
(Pont Senni)
Penpont
Llanfaes
Hermon
Llangadog
Cwmwysg
Defynnog
Llanspyddid
Felindre
Pont ar Hydfer
Manordeilo
A4067
400
Mynydd Illtyd
BRECKNOCK MUSEUM AND ART GALLERY
Cwmifor
Tai'r-Bull
MOUNTAIN CENTRE
Talsarn
Llanfr

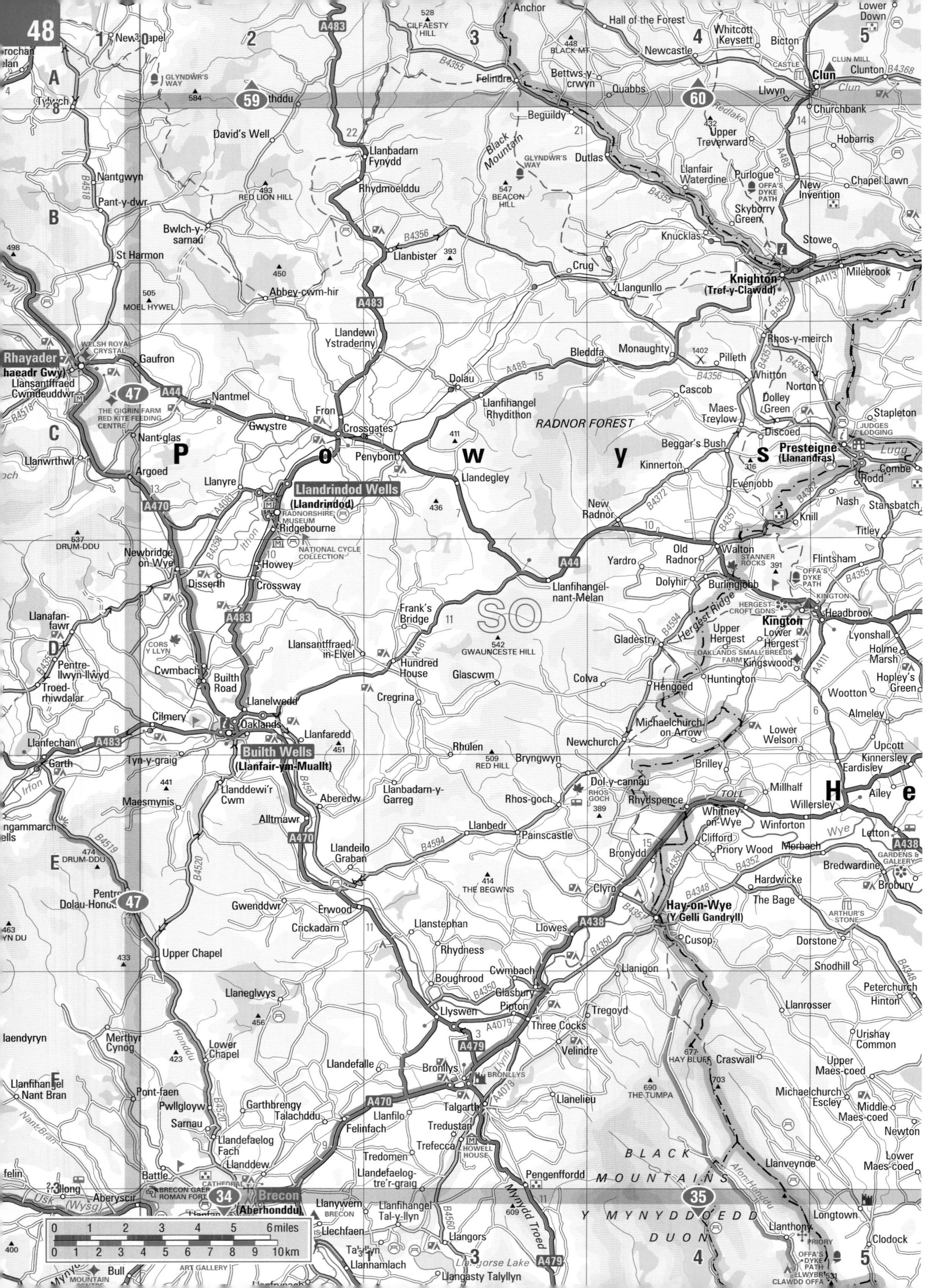

Anchor
Hall of the Forest
Whitcott Keysett
Bicton
Lower Down
CILFAESTY HILL
BLACK MT
Newcastle
Felindre
Bettws-y-crwyn
Quabbs
Clun
CLUN MILL
Clunton
Llwyn
Churchbank
New Chapel
GLYNDWR'S WAY
David's Well
Llanbadarn Fynydd
Black Mountain
Beguildy
Upper Treverward
Hobarris
Nantgwyn
RED LION HILL
Rhydmoelddu
BEACON HILL
Dutlas
Llanfair Waterdine
Purlogue
OFFA'S DYKE PATH
New Invention
Chapel Lawn
Pant-y-dwr
Bwlch-y-sarnau
Skyborry Green
Knucklas
Stowe
St Harmon
Llanbister
Crug
Knighton (Tref-y-Clawdd)
Milebrook
Abbey-cwm-hir
MOEL HYWEL
Llangunllo
Llandewi Ystradenny
Rhos-y-meirch
WELSH ROYAL CRYSTAL
Rhayader
Gaufron
Llansantffraed Cwmdeuddwr
THE GIGRIN FARM RED KITE FEEDING CENTRE
Bleddfa
Monaughty
Pilleth
Whitton
Norton
Dolau
Cascob
Nantmel
Llanfihangel Rhydithon
Dolley Green
Stapleton
JUDGES LODGING
Fron
Maes-Treylow
Nant-glas
Gwystre
Crossgates
RADNOR FOREST
Discoed
Presteigne (Llanandras)
Llanwrthwl
P
o
w
y
s
Penybont
Beggar's Bush
Lugg
Combe
Argoed
Llanyre
Llandegley
Kinnerton
Rodd
Llandrindod Wells (Llandrindod)
Evenjobb
RADNORSHIRE MUSEUM
Nash
Stansbatch
Ridgebourne
New Radnor
Knill
DRUM-DDU
NATIONAL CYCLE COLLECTION
Titley
Newbridge on Wye
Howey
Old Radnor
Walton
Yardro
STANNER ROCKS
Flintsham
Disserth
Crossway
Llanfihangel-nant-Melan
Dolyhir
Burlingjobb
OFFA'S DYKE PATH
KINGTON
Llanafan-fawr
Frank's Bridge
SO
HERGEST CROFT GDNS
Headbrook
Hergest Ridge
Kington
Lyonshall
CORS Y LLYN
Upper Hergest
Lower Hergest
Gladestry
Holme Marsh
Pentre-llwyn-llwyd
Llansantffraed-in-Elvel
GWAUNCESTE HILL
OAKLANDS SMALL BREEDS FARM
Kingswood
Troed-rhiwdalar
Cwmbach
Builth Road
Hundred House
Glascwm
Colva
Huntington
Hopley's Green
Hengoed
Wootton
Cregrina
Llanelwedd
Cilmery
Michaelchurch on Arrow
Almeley
Oaklands
Lower Welson
Llanfechan
Llanfaredd
Newchurch
Builth Wells (Llanfair-ym-Muallt)
Upcott
Garth
Tyn-y-graig
Rhulen
Bryngwyn
Brilley
Kinnersley
Eardisley
RED HILL
Irfon
Dol-y-cannau
Millhalf
Llanddewi'r Cwm
H
e
Ailey
Maesmynis
Aberedw
Llanbadarn-y-Garreg
Rhos-goch
RHOS GOCH
Rhydspence
TOLL
Willersley
Whitney-on-Wye
Alltmawr
Winforton
Llanbedr
Painscastle
Wye
Letton
Llandeilo Graban
Clifford
Priory Wood
Merbach
Bronydd
DRUM-DDU
GARDENS & GALLERY
Bredwardine
Hardwicke
THE BEGWNS
Clyro
Brobury
Pentre Dolau-Honddu
The Bage
Gwenddwr
Erwood
Hay-on-Wye (Y Gelli Gandryll)
ARTHUR'S STONE
Crickadarn
Llanstephan
Llowes
Cusop
Dorstone
Upper Chapel
Rhydness
Snodhill
Llanigon
Boughrood
Cwmbach
Glasbury
Peterchurch
Hinton
Llaneglwys
Pipton
Llanrosser
Tregoyd
Llyswen
Three Cocks
laendyryn
Merthyr Cynog
Lower Chapel
Honddu
Velindre
Urishay Common
HAY BLUFF
Craswall
Llandefalle
Bronllys
BRONLLYS
Upper Maes-coed
Llanfihangel Nant Bran
Pont-faen
THE TUMPA
Michaelchurch Escley
Pwllgloyw
Llanelieu
Talgarth
Middle Maes-coed
Garthbrengy
Talachddu
Llanfilo
Tredustan
Nant Bran
Sarnau
Felinfach
Newton
Llandefaelog Fach
HOWELL HOUSE
BLACK MOUNTAINS
Trefecca
Tredomen
Llanddew
Llandefaelog-tre'r-graig
Pengenffordd
Lower Maes-coed
Battle
Llanveynoe
BRECON GAER ROMAN FORT
CATHEDRAL
Usk (Wysg)
Aberyscir
Brecon (Aberhonddu)
Afon Honddu
Longtown
Llanywern
Llanfihangel Tal-y-llyn
Y MYNYDDOEDD DUON
Llanthony
PRIORY
Llechfaen
Llangors
Mynydd Troed
Clodock
Tal-y-llyn
OFFA'S DYKE PATH
Llannamlach
Llangorse Lake
Llangasty Talyllyn
LLWYBR CLAWDD OFFA
ART GALLERY
MOUNTAIN CENTRE
Bull
0 1 2 3 4 5 6 miles
0 1 2 3 4 5 6 7 8 9 10km

Craven Arms
Ludlow
Tenbury Wells
Leominster
Bromyard
Hereford
Ledbury
Cleobury Mortimer
Herefordshire
SO
Newent
Kington
Wigmore
Leintwardine
Clun
Aston on Clun
Stokesay
Onibury
Bromfield
Middleton
Ludford
Caynham
Woofferton
Burford
Brimfield
Orleton
Yarpole
Lucton
Luston
Eye
Kingsland
Shobdon
Pembridge
Eardisland
Weobley
Dilwyn
Bodenham
Marden
Sutton St Nicholas
Withington
Lugwardine
Tupsley
Holmer
Credenhill
Madley
Kingstone
Wormbridge
Kilpeck
Pontrilas
Ewyas Harold
Much Dewchurch
Holme Lacy
Mordiford
Fownhope
Much Marcle
Dymock
Colwall
Bosbury
Stoke Lacy
Much Cowarne
Bishops Frome
Acton Beauchamp
Whitbourne
Knightwick
Great Witley
Stanford Bridge
Stockton on Teme
Clows Top
Far Forest
Wyre Forest
Kinlet
Bewdley
Rock
Lindridge
Eardiston
Newnham Bridge
Kyre Magna
Docklow
Steens Bridge
Risbury
Humber
Stoke Prior
Hampton Court
Queenswood
Canon Pyon
Wellington
Burghill
Stretton Sugwas
Swainshill
Breinton
Clehonger
Allensmore
Wormelow Tump
Orcop Hill
Kentchurch
Garway
Llanwarne
Harewood End
Hoarwithy
King's Caple
Sellack
Foy
How Caple
Fawley Chapel
Brockhampton
Ballingham
Carey
Bolstone
Aconbury
Callow
Dewsall Court
Kivernoll
St Devereux
Didley
Thruxton
Cockyard
Vowchurch
Turnastone
Golden Valley
Peterchurch
St Margaret's
Bacton
Abbey Dore
Rowlestone
Llangua
Monmouth Cap
A49
A44
A4112
A4110
A417
A438
A465
A456
A4103
A480
A4113
A466
A449
M50
B4361
B4362
B4224
B4348
B4349
B4352
Teme
Lugg
Arrow
Frome
Wye
Rea
Leadon

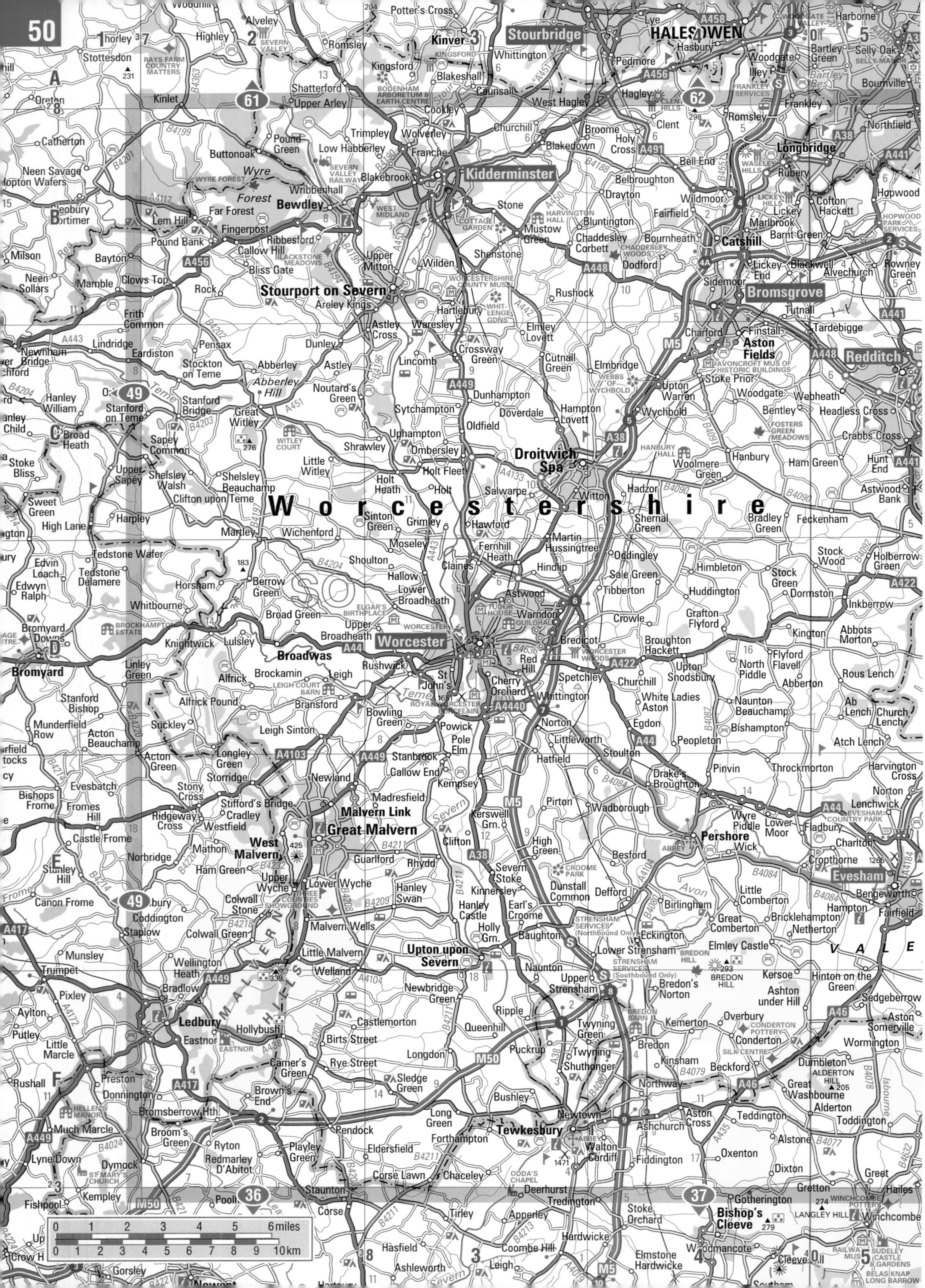
Worcestershire
Kidderminster
Stourbridge
HALESOWEN
Bromsgrove
Redditch
Droitwich Spa
Worcester
Evesham
Great Malvern
Malvern Link
West Malvern
Ledbury
Tewkesbury
Upton upon Severn
Pershore
Bromyard
Bewdley
Stourport on Severn
Bishop's Cleeve
Winchcombe
Kinver
Hagley
Catshill
Longbridge
Rubery
Alvechurch
Hartlebury
Ombersley
Broadwas
Eckington
Bredon
Wyre Forest
MALVERN HILLS
Severn
Teme
Avon
VALE
61
62
49
36
37
M5
M50
A38
A44
A449
A456
A422
A4440
A4103
A417
A46
A448
A441
6 miles
10 km

Sheldon
Butler's End
Moor
Keresley
Longford
Shilton
Ansty
Acock's Green
Sparkhill
Moseley
Springfield
King's Heath
Olton
Hall Green
Elmdon
Bickenhill
Elmdon Heath
Meriden
Hawkes End
Coundon
Little Heath
Foleshill
Walsgrave on Sowe
Allesley
Spon End
Wyken
Stretton under Fosse
Hampton in Arden
Four Oaks
Eastern Green
Coventry
Coombe Abbey
Brinklow
Easenhall
Cottendge
Shirley
Solihull
Eastcote
Berkswell
Whoberley
Earlsdon
Pinley
Binley
Binley Woods
King's Newnham
King's Norton
Hollywood
Copt Heath
Barston
Tile Hill
Stivichall
Willenhall
Bretford
Church Lawford
Drakes Cross
Whitlock's End
Monkspath
Knowle
Balsall Common
Brandon
Bentley Heath
Dorridge
Temple Balsall
Balsall
Fen End
Catchems Corner
Tollbar End
Wolston
Wythall
Earlswood Lakes Craft Centre
Burton Green
Baginton
Ryton-on-Dunsmore
Ryton Organic Gardens
Earlswood
Meer End
Crackley
Lunt Roman Fort
Midland Air Mus
Portway
Hockley Heath
Packwood House
Chadwick End
Baddesley Clinton
Kenilworth Castle
Honiley
Stoneleigh
Bubbenhall
Stretton-on-Dunsmore
Kingswood
Wroxall
National Agricultural Centre
Branson's Cross
Umberslade Farm
Wood End
Lapworth
Beausale
Kenilworth
Stareton
Ryton Pools
Princethorpe
Bourton on Dunsmore
Tanworth-in-Arden
Ashow
Beoley
Rowington
Weston under Wetherley
Wappenbury
Frankton
Draycote
Holt End
Forge Mill Needle Mus
Kemps Green
Marton
Eathorpe
Gorcott Hill
Lowsonford
Shrewley
Leek Wootton
Cubbington
Birdingbury
Arrow Valley
Ullenhall
Haseley
Hatton Country World
Old Milverton
Hunningham
Lillington
Leamington Hastings
Ipsley
Oldberrow
Henley-in-Arden
Preston Bagot
Hatton
Milverton
Royal Leamington Spa
Mappleborough Green
Budbrooke
Jephson Gardens
Offchurch
Long Itchington
Morton Bagot
Claverdon
Hampton on the Hill
St Mary's
Warwick Castle
Warwick
Radford Semele
Whitnash
Grand Union Canal
Bascote
Stockton
Studley
Wootton Wawen
Norton Lindsey
Longbridge
Shelfield
Langley
Edstone
Wolverton
Ufton
Southam
Napton on the Hill
Sambourne
Coughton Court
Little Alne
Heath End
Sherbourne
Bishop's Tachbrook
Coughton
Great Alne
Bearley
Barford
Harbury
Chapel Green
New End
Aston Cantlow
Snitterfield
Wasperton
Chesterton Windmill
Chesterton
Ladbroke
King's Coughton
Mary Arden's House
Warwick
Cookhill
Alcester
Walcote
Haselor
Wilmcote
Ingon
Hampton Lucy
Newbold Pacey
Ashorne
Warwick Services
Cross Green
Bishop's Itchington
Marston Doles
Overley Green
Billesley
Bishopton
Stratford-upon-Avon
Alveston
Charlecote Park
Charlecote
Moreton Morrell
Priors Hardwick
Arrow
Ragley Hall
Exhall
Temple Grafton
Shakespeare's Birthplace
Shottery
Tiddington
Wellesbourne
Lighthorne
Heritage Motor Centre
Knightcote
Oxford Canal
Weethley Gate
Wixford
Anne Hathaway's Cottage
Binton
Wellesbourne Watermill
Gaydon
Dunnington
Ardens Grafton
Stratford
Compton Verney
Chadshunt
Wormleighton
Iron Cross
Broom
Luddington
Shire Horse Centre
Loxley
Walton
Northend
Burton Dassett Hills
Fenny Compton
Salford Priors
Bidford-on-Avon
Welford-on-Avon
Clifford Chambers
Temple Herdewyke
Abbots Salford
Barton
Marlcliff
Atherstone on Stour
Ailstone
Combrook
Kineton
Burton Dassett
Little Kineton
Claydon
Dorsington
Preston on Stour
Ettington
Butlers Marston
Avon Dassett
Farnborough
Harvington
Cleeve Prior
Long Marston
Wimpstone
Alderminster
Pillerton Hersey
Radway
North Littleton
Lower Quinton
Warmington
Mollington
Middle Littleton
Pebworth
Pillerton Priors
Ratley
Edge Hill
Broad Marston
Newbold on Stour
Offenham
South Littleton
Upper Quinton
Admington
Oxhill
Shotteswell
Cropredy
All Things Wild Nature Centre
Honeybourne
Meon Hill
Armscote
Halford
Lower Tysoe
Upton House
Hornton
Aldington
Vale of Evesham
Mickleton
Kiftsgate Court Garden
Ilmington
Blackwell
Idlicote
Whatcote
Middle Tysoe
Horley
Bretforton
Hidcote Manor Garden
Tredington
Upper Tysoe
Alkerton
Hanwell
The Fleece Inn
Badsey
Honington Hall
Honington
Shenington
Wroxton
Drayton
Wickhamford
Aston Subedge
Hidcote Boyce
Darlingscott
Shipston-on-Stour
Winderton
Balscote
Neithrop
Weston-Sub-Edge
Ebrington
Epwell
Banbury
Willersey
Saintbury
Charingworth
Barcheston
Upper Brailes
Shutford
North Newington
Childswickham
Chipping Campden
Stretton-on-Fosse
Tidmington
Willington
Lower Brailes
Sutton under Brailes
Sibford Gower
Swalcliffe Barn
Broughton Castle
Easington
Broughton
Tadmarton
Broadway
Broad Campden
Paxford
Burmington
Swalcliffe
Bodicote
Sibford Ferris
Sor Brook
Buckland
Broadway Tower
Aston Magna
Todenham
Cherington
Stourton
Bloxham
West Adderbury
Laverton
Draycott
Little Wolford
Ascott
Milcombe
Snowshill Manor
Snowshill Lavender
Stanton
Snowshill
Blockley
Arboretum
Batsford
Lower Lemington
Great Wolford
Whichford
Hook Norton Brewery Visitors Centre
Milton
Barford St John
Moreton-in-Marsh
Bourton on the Hill
Barton on the Heath
Hook Norton
Wigginton
South Newington
Barford St Michael
Gloucestershire Warwickshire Steam Railway
Stanway
Stanway House
Sezincote
Wellington Aviation Museum
Long Compton
Great Rollright
Swerford
Hempton
Didbrook
Hailes Abbey
Cutsdean
Sezincote
Chastleton House
Little Compton
Rollright Stones
Nether Worton
Ford
Farmcote
Longborough
Evenlode
Great Tew
Over Worton
Condicote
Chastleton
Salford
Over Norton
Little Tew
Temple Guiting
Donnington
Adlestrop
Cornwell
Heythrop
Ledwell
Cotswold Farm Park
Broadwell
Chipping Norton
Sandford St Martin
Middle Barton
Kineton
Upper Swell
Lower Swell
Stow-on-the-Wold
Daylesford
Oddington
Church Enstone
Westcott Barton
Warwick
Vale of Evesham
M6
M42
M40
A45
A46
A452
A435
A448
A429
A422
A3400
A44
A424
A423
A425
A426
A428
A427
A4600
A4177
A4189
A4023
A361
62
63
52
37
38

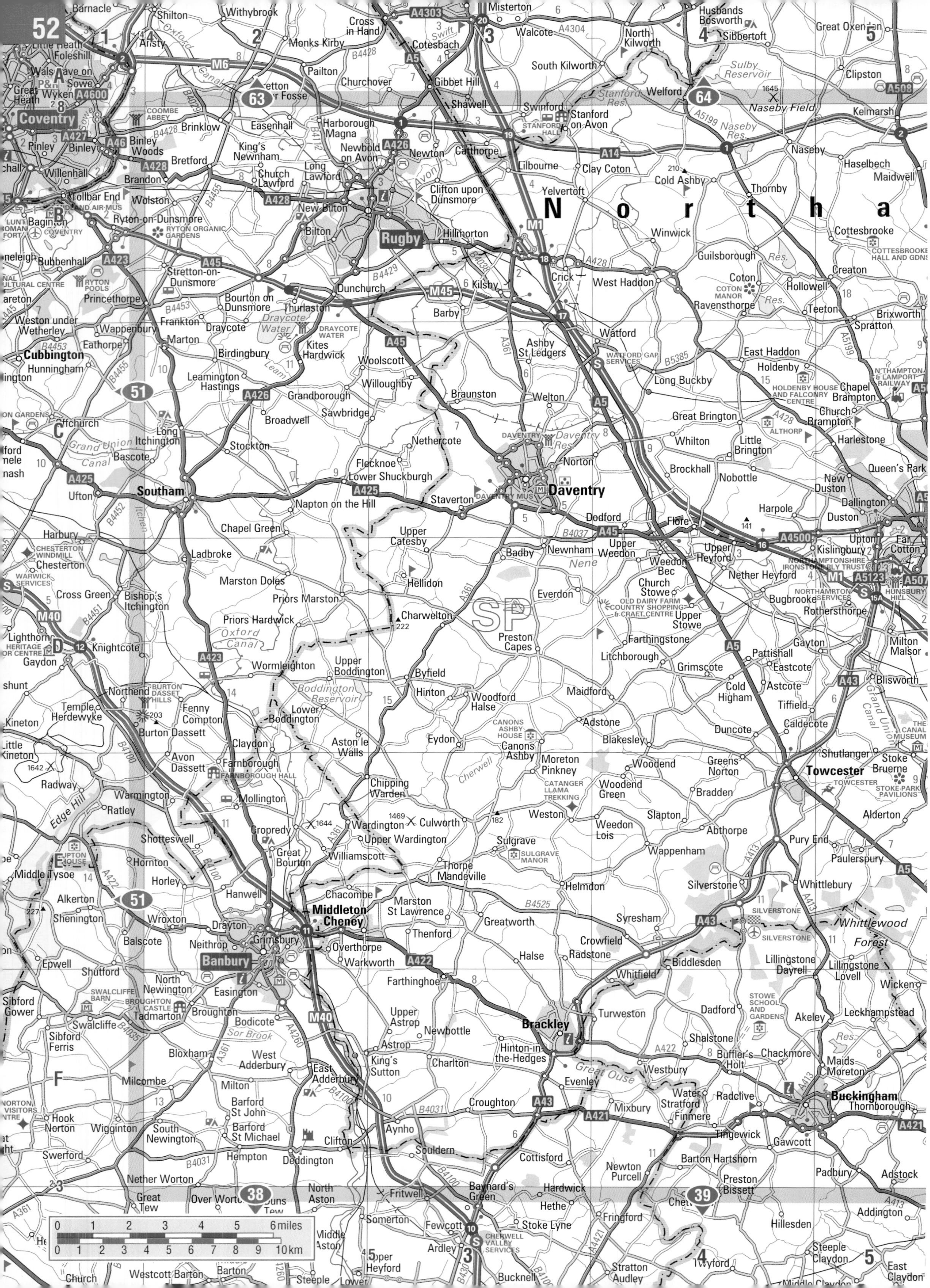

Barnacle
Shilton
Withybrook
Cross in Hand
A4303
Misterton
Walcote
A4304
North Kilworth
Husbands Bosworth
Sibbertoft
Great Oxendon
Little Heath
Foleshill
Ansty
Monks Kirby
Cotesbach
Swift
A5
Coventry
A4600
Wyken
Sowe
M6
Pailton
Churchover
Gibbet Hill
South Kilworth
Sulby Reservoir
Clipston
A508
Stretton under Fosse
63
Shawell
Stanford Res.
Welford
64
Naseby Field
Kelmarsh
Coombe Abbey
Brinklow
Easenhall
Harborough Magna
Swinford
Stanford on Avon
Stanford Hall
A5199
Naseby Res.
A427
Binley
Binley Woods
A46
King's Newnham
Newbold on Avon
A426
Newton
Catthorpe
Lilbourne
Clay Coton
A14
Naseby
Haselbech
Maidwell
Pinley
Willenhall
Bretford
Brandon
A428
Church Lawford
Long Lawford
Cold Ashby
Thornby
Tollbar End
Wolston
Clifton upon Dunsmore
Yelvertoft
Northa
New Bilton
Midland Air Mus
Baginton
Coventry
Ryton-on-Dunsmore
Ryton Organic Gardens
Bilton
Rugby
Hillmorton
M1
Winwick
Cottesbrooke
Cottesbrooke Hall and Gdns
Bubbenhall
A423
A45
Stretton-on-Dunsmore
Ryton Pools
B4429
Crick
A428
West Haddon
Guilsborough
Coton
Coton Manor
Hollowell
Creaton
Princethorpe
Bourton on Dunsmore
Dunchurch
Thurlaston
M45
Kilsby
Ravensthorpe
Teeton
Brixworth
Spratton
Weston under Wetherley
Frankton
Draycote
Draycote Water
Barby
Watford
Wappenbury
Eathorpe
Marton
Kites Hardwick
A45
Ashby St Ledgers
Cubbington
Hunningham
Birdingbury
Woolscott
Watford Gap Services
B5385
East Haddon
Holdenby
Leamington Hastings
Willoughby
Long Buckby
51
A426
Grandborough
Braunston
Welton
Holdenby House and Falconry Centre
Chapel Brampton
Church Brampton
Offchurch
Broadwell
Sawbridge
A5
Great Brington
Althorp
Long Itchington
Grand Union Canal
Stockton
Nethercote
Daventry Res.
Whilton
Little Brington
Harlestone
Bascote
Flecknoe
Norton
Brockhall
Queen's Park
A425
Lower Shuckburgh
Nobottle
New Duston
Southam
Ufton
Napton on the Hill
Staverton
Daventry Mus
Daventry
Dallington
Harpole
Dodford
Flore
Duston
B4037
Harbury
Chapel Green
Upper Catesby
A45
A4500
Upton
Far Cotton
Chesterton Windmill
Chesterton
Ladbroke
Badby
Newnham
Upper Weedon
Upper Heyford
Kislingbury
Nene
Weedon Bec
Nether Heyford
Northamptonshire Ironstone Rly Trust
Warwick Services
Marston Doles
Hellidon
Church Stowe
M1
A5123
Hunsbury Hill
Cross Green
Bishop's Itchington
Priors Marston
Everdon
Old Dairy Farm Country Shopping & Craft Centre
Northampton Services
Bugbrooke
Rothersthorpe
M40
Priors Hardwick
Charwelton
SP
Upper Stowe
Oxford Canal
Preston Capes
Farthingstone
Lighthorne
Heritage Motor Centre
Knightcote
Litchborough
Pattishall
Gayton
Milton Malsor
Gaydon
A423
Wormleighton
Upper Boddington
Byfield
Grimscote
Eastcote
Cold Higham
A43
Blisworth
Astcote
Northend
Burton Dassett Hills
Boddington Reservoir
Hinton
Woodford Halse
Maidford
Tiffield
Temple Herdewyke
Fenny Compton
Lower Boddington
Canons Ashby House
Adstone
Caldecote
Kineton
Burton Dassett
Aston le Walls
Eydon
Blakesley
Duncote
Canal Museum
Little Kineton
Claydon
Avon Dassett
Farnborough
Farnborough Hall
Canons Ashby
Moreton Pinkney
Woodend
Greens Norton
Shutlanger
Stoke Bruerne
Radway
Chipping Warden
Catanger Llama Trekking
Woodend Green
Towcester
Bradden
Stoke Park Pavilions
Warmington
Mollington
Edge Hill
Ratley
Cropredy
Wardington
Culworth
Weston
Slapton
Alderton
Upper Wardington
Sulgrave
Sulgrave Manor
Weedon Lois
Abthorpe
Pury End
Shotteswell
Hornton
Great Bourton
Williamscott
Thorpe Mandeville
Wappenham
Paulerspury
Middle Tysoe
Horley
A422
Silverstone
Whittlebury
Hanwell
Chacombe
Marston St Lawrence
Helmdon
A5
Alkerton
51
Middleton Cheney
B4525
Greatworth
Syresham
Silverstone
Whittlewood Forest
Shenington
Wroxton
Drayton
A43
Balscote
Neithrop
Grimsbury
Overthorpe
Thenford
Crowfield
Banbury
Warkworth
A422
Halse
Radstone
Biddlesden
Lillingstone Dayrell
Lillingstone Lovell
Epwell
Shutford
North Newington
Farthinghoe
Whitfield
Wicken
Swalcliffe Barn
Broughton Castle
Broughton
Easington
Stowe School and Gardens
Dadford
Akeley
Leckhampstead
Sibford Gower
Tadmarton
Upper Astrop
Turweston
Swalcliffe
Bodicote
M40
Brackley
Newbottle
Sibford Ferris
Sor Brook
Astrop
Shalstone
Bloxham
West Adderbury
King's Sutton
Charlton
Hinton-in-the-Hedges
A422
Buffler's Holt
Chackmore
Maids Moreton
East Adderbury
Great Ouse
Westbury
Milcombe
Milton
Evenley
Water Stratford
Radclive
Buckingham
Thornborough
Barford St John
Croughton
A43
Mixbury
Finmere
A421
Hook Norton
South Newington
Barford St Michael
B4031
Aynho
A421
Wigginton
Clifton
Tingewick
Gawcott
Swerford
Hempton
Deddington
Souldern
Cottisford
Barton Hartshorn
Newton Purcell
Padbury
Adstock
Nether Worton
B4031
North Aston
Bayard's Green
Hardwick
Preston Bissett
Great Tew
Over Worton
38
Fritwell
Hethe
Chetwode
39
Addington
Somerton
Fringford
Hillesden
Fewcott
Stoke Lyne
Cherwell Valley Services
Middle Aston
Upper Heyford
Ardley
Steeple Claydon
Twyford
East Claydon
Westcott Barton
Barton
Steeple
Lower
Bucknell
Stratton Audley
Middle Claydon
Church
0 1 2 3 4 5 6 miles
0 1 2 3 4 5 6 7 8 9 10 km

Braybrooke
Desborough
Rushton Triangular Lodge
Rushton
Newton
Geddington
Eleanor Cross
Sudborough
Lowick
Wadenhoe
Achurch
Aldwincle
Barnwell
All Saints
Wigsthorpe
Luddington in the Brook
Thurning
Great Gidding
Little Gidding
Steeple Gidding
Hamerton Zoo Park
Coppingford
Hamerton
Arthingworth
Rothwell
Harrington
Weekley
Boughton House
Warkton
Grafton Underwood
Thorpe Waterville
Clopton
Winwick
Titchmarsh
Orton
Loddington
Thorpe Malsor
Kettering
Barton Seagrave
Cranford St Andrew
Cranford St John
Slipton
Twywell
Islip
Thrapston
Woodford
Denford
Old Weston
Buckworth
Draughton
Great Cransley
Broughton
Mawsley
Wicksteed Park
Burton Latimer
Isham
Pytchley
Great Addington
Little Addington
Ringstead
Keyston
Bythorn
Brington
Molesworth
Leighton Bromswold
Barham
Lamport
Lamport Hall
Old
Scaldwell
Walgrave
Orlingbury
Finedon
Stanwick Lakes
Raunds
Catworth
Spaldwick
Easton
Ellington
Stow Longa
Hannington
Little Harrowden
Great Harrowden
Irthlingborough
Stanwick
Hargrave
Covington
Holcot
Hardwick
Higham Ferrers
Chelveston
Caldecott
Tilbrook
Pitsford Reservoir
Brixworth
Pitsford
Sywell
Wellingborough
Chichele College
Warmonds Hill
Shelton
Lower Dean
Upper Dean
Kimbolton
Grafham Water
Moulton
Mears Ashby
Little Irchester
Heritage Centre
Knuston
Rushden
Yeldon
West Perry
East Perry
Overstone
Sywell Reservoir
Wilby
Irchester
Little Wymington
Wymington
Newton Bromswold
Swineshead
Melchbourne
Pertenhall
Dillington
Stoughton Green
Boughton
Boothville
Kingsthorpe
Kingsley Park
Weston Favell
New Barton
Great Doddington
Narrow Gauge Railway Mus
Farndish
Knotting
Knotting Green
Riseley
Brook End
Great Staughton
Little Staughton
Hail Weston
Ecton
Earls Barton
Great Billing
Little Billing
Billing Aquadrome
Wollaston
Podington
Souldrop
Keysoe
Keysoe Row
Northampton
Little Houghton
Whiston
Cogenhoe
Strixton
Grendon
Hinwick
Santa Pod Raceway
Staploe
Duloe
Brafield-on-the-Green
Castle Ashby
Great Houghton
Denton
Easton Maudit
Bozeat
Sharnbrook
Bolnhurst
Bushmead Priory
Hardingstone
Yardley Hastings
Odell
Harrold
Harrold-Odell
Felmersham
Radwell
Bletsoe
Thurleigh
Rootham's Green
Colmworth
Wootton
Collingtree
Hackleton
Yardley Chase
Chellington
Milton Ernest
Duck's Cross
Chawston
Quinton
Piddington
Horton
Carlton
Pavenham
Colesden
Wilden
Ravensden
Roxton
Lavendon
Warrington
West End
Stevington
Oakley
Glenn Miller Museum
Bodyflight
Clapham
Renhold
Green End
Courteenhall
Salcey Forest
Cold Brayfield
Stevington Windmill
Salph End
Great Barford
Blunham
Roade
Eakley Lanes
Weston Underwood
Olney
Turvey
Bromham
Bedford
Hartwell
Clifton Reynes
Newton Blossomville
Bromham Mill
Goldington
Willington
Ravenstone
Emberton
Box End
Biddenham
Bedford Museum
Priory
Ashton
Stoke Goldington
Stagsden
Great Denham
Queen's Park
Fenlake
Moggerhanger
Cople
Moggerhanger Park
Long Street
Filgrave
Tyringham
Hardmead
Astwood
Kempston
Cardington
Hatch
Thorncote Green
Grafton Regis
Hanslope
Milton Keynes
Elstow Moot Hall
Harrowden
Shortstown
Tathall End
Gayhurst
Sherington
Chicheley
Chicheley Hall
North Crawley
Keeley Green
Elstow
Northill
Ickwell Green
Yardley Gobion
Castlethorpe
Lathbury
Bourne End
Wootton
Kempston Hardwick
Cotton End
Littleworth
Bird of Prey Centre
Old Warden
Potterspury
Newport Pagnell
Newport Pagnell Services
Haversham
Upper Shelton
Wilstead
Great Linford
Broad Green
Lower Shelton
Marston Vale Millennium
Stewartby
Haynes
Southill
Cosgrove
New Bradwell
Willen
Gullivers Land
Cranfield
Marston Moretaine
Houghton Conquest
Old Stratford
Moulsoe
Stony Stratford
Wolverton
How End
Houghton House
Haynes Church End
Passenham
Bradwell
Broughton
St Lawrence's
Salford
Central
Ampthill
Clophill
Shefford
Calverton
Woolstone
Milton Keynes Village
Lidlington
Millbrook
Maulden
Beadlow
Upper Weald
National Hockey
Woughton on the Green
Brogborough
Woburn Forest Village
De Grey Mausoleum
Campton
Beachampton
Loughton
Wavendon
Aspley Guise
Denel End
Flitton
Upper Gravenhurst
Meppershall
Shenley Church End
Simpson
Walton
Woburn Sands
Ridgmont
Steppingley
Silsoe
Wrest Park House
Thornton
Shenley Brook End
Bow Brickhill
Aspley Heath
Husborne Crawley
Flitwick
Greenfield
Upper Stondon
Shillington
Whaddon
Bletchley
Woburn Safari Park
Bedfordshire
Pulloxhill
Higham Gobion
Nash
Bletchley Park
Fenny Stratford
Woburn
Eversholt
Church End
Holwell
Tattenhoe
Far Bletchley
Woburn Abbey
Westoning
Apsley End
Pirton
Singleborough
Little Brickhill
Tingrith
Barton-le-Clay
Great Horwood
Little Horwood
Newton Longville
Great Brickhill
Milton Bryan
Harlington
Knocking Hoe
Hexton
Pegsdon
Sharpenhoe
Potsgrove
Kings Wood
Stockgrove Park
Battlesden
Toddington Services
Sundon Hills
Streatley
Barton Hills
Drayton Parslow
Stoke Hammond
Mursley
Toddington
Upper Sundon
Heath and Reach
Winslow
Swanbourne
Nash End
Soulbury
Hockliffe
Tebworth
Lower Sundon
Galley Hill
Lilley
Great Offley
Stewkley
South End
Leighton Buzzard
Eggington
Wingfield
Chalton
Sundon
SP
TL
Whaddon Chase
Great Ouse
Ouzel
Tove
Ise
Til
A6003
A43
A6116
A605
A6
A14
A509
A510
A45
A4500
A5076
B576
B574
B571
B645
B663
B662
B660
B645
A428
B526
B5388
B565
A508
A422
A603
A421
A600
A507
A4146
A5
H3
H5
H6
H7
H8
H9
V2
V3
V4
V6
V7
V8
V10
B4034
A5130
A4012
A5120
B530
B579
B4033
B4032
A505
M1
54
64
65
39
40
88
130
171
187
Amptheam
m p t o n
B e d f o r d
M i l t o n K e y n e s
C e n t r a l
B e d f o r d s h i r e

Luddington in the Brook
Sawtry
Church End
Upwood Meadows
Bury
Tick Fen
Ferry Hill
Langwood Fen
Wigsthorpe
Thurning
Great Gidding
Little Gidding
Steeple Gidding
Hamerton Zoo Park
Upwood
Wood Walton
Great Raveley
Wistow
Chapel Head
Horseley Fen
Pidley Fen
Mepal
Clopton
Winwick
Monks Wood
Little Raveley
Warboys
Fenton
Chatteris Fen
Sutton
Hamerton
Upton
Wennington
Cambrid
Old Weston
Alconbury Weston
Abbots Ripton
Broughton
Pidley
Somersham
Bythorn
Brington
Molesworth
Buckworth
Alconbury
Little Stukeley
King's Ripton
Old Hurst
Woodhurst
Colne
Bluntisham
Hill Row Doles
Leighton Bromswold
Barham
Great Stukeley
Earith
Catworth
Woolley
Sapley
Huntingdon
Hartford
Wyton
Aldreth
Spaldwick
Easton
Ellington
Brampton Hut Services
Hinchingbrooke
Cromwell Mus
Houghton
Houghton Mill
Hemingford Abbots
St Ives
Needingworth
Holywell
Great Ouse
Covington
Stow Longa
Brampton
Godmanchester
Hemingford Grey
Over
Willingham
Smithey
Tilbrook
Lower Dean
Upper Dean
Kimbolton
Grafham
Grafham Water
Buckden Towers
Buckden
Wood Green Animal Shelter
Galley Hill
Fenstanton
Fen Drayton
Swavesey
The Busway Guided Bus
Rampton
Cottenham
Longstanton
West Perry
East Perry
Offord Cluny
Offord Darcy
Hilton
Huntingdon Services
Boxworth End
Cambridge Services
Swineshead
Stonely
Dillington
Staughton Green
Staughton Highway
Diddington
Papworth St Agnes
Conington
Westwick
Oakington
Pertenhall
Great Staughton
Southoe
Great Paxton
Graveley
Boxworth
Lolworth
Histon
Impington
Brook End
Little Staughton
Little Paxton
Papworth Everard
Elsworth
Bar Hill
Dry Drayton
Girton
Keysoe
Hail Weston
Toseland
Yelling
Knapwell
Keysoe Row
Duloe
St Neots
Madingley
Staploe
Croxton
Bushmead Priory
Bolnhurst
Eltisley
Cambourne
Caxton
Highfields
Hardwick
Coton
Newnham
Thurleigh
Rootham's Green
Colmworth
Eaton Socon
Eynesbury
Little Barford
Wyboston
Caldecote
Toft
Comberton
Botanic Garden
Grantchester
Duck's Cross
Chawston
Abbotsley
Great Gransden
Little Gransden
Bourn
Kingston
Barton
Colesden
Wilden
Ravensden
Waresley
Longstowe
Renhold
Roxton
Tempsford
Great Eversden
Little Eversden
Rupert Brooke Museum
Salph End
Green End
Gamlingay
Harlton
Haslingfield
Hauxton
Bedford
Great Barford
Blunham
Hatley St George
Wimpole Hall and Home Farm
Harston
Everton
Goldington
Bedford Museum
Priory
Fenlake
Willington
Girtford
Sandy
Potton
East Hatley
Arrington
Orwell
Barrington
Newton
Moggerhanger
Moggerhanger Park
Cople
Cockayne Hatley
Croydon
New Wimpole
Kempston
Elstow Moot Hall
Harrowden
Shortstown
Cardington
Hatch
Beeston
Thorncote Green
Wrestlingworth
Tadlow
Shepreth
Shepreth Wildlife Park
Foxton
Elstow
Northill
Upper Caldecote
Sutton
Eyeworth
Cam or Rhee
Wendy
Meldreth
Thriplow
Ickwell Green
Cotton End
Whaddon
Chiswick End
Fowlmere
Littleworth
Bird of Prey Centre
Shuttleworth Collection
The Swiss Garden
Old Warden
Biggleswade
Dunton
Guilden Morden
Abington Pigotts
Kneesworth
Bassingbourn
Melbourn
Wilstead
Southill
Broom
Steeple Morden
Litlington
Haynes
Royston & District Mus
Houghton Conquest
Houghton House
Haynes Church End
Stanford
Langford
Edworth
Hinxworth
Royston
Heydon
Shefford
Clifton
Beadlow
Ampthill
Maulden
Clophill
Hoo Hill Maze
Henlow
Astwick
Caldecote
Ashwell
Great Chishill
Chrishall
Barley
Little Chishill
Campton
Church End
Newnham
Therfield
De Grey Mausoleum
Upper Gravenhurst
Meppershall
Stotfold
Arlesey
Slip End
Kelshall
Baldock Services
Bygrave
Flitton
Silsoe
Flitwick
Wrest Park House
Upper Stondon
Lower Stondon
Radwell
Langley Upper Green
Barkway
Nuthampstead
Reed
Greenfield
Shillington
Norton
Sandon
Langley Lower Green
Pulloxhill
Higham Gobion
Holwell
Baldock
Wallington
Roe Green
Mill End
Buckland
Westoning
Apsley End
Letchworth
Anstey
Chipping
Meesden
Barton-le-Clay
Pirton
Ickleford
Clothall
Rushden
Wyddial
Brent Pelham
Knocking Hoe
Willian
Weston
Throcking
Hare Street
Sharpenhoe
Hexton
Pegsdon
Hitchin
Walsworth
Sundon Hills
Barton Hills
Great Wymondley
Hall's Green
Cromer Windmill
Cromer
Cottered
Buntingford
Great Hormead
Streatley
Little Wymondley
Graveley
Aspenden
Ardeley
Furneaux Pelham
Galley Hill
Sundon
Ippollytts
Walkern
Westmill
Hay Street
Gravesend
Wood End
0 1 2 3 4 5 6 miles
0 1 2 3 4 5 6 7 8 9 10 km

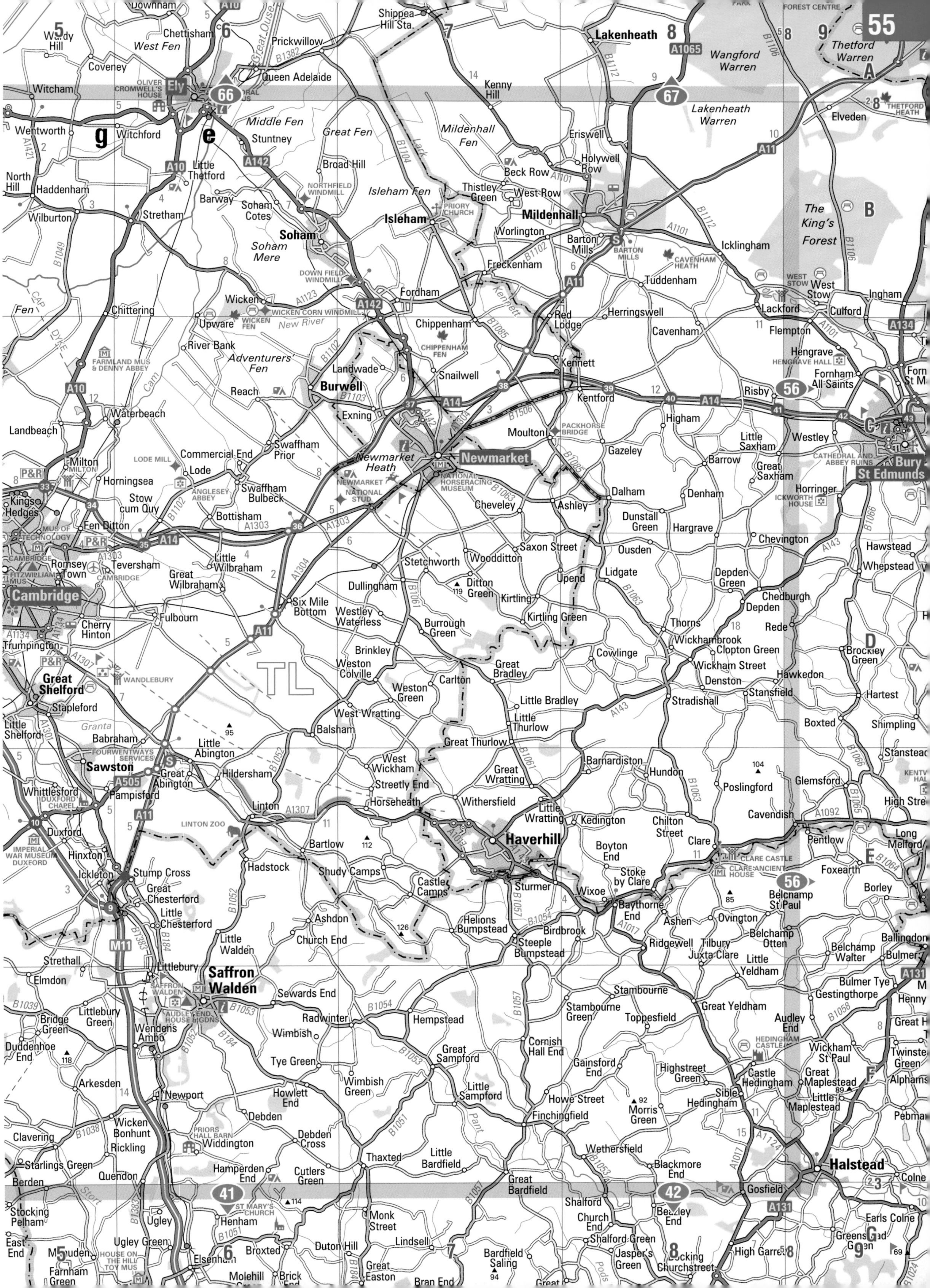
Downham
Witchy Hill
Chettisham
West Fen
Shippea Hill Sta.
Prickwillow
Lakenheath
A1065
Wangford Warren
Thetford Warren
FOREST CENTRE
Coveney
Queen Adelaide
B1382
Great Ouse
B1112
Kenny Hill
A
Witcham
OLIVER CROMWELL'S HOUSE
Ely
66
67
Lakenheath Warren
THETFORD HEATH
Elveden
Wentworth
Witchford
Middle Fen
Stuntney
Great Fen
Mildenhall Fen
Eriswell
A11
g
e
A1421
A142
A10
Little Thetford
Broad Hill
Lark
B1104
Holywell Row
Beck Row
A1101
North Hill
Haddenham
NORTHFIELD WINDMILL
Isleham Fen
Thistley Green
West Row
Wilburton
Stretham
Barway
Soham Cotes
PRIORY CHURCH
Isleham
Mildenhall
The King's Forest
B
Soham
Worlington
Barton Mills
BARTON MILLS
A1101
Icklingham
B1112
B1106
B1049
Soham Mere
B1102
Freckenham
CAVENHAM HEATH
DOWN FIELD WINDMILL
Tuddenham
WEST STOW
West Stow
Ingham
Wicken
A1123
Fordham
Kennett
CAP DYKE
Fen
Chittering
Upware
WICKEN FEN
WICKEN CORN WINDMILL
New River
A142
Chippenham
Red Lodge
Herringswell
Lackford
Culford
A134
B1085
Cavenham
Flempton
River Bank
Adventurers' Fen
FARMLAND MUS & DENNY ABBEY
CHIPPENHAM FEN
Hengrave
HENGRAVE HALL
Landwade
Kennett
Fornham All Saints
Cam
Snailwell
Burwell
B1103
Reach
38
39
Kentford
40
A14
Risby
56
A10
Waterbeach
Exning
37
A14
B1506
Higham
41
42
Landbeach
A1304
Moulton
PACKHORSE BRIDGE
Little Saxham
Westley
C
Milton
MILTON
LODE MILL
Commercial End
Lode
Swaffham Prior
Newmarket Heath
Newmarket
Gazeley
Barrow
CATHEDRAL AND ABBEY RUINS
Bury St Edmunds
P&R
33
Horningsea
ANGLESEY ABBEY
NEWMARKET
NATIONAL STUD
NATIONAL HORSERACING MUSEUM
B1085
Great Saxham
Kings Hedges
34
Stow cum Quy
Swaffham Bulbeck
B1063
Cheveley
Dalham
Denham
Ashley
Horringer
ICKWORTH HOUSE
Fen Ditton
Bottisham
Dunstall Green
Hargrave
MUS OF TECHNOLOGY
36
A1303
P&R
35
A14
Saxon Street
Ousden
Chevington
A143
Hawstead
CAMBRIDGE
Romsey Town
Teversham
CAMBRIDGE
Little Wilbraham
A1303
Stetchworth
Woodditton
Lidgate
Depden Green
Whepstead
FITZWILLIAM MUS
Great Wilbraham
A1304
Dullingham
Ditton Green
Upend
B1066
Cambridge
Six Mile Bottom
B1061
Kirtling
B1063
Chedburgh
Depden
Fulbourn
Westley Waterless
Burrough Green
Kirtling Green
Cherry Hinton
A1134
Thorns
Rede
Trumpington
A11
Wickhambrook
Clopton Green
D
Brockley Green
P&R
A1307
WANDLEBURY
Brinkley
Cowlinge
Great Bradley
Wickham Street
Hawkedon
Weston Colville
TL
Carlton
Denston
Great Shelford
Weston Green
Stansfield
Hartest
Stapleford
Little Bradley
Stradishall
West Wratting
Little Thurlow
A143
Granta
Little Shelford
A1301
Balsham
Boxted
Shimpling
Babraham
Great Thurlow
FOURWENTWAYS SERVICES
Little Abington
B1052
Sawston
West Wickham
Barnardiston
Stanstead
Great Abington
Hildersham
Great Wratting
B1061
Hundon
B1063
Poslingford
Glemsford
A505
Streetly End
Whittlesford
DUXFORD CHAPEL
Pampisford
Withersfield
Horseheath
High Street
Linton
A1307
Little Wratting
Cavendish
A1092
B1065
LINTON ZOO
Kedington
Chilton Street
Duxford
Long Melford
Haverhill
Clare
Pentlow
Boyton End
CLARE CASTLE
IMPERIAL WAR MUSEUM DUXFORD
Bartlow
A143
Hinxton
Foxearth
B1064
E
CLARE ANCIENT HOUSE
Hadstock
Stoke by Clare
Ickleton
Stump Cross
Shudy Camps
Castle Camps
Sturmer
Wixoe
56
Borley
Great Chesterford
B1052
B1057
Belchamp St Paul
Baythorne End
Ashen
A1017
Ovington
Little Chesterford
B1054
M11
Ashdon
Helions Bumpstead
Birdbrook
Belchamp Otten
Ballingdon
B1383
B184
Little Walden
Church End
Steeple Bumpstead
Ridgewell
Tilbury Juxta Clare
Belchamp Walter
Bulmer
Strethall
Little Yeldham
Littlebury
Saffron Walden
A131
Bulmer Tye
Elmdon
SAFFRON WALDEN
Sewards End
Stambourne
Gestingthorpe
B1039
Littlebury Green
AUDLEY END HOUSE & GDNS
B1053
B1054
Radwinter
Hempstead
Stambourne Green
Toppesfield
Great Yeldham
Audley End
Henny
Bridge Green
Wendens Ambo
B184
Wimbish
B1057
B1058
Great Henny
Duddenhoe End
Cornish Hall End
HEDINGHAM CASTLE
Wickham St Paul
Twinstead Green
Tye Green
Great Sampford
B1053
Gainsford End
Highstreet Green
Castle Hedingham
Great Maplestead
F
Alphamstone
Arkesden
Wimbish Green
Sible Hedingham
Little Maplestead
Newport
Howlett End
Little Sampford
Howe Street
Morris Green
Pebmarsh
Pant
Wicken Bonhunt
Debden
Finchingfield
Clavering
B1038
PRIORS HALL BARN
Rickling
Widdington
Debden Cross
B1051
Little Bardfield
Wethersfield
A1124
A1017
Starlings Green
Thaxted
Blackmore End
Halstead
Berden
Quendon
Hamperden End
Cutlers Green
B1053
Colne
Stort
Great Bardfield
Gosfield
41
ST MARY'S CHURCH
42
A131
B1383
Shalford
Stocking Pelham
Ugley
Henham
Monk Street
B1057
Church End
Beazley End
Earls Colne
B1051
Greenstead Green
Ugley Green
Lindsell
Shalford Green
East End
Manuden
HOUSE ON THE HILL TOY MUS
Elsenham
Broxted
Duton Hill
Bardfield Saling
Jasper's Green
Bocking Churchstreet
High Garrett
Farnham Green
Molehill
Brick End
Great Easton
Bran End
Pods
G
B184

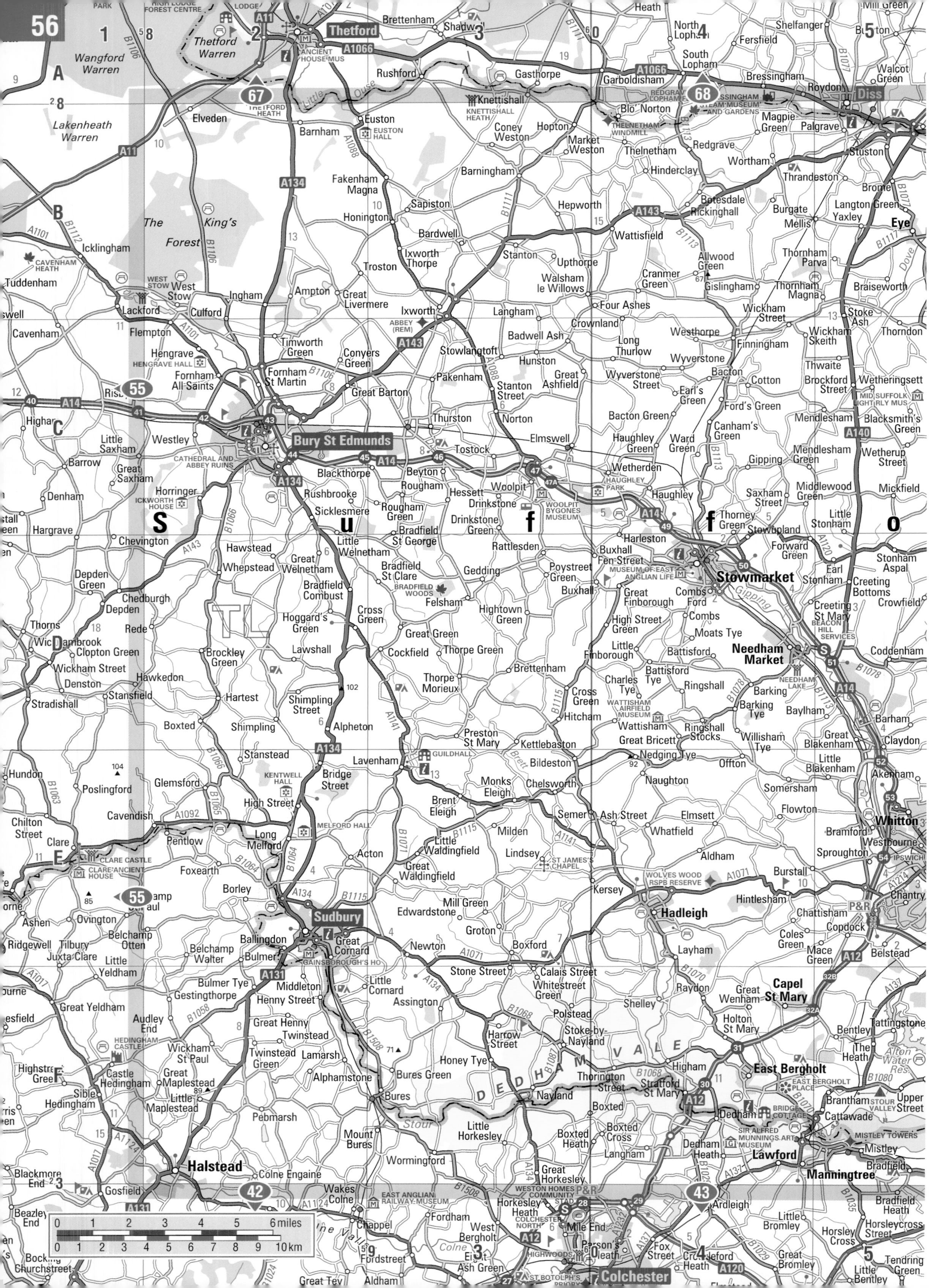
Thetford
Thetford Warren
Wangford Warren
Lakenheath Warren
The King's Forest
Brettenham
Shadwell
Rushford
Gasthorpe
Garboldisham
North Lopham
South Lopham
Fersfield
Shelfanger
Bressingham
Roydon
Diss
Elveden
Euston
Barnham
Knettishall
Coney Weston
Hopton
Market Weston
Blo' Norton
Thelnetham
Redgrave
Wortham
Palgrave
Stuston
Fakenham Magna
Barningham
Hinderclay
Botesdale
Rickinghall
Thrandeston
Brome
Sapiston
Honington
Hepworth
Wattisfield
Burgate
Mellis
Yaxley
Langton Green
Eye
Icklingham
Bardwell
Ixworth Thorpe
Stanton
Upthorpe
Allwood Green
Thornham Parva
Cavenham Heath
Tuddenham
Troston
Walsham le Willows
Cranmer Green
Gislingham
Thornham Magna
Braiseworth
West Stow
Lackford
Culford
Ingham
Ampton
Great Livermere
Ixworth
Langham
Four Ashes
Crownland
Wickham Street
Stoke Ash
Cavenham
Flempton
Timworth Green
Badwell Ash
Long Thurlow
Westhorpe
Finningham
Wickham Skeith
Thorndon
Hengrave
Conyers Green
Stowlangtoft
Hunston
Wyverstone
Fornham All Saints
Fornham St Martin
Pakenham
Great Ashfield
Stanton Street
Wyverstone Street
Bacton
Cotton
Thwaite
Brockford Street
Wetheringsett
Risby
Great Barton
Earl's Green
Ford's Green
Higham
Thurston
Norton
Bacton Green
Mendlesham
Blacksmith's Green
Little Saxham
Westley
Bury St Edmunds
Elmswell
Haughley Green
Ward Green
Canham's Green
Barrow
Great Saxham
Tostock
Beyton
Blackthorpe
Rougham
Hessett
Woolpit
Drinkstone
Wetherden
Haughley
Gipping
Mendlesham Green
Wetherup Street
Horringer
Ickworth House
Denham
Rushbrooke
Sicklesmere
Rougham Green
Drinkstone Green
Saxham Street
Middlewood Green
Mickfield
Hargrave
Chevington
Little Welnetham
Bradfield St George
Rattlesden
Harleston
Thorney Green
Stowupland
Little Stonham
Suffolk
Hawstead
Whepstead
Great Welnetham
Bradfield St Clare
Gedding
Buxhall
Fen Street
Poystreet Green
Forward Green
Stowmarket
Earl Stonham
Creeting Bottoms
Stonham Aspal
Depden Green
Bradfield Combust
Bradfield Woods
Felsham
Great Finborough
Combs Ford
Combs
Creeting St Mary
Crowfield
Chedburgh
Depden
Hoggard's Green
Cross Green
Hightown Green
High Street Green
Moats Tye
Rede
Thorns
Wickhambrook
Clopton Green
Brockley Green
Lawshall
Great Green
Cockfield
Thorpe Green
Little Finborough
Battisford
Needham Market
Coddenham
Wickham Street
Hawkedon
Stansfield
Stradishall
Denston
Hartest
Shimpling Street
Thorpe Morieux
Brettenham
Charles Tye
Battisford Tye
Ringshall
Barking
Barking Tye
Baylham
Cross Green
Hitcham
Wattisham
Ringshall Stocks
Willisham Tye
Barham
Boxted
Shimpling
Alpheton
Preston St Mary
Kettlebaston
Great Bricett
Nedging Tye
Offton
Great Blakenham
Claydon
Stanstead
Lavenham
Bildeston
Little Blakenham
Akenham
Hundon
Poslingford
Glemsford
Kentwell Hall
Bridge Street
Monks Eleigh
Chelsworth
Naughton
Somersham
Brent Eleigh
Cavendish
High Street
Semer
Ash Street
Elmsett
Flowton
Chilton Street
Clare
Pentlow
Long Melford
Melford Hall
Milden
Whatfield
Bramford
Whitton
Westbourne
Ipswich
Little Waldingfield
Lindsey
Aldham
Sproughton
Clare Castle
Foxearth
Acton
Great Waldingfield
St James's Chapel
Wolves Wood RSPB Reserve
Burstall
Borley
Kersey
Chantry
Ashen
Ovington
Sudbury
Mill Green
Edwardstone
Hadleigh
Hintlesham
Chattisham
Copdock
Ridgewell
Tilbury Juxta Clare
Belchamp Otten
Ballingdon
Great Cornard
Groton
Boxford
Coles Green
Belstead
Belchamp Walter
Bulmer
Gainsborough's House
Newton
Layham
Mace Green
Little Yeldham
Bulmer Tye
Middleton
Little Cornard
Stone Street
Calais Street
Whitestreet Green
Raydon
Great Wenham
Capel St Mary
Gestingthorpe
Henny Street
Assington
Shelley
Great Yeldham
Audley End
Great Henny
Twinstead
Polstead
Holton St Mary
Tattingstone
Hedingham Castle
Wickham St Paul
Twinstead Green
Lamarsh
Harrow Street
Stoke-by-Nayland
Bentley
Castle Hedingham
Great Maplestead
Alphamstone
Bures Green
Honey Tye
Thorington Street
Higham
East Bergholt
Sible Hedingham
Little Maplestead
Bures
Nayland
Stratford St Mary
Dedham Vale
Brantham
Cattawade
Pebmarsh
Little Horkesley
Boxted
Boxted Cross
Dedham
Bridge Cottage
Sir Alfred Munnings Art Museum
Mistley Towers
Mistley
Mount Bures
Boxted Heath
Dedham Heath
Langham
Lawford
Manningtree
Halstead
Colne Engaine
Wormingford
Great Horkesley
Bradfield
Blackmore End
Gosfield
Wakes Colne
East Anglian Railway Museum
Horkesley Heath
Ardleigh
Bradfield Heath
Beazley End
Chappel
Fordham
West Bergholt
Mile End
Little Bromley
Horsley Cross
Horsleycross Street
Bocking Churchstreet
Fordstreet
Eight Ash Green
Fox Street
Crockleford Heath
Great Bromley
Tendring Green
Little Bentley
Great Tey
Aldham
Colchester
0 1 2 3 4 5 6 miles
0 1 2 3 4 5 6 7 8 9 10 km

Garlic Street
Harleston
Redenhall
Wortwell
St Cross South Elmham
St Michael South Elmham
Ilketshall St Lawrence
Redisham
Sotterley
Benacre
Rushall
Shimpling
Mendham
St Margaret South Elmham
All Saints South Elmham
Stone Street
Shadingfield
West End
Wrentham
Benacre
Covehithe
Dickleburgh
Needham
100TH BOMB GROUP MEMORIAL MUS
SOUTH ELMHAM HALL
Cox Common
Brampton
Stoven
Clay Common
Frostenden
Thelveton
Withersdale Street
St James South Elmham
Rumburgh
Mill Common
South Cove
Thorpe Abbotts
Metfield
Spexhall
Westhall
Cove Bottom
Scole
Brockdish
Wissett
Broadway
Wangford
BILLINGFORD WINDMILL
Linstead Parva
Chediston
Reydon Smear
Oakley
Hoxne
Syleham
Fressingfield
WINGFIELD OLD COLLEGE
Little Whittingham Green
Halesworth
Holton
Blyford
Reydon
Brome Street
Cross Street
Wingfield
HEN REEDBED NATURE RESERVE
SOUTHWOLD MUSEUM
Southwold
Heckfield Green
Battlesea Green
Chippenhall Green
Silverley's Green
Cratfield
Cookley
Wenhaston
Blackheath
Blyth
Blythburgh
Denham
Swan Green
Pixey Green
Huntingfield
Thorington
Stradbroke
Walpole
Walberswick
Ashfield Green
Banyard's Green
Bramfield
Cranley
Wootten Green
SUFFOLK COAST
Denham Street
Horham
Wilby
Russel's Green
Laxfield
Heveningham
Sibton Green
Dunwich
Redlingfield
Athelington
Foals Green
Ubbeston Green
High Street
Forest
DUNWICH UNDERWATER EXPLORATION EXHIBITION
Brundish Street
Crown Corner
Darsham
Occold
Fingal Street
Stanway Green
Brundish
Owl's Green
Hemp Green
Sibton
Peasenhall
Yoxford
Southolt
WESTLETON HEATH
Westleton
Rishangles
Bedingfield
Worlingworth
Tannington
Badingham
Alde
Middleton Moor
MINSMERE RSPB NATURE RESERVE
Rotten End
Bedfield
Maypole Green
Dennington
North Green
Middleton
Kenton
Bruisyard
Theberton
Saxtead
Brabling Green
Curlew Green
Kelsale
Eastbridge
Monk Soham
SAXTEAD GREEN POST MILL
Cransford
Rendham
LEISTON ABBEY
Saxtead Green
Carlton
Debenham
Framlingham
Sweffling
Saxmundham
Leiston
Sizewell
Ashfield
Earl Soham
Great Glemham
Knodishall
Cole's Green
Benhall Street
Sternfield
Winston
Deben
Lampardbrook
Aldringham
Winston Green
Brandeston
Stratford St Andrew
Benhall Green
Coldfair Green
Peats Corner
Parham
Friston
Cretingham
Kettleburgh
Thorpeness
Framsden
Hacheston
Farnham
Pettaugh
Gromford
Easton
Marlesford
HELMINGHAM HALL GARDENS
Monewden
EASTON FARM PARK
Little Glemham
Snape
SNAPE MALTINGS
NORTH WARREN RSPB NATURE RESERVE
Helmingham
Letheringham
BLAXHALL
Aldeburgh
Charsfield
Lower Hacheston
Blaxhall
Iken
Gosbeck
Otley
Wickham Market
Campsey Ash
High Street
Aldeburgh Bay
Ashbocking
Clopton Corner
Dallinghoo
Debach
Pettistree
Tunstall
Rendlesham
Tunstall Forest
Hemingstone
Swilland
Bredfield
Sudbourne
Clopton
Ufford
Chillesford
Alde
Witnesham
Eyke
Butley
Henley
Grundisburgh
Burgh
Hasketon
Melton
Bromeswell
ORFORD CASTLE
Orford
Culpho
Great Bealings
Boot Street
Woodbridge
SUTTON HOO
Rendlesham Forest
Orford Ness
Tuddenham St Martin
Playford
Maidensgrave
Butley High Corner
ORFORDNESS-HAVERGATE
Westerfield
Rushmere St Andrew
Little Bealings
Capel St Andrew
Boyton
Martlesham
CHRISTCHURCH MANSION
Martlesham Heath
Waldringfield Heath
Sutton
Stores Corner
Duck Corner
Ipswich
Kesgrave
Waldringfield
Shottisham
Hollesley Bay
Rose Hill
MARTLESHAM HEATH CONTROL TOWER
Hollesley
Stoke
Brightwell
Maidenhall
Warren Heath
Newbourne
Shingle Street
Gainsborough
Bucklesham
Hemley
Alderton
Bawdsey
Wherstead
ORWELL
Nacton
Kirton
Deben
Freston
Woolverstone
Levington
Falkenham
Pin Mill
Orwell
Thorpe Common
Trimley St Martin
Chelmondiston
Trimley Lower Street
Felixstowe Ferry
Holbrook
Trimley St Mary
Old Felixstowe
Walton
Lower Holbrook
Stutton
Erwarton
Shotley
TRIMLEY MARSHES NATURE RESERVE
Harkstead
Shotley Gate
FELIXSTOWE
Holbrook Bay
Shop Corner
Stour
HARWICH
CHARLES MANNING'S AMUSEMENT PARK
HARWICH REDOUBT FORT
Parkeston
Wrabness
Dovercourt
Ramsey
Upper Dovercourt
Little Oakley
HOEK VAN HOLLAND
Wix
Great Oakley
Stone's Green
TM
A140 A143 A144 A145 A12 A1094 A1120 A1152 A1214 A14 A1156 A120 A154
B1116 B1123 B1124 B1126 B1127 B1095 B1387 B1125 B1118 B1117 B1122 B1121 B1119 B1120 B1069 B1353 B1077 B1078 B1079 B1438 B1084 B1083 B1080 B1456 B1352 B1414 B1122 B1125
68 69 43 56 57 58 59 60 61 62
A B C D E F G
5 6 7 8 9

TREMADOG BAY
BAE TREMADOG
Morfa Harlech
Harlech
Eisingrug
Glyn-cywarch
623 MOEL YSGYFARNOGOD
A470
Bronaber
Mynydd Bach
MOEL LLYFRANT
Mynydd Bryn-llech
Buarthmeini
Gwynedd
SNOWDONIA NATIONAL PARK
Llanfair
LLANFAIR SLATE CAVERNS
Llandanwg
Pen-sarn
Pen-y-bont
Pentre Gwynfryn
720 RHINOG FAWR
RHINOG
SARN HELEN
Bed-y-coedwr
RHAEADR MAWDDACH
Pont Aber-Geirw
Cwm-hesgen
COED Y BRENIN VISITOR CENTRE
Coed y Brenin Forest
Capel Hermon
734 RHOBELL FAWR
Pont Fronwydd
Afon Wnion
Llanbedr
Morfa Dyffryn
MORFA DYFFRYN
WALES COAST PATH
754 Y LLETHR
Coed Ystumgwern
Llanenddwyn
Dyffryn Ardudwy
DIFFWYS 750
Ganllwyd
COED GANLLWYD
ALLT Y BENGLOG
A494
Cors-y-Gedol
Llanddwywe
Llanfachreth
Rhydymain
Tal-y-bont
SH
Blaen-y-cwm
71
Llanelltyd
CYMER ABBEY
Pen-y-bryn
Plas-canol
Bontddu
PENMAENPOOL CENTRE
Bont Newydd
B4416
Brithdir
Caerdeon
TOLL
Penmaenpool
A470
Llanaber
Cutiau
Abergwynant
Dolgellau
Y Gribin
A496
Afon Mawddach
Rhydwen
KINGS
Afon Cerist
A470
Barmouth (Abermaw)
RNLI LIFEBOAT MUSEUM
BARMOUTH BAY
The Bar
Arthog
A493
Ynysgyfflog
PARC CENEDLAETHOL ERYRI
670 WAUN-OER
Mynydd Ceiswyn
Mynydd Dolgoed
MEIRION MILL
FAIRBOURNE STEAM RAILWAY
Fairbourne
BAE BERMO
893 CADAIR IDRIS
Friog
CADER IDRIS
Minffordd
Dyfi Forest
Llwyngwril
Tal-y-llyn
A487
Corris Uchaf
Aberllefenni
Aberangell
Afon Dysynni
Llanfihangel-y-pennant
CASTELL Y BERE
KING ARTHUR'S LABYRINTH & CRAFT CENTRE
A470
Corris
Cwm-Llinau
CORRIS RAILWAY AND MUSEUM
Llangelynin
A493
B4405
Abergynolwyn
Dol-fôr
Esgairgeiliog
Cemmaes
Rhoslefain
Llanegryn
Llanfendigaid
Peniarth
Plas Llwyngwern
Pantperthog
CENTRE FOR ALTERNATIVE TECHNOLOGY
B4404
Llanwrin
309
Tonfanau
633 TARRENHENDRE
Cemmaes Road
Bryncrug
Pandy
VALLEY DYFI
Pen-y-bont
A489
Abercegir
Commins Coch
SENEDD-DY-OWAIN GLYNDWR
Rhyd-yr-onen
TALYLLYN RAILWAY
Machynlleth
Darowen
Tywyn
Pennal
A493
Penegoes
FELIN CREWI WATER MILL
Tal-y-wern
Cwrt
DOVEY DYFI
Forge
Caethle
Melinbyrhedyn
Derwenlas
Glaspwll
Pant-glâs
468 MOELFRE
279
Aberhosan
Aberdovey
A493
Glandyfi
Dovey Dyfi
YNYS HIR RESERVE
Eglwys Fach
DYFI FURNACE
Aberdovey Bar
Bae Aberdyfi
A487
Glaslyn
DYFI
Fochno
B4353
Ynyslas
582
Llancynfelyn
Tre'r-ddôl
BORTH
Tre-Taliesin
521 MOEL-Y-LLYN
SN
Borth
Source of R. Severn Blaen Hafren
Upper Borth
Tal-y-bont
Dôl-y-Bont
Nant-y-Moch Reservoir
741
PLYNLIMON PUMLUMON FAWR
752
Source of R. Wye Blaen Gwy
Llandre
Pen-y-garn
Bont-goch
ARTS CENTRE
B4572
Bow Street
Salem
506
NATIONAL LIBRARY
Clarach
Penrhyn-coch
Pen-bont Rhydybeddau
CLIFF RAILWAY
148
Plas Gogerddan
A4159
Aberystwyth
Comins Coch
Capel Dewi
SILVER MOUNTAIN EXPERIENCE
Dyffryn Castell
P&R
Llanbadarn Fawr
Capel Bangor
Dollwen
Goginan
Trefechan
A44
Ponterwyd
CASTLE
564
Penparcau
Southgate
Glanrafon
Cwmbrwyno
Afon Rheidol
46
VALE OF RHEIDOL RAILWAY
RHEIDOL HYDRO ELECTRIC STATION
47
Rhydyfelin
Moriah
Capel Seion
Ystumtuen
A487
Aberffrwd
Ysbytycynfyn
COED RHEIDOL
Llanfarian
Gors
Pisgah
0 1 2 3 4 5 6 miles
0 1 2 3 4 5 6 7 8 9 10 km
New Cross
A4120
Llanfihangel-y-Creuddyn
Mynydd Bach
Devil's Bridge
610 PEN Y GARN
A485
Blaenplwyf
Trisant
Blaenycwm

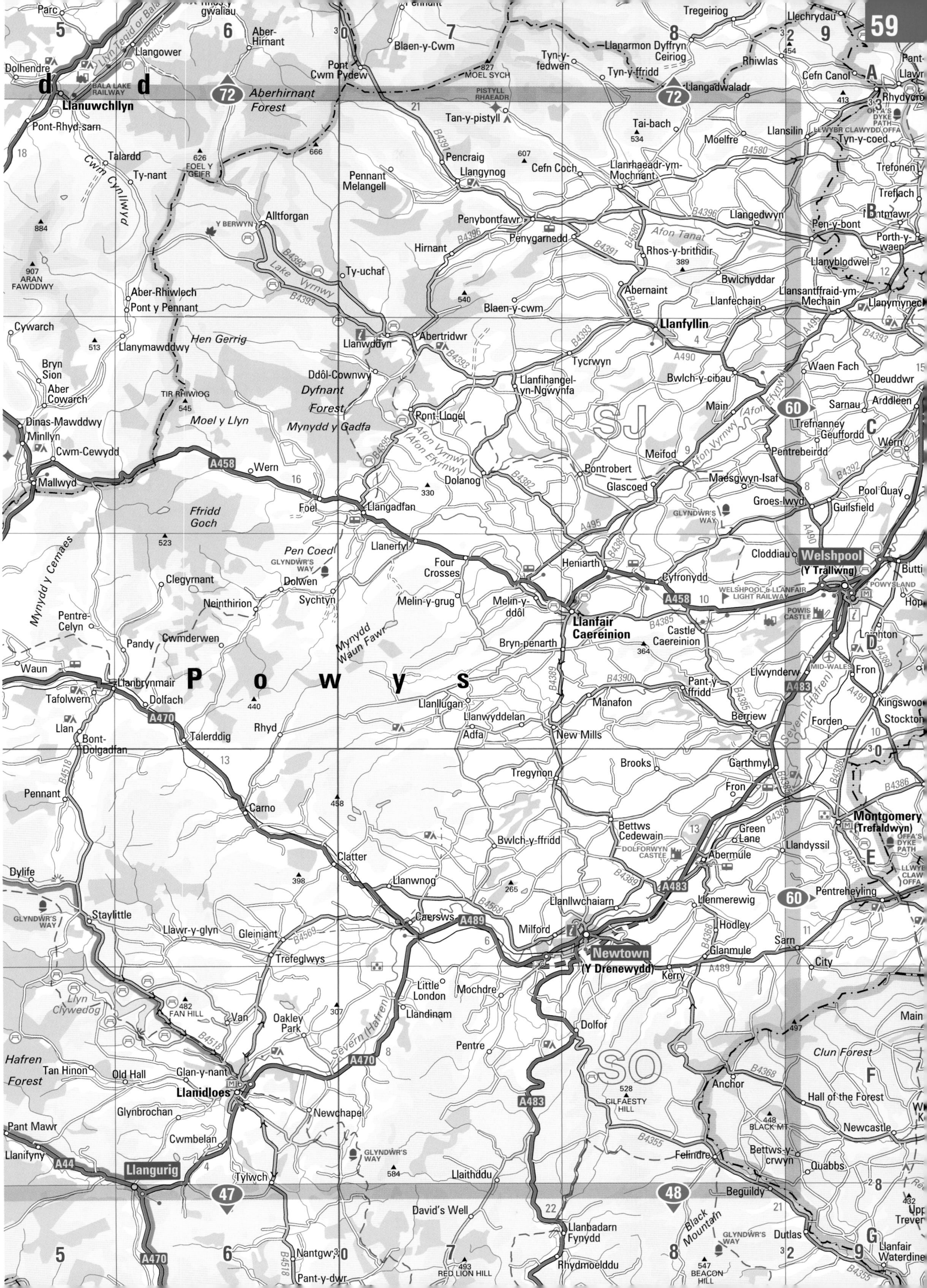
Parc
Llangower
Dolhendre
Lyn Tegid or Bala
Aber-Hirnant
Blaen-y-Cwm
Pont Cwm Pydew
827 MOEL SYCH
Tyn-y-fedwen
Llanarmon Dyffryn Ceiriog
Tregeiriog
Tyn-y-ffridd
Llechrydau
Rhiwlas
Cefn Canol
Llanuwchllyn
BALA LAKE RAILWAY
Aberhirnant Forest
72
PISTYLL RHAEADR
Tan-y-pistyll
Llangadwaladr
Rhydycroesau
Pont-Rhyd-sarn
Tai-bach
534
Llansilin
Moelfre
Tyn-y-coed
Talardd
626 FOEL Y GEIFR
666
Ty-nant
Cwm Cynllwyd
Pencraig
607
Cefn Coch
Llangynog
Pennant Melangell
Llanrhaeadr-ym-Mochnant
Trefonen
Treflach
884
Y BERWYN
Alltforgan
Penybontfawr
Penygarnedd
Llangedwyn
Pen-y-bont
Porth-y-waen
Afon Tanat
Hirnant
Rhos-y-brithdir
389
Llanyblodwel
907 ARAN FAWDDWY
Ty-uchaf
Lake Vyrnwy
Bwlchyddar
Abernaint
Llansantffraid-ym-Mechain
Aber-Rhiwlech
Pont y Pennant
540
Blaen-y-cwm
Llanfechain
Llanymynech
Cywarch
513
Llanymawddwy
Hen Gerrig
Llanwddyn
Abertridwr
Llanfyllin
Tycrwyn
Bryn Sion
Aber Cowarch
TIR RHIWIOG
545
Ddôl-Cownwy
Dyfnant Forest
Llanfihangel-yn-Ngwynfa
Bwlch-y-cibau
Waen Fach
Deuddwr
Dinas-Mawddwy
Minllyn
Moel y Llyn
Mynydd y Gadfa
Pont Llogel
SJ
Main
60
Sarnau
Arddleen
Trefnanney
Geufford
Cwm-Cewydd
A458
Wern
Afon Vyrnwy (Afon Efyrnwy)
Meifod
Pentrebeirdd
Mallwyd
16
330
Dolanog
Pontrobert
Glascoed
Maesgwyn-Isaf
Pool Quay
Foel
Llangadfan
GLYNDŴR'S WAY
Groes-lwyd
Guilsfield
Ffridd Goch
523
Llanerfyl
Heniarth
Cloddiau
Welshpool (Y Trallwng)
Pen Coed
Four Crosses
Mynydd y Cemaes
Clegyrnant
Dolwen
Cyfronydd
WELSHPOOL & LLANFAIR LIGHT RAILWAY
POWYSLAND
Sychtyn
Melin-y-grug
Melin-y-ddôl
Neinthirion
Llanfair Caereinion
POWIS CASTLE
Pentre-Celyn
Cwmderwen
Mynydd Waun Fawr
Castle Caereinion
Pandy
Bryn-penarth
364
Leighton
Waun
Llanbrynmair
Powys
MID-WALES
Fron
Llwynderw
Tafolwern
Dolfach
440
Llanllugan
Manafon
Pant-y-ffridd
A483
Kingswood
Llan
A470
Rhyd
Llanwyddelan
Adfa
Berriew
Forden
Stockton
Bont-Dolgadfan
Talerddig
New Mills
13
Brooks
Garthmyl
Pennant
Tregynon
Fron
458
Carno
Montgomery (Trefaldwyn)
Bettws Cedewain
Green Lane
DOLFORWYN CASTLE
Bwlch-y-ffridd
Llandyssil
OFFA'S DYKE PATH
Clatter
Abermule
Dylife
398
Llanwnog
265
Llenmerewig
Pentreheyling
Llanllwchaiarn
Staylittle
Caersws
Hodley
Llawr-y-glyn
Gleiniant
Milford
Sarn
Newtown (Y Drenewydd)
Glanmule
City
Trefeglwys
Kerry
Llyn Clywedog
Little London
Mochdre
482 FAN HILL
Llandinam
Van
Oakley Park
307
Dolfor
497
Main
Severn (Hafren)
Pentre
Hafren Forest
Tan Hinon
Old Hall
Glan-y-nant
SO
Clun Forest
Llanidloes
528 CILFAESTY HILL
Anchor
Glynbrochan
Newchapel
Hall of the Forest
448 BLACK MT
Pant Mawr
Cwmbelan
Newcastle
Llanifyny
GLYNDŴR'S WAY
Felindre
Bettws-y-crwyn
A44
Llangurig
Tylwch
584
Llaithddu
Quabbs
47
48
Beguildy
David's Well
Llanbadarn Fynydd
Black Mountain
Dutlas
Upper Treverward
Nantgwyn
493 RED LION HILL
547 BEACON HILL
Rhydmoelddu
Llanfair Waterdine
Pant-y-dwr

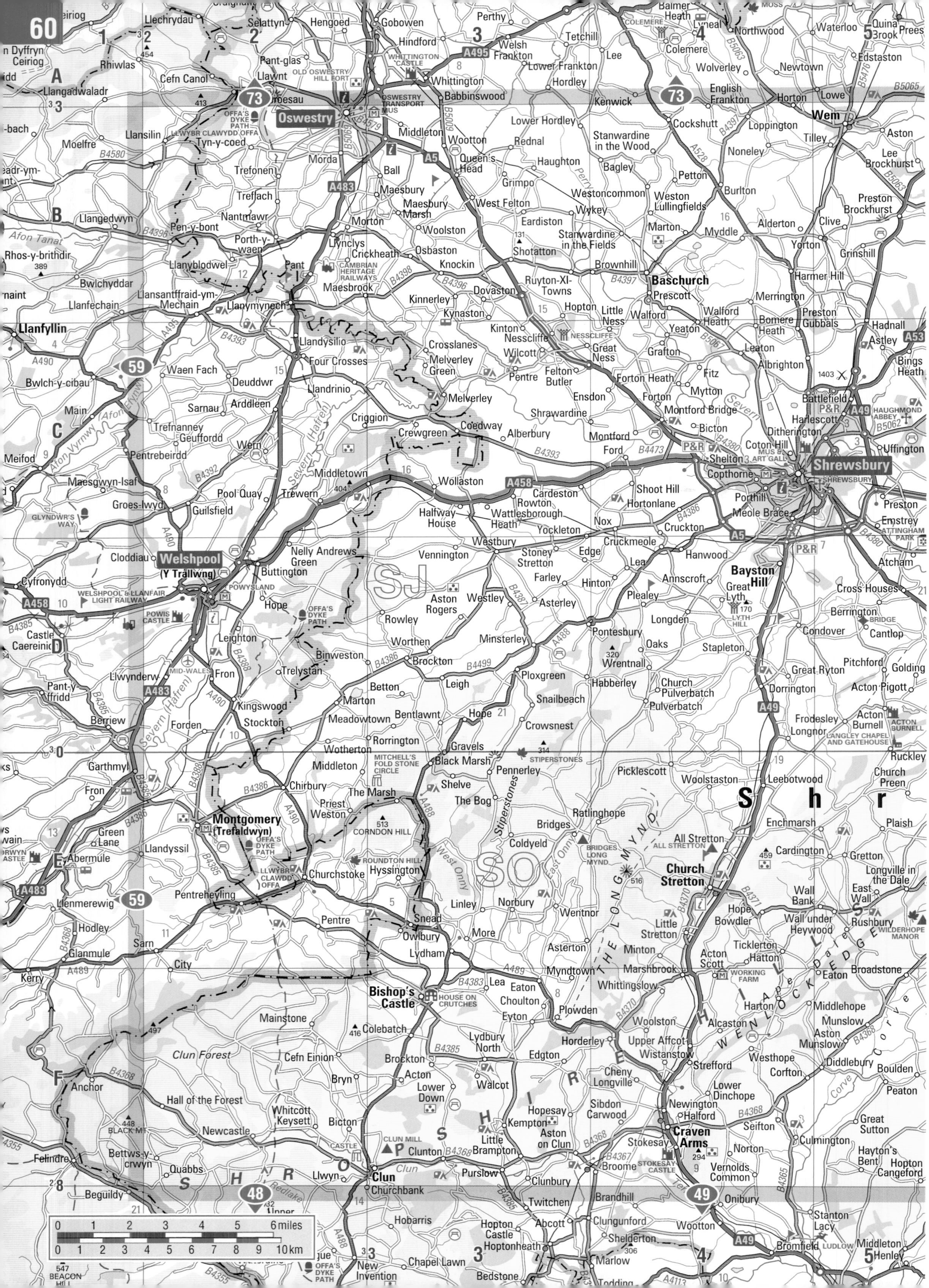
Dyffryn Ceiriog
Llechrydau
Selattyn
Hengoed
Gobowen
Perthy
Hindford
Welsh Frankton
Lower Frankton
Tetchill
Lee
Balmer Heath
Lyneal
Colemere
Northwood
Waterloo
Quina Brook
Prees
Rhiwlas
Pant-glas
Llawnt
Cefn Canol
Llangadwaladr
Gobowen
Whittington Castle
Whittington
Babbinswood
Hordley
Kenwick
Wolverley
Newtown
Edstaston
English Frankton
Horton
Lowe
Wem
Oswestry
Oswestry Transport Mus
Offa's Dyke Path
Llwybr Clawdd Offa
Llansilin
Tyn-y-coed
Moelfre
Middleton
Wootton
Lower Hordley
Rednal
Cockshutt
Loppington
Tilley
Aston
Stanwardine in the Wood
Noneley
Lee Brockhurst
Morda
Queen's Head
Haughton
Bagley
Petton
Trefonen
Ball
Grimpo
Burlton
Treflach
Maesbury
Westoncommon
Weston Lullingfields
Preston Brockhurst
Nantmawr
Maesbury Marsh
West Felton
Wykey
Llangedwyn
Pen-y-bont
Morton
Eardiston
Marton
Myddle
Alderton
Clive
Afon Tanat
Porth-y-waen
Llynclys
Woolston
Stanwardine in the Fields
Yorton
Rhos-y-brithdir
Crickheath
Osbaston
Shotatton
Grinshill
Llanyblodwel
Pant
Cambrian Heritage Railways
Knockin
Brownhill
Harmer Hill
Bwlchyddar
Maesbrook
Ruyton-XI-Towns
Baschurch
Llansantffraid-ym-Mechain
Dovaston
Prescott
Merrington
Llanfechain
Kinnerley
Hopton
Little Ness
Walford
Walford Heath
Preston Gubbals
Llanymynech
Kynaston
Llanfyllin
Kinton
Nesscliffe
Yeaton
Bomere Heath
Hadnall
Llandysilio
Crosslanes
Great Ness
Grafton
Leaton
Astley
Four Crosses
Melverley Green
Wilcott
Albrighton
Bings Heath
Bwlch-y-cibau
Waen Fach
Deuddwr
Pentre
Felton Butler
Fitz
Forton Heath
Llandrinio
Mytton
Sarnau
Arddleen
Melverley
Ensdon
Forton
Battlefield
Main
Afon Efyrnwy
Montford Bridge
Haughmond Abbey
Shrawardine
Harlescott
Trefnanney
Geuffordd
Criggion
Bicton
Ditherington
Crewgreen
Coedway
Alberbury
Montford
Uffington
Meifod
Afon Vyrnwy
Pentrebeirdd
Wern
Severn (Hafren)
Ford
Coton Hill
Shelton
Mus & Art Gall
Shrewsbury
Middletown
Wollaston
Copthorne
Maesgwyn-Isaf
Pool Quay
Trewern
Cardeston
Shoot Hill
Groes-lwyd
Guilsfield
Glyndŵr's Way
Rowton
Hortonlane
Porthill
Preston
Halfway House
Wattlesborough Heath
Meole Brace
Emstrey
Yockleton
Nox
Cruckton
Attingham Park
Cloddiau
Welshpool (Y Trallwng)
Nelly Andrews Green
Vennington
Westbury
Stoney Stretton
Edge
Cruckmeole
Hanwood
Bayston Hill
Atcham
Buttington
Farley
Hinton
Annscroft
Great Lyth
Cyfronydd
Powysland
Aston Rogers
Westley
Asterley
Plealey
Cross Houses
Welshpool & Llanfair Light Railway
Hope
Offa's Dyke Path
Rowley
Lyth Hill
Berrington
Powis Castle
Pontesbury
Longden
Condover
Bridge
Cantlop
Castle Caereinion
Leighton
Worthen
Minsterley
Oaks
Stapleton
Wrentnall
Binweston
Brockton
Pitchford
Golding
Mid-Wales
Fron
Trelystan
Ploxgreen
Habberley
Church Pulverbatch
Great Ryton
Llwynderw
Leigh
Acton Pigott
Pant-y-ffridd
Betton
Pulverbatch
Dorrington
Kingswood
Marton
Snailbeach
Frodesley
Acton Burnell
Berriew
Bentlawnt
Hope
Longnor
Forden
Stockton
Meadowtown
Crowsnest
Langley Chapel and Gatehouse
Rorrington
Gravels
Wotherton
Stiperstones
Ruckley
Garthmyl
Middleton
Mitchell's Fold Stone Circle
Black Marsh
Pennerley
Picklescott
Woolstaston
Leebotwood
Church Preen
Fron
Chirbury
Shelve
The Bog
Priest Weston
The Marsh
Montgomery (Trefaldwyn)
Ratlinghope
Stiperstones
Enchmarsh
Plaish
Green Lane
Llandyssil
Corndon Hill
Bridges
All Stretton
Abermule
Offa's Dyke Path
Coldyeld
Bridges Long Mynd
Cardington
Gretton
Roundton Hill
West Onny
East Onny
Church Stretton
Longville in the Dale
Llwybr Clawdd Offa
Churchstoke
Hyssington
The Long Mynd
Wall Bank
East Wall
Llanmerewig
Pentreheyling
Linley
Norbury
Wentnor
Hope Bowdler
Wall under Heywood
Rushbury
Hodley
Pentre
Snead
More
Little Stretton
Wilderhope Manor
Sarn
Owlbury
Asterton
Ticklerton
Glanmule
Lydham
Minton
Acton Scott
Hatton
Kerry
City
Myndtown
Marshbrook
Working Farm
Eaton
Broadstone
Bishop's Castle
House on Crutches
Lea
Eaton
Choulton
Whittingslow
Wenlock Edge
Ape Dale
Harton
Middlehope
Mainstone
Colebatch
Eyton
Plowden
Woolston
Alcaston
Munslow
Lydbury North
Horderley
Upper Affcot
Aston Munslow
Clun Forest
Cefn Einion
Brockton
Edgton
Wistanstow
Westhope
Diddlebury
Corve
Boulden
Anchor
Bryn
Acton
Walcot
Cheny Longville
Strefford
Corfton
Peaton
Lower Down
Lower Dinchope
Hall of the Forest
Whitcott Keysett
Sibdon Carwood
Newington
Halford
Black Mt
Hopesay
Kempton
Bicton
Aston on Clun
Seifton
Great Sutton
Newcastle
Clun Mill
Little Brampton
Craven Arms
Culmington
Felindre
Bettws-y-crwyn
Castle
Clunton
Stokesay
Norton
Hayton's Bent
Hopton Cangeford
Quabbs
Clun
Purslow
Broome
Stokesay Castle
Vernolds Common
Llwyn
Clunbury
Churchbank
Beguildy
Redlake
Twitchen
Brandhill
Onibury
Hobarris
Abcott
Clungunford
Wootton
Stanton Lacy
Hopton Castle
Shelderton
Hoptonheath
Bromfield
Ludlow
Middleton
Henley
Chapel Lawn
Marlow
New Invention
Bedstone
Beacon Hill
Shropshire
0 1 2 3 4 5 6 miles
0 1 2 3 4 5 6 7 8 9 10 km

Sandford
Longford
Market Drayton
Hales
Chatcull
Cotes
Stone
Prees Lower Heath
Darliston
Bletchley
Fauls
Ternhill
Fairoak
Wetwood
Croxtonbank
Croxton
Millmeece
Slindon
Yarnfield
Walton
Little Stoke
Milwich
Prees Green
Lostford
Sutton
The Four Alls
Woodseaves
Chipnall
Cheswardine
Bishop's Offley
Sugnall
Sturbridge
Norton Bridge
Aston-By-Stone
Burston
Sandon
Hawkstone Park
Wollerton
Wollerton Old Hall
Stoke Heath
Goldstone
Pershall
Eccleshall
Chebsey
Izaak Walton Cottage Museum
Whitgreave
Yarlet
Weston
Wixhill
Marchamley
Hodnet
Hodnet Hall
Wistanswick
Mill Green
Lockleywood
Goldstone Hall
Soudley
Adbaston
Great Bridgeford
Wootton
Ellenhall
Marston
Salt
Moston
Hopton
Stoke on Tern
Hinstock
Knighton
High Offley
Stafford Services
Stanton upon Hine Heath
High Hatton
Radmoor
Ollerton
Child's Ercall
Ellerton
Shebdon
Woodseaves
Weston Jones
Sambrook
Norbury
Lawnhead
Knightley Dale
Ranton
Seighford
Coton Clanford
Holmcroft
Stafford
Doxey
Derrington
Forebridge
Ancient High House
Moreton Corbet
Ellerdine Heath
Eaton on Tern
Howle
Pickstock
Puleston
Sutton
Long Compton
Gnosall
Whitecross
Weeping Cross
Moss Pit
Walton
Shawbury
Muckleton
Edgebolton
Great Bolas
Cold Hatton
Tibberton
Cherrington
Edgmond Marsh
Edgmond
Forton
Aqualate Mere
Coton
Gnosall Heath
Haughton
Allimore Green
Coppenhall
Acton Trussell
Bednall
Dunston
Great Wytheford
Rowton
Waters Upton
Walton
Crudgington
Adeney
Newport
Longford
Church Aston
Outwoods
Apeton
Bradley
Poynton Green
High Ercall
Telford and Wrekin
Kynnersley
Brockton
Chetwynd Aston
Moreton
Church Eaton
Levedale
Roden
Haughton
Longdon on Tern
Sleapford
Eyton upon the Weald Moors
Preston upon the Weald Moors
Lilleshall
Lilleshall Abbey
Hoo Farm Animal Kingdom
Orslow
High Onn
Shropshire Union Canal
Mitton
Longridge
Penkridge
Rodington
Great Chatwell
Muxton
Bratton
Donnington
Heath Hill
Brineton
Marston
Whiston
Congreve
Huntington
Withington
Admaston
Trench
Donnington Wood
Lilyhurst
Weston Heath
Blymhill
Mottey Meadows
Lapley
Upton Magna
Wrockwardine
Hadley
Granville
Sheriffhales
Wheaton Aston
Stretton
Walcot
Wellington
Ketley
Oakengates
Gailey
Charlton
Arleston
Ketley Bank
Crackleybank
Weston under Lizard
Belvide Res.
Hatherton
Norton
Priorslee
Telford Services
Weston Park
Bishop's Wood
Kiddemore Green
Horsebrook
Uppington
Aston
The Rock
Lawley
Haughton
Telford
Shifnal
Tong Norton
Brewood
Wroxeter Roman City
Rushton
Wroxeter
Donnington
The Wrekin
Telford Wonderland
Dawley
The Wyke
Tong
Boscobel House & The Royal Oak
White Ladies Priory
Chillington Hall
Standeford
Shareshill
Eaton
Constantine
Longwood
Little Wenlock
Telford Steam Railway
Stirchley
RAF Museum
Coven
Dryton
Leighton
Little Dawley
Rosehill
Halesfield
Featherstone
Hilton Park Services
Cound
Buildwas
Coalbrookdale
Kemberton
Albrighton
Codsall Wood
Buildwas Abbey
Mus of Iron
Mus of the Gorge
Madeley
Cressage
Sheinton
Ironbridge
Tollhouse
Blists Hill
Brockton
Ryton
David Austin Roses
Oaken
Codsall
Moseley Old Hall
Essington
Benthall Hall
Benthall
Coalport
Grindle
Boningale
Fordhouses
Bushbury
Wyke
Broseley
Jackfield Tile Mus
Sutton Maddock
Beckbury
Oxley
Wood Hayes
Homer
Harley
Much Wenlock
Norton
Burnhill Green
Wergs
Tettenhall
Bantock House
Wolverhampton
Wednesfield
Kenley
Willey
Stockton
Pattingham
Wightwick Manor
Stretton Westwood
Stableford
Badger
Perton
Willenhall
Hughley
Shropshire
Presthope
Callaughton
Ackleton
Rudge
Moseley
Bradmore
Blakenhall
Bilston
Bourton
Acton Round
Nordley
Astley Abbotts
Chesterton
Trescott
Lower Penn
Penn
Ettingshall
Easthope
Haughton
Worfield
Shipley
Cross Lane Head
Cliff Railway
Hilton
Seisdon
Hopstone
Trysull
Sedgley
Bradley
Brockton
Aston Eyre
Morville Hall
Morville
Tasley
Roughton
Claverley
Wombourne
Tipton
Weston
Monkhopton
Morville Heath
Bridgnorth
Stanmore
Heathton
Bagger
Upper Gornal
Wilderhope Manor
Shipton
Lower Netchwood
Upton Cressett
Oldbury
Watermill
Danesford
Farmcote
Halfpenny Green
Blakeley
Himley
Himley Hall
Gornalwood
Wrens Nest
Dudley Zoo & Castle
Stanton Long
Chetton
Quatford
Wolverhampton Halfpenny Green
Swindon
Highgate Common
Bobbington
Wall Heath
Dudley
Middleton Priors
Eardington
Holdgate
Ditton Priors
Glazeley
Dudmaston
Quatt
Six Ashes
Tuckhill
Four Ashes
Kingswinford
Bromley
Netherton
Tugford
Abdon
Neenton
Cleobury North
Chelmarsh
Middleton Scriven
Sutton
Hampton
Hampton Loade
Enville
Brierley Hill
Old Hill
Upper Heath
Brown Clee Hill
Borle Brook
Rea Brook
Sidbury
Billingsley
Wordsley
Amblecote
Red House Glass Cone
Quarry Bank
Cradley Heath
Clee St Margaret
Burwarton
Woodhill
Birdsgreen
Stourton
Potter's Cross
Wollescote
Aston Botterell
Alveley
Lye
Halesowen
Chorley
Highley
Severn Valley
Romsley
Kinver
Stourbridge
Hasbury
Stoke St Milborough
Loughton
Wheathill
Stottesdon
Rays Farm Country Matters
Kingsford
Whittington
Pedmore
Cleedownton
Farlow
Kinlet
Shatterford
Upper Arley
Bodenham Arboretum & Earth Centre
Blakeshall
Caunsall
Hagley
West Hagley
Clent Hills
Clent
Oreton
Silvington
Cookley
Churchill
Broome
Holy Cross
Cleeton St Mary
Catherton
Pound Green
Trimpley
Wolverley
Bitterley
Buttonoak
Low Habberley
Franche
Blakedown
Bell End
Foxwood
Doddington
Neen Savage
Wafers
Hopton
Wyre Forest
Severn Valley Railway
Blakebrook
Kidderminster
Belbroughton
Wribbenhall
Bewdley
Drayton
Farden
Wildmoor
Forest

S t a f f o r d
W e s t M i d l a n
Chatcull
Cotes
Stone
Dayhills
Garshall Green
Dods Leigh
Field
Bramshall
Uttoxeter
Doveridge
Wetwood
Croxton Bank
Millmeece
Slindon
Walton
Little Stoke
Milwich
Coton Hill
Blount's Green
Fairoak
Croxton
Yarnfield
Coton
Gratwich
Marchington
Sugnall
Norton Bridge
Aston-By-Stone
Fradswell
Bishop's Offley
Pershall
Burston
Sandon
Kingstone
Gorsty Hill
Eccleshall
Chebsey
Yarlet
Whitgreave
Gayton
Grindley
Marchington Woodlands
Adbaston
Great Bridgeford
Marston
Salt
Weston
Stowe-by-Chartley
Knighton
Wootton
Ellenhall
Drointon
High Offley
Hopton
Ingestre
Hixon
Newton
Newborough
Shebdon
Woodseaves
Holmcroft
Stafford
Abbots Bromley
Weston Jones
Lawnhead
Seighford
Coton Clanford
Great Haywood
Admaston
Norbury
Knightley Dale
Ranton
Derrington
Doxey
Tixall
Hoar Cross
Sutton
Puleston
Long Compton
Forebridge
Weeping Cross
Milford
Little Haywood
Colwich
Gnosall
Whitecross
Moss Pit
Woodlane
Forton
Aqualate Mere
Walton on the Hill
Colton
Hadley End
Haughton
TRENT VALE
Blithbury
Hamstall Ridware
Yoxall
Coton
Gnosall Heath
Brocton
Newport
Outwoods
Allimore Green
Coppenhall
Acton Trussell
Etchinghill
Rugeley
Hill Ridware
Morrey
Apeton
Bradley
Dunston
Bednall
CANNOCK CHASE
Chetwynd Aston
Moreton
Church Eaton
Levedale
Slitting Mill
Brereton
Handsacre
King's Bromley
Lilleshall
High Onn
Orslow
Mitton
Longridge
Armitage
Great Chatwell
Penkridge
Pye Green
Upper Longdon
Rileyhill
Heath Hill
Longdon
Lilyhurst
Weston Heath
Sheriffhales
Brineton
Marston
Whiston
Congreve
Huntington
Hazelslade
Longdon Green
Blymhill
Lapley
Hednesford
Cannock Wood
Wheaton Aston
Stretton
Littleworth
Elmhurst
Gentleshaw
Farewell
Oldfallow
Wimblebury
Chorley
Gailey
Weston under Lizard
Hatherton
Heath Hayes
Streethay
Belvide Res.
Kiddemore Green
Horsebrook
Cannock
Norton East
Burntwood
Lichfield
Bishop's Wood
Brewood
Bridgtown
Norton Canes
Chasetown
Leomansley
Shifnal
Tong Norton
Standeford
Churchbridge
Hammerwich
Tong
Great Wyrley
Muckley Corner
Wall
Coven
Shareshill
Cheslyn Hay
Little Wyrley
Brownhills
Featherstone
Springhill
Shenstone
Pemberton
Albrighton
Codsall Wood
Clayhanger
Walsall Wood
Stonnall
Oaken
Codsall
Essington
Pelsall
Grindle
Ryton
Fordhouses
Bushbury
Shelfield
Little Hay
Boningale
Oxley
Bloxwich
Leighswood
Beckbury
New Invention
Wood Hayes
Harden
Aldridge
Watford Gap
Rushall
Burnhill Green
Wergs
Short Heath
Little Aston
Hill
Wednesfield
Tettenhall
Heath Town
Roughley
Stockton
Pattingham
Willenhall
Walsall
Hardwick
Stableford
Badger
Perton
Wolverhampton
Streetly
Four Oaks
Ackleton
Rudge
Moseley
Palfrey
Mere Grn.
Chesterton
Trescott
Bradmore
Bilston
Darlaston
SUTTON COLDFIELD
Lower Penn
Penn
Blakenhall
Ettingshall
Worfield
Shipley
Great Barr
Moxley
Kingstanding
Bradley
Wednesbury
Wylde Green
Hilton
Seisdon
Trysull
Coseley
Hopstone
New Oscott
Roughton
Sedgley
Hill Top
Walmley
Wombourne
Grove Vale
Toll End
Tipton
Hamstead
Upper Witton
Heathton
Upper Gornal
Churchfield
Farmcote
Blakeley
Erdington
Gt. Bridge
Danesford
Halfpenny Green
Himley
Gornalwood
West Bromwich
Perry Barr
Gravelly Hill
Tyburn
Quatford
Swindon
Dudley Port
Tividale
Bobbington
Wall Heath
Dudley
Handsworth
Aston
Castle Bromwich
Oldbury
Sandwell
Winson Grn.
Six Ashes
Quatt
Kingswinford
Bromley
Netherton
Rowley Regis
SMETHWICK
Ward End
Tuckhill
Four Ashes
Brierley Hill
Enville
BIRMINGHAM
Old Hill
Hampton Loade
Bearwood
Wordsley
Amblecote
Blackheath
Yardley
Stourton
Quarry Bank
Cradley Heath
Quinton
Chad Valley
Birdsgreen
Wollescote
Potter's Cross
Harborne
Edgbaston
Balsall Hth.
Acock's Green
Alveley
Lye
HALESOWEN
Kinver
Stourbridge
Sparkhill
Romsley
Hasbury
Bartley Green
Selly Oak
Moseley
Whittington
Woodgate
Springfield
Olton
Kingsford
Pedmore
King's Heath
Hall Green
Blakeshall
Illey
Bournville
Shatterford
Caunsall
Upper Arley
West Hagley
Hagley
Frankley
Cookley
Churchill
Clent
Romsley
Northfield
Shirley
Solihull
Broome
Holy Cross
King's Norton
Blakedown
Longbridge
Hollywood
Bell End
Wribbenhall
Belbroughton
Rubery
Drakes Cross
Whitlock's End
Monkspath
Drayton
Wildmoor
Hopwood
Wyre Forest
M6
M54
M5
A34
A518
A5
A41
A449
A51
A513
A515
A38
A4041
A452
A461
A4148
A456
A458
A442
A454
A491
A441
A435
A45
A5190
A460
A464
A458
0 1 2 3 4 5 6 miles
0 1 2 3 4 5 6 7 8 9 10 km

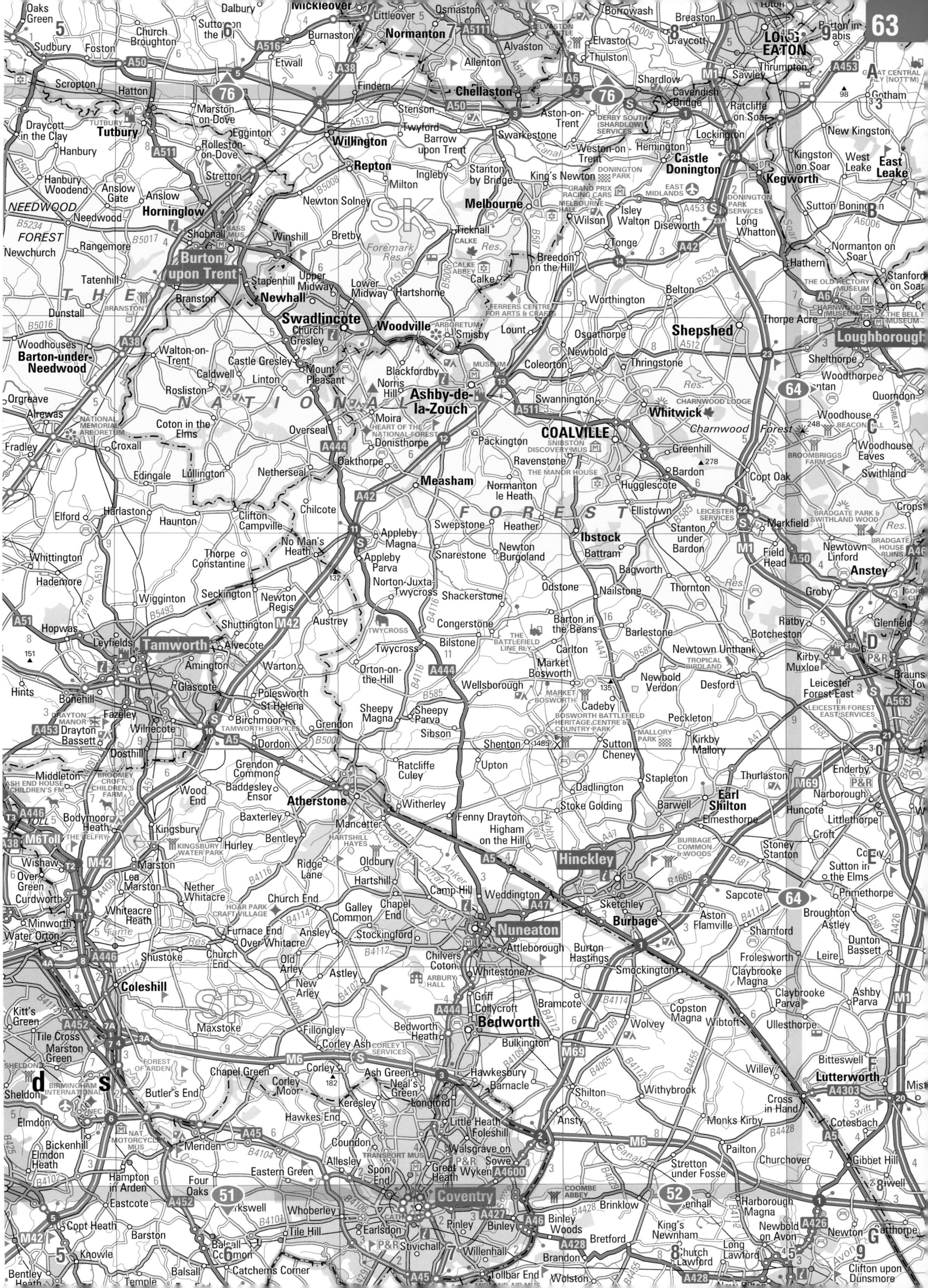
Oaks Green
Dalbury
Mickleover
Littleover
Osmaston
Borrowash
Breaston
Church Broughton
Sutton on the Hill
Burnaston
Normanton
Elvaston
Draycott
LONG EATON
Barton in Fabis
Sudbury
Foston
Etwall
Alvaston
Thulston
Allenton
Thrumpton
A50
Scropton
Hatton
Findern
Chellaston
Shardlow
Cavendish Bridge
Sawley
Gotham
Marston on Dove
Stenson
Aston-on-Trent
DERBY SOUTH (SHARDLOW) SERVICES
Ratcliffe on Soar
Draycott in the Clay
Tutbury
Egginton
Willington
Twyford
Barrow upon Trent
Swarkestone
Weston-on-Trent
Hemington
Lockington
New Kingston
Hanbury
Rolleston-on-Dove
Castle Donington
DONINGTON PARK
Kingston on Soar
West Leake
East Leake
Repton
Ingleby
Stanton by Bridge
King's Newton
Kegworth
Hanbury Woodend
Anslow Gate
Stretton
Milton
EAST MIDLANDS
Anslow
Newton Solney
Melbourne
DONINGTON PARK SERVICES
Sutton Bonington
NEEDWOOD
Needwood
Horninglow
SK
Isley Walton
Diseworth
Long Whatton
FOREST
Shobnall
Winshill
Bretby
Ticknall
Wilson
Rangemore
Newchurch
Burton upon Trent
Foremark Res.
CALKE ABBEY
Tonge
Breedon on the Hill
Normanton on Soar
Hathern
Tatenhill
Stapenhill
Upper Midway
Lower Midway
Hartshorne
Calke
Belton
Stanford on Soar
Branston
Newhall
FERRERS CENTRE FOR ARTS & CRAFTS
Worthington
THE OLD RECTORY MUSEUM
Dunstall
Swadlincote
Woodville
Church Gresley
Smisby
Lount
Osgathorpe
Shepshed
Thorpe Acre
CHARNWOOD MUSEUM
THE BELL FRY MUSEUM
Loughborough
Woodhouses
Barton-under-Needwood
Walton-on-Trent
Castle Gresley
Mount Pleasant
Blackfordby
Newbold
Coleorton
Thringstone
Shelthorpe
Woodthorpe
Rosliston
Caldwell
Linton
Norris Hill
Ashby-de-la-Zouch
Swannington
Whitwick
CHARNWOOD LODGE
Quorndon
Orgreave
Alrewas
NATIONAL
NATIONAL MEMORIAL ARBORETUM
Coton in the Elms
Moira
HEART OF THE NATIONAL FOREST
Overseal
COALVILLE
Charnwood Forest
Woodhouse
Woodhouse Eaves
Fradley
Croxall
Donisthorpe
Packington
SNIBSTON DISCOVERY MUS
Greenhill
BROOMBRIGGS FARM
Edingale
Lullington
Netherseal
Oakthorpe
Ravenstone
THE MANOR HOUSE
Bardon
Copt Oak
Swithland
Measham
Normanton le Heath
Hugglescote
Elford
Harlaston
Haunton
Clifton Campville
Chilcote
FOREST
Ellistown
LEICESTER SERVICES
Markfield
BRADGATE PARK & SWITHLAND WOOD
Cropston
Appleby Magna
Swepstone
Heather
Ibstock
Stanton under Bardon
Newtown Linford
Whittington
Thorpe Constantine
No Man's Heath
Appleby Parva
Snarestone
Newton Burgoland
Battram
Field Head
Anstey
Hademore
Norton-Juxta-Twycross
Bagworth
Thornton
Groby
Wigginton
Seckington
Newton Regis
Shackerstone
Odstone
Nailstone
Ratby
Glenfield
Hopwas
Shuttington
Austrey
TWYCROSS
Congerstone
Barton in the Beans
Barlestone
Botcheston
Leyfields
Tamworth
Alvecote
Twycross
Bilstone
THE BATTLEFIELD LINE RLY
Carlton
Newtown Unthank
Kirby Muxloe
Amington
Warton
Orton-on-the-Hill
Market Bosworth
TROPICAL BIRDLAND
Newbold Verdon
Desford
Leicester Forest East
Hints
Bonehill
Glascote
Wellsborough
Cadeby
Polesworth
St Helena
Sheepy Magna
Sheepy Parva
LEICESTER FOREST EAST SERVICES
DRAYTON MANOR
Fazeley
Wilnecote
Birchmoor
TAMWORTH SERVICES
Grendon
BOSWORTH BATTLEFIELD HERITAGE CENTRE & COUNTRY PARK
Peckleton
Drayton Bassett
Dordon
Sibson
MALLORY PARK
Kirkby Mallory
Dosthill
Shenton
Sutton Cheney
Enderby
Middleton
Grendon Common
Ratcliffe Culey
Upton
Stapleton
Thurlaston
ASH END HOUSE CHILDREN'S FM
BROOMEY CROFT CHILDREN'S FARM
Wood End
Baddesley Ensor
Atherstone
Dadlington
Earl Shilton
Narborough
Bodymoor Heath
Baxterley
Witherley
Fenny Drayton
Stoke Golding
Barwell
Huncote
THE BELFRY
Kingsbury
Mancetter
Higham on the Hill
Elmesthorpe
Littlethorpe
KINGSBURY WATER PARK
Hurley
Bentley
HARTSHILL HAYES
Croft
Wishaw
Marston
Ridge Lane
Oldbury
Hinckley
BURBAGE COMMON & WOODS
Stoney Stanton
Cosby
Over Green
Lea Marston
Hartshill
Camp Hill
Sutton in the Elms
Curdworth
Nether Whitacre
Church End
Weddington
Sketchley
Sapcote
Primethorpe
HOAR PARK CRAFT VILLAGE
Galley Common
Chapel End
Burbage
Aston Flamville
Broughton Astley
Whiteacre Heath
Minworth
Nuneaton
Water Orton
Furnace End
Over Whitacre
Ansley
Stockingford
Sharnford
Dunton Bassett
Attleborough
Burton Hastings
Shustoke
Church End
Old Arley
Chilvers Coton
Smockington
Frolesworth
Leire
Astley
Whitestone
Claybrooke Magna
Coleshill
ARBURY HALL
New Arley
Griff
Collycroft
Bramcote
Copston Magna
Claybrooke Parva
Ashby Parva
Kitt's Green
SP
Bedworth
Wolvey
Wibtoft
Ullesthorpe
Maxstoke
Fillongley
Bedworth Heath
Tile Cross
Marston Green
Corley Ash
CORLEY SERVICES
Bulkington
FOREST OF ARDEN
Bitteswell
SHELDON
Chapel Green
Corley
Ash Green
Hawkesbury
Willey
Lutterworth
BIRMINGHAM INTERNATIONAL
Corley Moor
Neal's Green
Barnacle
Sheldon
Butler's End
Longford
Shilton
Withybrook
Cross in Hand
Misterton
NEC
Keresley
Little Heath
Ansty
Monks Kirby
Cotesbach
Elmdon
Hawkes End
Foleshill
NAT MOTORCYCLE MUS
Coundon
Pailton
Bickenhill
Meriden
TRANSPORT MUS
Walsgrave on Sowe
Elmdon Heath
Allesley
Churchover
Gibbet Hill
Hampton in Arden
Eastern Green
Spon End
Great Heath
Wyken
Stretton under Fosse
Four Oaks
COOMBE ABBEY
Caldwell
Eastcote
Berkswell
Coventry
Brinklow
Harborough Magna
Whoberley
CATH
Copt Heath
Barston
Tile Hill
Earlsdon
Pinley
Binley
Binley Woods
King's Newnham
Newbold on Avon
Newton
Catthorpe
Stivichall
Willenhall
Bretford
Church Lawford
Long Lawford
Knowle
Balsall Common
Brandon
Bentley Heath
Balsall
Temple
Catchems Corner
Tollbar End
Wolston
Clifton upon Dunsmore
Avon
M1
M6
M42
M69
M6Toll
A38
A42
A444
A5
A47
A45
A46
A6
A453
A511
A452
A446
A426
A4303
A4600
A428
A427
A563
A50
A514
A516
A51
A513
A453

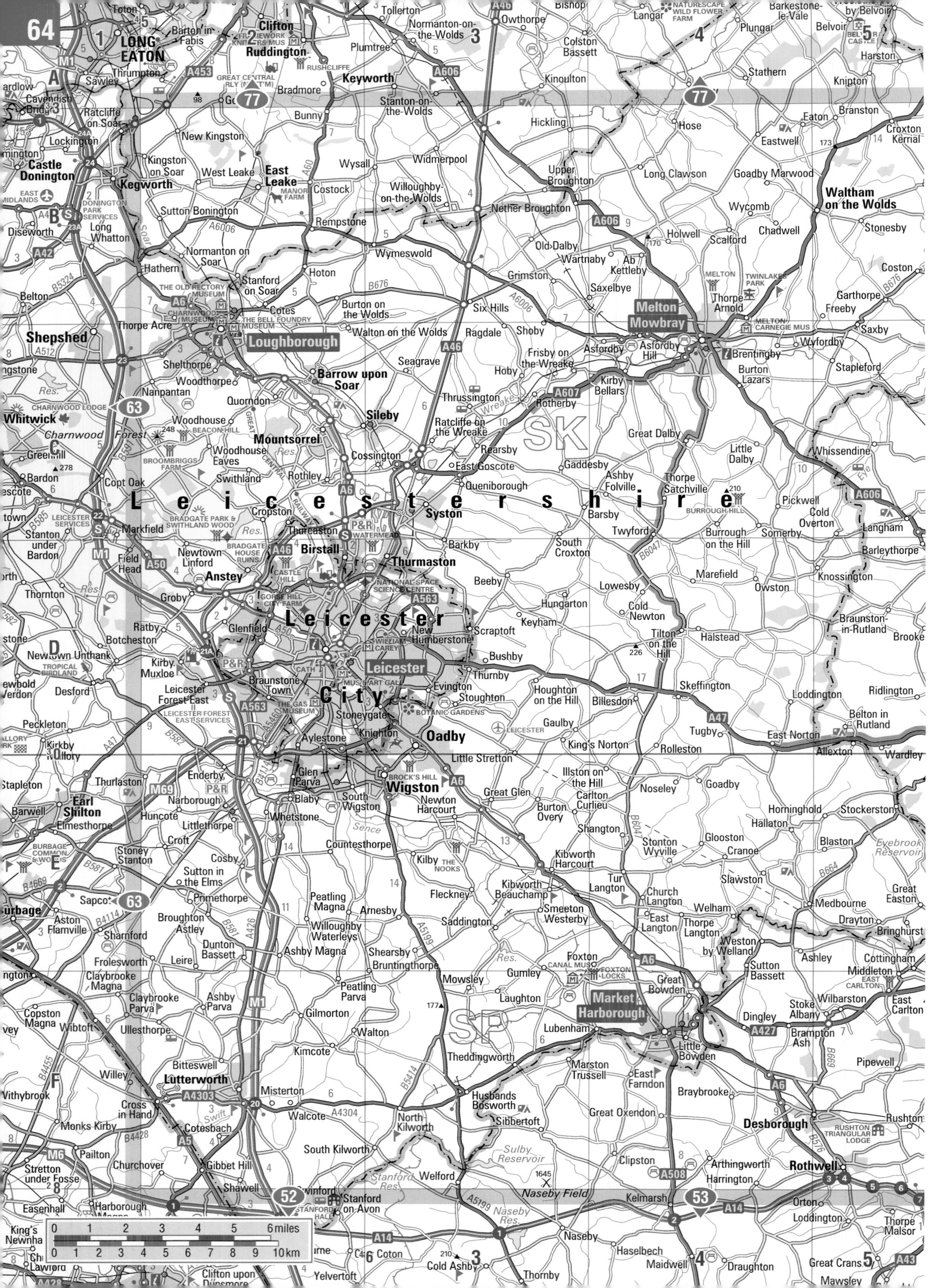
Long Eaton
Clifton
Ruddington
Tollerton
Normanton-on-the-Wolds
Owthorpe
Colston Bassett
Langar
Plungar
Barkestone-le-Vale
Belvoir
Harston
Stathern
Knipton
Barton in Fabis
Thrumpton
Sawley
Plumtree
Keyworth
Bradmore
Kinoulton
Cavendish Bridge
Ratcliffe on Soar
Bunny
Stanton-on-the-Wolds
Hickling
Hose
Eastwell
Eaton
Branston
Croxton Kerrial
Lockington
New Kingston
Castle Donington
Kingston on Soar
West Leake
East Leake
Wysall
Widmerpool
Upper Broughton
Long Clawson
Goadby Marwood
Waltham on the Wolds
Kegworth
Costock
Willoughby-on-the-Wolds
Nether Broughton
Wycomb
Chadwell
East Midlands
Donington Park Services
Sutton Bonington
Long Whatton
Rempstone
Holwell
Scalford
Stonesby
Diseworth
Normanton on Soar
Wymeswold
Old Dalby
Wartnaby
Ab Kettleby
Hathern
Stanford on Soar
Hoton
Grimston
Saxelbye
Coston
Belton
Cotes
Burton on the Wolds
Six Hills
Melton Mowbray
Thorpe Arnold
Garthorpe
Freeby
Shepshed
Thorpe Acre
Loughborough
Walton on the Wolds
Ragdale
Shoby
Asfordby
Asfordby Hill
Brentingby
Wyfordby
Saxby
Shelthorpe
Barrow upon Soar
Seagrave
Hoby
Frisby on the Wreake
Burton Lazars
Stapleford
Nanpantan
Woodthorpe
Whitwick
Quorndon
Thrussington
Rotherby
Kirby Bellars
Sileby
Ratcliffe on the Wreake
Woodhouse
Charnwood Forest
Mountsorrel
Woodhouse Eaves
Great Dalby
Little Dalby
Whissendine
Greenhill
Cossington
Rearsby
East Goscote
Gaddesby
Bardon
Copt Oak
Swithland
Rothley
Queniborough
Ashby Folville
Thorpe Satchville
Pickwell
Cold Overton
Leicestershire
Cropston
Syston
Barsby
Langham
Markfield
Leicester Services
Thurcaston
Twyford
Burrough on the Hill
Somerby
Stanton under Bardon
Birstall
Barkby
South Croxton
Barleythorpe
Newtown Linford
Field Head
Thurmaston
Marefield
Knossington
Thornton
Anstey
Beeby
Lowesby
Owston
Groby
Leicester
Hungarton
Cold Newton
Braunston-in-Rutland
Ratby
Glenfield
Scraptoft
Keyham
Tilton on the Hill
Halstead
Brooke
Botcheston
New Humberstone
Newtown Unthank
Kirby Muxloe
Bushby
Thurnby
Braunstone Town
Leicester City
Desford
Leicester Forest East
Evington
Stoughton
Houghton on the Hill
Billesdon
Skeffington
Loddington
Ridlington
Stoneygate
Peckleton
Gaulby
Tugby
Belton in Rutland
Kirkby Mallory
Aylestone
Knighton
Oadby
King's Norton
Rolleston
East Norton
Allexton
Wardley
Little Stretton
Stapleton
Thurlaston
Enderby
Glen Parva
Wigston
Illston on the Hill
Noseley
Goadby
Earl Shilton
Narborough
Blaby
South Wigston
Great Glen
Carlton Curlieu
Barwell
Huncote
Newton Harcourt
Burton Overy
Horninghold
Stockerston
Elmesthorpe
Littlethorpe
Whetstone
Shangton
Hallaton
Countesthorpe
Stonton Wyville
Glooston
Blaston
Eyebrook Reservoir
Croft
Stoney Stanton
Cosby
Kilby
Kibworth Harcourt
Cranoe
Sutton in the Elms
Tur Langton
Slawston
Great Easton
Burbage
Sapcote
Primethorpe
Peatling Magna
Fleckney
Kibworth Beauchamp
Church Langton
Medbourne
Aston Flamville
Broughton Astley
Arnesby
Smeeton Westerby
Welham
Drayton
Bringhurst
Sharnford
Dunton Bassett
Willoughby Waterleys
Saddington
East Langton
Thorpe Langton
Weston by Welland
Ashby Magna
Shearsby
Foxton
Frolesworth
Leire
Bruntingthorpe
Gumley
Sutton Bassett
Ashley
Cottingham
Middleton
Claybrooke Magna
Mowsley
Great Bowden
East Carlton
Claybrooke Parva
Ashby Parva
Peatling Parva
Laughton
Market Harborough
Wilbarston
Stoke Albany
Copston Magna
Gilmorton
Dingley
Brampton Ash
Wibtoft
Ullesthorpe
Walton
Lubenham
Little Bowden
Kimcote
Bitteswell
Theddingworth
Marston Trussell
Pipewell
Willey
Lutterworth
Misterton
Husbands Bosworth
East Farndon
Braybrooke
Withybrook
Cross in Hand
Walcote
North Kilworth
Sibbertoft
Great Oxendon
Desborough
Rushton
Monks Kirby
Cotesbach
South Kilworth
Pailton
Churchover
Gibbet Hill
Welford
Sulby Reservoir
Clipston
Arthingworth
Rothwell
Stretton under Fosse
Shawell
Swinford
Stanford Reservoir
Naseby Field
Harrington
Kelmarsh
Stanford on Avon
Orton
Loddington
Easenhall
Harborough Magna
Naseby
Thorpe Malsor
King's Newnham
Coton
Cold Ashby
Haselbech
Maidwell
Draughton
Great Cransley
Mawsley
Yelvertoft
Thornby
Clifton upon Dunsmore
SK
SP
M1
M6
M69
A6
A46
A47
A14
A606
A607
A563
A5
A4303
A427
A508
A453
A42
A50
A43
0 1 2 3 4 5 6 miles
0 1 2 3 4 5 6 7 8 9 10 km

Ropsley
Sapperton
Folkingham
Billingborough
Birthorpe
Pickworth
Old Somerby
Denton
Harlaxton
HARLAXTON MANOR
Little Ponton
Humby
Hanby
Laughton
Pointon
Boothby Pagnell
Westhorpe
Gosberton
Stroxton
Great Ponton
Lenton
Aslackby
Millthorpe
Gosberton Clough
Ingoldsby
Dowsby
Hungerton
Wyville
Keisby
Graby
Risegate
Bassingthorpe
Bitchfield
Kirkby Underwood
Surfleet
Hawthorpe
Rippingale
Stoke Rochford
Easton
Irnham
Crossgate
Saltby
Skillington
Bulby
Dunsby
Northgate
Pinchbeck
Pinchbeck Bars
WOOLSTHORPE MANOR
Burton-le-Coggles
Corby Glen
Stainfield
Haconby
Woolsthorpe
Colsterworth
Elsthorpe
Hanthorpe
Morton
Pinchbeck West
Sproxton
Twyford
Birkholme
Buckminster
GRANTHAM SOUTH SERVICES
Swinstead
Grimsthorpe
Dyke
Spalding
Stainby
Swayfield
GRIMSTHORPE CASTLE
Cawthorpe
Pode Hole
Sewstern
Gunby
North Witham
Edenham
Little London
Scottlethorpe
Twenty
Clay Lake
Bourne
NEW FOX
Creeton
Wymondham
South Witham
CRIBBS MEADOW
Castle Bytham
Little Bytham
Tongue End
Lound
Edmondthorpe
Thistleton
Witham on the Hill
Northorpe
Cowbit
Toft
Thurlby
Teigh
Market Overton
Clipsham
Careby
THURLBY
Deeping Fen
Deeping St Nicholas
Barrow
Stretton
Manthorpe
Thetford
THE LIVING IRONSTONE MUS
Obthorpe
Hop Pole
Brotherhouse Bar
Carlby
Wilsthorpe
Baston
Greetham
Pickworth
Ashwell
Cottesmore
Essendine
Braceborough
Langtoft
Greatford
Rutland
Exton
TOLETHORPE HALL RUTLAND OPEN AIR THEATRE
Ryhall
CROWLAND ABBEY
BARNSDALE GARDENS
Little Casterton
Barholm
Towngate
Market Deeping
Burley
FALCONRY CENTRE
Oakham
OAKHAM
Belmesthorpe
Frognall
Deeping St James
Crowland
Whitwell
Tickencote
Great Casterton
Deeping Gate
Empingham
Upper Hambleton
Northfields
Uffington
Tallington
West Deeping
Egleton
RUTLAND WATER
Maxey
Northborough
Stamford
Etton
Peakirk
RUTLAND WATER
Normanton
Tinwell
BURGHLEY
Newborough
Edith Weston
Glinton
Manton
Ketton
Easton on the Hill
Pilsgate
Bainton
Barnack
Helpston
Bedford Level (North)
Lyndon
North Luffenham
Ufford
Eye Green
Chater
BARNACK HILLS AND HOLES
Werrington
Gunthorpe
Preston
Pilton
Southorpe
Wing
South Luffenham
Collyweston
Wittering
Peterborough
Eye
Marholm
COLLYWESTON GREAT WOOD
CASTOR HANGLANDS
Walton
Ayston
Glaston
Morcott
Thornhaugh
SACREWELL FARM & COUNTRY CENTRE
Upton
Dogsthorpe
Newark
Stone
Duddington
Barrowden
Tixover
Bisbrooke
BEDFORD PURLIEUS
Wansford
Ailsworth
LONGTHORPE TOWER
Uppingham
Wakerley
Stibbington
Longthorpe
Fengate
Sutton
FERRY MEADOWS
Seaton
NENE VALLEY RAILWAY
Castor
FLAG FEN BRONZE AGE EXCAVATIONS
Stoke Dry
Lyddington
Harringworth
King's Cliffe
Yarwell
RAILWORLD
Old Fletton
BEDE HOUSE
Sibson
Water Newton
Orton Longueville
Stanground
Thorpe by Water
Laxton
Alwalton
Whittlesey
SIBSON
King's Delph
Blatherwycke
Apethorpe
Nassington
Orton Waterville
CROWN LAKES
Chesterton
Farcet
Gretton
Bulwick
Woodnewton
PETERBOROUGH SERVICES
Caldecott
KIRBY HALL
SOUTHWICK HALL
Fotheringhay
ELTON HALL
Elton
Haddon
Deene
Southwick
CASTLE SITE
Farcet Fen
Rockingham
ROCKINGHAM CASTLE
DEENE PARK
Deenethorpe
Morborne
Yaxley
ROCKINGHAM
Eaglethorpe
Warmington
Whittlesey Mere
Tansor
Glapthorn
Cotterstock
Norman Cross
Little Weldon
Folksworth
Corby
Great Weldon
Upper Benefield
Oundle
Ashton
Stilton
HOLME FEN
Lower Benefield
Caldecote
Rockingham Forest
Stanion
Polebrook
Lutton
Denton
Holme
BARNWELL
Stoke Doyle
Harper's Brook
Coningtown
Great Oakley
Little Oakley
Barnwell St Andrew
Glatton
Ramsey Heights
Brigstock
LYVEDEN NEW BIELD
Hemington
WOODWALTON FEN
HILL FARM HERBS
FERMYN WOODS
Pilton
Luddington in the Brook
Sawtry
Newton
Geddington
ELEANOR CROSS
Wadenhoe
Barnwell All Saints
Great Gidding
Church End
Achurch
Thurning
Little Gidding
UPWOOD MEADOWS
Sudborough
Wigsthorpe
Aldwincle
Steeple Gidding
Wood Walton
Weekley
BOUGHTON HOUSE
Grafton Underwood
Thorpe Waterville
Winwick
HAMERTON ZOO PARK
Coppingford
Great Raveley
Warkton
Lowick
Clopton
MONKS WOOD
Kettering
Titchmarsh
Islip
Thrapston
Hamerton
Twywell
Wennington
Upton
Cranford St Andrew
Cranford St John
Barton Seagrave
Old Weston
Alconbury Weston
Abbots Ripton
Woodford
Buckworth
Denford
Bythorn
Brington
Little Stukeley
WICKSTEED PARK
Molesworth
Alconbury

Donington South Ing
End
Quadring
Bicker Haven
Fosdyke
Holbeach St Matthew
Westhorpe
Gosberton
Holbeach St Marks
Lynn Channel
Gosberton Clough
79
Daws
79
Risegate
Surfleet Seas End
Surfleet
HOLBEACH MARSH
Gedney Marsh
Gedney Drove End
Moulton Seas End
Saracen's Head
Holbeach Hurn
THE WASH
Crossgate
Holbeach Bank
Northgate
Pinchbeck
Halesgate
Holbeach Clough
Gedney Dyke
Lutton
Guy's Head
Pinchbeck Bars
BAYTREE OWL CENTRE
Weston
Fleet Hargate
Chapelgate
Terrington
Pinchbeck West
Whaplode
Holbeach
Little London
Gedney
Spalding
SPRINGFIELDS
Moulton
MOULTON MILL
Fleet
Long Sutton
Pode Hole
Low Fulney
Austendike
Gedney Broadgate
Sutton Bridge
Orange Row
Twenty
Little London
Clay Lake
AYSCOUGHFEE HALL
Weston Hills
Sutton Crosses
Walpole Cross Keys
Whaplode St Catherine
Tydd St Mary
Tongue End
Moulton Chapel
Holbeach St Johns
Sutton St James
Tydd Gote
Walpole St Andrew
Hay Green
Cowbit
Four Gotes
Walpole Marsh
Walpole St Peter
65
Moulton Eaugate
Deeping St Nicholas
Tydd St Giles
Deeping Fen
TF
Newton
St John's Highway
Brotherhouse Bar
Ingleborough
Hop Pole
Whaplode Drove
Tydd St Giles Fen
West Walton
St John
Walpole Terrington Highway
Shepeau Stow
Sutton St Edmund
Fitton End
West Walton Highway
Holbeach Drove
Marshland
Gedney Hill
Gorefield
St John's Fen End
Market Deeping
CROWLAND ABBEY
Leverington
FENLAND & WEST NORFOLK AVIATION MUSEUM
Frognall
Dowsdale
Walsoken
Crowland
Throckenholt
Church End
PECKOVER HOUSE
Deeping St James
North Fen
Wisbech
Marshland St James
WISBECH & FENLAND MUS.
New Walsoken
Northborough
Parson Drove
Nene Terrace
Morris Fen
Wisbech St Mary
Emneth
Peakirk
Newborough
Murrow
Emneth Hungate
Glinton
Tholomas Drove
Elm
Rogue's Alley
Holly End
Bedford Level (North)
Thorney Toll
Outwell
Eye Green
Guyhirn Gull
Friday Bridge
Stow
Werrington
Gunthorpe
Thorney
Guyhirn
Waldersey
WELLE MANOR HALL
Eye
Ring's End
Coldham
Laddus Fens
Upwell
Walton
Dogsthorpe
Newark
Stone Bridge Corner
Chainbridge
Three Holes
Peterborough
LONGTHORPE TOWER
Fengate
FLAG FEN BRONZE AGE EXCAVATIONS
North Side
Eldernell
West Fen
Westry
Norwoodside
Euximoor Fen
Upwell
Longthorpe
Coates
Eximoor Drove
South District
FERRY MEADOWS
RAILWORLD
Old Fletton
Orton Longueville
Stanground
Whittlesey
Inham's End
Eastrea
March
Binnimoor Fen
Christchurch
Orton Waterville
CROWN LAKES
Farcet
King's Delph
Turves
TL
Town End
Tipsend
Lakesend
PETERBOROUGH SERVICES
Twenty Foot River
Upwell Fen
WILDLIFE TRUST WELNEY
65
Ranson Moor
Welney
BEDFORD LEVEL (MIDDLE)
Flood's Ferry
Yaxley
Farcet Fen
Wimblington
White Fen
Gold Hill
Whittlesey Mere
Pondersbridge
Doddington
Norman Cross
C a m b r i d g e
Benwick
Manea
Stilton
HOLME FEN
Middle Moor
Ramsey Mereside
Wimblington Fen
Sixteen Foot Drain
Holme
Ramsey St Mary's
Forty Foot Drain or Vermuden's Drain
Purls Bridge
Fodder Fen
Denton
Ramsey Forty Foot
Horseway
Chatteris
Conington
Ramsey Heights
Ramsey Hollow
Welches Dam
Pymoor
Glatton
Ramsey
RAMSEY RURAL MUSEUM
New Bedford River
Langwood Fen
Little Downham
WOODWALTON FEN
Bury
Sawtry
Tick Fen
Ferry Hill
Horseley Fen
Church End
Chettisham
UPWOOD MEADOWS
Upwood
Wardy Hill
West Fen
Gidding
Chapel Head
Coveney
Wood Walton
Great Raveley
Wistow
Mepal
Pidley Fen
CATHEDRAL AND MUS.
Coppingford
MONKS WOOD
Little Raveley
Witcham
OLIVER CROMWELL'S HOUSE
Ely
54
Warboys
Fenton
Chatteris Fen
55
Upton
Wennington
Sutton
Wentworth
Witchford
Pidley
Somersham
Hill Row Doles
North Hill
Little Thetford
Little Stukeley
Old Hurst
Ripton
Colne
Haddenham
Alconbury
Woodhurst
0 1 2 3 4 5 6 miles
0 1 2 3 4 5 6 7 8 9 10 km

Norfolk
TF
TL
THETFORD
B R E C K L A N D
FOREST
PARK
Snettisham Nature Reserve
Shepherd's Port
Snettisham Park
Ingoldisthorpe
Shernborne
Dersingham
Dersingham Bog
Sandringham
Wolferton
West Newton
Flitcham
Anmer
Great Bircham
Bircham Mill
Bircham Tofts
Newton
Barmer
Bagthorpe
Syderstone
Blenheim Park
Wicken Green Village
Sculthorpe
Barsham
East Barsham
Snoring
Fakenham
Dunton
Shereford
Hempton
Tattersett
Coxford
West Rudham
East Rudham
Tatterford
Toftrees
Little Ryburgh
Great Ryburgh
Houghton Hall
New Houghton
Harpley
Helhoughton
Colkirk
West Raynham
East Raynham
Oxwick
Hamrow
South Raynham
Horningtoft
Peddars Way & Norfolk Coast Path
Little Massingham
Great Massingham
Weasenham St Peter
Weasenham All Saints
Whissonsett
Wellingham
Brisley
Tittleshall
Extreme Adventure
Stanfield
Castle Rising
North Wootton
South Wootton
Ongar Hill
Marsh
Hillington
Congham
Congham Hall Herb Garden
Roydon
Roydon Common
Grimston
Pott Row
King's Lynn
Maritime Exhibition
Guildhall
Gaywood
Clenchwarton
Terrington St Clement
West Lynn
Fairstead
Massingham Heath
Gayton
Rougham
East Bilney
Mileham
Bittering
Gressenhall Farm & Workhouse
Hardwick
Leziate
Ashwicken
Tilney High End
Tilney All Saints
Fair Green
Tower End
Gayton Thorpe
West Lexham
Litcham
East Lexham
Middleton
East Walton
East Winch
West Bilney
Pentney
West Acre
Castle Acre
Castle Acre Priory
Newton
South Acre
Great Dunham
Drury Square
Beeston
Longham
Sparrow Green
Crane's Corner
Saddle Bow
West Winch
North Runcton
Wiggenhall St Germans
Setchey
Blackborough End
Tilney St Lawrence
Wiggenhall St Mary the Virgin
Tottenhill Row
Narborough
Little Dunham
Great Fransham
Wendling
Wiggenhall St Mary Magdalen
Watlington
Tottenhill
Wormegay
Great Palgrave
Sporle
Little Fransham
Hall Gdns & Arboretum
Daffy Green
Runcton Holme
Marham
Shouldham
Necton
West End
Swaffham
Marshland Fen
South Runcton
Shouldham Thorpe
Beachamwell Warren
North Pickenham
Bradenham
Stowbridge
Holme Hale
Stow Bardolph
Barton Bendish
Fincham
Crowshill
West Head
Wimbotsham
Beachamwell
Shingham
Downham Market
Stradsett
Iceni Village and Museums
South Pickenham
Ashill
Bardolph Fen
Broomhill
Crimplesham
Cockley Cley
Saham Hills
Barroway Drove
Bexwell
Eastmoor
Gooderstone Water Gardens
Saham Toney
Ovington
Nordelph
Denver
Boughton
Wereham
Oxborough
Gooderstone
Great Cressingham
Caudlesprings
West Dereham
Oxburgh Hall, Garden & Estate
Hilborough
Watton
Griston
Old Bedford River
Fen
Fordham
Wretton
Stoke Ferry
Whittington
Foulden
Bodney
Little Cressingham
Merton
Northacre
Hilgay
Wissey
Northwold
The Arms
Caston
Ten Mile Bank
Brookville
Thompson
Stow
Hilgay Fen
Southery
Cranwich
Ickburgh
Lynford Arboretum and Lakes
Methwold Hythe
Methwold
Mundford
Methwold Fens
Southery Fens
Queen's Ground
West Tofts
Brandon Creek
Great Hockham
Apes Hall
Feltwell
Wretham
Brandon Bank
Feltwell Fens
Grimes Graves
Weeting Castle
Mare Fen
Hockwold cum Wilton
Weeting
Burnt Fen
Hockwold Fens
Weeting Heath
Littleport
Brandon
Santon Downham
Croxton
Little Ouse
Bedford Level (South)
Brandon Park
High Lodge Forest Centre
Thetford Warren Lodge
Brettenham
Shadwell
Shippea Hill Sta.
Thetford
Ancient House Mus
Prickwillow
Lakenheath
Wangford Warren
Thetford Warren
Rushford
Great Ouse
Queen Adelaide
Kenny Hill
Lakenheath Warren
Knettishall Heath
Middle Fen
Elveden
Euston
Euston Hall
Barnham
Stuntney
Great Fen
Mildenhall Fen
Eriswell
Holywell Row
Beck Row
Broad Hill
Northfield Windmill
Isleham Fen
Thistley Green
West Row
Fakenham Magna
Sapiston
Barningham
Lark
A10
A47
A148
A149
A1078
A134
A1122
A1065
A11
A1066
A1075
A1088
A1101
A142
A1101
B1440
B1439
B1153
B1155
B1145
B1454
B1355
B1146
B1108
B1112
B1160
B1107
B1106
B1104
B1382
80
68
55
56

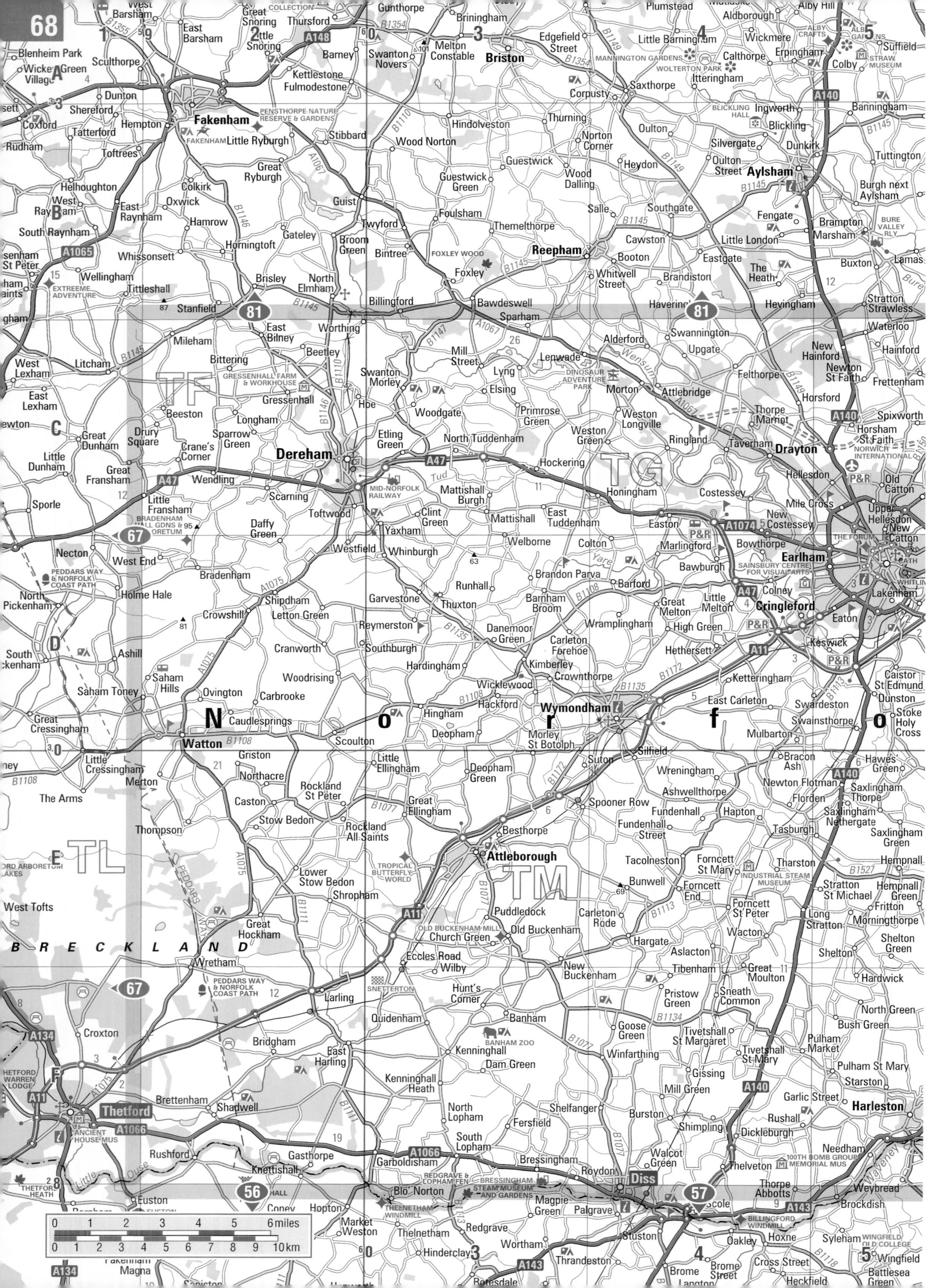
West Barsham
Great Snoring
Little Snoring
Thursford
Gunthorpe
Briningham
Plumstead
Aldborough
Alby Hill
East Barsham
Barney
Swanton Novers
Melton Constable
Briston
Edgefield Street
Little Barningham
Wickmere
Calthorpe
Erpingham
Suffield
Colby
Blenheim Park
Sculthorpe
Wicken Green Village
Kettlestone
Fulmodestone
Saxthorpe
Corpusty
Itteringham
Mannington Gardens
Wolterton Park
Alby Crafts
Straw Museum
Dunton
Shereford
Coxford
Tatterford
Hempton
Fakenham
Pensthorpe Nature Reserve & Gardens
Rudham
Toftrees
Little Ryburgh
Stibbard
Wood Norton
Hindolveston
Thurning
Norton Corner
Oulton
Ingworth
Blickling Hall
Blickling
Banningham
Silvergate
Dunkirk
Oulton Street
Aylsham
Tuttington
Burgh next Aylsham
Heydon
Guestwick
Wood Dalling
Guestwick Green
Helhoughton
Great Ryburgh
Colkirk
Oxwick
West Raynham
East Raynham
South Raynham
Hamrow
Guist
Foulsham
Salle
Southgate
Fengate
Brampton
Marsham
Bure Valley Rly
Themelthorpe
Twyford
Horningtoft
Gateley
Broom Green
Bintree
Foxley Wood
Reepham
Cawston
Little London
Booton
Eastgate
Buxton
Lamas
Whissonsett
Wellingham
Tittleshall
Extreme Adventure
Brisley
North Elmham
Foxley
Whitwell Street
Brandiston
The Heath
Billingford
Bawdeswell
Haveringland
Hevingham
Stratton Strawless
Stanfield
Sparham
Worthing
East Bilney
Mileham
Beetley
Mill Street
Alderford
Swannington
Upgate
Waterloo
New Hainford
Hainford
West Lexham
Litcham
Bittering
Gressenhall Farm & Workhouse
Swanton Morley
Lyng
Elsing
Lenwade
Dinosaur Adventure Park
Morton
Attlebridge
Felthorpe
Newton St Faith
Frettenham
Horsford
East Lexham
Gressenhall
Hoe
Woodgate
Primrose Green
Weston Longville
Thorpe Marriot
Spixworth
Horsham St Faith
Norwich International
Beeston
Longham
Etling Green
North Tuddenham
Weston Green
Ringland
Taverham
Drayton
Great Dunham
Drury Square
Sparrow Green
Crane's Corner
Dereham
Hockering
Little Dunham
Great Fransham
Wendling
Mid-Norfolk Railway
Mattishall Burgh
Honingham
Hellesdon
Old Catton
Costessey
Mile Cross
Upper Hellesdon
Sporle
Little Fransham
Scarning
Toftwood
Clint Green
Mattishall
East Tuddenham
Easton
New Costessey
New Catton
Bradenham Hall Gdns & Arboretum
Daffy Green
Yaxham
Welborne
Colton
Marlingford
Bowthorpe
The Forum
Earlham
Necton
West End
Westfield
Whinburgh
Bawburgh
Sainsbury Centre for Visual Arts
Peddars Way & Norfolk Coast Path
Bradenham
Brandon Parva
Barford
Colney
Whitlingham
Lakenham
North Pickenham
Holme Hale
Shipdham
Garvestone
Runhall
Barnham Broom
Great Melton
Little Melton
Cringleford
Eaton
Crowshill
Letton Green
Thuxton
Wramplingham
High Green
Reymerston
Danemoor Green
Carleton Forehoe
Hethersett
Keswick
South Pickenham
Ashill
Cranworth
Southburgh
Hardingham
Kimberley
Crownthorpe
Ketteringham
Caistor St Edmund
Saham Hills
Woodrising
Wicklewood
Dunston
Saham Toney
Ovington
Carbrooke
Hackford
Wymondham
East Carleton
Swardeston
Stoke Holy Cross
Great Cressingham
Caudlesprings
Hingham
Deopham
Morley St Botolph
Swainsthorpe
Mulbarton
Watton
Scoulton
Silfield
Bracon Ash
Hawes' Green
Little Cressingham
Griston
Little Ellingham
Suton
Wreningham
Newton Flotman
Saxlingham Thorpe
The Arms
Merton
Northacre
Rockland St Peter
Deopham Green
Ashwellthorpe
Flordon
Caston
Great Ellingham
Spooner Row
Fundenhall
Hapton
Saxlingham Nethergate
Thompson
Stow Bedon
Rockland All Saints
Besthorpe
Fundenhall Street
Tasburgh
Saxlingham Green
Attleborough
Tacolneston
Forncett St Mary
Tharston
Hempnall
Lower Stow Bedon
Tropical Butterfly World
Bunwell
Forncett End
Industrial Steam Museum
Stratton St Michael
Hempnall Green
West Tofts
Shropham
Puddledock
Carleton Rode
Forncett St Peter
Long Stratton
Fritton
Great Hockham
Old Buckenham Mill
Church Green
Old Buckenham
Hargate
Wacton
Morningthorpe
B R E C K L A N D
Wretham
Eccles Road
Wilby
Aslacton
Shelton Green
Shelton
Peddars Way & Norfolk Coast Path
Snetterton
Larling
Hunt's Corner
New Buckenham
Tibenham
Great Moulton
Hardwick
Pristow Green
Sneath Common
Croxton
Quidenham
Banham
Goose Green
Tivetshall St Margaret
North Green
Bush Green
Bridgham
Banham Zoo
Winfarthing
Tivetshall St Mary
Pulham Market
Thetford Warren Lodge
East Harling
Kenninghall
Dam Green
Gissing
Pulham St Mary
Kenninghall Heath
Mill Green
Starston
Thetford
Brettenham
Shadwell
North Lopham
Shelfanger
Burston
Garlic Street
Harleston
Ancient House Mus
Fersfield
Shimpling
Rushall
Dickleburgh
South Lopham
Rushford
Gasthorpe
Garboldisham
Bressingham
Walcot Green
Needham
Knettishall
Roydon
Thelveton
100th Bomb Group Memorial Mus
Redgrave & Lopham Fen
Bressingham Steam Museum and Gardens
Diss
Thetford Heath
Euston
Coney
Hopton
Blo' Norton
Thorpe Abbotts
Weybread
Brockdish
Scole
The Netham Windmill
Magpie Green
Palgrave
Billingford Windmill
Market Weston
Thelnetham
Redgrave
Stuston
Oakley
Hoxne
Syleham
Wingfield Old College
Hinderclay
Wortham
Thrandeston
Brome
Brome Street
Cross Street
Wingfield
Fakenham Magna
Botesdale
Langton
Heckfield
Battlesea Green
Norfolk
TF
TG
TL
TM
A148
A1065
A1067
A47
A1075
A11
A140
A1074
A134
A1066
A143
B1354
B1355
B1145
B1146
B1110
B1147
B1149
B1108
B1135
B1172
B1113
B1077
B1111
B1134
B1527
B1118
B1150
Wensum
Tud
Yare
Bure
Waveney
Little Ouse
0 1 2 3 4 5 6 miles
0 1 2 3 4 5 6 7 8 9 10 km

7
8
9
A
B
C
D
E
F
G
Knapton
Bacton
Bradfield
Broomholm
Keswick
Walcott
Antingham
Edingthorpe
Swafield
DAVENPORTS MAGIC KINGDOM
Edingthorpe Green
Witton Bridge
Happisburgh
Ridlington
North Walsham
Spa Common
Crostwight
Whimpwell Green
Eccles on Sea
Felmingham
Happisburgh Common
EAST RUSTON OLD VICARAGE GARDEN
Lessingham
Hempstead
Honing
Westwick
81
East Ruston
Sea Palling
Ingham Corner
Bengate
WAXHAM GREAT BARN
Waxham
Worstead
Skeyton
Ingham
Swanton Abbott
Sloley
Dilham
Stalham
Stalham Green
NORFOLK
Smallburgh
MUSEUM OF THE BROADS
Hickling
Scottow
Sutton
Hickling Green
COAST
Pennygate
Barton Turf
Little Hautbois
Tunstead
Wood Street
Hickling Heath
Horsey
ANT BROADS AND MARSHES
Hickling Broad
Sco Ruston
Neatishead
Barton Broad
Catfield
HORSEY WINDMILL
WINTERTON DUNES
WROXHAM BARNS
HICKLING BROAD
MARTHAM BROAD
Ashmanhaugh
RA BOAT TRIP
East Somerton
Coltishall
Irstead
Sharp Street
Potter Heigham
West Somerton
Winterton-on-Sea
Horstead
Threehammer Common
Hoveton
Belaugh
Thurne
Martham
Wroxham
Lower Street
Bastwick
Ludham
HILLSIDE ANIMAL SANCTUARY
Upper Street
Horning
LUDHAM MARSHES
Repps
Hemsby
Newport
Wroxham Broad
Upper Street
Thurne
Rollesby
BURE MARSHES
Scratby
Crostwick
Woodbastwick
Ormesby St Michael
California
TG
Ranworth
Rackheath
Salhouse
FAIRHAVEN WOODLAND & WATER GARDEN
Clippesby
Filby Broad
Ormesby St Margaret
Burgh St Margaret
New Rackheath
Panxworth
South Walsham
Billockby
Filby
Mautby
CAISTER ROMAN TOWN
P&R
Caister-on-Sea
Little Plumstead
Upton
THE CANDLEMAKER WORKSHOP
Thrigby
THRIGBY HALL WILDLIFE GARDENS
West Caister
Sprowston
Hemblington
Runham
Thorpe End
Blofield Heath
North Burlingham
Acle
Stokesby
West End
YARMOUTH
NORWICH
Great Plumstead
GREAT YARMOUTH GREAT DENES
Thorpe St Andrew
Blofield
Damgate
Bure
Brundall
Lingwood
A47
THE
Runham
Great Yarmouth
Beighton
Tunstall
Halvergate Marshes
Postwick
Moulton St Mary
Breydon Water
SEA LIFE GREAT YARMOUTH
Strumpshaw
South Burlingham
Surlingham
Cobholm Island
Trowse Newton
Halvergate
Buckenham
BROADS
Burgh Castle
ELIZABETHAN HOUSE, MARITIME NELSON/TOLHOUSE MUSEUMS
Kirby Bedon
Hassingham
Freethorpe
Southtown
EXHIBITION GALLERIES
Wickhampton
AMAZONIA-WORLD OF REPTILES
A146
Bramerton
MID YARE
Southwood
BERNEY ARMS WINDMILL
PLEASURE BEACH
Arminghall
Rockland St Mary
Cantley
Limpenhoe
Framingham Pigot
Claxton
Bradwell
Gorleston-on-Sea
Hellington
PETTITTS ANIMAL ADVENTURE PARK
Framingham Earl
Ashby St Mary
Belton
A143
Poringland
Yelverton
Bergh Apton
Langley Street
Hardley Street
Reedham
REDWINGS HORSE SANCTUARY
Ferry
A12
Howe
Thurton
ST OLAVES PRIORY
Fritton
Hopton on Sea
Shotesham
Brooke
Chedgrave
Lower Thurlton
The Dell
Lound
Stubb's Green
Sisland
Chet
Loddon
Thurlton
Thorpe
SOMERLEYTON HALL
Seething
Blundeston
Mundham
Hales
Herringfleet
Corton
Kirstead Green
Stubbs Green
Raveningham
Haddiscoe
Somerleyton
PLEASUREWOOD HILLS LEISURE PARK
HALES HALL BARN & GARDENS
RAVENINGHAM GARDENS
Maypole Green
TM
Thwaite St Mary
Toft Monks
Oulton
A1117
LOWESTOFT AND EAST SUFFOLK MARITIME MUSEUM
Road Green
Woodton
Kirby Cane
Stockton
Wheatacre
Normanstone
Hedenham
Burgh St Peter
HERITAGE/VISITOR CENTRE
Aldeby
Oulton Broad
Topcroft
Cobbler's Green
LOWESTOFT MUSEUM
Lowestoft
Topcroft Street
Ellingham
Kirby Row
CARLTON MARSHES NATURE RESERVE
Kirkley
Ditchingham
Broome
Geldeston
Gillingham
Waveney
Beccles
Shipmeadow
Barnby
Pakefield
Great Green
Earsham
Bungay
Mettingham
Worlingham
Carlton Colville
Barsham
North Cove
Denton
Mutford
Ringsfield
Gisleham
NORFOLK AND SUFFOLK AVIATION MUSEUM
Ilketshall St Andrew
Ringsfield Corner
Hulver Street
Rushmere
Alburgh
Flixton
Kessingland
Ilketshall St Margaret
Ellough
Kessingland Beach
Homersfield
Henstead
AFRICA ALIVE
Benacre
Sotterley
St Cross South Elmham
St Michael South Elmham
Ilketshall St Lawrence
Redisham
Redenhall
Wortwell
Shadingfield
Mendham
St Margaret South Elmham
Stone Street
West End
All Saints South Elmham
BENACRE
SOUTH ELMHAM HALL
Cox Common
Wrentham
Brampton
Stoven
Clay Common
Covehithe
Withersdale Street
Frostenden
Mill Common
South Cove
Rumburgh
St James South Elmham
Spexhall
Uggeshall
Metfield
Cove Bottom
Westhall
57
Broadway
Wangford
Linstead Parva
Chediston
Reydon Smear
Fressingfield
Reydon
Holton
Little Whittingham Green
Blyford
HEN REEDBED NATURE RESERVE
SOUTHWOLD MUSEUM
Halesworth
Southwold
Chippenhall Green
Silverley's Green
Cratfield
Cookley
Wenhaston
Blyth

CAERNARFON BAY
BAE CAERNARFON
SH
LLEYN
LLEYN
PENRHYN LLYN
Malltraeth Bay
Bae Malltraeth
Newborough Forest
MODEL VILLAGE
Llanddwyn I.
Ynys Llanddwyn
The Bar
Abermenai Pt.
Trwyn Abermenai
CASTLE & REGIMENTAL MUS.
CAERNARFON AIR MUSEUM
Morfa Dinlle
Dinas Dinlle
Llandwrog
GLYNLLIFON
Pontllyfni
Aberdesach
Clynnog-fawr
Tainlon
82
Gyrn-goch
Capel Uchaf
Bryn-yr-eryr
509
BWLCH MAWR
522
GYRN DDU
Trefor
564
YR EIFL
Llanaelhaearn
Pen-sarn
WALES COAST PATH
B4417
Llithfaen
Carreg Ddu
Porth Dinllaen
Pistyll
Nefyn
Morfa Nefyn
LLEYN MARITIME MUSEUM
Llwyndyrys
Pencaenewydd
Llangybi
Edern
Fron
B4354
Llanarmon
Tan-y-graig
Rhos-fawr
Y Ffôr
Chwilog
Porth Ysgadan
Glanrhyd
PENARTH FAWR MEDIEVAL HOUSE
Rhos-y-llan
CORS GEIRCH
Boduan
A497
Llannor
A499
Abererch
Tudweiliog
HAVEN
Dinas
Efailnewydd
Rhyd-y-clafdy
Denio
Pwllheli
Porth Golmon
Garnfadryn
B4415
Carreg yr Imbill
Bryn-mawr
Llaniestyn
Penrhos
South Beach
Pen-y-graig
Llangwnnadl
Rhedyn
Penrhyn Mawr
Sarn Meyllteyrn
Llanbedrog
Pen-y-groeslon
B4413
Ty-hen
Bryncroes
Botwnnog
Nanhoron
Mynytho
Trwyn Llanbedrog
Methlem
Rhydlios
Llandegwning
304
MYNYDD RHIW
PLAS-YN-RHIW
St Tudwal's Road
Angorfa St Tudwal
Capel Carmel
Rhoshirwaun
Llawrdref Bellaf
Llangian
Rhiw
Abersoch
191
Porth Neigwl or Hell's Mouth
Llanengan
Uwchmynydd
Aberdaron
Llanfaelrhys
Sarn Bach
St Tudwal's Island East
Ynys St Tudwal Dwyrain
Bwlchtocyn
Marchroes
St Tudwal's Island West
Ynys St Tudwal Gorllewin
Bodermid
Bardsey Sound
Swnt Enlli
Pen-y-cil
Cilan Uchaf
Trwyn Cilan
167
YNYS ENLLI
Bardsey Island
Ynys Enlli
0 1 2 3 4 5 6 miles
0 1 2 3 4 5 6 7 8 9 10 km

Caernarfon
Waterloo Port
Llanrug
Pont-rug
Segontium Fort
Cwm-y-glo
Brynrefail
Deiniolen
Clwt-y-bont
Dinorwic
Caeathro
Ceunant
Llanfaglan
Saron
Bontnewydd
Croesywaun
Groeslon
Waunfawr
Glan-rhyd
Rhostryfan
Rhosgadfan
Llanwnda
Ffrwd
Groeslon
Penyffridd
Fron
Betws-Garmon
Carmel
Cilgwyn
Penygroes
Nantlle
Talysarn
Tan-yr-allt
Rhyd-Ddu
Llanllyfni
Nebo
Nasareth
Pant-glas
Upper Clynnog
Dafarn Faig
Cenin
Bryncir
Glan- Dwyfach
Llecheiddior
Garndolbenmaen
Dolbenmaen
Golan
Llanfihangel-y-pennant
Tyddyn-mawr
Rhoslan
Penmorfa
Pentrefelin
Tremadog
Llanystumdwy
Porthmadog
Criccieth
Morfa Bychan
Borth-y-Gest
Minffordd
Portmeirion
Penrhyndeudraeth
Cilfor
Caerwych
Talsarnau
Ynys
Glan-y-wern
Eisingrug
Glyn-cywarch
Morfa Harlech
Harlech
TREMADOG BAY
BAE TREMADOG
Llanfair
Llandanwg
Pen-sarn
Pen-y-bont
Pentre Gwynfryn
Llanbedr
Morfa Dyffryn
Coed Ystumgwern
Llanenddwyn
Dyffryn Ardudwy
Cors-y-Gedol
Llanddwywe
Tal-y-bont
Plas-canol
Llanaber
Cutiau
Caerdeon
Bontddu
Penmaenpool
Abergwynant
Rhydwen
Barmouth (Abermaw)
BARMOUTH BAY
The Bar
BAE BERMO
Arthog
Ynysgyfflog
Fairbourne
Friog
Llwyngwril
Llanfihangel-y-pennant
Tal-y-llyn
Llangelynin
Llanegryn
Rhoslefain
Abergynolwyn
Corris Uchaf
Corris
Aberllefenni
Aberangell
Esgairgeiliog
Minffordd
Dolgellau
Llanelltyd
Pen-y-bryn
Nannau
Brithdir
Bont Newydd
Cywarch
Y Gribin
Dinas-Mawddwy
Cwm-Cewydd
Cwm-Llinau
Dol-fôr
Cemmaes
Blaen-y-cwm
Ganllwyd
Llanfachreth
Rhydymain
Capel Hermon
Pont Fronwydd
Coed y Brenin
Forest
Bed-y-coedwr
Pont Aber-Geirw
Cwm-hesgen
Pont-Rhyd-sarn
Dolhendre
Buarthmeini
Mynydd Bryn-llech
Mynydd Bach
Bronaber
Trawsfynydd
Pont Dolydd Prysor
Cwm Prysor
Llyn Trawsfynydd
Maentwrog
Gellilydan
Bont Newydd
Llan-Ffestiniog
Tan-y-bwlch
Rhyd-y-sarn
Rhyd
Llanfrothen
Tan-lan
Garreg
Prenteg
Croesor
Nantmor
Beddgelert
Pass of Aberglaslyn
Nantgwynant
Bethania
Ffridd-Uchaf
Beddgelert Forest
Tanygrisiau
Blaenau Ffestiniog
Rhiwbryfdir
Bethania
Congl-y-wal
Pont yr Afon-Gam
Migneint
Cwm Penmachno
Carrog
Penmachno
Gwydyr Forest
Pentre-bont
Dolwyddelan
Garnedd
Pont- y-pant
Mynydd Cribau
Pen-y-Gwryd Hotel
Pass of Llanberis
Nant Peris
Llanberis
Capel Curig
Pont Cyfyng
Betws-y-Coed
Pont Rhyd-goch
Pont Pen-y-benglog
Llyn Ogwen
Llyn Cowlyd
Llyn Crafnant
Trefriw
Tal-y-lan
Tai
Gwydyr Uchaf
Cornel
Llanrwst
Llanddoged
Pentre-tafarn-y-fedw
Melin-y-coed
Capel Garmon
Fairy Glen
Conwy Falls
Rhaeadr Conwy
Nebo
Glan-Conwy
Padog
Ysbyty Ifan
Llyn Conwy
Llyn Arenig fawr
Llidiardau
Snowdon
Yr Wyddfa
Gwynedd
SH

Llandudno
Conwy
Colwyn Bay (Bae Colwyn)
Llandudno Junction (Cyffordd Llandudno)
Abergele
Rhyl (Y Rhyl)
Prestatyn
Rhuddlan
Dyserth
St Asaph (Llanelwy)
Denbigh (Dinbych)
Ruthin (Rhuthun)
Llanrwst
Betws-y-Coed
Corwen
Bala (Y Bala)
Llanuwchllyn
Conwy
Denbighshire (Sir Ddinbych)
Gwynedd
Snowdonia National Park
Parc Cenedlaethol Eryri
Berwyn
Clwydian Range
Vale of Conwy
Dyffryn Conwy
Vale of Clwyd
Dyffryn Clwyd
Gwydyr Forest
Clocaenog Forest
Cynwyd Forest
Aberhirnant Forest
Llyn Tegid or Bala Lake
Alwen Reservoir
Llyn Brenig
Llyn Aled
Llyn Celyn
Llyn Conwy
Migneint
Conwy Sands
Traeth Conwy
Great Orme Copper Mines
Tramway
Toll
Penrhynside
Penrhyn Bay
Rhos-on-Sea
Llandrillo-yn-Rhos
Craig-y-don
Deganwy
Llanrhos
Tywyn
Mochdre
Welsh Mountain Zoo
Old Colwyn
Llanddulas
Llysfaen
Abergele Roads
Pensarn
Towyn
Kinmel Bay
Sealife Aquarium
Y-Ffrith
Gronant
Gwespyr
Ffynnongroyw
Picton
Meliden
Gwaenysgor
Llanasa
Offa's Dyke Path
Axton
Trelawnyd
Whitford
Cwm
Pant-y-Wacco
Rhuallt
Bodelwyddan
St George
Pen-y-cefn
Tremeirchion
Waen
Caerwys
Afon-Wen Craft and Antique Centre
Goleugoed
Glascoed
Groesffordd Marli
St Asaph Cathedral
Bodfari
Afon-wen
Plas-yn-Cefn
Trefnant
Bont-newydd
Cefn Berain
Green
Henllan
Castell
Fron
Llangwyfan
Llandyrnog
Llangynhafal
Llanynys
Gellifor
Moel Famau
Llanrhaeadr
Prion
Pentre Llanrhaeadr
Peniel
Rhewl
Hirwaen
Llanbedr-Dyffryn-Clwyd
Craft Centre
Llanfwrog
Bontuchel
Cyffylliog
Tai-Ucha
Nant Uchaf
Efenechtyd
Pwll-glas
Llanfair-Dyffryn-Clwyd
Nilig
Pennant
Clocaenog
Clawdd-newydd
Pentre-celyn
Derwen
Rhyd-y-meudwy
Llanelidan
Bryn Saith Marchog
Melin-y-Wig
Bryneglwys
Betws Gwerfil Goch
Gwyddelwern
Morfydd
Maerdy
Dinmael
Ty-nant
Druid
Carrog
Llangollen Steam Railway
Lidiart-y-parc
Glyndyfrdwy
Glan-yr-afon
Glassblobbery
Cynwyd
Wenallt
Foel Goch
Tai-mawr
Llangwm
Bethel
Sarnau
Cefn-ddwysarn
Llandderfel
Llandrillo
Pale
Cefn Coch
Pennant
Blaen-y-Cwm
Moel Sych
Pistyll Rhaeadr
Tyn-y-fedwen
Tyn-y-ffridd
Moel Fferna
Pentre
Bryn Du
Pencraig
Llangynog
Cefn Coch
Llanrhaeadr-ym-Mochnant
Pennant Melangell
Pont Cwm Pydew
Aber-Hirnant
Rhos-y-gwaliau
Llangower
Llanfor
Llanycil
Rhiwlas
Rhyd-uchaf
Frongoch
Ciltalgarth
Llidiardau
Llyn Arenig fawr
Arenig Fawr
Arenig Fach
Moel Llyfrant
Parc
Buarthmeini
Dolhendre
Mynydd Bryn-llech
Mynydd Bach
Bala Lake Rly
Talardd
Ty-nant
Foel y Geifr
Cwm Cynllwyd
Cwm-hesgen
Pont-Rhyd-y-fen
Bed-y-coedwr
Capel Hermon
Cwm Prysor
Pont yr Afon-Gam
Carnedd y Filiast
Pen-y-gop
Ty Mawr Cwm
Ffynnon Wen
Garn Prys
Afon Ceirw
Cerrigydrudion
Llanfihangel Glyn Myfyr
Glasfryn
Cefn-brith
Pentre-llyn cymmer
Rhydlydan
Pentrefoelas
Hafod-Dinbych
Mwdwl-eithin
Padog
Ysbyty Ifan
Penmachno
Cwm Penmachno
Carrog
Ty Mawr Wybrnant
Glan-Conwy
Conwy Falls
Rhaeadr Conwy
Fairy Glen
Capel Garmon
Burial Chamber
Nebo
Conwy Valley Railway Museum
Moel Seisiog
Swallow Falls
Mynydd Cribau
Ty-draw
Gwytherin
Tŷ'r-felin-isaf
Pandy Tudur
Llanddoged
Pentre-tafarn-y-fedw
Melin-y-coed
Gwydyr Uchaf Chapel
Cornel
Tai
Trefriw
Woollen Mill
Tan-lan
Bryn-glas
Hendre-ddu
Llangernyw
Pentre Isaf
Gell
Cefn-coch
Pentre'r Felin
Eglwysbach
Graig
Bodnant
Tal-y-cafn
Rowen
Ty'n-y-groes
Pontwgan
Tal-y-Bont
Dolgarrog
Surf Snowdonia
Coed Dolgarrog
Henryd
Felin Isaf Water Mill
Gyffin
Aberconwy House/Plas Mawr
Dolwyd
Glan-Conwy
Bryn-y-maen
Pentrefelin
Llanelian-yn-Rhos
Rhyd-y-foel
Dolwen
Betws-yn-Rhos
Dawn
Hafod-lom
Moelfre Uchaf
Moelfre Isaf
Llanfair Talhaiarn
Llannefydd
Bryn-nantllech
Bryn Rhyd-yr-Arian
Llansannan
Tan-y-fron
Clwt-grugoer
Bylchau
Waen
Nantglyn
Saron
Meifod
Groes
Castle & Town Walls
Bryn Trillyn
Gorsedd Bran
Mynydd Hiraethog
Hafod Elwy Moor
Llyn Brenig Visitor Centre
Brenig Res.
A55
A470
A5
A543
A544
A548
A525
A547
A541
A494
A4212
A5104
B5113
B5106
B5381
B5382
B5384
B5383
B5435
B4501
B5105
B5428
B5429
B5119
B4406
B4407
B4391
B4401
B4402
B4403
B5437
B5122
B5151
SH
83
85
71
59
0 1 2 3 4 5 6 miles
0 1 2 3 4 5 6 7 8 9 10 km

Flintshire
(Sir Y Fflint)
Wrexham
(Wrecsam)
Cheshire
West and Chester
Halton
Thurstaston
Irby
Thingwall
Storeton
Port Sunlight
Pensby
Barnston
Brimstage
Bromborough
Eastham
Eastham Ferry
Garston
Speke Hall
Speke
Liverpool John Lennon
Liverpool Airport
Runcorn
Hale
River Dee
Afon Dyfrdwy
Heswall
Thornton Hough
Mostyn Quay
Mostyn
Glan-y-don
Dawpool Bank
Gayton
Raby
Mersey
Weston
Preston Brook
Sutton Weaver
Ellesmere Port
Boat Museum
Ince Banks
Greenfield
Greenfield Valley Heritage Park
Holywell Bank
Gayton Sands
Parkgate
Hinderton
Willaston
Hooton
Childer Thornton
Carmel
Walwen
Neston
Newtown
Frodsham
Gorsedd
Holywell
(Treffynnon)
Little Neston
Ness
Ness Gardens
Little Sutton
Overpool
Stanlow
Ince
Elton
Chester Services
Overton
Fivecrosses
Bagillt
Great Sutton
Whitby
Whitbyheath
Cheshire Oak
Helsby
Wales Coast Path
Brynford
Dolphin
Burton
Two Mills
Ledsham
Little Stanney
Blue Planet Aquarium
Thornton-le-Moors
Elton Green
Hapsford
Alvanley
Newton
Kingsley
Babell
Puddington
Capenhurst
Backford Cross
Stoak
Birch Hill
Delamere
Pentre Halkyn
Flint (Y Fflint)
Mount Pleasant
Chester
Dunham-on-the-Hill
Manley
Delamere Forest
Ysceifiog
Lixwm
Shotwick
Wervin
Backford
Picton
Rhes-y-cae
Halkyn
Halkyn Mountain
Oakenholt
Connah's Quay
Saughall
Mollington
Mickle Trafford
Bridge Trafford
Mouldsworth
Visitor Centre
Flint Mountain
Garden City
Upton
Little Barrow
Nannerch
Rhosesmor
Sealand
Great Barrow
Ashton
Northop
Northop Hall
Shotton
Guilden Sutton
Hendre
Wepre
Queensferry
Blacon
Hoole
Stamford Bridge
Kelsall
Kelsall Hill
Rhydymwyn
Sandycroft
Littleton
Tarvin
Oscroft
Willington Corner
New Brighton
Ewloe Grn
Ewloe
Mancot
Greenacres
Hawarden
(Penarlâg)
Handbridge
Dewa
Grosvenor
Christleton
Duddon
Utkinton
Cotebrook
Cilcain
Buckley
(Bwcle)
Drury
Saltney
Brown Heath
Gwernaffield
Loggerheads
Mold
(Yr Wyddgrug)
Broughton
Bretton
Rowton
Waverton
Burton
Clotton
Moel Famau
Cadole
Mynydd-isa
Spon Green
Llong
Milner's Heath
Hargrave
Birch Heath
Tafarn-y-gelyn
Gwernymynydd
Lower Kinnerton
Eccleston
Saighton
Hatton Heath
Brassey Green
Maeshafn
Nercwys
Penyffordd
Dodleston
Balderton
Huxley
Higher Kinnerton
Shropshire Union Canal
Gatesheath
Pontbllyddyn
Llanferres
Leeswood
Bruera
Newton
Tiverton
Coed-Talon
Hope
(Yr Hôb)
Burton Green
Pulford
Aldford
Tattenhall
Beeston Castle
Waun-y-Llyn
Eryrys
Treuddyn
Lavister
Milton Green
Beeston
Bunbury Heath
Caergwrle
Rossett
Handley
Higher Burwardsley
Trevalyn
Aldersey Green
Burwardsley
Llanarmon-yn-Ial
Llanfynydd
Cefn-y-bedd
Llay
Marford
Churton
Chowley
Peckforton
Graianrhyd
Coddington
Harthill
Cheshire Candle Workshop
Rhydtalog
Ffrith
Farndon
Clutton
Barnhill
Graig-fechan
Brymbo
Alyn Waters
Moss
Gresford
Holt
Broxton
Bulkeley
Barton
Gwersyllt
Bwlchgwyn
Four Crosses
Borras Head
Crewe
Stretton
Fuller's Moor
Gallantry Bank
Llandegla
Gwynfryn
Rhosrobin
Garden Village
Bickerton
Minera
Lead Mines
Moss Valley
Acton
Ridleywood
Pen-y-stryt
Offa's Dyke Path
New Broughton
Llan-y-pwll
Tilston
Edge Green
Duckington
Cholmondeley Castle Gdns
Coedpoeth
Rhosnesni
Castletown
Horton Green
Wrexham
(Wrecsam)
Isycoed
Esclusham Mountain
Bersham
Llwybr Clawdd Offa
Cyrn y Brain
Wrexham Industrial Estate
Hampton Heath
Rhostyllen
King's Mills
Bowling Bank
Shocklach
Ebnal
Bickley Moss
Talwrn
Erddig
Chorlton Lane
No Man's Heath
Pentredwr
Eglwyseg Mountain
Malpas
Marchwiel
Cross Lanes
Farmworld
Llantysilio Mountain
Tai-nant
Johnstown
Sontley
Worthenbury
Rhosllanerchrugog
Cuddington Heath
Marbury
Llandynan
Ruabon Mountain
Stryt-issa
Cock Bank
Bangor-is-y-coed
Threapwood
Bell o' th' Hill
Rhewl
Penycae
Gyfelia
Eyton
Bangor
Eliseg's Pillar
Valle Crucis Abbey
Llangollen Motor Mus
Wirswall
Tallarn Green
Higher Wych
Canal Exhibition Centre
Acrefair
Overton Bridge
Cloy
Cefn-mawr
Ruabon
(Rhiwabon)
Overton
(Owrtyn)
Garth
Pont Cysyllte
Brook
Brooklands
Whitchurch
Llangollen
Llangollen Exhibition Centre
Plas Newydd
New Bridge
Rhos-y-Madoc
Erbistock
Lightwood Green
Chemistry
Eglwys Cross
Horseman's Green
Tŷ Mawr
Redbrook
Waymills
Froncysyllte
Pentre
Sandy Lane
The Chequer
Halton
Knolton Bryn
Knolton
Penley
Hanmer
Alkington
Street Lydan
Arowry
Bronington
Plas Nantyr
Glyn-Ceiriog
Pontfadog
Chirk Castle
Chirk
(Y Waun)
Dudleston
Street Dinas
Ifton Heath
Dudleston Heath
Fenn's, Whixall and Bettisfield Mosses
Tilstock
Tyn-y-celyn
Bronygarth
Chirk Bank
Llwynmawr
Breaden Heath
Hollinwood
Pandy
Preesgweene
Weston Rhyn
St Martin's
Elson
Llangollen Canal
Welsh End
New Marton
Ellesmere
Welshampton
The Mere
Bettisfield
Whixall
Tregeiriog
Craignant
Perthy
Balmer Heath
Wem Moss
Prees
Llechrydau
Selattyn
Hengoed
Gobowen
Colemere
Lyneal
Northwood
Waterloo
Quina Brook
Hindford
Tetchill
Llanarmon Dyffryn Ceiriog
Rhiwlas
Welsh Frankton
Colemere
Lee
Edstaston
Whittington Castle
Pant-glas
Old Oswestry Hill Fort
Llawnt
Lower Frankton
Wolverley
Newtown
Cefn Canol
Rhydycroesau
Whittington
Hordley
English Frankton
Llangadwaladr
Babbinswood
Oswestry
Oswestry Transport Mus
Kenwick
Horton
Lowe
Wem
Tai-bach
Llansilin
Tyn-y-coed
Middleton
Lower Hordley
Cockshutt
Loppington
Moelfre
Wootton
Rednal
Stanwardine in the Wood
Tilley
Aston
Morda
Queen's Head
Noneley
Lee Brockhurst
Trefonen
Ball
Haughton
Bagley
Pett
Treflach
Maesbury
Grimpo
Westoncommon
Weston
Burlton
Preston
West Felton

Halton
Runcorn
Hale
Weston
Halton
Norton
Daresbury
Hatton
Stretton
Lower Stretton
Appleton Thorn
Sworton Heath
High Legh
Rostherne Mere
Ashley
Thorns Green
Styal
Morley Green
New Mills
Tatton House
WILMSLOW
Davenport Green
Mobberley
Knolls Green
Alderley Edge
Knutsford
Over Knutsford
Ollerton
Nether Alderley
Marthall
Chelford
Over Peover
Peover Heath
Monks Heath
Capesthorne Hall
Withington Green
Siddington
Lower Withington
Jodrell Bank Visitor Centre
Blackden Heath
Goostrey
Twemlow Green
Cranage
Holmes Chapel
Gleadsmoss
Swettenham
Newsbank
Sandlow Green
Hulme Walfield
Brereton Green
Brereton Heath
West Heath
Arclid
Astbury
Brownlow
Brookhouse Green
Fourlanes End
Brownlow Heath
Little Moreton Hall
Hassall Green
Scholar Green
Thurlwood
Rode Heath
Mount Pleasant
Church Lawton
Alsager
Kidsgrove
Talke
Radway Green
Freeport Talke
Red Street
Audley
Chesterton
Bradwell
Alsagers Bank
Halmer End
Knutton
Silverdale
Madeley Heath
Keele
Newcastle-under-Lyme
Clayton
Keele Services
Madeley Park
Whitmore
Hanchurch
Baldwin's Gate
Stableford
Beech
Maer
Chapel Chorlton
Cranberry
Cotes
Standon
Millmeece
Slindon
Croxton
Sugnall
Sturbridge
Pershall
Eccleshall
Wootton
Ellenhall
High Offley
Adbaston
Knighton
Shebdon
Woodseaves
Sutton Weaver
Aston
Preston on the Hill
Dutton
Higher Whitley
Lower Whitley
Dones Green
Comberbach
Great Budworth
Arley
Arley Hall
Bate Heath
Holehouses
Cheshire County Showground
Pickmere
Higher Wincham
Tabley
Knutsford Services
Plumley
Smithy Green
Lower Peover
Swan Green
Peover Hall
Lostock Gralam
Lostock Green
Lach Dennis
Broken Cross
Rudheath
Northwich
Wincham
Marston
Anderton
Marbury
Anderton Boat Lift
Barnton
Little Leigh
Acton Bridge
Crowton
Weaverham
Hartford
Cuddington
Sandiway
Norley
Davenham
Moulton
Whitegate
Bostock Green
Puddinglake
Byley
Foxwist Green
Wharton Green
Wharton
Sproston Green
Middlewich
WINSFORD
Salterswall
Little Budworth
Over
Church Hill
School Green
Oulton Park
Rushton
Eaton
Tarporley
Rhuddall Heath
Occlestone Green
Bradwall Green
Elworth
Moston Green
Sandbach
Sandbach Services
Warmingham
Wettenhall
Church Minshull
Cholmondeston
Bradfield Green
Coppenhall Moss
Wheelock
Wheelock Heath
Barrows Green
Maw Green
Winterley
Hassall
Haslington
Crewe
Worleston
Woolstanwood
Wistaston Green
Wistaston
Wells Green
Gresty Green
Willaston
Weston
Shavington
Barthomley
Englesea-brook
Hough
Gorsteyhill
Balterley
Betley
Wybunbury
Walgherton
Stapeley
Butt Green
Nantwich
Acton
Burland
Burford
Faddiley
Ravensmoor
Larden Green
Chorley
Sound
Sound Heath
Broomhall
Wrenbury
Norbury
Aston
Newhall
Marley Green
Marbury
Hatherton
Hunsterson
Blakenhall
Wrinehill
Checkley
Madeley
Hankelow
Audlem
Buerton
Kinsey Heath
Lightwood Green
Coxbank
Woore
Ireland's Cross
Pipe Gate
Onneley
Knighton
Willoughbridge
The Dorothy Clive Garden
Bearstone
Blackbrook
Adderley
Norton in Hales
Mucklestone
Ashley Heath
Ashley
Podmore
Hookgate
Loggerheads
Almington
Betton
Market Drayton
Hales
Chatcull
Wetwood
Croxtonbank
Fairoak
Bishop's Offley
Chipnall
The Four Alls
Woodseaves
Cheswardine
Soudley
Goldstone Hall
Sutton
Rosehill
Ternhill
Longford
Moreton Say
Sandford
Bletchley
Darliston
Fauls
Lostford
Wollerton
Wollerton Old Hall
Stoke Heath
Wistanswick
Marchamley
Hodnet
Hodnet Hall
Mill Green
Lockleywood
Hinstock
Stoke on Tern
Hawkstone Park
Ellerton
Child's
Frodsham
Newtown
Overton
Fivecrosses
Helsby
Newton
Alvanley
Hapsford
Kingsley
Commonside
Birch Hill
Delamere Forest
Delamere Forest Park
Visitor Centre
Manley
Mouldsworth
Hatchmere
Ashton
Oakmere
Delamere
Kelsall
Kelsall Hill
Oscroft
Willington Corner
Little Budworth
Whitegate Way
Dunham-on-the-Hill
Bridge Trafford
Little Barrow
Great Barrow
Guilden Sutton
Stamford Bridge
Picton
Elton
Elton Green
Ince
Ince Banks
Chester Services
Cheshire
Cheshire West and Chester
Littleton
Christleton
Cotebrook
Utkinton
Duddon
Clotton
Burton
Waverton
Milner's Heath
Hargrave
Hatton Heath
Gatesheath
Huxley
Birch Heath
Brassey Green
Four Lane Ends
Tilstone Fearnall
Tiverton
Newton
Alpraham
Calveley
Wardle
Aston juxta Mondrum
Barbridge
Bunbury
Beeston
Beeston Castle
Bunbury Heath
Spurstow
Haughton Moss
Radmore Green
Tattenhall
Milton Green
Handley
Higher Burwardsley
Burwardsley
Cheshire Candle Workshops
Peckforton
Chowley
Harthill
Clutton
Barnhill
Broxton
Barton
Bulkeley
Gallantry Bank
Fuller's Moor
Bickerton
Duckington
Cholmondeley Castle Gdns
Edge Green
Tilston
Castletown
Horton Green
Hampton Heath
Bickley Moss
Shocklach
Ebnal
Chorlton Lane
Malpas
No Man's Heath
Cuddington Heath
Threapwood
Bell o' th' Hill
Higher Wych
Wirswall
Grindley Brook
Brooklands
Chemistry
Whitchurch
Eglwys Cross
Redbrook
Waymills
Broughall
Ash Magna
The Chequer
Hanmer
Arowry
Alkington
Bronington
Tilstock
Prees Heath
Ightfield
Newstreet Lane
Calverhall
Fenn's, Whixall and Bettisfield Mosses
Hollinwood
Welsh End
Prees Higher Heath
Llangollen Canal
Bettisfield
Wem Moss
Whixall
Lyneal
Northwood
Waterloo
Quina Brook
Prees
Prees Lower Heath
Edstaston
Newtown
Prees Green
Wolverley
English Frankton
Horton
Lowe
Wem
Cockshutt
Loppington
Petton
Burlton
Preston
Hopton
Shropshire Union Canal
Staffordshire
SJ
Weaver
0 1 2 3 4 5 6 miles
0 1 2 3 4 5 6 7 8 9 10 km

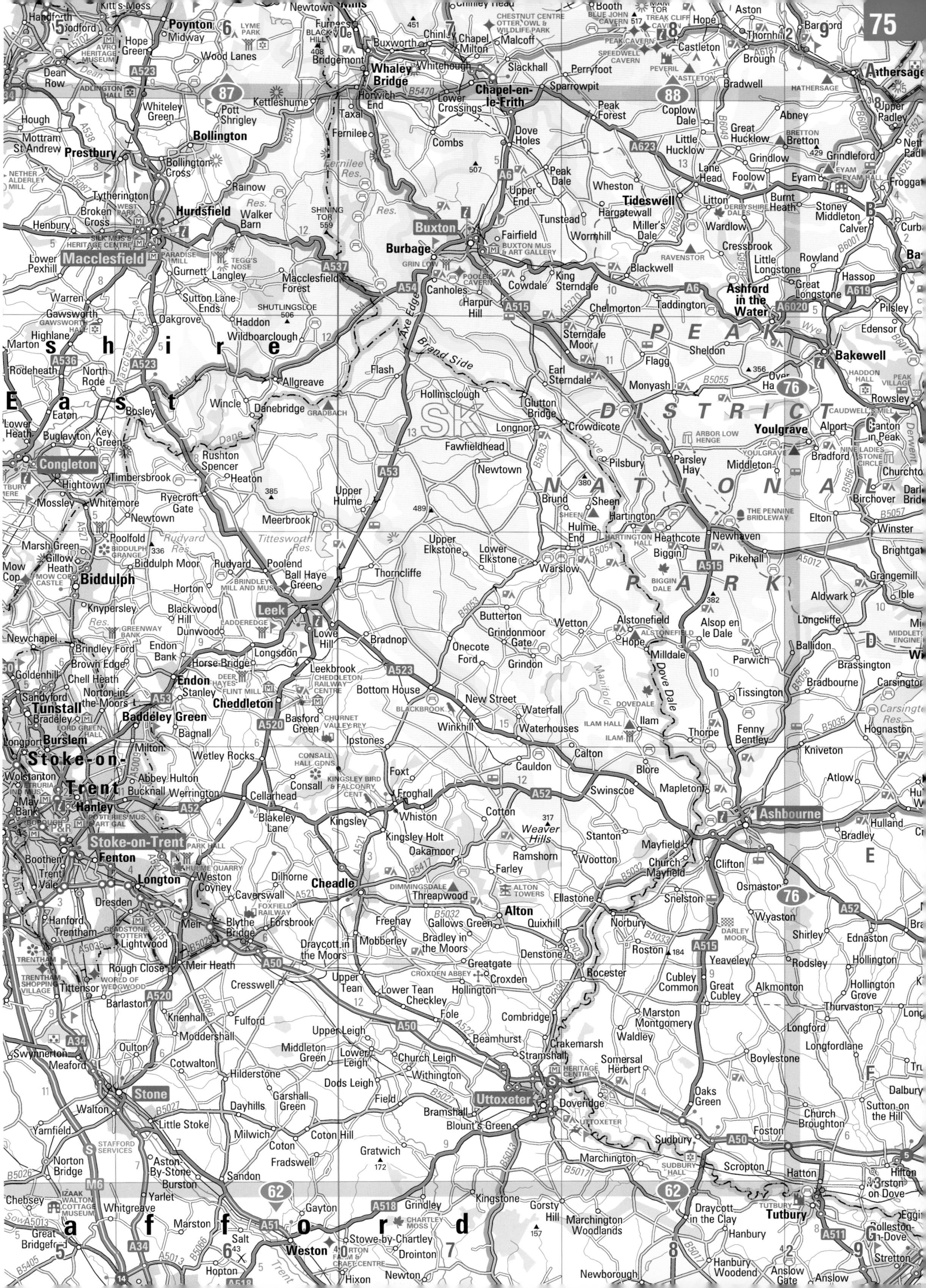

Handforth
Poynton
Lyme Park
Newtown
Furness Vale
Chinley
Chapel Milton
Malcoff
Booth
Aston
Bamford
Hope
Castleton
Brough
Bradwell
Hathersage
Peak Cavern
Speedwell Cavern
Blue John Cavern
Treak Cliff Cavern
Peveril Castle
Chestnut Centre Otter, Owl & Wildlife Park
Buxworth
Bridgemont
Whaley Bridge
Whitehough
Slackhall
Perryfoot
Sparrowpit
Chapel-en-le-Frith
Horwich End
Kettleshulme
Taxal
Fernilee
Fernilee Res.
Combs
Dove Holes
Peak Forest
Coplow Dale
Great Hucklow
Little Hucklow
Abney
Bretton
Grindleford
Upper Padley
Nether Padley
Froggatt
Eyam
Eyam Hall
Foolow
Grindlow
Lane Head
Wheston
Tideswell
Litton
Hargatewall
Miller's Dale
Tunstead
Wormhill
Fairfield
Peak Dale
Upper End
Burnt Heath
Stoney Middleton
Calver
Curbar
Wardlow
Cressbrook
Ravenstor
Little Longstone
Great Longstone
Rowland
Hassop
Ashford in the Water
Pilsley
Edensor
Bakewell
Haddon Hall
Over Haddon
Rowsley
Peak Village
Sheldon
Taddington
Blackwell
Chelmorton
King Sterndale
Cowdale
Harpur Hill
Canholes
Buxton
Buxton Mus & Art Gallery
Burbage
Grin Low
Poole's Cavern
Macclesfield Forest
Macclesfield
Silk Mus & Heritage Centre
Paradise Mill
Hurdsfield
Tytherington
Prestbury
Bollington
Bollington Cross
Rainow
Walker Barn
Shining Tor 559
Pott Shrigley
Whiteley Green
Hope Green
Wood Lanes
Adlington Hall
Dean Row
Hough
Mottram St Andrew
Nether Alderley Mill
Broken Cross
West Park
Henbury
Lower Pexhill
Gurnett
Langley
Tegg's Nose
Sutton Lane Ends
Warren
Gawsworth
Gawsworth Hall
Oakgrove
Haddon
Shutlingsloe 506
Wildboarclough
Highlane
Marton
Cheshire
Rodeheath
North Rode
Allgreave
Flash
Axe Edge
Brand Side
Wincle
Danebridge
Gradbach
Hollinsclough
Earl Sterndale
Sterndale Moor
Flagg
Monyash
Glutton Bridge
Longnor
Crowdicote
Peak District National Park
Youlgrave
Alport
Stanton in Peak
Bradford
Nine Ladies Stone Circle
Arbor Low Henge
Parsley Hay
Middleton
Pilsbury
Fawfieldhead
Newtown
Hartington
Hartington Hall
Sheen
Brund
Hulme End
Heathcote
Biggin
Newhaven
Elton
Winster
Birchover
Churchtown
Darley Bridge
The Pennine Bridleway
Brightgate
Pikehall
Grangemill
Aldwark
Ible
East Cheshire
Eaton
Bosley
Lower Heath
Buglawton
Key Green
Congleton
Hightown
Timbersbrook
Rushton Spencer
Heaton
Ryecroft Gate
Newtown
Mossley
Whitemore
Poolfold
Biddulph Grange
Rudyard Res.
Marsh Green
Gillow Heath
Mow Cop
Mow Cop Castle
Biddulph
Biddulph Moor
Rudyard
Horton
Poolend
Ball Haye Green
Brindley Mill and Mus
Upper Hulme
Meerbrook
Tittesworth Res.
Thorncliffe
Upper Elkstone
Lower Elkstone
Warslow
Knypersley
Blackwood Hill
Dunwood
Leek
Lowe Hill
Bradnop
Butterton
Grindonmoor Gate
Wetton
Alstonefield
Hope
Alsop en le Dale
Ballidon
Longcliffe
Newchapel
Brindley Ford
Greenway Bank
Brown Edge
Endon Bank
Horse Bridge
Longsdon
Leekbrook
Onecote
Ford
Grindon
Milldale
Dove Dale
Parwich
Brassington
Bradbourne
Carsington
Carsington Res.
Goldenhill
Chell Heath
Sandyford
Tunstall
Bradeley
Endon
Stanley
Norton-in-the-Moors
Deep Hayes
Flint Mill
Cheddleton
Cheddleton Railway Centre
Bottom House
Blackbrook
New Street
Waterfall
Waterhouses
Manifold
Dovedale
Ilam Hall
Ilam
Thorpe
Tissington
Fenny Bentley
Hognaston
Baddeley Green
Ford Green Hall
Bagnall
Basford Green
Churnet Valley Rly
Ipstones
Winkhill
Calton
Kniveton
Burslem
Longport
Milton
Wetley Rocks
Consall Hall Gdns
Stoke-on-Trent
Wolstanton
Etruria
Abbey Hulton
Bucknall
Werrington
Cellarhead
Consall
Kingsley Bird & Falconry Cent
Foxt
Froghall
Cauldon
Blore
Swinscoe
Mapleton
Atlow
Hanley
Potteries Mus & Art Gal
Blakeley Lane
Kingsley
Whiston
Cotton
Weaver Hills
Stanton
Ashbourne
Hulland
Bradley
Park Hall
Kingsley Holt
Oakamoor
Ramshorn
Wootton
Mayfield
Church Mayfield
Clifton
Boothen
Fenton
Trent Vale
Longton
Hulme Quarry
Weston Coyney
Dilhorne
Cheadle
Dimmingsdale
Threapwood
Farley
Alton Towers
Ellastone
Snelston
Osmaston
Wyaston
Ednaston
Shirley
Dresden
Caverswall
Foxfield Railway
Alton
Quixhill
Norbury
Darley Moor
Roston
Yeaveley
Rodsley
Hollington
Hanford
Trentham
Gladstone Pottery
Meir
Blythe Bridge
Forsbrook
Freehay
Gallows Green
Bradley in the Moors
Mobberley
Draycott in the Moors
Denstone
Lightwood
Meir Heath
Trentham Gardens
Trentham Shopping Village
Rough Close
Tittensor
World of Wedgwood
Cresswell
Upper Tean
Lower Tean
Checkley
Croxden Abbey
Croxden
Hollington
Greatgate
Rocester
Cubley Common
Great Cubley
Alkmonton
Hollington Grove
Thurvaston
Barlaston
Knenhall
Moddershall
Fulford
Fole
Combridge
Marston Montgomery
Waldley
Longford
Longfordlane
Swynnerton
Meaford
Oulton
Cotwalton
Hilderstone
Middleton Green
Upper Leigh
Lower Leigh
Church Leigh
Withington
Beamhurst
Crakemarsh
Stramshall
Somersal Herbert
Boylestone
Stone
Walton
Little Stoke
Dayhills
Garshall Green
Dods Leigh
Field
Uttoxeter
Doveridge
Bramshall
Blount's Green
Oaks Green
Church Broughton
Sutton on the Hill
Dalbury
Yarnfield
Stafford Services
Norton Bridge
Aston-By-Stone
Burston
Yarlet
Milwich
Coton
Coton Hill
Fradswell
Sandon
Gratwich
Marchington
Sudbury
Sudbury Hall
Foston
Scropton
Hatton
Hilton
Marston on Dove
Chebsey
Izaak Walton Cottage Museum
Whitgreave
Gayton
Grindley
Kingstone
Gorsty Hill
Marchington Woodlands
Draycott in the Clay
Tutbury
Tutbury Castle
Hanbury
Rolleston-on-Dove
Egginton
Great Bridgeford
Marston
Salt
Weston
Stowe-by-Chartley
Chartley Moss
Drointon
Hopton
Hixon
Newton
Newborough
Hanbury Woodend
Anslow Gate
Anslow
Stretton
Staffordshire
Trent
Sow
A523
A537
A54
A6
A515
A5270
A623
A619
A6020
A536
A53
A520
A52
A50
A34
A51
A518
A511
A5013
A5009
A5035
M6
B5470
B5032
B5033
B5027
B5017
B5013
B5066
B5026
B5405
B5053
B5054
B5055
B5056
B5057
B5035
B5417
B6049
B6001
B6012

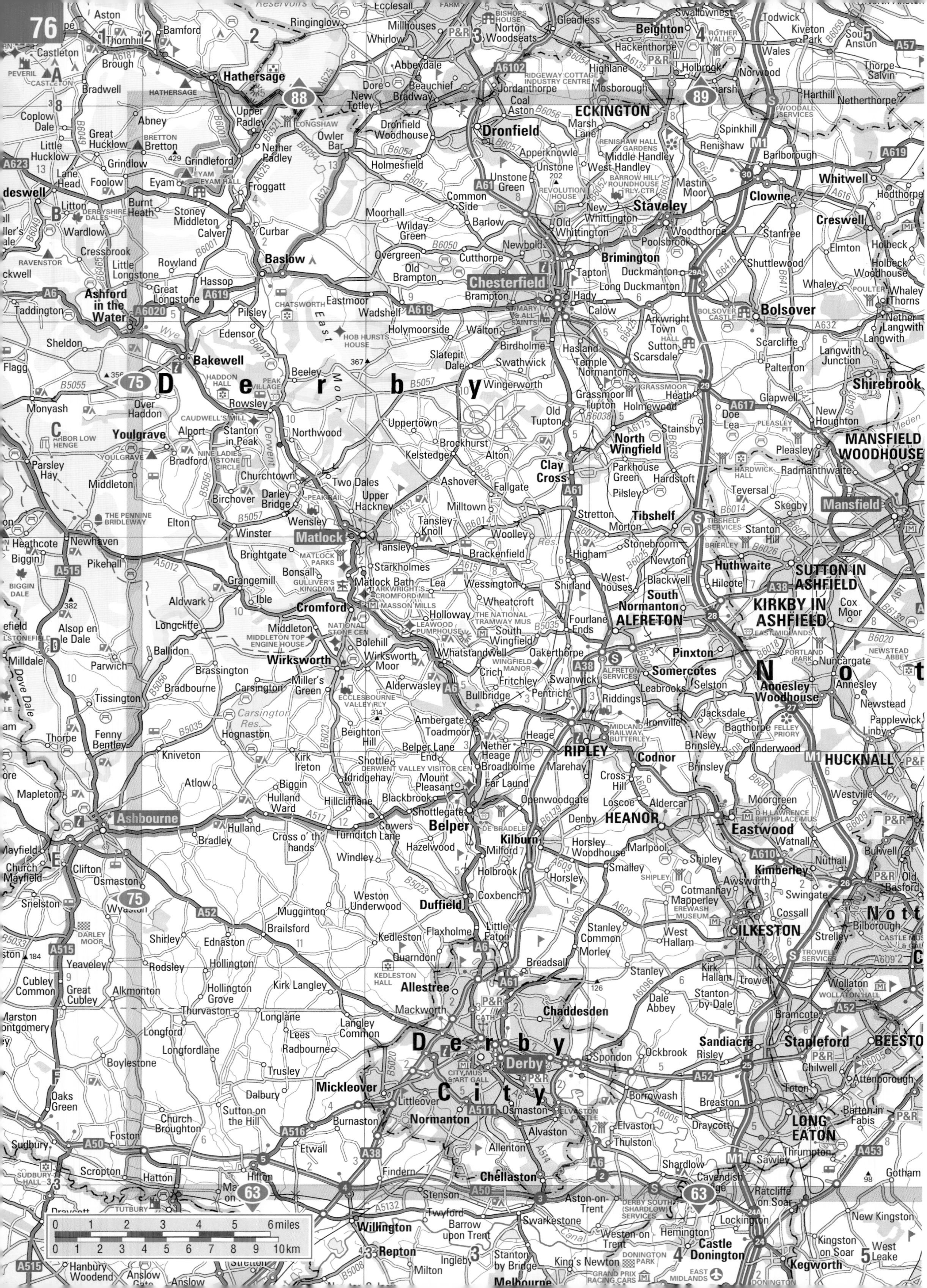
Derby
Derby City
Nott
Chesterfield
Matlock
Ashbourne
Mansfield
Bakewell
Dronfield
ECKINGTON
Staveley
Bolsover
Clowne
Whitwell
Creswell
Shirebrook
MANSFIELD WOODHOUSE
SUTTON IN ASHFIELD
KIRKBY IN ASHFIELD
ALFRETON
RIPLEY
HEANOR
Belper
Wirksworth
Cromford
Duffield
Allestree
ILKESTON
Eastwood
HUCKNALL
Kimberley
Stapleford
Sandiacre
LONG EATON
Castle Donington
Kegworth
Mickleover
Normanton
Chellaston
Hathersage
Baslow
Youlgrave
Clay Cross
Tibshelf
Codnor
Hatton
Willington
Repton
Melbourne
Beighton
Bolsover
0 1 2 3 4 5 6 miles
0 1 2 3 4 5 6 7 8 9 10 km

Woodsetts
Wigthorpe
Gateford
Shireoaks
Rhodesia
Darfoulds
Worksop
Manton
Kilton
Scofton
Ranby
Babworth
West Retford
RETFORD
Ordsall
BASSETLAW MUSEUM
Sutton
Hayton
Clarborough
Welham
North Leverton with Habblesthorpe
NORTH LEVERTON WINDMILL
Littleborough
Sturton le Steeple
Knaith
Gate Burton
Marton
Willingham by Stow
Normanby by Stow
Stow
Cammeringham
Thorpe in the Fallows
Brattleby
Coates
South Leverton
Sturton by Stow
Brampton
Torksey
Cottam
Aisthorpe
Scampton
Bransby
Broxholme
North Carlton
Grove
Eaton
Treswell
SUNDOWN ADVENTURELAND
Rampton
Woodbeck
Headon
Stokeham
Church Laneham
Fenton
Ingleby
South Carlton
Gamston
Upton
Laneham
Laughterton
Kettlethorpe
Saxilby
Odder
Burton
CLUMBER PARK
Hardwick Village
CRESWELL CRAGS MUSEUM
Elkesley
West Drayton
Askham
Markham Moor
East Drayton
Dunham
Newton on Trent
MUSEUM OF LINCOLNSHIRE LIFE
Poulter
Bothamsall
MARKHAM MOOR SERVICES
Darlton
Ragnall
Broadholme
Great Lake
Carburton
Haughton
Milton
West Markham
East Markham
Fledborough
Thorney
Norton
Bevercotes
Skellingthorpe
Perlethorpe
Walesby
Tuxford
WALKS OF LIFE
North Clifton
Harby
Cuckney
Trent
High Marnham
DODDINGTON HALL
Church Warsop
Budby
Meden Vale
HAMLYN LODGE COTTAGE INDUSTRY
Kirton
Normanton on Trent
South Clifton
Wigsley
Doddington
Birchwood
Boultham
SHERWOOD FOREST
Low Marnham
Spalford
HARTSHOLME
Market Warsop
Maun
New Ollerton
Egmanton
Weston
Grassthorpe
Eagle Moor
Bracebridge
LINCOLNSHIRE ROAD TRANSPORT MUSEUM
VISITORS CENTRE
Boughton
Laxton
Eagle
North Scarle
Whisby
WHISBY NATURE WORLD
Edwinstowe
Ollerton
Sutton on Trent
Lidgett
SHERWOOD FOREST
Wellow
BETH SHALOM HOLOCAUST CENTRE
Moorhouse
Girton
Eagle Barnsdale
Thorpe on the Hill
North Hykeham
Old Clipstone
Ompton
Carlton on Trent
Besthorpe
RUFFORD
Ossington
South Scarle
Morton
South Hykeham
Kneesall
Norwell Woodhouse
Swinderby
Haddington
SHERWOOD PINES FOREST PARK
SHERWOOD FOREST
Clipstone
Forest Town
Kersall
Cromwell
Aubourn
Eakring
Norwell
VINA'S DOLL GALLERY
Collingham
Thurlby
Harmston
Bilsthorpe
Maplebeck
Holme
Bassingham
Caunton
Bilsthorpe Moor
Knapthorpe
Bathley
Norton Disney
Rainworth
Winkburn
North Muskham
Langford
Brough
WHITE POST FARM CENTRE
WHEELGATE PARK
Kirklington
Little Carlton
Stapleford
Carlton le Moorland
White Post
Farnsfield
Hockerton
South Muskham
Winthorpe
NEWARK AIR MUSEUM
Bidworth
Kelham
Haywood Oaks
Edingley
Normanton
THE WORKHOUSE
Witham
Brant
Ravenshead
Halam
Upton
Averham
Coddington
Brant Broughton
Welbourn
Southwell
Staythorpe
Newark-on-Trent
Beckingham
Nottingham
LONGDALE RURAL CRAFT CENTRE
SOUTHWELL MINSTER
Easthorpe
SOUTHWELL
Rolleston
Farndon
Stragglethorpe
Barnby in the Willows
Leadenham
PAPPLEWICK PUMPING STATION
BURNTSTUMP
Halloughton
Park Hill
Morton
Balderton
Hawton
Oxton
Fiskerton
Fenton
Fulbeck
MANOR STABLES CRAFT WORKSHOPS
Calverton
Thurgarton
East Stoke
Thorpe
Claypole
Bleasby
BESTWOOD
Woodborough
Epperstone
Stubton
Caythorpe
Brandon
Bestwood Village
Gonalston
Elston
Syerston
Cotham
Frieston
Dry Doddington
Hough-on-the-Hill
Lowdham
Hoveringham
TUMBLE TOWN
Flintham
Bestwood
ARNOLD
Caythorpe
Kneeton
Long Bennington
Sibthorpe
Normanton
Lambley
Shelton
Gelston
Carlton Scroop
Hougham
Burton Joyce
Bulcote
Gunthorpe
Screveton
Staunton in the Vale
Westborough
West Willoughby
East Bridgford
Hawksworth
Porchester
Gedling
MARSTON
Marston
Flawborough
Honington
Car Colston
Thoroton
Kilvington
Foston
Mapperley Park
THE TALES OF ROBIN HOOD
GREENS MILL & SCIENCE CEN
Carlton
Shelford
Alverton
Stoke Bardolph
Newton
Scarrington
Orston
Barkston
BOUNDARY MILLS
GRANTHAM NORTH SERVICES
Syston
Colwick
Radcliffe on Trent
Saxondale
Bingham
Aslockton
Normanton
Lenton
Allington
Belton
BELTON HOUSE
Harlequin
Upper Saxondale
Whatton
Bottesford
Great Gonerby
Holme Pierrepont
HOLME PIERREPONT
Elton
Easthorpe
Sedgebrook
Manthorpe
TRENT BRIDGE CRICKET GRD
Cropwell Butler
Sutton
Muston
Londonthorpe
Bassingfield
MUSTON MEADOWS
Wilford
WEST BRIDGFORD
NOTTINGHAM
Tithby
Granby
Redmile
Stenwith
Barrowby
Earlsfield
Grantham
GRANTHAM MUSEUM
Cold Harbour
Edwalton
VALE OF BELVOIR
Barnstone
Cotgrave
Cropwell Bishop
Barkestone-le-Vale
Tollerton
NATURESCAPE WILD FLOWER FARM
Langar
Plungar
Belvoir
BELVOIR CASTLE
Woolsthorpe by Belvoir
Clifton
FRAMEWORK KNITTERS MUS
Owthorpe
Normanton-on-the-Wolds
Old Somerby
Ruddington
RUSHCLIFFE
Plumtree
Colston Bassett
Denton
Harlaxton
HARLAXTON MANOR
Little Ponton
GREAT CENTRAL RLY (NOTT'M)
Keyworth
Harston
Bradmore
Kinoulton
Stathern
Knipton
Stroxton
Great Ponton
Stanton-on-the-Wolds
Harby
Bunny
Hickling
Eaton
Branston
Croxton Kerrial
Hungerton
Wyville
Hose
Eastwell
Bassingthorpe
Wysall
Widmerpool
East Leake
Costock
MANOR FARM
Upper Broughton
Willoughby-on-the-Wolds
Long Clawson
Goadby Marwood
Waltham on the Wolds
Saltby
Stoke Rochford
Easton
Skillington
WOOLSTHORPE MANOR
SK

Willingham by Stow
Normanby by Stow
Ingham
Spridlington
Cold Hanworth
Friesthorpe
Lissington
Bleasby
East Torrington
South Willingham
Biscathorpe
Donington on Bain
Stow
Cammeringham
Hackthorn
Snarford
Wickenby
Holton cum Beckering
West Torrington
Benniworth
Thorpe in the Fallows
Brattleby
Welton Hill
East Barkwith
Sturton by Stow
Aisthorpe
DAMBUSTERS INN & HERITAGE CENTRE
Welton
Snelland
West Barkwith
Market Stainton
Brampton
Scampton
Dunholme
Fulnetby
Rand
RAND FARM PARK
Sotby
Torksey
Bransby
Stainton by Langworth
Wragby
Panton
Ranby
Broxholme
North Carlton
Scothern
Bullington
Fenton
Ingleby
Langworth
WOODSIDE WILDLIFE & FALCONRY PARK
Hatton
Saxilby
South Carlton
Sudbrooke
Langton by Wragby
Great Sturton
Kettlethorpe
Odder
Riseholme
Nettleham
Apley
Kingthorpe
Burton
Reepham
Hemingby
MUSEUM OF LINCOLNSHIRE LIFE
Bunker's Hill
North Greetwell
Cherry Willingham
Low Barlings
Baumber
Minting
Broadholme
Thorney
Ermine
ELLIS MILL
St Giles
Fiskerton
Stainfield
Skellingthorpe
CATH
Gautby
Wispington
Clifton
Lincoln
Washingborough
Young Wood
Edlington
Harby
DODDINGTON HALL
New Boultham
Wigsley
Spalford
Doddington
Birchwood
Boultham
HARTSHOLME
Canwick
Branston Booths
Heighington
Bardney
Bucknall
Thimbleby
Langton
Bracebridge
Horsington
Thornton
Eagle Moor
LINCOLNSHIRE ROAD TRANSPORT MUSEUM
Bracebridge Heath
Branston
Potterhanworth Booths
BARDNEY LIMEWOODS
Old Woodhall
North Scarle
Eagle
WHISBY NATURAL WORLD
Whisby
Southrey
Martin
Potterhanworth
Stixwould
Reeds Beck
Dalderby
Eagle Barnsdale
Thorpe on the Hill
North Hykeham
Bracebridge Low Fields
Roughton Moor
Roughton
South Hykeham
Waddington
Nocton
Wasps Nest
Sots Hole
COTTAGE MUSEUM
Haltham
South Scarle
Morton
Swinderby
Haddington
Dunston
Woodhall Spa
Kirkstead
Kirkby on Bain
Aubourn
Harmston
Metheringham
Toft Hill
Collingham
Thurlby
Coleby
Martin Dales
Martin
Bassingham
Boothby Graffoe
Blankney
METHERINGHAM AIRFIELD VISITOR CENTRE
Tattershall Thorpe
Norton Disney
Scopwick
Timberland
TATTERSHALL COLLEGE
Tattershall
Coningsby
Brough
Navenby
Kirkby Green
BATTLE OF BRITAIN MEMORIAL FLIGHT
Stapleford
Carlton le Moorland
SK
TF
Thorpe Tilney
Walcott
Tattershall Bridge
COLLEGIATE CHURCH OF THE HOLY TRINITY
Wellingore
Rowston
BILLINGHAY COTTAGE
Hawthorn Hill
NEWARK AIR MUSEUM
Ashby de la Launde
Dogdyke
Scrub Hill
New York
Digby
Billinghay
Coddington
Welbourn
Brant Broughton
Bloxholm
Chapel Hill
Beckingham
NORTH INGS FARM MUSEUM
Dorrington
North Kyme
Haven Bank
Stragglethorpe
Leadenham
Barnby in the Willows
Fenton
Fulbeck
Cranwell
Ruskington
Anwick
MANOR STABLES CRAFT WORKSHOPS
South Kyme
Holland Fen
Claypole
Caythorpe
Leasingham
Stubton
South Kyme Fen
Brandon
Evedon
Ewerby Thorpe
Dry Doddington
Frieston
North Rauceby
CRANWELL AVIATION HERITAGE CENTRE
Holdingham
COGGLESFORD WATERMILL
Ewerby
Amber Hill
Hough-on-the-Hill
Normanton
Kirkby la Thorpe
Long Bennington
Gelston
Carlton Scroop
South Rauceby
Howell
HOLLAND FEN
Sudbrook
Sleaford
Asgarby
East Heckington
Hougham
West Willoughby
Ancaster
Quarrington
Swineshead Bridge
Westborough
MARSTON HALL
Marston
Heckington
THE PEAROOM CENTRE
HECKINGTON WINDMILL
Great Hale
Foston
Honington
Wilsford
Silk Willoughby
Burton Pedwardine
Little Hale
North End
Kelby
Culverthorpe
Swarby
Northbeck
Helpringham
Swineshead
BOUNDARY MILLS
GRANTHAM NORTH SERVICES
Syston
Barkston
Scredington
Allington
Belton
Heydour
Aswarby
Drayton
Great Gonerby
BELTON HOUSE
Oasby
Sedgebrook
Aisby
Aunsby
Osbournby
Spanby
Bicker
Manthorpe
Welby
Dembleby
Londonthorpe
Swaton
Grantham
Newton
Northorpe
Barrowby
Haceby
Threekingham
Earlsfield
GRANTHAM MUSEUM
Cold Harbour
Braceby
Walcot
Bridge End
Donington
Horbling
Stow
Church End
Woolsthorpe by Belvoir
Ropsley
Sapperton
Pickworth
Billingborough
Donington South Ing
Folkingham
Birthorpe
HARLAXTON MANOR
Old Somerby
Quadring
Denton
Humby
Hanby
Harlaxton
Little Ponton
Laughton
Pointon
Gosberton
Boothby Pagnell
Stroxton
Great Ponton
Lenton
Aslackby
Millthorpe
Westhorpe
Hungerton
Ingoldsby
Dowsby
Gosberton Clough
Graby
Risegate
Croxton Kerrial
Keisby
Bitchfield
Kirkby Underwood
Hawthorpe
Irnham
Rippingale
Northgate
Saltby
Skillington
Bulby
Dunsby
Pinchbeck
Pinchbeck
Cossgate
WOOLSTHORPE MANOR
Witham
Brant
Till
ERMINE STREET
Wildmore
BUBBLE CAR MUSEUM
A1500
A156
A57
A46
A15
A158
A1434
A607
A17
A153
A52
A1
A151
A152
B1398
B1241
B1190
B1399
B1202
B1225
B1188
B1178
B1189
B1191
B1192
B1209
B1429
B6403
B1394
B1395
B1177
B1176
B1174
B1181
B1397
B1356
90
91
77
65
0 1 2 3 4 5 6 miles
0 1 2 3 4 5 6 7 8 9 10 km

Raithby
Withcall
Little Cawthorpe
South Reston
Gayton le Marsh
Trusthorpe
North Reston
Strubby
Sutton on Sea
Tathwell
Haugham
Muckton
Withern
Maltby le Marsh
Thorpe
Stenigot
CADWELL PARK
Tothill
Authorpe
Sandilands
Cawkwell
Maidenwell
Burwell
Woodthorpe
Beesby
WOODY'S TOP
Hannah
Goulceby
Scamblesby
Farforth
Ruckland
CLAYTHORPE WATER MILL AND WILDFOWL GARDENS
Saleby
Markby
Belleau
White Pit
Swaby
Aby
Asserby
Oxcombe
Ketsby
South Thoresby
ALFORD WINDMILL
ALFORD MANOR HOUSE
Bilsby
Huttoft
Belchford
South Ormsby
Haugh
Rigsby
Alford
Calceby
Anderby
ON YOUR MARQUES
Tetford
Driby
Farlesthorpe
Mumby
Authorpe Row
Fulletby
Brinkhill
Salmonby
Well
Cumberworth
Somersby
Ulceby
Helsey
Chapel St Leonards
West Ashby
Sutterby
Bonthorpe
Hogsthorpe
Bag Enderby
Claxby
Ashby Puerorum
Harrington
Willoughby
High Toynton
Langton
Sloothby
Greetham
Aswardby
HARDY'S ANIMAL FARM
Skendleby
Horncastle
Scrafield
Hagworthingham
Sausthorpe
Ingoldmells
Addlethorpe
FANTASY ISLAND
SNIPE DALES
Partney
Welton le Marsh
Lusby
Mareham on the Hill
Hameringham
Mavis Enderby
Raithby
Scremby
FUNCOAST WORLD
Candlesby
Orby
Orby Marsh
Scrivelsby
Asgarby
Ashby by Partney
GUNBY HALL
Spilsby
Burgh le Marsh
Seathorne
Winthorpe
Hundleby
Old Bolingbroke
Hareby
NORTHCOTE HEAVY HORSE CENTRE
Great Steeping
Bratoft
Wood Enderby
BOLINGBROKE
Halton Holegate
NATURELAND SEAL SANCTUARY
Moorby
Toynton All Saints
Irby in the Marsh
BURGH LE MARSH WINDMILL
THE VILLAGE CHURCH FARM
Skegness
Miningsby
West Keal
East Keal
OSLINC OSTRICH FARM
THE LIFEBOAT STATION
East Kirkby
Toynton St Peter
Little Steeping
Firsby
Toynton Fen Side
Mareham le Fen
Revesby
LINCOLNSHIRE AVIATION HERITAGE CENTRE
Keal Cotes
Thorpe Culvert
Thorpe St Peter
Croft
Seacroft
Croft Marsh
Revesby Bridge
Stickford
Thorpe Fendykes
Wainfleet All Saints
Wainfleet Bank
New Bolingbroke
Fen Side
MAGDALEN MUSEUM
Tumby Woodside
New Leake
Wainfleet Tofts
Wainfleet St Mary
GIBRALTAR POINT
Midville
Medlam
Stickney
Eastville
Friskney Eaudike
Wainfleet Sand
Sandy Bank
Carrington
East Fen
Friskney
Bunker's Hill
Lade Bank
West Fen
Wrangle Bank
Friskney Tofts
Hundle Houses
Northlands
SIBSEY TRADER MILL
Leake Commonside
Friskney Flats
Sibsey
Wrangle Lowgate
Gipsey Bridge
Frithville
Old Leake
Wrangle
Fishtoft Drove
Hurn's End
Langrick
Anton's Gowt
Hill Dyke
Boston Long Hedges
Leverton Outgate
Frith Bank
Leverton Highgate
Leverton
Cowbridge
Brothertoft
Benington
Leverton Lucasgate
BOSTON DEEPS
LYNN DEEPS
Boston West
Boston
Haltoft End
Butterwick
GUILDHALL
Freiston
TF
Chain Bridge
Skirbeck
Skirbeck Quarter
THE WASH
Kirton Holme
Wyberton
Fishtoft
Frampton West End
Fenhouses
Scrane End
Hunstan
Kirton End
Frampton
Asperton
Kirton
Sandholme
Heach
Skeldyke
Wigtoft
Seadyke
Sutterton
Bucklegate
Algarkirk
Fosdyke
Lynn Channel
SNETTISHAM NATURE RESERVE
Holbeach St Matthew
Holbeach St Marks
Dawsmere
Surfleet Seas End
HOLBEACH MARSH
Gedney Marsh
Gedney Drove End
DERSINGHAM
Surfleet
Moulton Seas End
Saracen's Head
Holbeach Hurn
Wolferton
Holbeach Bank
Holbeach Clough
Halesgate
THE WASH
Gedney Dyke
Lutton
Guy's
BAYTREE OWL CENTRE
Castle
A B C D E F G

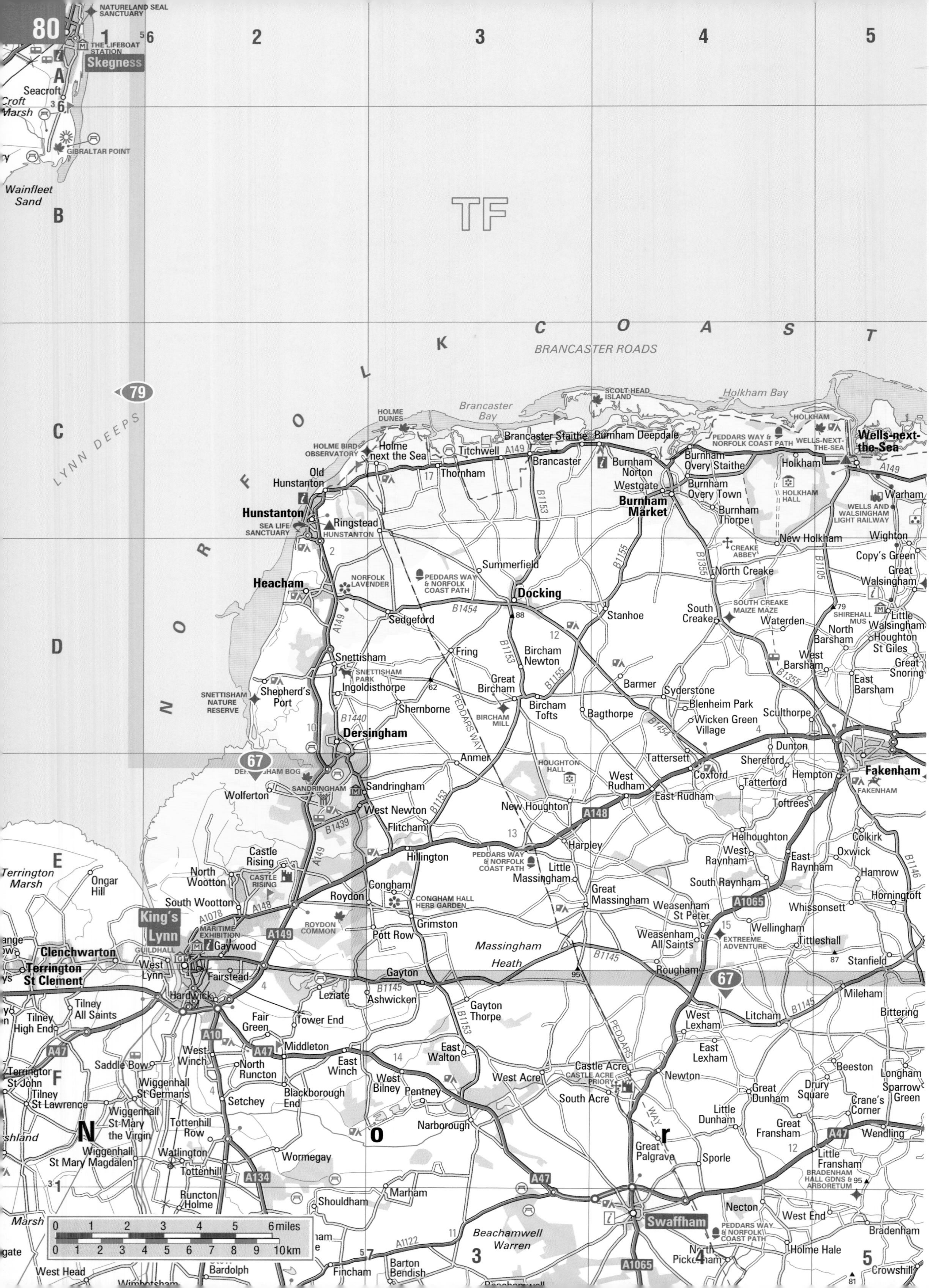

1
2
3
4
5
A
B
C
D
E
F
TF
NATURELAND SEAL SANCTUARY
THE LIFEBOAT STATION
Skegness
Seacroft
Croft Marsh
GIBRALTAR POINT
Wainfleet Sand
79
LYNN DEEPS
N O R F O L K C O A S T
BRANCASTER ROADS
Holkham Bay
SCOLT HEAD ISLAND
Brancaster Bay
HOLME DUNES
HOLME BIRD OBSERVATORY
Holme next the Sea
Titchwell
Brancaster Staithe
Burnham Deepdale
PEDDARS WAY & NORFOLK COAST PATH
HOLKHAM
WELLS-NEXT-THE-SEA
Wells-next-the-Sea
Old Hunstanton
Thornham
Brancaster
Burnham Norton
Burnham Overy Staithe
Holkham
Westgate
Burnham Overy Town
HOLKHAM HALL
Warham
Burnham Market
Burnham Thorpe
WELLS AND WALSINGHAM LIGHT RAILWAY
Hunstanton
Ringstead
SEA LIFE SANCTUARY
HUNSTANTON
New Holkham
Wighton
CREAKE ABBEY
Copy's Green
Summerfield
North Creake
Great Walsingham
Heacham
NORFOLK LAVENDER
PEDDARS WAY & NORFOLK COAST PATH
Docking
SOUTH CREAKE MAIZE MAZE
South Creake
SHIREHALL MUS
Little Walsingham
Sedgeford
Stanhoe
Waterden
North Barsham
Houghton St Giles
Snettisham
Fring
Bircham Newton
West Barsham
Great Snoring
SNETTISHAM PARK
Barmer
East Barsham
Ingoldisthorpe
Great Bircham
Syderstone
SNETTISHAM NATURE RESERVE
Shepherd's Port
Shernborne
BIRCHAM MILL
Bircham Tofts
Blenheim Park
Bagthorpe
Sculthorpe
Wicken Green Village
Dersingham
PEDDARS WAY
67
DERSINGHAM BOG
Anmer
Tattersett
Dunton
Shereford
HOUGHTON HALL
Coxford
Hempton
Fakenham
Wolferton
SANDRINGHAM
Sandringham
West Rudham
Tatterford
FAKENHAM
West Newton
New Houghton
East Rudham
Toftrees
Flitcham
Harpley
Helhoughton
Colkirk
Castle Rising
Hillington
PEDDARS WAY & NORFOLK COAST PATH
Little Massingham
West Raynham
Oxwick
East Raynham
Terrington Marsh
North Wootton
CASTLE RISING
Congham
Hamrow
Ongar Hill
Roydon
CONGHAM HALL HERB GARDEN
Great Massingham
South Raynham
Horningtoft
South Wootton
Weasenham St Peter
Whissonsett
King's Lynn
MARITIME EXHIBITION
ROYDON COMMON
Grimston
Wellingham
Weasenham All Saints
Tittleshall
EXTREME ADVENTURE
Clenchwarton
GUILDHALL
Gaywood
Pott Row
Massingham Heath
Stanfield
Terrington St Clement
West Lynn
Fairstead
Gayton
Rougham
Hardwick
Leziate
Ashwicken
Mileham
Tilney All Saints
Gayton Thorpe
Bittering
Tilney High End
Fair Green
Tower End
West Lexham
Litcham
Middleton
Saddle Bow
West Winch
East Walton
East Lexham
Terrington St John
North Runcton
East Winch
Castle Acre
CASTLE ACRE PRIORY
Beeston
Longham
Wiggenhall St Germans
West Bilney
Pentney
West Acre
Newton
Sparrow Green
Tilney St Lawrence
Setchey
Blackborough End
South Acre
Great Dunham
Drury Square
Crane's Corner
Wiggenhall St Mary the Virgin
Tottenhill Row
Narborough
Little Dunham
Great Fransham
Wendling
Marshland
N o r
Wiggenhall St Mary Magdalen
Watlington
Wormegay
Great Palgrave
Sporle
Little Fransham
Tottenhill
BRADENHAM HALL GDNS & ARBORETUM
Runcton Holme
Marham
Shouldham
Necton
West End
Swaffham
Bradenham
PEDDARS WAY & NORFOLK COAST PATH
Beachamwell Warren
North Pickenham
Holme Hale
Fincham
Barton Bendish
Bardolph
West Head
Crowshill
0 1 2 3 4 5 6 miles
0 1 2 3 4 5 6 7 8 9 10 km

5
6
7
8
9
60
63
A
B
C
D
E
F
G
36
TG
Blakeney Point
BLAKENEY
GUILDHALL
CLEY MILL
Cley next the Sea
PEDDARS WAY AND NORFOLK COAST PATH
Morston
Salthouse
MUCKLEBURGH COLLECTION
NORTH NORFOLK RAILWAY (THE POPPY LINE)
PRIORY MAZE & GARDENS
Sheringham
NORFOLK SHIRE HORSE CENTRE
CROMER MUSEUM
Cromer
Stiffkey
Blakeney
Wiveton
Newgate
Weybourne
West Runton
NORFOLK
Kelling
SHERINGHAM PARK
SHERINGHAM
Cockthorpe
Upper Sheringham
Beeston Regis
East Runton
Langham
Glandford
High Kelling
Overstrand
Westgate
Bodham
A148
A149
East Beckham
Aylmerton
Felbrigg
Binham
Saxlingham
Letheringsett
Holt
West Beckham
Northrepps
Sidestrand
WAYSIDE CROSS
Field Dalling
PICTURECRAFT GALLERY
Gresham
FELBRIGG HALL
Crossdale Street
COAST
Trimingham
THE TEXTILE CENTRE
Lower Green
LETHERINGSETT WATERMILL
BACONSTHORPE CASTLE
Frogshail
HOLT
Sustead
Bale
Sharrington
Hempstead
Baconsthorpe
Roughton
Southrepps
Gimingham
Mundesley
Hindringham
Brinton
Thornage
Hunworth
Bessingham
Hanworth
Thorpe Market
STOW WINDMILL
Lower Street
Trunch
Paston
THURSFORD COLLECTION
Stody
Edgefield
Plumstead
Matlaske
Thurgarton
A140
Alby Hill
Knapton
Bacton
ENGLAND CO...
Gunthorpe
Briningham
Aldborough
Bradfield
Thursford
Antingham
Broomholm
Keswick
Little Snoring
Melton Constable
Edgefield Street
Little Barningham
Wickmere
ALBY CRAFTS
ALBY GARDENS
Suffield
Swafield
Edingthorpe
Barney
Swanton Novers
Briston
MANNINGTON GARDENS
WOLTERTON PARK
Calthorpe
Erpingham
Colby
STRAW MUSEUM
Kettlestone
Fulmodestone
Itteringham
DAVENPORTS MAGIC KINGDOM
Edingthorpe Green
Witton Br...
Ridlingt...
Corpusty
Saxthorpe
North Walsham
Spa Common
Crostwight
PENSTHORPE NATURE RESERVE & GARDENS
BLICKLING HALL
Ingworth
Banningham
Happ...
Thurning
Hindolveston
Blickling
Felmingham
Stibbard
Norton Corner
Oulton
EAST RUSTON OLD VICARAGE GARDEN
Little Ryburgh
Wood Norton
Silvergate
Dunkirk
Honing
Great Ryburgh
Guestwick
Heydon
Oulton Street
Tuttington
Westwick
Bengate
East Ruston
Guestwick Green
Wood Dalling
Aylsham
Burgh next Aylsham
Skeyton
Worstead
Guist
Salle
Southgate
Fengate
Swanton Abbott
Sloley
Dilham
Smallburgh
Foulsham
Twyford
Themelthorpe
Marsham
Brampton
Gateley
Broom Green
Cawston
Little London
BURE VALLEY RAILWAY
Bintree
Reepham
Scottow
69
FOXLEY WOOD
Booton
Eastgate
Lamas
Pennygate
The Heath
Buxton
Little Hautbois
Tunstead
ANT BROADS AND MARSHES
Foxley
Whitwell Street
Brandiston
Brisley
North Elmham
Sco Ruston
WROXHAM BARNS
Neatishead
Billingford
Bawdeswell
Haveringland
Hevingham
Stratton Strawless
Ashmanhaugh
East Bilney
Worthing
Sparham
Coltishall
Threehamn Commo...
68
Waterloo
Beetley
Mill Street
Lenwade
Alderford
Swannington
New Hainford
Hainford
Belaugh
Hoveton
Upgate
Frettenham
Wroxham
Lower Str...
Swanton Morley
Lyng
DINOSAUR ADVENTURE PARK
Wensum
Felthorpe
HILLSIDE ANIMAL SANCTUARY
Upper Street
RURAL LIFE MUSEUM
Elsing
Morton
Attlebridge
Horning
Gressenhall
Hoe
Newton St Faith
BURE MARSHES
Woodgate
Primrose Green
Weston Longville
Thorpe Marriott
Horsford
Crostwick
Wroxham Broad
Woodbastwick
Etling Green
Weston Green
Horsham St Faith
Spixworth
Rackheath
Salhouse
North Tuddenham
Ringland
Taverham
NORWICH INTERNATIONAL
Dereham
A47
Hockering
Drayton
Panxworth
New Rackheath
MID-NORFOLK RAILWAY
Mattishall Burgh
Honingham
Hellesdon
Old Catton
Little Plumstead
Scarning
Costessey
Sprowston
Thorpe End
Hemblin...
Toftwood
Clint Green
Mattishall
Mile Cross
Upper Hellesdon
Blofield Heath
Daffy Green
Yaxham
East Tuddenham
Easton
A1074
New Costessey
Thorpe St Andrew
Great Plumstead
THE FORUM
New Catton
Westfield
Whinburgh
Welborne
Colton
Marlingford
Bowthorpe
Earlham
CATHEDRAL
Blofield
Brundall
63
Yare
Bawburgh
SAINSBURY CENTRE FOR VISUAL ARTS
NORWICH
Brandon Parva
WHITLINGHAM
Runhall
Barford
Colney
Postwick
Shipdham
Garvestone
Thuxton
Barnham Broom
Great Melton
Little Melton
Cringleford
Lakenham
Trowse Newton
Surlingham
Strum...
Letton Green
Kirby Bedon
Reymerston
Danemoor
Wramplingham
High Green
Eaton
P&R

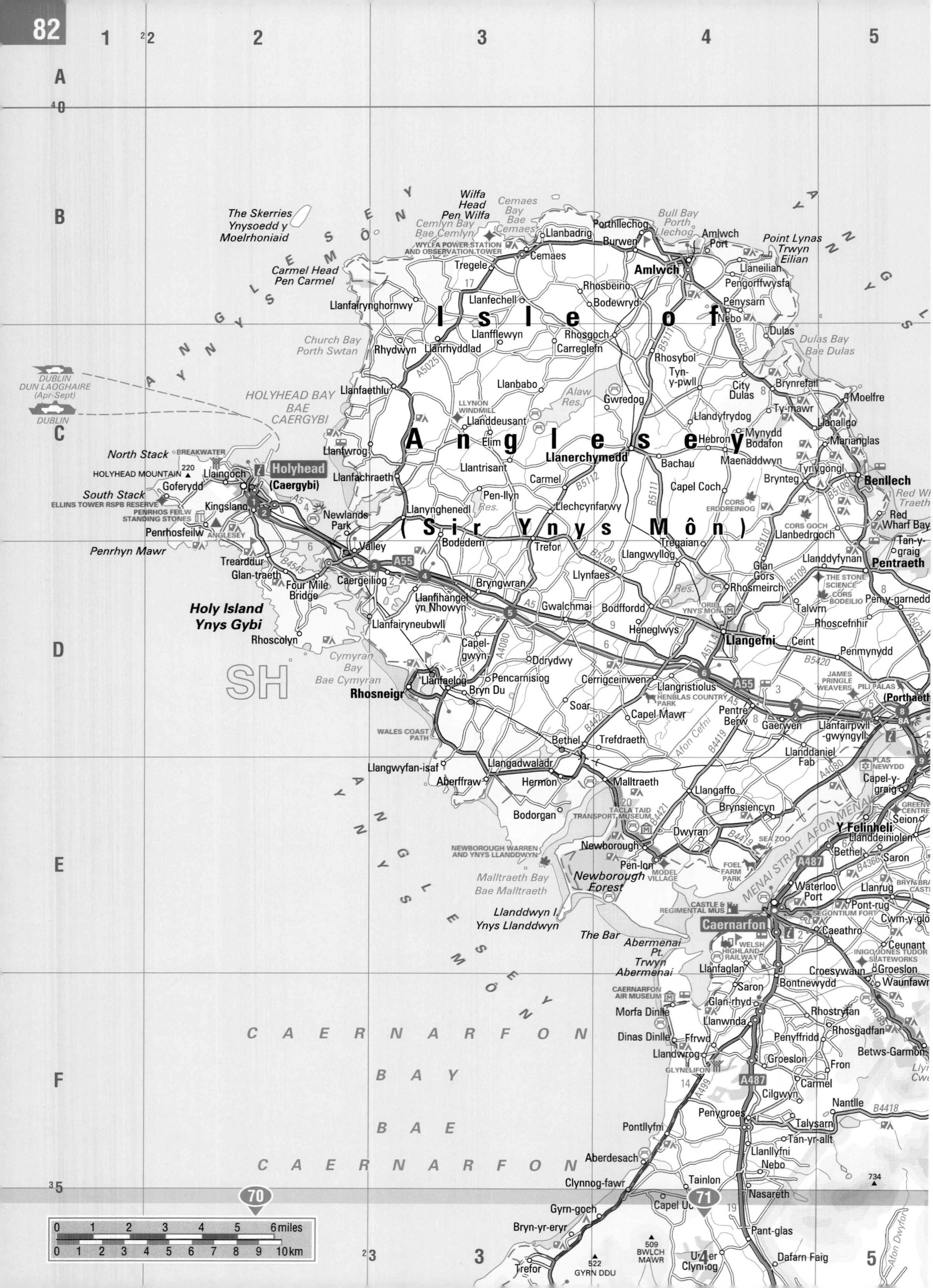

1
2
3
4
5
A
B
C
D
E
F
Isle of Anglesey (Sir Ynys Môn)
Holy Island
Ynys Gybi
The Skerries
Ynysoedd y Moelrhoniaid
Wilfa Head
Pen Wilfa
Cemaes Bay
Bae Cemaes
Cemlyn Bay
Bae Cemlyn
WYLFA POWER STATION AND OBSERVATION TOWER
Llanbadrig
Porthllechog
Bull Bay
Porth Llechog
Burwen
Amlwch Port
Amlwch
Point Lynas
Trwyn Eilian
Llaneilian
Pengorffwysfa
Penysarn
Nebo
Dulas
Dulas Bay
Bae Dulas
Carmel Head
Pen Carmel
Cemaes
Tregele
Llanfechell
Rhosbeirio
Bodewryd
Llanfairynghornwy
Llanfflewyn
Rhosgoch
Carreglefn
Rhosybol
Tyn-y-pwll
City Dulas
Brynrefail
Moelfre
Ty-mawr
Llanallgo
Marianglas
Church Bay
Porth Swtan
Rhydwyn
Llanrhyddlad
Llanfaethlu
Llanbabo
Alaw Res.
Gwredog
Llandyfrydog
Hebron
Mynydd Bodafon
HOLYHEAD BAY
BAE CAERGYBI
LLYNON WINDMILL
Llanddeusant
Elim
Llanfwrog
Llanerchymedd
Bachau
Maenaddwyn
Tynygongl
Benllech
Red Wharf Bay
North Stack
BREAKWATER
HOLYHEAD MOUNTAIN
220
Holyhead
(Caergybi)
Llaingoch
Goferydd
South Stack
ELLINS TOWER RSPB RESERVE
Kingsland
PENRHOS FEILW STANDING STONES
Penrhosfeilw
ANGLESEY
Penrhyn Mawr
Trearddur
Glan-traeth
Four Mile Bridge
Rhoscolyn
Llanfachraeth
Llantrisant
Carmel
Capel Coch
Brynteg
Pen-llyn
Llechcynfarwy
CORS ERDDREINIOG
CORS GOCH
Llanbedrgoch
Llanynghenedl
Newlands Park
Valley
Bodedern
Trefor
Tregaian
Tan-y-graig
Llangwyllog
Llanddyfnan
Pentraeth
Caergeiliog
Bryngwran
Llynfaes
Glan Gors
THE STONE SCIENCE
CORS BODEILIO
Pen-y-garnedd
Llanfihangel yn Nhowyn
Gwalchmai
Bodffordd
Rhosmeirch
ORIEL YNYS MON
Talwrn
Llanfairyneubwll
Heneglwys
Rhoscefnhir
Llangefni
Ceint
Penmynydd
Capel-gwyn
Ddrydwy
JAMES PRINGLE WEAVERS
PILI PALAS
(Porthaethwy)
Cymyran Bay
Bae Cymyran
Llanfaelog
Pencarnisiog
Rhosneigr
Bryn Du
Cerrigceinwen
Llangristiolus
HENBLAS COUNTRY PARK
Soar
Capel Mawr
Pentre Berw
Gaerwen
Llanfairpwll-gwyngyll
WALES COAST PATH
Bethel
Trefdraeth
Afon Cefni
Llanddaniel Fab
PLAS NEWYDD
Capel-y-graig
Llangwyfan-isaf
Aberffraw
Llangadwaladr
Hermon
Malltraeth
Llangaffo
Brynsiencyn
Bodorgan
TACLA TAID TRANSPORT MUSEUM
Dwyran
SEA ZOO
Y Felinheli
Seion
Llanddeiniolen
Bethel
Saron
NEWBOROUGH WARREN AND YNYS LLANDDWYN
Newborough
Pen-lon
MODEL VILLAGE
FOEL FARM PARK
MENAI STRAIT AFON MENAI
Malltraeth Bay
Bae Malltraeth
Newborough Forest
Waterloo Port
Llanrug
CASTLE & REGIMENTAL MUS
Caernarfon
SEGONTIUM FORT
Pont-rug
Llanddwyn I.
Ynys Llanddwyn
Caeathro
The Bar
Abermenai Pt.
Trwyn Abermenai
WELSH HIGHLAND RAILWAY
Ceunant
INIGO JONES TUDOR SLATEWORKS
Llanfaglan
Croesywaun
Groeslon
Saron
Bontnewydd
Waunfawr
CAERNARFON AIR MUSEUM
Glan-rhyd
Morfa Dinlle
Rhostryfan
Llanwnda
Dinas Dinlle
Ffrwd
Penyffridd
Rhosgadfan
Llandwrog
Betws-Garmon
GLYNLLIFON
Groeslon
Fron
Carmel
Cilgwyn
Nantlle
Penygroes
Talysarn
Pontllyfni
Tan-yr-allt
Llanllyfni
Aberdesach
Nebo
Tainlon
734
Clynnog-fawr
Nasareth
Capel Uchaf
Gyrn-goch
Pant-glas
Bryn-yr-eryr
509 BWLCH MAWR
522 GYRN DDU
Uwchaf Clynnog
Dafarn Faig
Trefor
Afon Dwyfor
CAERNARFON BAY
BAE CAERNARFON
ANGLESEY SEA
DUBLIN DUN LAOGHAIRE (Apr-Sept)
DUBLIN
SH
A55
A5
A5025
A4080
A5114
A5025
A487
A499
A4085
B5111
B5112
B5109
B5110
B5420
B4545
B4419
B4421
B4422
B4366
B4418
70
71
0 1 2 3 4 5 6 miles
0 1 2 3 4 5 6 7 8 9 10 km

Great Ormes Head
Pen-y-Gogarth
Llandudno
Puffin Island
Ynys Seiriol
CONWY BAY
BAE CONWY
Conwy Sands
Traeth Conwy
Penrhyn Bay
Rhos-on-Sea
COLWYN BAY
(BAE COLWYN)
Abergele Roads
Abergele
Llandudno Junction
(Cyffordd Llandudno)
Conwy
Penmaenmawr
Llanfairfechan
Beaumaris
Lavan Sands
Traeth Lafan
Menai Bridge
Bangor
Bethesda
Llanberis
SNOWDONIA NATIONAL PARK
PARC CENEDLAETHOL ERYRI
Aber Falls
Rhaeadr Aber
VALE OF CONWY
DYFFRYN CONWY
Llanrwst
Capel Curig
Betws-y-Coed
Conwy
Gwydyr Forest
Conwy Falls
Rhaeadr Conwy
Fairy Glen
Mynydd Cribau
Dolwyddelan
Blaenau Ffestiniog
Beddgelert
Pass of Llanberis
Pass of Aberglaslyn
Llyn Ogwen
Llyn Cowlyd
Llyn Crafnant
Llyn Eigiau
Marchlyn Mawr Res.
Llyn Padarn
Llyn Peris
Llyn Llydaw
Llyn Gwynant
Llyn Dinas
Llyn Aled
Llyn Alwen
Alwen Reservoir
Mynydd Hiraethog
Mwdwl-eithin
1085 SNOWDON YR WYDDFA
999 GLYDER FAWR
1064 CARNEDD LLYWELYN
1044 CARNEDD DAFYDD
942 FOEL FRAS
872 CARNEDD MOEL SIABOD
782 MOEL HEBOG
623 MOEL PENAMNEN
468 MOEL SEISIOG
Abergwyngregyn
Rowen
Tal-y-Bont
Dolgarrog
Trefriw
Gwytherin
Llangernyw
Llansannan
Pentrefoelas
Ysbyty Ifan
Cerrigydrudion
A55
A470
A5
A543
A548
A544
A4086
A498
A545
A4244
71
72

NX
SC
POINT OF AYRE
The Ayres
Rue Pt.
Glentruan
Cranstal
Dhowin
The Lhen
Bride
Andreas
MANX CROSSES
Jurby Head
JURBY SOUTH
Jurby East
Sandygate
Jurby West
Ballasalla
Regaby
The Cronk
St Judes
Dhoor
RAMSEY BAY
CURRAGHS WILDLIFE PARK
GROVE MUSEUM
Ramsey
Sulby
Churchtown
MANX ELECTRIC RAILWAY
Orrisdale
Ballaugh
T.T.Course
Port e Vullen
Glen Auldyn
Maughold
Maughold Head
Rhencullen
Ravensdale
Dreemskerry
Kirk Michael
565 NORTH BARRULE
Ballajora
CELTIC CRAFT CENTRE
Corrany
Cornaa
Ballaleigh
SNAEFELL 621
Glen Mona
Res.
Barregarrow
Druidale
Dhoon
MURRAYS MOTORCYCLE MUSEUM
Agneash
LAXEY WHEEL AND MINES
MANX TRANSPORT MUSEUM
Knocksharry
SNAEFELL MOUNTAIN RAILWAY
Bulgham Bay
Cronk-y-Voddy
544
Ballaquine
Laxey
St Patrick's I.
PEEL
Peel
487 COLDEN
LAXEY WOOLLEN MILLS
Old Laxey
Laxey Head
HOUSE OF MANANNAN
TYNWALD CRAFT CENTRE
BALLALHEANNAGH GARDENS
Fairy Cottage
Contrary Head
Laxey Bay
KIPPER MUSEUM
TYNWALD HILL
Isle of Man
Patrick
St John's
Greeba
Baldwin
Creg-ny-Baa
Ballacannel
Baldrine
Glenmaye
333
Clay Head
Lower Foxdale
Crosby
Dalby Pt.
Glen Vine
Strang
MANX CROSSES
Dalby
Onchan
GROUDLE GLEN RAILWAY
HEYSHAM
Niarbyl
Foxdale
Union Mills
Tromode
Eairy
ONCHAN PLEASURE PARK
LARNE
(TT race period only)
Niarbyl Bay
Braaid
Spring Valley
Douglas
483 SOUTH BARRULE
222
Cooil
Douglas Bay
Close Clark
Douglas Head
Ellenbrook
CAMERA OBSCURA
St Mark's
Ballaveare
Ballamodha
Newtown
LIVERPOOL
(March-Nov)
Lingague
Ronague
Little Ness
Fleshwick Bay
Grenaby
ISLE OF MAN STEAM RAILWAY
BIRKENHEAD
(Nov-March)
Surby
Ballabeg
RUSHEN ABBEY
Santon Head
Bradda Head
Bradda
Colby
Ballasalla
Port Greenaugh
Port Erin
BILLOWN
ISLE OF MAN
RAILWAY MUS
Four Roads
Castletown
Derbyhaven
The Howe
CASTLE RUSHEN
NAUTICAL MUS
Cregneash
SCARLETT VISITOR CENTRE
Port St Mary
OLD HOUSE OF KEYS
St Michael's I.
CREGNEASH VILLAGE FOLK MUSEUM
128
Calf of Man
Spanish Head
Scarlett Point
Dreswick Pt.
BELFAST (April-Sept)
DUBLIN (April-Sept)
Chicken Rock
A10
A19
B2
B6
A17
A16
B3
A9
B4
B7
A14
A13
B14
B9
A3
A15
A18
A2
B10
A4
A20
A1
B22
A30
A21
B21
B12
B20
A23
A24
B35
A22
B36
B32
A26
B37
A5
A6
A36
B39
B30
B41
A25
B44
B40
A34
B25
A31
0 1 2 3 4 5 6 miles
0 1 2 3 4 5 6 7 8 9 10 km

IRISH SEA
LIVERPOOL BAY
SD
SJ
Merseyside
South Shore
BLACKPOOL PLEASURE BEACH
Hawes Side
Mereside
Common Edge
Great Plumpton
Little Plumpton
Wesham
Kirkham
Dowbridge
Squires Gate
Westby
Moss Side
Wrea Green
Newton
Scales
TOY AND TEDDY BEAR MUSEUM
ROYAL LYTHAM & ST ANNES
LYTHAM HALL
St Annes
Lytham St Anne's
Ansdell
Lytham
Fairhaven
Salters Bank
Warton
Freckleton
Ribble
Banks Sands
Great Bank
RIBBLE MARSHES
WEST LANCASHIRE LIGHT RAILWAY
Hesketh Bank
Becconsall
Hundred End
Banks
Tarleton
Horse Bank
Crossens
Marshside
ECO VISITOR CENTRE
Southport
Churchtown
Mere Brow
Holmeswood
Blowick
Birkdale
Brown Edge
MARTIN MERE WILDFOWL AND WETLAND CENTRE
Rufford
Snape Green
Bescar
Scarisbrick
Hillside
ROYAL BIRKDALE
Ainsdale-on-Sea
Ainsdale
Shirdley Hill
New Lane
Pinfold
Burscough
Burscough Bridge
Woodvale
Halsall
Formby Hills
AINSDALE SAND DUNES
Barton
Haskayne
ORMSKIRK
Westhead
Freshfield
Formby
Formby Pt.
Downholland Cross
Little Altcar
Great Altcar
Aughton Park
Blaguegate
CABIN HILL
Stanley Gate
Aughton
Royal Oak
Hightown
Ince Blundell
Lydiate
Bickerstaffe
Maghull
Barrow Nook
Lunt
Little Crosby
Melling Mount
Sefton
Thornton
Netherton
Melling
BELFAST
Great Crosby
Kirkby
Crosby Channel
Aintree
DOUGLAS (Nov-March) DUBLIN
LITHERLAND
Southdene
Waterloo
Orrell
Seaforth
Fazakerley
Knowsley
Bootle
DOUGLAS (March-Nov)
New Brighton
Walton
Norris Green
CROXTETH
Kirkdale
Mockbeggar Wharf
NEW PALACE
Liscard
Anfield
West Derby
Egremont
Longview
WALKER GALL
Wallasey
Everton
Knotty Ash
Leasowe
Seacombe
LIVERPOOL
MARITIME MUS
Huyton
Meols
Moreton
Poulton
Edge Hill
Roby
HOYLAKE
HOYLAKE LIFEBOAT MUS
Bidston
West Hoyle Bank
Claughton
TATE
Wavertree
Childwall
Hilbre I.
Upton
Toxteth
Netherley
Tarbock Green
Greasby
ALBERT DOCK
Birkenhead
Mossley Hill
Grange
Woodchurch
Rock Ferry
Dingle
Gateacre
West Kirby
Frankby
Tranmere
SUDLEY
MENDIPS
Woolton
Welsh Channel
ARROWE
LADY LEVER ART GALLERY
Allerton
Point of Ayr
Yr Parlwr Du
Prenton
Aigburth
River Dee
Afon Dyfrdwy
Caldy
New Ferry
PORT SUNLIGHT MUS
Grassendale
Hunt's Cross
Talacre
Thurstaston
Irby
BEBINGTON
Thingwall
Storeton
Port Sunlight
Gwespyr
Pensby
Barnston
Garston
Speke
Gronant
Brimstage
SPEKE HALL
Prestatyn
Ffynnongroyw
WIRRAL
Bromborough
LIVERPOOL JOHN LENNON
Liverpool Airport
Gwaenysgor
Picton
Eastham
Eastham Ferry
OFFA'S DYKE PATH
LLWYBR CLAWDD OFFA
Llanasa
Mostyn Quay
Heswall
Thornton Hough
Dawpool Bank
Mostyn
WALES COAST PATH
Axton
Trelogan
Gayton
Mersey
Trelawnyd
Raby
Ince Banks
Ellesmere Port
Parkgate
Hinderton
Willaston
Hooton
Childer Thornton
RIVACRE
BOAT MUSEUM
GREENFIELD VALLEY HERITAGE PARK
Holywell Bank
Gayton Sands
Neston
Little Sutton
Overpool
Walwen
WIRRAL
Little Neston
Ness
NESS GARDENS
Great Sutton
Whitby
Whitbyheath
Stoak
Ince
Elton
Rhuallt
Holywell (Treffynnon)
Bagillt
CHESHIRE OAK
0 1 2 3 4 5 6 miles
0 1 2 3 4 5 6 7 8 9 10 km

Lancashire
Merseyside
Warrington
Halton
Blackburn with Darwen
Preston
Blackburn
Bolton
Wigan
Skelmersdale
St Helens
Huyton
Widnes
Runcorn
Speke
Garston
Liverpool John Lennon Airport
LIVERPOOL
Leigh
Kirkham
Fulwood
Ribbleton
Freckleton
Lytham
Warton
Penwortham
Bamber Bridge
LEYLAND
CHORLEY
DARWEN
Horwich
Standish
Blackrod
Adlington
Coppull
Orrell
ORMSKIRK
Burscough
Rufford
Tarleton
Banks
Crossens
Churchtown
Maghull
Kirkby
Knowsley
Prescot
Rainford
Billinge
Haydock
Golborne
ASHTON-IN-MAKERFIELD
Newton-le-Willows
WESTHOUGHTON
Hindley
ATHERTON
Tyldesley
Worsley
Irlam
Cadishead
Partington
Lymm
Culcheth
Frodsham
Helsby
Hale
Halewood
Woolton
Childwall
Wavertree
Aigburth
Port Sunlight
Bromborough
Eastham
Banks Sands
Chat Moss
Anglezarke Moor
Turton Moor
92
93
85
73
74
M6
M55
M58
M61
M62
M65
M56
M57
A59
A49
A580
A58
A57
0 1 2 3 4 5 6 miles
0 1 2 3 4 5 6 7 8 9 10 km

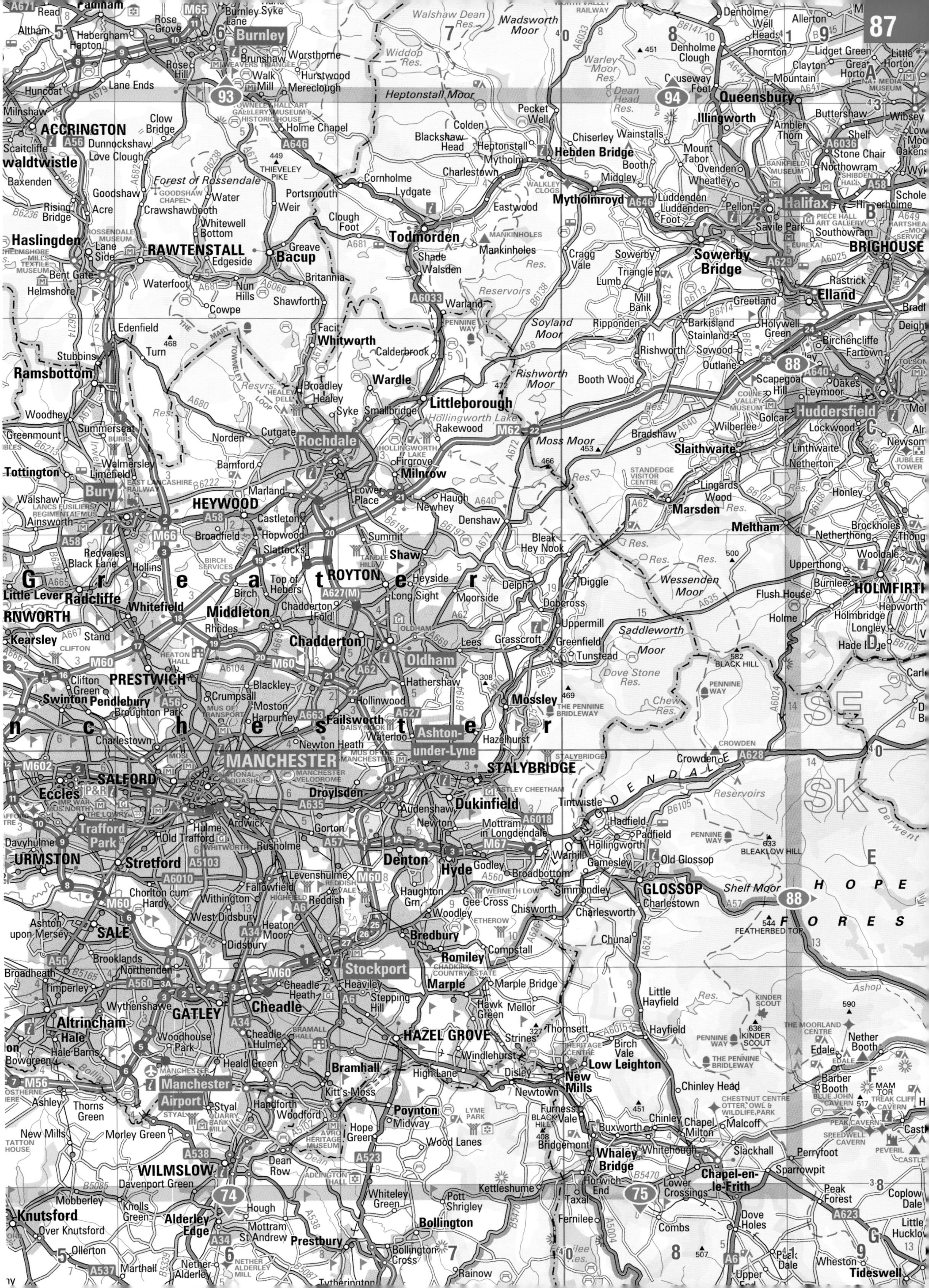
Burnley
Padiham
Read
Altham
Habergham
Hapton
Rose Grove
Burnley Lane
Worsthorne
Hurstwood
Mereclough
Huncoat
Lane Ends
Walsden Dean Res.
Wadsworth Moor
Widdop Res.
Heptonstall Moor
Walk Mill
Brunshaw
Holme Chapel
Denholme
Denholme Clough
Allerton
Thornton
Lidget Green
Clayton
Queensbury
Illingworth
Accrington
Clow Bridge
Dunnockshaw
Love Clough
Oswaldtwistle
Baxenden
Forest of Rossendale
Goodshaw
Water
Crawshawbooth
Rising Bridge
Acre
Whitewell Bottom
Haslingden
Lane Side
Rawtenstall
Edgeside
Helmshore
Bent Gate
Waterfoot
Bacup
Greave
Britannia
Nun Hills
Cowpe
Shawforth
Thieveley Pike
Portsmouth
Cornholme
Weir
Lydgate
Clough Foot
Todmorden
Shade
Walsden
Blackshaw Head
Heptonstall
Mytholm
Colden
Pecket Well
Charlestown
Hebden Bridge
Chiserley
Wainstalls
Midgley
Mytholmroyd
Eastwood
Mankinholes
Cragg Vale
Sowerby
Triangle
Sowerby Bridge
Luddenden
Luddenden Foot
Halifax
Savile Park
Southowram
Brighouse
Elland
Rastrick
Greetland
Mount Tabor
Ovenden
Wheatley
Pellon
Booth
Lumb
Mill Bank
Ripponden
Barkisland
Stainland
Holywell Green
Birchencliffe
Fartown
Rishworth
Sowood
Outlane
Soyland Moor
Rishworth Moor
Booth Wood
Warland
Edenfield
Stubbins
Turn
Ramsbottom
Facit
Whitworth
Calderbrook
Wardle
Broadley
Healey
Syke
Smallbridge
Littleborough
Hollingworth Lake
Rakewood
Woodhey
Summerseat
Greenmount
Tottington
Walmersley
Limefield
Bury
Norden
Cutgate
Rochdale
Bamford
Marland
Firgrove
Milnrow
Lower Place
Moss Moor
Scapegoat Hill
Leymoor
Oakes
Huddersfield
Golcar
Bradshaw
Wilberlee
Slaithwaite
Lockwood
Linthwaite
Netherton
Walshaw
Ainsworth
Heywood
Castleton
Hopwood
Broadfield
Haugh
Newhey
Denshaw
Summit
Lingards Wood
Marsden
Honley
Meltham
Netherthong
Brockholes
Redvales
Black Lane
Hollins
Slattocks
Shaw
Bleak Hey Nook
Wooldale
Upperthong
Greater Manchester
Royton
Heyside
Top of Hebers
Little Lever
Radcliffe
Whitefield
Birch
Long Sight
Delph
Diggle
Wessenden Moor
Burnlee
Holmfirth
Farnworth
Middleton
Chadderton Fold
Moorside
Dobcross
Flush House
Hepworth
Holmbridge
Holme
Longley
Kearsley
Stand
Rhodes
Chadderton
Lees
Grasscroft
Uppermill
Greenfield
Saddleworth Moor
Tunstead
Clifton
Prestwich
Oldham
Black Hill
Dove Stone Res.
Blackley
Hathershaw
Swinton
Pendlebury
Crumpsall
Moston
Hollinwood
Mossley
Chew Res.
Broughton Park
Harpurhey
Failsworth
Ashton-under-Lyne
Hazelhurst
Waterloo
Charlestown
Newton Heath
Manchester
Stalybridge
Crowden
Salford
Eccles
Droylsden
Dukinfield
Longdendale
Tintwistle
Audenshaw
Hadfield
Padfield
Trafford Park
Hulme
Ardwick
Gorton
Newton
Mottram in Longdendale
Hollingworth
Davyhulme
Old Trafford
Rusholme
Urmston
Stretford
Denton
Hyde
Godley
Broadbottom
Gamesley
Old Glossop
Bleaklow Hill
Levenshulme
Fallowfield
Reddish
Haughton Grn.
Simmondley
Glossop
Charlestown
Shelf Moor
Hope Forest
Chorlton cum Hardy
Withington
Gee Cross
Chisworth
Charlesworth
West Didsbury
Woodley
Ashton upon Mersey
Sale
Heaton Moor
Bredbury
Featherbed Top
Didsbury
Chunal
Brooklands
Romiley
Compstall
Broadheath
Northenden
Stockport
Marple
Marple Bridge
Timperley
Cheadle Heath
Heaviley
Stepping Hill
Little Hayfield
Wythenshawe
Gatley
Cheadle
Mellor
Hawk Green
Kinder Scout
Altrincham
Hale
Woodhouse Park
Cheadle Hulme
Hazel Grove
Strines
Thornsett
Birch Vale
Hayfield
Hale Barns
Bowgreen
Heald Green
Windlehurst
Nether Booth
Edale
Bramhall
High Lane
Disley
New Mills
Low Leighton
Manchester Airport
Ashley
Kitt's Moss
Newtown
Chinley Head
Barber Booth
Thorns Green
Styal
Handforth
Poynton
Furness Vale
Chinley
Chapel Milton
Malcoff
Woodford
Midway
Hope Green
Buxworth
New Mills
Morley Green
Wood Lanes
Whaley Bridge
Whitehough
Slackhall
Perryfoot
Dean Row
Bridgemont
Wilmslow
Davenport Green
Kettleshulme
Horwich End
Lower Crossings
Chapel-en-le-Frith
Sparrowpit
Mobberley
Whiteley Green
Pott Shrigley
Taxal
Peak Forest
Coplow Dale
Knutsford
Knolls Green
Alderley Edge
Hough
Bollington
Fernilee
Dove Holes
Little Hucklow
Over Knutsford
Mottram St Andrew
Prestbury
Combs
Ollerton
Bollington Cross
Peak Dale
Wheston
Tideswell
Marthall
Nether Alderley
Rainow
Tytherington
Upper End

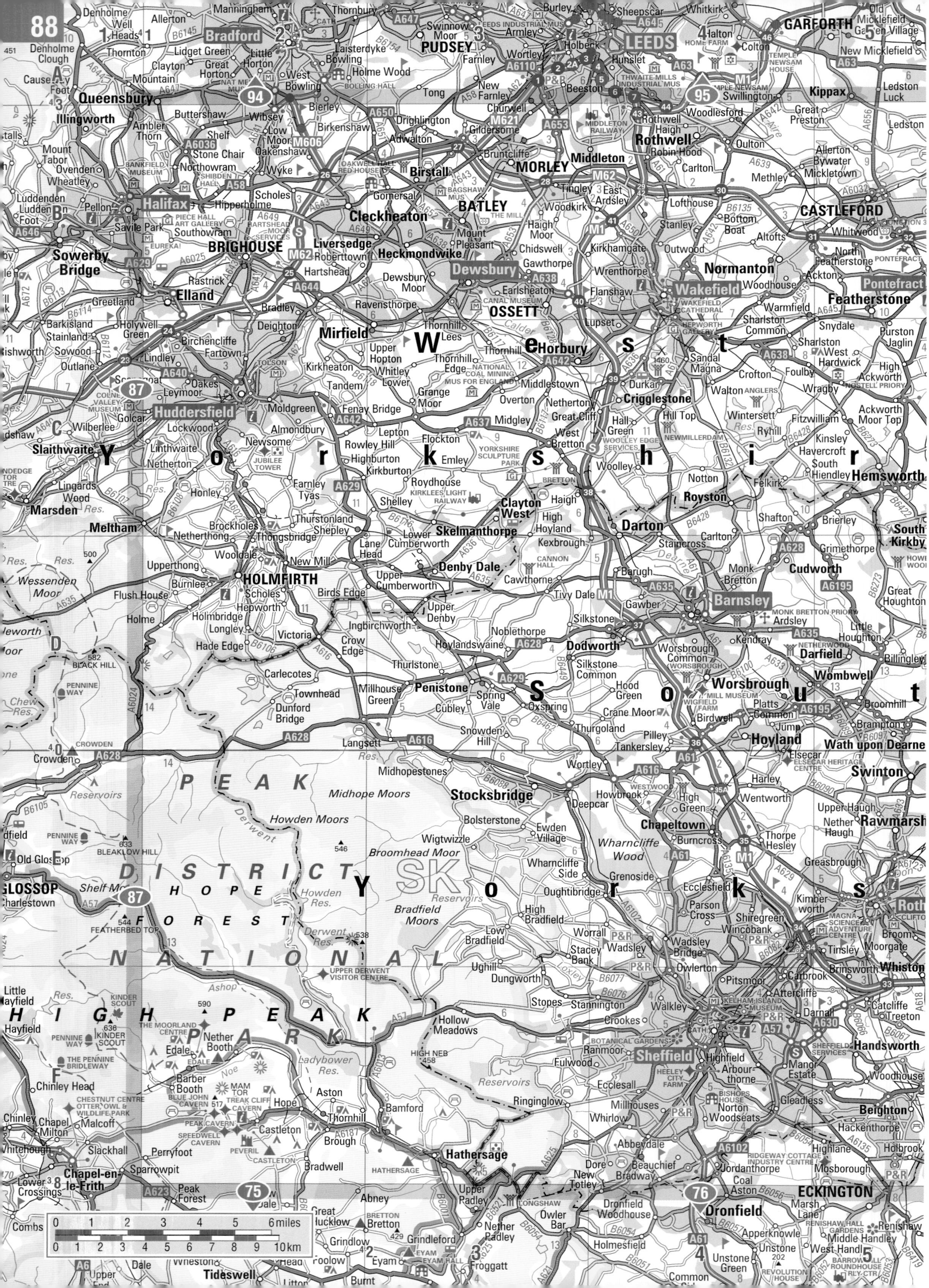

Bradford
LEEDS
PUDSEY
GARFORTH
Queensbury
Halifax
Sowerby Bridge
BRIGHOUSE
Elland
Cleckheaton
Heckmondwike
BATLEY
MORLEY
Rothwell
Dewsbury
OSSETT
Wakefield
Normanton
CASTLEFORD
Pontefract
Featherstone
Huddersfield
Mirfield
Horbury
Slaithwaite
Marsden
Meltham
HOLMFIRTH
Skelmanthorpe
Denby Dale
Darton
Royston
Barnsley
Hemsworth
South Kirkby
Cudworth
Penistone
Worsbrough
Wombwell
Hoyland
Wath upon Dearne
Swinton
Stocksbridge
Chapeltown
Rawmarsh
GLOSSOP
Sheffield
Handsworth
Dronfield
ECKINGTON
Hathersage
Chapel-en-le-Frith
Tideswell
West Yorkshire
South Yorkshire
PEAK DISTRICT NATIONAL PARK
HOPE FOREST
HIGH PEAK
SK
0 1 2 3 4 5 6 miles
0 1 2 3 4 5 6 7 8 9 10 km

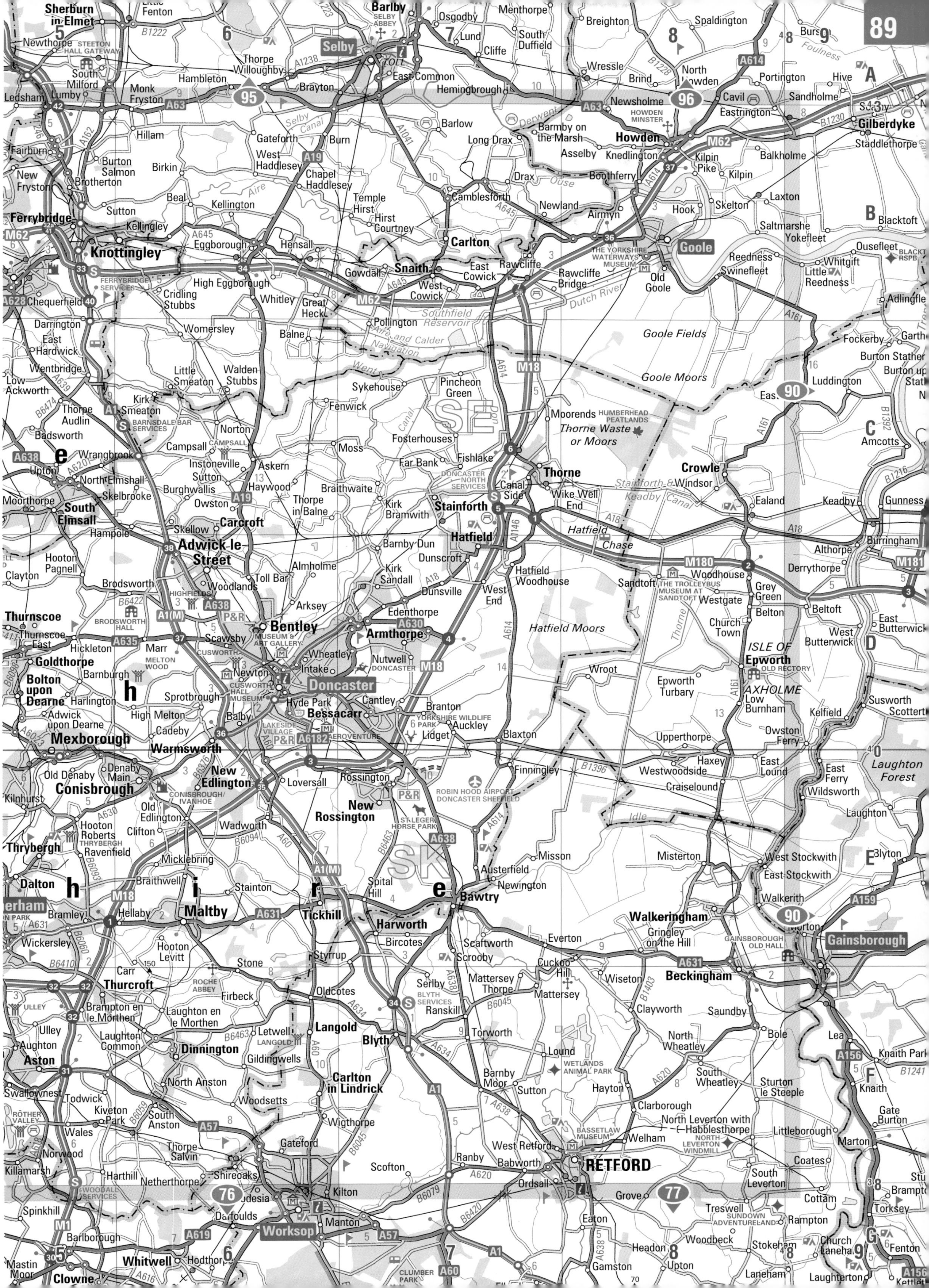

Sherburn in Elmet
Little Fenton
Barlby
Osgodby
Menthorpe
Breighton
Spaldington
Selby
Selby Abbey
Lund
South Duffield
Cliffe
Newthorpe
Steeton Hall Gateway
South Milford
Thorpe Willoughby
Hambleton
East Common
Wressle
Brind
North Howden
Portington
Hive
Ledsham
Lumby
Monk Fryston
Brayton
Hemingbrough
Newsholme
Cavil
Sandholme
Eastrington
Howden Minster
Gilberdyke
Hillam
Gateforth
Burn
Barlow
Barmby on the Marsh
Long Drax
Howden
Staddlethorpe
Fairburn
Burton Salmon
West Haddlesey
Asselby
Knedlington
Kilpin Pike
Balkholme
Birkin
Chapel Haddlesey
Drax
Boothferry
Kilpin
New Fryston
Brotherton
Temple Hirst
Camblesforth
Laxton
Beal
Kellington
Newland
Airmyn
Hook
Skelton
Sutton
Hirst Courtney
Saltmarshe
Blacktoft
Ferrybridge
Kellingley
Yokefleet
Eggborough
Hensall
Carlton
Knottingley
Goole
Reedness
Ousefleet
Blacktoft RSPB
The Yorkshire Waterways Museum
Gowdall
Snaith
East Cowick
Rawcliffe
Rawcliffe Bridge
Whitgift
Swinefleet
Little Reedness
Ferrybridge Services
High Eggborough
West Cowick
Old Goole
Cridling Stubbs
Whitley
Great Heck
Dutch River
Adlingfleet
Chequerfield
Southfield Reservoir
Pollington
Darrington
Balne
Aire and Calder Navigation
Goole Fields
East Hardwick
Womersley
Fockerby
Garthorpe
Wentbridge
Little Smeaton
Walden Stubbs
Burton Stather
Burton upon Stather
Low Ackworth
Sykehouse
Pincheon Green
Goole Moors
Luddington
Thorpe Audlin
Kirk Smeaton
Fenwick
Barnsdale Bar Services
Moorends
Humberhead Peatlands
Badsworth
Norton
Thorne Waste or Moors
Amcotts
Campsall
Moss
Fosterhouses
Wrangbrook
Instoneville
Fishlake
Upton
Askern
Far Bank
Thorne
Crowle
North Elmshall
Sutton
Doncaster North Services
Stainforth & Keadby Canal
Windsor
Haywood
Braithwaite
Canal Side
Moorthorpe
Skelbrooke
Burghwallis
Wike Well End
South Elmsall
Owston
Thorpe in Balne
Kirk Bramwith
Stainforth
Ealand
Keadby
Gunness
Carcroft
Hampole
Skellow
Hatfield
Hatfield Chase
Burringham
Adwick le Street
Barnby Dun
Althorpe
Hooton Pagnell
Almholme
Dunscroft
Derrythorpe
Clayton
Woodlands
Toll Bar
Kirk Sandall
Hatfield Woodhouse
Woodhouse
Brodsworth
Highfields
Dunsville
Sandtoft
The Trolleybus Museum at Sandtoft
Grey Green
West End
Westgate
Thurnscoe
Arksey
Edenthorpe
Belton
Beltoft
Thurnscoe East
Brodsworth Hall
Bentley
Church Town
East Butterwick
Hickleton
Marr
Scawsby
Museum & Art Gallery
Armthorpe
Hatfield Moors
West Butterwick
Cusworth
Isle of Axholme
Goldthorpe
Melton Wood
Wheatley
Nutwell
Epworth
Old Rectory
Bolton upon Dearne
Barnburgh
Intake
Doncaster
Wroot
Epworth Turbary
Harlington
Newton
Cusworth Hall Museum
Sprotbrough
Hyde Park
Cantley
Low Burnham
Susworth
Adwick upon Dearne
High Melton
Balby
Bessacarr
Branton
Yorkshire Wildlife Park
Kelfield
Scotter
Cadeby
Lakeside Village
Auckley
Owston Ferry
Mexborough
Warmsworth
Aeroventure
Lidget
Blaxton
Upperthorpe
Haxey
East Lound
Laughton Forest
Denaby Main
New Edlington
Loversall
Rossington
Finningley
Westwoodside
East Ferry
Old Denaby
Conisbrough
Conisbrough Ivanhoe
Robin Hood Airport Doncaster Sheffield
Craiselound
Wildsworth
Kilnhurst
Old Edlington
New Rossington
Idle
Laughton
Hooton Roberts
Thrybergh
Clifton
Wadworth
St. Leger Horse Park
Ravenfield
Misson
Misterton
West Stockwith
Blyton
Micklebring
Austerfield
East Stockwith
Dalton
Braithwell
Stainton
Spital Hill
Newington
Bawtry
Walkerith
Morton
Bramley
Hellaby
Maltby
Tickhill
Harworth
Walkeringham
Gainsborough
Wickersley
Hooton Levitt
Bircotes
Scaftworth
Everton
Gringley on the Hill
Gainsborough Old Hall
Stone
Styrrup
Scrooby
Carr
Roche Abbey
Cuckoo Hill
Wiseton
Beckingham
Thurcroft
Firbeck
Oldcotes
Serlby
Mattersey Thorpe
Mattersey
Ulley
Brampton en le Morthen
Laughton en le Morthen
Blyth Services
Ranskill
Clayworth
Saundby
Letwell
Langold
Langold
Torworth
North Wheatley
Bole
Lea
Aughton
Laughton Common
Dinnington
Blyth
Lound
Knaith Park
Aston
Gildingwells
Wetlands Animal Park
South Wheatley
Sturton le Steeple
North Anston
Carlton in Lindrick
Barnby Moor
Sutton
Hayton
Knaith
Swallownest
Todwick
Woodsetts
Clarborough
Kiveton Park
South Anston
Rother Valley
Wigthorpe
North Leverton with Habblesthorpe
Gate Burton
Wales
Littleborough
Bassetlaw Museum
Welham
Marton
Norwood
Thorpe Salvin
Gateford
West Retford
North Leverton Windmill
Killamarsh
Harthill
Shireoaks
Scofton
Ranby
Babworth
Retford
Coates
Netherthorpe
South Leverton
Brampton
Woodall Services
Rhodesia
Kilton
Ordsall
Grove
Cottam
Spinkhill
Darfoulds
Manton
Treswell
Sundown Adventureland
Torksey
Worksop
Eaton
Rampton
Barlborough
Woodbeck
Church Laneham
Headon
Stokeham
Fenton
Mastin Moor
Whitwell
Hodthorpe
Clumber Park
Gamston
Upton
Laneham
Laughterton
Clowne
Kettlethorpe

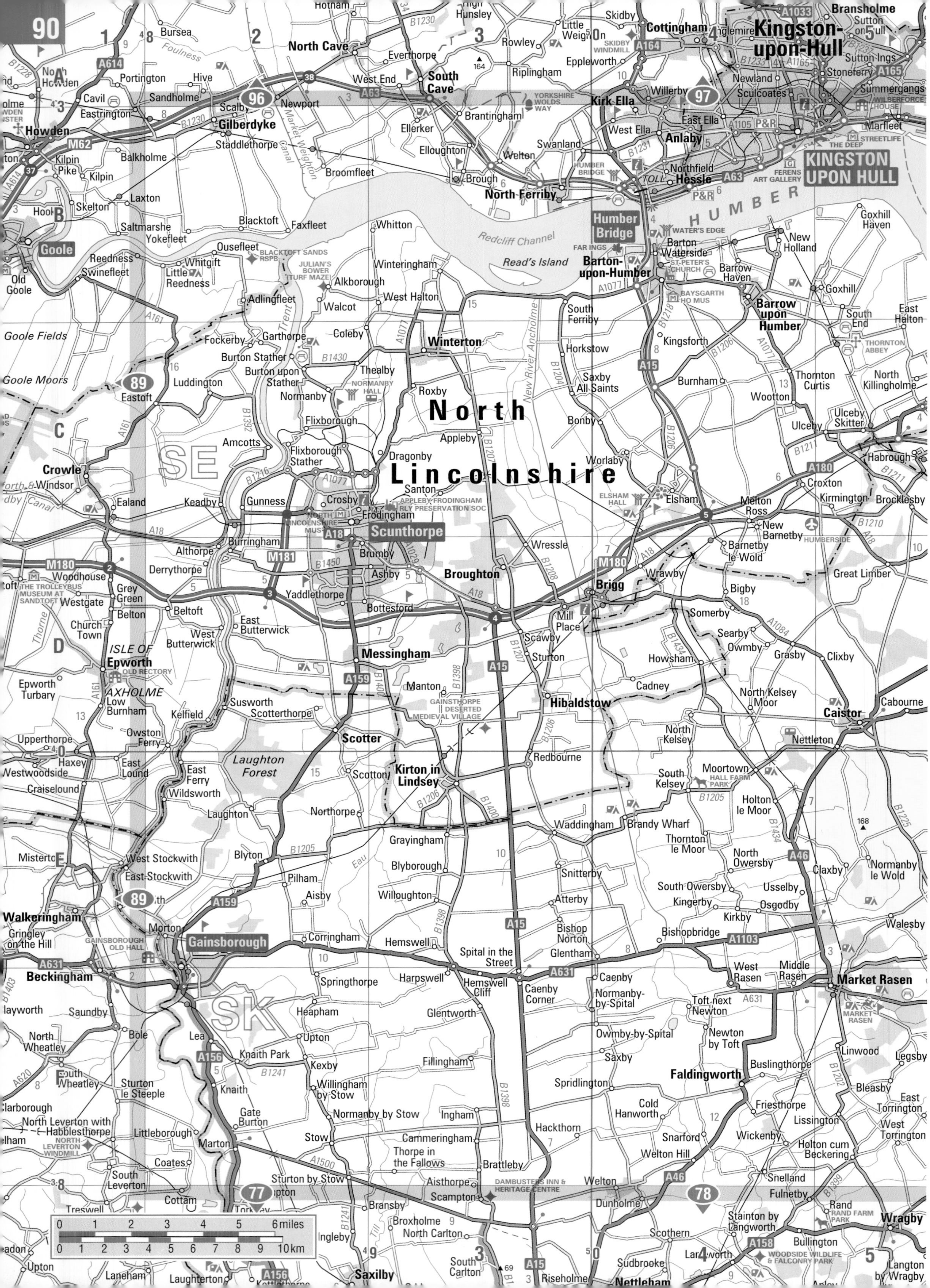
Kingston-upon-Hull
KINGSTON UPON HULL
North Lincolnshire
SE
SK
HUMBER
Redcliff Channel
Read's Island
Humber Bridge
Goole
Scunthorpe
Gainsborough
Howden
Gilberdyke
North Cave
South Cave
Cottingham
Kirk Ella
Anlaby
Hessle
North Ferriby
Brough
Barton-upon-Humber
Barrow upon Humber
Winterton
Crowle
Epworth
ISLE OF AXHOLME
Brigg
Broughton
Messingham
Scotter
Kirton in Lindsey
Hibaldstow
Caistor
Market Rasen
Walkeringham
Beckingham
Faldingworth
Wragby
Saxilby
Nettleham
Laughton Forest
Goole Fields
Goole Moors
Bransholme
Sutton Ings
Marfleet
Newland
Sculcoates
Willerby
West Ella
Swanland
Welton
Elloughton
Ellerker
Brantingham
Everthorpe
West End
Newport
Scalby
Staddlethorpe
Broomfleet
Blacktoft
Faxfleet
Whitton
Winteringham
Alkborough
West Halton
Walcot
Adlingfleet
Ousefleet
Whitgift
Reedness
Swinefleet
Saltmarshe
Yokefleet
Skelton
Hook
Laxton
Kilpin
Balkholme
Sandholme
Portington
Eastrington
Cavil
Hive
Bursea
Rowley
Riplingham
Little Weighton
Skidby
Eppleworth
Hotham
High Hunsley
Garthorpe
Fockerby
Luddington
Eastoft
Amcotts
Burton Stather
Burton upon Stather
Normanby
Thealby
Coleby
Roxby
Flixborough
Flixborough Stather
Appleby
Dragonby
Santon
Crosby
Frodingham
Gunness
Keadby
Ealand
Burringham
Althorpe
Derrythorpe
Brumby
Ashby
Yaddlethorpe
Bottesford
Wressle
Belton
Beltoft
Westgate
Woodhouse
Grey Green
Church Town
East Butterwick
West Butterwick
Manton
Susworth
Scotterthorpe
Kelfield
Owston Ferry
Haxey
Westwoodside
Craiseland
East Lound
East Ferry
Wildsworth
Laughton
Northorpe
Scotton
Redbourne
Waddingham
Brandy Wharf
Grayingham
Blyborough
Blyton
Pilham
Aisby
Willoughton
West Stockwith
East Stockwith
Morton
Corringham
Hemswell
Spital in the Street
Harpswell
Hemswell Cliff
Springthorpe
Heapham
Glentworth
Upton
Kexby
Fillingham
Knaith Park
Knaith
Lea
Gate Burton
Willingham by Stow
Normanby by Stow
Stow
Ingham
Cammeringham
Thorpe in the Fallows
Brattleby
Aisthorpe
Scampton
Sturton by Stow
Marton
Littleborough
Bole
Saundby
North Wheatley
South Wheatley
Sturton le Steeple
North Leverton with Habblesthorpe
South Leverton
Coates
Cottam
Treswell
Torksey
Bransby
Broxholme
North Carlton
South Carlton
Ingleby
Laneham
Riseholme
Welton
Dunholme
Scothern
Sudbrooke
Langworth
Stainton by Langworth
Bullington
Snarford
Welton Hill
Hackthorn
Cold Hanworth
Spridlington
Saxby
Owmby-by-Spital
Normanby-by-Spital
Caenby
Caenby Corner
Glentham
Bishop Norton
Atterby
Snitterby
Thornton le Moor
North Owersby
South Owersby
Kingerby
Kirkby
Osgodby
Usselby
Bishopbridge
West Rasen
Middle Rasen
Toft next Newton
Newton by Toft
Buslingthorpe
Friesthorpe
Wickenby
Lissington
Snelland
Holton cum Beckering
Fulnetby
Rand
Linwood
Legsby
Bleasby
East Torrington
West Torrington
Walesby
Claxby
Normanby le Wold
Holton le Moor
Moortown
South Kelsey
North Kelsey
Nettleton
Cabourne
North Kelsey Moor
Cadney
Howsham
Searby
Owmby
Grasby
Clixby
Somerby
Bigby
Great Limber
Barnetby le Wold
New Barnetby
Melton Ross
Wrawby
Mill Place
Scawby
Sturton
Elsham
Worlaby
Bonby
Saxby All Saints
Horkstow
South Ferriby
Kingsforth
Burnham
Wootton
Thornton Curtis
Ulceby
Ulceby Skitter
Habrough
Croxton
Kirmington
Brocklesby
North Killingholme
East Halton
South End
Goxhill
Goxhill Haven
New Holland
Barrow Haven
Barton Waterside
Little Reedness
Old Goole
Swinefleet
Rawcliffe
Upperthorpe
Misterton
Gringley on the Hill
Clarborough
Epworth Turbary
Low Burnham
Windsor
A63
A614
M62
A161
A18
M180
M181
A159
A15
A1077
A180
A1084
A1103
A631
A46
A158
A156
A1500
B1230
B1430
B1216
B1392
B1450
B1207
B1206
B1204
B1218
B1398
B1400
B1205
B1241
B1434
B1225
B1202
B1399
B1210
B1211
96
97
89
77
78
0 1 2 3 4 5 6 miles
0 1 2 3 4 5 6 7 8 9 10 km

Thirtleby
Ganstead
Sproatley
Humbleton
Fitling
Hilston
Bilton
Lelley
Owstwick
Elstronwick
Tunstall
Preston
Burton Pidsea
North End
West End
Roos
Waxholme
Salt End
A1033
Hedon
Owthorne
Haven Side
Rimswell
Withernsea
Burstwick
B1362
Halsham
Paull
East End
Thorngumbald
Camerton
FORT PAULL
Ryehill
Keyingham
Ottringham
Hollym
Winestead
Little Humber
Holmpton
Thorney Crofts
Patrington
B1445
Out Newton
Cherry Cob Sands
TA
Welwick
Weeton
Sunk Island
Skeffling
Easington
Kilnsea
A160
South Killingholme
Immingham
MUSEUM
SPURN
SPURN HEAD
Stallingborough
A180
Pyewipe
ROTTERDAM EUROPOORT ZEEBRUGGE
Grimsby
Keelby
Healing
West Marsh
Great Coates
CLEETHORPES
MOUTH OF THE HUMBER
Riby Cross Roads
FISHING HERITAGE CENTRE
Old Clee
Aylesby
Freshney
CLEETHORPES COAST LIGHT RAILWAY
Riby
Laceby
Nunsthorpe
A46
A16
PLEASURE ISLAND THEME PARK
Bradley
Scartho
A1098
CLEETHORPES
North East
Humberston
B1219
Irby upon Humber
A1173
Barnoldby le Beck
Waltham
New Waltham
A18
WALTHAM WINDMILL
Holton le Clay
Swallow
A46
Lincolnshire
Tetney Lock
Brigsley
Beelsby
B1203
Ashby cum Fenby
A1031
North Cotes
Hatcliffe
Cuxwold
Waithe
Tetney
East Ravendale
Grainsby
Marshchapel
Rothwell
Donna Nook
B1201
Eskham
Croxby
Wragholme
North Thoresby
Thoresway
Thorganby
Wold Newton
Grainthorpe
Swinhope
A16
Fulstow
North Somercotes
LINCOLNSHIRE WOLDS RLY
DONNA NOOK
Brookenby
Ludborough
Covenham St Bartholomew
Skidbrooke North End
Conisholme
South Somercotes
Saltfleet
Stainton le Vale
Binbrook
TF
Utterby
Covenham St Mary
A1031
Yarburgh
North Ormsby
Skidbrooke
ALVINGHAM MILL
Kirmond le Mire
B1203
Fotherby
Saltfleetby St Clements
Alvingham
SALTFLEETBY THEDDLETHORPE
Little Grimsby
North Cockerington
Tealby
Great Tows
North Elkington
Kelstern
RUSHMOOR
Saltfleetby All Saints
Theddlethorpe St Helen
A631
North Willingham
Ludford
South Elkington
South Cockerington
Saltfleetby St Peter
B1200
Keddington
Grimoldby
Welton le Wold
Louth
Theddlethorpe All Saints
Burgh on Bain
Stewton
SEAL SANCTUARY & NATURE CENTRE
Sixhills
Manby
ST JAMES
Meers Bridge
Grimblethorpe
Little Carlton
Mablethorpe
Gayton le Wold
Hallington
Great Carlton
Hainton
A157
Legbourne
Biscathorpe
Raithby
South Willingham
Trusthorpe
South Reston
Donington on Bain
Gayton le Marsh
A157
Little Cawthorpe
Withcall
A153
North Reston
A1104
Tathwell
Strubby
Sutton on Sea
Benniworth
Withern
Thorpe
Muckton
Tothill
A157
Maltby le Marsh
Haugham
B1373
East Barkwith
Stenigot
CADWELL PARK
Authorpe
Sandilands
B1225
Market Stainton
Beesby
West Barkwith
Cawkwell
A16
Woodthorpe
Maidenwell
Burwell
Sotby
Hannah
WOODY'S TOP
Gaulceby
Saleby
Panton
CLAYTHORPE WATER AND WILDFOWL GARDENS
Markby
Ranby
Scamblesby
Ruckland
Belleau
Farforth
White Pit
Aby
Swaby
A1111
Asserby
Oxcombe
ALFORD WINDMILL
Hatton
Ketsby
South Thoresby
A52
Bilsby
ALFORD MANOR HOUSE
Huttoft
Great Sturton
South Ormsby
Belchford
Rigsby
B1449
Haugh
Alford

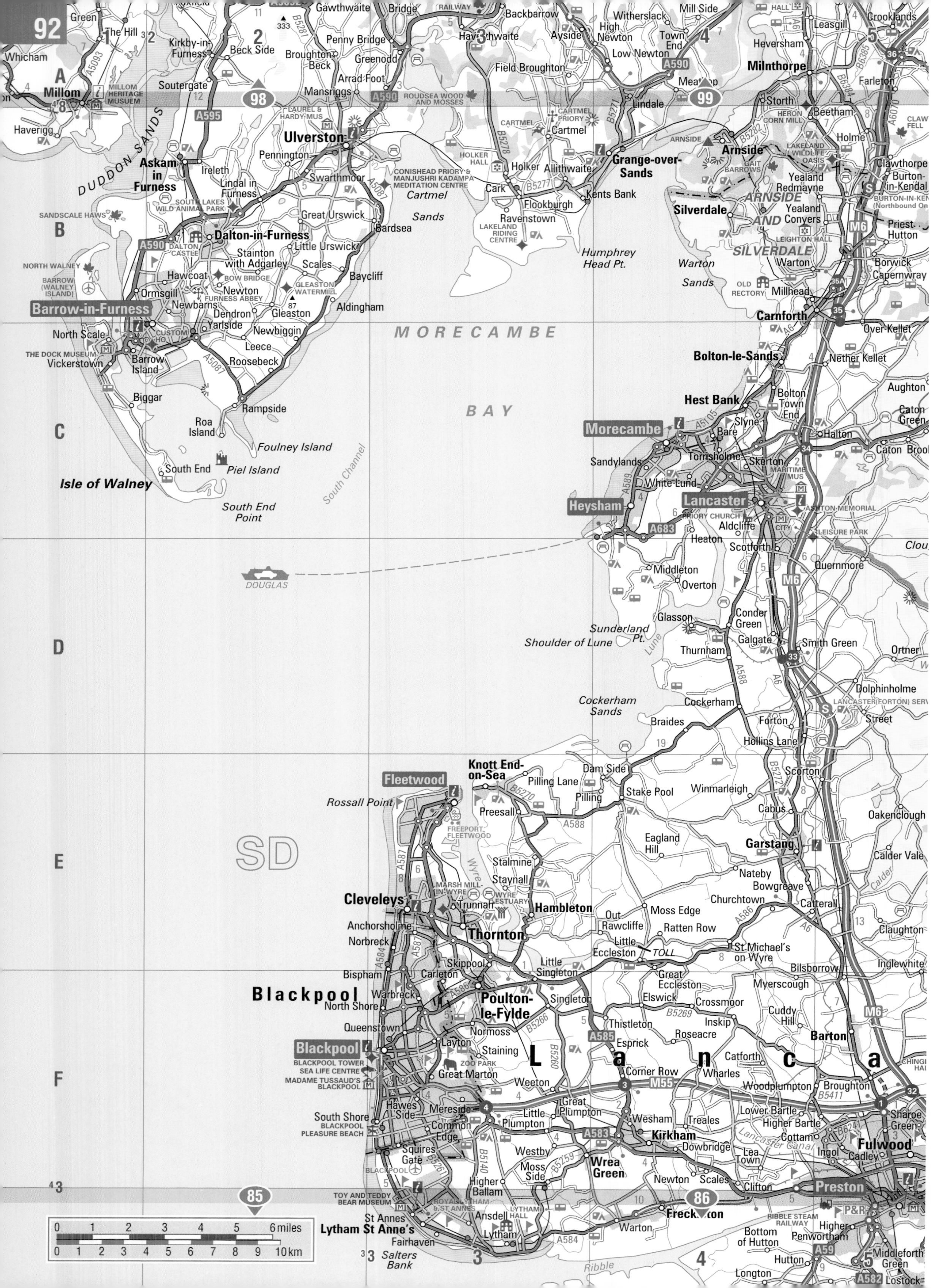

Green
The Hill
Whicham
Millom
MILLOM HERITAGE MUSEUM
Haverigg
Kirkby-in-Furness
Beck Side
Soutergate
Broughton Beck
Penny Bridge
Greenodd
Arrad Foot
Mansriggs
Gawthwaite
Bridge
RAILWAY
Backbarrow
Haverthwaite
Ayside
Witherslack
High Newton
Low Newton
Mill Side
Town End
Field Broughton
Heversham
Milnthorpe
Leasgill
Crooklands
Farleton
Meathop
ROUDSEA WOOD AND MOSSES
LAUREL & HARDY MUS
98
99
Lindale
Storth
HERON CORN MILL
Beetham
Holme
CLAW FELL
Ulverston
CARTMEL PRIORY
CARTMEL
Cartmel
HOLKER HALL
Holker
Allithwaite
Grange-over-Sands
ARNSIDE
Arnside
LAKELAND WILDLIFE OASIS
GAIT BARROWS
Clawthorpe
Burton-in-Kendal
Yealand Redmayne
Yealand Conyers
BURTON-IN-KENDAL (Northbound Only)
Priest Hutton
Pennington
Askam in Furness
Ireleth
Lindal in Furness
Swarthmoor
CONISHEAD PRIORY & MANJUSHRI KADAMPA MEDITATION CENTRE
Cartmel Sands
Cark
Flookburgh
Kents Bank
Ravenstown
LAKELAND RIDING CENTRE
DUDDON SANDS
SOUTH LAKES WILD ANIMAL PARK
SANDSCALE HAWS
Great Urswick
Bardsea
Dalton-in-Furness
DALTON CASTLE
Stainton with Adgarley
Little Urswick
Scales
Baycliff
Humphrey Head Pt.
Silverdale
ARNSIDE AND SILVERDALE
LEIGHTON HALL
Warton
Warton Sands
OLD RECTORY
Millhead
Borwick
Capernwray
NORTH WALNEY
BARROW (WALNEY ISLAND)
Hawcoat
BOW BRIDGE
Ormsgill
Newton
Newbarns
FURNESS ABBEY
GLEASTON WATERMILL
Barrow-in-Furness
Dendron
Gleaston
Aldingham
Yarlside
Newbiggin
North Scale
CUSTOM HO
THE DOCK MUSEUM
Vickerstown
Barrow Island
Leece
Roosebeck
MORECAMBE
BAY
Carnforth
Over Kellet
Bolton-le-Sands
Nether Kellet
Aughton
Biggar
Rampside
Roa Island
Foulney Island
Hest Bank
Bolton Town End
Slyne
Bare
Caton Green
Halton
Caton
Morecambe
Torrisholme
Skerton
MARITIME MUS
South End
Piel Island
Isle of Walney
South Channel
South End Point
Sandylands
White Lund
Heysham
Lancaster
PRIORY CHURCH
ASHTON MEMORIAL
Aldcliffe
CITY
LEISURE PARK
Heaton
Scotforth
Quernmore
DOUGLAS
Middleton
Overton
Glasson
Conder Green
Galgate
Sunderland Pt.
Shoulder of Lune
Thurnham
Lune
Smith Green
Ortner
Dolphinholme
Cockerham Sands
Cockerham
LANCASTER (FORTON) SERV
Forton
Street
Braides
Hollins Lane
Dam Side
Scorton
Knott End-on-Sea
Pilling Lane
Pilling
Stake Pool
Winmarleigh
Fleetwood
Rossall Point
Preesall
Cabus
Oakenclough
FREEPORT FLEETWOOD
Eagland Hill
Garstang
SD
Calder Vale
Stalmine
Wyre
Nateby
Bowgreave
Staynall
MARSH MILL-IN-WYRE
WYRE ESTUARY
Cleveleys
Trunnah
Hambleton
Churchtown
Moss Edge
Catterall
Anchorsholme
Out Rawcliffe
Ratten Row
Claughton
Norbreck
Thornton
Little Eccleston
TOLL
St Michael's on Wyre
Skippool
Bispham
Carleton
Little Singleton
Great Eccleston
Bilsborrow
Inglewhite
Blackpool
Warbreck
Poulton-le-Fylde
Singleton
Elswick
Myerscough
North Shore
Crossmoor
Cuddy Hill
Queenstown
Thistleton
Inskip
Normoss
Esprick
Roseacre
Barton
Layton
Staining
L
a
n
c
a
Catforth
BLACKPOOL TOWER
SEA LIFE CENTRE
MADAME TUSSAUD'S BLACKPOOL
ZOO PARK
Great Marton
Corner Row
Wharles
Weeton
Woodplumpton
Broughton
Hawes Side
Mereside
Great Plumpton
Lower Bartle
Higher Bartle
Sharoe Green
South Shore
BLACKPOOL PLEASURE BEACH
Common Edge
Little Plumpton
Wesham
Treales
Kirkham
Cottam
Fulwood
Lancaster Canal
Ingol
Cadley
Squires Gate
Westby
Dowbridge
Lea Town
Moss Side
Wrea Green
BLACKPOOL
Higher Ballam
Newton
Scales
Clifton
Preston
TOY AND TEDDY BEAR MUSEUM
ROYAL LYTHAM & ST ANNES
85
86
St Annes
Ansdell
LYTHAM HALL
Freckleton
RIBBLE STEAM RAILWAY
P&R
Lytham St Anne's
Lytham
Warton
Bottom of Hutton
Higher Penwortham
Fairhaven
Salters Bank
Ribble
Hutton
Middleforth Green
Longton
Lostock
0 1 2 3 4 5 6 miles
0 1 2 3 4 5 6 7 8 9 10 km
A
B
C
D
E
F
M6
M55
A590
A595
A5087
A6
A683
A588
A585
A583
A584
A586
A587
A589
A5105
A59
A582
A5093
B5281
B5278
B5277
B5271
B5282
B6385
B6384
A6070
B5270
B5272
B5266
B5260
B5269
B5259
B5140
B5261
B5411
B6241

YORKSHIRE DALES NATIONAL PARK
LANGSTROTHDALE CHASE
FOREST OF BOWLAND
Lancashire
SD
99
100
94
86
87
Kirkby Lonsdale
Casterton
Kearstwick
Barbon
Mansergh
Old Town
Lupton
Hutton Roof
Whittington
Cowan Bridge
Nether Burrow
Leck
Ireby
Masongill
Westhouse
Newton
Tunstall
Cantsfield
Arkholme
Melling
Wrayton
Burton in Lonsdale
Ingleton
Gressingham
Hornby
Tatham
Wennington
Low Bentham
High Bentham
Newby
Clapham
Austwick
Feizor
Lawkland
Farleton
Claughton
Wray
Mewith Head
Keasden
Lowgill
Eldroth
Caton Moor
Salter
Goodber Common
Tatham Fells
Burn Moor
Crossgill
Haylot Fell
Catlow Fell
Whernside
Blea Moor
Gayle Moor
Cam Fell
Oughtershaw
Cragdale Moor
Middle Tongue
Ribblehead
Scales Moor
Chapel-le-Dale
Ingleborough
Simon Fell
White Scar Caves
Ingleborough Common
Gaping Gill
Ingleborough Show Cave
The Pennine Bridleway
Pennine Way
Bentham Pottery
Yockenthwaite
Hubberholme
Buckden
Cray
Foxup
Halton Gill
High Birkwith
Horton Moor
Pen-y-ghent
New Houses
Horton in Ribblesdale
Litton
Scoska Wood
Arncliffe
Kettlewell
Hawkswick
Darnbrook Fell
Fountains Fell
Helwith Bridge
Wharfe
Little Stainforth
Stainforth
Malham Tarn
The Settle Loop
Stackhouse
Watershed Mill Visitor Centre
Langcliffe
Giggleswick
Giggleswick School Chapel
Settle
Malham Cove
Kirkby Fell
Malham
Bordley
New House Farm, Malham
Yorkshire Dales Falconry and Conservation Centre
Wham
Hanlith
Kirkby Malham
Mearbeck
Rathmell
Long Preston
Airton
Calton
Winterburn
Hetton
Otterburn
Hellifield
Bell Busk
Flasby
Eshton
Coniston Cold
Gargrave
Bank Newton
Wigglesworth
Tosside
Gisburn Forest
Stocks Reservoir
Ribblesdale
Grunsagill
Knotts
Halton West
Nappa
Paythorne
Newsholme
Horton
Broughton
East Marton
West Marton
Elslack
Thornton-in-Craven
Earby
Barnoldswick
Coates
Salterforth
Kelbrook
Foulridge
Colne Edge
Colne
Laneshaw Bridge
Winewall
Wycoller
Trawden
The Forest of Trawden
Boulsworth Hill
Walshaw Dean Res.
Widdop Res.
Heptonstall Moor
Ward's Stone
Mallowdale Fell
White Hill
Croasdale Fell
Lee Fell
Tarnbrook Fell
Tarnbrook
Lee
Abbeystead
Marshaw
Trough of Bowland
Whins Brow
Hawthornthwaite Fell
Fell Top
Sykes
Slaidburn
Newton
Hareden
Dunsop Bridge
Sykes Fell
Bleasdale Moors
Fair Snape Fell
Bleasdale
Whitewell
Easington Fell
Lane Ends
Holden
Forest Becks
Bolton-by-Bowland
Gisburn
Bracewell
Lane End
Sawley
Grindleton
West Bradford
Newby
Rimington
Twiston
Downham
Chatburn
Waddington
Bashall Eaves
Cow Ark
Chipping
Walker Fold
Beacon Fell
Whitechapel
Clitheroe
Low Moor
Clitheroe Castle Museum
Worston
Pendle Hill
Blacko
Roughlee
Barley
Pendle Heritage Centre
Hesketh Lane
Longridge Fell
Pendleton
Newchurch
Barrowford
Nelson
Little Marsden
Brierfield
Knowle Green
New Row
Great Mitton
Barrow
Longridge
Goosnargh
Hurst Green
Wiswell
Sabden
The Forest of Pendle
Fence
Higham
Whalley
Whalley Abbey
St Saviour's Church
Little Town
Old Langho
Ribchester
Roman Museum
Billington
Simonstone
Padiham
Gawthorpe Hall
Harle Syke
Haggate
Burnley
Haighton Green
Grimsargh
Langho
Read
Rose Grove
Copster Green
Great Harwood
Altham
Hapton
Habergham
Balderstone
Salesbury
Wilpshire
Clayton-le-Moors
Brunshaw
Worsthorne
Hurstwood
Ribbleton
Samlesbury Hall
Brockholes Nature Res
Osbaldeston
Samlesbury
Mellor Brook
Mellor
Brownhill
Rishton
Huncoat
Lane Ends
Mereclough
Walk Mill
Pleckgate
Church
Milnshaw
Accrington
Clow Bridge
Towneley Hall Art Gallery, Museum & Historic House
Holme Chapel
Samlesbury Bottoms
Walton-le-Dale
Higher Walton
Coup Green
Hoghton Tower
Blackburn
Shadsworth
West End
Scaitcliffe
Oswaldtwistle
Dunnockshaw
Love Clough
Thieveley Pike
Cornholme
Blackshaw Head
Charlestown
Bamber Bridge
Gregson Lane
Pleasington
Feniscowles
Riley Green
Hoghton
Lower Darwen
Guide
Baxenden
Goodshaw
Forest of Rossendale
Goodshaw Chapel
Water
Portsmouth
Lydgate
M6
M65
A65
A683
A687
A682
A59
A56
A6068
A671
A666
A646
A680
A678
B6480
B6479
B6478
B6255
B6254
B6243
B6245
B6246
B5269

YORKSHIRE
DALES
NATIONAL
PARK
NIDDERDALE
North
SD
SE
Cragdale Moor
Carlton Moor
West Scrafton
Ellingstring
High Ellington
Low Ellington
Low Burton
Masham
Walden
Gammersgill
Kidstones
Horsehouse
Coverdale
Colsterdale
Fearby
Healey
Uredale Glass
Theakston Brewery Visitor Centre
Swinton
Binsoe
643 Middle Tongue
Oughtershaw
100
101
Walden Head
Braidley
Hindlethwaite Moor
Colsterdale Moor
Woodale
544 Great Haw
Masham Moor
Leighton
Warthermarske
Leighton Res.
Ilton
Yockenthwaite
Cray
702 Buckden Pike
Hubberholme
Buckden
605 Little Whernside
Scar House Res.
Roundhill Res.
Foxup
Halton Gill
610
Starbotton
Angram Res.
Grewelthorpe
Kirkby Malzeard
Litton
Middlesmoor
Stean
Lofthouse
Carlesmoor
Scoska Wood
Kettlewell
704 Great Whernside
Riggs Moor
406 Hambleton Hill
Swetton
Laverton
Greygarth
Littondale
Darnbrook Fell
Arncliffe
Nidderdale
Bouthwaite
Dallowgill Moor
Dallow
Low Grantley
662 Fountains Fell
Hawkswick
Stean Moor
Ramsgill
Pennine Way
Conistone Moor
Gouthwaite Res.
Grantley
Kilnsey
Heathfield Moor
Wath
Pateley Moor
Eavestone
Risplith
Sawley
Kilnsey Park
Malham Tarn
93
Conistone
Nidderdale Museum
B6265
The Settle Loop
Hebden Moor
Grimwith Res.
Pateley Bridge
Bordley
Malham Cove
Grassington
Upper Wharfedale Museum
Greenhow Hill
Bewerley
Wilsill
Brimham Rocks
547 Kirkby Fell
New House Farm, Malham
Threshfield
Glasshouses
Malham
Linton
Hebden
Stump Cross Caverns
Low Laithe
New York
Dacre Banks
Summer Bridge
Parcevall Hall Gardens
Hanlith
Thorpe
Burnsall
Pockstones Moor
Kirkby Malham
Threapland
Skyreholme
Dacre
B6165
Cracoe
506 Upper Barden Res.
Appletreewick
Padside
Darley Head
Darley
Birstwith
Airton
Calton
Winterburn
Hetton
Rylstone
Drebley
449 Barden Fell
Thruscross Res.
Thornthwaite
Long Preston
Otterburn
West End
Kettlesing Bottom
Forest Moor
Hellifield
Bell Busk
Flasby
B6265
Barden Scale
Lower Barden Res.
Eshton
Bolton Abbey Estate
Blubberhouses
A59
Kettlesing Head
A65
Coniston Cold
Halton East
Bolton Abbey
Hill End
20
Fewston
Fewston Res.
A682
Halton West
Eastby
Embsay
Embsay & Bolton Abbey Steam Rly
Pace Gate
Bank Newton
Gargrave
Thorlby
A59
Buffers
Hazlewood
409
Swinsty Res.
Bland Hill
Nappa
219
Pennine Way
Skipton
Bolton Bridge
Beamsley
Timble
Jack Hill
Broughton
Draughton
Langbar
B6451
Newsholme
East Marton
A629
Horton
West Marton
Carleton
Addingham
Lindley Wood Res.
Lindley Green
Braythorn
Elslack
Middleton
Denton
Bracewell
A6034
Low Bradley
Cringles
Farnley
Stainburn
Lane End
Thornton-in-Craven
Askwith
Clifton
Coates
388
Earby
Cononley
Ilkley
B6382
Weston
Barnoldswick
Farnhill
Kildwick
Silsden
Newall
Leathley
A56
Rombalds Moor
Ilkley Moor
Burley in Wharfedale
Otley
Pool
Salterforth
Lothersdale
Glusburn
Eastburn
402
Kelbrook
Lane Ends
Steeton
Menston
Chevin Forest Park
Cowling
Sutton-in-Craven
Cliffe Castle
Riddlesden
East Riddlesden Hall
East Carlton
Old Bramhope
New Road Side
Utley
Guiseley
Keighley
East Morton
Micklethwaite
Hawksworth
Yeadon
Leeds Bradford International
Foulridge
Colne Edge
A6068
Braithwaite
Knowle Park
Thwaites
Crossflatts
Blacko
Roughlee
Laycock
Cookridge
Laneshaw Bridge
Goose Eye
Thwaites Brow
Eldwick
Esholt
Rawdon
Barrowford
Colne
Winewall
443
Exley Head
Vintage Railway Carriage Mus
Baildon
Tinshill
Wycoller
Oakworth
Ingrow
Bingley
A657
A658
Trawden
Keighley Moor
Saltaire
Apperley Bridge
Horsforth
British in India Mus
Dockroyd
Lees
Harden
A650
Shipley
Idle
Nelson
The Forest of Trawden
Parsonage Mus
Haworth
Cottingley
Moorhead
Calverley
A6120
Little Marsden
The Pennine Bridleway
Stanbury
Cullingworth
Wilsden
Frizinghall
Eccleshill
Rodley
Brierfield
517 Boulsworth Hill
Pennine Way
Haworth Moor
Marsh
Penistone Hill
Lingbob
Cartwright Hall Art Gallery
Bradford Ind Mus
Farsley
Bramley
Haggate
Keighley and Worth Valley Railway
Oxenhope
B6144
Heaton
Undercliffe
Stanningley
Harle Syke
Burnley Lane
Walshaw Dean Res.
A629
Denholme
Manningham
Thornbury
A647
Burnley
Wadsworth Moor
Well Heads
Allerton
B6145
Bradford
Swinnow Moor
Brunshaw
Worsthorne
A6033
451
Denholme Clough
Thornton
Little Horton
Laisterdyke
Pudsey
Widdop Res.
Lidget Green
Bowling
Walk Mill
Hurstwood
Warley Moor Res.
Clayton
Great Horton
Holme Wood
New Farnley
Mereclough
Causeway Foot
Mountain
West Bowling
Nat Media Museum
Bolling Hall
Tong
Heptonstall Moor
Dean Head Res.
A647
Towneley Hall Art Gallery, Museum & Historic House
Queensbury
Bierley
A650
87
88
Colden
Pecket Well
Illingworth
Butter
Wibsey
Drighlington
Gildersome
Holme Chapel
Chiserley
Wainstalls
Ambler Thorn
Shelf
Low Moor
Birkenshaw
Adwalton
Hebden Bridge
Mount Tabor
A6036
M606
Stone Chair
Oakenshaw
Booth
Ovenden
Bankfield Museum
Northowram
Wyke
Oakwell Hall Red House
Birstall
Portsmouth
Walkley Clogs
Midgley
Wheatley
Shibden Hall
A58
Lydgate
Water
Mytholmroyd
Luddenden
Halifax
Scholes
Gomersal
0 1 2 3 4 5 6 miles
0 1 2 3 4 5 6 7 8 9 10 km

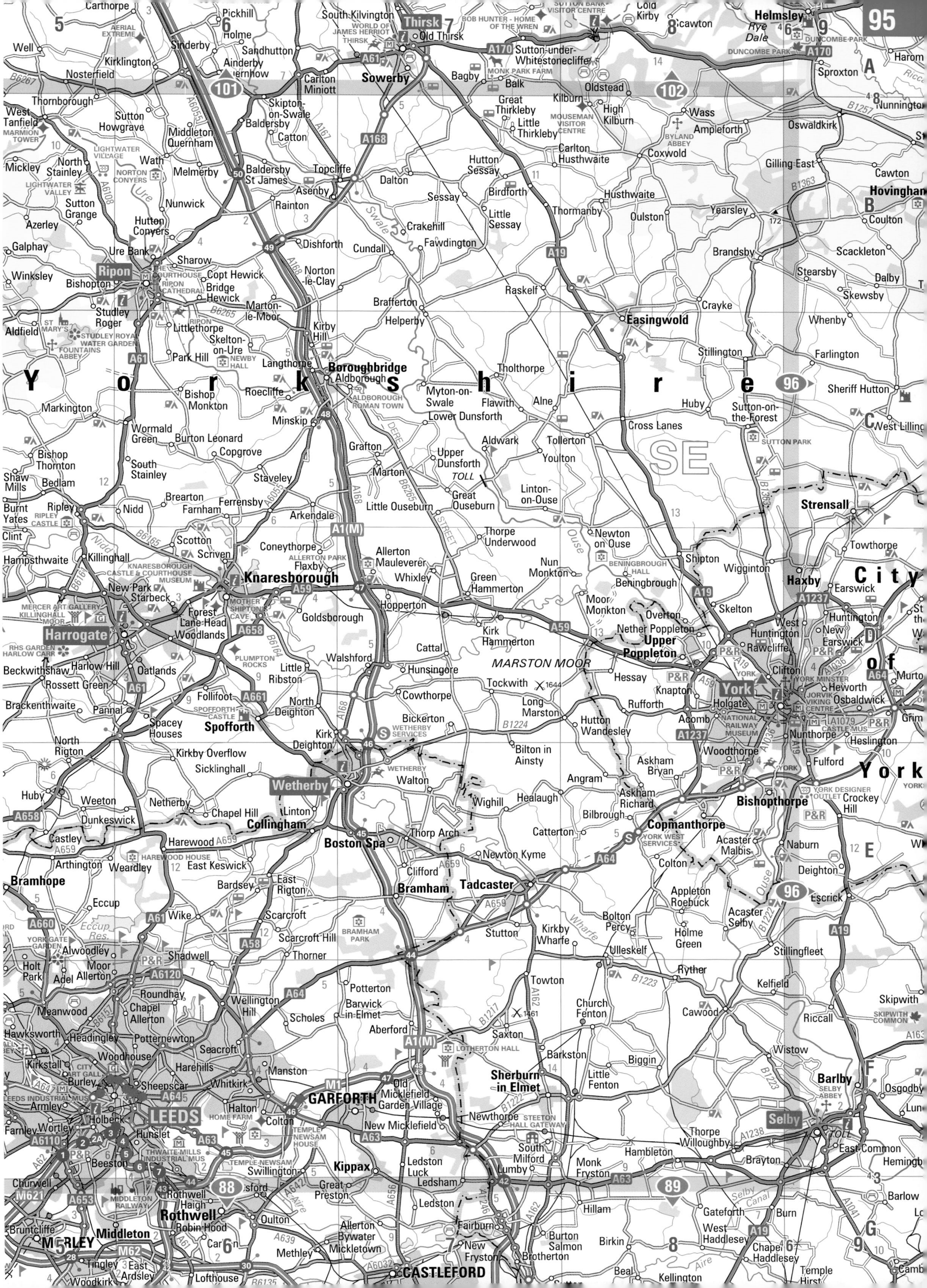
Carthorpe
Pickhill
South Kilvington
WORLD OF JAMES HERRIOT
Thirsk
BOB HUNTER - HOME OF THE WREN
SUTTON BANK VISITOR CENTRE
Cold Kirby
Helmsley
Rye Dale
DUNCOMBE PARK
AERIAL EXTREME
Holme
Sandhutton
Well
Sinderby
THIRSK
Old Thirsk
A170
Sutton-under-Whitestonecliffe
Harom
Kirklington
Ainderby Quernhow
Carlton Miniott
Sowerby
MONK PARK FARM
Bagby
Balk
Spraxton
Nosterfield
Oldstead
101
102
B6267
Thornborough
Great Thirkleby
Kilburn
High Kilburn
Wass
B1257
Nunnington
West Tanfield
MARMION TOWER
Sutton Howgrave
Middleton Quernham
Skipton-on-Swale
Baldersby
Catton
A168
Little Thirkleby
MOUSEMAN VISITOR CENTRE
BYLAND ABBEY
Ampleforth
Oswaldkirk
LIGHTWATER VILLAGE
Carlton Husthwaite
Coxwold
Mickley
North Stainley
NORTON CONYERS
Wath
Melmerby
Baldersby St James
Topcliffe
Hutton Sessay
Gilling East
Cawton
LIGHTWATER VALLEY
Asenby
Dalton
Birdforth
Hovingham
Sutton Grange
A6108
Ure
Nunwick
Rainton
Sessay
Husthwaite
B1363
Yearsley
Coulton
Azerley
Hutton Conyers
Swale
Crakehill
Little Sessay
Thormanby
Oulston
Galphay
Ure Bank
Dishforth
Cundall
Fawdington
A19
Brandsby
Scackleton
Ripon
Sharow
Winksley
Bishopton
THE COURTHOUSE
RIPON CATHEDRAL
Copt Hewick
Bridge Hewick
Norton-le-Clay
Stearsby
Dalby
Skewsby
Raskelf
Crayke
Studley Roger
Marton-le-Moor
Brafferton
Helperby
Easingwold
Whenby
B6265
Aldfield
ST MARY'S
STUDLEY ROYAL WATER GARDEN
FOUNTAINS ABBEY
Littlethorpe
RIPON
Skelton-on-Ure
Kirby Hill
NEWBY HALL
Stillington
Farlington
A61
Park Hill
Langthorpe
Boroughbridge
Aldborough
Tholthorpe
Yorkshire
96
Sheriff Hutton
Bishop Monkton
Roecliffe
ALDBOROUGH ROMAN TOWN
Myton-on-Swale
Flawith
Alne
Huby
Sutton-on-the-Forest
Markington
Minskip
Lower Dunsforth
Cross Lanes
West Lilling
SUTTON PARK
Wormald Green
Burton Leonard
Grafton
DERE STREET
Aldwark
Tollerton
Bishop Thornton
Copgrove
Upper Dunsforth
Youlton
SE
South Stainley
Marton
Shaw Mills
Bedlam
Staveley
TOLL
Linton-on-Ouse
Brearton
A6055
Great Ouseburn
Strensall
Burnt Yates
Ripley
Nidd
Farnham
Ferrensby
Arkendale
Little Ouseburn
RIPLEY CASTLE
A1(M)
Thorpe Underwood
Ouse
Newton on Ouse
Clint
B6165
Scotton
Scriven
Coneythorpe
ALLERTON PARK
Allerton Mauleverer
Towthorpe
Hampsthwaite
Killinghall
KNARESBOROUGH CASTLE & COURTHOUSE MUSEUM
Flaxby
Nun Monkton
BENINGBROUGH HALL
Shipton
Wigginton
Haxby
City of York
Knaresborough
Whixley
Green Hammerton
Beningbrough
Earswick
New Park
Starbeck
A59
Moor Monkton
Skelton
Huntington
MERCER ART GALLERY
Forest Lane Head
MOTHER SHIPTON'S CAVE
Goldsborough
Hopperton
Overton
KILLINGHALL MOOR
Woodlands
A658
Kirk Hammerton
Nether Poppleton
West Huntington
New Earswick
Harrogate
RHS GARDEN HARLOW CARR
Upper Poppleton
Rawcliffe
P&R
Cattal
Walshford
PLUMPTON ROCKS
Harlow Hill
Little Ribston
Hunsingore
MARSTON MOOR
Clifton
Beckwithshaw
Oatlands
Hessay
YORK MINSTER
Heworth
Rossett Green
Tockwith
Knapton
York
JORVIK VIKING CENTRE
Osbaldwick
Follifoot
A661
Cowthorpe
Long Marston
Rufforth
Holgate
Brackenthwaite
Pannal
SPOFFORTH CASTLE
North Deighton
Bickerton
Hutton Wandesley
Acomb
NATIONAL RAILWAY MUSEUM
Nunthorpe
CASTLE MUS
Spacey Houses
Spofforth
B1224
WETHERBY SERVICES
A1237
Heslington
North Rigton
Kirk Deighton
Bilton in Ainsty
Woodthorpe
Kirkby Overflow
Askham Bryan
Fulford
Sicklinghall
WETHERBY
Walton
YORK
Huby
Wetherby
Angram
Askham Richard
Bishopthorpe
YORK DESIGNER OUTLET
Crockey Hill
Weeton
Netherby
Wighill
Healaugh
A658
Dunkeswick
Chapel Hill
Linton
Bilbrough
Copmanthorpe
Collingham
Thorp Arch
Catterton
YORK WEST SERVICES
Acaster Malbis
Naburn
Castley
Harewood
A659
Boston Spa
HAREWOOD HOUSE
Newton Kyme
A64
Colton
Arthington
Weardley
East Keswick
Clifford
Deighton
Bramhope
Bardsey
East Rigton
Bramham
Tadcaster
Appleton Roebuck
Escrick
Eccup
Scarcroft
BRAMHAM PARK
Bolton Percy
Acaster Selby
Wike
Kirkby Wharfe
Wharfe
Holme Green
A660
Eccup Res.
Scarcroft Hill
Stutton
YORK GATE GARDEN
A58
Thorner
Ulleskelf
Stillingfleet
Alwoodley
Shadwell
Holt Park
Moor Allerton
A6120
Towton
Ryther
Adel
B1223
Kelfield
Roundhay
Potterton
A64
Chapel Allerton
Wellington Hill
Barwick in-Elmet
Church Fenton
Cawood
Skipwith
Meanwood
SKIPWITH COMMON
Scholes
Riccall
Hawksworth
Headingley
Potternewton
Aberford
Saxton
Wistow
Woodhouse
Seacroft
LOTHERTON HALL
Barkston
Kirkstall
CITY ART GALL
Harehills
Manston
Biggin
Little Fenton
Burley
Sheepscar
Whitkirk
Sherburn in Elmet
Barlby
SELBY ABBEY
Osgodby
LEEDS INDUSTRIAL MUS
M1
Old Micklefield
Garden Village
GARFORTH
Armley
A645
Halton
HOME FARM
Colton
Newthorpe
STEETON HALL GATEWAY
Selby
Farnley
Wortley
LEEDS
Holbeck
New Micklefield
TEMPLE NEWSAM HOUSE
Thorpe Willoughby
A1238
TOLL
A6110
Hunslet
A63
South Milford
Hambleton
East Common
THWAITE MILLS INDUSTRIAL MUS
Beeston
TEMPLE NEWSAM
Kippax
Ledston Luck
Monk Fryston
Brayton
Hemingbrough
Churwell
Swillington
Lumby
Ledsham
88
89
M621
A653
MIDDLETON RAILWAY
Rothwell Haigh
Great Preston
Ledston
Selby Canal
Barlow
Rothwell
Hillam
Gateforth
Burn
Bruntcliffe
Middleton
Robin Hood
Oulton
Allerton Bywater
Fairburn
Burton Salmon
West Haddlesey
MORLEY
M62
Carlton
A639
Mickletown
Methley
New Fryston
Birkin
Chapel Haddlesey
Tingley
East Ardsley
Brotherton
Woodkirk
Lofthouse
CASTLEFORD
Beal
Kellington
Aire
Temple Hirst

Helmsley
Rye Dale
DUNCOMBE PARK
A170
Nawton
Wombleton
Great Edstone
Marton
Pickering
PICKERING CASTLE
Ellerburn
Thornton-le-Dale
Wilton
Allerston
Ebberston
B1415
Snainton
Brompton
Harome
Sproxton
Riccal
Normanby
Costa Beck
Little Barugh
FLAMINGO LAND
102
103
Muscoates
NUNNINGTON HALL
Nunnington
West Ness
East Ness
Salton
Great Barugh
Kirby Misperton
A169
Wass
Ampleforth
BYLAND ABBEY
Coxwold
Oswaldkirk
B1257
Stonegrave
South Holme
Butterwick
Brawby
Little Habton
Great Habton
High Marishes
Derwent
Low Marishes
Ryton
Yedingham
East Heslerton
West Knapton
East Knapton
Scampston
SCAMPSTON HALL
A64
West Heslerton
Gilling East
Cawton
B1363
Hovingham
HOWARDIAN HILLS
Wath
HOVINGHAM HALL
Fryton
Slingsby
Barton-le-Street
Rye
EDEN CAMP MODERN HISTORY THEME MUSEUM
Wykeham
Rillington
WOLDS WAY LAVENDER
Thorpe Bassett
Wintringham
Yearsley
Coulton
Brandsby
Scackleton
Appleton-le-Street
Amotherby
Swinton
Broughton
Malton
Old Malton
Norton-on-Derwent
Scagglethorpe
Place Newton
Stearsby
Dalby
Skewsby
Terrington
YORKSHIRE LAVENDER
Ganthorpe
Coneysthorpe
CASTLE HOWARD
Settrington
Crayke
Whenby
Whitewall Corner
B1248
East Lutton
West Lutton
Stillington
Farlington
95
Bulmer
Welburn
High Hutton
Low Hutton
North Grimston
Sheriff Hutton
Whitwell-on-the-Hill
Firby
Langton
Duggleby
Kirby Grindalythe
Huby
Sutton-on-the-Forest
Thornton-le-Clay
Kirkham
KIRKHAM PRIORY
Kennythorpe
Birdsall
Wharram le Street
Sledmere
SUTTON PARK
West Lilling
Foston
Crambe
Westow
Burythorpe
WHARRAM PERCY MEDIEVAL VILLAGE
SLEDMERE HOUSE
Barton-le-Willows
Howsham
Leavening
B1251
Flaxton
Harton
Leppington
Acklam
Strensall
Bossall
Thixendale
Fimber
Claxton
Scrayingham
Towthorpe
Sand Hutton
Kirby Underdale
Fridaythorpe
Wetwang
Shipton
Wigginton
City of York
Haxby
Earswick
Moor End
Upper Helmsley
Buttercrambe
Bugthorpe
Painsthorpe
A166
YORKSHIRE WOLDS WAY
A19
A1237
Skelton
Huntington
Stockton on the Forest
Gate Helmsley
Stamford Bridge
Skirpenbeck
Youlthorpe
Huggate
Overton
Upper Poppleton
West Huntington
New Earswick
Warthill
Holtby
1066
Full Sutton
Bishop Wilton
Rawcliffe
Low Catton
Gowthorpe
Great Givendale
YORK
Clifton
A1036
Murton
High Catton
Fangfoss
Knapton
YORK MINSTER
Heworth
Dunnington
Meltonby
North Dalton
York
Holgate
JORVIK VIKING CENTRE
Osbaldwick
YORKSHIRE MUSEUM OF FARMING
Bolton
Millington
Acomb
NATIONAL RAILWAY MUSEUM
A1079
CASTLE MUS
Grimston
Wilberfoss
Yapham
B1246
Nunthorpe
Heslington
Kexby
Kilnwick Percy
Warter
Woodthorpe
Fulford
B1228
Barmby Moor
Middleton-on-the-Wolds
Bishopthorpe
YORK DESIGNER OUTLET
Crockey Hill
YORKSHIRE AIR MUSEUM
Elvington
Newton upon Derwent
Pocklington
STEWART'S BURNBY HALL GARDENS & MUSEUM
Nunburnholme
Copmanthorpe
YORK WEST SERVICES
Sutton upon Derwent
Allerthorpe
Burnby
Acaster Malbis
Naburn
Wheldrake
Thornton
Hayton
Londesborough
Colton
Deighton
Storwood
Pocklington Canal
Melbourne
Bielby
Thorpe le Street
Goodmanham
Appleton Roebuck
Escrick
LOWER DERWENT VALLEY
Shiptonthorpe
Market Weighton
Acaster Selby
Thorganby
East Cottingwith
Everingham
Seaton Ross
Holme Green
A614
Harswell
Stillingfleet
B1228
Ryther
Kelfield
Ellerton
Laytham
Water End
Sancton
B1222
Skipwith
SKIPWITH COMMON
North Duffield
Aughton
Harlthorpe
A163
Holme-on-Spalding-Moor
Moor End
Sand Hole
Cawood
Riccall
Foggathorpe
North Cliffe
North Newbald
Bubwith
Highfield
Rascal Moor
South Cliffe
South Newbald
Wistow
Gribthorpe
Willitoft
Gunby
A1034
B1223
Barlby
SELBY ABBEY
Osgodby
Menthorpe
Breighton
Spaldington
Hotham
Bursea
Lund
South Duffield
Foulness
North Cave
Selby
Cliffe
Everthorpe
Thorpe Willoughby
A1238
Wressle
Brind
North Howden
Portington
Hive
South Cave
East Common
West End
Brayton
Hemingbrough
Newsholme
Cavil
Sandholme
Newport
A63
89
HOWDEN MINSTER
Eastrington
Scalby
90
Gilberdyke
Brantingham
Selby Canal
Barmby on the Marsh
Howden
B1230
Market Weighton Canal
Ellerker
Asselby
Knedlington
M62
Staddlethorpe
Balkholme
Ellough ton
Kilpin Pike
Kilpin
Drax
Boothferry
Ouse
Brough
Broomfleet
Aire
Haddlesey
Temple
Camblesforth
Newland
Skelton
Laxton
THE YORKSHIRE WOLDS
EAST RIDING OF YORKSHIRE
0 1 2 3 4 5 6 miles
0 1 2 3 4 5 6 7 8 9 10 km

Seamer
Irton
Eastfield
Yons Nab
CLEVELAND WAY
Ruston
Wykeham
Cayton
Lebberston
Gristhorpe
PLAYDALE FARM PARK
Filey Brigg
Filey
Flixton
Folkton
Willerby
Staxton
Muston
Filey Bay
YORKSHIRE WOLDS WAY
Ganton
Primrose Valley
Sherburn
Hunmanby
Hunmanby Moor
Reighton Sands
Potter Brompton
Reighton Gap
Fordon
Reighton
Speeton
Wold Newton
Foxholes
Burton Fleming
Buckton
Bempton
Butterwick
Grindale
FLAMBOROUGH HEAD
Flamborough
Weaverthorpe
Helperthorpe
Octon
Thwing
Octon Cross Roads
SEWERBY HALL AND GARDENS
Sewerby
BONDVILLE MODEL VILLAGE
Boynton
PRIORY
BAYLE MUSEUM
Rudston
Bridlington
Langtoft
Bessingby
West Hill
OLD PENNY MEMORIES
Carnaby
Hilderthorpe
Haisthorpe
Cottam
BURTON AGNES HALL
Thornholme
Kilham
BURTON AGNES MANOR HOUSE
BRIDLINGTON BIRDS OF PREY & ANIMAL PARK
BRIDLINGTON BAY
Burton Agnes
Ruston Parva
Harpham
Fraisthorpe
Garton-on-the-Wolds
Lowthorpe
Gransmoor
Nafferton
Barmston
Great Kelk
Elmswell
Little Driffield
Driffield
Lissett
Gembling
Ulrome
Kelleythorpe
Foston on the Wolds
Tibthorpe
Wansford
SKIPSEA CASTLE
Kirkburn
Southburn
Skerne
Skipsea
Skipsea Brough
Church End
Beeford
Hutton
Brigham
North Frodingham
Bainton
Hutton Cranswick
Rotsea
Dunnington
Hempholme
Bewholme
Atwick
Watton
Kilnwick
North Cliff
Burshill
Lund
Beswick
Hornsea
Hornsea Mere
HORNSEA MUSEUM
Holme on the Wolds
Lockington
Baswick Steer
Brandesburton
Seaton
Thorpe
FREEPORT HORNSEA
Hornsea Bridge
South Dalton
Scorborough
Aike
Leven
Leven Canal
Sigglesthorpe
Rolston
Arram
Catwick
Goxhill
Etton
Mappleton
Leconfield
Eske
Little Hatfield
Gardham
Cherry Burton
Routh
Long Riston
Rise
Great Hatfield
Great Cowden
Tickton
Arnold
Withernwick
Molescroft
Beverley
Meaux
Skirlaugh
New Ellerby
Bishop Burton
Weel
Marton
West Newton
Aldbrough
East Newton
BEVERLEY FRIARY
MINSTER
Woodmansey
Walkington
Wawne
Old Ellerby
BURTON CONSTABLE HALL
Flinton
Thearne
Bentley
Swine
Coniston
Garton
High Hunsley
Dunswell
Grimston
Skidby
Bransholme
Thirtleby
Sproatley
Humbleton
Fitling
Hilston
Little Weighton
Ganstead
Rowley
SKIDBY WINDMILL
Kingston-upon-Hull
Sutton on Hull
Inglemire
Lelley
Cottingham
Bilton
Owstwick
Tunstall
Eppleworth
Sutton Ings
Elstronwick
Riplingham
Newland
Stoneferry
Preston
Burton Pidsea
North End
YORKSHIRE WOLDS WAY
Willerby
Sculcoates
Summergangs
Roos
Kirk Ella
WILBERFORCE HOUSE
West End
Waxholme
West Ella
Marfleet
Salt End
Owthorne
Swanland
Anlaby
STREETLIFE
THE DEEP
Hedon
Rimswell
Welton
Haven Side
Burstwick
Withernsea
HUMBER BRIDGE
Hessle
FERENS ART GALLERY
KINGSTON UPON HULL
Halsham
Camerton
Easington
North Ferriby
Paull
Thorngumbald
Ryehill
Keyingham
TA
CARRS
WOLDS
East Riding of Yorkshire
A170
A165
A64
A1039
B1261
A1039
B1249
B1229
B1255
B1259
A165
B1253
B1253
B1252
A614
A166
B1248
A165
B1249
B1249
B1242
A614
A164
B1244
B1248
A165
A1035
B1243
A1079
A1035
A1174
B1242
B1230
A164
A1033
B1238
B1240
B1239
B1233
A1165
A165
A1105
B1231
A63
A1033
B1362
B1242
103
90
91

1
2
3
4
A
B
C
D
E
F
Flimby
Broughton Moor
Standingstone
Dovenby
Bridekirk
Blindcrake
Bewaldeth
Orthwaite
LAKE DISTRICT WILDLIFE PARK
Siddick
Camerton
Great Broughton
Little Broughton
Papcastle
WORDSWORTH HO
Cockermouth
Embleton
Bassenthwaite
GREAT CALVA
SKIDDAW FOREST
SKIDDAW HOUSE
SKIDDAW
Seaton
Great Clifton
Brigham
CASTLEGATE HO
COCKERMOUTH
WYTHOP MILL
Wythop Mill
BASSENTHWAITE LAKE
MIREHOUSE
North Side
Workington
Stainburn
Bridgefoot
Greysouthen
Little Clifton
HELENA THOMPSON MUS
Eaglesfield
Westfield
Deanscales
Mossbay
Winscales
SANDYBECK MEADOW
Lorton Vale
Thornthwaite Forest
Low Lorton
Thornthwaite
THORNTHWAITE GALLERIES
CUMBERLAND PENCIL MUSEUM
Millbeck
Applethwaite
Harrington
High Harrington
Dean
Branthwaite
Mosser
Pardshaw
High Lorton
Whinlatter Pass
Braithwaite
Distington
Ullock
Mockerkin
Thackthwaite
HERITAGE/VISITOR CENTRE
WHINLATTER FOREST PARK
Portinscale
Keswick
GRISEDALE PIKE
Lowca
Pica
Moresby
Asby
Lamplugh
Loweswater
BRACKENTHWAITE FELL
Stair
DERWENT WATER
Parton
Bransty
Moresby Parks
Arlecdon
Rowrah
HIGH LEYS
Loweswater Fell
Crummock Water
Rannerdale
Little Town
THE RUM STORY
WALK MILL
Kirkland
Croasdale
Derwent Fells
Grange
HIGH SEAT
Whitehaven
HAIG COLLIERY MINING MUSEUM
Frizington
Ehen
GREAT BORNE
Buttermere
BUTTERMERE
Thirlmere
Watendlath
Saltom Bay
Hensingham
Cleator Moor
Ennerdale Bridge
Ennerdale Forest
HIGH STILE
Buttermere Fell
Mirehouse
Sandwith
Moor Row
Wath Brow
ENNERDALE
BORROWDALE
Borrowdale
Rosthwaite
ST BEES HEAD
Rottington
Ennerdale Water
Ennerdale Fell
Liza
BLACK SAIL
HONISTER HAUSE
Seatoller
Stonethwaite
Cleator
LONGLANDS LAKE
PILLAR
ULLSCARF
St Bees
Seathwaite
Egremont
Wilton
NY
L A K E
GREAT GABLE
HIGH WHITE STONES
Coulderton
Thornhill
SEATALLAN
Wasdale Head
Middletown
Haile
Calder
Bleng
N A T I O N
Stickle Tarn
Nethertown
Beckermet
COPELAND FOREST
C U M B R I A N
SCAFELL PIKE
Langdale Pikes
Braystones
Calder Bridge
BOW FELL
NX
A595
Wast Water
Burnmoor Tarn
High Sellafield
SELLAFIELD VISITORS CENTRE
Wellington
WASTWATER
C
Calder Hall
Nether Wasdale
The Screes
Gosforth
HARDKNOTT FORT
Hard Knott Pass
Wrynose Pass
Brathay
Santon Bridge
Boot
ESKDALE
Cockley Beck
Seascale
Eskdale Green
Beckfoot
Eskdale
FURNESS FELLS
Holmrook
Irt
HARTER FELL
Seathwaite Tarn
CONISTON COPPERMINES
Drigg
Mite
Esk
CONISTON HOLLY HOW
THE OLD MAN OF CONISTON
Birker Fell
Devoke Water
Saltcoats
RAVENGLASS AND ESKDALE RAILWAY & MUS
BATHHOUSE
Ravenglass
MUNCASTER CASTLE & WORLD OWL CENTRE
Woodend
Hall Dunnerdale
Seathwaite
Ulpha Fell
Broad Oak
CAW
Duddon
Torver
Newbiggin
Ulpha
Hoses
Lane End
WHITFELL
Corney Fell
Stub Place
Corney
Broughton Mills
High Nibthwaite
Water Yeat
Blawith
Hycemoor
Selker Bay
SC
Bootle
SD
Duddon Bridge
Lower Hawthwaite
Broughton in Furness
Lowick Bridge
Black Combe
Hallthwaites
DUDDON MOSSES
Foxfield
Grizebeck
Lowick Green
Gawthwaite
Whitbeck
The Green
The Hill
Kirkby-in-Furness
Beck Side
Broughton Beck
Silecroft
Whicham
Kirksanton
Millom
MILLOM HERITAGE MUSEUM
Soutergate
Mansriggs
LAUREL & HARDY MUS
Haverigg
DUDDON SANDS
Ulverston
Askam in Furness
Ireleth
Pennington
Lindal in Furness
Swarthmoor
0 1 2 3 4 5 6 miles
0 1 2 3 4 5 6 7 8 9 10 km

Hutton Roof
Mosedale
Johnby
Little Blencow
Catterlen
Laithes
Great Blencow
Newton Reigny
Langwathby
Edenhall
Ousby
Skirwith
Kirkland
Blencarn
Crowdundle Beck
Greystoke
Fair Hill
Penrith
Carleton
MAYBURGH HENGE
108
109
Mungrisdale
Berrier
Motherby
BECKSTONES ART GALLERY
Newbiggin
BROUGHAM CASTLE
Culgaith
Milburn
ACORN BANK
Newbiggin
SADDLEBACK OR BLENCATHRA
868
Scales
Penruddock
Stainton
Eamont Bridge
A66
CLIFTON HALL
Temple Sowerby
Knock
TARN MOSS
Troutbeck
DALEMAIN
Hutton
Dacre
RHEGED
Sockbridge
LILLIPUT LANE
Clifton
Tirril
Lowmoor Row
Threlkeld
CLIBURN MOSS
Cliburn
Dufton
Kirkby Thore
LAKELAND BIRD OF PREY CENTRE
Melkinthorpe
Long Marton
Brampton
CASTLERIGG STONE CIRCLE
Wreay
Pooley Bridge
Askham
Lowther
M6
Hackthorpe
Morland
Bolton
Matterdale End
Longthwaite
Watermillock
Helton
Great Strickland
Crackenthorpe
Dockray
AIRA FORCE
Knotts
ULLSWATER
Whale
King's Meaburn
Newby
Colby
Dowthwaitehead
Little Strickland
Appleby-in-Westmorland
Stanah
Fisher Place
Sandwick
Howtown
LOADPOT HILL
Sleagill
Burrells
Hoff
EDEN VALLEY RAILWAY
Bampton Grange
Bampton
HELVELLYN
Glenridding
Martindale Common
Bampton Common
Rosgill
Reagill
100
Patterdale
Dale Head
Maulds Meaburn
HELVELLYN
Grisedale Beck
Bridgend
Angle Tarn
Haweswater Reservoir
SHAP ABBEY
Shap
Crosby Ravensworth
Drybeck
Wythburn
Keld
Great Asby
Oddendale
Hartsop
Brothers Water
Ralfland Forest
Wythburn Fells
Grisedale Tarn
Swindale Beck
HIGH STREET
Res.
Crosby Ravensworth Fell
GREAT ASBY SCAR
D I S T R I C T
HARTER FELL
GRASMERE THORNEY HOW
Shap Fells
Little Asby
GRASMERE BUTHARLYP HOWE
Kirkstone Pass
Orton
DOVE COTTAGE AND WORDSWORTH MUSEUM
Inn
P A R K
Birk Beck
Raisbeck
Grasmere
Rydal
RYDAL MOUNT
TEBAY SERVICES
SMARDALE
Chapel Stile
NY
Sadgill
Greenholme
Gaisgill
Kelleth
Rydal Water
Long Sleddale
Bretherdale Head
Elterwater
LANGDALE
Ambleside
Kentmere
Lune
Tebay
A685
Little Langdale
Clappersgate
Waterhead
Bowderdale
Weasdale
Skelwith Bridge
ROMAN FORT
AMBLESIDE
Troutbeck
Borrowdale
TOWNEND
Kent
BROCKHOLE NAT PK VISITOR CENTRE
WINDERMERE
HOLEHIRD GARDENS
Lowbridge House
Forest Hall
Langdale Fell
Ravenstonedale Common
Outgate
Low Wray
Troutbeck Bridge
Elfhowe
HAWKSHEAD COURTHOUSE
High Wray
Garnett Bridge
Hawkshead Hill
Colthouse
WINDERMERE STEAMBOATS & MUS.
Ings
Staveley
Watchgate
Howgill Fell
Coniston
BEATRIX POTTER GALLERY
Windermere
Hawkshead
Bowston
Patton Bridge
Esthwaite Water
Bowness-on-Windermere
THE WORLD OF BEATRIX POTTER
Garth Row
Lowgill
THE CALF
Bowmanstead
HAWKSHEAD
Grayrigg
BRANTWOOD
Near Sawrey
A591
Meal Bank
Beck Foot
Brant Fell
Grizedale
GRIZEDALE FOREST PARK VISITOR CENTRE
Ferney Green
B5284
Burneside
Far Sawrey
HILL TOP
Crook
LAKELAND CLIMBING CENTRE
Lambrigg Fell
Cautley
Forest
Grizedale
Storrs
Winster
SD
GRIZEDALE FOREST PARK
Underbarrow
Kendal
Sedbergh
FARFIELD MILL ARTS & HERITAGE CENTRE
Satterthwaite
Crosthwaite
KENDAL
A684
New Hutton
KILLINGTON SERVICES (Southbound Only)
Millthrop
Force Mills
K VILLAGE
K VILLAGE HERITAGE CEN
Gregg Hall
Millholme
FOREST SPINNERS
Oxenholme
F U R N E S S
Brigsteer
Natland
Killington
Rusland
STOTT PARK BOBBIN MILL
Bowland Bridge
Row
Middleshaw
RUSLAND MOSS
Finsthwaite
Cartmel Fell
SIZERGH
Barrows Green
Old Hutton
Dee
Oxen Park
The Howe
Gawthrop
Lakeside
F E L L S
LAKES AQUARIUM
FELL FOOT
Cotes
Sedgwick
Dent
Colton
Bouth
WHITBARROW
Levens
Stainton
Gatebeck
Staveley
Newby Bridge
Middleton
Spark Bridge
LAKESIDE AND HAVERTHWAITE RAILWAY
Sampool Bridge
Hincaster
Endmoor
CALF TOP
Backbarrow
Mill Side
LEVENS HALL
Crooklands
Witherslack
Leasgill
Penny Bridge
Haverthwaite
Ayside
High Newton
Town End
Old Town
Barbon
CRAG HILL
Heversham
Greenodd
Low Newton
Mansergh
Field Broughton
A590
Milnthorpe
Lupton
Arrad Foot
Meathop
Farleton
ROUDSEA WOOD AND MOSSES
Lindale
Storth
Kearstwick
Casterton
HERON CORN MILL
Beetham
CLAWTHORPE FELL
Kirkby Lonsdale
CARTMEL
CARTMEL PRIORY
Cartmel
LECK FELL
ARNSIDE
Holme
Hutton Roof
HOLKER HALL
Arnside
LAKELAND WILDLIFE OASIS
Clawthorpe
CONISHEAD PRIORY & MANJUSHRI KADAMPA MEDITATION CENTRE
Holker
Allithwaite
Grange-over-Sands
GAIT BARROWS
Yealand Redmayne
Burton-in-Kendal
LAK WOOD
Leck
Cartmel Sands
Cark
Kents Bank
BURTON-IN-KENDAL SERVICES (Northbound Only)
Whittington
Cowan Bridge
Ireby
Masongill
92
93
100

Ousby
Skirwith
Kirkland
893 CROSS FELL
Tees
MILBURN FOREST
Trout Beck
MOOR HOUSE-UPPER TEESDALE
639 VIEWING HILL
Harwood Beck
Harwood
Langdon Common
696 CHAPELFELL TOP
Westernhope Moor
675
Bollihope Common
Blencarn
Crowdundle Beck
109
772
Widdybank Fell
Langdon Beck
LANGDON BECK
Forest
Ettersgill
110
Newbiggin Common
Middleton Common
Culgaith
Milburn
Cow Green Reservoir
Dufton Fell
767
CAULDRON SNOUT
HIGH FORCE
BOWLEES VISITOR CENTRE
Newbiggin
565
ACORN BANK
Newbiggin
Temple Sowerby
Knock
PENNINE WAY
Maize Beck
Cronkley Fell
TEESDALE
Holwick
Middleton-in-Teesdale
Lowmoor Row
BURN MOSS
Cliburn
Kirkby Thore
DUFTON
Dufton
Long Marton
Brampton
Murton Fell
673
NORTH
Mickle Fell
776
Lune Moor
Bowbank
Mickleton
EGGLESTON HALL
Eggleston
Hill Top
Morland
Bolton
Crackenthorpe
King's Meaburn
Murton
LUNE FOREST
Thringarth
B6276
Grassholme Reservoir
Romaldkirk
Newby
Colby
Appleby-in-Westmorland
Hilton
Warcop Fell
Lune
Grassholme
Hunderthwaite
Selset Reservoir
Hury
DOW CRAG 549
Hunderthwaite Moor
Lyvennet
Eden
Burrells
Hoff
EDEN VALLEY RAILWAY
Great Ormside
A66
PENNINES
Balder
Balderhead Reservoir
Clove Lodge
BALDERSDALE
Hury Reservoir
Reagill
99
B6260
Sandford
Stainmore Common
Cotherstone Moor
Maulds Meaburn
Drybeck
Warcop
Hillbeck
North Stainmore
Deep Dale
Deepdale Beck
Crosby Ravensworth
BROUGH CASTLE
Brough
South Stainmore
Bowes
PENNINE WAY
Oddendale
Great Asby
Bleatarn
Little Musgrave
Great Musgrave
Brough Sowerby
Kaber
Barras
Moudy Mea
Gilmonby
Soulby
A685
Bowes Moor
STAINMORE FOREST
Crosby Ravensworth Fell
GREAT ASBY SCAR
Winton
Heggerscales
Sleightholme
Crosby Garrett
Hartley
Belah
Scargill Moor
B6261
Orton
412
Little Asby
KIRKBY STEPHEN
Winton Fell
Sleightholme Moor
M6
Raisbeck
Smardale
Waitby
Kirkby Stephen
NY
Nateby
510 CLEASBY HILL
SERVICES
SMARDALE GILL
662
Arkengarthdale Moor
Lune
Gaisgill
Kelleth
Newbiggin-on-Lune
Ash Fell
B6270
38
Tebay
A685
Bowderdale
Coldbeck
385
A683
Stonesdale Moor
Whaw
Weasdale
Ravenstonedale
B6259
Ravenseat
ROGAN'S SEAT
671
Birkdale
Common
West Stonesdale
583 GREAT PINSEAT
Outhgill
709
Keld
Langdale Fell
Ravenstonedale Common
Melbecks Moor
494
587
THE PENNINE BRIDLEWAY
708
Mallerstang
Common
Angram
Angram Common
Kearton
Howgill Fell
Gunnerside
Feetham
Thwaite
Satron
Muker
Low Row
Lowgill
676 THE CALF
716
GREAT SHUNNER FELL
Crackpot
Beck Foot
Brant Fell
Abbotside Common
YORKSHIRE
BUTTERTUBS PASS
PENNINE WAY
Abbotside Common
Cautley
SD
Cotterdale
Askrigg Common
M6
B6257
Sedbergh
FARFIELD MILL ARTS & HERITAGE CENTRE
Baugh Fell
North Yorkshire
37
A684
676
Garsdale Head
High Shaw
Askrigg
LOW MILL OUTDOOR CENTRE
Newbiggin
KILLINGTON SERVICES (Southbound Only)
Millthrop
Garsdale
Mossdale Moor
Hardrow
Sedbusk
Appersett
DALES COUNTRYSIDE MUSEUM
Bainbridge
WENSLEYDALE POTTERY
Hawes
Worton
Woodhall
Killington
Garsdale
Dee
HAWES
Gayle
Burtersett
WENSLEYDALE
Cubeck
556 RISE HILL
Widdale Fell
Countersett
Thornton Rust
A683
Gawthrop
Dent
Cowgill
672
DALES
WENSLEYDALE CREAMERY
Semer Water
Dentdale
Wether Fell
Carpley Green
BISHOPDALE VALLEY
Middleton
614
Marsett
609 CALF TOP
Stone House
Wold Fell
Dodd Fell
Stalling Busk
Newbiggin
B6255
Deepdale
PENNINE WAY
668
Bishopdale Beck
B6160
Old Town
682 CRAG HILL
Barbon
Whernside
Gayle Moor
Cragdale Moor
Mansergh
NATIONAL
736
Blea Moor
Oughtershaw
Kidstones
643 MIDDLE TONGUE
Cam Fell
Walden Head
Casterton
93
Kirkby Lonsdale
627
Ribblehead
LANGSTROTHDALE CHASE
94
Yockenthwaite
702 BUCKDEN PIKE
Cray
Hubberholme
Buckden
Cam Beck
High Birkwith
Foxup
Halton Gill
610
Cowan Bridge
Ireby
Masongill
INGLEBOROUGH
B6479
636
PARK
0 1 2 3 4 5 6 miles
0 1 2 3 4 5 6 7 8 9 10 km

Fir Tree
Spennymoor
Ferryhill
Cornforth
Trimdon
Pikeston Fell
Bedburn
Hunwick
Newfield
Middlestone Moor
Byers Green
Ferryhill Station
Fishburn
Redford
Hamsterley
High Grange
Binchester Blocks
Westerton
Kirk Merrington
Mainsforth
Bishop Middleham
Butterwick
Hamsterley Forest
Witton Park
Toronto
Coundon
Middlestone
Leasingthorne
Chilton
Sedgefield
Escomb
Low Etherley
High Etherley
Bishop Auckland
Rushyford
Bradbury
Toft Hill
Morley
Coundon Grange
Eldon
Old Eldon
Woodland
Howle
Butterknowle
St Helen Auckland
Shildon
Middridge
Newton Aycliffe
Mordon
Woodland Fell
Copley
High Lands
Evenwood
West Auckland
Thorpe Larches
Foxton
Cockfield
Evenwood Gate
Bildershaw
Royal Oak
Redworth
Aycliffe
Stillington
Burnt Houses
Wackerfield
Bolam
Heighington
Elstob
Whitton
Carlton
Raby Castle
Hilton
Great Stainton
Redmarshall
Kinninvie
Houghton-le-Side
Brafferton
Bishopton
Staindrop
Ingleton
Walworth Gate
Coatham Mundeville
Little Stainton
Cotherstone
Langton
Killerby
Stainton
Cleatlam
Headlam
Summerhouse
Denton
Walworth
Beaumont Hill
Barmpton
Lartington
Barnard Castle
Little Newsham
Gainford
Harrowgate Hill
Great Burdon
Sadberge
The Bowes Museum
Startforth
Winston
High Coniscliffe
Darlington
Longnewton
Elton
Westwick
Whorlton
Piercebridge
Low Coniscliffe
Haughton Le-Skerne
Urlay Nook
Boldron
Egglestone Abbey
Rokeby Park
Ovington
Caldwell
Manfield
Head of Steam
Durham Tees Valley
Greta Bridge
Hutton Magna
Eppleby
Forcett
Carlton
Cleasby
Middleton St George
Egglescliffe
Brignall
Lane Head
Stanwick Iron Age Fortifications
Stanwick-St-John
Aldbrough St John
Stapleton
Blackwell
Middleton One Row
Aislaby
Scargill
West Layton
Low Dinsdale
Barningham
Newsham
East Layton
Newton Morrell
Croft-on-Tees
Hurworth Place
Neasham
Low Worsall
The Stang Forest
Barton
Eryholme
Girsby
Dalton
Ravensworth
Melsonby
Barton Park Services
Dalton-on-Tees
Gayles
Kirby Hill
Hartforth
Croft
Sockburn
Whashton
Middleton Tyas
Scotch Corner Services
Hornby
Appleton Wiske
Gilling West
Scotch Corner
Great Smeaton
Moulton
North Cowton
West Rounton
Langthwaite
Arkle Town
Washfold
Hurst
Atley Hill
East Cowton
Welbury
Birkby
Skeeby
Uckerby
Richmond
Deighton
Arkengarthdale
Skelton
Easby Abbey
Easby
Scorton
Marske
Richmond Castle
Healaugh
Swaledale Museum
Hudswell
Colburn
Brompton-on-Swale
Catterick
Bolton-on-Swale
Whitwell
Streetlam
Lovesome Hill
East Harlsey
Reeth
Fremington
Danby Wiske
Grinton
Marrick
Downholme
Hipswell
Walkerville
Catterick Bridge
Swale Dale
Grinton Lodge
Catterick Garrison
Brompton
Winton
Stainton
Great Langton
Kirby Sigston
Hipswell Moor
Scotton
Tunstall
East Appleton
Kirkby Fleetham
Yafforth
Stainton Moor
Bolton Moor
Redmire Moor
Barden
Hornby
Great Fencote
Bullamoor
East Hauxwell
Hackforth
Thrintoft
Northallerton
Garriston
Hunton
Arrathorne
Little Fencote
Ainderby Steeple
Romanby
Castle Bolton
Bellerby
Bolton Castle
Preston-under-Scar
Swineside Ceramics
Constable Burton
Patrick Brompton
Langthorne
Scruton
Warlaby
Redmire
Leyburn
Little Crakehall
Crakehall Water Mill
Morton-on-Swale
Carperby
Great Crakehall
Leeming Bar
North Otterington
Thornton-le-Beans
Aysgarth Falls
Swinithwaite
Wensley
Harmby
The Wensleydale Railway
Finghall
Newton-le-Willows
Leeming
Sowber Gate
Thornton-le-Moor
Aysgarth
West Witton
White Rose Candles
Spennithorne
Gatenby
Middleham
Cowling
Bedale
Aiskew
Newby Wiske
South Otterington
Thoralby
Penhill
Agglethorpe
Thornton Steward
Jervaulx Abbey
Burrill
Londonderry
Exelby
West Burton
Middleham Castle
Coverham
Maunby
Firby
Thornton-le-Street
Melmerby
East Witton
Thirn
Theakston
Carlton
Caldbergh
Thorp Perrow Arboretum
Thornton Watlass
Snape
Burneston
Kirby Wiske
Newsham
Sion Hill Hall & Birds of Prey Centre
Ellingstring
Carthorpe
Pickhill
Carlton Moor
High Ellington
Low Ellington
South Kilvington
Walden
Gammersgill
West Scrafton
Aerial Extreme
Holme
Well
Sinderby
Sandhutton
Horsehouse
Coverdale
Colsterdale
Low Burton
Kirklington
Ainderby Quernhow
Fearby
Uredale Glass
Bradley
Hindlethwaite Moor
Colsterdale Moor
Healey
Masham
Nosterfield
Carlton Miniott
Howe
Woodale
Theakston Brewery Visitor Centre
Leighton
Binsoe
Thornborough
Warthermarske
Swinton
Skipton-on-Swale
Great Haw
Masham Moor
West Tanfield
Sutton Howgrave
Middleton Quernham
Baldersby
Marmion Tower
Catton
Little Whernside
Scar House Res.
Leighton Res.
Ilton
Lightwater Village
Roundhill Res.
Mickley
North Stainley
Norton Conyers
Wath
Melmerby
Baldersby St James
Topcliffe
Angram Res.
Grewelthorpe
Lightwater Valley
Asenby
NZ
SE
Yorkshire Dales

Trimdon
High Throston
St Hilda's Parish Church
Hartlepool's Maritime Experience
Hartlepool Bay
Hartlepool
Elwick
West Park
Summerhill
Fishburn
Ferryhill Station
Mainsforth
Bishop Middleham
Chilton
Butterwick
Dalton Piercy
Rift House
Seaton Carew
Sedgefield
Hardwick Hall
Tees Bay
Greatham
Bradbury
Graythorp
Mordon
Wynyard Village
Newton Bewley
Thorpe Larches
Wynyard Woodland
Wolviston
Cowpen Bewley
Teesmouth
Salt Scar
REDCAR
Foxton
Stillington
Billingham Art Gallery
Coatham
Miniature Railway
Elstob
Thorpe Thewles
BILLINGHAM
Dormanstown
Marske-by-the-Sea
Saltburn-by-the-Sea
Stockton-on-Tees
Haverton Hill
Kirkleatham Old Hall Museum
Whitton
Carlton
Port Clarence
South Bank
Kirkleatham
Great Stainton
Redmarshall
Norton
Roseworth
Grangetown
Yearby
New Marske
Saltburn Valley
Brafferton
Bishopton
North Ormesby
Lazenby
Wilton
Brotton
Coatham Mundeville
Little Stainton
Fairfield
Middlesbrough
Upleatham
Dunsdale
Skelton
Stockton-on-Tees
Dorman Museum
Eston
Tocketts Water Mill
Beaumont Hill
Barmpton
Hartburn
Normanby
North Skelton
Middlesbrough
Redcar and Cleveland
Kilton Thorpe
Great Burdon
Sadberge
Thornaby-on-Tees
Acklam
Park End
Ormesby
Flatts Lane Woodland
Guisborough Priory
Boosbeck
Lingdale
Elton
Ormesby Hall
Guisborough
Margrove Park
Stanghow
Longnewton
Preston Hall Museum
Marton
Guisborough Forest
Hutton Gate
Charltons
Haughton Le Skerne
Urlay Nook
Eaglescliffe
Captain Cook Birthplace
Coulby Newham
Nunthorpe
Cleveland
Moorsholm
Durham Tees Valley
Ingleby Barwick
Stainton
Hemlington
Hutton Village
Gisborough Moor
Darlington
Middleton St George
Egglescliffe
Thornton
Newton under Roseberry
High Leven
Maltby
Aislaby
Middleton One Row
Yarm
Newby
Commondale Moor
Great Ayton
Low Dinsdale
Hilton
Seamer
Tanton
Little Ayton
New Row
Commondale
Neasham
Low Worsall
Kirklevington
Middleton-on-Leven
Stokesley
Easby
Kildale
Hurworth Place
Eryholme
Girsby
Tame Bridge
Kildale Moor
Castleton
Dalton-on-Tees
Sockburn
Picton
Crathorne
Rudby
Battersby
Hutton Rudby
Leven
Great Broughton
Ingleby Greenhow
Westerdale
Hornby
Appleton Wiske
Enterpen
Kirkby
Great Busby
Great Smeaton
West Rounton
Potto
Carlton in Cleveland
Cleveland Way
Wiske
Welbury
East Rounton
Faceby
Westerdale Moor
East Cowton
Birkby
Whorlton
Swainby
Urra
Deighton
Ingleby Arncliffe
Seave Green
Farndale Moor
Streetlam
Lovesome Hill
East Harlsey
Whorlton Moor
Chop Gate
Cockayne Ridge
Cockayne
Wake Lady Green
Danby Wiske
Mount Grace Priory
Osmotherley
Church Houses
Blakey Ridge
Brompton
Winton
Ellerbeck
Snilesworth Moor
Bilsdale West Moor
Bilsdale East Moor
Kirby Sigston
Thimbleby
Cleveland Way
Bransdale
Rudland Rigg
Low Mill
Yafforth
Fangdale Beck
Great Fencote
Bullamoor
Thrintoft
Northallerton
Romanby
Over Silton
Arden Great Moor
Scruton
Ainderby Steeple
East Moors
North York Moors
Morton-on-Swale
Warlaby
Nether Silton
Seph
Helmsley Moor
Skiplam Moor
Leeming Bar
Leeming
Leake
Kepwick
Thornton-le-Beans
Gillamoor
Sowber Gate
North Otterington
Thornton-le-Moor
Borrowby
Cowesby
Hawnby
Fadmoor
Gatenby
Rievaulx Moor
Londonderry
Newby Wiske
South Otterington
Knayton
Upsall
Hambleton Hills
Kirby Knowle
Rye
Carlton
Kirkbymoorside
Maunby
Thornton-le-Street
Boltby
Old Byland
Pockley
Kirby Wiske
Newsham
Rievaulx
Rievaulx Abbey
Helmsley
Beadlam
Welburn
Sion Hill Hall & Birds of Prey Centre
North Kilvington
Felixkirk
Thirlby
Sutton Bank Visitor Centre
Cleveland Way
Nawton
Burneston
Carthorpe
Pickhill
South Kilvington
Bob Hunter - Home of the Wren
Cold Kirby
Scawton
Rye Dale
Wombleton
Aerial Extreme
World of James Herriot
Thirsk
Duncombe Park
Sinderby
Holme
Sandhutton
Thirsk
Old Thirsk
Sutton-under-Whitestonecliffe
Harome
Kirklington
Ainderby Quernhow
Sowerby
Monk Park Farm
Sproxton
Muscoates
Carlton Miniott
Bagby
Balk
Riccal
Howe
Oldstead
Nunnington
Skipton-on-Swale
Great Thirkleby
Kilburn
High Kilburn
Wass
Nunnington
West Ness
Sutton Howgrave
Little Thirkleby
Mouseman Visitor Centre
Ampleforth
Oswaldkirk
East Ness
Byland Abbey
Stonegrave
Lightwater Valley
Carlton Husthwaite
Coxwold
Gilling East
South Holme
Norton Conyers
Hutton Sessay
Cawton
Dalton
St James
6 miles
10 km
NZ
SE

5
6
7
8
A
B
C
D
E
F
G
NZ
OV
SE
TA
CHRIS BIRKBECK INTERNATIONAL RALLY SCHOOL
Skinningrove
Carlin How
Boulby
Loftus
Staithes
A174
Easington
Port Mulgrave
Runswick Bay
Hinderwell
Runswick Bay
Liverton
Roxby
Newton Mulgrave
Kettleness
Goldsborough
B1366
Ellerby
Scaling
A174
Lythe
Sandsend
B1266
East Barnby
THE DRACULA EXPERIENCE
Mickleby
West Barnby
Sandsend Wyke
SUTCLIFFE GALLERY
Scaling Dam Res.
East Row
Whitby
Saltwick Bay
Dunsley
Danby Low Moor
Lealholm Moor
Ugthorpe
Newholm
P&R
WHITBY ABBEY
WHITBY
Danby
THE MOORS CENTRE
299
Stonegate
A171
13
Ruswarp
CAPTAIN COOK MEMORIAL MUSEUM
B1410
Ainthorpe
Houlsyke
Lealholm
Aislaby
Briggswath
Stainsacre
High Hawsker
Sleights
Sneaton
B1447
Esk
Ugglebarnby
Ness Pt.
CLEVELAND WAY
Low Garth
Egton
Grosmont
Sneatonthorpe
Raw
Robin Hood's Bay
Street
Glaisdale
MUSEUM OF VICTORIAN SCIENCE
Egton Bridge
A169
B1416
Littlebeck
Fylingthorpe
OLD COASTGUARD STATION
BOGGLE HOLE
Robin Hood's Bay
Esk Valley
Glaisdale
A171
Old Peak
Glaisdale Moor
432
Egton High Moor
Beck Hole
Goathland
Ravenscar
Flask Inn
Rosedale Moor
Fylingdales Moor
WHEELDALE MOOR ROMAN ROAD
299
20
Staintondale
YORK MOORS
Harwood Dale Forest
CLEVELAND WAY
Thorgill
Wheeldale Moor
Goathland Moor
Harwood Dale
Rosedale Abbey
20
Saltergate
Cloughton Newlands
Cloughton Wyke
PICKERING MOOR
Pickering Forest
ROSEDALE
NATIONAL PARK
Cloughton
Cropton
Hartoft End
Langdale Forest
Broxa Forest
A171
Burniston
Spaunton Moor
Stape
Derwent
Cromer Pt.
Seven
Forest
Newton Dale
A169
MOORLAND EXPERIENCE
TOLL
Silpho
A165
SCARBOROUGH SEA LIFE CENTRE
Scalby Ness Rocks
Lastingham
Levisham
Langdale End
Broxa
Suffield
Scalby
RYEDALE MUSEUM
Hackness
Newton-on-Rawcliffe
LOCKTON
North Bay
Hutton-le-Hole
Spaunton
Lockton
Staindale Forest
248
Wrench Green
Everley
Barrowcliff
Newby
SCARBOROUGH CASTLE
ROTUNDA MUSEUM
NORTH RIDING FOREST PARK
Trouts Dale
Wykeham Forest
Appleton-le-Moors
Cropton
Scarborough
NORTH YORKSHIRE MOORS RAILWAY
Low Dalby
South Bay
Falsgrave
Keldholme
FORGE VALLEY WOODLANDS
DALBY FOREST VISITOR CENTRE
Dalby Forest
East Ayton
P&R
Cayton Bay
Sinnington
Wrelton
Aislaby
ST PETER AND ST PAUL CHURCH
Kirkby Mills
West Ayton
THE HONEY FARM
Middleton
Sawdon
Osgodby
PICKERING CASTLE
Hutton Buscel
WORDSWORTH GALLERY
A170
Eastfield
Yons Nab
CLEVELAND WAY
Great Edstone
Pickering
Ellerburn
Irton
Ruston
A165
Wykeham
Seamer
17
B1261
Cayton
A170
Marton
Thornton-le-Dale
Wilton
Ebberston
Snainton
Allerston
B1415
A64
Normanby
B1261
Lebberston
Gristhorpe
Brompton
Costa Beck
PLAYDALE FARM PARK
Dove
Seven
Little Barugh
FLAMINGO LAND
THE CARRS
HALL
Salton
96
97
Flixton
Folkton
A1039
Kirby Misperton
Yedingham
Staxton
Muston
Great Barugh
A169
Derwent
YORKSHIRE WOLDS WAY
Brawby
High Marishes
B1258
East Heslerton
Ganton
Sherburn
Butterwick
Low Marishes
Hunmanby
Little Habton
Great Habton
East Knapton
West Knapton
16
Potter Brompton
Ryton
Scampston
SCAMPSTON
A64
West
Fordon

1
2
3
4
5
A
B
C
D
E
F
18
20
58
54
19
NW
CARLETON CASTLE
112
Bennane Hd.
Colmonell
Knockdolian
B734
265
Ballantrae Bay
Heronsford
Glen Tig
Ballantrae
Balkissock
Downan Pt.
Auchencrosh
439
BENERAIRD
LARNE
BELFAST
A77
Mark
Glen App
Milleur Pt.
17
257
Corsewall Pt.
Barnhills
Portencalzie
North Cairn
South Cairn
B738
Loch Connell
Corsewall
Kirkcolm
Dounan Bay
Cairnryan
Penwhirn Res.
Main Water of Luce
Mains of Airies
Ervie
Braid Fell
Low Salchrie
The Wig
B798
LOCH RYAN
6
Knocknain
B738
A77
Slouchnawen Bay
Leswalt
Craigencross
Innermessan
B7043
A718
A751
Black Loch
CASTLE KENNEDY GARDENS
Glenstockadale
White Loch
Stranraer
Aird
Castle Kennedy
Broadsea Bay
T H E R H I
CASTLE OF ST JOHN VISITOR CENTRE
STRANRAER MUSEUM
Knockglass
3
7
Soulseat Loch
A75
Mark
Black Hd.
Lochans
182
B738
B7077
Dunskey Ho.
5
A77
6
Torrs Wa
LITTLE WHEELS
Portpatrick
Awhirk
5
B7084
6
Stoneykirk
A716
Luce Sa
8
Port of Spittal Bay
B7042
Cairngarroch
Sandhead
KIRKMADRINE STONES
Sandhead Bay
Cairngarroch Bay
Money Hd.
Clachanmore
Hole Stone Bay
ARDWELL GDNS
Ardwell
Ardwell Mains
Chapel Rossan Bay
Ardwell Pt.
Logan Mains
10
LOGAN BOTANIC GARDEN
Balgowan Pt.
Mull of Logan
LOGAN FISH POND MARINE LIFE CENTRE
Port Nessock or Port Logan Bay
Port Logan
Cairnywellan Hd.
B7065
A716
Clanyard Bay
Low Clanyard
Kirkmaiden
Laggantalluch Hd.
Drummore
164
Damnaglaur
B7041
Crammag Hd.
Ma
Cairngaan
Port Kemin
0 1 2 3 4 5 6 miles
0 1 2 3 4 5 6 7 8 9 10 km

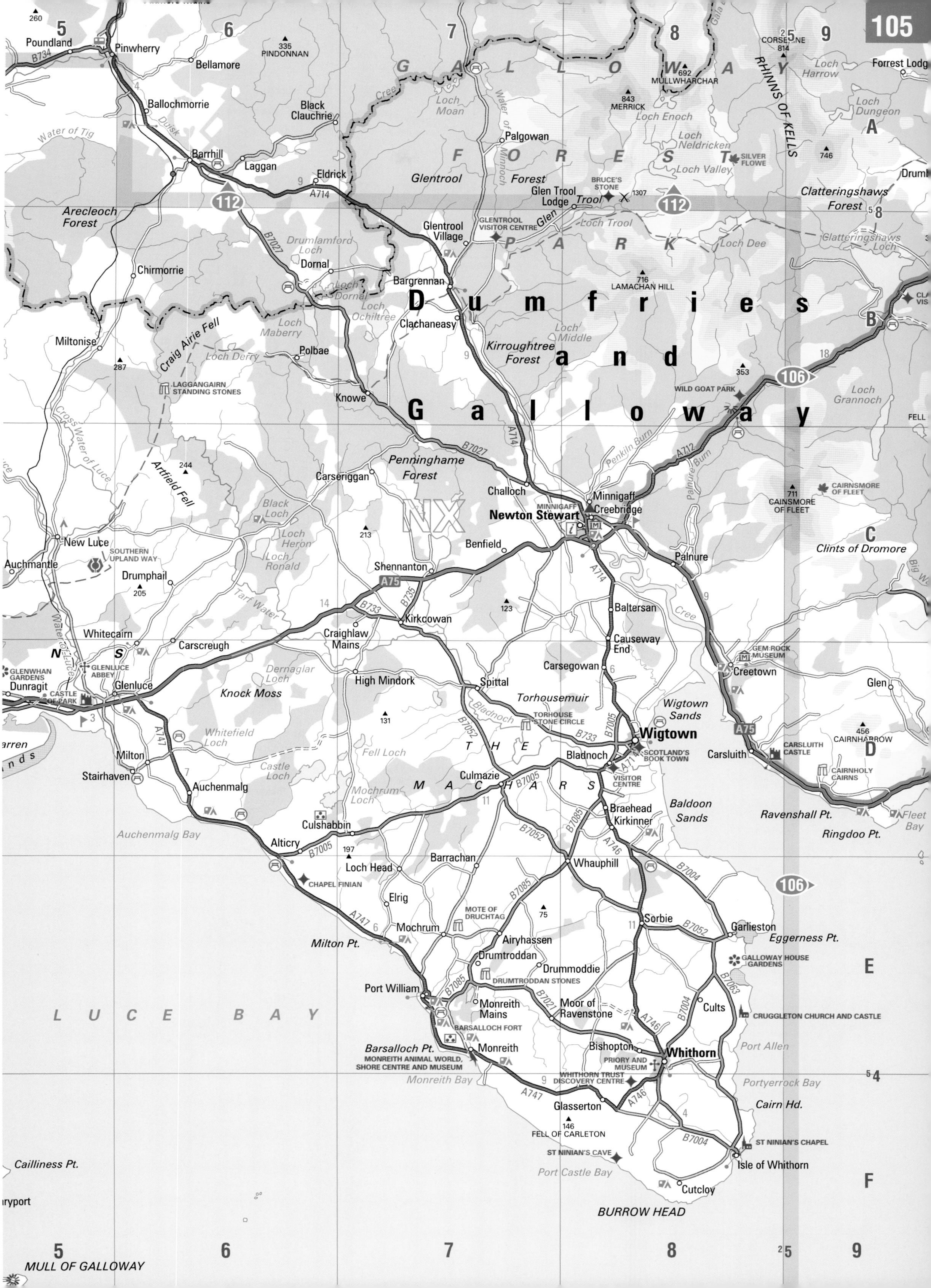
Dumfries and Galloway
GALLOWAY FOREST PARK
Poundland
Pinwherry
Bellamore
335 PINDONNAN
Ballochmorrie
Black Clauchrie
Barrhill
Laggan
Eldrick
A714
112
Arecleoch Forest
Drumlamford Loch
Dornal
Loch Dornal
Chirmorrie
Glentrool
Glentrool Village
GLENTROOL VISITOR CENTRE
Glen Trool Lodge
BRUCE'S STONE
Loch Trool
Palgowan
Water of Minnoch
Loch Moan
843 MERRICK
692 MULLWHARCHAR
Loch Enoch
Loch Neldricken
Loch Valley
SILVER FLOWE
RHINNS OF KELLS
CORSERINE 814
Loch Harrow
Loch Dungeon
Forrest Lodge
746
Clatteringshaws Forest
Clatteringshaws Loch
Loch Dee
716 LAMACHAN HILL
Bargrennan
Loch Ochiltree
Clachaneasy
Loch Maberry
Loch Middle
Kirroughtree Forest
Craig Airie Fell
Loch Derry
Polbae
Miltonise
287
LAGGANGAIRN STANDING STONES
Knowe
353
WILD GOAT PARK
106
A712
Loch Grannoch
Cross Water of Luce
Artfield Fell
244
B7027
A714
Penninghame Forest
Carseriggan
Challoch
Penkiln Burn
Palnure Burn
Minnigaff
MINNIGAFF
Creebridge
Newton Stewart
711 CAINSMORE OF FLEET
CAIRNSMORE OF FLEET
Black Loch
Loch Heron
Loch Ronald
213
NX
Benfield
Palnure
Clints of Dromore
New Luce
SOUTHERN UPLAND WAY
Auchmantle
Drumphail
205
Shennanton
A75
B733
B735
Tarf Water
Kirkcowan
123
Baltersan
Cree
Whitecairn
Carscreugh
Craighlaw Mains
Causeway End
GEM ROCK MUSEUM
Creetown
GLENWHAN GARDENS
GLENLUCE ABBEY
Dunragit
CASTLE OF PARK
Glenluce
Dernaglar Loch
High Mindork
Knock Moss
Spittal
Carsegowan
Torhousemuir
Wigtown Sands
Glen
A747
Whitefield Loch
131
Bladnoch
TORHOUSE STONE CIRCLE
B7052
B7005
Wigtown
SCOTLAND'S BOOK TOWN
Carsluith
CARSLUITH CASTLE
456 CAIRNHARROW
CAIRNHOLY CAIRNS
Milton
Stairhaven
Auchenmalg
Fell Loch
Castle Loch
Culmazie
THE MACHARS
VISITOR CENTRE
Braehead
Kirkinner
Baldoon Sands
Ravenshall Pt.
Fleet Bay
Ringdoo Pt.
Mochrum Loch
Culshabbin
Auchenmalg Bay
Alticry
197
Loch Head
Barrachan
Whauphill
A746
B7004
CHAPEL FINIAN
Elrig
B7085
MOTE OF DRUCHTAG
75
Sorbie
Garlieston
Eggerness Pt.
Mochrum
Milton Pt.
Airyhassen
Drumtroddan
Drummoddie
GALLOWAY HOUSE GARDENS
B7063
DRUMTRODDAN STONES
Port William
Monreith Mains
B7021
Moor of Ravenstone
Cults
CRUGGLETON CHURCH AND CASTLE
LUCE BAY
BARSALLOCH FORT
Barsalloch Pt.
Monreith
MONREITH ANIMAL WORLD, SHORE CENTRE AND MUSEUM
Bishopton
PRIORY AND MUSEUM
Whithorn
Port Allen
Monreith Bay
WHITHORN TRUST DISCOVERY CENTRE
Portyerrock Bay
Glasserton
Cairn Hd.
146 FELL OF CARLETON
ST NINIAN'S CHAPEL
ST NINIAN'S CAVE
Isle of Whithorn
Port Castle Bay
Cutcloy
Cailliness Pt.
BURROW HEAD
MULL OF GALLOWAY
5
6
7
8
9
A
B
C
D
E
F

Dumfries and Galloway
NX
Millquarter
St John's Town of Dalry
Bogue
Corriedoo Forest
Earlstoun Loch
Dungeon
Drumbuie
Silver Flowe
Loch Valley
Clatteringshaws Forest
Clatteringshaws Loch
Loch Dee
Garroch
Glenlee
New Galloway
Balmaclellan
Blackcraig
Knocklearn
Gibbshill
Sundaywell
Milton
Loch Urr
Glenkiln
Glen
Corsock
Ironmacannie
Craig
Merkland
Brooklands
Crocketford or Ninemile Bar
Auchenreoch Loch
Kirkpatrick Durham
Springholm
Clatteringshaws Forest Visitor Centre
Raiders Road Forest Drive
Wild Goat Park
Loch Grannoch
Bennan Forest
Cairn Edward Hill
Fell of Fleet
Drumrash
Mossdale
Parton
Stroan Loch
Loch Skerrow
Woodhall Loch
Loch Ken
Urr Water
Old Bridge of Urr
Crossmichael
Haugh of Urr
Clarebrand
Townhead of Greenlaw
Mote of Urr
Cairnsmore of Fleet
Fleet Forest
Lochenbreck Loch
Laurieston
Clints of Dromore
Palnure
Laurieston Forest
Loch Glentoo
Threave Castle
Castle Douglas
Old Buittle Tower
Barhill
Dalbeattie
Big Water of Fleet
Loch Whinyeon
Loch Mannoch
Glengap Forest
Bengray
Glengap
Loch Bargatton
Kelton Mains Open Farm
Threave Gardens
Carlingwark Loch
Bridge of Dee
Rhonehouse or Kelton Hill
Gelston
Gem Rock Museum
Creetown
Glen
Fleet Valley
Ringford
Palnackie
Barnbarroch
Wigtown Sands
Wigtown
Scotland's Book Town
Carsluith
Carsluith Castle
Cairnharrow
Anwoth
Cardoness Castle
Gatehouse of Fleet
Valleyfield
Airieland
Orchardton Tower
Kippford or Scaur
Mote of Mark
Rough Island
Cairnholy Cairns
Girthon
Twynholm
Galloway Hydro Visitor Centre
Tongland
Broughton House and Garden
Bengairn
East Stewartry Coast
Baldoon Sands
Ravenshall Pt.
Ringdoo Pt.
Fleet Bay
Sandgreen
Barharrow
Whinnieliggate
Stewartry Museum
Kirkcudbright
Auchencairn
Hestan
Knockbrex
Islands of Fleet
St Mary's Isle
Mutehill
Kirkcarswell
Rascarrel
Balcary Pt.
Kirkandrews
Borgue
Dundrennan
Rascarrel Bay
Wigtown Bay
Sorbie
Garlieston
Eggerness Pt.
Orroland
Galloway House Gardens
Borness
Ross
Kirkcudbright Bay
Townhead
Dundrennan Abbey
Netherlaw
Borness Pt.
Balmae
Port Mary
Abbey Hd.
Cults
Cruggleton Church and Castle
Little Ross
Whithorn
Port Allen
Portyerrock Bay
Cairn Hd.
St Ninian's Chapel
Isle of Whithorn
Cutcloy
0 1 2 3 4 5 6 miles
0 1 2 3 4 5 6 7 8 9 10 km

Duncow
Applegarthtown
A74(M)
Lochmaben
Marjoriebanks
Lockerbie
Bankshill
Galiaberry
Amisfield
Kirkton
Tinwald
A76
A701
Newtonairds
Holywood
114
Locharbriggs
Heathhall
LOCHMABEN CASTLE
Castle Loch
A709
Heck
B7068
Drumpark
Irongray
Newbridge
LINCLUDEN COLLEGE
The Grove
DUMFRIES AND GALLOWAY AVIATION MUS
Torthorwald
Hightae
BURNSWARK HILLFORT
Burnswark
Terregles Banks
Lincluden
OLD BRIDGE HOUSE MUS
Greystone
RAMMERSCALES HOUSE
Birkshaw Forest
Castlemilk
Waterbeck
Shawhead
Dumfries
Maxwelltown
Collin
Kettleholm
Middleshaw
Middlebie
A75
Greenlea
BURNS HOUSE
ROBERT BURNS CENTRE
Cargenbridge
DUMFRIES MUSEUM & CAMERA OBSCURA
Brae
Lochfoot
Lochrutton Loch
Racks
Dalton
Ecclefechan
THOMAS CARLYLE'S BIRTHPLACE
BIRRENS FORT
Eaglesfield
Cleughbrae
Hoddomcross
Kirtlebridge
Islesteps
Kingholm Quay
Mousewald
Carrutherstown
Hoddom Mains
Mabie Forest
Mabie
Kelton
Lochar Moss
Lochar Water
Brydekirk
Creca
KIRKCONNELL FLOW
Loch Arthur
Lochaber Loch
DRUMCOLTRAN TOWER
Beeswing
Glencaple
Bankend
Clarencefield
Charlesfield
Kirkconnell
RUTHWELL CROSS
108
Kirkgunzeon
River Nith
Ruthwell
DUNCAN SAVINGS BANK MUSEUM
Annan
New Abbey
New Abbey Pow
SWEETHEART ABBEY
NEW ABBEY CORN MILL
Shearington
Blackshaw
CAERLAVEROCK CASTLE
Eastpark
Bowhouse
Cummertrees
Powfoot
Welldale
Dornock
Eastriggs
Shawhill
NITH
Overton
WILDFOWL AND WETLAND CENTRE
CAERLAVEROCK
383 LONG FELL
Loch Kindar
Blackshaw Bank
ESTUARY
Bowness-on-Solway
Port Carlisle
Drumburn
569 CRIFFELL
SOLWAY FIRTH
SOLWAY COAST
Glasson
Bowness Common
Drumburgh
Carsethorn
Kirkbean
ARBIGLAND GARDENS
Cardurnock
Anthorn
DRUMBURGH MOSS
Drumstinchall
Caulkerbush
Prestonmill
Whitrigg
Mainsriddle
JOHN PAUL JONES COTTAGE MUSEUM
Skinburness
Newton Arlosh
Kirkbride
Sandyhills
Colvend
Southerness
Southerness Pt.
Rockcliffe
Portling
Mersehead Sands
Castlehill Pt.
Silloth
Greenrow
Calvo
Seaville
Wedholme Flow
Causewayhead
SOUTH SOLWAY MOSSES
Blitterlees
Kingside Hill
Abbey Town
Waver
Kelsick
Oulton
Lessonhall
Highlaws
Beckfoot
Pelutho
Dundraw
Waverbridge
Newtown
Wigton
NX
Blencogo
Bromfield
Holme St Cuthbert
Mawbray
Langrigg
Waverton
Waterside
Dubmill Pt.
Edderside
New Cowper
Westnewton
NY
Allonby
Watchhill
Aspatria
Allonby Bay
Hayton
Ellen
Mealsgate
Prospect
Blennerhasset
Boltongate
Oughterside
Torpenhow
Sandale
Allerby
Threapland
Crosscanonby
Crosby Villa
Parsonby
Plumbland
Whitrigg
Bothel
Ireby
Crosby
Bullgill
Gilcrux
MARYPORT MARITIME MUSEUM
Maryport
High Ireby
Uldale
Dearham
447 BINSEY
Over Water
Tallentire
Sunderland
Blindcrake
Bewaldeth
Flimby
Bridekirk
Dovenby
Broughton Moor
Standingstone
LAKE DISTRICT WILDLIFE PARK
Derwent
Little Broughton
Great Broughton
Siddick
Camerton
Papcastle
Bassenthwaite
WORDSWORTH HO
Embleton
Seaton
Great Clifton
Brigham
Cockermouth
CASTLEGATE HO
BASSENTHWAITE LAKE
Bassenthwaite Lake
North Side
98
Bridgefoot
Greysouthen
Wythop Mill
Workington
Stainburn
HELENA THOMPSON MUS
Little Clifton
MIREHOUSE
931 SKIDDAW
Westfield
A595
Eaglesfield
Thornthwaite Forest
Mossbay
A596
Deanscales
SANDYBECK MEADOW
Marron
Winscales
Low Lorton
Thornthwaite
THORNTHWAITE GALLERIES
Harrington
High
Dean
A66
A5086
B5292
CUMBERLAND PENCIL
Millbeck
5
6
7
8
9
A
B
C
D
E
F
G

Langholm
Malcolm Monument
Paddockhole
Lockerbie
Bankshill
Tinnisburn Forest
Kershopefoot
Kershope Forest
Bewcastle
Caulside
Kirtleton
Baileyhead
Gilnockie Tower
Claygate
Burnswark
Burnswark Hillfort
Waterbeck
Rowanburn
Catlowdy
Crossings
Blackpool Gate
Kirkconnel Churchyard
Evertown
Canonbie
Middlebie
Birrens Fort
Springkell
Milltown
Woodhouselees
Riddings
Roughsike
Roadhead
Ecclefechan
Thomas Carlyle's Birthplace
Eaglesfield
Haggbeck
Moat
Hoddomcross
Chapelknowe
Scots Dyke
Kirtlebridge
Merkland Cross
Netherby
Easton
Hoddom Mains
Kirkpatrick-Fleming
Stapleton
Brydekirk
Creca
Newton
Hollee
Gretna Green Services
Old Blacksmiths Shop Centre
Longtown
Charlesfield
Springfield
Gretna Green
Boltonfellend
Kirkcambeck
Annan
Rigg
Gretna
Gretna Gateway
Kirklinton
Hethersgill
Welldale
Powfoot
Shawhill
Dornock
Eastriggs
Browhouses
Sandysike
Westlinton
Smithfield
King Water
Walton
Scaleby Hill
Vallum
Bowness-on-Solway
NY
Todhills
Todhills Services
Scaleby
Newtown
Port Carlisle
Eden
Rockcliffe
Blackford
Laversdale
Irthington
Brampton
Glasson
Harker
Course of Hadrian's Wall
Carlisle
Walby Farm Park
Bowness Common
Drumburgh
Hadrian's Wall Path
Burgh by Sands
Beaumont
Cargo
Houghton
Low Crosby
Cardurnock
Anthon
Easton
Boustead Hill
Kingstown
Linstock
Newby East
Hayton
Drumburgh Moss
Kirkandrews upon Eden
Grinsdale
Edentown
Whitrigg
Warwick on Eden
Fingland
Finglandrigg Woods
Thurstonfield
Stanwix
Kirkbride
Moorhouse
Carlisle
Warwick Bridge
How
Castle Carrock
Newton Arlosh
Kirkbampton
Oughterby
Tullie House Mus. & Gall.
Cath.
Botcherby
Scotby
Heads Nook
Faugh
Little Bampton
Little Orton
Morton
Great Corby
Wedholme Flow
Great Orton
Newby West
Harraby
Wetheral
Wetheral Priory Gatehouse
Calvo
Seaville
Aikton
Upperby
Wiggonby
Cummersdale
Carleton
Cumwhitton
Kingside Hill
South Solway Mosses
Baldwinholme
Cumwhinton
Brisco
Durdar
Abbey Town
Waver
Kelsick
Oulton
Lessonhall
Dalston
Cotehill
Hornsby
Cumrew
Dundraw
Waverbridge
Thursby
Wreay
Buckabank
Blencogo
Wigton
West Curthwaite
East Curthwaite
Holmwrangle
Bromfield
Waverton
Gaitsgill
Aiketgate
Langrigg
Waterside
Brackenthwaite
Low Hesket
Ainstable
Armathwaite
Red Dial
Raughton Head
Southwaite Services
Stockdalewath
Rosley
Westward
Westnewton
Bolton Low Houses
Welton
High Hesket
Ruckcroft
Southwaite
Watchhill
Fletchertown
Old Town
Aspatria
Ivegill
Low Braithwaite
Brocklebank
Sebergham
Staffield
Ellen
Mealsgate
Blennerhasset
Boltongate
Cumbria
Inglewood Forest
Thomas Close
Sandale
Calthwaite
Lazonby
Threapland
Torpenhow
Caldbeck
Sowerby Row
Lazonby Fell
Townhead
Plumbland
Whitrigg
Bothel
Hesket Newmarket
Hutton End
Ireby
Uldale
Fell Side
Branthwaite
Millhouse
Plumpton
Brockleymoor
New Rent
Hutton-in-the-Forest
High Ireby
Low Row
Lamonby
Unthank
Skelton
Binsey
Over Water
Sunderland
Blindcrake
Bewaldeth
High Pike
High Row
Ellonby
Plumpton Head
Orthwaite
Hutton Roof
Little Blencow
Catterlen
Lake District Wildlife Park
Knott
Mosedale
Johnby
Laithes
Caldew
Derwent
Bassenthwaite
Great Blencow
Newton Reigny
Fair Hill
Embleton
Great Calva
Greystoke
Penrith
Skiddaw Forest
Bassenthwaite Lake
Mungrisdale
Carleton
Wythop Mill
Skiddaw House
Berrier
Newbiggin
Blakestones Art Gallery
Saddleback or Blencathra
Motherby
Eamont Bridge
Penruddock
Stainton
Rheged
Sockbridge
Clifton
Scales
Tarn Moss
Troutbeck
Hutton
Dacre
Dalemain
Tirril
Thornthwaite
Applethwaite
Threlkeld
Lorton
0 1 2 3 4 5 6 miles
0 1 2 3 4 5 6 7 8 9 10 km

Bellingham
Hesleyside
Ridsdale
Redesmouth
Hopehouse
Sighty Crag
Whitelyne Common
Paddaburn Moor
Kielder Mires
The Flatt
Churnsike Lodge
White Preston
Wark Forest
Birtley
Wark
Stonehaugh
Whygate
Colt Crag Reservoir
Great Swinburne
Gunnerton
Barrasford
Bewcastle
Butterburn
Park End
Simonburn
Spadeadam Forest
Black Fell
NORTHUMBERLAND NATIONAL PARK
Haughton Common
Haughton Castle
Chollerton
Humshaugh
Chollerford
Spadeadam Farm
Wiley Sike
Thirlwall Common
Whiteside
Greenlee Lough
Broomlee Lough
Course of Hadrian's Wall
Hadrian's Wall Path
Grindon
Walwick
Low Brunton
Brunton Turret
Chesters Roman Fort
Housesteads Roman Fort
Visitor Centre
West Hall
Gilsland Spa
Birdoswald Roman Fort
Roman Army Museum
Gilsland
Greenhead
Once Brewed
Chesterholm Museum (Vindolanda)
Wall
Hill Head
Fourstones
Newbrough
Warden
Acomb
Upper Denton
Banks
Lanercost
Haltwhistle
Henshaw
Bardon Mill
Chesterwood
Low Gate
Hexham
Melkridge
Redburn
Haydon Bridge
Low Row
Plenmeller
Denton Fell
Plenmellar Common
Border History Mus
Milton
Rowfoot
Langley
Talkin Tarn
Hallbankgate
Tindale
Midgeholme
Farlam
Halton Lea Gate
Lambley
Stonehouse
Whitfield
Dye House
Dalton
Talkin
Tindale Fells
Forest Head
Tindale Tarn
Maiden Way
Bearsbridge
Catton
Whitley Chapel
NY
Eals
Slaley Forest
Cold Fell
Glendue Fell
Allendale Town
Broadwell House
King's Forest of Geltsdale
Knarsdale
Whitfield Moor
Hexhamshire Common
Ninebanks
Slaggyford
South Tyne
Sinderhope
Blanchland Moor
Geltsdale Middle
Allendale Common
Blanchland
Newbiggin
Ayle
Spartylea
Hunstanworth
Croglin
Blagill
South Tynedale Railway
Gossipgate Gallery
Carrshield
Nookton Fell
Raise
Alston
Nenthall
Scale Houses
Watch Hill
Bayles
Dirt Pot
Allenheads
Coalcleugh
Bolt's Law
Gilderdale Forest
Middle Fell
Renwick
Nenthead
Haresceugh
Leadgate
Nenthead Mines Heritage Centre
North of England Lead Mining Museum
Rookhope
Rookhope Nurseries
High Bankhill
Lanehead
Middlehope Moor
Garrigill
NORTH PENNINES
Unthank
Cowshill
Wearhead
Weardale
Gamblesby
Burnhope Reservoir
Glassonby
Ireshopeburn
Westgate
Alston Moor
Great Salkeld
Melmerby
Melmerby Fell
Pennine Way
St John's Chapel
Daddry Shield
Burnhope Seat
Little Salkeld
Ireshope Moor
Hunsonby
Round Hill
Winskill
Ousby
Langwathby
Cross Fell
Tees
Harwood
Westernhope Moor
Briggle Beck
Skirwith
Kirkland
Milburn Forest
Langdon Common
Chapelfell Top
Edenhall
Viewing Hill
Harwood Beck
Moor House-Upper Teesdale
Newbiggin Common
Eden
Blencarn
Crowdundle Beck
Langdon Beck
Mayburgh Henge
Culgaith
Milburn
Widdybank Fell
Forest
Ettersgill
Brougham Castle
Cow Green Reservoir
Bowlees Visitor Centre
Acorn Bank
Newbiggin
Dufton Fell
Cauldron Snout
High Force
Temple Sowerby
Knock
Cronkley Fell
Middleton-in-Teesdale
Lowmoor Row
Holwick
Cliburn Moss
Kirkby Thore
Dufton

Northumberland
Durham
NORTH PENNINES
Ridsdale
Redesmouth
Sweethope Loughs
Wallington
Kirkharle
Bolam Lake
Bolam
Meldon
Molesden
Tranwell
Clifton
Choppington
Stakeford
Bedlington
Nedderton
Whalton
Shilvington
Saltwick
Great Bavington
Capheaton
Harnham
Belsay
Belsay Hall
Ogle
Stannington
Plessey Woods
Thockrington
Little Bavington
Kirkheaton
Birtley
Wark
Colt Crag Reservoir
Hallington Reservoir
Hallington
Great Swinburne
Colwell
Black Heddon
West Newham
Milbourne
Higham Dykes
Kirkley Hall
Berwick Hill
Northumberland Cheese Farm
Park End
Gunnerton
Ryal
Ingoe
Brenkley
Seaton Burn
Simonburn
Barrasford
Fenwick
Heugh
Dalton
Ponteland
Dinnington
Brunswick Village
Haughton Castle
Chollerton
Humshaugh
Bingfield
Matfen
Stamfordham
Prestwick
Darras Hall
Newcastle International
Hazlerigg
Chollerford
Great Whittington
Ouston
Eachwick
Medburn
High Callerton
Woolsington
Black Callerton
Kenton Bankfoot
Walwick
Low Brunton
Brunton Turret
Chesters Roman Fort
Hadrian's Wall Path
Course of Hadrian's Wall
Hill Head
Wall
Fourstones
Halton
Harlow Hill
North Walbottle
Westerhope
Gosforth
Kenton
Newbrough
Warden
Aydon Castle
Aydon
Acomb
Sandhoe
Tyne Green
Newton Hall
Horsley
Heddon-on-the-Wall
Throckley
Walbottle
NEWCASTLE UPON TYNE
Haydon Bridge
Low Gate
Moothall
Hexham
Abbey
Corbridge
Newton
George Stephenson's Birthplace
Wylam Railway Mus
Tyne Riverside
Newburn
Clara Vale
Scotswood
Wylam
West Wylam
Ovingham
Ryton
Crawcrook
Newcastle Discovery
Metroland
Dunston
Border History Mus
Dilston
Dilston Physic Gdn
Ovington
Cherryburn
Prudhoe
BLAYDON
Branch End
Mickley Square
High Mickley
Greenside
Winlaton
Whickham Thorns Centre
Riding Mill
Broomhaugh
Stocksfield
Coalburns
Barlow
Whickham
Painshawfield
Broomley
New Ridley
Leadgate
High Spen
Highfield
Derwent Walk
Sunniside
Street Gate
Chowdene
Dye House
Dalton
Hedley on the Hill
Chopwell
Rowlands Gill
Gibside
Byermoor
Marley Hill
Lamesley
Slaley
Healey
Whittonstall
Blackhall Mill
Derwentcote Steel Furnace
Whitley Chapel
St Andrew's Church
Hamsterley
Burnopfield
Tanfield Railway
Angel of the North
Kibblesworth
Leazes
Allendale Town
Slaley Forest
Kiln Pit Hill
Newlands
High Westwood
Hobson
Ebchester
Tanfield
Beamish
Urpeth
Broadwell House
Medomsley
Tantobie
Hexhamshire Common
Derwent Res.
Shotleyfield
Dipton
Tanfield Lea
Perkinsville
Sinderhope
Allendale Common
Blanchland Moor
Carterway Heads
Shotley Bridge
STANLEY
Catchgate
West Pelton
Leadgate
The Middles
Grange Villa
Bridgehill
Consett
Annfield Plain
Craghead
Pow Hill
Blanchland
Edmundbyers
Templetown
Iveston
Waldridge
Spartylea
Muggleswick
Allensford
Maiden Law
Hunstanworth
Castleside
Knitsley
Delves
Burnhope
Edmondsley
Nettlesworth
Nookton Fell
Muggleswick Common
Lanchester
Broom House Farm
Sacriston
Horsleyhope
Witton Gilbert
Dirt Pot
Allenheads
Bolt's Law
East Butsfield
Diggerland
Langley Park
Waskerley
Rookhope
Stanhope Common
Cornsay
Hall Hill Farm
Satley
Cornsay Colliery
Quebec
Esh
Bearpark
Rookhope Nurseries
Middlehope Moor
Ushaw Moor
Broompark
Lanehead
Collier Law
Tunstall Res.
Waterhouses
Esh Winning
New Brancepeth
Cowshill
Crawleyside
Wolsingham Park Moor
High Stoop
East Hedleyhope
Brandon
Wearhead
Weardale
Eastgate
Durham Dales Centre
Stanhope
Tow Law
Ireshopeburn
Westgate
Weardale Railway
Sunniside
Brancepeth
St John's Chapel
Daddry Shield
Frosterley
Wolsingham
Thornley
Billy Row
Oakenshaw
Page Bank
Ireshope Moor
Hill End
Crook
Helmington Row
Willington
Fir Tree
Byers Green
Westernhope Moor
Bollihope Common
Howden-le-Wear
Hunwick
Newfield
Middlestone Moor
Langdon Common
Chapelfell Top
Pikeston Fell
Witton-le-Wear
High Grange
Binchester Blocks
Binchester Fort
Newbiggin Common
Pawlaw Pike
Bedburn
Langdon Beck
Redford
Westerton
Middleton Common
Hamsterley
Witton Park
Toronto
Auckland Castle
Forest
Ettersgill
Escomb Church
Escomb
Coundon
Tees
High Force
Bowlees Visitor Centre
Hamsterley Forest
Low Etherley
Bishop Auckland
High Etherley
Eldon
Old Eldon
Cronkley Fell
Toft Hill
St Helen's
Coundon Grange
Shildon
Middleton-in-Teesdale
Woodland
Howle
Morley
Woodland Fell
Butterknowle
West Auckland
St Helen Auckland
0 1 2 3 4 5 6 miles
0 1 2 3 4 5 6 7 8 9 10 km

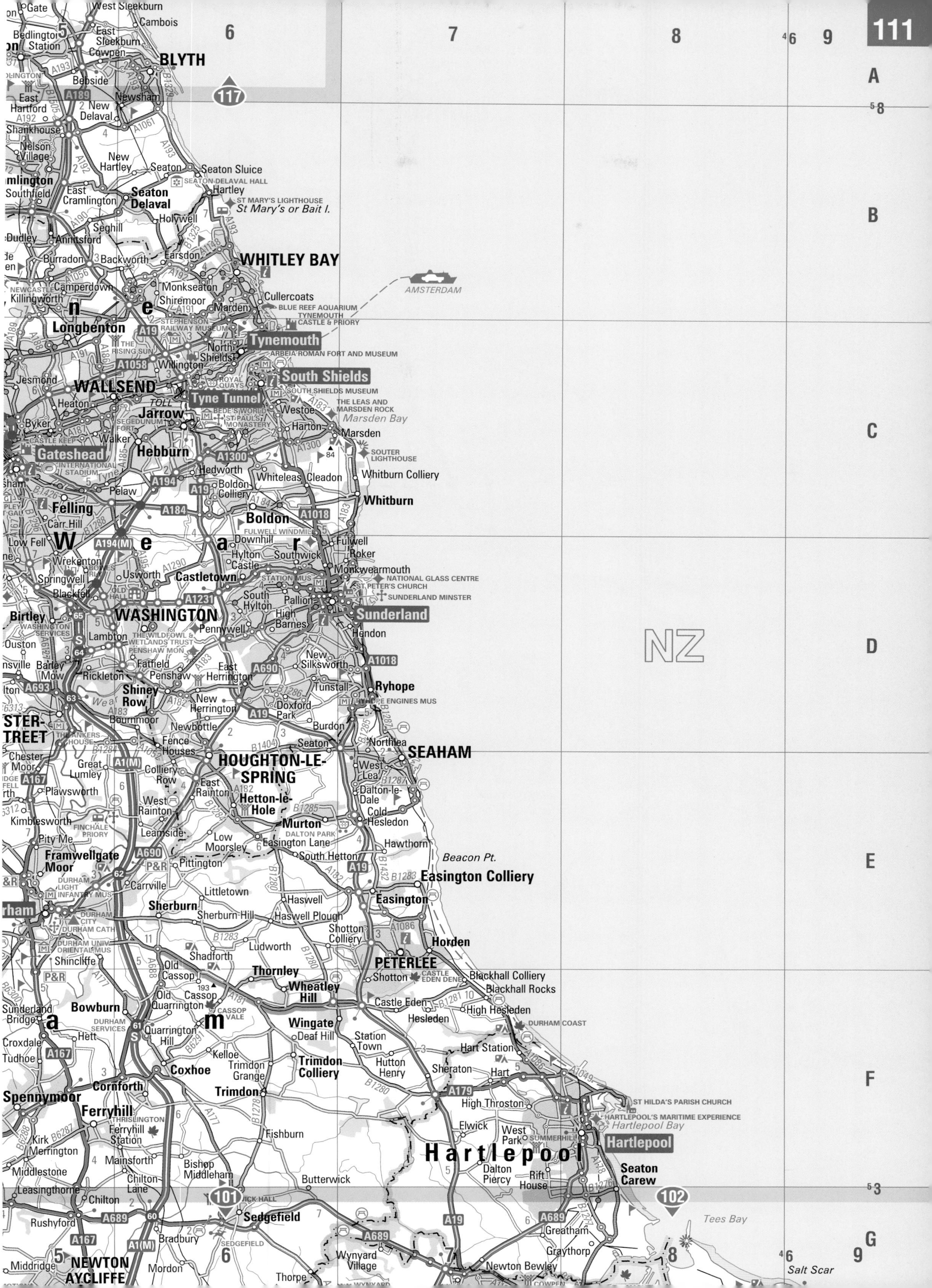
6
7
8
9
A
B
C
D
E
F
G
NZ
117
101
102
BLYTH
Bedlington Station
East Sleekburn
Cambois
West Sleekburn
Cowpen
Bebside
Newsham
East Hartford
New Delaval
Shankhouse
Nelson Village
Cramlington
Southfield
East Cramlington
New Hartley
Seaton
Seaton Sluice
SEATON DELAVAL HALL
Hartley
Seaton Delaval
ST MARY'S LIGHTHOUSE
St Mary's or Bait I.
Holywell
Seghill
Dudley
Annitsford
Burradon
Backworth
Earsdon
WHITLEY BAY
AMSTERDAM
Camperdown
Monkseaton
Killingworth
Shiremoor
Cullercoats
BLUE REEF AQUARIUM
TYNEMOUTH CASTLE & PRIORY
Marden
Longbenton
STEPHENSON RAILWAY MUSEUM
THE RISING SUN
Tynemouth
North Shields
ARBEIA ROMAN FORT AND MUSEUM
Willington
South Shields
ROYAL QUAYS
SOUTH SHIELDS MUSEUM
Jesmond
WALLSEND
Heaton
Tyne Tunnel
TOLL
THE LEAS AND MARSDEN ROCK
Marsden Bay
Westoe
Jarrow
BEDE'S WORLD
ST PAUL'S MONASTERY
SEGEDUNUM FORT
Byker
CASTLE KEEP
Walker
Harton
Marsden
SOUTER LIGHTHOUSE
Gateshead
Hebburn
INTERNATIONAL STADIUM
Hedworth
Whiteleas
Cleadon
Whitburn Colliery
Boldon Colliery
Whitburn
Pelaw
Felling
Boldon
FULWELL WINDMILL
Carr Hill
Low Fell
Downhill
Fulwell
Roker
Hylton Castle
Southwick
Monkwearmouth
Wrekenton
Usworth
Castletown
STATION MUS
NATIONAL GLASS CENTRE
ST PETER'S CHURCH
SUNDERLAND MINSTER
Springwell
Blackfell
OLD HALL
WASHINGTON
South Hylton
Pallion
High Barnes
Sunderland
Birtley
WASHINGTON SERVICES
Lambton
THE WILDFOWL & WETLANDS TRUST
PENSHAW MON
Pennywell
Hendon
Ouston
New Silksworth
Barley Mow
Fatfield
Rickleton
Penshaw
East Herrington
Shiney Row
Tunstall
Ryhope
RYHOPE ENGINES MUS
New Herrington
Doxford Park
Bournmoor
Newbottle
Burdon
THE ANKERS HOUSE
Fence Houses
Seaton
Northlea
SEAHAM
Chester Moor
Great Lumley
HOUGHTON-LE-SPRING
Colliery Row
West Lea
East Rainton
Dalton-le-Dale
Plawsworth
West Rainton
Hetton-le-Hole
Cold Hesledon
Kimblesworth
FINCHALE PRIORY
Murton
Leamside
DALTON PARK
Pity Me
Low Moorsley
Easington Lane
Hawthorn
Framwellgate Moor
South Hetton
Beacon Pt.
Pittington
Easington Colliery
DURHAM LIGHT INFANTRY MUS
Carrville
Littletown
Easington
Haswell
DURHAM CITY
DURHAM CATH
Sherburn
Sherburn Hill
Haswell Plough
Shotton Colliery
Horden
DURHAM UNIV ORIENTAL MUS
Ludworth
Shincliffe
Shadforth
PETERLEE
Old Cassop
Thornley
Shotton
CASTLE EDEN DENE
Blackhall Colliery
Blackhall Rocks
Cassop
Wheatley Hill
Old Quarrington
Castle Eden
High Hesleden
CASSOP VALE
Hesleden
Sunderland Bridge
Bowburn
DURHAM SERVICES
Wingate
DURHAM COAST
Hett
Quarrington Hill
Deaf Hill
Station Town
Croxdale
Hart Station
Tudhoe
Kelloe
Trimdon Grange
Trimdon Colliery
Hutton Henry
Sheraton
Hart
Coxhoe
Cornforth
Trimdon
Spennymoor
High Throston
ST HILDA'S PARISH CHURCH
HARTLEPOOL'S MARITIME EXPERIENCE
Hartlepool Bay
Ferryhill
THRISLINGTON
Ferryhill Station
Elwick
West Park
SUMMERHILL
Hartlepool
Fishburn
Kirk Merrington
Mainsforth
Middlestone
Bishop Middleham
Dalton Piercy
Rift House
Seaton Carew
Chilton Lane
Butterwick
Leasingthorne
Chilton
Sedgefield
Tees Bay
Rushyford
Bradbury
Greatham
SEDGEFIELD
Wynyard Village
Graythorp
Newton Bewley
Middridge
NEWTON AYCLIFFE
Mordon
Thorpe
Salt Scar
COWPEN
WYNYARD
A1(M)
A19
A689
A179
A167
A690
A1018
A1300
A194(M)
A184
A1231
A189
A193
A1058
A185
A194
A693
A182
A183
A186
A191
A192
A177
A181
A688
A1086
A1049
B1283
B1280
B1285
B1287
B1404
B1278
B6287
B6288
B6291
B1432
B1281
B1329
B1325

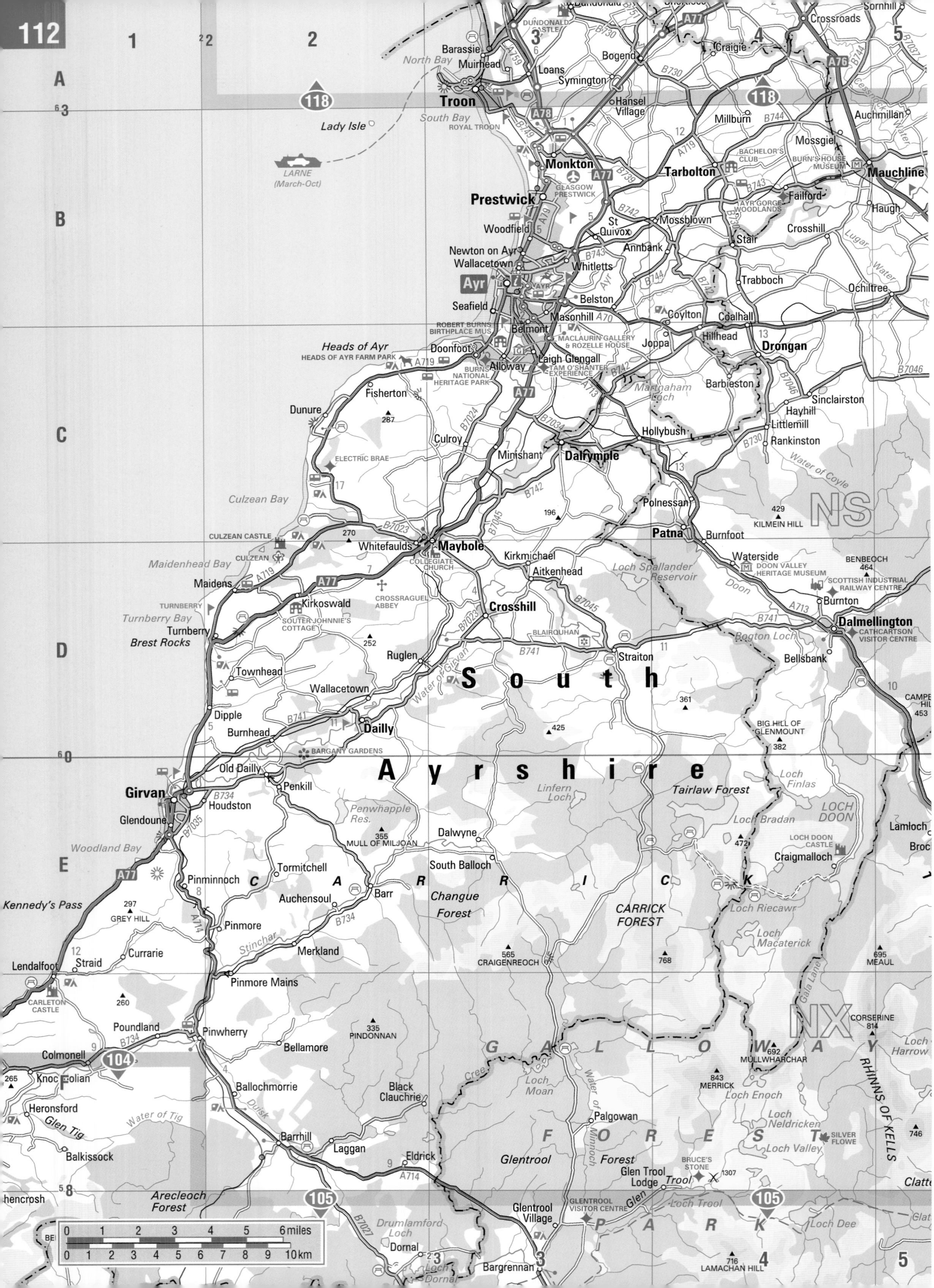
Troon
Barassie
Muirhead
North Bay
South Bay
ROYAL TROON
Lady Isle
LARNE
(March-Oct)
Loans
Symington
Bogend
Craigie
Crossroads
Sornhill
Hansel Village
Millburn
Auchmillan
Mossgiel
Mauchline
Monkton
GLASGOW PRESTWICK
Tarbolton
BACHELOR'S CLUB
BURNS HOUSE MUSEUM
Prestwick
Failford
AYR GORGE WOODLANDS
Haugh
Woodfield
St Quivox
Mossblown
Stair
Crosshill
Annbank
Newton on Ayr
Wallacetown
Whitletts
Ayr
Trabboch
Ochiltree
Seafield
Belston
Coylton
Coalhall
Masonhill
ROBERT BURNS BIRTHPLACE MUS
Belmont
MACLAURIN GALLERY & ROZELLE HOUSE
Joppa
Hillhead
Drongan
Heads of Ayr
HEADS OF AYR FARM PARK
Doonfoot
Alloway
Laigh Glengall
TAM O'SHANTER EXPERIENCE
BURNS NATIONAL HERITAGE PARK
Martnaham Loch
Barbieston
Fisherton
Sinclairston
Hayhill
Littlemill
Rankinston
Dunure
Culroy
Minishant
Dalrymple
Hollybush
ELECTRIC BRAE
Water of Coyle
Culzean Bay
Polnessan
KILMEIN HILL
NS
Patna
Burnfoot
CULZEAN CASTLE
CULZEAN
Whitefaulds
Maybole
COLLEGIATE CHURCH
Kirkmichael
Waterside
DOON VALLEY HERITAGE MUSEUM
BENBEOCH
Maidenhead Bay
Maidens
Aitkenhead
Loch Spallander Reservoir
SCOTTISH INDUSTRIAL RAILWAY CENTRE
Burnton
Kirkoswald
CROSSRAGUEL ABBEY
Crosshill
Dalmellington
CATHCARTSON VISITOR CENTRE
TURNBERRY
Turnberry Bay
Turnberry
Brest Rocks
SOUTER JOHNNIE'S COTTAGE
BLAIRQUHAN
Bogton Loch
Ruglen
Straiton
Bellsbank
Townhead
Water of Girvan
South
Wallacetown
CAMPBELL HILL
BIG HILL OF GLENMOUNT
Dipple
Burnhead
Dailly
BARGANY GARDENS
Ayrshire
Old Dailly
Loch Finlas
Girvan
Penkill
Linfern Loch
Tairlaw Forest
Houdston
Glendoune
Penwhapple Res.
Loch Bradan
LOCH DOON
Lamloch
MULL OF MILJOAN
Dalwyne
LOCH DOON CASTLE
Woodland Bay
Craigmalloch
South Balloch
Tormitchell
Pinminnoch
CARRICK
Barr
Changue Forest
Kennedy's Pass
Auchensoul
CARRICK FOREST
Loch Riecawr
GREY HILL
Pinmore
Stinchar
Loch Macaterick
Straid
Currarie
Merkland
CRAIGENREOCH
MEAUL
Lendalfoot
Pinmore Mains
CARLETON CASTLE
NX
Poundland
CORSERINE
PINDONNAN
Pinwherry
Bellamore
GALLOWAY
Loch Harrow
MULLWHARCHAR
Colmonell
Knockcolian
RHINNS OF KELLS
MERRICK
Ballochmorrie
Black Clauchrie
Loch Moan
Loch Enoch
Heronsford
Glen Tig
Water of Tig
Loch Neldricken
Palgowan
SILVER FLOWE
Water of Minnoch
FOREST
Barrhill
Laggan
Loch Valley
Balkissock
Eldrick
Glentrool
BRUCE'S STONE
Glen Trool Lodge
Trool
Arecleoch Forest
Loch Trool
Glentrool Village
GLENTROOL VISITOR CENTRE
PARK
Drumlamford Loch
Loch Dee
Dornal
Bargrennan
LAMACHAN HILL
Loch Dornal
0 1 2 3 4 5 6 miles
0 1 2 3 4 5 6 7 8 9 10 km

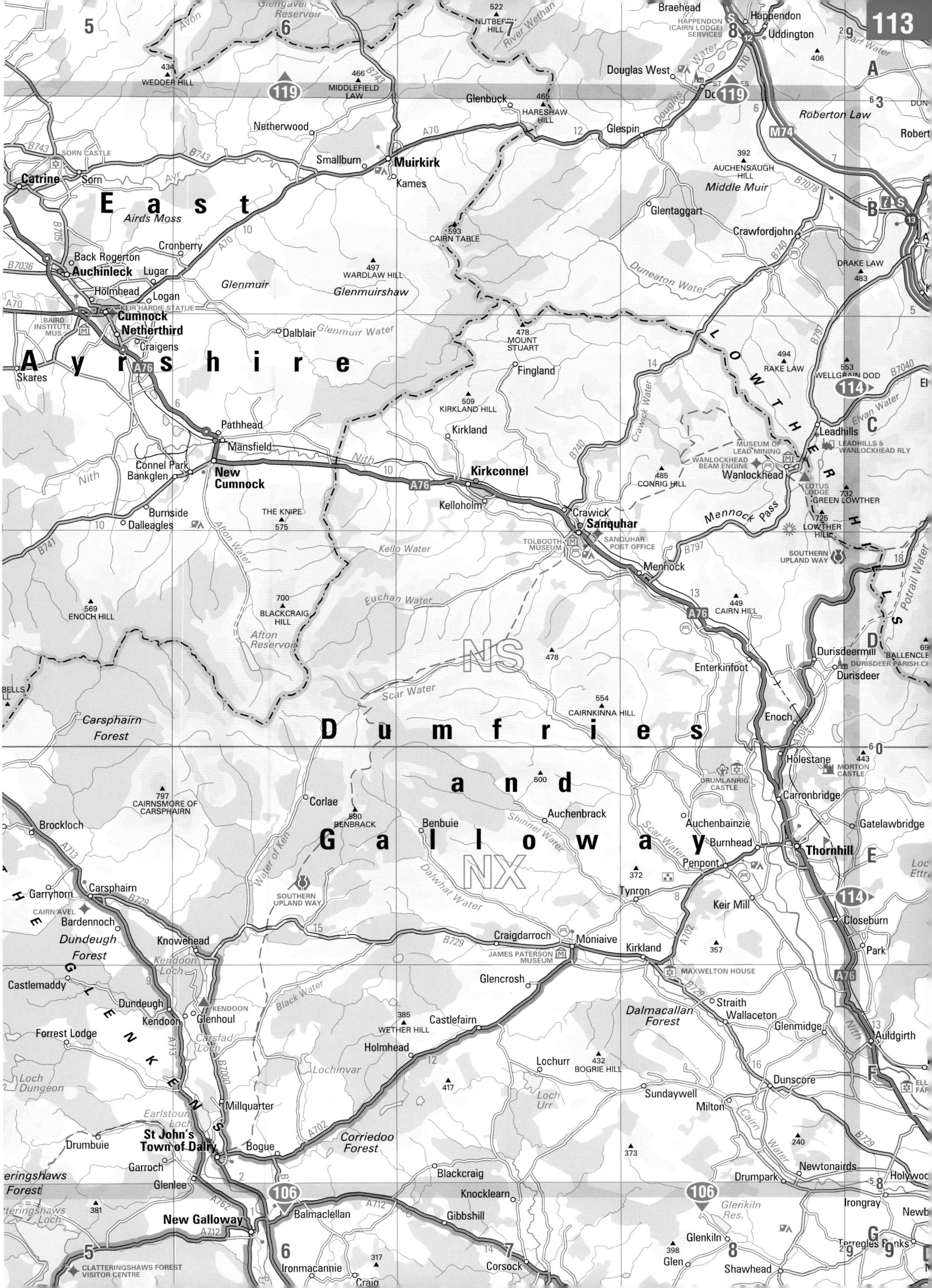
East Ayrshire
Dumfries and Galloway
NS
NX
Glengavel Reservoir
Avon
522 NUTBERRY HILL
River Wethan
Braehead
HAPPENDON (CAIRN LODGE) SERVICES
Happendon
Uddington
Garf Water
406
434 WEDDER HILL
466 MIDDLEFIELD LAW
119
Douglas West
Douglas Water
A70
Glenbuck
465 HARESHAW HILL
Roberton Law
Robert
Netherwood
Glespin
M74
B743
SORN CASTLE
Catrine
Sorn
Smallburn
Muirkirk
Kames
392 AUCHENSAUGH HILL
Middle Muir
B7078
Ayr
Glentaggart
Airds Moss
593 CAIRN TABLE
Crawfordjohn
B705
Cronberry
Back Rogerton
B7036
Auchinleck
Lugar
497 WARDLAW HILL
Duneaton Water
B740
DRAKE LAW 483
Holmhead
Logan
Glenmuir
Glenmuirshaw
KEIR HARDIE STATUE
BAIRD INSTITUTE MUS.
Cumnock
Netherthird
Dalblair
Glenmuir Water
478 MOUNT STUART
Craigens
LOWTHER HILLS
Skares
A76
Fingland
494 RAKE LAW
553 WELLGRAIN DOD
B7040
114
B797
509 KIRKLAND HILL
Crawick Water
Elvan Water
Pathhead
Kirkland
Leadhills
LEADHILLS & WANLOCKHEAD RLY
Mansfield
MUSEUM OF LEAD MINING
WANLOCKHEAD BEAM ENGINE
Wanlockhead
Connel Park
Bankglen
Nith
New Cumnock
Kirkconnel
485 CONRIG HILL
LOTUS LODGE
732 GREEN LOWTHER
Kelloholm
Crawick
Sanquhar
Mennock Pass
725 LOWTHER HILL
Burnside
Dalleagles
THE KNIPE 575
TOLBOOTH MUSEUM
SANQUHAR POST OFFICE
B741
Afton Water
Kello Water
Mennock
B797
SOUTHERN UPLAND WAY
Potrail Water
569 ENOCH HILL
700 BLACKCRAIG HILL
Euchan Water
449 CAIRN HILL
Afton Reservoir
478
Durisdeermill
BALLENCLEUCH
DURISDEER PARISH CH
Enterkinfoot
Durisdeer
Scar Water
554 CAIRNKINNA HILL
Enoch
Carsphairn Forest
A702
Holestane
443 MORTON CASTLE
797 CAIRNSMORE OF CARSPHAIRN
500
DRUMLANRIG CASTLE
Carronbridge
Corlae
580 BENBRACK
Benbuie
Auchenbrack
Shinnel Water
Auchenbainzie
Gatelawbridge
Brockloch
Scar Water
Burnhead
Thornhill
A713
Water of Ken
Dalwhat Water
372
Penpont
Carsphairn
Garryhorn
CAIRN AVEL
B729
SOUTHERN UPLAND WAY
Tynron
Keir Mill
Closeburn
Bardennoch
Dundeugh Forest
Knowehead
Craigdarroch
Moniaive
Kirkland
357
Park
Kendoon Loch
JAMES PATERSON MUSEUM
MAXWELTON HOUSE
Castlemaddy
Glencrosh
THE GLENKENS
Dundeugh
KENDOON
Black Water
385 WETHER HILL
Straith
Dalmacallan Forest
Kendoon
Glenhoul
Castlefairn
Wallaceton
Glenmidge
Forrest Lodge
Carsfad Loch
Holmhead
Auldgirth
B7000
Lochinvar
Lochurr
432 BOGRIE HILL
Loch Dungeon
417
Dunscore
Loch Urr
Sundaywell
Millquarter
Milton
Earlstoun Loch
Cairn Water
St John's Town of Dalry
Corriedoo Forest
240
Drumbuie
A702
Bogue
373
Garroch
Blackcraig
Newtonairds
Clatteringshaws Forest
Glenlee
Drumpark
Holywood
106
Knocklearn
Glenkiln Res.
381
A762
A712
Irongray
Clatteringshaws Loch
New Galloway
Balmaclellan
Gibbshill
Glenkiln
398
Glen
Terregles Banks
CLATTERINGSHAWS FOREST VISITOR CENTRE
Ironmacannie
317
Craig
Corsock
Shawhead

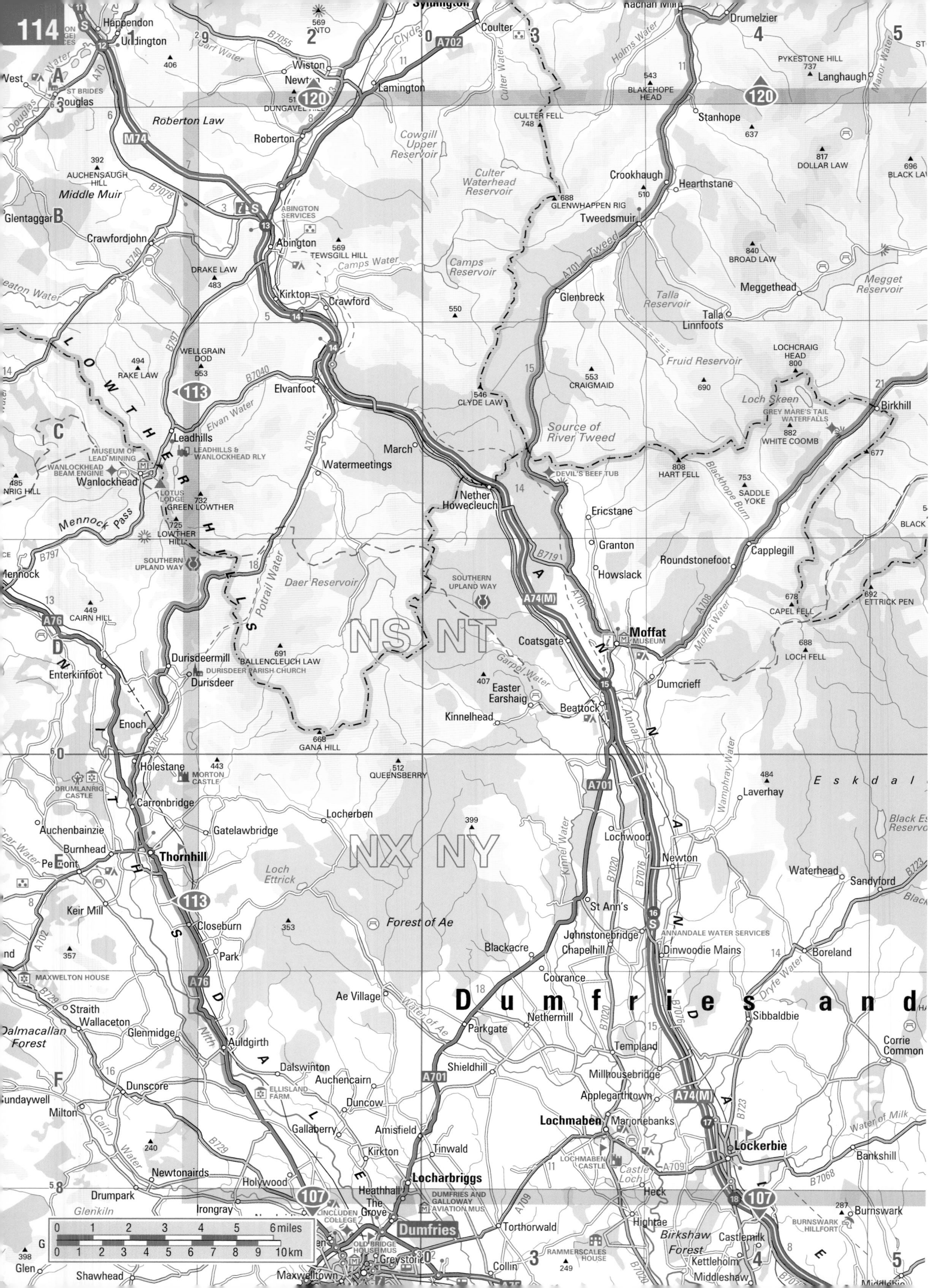

Happendon
Uddingston
Douglas
ST BRIDES
Robertson Law
M74
Wiston
Newton
Lamington
Coulter
A702
Clyde
Drumelzier
PYKESTONE HILL 737
Langhaugh
Manor Water
Holms Water
543 BLAKEHOPE HEAD
Stanhope
637
CULTER FELL 748
Culter Water
Cowgill Upper Reservoir
Culter Waterhead Reservoir
Roberton
DUNGAVEL HILL
120
392 AUCHENSAUGH HILL
Middle Muir
B7078
Glentaggart
ABINGTON SERVICES
Abington
569 TEWSGILL HILL
Camps Water
Camps Reservoir
Crawfordjohn
DRAKE LAW 483
Kirkton
Crawford
550
Crookhaugh
510
Hearthstane
688 GLENWHAPPEN RIG
Tweedsmuir
Tweed
A701
817 DOLLAR LAW
696 BLACK LAW
840 BROAD LAW
Meggethead
Megget Reservoir
Talla Reservoir
Talla Linnfoots
Glenbreck
Fruid Reservoir
LOCHCRAIG HEAD 800
690
553 CRAIGMAID
546 CLYDE LAW
Loch Skeen
GREY MARE'S TAIL WATERFALLS
882 WHITE COOMB
Birkhill
677
Source of River Tweed
808 HART FELL
753 SADDLE YOKE
Blackhope Burn
DEVIL'S BEEF TUB
LOWTHER HILLS
494 RAKE LAW
WELLGRAIN DOD 553
B797
B7040
113
Elvanfoot
Elvan Water
Leadhills
LEADHILLS & WANLOCKHEAD RLY
MUSEUM OF LEAD MINING
WANLOCKHEAD BEAM ENGINE
Wanlockhead
LOTUS LODGE
732 GREEN LOWTHER
725 LOWTHER HILL
485
Mennock Pass
Mennock
SOUTHERN UPLAND WAY
March
Watermeetings
A702
Nether Howecleuch
Ericstane
Granton
Howslack
Roundstonefoot
Capplegill
B719
A74(M)
Potrail Water
Daer Reservoir
SOUTHERN UPLAND WAY
678 CAPEL FELL
692 ETTRICK PEN
A708
Moffat Water
Moffat
MUSEUM
Coatsgate
688 LOCH FELL
NS NT
449 CAIRN HILL
A76
691 BALLENCLEUCH LAW
Durisdeermill
Durisdeer
DURISDEER PARISH CHURCH
Enterkinfoot
407
Garpol Water
Easter Earshaig
Kinnelhead
Beattock
Dumcrieff
Annan
668 GANA HILL
Enoch
Holestane
443 MORTON CASTLE
512 QUEENSBERRY
DRUMLANRIG CASTLE
Carronbridge
A701
484 Laverhay
Eskdale
Wamphray Water
Locherben
Gatelawbridge
Auchenbainzie
Burnhead
Penpont
Thornhill
399
NX NY
Kinnel Water
Lochwood
Newton
Black Esk Reservoir
Waterhead
Sandyford
B723
Loch Ettrick
Keir Mill
113
Closeburn
353
Forest of Ae
St Ann's
B7020
B7076
ANNANDALE WATER SERVICES
Johnstonebridge
Chapelhill
Dinwoodie Mains
Blackacre
357
Park
Boreland
Dryfe Water
MAXWELTON HOUSE
B729
Courance
Dumfries and
Ae Village
Water of Ae
Straith
Wallaceton
Glenmidge
Dalmacallan Forest
Auldgirth
Nith
Parkgate
Nethermill
Sibbaldbie
Corrie Common
Templand
Dalswinton
Auchencairn
Shieldhill
Millhousebridge
ELLISLAND FARM
Dunscore
Sundaywell
Milton
Cairn Water
Duncow
Applegarthtown
A74(M)
Lochmaben
Marjoriebanks
Water of Milk
Gallaberry
Amisfield
240
Kirkton
Tinwald
Lockerbie
Bankshill
LOCHMABEN CASTLE
Castle Loch
A709
B7068
Newtonairds
Holywood
Locharbriggs
Heck
Drumpark
Glenkiln
Irongray
Heathhall
The Grove
107
LINCLUDEN COLLEGE
DUMFRIES AND GALLOWAY AVIATION MUS
Dumfries
OLD BRIDGE HOUSE MUS
Torthorwald
Hightae
Birkshaw Forest
Castlemilk
287 Burnswark
BURNSWARK HILLFORT
RAMMERSCALES HOUSE
249
Greystone
Collin
Kettleholm
Middleshaw
398 Glen
Shawhead
Maxwelltown
0 1 2 3 4 5 6 miles
0 1 2 3 4 5 6 7 8 9 10 km

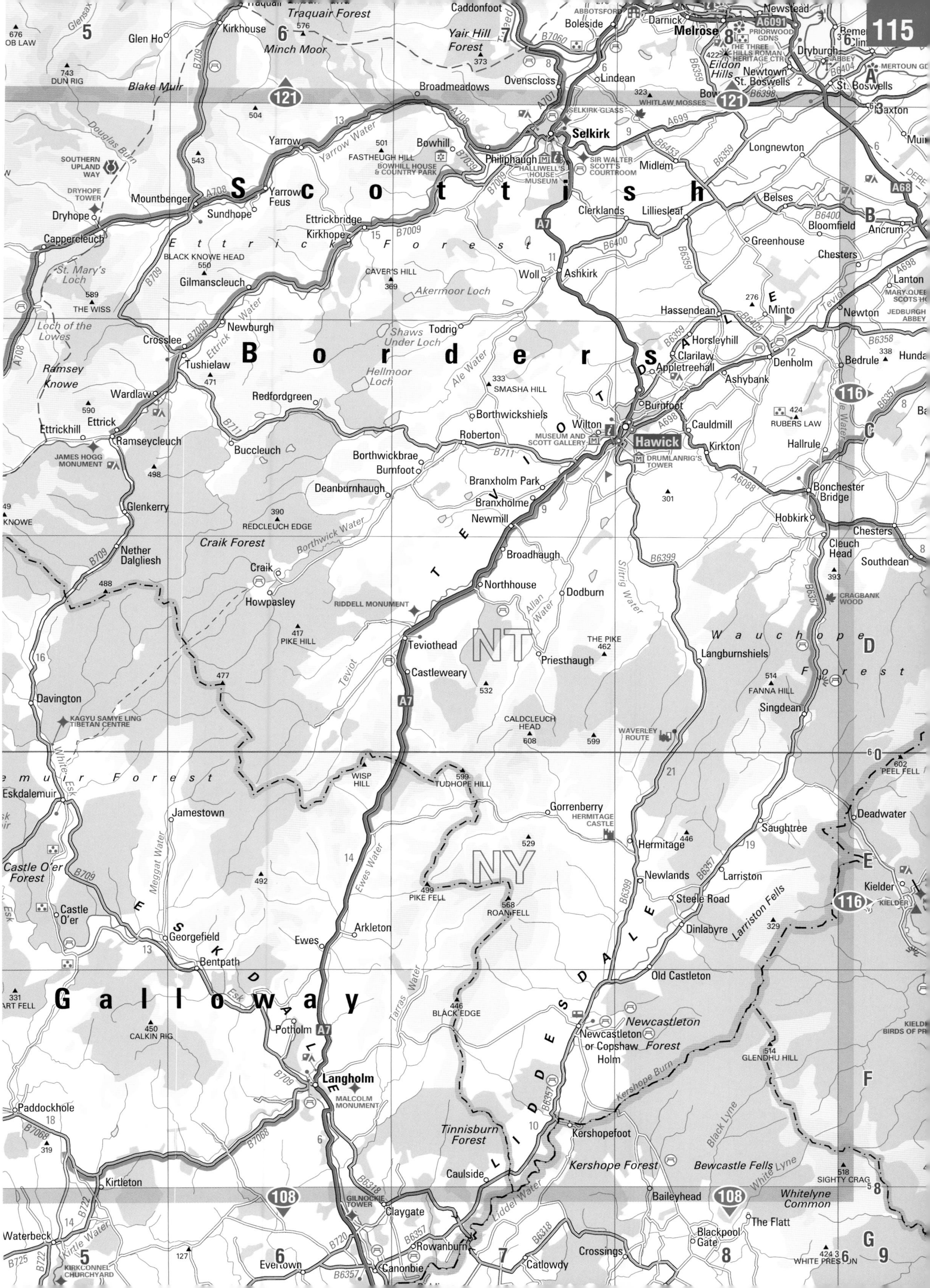

Traquair Forest
Caddonfoot
Abbotsford
Darnick
Newstead
Boleside
Melrose
A6091
Priorwood Gdns
Glensax
676
Glen Ho
Kirkhouse
576
Minch Moor
Yair Hill Forest
Tweed
B7060
The Three Hills Roman Heritage Ctr
Dryburgh Abbey
Bemersyde
Clintmains
743
Dun Rig
373
Eildon Hills
422
Newtown St. Boswells
Mertoun Gdns
B709
B6359
B6404
Lindean
Ovenscloss
Blake Muir
121
Broadmeadows
A707
323
Whitlaw Mosses
Bowden
B6398
St. Boswells
504
13
Selkirk Glass
A708
Selkirk
9
A699
Maxton
Douglas Burn
Yarrow Water
Yarrow
501
Fastheugh Hill
Bowhill
Bowhill House & Country Park
B7039
Philiphaugh
Halliwell's House Museum
Sir Walter Scott's Courtroom
Midlem
B6453
B6359
Longnewton
Muirhouselaw
Southern Upland Way
543
B7009
Dere Street
Dryhope Tower
Yarrow Feus
Scottish
A68
Mountbenger
A708
Sundhope
Clerklands
Lilliesleaf
Belses
Dryhope
Ettrickbridge
A7
B6400
Bloomfield
Ancrum
Cappercleuch
Kirkhope
15
B7009
Ettrick Forest
B6400
Greenhouse
Black Knowe Head
550
11
B6359
Chesters
St. Mary's Loch
Caver's Hill
369
Woll
Ashkirk
Lanton
A698
Gilmanscleuch
Akermoor Loch
B709
Mary Queen of Scots House
589
The Wiss
276
Minto
Teviot
Jedburgh Abbey
Loch of the Lowes
Ettrick Water
Newburgh
Shaws Under Loch
Todrig
Hassendean
B6405
Newton
Crosslee
B7009
B6359
Horsleyhill
B6358
A708
Borders
Clarilaw
Appletreehall
12
Denholm
Bedrule
338
Hundalee
Tushielaw
Hellmoor Loch
Ale Water
Ramsey Knowe
471
333
Smasha Hill
Ashybank
Teviotdale
116
B6357
Wardlaw
Redfordgreen
Burnfoot
424
Rubers Law
590
Ettrick
Borthwickshiels
Cauldmill
B711
A698
Wilton
Ettrickhill
Ramseycleuch
Roberton
Museum and Scott Gallery
Hawick
Kirkton
Rule Water
Hallrule
James Hogg Monument
Buccleuch
B711
Drumlanrig's Tower
Borthwickbrae
Burnfoot
498
7
A6088
Deanburnhaugh
Branxholm Park
Bonchester Bridge
Branxholme
9
301
Glenkerry
49
Knowe
Newmill
Hobkirk
390
Redcleuch Edge
Borthwick Water
Chesters
Craik Forest
Cleuch Head
B709
Nether Dalgliesh
Broadhaugh
B6399
Southdean
Craik
Slitrig Water
393
488
Northhouse
Dodburn
B6357
Howpasley
Cragbank Wood
Riddell Monument
Allan Water
NT
Wauchope Forest
417
Pike Hill
The Pike
462
16
Teviothead
Priesthaugh
Langburnshiels
Teviot
Castleweary
477
514
Fanna Hill
532
Davington
A7
Singdean
Kagyu Samye Ling Tibetan Centre
Caldcleuch Head
608
599
Waverley Route
White Esk
21
Wisp Hill
599
Tudhope Hill
602
Peel Fell
Eskdalemuir Forest
Eskdalemuir
Jamestown
Gorrenberry
Hermitage Castle
Deadwater
Saughtree
529
446
19
Hermitage
Meggat Water
14
Castle O'er Forest
B709
492
Ewes Water
NY
Newlands
Larriston
B6357
499
Pike Fell
568
Roan Fell
B6399
Steele Road
Kielder
116
Kielder
Castle O'er
Larriston Fells
329
Eskdale
Arkleton
Dinlabyre
Georgefield
Ewes
13
Bentpath
Tarras Water
Old Castleton
331
Hart Fell
Galloway
446
Black Edge
Newcastleton
Kielder Birds of Prey
450
Calkin Rig
Potholm
A7
Newcastleton or Copshaw Holm
Forest
514
Glendhu Hill
Liddesdale
B709
Langholm
Malcolm Monument
Kershope Burn
Black Lyne
Paddockhole
18
B6357
10
Tinnisburn Forest
Kershopefoot
B7068
319
B7068
6
Kershope Forest
Bewcastle Fells
White Lyne
518
Sighty Crag
Caulside
Kirtleton
B6318
Liddel Water
108
Gilnockie Tower
Baileyhead
Whitelyne Common
Claygate
The Flatt
14
B722
Kirtle Water
B6357
B6318
Waterbeck
B720
Rowanburn
Blackpool Gate
B725
Crossings
B722
127
Kirkconnel Churchyard
Evertown
Canonbie
B6357
Catlowdy
424
White Preston

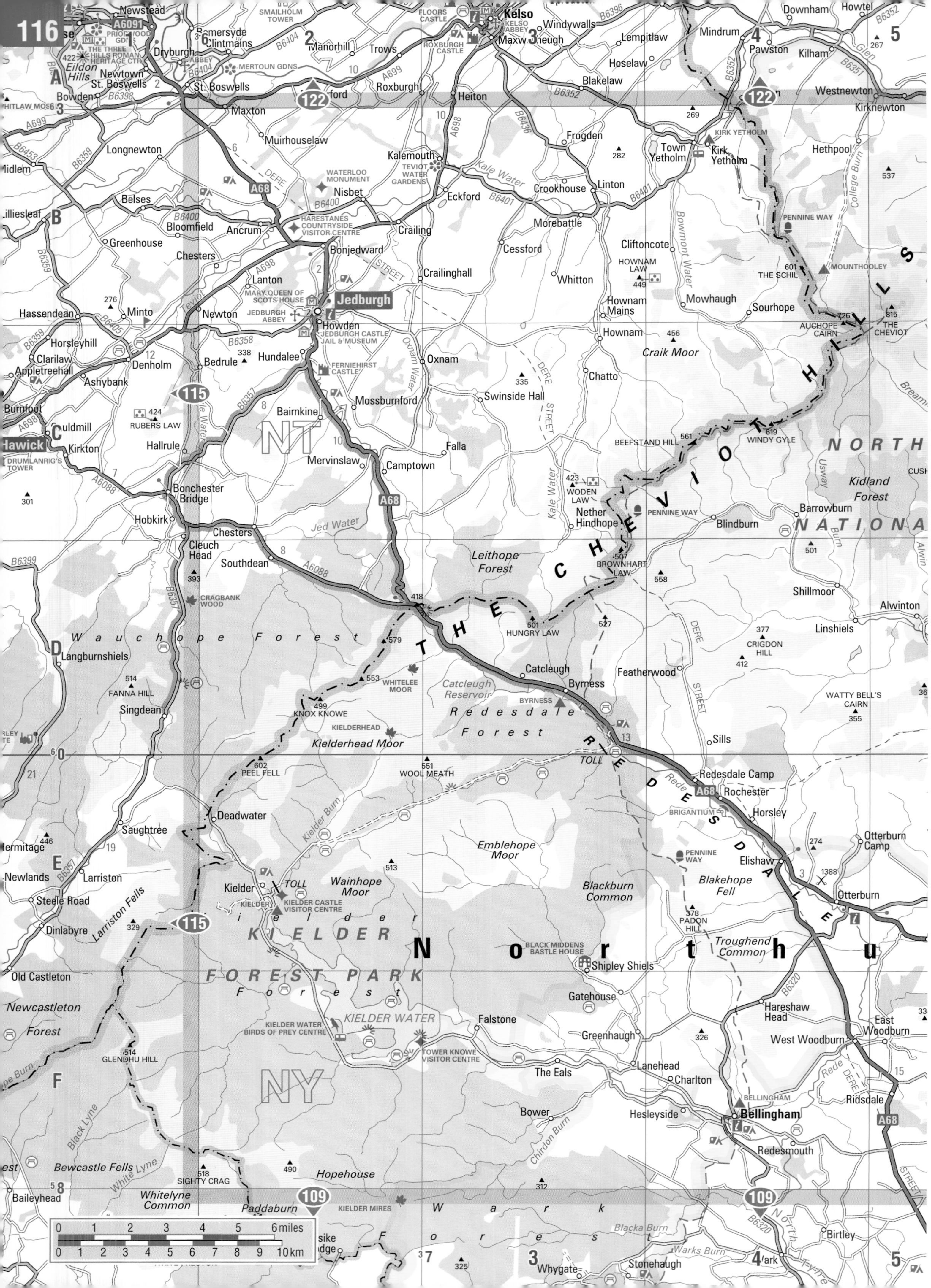

Newstead
Kelso
Windywalls
Downham
Howtel
Bemersyde
Clintmains
Manorhill
Trows
Maxwellheugh
Lempitlaw
Mindrum
Pawston
Kilham
Dryburgh
Eildon Hills
Newtown St. Boswells
St. Boswells
Hoselaw
Blakelaw
Bowden
Roxburgh
Heiton
Westnewton
Kirknewton
Maxton
Muirhouselaw
Frogden
Town Yetholm
Kirk Yetholm
Hethpool
Longnewton
Kalemouth
Midlem
Nisbet
Eckford
Crookhouse
Linton
Lilliesleaf
Belses
Bloomfield
Ancrum
Crailing
Morebattle
Greenhouse
Chesters
Bonjedward
Cessford
Clifton cote
Crailinghall
Whitton
Lanton
Jedburgh
Mowhaugh
Sourhope
Hassendean
Minto
Newton
Howden
Hownam Mains
Hownam
Craik Moor
Horsleyhill
Clarilaw
Appletreehall
Denholm
Bedrule
Hundalee
Oxnam
Chatto
Ashybank
Swinside Hall
Burnfoot
Mossburnford
Cauldmill
Bairnkine
Hawick
Kirkton
Hallrule
Falla
Mervinslaw
Camptown
Bonchester Bridge
Nether Hindhope
Blindburn
Barrowburn
Kidland Forest
Hobkirk
Chesters
Jed Water
Cleuch Head
Southdean
Leithope Forest
Shillmoor
Alwinton
Linshiels
Wauchope Forest
Langburnshiels
Catcleugh
Byrness
Featherwood
Catcleugh Reservoir
Singdean
Redesdale Forest
Kielderhead Moor
Sills
Redesdale Camp
Rochester
Deadwater
Horsley
Saughtree
Hermitage
Emblehope Moor
Otterburn Camp
Elishaw
Newlands
Larriston
Kielder
Wainhope Moor
Blackburn Common
Blakehope Fell
Otterburn
Steele Road
Dinlabyre
Larriston Fells
KIELDER FOREST PARK
Troughend Common
Shipley Shiels
Old Castleton
Newcastleton Forest
Gatehouse
Hareshaw Head
Falstone
East Woodburn
Greenhaugh
West Woodburn
The Eals
Lanehead
Charlton
Ridsdale
Bower
Hesleyside
Bellingham
Redesmouth
Bewcastle Fells
Hopehouse
Baileyhead
Whitelyne Common
Paddaburn
Birtley
Whygate
Stonehaugh
Wark
THE CHEVIOT HILLS
THE CHEVIOT
WINDY GYLE
NORTHUMBERLAND NATIONAL PARK
Wark Forest
NT
NY
0 1 2 3 4 5 6 miles
0 1 2 3 4 5 6 7 8 9 10 km

NORTHUMBERLAND COAST
N O R T H U M B E R L A N D
P A R K
R O T H B U R Y F O R E S T
m b e r l a n d
NT
NU
NY
NZ
123
110
Milfield
Fenton
Nesbit
Doddington
North Hazelrigg
Belford
Easington
Waren Mill
Burton
Seahouses
South Hazelrigg
Spindlestone
Glororum
Lanton
Coupland
Newtown
West Horton
East Horton
Mousen
Bradford
Bellshill
Warenton
Adderstone
Lucker
Elford
North Sunderland
Weetwood Hall
Akeld
Humbleton
Wooler
Chatton
Greendikes
Warenford
Newham Hall
Newham
Beadnell
Swinhoe
Benthall
Fleetham
Newstead
Beadnell Bay
Earle
Haugh Head
Chillingham
CHILLINGHAM CASTLE
WILD CATTLE OF CHILLINGHAM
Rosebrough
Chathill
Middleton Hall
Newtown
Ellingham
Preston
PRESTON TOWER
High Newton-by-the-Sea
Low Newton-by-the-Sea
Brunton
COLD LAW
North Middleton
Lilburn Tower
East Lilburn
Hepburn
Brownyside
North Charlton
Christon Bank
Embleton Bay
Embleton
South Middleton
Dunstan Steads
Castle Point
DUNSTANBURGH CASTLE
Ilderton
Langleeford
Old Bewick
West Ditchburn
South Charlton
Roseden
Roddam
Harehope
Rock
Craster
Wooperton
New Bewick
Eglingham
Dunstan
DUNMOOR HILL
Beanley
Rennington
Littlemill
Howick
Brandon
Greensidehill
Powburn
Shipley
Littlehoughton
Howick Haven
Ingram
Branton
HULNE PRIORY
Shill Moor
Titlington
Longhoughton
Glanton
Shawdon Hall
ALNWICK ABBEY
Alnwick
Denwick
Boulmer
Glanton Pike
Bolton
Abberwick
Boulmer Haven
HAT LAW
Great Ryle
Prendwick
Broome Park
Hawkhill
Lesbury
Whittingham
Lemmington Hall
ALN VALLEY RAILWAY
WILLOWTREE
Alnham
Little Ryle
Thrunton
Bilton
Alnmouth
Alnmouth Bay
Scrainwood
Yetlington
EDLINGHAM CASTLE
Callaly
Thrunton Wood
High Buston
Shilbottle
Biddlestone
Edlingham
Netherton
Lorbottle Hall
Low Buston
Birling
Burradon
Lorbottle
Newton-on-the-Moor
Eastfield Hall
Warkworth
High Trewhitt
Harbottle
Cartington
Amble
Coquet I.
Sharperton
Hazon
Gloster Hill
Hauxley
LADY'S WELL
Warton
Snitter
SHIRLAW PIKE
Swarland Estate
Brainshaugh
Guyzance
North Togston
Radcliffe
Holystone
Flotterton
Rothbury
CRAGSIDE HOUSE
Acklington
Togston
Caistron
Thropton
Swarland
Broomhill
Hepple
Newtown
Whitton
Longframlington
Felton
South Broomhill
Great Tosson
LONGFRAMLINGTON GARDENS
West Thirston
East Thirston
DRURIDGE BAY
BRINKBURN PRIORY
Weldon
Red Row
Low Hesleyhurst
Eshott
TOSSON HILL
Druridge Bay
West Chevington
Forestburn Gate
Helm
Harwood Forest
Widdrington
Wingates
Stobswood
Longhorsley
Causey Park Bridge
Widdrington Station
The Scars
Cresswell
Fontburn Res.
Nunnykirk
Fenrother
Tritlington
Elsdon
Ellington
Fallowlees Burn
Ewesley
Ulgham
Linton
Lynemouth
Raylees
THE SANCTUARY WILDLIFE CENTRE
Rothley Shield East
Netherwitton
COLLIERY MUSEUM
Stanton
Beacon Pt.
Hebron
Longhirst
QUEEN ELIZABETH II
Woodhorn
HERTERTON HOUSE GARDEN
Longwitton
Pegswood
Ashington
Rothley
Pigdon
NORTHUMBRIA CRAFT CENTRE
Bothal
WANSBECK
Hirst
Newbiggin-by-the-Sea
Hart Burn
Mitford
Hartburn
Throphill
Morpeth
Stakeford
North Seaton
Knowesgate
Cambo
Scots' Gap
High Angerton
Guide Post
Scotland Gate
Kirkwhelpington
Middleton
Choppington
West Sleekburn
Wansbeck
Meldon
Molesden
Hepscott
Cambois
WALLINGTON
Tranwell
BOLAM LAKE
Bolam
Clifton
Bedlington Station
East Sleekburn
Kirkharle
Bedlington
Cowpen
Sweethope Loughs
Whalton
BLYTH
Nedderton
Bebside
Great Bavington
Capheaton
Shilvington
BEDLINGTON
Harnham
Saltwick
East Hartford
Newsham
Thockrington
Blyth
New Delaval
Stannington
PLESSEY WOODS
Little Bavington
Belsay
BELSAY HALL
Ogle
Shankhouse
Colt Crag Reservoir
Nelson Village
New Hartley
KIRKLEY HALL
NORTHUMBERLAND CHEESE FARM
Seaton
Kirkheaton
West Newham
Higham Dykes
Berwick Hill
Cramlington
Seaton Delaval
Hallington Reservoir
Hallington
Black Heddon
Milbourne
Southfield
East Cramlington
SEATON
Coquet
Aln
Breamish
Blyth
Font
DEVIL'S CAUSEWAY
A1
A697
A696
A1068
A189
A192
A193
A196
A197
B1340
B1341
B1342
B1339
B6341
B6342
B6343
B6344
B6345
B6346
B6347
B6348
B6349
B6524
B6525
B1337
B1331
B1329
A1061
A Ⅰ B C D E F G

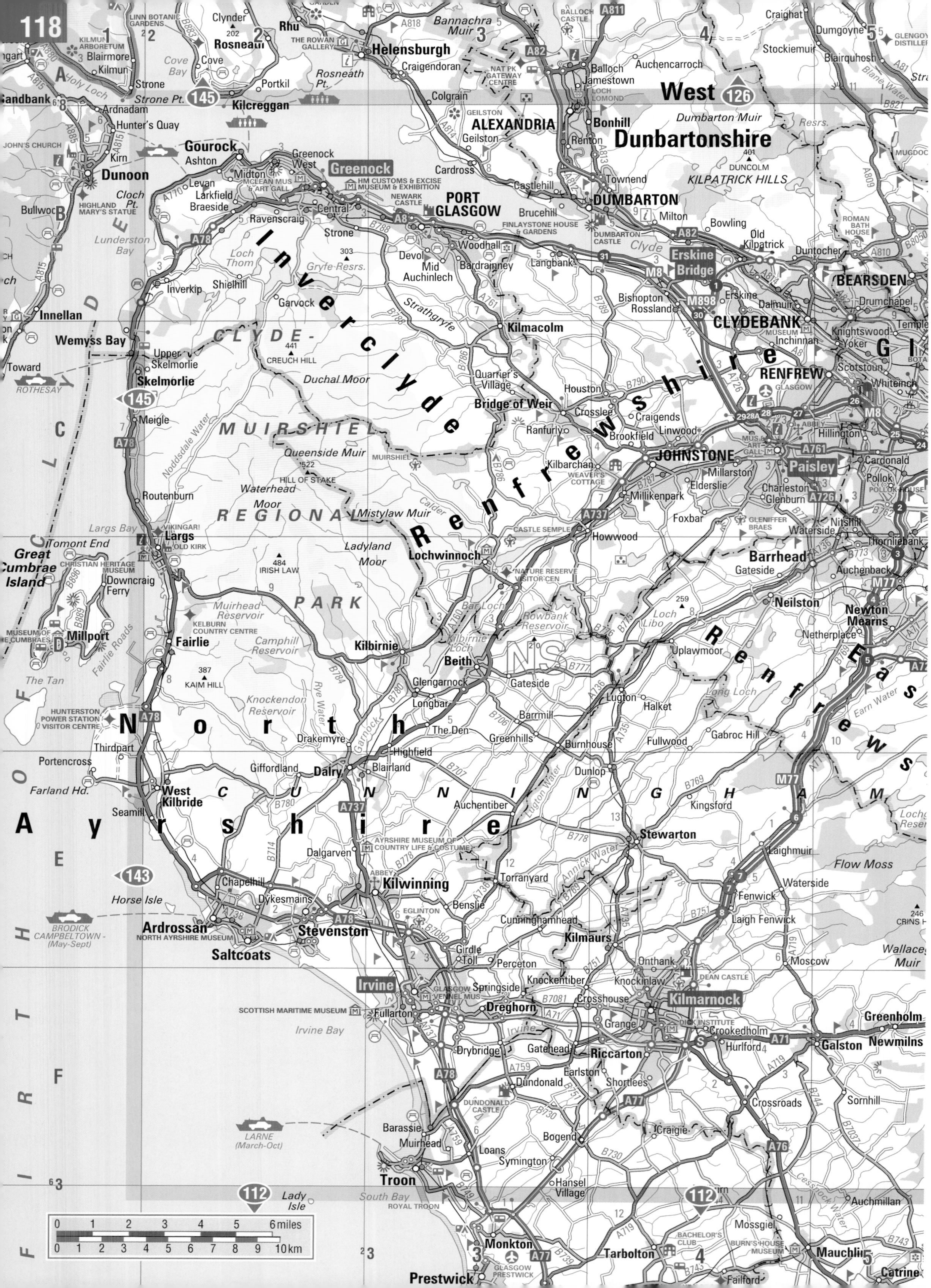
West Dunbartonshire
KILPATRICK HILLS
Inverclyde
Renfrewshire
East Renfrewshire
North Ayrshire
CUNNINGHAME
CLYDE-MUIRSHIEL REGIONAL PARK
FIRTH OF CLYDE
Helensburgh
Craigendoran
Rhu
Rosneath
Rosneath Pt.
Clynder
Kilcreggan
Cove
Cove Bay
Portkil
Strone
Strone Pt.
Kilmun
Blairmore
Holy Loch
Sandbank
Ardnadam
Hunter's Quay
Kirn
Dunoon
Cloch Pt.
Bullwood
Lunderston Bay
Innellan
Toward
Gourock
Ashton
Greenock
Greenock West
Midton
Levan
Larkfield
Braeside
Ravenscraig
Central
PORT GLASGOW
Newark Castle
Strone
Woodhall
Devol
Mid Auchinlech
Bardrainney
Langbank
Inverkip
Shielhill
Garvock
Loch Thom
Gryfe Resrs.
Wemyss Bay
Upper Skelmorlie
Skelmorlie
Meigle
Routenburn
Largs
Largs Bay
Tomont End
Great Cumbrae Island
Millport
Downcraig Ferry
Fairlie
Fairlie Roads
Kelburn Country Centre
Hunterston Power Station Visitor Centre
Portencross
Farland Hd.
Thirdpart
West Kilbride
Seamill
Chapelhill
Horse Isle
Ardrossan
Saltcoats
Stevenston
Dykesmains
Kilwinning
Dalgarven
Ayrshire Museum of Country Life & Costume
Irvine
Irvine Bay
Scottish Maritime Museum
Fullarton
Dreghorn
Springside
Girdle Toll
Perceton
Drybridge
Dundonald
Dundonald Castle
Barassie
Muirhead
Troon
Loans
Symington
Hansel Village
Lady Isle
South Bay
Royal Troon
Monkton
Prestwick
Glasgow Prestwick
Tarbolton
Mauchline
Mossgiel
Catrine
Failford
Auchmillan
Crossroads
Sornhill
Galston
Newmilns
Greenholm
Hurlford
Crookedholm
Kilmarnock
Riccarton
Gatehead
Earlston
Shortlees
Bogend
Craigie
Knockentiber
Knockinlaw
Crosshouse
Grange
Onthank
Dean Castle
Kilmaurs
Cunninghamhead
Benslie
Torranyard
Stewarton
Auchentiber
Kingsford
Dunlop
Fenwick
Laigh Fenwick
Laighmuir
Waterside
Moscow
Flow Moss
Fullwood
Gabroc Hill
Burnhouse
Greenhills
Barrmill
Lugton
Halket
Long Loch
Uplawmoor
Loch Libo
Neilston
Newton Mearns
Netherplace
Barrhead
Gateside
Auchenback
Thornliebank
Nitshill
Waterside
Glenburn
Charleston
Paisley
Pollok
Cardonald
Hillington
Millarston
Elderslie
Foxbar
Millikenpark
Howwood
Castle Semple
Lochwinnoch
Kilbarchan
Johnstone
Brookfield
Craigends
Linwood
Crosslee
Houston
Ranfurly
Bridge of Weir
Quarrier's Village
Kilmacolm
Strathgryfe
Bishopton
Rossland
Erskine
Erskine Bridge
Renfrew
Inchinnan
Clydebank
Dalmuir
Yoker
Knightswood
Scotstoun
Whiteinch
Drumchapel
Bearsden
Duntocher
Old Kilpatrick
Bowling
Milton
Dumbarton
Dumbarton Castle
Townend
Castlehill
Brucehill
Cardross
Renton
Bonhill
Alexandria
Geilston
Colgrain
Balloch
Jamestown
Auchencarroch
Bannachra Muir
Dumbarton Muir
Duncolm
Craighat
Dumgoyne
Stockiemuir
Blairquhosh
Kilbirnie
Beith
Glengarnock
Longbar
The Den
Highfield
Blairland
Dalry
Drakemyre
Giffordland
Kilbirnie Loch
Barr Loch
Rowbank Reservoir
Ladyland Moor
Mistylaw Muir
Muirhead Reservoir
Camphill Reservoir
Knockendon Reservoir
Irish Law
Kaim Hill
Hill of Stake
Creuch Hill
Duchal Moor
Queenside Muir
Waterhead Moor
Eglinton
BRODICK CAMPBELTOWN - (May-Sept)
LARNE (March-Oct)
ROTHESAY
0 1 2 3 4 5 6 miles
0 1 2 3 4 5 6 7 8 9 10 km

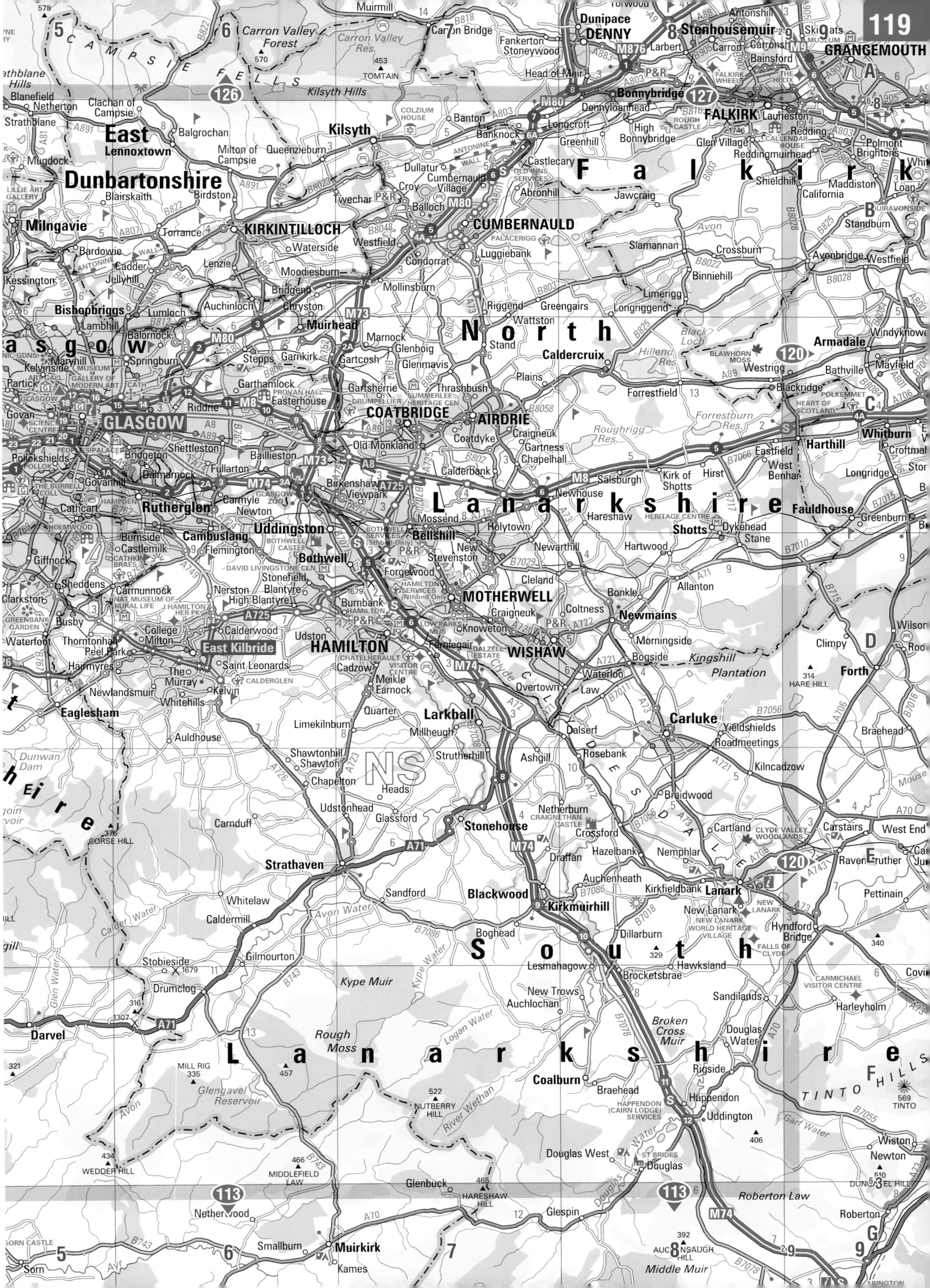
Campsie Fells
Carron Valley Forest
Carron Valley Res.
Kilsyth Hills
Denny
Dunipace
Stenhousemuir
Larbert
Grangemouth
Falkirk
Bonnybridge
Laurieston
Polmont
Brightons
Redding
Reddingmuirhead
Shieldhill
California
Maddiston
Falkirk
East Dunbartonshire
Lennoxtown
Strathblane
Blanefield
Mugdock
Milngavie
Kilsyth
Banton
Cumbernauld
Kirkintilloch
Lenzie
Bishopbriggs
Glasgow
Springburn
Maryhill
Kelvinside
Partick
Govan
Pollokshields
Govanhill
Bridgeton
Rutherglen
Cambuslang
Cathcart
Giffnock
Clarkston
Busby
East Kilbride
Stepps
Muirhead
Coatbridge
Airdrie
Easterhouse
Baillieston
Uddingston
Bellshill
Bothwell
Blantyre
Hamilton
Motherwell
Wishaw
Newmains
North Lanarkshire
Caldercruix
Harthill
Whitburn
Armadale
Shotts
Fauldhouse
Forth
Carluke
Larkhall
Stonehouse
Strathaven
Lanark
New Lanark
Lesmahagow
Kirkmuirhill
Blackwood
Coalburn
Douglas
Douglas West
South Lanarkshire
Eaglesham
Darvel
Glenbuck
Muirkirk
Sorn
Kames
Tinto Hills
Tinto
Kype Muir
Rough Moss
Glengavel Reservoir
Broken Cross Muir
Roberton Law
Middle Muir
Clydesdale
Kingshill Plantation
NS

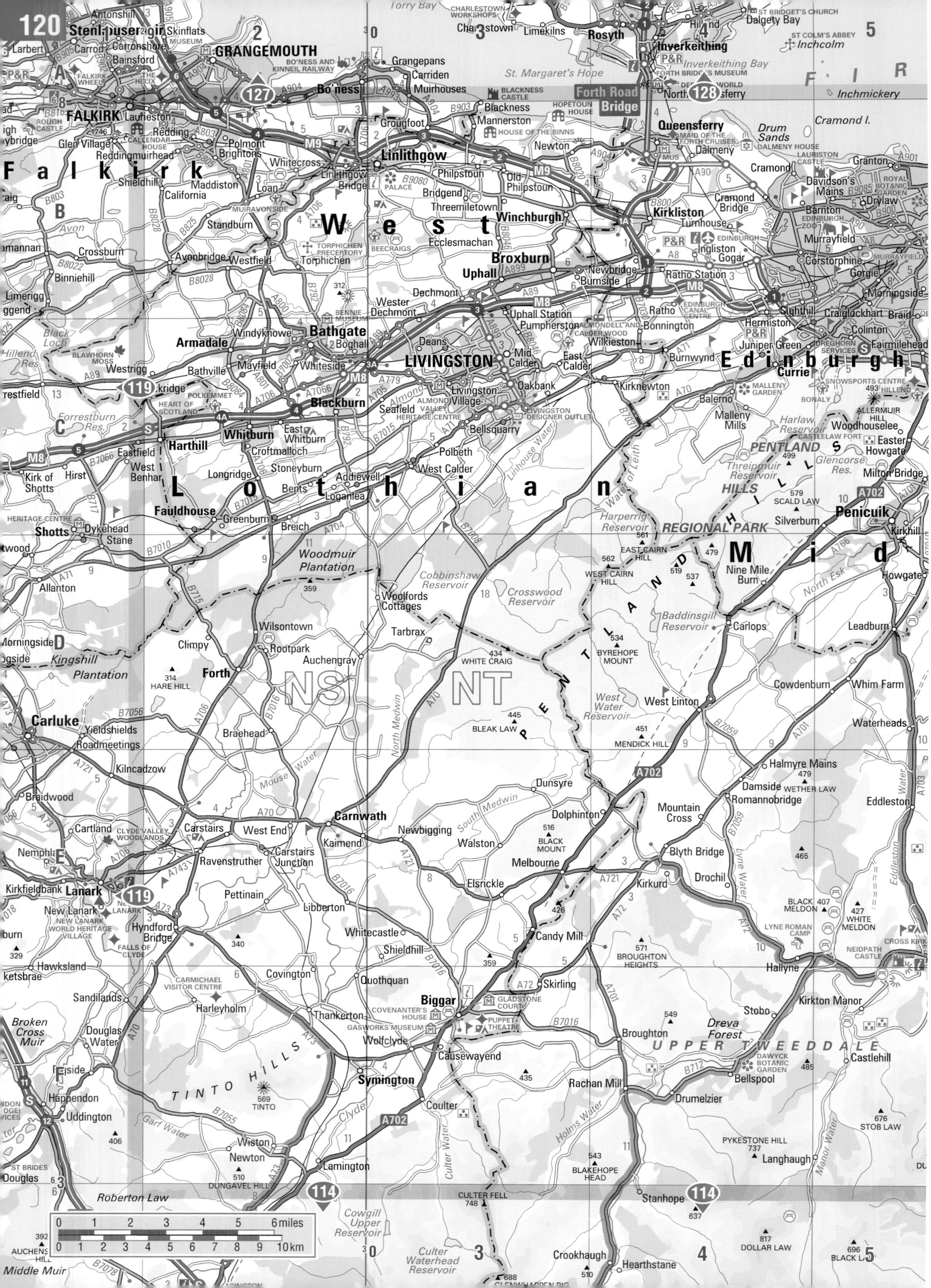

Falkirk
West Lothian
Edinburgh
Mid
GRANGEMOUTH
FALKIRK
Bo'ness
Linlithgow
Queensferry
Forth Road Bridge
Rosyth
Inverkeithing
Dalgety Bay
Inchcolm
Inchmickery
Cramond I.
Kirkliston
Winchburgh
Broxburn
Uphall
Bathgate
Armadale
LIVINGSTON
Whitburn
Blackburn
Harthill
Fauldhouse
Shotts
Stane
Ratho
Currie
Balerno
Penicuik
Carlops
West Linton
Carluke
Lanark
Carstairs
Carnwath
Forth
Biggar
Symington
Coulter
Lamington
Douglas
PENTLAND HILLS REGIONAL PARK
PENTLAND
TINTO HILLS
UPPER TWEEDDALE
NS
NT
Woodmuir Plantation
Kingshill Plantation
Cobbinshaw Reservoir
Crosswood Reservoir
Harperrig Reservoir
Baddinsgill Reservoir
West Water Reservoir
Dreva Forest
Roberton Law
Cowgill Upper Reservoir
Culter Waterhead Reservoir
Middle Muir
Broken Cross Muir
0 1 2 3 4 5 6 miles
0 1 2 3 4 5 6 7 8 9 10 km

FIRTH OF FORTH
Inchkeith
Gullane Bay
Gullane
Dirleton
West Fenton
Fenton Barns
Kingston
Whitekirk
Tyne Mouth
Aberlady Bay
Aberlady
Craigielaw
MYRETON MOTOR MUSEUM
Drem
THE CHESTERS FORT
MUSEUM OF FLIGHT
East Fortune
Tyninghame
Belhaven
West Barns
Preston
Gosford Bay
GOSFORD HOUSE
Spittal
Ballencrieff
Athelstaneford
East Linton
Black Rocks
HMY BRITANNIA
Newhaven
Leith
Cockenzie and Port Seton
SETON COLLEGIATE CHURCH
Longniddry
HOPETOUN MON
JANE WELSH CARLYLE MUSEUM
PRESTON MILL & PHANTASSIE DOOCOT
HAILES CASTLE
Traprain
Biel Water
Pitcox
EDINBURGH
MUSSELBURGH
Prestonpans
INDUSTRIAL HERITAGE MUSEUM
Huntington
Elvingston
PALACE OF HOLYROOD HOUSE
Portobello
Joppa
Fisherrow Sands
Musselburgh
Duddingston
NAT MUS OF SCOTLAND
ST MARY'S COLLEGIATE CH
Haddington
Luggate Burn
Stenton
Halls
Gladsmuir
NEWHAILES
INVERESK LODGE GDNS
Inveresk
Wallyford
Tranent
Penston
Macmerry
Papple
Craigmillar
Newcraighall
CRAIGMILLAR CASTLE
EDINBURGH SERVICES
ROYAL OBSERVATORY
Elphinstone
New Winton
New Town
Samuelston
East Lothian
Bolton
Garvald
Danderhall
Whitecraig
Dunbar Common
Liberton
Gilmerton
Millerhill
Crossgatehall
Ormiston
Carfrae
DALKEITH PARK
Kaimes
Dalkeith
Cousland
Pencaitland
Gifford
Danskine
GLENKINCHIE DISTILLERY
East Saltoun
West Saltoun
Peastonbank
Straiton
BUTTERFLY FARM
Eskbank
Loanhead
Newbattle
Easthouses
Mayfield
Gilchriston
Quarryford
Longyester
Long Newton
Bilston
Polton
Bonnyrigg and Lasswade
MINING MUSEUM
VOGRIE
Pathhead
Peaston
Roslin
Newtongrange
Newlandrig
Humbie
Stobshiel
Birns Water
Whiteadder Reservoir
ROSSLYN CHAPEL
ROSLIN GLEN
Rosewell
Auchendinny
Arniston
Crichton
Fala Dam
Blegbie
LAMMER LAW
Hopes Reservoir
MEIKLE SAYS LAW
LAMMERMUIR HILLS
Spartleton Edge
ARNISTON HOUSE
Gorebridge
CRICHTON CASTLE
Fala
Carrington
North Middleton
Tynehead
Temple
Middleton
Fala Moor
HUNT LAW
Dye Water
Gilston
Falahill
Rosebery Reservoir
Hillhouse
Watch Water Reservoir
Kirktonhill
HOG'S LAW
TORFICHEN HILL
MOORFOOT HILLS
Addinston
Oxton
Heriot
Carcant
Gladhouse Reservoir
Gala Water
Soonhope Burn
Wedderlie
COLLIE LAW
Leader Water
LAUDERDALE
Westruther
Blythe
Fountainhall
Torquhan
Portmore Loch
Dewar
BLACKHOPE SCAR
THIRLSTANE CASTLE
Lauder
Thornydykes
Whiteburn
Thirlestane
Houndslow
Scottish Borders
Lugate Water
Killochyett
Boon
Eden Water
WHITEHOPE LAW
Stow
Nether Blainslie
Legerwood
GREEN KNOWE TOWER
Gordon
Leithen Water
WINDLESTRAW LAW
Glentress Forest
TWEED
Peebles
BLACK LAW
Colquhar
Bow
THE JOHN BUCHAN STORY
GREAT LAW
SOUTHERN UPLAND WAY
West Morriston
Fans
Glentress
Caitha Bowland
Kings Muir
TWEEDDALE MUS & GALL
KAILZIE GARDENS
TWEED VALLEY
Langshaw
Blackhaugh
MELLERSTAIN HOUSE
Kirkburn
ROBERT SMAIL'S PRINTING WORKS
Buckholm
Earlston
Cardrona
ST RONAN'S WELL INTERPRETATIVE CENTRE
Galashiels
Cardrona Forest
Walkerburn
EILDON AND LEADERFOOT
Redpath
Brotherstone
Smailholm
Innerleithen
Clovenfords
OLD GALA HOUSE
Gattonside
ABBEY
SMAILHOLM TOWER
FOREST
TRAQUAIR HOUSE
Traquair
Elibank and Traquair Forest
Caddonfoot
ABBOTSFORD
Newstead
Darnick
Melrose
PRIORWOOD GDNS
Bemersyde
Clintmains
Glensax Burn
Kirkhouse
PARK
Yair Hill Forest
Boleside
THE THREE HILLS ROMAN HERITAGE CTR
Eildon Hills
Dryburgh
Manor
Glen Ho
Minch Moor
MERTOUN GDNS
Newtown St. Boswells
St. Boswells
IN RIG
Blake Muir
Ovenscloss
Lindean
Broadmeadows
WHITLAW MOSSES
Bowden
Rutherford
SELKIRK GLASS
Maxton
Yarrow
Selkirk
Yarrow Water
Bowhill
Longnewton
Muirhouselaw
Douglas Burn
FASTHEUGH HILL
BOWHILL HOUSE & COUNTRY PARK
Philiphaugh
HALLIWELL'S HOUSE MUSEUM
SIR WALTER SCOTT'S COURTROOM
Midlem
SOUTHERN UPLAND WAY
DRYHOPE TOWER
Mountbenger
Yarrow Feus
Belses
NT

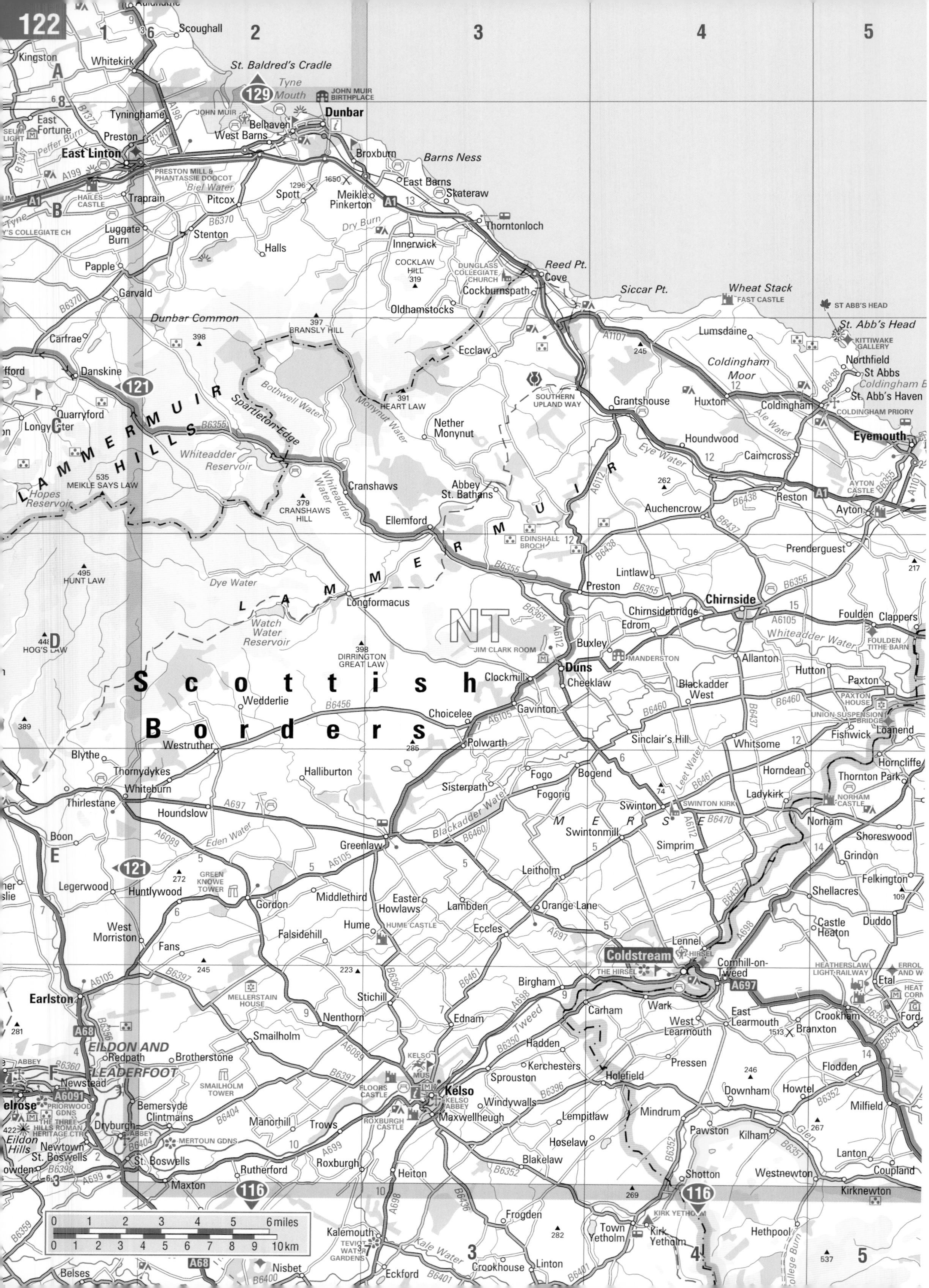
1
2
3
4
5
A
B
C
D
E
F
Scoughall
Kingston
Whitekirk
St. Baldred's Cradle
Tyne Mouth
129
JOHN MUIR BIRTHPLACE
Dunbar
East Fortune
Tyninghame
JOHN MUIR
Belhaven
West Barns
Preston
East Linton
Broxburn
Barns Ness
PRESTON MILL & PHANTASSIE DOOCOT
Biel Water
1650
1296
Spott
Meikle Pinkerton
East Barns
Skateraw
A1
13
HAILES CASTLE
Traprain
Pitcox
Thorntonloch
Dry Burn
Luggate Burn
B6370
Stenton
Innerwick
Halls
COCKLAW HILL 319
DUNGLASS COLLEGIATE CHURCH
Reed Pt.
Cove
Papple
Cockburnspath
Siccar Pt.
Wheat Stack
FAST CASTLE
ST ABB'S HEAD
Garvald
Oldhamstocks
Dunbar Common
397 BRANSLY HILL
398
Carfrae
Lumsdaine
St. Abb's Head
KITTIWAKE GALLERY
A1107
245
Ecclaw
Northfield
Danskine
121
Coldingham Moor
St Abbs
Coldingham B
St. Abb's Haven
391 HEART LAW
SOUTHERN UPLAND WAY
Grantshouse
Huxton
Coldingham
COLDINGHAM PRIORY
Quarryford
Bothwell Water
Monynut Water
Nether Monynut
Longyester
Spartleton Edge
B6355
Ale Water
Eyemouth
Houndwood
LAMMERMUIR HILLS
Whiteadder Reservoir
Eye Water
12
Cairncross
535 MEIKLE SAYS LAW
Hopes Reservoir
Cranshaws
Abbey St. Bathans
262
Reston
AYTON CASTLE
379 CRANSHAWS HILL
Whiteadder Water
A6112
Auchencrow
B6438
Ayton
Ellemford
EDINSHALL BROCH
B6437
Prenderguest
495 HUNT LAW
LAMMERMUIR
217
Lintlaw
Dye Water
Preston
B6355
Chirnside
Longformacus
B6365
Chirnsidebridge
15
Foulden
Clappers
Watch Water Reservoir
NT
Edrom
A6105
Whiteadder Water
FOULDEN TITHE BARN
448 HOG'S LAW
398 DIRRINGTON GREAT LAW
JIM CLARK ROOM
Buxley
MANDERSTON
Allanton
Duns
Hutton
Scottish Borders
Clockmill
Cheeklaw
Blackadder West
Paxton
Wedderlie
Gavinton
B6460
PAXTON HOUSE
B6456
Choicelee
UNION SUSPENSION BRIDGE
389
Loanend
Fishwick
Westruther
285
Polwarth
Sinclair's Hill
Whitsome
Blythe
Horncliffe
Thornydykes
Halliburton
6
Fogo
Bogend
Horndean
Thornton Park
74
Whiteburn
Sisterpath
Fogorig
Leet Water
B6461
Ladykirk
Thirlestane
A697
Swinton
SWINTON KIRK
NORHAM CASTLE
Houndslow
Blackadder Water
MERSE
B6470
Norham
Swintonmill
Boon
A6089
Eden Water
Greenlaw
Simprim
Shoreswood
14
272
GREEN KNOWE TOWER
Leitholm
Grindon
Felkington
109
Legerwood
Huntlywood
Gordon
Middlethird
Easter Howlaws
Lambden
Orange Lane
Shellacres
Duddo
West Morriston
Hume
HUME CASTLE
Eccles
Castle Heaton
A698
Falsidehill
A691
Lennel
Fans
245
223
Coldstream
HIRSEL
ERROL AND W
THE HIRSEL
Cornhill-on-Tweed
HEATHERSLAW LIGHT RAILWAY
B6397
B6364
Birgham
Etal
B6461
A697
Earlston
A6105
MELLERSTAIN HOUSE
Stichill
9
Carham
Wark
East Learmouth
Crookham
Ford
A68
Nenthorn
Ednam
West Learmouth
1513
Branxton
B6353
B6354
281
Smailholm
Tweed
Hadden
EILDON AND LEADERFOOT
Redpath
Brotherstone
B6350
Pressen
14
Kerchesters
246
Flodden
B6360
KELSO MUS
Holefield
Newstead
SMAILHOLM TOWER
FLOORS CASTLE
Sprouston
Downham
Howtel
A6091
Kelso
B6396
Milfield
Melrose
PRIORWOOD GDNS
KELSO ABBEY
Windywalls
B6352
Bemersyde
THE THREE HILLS ROMAN HERITAGE CTR
Clintmains
Manorhill
Trows
Maxwellheugh
Lempitlaw
Mindrum
422
Dryburgh
ABBEY
ROXBURGH CASTLE
267
Eildon Hills
MERTOUN GDNS
10
Pawston
Kilham
Glen
Newtown St. Boswells
A699
Hoselaw
B6351
Lanton
B6404
Roxburgh
Blakelaw
St. Boswells
B6398
Rutherford
Heiton
Shotton
Westnewton
Coupland
Bowden
Maxton
116
B6352
269
Kirknewton
10
A698
B6436
Frogden
KIRK YETHOLM
B6359
282
Town Yetholm
Kirk Yetholm
Hethpool
0 1 2 3 4 5 6 miles
0 1 2 3 4 5 6 7 8 9 10 km
Kalemouth
TEVIOT WATER GARDENS
Kale Water
Crookhouse
Linton
College Burn
537
A68
Belses
Nisbet
B6400
Eckford
B6401

NU
NORTHUMBERLAND COAST
EYEMOUTH MUSEUM
Burnmouth
Lamberton Beach
Lamberton
Highfields
Berwick-upon-Tweed
BERWICK-UPON-TWEED BARRACKS & MAIN GUARD
BERWICK
East Ord
Tweed
Tweedmouth
Spittal
Prior Park
Redshin Cove
Murton
Thornton
Scremerston
DEVIL'S CAUSEWAY
West Allerdean
Shoresdean
Cheswick
Goswick
Ancroft
North Low
Haggerston
South Low
Berrington
Beal
Bowsden
LINDISFARNE
Emmanuel Hd.
Holy Island (Lindisfarne)
Causeway
Holy Island Sands
Holy Island
LINDISFARNE CASTLE
Castle Pt.
HERITAGE CENTRE
LINDISFARNE PRIORY
Fenham
Guile Pt.
Barmoor Castle
Barmoor Lane End
Lowick
West Kyloe
East Kyloe
Fenwick
Kyloe Hills
Buckton
LADY WATERFORD HALL
Farne Islands
Staple Sound
FARNE ISLANDS
Inner Sound
Elwick
Ross
Budle Bay
BAMBURGH CASTLE
Holburn
Detchant
Middleton
Budle
Bamburgh
Kimmerston
Hetton Steads
North Hazelrigg
Belford
Easington
Waren Mill
Burton
Nesbit
Fenton Town
Spindlestone
Glororum
Doddington
South Hazelrigg
Mousen
Bradford
Seahouses
Newtown
West Horton
East Horton
Bellshill
Elford
North Sunderland
Akeld
Weetwood Hall
Warenton
Adderstone
ADDERSTONE
Lucker
Newham Hall
Beadnell
Humbleton
Wooler
Chatton
Greendikes
Warenford
Swinhoe
Benthall
Newham
Fleetham
Newstead
Beadnell Bay
Earle
Middleton Hall
Haugh Head
Chillingham
CHILLINGHAM CASTLE
WILD CATTLE OF CHILLINGHAM
Newtown
Rosebrough
Chathill
Ellingham
Preston
High Newton-by-the-Sea
Brunton
A1
A697
A698
A1167
B6461
B6354
B6525
B6353
B6349
B6348
B1342
B1340
B1341
117

ISLAND OF MULL
SOUND OF MULL
FIRTH OF LORN
LYNN OF LORN
LORN
BENDERLOCH
Claggan
Larachbeg
KINLOCHALINE CASTLE
ARDTORNISH GARDENS
Achranich
Loch Tearnait
Rannoch
Loch Aline
BEINN A' CHAISIL
Glensanda
Loch nan Clach
Shuna I.
Portnacroish
Appin
Port Appin
Port Ramsay
Clachan
Eriska
North Shian
South Shian
SCOTTISH SEA LIFE SANCTUARY
Lismore
Achnacroish
Achinduin
Kilcheran
Eilean Dubh
Baravullin
Kiel Crofts
Benderloch
Ledaig
Achnaba
Ardmucknish Bay
North Connel
Connel
Black Crofts
FALLS OF LORA
Eilean Mor
DUNSTAFFNAGE CASTLE
Dunbeg
Ganavan
Dunollie
OBAN LODGE
MCCAIG'S TOWER
OBAN DISTILLERY
Oban
Black Lochs
Fiunary
Savary
Lochaline
Aros Mains
Rubha Mor
Salen
Pennygown
Fishnish Bay
Killbeg
Corrynachenchy
Ardtornish Pt.
ARDTORNISH CASTLE
GLAIS BHEINN
AN SLEAGHACH
Eignaig
Inninmore Bay
Garbh Shlios
Camas Gorm
Garmony
Scallastle Bay
Rubha an Ridire
Bernera I.
Knock
Loch Bà
BEINN CHRAIG
Glen Cannel
Scallastle
Java
Craignure Bay
Craignure
DUN DA GHAOITHE
Duart Bay
Duart Pt.
DUART CASTLE
Eilean Musdile
BEINN TALAIDH
Lochdon
CASTLEBAY COLL LOCHBOISDALE TIREE
CORRA-BHEINN
Glen More
Lussa
Loch Don
Grass Pt.
Strathcoil
Coladoir
Loch Airdeglais
Loch Spelve
Kerrera
Balliemore
Altnacraig
Glenamachrie
BEN BUIE
CREACH BEINN
Loch Fuaron
Kinlochspelve
Croggan
Rubha nan Sailthean
Bach I.
Ardmore
Gallanach
Barran
Lochbuie
Barachandroman
Loch Uisg
BEINN NA CROISE
Rubha Seanach
Sound of Kerrera
Kilbride
Kilmore
Am Buth
Loch Feochan
Glen Feochan
GLENFEOCHAN HOUSE GARDENS
Carsaig
Loch Buie
Laggan Deer Forest
DRUIM FADA
LORD LOVAT'S CAVE
Carsaig Bay
Rubha Dubh
Kilninver
Barochreal
Glen Euchar
A'CHRUACH
Musdale
Bragleenmore
NM
CLACHAN BRIDGE
Frank Lockwood's Island
Insh I.
Sound of Insh
Clachan-Seil
Seil
Clachan
AN CALA GARDENS
Loch Scamadale
BEINN CHAPULL
CARN DEARG
Easdale
EASDALE ISLAND FOLK MUSEUM
Balvicar
Braes of Lorn
Blaran
CRUACH RAREY
Loch Tralaig
Drissaig
Lochavich Ho
Kilmun
Dubh-fheith
Cuan
Seil Sound
Cullipool
Torsa
Kilchoan
Ardanstur
Melfort
Kilmelford
Loch Avich
Garbh Eileach
Garvellachs
Luing
Loch Melfort
Glenmore
SCARBA, LUNGA AND THE GARVELLACHS
Eilean Dubh Mor
Eileach an Naoimh
ARDUAINE GARDEN
Arduaine
Kames
Lagalochan
Achafolla
CARN DUCHARA
Inverliever Forest
Kilmaha
Sound of Luing
Toberonochy
Garraron
COLONSAY
Lunga
Shuna
Craobh Haven
Barravullin
Shuna Sound
Shuna Pt.
Lunga
CRUACH AN EACHLAICH
Arichamish
CRUACH SCARBA
Rubha Aird Luing
Kintraw
Torran
Scarba
Ardfern
Ford
Finchairn
FINCHAIRN CASTLE
Ederline
CREAG MHOR
Gulf of Corryvreckan
Eilean Righ
CARNASSARIE CASTLE
CRUACH FHIONN
Aird
Loch Craignish
Rèisa an t-Sruith
Loch Gaineamhach
Kinuachdrachd
Kilmartin
GLEBE CAIRN
KILMARTIN HOUSE MUSEUM
Craignish Pt.
Island Macaskin
Glengarrisdale Bay
CRUACH NA SEILCHEIG
Kinuachdrachd Harbour
KILMARTIN SCULPTURED STONES
RI CRUIN CAIRN
Slockavullin
Poltalloch
Gleann Airigh
NR
Glendebadel Bay
Loch Crinan
DUN DUBH
BEN GARRISDALE
Crinan
CUP AND RING MARKS
Killmahumaig
Add
MOINE MHOR
DUNADD FORT
Kilmichael Glassary
Bridgend
Loch Glashan
Bellanoch
Mòine Mhòr
CAIRNBAAN CUP & RING MARKS
ROCK MARKINGS
Lussa
Lealt
Lochgair
Asknish
147
130
144
145
A828
A849
A884
A816
B844
B8003
B8002
B8025
B841
B8045
B840
B849
B8035
A848
A83
0 1 2 3 4 5 6 miles
0 1 2 3 4 5 6 7 8 9 10 km

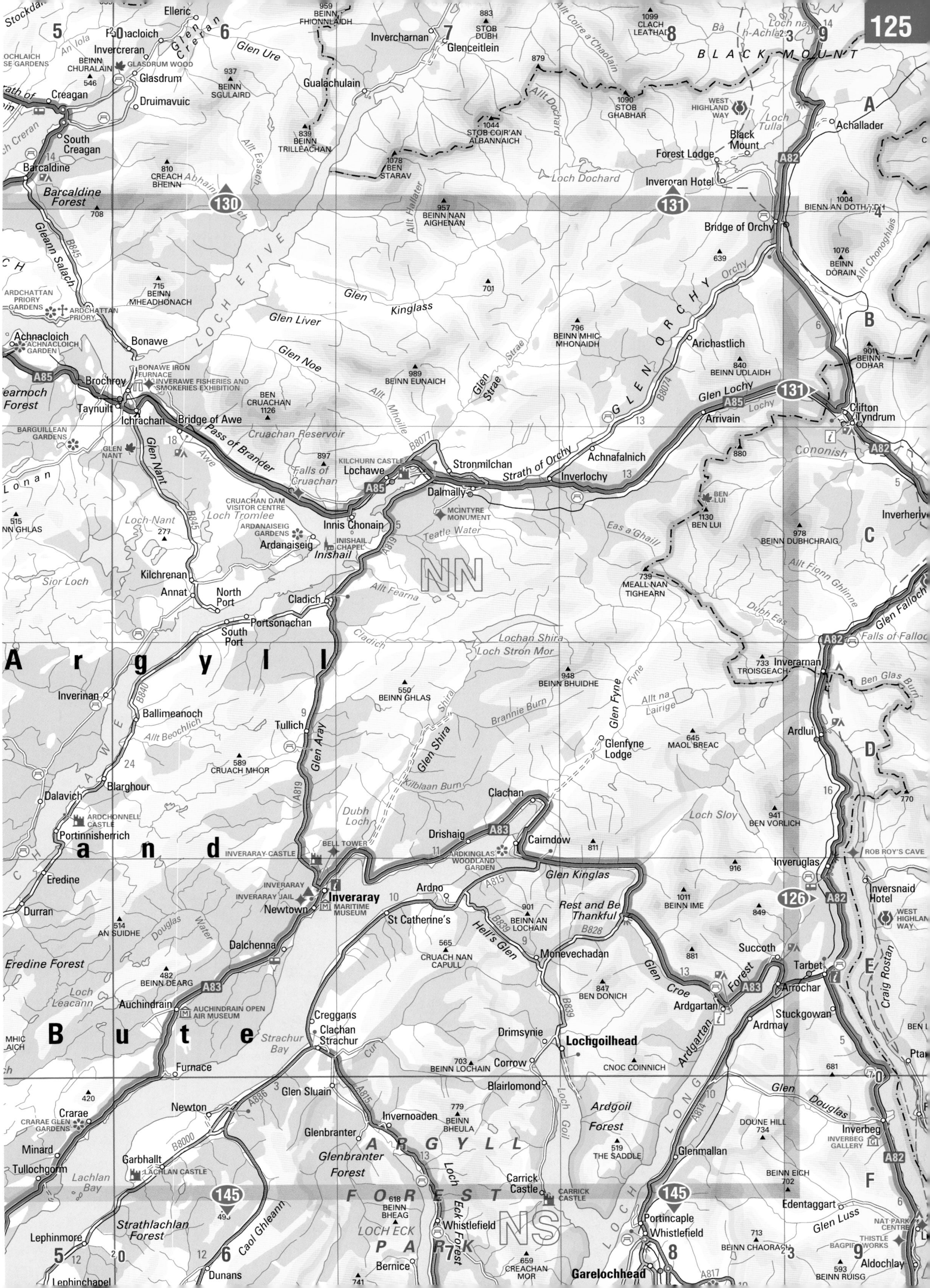

Elleric
Invercreran
Glen Creran
Glen Ure
Inverchamnan
Glenceitlein
STOB DUBH
CLACH LEATHAD
BLACK MOUNT
BEINN FHIONNLAIDH
BEINN CHURALAIN
GLASDRUM WOOD
Glasdrum
Druimavuic
BEINN SGULAIRD
Gualachulain
Creagan
South Creagan
Barcaldine
Barcaldine Forest
CREACH BHEINN
BEINN TRILLEACHAN
BEN STARAV
STOB COIR'AN ALBANNAICH
STOB GHABHAR
WEST HIGHLAND WAY
Loch Tulla
Achallader
Black Mount
Forest Lodge
Loch Dochard
Inveroran Hotel
Allt Coire a'Chaolain
Allt Dochard
130
131
BEINN NAN AIGHENAN
BIENN AN DOTHAIDH
Bridge of Orchy
BEINN DORAIN
Allt Chonoghlais
Gleann Salach
ARDCHATTAN PRIORY GARDENS
ARDCHATTAN PRIORY
BEINN MHEADHONACH
LOCH ETIVE
Glen Kinglass
Glen Liver
Glen Noe
GLEN ORCHY
BEINN MHIC-MHONAIDH
Arichastlich
BEINN UDLAIDH
BEINN ODHAR
Achnacloich
ACHNACLOICH GARDEN
Bonawe
BONAWE IRON FURNACE
INVERAWE FISHERIES AND SMOKERIES EXHIBITION
Brochroy
Taynuilt
Ichrachan
Bridge of Awe
BEN CRUACHAN
BEINN EUNAICH
Glen Strae
Glen Lochy
Arrivain
Clifton
Tyndrum
BARGUILLEAN GARDENS
GLEN NANT
Glen Nant
Pass of Brander
Cruachan Reservoir
Falls of Cruachan
KILCHURN CASTLE
Lochawe
Stronmilchan
Strath of Orchy
Achnafalnich
Inverlochy
Cononish
Dalmally
Glen Lonan
CRUACHAN DAM VISITOR CENTRE
Loch Tromlee
Loch-Nant
BEN LUI
Innis Chonain
MCINTYRE MONUMENT
ARDANAISEIG GARDENS
Ardanaiseig
INISHAIL CHAPEL
Inishail
Teatle Water
Eas a'Ghaill
BEINN DUBHCHRAIG
Inverherive
Allt Fionn Ghlinne
Kilchrenan
Sior Loch
Annat
North Port
Cladich
Allt Fearna
NN
MEALL NAN TIGHEARN
Dubh Eas
Glen Falloch
Portsonachan
South Port
Lochan Shira
Loch Stron Mor
Falls of Falloch
Argyll
TROISGEACH
Inverarnan
Ben Glas Burn
BEINN BHUIDHE
Inverinan
BEINN GHLAS
Allt na Lairige
Brannie Burn
Glen Fyne
Ballimeanoch
Allt Beochlich
Tullich
Glen Aray
Glen Shira
Glenfyne Lodge
MAOL BREAC
Ardlui
LOCH AWE
CRUACH MHOR
Kilblaan Burn
Dalavich
Blarghour
Clachan
Loch Sloy
BEN VORLICH
Dubh Loch
ARDCHONNELL CASTLE
Portinnisherrich
Drishaig
Cairndow
and
BELL TOWER
INVERARAY CASTLE
ARDKINGLAS WOODLAND GARDEN
ROB ROY'S CAVE
Inveruglas
Eredine
INVERARAY JAIL
Inveraray
Glen Kinglas
Ardno
Inversnaid Hotel
BEINN IME
Durran
Newtown
MARITIME MUSEUM
St Catherine's
BEINN AN LOCHAIN
Rest and Be Thankful
WEST HIGHLAND WAY
AN SUIDHE
Douglas Water
Dalchenna
CRUACH NAN CAPULL
Hell's Glen
Monevechadan
Glen Croe
Succoth
Tarbet
Eredine Forest
BEINN DEARG
Loch Leacann
Auchindrain
AUCHINDRAIN OPEN AIR MUSEUM
BEN DONICH
Ardgartan
Forest
Arrochar
Craig Rostan
Stuckgowan
Ardmay
Creggans
Clachan Strachur
Strachur Bay
Drimsynie
Lochgoilhead
Ardgartan
Bute
MHIC LAICH
Furnace
BEINN LOCHAIN
Corrow
CNOC COINNICH
Blairlomond
Glen Douglas
Glen Sluain
Newton
Caol Ghleann
Invernoaden
BEINN BHEULA
Ardgoil Forest
LOCH LONG
DOUNE HILL
Inverbeg
INVERBEG GALLERY
CRARAE GLEN GARDENS
Crarae
Minard
Glenbranter
Glenbranter Forest
ARGYLL FOREST PARK
THE SADDLE
Glenmallan
Tullochgorm
Garbhallt
LACHLAN CASTLE
Lachlan Bay
Loch Eck
Carrick Castle
CARRICK CASTLE
BEINN EICH
Edentaggart
145
BEINN BHEAG
Eck Forest
NS
Portincaple
Whistlefield
Glen Luss
NAT PARK CENTRE
Strathlachlan Forest
LOCH ECK
Whistlefield
BEINN CHAORACH
THISTLE BAGPIPE WORKS
Lephinmore
Dunans
Bernice
CREACHAN MOR
Garelochhead
BEINN RUISG
Aldochlay
Lephinchapel
126
A82
A85
A83
A819
A815
A886
A814
A817
B845
B840
B8077
B8074
B839
B828
B8000

Glen Lochy
Arrivain
Clifton
Tyndrum
131
132
Cononish
Strath Fillan
BEN LUI
BEINN ODHAR
BEINN UDLAIDH
BEN CHALLUM
BEINN CHEATHAICH
Allt Riobain
Auchlyne West Burn
Boreland
MOIRLANICH LONGHOUSE
Finlarig
Killin
Achmore
FALLS OF DOCHART
Dochart
Auchlyne
Ardchyle
GLEN DOCHART
Ledcharrie
Lochdochart House
Loch Iubhair
Glen Ogle
Beich Burn
Inverherive
Loch Dochart
Benmore
Portnellan
Crianlarich
CRIANLARICH
BEINN DUBHCHRAIG
BEN MORE
STOB BINNEIN
Dalveich
Lochearnhead
EDINAMPLE FALLS
Edinample
Ardvorlich
MEALL NAN TIGHEARN
Allt Fionn Ghlinne
WEST HIGHLAND WAY
Glen Falloch
Dubh Eas
LOCH LOMOND
AND THE
TROSSACHS
NATIONAL
PARK
Braes of Balquhidder
Balquhidder
ROB ROY'S GRAVE
Auchtubh
Monachylemore
Craigruie
Falls of Falloch
Fyne
TROISGEACH
Inverarnan
Ben Glas Burn
BEINN A'CHROIN
Loch Voil
Loch Doine
Inverlochlarig
Ballimore
Calair Burn
Strathyre
Strathyre Forest
BEN VORLICH
Allt na Lairige
125
Ardlui
MAOL BREAC
STOB A'CHOIN
NN
BEINN BHREAC
BENVANE
BEINN EACH
Ardchullarie More
Keltie Water
Loch Lubnaig
Loch Sloy
BEN VORLICH
Strath Gartney
Stirling
Glen Finglas Res.
Anie
Pass of Leny
ROB ROY'S CAVE
Stronachlachar
LOCH KATRINE
BEN LEDI
Leny Ho.
FALLS OF LENY
Kilmahog
Bochastle
Callander
Inveruglas
BEINN IME
Inversnaid Hotel
Loch Arklet
Loch Ard Forest
The Trossachs
TROSSACHS PIER COMPLEX
SS SIR WALTER SCOTT
Trossachs Hotel
Brig o'Turk
Coilantogle
Frenich
BEN VENUE
Duncraggan
Lendrick Lodge
Loch Achray
THE TROSSACHS
Succoth
Glen Croe
Forest
Tarbet
Arrochar
Ardgartan
Loch Chon
Craig Rostan
LOCH LOMOND
Loch Venachar
Achray Forest
Loch Drunkie
Menteith Hills
Torrie Forest
Loch Rusky
Stuckgowan
Ardmay
BEN LOMOND
Kinlochard
Altskeith
D. MARSHALL LODGE VISITOR CENTRE
SCOTTISH WOOL CENTRE
TROSSACHS DISCOVERY CENTRE
Port of Menteith
Milton
Aberfoyle
Kirkton
Loch Ard
INCHMAHOME PRIORY
Ruskie
Ptarmigan Lodge
QUEEN ELIZABETH
FOREST PARK
Malling
Lake of Menteith
Goodie Water
Glen Douglas
Duchray Water
Cobleland
Rowardennan
ROWARDENNAN LODGE
BEINN UIRD
FLANDERS MOSS
Flanders Moss
Loch Ard Forest
Dykehead
DOUNE HILL
Inverbeg
INVERBEG GALLERY
Gartmore
Forth
Rowardennan Forest
BEINN BHREAC
Glenmallan
Kelty Water
Flanders Moss
Dalmary
BEINN EICH
NS
Arnprior
Cauldhame
Edentaggart
Inchlonaig
NAT. PARK CENTRE
Milarrochy
Buchlyvie
Portincaple
Whistlefield
145
Glen Luss
Luss
THISTLE BAGPIPE WORKS
Moor Park
BEINN CHAORACH
NAT. PARK CENTRE
Garelochhead
Inchfad
Balmaha
Milton of Buchanan
Garadhban Forest
Buchlyvie Muir
Kippen
Muir
Aldochlay
BEINN RUISG
Inchcailloch
STRONE HOUSE GARDENS
Glen Fruin
LOMOND
LOCH LOMOND
Drymen
Balfron Station
Balfron
Harvieston
Fintry Hills
CULCREUCH CASTLE
Inchmurrin
Gartness
Boquhan
Endrick Water
Ballikinrain
Duchlage
Blairglas
Shandon
GARE LOCH
LOCH LOMOND & THE TROSSACHS
Gartocharn
Croftamie
Spittal
Killearn
Fintry
GLENARN GARDEN
THE HILL HOUSE
Arden
Rhu
Bannachra Muir
BALLOCH CASTLE
Craighat
EARL'S SEAT
Rosneath
THE ROWAN GALLERY
Helensburgh
Dumgoyne
GLENGOYNE DISTILLERY
CAMPSIE FELLS
Blairquhosh
Kilcreggan
Rosneath Pt.
Craigendoran
NAT PK GATEWAY CENTRE
Balloch
Jamestown
LOCH LOMOND
Auchencarroch
Stockiemuir
Strathblane Hills
Blane Water
Portkil
ALEXANDRIA
West
118
Dumbarton Muir
Resrs.
Netherton
Clachan of Campsie
119
Gourock
Greenock
Vest
Bonhill
Renton
Dunbartonshire
Blanefield
Strathblane
East
Lennoxtown
Balgrochan
Midton
MCLEAN MUS. & ART GALL.
Greenock
HM CUSTOMS & EXCISE MUSEUM & EXHIBITION
Cardross
DUNCOLM
KILPATRICK HILLS
MUGDOCK
Mugdock
Dunbartonshire
Castlehill
Townend
DUMBARTON
0 1 2 3 4 5 6 miles
0 1 2 3 4 5 6 7 8 9 10 km
A85
A82
A84
A83
A821
A81
A811
A809
A875
A873
A814
A817
A818
A813
A891
B8074
B829
B835
B837
B818
B834
B821
B822
B8034

Perth and Kinross
Clackmannanshire
Falkirk
NN
NS
STRATHALLAN
STRATHEARN
GLEN ALMOND
Little Glenshee
MEALL NAN CAORAICH
Logiealmond Lodge
Logiealmond
Harrietfield
Chapelhill
Almond
CREAG UCHDAG
BEN CHONZIE
Newton
Glen
MEALL TARSUINN
Shaggie Burn
Loch Lednock Reservoir
Loch Turret Reservoir
Invergeldie
Glen Lednock
Funtullich
Glen Turret
Buchanty
Methven
Almondbank
Keillour
Monzie
Monzie Castle
Fowlis Wester
STANDING STONES
Braegrum
Tibbermore
St Fillans
LOCH EARN
Ardtrostan
Dunira
RIVER EARN
MELVILLE MONUMENT
Lawers
COMRIE CROFT
Ochtertyre
FALLS OF TURRET
Hosh
Gilmerton
Keillour Forest
Pow Water
Comrie
Quoig
GLENTURRET DISTILLERY
Crieff
Tullybannocher
EARTHQUAKE HOUSE
Ross
Dalginross
Lochlane
Madderty
Findo Gask
Clathy
St David's
CRIEFF VISITORS' CENTRE
AUCHINGARRICH WILDLIFE & HIGHLAND CATTLE CENTRE
The Balloch
Forest of Glenartney
Allt Strath a' Ghlinne
Water of Ruchill
Culloch
Torlum Wood
DRUMMOND CASTLE GARDENS
OLD CHURCH & TOWER
Muthill
INNERPEFFRAY LIBRARY
Kirkton
Dupplin Castle
Kinkell Bridge
Dalchruin
Glen Artney
Tigh-na-Blair
Auchnashelloch
Ochtermuthill
Machany Water
Aberuthven
BEN CLACH
Langside
Tullibardine
TULLIBARDINE CHAPEL
Auchterarder
Dunning
Muirton
Milton
HERITAGE CENTRE
Glenlichorn
Knaik
Garrick
UAMH BHEAG
BLACKHALL ROMAN CAMPS
Gleneagles Hotel
GLENEAGLES
ARDOCH ROMAN CAMP
Braco
Blackford
Gleneagles House
Common of Dunning
Water of May
Middle Rig
Bullie Burn
Muckle Burn
Greenloaning
TULLIBARDINE DISTILLERY
Braes of Ogilvie
Glen Eagles
STEEL'S KNOWE
INNERDOUNY HILL
Braes of Doune
Ardoch Burn
Allan Water
Glendevon Resvrs.
Drumvaich
Kinbuck
Balhaldie
Glen Devon
Glendevon
South Queich
Burn of Cambus
Ashfield
Burnfoot
Castle Hill Reservoir
Sheriff Muir
Carnbo
Doune
Deanston
CATHEDRAL
Dunblane
Pisgah
LEIGHTON LIBRARY
BLAIRDENON HILL
BEN CLEUCH
Pool o' Muckhart
Yetts o' Muckhart
Thornhill
Blair Drummond
Easter Row
KING'S SEAT HILL
CASTLE CAMPBELL
DOLLAR GLEN
Crook of Devon
Drum
Rumbling Bridge
RUMBLING BRIDGE GORGE
BLAIR DRUMMOND SAFARI PARK
Sunnylaw
Bridge of Allan
MILL TRAIL VISITOR CENTRE
Blairdrummond Moss
Blairlogie
Menstrie
Tillicoultry
Dollar
Powmill
Alva
STERLING MILLS
Devonside
Blairingone
Drip Moss
Causewayhead
NATIONAL WALLACE MONUMENT
Tullibody
Fishcross
Hill End
Kippen
STIRLING CASTLE
Coalsnaughton
GARTMORN DAM
Glentirranmuir
Gargunnock
OLD TOWN JAIL
Raploch
Cambuskenneth
ABBEY
Branshill
Sauchie
Forest Mill
Balgonar
KNOCK HILL
Stirling
Cambus
Keilarsbrae
SMITH ART GALLERY & MUSEUM
CARLEATHERAN
Touch Hills
Cambusbarron
Torbrex
ALLOA
ALLOA TOWER
Saline
Gargunnock Hills
St Ninians
Fallin
Throsk
Clackmannan
South Alloa
Kennet
Kilbagie
Cowstrandburn
Bannockburn
BANNOCKBURN HERITAGE CENTRE
Earlsburn Reservoirs
Cowie
Dunmore
THE PINEAPPLE
Blairhall
Comrie
Oakley
Carnock
Devilla Forest
Craigend
STIRLING SERVICES
Airth
Kincardine
CULROSS ABBEY
High Valleyfield
Loch Walton
Loch Coulter
Plean
PLEAN
Easter Cringate
Letham
Kincardine Bridge
CULROSS PALACE
Culross
Low Torry
Torryburn
Cairneyhill
Torwood
Torry Bay
CHARLESTOWN WORKSHOPS
Charlestown
Muirmill
Carron
Carron Bridge
Dunipace
DENNY
Antonshill
Stenhousemuir
Skinflats
MUSEUM
Carron Valley Forest
Carron Valley Res.
Fankerton
Stoneywood
Larbert
Carron
Carronshore
Bainsford
GRANGEMOUTH
BO'NESS AND KINNEIL RAILWAY
Grangepans
Carriden
Muirhouses
TOMTAIN
Head of Muir
FALKIRK WHEEL
THE HELIX
Kilsyth Hills
Bonnybridge
Bo'ness
COLZIUM HOUSE
Dennyloanhead
FALKIRK
Laurieston
Grougfoot
Kilsyth
Banknock
Longcroft
High Bonnybridge
ROUGH CASTLE
Redding
CALLENDAR HOUSE
Polmont
Brightons
Linlithgow
Milton of Campsie
Queenzieburn
ANTONINE WALL
Greenhill
Glen Village
Reddingmuirhead
Whitecross
Dullatur
Cumbernauld
Castlecary
OLD INNS SERVICES
Shieldhill
Maddiston
Linlithgow Bridge
PALACE
Kilpstoun
Croy
Cumbernauld Village
Abronhill
Jawcraig
California
Loan
Bridgend

Little Glenshee
Tullybelton
Stanley
West Tofts
Wolfhill
Saucher
KING'S SEAT 377
Littleton
Fowlis
CAMPERDOWN AND TEMPLETON WOODS
Liff
Logiealmond Lodge
Logiealmond
Guildtown
Kinrossie
Collace
Kirkton of Collace
Abernyte
Knapp
Denhead of Gray
Benvie
Chapelhill
Harrietfield
Downhill
Newmiln
St Martins
Bandirran
Rossie Priory
Invergowrie
Longforgan
Kingoodie
Moneydie
Luncarty
Balbeggie
Ballindean
Castle Huntly
Inchture
Redgorton
PERTH
Kinnaird
BRAES OF THE CARSE
GOWRIE
CARSE OF GOWRIE
Pitcairngreen
SCONE PALACE
P&R
Rait
Almond
Tay
Methven
Almondbank
Huntingtower
PERTH MART VISITOR CENTRE
Scone
288 POLE HILL
Kilspindie
Grange
FIRTH OF TAY
Keillour
Lochty
Tulloch
Muirton
MUSEUM & ART GALLERY
MEGGINCH CASTLE GARDENS
Braegrum
Tibbermore
HUNTINGTOWER CASTLE
Letham
Gannochy
FERGUSSON GALLERY
Myreside
BALMERINO ABBEY
Pow Water
Keillour Forest
BROXDEN SERVICES
Cherrybank
Perth
BRANKLYN GARDEN
Kinfauns Forest
Glendoick
Kinfauns
Errol
Hazelton Walls
Craigie
Glencarse
Carthagena Bank
Creich
Friarton
BELL'S CHERRYBANK GARDENS
Findo Gask
Milltown of Aberdalgie
Tarsappie
ELCHO
St Madoes
Chapelhill
Brunton
Clathy
Aberdalgie
Elcho
Inchyra
St David's
Craigend
Rhynd
Mugdrum I.
LAING MUSEUM
Dupplin Castle
Newburgh
Glenduckie
Luthrie
Kirkton
Bridge of Earn
Easter Rhynd
Forteviot
Forgandenny
Dunbog
Moonzie
Earn
Kintillo
Lindores
Lindores Loch
Lindifferon
Aberuthven
Ardargie House Hotel
Dron
Aberargie
Abernethy
ROUND TOWER
Grange of Lindores
MOUNT HILL 221
DOUGLAS BADER GARDENS FOR THE DISABLED
Perth and Kinross
NO
Glenfoot
Pitmedden Forest
Fernie
Letham
Monimail
Dunning
Collessie
Bow of Fife
Milton
Auchterarder
AUCHTERARDER HERITAGE
Rossie Ochill
Pathstruie
Forest
Auchtermuchty
Kinloch
Giffordtown
SCOTTISH DEER CENTRE
Path of Condie
Glenfarg Res.
Newton of Balcanquhal
Springfield
Arngask
Glenfarg
Strathmiglo
Dunshalt
Howe of Fife
Ladybank
Eden
Pitlessie
Gleneagles House
Common of Dunning
Duncrievie
Gateside
Nether Urquhart
FALKLAND PALACE
Kingskettle
Middle Rigg
Newton of Falkland
Balmalcolm
485 STEEL'S KNOWE
Burnside
FIFE
Falkland
Kettlebridge
Kettlehill
497 INNERDOUNY HILL
WEST LOMOND 522
Middleton
LOMOND HILLS
FALKLAND
Freuchie
Rameldry Mill Bank
Craigow
Upper Tillyrie
Glasslie
REGIONAL PARK
Muirhead
Glendevon
BURLEIGH CASTLE
Res.
Langdyke
Glen Devon
Dalqueich
Milnathort
Wester Balgedie
Burnfoot
Castle Hill Reservoir
611
South Queich
Carnbo
KINROSS SERVICES
MICHAEL BRUCE'S COTTAGE
Pitkevy
Star
LOCH
Kinnesswood
Cadham
Kinross
LOCHLEVEN CASTLE
LOCH LEVEN
Markinch
BALGONIE CASTLE
Balcurvie
Pool o' Muckhart
Yetts o' Muckhart
KINROSS HOUSE
LEVEN
Scotlandwell
Auchmuirbridge
Leslie
Windygates
Drum
Coldrain
St Serf's Island
GLENROTHES
Milton of Balgonie
Gairney Bank
Crook of Devon
CASTLE CAMPBELL
DOLLAR GLEN
VANE FARM NATURE CENTRE
Kinglassie
Coaltown of Balgonie
Rumbling Bridge
RUMBLING BRIDGE GORGE
Stenton
Ballingry
Thornton
East Wemyss
Dollar
Powmill
Cleish
356 BENARTY HILL
DOGTON STONE
Lochore
FIFE
Blairingone
LOCHORE MEADOWS
Cleish Hills
Crosshill
Glencraig
Auchterderran
Cluny
Ore
Coaltown of Wemyss
Hill End
Loch Glow
Loch Ore
Forest Mill
Kelty
REG. PARK
Cardenden
Gallatown
West Wemyss
KNOCKHILL
364 KNOCK HILL
Lochgelly
Chapel
Balgonar
Templehall
Dysart
RAVENSCRAIG CASTLE
Lassodie
Lumphinnans
Loch Gelly
Hayfield
Pathhead
Saline
Loch Fitty
KIRKCALDY ART GALLERY AND MUSEUM
Cowdenbeath
Kirkcaldy
Bowershall
Cowstrandburn
Kingseat
Hill of Beath
Auchtertool
Linktown
TOWNHILL
Townhill
F
Comrie
Blairhall
Wellwood
Gowkhall
ABBOT HOUSE
Crossgates
Halbeath
FIFE COASTAL PATH
Devilla Forest
Oakley
Carnock
Milesmark
Donibristle
Fordell
Kincardine
CULROSS ABBEY
DUNFERMLINE
ABBEY
Balmule
High Valleyfield
ANDREW CARNEGIE BIRTHPLACE MUS
Kinghorn
CULROSS PALACE
Low Torry
Cairneyhill
Crossford
Pettycur
Burntisland
ALEXANDER III MONUMENT
Culross
Torryburn
Torry Bay
ABERDOUR CASTLE
Aberdour
CHARLESTOWN WORKSHOPS
Charlestown
Limekilns
ST BRIDGET'S CHURCH
Dalgety Bay
Hillend
NT
Inchkeith
FIRTH OF FORTH
Rosyth
Inverkeithing
ST COLM'S ABBEY
Inchcolm
GRANGEMOUTH
BO'NESS AND KINNEIL RAILWAY
Grangepans
Carriden
Inverkeithing Bay
FORTH BRIDGES MUSEUM
St. Margaret's Hope
DEEP SEA WORLD
Bo'ness
Muirhouses
BLACKNESS CASTLE
Forth Road Bridge
North Queensferry
Inchmickery
Blackness
HOPETOUN HOUSE
Abercorn
Grougfoot
Queensferry
Cramond I.
BINNS
MAID OF THE FORTH CRUISES
Drum Sands
DALMENY HOUSE
Black Rocks
HMY BRITANNIA
Polmont
Dalmeny
LAURISTON CASTLE
Granton
Newhaven
Leith
Cramond
Davidson's Mains
ROYAL BOTANIC GARDEN
EDINBURGH
Bridgend
Philpstoun
Loan
0 1 2 3 4 5 6 miles
0 1 2 3 4 5 6 7 8 9 10 km
127
133
134
120
121

Dundee
Downfield
Fintry
Douglas & Angus
Baldovie
Mains of Ardestie
Carnoustie
Barry Links
Monifieth
Lochee
Craigie
West Ferry
Broughty Ferry
Barnhill
Stannergate
FRIGATE UNICORN
BROUGHTY CASTLE MUSEUM
Buddon Ness
Tay Bridge
DISCOVERY POINT
Tayport
UNIVERSITY BOTANIC GARDENS
Newport-on-Tay
A92
Scotscraig
TENTSMUIR
Tentsmuir Forest
Woodhaven
Tay Rail Bridge
Wormit
Kirkton
Bottomcraig
Balmerino
Gauldry
Pickletillem
Rhynd
Carrick
Kilmany
Lucklawhill
Leuchars
LEUCHARS NORMAN CHURCH
Balmullo
Rathillet
Logie
Eden Mouth
Guardbridge
EDEN ESTUARY CENTRE
ST ANDREWS BAY
Dairsie or Osnaburgh
Kincaple
ST ANDREWS AQUARIUM
BRITISH GOLF MUS
St Andrews
CATH & ST RULE'S TOWER
Kilmaron Castle
Strathkinness
Newpark
Cupar
Kemback
Brownhills
Buddo Ness
Blebocraigs
Balone
ST ANDREWS BOTANIC GARDEN
Boarhills
Babbet Ness
Cupar Muir
CRAIGTOUN
Denhead
Prior Muir
HILL OF TARVIT MANSIONHOUSE
Pitscottie
Bridgend
Ceres
Baldinnie
Cameron Res.
Stravithie
Kingsbarns
Cambo Ness
CAMBO GARDENS
Carr Brigs
Tullybothy Craigs
SCOTSTARVIT TOWER
Craigrothie
FIFE FOLK MUSEUM
Peat Inn
Dunino
Balcomie
Craighead
Fife Ness
Radernie
Kingsmuir
Lochty
CRAIL TOLBOOTH
Woodside
Lathones
SCOTLAND'S SECRET BUNKER
Crail
New Gilston
CRAIL MUSEUM AND HERITAGE CENTRE
Montrave
Largoward
Pitcorthie
Carnbee
West Ness
Pitkierie
Wester Newburn
KELLIE CASTLE AND GARDEN
FIFE COASTAL PATH
Kilrenny
NO
Arncroach
Kirkton of Largo
Anstruther Easter
SCOTTISH FISHERIES MUSEUM
Bonnybank
Lundin Links
Drumeldrie
Colinsburgh
Kennoway
Abercrombie
Pittenweem
Anstruther Wester
ROBINSON CRUSOE STATUE
Scoonie
Lower Largo
Balchrystie
Kilconquhar
ST FILLAN'S CAVE
ST MONAN'S WINDMILL
SILVERBURN ESTATE
Leven
Ardross
St Monans
ST MONAN'S CHURCH
LETHAM GLEN
Largo Bay
Ruddons Pt.
Innerleven
Elie
Methil
Earlsferry
Sauchar Pt.
ISLE OF MAY
Isle of May
MUSEUM
Chapel Ness
Buckhaven
FIFE COASTAL PATH
F O R T H
Fidra
Craigleith
Bass Rock
SCOTTISH SEABIRD CENTRE
Eyebroughy
North Berwick
MUSEUM
DIRLETON CASTLE & GARDENS
TANTALLON CASTLE
NT
MUIRFIELD
Dirleton
Auldhame
Gullane Bay
Gullane
Scoughall
West Fenton
Kingston
Whitekirk
St. Baldred's Cradle
Fenton Barns
Aberlady Bay
Tyne Mouth
JOHN MUIR BIRTHPLACE
Aberlady
MYRETON MOTOR MUSEUM
Drem
JOHN MUIR
Dunbar
Craigielaw
THE CHESTERS FORT
East Fortune
Tyninghame
Belhaven
West Barns
MUSEUM OF FLIGHT
Preston
Gosford Bay
GOSFORD HOUSE
Ballencrieff
Athelstaneford
East Linton
Broxburn
Barns Ness
Spittal
Peffer Burn
Cockenzie and Port Seton
SETON COLLEGIATE CHURCH
HOPETOUN MON
PRESTON MILL & PHANTASSIE DOOCOT
Biel Water
Spott
East Barns
Longniddry
JANE WELSH CARLYLE MUSEUM
HAILES CASTLE
Traprain
Pitcox
Meikle Pinkerton
Skateraw

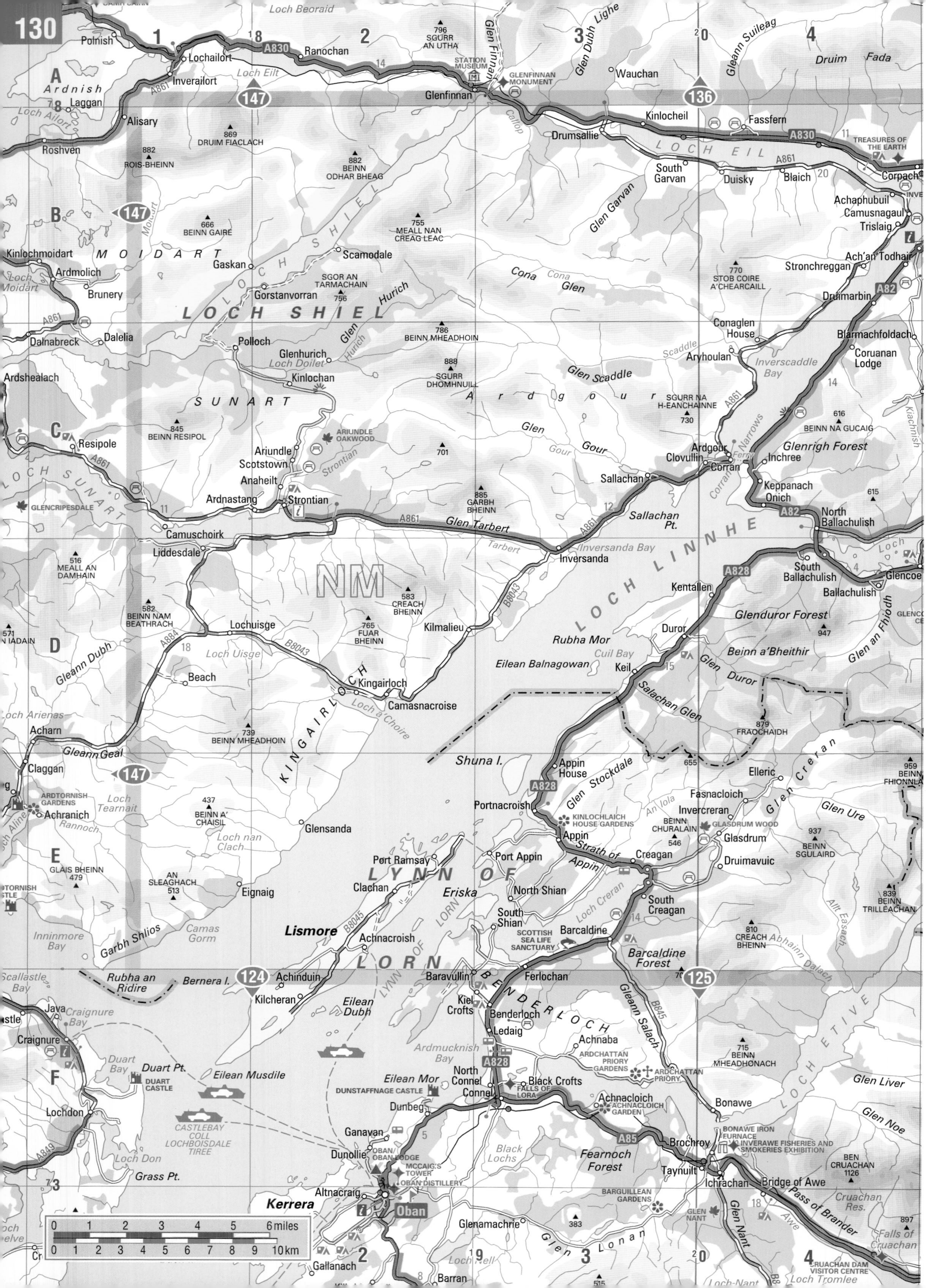
Loch Beoraid
Polnish
Lochailort
Inverailort
Loch Eilt
A830
Ranochan
796 SGURR AN UTHA
STATION MUSEUM
Glen Finnan
GLENFINNAN MONUMENT
Glenfinnan
Glen Dubh Lighe
Wauchan
Gleann Suileag
Druim Fada
147
136
Ardnish
Laggan
Loch Ailort
Alisary
Roshven
869 DRUIM FIACLACH
882 ROIS-BHEINN
882 BEINN ODHAR BHEAG
Callop
Drumsallie
Kinlocheil
Fassfern
LOCH EIL
A830
A861
TREASURES OF THE EARTH
South Garvan
Duisky
Blaich
Corpach
Achaphubuil
Camusnagaul
Trislaig
Moidart
666 BEINN GAIRE
755 MEALL NAN CREAG LEAC
Glen Garvan
Kinlochmoidart
MOIDART
LOCH SHIEL
Gaskan
Scamodale
Loch Moidart
Ardmolich
Brunery
SGOR AN TARMACHAIN 756
Gorstanvorran
Glen Hurich
Cona Glen
770 STOB COIRE A'CHEARCAILL
Stronchreggan
Ach'an Todhair
Druimarbin
A82
A861
Dalnabreck
Dalelia
Polloch
Glenhurich
Loch Doilet
786 BEINN MHEADHOIN
888 SGURR DHOMHNUILL
Conaglen House
Scaddle
Aryhoulan
Glen Scaddle
Inverscaddle Bay
Blarmachfoldach
Coruanan Lodge
Ardshealach
Kinlochan
SUNART
Ardgour
SGURR NA H-EANCHAINNE 730
616 BEINN NA GUCAIG
Kiachnish
Resipole
845 BEINN RESIPOL
ARIUNDLE OAKWOOD
Ariundle
Scotstown
Strontian
701
Glen Gour
Corran Narrows
Ardgour
Clovullin
Corran
Ferry
Glenrigh Forest
Inchree
LOCH SUNART
GLENCRIPESDALE
Anaheilt
Ardnastang
Strontian
885 GARBH BHEINN
Sallachan
Keppanach
Onich
615
Camuschoirk
Glen Tarbert
A861
Tarbert
Sallachan Pt.
A82
North Ballachulish
Liddesdale
Inversanda Bay
Inversanda
LOCH LINNHE
516 MEALL AN DAMHAIN
NM
583 CREACH BHEINN
B8043
A828
Kentallen
South Ballachulish
Loch Leven
Glencoe
Ballachulish
582 BEINN NAM BEATHRACH
Lochuisge
765 FUAR BHEINN
Kilmalieu
Glenduror Forest
Duror
947
Glen an Fhiodh
571 IADAIN
Gleann Dubh
A884
Loch Uisge
B8043
Rubha Mor
Cuil Bay
Beinn a'Bheithir
Beach
Kingairloch
Eilean Balnagowan
Keil
Glen Duror
Camasnacroise
Salachan Glen
Loch Arienas
Acharn
739 BEINN MHEADHOIN
Loch a'Choire
KINGAIRLOCH
879 FRAOCHAIDH
Gleann Geal
Claggan
Shuna I.
Appin House
655
Glen Stockdale
Elleric
Glen Creran
959 BEINN FHIONNLA
147
A828
Fasnacloich
ARDTORNISH GARDENS
Achranich
Loch Tearnait
Rannoch
437 BEINN A' CHAISIL
Portnacroish
KINLOCHLAICH HOUSE GARDENS
An Iola
Invercreran
BEINN CHURALAIN 546
GLASDRUM WOOD
Glasdrum
Glen Ure
937 BEINN SGULAIRD
Glensanda
Loch nan Clach
Appin
Strath of Appin
Port Ramsay
Port Appin
Creagan
Druimavuic
GLAIS BHEINN 479
AN SLEAGHACH 513
Eignaig
LYNN OF LORN
Clachan
Eriska
North Shian
South Creagan
839 BEINN TRILLEACHAN
Allt Easach
Loch Creran
South Shian
Barcaldine
Lismore
B8045
Achnacroish
SCOTTISH SEA LIFE SANCTUARY
Barcaldine Forest
810 CREACH BHEINN
Abhainn Dalach
Inninmore Bay
Garbh Shlios
Camas Gorm
LORN
Scallastle Bay
Rubha an Ridire
Bernera I.
124
Achinduin
Baravullin
Ferlochan
125
Kilcheran
Eilean Dubh
Kiel Crofts
BENDERLOCH
Benderloch
Gleann Salach
B845
LOCH ETIVE
Java
Craignure Bay
Craignure
Ledaig
Achnaba
715 BEINN MHEADHONACH
Duart Bay
Duart Pt.
DUART CASTLE
Eilean Musdile
Ardmucknish Bay
A828
North Connel
ARDCHATTAN PRIORY GARDENS
ARDCHATTAN PRIORY
Eilean Mor
DUNSTAFFNAGE CASTLE
Connel
Black Crofts
FALLS OF LORA
Glen Liver
Lochdon
Dunbeg
Achnacloich
ACHNACLOICH GARDEN
Bonawe
Glen Noe
CASTLEBAY COLL LOCHBOISDALE TIREE
Ganavan
BONAWE IRON FURNACE
INVERAWE FISHERIES AND SMOKERIES EXHIBITION
A849
Loch Don
Dunollie
OBAN/OBAN LODGE
Black Lochs
Fearnoch Forest
A85
Brochroy
BEN CRUACHAN 1126
MCCAIG'S TOWER
OBAN DISTILLERY
Taynuilt
Grass Pt.
Ichrachan
Bridge of Awe
Pass of Brander
Altnacraig
Kerrera
Oban
BARGUILLEAN GARDENS
GLEN NANT
Glen Nant
Cruachan Res.
Awe
897
Falls of Cruachan
0 1 2 3 4 5 6 miles
0 1 2 3 4 5 6 7 8 9 10 km
Glenamachrie
383
Glen Lonan
Loch Nell
Gallanach
Barran
CRUACHAN DAM VISITOR CENTRE
Loch Tromlee
Loch-Nant

Gairlochy
Stronaba
Moy Forest
Glen Loy
Kilmonivaig
COMMANDO MEMORIAL
Bohuntine
Bohenie
BEINN A' CHAORUINN
Moy
Moy Lodge
Brackletter
Spean Bridge
Inverroy
Roybridge
Achluachrach
Murlaggan
Roughburn
Glen Loy Forest
Strone
Highbridge
Muirshearlich
Killiechonate
A86
MONESSIE FALLS
Braes o'Lochaber
GLEN SPEAN
GEAL CHARN
TOR CASTLE
A82
Leanachan Forest
BEINN CHLIANAIG
Fersit
Allt Loraich
BEINN A'CHLACHAIR
Allt Cam
Banavie
NEPTUNE'S STAIRCASE LOCKS
Torlundy
NEVIS RANGE SKI CENTRE
The Cour
Caol
Lochyside
BEN NEVIS DISTILLERY VISITOR CENTRE
Inverlochy
Claggan
Allt Laire
Loch Ghuilbinn
Fort William
Achintee
WEST HIGHLAND MUSEUM
STOB CHOIRE CLAURIGH
Lairig Leacach
STOB COIRE EASAIN
CHNO DEARG
AONACH BEAG
GLEN NEVIS VISITOR CENTRE
GLEN NEVIS
Glen Nevis House
BEN NEVIS
AONACH BEAG
LOCH TREIG
Ossian
Uisge Labhair
BEN ALDER
Water of Nevis
Creaguaineach Lodge
BEINN NA LAP
Corrour Shooting Lodge
Prince Charlie's Cave
Achriabhach
Amhainn Rath
LOCH OSSIAN
Loch Ossian
Corrour Forest
SGOR GAIBHRE
Blar a'Chaorainn
SGURR A' MHAIM
BINNEIN MOR
Loch Eilde Beag
Allt na Cam
WEST HIGHLAND WAY
MAMORE FOREST
Loch Eilde Mor
LEUM UILLEIM
Rannoch Forest
Ciaran Water
MAM NA GUALAINN
Kinlochmore
Kinlochleven
B863
ALUMINIUM STORY VISITOR CENTRE
Leven
BLACKWATER RESERVOIR
Black Water
Ericht
GLENCOE AND NORTH LORN FOLK MUSEUM
AONACH
NN
Rannoch Station
B846
GLENCOE
GLENCOE VISITOR CENTRE
Glen Coe
Altnafeadh
BEINN A' CHRULAISTE
Black Corries Lodge
STOB NA CRUAICHE
Loch Eigheach
Gaur
Bridge of Gaur
BEN NEVIS AND GLEN COE
BIDEAN NAM BIAN
Coupall
Kingshouse Hotel
Loch Gaineamhach
Loch Laidon
Royal Forest
GLENCOE SKI CENTRE
Etive
RANNOCH MOOR
Allt Camghouran
SGOR NA H-ULAIDH
Dalness
Glen Etive
Alltchaorunn
Loch Bà
MEALL BUIDHE
STOB DUBH
Allt Coire a'Chaolain
CLACH LEATHAD
Bà
Loch na h-Achlaise
Water of Tulla
Invercharnan
Glenceitlein
BLACK MOUNT
Loch an Daimh
Eas Daimh
Gualachulain
Allt Dochard
STOB GHABHAR
WEST HIGHLAND WAY
Loch Tulla
Achallader
BEINN A' CHREACHAIN
MEALL BUIDHE
STUCHD AN LOCHAIN
STOB COIR'AN ALBANNAICH
Black Mount
Forest Lodge
Pubil
Cashlie
BEN STARAV
Loch Dochard
Inveroran Hotel
Loch Lyon
Stronuich Reservoir
Allt Hallater
BEINN NAN AIGHENAN
BIENN AN DOTHAIDH
BEINN MHANACH
Bridge of Orchy
BEINN HEASGARNICH
BEINN DORAIN
Allt Chonoghlais
Kenknock
Glen Lochay
Orchy
Glen Kinglass
CREAG MHOR
Breadalbane
BEINN MHIC-MHONAIDH
GLEN ORCHY
Arichastlich
BEINN ODHAR
Strae
BEINN EUNAICH
BEINN UDLAIDH
Glen Strae
B8074
BEINN CHEATHAICH
BEN CHALLUM
Glen Lochy
A85
Allt Mhoille
Lochy
Clifton
Tyndrum
Allt Ribbain
Auchlyne West Burn
Arrivain
B8077
Cononish
Strath Fillan
GLEN DOCHART
KILCHURN CASTLE
Lochawe
Stronmilchan
Strath of Orchy
Achnafalnich
Inverlochy
Lochdochart House
Dalmally
BEN LUI
Loch Dochart
Loch Iubhair
MCINTYRE MONUMENT
Inverherive
Crianlarich
Benmore
Innis Chonain

Moy
Moy Lodge
Lochan na h-Earba
674 BEINN EILDE
911
Gaick Forest
Loch Bhrodainn
Allt Gharbh Ghaig
A
A9
Ardverikie Forest
1049 GEAL CHARN
Pattack
Loch Ericht Forest
941 CARN NA CAIM
137
138
Loch an Duin
774 CREAGAN MOR
Allt Loraich
Loch Pattack
Ben Alder Lodge
Cama Choire
Sronphadruig Lodge
1087 BEINN A'CHLACHAIR
Allt Cam
917
936 A'BHUIDHEANACH BHEAG
Dail-na-Mine Forest
816 SRON A'CHLEIRICH
Allt a' Chaoil-reidhe
Ben Alder Forest
Allt Glas Choire
B
Loch Ghuilbinn
934 BEINN UDLAMAIN
803 THE SOW OF ATHOLL
FOREST
1114 AONACH BEAG
LOCH ERICHT
Dalnacardoch Forest
Edendon Water
Loch a' Bhealaich Bheithe
Dalnaspidal Lodge
ATHOLL
Ossian
Allt a' Chireachain
1148 BEN ALDER
Corrievarkie Lodge
Allt na Glaise
Dalnaspidal Forest
Loch Garry
775 MEALL NA LEITREACH
17
Dalnacardoch Lodge
Uisge Labhair
GLEN GARRY
Corrour Shooting Lodge
Loch Ossian
Prince Charlie's Cave
855
Garry
Loch Con
Corrour Forest
Talla Bheith Forest
GRAMPIAN
952 SGOR GAIBHRE
131
Loch Errochty
C
Rannoch Forest
Allt Ghlas
841 BEINN MHOLACH
612
Trinafour
Dalchalloch
B847
10 Errochty Water
GLEN ERROCHTY
515 SRON BHEAG
Aulich Burn
891 BEINN A'CHUALLAICH
Tummel Forest
477
Water
Erichd
Killichonan Burn
Craiganor Lodge
Kinloch Rannoch
Tummel Bridge
B846
B8019
G
Bridge of Ericht
Killichonan
19
Dunalastair
Tummel
Dunalastair Water
Rannoch Station
LOCH RANNOCH
Carie
Foss
Inverhadden
Loch Eigheach
Gaur
Bridge of Gaur
Finnart
Camghouran
Black Wood of Rannoch
Loch Kinardochy
Innerhadden Burn
TAY FOREST
D
Rannoch
Dall Burn
Allt na Bogair
1083 SCHIEHALLION
Allt Camghouran
Forest
Allt Mor
LOCH RANNOCH AND GLEN LYON
GLENGOULANDIE DEER PARK
13
Keltney Burn
1042 CARN MAIRG
745 MEALL A'MHUIC
1029 CARN GORM
931 MEALL BUIDHE
Appin of
Keltneyburn
Invervar
Camusvrachan
ST FILLAN'S CHURCH & FORTINGALL YEW
Loch an Daimh
GLEN LYON GALLERY
Innerwick
Lyon
Fortingall
Taymouth Castle
Eas Daimh
Bridge of Balgie
Allt Conait
Gallin
Kenmore
A827
E
907 MEALL BUIDHE
960 STUCHD AN LOCHAIN
Allt Bail a' Mhuilinn
Allt Gleann Da-Eig
Fearnan
SCOTTISH CRANNOG
Remony
131
780
1118
Acharn
Falls of Acharn
Pubil
Cashlie
Glen Lyon
Lawers Burn
LOCH TAY
Loch Lyon
Stronuich Reservoir
1214 BEN LAWERS
BEN LAWERS
25
716 BEINN BHREAC
Quaich
MEALL NAN TARMACHAN
Loch na Lairige
Lawers
BEINN HEASGARNICH
1076
1043
Ardtalnaig
Carie
Gleann a' Chilleine
888
Kenknock
Glen Lochay
Milton Morenish
F
Lochay
Morenish
Ardeonaig
FALLS OF LOCHAY AND FISH LIFT
Finglen Burn
Breadalbane
Boreland
MOIRLANICH LONGHOUSE
Finlarig
Killin
637
937 BEINN CHEATHAICH
Achmore
879 CREAG UCHDAG
Alm
Allt Ribhain
Auchlyne West Burn
Dochart
FALLS OF DOCHART
A821
Loch Lednock Reservoir
Invergeldie Burn
931 BEN CHONZIE
126
Auchlyne
A85
127
Ardchyle
Beich Burn
Glen Ogle
Glen Lednock
Invergeldie
Loch Iubhair
2
3
4
Funtullich
0 1 2 3 4 5 6 miles
0 1 2 3 4 5 6 7 8 9 10 km
Dochart
Benmore
672 SRON MHOR

CARN EALAR
AN SGARSOCH
CARN BHAC
Baddoch
UCHD A'CHLARSAIR
138
139
BEINN IUTHARN MHOR
Loch Vrotachan
GLENSHEE SKI CENTRE
THE CAIRNWELL
CARN AN TUIRC
GLAS MAOL
Devil's Elbow
Caenlochan Forest
Tarf Water
BRAIGH SRON GHORM
BEINN DEARG
Glen Bruar
Bruar Lodge
Loch nan Eun
Loch Loch
GLAS TULAICHEAN
Forest Lodge
BEINN A'GHLO
BEN GULABIN
Glen Diridh
Glenlochsie
MONAMEANACH
CARN LIATH
BEN VUIRICH
Gleann Fearnach
Spittal of Glenshee
BEN EARB
Auchavan
Loch Beanie
DUCHRAY HILL
BLAIR CASTLE
Falls of the Bruar
CLAN DONNACHAIDH MUSEUM
Pitagowan
Calvine
Struan
Old Bridge of Tilt
Lude House
Blair Atholl
BLAIR ATHOLL MILL
Ballentoul
BLAIR ATHOLL DISTILLERY
TULACH HILL
Glen Girnaig
MEALL UAINE
134
Dalnaglar Castle
Meikle Forter
Folda
Aldclune
ATHOLL COUNTRY COLLECTION
Killiecrankie
KILLIECRANKIE VISITOR CENTRE
Loch Bhac
BEN VRACKIE
Dalnavaid
Tarvie
Straloch
Glen Brerachan
Enochdhu
Cray
MOUNT BLAIR
Brewlands Bridge
Bonskeid House
LOCH
Tressait
Queen's View
QUEEN'S VIEW CENTRE
Falls of Tummel
LINN OF TUMMEL
TUMMEL
CREAG DHUBH
STRATHARDLE
Ashintully Castle
Kirkmichael
Blacklunans
CAIRN GIBBS
Moulin
PITLOCHRY
Pitlochry
EDRADOUR DISTILLERY
Milton of Edradour
Loch Faskally
Balmore
SCOTTISH PLANT COLLECTORS GARDEN
BLAIR ATHOLL DISTILLERY VISITOR CENTRE
Loch Broom
MEALL REAMHAR
KNOCK OF BALMYLE
Forest of Alyth
Black Water
NN
NO
Loch Derculich
FARRAGON HILL
FOREST PARK
Milton of Dalcapon
Ballintuim
Strathtay
Ballechin
Tulliemet
CREAG NAM MIAL
Edradynate
CLUNY HOUSE GARDENS
Grandtully
Little Ballinluig
Balnaguard
Logierait
Ballinluig
Blackcraig Forest
Netherton
Forest of Clunie
Loch Ordie
Loch Benachally
Bridge of Cally
CASTLE MENZIES
Weem
ST MARY'S CHURCH
Camserney
Dull
ABERFELDY DISTILLERY & DEWAR'S WORLD OF WHISKY
WADE'S BRIDGE
Aberfeldy
Balmacneil
Kindallachan
Riemore
Cochrage Muir
Tullyfergus
Falls of Moness
BOLFRACKS GARDEN
Bishopric
Kincraigie
Guay
Dowally
DEUCHARY HILL
Lornty Burn
Middleton
Loch Skiach
Riechip
Westfields of Rattray
Lornty
Dalguise
Urlar Burn
Loch Kennard
Craigvinean Forest
Butterstone
Achalader
Blairgowrie
Kinloch
Rattray
RIVER TAY
Forneth
SCOTTISH HORSE REGIMENTAL MUSEUM
Loch of Lowes
Concraigie
Loch of Clunie
Loch of Drumellie
Loch Hoil
Glen Cochill
LOCH OF LOWES NATURE RESERVE
Clunie
Craigie
Muirton of Blair
Rosemount
Dunkeld
Little Dunkeld
Snaigow House
Kirkton of Lethendy
THE HERMITAGE
WATERFALL
Inver
Birnam
Scotston
Ballinlick
Spittalfield
MEALL DEARG
Garrow
Trochry
Delvine
Caputh
Perth
Cablea
Strathbraan
Obney Hills
Meikleour
BEECH HEDGE
Kinclaven
Gellyburn
Murthly
Loch Freuchie
Glen Quaich
Braan
Upper Obney
Muir of Thorn
Ardoch
Woodside
Burrelton
Amulree
Balquharn
Waterloo
Cargill
MEALL NAM FUARAN
Corrymuckloch
Aimtully
Bankfoot
Ordie Burn
Whitefield
and
Little Glenshee
West Tofts
MEALL NAN CAORAICH
Milton Burn
Tullybelton
Stanley
Saucher
Wolfhill
Newton
Logiealmond Lodge
Shochie Burn
Guildtown
Kinrossie
Kirkton
Kinross
Logiealmond
Chapelhill
Downhill
Newmiln
St Martins
GLEN ALMOND
Sma' Glen
Harrietfield
Balbeggie
MEALL TARSUINN
127
Moneydie
128
Redgorton
Loch Turret Reservoir
Shaggie Burn
Buchanty
Almond
PERTH
Pitcairngreen
SCONE PALACE
Glen Turret
Methven
Almondbank
Huntingtower
PERTH MART VISITOR CENTRE
Scone
POLE HILL
Keillour
Lochty
Muirton

Angus
NO
Glen Callater
Loch Callater
Dubh Loch
Glas-allt Shiel
Spittal of Glenmuick
Glen Mark
Water of Mark
Burn of Branny
Water of Tarf
Loch Muick
Glen Lee
Invermark Lodge
Auchronie
Tarfside
Cairncross
Loch Lee
Inchgrundle
Baddoch
834
1012 CAIRN BANNOCH
998 BROAD CAIRN
939 AN SOCACH
1019 CARN AN TUIRC
958 TOLMOUNT
696 HAWEE
Water of Unich
832 LAIR OF ALDARARIE
Clunie Water
Loch Vrotachan
GLENSHEE SKI CENTRE
THE CAIRNWELL
Devil's Elbow
1068 GLAS MAOL
Caenlochan Forest
Glen Doll
Glendoll Lodge
Braedownie
Glendoll Forest
CORRIE FEE
MUCKLE CAIRN 826
Loch Brandy
Glen Effock
Water of Saughs
CRUYS 741
691 WEST KNOCK
905 FINALTY HILL
947 DRIESH
758
Clova
GLEN CLOVA
B955
778 WHITE HILL
Hunthill Lodge
BEN GULABIN 806
Isla
Wheen
808 MONAMEANACH
Spittal of Glenshee
Auchavan
Loch Beanie
Glen Prosen
Glenprosen Lodge
Kilburn
Rottal
756 FINBRACKS
794 MEALL UAINE
Glen Shee
A93
702 DUCHRAY HILL
740 BADENDUN HILL
Balnaboth
PROSEN
Glenprosen Village
512
Clachnabrain
545 AULD DARKNEY
Glenmoy
Dalnaglar Castle
Meikle Forter
Folda
Glenisla Forest
611
South Esk
Auchnacree
Cray
744 MOUNT BLAIR
B951
Brewlands Bridge
Backwater Res.
Glenhead Farm
Easter Lednathie
Glenogil
Glenquiech
Ogil
Fern
Ashintully Castle
Freuchies
Horniehaugh
Dykehead
668 CAT LAW
CAPTAIN SCOTT & DR WILSON CAIRN
Newmill of Inshewan
Noran
Kirkmichael
Blacklunans
Kirkton of Glenisla
Bellaty
497 CREIGH HILL
Balintore
Pearsie
Cortachy
Memus
Tannadice
B950
520 CAIRN GIBBS
Dykends
Balloch
Inverquharity
Murthill
Shielhill
Finavon
KNOCK OF BALMYLE 444
Forest of Alyth
Black Water
409 MILE HILL
Oathlaw
Loch of Lintrathen
PEEL FARM TRAIL
B954
B951
Kirkton of Kingoldrum
Northmuir
B957
Bintuim
Ardle
A924
Bridgend of Lintrathen
BALDUFF HILL 425
LOCH OF KINNORDY NATURE RESERVE
Kinnordy
Kirriemuir
BARRIE'S BIRTHPLACE
Carse Gray
REEKIE LINN WATERFALL
Bridge of Craigisla
Netherton
Tullymurdoch
Westmuir
GATEWAY TO THE GLENS MUS
Mosside
Lunanhead
RESTENNETH PRIORY
Blackcraig Forest
Auchrannie
Kirkton of Airlie
A926
Mains of Ballindarg
A90
Forfar
Bamff
Padanaram
FORFAR LOCH
Bridge of Cally
Shanzie
Craigton
A928
Drumgley
THE MEFFAN GALL & MUS
B9128
Cochrage Muir
Leys of Cossans
ST ORLAND'S STONE
Dean Water
Kingsmuir
Tullyfergus
Ruthven
Ruthven House
EASSIE SCULPTURED STONE
GLAMIS CASTLE
A94
A932
Caldhame
Lownie Moor
Lornty Burn
Middleton
308
Alyth
New Alyth
Glamis
Douglastown
Westfields of Rattray
Lornty
Balhary
Castleton
Thornton
Kirkton
B9127
Charleston
ANGUS FOLK MUSEUM
Achalader
A923
Blairgowrie
Kinloch
Rattray
Leitfie
MEIGLE MUSEUM
Balkeerie
Eassie
Foffarty
Inverarity
Loch of Clunie
Loch of Drumellie
B947
River Ericht
Kirkinch
Gateside
Whigstreet
Clunie
Craigie
Muirton
Ardblair
Rosemount
Kinloch
Meigle
Milton
Arthurstone
Wester Denoon
ARK HILL 340
Kirkton of Lethendy
Lunan Burn
Gallowfauld
Ardler
New-bigging
Newtyle
Nether Handwick
SIDLAW HILLS
Spittalfield
A984
Delvine
Keillor
259
Caputh
Coupar Angus
Coldstream
Tay
Meikleour
BEECH HEDGE
Kettins
Bonnyton
Tealing
Monikie
Murthly
Kinclaven
Markethill
Hallyburton House
B954
Balkemback
Kirkton of Auchterhouse
Newbigging
Ardoch
Woodside
Burrelton
Campmuir
Long Loch
Inveraldie
East March
Wellbank
B9099
Leys
Lundie
Auchterhouse
Leoch
Muir of Pert
Buckierheads
Newbigging
Cargill
Pitcur
Dronley
Bridgefoot
Burnside of Duntrune
Kellas
Drumsturdy
Whitefield
Muirhead
Birkhill
CLATTO
SOUTERRAIN ARDESTIE
West Tofts
Littleton
Fowlis
B961
Fintry
Stanley
Wolfhill
Saucher
KING'S SEAT 377
CAMPERDOWN AND TEMPLETON WOODS
Liff
Downfield
Baldovie
Douglas & Angus
Collace
Guildtown
Kinrossie
Kirkton of Collace
Denhead of Gray
Dundee
VERDANT WORKS
Lochee
MILLS OBSERVATORY
MUS AND ART GALL
MUS OF TRANSPORT
Craigie
A92
West Ferry
Monifieth
St Martins
B953
Abernyte
Knapp
BROUGHTY CASTLE
Stannergate
Broughty Ferry
Barnhill
BROUGHTY CASTLE MUSEUM
FRIGATE UNICORN
Newmiln
Bandirran
BRAES OF THE CARSE
Rossie Priory
Benvie
Invergowrie
Dowhill
A9
Balbeggie
Ballindean
Longforgan
Kingoodie
A85
Dundee
Tay Bridge
Tayport
Luncarty
Castle Huntly
UNIVERSITY BOTANIC GARDENS
DUNDEE
DISCOVERY POINT
Scotscraig
TENTSMUIR
PERTH
Kinnaird
Inchture
Newport-on-Tay
A92
Woodhaven
Tay Rail Bridge
B946
B945
Tentsmuir
PERTH MART VISITOR CENTRE
Scone
288 POLE HILL
Kilspindie
Grange
Wormit
0 1 2 3 4 5 6 miles
0 1 2 3 4 5 6 7 8 9 10 km
A B C D E F
1 2 3 4
133
139
140
128
129

Glen Dye
778 MOUNT BATTOCK
Drumtochty Forest
525 MELUNCART
464
Tannachie
Carmont
Nev Mill
Mains of Dellavaird
BURNS FAMILY MEMORIALS
Drumlithie
Glenfarquhar Lodge
Glenbervie
Fiddes
Mill of Uras
Barras
Thornyhive Bay
Crawton
FOWLSHEUGH NATURE RESERVE
140
141
Cairn o' Mount
Drumtochty Castle
Pitforthie
Roadside of Catterline
Crawton Bay
Catterline
Braidon Bay
Todhead Point
THE RETREAT - GLEN ESK FOLK MUS
Millden Lodge
Strath Finella
Clatterin Bridge
Glensaugh
Auchenblae
Monboddo House
Mondynes
Brownmuir
East Cairnbeg
Fordoun
B967
Parkneuk
Arbuthnott
Roadside of Kinneff
GRASSIC GIBBON CENTRE
ARBUTHNOTT CHURCH
Kinneff
Mains of Balnakettle
FASQUE HOUSE
Thainston
B966
FETTERCAIRN DISTILLERY VISITOR CENTRE
Fettercairn
Howe of the Mearns
Scotston
ARBUTHNOTT HOUSE GARDENS
Mains of Allardice
Little John's Haven
Auchmull
678 HILL OF WIRREN
North Esk
Bent
B9120
Inverbervie
Bervie Bay
Dalbog
Mains of Thornton
Meikle Strath
Inch of Arnhall
Laurencekirk
A90
Tulloch
DAMSIDE GARDEN HERBS & ARBORETUM
Gourdon
Witton
Gannochy
EDZELL CASTLE AND GARDENS
Sauchieburn
Garvock
Garvock Hill
Redford
Benholm
Bridgend
Balfield
Edzell
Luthermuir
Luther Water
MILL OF BENHOLM
Dykelands
440
Tillyarblet
West Water
Dunlappie
B966
North Water Bridge
B974
Johnshaven
BROWN CATERTHUN
WHITE CATERTHUN
North Esk
Kirkton of Menmuir
Tigerton
Inchbare
Newtonmill
Pert
Marykirk
Ecclesgreig
Craigo
Lochside
St Cyrus
Milton Ness
Mains of Balhall
Lochty
Belliehill
Little Brechin
Keithock
Logie Pert
Muirton of Ballochy
Logie
Morphie
ST CYRUS
Pathhead
West Muir
Trinity
A937
Hillside
Brechin
BRECHIN CASTLE CENTRE
HOUSE OF DUN
Dun
Kirkhill
A92
Careston Castle
PICTAVIA
A935
CATHEDRAL & ROUND TOWER
CALEDONIAN RAILWAY
South Esk
Montrose Basin
Montrose
MUSEUM AND ART GALLERY
Aldbar Castle
Bridge of Dun
Netherton
Mains of Melgund
Middle Drums
Kinnaird Castle
Barnhead
Inchbraoch
Scurdie Ness
WILLIAM LAMB MEMORIAL STUDIO
MONTROSE BASIN VISITOR CENTRE
Ferryden
ABERLEMNO SCULPTURED STONES
Aberlemno
Farnell
Bonnyton
A933
A934
Maryton
Kirkton of Craig
Montreathmont Forest
Pitkennedy
Carcary
Dunninald
Long Craig
Fishtown of Usan
B9134
Montreathmont Moor
Rossie Moor
Westerton
Boddin Pt.
252
Turin
B9113
Rescobie
Dubton
Braehead of Lunan
NO
Reswallie
Balgavies
Glasterlaw
Bolshan
Lunan
LUNAN BAY
Burnside
A932
Milldens
Guthrie
Kinnell
Redcastle
Dunnichen
Letham
Pitmuies
HOUSE OF PITMUIES GARDEN
Friockheim
Boysack
Inverkeilor
Lunan Water
Lang Craig
Chapelton
B965
Ethie Mains
Craichie
Idvies
Leysmill
Cauldcots
Red Head
Ethie Castle
Tulloes
B961
Drunkendub
Mosston
Colliston
Letham Grange
Auchmithie
B978
B9128
Greystone
Redford
St Vigeans
Marywell
Meg's Craig
Kirkbuddo
B9127
ST VIGEANS MUSEUM
Hayshead
Hayhillock
Carmyllie
Denhead of Arbilot
The Deil's Heid
Cliffburn
ARBROATH ABBEY
CROMBIE
Arbirlot
Arbroath
SIGNAL TOWER MUSEUM
Res.
Kirkton of Monikie
Balmirmer
Elliot
A92
Craigton
Salmond's Muir
Monikie Burn
CARLUNGIE SOUTERRAIN
Muirdrum
East Haven
BARRY MILL
Panbride
Barry
A930
Carnoustie
Mains of Ardestie
CARNOUSTIE
Barry Links
Buddon Ness
129
5
6
7
8
A
B
C
D
E
F
G

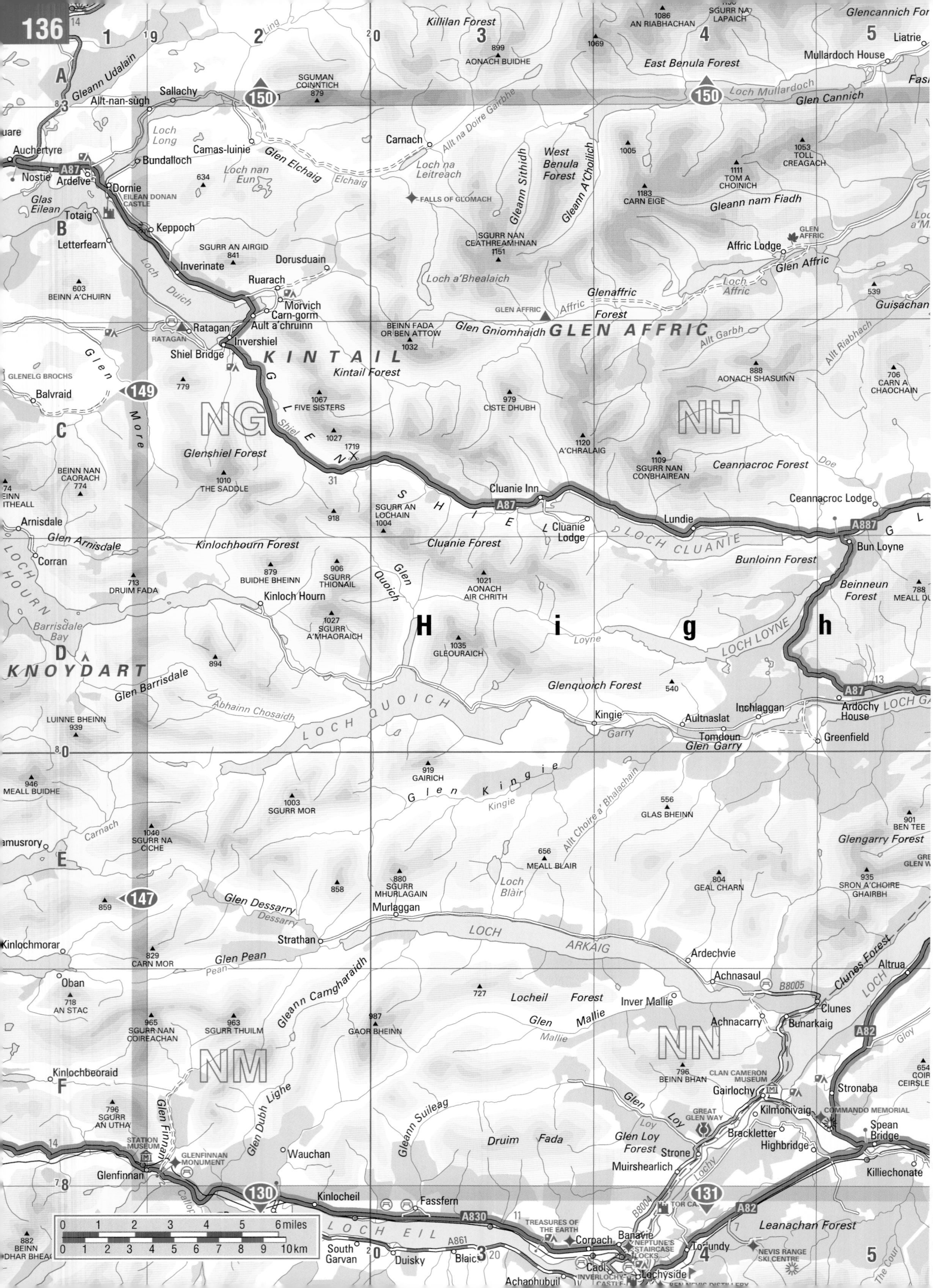

Gleann Udalain
Sallachy
Allt-nan-sùgh
Loch Long
Camas-luinie
Auchertyre
Bundalloch
Nostie
Ardelve
A87
Dornie
EILEAN DONAN CASTLE
Glas Eilean
Totaig
Letterfearn
Keppoch
Loch Duich
Invernate
SGURR AN AIRGID 841
Dorusduain
Ruarach
Morvich
Carn-gorm
Ault a'chruinn
603 BEINN A'CHUIRN
Ratagan
RATAGAN
Inversheil
Shiel Bridge
GLENELG BROCHS
Glen More
Balvraid
149
150
SGUMAN COINNTICH 879
Glen Elchaig
Elchaig
Loch nan Eun
634
Carnach
Allt na Doire Gairbhe
Loch na Leitreach
FALLS OF GLOMACH
Killilan Forest
899 AONACH BUIDHE
1086 AN RIABHACHAN
SGURR NA LAPAICH
1069
East Benula Forest
Glencannich Forest
Liatrie
Mullardoch House
Loch Mullardoch
Glen Cannich
Gleann Sithidh
West Benula Forest
Gleann A'Choilich
1005
1053 TOLL CREAGACH
1111 TOM A CHOINICH
1183 CARN EIGE
Gleann nam Fiadh
SGURR NAN CEATHREAMHNAN 1151
Loch a'Bhealaich
GLEN AFFRIC
Affric Lodge
Glen Affric
Loch Affric
Glenaffric Forest
Affric
539
Guisachan
BEINN FADA OR BEN ATTOW 1032
Glen Gniomhaidh
KINTAIL
Kintail Forest
Allt Garbh
Allt Riabhach
888 AONACH SHASUINN
706 CARN A CHAOCHAIN
NG
NH
1067 FIVE SISTERS
979 CISTE DHUBH
1027
1719
779
Glenshiel Forest
Glen Shiel
1120 A'CHRALAIG
1109 SGURR NAN CONBHAIREAN
Ceannacroc Forest
Doe
BEINN NAN CAORACH 774
1010 THE SADDLE
31
918
SGURR AN LOCHAIN 1004
Cluanie Inn
Cluanie Lodge
Lundie
Ceannacroc Lodge
LOCH CLUANIE
A887
Bun Loyne
Arnisdale
Glen Arnisdale
Corran
LOCH HOURN
Kinlochhourn Forest
879 BUIDHE BHEINN
906 SGURR THIONAIL
Cluanie Forest
Glen Quoich
1021 AONACH AIR CHRITH
Bunloinn Forest
Beinneun Forest
788 MEALL DU
713 DRUIM FADA
Kinloch Hourn
1027 SGURR A'MHAORAICH
Highland
1035 GLEOURAICH
Loyne
LOCH LOYNE
Barrisdale Bay
KNOYDART
894
Glen Barrisdale
Abhainn Chosaidh
LOCH QUOICH
Glenquoich Forest
540
13
A87
Kingie
Aultnaslat
Inchlaggan
Ardochy House
LOCH GARRY
Tomdoun
Glen Garry
Garry
Greenfield
LUINNE BHEINN 939
946 MEALL BUIDHE
919 GAIRICH
Glen Kingie
Kingie
1003 SGURR MOR
Allt Choire a' Bhalachain
556 GLAS BHEINN
901 BEN TEE
Glengarry Forest
Carnach
1040 SGURR NA CICHE
656 MEALL BLAIR
Loch Blàir
804 GEAL CHARN
935 SRON A'CHOIRE GHAIRBH
858
880 SGURR MHURLAGAIN
147
859
Glen Dessarry
Dessarry
Murlaggan
Kinlochmorar
Strathan
LOCH ARKAIG
Ardechvie
829 CARN MOR
Glen Pean
Pean
Oban
718 AN STAC
Gleann Camgharaidh
727
Locheil Forest
Achnasaul
B8005
Clunes Forest
Altrua
Inver Mallie
Clunes
Glen Mallie
Mallie
Achnacarry
Bunarkaig
A82
Gloy
965 SGURR NAN COIREACHAN
963 SGURR THUILM
987 GAOR BHEINN
NM
NN
796 BEINN BHAN
CLAN CAMERON MUSEUM
Gairlochy
Stronaba
654
Kinlochbeoraid
796 SGURR AN UTHA
Glen Finnan
Glen Dubh Lighe
Gleann Suileag
Druim Fada
Glen Loy
Loy
GREAT GLEN WAY
Kilmonivaig
COMMANDO MEMORIAL
Spean Bridge
Brackletter
Highbridge
Glen Loy Forest
Strone
Muirshearlich
Killiechonate
STATION MUSEUM
GLENFINNAN MONUMENT
Wauchan
Glenfinnan
130
Kinlocheil
Fassfern
131
Callop
A830
LOCH EIL
A861
B8004
TOR CA
A82
Leanachan Forest
TREASURES OF THE EARTH
Corpach
Banavie
NEPTUNE'S STAIRCASE LOCKS
Tomundy
NEVIS RANGE SKI CENTRE
882 BEINN DHAR BHEA
South Garvan
Duisky
Blaich
Achaphubuil
Caol
INVERLOCHY CASTLE
Lochyside
BEN NEVIS DISTILLERY
The Cour
0 1 2 3 4 5 6 miles
0 1 2 3 4 5 6 7 8 9 10 km

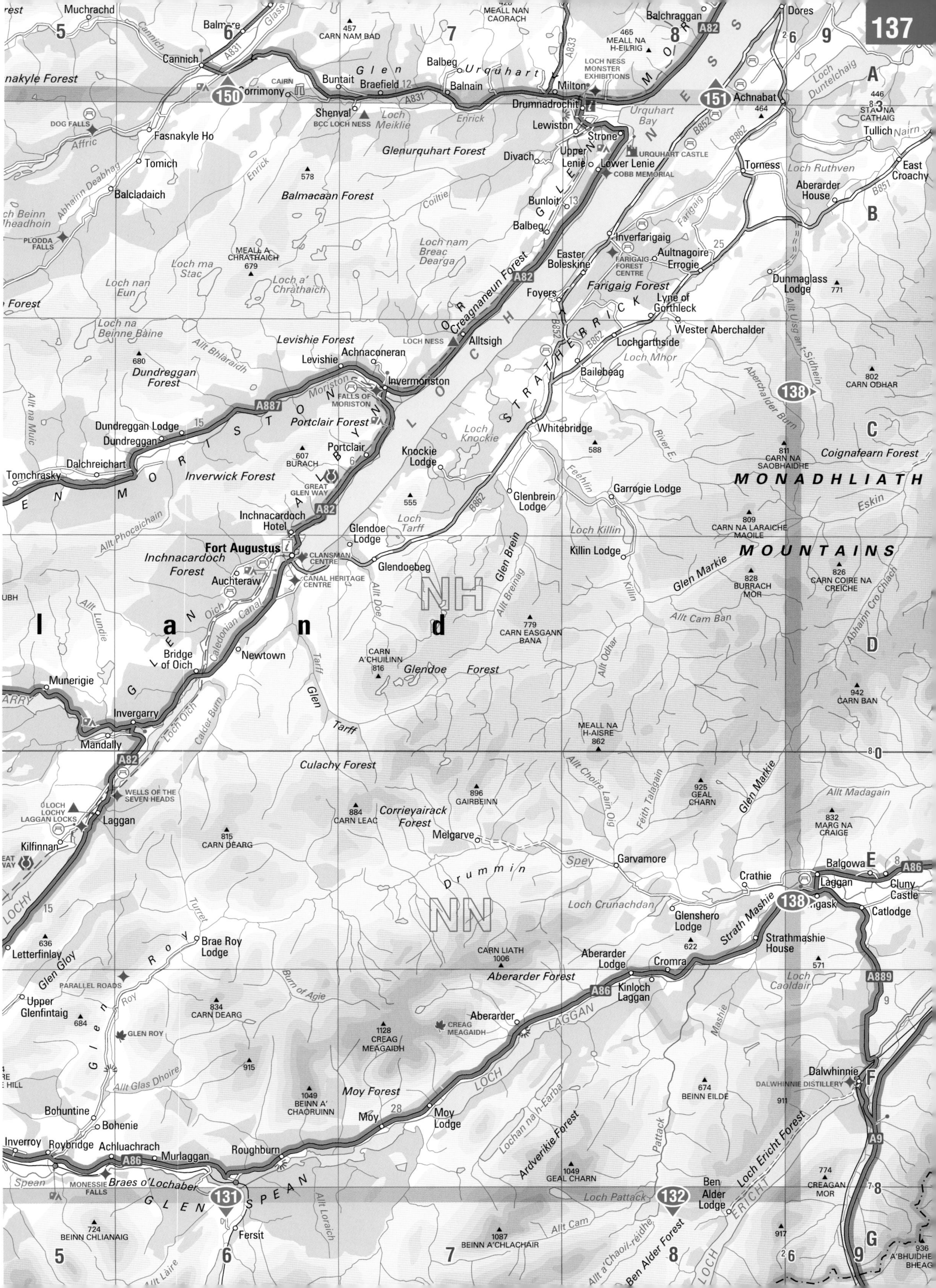
Muchrachd
Balmore
Cannich
Glass
457
CARN NAM BAD
MEALL NAN CAORACH
Balchraggan
A82
Dores
465
MEALL NA H-EILRIG
LOCH NESS MONSTER EXHIBITIONS
Nakyle Forest
150
CAIRN
Corrimony
Buntait
Glen
Braefield
Balbeg
Urquhart
Balnain
A831
A833
Milton
Drumnadrochit
151
Achnabat
Loch Duntelchaig
446
STA NA CATHAIG
464
Shenval
BCC LOCH NESS
Loch Meiklie
Enrick
Lewiston
Urquhart Bay
B852
B862
Tullich
Nairn
DOG FALLS
Affric
Fasnakyle Ho
Tomich
Glenurquhart Forest
Divach
Strone
Upper Lenie
Lower Lenie
URQUHART CASTLE
COBB MEMORIAL
Torness
East Croachy
Loch Ruthven
Abhainn Deabhag
Balcladaich
578
Balmacaan Forest
Coiltie
Bunloit
Balbeg
Aberarder House
B851
Loch Beinn a' Mheadhoin
PLODDA FALLS
MEALL A CHRATHAICH
679
Loch ma Stac
Loch nam Breac Dearga
Inverfarigaig
FARIGAIG FOREST CENTRE
Easter Boleskine
Aultnagoire
Errogie
Farigaig
Loch nan Eun
Loch a' Chràthaich
Creagnaneun Forest
A82
Foyers
Farigaig Forest
Dunmaglass Lodge
771
Lyne of Gorthleck
Wester Aberchalder
Forest
Loch na Beinne Bàine
Levishie Forest
LOCH NESS
Alltsigh
Lochgarthside
Loch Mhor
Allt Bhlàraidh
680
Dundreggan Forest
Levishie
Achnaconeran
Invermoriston
FALLS OF MORISTON
Bailebeag
Allt Uisg an t-Sidhein
Aberchalder Burn
138
802
CARN ODHAR
Allt na Muic
A887
Portclair Forest
Dundreggan Lodge
Dundreggan
Loch Knockie
Whitebridge
588
River E
Coignafearn Forest
Dalchreichart
607
BURACH
Portclair
Knockie Lodge
811
CARN NA SAOBHAIDHE
Tomchrasky
Inverwick Forest
GREAT GLEN WAY
555
Feehlin
Garrogie Lodge
MONADHLIATH
Glenbrein Lodge
Eskin
Allt Phocaichain
Inchnacardoch Hotel
A82
Loch Tarff
809
CARN NA LARAICHE MAOILE
Glendoe Lodge
Loch Killin
Fort Augustus
CLANSMAN CENTRE
Glendoebeg
Killin Lodge
MOUNTAINS
Inchnacardoch Forest
Auchteraw
CANAL HERITAGE CENTRE
Glen Brein
Glen Markie
826
CARN COIRE NA CREICHE
828
BURRACH MOR
Allt Doe
NH
Allt Breinag
Killin
Abhainn Cro Chlach
Allt Lundie
Oich
Caledonian Canal
Allt Cam Ban
779
CARN EASGANN BANA
Bridge of Oich
Newtown
Tarff
CARN A'CHUILINN
816
Glendoe Forest
Allt Odhar
Munerigie
Glen
942
CARN BAN
Invergarry
Loch Oich
Calder Burn
Tarff
MEALL NA H-AISRE
862
Mandally
A82
Culachy Forest
Allt Choire Lain Oig
Féith Talagain
Glen Markie
WELLS OF THE SEVEN HEADS
896
GAIRBEINN
925
GEAL CHARN
Allt Madagain
LOCH LOCHY
LAGGAN LOCKS
Laggan
884
CARN LEAC
Corrieyairack Forest
832
MARG NA CRAIGE
815
CARN DEARG
Melgarve
Kilfinnan
Spey
Garvamore
Balgowan
A86
Crathie
Laggan
Cluny Castle
Drummin
LOCHY
Loch Crunachdan
138
Catlodge
Glenshero Lodge
Strath Mashie
NN
Turret
Brae Roy Lodge
622
Strathmashie House
636
Letterfinlay
Roy
CARN LIATH
1006
Aberarder Lodge
Cromra
571
Glen Gloy
PARALLEL ROADS
Aberarder Forest
Loch Caoldair
A889
Burn of Agie
A86
Kinloch Laggan
Upper Glenfintaig
684
834
CARN DEARG
Aberarder
CREAG MEAGAIDH
LAGGAN
Mashie
GLEN ROY
1128
CREAG MEAGAIDH
Glen Roy
915
Allt Glas Dhoire
LOCH
Dalwhinnie
DALWHINNIE DISTILLERY
674
BEINN EILDE
1049
BEINN A' CHAORUINN
Moy Forest
911
Bohuntine
Moy
28
Moy Lodge
Bohenie
Lochan na h-Earba
Ardverikie Forest
Pattack
Loch Ericht Forest
A9
Inverroy
Roybridge
Achluachrach
Roughburn
A86
Murlaggan
1049
GEAL CHARN
774
CREAGAN MOR
Spean
MONESSIE FALLS
Braes o'Lochaber
GLEN SPEAN
131
Allt Loraich
Loch Pattack
132
Ben Alder Lodge
ERICHT
724
BEINN CHLIANAIG
Fersit
1087
BEINN A'CHLACHAIR
Allt Cam
Allt a' Chaoil-réidhe
Ben Alder Forest
917
936
A'BHUIDHE BHEAG
LOCH
Allt Làire
5
6
7
8
9
A
B
C
D
E
F
G

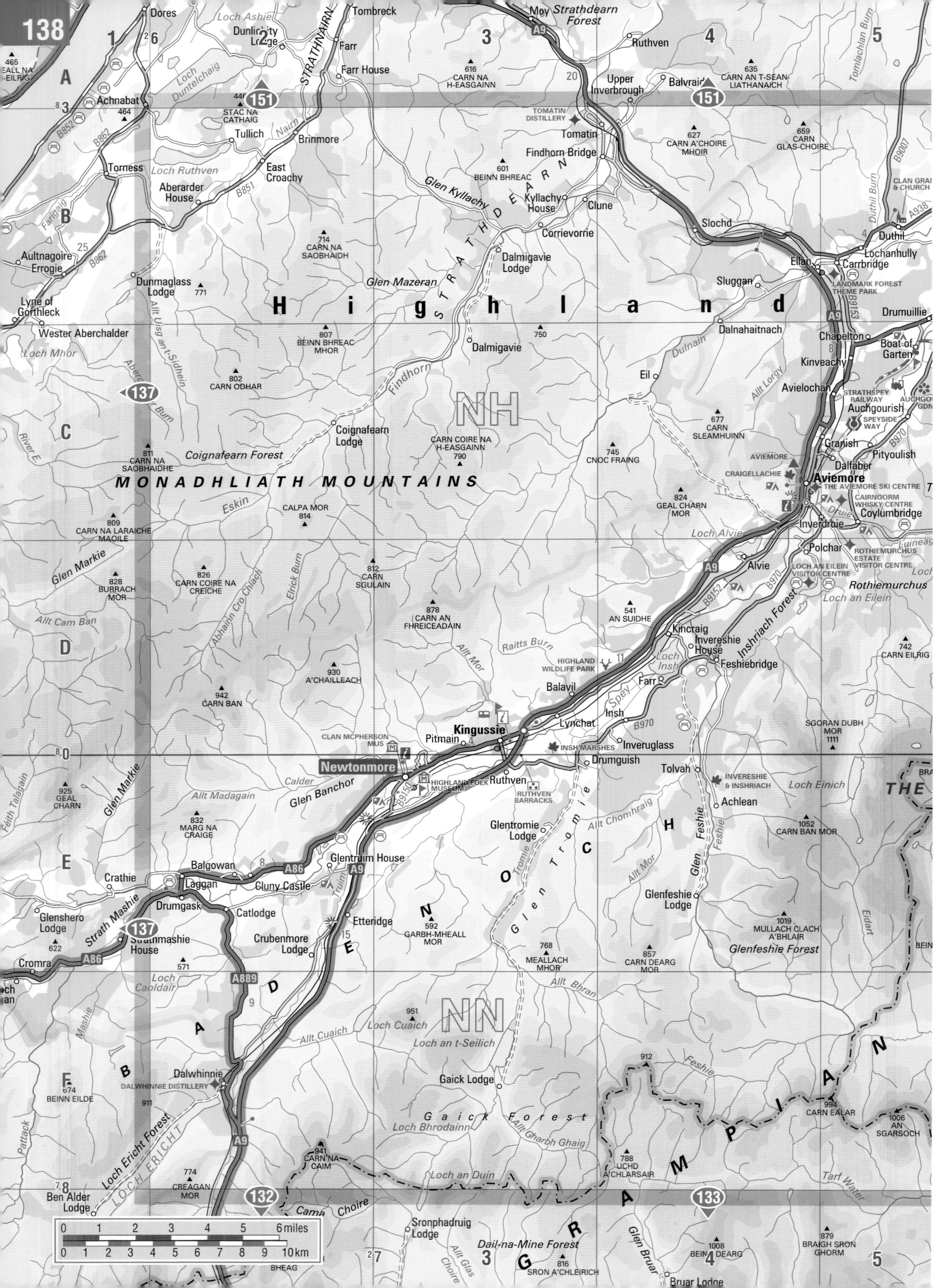
Dores
Loch Ashie
Dunlichity Lodge
STRATHNAIRN
Tombreck
Farr
Farr House
Moy
Strathdearn Forest
A9
Ruthven
616 CARN NA H-EASGAINN
635 CARN AN T-SEAN-LIATHANAICH
Tomlachlan Burn
465 EALL NA EILRIG
Loch Duntelchaig
Achnabat
464
446 STAC NA CATHAIG
151
Upper Inverbrough
Balvraid
TOMATIN DISTILLERY
Tomatin
627 CARN A'CHOIRE MHOIR
659 CARN GLAS-CHOIRE
B852
B862
Tullich
Nairn
Brinmore
Findhorn Bridge
601 BEINN BHREAC
Torness
Loch Ruthven
East Croachy
Aberarder House
B851
Glen Kyllachy
Kyllachy House
Clune
STRATHDEARN
Corrievorrie
Slochd
CLAN GRANT & CHURCH
B9007
Dulnain Burn
A938
Duthil
Lochanhully
Carrbridge
LANDMARK FOREST THEME PARK
Farigaig
Aultnagoire
Errogie
714 CARN NA SAOBHAIDH
Dalmigavie Lodge
Ellan
Sluggan
Dunmaglass Lodge
771
Glen Mazeran
Lyne of Gorthleck
Highland
B9153
Drumuillie
Wester Aberchalder
Loch Mhor
807 BEINN BHREAC MHOR
750
Dalmigavie
Dalnahaitnach
Chapelton
Boat of Garten
Dulnain
Kinveachy
Allt Usig an t-Sidhein
137
802 CARN ODHAR
Findhorn
NH
Eil
Allt Lorgy
Avielochan
STRATHSPEY RAILWAY
Auchgourish
SPEYSIDE WAY
River E
Coignafearn Lodge
677 CARN SLEAMHUINN
Granish
B970
Pityoulish
811 CARN NA SAOBHAIDHE
Coignafearn Forest
CARN COIRE NA H-EASGAINN 790
745 CNOC FRAING
AVIEMORE
Dalfaber
CRAIGELLACHIE
Aviemore
THE AVIEMORE SKI CENTRE
MONADHLIATH MOUNTAINS
824 GEAL CHARN MOR
CAIRNGORM WHISKY CENTRE
Eskin
CALPA MOR 814
809 CARN NA LARAICHE MAOILE
Coylumbridge
Druie
Inverdruie
Loch Alvie
Polchar
ROTHIEMURCHUS ESTATE VISITOR CENTRE
Glen Markie
826 CARN COIRE NA CREICHE
Abhainn Cro Chlach
Elrick Burn
812 CARN SGULAIN
Alvie
LOCH AN EILEIN VISITOR CENTRE
828 BURRACH MOR
B9152
B970
Rothiemurchus
Loch an Eilein
878 CARN AN FHREICEADAIN
541 AN SUIDHE
Inshriach Forest
Allt Cam Ban
Kincraig
Raitts Burn
Allt Mor
Inveshie House
742 CARN EILRIG
HIGHLAND WILDLIFE PARK
Loch Insh
Feshiebridge
930 A'CHAILLEACH
942 CARN BAN
Balavil
Farr
Spey
Insh
Lynchat
Kingussie
SGORAN DUBH MOR 1111
CLAN MCPHERSON MUS
Pitmain
INSH MARSHES
Inveruglass
Newtonmore
Drumguish
Tolvah
INVERESHIE & INSHRIACH
Loch Einich
THE
925 GEAL CHARN
Glen Markie
Calder
Glen Banchor
HIGHLAND FOLK MUSEUM
Ruthven
RUTHVEN BARRACKS
Achlean
Allt Madagain
832 MARG NA CRAIGE
Glentromie Lodge
Allt Chomhraig
Glen Feshie
1052 CARN BAN MOR
Glentruim House
Balgowan
A86
Crathie
Laggan
Cluny Castle
Drumgask
Catlodge
Allt Mor
Glenfeshie Lodge
Glenshero Lodge
Strath Mashie
Strathmashie House
Etteridge
Truim
592 GARBH-MHEALL MOR
Glen Tromie
1019 MULLACH CLACH A'BHLAIR
Glenfeshie Forest
Eidart
622
Crubenmore Lodge
768 MEALLACH MHOR
857 CARN DEARG MOR
Cromra
571
Loch Caoldair
A889
Allt Bhran
Mashie
951
Loch Cuaich
NN
Allt Cuaich
Loch an t-Seilich
GRAMPIAN
Dalwhinnie
DALWHINNIE DISTILLERY
674 BEINN EILDE
911
Gaick Lodge
912
Feshie
994 CARN EALAR
1006 AN SGARSOCH
Pattack
Loch Ericht Forest
LOCH ERICHT
Gaick Forest
Loch Bhrodainn
Allt Gharbh Ghaig
941 CARN NA CAIM
788 UCHD A'CHLARSAIR
774 CREAGAN MOR
Loch an Duin
Tarf Water
Ben Alder Lodge
132
133
Camas Choire
Sronphadruig Lodge
Glen Bruar
Allt Glas Choire
Dail-na-Mine Forest
816 SRON A'CHLEIRICH
1008 BEINN DEARG
879 BRAIGH SRON GHORM
Bruar Lodge
0 1 2 3 4 5 6 miles
0 1 2 3 4 5 6 7 8 9 10 km

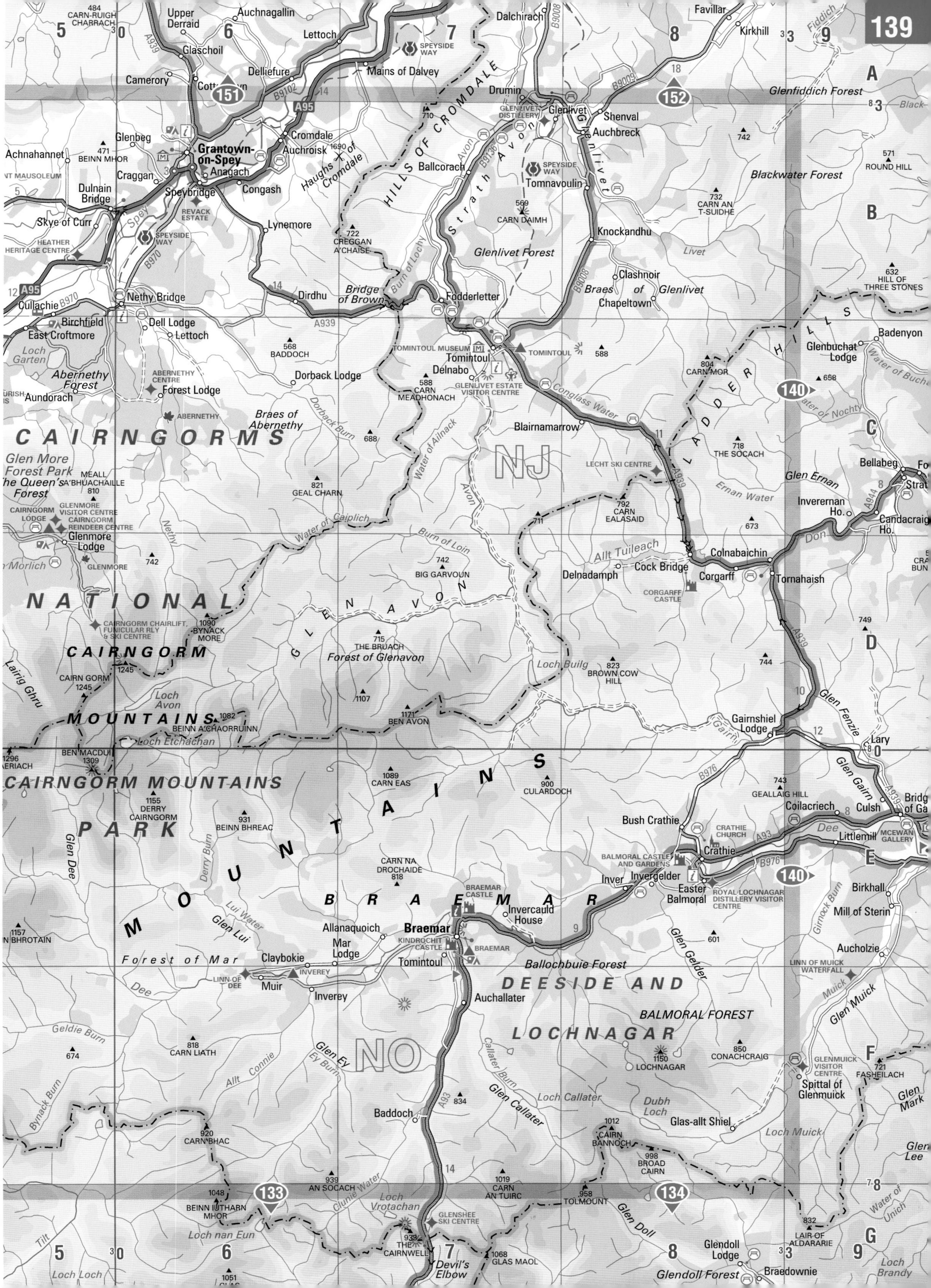

CARN-RUIGH CHARRACH
Upper Derraid
Auchnagallin
Lettoch
Dalchirach
Favillar
Kirkhill
Fiddich
Glaschoil
SPEYSIDE WAY
Mains of Dalvey
Dellefure
Camerory
Cottartown
151
152
Glenfiddich Forest
Black
A95
B9102
B9008
B9009
HILLS OF CROMDALE
Drumin
GLENLIVET DISTILLERY
Glenlivet
Shenval
Auchbreck
Glenbeg
Grantown-on-Spey
Cromdale
Auchroisk
Haughs of Cromdale
Achnahannet
BEINN MHOR
Anagach
Craggan
Ballcorach
Strath Avon
Tomnavoulin
Dulnain Bridge
Speybridge
Congash
ROUND HILL
Blackwater Forest
Skye of Curr
REVACK ESTATE
CARN DAIMH
CARN AN T-SUIDHE
Lynemore
HEATHER HERITAGE CENTRE
CREGGAN A'CHAISE
Knockandhu
Glenlivet Forest
Livet
B970
Burn of Lochy
Clashnoir
Braes of Glenlivet
Chapeltown
HILL OF THREE STONES
Cullachie
Nethy Bridge
Dirdhu
Bridge of Brown
Fodderletter
Birchfield
Dell Lodge
A939
East Croftmore
Lettoch
BADDOCH
TOMINTOUL MUSEUM
Tomintoul
TOMINTOUL
Badenyon
Loch Garten
Dorback Lodge
Delnabo
CARN MOR
Glenbuchat Lodge
Abernethy Forest
ABERNETHY CENTRE
Forest Lodge
CARN MEADHONACH
GLENLIVET ESTATE VISITOR CENTRE
LADDER HILLS
140
Water of Buchat
Water of Nochty
Aundorach
ABERNETHY
Dorback Burn
Conglass Water
Braes of Abernethy
CAIRNGORMS
Blairnamarrow
Water of Ailnack
NJ
THE SOCACH
Glen More Forest Park
The Queen's Forest
MEALL A'BHUACHAILLE
LECHT SKI CENTRE
Bellabeg
GEAL CHARN
Glen Ernan
Ernan Water
CAIRNGORM LODGE
GLENMORE VISITOR CENTRE
CAIRNGORM REINDEER CENTRE
CARN EALASAID
Inverernan Ho.
A944
Candacraig Ho.
Water of Caiplich
Glenmore Lodge
Nethy
Burn of Loin
Allt Tuileach
Don
Colnabaichin
Loch Morlich
GLENMORE
BIG GARVOUN
Cock Bridge
Delnadamph
Corgarff
Tornahaish
CORGARFF CASTLE
NATIONAL
GLEN AVON
CAIRNGORM CHAIRLIFT, FUNICULAR RLY & SKI CENTRE
BYNACK MORE
THE BRUACH
Forest of Glenavon
CAIRNGORM
Loch Builg
BROWN COW HILL
Lairig Ghru
CAIRN GORM
Glen Fenzie
Loch Avon
MOUNTAINS
BEINN A'CHAORRUINN
BEN AVON
Gairnshiel Lodge
Loch Etchachan
Gairn
Lary
BEN MACDUI
CARN EAS
CULARDOCH
B976
Glen Gairn
CAIRNGORM MOUNTAINS
DERRY CAIRNGORM
GEALLAIG HILL
Bridge of Gairn
Coilacriech
Culsh
PARK
BEINN BHREAC
Bush Crathie
CRATHIE CHURCH
Dee
Littlemill
MCEWAN GALLERY
A93
Glen Dee
Derry Burn
CARN NA DROCHAIDE
BALMORAL CASTLE AND GARDENS
Crathie
Invergelder
Inver
Easter Balmoral
ROYAL LOCHNAGAR DISTILLERY VISITOR CENTRE
Birkhall
BRAEMAR CASTLE
BRAEMAR
Invercauld House
Mill of Sterin
Lui Water
Glen Lui
Girnock Burn
BHROTAIN
Allanaquoich
Braemar
Glen Gelder
Aucholzie
KINDROCHIT CASTLE
Mar Lodge
Forest of Mar
Claybokie
Tomintoul
Ballochbuie Forest
LINN OF MUICK WATERFALL
LINN OF DEE
INVEREY
Muir
Inverey
DEESIDE AND
Auchallater
Glen Muick
BALMORAL FOREST
Geldie Burn
LOCHNAGAR
CARN LIATH
Glen Ey
Ey Burn
NO
CONACHCRAIG
GLENMUICK VISITOR CENTRE
FASHEILACH
Allt Connie
Callater Burn
Spittal of Glenmuick
Glen Mark
Bynack Burn
Glen Callater
Loch Callater
Dubh Loch
Baddoch
Glas-allt Shiel
Loch Muick
CARN BHAC
CAIRN BANNOCH
BROAD CAIRN
Glen Lee
AN SOCACH
Clunie Water
CARN AN TUIRC
TOLMOUNT
Loch Vrotachan
133
134
BEINN IUTHARN MHOR
GLENSHEE SKI CENTRE
Glen Doll
Water of Unich
Loch nan Eun
THE CAIRNWELL
LAIR OF ALDARARIE
Tilt
Glendoll Lodge
GLAS MAOL
Devil's Elbow
Glendoll Forest
Braedownie
Loch Loch
Loch Brandy

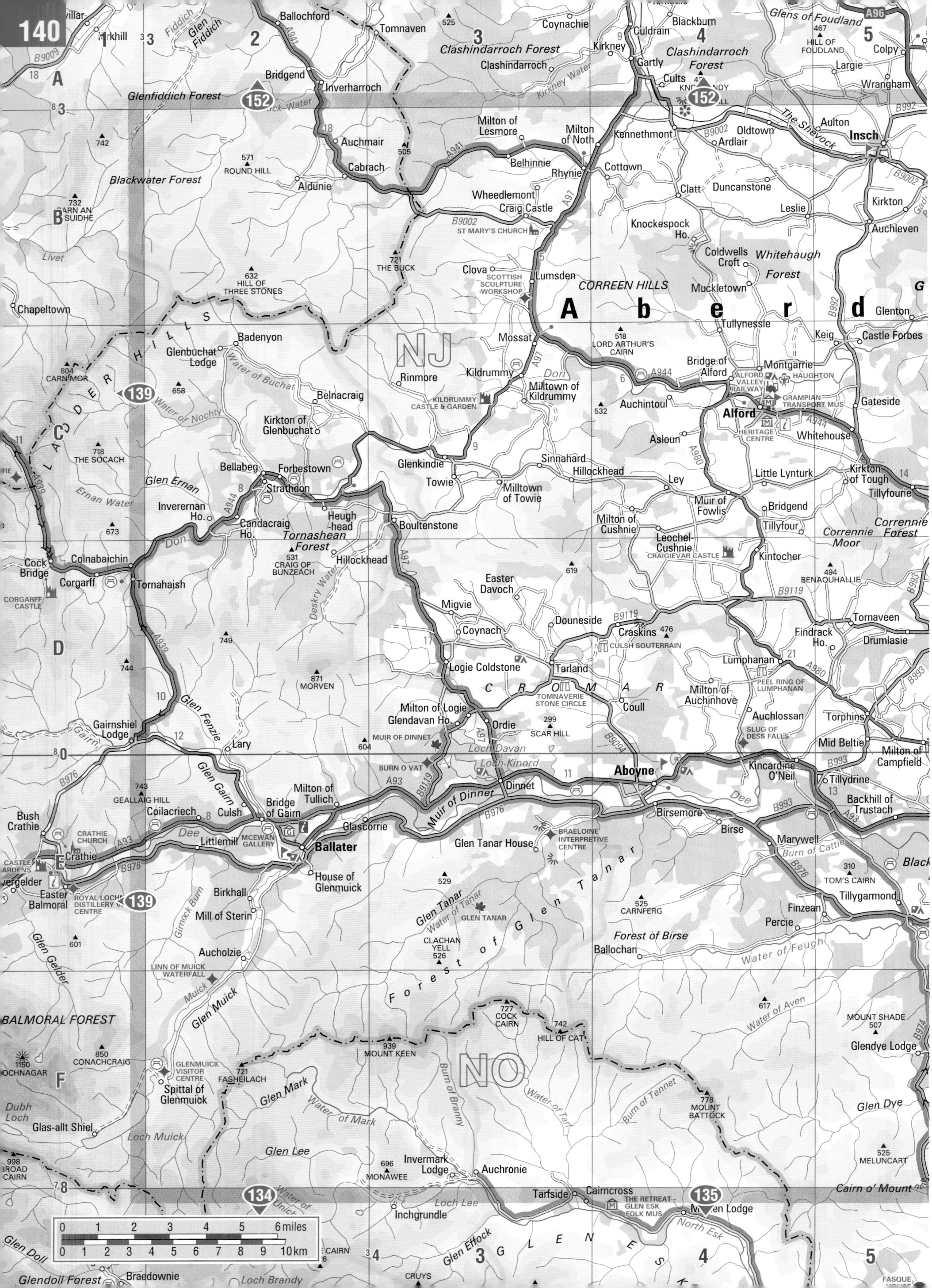

Ballochford
Tomnaven
Coynachie
Culdrain
Blackburn
Glens of Foudland
A96
Kirkhill
Glen Fiddich
Fiddich
525
3
Clashindarroch Forest
Kirkney
4
Clashindarroch Forest
467
HILL OF FOUDLAND
5
Colpy
B9009
A
Bridgend
Clashindarroch
Gartly
Largie
Cults
Wrangham
Inverharroch
Kirkney Water
Glenfiddich Forest
152
B992
Milton of Lesmore
Milton of Noth
Kennethmont
B9002
Oldtown
Aulton
The Shevock
Insch
742
Auchmair
505
Ardlair
571
ROUND HILL
A941
Belhinnie
Cabrach
Rhynie
Cottown
B9002
Blackwater Forest
Aldunie
Clatt
Duncanstone
732
CARN AN SUIDHE
B
Wheedlemont
Leslie
Kirkton
Craig Castle
B9002
ST MARY'S CHURCH
A97
Knockespock Ho.
Auchleven
Livet
721
THE BUCK
Coldwells Croft
Whitehaugh Forest
Clova
SCOTTISH SCULPTURE WORKSHOP
Lumsden
632
HILL OF THREE STONES
CORREEN HILLS
Muckletown
Chapeltown
A b e r d
Glenton
Tullynessle
LADDER HILLS
B992
Keig
Castle Forbes
Badenyon
NJ
518
LORD ARTHUR'S CAIRN
Mossat
Glenbuchat Lodge
Water of Buchat
Bridge of Alford
Montgarrie
804
CARN MOR
Rinmore
Kildrummy
A944
ALFORD VALLEY RAILWAY
HAUGHTON
139
658
Don
Milltown of Kildrummy
Water of Nochty
Belnacraig
KILDRUMMY CASTLE & GARDEN
Auchintoul
GRAMPIAN TRANSPORT MUS
Gateside
532
Alford
C
Kirkton of Glenbuchat
HERITAGE CENTRE
A944
Whitehouse
Asloun
718
THE SOCACH
A980
Bellabeg
Forbestown
Glenkindie
Sinnahard
Hillockhead
Little Lynturk
Kirkton of Tough
Glen Ernan
Strathdon
Towie
Ley
14
A939
Ernan Water
Milltown of Towie
Muir of Fowlis
Bridgend
Tillyfourie
Inverernan Ho.
A944
Heugh-head
Candacraig Ho.
Boultenstone
Milton of Cushnie
Tillyfour
Correnie Moor
Correnie Forest
673
Tornashean Forest
Leochel-Cushnie
Don
A97
CRAIGIEVAR CASTLE
Kintocher
Colnabaichin
531
CRAIG OF BUNZEACH
Hillockhead
619
Cock Bridge
Corgarff
Tornahaish
Deskry Water
494
BENAQUHALLIE
CORGARFF CASTLE
Easter Davoch
B9119
B993
Migvie
Tornaveen
Douneside
B9119
Coynach
Craskins
476
Findrack Ho.
Drumlasie
D
749
CULSH SOUTERRAIN
17
Lumphanan
A939
21
744
Logie Coldstone
Tarland
A980
B993
871
MORVEN
C R O M A R
PEEL RING OF LUMPHANAN
10
TOMNAVERIE STONE CIRCLE
Milton of Auchinhove
Glen Fenzie
Milton of Logie
Coull
Glendavan Ho.
Ordie
299
SCAR HILL
Auchlossan
Torphins
Gairnshiel Lodge
12
A97
B9094
SLUG OF DESS FALLS
Gairn
MUIR OF DINNET
Loch Davan
Mid Beltie
Lary
604
Milton of Campfield
0
B976
Loch Kinord
Aboyne
Kincardine O'Neil
B993
BURN O VAT
11
Tillydrine
Glen Gairn
B9119
Dinnet
13
743
GEALLAIG HILL
Milton of Tullich
A93
Dee
Backhill of Trustach
Muir of Dinnet
Bush
Crathie
Coilacriech
8
Culsh
Bridge of Gairn
B976
Birsemore
B993
Dee
Birse
A93
CRATHIE CHURCH
Glascorrie
BRAELOINE INTERPRETIVE CENTRE
Littlemill
MCEWAN GALLERY
Marywell
A93
Crathie
Ballater
Glen Tanar House
Burn of Cattie
CASTLE GARDENS
Black
E
B976
House of Glenmuick
B976
310
TOM'S CAIRN
Invergelder
529
Easter Balmoral
Birkhall
ROYAL LOCHNAGAR DISTILLERY VISITOR CENTRE
139
Glen Tanar
Tillygarmond
Water of Tanar
525
CARNFERG
Finzean
Girnock Burn
Mill of Sterin
GLEN TANAR
Percie
601
Forest of Glen Tanar
CLACHAN YELL
526
Forest of Birse
Glen Gelder
Aucholzie
Ballochan
Water of Feugh
LINN OF MUICK WATERFALL
Muick
Glen Muick
617
Water of Aven
727
COCK CAIRN
MOUNT SHADE
507
BALMORAL FOREST
742
HILL OF CAT
B974
939
MOUNT KEEN
Glendye Lodge
1150
LOCHNAGAR
850
CONACHCRAIG
GLENMUICK VISITOR CENTRE
721
FASHEILACH
Burn of Branny
NO
F
Spittal of Glenmuick
Glen Mark
Water of Tarf
Burn of Tennet
778
MOUNT BATTOCK
Glen Dye
Dubh Loch
Water of Mark
Glas-allt Shiel
Loch Muick
Glen Lee
525
MELUNCART
998
BROAD CAIRN
696
MONAWEE
Invermark Lodge
Auchronie
8
Cairn o' Mount
134
Water of Unich
Tarfside
Cairncross
135
THE RETREAT GLEN ESK FOLK MUS
Loch Lee
Millden Lodge
Inchgrundle
North Esk
0 1 2 3 4 5 6 miles
0 1 2 3 4 5 6 7 8 9 10 km
Glen Doll
CAIRN
Glen Effock
3
G L E N E S K
4
5
CRUYS
Glendoll Forest
Braedownie
Loch Brandy
FASQUE HOUSE

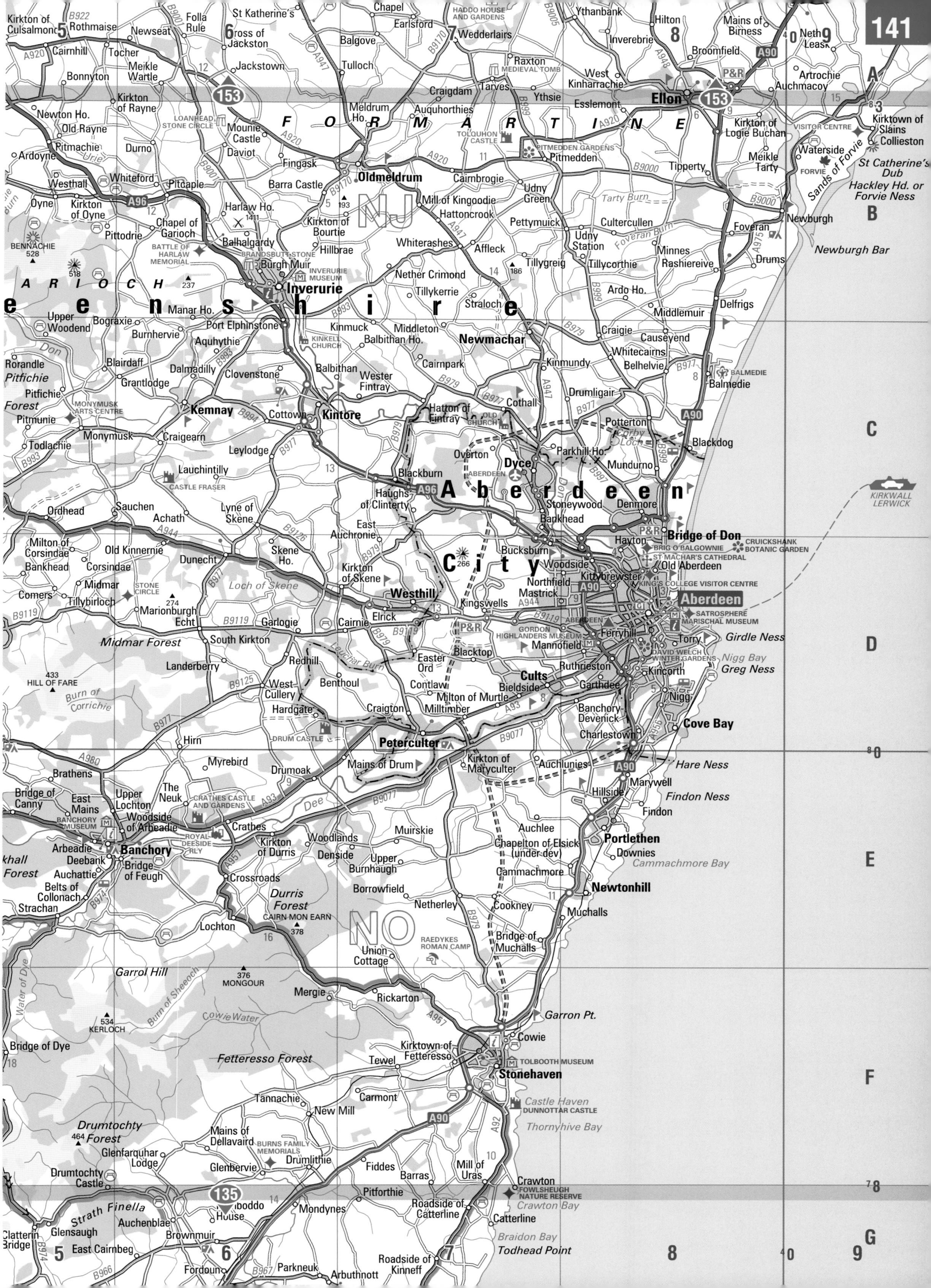
Kirkton of Culsalmond
Rothmaise
Newseat
Folla Rule
St Katherine's
Cross of Jackston
Chapel
Earlsford
HADDO HOUSE AND GARDENS
Ythanbank
Hilton
Mains of Birness
Neth Leask
Wedderlairs
Inverebrie
Broomfield
Cairnhill
Tocher
Meikle Wartle
Jackstown
Balgove
Tulloch
Raxton
MEDIEVAL TOMB
West Kinharrachie
Artrochie
Auchmacoy
Bonnyton
Kirkton of Rayne
Craigdam
Tarves
Ythsie
Esslemont
Ellon
Newton Ho.
Old Rayne
LOANHEAD STONE CIRCLE
Mounie Castle
Meldrum Ho.
Auquhorthies
F O R M A R T I N E
Kirkton of Logie Buchan
VISITOR CENTRE
Kirktown of Slains
Collieston
Pitmachie
Durno
Daviot
TOLQUHON CASTLE
PITMEDDEN GARDENS
Pitmedden
Waterside
Ardoyne
Fingask
Tipperty
Meikle Tarty
FORVIE
Sands of Forvie
St Catherine's Dub
Hackley Hd. or Forvie Ness
Westhall
Whiteford
Pitcaple
Barra Castle
Oldmeldrum
Cairnbrogie
Udny Green
Oyne
Kirkton of Oyne
Harlaw Ho.
Mill of Kingoodie
Hattoncrook
Tarty Burn
Chapel of Garioch
Kirkton of Bourtie
Pettymuick
Udny Station
Cultercullen
Foveran
Newburgh
BENNACHIE
Pittodrie
Balhalgardy
Whiterashes
Affleck
Foveran Burn
Minnes
Rashierieve
Drums
Newburgh Bar
BATTLE OF HARLAW MEMORIAL
BRANDSBUTT STONE
Hillbrae
Tillygreig
Tillycorthie
Burgh Muir
INVERURIE MUSEUM
Nether Crimond
A R I O C H
Inverurie
Tillykerrie
Ardo Ho.
Delfrigs
Manar Ho.
Straloch
Middlemuir
Upper Woodend
Bograxie
Port Elphinstone
Kinmuck
Middleton
Craigie
Causeyend
Burnhervie
Aquhythie
KINKELL CHURCH
Balbithan Ho.
Newmachar
Whitecairns
Belhelvie
Rorandle
Pitfichie
Blairdaff
Dalmadilly
Clovenstone
Balbithan
Wester Fintray
Cairnpark
Kinmundy
BALMEDIE
Balmedie
Pitfichie Forest
Grantlodge
Drumligair
Pitmunie
MONYMUSK ARTS CENTRE
Kemnay
Cottown
Kintore
Hatton of Fintray
Cothall
OLD CHURCH
Potterton
Todlachie
Monymusk
Craigearn
Leylodge
Overton
Parkhill Ho.
Corby Loch
Blackdog
Dyce
Mundurno
Lauchintilly
Blackburn
ABERDEEN
CASTLE FRASER
Haughs of Clinterty
Aberdeen City
Ordhead
Sauchen
Lyne of Skene
Achath
Stoneywood
Denmore
Bankhead
East Auchronie
Bridge of Don
Milton of Corsindae
Old Kinnernie
Skene Ho.
Bucksburn
Hayton
CRUICKSHANK BOTANIC GARDEN
BRIG O' BALGOWNIE
ST MACHAR'S CATHEDRAL
Bankhead
Corsindae
Dunecht
Kirkton of Skene
Woodside
Old Aberdeen
Kittybrewster
KING'S COLLEGE VISITOR CENTRE
Midmar
STONE CIRCLE
Loch of Skene
Northfield
Mastrick
Comers
Tillybirloch
Marionburgh
Echt
Westhill
Kingswells
Aberdeen
SATROSPHERE
MARISCHAL MUSEUM
Elrick
Garlogie
Cairnie
GORDON HIGHLANDERS MUSEUM
Ferryhill
Midmar Forest
South Kirkton
Mannofield
Torry
Girdle Ness
Landerberry
Redhill
Easter Ord
Blacktop
DAVID WELCH WINTER GARDENS
Nigg Bay
Greg Ness
HILL OF FARE
Leuchar Burn
Ruthrieston
Kincorth
West Cullery
Benthoul
Contlaw
Cults
Bieldside
Garthdee
Burn of Corrichie
Milton of Murtle
Nigg
Hardgate
Craigton
Milltimber
Banchory Devenick
Cove Bay
DRUM CASTLE
Peterculter
Charlestown
Hirn
Kirkton of Maryculter
Auchlunies
Hare Ness
Myrebird
Drumoak
Mains of Drum
Marywell
Brathens
Hillside
Findon Ness
Bridge of Canny
East Mains
Upper Lochton
The Neuk
CRATHES CASTLE AND GARDENS
Findon
Woodside of Arbeadie
BANCHORY MUSEUM
Crathes
Dee
Muirskie
Auchlee
Portlethen
ROYAL DEESIDE RLY
Arbeadie
Deebank
Banchory
Kirkton of Durris
Woodlands
Chapelton of Elsick (under dev)
Downies
Cammachmore Bay
Blackhall Forest
Auchattie
Bridge of Feugh
Denside
Upper Burnhaugh
Cammachmore
Belts of Collonach
Crossroads
Borrowfield
Newtonhill
Strachan
Durris Forest
Netherley
Cookney
Muchalls
Lochton
CAIRN-MON-EARN
NO
RAEDYKES ROMAN CAMP
Bridge of Muchalls
Union Cottage
Garrol Hill
MONGOUR
Mergie
Rickarton
Burn of Sheeoch
Water of Dye
Cowie Water
Garron Pt.
KERLOCH
Cowie
Bridge of Dye
Fetteresso Forest
Kirktown of Fetteresso
Tewel
TOLBOOTH MUSEUM
Stonehaven
Tannachie
Carmont
Castle Haven
DUNNOTTAR CASTLE
New Mill
Thornyhive Bay
Drumtochty Forest
Mains of Dellavaird
BURNS FAMILY MEMORIALS
Glenfarquhar Lodge
Drumlithie
Fiddes
Mill of Uras
Barras
Crawton
Drumtochty Castle
Glenbervie
Pitforthie
FOWLSHEUGH NATURE RESERVE
Crawton Bay
Strath Finella
Mondynes
Roadside of Catterline
Auchenblae
Catterline
Glensaugh
Brownmuir
Braidon Bay
Clatterin Bridge
East Cairnbeg
Todhead Point
Roadside of Kinneff
Fordoun
Parkneuk
Arbuthnott
KIRKWALL LERWICK

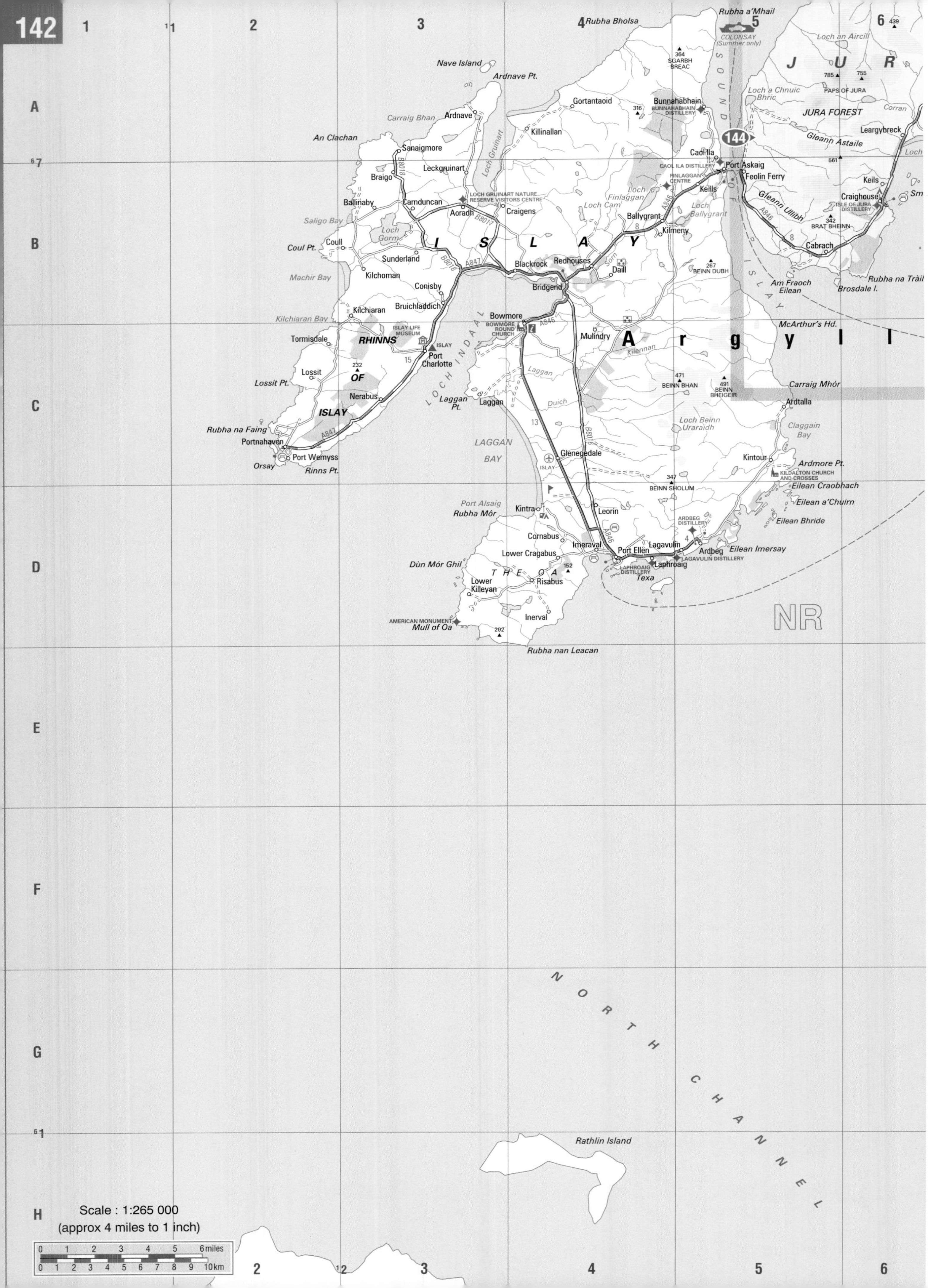
Rubha Bholsa
Rubha a'Mhail
COLONSAY (Summer only)
SOUND OF ISLAY
JURA
Loch an Aircill
364 SGARBH BREAC
785
755
PAPS OF JURA
Loch a Chnuic Bhric
JURA FOREST
Corran
Leargybreck
Gleann Astaile
144
Nave Island
Ardnave Pt.
Gortantaoid
Bunnahabhain
BUNNAHABHAIN DISTILLERY
316
Carraig Bhan
Ardnave
Killinallan
An Clachan
Sanaigmore
Caol Ila
CAOL ILA DISTILLERY
Port Askaig
Feolin Ferry
Braigo
Leckgruinart
Loch Gruinart
FINLAGGAN CENTRE
Loch Finlaggan
Keills
Keils
Craighouse
ISLE OF JURA DISTILLERY
LOCH GRUINART NATURE RESERVE VISITORS CENTRE
Ballinaby
Carnduncan
Aoradh
Craigens
Loch Cam
Ballygrant
Loch Ballygrant
Gleann Ullibh
342 BRAT BHEINN
Saligo Bay
Loch Gorm
ISLAY
Kilmeny
Cabrach
Coull
Coul Pt.
Sunderland
Blackrock
Redhouses
Daill
267 BEINN DUBH
Machir Bay
Kilchoman
Bridgend
Conisby
Am Fraoch Eilean
Brosdale I.
Rubha na Tràil
Bruichladdich
Kilchiaran
Kilchiaran Bay
Bowmore
BOWMORE ROUND CHURCH
ISLAY LIFE MUSEUM
Mulindry
McArthur's Hd.
Argyll
Tormisdale
RHINNS
ISLAY
Port Charlotte
Kilennan
LOCH INDAAL
232
Lossit
OF
Laggan
471 BEINN BHAN
491 BEINN BHEIGEIR
Lossit Pt.
Carraig Mhór
Nerabus
Laggan Pt.
Laggan
Duich
Ardtalla
ISLAY
Rubha na Faing
Loch Beinn Uraraidh
Claggain Bay
Portnahaven
LAGGAN BAY
Port Wemyss
Glenegedale
Kintour
Ardmore Pt.
Orsay
Rinns Pt.
ISLAY
KILDALTON CHURCH AND CROSSES
347 BEINN SHOLUM
Eilean Craobhach
Port Alsaig
Eilean a'Chuirn
Rubha Môr
Kintra
Leorin
ARDBEG DISTILLERY
Eilean Bhride
Cornabus
Lagavulin
Lower Cragabus
Imeraval
Port Ellen
Ardbeg
Eilean Imersay
Dùn Mór Ghil
THE OA
152
LAPHROAIG DISTILLERY
Laphroaig
LAGAVULIN DISTILLERY
Lower Killeyan
Risabus
Texa
NR
Inerval
AMERICAN MONUMENT
Mull of Oa
202
Rubha nan Leacan
A846
A847
B8016
B8017
B8018
NORTH CHANNEL
Rathlin Island
Scale : 1:265 000
(approx 4 miles to 1 inch)
0 1 2 3 4 5 6 miles
0 1 2 3 4 5 6 7 8 9 10km
1 2 3 4 5 6
A B C D E F G H

6
7
8
9
10
11
A
B
C
D
E
F
G
H
1
7
NS
Lagg
Loch Lesgamaill
An Dùnan
Knockrome
Lowlandman's Bay
Eilean Mór
St Cormac's Chapel
Kilmory Bay
Kilmory
Pt. of Knap
Island of Danna
Sween
Lochead
St Columba's Cave
Achahoish
Ellary
Clachbreck
Loch Caolisport
Baile Boidheach
Ormsary
Druimdrishaig
Cretshengan
Cruach Lagain
Coulaghailtro
Kilberry Hd.
Sculptured Stones
Kilberry
Miller's Bay
Loch nan Torran
Carse Ho.
Dunmore
Loch Stornoway
Ardpatrick
Kilchamaig
Ardpatrick Ho
Ardpatrick Pt.
Eilean Traighe
Portachoillan
K N A P D A L E
Stob Odhar
Erines
Loch Chaorain
Barmore I.
Ardmarnock Bay
Auchalick Bay
Kilfinan Bay
Kilfinan
Drum
Melldalloch
Beinn Bhreac
Kyles of Bute
Auchenlochan
Kames
Millhouse
Asgog Loch
Portavadie
Tignabruaich
Port Driseach
Blair's Ferry
Kyles of Bute
Asgog Bay
Kilbride Bay
Ardlamont Ho.
Ardlamont Pt.
Barfad
Tarbert
East Loch Tarbert
Glenan Bay
West Tarbert
Corranbuie
Rhu
Torinturk
Dun
West Loch Tarbert
Kennacraig
Redhouse
Whitehouse
Gartnagrenach
Cnoc A'Bhaileshios
Rubha Leathan
Glenreasdell Mains
Skipness
Skipness Castle
Skipness Pt.
Skipness Bay
Claonaig
Claonaig Bay
Cruach nam Fiadh
Clachan
Ronachan Pt.
Loch Ciaran
Argyll and Bute
Inchmarnock
Ardscalpsie Pt.
Scalpsie
Loch Quien
Scalpsie Bay
Stravanan Bay
Straad
Loch Fad
Island of Bute
Rothesay
Rothesay Castle
Rothesay Bay
Port Bannatyne
Kames B.
Ettrick Bay
St Colmac
Port Lamont
Windy Hill
Glen More
Ardentraive
Colintraive
Algaltraig
Loch Striven
Sound of Bute
Eilean Garbh
West Tarbert Bay
East Tarbert Bay
Tarbert
Gigha Island
Druimyeon More
Ardminish
Ardminish Bay
Achamore Gardens
Sound of Gigha
Gigalum Island
Cara Island
Balochroy
Crossaig Glen
Crossaig
Loch Garasdale
Cruach Mhic Gougan
Rhunahaorine
Tayinloan
Killean
Beacharr
Cnoc nan Craobh
Beinn Bhreac
Cruach Mhic-an-t-Saoir
Cruach nan Gabhar
Carradale Water
Cour Bay
Cour
Grogport
Brackley
Muasdale
Clachaig Water
Kintyre
Kilbrannan Sound
Carradale
Port Righ
Carradale Pt.
Carradale Bay
Amod
Belloch
Barr Water
Beinn Bhreac
Bridgend
Torrisdale-Square
Beinn an Tuirc
Glenacardoch Pt.
Glenbarr
Clan Macalister Centre
Cleongart
Bellochantuy Bay
Bellochantuy
Killocraw
Saddell Glen
Saddell
Saddell Abbey
A'Chruach
Saddell Bay
Lussa Loch
Tangy Loch
Sgreadan Hill
Ugadale
Skeroblingarry
Westport
Kilchenzie
Glenlussa Water
Peninver
Black Bay
Ardnacross Bay
West Darlochan
Kilmichael
Low Smerby
Machrihanish Bay
Campbeltown
Campbeltown Heritage Centre
Machrihanish
Trodigal
Campbeltown Loch
Island Davaar
Davaar Island Cave Painting
Drumlemble
Stewarton
Campbeltown Buckhouse
Kilkerran
Knocknaha
Kildalloig
Ardrossan (May-Sept)
Earadale Pt.
Beinn Ghuilean
Achinhoan Hd.
The Slate
Cnoc Moy
Woodbank
Feochaig
Rubh'a' Mharaiche
Glen Breackerie
Cnoc Odhar
Conie Glen
Johnston's Pt.
North Carrine
Keprigan
Strone Glen
Machariooch
Polliwilline Bay
Southend
Carskiey
Brunerican Bay
Cove Pt.
Mull of Kintyre
Port Mean
Rubha Chlachan
Sheep I.
Sanda Island
Cock of Arran
Lochranza Castle
Lochranza
Loch Ranza
Millstone Pt.
Catacol Bay
Catacol
Isle of Arran Distillery
Meall nan Damh
Thundergay
Sannox
Sannox Bay
Glen Sannox
North
Pirnmill
Loch Tanna
Cir Mhòr
Beinn Bharrain
Whitefarland
Corrie
Beinn Tarsuinn
Goat Fell
Imachar
Isle of Arran
Brodick
Brodick Castle
Ardrossan
Glen Rosa
Glen Iorsa
Dougarie
Brodick Bay
Isle of Arran Heritage Museum
Strathwhillan
Machrie Water
Auchagallon
Glenloig
A'Chruach
Glen Cloy
Machrie Bay
Clauchlands Pt.
Tormore
Machrie Moor Standing Stones
King's Cave
Balmichael
Blairbeg
Margnaheglish
Lamlash
Lamlash Bay
Holy Island
Cordon
Drumadoon Pt.
Torbeg
Shiskine
Blackwaterfoot
Drumadoon Bay
Kilpatrick
Kilpatrick Dun
Tighvein
Kingscross Pt.
Auchencairn
Kingscross
Knockenkelly
Whiting Bay
North Kiscadale
South Kiscadale
Largymore
Glenashdale Falls
Sliddery Water
Glenree
Brown Hd.
Carn Ban
Corriecravie
Kilmory Water
Largybeg
Dippin
Dippin Head
Sliddery
Lagg
Levencorroch
Kilmory
Torrylinn Cairn
Bennan
Bennan Hd.
Kildonan
Sound of Pladda
Pladda
A83
A846
A886
A8003
A844
A841
B8024
B8001
B842
B843
B8000
B880
B875
B878
B881
144
145

ARDMEANACH
Killiemore House
Aird of Kinloch
Kilfinichen Bay
THE BURG
LOCH SCRIDAIN
Pennycross
Torrans
BROLASS
Loch Airdeglais
BEN BUIE 717
698 CREACH BEINN
Kinlochspelve
Loch Spelve
Croggan
Rubha nan Sailthean
Bach I.
Ardmore
Rubha Seanach
Loch Fuaron
Lochbuie
Loch Uisg
Barachandroman
503 BEINN NA CROISE
Leidle
Carsaig
Loch Buie
405 DRUIM FADA
Laggan Deer Forest
LORD LOVAT'S CAVE
Rubha Dubh
Carsaig Bay
376 CRUACHAN MIN
Eilean Annraidh
MACLEAN'S CROSS
IONA ABBEY AND CATHEDRAL
Rubha nan Cearc
HERITAGE CENTRE
Iona
Beile Mor
Fionnphort
Kintra
ST COLUMBA EXHIBITION & WELCOME CENTRE
Aridhglas
Loch na Lathaich
Eorabus
Fidden
Tiraghoil
A849
Bunessan
Lee
Loch Assapol
Sound of Iona
Erraid
ROSS OF MULL
Ardalanish
Uisken
Scoor
Ardchiavaig
CARSAIG ARCHES
Malcolm's Pt.
Rubha nam Braithrean
Eilean a'Chalmain
Rubh Ardalanish
Frank Lockwood's Island
Insh I.
Sound of Insh
CLACHAN BRIDGE
Clachan-Seil
Clachan
Seil
AN CALA GARDENS
Easdale
EASDALE ISLAND FOLK MUSEUM
B844
Balvicar
Dubh-fheith
Cuan
Cullipool
Torsa
Kilchoan
Seil Sound
Luing
Achafolla
ARDUAINE GARDEN
Arduaine
Toberonochy
Craobh Haven
Shuna
Shuna Sound
Lunga
Shuna Pt.
Sound of Luing
F I R T H   O F   L O R N
Torran Rocks
NM
Garbh Eileach
Garvellachs
SCARBA, LUNGA AND THE GARVELLACHS
Eilean Dubh Mor
Eileach an Naoimh
OBAN
Lunga
CRUACH SCARBA 449
Scarba
Rubha Aird Luing
Gulf of Corryvreckan
B8002
Aird
Rèisa an t-Sruith
Sound of Craignish
Craignish Pt.
Island Macaskin
Rubh'a'Geadha
Balnahard
Kiloran Bay
KILORAN GARDENS
Kiloran
Kilchattan
B8086
B8087
COLONSAY
Scalasaig
Loch Staosnaig
B8085
Garvard
Rubha Dubh
PRIORY
Dubh Eilean
Oronsay
Eilean nan Ron
Kinuachdrachd
296 CRUACH NA SEILCHEIG
Kinuachdrachd Harbour
Glengarrisdale Bay
Glendebadel Bay
365 BEN GARRISDALE
Loch Crinan
Crinan
Kilmahumaig
B841
Bellanoch
Corpach Bay
Lealt Burn
Lussa
Lealt
467 BEINN BHREAC
Gallachoille
KNAPDALE
Carsaig
Tayvallich
Shian Bay
453 RAINBERG MOR
Ardlussa
Ardlussa Bay
Gleann Aoistail
Inverlussa
Lussagiven
Loch Righ Mòr
Achanamara
Kilmichael of Inverlussa
318
A846
Barrahormid
B8025
TAYNISH
Taynish
Loch Sween
486 CRUACH LUSACH
Rubh'an t-Sàilein
(Summer Only)
Tarbert
KEILLS CHAPEL
Dunrostan
Loch Tarbert
Rubha Lang-aoinidh
Keillmore
New Ulva
CASTLE SWEEN
Rubha a'Mhail
Rubha Bholsa
Lagg
Loch na Cille
Island of Danna
Lochead
439
Loch an Aircill
Loch Lesgamaill
241 ST COLUMBA'S CAVE
Achahoish
364 SGARBH BREAC
Nave Island
Ardnave Pt.
JURA
785
755
PAPS OF JURA
Eilean Mòr
ST CORMAC'S CHAPEL
CHAPEL
Kilmory
Ellary
Clachbreck
Kilmory Bay
Loch a Chnuic Bhric
JURA FOREST
Corran
An Dùnan
Baile Boidheach
Gortantaoid
Bunnahabhain
BUNNAHABHAIN DISTILLERY
316
Ardnave
Knockrome
Lowlandman's Bay
Ormsary
Killinallan
Leargybreck
Gleann Astaile
Pt. of Knap
Loch Caolisport
Loch Gruinart
Caol Ila
CAOL ILA DISTILLERY
Port Askaig
Feolin Ferry
561
Loch na Mile
Druimdrishaig
Leckgruinart
FINLAGGAN CENTRE
Loch Finlaggan
Keills
Keils
Small Isles
305
Loch nan Torran
LOCH GRUINART NATURE RESERVE VISITORS CENTRE
Craighouse
ISLE OF JURA DISTILLERY
Miller's Bay
Aoradh
B8017
Craigens
Loch Cam
Ballygrant
Loch Ballygrant
Gleann Ullibh
342 BRAT BHEINN
Cretshengan
Kilmeny
CRUACH LAGAIN 264
Coulaghailtro
ISLAY
142
NR
Kilberry Hd.
SCULPTURED STONES
Kilberry
B8024
A847
B8018
Blackrock
Redhouses
Daill
267 BEINN DUBH
Cabrach
Rubha na Tràille
Brosdale I.
Am Fraoch Eilean
Sound of Islay
DUN
Bridgend
Carse Ho.
Dunmore
Loch Indaal
Bowmore
BOWMORE ROUND CHURCH
A846
Mulindry
McArthur's Hd.
Loch Stornoway
Ardpatrick
Gartnagrenach
Ardpatrick Ho.
West Loch Tarbert
ISLAY
Port Charlotte
Kilennan
Laggan
Laggan Pt.
471 BEINN BHAN
491 BEINN BHEIGEIR
Carraig Mhòr
Portachoillan
Ardpatrick Pt.
Eilean Traighe
A83
Ronachan Pt.
Clachan
Loch Ciaran
Scale 1:265 000
(approx 4 miles to 1 inch)
0 1 2 3 4 5 6 miles
0 1 2 3 4 5 6 7 8 9 10 km
Ardtalla
Loch Beinn Uraraidh
Claggain Bay
143
Eilean Garbh
West Tarbert Bay
East Tarbert Bay
PORT ELLEN
Kintour
Ardmore Pt.
KILDALTON CHURCH
Gigha Island
Tarbert
Balochroy
Loch Garasdale
146
124

Argyll and Bute
Inverclyde
LOCH LOMOND AND THE TROSSACHS NATIONAL PARK
ARGYLL FOREST PARK
MUIRSHIEL REGIONAL PARK
NN
NS
Kerrera
Oban
Balliemore
Glenamachrie
Glen Lonan
Gallanach
Kilbride
Kilmore
Am Buth
Barran
Loch Nell
Glen Feochan
Loch Feochan
Glenfeochan House Gardens
Kilninver
Barochreal
Glen Euchar
Musdale
Bragleenmore
Loch Scamadale
Braes of Lorn
Blaran
Loch Tralaig
Melfort
Ardanstur
Kilmelford
Glenmore
Kames
Lagalochan
Garraron
Barravullin
Kintraw
Torran
Arichamish
Ardfern
Ford
Ederline
Finchairn
Finchairn Castle
Eilean Righ
Carnassarie Castle
Loch Gaineamhach
Kilmartin
Kilmartin House Museum
Slockavullin
Poltalloch
Glebe Cairn
Dun Dubh
Kilmichael Glassary
Bridgend
Moine Mhor
Dunadd Fort
Rock Markings
Cairnbaan
Cup and Ring Marks
Lochgilphead
Kilmory Castle Gardens
Kilmory Woodland Park
Ardrishaig
Loch Gilp
Castleton
Achnaba
Otter Ferry
Ballimore
Achabraid
Inverneill
Auchnaha
Kilfinan
Kilfinan Bay
Drum
Melldalloch
Erines
Auchalick Bay
Ardmarnock Bay
Barmore I.
Tarbert
East Loch Tarbert
West Tarbert
Barfad
Glenan Bay
Portavadie
Millhouse
Blair's Ferry
Corranbuie
Torinturk
Rhu
Kennacraig
Redhouse
Whitehouse
Kilchamaig
Glenreasdell Mains
Skipness
Skipness Castle
Skipness Pt.
Skipness Bay
Claonaig
Claonaig Bay
Crossaig Glen
Crossaig
Cock of Arran
Lochranza
Loch Ranza
Garroch Hd.
Inchmarnock
Ardscalpsie Pt.
Sound of Bute
Rubha Leathan
Ardlamont Pt.
Ardlamont Ho.
Kilbride Bay
Asgog Bay
Ettrick Bay
Kames
Auchenlochan
Tighnabruaich
Port Driseach
Kyles of Bute
Island of Bute
Colintraive
Ardentraive
Algaltraig
Port Bannatyne
Kames B.
St Colmac
Rothesay
Rothesay Castle
Rothesay Bay
Craigmore
Montford
Ardencraig Gardens
Victorian Fernery
Ascog
Kerrycroy
Scoulag
Mount Stuart House and Garden
Straad
Loch Fad
Loch Quien
Scalpsie
Scalpsie Bay
Stravanan Bay
Kingarth
Kilchattan Bay
St Blane's Chapel
Ardyne Pt.
Toward Pt.
Toward
Port Lamont
Loch Striven
Inverchaolain
Glenstriven
Corlarach Forest
Innellan
Wave Whisper Gallery
Newton Park
Bullwood
Highland Mary's Statue
Cloch Pt.
Lunderston Bay
Dunoon
Kirn
Hunter's Quay
St John's Church
Sandbank
Ardnadam
Holy Loch
Strone
Strone Pt.
Kilmun
Kilmun Arboretum
Blairmore
Ardbeg
Dalinlongart
Invereck
Clachaig
Glen Lean
Glen Kin
Benmore
Benmore Botanic Garden
Uig
Glen Massan
Glenmassan
Loch Tarsan
Balliemore
Craigendive
Auchenbreck
Loch Riddon
Glendaruel
Glendaruel Forest
Clachan of Glendaruel
Kilmodan Sculptured Stones
Conchra
Dunans
Lephinchapel
Lephinmore
Strathlachlan Forest
Caol Ghleann
Largiemore
Carrick
Port Ann
Asknish
Lochgair
Loch Glashan
Lachlan Bay
Lachlan Castle
Garbhallt
Tullochgorm
Minard
Crarae
Crarae Glen Gardens
Furnace
Newton
Glen Sluain
Strachur
Strachur Bay
Clachan Strachur
Creggans
Auchindrain
Auchindrain Open Air Museum
Loch Leacann
Eredine Forest
Dalchenna
Inveraray
Inveraray Jail
Inveraray Castle
Maritime Museum
Newtown
Bell Tower
Ardkinglas Woodland Garden
Cairndow
Drishaig
Clachan
Dubh Loch
Glen Aray
Tullich
Glen Shira
Lochan Shira
Loch Stron Mor
Kilblaan Burn
Brannie Burn
Glen Fyne
Glenfyne Lodge
Eredine
Durran
Kilmaha
Inverliever Forest
Portinnisherrich
Ardchonnell Castle
Dalavich
Blarghour
Loch Avich
Lochavich Ho
Kilmun
Drissaig
Ballimeanoch
Inverinan
South Port
Portsonachan
Cladich
North Port
Annat
Kilchrenan
Loch Nant
Glen Nant
Pass of Brander
Falls of Cruachan
Cruachan Reservoir
Cruachan Dam Visitor Centre
Loch Tromlee
Ardanaiseig Gardens
Ardanaiseig
Innis Chonain
Inishail
Inishail Chapel
Teatle Water
Lochawe
Kilchurn Castle
Dalmally
McIntyre Monument
Strath of Orchy
Inverlochy
Achnafalnich
Tyndrum
Ben Lui
Beinn Dubhchraig
Meall nan Tighearn
Allt Fionn Ghlinne
Dubh Eas
Inverarnan
Troisgeach
Ardlui
Maol Breac
Ben Vorlich
Loch Sloy
Inveruglas
Rob Roy
Beinn Ime
Succoth
Tarbet
Arrochar
Ardgartan
Glen Croe
Stuckgowan
Ardmay
Craig Rostan
Rest and Be Thankful
Glen Kinglas
Ardno
St Catherine's
Hell's Glen
Monevechadan
Beinn an Lochain
Cruach nan Capull
Ben Donich
Lochgoilhead
Drimsynie
Corrow
Blairlomond
Cnoc Coinnich
Ardgoil Forest
The Saddle
Doune Hill
Glen Douglas
Inverbeg
Inverbeg Gallery
Glenmallan
Beinn Eich
Edentaggart
Glen Luss
Invernoaden
Glenbranter
Glenbranter Forest
Beinn Bheula
Carrick Castle
Loch Eck
Whistlefield
Beinn Bheag
Bernice
Beinn Mhor
Creachan Mor
Beinn Ruadh
Glenfinart Deer Farm
Glen Finart
Ardentinny
Loch Long
Portincaple
Garelochhead
Beinn Chaorach
Aldochlay
Faslane Port
Strone House Gardens
Coulport
Rahane
Gare Loch
Shandon
Ardpeaton
Clynder
Rhu
Rosneath
Cove
Kilcreggan
Portkil
Rosneath Pt.
Glenarn Garden
The Hill House
Helensburgh
Craigendoran
Bannachra Muir
Duchlage
Blairglas
Colgrain
Linn Botanic Gardens
Gourock
Ashton
Greenock
Greenock West
Midton
McLean Museum & Art Gall.
HM Customs & Excise Museum & Exhibition
Levan
Larkfield
Braeside
Ravenscraig
Central
Newark Castle
Port Glasgow
Devol
Mid Auchinlech
Loch Thom
Gryfe Resrs.
Strathgryfe
Inverkip
Shielhill
Garvock
Wemyss Bay
Upper Skelmorlie
Skelmorlie
Creuch Hill
Duchal Moor
Meigle
Noddsdale Water
Queenside Muir
Hill of Stake
Waterhead Moor
Mistylaw Muir
Routenburn
Largs
Largs Bay
Vikingar!
Old Kirk
Tomont End
Great Cumbrae Island
Christian Heritage Museum
Downcraig Ferry
Millport
Museum of the Cumbraes
Fairlie
Fairlie Roads
Kelburn Country Centre
Muirhead Reservoir
Camphill Reservoir
Knockendon Reservoir
Kaim Hill
Irish Law
Ladyland Moor
Lochwinnoch
Kilbirnie
Glengarnock
Beith
Longbar
The Den
Rye Water
Hunterston Power Station Visitor Centre
The Tan
Little Cumbrae Island
A83
A85
A815
A819
A82
A78
A8
A886
B8000
B840
B828
B839
B836
B842
B8001
B8024
B845
B844
124
125
126
118
143

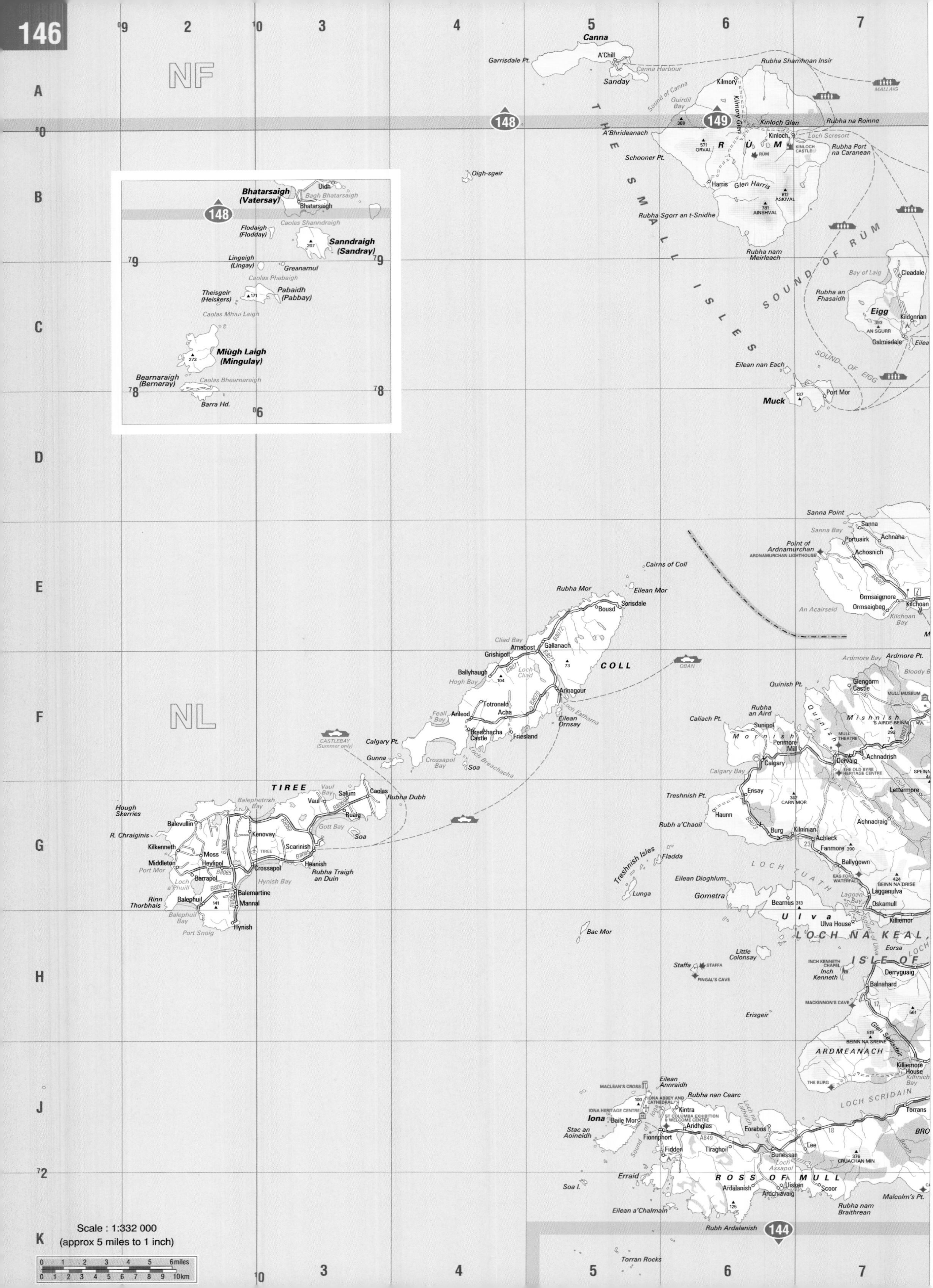
NF
NL
Canna
A'Chill
Garrisdale Pt.
Canna Harbour
Sanday
Sound of Canna
Guirdil Bay
Kilmory
Kilmory Glen
Rubha Shamhnan Insir
MALLAIG
Kinloch Glen
Rubha na Roinne
A'Bhrideanach
ORVAL
RÙM
Kinloch
Loch Scresort
KINLOCH CASTLE
Rubha Port na Caranean
Schooner Pt.
Harris
Glen Harris
ASKIVAL
AINSHVAL
Rubha Sgorr an t-Snidhe
Rubha nam Meirleach
THE SMALL ISLES
SOUND OF RÙM
Oigh-sgeir
Bay of Laig
Cleadale
Rubha an Fhasaidh
Eigg
AN SGURR
Kildonnan
Galmisdale
SOUND OF EIGG
Eilean nan Each
Muck
Port Mor
Bhatarsaigh (Vatersay)
Uidh
Bagh Bhatarsaigh
Bhatarsaigh
Caolas Shanndraigh
Flodaigh (Flodday)
Sanndraigh (Sandray)
Lingeigh (Lingay)
Greanamul
Caolas Phabaigh
Theisgeir (Heiskers)
Pabaidh (Pabbay)
Caolas Mhiui Laigh
Miùgh Laigh (Mingulay)
Bearnaraigh (Berneray)
Caolas Bhearnaraigh
Barra Hd.
Sanna Point
Sanna Bay
Sanna
Achnaha
Portuairk
Point of Ardnamurchan
ARDNAMURCHAN LIGHTHOUSE
Achosnich
Ormsaigmore
Ormsaigbeg
Kilchoan
Kilchoan Bay
An Acairseid
Cairns of Coll
Eilean Mor
Rubha Mor
Sorisdale
Bousd
Cliad Bay
Arnabost
Grishipoll
Gallanach
Ballyhaugh
Hogh Bay
Loch Cliad
COLL
OBAN
Arinagour
Totronald
Acha
Feall Bay
Arileod
Loch Eatharna
Eilean Ornsay
Breachacha Castle
Friesland
CASTLEBAY (Summer only)
Calgary Pt.
Gunna
Crossapol Bay
Soa
Loch Breachacha
TIREE
Vaul Bay
Salum
Caolas
Vaul
Rubha Dubh
Balephetrish Bay
Hough Skerries
Balevullin
Ruaig
Gott Bay
Soa
R. Chraiginis
Kenovay
Kilkenneth
Scarinish
Moss
Middleton
Heylipol
Crossapol
Heanish
Port Mor
Barrapol
Hynish Bay
Rubha Traigh an Duin
Loch a'Phuill
Balemartine
Rinn Thorbhais
Balephuil
Mannal
Balephuil Bay
Port Snoig
Hynish
Ardmore Bay
Ardmore Pt.
Bloody B
Quinish Pt.
Glengorm Castle
MULL MUSEUM
Rubha an Aird
Caliach Pt.
Sunipol
Mishnish
Quinish
Mornish
Penmore Mill
MULL THEATRE
Dervaig
Achnadrish
Calgary
Calgary Bay
THE OLD BYRE HERITAGE CENTRE
Treshnish Pt.
Ensay
CARN MOR
Lettermore
Haunn
Bellart
Achnacraig
Rubh a'Chaoil
Burg
Kilninian
Achleck
Fanmore
Treshnish Isles
Fladda
Ballygown
LOCH TUATH
EAS FORS WATERFALL
BEINN NA DRISE
Eilean Dioghlum
Lunga
Gometra
Laggan Bay
Lagganulva
Beamus
Oskamull
Ulva
Ulva House
Killiemor
Bac Mor
LOCH NA KEAL
Eorsa
Little Colonsay
INCH KENNETH CHAPEL
Inch Kenneth
ISLE OF
Staffa
STAFFA
FINGAL'S CAVE
Derryguaig
Balnahard
MACKINNON'S CAVE
Erisgeir
Glen Seilisdeir
BEINN NA SREINE
ARDMEANACH
Killiemore House
Kilfinichen Bay
THE BURG
Eilean Annraidh
MACLEAN'S CROSS
IONA ABBEY AND CATHEDRAL
Rubha nan Cearc
Loch na Lathaich
IONA HERITAGE CENTRE
Kintra
LOCH SCRIDAIN
Torrans
Iona
Baile Mor
ST COLUMBA EXHIBITION & WELCOME CENTRE
Ardhglas
Eorabus
Stac an Aoineidh
Fionnphort
Sound of Iona
Fidden
Tiraghoil
Bunessan
Lee
CRUACHAN MIN
Loch Assapol
Erraid
ROSS OF MULL
Soa I.
Ardalanish
Uisken
Ardchiavaig
Scoor
Malcolm's Pt.
Rubha nam Braithrean
Eilean a'Chalmain
Rubh Ardalanish
Torran Rocks
148
149
144
Scale : 1:332 000
(approx 5 miles to 1 inch)
0 1 2 3 4 5 6 miles
0 1 2 3 4 5 6 7 8 9 10 km

NG
NH
NM
NN
SOUND OF SLEAT
KNOYDART
Highland
Argyll and Bute
ISLAND OF MULL
MORAR, MOIDART AND ARDNAMURCHAN
ARDNAMURCHAN
MORVERN
SUNART
LOCH SHIEL
MOIDART
SOUND OF ARISAIG
SOUND OF MULL
LOCH LINNHE
LYNN OF LORN
FIRTH OF LORN
LOCH NEVIS
LOCH MORAR
LOCH ARKAIG
LOCH QUOICH
LOCH EIL
LOCH SUNART
LOCH ETIVE
LOCH AWE
Mallaig
Fort William
Oban
Tobermory
Craignure
Arisaig
Glenfinnan
Lochailort
Acharacle
Strontian
Salen
Lochaline
Corpach
Ballachulish
Glencoe
Kentallen
Appin
Connel
Taynuilt
Kilmore
Kilninver
Seil
Easdale
Luing
Lismore
Kerrera
Dalmally
Lochawe
Inveraray
Ben Nevis
A830
A82
A828
A861
A884
A849
A85
A816
149
136
130
124
8
9
10
11
12
13
14
A
B
C
D
E
F
G
H
J
K

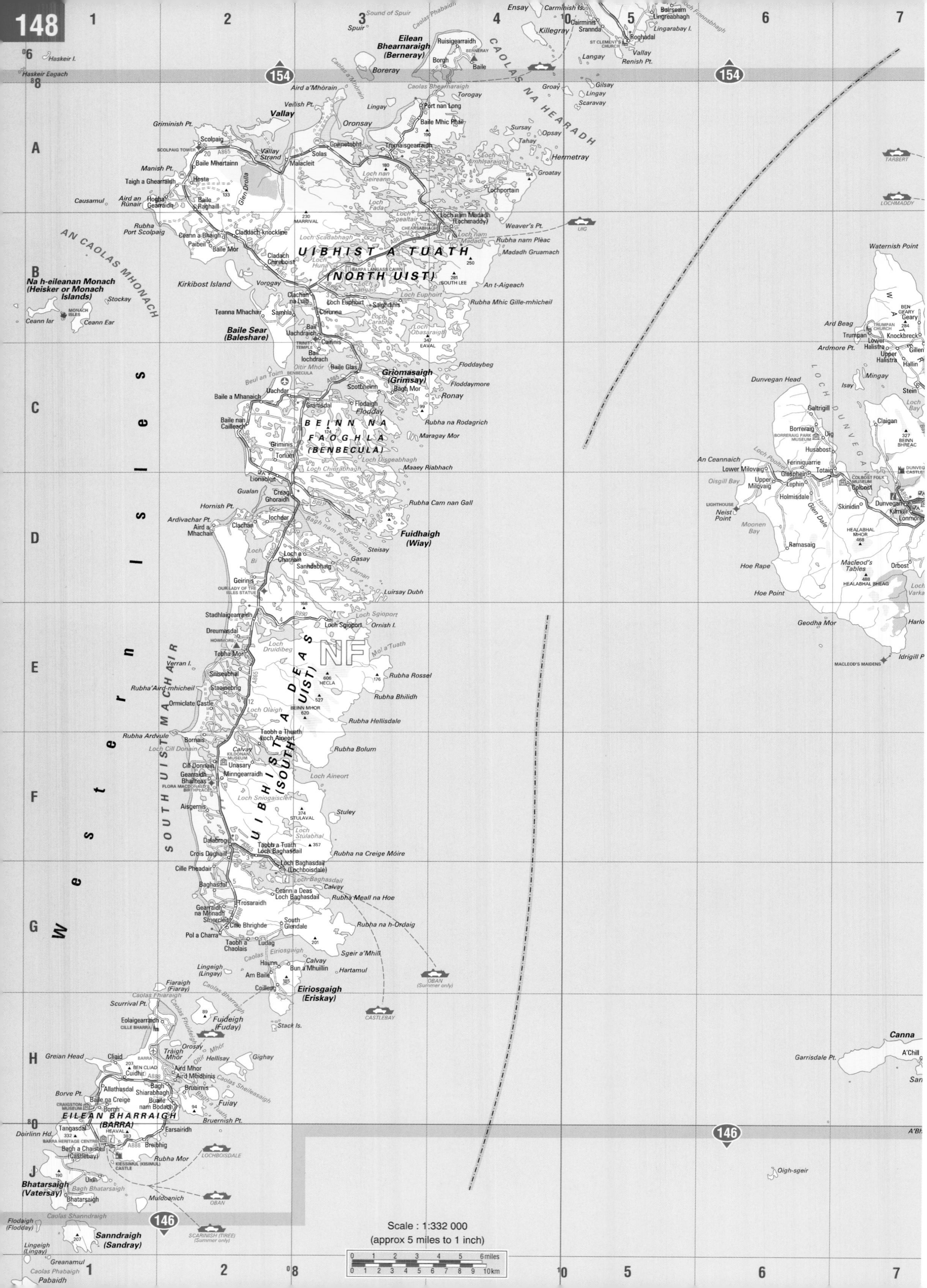
Sound of Spuir
Spuir
Eilean Bhearnaraigh (Berneray)
Ruisigearraidh
Borgh
Baile
Boreray
CAOLAS NA HEARADH
Ensay
Carminish Is.
Killegray
Cairminis
Srannda
Roghadal
Lingarabay I.
Langay
Renish Pt.
Vallay
Gilsay
Lingay
Scaravay
Groay
Haskeir I.
Haskeir Eagach
154
Aird a'Mhòrain
Veilish Pt.
Vallay
Oronsay
Lingay
Port nan Long
Baile Mhic Phàil
Sursay
Tahay
Opsay
Hermetray
Groatay
Griminish Pt.
Scolpaig
Vallay Strand
Solas
Malacleit
Greinetobht
Trumaisgearraidh
Baile Mhartainn
Manish Pt.
Hosta
Taigh a Ghearraidh
Glen Drolla
Loch nan Geireann
Lochportain
Causamul
Aird an Rùnair
Hogha Gearraidh
Baile Raghaill
Loch Fada
MARRIVAL
Loch nam Madadh (Lochmaddy)
Weaver's Pt.
Rubha nam Plèac
Madadh Gruamach
UIG
Rubha Port Scolpaig
Ceann a Bhàigh
Claddach-knockline
Paibeil
Baile Mor
Loch Scadabhagh
AN CAOLAS MHONACH
UIBHIST A TUATH (NORTH UIST)
Cladach Chireboist
Loch Hunda
BARPA LANGASS CAIRN
SOUTH LEE
Na h-eileanan Monach (Heisker or Monach Islands)
Stockay
Kirkibost Island
Vorogay
An t-Aigeach
Ceann Iar
Ceann Ear
Clachan na Luib
Loch Euphort
Saighdinis
Rubha Mhic Gille-mhicheil
Teanna Mhachair
Samhla
Corùnna
Baile Sear (Baleshare)
Uachdraich
Cairinis
EAVAL
TRINITY TEMPLE
Baile Iochdrach
Baile Glas
Oitir Mhòr
Beul an Toim
Griomasaigh (Grimsay)
Floddaybeg
Floddaymore
Bagh Mor
Ronay
Uachdar
Baile a Mhanaich
Gramsdal
Flodaigh
Flodday
Baile nan Cailleach
BEINN NA FAOGHLA (BENBECULA)
Rubha na Rodagrich
Maragay Mor
Griminis
Torlum
Loch Uisgeabhagh
Loch Chiarabhagh
Maaey Riabhach
Lionacleit
Guaelan
Creag Ghoraidh
Rubha Cam nan Gall
Hornish Pt.
Ardivachar Pt.
Aird a Mhachair
Iochdar
Clachan
Fuidhaigh (Wiay)
Bagh nam Faoileann
Steisay
Loch Bi
Loch a Charnain
Sanndabhaig
Gasay
Loch Carnan
Geirinis
OUR LADY OF THE ISLES STATUE
Luirsay Dubh
Western Isles
Stadhlaigearraidh
Loch Sgioport
Ornish I.
Dreumasdal
HOWMORE
Loch Druidibeg
NF
Mol a'Tuath
Tobha Mor
Verran I.
Sniseabhal
SOUTH UIST MACHAIR
HECLA
Rubha Rossel
Rubha'Aird-mhicheil
Staoinebrig
UIBHIST A DEAS (SOUTH UIST)
Rubha Bhilidh
Ormiclate Castle
Loch Olaigh
BEINN MHOR
Rubha Hellisdale
Taobh a Tuath Loch Aineort
Rubha Ardvule
Bornais
Loch Cill Donain
Calvay
KILDONAN MUSEUM
Rubha Bolum
Cill Donnain
Unasary
Gearraidh Bhailteas
Minngearraidh
Loch Aineort
FLORA MACDONALD'S BIRTHPLACE
Loch Sniogaiscleit
Aisgernis
STULAVAL
Stuley
Loch Stùlabhal
Dalabrog
Taobh a Tuath Loch Baghasdail
Crois Dughaill
Rubha na Creige Móire
Cille Pheadair
Loch Baghasdail (Lochboisdale)
Loch Baghasdail
Baghasdal
Calvay
Ceann a Deas Loch Baghasdail
Rubha Meall na Hoe
Gearraidh na Mònadh
Trosaraidh
Smercleit
Cille Bhrighde
South Glendale
Rubha na h-Ordaig
Pol a Charra
Taobh a Chaolais
Ludag
Caolas Eiriosgaigh
Sgeir a'Mhill
Lingeigh (Lingay)
Haunn
Am Baile
Bun a'Mhuillin
Calvay
Hartamul
OBAN (Summer only)
Fiaraigh (Fiaray)
Caolas Fhiaraigh
Coilleag
Eiriosgaigh (Eriskay)
Caolas Bharraigh
Scurrival Pt.
CASTLEBAY
Fuideigh (Fuday)
Eolaigearraidh
CILLE BHARRA
Stack Is.
Orosay
Traigh Mhor
Oitir Mhòr
Hellisay
Gighay
Greian Head
Claid
BARRA
BEN CLIAD
Cuidhir
Aird Mhor
Aird Mhidhinis
Caolas Sheileasaigh
Borve Pt.
Allathasdal
Bagh Shiarabhagh
Bruairnis
Baile na Creige
Buaile nam Bodach
Fuiay
CRAIGSTON MUSEUM
Borgh
Bruernish Pt.
EILEAN BHARRAIGH (BARRA)
Doirlinn Hd.
Tangasdal
HEAVAL
Earsairidh
BARRA HERITAGE CENTRE
Bagh a Chaisteil (Castlebay)
Breibhig
KIESSIMUL (KISIMUL) CASTLE
Rubha Mor
LOCHBOISDALE
Bhatarsaigh (Vatersay)
Uidh
Bagh Bhatarsaigh
Bhatarsaigh
Muldoanich
OBAN
Caolas Shanndraigh
146
Flodaigh (Flodday)
Sanndraigh (Sandray)
SCARINISH (TIREE) (Summer only)
Lingeigh (Lingay)
Greanamul
Caolas Phabaigh
Pabaidh
Scale : 1:332 000
(approx 5 miles to 1 inch)
0 1 2 3 4 5 6 miles
0 1 2 3 4 5 6 7 8 9 10 km
TARBERT
LOCHMADDY
Waternish Point
Ard Beag
Trumpan
Knockbreck
Geary
Ardmore Pt.
Lower Halistra
Upper Halistra
Hallin
Gillen
Mingay
Dunvegan Head
Isay
Stein
LOCH DUNVEGAN
Galtrigill
Claigan
Borreraig
BORRERAIG PARK MUSEUM
Uig
BEINN BHREAC
Husabost
An Ceannaich
Loch Pooltiel
Lower Milovaig
Feriniquarrie
Totaig
Upper Milovaig
Glasphein
Oisgill Bay
Lephin
COLBOST FOLK MUSEUM
Colbost
DUNVEGAN CASTLE
Holmisdale
LIGHTHOUSE
Neist Point
Glen Dale
Skinidin
Dunvegan
Kilmuir
Lonmore
Moonen Bay
HEALABHAL MHOR
Ramasaig
Macleod's Tables
HEALABHAL BHEAG
Hoe Rape
Orbost
Hoe Point
Geodha Mor
MACLEOD'S MAIDENS
Idrigill Pt
Canna
A'Chill
Garrisdale Pt.
Oigh-sgeir

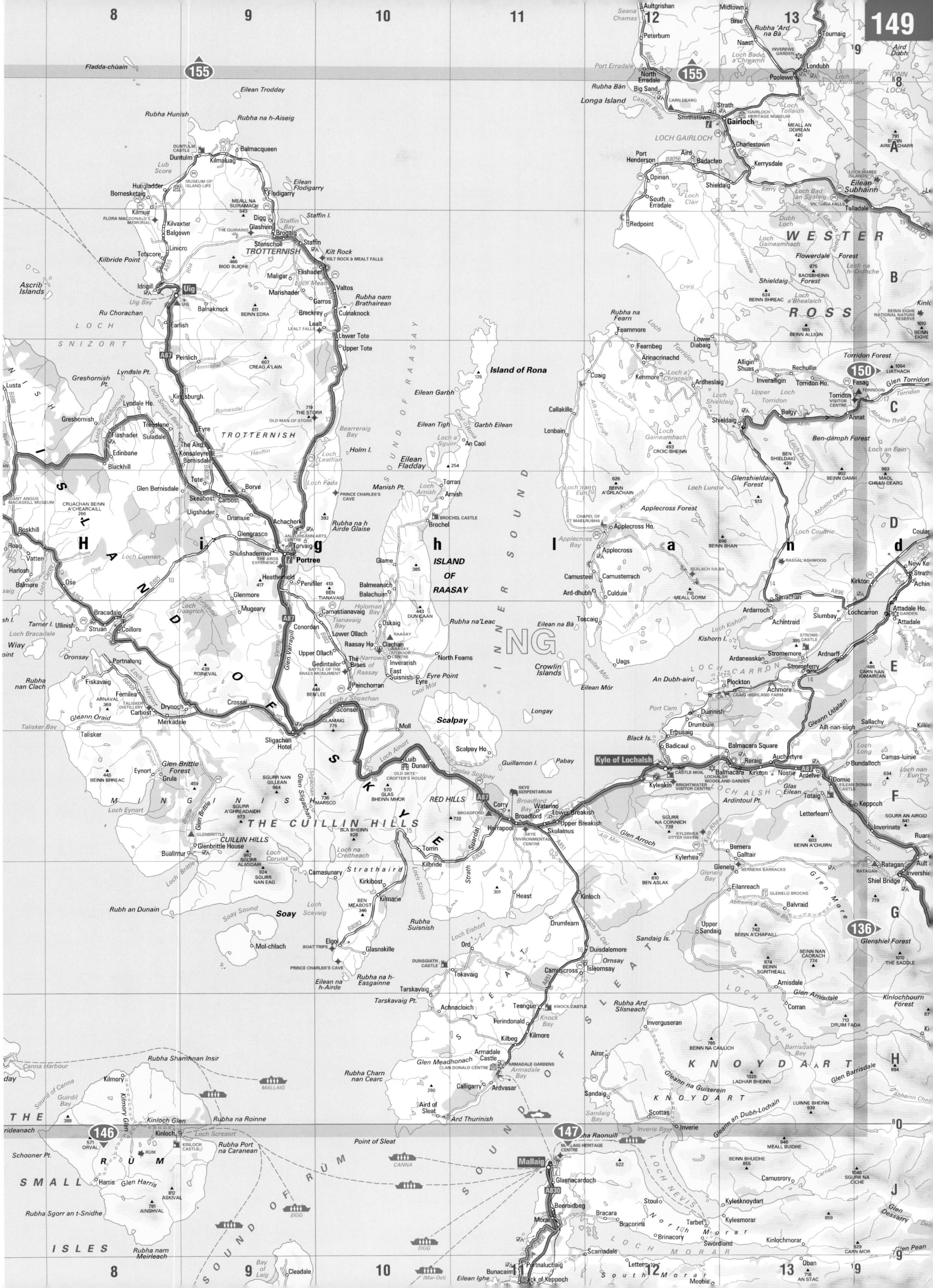
Fladda-chùain
Eilean Trodday
Rubha Hunish
Rubha na h-Aiseig
Duntulm
Kilmaluag
Balmacqueen
Lub Score
Hunglader
Borneskeitaig
Eilean Flodigarry
Flodigarry
Kilmuir
Digg
Kilvaxter
Glashvin
Brogaig
Staffin Bay
Staffin I.
Balgown
Staffin
Stenscholl
Kilt Rock
Linicro
TROTTERNISH
Totscore
Kilbride Point
Maligar
Elishader
Ascrib Islands
Idrigill
Uig
Uig Bay
Marishader
Valtos
Rubha nam Brathairean
Balnaknock
Garros
Ru Chorachan
Breckrey
Culnaknock
Earlish
Lealt
Lower Tote
Upper Tote
LOCH SNIZORT
Peinlich
Lyndale Pt.
Greshornish Pt.
Lusta
Kingsburgh
Lyndale Ho.
Greshornish
Treaslane
Suladale
Flashader
Eyre
TROTTERNISH
Edinbane
The Aird
Kensaleyre
Bernisdale
Blackhill
Holm I.
Tote
Borve
Glen Bernisdale
Skeabost
Carbost
Uigshader
Drumuie
Achachork
Prince Charles's Cave
Rubha na h Airde Glaise
Roskhill
Glengrasco
Roag
Vatten
Shulishadermor
Portree
Harlosh
Balmore
Ose
Heatherfield
Penifiler
Glenmore
Mugeary
Bracadale
Struan
Coillore
Ullinish
Tarner I.
Loch Bracadale
Wiay
Oronsay
Portnalong
Rubha nan Clach
Fiskavaig
Fernilea
Carbost
Drynoch
Crossal
Merkadale
Talisker Bay
Talisker
Gleann Oraid
Sligachan Hotel
Sconser
Glen Brittle Forest
Eynort
Grula
Loch Eynort
Glenbrittle House
CUILLIN HILLS
THE CUILLIN HILLS
Bualintur
Camasunary
Kirkibost
Kilmarie
Rubh an Dunain
Soay Sound
Soay
Loch Scavaig
Elgol
Glasnakille
Mol-chlach
Rubha na h-Easgainne
Eilean na h-Airde
Island of Rona
Eilean Garbh
Eilean Tigh
Garbh Eilean
An Caol
Eilean Fladday
Torran
Arnish
Brochel
ISLAND OF RAASAY
Manish Pt.
Glame
Balmeanach
Balachuirn
Camastianavaig
Conordan
Lower Ollach
Upper Ollach
Oskaig
Raasay Ho.
Clachan
Inverarish
East Suisnish
Eyre
Eyre Point
Gedintailor
The Braes
Peinchorran
North Fearns
Rubha na'Leac
SOUND OF RAASAY
INNER SOUND
Moll
Scalpay
Scalpay Ho.
Luib
Dunan
Loch Ainort
Guillamon I.
Pabay
RED HILLS
Corry
Waterloo
Broadford
Broadford Bay
Lower Breakish
Upper Breakish
Harrapool
Skulamus
Torrin
Kilbride
Strath Suardal
Heast
Kinloch
Drumfearn
Rubha Suisnish
Loch Eishort
Ord
Tokavaig
Tarskavaig
Tarskavaig Pt.
Achnacloich
Duisdalemore
Ornsay
Isleornsay
Camuscross
Teangue
Knock Bay
Ferindonald
Kilbeg
Kilmore
Rubha Ard Slisneach
Glen Meadhonach
Armadale Castle
Armadale Bay
Calligarry
Ardvasar
Aird of Sleat
Ard Thurinish
Point of Sleat
Rubha Charn nan Cearc
SLEAT
SOUND OF SLEAT
Kilmory
Canna Harbour
Sound of Canna
Guirdil Bay
Kinloch Glen
Kinloch
Loch Scresort
Rubha na Roinne
Rubha Port na Caranean
Schooner Pt.
RÙM
Harris
Glen Harris
Rubha Sgorr an t-Snidhe
Rubha nam Meirleach
SMALL ISLES
SOUND OF RÙM
Bay of Laig
Cleadale
Eilean Ighe
Mallaig
Glasnacardoch
Beoraidbeg
Morar
Bracara
Bracorina
Brinacory
Tarbet
Stoul
Kyleknoydart
Kylesmorar
Swordland
Kinlochmorar
North Morar
LOCH MORAR
LOCH NEVIS
Scamadale
Portnaluchaig
Back of Keppoch
Bunacaimb
Letterm
Meoble
Oban
Glen Pean
Inverie
Inverie Bay
Scottas
Sandaig
Airor
KNOYDART
Gleann na Guiserein
Gleann an Dubh-Lochain
Glen Barrisdale
Barrisdale Bay
LOCH HOURN
Inverguseran
Corran
Arnisdale
Glen Arnisdale
Kinlochhourn Forest
Sandaig Is.
Upper Sandaig
Eilanreach
Glenelg
Glenelg Bay
Balvraid
Glen More
Bernera
Galltair
Kylerhea
Glen Arroch
Kyleakin
Kyle of Lochalsh
Erbusaig
Badicaul
Balmacara Square
Balmacara
Reraig
Kirkton
Auchtertyre
Nostie
Ardelve
Dornie
Totaig
Letterfearn
LOCH ALSH
Ardintoul Pt.
Glas Eilean
Keppoch
Inverinate
Ratagan
Shiel Bridge
Glenshiel Forest
Loch Duich
Duirinish
Drumbuie
Plockton
Achmore
Port Cam
Black Is.
Sallachy
Allt-nan-sugh
Gleann Udalain
Camas-luinie
Bundalloch
Stromeferry
Stromemore
Ardnarff
Ardaneaskan
LOCH CARRON
An Dubh-aird
Kishorn I.
Eilean Mór
Crowlin Islands
Longay
Uags
Toscaig
Eilean na Bà
Ard-dhubh
Culduie
Camusteel
Camusterrach
Applecross
Applecross Ho.
Applecross Bay
Applecross Forest
Glenshieldaig Forest
Sanachan
Ardarroch
Achintraid
Loch Kishorn
Slumbay
Lochcarron
Kirkton
Attadale Ho.
Attadale
Strath
Achin
New Ke
Coulag
Callakille
Lonbain
Cuaig
Kenmore
Ardheslaig
Loch a' Chracaich
Shieldaig
Loch Shieldaig
Balgy
Annat
Torridon
Fasag
Glen Torridon
Torridon Forest
Ben-damph Forest
Upper Loch Torridon
Inveralligin
Alligin Shuas
Rechullin
Torridon Ho.
Loch Torridon
Fearnmore
Fearnbeg
Arinacrinachd
Lower Diabaig
Rubha na Fearn
Craig
Redpoint
South Erradale
Opinan
Port Henderson
Aird
Badachro
Charlestown
Kerrysdale
LOCH GAIRLOCH
Gairloch
Strath
Smithstown
Big Sand
North Erradale
Rubha Bàn
Longa Island
Port Erradale
Peterburn
Aultgrishan
Seana Chamas
Midtown
Brae
Naast
Rubha 'Ard na Bà
Tournaig
Poolewe
Londubh
Aird Dubh
LOCH MAREE
Eilean Subhainn
Talladale
Loch Clàir
Sheildaig
WESTER ROSS
Flowerdale Forest
Shieldaig Forest
Loch Gaineamhach
NG
Kyle Rhea
Mallaig
155
150
136
146
147
8
9
10
11
12
13

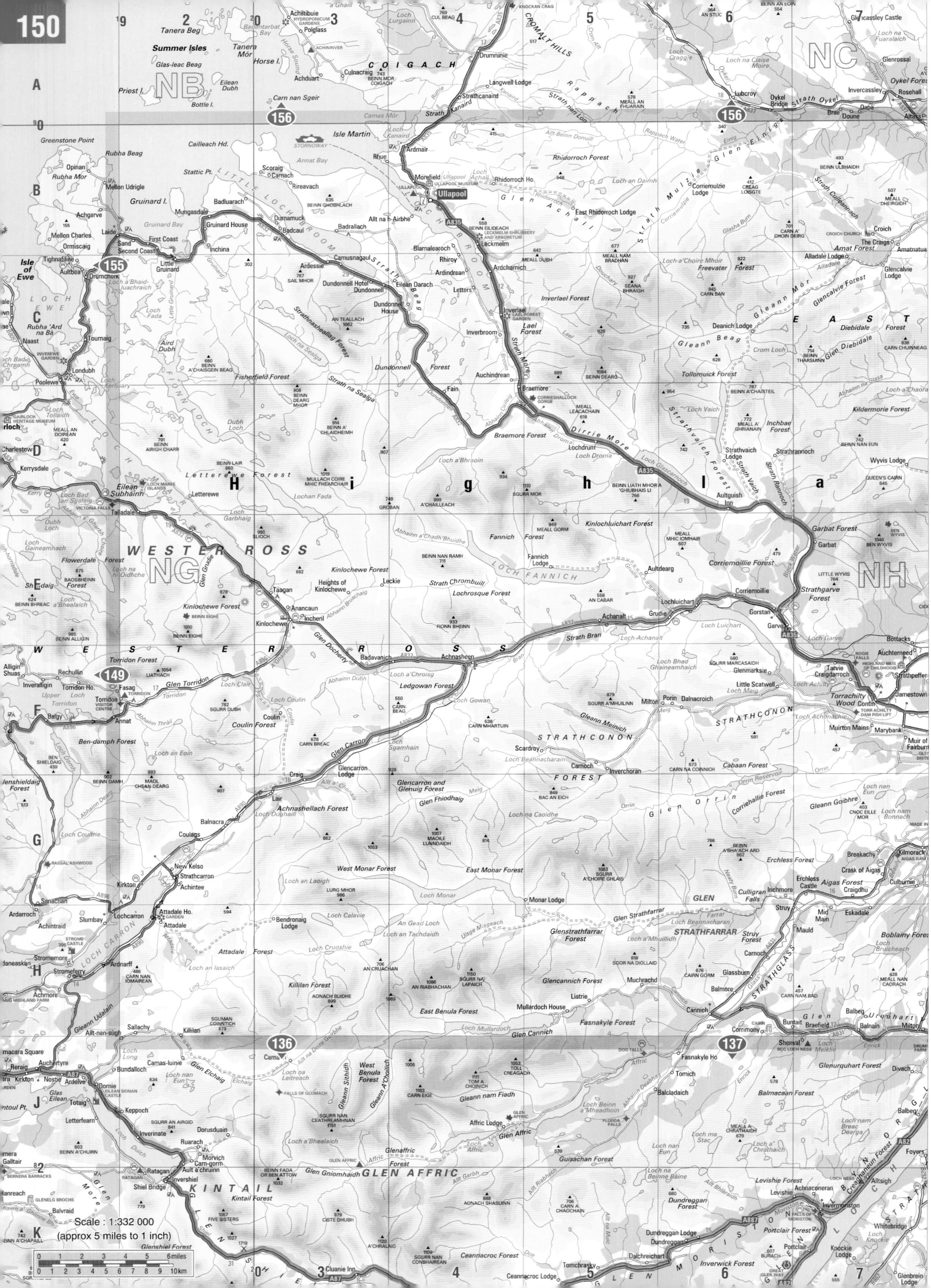
NB
NC
NG
NH
Summer Isles
Tanera Beg
Tanera Mór
Horse I.
Isle Martin
Priest I.
Bottle I.
Glas-leac Beag
Eilean Dubh
Achiltibuie
Polglass
Achduart
Culnacraig
COIGACH
CROMALT HILLS
Drumrunie
Strathcanaird
Strath Kanaird
Langwell Lodge
Rappach
Strath nan Lon
Loch Craggie
Lubcroy
Oykel Bridge
Strath Oykel
Invercassley
Rosehall
Altass
Doune
Glenrossal
Glencassley Castle
Greenstone Point
Rubha Beag
Opinan
Rubha Mor
Mellon Udrigle
Cailleach Hd.
Stattic Pt.
Scoraig
Carnach
Rireavach
Annat Bay
LITTLE LOCH BROOM
Ardmair
Rhue
Morefield
Ullapool
Rhidorroch Forest
Rhidorroch Ho.
Glen Achall
East Rhidorroch Lodge
Strath Mulzie
Corriemulzie Lodge
Glen Einig
Strath Cuileannach
Gruinard I.
Badluarach
Mungasdale
Gruinard Bay
Gruinard House
Achgarve
Mellon Charles
Laide
Sand
First Coast
Second Coast
Ormiscaig
Inchina
Dundonnell Hotel
Dundonnell
Camusnagaul
Strath Beag
Eilean Darach
Badrallach
Allt na h-Airbhe
LOCH BROOM
Leckmelm
Ardcharnich
Letters
Inverlael
Inverlael Forest
Lael Forest
Isle of Ewe
Tighnafiline
Aultbea
Drumchork
Loch Ewe
Rubha 'Ard na Bà
Naast
Tournaig
Londubh
Poolewe
Strathnasheallag Forest
Fisherfield Forest
Dundonnell Forest
Strath na Sealga
Fain
Braemore
Auchindrean
Inverbroom
Strath More
Braemore Forest
Dirrie More
Lochdrum
Loch Droma
Loch Glascarnoch
Amat Forest
Alladale Lodge
Freevater Forest
Deanich Lodge
Gleann Beag
Gleann Mór
Glencalvie Forest
Glencalvie Lodge
EAST
Diebidale
Glen Diebidale
Forest
Tollomuick Forest
Kildermorie Forest
Inchbae Forest
Strathvaich Lodge
Strathvaich Forest
Strath Vaich
Strathrannoch
Wyvis Lodge
Strath Rannoch
Aultguish Inn
Garbat Forest
Garbat
Highland
Letterewe Forest
Letterewe
Eilean Subhainn
Loch Maree
Kerrysdale
Charlestown
Talladale
Dubh Loch
Kinlochewe Forest
Kinlochewe
Heights of Kinlochewe
Leckie
Strath Chrombuill
Lochrosque Forest
Loch Fannich
Fannich Forest
Fannich Lodge
Kinlochluichart Forest
Aultdearg
Corriemoillie Forest
Corriemoillie
Lochluichart
Gorstan
Garve
Strathgarve Forest
WESTER ROSS
Flowerdale Forest
Shieldaig
Taagan
Anancaun
Incheril
Glen Docherty
Badavanich
Achnasheen
Achanalt
Grudie
Strath Bran
Loch Luichart
Loch Garve
Bottacks
Auchterneed
Strathpeffer
Tarvie
Craigdarroch
Glenmarksie
Little Scatwell
Jamestown
Torrachilty Wood
Contin
Marybank
Muirton Mains
Muir of Fairburn
Torridon Forest
Rechullin
Inveralligin
Torridon Ho.
Glen Torridon
Torridon
Fasag
Annat
Balgy
Loch Clair
Ledgowan Forest
Loch Coulin
Coulin
Coulin Forest
Ben-damph Forest
Milton
Porin
Dalnacroich
Gleann Meinich
STRATHCONON
STRATHCONON FOREST
Scardroy
Carnoch
Inverchoran
Cabaan Forest
Orrin Reservoir
Corriehallie Forest
Glen Orrin
Gleann Goibhre
Glen Carron
Glencarron Lodge
Glencarron and Glenuig Forest
Craig
Lair
Achnashellach Forest
Glen Fhiodhaig
Balnacra
Coulags
Loch Coultrie
New Kelso
Strathcarron
Achintee
Kirkton
West Monar Forest
East Monar Forest
Loch Monar
Monar Lodge
Erchless Forest
Breakachy
Crask of Aigas
Kilmorack
Erchless Castle
Aigas Forest
Inchmore
Craigdhu
Culburnie
Culligran Falls
GLEN STRATHFARRAR
Glen Strathfarrar
Glenstrathfarrar Forest
Struy
Struy Forest
Mid Main
Eskadale
Mauld
Boblainy Forest
Sanachan
Ardarroch
Achintraid
Slumbay
Lochcarron
Attadale Ho.
Attadale
Bendronaig Lodge
Loch Calavie
An Gead Loch
Loch an Tachdaidh
Attadale Forest
Loch Cruoshie
Stromemore
Stromeferry
LOCH CARRON
Ardnarff
Achmore
Killilan Forest
East Benula Forest
Glencannich Forest
Muchrachd
Liatrie
Mullardoch House
Fasnakyle Forest
Cannich
Glassburn
Balmore
Carnoch
STRATHGLASS
Glen Urquhart
Buntait
Braefield
Balbeg
Balnain
Milton
Corrimony
Shenval
Gleann Udalain
Sallachy
Allt-nan-sùgh
Killilan
Loch Mullardoch
Glen Cannich
Plockton
Auchertyre
Reraig
Kirkton
Nostie
Ardelve
Dornie
Glas Eilean
Totaig
Camas-luinie
Bundalloch
Glen Elchaig
Camas
West Benula Forest
Gleann Sithidh
Gleann a' Chaoruinn
Gleann nam Fiadh
Affric Lodge
Glen Affric
Tomich
Fasnakyle Ho
Balcladaich
Glenurquhart Forest
Divach
Balmacaan Forest
Keppoch
Letterfearn
Inverinate
Dorusduain
Ruarach
Morvich
Ault a'chruinn
Ratagan
Shiel Bridge
Invershiel
Glenaffric Forest
GLEN AFFRIC
Glen Gniomhaidh
KINTAIL
Kintail Forest
Glen More
Balvraid
Guisachan Forest
Levishie Forest
Levishie
Dundreggan Forest
Achnaconeran
Invermoriston
GLEN MORISTON
Portclair Forest
Dundreggan Lodge
Dundreggan
Dalchreichart
Inverwick Forest
Tomchrasky
Ceannacroc Forest
Ceannacroc Lodge
Cluanie Inn
Glenshiel Forest
GLEN SHIEL
Achlain
Knockie Lodge
Whitebridge
Glenbrein Lodge
Foyers
Creag nan Forest
Allt Saigh
Scale : 1:332 000
(approx 5 miles to 1 inch)
0 1 2 3 4 5 6 miles
0 1 2 3 4 5 6 7 8 9 10 km
A
B
C
D
E
F
G
H
J
K
2
3
4
5
6
7
155
156
149
136
137
A835
A832
A837
A890
A896
A87
A887
A831
A82

ND
NJ
157
152
138
139
Lairg
Brora
Golspie
Bonar Bridge
Dornoch
DORNOCH FIRTH
Tarbat Ness
Portmahomack
Tain
Morangie Forest
Balintore
Alness
Invergordon
Cromarty
Cromarty Firth
MORAY FIRTH
BLACK ISLE
Dingwall
Conon Bridge
Fortrose
Rosemarkie
Burghead
Burghead Bay
Findhorn
Forres
Nairn
Culbin Forest
Moray
Dallas
Muir of Ord
Beauly
Beauly Firth
Inverness
Culloden Forest
Drumnadrochit
Loch Ness
Strathdearn Forest
Tomatin
Carrbridge
Grantown-on-Spey
Nethy Bridge
Boat of Garten
Aviemore
Abernethy Forest
CAIRNGORMS NATIONAL PARK
HILLS OF CROMDALE
MONADHLIATH MOUNTAINS
Glen More Forest Park
Tomintoul
Coignafearn Forest
A B C D E F G H J K
8 9 10 11 12 13 14

Halliman Skerries
Covesea Skerries
LOSSIEMOUTH FISHERIES & COMMUNITY MUSEUM
Branderburgh
Stotfield
Lossiemouth
Covesea
Burghead
BURGHEAD MUSEUM
Hopeman
Duffus
Gordonstoun
Cummingston
Roseisle
Roseisle Forest
DUFFUS CASTLE
PALACE OF SPYNIE
Loch Spynie
Lossie Forest
Spynie
Lower Hempriggs
Quarrywood
Bishopmill
Elgin
ELGIN MUSEUM
CATHEDRAL
CASHMERE VISITOR CENTRE
OLD MILLS
MORAY MOTOR MUSEUM
New Elgin
Newton
Coltfield
Alves
Miltonhill
Pittendreich
Miltonduff
Urquhart
Lhanbryde
Lochs Crofts
Moss of Barmuckity
COXTON TOWER
Mosstodloch
Mains of Burgie
Monaughty Forest
PLUSCARDEN ABBEY
Barnhill
Foresterseat
Auchtertyre
Paddockhaugh
BIRNIE CHURCH
Thornhill
Longmorn
Blackhills
MILLBUIES
Califer
Kellas
Glenlatterach
Dallas Forest
Brodie
Briach
Branchill
Dallas
Moray
Craigroy
MILL BUIE
CAIRN UISH
S P E Y B A Y
THE BUCKIE DRIFTER
Gordonsburgh
Portknockie
Findochty
Portessie
Buckie
Buckpool
Rathven
Kingston
TUGNET ICE HOUSE
Spey Bay
DOLPHIN CENTRE
Garmouth
Leuchars Ho.
Lochhill
Porttannachy
Nether Dallachy
Upper Dallachy
Slackhead
Portgordon
Cairnfield Ho.
Drybridge
Bogmoor
SPEYSIDE WAY
Auchenhalrig
Newlands of Tynet
BAXTERS HIGHLAND VILLAGE
FOCHABERS FOLK MUSEUM
Fochabers
Dipple
Braes of Enzie
Broadley
ST. GREGORY'S CHAPEL
Clochan
Shiel Muir
Speymouth Forest
Orbliston
Ordiequish
Teindland Forest
Wood of Ordiequish
Inchberry
Glen of Rothes
Auchinroath
Newlands
Rothes
GLEN GRANT DISTILLERY
Cullen Bay
Logie Hd.
FINDLATER CASTLE
Sandend Bay
Sandend
Redhythe Pt.
Cullen
Portsoy
Seatown
Lintmill
Milton
JOINER'S WORKSHOP
Fordyce
Easter Whyntie
Kirktown of Deskford
DESKFORD CHURCH
Ardiecow
Berryhillock
Craibstone
Little Toux
Newmills of Boyne
Oldtown of Ord
Cornhill
MILLSTONE HILL
Mains of Edingight
Edingight Ho.
Gordonstown
KNOCK HILL
Finnygaud
Deerhill
Grange Crossroads
Broadrashes
Forgie
Aultmore
Newmill
Crannoch
Sillyearn
Bracobrae
Davoch of Grange
Knock
Drumnagorrach
Knowes of Elrick
Aberchirder
Farmtown
Old Crombie
Knauchland
Marnoch
Mulben
Keith
STRATHISLA DISTILLERY
Rosarie Forest
SPEYSIDE WAY
BEN AIGAN
Burn of Rothes
Elchies Forest
CARN NA CAILLICHE
Whiteacen
Dandaleith
MACALLAN DISTILLERY
Maggieknockater
KEITH AND DUFFTOWN RLY
Towiemore
Balloch Wood
Edintore
Little Pitlurg
Coachford
Glen of Coachford
Cairnie
Ruthven
Millown of Rothiemay
Mains of Mayen
Yonder Bognie
Bogniebrae
FOURMAN HILL
Hillbrae
Archiestown
CARDHU DISTILLERY
Cardow
Upper Knockando
CARN KITTY
Ringorm
Craigellachie
SPEYSIDE COOPERAGE VISITOR CENTRE
Kininvie Ho.
Drummuir Castle
Drummuir
NJ
THE BIN
The Bin Forest
NORDIC SKI CENTRE
HUNTLY CASTLE
Corse of Kinnoir
GLENDRONACH DISTILLERY
SPEYSIDE WAY VISITOR CENTRE
Knockando Ho.
Knockando
Carron
Speyview
Charlestown of Aberlour
Midtown of Buchromb
Daugh of Cairnborrow
Cairnborrow
Daugh of Kinermony
Milltown of Edinvillie
BALVENIE CASTLE
GLENFIDDICH DISTILLERY
Dufftown
Milltown of Auchindoun
Huntly
BRANDER MUSEUM
Lessendrum
Drumblade
Corse
Brideswell
Slioch
LARIG HILL
Burn of Tulchan
Marypark
GLENFARCLAS DISTILLERY
Bellehiglash
CRAGGANMORE DISTILLERY
Kirktown of Mortlach
MEIKLE CONVAL
AUCHINDOUN CASTLE
THE SCALP
Torry
Haugh of Glass
Deveron
S T R A T H B O G I E
Bailiesward
Bridgend
Thomastown
Denend
Hillhead
Bainshole
Advie
Bridge of Avon
Dalchirach
BEN RINNES
Glen Rinnes
Favillar
Kirkhill
Dullan Water
Glen Fiddich
Ballochford
Succoth
Tillathrowie
Coynachie
Kirkstile
Shanquhar
Blackburn
Glens of Foudland
Lettoch
Mains of Dalvey
Tomnaven
Clashindarroch Forest
Clashindarroch
Culdrain
Kirkney
Gartly
Clashindarroch Forest
HILL OF FOUDLAND
Cults
KNOCKANDY HILL
LEITH HALL
Largie
Cromdale
Drumin
GLENLIVET DISTILLERY
Glenlivet
Shenval
Auchbreck
Glenfiddich Forest
Black Water
Bridgend
Inverharroch
Milton of Lesmore
Kennethmont
Milton of Noth
Ardlair
Oldtown
Aulton
The Shevock
HILLS OF CROMDALE
Haughs of Cromdale
Ballcorach
Tomnavoulin
Livet
Blackwater Forest
ROUND HILL
Auchmair
Cabrach
Aldunie
Belhinnie
Rhynie
Cottown
Clatt
Duncanstone
CARN AN T-SUIDHE
CARN DAIMH
Knockandhu
Wheedlemont
Craig Castle
ST MARY'S CHURCH
Knockespock Ho.
Leslie
Glenlivet Forest
CREGGAN A'CHAISE
Clashnoir
Braes of Glenlivet
Chapeltown
HILL OF THREE STONES
THE BUCK
Clova
SCOTTISH SCULPTURE WORKSHOP
Lumsden
CORREEN HILLS
Coldwells Croft
Whitehaugh Forest
Muckletown
Dirdhu
Bridge of Brown
Fodderletter
L A D D E R H I L L S
Aberd
Mossat
LORD ARTHUR'S CAIRN
Tullynessle
Keig
Castle Forbes
DORBACK
Dorback Lodge
TOMINTOUL MUSEUM
Tomintoul
Delnabo
CARN MEADHONACH
GLENLIVET ESTATE VISITOR CENTRE
CARN MOR
Glenbuchat Lodge
Badenyon
Water of Buchat
Belnacraig
Rinmore
Kildrummy
KILDRUMMY CASTLE & GARDEN
Milltown of Kildrummy
Don
Bridge of Alford
Montgarrie
ALFORD VALLEY RAILWAY
HAUGHTON
GRAMPIAN TRANSPORT MUS.
Gateside
Alford
HERITAGE CENTRE
Auchintoul
Asloun
Whitehouse
Conglass Water
Blairnamarrow
Water of Nochty
Kirkton of Glenbuchat
Glenkindie
Towie
Milltown of Towie
Sinnahard
Hillockhead
Ley
Little Lynturk
Kirkton of Tough
GEAL CHARN
C A I R N G O R M S
LECHT SKI CENTRE
THE SOCACH
Bellabeg
Forbestown
Strathdon
Glen Ernan
Ernan Water
Inverernan Ho.
Candacraig Ho.
Heugh-head
Tornashean Forest
Boultenstone
Muir of Fowlis
Bridgend
Tillyfour
Milton of Cushnie
Leochel Cushnie
CRAIGIEVAR CASTLE
Corrennie Moor
Kintocher
N A T I O N A L
P A R K
BIG GARVOUN
CARN EALASAID
Allt Tuileach
Colnabaichin
Cock Bridge
Delnadamph
Corgarff
CORGARFF CASTLE
Tornahaish
CRAIG OF BUNZEACH
Hillockhead
Deskry Water
Easter Davoch
BENAQUHALLIE
G L E N A V O N
Scale : 1:265 000
(approx 4 miles to 1 inch)
Loch Builg
BROWN COW HILL
Migvie
Coynach
Douneside
Craskins
CULSH SOUTERRAIN
Tornaveen
Findrack Ho.
Logie Coldstone
Tarland
C R O M A R
TOMNAVERIE STONE CIRCLE
Lumphanan
PEEL RING OF LUMPHANAN
Milton of Logie
Glendavan Ho.
Ordie
Coull
Milton of Auchinhove
Auchlossan
Torphins
MORVEN
Glen Fenzie
Gairnshiel
BEN AVON
0 1 2 3 4 5 6 miles
0 1 2 3 4 5 6 7 8 9 10 km
151
139
140

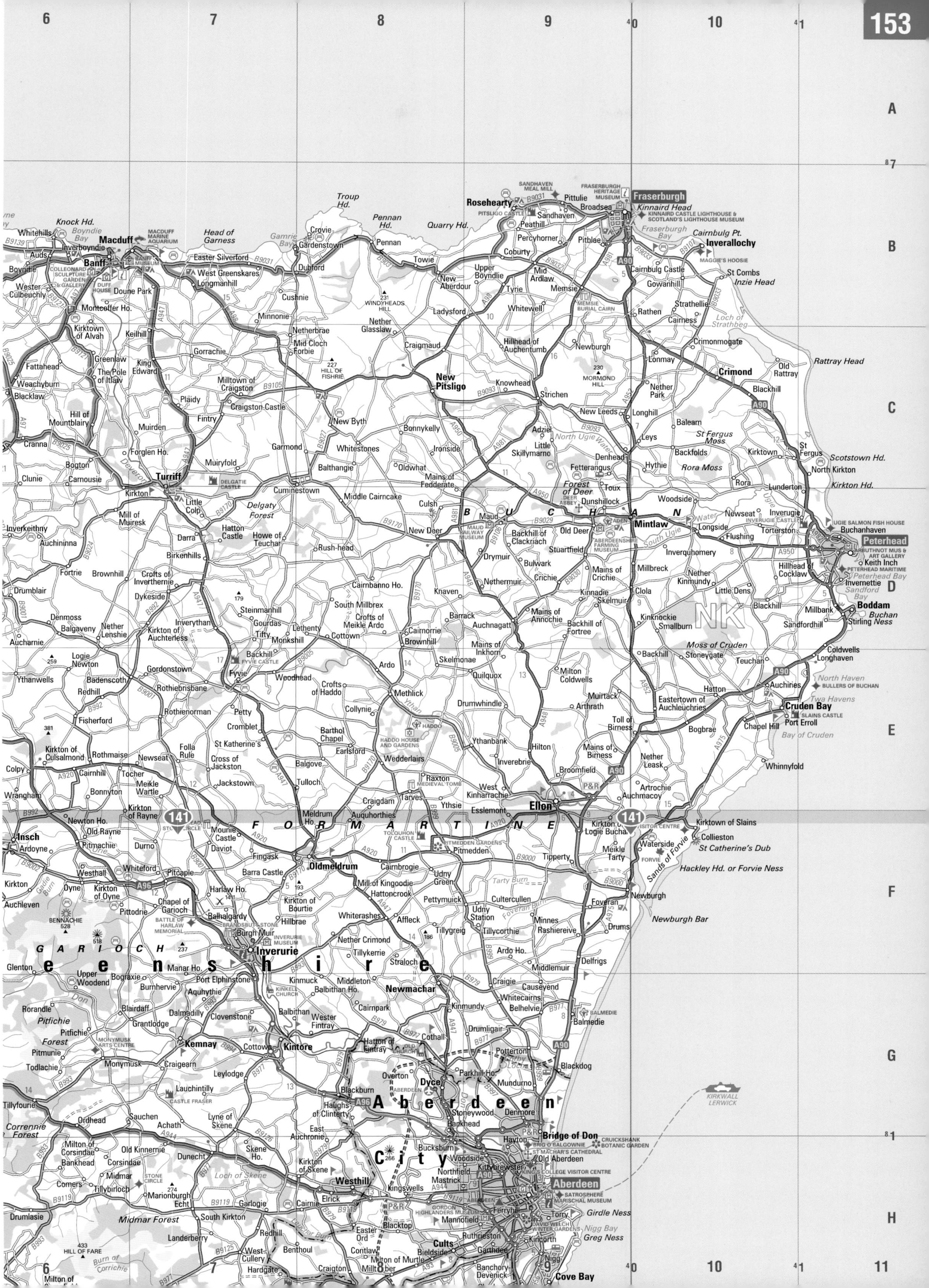

6
7
8
9
10
A
B
C
D
E
F
G
H
11
Fraserburgh
Kinnaird Head
KINNAIRD CASTLE LIGHTHOUSE & SCOTLAND'S LIGHTHOUSE MUSEUM
FRASERBURGH HERITAGE MUSEUM
SANDHAVEN MEAL MILL
Rosehearty
Pittulie
Sandhaven
Broadsea
PITSLIGO CASTLE
Peathill
Fraserburgh Bay
Cairnbulg Pt.
Inverallochy
MAGGIE'S HOOSIE
Cairnbulg Castle
St Combs
Inzie Head
Gowanhill
Rathen
Strathellie
Cairness
Loch of Strathbeg
Crimonmogate
Rattray Head
Old Rattray
Crimond
Blackhill
Troup Hd.
Pennan Hd.
Quarry Hd.
Knock Hd.
Boyndie Bay
Whitehills
Macduff
MACDUFF MARINE AQUARIUM
Head of Garness
Gamrie Bay
Crovie
Gardenstown
Pennan
Towie
Banff
BANFF MUSEUM
DUFF HOUSE
Inverboyndie
Auds
Boyndie
Western Culbeuchly
Easter Silverford
West Greenskares
Longmanhill
Dubford
Cushnie
Doune Park
Montcoffer Ho.
Kirktown of Alvah
Keilhill
Minnonie
Netherbrae
Mid Cloch Forbie
Nether Glasslaw
WINDYHEADS HILL
New Aberdour
Upper Boyndlie
Coburty
Percyhorner
Pitblae
Mid Ardlaw
Memsie
MEMSIE BURIAL CAIRN
Tyrie
Whitewell
Ladysford
Hillhead of Auchentumb
Newburgh
MORMOND HILL
Lonmay
Craigmaud
HILL OF FISHRIE
Gorrachie
Greenlaw
King Edward
The Pole of Itlaw
Fattahead
Weachyburn
Blacklaw
Milltown of Craigston
Craigston Castle
Plaidy
Fintry
Hill of Mountblairy
New Pitsligo
Knowhead
Strichen
Nether Park
New Leeds
Longhill
Balearn
New Byth
Bonnykelly
Muirden
Forglen Ho.
Cranna
Garmond
Whitestones
Ironside
Adziel
North Ugie Water
Little Skillymarno
Leys
St Fergus Moss
Backfolds
Kirktown
St Fergus
Scotstown Hd.
North Kirkton
Rora Moss
Rora
Lunderton
Kirkton Hd.
Denhead
Hythie
Fetterangus
Forest of Deer
DEER ABBEY
Toux
Dunshillock
Bogton
Muiryfold
Balthangie
Oldwhat
Mains of Fedderate
Clunie
Carnousie
Turriff
DELGATIE CASTLE
Kirkton
Cuminestown
Middle Cairncake
Culsh
Little Colp
Delgaty Forest
Mill of Muiresk
Inverkeithny
Auchininna
Darra
Hatton Castle
Howe of Teuchar
New Deer
Maud
MAUD RAILWAY MUSEUM
B U C H A N
Backhill of Clackriach
Old Deer
ADEN
ABERDEENSHIRE FARMING MUSEUM
Mintlaw
South Ugie Water
Woodside
Newseat
Inverugie
INVERUGIE CASTLE
UGIE SALMON FISH HOUSE
Buchanhaven
Longside
Flushing
Torterston
Peterhead
ARBUTHNOT MUS & ART GALLERY
Keith Inch
PETERHEAD MARITIME
Peterhead Bay
Inverquhomery
Millbreck
Hillhead of Cocklaw
Invernettie
Sandford Bay
Stuartfield
Bulwark
Drymuir
Rush-head
Birkenhills
Fortrie
Brownhill
Crofts of Inverthernie
Dykeside
Drumblair
Cairnbanno Ho.
Knaven
Nethermuir
Crichie
Mains of Crichie
Kinnadie
Skelmuir
Clola
Nether Kinmundy
Little Dens
Boddam
Buchan Ness
Stirling Ness
Millbank
Sandfordhill
Denmoss
Balgaveny
Nether Lenshie
Kirkton of Auchterless
Inverythan
Steinmanhill
South Millbrex
Crofts of Meikle Ardo
Gourdas
Tifty
Lethenty
Monkshill
Cottown
Cairnorrie
Brownhill
Barrack
Auchnagatt
Mains of Annochie
Backhill of Fortree
Kinknockie
Smallburn
NK
Moss of Cruden
Backhill
Stoneygate
Teuchan
Coldwells
Longhaven
Aucharnie
Logie Newton
Ythanwells
Badenscoth
Gordonstown
Backhill
FYVIE CASTLE
Fyvie
Woodhead
Ardo
Skelmonae
Mains of Inkhorn
Quilquox
Milton Coldwells
North Haven
BULLERS OF BUCHAN
Auchiries
Two Havens
Redhill
Rothiebrisbane
Crofts of Haddo
Methlick
Collynie
Ythan
HADDO
HADDO HOUSE AND GARDENS
Drumwhindle
Muirtack
Arthrath
Hatton
Eastertown of Auchleuchries
Cruden Bay
SLAINS CASTLE
Port Erroll
Bay of Cruden
Fisherford
Rothienorman
Petty
Cromblet
Barthol Chapel
St Katherine's
Earlsford
Ythanbank
Toll of Birness
Bogbrae
Chapel Hill
Kirkton of Culsalmond
Rothmaise
Folla Rule
Newseat
Cross of Jackston
Balgove
Wedderlairs
Hilton
Inverebrie
Mains of Birness
Nether Leask
Whinnyfold
Colpy
Cairnhill
Tocher
Meikle Wartle
Jackstown
Tulloch
Raxton
MEDIEVAL TOMB
Broomfield
Artrochie
Auchmacoy
Wrangham
Bonnyton
Craigdam
Tarves
West Kinharrachie
Ythsie
Esslemont
Ellon
Insch
Newton Ho.
Old Rayne
Kirkton of Rayne
Meldrum Ho.
Auquhorthies
F O R M A R T I N E
Kirkton of Logie Buchan
VISITOR CENTRE
Kirktown of Slains
Collieston
St Catherine's Dub
Waterside
FORVIE
Sands of Forvie
Hackley Hd. or Forvie Ness
Ardoyne
Pitmachie
Durno
Mounie Castle
Daviot
TOLQUHON CASTLE
PITMEDDEN GARDENS
Pitmedden
Tipperty
Meikle Tarty
Fingask
Oldmeldrum
Cairnbrogie
Udny Green
Westhall
Whiteford
Pitcaple
Barra Castle
Harlaw Ho.
Mill of Kingoodie
Hattoncrook
Culterculleen
Tarty Burn
Foveran
Newburgh
Kirkton
Oyne
Kirkton of Oyne
Auchleven
Chapel of Garioch
Pittodrie
Kirkton of Bourtie
Pettymuick
Udny Station
Foveran Burn
Minnes
Drums
Newburgh Bar
BENNACHIE
BATTLE OF HARLAW MEMORIAL
Balhalgardy
BRANDSBUTT STONE
Hillbrae
Whiterashes
Affleck
Tillygreig
Tillycorthie
Rashiereive
Burgh Muir
INVERURIE MUSEUM
Nether Crimond
G A R I O C H
Inverurie
Tillykerrie
Straloch
Ardo Ho.
Delfrigs
Glenton
Manar Ho.
Port Elphinstone
Kinmuck
Middleton
Middlemuir
Upper Woodend
Bograxie
Burnhervie
Aquhythie
KINKELL CHURCH
Balbithan Ho.
Newmachar
Craigie
Causeyend
e n s h i r e
Rorandle
Pitfichie
Blairdaff
Dalmadilly
Clovenstone
Balbithan
Wester Fintray
Cairnpark
Kinmundy
Whitecairns
Belhelvie
BALMEDIE
Balmedie
Forest
Pitfichie
Grantlodge
MONYMUSK ARTS CENTRE
Kemnay
Kintore
Hatton of Fintray
Cothall
Drumligair
Pitmunie
Cottown
Potterton
Todlachie
Monymusk
Craigearn
Leylodge
Parkhill Ho.
Blackdog
Overton
Dyce
Mundurno
Lauchintilly
CASTLE FRASER
Blackburn
ABERDEEN
KIRKWALL LERWICK
Tillyfourie
Haughs of Clinterty
A b e r d e e n
Stoneywood
Denmore
Bankhead
Corrennie Forest
Ordhead
Sauchen
Achath
Lyne of Skene
East Auchronie
Hayton
Bridge of Don
CRUICKSHANK BOTANIC GARDEN
BRIG O' BALGOWNIE
ST MACHAR'S CATHEDRAL
Milton of Corsindae
Old Kinnernie
Dunecht
Skene Ho.
Bucksburn
Woodside
Old Aberdeen
Bankhead
Corsindae
Kirkton of Skene
C i t y
Kittybrewster
KING'S COLLEGE VISITOR CENTRE
Northfield
Mastrick
Aberdeen
Comers
Midmar
STONE CIRCLE
Loch of Skene
Westhill
Kingswells
SATROSPHERE
MARISCHAL MUSEUM
Tillybirloch
Marionburgh
Echt
Garlogie
Cairnie
Elrick
GORDON HIGHLANDERS MUSEUM
Mannofield
Ferryhill
Torry
Girdle Ness
Drumlasie
Midmar Forest
South Kirkton
Blacktop
DAVID WELCH WINTER GARDENS
Nigg Bay
Greg Ness
Landerberry
Redhill
Easter Ord
Ruthrieston
Kincorth
HILL OF FARE
Benthoul
West Cullery
Contlaw
Cults
Bieldside
Garthdee
Nigg
Burn of Corrichie
Hardgate
Craigton
Milltimber
Milton of Murtle
Banchory-Devenick
Cove Bay
Milton of

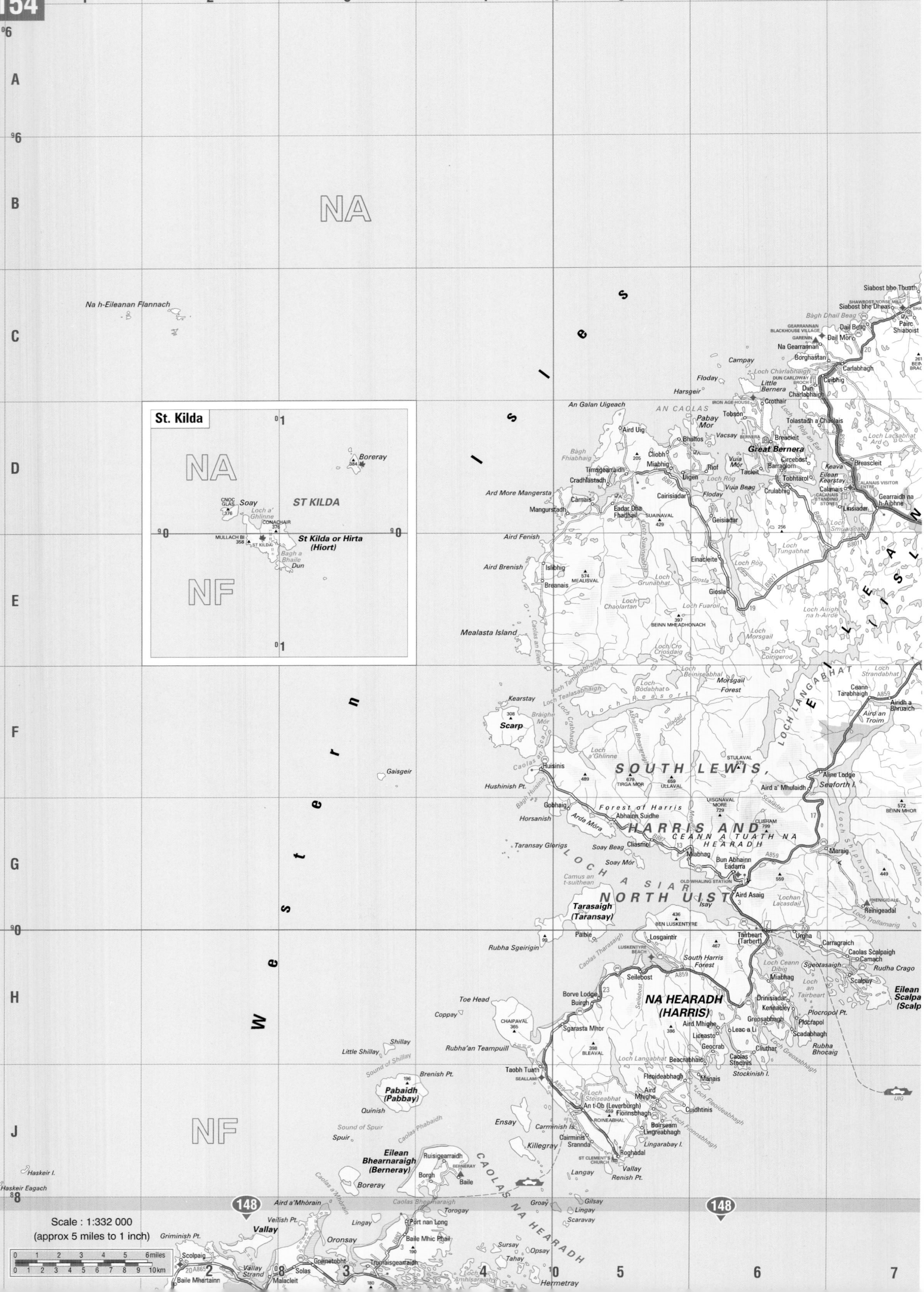
NA
NF
Western Isles
Na h-Eileanan Flannach
St. Kilda
Boreray
ST KILDA
Soay
CNOC GLAS
Loch a' Ghlinne
CONACHAIR
MULLACH BI
St Kilda or Hirta
(Hiort)
Bagh a Bhaile
Dun
Siabost bho Thuath
Siabost bho Dheas
Bàgh Dhail Beag
Dail Beag
Pairc Shiaboist
GEARRANNAN BLACKHOUSE VILLAGE
GARENIN
Dail Mòr
Na Gearrannan
Borghastan
Carlabhagh
Campay
Loch Chàrlabhaigh
DUN CARLOWAY BROCH
Dun Chàrlabhaigh
Little Bernera
Floday
Harsgeir
Cirbhig
IRON AGE HOUSE
Crothair
An Galan Uigeach
AN CAOLAS
Pabay Mor
Tobson
Tolastadh a Chaolais
Aird Uig
Bhaltos
Vacsay
BERNERA
Breacleit
Great Bernera
Bàgh Fhiabhaig
Cliobh
Miabhig
Vuia Mòr
Circebost
Barraglom
Tacleit
Riof
Uigen
Timsgearraidh
Cradhlastadh
Loch Ròg
Vuia Beag
Crulabhig
Tobhtarol
Keava
Eilean Kearstay
Calanais
CALANAIS VISITOR CENTRE
CALANAIS STANDING STONES
Linsiadar
Breascleit
Gearraidh na h-Aibhne
Ard More Mangersta
Càrnais
Eadar Dha Fhadhail
SUAINAVAL
Cairisiadar
Floday
Mangurstadh
Geisiadar
Loch Smuaisebhal
Aird Fenish
Loch Tungabhat
Einacleite
Aird Brenish
Islibhig
Breanais
MEALISVAL
Loch Grunabhat
Loch Ròg
Giosla
Loch Chaolartan
Loch Fuaroil
Loch Airigh na h-Airde
BEINN MHEADHONACH
Mealasta Island
Caolas an Eilein
Loch Morsgail
Loch Cro Criosdaig
Loch Coirgerod
Loch Beiniseabhal
Morsgail Forest
Loch Bòdabhat
Loch Strandabhat
Ceann Tarabhaigh
LOCH LANGABHAT
Airidh a Bhruaich
Aird an Troim
Kearstay
Scarp
Bràighe Mòr
Loch Tamanabhaigh
Loch Tealasabhaigh
Loch Reasort
Gaisgeir
Loch a'Ghlinne
STULAVAL
Caolas an Scarp
Huisinis
SOUTH LEWIS,
HARRIS AND
NORTH UIST
Hushinish Pt.
TIRGA MOR
ULLAVAL
Aline Lodge
Seaforth I.
Aird a' Mhulaidh
Bagh Huisinis
Gobhaig
Forest of Harris
Abhainn Suidhe
UISGNAVAL MORE
BEINN MHOR
Horsanish
Ardа Mòra
CLISHAM
CEANN A TUATH NA HEARADH
Taransay Glorigs
Soay Beag
Cliasmol
Miabhag
Maraig
LOCH A SIAR
Soay Mòr
Bun Abhainn Eadarra
OLD WHALING STATION
Camus an t-suithean
Aird Asaig
Isay
RHENIGIDALE
Reinigeadal
Tarasaigh (Taransay)
Lochan Lacasdail
Loch Trollamarig
BEN LUSKENTYRE
Paible
Losgaintir
Tairbeart (Tarbert)
Urgha
Carragraich
Rubha Sgeirigin
LUSKENTYRE BEACH
South Harris Forest
Caolas Tharasaigh
Loch Ceann Dibig
Sgeotasaigh
Caolas Scalpaigh
Camach
Rubha Crago
Seilebost
Miabhag
Scalpay
Eilean Scalpa (Scalp
Toe Head
Borve Lodge
Buirgh
NA HEARADH (HARRIS)
Drinisiadar
Loch an Tairbeart
Kennacley
Plocropol Pt.
Coppay
CHAIPAVAL
Sgarasta Mhor
Aird Mhighe
Greosabhagh
Plocrapol
Leac a Li
Scadabhagh
Lìceasto
Rubha Bhocaig
Geocrab
Cluthar
Shillay
Little Shillay
Rubha'an Teampuill
BLEAVAL
Loch Langabhat
Beacrabhaic
Caolas Stocinis
Loch Greosabhagh
Sound of Shillay
Brenish Pt.
Taobh Tuath
SEALLAM
Fleoideabhagh
Manais
Stockinish I.
Pabaidh (Pabbay)
Loch Steiseabhat
Aird Mhighe
UIG
Quinish
An t-Ob (Leverburgh)
Fionnsbhagh
Cuidhtinis
ROINEABHAL
Loch Fleoideabhagh
Ensay
Carminish Is.
Boirseam
Lingreabhagh
Loch Fionnsbhagh
Sound of Spuir
Spuir
Caolas Phabaidh
Cairminis
Srannda
Killegray
Lingarabay I.
Eilean Bhearnaraigh (Berneray)
Ruisigearraidh
Borgh
BERNERAY
Baile
ST CLEMENT'S CHURCH
Roghadal
Vallay
Renish Pt.
Langay
CAOLAS NA HEARADH
Boreray
Caolas a Mhòrain
Haskeir I.
Haskeir Eagach
Aird a'Mhòrain
Caolas Bhearnaraigh
Torogay
Groay
Gilsay
Lingay
Scaravay
148
Veilish Pt.
Lingay
Port nan Long
Griminish Pt.
Vallay
Oronsay
Baile Mhic Phail
Sursay
Opsay
Tahay
Scolpaig
Vallay Strand
Solas
Greinetobht
Trumaisgearraidh
Loch Aimhsaraigh
Baile Mhartainn
Malacleit
Hermetray
Scale : 1:332 000
(approx 5 miles to 1 inch)
0 1 2 3 4 5 6 miles
0 1 2 3 4 5 6 7 8 9 10 km

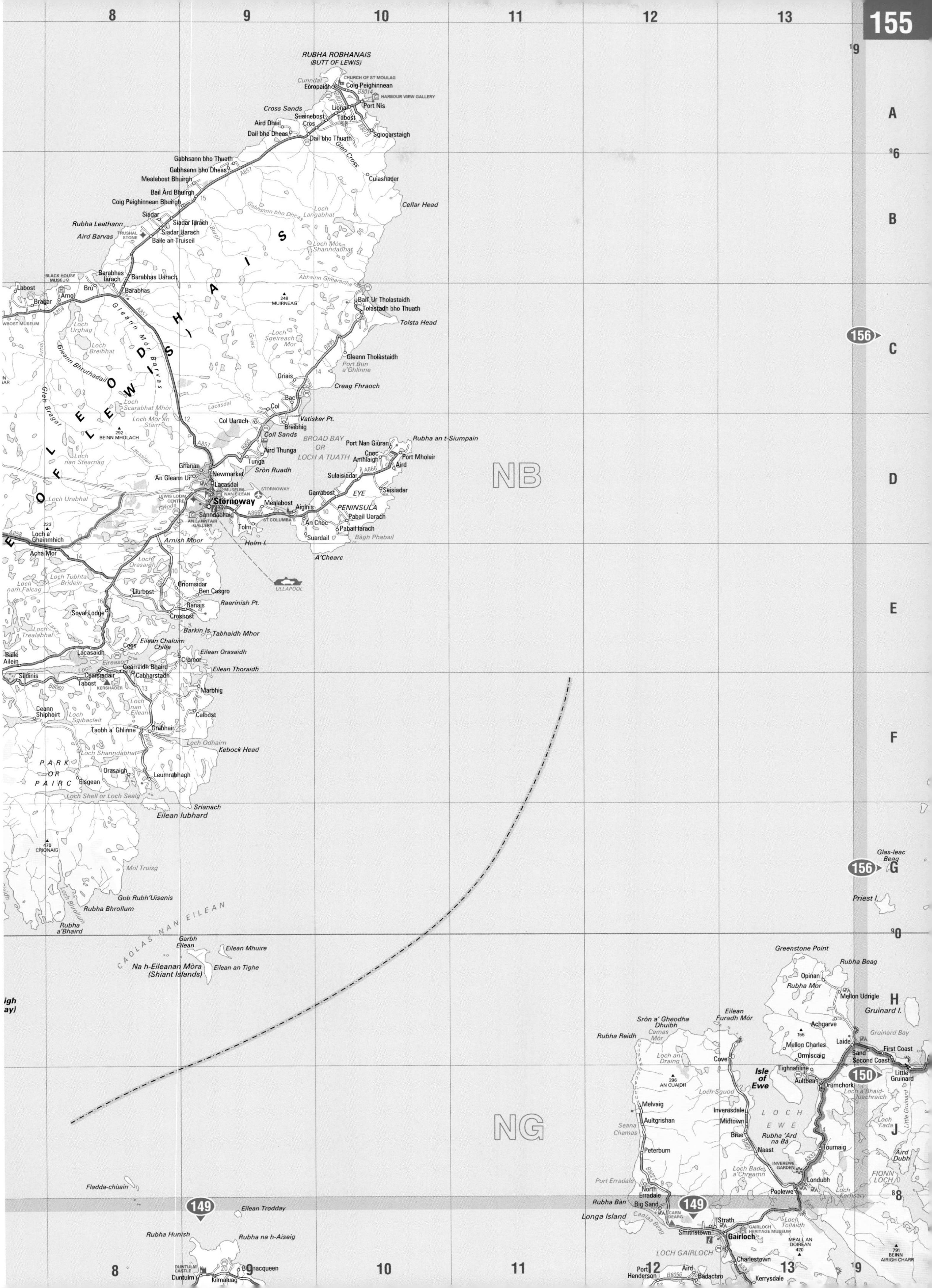
RUBHA ROBHANAIS
(BUTT OF LEWIS)
Cunndal
CHURCH OF ST MOULAG
Eòropaidh
Coig Peighinnean
HARBOUR VIEW GALLERY
Cross Sands
Lional
Port Nis
Suainebost
Tabost
Aird Dhail
Cros
Dail bho Dheas
Dail bho Thuath
Sgiogarstaigh
Glen Cross
Gabhsann bho Thuath
Gabhsann bho Dheas
Cuiashader
Mealabost Bhuirgh
Bail Àrd Bhuirgh
Coig Peighinnean Bhuirgh
Cellar Head
Gabhsann bho Dheas
Loch Langabhat
Siadar
Rubha Leathann
Siadar Iarach
TRUSHAL STONE
Aird Barvas
Siadar Uarach
Baile an Truiseil
Loch Mòr Shanndabhat
BLACK HOUSE MUSEUM
Barabhas Iarach
Barabhas Uarach
Labost
Brù
Barabhas
Abhainn Ghearadha
Bragar
Arnol
248 MUIRNEAG
Baile Ur Tholastaidh
Tolastadh bho Thuath
Tolsta Head
Loch Urghag
Loch Breibhat
Loch Sgeireach Mor
Gleann Tholàstaidh
Port Bun a'Ghlinne
Gleann Bhruthadail
Gleann Mòr Barvas
Griais
Creag Fhraoch
Glen Bragar
Loch Scarabhat Mhòr
Lacasdal
Bac
Col
Loch Mòr an Stàirr
Col Uarach
Vatisker Pt.
292 BEINN MHOLACH
Breibhig
Coll Sands
BROAD BAY OR LOCH A TUATH
Port Nan Giùran
Rubha an t-Siumpain
Aird Thunga
Cnoc
Port Mholair
Loch nan Stearnag
Tunga
Amhlaigh
Aird
Grianan
Sròn Ruadh
An Gleann Ur
Newmarket
Sulaisiadar
NB
Lacasdal
STORNOWAY
LEWIS LOOM CENTRE
MUSEUM NAN EILEAN
Garrabost
EYE PENINSULA
Seisiadar
Loch Urabhal
Stornoway
Mealabost
Aiginis
Sanndabhaig
Pabail Uarach
ST COLUMBA'S
AN LANNTAIR GALLERY
An Cnoc
Pabail Iarach
223
Loch a' Ghainmhich
Tolm
Bàgh Phabail
Suardail
Arnish Moor
Holm I.
Acha Mòr
A'Chearc
Loch Orasaigh
Loch Tobhta Bridein
Loch nam Falcag
Griomsidar
Ben Casgro
ULLAPOOL
Liurbost
Raerinish Pt.
Ranais
Soval Lodge
Crosbost
Loch Trealabhal
Barkin Is.
Tabhaidh Mhor
Eilean Chaluim Chille
Baile Ailein
Ceos
Eilean Orasaidh
Lacasaidh
Cromor
Gearraidh Bhaird
Eilean Thoraidh
Sildinis
Cearsiadar
Cabharstadh
Tabost
KERSHADER
Marbhig
Loch nan Eilean
Ceann Shìphoirt
Loch Sgibacleit
Calbost
Taobh a' Ghlinne
Grabhair
Loch Odhairn
Kebock Head
Loch Shanndabhat
PARK OR PAIRC
Orasaigh
Leumrabhagh
Eisgean
Loch Shell or Loch Sealg
Srianach
Eilean Iubhard
470 CRÌONAIG
Mol Truisg
Loch Bhrollum
Gob Rubh'Uisenis
Rubha Bhrollum
Rubha a'Bhaird
CAOLAS NAN EILEAN
Garbh Eilean
Eilean Mhuire
Na h-Eileanan Mòra (Shiant Islands)
Eilean an Tighe
NG
Fladda-chùain
Eilean Trodday
Rubha Hunish
Rubha na h-Aiseig
DUNTULM CASTLE
Duntulm
Kilmaluag
Bornacqueen
Glas-leac Beag
Priest I.
Greenstone Point
Rubha Beag
Opinan
Rubha Mor
Mellon Udrigle
Gruinard I.
Sròn a' Gheodha Dhuibh
Eilean Furadh Mór
Achgarve
Rubha Reidh
Camas Mór
155
Gruinard Bay
Laide
Mellon Charles
First Coast
Loch an Draing
Ormiscaig
Sand
Second Coast
Cove
Tighnafiline
Isle of Ewe
Little Gruinard
296 AN CUAIDH
Aultbea
Drumchork
Loch a' Bhaid-luachraich
Loch Sguod
Melvaig
LOCH EWE
Inverasdale
Aultgrishan
Midtown
Loch Fada
Seana Chamas
Brae
Rubha 'Ard na Bà
Tournaig
Peterburn
Naast
Aird Dubh
INVEREWE GARDEN
Loch Bad a'Chreamh
Port Erradale
North Erradale
Londubh
FIONN LOCH
Poolewe
Loch Kernsary
Rubha Bàn
Big Sand
Longa Island
Caolas Beag
CARN DEARG
Strath
Loch Tollaidh
Smithstown
GAIRLOCH HERITAGE MUSEUM
Gairloch
MEALL AN DOIREAN 420
LOCH GAIRLOCH
791 BEINN AIRIGH CHARR
Port Henderson
Aird
Charlestown
Badachro
Kerrysdale
149
150
156

CAPE WRATH
Kearvaig
371 SGRIBHIS-BHEINN
Faraid Head
Geodha Ruadh na Fola
Bay of Keisgaig
Loch Keisgaig
Inshore
Balnakeil Bay
BALNAKEIL CHURCH
BALNAKEIL CRAFT VILLAGE
Balnakeil
DURNESS VISITOR CENTRE
SMOO CAVE
Durness
Whiten
Geodh'a' Bhrideoin
Eilean Hoan
Eilean Clùimhrig
Geodha Ruadh
Achiemore
Sangomore
Leirinmore
Keoldale
457 FASHVEN
Loch Airigh na Beinne
Kyle of Durness
Sangobeg
Rispond
Am Balg
423 BEINN DEARG
Sandwood Loch
485 CREAG RIABHACH
Sarsgrum
Grudie
Rubh'an Fhir Léithe
422 MEALL MEADHONACH
LOCH ERIBOLL
Loch na Gainimh
Strath Shinary
332 GHLAS BHEINN
Sheigra
Balchrick
Portnancon
Heilam
Hope
Droman
Oldshore Beg
Oldshoremore
Eilean Roin Mor
521 FARRMHEALL
A838
772 BEINN SPIONNAIDH
Eilean Choraidh
230
Lochside
Loch Clash
Kinlochbervie
Gualin Ho.
Eriboll
Badcall
Bagh Loch an Roin
Achriesgill
800 CRANSTACKIE
Strath Dionard
Polla
Strath Beag
Loch Hope
Loch Dughaill
Achlyness
L. na Claise Carnaich
Ardmore Pt.
Ceathramh Garbh
Rhiconich
521 AN LEAN-CHARN
Rubha Ruadh
Ardmore
GANU MOR 908
Foinaven
NORTH-WEST SUTHERLAND
Fanagmore
Tarbet
Loch a' Garbh-bhaid Mòr
Loch Dionard
Loch Crocach
927 BEN HOPE
Handa Island
Foindle
Loch nam Brac
Laxford Bridge
Loch an Easain Uaine
FEINNE-BHEINN MOR 465
787 ARKLE
Alltnacaillich
DUN DORNAIGIL BROCH
Scourie Bay
Gorm Loch
777
Scourie More
Rubh' Aird an t-Sionnaich
Scourie
Lochstack Lodge
Glen Golly
Strathmore
Upper Badcall
Lower Badcall
719 BEN STACK
Loch Stack
Gobernuisgach Lodge
Badcall Bay
BENN AUSKAIRD 386
Strath Stack
Eil. a' Bhreitheimh
Achfary
332
REAY FOREST
759
Rubha a' Mhucard
Loch Crocach
Lochmore Lodge
A894
Meall Mór
Calbha Mór
Loch More
Alt a' Chraois
Calbha Beag
Eddrachillis Bay
Duartmore Forest
Loch na Creige Duibhe
Loch Coire na Saidhe Duibhe
Oldany Island
Loch an Leathaid Bhuain
Aultanrynie
Point of Stoer
R. nan Còsan
Kylestrome
547 Forest
Kinloch
Cirean Geardail
161
Eilean Chrona
Culkein Drumbeg
Kylesku
Glendhu
Culkein
Clashnessie Bay
Oldany
Unapool
Loch Glendhu
Gleann Dubh
873 BEN HEE
Loch a' Ghorm-choire
Cluas Deas
Achnacarnin
Drumbeg
Nedd
B869
Newton
530 BEINN AIRD DA LOCH
566
Clashmore
Loch Poll
Gleann Leireag
Glen Coul
Loch Merkland
Clashnessie
Balchladich
Rienachait
Loch an Leothaid
792 BEINN LEOID
Merkland Lodge
Loch Fiag
Rubh'a' Mhill Dheirg
Stoer
808 QUINAG
EAS COUL AULIN WATERFALL
H
Loch Dubh a' Chuail
Loch an Eircill
i
404
g
Bay of Stoer
Clachtoll
Loch Crocach
Loch Beannach
Lochassynt Lodge
R. Leumair
Achmelvich Bay
776
BEINN UIDHE 740
Loch a' Ghriama
Corrykinloch
312 CNOC A' ALASK
Rhicarn
LOCH ASSYNT
Fiag Plantation
Achmelvich
ACHMELVICH BEACH
A837
Inver
Little Assynt
Skiag Bridge
Gorm Loch Mor
Glen Fiag
ASSYNT VISITOR CENTRE
ARDVRECK CASTLE
Overscaig Hotel
Rubha Rodha
Baddidarach
Brackloch
Loch Feith an Leothaid
Fionn Loch Mor
Lochinver
Glencanisp Lodge
Soyea I.
Loch Inver
540
Inchnadamph
Kirkaig Pt.
Badnaban
Strathan
ASSYNT-
Inchnadamph Forest
512 MAOVALLY
Fiag Bridge
A'Chleit
Loch Kirkaig
Inverkirkaig
998 BEN MORE ASSYNT
Rubha Coigeach
Glencanisp Forest
Stronchrubie
391
Rubha na Breige
SUILVEN 731
846 CANISP
LOCH
Eilean Mór
Kirkaig
Falls
Fionn Loch
Loch na Gainimh
718 BREABAG
MEALLAN AONAICH 715
Allt Car
Strath an Lòin
ENARD BAY
Camas Eilean Ghlais
Rubh'a' Choin
COIGACH
Duchally
Rubha Mor
Reiff
Inverpolly Lodge
Loch Awe
Benmore Forest
Brae of Achnahaird
Loch Veyatie
Cam Loch
Altandhu
SUMMER ISLES SMOKEHOUSE
Loch Sionascaig
Ledbeg
Glen Oykel
Glen Cassley
Eilean Mullagrach
Polly
Aird of Coigach
Inverpolly Forest
849 CUL MOR
HIGHLAND & RARE BREEDS FARM
Ledmore
Altnacealgach Hotel
Loch Ailsh
Benmore Lodge
BEINN SGEIREACH
Allt a' Bh
Isle Ristol
Loch Vatachan
Loch Osgaig
613 STAC POLLAIDH
Drumrunie Forest
Elphin
Glas-leac Mór
Polbain
Loch an Doire Dhuibh
Knockan
Loch Urigill
Loch Bad a' Ghaill
KNOCKAN CRAG
Achiltibuie
HYDROPONICUM GARDENS
769 CUL BEAG
Loch Lurgainn
CROMALT HILLS
364 AN STUC
BEINN AN EOIN 554
Tanera Beg
Badentarbat Bay
Polglass
A835
Glencassley Castle
Loch na Fuaralaich
Summer Isles
Tanera Mór
ACHININVER
517
Oykel
Glas-leac Beag
Horse I.
Horse Sound
COIGACH
Drumrunie
Loch Craggie
Loch na Claise Moire
Glenrossal
Achduart
Culnacraig
743 BEINN MOR COIGACH
Eilean Dubh
Langwell Lodge
Priest I.
Carn nan Sgeir
Strathcanaird
Rappach
578 MEALL AN FHUARAIN
Lubcroy
Oykel Bridge
Strath Oykel
Invercassley
Oykel Fore
Rosehall
Bottle I.
Strath Kanaird
Strath nan Lon
Brae
Doune
Altass
Camas Mór
415
Greenstone Point
Isle Martin
Rubha Beag
Cailleach Hd.
STORNOWAY
Rappach Water
Glen Einig
Opinan
NG
Annat Bay
Ardmair
Rhidorroch Forest
493 BEINN ULBHAIDH
Scaraig
Cadh
Rhue
Staffic Pt.
Carnach
Morefield
Ullapool
ULLAPOOL MUSEUM
Rhidorroch Ho.
548
Loch an Daimh
Corriemulzie Lodge
412 CREAG LOISGTE
Strath Cuileannach
507 MEALL DHEIRGIDH
Rireavach
635 BEINN GHOBHLACH
Glen Achall
Strath Mulzie
Badluarach
Little Loch Broom
Scale 1:332 000
(approx 5 miles to 1 inch)
0 1 2 3 4 5 6 miles
0 1 2 3 4 5 6 7 8 9 10 km
Gruinard House
Dumamuck
Badcaul
Badrallach
Allt na h-Airbhe
A835
558 BEINN EILIDEACH
LECKMELM SHRUBBERY AND ARBORETUM
East Rhidorroch Lodge
Glasha Burn
701 CARN A' CHOIN DEIRG
CROICH CHURCH
Croich
First Coast
NB
155
150

Head
Rubha Thormaid
Strathen
Midfield
Port Vasgo
Eilean nan Ron
Neave I. or Coombe I.
Farr Pt.
Kirtomy Pt.
Ardmore Pt.
Armadale Bay
Strathy Point
Totegan
Strathy Bay
Melvich Bay
Red Pt.
Brims Ness
ST MARY'S CHAPEL
Crosskirk
Spear Hd.
Holborn Hd.
STROMNESS
Thurso Bay
Clardon Hd.
Scrabster
THURSO CASTLE
THURSO FOLK MUSEUM
Clardon
Murkle
Castletown
Thurso
Millbank
Thurso East
Haimer
Olrig Ho.
Hillclia
Dunnet
Dounreay
Buldoo
Achreamie
Bridge of Forss
Newlands of Geise
Geise
Weydale
Achingills
Fresgoe
Sandside Ho.
Isauld
Reay
Achvarasdal
CNOC FREKEDAIN CHAMBERED CAIRN
Westfield
Shebster
Lieurary
Buckies
Sordale
Knockdee
Braal Castle
Roadside
Clayock
Halkirk
Banniskirk Ho.
Calder Mains
Broubster
Shurrery
Shurrery Lodge
Brawlbin
Scotscalder Station
Harpsdale
Olgrinmore
Dorrery
Spittal
Mybster
Westerdale
Strathmore Lodge
Lochmore Cottage
Altnabreac Station
Lochdhu
Dalnawillan Lodge
Glutt Lodge
Braehungie
CNOCAN CONACHREAG
Houstry
Smerral
Latheronwheel Ho.
Braemore
Balnabruich
Dunbeath
DUNBEATH CASTLE
Knockally
Ramscraigs
Borgue
Newport
Berriedale
Langwell Ho.
BADBEA CLEARANCE VILLAGE
Ousdale
Ord Point
Navidale
TIMESPAN HERITAGE CENTRE
Helmsdale
Marrel
West Helmsdale
Gartymore
Portgower
Lothmore
Lothbeg
Lothbeg Pt.
Torrish
Kilphedir
Kildonan Lodge
BAILE AN OR GOLDRUSH SITE
Craggie
STRATH OF KILDONAN
Glen Loth
Glen Sletdale
Langwell Forest
Wag
Aultibea
MORVEN
SCARABEN
BEN ALISKY
CNOC LOCH MHADADH
CNOC COIRE NA PEARNA
CNOC AN EIREANNAICH
CREAG SCALABSDALE
BEINN DUBHAIN
BEINN DHORAIN
COL-BHEINN
EILDRABLE HILL
Brawl
Aultiphurst
Baligill
Portskerra
Bighouse
Strathy
Melvich
Golval
Lednagullin
Armadale
Kirtomy
Swordly
Farr
STRATHNAVER MUSEUM
Bettyhill
Achina
Invernaver
Skerray
Achtoty
Airdtorrisdale
Torrisdale
Borgie
Coldbackie
Skullomie
Rabbit Is.
Talmine
Skinnet
Midtown
West Strathan
BEN HUTIG
A'Mhoine
Achuvoldrach
TONGUE
Kirkiboll
CASTLE VARRICH
Tongue
KYLE OF TONGUE
Kinloch Lodge
Ribigill
Borgie Forest
Leckfurin
ACHANLOCHY CLEARANCE VILLAGE
Skelpick
Achagary
Carnachy
Rhifail
BEINN RIFA-GIL
Skail
STRATHNAVER
Strathy Forest
Bowside Lodge
Upper Bighouse
Achiemore
Craigtown
Dalhalvaig
Trantlemore
Trantlebeg
STRATH HALLADALE
Forsinain
SLETILL HILL
Forsinard
Forsinard Station
THE FLOWS
BEINN NAM BAD MOR
BEN LOYAL
BEINN STUMANADH
Loch Loyal Lodge
CNOC NAN CULLEAN
Inchkinloch
Langdale
Syre
Dalvina Lo.
ROSAL CLEARANCE TRAIL
POLE HILL
BEN GRIAM BEG
BEN GRIAM MORE
Garvault Hotel
Achentoul Forest
Badanloch Forest
Naver Forest
Mudale
Altnaharra
Clebrig
Badanloch Lodge
Strath Beg
Kinbrace
Achentoul
Lochside
Knockfin Heights
BEN KLIBRECK
MEALL NAN CON
Loch Choire Lodge
Loch Choire Forest
Strath Vagastie
Highland
Borrobol Forest
Borrobol Lodge
Altanduin
BEN ARMINE
MEALL A'BHATA
Crask Inn
CREAG MHOR
CREAG NAM FIADH
BEN ARMINE FOREST
Ben Armine Lodge
Strath na Seilge
Strath Skinsdale
MEALLAN LIATH MOR
Strath Tirry
Rhian
Shinness
Dalnessie
Achnairn
Dalchork
Dalchork Wood
Colaboll
Achnaluachrach
West Langwell
Strath Brora
Balnacoil
Gordonbush
Dalreavoch
Rhilochan
Sallachy
Saval
Lairg Lodge
Lairg Muir
Lairg
FERRYCROFT COUNTRYSIDE CENTRE
East Langwell
Farlary
BEN HORN
Achrimsdale
East Clyne
West Clyne
Clynelish
CLYNELISH DISTILLERY
Dalchalm
Brora
Doll
CAGAR FEOSAIG
Claonel
Gruids
Torroble
Muie
Strath Fleet
Ardachu
Rogart
Pittentrail
HECTOR MACDONALD MONUMENT
Rogart Station
BEINN LUNNDAIDH
Backies
DUNROBIN CASTLE MUSEUM & GARDENS
Achany
Shin Forest
Achinduich
Morvich
Golspie
Linsidemore
FALLS OF SHIN VISITOR CENTRE
Torboll Farm
Culmaily
Kirkton
Achnahanat
Inveran
Invershin
Little Torboll
Cambusmore Lodge
Loch Fleet
LOCH FLEET
Cambusavie Farm
Littleferry
Skelbo
SKELBO CASTLE
Fourpenny
BEINN DOMHNAILL
Craigton
CARBISDALE CASTLE
Culrain
Balblair
Airdens
Achvaich
Badninish
Clashcoig
Braelangwell Lodge
Rearquhar
Poles
Embo
Proncy
Embo Street
Migdale
Bonar Bridge
Gablon
Pitgrudy
Westerd Gruinards
Soyal
Lower Gledfield
NC
ND
NH
NJ
151
158

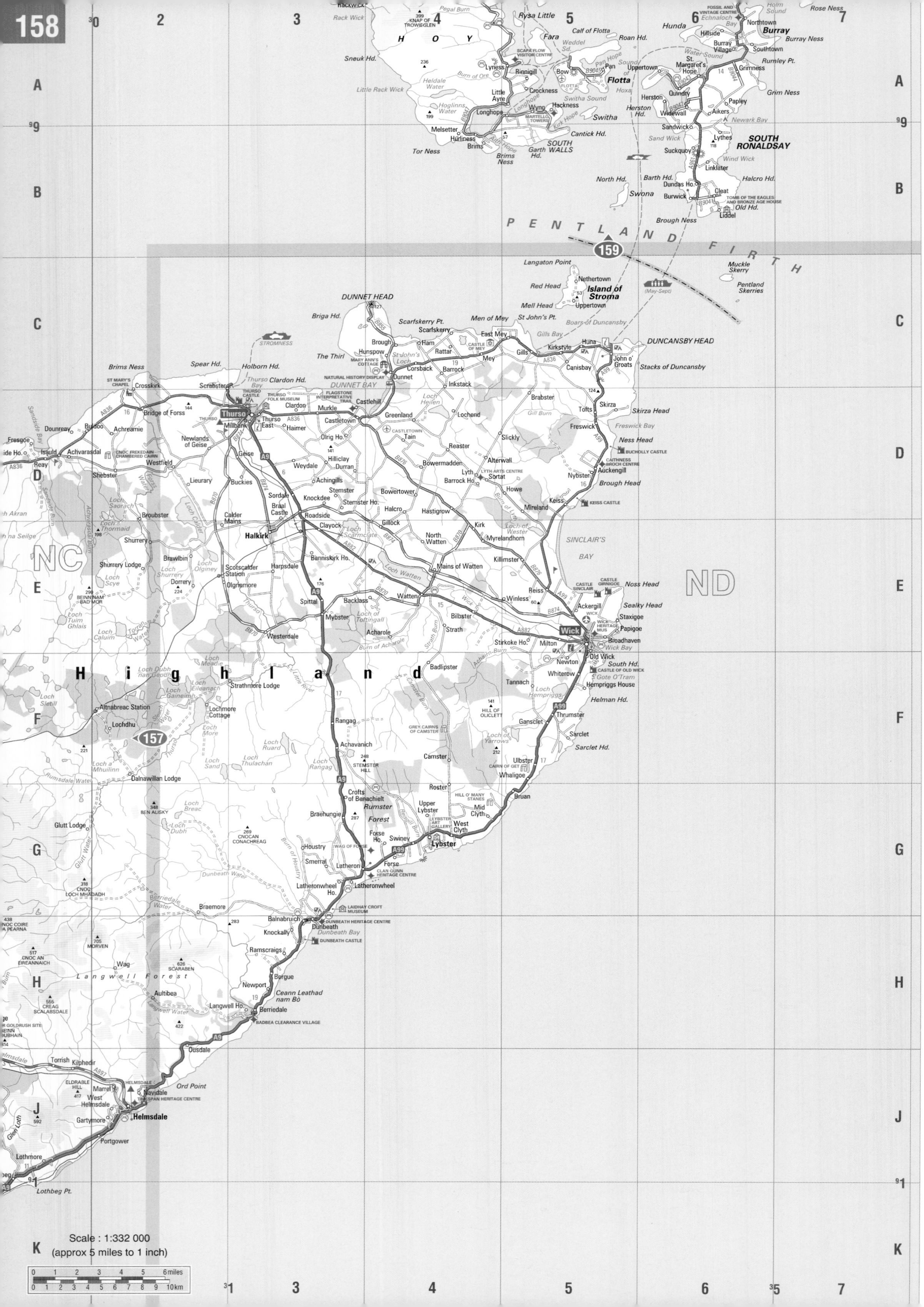

HOY
Burray
SOUTH RONALDSAY
Flotta
Swona
Island of Stroma
PENTLAND FIRTH
159
157
DUNNET HEAD
DUNNET BAY
DUNCANSBY HEAD
John o' Groats
Thurso
Scrabster
Castletown
Dunnet
Wick
SINCLAIR'S BAY
Noss Head
Halkirk
Watten
Lybster
Dunbeath
Berriedale
Helmsdale
Highland
NC
ND
Langwell Forest
Rumster Forest
Lyness
Longhope
St. Margaret's Hope
Melsetter
Reay
Dounreay
Keiss
Thrumster
Latheron
Ord Point
Brora
Scale : 1:332 000
(approx 5 miles to 1 inch)
0 1 2 3 4 5 6 miles
0 1 2 3 4 5 6 7 8 9 10 km

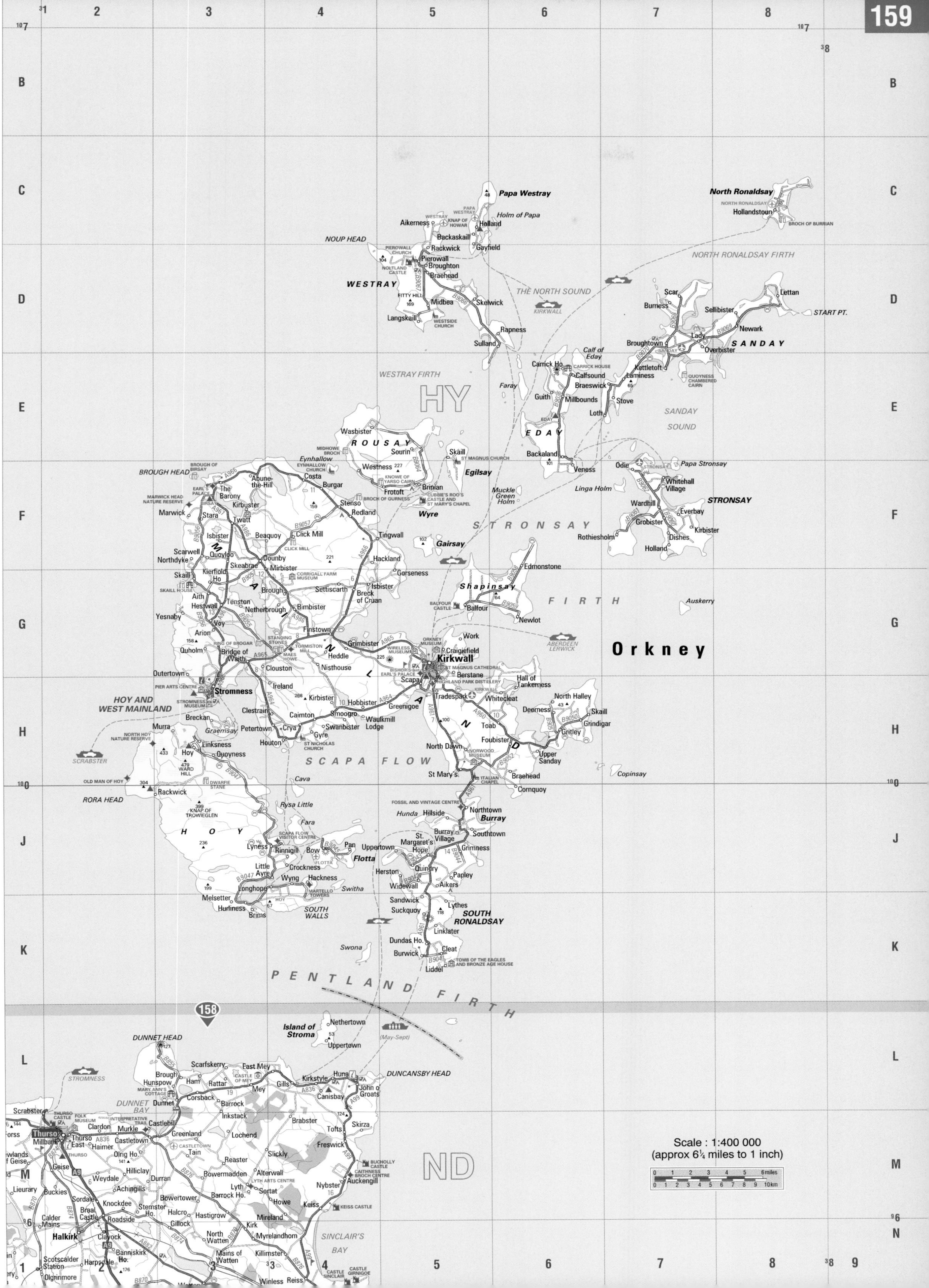

Papa Westray
Holm of Papa
Holland
Aikerness
Backaskaill
Rackwick
Gayfield
NOUP HEAD
Pierowall
Broughton
Braehead
WESTRAY
Midbea
Skelwick
Langskaill
Rapness
Sulland
North Ronaldsay
Hollandstoun
BROCH OF BURRIAN
NORTH RONALDSAY FIRTH
THE NORTH SOUND
KIRKWALL
Scar
Burness
Lettan
Sellibister
START PT.
Newark
Lady
Overbister
SANDAY
Broughtown
Calf of Eday
Carrick Ho.
Calfsound
Kettletoft
Laminess
Braeswick
Millbounds
Guith
Stove
Loth
EDAY
SANDAY SOUND
Backaland
Veness
WESTRAY FIRTH
Faray
HY
Wasbister
ROUSAY
Sourin
Westness
Skaill
Egilsay
Frotoft
Brinian
Wyre
Muckle Green Holm
Odie
Papa Stronsay
Whitehall Village
Linga Holm
STRONSAY
Wardhill
Everbay
Grobister
Rothiesholm
Kirbister
Dishes
Holland
S T R O N S A Y
BROUGH HEAD
Abune-the-Hill
Costa
Burgar
Stenso
Redland
The Barony
Kirbuster
Marwick
Stara
Twatt
Isbister
Beaquoy
Click Mill
Tingwall
Gairsay
Scarwell
Northdyke
Quoyloo
Skeabrae
Mirbister
Dounby
Hackland
Skaill
Kierfiold Ho
Gorseness
Edmonstone
Shapinsay
Aith
Brough
Settiscarth
Isbister
Breck of Cruan
Hestwall
Tenston
Netherbrough
Bimbister
Balfour
Newlot
F I R T H
Auskerry
Yesnaby
Voy
Finstown
Arion
Work
Grimbister
Craigiefield
Kirkwall
Orkney
Quholm
Bridge of Waith
Heddle
Nisthouse
Berstane
Outertown
Clouston
Scapa
Hall of Tankerness
Ireland
Stromness
Kirbister
Tradespark
Whitecleat
North Halley
HOY AND WEST MAINLAND
Hobbister
Greenigoe
Deerness
Skaill
Clestrain
Caimton
Smoogro
Waulkmill Lodge
Grindigar
Breckan
Toab
Gritley
Murra
Graemsay
Peterstown
Cryva
Swanbister
Gyre
Foubister
Houton
North Dawn
Upper Sandays
Linksness
Hoy
Quoyness
SCRABSTER
S C A P A   F L O W
St Mary's
Braehead
Copinsay
OLD MAN OF HOY
Rackwick
Cava
Cornquoy
RORA HEAD
Rysa Little
Northtown
Hunda
Hillside
Burray
Fara
H O Y
Burray Village
Southtown
Lyness
Pan
Uppertown
St. Margaret's Hope
Grimness
Rinnigill
Bow
Flotta
Little Ayre
Crockness
Herston
Quindry
Papley
Wyng
Hackness
Widewall
Aikers
Longhope
Switha
Melsetter
Hurliness
Brims
SOUTH WALLS
Sandwick
Lythes
Suckquoy
SOUTH RONALDSAY
Linklater
Swona
Dundas Ho.
Burwick
Cleat
Liddel
P E N T L A N D   F I R T H
158
Nethertown
Island of Stroma
Uppertown
(May-Sept)
DUNNET HEAD
DUNCANSBY HEAD
STROMNESS
Scarfskerry
East Mey
Brough
Hunspow
Ham
Rattar
Mey
Gills
Kirkstyle
Huna
John o' Groats
Canisbay
Dunnet
Corsback
Barrock
DUNNET BAY
Scrabster
Inkstack
Brabster
Castlehill
Skirza
Forss
Clardon
Murkle
Greenland
Lochend
Tofts
Thurso
Castletown
Millbank
East Haimer
Freswick
Tain
Slickly
Olrig Ho.
Reaster
Geise
Hilliclay
Durran
Bowermadden
Alterwall
Weydale
Lyth
Sortat
Nybster
Auckengill
Achingills
ND
Lieurary
Buckies
Sordale
Knockdee
Bowertower
Barrock Ho.
Howe
Keiss
Stemster Ho.
Braal Castle
Halcro
Hastigrow
Mireland
Calder Mains
Roadside
Gillock
Halkirk
Kirk
Clayock
North Watten
Myrelandhorn
SINCLAIR'S BAY
Scotscalder Station
Harpsdale
Banniskirk Ho.
Mains of Watten
Killimster
Olgrinmore
Winless
Reiss
Scale : 1:400 000
(approx 6¼ miles to 1 inch)

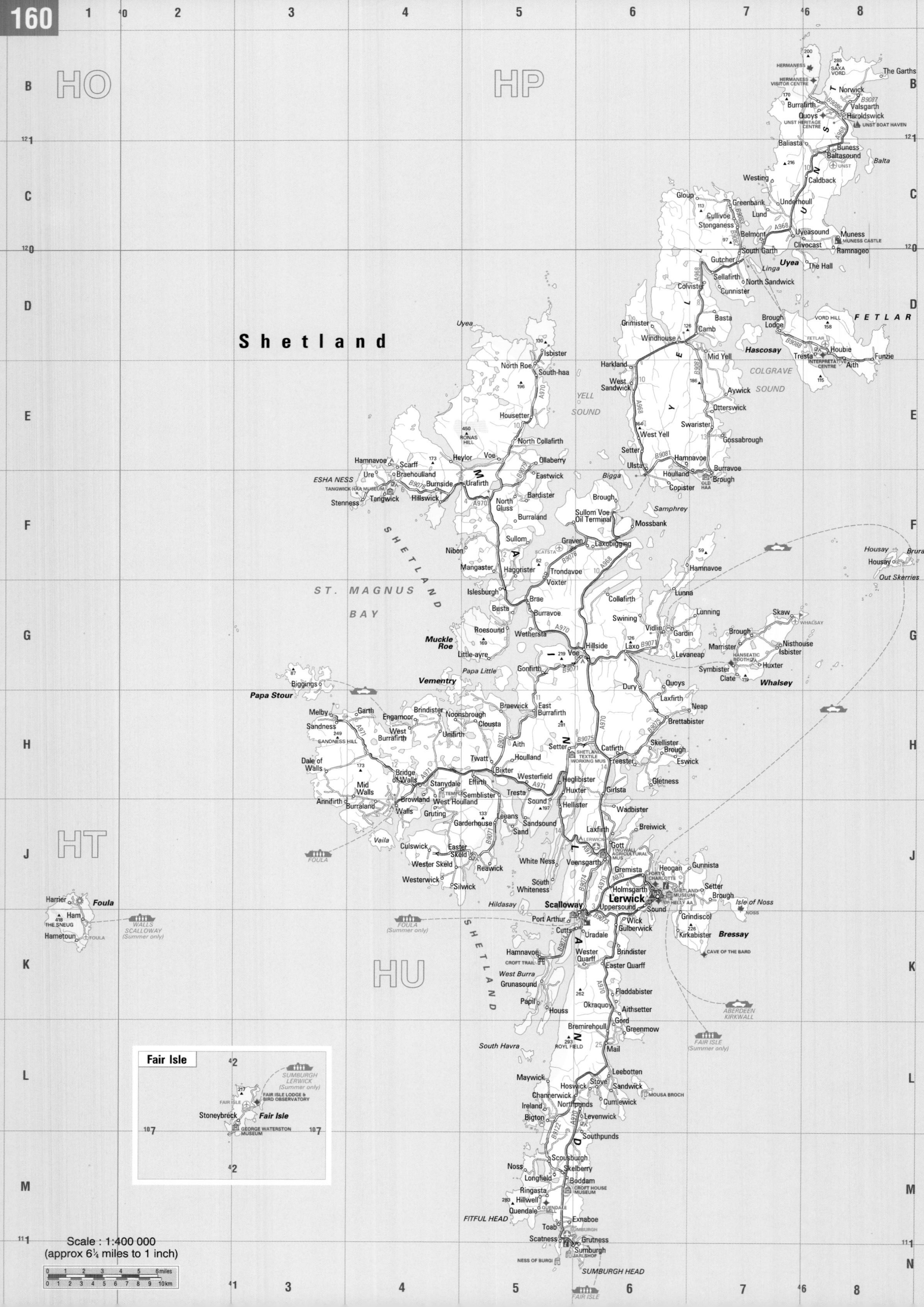
Shetland
HO
HP
HT
HU
Unst
Yell
Mainland
Fetlar
Hascosay
Uyea
Linga
Whalsey
Bressay
Isle of Noss
Foula
Papa Stour
Muckle Roe
Vementry
Papa Little
Vaila
Hildasay
West Burra
South Havra
Samphrey
Bigga
Out Skerries
Housay
Bruray
Balta
ST. MAGNUS BAY
SHETLAND
YELL SOUND
COLGRAVE SOUND
ESHA NESS
FITFUL HEAD
SUMBURGH HEAD
NESS OF BURGI
Hermaness
Hermaness Visitor Centre
Saxa Vord
The Garths
Norwick
Burrafirth
Valsgarth
Haroldswick
Quoys
Unst Heritage Centre
Unst Boat Haven
Baliasta
Buness
Baltasound
Westing
Caldback
Underhoull
Gloup
Greenbank
Cullivoe
Stonganess
Lund
Belmont
Uyeasound
Muness
Muness Castle
Clivocast
Ramnageo
South Garth
Gutcher
The Hall
Sellafirth
North Sandwick
Cunnister
Colvister
Basta
Grimister
Camb
Windhouse
Brough Lodge
Vord Hill
Houbie
Tresta
Funzie
Aith
Interpretative Centre
Mid Yell
Harkland
West Sandwick
Aywick
Otterswick
Swarister
Gossabrough
West Yell
Setter
Ulsta
Hamnavoe
Burravoe
Brough
Old Haa
Houlland
Copister
Isbister
North Roe
South-haa
Housetter
Ronas Hill
North Collafirth
Heylor
Voe
Ollaberry
Hamnavoe
Scarff
Ure
Braehoulland
Eastwick
Urafirth
Tangwick Haa Museum
Burnside
Stenness
Tangwick
Hillswick
Bardister
North Gluss
Burraland
Sullom Voe Oil Terminal
Mossbank
Sullom
Graven
Scatsta
Laxobigging
Nibon
Mangaster
Haggrister
Trondavoe
Voxter
Isbister
Hamnavoe
Isleburgh
Brae
Collafirth
Lunna
Busta
Burravoe
Swining
Lunning
Skaw
Roesound
Wethersta
Vidlin
Gardin
Brough
Nisthouse
Isbister
Little-ayre
Voe
Hillside
Laxo
Levaneap
Marrister
Hanseatic Booth
Symbister
Huxter
Clate
Gonfirth
Dury
Quoys
Biggings
Laxfirth
Neap
Melby
Garth
Brindister
Engamoor
Noonsbrough
Braewick
East Burrafirth
Brettabister
Sandness
Sandness Hill
West Burrafirth
Clousta
Unifirth
Aith
Setter
Shetland Textile Working Mus
Catfirth
Skellister
Brough
Eswick
Dale of Walls
Twatt
Houlland
Freester
Bixter
Westerfield
Bridge of Walls
Stanydale
Effirth
Gletness
Mid Walls
Temple
Heglibister
Huxter
Girlsta
Semblister
Tresta
Annifirth
Burraland
Browland
West Houlland
Sound
Hellister
Walls
Gruting
Wadbister
Garderhouse
Leeans
Sandsound
Sand
Breiwick
Laxfirth
Culswick
Easter Skeld
Gott
Tingwall Agricultural Mus
Wester Skeld
Reawick
White Ness
Veensgarth
Gremista
Heogan
Gunnista
Westerwick
Silwick
South Whiteness
Fort Charlotte
Holmsgarth
Shetland Museum
Setter
Brough
Lerwick
Up Helly Aa
Scalloway
Uppersound
Sound
Noss
Harrier
Ham
The Sneug
Hametoun
Port Arthur
Wick
Grindiscol
Cutts
Gulberwick
Kirkabister
Uradale
Cave of the Bard
Hamnavoe
Croft Trail
Wester Quarff
Brindister
Easter Quarff
Grunasound
Fladdabister
Papil
Okraquoy
Aithsetter
Houss
Gord
Bremirehoull
Greenmow
Royl Field
Mail
Leebotten
Maywick
Stove
Sandwick
Hoswick
Mousa Broch
Channerwick
Northpunds
Cumlewick
Ireland
Bigton
Levenwick
Southpunds
Scousburgh
Noss
Skelberry
Longfield
Boddam
Croft House Museum
Ringasta
Hillwell
Quendale
Quendale Mill
Exnaboe
Toab
Sumburgh
Scatness
Grutness
Jarlshof
Foula
Walls
Scalloway (Summer only)
Foula (Summer only)
Aberdeen
Kirkwall
Fair Isle (Summer only)
Fair Isle
Fair Isle
Sumburgh
Lerwick
(Summer only)
Fair Isle Lodge & Bird Observatory
Stoneybreck
Fair Isle
George Waterston Museum
A968
A970
A971
B9081
B9082
B9083
B9084
B9085
B9086
B9087
B9088
B9071
B9074
B9075
B9076
B9077
B9078
B9122
Scale : 1:400 000
(approx 6¼ miles to 1 inch)
miles
km

GLASGOW
Moodiesburn
Muirhead
Gartcosh
Chryston
Auchinloch
Stepps
Craigend
Easterhouse
Bargeddie
Swinton
Muirhead
Broomhouse
Uddingston
Springboig
Mont Vernon
Westburn
Flemington
Dechmont Hill
Robroyston
Balornock
Riddrie
Carntyne
Braidfauld
Clyde Gateway East
Cambuslang
Bishopbriggs
Springburn
Dennistoun
Gallowgate
Rutherglen
Castlemilk
Croftfoot
Milton
Firhill
Govanhill
Cathcart
Netherlee
Muirend
Langside
Pollokshields
Crossmyloof
Kelvinside
Partick
Ibrox
Govan
Hillpark
Giffnock
Orchard Park
Knightswood
Jordanhill
Hillington
Crookston
Priesthill
Nitshill
River Clyde
M8
M73
M74
M77
M80
2 miles
3 km

WOLVERHAMPTON
MOLINEUX
West Park
Town Hall
THE ROYAL
ST GEORGES
P&R
RING RD
PENN ROAD
DUDLEY ROAD
WILLENHALL
WILLENHALL ROAD
Bentley
BIRCHILLS CANAL MUSEUM
MELLISH RD
ARBORETUM
WALSALL
BROADWAY NORTH
BROADWAY WEST
BANKS'S STADIUM
BESCOT STADIUM
WOLVERHAMPTON RD
BOUNDARY MILL
BILSTON
PRIESTFIELD
WELLINGTON RD
THE CRESCENT
BILSTON CENTRAL
THE KEYWAY
BLACK COUNTRY ROUTE
DARLASTON
MOXLEY
GOLDTHORN HILL
PARKFIELD RD
MILLFIELDS ROAD
WOLVERHAMPTON ROAD
SPRING ROAD
ETTINGSHALL RD
OXFORD ST
LOXDALE
SALOP ST
BRADLEY LANE
COSELEY
WEDNESBURY
WEDNESBURY PARKWAY
WEDNESBURY GREAT WESTERN ST
Tame Valley Canal
TAME BRIDGE PARKWAY
FRIAR PARK RD
SEDGLEY
GOSPEL END ROAD
BILSTON ST
BAGGERIDGE COUNTRY PARK
Nature Centre
Upper Gornal
TIPTON ROAD
TIPTON
BIRMINGHAM NEW ROAD
BLOOMFIELD RD
HIGH ST
ALEXANDRA RD
OWEN ST
HORSELEY HEATH
DUDLEY PORT
BLACK LAKE
SWAN LA
Lyndon
NEWTON
ALL SAINTS WAY
THE EXPRESSWAY
SANDWELL VALLEY COUNTRY PARK
WEST BROMWICH
DUDLEY ST GUNS VILLAGE
DARTMOUTH ST
LODGE RD WEST BROM
WEST BROMWICH CENTRAL
TRINITY WAY
KENRICK PARK
KELVIN WAY
BIRMINGHAM RD
THE HAWTHORNS
Sandwell
SANDWELL & DUDLEY
The Black Country
Wren's Nest NNR
BLACK COUNTRY MUSEUM
DUDLEY ZOO & CASTLE
Univ
DUDLEY
Gornalwood
HIMLEY ROAD
CINDER ROAD
DUDLEY ROAD WEST
Oakham
NEW BIRMINGHAM ROAD
OLDBURY
OLDBURY ROAD
LANGLEY GREEN
Langley Green
SMETHWICK GALTON BRIDGE
SMETHWICK ROLFE STREET
SOHO WAY
SMETHWICK
THIMBLEMILL RD
Warley Woods
HIGH STREET
Pensnett
Netherton
ROWLEY REGIS
Blackheath
Old Hill
BRIERLEY HILL
Merry Hill Centre
MERRY HILL
AMBLECOTE
CRADLEY HEATH
OLD HILL
Dudley Canal
Hurst Green
HALESOWEN ROAD
WOLVERHAMPTON ROAD
Lye
Cradley
STOURBRIDGE ROAD
HAGLEY ROAD WEST
COURT OAK ROAD
World's End
QUINTON RD WEST
BIRMINGHAM STREET STOURBRIDGE TOWN
STOURBRIDGE JUNCTION
HALESOWEN
MANOR WAY
HALESOWEN ABBEY (REMS)
WOODGATE VALLEY COUNTRY PARK
Woodgate
CLAPGATE LANE
Weoley Castle
Pedmore
Wychbury Hill
HAGLEY CAUSEWAY
Hagley Wood
Uffmoor Wood
Twiland Wood
FRANKLEY SERVICES
Bartley Resr
Shenley
Fields
Hagley
Hagley Park

Hardwick
Four Oaks
Streetly
Upper Nut Hurst
Sutton Park National Nature Reserve
Doe Bank Wood
Westwood Coppice
Holly Hurst
Pheasey
SUTTON COLDFIELD
Reddicap Heath
Kingstanding
Over Green
Short Heath
Walmley
Nature Centre
Hamstead
Perry Park
Witton Lakes
Erdington
Bromford
Aston
Winson Green
BIRMINGHAM
Lea Hall
Bordesley Green
Yardley
Lyndon Green
Sheldon
Moseley
Acock's Green
Cannon Hill Park
Nature Centre
Selly Park
Selly Oak
Moor Green
Ulverley Green
Stirchley
Bournville
Lode Heath
New Park Wood
Elmdon Park
Edgbaston Resr
BIRMINGHAM BOTANICAL GARDENS
CASTLE BROMWICH HALL
NEW HALL COUNTRY PARK
SHELDON COUNTRY PARK
BIRMINGHAM ECO PARK
Birmingham & Fazeley Canal
Grand Union Canal
River Tame
River Cole
M6
M6 Toll
A38
A34
A452
A4540
A45
A41
0 1 2 miles
0 1 2 3 km

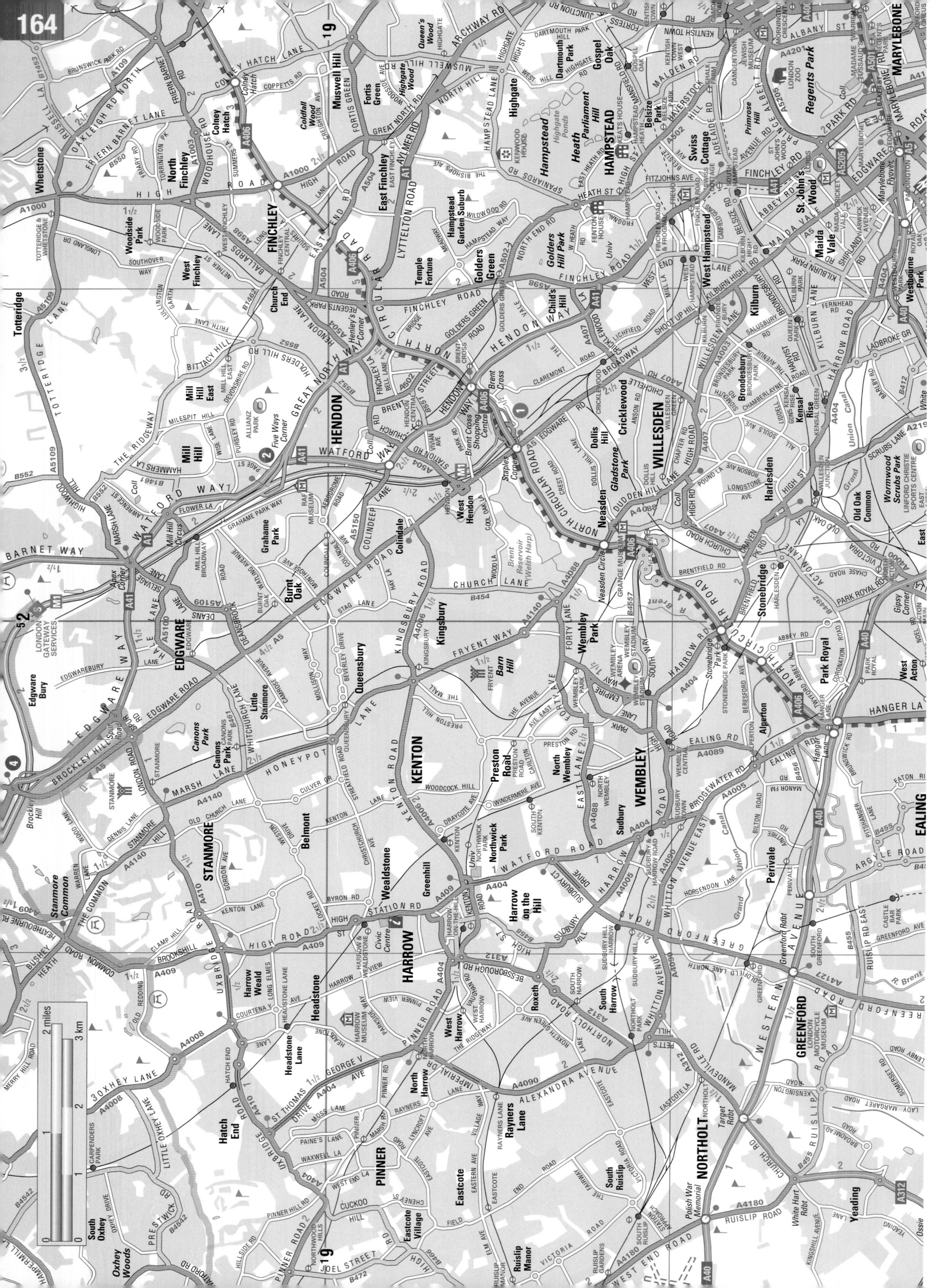
Whetstone
North Finchley
Colney Hatch
Muswell Hill
Fortis Green
Highgate
Hampstead Heath
Hampstead
Dartmouth Park
Gospel Oak
Belsize Park
Swiss Cottage
Primrose Hill
Regents Park
Marylebone
Totteridge
Woodside Park
West Finchley
Finchley
Church End
East Finchley
Hampstead Garden Suburb
Temple Fortune
Golders Green
Golders Hill Park
West Hampstead
St. John's Wood
Maida Vale
Kilburn
Child's Hill
Cricklewood
Willesden
Brondesbury
Kensal Rise
Harlesden
Mill Hill East
Mill Hill
Hendon
Brent Cross
Dollis Hill
Gladstone Park
Neasden
West Hendon
Colindale
Grahame Park
Burnt Oak
Edgware
Edgware Bury
Kingsbury
Queensbury
Little Stanmore
Canons Park
Wembley Park
Barn Hill
Stonebridge
Park Royal
West Acton
Old Oak Common
Wormwood Scrubs Park
Kenton
Preston Road
North Wembley
Wembley
Sudbury
Alperton
Stanmore
Belmont
Wealdstone
Greenhill
Harrow on the Hill
Harrow
Northwick Park
Perivale
Ealing
Stanmore Common
Harrow Weald
Headstone
Headstone Lane
West Harrow
Roxeth
South Harrow
North Harrow
Hatch End
Pinner
Rayners Lane
Eastcote
Eastcote Village
Ruislip Manor
South Ruislip
Northolt
Greenford
Yeading
South Oxhey
Oxhey Woods
NORTH CIRCULAR ROAD
WATFORD WAY
EDGWARE ROAD
FINCHLEY ROAD
WESTERN AVENUE
2 miles
3 km

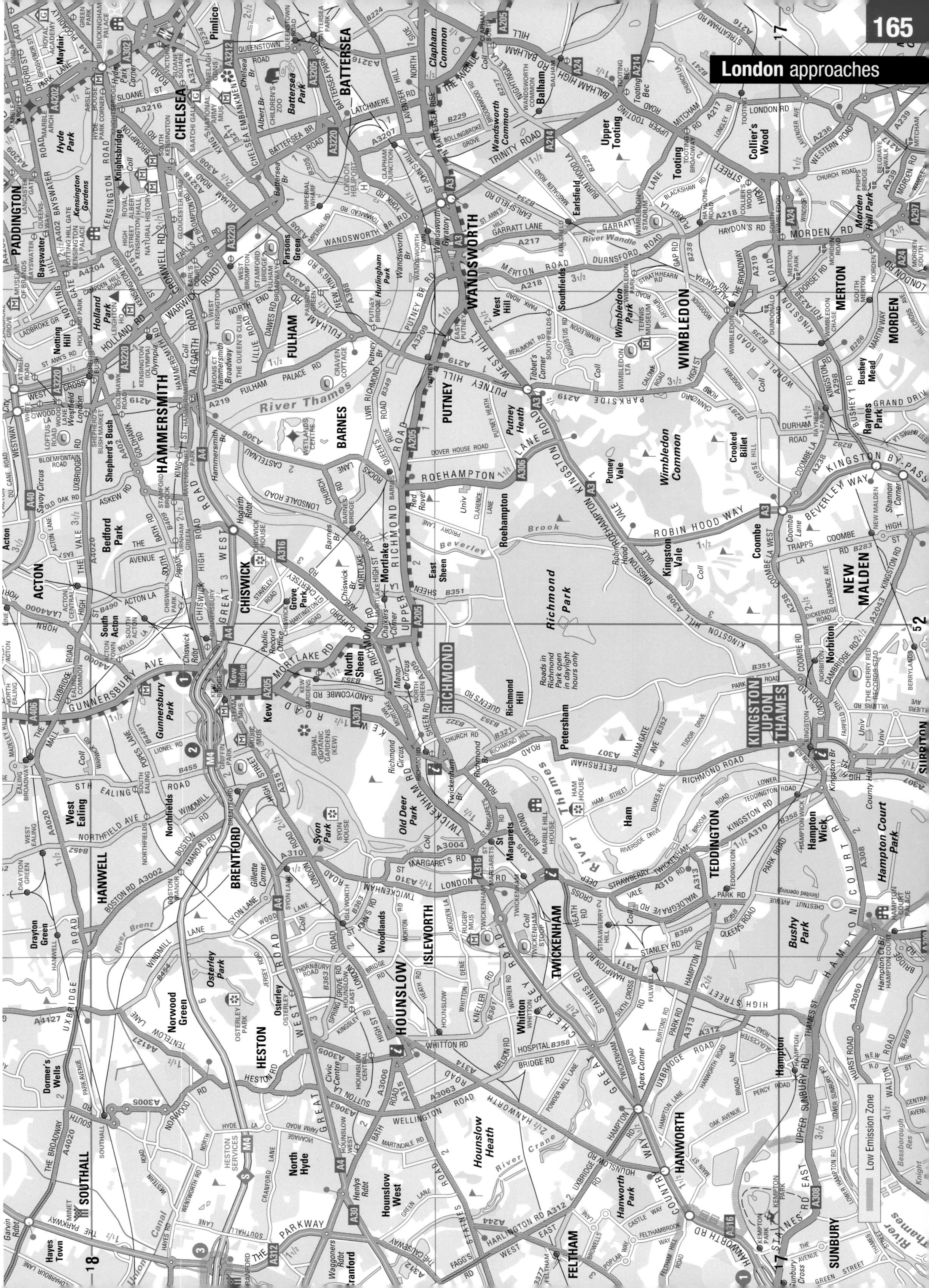
PADDINGTON
CHELSEA
BATTERSEA
Clapham Common
Pimlico
Mayfair
Hyde Park
Kensington Gardens
Knightsbridge
Notting Hill
Holland Park
Bayswater
FULHAM
HAMMERSMITH
Shepherd's Bush
Wandsworth Common
Balham
Upper Tooting
Tooting
Collier's Wood
Earlsfield
WANDSWORTH
Southfields
West Hill
Wimbledon Park
WIMBLEDON
MERTON
MORDEN
Morden Hall Park
PUTNEY
Putney Heath
Putney Vale
Wimbledon Common
Crooked Billet
Raynes Park
Bushey Mead
BARNES
Roehampton
Richmond Park
Kingston Vale
Coombe
NEW MALDEN
Norbiton
KINGSTON UPON THAMES
ACTON
South Acton
Bedford Park
CHISWICK
Mortlake
East Sheen
North Sheen
Kew
Gunnersbury Park
RICHMOND
Richmond Hill
Petersham
Ham
Old Deer Park
Syon Park
St Margarets
TEDDINGTON
Hampton Wick
Hampton Court Park
Bushy Park
West Ealing
Northfields
HANWELL
BRENTFORD
Drayton Green
Osterley Park
Norwood Green
ISLEWORTH
Woodlands
TWICKENHAM
Whitton
HOUNSLOW
HESTON
Hounslow Heath
Hounslow West
North Hyde
Dormer's Wells
SOUTHALL
Hayes Town
Cranford
FELTHAM
Hanworth Park
HANWORTH
Hampton
SUNBURY
River Thames
Low Emission Zone

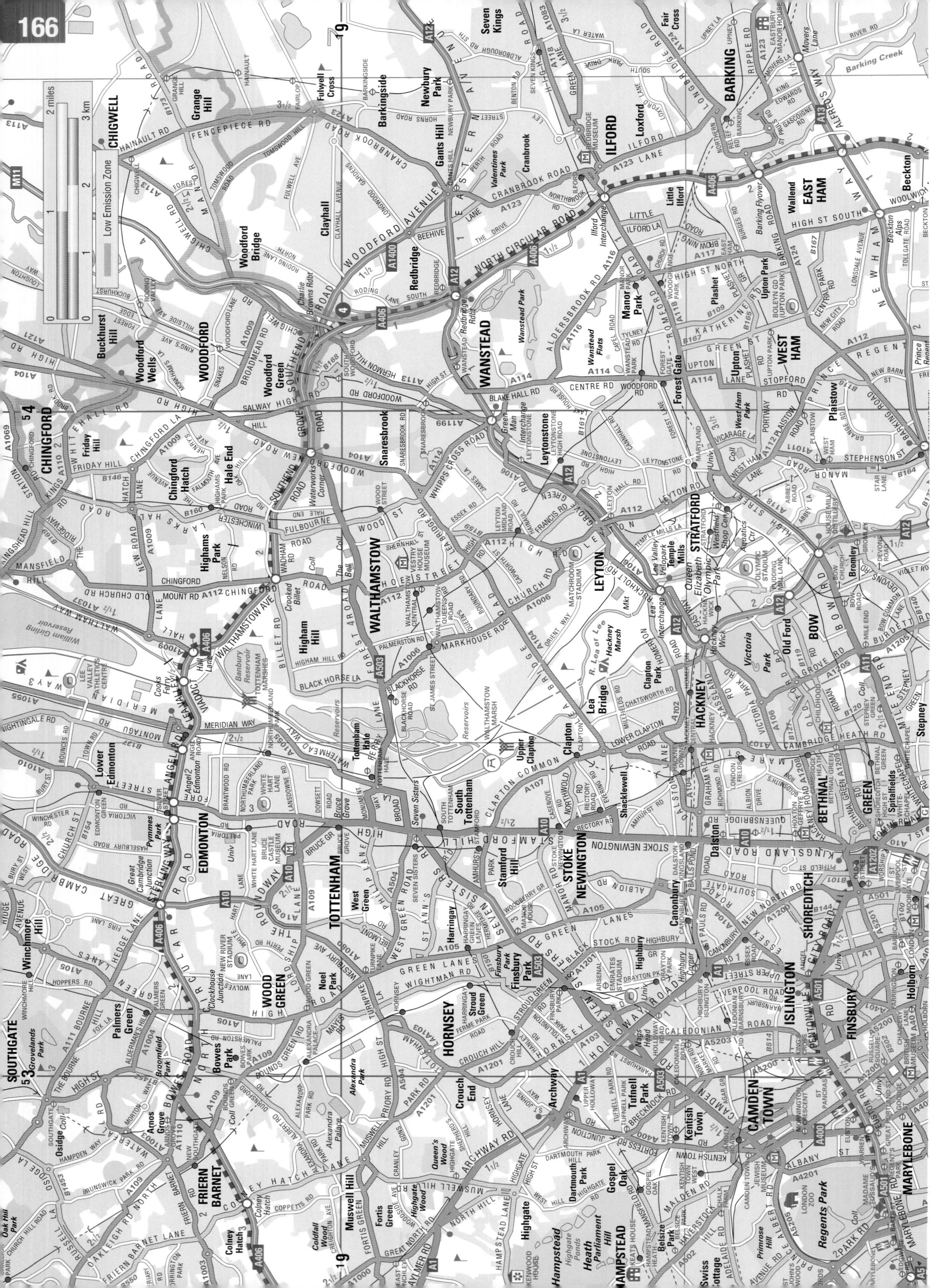
Low Emission Zone
2 miles
3 km
CHIGWELL
Grange Hill
Fulwell Cross
Barkingside
Newbury Park
Seven Kings
Fair Cross
BARKING
ILFORD
Loxford
Gants Hill
Cranbrook
Valentines Park
Clayhall
Woodford Bridge
Redbridge
Little Ilford
EAST HAM
Wallend
Beckton
Buckhurst Hill
Woodford Wells
WOODFORD
Woodford Green
WANSTEAD
Wanstead Park
Wanstead Flats
Manor Park
Plashet
Upton Park
WEST HAM
Upton
Forest Gate
Plaistow
CHINGFORD
Friday Hill
Chingford Hatch
Hale End
Snaresbrook
Leytonstone
STRATFORD
Highams Park
WALTHAMSTOW
LEYTON
Temple Mills
Queen Elizabeth Olympic Park
Bromley
BOW
Old Ford
Victoria Park
Higham Hill
Hackney Marsh
Clapton Park
HACKNEY
Lea Bridge
Clapton
Upper Clapton
Tottenham Hale
Lower Edmonton
EDMONTON
South Tottenham
Shacklewell
Dalston
BETHNAL GREEN
Stepney
Spitalfields
Stamford Hill
STOKE NEWINGTON
TOTTENHAM
West Green
Harringay
Canonbury
SHOREDITCH
Winchmore Hill
WOOD GREEN
Noel Park
Finsbury Park
Highbury
ISLINGTON
FINSBURY
Holborn
SOUTHGATE
Grovelands Park
Palmers Green
Bowes Park
HORNSEY
Stroud Green
Tufnell Park
CAMDEN TOWN
Kentish Town
Crouch End
Archway
Arnos Grove
FRIERN BARNET
Muswell Hill
Fortis Green
Highgate
Gospel Oak
Dartmouth Park
Hampstead Heath
Parliament Hill
Belsize Park
Primrose Hill
Regents Park
MARYLEBONE
Colney Hatch
Osidge
Oak Hill Park
Alexandra Palace
Alexandra Park
Queen's Wood
Highgate Wood
Coldfall Wood
William Girling Reservoir
Banbury Reservoir
Barking Creek

River Thames
North Woolwich
Plumstead
Shooters Hill
East Wickham
Falconwood
Oxleas Wood
New Eltham
Avery Hill
Longlands
CHISLEHURST
Chislehurst Common
Petts Wood
WOOLWICH
Woolwich Ferry
Eltham Common
ELTHAM
Woolwich Common
Charlton
Kidbrooke
Silvertown
Thames Barrier
City Airport
Royal Albert Dock
King George V Dock
Royal Victoria Dock
Custom House
Canning Town
North Greenwich
Blackheath Park
Mottingham
Grove Park
Elmstead Wood
Widmore
Bickley
Sundridge Park
BROMLEY
GREENWICH
Greenwich Park
Blackwall Tunnel
Blackwall
BLACKHEATH
LEWISHAM
Hither Green
Lee
Plaistow
Downham
Shortlands
POPLAR
Canary Wharf
ISLE OF DOGS
Millwall
CATFORD
Bellingham
Bell Green
Beckenham Place Park
BECKENHAM
Eden Park
Brockley
Ladywell
Limehouse
Rotherhithe
Surrey Quays
DEPTFORD
New Cross
Forest Hill
PENGE
Elmers End
Nunhead
Honor Oak
Wapping
BERMONDSEY
Peckham
Peckham Rye Park
Aldgate
Tower Br.
East Dulwich
Dulwich
Anerley
Walworth
CAMBERWELL
Elephant & Castle
Dulwich Park
South Norwood
West Dulwich
Kennington
Camberwell Green
LAMBETH
Brockwell Park
Tulse Hill
STREATHAM
Norbury
BRIXTON
Streatham Common
Vauxhall
Pimlico
Green Park
Mayfair
CLAPHAM
Streatham Vale
Mitcham Common
BATTERSEA
Battersea Park
Grange Mills
Tooting Bec Common
Furzedown
MITCHAM
Clapham Common
Balham
Hyde Park
CHELSEA
Wandsworth Common
Upper Tooting
Tooting Bec
Collier's Wood

Outwood
Ringley
WHITEFIELD
Besses o' th' Barn
Simister
Rhodes
Moorclose
Alkrington Garden Village
Park Lane
Heaton Park
Higher Blackley
Clifton Country Park
PRESTWICH
Charlestown
Clifton Green
Newtown
Prestwich Forest Park
Crumpsall
Boggart Hole Clough
New Moston
SWINTON
Kersal
Broughton Park
Moston
River Irwell
PENDLEBURY
Harpurhey
Newton Heath
Ellesmere Park
Strangeways
Miles Platting
Little Bolton
Seedley
SALFORD
Clayton
Patricroft
ECCLES
MANCHESTER
Openshaw
Manchester Ship Canal
Ardwick
Salford Quays
Hulme
TRAFFORD PARK
Gorton
Old Trafford
Moss Side
Rusholme
Ryder Brow
Firswood
Whalley Range
Levenshulme
STRETFORD
Longford Park
North Reddish
REDDISH
Chorlton-cum-Hardy
Ashton upon Mersey
Withington
River Mersey
Barlow Moor
Burnage
South Reddish
West Didsbury
SALE
Woodhouses
Brooklands
Heaton Mersey
Heaton Norris
Northern Moor
Fletcher Moss
Timperley
Roundthorn
GATLEY
WYTHENSHAWE
ALTRINCHAM
Newall Green
CHEADLE
0 1 2 miles
0 1 2 3 km

Town plan symbols

- Motorway
- **Primary route** – dual, single carriageway
- **A road** – dual, single carriageway
- **B road** – dual, single carriageway
- Minor through road
- One-way street
- Pedestrian roads
- Shopping streets
- Railway with station
- Tramway with station (City Hall)
- Underground or Metro station (Bank, West St)
- Hospital
- Parking
- Police, Post Office
- Shopmobility
- Youth hostel
- Bus or railway station building
- Shopping precinct or retail park
- Park
- Congestion charge zone
- Abbey or cathedral
- Ancient monument
- Aquarium
- Art gallery
- Bird collection or aviary
- Building of interest
- Castle
- Church of interest
- Cinema
- Garden
- Historic ship
- House
- House and garden
- Museum
- Preserved railway
- Roman antiquity
- Safari park
- Theatre
- Tourist information centre
- Zoo
- Other place of interest

Aberdeen

0 Miles ¼

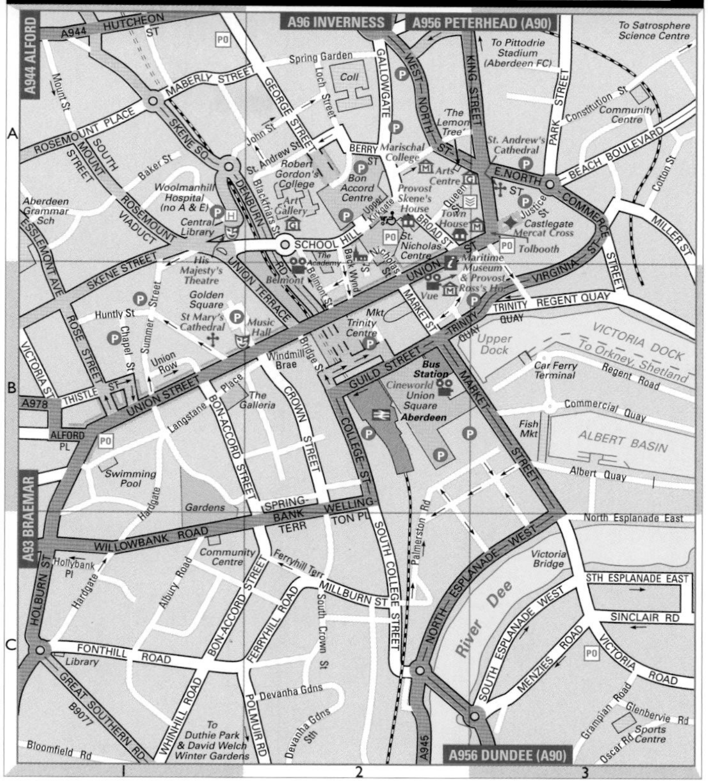

Birmingham

0 Miles ¼

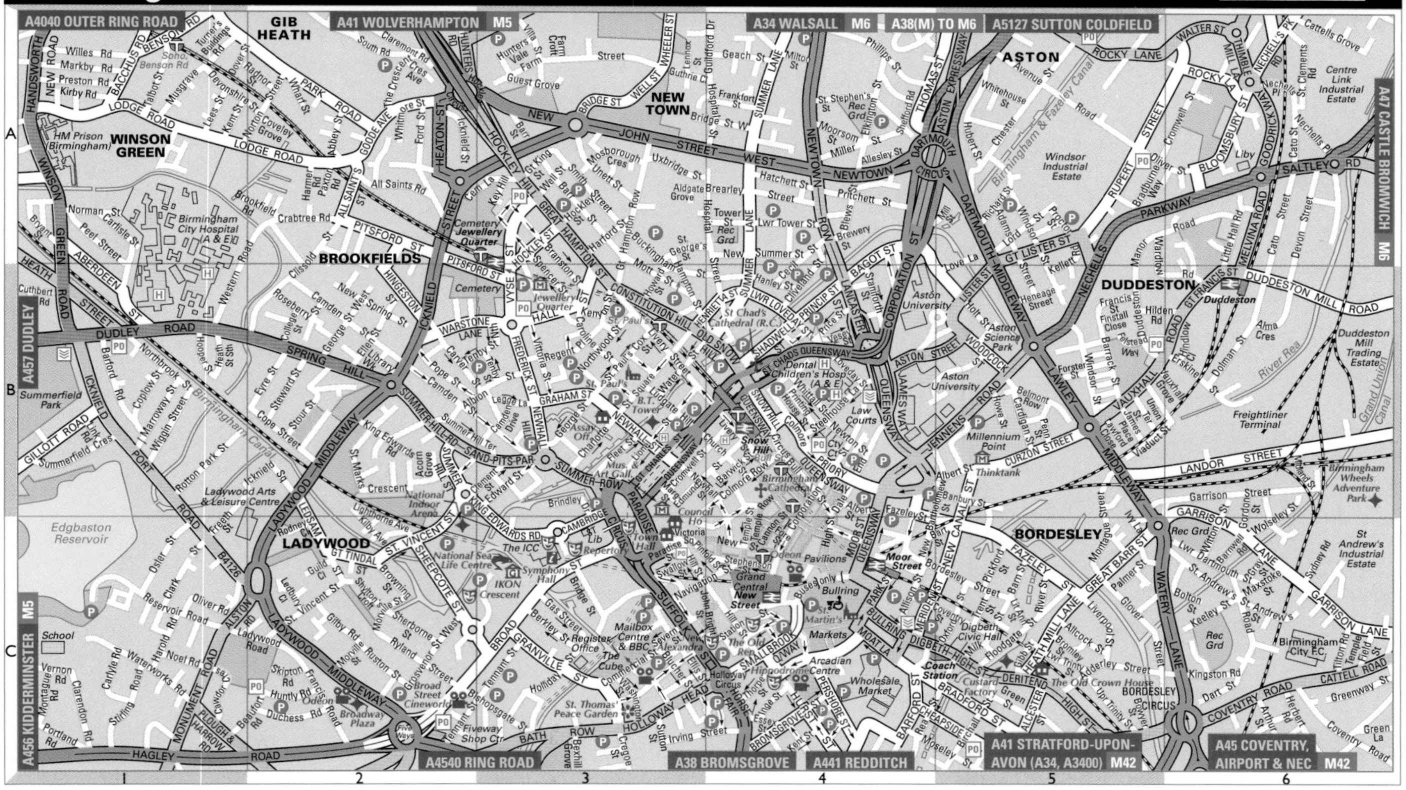

Bath

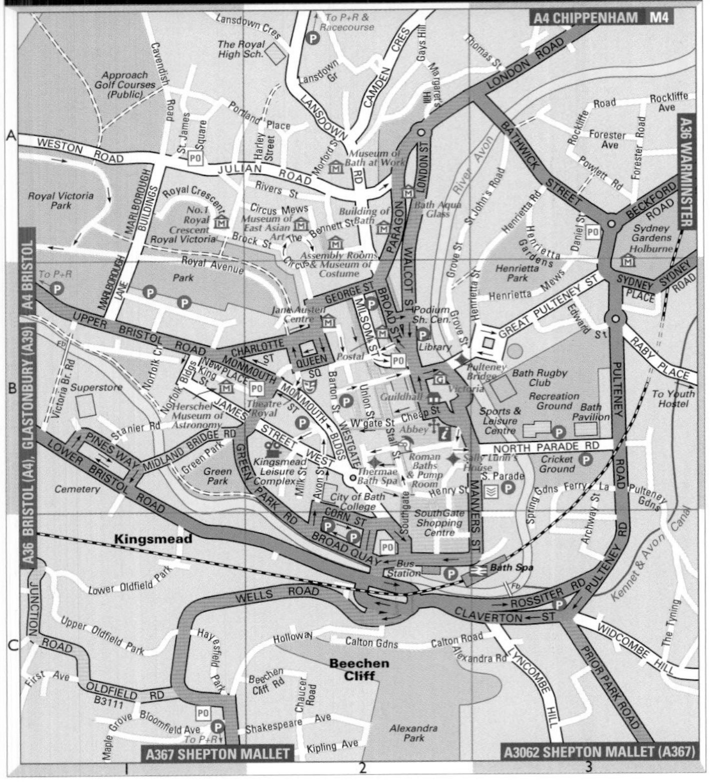

Bradford

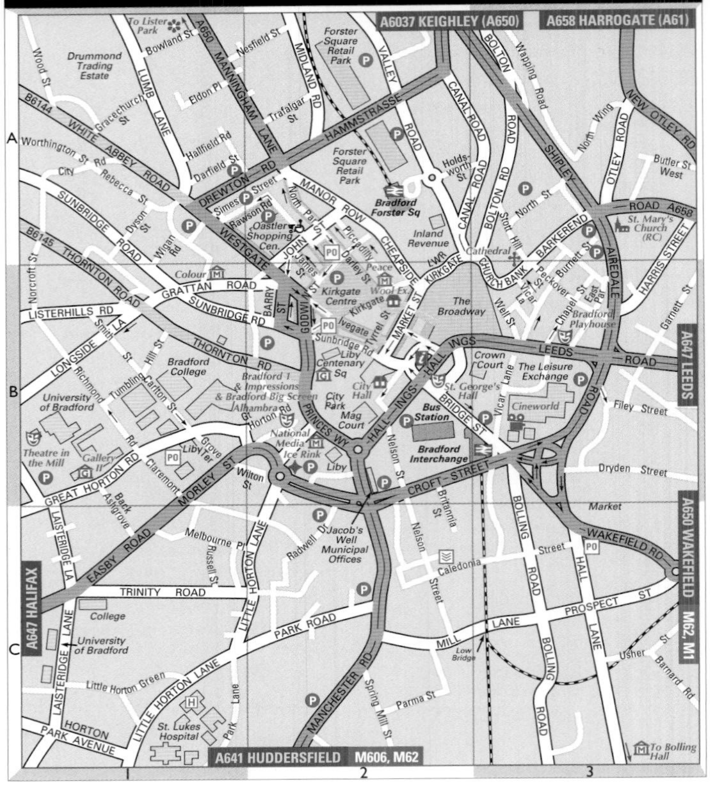

Bristol

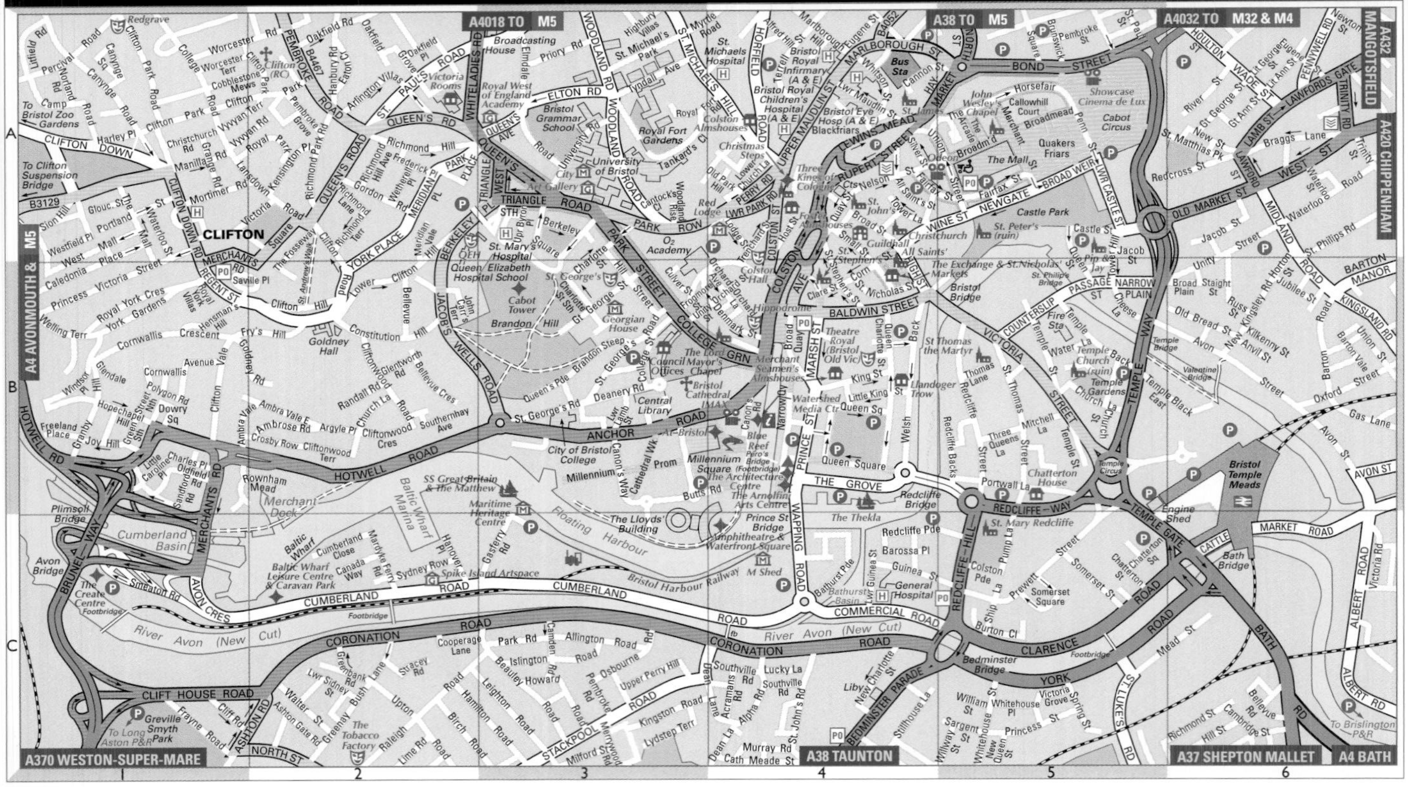

Cambridge

0 Miles ¼

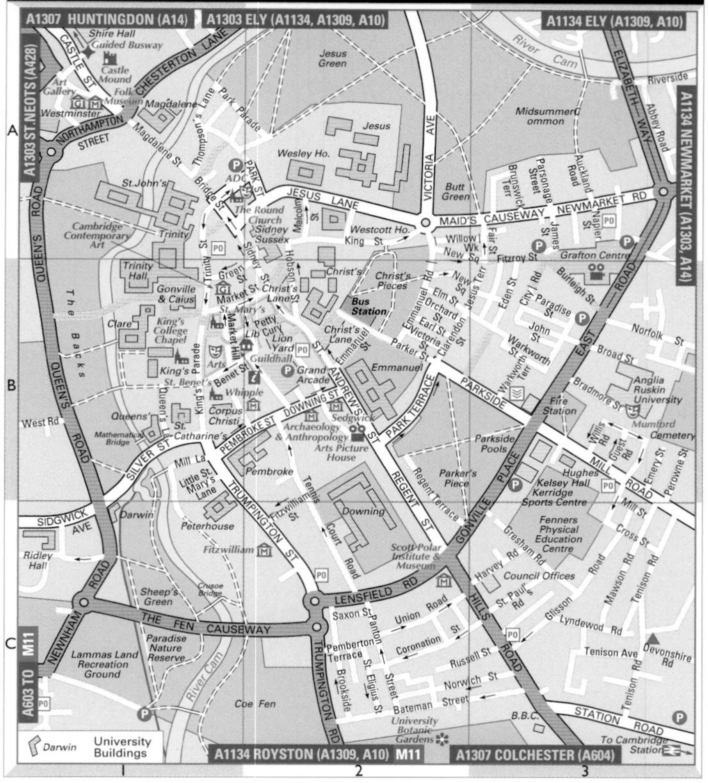

Cardiff / Caerdydd

0 Miles ¼

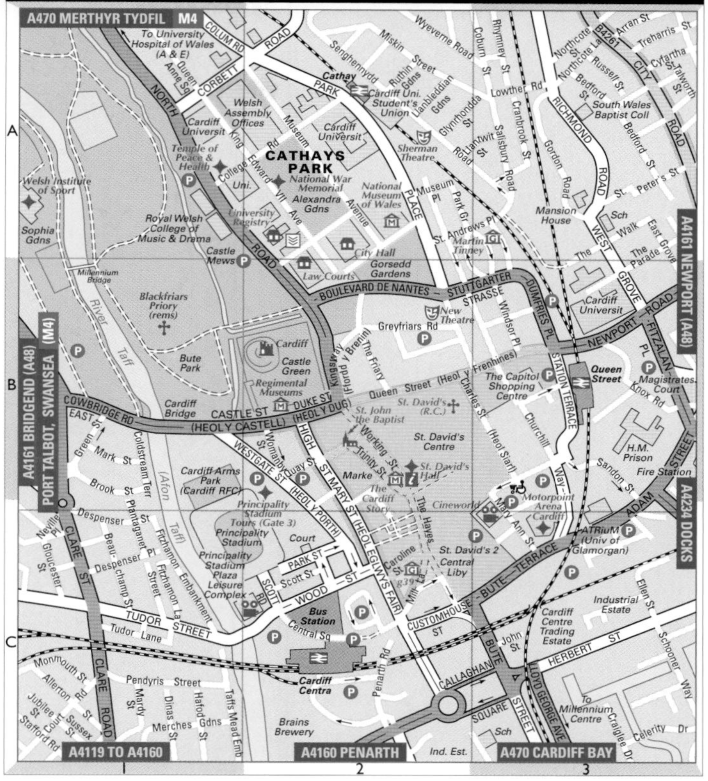

Coventry

0 Miles ¼

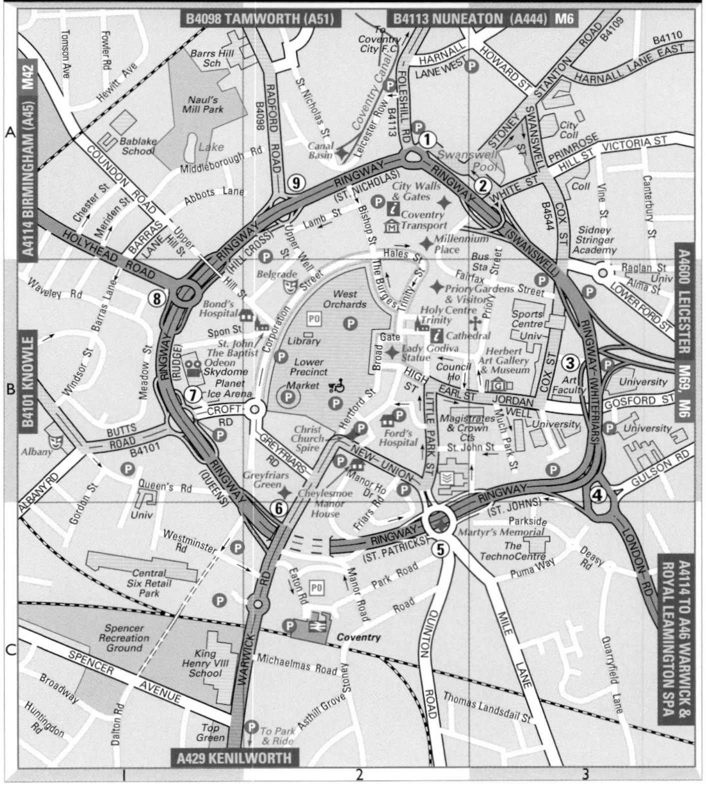

Derby

0 Miles ¼

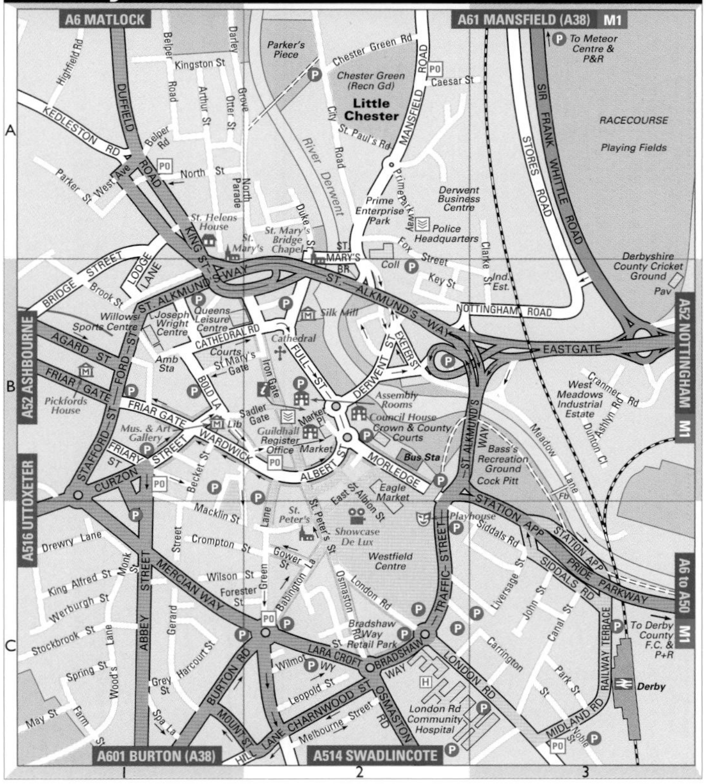

Edinburgh

0 Miles ¼

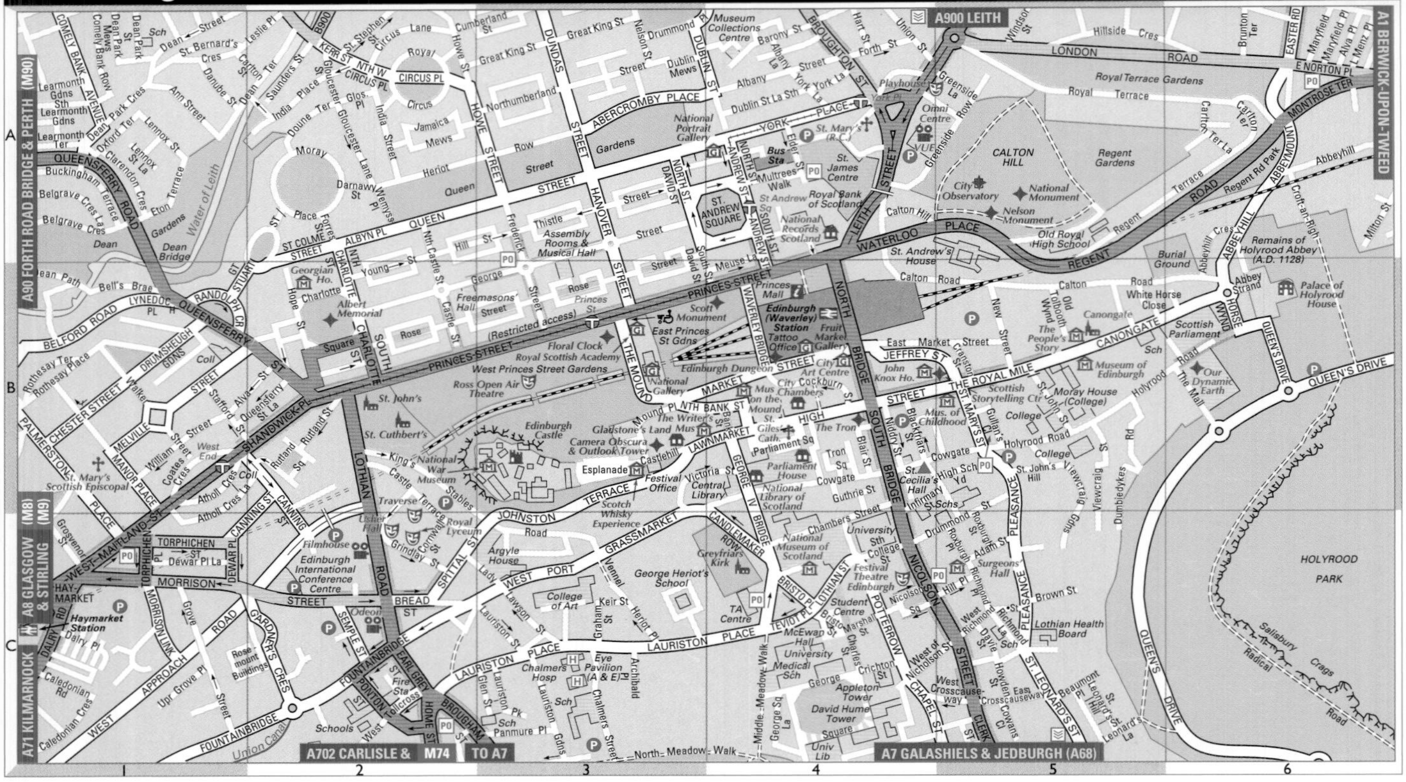

Glasgow

0 Miles ¼

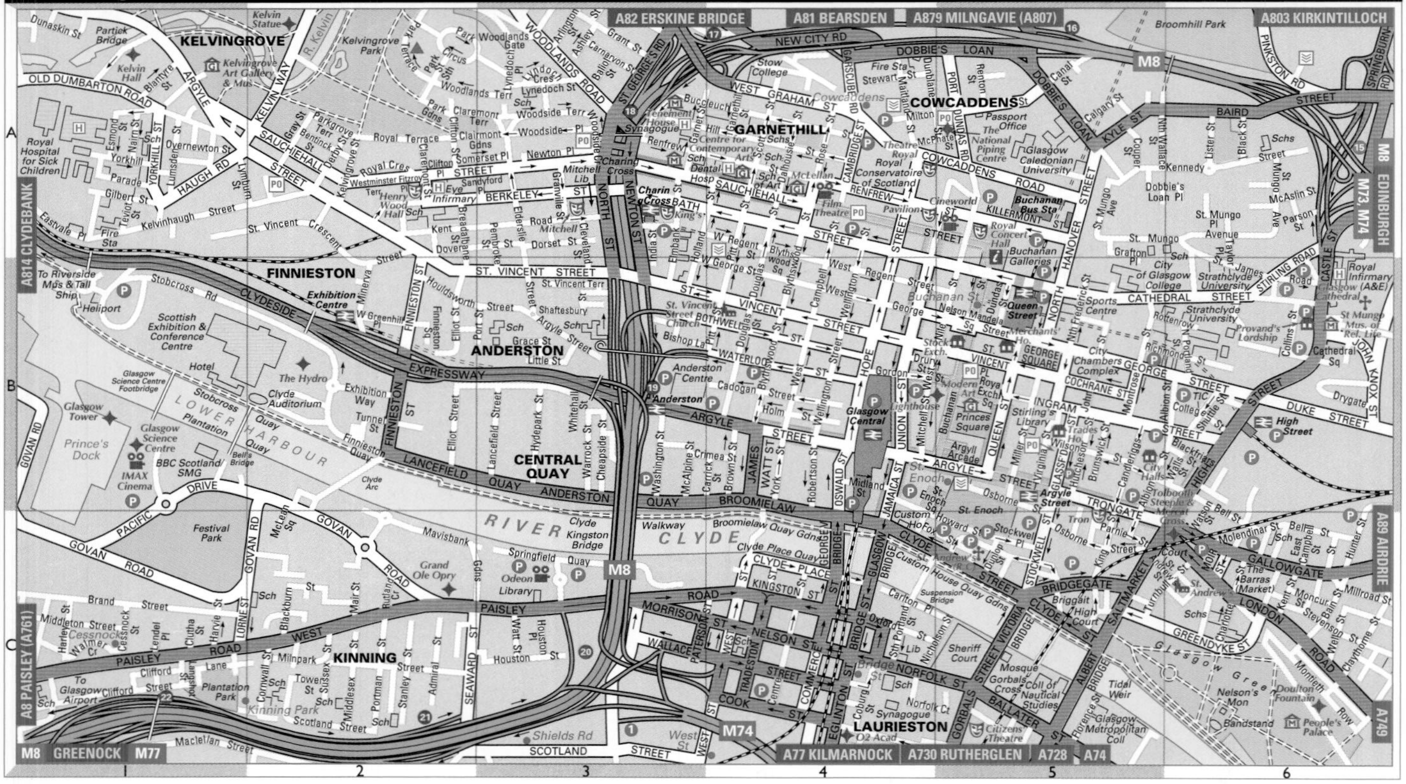

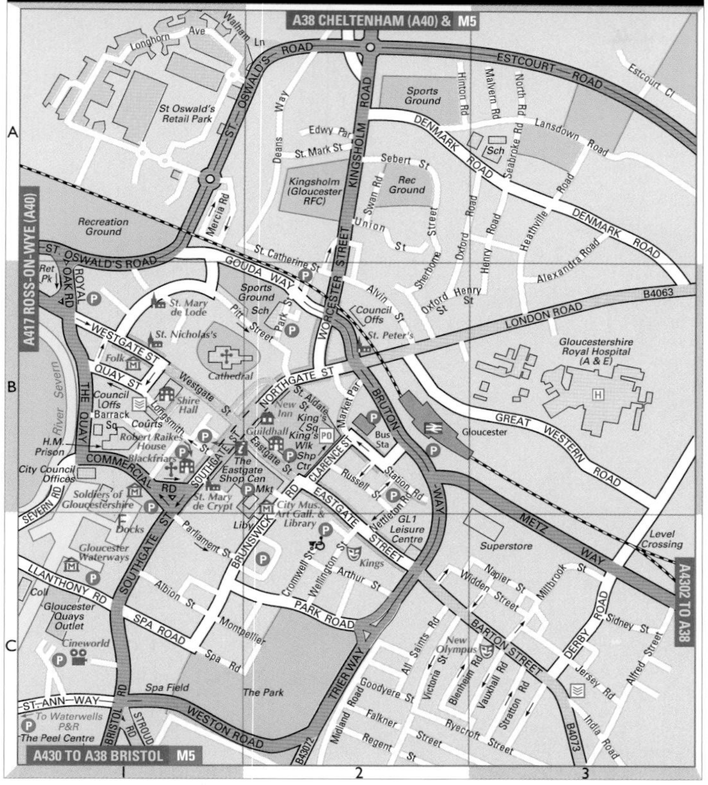
Gloucester
0 Miles ¼
A38 CHELTENHAM (A40) & M5
A417 ROSS-ON-WYE (A40)
A4302 TO A38
A430 TO A38 BRISTOL M5
St Oswald's Retail Park
Sports Ground
Kingsholm (Gloucester RFC)
Rec Ground
Recreation Ground
ESTCOURT ROAD
DENMARK ROAD
LONDON ROAD
GREAT WESTERN ROAD
METZ WAY
Gloucestershire Royal Hospital (A & E)
Cathedral
Gloucester
Superstore
Level Crossing
Gloucester Quays Outlet
Cineworld
Spa Field
The Park
The Peel Centre
ST ANN WAY
WESTON ROAD
SOUTHGATE
EASTGATE
NORTHGATE ST
WESTGATE ST
BRUTON WAY
TRIER WAY
BARTON STREET
PARK ROAD
SPA ROAD
LLANTHONY RD
COMMERCIAL RD
THE QUAY
A
B
C
1
2
3

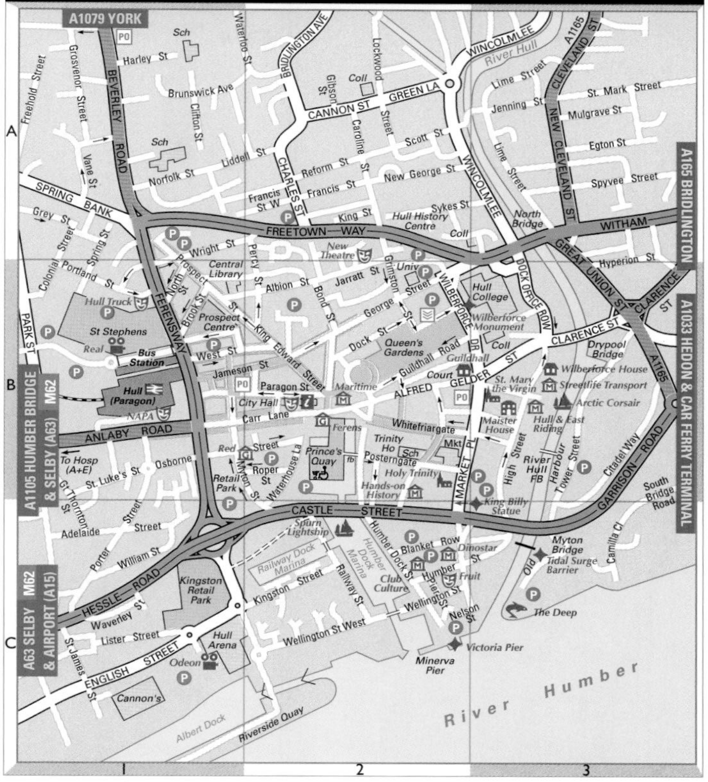
Hull
0 Miles ¼
A1079 YORK
A165 BRIDLINGTON
A1033 HEDON & CAR FERRY TERMINAL
A1105 HUMBER BRIDGE & SELBY (A63) M62
A63 SELBY M62 & AIRPORT (A15)
BEVERLEY ROAD
FREETOWN WAY
WINCOLMLEE
NEW CLEVELAND ST
GREAT UNION ST
CLARENCE ST
GARRISON ROAD
CASTLE STREET
ANLABY ROAD
HESSLE ROAD
ENGLISH STREET
FERENSWAY
Hull (Paragon)
Bus Station
Hull College
Queen's Gardens
Prince's Quay
Kingston Retail Park
Hull Arena
The Deep
Victoria Pier
Minerva Pier
Myton Bridge
Tidal Surge Barrier
River Hull
River Humber
A
B
C
1
2
3

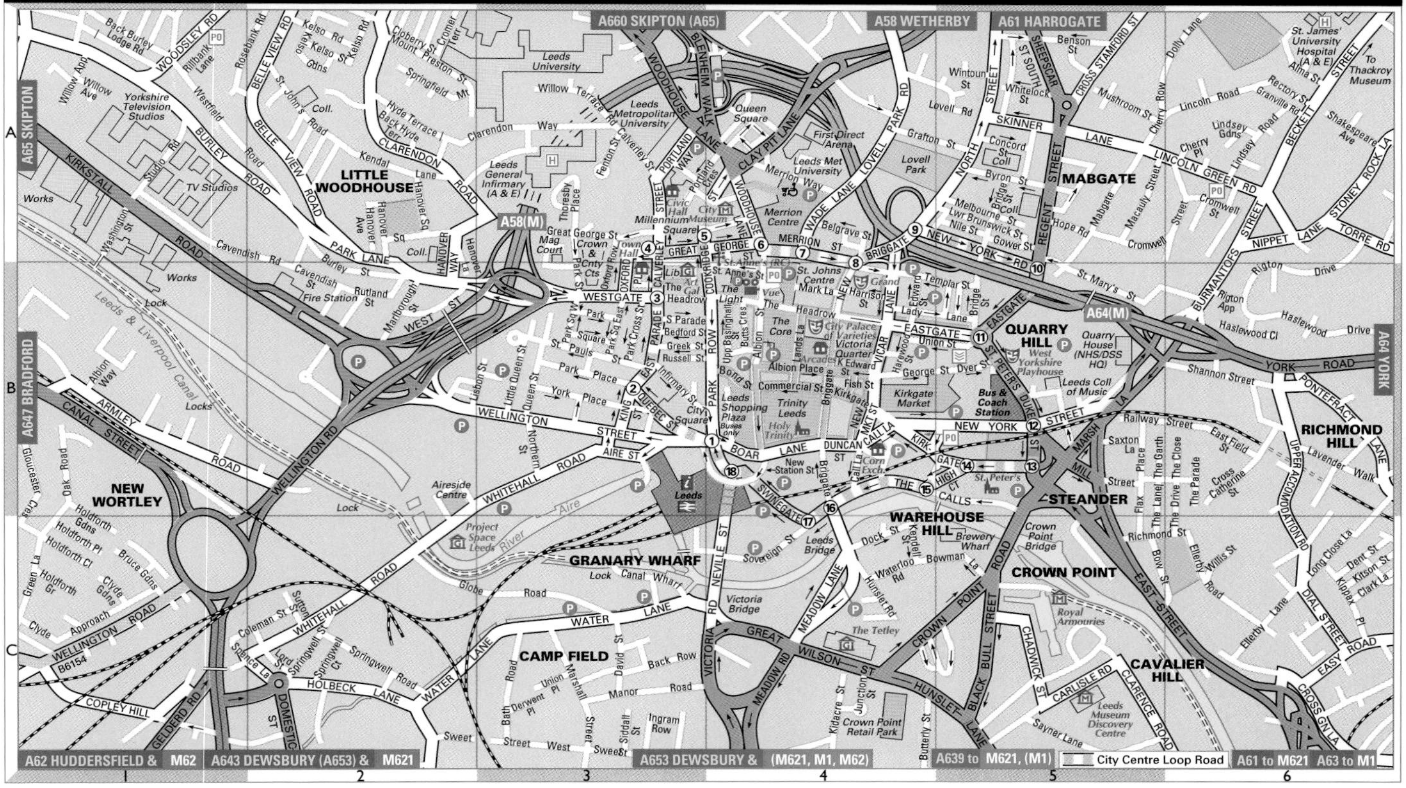
Leeds
0 Miles ¼
A660 SKIPTON (A65)
A58 WETHERBY
A61 HARROGATE
A65 SKIPTON
A647 BRADFORD
A64 YORK
A62 HUDDERSFIELD & M62
A643 DEWSBURY (A653) & M621
A653 DEWSBURY & (M621, M1, M62)
A639 to M621, (M1)
City Centre Loop Road
A61 to M621 A63 to M1
LITTLE WOODHOUSE
MABGATE
QUARRY HILL
RICHMOND HILL
NEW WORTLEY
GRANARY WHARF
WAREHOUSE HILL
CROWN POINT
STEANDER
CAMP FIELD
CAVALIER HILL
Leeds University
Leeds General Infirmary (A & E)
Leeds Met University
Yorkshire Television Studios
TV Studios
St. James' University Hospital (A & E)
To Thackray Museum
Kirkgate Market
Bus & Coach Station
Leeds Shopping Plaza
Leeds
Royal Armouries
The Tetley
Crown Point Retail Park
Leeds Museum Discovery Centre
KIRKSTALL ROAD
WELLINGTON ROAD
WELLINGTON STREET
WHITEHALL ROAD
WATER LANE
HOLBECK LANE
NEVILLE ST
VICTORIA RD
MEADOW LANE
CROWN POINT ROAD
EAST STREET
YORK ROAD
REGENT STREET
Leeds & Liverpool Canal
River Aire
A
B
C
1
2
3
4
5
6

REGENT'S PARK
SOMERS TOWN
BLOOMSBURY
FITZROVIA
SOHO
MAYFAIR
ST. JAMES'S
HYDE PARK
GREEN PARK
ST. JAMES'S PARK
WESTMINSTER
BELGRAVIA
Buckingham Palace
Houses of Parliament
Westminster Abbey
British Museum
Euston
Victoria
Charing Cross
St. Pancras International
King's Cross
0 Miles 1/2

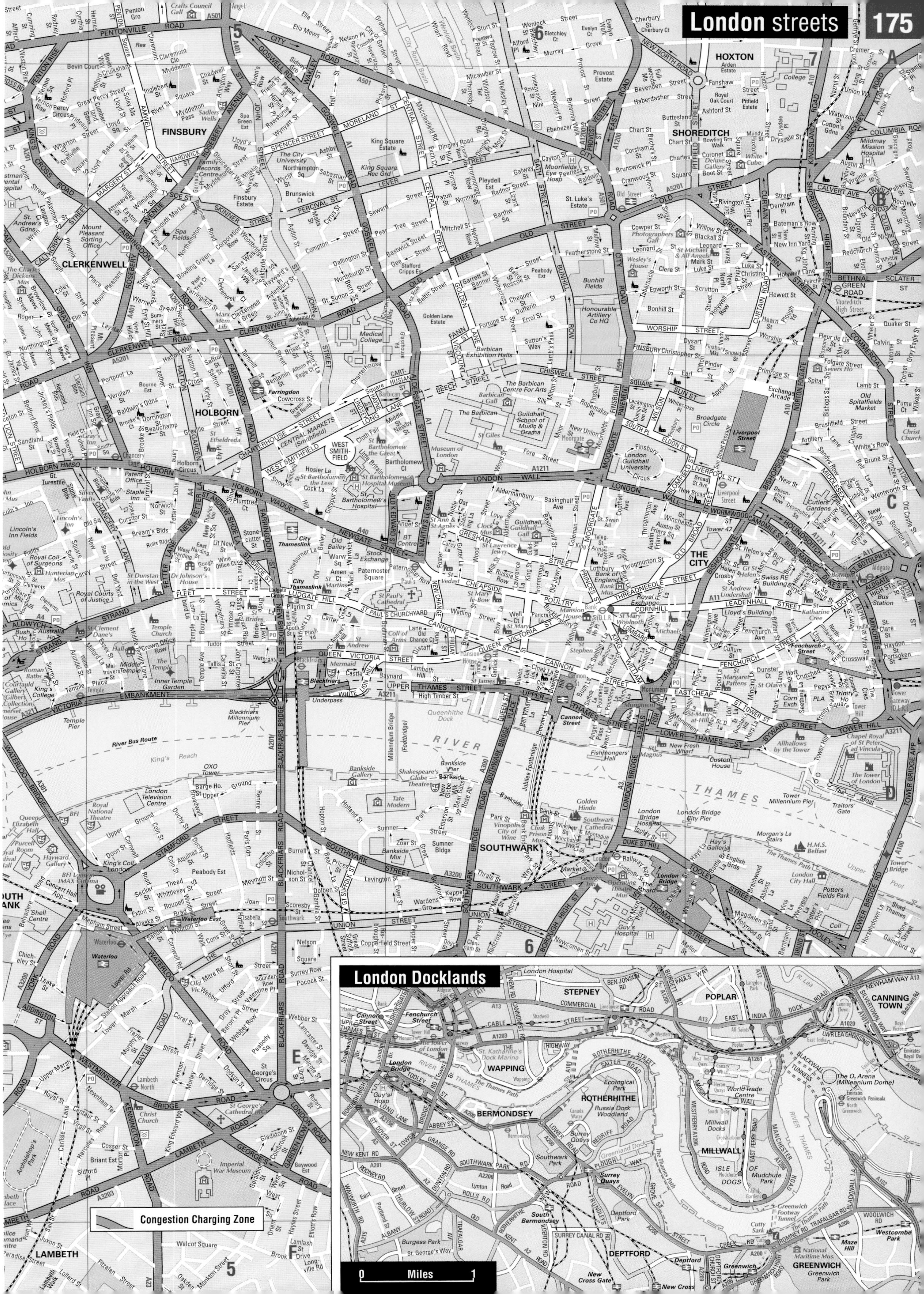
FINSBURY
CLERKENWELL
HOLBORN
HOXTON
SHOREDITCH
THE CITY
SOUTHWARK
LAMBETH
RIVER THAMES
The Barbican
St Paul's Cathedral
Bank of England
The Tower of London
Tate Modern
Shakespeare's Globe Theatre
Imperial War Museum
Waterloo
Congestion Charging Zone
London Docklands
STEPNEY
POPLAR
CANNING TOWN
WAPPING
ROTHERHITHE
BERMONDSEY
MILLWALL
ISLE OF DOGS
DEPTFORD
GREENWICH
The O2 Arena (Millennium Dome)
Miles

Liverpool

0 Miles ¼

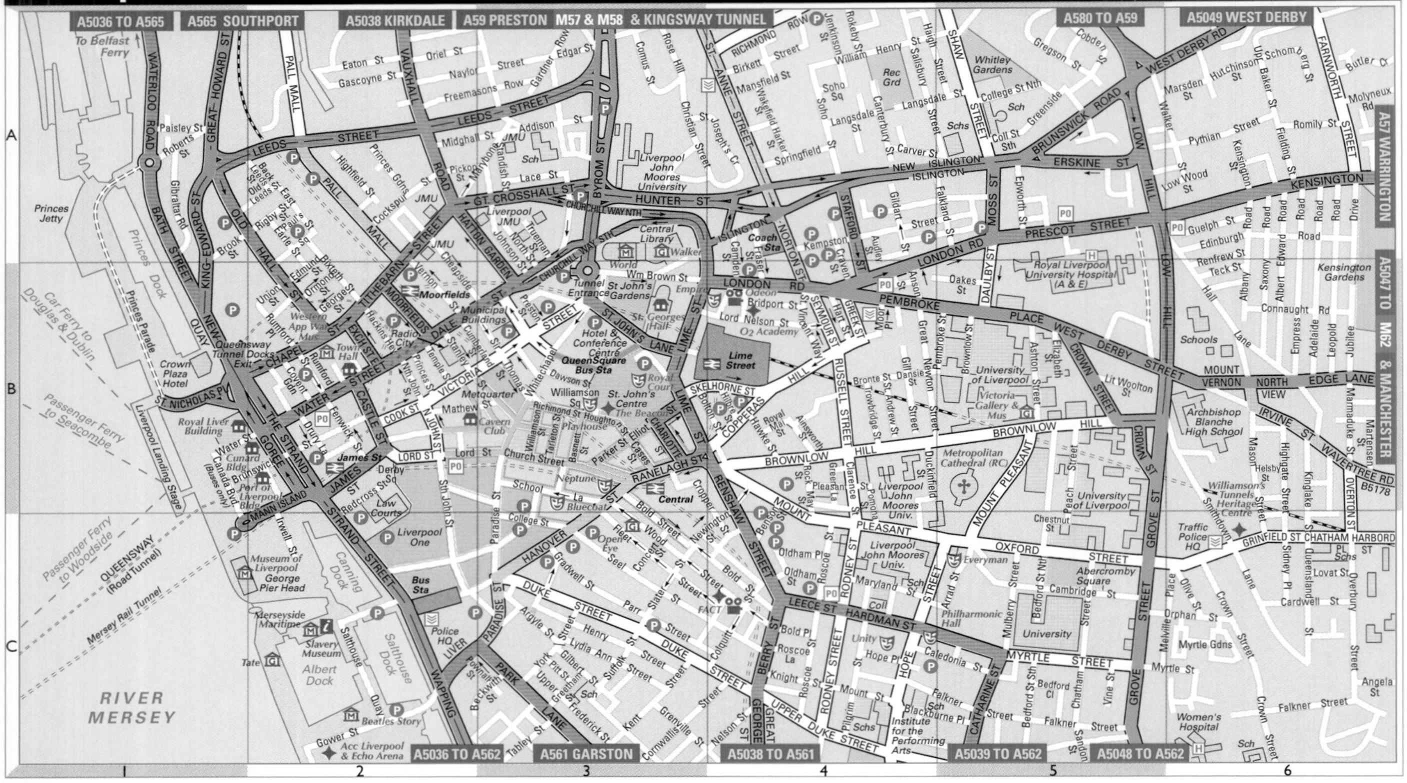

Manchester

0 Miles ¼

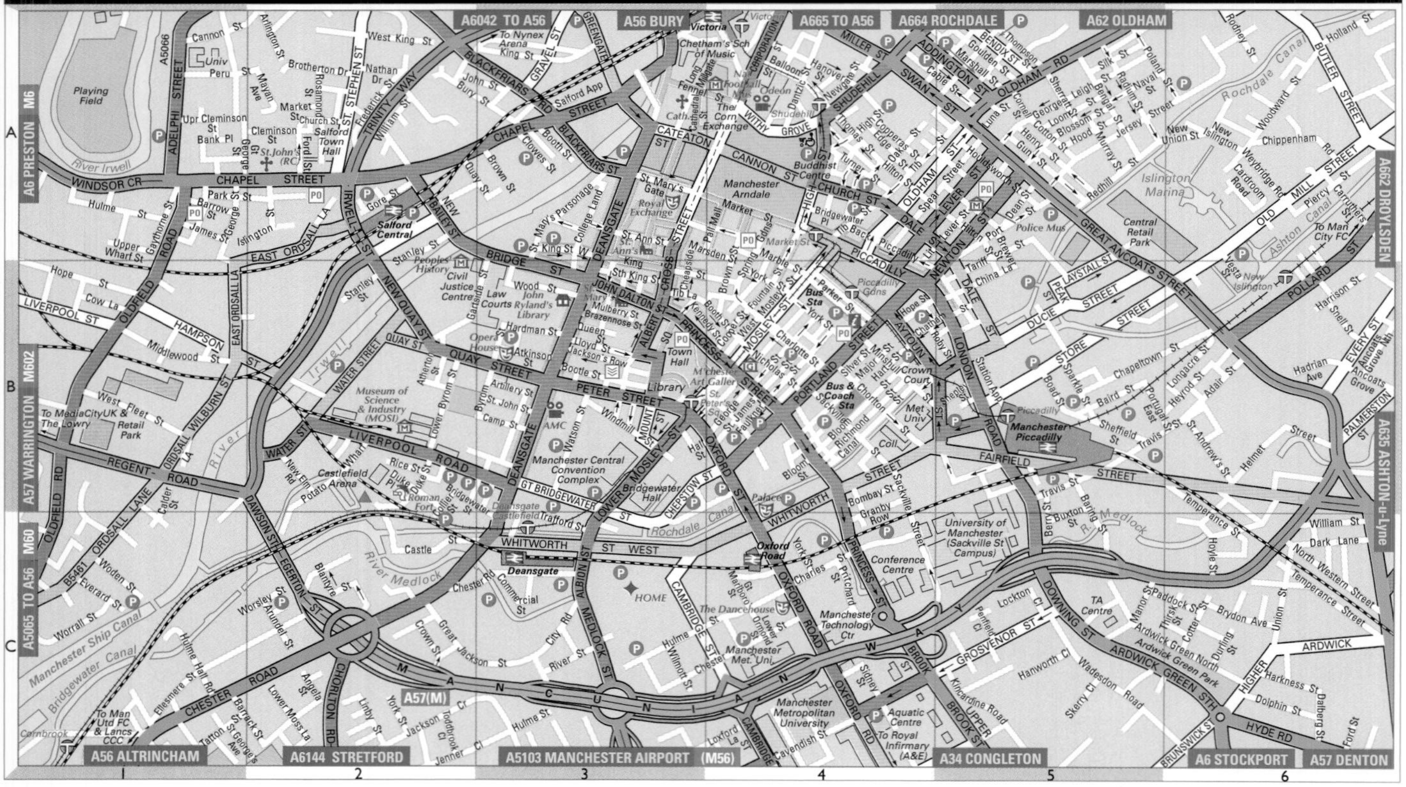

Leicester

0 Miles ¼

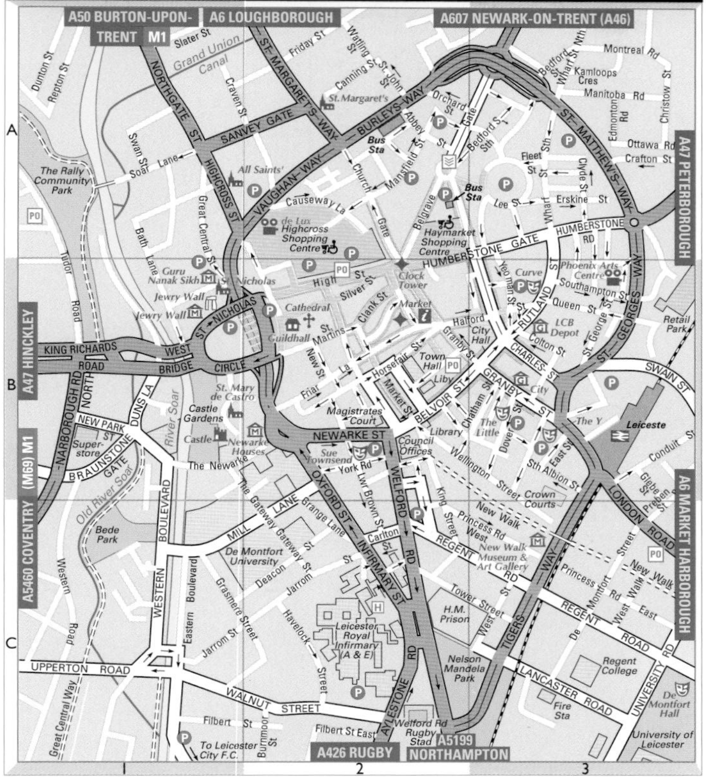

Middlesbrough

0 Miles ¼

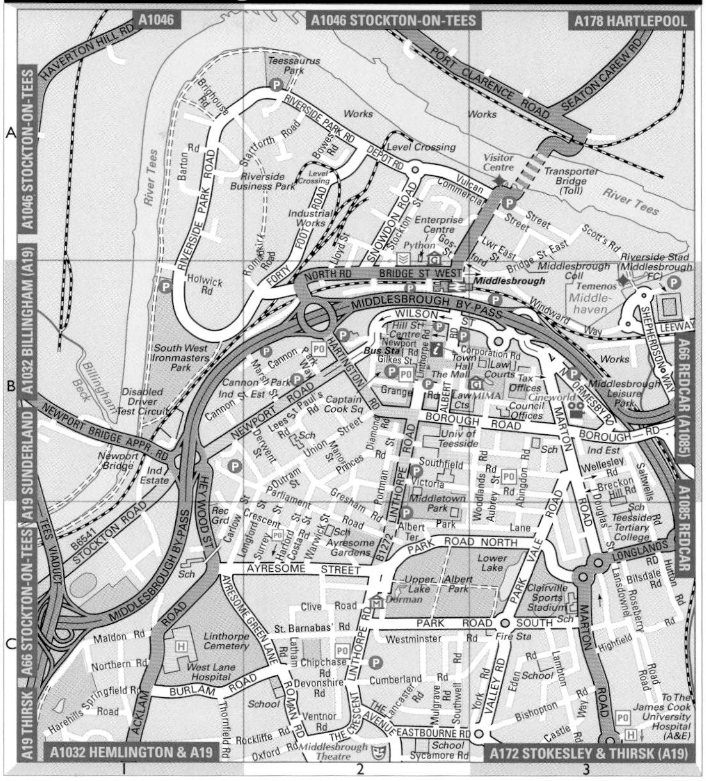

Newcastle upon Tyne

0 Miles ¼

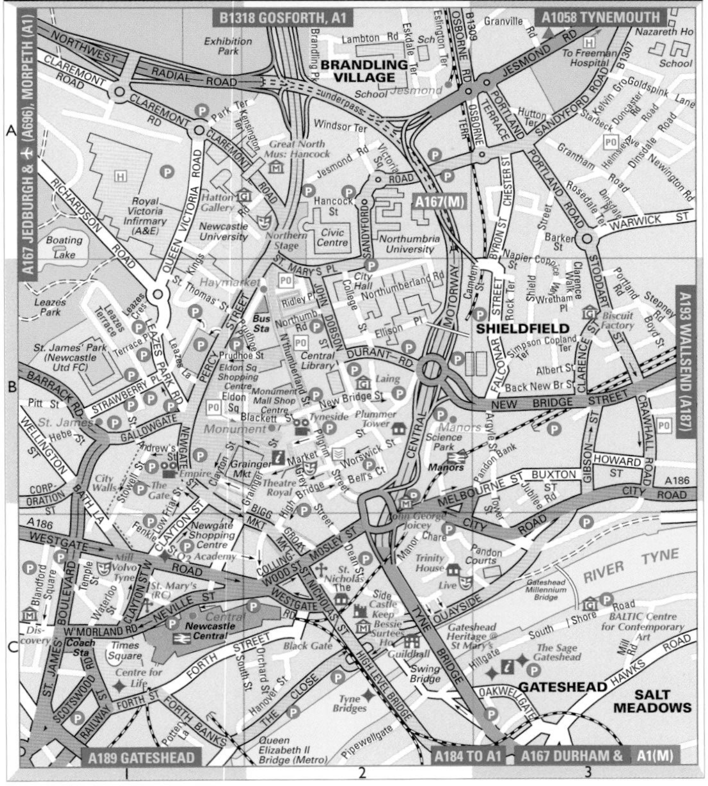

Norwich

0 Miles ¼

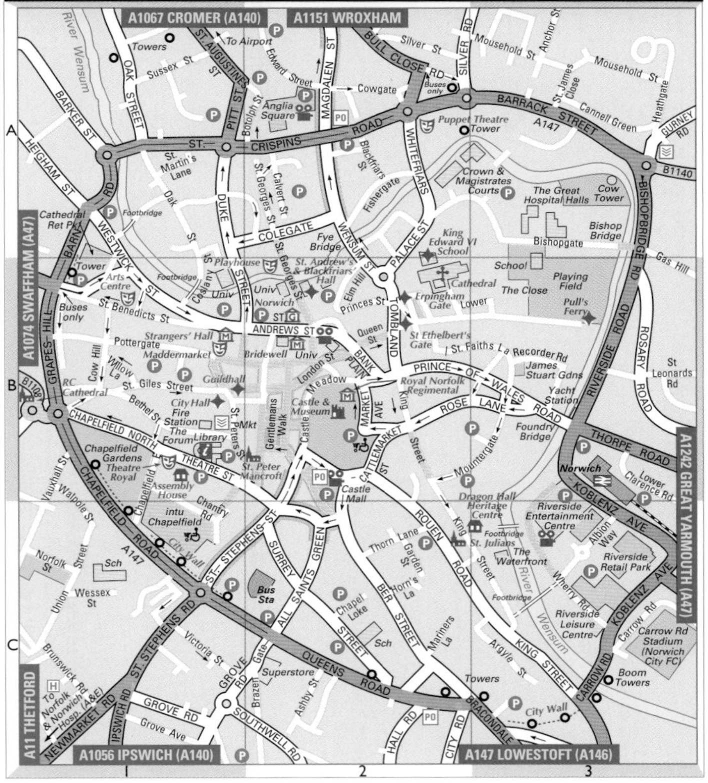

Nottingham

0 Miles ¼

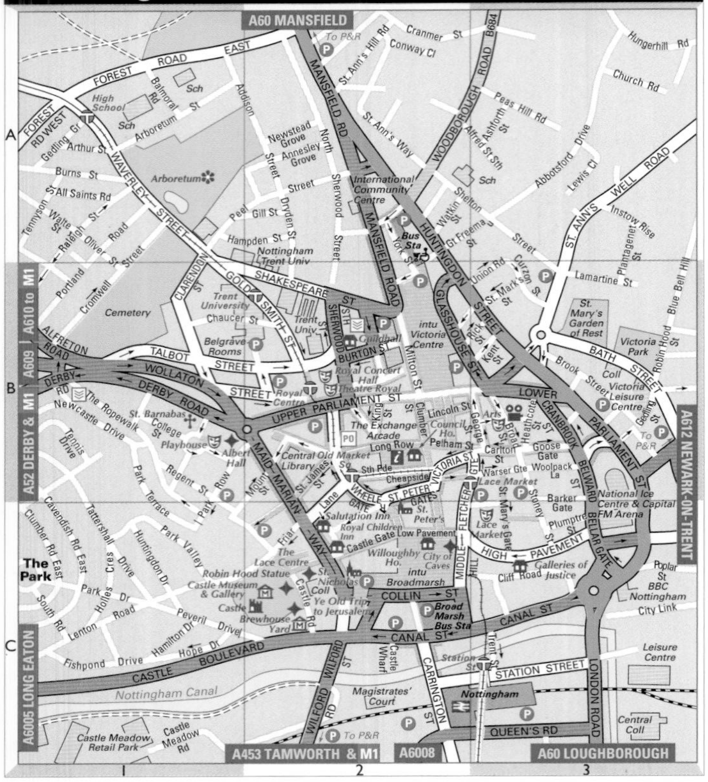

Oxford

0 Miles ¼

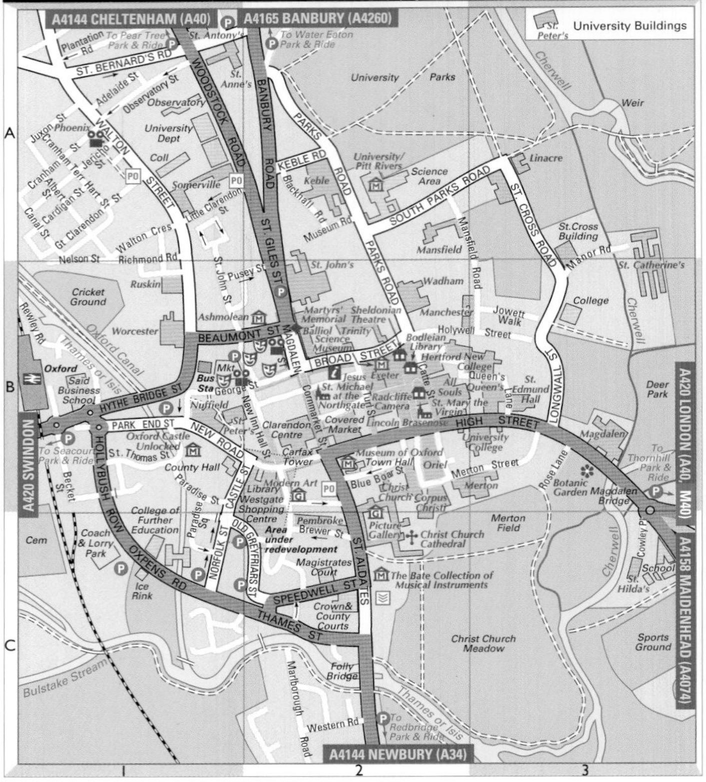

Plymouth

0 Miles ¼

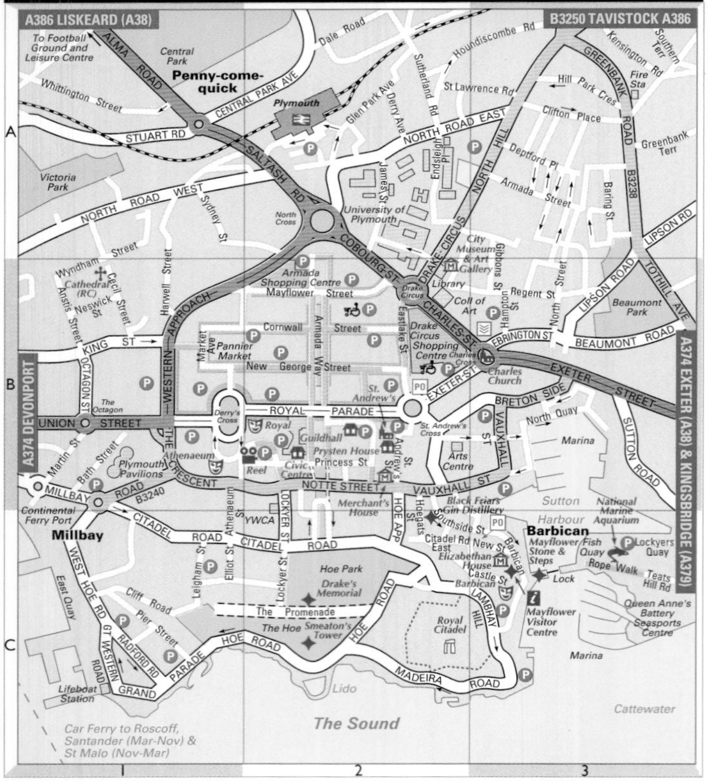

Portsmouth

0 Miles ¼

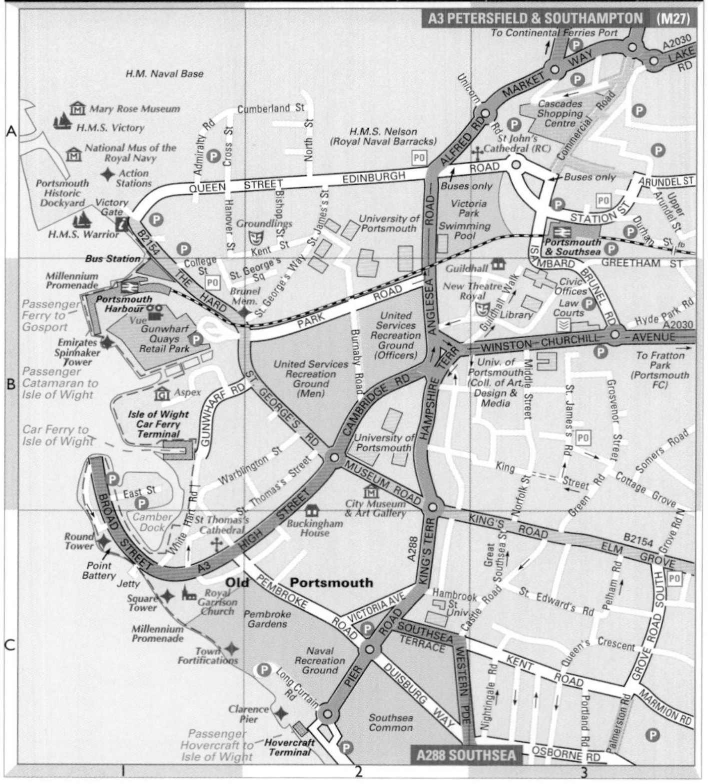

Reading

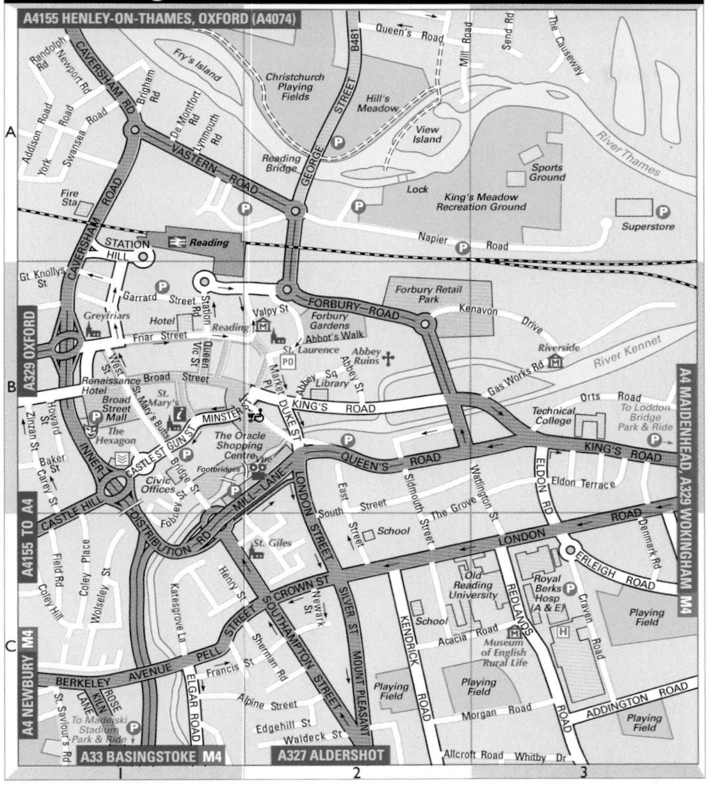

Southampton

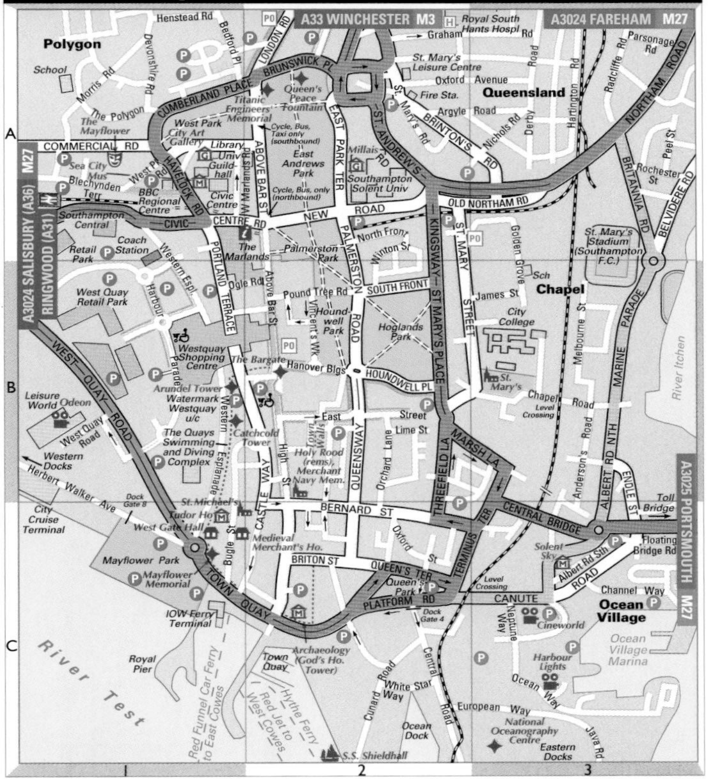

Sheffield

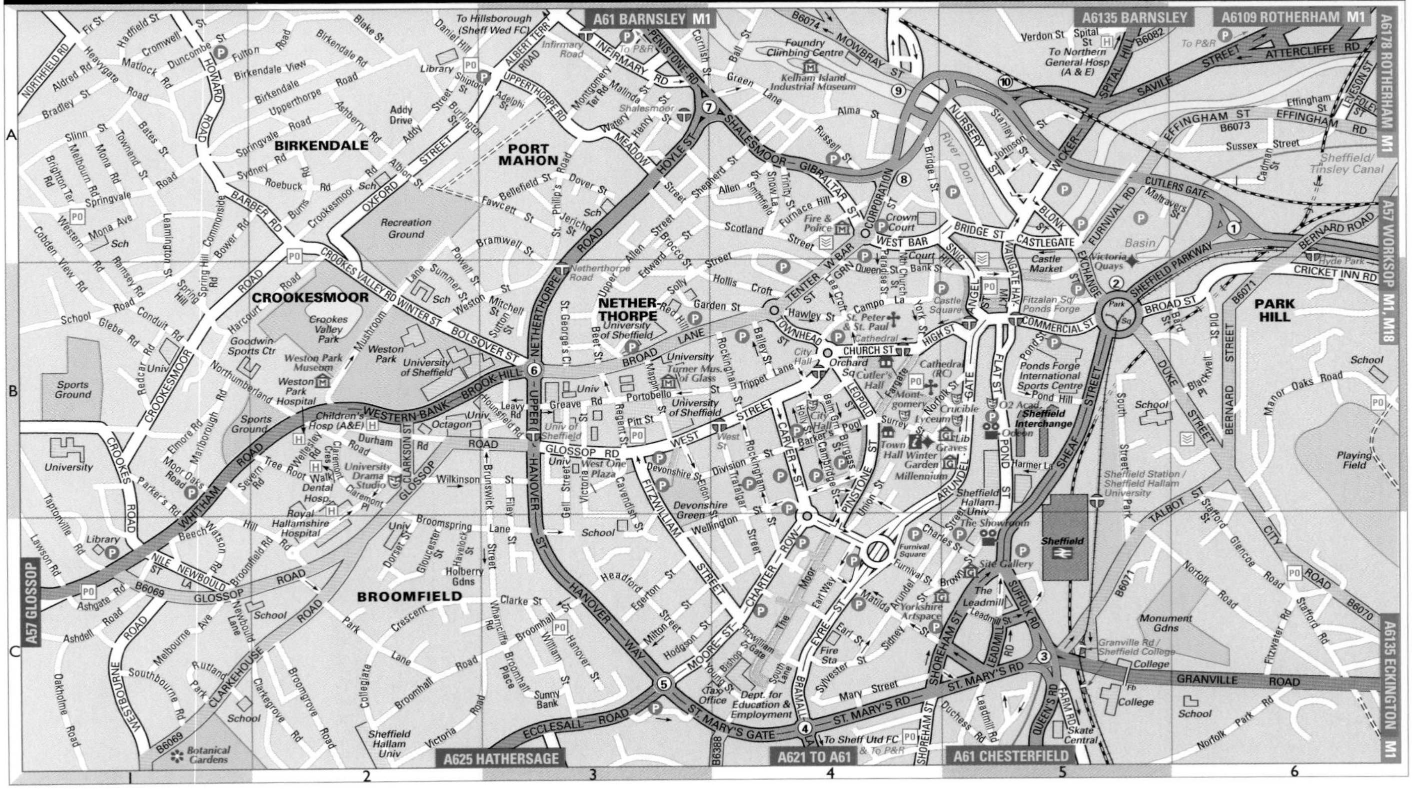

Stoke-on-Trent (Hanley)

0 Miles ¼

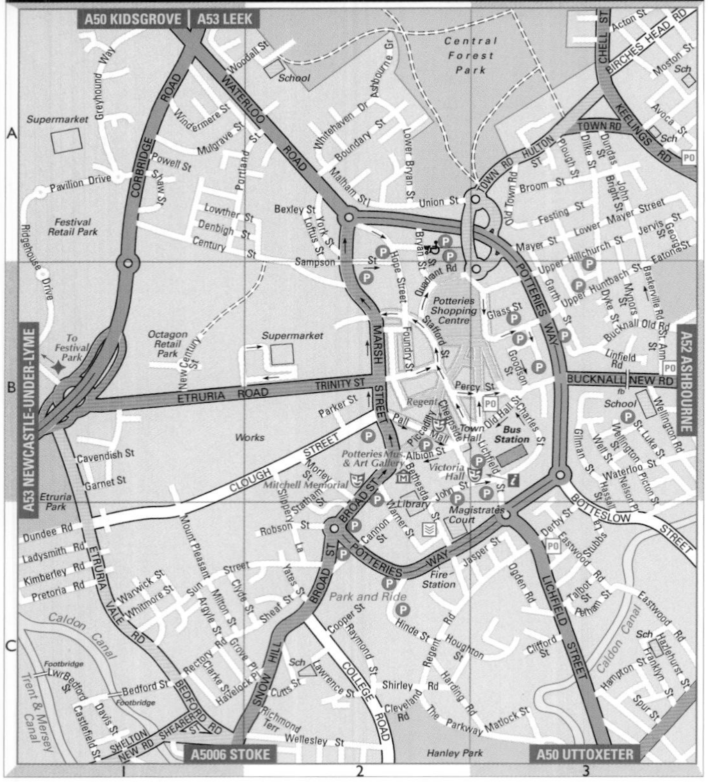

Swansea / Abertawe

0 Miles ¼

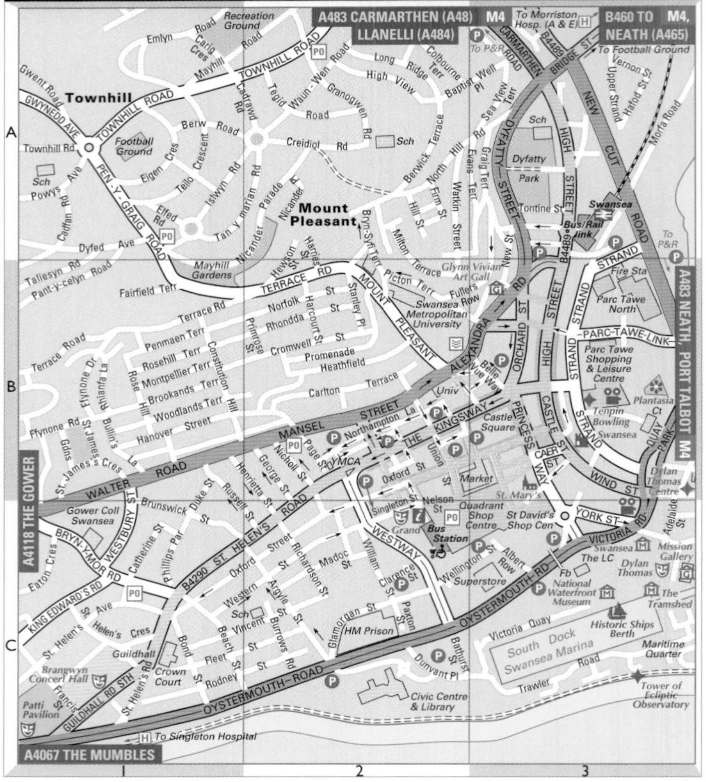

Worcester

0 Miles ¼

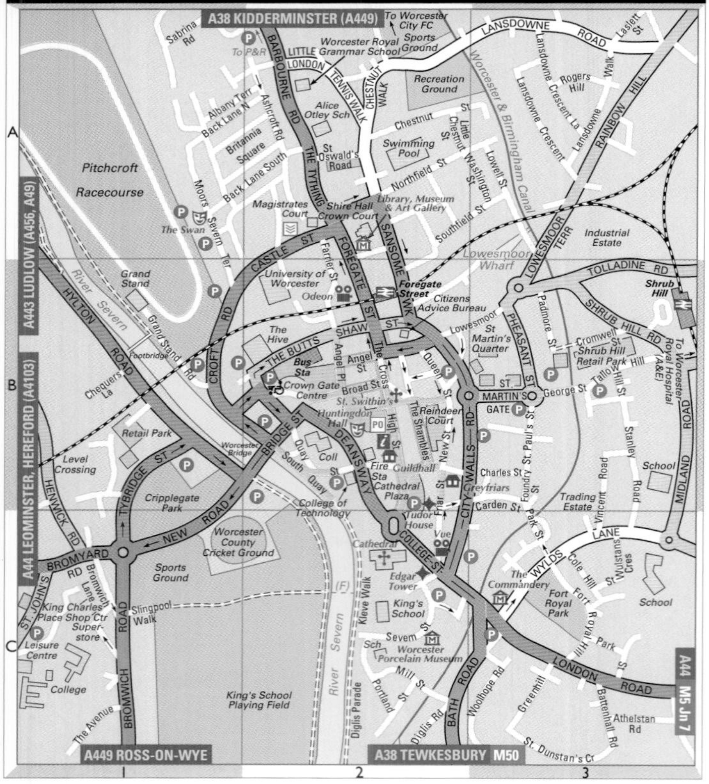

York

0 Miles ¼

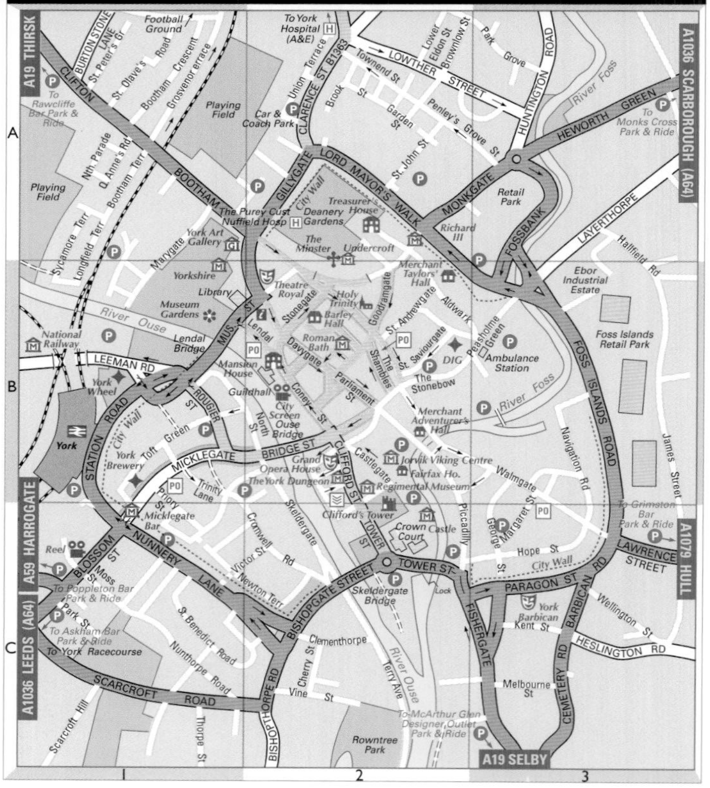

Index to road maps of Britain

Abbreviations used in the index

Aberdeen **Aberdeen City**
Aberds **Aberdeenshire**
Ald **Alderney**
Anglesey **Isle of Anglesey**
Angus **Angus**
Argyll **Argyll and Bute**
Bath **Bath and North East Somerset**
Bedford **Bedford**
Bl Gwent **Blaenau Gwent**
Blackburn **Blackburn with Darwen**
Blackpool **Blackpool**
Bmouth **Bournemouth**
Borders **Scottish Borders**
Brack **Bracknell**
Bridgend **Bridgend**
Brighton **City of Brighton and Hove**
Bristol **City and County of Bristol**
Bucks **Buckinghamshire**
C Beds **Central Bedfordshire**
Caerph **Caerphilly**
Cambs **Cambridgeshire**
Cardiff **Cardiff**
Carms **Carmarthenshire**
Ceredig **Ceredigion**
Ches E **Cheshire East**
Ches W **Cheshire West and Chester**
Clack **Clackmannanshire**
Conwy **Conwy**
Corn **Cornwall**
Cumb **Cumbria**
Darl **Darlington**
Denb **Denbighshire**
Derby **City of Derby**
Derbys **Derbyshire**
Devon **Devon**
Dorset **Dorset**
Dumfries **Dumfries and Galloway**
Dundee **Dundee City**
Durham **Durham**
E Ayrs **East Ayrshire**
E Dunb **East Dunbartonshire**
E Loth **East Lothian**
E Renf **East Renfrewshire**
E Sus **East Sussex**
E Yorks **East Riding of Yorkshire**
Edin **City of Edinburgh**
Essex **Essex**
Falk **Falkirk**
Fife **Fife**
Flint **Flintshire**
Glasgow **City of Glasgow**
Glos **Gloucestershire**
Gtr Man **Greater Manchester**
Guern **Guernsey**
Gwyn **Gwynedd**
Halton **Halton**
Hants **Hampshire**
Hereford **Herefordshire**
Herts **Hertfordshire**
Highld **Highland**
Hrtlpl **Hartlepool**
Hull **Hull**
IoM **Isle of Man**
IoW **Isle of Wight**
Invclyd **Inverclyde**
Jersey **Jersey**
Kent **Kent**
Lancs **Lancashire**
Leicester **City of Leicester**
Leics **Leicestershire**
Lincs **Lincolnshire**
London **Greater London**
Luton **Luton**
M Keynes **Milton Keynes**
M Tydf **Merthyr Tydfil**
Mbro **Middlesbrough**
Medway **Medway**
Mers **Merseyside**
Midloth **Midlothian**
Mon **Monmouthshire**
Moray **Moray**
N Ayrs **North Ayrshire**
N Lincs **North Lincolnshire**
N Lanark **North Lanarkshire**
N Som **North Somerset**
N Yorks **North Yorkshire**
NE Lincs **North East Lincolnshire**
Neath **Neath Port Talbot**
Newport **City and County of Newport**
Norf **Norfolk**
Northants **Northamptonshire**
Northumb **Northumberland**
Nottingham **City of Nottingham**
Notts **Nottinghamshire**
Orkney **Orkney**
Oxon **Oxfordshire**
Pboro **Peterborough**
Pembs **Pembrokeshire**
Perth **Perth and Kinross**
Plym **Plymouth**
Poole **Poole**
Powys **Powys**
Ptsmth **Portsmouth**
Reading **Reading**
Redcar **Redcar and Cleveland**
Renfs **Renfrewshire**
Rhondda **Rhondda Cynon Taff**
Rutland **Rutland**
S Ayrs **South Ayrshire**
S Glos **South Gloucestershire**
S Lanark **South Lanarkshire**
S Yorks **South Yorkshire**
Scilly **Scilly**
Shetland **Shetland**
Shrops **Shropshire**
Slough **Slough**
Som **Somerset**
Soton **Southampton**
Staffs **Staffordshire**
Southend **Southend-on-Sea**
Stirling **Stirling**
Stockton **Stockton-on-Tees**
Stoke **Stoke-on-Trent**
Suff **Suffolk**
Sur **Surrey**
Swansea **Swansea**
Swindon **Swindon**
T&W **Tyne and Wear**
Telford **Telford and Wrekin**
Thurrock **Thurrock**
Torbay **Torbay**
Torf **Torfaen**
V Glam **The Vale of Glamorgan**
W Berks **West Berkshire**
W Dunb **West Dunbartonshire**
W Isles **Western Isles**
W Loth **West Lothian**
W Mid **West Midlands**
W Sus **West Sussex**
W Yorks **West Yorkshire**
Warks **Warwickshire**
Warr **Warrington**
Wilts **Wiltshire**
Windsor **Windsor and Maidenhead**
Wokingham **Wokingham**
Worcs **Worcestershire**
Wrex **Wrexham**
York **City of York**

How to use the index

Example

Trudoxhill Som **24** E2

- grid square
- page number
- county or unitary authority

A

Ab Kettleby Leics 64 B4
Ab Lench Worcs 50 D5
Abbas Combe Som 12 B5
Abberley Worcs 50 C2
Abberton Essex 43 C6
Abberton Worcs 50 D4
Abberwick Northumb 117 C7
Abbess Roding Essex 42 C1
Abbey Devon 11 C6
Abbey-cwm-hir Powys 48 B2
Abbey Dore Hereford 49 F5
Abbey Field Essex 43 B5
Abbey Hulton Stoke 75 E6
Abbey St Bathans Borders 122 C3
Abbey Town Cumb 107 D8
Abbey Village Lancs 86 B4
Abbey Wood London 29 B5
Abbeydale S Yorks 88 F4
Abbeystead Lancs 93 D5
Abbots Bickington Devon 9 C5
Abbots Bromley Staffs 62 B4
Abbots Langley Herts 40 D3
Abbots Leigh N Som 23 B7
Abbots Morton Worcs 50 D5
Abbots Ripton Cambs 54 B3
Abbots Salford Warks 51 D5
Abbotsbury Dorset 12 F3
Abbotsham Devon 9 B6
Abbotskerswell Devon 7 C6
Abbotsley Cambs 54 D3
Abbotswood Hants 14 B4
Abbotts Ann Hants 25 E8
Abcott Shrops 49 B5
Abdon Shrops 61 F5
Aber Ceredig 46 E3
Aber-Arad Carms 46 F2
Aber-banc Ceredig 46 E2
Aber Cowarch Gwyn 59 C5
Aber-Giâr Carms 46 E4
Aber-gwynfi Neath 34 E2
Aber-Hirnant Gwyn 72 F3
Aber-nant Rhondda 34 D4
Aber-Rhiwlech Gwyn 59 B6
Aber-Village Powys 35 B5
Aberaeron Ceredig 46 C3
Aberaman Rhondda 34 D4
Aberangell Gwyn 58 C5
Aberarder Highld 137 F7
Aberarder House Highld 138 B2
Aberarder Lodge Highld 137 F8
Aberargie Perth 128 C3
Aberarth Ceredig 46 C3
Aberavon Neath 33 E8
Aberbeeg Bl Gwent 35 D6
Abercanaid M Tydf 34 D4
Abercarn Caerph 35 E6
Abercastle Pembs 44 B3
Abercegir Powys 58 D5
Aberchirder Aberds 152 C6
Abercraf Powys 34 C2
Abercrombie Fife 129 D7
Abercych Pembs 45 E4
Abercynafon Powys 34 C4
Abercynon Rhondda 34 E4
Aberdalgie Perth 128 B2
Aberdâr = Aberdare Rhondda 34 D3
Aberdare = Aberdâr Rhondda 34 D3
Aberdaron Gwyn 70 E2
Aberdaugleddau = Milford Haven Pembs 44 E4
Aberdeen Aberdeen 141 D8
Aberdesach Gwyn 82 F4
Aberdour Fife 128 F3
Aberdovey Gwyn 58 E3
Aberdulais Neath 34 D1
Aberedw Powys 48 E2
Abereiddy Pembs 44 B2
Abererch Gwyn 70 D4
Aberfan M Tydf 34 D4
Aberfeldy Perth 133 E5
Aberffraw Anglesey 82 E3
Aberffrwd Ceredig 47 B5
Aberford W Yorks 95 F7
Aberfoyle Stirling 126 D4
Abergavenny = Y Fenni Mon 35 C6
Abergele Conwy 72 B3
Abergorlech Carms 46 F4
Abergwaun = Fishguard Pembs 44 B4
Abergwesyn Powys 47 D7
Abergwili Carms 33 B5
Abergwynant Gwyn 58 C3
Abergwyngregyn Gwyn 83 D6
Abergynolwyn Gwyn 58 D3
Aberhonddu = Brecon Powys 34 B4
Aberhosan Powys 58 E5
Aberkenfig Bridgend 34 F2
Aberlady E Loth 129 F6
Aberlemno Angus 135 D5
Aberllefenni Gwyn 58 D4
Abermagwr Ceredig 47 B5
Abermaw = Barmouth Gwyn 58 C3
Abermeurig Ceredig 46 D4
Abermule Powys 59 E8
Abernaint Powys 59 B8
Abernant Carms 32 B4
Abernethy Perth 128 C3
Abernyte Perth 134 F2
Aberpennar = Mountain Ash Rhondda 34 E4
Aberporth Ceredig 45 D4
Abersoch Gwyn 70 E4
Abersychan Torf 35 D6
Abertawe = Swansea Swansea 33 E7
Aberteifi = Cardigan Ceredig 45 E3
Aberthin V Glam 22 B2
Abertillery = Abertyleri Bl Gwent 35 D6
Abertridwr Caerph 35 F5
Abertridwr Powys 59 C7
Abertyleri = Abertillery Bl Gwent 35 D6
Abertysswg Caerph 35 D5
Aberuthven Perth 127 C8
Aberyscir Powys 34 B3
Aberystwyth Ceredig 58 F2
Abhainn Suidhe W Isles 154 G5
Abingdon-on-Thames Oxon 38 E4
Abinger Common Sur 28 E2
Abinger Hammer Sur 27 E8
Abington S Lanark 114 B2
Abington Pigotts Cambs 54 E4
Ablington Glos 37 D8
Ablington Wilts 25 E6
Abney Derbys 75 B8
Aboyne Aberds 140 E4
Abram Gtr Man 86 D4
Abriachan Highld 151 H8
Abridge Essex 41 E7
Abronhill N Lanark 119 B7
Abson S Glos 24 B2
Abthorpe Northants 52 E4
Abune-the-Hill Orkney 159 F3
Aby Lincs 79 B7
Acaster Malbis York 95 E8
Acaster Selby N Yorks 95 E8
Accrington Lancs 87 B5
Acha Argyll 146 F4
Acha Mor W Isles 155 E8
Achabraid Argyll 145 E7
Achachork Highld 149 D9
Achafolla Argyll 124 D3
Achagary Highld 157 D10
Achahoish Argyll 144 F6
Achalader Perth 133 E8
Achallader Argyll 131 E7
Ach'an Todhair Highld 130 B4
Achanalt Highld 150 E5
Achanamara Argyll 144 E6
Achandunie Highld 151 D9
Achany Highld 157 J8
Achaphubuil Highld 130 B4
Acharacle Highld 147 E9
Acharn Highld 147 F10
Acharn Perth 132 E4
Acharole Highld 158 E4
Achath Aberds 141 C6
Achavanich Highld 158 F3
Achavraat Highld 151 G12
Achddu Carms 33 D5
Achduart Highld 156 J3
Achentoul Highld 157 F11
Achfary Highld 156 F5
Achgarve Highld 155 H13
Achiemore Highld 156 C6
Achiemore Highld 157 D11
A'Chill Highld 148 H7
Achiltibuie Highld 156 J3
Achina Highld 157 C10
Achinduich Highld 157 J8
Achinduin Argyll 124 B4
Achingills Highld 158 D3
Achintee Highld 131 B5
Achintee Highld 150 G2
Achintraid Highld 149 E13
Achlean Highld 138 E4
Achleck Argyll 146 G7
Achluachrach Highld 137 F5
Achlyness Highld 156 D5
Achmelvich Highld 156 G3
Achmore Highld 149 E13
Achmore Stirling 132 F2
Achnaba Argyll 124 B5
Achnaba Argyll 145 E8
Achnabat Highld 151 H8
Achnacarnin Highld 156 F3
Achnacarry Highld 136 F4
Achnacloich Argyll 125 B5
Achnacloich Highld 149 H10
Achnaconeran Highld 137 C7
Achnacraig Argyll 146 G7
Achnacroish Argyll 130 E2
Achnadrish Argyll 146 F7
Achnafalnich Argyll 125 C8
Achnagarron Highld 151 E9
Achnaha Highld 146 E7
Achnahanat Highld 151 B8
Achnahannet Highld 139 B5
Achnairn Highld 157 H8
Achnaluachrach Highld 157 J9
Achnasaul Highld 136 F4
Achnasheen Highld 150 F4
Achosnich Highld 146 E7
Achranich Highld 147 G10
Achreamie Highld 157 C13
Achriabhach Highld 131 C5
Achriesgill Highld 156 D5
Achrimsdale Highld 157 J12
Achtoty Highld 157 C9
Achurch Northants 65 F7
Achuvoldrach Highld 157 D8
Achvaich Highld 151 B10
Achvarasdal Highld 157 C12
Ackergill Highld 158 E5
Acklam Mbro 102 C2
Acklam N Yorks 96 C3
Ackleton Shrops 61 E7
Acklington Northumb 117 D8
Ackton W Yorks 88 B5
Ackworth Moor Top W Yorks 88 C5
Acle Norf 69 C7
Acock's Green W Mid 62 F5
Acol Kent 31 C7
Acomb Northumb 110 C2
Acomb York 95 D8
Aconbury Hereford 49 F7
Acre Lancs 87 B5
Acre Street W Sus 15 E8
Acrefair Wrex 73 E6
Acton Ches E 74 D3
Acton Dorset 13 G7
Acton London 41 F5
Acton Shrops 60 F3
Acton Suff 56 E2
Acton Wrex 73 D7
Acton Beauchamp Hereford 49 D8
Acton Bridge Ches W 74 B2
Acton Burnell Shrops 60 D5
Acton Green Hereford 49 D8
Acton Pigott Shrops 60 D5
Acton Round Shrops 61 E6
Acton Scott Shrops 60 F4
Acton Trussell Staffs 62 C3
Acton Turville S Glos 37 F5
Adbaston Staffs 61 B7
Adber Dorset 12 B3
Adderley Shrops 74 E3
Adderstone Northumb 123 F7
Addiewell W Loth 120 C2
Addingham W Yorks 94 E3
Addington Bucks 39 B7
Addington Kent 29 D7
Addington London 28 C4
Addinston Borders 121 D8
Addiscombe London 28 C4
Addlestone Sur 27 C8
Addlethorpe Lincs 79 C8
Adel W Yorks 95 F5
Adeney Telford 61 C7
Adfa Powys 59 D7
Adforton Hereford 49 B6
Adisham Kent 31 D6
Adlestrop Glos 38 B2
Adlingfleet E Yorks 90 B2
Adlington Lancs 86 C4
Admaston Staffs 62 B4
Admaston Telford 61 C6
Admington Warks 51 E7
Adstock Bucks 52 F5
Adstone Northants 52 D3
Adversane W Sus 16 B4
Advie Highld 152 E1
Adwalton W Yorks 88 B3
Adwell Oxon 39 E6
Adwick le Street S Yorks 89 D6
Adwick upon Dearne S Yorks 89 D5
Adziel Aberds 153 C9
Ae Village Dumfries 114 F2
Affleck Aberds 141 B7
Affpuddle Dorset 13 E6
Affric Lodge Highld 136 B4
Afon-wen Flint 72 B5
Afton IoW 14 F4
Agglethorpe N Yorks 101 F5
Agneash IoM 84 D4
Aigburth Mers 85 F4
Aiginis W Isles 155 D9
Aike E Yorks 97 E6
Aikerness Orkney 159 C5
Aikers Orkney 159 J5
Aiketgate Cumb 108 E4
Aikton Cumb 108 D2
Ailey Hereford 48 E5
Ailstone Warks 51 D7
Ailsworth Pboro 65 E8
Ainderby Quernhow N Yorks 102 F1
Ainderby Steeple N Yorks 101 E8
Aingers Green Essex 43 B7
Ainsdale Mers 85 C4
Ainsdale-on-Sea Mers 85 C4
Ainstable Cumb 108 E5
Ainsworth Gtr Man 87 C5
Ainthorpe N Yorks 103 D5
Aintree Mers 85 E4
Aird Argyll 124 E3
Aird Dumfries 104 C4
Aird Highld 149 A12
Aird W Isles 155 D10
Aird a Mhachair W Isles 148 D2
Aird a' Mhulaidh W Isles 154 F6
Aird Asaig W Isles 154 G6
Aird Dhail W Isles 155 A9
Aird Mhidhinis W Isles 148 H2
Aird Mhighe W Isles 154 H6
Aird Mhighe W Isles 154 J5
Aird Mhor W Isles 148 H2
Aird of Sleat Highld 149 H10
Aird Thunga W Isles 155 D9
Aird Uig W Isles 154 D5
Airdens Highld 151 B9
Airdrie N Lanark 119 C7
Airdtorrisdale Highld 157 C9
Airidh a Bhruaich W Isles 154 F7
Airieland Dumfries 106 D4
Airmyn E Yorks 89 B8
Airntully Perth 133 F7
Airor Highld 149 H12
Airth Falk 127 F7
Airton N Yorks 94 D2
Airyhassen Dumfries 105 E7
Aisby Lincs 78 F3
Aisby Lincs 90 E2
Aisgernis W Isles 148 F2
Aiskew N Yorks 101 F7
Aislaby N Yorks 103 D6
Aislaby N Yorks 103 F5
Aislaby Stockton 102 C2
Aisthorpe Lincs 78 A2
Aith Orkney 159 G3
Aith Shetland 160 D8
Aith Shetland 160 H5
Aithsetter Shetland 160 K6
Aitkenhead S Ayrs 112 D3
Aitnoch Highld 151 H12
Akeld Northumb 117 B5
Akeley Bucks 52 F5
Akenham Suff 56 E5
Albaston Corn 6 B2
Alberbury Shrops 60 C3
Albourne W Sus 17 C6
Albrighton Shrops 60 C4
Albrighton Shrops 62 D2
Alburgh Norf 69 F5
Albury Herts 41 B7
Albury Sur 27 E8
Albury End Herts 41 B7
Alby Hill Norf 81 D7
Alcaig Highld 151 F8
Alcaston Shrops 60 F4
Alcester Warks 51 D5
Alciston E Sus 18 E2
Alcombe Som 21 E8
Alcombe Wilts 24 C3
Alconbury Cambs 54 B2
Alconbury Weston Cambs 54 B2
Aldbar Castle Angus 135 D5
Aldborough N Yorks 95 C7
Aldborough Norf 81 D7
Aldbourne Wilts 25 B7
Aldbrough E Yorks 97 F8
Aldbrough St John N Yorks 101 C7
Aldbury Herts 40 C2
Aldcliffe Lancs 92 C4
Aldclune Perth 133 C6
Aldeburgh Suff 57 D8
Aldeby Norf 69 E7
Aldenham Herts 40 E4
Alderbury Wilts 14 B2
Aldercar Derbys 76 E4
Alderford Norf 68 C4
Alderholt Dorset 14 C2
Alderley Glos 36 E4
Alderley Edge Ches E 74 B5
Aldermaston W Berks 26 C3
Aldermaston Wharf W Berks 26 C4
Alderminster Warks 51 E7
Alder's End Hereford 49 E8
Aldersey Green Ches W 73 D8
Aldershot Hants 27 D6
Alderton Glos 50 F5
Alderton Northants 52 E5
Alderton Shrops 60 B4
Alderton Suff 57 E7
Alderton Wilts 37 F5
Alderwasley Derbys 76 D3
Aldfield N Yorks 95 C5
Aldford Ches W 73 D8
Aldham Essex 43 B5
Aldham Suff 56 E4
Aldie Highld 151 C10
Aldingbourne W Sus 16 D3
Aldingham Cumb 92 B2
Aldington Kent 19 B7
Aldington Worcs 51 E5
Aldington Frith Kent 19 B7
Aldochlay Argyll 126 E2
Aldreth Cambs 54 B5
Aldridge W Mid 62 D4
Aldringham Suff 57 C8
Aldsworth Glos 38 C1
Aldunie Moray 140 B2
Aldwark Derbys 76 D2
Aldwark N Yorks 95 C7
Aldwick W Sus 16 E3
Aldwincle Northants 65 F7
Aldworth W Berks 26 B3
Alexandria W Dunb 118 B3
Alfardisworthy Devon 8 C4
Alfington Devon 11 E6
Alfold Sur 27 F8
Alfold Bars W Sus 27 F8
Alfold Crossways Sur 27 F8
Alford Aberds 140 C4
Alford Lincs 79 B7
Alford Som 23 F8
Alfreton Derbys 76 D4
Alfrick Worcs 50 D2
Alfrick Pound Worcs 50 D2
Alfriston E Sus 18 E2
Algaltraig Argyll 145 F9
Algarkirk Lincs 79 F5
Alhampton Som 23 F8
Aline Lodge W Isles 154 F6
Alisary Highld 147 D10
Alkborough N Lincs 90 B2
Alkerton Oxon 51 E8
Alkham Kent 31 E6
Alkington Shrops 74 F2
Alkmonton Derbys 75 F8
All Cannings Wilts 25 C5
All Saints South Elmham Suff 69 F6
All Stretton Shrops 60 E4
Alladale Lodge Highld 150 C7
Allaleigh Devon 7 D6
Allanaquoich Aberds 139 E7
Allangrange Mains Highld 151 F9
Allanton Borders 122 D4
Allanton N Lanark 119 D8
Allathasdal W Isles 148 H1
Allendale Town Northumb 109 D8
Allenheads Northumb 109 E8
Allens Green Herts 41 C7
Allensford Durham 110 D3
Allensmore Hereford 49 F6
Allenton Derby 76 F3
Aller Som 12 B2
Allerby Cumb 107 F7
Allerford Som 21 E8
Allerston N Yorks 103 F6
Allerthorpe E Yorks 96 E3
Allerton Mers 86 F2
Allerton W Yorks 94 F4
Allerton Bywater W Yorks 88 B5
Allerton Mauleverer N Yorks 95 D7
Allesley W Mid 63 F7
Allestree Derby 76 F3
Allet Corn 3 B6
Allexton Leics 64 D5
Allgreave Ches E 75 C6
Allhallows Medway 30 B2
Allhallows-on-Sea Medway 30 B2
Alligin Shuas Highld 149 C13
Allimore Green Staffs 62 C2
Allington Lincs 77 E8
Allington Wilts 25 C5
Allington Wilts 25 F7
Allithwaite Cumb 92 B3
Alloa Clack 127 E7
Allonby Cumb 107 E7
Alloway S Ayrs 112 C3
Allt Carms 33 D6
Allt na h-Airbhe Highld 150 B4
Allt-nan-sùgh Highld 136 B2
Alltchaorunn Highld 131 D5
Alltforgan Powys 59 B6
Alltmawr Powys 48 E2
Alltnacaillich Highld 156 E7
Alltsigh Highld 137 C7
Alltwalis Carms 46 F3
Alltwen Neath 33 D8
Alltyblaca Ceredig 46 E4
Allwood Green Suff 56 B4
Almeley Hereford 48 D5
Almer Dorset 13 E7
Almholme S Yorks 89 D6
Almington Staffs 74 F4
Alminstone Cross Devon 8 B5
Almondbank Perth 128 B2
Almondbury W Yorks 88 C2
Almondsbury S Glos 36 F3
Alne N Yorks 95 C7
Alness Highld 151 E9
Alnham Northumb 117 C5
Alnmouth Northumb 117 C8
Alnwick Northumb 117 C7
Alperton London 40 F4
Alphamstone Essex 56 F2
Alpheton Suff 56 D2
Alphington Devon 10 E4
Alport Derbys 76 C2
Alpraham Ches E 74 D2
Alresford Essex 43 B6
Alrewas Staffs 63 C5
Alsager Ches E 74 D4
Alsagers Bank Staffs 74 E5
Alsop en le Dale Derbys 75 D8
Alston Cumb 109 E7
Alston Devon 11 D8
Alstone Glos 50 F4
Alstonefield Staffs 75 D8
Alswear Devon 10 B2
Altandhu Highld 156 H2
Altanduin Highld 157 G11
Altarnun Corn 8 F4
Altass Highld 156 J7
Alterwall Highld 158 D4
Altham Lancs 93 F7
Althorne Essex 43 E5
Althorpe N Lincs 90 D2
Alticry Dumfries 105 D6
Altnabreac Station Highld 157 E13
Altnacealgach Hotel Highld 156 H5
Altnacraig Argyll 124 C4
Altnafeadh Highld 131 D6
Altnaharra Highld 157 F8
Altofts W Yorks 88 B4
Alton Derbys 76 C3
Alton Hants 26 F5
Alton Staffs 75 E7
Alton Pancras Dorset 12 D5
Alton Priors Wilts 25 C6
Altrincham Gtr Man 87 F5
Altrua Highld 136 F5
Altskeith Stirling 126 D3
Altyre Ho. Moray 151 F13
Alva Clack 127 E7
Alvanley Ches W 73 B8
Alvaston Derby 76 F3
Alvechurch Worcs 50 B5
Alvecote Warks 63 D6
Alvediston Wilts 13 B7
Alveley Shrops 61 F7
Alverdiscott Devon 9 B7
Alverstoke Hants 15 E7
Alverstone IoW 15 F6
Alverton Notts 77 E7
Alves Moray 152 B1
Alvescot Oxon 38 D2
Alveston S Glos 36 F3
Alveston Warks 51 D7
Alvie Highld 138 D4
Alvingham Lincs 91 E7
Alvington Glos 36 D3
Alwalton Cambs 65 E8
Alweston Dorset 12 C4
Alwinton Northumb 116 D5
Alwoodley W Yorks 95 E5
Alyth Perth 134 E2
Am Baile W Isles 148 G2
Am Buth Argyll 124 C4
Amatnatua Highld 150 B7
Amber Hill Lincs 78 E5
Ambergate Derbys 76 D3
Amberley Glos 37 D5
Amberley W Sus 16 C4
Amble Northumb 117 D8
Amblecote W Mid 62 F2
Ambler Thorn W Yorks 87 B8
Ambleside Cumb 99 D5
Ambleston Pembs 44 C5
Ambrosden Oxon 39 C6
Amcotts N Lincs 90 C2
Amersham Bucks 40 E2
Amesbury Wilts 25 E6
Amington Staffs 63 D6
Amisfield Dumfries 114 F2
Amlwch Anglesey 82 B4
Amlwch Port Anglesey 82 B4
Ammanford = Rhydaman Carms 33 C7
Amod Argyll 143 E8
Amotherby N Yorks 96 B3
Ampfield Hants 14 B5
Ampleforth N Yorks 95 B8
Ampney Crucis Glos 37 D7
Ampney St Mary Glos 37 D7
Ampney St Peter Glos 37 D7
Amport Hants 25 E7
Ampthill C Beds 53 F8
Ampton Suff 56 B2
Amroth Pembs 32 D2
Amulree Perth 133 F5
An Caol Highld 149 C11
An Cnoc W Isles 155 D9
An Gleann Ur W Isles 155 D9
An t-Ob = Leverburgh W Isles 154 J5
Anagach Highld 139 B6
Anaheilt Highld 130 C2
Anancaun Highld 150 E3
Ancaster Lincs 78 E2
Anchor Shrops 59 F8
Anchorsholme Blackpool 92 E3
Ancroft Northumb 123 E5
Ancrum Borders 116 B2
Anderby Lincs 79 B8
Anderson Dorset 13 E6
Anderton Ches W 74 B3
Andover Hants 25 E8
Andover Down Hants 25 E8
Andoversford Glos 37 C7
Andreas IoM 84 C4
Anfield Mers 85 E4
Angersleigh Som 11 C6
Angle Pembs 44 E3
Angmering W Sus 16 D4
Angram N Yorks 95 E8
Angram N Yorks 100 E3
Anie Stirling 126 C4
Ankerville Highld 151 D11
Anlaby E Yorks 90 B4
Anmer Norf 80 E3
Anna Valley Hants 25 E8
Annan Dumfries 107 C8
Annat Argyll 125 C6
Annat Highld 149 C13
Annbank S Ayrs 112 B4
Annesley Notts 76 D5
Annesley Woodhouse Notts 76 D4
Annfield Plain Durham 110 D4
Annifirth Shetland 160 J3
Annitsford T&W 111 B5
Annscroft Shrops 60 D4
Ansdell Lancs 85 B4
Ansford Som 23 F8
Ansley Warks 63 E6
Anslow Staffs 63 B6
Anslow Gate Staffs 63 B5
Anstey Herts 54 F5
Anstey Leics 64 D2
Anstruther Easter Fife 129 D7
Anstruther Wester Fife 129 D7
Ansty Hants 26 E5
Ansty W Sus 17 B6
Ansty Warks 63 F7

Ansty Wilts 13 B7
Anthill Common Hants 15 C7
Anthorn Cumb 107 D8
Antingham Norf 81 D8
Anton's Gowt Lincs 79 E5
Antonshill Falk 127 F7
Antony Corn 5 D8
Anwick Lincs 78 D4
Anwoth Dumfries 106 D2
Aoradh Argyll 142 B3
Apes Hall Cambs 67 E5
Apethorpe Northants 65 E7
Apeton Staffs 62 C2
Apley Lincs 78 B4
Apperknowle Derbys 76 B3
Apperley Glos 37 B5
Apperley Bridge W Yorks 94 F4
Appersett N Yorks 100 E3
Appin Argyll 130 E3
Appin House Argyll 130 E3
Appleby N Lincs 90 C3
Appleby-in-Westmorland Cumb 100 B1
Appleby Magna Leics 63 D7
Appleby Parva Leics 63 D7
Applecross Highld 149 D12
Applecross Ho. Highld 149 D12
Appledore Devon 11 C5
Appledore Devon 20 F3
Appledore Kent 19 C6
Appledore Heath Kent 19 B6
Appleford Oxon 39 E5
Applegarthtown Dumfries 114 F4
Appleshaw Hants 25 E8
Applethwaite Cumb 98 B4
Appleton Halton 86 F3
Appleton Oxon 38 D4
Appleton-le-Moors N Yorks 103 F5
Appleton-le-Street N Yorks 96 B3
Appleton Roebuck N Yorks 95 E8
Appleton Thorn Warr 86 F4
Appleton Wiske N Yorks 102 D1
Appletreehall Borders 115 C8
Appletreewick N Yorks 94 C3
Appley Som 11 B5
Appley Bridge Lancs 86 D3
Apse Heath IoW 15 F6
Apsley End C Beds 54 F2
Apuldram W Sus 16 D2
Aquhythie Aberds 141 C6
Arabella Highld 151 D11
Arbeadie Aberds 141 E5
Arberth = Narberth Pembs 32 C2
Arbirlot Angus 135 E6
Arboll Highld 151 C11
Arborfield Wokingham 27 C5
Arborfield Cross Wokingham 27 C5
Arborfield Garrison Wokingham 27 C5
Arbour-thorne S Yorks 88 F4
Arbroath Angus 135 E6
Arbuthnott Aberds 135 B7
Archiestown Moray 152 D2
Arclid Ches E 74 C4
Ard-dhubh Highld 149 D12
Ardachu Highld 157 J9
Ardalanish Argyll 146 K6
Ardanaiseig Argyll 125 C6
Ardaneaskan Highld 149 E13
Ardanstur Argyll 124 D4
Ardargie House Hotel Perth 128 C2
Ardarroch Highld 149 E13
Ardbeg Argyll 142 D5
Ardbeg Argyll 145 E10
Ardcharnich Highld 150 C4
Ardchiavaig Argyll 146 K6
Ardchullarie More Stirling 126 C4
Ardchyle Stirling 126 B4
Arddleen Powys 60 C2
Ardechvie Highld 136 E4
Ardeley Herts 41 B6
Ardelve Highld 149 F13
Arden Argyll 126 F2
Ardens Grafton Warks 51 D6
Ardentinny Argyll 145 E10
Ardentraive Argyll 145 F9
Ardeonaig Stirling 132 F3
Ardersier Highld 151 F10
Ardessie Highld 150 C3
Ardfern Argyll 124 E4
Ardgartan Argyll 125 E8
Ardgay Highld 151 B8
Ardgour Highld 130 C4
Ardheslaig Highld 149 C12
Ardiecow Moray 152 B5
Ardindrean Highld 150 C4
Ardingly W Sus 17 B7
Ardington Oxon 38 F4
Ardlair Aberds 140 B4
Ardlamont Ho. Argyll 145 G8
Ardleigh Essex 43 B6
Ardler Perth 134 E2
Ardley Oxon 39 B5
Ardlui Argyll 126 C2
Ardlussa Argyll 144 E5
Ardmair Highld 150 B4
Ardmay Argyll 125 E8
Ardminish Argyll 143 D7
Ardmolich Highld 147 D10
Ardmore Argyll 124 C3
Ardmore Highld 151 C10
Ardmore Highld 156 D5
Ardnacross Argyll 147 G8
Ardnadam Argyll 145 F10
Ardnagrask Highld 151 G8
Ardnarff Highld 149 E13
Ardnastang Highld 130 C2
Ardnave Argyll 142 A3
Ardno Argyll 125 E7
Ardo Aberds 153 E8
Ardo Ho. Aberds 141 B8
Ardoch Perth 133 F7
Ardochy House Highld 136 D5
Ardoyne Aberds 141 B5
Ardpatrick Argyll 144 G6
Ardpatrick Ho. Argyll 144 H6
Ardpeaton Argyll 145 E11
Ardrishaig Argyll 145 E7
Ardross Fife 129 D7
Ardross Highld 151 D9
Ardross Castle Highld 151 D9
Ardrossan N Ayrs 118 E2
Ardshealach Highld 147 E9
Ardsley S Yorks 88 D4
Ardslignish Highld 147 E8
Ardtalla Argyll 142 C5
Ardtalnaig Perth 132 F4
Ardtoe Highld 147 D9
Ardtrostan Perth 127 B5
Arduaine Argyll 124 D3
Ardullie Highld 151 E8
Ardvasar Highld 149 H11
Ardvorlich Perth 126 B5
Ardwell Dumfries 104 E5
Ardwell Mains Dumfries 104 E5
Ardwick Gtr Man 87 E6
Areley Kings Worcs 50 B3
Arford Hants 27 F6
Argoed Caerph 35 E5
Argoed Mill Powys 47 C8
Arichamish Argyll 124 E5
Arichastlich Argyll 125 B8
Aridhglas Argyll 146 J6
Arileod Argyll 146 F4
Arinacrinachd Highld 149 C12
Arinagour Argyll 146 F5
Arion Orkney 159 G3
Arisaig Highld 147 C9
Ariundle Highld 130 C2
Arkendale N Yorks 95 C6
Arkesden Essex 55 F5
Arkholme Lancs 93 B5
Arkle Town N Yorks 101 D5
Arkleton Dumfries 115 E6
Arkley London 41 E5
Arksey S Yorks 89 D6
Arkwright Town Derbys 76 B4
Arle Glos 37 B6
Arlecdon Cumb 98 C2
Arlesey C Beds 54 F2
Arleston Telford 61 C6
Arley Ches E 86 F4
Arlingham Glos 36 C4
Arlington Devon 20 E5
Arlington E Sus 18 E2
Arlington Glos 37 D8
Armadale Highld 157 C10
Armadale W Loth 120 C2
Armadale Castle Highld 149 H11
Armathwaite Cumb 108 E5
Arminghall Norf 69 D5
Armitage Staffs 62 C4
Armley W Yorks 95 F5
Armscote Warks 51 E7
Armthorpe S Yorks 89 D7
Arnabost Argyll 146 F5
Arncliffe N Yorks 94 B2
Arncroach Fife 129 D7
Arne Dorset 13 F7
Arnesby Leics 64 E3
Arngask Perth 128 C3
Arnisdale Highld 149 G13
Arnish Highld 149 D10
Arniston Engine Midloth 121 C6
Arnol W Isles 155 C8
Arnold E Yorks 97 E7
Arnold Notts 77 E5
Arnprior Stirling 126 E5
Arnside Cumb 92 B4
Aros Mains Argyll 147 G8
Arowry Wrex 73 F8
Arpafeelie Highld 151 F9
Arrad Foot Cumb 99 F5
Arram E Yorks 97 E6
Arrathorne N Yorks 101 E7
Arreton IoW 15 F6
Arrington Cambs 54 D4
Arrivain Argyll 125 B8
Arrochar Argyll 125 E8
Arrow Warks 51 D5
Arthington W Yorks 95 E5
Arthingworth Northants 64 F4
Arthog Gwyn 58 C3
Arthrath Aberds 153 E9
Arthurstone Perth 134 E2
Artrochie Aberds 153 E10
Arundel W Sus 16 D4
Aryhoulan Highld 130 C4
Asby Cumb 98 B2
Ascog Argyll 145 G10
Ascot Windsor 27 C7
Ascott Warks 51 F8
Ascott-under-Wychwood Oxon 38 C3
Asenby N Yorks 95 B6
Asfordby Leics 64 C4
Asfordby Hill Leics 64 C4
Asgarby Lincs 78 E4
Asgarby Lincs 79 C6
Ash Kent 29 C6
Ash Kent 31 D6
Ash Som 12 B2
Ash Sur 27 D6
Ash Bullayne Devon 10 D2
Ash Green Warks 63 F7
Ash Magna Shrops 74 F2
Ash Mill Devon 10 B2
Ash Priors Som 11 B6
Ash Street Suff 56 E4
Ash Thomas Devon 10 C5
Ash Vale Sur 27 D6
Ashampstead W Berks 26 B3
Ashbocking Suff 57 D5
Ashbourne Derbys 75 E8
Ashbrittle Som 11 B5
Ashburton Devon 7 C5
Ashbury Devon 9 E7
Ashbury Oxon 38 F2
Ashby N Lincs 90 D3
Ashby by Partney Lincs 79 C7
Ashby cum Fenby NE Lincs 91 D6
Ashby de la Launde Lincs 78 D3
Ashby-de-la-Zouch Leics 63 C7
Ashby Folville Leics 64 C4
Ashby Magna Leics 64 E2
Ashby Parva Leics 64 F2
Ashby Puerorum Lincs 79 B6
Ashby St Ledgers Northants 52 C3
Ashby St Mary Norf 69 D6
Ashchurch Glos 50 F4
Ashcombe Devon 7 B7
Ashcott Som 23 F6
Ashdon Essex 55 E6
Ashe Hants 26 E3
Asheldham Essex 43 D5
Ashen Essex 55 E8
Ashendon Bucks 39 C7
Ashfield Carms 33 B7
Ashfield Stirling 127 D6
Ashfield Suff 57 C6
Ashfield Green Suff 57 B6
Ashfold Crossways W Sus 17 B6
Ashford Devon 20 F4
Ashford Hants 14 C2
Ashford Kent 30 E4
Ashford Sur 27 B8
Ashford Bowdler Shrops 49 B7
Ashford Carbonell Shrops 49 B7
Ashford Hill Hants 26 C3
Ashford in the Water Derbys 75 C8
Ashgill S Lanark 119 E7
Ashill Devon 11 C5
Ashill Norf 67 D8
Ashill Som 11 C8
Ashingdon Essex 42 E4
Ashington Northumb 117 F8
Ashington Som 12 B3
Ashington W Sus 16 C5
Ashintully Castle Perth 133 C8
Ashkirk Borders 115 B7
Ashlett Hants 15 D5
Ashleworth Glos 37 B5
Ashley Cambs 55 C7
Ashley Ches E 87 F5
Ashley Devon 9 C8
Ashley Dorset 14 D2
Ashley Glos 37 E6
Ashley Hants 14 E3
Ashley Hants 25 F8
Ashley Northants 64 E4
Ashley Staffs 74 F4
Ashley Green Bucks 40 D2
Ashley Heath Dorset 14 D2
Ashley Heath Staffs 74 F4
Ashmanhaugh Norf 69 B6
Ashmansworth Hants 26 D2
Ashmansworthy Devon 8 C5
Ashmore Dorset 13 C7
Ashorne Warks 51 D8
Ashover Derbys 76 C3
Ashow Warks 51 B8
Ashprington Devon 7 D6
Ashreigney Devon 9 C8
Ashtead Sur 28 D2
Ashton Ches W 74 C2
Ashton Corn 2 D5
Ashton Hants 15 C6
Ashton Hereford 49 C7
Ashton Involyd 118 B2
Ashton Northants 53 E5
Ashton Northants 65 F7
Ashton Common Wilts 24 D3
Ashton-In-Makerfield Gtr Man 86 E3
Ashton Keynes Wilts 37 E7
Ashton under Hill Worcs 50 F4
Ashton-under-Lyne Gtr Man 87 E7
Ashton upon Mersey Gtr Man 87 E5
Ashurst Hants 14 C4
Ashurst Kent 18 B2
Ashurst W Sus 17 C5
Ashurstwood W Sus 28 F5
Ashwater Devon 9 E5
Ashwell Herts 54 F3
Ashwell Rutland 65 C5
Ashwell Som 11 C8
Ashwellthorpe Norf 68 E4
Ashwick Som 23 E8
Ashwicken Norf 67 C7
Ashybank Borders 115 C8
Askam in Furness Cumb 92 B2
Askern S Yorks 89 C6
Askerswell Dorset 12 E3
Askett Bucks 39 D8
Askham Cumb 99 B7
Askham Notts 77 B7
Askham Bryan York 95 E8
Askham Richard York 95 E8
Asknish Argyll 145 D8
Askrigg N Yorks 100 E4
Askwith N Yorks 94 E4
Aslackby Lincs 78 F3
Aslacton Norf 68 E4
Aslockton Notts 77 F7
Asloun Aberds 140 C4
Aspatria Cumb 107 E8
Aspenden Herts 41 B6
Asperton Lincs 79 F5
Aspley Guise C Beds 53 F7
Aspley Heath C Beds 53 F7
Aspull Gtr Man 86 D4
Asselby E Yorks 89 B8
Asserby Lincs 79 B7
Assington Suff 56 F3
Assynt Ho. Highld 151 E8
Astbury Ches E 74 C5
Astcote Northants 52 D4
Asterley Shrops 60 D3
Asterton Shrops 60 E3
Asthall Oxon 38 C2
Asthall Leigh Oxon 38 C3
Astley Shrops 60 C5
Astley Warks 63 F7
Astley Worcs 50 C2
Astley Abbotts Shrops 61 E7
Astley Bridge Gtr Man 86 C5
Astley Cross Worcs 50 C3
Astley Green Gtr Man 86 E5
Aston Ches E 74 E3
Aston Ches W 74 B2
Aston Derbys 88 F2
Aston Hereford 49 B6
Aston Herts 41 B5
Aston Oxon 38 D3
Aston S Yorks 89 F5
Aston Shrops 60 B5
Aston Staffs 74 E4
Aston Telford 61 D6
Aston W Mid 62 F4
Aston Wokingham 39 F7
Aston Abbotts Bucks 39 B8
Aston Botterell Shrops 61 F6
Aston-By-Stone Staffs 75 F6
Aston Cantlow Warks 51 D6
Aston Clinton Bucks 40 C1
Aston Crews Hereford 36 B3
Aston Cross Glos 50 F4
Aston End Herts 41 B5
Aston Eyre Shrops 61 E6
Aston Fields Worcs 50 C4
Aston Flamville Leics 63 E8
Aston Ingham Hereford 36 B3
Aston juxta Mondrum Ches E 74 D3
Aston le Walls Northants 52 D2
Aston Magna Glos 51 F6
Aston Munslow Shrops 60 F5
Aston on Clun Shrops 60 F3
Aston-on-Trent Derbys 63 B8
Aston Rogers Shrops 60 D3
Aston Rowant Oxon 39 E7
Aston Sandford Bucks 39 D7
Aston Somerville Worcs 50 F5
Aston Subedge Glos 51 E6
Aston Tirrold Oxon 39 F5
Aston Upthorpe Oxon 39 F5
Astrop Northants 52 F3
Astwick C Beds 54 F3
Astwood M Keynes 53 E7
Astwood Worcs 50 D3
Astwood Bank Worcs 50 C5
Aswarby Lincs 78 F3
Aswardby Lincs 79 B6
Atch Lench Worcs 50 D5
Atcham Shrops 60 D5
Athelhampton Dorset 13 E5
Athelington Suff 57 B6
Athelney Som 11 B8
Athelstaneford E Loth 121 B8
Atherington Devon 9 B7
Atherstone Warks 63 E7
Atherstone on Stour Warks 51 D7
Atherton Gtr Man 86 D4
Atley Hill N Yorks 101 D7
Atlow Derbys 76 E2
Attadale Highld 150 H2
Attadale Ho. Highld 150 H2
Attenborough Notts 76 F5
Atterby Lincs 90 E3
Attercliffe S Yorks 88 F4
Attleborough Norf 68 E3
Attleborough Warks 63 E7
Attlebridge Norf 68 C4
Atwick E Yorks 97 D7
Atworth Wilts 24 C3
Aubourn Lincs 78 C2
Auchagallon N Ayrs 143 E9
Auchallater Aberds 139 F7
Aucharnie Aberds 153 D6
Auchattie Aberds 141 E5
Auchavan Angus 134 C1
Auchbreck Moray 139 B8
Auchenback E Renf 118 D5
Auchenbainzie Dumfries 113 E8
Auchenblae Aberds 135 B7
Auchenbrack Dumfries 113 E7
Auchenbreck Argyll 145 E9
Auchencairn Dumfries 106 D4
Auchencairn Dumfries 114 F2
Auchencairn N Ayrs 143 F11
Auchencrosh S Ayrs 104 B5
Auchencrow Borders 122 C4
Auchendinny Midloth 121 C5
Auchengray S Lanark 120 D2
Auchenhalrig Moray 152 B3
Auchenheath S Lanark 119 E8
Auchenlochan Argyll 145 F8
Auchenmalg Dumfries 105 D6
Auchensoul S Ayrs 112 E2
Auchentiber N Ayrs 118 E3
Auchertyre Highld 149 F13
Auchgourish Highld 138 C5
Auchincarroch W Dunb 126 F3
Auchindrain Argyll 125 E6
Auchindrean Highld 150 C4
Auchininna Aberds 153 D6
Auchinleck E Ayrs 113 B5
Auchinloch N Lanark 119 B6
Auchinroath Moray 152 C2
Auchintoul Aberds 140 C4
Auchiries Aberds 153 E10
Auchlee Aberds 141 E7
Auchleven Aberds 140 B5
Auchlochan S Lanark 119 F8
Auchlossan Aberds 140 D4
Auchlunies Aberds 141 E7
Auchlyne Stirling 126 B4
Auchmacoy Aberds 153 E9
Auchmair Moray 140 B2
Auchmantle Dumfries 105 C5
Auchmillan E Ayrs 112 B5
Auchmithie Angus 135 E6
Auchmuirbridge Fife 128 D4
Auchmull Angus 135 B5
Auchnacree Angus 134 C4
Auchnagallin Highld 151 H13
Auchnagatt Aberds 153 D9
Auchnaha Argyll 145 E8
Auchnashelloch Perth 127 C6
Aucholzie Aberds 140 E2
Auchrannie Angus 134 D2
Auchroisk Highld 139 B6
Auchronie Angus 140 F3
Auchterarder Perth 127 C8
Auchteraw Highld 137 D6
Auchterderran Fife 128 E4
Auchterhouse Angus 134 F3
Auchtermuchty Fife 128 C4
Auchterneed Highld 150 F7
Auchtertool Fife 128 E4
Auchtertyre Moray 152 C1
Auchtubh Stirling 126 B4
Auckengill Highld 158 D5
Auckley S Yorks 89 D7
Audenshaw Gtr Man 87 E7
Audlem Ches E 74 E3
Audley Staffs 74 D4
Audley End Essex 56 F2
Auds Aberds 153 B6
Aughton E Yorks 96 F3
Aughton Lancs 85 D4
Aughton Lancs 93 C5
Aughton S Yorks 89 F5
Aughton Wilts 25 D7
Aughton Park Lancs 86 D2
Auldearn Highld 151 F12
Aulden Hereford 49 D6
Auldgirth Dumfries 114 F2
Auldhame E Loth 129 F7
Auldhouse S Lanark 119 D6
Ault a'chruinn Highld 136 B2
Aultanrynie Highld 156 F6
Aultbea Highld 155 J13
Aultdearg Highld 150 E5
Aultgrishan Highld 155 J12
Aultguish Inn Highld 150 D6
Aultibea Highld 157 G13
Aultiphurst Highld 157 C11
Aultmore Moray 152 C4
Aultnagoire Highld 137 B8
Aultnamain Inn Highld 151 C9
Aultnaslat Highld 136 D4
Aulton Aberds 140 B5
Aundorach Highld 139 C5
Aunsby Lincs 78 F3
Auquhorthies Aberds 141 B7
Aust S Glos 36 F2
Austendike Lincs 66 B2
Austerfield S Yorks 89 E7
Austrey Warks 63 D6
Austwick N Yorks 93 C7
Authorpe Lincs 91 F8
Authorpe Row Lincs 79 B8
Avebury Wilts 25 C6
Aveley Thurrock 42 F1
Avening Glos 37 E5
Averham Notts 77 D7
Aveton Gifford Devon 6 E4
Avielochan Highld 138 C5
Aviemore Highld 138 C4
Avington Hants 26 F3
Avington W Berks 25 C8
Avoch Highld 151 F10
Avon Hants 14 E2
Avon Dassett Warks 52 E2
Avonbridge Falk 120 B2
Avonmouth Bristol 23 B7
Avonwick Devon 6 D5
Awbridge Hants 14 B4
Awhirk Dumfries 104 D4
Awkley S Glos 36 F2
Awliscombe Devon 11 D6
Awre Glos 36 D4
Awsworth Notts 76 E4
Axbridge Som 23 D6
Axford Hants 26 E4
Axford Wilts 25 B7
Axminster Devon 11 E7
Axmouth Devon 11 E7
Axton Flint 85 F2
Aycliff Kent 31 E7
Aycliffe Durham 101 B7
Aydon Northumb 110 C3
Aylburton Glos 36 D3
Ayle Northumb 109 E7
Aylesbeare Devon 10 E5
Aylesbury Bucks 39 C8
Aylesby NE Lincs 91 D6
Aylesford Kent 29 D8
Aylesham Kent 31 D6
Aylestone Leicester 64 D2
Aylmerton Norf 81 D7
Aylsham Norf 81 E7
Aylton Hereford 49 F8
Aymestrey Hereford 49 C6
Aynho Northants 52 F3
Ayot St Lawrence Herts 40 C4
Ayot St Peter Herts 41 C5
Ayr S Ayrs 112 B3
Aysgarth N Yorks 101 F5
Ayside Cumb 99 F5
Ayston Rutland 65 D5
Aythorpe Roding Essex 42 C1
Ayton Borders 122 C5
Aywick Shetland 160 E7
Azerley N Yorks 95 B5

B

Babbacombe Torbay 7 C7
Babbinswood Shrops 73 F7
Babcary Som 12 B3
Babel Carms 47 F7
Babell Flint 73 B5
Babraham Cambs 55 D6
Babworth Notts 89 F7
Bac W Isles 155 C9
Bachau Anglesey 82 C4
Back of Keppoch Highld 147 C9
Back Rogerton E Ayrs 113 B5
Backaland Orkney 159 E6
Backaskaill Orkney 159 C5
Backbarrow Cumb 99 F5
Backe Carms 32 C3
Backfolds Aberds 153 C10
Backford Ches W 73 B8
Backford Cross Ches W 73 B7
Backhill Aberds 153 E7
Backhill Aberds 153 E10
Backhill of Clackriach Aberds 153 D9
Backhill of Fortree Aberds 153 D9
Backhill of Trustach Aberds 140 E5
Backies Highld 157 J11
Backlass Highld 158 E4
Backwell N Som 23 C6
Backworth T&W 111 B6
Bacon End Essex 42 C2
Baconsthorpe Norf 81 D7
Bacton Hereford 49 F5
Bacton Norf 81 D9
Bacton Suff 56 C4
Bacton Green Suff 56 C4
Bacup Lancs 87 B6
Badachro Highld 149 A12
Badanloch Lodge Highld 157 F10
Badavanich Highld 150 F4
Badbury Swindon 38 F1
Badby Northants 52 D3
Badcall Highld 156 D5
Badcaul Highld 150 B3
Baddeley Green Stoke 75 D6
Baddesley Clinton Warks 51 B7
Baddesley Ensor Warks 63 E6
Baddidarach Highld 156 G3
Baddoch Aberds 139 F7
Baddock Highld 151 F10
Badenscoth Aberds 153 E7
Badenyon Aberds 140 C2
Badger Shrops 61 E7
Badger's Mount Kent 29 C5
Badgeworth Glos 37 C6
Badgworth Som 23 D5
Badicaul Highld 149 F12
Badingham Suff 57 C7
Badlesmere Kent 30 D4
Badlipster Highld 158 F4
Badluarach Highld 150 B2
Badminton S Glos 37 F5
Badnaban Highld 156 G3
Badninish Highld 151 B10
Badrallach Highld 150 B3
Badsey Worcs 51 E5
Badshot Lea Sur 27 E6
Badsworth W Yorks 89 C5
Badwell Ash Suff 56 C3
Bae Colwyn = Colwyn Bay Conwy 83 D8
Bag Enderby Lincs 79 B6
Bagby N Yorks 102 F2
Bagendon Glos 37 D7
Bagh a Chaisteil = Castlebay W Isles 148 J1
Bagh Mor W Isles 148 C3
Bagh Shiarabhagh W Isles 148 H2
Baghasdal W Isles 148 G2
Bagillt Flint 73 B6
Baginton Warks 51 B8
Baglan Neath 33 E8
Bagley Shrops 60 B4
Bagnall Staffs 75 D6
Bagnor W Berks 26 C2
Bagshot Sur 27 C7
Bagshot Wilts 25 C8
Bagthorpe Norf 80 D3
Bagthorpe Notts 76 D4
Bagworth Leics 63 D8
Bagwy Llydiart Hereford 35 B8
Bail Àrd Bhuirgh W Isles 155 B9
Bail Uachdraich W Isles 148 B3
Baildon W Yorks 94 F4
Baile W Isles 154 J4
Baile a Mhanaich W Isles 148 C2
Baile Ailein W Isles 155 E7
Baile an Truiseil W Isles 155 B8
Baile Boidheach Argyll 144 F6
Baile Glas W Isles 148 C3
Baile Mhartainn W Isles 148 A2
Baile Mhic Phail W Isles 148 A3
Baile Mor Argyll 146 J5
Baile Mor W Isles 148 B2
Baile na Creige W Isles 148 H1
Baile nan Cailleach W Isles 148 C2
Baile Raghaill W Isles 148 A2
Bailebeag Highld 137 C8
Baileyhead Cumb 108 B5
Bailiesward Aberds 152 E4
Baillieston Glasgow 119 C6
Bail'lochdrach W Isles 148 C3
Bail'Ur Tholastaidh W Isles 155 C10
Bainbridge N Yorks 100 E4
Bainsford Falk 127 F7
Bainshole Aberds 152 E6
Bainton E Yorks 97 D5
Bainton Pboro 65 D7
Bairnkine Borders 116 C2
Baker Street Thurrock 42 F2
Baker's End Herts 41 C6
Bakewell Derbys 76 C2
Bala = Y Bala Gwyn 72 F3
Balachuirn Highld 149 D10
Balavil Highld 138 D3
Balbeg Highld 137 B7
Balbeg Highld 150 H7
Balbeggie Perth 128 B3
Balbithan Aberds 141 C6
Balbithan Ho. Aberds 141 C7
Balblair Highld 151 B8
Balblair Highld 151 E10
Balby S Yorks 89 D6
Balchladich Highld 156 F3
Balchraggan Highld 151 G8
Balchraggan Highld 151 H8
Balchrick Highld 156 D4
Balchrystie Fife 129 D6
Balcladaich Highld 137 B5
Balcombe W Sus 28 F4
Balcombe Lane W Sus 28 F4
Balcomie Fife 129 C8
Balcurvie Fife 128 D5
Baldersby N Yorks 95 B6
Baldersby St James N Yorks 95 B6
Balderstone Lancs 93 F6
Balderton Ches W 73 C7
Balderton Notts 77 D8
Baldhu Corn 3 B6
Baldinnie Fife 129 C6
Baldock Herts 54 F3
Baldovie Dundee 134 F4
Baldrine IoM 84 D4
Baldslow E Sus 18 D4
Baldwin IoM 84 D3
Baldwinholme Cumb 108 D3
Baldwin's Gate Staffs 74 E4
Bale Norf 81 D6
Balearn Aberds 153 C10
Balemartine Argyll 146 G2
Balephuil Argyll 146 G2
Balerno Edin 120 C4
Balevullin Argyll 146 G2
Balfield Angus 135 C5
Balfour Orkney 159 G5
Balfron Stirling 126 F4
Balfron Station Stirling 126 F4
Balgaveny Aberds 153 D6
Balgavies Angus 135 D5
Balgonar Fife 128 E2
Balgove Aberds 153 E8
Balgowan Highld 138 E2
Balgown Highld 149 B8
Balgrochan E Dunb 119 B6
Balgy Highld 149 C13
Balhaldie Stirling 127 D7
Balhalgardy Aberds 141 B6
Balham London 28 B3
Balhary Perth 134 E2
Baliasta Shetland 160 C8
Baligill Highld 157 C11
Balintore Angus 134 D2
Balintore Highld 151 D11
Balintraid Highld 151 D10
Balk N Yorks 102 F2
Balkeerie Angus 134 E3
Balkemback Angus 134 F3
Balkholme E Yorks 89 B8
Balkissock S Ayrs 104 A5
Ball Shrops 60 B3
Ball Haye Green Staffs 75 D6
Ball Hill Hants 26 C2
Ballabeg IoM 84 E2
Ballacannel IoM 84 D4
Ballachulish Highld 130 D4
Ballajora IoM 84 C4
Ballaleigh IoM 84 D3
Ballamodha IoM 84 E2
Ballantrae S Ayrs 104 A4
Ballaquine IoM 84 D4
Ballards Gore Essex 43 E5
Ballasalla IoM 84 C3
Ballasalla IoM 84 E2
Ballater Aberds 140 E2
Ballaugh IoM 84 C3
Ballaveare IoM 84 E3
Ballcorach Moray 139 B7
Ballechin Perth 133 D6
Balleigh Highld 151 C10
Ballencrieff E Loth 121 B7
Ballentoul Perth 133 C5
Ballidon Derbys 76 D2
Balliemore Argyll 124 C4
Balliemore Argyll 145 E9
Ballikinrain Stirling 126 F4
Ballimeanoch Argyll 125 D6
Ballimore Argyll 145 E8
Ballimore Stirling 126 C4
Ballinaby Argyll 142 B3
Ballindean Perth 128 B4
Ballingdon Suff 56 E2
Ballinger Common Bucks 40 D2
Ballingham Hereford 49 F7
Ballingry Fife 128 E3
Ballinlick Perth 133 E6
Ballinluig Perth 133 D6
Ballintuim Perth 133 D8
Balloch Angus 134 D3
Balloch Highld 151 G10
Balloch N Lanark 119 B7
Balloch W Dunb 126 F2
Ballochan Aberds 140 E4
Ballochford Moray 152 E3
Ballochmorrie S Ayrs 112 F2
Balls Cross W Sus 16 B3
Balls Green Essex 43 B6
Ballygown Argyll 146 G7
Ballygrant Argyll 142 B4
Ballyhaugh Argyll 146 F4
Balmacara Highld 149 F13
Balmacara Square Highld 149 F13
Balmaclellan Dumfries 106 B3
Balmacneil Perth 133 D6
Balmacqueen Highld 149 A9
Balmae Dumfries 106 E3
Balmaha Stirling 126 E3
Balmalcolm Fife 128 D5
Balmeanach Highld 149 D10
Balmedie Aberds 141 C8
Balmer Heath Shrops 73 F8
Balmerino Fife 129 B5
Balmerlawn Hants 14 D4
Balmichael N Ayrs 143 E10
Balmirmer Angus 135 F5
Balmore Highld 149 D7
Balmore Highld 150 H6
Balmore Highld 151 G11
Balmore Perth 133 D6
Balmule Fife 128 F4
Balmullo Fife 129 B6
Balmungie Highld 151 F10
Balnaboth Angus 134 C3
Balnabruaich Highld 151 E10
Balnabruich Highld 158 H3
Balnacoil Highld 157 H11
Balnacra Highld 150 G2
Balnafoich Highld 151 H9
Balnagall Highld 151 C11
Balnaguard Perth 133 D6
Balnahard Argyll 144 D3
Balnahard Argyll 146 H7
Balnain Highld 150 H7
Balnakeil Highld 156 C6
Balnaknock Highld 149 B9
Balnapaling Highld 151 E10
Balne N Yorks 89 C6
Balochroy Argyll 143 C8
Balone Fife 129 C6
Balornock Glasgow 119 C6
Balquharn Perth 133 F7
Balquhidder Stirling 126 B4
Balsall W Mid 51 B7
Balsall Common W Mid 51 B7
Balsall Heath W Mid 62 F4
Balscott Oxon 51 E8
Balsham Cambs 55 D6
Baltasound Shetland 160 C8
Balterley Staffs 74 D4
Baltersan Dumfries 105 C8
Balthangie Aberds 153 C8
Baltonsborough Som 23 F7
Balvaird Highld 151 F8
Balvicar Argyll 124 D3
Balvraid Highld 149 G13
Balvraid Highld 151 H11
Bamber Bridge Lancs 86 B3
Bambers Green Essex 42 B1
Bamburgh Northumb 123 F7
Bamff Perth 134 D2
Bamford Derbys 88 F3
Bamford Gtr Man 87 C6
Bampton Cumb 99 C7
Bampton Devon 10 B4
Bampton Oxon 38 D3
Bampton Grange Cumb 99 C7
Banavie Highld 131 B5
Banbury Oxon 52 E2
Bancffosfelen Carms 33 C5
Banchory Aberds 141 E5
Banchory-Devenick Aberds 141 D8
Bancycapel Carms 33 C5
Bancyfelin Carms 32 C4
Bancyffordd Carms 46 F3
Bandirran Perth 134 F2
Banff Aberds 153 B6
Bangor Gwyn 83 D5
Bangor-is-y-coed Wrex 73 E7
Banham Norf 68 F3
Bank Hants 14 D3
Bank Newton N Yorks 94 D2
Bank Street Worcs 49 C8
Bankend Dumfries 107 C7
Bankfoot Perth 133 F7
Bankglen E Ayrs 113 C6
Bankhead Aberdeen 141 C7
Bankhead Aberds 141 D5
Banknock Falk 119 B7
Banks Cumb 109 C5
Banks Lancs 85 B4
Bankshill Dumfries 114 F4
Banningham Norf 81 E8
Banniskirk Ho. Highld 158 E3
Bannister Green Essex 42 B2
Bannockburn Stirling 127 E7
Banstead Sur 28 D3
Bantham Devon 6 E4
Banton N Lanark 119 B7
Banwell N Som 23 D5
Banyard's Green Suff 57 B6
Bapchild Kent 30 C3
Bar Hill Cambs 54 C4
Barabhas W Isles 155 C8
Barabhas Iarach W Isles 155 C8
Barabhas Uarach W Isles 155 B8
Barachandroman Argyll 124 C2
Barassie S Ayrs 118 F3
Baravullin Argyll 124 E4
Barbaraville Highld 151 D10
Barber Booth Derbys 88 F2
Barbieston S Ayrs 112 C4
Barbon Cumb 99 F8
Barbridge Ches E 74 D3
Barbrook Devon 21 E6
Barby Northants 52 B3
Barcaldine Argyll 130 E3
Barcheston Warks 51 F7
Barcombe E Sus 17 C8
Barcombe Cross E Sus 17 C8
Barden N Yorks 101 E6
Barden Scale N Yorks 94 D3
Bardennoch Dumfries 113 E5
Bardfield Saling Essex 42 B2
Bardister Shetland 160 F5
Bardney Lincs 78 C4
Bardon Leics 63 C8
Bardon Mill Northumb 109 C7
Bardowie E Dunb 119 B5
Bardrainney Involyd 118 B3
Bardsea Cumb 92 B3
Bardsey W Yorks 95 E6
Bardwell Suff 56 B3
Bare Lancs 92 C4
Barfad Argyll 145 G7
Barford Norf 68 D4
Barford Warks 51 C7
Barford St John Oxon 52 F2
Barford St Martin Wilts 25 F5
Barford St Michael Oxon 52 F2
Barfrestone Kent 31 D6
Bargod = Bargoed Caerph 35 E5
Bargoed = Bargod Caerph 35 E5
Bargrennan Dumfries 105 B7
Barham Cambs 54 B2
Barham Kent 31 D6
Barham Suff 56 D5
Barharrow Dumfries 106 D3
Barhill Dumfries 106 C5
Barholm Lincs 65 C7
Barkby Leics 64 D3
Barkestone-le-Vale Leics 77 F7
Barkham Wokingham 27 C5
Barking London 41 F7
Barking Suff 56 D4
Barking Tye Suff 56 D4
Barkingside London 41 F7
Barkisland W Yorks 87 C8
Barkston Lincs 78 E2
Barkston N Yorks 95 F7
Barkway Herts 54 F4
Barlaston Staffs 75 F5
Barlavington W Sus 16 C3
Barlborough Derbys 76 B4
Barlby N Yorks 96 F2
Barlestone Leics 63 D8
Barley Herts 54 F4
Barley Lancs 93 E8
Barley Mow T&W 111 D5
Barleythorpe Rutland 64 D5
Barling Essex 43 F5
Barlow Derbys 76 B3
Barlow N Yorks 89 B7
Barlow T&W 110 C4
Barmby Moor E Yorks 96 E3
Barmby on the Marsh E Yorks 89 B7
Barmer Norf 80 D4
Barmoor Castle Northumb 123 F5
Barmoor Lane End Northumb 123 F6
Barmouth = Abermaw Gwyn 58 C3
Barmpton Darl 101 C8
Barmston E Yorks 97 D7
Barnack Pboro 65 D7
Barnacle Warks 63 F7
Barnard Castle Durham 101 C5
Barnard Gate Oxon 38 C4
Barnardiston Suff 55 E8
Barnbarroch Dumfries 106 D5
Barnburgh S Yorks 89 D5
Barnby Suff 69 F7
Barnby Dun S Yorks 89 D7
Barnby in the Willows Notts 77 D8
Barnby Moor Notts 89 F7
Barnes Street Kent 29 E7
Barnet London 41 E5
Barnetby le Wold N Lincs 90 D4
Barney Norf 81 D5
Barnham Suff 56 B2
Barnham W Sus 16 D3
Barnham Broom Norf 68 D3
Barnhead Angus 135 D6
Barnhill Ches W 73 D8
Barnhill Dundee 134 F4
Barnhill Moray 152 C1
Barnhills Dumfries 104 B3
Barningham Durham 101 C5
Barningham Suff 56 B3
Barnoldby le Beck NE Lincs 91 D6
Barnoldswick Lancs 93 E8
Barns Green W Sus 16 B5
Barnsley Glos 38 D1
Barnsley S Yorks 88 D4
Barnstaple Devon 20 F4
Barnston Essex 42 C2
Barnston Mers 85 F3
Barnstone Notts 77 F7
Barnt Green Worcs 50 B5
Barnton Ches W 74 B3
Barnton Edin 120 B4
Barnwell All Saints Northants 65 F7
Barnwell St Andrew Northants 65 F7
Barnwood Glos 37 C5
Barochreal Argyll 124 C4
Barons Cross Hereford 49 D6
Barr S Ayrs 112 E2
Barra Castle Aberds 141 B6
Barrachan Dumfries 105 E7
Barrack Aberds 153 D8
Barraglom W Isles 154 D6
Barrahormid Argyll 144 E6
Barran Argyll 124 C4
Barrapol Argyll 146 G2
Barras Aberds 141 F7
Barras Cumb 100 C3
Barrasford Northumb 110 B2
Barravullin Argyll 124 E4
Barregarrow IoM 84 D3
Barrhead E Renf 118 D4
Barrhill S Ayrs 112 F2
Barrington Cambs 54 E4
Barrington Som 11 C8
Barripper Corn 2 C5
Barrmill N Ayrs 118 D3
Barrock Highld 158 C4
Barrock Ho. Highld 158 D4
Barrow Lancs 93 F7
Barrow Rutland 65 C5
Barrow Suff 55 C8
Barrow Green Kent 30 C3
Barrow Gurney N Som 23 C7
Barrow Haven N Lincs 90 B4
Barrow-in-Furness Cumb 92 C2
Barrow Island Cumb 92 C1
Barrow Nook Lancs 86 D2
Barrow Street Wilts 24 F3
Barrow upon Humber N Lincs 90 B4
Barrow upon Soar Leics 64 C2
Barrow upon Trent Derbys 63 B7
Barroway Drove Norf 67 D5
Barrowburn Northumb 116 C4
Barrowby Lincs 77 F8
Barrowcliff N Yorks 103 F8
Barrowden Rutland 65 D6
Barrowford Lancs 93 F8
Barrows Green Ches E 74 D3
Barrows Green Cumb 99 F7
Barrow's Green Mers 86 F3
Barry Angus 135 F5
Barry = Y Barri V Glam 22 C3
Barry Island V Glam 22 C3
Barsby Leics 64 C3
Barsham Suff 69 F6
Barston W Mid 51 B7
Bartestree Hereford 49 E7
Barthol Chapel Aberds 153 E8
Barthomley Ches E 74 D4
Bartley Hants 14 C4
Bartley Green W Mid 62 F4
Bartlow Cambs 55 E6
Barton Cambs 54 D5
Barton Ches W 73 D8
Barton Glos 37 B8
Barton Lancs 85 D4
Barton Lancs 92 F5
Barton N Yorks 101 D7
Barton Oxon 39 D5
Barton Torbay 7 C7
Barton Warks 51 D6
Barton Bendish Norf 67 D7
Barton Hartshorn Bucks 52 F4
Barton in Fabis Notts 76 F5
Barton in the Beans Leics 63 D7
Barton-le-Clay C Beds 53 F8
Barton-le-Street N Yorks 96 B3
Barton-le-Willows N Yorks 96 C3
Barton Mills Suff 55 B8
Barton on Sea Hants 14 E3
Barton on the Heath Warks 51 F7
Barton St David Som 23 F7
Barton Seagrave Northants 53 B6
Barton Stacey Hants 26 E2
Barton Turf Norf 69 B6
Barton-under-Needwood Staffs 63 C5
Barton-upon-Humber N Lincs 90 B4
Barton Waterside N Lincs 90 B4
Barugh S Yorks 88 D4
Barway Cambs 55 B6
Barwell Leics 63 E8
Barwick Herts 41 C6
Barwick Som 12 C3
Barwick in Elmet W Yorks 95 F6
Baschurch Shrops 60 B4
Bascote Warks 52 C2
Basford Green Staffs 75 D6
Bashall Eaves Lancs 93 E6
Bashley Hants 14 E3
Basildon Essex 42 F3
Basingstoke Hants 26 D4
Baslow Derbys 76 B2
Bason Bridge Som 22 E5
Bassaleg Newport 35 F6
Bassenthwaite Cumb 108 F2
Bassett Soton 14 C5
Bassingbourn Cambs 54 E4
Bassingfield Notts 77 F6
Bassingham Lincs 78 C2
Bassingthorpe Lincs 65 B6
Basta Shetland 160 D7
Baston Lincs 65 C8
Bastwick Norf 69 C7
Baswick Steer E Yorks 97 E6
Batchworth Heath Herts 40 E3
Batcombe Dorset 12 D4
Batcombe Som 23 F8
Bate Heath Ches E 74 B3
Batford Herts 40 C4
Bath Bath 24 C2
Bathampton Bath 24 C2
Bathealton Som 11 B5
Batheaston Bath 24 C2
Bathford Bath 24 C2
Bathgate W Loth 120 C2
Bathley Notts 77 D7
Bathpool Corn 5 B7
Bathpool Som 11 B7
Bathville W Loth 120 C2
Batley W Yorks 88 B3
Batsford Glos 51 F6
Battersby N Yorks 102 D3
Battersea London 28 B3
Battisborough Cross Devon 6 E3
Battisford Suff 56 D4
Battisford Tye Suff 56 D4
Battle E Sus 18 D4
Battle Powys 48 F2
Battledown Glos 37 B6
Battlefield Shrops 60 C5
Battlesbridge Essex 42 E3
Battlesden C Beds 40 B2
Battlesea Green Suff 57 B6
Battleton Som 10 B4
Battram Leics 63 D8
Battramsley Hants 14 E4
Baughton Worcs 50 E3
Baughurst Hants 26 D3

Baulking Oxon 38 E3
Baumber Lincs 78 B5
Baunton Glos 37 D7
Baverstock Wilts 24 F5
Bawburgh Norf 68 D4
Bawdeswell Norf 81 E6
Bawdrip Som 22 F5
Bawdsey Suff 57 E7
Bawtry S Yorks 89 E7
Baxenden Lancs 87 B5
Baxterley Warks 63 E6
Baybridge Hants 15 B6
Baycliff Cumb 92 B2
Baydon Wilts 25 B7
Bayford Herts 41 D6
Bayford Som 12 B5
Bayles Cumb 109 E7
Baylham Suff 56 D5
Baynard's Green Oxon 39 B5
Bayston Hill Shrops 60 D4
Baythorn End Essex 55 E8
Bayton Worcs 49 B8
Beach Highld 130 D1
Beachampton Bucks 53 F5
Beachamwell Norf 67 D7
Beachans Moray 151 G13
Beacharr Argyll 143 D7
Beachborough Kent 19 B8
Beachley Glos 36 E2
Beacon Devon 11 D6
Beacon End Essex 43 B5
Beacon Hill Sur 27 F6
Beacon's Bottom Bucks 39 E7
Beaconsfield Bucks 40 F2
Beacrabhaic W Isles 154 H6
Beadlam N Yorks 102 F4
Beadlow C Beds 54 F2
Beadnell Northumb 117 B8
Beaford Devon 9 C7
Beal N Yorks 89 B6
Beal Northumb 123 E6
Beamhurst Staffs 75 F7
Beaminster Dorset 12 D2
Beamish Durham 110 D5
Beamsley N Yorks 94 D3
Bean Kent 29 B6
Beanacre Wilts 24 C4
Beanley Northumb 117 C6
Beaquoy Orkney 159 F4
Bear Cross Bmouth 13 E8
Beardwood Blackburn 86 B4
Beare Green Sur 28 E2
Bearley Warks 51 C6
Bearnus Argyll 146 G6
Bearpark Durham 110 E5
Bearsbridge Northumb 109 D7
Bearsden E Dunb 118 B5
Bearsted Kent 29 D8
Bearstone Shrops 74 F4
Bearwood Hereford 49 D5
Bearwood Poole 13 E8
Bearwood W Mid 62 F4
Beattock Dumfries 114 D3
Beauchamp Roding Essex 42 C1
Beauchief S Yorks 88 F4
Beaufort Bl Gwent 35 C5
Beaufort Castle Highld 151 G8
Beaulieu Hants 14 D4
Beauly Highld 151 G8
Beaumaris Anglesey 83 D6
Beaumont Cumb 108 D3
Beaumont Essex 43 B7
Beaumont Hill Darl 101 C7
Beausale Warks 51 B7
Beauworth Hants 15 B6
Beaworthy Devon 9 E6
Beazley End Essex 42 B3
Bebington Mers 85 F4
Bebside Northumb 117 F8
Beccles Suff 69 E7
Becconsall Lancs 86 B2
Beck Foot Cumb 99 E8
Beck Hole N Yorks 103 D6
Beck Row Suff 55 B7
Beck Side Cumb 98 F4
Beckbury Shrops 61 D7
Beckenham London 28 C4
Beckermet Cumb 98 D2
Beckfoot Cumb 98 D3
Beckfoot Cumb 107 E7
Beckford Worcs 50 F4
Beckhampton Wilts 25 C5
Beckingham Lincs 77 D8
Beckingham Notts 89 F8
Beckington Som 24 D3
Beckley E Sus 19 C5
Beckley Hants 14 E3
Beckley Oxon 39 C5
Beckton London 41 F7
Beckwithshaw N Yorks 95 D5
Becontree London 41 F7
Bed-y-coedwr Gwyn 71 E8
Bedale N Yorks 101 F7
Bedburn Durham 110 F4
Bedchester Dorset 13 C6
Beddau Rhondda 34 F4
Beddgelert Gwyn 71 C6
Beddingham E Sus 17 D8
Beddington London 28 C4
Bedfield Suff 57 C6
Bedford Bedford 53 D8
Bedham W Sus 16 B4
Bedhampton Hants 15 D8
Bedingfield Suff 57 C5
Bedlam N Yorks 95 C5
Bedlington Northumb 117 F8
Bedlington Station Northumb 117 F8
Bedlinog M Tydf 34 D4
Bedminster Bristol 23 B7
Bedmond Herts 40 D3
Bednall Staffs 62 C3
Bedrule Borders 116 C2
Bedstone Shrops 49 B5
Bedwas Caerph 35 F5
Bedworth Warks 63 F7
Bedworth Heath Warks 63 F7
Beeby Leics 64 D3
Beech Hants 26 F4
Beech Staffs 75 F5
Beech Hill Gtr Man 86 D3
Beech Hill W Berks 26 C4
Beechingstoke Wilts 25 D5
Beedon W Berks 26 B2
Beeford E Yorks 97 D7
Beeley Derbys 76 C2
Beelsby NE Lincs 91 D6
Beenham W Berks 26 C3
Beeny Corn 8 E3
Beer Devon 11 F7
Beer Hackett Dorset 12 C3
Beercrocombe Som 11 B8
Beesands Devon 7 E6
Beesby Lincs 91 F8
Beeson Devon 7 E6
Beeston C Beds 54 E2
Beeston Ches W 74 D2
Beeston Norf 68 C2
Beeston Notts 76 F5
Beeston W Yorks 95 F5
Beeston Regis Norf 81 C7
Beeswing Dumfries 107 C5
Beetham Cumb 92 B4
Beetley Norf 68 C2
Begbroke Oxon 38 C4
Begelly Pembs 32 D2
Beggar's Bush Powys 48 C4
Beguildy Powys 48 B3
Beighton Norf 69 D6
Beighton S Yorks 88 F5
Beighton Hill Derbys 76 D2
Beith N Ayrs 118 D3
Bekesbourne Kent 31 D5
Belaugh Norf 69 C5
Belbroughton Worcs 50 B4
Belchamp Otten Essex 56 E2
Belchamp St Paul Essex 55 E8
Belchamp Walter Essex 56 E2
Belchford Lincs 79 B5
Belford Northumb 123 F7
Belhaven E Loth 122 B2
Belhelvie Aberds 141 C8
Belhinnie Aberds 140 B3
Bell Bar Herts 41 D5
Bell Busk N Yorks 94 D2
Bell End Worcs 50 B4
Bell o'th'Hill Ches W 74 E2
Bellabeg Aberds 140 C2
Bellamore S Ayrs 112 F2
Bellanoch Argyll 144 D6
Bellaty Angus 134 D2
Belleau Lincs 79 B7
Bellehiglash Moray 152 E1
Bellerby N Yorks 101 E6
Bellever Devon 6 B4
Belliehill Angus 135 C5
Bellingdon Bucks 40 D2
Bellingham Northumb 116 F4
Belloch Argyll 143 E7
Bellochantuy Argyll 143 E7
Bells Yew Green E Sus 18 B3
Bellsbank E Ayrs 112 D4
Bellshill N Lanark 119 C7
Bellshill Northumb 123 F7
Bellspool Borders 120 F4
Bellsquarry W Loth 120 C3
Belmaduthy Highld 151 F9
Belmesthorpe Rutland 65 C7
Belmont Blackburn 86 C4
Belmont London 28 C3
Belmont S Ayrs 112 B3
Belmont Shetland 160 C7
Belnacraig Aberds 140 C2
Belowda Corn 4 C4
Belper Derbys 76 E3
Belper Lane End Derbys 76 E3
Belsay Northumb 110 B4
Belses Borders 115 B8
Belsford Devon 7 D5
Belstead Suff 56 E5
Belston S Ayrs 112 B3
Belstone Devon 9 E8
Belthorn Blackburn 86 B5
Beltinge Kent 31 C5
Beltoft N Lincs 90 D2
Belton Leics 63 B8
Belton Lincs 78 F2
Belton N Lincs 89 D8
Belton Norf 69 D7
Belton in Rutland Rutland 64 D5
Beltring Kent 29 E7
Belts of Collonach Aberds 141 E5
Belvedere London 29 B5
Belvoir Leics 77 F8
Bembridge IoW 15 F7
Bemersyde Borders 121 F8
Bemerton Wilts 25 F6
Bempton E Yorks 97 B7
Ben Alder Lodge Highld 132 B2
Ben Armine Lodge Highld 157 H10
Ben Casgro W Isles 155 E9
Benacre Suff 69 F8
Benbuie Dumfries 113 E7
Benderloch Argyll 124 B5
Bendronaig Lodge Highld 150 H3
Benenden Kent 18 B5
Benfield Dumfries 105 C7
Bengate Norf 69 B6
Bengeworth Worcs 50 E5
Benhall Green Suff 57 C7
Benhall Street Suff 57 C7
Benholm Aberds 135 C8
Beningbrough N Yorks 95 D8
Benington Herts 41 B5
Benington Lincs 79 E6
Benllech Anglesey 82 C5
Benmore Argyll 145 E10
Benmore Stirling 126 B3
Benmore Lodge Highld 156 H6
Bennacott Corn 8 E4
Bennan N Ayrs 143 F10
Benniworth Lincs 91 F6
Benover Kent 29 E8
Bensham T&W 110 C5
Benslie N Ayrs 118 E3
Benson Oxon 39 E6
Bent Aberds 135 B6
Bent Gate Lancs 87 B5
Benthall Northumb 117 B8
Benthall Shrops 61 D6
Bentham Glos 37 C6
Benthoul Aberdeen 141 D7
Bentlawnt Shrops 60 D3
Bentley E Yorks 97 F6
Bentley Hants 27 E5
Bentley S Yorks 89 D6
Bentley Suff 56 F5
Bentley Warks 63 E6
Bentley Worcs 50 C4
Bentley Heath W Mid 51 B6
Benton Devon 21 F5
Bentpath Dumfries 115 E6
Bents W Loth 120 C2
Bentworth Hants 26 E4
Benvie Dundee 134 F3
Benwick Cambs 66 E3
Beoley Worcs 51 C5
Beoraidbeg Highld 147 B9
Bepton W Sus 16 C2
Berden Essex 41 B7
Bere Alston Devon 6 C2
Bere Ferrers Devon 6 C2
Bere Regis Dorset 13 E6
Berepper Corn 3 D5
Bergh Apton Norf 69 D6
Berinsfield Oxon 39 E5
Berkeley Glos 36 E3
Berkhamsted Herts 40 D2
Berkley Som 24 E3
Berkswell W Mid 51 B7
Bermondsey London 28 B4
Bernera Highld 149 F13
Bernice Argyll 145 D10
Bernisdale Highld 149 C9
Berrick Salome Oxon 39 E6
Berriedale Highld 158 H3
Berrier Cumb 99 B5
Berriew Powys 59 D8
Berrington Northumb 123 E6
Berrington Shrops 60 D5
Berrow Som 22 D5
Berrow Green Worcs 50 D2
Berry Down Cross Devon 20 E4
Berry Hill Glos 36 C2
Berry Hill Pembs 45 E2
Berry Pomeroy Devon 7 C6
Berryhillock Moray 152 B5
Berrynarbor Devon 20 E4
Bersham Wrex 73 E7
Berstane Orkney 159 G5
Berwick E Sus 18 E2
Berwick Bassett Wilts 25 B5
Berwick Hill Northumb 110 B4
Berwick St James Wilts 25 F5
Berwick St John Wilts 13 B7
Berwick St Leonard Wilts 24 F4
Berwick-upon-Tweed Northumb 123 D5
Bescar Lancs 85 C4
Besford Worcs 50 E4
Bessacarr S Yorks 89 D7
Bessels Leigh Oxon 38 D4
Bessingby E Yorks 97 C7
Bessingham Norf 81 D7
Bestbeech Hill E Sus 18 B3
Besthorpe Norf 68 E3
Besthorpe Notts 77 C8
Bestwood Nottingham 77 E5
Bestwood Village Notts 77 E5
Beswick E Yorks 97 E6
Betchworth Sur 28 E3
Bethania Ceredig 46 C4
Bethania Gwyn 71 C8
Bethania Gwyn 83 F6
Bethel Anglesey 82 D3
Bethel Gwyn 72 F3
Bethel Gwyn 82 E5
Bethersden Kent 30 E3
Bethesda Gwyn 83 E6
Bethesda Pembs 32 C1
Bethlehem Carms 33 B7
Bethnal Green London 41 F6
Betley Staffs 74 E4
Betsham Kent 29 B7
Betteshanger Kent 31 D7
Bettiscombe Dorset 11 E8
Bettisfield Wrex 73 F8
Betton Shrops 60 D3
Betton Shrops 74 F3
Bettws Bridgend 34 F3
Bettws Mon 35 C6
Bettws Newport 35 E6
Bettws Cedewain Powys 59 E8
Bettws Gwerfil Goch Denb 72 E4
Bettws Ifan Ceredig 46 E2
Bettws Newydd Mon 35 D7
Bettws-y-crwyn Shrops 60 F2
Bettyhill Highld 157 C10
Betws Carms 33 C7
Betws Bledrws Ceredig 46 D4
Betws-Garmon Gwyn 82 F5
Betws-y-Coed Conwy 83 F7
Betws-yn-Rhos Conwy 72 B3
Beulah Ceredig 45 E4
Beulah Powys 47 D8
Bevendean Brighton 17 D7
Bevercotes Notts 77 B6
Beverley E Yorks 97 F6
Beverston Glos 37 E5
Bevington Glos 36 E3
Bewaldeth Cumb 108 F2
Bewcastle Cumb 109 B5
Bewdley Worcs 50 B2
Bewerley N Yorks 94 C4
Bewholme E Yorks 97 D7
Bexhill E Sus 18 E4
Bexley London 29 B5
Bexleyheath London 29 B5
Bexwell Norf 67 D6
Beyton Suff 56 C3
Bhaltos W Isles 154 D5
Bhatarsaigh W Isles 148 J1
Bibury Glos 37 D8
Bicester Oxon 39 B5
Bickenhall Som 11 C7
Bickenhill W Mid 63 F5
Bicker Lincs 78 F5
Bickershaw Gtr Man 86 D4
Bickerstaffe Lancs 86 D2
Bickerton Ches E 74 D2
Bickerton N Yorks 95 D7
Bickington Devon 7 B5
Bickington Devon 20 F4
Bickleigh Devon 6 C3
Bickleigh Devon 10 D4
Bickleton Devon 20 F4
Bickley London 28 C5
Bickley Moss Ches W 74 E2
Bicknacre Essex 42 D3
Bicknoller Som 22 F3
Bicknor Kent 30 D2
Bickton Hants 14 C2
Bicton Shrops 60 C4
Bicton Shrops 60 F2
Bidborough Kent 29 E6
Biddenden Kent 19 B5
Biddenham Bedford 53 E8
Biddestone Wilts 24 B3
Biddisham Som 23 D5
Biddlesden Bucks 52 E4
Biddlestone Northumb 117 D5
Biddulph Staffs 75 D5
Biddulph Moor Staffs 75 D6
Bideford Devon 9 B6
Bidford-on-Avon Warks 51 D6
Bidston Mers 85 E3
Bielby E Yorks 96 E3
Bieldside Aberdeen 141 D7
Bierley IoW 15 G6
Bierley W Yorks 94 F4
Bierton Bucks 39 C8
Big Sand Highld 149 A12
Bigbury Devon 6 E4
Bigbury on Sea Devon 6 E4
Bigby Lincs 90 D4
Biggar Cumb 92 C1
Biggar S Lanark 120 F3
Biggin Derbys 75 D8
Biggin Derbys 76 E2
Biggin N Yorks 95 F8
Biggin Hill London 28 D5
Biggings Shetland 160 G3
Biggleswade C Beds 54 E2
Bighouse Highld 157 C11
Bighton Hants 26 F4
Bignor W Sus 16 C3
Bigton Shetland 160 L5
Bilberry Corn 4 C5
Bilborough Nottingham 76 E5
Bilbrook Som 22 E2
Bilbrough N Yorks 95 E8
Bilbster Highld 158 E4
Bildershaw Durham 101 B7
Bildeston Suff 56 E3
Billericay Essex 42 E2
Billesdon Leics 64 D4
Billesley Warks 51 D6
Billingborough Lincs 78 F4
Billinge Mers 86 D3
Billingford Norf 81 E6
Billingham Stockton 102 B2
Billinghay Lincs 78 D4
Billingley S Yorks 88 D5
Billingshurst W Sus 16 B4
Billingsley Shrops 61 F7
Billington C Beds 40 B2
Billington Lancs 93 F7
Billockby Norf 69 C7
Billy Row Durham 110 F4
Bilsborrow Lancs 92 F5
Bilsby Lincs 79 B7
Bilsham W Sus 16 D3
Bilsington Kent 19 B7
Bilson Green Glos 36 C3
Bilsthorpe Notts 77 C6
Bilsthorpe Moor Notts 77 D6
Bilston Midloth 121 C5
Bilston W Mid 62 E3
Bilstone Leics 63 D7
Bilting Kent 30 E4
Bilton E Yorks 97 F7
Bilton Northumb 117 C8
Bilton Warks 52 B2
Bilton in Ainsty N Yorks 95 E7
Bimbister Orkney 159 G4
Binbrook Lincs 91 E6
Binchester Blocks Durham 110 F5
Bincombe Dorset 12 F4
Bindal Highld 151 C12
Binegar Som 23 E8
Binfield Brack 27 B6
Binfield Heath Oxon 26 B5
Bingfield Northumb 110 B2
Bingham Notts 77 F7
Bingley W Yorks 94 F4
Bings Heath Shrops 60 C5
Binham Norf 81 D5
Binley Hants 26 D2
Binley W Mid 51 B8
Binley Woods Warks 51 B8
Binniehill Falk 119 B8
Binsoe N Yorks 94 B5
Binstead IoW 15 E6
Binsted Hants 27 E5
Binton Warks 51 D6
Bintree Norf 81 E6
Binweston Shrops 60 D3
Birch Essex 43 C5
Birch Gtr Man 87 D6
Birch Green Essex 43 C5
Birch Heath Ches W 74 C2
Birch Hill Ches W 74 B2
Birch Vale Derbys 87 F8
Bircham Newton Norf 80 D3
Bircham Tofts Norf 80 D3
Birchanger Essex 41 B8
Birchencliffe W Yorks 88 C2
Bircher Hereford 49 C6
Birchgrove Cardiff 22 B3
Birchgrove Swansea 33 E8
Birchington Kent 31 C6
Birchmoor Warks 63 D6
Birchover Derbys 76 C2
Birchwood Lincs 78 C2
Birchwood Warr 86 E4
Bircotes Notts 89 E7
Birdbrook Essex 55 E8
Birdforth N Yorks 95 B7
Birdham W Sus 16 E2
Birdholme Derbys 76 C3
Birdingbury Warks 52 C2
Birdlip Glos 37 C6
Birds Edge W Yorks 88 D3
Birdsall N Yorks 96 C4
Birdsgreen Shrops 61 F7
Birdsmoor Gate Dorset 11 D8
Birdston E Dunb 119 B6
Birdwell S Yorks 88 D4
Birdwood Glos 36 C4
Birgham Borders 122 F3
Birkby N Yorks 101 D8
Birkdale Mers 85 C4
Birkenhead Mers 85 F4
Birkenhills Aberds 153 D7
Birkenshaw N Lanark 119 C6
Birkenshaw W Yorks 88 B3
Birkhall Aberds 140 E2
Birkhill Angus 134 F3
Birkhill Borders 114 C5
Birkholme Lincs 65 B6
Birkin N Yorks 89 B6
Birley Hereford 49 D6
Birling Kent 29 C7
Birling Northumb 117 D8
Birling Gap E Sus 18 F2
Birlingham Worcs 50 E4
Birmingham W Mid 62 F4
Birnam Perth 133 E7
Birse Aberds 140 E4
Birsemore Aberds 140 E4
Birstall Leics 64 D2
Birstall W Yorks 88 B3
Birstwith N Yorks 94 D5
Birthorpe Lincs 78 F4
Birtley Hereford 49 C5
Birtley Northumb 109 B8
Birtley T&W 111 D5
Birts Street Worcs 50 F2
Bisbrooke Rutland 65 E5
Biscathorpe Lincs 91 F6
Biscot Luton 40 B3
Bish Mill Devon 10 B2
Bisham Windsor 39 F8
Bishampton Worcs 50 D4
Bishop Auckland Durham 101 B7
Bishop Burton E Yorks 97 F5
Bishop Middleham Durham 111 F6
Bishop Monkton N Yorks 95 C6
Bishop Norton Lincs 90 E3
Bishop Sutton Bath 23 D7
Bishop Thornton N Yorks 95 C5
Bishop Wilton E Yorks 96 D3
Bishopbridge Lincs 90 E4
Bishopbriggs E Dunb 119 C6
Bishopmill Moray 152 B2
Bishops Cannings Wilts 24 C5
Bishop's Castle Shrops 60 F3
Bishop's Caundle Dorset 12 C4
Bishop's Cleeve Glos 37 B6
Bishops Frome Hereford 49 E8
Bishop's Green Essex 42 C2
Bishop's Hull Som 11 B7
Bishop's Itchington Warks 51 D8
Bishops Lydeard Som 11 B6
Bishops Nympton Devon 10 B2
Bishop's Offley Staffs 61 B7
Bishop's Stortford Herts 41 B7
Bishop's Sutton Hants 26 F4
Bishop's Tachbrook Warks 51 C8
Bishops Tawton Devon 20 F4
Bishop's Waltham Hants 15 C6
Bishop's Wood Staffs 62 D2
Bishopsbourne Kent 31 D5
Bishopsteignton Devon 7 B7
Bishopstoke Hants 15 C5
Bishopston Swansea 33 F6
Bishopstone Bucks 39 C8
Bishopstone E Sus 17 D8
Bishopstone Hereford 49 E6
Bishopstone Swindon 38 F2
Bishopstone Wilts 13 B8
Bishopstrow Wilts 24 E3
Bishopswood Som 11 C7
Bishopsworth Bristol 23 C7
Bishopthorpe York 95 E8
Bishopton Darl 102 B1
Bishopton Dumfries 105 E8
Bishopton N Yorks 95 B6
Bishopton Renfs 118 B4
Bishopton Warks 51 D6
Bishton Newport 35 F7
Bisley Glos 37 D6
Bisley Sur 27 D7
Bispham Blackpool 92 E3
Bispham Green Lancs 86 C2
Bissoe Corn 3 B6
Bisterne Close Hants 14 D3
Bitchfield Lincs 65 B6
Bittadon Devon 20 E4
Bittaford Devon 6 D4
Bittering Norf 68 C2
Bitterley Shrops 49 B7
Bitterne Soton 15 C5
Bitteswell Leics 64 F2
Bitton S Glos 23 C8
Bix Oxon 39 F7
Bixter Shetland 160 H5
Blaby Leics 64 E2
Black Bourton Oxon 38 D2
Black Callerton T&W 110 C4
Black Clauchrie S Ayrs 112 F2
Black Corries Lodge Highld 131 D6
Black Crofts Argyll 124 B5
Black Dog Devon 10 D3
Black Heddon Northumb 110 B3
Black Lane Gtr Man 87 D5
Black Marsh Shrops 60 E3
Black Mount Argyll 131 E6
Black Notley Essex 42 B3
Black Pill Swansea 33 E7
Black Tar Pembs 44 E4
Black Torrington Devon 9 D6
Blackacre Dumfries 114 E3
Blackadder West Borders 122 D4
Blackawton Devon 7 D6
Blackborough Devon 11 D5
Blackborough End Norf 67 C6
Blackboys E Sus 18 C2
Blackbrook Derbys 76 E3
Blackbrook Mers 86 E3
Blackbrook Staffs 74 F4
Blackburn Aberds 141 C7
Blackburn Aberds 152 E5
Blackburn Blackburn 86 B4
Blackburn W Loth 120 C2
Blackcraig Dumfries 113 F7
Blackden Heath Ches E 74 B4
Blackdog Aberds 141 C8
Blackfell T&W 111 D5
Blackfield Hants 14 D5
Blackford Cumb 108 C3
Blackford Perth 127 D7
Blackford Som 12 B4
Blackford Som 23 E6
Blackfordby Leics 63 C7
Blackgang IoW 15 G5
Blackhall Colliery Durham 111 F7
Blackhall Mill T&W 110 D4
Blackhall Rocks Durham 111 F7
Blackham E Sus 29 F5
Blackhaugh Borders 121 F7
Blackheath Essex 43 B6
Blackheath Suff 57 B8
Blackheath Sur 27 E8
Blackheath W Mid 62 F3
Blackhill Aberds 153 C10
Blackhill Aberds 153 D10
Blackhill Highld 149 C8
Blackhills Highld 151 F12
Blackhills Moray 152 C2
Blackhorse S Glos 23 B8
Blackland Wilts 24 C5
Blacklaw Aberds 153 C6
Blackley Gtr Man 87 D6
Blacklunans Perth 134 C1
Blackmill Bridgend 34 F3
Blackmoor Hants 27 F5
Blackmoor Gate Devon 21 E5
Blackmore Essex 42 D2
Blackmore End Essex 55 F8
Blackmore End Herts 40 C4
Blackness Falk 120 B3
Blacknest Hants 27 E5
Blacko Lancs 93 E8
Blackpool Blackpool 92 F3
Blackpool Devon 7 E6
Blackpool Pembs 32 C1
Blackpool Gate Cumb 108 B5
Blackridge W Loth 119 C8
Blackrock Argyll 142 B4
Blackrock Mon 35 C6
Blackrod Gtr Man 86 C4
Blackshaw Dumfries 107 C7
Blackshaw Head W Yorks 87 B7
Blacksmith's Green Suff 56 C5
Blackstone W Sus 17 C6
Blackthorn Oxon 39 C6
Blackthorpe Suff 56 C3
Blacktoft E Yorks 90 B2
Blacktop Aberdeen 141 D7
Blacktown Newport 35 F6
Blackwall Tunnel London 41 F6
Blackwater Corn 3 B6
Blackwater Hants 27 D6
Blackwater IoW 15 F6
Blackwaterfoot N Ayrs 143 F9
Blackwell Darl 101 C7
Blackwell Derbys 75 B8
Blackwell Derbys 76 D4
Blackwell W Sus 28 F4
Blackwell Warks 51 E7
Blackwell Worcs 50 B4
Blackwood = Coed Duon Caerph 35 E5
Blackwood S Lanark 119 E7
Blackwood Hill Staffs 75 D6
Blacon Ches W 73 C7
Bladnoch Dumfries 105 D8
Bladon Oxon 38 C4
Blaen-gwynfi Neath 34 E2
Blaen-waun Carms 32 B3
Blaen-y-coed Carms 32 B4
Blaen-y-Cwm Denb 72 F4
Blaen-y-cwm Gwyn 71 E8
Blaen-y-cwm Powys 59 B7
Blaenannerch Ceredig 45 E4
Blaenau Ffestiniog Gwyn 71 C8
Blaenavon Torf 35 D6
Blaencelyn Ceredig 46 D2
Blaendyryn Powys 47 F8
Blaenffos Pembs 45 F3
Blaengarw Bridgend 34 E3
Blaengwrach Neath 34 D2
Blaenpennal Ceredig 46 C5
Blaenplwyf Ceredig 46 B4
Blaenporth Ceredig 45 E4
Blaenrhondda Rhondda 34 D3
Blaenycwm Ceredig 47 B7
Blagdon N Som 23 D7
Blagdon Torbay 7 C6
Blagdon Hill Som 11 C7
Blagill Cumb 109 E7
Blaguegate Lancs 86 D2
Blaich Highld 130 B4
Blain Highld 147 E9
Blaina Bl Gwent 35 D6
Blair Atholl Perth 133 C5
Blair Drummond Stirling 127 E6
Blairbeg N Ayrs 143 E11
Blairdaff Aberds 141 C5
Blairglas Argyll 126 F2
Blairgowrie Perth 134 E1
Blairhall Fife 128 F2
Blairingone Perth 127 E8
Blairland N Ayrs 118 E3
Blairlogie Stirling 127 E7
Blairlomond Argyll 125 F7
Blairmore Argyll 145 E10
Blairnamarrow Moray 139 C8
Blairquhosh Stirling 126 F4
Blair's Ferry Argyll 145 G8
Blairskaith E Dunb 119 B5
Blaisdon Glos 36 C4
Blakebrook Worcs 50 B3
Blakedown Worcs 50 B3
Blakelaw Borders 122 F3
Blakeley Staffs 62 E2
Blakeley Lane Staffs 75 E6
Blakemere Hereford 49 E5
Blakeney Glos 36 D3
Blakeney Norf 81 C6
Blakenhall Ches E 74 E4
Blakenhall W Mid 62 E3
Blakeshall Worcs 62 F2
Blakesley Northants 52 D4
Blanchland Northumb 110 D2
Bland Hill N Yorks 94 D5
Blandford Forum Dorset 13 D6
Blandford St Mary Dorset 13 D6
Blanefield Stirling 119 B5
Blankney Lincs 78 C3
Blantyre S Lanark 119 D6
Blar a'Chaorainn Highld 131 C5
Blaran Argyll 124 D4
Blarghour Argyll 125 D5
Blarmachfoldach Highld 130 C4
Blarnalearoch Highld 150 B4
Blashford Hants 14 D2
Blaston Leics 64 E5
Blatherwycke Northants 65 E6
Blawith Cumb 98 F4
Blaxhall Suff 57 D7
Blaxton S Yorks 89 D7
Blaydon T&W 110 C4
Bleadon N Som 22 D5
Bleak Hey Nook Gtr Man 87 D8
Blean Kent 30 C5
Bleasby Lincs 90 F5
Bleasby Notts 77 E7
Bleasdale Lancs 93 E5
Bleatarn Cumb 100 C2
Blebocraigs Fife 129 C6
Bleddfa Powys 48 C4
Bledington Glos 38 B2
Bledlow Bucks 39 D7
Bledlow Ridge Bucks 39 E7
Blegbie E Loth 121 C7
Blencarn Cumb 109 F6
Blencogo Cumb 107 E8
Blendworth Hants 15 C8
Blenheim Park Norf 80 D4
Blennerhasset Cumb 107 E8
Blervie Castle Moray 151 F13
Bletchingdon Oxon 39 C5
Bletchingley Sur 28 D4
Bletchley M Keynes 53 F6
Bletchley Shrops 74 F3
Bletherston Pembs 32 B1
Bletsoe Bedford 53 D8
Blewbury Oxon 39 F5
Blickling Norf 81 E7
Blidworth Notts 77 D5
Blindburn Northumb 116 C4
Blindcrake Cumb 107 F8
Blindley Heath Sur 28 E4
Blisland Corn 5 B6
Bliss Gate Worcs 50 B2
Blissford Hants 14 C2
Blisworth Northants 52 D5
Blithbury Staffs 62 B4
Blitterlees Cumb 107 D8
Blockley Glos 51 F6
Blofield Norf 69 D6
Blofield Heath Norf 69 C6
Blo' Norton Norf 56 B4
Bloomfield Borders 115 B8
Blore Staffs 75 E8
Blount's Green Staffs 75 F7
Blowick Mers 85 C4
Bloxham Oxon 52 F2
Bloxholm Lincs 78 D3
Bloxwich W Mid 62 D3
Bloxworth Dorset 13 E6
Blubberhouses N Yorks 94 D4
Blue Anchor Som 22 E2
Blue Anchor Swansea 33 E6
Blue Row Essex 43 C6
Blundeston Suff 69 E8
Blunham C Beds 54 D2
Blunsdon St Andrew Swindon 37 F8
Bluntington Worcs 50 B3
Bluntisham Cambs 54 B4
Blunts Corn 5 C8
Blyborough Lincs 90 E3
Blyford Suff 57 B8
Blymhill Staffs 62 C2
Blyth Northumb 117 F9
Blyth Notts 89 F7
Blyth Bridge Borders 120 E4
Blythburgh Suff 57 B8
Blythe Borders 121 E8
Blythe Bridge Staffs 75 E6
Blyton Lincs 90 E2
Boarhills Fife 129 C7
Boarhunt Hants 15 D7
Boars Head Gtr Man 86 D3
Boars Hill Oxon 38 D4
Boarshead E Sus 18 B2
Boarstall Bucks 39 C6
Boasley Cross Devon 9 E6
Boat of Garten Highld 138 C5
Boath Highld 151 D8
Bobbing Kent 30 C2
Bobbington Staffs 62 E2
Bobbingworth Essex 41 D8
Bocaddon Corn 5 D6
Bochastle Stirling 126 D5
Bocking Essex 42 B3
Bocking Churchstreet Essex 42 B3
Boddam Aberds 153 D11
Boddam Shetland 160 M5
Boddington Glos 37 B5
Bodedern Anglesey 82 C3
Bodelwyddan Denb 72 B4
Bodenham Hereford 49 D7
Bodenham Wilts 14 B2
Bodenham Moor Hereford 49 D7
Bodermid Gwyn 70 E2
Bodewryd Anglesey 82 B3
Bodfari Denb 72 B4
Bodffordd Anglesey 82 D4
Bodham Norf 81 C7
Bodiam E Sus 18 C4
Bodicote Oxon 52 F2
Bodieve Corn 4 B4
Bodinnick Corn 5 D6
Bodle Street Green E Sus 18 D3
Bodmin Corn 5 C5
Bodney Norf 67 E8
Bodorgan Anglesey 82 E3
Bodsham Kent 30 E5
Boduan Gwyn 70 D4
Bodymoor Heath Warks 63 E5
Bogallan Highld 151 F9
Bogbrae Aberds 153 E10
Bogend Borders 122 E3
Bogend S Ayrs 118 F3
Boghall W Loth 120 C2
Boghead S Lanark 119 E7
Bogmoor Moray 152 B3
Bogniebrae Aberds 152 D5
Bognor Regis W Sus 16 E3
Bograxie Aberds 141 C6
Bogside N Lanark 119 D8
Bogton Aberds 153 C6
Bogue Dumfries 113 F6
Bohenie Highld 137 F5
Bohortha Corn 3 C7
Bohuntine Highld 137 F5
Boirseam W Isles 154 J5
Bojewyan Corn 2 C2
Bolam Durham 101 B6
Bolam Northumb 117 F6
Bolberry Devon 6 F4
Bold Heath Mers 86 F3
Boldon T&W 111 C6
Boldon Colliery T&W 111 C6
Boldre Hants 14 E4
Boldron Durham 101 C5
Bole Notts 89 F8
Bolehill Derbys 76 D2
Boleside Borders 121 F7
Bolham Devon 10 C4
Bolham Water Devon 11 C6
Bolingey Corn 4 D2
Bollington Ches E 75 B6
Bollington Cross Ches E 75 B6
Bolney W Sus 17 B6
Bolnhurst Bedford 53 D8
Bolshan Angus 135 D6
Bolsover Derbys 76 B4
Bolsterstone S Yorks 88 E3
Bolstone Hereford 49 F7
Boltby N Yorks 102 F2
Bolter End Bucks 39 E7
Bolton Cumb 99 B8
Bolton E Loth 121 B8
Bolton E Yorks 96 D3
Bolton Gtr Man 86 D5
Bolton Northumb 117 C7
Bolton Abbey N Yorks 94 D3
Bolton Bridge N Yorks 94 D3
Bolton-by-Bowland Lancs 93 E7
Bolton-le-Sands Lancs 92 C4
Bolton Low Houses Cumb 108 E2
Bolton-on-Swale N Yorks 101 E7
Bolton Percy N Yorks 95 E8
Bolton Town End Lancs 92 C4
Bolton upon Dearne S Yorks 89 D5
Boltonfellend Cumb 108 C4
Boltongate Cumb 108 E2
Bolventor Corn 5 B6
Bomere Heath Shrops 60 C4
Bon-y-maen Swansea 33 E7
Bonar Bridge Highld 151 B9
Bonawe Argyll 125 B6
Bonby N Lincs 90 C4
Boncath Pembs 45 F4
Bonchester Bridge Borders 115 C8
Bonchurch IoW 15 G6
Bondleigh Devon 9 D8
Bonehill Devon 6 B5
Bonehill Staffs 63 D5
Bo'ness Falk 127 F8
Bonhill W Dunb 118 B3
Boningale Shrops 62 D2
Bonjedward Borders 116 B2
Bonkle N Lanark 119 D8
Bonnavoulin Highld 147 F8
Bonnington Edin 120 C4
Bonnington Kent 19 B7
Bonnybank Fife 129 D5
Bonnybridge Falk 127 F7
Bonnykelly Aberds 153 C8
Bonnyrigg and Lasswade Midloth 121 C6
Bonnyton Aberds 153 E6
Bonnyton Angus 134 F3
Bonnyton Angus 135 D6
Bonsall Derbys 76 D2
Bonskeid House Perth 133 C5
Bont Mon 35 C7
Bont-Dolgadfan Powys 59 D5
Bont-goch Ceredig 58 F3
Bont-newydd Conwy 72 B4
Bont Newydd Gwyn 71 C8
Bont Newydd Gwyn 71 E8
Bontddu Gwyn 58 C3
Bonthorpe Lincs 79 B7
Bontnewydd Ceredig 46 C5
Bontnewydd Gwyn 82 F4
Bontuchel Denb 72 D4
Bonvilston V Glam 22 B2
Booker Bucks 39 E8
Boon Borders 121 E8
Boosbeck Redcar 102 C4
Boot Cumb 98 D3
Boot Street Suff 57 E6
Booth W Yorks 87 B8
Booth Wood W Yorks 87 C8
Boothby Graffoe Lincs 78 D2
Boothby Pagnell Lincs 78 F2
Boothen Stoke 75 E5
Boothferry E Yorks 89 B8
Boothville Northants 53 C5
Bootle Cumb 98 F3
Bootle Mers 85 E4
Booton Norf 81 E7
Boquhan Stirling 126 F4
Boraston Shrops 49 B8
Borden Kent 30 C2
Borden W Sus 16 B2
Bordley N Yorks 94 C2
Bordon Hants 27 F6
Bordon Camp Hants 27 F5
Boreham Essex 42 D3
Boreham Wilts 24 E3
Boreham Street E Sus 18 D3
Borehamwood Herts 40 E4
Boreland Dumfries 114 E4
Boreland Stirling 132 F2
Borgh W Isles 148 H1
Borgh W Isles 154 J4
Borghastan W Isles 154 C7
Borgie Highld 157 D9
Borgue Dumfries 106 E3
Borgue Highld 158 H3
Borley Essex 56 E2
Bornais W Isles 148 F2
Bornesketaig Highld 149 A8
Borness Dumfries 106 E3
Borough Green Kent 29 D7
Boroughbridge N Yorks 95 C6
Borras Head Wrex 73 D7
Borreraig Highld 148 C6
Borrobol Lodge Highld 157 G11
Borrowash Derbys 76 F4
Borrowby N Yorks 102 F2
Borrowdale Cumb 98 C4
Borrowfield Aberds 141 E7
Borth Ceredig 58 E3
Borth-y-Gest Gwyn 71 D6
Borthwickbrae Borders 115 C7
Borthwickshiels Borders 115 C7
Borve Highld 149 D9
Borve Lodge W Isles 154 H5
Borwick Lancs 92 B5
Bosavern Corn 2 C2
Bosbury Hereford 49 E8
Boscastle Corn 8 E3
Boscombe Bmouth 14 E2
Boscombe Wilts 25 F7
Boscoppa Corn 4 D5
Bosham W Sus 16 D2
Bosherston Pembs 44 F4
Boskenna Corn 2 D3
Bosley Ches E 75 C6
Bossall N Yorks 96 C3
Bossiney Corn 8 F2
Bossingham Kent 31 E5
Bossington Som 21 E7
Bostock Green Ches W 74 C3
Boston Lincs 79 E6
Boston Long Hedges Lincs 79 E6
Boston Spa W Yorks 95 E7
Boston West Lincs 79 E5
Boswinger Corn 3 B8
Botallack Corn 2 C2
Botany Bay London 41 E5
Botcherby Cumb 108 D4
Botcheston Leics 63 D8
Botesdale Suff 56 B4
Bothal Northumb 117 F8
Bothamsall Notts 77 B6
Bothel Cumb 107 F8
Bothenhampton Dorset 12 E2
Bothwell S Lanark 119 D7
Botley Bucks 40 D2
Botley Hants 15 C6
Botley Oxon 38 D4
Botolph Claydon Bucks 39 B7
Botolphs W Sus 17 D5
Bottacks Highld 150 E7
Bottesford Leics 77 F8
Bottesford N Lincs 90 D2
Bottisham Cambs 55 C6
Bottlesford Wilts 25 D6
Bottom Boat W Yorks 88 B4
Bottom House Staffs 75 D7
Bottom o'th'Moor Gtr Man 86 C4
Bottom of Hutton Lancs 86 B2
Bottomcraig Fife 129 B5
Botusfleming Corn 6 C2
Botwnnog Gwyn 70 D3
Bough Beech Kent 29 E5
Boughrood Powys 48 F3
Boughspring Glos 36 E2
Boughton Norf 67 D6
Boughton Northants 53 C5
Boughton Notts 77 C6
Boughton Aluph Kent 30 E4
Boughton Lees Kent 30 E4
Boughton Malherbe Kent 30 E2
Boughton Monchelsea Kent 29 D8
Boughton Street Kent 30 D4
Boulby Redcar 103 C5
Boulden Shrops 60 F5
Boulmer Northumb 117 C8
Boulston Pembs 44 D4
Boultenstone Aberds 140 C3
Boultham Lincs 78 C2
Bourn Cambs 54 D4
Bourne Lincs 65 B7
Bourne End Bucks 40 F1
Bourne End C Beds 53 E7
Bourne End Herts 40 D3
Bournemouth Bmouth 13 E8
Bournes Green Glos 37 D6
Bournes Green Southend 43 F5
Bournheath Worcs 50 B4
Bournmoor Durham 111 D6
Bournville W Mid 62 F4
Bourton Dorset 24 F2
Bourton N Som 23 C5
Bourton Oxon 38 F2
Bourton Shrops 61 E5
Bourton on Dunsmore Warks 52 B2
Bourton on the Hill Glos 51 F6
Bourton-on-the-Water Glos 38 B1
Bousd Argyll 146 E5
Boustead Hill Cumb 108 D2
Bouth Cumb 99 F5
Bouthwaite N Yorks 94 B4
Boveney Bucks 27 B7
Boverton V Glam 21 C8
Bovey Tracey Devon 7 B6
Bovingdon Herts 40 D3
Bovingdon Green Bucks 39 F8
Bovingdon Green Herts 40 D3
Bovinger Essex 41 D8
Bovington Camp Dorset 13 F6
Bow Borders 121 E7
Bow Devon 10 D2
Bow Orkney 159 J4
Bow Brickhill M Keynes 53 F7
Bow of Fife Fife 128 C5
Bow Street Ceredig 58 F3
Bowbank Durham 100 B4
Bowburn Durham 111 F6
Bowcombe IoW 15 F5
Bowd Devon 11 E6
Bowden Borders 121 F8
Bowden Devon 7 E6
Bowden Hill Wilts 24 C4
Bowderdale Cumb 100 D1
Bowdon Gtr Man 87 F5
Bower Northumb 116 F3
Bower Hinton Som 12 C2
Bowerchalke Wilts 13 B8
Bowerhill Wilts 24 C4
Bowermadden Highld 158 D4
Bowers Gifford Essex 42 F3
Bowershall Fife 128 E2
Bowertower Highld 158 D4
Bowes Durham 100 C4
Bowgreave Lancs 92 E4
Bowgreen Gtr Man 87 F5
Bowhill Borders 115 B7
Bowhouse Dumfries 107 C7
Bowland Bridge Cumb 99 F6
Bowley Hereford 49 D7
Bowlhead Green Sur 27 F7
Bowling W Dunb 118 B4
Bowling W Yorks 94 F4
Bowling Bank Wrex 73 E7
Bowling Green Worcs 50 D3
Bowmanstead Cumb 99 E5
Bowmore Argyll 142 C4
Bowness-on-Solway Cumb 108 C2
Bowness-on-Windermere Cumb 99 E6
Bowsden Northumb 123 E5
Bowside Lodge Highld 157 C11
Bowston Cumb 99 E6
Bowthorpe Norf 68 D4
Box Glos 37 D5
Box Wilts 24 C3
Box End Bedford 53 E8
Boxbush Glos 36 C4
Boxford Suff 56 E3
Boxford W Berks 26 B2
Boxgrove W Sus 16 D3
Boxley Kent 29 D8
Boxmoor Herts 40 D3
Boxted Essex 56 F4
Boxted Suff 56 D2
Boxted Cross Essex 56 F4
Boxted Heath Essex 56 F4
Boxworth Cambs 54 C4
Boxworth End Cambs 54 C4
Boyden Gate Kent 31 C6
Boylestone Derbys 75 F8
Boyndie Aberds 153 B6
Boynton E Yorks 97 C7
Boysack Angus 135 E6
Boyton Corn 8 E5
Boyton Suff 57 E7
Boyton Wilts 24 F4
Boyton Cross Essex 42 D2
Boyton End Suff 55 E8
Bozeat Northants 53 D7

Braaid IoM 84 E3
Braal Castle Highld 158 D3
Brabling Green Suff 57 C6
Brabourne Kent 30 E4
Brabourne Lees Kent 30 E4
Brabster Highld 158 D5
Bracadale Highld 149 E8
Bracara Highld 147 B10
Braceborough Lincs 65 C7
Bracebridge Lincs 78 C2
Bracebridge Heath Lincs 78 C2
Bracebridge Low Fields Lincs 78 C2
Braceby Lincs 78 F3
Bracewell Lancs 93 E8
Brackenfield Derbys 76 D3
Brackenthwaite Cumb 108 E2
Brackenthwaite N Yorks 95 D5
Bracklesham W Sus 16 E2
Brackletter Highld 136 F4
Brackley Argyll 143 D8
Brackley Northants 52 F3
Brackloch Highld 156 G4
Bracknell Brack 27 C6
Braco Perth 127 D7
Bracobrae Moray 152 C5
Bracon Ash Norf 68 E4
Bracorina Highld 147 B10
Bradbourne Derbys 76 D2
Bradbury Durham 101 B8
Bradda IoM 84 F1
Bradden Northants 52 E4
Braddock Corn 5 C6
Bradeley Stoke 75 D5
Bradenham Bucks 39 E8
Bradenham Norf 68 D2
Bradenstoke Wilts 24 B5
Bradfield Essex 56 F5
Bradfield Norf 81 D8
Bradfield W Berks 26 B4
Bradfield Combust Suff 56 D2
Bradfield Green Ches E 74 D3
Bradfield Heath Essex 43 B7
Bradfield St Clare Suff 56 D3
Bradfield St George Suff 56 C3
Bradford Corn 5 B6
Bradford Derbys 76 C2
Bradford Devon 9 D6
Bradford Northumb 123 F7
Bradford W Yorks 94 F4
Bradford Abbas Dorset 12 C3
Bradford Leigh Wilts 24 C3
Bradford-on-Avon Wilts 24 C3
Bradford-on-Tone Som 11 B6
Bradford Peverell Dorset 12 E4
Brading IoW 15 F7
Bradley Derbys 76 E2
Bradley Hants 26 E4
Bradley NE Lincs 91 D6
Bradley Staffs 62 C2
Bradley W Mid 62 E3
Bradley W Yorks 88 B2
Bradley Green Worcs 50 C4
Bradley in the Moors Staffs 75 E7
Bradley Stoke S Glos 36 F3
Bradlow Hereford 50 F2
Bradmore Notts 77 F5
Bradmore W Mid 62 E2
Bradninch Devon 10 D5
Bradnop Staffs 75 D7
Bradpole Dorset 12 E2
Bradshaw Gtr Man 86 C5
Bradshaw W Yorks 87 C8
Bradstone Devon 9 F5
Bradwall Green Ches E 74 C4
Bradway S Yorks 88 F4
Bradwell Derbys 88 F2
Bradwell Essex 42 B4
Bradwell M Keynes 53 F6
Bradwell Norf 69 D8
Bradwell Staffs 74 E5
Bradwell Grove Oxon 38 D2
Bradwell on Sea Essex 43 D6
Bradwell Waterside Essex 43 D5
Bradworthy Devon 8 C5
Bradworthy Cross Devon 8 C5
Brae Dumfries 107 B5
Brae Highld 155 J13
Brae Highld 156 J7
Brae Shetland 160 G5
Brae of Achnahaird Highld 156 H3
Brae Roy Lodge Highld 137 E6
Braeantra Highld 151 D8
Braedownie Angus 134 B2
Braefield Highld 150 H7
Braegrum Perth 128 B2
Braehead Dumfries 105 D8
Braehead Orkney 159 D5
Braehead Orkney 159 H6
Braehead S Lanark 119 F8
Braehead S Lanark 120 D2
Braehead of Lunan Angus 135 D6
Braehoulland Shetland 160 F4
Braehungie Highld 158 G3
Braelangwell Lodge Highld 151 B8
Braemar Aberds 139 E7
Braemore Highld 150 D4
Braemore Highld 158 G2
Braes of Enzie Moray 152 C3
Braeside Invclyd 118 B2
Braeswick Orkney 159 E7
Braewick Shetland 160 H5
Brafferton Darl 101 B7
Brafferton N Yorks 95 B7
Brafield-on-the-Green Northants 53 D6
Bragar W Isles 155 C7
Bragbury End Herts 41 B5
Bragleenmore Argyll 124 C5
Braichmelyn Gwyn 83 E6
Braid Edin 120 C5
Braides Lancs 92 D4
Braidley N Yorks 101 F5
Braidwood S Lanark 119 E8
Braigo Argyll 142 B3
Brailsford Derbys 76 E2
Brainshaugh Northumb 117 D8
Braintree Essex 42 B3
Braiseworth Suff 56 B5
Braishfield Hants 14 B4
Braithwaite Cumb 98 B4
Braithwaite S Yorks 89 C7
Braithwaite W Yorks 94 E3
Braithwell S Yorks 89 E6
Bramber W Sus 17 C5
Bramcote Notts 76 F5
Bramcote Warks 63 F8
Bramdean Hants 15 B7
Bramerton Norf 69 D5
Bramfield Herts 41 C5
Bramfield Suff 57 B7
Bramford Suff 56 E5
Bramhall Gtr Man 87 F6
Bramham W Yorks 95 E7
Bramhope W Yorks 95 E5
Bramley Hants 26 D4
Bramley S Yorks 89 E5
Bramley Sur 27 E8
Bramley W Yorks 94 F5
Bramling Kent 31 D6
Brampford Speke Devon 10 E4
Brampton Cambs 54 B3
Brampton Cumb 100 B1
Brampton Cumb 108 C5
Brampton Derbys 76 B3
Brampton Hereford 49 F6
Brampton Lincs 77 B8
Brampton Norf 81 E8
Brampton S Yorks 88 D5
Brampton Suff 69 F7
Brampton Abbotts Hereford 36 B3
Brampton Ash Northants 64 F4
Brampton Bryan Hereford 49 B5
Brampton en le Morthen S Yorks 89 F5
Bramshall Staffs 75 F7
Bramshaw Hants 14 C3
Bramshill Hants 26 C5
Bramshott Hants 27 F6
Bran End Essex 42 B2
Branault Highld 147 E8
Brancaster Norf 80 C3
Brancaster Staithe Norf 80 C3
Brancepeth Durham 110 F5
Branch End Northumb 110 C3
Branchill Moray 151 F13
Brand Green Glos 36 B4
Branderburgh Moray 152 A2
Brandesburton E Yorks 97 E7
Brandeston Suff 57 C6
Brandhill Shrops 49 B6
Brandis Corner Devon 9 D6
Brandiston Norf 81 E7
Brandon Durham 110 F5
Brandon Lincs 78 E2
Brandon Northumb 117 C6
Brandon Suff 67 F7
Brandon Warks 52 B2
Brandon Bank Cambs 67 F6
Brandon Creek Norf 67 E6
Brandon Parva Norf 68 D3
Brandsby N Yorks 95 B8
Brandy Wharf Lincs 90 E4
Brane Corn 2 D3
Branksome Poole 13 E8
Branksome Park Poole 13 E8
Bransby Lincs 77 B8
Branscombe Devon 11 F6
Bransford Worcs 50 D2
Bransgore Hants 14 E2
Branshill Clack 127 E7
Bransholme Hull 97 F7
Branson's Cross Worcs 51 B5
Branston Leics 64 B5
Branston Lincs 78 C3
Branston Staffs 63 B6
Branston Booths Lincs 78 C3
Branstone IoW 15 F6
Bransty Cumb 98 C1
Brant Broughton Lincs 78 D2
Brantham Suff 56 F5
Branthwaite Cumb 98 B2
Branthwaite Cumb 108 F2
Brantingham E Yorks 90 B3
Branton Northumb 117 C6
Branton S Yorks 89 D7
Branxholm Park Borders 115 C7
Branxholme Borders 115 C7
Branxton Northumb 122 F4
Brassey Green Ches W 74 C2
Brassington Derbys 76 D2
Brasted Kent 29 D5
Brasted Chart Kent 29 D5
Brathens Aberds 141 E5
Bratoft Lincs 79 C7
Brattleby Lincs 90 F3
Bratton Telford 61 C6
Bratton Wilts 24 D4
Bratton Clovelly Devon 9 E6
Bratton Fleming Devon 20 F5
Bratton Seymour Som 12 B4
Braughing Herts 41 B6
Braunston Northants 52 C3
Braunston-in-Rutland Rutland 64 D5
Braunstone Town Leicester 64 D2
Braunton Devon 20 F3
Brawby N Yorks 96 B3
Brawl Highld 157 C11
Brawlbin Highld 158 E2
Bray Windsor 27 B7
Bray Shop Corn 5 B8
Bray Wick Windsor 27 B6
Braybrooke Northants 64 F4
Braye Ald 16
Brayford Devon 21 F5
Braystones Cumb 98 D2
Braythorn N Yorks 94 E5
Brayton N Yorks 95 F9
Brazacott Corn 8 E4
Breach Kent 30 C2
Breachacha Castle Argyll 146 F4
Breachwood Green Herts 40 B4
Breacleit W Isles 154 D6
Breaden Heath Shrops 73 F8
Breadsall Derbys 76 F3
Breadstone Glos 36 D4
Breage Corn 2 D5
Breakachy Highld 150 G7
Bream Glos 36 D3
Breamore Hants 14 C2
Brean Som 22 D4
Breanais W Isles 154 E4
Brearton N Yorks 95 C6
Breascleit W Isles 154 D7
Breaston Derbys 76 F4
Brechfa Carms 46 F4
Brechin Angus 135 C5
Breck of Cruan Orkney 159 G4
Breckan Orkney 159 H3
Breckrey Highld 149 B10
Brecon = Aberhonddu Powys 34 B4
Bredbury Gtr Man 87 E7
Brede E Sus 18 D5
Bredenbury Hereford 49 D8
Bredfield Suff 57 D6
Bredgar Kent 30 C2
Bredhurst Kent 29 C8
Bredicot Worcs 50 D4
Bredon Worcs 50 F4
Bredon's Norton Worcs 50 F4
Bredwardine Hereford 48 E5
Breedon on the Hill Leics 63 B8
Breibhig W Isles 148 J1
Breibhig W Isles 155 D9
Breich W Loth 120 C2
Breightmet Gtr Man 86 D5
Breighton E Yorks 96 F3
Breinton Hereford 49 F6
Breinton Common Hereford 49 E6
Breiwick Shetland 160 J6
Bremhill Wilts 24 B4
Bremirehoull Shetland 160 L6
Brenchley Kent 29 E7
Brendon Devon 21 E6
Brenkley T&W 110 B5
Brent Eleigh Suff 56 E3
Brent Knoll Som 22 D5
Brent Pelham Herts 54 F5
Brentford London 28 B2
Brentingby Leics 64 C4
Brentwood Essex 42 E1
Brenzett Kent 19 C7
Brereton Staffs 62 C4
Brereton Green Ches E 74 C4
Brereton Heath Ches E 74 C5
Bressingham Norf 68 F3
Bretby Derbys 63 B6
Bretford Warks 52 B2
Bretforton Worcs 51 E5
Bretherdale Head Cumb 99 D7
Bretherton Lancs 86 B2
Brettabister Shetland 160 H6
Brettenham Norf 68 F2
Brettenham Suff 56 D3
Bretton Derbys 76 B2
Bretton Flint 73 C7
Brewer Street Sur 28 D4
Brewlands Bridge Angus 134 C1
Brewood Staffs 62 D2
Briach Moray 151 F13
Briants Puddle Dorset 13 E6
Brick End Essex 42 B1
Brickendon Herts 41 D6
Bricket Wood Herts 40 D4
Bricklehampton Worcs 50 E4
Bride IoM 84 B4
Bridekirk Cumb 107 F8
Bridell Pembs 45 E3
Bridestowe Devon 9 F7
Brideswell Aberds 152 E5
Bridford Devon 10 F3
Bridfordmills Devon 10 F3
Bridge Kent 31 D5
Bridge End Lincs 78 F4
Bridge Green Essex 55 F5
Bridge Hewick N Yorks 95 B6
Bridge of Alford Aberds 140 C4
Bridge of Allan Stirling 127 E6
Bridge of Avon Moray 152 E1
Bridge of Awe Argyll 125 C6
Bridge of Balgie Perth 132 E2
Bridge of Cally Perth 133 D8
Bridge of Canny Aberds 141 E5
Bridge of Craigisla Angus 134 D2
Bridge of Dee Dumfries 106 D4
Bridge of Don Aberdeen 141 C8
Bridge of Dun Angus 135 D6
Bridge of Dye Aberds 141 F5
Bridge of Earn Perth 128 C3
Bridge of Ericht Perth 132 D2
Bridge of Feugh Aberds 141 E6
Bridge of Forss Highld 157 C13
Bridge of Gairn Aberds 140 E2
Bridge of Gaur Perth 132 D2
Bridge of Muchalls Aberds 141 E7
Bridge of Oich Highld 137 D6
Bridge of Orchy Argyll 125 B8
Bridge of Waith Orkney 159 G3
Bridge of Walls Shetland 160 H4
Bridge of Weir Renfs 118 C3
Bridge Sollers Hereford 49 E6
Bridge Street Suff 56 E2
Bridge Trafford Ches W 73 B8
Bridge Yate S Glos 23 B8
Bridgefoot Angus 134 F3
Bridgefoot Cumb 98 B2
Bridgehampton Som 12 B3
Bridgehill Durham 110 D3
Bridgemary Hants 15 D6
Bridgemont Derbys 87 F8
Bridgend Aberds 140 C4
Bridgend Aberds 152 E5
Bridgend Angus 135 C5
Bridgend Argyll 142 B4
Bridgend Argyll 143 E8
Bridgend Argyll 145 D7
Bridgend = Pen-Y-Bont Ar Ogwr Bridgend 21 B8
Bridgend Cumb 99 C5
Bridgend Fife 129 C5
Bridgend Moray 152 E3
Bridgend N Lanark 119 B6
Bridgend Pembs 45 E3
Bridgend W Loth 120 B3
Bridgend of Lintrathen Angus 134 D2
Bridgerule Devon 8 D4
Bridges Shrops 60 E3
Bridgeton Glasgow 119 C6
Bridgetown Corn 8 F5
Bridgetown Som 21 F8
Bridgham Norf 68 F2
Bridgnorth Shrops 61 E7
Bridgtown Staffs 62 D3
Bridgwater Som 22 F5
Bridlington E Yorks 97 C7
Bridport Dorset 12 E2
Bridstow Hereford 36 B2
Brierfield Lancs 93 F8
Brierley Glos 36 C3
Brierley Hereford 49 D6
Brierley S Yorks 88 C5
Brierley Hill W Mid 62 F3
Briery Hill Bl Gwent 35 D5
Brig o'Turk Stirling 126 D4
Brigg N Lincs 90 D4
Briggswath N Yorks 103 D6
Brigham Cumb 107 F7
Brigham E Yorks 97 D6
Brighouse W Yorks 88 B2
Brighstone IoW 14 F5
Brightgate Derbys 76 D2
Brighthampton Oxon 38 D3
Brightling E Sus 18 C3
Brightlingsea Essex 43 C6
Brighton Brighton 17 D7
Brighton Corn 4 D4
Brighton Hill Hants 26 E4
Brightons Falk 120 B2
Brightwalton W Berks 26 B2
Brightwell Suff 57 E6
Brightwell Baldwin Oxon 39 E6
Brightwell cum Sotwell Oxon 39 E5
Brignall Durham 101 C5
Brigsley NE Lincs 91 D6
Brigsteer Cumb 99 F6
Brigstock Northants 65 F6
Brill Bucks 39 C6
Brilley Hereford 48 E4
Brimaston Pembs 44 C4
Brimfield Hereford 49 C7
Brimington Derbys 76 B4
Brimley Devon 7 B5
Brimpsfield Glos 37 C6
Brimpton W Berks 26 C3
Brims Orkney 159 K3
Brimscombe Glos 37 D5
Brimstage Mers 85 F4
Brinacory Highld 147 B10
Brind E Yorks 96 F3
Brindister Shetland 160 H4
Brindister Shetland 160 K6
Brindle Lancs 86 B4
Brindley Ford Stoke 75 D5
Brineton Staffs 62 C2
Bringhurst Leics 64 E5
Brington Cambs 53 B8
Brinian Orkney 159 F5
Briningham Norf 81 D6
Brinkhill Lincs 79 B6
Brinkley Cambs 55 D7
Brinklow Warks 52 B2
Brinkworth Wilts 37 F7
Brinmore Highld 138 B2
Brinscall Lancs 86 B4
Brinsea N Som 23 C6
Brinsley Notts 76 E4
Brinsop Hereford 49 E6
Brinsworth S Yorks 88 F5
Brinton Norf 81 D6
Brisco Cumb 108 D4
Brisley Norf 81 E5
Brislington Bristol 23 B8
Bristol Bristol 23 B7
Briston Norf 81 D6
Britannia Lancs 87 B6
Britford Wilts 14 B2
Brithdir Gwyn 58 C4
British Legion Village Kent 29 D8
Briton Ferry Neath 33 E8
Britwell Salome Oxon 39 E6
Brixham Torbay 7 D7
Brixton Devon 6 D3
Brixton London 28 B4
Brixton Deverill Wilts 24 F3
Brixworth Northants 52 B5
Brize Norton Oxon 38 D3
Broad Blunsdon Swindon 38 E1
Broad Campden Glos 51 F6
Broad Chalke Wilts 13 B8
Broad Green C Beds 53 E7
Broad Green Essex 42 B4
Broad Green Worcs 50 D2
Broad Haven Pembs 44 D3
Broad Heath Worcs 49 C8
Broad Hill Cambs 55 B6
Broad Hinton Wilts 25 B6
Broad Laying Hants 26 C2
Broad Marston Worcs 51 E6
Broad Oak Carms 33 B6
Broad Oak Cumb 98 E3
Broad Oak Dorset 12 E2
Broad Oak Dorset 13 C5
Broad Oak E Sus 18 C3
Broad Oak E Sus 18 D5
Broad Oak Hereford 36 B1
Broad Oak Mers 86 E3
Broad Street Kent 30 D2
Broad Street Green Essex 42 D4
Broad Town Wilts 25 B5
Broadbottom Gtr Man 87 E7
Broadbridge W Sus 16 D2
Broadbridge Heath W Sus 28 F2
Broadclyst Devon 10 E4
Broadfield Gtr Man 87 C6
Broadfield Lancs 86 B3
Broadfield Pembs 32 D2
Broadfield W Sus 28 F3
Broadford Highld 149 F11
Broadford Bridge W Sus 16 B4
Broadhaugh Borders 115 D7
Broadhaven Highld 158 E5
Broadheath Gtr Man 87 F5
Broadhembury Devon 11 D6
Broadhempston Devon 7 C6
Broadholme Derbys 76 E3
Broadholme Lincs 77 B8
Broadland Row E Sus 18 D5
Broadlay Carms 32 D4
Broadley Lancs 87 C6
Broadley Moray 152 B3
Broadley Common Essex 41 D7
Broadmayne Dorset 12 F5
Broadmeadows Borders 121 F7
Broadmere Hants 26 E4
Broadmoor Pembs 32 D1
Broadoak Kent 31 C5
Broadrashes Moray 152 C4
Broadsea Aberds 153 B9
Broadstairs Kent 31 C7
Broadstone Poole 13 E8
Broadstone Shrops 60 F5
Broadtown Lane Wilts 25 B5
Broadwas Worcs 50 D2
Broadwater Herts 41 B5
Broadwater W Sus 17 D5
Broadway Carms 32 D3
Broadway Pembs 44 D3
Broadway Som 11 C8
Broadway Suff 57 B7
Broadway Worcs 51 F5
Broadwell Glos 36 C2
Broadwell Glos 38 B2
Broadwell Oxon 38 D2
Broadwell Warks 52 C2
Broadwell House Northumb 110 D2
Broadwey Dorset 12 F4
Broadwindsor Dorset 12 D2
Broadwood Kelly Devon 9 D8
Broadwoodwidger Devon 9 F6
Brobury Hereford 48 E5
Brochel Highld 149 D10
Brochloch Dumfries 113 E5
Brochroy Argyll 125 B6
Brockamin Worcs 50 D2
Brockbridge Hants 15 C7
Brockdam Northumb 117 B7
Brockdish Norf 57 B6
Brockenhurst Hants 14 D4
Brocketsbrae S Lanark 119 F8
Brockford Street Suff 56 C5
Brockhall Northants 52 C4
Brockham Sur 28 E2
Brockhampton Glos 37 B7
Brockhampton Hereford 49 F7
Brockholes W Yorks 88 C2
Brockhurst Derbys 76 C3
Brockhurst Hants 15 D7
Brocklebank Cumb 108 E3
Brocklesby Lincs 90 C5
Brockley N Som 23 C6
Brockley Green Suff 56 D2
Brockleymoor Cumb 108 F4
Brockton Shrops 60 D3
Brockton Shrops 60 F3
Brockton Shrops 61 D7
Brockton Shrops 61 E5
Brockton Telford 61 C7
Brockweir Glos 36 D2
Brockwood Hants 15 B7
Brockworth Glos 37 C5
Brocton Staffs 62 C3
Brodick N Ayrs 143 E11
Brodsworth S Yorks 89 D6
Brogaig Highld 149 B9
Brogborough C Beds 53 F7
Broken Cross Ches E 75 B5
Broken Cross Ches W 74 B3
Brokenborough Wilts 37 F6
Bromborough Mers 85 F4
Brome Suff 56 B5
Brome Street Suff 57 B5
Bromeswell Suff 57 D7
Bromfield Cumb 107 E8
Bromfield Shrops 49 B6
Bromham Bedford 53 D8
Bromham Wilts 24 C4
Bromley London 28 C5
Bromley W Mid 62 F3
Bromley Common London 28 C5
Bromley Green Kent 19 B6
Brompton Medway 29 C8
Brompton N Yorks 102 E1
Brompton N Yorks 103 F7
Brompton-on-Swale N Yorks 101 E7
Brompton Ralph Som 22 F2
Brompton Regis Som 21 F8
Bromsash Hereford 36 B3
Bromsberrow Heath Glos 50 F2
Bromsgrove Worcs 50 B4
Bromyard Hereford 49 D8
Bromyard Downs Hereford 49 D8
Bronaber Gwyn 71 D8
Brongest Ceredig 46 E2
Bronington Wrex 73 F8
Bronllys Powys 48 F3
Bronnant Ceredig 46 C5
Bronwydd Arms Carms 33 B5
Bronydd Powys 48 E4
Bronygarth Shrops 73 F6
Brook Carms 32 D3
Brook Hants 14 B4
Brook Hants 14 C3
Brook IoW 14 F4
Brook Kent 30 E4
Brook Sur 27 E8
Brook Sur 27 F7
Brook End Bedford 53 C8
Brook Hill Hants 14 C3
Brook Street Kent 19 B6
Brook Street Kent 29 E6
Brook Street W Sus 17 B7
Brooke Norf 69 E5
Brooke Rutland 64 D5
Brookenby Lincs 91 E6
Brookend Glos 36 E2
Brookfield Renfs 118 C4
Brookhouse Lancs 92 C5
Brookhouse Green Ches E 74 C5
Brookland Kent 19 C6
Brooklands Dumfries 106 B5
Brooklands Gtr Man 87 E5
Brooklands Shrops 74 E2
Brookmans Park Herts 41 D5
Brooks Powys 59 E8
Brooks Green W Sus 16 B5
Brookthorpe Glos 37 C5
Brookville Norf 67 E7
Brookwood Sur 27 D7
Broom C Beds 54 E2
Broom S Yorks 88 E5
Broom Warks 51 D5
Broom Worcs 50 B4
Broom Green Norf 81 E5
Broom Hill Dorset 13 D8
Broome Norf 69 E6
Broome Shrops 60 F4
Broome Park Northumb 117 C7
Broomedge Warr 86 F5
Broomer's Corner W Sus 16 B5
Broomfield Aberds 153 E9
Broomfield Essex 42 C3
Broomfield Kent 30 D2
Broomfield Kent 31 C5
Broomfield Som 22 F4
Broomfleet E Yorks 90 B2
Broomhall Ches E 74 E3
Broomhall Windsor 27 C7
Broomhaugh Northumb 110 C3
Broomhill Norf 67 D6
Broomhill Northumb 117 D8
Broomhill S Yorks 88 D5
Broomholm Norf 81 D9
Broomley Northumb 110 C3
Broompark Durham 110 E5
Broom's Green Glos 50 F2
Broomy Lodge Hants 14 C3
Brora Highld 157 J12
Broseley Shrops 61 D6
Brotherhouse Bar Lincs 66 C2
Brotherstone Borders 122 F2
Brothertoft Lincs 79 E5
Brotherton N Yorks 89 B5
Brotton Redcar 102 C4
Broubster Highld 157 C13
Brough Cumb 100 C2
Brough Derbys 88 F2
Brough E Yorks 90 B3
Brough Highld 158 C4
Brough Notts 77 D8
Brough Orkney 159 G4
Brough Shetland 160 F6
Brough Shetland 160 F7
Brough Shetland 160 G7
Brough Shetland 160 H6
Brough Shetland 160 J7
Brough Lodge Shetland 160 D7
Brough Sowerby Cumb 100 C2
Broughall Shrops 74 E2
Broughton Borders 120 F4
Broughton Cambs 54 B3
Broughton Flint 73 C7
Broughton Hants 25 F8
Broughton Lancs 92 F5
Broughton M Keynes 53 E6
Broughton N Lincs 90 D3
Broughton N Yorks 94 D2
Broughton N Yorks 96 B3
Broughton Northants 53 B6
Broughton Orkney 159 D5
Broughton Oxon 52 F2
Broughton V Glam 21 B8
Broughton Astley Leics 64 E2
Broughton Beck Cumb 98 F4
Broughton Common Wilts 24 C3
Broughton Gifford Wilts 24 C3
Broughton Hackett Worcs 50 D4
Broughton in Furness Cumb 98 F4
Broughton Mills Cumb 98 E4
Broughton Moor Cumb 107 F7
Broughton Park Gtr Man 87 D6
Broughton Poggs Oxon 38 D2
Broughtown Orkney 159 D7
Broughty Ferry Dundee 134 F4
Browhouses Dumfries 108 C2
Browland Shetland 160 H4
Brown Candover Hants 26 F3
Brown Edge Lancs 85 C4
Brown Edge Staffs 75 D6
Brown Heath Ches W 73 C8
Brownhill Aberds 153 D6
Brownhill Aberds 153 D8
Brownhill Blackburn 93 F6
Brownhill Shrops 60 B4
Brownhills Fife 129 C7
Brownhills W Mid 62 D4
Brownlow Ches E 74 C5
Brownlow Heath Ches E 74 C5
Brownmuir Aberds 135 B7
Brown's End Glos 50 F2
Brownshill Glos 37 D5
Brownston Devon 6 D4
Brownyside Northumb 117 B7
Broxa N Yorks 103 E7
Broxbourne Herts 41 D6
Broxburn E Loth 122 B2
Broxburn W Loth 120 B3
Broxholme Lincs 78 B2
Broxted Essex 42 B1
Broxton Ches W 73 D8
Broxwood Hereford 49 D5
Broyle Side E Sus 17 C8
Brù W Isles 155 C8
Bruairnis W Isles 148 H2
Bruan Highld 158 G5
Bruar Lodge Perth 133 B5
Brucehill W Dunb 118 B3
Bruera Ches W 73 C8
Bruern Abbey Oxon 38 B2
Bruichladdich Argyll 142 B3
Bruisyard Suff 57 C7
Brumby N Lincs 90 D2
Brund Staffs 75 C8
Brundall Norf 69 D6
Brundish Suff 57 C6
Brundish Street Suff 57 B6
Brunery Highld 147 D10
Brunshaw Lancs 93 F8
Brunswick Village T&W 110 B5
Bruntcliffe W Yorks 88 B3
Bruntingthorpe Leics 64 E3
Brunton Fife 128 B5
Brunton Northumb 117 B8
Brunton Wilts 25 D7
Brushford Devon 9 D8
Brushford Som 10 B4
Bruton Som 23 F8
Bryanston Dorset 13 D6
Brydekirk Dumfries 107 B8
Bryher Scilly 2 E3
Brymbo Wrex 73 D6
Brympton Som 12 C3
Bryn Carms 33 D6
Bryn Gtr Man 86 D3
Bryn Neath 34 E2
Bryn Shrops 60 F2
Bryn-coch Neath 33 E8
Bryn Du Anglesey 82 D3
Bryn Gates Gtr Man 86 D3
Bryn-glas Conwy 83 E8
Bryn Golau Rhondda 34 F3
Bryn-Iwan Carms 46 F2
Bryn-mawr Gwyn 70 D3
Bryn-nantllech Conwy 72 C3
Bryn-penarth Powys 59 D8
Bryn Rhyd-yr-Arian Conwy 72 C3
Bryn Saith Marchog Denb 72 D4
Bryn Sion Gwyn 59 C5
Bryn-y-gwenin Mon 35 C7
Bryn-y-maen Conwy 83 D8
Bryn-yr-eryr Gwyn 70 C4
Brynamman Carms 33 C8
Brynberian Pembs 45 F3
Brynbryddan Neath 34 E1
Brynbuga = Usk Mon 35 D7
Bryncae Rhondda 34 F3
Bryncethin Bridgend 34 F3
Bryncir Gwyn 71 C5
Bryncroes Gwyn 70 D3
Bryncrug Gwyn 58 D3
Bryneglwys Denb 72 E5
Brynford Flint 73 B5
Bryngwran Anglesey 82 D3
Bryngwyn Ceredig 45 E4
Bryngwyn Mon 35 D7
Bryngwyn Powys 48 E3
Brynhenllan Pembs 45 F2
Brynhoffnant Ceredig 46 D2
Brynithel Bl Gwent 35 D6
Brynmawr Bl Gwent 35 C5
Brynmenyn Bridgend 34 F3
Brynmill Swansea 33 E7
Brynna Rhondda 34 F3
Brynrefail Anglesey 82 C4
Brynrefail Gwyn 83 E5
Brynsadler Rhondda 34 F4
Brynsiencyn Anglesey 82 E4
Brynteg Anglesey 82 C4
Brynteg Ceredig 46 E3
Buaile nam Bodach W Isles 148 H2
Bualintur Highld 149 F9
Buarthmeini Gwyn 72 F2
Bubbenhall Warks 51 B8
Bubwith E Yorks 96 F3
Buccleuch Borders 115 C6
Buchanhaven Aberds 153 D11
Buchanty Perth 127 B8
Buchlyvie Stirling 126 E4
Buckabank Cumb 108 E3
Buckden Cambs 54 C2
Buckden N Yorks 94 B2
Buckenham Norf 69 D6
Buckerell Devon 11 D6
Buckfast Devon 6 C5
Buckfastleigh Devon 6 C5
Buckhaven Fife 129 E5
Buckholm Borders 121 F7
Buckholt Mon 36 C2
Buckhorn Weston Dorset 13 B5
Buckhurst Hill Essex 41 E7
Buckie Moray 152 B4
Buckies Highld 158 D3
Buckingham Bucks 52 F4
Buckland Bucks 40 C1
Buckland Devon 6 E4
Buckland Glos 51 F5
Buckland Hants 14 E4
Buckland Herts 54 F4
Buckland Kent 31 E7
Buckland Oxon 38 E3
Buckland Sur 28 D3
Buckland Brewer Devon 9 B6
Buckland Common Bucks 40 D2
Buckland Dinham Som 24 D2
Buckland Filleigh Devon 9 D6
Buckland in the Moor Devon 6 B5
Buckland Monachorum Devon 6 C2
Buckland Newton Dorset 12 D4
Buckland St Mary Som 11 C7
Bucklebury W Berks 26 B3
Bucklegate Lincs 79 F6
Bucklerheads Angus 134 F4
Bucklers Hard Hants 14 E5
Bucklesham Suff 57 E6
Buckley = Bwcle Flint 73 C6
Bucklow Hill Ches E 86 F5
Buckminster Leics 65 B5
Bucknall Lincs 78 C4
Bucknall Stoke 75 E6
Bucknell Oxon 39 B5
Bucknell Shrops 49 B5
Buckpool Moray 152 B4
Buck's Cross Devon 8 B5
Bucks Green W Sus 27 F8
Bucks Horn Oak Hants 27 E6
Buck's Mills Devon 9 B5
Bucksburn Aberdeen 141 D7
Buckshaw Village Lancs 86 B3
Buckskin Hants 26 D4
Buckton E Yorks 97 B7
Buckton Hereford 49 B5
Buckton Northumb 123 F6
Buckworth Cambs 54 B2
Budbrooke Warks 51 C7
Budby Notts 77 C6
Budd's Titson Corn 8 D4
Bude Corn 8 D4
Budlake Devon 10 E4
Budle Northumb 123 F7
Budleigh Salterton Devon 11 F5
Budock Water Corn 3 C6
Buerton Ches E 74 E3
Buffler's Holt Bucks 52 F4
Bugbrooke Northants 52 D4
Buglawton Ches E 75 C5
Bugle Corn 4 D5
Bugley Wilts 24 E3
Bugthorpe E Yorks 96 D3
Buildwas Shrops 61 D6
Builth Road Powys 48 D2
Builth Wells = Llanfair-Ym-Muallt Powys 48 D2
Buirgh W Isles 154 H5
Bulby Lincs 65 B7
Bulcote Notts 77 E6
Buldoo Highld 157 C12
Bulford Wilts 25 E6
Bulford Camp Wilts 25 E6
Bulkeley Ches E 74 D2
Bulkington Warks 63 F7
Bulkington Wilts 24 D4
Bulkworthy Devon 9 C5
Bull Hill Hants 14 E4
Bullamoor N Yorks 102 E1
Bullbridge Derbys 76 D3
Bullbrook Brack 27 C6
Bulley Glos 36 C4
Bullgill Cumb 107 F7
Bullington Hants 26 E2
Bullington Lincs 78 B3
Bull's Green Herts 41 C5
Bullwood Argyll 145 F10
Bulmer Essex 56 E2
Bulmer N Yorks 96 C2
Bulmer Tye Essex 56 F2
Bulphan Thurrock 42 F2
Bulverhythe E Sus 18 E4
Bulwark Aberds 153 D9
Bulwell Nottingham 76 E5
Bulwick Northants 65 E6
Bumble's Green Essex 41 D7
Bun a'Mhuillin W Isles 148 G2
Bun Abhainn Eadarra W Isles 154 G6
Bun Loyne Highld 136 D5
Bunacaimb Highld 147 C9
Bunarkaig Highld 136 F4
Bunbury Ches E 74 D2
Bunbury Heath Ches E 74 D2
Bunchrew Highld 151 G9
Bundalloch Highld 149 F13
Buness Shetland 160 C8
Bunessan Argyll 146 J6
Bungay Suff 69 F6
Bunker's Hill Lincs 78 B2
Bunker's Hill Lincs 79 D5
Bunkers Hill Oxon 38 C4
Bunloit Highld 137 B8
Bunnahabhain Argyll 142 A5
Bunny Notts 64 B2
Buntait Highld 150 H6
Buntingford Herts 41 B6
Bunwell Norf 68 E4
Burbage Derbys 75 B7
Burbage Leics 63 E8
Burbage Wilts 25 C7
Burchett's Green Windsor 39 F8
Burcombe Wilts 25 F5
Burcot Oxon 39 E5
Burcott Bucks 40 B1
Burdon T&W 111 D6
Bures Suff 56 F3
Bures Green Suff 56 F3
Burford Ches E 74 D3
Burford Oxon 38 C2
Burford Shrops 49 C7
Burg Argyll 146 G6
Burgar Orkney 159 F4
Burgate Hants 14 C2
Burgate Suff 56 B4
Burgess Hill W Sus 17 C7
Burgh Suff 57 D6
Burgh by Sands Cumb 108 D3
Burgh Castle Norf 69 D7
Burgh Heath Sur 28 D3
Burgh le Marsh Lincs 79 C8
Burgh Muir Aberds 141 B6
Burgh next Aylsham Norf 81 E8
Burgh on Bain Lincs 91 F6
Burgh St Margaret Norf 69 C7
Burgh St Peter Norf 69 E7
Burghclere Hants 26 C2
Burghead Moray 151 E14
Burghfield W Berks 26 C4
Burghfield Common W Berks 26 C4
Burghfield Hill W Berks 26 C4
Burghill Hereford 49 E6
Burghwallis S Yorks 89 C6
Burham Kent 29 C8
Buriton Hants 15 B8
Burland Ches E 74 D3
Burlawn Corn 4 B4
Burleigh Brack 27 C6
Burlescombe Devon 11 C5
Burleston Dorset 13 E5
Burley Hants 14 D3
Burley Rutland 65 C5
Burley W Yorks 95 F5
Burley Gate Hereford 49 E7
Burley in Wharfedale W Yorks 94 E4
Burley Lodge Hants 14 D3
Burley Street Hants 14 D3
Burleydam Ches E 74 E3
Burlingjobb Powys 48 D4
Burlow E Sus 18 D2
Burlton Shrops 60 B4
Burmarsh Kent 19 B7
Burmington Warks 51 F7
Burn N Yorks 89 B6
Burn of Cambus Stirling 127 D6
Burnaston Derbys 76 F2
Burnbank S Lanark 119 D7
Burnby E Yorks 96 E4
Burncross S Yorks 88 E4
Burneside Cumb 99 E7
Burness Orkney 159 D7
Burneston N Yorks 101 F8
Burnett Bath 23 C8
Burnfoot Borders 115 C7
Burnfoot Borders 115 C8
Burnfoot E Ayrs 112 D4
Burnfoot Perth 127 D8
Burnham Bucks 40 F2
Burnham N Lincs 90 C4
Burnham Deepdale Norf 80 C4
Burnham Green Herts 41 C5
Burnham Market Norf 80 C4
Burnham Norton Norf 80 C4
Burnham-on-Crouch Essex 43 E5
Burnham-on-Sea Som 22 E5
Burnham Overy Staithe Norf 80 C4
Burnham Overy Town Norf 80 C4
Burnham Thorpe Norf 80 C4
Burnhead Dumfries 113 E8
Burnhead S Ayrs 112 D2
Burnhervie Aberds 141 C6
Burnhill Green Staffs 61 D7
Burnhope Durham 110 E4
Burnhouse N Ayrs 118 D3
Burniston N Yorks 103 E8
Burnlee W Yorks 88 D2
Burnley Lancs 93 F8
Burnley Lane Lancs 93 F8
Burnmouth Borders 123 C5
Burnopfield Durham 110 D4
Burnsall N Yorks 94 C3
Burnside Angus 135 D5
Burnside E Ayrs 113 C5
Burnside Fife 128 D3
Burnside S Lanark 119 C6
Burnside Shetland 160 F4
Burnside W Loth 120 B3
Burnside of Duntrune Angus 134 F4
Burnswark Dumfries 107 B8
Burnt Heath Derbys 76 B2
Burnt Houses Durham 101 B6
Burnt Yates N Yorks 95 C5
Burntcommon Sur 27 D8
Burnthouse Corn 3 C6
Burntisland Fife 128 F4
Burnton E Ayrs 112 D4
Burntwood Staffs 62 D4
Burnwynd Edin 120 C4
Burpham Sur 27 D8
Burpham W Sus 16 D4
Burradon Northumb 117 D5
Burradon T&W 111 B5
Burrafirth Shetland 160 B8
Burraland Shetland 160 F5
Burraland Shetland 160 J4
Burras Corn 3 C5
Burravoe Shetland 160 F7
Burravoe Shetland 160 G5
Burray Village Orkney 159 J5
Burrells Cumb 100 C1
Burrelton Perth 134 F2
Burridge Devon 20 F4
Burridge Hants 15 C6
Burrill N Yorks 101 F7
Burringham N Lincs 90 D2
Burrington Devon 9 C8
Burrington Hereford 49 B6
Burrington N Som 23 D6
Burrough Green Cambs 55 D7
Burrough on the Hill Leics 64 C4
Burrow-bridge Som 11 B8
Burrowhill Sur 27 C7
Burry Swansea 33 E5
Burry Green Swansea 33 E5
Burry Port = Porth Tywyn Carms 33 D5
Burscough Lancs 86 C2
Burscough Bridge Lancs 86 C2
Bursea E Yorks 96 F4
Burshill E Yorks 97 E6
Bursledon Hants 15 D5
Burslem Stoke 75 E5
Burstall Suff 56 E4
Burstock Dorset 12 D2
Burston Norf 68 F4
Burston Staffs 75 F6
Burstow Sur 28 E4
Burstwick E Yorks 91 B6
Burtersett N Yorks 100 F3
Burtle Som 23 E5
Burton Ches W 73 B7
Burton Ches W 74 C2
Burton Dorset 14 E2
Burton Lincs 78 B2
Burton Northumb 123 F7
Burton Pembs 44 E4
Burton Som 22 E3
Burton Wilts 24 B3
Burton Agnes E Yorks 97 C7
Burton Bradstock Dorset 12 F2
Burton Dassett Warks 51 D8
Burton Fleming E Yorks 97 B6
Burton Green W Mid 51 B7
Burton Green Wrex 73 D7
Burton Hastings Warks 63 E8
Burton-in-Kendal Cumb 92 B5
Burton in Lonsdale N Yorks 93 B6
Burton Joyce Notts 77 E6
Burton Latimer Northants 53 B7
Burton Lazars Leics 64 C4
Burton-le-Coggles Lincs 65 B6
Burton Leonard N Yorks 95 C6
Burton on the Wolds Leics 64 B2
Burton Overy Leics 64 E3
Burton Pedwardine Lincs 78 E4
Burton Pidsea E Yorks 97 F8
Burton Salmon N Yorks 89 B5
Burton Stather N Lincs 90 C2
Burton upon Stather N Lincs 90 C2
Burton upon Trent Staffs 63 B6
Burtonwood Warr 86 E3
Burwardsley Ches W 74 D2
Burwarton Shrops 61 F6
Burwash E Sus 18 C3
Burwash Common E Sus 18 C3
Burwash Weald E Sus 18 C3
Burwell Cambs 55 C6
Burwell Lincs 79 B6
Burwen Anglesey 82 B4
Burwick Orkney 159 K5
Bury Cambs 66 F2
Bury Gtr Man 87 C6
Bury Som 10 B4
Bury W Sus 16 C4
Bury Green Herts 41 B7
Bury St Edmunds Suff 56 C2
Burythorpe N Yorks 96 C3
Busby E Renf 119 D5
Buscot Oxon 38 E2
Bush Bank Hereford 49 D6
Bush Crathie Aberds 139 E8
Bush Green Norf 68 F5
Bushbury W Mid 62 D3
Bushby Leics 64 D3
Bushey Herts 40 E4
Bushey Heath Herts 40 E4
Bushley Worcs 50 F3
Bushton Wilts 25 B5
Buslingthorpe Lincs 90 F4
Busta Shetland 160 G5
Butcher's Cross E Sus 18 C2
Butcombe N Som 23 C7
Butetown Cardiff 22 B3
Butleigh Som 23 F7
Butleigh Wootton Som 23 F7
Butler's Cross Bucks 39 D8
Butler's End Warks 63 F6
Butlers Marston Warks 51 E8
Butley Suff 57 D7
Butley High Corner Suff 57 E7
Butt Green Ches E 74 D3
Butterburn Cumb 109 B6
Buttercrambe N Yorks 96 D3
Butterknowle Durham 101 B6
Butterleigh Devon 10 D4
Buttermere Cumb 98 C3
Buttermere Wilts 25 C8
Buttershaw W Yorks 88 B2
Butterstone Perth 133 E7
Butterton Staffs 75 D7
Butterwick Durham 102 B1
Butterwick Lincs 79 E6
Butterwick N Yorks 96 B3
Butterwick N Yorks 97 B5
Buttington Powys 60 D2
Buttonoak Worcs 50 B2
Butt's Green Hants 14 B4
Buttsash Hants 14 D5
Buxhall Suff 56 D4
Buxhall Fen Street Suff 56 D4
Buxley Borders 122 D4
Buxted E Sus 17 B8
Buxton Derbys 75 B7

Buxton Norf 81 E8
Buxworth Derbys 87 F8
Bwcle = Buckley Flint 73 C6
Bwlch Powys 35 B5
Bwlch-Llan Ceredig 46 D4
Bwlch-y-cibau Powys 59 C8
Bwlch-y-fadfa Ceredig 46 E3
Bwlch-y-ffridd Powys 59 E7
Bwlch-y-sarnau Powys 48 B2
Bwlchgwyn Wrex 73 D6
Bwlchnewydd Carms 32 B4
Bwlchtocyn Gwyn 70 E4
Bwlchyddar Powys 59 B8
Bwlchygroes Pembs 45 F4
Byermoor T&W 110 D4
Byers Green Durham 110 F5
Byfield Northants 52 D3
Byfleet Sur 27 C8
Byford Hereford 49 E5
Bygrave Herts 54 F3
Byker T&W 111 C5
Bylchau Conwy 72 C3
Byley Ches W 74 C4
Bynea Carms 33 E6
Byrness Northumb 116 D3
Bythorn Cambs 53 B8
Byton Hereford 49 C5
Byworth W Sus 16 B3

C

Cabharstadh W Isles 155 E8
Cablea Perth 133 F6
Cabourne Lincs 90 D5
Cabrach Argyll 144 G3
Cabrach Moray 140 B2
Cabrich Highld 151 G8
Cabus Lancs 92 E4
Cackle Street E Sus 17 B8
Cadbury Devon 10 D4
Cadbury Barton Devon 9 C8
Cadder E Dunb 119 B6
Caddington C Beds 40 C3
Caddonfoot Borders 121 F7
Cade Street E Sus 18 C3
Cadeby Leics 63 D8
Cadeby S Yorks 89 D6
Cadeleigh Devon 10 D4
Cadgwith Corn 3 E6
Cadham Fife 128 D4
Cadishead Gtr Man 86 E5
Cadle Swansea 33 E7
Cadley Lancs 92 F5
Cadley Wilts 25 C7
Cadley Wilts 25 D7
Cadmore End Bucks 39 E7
Cadnam Hants 14 C3
Cadney N Lincs 90 D4
Cadole Flint 73 C6
Cadoxton V Glam 22 C3
Cadoxton-Juxta-Neath Neath 34 E1
Cadshaw Blackburn 86 C5
Cadzow S Lanark 119 D7
Caeathro Gwyn 82 E5
Caehopkin Powys 34 C2
Caenby Lincs 90 F4
Caenby Corner Lincs 90 F3
Caér-bryn Carms 33 C6
Caer Llan Mon 36 D1
Caerau Bridgend 34 E2
Caerau Cardiff 22 B3
Caerdeon Gwyn 58 C3
Caerdydd = Cardiff Cardiff 22 B3
Caerfarchell Pembs 44 C2
Caerffili = Caerphilly Caerph 35 F5
Caerfyrddin = Carmarthen Carms 33 B5
Caergeiliog Anglesey 82 D3
Caergwrle Flint 73 D7
Caergybi = Holyhead Anglesey 82 C2
Caerleon = Caerllion Newport 35 E7
Caerllion = Caerleon Newport 35 E7
Caernarfon Gwyn 82 E4
Caerphilly = Caerffili Caerph 35 F5
Caersws Powys 59 E7
Caerwedros Ceredig 46 D2
Caerwent Mon 36 E1
Caerwych Gwyn 71 D7
Caerwys Flint 72 B5
Caethle Gwyn 58 E3
Caim Anglesey 83 C6
Caio Carms 47 F5
Cairinis W Isles 148 B3
Cairisiadar W Isles 154 D5
Cairminis W Isles 154 J5
Cairnbaan Argyll 145 D7
Cairnbanno Ho. Aberds 153 D8
Cairnborrow Aberds 152 D4
Cairnbrogie Aberds 141 B7
Cairnbulg Castle Aberds 153 B10
Cairncross Angus 134 B4
Cairncross Borders 122 C4
Cairndow Argyll 125 D7
Cairness Aberds 153 B10
Cairneyhill Fife 128 F2
Cairnfield Ho. Moray 152 B4
Cairngaan Dumfries 104 F5
Cairngarroch Dumfries 104 E4
Cairnhill Aberds 153 E6
Cairnie Aberds 141 D7
Cairnie Aberds 152 D4
Cairnorrie Aberds 153 D8
Cairnpark Aberds 141 C7
Cairnryan Dumfries 104 C4
Cairnton Orkney 159 H4
Caister-on-Sea Norf 69 C8
Caistor Lincs 90 D5
Caistor St Edmund Norf 68 D5
Caistron Northumb 117 D5
Caitha Bowland Borders 121 E7
Calais Street Suff 56 F3
Calanais W Isles 154 D7
Calbost W Isles 155 F9
Calbourne IoW 14 F5
Calceby Lincs 79 B6
Calcot Row W Berks 26 B4
Calcott Kent 31 C5
Caldback Shetland 160 C8
Caldbeck Cumb 108 F3
Caldbergh N Yorks 101 F5
Caldecote Cambs 54 D4
Caldecote Cambs 65 F8
Caldecote Herts 54 F3
Caldecote Northants 52 D4
Caldecott Northants 53 C7
Caldecott Oxon 38 E4
Caldecott Rutland 65 E5
Calder Bridge Cumb 98 D2
Calder Hall Cumb 98 D2
Calder Mains Highld 158 E2
Calder Vale Lancs 92 E5
Calderbank N Lanark 119 C7
Calderbrook Gtr Man 87 C7
Caldercruix N Lanark 119 C8
Caldermill S Lanark 119 E6
Calderwood S Lanark 119 D6
Caldhame Angus 134 E4
Caldicot Mon 36 F1
Caldwell Derbys 63 C6
Caldwell N Yorks 101 C6
Caldy Mers 85 F3
Caledrhydiau Ceredig 46 D3
Calfsound Orkney 159 E6
Calgary Argyll 146 F6
Califer Moray 151 F13
California Falk 120 B2
California Norf 69 C8
Calke Derbys 63 B7
Callakille Highld 149 C11
Callaly Northumb 117 D6
Callander Stirling 126 D5
Callaughton Shrops 61 E6
Callestick Corn 4 D2
Calligarry Highld 149 H11
Callington Corn 5 C8
Callow Hereford 49 F6
Callow End Worcs 50 E3
Callow Hill Wilts 37 F7
Callow Hill Worcs 50 B2
Callows Grave Worcs 49 C7
Calmore Hants 14 C4
Calmsden Glos 37 D7
Calne Wilts 24 B5
Calow Derbys 76 B4
Calshot Hants 15 D5
Calstock Corn 6 C2
Calstone Wellington Wilts 24 C5
Calthorpe Norf 81 D7
Calthwaite Cumb 108 E4
Calton N Yorks 94 D2
Calton Staffs 75 D8
Calveley Ches E 74 D2
Calver Derbys 76 B2
Calver Hill Hereford 49 E5
Calverhall Shrops 74 F3
Calverleigh Devon 10 C4
Calverley W Yorks 94 F5
Calvert Bucks 39 B6
Calverton M Keynes 53 F5
Calverton Notts 77 E6
Calvine Perth 133 C5
Calvo Cumb 107 D8
Cam Glos 36 E4
Camas-luinie Highld 136 B2
Camasnacroise Highld 130 D2
Camastianavaig Highld 149 E10
Camasunary Highld 149 G10
Camault Muir Highld 151 G8
Camb Shetland 160 D7
Camber E Sus 19 D6
Camberley Sur 27 C6
Camberwell London 28 B4
Camblesforth N Yorks 89 B7
Cambo Northumb 117 F6
Cambois Northumb 117 F9
Camborne Corn 3 B5
Cambourne Cambs 54 D4
Cambridge Cambs 55 D5
Cambridge Glos 36 D4
Cambridge Town Southend 43 F5
Cambus Clack 127 E7
Cambusavie Farm Highld 151 B10
Cambusbarron Stirling 127 E6
Cambuskenneth Stirling 127 E7
Cambuslang S Lanark 119 C6
Cambusmore Lodge Highld 151 B10
Camden London 41 F5
Camelford Corn 8 F3
Camelsdale Sur 27 F6
Camerory Highld 151 H13
Camer's Green Worcs 50 F2
Camerton Bath 23 D8
Camerton Cumb 107 F7
Camerton E Yorks 91 B6
Camghouran Perth 132 D2
Cammachmore Aberds 141 E8
Cammeringham Lincs 90 F3
Camore Highld 151 B10
Camp Hill Warks 63 E7
Campbeltown Argyll 143 F8
Camperdown T&W 111 B5
Campmuir Perth 134 F2
Campsall S Yorks 89 C6
Campsey Ash Suff 57 D7
Campton C Beds 54 F2
Camptown Borders 116 C2
Camrose Pembs 44 C4
Camserney Perth 133 E5
Camster Highld 158 F4
Camuschoirk Highld 130 C1
Camuscross Highld 149 G11
Camusnagaul Highld 130 B4
Camusnagaul Highld 150 C3
Camusrory Highld 147 B11
Camusteel Highld 149 D12
Camusterrach Highld 149 D12
Camusvrachan Perth 132 E3
Canada Hants 14 C3
Canadia E Sus 18 D4
Canal Side S Yorks 89 C7
Candacraig Ho. Aberds 140 C2
Candlesby Lincs 79 C7
Candy Mill S Lanark 120 E3
Cane End Oxon 26 B4
Canewdon Essex 42 E4
Canford Bottom Dorset 13 D8
Canford Cliffs Poole 13 F8
Canford Magna Poole 13 E8
Canham's Green Suff 56 C4
Canholes Derbys 75 B7
Canisbay Highld 158 C5
Cann Dorset 13 B6
Cann Common Dorset 13 B6
Cannard's Grave Som 23 E8
Cannich Highld 150 H6
Cannington Som 22 F4
Cannock Staffs 62 D3
Cannock Wood Staffs 62 C4
Canon Bridge Hereford 49 E6
Canon Frome Hereford 49 E8
Canon Pyon Hereford 49 E6
Canonbie Dumfries 108 B3
Canons Ashby Northants 52 D3
Canonstown Corn 2 C4
Canterbury Kent 30 D5
Cantley Norf 69 D6
Cantley S Yorks 89 D7
Cantlop Shrops 60 D5
Canton Cardiff 22 B3
Cantraybruich Highld 151 G10
Cantraydoune Highld 151 G10
Cantraywood Highld 151 G10
Cantsfield Lancs 93 B6
Canvey Island Essex 42 F3
Canwick Lincs 78 C2
Canworthy Water Corn 8 E4
Caol Highld 131 B5
Caol Ila Argyll 142 A5
Caolas Argyll 146 G3
Caolas Scalpaigh W Isles 154 H7
Caolas Stocinis W Isles 154 H6
Capel Sur 28 E2
Capel Bangor Ceredig 58 F3
Capel Betws Lleucu Ceredig 46 D5
Capel Carmel Gwyn 70 E2
Capel Coch Anglesey 82 C4
Capel Curig Conwy 83 F7
Capel Cynon Ceredig 46 E2
Capel Dewi Carms 33 B5
Capel Dewi Ceredig 46 E3
Capel Dewi Ceredig 58 F3
Capel Garmon Conwy 83 F8
Capel-gwyn Anglesey 82 D3
Capel Gwyn Carms 33 B5
Capel Gwynfe Carms 33 B8
Capel Hendre Carms 33 C6
Capel Hermon Gwyn 71 E8
Capel Isaac Carms 33 B6
Capel Iwan Carms 45 F4
Capel le Ferne Kent 31 F6
Capel Llanilltern Cardiff 34 F4
Capel Mawr Anglesey 82 D4
Capel St Andrew Suff 57 E7
Capel St Mary Suff 56 F4
Capel Seion Ceredig 46 B5
Capel Tygwydd Ceredig 45 E4
Capel Uchaf Gwyn 70 C5
Capel-y-graig Gwyn 82 E5
Capelulo Conwy 83 D7
Capenhurst Ches W 73 B7
Capernwray Lancs 92 B5
Capheaton Northumb 117 F6
Cappercleuch Borders 115 B5
Capplegill Dumfries 114 D4
Capton Devon 7 D6
Caputh Perth 133 F7
Car Colston Notts 77 E7
Carbis Bay Corn 2 C4
Carbost Highld 149 D9
Carbost Highld 149 E8
Carbrook S Yorks 88 F4
Carbrooke Norf 68 D2
Carburton Notts 77 B6
Carcant Borders 121 D6
Carcary Angus 135 D6
Carclaze Corn 4 D5
Carcroft S Yorks 89 C6
Cardenden Fife 128 E4
Cardeston Shrops 60 C3
Cardiff = Caerdydd Cardiff 22 B3
Cardigan = Aberteifi Ceredig 45 E3
Cardington Bedford 53 E8
Cardington Shrops 60 E5
Cardinham Corn 5 C6
Cardonald Glasgow 118 C5
Cardow Moray 152 D1
Cardrona Borders 121 F6
Cardross Argyll 118 B3
Cardurnock Cumb 107 D8
Careby Lincs 65 C7
Careston Castle Angus 135 D5
Carew Pembs 32 D1
Carew Cheriton Pembs 32 D1
Carew Newton Pembs 32 D1
Carey Hereford 49 F7
Carfrae E Loth 121 C8
Cargenbridge Dumfries 107 B6
Cargill Perth 134 F1
Cargo Cumb 108 D3
Cargreen Corn 6 C2
Carham Northumb 122 F4
Carhampton Som 22 E2
Carharrack Corn 3 B6
Carie Perth 132 D3
Carie Perth 132 F3
Carines Corn 4 D2
Carisbrooke IoW 15 F5
Cark Cumb 92 B3
Carlabhagh W Isles 154 C7
Carland Cross Corn 4 D3
Carlby Lincs 65 C7
Carlecotes S Yorks 88 D2
Carlesmoor N Yorks 94 B4
Carleton Cumb 99 B7
Carleton Cumb 108 D4
Carleton Lancs 92 F3
Carleton N Yorks 94 E2
Carleton Forehoe Norf 68 D3
Carleton Rode Norf 68 E4
Carlin How Redcar 103 C5
Carlingcott Bath 23 D8
Carlisle Cumb 108 D4
Carlops Borders 120 D4
Carlton Bedford 53 D7
Carlton Cambs 55 D7
Carlton Leics 63 D7
Carlton N Yorks 89 B7
Carlton N Yorks 101 C6
Carlton N Yorks 101 F5
Carlton N Yorks 102 F4
Carlton Notts 77 E6
Carlton S Yorks 88 C4
Carlton Stockton 102 B1
Carlton Suff 57 C7
Carlton W Yorks 88 B4
Carlton Colville Suff 69 F8
Carlton Curlieu Leics 64 E3
Carlton Husthwaite N Yorks 95 B7
Carlton in Cleveland N Yorks 102 D3
Carlton in Lindrick Notts 89 F6
Carlton le Moorland Lincs 78 D2
Carlton Miniott N Yorks 102 F1
Carlton on Trent Notts 77 C7
Carlton Scroop Lincs 78 E2
Carluke S Lanark 119 D8
Carmarthen = Caerfyrddin Carms 33 B5
Carmel Anglesey 82 C3
Carmel Carms 33 C6
Carmel Flint 73 B5
Carmel Guern 16
Carmel Gwyn 82 F4
Carmont Aberds 141 F7
Carmunnock Glasgow 119 D6
Carmyle Glasgow 119 C6
Carmyllie Angus 135 E5
Carn-gorm Highld 136 B2
Carnaby E Yorks 97 C7
Carnach Highld 136 B3
Carnach Highld 150 B3
Carnach W Isles 154 H7
Carnachy Highld 157 D10
Càrnais W Isles 154 D5
Carnbee Fife 129 D7
Carnbo Perth 128 D2
Carnbrea Corn 3 B5
Carnduff S Lanark 119 E6
Carnduncan Argyll 142 B3
Carne Corn 3 C8
Carnforth Lancs 92 B4
Carnhedryn Pembs 44 C3
Carnhell Green Corn 2 C5
Carnkie Corn 3 C5
Carnkie Corn 3 C6
Carno Powys 59 E6
Carnoch Highld 150 F5
Carnoch Highld 150 H6
Carnock Fife 128 F2
Carnon Downs Corn 3 B6
Carnousie Aberds 153 C6
Carnoustie Angus 135 F5
Carnwath S Lanark 120 E2
Carnyorth Corn 2 C2
Carperby N Yorks 101 F5
Carpley Green N Yorks 100 F4
Carr S Yorks 89 E6
Carr Hill T&W 111 C5
Carradale Argyll 143 E9
Carragraich W Isles 154 H6
Carrbridge Highld 138 B5
Carrefour Selous Jersey 17
Carreg-wen Pembs 45 E4
Carreglefn Anglesey 82 C3
Carrick Argyll 145 E8
Carrick Fife 129 B6
Carrick Castle Argyll 145 D10
Carrick Ho. Orkney 159 E6
Carriden Falk 128 F2
Carrington Gtr Man 86 E5
Carrington Lincs 79 D6
Carrington Midloth 121 C6
Carrog Conwy 71 C8
Carrog Denb 72 E5
Carron Falk 127 F7
Carron Moray 152 D2
Carron Bridge Stirling 127 F6
Carronbridge Dumfries 113 E8
Carronshore Falk 127 F7
Carrshield Northumb 109 E8
Carrutherstown Dumfries 107 B8
Carrville Durham 111 E6
Carsaig Argyll 144 E6
Carsaig Argyll 147 J8
Carscreugh Dumfries 105 D6
Carse Gray Angus 134 D4
Carse Ho. Argyll 144 G6
Carsegowan Dumfries 105 D8
Carseriggan Dumfries 105 C7
Carsethorn Dumfries 107 D6
Carshalton London 28 C3
Carsington Derbys 76 D2
Carskiey Argyll 143 H7
Carsluith Dumfries 105 D8
Carsphairn Dumfries 113 E5
Carstairs S Lanark 120 E2
Carstairs Junction S Lanark 120 E2
Carswell Marsh Oxon 38 E3
Carter's Clay Hants 14 B4
Carterton Oxon 38 D2
Carterway Heads Northumb 110 D3
Carthew Corn 4 D5
Carthorpe N Yorks 101 F8
Cartington Northumb 117 D6
Cartland S Lanark 119 E8
Cartmel Cumb 92 B3
Cartmel Fell Cumb 99 F6
Carway Carms 33 D5
Cary Fitzpaine Som 12 B3
Cas-gwent = Chepstow Mon 36 E2
Cascob Powys 48 C4
Cashlie Perth 132 E1
Cashmoor Dorset 13 C7
Casnewydd = Newport Newport 35 F7
Cassey Compton Glos 37 C7
Cassington Oxon 38 C4
Cassop Durham 111 F6
Castell Denb 72 C5
Castell-Howell Ceredig 46 E3
Castell-Nedd = Neath Neath 33 E8
Castell Newydd Emlyn = Newcastle Emlyn Carms 46 E2
Castell-y-bwch Torf 35 E6
Castellau Rhondda 34 F4
Casterton Cumb 93 B6
Castle Acre Norf 67 C8
Castle Ashby Northants 53 D6
Castle Bolton N Yorks 101 E5
Castle Bromwich W Mid 62 F5
Castle Bytham Lincs 65 C6
Castle Caereinion Powys 59 D8
Castle Camps Cambs 55 E7
Castle Carrock Cumb 108 D5
Castle Cary Som 23 F8
Castle Combe Wilts 24 B3
Castle Donington Leics 63 B8
Castle Douglas Dumfries 106 C4
Castle Eaton Swindon 37 E8
Castle Eden Durham 111 F7
Castle Forbes Aberds 140 C5
Castle Frome Hereford 49 E8
Castle Green Sur 27 C7
Castle Gresley Derbys 63 C6
Castle Heaton Northumb 122 E5
Castle Hedingham Essex 55 F8
Castle Hill Kent 29 E7
Castle Huntly Perth 128 B5
Castle Kennedy Dumfries 104 D5
Castle O'er Dumfries 115 E5
Castle Pulverbatch Shrops 60 D4
Castle Rising Norf 67 B6
Castle Stuart Highld 151 G10
Castlebay = Bagh a Chaisteil W Isles 148 J1
Castlebythe Pembs 32 B1
Castlecary N Lanark 119 B7
Castlecraig Highld 151 E11
Castlefairn Dumfries 113 F7
Castleford W Yorks 88 B5
Castlehill Borders 120 F5
Castlehill Highld 158 D3
Castlehill W Dunb 118 B3
Castlemaddy Dumfries 113 F5
Castlemartin Pembs 44 F4
Castlemilk Dumfries 107 B8
Castlemilk Glasgow 119 D6
Castlemorris Pembs 44 B4
Castlemorton Worcs 50 F2
Castleside Durham 110 E3
Castlethorpe M Keynes 53 E6
Castleton Angus 134 E3
Castleton Argyll 145 E7
Castleton Derbys 88 F2
Castleton Gtr Man 87 C6
Castleton N Yorks 102 D4
Castleton Newport 35 F6
Castletown Ches W 73 D8
Castletown Highld 151 G10
Castletown Highld 158 D3
Castletown IoM 84 F2
Castletown T&W 111 D6
Castleweary Borders 115 D7
Castley N Yorks 95 E5
Caston Norf 68 E2
Castor Pboro 65 E8
Catacol N Ayrs 143 D10
Catbrain S Glos 36 F2
Catbrook Mon 36 D2
Catchall Corn 2 D3
Catchems Corner W Mid 51 B7
Catchgate Durham 110 D4
Catcleugh Northumb 116 D3
Catcliffe S Yorks 88 F5
Catcott Som 23 F5
Caterham Sur 28 D4
Catfield Norf 69 B6
Catfirth Shetland 160 H6
Catford London 28 B4
Catforth Lancs 92 F4
Cathays Cardiff 22 B3
Cathcart Glasgow 119 C5
Cathedine Powys 35 B5
Catherington Hants 15 C7
Catherton Shrops 49 B8
Catlodge Highld 138 E2
Catlowdy Cumb 108 B4
Catmore W Berks 38 F4
Caton Lancs 92 C5
Caton Green Lancs 92 C5
Catrine E Ayrs 113 B5
Cat's Ash Newport 35 E7
Catsfield E Sus 18 D4
Catshill Worcs 50 B4
Cattal N Yorks 95 D7
Cattawade Suff 56 F5
Catterall Lancs 92 E4
Catterick N Yorks 101 E7
Catterick Bridge N Yorks 101 E7
Catterick Garrison N Yorks 101 E6
Catterlen Cumb 108 F4
Catterline Aberds 135 B8
Catterton N Yorks 95 E8
Catthorpe Leics 52 B3
Cattistock Dorset 12 E3
Catton N Yorks 95 B6
Catton Northumb 109 D8
Catwick E Yorks 97 E7
Catworth Cambs 53 B8
Caudlesprings Norf 68 D2
Caulcott Oxon 39 B5
Cauldcots Angus 135 E6
Cauldhame Stirling 126 E5
Cauldmill Borders 115 C8
Cauldon Staffs 75 E7
Caulkerbush Dumfries 107 D6
Caulside Dumfries 115 F7
Caunsall Worcs 62 F2
Caunton Notts 77 D7
Causeway End Dumfries 105 C8
Causeway Foot W Yorks 94 F3
Causeway-head Stirling 127 E6
Causewayend S Lanark 120 F3
Causewayhead Cumb 107 D8
Causey Park Bridge Northumb 117 E7
Causeyend Aberds 141 C8
Cautley Cumb 100 E1
Cavendish Suff 56 E2
Cavendish Bridge Leics 63 B8
Cavenham Suff 55 C8
Caversfield Oxon 39 B5
Caversham Reading 26 B5
Caverswall Staffs 75 E6
Cavil E Yorks 96 F3
Cawdor Highld 151 F11
Cawkwell Lincs 79 B5
Cawood N Yorks 95 F8
Cawsand Corn 6 D2
Cawston Norf 81 E7
Cawthorne S Yorks 88 D3
Cawthorpe Lincs 65 B7
Cawton N Yorks 96 B2
Caxton Cambs 54 D4
Caynham Shrops 49 B7
Caythorpe Lincs 78 E2
Caythorpe Notts 77 E6
Cayton N Yorks 103 F8
Ceann a Bhaigh W Isles 148 B2
Ceann a Deas Loch Baghasdail W Isles 148 G2
Ceann Shiphoirt W Isles 155 F7
Ceann Tarabhaigh W Isles 154 F7
Ceannacroc Lodge Highld 136 C5
Cearsiadair W Isles 155 E8
Cefn Berain Conwy 72 C3
Cefn-brith Conwy 72 D3
Cefn Canol Powys 73 F6
Cefn-coch Conwy 83 E8
Cefn Coch Powys 59 B8
Cefn-coed-y-cymmer M Tydf 34 D4
Cefn Cribbwr Bridgend 34 F2
Cefn Cross Bridgend 34 F2
Cefn-ddwysarn Gwyn 72 F3
Cefn Einion Shrops 60 F2
Cefn-gorwydd Powys 47 E8
Cefn-mawr Wrex 73 E6
Cefn-y-bedd Flint 73 D7
Cefn-y-pant Carms 32 B2
Cefneithin Carms 33 C6
Cei-bach Ceredig 46 D3
Ceinewydd = New Quay Ceredig 46 D2
Ceint Anglesey 82 D4
Cellan Ceredig 46 E5
Cellarhead Staffs 75 E6
Cemaes Anglesey 82 B3
Cemmaes Powys 58 D5
Cemmaes Road Powys 58 D5
Cenarth Carms 45 E4
Cenin Gwyn 71 C5
Central Invclyd 118 B2
Ceos W Isles 155 E8
Ceres Fife 129 C6
Cerne Abbas Dorset 12 D4
Cerney Wick Glos 37 E7
Cerrigceinwen Anglesey 82 D4
Cerrigydrudion Conwy 72 E3
Cessford Borders 116 B3
Ceunant Gwyn 82 E5
Chaceley Glos 50 F3
Chacewater Corn 3 B6
Chackmore Bucks 52 F4
Chacombe Northants 52 E2
Chad Valley W Mid 62 F4
Chadderton Gtr Man 87 D7
Chadderton Fold Gtr Man 87 D6
Chaddesden Derby 76 F3
Chaddesley Corbett Worcs 50 B3
Chaddleworth W Berks 26 B2
Chadlington Oxon 38 B3
Chadshunt Warks 51 D8
Chadwell Leics 64 B4
Chadwell St Mary Thurrock 29 B7
Chadwick End W Mid 51 B7
Chadwick Green Mers 86 E3
Chaffcombe Som 11 C8
Chagford Devon 10 F2
Chailey E Sus 17 C7
Chain Bridge Lincs 79 E6
Chainbridge Cambs 66 D4
Chainhurst Kent 29 E8
Chalbury Dorset 13 D8
Chalbury Common Dorset 13 D8
Chaldon Sur 28 D4
Chaldon Herring Dorset 13 F5
Chale IoW 15 G5
Chale Green IoW 15 G5
Chalfont Common Bucks 40 E3
Chalfont St Giles Bucks 40 E2
Chalfont St Peter Bucks 40 E3
Chalford Glos 37 D5
Chalgrove Oxon 39 E6
Chalk Kent 29 B7
Challacombe Devon 21 E5
Challoch Dumfries 105 C7
Challock Kent 30 D4
Chalton C Beds 40 B3
Chalton Hants 15 C8
Chalvington E Sus 18 E2
Chancery Ceredig 46 B4
Chandler's Ford Hants 14 B5
Channel Tunnel Kent 19 B8
Channerwick Shetland 160 L6
Chantry Som 24 E2
Chantry Suff 56 E5
Chapel Fife 128 E4
Chapel Allerton Som 23 D6
Chapel Allerton W Yorks 95 F6
Chapel Amble Corn 4 B4
Chapel Brampton Northants 52 C5
Chapel Chorlton Staffs 74 F5
Chapel-en-le-Frith Derbys 87 F8
Chapel End Warks 63 E7
Chapel Green Warks 52 C2
Chapel Green Warks 63 F6
Chapel Haddlesey N Yorks 89 B6
Chapel Head Cambs 66 F3
Chapel Hill Aberds 153 E10
Chapel Hill Lincs 78 D5
Chapel Hill Mon 36 E2
Chapel Hill N Yorks 95 E6
Chapel Lawn Shrops 48 B5
Chapel-le-Dale N Yorks 93 B7
Chapel Milton Derbys 87 F8
Chapel of Garioch Aberds 141 B6
Chapel Row W Berks 26 C3
Chapel St Leonards Lincs 79 B8
Chapel Stile Cumb 99 D5
Chapelgate Lincs 66 B4
Chapelhall N Lanark 119 C7
Chapelhill Dumfries 114 E3
Chapelhill Highld 151 D11
Chapelhill N Ayrs 118 E2
Chapelhill Perth 128 B4
Chapelhill Perth 133 F7
Chapelknowe Dumfries 108 B3
Chapelton Angus 135 E6
Chapelton Devon 9 B7
Chapelton Highld 138 C5
Chapelton S Lanark 119 E6
Chapeltown Blackburn 86 C5
Chapeltown Moray 139 B8
Chapeltown S Yorks 88 E4
Chapmans Well Devon 9 E5
Chapmanslade Wilts 24 E3
Chapmore End Herts 41 C6
Chappel Essex 42 B4
Chard Som 11 D8
Chardstock Devon 11 D8
Charfield S Glos 36 E4
Charford Worcs 50 C4
Charing Kent 30 E3
Charing Cross Dorset 14 C2
Charing Heath Kent 30 E3
Charingworth Glos 51 F7
Charlbury Oxon 38 C3
Charlcombe Bath 24 C2
Charlecote Warks 51 D7
Charles Devon 21 F5
Charles Tye Suff 56 D4
Charlesfield Dumfries 107 C8
Charleston Angus 134 E3
Charleston Renfs 118 C4
Charlestown Aberdeen 141 D8
Charlestown Corn 4 D5
Charlestown Derbys 87 E8
Charlestown Dorset 12 G4
Charlestown Fife 128 F2
Charlestown Gtr Man 87 D6
Charlestown Highld 149 A13
Charlestown Highld 151 G9
Charlestown W Yorks 87 B7
Charlestown of Aberlour Moray 152 D2
Charlesworth Derbys 87 E8
Charleton Devon 7 E5
Charlton Hants 25 E8
Charlton Herts 40 B4
Charlton London 28 B5
Charlton Northants 52 F3
Charlton Northumb 116 F4
Charlton Som 23 D8
Charlton Telford 61 C5
Charlton W Sus 16 C2
Charlton Wilts 13 B7
Charlton Wilts 25 D6
Charlton Wilts 37 F6
Charlton Worcs 50 E5
Charlton Abbots Glos 37 B7
Charlton Adam Som 12 B3
Charlton-All-Saints Wilts 14 B2
Charlton Down Dorset 12 E4
Charlton Horethorne Som 12 B4
Charlton Kings Glos 37 B6
Charlton Mackerell Som 12 B3
Charlton Marshall Dorset 13 D6
Charlton Musgrove Som 12 B5
Charlton on Otmoor Oxon 39 C5
Charltons Redcar 102 C4
Charlwood Sur 28 E3
Charlynch Som 22 F4
Charminster Dorset 12 E4
Charmouth Dorset 11 E8
Charndon Bucks 39 B6
Charney Bassett Oxon 38 E3
Charnock Richard Lancs 86 C3
Charsfield Suff 57 D6
Chart Corner Kent 29 D8
Chart Sutton Kent 30 E2
Charter Alley Hants 26 D3
Charterhouse Som 23 D6
Charterville Allotments Oxon 38 C3
Chartham Kent 30 D5
Chartham Hatch Kent 30 D5
Chartridge Bucks 40 D2
Charvil Wokingham 27 B5
Charwelton Northants 52 D3
Chasetown Staffs 62 D4
Chastleton Oxon 38 B2
Chasty Devon 8 D5
Chatburn Lancs 93 E7
Chatcull Staffs 74 F4
Chatham Medway 29 C8
Chathill Northumb 117 B7
Chattenden Medway 29 B8
Chatteris Cambs 66 F3
Chattisham Suff 56 E4
Chatto Borders 116 C3
Chatton Northumb 117 B6
Chawleigh Devon 10 C2
Chawley Oxon 38 D4
Chawston Bedford 54 D2
Chawton Hants 26 F5
Cheadle Gtr Man 87 F6
Cheadle Staffs 75 E7
Cheadle Heath Gtr Man 87 F6
Cheadle Hulme Gtr Man 87 F6
Cheam London 28 C3
Cheapside Sur 27 D8
Chearsley Bucks 39 C7
Chebsey Staffs 62 B2
Checkendon Oxon 39 F6
Checkley Ches E 74 E4
Checkley Hereford 49 F7
Checkley Staffs 75 F7
Chedburgh Suff 55 D8
Cheddar Som 23 D6
Cheddington Bucks 40 C2
Cheddleton Staffs 75 D6
Cheddon Fitzpaine Som 11 B7
Chedglow Wilts 37 E6
Chedgrave Norf 69 E6
Chedington Dorset 12 D2
Chediston Suff 57 B7
Chedworth Glos 37 C7
Chedzoy Som 22 F5
Cheeklaw Borders 122 D3
Cheeseman's Green Kent 19 B7
Cheglinch Devon 20 E4
Cheldon Devon 10 C2
Chelford Ches E 74 B5
Chell Heath Stoke 75 D5
Chellaston Derby 76 F3
Chellington Bedford 53 D7
Chelmarsh Shrops 61 F7
Chelmer Village Essex 42 D3
Chelmondiston Suff 57 F6
Chelmorton Derbys 75 C8
Chelmsford Essex 42 D3
Chelsea London 28 B3
Chelsfield London 29 C5
Chelsworth Suff 56 E3
Cheltenham Glos 37 B6
Chelveston Northants 53 C7
Chelvey N Som 23 C6
Chelwood Bath 23 C8
Chelwood Common E Sus 17 B8
Chelwood Gate E Sus 17 B8
Chelworth Wilts 37 E6
Chelworth Green Wilts 37 E7
Chemistry Shrops 74 E2
Chenies Bucks 40 E3
Cheny Longville Shrops 60 F4
Chepstow = Cas-gwent Mon 36 E2
Chequerfield W Yorks 89 B5
Cherhill Wilts 24 B5
Cherington Glos 37 E6
Cherington Warks 51 F7
Cheriton Devon 21 E6
Cheriton Hants 15 B6
Cheriton Kent 19 B8
Cheriton Swansea 33 E5
Cheriton Bishop Devon 10 E2
Cheriton Fitzpaine Devon 10 D3
Cheriton or Stackpole Elidor Pembs 44 F4
Cherrington Telford 61 B6
Cherry Burton E Yorks 97 E5
Cherry Hinton Cambs 55 D5
Cherry Orchard Worcs 50 D3
Cherry Willingham Lincs 78 B3
Cherrybank Perth 128 B3
Chertsey Sur 27 C8
Cheselbourne Dorset 13 E5
Chesham Bucks 40 D2
Chesham Bois Bucks 40 E2
Cheshunt Herts 41 D6
Cheslyn Hay Staffs 62 D3
Chessington London 28 C2
Chester Ches W 73 C8
Chester-Le-Street Durham 111 D5
Chester Moor Durham 111 E5
Chesterblade Som 23 E8
Chesterfield Derbys 76 B3
Chesters Borders 116 B2
Chesters Borders 116 C2
Chesterton Cambs 55 C5
Chesterton Cambs 65 E8
Chesterton Glos 37 D7
Chesterton Oxon 39 B5
Chesterton Shrops 61 E7
Chesterton Staffs 74 E5
Chesterton Warks 51 D8
Chesterwood Northumb 109 C8
Chestfield Kent 30 C5
Cheston Devon 6 D4
Cheswardine Shrops 61 B7
Cheswick Northumb 123 E6
Chetnole Dorset 12 D4
Chettiscombe Devon 10 C4
Chettisham Cambs 66 F5
Chettle Dorset 13 C7
Chetton Shrops 61 E6
Chetwode Bucks 39 B6
Chetwynd Aston Telford 61 C7
Cheveley Cambs 55 C7
Chevening Kent 29 D5
Chevington Suff 55 D8
Chevithorne Devon 10 C4
Chew Magna Bath 23 C7
Chew Stoke Bath 23 C7
Chewton Keynsham Bath 23 C8
Chewton Mendip Som 23 D7
Chicheley M Keynes 53 E7
Chichester W Sus 16 D2
Chickerell Dorset 12 F4
Chicklade Wilts 24 F4
Chicksgrove Wilts 24 F4
Chidden Hants 15 C7
Chiddingfold Sur 27 F7
Chiddingly E Sus 18 D2
Chiddingstone Kent 29 E5
Chiddingstone Causeway Kent 29 E6
Chiddingstone Hoath Kent 29 E5
Chideock Dorset 12 E2
Chidham W Sus 15 D8
Chidswell W Yorks 88 B3
Chieveley W Berks 26 B2
Chignall Smealy Essex 42 C2
Chignall St James Essex 42 D2
Chigwell Essex 41 E7
Chigwell Row Essex 41 E7
Chilbolton Hants 25 F8
Chilcomb Hants 15 B6
Chilcombe Dorset 12 E3
Chilcompton Som 23 D8
Chilcote Leics 63 C6
Child Okeford Dorset 13 C6
Childer Thornton Ches W 73 B7
Childrey Oxon 38 F3
Child's Ercall Shrops 61 B6
Childswickham Worcs 51 F5
Childwall Mers 86 F2
Childwick Green Herts 40 C4
Chilfrome Dorset 12 E3
Chilgrove W Sus 16 C2
Chilham Kent 30 D4
Chilhampton Wilts 25 F5
Chilla Devon 9 D6
Chillaton Devon 9 F6
Chillenden Kent 31 D6
Chillerton IoW 15 F5
Chillesford Suff 57 D7
Chillingham Northumb 117 B6
Chillington Devon 7 E5
Chillington Som 11 C8
Chilmark Wilts 24 F4
Chilson Oxon 38 C3
Chilsworthy Corn 6 B2
Chilsworthy Devon 8 D5
Chilthorne Domer Som 12 C3
Chiltington E Sus 17 C7
Chilton Bucks 39 C6
Chilton Durham 101 B7
Chilton Oxon 38 F4
Chilton Cantelo Som 12 B3
Chilton Foliat Wilts 25 B8
Chilton Lane Durham 111 F6
Chilton Polden Som 23 F5
Chilton Street Suff 55 E8
Chilton Trinity Som 22 F4
Chilvers Coton Warks 63 E7
Chilwell Notts 76 F5
Chilworth Hants 14 C5
Chilworth Sur 27 E8
Chimney Oxon 38 D3
Chineham Hants 26 D4
Chingford London 41 E6
Chinley Derbys 87 F8
Chinley Head Derbys 87 F8
Chinnor Oxon 39 D7
Chipnall Shrops 74 F4
Chippenhall Green Suff 57 B6
Chippenham Cambs 55 C7
Chippenham Wilts 24 B4
Chipperfield Herts 40 D3
Chipping Herts 54 F4
Chipping Lancs 93 E6
Chipping Campden Glos 51 F6
Chipping Hill Essex 42 C4
Chipping Norton Oxon 38 B3
Chipping Ongar Essex 42 D1
Chipping Sodbury S Glos 36 F4
Chipping Warden Northants 52 E2
Chipstable Som 10 B5
Chipstead Kent 29 D5
Chipstead Sur 28 D3
Chirbury Shrops 60 E2
Chirk = Y Waun Wrex 73 F6
Chirk Bank Shrops 73 F6
Chirmorrie S Ayrs 105 B6
Chirnside Borders 122 D4
Chirnsidebridge Borders 122 D4
Chirton Wilts 25 D5
Chisbury Wilts 25 C7
Chiselborough Som 12 C2
Chiseldon Swindon 25 B6
Chiserley W Yorks 87 B8
Chislehampton Oxon 39 E5
Chislehurst London 28 B5
Chislet Kent 31 C6
Chiswell Green Herts 40 D4
Chiswick London 28 B3
Chiswick End Cambs 54 E4
Chisworth Derbys 87 E7
Chithurst W Sus 16 B2
Chittering Cambs 55 B5
Chitterne Wilts 24 E4
Chittlehamholt Devon 9 B8
Chittlehampton Devon 9 B8
Chittoe Wilts 24 C4
Chivenor Devon 20 F4
Chobham Sur 27 C7
Choicelee Borders 122 D3
Cholderton Wilts 25 E7
Cholesbury Bucks 40 D2
Chollerford Northumb 110 B2
Chollerton Northumb 110 B2
Cholmondeston Ches E 74 C3
Cholsey Oxon 39 F5
Cholstrey Hereford 49 D6
Chop Gate N Yorks 102 E3
Choppington Northumb 117 F8
Chopwell T&W 110 D4
Chorley Ches E 74 D2
Chorley Lancs 86 C3
Chorley Shrops 61 F6
Chorley Staffs 62 C4
Chorleywood Herts 40 E3
Chorlton cum Hardy Gtr Man 87 E6
Chorlton Lane Ches W 73 E8
Choulton Shrops 60 F3
Chowdene T&W 111 D5
Chowley Ches W 73 D8
Chrishall Essex 54 F5
Christchurch Cambs 66 E4
Christchurch Dorset 14 E2
Christchurch Glos 36 C2
Christchurch Newport 35 F7
Christian Malford Wilts 24 B4
Christleton Ches W 73 C8
Christmas Common Oxon 39 E7
Christon N Som 23 D5
Christon Bank Northumb 117 B8
Christow Devon 10 F3
Chryston N Lanark 119 B6
Chudleigh Devon 7 B6
Chudleigh Knighton Devon 7 B6
Chulmleigh Devon 9 C8
Chunal Derbys 87 E8
Church Lancs 86 B5
Church Aston Telford 61 C7
Church Brampton Northants 52 C5
Church Broughton Derbys 76 F2
Church Crookham Hants 27 D6
Church Eaton Staffs 62 C2
Church End C Beds 40 B2
Church End C Beds 53 F7
Church End C Beds 54 F2
Church End Cambs 66 D3
Church End Cambs 66 F2
Church End E Yorks 97 D6
Church End Essex 42 B3
Church End Essex 55 E6
Church End Hants 26 D4
Church End Lincs 78 F5
Church End Warks 63 E6
Church End Warks 63 E6
Church End Wilts 24 B5
Church Enstone Oxon 38 B3
Church Fenton N Yorks 95 F8
Church Green Devon 11 E6
Church Green Norf 68 E3
Church Gresley Derbys 63 C6
Church Hanborough Oxon 38 C4
Church Hill Ches W 74 C3
Church Houses N Yorks 102 E4
Church Knowle Dorset 13 F7
Church Laneham Notts 77 B8
Church Langton Leics 64 E4
Church Lawford Warks 52 B2
Church Lawton Ches E 74 D5
Church Leigh Staffs 75 F7
Church Lench Worcs 50 D5
Church Mayfield Staffs 75 E8
Church Minshull Ches E 74 C3
Church Norton W Sus 16 E2
Church Preen Shrops 60 E5
Church Pulverbatch Shrops 60 D4
Church Stoke Powys 60 E2
Church Stowe Northants 52 D4
Church Street Kent 29 B8
Church Stretton Shrops 60 E4
Church Town N Lincs 89 D8
Church Town Sur 28 D4
Church Village Rhondda 34 F4
Church Warsop Notts 77 C5
Churcham Glos 36 C4
Churchbank Shrops 48 B4
Churchbridge Staffs 62 D3
Churchdown Glos 37 C5
Churchend Essex 42 B2
Churchend Essex 43 E6
Churchend S Glos 36 E4
Churchfield W Mid 62 E4
Churchgate Street Essex 41 C7
Churchill Devon 11 D8
Churchill Devon 20 E4
Churchill N Som 23 D6
Churchill Oxon 38 B2
Churchill Worcs 50 B3
Churchill Worcs 50 D4
Churchinford Som 11 C7
Churchover Warks 64 F2
Churchstanton Som 11 C6
Churchstow Devon 6 E5
Churchtown Derbys 76 C2
Churchtown IoM 84 C4
Churchtown Lancs 92 E4

Churchtown Mers 85 C4
Churnsike Lodge Northumb 109 B6
Churston Ferrers Torbay 7 D7
Churt Sur 27 F6
Churton Ches W 73 D8
Churwell W Yorks 88 B3
Chute Standen Wilts 25 D8
Chwilog Gwyn 70 D5
Chyandour Corn 2 C3
Cilan Uchaf Gwyn 70 E3
Cilcain Flint 73 C5
Cilcennin Ceredig 46 C4
Cilfor Gwyn 71 D7
Cilfrew Neath 34 D1
Cilfynydd Rhondda 34 E4
Cilgerran Pembs 45 E3
Cilgwyn Carms 33 B8
Cilgwyn Gwyn 82 F4
Cilgwyn Pembs 45 F2
Ciliau Aeron Ceredig 46 D3
Cill Donnain W Isles 148 F2
Cille Bhrighde W Isles 148 G2
Cille Pheadair W Isles 148 G2
Cilmery Powys 48 D2
Cilsan Carms 33 B6
Ciltalgarth Gwyn 72 E2
Cilwendeg Pembs 45 F4
Cilybebyll Neath 33 D8
Cilycwm Carms 47 F6
Cimla Neath 34 E1
Cinderford Glos 36 C3
Cippyn Pembs 45 E3
Circebost W Isles 154 D6
Cirencester Glos 37 D7
Ciribhig W Isles 154 C6
City London 41 F6
City Powys 60 F2
City Dulas Anglesey 82 C4
Clachaig Argyll 145 E10
Clachan Argyll 124 D3
Clachan Argyll 125 D7
Clachan Argyll 130 E2
Clachan Argyll 144 H6
Clachan Highld 149 E10
Clachan W Isles 148 D2
Clachan na Luib W Isles 148 B3
Clachan of Campsie E Dunb 119 B6
Clachan of Glendaruel Argyll 145 E8
Clachan-Seil Argyll 124 D3
Clachan Strachur Argyll 125 E6
Clachaneasy Dumfries 105 B7
Clachanmore Dumfries 104 E4
Clachbreck Argyll 144 F6
Clachnabrain Angus 134 C3
Clachtoll Highld 156 G3
Clackmannan Clack 127 E8
Clacton-on-Sea Essex 43 C7
Cladach Chireboist W Isles 148 B2
Claddach-knockline W Isles 148 B2
Cladich Argyll 125 C6
Claggan Highld 131 B5
Claggan Highld 147 G9
Claigan Highld 148 C7
Claines Worcs 50 D3
Clandown Bath 23 D8
Clanfield Hants 15 C7
Clanfield Oxon 38 D2
Clanville Hants 25 E8
Claonaig Argyll 145 H7
Claonel Highld 157 J8
Clap Hill Kent 19 B7
Clapgate Dorset 13 D8
Clapgate Herts 41 B7
Clapham Bedford 53 D8
Clapham London 28 B3
Clapham N Yorks 93 C7
Clapham W Sus 16 D4
Clappers Borders 122 D5
Clappersgate Cumb 99 D5
Clapton Som 12 D2
Clapton-in-Gordano N Som 23 B6
Clapton-on-the-Hill Glos 38 C1
Clapworthy Devon 9 B8
Clara Vale T&W 110 C4
Clarach Ceredig 58 F3
Clarbeston Pembs 32 B1
Clarbeston Road Pembs 32 B1
Clarborough Notts 89 F8
Clardon Highld 158 D3
Clare Suff 55 E8
Clarebrand Dumfries 106 C4
Clarencefield Dumfries 107 C7
Clarilaw Borders 115 C8
Clark's Green Sur 28 F2
Clarkston E Renf 119 D5
Clashandorran Highld 151 G8
Clashcoig Highld 151 B9
Clashindarroch Aberds 152 E4
Clashmore Highld 151 C10
Clashmore Highld 156 F3
Clashnessie Highld 156 F3
Clashnoir Moray 139 B8
Clate Shetland 160 G7
Clathy Perth 127 C8
Clatt Aberds 140 B4
Clatter Powys 59 E6
Clatterford IoW 15 F5
Clatterin Bridge Aberds 135 B6
Clatworthy Som 22 F2
Claughton Lancs 92 E5
Claughton Lancs 93 C5
Claughton Mers 85 F4
Claverdon Warks 51 C6
Claverham N Som 23 C6
Clavering Essex 55 F5
Claverley Shrops 61 E7
Claverton Bath 24 C2
Clawdd-newydd Denb 72 D4
Clawthorpe Cumb 92 B5
Clawton Devon 9 E5
Claxby Lincs 79 B7
Claxby Lincs 90 E5
Claxton N Yorks 96 C2
Claxton Norf 69 D6
Clay Common Suff 69 F7
Clay Coton Northants 52 B3
Clay Cross Derbys 76 C3
Clay Hill W Berks 26 B3
Clay Lake Lincs 66 B2
Claybokie Aberds 139 E6
Claybrooke Magna Leics 63 F8
Claybrooke Parva Leics 63 F8
Claydon Oxon 52 D2
Claydon Suff 56 D5
Claygate Dumfries 108 B3
Claygate Kent 29 E8
Claygate Sur 28 C2
Claygate Cross Kent 29 D7
Clayhanger Devon 10 B5
Clayhanger W Mid 62 D4
Clayhidon Devon 11 C6
Clayhill E Sus 18 C5
Clayhill Hants 14 D4
Clayock Highld 158 E3
Claypole Lincs 77 E8
Clayton S Yorks 89 D5
Clayton Staffs 75 E5
Clayton W Sus 17 C6
Clayton W Yorks 94 F4
Clayton Green Lancs 86 B3
Clayton-le-Moors Lancs 93 F7
Clayton-le-Woods Lancs 86 B3
Clayton West W Yorks 88 C3
Clayworth Notts 89 F8
Cleadale Highld 146 C7
Cleadon T&W 111 C6
Clearbrook Devon 6 C3
Clearwell Glos 36 D2
Cleasby N Yorks 101 C7
Cleat Orkney 159 K5
Cleatlam Durham 101 C6
Cleator Cumb 98 C2
Cleator Moor Cumb 98 C2
Clebrig Highld 157 F8
Cleckheaton W Yorks 88 B2
Clee St Margaret Shrops 61 F5
Cleedownton Shrops 61 F5
Cleehill Shrops 49 B7
Cleethorpes NE Lincs 91 D7
Cleeton St Mary Shrops 49 B8
Cleeve N Som 23 C6
Cleeve Hill Glos 37 B6
Cleeve Prior Worcs 51 E5
Clegyrnant Powys 59 D6
Clehonger Hereford 49 F6
Cleish Perth 128 E2
Cleland N Lanark 119 D8
Clench Common Wilts 25 C6
Clenchwarton Norf 67 B5
Clent Worcs 50 B4
Cleobury Mortimer Shrops 49 B8
Cleobury North Shrops 61 F6
Cleongart Argyll 143 E7
Clephanton Highld 151 F11
Clerklands Borders 115 B8
Clestrain Orkney 159 H4
Cleuch Head Borders 115 C8
Cleughbrae Dumfries 107 B7
Clevancy Wilts 25 B5
Clevedon N Som 23 B6
Cleveley Oxon 38 B3
Cleveleys Lancs 92 E3
Cleverton Wilts 37 F6
Clevis Bridgend 21 B7
Clewer Som 23 D6
Cley next the Sea Norf 81 C6
Cliaid W Isles 148 H1
Cliasmol W Isles 154 G5
Cliburn Cumb 99 B7
Click Mill Orkney 159 F4
Cliddesden Hants 26 E4
Cliff End E Sus 19 D5
Cliffburn Angus 135 E6
Cliffe Medway 29 B8
Cliffe N Yorks 96 F2
Cliffe Woods Medway 29 B8
Clifford Hereford 48 E4
Clifford W Yorks 95 E7
Clifford Chambers Warks 51 D6
Clifford's Mesne Glos 36 B4
Cliffsend Kent 31 C7
Clifton Bristol 23 B7
Clifton C Beds 54 F2
Clifton Cumb 99 B7
Clifton Derbys 75 E8
Clifton Lancs 92 F4
Clifton N Yorks 94 E4
Clifton Northumb 117 F8
Clifton Nottingham 77 F5
Clifton Oxon 52 F2
Clifton S Yorks 89 E6
Clifton Stirling 131 F7
Clifton Worcs 50 E3
Clifton York 95 D8
Clifton Campville Staffs 63 C6
Clifton Green Gtr Man 87 D5
Clifton Hampden Oxon 39 E5
Clifton Reynes M Keynes 53 D7
Clifton upon Dunsmore Warks 52 B3
Clifton upon Teme Worcs 50 C2
Cliftoncote Borders 116 B4
Cliftonville Kent 31 B7
Climaen gwyn Neath 33 D8
Climping W Sus 16 D4
Climpy S Lanark 120 D2
Clink Som 24 E2
Clint N Yorks 95 D5
Clint Green Norf 68 C3
Clintmains Borders 122 F2
Cliobh W Isles 154 D5
Clippesby Norf 69 C7
Clipsham Rutland 65 C6
Clipston Northants 64 F4
Clipstone Notts 77 C5
Clitheroe Lancs 93 E7
Cliuthar W Isles 154 H6
Clive Shrops 60 B5
Clivocast Shetland 160 C8
Clixby Lincs 90 D5
Clocaenog Denb 72 D4
Clochan Moray 152 B4
Clock Face Mers 86 E3
Clockmill Borders 122 D3
Cloddiau Powys 60 D2
Clodock Hereford 35 B7
Clola Aberds 153 D10
Clophill C Beds 53 F8
Clopton Northants 65 F7
Clopton Suff 57 D6
Clopton Corner Suff 57 D6
Clopton Green Suff 55 D8
Close Clark IoM 84 E2
Closeburn Dumfries 113 E8
Closworth Som 12 C3
Clothall Herts 54 F3
Clotton Ches W 74 C2
Clough Foot W Yorks 87 B7
Cloughton N Yorks 103 E8
Cloughton Newlands N Yorks 103 E8
Clousta Shetland 160 H5
Clouston Orkney 159 G3
Clova Aberds 140 B3
Clova Angus 134 B3
Clove Lodge Durham 100 C4
Clovelly Devon 8 B5
Clovenfords Borders 121 F7
Clovenstone Aberds 141 C6
Clovullin Highld 130 C4
Clow Bridge Lancs 87 B6
Clowne Derbys 76 B4
Clows Top Worcs 50 B2
Cloy Wrex 73 E7
Cluanie Inn Highld 136 C3
Cluanie Lodge Highld 136 C3
Clun Shrops 60 F3
Clunbury Shrops 60 F3
Clunderwen Carms 32 C2
Clune Highld 138 B3
Clunes Highld 136 F5
Clungunford Shrops 49 B5
Clunie Aberds 153 C6
Clunie Perth 133 E8
Clunton Shrops 60 F3
Cluny Fife 128 E4
Cluny Castle Highld 138 E2
Clutton Bath 23 D8
Clutton Ches W 73 D8
Clwt-grugoer Conwy 72 C3
Clwt-y-bont Gwyn 83 E5
Clydach Mon 35 C6
Clydach Swansea 33 D7
Clydach Vale Rhondda 34 E3
Clydebank W Dunb 118 B4
Clydey Pembs 45 F4
Clyffe Pypard Wilts 25 B5
Clynder Argyll 145 E11
Clyne Neath 34 D2
Clynelish Highld 157 J11
Clynnog-fawr Gwyn 82 F4
Clyro Powys 48 E4
Clyst Honiton Devon 10 E4
Clyst Hydon Devon 10 D5
Clyst St George Devon 10 F4
Clyst St Lawrence Devon 10 D5
Clyst St Mary Devon 10 E4
Cnoc Amhlaigh W Isles 155 D10
Cnwch-coch Ceredig 47 B5
Coachford Aberds 152 D4
Coad's Green Corn 5 B7
Coal Aston Derbys 76 B3
Coalbrookdale Telford 61 D6
Coalbrookvale Bl Gwent 35 D5
Coalburn S Lanark 119 F8
Coalburns T&W 110 C4
Coalcleugh Northumb 109 E8
Coaley Glos 36 D4
Coalhall E Ayrs 112 C4
Coalhill Essex 42 E3
Coalpit Heath S Glos 36 F3
Coalport Telford 61 D6
Coalsnaughton Clack 127 E8
Coaltown of Balgonie Fife 128 E4
Coaltown of Wemyss Fife 128 E5
Coalville Leics 63 C8
Coalway Glos 36 C2
Coat Som 12 B2
Coatbridge N Lanark 119 C7
Coatdyke N Lanark 119 C7
Coate Swindon 38 F1
Coate Wilts 24 C5
Coates Cambs 66 E3
Coates Glos 37 D6
Coates Lancs 93 E8
Coates Notts 90 F2
Coates W Sus 16 C3
Coatham Redcar 102 B3
Coatham Mundeville Darl 101 B7
Coatsgate Dumfries 114 D3
Cobbaton Devon 9 B8
Cobbler's Green Norf 69 E5
Coberley Glos 37 C6
Cobham Kent 29 C7
Cobham Sur 28 C2
Cobholm Island Norf 69 D8
Cobleland Stirling 126 E4
Cobnash Hereford 49 C6
Coburty Aberds 153 B9
Cock Bank Wrex 73 E7
Cock Bridge Aberds 139 D8
Cock Clarks Essex 42 D4
Cockayne N Yorks 102 E4
Cockayne Hatley Cambs 54 E3
Cockburnspath Borders 122 B3
Cockenzie and Port Seton E Loth 121 B7
Cockerham Lancs 92 D4
Cockermouth Cumb 107 F8
Cockernhoe Green Herts 40 B4
Cockfield Durham 101 B6
Cockfield Suff 56 D3
Cockfosters London 41 E5
Cocking W Sus 16 C2
Cockington Torbay 7 C6
Cocklake Som 23 E6
Cockley Beck Cumb 98 D4
Cockley Cley Norf 67 D7
Cockshutt Shrops 60 B4
Cockthorpe Norf 81 C5
Cockwood Devon 10 F4
Cockyard Hereford 49 F6
Codda Corn 5 B6
Coddenham Suff 56 D5
Coddington Ches W 73 D8
Coddington Hereford 50 E2
Coddington Notts 77 D8
Codford St Mary Wilts 24 F4
Codford St Peter Wilts 24 F4
Codicote Herts 41 C5
Codmore Hill W Sus 16 B4
Codnor Derbys 76 E4
Codrington S Glos 24 B2
Codsall Staffs 62 D2
Codsall Wood Staffs 62 D2
Coed Duon = Blackwood Caerph 35 E5
Coed Mawr Gwyn 83 D5
Coed Morgan Mon 35 C7
Coed-Talon Flint 73 D6
Coed-y-bryn Ceredig 46 E2
Coed-y-paen Mon 35 E7
Coed-yr-ynys Powys 35 B5
Coed Ystumgwern Gwyn 71 E6
Coedely Rhondda 34 F4
Coedkernew Newport 35 F6
Coedpoeth Wrex 73 D6
Coedway Powys 60 C3
Coelbren Powys 34 C2
Coffinswell Devon 7 C6
Cofton Hackett Worcs 50 B5
Cogan V Glam 22 B3
Cogenhoe Northants 53 C6
Cogges Oxon 38 D3
Coggeshall Essex 42 B4
Coggeshall Hamlet Essex 42 B4
Coggins Mill E Sus 18 C2
Coig Peighinnean W Isles 155 A10
Coig Peighinnean Bhuirgh W Isles 155 B9
Coignafearn Lodge Highld 138 C2
Coilacriech Aberds 140 E2
Coilantogle Stirling 126 D4
Coilleag W Isles 148 G2
Coillore Highld 149 E8
Coity Bridgend 34 F3
Col W Isles 155 C9
Col Uarach W Isles 155 D9
Colaboll Highld 157 H8
Colan Corn 4 C3
Colaton Raleigh Devon 11 F5
Colbost Highld 148 D7
Colburn N Yorks 101 E6
Colby Cumb 100 B1
Colby IoM 84 E2
Colby Norf 81 D8
Colchester Essex 43 B6
Colcot V Glam 22 C3
Cold Ash W Berks 26 C3
Cold Ashby Northants 52 B4
Cold Ashton S Glos 24 B2
Cold Aston Glos 37 C8
Cold Blow Pembs 32 C2
Cold Brayfield M Keynes 53 D7
Cold Hanworth Lincs 90 F4
Cold Harbour Lincs 78 F2
Cold Hatton Telford 61 B6
Cold Hesledon Durham 111 E7
Cold Higham Northants 52 D4
Cold Kirby N Yorks 102 F3
Cold Newton Leics 64 D4
Cold Northcott Corn 8 F4
Cold Norton Essex 42 D4
Cold Overton Leics 64 C5
Coldbackie Highld 157 D9
Coldbeck Cumb 100 D2
Coldblow London 29 B6
Coldean Brighton 17 D7
Coldeast Devon 7 B6
Colden W Yorks 87 B7
Colden Common Hants 15 B5
Coldfair Green Suff 57 C8
Coldham Cambs 66 D4
Coldharbour Glos 36 D2
Coldharbour Kent 29 D6
Coldharbour Sur 28 E2
Coldingham Borders 122 C5
Coldrain Perth 128 D2
Coldred Kent 31 E6
Coldridge Devon 9 D8
Coldstream Angus 134 F3
Coldstream Borders 122 F4
Coldwaltham W Sus 16 C4
Coldwells Aberds 153 D11
Coldwells Croft Aberds 140 B4
Coldyeld Shrops 60 E3
Cole Som 23 F8
Cole Green Herts 41 C5
Cole Henley Hants 26 D2
Colebatch Shrops 60 F3
Colebrook Devon 10 D5
Colebrooke Devon 10 E2
Coleby Lincs 78 C2
Coleby N Lincs 90 C2
Coleford Devon 10 D2
Coleford Glos 36 C2
Coleford Som 23 E8
Colehill Dorset 13 D8
Coleman's Hatch E Sus 29 F5
Colemere Shrops 73 F8
Colemore Hants 26 F5
Coleorton Leics 63 C8
Colerne Wilts 24 B3
Cole's Green Suff 57 C6
Coles Green Suff 56 E4
Colesbourne Glos 37 C6
Colesden Bedford 54 D2
Coleshill Bucks 40 E2
Coleshill Oxon 38 E2
Coleshill Warks 63 F6
Colestocks Devon 11 D5
Colgate W Sus 28 F3
Colgrain Argyll 126 F2
Colinsburgh Fife 129 D6
Colinton Edin 120 C5
Colintraive Argyll 145 F9
Colkirk Norf 80 E5
Collace Perth 134 F2
Collafirth Shetland 160 G6
Collaton St Mary Torbay 7 D6
College Milton S Lanark 119 D6
Collessie Fife 128 C4
Collier Row London 41 E8
Collier Street Kent 29 E8
Collier's End Herts 41 B6
Collier's Green Kent 18 B4
Colliery Row T&W 111 E6
Collieston Aberds 141 B9
Collin Dumfries 107 B7
Collingbourne Ducis Wilts 25 D7
Collingbourne Kingston Wilts 25 D7
Collingham Notts 77 C8
Collingham W Yorks 95 E6
Collington Hereford 49 C8
Collingtree Northants 53 D5
Collins Green Warr 86 E3
Colliston Angus 135 E6
Collycroft Warks 63 F7
Collynie Aberds 153 E8
Collyweston Northants 65 D6
Colmonell S Ayrs 104 A5
Colmworth Bedford 54 D2
Coln Rogers Glos 37 D7
Coln St Aldwyn's Glos 37 D8
Coln St Dennis Glos 37 C7
Colnabaichin Aberds 139 D8
Colnbrook Slough 27 B8
Colne Cambs 54 B4
Colne Lancs 93 E8
Colne Edge Lancs 93 E8
Colne Engaine Essex 56 F2
Colney Norf 68 D4
Colney Heath Herts 41 D5
Colney Street Herts 40 D4
Colpy Aberds 153 E6
Colquhar Borders 121 E6
Colsterdale N Yorks 101 F6
Colsterworth Lincs 65 B6
Colston Bassett Notts 77 F6
Coltfield Moray 151 E14
Colthouse Cumb 99 E5
Coltishall Norf 69 C5
Coltness N Lanark 119 D8
Colton Cumb 99 F5
Colton N Yorks 95 E8
Colton Norf 68 D4
Colton Staffs 62 B4
Colton W Yorks 95 F6
Colva Powys 48 D4
Colvend Dumfries 107 D5
Colvister Shetland 160 D7
Colwall Green Hereford 50 E2
Colwall Stone Hereford 50 E2
Colwell Northumb 110 B2
Colwich Staffs 62 B4
Colwick Notts 77 E6
Colwinston V Glam 21 B8
Colworth W Sus 16 D3
Colwyn Bay = Bae Colwyn Conwy 83 D8
Colyford Devon 11 E7
Colyton Devon 11 E7
Combe Hereford 48 C5
Combe Oxon 38 C4
Combe W Berks 25 C8
Combe Common Sur 27 F7
Combe Down Bath 24 C2
Combe Florey Som 22 F3
Combe Hay Bath 24 D2
Combe Martin Devon 20 E4
Combe Moor Hereford 49 C5
Combe Raleigh Devon 11 D6
Combe St Nicholas Som 11 C8
Combeinteignhead Devon 7 B7
Comberbach Ches W 74 B3
Comberton Cambs 54 D4
Comberton Hereford 49 C6
Combpyne Devon 11 E7
Combridge Staffs 75 F7
Combrook Warks 51 D8
Combs Derbys 75 B7
Combs Suff 56 D4
Combs Ford Suff 56 D4
Combwich Som 22 E4
Comers Aberds 141 D5
Comins Coch Ceredig 58 F3
Commercial End Cambs 55 C6
Commins Capel Betws Ceredig 46 D5
Commins Coch Powys 58 D5
Common Edge Blackpool 92 F3
Common Side Derbys 76 B3
Commondale N Yorks 102 C4
Commonmoor Corn 5 C7
Commonside Ches W 74 B2
Compstall Gtr Man 87 E7
Compton Devon 7 C6
Compton Hants 15 B5
Compton Sur 27 E6
Compton Sur 27 E7
Compton W Berks 26 B3
Compton W Sus 15 C8
Compton Wilts 25 D6
Compton Abbas Dorset 13 C6
Compton Abdale Glos 37 C7
Compton Bassett Wilts 24 B5
Compton Beauchamp Oxon 38 F2
Compton Bishop Som 23 D5
Compton Chamberlayne Wilts 13 B8
Compton Dando Bath 23 C8
Compton Dundon Som 23 F6
Compton Martin Bath 23 D7
Compton Pauncefoot Som 12 B4
Compton Valence Dorset 12 E3
Comrie Fife 128 F2
Comrie Perth 127 B6
Conaglen House Highld 130 C4
Conchra Argyll 145 E9
Concraigie Perth 133 E8
Conder Green Lancs 92 D4
Conderton Worcs 50 F4
Condicote Glos 38 B1
Condorrat N Lanark 119 B7
Condover Shrops 60 D4
Coney Weston Suff 56 B3
Coneyhurst W Sus 16 B5
Coneysthorpe N Yorks 96 B3
Coneythorpe N Yorks 95 D6
Conford Hants 27 F6
Congash Highld 139 B6
Congdon's Shop Corn 5 B7
Congerstone Leics 63 D7
Congham Norf 80 E3
Congl-y-wal Gwyn 71 C8
Congleton Ches E 75 C5
Congresbury N Som 23 C6
Congreve Staffs 62 C3
Conicavel Moray 151 F12
Coningsby Lincs 78 D5
Conington Cambs 54 C4
Conington Cambs 65 F8
Conisbrough S Yorks 89 E6
Conisby Argyll 142 B3
Conisholme Lincs 91 E8
Coniston Cumb 99 E5
Coniston E Yorks 97 F7
Coniston Cold N Yorks 94 D2
Conistone N Yorks 94 C2
Connah's Quay Flint 73 C6
Connel Argyll 124 B5
Connel Park E Ayrs 113 C6
Connor Downs Corn 2 C4
Conon Bridge Highld 151 F8
Conon House Highld 151 F8
Cononley N Yorks 94 E2
Conordan Highld 149 E10
Consall Staffs 75 E6
Consett Durham 110 D4
Constable Burton N Yorks 101 E6
Constantine Corn 3 D6
Constantine Bay Corn 4 B3
Contin Highld 150 F7
Contlaw Aberdeen 141 D7
Conwy Conwy 83 D7
Conyer Kent 30 C3
Conyers Green Suff 56 C2
Cooden E Sus 18 E4
Cooil IoM 84 E3
Cookbury Devon 9 D6
Cookham Windsor 40 F1
Cookham Dean Windsor 40 F1
Cookham Rise Windsor 40 F1
Cookhill Worcs 51 D5
Cookley Suff 57 B7
Cookley Worcs 62 F2
Cookley Green Oxon 39 E6
Cookney Aberds 141 E7
Cookridge W Yorks 95 E5
Cooksbridge E Sus 17 C8
Cooksmill Green Essex 42 D2
Coolham W Sus 16 B5
Cooling Medway 29 B8
Coombe Corn 4 D4
Coombe Corn 8 C4
Coombe Hants 15 B7
Coombe Wilts 25 D6
Coombe Bissett Wilts 14 B2
Coombe Hill Glos 37 B5
Coombe Keynes Dorset 13 F6
Coombes W Sus 17 D5
Coopersale Common Essex 41 D7
Cootham W Sus 16 C4
Copdock Suff 56 E5
Copford Green Essex 43 B5
Copgrove N Yorks 95 C6
Copister Shetland 160 F6
Cople Bedford 54 E2
Copley Durham 101 B5
Coplow Dale Derbys 75 B8
Copmanthorpe York 95 E8
Coppathorne Corn 8 D4
Coppenhall Staffs 62 C3
Coppenhall Moss Ches E 74 D4
Copperhouse Corn 2 C4
Coppingford Cambs 65 F8
Copplestone Devon 10 D2
Coppull Lancs 86 C3
Coppull Moor Lancs 86 C3
Copsale W Sus 17 B5
Copster Green Lancs 93 F6
Copston Magna Warks 63 F8
Copt Heath W Mid 51 B6
Copt Hewick N Yorks 95 B6
Copt Oak Leics 63 C8
Copthorne Shrops 60 C4
Copthorne Sur 28 F4
Copy's Green Norf 80 D5
Copythorne Hants 14 C4
Corbets Tey London 42 F1
Corbridge Northumb 110 C2
Corby Northants 65 F5
Corby Glen Lincs 65 B6
Cordon N Ayrs 143 E11
Coreley Shrops 49 B8
Cores End Bucks 40 F2
Corfe Som 11 C7
Corfe Castle Dorset 13 F7
Corfe Mullen Dorset 13 E7
Corfton Shrops 60 F4
Corgarff Aberds 139 D8
Corhampton Hants 15 B7
Corlae Dumfries 113 E6
Corley Warks 63 F7
Corley Ash Warks 63 F6
Corley Moor Warks 63 F6
Cornaa IoM 84 D4
Cornabus Argyll 142 D4
Cornel Conwy 83 E7
Corner Row Lancs 92 F4
Corney Cumb 98 E3
Cornforth Durham 111 F6
Cornhill Aberds 152 C5
Cornhill-on-Tweed Northumb 122 F4
Cornholme W Yorks 87 B7
Cornish Hall End Essex 55 F7
Cornquoy Orkney 159 J6
Cornsay Durham 110 E4
Cornsay Colliery Durham 110 E4
Corntown Highld 151 F8
Corntown V Glam 21 B8
Cornwell Oxon 38 B2
Cornwood Devon 6 D4
Cornworthy Devon 7 D6
Corpach Highld 130 B4
Corpusty Norf 81 D7
Corran Highld 130 C4
Corran Highld 149 H13
Corranbuie Argyll 145 G7
Corrany IoM 84 D4
Corrie N Ayrs 143 D11
Corrie Common Dumfries 114 F5
Corriecravie N Ayrs 143 F10
Corriemoillie Highld 150 E6
Corriemulzie Lodge Highld 150 B6
Corrievarkie Lodge Perth 132 B2
Corrievorrie Highld 138 B3
Corrimony Highld 150 H6
Corringham Lincs 90 E2
Corringham Thurrock 42 F3
Corris Gwyn 58 D4
Corris Uchaf Gwyn 58 D4
Corrour Shooting Lodge Highld 131 C8
Corrow Argyll 125 E7
Corry Highld 149 F11
Corry of Ardnagrask Highld 151 G8
Corrykinloch Highld 156 G6
Corrymuckloch Perth 133 F5
Corrynachenchy Argyll 147 G9
Cors-y-Gedol Gwyn 71 E6
Corsback Highld 158 C4
Corscombe Dorset 12 D3
Corse Aberds 152 D6
Corse Glos 36 B4
Corse Lawn Worcs 50 F3
Corse of Kinnoir Aberds 152 D5
Corsewall Dumfries 104 C4
Corsham Wilts 24 B3
Corsindae Aberds 141 D5
Corsley Wilts 24 E3
Corsley Heath Wilts 24 E3
Corsock Dumfries 106 B4
Corston Bath 23 C8
Corston Wilts 37 F6
Corstorphine Edin 120 B4
Cortachy Angus 134 D3
Corton Suff 69 E8
Corton Wilts 24 E4
Corton Denham Som 12 B4
Coruanan Lodge Highld 130 C4
Corunna W Isles 148 B3
Corwen Denb 72 E4
Coryton Devon 9 F6
Coryton Thurrock 42 F3
Cosby Leics 64 E2
Coseley W Mid 62 E3
Cosgrove Northants 53 E5
Cosham Ptsmth 15 D7
Cosheston Pembs 32 D1
Cossall Notts 76 E4
Cossington Leics 64 C3
Cossington Som 23 E5
Costa Orkney 159 F4
Costessey Norf 68 C4
Costock Notts 64 B2
Coston Leics 64 B5
Cote Oxon 38 D3
Cotebrook Ches W 74 C2
Cotehill Cumb 108 D4
Cotes Cumb 99 F6
Cotes Leics 64 B2
Cotes Staffs 74 F5
Cotesbach Leics 64 F2
Cotgrave Notts 77 F6
Cothall Aberds 141 C7
Cotham Notts 77 E7
Cothelstone Som 22 F3
Cotherstone Durham 101 C5
Cothill Oxon 38 E4
Cotleigh Devon 11 D7
Cotmanhay Derbys 76 E4
Cotmaton Devon 11 F6
Coton Cambs 54 D5
Coton Northants 52 B4
Coton Staffs 62 B2
Coton Staffs 75 F6
Coton Clanford Staffs 62 B2
Coton Hill Shrops 60 C4
Coton Hill Staffs 75 F6
Coton in the Elms Derbys 63 C6
Cott Devon 7 C5
Cottam E Yorks 97 C5
Cottam Lancs 92 F5
Cottam Notts 77 B8
Cottartown Highld 151 H13
Cottenham Cambs 54 C5
Cotterdale N Yorks 100 E3
Cottered Herts 41 B6
Cotteridge W Mid 50 B5
Cotterstock Northants 65 E7
Cottesbrooke Northants 52 B5
Cottesmore Rutland 65 C6
Cotteylands Devon 10 C4
Cottingham E Yorks 97 F6
Cottingham Northants 64 E5
Cottingley W Yorks 94 F4
Cottisford Oxon 52 F3
Cotton Staffs 75 E7
Cotton Suff 56 C4
Cotton End Bedford 53 E8
Cottown Aberds 140 B4
Cottown Aberds 141 C6
Cottown Aberds 153 D8
Cotwalton Staffs 75 F6
Couch's Mill Corn 5 D6
Coughton Hereford 36 B2
Coughton Warks 51 C5
Coulaghailtro Argyll 144 G6
Coulags Highld 150 G2
Coulby Newham Mbro 102 C3
Coulderton Cumb 98 D1
Coulin Highld 150 F3
Coull Aberds 140 D4
Coull Argyll 142 B3
Coulport Argyll 145 E11
Coulsdon London 28 D3
Coulston Wilts 24 D4
Coulter S Lanark 120 F3
Coulton N Yorks 96 B2
Cound Shrops 61 D5
Coundon Durham 101 B7
Coundon W Mid 63 F7
Coundon Grange Durham 101 B7
Countersett N Yorks 100 F4
Countess Wilts 25 E6
Countess Wear Devon 10 F4
Countesthorpe Leics 64 E2
Countisbury Devon 21 E6
County Oak W Sus 28 F3
Coup Green Lancs 86 B3
Coupar Angus Perth 134 E2
Coupland Northumb 122 F5
Cour Argyll 143 D9
Courance Dumfries 114 E3
Court-at-Street Kent 19 B7
Court Henry Carms 33 B6
Courteenhall Northants 53 D5
Courtsend Essex 43 E6
Courtway Som 22 F4
Cousland Midloth 121 C6
Cousley Wood E Sus 18 B3
Cove Argyll 145 E11
Cove Borders 122 B3
Cove Devon 10 C4
Cove Hants 27 D6
Cove Highld 155 H13
Cove Bay Aberdeen 141 D8
Cove Bottom Suff 57 B8
Covehithe Suff 69 F8
Coven Staffs 62 D3
Coveney Cambs 66 F4
Covenham St Bartholomew Lincs 91 E7
Covenham St Mary Lincs 91 E7
Coventry W Mid 51 B8
Coverack Corn 3 E6
Coverham N Yorks 101 F6
Covesea Moray 152 A1
Covington Cambs 53 B8
Covington S Lanark 120 F2
Cow Ark Lancs 93 E6
Cowan Bridge Lancs 93 B6
Cowbeech E Sus 18 D3
Cowbit Lincs 66 C2
Cowbridge Lincs 79 E6
Cowbridge Som 21 E8
Cowbridge = Y Bont-Faen V Glam 21 B8
Cowdale Derbys 75 B7
Cowden Kent 29 E5
Cowdenbeath Fife 128 E3
Cowdenburn Borders 120 D5
Cowers Lane Derbys 76 E3
Cowes IoW 15 E5
Cowesby N Yorks 102 F2
Cowfold W Sus 17 B6
Cowgill Cumb 100 F2
Cowie Aberds 141 F7
Cowie Stirling 127 F7
Cowley Devon 10 E4
Cowley Glos 37 C6
Cowley London 40 F3
Cowley Oxon 39 D5
Cowleymoor Devon 10 C4
Cowling Lancs 86 C3
Cowling N Yorks 94 E2
Cowling N Yorks 101 F7
Cowlinge Suff 55 D8
Cowpe Lancs 87 B6
Cowpen Northumb 117 F8
Cowpen Bewley Stockton 102 B2
Cowplain Hants 15 C7
Cowshill Durham 109 E8
Cowslip Green N Som 23 C6
Cowstrandburn Fife 128 E2
Cowthorpe N Yorks 95 D7
Cox Common Suff 69 F6
Cox Green Windsor 27 B6
Cox Moor Notts 76 D5
Coxbank Ches E 74 E3
Coxbench Derbys 76 E3
Coxford Norf 80 E4
Coxford Soton 14 C4
Coxheath Kent 29 D8
Coxhill Kent 31 E6
Coxhoe Durham 111 F6
Coxley Som 23 E7
Coxwold N Yorks 95 B8
Coychurch Bridgend 21 B8
Coylton S Ayrs 112 B4
Coylumbridge Highld 138 C5
Coynach Aberds 140 D3
Coynachie Aberds 152 E4
Coytrahen Bridgend 34 F2
Crabadon Devon 7 D5
Crabbs Cross Worcs 50 C5
Crabtree W Sus 17 B6
Crackenthorpe Cumb 100 B1
Crackington Haven Corn 8 E3
Crackley Warks 51 B7
Crackleybank Shrops 61 C7
Crackpot N Yorks 100 E4
Cracoe N Yorks 94 C2
Craddock Devon 11 C5
Cradhlastadh W Isles 154 D5
Cradley Hereford 50 E2
Cradley Heath W Mid 62 F3
Crafthole Corn 5 D8
Cragg Vale W Yorks 87 B8
Craggan Highld 139 B6
Craggie Highld 151 H10
Craggie Highld 157 H11
Craghead Durham 110 D5
Crai Powys 34 B2
Craibstone Moray 152 C4
Craichie Angus 135 E5
Craig Dumfries 106 B3
Craig Dumfries 106 C3
Craig Highld 150 G3
Craig Castle Aberds 140 B3
Craig-cefn-parc Swansea 33 D7
Craig Penllyn V Glam 21 B8
Craig-y-don Conwy 83 C7
Craig-y-nos Powys 34 C2
Craiganor Lodge Perth 132 D3
Craigdam Aberds 153 E8
Craigdarroch Dumfries 113 E7
Craigdarroch Highld 150 F7
Craigdhu Highld 150 G7
Craigearn Aberds 141 C6
Craigellachie Moray 152 D2
Craigencross Dumfries 104 C4
Craigend Perth 128 B3
Craigend Stirling 127 F6
Craigendive Argyll 145 E9
Craigendoran Argyll 126 F2
Craigends Renfs 118 C4
Craigens Argyll 142 B3
Craigens E Ayrs 113 C5
Craighat Stirling 126 F3
Craighead Fife 129 D8
Craighlaw Mains Dumfries 105 C7
Craighouse Argyll 144 G4
Craigie Aberds 141 C8
Craigie Dundee 134 F4
Craigie Perth 128 B3
Craigie Perth 133 E8
Craigie S Ayrs 118 F4
Craigiefield Orkney 159 G5
Craigielaw E Loth 121 B7
Craiglockhart Edin 120 B5
Craigmalloch E Ayrs 112 E4
Craigmaud Aberds 153 C8
Craigmillar Edin 121 B5
Craigmore Argyll 145 G10
Craignant Shrops 73 F6
Craigneuk N Lanark 119 C7
Craigneuk N Lanark 119 D7
Craignure Argyll 124 B3
Craigo Angus 135 C6
Craigow Perth 128 D2
Craigrothie Fife 129 C5
Craigroy Moray 151 F14
Craigruie Stirling 126 B3
Craigston Castle Aberds 153 C7
Craigton Aberdeen 141 D7
Craigton Angus 134 D3
Craigton Angus 135 F5
Craigton Highld 151 B9
Craigtown Highld 157 D11
Craik Borders 115 D6
Crail Fife 129 D8
Crailing Borders 116 B2
Crailinghall Borders 116 B2
Craiselound N Lincs 89 E8
Crakehill N Yorks 95 B7
Crakemarsh Staffs 75 F7
Crambe N Yorks 96 C3
Cramlington Northumb 111 B5
Cramond Edin 120 B4
Cramond Bridge Edin 120 B4
Cranage Ches E 74 C4
Cranberry Staffs 74 F5
Cranborne Dorset 13 C8
Cranbourne Brack 27 B7
Cranbrook, Devon 10 E5
Cranbrook Kent 18 B4
Cranbrook Common Kent 18 B4
Crane Moor S Yorks 88 D4
Crane's Corner Norf 68 C2
Cranfield C Beds 53 E7
Cranford London 28 B2
Cranford St Andrew Northants 53 B7
Cranford St John Northants 53 B7
Cranham Glos 37 C5
Cranham London 42 F1
Crank Mers 86 E3
Crank Wood Gtr Man 86 D4
Cranleigh Sur 27 F8
Cranley Suff 57 B5
Cranmer Green Suff 56 B4
Cranmore IoW 14 E4
Cranna Aberds 153 C6
Crannich Argyll 147 G8
Crannoch Moray 152 C4
Cranoe Leics 64 E4
Cransford Suff 57 C7
Cranshaws Borders 122 C2
Cranstal IoM 84 B4
Crantock Corn 4 C2
Cranwell Lincs 78 E3
Cranwich Norf 67 E7
Cranworth Norf 68 D2
Craobh Haven Argyll 124 E3
Crapstone Devon 6 C3
Crarae Argyll 125 F5
Crask Inn Highld 157 G8
Crask of Aigas Highld 150 G7
Craskins Aberds 140 D4
Craster Northumb 117 C8
Craswall Hereford 48 F4
Cratfield Suff 57 B7
Crathes Aberds 141 E6
Crathie Aberds 139 E8
Crathie Highld 137 E8
Crathorne N Yorks 102 D2
Craven Arms Shrops 60 F4
Crawcrook T&W 110 C4
Crawford Lancs 86 D2
Crawford S Lanark 114 B2
Crawfordjohn S Lanark 113 B8
Crawick Dumfries 113 C7
Crawley Hants 26 F2
Crawley Oxon 38 C3
Crawley W Sus 28 F3
Crawley Down W Sus 28 F4
Crawleyside Durham 110 E2
Crawshawbooth Lancs 87 B6
Crawton Aberds 135 B8
Cray N Yorks 94 B2
Cray Perth 133 C8
Crayford London 29 B6
Crayke N Yorks 95 B8
Crays Hill Essex 42 E3
Cray's Pond Oxon 39 F6
Creacombe Devon 10 C3
Creag Ghoraidh W Isles 148 D2
Creagan Argyll 130 E3
Creaguaineach Lodge Highld 131 C7
Creaksea Essex 43 E5
Creaton Northants 52 B5
Creca Dumfries 108 B2
Credenhill Hereford 49 E6
Crediton Devon 10 D3
Creebridge Dumfries 105 C8
Creech Heathfield Som 11 B7
Creech St Michael Som 11 B7
Creed Corn 3 B8
Creekmouth London 41 F7
Creeting Bottoms Suff 56 D5
Creeting St Mary Suff 56 D4
Creeton Lincs 65 B7
Creetown Dumfries 105 D8
Creg-ny-Baa IoM 84 D3
Creggans Argyll 125 E6
Cregneash IoM 84 F1
Cregrina Powys 48 D3
Creich Fife 128 B5
Creigiau Cardiff 34 F4
Cremyll Corn 6 D2
Creslow Bucks 39 B8
Cressage Shrops 61 D5
Cressbrook Derbys 75 B8
Cresselly Pembs 32 D1
Cressing Essex 42 B3
Cresswell Northumb 117 E8
Cresswell Staffs 75 F6
Cresswell Quay Pembs 32 D1
Creswell Derbys 76 B5
Cretingham Suff 57 C6
Cretshengan Argyll 144 G6
Crewe Ches E 74 D4
Crewe Ches W 73 D8
Crewgreen Powys 60 C3
Crewkerne Som 12 D2
Crianlarich Stirling 126 B2
Cribyn Ceredig 46 D4
Criccieth Gwyn 71 D5
Crich Derbys 76 D3
Crichie Aberds 153 D9
Crichton Midloth 121 C6
Crick Mon 36 E1
Crick Northants 52 B3
Crickadarn Powys 48 E2
Cricket Malherbie Som 11 C8
Cricket St Thomas Som 11 D8
Crickheath Shrops 60 B2
Crickhowell Powys 35 C6
Cricklade Wilts 37 E8
Cricklewood London 41 F5
Cridling Stubbs N Yorks 89 B6
Crieff Perth 127 B7
Criggion Powys 60 C2
Crigglestone W Yorks 88 C4
Crimond Aberds 153 C10
Crimonmogate Aberds 153 C10
Crimplesham Norf 67 D6
Crinan Argyll 144 D6
Cringleford Norf 68 D4
Cringles W Yorks 94 E3
Crinow Pembs 32 C2
Cripplesease Corn 2 C4
Cripplestyle Dorset 13 C8
Cripp's Corner E Sus 18 C4
Croasdale Cumb 98 C2
Crock Street Som 11 C8
Crockenhill Kent 29 C6
Crockernwell Devon 10 E2
Crockerton Wilts 24 E3
Crocketford or Ninemile Bar Dumfries 106 B5
Crockey Hill York 96 E2
Crockham Hill Kent 28 D5
Crockleford Heath Essex 43 B6
Crockness Orkney 159 J4
Croes-goch Pembs 44 B3
Croes-lan Ceredig 46 E2
Croes-y-mwyalch Torf 35 E7
Croeserw Neath 34 E2
Croesor Gwyn 71 C7
Croesyceiliog Carms 33 C5
Croesyceiliog Torf 35 E7
Croesywaun Gwyn 82 F5
Croft Leics 64 E2
Croft Lincs 79 C8
Croft Pembs 45 E3
Croft Warr 86 E4
Croft-on-Tees N Yorks 101 D7
Croftamie Stirling 126 F3
Croftmalloch W Loth 120 C2
Crofton W Yorks 88 C4

Crofton Wilts 25 C7
Crofts of Benachielt Highld 158 G3
Crofts of Haddo Aberds 153 E8
Crofts of Inverthernie Aberds 153 D7
Crofts of Meikle Ardo Aberds 153 D8
Crofty Swansea 33 E6
Croggan Argyll 124 C3
Croglin Cumb 109 E5
Croich Highld 150 B7
Crois Dughaill W Isles 148 F2
Cromarty Highld 151 E10
Cromblet Aberds 153 E7
Cromdale Highld 139 B6
Cromer Herts 41 B5
Cromer Norf 81 C8
Cromford Derbys 76 D2
Cromhall S Glos 36 E3
Cromhall Common S Glos 36 F3
Cromor W Isles 155 E9
Cromra Highld 137 E8
Cromwell Notts 77 C7
Cronberry E Ayrs 113 B6
Crondall Hants 27 E5
Cronk-y-Voddy IoM 84 D3
Cronton Mers 86 F2
Crook Cumb 99 E6
Crook Durham 110 F4
Crook of Devon Perth 128 D2
Crookedholm E Ayrs 118 F4
Crookes S Yorks 88 F4
Crookham Northumb 122 F5
Crookham W Berks 26 C3
Crookham Village Hants 27 D5
Crookhaugh Borders 114 B4
Crookhouse Borders 116 B3
Crooklands Cumb 99 F7
Cropredy Oxon 52 E2
Cropston Leics 64 C2
Cropthorne Worcs 50 E4
Cropton N Yorks 103 F5
Cropwell Bishop Notts 77 F6
Cropwell Butler Notts 77 F6
Cros W Isles 155 A10
Crosbost W Isles 155 E8
Crosby Cumb 107 F7
Crosby IoM 84 E3
Crosby N Lincs 90 C2
Crosby Garrett Cumb 100 D2
Crosby Ravensworth Cumb 99 C8
Crosby Villa Cumb 107 F7
Croscombe Som 23 E7
Cross Som 23 D6
Cross Ash Mon 35 C8
Cross-at-Hand Kent 29 E8
Cross Green Devon 9 F5
Cross Green Suff 56 D2
Cross Green Suff 56 D3
Cross Green Warks 51 D8
Cross-hands Carms 32 B2
Cross Hands Carms 33 C6
Cross Hands Pembs 32 C1
Cross Hill Derbys 76 E4
Cross Houses Shrops 60 D5
Cross in Hand E Sus 18 C2
Cross in Hand Leics 64 F2
Cross Inn Ceredig 46 C4
Cross Inn Ceredig 46 D2
Cross Inn Rhondda 34 F4
Cross Keys Kent 29 D6
Cross Lane Head Shrops 61 E7
Cross Lanes Corn 3 D5
Cross Lanes N Yorks 95 C8
Cross Lanes Wrex 73 E7
Cross Oak Powys 35 B5
Cross of Jackston Aberds 153 E7
Cross o'th'hands Derbys 76 E2
Cross Street Suff 57 B5
Crossaig Argyll 143 C9
Crossal Highld 149 E9
Crossapol Argyll 146 G2
Crossburn Falk 119 B8
Crossbush W Sus 16 D4
Crosscanonby Cumb 107 F7
Crossdale Street Norf 81 D8
Crossens Mers 85 C4
Crossflatts W Yorks 94 E4
Crossford Fife 128 F2
Crossford S Lanark 119 E8
Crossgate Lincs 66 B2
Crossgatehall E Loth 121 C6
Crossgates Fife 128 F3
Crossgates Powys 48 C2
Crossgill Lancs 93 C5
Crosshill E Ayrs 112 B4
Crosshill Fife 128 E3
Crosshill S Ayrs 112 D3
Crosshouse E Ayrs 118 F3
Crossings Cumb 108 B5
Crosskeys Caerph 35 E6
Crosskirk Highld 157 B13
Crosslanes Shrops 60 C3
Crosslee Borders 115 C6
Crosslee Renfs 118 C4
Crossmichael Dumfries 106 C4
Crossmoor Lancs 92 F4
Crossroads Aberds 141 E6
Crossroads E Ayrs 118 F4
Crossway Hereford 49 F8
Crossway Mon 35 C8
Crossway Powys 48 D2
Crossway Green Worcs 50 C3
Crossways Dorset 13 F5
Crosswell Pembs 45 F3
Crosswood Ceredig 47 B5
Crosthwaite Cumb 99 E6
Croston Lancs 86 C2
Crostwick Norf 69 C5
Crostwight Norf 69 B6
Crothair W Isles 154 D6
Crouch Kent 29 D7
Crouch Hill Dorset 12 C5
Crouch House Green Kent 28 E5
Croucheston Wilts 13 B8
Croughton Northants 52 F3
Crovie Aberds 153 B8
Crow Edge S Yorks 88 D2
Crow Hill Hereford 36 B3
Crowan Corn 2 C5
Crowborough E Sus 18 B2
Crowcombe Som 22 F3
Crowdecote Derbys 75 C8
Crowden Derbys 87 E8
Crowell Oxon 39 E7
Crowfield Northants 52 E4
Crowfield Suff 56 D5
Crowhurst E Sus 18 D4
Crowhurst Sur 28 E4
Crowhurst Lane End Sur 28 E4
Crowland Lincs 66 C2
Crowlas Corn 2 C4
Crowle N Lincs 89 C8
Crowle Worcs 50 D4
Crowmarsh Gifford Oxon 39 F6
Crown Corner Suff 57 B6
Crownhill Plym 6 D2
Crownland Suff 56 C4
Crownthorpe Norf 68 D3
Crowntown Corn 2 C5
Crows-an-wra Corn 2 D2
Crowshill Norf 68 D2
Crowsnest Shrops 60 D3
Crowthorne Brack 27 C6
Crowton Ches W 74 B2
Croxall Staffs 63 C5
Croxby Lincs 91 E5
Croxdale Durham 111 F5
Croxden Staffs 75 F7
Croxley Green Herts 40 E3
Croxton Cambs 54 C3
Croxton N Lincs 90 C4
Croxton Norf 67 F8
Croxton Staffs 74 F4
Croxton Kerrial Leics 64 B5
Croxtonbank Staffs 74 F4
Croy Highld 151 G10
Croy N Lanark 119 B7
Croyde Devon 20 F3
Croydon Cambs 54 E4
Croydon London 28 C4
Crubenmore Lodge Highld 138 E2
Cruckmeole Shrops 60 D4
Cruckton Shrops 60 C4
Cruden Bay Aberds 153 E10
Crudgington Telford 61 C6
Crudwell Wilts 37 E6
Crug Powys 48 B3
Crugmeer Corn 4 B4
Crugybar Carms 47 F5
Crulabhig W Isles 154 D6
Crumlin = Crymlyn Caerph 35 E6
Crumpsall Gtr Man 87 D6
Crundale Kent 30 E4
Crundale Pembs 44 D4
Cruwys Morchard Devon 10 C3
Crux Easton Hants 26 D2
Crwbin Carms 33 C5
Crya Orkney 159 H4
Cryers Hill Bucks 40 E1
Crymlyn = Crumlin Caerph 35 E6
Crymlyn Gwyn 83 D6
Crymych Pembs 45 F3
Crynant Neath 34 D1
Crynfryn Ceredig 46 C4
Cuaig Highld 149 C12
Cuan Argyll 124 D3
Cubbington Warks 51 C8
Cubeck N Yorks 100 F4
Cubert Corn 4 D2
Cubley S Yorks 88 D3
Cubley Common Derbys 75 F8
Cublington Bucks 39 B8
Cublington Hereford 49 F6
Cuckfield W Sus 17 B7
Cucklington Som 13 B5
Cuckney Notts 77 B5
Cuckoo Hill Notts 89 E8
Cuddesdon Oxon 39 D6
Cuddington Bucks 39 C7
Cuddington Ches W 74 B3
Cuddington Heath Ches W 73 E8
Cuddy Hill Lancs 92 F4
Cudham London 28 D5
Cudliptown Devon 6 B3
Cudworth S Yorks 88 D4
Cudworth Som 11 C8
Cuffley Herts 41 D6
Cuiashader W Isles 155 B10
Cuidhir W Isles 148 H1
Cuidhtinis W Isles 154 J5
Culbo Highld 151 E9
Culbokie Highld 151 F9
Culburnie Highld 150 G7
Culcabock Highld 151 G9
Culcairn Highld 151 E9
Culcharry Highld 151 F11
Culcheth Warr 86 E4
Culdrain Aberds 152 E5
Culduie Highld 149 D12
Culford Suff 56 B2
Culgaith Cumb 99 B8
Culham Oxon 39 E5
Culkein Highld 156 F3
Culkein Drumbeg Highld 156 F4
Culkerton Glos 37 E6
Cullachie Highld 139 B5
Cullen Moray 152 B5
Cullercoats T&W 111 B6
Cullicudden Highld 151 E9
Cullingworth W Yorks 94 F3
Cullipool Argyll 124 D3
Cullivoe Shetland 160 C7
Culloch Perth 127 C6
Culloden Highld 151 G10
Cullompton Devon 10 D5
Culmaily Highld 151 B11
Culmazie Dumfries 105 D7
Culmington Shrops 60 F4
Culmstock Devon 11 C6
Culnacraig Highld 156 J3
Culnaknock Highld 149 B10
Culpho Suff 57 E6
Culrain Highld 151 B8
Culross Fife 127 F8
Culroy S Ayrs 112 C3
Culsh Aberds 140 E2
Culsh Aberds 153 D8
Culshabbin Dumfries 105 D7
Culswick Shetland 160 J4
Cultercullen Aberds 141 B8
Cults Aberdeen 141 D7
Cults Aberds 152 E5
Cults Dumfries 105 E8
Culverstone Green Kent 29 C7
Culverthorpe Lincs 78 E3
Culworth Northants 52 E3
Culzie Lodge Highld 151 D8
Cumbernauld N Lanark 119 B7
Cumbernauld Village N Lanark 119 B7
Cumberworth Lincs 79 B8
Cuminestown Aberds 153 C8
Cumlewick Shetland 160 L6
Cummersdale Cumb 108 D3
Cummertrees Dumfries 107 C8
Cummingston Moray 152 B1
Cumnock E Ayrs 113 B5
Cumnor Oxon 38 D4
Cumrew Cumb 108 D5
Cumwhinton Cumb 108 D4
Cumwhitton Cumb 108 D5
Cundall N Yorks 95 B7
Cunninghamhead N Ayrs 118 E3
Cunnister Shetland 160 D7
Cupar Fife 129 C5
Cupar Muir Fife 129 C5
Cupernham Hants 14 B4
Curbar Derbys 76 B2
Curbridge Hants 15 C6
Curbridge Oxon 38 D3
Curdridge Hants 15 C6
Curdworth Warks 63 E5
Curland Som 11 C7
Curlew Green Suff 57 C7
Currarie S Ayrs 112 E1
Curridge W Berks 26 B2
Currie Edin 120 C4
Curry Mallet Som 11 B8
Curry Rivel Som 11 B8
Curtisden Green Kent 29 E8
Curtisknowle Devon 6 D5
Cury Corn 3 D5
Cushnie Aberds 153 B7
Cushuish Som 22 F3
Cusop Hereford 48 E4
Cutcloy Dumfries 105 F8
Cutcombe Som 21 F8
Cutgate Gtr Man 87 C6
Cutiau Gwyn 58 C3
Cutlers Green Essex 55 F6
Cutnall Green Worcs 50 C3
Cutsdean Glos 51 F5
Cutthorpe Derbys 76 B3
Cutts Shetland 160 K6
Cuxham Oxon 39 E6
Cuxton Medway 29 C8
Cuxwold Lincs 91 D5
Cwm Bl Gwent 35 D5
Cwm Denb 72 B4
Cwm Swansea 33 E7
Cwm-byr Carms 46 F5
Cwm-Cewydd Gwyn 59 C5
Cwm-cou Ceredig 45 E4
Cwm-Dulais Swansea 33 D7
Cwm-felin-fach Caerph 35 E5
Cwm Ffrwd-oer Torf 35 D6
Cwm-hesgen Gwyn 71 E8
Cwm-hwnt Rhondda 34 D3
Cwm Irfon Powys 47 E7
Cwm-Llinau Powys 58 D5
Cwm-mawr Carms 33 C6
Cwm-parc Rhondda 34 E3
Cwm Penmachno Conwy 71 C8
Cwm-y-glo Carms 33 C6
Cwm-y-glo Gwyn 82 E5
Cwmafan Neath 34 E1
Cwmaman Rhondda 34 E4
Cwmann Carms 46 E4
Cwmavon Torf 35 D6
Cwmbâch Rhondda 34 D4
Cwmbach Carms 32 B3
Cwmbach Carms 33 D5
Cwmbach Powys 48 D2
Cwmbach Powys 48 F3
Cwmbelan Powys 59 F6
Cwmbrân = Cwmbran Torf 35 E6
Cwmbran = Cwmbrân Torf 35 E6
Cwmbrwyno Ceredig 58 F4
Cwmcarn Caerph 35 E6
Cwmcarvan Mon 36 D1
Cwmcych Carms 45 F4
Cwmdare Rhondda 34 D3
Cwmderwen Powys 59 D6
Cwmdu Carms 46 F5
Cwmdu Powys 35 B5
Cwmdu Swansea 33 E7
Cwmduad Carms 46 F2
Cwmdwr Carms 47 F6
Cwmfelin Bridgend 34 F2
Cwmfelin M Tydf 34 D4
Cwmfelin Boeth Carms 32 C2
Cwmfelin Mynach Carms 32 B3
Cwmffrwd Carms 33 C5
Cwmgiedd Powys 34 C1
Cwmgors Neath 33 C8
Cwmgwili Carms 33 C6
Cwmgwrach Neath 34 D2
Cwmhiraeth Carms 46 F2
Cwmifor Carms 33 B7
Cwmisfael Carms 33 C5
Cwmllynfell Neath 33 C8
Cwmorgan Pembs 45 F4
Cwmpengraig Carms 46 F2
Cwmrhos Powys 35 B5
Cwmsychpant Ceredig 46 E3
Cwmtillery Bl Gwent 35 D6
Cwmwysg Powys 34 B2
Cwmyoy Mon 35 B6
Cwmystwyth Ceredig 47 B6
Cwrt Gwyn 58 D3
Cwrt-newydd Ceredig 46 E3
Cwrt-y-cadno Carms 47 E5
Cwrt-y-gollen Powys 35 C6
Cydweli = Kidwelly Carms 33 D5
Cyffordd Llandudno = Llandudno Junction Conwy 83 D7
Cyffylliog Denb 72 D4
Cyfronydd Powys 59 D8
Cymer Neath 34 E2
Cyncoed Cardiff 35 F5
Cynghordy Carms 47 E7
Cynheidre Carms 33 D5
Cynwyd Denb 72 E4
Cynwyl Elfed Carms 32 B4
Cywarch Gwyn 59 C5

D

Dacre Cumb 99 B6
Dacre N Yorks 94 C4
Dacre Banks N Yorks 94 C4
Daddry Shield Durham 109 F8
Dadford Bucks 52 F4
Dadlington Leics 63 E8
Dafarn Faig Gwyn 71 C5
Dafen Carms 33 D6
Daffy Green Norf 68 D2
Dagenham London 41 F7
Daglingworth Glos 37 D6
Dagnall Bucks 40 C2
Dail Beag W Isles 154 C7
Dail bho Dheas W Isles 155 A9
Dail bho Thuath W Isles 155 A9
Dail Mor W Isles 154 C7
Daill Argyll 142 B4
Dailly S Ayrs 112 D2
Dairsie or Osnaburgh Fife 129 C6
Daisy Hill Gtr Man 86 D4
Dalabrog W Isles 148 F2
Dalavich Argyll 125 D5
Dalbeattie Dumfries 106 C5
Dalblair E Ayrs 113 C6
Dalbog Angus 135 B5
Dalbury Derbys 76 F2
Dalby IoM 84 E2
Dalby N Yorks 96 B2
Dalchalloch Perth 132 C4
Dalchalm Highld 157 J12
Dalchenna Argyll 125 E6
Dalchirach Moray 152 E1
Dalchork Highld 157 H8
Dalchreichart Highld 137 C5
Dalchruin Perth 127 C6
Dalderby Lincs 78 C5
Dale Pembs 44 E3
Dale Abbey Derbys 76 F4
Dale Head Cumb 99 C6
Dale of Walls Shetland 160 H3
Dalelia Highld 147 E10
Daless Highld 151 H11
Dalfaber Highld 138 C5
Dalgarven N Ayrs 118 E2
Dalgety Bay Fife 128 F3
Dalginross Perth 127 B6
Dalguise Perth 133 E6
Dalhalvaig Highld 157 D11
Dalham Suff 55 C8
Dalinlongart Argyll 145 E10
Dalkeith Midloth 121 C6
Dallam Warr 86 E3
Dallas Moray 151 F14
Dalleagles E Ayrs 113 C5
Dallinghoo Suff 57 D6
Dallington E Sus 18 D3
Dallington Northants 52 C5
Dallow N Yorks 94 B4
Dalmadilly Aberds 141 C6
Dalmally Argyll 125 C7
Dalmarnock Glasgow 119 C6
Dalmary Stirling 126 E4
Dalmellington E Ayrs 112 D4
Dalmeny Edin 120 B4
Dalmigavie Highld 138 C3
Dalmigavie Lodge Highld 138 B3
Dalmore Highld 151 E9
Dalmuir W Dunb 118 B4
Dalnabreck Highld 147 E9
Dalnacardoch Lodge Perth 132 B4
Dalnacroich Highld 150 F6
Dalnaglar Castle Perth 133 C8
Dalnahaitnach Highld 138 B4
Dalnaspidal Lodge Perth 132 B3
Dalnavaid Perth 133 C7
Dalnavie Highld 151 D9
Dalnawillan Lodge Highld 157 E13
Dalness Highld 131 D5
Dalnessie Highld 157 H9
Dalqueich Perth 128 D2
Dalreavoch Highld 157 J10
Dalry N Ayrs 118 E2
Dalrymple E Ayrs 112 C3
Dalserf S Lanark 119 D8
Dalston Cumb 108 D3
Dalswinton Dumfries 114 F2
Dalton Dumfries 107 B8
Dalton Lancs 86 D2
Dalton N Yorks 95 B7
Dalton N Yorks 101 D6
Dalton Northumb 110 B4
Dalton Northumb 110 D2
Dalton S Yorks 89 E5
Dalton-in-Furness Cumb 92 B2
Dalton-le-Dale Durham 111 E7
Dalton-on-Tees N Yorks 101 D7
Dalton Piercy Hrtlpl 111 F7
Dalveich Stirling 126 B5
Dalvina Lodge Highld 157 E9
Dalwhinnie Highld 138 F2
Dalwood Devon 11 D7
Dalwyne S Ayrs 112 E3
Dam Green Norf 68 F3
Dam Side Lancs 92 E4
Damerham Hants 14 C2
Damgate Norf 69 D7
Damnaglaur Dumfries 104 F5
Damside Borders 120 E4
Danbury Essex 42 D3
Danby N Yorks 103 D5
Danby Wiske N Yorks 101 E8
Dandaleith Moray 152 D2
Danderhall Midloth 121 C6
Dane End Herts 41 B6
Danebridge Ches E 75 C6
Danehill E Sus 17 B8
Danemoor Green Norf 68 D3
Danesford Shrops 61 E7
Daneshill Hants 26 D4
Dangerous Corner Lancs 86 C3
Danskine E Loth 121 C8
Darcy Lever Gtr Man 86 D5
Darenth Kent 29 B6
Daresbury Halton 86 F3
Darfield S Yorks 88 D5
Darfoulds Notts 77 B5
Dargate Kent 30 C4
Darite Corn 5 C7
Darlaston W Mid 62 E3
Darley N Yorks 94 D5
Darley Bridge Derbys 76 C2
Darley Head N Yorks 94 D4
Darlingscott Warks 51 E7
Darlington Darl 101 C7
Darliston Shrops 74 F2
Darlton Notts 77 B7
Darnall S Yorks 88 F4
Darnick Borders 121 F8
Darowen Powys 58 D5
Darra Aberds 153 D7
Darracott Devon 20 F3
Darras Hall Northumb 110 B4
Darrington W Yorks 89 B5
Darsham Suff 57 C8
Dartford Kent 29 B6
Dartford Crossing Kent 29 B6
Dartington Devon 7 C5
Dartmeet Devon 6 B4
Dartmouth Devon 7 D6
Darton S Yorks 88 D4
Darvel E Ayrs 119 F5
Darwell Hole E Sus 18 D3
Darwen Blackburn 86 B4
Datchet Windsor 27 B7
Datchworth Herts 41 C5
Datchworth Green Herts 41 C5
Daubhill Gtr Man 86 D5
Daugh of Kinermony Moray 152 D2
Dauntsey Wilts 37 F6
Dava Moray 151 H13
Davenham Ches W 74 B3
Davenport Green Ches E 74 B5
Daventry Northants 52 C3
David's Well Powys 48 B2
Davidson's Mains Edin 120 B5
Davidstow Corn 8 F3
Davington Dumfries 115 D5
Daviot Aberds 141 B6
Daviot Highld 151 H10
Davoch of Grange Moray 152 C4
Davyhulme Gtr Man 87 E5
Daw's House Corn 8 F5
Dawley Telford 61 D6
Dawlish Devon 7 B7
Dawlish Warren Devon 7 B7
Dawn Conwy 83 D8
Daws Heath Essex 42 F4
Daw's House Corn 8 F5
Dawsmere Lincs 79 F7
Dayhills Staffs 75 F6
Daylesford Glos 38 B2
Ddôl-Cownwy Powys 59 C7
Ddrydwy Anglesey 82 D3
Deadwater Northumb 116 E2
Deaf Hill Durham 111 F6
Deal Kent 31 D7
Deal Hall Essex 43 E6
Dean Cumb 98 B2
Dean Devon 6 C5
Dean Devon 20 E4
Dean Dorset 13 C7
Dean Hants 15 C6
Dean Som 23 E8
Dean Prior Devon 6 C5
Dean Row Ches E 87 F6
Deanburnhaugh Borders 115 C6
Deane Gtr Man 86 D4
Deane Hants 26 D3
Deanich Lodge Highld 150 C6
Deanland Dorset 13 C7
Deans W Loth 120 C3
Deanscales Cumb 98 B2
Deanshanger Northants 53 F5
Deanston Stirling 127 D6
Dearham Cumb 107 F7
Debach Suff 57 D6
Debden Essex 41 E7
Debden Essex 55 F6
Debden Cross Essex 55 F6
Debenham Suff 57 C5
Dechmont W Loth 120 B3
Deddington Oxon 52 F2
Dedham Essex 56 F4
Dedham Heath Essex 56 F4
Deebank Aberds 141 E5
Deene Northants 65 E6
Deenethorpe Northants 65 E6
Deepcar S Yorks 88 E3
Deepcut Sur 27 D7
Deepdale Cumb 100 F2
Deeping Gate Lincs 65 D8
Deeping St James Lincs 65 D8
Deeping St Nicholas Lincs 66 C2
Deerhill Moray 152 C4
Deerhurst Glos 37 B5
Deerness Orkney 159 H6
Defford Worcs 50 E4
Defynnog Powys 34 B3
Deganwy Conwy 83 D7
Deighton N Yorks 102 D1
Deighton W Yorks 88 C2
Deighton York 96 E2
Deiniolen Gwyn 83 E5
Delabole Corn 8 F2
Delamere Ches W 74 C2
Delfrigs Aberds 141 B8
Dell Lodge Highld 139 C6
Delliefure Highld 151 H13
Delnabo Moray 139 C7
Delnadamph Aberds 139 D8
Delph Gtr Man 87 D7
Delves Durham 110 E4
Delvine Perth 133 E8
Dembleby Lincs 78 F3
Denaby Main S Yorks 89 E5
Denbigh = Dinbych Denb 72 C4
Denbury Devon 7 C6
Denby Derbys 76 E3
Denby Dale W Yorks 88 D3
Denchworth Oxon 38 E3
Dendron Cumb 92 B2
Denel End C Beds 53 F8
Denend Aberds 152 E6
Denford Northants 53 B7
Dengie Essex 43 D5
Denham Bucks 40 F3
Denham Suff 55 C8
Denham Suff 57 B5
Denham Street Suff 57 B5
Denhead Aberds 153 C9
Denhead Fife 129 C6
Denhead of Arbilot Angus 135 E5
Denhead of Gray Dundee 134 F3
Denholm Borders 115 C8
Denholme W Yorks 94 F3
Denholme Clough W Yorks 94 F3
Denio Gwyn 70 D4
Denmead Hants 15 C7
Denmore Aberdeen 141 C8
Denmoss Aberds 153 D6
Dennington Suff 57 C6
Denny Falk 127 F7
Denny Lodge Hants 14 D4
Dennyloanhead Falk 127 F7
Denshaw Gtr Man 87 C7
Denside Aberds 141 E7
Densole Kent 31 E6
Denston Suff 55 D8
Denstone Staffs 75 E8
Dent Cumb 100 F2
Denton Cambs 65 F8
Denton Darl 101 C7
Denton E Sus 17 D8
Denton Gtr Man 87 E7
Denton Kent 31 E6
Denton Lincs 77 F8
Denton N Yorks 94 E4
Denton Norf 69 F5
Denton Northants 53 D6
Denton Oxon 39 D5
Denton's Green Mers 86 E2
Denver Norf 67 D6
Denwick Northumb 117 C8
Deopham Norf 68 D3
Deopham Green Norf 68 E3
Depden Suff 55 D8
Depden Green Suff 55 D8
Deptford London 28 B4
Deptford Wilts 24 F5
Derby Derby 76 F3
Derbyhaven IoM 84 F2
Dereham Norf 68 C2
Deri Caerph 35 D5
Derril Devon 8 D5
Derringstone Kent 31 E6
Derrington Staffs 62 B2
Derriton Devon 8 D5
Derry Hill Wilts 24 B4
Derryguaig Argyll 146 H7
Derrythorpe N Lincs 90 D2
Dersingham Norf 80 D2
Dervaig Argyll 146 F7
Derwen Denb 72 D4
Derwenlas Powys 58 E4
Desborough Northants 64 F5
Desford Leics 63 D8
Detchant Northumb 123 F6
Detling Kent 29 D8
Deuddwr Powys 60 C2
Devauden Mon 36 E1
Devil's Bridge Ceredig 47 B6
Devizes Wilts 24 C5
Devol Invclyd 118 B3
Devonport Plym 6 D2
Devonside Clack 127 E8
Devoran Corn 3 C6
Dewar Borders 121 E6
Dewlish Dorset 13 E5
Dewsbury W Yorks 88 B3
Dewsbury Moor W Yorks 88 B3
Dewshall Court Hereford 49 F6
Dhoon IoM 84 D4
Dhoor IoM 84 C4
Dhowin IoM 84 B4
Dial Post W Sus 17 C5
Dibden Hants 14 D5
Dibden Purlieu Hants 14 D5
Dickleburgh Norf 68 F4
Didbrook Glos 51 F5
Didcot Oxon 39 F5
Diddington Cambs 54 C2
Diddlebury Shrops 60 F5
Didley Hereford 49 F6
Didling W Sus 16 C2
Didmarton Glos 37 F5
Didsbury Gtr Man 87 E6
Didworthy Devon 6 C4
Digby Lincs 78 D3
Digg Highld 149 B9
Diggle Gtr Man 87 D8
Digmoor Lancs 86 D2
Digswell Park Herts 41 C5
Dihewyd Ceredig 46 D3
Dilham Norf 69 B6
Dilhorne Staffs 75 E6
Dillarburn S Lanark 119 E8
Dillington Cambs 54 C2
Dilston Northumb 110 C2
Dilton Marsh Wilts 24 E3
Dilwyn Hereford 49 D6
Dinas Carms 45 F4
Dinas Gwyn 70 D3
Dinas Cross Pembs 45 F2
Dinas Dinlle Gwyn 82 F4
Dinas-Mawddwy Gwyn 59 C5
Dinas Powys V Glam 22 B3
Dinbych = Denbigh Denb 72 C4
Dinbych-Y-Pysgod = Tenby Pembs 32 D2
Dinder Som 23 E7
Dinedor Hereford 49 F7
Dingestow Mon 36 C1
Dingle Mers 85 F4
Dingleden Kent 18 B5
Dingley Northants 64 F4
Dingwall Highld 151 F8
Dinlabyre Borders 115 E8
Dinmael Conwy 72 E4
Dinnet Aberds 140 E3
Dinnington S Yorks 89 F6
Dinnington Som 12 C2
Dinnington T&W 110 B5
Dinorwic Gwyn 83 E5
Dinton Bucks 39 C7
Dinton Wilts 24 F5
Dinwoodie Mains Dumfries 114 E4
Dinworthy Devon 8 C5
Dippen N Ayrs 143 F11
Dippenhall Sur 27 E6
Dipple Moray 152 C3
Dipple S Ayrs 112 D2
Diptford Devon 6 D5
Dipton Durham 110 D4
Dirdhu Highld 139 B6
Dirleton E Loth 129 F7
Dirt Pot Northumb 109 E8
Discoed Powys 48 C4
Diseworth Leics 63 B8
Dishes Orkney 159 F7
Dishforth N Yorks 95 B6
Disley Ches E 87 F7
Diss Norf 56 B5
Disserth Powys 48 D2
Distington Cumb 98 B2
Ditchampton Wilts 25 F5
Ditcheat Som 23 F8
Ditchingham Norf 69 E6
Ditchling E Sus 17 C7
Ditherington Shrops 60 C5
Dittisham Devon 7 D6
Ditton Halton 86 F2
Ditton Kent 29 D8
Ditton Green Cambs 55 D7
Ditton Priors Shrops 61 F6
Divach Highld 137 B7
Divlyn Carms 47 F6
Dixton Glos 50 F4
Dixton Mon 36 C2
Dobcross Gtr Man 87 D7
Dobwalls Corn 5 C7
Doc Penfro = Pembroke Dock Pembs 44 E4
Doccombe Devon 10 F2
Dochfour Ho. Highld 151 H9
Dochgarroch Highld 151 G9
Docking Norf 80 D3
Docklow Hereford 49 D7
Dockray Cumb 99 B5
Dockroyd W Yorks 94 F3
Dodburn Borders 115 D7
Doddinghurst Essex 42 E1
Doddington Cambs 66 E3
Doddington Kent 30 D3
Doddington Lincs 78 B2
Doddington Northumb 123 F5
Doddington Shrops 49 B8
Doddiscombsleigh Devon 10 F3
Dodford Northants 52 C4
Dodford Worcs 50 B4
Dodington S Glos 24 A2
Dodleston Ches W 73 C7
Dods Leigh Staffs 75 F7
Dodworth S Yorks 88 D4
Doe Green Warr 86 F3
Doe Lea Derbys 76 C4
Dog Village Devon 10 E4
Dogdyke Lincs 78 D5
Dogmersfield Hants 27 D5
Dogridge Wilts 37 F7
Dogsthorpe Pboro 65 D8
Dol-fôr Powys 58 D5
Dôl-y-Bont Ceredig 58 F3
Dol-y-cannau Powys 48 E4
Dolanog Powys 59 C7
Dolau Powys 48 C3
Dolau Rhondda 34 F3
Dolbenmaen Gwyn 71 C6
Dolfach Powys 59 D6
Dolfor Powys 59 F8
Dolgarrog Conwy 83 E7
Dolgellau Gwyn 58 C4
Dolgran Carms 46 F3
Dolhendre Gwyn 72 F2
Doll Highld 157 J11
Dollar Clack 127 E8
Dolley Green Powys 48 C4
Dollwen Ceredig 58 F3
Dolphin Flint 73 B5
Dolphinholme Lancs 92 D5
Dolphinton S Lanark 120 E4
Dolton Devon 9 C7
Dolwen Conwy 83 D8
Dolwen Powys 59 D6
Dolwyd Conwy 83 D8
Dolwyddelan Conwy 83 F7
Dolyhir Powys 48 D4
Doncaster S Yorks 89 D6
Dones Green Ches W 74 B3
Donhead St Andrew Wilts 13 B7
Donhead St Mary Wilts 13 B7
Donibristle Fife 128 F3
Donington Lincs 78 F5
Donington on Bain Lincs 91 F6
Donington South Ing Lincs 78 F5
Donisthorpe Leics 63 C7
Donkey Town Sur 27 C7
Donnington Glos 38 B1
Donnington Hereford 50 F2
Donnington Shrops 61 D5
Donnington Telford 61 C7
Donnington W Berks 26 C2
Donnington W Sus 16 D2
Donnington Wood Telford 61 C7
Donyatt Som 11 C8
Doonfoot S Ayrs 112 C3
Dorback Lodge Highld 139 C6
Dorchester Dorset 12 E4
Dorchester Oxon 39 E5
Dordon Warks 63 D6
Dore S Yorks 88 F4
Dores Highld 151 H8
Dorking Sur 28 E2
Dormansland Sur 28 E5
Dormanstown Redcar 102 B3
Dormington Hereford 49 E7
Dormston Worcs 50 D4
Dornal S Ayrs 105 B6
Dorney Bucks 27 B7
Dornie Highld 149 F13
Dornoch Highld 151 C10
Dornock Dumfries 108 C2
Dorrery Highld 158 E2
Dorridge W Mid 51 B6
Dorrington Lincs 78 D3
Dorrington Shrops 60 D4
Dorsington Warks 51 E6
Dorstone Hereford 48 E5
Dorton Bucks 39 C6
Dorusduain Highld 136 B2
Dosthill Staffs 63 E6
Dottery Dorset 12 E2
Doublebois Corn 5 C6
Dougarie N Ayrs 143 E9
Doughton Glos 37 E5
Douglas IoM 84 E3
Douglas S Lanark 119 F8
Douglas & Angus Dundee 134 F4
Douglas Water S Lanark 119 F8
Douglas West S Lanark 119 F8
Douglastown Angus 134 E4
Doulting Som 23 E8
Dounby Orkney 159 F3
Doune Highld 156 J7
Doune Stirling 127 D6
Doune Park Aberds 153 B7
Douneside Aberds 140 D3
Dounie Highld 151 B8
Dounreay Highld 157 C12
Dousland Devon 6 C3
Dovaston Shrops 60 B3
Dove Holes Derbys 75 B7
Dovenby Cumb 107 F7
Dover Kent 31 E7
Dovercourt Essex 57 F6
Doverdale Worcs 50 C3
Doveridge Derbys 75 F8
Doversgreen Sur 28 E3
Dowally Perth 133 E7
Dowbridge Lancs 92 F4
Dowdeswell Glos 37 C6
Dowlais M Tydf 34 D4
Dowland Devon 9 C7
Dowlish Wake Som 11 C8
Down Ampney Glos 37 E8
Down Hatherley Glos 37 B5
Down St Mary Devon 10 D2
Down Thomas Devon 6 D3
Downcraig Ferry N Ayrs 145 H10
Downderry Corn 5 D8
Downe London 28 C5
Downend IoW 15 F6
Downend S Glos 23 B8
Downend W Berks 26 B2
Downfield Dundee 134 F3
Downgate Corn 5 B8
Downham Essex 42 E3
Downham Lancs 93 E7
Downham Northumb 122 F4
Downham Market Norf 67 D6
Downhead Som 23 E8
Downhill Perth 133 F7
Downhill T&W 111 D6
Downholland Cross Lancs 85 D4
Downholme N Yorks 101 E6
Downies Aberds 141 E8
Downley Bucks 39 E8
Downside Som 23 E8
Downside Sur 28 D2
Downton Hants 14 E3
Downton Wilts 14 B2
Downton on the Rock Hereford 49 B6
Dowsby Lincs 65 B8
Dowsdale Lincs 66 C2
Dowthwaitehead Cumb 99 B5
Doxey Staffs 62 B3
Doxford Northumb 117 B7
Doxford Park T&W 111 D6
Doynton S Glos 24 B2
Draffan S Lanark 119 E7
Dragonby N Lincs 90 C3
Drakeland Corner Devon 6 D3
Drakemyre N Ayrs 118 D2
Drake's Broughton Worcs 50 E4
Drakes Cross Worcs 51 B5
Drakewalls Corn 6 B2
Draughton N Yorks 94 D3
Draughton Northants 53 B5
Drax N Yorks 89 B7
Draycote Warks 52 B2
Draycott Derbys 76 F4
Draycott Glos 51 F6
Draycott Som 23 D6
Draycott in the Clay Staffs 63 B5
Draycott in the Moors Staffs 75 E6
Drayford Devon 10 C2
Drayton Leics 64 E5
Drayton Lincs 78 F5
Drayton Norf 68 C4
Drayton Oxon 38 E4
Drayton Oxon 52 E2
Drayton Ptsmth 15 D7
Drayton Som 12 B2
Drayton Worcs 50 B4
Drayton Bassett Staffs 63 D5
Drayton Beauchamp Bucks 40 C2
Drayton Parslow Bucks 39 B8
Drayton St Leonard Oxon 39 E5
Dre-fach Carms 33 C7
Dre-fach Ceredig 46 E4
Drebley N Yorks 94 D3
Dreemskerry IoM 84 C4
Dreenhill Pembs 44 D4
Drefach Carms 33 C6
Drefach Carms 46 F2
Drefelin Carms 46 F2
Dreghorn N Ayrs 118 F3
Drellingore Kent 31 E6
Drem E Loth 121 B8
Dresden Stoke 75 E6
Dreumasdal W Isles 148 E2
Drewsteignton Devon 10 E2
Driby Lincs 79 B6
Driffield E Yorks 97 D6
Driffield Glos 37 E7
Drigg Cumb 98 E2
Drighlington W Yorks 88 B3
Drimnin Highld 147 F8
Drimpton Dorset 12 D2
Drimsynie Argyll 125 E7
Drinisiadar W Isles 154 H6
Drinkstone Suff 56 C3
Drinkstone Green Suff 56 C3
Drishaig Argyll 125 D7
Drissaig Argyll 124 D5
Drochil Borders 120 E4
Drointon Staffs 62 B4
Droitwich Spa Worcs 50 C3
Droman Highld 156 D4
Dron Perth 128 C3
Dronfield Derbys 76 B3
Dronfield Woodhouse Derbys 76 B3
Drongan E Ayrs 112 C4
Dronley Angus 134 F3
Droxford Hants 15 C7
Droylsden Gtr Man 87 E7
Druid Denb 72 E4
Druidston Pembs 44 D3
Druimarbin Highld 130 B4
Druimavuic Argyll 130 E4
Druimdrishaig Argyll 144 F6
Druimindarroch Highld 147 C9
Druimyeon More Argyll 143 C7
Drum Argyll 145 F8
Drum Perth 128 D2
Drumbeg Highld 156 F4
Drumblade Aberds 152 D5
Drumblair Aberds 153 D6
Drumbuie Dumfries 113 F5
Drumbuie Highld 149 E12
Drumburgh Cumb 108 D2
Drumburn Dumfries 107 C6
Drumchapel Glasgow 118 B5
Drumchardine Highld 151 G8
Drumchork Highld 155 J13
Drumclog S Lanark 119 F6
Drumderfit Highld 151 F9
Drumeldrie Fife 129 D6
Drumelzier Borders 120 F4
Drumfearn Highld 149 G11
Drumgask Highld 138 E2
Drumgley Angus 134 D4
Drumguish Highld 138 E3
Drumin Moray 152 E1
Drumlasie Aberds 140 D5
Drumlemble Argyll 143 G7
Drumligair Aberds 141 C8
Drumlithie Aberds 141 F6
Drummoddie Dumfries 105 E7
Drummond Highld 151 E9
Drummore Dumfries 104 F5
Drummuir Moray 152 D3
Drummuir Castle Moray 152 D3
Drumnadrochit Highld 137 B8
Drumnagorrach Moray 152 C5
Drumoak Aberds 141 E6
Drumpark Dumfries 107 A5
Drumphail Dumfries 105 C6
Drumrash Dumfries 106 B3
Drumrunie Highld 156 J4
Drums Aberds 141 B8
Drumsallie Highld 130 B3
Drumstinchall Dumfries 107 D5
Drumsturdy Angus 134 F4
Drumtochty Castle Aberds 135 B6
Drumtroddan Dumfries 105 E7
Drumuie Highld 149 D9
Drumuillie Highld 138 B5
Drumvaich Stirling 127 D5
Drumwhindle Aberds 153 E9
Drunkendub Angus 135 E6
Drury Flint 73 C6
Drury Square Norf 68 C2
Dry Doddington Lincs 77 E8
Dry Drayton Cambs 54 C4
Drybeck Cumb 100 C1
Drybridge Moray 152 B4
Drybridge N Ayrs 118 F3
Drybrook Glos 36 C3
Dryburgh Borders 121 F8
Dryhope Borders 115 B5
Drylaw Edin 120 B5
Drym Corn 2 C5
Drymen Stirling 126 F3
Drymuir Aberds 153 D9
Drynoch Highld 149 E9
Dryslwyn Carms 33 B6
Dryton Shrops 61 D5
Dubford Aberds 153 B8
Dubton Angus 135 D5
Duchally Highld 156 H6
Duchlage Argyll 126 F2
Duck Corner Suff 57 E7
Duckington Ches W 73 D8
Ducklington Oxon 38 D3
Duckmanton Derbys 76 B4
Duck's Cross Bedford 54 D2
Duddenhoe End Essex 55 F5
Duddingston Edin 121 B5
Duddington Northants 65 D6
Duddleswell E Sus 17 B8
Duddo Northumb 122 E5
Duddon Ches W 74 C2
Duddon Bridge Cumb 98 F4
Dudleston Shrops 73 F7
Dudleston Heath Shrops 73 F7
Dudley T&W 111 B5
Dudley W Mid 62 E3
Dudley Port W Mid 62 E3
Duffield Derbys 76 E3
Duffryn Neath 34 E2
Duffryn Newport 35 F6
Dufftown Moray 152 E3
Duffus Moray 152 B1
Dufton Cumb 100 B1
Duggleby N Yorks 96 C4
Duirinish Highld 149 E12
Duisdalemore Highld 149 G12
Duisky Highld 130 B4
Dukestown Bl Gwent 35 C5
Dukinfield Gtr Man 87 E7
Dulas Anglesey 82 C4
Dulcote Som 23 E7
Dulford Devon 11 D5
Dull Perth 133 E5
Dullatur N Lanark 119 B7
Dullingham Cambs 55 D7
Dulnain Bridge Highld 139 B5
Duloe Bedford 54 C2
Duloe Corn 5 D7
Dulsie Highld 151 G12
Dulverton Som 10 B4
Dulwich London 28 B4
Dumbarton W Dunb 118 B3
Dumbleton Glos 50 F5
Dumcrieff Dumfries 114 D4
Dumfries Dumfries 107 B6
Dumgoyne Stirling 126 F4
Dummer Hants 26 E3
Dumpford W Sus 16 B2
Dumpton Kent 31 C7
Dun Angus 135 D6
Dun Charlabhaigh W Isles 154 C6
Dunain Ho. Highld 151 G9
Dunalastair Perth 132 D4
Dunan Highld 149 F10
Dunans Argyll 145 D9
Dunball Som 22 E5
Dunbar E Loth 122 B2
Dunbeath Highld 158 H3
Dunbeg Argyll 124 B4
Dunblane Stirling 127 D6
Dunbog Fife 128 C4
Duncanston Highld 151 F8
Duncanstone Aberds 140 B4
Dunchurch Warks 52 B2
Duncote Northants 52 D4
Duncow Dumfries 114 F2
Duncraggan Stirling 126 D4
Duncrievie Perth 128 D3
Duncton W Sus 16 C3
Dundas Ho. Orkney 159 K5
Dundee Dundee 134 F4
Dundeugh Dumfries 113 F5
Dundon Som 23 F6
Dundonald S Ayrs 118 F3
Dundonnell Highld 150 C3
Dundonnell Hotel Highld 150 C3
Dundonnell House Highld 150 C4
Dundraw Cumb 108 E2
Dundreggan Highld 137 C6
Dundreggan Lodge Highld 137 C6
Dundrennan Dumfries 106 E4
Dundry N Som 23 C7
Dunecht Aberds 141 D6
Dunfermline Fife 128 F2
Dunfield Glos 37 E8
Dunford Bridge S Yorks 88 D2
Dungworth S Yorks 88 F3
Dunham Notts 77 B8
Dunham-on-the-Hill Ches W 73 B8

Dunham Town Gtr Man 86 F5
Dunhampton Worcs 50 C3
Dunholme Lincs 78 B3
Dunino Fife 129 C7
Dunipace Falk 127 F7
Dunira Perth 127 B6
Dunkeld Perth 133 E7
Dunkerton Bath 24 D2
Dunkeswell Devon 11 D6
Dunkeswick N Yorks 95 E6
Dunkirk Kent 30 D4
Dunkirk Norf 81 E8
Dunk's Green Kent 29 D7
Dunlappie Angus 135 C5
Dunley Hants 26 D2
Dunley Worcs 50 C2
Dunlichity Lodge Highld 151 H9
Dunlop E Ayrs 118 E4
Dunmaglass Lodge Highld 137 B8
Dunmore Argyll 144 G6
Dunmore Falk 127 F7
Dunnet Highld 158 C4
Dunnichen Angus 135 E5
Dunninald Angus 135 D7
Dunning Perth 128 C2
Dunnington E Yorks 97 D7
Dunnington Warks 51 D5
Dunnington York 96 D2
Dunnockshaw Lancs 87 B6
Dunollie Argyll 124 B4
Dunoon Argyll 145 F10
Dunragit Dumfries 105 D5
Dunrostan Argyll 144 E6
Duns Borders 122 D3
Duns Tew Oxon 38 B4
Dunsby Lincs 65 B8
Dunscore Dumfries 113 F8
Dunscroft S Yorks 89 D7
Dunsdale Redcar 102 C4
Dunsden Green Oxon 26 B5
Dunsfold Sur 27 F8
Dunsford Devon 10 F3
Dunshalt Fife 128 C4
Dunshillock Aberds 153 D9
Dunskey Ho. Dumfries 104 D4
Dunsley N Yorks 103 C6
Dunsmore Bucks 40 D1
Dunsop Bridge Lancs 93 D6
Dunstable C Beds 40 B3
Dunstall Staffs 63 B5
Dunstall Common Worcs 50 E3
Dunstall Green Suff 55 C8
Dunstan Northumb 117 C8
Dunstan Steads Northumb 117 B8
Dunster Som 21 E8
Dunston Lincs 78 C3
Dunston Norf 68 D5
Dunston Staffs 62 C3
Dunston T&W 110 C5
Dunsville S Yorks 89 D7
Dunswell E Yorks 97 F6
Dunsyre S Lanark 120 E3
Dunterton Devon 5 B8
Duntisbourne Abbots Glos 37 D6
Duntisbourne Leer Glos 37 D6
Duntisbourne Rouse Glos 37 D6
Duntish Dorset 12 D4
Duntocher W Dunb 118 B4
Dunton Bucks 39 B8
Dunton C Beds 54 E3
Dunton Norf 80 D4
Dunton Bassett Leics 64 E2
Dunton Green Kent 29 D6
Dunton Wayletts Essex 42 E2
Duntulm Highld 149 A9
Dunure S Ayrs 112 C2
Dunvant Swansea 33 E6
Dunvegan Highld 148 D7
Dunwich Suff 57 B8
Dunwood Staffs 75 D6
Dupplin Castle Perth 128 C2
Durdar Cumb 108 D4
Durgates E Sus 18 B3
Durham Durham 111 E5
Durisdeer Dumfries 113 D8
Durisdeermill Dumfries 113 D8
Durkar W Yorks 88 C4
Durleigh Som 22 F4
Durley Hants 15 C6
Durley Wilts 25 C7
Durnamuck Highld 150 B3
Durness Highld 156 C7
Durno Aberds 141 B6
Duror Highld 130 D3
Durran Argyll 125 E5
Durran Highld 158 D3
Durrington W Sus 16 D5
Durrington Wilts 25 E6
Dursley Glos 36 E4
Durston Som 11 B7
Durweston Dorset 13 D6
Dury Shetland 160 G6
Duston Northants 52 C5
Duthil Highld 138 B5
Dutlas Powys 48 B4
Duton Hill Essex 42 B2
Dutson Corn 8 F5
Dutton Ches W 74 B2
Duxford Cambs 55 E5
Duxford Oxon 38 E3
Dwygyfylchi Conwy 83 D7
Dwyran Anglesey 82 E4
Dyce Aberdeen 141 C7
Dye House Northumb 110 D2
Dyffryn Bridgend 34 E2
Dyffryn Carms 32 B4
Dyffryn Pembs 44 B4
Dyffryn Ardudwy Gwyn 71 E6
Dyffryn Castell Ceredig 58 F4
Dyffryn Ceidrych Carms 33 B8
Dyffryn Cellwen Neath 34 D2
Dyke Lincs 65 B8
Dyke Moray 151 F12
Dykehead Angus 134 C3
Dykehead N Lanark 119 D8
Dykehead Stirling 126 E4
Dykelands Aberds 135 C7
Dykends Angus 134 D2
Dykeside Aberds 153 D7
Dykesmains N Ayrs 118 E2
Dylife Powys 59 E5
Dymchurch Kent 19 C7
Dymock Glos 50 F2
Dyrham S Glos 24 B2
Dysart Fife 128 E5
Dyserth Denb 72 B4

E

Eachwick Northumb 110 B4
Eadar Dha Fhadhail W Isles 154 D5
Eagland Hill Lancs 92 E4
Eagle Lincs 77 C8
Eagle Barnsdale Lincs 77 C8
Eagle Moor Lincs 77 C8
Eaglescliffe Stockton 102 C2
Eaglesfield Cumb 98 B2
Eaglesfield Dumfries 108 B2
Eaglesham E Renf 119 D5
Eaglethorpe Northants 65 E7
Eairy IoM 84 E2
Eakley Lanes M Keynes 53 D6
Eakring Notts 77 C6
Ealand N Lincs 89 C8
Ealing London 40 F4
Eals Northumb 109 D6
Eamont Bridge Cumb 99 B7
Earby Lancs 94 E2
Earcroft Blackburn 86 B4
Eardington Shrops 61 E7
Eardisland Hereford 49 D6
Eardisley Hereford 48 E5
Eardiston Shrops 60 B3
Eardiston Worcs 49 C8
Earith Cambs 54 B4
Earl Shilton Leics 63 E8
Earl Soham Suff 57 C6
Earl Sterndale Derbys 75 C7
Earl Stonham Suff 56 D5
Earle Northumb 117 B5
Earley Wokingham 27 B5
Earlham Norf 68 D5
Earlish Highld 149 B8
Earls Barton Northants 53 C6
Earls Colne Essex 42 B4
Earl's Croome Worcs 50 E3
Earl's Green Suff 56 C4
Earlsdon W Mid 51 B8
Earlsferry Fife 129 E6
Earlsfield Lincs 78 F2
Earlsford Aberds 153 E8
Earlsheaton W Yorks 88 B3
Earlsmill Moray 151 F12
Earlston Borders 121 F8
Earlston E Ayrs 118 F4
Earlswood Mon 36 E1
Earlswood Sur 28 E3
Earlswood Warks 51 B6
Earnley W Sus 16 E2
Earsairidh W Isles 148 J2
Earsdon T&W 111 B6
Earsham Norf 69 F6
Earswick York 96 D2
Eartham W Sus 16 D3
Easby N Yorks 101 D6
Easby N Yorks 102 D3
Easdale Argyll 124 D3
Easebourne W Sus 16 B2
Easenhall Warks 52 B2
Eashing Sur 27 E7
Easington Bucks 39 C6
Easington Durham 111 E7
Easington E Yorks 91 C7
Easington Northumb 123 F7
Easington Oxon 39 E6
Easington Oxon 52 F2
Easington Redcar 103 C5
Easington Colliery Durham 111 E7
Easington Lane T&W 111 E6
Easingwold N Yorks 95 C8
Easole Street Kent 31 D6
Eassie Angus 134 E3
East Aberthaw V Glam 22 C2
East Adderbury Oxon 52 F2
East Allington Devon 7 E5
East Anstey Devon 10 B3
East Appleton N Yorks 101 E7
East Ardsley W Yorks 88 B4
East Ashling W Sus 16 D2
East Auchronie Aberds 141 D7
East Ayton N Yorks 103 F7
East Bank Bl Gwent 35 D6
East Barkwith Lincs 91 F5
East Barming Kent 29 D8
East Barnby N Yorks 103 C6
East Barnet London 41 E5
East Barns E Loth 122 B3
East Barsham Norf 80 D5
East Beckham Norf 81 D7
East Bedfont London 27 B8
East Bergholt Suff 56 F4
East Bilney Norf 68 C2
East Blatchington E Sus 17 D8
East Boldre Hants 14 D4
East Brent Som 22 D5
East Bridgford Notts 77 E6
East Buckland Devon 21 F5
East Budleigh Devon 11 F5
East Burrafirth Shetland 160 H5
East Burton Dorset 13 F6
East Butsfield Durham 110 E4
East Butterwick N Lincs 90 D2
East Cairnbeg Aberds 135 B7
East Calder W Loth 120 C3
East Carleton Norf 68 D4
East Carlton Northants 64 F5
East Carlton W Yorks 94 E5
East Chaldon Dorset 13 F5
East Challow Oxon 38 F3
East Chiltington E Sus 17 C7
East Chinnock Som 12 C2
East Chisenbury Wilts 25 D6
East Clandon Sur 27 D8
East Claydon Bucks 39 B7
East Clyne Highld 157 J12
East Coker Som 12 C3
East Combe Som 22 F3
East Common N Yorks 96 F2
East Compton Som 23 E8
East Cottingwith E Yorks 96 E3
East Cowes IoW 15 E6
East Cowick E Yorks 89 B7
East Cowton N Yorks 101 D8
East Cramlington Northumb 111 B5
East Cranmore Som 23 E8
East Creech Dorset 13 F7
East Croachy Highld 138 B2
East Croftmore Highld 139 C5
East Curthwaite Cumb 108 E3
East Dean E Sus 18 F2
East Dean Hants 14 B3
East Dean W Sus 16 C3
East Down Devon 20 E5
East Drayton Notts 77 B7
East Ella Hull 90 B4
East End Dorset 13 E7
East End E Yorks 91 B6
East End Hants 14 E4
East End Hants 15 B7
East End Hants 26 C2
East End Herts 41 B7
East End Kent 18 B5
East End N Som 23 B6
East End Oxon 38 C3
East Farleigh Kent 29 D8
East Farndon Northants 64 F4
East Ferry Lincs 90 E2
East Fortune E Loth 121 B8
East Garston W Berks 25 B8
East Ginge Oxon 38 F4
East Goscote Leics 64 C3
East Grafton Wilts 25 C7
East Grimstead Wilts 14 B3
East Grinstead W Sus 28 F4
East Guldeford E Sus 19 C6
East Haddon Northants 52 C4
East Hagbourne Oxon 39 F5
East Halton N Lincs 90 C5
East Ham London 41 F7
East Hanney Oxon 38 E4
East Hanningfield Essex 42 D3
East Hardwick W Yorks 89 C5
East Harling Norf 68 F2
East Harlsey N Yorks 102 E2
East Harnham Wilts 14 B2
East Harptree Bath 23 D7
East Hartford Northumb 111 B5
East Harting W Sus 15 C8
East Hatley Cambs 54 D3
East Hauxwell N Yorks 101 E6
East Haven Angus 135 F5
East Heckington Lincs 78 E4
East Hedleyhope Durham 110 E4
East Hendred Oxon 38 F4
East Herrington T&W 111 D6
East Heslerton N Yorks 96 B5
East Hoathly E Sus 18 D2
East Horrington Som 23 E7
East Horsley Sur 27 D8
East Horton Northumb 123 F6
East Huntspill Som 22 E5
East Hyde C Beds 40 C4
East Ilkerton Devon 21 E6
East Ilsley W Berks 38 F4
East Keal Lincs 79 C6
East Kennett Wilts 25 C6
East Keswick W Yorks 95 E6
East Kilbride S Lanark 119 D6
East Kirkby Lincs 79 C6
East Knapton N Yorks 96 B4
East Knighton Dorset 13 F6
East Knoyle Wilts 24 F3
East Kyloe Northumb 123 F6
East Lambrook Som 12 C2
East Lamington Highld 151 D10
East Langdon Kent 31 E7
East Langton Leics 64 E4
East Langwell Highld 157 J10
East Lavant W Sus 16 D2
East Lavington W Sus 16 C3
East Layton N Yorks 101 D6
East Leake Notts 64 B2
East Learmouth Northumb 122 F4
East Leigh Devon 9 D8
East Lexham Norf 67 C8
East Lilburn Northumb 117 B6
East Linton E Loth 121 B8
East Liss Hants 15 B8
East Looe Corn 5 D7
East Lound N Lincs 89 E8
East Lulworth Dorset 13 F6
East Lutton N Yorks 96 C5
East Lydford Som 23 F7
East Mains Aberds 141 E5
East Malling Kent 29 D8
East March Angus 134 F4
East Marden W Sus 16 C2
East Markham Notts 77 B7
East Marton N Yorks 94 D2
East Meon Hants 15 B7
East Mere Devon 10 C4
East Mersea Essex 43 C6
East Mey Highld 158 C5
East Molesey Sur 28 C2
East Morden Dorset 13 E7
East Morton W Yorks 94 E3
East Ness N Yorks 96 B2
East Newton E Yorks 97 F8
East Norton Leics 64 D4
East Nynehead Som 11 B6
East Oakley Hants 26 D3
East Ogwell Devon 7 B6
East Orchard Dorset 13 C6
East Ord Northumb 123 D5
East Panson Devon 9 E5
East Peckham Kent 29 E7
East Pennard Som 23 F7
East Perry Cambs 54 C2
East Portlemouth Devon 6 F5
East Prawle Devon 7 F5
East Preston W Sus 16 D4
East Putford Devon 9 C5
East Quantoxhead Som 22 E3
East Rainton T&W 111 E6
East Ravendale NE Lincs 91 E6
East Raynham Norf 80 E4
East Rhidorroch Lodge Highld 150 B5
East Rigton W Yorks 95 E6
East Rounton N Yorks 102 D2
East Row N Yorks 103 C6
East Rudham Norf 80 E4
East Runton Norf 81 C7
East Ruston Norf 69 B6
East Saltoun E Loth 121 C7
East Sleekburn Northumb 117 F8
East Somerton Norf 69 C7
East Stockwith Lincs 89 E8
East Stoke Dorset 13 F6
East Stoke Notts 77 E7
East Stour Dorset 13 B6
East Stourmouth Kent 31 C6
East Stowford Devon 9 B8
East Stratton Hants 26 F3
East Studdal Kent 31 E7
East Suisnish Highld 149 E10
East Taphouse Corn 5 C6
East-the-Water Devon 9 B6
East Thirston Northumb 117 E7
East Tilbury Thurrock 29 B7
East Tisted Hants 26 F5
East Torrington Lincs 90 F5
East Tuddenham Norf 68 C3
East Tytherley Hants 14 B3
East Tytherton Wilts 24 B4
East Village Devon 10 D3
East Wall Shrops 60 E5
East Walton Norf 67 C7
East Wellow Hants 14 B4
East Wemyss Fife 128 E5
East Whitburn W Loth 120 C2
East Williamston Pembs 32 D1
East Winch Norf 67 C6
East Winterslow Wilts 25 F7
East Wittering W Sus 15 E8
East Witton N Yorks 101 F6
East Woodburn Northumb 116 F5
East Woodhay Hants 26 C2
East Worldham Hants 26 F5
East Worlington Devon 10 C2
East Worthing W Sus 17 D5
Eastbourne E Sus 18 F3
Eastbridge Suff 57 C8
Eastburn W Yorks 94 E3
Eastbury London 40 E3
Eastbury W Berks 25 B8
Eastby N Yorks 94 D3
Eastchurch Kent 30 B3
Eastcombe Glos 37 D5
Eastcote London 40 F4
Eastcote Northants 52 D4
Eastcote W Mid 51 B6
Eastcott Corn 8 C4
Eastcott Wilts 24 D5
Eastcourt Wilts 25 C7
Eastcourt Wilts 37 E6
Easter Ardross Highld 151 D9
Easter Balmoral Aberds 139 E8
Easter Boleskine Highld 137 B8
Easter Compton S Glos 36 F2
Easter Cringate Stirling 127 F6
Easter Davoch Aberds 140 D3
Easter Earshaig Dumfries 114 D3
Easter Fearn Highld 151 C9
Easter Galcantray Highld 151 G11
Easter Howgate Midloth 120 C5
Easter Howlaws Borders 122 E3
Easter Kinkell Highld 151 F8
Easter Lednathie Angus 134 C3
Easter Milton Highld 151 F12
Easter Moniack Highld 151 G8
Easter Ord Aberdeen 141 D7
Easter Quarff Shetland 160 K6
Easter Rhynd Perth 128 C3
Easter Row Stirling 127 E6
Easter Silverford Aberds 153 B7
Easter Skeld Shetland 160 J5
Easter Whyntie Aberds 152 B6
Eastergate W Sus 16 D3
Easterhouse Glasgow 119 C6
Eastern Green W Mid 63 F6
Easterton Wilts 24 D5
Eastertown Som 22 D5
Eastertown of Auchleuchries Aberds 153 E10
Eastfield N Lanark 119 C8
Eastfield N Yorks 103 F8
Eastfield Hall Northumb 117 D8
Eastgate Durham 110 F2
Eastgate Norf 81 E7
Eastham Mers 85 F4
Eastham Ferry Mers 85 F4
Easthampstead Brack 27 C6
Eastheath Wokingham 27 C6
Easthope Shrops 61 E5
Easthorpe Essex 43 B5
Easthorpe Leics 77 F8
Easthorpe Notts 77 D7
Easthouses Midloth 121 C6
Eastington Devon 10 D2
Eastington Glos 36 D4
Eastington Glos 37 C8
Eastleach Martin Glos 38 D2
Eastleach Turville Glos 38 D1
Eastleigh Devon 9 B6
Eastleigh Hants 14 C5
Eastling Kent 30 D3
Eastmoor Derbys 76 B3
Eastmoor Norf 67 D7
Eastney Ptsmth 15 E7
Eastnor Hereford 50 F2
Eastoft N Lincs 90 C2
Eastoke Hants 15 E8
Easton Cambs 54 B2
Easton Cumb 108 B4
Easton Cumb 108 D2
Easton Devon 10 F2
Easton Dorset 12 G4
Easton Hants 26 F3
Easton Lincs 65 B6
Easton Norf 68 C4
Easton Som 23 E7
Easton Suff 57 D6
Easton Wilts 24 B3
Easton Grey Wilts 37 F5
Easton-in-Gordano N Som 23 B7
Easton Maudit Northants 53 D6
Easton on the Hill Northants 65 D7
Easton Royal Wilts 25 C7
Eastpark Dumfries 107 C7
Eastrea Cambs 66 E2
Eastriggs Dumfries 108 C2
Eastrington E Yorks 89 B8
Eastry Kent 31 D7
Eastville Bristol 23 B8
Eastville Lincs 79 D7
Eastwell Leics 64 B4
Eastwick Herts 41 C7
Eastwick Shetland 160 F5
Eastwood Notts 76 E4
Eastwood Southend 42 F4
Eastwood W Yorks 87 B7
Eathorpe Warks 51 C8
Eaton Ches E 75 C5
Eaton Ches W 74 C2
Eaton Leics 64 B4
Eaton Norf 68 D5
Eaton Notts 77 B7
Eaton Oxon 38 D4
Eaton Shrops 60 F3
Eaton Shrops 60 F5
Eaton Bishop Hereford 49 F6
Eaton Bray C Beds 40 B2
Eaton Constantine Shrops 61 D5
Eaton Green C Beds 40 B2
Eaton Hastings Oxon 38 E2
Eaton on Tern Shrops 61 B6
Eaton Socon Cambs 54 D2
Eavestone N Yorks 94 C5
Ebberston N Yorks 103 F6
Ebbesbourne Wake Wilts 13 B7
Ebbw Vale = Glyn Ebwy Bl Gwent 35 D5
Ebchester Durham 110 D4
Ebford Devon 10 F4
Ebley Glos 37 D5
Ebnal Ches W 73 E8
Ebrington Glos 51 E6
Ecchinswell Hants 26 D2
Ecclaw Borders 122 C3
Ecclefechan Dumfries 107 B8
Eccles Borders 122 E3
Eccles Gtr Man 87 E5
Eccles Kent 29 C8
Eccles on Sea Norf 69 B7
Eccles Road Norf 68 E3
Ecclesall S Yorks 88 F4
Ecclesfield S Yorks 88 E4
Ecclesgreig Aberds 135 C7
Eccleshall Staffs 62 B2
Eccleshill W Yorks 94 F4
Ecclesmachan W Loth 120 B3
Eccleston Ches W 73 C8
Eccleston Lancs 86 C3
Eccleston Mers 86 E2
Eccleston Park Mers 86 E2
Eccup W Yorks 95 E5
Echt Aberds 141 D6
Eckford Borders 116 B3
Eckington Derbys 76 B4
Eckington Worcs 50 E4
Ecton Northants 53 C6
Edale Derbys 88 F2
Edburton W Sus 17 C6
Edderside Cumb 107 E7
Edderton Highld 151 C10
Eddistone Devon 8 B4
Eddleston Borders 120 E5
Eden Park London 28 C4
Edenbridge Kent 28 E5
Edenfield Lancs 87 C5
Edenhall Cumb 109 F5
Edenham Lincs 65 B7
Edensor Derbys 76 C2
Edentaggart Argyll 126 E2
Edenthorpe S Yorks 89 D7
Edentown Cumb 108 D3
Ederline Argyll 124 E4
Edern Gwyn 70 D3
Edgarley Som 23 F7
Edgbaston W Mid 62 F4
Edgcott Bucks 39 B6
Edgcott Som 21 F7
Edge Shrops 60 D3
Edge End Glos 36 C2
Edge Green Ches W 73 D8
Edge Hill Mers 85 F4
Edgebolton Shrops 61 B5
Edgefield Norf 81 D6
Edgefield Street Norf 81 D6
Edgeside Lancs 87 B6
Edgeworth Glos 37 D6
Edgmond Telford 61 C7
Edgmond Marsh Telford 61 B7
Edgton Shrops 60 F3
Edgware London 40 E4
Edgworth Blackburn 86 C5
Edinample Stirling 126 B4
Edinbane Highld 149 C8
Edinburgh Edin 121 B5
Edingale Staffs 63 C6
Edingight Ho. Moray 152 C5
Edingley Notts 77 D6
Edingthorpe Norf 69 A6
Edingthorpe Green Norf 69 A6
Edington Som 23 F5
Edington Wilts 24 D4
Edintore Moray 152 D4
Edith Weston Rutland 65 D6
Edithmead Som 22 E5
Edlesborough Bucks 40 C2
Edlingham Northumb 117 D7
Edlington Lincs 78 B5
Edmondsham Dorset 13 C8
Edmondsley Durham 110 E5
Edmondthorpe Leics 65 C5
Edmonstone Orkney 159 F6
Edmonton London 41 E6
Edmundbyers Durham 110 D3
Ednam Borders 122 F3
Ednaston Derbys 76 E2
Edradynate Perth 133 D5
Edrom Borders 122 D4
Edstaston Shrops 74 F2
Edstone Warks 51 C6
Edvin Loach Hereford 49 D8
Edwalton Notts 77 F5
Edwardstone Suff 56 E3
Edwinsford Carms 46 F5
Edwinstowe Notts 77 C6
Edworth C Beds 54 E3
Edwyn Ralph Hereford 49 D8
Edzell Angus 135 C5
Efail Isaf Rhondda 34 F4
Efailnewydd Gwyn 70 D4
Efailwen Carms 32 B2
Efenechtyd Denb 72 D5
Effingham Sur 28 D2
Effirth Shetland 160 H5
Efford Devon 10 D3
Egdon Worcs 50 D4
Egerton Gtr Man 86 C5
Egerton Kent 30 E3
Egerton Forstal Kent 30 E2
Eggborough N Yorks 89 B6
Eggbuckland Plym 6 D3
Eggington C Beds 40 B2
Egginton Derbys 63 B6
Egglescliffe Stockton 102 C2
Eggleston Durham 100 B4
Egham Sur 27 B8
Egleton Rutland 65 D5
Eglingham Northumb 117 C7
Egloshayle Corn 4 B5
Egloskerry Corn 8 F4
Eglwys-Brewis V Glam 22 C2
Eglwys Cross Wrex 73 E8
Eglwys Fach Ceredig 58 E3
Eglwysbach Conwy 83 D8
Eglwyswen Pembs 45 F3
Eglwyswrw Pembs 45 F3
Egmanton Notts 77 C7
Egremont Cumb 98 C2
Egremont Mers 85 E4
Egton N Yorks 103 D6
Egton Bridge N Yorks 103 D6
Eight Ash Green Essex 43 B5
Eignaig Highld 130 E1
Eil Highld 138 C4
Eilanreach Highld 149 G13
Eilean Darach Highld 150 C4
Eileanach Lodge Highld 151 E8
Einacleite W Isles 154 E6
Eisgean W Isles 155 F8
Eisingrug Gwyn 71 D7
Elan Village Powys 47 C8
Elberton S Glos 36 F3
Elburton Plym 6 D3
Elcho Perth 128 B3
Elcombe Swindon 37 F8
Eldernell Cambs 66 E3
Eldersfield Worcs 50 F3
Elderslie Renfs 118 C4
Eldon Durham 101 B7
Eldrick S Ayrs 112 F2
Eldroth N Yorks 93 C7
Eldwick W Yorks 94 E4
Elfhowe Cumb 99 E6
Elford Northumb 123 F7
Elford Staffs 63 C5
Elgin Moray 152 B2
Elgol Highld 149 G10
Elham Kent 31 E5
Elie Fife 129 D6
Elim Anglesey 82 C3
Eling Hants 14 C4
Elishader Highld 149 B10
Elishaw Northumb 116 E4
Elkesley Notts 77 B6
Elkstone Glos 37 C6
Ellan Highld 138 B4
Elland W Yorks 88 B2
Ellary Argyll 144 F6
Ellastone Staffs 75 E8
Ellemford Borders 122 C3
Ellenbrook IoM 84 E3
Ellenhall Staffs 62 B2
Ellen's Green Sur 27 F8
Ellerbeck N Yorks 102 E2
Ellerburn N Yorks 103 F6
Ellerby N Yorks 103 C5
Ellerdine Heath Telford 61 B6
Ellerhayes Devon 10 D4
Elleric Argyll 130 E4
Ellerker E Yorks 90 B3
Ellerton E Yorks 96 F3
Ellerton Shrops 61 B7
Ellesborough Bucks 39 D8
Ellesmere Shrops 73 F8
Ellesmere Port Ches W 73 B8
Ellingham Norf 69 E6
Ellingham Northumb 117 B7
Ellingstring N Yorks 101 F6
Ellington Cambs 54 B2
Ellington Northumb 117 E8
Elliot Angus 135 F6
Ellisfield Hants 26 E4
Ellistown Leics 63 C8
Ellon Aberds 153 E9
Ellonby Cumb 108 F4
Ellough Suff 69 F7
Elloughton E Yorks 90 B3
Ellwood Glos 36 D2
Elm Cambs 66 D4
Elm Hill Dorset 13 B6
Elm Park London 41 F8
Elmbridge Worcs 50 C4
Elmdon Essex 55 F5
Elmdon W Mid 63 F5
Elmdon Heath W Mid 63 F5
Elmers End London 28 C4
Elmesthorpe Leics 63 E8
Elmfield IoW 15 E7
Elmhurst Staffs 62 C5
Elmley Castle Worcs 50 E4
Elmley Lovett Worcs 50 C3
Elmore Glos 36 C4
Elmore Back Glos 36 C4
Elmscott Devon 8 B4
Elmsett Suff 56 E4
Elmstead Market Essex 43 B6
Elmsted Kent 30 E5
Elmstone Kent 31 C6
Elmstone Hardwicke Glos 37 B6
Elmswell E Yorks 97 D5
Elmswell Suff 56 C3
Elmton Derbys 76 B5
Elphin Highld 156 H5
Elphinstone E Loth 121 B6
Elrick Aberds 141 D7
Elrig Dumfries 105 E7
Elsdon Northumb 117 E5
Elsecar S Yorks 88 E4
Elsenham Essex 41 B8
Elsfield Oxon 39 C5
Elsham N Lincs 90 C4
Elsing Norf 68 C3
Elslack N Yorks 94 E2
Elson Shrops 73 F7
Elsrickle S Lanark 120 E3
Elstead Sur 27 E7
Elsted W Sus 16 C2
Elsthorpe Lincs 65 B7
Elstob Durham 101 B8
Elston Notts 77 E7
Elston Wilts 25 E5
Elstone Devon 9 C8
Elstow Bedford 53 E8
Elstree Herts 40 E4
Elstronwick E Yorks 97 F8
Elswick Lancs 92 F4
Elsworth Cambs 54 C4
Elterwater Cumb 99 D5
Eltham London 28 B5
Eltisley Cambs 54 D3
Elton Cambs 65 E7
Elton Ches W 73 B8
Elton Derbys 76 C2
Elton Glos 36 C4
Elton Hereford 49 B6
Elton Notts 77 F7
Elton Stockton 102 C2
Elton Green Ches W 73 B8
Elvanfoot S Lanark 114 C2
Elvaston Derbys 76 F4
Elveden Suff 56 B2
Elvingston E Loth 121 B7
Elvington Kent 31 D6
Elvington York 96 E2
Elwick Hrtlpl 111 F7
Elwick Northumb 123 F7
Elworth Ches E 74 C4
Elworthy Som 22 F2
Ely Cambs 66 F5
Ely Cardiff 22 B3
Emberton M Keynes 53 E6
Embleton Cumb 107 F8
Embleton Northumb 117 B8
Embo Highld 151 B11
Embo Street Highld 151 B11
Emborough Som 23 D8
Embsay N Yorks 94 D3
Emery Down Hants 14 D3
Emersons Green S Glos 23 B8
Emley W Yorks 88 C3
Emmbrook Wokingham 27 C5
Emmer Green Reading 26 B5
Emmington Oxon 39 D7
Emneth Norf 66 D4
Emneth Hungate Norf 66 D5
Empingham Rutland 65 D6
Empshott Hants 27 F5
Emstrey Shrops 60 C5
Emsworth Hants 15 D8
Enborne W Berks 26 C2
Enchmarsh Shrops 60 E5
Enderby Leics 64 E2
Endmoor Cumb 99 F7
Endon Staffs 75 D6
Endon Bank Staffs 75 D6
Enfield London 41 E6
Enfield Wash London 41 E6
Enford Wilts 25 D6
Engamoor Shetland 160 H4
Engine Common S Glos 36 F3
Englefield W Berks 26 B4
Englefield Green Sur 27 B7
Englesea-brook Ches E 74 D4
English Bicknor Glos 36 C2
English Frankton Shrops 60 B4
Englishcombe Bath 24 C2
Enham Alamein Hants 25 E8
Enmore Som 22 F4
Ennerdale Bridge Cumb 98 C2
Enoch Dumfries 113 D8
Enochdhu Perth 133 C7
Ensay Argyll 146 G6
Ensbury Bmouth 13 E8
Ensdon Shrops 60 C4
Ensis Devon 9 B7
Enstone Oxon 38 B3
Enterkinfoot Dumfries 113 D8
Enterpen N Yorks 102 D2
Enville Staffs 62 F2
Eolaigearraidh W Isles 148 H2
Eorabus Argyll 146 J6
Eòropaidh W Isles 155 A10
Epperstone Notts 77 E6
Epping Essex 41 D7
Epping Green Essex 41 D7
Epping Green Herts 41 D5
Epping Upland Essex 41 D7
Eppleby N Yorks 101 C6
Eppleworth E Yorks 97 F6
Epsom Sur 28 C3
Epwell Oxon 51 E8
Epworth N Lincs 89 D8
Epworth Turbary N Lincs 89 D8
Erbistock Wrex 73 E7
Erbusaig Highld 149 F12
Erchless Castle Highld 150 G7
Erdington W Mid 62 E5
Eredine Argyll 125 E5
Eriboll Highld 156 D7
Ericstane Dumfries 114 C3
Eridge Green E Sus 18 B2
Erines Argyll 145 F7
Eriswell Suff 55 B8
Erith London 29 B6
Erlestoke Wilts 24 D4
Ermine Lincs 78 B2
Ermington Devon 6 D4
Erpingham Norf 81 D7
Errogie Highld 137 B8
Errol Perth 128 B4
Erskine Renfs 118 B4
Erskine Bridge Renfs 118 B4
Ervie Dumfries 104 C4
Erwarton Suff 57 F6
Erwood Powys 48 E2
Eryholme N Yorks 101 D8
Eryrys Denb 73 D6
Escomb Durham 101 B6
Escrick N Yorks 96 E2
Esgairdawe Carms 46 E5
Esgairgeiliog Powys 58 D4
Esh Durham 110 E4
Esh Winning Durham 110 E4
Esher Sur 28 C2
Esholt W Yorks 94 E4
Eshott Northumb 117 E8
Eshton N Yorks 94 D2
Esk Valley N Yorks 103 D6
Eskadale Highld 150 H7
Eskbank Midloth 121 C6
Eskdale Green Cumb 98 D3
Eskdalemuir Dumfries 115 E5
Eske E Yorks 97 E6
Eskham Lincs 91 E7
Esprick Lancs 92 F4
Essendine Rutland 65 C7
Essendon Herts 41 D5
Essich Highld 151 H9
Essington Staffs 62 D3
Esslemont Aberds 141 B8
Eston Redcar 102 C3
Eswick Shetland 160 H6
Etal Northumb 122 F5
Etchilhampton Wilts 24 C5
Etchingham E Sus 18 C4
Etchinghill Kent 19 B8
Etchinghill Staffs 62 C4
Ethie Castle Angus 135 E6
Ethie Mains Angus 135 E6
Etling Green Norf 68 C3
Eton Windsor 27 B7
Eton Wick Windsor 27 B7
Etteridge Highld 138 E2
Ettersgill Durham 100 B3
Ettingshall W Mid 62 E3
Ettington Warks 51 E7
Etton E Yorks 97 E5
Etton Pboro 65 D8
Ettrick Borders 115 C5
Ettrickbridge Borders 115 B6
Ettrickhill Borders 115 C5
Etwall Derbys 76 F2
Euston Suff 56 B2
Euximoor Drove Cambs 66 E4
Euxton Lancs 86 C3
Evanstown Bridgend 34 F3
Evanton Highld 151 E9
Evedon Lincs 78 E3
Evelix Highld 151 B10
Evenjobb Powys 48 C4
Evenley Northants 52 F3
Evenlode Glos 38 B2
Evenwood Durham 101 B6
Evenwood Gate Durham 101 B6
Everbay Orkney 159 F7
Evercreech Som 23 F8
Everdon Northants 52 D3
Everingham E Yorks 96 E4
Everleigh Wilts 25 D7
Everley N Yorks 103 F7
Eversholt C Beds 53 F7
Evershot Dorset 12 D3
Eversley Hants 27 C5
Eversley Cross Hants 27 C5
Everthorpe E Yorks 96 F5
Everton C Beds 54 D3
Everton Hants 14 E3
Everton Mers 85 E4
Everton Notts 89 E7
Evertown Dumfries 108 B3
Evesbatch Hereford 49 E8
Evesham Worcs 50 E5
Evington Leicester 64 D3
Ewden Village S Yorks 88 E3
Ewell Sur 28 C3
Ewell Minnis Kent 31 E6
Ewelme Oxon 39 E6
Ewen Glos 37 E7
Ewenny V Glam 21 B8
Ewerby Lincs 78 E4
Ewerby Thorpe Lincs 78 E4
Ewes Dumfries 115 E6
Ewesley Northumb 117 E6
Ewhurst Sur 27 E8
Ewhurst Green E Sus 18 C4
Ewhurst Green Sur 27 F8
Ewloe Flint 73 C7
Ewloe Green Flint 73 C6
Ewood Blackburn 86 B4
Eworthy Devon 9 E6
Ewshot Hants 27 E6
Ewyas Harold Hereford 35 B7
Exbourne Devon 9 D8
Exbury Hants 14 E5
Exebridge Devon 10 B4
Exelby N Yorks 101 F7
Exeter Devon 10 E4
Exford Som 21 F7
Exhall Warks 51 D6
Exley Head W Yorks 94 F3
Exminster Devon 10 F4
Exmouth Devon 10 F5
Exnaboe Shetland 160 M5
Exning Suff 55 C7
Exton Devon 10 F4
Exton Hants 15 B7
Exton Rutland 65 C6
Exton Som 21 F8
Exwick Devon 10 E4
Eyam Derbys 76 B2
Eydon Northants 52 D3
Eye Hereford 49 C6
Eye Pboro 66 D2
Eye Suff 56 B5
Eye Green Pboro 66 D2
Eyemouth Borders 122 C5
Eyeworth C Beds 54 E3
Eyhorne Street Kent 30 D2
Eyke Suff 57 D7
Eynesbury Cambs 54 D2
Eynort Highld 149 F8
Eynsford Kent 29 C6
Eynsham Oxon 38 D4
Eype Dorset 12 E2
Eyre Highld 149 C9
Eyre Highld 149 E10
Eythorne Kent 31 E6
Eyton Hereford 49 C6
Eyton Shrops 60 F3
Eyton Wrex 73 E7
Eyton upon the Weald Moors Telford 61 C6

F

Faccombe Hants 25 D8
Faceby N Yorks 102 D2
Facit Lancs 87 C6
Faddiley Ches E 74 D2
Fadmoor N Yorks 102 F4
Faerdre Swansea 33 D7
Failand N Som 23 B7
Failford S Ayrs 112 B4
Failsworth Gtr Man 87 D6
Fain Highld 150 D4
Fair Green Norf 67 C6
Fair Hill Cumb 108 F5
Fair Oak Hants 15 C5
Fair Oak Green Hants 26 C4
Fairbourne Gwyn 58 C3
Fairburn N Yorks 89 B5
Fairfield Derbys 75 B7
Fairfield Stockton 102 C2
Fairfield Worcs 50 B4
Fairfield Worcs 50 E5
Fairford Glos 38 D1
Fairhaven Lancs 85 B4
Fairlie N Ayrs 118 D2
Fairlight E Sus 19 D5
Fairlight Cove E Sus 19 D5
Fairmile Devon 11 E5
Fairmilehead Edin 120 C5
Fairoak Staffs 74 F4
Fairseat Kent 29 C7
Fairstead Essex 42 C3
Fairstead Norf 67 C6
Fairwarp E Sus 17 B8
Fairy Cottage IoM 84 D4
Fairy Cross Devon 9 B6
Fakenham Norf 80 E5
Fakenham Magna Suff 56 B3
Fala Midloth 121 C7
Fala Dam Midloth 121 C7
Falahill Borders 121 D6
Falcon Hereford 49 F8
Faldingworth Lincs 90 F4
Falfield S Glos 36 E3
Falkenham Suff 57 F6
Falkirk Falk 119 B8
Falkland Fife 128 D4
Falla Borders 116 C3
Fallgate Derbys 76 C3
Fallin Stirling 127 E7
Fallowfield Gtr Man 87 E6
Fallsidehill Borders 122 E2
Falmer E Sus 17 D7
Falmouth Corn 3 C7
Falsgrave N Yorks 103 F8
Falstone Northumb 116 F3
Fanagmore Highld 156 E4
Fangdale Beck N Yorks 102 E3
Fangfoss E Yorks 96 D3
Fankerton Falk 127 F6
Fanmore Argyll 146 G7
Fannich Lodge Highld 150 E5
Fans Borders 122 E2
Far Bank S Yorks 89 C7
Far Bletchley M Keynes 53 F6
Far Cotton Northants 52 D5
Far Forest Worcs 50 B2
Far Laund Derbys 76 E3
Far Sawrey Cumb 99 E5
Farcet Cambs 66 E2
Farden Shrops 49 B7
Fareham Hants 15 D6
Farewell Staffs 62 C4
Farforth Lincs 79 B6
Faringdon Oxon 38 E2
Farington Lancs 86 B3
Farlam Cumb 109 D5
Farlary Highld 157 J10
Farleigh N Som 23 C6
Farleigh Sur 28 C4
Farleigh Hungerford Som 24 D3
Farleigh Wallop Hants 26 E4
Farlesthorpe Lincs 79 B7
Farleton Cumb 99 F7
Farleton Lancs 93 C5
Farley Shrops 60 D3
Farley Staffs 75 E7
Farley Wilts 14 B3
Farley Green Sur 27 E8
Farley Hill Luton 40 B3
Farley Hill Wokingham 26 C5
Farleys End Glos 36 C4
Farlington N Yorks 96 C2
Farlow Shrops 61 F6
Farmborough Bath 23 C8
Farmcote Glos 37 B7
Farmcote Shrops 61 E7
Farmington Glos 37 C8
Farmoor Oxon 38 D4
Farmtown Moray 152 C5
Farnborough Hants 27 D6
Farnborough London 28 C5
Farnborough W Berks 38 F4
Farnborough Warks 52 E2
Farnborough Green Hants 27 D6
Farncombe Sur 27 E7
Farndish Bedford 53 C7
Farndon Ches W 73 D8
Farndon Notts 77 D7
Farnell Angus 135 D6
Farnham Dorset 13 C7
Farnham Essex 41 B7
Farnham N Yorks 95 C6
Farnham Suff 57 C7
Farnham Sur 27 E6
Farnham Common Bucks 40 F2
Farnham Green Essex 41 B7
Farnham Royal Bucks 40 F2
Farnhill N Yorks 94 E3
Farningham Kent 29 C6
Farnley N Yorks 94 E5
Farnley W Yorks 95 F5
Farnley Tyas W Yorks 88 C2
Farnsfield Notts 77 D6
Farnworth Gtr Man 86 D5
Farnworth Halton 86 F3
Farr Highld 138 D4
Farr Highld 151 H9
Farr Highld 157 C10
Farr House Highld 151 H9
Farringdon Devon 10 E5
Farrington Gurney Bath 23 D8
Farsley W Yorks 94 F5
Farthinghoe Northants 52 F3
Farthingloe Kent 31 E6
Farthingstone Northants 52 D4
Fartown W Yorks 88 C2
Farway Devon 11 E6
Fasag Highld 149 C13
Fascadale Highld 147 D8
Faslane Port Argyll 145 E11
Fasnacloich Argyll 130 E4
Fasnakyle Ho Highld 137 B6
Fassfern Highld 130 B4
Fatfield T&W 111 D6
Fattahead Aberds 153 C6
Faugh Cumb 108 D5
Fauldhouse W Loth 120 C2
Faulkbourne Essex 42 C3
Faulkland Som 24 D2
Fauls Shrops 74 F2
Faversham Kent 30 C4
Favillar Moray 152 E2
Fawdington N Yorks 95 B7
Fawfieldhead Staffs 75 C7
Fawkham Green Kent 29 C6
Fawler Oxon 38 C3
Fawley Bucks 39 F7
Fawley Hants 15 D5
Fawley W Berks 38 F3
Fawley Chapel Hereford 36 B2
Faxfleet E Yorks 90 B2
Faygate W Sus 28 F3
Fazakerley Mers 85 E4
Fazeley Staffs 63 D6
Fearby N Yorks 101 F6
Fearn Highld 151 D11
Fearn Lodge Highld 151 C9
Fearn Station Highld 151 D11
Fearnan Perth 132 E4
Fearnbeg Highld 149 C12
Fearnhead Warr 86 E4
Fearnmore Highld 149 B12
Featherstone Staffs 62 D3
Featherstone W Yorks 88 B5
Featherwood Northumb 116 D4
Feckenham Worcs 50 C5
Feering Essex 42 B4
Feetham N Yorks 100 E4
Feizor N Yorks 93 C7
Felbridge Sur 28 F4
Felbrigg Norf 81 D8
Felcourt Sur 28 E4
Felden Herts 40 D3
Felin-Crai Powys 34 B2
Felindre Carms 33 B6
Felindre Carms 33 B8
Felindre Carms 46 F2
Felindre Carms 47 F5
Felindre Ceredig 46 D4
Felindre Powys 59 F8
Felindre Swansea 33 D7
Felindre Farchog Pembs 45 F3
Felinfach Ceredig 46 D4
Felinfach Powys 48 F2
Felinfoel Carms 33 D6
Felingwm isaf Carms 33 B6

Felingwm uchaf Carms 33 B6
Felinwynt Ceredig 45 D4
Felixkirk N Yorks 102 F2
Felixstowe Suff 57 F6
Felixstowe Ferry Suff 57 F7
Felkington Northumb 122 E5
Felkirk W Yorks 88 C4
Fell Side Cumb 108 F3
Felling T&W 111 C5
Felmersham Bedford 53 D7
Felmingham Norf 81 E8
Felpham W Sus 16 E3
Felsham Suff 56 D3
Felsted Essex 42 B2
Feltham London 28 B2
Felthorpe Norf 68 C4
Felton Hereford 49 E7
Felton N Som 23 C7
Felton Northumb 117 D7
Felton Butler Shrops 60 C3
Feltwell Norf 67 E7
Fen Ditton Cambs 55 C5
Fen Drayton Cambs 54 C4
Fen End W Mid 51 B7
Fen Side Lincs 79 D6
Fenay Bridge W Yorks 88 C2
Fence Lancs 93 F8
Fence Houses T&W 111 D6
Fengate Norf 81 E7
Fengate Pboro 66 E2
Fenham Northumb 123 E6
Fenhouses Lincs 79 E5
Feniscliffe Blackburn 86 B4
Feniscowles Blackburn 86 B4
Feniton Devon 11 E6
Fenlake Bedford 53 E8
Fenny Bentley Derbys 75 D8
Fenny Bridges Devon 11 E6
Fenny Compton Warks 52 D2
Fenny Drayton Leics 63 E7
Fenny Stratford M Keynes 53 F6
Fenrother Northumb 117 E7
Fenstanton Cambs 54 C4
Fenton Cambs 54 B4
Fenton Lincs 77 B8
Fenton Lincs 77 D8
Fenton Stoke 75 E5
Fenton Barns E Loth 129 F7
Fenton Town Northumb 123 F5
Fenwick E Ayrs 118 E4
Fenwick Northumb 110 B3
Fenwick Northumb 123 E6
Fenwick S Yorks 89 C6
Feochaig Argyll 143 G8
Feock Corn 3 C7
Feolin Ferry Argyll 144 G3
Ferindonald Highld 149 H11
Feriniquarrie Highld 148 C6
Ferlochan Argyll 130 E3
Fern Angus 134 C4
Ferndale Rhondda 34 E4
Ferndown Dorset 13 D8
Ferness Highld 151 G12
Ferney Green Cumb 99 E6
Fernham Oxon 38 E2
Fernhill Heath Worcs 50 D3
Fernhurst W Sus 16 B2
Fernie Fife 128 C5
Ferniegair S Lanark 119 D7
Fernilea Highld 149 E8
Fernilee Derbys 75 B7
Ferrensby N Yorks 95 C6
Ferring W Sus 16 D4
Ferry Hill Cambs 66 F3
Ferry Point Highld 151 C10
Ferrybridge W Yorks 89 B5
Ferryden Angus 135 D7
Ferryhill Aberdeen 141 D8
Ferryhill Durham 111 F5
Ferryhill Station Durham 111 F6
Ferryside Carms 32 C4
Fersfield Norf 68 F3
Fersit Highld 131 B7
Ferwig Ceredig 45 E3
Feshiebridge Highld 138 D4
Fetcham Sur 28 D2
Fetterangus Aberds 153 C9
Fettercairn Aberds 135 B6
Fettes Highld 151 F8
Fewcott Oxon 39 B5
Fewston N Yorks 94 D4
Ffair-Rhos Ceredig 47 C6
Ffairfach Carms 33 B7
Ffaldybrenin Carms 46 E5
Ffarmers Carms 47 E5
Ffawyddog Powys 35 C6
Fforest Carms 33 D6
Fforest-fâch Swansea 33 E7
Ffos-y-ffin Ceredig 46 C3
Ffostrasol Ceredig 46 E2
Ffridd-Uchaf Gwyn 83 F5
Ffrith Wrex 73 D6
Ffrwd Gwyn 82 F4
Ffynnon ddrain Carms 33 B5
Ffynnon-oer Ceredig 46 D4
Ffynnongroyw Flint 85 F2
Fidden Argyll 146 J6
Fiddes Aberds 141 F7
Fiddington Glos 50 F4
Fiddington Som 22 E4
Fiddleford Dorset 13 C6
Fiddlers Hamlet Essex 41 D7
Field Staffs 75 F7
Field Broughton Cumb 99 F5
Field Dalling Norf 81 D6
Field Head Leics 63 D8
Fifehead Magdalen Dorset 13 B5
Fifehead Neville Dorset 13 C5
Fifield Oxon 38 C2
Fifield Wilts 25 D6
Fifield Windsor 27 B7
Fifield Bavant Wilts 13 B8
Figheldean Wilts 25 E6
Filands Wilts 37 F6
Filby Norf 69 C7
Filey N Yorks 97 A7
Filgrave M Keynes 53 E6
Filkins Oxon 38 D2
Filleigh Devon 9 B8
Filleigh Devon 10 C2
Fillingham Lincs 90 F3
Fillongley Warks 63 F6
Filton S Glos 23 B8
Fimber E Yorks 96 C4
Finavon Angus 134 D4
Finchairn Argyll 124 E5
Fincham Norf 67 D6
Finchampstead Wokingham 27 C5
Finchdean Hants 15 C8
Finchingfield Essex 55 F7
Finchley London 41 E5
Findern Derbys 76 F3
Findhorn Moray 151 E13
Findhorn Bridge Highld 138 B4
Findo Gask Perth 128 B2
Findochty Moray 152 B4
Findon Aberds 141 E8
Findon W Sus 16 D5
Findon Mains Highld 151 E9
Findrack Ho. Aberds 140 D5
Finedon Northants 53 B7
Fingal Street Suff 57 C6
Fingask Aberds 141 B6
Fingerpost Worcs 50 B2
Fingest Bucks 39 E7
Finghall N Yorks 101 F6
Fingland Cumb 108 D2
Fingland Dumfries 113 C7
Finglesham Kent 31 D7
Fingringhoe Essex 43 B6
Finlarig Stirling 132 F2
Finmere Oxon 52 F4
Finnart Perth 132 D2
Finningham Suff 56 C4
Finningley S Yorks 89 E7
Finnygaud Aberds 152 C5
Finsbury London 41 F6
Finstall Worcs 50 C4
Finsthwaite Cumb 99 F5
Finstock Oxon 38 C3
Finstown Orkney 159 G4
Fintry Aberds 153 C7
Fintry Dundee 134 F4
Fintry Stirling 126 F5
Finzean Aberds 140 E5
Fionnphort Argyll 146 J6
Fionnsbhagh W Isles 154 J5
Fir Tree Durham 110 F4
Firbeck S Yorks 89 F6
Firby N Yorks 96 C3
Firby N Yorks 101 F7
Firgrove Gtr Man 87 C7
Firsby Lincs 79 C7
Firsdown Wilts 25 F7
First Coast Highld 150 B2
Fishbourne IoW 15 E6
Fishbourne W Sus 16 D2
Fishburn Durham 111 F6
Fishcross Clack 127 E7
Fisher Place Cumb 99 C5
Fisherford Aberds 153 E6
Fisher's Pond Hants 15 B5
Fisherstreet W Sus 27 F7
Fisherton Highld 151 F10
Fisherton S Ayrs 112 C2
Fishguard = Abergwaun Pembs 44 B4
Fishlake S Yorks 89 C7
Fishleigh Barton Devon 9 B7
Fishponds Bristol 23 B8
Fishpool Glos 36 B3
Fishtoft Lincs 79 E6
Fishtoft Drove Lincs 79 E6
Fishtown of Usan Angus 135 D7
Fishwick Borders 122 D5
Fiskavaig Highld 149 E8
Fiskerton Lincs 78 B3
Fiskerton Notts 77 D7
Fitling E Yorks 97 F8
Fittleton Wilts 25 E6
Fittleworth W Sus 16 C4
Fitton End Cambs 66 C4
Fitz Shrops 60 C4
Fitzhead Som 11 B6
Fitzwilliam W Yorks 88 C5
Fiunary Highld 147 G9
Five Acres Glos 36 C2
Five Ashes E Sus 18 C2
Five Oak Green Kent 29 E7
Five Oaks Jersey 17
Five Oaks W Sus 16 B4
Five Roads Carms 33 D5
Fivecrosses Ches W 74 B2
Fivehead Som 11 B8
Flack's Green Essex 42 C3
Flackwell Heath Bucks 40 F1
Fladbury Worcs 50 E4
Fladdabister Shetland 160 K6
Flagg Derbys 75 C8
Flamborough E Yorks 97 B8
Flamstead Herts 40 C3
Flamstead End Herts 41 D6
Flansham W Sus 16 D3
Flanshaw W Yorks 88 B4
Flasby N Yorks 94 D2
Flash Staffs 75 C7
Flashader Highld 149 C8
Flask Inn N Yorks 103 D7
Flaunden Herts 40 D3
Flawborough Notts 77 E7
Flawith N Yorks 95 C7
Flax Bourton N Som 23 C7
Flaxby N Yorks 95 D6
Flaxholme Derbys 76 E3
Flaxley Glos 36 C3
Flaxpool Som 22 F3
Flaxton N Yorks 96 C2
Fleckney Leics 64 E3
Flecknoe Warks 52 C3
Fledborough Notts 77 B8
Fleet Hants 15 D8
Fleet Hants 27 D6
Fleet Lincs 66 B3
Fleet Hargate Lincs 66 B3
Fleetham Northumb 117 B7
Fleetlands Hants 15 D6
Fleetville Herts 40 D4
Fleetwood Lancs 92 E3
Flemingston V Glam 22 C2
Flemington S Lanark 119 D6
Flempton Suff 56 C2
Fleoideabhagh W Isles 154 J5
Fletchertown Cumb 108 E2
Fletching E Sus 17 B8
Flexbury Corn 8 D4
Flexford Sur 27 E7
Flimby Cumb 107 F7
Flimwell E Sus 18 B4
Flint = Y Fflint Flint 73 B6
Flint Mountain Flint 73 B6
Flintham Notts 77 E7
Flinton E Yorks 97 F8
Flintsham Hereford 48 D5
Flitcham Norf 80 E3
Flitton C Beds 53 F8
Flitwick C Beds 53 F8
Flixborough N Lincs 90 C2
Flixborough Stather N Lincs 90 C2
Flixton Gtr Man 86 E5
Flixton N Yorks 97 B6
Flixton Suff 69 F6
Flockton W Yorks 88 C3
Flodaigh W Isles 148 C3
Flodden Northumb 122 F5
Flodigarry Highld 149 A9
Flood's Ferry Cambs 66 E3
Flookburgh Cumb 92 B3
Florden Norf 68 E4
Flore Northants 52 C4
Flotterton Northumb 117 D5
Flowton Suff 56 E4
Flush House W Yorks 88 D2
Flushing Aberds 153 D10
Flushing Corn 3 C7
Flyford Flavell Worcs 50 D4
Foals Green Suff 57 B6
Fobbing Thurrock 42 F3
Fochabers Moray 152 C3
Fochriw Caerph 35 D5
Fockerby N Lincs 90 C2
Fodderletter Moray 139 B7
Fodderty Highld 151 F8
Foel Powys 59 C6
Foel-gastell Carms 33 C6
Foffarty Angus 134 E4
Foggathorpe E Yorks 96 F3
Fogo Borders 122 E3
Fogorig Borders 122 E3
Foindle Highld 156 E4
Folda Angus 134 C1
Fole Staffs 75 F7
Foleshill W Mid 63 F7
Folke Dorset 12 C4
Folkestone Kent 31 F6
Folkingham Lincs 78 F3
Folkington E Sus 18 E2
Folksworth Cambs 65 F8
Folkton N Yorks 97 B6
Folla Rule Aberds 153 E7
Follifoot N Yorks 95 D6
Folly Gate Devon 9 E7
Fonthill Bishop Wilts 24 F4
Fonthill Gifford Wilts 24 F4
Fontmell Magna Dorset 13 C6
Fontwell W Sus 16 D3
Foolow Derbys 75 B8
Foots Cray London 29 B5
Forbestown Aberds 140 C2
Force Mills Cumb 99 E5
Forcett N Yorks 101 C6
Ford Argyll 124 E4
Ford Bucks 39 D7
Ford Devon 9 B6
Ford Glos 37 B7
Ford Northumb 122 F5
Ford Shrops 60 C4
Ford Staffs 75 D7
Ford W Sus 16 D3
Ford Wilts 24 B3
Ford End Essex 42 C2
Ford Street Som 11 C6
Fordcombe Kent 29 E6
Fordell Fife 128 F3
Forden Powys 60 D2
Forder Green Devon 7 C5
Fordham Cambs 55 B7
Fordham Essex 43 B5
Fordham Norf 67 E6
Fordhouses W Mid 62 D3
Fordingbridge Hants 14 C2
Fordon E Yorks 97 B6
Fordoun Aberds 135 B7
Ford's Green Suff 56 C4
Fordstreet Essex 43 B5
Fordwells Oxon 38 C3
Fordwich Kent 31 D5
Fordyce Aberds 152 B5
Forebridge Staffs 62 B3
Forest Durham 109 F8
Forest Becks Lancs 93 D7
Forest Gate London 41 F7
Forest Green Sur 28 E2
Forest Hall Cumb 99 D7
Forest Head Cumb 109 D5
Forest Hill Oxon 39 D5
Forest Lane Head N Yorks 95 D6
Forest Lodge Argyll 131 E6
Forest Lodge Highld 139 C6
Forest Lodge Perth 133 B6
Forest Mill Clack 127 E8
Forest Row E Sus 28 F5
Forest Town Notts 77 C5
Forestburn Gate Northumb 117 E6
Foresterseat Moray 152 C1
Forestside W Sus 15 C8
Forfar Angus 134 D4
Forgandenny Perth 128 C2
Forge Powys 58 E4
Forge Side Torf 35 D6
Forgewood N Lanark 119 D7
Forgie Moray 152 C3
Forglen Ho. Aberds 153 C6
Formby Mers 85 D4
Forncett End Norf 68 E4
Forncett St Mary Norf 68 E4
Forncett St Peter Norf 68 E4
Forneth Perth 133 E7
Fornham All Saints Suff 56 C2
Fornham St Martin Suff 56 C2
Forres Moray 151 F13
Forrest Lodge Dumfries 113 F5
Forrestfield N Lanark 119 C8
Forsbrook Staffs 75 E6
Forse Highld 158 G4
Forse Ho. Highld 158 G4
Forsinain Highld 157 E12
Forsinard Highld 157 E11
Forsinard Station Highld 157 E11
Forston Dorset 12 E4
Fort Augustus Highld 137 D6
Fort George Guern 16
Fort George Highld 151 F10
Fort William Highld 131 B5
Forteviot Perth 128 C2
Forth S Lanark 120 D2
Forth Road Bridge Edin 120 B4
Forthampton Glos 50 F3
Fortingall Perth 132 E4
Forton Hants 26 E2
Forton Lancs 92 D4
Forton Shrops 60 C4
Forton Som 11 D8
Forton Staffs 61 B7
Forton Heath Shrops 60 C4
Fortrie Aberds 153 D6
Fortrose Highld 151 F10
Fortuneswell Dorset 12 G4
Forty Green Bucks 40 E2
Forty Hill London 41 E6
Forward Green Suff 56 D4
Fosbury Wilts 25 D8
Fosdyke Lincs 79 F6
Foss Perth 132 D4
Foss Cross Glos 37 D7
Fossebridge Glos 37 C7
Foster Street Essex 41 D7
Fosterhouses S Yorks 89 C7
Foston Derbys 75 F8
Foston Lincs 77 E8
Foston N Yorks 96 C2
Foston on the Wolds E Yorks 97 D7
Fotherby Lincs 91 E7
Fotheringhay Northants 65 E7
Foubister Orkney 159 H6
Foul Mile E Sus 18 D3
Foulby W Yorks 88 C4
Foulden Borders 122 D5
Foulden Norf 67 E7
Foulis Castle Highld 151 E8
Foulridge Lancs 93 E8
Foulsham Norf 81 E6
Fountainhall Borders 121 E7
Four Ashes Staffs 62 F2
Four Ashes Suff 56 B4
Four Crosses Powys 59 D7
Four Crosses Powys 60 C2
Four Crosses Wrex 73 D6
Four Elms Kent 29 E5
Four Forks Som 22 F4
Four Gotes Cambs 66 C4
Four Lane Ends Ches W 74 C2
Four Lanes Corn 3 C5
Four Marks Hants 26 F4
Four Mile Bridge Anglesey 82 D2
Four Oaks E Sus 19 C5
Four Oaks W Mid 62 E5
Four Oaks W Mid 63 F6
Four Roads Carms 33 D5
Four Roads IoM 84 F2
Four Throws Kent 18 C4
Fourlane Ends Derbys 76 D3
Fourlanes End Ches E 74 D5
Fourpenny Highld 151 B11
Fourstones Northumb 109 C8
Fovant Wilts 13 B8
Foveran Aberds 141 B8
Fowey Corn 5 D6
Fowley Common Warr 86 E4
Fowlis Angus 134 F3
Fowlis Wester Perth 127 B8
Fowlmere Cambs 54 E5
Fownhope Hereford 49 F7
Fox Corner Sur 27 D7
Fox Lane Hants 27 D6
Fox Street Essex 43 B6
Foxbar Renfs 118 C4
Foxcombe Hill Oxon 38 D4
Foxdale IoM 84 E2
Foxearth Essex 56 E2
Foxfield Cumb 98 F4
Foxham Wilts 24 B4
Foxhole Corn 4 D4
Foxhole Swansea 33 E7
Foxholes N Yorks 97 B6
Foxhunt Green E Sus 18 D2
Foxley Norf 81 E6
Foxley Wilts 37 F5
Foxt Staffs 75 E7
Foxton Cambs 54 E5
Foxton Durham 102 B1
Foxton Leics 64 E4
Foxup N Yorks 93 B8
Foxwist Green Ches W 74 C3
Foxwood Shrops 49 B8
Foy Hereford 36 B2
Foyers Highld 137 B7
Fraddam Corn 2 C4
Fraddon Corn 4 D4
Fradley Staffs 63 C5
Fradswell Staffs 75 F6
Fraisthorpe E Yorks 97 C7
Framfield E Sus 17 B8
Framingham Earl Norf 69 D5
Framingham Pigot Norf 69 D5
Framlingham Suff 57 C6
Frampton Dorset 12 E4
Frampton Lincs 79 F6
Frampton Cotterell S Glos 36 F3
Frampton Mansell Glos 37 D6
Frampton on Severn Glos 36 D4
Frampton West End Lincs 79 E5
Framsden Suff 57 D5
Framwellgate Moor Durham 111 E5
Franche Worcs 50 B3
Frankby Mers 85 F3
Frankley Worcs 62 F3
Frank's Bridge Powys 48 D3
Frankton Warks 52 B2
Frant E Sus 18 B2
Fraserburgh Aberds 153 B9
Frating Green Essex 43 B6
Fratton Ptsmth 15 E7
Freathy Corn 5 D8
Freckenham Suff 55 B7
Freckleton Lancs 86 B2
Freeby Leics 64 B5
Freehay Staffs 75 E7
Freeland Oxon 38 C4
Freester Shetland 160 H6
Freethorpe Norf 69 D7
Freiston Lincs 79 E6
Fremington Devon 20 F4
Fremington N Yorks 101 E5
Frenchay S Glos 23 B8
Frenchbeer Devon 9 F8
Frenich Stirling 126 D3
Frensham Sur 27 E6
Fresgoe Highld 157 C12
Freshfield Mers 85 D3
Freshford Bath 24 C2
Freshwater IoW 14 F4
Freshwater Bay IoW 14 F4
Freshwater East Pembs 32 E1
Fressingfield Suff 57 B6
Freston Suff 57 F5
Freswick Highld 158 D5
Fretherne Glos 36 D4
Frettenham Norf 68 C5
Freuchie Fife 128 D4
Freuchies Angus 134 C2
Freystrop Pembs 44 D4
Friar's Gate E Sus 29 F5
Friarton Perth 128 B3
Friday Bridge Cambs 66 D4
Friday Street E Sus 18 E3
Fridaythorpe E Yorks 96 D4
Friern Barnet London 41 E5
Friesland Argyll 146 F4
Friesthorpe Lincs 90 F4
Frieston Lincs 78 E2
Frieth Bucks 39 E7
Frilford Oxon 38 E4
Frilsham W Berks 26 B3
Frimley Sur 27 D6
Frimley Green Sur 27 D6
Frindsbury Medway 29 B8
Fring Norf 80 D3
Fringford Oxon 39 B6
Frinsted Kent 30 D2
Frinton-on-Sea Essex 43 B8
Friockheim Angus 135 E5
Friog Gwyn 58 C3
Frisby on the Wreake Leics 64 C3
Friskney Lincs 79 D7
Friskney Eaudike Lincs 79 D7
Friskney Tofts Lincs 79 D7
Friston E Sus 18 F2
Friston Suff 57 C8
Fritchley Derbys 76 D3
Frith Bank Lincs 79 E6
Frith Common Worcs 49 C8
Fritham Hants 14 C3
Frithelstock Devon 9 C6
Frithelstock Stone Devon 9 C6
Frithville Lincs 79 D6
Frittenden Kent 30 E2
Frittiscombe Devon 7 E6
Fritton Norf 68 E5
Fritton Norf 69 D7
Fritwell Oxon 39 B5
Frizinghall W Yorks 94 F4
Frizington Cumb 98 C2
Frocester Glos 36 D4
Frodesley Shrops 60 D5
Frodingham N Lincs 90 C2
Frodsham Ches W 74 B2
Frogden Borders 116 B3
Froggatt Derbys 76 B2
Froghall Staffs 75 E7
Frogmore Devon 7 E5
Frogmore Hants 27 D6
Frognall Lincs 65 C8
Frogshail Norf 81 D8
Frolesworth Leics 64 E2
Frome Som 24 E2
Frome St Quintin Dorset 12 D3
Fromes Hill Hereford 49 E8
Fron Denb 72 C4
Fron Gwyn 70 D4
Fron Gwyn 82 F5
Fron Powys 48 C2
Fron Powys 59 E8
Fron Powys 60 D2
Froncysyllte Wrex 73 E6
Frongoch Gwyn 72 F3
Frostenden Suff 69 F7
Frosterley Durham 110 F3
Frotoft Orkney 159 F5
Froxfield Wilts 25 C7
Froxfield Green Hants 15 B8
Froyle Hants 27 E5
Fryerning Essex 42 D2
Fryton N Yorks 96 B2
Fulbeck Lincs 78 D2
Fulbourn Cambs 55 D6
Fulbrook Oxon 38 C2
Fulford Som 11 B7
Fulford Staffs 75 F6
Fulford York 96 E2
Fulham London 28 B3
Fulking W Sus 17 C6
Full Sutton E Yorks 96 D3
Fullarton Glasgow 119 C6
Fullarton N Ayrs 118 F3
Fuller Street Essex 42 C3
Fuller's Moor Ches W 73 D8
Fullerton Hants 25 F8
Fulletby Lincs 79 B5
Fullwood E Ayrs 118 D4
Fulmer Bucks 40 F2
Fulmodestone Norf 81 D5
Fulnetby Lincs 78 B3
Fulstow Lincs 91 E7
Fulwell T&W 111 D6
Fulwood Lancs 92 F5
Fulwood S Yorks 88 F4
Fundenhall Norf 68 E4
Fundenhall Street Norf 68 E4
Funtington W Sus 15 D8
Funtley Hants 15 D6
Funtullich Perth 127 B6
Funzie Shetland 160 D8
Furley Devon 11 D7
Furnace Argyll 125 E6
Furnace Carms 33 D6
Furnace End Warks 63 E6
Furneaux Pelham Herts 41 B7
Furness Vale Derbys 87 F8
Furze Platt Windsor 40 F1
Furzehill Devon 21 E6
Fyfett Som 11 C7
Fyfield Essex 42 D1
Fyfield Glos 38 D2
Fyfield Hants 25 E7
Fyfield Oxon 38 E4
Fyfield Wilts 25 C6
Fylingthorpe N Yorks 103 D7
Fyvie Aberds 153 E7

G

Gabhsann bho Dheas W Isles 155 B9
Gabhsann bho Thuath W Isles 155 B9
Gablon Highld 151 B10
Gabroc Hill E Ayrs 118 D4
Gaddesby Leics 64 C3
Gadebridge Herts 40 D3
Gaer Powys 35 B5
Gaerllwyd Mon 35 E8
Gaerwen Anglesey 82 D4
Gagingwell Oxon 38 B4
Gaick Lodge Highld 138 F3
Gailey Staffs 62 C3
Gainford Durham 101 C6
Gainsborough Lincs 90 E2
Gainsborough Suff 57 E5
Gainsford End Essex 55 F8
Gairloch Highld 149 A13
Gairlochy Highld 136 F4
Gairney Bank Perth 128 E3
Gairnshiel Lodge Aberds 139 D8
Gaisgill Cumb 99 D8
Gaitsgill Cumb 108 E3
Galashiels Borders 121 F7
Galgate Lancs 92 D4
Galhampton Som 12 B4
Gallaberry Dumfries 114 F2
Gallachoille Argyll 144 E6
Gallanach Argyll 124 C4
Gallanach Argyll 146 E5
Gallantry Bank Ches E 74 D2
Gallatown Fife 128 E4
Galley Common Warks 63 E7
Galley Hill Cambs 54 C4
Galleyend Essex 42 D3
Galleywood Essex 42 D3
Gallin Perth 132 E2
Gallowfauld Angus 134 E4
Gallows Green Staffs 75 E7
Galltair Highld 149 F13
Galmisdale Highld 146 C7
Galmpton Devon 6 E4
Galmpton Torbay 7 D6
Galphay N Yorks 95 B5
Galston E Ayrs 118 F5
Galtrigill Highld 148 C6
Gamblesby Cumb 109 F6
Gamesley Derbys 87 E8
Gamlingay Cambs 54 D3
Gammersgill N Yorks 101 F5
Gamston Notts 77 B7
Ganarew Hereford 36 C2
Ganavan Argyll 124 B4
Gang Corn 5 C8
Ganllwyd Gwyn 71 E8
Gannochy Angus 135 B5
Gannochy Perth 128 B3
Gansclet Highld 158 F5
Ganstead E Yorks 97 F7
Ganthorpe N Yorks 96 B2
Ganton N Yorks 97 B5
Garbat Highld 150 E7
Garbhallt Argyll 125 F6
Garboldisham Norf 68 F3
Garden City Flint 73 C7
Garden Village W Yorks 95 F7
Garden Village Wrex 73 D7
Gardenstown Aberds 153 B7
Garderhouse Shetland 160 J5
Gardham E Yorks 97 E5
Gardin Shetland 160 G6
Gare Hill Som 24 E2
Garelochhead Argyll 145 D11
Garford Oxon 38 E4
Garforth W Yorks 95 F7
Gargrave N Yorks 94 D2
Gargunnock Stirling 127 E6
Garlic Street Norf 68 F5
Garlieston Dumfries 105 E8
Garlinge Green Kent 30 D5
Garlogie Aberds 141 D6
Garmond Aberds 153 C8
Garmony Argyll 147 G9
Garmouth Moray 152 B3
Garn-yr-erw Torf 35 C6
Garnant Carms 33 C7
Garndiffaith Torf 35 D6
Garndolbenmaen Gwyn 71 C5
Garnedd Conwy 83 F7
Garnett Bridge Cumb 99 E7
Garnfadryn Gwyn 70 D3
Garnkirk N Lanark 119 C6
Garnlydan Bl Gwent 35 C5
Garnswllt Swansea 33 D7
Garrabost W Isles 155 D10
Garraron Argyll 124 E4
Garras Corn 3 D6
Garreg Gwyn 71 C7
Garrick Perth 127 C7
Garrigill Cumb 109 E7
Garriston N Yorks 101 E6
Garroch Dumfries 113 F5
Garrogie Lodge Highld 137 C8
Garros Highld 149 B9
Garrow Perth 133 E5
Garryhorn Dumfries 113 E5
Garsdale Cumb 100 F2
Garsdale Head Cumb 100 E2
Garsdon Wilts 37 F6
Garshall Green Staffs 75 F6
Garsington Oxon 39 D5
Garstang Lancs 92 E4
Garston Mers 86 F2
Garswood Mers 86 E3
Gartcosh N Lanark 119 C6
Garth Bridgend 34 E2
Garth Gwyn 83 D5
Garth Powys 47 E8
Garth Shetland 160 H4
Garth Wrex 73 E6
Garth Row Cumb 99 E7
Garthamlock Glasgow 119 C6
Garthbrengy Powys 48 F2
Gartheli Ceredig 46 D4
Garthmyl Powys 59 E8
Garthorpe Leics 64 B5
Garthorpe N Lincs 90 C2
Gartly Aberds 152 E5
Gartmore Stirling 126 E4
Gartnagrenach Argyll 144 H6
Gartness N Lanark 119 C7
Gartness Stirling 126 F4
Gartocharn W Dunb 126 F3
Garton E Yorks 97 F8
Garton-on-the-Wolds E Yorks 97 D5
Gartsherrie N Lanark 119 C7
Gartymore Highld 157 H13
Garvald E Loth 121 B8
Garvamore Highld 137 E8
Garvard Argyll 144 D2
Garvault Hotel Highld 157 F10
Garve Highld 150 E6
Garvestone Norf 68 D3
Garvock Aberds 135 B7
Garvock Invclyd 118 B2
Garway Hereford 36 B1
Garway Hill Hereford 35 B8
Gaskan Highld 130 B1
Gastard Wilts 24 C3
Gasthorpe Norf 68 F2
Gatcombe IoW 15 F5
Gate Burton Lincs 90 F2
Gate Helmsley N Yorks 96 D2
Gateacre Mers 86 F2
Gatebeck Cumb 99 F7
Gateford Notts 89 F6
Gateforth N Yorks 89 B6
Gatehead E Ayrs 118 F3
Gatehouse Northumb 116 F3
Gatehouse of Fleet Dumfries 106 D3
Gatelawbridge Dumfries 114 E2
Gateley Norf 81 E5
Gatenby N Yorks 101 F8
Gateshead T&W 111 C5
Gatesheath Ches W 73 C8
Gateside Aberds 140 C5
Gateside Angus 134 E4
Gateside E Renf 118 D4
Gateside Fife 128 D3
Gateside N Ayrs 118 D3
Gathurst Gtr Man 86 D3
Gatley Gtr Man 87 F6
Gattonside Borders 121 F8
Gatwick Airport W Sus 28 E3
Gaufron Powys 47 C8
Gaulby Leics 64 D3
Gauldry Fife 129 B5
Gaunt's Common Dorset 13 D8
Gautby Lincs 78 B4
Gavinton Borders 122 D3
Gawber S Yorks 88 D4
Gawcott Bucks 52 F4
Gawsworth Ches E 75 C5
Gawthorpe W Yorks 88 B3
Gawthrop Cumb 100 F1
Gawthwaite Cumb 98 F4
Gay Street W Sus 16 B4
Gaydon Warks 51 D8
Gayfield Orkney 159 C5
Gayhurst M Keynes 53 E6
Gayle N Yorks 100 F3
Gayles N Yorks 101 D6
Gayton Mers 85 F3
Gayton Norf 67 C7
Gayton Northants 52 D5
Gayton Staffs 62 B3
Gayton le Marsh Lincs 91 F8
Gayton le Wold Lincs 91 F6
Gayton Thorpe Norf 67 C7
Gaywood Norf 67 B6
Gazeley Suff 55 C8
Geanies House Highld 151 D11
Gearraidh Bhailteas W Isles 148 F2
Gearraidh Bhaird W Isles 155 E8
Gearraidh na h-Aibhne W Isles 154 D7
Gearraidh na Monadh W Isles 148 G2
Geary Highld 148 B7
Geddes House Highld 151 F11
Gedding Suff 56 D3
Geddington Northants 65 F5
Gedintailor Highld 149 E10
Gedling Notts 77 E6
Gedney Lincs 66 B4
Gedney Broadgate Lincs 66 B4
Gedney Drove End Lincs 66 B4
Gedney Dyke Lincs 66 B4
Gedney Hill Lincs 66 C3
Gee Cross Gtr Man 87 E7
Geilston Argyll 118 B3
Geirinis W Isles 148 D2
Geise Highld 158 D3
Geisiadar W Isles 154 D6
Geldeston Norf 69 E6
Gell Conwy 83 E8
Gelli Pembs 32 C1
Gelli Rhondda 34 E3
Gellideg M Tydf 34 D4
Gellifor Denb 72 C5
Gelligaer Caerph 35 E5
Gellilydan Gwyn 71 D7
Gellinudd Neath 33 D8
Gellyburn Perth 133 F7
Gellywen Carms 32 B3
Gelston Dumfries 106 D4
Gelston Lincs 78 E2
Gembling E Yorks 97 D7
Gentleshaw Staffs 62 C4
Geocrab W Isles 154 H6
George Green Bucks 40 F3
George Nympton Devon 10 B2
Georgefield Dumfries 115 E5
Georgeham Devon 20 F3
Georgetown Bl Gwent 35 D5
Gerlan Gwyn 83 E6
Germansweek Devon 9 E6
Germoe Corn 2 D4
Gerrans Corn 3 C7
Gerrards Cross Bucks 40 F3
Gestingthorpe Essex 56 F2
Geuffordd Powys 60 C2
Gib Hill Ches W 74 B3
Gibbet Hill Warks 64 F2
Gibbshill Dumfries 106 B4
Gidea Park London 41 F8
Gidleigh Devon 9 F8
Giffnock E Renf 119 D5
Gifford E Loth 121 C8
Giffordland N Ayrs 118 E2
Giffordtown Fife 128 C4
Giggleswick N Yorks 93 C8
Gilberdyke E Yorks 90 B2
Gilchriston E Loth 121 C7
Gilcrux Cumb 107 F8
Gildersome W Yorks 88 B3
Gildingwells S Yorks 89 F6
Gileston V Glam 22 C2
Gilfach Caerph 35 E5
Gilfach Goch Rhondda 34 F3
Gilfachrheda Ceredig 46 D3
Gillamoor N Yorks 102 F4
Gillar's Green Mers 86 E2
Gillen Highld 148 C7
Gilling East N Yorks 96 B2
Gilling West N Yorks 101 D6
Gillingham Dorset 13 B6
Gillingham Medway 29 C8
Gillingham Norf 69 E7
Gillock Highld 158 E4
Gillow Heath Staffs 75 D5
Gills Highld 158 C5
Gill's Green Kent 18 B4
Gilmanscleuch Borders 115 B6
Gilmerton Edin 121 C5
Gilmerton Perth 127 B7
Gilmonby Durham 100 C4
Gilmorton Leics 64 F2
Gilmourton S Lanark 119 E6
Gilsland Northumb 109 C6
Gilsland Spa Cumb 109 C6
Gilston Borders 121 D7
Gilston Herts 41 C7
Gilwern Mon 35 C6
Gimingham Norf 81 D8
Giosla W Isles 154 E6
Gipping Suff 56 C4
Gipsey Bridge Lincs 79 E5
Girdle Toll N Ayrs 118 E3
Girlsta Shetland 160 H6
Girsby N Yorks 102 D1
Girtford C Beds 54 D2
Girthon Dumfries 106 D3
Girton Cambs 54 C5
Girton Notts 77 C8
Girvan S Ayrs 112 E1
Gisburn Lancs 93 E8
Gisleham Suff 69 F8
Gislingham Suff 56 B4
Gissing Norf 68 F4
Gittisham Devon 11 E6
Gladestry Powys 48 D4
Gladsmuir E Loth 121 B7
Glais Swansea 33 D8
Glaisdale N Yorks 103 D5
Glame Highld 149 D10
Glamis Angus 134 E3
Glan Adda Gwyn 83 D5
Glan Conwy Conwy 83 D8
Glan-Conwy Conwy 83 F8
Glan-Duar Carms 46 E4
Glan-Dwyfach Gwyn 71 C5
Glan Gors Anglesey 82 D4
Glan-rhyd Gwyn 82 F4
Glan-traeth Anglesey 82 D2
Glan-y-don Flint 73 B5
Glan-y-nant Powys 59 F6
Glan-y-wern Gwyn 71 D7
Glan-yr-afon Anglesey 83 C6
Glan-yr-afon Gwyn 72 E3
Glan-yr-afon Gwyn 72 E4
Glanaman Carms 33 C7
Glandford Norf 81 C6
Glandwr Pembs 32 B2
Glandy Cross Carms 32 B2
Glandyfi Ceredig 58 E3
Glangrwyney Powys 35 C6
Glanmule Powys 59 E8
Glanrafon Ceredig 58 F3
Glanrhyd Gwyn 70 D3
Glanrhyd Pembs 45 E3
Glanton Northumb 117 C6
Glanton Pike Northumb 117 C6
Glanvilles Wootton Dorset 12 D4
Glapthorn Northants 65 E7
Glapwell Derbys 76 C4
Glas-allt Shiel Aberds 139 F8
Glasbury Powys 48 F3
Glaschoil Highld 151 H13
Glascoed Denb 72 B3
Glascoed Mon 35 D7
Glascoed Powys 59 C8
Glascorrie Aberds 140 E2
Glascote Staffs 63 D6
Glascwm Powys 48 D3
Glasdrum Argyll 130 E4
Glasfryn Conwy 72 D3
Glasgow Glasgow 119 C5
Glashvin Highld 149 B9
Glasinfryn Gwyn 83 E5
Glasnacardoch Highld 147 B9
Glasnakille Highld 149 G10
Glasphein Highld 148 D6
Glaspwll Powys 58 E4
Glassburn Highld 150 H6
Glasserton Dumfries 105 F8
Glassford S Lanark 119 E7
Glasshouse Hill Glos 36 B4
Glasshouses N Yorks 94 C4
Glasslie Fife 128 D4
Glasson Cumb 108 C2
Glasson Lancs 92 D4
Glassonby Cumb 109 F5
Glasterlaw Angus 135 D5
Glaston Rutland 65 D5
Glastonbury Som 23 F7
Glatton Cambs 65 F8
Glazebrook Warr 86 E4
Glazebury Warr 86 E4
Glazeley Shrops 61 F7
Gleadless S Yorks 88 F4
Gleadsmoss Ches E 74 C5
Gleann Tholàstaidh W Isles 155 C10
Gleaston Cumb 92 B2
Gleiniant Powys 59 E6
Glemsford Suff 56 E2
Glen Dumfries 106 B5
Glen Dumfries 106 D2
Glen Auldyn IoM 84 C4
Glen Bernisdale Highld 149 D9
Glen Ho Borders 121 F5
Glen Mona IoM 84 D4
Glen Nevis House Highld 131 B5
Glen Parva Leics 64 E2
Glen Sluain Argyll 125 F6
Glen Tanar House Aberds 140 E3
Glen Trool Lodge Dumfries 112 F4
Glen Village Falk 119 B8
Glen Vine IoM 84 E3
Glenamachrie Argyll 124 C5
Glenbarr Argyll 143 E7
Glenbeg Highld 139 B6
Glenbeg Highld 147 E8
Glenbervie Aberds 141 F6
Glenboig N Lanark 119 C7
Glenborrodale Highld 147 E9
Glenbranter Argyll 125 F7
Glenbreck Borders 114 B3
Glenbrein Lodge Highld 137 C7
Glenbrittle House Highld 149 F9
Glenbuchat Lodge Aberds 140 C2
Glenbuck E Ayrs 113 B7
Glenburn Renfs 118 C4
Glencalvie Lodge Highld 150 C7
Glencanisp Lodge Highld 156 G4
Glencaple Dumfries 107 C6
Glencarron Lodge Highld 150 F3
Glencarse Perth 128 B3
Glencassley Castle Highld 156 J7
Glenceitlein Highld 131 E5
Glencoe Highld 130 D4
Glencraig Fife 128 E3
Glencripesdale Highld 147 F9
Glencrosh Dumfries 113 F7
Glendavan Ho. Aberds 140 D3
Glendevon Perth 127 D8
Glendoe Lodge Highld 137 D7
Glendoebeg Highld 137 D7
Glendoick Perth 128 B4
Glendoll Lodge Angus 134 B2
Glendoune S Ayrs 112 E1
Glenduckie Fife 128 C4
Glendye Lodge Aberds 140 F5
Gleneagles Hotel Perth 127 C8
Gleneagles House Perth 127 D8
Glenegedale Argyll 142 C4
Glenelg Highld 149 G13
Glenernie Moray 151 G13
Glenfarg Perth 128 C3
Glenfarquhar Lodge Aberds 141 F6
Glenferness House Highld 151 G12
Glenfeshie Lodge Highld 138 E4
Glenfield Leics 64 D2
Glenfinnan Highld 147 C11
Glenfoot Perth 128 C3
Glenfyne Lodge Argyll 125 D8
Glengap Dumfries 106 D3
Glengarnock N Ayrs 118 D3
Glengorm Castle Argyll 146 F7
Glengrasco Highld 149 D9
Glenhead Farm Angus 134 C2
Glenhoul Dumfries 113 F5
Glenhurich Highld 130 C2
Glenkerry Borders 115 C5
Glenkiln Dumfries 106 B5
Glenkindie Aberds 140 C3
Glenlatterach Moray 152 C1
Glenlee Dumfries 113 F6
Glenlichorn Perth 127 C6
Glenlivet Moray 139 B7
Glenlochsie Perth 133 B7
Glenloig N Ayrs 143 E10
Glenluce Dumfries 105 D6
Glenmallan Argyll 125 F8
Glenmarksie Highld 150 F6
Glenmassan Argyll 145 E10
Glenmavis N Lanark 119 C7
Glenmaye IoM 84 E2
Glenmidge Dumfries 113 F8
Glenmore Argyll 124 D4
Glenmore Highld 149 D9
Glenmore Lodge Highld 139 D5
Glenmoy Angus 134 C4
Glenogil Angus 134 C4
Glenprosen Lodge Angus 134 C2
Glenprosen Village Angus 134 C3
Glenquiech Angus 134 C4
Glenreasdell Mains Argyll 145 H7
Glenree N Ayrs 143 F10
Glenridding Cumb 99 C5
Glenrossal Highld 156 J7
Glenrothes Fife 128 D4
Glensanda Highld 130 E2
Glensaugh Aberds 135 B6
Glenshero Lodge Highld 137 E8
Glenstockadale Dumfries 104 C4
Glenstriven Argyll 145 F9
Glentaggart S Lanark 113 B8
Glentham Lincs 90 E4
Glentirranmuir Stirling 127 E5
Glenton Aberds 140 B5
Glentress Borders 121 F5
Glentromie Lodge Highld 138 E3
Glentrool Village Dumfries 105 B7
Glentruan IoM 84 B4
Glentruim House Highld 138 E2
Glentworth Lincs 90 F3
Glenuig Highld 147 D9
Glenurquhart Highld 151 E10
Glespin S Lanark 113 B8
Gletness Shetland 160 H6
Glewstone Hereford 36 B2
Glinton Pboro 65 D8
Glooston Leics 64 E4
Glororum Northumb 123 F7
Glossop Derbys 87 E8
Gloster Hill Northumb 117 D8
Gloucester Glos 37 C5
Gloup Shetland 160 C7
Glusburn N Yorks 94 E3
Glutt Lodge Highld 157 F12
Glutton Bridge Staffs 75 C7
Glympton Oxon 38 B4
Glyn-Ceiriog Wrex 73 F6
Glyn-cywarch Gwyn 71 D7
Glyn Ebwy = Ebbw Vale Bl Gwent 35 D5
Glyn-neath = Glynedd Neath 34 D2
Glynarthen Ceredig 46 E2
Glynbrochan Powys 59 F6
Glyncoch Rhondda 34 E4
Glyncorrwg Neath 34 E2
Glynde E Sus 17 D8
Glyndebourne E Sus 17 C8
Glyndyfrdwy Denb 72 E5
Glynedd = Glyn-neath Neath 34 D2
Glynogwr Bridgend 34 F3
Glyntaff Rhondda 34 F4
Glyntawe Powys 34 C2
Gnosall Staffs 62 B2
Gnosall Heath Staffs 62 B2
Goadby Leics 64 E4
Goadby Marwood Leics 64 B4
Goat Lees Kent 30 E4
Goatacre Wilts 24 B5
Goathill Dorset 12 C4
Goathland N Yorks 103 D6
Goathurst Som 22 F4
Gobernuisgach Lodge Highld 156 E7
Gobhaig W Isles 154 G5
Gobowen Shrops 73 F7
Godalming Sur 27 E7
Godley Gtr Man 87 E7
Godmanchester Cambs 54 B3
Godmanstone Dorset 12 E4
Godmersham Kent 30 D4
Godney Som 23 E6
Godolphin Cross Corn 2 C5
Godre'r-graig Neath 34 D1
Godshill Hants 14 C2
Godshill IoW 15 F6
Godstone Sur 28 D4
Godwinscroft Hants 14 E2
Goetre Mon 35 D7
Goferydd Anglesey 82 C2
Goff's Oak Herts 41 D6
Gogar Edin 120 B4
Goginan Ceredig 58 F3
Golan Gwyn 71 C6
Golant Corn 5 D6
Golberdon Corn 5 B8
Golborne Gtr Man 86 E4
Golcar W Yorks 88 C2
Gold Hill Norf 66 E5
Goldcliff Newport 35 F7
Golden Cross E Sus 18 D2
Golden Green Kent 29 E7
Golden Grove Carms 33 C6

Golden Hill Hants 14 E3
Golden Pot Hants 26 E5
Golden Valley Glos 37 B6
Goldenhill Stoke 75 D5
Golders Green London 41 F5
Goldhanger Essex 43 D5
Golding Shrops 60 D5
Goldington Bedford 53 D8
Goldsborough N Yorks 95 D6
Goldsborough N Yorks 103 C6
Goldsithney Corn 2 C4
Goldsworthy Devon 9 B5
Goldthorpe S Yorks 89 D5
Gollanfield Highld 151 F11
Golspie Highld 157 J11
Golval Highld 157 C11
Gomeldon Wilts 25 F6
Gomersal W Yorks 88 B3
Gomshall Sur 27 E8
Gonalston Notts 77 E6
Gonfirth Shetland 160 G5
Good Easter Essex 42 C2
Gooderstone Norf 67 D7
Goodleigh Devon 20 F5
Goodmanham E Yorks 96 E4
Goodnestone Kent 30 C4
Goodnestone Kent 31 D6
Goodrich Hereford 36 C2
Goodrington Torbay 7 D6
Goodshaw Lancs 87 B6
Goodwick = Wdig Pembs 44 B4
Goodworth Clatford Hants 25 E8
Goole E Yorks 89 B8
Goonbell Corn 3 B6
Goonhavern Corn 4 D2
Goose Eye W Yorks 94 E3
Goose Green Gtr Man 86 D3
Goose Green Norf 68 F4
Goose Green W Sus 16 C5
Gooseham Corn 8 C4
Goosey Oxon 38 E3
Goosnargh Lancs 93 F5
Goostrey Ches E 74 B4
Gorcott Hill Warks 51 C5
Gord Shetland 160 L6
Gordon Borders 122 E2
Gordonbush Highld 157 J11
Gordonsburgh Moray 152 B4
Gordonstoun Moray 152 B1
Gordonstown Aberds 152 C5
Gordonstown Aberds 153 E7
Gore Kent 31 D7
Gore Cross Wilts 24 D5
Gore Pit Essex 42 C4
Gorebridge Midloth 121 C6
Gorefield Cambs 66 C4
Gorey Jersey 17
Gorgie Edin 120 B5
Goring Oxon 39 F6
Goring-by-Sea W Sus 16 D5
Goring Heath Oxon 26 B4
Gorleston-on-Sea Norf 69 D8
Gornalwood W Mid 62 E3
Gorrachie Aberds 153 C7
Gorran Churchtown Corn 3 B8
Gorran Haven Corn 3 B9
Gorrenberry Borders 115 E7
Gors Ceredig 46 B5
Gorse Hill Swindon 38 F1
Gorsedd Flint 73 B5
Gorseinon Swansea 33 E6
Gorseness Orkney 159 G5
Gorsgoch Ceredig 46 D3
Gorslas Carms 33 C6
Gorsley Glos 36 B3
Gorstan Highld 150 E6
Gorstanvorran Highld 130 B2
Gorsteyhill Staffs 74 D4
Gorsty Hill Staffs 62 B5
Gortantaoid Argyll 142 A4
Gorton Gtr Man 87 E6
Gosbeck Suff 57 D5
Gosberton Lincs 78 F5
Gosberton Clough Lincs 65 B8
Gosfield Essex 42 B3
Gosford Hereford 49 C7
Gosforth Cumb 98 D2
Gosforth T&W 110 C5
Gosmore Herts 40 B4
Gosport Hants 15 E7
Gossabrough Shetland 160 E7
Gossington Glos 36 D4
Goswick Northumb 123 E6
Gotham Notts 76 F5
Gotherington Glos 37 B6
Gott Shetland 160 J6
Goudhurst Kent 18 B4
Goulceby Lincs 79 B5
Gourdas Aberds 153 D7
Gourdon Aberds 135 B8
Gourock Invclyd 118 B2
Govan Glasgow 119 C5
Govanhill Glasgow 119 C5
Goveton Devon 7 E5
Govilon Mon 35 C6
Gowanhill Aberds 153 B10
Gowdall E Yorks 89 B7
Gowerton Swansea 33 E6
Gowkhall Fife 128 F2
Gowthorpe E Yorks 96 D3
Goxhill E Yorks 97 E7
Goxhill N Lincs 90 B5
Goxhill Haven N Lincs 90 B5
Goytre Neath 34 F1
Grabhair W Isles 155 F8
Graby Lincs 65 B7
Grade Corn 3 E6
Graffham W Sus 16 C3
Grafham Cambs 54 C2
Grafham Sur 27 E8
Grafton Hereford 49 F6
Grafton N Yorks 95 C7
Grafton Oxon 38 D2
Grafton Shrops 60 C4
Grafton Worcs 49 C7
Grafton Flyford Worcs 50 D4
Grafton Regis Northants 53 E5
Grafton Underwood Northants 65 F6
Grafty Green Kent 30 E2
Graianrhyd Denb 73 D6
Graig Conwy 83 D8
Graig Denb 72 B4
Graig-fechan Denb 72 D5
Grain Medway 30 B2
Grainsby Lincs 91 E6
Grainthorpe Lincs 91 E7
Grampound Corn 3 B8
Grampound Road Corn 4 D4
Gramsdal W Isles 148 C3
Granborough Bucks 39 B7
Granby Notts 77 F7
Grandborough Warks 52 C2
Grandtully Perth 133 D6
Grange Cumb 98 C4
Grange E Ayrs 118 F4
Grange Medway 29 C8
Grange Mers 85 F3
Grange Perth 128 B4
Grange Crossroads Moray 152 C4
Grange Hall Moray 151 E13
Grange Hill Essex 41 E7
Grange Moor W Yorks 88 C3
Grange of Lindores Fife 128 C4
Grange-over-Sands Cumb 92 B4
Grange Villa Durham 110 D5
Grangemill Derbys 76 D2
Grangemouth Falk 127 F8
Grangepans Falk 128 F2
Grangetown Cardiff 22 B3
Grangetown Redcar 102 B3
Granish Highld 138 C5
Gransmoor E Yorks 97 D7
Granston Pembs 44 B3
Grantchester Cambs 54 D5
Grantham Lincs 78 F2
Grantley N Yorks 94 C5
Grantlodge Aberds 141 C6
Granton Dumfries 114 D3
Granton Edin 120 B5
Grantown-on-Spey Highld 139 B6
Grantshouse Borders 122 C4
Grappenhall Warr 86 F4
Grasby Lincs 90 D4
Grasmere Cumb 99 D5
Grasscroft Gtr Man 87 D7
Grassendale Mers 85 F4
Grassholme Durham 100 B4
Grassington N Yorks 94 C3
Grassmoor Derbys 76 C4
Grassthorpe Notts 77 C7
Grateley Hants 25 E7
Gratwich Staffs 75 F7
Graveley Cambs 54 C3
Graveley Herts 41 B5
Gravelly Hill W Mid 62 E5
Gravels Shrops 60 D3
Graven Shetland 160 F6
Graveney Kent 30 C4
Gravesend Herts 41 B7
Gravesend Kent 29 B7
Grayingham Lincs 90 E3
Grayrigg Cumb 99 E7
Grays Thurrock 29 B7
Grayshott Hants 27 F6
Grayswood Sur 27 F7
Graythorp Hrtlpl 102 B3
Grazeley Wokingham 26 C4
Greasbrough S Yorks 88 E5
Greasby Mers 85 F3
Great Abington Cambs 55 E6
Great Addington Northants 53 B7
Great Alne Warks 51 D6
Great Altcar Lancs 85 D4
Great Amwell Herts 41 C6
Great Asby Cumb 100 C1
Great Ashfield Suff 56 C3
Great Ayton N Yorks 102 C3
Great Baddow Essex 42 D3
Great Bardfield Essex 55 F7
Great Barford Bedford 54 D2
Great Barr W Mid 62 E4
Great Barrington Glos 38 C2
Great Barrow Ches W 73 C8
Great Barton Suff 56 C2
Great Barugh N Yorks 96 B3
Great Bavington Northumb 117 F5
Great Bealings Suff 57 E6
Great Bedwyn Wilts 25 C7
Great Bentley Essex 43 B7
Great Billing Northants 53 C6
Great Bircham Norf 80 D3
Great Blakenham Suff 56 D5
Great Blencow Cumb 108 F4
Great Bolas Telford 61 B6
Great Bookham Sur 28 D2
Great Bourton Oxon 52 E2
Great Bowden Leics 64 F4
Great Bradley Suff 55 D7
Great Braxted Essex 42 C4
Great Bricett Suff 56 D4
Great Brickhill Bucks 53 F7
Great Bridge W Mid 62 E3
Great Bridgeford Staffs 62 B2
Great Brington Northants 52 C4
Great Bromley Essex 43 B6
Great Broughton Cumb 107 F7
Great Broughton N Yorks 102 D3
Great Budworth Ches W 74 B3
Great Burdon Darl 101 C8
Great Burgh Sur 28 D3
Great Burstead Essex 42 E2
Great Busby N Yorks 102 D3
Great Canfield Essex 42 C1
Great Carlton Lincs 91 F8
Great Casterton Rutland 65 D7
Great Chart Kent 30 E3
Great Chatwell Staffs 61 C7
Great Chesterford Essex 55 E6
Great Cheverell Wilts 24 D4
Great Chishill Cambs 54 F5
Great Clacton Essex 43 C7
Great Cliff W Yorks 88 C4
Great Clifton Cumb 98 B2
Great Coates NE Lincs 91 D6
Great Comberton Worcs 50 E4
Great Corby Cumb 108 D4
Great Cornard Suff 56 E2
Great Cowden E Yorks 97 E8
Great Coxwell Oxon 38 E2
Great Crakehall N Yorks 101 E7
Great Cransley Northants 53 B6
Great Cressingham Norf 67 D8
Great Crosby Mers 85 E4
Great Cubley Derbys 75 F8
Great Dalby Leics 64 C4
Great Denham Bedford 53 E8
Great Doddington Northants 53 C6
Great Dunham Norf 67 C8
Great Dunmow Essex 42 B2
Great Durnford Wilts 25 F6
Great Easton Essex 42 B2
Great Easton Leics 64 E5
Great Eccleston Lancs 92 E4
Great Edstone N Yorks 103 F5
Great Ellingham Norf 68 E3
Great Elm Som 24 E2
Great Eversden Cambs 54 D4
Great Fencote N Yorks 101 E7
Great Finborough Suff 56 D4
Great Fransham Norf 67 C8
Great Gaddesden Herts 40 C3
Great Gidding Cambs 65 F8
Great Givendale E Yorks 96 D4
Great Glemham Suff 57 C7
Great Glen Leics 64 E3
Great Gonerby Lincs 77 F8
Great Gransden Cambs 54 D3
Great Green Norf 69 F5
Great Green Suff 56 D3
Great Habton N Yorks 96 B3
Great Hale Lincs 78 E4
Great Hallingbury Essex 41 C8
Great Hampden Bucks 39 D8
Great Harrowden Northants 53 B6
Great Harwood Lancs 93 F7
Great Haseley Oxon 39 D6
Great Hatfield E Yorks 97 E7
Great Haywood Staffs 62 B4
Great Heath W Mid 63 F7
Great Heck N Yorks 89 B6
Great Henny Essex 56 F2
Great Hinton Wilts 24 D4
Great Hockham Norf 68 E2
Great Holland Essex 43 C8
Great Horkesley Essex 56 F3
Great Hormead Herts 41 B6
Great Horton W Yorks 94 F4
Great Horwood Bucks 53 F5
Great Houghton Northants 53 D5
Great Houghton S Yorks 88 D5
Great Hucklow Derbys 75 B8
Great Kelk E Yorks 97 D7
Great Kimble Bucks 39 D8
Great Kingshill Bucks 40 E1
Great Langton N Yorks 101 E7
Great Leighs Essex 42 C3
Great Lever Gtr Man 86 D5
Great Limber Lincs 90 D5
Great Linford M Keynes 53 E6
Great Livermere Suff 56 B2
Great Longstone Derbys 76 B2
Great Lumley Durham 111 E5
Great Lyth Shrops 60 D4
Great Malvern Worcs 50 E2
Great Maplestead Essex 56 F2
Great Marton Blackpool 92 F3
Great Massingham Norf 80 E3
Great Melton Norf 68 D4
Great Milton Oxon 39 D6
Great Missenden Bucks 40 D1
Great Mitton Lancs 93 F7
Great Mongeham Kent 31 D7
Great Moulton Norf 68 E4
Great Munden Herts 41 B6
Great Musgrave Cumb 100 C2
Great Ness Shrops 60 C3
Great Notley Essex 42 B3
Great Oakley Essex 43 B7
Great Oakley Northants 65 F5
Great Offley Herts 40 B4
Great Ormside Cumb 100 C2
Great Orton Cumb 108 D3
Great Ouseburn N Yorks 95 C7
Great Oxendon Northants 64 F4
Great Oxney Green Essex 42 D2
Great Palgrave Norf 67 C8
Great Parndon Essex 41 D7
Great Paxton Cambs 54 C3
Great Plumpton Lancs 92 F3
Great Plumstead Norf 69 C6
Great Ponton Lincs 78 F2
Great Preston W Yorks 88 B5
Great Raveley Cambs 66 F2
Great Rissington Glos 38 C1
Great Rollright Oxon 51 F8
Great Ryburgh Norf 81 E5
Great Ryle Northumb 117 C6
Great Ryton Shrops 60 D4
Great Saling Essex 42 B3
Great Salkeld Cumb 109 F5
Great Sampford Essex 55 F7
Great Sankey Warr 86 F3
Great Saxham Suff 55 C8
Great Shefford W Berks 25 B8
Great Shelford Cambs 55 D5
Great Smeaton N Yorks 101 D8
Great Snoring Norf 80 D5
Great Somerford Wilts 37 F6
Great Stainton Darl 101 B8
Great Stambridge Essex 42 E4
Great Staughton Cambs 54 C2
Great Steeping Lincs 79 C7
Great Stonar Kent 31 D7
Great Strickland Cumb 99 B7
Great Stukeley Cambs 54 B3
Great Sturton Lincs 78 B5
Great Sutton Ches W 73 B7
Great Sutton Shrops 60 F5
Great Swinburne Northumb 110 B2
Great Tew Oxon 38 B3
Great Tey Essex 42 B4
Great Thurkleby N Yorks 95 B7
Great Thurlow Suff 55 D7
Great Torrington Devon 9 C6
Great Tosson Northumb 117 D6
Great Totham Essex 42 C4
Great Totham Essex 42 C4
Great Tows Lincs 91 E6
Great Urswick Cumb 92 B2
Great Wakering Essex 43 F5
Great Waldingfield Suff 56 E3
Great Walsingham Norf 80 D5
Great Waltham Essex 42 C2
Great Warley Essex 42 E1
Great Washbourne Glos 50 F4
Great Weldon Northants 65 F6
Great Welnetham Suff 56 D2
Great Wenham Suff 56 F4
Great Whittington Northumb 110 B3
Great Wigborough Essex 43 C5
Great Wilbraham Cambs 55 D6
Great Wishford Wilts 25 F5
Great Witcombe Glos 37 C6
Great Witley Worcs 50 C2
Great Wolford Warks 51 F7
Great Wratting Suff 55 E7
Great Wymondley Herts 41 B5
Great Wyrley Staffs 62 D3
Great Wytheford Shrops 61 C5
Great Yarmouth Norf 69 D8
Great Yeldham Essex 55 F8
Greater Doward Hereford 36 C2
Greatford Lincs 65 C7
Greatgate Staffs 75 E7
Greatham Hants 27 F5
Greatham Hrtlpl 102 B2
Greatham W Sus 16 C4
Greatstone on Sea Kent 19 C7
Greatworth Northants 52 E3
Greave Lancs 87 B6
Greeba IoM 84 D3
Green Denb 72 C4
Green End Bedford 54 D2
Green Hammerton N Yorks 95 D7
Green Lane Powys 59 E8
Green Ore Som 23 D7
Green St Green London 29 C5
Green Street Herts 40 E4
Greenbank Shetland 160 C7
Greenburn W Loth 120 C2
Greendikes Northumb 117 B6
Greenfield C Beds 53 F8
Greenfield Flint 73 B5
Greenfield Gtr Man 87 D7
Greenfield Highld 136 D5
Greenfield Oxon 39 E7
Greenford London 40 F4
Greengairs N Lanark 119 B7
Greenham W Berks 26 C2
Greenhaugh Northumb 116 F3
Greenhead Northumb 109 C6
Greenhill Falk 119 B8
Greenhill Kent 31 C5
Greenhill Leics 63 C8
Greenhill London 40 F4
Greenhills N Ayrs 118 D3
Greenhithe Kent 29 B6
Greenholm E Ayrs 118 F5
Greenholme Cumb 99 D7
Greenhouse Borders 115 B8
Greenhow Hill N Yorks 94 C4
Greenigoe Orkney 159 H5
Greenland Highld 158 D4
Greenlands Bucks 39 F7
Greenlaw Aberds 153 C6
Greenlaw Borders 122 E3
Greenlea Dumfries 107 B7
Greenloaning Perth 127 D7
Greenmount Gtr Man 87 C5
Greenmow Shetland 160 L6
Greenock Invclyd 118 B2
Greenock West Invclyd 118 B2
Greenodd Cumb 99 F5
Greenrow Cumb 107 D8
Greens Norton Northants 52 E4
Greenside T&W 110 C4
Greensidehill Northumb 117 C5
Greenstead Green Essex 42 B4
Greensted Essex 41 D8
Greenwich London 28 B4
Greet Glos 50 F5
Greete Shrops 49 B7
Greetham Lincs 79 B6
Greetham Rutland 65 C6
Greetland W Yorks 87 B8
Gregg Hall Cumb 99 E6
Gregson Lane Lancs 86 B3
Greinetobht W Isles 148 A3
Greinton Som 23 F6
Gremista Shetland 160 J6
Grenaby IoM 84 E2
Grendon Northants 53 C6
Grendon Warks 63 D6
Grendon Common Warks 63 E6
Grendon Green Hereford 49 D7
Grendon Underwood Bucks 39 B6
Grenofen Devon 6 B2
Grenoside S Yorks 88 E4
Greosabhagh W Isles 154 H6
Gresford Wrex 73 D7
Gresham Norf 81 D7
Greshornish Highld 149 C8
Gressenhall Norf 68 C2
Gressingham Lancs 93 C5
Gresty Green Ches E 74 D4
Greta Bridge Durham 101 C5
Gretna Dumfries 108 C3
Gretna Green Dumfries 108 C3
Gretton Glos 50 F5
Gretton Northants 65 E5
Gretton Shrops 60 E5
Grewelthorpe N Yorks 94 B5
Grey Green N Lincs 89 D8
Greygarth N Yorks 94 B4
Greynor Carms 33 D6
Greysouthen Cumb 98 B2
Greystoke Cumb 108 F4
Greystone Angus 135 E5
Greystone Dumfries 107 B6
Greywell Hants 26 D5
Griais W Isles 155 C9
Grianan W Isles 155 D9
Gribthorpe E Yorks 96 F3
Gridley Corner Devon 9 E5
Griff Warks 63 F7
Griffithstown Torf 35 E6
Grimbister Orkney 159 G4
Grimblethorpe Lincs 91 F6
Grimeford Village Lancs 86 C4
Grimethorpe S Yorks 88 D5
Griminis W Isles 148 C2
Grimister Shetland 160 D6
Grimley Worcs 50 C3
Grimness Orkney 159 J5
Grimoldby Lincs 91 F7
Grimpo Shrops 60 B3
Grimsargh Lancs 93 F5
Grimsbury Oxon 52 E2
Grimsby NE Lincs 91 C6
Grimscote Northants 52 D4
Grimscott Corn 8 D4
Grimsthorpe Lincs 65 B7
Grimston E Yorks 97 F8
Grimston Leics 64 B3
Grimston Norf 80 E3
Grimston York 96 D2
Grimstone Dorset 12 E4
Grinacombe Moor Devon 9 E6
Grindale E Yorks 97 B7
Grindigar Orkney 159 H6
Grindiscol Shetland 160 K6
Grindle Shrops 61 D7
Grindleford Derbys 76 B2
Grindleton Lancs 93 E7
Grindley Staffs 62 B4
Grindley Brook Shrops 74 E2
Grindlow Derbys 75 B8
Grindon Northumb 122 E5
Grindon Staffs 75 D7
Grindonmoor Gate Staffs 75 D7
Gringley on the Hill Notts 89 E8
Grinsdale Cumb 108 D3
Grinshill Shrops 60 B5
Grinton N Yorks 101 E5
Griomsidar W Isles 155 E8
Grishipoll Argyll 146 F4
Grisling Common E Sus 17 B8
Gristhorpe N Yorks 103 F8
Griston Norf 68 E2
Gritley Orkney 159 H6
Grittenham Wilts 37 F7
Grittleton Wilts 37 F5
Grizebeck Cumb 98 F4
Grizedale Cumb 99 E5
Grobister Orkney 159 F7
Groby Leics 64 D2
Groes Conwy 72 C4
Groes Neath 34 F1
Groes-faen Rhondda 34 F4
Groes-lwyd Powys 60 C2
Groesffordd Marli Denb 72 B4
Groeslon Gwyn 82 E5
Groeslon Gwyn 82 F4
Grogport Argyll 143 D9
Gromford Suff 57 D7
Gronant Flint 72 A4
Groombridge E Sus 18 B2
Grosmont Mon 35 B8
Grosmont N Yorks 103 D6
Groton Suff 56 E3
Grougfoot Falk 120 B3
Grouville Jersey 17
Grove Dorset 12 G5
Grove Kent 31 C6
Grove Notts 77 B7
Grove Oxon 38 E4
Grove Park London 28 B5
Grove Vale W Mid 62 E4
Grovesend Swansea 33 D6
Grudie Highld 150 E6
Gruids Highld 157 J8
Gruinard House Highld 150 B2
Grula Highld 149 F8
Gruline Argyll 147 G8
Grunasound Shetland 160 K5
Grundisburgh Suff 57 D6
Grunsagill Lancs 93 D7
Gruting Shetland 160 J4
Grutness Shetland 160 N6
Gualachulain Highld 131 E5
Gualin Ho. Highld 156 D6
Guardbridge Fife 129 C6
Guarlford Worcs 50 E3
Guay Perth 133 E7
Guestling Green E Sus 19 D5
Guestling Thorn E Sus 18 D5
Guestwick Norf 81 E6
Guestwick Green Norf 81 E6
Guide Blackburn 86 B5
Guide Post Northumb 117 F8
Guilden Morden Cambs 54 E3
Guilden Sutton Ches W 73 C8
Guildford Sur 27 E7
Guildtown Perth 133 F8
Guilsborough Northants 52 B4
Guilsfield Powys 60 C2
Guilton Kent 31 D6
Guineaford Devon 20 F4
Guisborough Redcar 102 C4
Guiseley W Yorks 94 E4
Guist Norf 81 E5
Guith Orkney 159 E6
Guiting Power Glos 37 B7
Gulberwick Shetland 160 K6
Gullane E Loth 129 F6
Gulval Corn 2 C3
Gulworthy Devon 6 B2
Gumfreston Pembs 32 D2
Gumley Leics 64 E3
Gummow's Shop Corn 4 D3
Gun Hill E Sus 18 D2
Gunby E Yorks 96 F3
Gunby Lincs 65 B6
Gundleton Hants 26 F4
Gunn Devon 20 F5
Gunnerside N Yorks 100 E4
Gunnerton Northumb 110 B2
Gunness N Lincs 90 C2
Gunnislake Corn 6 B2
Gunnista Shetland 160 J7
Gunthorpe Norf 81 D6
Gunthorpe Notts 77 E6
Gunthorpe Pboro 65 D8
Gunville IoW 15 F5
Gunwalloe Corn 3 D5
Gurnard IoW 15 E5
Gurnett Ches E 75 B6
Gurney Slade Som 23 E8
Gurnos Powys 34 D1
Gussage All Saints Dorset 13 C8
Gussage St Michael Dorset 13 C7
Guston Kent 31 E7
Gutcher Shetland 160 D7
Guthrie Angus 135 D5
Guyhirn Cambs 66 D3
Guyhirn Gull Cambs 66 D3
Guy's Head Lincs 66 B4
Guy's Marsh Dorset 13 B6
Guyzance Northumb 117 D8
Gwaenysgor Flint 72 A4
Gwalchmai Anglesey 82 D3
Gwaun-Cae-Gurwen Neath 33 C8
Gwaun-Leision Neath 33 C8
Gwbert Ceredig 45 E3
Gweek Corn 3 D6
Gwehelog Mon 35 D7
Gwenddwr Powys 48 E2
Gwennap Corn 3 C6
Gwenter Corn 3 E6
Gwernaffield Flint 73 C6
Gwernesney Mon 35 D8
Gwernogle Carms 46 F4
Gwernymynydd Flint 73 C6
Gwersyllt Wrex 73 D7
Gwespyr Flint 85 F2
Gwithian Corn 2 B4
Gwredog Anglesey 82 C4
Gwyddelwern Denb 72 E4
Gwyddgrug Carms 46 F3
Gwydyr Uchaf Conwy 83 E7
Gwynfryn Wrex 73 D6
Gwystre Powys 48 C2
Gwytherin Conwy 83 E8
Gyfelia Wrex 73 E7
Gyffin Conwy 83 D7
Gyre Orkney 159 H4
Gyrn-goch Gwyn 70 C5

H

Habberley Shrops 60 D3
Habergham Lancs 93 F8
Habrough NE Lincs 90 C5
Haceby Lincs 78 F3
Hacheston Suff 57 D7
Hackbridge London 28 C3
Hackenthorpe S Yorks 88 F5
Hackford Norf 68 D3
Hackforth N Yorks 101 E7
Hackland Orkney 159 F4
Hackleton Northants 53 D6
Hackness N Yorks 103 E7
Hackness Orkney 159 J4
Hackney London 41 F6
Hackthorn Lincs 90 F3
Hackthorpe Cumb 99 B7
Haconby Lincs 65 B8
Hacton London 41 F8
Hadden Borders 122 F3
Haddenham Bucks 39 D7
Haddenham Cambs 55 B5
Haddington E Loth 121 B8
Haddington Lincs 78 C2
Haddiscoe Norf 69 E7
Haddon Cambs 65 E8
Haddon Ches E 75 C6
Hade Edge W Yorks 88 D2
Hademore Staffs 63 D5
Hadfield Derbys 87 E8
Hadham Cross Herts 41 C7
Hadham Ford Herts 41 B7
Hadleigh Essex 42 F4
Hadleigh Suff 56 E4
Hadley Telford 61 C6
Hadley End Staffs 62 B5
Hadlow Kent 29 E7
Hadlow Down E Sus 18 C2
Hadnall Shrops 60 C5
Hadstock Essex 55 E6
Hady Derbys 76 B3
Hadzor Worcs 50 C4
Haffenden Quarter Kent 30 E2
Hafod-Dinbych Conwy 83 F8
Hafod-Iom Conwy 83 D8
Haggate Lancs 93 F8
Haggbeck Cumb 108 B4
Haggerston Northumb 123 E6
Haggrister Shetland 160 F5
Hagley Hereford 49 E7
Hagley Worcs 62 F3
Hagworthingham Lincs 79 C6
Haigh Gtr Man 86 D4
Haigh S Yorks 88 C3
Haigh Moor W Yorks 88 B3
Haighton Green Lancs 93 F5
Hail Weston Cambs 54 C2
Haile Cumb 98 D2
Hailes Glos 50 F5
Hailey Herts 41 C6
Hailey Oxon 38 C3
Hailsham E Sus 18 E2
Haimer Highld 158 D3
Hainault London 41 E7
Hainford Norf 68 C5
Hainton Lincs 91 F5
Hairmyres S Lanark 119 D6
Haisthorpe E Yorks 97 C7
Hakin Pembs 44 E3
Halam Notts 77 D6
Halbeath Fife 128 F3
Halberton Devon 10 C5
Halcro Highld 158 D4
Hale Gtr Man 87 F5
Hale Halton 86 F2
Hale Hants 14 C2
Hale Bank Halton 86 F2
Hale Street Kent 29 E7
Halebarns Gtr Man 87 F5
Hales Norf 69 E6
Hales Staffs 74 F4
Hales Place Kent 30 D5
Halesfield Telford 61 D7
Halesgate Lincs 66 B3
Halesowen W Mid 62 F3
Halesworth Suff 57 B7
Halewood Mers 86 F2
Halford Shrops 60 F4
Halford Warks 51 E7
Halfpenny Furze Carms 32 C3
Halfpenny Green Staffs 62 E2
Halfway Carms 46 F5
Halfway Carms 47 F7
Halfway W Berks 26 C2
Halfway Bridge W Sus 16 B3
Halfway House Shrops 60 C3
Halfway Houses Kent 30 B3
Halifax W Yorks 87 B8
Halket E Ayrs 118 D4
Halkirk Highld 158 E3
Halkyn Flint 73 B6
Hall Dunnerdale Cumb 98 E4
Hall Green W Mid 62 F5
Hall Green W Yorks 88 C4
Hall Grove Herts 41 C5
Hall of Tankerness Orkney 159 H6
Hall of the Forest Shrops 60 F2
Halland E Sus 18 D2
Hallaton Leics 64 E4
Hallatrow Bath 23 D8
Hallbankgate Cumb 109 D5
Hallen S Glos 36 F2
Halliburton Borders 122 E2
Hallin Highld 148 C7
Halling Medway 29 C8
Hallington Lincs 91 F7
Hallington Northumb 110 B2
Halliwell Gtr Man 86 C5
Halloughton Notts 77 D6
Hallow Worcs 50 D3
Hallrule Borders 115 C8
Halls E Loth 122 B2
Hall's Green Herts 41 B5
Hallsands Devon 7 F6
Hallthwaites Cumb 98 F3
Hallworthy Corn 8 F3
Hallyburton House Perth 134 F2
Hallyne Borders 120 E4
Halmer End Staffs 74 E4
Halmore Glos 36 D3
Halmyre Mains Borders 120 E4
Halnaker W Sus 16 D3
Halsall Lancs 85 C4
Halse Northants 52 E3
Halse Som 11 B6
Halsetown Corn 2 C4
Halsham E Yorks 91 B6
Halsinger Devon 20 F4
Halstead Essex 56 F2
Halstead Kent 29 C5
Halstead Leics 64 D4
Halstock Dorset 12 D3
Haltham Lincs 78 C5
Haltoft End Lincs 79 E6
Halton Bucks 40 C1
Halton Halton 86 F3
Halton Lancs 92 C5
Halton Northumb 110 C2
Halton W Yorks 95 F6
Halton Wrex 73 F7
Halton East N Yorks 94 D3
Halton Gill N Yorks 93 B8
Halton Holegate Lincs 79 C7
Halton Lea Gate Northumb 109 D6
Halton West N Yorks 93 D8
Haltwhistle Northumb 109 C7
Halvergate Norf 69 D7
Halwell Devon 7 D5
Halwill Devon 9 E6
Halwill Junction Devon 9 D6
Ham Devon 11 D7
Ham Glos 36 E3
Ham Highld 158 C4
Ham Kent 31 D7
Ham London 28 B2
Ham Shetland 160 K1
Ham Wilts 25 C8
Ham Common Dorset 13 B6
Ham Green Hereford 50 E2
Ham Green Kent 19 C5
Ham Green Kent 30 C2
Ham Green N Som 23 B7
Ham Green Worcs 50 C5
Ham Street Som 23 F7
Hamble-le-Rice Hants 15 D5
Hambleden Bucks 39 F7
Hambledon Hants 15 C7
Hambledon Sur 27 F7
Hambleton Lancs 92 E3
Hambleton N Yorks 95 F8
Hambridge Som 11 B8
Hambrook S Glos 23 B8
Hambrook W Sus 15 D8
Hameringham Lincs 79 C6
Hamerton Cambs 54 B2
Hametoun Shetland 160 K1
Hamilton S Lanark 119 D7
Hammer W Sus 27 F6
Hammerpot W Sus 16 D4
Hammersmith London 28 B3
Hammerwich Staffs 62 D4
Hammerwood E Sus 28 F5
Hammond Street Herts 41 D6
Hammoon Dorset 13 C6
Hamnavoe Shetland 160 E4
Hamnavoe Shetland 160 E6
Hamnavoe Shetland 160 F6
Hamnavoe Shetland 160 K5
Hampden Park E Sus 18 E3
Hamperden End Essex 55 F6
Hampnett Glos 37 C7
Hampole S Yorks 89 C6
Hampreston Dorset 13 E8
Hampstead London 41 F5
Hampstead Norreys W Berks 26 B3
Hampsthwaite N Yorks 95 D5
Hampton London 28 C2
Hampton Shrops 61 F7
Hampton Worcs 50 E5
Hampton Bishop Hereford 49 F7
Hampton Heath Ches W 73 E8
Hampton in Arden W Mid 63 F6
Hampton Loade Shrops 61 F7
Hampton Lovett Worcs 50 C3
Hampton Lucy Warks 51 D7
Hampton on the Hill Warks 51 C7
Hampton Poyle Oxon 39 C5
Hamrow Norf 80 E5
Hamsey E Sus 17 C8
Hamsey Green London 28 D4
Hamstall Ridware Staffs 62 C5
Hamstead IoW 14 E5
Hamstead W Mid 62 E4
Hamstead Marshall W Berks 26 C2
Hamsterley Durham 110 D4
Hamsterley Durham 110 F4
Hamstreet Kent 19 B7
Hamworthy Poole 13 E7
Hanbury Staffs 63 B5
Hanbury Worcs 50 C4
Hanbury Woodend Staffs 63 B5
Hanby Lincs 78 F3
Hanchurch Staffs 74 E5
Handbridge Ches W 73 C8
Handcross W Sus 17 B6
Handforth Ches E 87 F6
Handley Ches W 73 D8
Handsacre Staffs 62 C4
Handsworth S Yorks 88 F5
Handsworth W Mid 62 E4
Handy Cross Devon 9 B6
Hanford Stoke 75 E5
Hanging Langford Wilts 24 F5
Hangleton W Sus 16 D4
Hanham S Glos 23 B8
Hankelow Ches E 74 E3
Hankerton Wilts 37 E6
Hankham E Sus 18 E3
Hanley Stoke 75 E5
Hanley Castle Worcs 50 E3
Hanley Child Worcs 49 C8
Hanley Swan Worcs 50 E3
Hanley William Worcs 49 C8
Hanlith N Yorks 94 C2
Hanmer Wrex 73 F8
Hannah Lincs 79 B8
Hannington Hants 26 D3
Hannington Northants 53 B6
Hannington Swindon 38 E1
Hannington Wick Swindon 38 E1
Hansel Village S Ayrs 118 F3
Hanslope M Keynes 53 E6
Hanthorpe Lincs 65 B7
Hanwell London 40 F4
Hanwell Oxon 52 E2
Hanwood Shrops 60 D4
Hanworth London 28 B2
Hanworth Norf 81 D7
Happendon S Lanark 119 F8
Happisburgh Norf 69 A6
Happisburgh Common Norf 69 B6
Hapsford Ches W 73 B8
Hapton Lancs 93 F7
Hapton Norf 68 E4
Harberton Devon 7 D5
Harbertonford Devon 7 D5
Harbledown Kent 30 D5
Harborne W Mid 62 F4
Harborough Magna Warks 52 B2
Harbottle Northumb 117 D5
Harbury Warks 51 D8
Harby Leics 77 F7
Harby Notts 77 B8
Harcombe Devon 11 E6
Harden W Mid 62 D4
Harden W Yorks 94 F3
Hardenhuish Wilts 24 B4
Hardgate Aberds 141 D6
Hardham W Sus 16 C4
Hardingham Norf 68 D3
Hardingstone Northants 53 D5
Hardington Som 24 D2
Hardington Mandeville Som 12 C3
Hardington Marsh Som 12 D3
Hardley Hants 14 D5
Hardley Street Norf 69 D6
Hardmead M Keynes 53 E7
Hardrow N Yorks 100 E3
Hardstoft Derbys 76 C4
Hardway Hants 15 D7
Hardway Som 24 F2
Hardwick Bucks 39 C8
Hardwick Cambs 54 D4
Hardwick Norf 67 C6
Hardwick Norf 68 F5
Hardwick Northants 53 C6
Hardwick Notts 77 B6
Hardwick Oxon 38 D3
Hardwick Oxon 39 B5
Hardwick W Mid 62 E4
Hardwicke Glos 36 C4
Hardwicke Glos 37 B6
Hardwicke Hereford 48 E4
Hardy's Green Essex 43 B5
Hare Green Essex 43 B6
Hare Hatch Wokingham 27 B6
Hare Street Herts 41 B6
Hareby Lincs 79 C6
Hareden Lancs 93 D6
Harefield London 40 E3
Harehills W Yorks 95 F6
Harehope Northumb 117 B6
Haresceugh Cumb 109 E6
Harescombe Glos 37 C5
Haresfield Glos 37 C5
Hareshaw N Lanark 119 C8
Hareshaw Head Northumb 116 F4
Harewood W Yorks 95 E6
Harewood End Hereford 36 B2
Harford Carms 46 E5
Harford Devon 6 D4
Hargate Norf 68 E4
Hargatewall Derbys 75 B8
Hargrave Ches W 73 C8
Hargrave Northants 53 B8
Hargrave Suff 55 D8
Harker Cumb 108 C3
Harkland Shetland 160 E6
Harkstead Suff 57 F5
Harlaston Staffs 63 C6
Harlaw Ho. Aberds 141 B6
Harlaxton Lincs 77 F8
Harle Syke Lancs 93 F8
Harlech Gwyn 71 D6
Harlequin Notts 77 F6
Harlescott Shrops 60 C5
Harlesden London 41 F5
Harleston Devon 7 E5
Harleston Norf 68 F5
Harleston Suff 56 D4
Harlestone Northants 52 C5
Harley S Yorks 88 E4
Harley Shrops 61 D5
Harleyholm S Lanark 120 F2
Harlington C Beds 53 F8
Harlington London 27 B8
Harlington S Yorks 89 D5
Harlosh Highld 149 D7
Harlow Essex 41 C7
Harlow Hill N Yorks 95 D5
Harlow Hill Northumb 110 C3
Harlthorpe E Yorks 96 F3
Harlton Cambs 54 D4
Harman's Cross Dorset 13 F7
Harmby N Yorks 101 F6
Harmer Green Herts 41 C5
Harmer Hill Shrops 60 B4
Harmondsworth London 27 B8
Harmston Lincs 78 C2
Harnham Northumb 110 B3
Harnhill Glos 37 D7
Harold Hill London 41 E8
Harold Wood London 41 E8
Haroldston West Pembs 44 D3
Haroldswick Shetland 160 B8
Harome N Yorks 102 F4
Harpenden Herts 40 C4
Harpford Devon 11 E5
Harpham E Yorks 97 C6
Harpley Norf 80 E3
Harpley Worcs 49 C8
Harpole Northants 52 C4
Harpsdale Highld 158 E3
Harpsden Oxon 39 F7
Harpswell Lincs 90 F3
Harpur Hill Derbys 75 B7
Harpurhey Gtr Man 87 D6
Harraby Cumb 108 D4
Harrapool Highld 149 F11
Harrier Shetland 160 J1
Harrietfield Perth 127 B8
Harrietsham Kent 30 D2
Harrington Cumb 98 B1
Harrington Lincs 79 B6
Harrington Northants 64 F4
Harringworth Northants 65 E6
Harris Highld 146 B6
Harrogate N Yorks 95 D6
Harrold Bedford 53 D7
Harrow London 40 F4
Harrow on the Hill London 40 F4
Harrow Street Suff 56 F3
Harrow Weald London 40 E4
Harrowbarrow Corn 5 C8
Harrowden Bedford 53 E8
Harrowgate Hill Darl 101 C7
Harston Cambs 54 D5
Harston Leics 77 F8
Harswell E Yorks 96 E4
Hart Hrtlpl 111 F7
Hart Common Gtr Man 86 D4
Hart Hill Luton 40 B4
Hart Station Hrtlpl 111 F7
Hartburn Northumb 117 F6
Hartburn Stockton 102 C2
Hartest Suff 56 D2
Hartfield E Sus 29 F5
Hartford Cambs 54 B3
Hartford Ches W 74 B3
Hartford End Essex 42 C2
Hartfordbridge Hants 27 D5
Hartforth N Yorks 101 D6
Harthill Ches W 74 D2
Harthill N Lanark 120 C2
Harthill S Yorks 89 F5
Hartington Derbys 75 C8
Hartland Devon 8 B4
Hartlebury Worcs 50 B3
Hartlepool Hrtlpl 111 F8
Hartley Cumb 100 D2
Hartley Kent 18 B4
Hartley Kent 29 C7
Hartley Northumb 111 B6
Hartley Westpall Hants 26 D4
Hartley Wintney Hants 27 D5
Hartlip Kent 30 C2
Hartoft End N Yorks 103 E5
Harton N Yorks 96 C3
Harton Shrops 60 F4
Harton T&W 111 C6
Hartpury Glos 36 B4
Hartshead W Yorks 88 B2
Hartshill Warks 63 E7
Hartshorne Derbys 63 B7
Hartsop Cumb 99 C6
Hartwell Northants 53 D5
Hartwood N Lanark 119 D8
Harvieston Stirling 126 F4
Harvington Worcs 51 E5
Harvington Cross Worcs 51 E5
Harwell Oxon 38 F4
Harwich Essex 57 F6
Harwood Durham 109 F8
Harwood Gtr Man 86 C5
Harwood Dale N Yorks 103 E7
Harworth Notts 89 E7
Hasbury W Mid 62 F3
Hascombe Sur 27 E7
Haselbech Northants 52 B5
Haselbury Plucknett Som 12 C2
Haseley Warks 51 C7
Haselor Warks 51 D6
Hasfield Glos 37 B5
Hasguard Pembs 44 E3
Haskayne Lancs 85 D4
Hasketon Suff 57 D6
Hasland Derbys 76 C3
Haslemere Sur 27 F7
Haslingden Lancs 87 B5
Haslingfield Cambs 54 D5
Haslington Ches E 74 D4
Hassall Ches E 74 D4
Hassall Green Ches E 74 D4
Hassell Street Kent 30 E4
Hassendean Borders 115 B8
Hassingham Norf 69 D6
Hassocks W Sus 17 C6
Hassop Derbys 76 B2
Hastigrow Highld 158 D4
Hastingleigh Kent 30 E4
Hastings E Sus 18 E5
Hastingwood Essex 41 D7
Hastoe Herts 40 D2
Haswell Durham 111 E6
Haswell Plough Durham 111 E6
Hatch C Beds 54 E2
Hatch Hants 26 D4
Hatch Wilts 13 B7
Hatch Beauchamp Som 11 B8
Hatch End London 40 E4
Hatch Green Som 11 C8
Hatchet Gate Hants 14 D4
Hatching Green Herts 40 C4
Hatchmere Ches W 74 B2
Hatcliffe NE Lincs 91 D6
Hatfield Hereford 49 D7
Hatfield Herts 41 D5
Hatfield S Yorks 89 D7
Hatfield Worcs 50 D3
Hatfield Broad Oak Essex 41 C8
Hatfield Garden Village Herts 41 D5
Hatfield Heath Essex 41 C8
Hatfield Hyde Herts 41 C5
Hatfield Peverel Essex 42 C3
Hatfield Woodhouse S Yorks 89 D7
Hatford Oxon 38 E3
Hatherden Hants 25 D8
Hatherleigh Devon 9 D7
Hathern Leics 63 B8
Hatherop Glos 38 D1
Hathersage Derbys 88 F3
Hathershaw Gtr Man 87 D7

Hatherton Ches E 74 E3
Hatherton Staffs 62 C3
Hatley St George Cambs 54 D3
Hatt Corn 5 C8
Hattingley Hants 26 F4
Hatton Aberds 153 E10
Hatton Derbys 63 B6
Hatton Lincs 78 B4
Hatton Shrops 60 E4
Hatton Warks 51 C7
Hatton Warr 86 F3
Hatton Castle Aberds 153 D7
Hatton Heath Ches W 73 C8
Hatton of Fintray Aberds 141 C7
Hattoncrook Aberds 141 B7
Haugh E Ayrs 112 B4
Haugh Gtr Man 87 C7
Haugh Lincs 79 B7
Haugh Head Northumb 117 B6
Haugh of Glass Moray 152 E4
Haugh of Urr Dumfries 106 C5
Haugham Lincs 91 F7
Haughley Suff 56 C4
Haughley Green Suff 56 C4
Haughs of Clinterty Aberdeen 141 C7
Haughton Notts 77 B6
Haughton Shrops 60 B3
Haughton Shrops 61 C5
Haughton Shrops 61 D7
Haughton Shrops 61 E6
Haughton Staffs 62 B2
Haughton Castle Northumb 110 B2
Haughton Green Gtr Man 87 E7
Haughton Moss Ches E 74 D2
Haultwick Herts 41 B6
Haunn Argyll 146 G6
Haunn W Isles 148 G2
Haunton Staffs 63 C6
Hauxley Northumb 117 D8
Hauxton Cambs 54 D5
Havant Hants 15 D8
Haven Hereford 49 D6
Haven Bank Lincs 78 D5
Haven Side E Yorks 91 B5
Havenstreet IoW 15 E6
Havercroft W Yorks 88 C4
Haverfordwest = Hwlffordd Pembs 44 D4
Haverhill Suff 55 E7
Haverigg Cumb 92 B1
Havering-atte-Bower London 41 E8
Haveringland Norf 81 E7
Haversham M Keynes 53 E6
Haverthwaite Cumb 99 F5
Haverton Hill Stockton 102 B2
Hawarden = Penarlâg Flint 73 C7
Hawcoat Cumb 92 B2
Hawen Ceredig 46 E2
Hawes N Yorks 100 F3
Hawes' Green Norf 68 E5
Hawes Side Blackpool 92 F3
Hawford Worcs 50 C3
Hawick Borders 115 C8
Hawk Green Gtr Man 87 F7
Hawkchurch Devon 11 D8
Hawkedon Suff 55 D8
Hawkenbury Kent 18 B2
Hawkenbury Kent 30 E2
Hawkeridge Wilts 24 D3
Hawkerland Devon 11 F5
Hawkes End W Mid 63 F7
Hawkesbury S Glos 36 F4
Hawkesbury Warks 63 F7
Hawkesbury Upton S Glos 36 F4
Hawkhill Northumb 117 C8
Hawkhurst Kent 18 B4
Hawkinge Kent 31 F6
Hawkley Hants 15 B8
Hawkridge Som 21 F7
Hawkshead Cumb 99 E5
Hawkshead Hill Cumb 99 E5
Hawksland S Lanark 119 F8
Hawkswick N Yorks 94 B2
Hawksworth Notts 77 E7
Hawksworth W Yorks 94 E4
Hawksworth W Yorks 95 F5
Hawkwell Essex 42 E4
Hawley Hants 27 D6
Hawley Kent 29 B6
Hawling Glos 37 B7
Hawnby N Yorks 102 F3
Haworth W Yorks 94 F3
Hawstead Suff 56 D2
Hawthorn Durham 111 E7
Hawthorn Rhondda 35 F5
Hawthorn Wilts 24 C3
Hawthorn Hill Brack 27 B6
Hawthorn Hill Lincs 78 D5
Hawthorpe Lincs 65 B7
Hawton Notts 77 D7
Haxby York 96 D2
Haxey N Lincs 89 D8
Hay Green Norf 66 C5
Hay-on-Wye = Y Gelli Gandryll Powys 48 E4
Hay Street Herts 41 B6
Haydock Mers 86 E3
Haydon Dorset 12 C4
Haydon Bridge Northumb 109 C8
Haydon Wick Swindon 37 F8
Haye Corn 5 C8
Hayes London 28 C5
Hayes London 40 F4
Hayfield Derbys 87 F8
Hayfield Fife 128 E4
Hayhill E Ayrs 112 C4
Hayhillock Angus 135 E5
Hayle Corn 2 C4
Haynes C Beds 53 E8
Haynes Church End C Beds 53 E8
Hayscastle Pembs 44 C3
Hayscastle Cross Pembs 44 C4
Hayshead Angus 135 E6
Hayton Aberdeen 141 D8
Hayton Cumb 107 E8
Hayton Cumb 108 D5
Hayton E Yorks 96 E4
Hayton Notts 89 F8
Hayton's Bent Shrops 60 F5
Haytor Vale Devon 7 B5
Haywards Heath W Sus 17 B7
Haywood S Yorks 89 C6
Haywood Oaks Notts 77 D6
Hazel Grove Gtr Man 87 F7
Hazel Street Kent 18 B3
Hazelbank S Lanark 119 E8
Hazelbury Bryan Dorset 12 D5
Hazeley Hants 26 D5
Hazelhurst Gtr Man 87 D7
Hazelslade Staffs 62 C4
Hazelton Glos 37 C7
Hazelton Walls Fife 128 B5
Hazelwood Derbys 76 E3
Hazlemere Bucks 40 E1
Hazlerigg T&W 110 B5
Hazlewood N Yorks 94 D3
Hazon Northumb 117 D7
Heacham Norf 80 D2
Head of Muir Falk 127 F7
Headbourne Worthy Hants 26 F2
Headbrook Hereford 48 D5
Headcorn Kent 30 E2
Headingley W Yorks 95 F5
Headington Oxon 39 D5
Headlam Durham 101 C6
Headless Cross Worcs 50 C5
Headley Hants 26 C3
Headley Hants 27 F6
Headley Sur 28 D3
Headon Notts 77 B7
Heads S Lanark 119 E7
Heads Nook Cumb 108 D4
Heage Derbys 76 D3
Healaugh N Yorks 95 E7
Healaugh N Yorks 101 E5
Heald Green Gtr Man 87 F6
Heale Devon 20 E5
Heale Som 23 E8
Healey Gtr Man 87 C6
Healey N Yorks 101 F6
Healey Northumb 110 D3
Healing NE Lincs 91 C6
Heamoor Corn 2 C3
Heanish Argyll 146 G3
Heanor Derbys 76 E4
Heanton Punchardon Devon 20 F4
Heapham Lincs 90 F2
Hearthstane Borders 114 B4
Heasley Mill Devon 21 F6
Heast Highld 149 G11
Heath Cardiff 22 B3
Heath Derbys 76 C4
Heath and Reach C Beds 40 B2
Heath End Hants 26 C3
Heath End Sur 27 E6
Heath End Warks 51 C7
Heath Hayes Staffs 62 C4
Heath Hill Shrops 61 C7
Heath House Som 23 E6
Heath Town W Mid 62 E3
Heathcote Derbys 75 C8
Heather Leics 63 C7
Heatherfield Highld 149 D9
Heathfield Devon 7 B6
Heathfield E Sus 18 C2
Heathfield Som 11 B6
Heathhall Dumfries 107 B6
Heathrow Airport London 27 B8
Heathstock Devon 11 D7
Heathton Shrops 62 E2
Heatley Warr 86 F5
Heaton Lancs 92 C4
Heaton Staffs 75 C6
Heaton T&W 111 C5
Heaton W Yorks 94 F4
Heaton Moor Gtr Man 87 E6
Heaverham Kent 29 D6
Heaviley Gtr Man 87 F7
Heavitree Devon 10 E4
Hebburn T&W 111 C6
Hebden N Yorks 94 C3
Hebden Bridge W Yorks 87 B7
Hebron Anglesey 82 C4
Hebron Carms 32 B2
Hebron Northumb 117 F7
Heck Dumfries 114 F3
Heckfield Hants 26 C5
Heckfield Green Suff 57 B5
Heckfordbridge Essex 43 B5
Heckington Lincs 78 E4
Heckmondwike W Yorks 88 B3
Heddington Wilts 24 C4
Heddle Orkney 159 G4
Heddon-on-the-Wall Northumb 110 C4
Hedenham Norf 69 E6
Hedge End Hants 15 C5
Hedgerley Bucks 40 F2
Hedging Som 11 B8
Hedley on the Hill Northumb 110 D3
Hednesford Staffs 62 C4
Hedon E Yorks 91 B5
Hedsor Bucks 40 F2
Hedworth T&W 111 C6
Hegdon Hill Hereford 49 D7
Heggerscales Cumb 100 C3
Heglibister Shetland 160 H5
Heighington Darl 101 B7
Heighington Lincs 78 C3
Heights of Brae Highld 151 E8
Heights of Kinlochewe Highld 150 E3
Heilam Highld 156 C7
Heiton Borders 122 F3
Hele Devon 10 D4
Hele Devon 20 E4
Helensburgh Argyll 145 E11
Helford Corn 3 D6
Helford Passage Corn 3 D6
Helhoughton Norf 80 E4
Helions Bumpstead Essex 55 E7
Hellaby S Yorks 89 E6
Helland Corn 5 B5
Hellesdon Norf 68 C5
Hellidon Northants 52 D3
Hellifield N Yorks 93 D8
Hellingly E Sus 18 D2
Hellington Norf 69 D6
Hellister Shetland 160 J5
Helm Northumb 117 E7
Helmdon Northants 52 E3
Helmingham Suff 57 D5
Helmington Row Durham 110 F4
Helmsdale Highld 157 H13
Helmshore Lancs 87 B5
Helmsley N Yorks 102 F4
Helperby N Yorks 95 C7
Helperthorpe N Yorks 97 B5
Helpringham Lincs 78 E4
Helpston Pboro 65 D8
Helsby Ches W 73 B8
Helsey Lincs 79 B8
Helston Corn 3 D5
Helstone Corn 8 F2
Helton Cumb 99 B7
Helwith Bridge N Yorks 93 C8
Hemblington Norf 69 C6
Hemel Hempstead Herts 40 D3
Hemingbrough N Yorks 96 F2
Hemingby Lincs 78 B5
Hemingford Abbots Cambs 54 B3
Hemingford Grey Cambs 54 B3
Hemingstone Suff 57 D5
Hemington Leics 63 B8
Hemington Northants 65 F7
Hemington Som 24 D2
Hemley Suff 57 E6
Hemlington Mbro 102 C3
Hemp Green Suff 57 C7
Hempholme E Yorks 97 D6
Hempnall Norf 68 E5
Hempnall Green Norf 68 E5
Hempriggs House Highld 158 F5
Hempstead Essex 55 F7
Hempstead Medway 29 C8
Hempstead Norf 69 B7
Hempstead Norf 81 D7
Hempsted Glos 37 C5
Hempton Norf 80 E5
Hempton Oxon 52 F2
Hemsby Norf 69 C7
Hemswell Lincs 90 E3
Hemswell Cliff Lincs 90 F3
Hemsworth W Yorks 88 C5
Hemyock Devon 11 C6
Hen-feddau fawr Pembs 45 F4
Henbury Bristol 23 B7
Henbury Ches E 75 B5
Hendon London 41 F5
Hendon T&W 111 D7
Hendre Flint 73 C5
Hendre-ddu Conwy 83 E8
Hendreforgan Rhondda 34 F3
Hendy Carms 33 D6
Heneglwys Anglesey 82 D4
Henfield W Sus 17 C6
Henford Devon 9 E5
Henghurst Kent 19 B6
Hengoed Caerph 35 E5
Hengoed Powys 48 D4
Hengoed Shrops 73 F6
Hengrave Suff 56 C2
Henham Essex 41 B8
Heniarth Powys 59 D8
Henlade Som 11 B7
Henley Shrops 49 B7
Henley Som 23 F6
Henley Suff 57 D5
Henley W Sus 16 B2
Henley-in-Arden Warks 51 C6
Henley-on-Thames Oxon 39 F7
Henley's Down E Sus 18 D4
Henllan Ceredig 46 E2
Henllan Denb 72 C4
Henllan Amgoed Carms 32 B2
Henllys Torf 35 E6
Henlow C Beds 54 F2
Hennock Devon 10 F3
Henny Street Essex 56 F2
Henryd Conwy 83 D7
Henry's Moat Pembs 32 B1
Hensall N Yorks 89 B6
Henshaw Northumb 109 C7
Hensingham Cumb 98 C1
Henstead Suff 69 F7
Henstridge Som 12 C5
Henstridge Ash Som 12 B5
Henstridge Marsh Som 12 B5
Henton Oxon 39 D7
Henton Som 23 E6
Henwood Corn 5 B7
Heogan Shetland 160 J6
Heol-las Swansea 33 E7
Heol Senni Powys 34 B3
Heol-y-Cyw Bridgend 34 F3
Hepburn Northumb 117 B6
Hepple Northumb 117 D5
Hepscott Northumb 117 F8
Heptonstall W Yorks 87 B7
Hepworth Suff 56 B3
Hepworth W Yorks 88 D2
Herbrandston Pembs 44 E3
Hereford Hereford 49 E7
Heriot Borders 121 D6
Hermiston Edin 120 B4
Hermitage Borders 115 E8
Hermitage Dorset 12 D4
Hermitage W Berks 26 B3
Hermitage W Sus 15 D8
Hermon Anglesey 82 E3
Hermon Carms 33 B7
Hermon Carms 46 F2
Hermon Pembs 45 F4
Herne Kent 31 C5
Herne Bay Kent 31 C5
Herner Devon 9 B7
Hernhill Kent 30 C4
Herodsfoot Corn 5 C7
Herongate Essex 42 E2
Heronsford S Ayrs 104 A5
Herriard Hants 26 E4
Herringfleet Suff 69 E7
Herringswell Suff 55 B8
Hersden Kent 31 C6
Hersham Corn 8 D4
Hersham Sur 28 C2
Herstmonceux E Sus 18 D3
Herston Orkney 159 J5
Hertford Herts 41 C6
Hertford Heath Herts 41 C6
Hertingfordbury Herts 41 C6
Hesket Newmarket Cumb 108 F3
Hesketh Bank Lancs 86 B2
Hesketh Lane Lancs 93 E6
Heskin Green Lancs 86 C3
Hesleden Durham 111 F7
Hesleyside Northumb 116 F4
Heslington York 96 D2
Hessay York 95 D8
Hessenford Corn 5 D8
Hessett Suff 56 C3
Hessle E Yorks 90 B4
Hest Bank Lancs 92 C4
Heston London 28 B2
Hestwall Orkney 159 G3
Heswall Mers 85 F3
Hethe Oxon 39 B5
Hethersett Norf 68 D4
Hethersgill Cumb 108 C4
Hethpool Northumb 116 B4
Hett Durham 111 F5
Hetton N Yorks 94 D2
Hetton-le-Hole T&W 111 E6
Hetton Steads Northumb 123 F6
Heugh Northumb 110 B3
Heugh-head Aberds 140 C2
Heveningham Suff 57 B7
Hever Kent 29 E5
Heversham Cumb 99 F6
Hevingham Norf 81 E7
Hewas Water Corn 3 B8
Hewelsfield Glos 36 D2
Hewish N Som 23 C6
Hewish Som 12 D2
Heworth York 96 D2
Hexham Northumb 110 C2
Hextable Kent 29 B6
Hexton Herts 54 F2
Hexworthy Devon 6 B4
Hey Lancs 93 E8
Heybridge Essex 42 D4
Heybridge Essex 42 E2
Heybridge Basin Essex 42 D4
Heybrook Bay Devon 6 E3
Heydon Cambs 54 E5
Heydon Norf 81 E7
Heydour Lincs 78 F3
Heylipol Argyll 146 G2
Heylor Shetland 160 E4
Heysham Lancs 92 C4
Heyshott W Sus 16 C2
Heyside Gtr Man 87 D7
Heytesbury Wilts 24 E4
Heythrop Oxon 38 B3
Heywood Gtr Man 87 C6
Heywood Wilts 24 D3
Hibaldstow N Lincs 90 D3
Hickleton S Yorks 89 D5
Hickling Norf 69 B7
Hickling Notts 64 B3
Hickling Green Norf 69 B7
Hickling Heath Norf 69 B7
Hickstead W Sus 17 B6
Hidcote Boyce Glos 51 E6
High Ackworth W Yorks 88 C5
High Angerton Northumb 117 F6
High Bankhill Cumb 109 E5
High Barnes T&W 111 D6
High Beach Essex 41 E7
High Bentham N Yorks 93 C6
High Bickington Devon 9 B8
High Birkwith N Yorks 93 B7
High Blantyre S Lanark 119 D6
High Bonnybridge Falk 119 B8
High Bradfield S Yorks 88 E3
High Bray Devon 21 F5
High Brooms Kent 29 E6
High Bullen Devon 9 B7
High Buston Northumb 117 D8
High Callerton Northumb 110 B4
High Catton E Yorks 96 D3
High Cogges Oxon 38 D3
High Coniscliffe Darl 101 C7
High Cross Hants 15 B8
High Cross Herts 41 C6
High Easter Essex 42 C2
High Eggborough N Yorks 89 B6
High Ellington N Yorks 101 F6
High Ercall Telford 61 C5
High Etherley Durham 101 B6
High Garrett Essex 42 B3
High Grange Durham 110 F4
High Green Norf 68 D4
High Green S Yorks 88 E4
High Green Worcs 50 E3
High Halden Kent 19 B5
High Halstow Medway 29 B8
High Ham Som 23 F6
High Harrington Cumb 98 B2
High Hatton Shrops 61 B6
High Hawsker N Yorks 103 D7
High Hesket Cumb 108 E4
High Hesleden Durham 111 F7
High Hoyland S Yorks 88 C3
High Hunsley E Yorks 97 F5
High Hurstwood E Sus 17 B8
High Hutton N Yorks 96 C3
High Ireby Cumb 108 F2
High Kelling Norf 81 C7
High Kilburn N Yorks 95 B8
High Lands Durham 101 B6
High Lane Gtr Man 87 F7
High Lane Worcs 49 C8
High Laver Essex 41 D8
High Legh Ches E 86 F5
High Leven Stockton 102 C2
High Littleton Bath 23 D8
High Lorton Cumb 98 B3
High Marishes N Yorks 96 B4
High Marnham Notts 77 B8
High Melton S Yorks 89 D6
High Mickley Northumb 110 C3
High Mindork Dumfries 105 D7
High Newton Cumb 99 F6
High Newton-by-the-Sea Northumb 117 B8
High Nibthwaite Cumb 98 F4
High Offley Staffs 61 B7
High Ongar Essex 42 D1
High Onn Staffs 62 C2
High Roding Essex 42 C2
High Row Cumb 108 F3
High Salvington W Sus 16 D5
High Sellafield Cumb 98 D2
High Shaw N Yorks 100 E3
High Spen T&W 110 D4
High Stoop Durham 110 E4
High Street Corn 4 D4
High Street Kent 18 B4
High Street Suff 56 E2
High Street Suff 57 B8
High Street Suff 57 D8
High Street Green Suff 56 D4
High Throston Hrtlpl 111 F7
High Toynton Lincs 79 C5
High Trewhitt Northumb 117 D6
High Valleyfield Fife 128 F2
High Westwood Durham 110 D4
High Wray Cumb 99 E5
High Wych Herts 41 C7
High Wycombe Bucks 40 E1
Higham Derbys 76 D3
Higham Kent 29 B8
Higham Lancs 93 F8
Higham Suff 55 C8
Higham Suff 56 F4
Higham Dykes Northumb 110 B4
Higham Ferrers Northants 53 C7
Higham Gobion C Beds 54 F2
Higham on the Hill Leics 63 E7
Higham Wood Kent 29 E6
Highampton Devon 9 D6
Highbridge Highld 136 F4
Highbridge Som 22 E5
Highbrook W Sus 28 F4
Highburton W Yorks 88 C2
Highbury Som 23 E8
Highclere Hants 26 C2
Highcliffe Dorset 14 E3
Higher Ansty Dorset 13 D5
Higher Ashton Devon 10 F3
Higher Ballam Lancs 92 F3
Higher Bartle Lancs 92 F5
Higher Boscaswell Corn 2 C2
Higher Burwardsley Ches W 74 D2
Higher Clovelly Devon 8 B5
Higher End Gtr Man 86 D3
Higher Kinnerton Flint 73 C7
Higher Penwortham Lancs 86 B3
Higher Town Scilly 2 E4
Higher Walreddon Devon 6 B2
Higher Walton Lancs 86 B3
Higher Walton Warr 86 F3
Higher Wheelton Lancs 86 B4
Higher Whitley Ches W 86 F4
Higher Wincham Ches W 74 B3
Higher Wych Ches W 73 E8
Highfield E Yorks 96 F3
Highfield Gtr Man 86 D5
Highfield N Ayrs 118 D3
Highfield Oxon 39 B5
Highfield S Yorks 88 F4
Highfield T&W 110 D4
Highfields Cambs 54 D4
Highfields Northumb 123 D5
Highgate London 41 F5
Highlane Ches E 75 C5
Highlane Derbys 88 F5
Highlaws Cumb 107 E8
Highleadon Glos 36 B4
Highleigh W Sus 16 E2
Highley Shrops 61 F7
Highmoor Cross Oxon 39 F7
Highmoor Hill Mon 36 F1
Highnam Glos 36 C4
Highnam Green Glos 36 B4
Highsted Kent 30 C3
Highstreet Green Essex 55 F8
Hightae Dumfries 107 B7
Hightown Ches E 75 C5
Hightown Mers 85 D4
Hightown Green Suff 56 D3
Highway Wilts 24 B5
Highweek Devon 7 B6
Highworth Swindon 38 E2
Hilborough Norf 67 D8
Hilcote Derbys 76 D4
Hilcott Wilts 25 D6
Hilden Park Kent 29 E6
Hildenborough Kent 29 E6
Hildersham Cambs 55 E6
Hilderstone Staffs 75 F6
Hilderthorpe E Yorks 97 C7
Hilfield Dorset 12 D4
Hilgay Norf 67 E6
Hill Pembs 32 D2
Hill S Glos 36 E3
Hill W Mid 62 E5
Hill Brow W Sus 15 B8
Hill Dale Lancs 86 C2
Hill Dyke Lincs 79 E6
Hill End Durham 110 F3
Hill End Fife 128 E2
Hill End N Yorks 94 D3
Hill Head Hants 15 D6
Hill Head Northumb 110 C2
Hill Mountain Pembs 44 E4
Hill of Beath Fife 128 E3
Hill of Fearn Highld 151 D11
Hill of Mountblairy Aberds 153 C6
Hill Ridware Staffs 62 C4
Hill Top Durham 100 B4
Hill Top Hants 14 D5
Hill Top W Mid 62 E3
Hill Top W Yorks 88 C4
Hill View Dorset 13 E7
Hillam N Yorks 89 B6
Hillbeck Cumb 100 C2
Hillborough Kent 31 C6
Hillbrae Aberds 141 B6
Hillbrae Aberds 152 D6
Hillbutts Dorset 13 D7
Hillcliffelane Derbys 76 E2
Hillcommon Som 11 B6
Hillend Fife 128 F3
Hillerton Devon 10 E2
Hillesden Bucks 39 B6
Hillesley Glos 36 F4
Hillfarance Som 11 B6
Hillhead Aberds 152 E5
Hillhead Devon 7 D7
Hillhead S Ayrs 112 C4
Hillhead of Auchentumb Aberds 153 C9
Hillhead of Cocklaw Aberds 153 D10
Hillhouse Borders 121 D8
Hilliclay Highld 158 D3
Hillingdon London 40 F3
Hillington Glasgow 118 C5
Hillington Norf 80 E3
Hillmorton Warks 52 B3
Hillockhead Aberds 140 C3
Hillockhead Aberds 140 D2
Hillside Aberds 141 E8
Hillside Angus 135 C7
Hillside Mers 85 C4
Hillside Orkney 159 J5
Hillside Shetland 160 G6
Hillswick Shetland 160 F4
Hillway IoW 15 F7
Hillwell Shetland 160 M5
Hilmarton Wilts 24 B5
Hilperton Wilts 24 D3
Hilsea Ptsmth 15 D7
Hilston E Yorks 97 F8
Hilton Aberds 153 E9
Hilton Cambs 54 C3
Hilton Cumb 100 B2
Hilton Derbys 76 F2
Hilton Dorset 13 D5
Hilton Durham 101 B6
Hilton Highld 151 C10
Hilton Shrops 61 E7
Hilton Stockton 102 C2
Hilton of Cadboll Highld 151 D11
Himbleton Worcs 50 D4
Himley Staffs 62 E2
Hincaster Cumb 99 F7
Hinckley Leics 63 E8
Hinderclay Suff 56 B4
Hinderton Ches W 73 B7
Hinderwell N Yorks 103 C5
Hindford Shrops 73 F7
Hindhead Sur 27 F6
Hindley Gtr Man 86 D4
Hindley Green Gtr Man 86 D4
Hindlip Worcs 50 D3
Hindolveston Norf 81 E6
Hindon Wilts 24 F4
Hindringham Norf 81 D5
Hingham Norf 68 D3
Hinstock Shrops 61 B6
Hintlesham Suff 56 E4
Hinton Hants 14 E3
Hinton Hereford 49 F5
Hinton Northants 52 D3
Hinton S Glos 24 B2
Hinton Shrops 60 D4
Hinton Ampner Hants 15 B6
Hinton Blewett Bath 23 D7
Hinton Charterhouse Bath 24 D2
Hinton-in-the-Hedges Northants 52 F3
Hinton Martell Dorset 13 D8
Hinton on the Green Worcs 50 E5
Hinton Parva Swindon 38 F2
Hinton St George Som 12 C2
Hinton St Mary Dorset 13 C5
Hinton Waldrist Oxon 38 E3
Hints Shrops 49 B8
Hints Staffs 63 D5
Hinwick Bedford 53 C7
Hinxhill Kent 30 E4
Hinxton Cambs 55 E5
Hinxworth Herts 54 E3
Hipperholme W Yorks 88 B2
Hipswell N Yorks 101 E6
Hirael Gwyn 83 D5
Hiraeth Carms 32 B2
Hirn Aberds 141 D6
Hirnant Powys 59 B7
Hirst N Lanark 119 C8
Hirst Northumb 117 F8
Hirst Courtney N Yorks 89 B7
Hirwaen Denb 72 C5
Hirwaun Rhondda 34 D3
Hiscott Devon 9 B7
Histon Cambs 54 C5
Hitcham Suff 56 D3
Hitchin Herts 40 B4
Hither Green London 28 B4
Hittisleigh Devon 10 E2
Hive E Yorks 96 F4
Hixon Staffs 62 B4
Hoaden Kent 31 D6
Hoaldalbert Mon 35 B7
Hoar Cross Staffs 62 B5
Hoarwithy Hereford 36 B2
Hoath Kent 31 C6
Hobarris Shrops 48 B5
Hobbister Orkney 159 H4
Hobkirk Borders 115 C8
Hobson Durham 110 D4
Hoby Leics 64 C3
Hockering Norf 68 C3
Hockerton Notts 77 D7
Hockley Essex 42 E4
Hockley Heath W Mid 51 B6
Hockliffe C Beds 40 B2
Hockwold cum Wilton Norf 67 F7
Hockworthy Devon 10 C5
Hoddesdon Herts 41 D6
Hoddlesden Blackburn 86 B5
Hoddom Mains Dumfries 107 B8
Hoddomcross Dumfries 107 B8
Hodgeston Pembs 32 E1
Hodley Powys 59 E8
Hodnet Shrops 61 B6
Hodthorpe Derbys 76 B5
Hoe Hants 15 C6
Hoe Norf 68 C2
Hoe Gate Hants 15 C7
Hoff Cumb 100 C1
Hog Patch Sur 27 E6
Hoggard's Green Suff 56 D2
Hoggeston Bucks 39 B8
Hogha Gearraidh W Isles 148 A2
Hoghton Lancs 86 B4
Hognaston Derbys 76 D2
Hogsthorpe Lincs 79 B8
Holbeach Lincs 66 B3
Holbeach Bank Lincs 66 B3
Holbeach Clough Lincs 66 B3
Holbeach Drove Lincs 66 C3
Holbeach Hurn Lincs 66 B3
Holbeach St Johns Lincs 66 C3
Holbeach St Marks Lincs 79 F6
Holbeach St Matthew Lincs 79 F7
Holbeck Notts 76 B5
Holbeck W Yorks 95 F5
Holbeck Woodhouse Notts 76 B5
Holberrow Green Worcs 50 D5
Holbeton Devon 6 D4
Holborn London 41 F6
Holbrook Derbys 76 E3
Holbrook S Yorks 88 F5
Holbrook Suff 57 F5
Holburn Northumb 123 F6
Holbury Hants 14 D5
Holcombe Devon 7 B7
Holcombe Som 23 E8
Holcombe Rogus Devon 11 C5
Holcot Northants 53 C5
Holden Lancs 93 E7
Holdenby Northants 52 C4
Holdenhurst Bmouth 14 E2
Holdgate Shrops 61 F5
Holdingham Lincs 78 E3
Holditch Dorset 11 D8
Hole-in-the-Wall Hereford 36 B3
Holefield Borders 122 F4
Holehouses Ches E 74 B4
Holemoor Devon 9 D6
Holestane Dumfries 113 E8
Holford Som 22 E3
Holgate York 95 D8
Holker Cumb 92 B3
Holkham Norf 80 C4
Hollacombe Devon 9 D5
Holland Orkney 159 C5
Holland Orkney 159 F7
Holland Fen Lincs 78 E5
Holland-on-Sea Essex 43 C8
Hollandstoun Orkney 159 C8
Hollee Dumfries 108 C2
Hollesley Suff 57 E7
Hollicombe Torbay 7 C6
Hollingbourne Kent 30 D2
Hollington Derbys 76 F2
Hollington E Sus 18 D4
Hollington Staffs 75 F7
Hollington Grove Derbys 76 F2
Hollingworth Gtr Man 87 E8
Hollins Gtr Man 87 D6
Hollins Green Warr 86 E4
Hollins Lane Lancs 92 D4
Hollinsclough Staffs 75 C7
Hollinwood Gtr Man 87 D7
Hollinwood Shrops 74 F2
Hollocombe Devon 9 C8
Hollow Meadows S Yorks 88 F3
Holloway Derbys 76 D3
Hollowell Northants 52 B4
Holly End Norf 66 D4
Holly Green Worcs 50 E3
Hollybush Caerph 35 D5
Hollybush E Ayrs 112 C3
Hollybush Worcs 50 F2
Hollym E Yorks 91 B7
Hollywood Worcs 51 B5
Holmbridge W Yorks 88 D2
Holmbury St Mary Sur 28 E2
Holmbush Corn 4 D5
Holmcroft Staffs 62 B3
Holme Cambs 65 F8
Holme Cumb 92 B5
Holme N Yorks 102 F1
Holme Notts 77 D8
Holme W Yorks 88 D2
Holme Chapel Lancs 87 B6
Holme Green N Yorks 95 E8
Holme Hale Norf 67 D8
Holme Lacy Hereford 49 F7
Holme Marsh Hereford 48 D5
Holme next the Sea Norf 80 C3
Holme-on-Spalding-Moor E Yorks 96 F4
Holme on the Wolds E Yorks 97 E5
Holme Pierrepont Notts 77 F6
Holme St Cuthbert Cumb 107 E8
Holme Wood W Yorks 94 F4
Holmer Hereford 49 E7
Holmer Green Bucks 40 E2
Holmes Chapel Ches E 74 C4
Holmesfield Derbys 76 B3
Holmeswood Lancs 86 C2
Holmewood Derbys 76 C4
Holmfirth W Yorks 88 D2
Holmhead Dumfries 113 F7
Holmhead E Ayrs 113 B5
Holmisdale Highld 148 D6
Holmpton E Yorks 91 B7
Holmrook Cumb 98 E2
Holmsgarth Shetland 160 J6
Holmwrangle Cumb 108 E5
Holne Devon 6 C5
Holnest Dorset 12 D4
Holsworthy Devon 8 D5
Holsworthy Beacon Devon 9 D5
Holt Dorset 13 D8
Holt Norf 81 D6
Holt Wilts 24 C3
Holt Worcs 50 C3
Holt Wrex 73 D8
Holt End Hants 26 F4
Holt End Worcs 51 C5
Holt Fleet Worcs 50 C3
Holt Heath Worcs 50 C3
Holt Park W Yorks 95 E5
Holtby York 96 D2
Holton Oxon 39 D6
Holton Som 12 B4
Holton Suff 57 B7
Holton cum Beckering Lincs 90 F5
Holton Heath Dorset 13 E7
Holton le Clay Lincs 91 D6
Holton le Moor Lincs 90 E4
Holton St Mary Suff 56 F4
Holwell Dorset 12 C5
Holwell Herts 54 F2
Holwell Leics 64 B4
Holwell Oxon 38 D2
Holwick Durham 100 B4
Holworth Dorset 13 F5
Holy Cross Worcs 50 B4
Holy Island Northumb 123 E7
Holybourne Hants 26 E5
Holyhead = Caergybi Anglesey 82 C2
Holymoorside Derbys 76 C3
Holyport Windsor 27 B6
Holystone Northumb 117 D5
Holytown N Lanark 119 C7
Holywell Cambs 54 B4
Holywell Corn 4 D2
Holywell Dorset 12 D3
Holywell E Sus 18 F2
Holywell = Treffynnon Flint 73 B5
Holywell Northumb 111 B6
Holywell Green W Yorks 87 C8
Holywell Lake Som 11 B6
Holywell Row Suff 55 B8
Holywood Dumfries 114 F2
Hom Green Hereford 36 B2
Homer Shrops 61 D6
Homersfield Suff 69 F5
Homington Wilts 14 B2
Honey Hill Kent 30 C5
Honey Street Wilts 25 C6
Honey Tye Suff 56 F3
Honeyborough Pembs 44 E4
Honeybourne Worcs 51 E6
Honeychurch Devon 9 D8
Honiley Warks 51 B7
Honing Norf 69 B6
Honingham Norf 68 C4
Honington Lincs 78 E2
Honington Suff 56 B3
Honington Warks 51 E7
Honiton Devon 11 D6
Honley W Yorks 88 C2
Hoo Green Ches E 86 F5
Hoo St Werburgh Medway 29 B8
Hood Green S Yorks 88 D4
Hooe E Sus 18 E3
Hooe Plym 6 D3
Hooe Common E Sus 18 D3
Hook E Yorks 89 B8
Hook Hants 26 D5
Hook London 28 C2
Hook Pembs 44 D4
Hook Wilts 37 F7
Hook Green Kent 18 B3
Hook Green Kent 29 C7
Hook Norton Oxon 51 F8
Hooke Dorset 12 E3
Hookgate Staffs 74 F4
Hookway Devon 10 E3
Hookwood Sur 28 E3
Hoole Ches W 73 C8
Hooley Sur 28 D3
Hoop Mon 36 D2
Hooton Ches W 73 B7
Hooton Levitt S Yorks 89 E6
Hooton Pagnell S Yorks 89 D5
Hooton Roberts S Yorks 89 E5
Hop Pole Lincs 65 C8
Hope Derbys 88 F2
Hope Devon 6 F4
Hope Highld 156 B7
Hope Powys 60 D2
Hope Shrops 60 D3
Hope Staffs 75 D8
Hope = Yr Hôb Flint 73 D7
Hope Bagot Shrops 49 B7
Hope Bowdler Shrops 60 E4
Hope End Green Essex 42 B1
Hope Green Ches E 87 F7
Hope Mansell Hereford 36 C3
Hope under Dinmore Hereford 49 D7
Hopeman Moray 152 B1
Hope's Green Essex 42 F3
Hopesay Shrops 60 F3
Hopley's Green Hereford 48 D5
Hopperton N Yorks 95 D7
Hopstone Shrops 61 E7
Hopton Shrops 60 B3
Hopton Shrops 61 B5
Hopton Staffs 62 B3
Hopton Suff 56 B3
Hopton Cangeford Shrops 60 F5
Hopton Castle Shrops 49 B5
Hopton on Sea Norf 69 D8
Hopton Wafers Shrops 49 B8
Hoptonheath Shrops 49 B5
Hopwas Staffs 63 D5
Hopwood Gtr Man 87 D6
Hopwood Worcs 50 B5
Horam E Sus 18 D2
Horbling Lincs 78 F4
Horbury W Yorks 88 C3
Horcott Glos 38 D1
Horden Durham 111 E7
Horderley Shrops 60 F4
Hordle Hants 14 E3
Hordley Shrops 73 F7
Horeb Carms 33 B6
Horeb Carms 33 D5
Horeb Ceredig 46 E2
Horfield Bristol 23 B8
Horham Suff 57 B6
Horkesley Heath Essex 43 B5
Horkstow N Lincs 90 C3
Horley Oxon 52 E2
Horley Sur 28 E3
Hornblotton Green Som 23 F7
Hornby Lancs 93 C5
Hornby N Yorks 101 E7
Hornby N Yorks 102 D1
Horncastle Lincs 79 C5
Hornchurch London 41 F8
Horncliffe Northumb 122 E5
Horndean Borders 122 E4
Horndean Hants 15 C8
Horndon Devon 6 B3
Horndon on the Hill Thurrock 42 F2
Horne Sur 28 E4
Horniehaugh Angus 134 C4
Horning Norf 69 C6
Horninghold Leics 64 E5
Horninglow Staffs 63 B6
Horningsea Cambs 55 C5
Horningsham Wilts 24 E3
Horningtoft Norf 80 E5
Hornsby Cumb 108 D5
Horns Corner Kent 18 C4
Horns Cross Devon 9 B5
Horns Cross E Sus 18 C5
Hornsea E Yorks 97 E8
Hornsea Bridge E Yorks 97 E8
Hornsey London 41 F6
Hornton Oxon 51 E8
Horrabridge Devon 6 C3
Horringer Suff 56 C2
Horringford IoW 15 F6
Horse Bridge Staffs 75 D6
Horsebridge Devon 6 B2
Horsebridge Hants 25 F8
Horsebrook Staffs 62 C2
Horsehay Telford 61 D6
Horseheath Cambs 55 E7
Horsehouse N Yorks 101 F5
Horsell Sur 27 D7
Horseman's Green Wrex 73 E8
Horseway Cambs 66 F4
Horsey Norf 69 B7
Horsford Norf 68 C4
Horsforth W Yorks 94 F5
Horsham W Sus 28 F2
Horsham Worcs 50 D2
Horsham St Faith Norf 68 C5
Horsington Lincs 78 C4
Horsington Som 12 B5
Horsley Derbys 76 E3
Horsley Glos 37 E5
Horsley Northumb 110 C3
Horsley Northumb 116 E4
Horsley Cross Essex 43 B7
Horsley Woodhouse Derbys 76 E3
Horsleycross Street Essex 43 B7
Horsleyhill Borders 115 C8
Horsleyhope Durham 110 E3
Horsmonden Kent 29 E7
Horspath Oxon 39 D5
Horstead Norf 69 C5
Horsted Keynes W Sus 17 B7
Horton Bucks 40 C2
Horton Dorset 13 D8
Horton Lancs 93 D8
Horton Northants 53 D6
Horton S Glos 36 F4
Horton Shrops 60 B4
Horton Som 11 C8
Horton Staffs 75 D6
Horton Swansea 33 F5
Horton Wilts 25 C5
Horton Windsor 27 B8
Horton-cum-Studley Oxon 39 C5
Horton Green Ches W 73 E8
Horton Heath Hants 15 C5
Horton in Ribblesdale N Yorks 93 B8
Horton Kirby Kent 29 C6
Hortonlane Shrops 60 C4
Horwich Gtr Man 86 C4
Horwich End Derbys 87 F8
Horwood Devon 9 B7
Hose Leics 64 B4
Hoselaw Borders 122 F4
Hoses Cumb 98 E4
Hosh Perth 127 B7
Hosta W Isles 148 A2
Hoswick Shetland 160 L6
Hotham E Yorks 96 F4
Hothfield Kent 30 E3
Hoton Leics 64 B2
Houbie Shetland 160 D8
Houdston S Ayrs 112 E1
Hough Ches E 74 D4
Hough Ches E 75 B5
Hough Green Halton 86 F2
Hough-on-the-Hill Lincs 78 E2
Hougham Lincs 77 E8
Houghton Cambs 54 B3
Houghton Cumb 108 D4
Houghton Hants 25 F8
Houghton Pembs 44 E4
Houghton W Sus 16 C4
Houghton Conquest C Beds 53 E8
Houghton Green E Sus 19 C6
Houghton Green Warr 86 E4
Houghton-le-Side Darl 101 B7
Houghton-Le-Spring T&W 111 E6
Houghton on the Hill Leics 64 D3
Houghton Regis C Beds 40 B3
Houghton St Giles Norf 80 D5
Houlland Shetland 160 F7
Houlland Shetland 160 H5
Houlsyke N Yorks 103 D5
Hound Hants 15 D5
Hound Green Hants 26 D5
Houndslow Borders 122 E2
Houndwood Borders 122 C4
Hounslow London 28 B2
Hounslow Green Essex 42 C2
Housay Shetland 160 F8
House of Daviot Highld 151 G10
House of Glenmuick Aberds 140 E2
Housetter Shetland 160 E5
Houss Shetland 160 K5
Houston Renfs 118 C4
Houstry Highld 158 G3
Houton Orkney 159 H4
Hove Brighton 17 D6
Hoveringham Notts 77 E6
Hoveton Norf 69 C6
Hovingham N Yorks 96 B2
How Cumb 108 D5
How Caple Hereford 49 F8
How End C Beds 53 E8
How Green Kent 29 E5
Howbrook S Yorks 88 E4
Howden Borders 116 B2
Howden E Yorks 89 B8
Howden-le-Wear Durham 110 F4
Howe Highld 158 D5
Howe N Yorks 101 F8
Howe Norf 69 D5
Howe Bridge Gtr Man 86 D4
Howe Green Essex 42 D3
Howe of Teuchar Aberds 153 D7
Howe Street Essex 42 C2
Howe Street Essex 55 F7
Howell Lincs 78 E4
Howey Powys 48 D2
Howgate Midloth 120 D5
Howick Northumb 117 C8
Howle Durham 101 B5
Howle Telford 61 B6
Howlett End Essex 55 F6
Howley Som 11 D7
Hownam Borders 116 C3
Hownam Mains Borders 116 B3
Howpasley Borders 115 D6
Howsham N Lincs 90 D4
Howsham N Yorks 96 C3
Howslack Dumfries 114 D3
Howtel Northumb 122 F4
Howton Hereford 35 B8
Howtown Cumb 99 C6
Howwood Renfs 118 C3
Hoxne Suff 57 B5
Hoy Orkney 159 H3
Hoylake Mers 85 F3
Hoyland S Yorks 88 D4
Hoylandswaine S Yorks 88 D3
Hubberholme N Yorks 94 B2
Hubbert's Bridge Lincs 79 E5
Huby N Yorks 95 C8
Huby N Yorks 95 E5
Hucclecote Glos 37 C5
Hucking Kent 30 D2
Hucknall Notts 76 E5
Huddersfield W Yorks 88 C2
Huddington Worcs 50 D4
Hudswell N Yorks 101 D6
Huggate E Yorks 96 D4
Hugglescote Leics 63 C8
Hugh Town Scilly 2 E4
Hughenden Valley Bucks 40 E1
Hughley Shrops 61 E5
Huish Devon 9 C7
Huish Wilts 25 C6
Huish Champflower Som 11 B5
Huish Episcopi Som 12 B2
Huisinis W Isles 154 F4
Hulcott Bucks 40 C1
Hulland Derbys 76 E2
Hulland Ward Derbys 76 E2
Hullavington Wilts 37 F5
Hullbridge Essex 42 E4
Hulme Gtr Man 87 E6

Hulme End Staffs 75 D8
Hulme Walfield Ches E 74 C5
Hulver Street Suff 69 F7
Hulverstone IoW 14 F4
Humber Hereford 49 D7
Humber Bridge N Lincs 90 B4
Humberston NE Lincs 91 D7
Humbie E Loth 121 C7
Humbleton E Yorks 97 F8
Humbleton Northumb 117 B5
Humby Lincs 78 F3
Hume Borders 122 E3
Humshaugh Northumb 110 B2
Huna Highld 158 C5
Huncoat Lancs 93 F7
Huncote Leics 64 E2
Hundalee Borders 116 C2
Hunderthwaite Durham 100 B4
Hundle Houses Lincs 79 D5
Hundleby Lincs 79 C6
Hundleton Pembs 44 E4
Hundon Suff 55 E8
Hundred Acres Hants 15 C6
Hundred End Lancs 86 B2
Hundred House Powys 48 D3
Hungarton Leics 64 D3
Hungerford Hants 14 C2
Hungerford W Berks 25 C8
Hungerford Newtown W Berks 25 B8
Hungerton Lincs 65 B5
Hungladder Highld 149 A8
Hunmanby N Yorks 97 B6
Hunmanby Moor N Yorks 97 B7
Hunningham Warks 51 C8
Hunny Hill IoW 15 F5
Hunsdon Herts 41 C7
Hunsingore N Yorks 95 D7
Hunslet W Yorks 95 F6
Hunsonby Cumb 109 F5
Hunspow Highld 158 C4
Hunstanton Norf 80 C2
Hunstanworth Durham 110 E2
Hunsterson Ches E 74 E3
Hunston Suff 56 C3
Hunston W Sus 16 D2
Hunstrete Bath 23 C8
Hunt End Worcs 50 C5
Hunter's Quay Argyll 145 F10
Hunthill Lodge Angus 134 B4
Hunting-tower Perth 128 B2
Huntingdon Cambs 54 B3
Huntingfield Suff 57 B7
Huntingford Dorset 24 F3
Huntington E Loth 121 B7
Huntington Hereford 48 D4
Huntington Staffs 62 C3
Huntington York 96 D2
Huntley Glos 36 C4
Huntly Aberds 152 E5
Huntlywood Borders 122 E2
Hunton Kent 29 E8
Hunton N Yorks 101 E6
Hunt's Corner Norf 68 F3
Hunt's Cross Mers 86 F2
Huntsham Devon 10 B5
Huntspill Som 22 E5
Huntworth Som 22 F5
Hunwick Durham 110 F4
Hunworth Norf 81 D6
Hurdsfield Ches E 75 B6
Hurley Warks 63 E6
Hurley Windsor 39 F8
Hurlford E Ayrs 118 F4
Hurliness Orkney 159 K3
Hurn Dorset 14 E2
Hurn's End Lincs 79 E7
Hursley Hants 14 B5
Hurst N Yorks 101 D5
Hurst Som 12 C2
Hurst Wokingham 27 B5
Hurst Green E Sus 18 C4
Hurst Green Lancs 93 F6
Hurst Wickham W Sus 17 C6
Hurstbourne Priors Hants 26 E2
Hurstbourne Tarrant Hants 25 D8
Hurstpierpoint W Sus 17 C6
Hurstwood Lancs 93 F8
Hurtmore Sur 27 E7
Hurworth Place Darl 101 D7
Hury Durham 100 C4
Husabost Highld 148 C7
Husbands Bosworth Leics 64 F3
Husborne Crawley C Beds 53 F7
Husthwaite N Yorks 95 B8
Hutchwns Bridgend 21 B7
Huthwaite Notts 76 D4
Huttoft Lincs 79 B8
Hutton Borders 122 D5
Hutton Cumb 99 B6
Hutton E Yorks 97 D6
Hutton Essex 42 E2
Hutton Lancs 86 B2
Hutton N Som 22 D5
Hutton Buscel N Yorks 103 F7
Hutton Conyers N Yorks 95 B6
Hutton Cranswick E Yorks 97 D6
Hutton End Cumb 108 F4
Hutton Gate Redcar 102 C3
Hutton Henry Durham 111 F7
Hutton-le-Hole N Yorks 103 E5
Hutton Magna Durham 101 C6
Hutton Roof Cumb 93 B5
Hutton Roof Cumb 108 F3
Hutton Rudby N Yorks 102 D2
Hutton Sessay N Yorks 95 B7
Hutton Village Redcar 102 C3
Hutton Wandesley N Yorks 95 D8
Huxley Ches W 74 C2
Huxter Shetland 160 G7
Huxter Shetland 160 H5
Huxton Borders 122 C4
Huyton Mers 86 E2
Hwlffordd = Haverfordwest Pembs 44 D4
Hycemoor Cumb 98 F2
Hyde Glos 37 D5
Hyde Gtr Man 87 E7
Hyde Hants 14 C2
Hyde Heath Bucks 40 D2
Hyde Park S Yorks 89 D6
Hydestile Sur 27 E7
Hylton Castle T&W 111 D6
Hyndford Bridge S Lanark 120 E2
Hynish Argyll 146 H2
Hyssington Powys 60 E3
Hythe Hants 14 D5
Hythe Kent 19 B8
Hythe End Windsor 27 B8
Hythie Aberds 153 C10

I

Ibberton Dorset 13 D5
Ible Derbys 76 D2
Ibsley Hants 14 D2
Ibstock Leics 63 C8
Ibstone Bucks 39 E7
Ibthorpe Hants 25 D8
Ibworth Hants 26 D3
Ichrachan Argyll 125 B6
Ickburgh Norf 67 E8
Ickenham London 40 F3
Ickford Bucks 39 D6
Ickham Kent 31 D6
Ickleford Herts 54 F2
Icklesham E Sus 19 D5
Ickleton Cambs 55 E5
Icklingham Suff 55 B8
Ickwell Green C Beds 54 E2
Icomb Glos 38 B2
Idbury Oxon 38 C2
Iddesleigh Devon 9 D7
Ide Devon 10 E3
Ide Hill Kent 29 D5
Ideford Devon 7 B6
Iden E Sus 19 C6
Iden Green Kent 18 B4
Iden Green Kent 18 B5
Idle W Yorks 94 F4
Idlicote Warks 51 E7
Idmiston Wilts 25 F6
Idole Carms 33 C5
Idridgehay Derbys 76 E2
Idrigill Highld 149 B8
Idstone Oxon 38 F2
Idvies Angus 135 E5
Iffley Oxon 39 D5
Ifield W Sus 28 F3
Ifold W Sus 27 F8
Iford E Sus 17 D8
Ifton Heath Shrops 73 F7
Ightfield Shrops 74 F2
Ightham Kent 29 D6
Iken Suff 57 D8
Ilam Staffs 75 D8
Ilchester Som 12 B3
Ilderton Northumb 117 B6
Ilford London 41 F7
Ilfracombe Devon 20 E4
Ilkeston Derbys 76 E4
Ilketshall St Andrew Suff 69 F6
Ilketshall St Lawrence Suff 69 F6
Ilketshall St Margaret Suff 69 F6
Ilkley W Yorks 94 E4
Illey W Mid 62 F3
Illingworth W Yorks 87 B8
Illogan Corn 3 B5
Illston on the Hill Leics 64 E4
Ilmer Bucks 39 D7
Ilmington Warks 51 E7
Ilminster Som 11 C8
Ilsington Devon 7 B5
Ilston Swansea 33 E6
Ilton N Yorks 94 B4
Ilton Som 11 C8
Imachar N Ayrs 143 D9
Imeraval Argyll 142 D4
Immingham NE Lincs 91 C5
Impington Cambs 54 C5
Ince Ches W 73 B8
Ince Blundell Mers 85 D4
Ince in Makerfield Gtr Man 86 D3
Inch of Arnhall Aberds 135 B6
Inchbare Angus 135 C6
Inchberry Moray 152 C3
Inchbraoch Angus 135 D7
Incheril Highld 150 E3
Inchgrundle Angus 134 B4
Inchina Highld 150 B2
Inchinnan Renfs 118 C4
Inchkinloch Highld 157 E8
Inchlaggan Highld 136 D4
Inchlumpie Highld 151 D8
Inchmore Highld 150 G6
Inchnacardoch Hotel Highld 137 C6
Inchnadamph Highld 156 G5
Inchree Highld 130 C4
Inchture Perth 128 B4
Inchyra Perth 128 B3
Indian Queens Corn 4 D4
Inerval Argyll 142 D4
Ingatestone Essex 42 E2
Ingbirchworth S Yorks 88 D3
Ingestre Staffs 62 B3
Ingham Lincs 90 F3
Ingham Norf 69 B6
Ingham Suff 56 B2
Ingham Corner Norf 69 B6
Ingleborough Norf 66 C4
Ingleby Derbys 63 B7
Ingleby Lincs 77 B8
Ingleby Arncliffe N Yorks 102 D2
Ingleby Barwick Stockton 102 C2
Ingleby Greenhow N Yorks 102 D3
Inglemire Hull 97 F6
Inglesbatch Bath 24 C2
Inglesham Swindon 38 E2
Ingleton Durham 101 B6
Ingleton N Yorks 93 B6
Inglewhite Lancs 92 E5
Ingliston Edin 120 B4
Ingoe Northumb 110 B3
Ingol Lancs 92 F5
Ingoldisthorpe Norf 80 D2
Ingoldmells Lincs 79 C8
Ingoldsby Lincs 78 F3
Ingon Warks 51 D7
Ingram Northumb 117 C6
Ingrow W Yorks 94 F3
Ings Cumb 99 E6
Ingst S Glos 36 F2
Ingworth Norf 81 E7
Inham's End Cambs 66 E2
Inkberrow Worcs 50 D5
Inkpen W Berks 25 C8
Inkstack Highld 158 C4
Inn Cumb 99 D6
Innellan Argyll 145 F10
Innerleithen Borders 121 F6
Innerleven Fife 129 D5
Innermessan Dumfries 104 C4
Innerwick E Loth 122 B3
Innerwick Perth 132 E2
Innis Chonain Argyll 125 C7
Insch Aberds 140 B5
Insh Highld 138 D4
Inshore Highld 156 C6
Inskip Lancs 92 F4
Instoneville S Yorks 89 C6
Instow Devon 20 F3
Intake S Yorks 89 D6
Inver Aberds 139 E8
Inver Highld 151 C11
Inver Perth 133 E7
Inver Mallie Highld 136 F4
Inverailort Highld 147 C10
Inveraldie Angus 134 F4
Inverallighin Highld 149 C13
Inverallochy Aberds 153 B10
Inveran Highld 151 B8
Inveraray Argyll 125 E6
Inverarish Highld 149 E10
Inverarity Angus 134 E4
Inverarnan Stirling 126 C2
Inverasdale Highld 155 J13
Inverbeg Argyll 126 E2
Inverbervie Aberds 135 B8
Inverboyndie Aberds 153 B6
Inverbroom Highld 150 C4
Invercassley Highld 156 J7
Invercauld House Aberds 139 E7
Inverchaolain Argyll 145 F9
Invercharnan Highld 131 E5
Inverchoran Highld 150 F5
Invercreran Argyll 130 E4
Inverdruie Highld 138 C5
Inverebrie Aberds 153 E9
Invereck Argyll 145 E10
Inverernan Ho. Aberds 140 C2
Invereshie House Highld 138 D4
Inveresk E Loth 121 B6
Inverey Aberds 139 F6
Inverfarigaig Highld 137 B8
Invergarry Highld 137 D6
Invergelder Aberds 139 E8
Invergeldie Perth 127 B6
Invergordon Highld 151 E10
Invergowrie Perth 134 F3
Inverguseran Highld 149 H12
Inverhadden Perth 132 D3
Inverharroch Moray 152 E3
Inverherive Stirling 126 B2
Inverie Highld 147 B10
Inverinan Argyll 125 D5
Inverinate Highld 136 B2
Inverkeilor Angus 135 E6
Inverkeithing Fife 128 F3
Inverkeithny Aberds 153 D6
Inverkip Invclyd 118 B2
Inverkirkaig Highld 156 H3
Inverlael Highld 150 C4
Inverlochlarig Stirling 126 C3
Inverlochy Argyll 125 C7
Inverlochy Highld 131 B5
Inverlussa Argyll 144 E5
Invermark Lodge Angus 140 F3
Invermoidart Highld 147 D9
Invermoriston Highld 137 C7
Invernaver Highld 157 C10
Inverneill Argyll 145 E7
Inverness Highld 151 G9
Invernettie Aberds 153 D11
Invernoaden Argyll 125 F7
Inveroran Hotel Argyll 131 E6
Inverpolly Lodge Highld 156 H3
Inverquharity Angus 134 D4
Inverquhomery Aberds 153 D10
Inverroy Highld 137 F5
Inversanda Highld 130 D3
Invershiel Highld 136 C2
Invershin Highld 151 B8
Inversnaid Hotel Stirling 126 D2
Inverugie Aberds 153 D11
Inveruglas Argyll 126 D2
Inveruglass Highld 138 D4
Inverurie Aberds 141 B6
Invervar Perth 132 E3
Inverythan Aberds 153 D7
Inwardleigh Devon 9 E7
Inworth Essex 42 C4
Iochdar W Isles 148 D2
Iping W Sus 16 B2
Ipplepen Devon 7 C6
Ipsden Oxon 39 F6
Ipsley Worcs 51 C5
Ipstones Staffs 75 D7
Ipswich Suff 57 E5
Irby Mers 85 F3
Irby in the Marsh Lincs 79 C7
Irby upon Humber NE Lincs 91 D5
Irchester Northants 53 C7
Ireby Cumb 108 F2
Ireby Lancs 93 B6
Ireland Orkney 159 H4
Ireland Shetland 160 L5
Ireland's Cross Shrops 74 E4
Ireleth Cumb 92 B2
Ireshopeburn Durham 109 F8
Irlam Gtr Man 86 E5
Irnham Lincs 65 B7
Iron Acton S Glos 36 F3
Iron Cross Warks 51 D5
Ironbridge Telford 61 D6
Irongray Dumfries 107 B6
Ironmacannie Dumfries 106 B3
Ironside Aberds 153 C8
Ironville Derbys 76 D4
Irstead Norf 69 B6
Irthington Cumb 108 C4
Irthlingborough Northants 53 B7
Irton N Yorks 103 F8
Irvine N Ayrs 118 F3
Isauld Highld 157 C12
Isbister Orkney 159 F3
Isbister Orkney 159 G4
Isbister Shetland 160 D5
Isbister Shetland 160 G7
Isfield E Sus 17 C8
Isham Northants 53 B6
Isle Abbotts Som 11 B8
Isle Brewers Som 11 B8
Isle of Whithorn Dumfries 105 F8
Isleham Cambs 55 B7
Isleornsay Highld 149 G12
Islesburgh Shetland 160 G5
Islesteps Dumfries 107 B6
Isleworth London 28 B2
Isley Walton Leics 63 B8
Islibhig W Isles 154 E4
Islington London 41 F6
Islip Northants 53 B7
Islip Oxon 39 C5
Istead Rise Kent 29 C7
Isycoed Wrex 73 D8
Itchen Soton 14 C5
Itchen Abbas Hants 26 F3
Itchen Stoke Hants 26 F3
Itchingfield W Sus 16 B5
Itchington S Glos 36 F3
Itteringham Norf 81 D7
Itton Devon 9 E8
Itton Common Mon 36 E1
Ivegill Cumb 108 E4
Iver Bucks 40 F3
Iver Heath Bucks 40 F3
Iveston Durham 110 D4
Ivinghoe Bucks 40 C2
Ivinghoe Aston Bucks 40 C2
Ivington Hereford 49 D6
Ivington Green Hereford 49 D6
Ivy Chimneys Essex 41 D7
Ivy Cross Dorset 13 B6
Ivy Hatch Kent 29 D6
Ivybridge Devon 6 D4
Ivychurch Kent 19 C7
Iwade Kent 30 C3
Iwerne Courtney or Shroton Dorset 13 C6
Iwerne Minster Dorset 13 C6
Ixworth Suff 56 B3
Ixworth Thorpe Suff 56 B3

J

Jack Hill N Yorks 94 D5
Jack in the Green Devon 10 E5
Jacksdale Notts 76 D4
Jackstown Aberds 153 E7
Jacobstow Corn 8 E3
Jacobstowe Devon 9 D7
Jameston Pembs 32 E1
Jamestown Dumfries 115 E6
Jamestown Highld 150 F7
Jamestown W Dunb 126 F2
Jarrow T&W 111 C6
Jarvis Brook E Sus 18 C2
Jasper's Green Essex 42 B3
Java Argyll 124 B3
Jawcraig Falk 119 B8
Jaywick Essex 43 C7
Jealott's Hill Brack 27 B6
Jedburgh Borders 116 B2
Jeffreyston Pembs 32 D1
Jellyhill E Dunb 119 B6
Jemimaville Highld 151 E10
Jersey Farm Herts 40 D4
Jesmond T&W 111 C5
Jevington E Sus 18 E2
Jockey End Herts 40 C3
John o'Groats Highld 158 C5
Johnby Cumb 108 F4
John's Cross E Sus 18 C4
Johnshaven Aberds 135 C7
Johnston Pembs 44 D4
Johnstone Renfs 118 C4
Johnstonebridge Dumfries 114 E3
Johnstown Carms 33 C5
Johnstown Wrex 73 E7
Joppa Edin 121 B6
Joppa S Ayrs 112 C4
Jordans Bucks 40 E2
Jordanthorpe S Yorks 88 F4
Jump S Yorks 88 D4
Jumpers Green Dorset 14 E2
Juniper Green Edin 120 C4
Jurby East IoM 84 C3
Jurby West IoM 84 C3

K

Kaber Cumb 100 C2
Kaimend S Lanark 120 E2
Kaimes Edin 121 C5
Kalemouth Borders 116 B3
Kames Argyll 124 D4
Kames Argyll 145 F8
Kames E Ayrs 113 B6
Kea Corn 3 B7
Keadby N Lincs 90 C2
Keal Cotes Lincs 79 C6
Kearsley Gtr Man 87 D5
Kearstwick Cumb 99 F8
Kearton N Yorks 100 E4
Kearvaig Highld 156 B5
Keasden N Yorks 93 C7
Keckwick Halton 86 F3
Keddington Lincs 91 F7
Kedington Suff 55 E8
Kedleston Derbys 76 E3
Keelby Lincs 91 C5
Keele Staffs 74 E5
Keeley Green Bedford 53 E8
Keeston Pembs 44 D4
Keevil Wilts 24 D4
Kegworth Leics 63 B8
Kehelland Corn 2 B5
Keig Aberds 140 C5
Keighley W Yorks 94 E3
Keil Highld 130 D3
Keilarsbrae Clack 127 E7
Keilhill Aberds 153 C7
Keillmore Argyll 144 E5
Keillor Perth 134 E2
Keillour Perth 127 B8
Keills Argyll 142 B5
Keils Argyll 144 G4
Keinton Mandeville Som 23 F7
Keir Mill Dumfries 113 E8
Keisby Lincs 65 B7
Keiss Highld 158 D5
Keith Moray 152 C4
Keith Inch Aberds 153 D11
Keithock Angus 135 C6
Kelbrook Lancs 94 E2
Kelby Lincs 78 E3
Keld Cumb 99 C7
Keld N Yorks 100 D3
Keldholme N Yorks 103 F5
Kelfield N Lincs 90 D2
Kelfield N Yorks 95 F8
Kelham Notts 77 D7
Kellan Argyll 147 G8
Kellas Angus 134 F4
Kellas Moray 152 C1
Kellaton Devon 7 F6
Kelleth Cumb 100 D1
Kelleythorpe E Yorks 97 D5
Kelling Norf 81 C6
Kellingley N Yorks 89 B6
Kellington N Yorks 89 B6
Kelloe Durham 111 F6
Kelloholm Dumfries 113 C7
Kelly Devon 9 F5
Kelly Bray Corn 5 B8
Kelmarsh Northants 52 B5
Kelmscot Oxon 38 E2
Kelsale Suff 57 C7
Kelsall Ches W 74 C2
Kelsall Hill Ches W 74 C2
Kelshall Herts 54 F4
Kelsick Cumb 107 D8
Kelso Borders 122 F3
Kelstedge Derbys 76 C3
Kelstern Lincs 91 E6
Kelston Bath 24 C2
Keltneyburn Perth 132 E4
Kelton Dumfries 107 B6
Kelty Fife 128 E3
Kelvedon Essex 42 C4
Kelvedon Hatch Essex 42 E1
Kelvin S Lanark 119 D6
Kelvinside Glasgow 119 C5
Kelynack Corn 2 C2
Kemback Fife 129 C6
Kemberton Shrops 61 D7
Kemble Glos 37 E6
Kemerton Worcs 50 F4
Kemeys Commander Mon 35 D7
Kemnay Aberds 141 C6
Kemp Town Brighton 17 D7
Kempley Glos 36 B3
Kemps Green Warks 51 B6
Kempsey Worcs 50 E3
Kempsford Glos 38 E1
Kempshott Hants 26 D4
Kempston Bedford 53 E8
Kempston Hardwick Bedford 53 E8
Kempton Shrops 60 F3
Kemsing Kent 29 D6
Kemsley Kent 30 C3
Kenardington Kent 19 B6
Kenchester Hereford 49 E6
Kencot Oxon 38 D2
Kendal Cumb 99 E7
Kendoon Dumfries 113 F6
Kendray S Yorks 88 D4
Kenfig Bridgend 34 F2
Kenfig Hill Bridgend 34 F2
Kenilworth Warks 51 B7
Kenknock Stirling 132 F1
Kenley London 28 D4
Kenley Shrops 61 D5
Kenmore Highld 149 C12
Kenmore Perth 132 E4
Kenn Devon 10 F4
Kenn N Som 23 C6
Kennacley W Isles 154 H6
Kennacraig Argyll 145 G7
Kennerleigh Devon 10 D3
Kennet Clack 127 E8
Kennethmont Aberds 140 B4
Kennett Cambs 55 C7
Kennford Devon 10 F4
Kenninghall Norf 68 F3
Kenninghall Heath Norf 68 F3
Kennington Kent 30 E4
Kennington Oxon 39 D5
Kennoway Fife 129 D5
Kenny Hill Suff 55 B7
Kennythorpe N Yorks 96 C3
Kenovay Argyll 146 G2
Kensaleyre Highld 149 C9
Kensington London 28 B3
Kensworth C Beds 40 C3
Kensworth Common C Beds 40 C3
Kent Street E Sus 18 D4
Kent Street Kent 29 D7
Kent Street W Sus 17 B6
Kentallen Highld 130 D4
Kentchurch Hereford 35 B8
Kentford Suff 55 C8
Kentisbeare Devon 11 D5
Kentisbury Devon 20 E5
Kentisbury Ford Devon 20 E5
Kentmere Cumb 99 D6
Kenton Devon 10 F4
Kenton Suff 57 C5
Kenton T&W 110 C5
Kenton Bankfoot T&W 110 C5
Kentra Highld 147 E9
Kents Bank Cumb 92 B3
Kent's Green Glos 36 B4
Kent's Oak Hants 14 B4
Kenwick Shrops 73 F8
Kenwyn Corn 3 B7
Keoldale Highld 156 C6
Keppanach Highld 130 C4
Keppoch Highld 136 B2
Keprigan Argyll 143 G7
Kepwick N Yorks 102 E2
Kerchesters Borders 122 F3
Keresley W Mid 63 F7
Kernborough Devon 7 E5
Kerne Bridge Hereford 36 C2
Kerris Corn 2 D3
Kerry Powys 59 F8
Kerrycroy Argyll 145 G10
Kerry's Gate Hereford 49 F5
Kerrysdale Highld 149 A13
Kersall Notts 77 C7
Kersey Suff 56 E4
Kershopefoot Cumb 115 F7
Kersoe Worcs 50 F4
Kerswell Devon 11 D5
Kerswell Green Worcs 50 E3
Kesgrave Suff 57 E6
Kessingland Suff 69 F8
Kessingland Beach Suff 69 F8
Kessington E Dunb 119 B5
Kestle Corn 3 B8
Kestle Mill Corn 4 D3
Keston London 28 C5
Keswick Cumb 98 B4
Keswick Norf 68 D5
Keswick Norf 81 D9
Ketley Telford 61 C6
Ketley Bank Telford 61 C6
Ketsby Lincs 79 B6
Kettering Northants 53 B6
Ketteringham Norf 68 D4
Kettins Perth 134 F2
Kettlebaston Suff 56 D3
Kettlebridge Fife 128 D5
Kettleburgh Suff 57 C6
Kettlehill Fife 128 D5
Kettleholm Dumfries 107 B8
Kettleness N Yorks 103 C6
Kettleshume Ches E 75 B6
Kettlesing Bottom N Yorks 94 D5
Kettlesing Head N Yorks 94 D5
Kettlestone Norf 81 D5
Kettlethorpe Lincs 77 B8
Kettletoft Orkney 159 E7
Kettlewell N Yorks 94 B2
Ketton Rutland 65 D6
Kew London 28 B2
Kew Br. London 28 B2
Kewstoke N Som 22 C5
Kexbrough S Yorks 88 D4
Kexby Lincs 90 F2
Kexby York 96 D3
Key Green Ches E 75 C5
Keyham Leics 64 D3
Keyhaven Hants 14 E4
Keyingham E Yorks 91 B6
Keymer W Sus 17 C7
Keynsham Bath 23 C8
Keysoe Bedford 53 C8
Keysoe Row Bedford 53 C8
Keyston Cambs 53 B8
Keyworth Notts 77 F6
Kibblesworth T&W 110 D5
Kibworth Beauchamp Leics 64 E3
Kibworth Harcourt Leics 64 E3
Kidbrooke London 28 B5
Kiddemore Green Staffs 62 D2
Kidderminster Worcs 50 B3
Kiddington Oxon 38 B4
Kidlington Oxon 38 C4
Kidmore End Oxon 26 B4
Kidsgrove Staffs 74 D5
Kidstones N Yorks 100 F4
Kidwelly = Cydweli Carms 33 D5
Kiel Crofts Argyll 124 B5
Kielder Northumb 116 E2
Kierfiold Ho Orkney 159 G3
Kilbagie Fife 127 F8
Kilbarchan Renfs 118 C4
Kilbeg Highld 149 H11
Kilberry Argyll 144 G6
Kilbirnie N Ayrs 118 D3
Kilbride Argyll 124 C4
Kilbride Argyll 124 C5
Kilbride Highld 149 F10
Kilburn Angus 134 C3
Kilburn Derbys 76 E3
Kilburn London 41 F5
Kilburn N Yorks 95 B8
Kilby Leics 64 E3
Kilchamaig Argyll 145 G7
Kilchattan Argyll 144 D2
Kilchattan Bay Argyll 145 H10
Kilchenzie Argyll 143 F7
Kilcheran Argyll 124 B4
Kilchiaran Argyll 142 B3
Kilchoan Argyll 124 D3
Kilchoan Highld 146 E7
Kilchoman Argyll 142 B3
Kilchrenan Argyll 125 C6
Kilconquhar Fife 129 D6
Kilcot Glos 36 B3
Kilcoy Highld 151 F8
Kilcreggan Argyll 145 E11
Kildale N Yorks 102 D4
Kildalloig Argyll 143 G8
Kildary Highld 151 D10
Kildermorie Lodge Highld 151 D8
Kildonan N Ayrs 143 F11
Kildonan Lodge Highld 157 G12
Kildonnan Highld 146 C7
Kildrummy Aberds 140 C3
Kildwick N Yorks 94 E3
Kilfinan Argyll 145 F8
Kilfinnan Highld 137 E5
Kilgetty Pembs 32 D2
Kilgwrrwg Common Mon 36 E1
Kilham E Yorks 97 C6
Kilham Northumb 122 F4
Kilkenneth Argyll 146 G2
Kilkerran Argyll 143 G8
Kilkhampton Corn 9 E6
Killamarsh Derbys 89 F5
Killay Swansea 33 E7
Killbeg Argyll 147 G9
Killean Argyll 143 D7
Killearn Stirling 126 F4
Killen Highld 151 F9
Killerby Darl 101 C6
Killichonan Perth 132 D2
Killiechonate Highld 136 F5
Killiechronan Argyll 147 G8
Killiecrankie Perth 133 C6
Killiemor Argyll 146 H7
Killiemore House Argyll 146 J7
Killilan Highld 150 H2
Killimster Highld 158 E5
Killin Stirling 132 F2
Killin Lodge Highld 137 D8
Killinallan Argyll 142 A4
Killinghall N Yorks 95 D5
Killington Cumb 99 F8
Killingworth T&W 111 B5
Killmahumaig Argyll 144 D6
Killochyett Borders 121 E7
Killocraw Argyll 143 E7
Killundine Highld 147 G8
Kilmacolm Invclyd 118 C3
Kilmaha Argyll 124 E5
Kilmahog Stirling 126 D5
Kilmalieu Highld 130 D2
Kilmaluag Highld 149 A9
Kilmany Fife 129 B5
Kilmarie Highld 149 G10
Kilmarnock E Ayrs 118 F4
Kilmaron Castle Fife 129 C5
Kilmartin Argyll 124 F4
Kilmaurs E Ayrs 118 E4
Kilmelford Argyll 124 D4
Kilmeny Argyll 142 B4
Kilmersdon Som 23 D8
Kilmeston Hants 15 B6
Kilmichael Argyll 143 F7
Kilmichael Glassary Argyll 145 D7
Kilmichael of Inverlussa Argyll 144 E6
Kilmington Devon 11 E7
Kilmington Wilts 24 F2
Kilmonivaig Highld 136 F4
Kilmorack Highld 150 G7
Kilmore Argyll 124 C4
Kilmore Highld 149 H11
Kilmory Argyll 144 F6
Kilmory Highld 147 D8
Kilmory Highld 149 H8
Kilmory N Ayrs 143 F10
Kilmuir Highld 148 D7
Kilmuir Highld 149 A8
Kilmuir Highld 151 D10
Kilmuir Highld 151 G9
Kilmun Argyll 124 D5
Kilmun Argyll 145 E10
Kiln Pit Hill Northumb 110 D3
Kilncadzow S Lanark 119 E8
Kilndown Kent 18 B4
Kilnhurst S Yorks 89 E5
Kilninian Argyll 146 G6
Kilninver Argyll 124 C4
Kilnsea E Yorks 91 C8
Kilnsey N Yorks 94 C2
Kilnwick E Yorks 97 E5
Kilnwick Percy E Yorks 96 D4
Kiloran Argyll 144 D2
Kilpatrick N Ayrs 143 F10
Kilpeck Hereford 49 F6
Kilphedir Highld 157 H12
Kilpin E Yorks 89 B8
Kilpin Pike E Yorks 89 B8
Kilrenny Fife 129 D7
Kilsby Northants 52 B3
Kilspindie Perth 128 B4
Kilsyth N Lanark 119 B7
Kiltarlity Highld 151 G8
Kilton Notts 77 B5
Kilton Som 22 E3
Kilton Thorpe Redcar 102 C4
Kilvaxter Highld 149 B8
Kilve Som 22 E3
Kilvington Notts 77 E7
Kilwinning N Ayrs 118 E3
Kimber worth S Yorks 88 E5
Kimberley Norf 68 D3
Kimberley Notts 76 E5
Kimble Wick Bucks 39 D8
Kimblesworth Durham 111 E5
Kimbolton Cambs 53 C8
Kimbolton Hereford 49 C7
Kimcote Leics 64 F2
Kimmeridge Dorset 13 G7
Kimmerston Northumb 123 F5
Kimpton Hants 25 E7
Kimpton Herts 40 C4
Kinbrace Highld 157 F11
Kinbuck Stirling 127 D6
Kincaple Fife 129 C6
Kincardine Fife 127 F8
Kincardine Highld 151 C9
Kincardine Bridge Falk 127 F8
Kincardine O'Neil Aberds 140 E4
Kinclaven Perth 134 F1
Kincorth Aberdeen 141 D8
Kincorth Ho. Moray 151 E13
Kincraig Highld 138 D4
Kincraigie Perth 133 E6
Kindallachan Perth 133 E6
Kineton Glos 37 B7
Kineton Warks 51 D8
Kinfauns Perth 128 B3
King Edward Aberds 153 C7
King Sterndale Derbys 75 B7
Kingairloch Highld 130 D2
Kingarth Argyll 145 H9
Kingcoed Mon 35 D8
Kingerby Lincs 90 E4
Kingham Oxon 38 B2
Kingholm Quay Dumfries 107 B6
Kinghorn Fife 128 F4
Kingie Highld 136 D4
Kinglassie Fife 128 E4
Kingoodie Perth 128 B5
King's Acre Hereford 49 E6
King's Bromley Staffs 62 C5
King's Caple Hereford 36 B2
King's Cliffe Northants 65 E7
King's Coughton Warks 51 D5
King's Heath W Mid 62 F4
Kings Hedges Cambs 55 C5
Kings Langley Herts 40 D3
King's Hill Kent 29 D7
King's Lynn Norf 67 B6
King's Meaburn Cumb 99 B8
King's Mills Wrex 73 E7
Kings Muir Borders 121 F5
King's Newnham Warks 52 B2
King's Newton Derbys 63 B7
King's Norton Leics 64 D3
King's Norton W Mid 51 B5
King's Nympton Devon 9 C8
King's Pyon Hereford 49 D6
King's Ripton Cambs 54 B3
King's Somborne Hants 25 F8
King's Stag Dorset 12 C5
King's Stanley Glos 37 D5
King's Sutton Northants 52 F2
King's Thorn Hereford 49 F7
King's Walden Herts 40 B4
Kings Worthy Hants 26 F2
Kingsand Corn 6 D2
Kingsbarns Fife 129 C7
Kingsbridge Devon 6 E5
Kingsbridge Som 21 F8
Kingsburgh Highld 149 C8
Kingsbury London 41 F5
Kingsbury Warks 63 E6
Kingsbury Episcopi Som 12 B2
Kingsclere Hants 26 D3
Kingscote Glos 37 E5
Kingscott Devon 9 C7
Kingscross N Ayrs 143 F11
Kingsdon Som 12 B3
Kingsdown Kent 31 E7
Kingseat Fife 128 E3
Kingsey Bucks 39 D7
Kingsfold W Sus 28 F2
Kingsford E Ayrs 118 E4
Kingsford Worcs 62 F2
Kingsforth N Lincs 90 C4
Kingsgate Kent 31 B7
Kingsheanton Devon 20 F4
Kingshouse Hotel Highld 131 D6
Kingside Hill Cumb 107 D8
Kingskerswell Devon 7 C6
Kingskettle Fife 128 D5
Kingsland Anglesey 82 C2
Kingsland Hereford 49 C6
Kingsley Ches W 74 B2
Kingsley Hants 27 F5
Kingsley Staffs 75 E7
Kingsley Green W Sus 27 F6
Kingsley Holt Staffs 75 E7
Kingsley Park Northants 53 C5
Kingsmuir Angus 134 E4
Kingsmuir Fife 129 D7
Kingsnorth Kent 19 B7
Kingstanding W Mid 62 E4
Kingsteignton Devon 7 B6
Kingsthorpe Northants 53 C5
Kingston Cambs 54 D4
Kingston Devon 6 E4
Kingston Dorset 13 D5
Kingston Dorset 13 G7
Kingston E Loth 129 F7
Kingston Hants 14 D2
Kingston IoW 15 F5
Kingston Kent 31 D5
Kingston Moray 152 B3
Kingston Bagpuize Oxon 38 E4
Kingston Blount Oxon 39 E7
Kingston by Sea W Sus 17 D6
Kingston Deverill Wilts 24 F3
Kingston Gorse W Sus 16 D4
Kingston Lisle Oxon 38 F3
Kingston Maurward Dorset 12 E5
Kingston near Lewes E Sus 17 D7
Kingston on Soar Notts 64 B2
Kingston Russell Dorset 12 E3
Kingston Seymour N Som 23 C6
Kingston St Mary Som 11 B7
Kingston Upon Hull Hull 90 B4
Kingston upon Thames London 28 C2
Kingston Vale London 28 B3
Kingstone Hereford 49 F6
Kingstone Som 11 C8
Kingstone Staffs 62 B4
Kingstown Cumb 108 D3
Kingswear Devon 7 D6
Kingswells Aberdeen 141 D7
Kingswinford W Mid 62 F2
Kingswood Bucks 39 C6
Kingswood Glos 36 E4
Kingswood Hereford 48 D4
Kingswood Kent 30 D2
Kingswood Powys 60 D2
Kingswood S Glos 23 B8
Kingswood Sur 28 D3
Kingswood Warks 51 B6
Kingthorpe Lincs 78 B4
Kington Hereford 48 D4
Kington Worcs 50 D4
Kington Langley Wilts 24 B4
Kington Magna Dorset 13 B5
Kington St Michael Wilts 24 B4
Kingussie Highld 138 D3
Kingweston Som 23 F7
Kininvie Ho. Moray 152 D3
Kinkell Bridge Perth 127 C8
Kinknockie Aberds 153 D10
Kinlet Shrops 61 F7
Kinloch Fife 128 C4
Kinloch Highld 146 B6
Kinloch Highld 149 G11
Kinloch Highld 156 F6
Kinloch Perth 133 E8
Kinloch Perth 134 E2
Kinloch Hourn Highld 136 D2
Kinloch Laggan Highld 137 F8
Kinloch Lodge Highld 157 D8
Kinloch Rannoch Perth 132 D3
Kinlochan Highld 130 C2
Kinlochard Stirling 126 D3
Kinlochbeoraid Highld 147 C11
Kinlochbervie Highld 156 D5
Kinlocheil Highld 130 B3
Kinlochewe Highld 150 E3
Kinlochleven Highld 131 C5
Kinlochmoidart Highld 147 D10
Kinlochmorar Highld 147 B11
Kinlochmore Highld 131 C5
Kinlochspelve Argyll 124 C2
Kinloid Highld 147 C9
Kinloss Moray 151 E13
Kinmel Bay Conwy 72 A3
Kinmuck Aberds 141 C7
Kinmundy Aberds 141 C7
Kinnadie Aberds 153 D9
Kinnaird Perth 128 B4
Kinnaird Castle Angus 135 D6
Kinneff Aberds 135 B8
Kinnelhead Dumfries 114 D3
Kinnell Angus 135 D6
Kinnerley Shrops 60 B3
Kinnersley Hereford 48 E5
Kinnersley Worcs 50 E3
Kinnerton Powys 48 C4
Kinnesswood Perth 128 D3
Kinninvie Durham 101 B5
Kinnordy Angus 134 D3
Kinoulton Notts 77 F6
Kinross Perth 128 D3
Kinrossie Perth 134 F1
Kinsbourne Green Herts 40 C4
Kinsey Heath Ches E 74 E3
Kinsham Hereford 49 C5
Kinsham Worcs 50 F4
Kinsley W Yorks 88 C5
Kinson Bmouth 13 E8
Kintbury W Berks 25 C8
Kintessack Moray 151 E12
Kintillo Perth 128 C3
Kintocher Aberds 140 D4
Kinton Hereford 49 B6
Kinton Shrops 60 C3
Kintore Aberds 141 C6
Kintour Argyll 142 C5
Kintra Argyll 142 D4
Kintra Argyll 146 J6
Kintraw Argyll 124 E4
Kinuachdrachd Argyll 124 F3
Kinveachy Highld 138 C5
Kinver Staffs 62 F2
Kippax W Yorks 95 F7
Kippen Stirling 127 E5
Kippford or Scaur Dumfries 106 D5
Kirbister Orkney 159 F7
Kirbister Orkney 159 H4
Kirbuster Orkney 159 F3
Kirby Bedon Norf 69 D5
Kirby Bellars Leics 64 C4
Kirby Cane Norf 69 E6
Kirby Cross Essex 43 B8
Kirby Grindalythe N Yorks 96 C5
Kirby Hill N Yorks 95 C6
Kirby Hill N Yorks 101 D6
Kirby Knowle N Yorks 102 F2
Kirby-le-Soken Essex 43 B8
Kirby Misperton N Yorks 96 B3
Kirby Muxloe Leics 64 D2
Kirby Row Norf 69 E6
Kirby Sigston N Yorks 102 E2
Kirby Underdale E Yorks 96 D4
Kirby Wiske N Yorks 102 F1
Kirdford W Sus 16 B4
Kirk Highld 158 E4
Kirk Bramwith S Yorks 89 C7
Kirk Deighton N Yorks 95 D6
Kirk Ella E Yorks 90 B4
Kirk Hallam Derbys 76 E4
Kirk Hammerton N Yorks 95 D7
Kirk Ireton Derbys 76 D2
Kirk Langley Derbys 76 F2
Kirk Merrington Durham 111 F5
Kirk Michael IoM 84 C3
Kirk of Shotts N Lanark 119 C8
Kirk Sandall S Yorks 89 D7
Kirk Smeaton N Yorks 89 C6
Kirk Yetholm Borders 116 B4
Kirkabister Shetland 160 K6
Kirkandrews Dumfries 106 E3
Kirkandrews upon Eden Cumb 108 D3
Kirkbampton Cumb 108 D3
Kirkbean Dumfries 107 D6
Kirkbride Cumb 108 D2
Kirkbuddo Angus 135 E5
Kirkburn Borders 121 F5
Kirkburn E Yorks 97 D5
Kirkburton W Yorks 88 C2
Kirkby Lincs 90 E4
Kirkby Mers 86 E2
Kirkby N Yorks 102 D3
Kirkby Fleetham N Yorks 101 E7
Kirkby Green Lincs 78 D3
Kirkby In Ashfield Notts 76 D5
Kirkby-in-Furness Cumb 98 F4
Kirkby la Thorpe Lincs 78 E3
Kirkby Lonsdale Cumb 93 B6
Kirkby Malham N Yorks 93 C8
Kirkby Mallory Leics 63 D8
Kirkby Malzeard N Yorks 94 B5
Kirkby Mills N Yorks 103 F5
Kirkby on Bain Lincs 78 C5
Kirkby Overflow N Yorks 95 E6
Kirkby Stephen Cumb 100 D2
Kirkby Thore Cumb 99 B8
Kirkby Underwood Lincs 65 B7
Kirkby Wharfe N Yorks 95 E8
Kirkbymoorside N Yorks 102 F4
Kirkcaldy Fife 128 E4
Kirkcambeck Cumb 108 C5
Kirkcarswell Dumfries 106 E4
Kirkcolm Dumfries 104 C4
Kirkconnel Dumfries 113 C7
Kirkconnell Dumfries 107 C6
Kirkcowan Dumfries 105 C7
Kirkcudbright Dumfries 106 D3
Kirkdale Mers 85 E4
Kirkfieldbank S Lanark 119 E8
Kirkgunzeon Dumfries 107 C5
Kirkham Lancs 92 F4
Kirkham N Yorks 96 C3
Kirkhamgate W Yorks 88 B3
Kirkharle Northumb 117 F6
Kirkheaton Northumb 110 B3
Kirkheaton W Yorks 88 C2
Kirkhill Angus 135 C6
Kirkhill Highld 151 G8
Kirkhill Midloth 120 C5
Kirkhill Moray 152 E2
Kirkhope Borders 115 B6
Kirkhouse Borders 121 F6
Kirkiboll Highld 157 D8
Kirkibost Highld 149 G10
Kirkinch Angus 134 E3
Kirkinner Dumfries 105 D8
Kirkintilloch E Dunb 119 B6
Kirkland Cumb 98 C2
Kirkland Cumb 109 F6
Kirkland Dumfries 113 C7
Kirkland Dumfries 113 E8
Kirkleatham Redcar 102 B3
Kirklevington Stockton 102 D2
Kirkley Suff 69 E8
Kirklington N Yorks 101 F8
Kirklington Notts 77 D6
Kirklinton Cumb 108 C4
Kirkliston Edin 120 B4
Kirkmaiden Dumfries 104 F5
Kirkmichael Perth 133 D7
Kirkmichael S Ayrs 112 D3
Kirkmuirhill S Lanark 119 E7
Kirknewton Northumb 122 F5
Kirknewton W Loth 120 C4
Kirkney Aberds 152 E5
Kirkoswald Cumb 109 E5
Kirkoswald S Ayrs 112 D2
Kirkpatrick Durham Dumfries 106 B4
Kirkpatrick-Fleming Dumfries 108 B2
Kirksanton Cumb 98 F3
Kirkstall W Yorks 95 F5
Kirkstead Lincs 78 C4
Kirkstile Aberds 152 E5
Kirkstyle Highld 158 C5
Kirkton Aberds 140 B5
Kirkton Aberds 153 D6
Kirkton Angus 134 E4
Kirkton Angus 134 F4
Kirkton Borders 115 C8
Kirkton Dumfries 114 F2
Kirkton Fife 129 B5
Kirkton Highld 149 F13
Kirkton Highld 150 G2
Kirkton Highld 151 B10
Kirkton Highld 151 F10
Kirkton Perth 127 C8
Kirkton S Lanark 114 B2
Kirkton Stirling 126 D4
Kirkton Manor Borders 120 F5
Kirkton of Airlie Angus 134 D3

Kirkton of Auchterhouse Angus 134 F3
Kirkton of Auchterless Aberds 153 D7
Kirkton of Barevan Highld 151 G11
Kirkton of Bourtie Aberds 141 B7
Kirkton of Collace Perth 134 F1
Kirkton of Craig Angus 135 D7
Kirkton of Culsalmond Aberds 153 E6
Kirkton of Durris Aberds 141 E6
Kirkton of Glenbuchat Aberds 140 C2
Kirkton of Glenisla Angus 134 C2
Kirkton of Kingoldrum Angus 134 D3
Kirkton of Largo Fife 129 D6
Kirkton of Lethendy Perth 133 E8
Kirkton of Logie Buchan Aberds 141 B8
Kirkton of Maryculter Aberds 141 E7
Kirkton of Menmuir Angus 135 C5
Kirkton of Monikie Angus 135 F5
Kirkton of Oyne Aberds 141 B5
Kirkton of Rayne Aberds 153 F6
Kirkton of Skene Aberds 141 D7
Kirkton of Tough Aberds 140 C5
Kirktonhill Borders 121 D7
Kirktown Aberds 153 C10
Kirktown of Alvah Aberds 153 B6
Kirktown of Deskford Moray 152 B5
Kirktown of Fetteresso Aberds 141 F7
Kirktown of Mortlach Moray 152 E3
Kirktown of Slains Aberds 141 B9
Kirkurd Borders 120 E4
Kirkwall Orkney 159 G5
Kirkwhelpington Northumb 117 F5
Kirmington N Lincs 90 C5
Kirmond le Mire Lincs 91 E5
Kirn Argyll 145 F10
Kirriemuir Angus 134 D3
Kirstead Green Norf 69 E5
Kirtlebridge Dumfries 108 B2
Kirtleton Dumfries 115 F5
Kirtling Cambs 55 D7
Kirtling Green Cambs 55 D7
Kirtlington Oxon 38 C4
Kirtomy Highld 157 C10
Kirton Lincs 79 F6
Kirton Notts 77 C6
Kirton Suff 57 F6
Kirton End Lincs 79 E5
Kirton Holme Lincs 79 E5
Kirton in Lindsey N Lincs 90 E3
Kislingbury Northants 52 D4
Kites Hardwick Warks 52 C2
Kittisford Som 11 B5
Kittle Swansea 33 F6
Kitt's Green W Mid 63 F5
Kitt's Moss Gtr Man 87 F6
Kittybrewster Aberdeen 141 D8
Kitwood Hants 26 F4
Kivernoll Hereford 49 F6
Kiveton Park S Yorks 89 F5
Knaith Lincs 90 F2
Knaith Park Lincs 90 F2
Knap Corner Dorset 13 B6
Knaphill Sur 27 D7
Knapp Perth 134 F2
Knapp Som 11 B8
Knapthorpe Notts 77 D7
Knapton Norf 81 D9
Knapton York 95 D8
Knapton Green Hereford 49 D6
Knapwell Cambs 54 C4
Knaresborough N Yorks 95 D6
Knarsdale Northumb 109 D6
Knauchland Moray 152 C5
Knaven Aberds 153 D8
Knayton N Yorks 102 F2
Knebworth Herts 41 B5
Knedlington E Yorks 89 B8
Kneesall Notts 77 C7
Kneesworth Cambs 54 E4
Kneeton Notts 77 E7
Knelston Swansea 33 F5
Knenhall Staffs 75 F6
Knettishall Suff 68 F2
Knightacott Devon 21 F5
Knightcote Warks 51 D8
Knightley Dale Staffs 62 B2
Knighton Devon 6 E3
Knighton Leicester 64 D2
Knighton = Tref-Y-Clawdd Powys 48 B4
Knighton Staffs 61 B7
Knighton Staffs 74 E4
Knightswood Glasgow 118 C5
Knightwick Worcs 50 D2
Knill Hereford 48 C4
Knipton Leics 77 F8
Knitsley Durham 110 E4
Kniveton Derbys 76 D2
Knock Argyll 147 H8
Knock Cumb 100 B1
Knock Moray 152 C5
Knockally Highld 158 H3
Knockan Highld 156 H5
Knockandhu Moray 139 B8
Knockando Moray 152 D1
Knockando Ho. Moray 152 D2
Knockbain Highld 151 F9
Knockbreck Highld 148 C7
Knockbrex Dumfries 106 E2
Knockdee Highld 158 D3
Knockdolian S Ayrs 104 A5
Knockenkelly N Ayrs 143 F11
Knockentiber E Ayrs 118 F3
Knockespock Ho. Aberds 140 B4
Knockfarrel Highld 151 F8
Knockglass Dumfries 104 D4
Knockholt Kent 29 D5
Knockholt Pound Kent 29 D5
Knockie Lodge Highld 137 C7
Knockin Shrops 60 B3
Knockinlaw E Ayrs 118 F4
Knocklearn Dumfries 106 B4
Knocknaha Argyll 143 G7
Knocknain Dumfries 104 C3
Knockrome Argyll 144 F4
Knocksharry IoM 84 D2
Knodishall Suff 57 C8
Knolls Green Ches E 74 B5
Knolton Wrex 73 F7
Knolton Bryn Wrex 73 F7
Knook Wilts 24 E4
Knossington Leics 64 D5
Knott End-on-Sea Lancs 92 E3
Knotting Bedford 53 C8
Knotting Green Bedford 53 C8
Knottingley W Yorks 89 B5
Knotts Cumb 99 B6
Knotts Lancs 93 D7
Knotty Ash Mers 86 E2
Knotty Green Bucks 40 E2
Knowbury Shrops 49 B7
Knowe Dumfries 105 B7
Knowehead Dumfries 113 E6
Knowes of Elrick Aberds 152 C6
Knowesgate Northumb 117 F5
Knoweton N Lanark 119 D7
Knowhead Aberds 153 C9
Knowl Hill Windsor 27 B6
Knowle Bristol 23 B8
Knowle Devon 10 D2
Knowle Devon 11 F5
Knowle Devon 20 F3
Knowle Shrops 49 B7
Knowle W Mid 51 B6
Knowle Green Lancs 93 F6
Knowle Park W Yorks 94 E3
Knowlton Dorset 13 C8
Knowlton Kent 31 D6
Knowsley Mers 86 E2
Knowstone Devon 10 B3
Knox Bridge Kent 29 E8
Knucklas Powys 48 B4
Knuston Northants 53 C7
Knutsford Ches E 74 B4
Knutton Staffs 74 E5
Knypersley Staffs 75 D5
Kuggar Corn 3 E6
Kyle of Lochalsh Highld 149 F12
Kyleakin Highld 149 F12
Kylerhea Highld 149 F12
Kylesknoydart Highld 147 B11
Kylesku Highld 156 F5
Kylesmorar Highld 147 B11
Kylestrome Highld 156 F5
Kyllachy House Highld 138 B3
Kynaston Shrops 60 B3
Kynnersley Telford 61 C6
Kyre Magna Worcs 49 C8

L

La Fontenelle Guern 16
La Planque Guern 16
Labost W Isles 155 C7
Lacasaidh W Isles 155 E8
Lacasdal W Isles 155 D9
Laceby NE Lincs 91 D6
Lacey Green Bucks 39 E8
Lach Dennis Ches W 74 B4
Lackford Suff 55 B8
Lacock Wilts 24 C4
Ladbroke Warks 52 D2
Laddingford Kent 29 E7
Lade Bank Lincs 79 D6
Ladock Corn 4 D3
Lady Orkney 159 D7
Ladybank Fife 128 C5
Ladykirk Borders 122 E4
Ladysford Aberds 153 B9
Laga Highld 147 E9
Lagalochan Argyll 124 D4
Lagavulin Argyll 142 D5
Lagg Argyll 144 F4
Lagg N Ayrs 143 F10
Laggan Argyll 142 C3
Laggan Highld 137 E5
Laggan Highld 138 E2
Laggan Highld 147 D10
Laggan S Ayrs 112 F2
Lagganulva Argyll 146 G7
Laide Highld 155 H13
Laigh Fenwick E Ayrs 118 E4
Laigh Glengall S Ayrs 112 C3
Laighmuir E Ayrs 118 E4
Laindon Essex 42 F2
Lair Highld 150 G3
Lairg Highld 157 J8
Lairg Lodge Highld 157 J8
Lairg Muir Highld 157 J8
Lairgmore Highld 151 H8
Laisterdyke W Yorks 94 F4
Laithes Cumb 108 F4
Lake IoW 15 F6
Lake Wilts 25 F6
Lakenham Norf 68 D5
Lakenheath Suff 67 F7
Lakesend Norf 66 E5
Lakeside Cumb 99 F5
Laleham Sur 27 C8
Laleston Bridgend 21 B7
Lamarsh Essex 56 F2
Lamas Norf 81 E8
Lambden Borders 122 E3
Lamberhurst Kent 18 B3
Lamberhurst Quarter Kent 18 B3
Lamberton Borders 123 D5
Lambeth London 28 B4
Lambhill Glasgow 119 C5
Lambley Northumb 109 D6
Lambley Notts 77 E6
Lamborough Hill Oxon 38 D4
Lambourn W Berks 25 B8
Lambourne End Essex 41 E7
Lambs Green W Sus 28 F3
Lambston Pembs 44 D4
Lambton T&W 111 D5
Lamerton Devon 6 B2
Lamesley T&W 111 D5
Laminess Orkney 159 E7
Lamington Highld 151 D10
Lamington S Lanark 120 F2
Lamlash N Ayrs 143 E11
Lamloch Dumfries 112 E5
Lamonby Cumb 108 F4
Lamorna Corn 2 D3
Lamorran Corn 3 B7
Lampardbrook Suff 57 C6
Lampeter = Llanbedr Pont Steffan Ceredig 46 E4
Lampeter Velfrey Pembs 32 C2
Lamphey Pembs 32 D1
Lamplugh Cumb 98 B2
Lamport Northants 53 B5
Lamyatt Som 23 F8
Lana Devon 8 E5
Lanark S Lanark 119 E8
Lancaster Lancs 92 C4
Lanchester Durham 110 E4
Lancing W Sus 17 D5
Landbeach Cambs 55 C5
Landcross Devon 9 B6
Landerberry Aberds 141 D6
Landford Wilts 14 C3
Landford Manor Wilts 14 B3
Landimore Swansea 33 E5
Landkey Devon 20 F4
Landore Swansea 33 E7
Landrake Corn 5 C8
Landscove Devon 7 C5
Landshipping Pembs 32 C1
Landshipping Quay Pembs 32 C1
Landulph Corn 6 C2
Landwade Suff 55 C7
Lane Corn 4 C3
Lane End Bucks 39 E8
Lane End Cumb 98 E3
Lane End Dorset 13 E6
Lane End Hants 15 B6
Lane End IoW 15 F7
Lane End Lancs 93 E8
Lane Ends Lancs 93 D7
Lane Ends Lancs 93 F7
Lane Ends N Yorks 94 E2
Lane Head Derbys 75 B8
Lane Head Durham 101 C6
Lane Head Gtr Man 86 E4
Lane Head W Yorks 88 D2
Lane Side Lancs 87 B5
Laneast Corn 8 F4
Laneham Notts 77 B8
Lanehead Durham 109 E8
Lanehead Northumb 116 F3
Lanercost Cumb 109 C5
Laneshaw Bridge Lancs 94 E2
Lanfach Caerph 35 E6
Langar Notts 77 F7
Langbank Renfs 118 B3
Langbar N Yorks 94 D3
Langburnshiels Borders 115 D8
Langcliffe N Yorks 93 C8
Langdale Highld 157 E9
Langdale End N Yorks 103 E7
Langdon Corn 8 F5
Langdon Beck Durham 109 F8
Langdon Hills Essex 42 F2
Langdyke Fife 128 D5
Langenhoe Essex 43 C6
Langford C Beds 54 E2
Langford Devon 10 D5
Langford Essex 42 D4
Langford Notts 77 D8
Langford Oxon 38 D2
Langford Budville Som 11 B6
Langham Essex 56 F4
Langham Norf 81 C6
Langham Rutland 64 C5
Langham Suff 56 C3
Langhaugh Borders 120 F5
Langho Lancs 93 F7
Langholm Dumfries 115 F6
Langleeford Northumb 117 B5
Langley Ches E 75 B6
Langley Hants 14 D5
Langley Herts 41 B5
Langley Kent 30 D2
Langley Northumb 109 C8
Langley Slough 27 B8
Langley W Sus 16 B2
Langley Warks 51 C6
Langley Burrell Wilts 24 B4
Langley Common Derbys 76 F2
Langley Heath Kent 30 D2
Langley Lower Green Essex 54 F5
Langley Marsh Som 11 B5
Langley Park Durham 110 E5
Langley Street Norf 69 D6
Langley Upper Green Essex 54 F5
Langney E Sus 18 E3
Langold Notts 89 F6
Langore Corn 8 F5
Langport Som 12 B2
Langrick Lincs 79 E5
Langridge Bath 24 C2
Langridge Ford Devon 9 B7
Langrigg Cumb 107 E8
Langrish Hants 15 B8
Langsett S Yorks 88 D3
Langshaw Borders 121 F8
Langside Perth 127 C6
Langskaill Orkney 159 D5
Langstone Hants 15 D8
Langstone Newport 35 E7
Langthorne N Yorks 101 E7
Langthorpe N Yorks 95 C6
Langthwaite N Yorks 101 D5
Langtoft E Yorks 97 C6
Langtoft Lincs 65 C8
Langton Durham 101 C6
Langton Lincs 78 C5
Langton Lincs 79 B6
Langton N Yorks 96 C3
Langton by Wragby Lincs 78 B4
Langton Green Kent 18 B2
Langton Green Suff 56 B5
Langton Herring Dorset 12 F4
Langton Matravers Dorset 13 G8
Langtree Devon 9 C6
Langwathby Cumb 109 F5
Langwell Ho. Highld 158 H3
Langwell Lodge Highld 156 J4
Langwith Derbys 76 B5
Langwith Junction Derbys 76 C5
Langworth Lincs 78 B3
Lanivet Corn 4 C5
Lanlivery Corn 5 D5
Lanner Corn 3 C6
Lanreath Corn 5 D6
Lansallos Corn 5 D6
Lansdown Glos 37 B6
Lanteglos Highway Corn 5 D6
Lanton Borders 116 B2
Lanton Northumb 122 F5
Lapford Devon 10 D2
Laphroaig Argyll 142 D4
Lapley Staffs 62 C2
Lapworth Warks 51 B6
Larachbeg Highld 147 G9
Larbert Falk 127 F7
Larden Green Ches E 74 D2
Largie Aberds 152 E6
Largiemore Argyll 145 E8
Largoward Fife 129 D6
Largs N Ayrs 118 D2
Largybeg N Ayrs 143 F11
Largymore N Ayrs 143 F11
Larkfield Invclyd 118 B2
Larkhall S Lanark 119 D7
Larkhill Wilts 25 E6
Larling Norf 68 F2
Larriston Borders 115 E8
Lartington Durham 101 C5
Lary Aberds 140 D2
Lasham Hants 26 E4
Lashenden Kent 30 E2
Lassington Glos 36 B4
Lassodie Fife 128 E3
Lastingham N Yorks 103 E5
Latcham Som 23 E6
Latchford Herts 41 B6
Latchford Warr 86 F4
Latchingdon Essex 42 D4
Latchley Corn 6 B2
Lately Common Warr 86 E4
Lathbury M Keynes 53 E6
Latheron Highld 158 G3
Latheronwheel Highld 158 G3
Latheronwheel Ho. Highld 158 G3
Lathones Fife 129 D6
Latimer Bucks 40 E3
Latteridge S Glos 36 F3
Lattiford Som 12 B4
Latton Wilts 37 E7
Latton Bush Essex 41 D7
Lauchintilly Aberds 141 C6
Lauder Borders 121 E8
Laugharne Carms 32 C4
Laughterton Lincs 77 B8
Laughton E Sus 18 D2
Laughton Leics 64 F3
Laughton Lincs 78 F3
Laughton Lincs 90 E2
Laughton Common S Yorks 89 F6
Laughton en le Morthen S Yorks 89 F6
Launcells Corn 8 D4
Launceston Corn 8 F5
Launton Oxon 39 B6
Laurencekirk Aberds 135 B7
Laurieston Dumfries 106 C3
Laurieston Falk 120 B2
Lavendon M Keynes 53 D7
Lavenham Suff 56 E3
Laverhay Dumfries 114 E4
Laversdale Cumb 108 C4
Laverstock Wilts 25 F6
Laverstoke Hants 26 E2
Laverton Glos 51 F5
Laverton N Yorks 94 B5
Laverton Som 24 D2
Lavister Wrex 73 D7
Law S Lanark 119 D8
Lawers Perth 127 B6
Lawers Perth 132 F3
Lawford Essex 56 F4
Lawhitton Corn 9 F5
Lawkland N Yorks 93 C7
Lawley Telford 61 D6
Lawnhead Staffs 62 B2
Lawrenny Pembs 32 D1
Lawshall Suff 56 D2
Lawton Hereford 49 D6
Laxey IoM 84 D4
Laxfield Suff 57 B6
Laxfirth Shetland 160 H6
Laxfirth Shetland 160 J6
Laxford Bridge Highld 156 E5
Laxo Shetland 160 G6
Laxobigging Shetland 160 F6
Laxton E Yorks 89 B8
Laxton Northants 65 E6
Laxton Notts 77 C7
Laycock W Yorks 94 E3
Layer Breton Essex 43 C5
Layer de la Haye Essex 43 C5
Layer Marney Essex 43 C5
Layham Suff 56 E4
Laylands Green W Berks 25 C8
Laytham E Yorks 96 F3
Layton Blackpool 92 F3
Lazenby Redcar 102 B3
Lazonby Cumb 108 F5
Le Planel Guern 16
Le Skerne Haughton Darl 101 C8
Le Villocq Guern 16
Lea Derbys 76 D3
Lea Hereford 36 B3
Lea Lincs 90 F2
Lea Shrops 60 D4
Lea Shrops 60 F3
Lea Wilts 37 F6
Lea Marston Warks 63 E6
Lea Town Lancs 92 F4
Leabrooks Derbys 76 D4
Leac a Li W Isles 154 H6
Leachkin Highld 151 G9
Leadburn Midloth 120 D5
Leaden Roding Essex 42 C1
Leadenham Lincs 78 D2
Leadgate Cumb 109 E7
Leadgate Durham 110 D4
Leadgate T&W 110 D4
Leadhills S Lanark 113 C8
Leafield Oxon 38 C3
Leagrave Luton 40 B3
Leake N Yorks 102 E2
Leake Commonside Lincs 79 D6
Lealholm N Yorks 103 D5
Lealt Argyll 144 D5
Lealt Highld 149 B10
Leamington Hastings Warks 52 C2
Leamonsley Staffs 62 D5
Leamside Durham 111 E6
Leanaig Highld 151 F8
Leargybreck Argyll 144 F4
Leasgill Cumb 99 F6
Leasingham Lincs 78 E3
Leasingthorne Durham 101 B7
Leasowe Mers 85 E3
Leatherhead Sur 28 D2
Leatherhead Common Sur 28 D2
Leathley N Yorks 94 E5
Leaton Shrops 60 C4
Leaveland Kent 30 D4
Leavening N Yorks 96 C3
Leaves Green London 28 C5
Leazes Durham 110 D4
Lebberston N Yorks 103 F8
Lechlade-on-Thames Glos 38 E2
Leck Lancs 93 B6
Leckford Hants 25 F8
Leckfurin Highld 157 D10
Leckgruinart Argyll 142 B3
Leckhampstead Bucks 52 F5
Leckhampstead W Berks 26 B2
Leckhampstead Thicket W Berks 26 B2
Leckhampton Glos 37 C6
Leckie Highld 150 E3
Leckmelm Highld 150 B4
Leckwith V Glam 22 B3
Leconfield E Yorks 97 E6
Ledaig Argyll 124 B5
Ledburn Bucks 40 B2
Ledbury Hereford 50 F2
Ledcharrie Stirling 126 B4
Ledgemoor Hereford 49 D6
Ledicot Hereford 49 C6
Ledmore Highld 156 H5
Lednagullin Highld 157 C10
Ledsham Ches W 73 B7
Ledsham W Yorks 89 B5
Ledston W Yorks 88 B5
Ledston Luck W Yorks 95 F7
Ledwell Oxon 38 B4
Lee Argyll 146 J7
Lee Devon 20 E3
Lee Hants 14 C4
Lee Lancs 93 D5
Lee Shrops 73 F8
Lee Brockhurst Shrops 60 B5
Lee Clump Bucks 40 D2
Lee Mill Devon 6 D4
Lee Moor Devon 6 C3
Lee-on-the-Solent Hants 15 D6
Leeans Shetland 160 J5
Leebotten Shetland 160 L6
Leebotwood Shrops 60 E4
Leece Cumb 92 C2
Leechpool Pembs 44 D4
Leeds Kent 30 D2
Leeds W Yorks 95 F5
Leedstown Corn 2 C5
Leek Staffs 75 D6
Leek Wootton Warks 51 C7
Leekbrook Staffs 75 D6
Leeming N Yorks 101 F7
Leeming Bar N Yorks 101 E7
Lees Derbys 76 F2
Lees Gtr Man 87 D7
Lees W Yorks 94 F3
Leeswood Flint 73 C6
Legbourne Lincs 91 F7
Legerwood Borders 121 E8
Legsby Lincs 90 F5
Leicester Leicester 64 D2
Leicester Forest East Leics 64 D2
Leigh Dorset 12 D4
Leigh Glos 37 B5
Leigh Gtr Man 86 D4
Leigh Kent 29 E6
Leigh Shrops 60 D3
Leigh Sur 28 E3
Leigh Wilts 37 E7
Leigh Worcs 50 D2
Leigh Beck Essex 42 F4
Leigh Common Som 12 B5
Leigh Delamere Wilts 24 B3
Leigh Green Kent 19 B6
Leigh on Sea Southend 42 F4
Leigh Park Hants 15 D8
Leigh Sinton Worcs 50 D2
Leigh upon Mendip Som 23 E8
Leigh Woods N Som 23 B7
Leighswood W Mid 62 D4
Leighterton Glos 37 E5
Leighton N Yorks 94 B4
Leighton Powys 60 D2
Leighton Shrops 61 D6
Leighton Som 24 E2
Leighton Bromswold Cambs 54 B2
Leighton Buzzard C Beds 40 B2
Leinthall Earls Hereford 49 C6
Leinthall Starkes Hereford 49 C6
Leintwardine Hereford 49 B6
Leire Leics 64 E2
Leirinmore Highld 156 C7
Leiston Suff 57 C8
Leitfie Perth 134 E2
Leith Edin 121 B5
Leitholm Borders 122 E3
Lelant Corn 2 C4
Lelley E Yorks 97 F8
Lem Hill Worcs 50 B2
Lemmington Hall Northumb 117 C7
Lempitlaw Borders 122 F3
Lenchwick Worcs 50 E5
Lendalfoot S Ayrs 112 F1
Lendrick Lodge Stirling 126 D4
Lenham Kent 30 D2
Lenham Heath Kent 30 E3
Lennel Borders 122 E4
Lennoxtown E Dunb 119 B6
Lenton Lincs 78 F3
Lenton Nottingham 77 F5
Lentran Highld 151 G8
Lenwade Norf 68 C3
Leny Ho. Stirling 126 D5
Lenzie E Dunb 119 B6
Leoch Angus 134 F3
Leochel-Cushnie Aberds 140 C4
Leominster Hereford 49 D6
Leonard Stanley Glos 37 D5
Leorin Argyll 142 D4
Lepe Hants 15 E5
Lephin Highld 148 D6
Lephinchapel Argyll 145 D8
Lephinmore Argyll 145 D8
Leppington N Yorks 96 C3
Lepton W Yorks 88 C3
Lerryn Corn 5 D6
Lerwick Shetland 160 J6
Lesbury Northumb 117 C8
Leslie Aberds 140 B4
Leslie Fife 128 D4
Lesmahagow S Lanark 119 F8
Lesnewth Corn 8 E3
Lessendrum Aberds 152 D5
Lessingham Norf 69 B6
Lessonhall Cumb 108 D2
Leswalt Dumfries 104 C4
Letchmore Heath Herts 40 E4
Letchworth Herts 54 F3
Letcombe Bassett Oxon 38 F3
Letcombe Regis Oxon 38 F3
Letham Angus 135 E5
Letham Falk 127 F7
Letham Fife 128 C5
Letham Perth 128 B2
Letham Grange Angus 135 E6
Lethenty Aberds 153 D8
Letheringham Suff 57 D6
Letheringsett Norf 81 D6
Lettaford Devon 10 F2
Lettan Orkney 159 D8
Letterewe Highld 150 D2
Letterfearn Highld 149 F13
Letterfinlay Highld 137 E5
Lettermorar Highld 147 C10
Lettermore Argyll 146 G7
Letters Highld 150 C4
Letterston Pembs 44 C4
Lettoch Highld 139 C6
Lettoch Highld 151 H13
Letton Hereford 48 E5
Letton Hereford 49 B5
Letton Green Norf 68 D2
Letty Green Herts 41 C5
Letwell S Yorks 89 F6
Leuchars Fife 129 B6
Leuchars Ho. Moray 152 B2
Leumrabhagh W Isles 155 F8
Levan Invclyd 118 B2
Levaneap Shetland 160 G6
Levedale Staffs 62 C2
Leven E Yorks 97 E7
Leven Fife 129 D5
Levencorroch N Ayrs 143 F11
Levens Cumb 99 F6
Levens Green Herts 41 B6
Levenshulme Gtr Man 87 E6
Levenwick Shetland 160 L6
Leverburgh = An t-Ob W Isles 154 J5
Leverington Cambs 66 C4
Leverton Lincs 79 E7
Leverton Highgate Lincs 79 E7
Leverton Lucasgate Lincs 79 E7
Leverton Outgate Lincs 79 E7
Levington Suff 57 F6
Levisham N Yorks 103 E6
Levishie Highld 137 C7
Lew Oxon 38 D3
Lewannick Corn 8 F4
Lewdown Devon 9 F6
Lewes E Sus 17 C8
Leweston Pembs 44 C4
Lewisham London 28 B4
Lewiston Highld 137 B8
Lewistown Bridgend 34 F3
Lewknor Oxon 39 E7
Leworthy Devon 8 D5
Leworthy Devon 21 F5
Lewtrenchard Devon 9 F6
Lexden Essex 43 B5
Ley Aberds 140 C4
Ley Corn 5 C6
Leybourne Kent 29 D7
Leyburn N Yorks 101 E6
Leyfields Staffs 63 D6
Leyhill Bucks 40 D2
Leyland Lancs 86 B3
Leylodge Aberds 141 C6
Leymoor W Yorks 88 C2
Leys Aberds 153 C10
Leys Perth 134 F2
Leys Castle Highld 151 G9
Leys of Cossans Angus 134 E3
Leysdown-on-Sea Kent 30 B4
Leysmill Angus 135 E6
Leysters Pole Hereford 49 C7
Leyton London 41 F6
Leytonstone London 41 F6
Lezant Corn 5 B8
Leziate Norf 67 C6
Lhanbryde Moray 152 B2
Liatrie Highld 150 H5
Libanus Powys 34 B3
Libberton S Lanark 120 E2
Liberton Edin 121 C5
Liceasto W Isles 154 H6
Lichfield Staffs 62 D5
Lickey Worcs 50 B4
Lickey End Worcs 50 B4
Lickfold W Sus 16 B3
Liddel Orkney 159 K5
Liddesdale Highld 130 D1
Liddington Swindon 38 F2
Lidgate Suff 55 D8
Lidget S Yorks 89 D7
Lidget Green W Yorks 94 F4
Lidgett Notts 77 C6
Lidlington C Beds 53 F7
Lidstone Oxon 38 B3
Lieurary Highld 158 D2
Liff Angus 134 F3
Lifton Devon 9 F5
Liftondown Devon 9 F5
Lighthorne Warks 51 D8
Lightwater Sur 27 C7
Lightwood Stoke 75 E6
Lightwood Green Ches E 74 E3
Lightwood Green Wrex 73 E7
Lilbourne Northants 52 B3
Lilburn Tower Northumb 117 B6
Lilleshall Telford 61 C7
Lilley Herts 40 B4
Lilley W Berks 26 B2
Lilliesleaf Borders 115 B8
Lillingstone Dayrell Bucks 52 F5
Lillingstone Lovell Bucks 52 E5
Lillington Dorset 12 C4
Lillington Warks 51 C8
Lilliput Poole 13 E8
Lilstock Som 22 E3
Lilyhurst Shrops 61 C7
Limbury Luton 40 B3
Limebrook Hereford 49 C5
Limefield Gtr Man 87 C6
Limekilnburn S Lanark 119 D7
Limekilns Fife 128 F2
Limerigg Falk 119 B8
Limerstone IoW 14 F5
Limington Som 12 B3
Limpenhoe Norf 69 D6
Limpley Stoke Wilts 24 C2
Limpsfield Sur 28 D5
Limpsfield Chart Sur 28 D5
Linby Notts 76 D5
Linchmere W Sus 27 F6
Lincluden Dumfries 107 B6
Lincoln Lincs 78 B2
Lincomb Worcs 50 C3
Lincombe Devon 6 D5
Lindal in Furness Cumb 92 B2
Lindale Cumb 99 F6
Lindean Borders 121 F7
Lindfield W Sus 17 B7
Lindford Hants 27 F6
Lindifferon Fife 128 C5
Lindley W Yorks 88 C2
Lindley Green N Yorks 94 E5
Lindores Fife 128 C4
Lindridge Worcs 49 C8
Lindsell Essex 42 B2
Lindsey Suff 56 E3
Linford Hants 14 D2
Linford Thurrock 29 B7
Lingague IoM 84 E2
Lingards Wood W Yorks 87 C8
Lingbob W Yorks 94 F3
Lingdale Redcar 102 C4
Lingen Hereford 49 C5
Lingfield Sur 28 E4
Lingreabhagh W Isles 154 J5
Lingwood Norf 69 D6
Linicro Highld 149 B8
Linkenholt Hants 25 D8
Linkhill Kent 18 C5
Linkinhorne Corn 5 B8
Linklater Orkney 159 K5
Linksness Orkney 159 H3
Linktown Fife 128 E4
Linley Shrops 60 E3
Linley Green Hereford 49 D8
Linlithgow W Loth 120 B3
Linlithgow Bridge W Loth 120 B2
Linshiels Northumb 116 D4
Linsiadar W Isles 154 D7
Linsidemore Highld 151 B8
Linslade C Beds 40 B2
Linstead Parva Suff 57 B7
Linstock Cumb 108 D4
Linthwaite W Yorks 88 C2
Lintlaw Borders 122 D4
Lintmill Moray 152 B5
Linton Borders 116 B3
Linton Cambs 55 E6
Linton Derbys 63 C6
Linton Hereford 36 B3
Linton Kent 29 E8
Linton N Yorks 94 C2
Linton Northumb 117 E8
Linton W Yorks 95 E6
Linton-on-Ouse N Yorks 95 C7
Linwood Hants 14 D2
Linwood Lincs 90 F5
Linwood Renfs 118 C4
Lionacleit W Isles 148 D2
Lional W Isles 155 A10
Liphook Hants 27 F6
Liscard Mers 85 E4
Liscombe Som 21 F7
Liskeard Corn 5 C7
L'Islet Guern 16
Liss Hants 15 B8
Liss Forest Hants 15 B8
Lissett E Yorks 97 D7
Lissington Lincs 90 F5
Lisvane Cardiff 35 F5
Liswerry Newport 35 F7
Litcham Norf 67 C8
Litchborough Northants 52 D4
Litchfield Hants 26 D2
Litherland Mers 85 E4
Litlington Cambs 54 E4
Litlington E Sus 18 E2
Little Abington Cambs 55 E6
Little Addington Northants 53 B7
Little Alne Warks 51 C6
Little Altcar Mers 85 D4
Little Asby Cumb 100 D1
Little Assynt Highld 156 G4
Little Aston Staffs 62 D4
Little Atherfield IoW 15 G5
Little Ayre Orkney 159 J4
Little-ayre Shetland 160 G5
Little Ayton N Yorks 102 C3
Little Baddow Essex 42 D3
Little Badminton S Glos 37 F5
Little Ballinluig Perth 133 D6
Little Bampton Cumb 108 D2
Little Bardfield Essex 55 F7
Little Barford Bedford 54 D2
Little Barningham Norf 81 D7
Little Barrington Glos 38 C2
Little Barrow Ches W 73 B8
Little Barugh N Yorks 96 B3
Little Bavington Northumb 110 B2
Little Bealings Suff 57 E6
Little Bedwyn Wilts 25 C7
Little Bentley Essex 43 B7
Little Berkhamsted Herts 41 D5
Little Billing Northants 53 C6
Little Birch Hereford 49 F7
Little Blakenham Suff 56 E5
Little Blencow Cumb 108 F4
Little Bollington Ches E 86 F5
Little Bookham Sur 28 D2
Little Bowden Leics 64 F4
Little Bradley Suff 55 D7
Little Brampton Shrops 60 F3
Little Brechin Angus 135 C5
Little Brickhill M Keynes 53 F7
Little Brington Northants 52 C4
Little Bromley Essex 43 B6
Little Broughton Cumb 107 F7
Little Budworth Ches W 74 C2
Little Burstead Essex 42 E2
Little Bytham Lincs 65 C7
Little Carlton Lincs 91 F7
Little Carlton Notts 77 D7
Little Casterton Rutland 65 D7
Little Cawthorpe Lincs 91 F7
Little Chalfont Bucks 40 E2
Little Chart Kent 30 E3
Little Chesterford Essex 55 E6
Little Cheverell Wilts 24 D4
Little Chishill Cambs 54 F5
Little Clacton Essex 43 C7
Little Clifton Cumb 98 B2
Little Colp Aberds 153 D7
Little Comberton Worcs 50 E4
Little Common E Sus 18 E4
Little Compton Warks 51 F7
Little Cornard Suff 56 F2
Little Cowarne Hereford 49 D8
Little Coxwell Oxon 38 E2
Little Crakehall N Yorks 101 E7
Little Cressingham Norf 67 D8
Little Crosby Mers 85 D4
Little Dalby Leics 64 C4
Little Dawley Telford 61 D6
Little Dens Aberds 153 D10
Little Dewchurch Hereford 49 F7
Little Downham Cambs 66 F5
Little Driffield E Yorks 97 D6
Little Dunham Norf 67 C8
Little Dunkeld Perth 133 E7
Little Dunmow Essex 42 B2
Little Easton Essex 42 B2
Little Eaton Derbys 76 E3
Little Eccleston Lancs 92 E4
Little Ellingham Norf 68 E3
Little End Essex 41 D8
Little Eversden Cambs 54 D4
Little Faringdon Oxon 38 D2
Little Fencote N Yorks 101 E7
Little Fenton N Yorks 95 F8
Little Finborough Suff 56 D4
Little Fransham Norf 68 C2
Little Gaddesden Herts 40 C2
Little Gidding Cambs 65 F8
Little Glemham Suff 57 D7
Little Glenshee Perth 133 F6
Little Gransden Cambs 54 D3
Little Green Som 24 E2
Little Grimsby Lincs 91 E7
Little Gruinard Highld 150 C2
Little Habton N Yorks 96 B3
Little Hadham Herts 41 B7
Little Hale Lincs 78 E4
Little Hallingbury Essex 41 C7
Little Hampden Bucks 40 D1
Little Harrowden Northants 53 B6
Little Haseley Oxon 39 D6
Little Hatfield E Yorks 97 E7
Little Hautbois Norf 81 E8
Little Haven Pembs 44 D3
Little Hay Staffs 62 D5
Little Hayfield Derbys 87 F8
Little Haywood Staffs 62 B4
Little Heath W Mid 63 F7
Little Hereford Hereford 49 C7
Little Horkesley Essex 56 F3
Little Horsted E Sus 17 C8
Little Horton W Yorks 94 F4
Little Horwood Bucks 53 F5
Little Houghton Northants 53 D6
Little Houghton S Yorks 88 D5
Little Hucklow Derbys 75 B8
Little Hulton Gtr Man 86 D5
Little Humber E Yorks 91 B5
Little Hungerford W Berks 26 B3
Little Irchester Northants 53 C7
Little Kimble Bucks 39 D8
Little Kineton Warks 51 D8
Little Kingshill Bucks 40 E1
Little Langdale Cumb 99 D5
Little Langford Wilts 25 F5
Little Laver Essex 41 D8
Little Leigh Ches W 74 B3
Little Leighs Essex 42 C3
Little Lever Gtr Man 87 D5
Little London Bucks 39 C6
Little London E Sus 18 D2
Little London Hants 25 E8
Little London Hants 26 D4
Little London Lincs 66 B2
Little London Lincs 66 B4
Little London Norf 81 E7
Little London Powys 59 F7
Little Longstone Derbys 75 B8
Little Lynturk Aberds 140 C4
Little Malvern Worcs 50 E2
Little Maplestead Essex 56 F2
Little Marcle Hereford 49 F8
Little Marlow Bucks 40 F1
Little Marsden Lancs 93 F8
Little Massingham Norf 80 E3
Little Melton Norf 68 D4
Little Mill Mon 35 D7
Little Milton Oxon 39 D6
Little Missenden Bucks 40 E2
Little Musgrave Cumb 100 C2
Little Ness Shrops 60 C4
Little Neston Ches W 73 B6
Little Newcastle Pembs 44 C4
Little Newsham Durham 101 C6
Little Oakley Essex 43 B8
Little Oakley Northants 65 F5
Little Orton Cumb 108 D3
Little Ouseburn N Yorks 95 C7
Little Paxton Cambs 54 C2
Little Petherick Corn 4 B4
Little Pitlurg Moray 152 D4
Little Plumpton Lancs 92 F3
Little Plumstead Norf 69 C6
Little Ponton Lincs 78 F2
Little Raveley Cambs 54 B3
Little Reedness E Yorks 90 B2
Little Ribston N Yorks 95 D6
Little Rissington Glos 38 C1
Little Ryburgh Norf 81 E5
Little Ryle Northumb 117 C6
Little Salkeld Cumb 109 F5
Little Sampford Essex 55 F7
Little Sandhurst Brack 27 C6
Little Saxham Suff 55 C8
Little Scatwell Highld 150 F6
Little Sessay N Yorks 95 B7
Little Shelford Cambs 54 D5
Little Singleton Lancs 92 F3
Little Skillymarno Aberds 153 C9
Little Smeaton N Yorks 89 C6
Little Snoring Norf 81 D5
Little Sodbury S Glos 36 F4
Little Somborne Hants 25 F8
Little Somerford Wilts 37 F6
Little Stainforth N Yorks 93 C8
Little Stainton Darl 101 B8
Little Stanney Ches W 73 B8
Little Staughton Bedford 54 C2
Little Steeping Lincs 79 C7
Little Stoke Staffs 75 F6
Little Stonham Suff 56 C5
Little Stretton Leics 64 D3
Little Stretton Shrops 60 E4
Little Strickland Cumb 99 C7
Little Stukeley Cambs 54 B3
Little Sutton Ches W 73 B7
Little Tew Oxon 38 B3
Little Thetford Cambs 55 B6
Little Thirkleby N Yorks 95 B7
Little Thurlow Suff 55 D7
Little Thurrock Thurrock 29 B7
Little Torboll Highld 151 B10
Little Torrington Devon 9 C6
Little Totham Essex 42 C4
Little Toux Aberds 152 C5
Little Town Cumb 98 C4
Little Town Lancs 93 F6
Little Urswick Cumb 92 B2
Little Wakering Essex 43 F5
Little Walden Essex 55 E6
Little Waldingfield Suff 56 E3
Little Walsingham Norf 80 D5
Little Waltham Essex 42 C3
Little Warley Essex 42 E2
Little Weighton E Yorks 97 F5
Little Weldon Northants 65 F6
Little Welnetham Suff 56 C2
Little Wenlock Telford 61 D6
Little Whittingham Green Suff 57 B6
Little Wilbraham Cambs 55 D6
Little Wishford Wilts 25 F5
Little Witley Worcs 50 C2
Little Wittenham Oxon 39 E5
Little Wolford Warks 51 F7
Little Wratting Suff 55 E7
Little Wymington Bedford 53 C7
Little Wymondley Herts 41 B5
Little Wyrley Staffs 62 D4
Little Yeldham Essex 55 F8
Littlebeck N Yorks 103 D6
Littleborough Gtr Man 87 C7
Littleborough Notts 90 F2
Littlebourne Kent 31 D6
Littlebredy Dorset 12 F3
Littlebury Essex 55 F6
Littlebury Green Essex 55 F5
Littledean Glos 36 C3
Littleferry Highld 151 B11
Littleham Devon 9 B6
Littleham Devon 10 F5
Littlehampton W Sus 16 D4
Littlehempston Devon 7 C6
Littlehoughton Northumb 117 C8
Littlemill Aberds 140 E2
Littlemill E Ayrs 112 C4
Littlemill Highld 151 F12
Littlemill Northumb 117 C8
Littlemoor Dorset 12 F4
Littlemore Oxon 39 D5
Littleover Derby 76 F3
Littleport Cambs 67 F5
Littlestone on Sea Kent 19 C7
Littlethorpe Leics 64 E2
Littlethorpe N Yorks 95 C6
Littleton Ches W 73 C8
Littleton Hants 26 F2
Littleton Perth 134 F2
Littleton Som 23 F6
Littleton Sur 27 C8
Littleton Sur 27 E7
Littleton Drew Wilts 37 F5
Littleton-on-Severn S Glos 36 F2
Littleton Pannell Wilts 24 D5
Littletown Durham 111 E6
Littlewick Green Windsor 27 B6
Littleworth Bedford 53 E8
Littleworth Glos 37 D5
Littleworth Oxon 38 E3
Littleworth Staffs 62 C4
Littleworth Worcs 50 D3
Litton Derbys 75 B8
Litton N Yorks 94 B2
Litton Som 23 D7
Litton Cheney Dorset 12 E3
Liurbost W Isles 155 E8
Liverpool Mers 85 E4
Liverpool Airport Mers 86 F2
Liversedge W Yorks 88 B3
Liverton Devon 7 B6
Liverton Redcar 103 C5
Livingston W Loth 120 C3
Livingston Village W Loth 120 C3
Lixwm Flint 73 B5
Lizard Corn 3 E6
Llaingoch Anglesey 82 C2
Llaithddu Powys 59 F7
Llan Powys 59 D5
Llan Ffestiniog Gwyn 71 C8
Llan-y-pwll Wrex 73 D7
Llanaber Gwyn 58 C3
Llanaelhaearn Gwyn 70 C4
Llanafan Ceredig 47 B5
Llanafan-fawr Powys 47 D8
Llanallgo Anglesey 82 C4
Llanandras = Presteigne Powys 48 C5
Llanarmon Gwyn 70 D5
Llanarmon Dyffryn Ceiriog Wrex 73 F5
Llanarmon-yn-Ial Denb 73 D5
Llanarth Ceredig 46 D3
Llanarth Mon 35 C7
Llanarthne Carms 33 B6
Llanasa Flint 85 F2
Llanbabo Anglesey 82 C3
Llanbadarn Fawr Ceredig 58 F3

Llanbadarn Fynydd Powys 48 B3
Llanbadarn-y-Garreg Powys 48 E3
Llanbadoc Mon 35 E7
Llanbadrig Anglesey 82 B3
Llanbeder Newport 35 E7
Llanbedr Gwyn 71 E6
Llanbedr Powys 35 B6
Llanbedr Powys 48 E3
Llanbedr-Dyffryn-Clwyd Denb 72 D5
Llanbedr Pont Steffan = Lampeter Ceredig 46 E4
Llanbedr-y-cennin Conwy 83 E7
Llanbedrgoch Anglesey 82 C5
Llanbedrog Gwyn 70 D4
Llanberis Gwyn 83 E5
Llanbethêry V Glam 22 C2
Llanbister Powys 48 B3
Llanblethian V Glam 21 B8
Llanboidy Carms 32 B3
Llanbradach Caerph 35 E5
Llanbrynmair Powys 59 D5
Llancarfan V Glam 22 B2
Llancayo Mon 35 D7
Llancloudy Hereford 36 B1
Llancynfelyn Ceredig 58 E3
Llandaff Cardiff 22 B3
Llandanwg Gwyn 71 E6
Llandarcy Neath 33 E8
Llandawke Carms 32 C3
Llanddaniel Fab Anglesey 82 D4
Llanddarog Carms 33 C6
Llanddeiniol Ceredig 46 B4
Llanddeiniolen Gwyn 82 E5
Llandderfel Gwyn 72 F3
Llanddeusant Anglesey 82 C3
Llanddeusant Carms 34 B1
Llanddew Powys 48 F2
Llanddewi Swansea 33 F5
Llanddewi-Brefi Ceredig 47 D5
Llanddewi Rhydderch Mon 35 C7
Llanddewi Velfrey Pembs 32 C2
Llanddewi'r Cwm Powys 48 E2
Llanddoged Conwy 83 E8
Llanddona Anglesey 83 D5
Llanddowror Carms 32 C3
Llanddulas Conwy 72 B3
Llanddwywe Gwyn 71 E6
Llanddyfynan Anglesey 82 D5
Llandefaelog Fach Powys 48 F2
Llandefaelog-tre'r-graig Powys 35 B5
Llandefalle Powys 48 F3
Llandegai Gwyn 83 D5
Llandegfan Anglesey 83 D5
Llandegla Denb 73 D5
Llandegley Powys 48 C3
Llandegveth Mon 35 E7
Llandegwning Gwyn 70 D3
Llandeilo Carms 33 B7
Llandeilo Graban Powys 48 E2
Llandeilo'r Fan Powys 47 F7
Llandeloy Pembs 44 C3
Llandenny Mon 35 D8
Llandevenny Mon 35 F8
Llandewednock Corn 3 E6
Llandewi Ystradenny Powys 48 C3
Llandinabo Hereford 36 B2
Llandinam Powys 59 F7
Llandissilio Pembs 32 B2
Llandogo Mon 36 D2
Llandough V Glam 21 B8
Llandough V Glam 22 B3
Llandovery = Llanymddyfri Carms 47 F6
Llandow V Glam 21 B8
Llandre Carms 47 E5
Llandre Ceredig 58 F3
Llandrillo Denb 72 F4
Llandrillo-yn-Rhos Conwy 83 C8
Llandrindod = Llandrindod Wells Powys 48 C2
Llandrindod Wells = Llandrindod Powys 48 C2
Llandrinio Powys 60 C2
Llandudno Conwy 83 C7
Llandudno Junction = Cyffordd Llandudno Conwy 83 D7
Llandwrog Gwyn 82 F4
Llandybie Carms 33 C7
Llandyfaelog Carms 33 C5
Llandyfan Carms 33 C7
Llandyfriog Ceredig 46 E2
Llandyfrydog Anglesey 82 C4
Llandygwydd Ceredig 45 E4
Llandynan Denb 73 E5
Llandyrnog Denb 72 C5
Llandysilio Powys 60 C2
Llandyssil Powys 59 E8
Llandysul Ceredig 46 E3
Llanedeyrn Cardiff 35 F6
Llanedi Carms 33 D6
Llaneglwys Powys 48 F2
Llanegryn Gwyn 58 D2
Llanegwad Carms 33 B6
Llaneilian Anglesey 82 B4
Llanelian-yn-Rhos Conwy 83 D8
Llanelidan Denb 72 D5
Llanelieu Powys 48 F3
Llanellen Mon 35 C7
Llanelli Carms 33 E6
Llanelltyd Gwyn 58 C4
Llanelly Mon 35 C6
Llanelly Hill Mon 35 C6
Llanelwedd Powys 48 D2
Llanelwy = St Asaph Denb 72 B4
Llanenddwyn Gwyn 71 E6
Llanengan Gwyn 70 E3
Llanerchymedd Anglesey 82 C4
Llanerfyl Powys 59 D7
Llanfachraeth Anglesey 82 C3
Llanfachreth Gwyn 71 E8
Llanfaelog Anglesey 82 D3
Llanfaelrhys Gwyn 70 E3
Llanfaenor Mon 35 C8
Llanfaes Anglesey 83 D6
Llanfaes Powys 34 B4
Llanfaethlu Anglesey 82 C3
Llanfaglan Gwyn 82 E4
Llanfair Gwyn 71 E6
Llanfair-ar-y-bryn Carms 47 F7
Llanfair Caereinion Powys 59 D8
Llanfair Clydogau Ceredig 46 D5
Llanfair-Dyffryn-Clwyd Denb 72 D5
Llanfair Kilgheddin Mon 35 D7
Llanfair-Nant-Gwyn Pembs 45 F3
Llanfair Talhaiarn Conwy 72 B3
Llanfair Waterdine Shrops 48 B4
Llanfair-Ym-Muallt = Builth Wells Powys 48 D2
Llanfairfechan Conwy 83 D6
Llanfairpwll-gwyngyll Anglesey 82 D5
Llanfairyneubwll Anglesey 82 D3
Llanfairynghornwy Anglesey 82 B3
Llanfallteg Carms 32 C2
Llanfaredd Powys 48 D2
Llanfarian Ceredig 46 B4
Llanfechain Powys 59 B8
Llanfechan Powys 47 D8
Llanfechell Anglesey 82 B3
Llanfendigaid Gwyn 58 D2
Llanferres Denb 73 C5
Llanfflewyn Anglesey 82 C3
Llanfihangel-ar-arth Carms 46 F3
Llanfihangel-Crucorney Mon 35 B7
Llanfihangel Glyn Myfyr Conwy 72 E3
Llanfihangel Nant Bran Powys 47 F8
Llanfihangel-nant-Melan Powys 48 D3
Llanfihangel Rhydithon Powys 48 C3
Llanfihangel Rogiet Mon 35 F8
Llanfihangel Tal-y-llyn Powys 35 B5
Llanfihangel-uwch-Gwili Carms 33 B5
Llanfihangel-y-Creuddyn Ceredig 47 B5
Llanfihangel-y-pennant Gwyn 58 D3
Llanfihangel-y-pennant Gwyn 71 C6
Llanfihangel-y-traethau Gwyn 71 D6
Llanfihangel-yn-Ngwynfa Powys 59 C7
Llanfihangel yn Nhowyn Anglesey 82 D3
Llanfilo Powys 48 F3
Llanfoist Mon 35 C6
Llanfor Gwyn 72 F3
Llanfrechfa Torf 35 E7
Llanfrothen Gwyn 71 C7
Llanfrynach Powys 34 B4
Llanfwrog Anglesey 82 C3
Llanfwrog Denb 72 D5
Llanfyllin Powys 59 C8
Llanfynydd Carms 33 B6
Llanfynydd Flint 73 D6
Llanfyrnach Pembs 45 F4
Llangadfan Powys 59 C7
Llangadog Carms 33 B8
Llangadwaladr Anglesey 82 E3
Llangadwaladr Powys 73 F5
Llangaffo Anglesey 82 E4
Llangain Carms 32 C4
Llangammarch Wells Powys 47 E8
Llangan V Glam 21 B8
Llangarron Hereford 36 B2
Llangasty Talyllyn Powys 35 B5
Llangathen Carms 33 B6
Llangattock Powys 35 C6
Llangattock Lingoed Mon 35 B7
Llangattock nigh Usk Mon 35 D7
Llangattock-Vibon-Avel Mon 36 C1
Llangedwyn Powys 59 B8
Llangefni Anglesey 82 D4
Llangeinor Bridgend 34 F3
Llangeitho Ceredig 46 D5
Llangeler Carms 46 F2
Llangelynin Gwyn 58 D2
Llangendeirne Carms 33 C5
Llangennech Carms 33 D6
Llangennith Swansea 33 E5
Llangenny Powys 35 C6
Llangernyw Conwy 83 E8
Llangian Gwyn 70 E3
Llanglydwen Carms 32 B2
Llangoed Anglesey 83 D6
Llangoedmor Ceredig 45 E3
Llangollen Denb 73 E6
Llangolman Pembs 32 B2
Llangors Powys 35 B5
Llangovan Mon 36 D1
Llangower Gwyn 72 F3
Llangrannog Ceredig 46 D2
Llangristiolus Anglesey 82 D4
Llangrove Hereford 36 C2
Llangua Mon 35 B7
Llangunllo Powys 48 B4
Llangunnor Carms 33 C5
Llangurig Powys 47 B8
Llangwm Conwy 72 E3
Llangwm Mon 35 D8
Llangwm Pembs 44 E4
Llangwnnadl Gwyn 70 D3
Llangwyfan Denb 72 C5
Llangwyfan-isaf Anglesey 82 E3
Llangwyllog Anglesey 82 D4
Llangwyryfon Ceredig 46 B4
Llangybi Ceredig 46 D5
Llangybi Gwyn 70 C5
Llangybi Mon 35 E7
Llangyfelach Swansea 33 E7
Llangynhafal Denb 72 C5
Llangynidr Powys 35 C5
Llangynin Carms 32 C3
Llangynog Carms 32 C4
Llangynog Powys 59 B7
Llangynwyd Bridgend 34 F2
Llanhamlach Powys 34 B4
Llanharan Rhondda 34 F4
Llanharry Rhondda 34 F4
Llanhennock Mon 35 E7
Llanhiledd = Llanhilleth Bl Gwent 35 D6
Llanhilleth = Llanhiledd Bl Gwent 35 D6
Llanidloes Powys 59 F6
Llaniestyn Gwyn 70 D3
Llanifyny Powys 59 F5
Llanigon Powys 48 F4
Llanilar Ceredig 46 B5
Llanilid Rhondda 34 F3
Llanilltud Fawr = Llantwit Major V Glam 21 C8
Llanishen Cardiff 35 F5
Llanishen Mon 36 D1
Llanllawddog Carms 33 B5
Llanllechid Gwyn 83 E6
Llanllowell Mon 35 E7
Llanllugan Powys 59 D7
Llanllwch Carms 32 C4
Llanllwchaiarn Powys 59 E8
Llanllwni Carms 46 F3
Llanllyfni Gwyn 82 F4
Llanmadoc Swansea 33 E5
Llanmaes V Glam 21 C8
Llanmartin Newport 35 F7
Llanmihangel V Glam 21 B8
Llanmorlais Swansea 33 E6
Llannefydd Conwy 72 B3
Llannon Carms 33 D6
Llannor Gwyn 70 D4
Llanon Ceredig 46 C4
Llanover Mon 35 D7
Llanpumsaint Carms 33 B5
Llanreithan Pembs 44 C3
Llanrhaeadr Denb 72 C4
Llanrhaeadr-ym-Mochnant Powys 59 B8
Llanrhian Pembs 44 B3
Llanrhidian Swansea 33 E5
Llanrhos Conwy 83 C7
Llanrhyddlad Anglesey 82 C3
Llanrhystud Ceredig 46 C4
Llanrosser Hereford 48 F4
Llanrothal Hereford 36 C1
Llanrug Gwyn 82 E5
Llanrumney Cardiff 35 F6
Llanrwst Conwy 83 E8
Llansadurnen Carms 32 C3
Llansadwrn Anglesey 83 D5
Llansadwrn Carms 47 F5
Llansaint Carms 32 D4
Llansamlet Swansea 33 E7
Llansanffraid-ym-Mechain Powys 60 B2
Llansannan Conwy 72 C3
Llansannor V Glam 21 B8
Llansantffraed Ceredig 46 C4
Llansantffraed Powys 35 B5
Llansantffraed Cwmdeuddwr Powys 47 C8
Llansantffraed-in-Elvel Powys 48 D2
Llansawel Carms 46 F5
Llansilin Powys 60 B2
Llansoy Mon 35 D8
Llanspyddid Powys 34 B4
Llanstadwell Pembs 44 E4
Llansteffan Carms 32 C4
Llanstephan Powys 48 E3
Llantarnam Torf 35 E7
Llanteg Pembs 32 C2
Llanthony Mon 35 B6
Llantilio Crossenny Mon 35 C7
Llantilio Pertholey Mon 35 C7
Llantood Pembs 45 E3
Llantrisant Anglesey 82 C3
Llantrisant Mon 35 E7
Llantrisant Rhondda 34 F4
Llantrithyd V Glam 22 B2
Llantwit Fardre Rhondda 34 F4
Llantwit Major = Llanilltud Fawr V Glam 21 C8
Llanuwchllyn Gwyn 72 F2
Llanvaches Newport 35 E8
Llanvair Discoed Mon 35 E8
Llanvapley Mon 35 C7
Llanvetherine Mon 35 C7
Llanveynoe Hereford 48 F5
Llanvihangel Gobion Mon 35 D7
Llanvihangel-Ystern-Llewern Mon 35 C8
Llanwarne Hereford 36 B2
Llanwddyn Powys 59 C7
Llanwenog Ceredig 46 E3
Llanwern Newport 35 F7
Llanwinio Carms 32 B3
Llanwnda Gwyn 82 F4
Llanwnda Pembs 44 B4
Llanwnnen Ceredig 46 E4
Llanwnog Powys 59 E7
Llanwrda Carms 47 F6
Llanwrin Powys 58 D4
Llanwrthwl Powys 47 C8
Llanwrtud = Llanwrtyd Wells Powys 47 E7
Llanwrtyd Powys 47 E7
Llanwrtyd Wells = Llanwrtud Powys 47 E7
Llanwyddelan Powys 59 D7
Llanyblodwel Shrops 60 B2
Llanybri Carms 32 C4
Llanybydder Carms 46 E4
Llanycefn Pembs 32 B1
Llanychaer Pembs 44 B4
Llanycil Gwyn 72 F3
Llanycrwys Carms 46 E5
Llanymawddwy Gwyn 59 C6
Llanymddyfri = Llandovery Carms 47 F6
Llanymynech Powys 60 B2
Llanynghenedl Anglesey 82 C3
Llanynys Denb 72 C5
Llanyre Powys 48 C2
Llanystumdwy Gwyn 71 D5
Llanywern Powys 35 B5
Llawhaden Pembs 32 C1
Llawnt Shrops 73 F6
Llawr Dref Gwyn 70 E3
Llawryglyn Powys 59 E6
Llay Wrex 73 D7
Llechcynfarwy Anglesey 82 C3
Llecheiddior Gwyn 71 C5
Llechfaen Powys 34 B4
Llechryd Caerph 35 D5
Llechryd Ceredig 45 E4
Llechrydau Powys 73 F6
Lledrod Ceredig 46 B5
Llenmerewig Powys 59 E8
Llethrid Swansea 33 E6
Llidiad Nenog Carms 46 F4
Llidiardau Gwyn 72 F2
Llidiart-y-parc Denb 72 E5
Llithfaen Gwyn 70 C4
Llong Flint 73 C6
Llowes Powys 48 E3
Llundain-fach Ceredig 46 D4
Llwydcoed Rhondda 34 D3
Llwyn Shrops 60 F2
Llwyn-du Mon 35 C6
Llwyn-hendy Carms 33 E6
Llwyn-têg Carms 33 D6
Llwyn-y-brain Carms 32 C2
Llwyn-y-groes Ceredig 46 D4
Llwyncelyn Ceredig 46 D3
Llwyndafydd Ceredig 46 D2
Llwynderw Powys 60 D2
Llwyndyrys Gwyn 70 C4
Llwyngwril Gwyn 58 D2
Llwynmawr Wrex 73 F6
Llwynypia Rhondda 34 E3
Llynclys Shrops 60 B2
Llynfaes Anglesey 82 D4
Llys-y-frân Pembs 32 B1
Llysfaen Conwy 83 D8
Llyswen Powys 48 F3
Llysworney V Glam 21 B8
Llywel Powys 47 F7
Loan Falk 120 B2
Loanend Northumb 122 D5
Loanhead Midloth 121 C5
Loans S Ayrs 118 F3
Loans of Tullich Highld 151 D11
Lobb Devon 20 F3
Loch a Charnain W Isles 148 D3
Loch a' Ghainmhich W Isles 155 E7
Loch Baghasdail = Lochboisdale W Isles 148 G2
Loch Choire Lodge Highld 157 F9
Loch Euphoirt W Isles 148 B3
Loch Head Dumfries 105 E7
Loch Loyal Lodge Highld 157 E9
Loch nam Madadh = Lochmaddy W Isles 148 B4
Loch Sgioport W Isles 148 E3
Lochailort Highld 147 C10
Lochaline Highld 147 G9
Lochanhully Highld 138 B5
Lochans Dumfries 104 D4
Locharbriggs Dumfries 114 F2
Lochassynt Lodge Highld 156 G4
Lochavich Ho Argyll 124 D5
Lochawe Argyll 125 C7
Lochboisdale = Loch Baghasdail W Isles 148 G2
Lochbuie Argyll 124 C2
Lochcarron Highld 149 E13
Lochdhu Highld 157 E13
Lochdochart House Stirling 126 B3
Lochdon Argyll 124 B3
Lochdrum Highld 150 D5
Lochead Argyll 144 F6
Lochearnhead Stirling 126 B4
Lochee Dundee 134 F3
Lochend Highld 151 H8
Lochend Highld 158 D4
Locherben Dumfries 114 E2
Lochfoot Dumfries 107 B5
Lochgair Argyll 145 D8
Lochgarthside Highld 137 C8
Lochgelly Fife 128 E3
Lochgilphead Argyll 145 E7
Lochgoilhead Argyll 125 E8
Lochhill Moray 152 B2
Lochindorb Lodge Highld 151 H12
Lochinver Highld 156 G3
Lochlane Perth 127 B7
Lochluichart Highld 150 E6
Lochmaben Dumfries 114 F3
Lochmaddy = Loch nam Madadh W Isles 148 B4
Lochmore Cottage Highld 158 F2
Lochmore Lodge Highld 156 F5
Lochore Fife 128 E3
Lochportain W Isles 148 A4
Lochranza N Ayrs 143 C10
Lochs Crofts Moray 152 B3
Lochside Aberds 135 C7
Lochside Highld 151 F11
Lochside Highld 156 D7
Lochside Highld 157 F11
Lochslin Highld 151 C11
Lochstack Lodge Highld 156 E5
Lochton Aberds 141 E6
Lochty Angus 135 C5
Lochty Fife 129 D7
Lochty Perth 128 B2
Lochuisge Highld 130 D1
Lochurr Dumfries 113 F7
Lochwinnoch Renfs 118 D3
Lochwood Dumfries 114 E3
Lochyside Highld 131 B5
Lockengate Corn 4 C5
Lockerbie Dumfries 114 F4
Lockeridge Wilts 25 C6
Lockerley Hants 14 B3
Locking N Som 23 D5
Lockinge Oxon 38 F4
Lockington E Yorks 97 E5
Lockington Leics 63 B8
Lockleywood Shrops 61 B6
Locks Heath Hants 15 D6
Lockton N Yorks 103 E6
Lockwood W Yorks 88 C2
Loddington Leics 64 D4
Loddington Northants 53 B6
Loddiswell Devon 6 E5
Loddon Norf 69 E6
Lode Cambs 55 C6
Loders Dorset 12 E2
Lodsworth W Sus 16 B3
Lofthouse N Yorks 94 B4
Lofthouse W Yorks 88 B4
Loftus Redcar 103 C5
Logan E Ayrs 113 B5
Logan Mains Dumfries 104 E4
Loganlea W Loth 120 C2
Loggerheads Staffs 74 F4
Logie Angus 135 C6
Logie Fife 129 B6
Logie Moray 151 F13
Logie Coldstone Aberds 140 D3
Logie Hill Highld 151 D10
Logie Newton Aberds 153 E6
Logie Pert Angus 135 C6
Logiealmond Lodge Perth 133 F6
Logierait Perth 133 D6
Login Carms 32 B2
Lolworth Cambs 54 C4
Lonbain Highld 149 C11
Londesborough E Yorks 96 E4
London Colney Herts 40 D4
Londonderry N Yorks 101 F8
Londonthorpe Lincs 78 F2
Londubh Highld 155 J13
Lonemore Highld 151 C10
Long Ashton N Som 23 B7
Long Bennington Lincs 77 E8
Long Bredy Dorset 12 E3
Long Buckby Northants 52 C4
Long Clawson Leics 64 B4
Long Common Hants 15 C6
Long Compton Staffs 62 B2
Long Compton Warks 51 F7
Long Crendon Bucks 39 D6
Long Crichel Dorset 13 C7
Long Ditton Sur 28 C2
Long Drax N Yorks 89 B7
Long Duckmanton Derbys 76 B4
Long Eaton Derbys 76 F4
Long Green Worcs 50 F3
Long Hanborough Oxon 38 C4
Long Itchington Warks 52 C2
Long Lawford Warks 52 B2
Long Load Som 12 B2
Long Marston Herts 40 C1
Long Marston N Yorks 95 D8
Long Marston Warks 51 E6
Long Marton Cumb 100 B1
Long Melford Suff 56 E2
Long Newnton Glos 37 E6
Long Newton E Loth 121 C8
Long Preston N Yorks 93 D8
Long Riston E Yorks 97 E7
Long Sight Gtr Man 87 D7
Long Stratton Norf 68 E4
Long Street M Keynes 53 E5
Long Sutton Hants 26 E5
Long Sutton Lincs 66 B4
Long Sutton Som 12 B2
Long Thurlow Suff 56 C4
Long Whatton Leics 63 B8
Long Wittenham Oxon 39 E5
Longbar N Ayrs 118 D3
Longbenton T&W 111 C5
Longborough Glos 38 B1
Longbridge W Mid 50 B5
Longbridge Warks 51 C7
Longbridge Deverill Wilts 24 E3
Longburton Dorset 12 C4
Longcliffe Derbys 76 D2
Longcot Oxon 38 E2
Longcroft Falk 119 B7
Longden Shrops 60 D4
Longdon Staffs 62 C4
Longdon Worcs 50 F3
Longdon Green Staffs 62 C4
Longdon on Tern Telford 61 C6
Longdown Devon 10 E3
Longdowns Corn 3 C6
Longfield Kent 29 C7
Longfield Shetland 160 M5
Longford Derbys 76 F2
Longford Glos 37 B5
Longford London 27 B8
Longford Shrops 74 F3
Longford Telford 61 C7
Longford W Mid 63 F7
Longfordlane Derbys 76 F2
Longforgan Perth 128 B5
Longformacus Borders 122 D2
Longframlington Northumb 117 D7
Longham Dorset 13 E8
Longham Norf 68 C2
Longhaven Aberds 153 E11
Longhill Aberds 153 C9
Longhirst Northumb 117 F8
Longhope Glos 36 C3
Longhope Orkney 159 J4
Longhorsley Northumb 117 E7
Longhoughton Northumb 117 C8
Longlane Derbys 76 F2
Longlane W Berks 26 B2
Longlevens Glos 37 B5
Longley W Yorks 88 D2
Longley Green Worcs 50 D2
Longmanhill Aberds 153 B7
Longmoor Camp Hants 27 F5
Longmorn Moray 152 C2
Longnewton Borders 115 B8
Longnewton Stockton 102 C1
Longney Glos 36 C4
Longniddry E Loth 121 B7
Longnor Shrops 60 D4
Longnor Staffs 75 C7
Longparish Hants 26 E2
Longport Stoke 75 E5
Longridge Lancs 93 F6
Longridge Staffs 62 C3
Longridge W Loth 120 C2
Longriggend N Lanark 119 B8
Longsdon Staffs 75 D6
Longshaw Gtr Man 86 D3
Longside Aberds 153 D10
Longstanton Cambs 54 C4
Longstock Hants 25 F8
Longstone Pembs 32 D2
Longstowe Cambs 54 D4
Longthorpe Pboro 65 E8
Longthwaite Cumb 99 B6
Longton Lancs 86 B2
Longton Stoke 75 E6
Longtown Cumb 108 C3
Longtown Hereford 35 B7
Longview Mers 86 E2
Longville in the Dale Shrops 60 E5
Longwick Bucks 39 D7
Longwitton Northumb 117 F6
Longwood Shrops 61 D6
Longworth Oxon 38 E3
Longyester E Loth 121 C8
Lonmay Aberds 153 C10
Lonmore Highld 148 D7
Looe Corn 5 D7
Loose Kent 29 D8
Loosley Row Bucks 39 D8
Lopcombe Corner Wilts 25 F7
Lopen Som 12 C2
Loppington Shrops 60 B4
Lopwell Devon 6 C2
Lorbottle Northumb 117 D6
Lorbottle Hall Northumb 117 D6
Lornty Perth 134 E1
Loscoe Derbys 76 E4
Losgaintir W Isles 154 H5
Lossiemouth Moray 152 A2
Lossit Argyll 142 C2
Lostford Shrops 74 F3
Lostock Gralam Ches W 74 B3
Lostock Green Ches W 74 B3
Lostock Hall Lancs 86 B3
Lostock Junction Gtr Man 86 D4
Lostwithiel Corn 5 D6
Loth Orkney 159 E7
Lothbeg Highld 157 H12
Lothersdale N Yorks 94 E2
Lothmore Highld 157 H12
Loudwater Bucks 40 E2
Loughborough Leics 64 C2
Loughor Swansea 33 E6
Loughton Essex 41 E7
Loughton M Keynes 53 F6
Loughton Shrops 61 F6
Lound Lincs 65 C7
Lound Notts 89 F7
Lound Suff 69 E8
Lount Leics 63 C7
Louth Lincs 91 F7
Love Clough Lancs 87 B6
Lovedean Hants 15 C7
Lover Wilts 14 B3
Loversall S Yorks 89 E6
Loves Green Essex 42 D2
Lovesome Hill N Yorks 102 E1
Loveston Pembs 32 D1
Lovington Som 23 F7
Low Ackworth W Yorks 89 C5
Low Barlings Lincs 78 B3
Low Bentham N Yorks 93 C6
Low Bradfield S Yorks 88 E3
Low Bradley N Yorks 94 E3
Low Braithwaite Cumb 108 E4
Low Brunton Northumb 110 B2
Low Burnham N Lincs 89 D8
Low Burton N Yorks 101 F7
Low Buston Northumb 117 D8
Low Catton E Yorks 96 D3
Low Clanyard Dumfries 104 F5
Low Coniscliffe Darl 101 C7
Low Crosby Cumb 108 D4
Low Dalby N Yorks 103 F6
Low Dinsdale Darl 101 C8
Low Ellington N Yorks 101 F7
Low Etherley Durham 101 B6
Low Fell T&W 111 D5
Low Fulney Lincs 66 B2
Low Garth N Yorks 103 D5
Low Gate Northumb 110 C2
Low Grantley N Yorks 94 B5
Low Habberley Worcs 50 B3
Low Ham Som 12 B2
Low Hesket Cumb 108 E4
Low Hesleyhurst Northumb 117 E6
Low Hutton N Yorks 96 C3
Low Laithe N Yorks 94 C4
Low Leighton Derbys 87 F8
Low Lorton Cumb 98 B3
Low Marishes N Yorks 96 B4
Low Marnham Notts 77 C8
Low Mill N Yorks 102 E4
Low Moor Lancs 93 E7
Low Moor W Yorks 88 B2
Low Moorsley T&W 111 E6
Low Newton Cumb 99 F6
Low Newton-by-the-Sea Northumb 117 B8
Low Row Cumb 108 F3
Low Row Cumb 109 C5
Low Row N Yorks 100 E4
Low Salchrie Dumfries 104 C4
Low Smerby Argyll 143 F8
Low Torry Fife 128 F2
Low Worsall N Yorks 102 D1
Low Wray Cumb 99 D5
Lowbridge House Cumb 99 D7
Lowca Cumb 98 B1
Lowdham Notts 77 E6
Lowe Shrops 74 F2
Lowe Hill Staffs 75 D6
Lower Aisholt Som 22 F4
Lower Arncott Oxon 39 C6
Lower Ashton Devon 10 F3
Lower Assendon Oxon 39 F7
Lower Badcall Highld 156 E4
Lower Bartle Lancs 92 F4
Lower Basildon W Berks 26 B4
Lower Beeding W Sus 17 B6
Lower Benefield Northants 65 F6
Lower Boddington Northants 52 D2
Lower Brailes Warks 51 F8
Lower Breakish Highld 149 F11
Lower Broadheath Worcs 50 D3
Lower Bullingham Hereford 49 F7
Lower Cam Glos 36 D4
Lower Chapel Powys 48 F2
Lower Chute Wilts 25 D8
Lower Cragabus Argyll 142 D4
Lower Crossings Derbys 87 F8
Lower Cumberworth W Yorks 88 D3
Lower Cwm-twrch Powys 34 C1
Lower Darwen Blackburn 86 B4
Lower Dean Bedford 53 C8
Lower Diabaig Highld 149 B12
Lower Dicker E Sus 18 D2
Lower Dinchope Shrops 60 F4
Lower Down Shrops 60 F3
Lower Drift Corn 2 D3
Lower Dunsforth N Yorks 95 C7
Lower Egleton Hereford 49 E8
Lower Elkstone Staffs 75 D7
Lower End C Beds 40 B2
Lower Everleigh Wilts 25 D6
Lower Farringdon Hants 26 F5
Lower Foxdale IoM 84 E2
Lower Frankton Shrops 73 F7
Lower Froyle Hants 27 E5
Lower Gledfield Highld 151 B8
Lower Green Norf 81 D5
Lower Hacheston Suff 57 D7
Lower Halistra Highld 148 C7
Lower Halstow Kent 30 C2
Lower Hardres Kent 31 D5
Lower Hawthwaite Cumb 98 F4
Lower Heath Ches E 75 C5
Lower Hempriggs Moray 151 E14
Lower Hergest Hereford 48 D4
Lower Heyford Oxon 38 B4
Lower Higham Kent 29 B8
Lower Holbrook Suff 57 F5
Lower Hordley Shrops 60 B3
Lower Horsebridge E Sus 18 D2
Lower Killeyan Argyll 142 D3
Lower Kingswood Sur 28 D3
Lower Kinnerton Ches W 73 C7
Lower Langford N Som 23 C6
Lower Largo Fife 129 D6
Lower Leigh Staffs 75 F7
Lower Lemington Glos 51 F7
Lower Lenie Highld 137 B8
Lower Lydbrook Glos 36 C2
Lower Lye Hereford 49 C6
Lower Machen Newport 35 F6
Lower Maes-coed Hereford 48 F5
Lower Mayland Essex 43 D5
Lower Midway Derbys 63 B7
Lower Milovaig Highld 148 C6
Lower Moor Worcs 50 E4
Lower Nazeing Essex 41 D6
Lower Netchwood Shrops 61 E6
Lower Ollach Highld 149 E10
Lower Penarth V Glam 22 B3
Lower Penn Staffs 62 E2
Lower Pennington Hants 14 E4
Lower Peover Ches W 74 B4
Lower Pexhill Ches E 75 B5
Lower Place Gtr Man 87 C7
Lower Quinton Warks 51 E6
Lower Rochford Worcs 49 C8
Lower Seagry Wilts 37 F6
Lower Shelton C Beds 53 E7
Lower Shiplake Oxon 27 B5
Lower Shuckburgh Warks 52 C2
Lower Slaughter Glos 38 B1
Lower Stanton St Quintin Wilts 37 F6
Lower Stoke Medway 30 B2
Lower Stondon C Beds 54 F2
Lower Stow Bedon Norf 68 E2
Lower Street Norf 69 C6
Lower Street Norf 81 D8
Lower Strensham Worcs 50 E4
Lower Stretton Warr 86 F4
Lower Sundon C Beds 40 B3
Lower Swanwick Hants 15 D5
Lower Swell Glos 38 B1
Lower Tean Staffs 75 F7
Lower Thurlton Norf 69 E7
Lower Tote Highld 149 B10
Lower Town Pembs 44 B4
Lower Tysoe Warks 51 E8
Lower Upham Hants 15 C6
Lower Vexford Som 22 F3
Lower Weare Som 23 D6
Lower Welson Hereford 48 D4
Lower Whitley Ches W 74 B3
Lower Wield Hants 26 E4
Lower Winchendon Bucks 39 C7
Lower Withington Ches E 74 C5
Lower Woodend Bucks 39 F8
Lower Woodford Wilts 25 F6
Lower Wyche Worcs 50 E2
Lowesby Leics 64 D4
Lowestoft Suff 69 E8
Loweswater Cumb 98 B3
Lowford Hants 15 C5
Lowgill Cumb 99 E8
Lowgill Lancs 93 C6
Lowick Northants 65 F6
Lowick Northumb 123 F6
Lowick Bridge Cumb 98 F4
Lowick Green Cumb 98 F4
Lowlands Torf 35 E6
Lowmoor Row Cumb 99 B8
Lownie Moor Angus 134 E4
Lowsonford Warks 51 C6
Lowther Cumb 99 B7
Lowthorpe E Yorks 97 C6
Lowton Gtr Man 86 E4
Lowton Common Gtr Man 86 E4
Loxbeare Devon 10 C4
Loxhill Sur 27 F8
Loxhore Devon 20 F5
Loxley Warks 51 D7
Loxton N Som 23 D5
Loxwood W Sus 27 F8
Lubcroy Highld 156 J6
Lubenham Leics 64 F4
Luccombe Som 21 E8
Luccombe Village IoW 15 G6
Lucker Northumb 123 F7
Luckett Corn 5 B8
Luckington Wilts 37 F5
Lucklawhill Fife 129 B6
Luckwell Bridge Som 21 F8
Lucton Hereford 49 C6
Ludag W Isles 148 G2
Ludborough Lincs 91 E6
Ludchurch Pembs 32 C2
Luddenden W Yorks 87 B8
Luddenden Foot W Yorks 87 B8
Luddesdown Kent 29 C7
Luddington N Lincs 90 C2
Luddington Warks 51 D6
Luddington in the Brook Northants 65 F8
Lude House Perth 133 C5
Ludford Lincs 91 F6
Ludford Shrops 49 B7
Ludgershall Bucks 39 C6
Ludgershall Wilts 25 D7
Ludgvan Corn 2 C4
Ludham Norf 69 C6
Ludlow Shrops 49 B7
Ludwell Wilts 13 B7
Ludworth Durham 111 E6
Luffincott Devon 8 E5
Lugar E Ayrs 113 B5
Lugg Green Hereford 49 C6
Luggate Burn E Loth 122 B2
Luggiebank N Lanark 119 B7
Lugton E Ayrs 118 D4
Lugwardine Hereford 49 E7
Luib Highld 149 F10
Lulham Hereford 49 E6
Lullenden Sur 28 E5
Lullington Derbys 63 C6
Lullington Som 24 D2
Lulsgate Bottom N Som 23 C7
Lulsley Worcs 50 D2
Lumb W Yorks 87 B8
Lumby N Yorks 95 F7
Lumloch E Dunb 119 C6
Lumphanan Aberds 140 D4
Lumphinnans Fife 128 E3
Lumsdaine Borders 122 C4
Lumsden Aberds 140 B3
Lunan Angus 135 D6
Lunanhead Angus 134 D4
Luncarty Perth 128 B2
Lund E Yorks 97 E5
Lund N Yorks 96 F2
Lund Shetland 160 C7
Lunderton Aberds 153 D11
Lundie Angus 134 F2
Lundie Highld 136 C4
Lundin Links Fife 129 D6
Lunga Argyll 124 E3
Lunna Shetland 160 G6
Lunning Shetland 160 G7
Lunnon Swansea 33 F6
Lunsford's Cross E Sus 18 D4
Lunt Mers 85 D4
Luntley Hereford 49 D5
Luppitt Devon 11 D6
Lupset W Yorks 88 C4
Lupton Cumb 99 F7
Lurgashall W Sus 16 B3
Lusby Lincs 79 C6
Luson Devon 6 E4
Luss Argyll 126 E2
Lussagiven Argyll 144 E5
Lusta Highld 149 C7
Lustleigh Devon 10 F2
Luston Hereford 49 C6
Luthermuir Aberds 135 C6
Luthrie Fife 128 C5
Luton Devon 7 B7
Luton Luton 40 B3
Luton Medway 29 C8
Lutterworth Leics 64 F2
Lutton Devon 6 D3
Lutton Lincs 66 B4
Lutton Northants 65 F8
Lutworthy Devon 10 C2
Luxborough Som 21 F8
Luxulyan Corn 5 D5
Lybster Highld 158 G4
Lydbury North Shrops 60 F3
Lydcott Devon 21 F5
Lydd Kent 19 C7
Lydd on Sea Kent 19 C7
Lydden Kent 31 E6
Lyddington Rutland 65 E5
Lyde Green Hants 26 D5
Lydeard St Lawrence Som 22 F3
Lydford Devon 9 F7
Lydford-on-Fosse Som 23 F7
Lydgate W Yorks 87 B7
Lydham Shrops 60 E3
Lydiard Green Wilts 37 F7
Lydiard Millicent Wilts 37 F7
Lydiate Mers 85 D4
Lydlinch Dorset 12 C5
Lydney Glos 36 D3
Lydstep Pembs 32 E1
Lye W Mid 62 F3
Lye Green Bucks 40 D2
Lye Green E Sus 18 B2
Lyford Oxon 38 E3
Lymbridge Green Kent 30 E5
Lyme Regis Dorset 11 E8
Lyminge Kent 31 E5
Lymington Hants 14 E4
Lyminster W Sus 16 D4
Lymm Warr 86 F4
Lymore Hants 14 E3
Lympne Kent 19 B8
Lympsham Som 22 D5
Lympstone Devon 10 F4
Lynchat Highld 138 D3
Lyndale Ho. Highld 149 C8
Lyndhurst Hants 14 D4
Lyndon Rutland 65 D6
Lyne Sur 27 C8
Lyne Down Hereford 49 F8
Lyne of Gorthleck Highld 137 B8
Lyne of Skene Aberds 141 C6
Lyneal Shrops 73 F8
Lyneham Oxon 38 B2
Lyneham Wilts 24 B5
Lynemore Highld 139 B6
Lynemouth Northumb 117 E8
Lyness Orkney 159 J4
Lyng Norf 68 C3
Lyng Som 11 B8
Lynmouth Devon 21 E6
Lynsted Kent 30 C3
Lynton Devon 21 E6
Lyon's Gate Dorset 12 D4
Lyonshall Hereford 48 D5
Lytchett Matravers Dorset 13 E7
Lytchett Minster Dorset 13 E7
Lyth Highld 158 D4
Lytham Lancs 85 B4
Lytham St Anne's Lancs 85 B4
Lythe N Yorks 103 C6
Lythes Orkney 159 K5

M

Mabe Burnthouse Corn 3 C6
Mabie Dumfries 107 B6
Mablethorpe Lincs 91 F9
Macclesfield Ches E 75 B6
Macclesfield Forest Ches E 75 B6
Macduff Aberds 153 B7
Mace Green Suff 56 E5
Macharioch Argyll 143 H8
Machen Caerph 35 F6
Machrihanish Argyll 143 F7
Machynlleth Powys 58 D4
Machynys Carms 33 E6
Mackerel's Common W Sus 16 B4
Mackworth Derbys 76 F3
Macmerry E Loth 121 B7
Madderty Perth 127 B8
Maddiston Falk 120 B2
Madehurst W Sus 16 C3
Madeley Staffs 74 E4
Madeley Telford 61 D6
Madeley Heath Staffs 74 E4
Madeley Park Staffs 74 E4
Madingley Cambs 54 C4
Madley Hereford 49 F6
Madresfield Worcs 50 E3
Madron Corn 2 C3
Maen-y-groes Ceredig 46 D2
Maenaddwyn Anglesey 82 C4
Maenclochog Pembs 32 B1
Maendy V Glam 22 B2
Maentwrog Gwyn 71 C7
Maer Staffs 74 F4
Maerdy Conwy 72 E4
Maerdy Rhondda 34 E3
Maes-Treylow Powys 48 C4
Maesbrook Shrops 60 B2
Maesbury Shrops 60 B3
Maesbury Marsh Shrops 60 B3
Maesgwyn-Isaf Powys 59 C8
Maesgwynne Carms 32 B3
Maeshafn Denb 73 C6
Maesllyn Ceredig 46 E2
Maesmynis Powys 48 E2
Maesteg Bridgend 34 E2
Maestir Ceredig 46 E4
Maesy cwmmer Caerph 35 E5
Maesybont Carms 33 C6
Maesycrugiau Carms 46 E3
Maesymeillion Ceredig 46 E3
Magdalen Laver Essex 41 D8
Maggieknockater Moray 152 D3
Magham Down E Sus 18 D3
Maghull Mers 85 D4
Magor Mon 35 F8
Magpie Green Suff 56 B4
Maiden Bradley Wilts 24 F3
Maiden Law Durham 110 E4
Maiden Newton Dorset 12 E3
Maiden Wells Pembs 44 F4
Maidencombe Torbay 7 C7
Maidenhall Suff 57 E5
Maidenhead Windsor 40 F1
Maidens S Ayrs 112 D2
Maiden's Green Brack 27 B6
Maidensgrave Suff 57 E6
Maidenwell Corn 5 B6
Maidenwell Lincs 79 B6
Maidford Northants 52 D4
Maids Moreton Bucks 52 F5
Maidstone Kent 29 D8
Maidwell Northants 52 B5
Mail Shetland 160 L6
Main Powys 59 C8
Maindee Newport 35 F7
Mains of Airies Dumfries 104 C3
Mains of Allardice Aberds 135 B8
Mains of Annochie Aberds 153 D9
Mains of Ardestie Angus 135 F5
Mains of Balhall Angus 135 C5
Mains of Ballindarg Angus 134 D4
Mains of Balnakettle Aberds 135 B6
Mains of Birness Aberds 153 E9
Mains of Burgie Moray 151 F13
Mains of Clunas Highld 151 G11
Mains of Crichie Aberds 153 D9
Mains of Dalvey Highld 151 H14
Mains of Dellavaird Aberds 141 F6
Mains of Drum Aberds 141 E7
Mains of Edingight Moray 152 C5
Mains of Fedderate Aberds 153 D8
Mains of Inkhorn Aberds 153 E9
Mains of Mayen Moray 152 D5
Mains of Melgund Angus 135 D5
Mains of Thornton Aberds 135 B6
Mains of Watten Highld 158 E4
Mainsforth Durham 111 F6
Mainsriddle Dumfries 107 D6
Mainstone Shrops 60 F2
Maisemore Glos 37 B5
Malacleit W Isles 148 A2
Malborough Devon 6 F5
Malcoff Derbys 87 F8
Maldon Essex 42 D4
Malham N Yorks 94 C2
Maligar Highld 149 B9
Mallaig Highld 147 B9
Malleny Mills Edin 120 C4
Malling Stirling 126 D4
Malltraeth Anglesey 82 E4
Mallwyd Gwyn 59 C5
Malmesbury Wilts 37 F6
Malmsmead Devon 21 E6
Malpas Ches W 73 E8
Malpas Corn 3 B7
Malpas Newport 35 E7
Malswick Glos 36 B4
Maltby S Yorks 89 E6
Maltby Stockton 102 C2
Maltby le Marsh Lincs 91 F8
Malting Green Essex 43 B5
Maltman's Hill Kent 30 E3
Malton N Yorks 96 B3
Malvern Link Worcs 50 E2
Malvern Wells Worcs 50 E2
Mamble Worcs 49 B8
Man-moel Caerph 35 D5
Manaccan Corn 3 D6
Manafon Powys 59 D8
Manais W Isles 154 J6

Manar Ho. Aberds 141 B6
Manaton Devon 10 F2
Manby Lincs 91 F7
Mancetter Warks 63 E7
Manchester Gtr Man 87 E6
Manchester Airport Gtr Man 87 F6
Mancot Flint 73 C7
Mandally Highld 137 D5
Manea Cambs 66 F4
Manfield N Yorks 101 C7
Mangaster Shetland 160 F5
Mangotsfield S Glos 23 B8
Mangurstadh W Isles 154 D5
Mankinholes W Yorks 87 B7
Manley Ches W 74 B2
Mannal Argyll 146 G2
Mannerston W Loth 120 B3
Manningford Bohune Wilts 25 D6
Manningford Bruce Wilts 25 D6
Manningham W Yorks 94 F4
Mannings Heath W Sus 17 B6
Mannington Dorset 13 D8
Manningtree Essex 56 F4
Mannofield Aberdeen 141 D8
Manor London 41 F7
Manor Estate S Yorks 88 F4
Manorbier Pembs 32 E1
Manordeilo Carms 33 B7
Manorhill Borders 122 F2
Manorowen Pembs 44 B4
Mansel Lacy Hereford 49 E6
Manselfield Swansea 33 F6
Mansell Gamage Hereford 49 E5
Mansergh Cumb 99 F8
Mansfield E Ayrs 113 C6
Mansfield Notts 76 C5
Mansfield Woodhouse Notts 76 C5
Mansriggs Cumb 98 F4
Manston Dorset 13 C6
Manston Kent 31 C7
Manston W Yorks 95 F6
Manswood Dorset 13 D7
Manthorpe Lincs 65 C7
Manthorpe Lincs 78 F2
Manton N Lincs 90 D3
Manton Notts 77 B5
Manton Rutland 65 D5
Manton Wilts 25 C6
Manuden Essex 41 B7
Maperton Som 12 B4
Maple Cross Herts 40 E3
Maplebeck Notts 77 C7
Mapledurham Oxon 26 B4
Mapledurwell Hants 26 D4
Maplehurst W Sus 17 B5
Maplescombe Kent 29 C6
Mapleton Derbys 75 E8
Mapperley Derbys 76 E4
Mapperley Park Nottingham 77 E5
Mapperton Dorset 12 E3
Mappleborough Green Warks 51 C5
Mappleton E Yorks 97 E8
Mappowder Dorset 12 D5
Mar Lodge Aberds 139 E6
Maraig W Isles 154 G6
Marazanvose Corn 4 D3
Marazion Corn 2 C4
Marbhig W Isles 155 F9
Marbury Ches E 74 E2
March Cambs 66 E4
March S Lanark 114 C2
Marcham Oxon 38 E4
Marchamley Shrops 61 B5
Marchington Staffs 75 F8
Marchington Woodlands Staffs 62 B5
Marchroes Gwyn 70 E4
Marchwiel Wrex 73 E7
Marchwood Hants 14 C4
Marcross V Glam 21 C8
Marden Hereford 49 E7
Marden Kent 29 E8
Marden T&W 111 B6
Marden Wilts 25 D5
Marden Beech Kent 29 E8
Marden Thorn Kent 29 E8
Mardy Mon 35 C7
Marefield Leics 64 D4
Mareham le Fen Lincs 79 C5
Mareham on the Hill Lincs 79 C5
Marehay Derbys 76 E3
Marehill W Sus 16 C4
Maresfield E Sus 17 B8
Marfleet Hull 90 B5
Marford Wrex 73 D7
Margam Neath 34 F1
Margaret Marsh Dorset 13 C6
Margaret Roding Essex 42 C1
Margaretting Essex 42 D2
Margate Kent 31 B7
Margnaheglish N Ayrs 143 E11
Margrove Park Redcar 102 C4
Marham Norf 67 C7
Marhamchurch Corn 8 D4
Marholm Pboro 65 D8
Mariandyrys Anglesey 83 C6
Marianglas Anglesey 82 C5
Mariansleigh Devon 10 B2
Marionburgh Aberds 141 D6
Marishader Highld 149 B9
Marjoriebanks Dumfries 114 F3
Mark Dumfries 104 D5
Mark S Ayrs 104 B4
Mark Som 23 E5
Mark Causeway Som 23 E5
Mark Cross E Sus 17 C8
Mark Cross E Sus 18 B2
Markbeech Kent 29 E5
Markby Lincs 79 B7
Market Bosworth Leics 63 D8
Market Deeping Lincs 65 D8
Market Drayton Shrops 74 F3
Market Harborough Leics 64 F4
Market Lavington Wilts 24 D5
Market Overton Rutland 65 C5
Market Rasen Lincs 90 F5
Market Stainton Lincs 78 B5
Market Warsop Notts 77 C5
Market Weighton E Yorks 96 E4
Market Weston Suff 56 B3
Markethill Perth 134 F2
Markfield Leics 63 C8
Markham Caerph 35 D5
Markham Moor Notts 77 B7
Markinch Fife 128 D4
Markington N Yorks 95 C5
Marks Tey Essex 43 B5
Marksbury Bath 23 C8
Markyate Herts 40 C3
Marland Gtr Man 87 C6
Marlborough Wilts 25 C6
Marlbrook Hereford 49 D7
Marlbrook Worcs 50 B4
Marlcliff Warks 51 D5
Marldon Devon 7 C6
Marlesford Suff 57 D7
Marley Green Ches E 74 E2
Marley Hill T&W 110 D5
Marley Mount Hants 14 E3
Marlingford Norf 68 D4
Marloes Pembs 44 E2
Marlow Bucks 39 F8
Marlow Hereford 49 B6
Marlow Bottom Bucks 40 F1
Marlpit Hill Kent 28 E5
Marlpool Derbys 76 E4
Marnhull Dorset 13 C5
Marnoch Aberds 152 C5
Marnock N Lanark 119 C7
Marple Gtr Man 87 F7
Marple Bridge Gtr Man 87 F7
Marr S Yorks 89 D6
Marrel Highld 157 H13
Marrick N Yorks 101 E5
Marrister Shetland 160 G7
Marros Carms 32 D3
Marsden T&W 111 C6
Marsden W Yorks 87 C8
Marsett N Yorks 100 F4
Marsh Devon 11 C7
Marsh W Yorks 94 F3
Marsh Baldon Oxon 39 E5
Marsh Gibbon Bucks 39 B6
Marsh Green Devon 10 E5
Marsh Green Kent 28 E5
Marsh Green Staffs 75 D5
Marsh Lane Derbys 76 B4
Marsh Street Som 21 E8
Marshall's Heath Herts 40 C4
Marshalsea Dorset 11 D8
Marshalswick Herts 40 D4
Marsham Norf 81 E7
Marshaw Lancs 93 D5
Marshborough Kent 31 D7
Marshbrook Shrops 60 F4
Marshchapel Lincs 91 E7
Marshfield Newport 35 F6
Marshfield S Glos 24 B2
Marshgate Corn 8 E3
Marshland St James Norf 66 D5
Marshside Mers 85 C4
Marshwood Dorset 11 E8
Marske N Yorks 101 D6
Marske-by-the-Sea Redcar 102 B4
Marston Ches W 74 B3
Marston Hereford 49 D5
Marston Lincs 77 E8
Marston Oxon 39 D5
Marston Staffs 62 B3
Marston Staffs 62 C2
Marston Warks 63 E6
Marston Wilts 24 D4
Marston Doles Warks 52 D2
Marston Green W Mid 63 F5
Marston Magna Som 12 B3
Marston Meysey Wilts 37 E8
Marston Montgomery Derbys 75 F8
Marston Moretaine C Beds 53 E7
Marston on Dove Derbys 63 B6
Marston St Lawrence Northants 52 E3
Marston Stannett Hereford 49 D7
Marston Trussell Northants 64 F3
Marstow Hereford 36 C2
Marsworth Bucks 40 C2
Marten Wilts 25 D7
Marthall Ches E 74 B5
Martham Norf 69 C7
Martin Hants 13 C8
Martin Kent 31 E7
Martin Lincs 78 C5
Martin Lincs 78 D4
Martin Dales Lincs 78 C4
Martin Drove End Hants 13 B8
Martin Hussingtree Worcs 50 C3
Martin Mill Kent 31 E7
Martinhoe Devon 21 E5
Martinhoe Cross Devon 21 E5
Martinscroft Warr 86 F4
Martinstown Dorset 12 F4
Martlesham Suff 57 E6
Martlesham Heath Suff 57 E6
Martletwy Pembs 32 C1
Martley Worcs 50 D2
Martock Som 12 C2
Marton Ches E 75 C5
Marton E Yorks 97 F7
Marton Lincs 90 F2
Marton Mbro 102 C3
Marton N Yorks 95 C7
Marton N Yorks 103 F5
Marton Shrops 60 B4
Marton Shrops 60 D2
Marton Warks 52 C2
Marton-le-Moor N Yorks 95 B6
Martyr Worthy Hants 26 F3
Martyr's Green Sur 27 D8
Marwick Orkney 159 F3
Marwood Devon 20 F4
Mary Tavy Devon 6 B3
Marybank Highld 150 F7
Maryburgh Highld 151 F8
Maryhill Glasgow 119 C5
Marykirk Aberds 135 C6
Marylebone Gtr Man 86 D3
Marypark Moray 152 E1
Maryport Cumb 107 F7
Maryport Dumfries 104 F5
Maryton Angus 135 D6
Marywell Aberds 140 E4
Marywell Aberds 141 E8
Marywell Angus 135 E6
Masham N Yorks 101 F7
Mashbury Essex 42 C2
Masongill N Yorks 93 B6
Masonhill S Ayrs 112 B3
Mastin Moor Derbys 76 B4
Mastrick Aberdeen 141 D7
Matching Essex 41 C8
Matching Green Essex 41 C8
Matching Tye Essex 41 C8
Matfen Northumb 110 B3
Matfield Kent 29 E7
Mathern Mon 36 E2
Mathon Hereford 50 E2
Mathry Pembs 44 B3
Matlaske Norf 81 D7
Matlock Derbys 76 C2
Matlock Bath Derbys 76 D2
Matson Glos 37 C5
Matterdale End Cumb 99 B5
Mattersey Notts 89 F7
Mattersey Thorpe Notts 89 F7
Mattingley Hants 26 D5
Mattishall Norf 68 C3
Mattishall Burgh Norf 68 C3
Mauchline E Ayrs 112 B4
Maud Aberds 153 D9
Maugersbury Glos 38 B2
Maughold IoM 84 C4
Mauld Highld 150 H7
Maulden C Beds 53 F8
Maulds Meaburn Cumb 99 C8
Maunby N Yorks 102 F1
Maund Bryan Hereford 49 D7
Maundown Som 11 B5
Mautby Norf 69 C7
Mavis Enderby Lincs 79 C6
Maw Green Ches E 74 D4
Mawbray Cumb 107 E7
Mawdesley Lancs 86 C2
Mawdlam Bridgend 34 F2
Mawgan Corn 3 D6
Mawla Corn 3 B6
Mawnan Corn 3 D6
Mawnan Smith Corn 3 D6
Mawsley Northants 53 B6
Maxey Pboro 65 D8
Maxstoke Warks 63 F6
Maxton Borders 122 F2
Maxton Kent 31 E7
Maxwellheugh Borders 122 F3
Maxwelltown Dumfries 107 B6
Maxworthy Corn 8 E4
May Bank Staffs 75 E5
Mayals Swansea 33 E7
Maybole S Ayrs 112 D3
Mayfield E Sus 18 C2
Mayfield Midloth 121 C6
Mayfield Staffs 75 E8
Mayfield W Loth 120 C2
Mayford Sur 27 D7
Mayland Essex 43 D5
Maynard's Green E Sus 18 D2
Maypole Mon 36 C1
Maypole Scilly 2 E4
Maypole Green Essex 43 B5
Maypole Green Norf 69 E7
Maypole Green Suff 57 C6
Maywick Shetland 160 L5
Meadle Bucks 39 D8
Meadowtown Shrops 60 D3
Meaford Staffs 75 F5
Meal Bank Cumb 99 E7
Mealabost W Isles 155 D9
Mealabost Bhuirgh W Isles 155 B9
Mealsgate Cumb 108 E2
Meanwood W Yorks 95 F5
Mearbeck N Yorks 93 C8
Meare Som 23 E6
Meare Green Som 11 B8
Mears Ashby Northants 53 C6
Measham Leics 63 C7
Meath Green Sur 28 E3
Meathop Cumb 99 F6
Meaux E Yorks 97 F6
Meavy Devon 6 C3
Medbourne Leics 64 E4
Medburn Northumb 110 B4
Meddon Devon 8 C4
Meden Vale Notts 77 C5
Medlam Lincs 79 D6
Medmenham Bucks 39 F8
Medomsley Durham 110 D4
Medstead Hants 26 F4
Meer End W Mid 51 B7
Meerbrook Staffs 75 C6
Meers Bridge Lincs 91 F8
Meesden Herts 54 F5
Meeth Devon 9 D7
Meggethead Borders 114 B4
Meidrim Carms 32 B3
Meifod Denb 72 D4
Meifod Powys 59 C8
Meigle N Ayrs 118 C1
Meigle Perth 134 E2
Meikle Earnock S Lanark 119 D7
Meikle Ferry Highld 151 C10
Meikle Forter Angus 134 C1
Meikle Gluich Highld 151 C9
Meikle Pinkerton E Loth 122 B3
Meikle Strath Aberds 135 B6
Meikle Tarty Aberds 141 B8
Meikle Wartle Aberds 153 E7
Meikleour Perth 134 F1
Meinciau Carms 33 C5
Meir Stoke 75 E6
Meir Heath Staffs 75 E6
Melbourn Cambs 54 E4
Melbourne Derbys 63 B7
Melbourne E Yorks 96 E3
Melbourne S Lanark 120 E3
Melbury Abbas Dorset 13 B6
Melbury Bubb Dorset 12 D3
Melbury Osmond Dorset 12 D3
Melbury Sampford Dorset 12 D3
Melby Shetland 160 H3
Melchbourne Bedford 53 C8
Melcombe Bingham Dorset 13 D5
Melcombe Regis Dorset 12 F4
Meldon Devon 9 E7
Meldon Northumb 117 F7
Meldreth Cambs 54 E4
Meldrum Ho. Aberds 141 B7
Melfort Argyll 124 D4
Melgarve Highld 137 E7
Meliden Denb 72 A4
Melin-y-coed Conwy 83 E8
Melin-y-ddôl Powys 59 D7
Melin-y-grug Powys 59 D7
Melin-y-Wig Denb 72 E4
Melinbyrhedyn Powys 58 E5
Melincourt Neath 34 D2
Melkinthorpe Cumb 99 B7
Melkridge Northumb 109 C7
Melksham Wilts 24 C4
Melldalloch Argyll 145 F8
Melling Lancs 93 B5
Melling Mers 85 D4
Melling Mount Mers 86 D2
Mellis Suff 56 B5
Mellon Charles Highld 155 H13
Mellon Udrigle Highld 155 H13
Mellor Gtr Man 87 F7
Mellor Lancs 93 F6
Mellor Brook Lancs 93 F6
Mells Som 24 E2
Melmerby Cumb 109 F6
Melmerby N Yorks 95 B6
Melmerby N Yorks 101 F5
Melplash Dorset 12 E2
Melrose Borders 121 F8
Melsetter Orkney 159 K3
Melsonby N Yorks 101 D6
Meltham W Yorks 88 C2
Melton Suff 57 D6
Melton Constable Norf 81 D6
Melton Mowbray Leics 64 C4
Melton Ross N Lincs 90 C4
Meltonby E Yorks 96 D3
Melvaig Highld 155 J12
Melverley Shrops 60 C3
Melverley Green Shrops 60 C3
Melvich Highld 157 C11
Membury Devon 11 D7
Memsie Aberds 153 B9
Memus Angus 134 D4
Menabilly Corn 5 D5
Menai Bridge = Porthaethwy Anglesey 83 D5
Mendham Suff 69 F5
Mendlesham Suff 56 C5
Mendlesham Green Suff 56 C4
Menheniot Corn 5 C7
Mennock Dumfries 113 D8
Menston W Yorks 94 E4
Menstrie Clack 127 E7
Menthorpe N Yorks 96 F2
Mentmore Bucks 40 C2
Meoble Highld 147 C10
Meole Brace Shrops 60 C4
Meols Mers 85 E3
Meonstoke Hants 15 C7
Meopham Kent 29 C7
Meopham Station Kent 29 C7
Mepal Cambs 66 F4
Meppershall C Beds 54 F2
Merbach Hereford 48 E5
Mere Ches E 86 F5
Mere Wilts 24 F3
Mere Brow Lancs 86 C2
Mere Green W Mid 62 E5
Mereclough Lancs 93 F8
Mereside Blackpool 92 F3
Mereworth Kent 29 D7
Mergie Aberds 141 F6
Meriden W Mid 63 F6
Merkadale Highld 149 E8
Merkland Dumfries 106 B4
Merkland S Ayrs 112 E2
Merkland Lodge Highld 156 G7
Merley Poole 13 E8
Merlin's Bridge Pembs 44 D4
Merrington Shrops 60 B4
Merrion Pembs 44 F4
Merriott Som 12 C2
Merrivale Devon 6 B3
Merrow Sur 27 D8
Merrymeet Corn 5 C7
Mersham Kent 19 B7
Merstham Sur 28 D3
Merston W Sus 16 D2
Merstone IoW 15 F6
Merther Corn 3 B7
Merthyr Carms 32 B4
Merthyr Cynog Powys 47 F8
Merthyr-Dyfan V Glam 22 C3
Merthyr Mawr Bridgend 21 B7
Merthyr Tudful = Merthyr Tydfil M Tydf 34 D4
Merthyr Tydfil = Merthyr Tudful M Tydf 34 D4
Merthyr Vale M Tydf 34 E4
Merton Devon 9 C7
Merton London 28 B3
Merton Norf 68 E2
Merton Oxon 39 C5
Mervinslaw Borders 116 C2
Meshaw Devon 10 C2
Messing Essex 42 C4
Messingham N Lincs 90 D2
Metfield Suff 69 F5
Metheringham Lincs 78 C3
Methil Fife 129 E5
Methlem Gwyn 70 D2
Methley W Yorks 88 B4
Methlick Aberds 153 E8
Methven Perth 128 B2
Methwold Norf 67 E7
Methwold Hythe Norf 67 E7
Mettingham Suff 69 F6
Mevagissey Corn 3 B9
Mewith Head N Yorks 93 C7
Mexborough S Yorks 89 D5
Mey Highld 158 C4
Meysey Hampton Glos 37 E8
Miabhag W Isles 154 G5
Miabhag W Isles 154 H6
Miabhig W Isles 154 D5
Michaelchurch Hereford 36 B2
Michaelchurch Escley Hereford 48 F5
Michaelchurch on Arrow Powys 48 D4
Michaelston-le-Pit V Glam 22 B3
Michaelston-y-Fedw Newport 35 F6
Michaelstow Corn 5 B5
Michealston-super-Ely Cardiff 22 B3
Micheldever Hants 26 F3
Michelmersh Hants 14 B4
Mickfield Suff 56 C5
Mickle Trafford Ches W 73 C8
Micklebring S Yorks 89 E6
Mickleby N Yorks 103 C6
Mickleham Sur 28 D2
Mickleover Derby 76 F3
Micklethwaite W Yorks 94 E4
Mickleton Durham 100 B4
Mickleton Glos 51 E6
Mickletown W Yorks 88 B4
Mickley N Yorks 95 B5
Mickley Square Northumb 110 C3
Mid Ardlaw Aberds 153 B9
Mid Auchinlech Involyd 118 B3
Mid Beltie Aberds 140 D5
Mid Calder W Loth 120 C3
Mid Cloch Forbie Aberds 153 C7
Mid Clyth Highld 158 G4
Mid Lavant W Sus 16 D2
Mid Main Highld 150 H7
Mid Urchany Highld 151 G11
Mid Walls Shetland 160 H4
Mid Yell Shetland 160 D7
Midbea Orkney 159 D5
Middle Assendon Oxon 39 F7
Middle Aston Oxon 38 B4
Middle Barton Oxon 38 B4
Middle Cairncake Aberds 153 D8
Middle Claydon Bucks 39 B7
Middle Drums Angus 135 D5
Middle Handley Derbys 76 B4
Middle Littleton Worcs 51 E5
Middle Maes-coed Hereford 48 F5
Middle Mill Pembs 44 C3
Middle Rasen Lincs 90 F4
Middle Rigg Perth 128 D2
Middle Tysoe Warks 51 E8
Middle Wallop Hants 25 F7
Middle Winterslow Wilts 25 F7
Middle Woodford Wilts 25 F6
Middlebie Dumfries 108 B2
Middleforth Green Lancs 86 B3
Middleham N Yorks 101 F6
Middlehope Shrops 60 F4
Middlemarsh Dorset 12 D4
Middlemuir Aberds 141 B8
Middlesbrough Mbro 102 B2
Middleshaw Cumb 99 F7
Middleshaw Dumfries 107 B8
Middlesmoor N Yorks 94 B3
Middlestone Durham 111 F5
Middlestone Moor Durham 110 F5
Middlestown W Yorks 88 C3
Middlethird Borders 122 E2
Middleton Aberds 141 C7
Middleton Argyll 146 G2
Middleton Cumb 99 F8
Middleton Derbys 75 C8
Middleton Derbys 76 D2
Middleton Essex 56 F2
Middleton Gtr Man 87 D6
Middleton Hants 26 E2
Middleton Hereford 49 C7
Middleton Lancs 92 D4
Middleton Midloth 121 D6
Middleton N Yorks 94 E4
Middleton N Yorks 103 F5
Middleton Norf 67 C6
Middleton Northants 64 F5
Middleton Northumb 117 F6
Middleton Northumb 123 F7
Middleton Perth 128 D3
Middleton Perth 133 E8
Middleton Shrops 49 B7
Middleton Shrops 60 B3
Middleton Shrops 60 E2
Middleton Suff 57 C8
Middleton Swansea 33 F5
Middleton W Yorks 88 B3
Middleton Warks 63 E5
Middleton Cheney Northants 52 E2
Middleton Green Staffs 75 F6
Middleton Hall Northumb 117 B5
Middleton-in-Teesdale Durham 100 B4
Middleton Moor Suff 57 C8
Middleton-on-Leven N Yorks 102 D2
Middleton-on-Sea W Sus 16 D3
Middleton on the Hill Hereford 49 C7
Middleton-on-the-Wolds E Yorks 96 E5
Middleton One Row Darl 102 C1
Middleton Priors Shrops 61 E6
Middleton Quernham N Yorks 95 B6
Middleton Scriven Shrops 61 F6
Middleton St George Darl 101 C8
Middleton Stoney Oxon 39 B5
Middleton Tyas N Yorks 101 D7
Middletown Cumb 98 D1
Middletown Powys 60 C3
Middlewich Ches E 74 C3
Middlewood Green Suff 56 C4
Middlezoy Som 23 F5
Middridge Durham 101 B7
Midfield Highld 157 C8
Midge Hall Lancs 86 B3
Midgeholme Cumb 109 D6
Midgham W Berks 26 C3
Midgley W Yorks 87 B8
Midgley W Yorks 88 C3
Midhopestones S Yorks 88 E3
Midhurst W Sus 16 B2
Midlem Borders 115 B8
Midmar Aberds 141 D5
Midsomer Norton Bath 23 D8
Midton Involyd 118 B2
Midtown Highld 155 J13
Midtown Highld 157 C8
Midtown of Buchromb Moray 152 D3
Midville Lincs 79 D6
Midway Ches E 87 F7
Migdale Highld 151 B9
Migvie Aberds 140 D3
Milarrochy Stirling 126 E3
Milborne Port Som 12 C4
Milborne St Andrew Dorset 13 E6
Milborne Wick Som 12 B4
Milbourne Northumb 110 B4
Milburn Cumb 100 B1
Milbury Heath S Glos 36 E3
Milcombe Oxon 52 F2
Milden Suff 56 E3
Mildenhall Suff 55 B8
Mildenhall Wilts 25 C7
Mile Cross Norf 68 C5
Mile Elm Wilts 24 C4
Mile End Essex 43 B5
Mile End Glos 36 C2
Mile Oak Brighton 17 D6
Milebrook Powys 48 B5
Milebush Kent 29 E8
Mileham Norf 68 C2
Milesmark Fife 128 F2
Milfield Northumb 122 F5
Milford Derbys 76 E3
Milford Devon 8 B4
Milford Powys 59 E7
Milford Staffs 62 B3
Milford Sur 27 E7
Milford Wilts 14 B2
Milford Haven = Aberdaugleddau Pembs 44 E4
Milford on Sea Hants 14 E3
Milkwall Glos 36 D2
Milkwell Wilts 13 B7
Mill Bank W Yorks 87 B8
Mill Common Suff 69 F7
Mill End Bucks 39 F7
Mill End Herts 54 F4
Mill Green Essex 42 D2
Mill Green Norf 68 F4
Mill Green Suff 56 E3
Mill Hill London 41 E5
Mill Lane Hants 27 D5
Mill of Kingoodie Aberds 141 B7
Mill of Muiresk Aberds 153 D6
Mill of Sterin Aberds 140 E2
Mill of Uras Aberds 141 F7
Mill Place N Lincs 90 D3
Mill Side Cumb 99 F6
Mill Street Norf 68 C3
Milland W Sus 16 B2
Millarston Renfs 118 C4
Millbank Aberds 153 D11
Millbank Highld 158 D3
Millbeck Cumb 98 B4
Millbounds Orkney 159 E6
Millbreck Aberds 153 D10
Millbridge Sur 27 E6
Millbrook C Beds 53 F8
Millbrook Corn 6 D2
Millbrook Soton 14 C4
Millburn S Ayrs 112 B4
Millcombe Devon 7 E6
Millcorner E Sus 18 C5
Milldale Staffs 75 D8
Millden Lodge Angus 135 B5
Milldens Angus 135 D5
Millerhill Midloth 121 C6
Miller's Dale Derbys 75 B8
Miller's Green Derbys 76 D2
Millgreen Shrops 61 B6
Millhalf Hereford 48 E4
Millhayes Devon 11 D7
Millhead Lancs 92 B4
Millheugh S Lanark 119 D7
Millholme Cumb 99 E7
Millhouse Argyll 145 F8
Millhouse Cumb 108 F3
Millhouse Green S Yorks 88 D3
Millhousebridge Dumfries 114 F4
Millhouses S Yorks 88 F4
Millikenpark Renfs 118 C4
Millin Cross Pembs 44 D4
Millington E Yorks 96 D4
Millmeece Staffs 74 F5
Millom Cumb 98 F3
Millook Corn 8 E3
Millpool Corn 5 B6
Millport N Ayrs 145 H10
Millquarter Dumfries 113 F6
Millthorpe Lincs 78 F4
Millthrop Cumb 100 E1
Milltimber Aberdeen 141 D7
Milltown Corn 5 D6
Milltown Derbys 76 C3
Milltown Devon 20 F4
Milltown Dumfries 108 B3
Milltown of Aberdalgie Perth 128 B2
Milltown of Auchindoun Moray 152 D3
Milltown of Craigston Aberds 153 C7
Milltown of Edinvillie Moray 152 D2
Milltown of Kildrummy Aberds 140 C3
Milltown of Rothiemay Moray 152 D5
Milltown of Towie Aberds 140 C3
Milnathort Perth 128 D3
Milner's Heath Ches W 73 C8
Milngavie E Dunb 119 B5
Milnrow Gtr Man 87 C7
Milnshaw Lancs 87 B5
Milnthorpe Cumb 99 F6
Milo Carms 33 C6
Milson Shrops 49 B8
Milstead Kent 30 D3
Milston Wilts 25 E6
Milton Angus 134 E3
Milton Cambs 55 C5
Milton Cumb 109 C5
Milton Derbys 63 B7
Milton Dumfries 105 D6
Milton Dumfries 106 B5
Milton Dumfries 113 F8
Milton Highld 150 F6
Milton Highld 150 H7
Milton Highld 151 D10
Milton Highld 151 G8
Milton Highld 158 E5
Milton Moray 152 B5
Milton N Som 22 C5
Milton Notts 77 B7
Milton Oxon 38 E4
Milton Oxon 52 F2
Milton Pembs 32 D1
Milton Perth 127 C8
Milton Ptsmth 15 E7
Milton Stirling 126 D4
Milton Stoke 75 D6
Milton W Dunb 118 B4
Milton Abbas Dorset 13 D6
Milton Abbot Devon 6 B2
Milton Bridge Midloth 120 C5
Milton Bryan C Beds 53 F7
Milton Clevedon Som 23 F8
Milton Coldwells Aberds 153 E9
Milton Combe Devon 6 C2
Milton Damerel Devon 9 C5
Milton End Glos 37 D8
Milton Ernest Bedford 53 D8
Milton Green Ches W 73 D8
Milton Hill Oxon 38 E4
Milton Keynes M Keynes 53 F6
Milton Keynes Village M Keynes 53 F6
Milton Lilbourne Wilts 25 C6
Milton Malsor Northants 52 D5
Milton Morenish Perth 132 F3
Milton of Auchinhove Aberds 140 D4
Milton of Balgonie Fife 128 D5
Milton of Buchanan Stirling 126 E3
Milton of Campfield Aberds 140 D5
Milton of Campsie E Dunb 119 B6
Milton of Corsindae Aberds 141 D5
Milton of Cushnie Aberds 140 C4
Milton of Dalcapon Perth 133 D6
Milton of Edradour Perth 133 D6
Milton of Gollanfield Highld 151 F10
Milton of Lesmore Aberds 140 B3
Milton of Logie Aberds 140 D3
Milton of Murtle Aberdeen 141 D7
Milton of Noth Aberds 140 B4
Milton of Tullich Aberds 140 E2
Milton on Stour Dorset 13 B5
Milton Regis Kent 30 C3
Milton under Wychwood Oxon 38 C2
Miltonduff Moray 152 B1
Miltonhill Moray 151 E13
Miltonise Dumfries 105 B5
Milverton Som 11 B6
Milverton Warks 51 C8
Milwich Staffs 75 F6
Minard Argyll 125 F5
Minchinhampton Glos 37 D5
Mindrum Northumb 122 F4
Minehead Som 21 E8
Minera Wrex 73 D6
Minety Wilts 37 E7
Minffordd Gwyn 58 C4
Minffordd Gwyn 71 D6
Minffordd Gwyn 83 D5
Miningsby Lincs 79 C6
Minions Corn 5 B7
Minishant S Ayrs 112 C3
Minllyn Gwyn 59 C5
Minnes Aberds 141 B8
Minngearraidh W Isles 148 F2
Minnigaff Dumfries 105 C8
Minnonie Aberds 153 B7
Minskip N Yorks 95 C6
Minstead Hants 14 C3
Minsted W Sus 16 B2
Minster Kent 30 B3
Minster Kent 31 C7
Minster Lovell Oxon 38 C3
Minsterley Shrops 60 D3
Minsterworth Glos 36 C4
Minterne Magna Dorset 12 D4
Minting Lincs 78 B4
Mintlaw Aberds 153 D9
Minto Borders 115 B8
Minton Shrops 60 E4
Minwear Pembs 32 C1
Minworth W Mid 63 E5
Mirbister Orkney 159 F4
Mirehouse Cumb 98 C1
Mireland Highld 158 D5
Mirfield W Yorks 88 C3
Miserden Glos 37 D6
Miskin Rhondda 34 F4
Misson Notts 89 E7
Misterton Leics 64 F2
Misterton Notts 89 E8
Misterton Som 12 D2
Mistley Essex 56 F5
Mitcham London 28 C3
Mitchel Troy Mon 36 C1
Mitcheldean Glos 36 C3
Mitchell Corn 4 D3
Mitcheltroy Common Mon 36 D1
Mitford Northumb 117 F7
Mithian Corn 4 D2
Mitton Staffs 62 C2
Mixbury Oxon 52 F4
Moat Cumb 108 B4
Moats Tye Suff 56 D4
Mobberley Ches E 74 B4
Mobberley Staffs 75 E7
Moccas Hereford 49 E5
Mochdre Conwy 83 D8
Mochdre Powys 59 F7
Mochrum Dumfries 105 E7
Mockbeggar Hants 14 D2
Mockerkin Cumb 98 B2
Modbury Devon 6 D4
Moddershall Staffs 75 F6
Moelfre Anglesey 82 C5
Moelfre Powys 59 B8
Moffat Dumfries 114 D3
Moggerhanger C Beds 54 E2
Moira Leics 63 C7
Mol-chlach Highld 149 G9
Molash Kent 30 D4
Mold = Yr Wyddgrug Flint 73 C6
Moldgreen W Yorks 88 C2
Molehill Green Essex 42 B1
Molescroft E Yorks 97 E6
Molesden Northumb 117 F7
Molesworth Cambs 53 B8
Moll Highld 149 E10
Molland Devon 10 B3
Mollington Ches W 73 B7
Mollington Oxon 52 E2
Mollinsburn N Lanark 119 B7
Monachty Ceredig 46 C4
Monachylemore Stirling 126 C3
Monar Lodge Highld 150 G5
Monaughty Powys 48 C4
Monboddo House Aberds 135 B7
Mondynes Aberds 135 B7
Monevechadan Argyll 125 E7
Monewden Suff 57 D6
Moneydie Perth 128 B2
Moniaive Dumfries 113 E7
Monifieth Angus 134 F4
Monikie Angus 135 F4
Monimail Fife 128 C4
Monington Pembs 45 E3
Monk Bretton S Yorks 88 D4
Monk Fryston N Yorks 89 B6
Monk Sherborne Hants 26 D4
Monk Soham Suff 57 C6
Monk Street Essex 42 B2
Monken Hadley London 41 E5
Monkhopton Shrops 61 E6
Monkland Hereford 49 D6
Monkleigh Devon 9 B6
Monknash V Glam 21 B8
Monkokehampton Devon 9 D7
Monks Eleigh Suff 56 E3
Monk's Gate W Sus 17 B6
Monks Heath Ches E 74 B5
Monks Kirby Warks 63 F8
Monks Risborough Bucks 39 D8
Monkseaton T&W 111 B6
Monkshill Aberds 153 D7
Monksilver Som 22 F2
Monkspath W Mid 51 B6
Monkswood Mon 35 D7
Monkton Devon 11 D6
Monkton Kent 31 C6
Monkton Pembs 44 E4
Monkton S Ayrs 112 B3
Monkton Combe Bath 24 C2
Monkton Deverill Wilts 24 F3
Monkton Farleigh Wilts 24 C3
Monkton Heathfield Som 11 B7
Monkton Up Wimborne Dorset 13 C8
Monkwearmouth T&W 111 D6
Monkwood Hants 26 F4
Monmouth = Trefynwy Mon 36 C2
Monmouth Cap Mon 35 B7
Monnington on Wye Hereford 49 E5
Monreith Dumfries 105 E7
Monreith Mains Dumfries 105 E7
Mont Saint Guern 16
Montacute Som 12 C2
Montcoffer Ho. Aberds 153 B6
Montford Argyll 145 G10
Montford Shrops 60 C4
Montford Bridge Shrops 60 C4
Montgarrie Aberds 140 C4
Montgomery = Trefaldwyn Powys 60 E2
Montrave Fife 129 D5
Montrose Angus 135 D7
Montsale Essex 43 E6
Monxton Hants 25 E8
Monyash Derbys 75 C8
Monymusk Aberds 141 C5
Monzie Perth 127 B7
Monzie Castle Perth 127 B7
Moodiesburn N Lanark 119 B6
Moonzie Fife 128 C5
Moor Allerton W Yorks 95 F5
Moor Crichel Dorset 13 D7
Moor End E Yorks 96 F4
Moor End York 96 D2
Moor Monkton N Yorks 95 D8
Moor of Granary Moray 151 F13
Moor of Ravenstone Dumfries 105 E7
Moor Row Cumb 98 C2
Moor Street Kent 30 C2
Moorby Lincs 79 C5
Moordown Bmouth 13 E8
Moore Halton 86 F3
Moorend Glos 36 D4
Moorends S Yorks 89 C7
Moorgreen Notts 76 E4
Moorhall Derbys 76 B3
Moorhampton Hereford 49 E5
Moorhead W Yorks 94 F4
Moorhouse Cumb 108 D3
Moorhouse Notts 77 C7
Moorlinch Som 23 F5
Moorsholm Redcar 102 C4
Moorside Gtr Man 87 D7
Moorthorpe W Yorks 89 C5
Moortown Hants 14 D2
Moortown IoW 14 F5
Moortown Lincs 90 E4
Morangie Highld 151 C10
Morar Highld 147 B9
Morborne Cambs 65 E8
Morchard Bishop Devon 10 D2
Morcombelake Dorset 12 E2
Morcott Rutland 65 D6
Morda Shrops 60 B2
Morden Dorset 13 E7
Morden London 28 C3
Mordiford Hereford 49 F7
Mordon Durham 101 B8
More Shrops 60 E3
Morebath Devon 10 B4
Morebattle Borders 116 B3
Morecambe Lancs 92 C4
Morefield Highld 150 B4
Moreleigh Devon 7 D5
Morenish Perth 132 F2
Moresby Cumb 98 B1
Moresby Parks Cumb 98 C1
Morestead Hants 15 B6
Moreton Dorset 13 F6
Moreton Essex 41 D8
Moreton Mers 85 E3
Moreton Oxon 39 D6
Moreton Staffs 61 C7
Moreton Corbet Shrops 61 B5
Moreton-in-Marsh Glos 51 F7
Moreton Jeffries Hereford 49 E8
Moreton Morrell Warks 51 D8
Moreton on Lugg Hereford 49 E7
Moreton Pinkney Northants 52 E3
Moreton Say Shrops 74 F3
Moreton Valence Glos 36 D4
Moretonhampstead Devon 10 F2
Morfa Carms 33 C6
Morfa Carms 33 E6
Morfa Bach Carms 32 C4
Morfa Bychan Gwyn 71 D6
Morfa Dinlle Gwyn 82 F4
Morfa Glas Neath 34 D2
Morfa Nefyn Gwyn 70 C3
Morfydd Denb 72 E5
Morgan's Vale Wilts 14 B2
Moriah Ceredig 46 B5
Morland Cumb 99 B7
Morley Derbys 76 E3
Morley Durham 101 B6
Morley W Yorks 88 B3
Morley Green Ches E 87 F6
Morley St Botolph Norf 68 E3
Morningside Edin 120 B5
Morningside N Lanark 119 D8
Morningthorpe Norf 68 E5
Morpeth Northumb 117 F8
Morphie Aberds 135 C7
Morrey Staffs 62 C5
Morris Green Essex 55 F8
Morriston Swansea 33 E7
Morston Norf 81 C6
Mortehoe Devon 20 E3
Mortimer W Berks 26 C4
Mortimer West End Hants 26 C4
Mortimer's Cross Hereford 49 C6
Mortlake London 28 B3
Morton Cumb 108 D3
Morton Derbys 76 C4
Morton Lincs 65 B7
Morton Lincs 77 C8
Morton Lincs 90 E2
Morton Norf 68 C4
Morton Notts 77 D7
Morton S Glos 36 E3
Morton Shrops 60 B2
Morton Bagot Warks 51 C6
Morton-on-Swale N Yorks 101 E8
Morvah Corn 2 C3
Morval Corn 5 D7
Morvich Highld 136 B2
Morvich Highld 157 J10
Morville Shrops 61 E6
Morville Heath Shrops 61 E6
Morwenstow Corn 8 C4
Mosborough S Yorks 88 F5
Moscow E Ayrs 118 E4
Mosedale Cumb 108 F3
Moseley W Mid 62 E3
Moseley W Mid 62 F4
Moseley Worcs 50 D3
Moss Argyll 146 G2
Moss Highld 147 E9
Moss S Yorks 89 C6
Moss Wrex 73 D7
Moss Bank Mers 86 E3
Moss Edge Lancs 92 E4
Moss End Brack 27 B6
Moss of Barmuckity Moray 152 B2
Moss Pit Staffs 62 B3
Moss-side Highld 151 F11
Moss Side Lancs 92 F3
Mossat Aberds 140 C3
Mossbank Shetland 160 F6
Mossbay Cumb 98 B1
Mossblown S Ayrs 112 B4
Mossbrow Gtr Man 86 F5
Mossburnford Borders 116 C2
Mossdale Dumfries 106 B3
Mossend N Lanark 119 C7
Mosser Cumb 98 B3
Mossfield Highld 151 D9
Mossgiel E Ayrs 112 B4
Mosside Angus 134 D4
Mossley Ches E 75 C5
Mossley Gtr Man 87 D7
Mossley Hill Mers 85 F4
Mosstodloch Moray 152 B3
Mosston Angus 135 E5
Mossy Lea Lancs 86 C3
Mosterton Dorset 12 D2
Moston Gtr Man 87 D6
Moston Shrops 61 B5
Moston Green Ches E 74 C4
Mostyn Flint 85 F2
Mostyn Quay Flint 85 F2
Motcombe Dorset 13 B6
Mothecombe Devon 6 E4
Motherby Cumb 99 B6
Motherwell N Lanark 119 D7
Mottingham London 28 B5
Mottisfont Hants 14 B4
Mottistone IoW 14 F5
Mottram in Longdendale Gtr Man 87 E7
Mottram St Andrew Ches E 75 B5
Mouilpied Guern 16
Mouldsworth Ches W 74 B2
Moulin Perth 133 D6
Moulsecoomb Brighton 17 D7
Moulsford Oxon 39 F5
Moulsoe M Keynes 53 E7
Moulton Ches W 74 C3
Moulton Lincs 66 B3
Moulton N Yorks 101 D7
Moulton Northants 53 C5
Moulton Suff 55 C7
Moulton V Glam 22 B2
Moulton Chapel Lincs 66 C2
Moulton Eaugate Lincs 66 C3
Moulton Seas End Lincs 66 B3
Moulton St Mary Norf 69 D6
Mounie Castle Aberds 141 B6
Mount Corn 4 D2
Mount Corn 5 C6
Mount Highld 151 G12
Mount Bures Essex 56 F3
Mount Canisp Highld 151 D10
Mount Hawke Corn 3 B6
Mount Pleasant Ches E 74 D5
Mount Pleasant Derbys 63 C6
Mount Pleasant Derbys 76 E3
Mount Pleasant Flint 73 B6
Mount Pleasant Hants 14 E3
Mount Pleasant W Yorks 88 B3
Mount Sorrel Wilts 13 B8
Mount Tabor W Yorks 87 B8
Mountain W Yorks 94 F3
Mountain Ash = Aberpennar Rhondda 34 E4
Mountain Cross Borders 120 E4

Mountain Water Pembs 44 C4
Mountbenger Borders 115 B6
Mountfield E Sus 18 C4
Mountgerald Highld 151 E8
Mountjoy Corn 4 C3
Mountnessing Essex 42 E2
Mounton Mon 36 E2
Mountsorrel Leics 64 C2
Mousehole Corn 2 D3
Mousen Northumb 123 F7
Mouswald Dumfries 107 B7
Mow Cop Ches E 75 D5
Mowhaugh Borders 116 B4
Mowsley Leics 64 F3
Moxley W Mid 62 E3
Moy Highld 137 F7
Moy Highld 151 H10
Moy Hall Highld 151 H10
Moy Ho. Moray 151 E13
Moy Lodge Highld 137 F7
Moyles Court Hants 14 D2
Moylgrove Pembs 45 E3
Muasdale Argyll 143 D7
Much Birch Hereford 49 F7
Much Cowarne Hereford 49 E8
Much Dewchurch Hereford 49 F6
Much Hadham Herts 41 C7
Much Hoole Lancs 86 B2
Much Marcle Hereford 49 F8
Much Wenlock Shrops 61 D6
Muchalls Aberds 141 E8
Muchelney Som 12 B2
Muchlarnick Corn 5 D7
Muchrachd Highld 150 H5
Muckernich Highld 151 F8
Mucking Thurrock 42 F2
Muckleford Dorset 12 E4
Mucklestone Staffs 74 F4
Muckleton Shrops 61 B5
Muckletown Aberds 140 B4
Muckley Corner Staffs 62 D4
Muckton Lincs 91 F7
Mudale Highld 157 F8
Muddiford Devon 20 F4
Mudeford Dorset 14 E2
Mudford Som 12 C3
Mudgley Som 23 E6
Mugdock Stirling 119 B5
Mugeary Highld 149 E9
Mugginton Derbys 76 E2
Muggleswick Durham 110 E3
Muie Highld 157 J9
Muir Aberds 139 F6
Muir of Fairburn Highld 150 F7
Muir of Fowlis Aberds 140 C4
Muir of Ord Highld 151 F8
Muir of Pert Angus 134 F4
Muirden Aberds 153 C7
Muirdrum Angus 135 F5
Muirhead Angus 134 F3
Muirhead Fife 128 D4
Muirhead N Lanark 119 C6
Muirhead S Ayrs 118 F3
Muirhouselaw Borders 116 B2
Muirhouses Falk 128 F2
Muirkirk E Ayrs 113 B6
Muirmill Stirling 127 F6
Muirshearlich Highld 136 F4
Muirskie Aberds 141 E7
Muirtack Aberds 153 E9
Muirton Highld 151 E10
Muirton Perth 127 C8
Muirton Perth 128 B3
Muirton Mains Highld 150 F7
Muirton of Ardblair Perth 134 E1
Muirton of Ballochy Angus 135 C6
Muiryfold Aberds 153 C7
Muker N Yorks 100 E4
Mulbarton Norf 68 D4
Mulben Moray 152 C3
Mulindry Argyll 142 C4
Mullardoch House Highld 150 H5
Mullion Corn 3 E5
Mullion Cove Corn 3 E5
Mumby Lincs 79 B8
Munderfield Row Hereford 49 D8
Munderfield Stocks Hereford 49 D8
Mundesley Norf 81 D9
Mundford Norf 67 E8
Mundham Norf 69 E6
Mundon Essex 42 D4
Mundurno Aberdeen 141 C8
Munerigie Highld 137 D5
Muness Shetland 160 C8
Mungasdale Highld 150 B2
Mungrisdale Cumb 108 F3
Munlochy Highld 151 F9
Munsley Hereford 49 E8
Munslow Shrops 60 F5
Murchington Devon 9 F8
Murcott Oxon 39 C5
Murkle Highld 158 D3
Murlaggan Highld 136 E3
Murlaggan Highld 137 F6
Murra Orkney 159 H3
Murrayfield Edin 120 B5
Murrow Cambs 66 D3
Mursley Bucks 39 B8
Murthill Angus 134 D4
Murthly Perth 133 F7
Murton Cumb 100 B2
Murton Durham 111 E6
Murton Northumb 123 E5
Murton York 96 D2
Musbury Devon 11 E7
Muscoates N Yorks 102 F4
Musdale Argyll 124 C5
Musselburgh E Loth 121 B6
Muston Leics 77 F8
Muston N Yorks 97 B6
Mustow Green Worcs 50 B3
Mutehill Dumfries 106 E3
Mutford Suff 69 F7
Muthill Perth 127 C7
Mutterton Devon 10 D5
Muxton Telford 61 C7
Mybster Highld 158 E3
Myddfai Carms 34 B1
Myddle Shrops 60 B4
Mydroilyn Ceredig 46 D3
Myerscough Lancs 92 F4
Mylor Bridge Corn 3 C7
Mynachlog-ddu Pembs 45 F3
Myndtown Shrops 60 F3
Mynydd Bach Ceredig 47 B6
Mynydd-bach Mon 36 E1
Mynydd Bodafon Anglesey 82 C4
Mynydd-isa Flint 73 C6
Mynyddygarreg Carms 33 D5
Mynytho Gwyn 70 D4
Myrebird Aberds 141 E6
Myrelandhorn Highld 158 E4
Myreside Perth 128 B4
Myrtle Hill Carms 47 F6
Mytchett Sur 27 D6
Mytholm W Yorks 87 B7
Mytholmroyd W Yorks 87 B8
Myton-on-Swale N Yorks 95 C7
Mytton Shrops 60 C4

N

Na Gearrannan W Isles 154 C6
Naast Highld 155 J13
Naburn York 95 E8
Nackington Kent 31 D5
Nacton Suff 57 E6
Nafferton E Yorks 97 D6
Nailbridge Glos 36 C3
Nailsbourne Som 11 B7
Nailsea N Som 23 B6
Nailstone Leics 63 D8
Nailsworth Glos 37 E5
Nairn Highld 151 F11
Nalderswood Sur 28 E3
Nancegollan Corn 2 C5
Nancledra Corn 2 C3
Nanhoron Gwyn 70 D3
Nannau Gwyn 71 E8
Nannerch Flint 73 C5
Nanpantan Leics 64 C2
Nanpean Corn 4 D4
Nanstallon Corn 4 C5
Nant-ddu Powys 34 C4
Nant-glas Powys 47 C8
Nant Peris Gwyn 83 F6
Nant Uchaf Denb 72 D4
Nant-y-Bai Carms 47 E6
Nant-y-cafn Neath 34 D2
Nant-y-derry Mon 35 D7
Nant-y-ffin Carms 46 F4
Nant-y-moel Bridgend 34 E3
Nant-y-pandy Conwy 83 D6
Nanternis Ceredig 46 D2
Nantgaredig Carms 33 B5
Nantgarw Rhondda 35 F5
Nantglyn Denb 72 C4
Nantgwyn Powys 47 B8
Nantlle Gwyn 82 F5
Nantmawr Shrops 60 B2
Nantmel Powys 48 C2
Nantmor Gwyn 71 C7
Nantwich Ches E 74 D3
Nantycaws Carms 33 C5
Nantyffyllon Bridgend 34 E2
Nantyglo Bl Gwent 35 C5
Naphill Bucks 39 E8
Nappa N Yorks 93 D8
Napton on the Hill Warks 52 C2
Narberth = Arberth Pembs 32 C2
Narborough Leics 64 E2
Narborough Norf 67 C7
Nasareth Gwyn 82 F4
Naseby Northants 52 B4
Nash Bucks 53 F5
Nash Hereford 48 C5
Nash Newport 35 F7
Nash Shrops 49 B8
Nash Lee Bucks 39 D8
Nassington Northants 65 E7
Nasty Herts 41 B6
Nateby Cumb 100 D2
Nateby Lancs 92 E4
Natland Cumb 99 F7
Naughton Suff 56 E4
Naunton Glos 37 B8
Naunton Worcs 50 F3
Naunton Beauchamp Worcs 50 D4
Navenby Lincs 78 D2
Navestock Heath Essex 41 E8
Navestock Side Essex 42 E1
Navidale Highld 157 H13
Nawton N Yorks 102 F4
Nayland Suff 56 F3
Nazeing Essex 41 D7
Neacroft Hants 14 E2
Neal's Green Warks 63 F7
Neap Shetland 160 H7
Near Sawrey Cumb 99 E5
Neasham Darl 101 C8
Neath = Castell-Nedd Neath 33 E8
Neath Abbey Neath 33 E8
Neatishead Norf 69 B6
Nebo Anglesey 82 B4
Nebo Ceredig 46 C4
Nebo Conwy 83 F8
Nebo Gwyn 82 F4
Necton Norf 67 D8
Nedd Highld 156 F4
Nedderton Northumb 117 F8
Nedging Tye Suff 56 E4
Needham Norf 68 F5
Needham Market Suff 56 D4
Needingworth Cambs 54 B4
Needwood Staffs 63 B5
Neen Savage Shrops 49 B8
Neen Sollars Shrops 49 B8
Neenton Shrops 61 F6
Nefyn Gwyn 70 C4
Neilston E Renf 118 D4
Neinthirion Powys 59 D6
Neithrop Oxon 52 E2
Nelly Andrews Green Powys 60 D2
Nelson Caerph 35 E5
Nelson Lancs 93 F8
Nelson Village Northumb 111 B5
Nemphlar S Lanark 119 E8
Nempnett Thrubwell N Som 23 C7
Nene Terrace Lincs 66 D2
Nenthall Cumb 109 E7
Nenthead Cumb 109 E7
Nenthorn Borders 122 F2
Nerabus Argyll 142 C3
Nercwys Flint 73 C6
Nerston S Lanark 119 D6
Nesbit Northumb 123 F5
Ness Ches W 73 B7
Nesscliffe Shrops 60 C3
Neston Ches W 73 B6
Neston Wilts 24 C3
Nether Alderley Ches E 74 B5
Nether Blainslie Borders 121 E8
Nether Booth Derbys 88 F2
Nether Broughton Leics 64 B3
Nether Burrow Lancs 93 B6
Nether Cerne Dorset 12 E4
Nether Compton Dorset 12 C3
Nether Crimond Aberds 141 B7
Nether Dalgliesh Borders 115 D5
Nether Dallachy Moray 152 B3
Nether Exe Devon 10 D4
Nether Glasslaw Aberds 153 C8
Nether Handwick Angus 134 E3
Nether Haugh S Yorks 88 E5
Nether Heage Derbys 76 D3
Nether Heyford Northants 52 D4
Nether Hindhope Borders 116 C3
Nether Howecleuch S Lanark 114 C3
Nether Kellet Lancs 92 C5
Nether Kinmundy Aberds 153 D10
Nether Langwith Notts 76 B5
Nether Leask Aberds 153 E10
Nether Lenshie Aberds 153 D6
Nether Monynut Borders 122 C3
Nether Padley Derbys 76 B2
Nether Park Aberds 153 C10
Nether Poppleton York 95 D8
Nether Silton N Yorks 102 E2
Nether Stowey Som 22 F3
Nether Urquhart Fife 128 D3
Nether Wallop Hants 25 F8
Nether Wasdale Cumb 98 D3
Nether Whitacre Warks 63 E6
Nether Worton Oxon 52 F2
Netheravon Wilts 25 E6
Netherbrae Aberds 153 C7
Netherbrough Orkney 159 G4
Netherburn S Lanark 119 E8
Netherbury Dorset 12 E2
Netherby Cumb 108 B3
Netherby N Yorks 95 E6
Nethercote Warks 52 C3
Nethercott Devon 20 F3
Netherend Glos 36 D2
Netherfield E Sus 18 D4
Netherhampton Wilts 14 B2
Netherlaw Dumfries 106 E4
Netherley Aberds 141 E7
Netherley Mers 86 F2
Nethermill Dumfries 114 F3
Nethermuir Aberds 153 D9
Netherplace E Renf 118 D5
Netherseal Derbys 63 C6
Netherthird E Ayrs 113 C5
Netherthong W Yorks 88 D2
Netherthorpe S Yorks 89 F6
Netherton Angus 135 D5
Netherton Devon 7 B6
Netherton Hants 25 D8
Netherton Mers 85 D4
Netherton Northumb 117 D5
Netherton Oxon 38 E4
Netherton Perth 133 D8
Netherton Stirling 119 B5
Netherton W Mid 62 F3
Netherton W Yorks 88 C2
Netherton W Yorks 88 C3
Netherton Worcs 50 E4
Nethertown Cumb 98 D1
Nethertown Highld 158 C5
Netherwitton Northumb 117 E7
Netherwood E Ayrs 113 B6
Nethy Bridge Highld 139 B6
Netley Hants 15 D5
Netley Marsh Hants 14 C4
Netteswell Essex 41 C7
Nettlebed Oxon 39 F7
Nettlebridge Som 23 E8
Nettlecombe Dorset 12 E3
Nettleden Herts 40 C3
Nettleham Lincs 78 B3
Nettlestead Kent 29 D7
Nettlestead Green Kent 29 D7
Nettlestone IoW 15 E7
Nettlesworth Durham 111 E5
Nettleton Lincs 90 D5
Nettleton Wilts 24 B3
Neuadd Carms 33 B7
Nevendon Essex 42 E3
Nevern Pembs 45 E2
New Abbey Dumfries 107 C6
New Aberdour Aberds 153 B8
New Addington London 28 C4
New Alresford Hants 26 F3
New Alyth Perth 134 E2
New Arley Warks 63 F6
New Ash Green Kent 29 C7
New Barn Kent 29 C7
New Barnetby N Lincs 90 C4
New Barton Northants 53 C6
New Bewick Northumb 117 B6
New-bigging Angus 134 E3
New Bilton Warks 52 B2
New Bolingbroke Lincs 79 D6
New Boultham Lincs 78 B2
New Bradwell M Keynes 53 E6
New Brancepeth Durham 110 E5
New Bridge Wrex 73 E6
New Brighton Flint 73 C6
New Brighton Mers 85 E4
New Brinsley Notts 76 D4
New Broughton Wrex 73 D7
New Buckenham Norf 68 E3
New Byth Aberds 153 C8
New Catton Norf 68 C5
New Cheriton Hants 15 B6
New Costessey Norf 68 C4
New Cowper Cumb 107 E8
New Cross Ceredig 46 B5
New Cross London 28 B4
New Cumnock E Ayrs 113 C6
New Deer Aberds 153 D8
New Delaval Northumb 111 B5
New Duston Northants 52 C5
New Earswick York 96 D2
New Edlington S Yorks 89 E6
New Elgin Moray 152 B2
New Ellerby E Yorks 97 F7
New Eltham London 28 B5
New End Worcs 51 D5
New Farnley W Yorks 94 F5
New Ferry Mers 85 F4
New Fryston W Yorks 89 B5
New Galloway Dumfries 106 B3
New Gilston Fife 129 D6
New Grimsby Scilly 2 E3
New Hainford Norf 68 C5
New Hartley Northumb 111 B6
New Haw Sur 27 C8
New Hedges Pembs 32 D2
New Herrington T&W 111 D6
New Hinksey Oxon 39 D5
New Holkham Norf 80 D4
New Holland N Lincs 90 B4
New Houghton Derbys 76 C4
New Houghton Norf 80 E3
New Houses N Yorks 93 B8
New Humberstone Leicester 64 D3
New Hutton Cumb 99 E7
New Hythe Kent 29 D8
New Inn Carms 46 F3
New Inn Mon 36 D1
New Inn Pembs 45 F2
New Inn Torf 35 E7
New Invention Shrops 48 B4
New Invention W Mid 62 D3
New Kelso Highld 150 G2
New Kingston Notts 64 B2
New Lanark S Lanark 119 E8
New Lane Lancs 86 C2
New Lane End Warr 86 E4
New Leake Lincs 79 D7
New Leeds Aberds 153 C9
New Longton Lancs 86 B3
New Luce Dumfries 105 C5
New Malden London 28 C3
New Marske Redcar 102 B4
New Marton Shrops 73 F7
New Micklefield W Yorks 95 F7
New Mill Aberds 141 F6
New Mill Herts 40 C2
New Mill W Yorks 88 D2
New Mill Wilts 25 C6
New Mills Ches E 87 F5
New Mills Corn 4 D3
New Mills Derbys 87 F7
New Mills Powys 59 D7
New Milton Hants 14 E3
New Moat Pembs 32 B1
New Ollerton Notts 77 C6
New Oscott W Mid 62 E4
New Park N Yorks 95 D5
New Pitsligo Aberds 153 C8
New Polzeath Corn 4 B4
New Quay = Ceinewydd Ceredig 46 D2
New Rackheath Norf 69 C5
New Radnor Powys 48 C4
New Rent Cumb 108 F4
New Ridley Northumb 110 D3
New Road Side N Yorks 94 E2
New Romney Kent 19 C7
New Rossington S Yorks 89 E7
New Row Ceredig 47 B6
New Row Lancs 93 F6
New Row N Yorks 102 C4
New Sarum Wilts 25 F6
New Silksworth T&W 111 D6
New Stevenston N Lanark 119 D7
New Street Staffs 75 D7
New Street Lane Shrops 74 F3
New Swanage Dorset 13 F8
New Totley S Yorks 76 B3
New Town E Loth 121 B7
New Tredegar = Tredegar Newydd Caerph 35 D5
New Trows S Lanark 119 F8
New Ulva Argyll 144 E6
New Walsoken Cambs 66 D4
New Waltham NE Lincs 91 D6
New Whittington Derbys 76 B3
New Wimpole Cambs 54 E4
New Winton E Loth 121 B7
New Yatt Oxon 38 C3
New York Lincs 78 D5
New York N Yorks 94 C4
Newall W Yorks 94 E4
Newark Orkney 159 D8
Newark Pboro 66 D2
Newark-on-Trent Notts 77 D7
Newarthill N Lanark 119 D7
Newbarns Cumb 92 B2
Newbattle Midloth 121 C6
Newbiggin Cumb 92 C2
Newbiggin Cumb 98 E2
Newbiggin Cumb 99 B6
Newbiggin Cumb 99 B8
Newbiggin Cumb 109 E5
Newbiggin Durham 100 B4
Newbiggin N Yorks 100 E4
Newbiggin N Yorks 100 F4
Newbiggin-by-the-Sea Northumb 117 F9
Newbiggin-on-Lune Cumb 100 D2
Newbigging Angus 134 F4
Newbigging Angus 134 F4
Newbigging S Lanark 120 E3
Newbold Derbys 76 B3
Newbold Leics 63 C8
Newbold on Avon Warks 52 B2
Newbold on Stour Warks 51 E7
Newbold Pacey Warks 51 D7
Newbold Verdon Leics 63 D8
Newborough Anglesey 82 E4
Newborough Pboro 66 D2
Newborough Staffs 62 B5
Newbottle Northants 52 F3
Newbottle T&W 111 D6
Newbourne Suff 57 E6
Newbridge Caerph 35 E6
Newbridge Ceredig 46 D4
Newbridge Corn 2 C3
Newbridge Corn 5 C8
Newbridge Dumfries 107 B6
Newbridge Edin 120 B4
Newbridge Hants 14 C3
Newbridge IoW 14 F5
Newbridge Pembs 44 B4
Newbridge Green Worcs 50 F3
Newbridge-on-Usk Mon 35 E7
Newbridge on Wye Powys 48 D2
Newbrough Northumb 109 C8
Newbuildings Devon 10 D2
Newburgh Aberds 141 B8
Newburgh Aberds 153 C9
Newburgh Borders 115 C6
Newburgh Fife 128 C4
Newburgh Lancs 86 C2
Newburn T&W 110 C4
Newbury W Berks 26 C2
Newbury Park London 41 F7
Newby Cumb 99 B7
Newby Lancs 93 E8
Newby N Yorks 93 B7
Newby N Yorks 102 C3
Newby N Yorks 103 E8
Newby Bridge Cumb 99 F5
Newby East Cumb 108 D4
Newby West Cumb 108 D3
Newby Wiske N Yorks 102 F1
Newcastle Mon 35 C8
Newcastle Shrops 60 F2
Newcastle Emlyn = Castell Newydd Emlyn Carms 46 E2
Newcastle-under-Lyme Staffs 74 E5
Newcastle Upon Tyne T&W 110 C5
Newcastleton or Copshaw Holm Borders 115 F7
Newchapel Pembs 45 F4
Newchapel Powys 59 F6
Newchapel Staffs 75 D5
Newchapel Sur 28 E4
Newchurch Carms 32 B4
Newchurch IoW 15 F6
Newchurch Kent 19 B7
Newchurch Lancs 93 F8
Newchurch Mon 36 E1
Newchurch Powys 48 D4
Newchurch Staffs 62 B5
Newcott Devon 11 D7
Newcraighall Edin 121 B6
Newdigate Sur 28 E2
Newell Green Brack 27 B6
Newenden Kent 18 C5
Newent Glos 36 B4
Newerne Glos 36 D3
Newfield Durham 110 F5
Newfield Highld 151 D10
Newford Scilly 2 E4
Newfound Hants 26 D3
Newgale Pembs 44 C3
Newgate Norf 81 C6
Newgate Street Herts 41 D6
Newhall Ches E 74 E3
Newhall Derbys 63 B6
Newhall House Highld 151 E9
Newhall Point Highld 151 E10
Newham Northumb 117 B7
Newham Hall Northumb 117 B7
Newhaven Derbys 75 D8
Newhaven E Sus 17 D8
Newhaven Edin 121 B5
Newhey Gtr Man 87 C7
Newholm N Yorks 103 C6
Newhouse N Lanark 119 C7
Newick E Sus 17 B8
Newingreen Kent 19 B8
Newington Kent 19 B8
Newington Kent 30 C2
Newington Kent 31 C7
Newington Notts 89 E7
Newington Oxon 39 E6
Newington Shrops 60 F4
Newland Glos 36 D2
Newland Hull 97 F6
Newland N Yorks 89 B7
Newland Worcs 50 E2
Newlandrig Midloth 121 C6
Newlands Borders 115 E8
Newlands Highld 151 G10
Newlands Moray 152 C3
Newlands Northumb 110 D3
Newland's Corner Sur 27 E8
Newlands of Geise Highld 158 D2
Newlands of Tynet Moray 152 B3
Newlands Park Anglesey 82 C2
Newlandsmuir S Lanark 119 D6
Newlot Orkney 159 G6
Newlyn Corn 2 D3
Newmachar Aberds 141 C7
Newmains N Lanark 119 D8
Newmarket Suff 55 C7
Newmarket W Isles 155 D9
Newmill Borders 115 C7
Newmill Corn 2 C3
Newmill Moray 152 C4
Newmill of Inshewan Angus 134 C4
Newmills of Boyne Aberds 152 C5
Newmiln Perth 133 F8
Newmilns E Ayrs 118 F5
Newnham Cambs 54 D5
Newnham Glos 36 C3
Newnham Hants 26 D5
Newnham Herts 54 F3
Newnham Kent 30 D3
Newnham Northants 52 D3
Newnham Bridge Worcs 49 C8
Newpark Fife 129 C6
Newport Devon 20 F4
Newport E Yorks 96 F4
Newport Essex 55 F6
Newport Highld 158 H3
Newport IoW 15 F6
Newport = Casnewydd Newport 35 F7
Newport Norf 69 C8
Newport = Trefdraeth Pembs 45 F2
Newport Telford 61 C7
Newport-on-Tay Fife 129 B6
Newport Pagnell M Keynes 53 E6
Newpound Common W Sus 16 B4
Newquay Corn 4 C3
Newsbank Ches E 74 C5
Newseat Aberds 153 D10
Newseat Aberds 153 E7
Newsham N Yorks 101 C6
Newsham N Yorks 102 F1
Newsham Northumb 111 B6
Newsholme E Yorks 89 B8
Newsholme Lancs 93 D8
Newsome W Yorks 88 C2
Newstead Borders 121 F8
Newstead Northumb 117 B7
Newstead Notts 76 D5
Newthorpe N Yorks 95 F7
Newton Argyll 125 F6
Newton Borders 116 B2
Newton Bridgend 21 B7
Newton Cambs 54 E5
Newton Cambs 66 C4
Newton Cardiff 22 B4
Newton Ches W 73 C8
Newton Ches W 74 B2
Newton Ches W 74 D2
Newton Cumb 92 B2
Newton Derbys 76 D4
Newton Dorset 13 C5
Newton Dumfries 108 B2
Newton Dumfries 114 E4
Newton Gtr Man 87 E7
Newton Hereford 48 F5
Newton Hereford 49 D7
Newton Highld 151 E10
Newton Highld 151 G10
Newton Highld 156 F5
Newton Highld 158 F5
Newton Lancs 92 F4
Newton Lancs 93 B5
Newton Lancs 93 D6
Newton Lincs 78 F3
Newton Moray 152 B1
Newton Norf 67 C8
Newton Northants 65 F5
Newton Northumb 110 C3
Newton Notts 77 E6
Newton Perth 133 F5
Newton S Lanark 119 C6
Newton S Lanark 120 F2
Newton S Yorks 89 D6
Newton Staffs 62 B4
Newton Suff 56 E3
Newton Swansea 33 F7
Newton W Loth 120 B3
Newton Warks 52 B3
Newton Wilts 14 B3
Newton Abbot Devon 7 B6
Newton Arlosh Cumb 107 D8
Newton Aycliffe Durham 101 B7
Newton Bewley Hrtlpl 102 B2
Newton Blossomville M Keynes 53 D7
Newton Bromswold Northants 53 C7
Newton Burgoland Leics 63 D7
Newton by Toft Lincs 90 F4
Newton Ferrers Devon 6 E3
Newton Flotman Norf 68 E5
Newton Hall Northumb 110 C3
Newton Harcourt Leics 64 E3
Newton Heath Gtr Man 87 D6
Newton Ho. Aberds 141 B5
Newton Kyme N Yorks 95 E7
Newton-le-Willows Mers 86 E3
Newton-le-Willows N Yorks 101 F7
Newton Longville Bucks 53 F6
Newton Mearns E Renf 118 D5
Newton Morrell N Yorks 101 D7
Newton Mulgrave N Yorks 103 C5
Newton of Ardtoe Highld 147 D9
Newton of Balcanquhal Perth 128 C3
Newton of Falkland Fife 128 D4
Newton on Ayr S Ayrs 112 B3
Newton on Ouse N Yorks 95 D8
Newton-on-Rawcliffe N Yorks 103 E6
Newton-on-the-Moor Northumb 117 D7
Newton on Trent Lincs 77 B8
Newton Park Argyll 145 G10
Newton Poppleford Devon 11 F5
Newton Purcell Oxon 52 F4
Newton Regis Warks 63 D6
Newton Reigny Cumb 108 F4
Newton St Cyres Devon 10 E3
Newton St Faith Norf 68 C5
Newton St Loe Bath 24 C2
Newton St Petrock Devon 9 C6
Newton Stacey Hants 26 E2
Newton Stewart Dumfries 105 C8
Newton Tony Wilts 25 E7
Newton Tracey Devon 9 B7
Newton under Roseberry Redcar 102 C3
Newton upon Derwent E Yorks 96 E3
Newton Valence Hants 26 F5
Newtonairds Dumfries 113 F8
Newtongrange Midloth 121 C6
Newtonhill Aberds 141 E8
Newtonhill Highld 151 G8
Newtonmill Angus 135 C6
Newtonmore Highld 138 E3
Newtown Argyll 125 E6
Newtown Ches W 74 B2
Newtown Corn 3 D6
Newtown Cumb 107 E7
Newtown Cumb 108 C5
Newtown Derbys 87 F7
Newtown Devon 10 B2
Newtown Glos 36 D3
Newtown Glos 50 F4
Newtown Hants 14 B4
Newtown Hants 14 C3
Newtown Hants 15 C6
Newtown Hants 15 C7
Newtown Hants 15 D5
Newtown Hants 26 C2
Newtown Hereford 49 E8
Newtown Highld 137 D6
Newtown IoM 84 E3
Newtown IoW 14 E5
Newtown Northumb 117 B6
Newtown Northumb 117 D6
Newtown Northumb 123 F5
Newtown Poole 13 E8
Newtown = Y Drenewydd Powys 59 E8
Newtown Shrops 73 F8
Newtown Staffs 75 C6
Newtown Staffs 75 C7
Newtown Wilts 13 B7
Newtown Linford Leics 64 D2
Newtown St Boswells Borders 121 F8
Newtown Unthank Leics 63 D8
Newtyle Angus 134 E2
Neyland Pembs 44 E4
Niarbyl IoM 84 E2
Nibley S Glos 36 F3
Nibley Green Glos 36 E4
Nibon Shetland 160 F5
Nicholashayne Devon 11 C6
Nicholaston Swansea 33 F6
Nidd N Yorks 95 C6
Nigg Aberdeen 141 D8
Nigg Highld 151 D11
Nigg Ferry Highld 151 E10
Nightcott Som 10 B3
Nilig Denb 72 D4
Nine Ashes Essex 42 D1
Nine Mile Burn Midloth 120 D4
Nine Wells Pembs 44 C2
Ninebanks Northumb 109 D7
Ninfield E Sus 18 D4
Ningwood IoW 14 F4
Nisbet Borders 116 B2
Nisthouse Orkney 159 G4
Nisthouse Shetland 160 G7
Niton IoW 15 G6
Nitshill Glasgow 118 C5
No Man's Heath Ches W 74 E2
No Man's Heath Warks 63 D6
Noak Hill London 41 E8
Noblethorpe S Yorks 88 D3
Nobottle Northants 52 C4
Nocton Lincs 78 C3
Noke Oxon 39 C5
Nolton Pembs 44 D3
Nolton Haven Pembs 44 D3
Nomansland Devon 10 C3
Nomansland Wilts 14 C3
Noneley Shrops 60 B4
Nonikiln Highld 151 D9
Nonington Kent 31 D6
Noonsbrough Shetland 160 H4
Norbreck Blackpool 92 E3
Norbridge Hereford 50 E2
Norbury Ches E 74 E2
Norbury Derbys 75 E8
Norbury Shrops 60 E3
Norbury Staffs 61 B7
Nordelph Norf 67 D5
Norden Gtr Man 87 C6
Norden Heath Dorset 13 F7
Nordley Shrops 61 E6
Norham Northumb 122 E5
Norley Ches W 74 B2
Norleywood Hants 14 E4
Norman Cross Cambs 65 E8
Normanby N Lincs 90 C2
Normanby N Yorks 103 F5
Normanby Redcar 102 C3
Normanby-by-Spital Lincs 90 F4
Normanby by Stow Lincs 90 F2
Normanby le Wold Lincs 90 E5
Normandy Sur 27 D7
Norman's Bay E Sus 18 E3
Norman's Green Devon 11 D5
Normanstone Suff 69 E8
Normanton Derby 76 F3
Normanton Leics 77 E8
Normanton Lincs 78 E2
Normanton Notts 77 D7
Normanton Rutland 65 D6
Normanton W Yorks 88 B4
Normanton le Heath Leics 63 C7
Normanton on Soar Notts 64 B2
Normanton-on-the-Wolds Notts 77 F6
Normanton on Trent Notts 77 C7
Normoss Lancs 92 F3
Norney Sur 27 E7
Norrington Common Wilts 24 C3
Norris Green Mers 85 E4
Norris Hill Leics 63 C7
North Anston S Yorks 89 F6
North Aston Oxon 38 B4
North Baddesley Hants 14 C4
North Ballachulish Highld 130 C4
North Barrow Som 12 B4
North Barsham Norf 80 D5
North Benfleet Essex 42 F3
North Bersted W Sus 16 D3
North Berwick E Loth 129 F7
North Boarhunt Hants 15 C7
North Bovey Devon 10 F2
North Bradley Wilts 24 D3
North Brentor Devon 9 F6
North Brewham Som 24 F2
North Buckland Devon 20 E3
North Burlingham Norf 69 C6
North Cadbury Som 12 B4
North Cairn Dumfries 104 B3
North Carlton Lincs 78 B2
North Carrine Argyll 143 H7
North Cave E Yorks 96 F4
North Cerney Glos 37 D7
North Charford Wilts 14 C2
North Charlton Northumb 117 B7
North Cheriton Som 12 B4
North Cliff E Yorks 97 E8
North Cliffe E Yorks 96 F4
North Clifton Notts 77 B8
North Cockerington Lincs 91 E7
North Coker Som 12 C3
North Collafirth Shetland 160 E5
North Common E Sus 17 B7
North Connel Argyll 124 B5
North Cornelly Bridgend 34 F2
North Cotes Lincs 91 D7
North Cove Suff 69 F7
North Cowton N Yorks 101 D7
North Crawley M Keynes 53 E7
North Cray London 29 B5
North Creake Norf 80 D4
North Curry Som 11 B8
North Dalton E Yorks 96 D5
North Dawn Orkney 159 H5
North Deighton N Yorks 95 D6
North Duffield N Yorks 96 F2
North Elkington Lincs 91 E6
North Elmham Norf 81 E5
North Elmshall W Yorks 89 C5
North End Bucks 39 B8
North End E Yorks 97 F8
North End Essex 42 C2
North End Hants 26 C2
North End Lincs 78 E5
North End N Som 23 C6
North End Ptsmth 15 D7
North End Som 11 B7
North End W Sus 16 D5
North Erradale Highld 155 J12
North Fambridge Essex 42 E4
North Fearns Highld 149 E10
North Featherstone W Yorks 88 B5
North Ferriby E Yorks 90 B3
North Frodingham E Yorks 97 D7
North Gluss Shetland 160 F5
North Gorley Hants 14 C2
North Green Norf 68 F5
North Green Suff 57 C7
North Greetwell Lincs 78 B3
North Grimston N Yorks 96 C4
North Halley Orkney 159 H6
North Halling Medway 29 C8
North Hayling Hants 15 D8
North Hazelrigg Northumb 123 F6
North Heasley Devon 21 F6
North Heath W Sus 16 B4
North Hill Cambs 55 B5
North Hill Corn 5 B7
North Hinksey Oxon 38 D4
North Holmwood Sur 28 E2
North Howden E Yorks 96 F3
North Huish Devon 6 D5
North Hykeham Lincs 78 C2
North Johnston Pembs 44 D4
North Kelsey Lincs 90 D4
North Kelsey Moor Lincs 90 D4
North Kessock Highld 151 G9
North Killingholme N Lincs 90 C5
North Kilvington N Yorks 102 F2
North Kilworth Leics 64 F3
North Kirkton Aberds 153 C11
North Kiscadale N Ayrs 143 F11
North Kyme Lincs 78 D4
North Lancing W Sus 17 D5
North Lee Bucks 39 D8
North Leigh Oxon 38 C3
North Leverton with Habblesthorpe Notts 89 F8
North Littleton Worcs 51 E5
North Lopham Norf 68 F3
North Luffenham Rutland 65 D6
North Marden W Sus 16 C2
North Marston Bucks 39 B7
North Middleton Midloth 121 D6
North Middleton Northumb 117 B6
North Molton Devon 10 B2
North Moreton Oxon 39 F5
North Mundham W Sus 16 D2
North Muskham Notts 77 D7
North Newbald E Yorks 96 F5
North Newington Oxon 52 F2
North Newnton Wilts 25 D6
North Newton Som 22 F4
North Nibley Glos 36 E4
North Oakley Hants 26 D3
North Ockendon London 42 F1
North Ormesby Mbro 102 B3
North Ormsby Lincs 91 E6
North Otterington N Yorks 102 F1
North Owersby Lincs 90 E4
North Perrott Som 12 D2
North Petherton Som 22 F4
North Petherwin Corn 8 F4
North Pickenham Norf 67 D8
North Piddle Worcs 50 D4
North Poorton Dorset 12 E3
North Port Argyll 125 C6
North Queensferry Fife 128 F3
North Radworthy Devon 21 F6
North Rauceby Lincs 78 E3
North Reston Lincs 91 F7
North Rigton N Yorks 95 E5
North Rode Ches E 75 C5
North Roe Shetland 160 E5
North Runcton Norf 67 C6
North Sandwick Shetland 160 D7
North Scale Cumb 92 C1
North Scarle Lincs 77 C8
North Seaton Northumb 117 F8
North Shian Argyll 130 E3
North Shields T&W 111 C6
North Shoebury Southend 43 F5
North Shore Blackpool 92 F3
North Side Cumb 98 B2
North Side Pboro 66 E2
North Skelton Redcar 102 C4
North Somercotes Lincs 91 E8
North Stainley N Yorks 95 B5
North Stainmore Cumb 100 C3
North Stifford Thurrock 42 F2
North Stoke Bath 24 C2
North Stoke Oxon 39 F6
North Stoke W Sus 16 C4
North Street Hants 26 F4
North Street Kent 30 D4
North Street Medway 30 B2
North Street W Berks 26 B4
North Sunderland Northumb 123 F8
North Tamerton Corn 8 E5
North Tawton Devon 9 D8
North Thoresby Lincs 91 E6
North Tidworth Wilts 25 E7
North Togston Northumb 117 D8
North Tuddenham Norf 68 C3
North Walbottle T&W 110 C4
North Walsham Norf 81 D8
North Waltham Hants 26 E3
North Warnborough Hants 26 D5
North Water Bridge Angus 135 C6
North Watten Highld 158 E4
North Weald Bassett Essex 41 D7
North Wheatley Notts 89 F8
North Whilborough Devon 7 C6
North Wick Bath 23 C7
North Willingham Lincs 91 F5
North Wingfield Derbys 76 C4
North Witham Lincs 65 B6
North Woolwich London 28 B5
North Wootton Dorset 12 C4
North Wootton Norf 67 B6
North Wootton Som 23 E7
North Wraxall Wilts 24 B3
North Wroughton Swindon 38 F1
Northacre Norf 68 E2
Northallerton N Yorks 102 E1
Northam Devon 9 B6
Northam Soton 14 C5
Northampton Northants 53 C5
Northaw Herts 41 D5
Northbeck Lincs 78 E3
Northborough Pboro 65 D8
Northbourne Kent 31 D7
Northbridge Street E Sus 18 C4
Northchapel W Sus 16 B3
Northchurch Herts 40 D2
Northcott Devon 8 E5
Northdown Kent 31 B7
Northdyke Orkney 159 F3
Northend Bath 24 C2
Northend Bucks 39 E7
Northend Warks 51 D8
Northenden Gtr Man 87 E6
Northfield Aberdeen 141 D8
Northfield Borders 122 C5
Northfield E Yorks 90 B4
Northfield W Mid 50 B5
Northfields Lincs 65 D7
Northfleet Kent 29 B7
Northgate Lincs 65 B8
Northhouse Borders 115 D7
Northiam E Sus 18 C5
Northill C Beds 54 E2
Northington Hants 26 F3
Northlands Lincs 79 D6
Northlea Durham 111 D7
Northleach Glos 37 C8
Northleigh Devon 11 E6
Northlew Devon 9 E7
Northmoor Oxon 38 D4
Northmoor Green or Moorland Som 22 F5
Northmuir Angus 134 D3
Northney Hants 15 D8
Northolt London 40 F4
Northop Flint 73 C6
Northop Hall Flint 73 C6
Northorpe Lincs 65 C7
Northorpe Lincs 78 F5
Northorpe Lincs 90 E2
Northover Som 12 B3
Northover Som 23 F6
Northowram W Yorks 88 B2
Northport Dorset 13 F7
Northpunds Shetland 160 L6
Northrepps Norf 81 D8
Northtown Orkney 159 J5
Northway Glos 50 F4
Northwich Ches W 74 B3
Northwick S Glos 36 F2
Northwold Norf 67 E7
Northwood Derbys 76 C2
Northwood IoW 15 E5
Northwood Kent 31 C7
Northwood London 40 E3
Northwood Shrops 73 F8
Northwood Green Glos 36 C4
Norton E Sus 17 D8
Norton Glos 37 B5
Norton Halton 86 F3
Norton Herts 54 F3
Norton IoW 14 F4
Norton Mon 35 C8
Norton Northants 52 C4
Norton Notts 77 B5
Norton Powys 48 C5
Norton S Yorks 89 C6
Norton Shrops 60 F4
Norton Shrops 61 D5
Norton Shrops 61 D7
Norton Stockton 102 B2
Norton Suff 56 C3
Norton W Sus 16 D3
Norton W Sus 16 E2
Norton Wilts 37 F5
Norton Worcs 50 D3
Norton Worcs 50 E5
Norton Bavant Wilts 24 E4
Norton Bridge Staffs 75 F5
Norton Canes Staffs 62 D4
Norton Canon Hereford 49 E5
Norton Corner Norf 81 E6
Norton Disney Lincs 77 D8
Norton East Staffs 62 D4
Norton Ferris Wilts 24 F2
Norton Fitzwarren Som 11 B6
Norton Green IoW 14 F4
Norton Hawkfield Bath 23 C7
Norton Heath Essex 42 D2
Norton in Hales Shrops 74 F4
Norton-in-the-Moors Stoke 75 D5
Norton-Juxta-Twycross Leics 63 D7
Norton-le-Clay N Yorks 95 B7
Norton Lindsey Warks 51 C7
Norton Malreward Bath 23 C8
Norton Mandeville Essex 42 D1
Norton-on-Derwent N Yorks 96 B3
Norton St Philip Som 24 D2
Norton sub Hamdon Som 12 C2
Norton Woodseats S Yorks 88 F4

Norwell Notts 77 C7
Norwell Woodhouse Notts 77 C7
Norwich Norf 68 D5
Norwick Shetland 160 B8
Norwood Derbys 89 F5
Norwood Hill Sur 28 E3
Norwoodside Cambs 66 E4
Noseley Leics 64 E4
Noss Shetland 160 M5
Noss Mayo Devon 6 E3
Nosterfield N Yorks 101 F7
Nostie Highld 149 F13
Notgrove Glos 37 B8
Nottage Bridgend 21 B7
Nottingham Nottingham 77 F5
Nottington Dorset 12 F4
Notton W Yorks 88 C4
Notton Wilts 24 C4
Nounsley Essex 42 C3
Noutard's Green Worcs 50 C2
Novar House Highld 151 E9
Nox Shrops 60 C4
Nuffield Oxon 39 F6
Nun Hills Lancs 87 B6
Nun Monkton N Yorks 95 D8
Nunburnholme E Yorks 96 E4
Nuncargate Notts 76 D5
Nuneaton Warks 63 E7
Nuneham Courtenay Oxon 39 E5
Nunney Som 24 E2
Nunnington N Yorks 96 B2
Nunnykirk Northumb 117 E6
Nunsthorpe NE Lincs 91 D6
Nunthorpe Mbro 102 C3
Nunthorpe York 96 D2
Nunton Wilts 14 B2
Nunwick N Yorks 95 B6
Nupend Glos 36 D4
Nursling Hants 14 C4
Nursted Hants 15 B8
Nutbourne W Sus 15 D8
Nutbourne W Sus 16 C4
Nutfield Sur 28 D4
Nuthall Notts 76 E5
Nuthampstead Herts 54 F5
Nuthurst W Sus 17 B5
Nutley E Sus 17 B8
Nutley Hants 26 E4
Nutwell S Yorks 89 D7
Nybster Highld 158 D5
Nyetimber W Sus 16 E2
Nyewood W Sus 16 B2
Nymet Rowland Devon 10 D2
Nymet Tracey Devon 10 D2
Nympsfield Glos 37 D5
Nynehead Som 11 B6
Nyton W Sus 16 D3

O

Oad Street Kent 30 C2
Oadby Leics 64 D3
Oak Cross Devon 9 E7
Oakamoor Staffs 75 E7
Oakbank W Loth 120 C3
Oakdale Caerph 35 E5
Oake Som 11 B6
Oaken Staffs 62 D2
Oakenclough Lancs 92 E5
Oakengates Telford 61 C7
Oakenholt Flint 73 B6
Oakenshaw Durham 110 F5
Oakenshaw W Yorks 88 B2
Oakerthorpe Derbys 76 D3
Oakes W Yorks 88 C2
Oakfield Torf 35 E7
Oakford Ceredig 46 D3
Oakford Devon 10 B4
Oakfordbridge Devon 10 B4
Oakgrove Ches E 75 C6
Oakham Rutland 65 D5
Oakhanger Hants 27 F5
Oakhill Som 23 E8
Oakhurst Kent 29 D6
Oakington Cambs 54 C5
Oaklands Herts 41 C5
Oaklands Powys 48 D2
Oakle Street Glos 36 C4
Oakley Bedford 53 D8
Oakley Bucks 39 C6
Oakley Fife 128 F2
Oakley Hants 26 D3
Oakley Oxon 39 D7
Oakley Poole 13 E8
Oakley Suff 57 B5
Oakley Green Windsor 27 B7
Oakley Park Powys 59 F6
Oakmere Ches W 74 C2
Oakridge Glos 37 D6
Oakridge Hants 26 D4
Oaks Shrops 60 D4
Oaks Green Derbys 75 F8
Oaksey Wilts 37 E6
Oakthorpe Leics 63 C7
Oakwoodhill Sur 28 F2
Oakworth W Yorks 94 F3
Oape Highld 156 J7
Oare Kent 30 C4
Oare Som 21 E7
Oare W Berks 26 B3
Oare Wilts 25 C6
Oasby Lincs 78 F3
Oathlaw Angus 134 D4
Oatlands N Yorks 95 D6
Oban Argyll 124 C4
Oban Highld 147 C11
Oborne Dorset 12 C4
Obthorpe Lincs 65 C7
Occlestone Green Ches W 74 C3
Occold Suff 57 B5
Ochiltree E Ayrs 112 B5
Ochtermuthill Perth 127 C7
Ochtertyre Perth 127 B7
Ockbrook Derbys 76 F4
Ockham Sur 27 D8
Ockle Highld 147 D8
Ockley Sur 28 F2
Ocle Pychard Hereford 49 E7
Octon E Yorks 97 C6
Octon Cross Roads E Yorks 97 C6
Odcombe Som 12 C3
Odd Down Bath 24 C2
Oddendale Cumb 99 C7
Odder Lincs 78 B2
Oddingley Worcs 50 D4
Oddington Glos 38 B2
Oddington Oxon 39 C5
Odell Bedford 53 D7
Odie Orkney 159 F7
Odiham Hants 26 D5
Odstock Wilts 14 B2
Odstone Leics 63 D7
Offchurch Warks 51 C8
Offenham Worcs 51 E5
Offham E Sus 17 C7
Offham Kent 29 D7
Offham W Sus 16 D4
Offord Cluny Cambs 54 C3
Offord Darcy Cambs 54 C3
Offton Suff 56 E4
Offwell Devon 11 E6
Ogbourne Maizey Wilts 25 B6
Ogbourne St Andrew Wilts 25 B6
Ogbourne St George Wilts 25 B7
Ogil Angus 134 C4
Ogle Northumb 110 B4
Ogmore V Glam 21 B7
Ogmore-by-Sea V Glam 21 B7
Ogmore Vale Bridgend 34 E3
Okeford Fitzpaine Dorset 13 C6
Okehampton Devon 9 E7
Okehampton Camp Devon 9 E7
Okraquoy Shetland 160 K6
Old Northants 53 B5
Old Aberdeen Aberdeen 141 D8
Old Alresford Hants 26 F3
Old Arley Warks 63 E6
Old Basford Nottingham 76 E5
Old Basing Hants 26 D4
Old Bewick Northumb 117 B6
Old Bolingbroke Lincs 79 C6
Old Bramhope W Yorks 94 E5
Old Brampton Derbys 76 B3
Old Bridge of Tilt Perth 133 C5
Old Bridge of Urr Dumfries 106 C4
Old Buckenham Norf 68 E3
Old Burghclere Hants 26 D2
Old Byland N Yorks 102 F3
Old Cassop Durham 111 F6
Old Castleton Borders 115 E8
Old Catton Norf 68 C5
Old Clee NE Lincs 91 D6
Old Cleeve Som 22 E2
Old Clipstone Notts 77 C6
Old Colwyn Conwy 83 D8
Old Coulsdon London 28 D4
Old Crombie Aberds 152 C5
Old Dailly S Ayrs 112 E2
Old Dalby Leics 64 B3
Old Deer Aberds 153 D9
Old Denaby S Yorks 89 E5
Old Edlington S Yorks 89 E6
Old Eldon Durham 101 B7
Old Ellerby E Yorks 97 F7
Old Felixstowe Suff 57 F7
Old Fletton Pboro 65 E8
Old Glossop Derbys 87 E8
Old Goole E Yorks 89 B8
Old Hall Powys 59 F6
Old Heath Essex 43 B6
Old Heathfield E Sus 18 C2
Old Hill W Mid 62 F3
Old Hunstanton Norf 80 C2
Old Hurst Cambs 54 B3
Old Hutton Cumb 99 F7
Old Kea Corn 3 B7
Old Kilpatrick W Dunb 118 B4
Old Kinnernie Aberds 141 D6
Old Knebworth Herts 41 B5
Old Langho Lancs 93 F7
Old Laxey IoM 84 D4
Old Leake Lincs 79 D7
Old Malton N Yorks 96 B3
Old Micklefield W Yorks 95 F7
Old Milton Hants 14 E3
Old Milverton Warks 51 C7
Old Monkland N Lanark 119 C7
Old Netley Hants 15 D5
Old Philpstoun W Loth 120 B3
Old Quarrington Durham 111 F6
Old Radnor Powys 48 D4
Old Rattray Aberds 153 C10
Old Rayne Aberds 141 B5
Old Romney Kent 19 C7
Old Sodbury S Glos 36 F4
Old Somerby Lincs 78 F2
Old Stratford Northants 53 E5
Old Thirsk N Yorks 102 F2
Old Town Cumb 99 F7
Old Town Cumb 108 E4
Old Town Northumb 116 E4
Old Town Scilly 2 E4
Old Trafford Gtr Man 87 E6
Old Tupton Derbys 76 C3
Old Warden C Beds 54 E2
Old Weston Cambs 53 B8
Old Whittington Derbys 76 B3
Old Wick Highld 158 E5
Old Windsor Windsor 27 B7
Old Wives Lees Kent 30 D4
Old Woking Sur 27 D8
Old Woodhall Lincs 78 C5
Oldany Highld 156 F4
Oldberrow Warks 51 C6
Oldborough Devon 10 D2
Oldbury Shrops 61 E7
Oldbury W Mid 62 F3
Oldbury Warks 63 E7
Oldbury-on-Severn S Glos 36 E3
Oldbury on the Hill Glos 37 F5
Oldcastle Bridgend 21 B8
Oldcastle Mon 35 B7
Oldcotes Notts 89 F6
Oldfallow Staffs 62 C3
Oldfield Worcs 50 C3
Oldford Som 24 D2
Oldham Gtr Man 87 D7
Oldhamstocks E Loth 122 B3
Oldland S Glos 23 B8
Oldmeldrum Aberds 141 B7
Oldshore Beg Highld 156 D4
Oldshoremore Highld 156 D5
Oldstead N Yorks 102 F3
Oldtown Aberds 140 B4
Oldtown of Ord Aberds 152 C6
Oldway Swansea 33 F6
Oldways End Devon 10 B3
Oldwhat Aberds 153 C8
Olgrinmore Highld 158 E2
Oliver's Battery Hants 15 B5
Ollaberry Shetland 160 E5
Ollerton Ches E 74 B4
Ollerton Notts 77 C6
Ollerton Shrops 61 B6
Olmarch Ceredig 46 D5
Olney M Keynes 53 D6
Olrig Ho. Highld 158 D3
Olton W Mid 62 F5
Olveston S Glos 36 F3
Olwen Ceredig 46 E4
Ombersley Worcs 50 C3
Ompton Notts 77 C6
Onchan IoM 84 E3
Onecote Staffs 75 D7
Onen Mon 35 C8
Ongar Hill Norf 67 B5
Ongar Street Hereford 49 C5
Onibury Shrops 49 B6
Onich Highld 130 C4
Onllwyn Neath 34 C2
Onneley Staffs 74 E4
Onslow Village Sur 27 E7
Onthank E Ayrs 118 E4
Openwoodgate Derbys 76 E3
Opinan Highld 149 A12
Opinan Highld 155 H13
Orange Lane Borders 122 E3
Orange Row Norf 66 B5
Orasaigh W Isles 155 F8
Orbliston Moray 152 C3
Orbost Highld 148 D7
Orby Lincs 79 C7
Orchard Hill Devon 9 B6
Orchard Portman Som 11 B7
Orcheston Wilts 25 E5
Orcop Hereford 36 B1
Orcop Hill Hereford 36 B1
Ord Highld 149 G11
Ordhead Aberds 141 C5
Ordie Aberds 140 D3
Ordiequish Moray 152 C3
Ordsall Notts 89 F7
Ore E Sus 18 D5
Oreton Shrops 61 F6
Orford Suff 57 E8
Orford Warr 86 E4
Orgreave Staffs 63 C5
Orlestone Kent 19 B6
Orleton Hereford 49 C6
Orleton Worcs 49 C8
Orlingbury Northants 53 B6
Ormesby Redcar 102 C3
Ormesby St Margaret Norf 69 C7
Ormesby St Michael Norf 69 C7
Ormiclate Castle W Isles 148 E2
Ormiscaig Highld 155 H13
Ormiston E Loth 121 C7
Ormsaigbeg Highld 146 E7
Ormsaigmore Highld 146 E7
Ormsary Argyll 144 F6
Ormsgill Cumb 92 B1
Ormskirk Lancs 86 D2
Orpington London 29 C5
Orrell Gtr Man 86 D3
Orrell Mers 85 E4
Orrisdale IoM 84 C3
Orroland Dumfries 106 E4
Orsett Thurrock 42 F2
Orslow Staffs 62 C2
Orston Notts 77 E7
Orthwaite Cumb 108 F2
Ortner Lancs 92 D5
Orton Cumb 99 D8
Orton Northants 53 B6
Orton Longueville Pboro 65 E8
Orton-on-the-Hill Leics 63 D7
Orton Waterville Pboro 65 E8
Orwell Cambs 54 D4
Osbaldeston Lancs 93 F6
Osbaldwick York 96 D2
Osbaston Shrops 60 B3
Osbournby Lincs 78 F3
Oscroft Ches W 74 C2
Ose Highld 149 D8
Osgathorpe Leics 63 C8
Osgodby Lincs 90 E4
Osgodby N Yorks 96 F2
Osgodby N Yorks 103 F8
Oskaig Highld 149 E10
Oskamull Argyll 146 G7
Osmaston Derby 76 F3
Osmaston Derbys 76 E2
Osmington Dorset 12 F5
Osmington Mills Dorset 12 F5
Osmotherley N Yorks 102 E2
Ospisdale Highld 151 C10
Ospringe Kent 30 C4
Ossett W Yorks 88 B3
Ossington Notts 77 C7
Ostend Essex 43 E5
Oswaldkirk N Yorks 96 B2
Oswaldtwistle Lancs 86 B5
Oswestry Shrops 60 B2
Otford Kent 29 D6
Otham Kent 29 D8
Othery Som 23 F5
Otley Suff 57 D6
Otley W Yorks 94 E5
Otter Ferry Argyll 145 E8
Otterbourne Hants 15 B5
Otterburn N Yorks 93 D8
Otterburn Northumb 116 E4
Otterburn Camp Northumb 116 E4
Otterham Corn 8 E3
Otterhampton Som 22 E4
Ottershaw Sur 27 C8
Otterswick Shetland 160 E7
Otterton Devon 11 F5
Ottery St Mary Devon 11 E6
Ottinge Kent 31 E5
Ottringham E Yorks 91 B6
Oughterby Cumb 108 D2
Oughtershaw N Yorks 100 F3
Oughterside Cumb 107 E8
Oughtibridge S Yorks 88 E4
Oughtrington Warr 86 F4
Oulston N Yorks 95 B8
Oulton Cumb 108 D2
Oulton Norf 81 E7
Oulton Staffs 75 F6
Oulton Suff 69 E8
Oulton W Yorks 88 B4
Oulton Broad Suff 69 E8
Oulton Street Norf 81 E7
Oundle Northants 65 F7
Ousby Cumb 109 F6
Ousdale Highld 158 H2
Ousden Suff 55 D8
Ousefleet E Yorks 90 B2
Ouston Durham 111 D5
Ouston Northumb 110 B3
Out Newton E Yorks 91 B7
Out Rawcliffe Lancs 92 E4
Outertown Orkney 159 G3
Outgate Cumb 99 E5
Outhgill Cumb 100 D2
Outlane W Yorks 87 C8
Outwell Norf 66 D5
Outwick Hants 14 C2
Outwood Sur 28 E4
Outwood W Yorks 88 B4
Outwoods Staffs 61 C7
Ovenden W Yorks 87 B8
Ovenscloss Borders 121 F7
Over Cambs 54 B4
Over Ches W 74 C3
Over S Glos 36 F2
Over Compton Dorset 12 C3
Over Green W Mid 63 E5
Over Haddon Derbys 76 C2
Over Hulton Gtr Man 86 D4
Over Kellet Lancs 92 B5
Over Kiddington Oxon 38 B4
Over Knutsford Ches E 74 B4
Over Monnow Mon 36 C2
Over Norton Oxon 38 B3
Over Peover Ches E 74 B4
Over Silton N Yorks 102 E2
Over Stowey Som 22 F3
Over Stratton Som 12 C2
Over Tabley Ches E 86 F5
Over Wallop Hants 25 F7
Over Whitacre Warks 63 E6
Over Worton Oxon 38 B4
Overbister Orkney 159 D7
Overbury Worcs 50 F4
Overcombe Dorset 12 F4
Overgreen Derbys 76 B3
Overleigh Som 23 F6
Overley Green Warks 51 D5
Overpool Ches W 73 B7
Overscaig Hotel Highld 156 G7
Overseal Derbys 63 C6
Oversland Kent 30 D4
Overstone Northants 53 C6
Overstrand Norf 81 C8
Overthorpe Northants 52 E2
Overton Aberdeen 141 C7
Overton Ches W 74 B2
Overton Dumfries 107 C6
Overton Hants 26 E3
Overton Lancs 92 D4
Overton N Yorks 95 D8
Overton Shrops 49 B7
Overton Swansea 33 F5
Overton W Yorks 88 C3
Overton = Owrtyn Wrex 73 E7
Overton Bridge Wrex 73 E7
Overtown N Lanark 119 D8
Oving Bucks 39 B7
Oving W Sus 16 D3
Ovingdean Brighton 17 D7
Ovingham Northumb 110 C3
Ovington Durham 101 C6
Ovington Essex 55 E8
Ovington Hants 26 F3
Ovington Norf 68 D2
Ovington Northumb 110 C3
Ower Hants 14 C4
Owermoigne Dorset 13 F5
Owlbury Shrops 60 E3
Owler Bar Derbys 76 B2
Owlerton S Yorks 88 F4
Owl's Green Suff 57 C6
Owlswick Bucks 39 D7
Owmby Lincs 90 D4
Owmby-by-Spital Lincs 90 F4
Owrtyn = Overton Wrex 73 E7
Owslebury Hants 15 B6
Owston Leics 64 D4
Owston S Yorks 89 C6
Owston Ferry N Lincs 90 D2
Owstwick E Yorks 97 F8
Owthorne E Yorks 91 B7
Owthorpe Notts 77 F6
Oxborough Norf 67 D7
Oxcombe Lincs 79 B6
Oxen Park Cumb 99 F5
Oxenholme Cumb 99 F7
Oxenhope W Yorks 94 F3
Oxenton Glos 50 F4
Oxenwood Wilts 25 D8
Oxford Oxon 39 D5
Oxhey Herts 40 E4
Oxhill Warks 51 E8
Oxley W Mid 62 D3
Oxley Green Essex 43 C5
Oxley's Green E Sus 18 C3
Oxnam Borders 116 C2
Oxshott Sur 28 C2
Oxspring S Yorks 88 D3
Oxted Sur 28 D4
Oxton Borders 121 D7
Oxton Notts 77 D6
Oxwich Swansea 33 F5
Oxwick Norf 80 E5
Oykel Bridge Highld 156 J6
Oyne Aberds 141 B5

P

Pabail Iarach W Isles 155 D10
Pabail Uarach W Isles 155 D10
Pace Gate N Yorks 94 D4
Packington Leics 63 C7
Padanaram Angus 134 D4
Padbury Bucks 52 F5
Paddington London 41 F5
Paddlesworth Kent 19 B8
Paddock Wood Kent 29 E7
Paddockhaugh Moray 152 C2
Paddockhole Dumfries 115 F5
Padfield Derbys 87 E8
Padiham Lancs 93 F7
Padog Conwy 83 F8
Padside N Yorks 94 D4
Padstow Corn 4 B4
Padworth W Berks 26 C4
Page Bank Durham 110 F5
Pagham W Sus 16 E2
Paglesham Churchend Essex 43 E5
Paglesham Eastend Essex 43 E5
Paibeil W Isles 148 B2
Paible W Isles 154 H5
Paignton Torbay 7 C6
Pailton Warks 63 F8
Painscastle Powys 48 E3
Painshawfield Northumb 110 C3
Painsthorpe E Yorks 96 D4
Painswick Glos 37 D5
Pairc Shiaboist W Isles 154 C7
Paisley Renfs 118 C4
Pakefield Suff 69 E8
Pakenham Suff 56 C3
Pale Gwyn 72 F3
Palestine Hants 25 E7
Paley Street Windsor 27 B6
Palfrey W Mid 62 E4
Palgowan Dumfries 112 F3
Palgrave Suff 56 B5
Pallion T&W 111 D6
Palmarsh Kent 19 B8
Palnackie Dumfries 106 D5
Palnure Dumfries 105 C8
Palterton Derbys 76 C4
Pamber End Hants 26 D4
Pamber Green Hants 26 D4
Pamber Heath Hants 26 C4
Pamphill Dorset 13 D7
Pampisford Cambs 55 E5
Pan Orkney 159 J4
Panbride Angus 135 F5
Pancrasweek Devon 8 D4
Pandy Gwyn 58 D3
Pandy Mon 35 B7
Pandy Powys 59 D6
Pandy Wrex 73 F5
Pandy Tudur Conwy 83 E8
Panfield Essex 42 B3
Pangbourne W Berks 26 B4
Pannal N Yorks 95 D6
Panshanger Herts 41 C5
Pant Shrops 60 B2
Pant-glas Powys 58 E4
Pant-glas Carms 33 B6
Pant-glas Gwyn 71 C5
Pant-glas Shrops 73 F6
Pant-lasau Swansea 33 E7
Pant Mawr Powys 59 F5
Pant-teg Carms 33 B5
Pant-y-Caws Carms 32 B2
Pant-y-dwr Powys 47 B8
Pant-y-ffridd Powys 59 D8
Pant-y-Wacco Flint 72 B5
Pant-yr-awel Bridgend 34 F3
Pantgwyn Carms 33 B6
Pantgwyn Ceredig 45 E4
Panton Lincs 78 B4
Pantperthog Gwyn 58 D4
Pantyffynnon Carms 33 C7
Pantymwyn Flint 73 C5
Panxworth Norf 69 C6
Papcastle Cumb 107 F8
Papigoe Highld 158 E5
Papil Shetland 160 K5
Papley Orkney 159 J5
Papple E Loth 121 B8
Papplewick Notts 76 D5
Papworth Everard Cambs 54 C3
Papworth St Agnes Cambs 54 C3
Par Corn 5 D5
Parbold Lancs 86 C2
Parbrook Som 23 F7
Parbrook W Sus 16 B4
Parc Gwyn 72 F2
Parc-Seymour Newport 35 E8
Parc-y-rhôs Carms 46 E4
Parcllyn Ceredig 45 D4
Pardshaw Cumb 98 B2
Parham Suff 57 C7
Park Dumfries 114 E2
Park Corner Oxon 39 F6
Park Corner Windsor 40 F1
Park End Mbro 102 C3
Park End Northumb 109 B8
Park Gate Hants 15 D6
Park Hill N Yorks 95 C6
Park Hill Notts 77 D6
Park Street W Sus 28 F2
Parkend Glos 36 D3
Parkeston Essex 57 F6
Parkgate Ches W 73 B6
Parkgate Dumfries 114 F3
Parkgate Kent 19 B5
Parkgate Sur 28 E3
Parkham Devon 9 B5
Parkham Ash Devon 9 B5
Parkhill Ho. Aberds 141 C7
Parkhouse Mon 36 D1
Parkhouse Green Derbys 76 C4
Parkhurst IoW 15 E5
Parkmill Swansea 33 F6
Parkneuk Aberds 135 B7
Parkstone Poole 13 E8
Parley Cross Dorset 13 E8
Parracombe Devon 21 E5
Parrog Pembs 45 F2
Parsley Hay Derbys 75 C8
Parson Cross S Yorks 88 E4
Parson Drove Cambs 66 D3
Parsonage Green Essex 42 D3
Parsonby Cumb 107 F8
Parson's Heath Essex 43 B6
Partick Glasgow 119 C5
Partington Gtr Man 86 E5
Partney Lincs 79 C7
Parton Cumb 98 B1
Parton Dumfries 106 B3
Parton Glos 37 B5
Partridge Green W Sus 17 C5
Parwich Derbys 75 D8
Passenham Northants 53 F5
Paston Norf 81 D9
Patchacott Devon 9 E6
Patcham Brighton 17 D7
Patching W Sus 16 D4
Patchole Devon 20 E5
Pateley Bridge N Yorks 94 C4
Paternoster Heath Essex 43 C5
Path of Condie Perth 128 C2
Pathe Som 23 F5
Pathhead Aberds 135 C7
Pathhead E Ayrs 113 C6
Pathhead Fife 128 E4
Pathhead Midloth 121 C6
Pathstruie Perth 128 C2
Patna E Ayrs 112 C4
Patney Wilts 25 D5
Patrick IoM 84 D2
Patrick Brompton N Yorks 101 E7
Patrington E Yorks 91 B7
Patrixbourne Kent 31 D5
Patterdale Cumb 99 C5
Pattingham Staffs 62 E2
Pattishall Northants 52 D4
Pattiswick Green Essex 42 B4
Patton Bridge Cumb 99 E7
Paul Corn 2 D3
Paulerspury Northants 52 E5
Paull E Yorks 91 B5
Paulton Bath 23 D8
Pavenham Bedford 53 D7
Pawlett Som 22 E5
Pawston Northumb 122 F4
Paxford Glos 51 F6
Paxton Borders 122 D5
Payhembury Devon 11 D5
Paythorne Lancs 93 D8
Peacehaven E Sus 17 D8
Peak Dale Derbys 75 B7
Peak Forest Derbys 75 B8
Peakirk Pboro 65 D8
Pearsie Angus 134 D3
Pease Pottage W Sus 28 F3
Peasedown St John Bath 24 D2
Peasemore W Berks 26 B2
Peasenhall Suff 57 C7
Peaslake Sur 27 E8
Peasley Cross Mers 86 E3
Peasmarsh E Sus 19 C5
Peaston E Loth 121 C7
Peastonbank E Loth 121 C7
Peat Inn Fife 129 D6
Peathill Aberds 153 B9
Peatling Magna Leics 64 E2
Peatling Parva Leics 64 F2
Peaton Shrops 60 F5
Peats Corner Suff 57 C5
Pebmarsh Essex 56 F2
Pebworth Worcs 51 E6
Pecket Well W Yorks 87 B7
Peckforton Ches E 74 D2
Peckham London 28 B4
Peckleton Leics 63 D8
Pedlinge Kent 19 B8
Pedmore W Mid 62 F3
Pedwell Som 23 F6
Peebles Borders 121 E5
Peel IoM 84 D2
Peel Common Hants 15 D6
Peel Park S Lanark 119 D6
Peening Quarter Kent 19 C5
Pegsdon C Beds 54 F2
Pegswood Northumb 117 F8
Pegwell Kent 31 C7
Peinchorran Highld 149 E10
Peinlich Highld 149 C9
Pelaw T&W 111 C5
Pelcomb Bridge Pembs 44 D4
Pelcomb Cross Pembs 44 D4
Peldon Essex 43 C5
Pellon W Yorks 87 B8
Pelsall W Mid 62 D4
Pelton Durham 111 D5
Pelutho Cumb 107 E8
Pelynt Corn 5 D7
Pemberton Gtr Man 86 D3
Pembrey Carms 33 D5
Pembridge Hereford 49 D5
Pembroke = Penfro Pembs 44 E4
Pembroke Dock = Doc Penfro Pembs 44 E4
Pembury Kent 29 E7
Pen-bont Rhydybeddau Ceredig 58 F3
Pen-clawdd Swansea 33 E6
Pen-ffordd Pembs 32 B1
Pen-groes-oped Mon 35 D7
Pen-llyn Anglesey 82 C3
Pen-lon Anglesey 82 E4
Pen-sarn Gwyn 70 C5
Pen-sarn Gwyn 71 E6
Pen-twyn Mon 36 D2
Pen-y-banc Carms 33 B7
Pen-y-bont Carms 32 B4
Pen-y-bont Gwyn 58 D4
Pen-y-bont Gwyn 71 E7
Pen-y-bont Powys 60 B2
Pen-Y-Bont Ar Ogwr = Bridgend Bridgend 21 B8
Pen-y-bryn Gwyn 58 C3
Pen-y-bryn Pembs 45 E3
Pen-y-cae Powys 34 C2
Pen-y-cae-mawr Mon 35 E8
Pen-y-cefn Flint 72 B5
Pen-y-clawdd Mon 36 D1
Pen-y-coedcae Rhondda 34 F4
Pen-y-fai Bridgend 34 F2
Pen-y-garn Carms 46 F4
Pen-y-garn Ceredig 58 F3
Pen-y-garnedd Anglesey 82 D5
Pen-y-gop Conwy 72 E3
Pen-y-graig Gwyn 70 D2
Pen-y-groes Carms 33 C6
Pen-y-groeslon Gwyn 70 D3
Pen-y-Gwryd Hotel Gwyn 83 F6
Pen-y-stryt Denb 73 D5
Pen-yr-heol Mon 35 C8
Pen-yr-Heolgerrig M Tydf 34 D4
Penallt Mon 36 C2
Penally Pembs 32 E2
Penalt Hereford 36 B2
Penare Corn 3 B8
Penarlâg = Hawarden Flint 73 C7
Penarth V Glam 22 B3
Penbryn Ceredig 45 D4
Pencader Carms 46 F3
Pencaenewydd Gwyn 70 C5
Pencaitland E Loth 121 C7
Pencarnisiog Anglesey 82 D3
Pencarreg Carms 46 E4
Pencelli Powys 34 B4
Pencoed Bridgend 34 F3
Pencombe Hereford 49 D7
Pencoyd Hereford 36 B2
Pencraig Hereford 36 B2
Pencraig Powys 59 B7
Pendeen Corn 2 C2
Penderyn Rhondda 34 D3
Pendine Carms 32 D3
Pendlebury Gtr Man 87 D5
Pendleton Lancs 93 F7
Pendock Worcs 50 F2
Pendoggett Corn 4 B5
Pendomer Som 12 C3
Pendoylan V Glam 22 B2
Pendre Bridgend 34 F3
Penegoes Powys 58 D4
Penfro = Pembroke Pembs 44 E4
Pengam Caerph 35 E5
Penge London 28 B4
Pengenffordd Powys 48 F3
Pengorffwysfa Anglesey 82 B4
Pengover Green Corn 5 C7
Penhale Corn 3 E5
Penhale Corn 4 D4
Penhalvaen Corn 3 C6
Penhill Swindon 38 F1
Penhow Newport 35 E8
Penhurst E Sus 18 D3
Peniarth Gwyn 58 D3
Penicuik Midloth 120 C5
Peniel Carms 33 B5
Peniel Denb 72 C4
Penifiler Highld 149 D9
Peninver Argyll 143 F8
Penisarwaun Gwyn 83 E5
Penistone S Yorks 88 D3
Penjerrick Corn 3 C6
Penketh Warr 86 F3
Penkill S Ayrs 112 E2
Penkridge Staffs 62 C3
Penley Wrex 73 F8
Penllergaer Swansea 33 E7
Penllyn V Glam 21 B8
Penmachno Conwy 83 F7
Penmaen Swansea 33 F6
Penmaenan Conwy 83 D7
Penmaenmawr Conwy 83 D7
Penmaenpool Gwyn 58 C3
Penmark V Glam 22 C2
Penmarth Corn 3 C6
Penmon Anglesey 83 C6
Penmore Mill Argyll 146 F7
Penmorfa Ceredig 46 D2
Penmorfa Gwyn 71 C6
Penmynydd Anglesey 82 D5
Penn Bucks 40 E2
Penn W Mid 62 E2
Penn Street Bucks 40 E2
Pennal Gwyn 58 D4
Pennan Aberds 153 B8
Pennant Ceredig 46 C4
Pennant Denb 72 D4
Pennant Denb 72 F4
Pennant Powys 59 E5
Pennant Melangell Powys 59 B7
Pennar Pembs 44 E4
Pennard Swansea 33 F6
Pennerley Shrops 60 E3
Pennington Cumb 92 B2
Pennington Gtr Man 86 E4
Pennington Hants 14 E4
Penny Bridge Cumb 99 F5
Pennycross Argyll 147 J8
Pennygate Norf 69 B6
Pennygown Argyll 147 G8
Pennymoor Devon 10 C3
Pennywell T&W 111 D6
Penparc Ceredig 45 E4
Penparc Pembs 44 B3
Penparcau Ceredig 58 F2
Penperlleni Mon 35 D7
Penpillick Corn 5 D5
Penpol Corn 3 C7
Penpoll Corn 5 D6
Penpont Dumfries 113 E8
Penpont Powys 34 B3
Penrhôs Mon 35 C8
Penrherber Carms 45 F4
Penrhiw goch Carms 33 C6
Penrhiw-llan Ceredig 46 E2
Penrhiw-pâl Ceredig 46 E2
Penrhiwceiber Rhondda 34 E4
Penrhos Gwyn 70 D4
Penrhos Powys 34 C1
Penrhosfeilw Anglesey 82 C2
Penrhyn Bay Conwy 83 C8
Penrhyn-coch Ceredig 58 F3
Penrhyndeudraeth Gwyn 71 D7
Penrhynside Conwy 83 C8
Penrice Swansea 33 F5
Penrith Cumb 108 F5
Penrose Corn 4 B3
Penruddock Cumb 99 B6
Penryn Corn 3 C6
Pensarn Carms 33 C5
Pensarn Conwy 72 B3
Pensax Worcs 50 C2
Pensby Mers 85 F3
Penselwood Som 24 F2
Pensford Bath 23 C8
Penshaw T&W 111 D6
Penshurst Kent 29 E6
Pensilva Corn 5 C7
Penston E Loth 121 B7
Pentewan Corn 3 B9
Pentir Gwyn 83 E5
Pentire Corn 4 C2
Pentlow Essex 56 E2
Pentney Norf 67 C7
Penton Mewsey Hants 25 E8
Pentraeth Anglesey 82 D5
Pentre Carms 33 C6
Pentre Powys 59 F7
Pentre Powys 60 E2
Pentre Rhondda 34 E3
Pentre Shrops 60 C3
Pentre Wrex 72 F5
Pentre Wrex 73 E6
Pentre-bâch Ceredig 46 E4
Pentre-bach Powys 47 F8
Pentre Berw Anglesey 82 D4
Pentre-bont Conwy 83 F7
Pentre-celyn Denb 72 D5
Pentre-Celyn Powys 59 D5
Pentre-chwyth Swansea 33 E7
Pentre-cwrt Carms 46 F2
Pentre Dolau-Honddu Powys 47 E8
Pentre-dwr Swansea 33 E7
Pentre-galar Pembs 45 F3
Pentre-Gwenlais Carms 33 C7
Pentre Gwynfryn Gwyn 71 E6
Pentre Halkyn Flint 73 B6
Pentre-Isaf Conwy 83 E8
Pentre Llanrhaeadr Denb 72 C4
Pentre-llwyn-llŵyd Powys 47 D8
Pentre-llyn Ceredig 46 B5
Pentre-llyn cymmer Conwy 72 D3
Pentre Meyrick V Glam 21 B8
Pentre-poeth Newport 35 F6
Pentre-rhew Ceredig 47 D5
Pentre-tafarn-y-fedw Conwy 83 E8
Pentre-ty-gwyn Carms 47 F7
Pentrebach M Tydf 34 D4
Pentrebach Swansea 33 D7
Pentrebeirdd Powys 59 C8
Pentrecagal Carms 46 E2
Pentredwr Denb 73 E5
Pentrefelin Carms 33 B6
Pentrefelin Ceredig 46 E5
Pentrefelin Conwy 83 D8
Pentrefelin Gwyn 71 D6
Pentrefoelas Conwy 83 F8
Pentregat Ceredig 46 D2
Pentreheyling Shrops 60 E2
Pentre'r Felin Conwy 83 E8
Pentre'r-felin Powys 47 F8
Pentrich Derbys 76 D3
Pentridge Dorset 13 C8
Pentyrch Cardiff 35 F5
Penuchadre V Glam 21 B7
Penuwch Ceredig 46 C4
Penwithick Corn 4 D5
Penwyllt Powys 34 C2
Penybanc Carms 33 C7
Penybont Powys 48 C3
Penybontfawr Powys 59 B7
Penycae Wrex 73 E6
Penycwm Pembs 44 C3
Penyffordd Flint 73 C7
Penyffridd Gwyn 82 F5
Penygarnedd Powys 59 B8
Penygraig Rhondda 34 E3
Penygroes Gwyn 82 F4
Penygroes Pembs 45 F3
Penyrheol Caerph 35 F5
Penysarn Anglesey 82 B4
Penywaun Rhondda 34 D3
Penzance Corn 2 C3
Peopleton Worcs 50 D4
Peover Heath Ches E 74 B4
Peper Harow Sur 27 E7
Perceton N Ayrs 118 E3
Percie Aberds 140 E4
Percyhorner Aberds 153 B9
Periton Som 21 E8
Perivale London 40 F4
Perkinsville Durham 111 D5
Perlethorpe Notts 77 B6
Perranarworthal Corn 3 C6
Perranporth Corn 4 D2
Perranuthnoe Corn 2 D4
Perranzabuloe Corn 4 D2
Perry Barr W Mid 62 E4
Perry Green Herts 41 C7
Perry Green Wilts 37 F6
Perry Street Kent 29 B7
Perryfoot Derbys 88 F2
Pershall Staffs 74 F5
Pershore Worcs 50 E4
Pert Angus 135 C6
Pertenhall Bedford 53 C8
Perth Perth 128 B3
Perthy Shrops 73 F7
Perton Staffs 62 E2
Pertwood Wilts 24 F3
Peter Tavy Devon 6 B3
Peterborough Pboro 65 E8
Peterburn Highld 155 J12
Peterchurch Hereford 48 F5
Peterculter Aberdeen 141 D7
Peterhead Aberds 153 D11
Peterlee Durham 111 E7
Peter's Green Herts 40 C4
Peters Marland Devon 9 C6
Petersfield Hants 15 B8
Peterston super-Ely V Glam 22 B2
Peterstone Wentlooge Newport 35 F6
Peterstow Hereford 36 B2
Petertown Orkney 159 H4
Petham Kent 30 D5
Petrockstow Devon 9 D7
Pett E Sus 19 D5
Pettaugh Suff 57 D5
Petteridge Kent 29 E7
Pettinain S Lanark 120 E2
Pettistree Suff 57 D6
Petton Devon 10 B5
Petton Shrops 60 B4
Petts Wood London 28 C5
Petty Aberds 153 E7
Pettycur Fife 128 F4
Pettymuick Aberds 141 B8
Petworth W Sus 16 B3
Pevensey E Sus 18 E3
Pevensey Bay E Sus 18 E3
Pewsey Wilts 25 C6
Philham Devon 8 B4
Philiphaugh Borders 115 B7
Phillack Corn 2 C4
Philleigh Corn 3 C7
Philpstoun W Loth 120 B3
Phocle Green Hereford 36 B3
Phoenix Green Hants 27 D5
Pica Cumb 98 B2
Piccotts End Herts 40 D3
Pickering N Yorks 103 F5
Picket Piece Hants 25 E8
Picket Post Hants 14 D2
Pickhill N Yorks 101 F8
Picklescott Shrops 60 E4
Pickletillem Fife 129 B6
Pickmere Ches E 74 B3
Pickney Som 11 B6
Pickstock Telford 61 B7
Pickwell Devon 20 E3
Pickwell Leics 64 C4
Pickworth Lincs 78 F3
Pickworth Rutland 65 C6
Picton Ches W 73 B8
Picton Flint 85 F2
Picton N Yorks 102 D2
Piddinghoe E Sus 17 D8
Piddington Northants 53 D6
Piddington Oxon 39 C6
Piddlehinton Dorset 12 E5
Piddletrenthide Dorset 12 E5
Pidley Cambs 54 B4
Piercebridge Darl 101 C7
Pierowall Orkney 159 D5
Pigdon Northumb 117 F7
Pikehall Derbys 75 D8
Pilgrims Hatch Essex 42 E1
Pilham Lincs 90 E2
Pill N Som 23 B7
Pillaton Corn 5 C8
Pillerton Hersey Warks 51 E8
Pillerton Priors Warks 51 E7
Pilleth Powys 48 C4
Pilley Hants 14 E4
Pilley S Yorks 88 D4
Pilling Lancs 92 E4
Pilling Lane Lancs 92 E3
Pillowell Glos 36 D3
Pillwell Dorset 13 C5
Pilning S Glos 36 F2
Pilsbury Derbys 75 C8
Pilsdon Dorset 12 E2
Pilsgate Pboro 65 D7
Pilsley Derbys 76 B2
Pilsley Derbys 76 C4
Pilton Devon 20 F4
Pilton Northants 65 F7
Pilton Rutland 65 D6
Pilton Som 23 E7
Pilton Green Swansea 33 F5
Pimperne Dorset 13 D7
Pin Mill Suff 57 F6
Pinchbeck Lincs 66 B2
Pinchbeck Bars Lincs 65 B8
Pinchbeck West Lincs 66 B2
Pincheon Green S Yorks 89 C7
Pinehurst Swindon 38 F1
Pinfold Lancs 85 C4
Pinged Carms 33 D5
Pinhoe Devon 10 E4
Pinkneys Green Windsor 40 F1
Pinley W Mid 51 B8
Pinminnoch S Ayrs 112 E1
Pinmore S Ayrs 112 E2
Pinmore Mains S Ayrs 112 E2
Pinner London 40 F4
Pinvin Worcs 50 E4
Pinwherry S Ayrs 112 F1
Pinxton Derbys 76 D4
Pipe and Lyde Hereford 49 E7
Pipe Gate Shrops 74 E4
Piperhill Highld 151 F11
Piper's Pool Corn 8 F4
Pipewell Northants 64 F5
Pippacott Devon 20 F4
Pipton Powys 48 F3
Pirbright Sur 27 D7
Pirnmill N Ayrs 143 D9
Pirton Herts 54 F2
Pirton Worcs 50 E3
Pisgah Ceredig 47 B5
Pisgah Stirling 127 D6
Pishill Oxon 39 F7
Pistyll Gwyn 70 C4
Pitagowan Perth 133 C5
Pitblae Aberds 153 B9
Pitcairngreen Perth 128 B2
Pitcalnie Highld 151 D11
Pitcaple Aberds 141 B6
Pitch Green Bucks 39 D7
Pitch Place Sur 27 D7
Pitchcombe Glos 37 D5
Pitchcott Bucks 39 B7
Pitchford Shrops 60 D5
Pitcombe Som 23 F8
Pitcorthie Fife 129 D7
Pitcox E Loth 122 B2
Pitcur Perth 134 F2
Pitfichie Aberds 141 C5
Pitforthie Aberds 135 B8
Pitgrudy Highld 151 B10
Pitkennedy Angus 135 D5
Pitkevy Fife 128 D4
Pitkierie Fife 129 D7
Pitlessie Fife 128 D5
Pitlochry Perth 133 D6
Pitmachie Aberds 141 B5
Pitmain Highld 138 D3
Pitmedden Aberds 141 B7
Pitminster Som 11 C7
Pitmuies Angus 135 E5
Pitmunie Aberds 141 C5
Pitney Som 12 B2
Pitscottie Fife 129 C6
Pitsea Essex 42 F3
Pitsford Northants 53 C5
Pitsmoor S Yorks 88 F4
Pitstone Bucks 40 C2
Pitstone Green Bucks 40 C2
Pittendreich Moray 152 B1
Pittentrail Highld 157 J10
Pittenweem Fife 129 D7
Pittington Durham 111 E6
Pittodrie Aberds 141 B5
Pitton Wilts 25 F7
Pittswood Kent 29 E7
Pittulie Aberds 153 B9
Pity Me Durham 111 E5
Pityme Corn 4 B4
Pityoulish Highld 138 C5
Pixey Green Suff 57 B6
Pixham Sur 28 D2
Pixley Hereford 49 F8
Place Newton N Yorks 96 B4
Plaidy Aberds 153 C7
Plains N Lanark 119 C7
Plaish Shrops 60 E5
Plaistow W Sus 27 F8
Plaitford Wilts 14 C3
Plank Lane Gtr Man 86 E4
Plas-canol Gwyn 58 C2
Plas Gogerddan Ceredig 58 F3
Plas Llwyngwern Powys 58 D4
Plas Nantyr Wrex 73 F5
Plas-yn-Cefn Denb 72 B4
Plastow Green Hants 26 C3
Platt Kent 29 D7
Platt Bridge Gtr Man 86 D4
Platts Common S Yorks 88 D4
Plawsworth Durham 111 E5
Plaxtol Kent 29 D7
Play Hatch Oxon 26 B5
Playden E Sus 19 C6
Playford Suff 57 E6
Playing Place Corn 3 B7
Playley Green Glos 50 F2
Plealey Shrops 60 D4
Plean Stirling 127 F7
Pleasington Blackburn 86 B4
Pleasley Derbys 76 C5
Pleckgate Blackburn 93 F6
Plenmeller Northumb 109 C7
Pleshey Essex 42 C2
Plockton Highld 149 E13
Plocrapol W Isles 154 H6
Ploughfield Hereford 49 E5
Plowden Shrops 60 F3
Ploxgreen Shrops 60 D3
Pluckley Kent 30 E3
Pluckley Thorne Kent 30 E3
Plumbland Cumb 107 F8
Plumley Ches E 74 B4
Plumpton Cumb 108 F4
Plumpton E Sus 17 C7
Plumpton Green E Sus 17 C7
Plumpton Head Cumb 108 F5
Plumstead London 29 B5
Plumstead Norf 81 D7
Plumtree Notts 77 F6
Plungar Leics 77 F7
Plush Dorset 12 D5
Plwmp Ceredig 46 D2
Plymouth Plym 6 D2
Plympton Plym 6 D3

Plymstock Plym 6 D3
Plymtree Devon 11 D5
Pockley N Yorks 102 F4
Pocklington E Yorks 96 E4
Pode Hole Lincs 66 B2
Podimore Som 12 B3
Podington Bedford 53 C7
Podmore Staffs 74 F4
Point Clear Essex 43 C6
Pointon Lincs 78 F4
Pokesdown Bmouth 14 E2
Pol a Charra W Isles 148 G2
Polbae Dumfries 105 B6
Polbain Highld 156 H2
Polbathic Corn 5 D8
Polbeth W Loth 120 C3
Polchar Highld 138 D4
Pole Elm Worcs 50 E3
Polebrook Northants 65 F7
Polegate E Sus 18 E2
Poles Highld 151 B10
Polesworth Warks 63 D6
Polgigga Corn 2 D2
Polglass Highld 156 J3
Polgooth Corn 4 D4
Poling W Sus 16 D4
Polkerris Corn 5 D5
Polla Highld 156 D6
Pollington E Yorks 89 C7
Polloch Highld 130 C1
Pollok Glasgow 118 C5
Pollokshields Glasgow 119 C5
Polmassick Corn 3 B8
Polmont Falk 120 B2
Polnessan E Ayrs 112 C4
Polnish Highld 147 C10
Polperro Corn 5 D7
Polruan Corn 5 D6
Polsham Som 23 E7
Polstead Suff 56 F3
Poltalloch Argyll 124 F4
Poltimore Devon 10 E4
Polton Midloth 121 C5
Polwarth Borders 122 D3
Polyphant Corn 8 F4
Polzeath Corn 4 B4
Ponders End London 41 E6
Pondersbridge Cambs 66 E2
Pondtail Hants 27 D6
Ponsanooth Corn 3 C6
Ponsworthy Devon 6 B5
Pont Aber Carms 33 B8
Pont Aber-Geirw Gwyn 71 E8
Pont-ar-gothi Carms 33 B6
Pont ar Hydfer Powys 34 B2
Pont-ar-llechau Carms 33 B8
Pont Cwm Pydew Denb 72 F4
Pont Cyfyng Conwy 83 F7
Pont Cysyllte Wrex 73 E6
Pont Dolydd Prysor Gwyn 71 D8
Pont-faen Powys 47 F8
Pont Fronwydd Gwyn 58 B5
Pont-gareg Pembs 45 E3
Pont-Henri Carms 33 D5
Pont-Llogel Powys 59 C7
Pont Pen-y-benglog Gwyn 83 E6
Pont Rhyd-goch Conwy 83 E6
Pont-Rhyd-sarn Gwyn 59 B5
Pont Rhyd-y-cyff Bridgend 34 F2
Pont-rhyd-y-groes Ceredig 47 B6
Pont-rug Gwyn 82 E5
Pont Senni = Sennybridge Powys 34 B3
Pont-siân Ceredig 46 E3
Pont-y-gwaith Rhondda 34 E4
Pont-Y-Pŵl = Pontypool Torf 35 D6
Pont-y-pant Conwy 83 F7
Pont y Pennant Gwyn 59 B6
Pont yr Afon-Gam Gwyn 71 C8
Pont-yr-hafod Pembs 44 C4
Pontamman Carms 33 C7
Pontantwn Carms 33 C5
Pontardawe Neath 33 D8
Pontarddulais Swansea 33 D6
Pontarsais Carms 33 B5
Pontblyddyn Flint 73 C6
Pontbren Araeth Carms 33 B7
Pontbren Llwyd Rhondda 34 D3
Pontefract W Yorks 89 B5
Ponteland Northumb 110 B4
Ponterwyd Ceredig 58 F4
Pontesbury Shrops 60 D3
Pontfadog Wrex 73 F6
Pontfaen Pembs 45 F2
Pontgarreg Ceredig 46 D2
Ponthir Torf 35 E7
Ponthirwaun Ceredig 45 E4
Pontllanfraith Caerph 35 E5
Pontlliw Swansea 33 D7
Pontllyfni Gwyn 82 F4
Pontlottyn Caerph 35 D5
Pontneddfechan Powys 34 D3
Pontnewydd Torf 35 E6
Pontrhydfendigaid Ceredig 47 C6
Pontrhydyfen Neath 34 E1
Pontrilas Hereford 35 B7
Pontrobert Powys 59 C8
Ponts Green E Sus 18 D3
Pontshill Hereford 36 B3
Pontsticill M Tydf 34 C4
Pontwgan Conwy 83 D7
Pontyates Carms 33 D5
Pontyberem Carms 33 C6
Pontyclun Rhondda 34 F4
Pontycymer Bridgend 34 E3
Pontyglasier Pembs 45 F3
Pontypool = Pont-Y-Pŵl Torf 35 D6
Pontypridd Rhondda 34 F4
Pontywaun Caerph 35 E6
Pooksgreen Hants 14 C4
Pool Corn 3 B5
Pool W Yorks 94 E5
Pool o'Muckhart Clack 128 D2
Pool Quay Powys 60 C2
Poole Poole 13 E8
Poole Keynes Glos 37 E6
Poolend Staffs 75 D6
Poolewe Highld 155 J13
Pooley Bridge Cumb 99 B6
Poolfold Staffs 75 D5
Poolhill Glos 36 B4
Poolsbrook Derbys 76 B4
Pootings Kent 29 E5
Pope Hill Pembs 44 D4
Popeswood Brack 27 C6
Popham Hants 26 E3
Poplar London 41 F6
Popley Hants 26 D4
Porchester Nottingham 77 E5
Porchfield IoW 14 E5
Porin Highld 150 F6
Poringland Norf 69 D5
Porkellis Corn 3 C5
Porlock Som 21 E7
Porlock Weir Som 21 E7
Port Ann Argyll 145 E8
Port Appin Argyll 130 E3
Port Arthur Shetland 160 K5
Port Askaig Argyll 142 B5
Port Bannatyne Argyll 145 G9
Port Carlisle Cumb 108 C2
Port Charlotte Argyll 142 C3
Port Clarence Stockton 102 B2
Port Driseach Argyll 145 F8
Port e Vullen IoM 84 C4
Port Ellen Argyll 142 D4
Port Elphinstone Aberds 141 C6
Port Erin IoM 84 F1
Port Erroll Aberds 153 E10
Port-Eynon Swansea 33 F5
Port Gaverne Corn 8 F2
Port Glasgow Invclyd 118 B3
Port Henderson Highld 149 A12
Port Isaac Corn 4 A4
Port Lamont Argyll 145 F9
Port Lion Pembs 44 E4
Port Logan Dumfries 104 E4
Port Mholair W Isles 155 D10
Port Mor Highld 146 D7
Port Mulgrave N Yorks 103 C5
Port Nan Giùran W Isles 155 D10
Port nan Long W Isles 148 A3
Port Nis W Isles 155 A10
Port of Menteith Stirling 126 D4
Port Quin Corn 4 A4
Port Ramsay Argyll 130 E2
Port St Mary IoM 84 F2
Port Sunlight Mers 85 F4
Port Talbot Neath 34 E1
Port Tennant Swansea 33 E7
Port Wemyss Argyll 142 C2
Port William Dumfries 105 E7
Portachoillan Argyll 144 H6
Portavadie Argyll 145 G8
Portbury N Som 23 B7
Portchester Hants 15 D7
Portclair Highld 137 C7
Portencalzie Dumfries 104 B4
Portencross N Ayrs 118 E1
Portesham Dorset 12 F4
Portessie Moray 152 B4
Portfield Gate Pembs 44 D4
Portgate Devon 9 F6
Portgordon Moray 152 B3
Portgower Highld 157 H13
Porth Corn 4 C3
Porth Rhondda 34 E4
Porth Navas Corn 3 D6
Porth Tywyn = Burry Port Carms 33 D5
Porth-y-waen Shrops 60 B2
Porthaethwy = Menai Bridge Anglesey 83 D5
Porthallow Corn 3 D6
Porthallow Corn 5 D7
Porthcawl Bridgend 21 B7
Porthcothan Corn 4 B3
Porthcurno Corn 2 D2
Porthgain Pembs 44 B3
Porthill Shrops 60 C4
Porthkerry V Glam 22 C2
Porthleven Corn 2 D5
Porthllechog Anglesey 82 B4
Porthmadog Gwyn 71 D6
Porthmeor Corn 2 C3
Portholland Corn 3 B8
Porthoustock Corn 3 D7
Porthpean Corn 4 D5
Porthtowan Corn 3 B5
Porthyrhyd Carms 33 C6
Porthyrhyd Carms 47 F6
Portincaple Argyll 145 D11
Portington E Yorks 96 F3
Portinnisherrich Argyll 125 D5
Portinscale Cumb 98 B4
Portishead N Som 23 B6
Portkil Argyll 145 E11
Portknockie Moray 152 B4
Portlethen Aberds 141 E8
Portling Dumfries 107 D5
Portloe Corn 3 C8
Portmahomack Highld 151 C12
Portmeirion Gwyn 71 D6
Portmellon Corn 3 B9
Portmore Hants 14 E4
Portnacroish Argyll 130 E3
Portnahaven Argyll 142 C2
Portnalong Highld 149 E8
Portnaluchaig Highld 147 C9
Portnancon Highld 156 C7
Portnellan Stirling 126 B3
Portobello Edin 121 B6
Porton Wilts 25 F6
Portpatrick Dumfries 104 D4
Portreath Corn 3 B5
Portree Highld 149 D9
Portscatho Corn 3 C7
Portsea Ptsmth 15 D7
Portskerra Highld 157 C11
Portskewett Mon 36 F2
Portslade Brighton 17 D6
Portslade-by-Sea Brighton 17 D6
Portsmouth Ptsmth 15 D7
Portsmouth W Yorks 87 B7
Portsonachan Argyll 125 C6
Portsoy Aberds 152 B5
Portswood Soton 14 C5
Portuairk Highld 146 E7
Portway Hereford 49 F6
Portway Worcs 51 B5
Portwrinkle Corn 5 D8
Poslingford Suff 55 E8
Postbridge Devon 6 B4
Postcombe Oxon 39 E7
Postling Kent 19 B8
Postwick Norf 69 D5
Potholm Dumfries 115 F6
Potsgrove C Beds 40 B2
Pott Row Norf 80 E3
Pott Shrigley Ches E 75 B6
Potten End Herts 40 D3
Potter Brompton N Yorks 97 B5
Potter Heigham Norf 69 C7
Potter Street Essex 41 D7
Potterhanworth Lincs 78 C3
Potterhanworth Booths Lincs 78 C3
Potterne Wilts 24 D4
Potterne Wick Wilts 24 D5
Potternewton W Yorks 95 F6
Potters Bar Herts 41 D5
Potter's Cross Staffs 62 F2
Potterspury Northants 53 E5
Potterton Aberds 141 C8
Potterton W Yorks 95 F7
Potto N Yorks 102 D2
Potton C Beds 54 E3
Poughill Corn 8 D4
Poughill Devon 10 D3
Poulshot Wilts 24 D4
Poulton Glos 37 D8
Poulton Mers 85 E4
Poulton-le-Fylde Lancs 92 F3
Pound Bank Worcs 50 B2
Pound Green E Sus 18 C2
Pound Green IoW 14 F4
Pound Green Worcs 50 B2
Pound Hill W Sus 28 F3
Poundfield E Sus 18 B2
Poundland S Ayrs 112 F1
Poundon Bucks 39 B6
Poundsgate Devon 6 B5
Poundstock Corn 8 E4
Powburn Northumb 117 C6
Powderham Devon 10 F4
Powerstock Dorset 12 E3
Powfoot Dumfries 107 C8
Powick Worcs 50 D3
Powmill Perth 128 E2
Poxwell Dorset 12 F5
Poyle Slough 27 B8
Poynings W Sus 17 C6
Poyntington Dorset 12 C4
Poynton Ches E 87 F7
Poynton Green Telford 61 C5
Poystreet Green Suff 56 D3
Praa Sands Corn 2 D4
Pratt's Bottom London 29 C5
Praze Corn 2 C4
Praze-an-Beeble Corn 2 C5
Predannack Wollas Corn 3 E5
Prees Shrops 74 F2
Prees Green Shrops 74 F2
Prees Heath Shrops 74 F2
Prees Higher Heath Shrops 74 F2
Prees Lower Heath Shrops 74 F2
Preesall Lancs 92 E3
Preesgweene Shrops 73 F6
Prenderguest Borders 122 D5
Prendwick Northumb 117 C6
Prengwyn Ceredig 46 E3
Prenteg Gwyn 71 C6
Prenton Mers 85 F4
Prescot Mers 86 E2
Prescott Shrops 60 B4
Pressen Northumb 122 F4
Prestatyn Denb 72 A4
Prestbury Ches E 75 B6
Prestbury Glos 37 B6
Presteigne = Llanandras Powys 48 C5
Presthope Shrops 61 E5
Prestleigh Som 23 E8
Preston Borders 122 D3
Preston Brighton 17 D7
Preston Devon 7 B6
Preston Dorset 12 F5
Preston E Loth 121 B8
Preston E Yorks 97 F7
Preston Glos 37 D7
Preston Glos 49 F8
Preston Herts 40 B4
Preston Kent 30 C4
Preston Kent 31 C6
Preston Lancs 86 B3
Preston Northumb 117 B7
Preston Rutland 65 D5
Preston Shrops 60 C5
Preston Wilts 24 B5
Preston Wilts 25 B7
Preston Bagot Warks 51 C6
Preston Bissett Bucks 39 B6
Preston Bowyer Som 11 B6
Preston Brockhurst Shrops 60 B5
Preston Brook Halton 86 F3
Preston Candover Hants 26 E4
Preston Capes Northants 52 D3
Preston Crowmarsh Oxon 39 E6
Preston Gubbals Shrops 60 C4
Preston on Stour Warks 51 E7
Preston on the Hill Halton 86 F3
Preston on Wye Hereford 49 E5
Preston Plucknett Som 12 C3
Preston St Mary Suff 56 D3
Preston-under-Scar N Yorks 101 E5
Preston upon the Weald Moors Telford 61 C6
Preston Wynne Hereford 49 E7
Prestonmill Dumfries 107 D6
Prestonpans E Loth 121 B6
Prestwich Gtr Man 87 D6
Prestwick Northumb 110 B4
Prestwick S Ayrs 112 B3
Prestwood Bucks 40 D1
Price Town Bridgend 34 E3
Prickwillow Cambs 67 F5
Priddy Som 23 D7
Priest Hutton Lancs 92 B5
Priest Weston Shrops 60 E2
Priesthaugh Borders 115 D7
Primethorpe Leics 64 E2
Primrose Green Norf 68 C3
Primrose Valley N Yorks 97 B7
Primrosehill Herts 40 D3
Princes Gate Pembs 32 C2
Princes Risborough Bucks 39 D8
Princethorpe Warks 52 B2
Princetown Caerph 35 C5
Princetown Devon 6 B3
Prion Denb 72 C4
Prior Muir Fife 129 C7
Prior Park Northumb 123 D5
Priors Frome Hereford 49 F7
Priors Hardwick Warks 52 D2
Priors Marston Warks 52 D2
Priorslee Telford 61 C7
Priory Wood Hereford 48 E4
Priston Bath 23 C8
Pristow Green Norf 68 F4
Prittlewell Southend 42 F4
Privett Hants 15 B7
Prixford Devon 20 F4
Probus Corn 3 B7
Proncy Highld 151 B10
Prospect Cumb 107 E8
Prudhoe Northumb 110 C3
Ptarmigan Lodge Stirling 126 D2
Pubil Perth 132 E1
Puckeridge Herts 41 B6
Puckington Som 11 C8
Pucklechurch S Glos 23 B8
Pucknall Hants 14 B4
Puckrup Glos 50 F3
Puddinglake Ches W 74 C4
Puddington Ches W 73 B7
Puddington Devon 10 C3
Puddledock Norf 68 E3
Puddletown Dorset 13 E5
Pudleston Hereford 49 D7
Pudsey W Yorks 94 F5
Pulborough W Sus 16 C4
Puleston Telford 61 B7
Pulford Ches W 73 D7
Pulham Dorset 12 D5
Pulham Market Norf 68 F4
Pulham St Mary Norf 68 F5
Pulloxhill C Beds 53 F8
Pumpherston W Loth 120 C3
Pumsaint Carms 47 E5
Puncheston Pembs 32 B1
Puncknowle Dorset 12 F3
Punnett's Town E Sus 18 C3
Purbrook Hants 15 D7
Purewell Dorset 14 E2
Purfleet Thurrock 29 B6
Puriton Som 22 E5
Purleigh Essex 42 D4
Purley London 28 C4
Purley W Berks 26 B4
Purlogue Shrops 48 B4
Purls Bridge Cambs 66 F4
Purse Caundle Dorset 12 C4
Purslow Shrops 60 F3
Purston Jaglin W Yorks 88 C5
Purton Glos 36 D3
Purton Glos 36 D3
Purton Wilts 37 F7
Purton Stoke Wilts 37 E7
Pury End Northants 52 E5
Pusey Oxon 38 E3
Putley Hereford 49 F8
Putney London 28 B3
Putsborough Devon 20 E3
Puttenham Herts 40 C1
Puttenham Sur 27 E7
Puxton N Som 23 C6
Pwll Carms 33 D5
Pwll-glas Denb 72 D5
Pwll-trap Carms 32 C3
Pwll-y-glaw Neath 34 E1
Pwllcrochan Pembs 44 E4
Pwllgloyw Powys 48 F2
Pwllheli Gwyn 70 D4
Pwllmeyric Mon 36 E2
Pye Corner Newport 35 F7
Pye Green Staffs 62 C3
Pyecombe W Sus 17 C6
Pyewipe NE Lincs 91 C6
Pyle = Y Pîl Bridgend 34 F2
Pyle IoW 15 G5
Pylle Som 23 F8
Pymoor Cambs 66 F4
Pyrford Sur 27 D8
Pyrton Oxon 39 E6
Pytchley Northants 53 B6
Pyworthy Devon 8 D5

Q

Quabbs Shrops 60 F2
Quadring Lincs 78 F5
Quainton Bucks 39 C7
Quarley Hants 25 E7
Quarndon Derbys 76 E3
Quarrier's Homes Invclyd 118 C3
Quarrington Lincs 78 E3
Quarrington Hill Durham 111 F6
Quarry Bank W Mid 62 F3
Quarryford E Loth 121 C8
Quarryhill Highld 151 C10
Quarrywood Moray 152 B1
Quarter S Lanark 119 D7
Quatford Shrops 61 E7
Quatt Shrops 61 F7
Quebec Durham 110 E4
Quedgeley Glos 37 C5
Queen Adelaide Cambs 67 F5
Queen Camel Som 12 B3
Queen Charlton Bath 23 C8
Queen Dart Devon 10 C3
Queen Oak Dorset 24 F2
Queen Street Kent 29 E7
Queen Street Wilts 37 F7
Queenborough Kent 30 B3
Queenhill Worcs 50 F3
Queen's Head Shrops 60 B3
Queen's Park Bedford 53 E8
Queen's Park Northants 53 C5
Queensbury W Yorks 94 F4
Queensferry Edin 120 B4
Queensferry Flint 73 C7
Queenstown Blackpool 92 F3
Queenzieburn N Lanark 119 B6
Quemerford Wilts 24 C5
Quendale Shetland 160 M5
Quendon Essex 55 F6
Queniborough Leics 64 C3
Quenington Glos 37 D8
Quernmore Lancs 92 D5
Quethiock Corn 5 C8
Quholm Orkney 159 G3
Quicks Green W Berks 26 B3
Quidenham Norf 68 F3
Quidhampton Hants 26 D3
Quidhampton Wilts 25 F6
Quilquox Aberds 153 E9
Quina Brook Shrops 74 F2
Quindry Orkney 159 J5
Quinton Northants 53 D5
Quinton W Mid 62 F3
Quintrell Downs Corn 4 C3
Quixhill Staffs 75 E8
Quoditch Devon 9 E6
Quoig Perth 127 B7
Quorndon Leics 64 C2
Quothquan S Lanark 120 F2
Quoyloo Orkney 159 F3
Quoyness Orkney 159 H3
Quoys Shetland 160 B8
Quoys Shetland 160 G6

R

Raasay Ho. Highld 149 E10
Rabbit's Cross Kent 29 E8
Raby Mers 73 B7
Rachan Mill Borders 120 F4
Rachub Gwyn 83 E6
Rackenford Devon 10 C3
Rackham W Sus 16 C4
Rackheath Norf 69 C5
Racks Dumfries 107 B7
Rackwick Orkney 159 D5
Rackwick Orkney 159 J3
Radbourne Derbys 76 F2
Radcliffe Gtr Man 87 D5
Radcliffe Northumb 117 D8
Radcliffe on Trent Notts 77 F6
Radclive Bucks 52 F4
Radcot Oxon 38 E2
Raddery Highld 151 F10
Radernie Fife 129 D6
Radford Semele Warks 51 C8
Radipole Dorset 12 F4
Radlett Herts 40 E4
Radley Oxon 39 E5
Radmanthwaite Notts 76 C5
Radmoor Shrops 61 B6
Radmore Green Ches E 74 D2
Radnage Bucks 39 E7
Radstock Bath 23 D8
Radstone Northants 52 E3
Radway Warks 51 E8
Radway Green Ches E 74 D4
Radwell Bedford 53 D8
Radwell Herts 54 F3
Radwinter Essex 55 F7
Radyr Cardiff 35 F5
Rafford Moray 151 F13
Ragdale Leics 64 C3
Raglan Mon 35 D8
Ragnall Notts 77 B8
Rahane Argyll 145 E11
Rainford Mers 86 D2
Rainford Junction Mers 86 D2
Rainham London 41 F8
Rainham Medway 30 C2
Rainhill Mers 86 E2
Rainhill Stoops Mers 86 E3
Rainow Ches E 75 B6
Rainton N Yorks 95 B6
Rainworth Notts 77 D5
Raisbeck Cumb 99 D8
Raise Cumb 109 E7
Rait Perth 128 B4
Raithby Lincs 79 C6
Raithby Lincs 91 F7
Rake W Sus 16 B2
Rakewood Gtr Man 87 C7
Ram Carms 46 E4
Ram Lane Kent 30 E3
Ramasaig Highld 148 D6
Rame Corn 3 C6
Rame Corn 6 E2
Rameldry Mill Bank Fife 128 D5
Ramnageo Shetland 160 C8
Rampisham Dorset 12 D3
Rampside Cumb 92 C2
Rampton Cambs 54 C5
Rampton Notts 77 B7
Ramsbottom Gtr Man 87 C5
Ramsbury Wilts 25 B7
Ramscraigs Highld 158 H3
Ramsdean Hants 15 B8
Ramsdell Hants 26 D3
Ramsden Oxon 38 C3
Ramsden Bellhouse Essex 42 E3
Ramsden Heath Essex 42 E3
Ramsey Cambs 66 F2
Ramsey Essex 57 F6
Ramsey IoM 84 C4
Ramsey Forty Foot Cambs 66 F3
Ramsey Heights Cambs 66 F2
Ramsey Island Essex 43 D5
Ramsey Mereside Cambs 66 F2
Ramsey St Mary's Cambs 66 F2
Ramseycleuch Borders 115 C5
Ramsgate Kent 31 C7
Ramsgill N Yorks 94 B4
Ramshorn Staffs 75 E7
Ramsnest Common Sur 27 F7
Ranais W Isles 155 E9
Ranby Lincs 78 B5
Ranby Notts 89 F7
Rand Lincs 78 B4
Randwick Glos 37 D5
Ranfurly Renfs 118 C3
Rangag Highld 158 F3
Rangemore Staffs 63 B5
Rangeworthy S Glos 36 F3
Rankinston E Ayrs 112 C4
Ranmoor S Yorks 88 F4
Ranmore Common Sur 28 D2
Rannerdale Cumb 98 C3
Rannoch Station Perth 131 D8
Ranochan Highld 147 C11
Ranskill Notts 89 F7
Ranton Staffs 62 B2
Ranworth Norf 69 C6
Raploch Stirling 127 E6
Rapness Orkney 159 D6
Rascal Moor E Yorks 96 F4
Rascarrel Dumfries 106 E4
Rashiereive Aberds 141 B8
Raskelf N Yorks 95 B7
Rassau Bl Gwent 35 C5
Rastrick W Yorks 88 B2
Ratagan Highld 136 C2
Ratby Leics 64 D2
Ratcliffe Culey Leics 63 E7
Ratcliffe on Soar Leics 63 B8
Ratcliffe on the Wreake Leics 64 C3
Rathen Aberds 153 B10
Rathillet Fife 129 B5
Rathmell N Yorks 93 D8
Ratho Edin 120 B4
Ratho Station Edin 120 B4
Rathven Moray 152 B4
Ratley Warks 51 E8
Ratlinghope Shrops 60 E4
Rattar Highld 158 C4
Ratten Row Lancs 92 E4
Rattery Devon 6 C5
Rattlesden Suff 56 D3
Rattray Perth 134 E1
Raughton Head Cumb 108 E3
Raunds Northants 53 B7
Ravenfield S Yorks 89 E5
Ravenglass Cumb 98 E2
Raveningham Norf 69 E6
Ravenscar N Yorks 103 D7
Ravenscraig Invclyd 118 B2
Ravensdale IoM 84 C3
Ravensden Bedford 53 D8
Ravenseat N Yorks 100 D3
Ravenshead Notts 77 D5
Ravensmoor Ches E 74 D3
Ravensthorpe Northants 52 B4
Ravensthorpe W Yorks 88 B3
Ravenstone Leics 63 C8
Ravenstone M Keynes 53 D6
Ravenstonedale Cumb 100 D2
Ravenstown Cumb 92 B3
Ravenstruther S Lanark 120 E2
Ravensworth N Yorks 101 D6
Raw N Yorks 103 D7
Rawcliffe E Yorks 89 B7
Rawcliffe York 95 D8
Rawcliffe Bridge E Yorks 89 B7
Rawdon W Yorks 94 F5
Rawmarsh S Yorks 88 E5
Rawreth Essex 42 E3
Rawridge Devon 11 D7
Rawtenstall Lancs 87 B6
Raxton Aberds 153 E8
Raydon Suff 56 F4
Raylees Northumb 117 E5
Rayleigh Essex 42 E4
Rayne Essex 42 B3
Rayners Lane London 40 F4
Raynes Park London 28 C3
Reach Cambs 55 C6
Read Lancs 93 F7
Reading Reading 26 B5
Reading Street Kent 19 B6
Reagill Cumb 99 C8
Rearquhar Highld 151 B10
Rearsby Leics 64 C3
Reaster Highld 158 D4
Reawick Shetland 160 J5
Reay Highld 157 C12
Rechullin Highld 149 C13
Reculver Kent 31 C6
Red Dial Cumb 108 E2
Red Hill Worcs 50 D3
Red Houses Jersey 17
Red Lodge Suff 55 B7
Red Rail Hereford 36 B2
Red Rock Gtr Man 86 D3
Red Roses Carms 32 C3
Red Row Northumb 117 E8
Red Street Staffs 74 D5
Red Wharf Bay Anglesey 82 C5
Redberth Pembs 32 D1
Redbourn Herts 40 C4
Redbourne N Lincs 90 E3
Redbrook Mon 36 C2
Redbrook Wrex 74 E2
Redburn Highld 151 E8
Redburn Highld 151 G12
Redburn Northumb 109 C7
Redcar Redcar 102 B4
Redcastle Angus 135 D6
Redcastle Highld 151 G8
Redcliff Bay N Som 23 B6
Redding Falk 120 B2
Reddingmuirhead Falk 120 B2
Reddish Gtr Man 87 E6
Redditch Worcs 50 C5
Rede Suff 56 D2
Redenhall Norf 69 F5
Redesdale Camp Northumb 116 E4
Redesmouth Northumb 116 F4
Redford Aberds 135 B7
Redford Angus 135 E5
Redford Durham 110 F3
Redfordgreen Borders 115 C6
Redgorton Perth 128 B2
Redgrave Suff 56 B4
Redhill Aberds 141 D6
Redhill Aberds 153 E6
Redhill N Som 23 C7
Redhill Sur 28 D3
Redhouse Argyll 145 G7
Redhouses Argyll 142 B4
Redisham Suff 69 F7
Redland Bristol 23 B7
Redland Orkney 159 F4
Redlingfield Suff 57 B5
Redlynch Som 23 F9
Redlynch Wilts 14 B3
Redmarley D'Abitot Glos 50 F2
Redmarshall Stockton 102 B1
Redmile Leics 77 F7
Redmire N Yorks 101 E5
Redmoor Corn 5 C5
Rednal Shrops 60 B3
Redpath Borders 121 F8
Redpoint Highld 149 B12
Redruth Corn 3 B5
Redvales Gtr Man 87 D6
Redwick Newport 35 F8
Redwick S Glos 36 F2
Redworth Darl 101 B7
Reed Herts 54 F4
Reedham Norf 69 D7
Reedness E Yorks 89 B8
Reeds Beck Lincs 78 C5
Reepham Lincs 78 B3
Reepham Norf 81 E6
Reeth N Yorks 101 E5
Regaby IoM 84 C4
Regoul Highld 151 F11
Reiff Highld 156 H2
Reigate Sur 28 D3
Reighton N Yorks 97 B7
Reighton Gap N Yorks 97 B7
Reinigeadal W Isles 154 G7
Reiss Highld 158 E5
Rejerrah Corn 4 D2
Releath Corn 3 C5
Relubbus Corn 2 C4
Relugas Moray 151 G12
Remenham Wokingham 39 F7
Remenham Hill Wokingham 39 F7
Remony Perth 132 E4
Rempstone Notts 64 B2
Rendcomb Glos 37 D7
Rendham Suff 57 C7
Rendlesham Suff 57 D7
Renfrew Renfs 118 C5
Renhold Bedford 53 D8
Renishaw Derbys 76 B4
Rennington Northumb 117 C8
Renton W Dunb 118 B3
Renwick Cumb 109 E5
Repps Norf 69 C7
Repton Derbys 63 B7
Reraig Highld 149 F13
Rescobie Angus 135 D5
Resipole Highld 147 E10
Resolis Highld 151 E9
Resolven Neath 34 D2
Reston Borders 122 C4
Reswallie Angus 135 D5
Retew Corn 4 D4
Retford Notts 89 F8
Rettendon Essex 42 E3
Rettendon Place Essex 42 E3
Revesby Lincs 79 C5
Revesby Bridge Lincs 79 C6
Rew Street IoW 15 E5
Rewe Devon 10 E4
Reydon Suff 57 B8
Reydon Smear Suff 57 B8
Reymerston Norf 68 D3
Reynalton Pembs 32 D1
Reynoldston Swansea 33 E5
Rezare Corn 5 B8
Rhaeadr Gwy = Rhayader Powys 47 C8
Rhandirmwyn Carms 47 E6
Rhayader = Rhaeadr Gwy Powys 47 C8
Rhedyn Gwyn 70 D3
Rhemore Highld 147 F8
Rhencullen IoM 84 C3
Rhes-y-cae Flint 73 B5
Rhewl Denb 72 C5
Rhewl Denb 73 E5
Rhian Highld 157 H8
Rhicarn Highld 156 G3
Rhiconich Highld 156 D5
Rhicullen Highld 151 D9
Rhidorroch Ho. Highld 150 B4
Rhifail Highld 157 E10
Rhigos Rhondda 34 D3
Rhilochan Highld 157 J10
Rhiroy Highld 150 C4
Rhisga = Risca Caerph 35 E6
Rhiw Gwyn 70 E3
Rhiwabon = Ruabon Wrex 73 E7
Rhiwbina Cardiff 35 F5
Rhiwbryfdir Gwyn 71 C7
Rhiwderin Newport 35 F6
Rhiwlas Gwyn 72 F3
Rhiwlas Gwyn 83 E5
Rhiwlas Powys 73 F5
Rhodes Gtr Man 87 D6
Rhodes Minnis Kent 31 E5
Rhodesia Notts 77 B5
Rhodiad Pembs 44 C2
Rhonehouse or Kelton Hill Dumfries 106 D4
Rhoose = Y Rhws V Glam 22 C2
Rhôs Carms 46 F2
Rhôs Neath 33 D8
Rhos-fawr Gwyn 70 D4
Rhos-goch Powys 48 E3
Rhos-hill Pembs 45 E3
Rhos-on-Sea Conwy 83 C8
Rhos-y-brithdir Powys 59 B8
Rhos-y-garth Ceredig 46 B5
Rhos-y-gwaliau Gwyn 72 F3
Rhos-y-llan Gwyn 70 D3
Rhos-y-Madoc Wrex 73 E7
Rhos-y-meirch Powys 48 C4
Rhosaman Carms 33 C8
Rhosbeirio Anglesey 82 B3
Rhoscefnhir Anglesey 82 D5
Rhoscolyn Anglesey 82 D2
Rhoscrowther Pembs 44 E4
Rhosesmor Flint 73 C6
Rhosgadfan Gwyn 82 F5
Rhosgoch Anglesey 82 C4
Rhoshirwaun Gwyn 70 E2
Rhoslan Gwyn 71 C5
Rhoslefain Gwyn 58 D2
Rhosllanerchrugog Wrex 73 E6
Rhosmaen Carms 33 B7
Rhosmeirch Anglesey 82 D4
Rhosneigr Anglesey 82 D3
Rhosnesni Wrex 73 D7
Rhosrobin Wrex 73 D7
Rhossili Swansea 33 F5
Rhosson Pembs 44 C2
Rhostryfan Gwyn 82 F4
Rhostyllen Wrex 73 E7
Rhosybol Anglesey 82 C4
Rhu Argyll 145 E11
Rhu Argyll 145 G7
Rhuallt Denb 72 B4
Rhuddall Heath Ches W 74 C2
Rhuddlan Ceredig 46 E3
Rhuddlan Denb 72 B4
Rhue Highld 150 B3
Rhulen Powys 48 E3
Rhunahaorine Argyll 143 D8
Rhuthun = Ruthin Denb 72 D5
Rhyd Gwyn 71 C7
Rhyd Powys 59 D6
Rhyd-Ddu Gwyn 83 F5
Rhyd-moel-ddu Powys 48 B2
Rhyd-Rosser Ceredig 46 C4
Rhyd-uchaf Gwyn 72 F3
Rhyd-wen Gwyn 58 C4
Rhyd-y-clafdy Gwyn 70 D4
Rhyd-y-foel Conwy 72 B3
Rhyd-y-fro Neath 33 D8
Rhyd-y-gwin Swansea 33 D7
Rhyd-y-meirch Mon 35 D7
Rhyd-y-meudwy Denb 72 D5
Rhyd-y-pandy Swansea 33 D7
Rhyd-y-sarn Gwyn 71 C7
Rhyd-yr-onen Gwyn 58 D3
Rhydaman = Ammanford Carms 33 C7
Rhydargaeau Carms 33 B5
Rhydcymerau Carms 46 F4
Rhydd Worcs 50 E3
Rhydding Neath 33 E8
Rhydfudr Ceredig 46 C4
Rhydlewis Ceredig 46 E2
Rhydlios Gwyn 70 D2
Rhydlydan Conwy 83 F8
Rhydness Powys 48 E3
Rhydowen Ceredig 46 E3
Rhydspence Hereford 48 E4
Rhydtalog Flint 73 D6
Rhydwyn Anglesey 82 C3
Rhydycroesau Powys 73 F6
Rhydyfelin Ceredig 46 B4
Rhydyfelin Rhondda 34 F4
Rhydymain Gwyn 58 B5
Rhydymwyn Flint 73 C6
Rhyl = Y Rhyl Denb 72 A4
Rhymney = Rhymni Caerph 35 D5
Rhymni = Rhymney Caerph 35 D5
Rhynd Fife 129 B6
Rhynd Perth 128 B3
Rhynie Aberds 140 B3
Rhynie Highld 151 D11
Ribbesford Worcs 50 B2
Ribblehead N Yorks 93 B7
Ribbleton Lancs 93 F5
Ribchester Lancs 93 F6
Ribigill Highld 157 D8
Riby Lincs 91 D5
Riby Cross Roads Lincs 91 D5
Riccall N Yorks 96 F2
Riccarton E Ayrs 118 F4
Richards Castle Hereford 49 C6
Richings Park Bucks 27 B8
Richmond London 28 B2
Richmond N Yorks 101 D6
Rickarton Aberds 141 F7
Rickinghall Suff 56 B4
Rickleton T&W 111 D5
Rickling Essex 55 F5
Rickmansworth Herts 40 E3
Riddings Cumb 108 B4
Riddings Derbys 76 D4
Riddlecombe Devon 9 C8
Riddlesden W Yorks 94 E3
Riddrie Glasgow 119 C6
Ridge Dorset 13 F7
Ridge Hants 14 C4
Ridge Wilts 24 F4
Ridge Green Sur 28 E4
Ridge Lane Warks 63 E6
Ridgebourne Powys 48 C2
Ridgehill N Som 23 C7
Ridgeway Cross Hereford 50 E2
Ridgewell Essex 55 E8
Ridgewood E Sus 17 C8
Ridgmont C Beds 53 F7
Riding Mill Northumb 110 C3
Ridleywood Wrex 73 D8
Ridlington Norf 69 A6
Ridlington Rutland 64 D5
Ridsdale Northumb 116 F5
Riechip Perth 133 E7
Riemore Perth 133 E7
Rienachait Highld 156 F3
Rievaulx N Yorks 102 F3
Rift House Hrtlpl 111 F7
Rigg Dumfries 108 C2
Riggend N Lanark 119 B7
Rigsby Lincs 79 B7
Rigside S Lanark 119 F8
Riley Green Lancs 86 B4
Rileyhill Staffs 62 C5
Rilla Mill Corn 5 B7
Rillington N Yorks 96 B4
Rimington Lancs 93 E8
Rimpton Som 12 B4
Rimswell E Yorks 91 B7
Rinaston Pembs 44 C4
Ringasta Shetland 160 M5
Ringford Dumfries 106 D3
Ringinglow S Yorks 88 F3
Ringland Norf 68 C4
Ringles Cross E Sus 17 B8
Ringmer E Sus 17 C8
Ringmore Devon 6 E4
Ringorm Moray 152 D2
Ring's End Cambs 66 D3
Ringsfield Suff 69 F7
Ringsfield Corner Suff 69 F7
Ringshall Herts 40 C2
Ringshall Suff 56 D4
Ringshall Stocks Suff 56 D4
Ringstead Norf 80 C3
Ringstead Northants 53 B7
Ringwood Hants 14 D2
Ringwould Kent 31 E7
Rinmore Aberds 140 C3
Rinnigill Orkney 159 J4
Rinsey Corn 2 D4
Riof W Isles 154 D6
Ripe E Sus 18 D2
Ripley Derbys 76 D3
Ripley Hants 14 E2
Ripley N Yorks 95 C5
Ripley Sur 27 D8
Riplingham E Yorks 97 F5
Ripon N Yorks 95 B6
Rippingale Lincs 65 B7
Ripple Kent 31 E7
Ripple Worcs 50 F3
Ripponden W Yorks 87 C8
Rireavach Highld 150 B3
Risabus Argyll 142 D4
Risbury Hereford 49 D7
Risby Suff 55 C8
Risca = Rhisga Caerph 35 E6
Rise E Yorks 97 E7
Riseden E Sus 18 B3
Risegate Lincs 66 B2
Riseholme Lincs 78 B2
Riseley Bedford 53 C8
Riseley Wokingham 26 C5
Rishangles Suff 57 C5
Rishton Lancs 93 F7
Rishworth W Yorks 87 C8
Rising Bridge Lancs 87 B5
Risley Derbys 76 F4
Risley Warr 86 E4
Risplith N Yorks 94 C5
Rispond Highld 156 C7
Rivar Wilts 25 C8
Rivenhall End Essex 42 C4
River Bank Cambs 55 C6
Riverhead Kent 29 D6
Rivington Lancs 86 C4
Roa Island Cumb 92 C2
Roachill Devon 10 B3
Road Green Norf 69 E5
Roade Northants 53 D5
Roadhead Cumb 108 B5
Roadmeetings S Lanark 119 E8
Roadside Highld 158 D3
Roadside of Catterline Aberds 135 B8
Roadside of Kinneff Aberds 135 B8
Roadwater Som 22 F2
Roag Highld 149 D7
Roath Cardiff 22 B3
Roberton Borders 115 C7
Roberton S Lanark 114 B2
Robertsbridge E Sus 18 C4
Roberttown W Yorks 88 B2
Robeston Cross Pembs 44 E3
Robeston Wathen Pembs 32 C1
Robin Hood W Yorks 88 B4
Robin Hood's Bay N Yorks 103 D7
Roborough Devon 6 C3
Roborough Devon 9 C7
Roby Mers 86 E2
Roby Mill Lancs 86 D3
Rocester Staffs 75 F8
Roch Pembs 44 C3
Roch Gate Pembs 44 C3
Rochdale Gtr Man 87 C6
Roche Corn 4 C4
Rochester Medway 29 C8
Rochester Northumb 116 E4
Rochford Essex 42 E4
Rock Corn 4 B4
Rock Northumb 117 B8
Rock W Sus 16 C5
Rock Worcs 50 B2
Rock Ferry Mers 85 F4
Rockbeare Devon 10 E5
Rockbourne Hants 14 C2
Rockcliffe Cumb 108 C3
Rockcliffe Dumfries 107 D5
Rockfield Highld 151 C12
Rockfield Mon 36 C1
Rockford Hants 14 D2
Rockhampton S Glos 36 E3
Rockingham Northants 65 E5
Rockland All Saints Norf 68 E2
Rockland St Mary Norf 69 D6
Rockland St Peter Norf 68 E2
Rockley Wilts 25 B6
Rockwell End Bucks 39 F7
Rockwell Green Som 11 B6
Rodborough Glos 37 D5
Rodbourne Swindon 37 F8
Rodbourne Wilts 37 F6
Rodbourne Cheney Swindon 37 F8
Rodd Hereford 48 C5
Roddam Northumb 117 B6
Rodden Dorset 12 F4
Rode Som 24 D3
Rode Heath Ches E 74 D5
Rodeheath Ches E 75 C5
Roden Telford 61 C5
Rodhuish Som 22 F2
Rodington Telford 61 C5
Rodley Glos 36 C4
Rodley W Yorks 94 F5
Rodmarton Glos 37 E6
Rodmell E Sus 17 D8
Rodmersham Kent 30 C3
Rodney Stoke Som 23 D6
Rodsley Derbys 76 E2
Rodway Som 22 F4
Rodwell Dorset 12 G4
Roe Green Herts 54 F4
Roecliffe N Yorks 95 C6
Roehampton London 28 B3
Roesound Shetland 160 G5
Roffey W Sus 28 F2
Rogart Highld 157 J10
Rogart Station Highld 157 J10
Rogate W Sus 16 B2
Rogerstone Newport 35 F6
Roghadal W Isles 154 J5
Rogiet Mon 36 F1
Rogue's Alley Cambs 66 D3
Roke Oxon 39 E6
Roker T&W 111 D7
Rollesby Norf 69 C7
Rolleston Leics 64 D4
Rolleston Notts 77 D7
Rolleston-on-Dove Staffs 63 B6
Rolston E Yorks 97 E8
Rolvenden Kent 18 B5
Rolvenden Layne Kent 19 B5
Romaldkirk Durham 100 B4
Romanby N Yorks 102 E1
Romannobridge Borders 120 E4
Romansleigh Devon 10 B2
Romford London 41 F8
Romiley Gtr Man 87 E7
Romsey Hants 14 B4
Romsey Town Cambs 55 D5
Romsley Shrops 61 F7
Romsley Worcs 50 B4
Ronague IoM 84 E2
Rookhope Durham 110 E2
Rookley IoW 15 F6
Rooks Bridge Som 23 D5
Roos E Yorks 97 F8
Roosebeck Cumb 92 C2
Rootham's Green Bedford 54 D2
Rootpark S Lanark 120 D2
Ropley Hants 26 F4
Ropley Dean Hants 26 F4
Ropsley Lincs 78 F2
Rora Aberds 153 C10
Rorandle Aberds 141 C5
Rorrington Shrops 60 D3
Roscroggan Corn 3 B5
Rose Corn 4 D2
Rose Ash Devon 10 B2
Rose Green W Sus 16 E3
Rose Grove Lancs 93 F8
Rose Hill E Sus 17 C8
Rose Hill Lancs 93 F8
Rose Hill Suff 57 E5
Roseacre Kent 29 D8
Roseacre Lancs 92 F4
Rosebank S Lanark 119 E8
Rosebrough Northumb 117 B7
Rosebush Pembs 32 B1
Rosecare Corn 8 E3
Rosedale Abbey N Yorks 103 E5
Roseden Northumb 117 B6
Rosefield Highld 151 F11

Rosehall Highld 156 J7
Rosehaugh Mains Highld 151 F9
Rosehearty Aberds 153 B9
Rosehill Shrops 74 F3
Roseisle Moray 152 B1
Roselands E Sus 18 E3
Rosemarket Pembs 44 E4
Rosemarkie Highld 151 F10
Rosemary Lane Devon 11 C6
Rosemount Perth 134 E1
Rosenannon Corn 4 C4
Rosewell Midloth 121 C5
Roseworth Stockton 102 B2
Roseworthy Corn 2 C5
Rosgill Cumb 99 C7
Roshven Highld 147 D10
Roskhill Highld 149 D7
Roskill House Highld 151 F9
Rosley Cumb 108 E3
Roslin Midloth 121 C5
Rosliston Derbys 63 C6
Rosneath Argyll 145 E11
Ross Dumfries 106 E3
Ross Northumb 123 F7
Ross Perth 127 B6
Ross-on-Wye Hereford 36 B3
Rossett Wrex 73 D7
Rossett Green N Yorks 95 D6
Rossie Ochill Perth 128 C2
Rossie Priory Perth 134 F2
Rossington S Yorks 89 E7
Rosskeen Highld 151 E9
Rossland Renfs 118 B4
Roster Highld 158 G4
Rostherne Ches E 86 F5
Rosthwaite Cumb 98 C4
Roston Derbys 75 E8
Rosyth Fife 128 F3
Rothbury Northumb 117 D6
Rotherby Leics 64 C3
Rotherfield E Sus 18 C2
Rotherfield Greys Oxon 39 F7
Rotherfield Peppard Oxon 39 F7
Rotherham S Yorks 88 E5
Rothersthorpe Northants 52 D5
Rotherwick Hants 26 D5
Rothes Moray 152 D2
Rothesay Argyll 145 G9
Rothiebrisbane Aberds 153 E7
Rothienorman Aberds 153 E7
Rothiesholm Orkney 159 F7
Rothley Leics 64 C2
Rothley Northumb 117 F6
Rothley Shield East Northumb 117 E6
Rothmaise Aberds 153 E6
Rothwell Lincs 91 E5
Rothwell Northants 64 F5
Rothwell W Yorks 88 B4
Rothwell Haigh W Yorks 88 B4
Rotsea E Yorks 97 D6
Rottal Angus 134 C3
Rotten End Suff 57 C7
Rottingdean Brighton 17 D7
Rottington Cumb 98 C1
Roud IoW 15 F6
Rough Close Staffs 75 F6
Rough Common Kent 30 D5
Rougham Norf 80 E4
Rougham Suff 56 C3
Rougham Green Suff 56 C3
Roughburn Highld 137 F6
Roughlee Lancs 93 E8
Roughley W Mid 62 E5
Roughsike Cumb 108 B5
Roughton Lincs 78 C5
Roughton Norf 81 D8
Roughton Shrops 61 E7
Roughton Moor Lincs 78 C5
Roundhay W Yorks 95 F6
Roundstonefoot Dumfries 114 D4
Roundstreet Common W Sus 16 B4
Roundway Wilts 24 C5
Rous Lench Worcs 50 D5
Rousdon Devon 11 E7
Routenburn N Ayrs 118 C1
Routh E Yorks 97 E6
Row Corn 5 B5
Row Cumb 99 F6
Row Heath Essex 43 C7
Rowanburn Dumfries 108 B4
Rowardennan Stirling 126 E2
Rowde Wilts 24 C4
Rowen Conwy 83 D7
Rowfoot Northumb 109 C6
Rowhedge Essex 43 B6
Rowhook W Sus 28 F2
Rowington Warks 51 C7
Rowland Derbys 76 B2
Rowlands Castle Hants 15 C8
Rowlands Gill T&W 110 D4
Rowledge Sur 27 E6
Rowlestone Hereford 35 B7
Rowley E Yorks 97 F5
Rowley Shrops 60 D3
Rowley Hill W Yorks 88 C2
Rowley Regis W Mid 62 F3
Rowly Sur 27 E8
Rowney Green Worcs 50 B5
Rownhams Hants 14 C4
Rowrah Cumb 98 C2
Rowsham Bucks 39 C8
Rowsley Derbys 76 C2
Rowstock Oxon 38 F4
Rowston Lincs 78 D3
Rowton Ches W 73 C8
Rowton Shrops 60 C3
Rowton Telford 61 C6
Roxburgh Borders 122 F3
Roxby N Lincs 90 C3
Roxby N Yorks 103 C5
Roxton Bedford 54 D2
Roxwell Essex 42 D2
Royal Leamington Spa Warks 51 C8
Royal Oak Darl 101 B7
Royal Oak Lancs 86 D2
Royal Tunbridge Wells Kent 18 B2
Royal Wootton Bassett Wilts 37 F7
Roybridge Highld 137 F5
Roydhouse W Yorks 88 C3
Roydon Essex 41 D7
Roydon Norf 68 F3
Roydon Norf 80 E3
Roydon Hamlet Essex 41 D7
Royston Herts 54 E4
Royston S Yorks 88 C4
Royton Gtr Man 87 D7
Rozel Jersey 17
Ruabon = Rhiwabon Wrex 73 E7
Ruaig Argyll 146 G3
Ruan Lanihorne Corn 3 B7
Ruan Minor Corn 3 E6
Ruarach Highld 136 B2
Ruardean Glos 36 C3
Ruardean Woodside Glos 36 C3
Rubery Worcs 50 B4
Ruckcroft Cumb 108 E5
Ruckhall Hereford 49 F6
Ruckinge Kent 19 B7
Ruckland Lincs 79 B6
Ruckley Shrops 60 D5
Rudbaxton Pembs 44 C4
Rudby N Yorks 102 D2
Ruddington Notts 77 F5
Rudford Glos 36 B4
Rudge Shrops 62 E2
Rudge Som 24 D3
Rudgeway S Glos 36 F3
Rudgwick W Sus 27 F8
Rudhall Hereford 36 B3
Rudheath Ches W 74 B3
Rudley Green Essex 42 D4
Rudry Caerph 35 F5
Rudston E Yorks 97 C6
Rudyard Staffs 75 D6
Rufford Lancs 86 C2
Rufforth York 95 D8
Rugby Warks 52 B3
Rugeley Staffs 62 C4
Ruglen S Ayrs 112 D2
Ruilick Highld 151 G8
Ruishton Som 11 B7
Ruisigearraidh W Isles 154 J4
Ruislip London 40 F3
Ruislip Common London 40 F3
Rumbling Bridge Perth 128 E2
Rumburgh Suff 69 F6
Rumford Corn 4 B3
Rumney Cardiff 22 B4
Runcorn Halton 86 F3
Runcton W Sus 16 D2
Runcton Holme Norf 67 D6
Rundlestone Devon 6 B3
Runfold Sur 27 E6
Runhall Norf 68 D3
Runham Norf 69 C7
Runham Norf 69 D8
Runnington Som 11 B6
Runsell Green Essex 42 D3
Runswick Bay N Yorks 103 C6
Runwell Essex 42 E3
Ruscombe Wokingham 27 B5
Rush Green London 41 F8
Rush-head Aberds 153 D8
Rushall Hereford 49 F8
Rushall Norf 68 F4
Rushall W Mid 62 D4
Rushall Wilts 25 D6
Rushbrooke Suff 56 C2
Rushbury Shrops 60 E5
Rushden Herts 54 F4
Rushden Northants 53 C7
Rushenden Kent 30 B3
Rushford Norf 68 F2
Rushlake Green E Sus 18 D3
Rushmere Suff 69 F7
Rushmere St Andrew Suff 57 E6
Rushmoor Sur 27 E6
Rushock Worcs 50 B3
Rusholme Gtr Man 87 E6
Rushton Ches W 74 C2
Rushton Northants 64 F5
Rushton Shrops 61 D6
Rushton Spencer Staffs 75 C6
Rushwick Worcs 50 D3
Rushyford Durham 101 B7
Ruskie Stirling 126 D5
Ruskington Lincs 78 D3
Rusland Cumb 99 F5
Rusper W Sus 28 F3
Ruspidge Glos 36 C3
Russell's Water Oxon 39 F7
Russel's Green Suff 57 B6
Rusthall Kent 18 B2
Rustington W Sus 16 D4
Ruston N Yorks 103 F7
Ruston Parva E Yorks 97 C6
Ruswarp N Yorks 103 D6
Rutherford Borders 122 F2
Rutherglen S Lanark 119 C6
Ruthernbridge Corn 4 C5
Ruthin = Rhuthun Denb 72 D5
Ruthrieston Aberdeen 141 D8
Ruthven Aberds 152 D5
Ruthven Angus 134 E2
Ruthven Highld 138 E3
Ruthven Highld 151 H11
Ruthven House Angus 134 E3
Ruthvoes Corn 4 C4
Ruthwell Dumfries 107 C7
Ruyton-XI-Towns Shrops 60 B3
Ryal Northumb 110 B3
Ryal Fold Blackburn 86 B4
Ryall Dorset 12 E2
Ryarsh Kent 29 D7
Rydal Cumb 99 D5
Ryde IoW 15 E6
Rye E Sus 19 C6
Rye Foreign E Sus 19 C5
Rye Harbour E Sus 19 D6
Rye Park Herts 41 C6
Rye Street Worcs 50 F2
Ryecroft Gate Staffs 75 C6
Ryehill E Yorks 91 B6
Ryhall Rutland 65 C7
Ryhill W Yorks 88 C4
Ryhope T&W 111 D7
Rylstone N Yorks 94 D2
Ryme Intrinseca Dorset 12 C3
Ryther N Yorks 95 F8
Ryton Glos 50 F2
Ryton N Yorks 96 B3
Ryton Shrops 61 D7
Ryton T&W 110 C4
Ryton-on-Dunsmore Warks 51 B8

S

Sabden Lancs 93 F7
Sacombe Herts 41 C6
Sacriston Durham 110 E5
Sadberge Darl 101 C8
Saddell Argyll 143 E8
Saddington Leics 64 E3
Saddle Bow Norf 67 C6
Saddlescombe W Sus 17 C6
Sadgill Cumb 99 D6
Saffron Walden Essex 55 F6
Sageston Pembs 32 D1
Saham Hills Norf 68 D2
Saham Toney Norf 68 D2
Saighdinis W Isles 148 B3
Saighton Ches W 73 C8
St Abbs Borders 122 C5
St Abb's Haven Borders 122 C5
St Agnes Corn 4 D2
St Agnes Scilly 2 F3
St Albans Herts 40 D4
St Allen Corn 4 D3
St Andrews Fife 129 C7
St Andrew's Major V Glam 22 B3
St Anne Ald 16
St Annes Lancs 85 B4
St Ann's Dumfries 114 E3
St Ann's Chapel Corn 6 B2
St Ann's Chapel Devon 6 E4
St Anthony-in-Meneage Corn 3 D6
St Anthony's Hill E Sus 18 E3
St Arvans Mon 36 E2
St Asaph = Llanelwy Denb 72 B4
St Athan V Glam 22 C2
St Aubin Jersey 17
St Austell Corn 4 D5
St Bees Cumb 98 C1
St Blazey Corn 5 D5
St Boswells Borders 121 F8
St Brelade Jersey 17
St Breock Corn 4 B4
St Breward Corn 5 B5
St Briavels Glos 36 D2
St Bride's Pembs 44 D3
St Brides Major V Glam 21 B7
St Bride's Netherwent Mon 35 F8
St Brides super Ely V Glam 22 B2
St Brides Wentlooge Newport 35 F6
St Budeaux Plym 6 D2
St Buryan Corn 2 D3
St Catherine Bath 24 B2
St Catherine's Argyll 125 E7
St Clears = Sanclêr Carms 32 C3
St Cleer Corn 5 C7
St Clement Corn 3 B7
St Clements Jersey 17
St Clether Corn 8 F4
St Colmac Argyll 145 G9
St Columb Major Corn 4 C4
St Columb Minor Corn 4 C3
St Columb Road Corn 4 D4
St Combs Aberds 153 B10
St Cross South Elmham Suff 69 F5
St Cyrus Aberds 135 C7
St David's Perth 127 B8
St David's = Tyddewi Pembs 44 C2
St Day Corn 3 B6
St Dennis Corn 4 D4
St Devereux Hereford 49 F6
St Dogmaels Pembs 45 E3
St Dogwells Pembs 44 C4
St Dominick Corn 6 C2
St Donat's V Glam 21 C8
St Edith's Wilts 24 C4
St Endellion Corn 4 B4
St Enoder Corn 4 D3
St Erme Corn 4 D3
St Erney Corn 5 D8
St Erth Corn 2 C4
St Ervan Corn 4 B3
St Eval Corn 4 C3
St Ewe Corn 3 B8
St Fagans Cardiff 22 B3
St Fergus Aberds 153 C10
St Fillans Perth 127 B5
St Florence Pembs 32 D1
St Genny's Corn 8 E3
St George Conwy 72 B3
St George's V Glam 22 B2
St Germans Corn 5 D8
St Giles Lincs 78 B2
St Giles in the Wood Devon 9 C7
St Giles on the Heath Devon 9 E5
St Harmon Powys 47 B8
St Helen Auckland Durham 101 B6
St Helena Warks 63 D6
St Helen's E Sus 18 D5
St Helens IoW 15 F7
St Helens Mers 86 E3
St Helier Jersey 17
St Helier London 28 C3
St Hilary Corn 2 C4
St Hilary V Glam 22 B2
Saint Hill W Sus 28 F4
St Illtyd Bl Gwent 35 D6
St Ippollytts Herts 40 B4
St Ishmael's Pembs 44 E3
St Issey Corn 4 B4
St Ive Corn 5 C8
St Ives Cambs 54 B4
St Ives Corn 2 B4
St Ives Dorset 14 D2
St James South Elmham Suff 69 F6
St Jidgey Corn 4 C4
St John Corn 6 D2
St John's IoM 84 D2
St John's Jersey 17
St John's Sur 27 D7
St John's Worcs 50 D3
St John's Chapel Durham 109 F8
St John's Fen End Norf 66 C5
St John's Highway Norf 66 C5
St John's Town of Dalry Dumfries 113 F6
St Judes IoM 84 C3
St Just Corn 2 C2
St Just in Roseland Corn 3 C7
St Katherine's Aberds 153 E7
St Keverne Corn 3 D6
St Kew Corn 4 B5
St Kew Highway Corn 4 B5
St Keyne Corn 5 C7
St Lawrence Corn 4 C5
St Lawrence Essex 43 D5
St Lawrence IoW 15 G6
St Leonard's Bucks 40 D2
St Leonards Dorset 14 D2
St Leonards E Sus 18 E4
Saint Leonards S Lanark 119 D6
St Levan Corn 2 D2
St Lythans V Glam 22 B3
St Mabyn Corn 4 B5
St Madoes Perth 128 B3
St Margaret's Hereford 49 F5
St Margarets Herts 41 C6
St Margaret's at Cliffe Kent 31 E7
St Margaret's Hope Orkney 159 J5
St Margaret South Elmham Suff 69 F6
St Mark's IoM 84 E2
St Martin Corn 5 D7
St Martins Corn 3 D6
St Martin's Jersey 17
St Martins Perth 134 F1
St Martin's Shrops 73 F7
St Mary Bourne Hants 26 D2
St Mary Church V Glam 22 B2
St Mary Cray London 29 C5
St Mary Hill V Glam 21 B8
St Mary Hoo Medway 30 B2
St Mary in the Marsh Kent 19 C7
St Mary's Jersey 17
St Mary's Orkney 159 H5
St Mary's Bay Kent 19 C7
St Maughans Mon 36 C1
St Mawes Corn 3 C7
St Mawgan Corn 4 C3
St Mellion Corn 5 C8
St Mellons Cardiff 35 F6
St Merryn Corn 4 B3
St Mewan Corn 4 D4
St Michael Caerhays Corn 3 B8
St Michael Penkevil Corn 3 B7
St Michael South Elmham Suff 69 F6
St Michael's Kent 19 B5
St Michaels Worcs 49 C7
St Michael's on Wyre Lancs 92 E4
St Minver Corn 4 B4
St Monans Fife 129 D7
St Neot Corn 5 C6
St Neots Cambs 54 C2
St Newlyn East Corn 4 D3
St Nicholas Pembs 44 B3
St Nicholas V Glam 22 B2
St Nicholas at Wade Kent 31 C6
St Ninians Stirling 127 E6
St Osyth Essex 43 C7
St Osyth Heath Essex 43 C7
St Ouens Jersey 17
St Owens Cross Hereford 36 B2
St Paul's Cray London 29 C5
St Paul's Walden Herts 40 B4
St Peter Port Guern 16
St Peter's Jersey 17
St Peter's Kent 31 C7
St Petrox Pembs 44 F4
St Pinnock Corn 5 C7
St Quivox S Ayrs 112 B3
St Ruan Corn 3 E6
St Sampson Guern 16
St Stephen Corn 4 D4
St Stephen's Corn 8 F5
St Stephens Corn 6 D2
St Stephens Herts 40 D4
St Teath Corn 8 F2
St Thomas Devon 10 E4
St Tudy Corn 5 B5
St Twynnells Pembs 44 F4
St Veep Corn 5 D6
St Vigeans Angus 135 E6
St Wenn Corn 4 C4
St Weonards Hereford 36 B1
Saintbury Glos 51 F6
Salcombe Devon 6 F5
Salcombe Regis Devon 11 F6
Salcott Essex 43 C5
Sale Gtr Man 87 E5
Sale Green Worcs 50 D4
Saleby Lincs 79 B7
Salehurst E Sus 18 C4
Salem Carms 33 B7
Salem Ceredig 58 F3
Salen Argyll 147 G8
Salen Highld 147 E9
Salesbury Lancs 93 F6
Salford C Beds 53 F7
Salford Gtr Man 87 E6
Salford Oxon 38 B2
Salford Priors Warks 51 D5
Salfords Sur 28 E3
Salhouse Norf 69 C6
Saline Fife 128 E2
Salisbury Wilts 14 B2
Sallachan Highld 130 C3
Sallachy Highld 150 H2
Sallachy Highld 157 J8
Salle Norf 81 E7
Salmonby Lincs 79 B6
Salmond's Muir Angus 135 F5
Salperton Glos 37 B7
Salph End Bedford 53 D8
Salsburgh N Lanark 119 C8
Salt Staffs 62 B3
Salt End E Yorks 91 B5
Saltaire W Yorks 94 F4
Saltash Corn 6 D2
Saltburn Highld 151 E10
Saltburn-by-the-Sea Redcar 102 B4
Saltby Leics 65 B5
Saltcoats Cumb 98 E2
Saltcoats N Ayrs 118 E2
Saltdean Brighton 17 D7
Salter Lancs 93 C6
Salterforth Lancs 93 E8
Salterswall Ches W 74 C3
Saltfleet Lincs 91 E8
Saltfleetby All Saints Lincs 91 E8
Saltfleetby St Clements Lincs 91 E8
Saltfleetby St Peter Lincs 91 F8
Saltford Bath 23 C8
Salthouse Norf 81 C6
Saltmarshe E Yorks 89 B8
Saltney Flint 73 C7
Salton N Yorks 96 B3
Saltwick Northumb 110 B4
Saltwood Kent 19 B8
Salum Argyll 146 G3
Salvington W Sus 16 D5
Salwarpe Worcs 50 C3
Salwayash Dorset 12 E2
Sambourne Warks 51 C5
Sambrook Telford 61 B7
Samhla W Isles 148 B2
Samlesbury Lancs 93 F5
Samlesbury Bottoms Lancs 86 B4
Sampford Arundel Som 11 C6
Sampford Brett Som 22 E2
Sampford Courtenay Devon 9 D8
Sampford Peverell Devon 10 C5
Sampford Spiney Devon 6 B3
Sampool Bridge Cumb 99 F6
Samuelston E Loth 121 B7
Sanachan Highld 149 D13
Sanaigmore Argyll 142 A3
Sanclêr = St Clears Carms 32 C3
Sancreed Corn 2 D3
Sancton E Yorks 96 F5
Sand Highld 150 B2
Sand Shetland 160 J5
Sand Hole E Yorks 96 F4
Sand Hutton N Yorks 96 D2
Sandaig Highld 149 H12
Sandal Magna W Yorks 88 C4
Sandale Cumb 108 E2
Sandbach Ches E 74 C4
Sandbank Argyll 145 E10
Sandbanks Poole 13 F8
Sandend Aberds 152 B5
Sanderstead London 28 C4
Sandfields Glos 37 B6
Sandford Cumb 100 C2
Sandford Devon 10 D3
Sandford Dorset 13 F7
Sandford IoW 15 F6
Sandford N Som 23 D6
Sandford S Lanark 119 E7
Sandford Shrops 74 F2
Sandford on Thames Oxon 39 D5
Sandford Orcas Dorset 12 B4
Sandford St Martin Oxon 38 B4
Sandfordhill Aberds 153 D11
Sandgate Kent 19 B8
Sandgreen Dumfries 106 D2
Sandhaven Aberds 153 B9
Sandhead Dumfries 104 E4
Sandhills Sur 27 F7
Sandhoe Northumb 110 C2
Sandholme E Yorks 96 F4
Sandholme Lincs 79 F6
Sandhurst Brack 27 C6
Sandhurst Glos 37 B5
Sandhurst Kent 18 C4
Sandhurst Cross Kent 18 C4
Sandhutton N Yorks 102 F1
Sandiacre Derbys 76 F4
Sandilands Lincs 91 F9
Sandilands S Lanark 119 F8
Sandiway Ches W 74 B3
Sandleheath Hants 14 C2
Sandling Kent 29 D8
Sandlow Green Ches E 74 C4
Sandness Shetland 160 H3
Sandon Essex 42 D3
Sandon Herts 54 F4
Sandon Staffs 75 F6
Sandown IoW 15 F6
Sandplace Corn 5 D7
Sandridge Herts 40 C4
Sandridge Wilts 24 C4
Sandringham Norf 67 B6
Sandsend N Yorks 103 C6
Sandside Ho. Highld 157 C12
Sandsound Shetland 160 J5
Sandtoft N Lincs 89 D8
Sandway Kent 30 D2
Sandwell W Mid 62 F4
Sandwich Kent 31 D7
Sandwick Cumb 99 C6
Sandwick Orkney 159 K5
Sandwick Shetland 160 L6
Sandwith Cumb 98 C1
Sandy C Beds 54 E2
Sandy Carms 33 D5
Sandy Bank Lincs 79 D5
Sandy Haven Pembs 44 E3
Sandy Lane Wilts 24 C4
Sandy Lane Wrex 73 E7
Sandycroft Flint 73 C7
Sandyford Dumfries 114 E5
Sandyford Stoke 75 D5
Sandygate IoM 84 C3
Sandyhills Dumfries 107 D5
Sandylands Lancs 92 C4
Sandypark Devon 10 F2
Sandysike Cumb 108 C3
Sangobeg Highld 156 C7
Sangomore Highld 156 C7
Sanna Highld 146 E7
Sanndabhaig W Isles 148 D3
Sanndabhaig W Isles 155 D9
Sannox N Ayrs 143 D11
Sanquhar Dumfries 113 D7
Santon N Lincs 90 C3
Santon Bridge Cumb 98 D3
Santon Downham Suff 67 F8
Sapcote Leics 63 E8
Sapey Common Hereford 50 C2
Sapiston Suff 56 B3
Sapley Cambs 54 B3
Sapperton Glos 37 D6
Sapperton Lincs 78 F3
Saracen's Head Lincs 66 B3
Sarclet Highld 158 F5
Sardis Carms 33 D6
Sarn Bridgend 34 F3
Sarn Powys 60 E2
Sarn Bach Gwyn 70 E4
Sarn Meyllteyrn Gwyn 70 D3
Sarnau Carms 32 C4
Sarnau Ceredig 46 D2
Sarnau Gwyn 72 F3
Sarnau Powys 48 F2
Sarnau Powys 60 C2
Sarnesfield Hereford 49 D5
Saron Carms 33 C7
Saron Carms 46 F2
Saron Denb 72 C4
Saron Gwyn 82 E5
Saron Gwyn 82 F4
Sarratt Herts 40 E3
Sarre Kent 31 C6
Sarsden Oxon 38 B2
Sarsgrum Highld 156 C6
Satley Durham 110 E4
Satron N Yorks 100 E4
Satterleigh Devon 9 B8
Satterthwaite Cumb 99 E5
Satwell Oxon 39 F7
Sauchen Aberds 141 C5
Saucher Perth 134 F1
Sauchie Clack 127 E7
Sauchieburn Aberds 135 C6
Saughall Ches W 73 B7
Saughtree Borders 115 E8
Saul Glos 36 D4
Saundby Notts 89 F8
Saundersfoot Pembs 32 D2
Saunderton Bucks 39 D7
Saunton Devon 20 F3
Sausthorpe Lincs 79 C6
Saval Highld 157 J8
Savary Highld 147 G9
Savile Park W Yorks 87 B8
Sawbridge Warks 52 C3
Sawbridgeworth Herts 41 C7
Sawdon N Yorks 103 F7
Sawley Derbys 76 F4
Sawley Lancs 93 E7
Sawley N Yorks 94 C5
Sawston Cambs 55 E5
Sawtry Cambs 65 F8
Saxby Leics 64 C5
Saxby Lincs 90 F4
Saxby All Saints N Lincs 90 C3
Saxelbye Leics 64 B4
Saxham Street Suff 56 C4
Saxilby Lincs 77 B8
Saxlingham Norf 81 D6
Saxlingham Green Norf 68 E5
Saxlingham Nethergate Norf 68 E5
Saxlingham Thorpe Norf 68 E5
Saxmundham Suff 57 C7
Saxon Street Cambs 55 D7
Saxondale Notts 77 F6
Saxtead Suff 57 C6
Saxtead Green Suff 57 C6
Saxthorpe Norf 81 D7
Saxton N Yorks 95 F7
Sayers Common W Sus 17 C6
Scackleton N Yorks 96 B2
Scadabhagh W Isles 154 H6
Scaftworth Notts 89 E7
Scagglethorpe N Yorks 96 B4
Scaitcliffe Lancs 87 B5
Scalasaig Argyll 144 D2
Scalby E Yorks 90 B2
Scalby N Yorks 103 E8
Scaldwell Northants 53 B5
Scale Houses Cumb 109 E5
Scaleby Cumb 108 C4
Scaleby Hill Cumb 108 C4
Scales Cumb 92 B2
Scales Cumb 99 B5
Scales Lancs 92 F4
Scalford Leics 64 B4
Scaling Redcar 103 C5
Scallastle Argyll 124 B2
Scalloway Shetland 160 K6
Scalpay W Isles 154 H7
Scalpay Ho. Highld 149 F11
Scalpsie Argyll 145 H9
Scamadale Highld 147 B10
Scamblesby Lincs 79 B5
Scamodale Highld 130 B2
Scampston N Yorks 96 B4
Scampton Lincs 78 B2
Scapa Orkney 159 H5
Scapegoat Hill W Yorks 87 C8
Scar Orkney 159 D7
Scarborough N Yorks 103 F8
Scarcliffe Derbys 76 C4
Scarcroft W Yorks 95 E6
Scarcroft Hill W Yorks 95 E6
Scardroy Highld 150 F5
Scarff Shetland 160 E4
Scarfskerry Highld 158 C4
Scargill Durham 101 C5
Scarinish Argyll 146 G3
Scarisbrick Lancs 85 C4
Scarning Norf 68 C2
Scarrington Notts 77 E7
Scartho NE Lincs 91 D6
Scarwell Orkney 159 F3
Scatness Shetland 160 M5
Scatraig Highld 151 H10
Scawby N Lincs 90 D3
Scawsby S Yorks 89 D6
Scawton N Yorks 102 F3
Scayne's Hill W Sus 17 B7
Scethrog Powys 35 B5
Scholar Green Ches E 74 D5
Scholes W Yorks 88 B2
Scholes W Yorks 88 D2
Scholes W Yorks 95 F6
School Green Ches W 74 C3
Scleddau Pembs 44 B4
Sco Ruston Norf 81 E8
Scofton Notts 89 F7
Scole Norf 56 B5
Scolpaig W Isles 148 A2
Scone Perth 128 B3
Sconser Highld 149 E10
Scoonie Fife 129 D5
Scoor Argyll 146 K7
Scopwick Lincs 78 D3
Scoraig Highld 150 B3
Scorborough E Yorks 97 E6
Scorrier Corn 3 B6
Scorton Lancs 92 E5
Scorton N Yorks 101 D7
Scotbheinn W Isles 148 C3
Scotby Cumb 108 D4
Scotch Corner N Yorks 101 D7
Scotforth Lancs 92 D4
Scothern Lincs 78 B3
Scotland Gate Northumb 117 F8
Scotlandwell Perth 128 D3
Scotsburn Highld 151 D10
Scotscalder Station Highld 158 E2
Scotscraig Fife 129 B6
Scots' Gap Northumb 117 F6
Scotston Aberds 135 B7
Scotston Perth 133 E6
Scotstoun Glasgow 118 C5
Scotstown Highld 130 C2
Scotswood T&W 110 C4
Scottas Highld 149 H12
Scotter Lincs 90 D2
Scotterthorpe Lincs 90 D2
Scottlethorpe Lincs 65 B7
Scotton Lincs 90 E2
Scotton N Yorks 95 D6
Scotton N Yorks 101 E6
Scottow Norf 81 E8
Scoughall E Loth 129 F8
Scoulag Argyll 145 H10
Scoulton Norf 68 D2
Scourie Highld 156 E4
Scourie More Highld 156 E4
Scousburgh Shetland 160 M5
Scrabster Highld 158 C2
Scrafield Lincs 79 C6
Scrainwood Northumb 117 D5
Scrane End Lincs 79 E6
Scraptoft Leics 64 D3
Scratby Norf 69 C8
Scrayingham N Yorks 96 C3
Scredington Lincs 78 E3
Scremby Lincs 79 C7
Scremerston Northumb 123 E6
Screveton Notts 77 E7
Scrivelsby Lincs 79 C5
Scriven N Yorks 95 D6
Scrooby Notts 89 E7
Scropton Derbys 75 F8
Scrub Hill Lincs 78 D5
Scruton N Yorks 101 E7
Sculcoates Hull 97 F6
Sculthorpe Norf 80 D4
Scunthorpe N Lincs 90 C2
Scurlage Swansea 33 F5
Sea Palling Norf 69 B7
Seaborough Dorset 12 D2
Seacombe Mers 85 E4
Seacroft Lincs 79 C8
Seacroft W Yorks 95 F6
Seadyke Lincs 79 F6
Seafield S Ayrs 112 B3
Seafield W Loth 120 C3
Seaford E Sus 17 E8
Seaforth Mers 85 E4
Seagrave Leics 64 C3
Seaham Durham 111 E7
Seahouses Northumb 123 F8
Seal Kent 29 D6
Sealand Flint 73 C7
Seale Sur 27 E6
Seamer N Yorks 102 C2
Seamer N Yorks 103 F8
Seamill N Ayrs 118 E2
Searby Lincs 90 D4
Seasalter Kent 30 C4
Seascale Cumb 98 D2
Seathorne Lincs 79 C8
Seathwaite Cumb 98 C4
Seathwaite Cumb 98 E4
Seatoller Cumb 98 C4
Seaton Corn 5 D8
Seaton Cumb 107 F7
Seaton Devon 11 F7
Seaton Durham 111 D6
Seaton E Yorks 97 E7
Seaton Northumb 111 B6
Seaton Rutland 65 E6
Seaton Burn T&W 110 B5
Seaton Carew Hrtlpl 102 B3
Seaton Delaval Northumb 111 B6
Seaton Ross E Yorks 96 E3
Seaton Sluice Northumb 111 B6
Seatown Aberds 152 B5
Seatown Dorset 12 E2
Seave Green N Yorks 102 D3
Seaview IoW 15 E7
Seaville Cumb 107 D8
Seavington St Mary Som 12 C2
Seavington St Michael Som 12 C2
Sebergham Cumb 108 E3
Seckington Warks 63 D6
Second Coast Highld 150 B2
Sedbergh Cumb 100 E1
Sedbury Glos 36 E2
Sedbusk N Yorks 100 E3
Sedgeberrow Worcs 50 F5
Sedgebrook Lincs 77 F8
Sedgefield Durham 102 B1
Sedgeford Norf 80 D3
Sedgehill Wilts 13 B6
Sedgley W Mid 62 E3
Sedgwick Cumb 99 F7
Sedlescombe E Sus 18 D4
Sedlescombe Street E Sus 18 D4
Seend Wilts 24 C4
Seend Cleeve Wilts 24 C4
Seer Green Bucks 40 E2
Seething Norf 69 E6
Sefton Mers 85 D4
Seghill Northumb 111 B5
Seifton Shrops 60 F4
Seighford Staffs 62 B2
Seilebost W Isles 154 H5
Seion Gwyn 82 E5
Seisdon Staffs 62 E2
Seisiadar W Isles 155 D10
Selattyn Shrops 73 F6
Selborne Hants 26 F5
Selby N Yorks 96 F2
Selham W Sus 16 B3
Selhurst London 28 C4
Selkirk Borders 115 B7
Sellack Hereford 36 B2
Sellafirth Shetland 160 D7
Sellibister Orkney 159 D8
Sellindge Kent 19 B7
Sellindge Lees Kent 19 B8
Selling Kent 30 D4
Sells Green Wilts 24 C4
Selly Oak W Mid 62 F4
Selmeston E Sus 18 E2
Selsdon London 28 C4
Selsey W Sus 16 E2
Selsfield Common W Sus 28 F4
Selsted Kent 31 E6
Selston Notts 76 D4
Selworthy Som 21 E8
Semblister Shetland 160 H5
Semer Suff 56 E3
Semington Wilts 24 C3
Semley Wilts 13 B6
Send Sur 27 D8
Send Marsh Sur 27 D8
Senghenydd Caerph 35 E5
Sennen Corn 2 D2
Sennen Cove Corn 2 D2
Sennybridge = Pont Senni Powys 34 B3
Serlby Notts 89 F7
Sessay N Yorks 95 B7
Setchey Norf 67 C6
Setley Hants 14 D4
Setter Shetland 160 E6
Setter Shetland 160 H5
Setter Shetland 160 J7
Settiscarth Orkney 159 G4
Settle N Yorks 93 C8
Settrington N Yorks 96 B4
Seven Kings London 41 F7
Seven Sisters Neath 34 D2
Sevenhampton Glos 37 B7
Sevenoaks Kent 29 D6
Sevenoaks Weald Kent 29 D6
Severn Beach S Glos 36 F2
Severn Stoke Worcs 50 E3
Severnhampton Swindon 38 E2
Sevington Kent 30 E4
Sewards End Essex 55 F6
Sewardstone Essex 41 E6
Sewardstonebury Essex 41 E6
Sewerby E Yorks 97 C7
Seworgan Corn 3 C6
Sewstern Leics 65 B5
Sezincote Glos 51 F6
Sgarasta Mhor W Isles 154 H5
Sgiogarstaigh W Isles 155 A10
Shabbington Bucks 39 D6
Shackerstone Leics 63 D7
Shackleford Sur 27 E7
Shade W Yorks 87 B7
Shadforth Durham 111 E6
Shadingfield Suff 69 F7
Shadoxhurst Kent 19 B6
Shadsworth Blackburn 86 B5
Shadwell Norf 68 F2
Shadwell W Yorks 95 F6
Shaftesbury Dorset 13 B6
Shafton S Yorks 88 C4
Shalbourne Wilts 25 C8
Shalcombe IoW 14 F4
Shalden Hants 26 E4
Shaldon Devon 7 B7
Shalfleet IoW 14 F5
Shalford Essex 42 B3
Shalford Sur 27 E8
Shalford Green Essex 42 B3
Shallowford Devon 21 E6
Shalmsford Street Kent 30 D4
Shalstone Bucks 52 F4
Shamley Green Sur 27 E8
Shandon Argyll 145 E11
Shandwick Highld 151 D11
Shangton Leics 64 E4
Shankhouse Northumb 111 B5
Shanklin IoW 15 F6
Shanquhar Aberds 152 E5
Shanzie Perth 134 D2
Shap Cumb 99 C7
Shapwick Dorset 13 D7
Shapwick Som 23 F6
Shardlow Derbys 76 F4
Shareshill Staffs 62 D3
Sharlston W Yorks 88 C4
Sharlston Common W Yorks 88 C4
Sharnbrook Bedford 53 D7
Sharnford Leics 63 E8
Sharoe Green Lancs 92 F5
Sharow N Yorks 95 B6
Sharp Street Norf 69 B6
Sharpenhoe C Beds 53 F8
Sharperton Northumb 117 D5
Sharpness Glos 36 D3
Sharpthorne W Sus 28 F4
Sharrington Norf 81 D6
Shatterford Worcs 61 F7
Shaugh Prior Devon 6 C3
Shavington Ches E 74 D4
Shaw Gtr Man 87 D7
Shaw W Berks 26 C2
Shaw Wilts 24 C3
Shaw Green Lancs 86 C3
Shaw Mills N Yorks 95 C5
Shawbury Shrops 61 B5
Shawdon Hall Northumb 117 C6
Shawell Leics 64 F2
Shawford Hants 15 B5
Shawforth Lancs 87 B6
Shawhead Dumfries 107 B5
Shawhill Dumfries 108 C2
Shawton S Lanark 119 E6
Shawtonhill S Lanark 119 E6
Shear Cross Wilts 24 E3
Shearington Dumfries 107 C7
Shearsby Leics 64 E3
Shebbear Devon 9 D6
Shebdon Staffs 61 B7
Shebster Highld 157 C13
Sheddens E Renf 119 D5
Shedfield Hants 15 C6
Sheen Staffs 75 C8
Sheepscar W Yorks 95 F6
Sheepscombe Glos 37 C5
Sheepstor Devon 6 C3
Sheepwash Devon 9 D6
Sheepway N Som 23 B6
Sheepy Magna Leics 63 D7
Sheepy Parva Leics 63 D7
Sheering Essex 41 C8
Sheerness Kent 30 B3
Sheet Hants 15 B8
Sheffield S Yorks 88 F4
Sheffield Bottom W Berks 26 C4
Sheffield Green E Sus 17 B8
Shefford C Beds 54 F2
Shefford Woodlands W Berks 25 B8
Sheigra Highld 156 C4
Sheinton Shrops 61 D6
Shelderton Shrops 49 B6
Sheldon Derbys 75 C8
Sheldon Devon 11 D6
Sheldon W Mid 63 F5
Sheldwich Kent 30 D4
Shelf W Yorks 88 B2
Shelfanger Norf 68 F4
Shelfield W Mid 62 D4
Shelfield Warks 51 C6
Shelford Notts 77 E6
Shellacres Northumb 122 E4
Shelley Essex 42 D1
Shelley Suff 56 F4
Shelley W Yorks 88 C3
Shellingford Oxon 38 E3
Shellow Bowells Essex 42 D2
Shelsley Beauchamp Worcs 50 C2
Shelsley Walsh Worcs 50 C2
Shelthorpe Leics 64 C2
Shelton Bedford 53 C8
Shelton Norf 68 E5
Shelton Notts 77 E7
Shelton Shrops 60 C4
Shelton Green Norf 68 E5
Shelve Shrops 60 E3
Shelwick Hereford 49 E7
Shenfield Essex 42 E2
Shenington Oxon 51 E8
Shenley Herts 40 D4
Shenley Brook End M Keynes 53 F6
Shenley Church End M Keynes 53 F6
Shenleybury Herts 40 D4
Shenmore Hereford 49 F5
Shennanton Dumfries 105 C7
Shenstone Staffs 62 D5
Shenstone Worcs 50 B3
Shenton Leics 63 D7
Shenval Highld 137 B7
Shenval Moray 139 B8
Shepeau Stow Lincs 66 C3
Shephall Herts 41 B5
Shepherd's Green Oxon 39 F7
Shepherd's Port Norf 80 D2
Shepherdswell Kent 31 E6
Shepley W Yorks 88 D2
Shepperdine S Glos 36 E3
Shepperton Sur 27 C8
Shepreth Cambs 54 E4
Shepshed Leics 63 C8
Shepton Beauchamp Som 12 C2
Shepton Mallet Som 23 E8
Shepton Montague Som 23 F8
Shepway Kent 29 D8
Sheraton Durham 111 F7
Sherborne Dorset 12 C4
Sherborne Glos 38 C1
Sherborne St John Hants 26 D4
Sherbourne Warks 51 C7
Sherburn Durham 111 E6
Sherburn N Yorks 97 B5
Sherburn Hill Durham 111 E6
Sherburn in Elmet N Yorks 95 F7
Shere Sur 27 E8
Shereford Norf 80 E4
Sherfield English Hants 14 B3
Sherfield on Loddon Hants 26 D4
Sherford Devon 7 E5
Sheriff Hutton N Yorks 96 C2
Sheriffhales Shrops 61 C7
Sheringham Norf 81 C7
Sherington M Keynes 53 E6
Shernal Green Worcs 50 C4
Shernborne Norf 80 D3
Sherrington Wilts 24 F4
Sherston Wilts 37 F5
Sherwood Green Devon 9 B7
Shettleston Glasgow 119 C6
Shevington Gtr Man 86 D3
Shevington Moor Gtr Man 86 C3
Shevington Vale Gtr Man 86 D3
Sheviock Corn 5 D8
Shide IoW 15 F5
Shiel Bridge Highld 136 C2
Shieldaig Highld 149 A13
Shieldaig Highld 149 C13
Shieldhill Dumfries 114 F3
Shieldhill Falk 119 B8
Shieldhill S Lanark 120 E3
Shielfoot Highld 147 E9
Shielhill Angus 134 D4
Shielhill Invclyd 118 B2
Shifford Oxon 38 D3
Shifnal Shrops 61 D7
Shilbottle Northumb 117 D7
Shildon Durham 101 B7
Shillingford Devon 10 B4
Shillingford Oxon 39 E5
Shillingford St George Devon 10 F4
Shillingstone Dorset 13 C6
Shillington C Beds 54 F2
Shillmoor Northumb 116 D4
Shilton Oxon 38 D2
Shilton Warks 63 F8
Shilvington Northumb 117 F7
Shimpling Norf 68 F4
Shimpling Suff 56 D2
Shimpling Street Suff 56 D2
Shincliffe Durham 111 E5
Shiney Row T&W 111 D6
Shinfield Wokingham 26 C5
Shingham Norf 67 D7
Shingle Street Suff 57 E7
Shinner's Bridge Devon 7 C5
Shinness Highld 157 H8
Shipbourne Kent 29 D6
Shipdham Norf 68 D2
Shipham Som 23 D6
Shiphay Torbay 7 C6
Shiplake Oxon 27 B5
Shipley Derbys 76 E4
Shipley Northumb 117 C7
Shipley Shrops 62 E2
Shipley W Sus 16 B5
Shipley W Yorks 94 F4
Shipley Shiels Northumb 116 E3
Shipmeadow Suff 69 F6
Shippea Hill Station Cambs 67 F6
Shippon Oxon 38 E4
Shipston-on-Stour Warks 51 E7
Shipton Glos 37 C7
Shipton N Yorks 95 D8
Shipton Shrops 61 E5
Shipton Bellinger Hants 25 E7
Shipton Gorge Dorset 12 E2
Shipton Green W Sus 16 D2
Shipton Moyne Glos 37 F5
Shipton on Cherwell Oxon 38 C4
Shipton Solers Glos 37 C7
Shipton-under-Wychwood Oxon 38 C2
Shiptonthorpe E Yorks 96 E4
Shirburn Oxon 39 E6
Shirdley Hill Lancs 85 C4
Shirebrook Derbys 76 C5

Shiregreen S Yorks 88 E4
Shirehampton Bristol 23 B7
Shiremoor T&W 111 B6
Shirenewton Mon 36 E1
Shireoaks Notts 89 F6
Shirkoak Kent 19 B6
Shirl Heath Hereford 49 D6
Shirland Derbys 76 D3
Shirley Derbys 76 E2
Shirley London 28 C4
Shirley Soton 14 C5
Shirley W Mid 51 B6
Shirrell Heath Hants 15 C6
Shirwell Devon 20 F4
Shirwell Cross Devon 20 F4
Shiskine N Ayrs 143 F10
Shobdon Hereford 49 C6
Shobnall Staffs 63 B6
Shobrooke Devon 10 D3
Shoby Leics 64 C3
Shocklach Ches W 73 E8
Shoeburyness Southend 43 F5
Sholden Kent 31 D7
Sholing Soton 14 C5
Shoot Hill Shrops 60 C4
Shop Corn 4 B3
Shop Corn 8 C4
Shop Corner Suff 57 F6
Shore Mill Highld 151 E10
Shoreditch London 41 F6
Shoreham Kent 29 C6
Shoreham-By-Sea W Sus 17 D6
Shoresdean Northumb 123 E5
Shoreswood Northumb 122 E5
Shoreton Highld 151 E9
Shorncote Glos 37 E7
Shorne Kent 29 B7
Short Heath W Mid 62 D3
Shortacombe Devon 9 F7
Shortgate E Sus 17 C8
Shortlanesend Corn 3 B7
Shortlees E Ayrs 118 F4
Shortstown Bedford 53 E8
Shorwell IoW 15 F5
Shoscombe Bath 24 D2
Shotatton Shrops 60 B3
Shotesham Norf 69 E5
Shotgate Essex 42 E3
Shotley Suff 57 F6
Shotley Bridge Durham 110 D3
Shotley Gate Suff 57 F6
Shotleyfield Northumb 110 D3
Shottenden Kent 30 D4
Shottermill Sur 27 F6
Shottery Warks 51 D6
Shotteswell Warks 52 E2
Shottisham Suff 57 E7
Shottle Derbys 76 E3
Shottlegate Derbys 76 E3
Shotton Durham 111 F7
Shotton Flint 73 C7
Shotton Northumb 122 F4
Shotton Colliery Durham 111 E6
Shotts N Lanark 119 C8
Shotwick Ches W 73 B7
Shouldham Norf 67 D6
Shouldham Thorpe Norf 67 D6
Shoulton Worcs 50 D3
Shover's Green E Sus 18 B3
Shrawardine Shrops 60 C4
Shrawley Worcs 50 C3
Shrewley Common Warks 51 C7
Shrewsbury Shrops 60 C4
Shrewton Wilts 25 E5
Shripney W Sus 16 D3
Shrivenham Oxon 38 F2
Shropham Norf 68 E2
Shrub End Essex 43 B5
Shucknall Hereford 49 E7
Shudy Camps Cambs 55 E7
Shulishadermor Highld 149 D9
Shurdington Glos 37 C6
Shurlock Row Windsor 27 B6
Shurrery Highld 157 D13
Shurrery Lodge Highld 157 D13
Shurton Som 22 E4
Shustoke Warks 63 E6
Shute Devon 10 D3
Shute Devon 11 E7
Shutford Oxon 51 E8
Shuthonger Glos 50 F3
Shutlanger Northants 52 D5
Shuttington Warks 63 D6
Shuttlewood Derbys 76 B4
Siabost bho Dheas W Isles 154 C7
Siabost bho Thuath W Isles 154 C7
Siadar W Isles 155 B8
Siadar Iarach W Isles 155 B8
Siadar Uarach W Isles 155 B8
Sibbaldbie Dumfries 114 F4
Sibbertoft Northants 64 F3
Sibdon Carwood Shrops 60 F4
Sibford Ferris Oxon 51 F8
Sibford Gower Oxon 51 F8
Sible Hedingham Essex 55 F8
Sibsey Lincs 79 D6
Sibson Cambs 65 E7
Sibson Leics 63 D7
Sibthorpe Notts 77 E7
Sibton Suff 57 C7
Sibton Green Suff 57 B7
Sicklesmere Suff 56 C2
Sicklinghall N Yorks 95 E6
Sid Devon 11 F6
Sidbury Devon 11 E6
Sidbury Shrops 61 F6
Sidcot N Som 23 D6
Sidcup London 29 B5
Siddick Cumb 107 F7
Siddington Ches E 74 B5
Siddington Glos 37 E7
Sidemoor Worcs 50 B4
Sidestrand Norf 81 D8
Sidford Devon 11 E6
Sidlesham W Sus 16 E2
Sidley E Sus 18 E4
Sidlow Sur 28 E3
Sidmouth Devon 11 F6
Sigford Devon 7 B5
Sigglesthorne E Yorks 97 E7
Sighthill Edin 120 B4
Sigingstone V Glam 21 B8
Signet Oxon 38 C2
Silchester Hants 26 C4
Sildinis W Isles 155 F7
Sileby Leics 64 C2
Silecroft Cumb 98 F3
Silfield Norf 68 E4
Silian Ceredig 46 D4
Silk Willoughby Lincs 78 E3
Silkstone S Yorks 88 D3
Silkstone Common S Yorks 88 D3
Silloth Cumb 107 D8
Sills Northumb 116 D4
Sillyearn Moray 152 C5
Siloh Carms 47 F6
Silpho N Yorks 103 E7
Silsden W Yorks 94 E3
Silsoe C Beds 53 F8
Silver End Essex 42 C4
Silverburn Midloth 120 C5
Silverdale Lancs 92 B4
Silverdale Staffs 74 E5
Silvergate Norf 81 E7
Silverhill E Sus 18 D4
Silverley's Green Suff 57 B6
Silverstone Northants 52 E4
Silverton Devon 10 D4
Silvington Shrops 49 B8
Silwick Shetland 160 J4
Simmondley Derbys 87 E8
Simonburn Northumb 109 B8
Simonsbath Som 21 F6
Simonstone Lancs 93 F7
Simprim Borders 122 E4
Simpson M Keynes 53 F6
Simpson Cross Pembs 44 D3
Sinclair's Hill Borders 122 D4
Sinclairston E Ayrs 112 C4
Sinderby N Yorks 101 F8
Sinderhope Northumb 109 D8
Sindlesham Wokingham 27 C5
Singdean Borders 115 D8
Singleborough Bucks 53 F5
Singleton Lancs 92 F3
Singleton W Sus 16 C2
Singlewell Kent 29 B7
Sinkhurst Green Kent 30 E2
Sinnahard Aberds 140 C3
Sinnington N Yorks 103 F5
Sinton Green Worcs 50 C3
Sipson London 27 B8
Sirhowy Bl Gwent 35 C5
Sisland Norf 69 E6
Sissinghurst Kent 18 B4
Sisterpath Borders 122 E3
Siston S Glos 23 B8
Sithney Corn 2 D5
Sittingbourne Kent 30 C2
Six Ashes Staffs 61 F7
Six Hills Leics 64 B3
Six Mile Bottom Cambs 55 D6
Sixhills Lincs 91 F5
Sixpenny Handley Dorset 13 C7
Sizewell Suff 57 C8
Skail Highld 157 E10
Skaill Orkney 159 E5
Skaill Orkney 159 G3
Skaill Orkney 159 H6
Skares E Ayrs 113 C5
Skateraw E Loth 122 B3
Skaw Shetland 160 G7
Skeabost Highld 149 D9
Skeabrae Orkney 159 F3
Skeeby N Yorks 101 D7
Skeffington Leics 64 D4
Skeffling E Yorks 91 C7
Skegby Notts 76 C4
Skegness Lincs 79 C8
Skelberry Shetland 160 M5
Skelbo Highld 151 B10
Skelbrooke S Yorks 89 C6
Skeldyke Lincs 79 F6
Skellingthorpe Lincs 78 B2
Skellister Shetland 160 H6
Skellow S Yorks 89 C6
Skelmanthorpe W Yorks 88 C3
Skelmersdale Lancs 86 D2
Skelmonae Aberds 153 E8
Skelmorlie N Ayrs 118 C1
Skelmuir Aberds 153 D9
Skelpick Highld 157 D10
Skelton Cumb 108 F4
Skelton E Yorks 89 B8
Skelton N Yorks 101 D5
Skelton Redcar 102 C4
Skelton York 95 D8
Skelton-on-Ure N Yorks 95 C6
Skelwick Orkney 159 D5
Skelwith Bridge Cumb 99 D5
Skendleby Lincs 79 C7
Skene Ho. Aberds 141 D6
Skenfrith Mon 36 B1
Skerne E Yorks 97 D6
Skeroblingarry Argyll 143 F8
Skerray Highld 157 C9
Skerton Lancs 92 C4
Sketchley Leics 63 E8
Sketty Swansea 33 E7
Skewen Neath 33 E8
Skewsby N Yorks 96 B2
Skeyton Norf 81 E8
Skiag Bridge Highld 156 G5
Skibo Castle Highld 151 C10
Skidbrooke Lincs 91 E8
Skidbrooke North End Lincs 91 E8
Skidby E Yorks 97 F6
Skilgate Som 10 B4
Skillington Lincs 65 B5
Skinburness Cumb 107 D8
Skinflats Falk 127 F8
Skinidin Highld 148 D7
Skinnet Highld 157 C8
Skinningrove Redcar 103 B5
Skipness Argyll 145 H7
Skippool Lancs 92 E3
Skipsea E Yorks 97 D7
Skipsea Brough E Yorks 97 D7
Skipton N Yorks 94 D2
Skipton-on-Swale N Yorks 95 B6
Skipwith N Yorks 96 F2
Skirbeck Lincs 79 E6
Skirbeck Quarter Lincs 79 E6
Skirlaugh E Yorks 97 F7
Skirling Borders 120 F3
Skirmett Bucks 39 F7
Skirpenbeck E Yorks 96 D3
Skirwith Cumb 109 F6
Skirza Highld 158 D5
Skulamus Highld 149 F11
Skullomie Highld 157 C9
Skyborry Green Shrops 48 B4
Skye of Curr Highld 139 B5
Skyreholme N Yorks 94 C3
Slackhall Derbys 87 F8
Slackhead Moray 152 B4
Slad Glos 37 D5
Slade Devon 20 E4
Slade Pembs 44 D4
Slade Green London 29 B6
Slaggyford Northumb 109 D6
Slaidburn Lancs 93 D7
Slaithwaite W Yorks 87 C8
Slaley Northumb 110 D2
Slamannan Falk 119 B8
Slapton Bucks 40 B2
Slapton Devon 7 E6
Slapton Northants 52 E4
Slatepit Dale Derbys 76 C3
Slattocks Gtr Man 87 D6
Slaugham W Sus 17 B6
Slaughterford Wilts 24 B3
Slawston Leics 64 E4
Sleaford Hants 27 F6
Sleaford Lincs 78 E3
Sleagill Cumb 99 C7
Sleapford Telford 61 C6
Sledge Green Worcs 50 F3
Sledmere E Yorks 96 C5
Sleightholme Durham 100 C4
Sleights N Yorks 103 D6
Slepe Dorset 13 E7
Slickly Highld 158 D4
Sliddery N Ayrs 143 F10
Sligachan Hotel Highld 149 F9
Slimbridge Glos 36 D4
Slindon Staffs 74 F5
Slindon W Sus 16 D3
Slinfold W Sus 28 F2
Sling Gwyn 83 E6
Slingsby N Yorks 96 B2
Slioch Aberds 152 E5
Slip End C Beds 40 C3
Slip End Herts 54 F3
Slipton Northants 53 B7
Slitting Mill Staffs 62 C4
Slochd Highld 138 B4
Slockavullin Argyll 124 F4
Sloley Norf 81 E8
Sloothby Lincs 79 B7
Slough Slough 27 B7
Slough Green W Sus 17 B6
Sluggan Highld 138 B4
Slumbay Highld 149 E13
Slyfield Sur 27 D7
Slyne Lancs 92 C4
Smailholm Borders 122 F2
Small Dole W Sus 17 C6
Small Hythe Kent 19 B5
Smallbridge Gtr Man 87 C7
Smallburgh Norf 69 B6
Smallburn Aberds 153 D10
Smallburn E Ayrs 113 B6
Smalley Derbys 76 E4
Smallfield Sur 28 E4
Smallridge Devon 11 D8
Smannell Hants 25 E8
Smardale Cumb 100 D2
Smarden Kent 30 E2
Smarden Bell Kent 30 E2
Smeatharpe Devon 11 C6
Smeeth Kent 19 B7
Smeeton Westerby Leics 64 E3
Smercleit W Isles 148 G2
Smerral Highld 158 G3
Smethwick W Mid 62 F4
Smirisary Highld 147 D9
Smisby Derbys 63 C7
Smith Green Lancs 92 D4
Smithfield Cumb 108 C4
Smithincott Devon 11 C5
Smith's Green Essex 42 B1
Smithstown Highld 149 A12
Smithton Highld 151 G10
Smithy Green Ches E 74 B4
Smockington Leics 63 F8
Smoogro Orkney 159 H4
Smythe's Green Essex 43 C5
Snaigow House Perth 133 E7
Snailbeach Shrops 60 D3
Snailwell Cambs 55 C7
Snainton N Yorks 103 F7
Snaith E Yorks 89 B7
Snape N Yorks 101 F7
Snape Suff 57 D7
Snape Green Lancs 85 C4
Snarestone Leics 63 D7
Snarford Lincs 90 F4
Snargate Kent 19 C6
Snave Kent 19 C7
Snead Powys 60 E3
Sneath Common Norf 68 F4
Sneaton N Yorks 103 D6
Sneatonthorpe N Yorks 103 D7
Snelland Lincs 90 F4
Snelston Derbys 75 E8
Snettisham Norf 80 D2
Sniseabhal W Isles 148 E2
Snitter Northumb 117 D6
Snitterby Lincs 90 E3
Snitterfield Warks 51 D7
Snitton Shrops 49 B7
Snodhill Hereford 48 E5
Snodland Kent 29 C7
Snowden Hill S Yorks 88 D3
Snowdown Kent 31 D6
Snowshill Glos 51 F5
Snydale W Yorks 88 C5
Soar Anglesey 82 D3
Soar Carms 33 B7
Soar Devon 6 F5
Soar-y-Mynydd Ceredig 47 D6
Soberton Hants 15 C7
Soberton Heath Hants 15 C7
Sockbridge Cumb 99 B7
Sockburn Darl 101 D8
Soham Cambs 55 B6
Soham Cotes Cambs 55 B6
Solas W Isles 148 A3
Soldon Cross Devon 8 C5
Soldridge Hants 26 F4
Sole Street Kent 29 C7
Sole Street Kent 30 E4
Solihull W Mid 51 B6
Sollers Dilwyn Hereford 49 D6
Sollers Hope Hereford 49 F8
Sollom Lancs 86 C2
Solva Pembs 44 C2
Somerby Leics 64 C4
Somerby Lincs 90 D4
Somercotes Derbys 76 D4
Somerford Dorset 14 E2
Somerford Keynes Glos 37 E7
Somerley W Sus 16 E2
Somerleyton Suff 69 E7
Somersal Herbert Derbys 75 F8
Somersby Lincs 79 B6
Somersham Cambs 54 B4
Somersham Suff 56 E4
Somerton Oxon 38 B4
Somerton Som 12 B2
Sompting W Sus 17 D5
Sonning Wokingham 27 B5
Sonning Common Oxon 39 F7
Sonning Eye Oxon 27 B5
Sontley Wrex 73 E7
Sopley Hants 14 E2
Sopwell Herts 40 D4
Sopworth Wilts 37 F5
Sorbie Dumfries 105 E8
Sordale Highld 158 D3
Sorisdale Argyll 146 E5
Sorn E Ayrs 113 B5
Sornhill E Ayrs 118 F5
Sortat Highld 158 D4
Sotby Lincs 78 B5
Sots Hole Lincs 78 C4
Sotterley Suff 69 F7
Soudley Shrops 61 B7
Soughton Flint 73 C6
Soulbury Bucks 40 B1
Soulby Cumb 100 C2
Souldern Oxon 52 F3
Souldrop Bedford 53 C7
Sound Ches E 74 E3
Sound Shetland 160 H5
Sound Shetland 160 J6
Sound Heath Ches E 74 E3
Soundwell S Glos 23 B8
Sourhope Borders 116 B4
Sourin Orkney 159 E5
Sourton Devon 9 E7
Soutergate Cumb 98 F4
South Acre Norf 67 C8
South Allington Devon 7 F5
South Alloa Falk 127 E7
South Ambersham W Sus 16 B3
South Anston S Yorks 89 F6
South Ascot Windsor 27 C7
South Ballachulish Highld 130 D4
South Balloch S Ayrs 112 E3
South Bank Redcar 102 B3
South Barrow Som 12 B4
South Beach Gwyn 70 D4
South Benfleet Essex 42 F3
South Bersted W Sus 16 D3
South Brent Devon 6 C4
South Brewham Som 24 F2
South Broomhill Northumb 117 E8
South Burlingham Norf 69 D6
South Cadbury Som 12 B4
South Cairn Dumfries 104 C3
South Carlton Lincs 78 B2
South Cave E Yorks 96 F5
South Cerney Glos 37 E7
South Chard Som 11 D8
South Charlton Northumb 117 B7
South Cheriton Som 12 B4
South Cliffe E Yorks 96 F4
South Clifton Notts 77 B8
South Cockerington Lincs 91 F7
South Cornelly Bridgend 34 F2
South Cove Suff 69 F7
South Creagan Argyll 130 E3
South Creake Norf 80 D4
South Croxton Leics 64 C3
South Croydon London 28 C4
South Dalton E Yorks 97 E5
South Darenth Kent 29 C6
South Duffield N Yorks 96 F2
South Elkington Lincs 91 F6
South Elmsall W Yorks 89 C5
South End Bucks 40 B1
South End Cumb 92 C2
South End N Lincs 90 B5
South Erradale Highld 149 A12
South Fambridge Essex 42 E4
South Fawley W Berks 38 F3
South Ferriby N Lincs 90 B3
South Garth Shetland 160 D7
South Garvan Highld 130 B3
South Glendale W Isles 148 G2
South Godstone Sur 28 E4
South Gorley Hants 14 C2
South Green Essex 42 E2
South Green Kent 30 C2
South-haa Shetland 160 E5
South Ham Hants 26 D4
South Hanningfield Essex 42 E3
South Harting W Sus 15 C8
South Hatfield Herts 41 D5
South Hayling Hants 15 E8
South Hazelrigg Northumb 123 F6
South Heath Bucks 40 D2
South Heighton E Sus 17 D8
South Hetton Durham 111 E6
South Hiendley W Yorks 88 C4
South Hill Corn 5 B8
South Hinksey Oxon 39 D5
South Hole Devon 8 B4
South Holme N Yorks 96 B2
South Holmwood Sur 28 E2
South Hornchurch London 41 F8
South Hykeham Lincs 78 C2
South Hylton T&W 111 D6
South Kelsey Lincs 90 E4
South Kessock Highld 151 G9
South Killingholme N Lincs 91 C5
South Kilvington N Yorks 102 F2
South Kilworth Leics 64 F3
South Kirkby W Yorks 88 C5
South Kirkton Aberds 141 D6
South Kiscadale N Ayrs 143 F11
South Kyme Lincs 78 E4
South Lancing W Sus 17 D5
South Leigh Oxon 38 D3
South Leverton Notts 89 F8
South Littleton Worcs 51 E5
South Lopham Norf 68 F3
South Luffenham Rutland 65 D6
South Malling E Sus 17 C8
South Marston Swindon 38 F1
South Middleton Northumb 117 B5
South Milford N Yorks 95 F7
South Millbrex Aberds 153 D8
South Milton Devon 6 E5
South Mimms Herts 41 D5
South Molton Devon 10 B2
South Moreton Oxon 39 F5
South Mundham W Sus 16 D2
South Muskham Notts 77 D7
South Newbald E Yorks 96 F5
South Newington Oxon 52 F2
South Newton Wilts 25 F5
South Normanton Derbys 76 D4
South Norwood London 28 C4
South Nutfield Sur 28 E4
South Ockendon Thurrock 42 F1
South Ormsby Lincs 79 B6
South Otterington N Yorks 102 F1
South Owersby Lincs 90 E4
South Oxhey Herts 40 E4
South Perrott Dorset 12 D2
South Petherton Som 12 C2
South Petherwin Corn 8 F5
South Pickenham Norf 67 D8
South Pool Devon 7 E5
South Port Argyll 125 C6
South Radworthy Devon 21 F6
South Rauceby Lincs 78 E3
South Raynham Norf 80 E4
South Reston Lincs 91 F8
South Runcton Norf 67 D6
South Scarle Notts 77 C8
South Shian Argyll 130 E3
South Shields T&W 111 C6
South Shore Blackpool 92 F3
South Somercotes Lincs 91 E8
South Stainley N Yorks 95 C6
South Stainmore Cumb 100 C3
South Stifford Thurrock 29 B7
South Stoke Oxon 39 F5
South Stoke W Sus 16 D4
South Street E Sus 17 C7
South Street Kent 30 C5
South Street Kent 30 D4
South Street London 28 D5
South Tawton Devon 9 E8
South Thoresby Lincs 79 B7
South Tidworth Wilts 25 E7
South Town Hants 26 F4
South View Hants 26 D4
South Walsham Norf 69 C6
South Warnborough Hants 26 E5
South Weald Essex 42 E1
South Weston Oxon 39 E7
South Wheatley Corn 8 E4
South Wheatley Notts 89 F8
South Whiteness Shetland 160 J5
South Widcombe Bath 23 D7
South Wigston Leics 64 E2
South Willingham Lincs 91 F5
South Wingfield Derbys 76 D3
South Witham Lincs 65 C6
South Wonston Hants 26 F2
South Woodham Ferrers Essex 42 E4
South Wootton Norf 67 B6
South Wraxall Wilts 24 C3
South Zeal Devon 9 E8
Southall London 40 F4
Southam Glos 37 B6
Southam Warks 52 C2
Southampton Soton 14 C5
Southborough Kent 29 E6
Southbourne Bmouth 14 E2
Southbourne W Sus 15 D8
Southburgh Norf 68 D2
Southburn E Yorks 97 D5
Southchurch Southend 43 F5
Southcott Wilts 25 D6
Southcourt Bucks 39 C8
Southdean Borders 116 D2
Southdene Mers 86 E2
Southease E Sus 17 D8
Southend Argyll 143 H7
Southend W Berks 26 B3
Southend Wilts 25 B6
Southend-on-Sea Southend 42 F4
Southernden Kent 30 E2
Southerndown V Glam 21 B7
Southerness Dumfries 107 D6
Southery Norf 67 E6
Southfield Northumb 111 B5
Southfleet Kent 29 B7
Southgate Ceredig 46 B4
Southgate London 41 E5
Southgate Norf 81 E7
Southgate Swansea 33 F6
Southill C Beds 54 E2
Southleigh Devon 11 E7
Southminster Essex 43 E5
Southmoor Oxon 38 E3
Southoe Cambs 54 C2
Southolt Suff 57 C5
Southorpe Pboro 65 D7
Southowram W Yorks 88 B2
Southport Mers 85 C4
Southpunds Shetland 160 L6
Southrepps Norf 81 D8
Southrey Lincs 78 C4
Southrop Glos 38 D1
Southrope Hants 26 E4
Southsea Ptsmth 15 E7
Southstoke Bath 24 C2
Southtown Norf 69 D8
Southtown Orkney 159 J5
Southwaite Cumb 108 E4
Southwark London 28 B4
Southwater W Sus 17 B5
Southwater Street W Sus 17 B5
Southway Som 23 E7
Southwell Dorset 12 G4
Southwell Notts 77 D6
Southwick Hants 15 D7
Southwick Northants 65 E7
Southwick T&W 111 D6
Southwick W Sus 17 D6
Southwick Wilts 24 D3
Southwold Suff 57 B9
Southwood Norf 69 D6
Southwood Som 23 F7
Soval Lodge W Isles 155 E8
Sowber Gate N Yorks 102 F1
Sowerby N Yorks 102 F2
Sowerby W Yorks 87 B8
Sowerby Bridge W Yorks 87 B8
Sowerby Row Cumb 108 F3
Sowood W Yorks 87 C8
Sowton Devon 10 E4
Soyal Highld 151 B8
Spa Common Norf 81 D8
Spacey Houses N Yorks 95 D6
Spadeadam Farm Cumb 109 B5
Spalding Lincs 66 B2
Spaldington E Yorks 96 F3
Spaldwick Cambs 54 B2
Spalford Notts 77 C8
Spanby Lincs 78 F3
Sparham Norf 68 C3
Spark Bridge Cumb 99 F5
Sparkford Som 12 B4
Sparkhill W Mid 62 F4
Sparkwell Devon 6 D3
Sparrow Green Norf 68 C2
Sparrowpit Derbys 87 F8
Sparsholt Hants 26 F2
Sparsholt Oxon 38 F3
Spartylea Northumb 109 E8
Spaunton N Yorks 103 F5
Spaxton Som 22 F4
Spean Bridge Highld 136 F5
Spear Hill W Sus 16 C5
Speen Bucks 39 E8
Speen W Berks 26 C2
Speeton N Yorks 97 B7
Speke Mers 86 F2
Speldhurst Kent 29 E6
Spellbrook Herts 41 C7
Spelsbury Oxon 38 B3
Spelter Bridgend 34 E2
Spencers Wood Wokingham 26 C5
Spennithorne N Yorks 101 F6
Spennymoor Durham 111 F5
Spetchley Worcs 50 D3
Spetisbury Dorset 13 D7
Spexhall Suff 69 F6
Spey Bay Moray 152 B3
Speybridge Highld 139 B6
Speyview Moray 152 D2
Spilsby Lincs 79 C7
Spindlestone Northumb 123 F7
Spinkhill Derbys 76 B4
Spinningdale Highld 151 C9
Spirthill Wilts 24 B4
Spital Hill S Yorks 89 E7
Spital in the Street Lincs 90 F3
Spithurst E Sus 17 C8
Spittal Dumfries 105 D7
Spittal E Loth 121 B7
Spittal Highld 158 E3
Spittal Northumb 123 D6
Spittal Pembs 44 C4
Spittal Stirling 126 F4
Spittal of Glenmuick Aberds 140 F2
Spittal of Glenshee Perth 133 B8
Spittalfield Perth 133 E8
Spixworth Norf 68 C5
Splayne's Green E Sus 17 B8
Spofforth N Yorks 95 D6
Spon End W Mid 51 B8
Spon Green Flint 73 C6
Spondon Derby 76 F4
Spooner Row Norf 68 E3
Sporle Norf 67 C8
Spott E Loth 122 B2
Spratton Northants 52 B5
Spreakley Sur 27 E6
Spreyton Devon 9 E8
Spridlington Lincs 90 F4
Spring Vale S Yorks 88 D3
Spring Valley IoM 84 E3
Springburn Glasgow 119 C6
Springfield Dumfries 108 C3
Springfield Essex 42 D3
Springfield Fife 128 C5
Springfield Moray 151 F13
Springfield W Mid 62 F4
Springhill Staffs 62 D3
Springholm Dumfries 106 C5
Springkell Dumfries 108 B2
Springside N Ayrs 118 F3
Springthorpe Lincs 90 F2
Springwell T&W 111 D5
Sproatley E Yorks 97 F7
Sproston Green Ches W 74 C4
Sprotbrough S Yorks 89 D6
Sproughton Suff 56 E5
Sprouston Borders 122 F3
Sprowston Norf 68 C5
Sproxton Leics 65 B5
Sproxton N Yorks 102 F4
Spurstow Ches E 74 D2
Spynie Moray 152 B2
Squires Gate Blackpool 92 F3
Srannda W Isles 154 J5
Sronphadruig Lodge Perth 132 B4
Stableford Shrops 61 E7
Stableford Staffs 74 F5
Stacey Bank S Yorks 88 E3
Stackhouse N Yorks 93 C8
Stackpole Pembs 44 F4
Staddiscombe Plym 6 D3
Staddlethorpe E Yorks 90 B2
Stadhampton Oxon 39 E6
Stadhlaigearraidh W Isles 148 E2
Staffield Cumb 108 E5
Staffin Highld 149 B9
Stafford Staffs 62 B3
Stagsden Bedford 53 E7
Stainburn Cumb 98 B2
Stainburn N Yorks 94 E5
Stainby Lincs 65 B6
Staincross S Yorks 88 C4
Staindrop Durham 101 B6
Staines-upon-Thames Sur 27 B8
Stainfield Lincs 65 B7
Stainfield Lincs 78 B4
Stainforth N Yorks 93 C8
Stainforth S Yorks 89 C7
Staining Lancs 92 F3
Stainland W Yorks 87 C8
Stainsacre N Yorks 103 D7
Stainsby Derbys 76 C4
Stainton Cumb 99 B6
Stainton Cumb 99 F7
Stainton Durham 101 C5
Stainton Mbro 102 C2
Stainton N Yorks 101 E6
Stainton S Yorks 89 E6
Stainton by Langworth Lincs 78 B3
Stainton le Vale Lincs 91 E5
Stainton with Adgarley Cumb 92 B2
Staintondale N Yorks 103 E7
Stair Cumb 98 B4
Stair E Ayrs 112 B4
Stairhaven Dumfries 105 D6
Staithes N Yorks 103 C5
Stake Pool Lancs 92 E4
Stakeford Northumb 117 F8
Stalbridge Dorset 12 C5
Stalbridge Weston Dorset 12 C5
Stalham Norf 69 B6
Stalham Green Norf 69 B6
Stalisfield Green Kent 30 D3
Stalling Busk N Yorks 100 F4
Stallingborough NE Lincs 91 C5
Stalmine Lancs 92 E3
Stalybridge Gtr Man 87 E7
Stambourne Essex 55 F8
Stambourne Green Essex 55 F8
Stamford Lincs 65 D7
Stamford Bridge Ches W 73 C8
Stamford Bridge E Yorks 96 D3
Stamfordham Northumb 110 B3
Stanah Cumb 99 C5
Stanborough Herts 41 C5
Stanbridge C Beds 40 B2
Stanbridge Dorset 13 D8
Stanbrook Worcs 50 E3
Stanbury W Yorks 94 F3
Stand Gtr Man 87 D5
Stand N Lanark 119 C7
Standburn Falk 120 B2
Standeford Staffs 62 D3
Standen Kent 30 E2
Standford Hants 27 F6
Standingstone Cumb 107 F7
Standish Gtr Man 86 C3
Standlake Oxon 38 D3
Standon Hants 14 B5
Standon Herts 41 B6
Standon Staffs 74 F5
Stane N Lanark 119 D8
Stanfield Norf 80 E5
Stanford C Beds 54 E2
Stanford Kent 19 B8
Stanford Bishop Hereford 49 D8
Stanford Bridge Worcs 50 C2
Stanford Dingley W Berks 26 B3
Stanford in the Vale Oxon 38 E3
Stanford-le-Hope Thurrock 42 F2
Stanford on Avon Northants 52 B3
Stanford on Soar Notts 64 B2
Stanford on Teme Worcs 50 C2
Stanford Rivers Essex 41 D8
Stanfree Derbys 76 B4
Stanghow Redcar 102 C4
Stanground Pboro 66 E2
Stanhoe Norf 80 D4
Stanhope Borders 114 B4
Stanhope Durham 110 F2
Stanion Northants 65 F6
Stanley Derbys 76 E4
Stanley Durham 110 D4
Stanley Lancs 86 D2
Stanley Perth 133 F8
Stanley Staffs 75 D6
Stanley W Yorks 88 B4
Stanley Common Derbys 76 E4
Stanley Gate Lancs 86 D2
Stanley Hill Hereford 49 E8
Stanlow Ches W 73 B8
Stanmer Brighton 17 D7
Stanmore Hants 15 B5
Stanmore London 40 E4
Stanmore W Berks 26 B2
Stannergate Dundee 134 F4
Stanningley W Yorks 94 F5
Stannington Northumb 110 B5
Stannington S Yorks 88 F4
Stansbatch Hereford 48 C5
Stansfield Suff 55 D8
Stanstead Suff 56 E2
Stanstead Abbotts Herts 41 C6
Stansted Kent 29 C7
Stansted Airport Essex 42 B1
Stansted Mountfitchet Essex 41 B8
Stanton Glos 51 F5
Stanton Mon 35 B7
Stanton Northumb 117 F7
Stanton Staffs 75 E8
Stanton Suff 56 B3
Stanton by Bridge Derbys 63 B7
Stanton-by-Dale Derbys 76 F4
Stanton Drew Bath 23 C7
Stanton Fitzwarren Swindon 38 E1
Stanton Harcourt Oxon 38 D4
Stanton Hill Notts 76 C4
Stanton in Peak Derbys 76 C2
Stanton Lacy Shrops 49 B6
Stanton Long Shrops 61 E5
Stanton-on-the-Wolds Notts 77 F6
Stanton Prior Bath 23 C8
Stanton St Bernard Wilts 25 C5
Stanton St John Oxon 39 D5
Stanton St Quintin Wilts 24 B4
Stanton Street Suff 56 C3
Stanton under Bardon Leics 63 C8
Stanton upon Hine Heath Shrops 61 B5
Stanton Wick Bath 23 C8
Stanwardine in the Fields Shrops 60 B4
Stanwardine in the Wood Shrops 60 B4
Stanway Essex 43 B5
Stanway Glos 51 F5
Stanway Green Suff 57 B6
Stanwell Sur 27 B8
Stanwell Moor Sur 27 B8
Stanwick Northants 53 B7
Stanwick-St-John N Yorks 101 C6
Stanwix Cumb 108 D4
Stanydale Shetland 160 H4
Staoinebrig W Isles 148 E2
Stape N Yorks 103 E5
Stapehill Dorset 13 D8
Stapeley Ches E 74 E3
Stapenhill Staffs 63 B6
Staple Kent 31 D6
Staple Som 22 E3
Staple Cross E Sus 18 C4
Staple Fitzpaine Som 11 C7
Staplefield W Sus 17 B6
Stapleford Cambs 55 D5
Stapleford Herts 41 C6
Stapleford Leics 64 C5
Stapleford Lincs 77 D8
Stapleford Notts 76 F4
Stapleford Wilts 25 F5
Stapleford Abbotts Essex 41 E8
Stapleford Tawney Essex 41 E8
Staplegrove Som 11 B7
Staplehay Som 11 B7
Staplehurst Kent 29 E8
Staplers IoW 15 F6
Stapleton Bristol 23 B8
Stapleton Cumb 108 B5
Stapleton Hereford 48 C5
Stapleton Leics 63 E8
Stapleton N Yorks 101 C7
Stapleton Shrops 60 D4
Stapleton Som 12 B2
Stapley Som 11 C6
Staploe Bedford 54 C2
Staplow Hereford 49 E8
Star Fife 128 D5
Star Pembs 45 F4
Star Som 23 D6
Stara Orkney 159 F3
Starbeck N Yorks 95 D6
Starbotton N Yorks 94 B2
Starcross Devon 10 F4
Stareton Warks 51 B8
Starkholmes Derbys 76 D3
Starlings Green Essex 55 F5
Starston Norf 68 F5
Startforth Durham 101 C5
Startley Wilts 37 F6
Stathe Som 11 B8
Stathern Leics 77 F7
Station Town Durham 111 F7
Staughton Green Cambs 54 C2
Staughton Highway Cambs 54 C2
Staunton Glos 36 B4
Staunton Glos 36 C2
Staunton in the Vale Notts 77 E8
Staunton on Arrow Hereford 49 C5
Staunton on Wye Hereford 49 E5
Staveley Cumb 99 E6
Staveley Cumb 99 F5
Staveley Derbys 76 B4
Staveley N Yorks 95 C6
Staverton Devon 7 C5
Staverton Glos 37 B5
Staverton Northants 52 C3
Staverton Wilts 24 C3
Staverton Bridge Glos 37 B5
Stawell Som 23 F5
Staxigoe Highld 158 E5
Staxton N Yorks 97 B6
Staylittle Powys 59 E5
Staynall Lancs 92 E3
Staythorpe Notts 77 D7
Stean N Yorks 94 B3
Stearsby N Yorks 96 B2
Steart Som 22 E4
Stebbing Essex 42 B2
Stebbing Green Essex 42 B2
Stedham W Sus 16 B2
Steele Road Borders 115 E8
Steen's Bridge Hereford 49 D7
Steep Hants 15 B8
Steep Marsh Hants 15 B8
Steeple Dorset 13 F7
Steeple Essex 43 D5
Steeple Ashton Wilts 24 D4
Steeple Aston Oxon 38 B4
Steeple Barton Oxon 38 B4
Steeple Bumpstead Essex 55 E7
Steeple Claydon Bucks 39 B6
Steeple Gidding Cambs 65 F8
Steeple Langford Wilts 24 F5
Steeple Morden Cambs 54 E3
Steeton W Yorks 94 E3
Stein Highld 148 C7
Steinmanhill Aberds 153 D7
Stelling Minnis Kent 30 E5
Stemster Highld 158 D3
Stemster Ho. Highld 158 D3
Stenalees Corn 4 D5
Stenhousemuir Falk 127 F7
Stenigot Lincs 91 F6
Stenness Shetland 160 F4
Stenscholl Highld 149 B9
Stenso Orkney 159 F4
Stenson Derbys 63 B7
Stenton E Loth 122 B2
Stenton Fife 128 E4
Stenwith Lincs 77 F8
Stepaside Pembs 32 D2
Stepping Hill Gtr Man 87 F7
Steppingley C Beds 53 F8
Stepps N Lanark 119 C6
Sterndale Moor Derbys 75 C8
Sternfield Suff 57 C7
Sterridge Devon 20 E4
Stert Wilts 24 D5
Stetchworth Cambs 55 D7
Stevenage Herts 41 B5
Stevenston N Ayrs 118 E2
Steventon Hants 26 E3
Steventon Oxon 38 E4
Stevington Bedford 53 D7
Stewartby Bedford 53 E8
Stewarton Argyll 143 G7
Stewarton E Ayrs 118 E4
Stewkley Bucks 40 B1
Stewton Lincs 91 F7
Steyne Cross IoW 15 F7
Steyning W Sus 17 C5
Steynton Pembs 44 E4
Stibb Corn 8 C4
Stibb Cross Devon 9 C6
Stibb Green Wilts 25 C7
Stibbard Norf 81 E5
Stibbington Cambs 65 E7
Stichill Borders 122 F3
Sticker Corn 4 D4
Stickford Lincs 79 D6
Sticklepath Devon 9 E8
Stickney Lincs 79 D6
Stiffkey Norf 81 C5
Stifford's Bridge Hereford 50 E2
Stillingfleet N Yorks 95 E8
Stillington N Yorks 95 C8
Stillington Stockton 102 B1
Stilton Cambs 65 F8
Stinchcombe Glos 36 E4
Stinsford Dorset 12 E5
Stirchley Telford 61 D7
Stirkoke Ho. Highld 158 E5
Stirling Aberds 153 D11
Stirling Stirling 127 E6
Stisted Essex 42 B3
Stithians Corn 3 C6
Stittenham Highld 151 D9
Stivichall W Mid 51 B8
Stixwould Lincs 78 C4
Stoak Ches W 73 B8
Stobieside S Lanark 119 F6
Stobo Borders 120 F4
Stoborough Dorset 13 F7
Stoborough Green Dorset 13 F7
Stobshiel E Loth 121 C7
Stobswood Northumb 117 E8
Stock Essex 42 E2
Stock Green Worcs 50 D4
Stock Wood Worcs 50 D5
Stockbridge Hants 25 F8
Stockbury Kent 30 C2
Stockcross W Berks 26 C2
Stockdalewath Cumb 108 E3
Stockerston Leics 64 E5
Stockheath Hants 15 D8
Stockiemuir Stirling 126 F4
Stocking Pelham Herts 41 B7
Stockingford Warks 63 E7
Stockland Devon 11 D7
Stockland Bristol Som 22 E4
Stockleigh English Devon 10 D3
Stockleigh Pomeroy Devon 10 D3
Stockley Wilts 24 C5
Stocklinch Som 11 C8
Stockport Gtr Man 87 E6
Stocksbridge S Yorks 88 E3
Stocksfield Northumb 110 C3
Stockton Hereford 49 C7
Stockton Norf 69 E6
Stockton Shrops 60 D2
Stockton Shrops 61 E7
Stockton Warks 52 C2
Stockton Wilts 24 F4
Stockton Heath Warr 86 F4
Stockton-on-Tees Stockton 102 C2
Stockton on Teme Worcs 50 C2
Stockton on the Forest York 96 D2
Stodmarsh Kent 31 C6
Stody Norf 81 D6
Stoer Highld 156 G3
Stoford Som 12 C3
Stoford Wilts 25 F5
Stogumber Som 22 F2
Stogursey Som 22 E4
Stoke Devon 8 B4
Stoke Hants 15 D8
Stoke Hants 26 D2
Stoke Medway 30 B2
Stoke Suff 57 E5
Stoke Abbott Dorset 12 D2
Stoke Albany Northants 64 F5
Stoke Ash Suff 56 B5
Stoke Bardolph Notts 77 E6
Stoke Bliss Worcs 49 C8
Stoke Bruerne Northants 52 E5
Stoke by Clare Suff 55 E8
Stoke-by-Nayland Suff 56 F3
Stoke Canon Devon 10 E4
Stoke Charity Hants 26 F2
Stoke Climsland Corn 5 B8
Stoke D'Abernon Sur 28 D2
Stoke Doyle Northants 65 F7
Stoke Dry Rutland 65 E5
Stoke Farthing Wilts 13 B8
Stoke Ferry Norf 67 E7
Stoke Fleming Devon 7 E6
Stoke Gabriel Devon 7 D6
Stoke Gifford S Glos 23 B8
Stoke Golding Leics 63 E7
Stoke Goldington M Keynes 53 E6
Stoke Green Bucks 40 F2
Stoke Hammond Bucks 40 B1
Stoke Heath Shrops 61 B6
Stoke Holy Cross Norf 68 D5
Stoke Lacy Hereford 49 E8
Stoke Lyne Oxon 39 B5
Stoke Mandeville Bucks 39 C8
Stoke Newington London 41 F6
Stoke on Tern Shrops 61 B6
Stoke-on-Trent Stoke 75 E5
Stoke Orchard Glos 37 B6
Stoke Poges Bucks 40 F2
Stoke Prior Hereford 49 D7
Stoke Prior Worcs 50 C4
Stoke Rivers Devon 20 F5
Stoke Rochford Lincs 65 B6
Stoke Row Oxon 39 F6
Stoke St Gregory Som 11 B8
Stoke St Mary Som 11 B7
Stoke St Michael Som 23 E8
Stoke St Milborough Shrops 61 F5

Stoke sub Hamdon Som 12 C2
Stoke Talmage Oxon 39 E6
Stoke Trister Som 12 B5
Stoke Wake Dorset 13 D5
Stokeford Dorset 13 F6
Stokeham Notts 77 E7
Stokeinteignhead Devon 7 B7
Stokenchurch Bucks 39 E7
Stokenham Devon 7 E6
Stokesay Shrops 60 F4
Stokesby Norf 69 C7
Stokesley N Yorks 102 D3
Stolford Som 22 E4
Ston Easton Som 23 D8
Stondon Massey Essex 42 D1
Stone Bucks 39 C7
Stone Glos 36 E3
Stone Kent 19 C6
Stone Kent 29 B6
Stone S Yorks 89 F6
Stone Staffs 75 F6
Stone Worcs 50 B3
Stone Allerton Som 23 D6
Stone Bridge Corner Pboro 66 D2
Stone Chair W Yorks 88 B2
Stone Cross E Sus 18 E3
Stone Cross Kent 31 D7
Stone-edge Batch N Som 23 B6
Stone House Cumb 100 F2
Stone Street Kent 29 D6
Stone Street Suff 56 F3
Stone Street Suff 69 F6
Stonebroom Derbys 76 D4
Stoneferry Hull 97 F7
Stonefield S Lanark 119 D6
Stonegate E Sus 18 C3
Stonegate N Yorks 103 D5
Stonegrave N Yorks 96 B2
Stonehaugh Northumb 109 B7
Stonehaven Aberds 141 F7
Stonehouse Glos 37 D5
Stonehouse Northumb 109 D6
Stonehouse S Lanark 119 E7
Stoneleigh Warks 51 B8
Stonely Cambs 54 C2
Stoner Hill Hants 15 B8
Stone's Green Essex 43 B7
Stonesby Leics 64 B5
Stonesfield Oxon 38 C3
Stonethwaite Cumb 98 C4
Stoney Cross Hants 14 C3
Stoney Middleton Derbys 76 B2
Stoney Stanton Leics 63 E8
Stoney Stoke Som 24 F2
Stoney Stratton Som 23 F8
Stoney Stretton Shrops 60 D3
Stoneybreck Shetland 160 N8
Stoneyburn W Loth 120 C2
Stoneygate Aberds 153 E10
Stoneygate Leicester 64 D3
Stoneyhills Essex 43 E5
Stoneykirk Dumfries 104 D4
Stoneywood Aberdeen 141 C7
Stoneywood Falk 127 F6
Stonganess Shetland 160 C7
Stonham Aspal Suff 56 D5
Stonnall Staffs 62 D4
Stonor Oxon 39 F7
Stonton Wyville Leics 64 E4
Stony Cross Hereford 50 E2
Stony Stratford M Keynes 53 E5
Stonyfield Highld 151 D9
Stoodleigh Devon 10 C4
Stopes S Yorks 88 F3
Stopham W Sus 16 C4
Stopsley Luton 40 B4
Stores Corner Suff 57 E7
Storeton Mers 85 F4
Stornoway W Isles 155 D9
Storridge Hereford 50 E2
Storrington W Sus 16 C4
Storrs Cumb 99 E5
Storth Cumb 99 F6
Storwood E Yorks 96 E3
Stotfield Moray 152 A2
Stotfold C Beds 54 F3
Stottesdon Shrops 61 F6
Stoughton Leics 64 D3
Stoughton Sur 27 D7
Stoughton W Sus 16 C2
Stoul Highld 147 B10
Stoulton Worcs 50 E4
Stour Provost Dorset 13 B5
Stour Row Dorset 13 B6
Stourbridge W Mid 62 F3
Stourpaine Dorset 13 D6
Stourport on Severn Worcs 50 B3
Stourton Staffs 62 F2
Stourton Warks 51 F7
Stourton Wilts 24 F2
Stourton Caundle Dorset 12 C5
Stove Orkney 159 E7
Stove Shetland 160 L6
Stoven Suff 69 F7
Stow Borders 121 E7
Stow Lincs 78 F3
Stow Lincs 90 F2
Stow Bardolph Norf 67 D6
Stow Bedon Norf 68 E2
Stow cum Quy Cambs 55 C6
Stow Longa Cambs 54 B2
Stow Maries Essex 42 E4
Stow-on-the-Wold Glos 38 B1
Stowbridge Norf 67 D6
Stowe Shrops 48 B5
Stowe-by-Chartley Staffs 62 B4
Stowe Green Glos 36 D2
Stowell Som 12 B4
Stowford Devon 9 F6
Stowlangtoft Suff 56 C3
Stowmarket Suff 56 D4
Stowting Kent 30 E5
Stowupland Suff 56 D4
Straad Argyll 145 G9
Strachan Aberds 141 E5
Stradbroke Suff 57 B6
Stradishall Suff 55 D8
Stradsett Norf 67 D6
Stragglethorpe Lincs 78 D2
Straid S Ayrs 112 E1
Straith Dumfries 113 F8
Straiton Edin 121 C5
Straiton S Ayrs 112 D3
Straloch Aberds 141 B7
Straloch Perth 133 C7
Stramshall Staffs 75 F7
Strang IoM 84 E3
Stranraer Dumfries 104 C4
Stratfield Mortimer W Berks 26 C4
Stratfield Saye Hants 26 C4
Stratfield Turgis Hants 26 D4
Stratford London 41 F6
Stratford St Andrew Suff 57 C7
Stratford St Mary Suff 56 F4
Stratford Sub Castle Wilts 25 F6
Stratford Tony Wilts 13 B8
Stratford-upon-Avon Warks 51 D6
Strath Highld 149 A12
Strath Highld 158 E4
Strathan Highld 136 E2
Strathan Highld 156 G3
Strathan Highld 157 C8
Strathaven S Lanark 119 E7
Strathblane Stirling 119 B5
Strathcanaird Highld 156 J4
Strathcarron Highld 150 G2
Strathcoil Argyll 124 B2
Strathdon Aberds 140 C2
Strathellie Aberds 153 B10
Strathkinness Fife 129 C6
Strathmashie House Highld 137 E8
Strathmiglo Fife 128 C4
Strathmore Lodge Highld 158 F3
Strathpeffer Highld 150 F7
Strathrannoch Highld 150 D6
Strathtay Perth 133 D6
Strathvaich Lodge Highld 150 D6
Strathwhillan N Ayrs 143 E11
Strathy Highld 157 C11
Strathyre Stirling 126 C4
Stratton Corn 8 D4
Stratton Dorset 12 E4
Stratton Glos 37 D7
Stratton Audley Oxon 39 B6
Stratton on the Fosse Som 23 D8
Stratton St Margaret Swindon 38 F1
Stratton St Michael Norf 68 E5
Stratton Strawless Norf 81 E8
Stravithie Fife 129 C7
Streat E Sus 17 C7
Streatham London 28 B4
Streatley C Beds 40 B3
Streatley W Berks 39 F5
Street Lancs 92 D5
Street N Yorks 103 D5
Street Som 23 F6
Street Dinas Shrops 73 F7
Street End Kent 30 D5
Street End W Sus 16 E2
Street Gate T&W 110 D5
Street Lydan Wrex 73 F8
Streethay Staffs 62 C5
Streetlam N Yorks 101 E8
Streetly W Mid 62 E4
Streetly End Cambs 55 E7
Strefford Shrops 60 F4
Strelley Notts 76 E5
Strensall York 96 C2
Stretcholt Som 22 E4
Strete Devon 7 E6
Stretford Gtr Man 87 E6
Strethall Essex 55 F5
Stretham Cambs 55 B6
Strettington W Sus 16 D2
Stretton Ches W 73 D8
Stretton Derbys 76 C3
Stretton Rutland 65 C6
Stretton Staffs 62 C2
Stretton Staffs 63 B6
Stretton Warr 86 F4
Stretton Grandison Hereford 49 E8
Stretton-on-Dunsmore Warks 52 B2
Stretton-on-Fosse Warks 51 F7
Stretton Sugwas Hereford 49 E6
Stretton under Fosse Warks 63 F8
Stretton Westwood Shrops 61 E5
Strichen Aberds 153 C9
Strines Gtr Man 87 F7
Stringston Som 22 E3
Strixton Northants 53 C7
Stroat Glos 36 E2
Stromeferry Highld 149 E13
Stromemore Highld 149 E13
Stromness Orkney 159 H3
Stronaba Highld 136 F5
Stronachlachar Stirling 126 C3
Stronchreggan Highld 130 B4
Stronchrubie Highld 156 H5
Strone Argyll 145 E10
Strone Highld 136 F4
Strone Highld 137 B8
Strone Invclyd 118 B2
Stronmilchan Argyll 125 C7
Strontian Highld 130 C2
Strood Medway 29 C8
Strood Green Sur 28 E3
Strood Green W Sus 16 B4
Strood Green W Sus 28 F2
Stroud Glos 37 D5
Stroud Hants 15 B8
Stroud Green Essex 42 E4
Stroxton Lincs 78 F2
Struan Highld 149 E8
Struan Perth 133 C5
Strubby Lincs 91 F8
Strumpshaw Norf 69 D6
Strutherhill S Lanark 119 E7
Struy Highld 150 H6
Stryt-issa Wrex 73 E6
Stuartfield Aberds 153 D9
Stub Place Cumb 98 E2
Stubbington Hants 15 D6
Stubbins Lancs 87 C5
Stubbs Cross Kent 19 B6
Stubb's Green Norf 69 E5
Stubbs Green Norf 69 E6
Stubhampton Dorset 13 C7
Stubton Lincs 77 E8
Stuckgowan Argyll 126 D2
Stuckton Hants 14 C2
Stud Green Windsor 27 B6
Studham C Beds 40 C3
Studland Dorset 13 F8
Studley Warks 51 C5
Studley Wilts 24 B4
Studley Roger N Yorks 95 B5
Stump Cross Essex 55 E6
Stuntney Cambs 55 B6
Sturbridge Staffs 74 F5
Sturmer Essex 55 E7
Sturminster Marshall Dorset 13 D7
Sturminster Newton Dorset 13 C5
Sturry Kent 31 C5
Sturton N Lincs 90 D3
Sturton by Stow Lincs 90 F2
Sturton le Steeple Notts 89 F8
Stuston Suff 56 B5
Stutton N Yorks 95 E7
Stutton Suff 57 F5
Styal Ches E 87 F6
Styrrup Notts 89 E7
Suainebost W Isles 155 A10
Suardail W Isles 155 D9
Succoth Aberds 152 E4
Succoth Argyll 125 E8
Suckley Worcs 50 D2
Suckquoy Orkney 159 K5
Sudborough Northants 65 F6
Sudbourne Suff 57 D8
Sudbrook Lincs 78 E2
Sudbrook Mon 36 F2
Sudbrooke Lincs 78 B3
Sudbury Derbys 75 F8
Sudbury London 40 F4
Sudbury Suff 56 E2
Suddie Highld 151 F9
Sudgrove Glos 37 D6
Suffield N Yorks 103 E7
Suffield Norf 81 D8
Sugnall Staffs 74 F4
Suladale Highld 149 C8
Sulaisiadar W Isles 155 D10
Sulby IoM 84 C3
Sulgrave Northants 52 E3
Sulham W Berks 26 B4
Sulhamstead W Berks 26 C4
Sulland Orkney 159 D6
Sullington W Sus 16 C4
Sullom Shetland 160 F5
Sullom Voe Oil Terminal Shetland 160 F5
Sully V Glam 22 C3
Sumburgh Shetland 160 N6
Summer Bridge N Yorks 94 C5
Summer-house Darl 101 C7
Summercourt Corn 4 D3
Summerfield Norf 80 D3
Summergangs Hull 97 F7
Summerleaze Mon 35 F8
Summersdale W Sus 16 D2
Summerseat Gtr Man 87 C5
Summertown Oxon 39 D5
Summit Gtr Man 87 D7
Sunbury-on-Thames Sur 28 C2
Sundaywell Dumfries 113 F8
Sunderland Argyll 142 B3
Sunderland Cumb 107 F8
Sunderland T&W 111 D6
Sunderland Bridge Durham 111 F5
Sundhope Borders 115 B6
Sundon Park Luton 40 B3
Sundridge Kent 29 D5
Sunipol Argyll 146 F6
Sunk Island E Yorks 91 C6
Sunningdale Windsor 27 C7
Sunninghill Windsor 27 C7
Sunningwell Oxon 38 D4
Sunniside Durham 110 F4
Sunniside T&W 110 D5
Sunnyhurst Blackburn 86 B4
Sunnylaw Stirling 127 E6
Sunnyside W Sus 28 F4
Sunton Wilts 25 D7
Surbiton London 28 C2
Surby IoM 84 E2
Surfleet Lincs 66 B2
Surfleet Seas End Lincs 66 B2
Surlingham Norf 69 D6
Sustead Norf 81 D7
Susworth Lincs 90 D2
Sutcombe Devon 8 C5
Suton Norf 68 E3
Sutors of Cromarty Highld 151 E11
Sutterby Lincs 79 B6
Sutterton Lincs 79 F5
Sutton C Beds 54 E3
Sutton Cambs 54 B5
Sutton Kent 31 E7
Sutton London 28 C3
Sutton Mers 86 E3
Sutton N Yorks 89 B5
Sutton Norf 69 B6
Sutton Notts 77 F7
Sutton Notts 89 F7
Sutton Oxon 38 D4
Sutton Pboro 65 E7
Sutton S Yorks 89 C6
Sutton Shrops 61 F7
Sutton Shrops 74 F3
Sutton Som 23 F8
Sutton Staffs 61 B7
Sutton Suff 57 E7
Sutton Sur 27 E8
Sutton W Sus 16 C3
Sutton at Hone Kent 29 B6
Sutton Bassett Northants 64 E4
Sutton Benger Wilts 24 B4
Sutton Bonington Notts 64 B2
Sutton Bridge Lincs 66 B4
Sutton Cheney Leics 63 D8
Sutton Coldfield W Mid 62 E5
Sutton Courtenay Oxon 39 E5
Sutton Crosses Lincs 66 B4
Sutton Grange N Yorks 95 B5
Sutton Green Sur 27 D8
Sutton Howgrave N Yorks 95 B6
Sutton In Ashfield Notts 76 D4
Sutton-in-Craven N Yorks 94 E3
Sutton in the Elms Leics 64 E2
Sutton Ings Hull 97 F7
Sutton Lane Ends Ches E 75 B6
Sutton Leach Mers 86 E3
Sutton Maddock Shrops 61 D7
Sutton Mallet Som 23 F5
Sutton Mandeville Wilts 13 B7
Sutton Manor Mers 86 E3
Sutton Montis Som 12 B4
Sutton on Hull Hull 97 F7
Sutton on Sea Lincs 91 F9
Sutton-on-the-Forest N Yorks 95 C8
Sutton on the Hill Derbys 76 F2
Sutton on Trent Notts 77 C7
Sutton Scarsdale Derbys 76 C4
Sutton Scotney Hants 26 F2
Sutton St Edmund Lincs 66 C3
Sutton St James Lincs 66 C3
Sutton St Nicholas Hereford 49 E7
Sutton under Brailes Warks 51 F8
Sutton-under-Whitestonecliffe N Yorks 102 F2
Sutton upon Derwent E Yorks 96 E3
Sutton Valence Kent 30 E2
Sutton Veny Wilts 24 E3
Sutton Waldron Dorset 13 C6
Sutton Weaver Ches W 74 B2
Sutton Wick Bath 23 D7
Swaby Lincs 79 B6
Swadlincote Derbys 63 C7
Swaffham Norf 67 D8
Swaffham Bulbeck Cambs 55 C6
Swaffham Prior Cambs 55 C6
Swafield Norf 81 D8
Swainby N Yorks 102 D2
Swainshill Hereford 49 E6
Swainsthorpe Norf 68 D5
Swainswick Bath 24 C2
Swalcliffe Oxon 51 F8
Swalecliffe Kent 30 C5
Swallow Lincs 91 D5
Swallowcliffe Wilts 13 B7
Swallowfield Wokingham 26 C5
Swallownest S Yorks 89 F5
Swallows Cross Essex 42 E2
Swan Green Ches W 74 B4
Swan Green Suff 57 B6
Swanage Dorset 13 G8
Swanbister Orkney 159 H4
Swanbourne Bucks 39 B8
Swanland E Yorks 90 B3
Swanley Kent 29 C6
Swanley Village Kent 29 C6
Swanmore Hants 15 C6
Swannington Leics 63 C8
Swannington Norf 68 C4
Swanscombe Kent 29 B7
Swansea = Abertawe Swansea 33 E7
Swanton Abbott Norf 81 E8
Swanton Morley Norf 68 C3
Swanton Novers Norf 81 D6
Swanton Street Kent 30 D2
Swanwick Derbys 76 D4
Swanwick Hants 15 D6
Swarby Lincs 78 E3
Swardeston Norf 68 D5
Swarister Shetland 160 E7
Swarkestone Derbys 63 B7
Swarland Northumb 117 D7
Swarland Estate Northumb 117 D7
Swarthmoor Cumb 92 B2
Swathwick Derbys 76 C3
Swaton Lincs 78 F4
Swavesey Cambs 54 C4
Sway Hants 14 E3
Swayfield Lincs 65 B6
Swaythling Soton 14 C5
Sweet Green Worcs 49 C8
Sweetham Devon 10 E3
Sweethouse Corn 5 C5
Sweffling Suff 57 C7
Swepstone Leics 63 C7
Swerford Oxon 51 F8
Swettenham Ches E 74 C5
Swetton N Yorks 94 B4
Swffryd Caerph 35 E6
Swiftsden E Sus 18 C4
Swilland Suff 57 D5
Swillington W Yorks 95 F6
Swimbridge Devon 9 B8
Swimbridge Newland Devon 20 F5
Swinbrook Oxon 38 C2
Swinderby Lincs 77 C8
Swindon Glos 37 B6
Swindon Staffs 62 E2
Swindon Swindon 38 F1
Swine E Yorks 97 F7
Swinefleet E Yorks 89 B8
Swineshead Bedford 53 C8
Swineshead Lincs 78 E5
Swineshead Bridge Lincs 78 E5
Swiney Highld 158 G4
Swinford Leics 52 B3
Swinford Oxon 38 D4
Swingate Notts 76 E5
Swingfield Minnis Kent 31 E6
Swingfield Street Kent 31 E6
Swinhoe Northumb 117 B8
Swinhope Lincs 91 E6
Swining Shetland 160 G6
Swinithwaite N Yorks 101 F5
Swinnow Moor W Yorks 94 F5
Swinscoe Staffs 75 E8
Swinside Hall Borders 116 C3
Swinstead Lincs 65 B7
Swinton Borders 122 E4
Swinton Gtr Man 87 D5
Swinton N Yorks 94 B5
Swinton N Yorks 96 B3
Swinton S Yorks 88 E5
Swintonmill Borders 122 E4
Swithland Leics 64 C2
Swordale Highld 151 E8
Swordland Highld 147 B10
Swordly Highld 157 C10
Sworton Heath Ches E 86 F4
Swydd-ffynnon Ceredig 47 C5
Swynnerton Staffs 75 F5
Swyre Dorset 12 F3
Sychtyn Powys 59 D6
Syde Glos 37 C6
Sydenham London 28 B4
Sydenham Oxon 39 D7
Sydenham Damerel Devon 6 B2
Syderstone Norf 80 D4
Sydling St Nicholas Dorset 12 E4
Sydmonton Hants 26 D2
Syerston Notts 77 E7
Syke Gtr Man 87 C6
Sykehouse S Yorks 89 C7
Sykes Lancs 93 D6
Syleham Suff 57 B6
Sylen Carms 33 D6
Symbister Shetland 160 G7
Symington S Ayrs 118 F3
Symington S Lanark 120 F2
Symonds Yat Hereford 36 C2
Symondsbury Dorset 12 E2
Synod Inn Ceredig 46 D3
Syre Highld 157 E9
Syreford Glos 37 B7
Syresham Northants 52 E4
Syston Leics 64 C3
Syston Lincs 78 E2
Sytchampton Worcs 50 C3
Sywell Northants 53 C6

T

Taagan Highld 150 E3
Tàbost W Isles 155 A10
Tabost W Isles 155 F8
Tackley Oxon 38 B4
Tacleit W Isles 154 D6
Tacolneston Norf 68 E4
Tadcaster N Yorks 95 E7
Taddington Derbys 75 B8
Taddiport Devon 9 C6
Tadley Hants 26 C4
Tadlow C Beds 54 E3
Tadmarton Oxon 51 F8
Tadworth Sur 28 D3
Tafarn-y-gelyn Denb 73 C5
Tafarnau-bach Bl Gwent 35 C5
Taff's Well Rhondda 35 F5
Tafolwern Powys 59 D5
Tai Conwy 83 E7
Tai-bach Powys 59 B8
Tai-mawr Conwy 72 E3
Tai-Ucha Denb 72 D4
Taibach Neath 34 F1
Taigh a Ghearraidh W Isles 148 A2
Tain Highld 151 C10
Tain Highld 158 D4
Tainant Wrex 73 E6
Tainlon Gwyn 82 F4
Tairbeart = Tarbert W Isles 154 G6
Tai'r-Bull Powys 34 B3
Tairgwaith Neath 33 C8
Takeley Essex 42 B1
Takeley Street Essex 41 B8
Tal-sarn Ceredig 46 D4
Tal-y-bont Ceredig 58 F3
Tal-y-Bont Conwy 83 E7
Tal-y-bont Gwyn 71 E6
Tal-y-bont Gwyn 83 D6
Tal-y-cafn Conwy 83 D7
Tal-y-llyn Gwyn 58 D4
Tal-y-wern Powys 58 D5
Talachddu Powys 48 F2
Talacre Flint 85 F2
Talardd Gwyn 59 B5
Talaton Devon 11 E5
Talbenny Pembs 44 D3
Talbot Green Rhondda 34 F4
Talbot Village Poole 13 E8
Tale Devon 11 D5
Talerddig Powys 59 D6
Talgarreg Ceredig 46 D3
Talgarth Powys 48 F3
Talisker Highld 149 E8
Talke Staffs 74 D5
Talkin Cumb 109 D5
Talla Linnfoots Borders 114 B4
Talladale Highld 150 D2
Tallarn Green Wrex 73 E8
Tallentire Cumb 107 F8
Talley Carms 46 F5
Tallington Lincs 65 D7
Talmine Highld 157 C8
Talog Carms 32 B4
Talsarn Carms 34 B1
Talsarnau Gwyn 71 D7
Talskiddy Corn 4 C4
Talwrn Anglesey 82 D4
Talwrn Wrex 73 E6
Talybont-on-Usk Powys 35 B5
Talygarn Rhondda 34 F4
Talyllyn Powys 35 B5
Talysarn Gwyn 82 F4
Talywain Torf 35 D6
Tame Bridge N Yorks 102 D3
Tamerton Foliot Plym 6 C2
Tamworth Staffs 63 D6
Tan Hinon Powys 59 F5
Tan-lan Conwy 83 E7
Tan-lan Gwyn 71 C7
Tan-y-bwlch Gwyn 71 C7
Tan-y-fron Conwy 72 C3
Tan-y-graig Anglesey 82 D5
Tan-y-graig Gwyn 70 D4
Tan-y-groes Ceredig 45 E4
Tan-y-pistyll Powys 59 B7
Tan-yr-allt Gwyn 82 F4
Tandem W Yorks 88 C2
Tanden Kent 19 B6
Tandridge Sur 28 D4
Tanerdy Carms 33 B5
Tanfield Durham 110 D4
Tanfield Lea Durham 110 D4
Tangasdal W Isles 148 J1
Tangiers Pembs 44 D4
Tangley Hants 25 D8
Tanglwst Carms 46 F2
Tangmere W Sus 16 D3
Tangwick Shetland 160 F4
Tankersley S Yorks 88 D4
Tankerton Kent 30 C5
Tannach Highld 158 F5
Tannachie Aberds 141 F6
Tannadice Angus 134 D4
Tannington Suff 57 C6
Tansley Derbys 76 D3
Tansley Knoll Derbys 76 C3
Tansor Northants 65 E7
Tantobie Durham 110 D4
Tanton N Yorks 102 C3
Tanworth-in-Arden Warks 51 B6
Tanygrisiau Gwyn 71 C7
Tanyrhydiau Ceredig 47 C6
Taobh a Chaolais W Isles 148 G2
Taobh a Thuath Loch Aineort W Isles 148 F2
Taobh a Tuath Loch Baghasdail W Isles 148 F2
Taobh a'Ghlinne W Isles 155 F8
Taobh Tuath W Isles 154 J4
Taplow Bucks 40 F2
Tapton Derbys 76 B3
Tarbat Ho. Highld 151 D10
Tarbert Argyll 143 C7
Tarbert Argyll 144 E5
Tarbert Argyll 145 G7
Tarbert = Tairbeart W Isles 154 G6
Tarbet Argyll 126 D2
Tarbet Highld 147 B10
Tarbet Highld 156 E4
Tarbock Green Mers 86 F2
Tarbolton S Ayrs 112 B4
Tarbrax S Lanark 120 D3
Tardebigge Worcs 50 C5
Tarfside Angus 134 B4
Tarland Aberds 140 D3
Tarleton Lancs 86 B2
Tarlogie Highld 151 C10
Tarlscough Lancs 86 C2
Tarlton Glos 37 E6
Tarnbrook Lancs 93 D5
Tarporley Ches W 74 C2
Tarr Som 22 F3
Tarrant Crawford Dorset 13 D7
Tarrant Gunville Dorset 13 C7
Tarrant Hinton Dorset 13 C7
Tarrant Keyneston Dorset 13 D7
Tarrant Launceston Dorset 13 D7
Tarrant Monkton Dorset 13 D7
Tarrant Rawston Dorset 13 D7
Tarrant Rushton Dorset 13 D7
Tarrel Highld 151 C11
Tarring Neville E Sus 17 D8
Tarrington Hereford 49 E8
Tarsappie Perth 128 B3
Tarskavaig Highld 149 H10
Tarves Aberds 153 E8
Tarvie Highld 150 F7
Tarvie Perth 133 C7
Tarvin Ches W 73 C8
Tasburgh Norf 68 E5
Tasley Shrops 61 E6
Taston Oxon 38 B3
Tatenhill Staffs 63 B6
Tathall End M Keynes 53 E6
Tatham Lancs 93 C6
Tathwell Lincs 91 F7
Tatling End Bucks 40 F3
Tatsfield Sur 28 D5
Tattenhall Ches W 73 D8
Tattenhoe M Keynes 53 F6
Tatterford Norf 80 E4
Tattersett Norf 80 D4
Tattershall Lincs 78 D5
Tattershall Bridge Lincs 78 D4
Tattershall Thorpe Lincs 78 D5
Tattingstone Suff 56 F5
Tatworth Som 11 D8
Taunton Som 11 B7
Taverham Norf 68 C4
Tavernspite Pembs 32 C2
Tavistock Devon 6 B2
Taw Green Devon 9 E8
Tawstock Devon 9 B7
Taxal Derbys 75 B7
Tay Bridge Dundee 129 B6
Tayinloan Argyll 143 D7
Taymouth Castle Perth 132 E4
Taynish Argyll 144 E6
Taynton Glos 36 B4
Taynton Oxon 38 C2
Taynuilt Argyll 125 B6
Tayport Fife 129 B6
Tayvallich Argyll 144 E6
Tealby Lincs 91 E5
Tealing Angus 134 F4
Teangue Highld 149 H11
Teanna Mhachair W Isles 148 B2
Tebay Cumb 99 D8
Tebworth C Beds 40 B2
Tedburn St Mary Devon 10 E3
Teddington Glos 50 F4
Teddington London 28 B2
Tedstone Delamere Hereford 49 D8
Tedstone Wafre Hereford 49 D8
Teeton Northants 52 B4
Teffont Evias Wilts 24 F4
Teffont Magna Wilts 24 F4
Tegryn Pembs 45 F4
Teigh Rutland 65 C5
Teigncombe Devon 9 F8
Teigngrace Devon 7 B6
Teignmouth Devon 7 B7
Telford Telford 61 D6
Telham E Sus 18 D4
Tellisford Som 24 D3
Telscombe E Sus 17 D8
Telscombe Cliffs E Sus 17 D7
Templand Dumfries 114 F3
Temple Corn 5 B6
Temple Glasgow 118 C5
Temple Midloth 121 D6
Temple Balsall W Mid 51 B7
Temple Bar Carms 33 C6
Temple Bar Ceredig 46 D4
Temple Cloud Bath 23 D8
Temple Combe Som 12 B5
Temple Ewell Kent 31 E6
Temple Grafton Warks 51 D6
Temple Guiting Glos 37 B7
Temple Herdewyke Warks 51 D8
Temple Hirst N Yorks 89 B7
Temple Normanton Derbys 76 C4
Temple Sowerby Cumb 99 B8
Templehall Fife 128 E4
Templeton Devon 10 C3
Templeton Pembs 32 C2
Templeton Bridge Devon 10 C3
Templetown Durham 110 D4
Tempsford C Beds 54 D2
Ten Mile Bank Norf 67 E6
Tenbury Wells Worcs 49 C7
Tenby = Dinbych-Y-Pysgod Pembs 32 D2
Tendring Essex 43 B7
Tendring Green Essex 43 B7
Tenston Orkney 159 G3
Tenterden Kent 19 B5
Terling Essex 42 C3
Ternhill Shrops 74 F3
Terregles Banks Dumfries 107 B6
Terrick Bucks 39 D8
Terrington N Yorks 96 B2
Terrington St Clement Norf 66 C5
Terrington St John Norf 66 C5
Teston Kent 29 D8
Testwood Hants 14 C4
Tetbury Glos 37 E5
Tetbury Upton Glos 37 E5
Tetchill Shrops 73 F7
Tetcott Devon 8 E5
Tetford Lincs 79 B6
Tetney Lincs 91 D7
Tetney Lock Lincs 91 D7
Tetsworth Oxon 39 D6
Tettenhall W Mid 62 E2
Teuchan Aberds 153 E10
Teversal Notts 76 C4
Teversham Cambs 55 D5
Teviothead Borders 115 D7
Tewel Aberds 141 F7
Tewin Herts 41 C5
Tewkesbury Glos 50 F3
Teynham Kent 30 C3
Thackthwaite Cumb 98 B3
Thainston Aberds 135 B6
Thakeham W Sus 16 C5
Thame Oxon 39 D7
Thames Ditton Sur 28 C2
Thames Haven Thurrock 42 F3
Thamesmead London 41 F7
Thanington Kent 30 D5
Thankerton S Lanark 120 F2
Tharston Norf 68 E4
Thatcham W Berks 26 C3
Thatto Heath Mers 86 E3
Thaxted Essex 55 F7
The Aird Highld 149 C9
The Arms Norf 67 E8
The Bage Hereford 48 E4
The Balloch Perth 127 C7
The Barony Orkney 159 F3
The Bog Shrops 60 E3
The Bourne Sur 27 E6
The Braes Highld 149 E10
The Broad Hereford 49 C6
The Butts Som 24 E2
The Camp Glos 37 D6
The Camp Herts 40 D4
The Chequer Wrex 73 E8
The City Bucks 39 E7
The Common Wilts 25 F7
The Craigs Highld 150 B7
The Cronk IoM 84 C3
The Dell Suff 69 E7
The Den N Ayrs 118 D3
The Eals Northumb 116 F3
The Eaves Glos 36 D3
The Flatt Cumb 109 B5
The Four Alls Shrops 74 F3
The Garths Shetland 160 B8
The Green Cumb 98 F3
The Green Wilts 24 F3
The Grove Dumfries 107 B6
The Hall Shetland 160 D8
The Haven W Sus 27 F8
The Heath Norf 81 E7
The Heath Suff 56 F5
The Hill Cumb 98 F3
The Howe Cumb 99 F6
The Howe IoM 84 F1
The Hundred Hereford 49 C7
The Lee Bucks 40 D2
The Lhen IoM 84 B3
The Marsh Powys 60 E3
The Marsh Wilts 37 F7
The Middles Durham 110 D5
The Moor Kent 18 C4
The Mumbles = Y Mwmbwls Swansea 33 F7
The Murray S Lanark 119 D6
The Neuk Aberds 141 E6
The Oval Bath 24 C2
The Pole of Itlaw Aberds 153 C6
The Quarry Glos 36 E4
The Rhos Pembs 32 C1
The Rock Telford 61 D6
The Ryde Herts 41 D5
The Sands Sur 27 E6
The Stocks Kent 19 C6
The Throat Wokingham 27 C6
The Vauld Hereford 49 E7
The Wyke Shrops 61 D7
Theakston N Yorks 101 F8
Thealby N Lincs 90 C2
Theale Som 23 E6
Theale W Berks 26 B4
Thearne E Yorks 97 F6
Theberton Suff 57 C8
Theddingworth Leics 64 F3
Theddlethorpe All Saints Lincs 91 F8
Theddlethorpe St Helen Lincs 91 F8
Thelbridge Barton Devon 10 C2
Thelnetham Suff 56 B4
Thelveton Norf 68 F4
Thelwall Warr 86 F4
Themelthorpe Norf 81 E6
Thenford Northants 52 E3
Therfield Herts 54 F4
Thetford Lincs 65 C8
Thetford Norf 67 F8
Theydon Bois Essex 41 E7
Thickwood Wilts 24 B3
Thimbleby Lincs 78 C5
Thimbleby N Yorks 102 E2
Thingwall Mers 85 F3
Thirdpart N Ayrs 118 E1
Thirlby N Yorks 102 F2
Thirlestane Borders 121 E8
Thirn N Yorks 101 F7
Thirsk N Yorks 102 F2
Thirtleby E Yorks 97 F7
Thistleton Lancs 92 F4
Thistleton Rutland 65 C6
Thistley Green Suff 55 B7
Thixendale N Yorks 96 C4
Thockrington Northumb 110 B2
Tholomas Drove Cambs 66 D3
Tholthorpe N Yorks 95 C7
Thomas Chapel Pembs 32 D2
Thomas Close Cumb 108 E4
Thomastown Aberds 152 E5
Thompson Norf 68 E2
Thomshill Moray 152 C2
Thong Kent 29 B7
Thongsbridge W Yorks 88 D2
Thoralby N Yorks 101 F5
Thoresway Lincs 91 E5
Thorganby Lincs 91 E6
Thorganby N Yorks 96 E2
Thorgill N Yorks 103 E5
Thorington Suff 57 B8
Thorington Street Suff 56 F4
Thorlby N Yorks 94 D2
Thorley Herts 41 C7
Thorley Street Herts 41 C7
Thorley Street IoW 14 F4
Thormanby N Yorks 95 B7
Thornaby-on-Tees Stockton 102 C2
Thornage Norf 81 D6
Thornborough Bucks 52 F5
Thornborough N Yorks 95 B5
Thornbury Devon 9 D6
Thornbury Hereford 49 D8
Thornbury S Glos 36 E3
Thornbury W Yorks 94 F4
Thornby Northants 52 B4
Thorncliffe Staffs 75 D7
Thorncombe Dorset 11 D8
Thorncombe Dorset 13 D6
Thorncombe Street Sur 27 E8
Thorncote Green C Beds 54 E2
Thorncross IoW 14 F5
Thorndon Suff 56 C5
Thorndon Cross Devon 9 E7
Thorne S Yorks 89 C7
Thorne St Margaret Som 11 B5
Thorner W Yorks 95 E6
Thorney Notts 77 B8
Thorney Pboro 66 D2
Thorney Crofts E Yorks 91 B6
Thorney Green Suff 56 C4
Thorney Hill Hants 14 E2
Thorney Toll Pboro 66 D3
Thornfalcon Som 11 B7
Thornford Dorset 12 C4
Thorngumbald E Yorks 91 B6
Thornham Norf 80 C3
Thornham Magna Suff 56 B5
Thornham Parva Suff 56 B5
Thornhaugh Pboro 65 D7
Thornhill Cardiff 35 F5
Thornhill Cumb 98 D2
Thornhill Derbys 88 F2
Thornhill Dumfries 113 E8
Thornhill Soton 15 C5
Thornhill Stirling 127 E5
Thornhill W Yorks 88 C3
Thornhill Edge W Yorks 88 C3
Thornhill Lees W Yorks 88 C3
Thornholme E Yorks 97 C7
Thornley Durham 110 F4
Thornley Durham 111 F6
Thornliebank E Renf 118 D5
Thorns Suff 55 D8
Thorns Green Ches E 87 F5
Thornsett Derbys 87 F8
Thornthwaite Cumb 98 B4
Thornthwaite N Yorks 94 D4
Thornton Angus 134 E3
Thornton Bucks 53 F5
Thornton E Yorks 96 E3
Thornton Fife 128 E4
Thornton Lancs 92 E3
Thornton Leics 63 D8
Thornton Lincs 78 C5
Thornton Mbro 102 C2
Thornton Mers 85 D4
Thornton Northumb 123 E5
Thornton Pembs 44 E4
Thornton W Yorks 94 F4
Thornton Curtis N Lincs 90 C4
Thornton Heath London 28 C4
Thornton Hough Mers 85 F4
Thornton in Craven N Yorks 94 E2
Thornton-le-Beans N Yorks 102 E1
Thornton-le-Clay N Yorks 96 C2
Thornton-le-Dale N Yorks 103 F6
Thornton le Moor Lincs 90 E4
Thornton-le-Moor N Yorks 102 F1
Thornton-le-Moors Ches W 73 B8
Thornton-le-Street N Yorks 102 F2
Thornton Rust N Yorks 100 F4
Thornton Steward N Yorks 101 F6
Thornton Watlass N Yorks 101 F7
Thorntonhall S Lanark 119 D5
Thorntonloch E Loth 122 B3
Thorntonpark Northumb 122 E5
Thornwood Common Essex 41 D7
Thornydykes Borders 122 E2
Thoroton Notts 77 E7
Thorp Arch W Yorks 95 E7
Thorpe Derbys 75 D8
Thorpe E Yorks 97 E5
Thorpe Lincs 91 F8
Thorpe N Yorks 94 C3
Thorpe Norf 69 E7
Thorpe Notts 77 E7
Thorpe Sur 27 C8
Thorpe Abbotts Norf 57 B5
Thorpe Acre Leics 64 B2
Thorpe Arnold Leics 64 B4
Thorpe Audlin W Yorks 89 C5
Thorpe Bassett N Yorks 96 B4
Thorpe Bay Southend 43 F5
Thorpe by Water Rutland 65 E5
Thorpe Common Suff 57 F6
Thorpe Constantine Staffs 63 D6
Thorpe Culvert Lincs 79 C7
Thorpe End Norf 69 C5
Thorpe Fendykes Lincs 79 C7
Thorpe Green Essex 43 B7
Thorpe Green Suff 56 D3
Thorpe Hesley S Yorks 88 E4
Thorpe in Balne S Yorks 89 C6
Thorpe in the Fallows Lincs 90 F3
Thorpe Langton Leics 64 E4
Thorpe Larches Durham 102 B1
Thorpe-le-Soken Essex 43 B7
Thorpe le Street E Yorks 96 E4
Thorpe Malsor Northants 53 B6
Thorpe Mandeville Northants 52 E3
Thorpe Market Norf 81 D8
Thorpe Marriot Norf 68 C4
Thorpe Morieux Suff 56 D3
Thorpe on the Hill Lincs 78 C2
Thorpe Salvin S Yorks 89 F6
Thorpe Satchville Leics 64 C4
Thorpe St Andrew Norf 69 D5
Thorpe St Peter Lincs 79 C7
Thorpe Thewles Stockton 102 B2
Thorpe Tilney Lincs 78 D4
Thorpe Underwood N Yorks 95 D7
Thorpe Waterville Northants 65 F7
Thorpe Willoughby N Yorks 95 F8
Thorpeness Suff 57 D8
Thorrington Essex 43 C6
Thorverton Devon 10 D4
Thrandeston Suff 56 B5
Thrapston Northants 53 B7
Thrashbush N Lanark 119 C7
Threapland Cumb 107 F8
Threapland N Yorks 94 C2
Threapwood Ches W 73 E8
Threapwood Staffs 75 E7
Three Ashes Hereford 36 B2
Three Bridges W Sus 28 F3
Three Burrows Corn 3 B6
Three Chimneys Kent 18 B5
Three Cocks Powys 48 F3
Three Crosses Swansea 33 E6
Three Cups Corner E Sus 18 C3
Three Holes Norf 66 D5
Three Leg Cross E Sus 18 B3
Three Legged Cross Dorset 13 D8
Three Oaks E Sus 18 D5
Threehammer Common Norf 69 C6
Threekingham Lincs 78 F3
Threemile Cross Wokingham 26 C5
Threemilestone Corn 3 B6
Threemiletown W Loth 120 B3
Threlkeld Cumb 99 B5
Threshfield N Yorks 94 C2
Thrigby Norf 69 C7
Thringarth Durham 100 B4
Thringstone Leics 63 C8
Thrintoft N Yorks 101 E8
Thriplow Cambs 54 E5
Throckenholt Lincs 66 D3
Throcking Herts 54 F4
Throckley T&W 110 C4
Throckmorton Worcs 50 E4
Throphill Northumb 117 F7
Thropton Northumb 117 D6
Throsk Stirling 127 E7
Throwleigh Devon 9 E8
Throwley Kent 30 D3
Thrumpton Notts 76 F5
Thrumster Highld 158 F5
Thrunton Northumb 117 C6
Thrupp Glos 37 D5
Thrupp Oxon 38 C4
Thrushelton Devon 9 F6
Thrussington Leics 64 C3
Thruxton Hants 25 E7
Thruxton Hereford 49 F6
Thrybergh S Yorks 89 E5
Thulston Derbys 76 F4
Thundergay N Ayrs 143 D9
Thundersley Essex 42 F3
Thundridge Herts 41 C6
Thurcaston Leics 64 C2
Thurcroft S Yorks 89 F5
Thurgarton Norf 81 D7
Thurgarton Notts 77 E6
Thurgoland S Yorks 88 D3
Thurlaston Leics 64 E2
Thurlaston Warks 52 B2
Thurlbear Som 11 B7
Thurlby Lincs 65 C8
Thurlby Lincs 78 C2
Thurleigh Bedford 53 D8
Thurlestone Devon 6 E4
Thurloxton Som 22 F4
Thurlstone S Yorks 88 D3
Thurlton Norf 69 E7
Thurlwood Ches E 74 D5
Thurmaston Leics 64 D3
Thurnby Leics 64 D3
Thurne Norf 69 C7
Thurnham Kent 30 D2
Thurnham Lancs 92 D4
Thurning Norf 81 E6
Thurning Northants 65 F7
Thurnscoe S Yorks 89 D5
Thurnscoe East S Yorks 89 D5
Thursby Cumb 108 D3
Thursford Norf 81 D5
Thursley Sur 27 F7
Thurso Highld 158 D3
Thurso East Highld 158 D3
Thurstaston Mers 85 F3
Thurston Suff 56 C3
Thurstonfield Cumb 108 D3
Thurstonland W Yorks 88 C2
Thurton Norf 69 D6
Thurvaston Derbys 76 F2
Thuxton Norf 68 D3
Thwaite N Yorks 100 E3

Thwaite Suff 56 C5
Thwaite St Mary Norf 69 E6
Thwaites W Yorks 94 E3
Thwaites Brow W Yorks 94 E3
Thwing E Yorks 97 B6
Tibbermore Perth 128 B2
Tibberton Glos 36 B4
Tibberton Telford 61 B6
Tibberton Worcs 50 D4
Tibenham Norf 68 F4
Tibshelf Derbys 76 C4
Tibthorpe E Yorks 97 D5
Ticehurst E Sus 18 B3
Tichborne Hants 26 F3
Tickencote Rutland 65 D6
Tickenham N Som 23 B6
Tickhill S Yorks 89 E6
Ticklerton Shrops 60 E4
Ticknall Derbys 63 B7
Tickton E Yorks 97 E6
Tidcombe Wilts 25 D7
Tiddington Oxon 39 D6
Tiddington Warks 51 D7
Tidebrook E Sus 18 C3
Tideford Corn 5 D8
Tideford Cross Corn 5 C8
Tidenham Glos 36 E2
Tideswell Derbys 75 B8
Tidmarsh W Berks 26 B4
Tidmington Warks 51 F7
Tidpit Hants 13 C8
Tidworth Wilts 25 E7
Tiers Cross Pembs 44 D4
Tiffield Northants 52 D4
Tifty Aberds 153 D7
Tigerton Angus 135 C5
Tigh-na-Blair Perth 127 C6
Tighnabruaich Argyll 145 F8
Tighnafiline Highld 155 J13
Tigley Devon 7 C5
Tilbrook Cambs 53 C8
Tilbury Thurrock 29 B7
Tilbury Juxta Clare Essex 55 E8
Tile Cross W Mid 63 F5
Tile Hill W Mid 51 B7
Tilehurst Reading 26 B4
Tilford Sur 27 E6
Tilgate W Sus 28 F3
Tilgate Forest Row W Sus 28 F3
Tillathrowie Aberds 152 E4
Tilley Shrops 60 B5
Tillicoultry Clack 127 E8
Tillingham Essex 43 D5
Tillington Hereford 49 E6
Tillington W Sus 16 B3
Tillington Common Hereford 49 E6
Tillyarblet Angus 135 C5
Tillybirloch Aberds 141 D5
Tillycorthie Aberds 141 B8
Tillydrine Aberds 140 E5
Tillyfour Aberds 140 C4
Tillyfourie Aberds 140 C5
Tillygarmond Aberds 140 E5
Tillygreig Aberds 141 B7
Tillykerrie Aberds 141 B7
Tilmanstone Kent 31 D7
Tilney All Saints Norf 67 C5
Tilney High End Norf 67 C5
Tilney St Lawrence Norf 66 C5
Tilshead Wilts 24 E5
Tilstock Shrops 74 F2
Tilston Ches W 73 D8
Tilstone Fearnall Ches W 74 C2
Tilsworth C Beds 40 B2
Tilton on the Hill Leics 64 D4
Timberland Lincs 78 D4
Timbersbrook Ches E 75 C5
Timberscombe Som 21 E8
Timble N Yorks 94 D4
Timperley Gtr Man 87 F5
Timsbury Bath 23 D8
Timsbury Hants 14 B4
Timsgearraidh W Isles 154 D5
Timworth Green Suff 56 C2
Tincleton Dorset 13 E5
Tindale Cumb 109 D6
Tingewick Bucks 52 F4
Tingley W Yorks 88 B3
Tingrith C Beds 53 F8
Tingwall Orkney 159 F4
Tinhay Devon 9 F5
Tinshill W Yorks 95 F5
Tinsley S Yorks 88 E5
Tintagel Corn 8 F2
Tintern Parva Mon 36 D2
Tintinhull Som 12 C3
Tintwistle Derbys 87 E8
Tinwald Dumfries 114 F3
Tinwell Rutland 65 D7
Tipperty Aberds 141 B8
Tipsend Norf 66 E5
Tipton W Mid 62 E3
Tipton St John Devon 11 E5
Tiptree Essex 42 C4
Tir-y-dail Carms 33 C7
Tirabad Powys 47 E7
Tiraghoil Argyll 146 J6
Tirley Glos 37 B5
Tirphil Caerph 35 D5
Tirril Cumb 99 B7
Tisbury Wilts 13 B7
Tisman's Common W Sus 27 F8
Tissington Derbys 75 D8
Titchberry Devon 8 B4
Titchfield Hants 15 D6
Titchmarsh Northants 53 B8
Titchwell Norf 80 C3
Tithby Notts 77 F6
Titley Hereford 48 C5
Titlington Northumb 117 C7
Titsey Sur 28 D5
Tittensor Staffs 75 F5
Tittleshall Norf 80 E4
Tiverton Ches W 74 C2
Tiverton Devon 10 C4
Tivetshall St Margaret Norf 68 F4
Tivetshall St Mary Norf 68 F4
Tividale W Mid 62 E3
Tivy Dale S Yorks 88 D3
Tixall Staffs 62 B3
Tixover Rutland 65 D6
Toab Orkney 159 H6
Toab Shetland 160 M5
Toadmoor Derbys 76 D3
Tobermory Argyll 147 F8
Toberonochy Argyll 124 E3
Tobha Mor W Isles 148 E2
Tobhtarol W Isles 154 D6
Tobson W Isles 154 D6
Tocher Aberds 153 E6
Tockenham Wilts 24 B5
Tockenham Wick Wilts 37 F7
Tockholes Blackburn 86 B4
Tockington S Glos 36 F3
Tockwith N Yorks 95 D7
Todber Dorset 13 B6
Todding Hereford 49 B6
Toddington C Beds 40 B3
Toddington Glos 50 F5
Todenham Glos 51 F7
Todhills Cumb 108 C3
Todlachie Aberds 141 C5
Todmorden W Yorks 87 B7
Todrig Borders 115 C7
Todwick S Yorks 89 F5
Toft Cambs 54 D4
Toft Lincs 65 C7
Toft Hill Durham 101 B6
Toft Hill Lincs 78 C5
Toft Monks Norf 69 E7
Toft next Newton Lincs 90 F4
Toftrees Norf 80 E4
Tofts Highld 158 D5
Toftwood Norf 68 C2
Togston Northumb 117 D8
Tokavaig Highld 149 G11
Tokers Green Oxon 26 B5
Tolastadh a Chaolais W Isles 154 D6
Tolastadh bho Thuath W Isles 155 C10
Toll Bar S Yorks 89 D6
Toll End W Mid 62 E3
Toll of Birness Aberds 153 E10
Tolland Som 22 F3
Tollard Royal Wilts 13 C7
Tollbar End W Mid 51 B8
Toller Fratrum Dorset 12 E3
Toller Porcorum Dorset 12 E3
Tollerton N Yorks 95 C8
Tollerton Notts 77 F6
Tollesbury Essex 43 C5
Tolleshunt D'Arcy Essex 43 C5
Tolleshunt Major Essex 43 C5
Tolm W Isles 155 D9
Tolpuddle Dorset 13 E5
Tolvah Highld 138 E4
Tolworth London 28 C2
Tomatin Highld 138 B4
Tombreck Highld 151 H9
Tomchrasky Highld 137 C5
Tomdoun Highld 136 D4
Tomich Highld 137 B6
Tomich Highld 151 D9
Tomich House Highld 151 G8
Tomintoul Aberds 139 E7
Tomintoul Moray 139 C7
Tomnaven Moray 152 E4
Tomnavoulin Moray 139 B8
Ton-Pentre Rhondda 34 E3
Tonbridge Kent 29 E6
Tondu Bridgend 34 F2
Tonfanau Gwyn 58 D2
Tong Shrops 61 D7
Tong W Yorks 94 F5
Tong Norton Shrops 61 D7
Tonge Leics 63 B8
Tongham Sur 27 E6
Tongland Dumfries 106 D3
Tongue Highld 157 D8
Tongue End Lincs 65 C8
Tongwynlais Cardiff 35 F5
Tonna Neath 34 E1
Tonwell Herts 41 C6
Tonypandy Rhondda 34 E3
Tonyrefail Rhondda 34 F4
Toot Baldon Oxon 39 D5
Toot Hill Essex 41 D8
Toothill Hants 14 C4
Top of Hebers Gtr Man 87 D6
Topcliffe N Yorks 95 B7
Topcroft Norf 69 E5
Topcroft Street Norf 69 E5
Toppesfield Essex 55 F8
Toppings Gtr Man 86 C5
Topsham Devon 10 F4
Torbay Torbay 7 D7
Torbeg N Ayrs 143 F10
Torboll Farm Highld 151 B10
Torbrex Stirling 127 E6
Torbryan Devon 7 C6
Torcross Devon 7 E6
Tore Highld 151 F9
Torinturk Argyll 145 G7
Torksey Lincs 77 B8
Torlum W Isles 148 C2
Torlundy Highld 131 B5
Tormarton S Glos 24 B2
Tormisdale Argyll 142 C2
Tormitchell S Ayrs 112 E2
Tormore N Ayrs 143 E9
Tornagrain Highld 151 G10
Tornahaish Aberds 139 D8
Tornaveen Aberds 140 D5
Torness Highld 137 B8
Toronto Durham 110 F4
Torpenhow Cumb 108 F2
Torphichen W Loth 120 B2
Torphins Aberds 140 D5
Torpoint Corn 6 D2
Torquay Torbay 7 C7
Torquhan Borders 121 E7
Torran Argyll 124 E4
Torran Highld 149 D10
Torran Highld 151 D10
Torrance E Dunb 119 B6
Torrans Argyll 146 J7
Torranyard N Ayrs 118 E3
Torre Torbay 7 C7
Torridon Highld 150 F2
Torridon Ho. Highld 149 C13
Torrin Highld 149 F10
Torrisdale Highld 157 C9
Torrisdale-Square Argyll 143 E8
Torrish Highld 157 H12
Torrisholme Lancs 92 C4
Torroble Highld 157 J8
Torry Aberdeen 141 D8
Torry Aberds 152 E4
Torryburn Fife 128 F2
Torterston Aberds 153 D10
Torthorwald Dumfries 107 B7
Tortington W Sus 16 D4
Tortworth S Glos 36 E4
Torvaig Highld 149 D9
Torver Cumb 98 E4
Torwood Falk 127 F7
Torworth Notts 89 F7
Tosberry Devon 8 B4
Toscaig Highld 149 E12
Toseland Cambs 54 C3
Tosside N Yorks 93 D7
Tostock Suff 56 C3
Totaig Highld 148 C7
Totaig Highld 149 F13
Tote Highld 149 D9
Totegan Highld 157 C11
Tothill Lincs 91 F8
Totland IoW 14 F4
Totnes Devon 7 C6
Toton Notts 76 F5
Totronald Argyll 146 F4
Totscore Highld 149 B8
Tottenham London 41 E6
Tottenhill Norf 67 C6
Tottenhill Row Norf 67 C6
Totteridge London 41 E5
Totternhoe C Beds 40 B2
Tottington Gtr Man 87 C5
Totton Hants 14 C4
Touchen End Windsor 27 B6
Tournaig Highld 155 J13
Toux Aberds 153 C9
Tovil Kent 29 D8
Tow Law Durham 110 F4
Toward Argyll 145 G10
Towcester Northants 52 E4
Towednack Corn 2 C3
Tower End Norf 67 C6
Towersey Oxon 39 D7
Towie Aberds 140 C3
Towie Aberds 153 B8
Towiemore Moray 152 D3
Town End Cambs 66 E4
Town End Cumb 99 F6
Town Row E Sus 18 B2
Town Yetholm Borders 116 B4
Townend W Dunb 118 B4
Towngate Lincs 65 C8
Townhead Cumb 108 F5
Townhead Dumfries 106 E3
Townhead S Ayrs 112 D2
Townhead S Yorks 88 D2
Townhead of Greenlaw Dumfries 106 C4
Townhill Fife 128 F3
Townsend Bucks 39 D7
Townsend Herts 40 D4
Townshend Corn 2 C4
Towthorpe York 96 D2
Towton N Yorks 95 F7
Towyn Conwy 72 B3
Toxteth Mers 85 F4
Toynton All Saints Lincs 79 C6
Toynton Fen Side Lincs 79 C6
Toynton St Peter Lincs 79 C7
Toy's Hill Kent 29 D5
Trabboch E Ayrs 112 B4
Traboe Corn 3 D6
Tradespark Highld 151 F11
Tradespark Orkney 159 H5
Trafford Park Gtr Man 87 E5
Trallong Powys 34 B3
Tranent E Loth 121 B7
Tranmere Mers 85 F4
Trantlebeg Highld 157 D11
Trantlemore Highld 157 D11
Tranwell Northumb 117 F7
Trapp Carms 33 C7
Traprain E Loth 121 B8
Traquair Borders 121 F6
Trawden Lancs 94 F2
Trawsfynydd Gwyn 71 D8
Tre-Gibbon Rhondda 34 D3
Tre-Taliesin Ceredig 58 E3
Tre-vaughan Carms 32 B4
Tre-wyn Mon 35 B7
Trealaw Rhondda 34 E4
Treales Lancs 92 F4
Trearddur Anglesey 82 D2
Treaslane Highld 149 C8
Trebanog Rhondda 34 E4
Trebanos Neath 33 D8
Trebartha Corn 5 B7
Trebarwith Corn 8 F2
Trebetherick Corn 4 B4
Treborough Som 22 F2
Trebudannon Corn 4 C3
Trebullett Corn 5 B8
Treburley Corn 5 B8
Trebyan Corn 5 C5
Trecastle Powys 34 B2
Trecenydd Caerph 35 F5
Trecwn Pembs 44 B4
Trecynon Rhondda 34 D3
Tredavoe Corn 2 D3
Treddiog Pembs 44 C3
Tredegar Bl Gwent 35 D5
Tredegar = Newydd New Tredegar Caerph 35 D5
Tredington Glos 37 B6
Tredington Warks 51 E7
Tredinnick Corn 4 B4
Tredomen Powys 48 F3
Tredunnock Mon 35 E7
Tredustan Powys 48 F3
Treen Corn 2 D2
Treeton S Yorks 88 F5
Tref-Y-Clawdd = Knighton Powys 48 B4
Trefaldwyn = Montgomery Powys 60 E2
Trefasser Pembs 44 B3
Trefdraeth Anglesey 82 D4
Trefdraeth = Newport Pembs 45 F2
Trefecca Powys 48 F3
Trefechan Ceredig 58 F2
Trefeglwys Powys 59 E6
Trefenter Ceredig 46 C5
Treffgarne Pembs 44 C4
Treffynnon = Holywell Flint 73 B5
Treffynnon Pembs 44 C3
Trefgarn Owen Pembs 44 C3
Trefil Bl Gwent 35 C5
Trefilan Ceredig 46 D4
Trefin Pembs 44 B3
Treflach Shrops 60 B2
Trefnanney Powys 60 C2
Trefnant Denb 72 B4
Trefonen Shrops 60 B2
Trefor Anglesey 82 C3
Trefor Gwyn 70 C4
Treforest Rhondda 34 F4
Trefriw Conwy 83 E7
Trefynwy = Monmouth Mon 36 C2
Tregadillett Corn 8 F4
Tregaian Anglesey 82 D4
Tregare Mon 35 C8
Tregaron Ceredig 47 D5
Tregarth Gwyn 83 E6
Tregeare Corn 8 F4
Tregeiriog Wrex 73 F5
Tregele Anglesey 82 B3
Tregidden Corn 3 D6
Treglemais Pembs 44 C3
Tregole Corn 8 E3
Tregonetha Corn 4 C4
Tregony Corn 3 B8
Tregoss Corn 4 C4
Tregoyd Powys 48 F4
Tregroes Ceredig 46 E3
Tregurrian Corn 4 C3
Tregynon Powys 59 E7
Trehafod Rhondda 34 E4
Treharris M Tydf 34 E4
Treherbert Rhondda 34 E3
Trekenner Corn 5 B8
Treknow Corn 8 F2
Trelan Corn 3 E6
Trelash Corn 8 E3
Trelassick Corn 4 D3
Trelawnyd Flint 72 B4
Trelech Carms 45 F4
Treleddyd-fawr Pembs 44 C2
Trelewis M Tydf 35 E5
Treligga Corn 8 F2
Trelights Corn 4 B4
Trelill Corn 4 B5
Trelissick Corn 3 C7
Trellech Mon 36 D2
Trelleck Grange Mon 36 D1
Trelogan Flint 85 F2
Trelystan Powys 60 D2
Tremadog Gwyn 71 C6
Tremail Corn 8 F3
Tremain Ceredig 45 E4
Tremaine Corn 8 F4
Tremar Corn 5 C7
Trematon Corn 5 D8
Tremeirchion Denb 72 B4
Trenance Corn 4 C3
Trenarren Corn 3 B9
Trench Telford 61 C6
Treneglos Corn 8 F4
Trenewan Corn 5 D6
Trent Dorset 12 C3
Trent Vale Stoke 75 E5
Trentham Stoke 75 E5
Trentishoe Devon 20 E5
Treoes V Glam 21 B8
Treorchy = Treorci Rhondda 34 E3
Treorci = Treorchy Rhondda 34 E3
Tre'r-ddôl Ceredig 58 E3
Trerulefoot Corn 5 D8
Tresaith Ceredig 45 D4
Trescott Staffs 62 E2
Trescowe Corn 2 C4
Tresham Glos 36 E4
Tresillian Corn 3 B7
Tresinwen Pembs 44 A4
Treskinnick Cross Corn 8 E4
Tresmeer Corn 8 F4
Tresparrett Corn 8 E3
Tresparrett Posts Corn 8 E3
Tressait Perth 133 C5
Tresta Shetland 160 D8
Tresta Shetland 160 H5
Treswell Notts 77 B7
Trethosa Corn 4 D4
Trethurgy Corn 4 D5
Tretio Pembs 44 C2
Tretire Hereford 36 B2
Tretower Powys 35 B5
Treuddyn Flint 73 D6
Trevalga Corn 8 F2
Trevalyn Wrex 73 D7
Trevanson Corn 4 B4
Trevarren Corn 4 C4
Trevarrian Corn 4 C3
Trevarrick Corn 3 B8
Trevaughan Carms 32 C2
Treveighan Corn 5 B5
Trevellas Corn 4 D2
Treverva Corn 3 C6
Trevethin Torf 35 D6
Trevigro Corn 5 C8
Treviscoe Corn 4 D4
Trevone Corn 4 B3
Trewarmett Corn 8 F2
Trewassa Corn 8 F3
Trewellard Corn 2 C2
Trewen Corn 8 F4
Trewennack Corn 3 D5
Trewern Powys 60 C2
Trewethern Corn 4 B5
Trewidland Corn 5 D7
Trewint Corn 8 E3
Trewint Corn 8 F4
Trewithian Corn 3 C7
Trewoofe Corn 2 D3
Trewoon Corn 4 D4
Treworga Corn 3 B7
Treworlas Corn 3 C7
Treyarnon Corn 4 B3
Treyford W Sus 16 C2
Trezaise Corn 4 D4
Triangle W Yorks 87 B8
Trickett's Cross Dorset 13 D8
Triffleton Pembs 44 C4
Trimdon Durham 111 F6
Trimdon Colliery Durham 111 F6
Trimdon Grange Durham 111 F6
Trimingham Norf 81 D8
Trimley Lower Street Suff 57 F6
Trimley St Martin Suff 57 F6
Trimley St Mary Suff 57 F6
Trimpley Worcs 50 B2
Trimsaran Carms 33 D5
Trimstone Devon 20 E3
Trinafour Perth 132 C4
Trinant Caerph 35 D6
Tring Herts 40 C2
Tring Wharf Herts 40 C2
Trinity Angus 135 C6
Trinity Jersey 17
Trisant Ceredig 47 B6
Trislaig Highld 130 B4
Trispen Corn 4 D3
Tritlington Northumb 117 E8
Trochry Perth 133 E6
Trodigal Argyll 143 F7
Troed-rhiwdalar Powys 47 D8
Troedyraur Ceredig 46 E2
Troedyrhiw M Tydf 34 D4
Tromode IoM 84 E3
Trondavoe Shetland 160 F5
Troon Corn 3 C5
Troon S Ayrs 118 F3
Trosaraidh W Isles 148 G2
Trossachs Hotel Stirling 126 D4
Troston Suff 56 B2
Trottiscliffe Kent 29 C7
Trotton W Sus 16 B2
Troutbeck Cumb 99 B5
Troutbeck Cumb 99 D6
Troutbeck Bridge Cumb 99 D6
Trow Green Glos 36 D2
Trowbridge Wilts 24 D3
Trowell Notts 76 F4
Trowle Common Wilts 24 D3
Trowley Bottom Herts 40 C3
Trows Borders 122 F2
Trowse Newton Norf 68 D5
Trudoxhill Som 24 E2
Trull Som 11 B7
Trumaisgearraidh W Isles 148 A3
Trumpan Highld 148 B7
Trumpet Hereford 49 F8
Trumpington Cambs 54 D5
Trunch Norf 81 D8
Trunnah Lancs 92 E3
Truro Corn 3 B7
Trusham Devon 10 F3
Trusley Derbys 76 F2
Trusthorpe Lincs 91 F9
Trysull Staffs 62 E2
Tubney Oxon 38 E4
Tuckenhay Devon 7 D6
Tuckhill Shrops 61 F7
Tuckingmill Corn 3 B5
Tuddenham Suff 55 B8
Tuddenham St Martin Suff 57 E5
Tudeley Kent 29 E7
Tudhoe Durham 111 F5
Tudorville Hereford 36 B2
Tudweiliog Gwyn 70 D3
Tuesley Sur 27 E7
Tuffley Glos 37 C5
Tufton Hants 26 E2
Tufton Pembs 32 B1
Tugby Leics 64 D4
Tugford Shrops 61 F5
Tullibardine Perth 127 C8
Tullibody Clack 127 E7
Tullich Argyll 125 D6
Tullich Highld 138 B2
Tullich Muir Highld 151 D10
Tulliemet Perth 133 D6
Tulloch Aberds 135 B7
Tulloch Aberds 153 E8
Tulloch Perth 128 B2
Tulloch Castle Highld 151 E8
Tullochgorm Argyll 125 F5
Tulloes Angus 135 E5
Tullybannocher Perth 127 B6
Tullybelton Perth 133 F7
Tullyfergus Perth 134 E2
Tullymurdoch Perth 134 D1
Tullynessle Aberds 140 C4
Tumble Carms 33 C6
Tumby Woodside Lincs 79 D5
Tummel Bridge Perth 132 D4
Tunga W Isles 155 D9
Tunstall E Yorks 97 F9
Tunstall Kent 30 C2
Tunstall Lancs 93 B6
Tunstall N Yorks 101 E7
Tunstall Norf 69 D7
Tunstall Stoke 75 D5
Tunstall Suff 57 D7
Tunstall T&W 111 D6
Tunstead Derbys 75 B8
Tunstead Gtr Man 87 D8
Tunstead Norf 81 E8
Tunworth Hants 26 E4
Tupsley Hereford 49 E7
Tupton Derbys 76 C3
Tur Langton Leics 64 E4
Turgis Green Hants 26 D4
Turin Angus 135 D5
Turkdean Glos 37 C8
Turleigh Wilts 24 C3
Turn Lancs 87 C6
Turnastone Hereford 49 F5
Turnberry S Ayrs 112 D2
Turnditch Derbys 76 E2
Turners Hill W Sus 28 F4
Turners Puddle Dorset 13 E6
Turnford Herts 41 D6
Turnhouse Edin 120 B4
Turnworth Dorset 13 D6
Turriff Aberds 153 C7
Turton Bottoms Blackburn 86 C5
Turves Cambs 66 E3
Turvey Bedford 53 D7
Turville Bucks 39 E7
Turville Heath Bucks 39 E7
Turweston Bucks 52 F4
Tushielaw Borders 115 C6
Tutbury Staffs 63 B6
Tutnall Worcs 50 B4
Tutshill Glos 36 E2
Tuttington Norf 81 E8
Tutts Clump W Berks 26 B3
Tuxford Notts 77 B7
Twatt Orkney 159 F3
Twatt Shetland 160 H5
Twechar E Dunb 119 B7
Tweedmouth Northumb 123 D5
Tweedsmuir Borders 114 B3
Twelve Heads Corn 3 B6
Twemlow Green Ches E 74 C4
Twenty Lincs 65 B8
Twerton Bath 24 C2
Twickenham London 28 B2
Twigworth Glos 37 B5
Twineham W Sus 17 C6
Twinhoe Bath 24 D2
Twinstead Essex 56 F2
Twinstead Green Essex 56 F2
Twiss Green Warr 86 E4
Twiston Lancs 93 E8
Twitchen Devon 21 F6
Twitchen Shrops 49 B5
Two Bridges Devon 6 B4
Two Dales Derbys 76 C2
Two Mills Ches W 73 B7
Twycross Leics 63 D7
Twyford Bucks 39 B6
Twyford Derbys 63 B7
Twyford Hants 15 B5
Twyford Leics 64 C4
Twyford Lincs 65 B6
Twyford Norf 81 E6
Twyford Wokingham 27 B5
Twyford Common Hereford 49 F7
Twyn-y-Sheriff Mon 35 D8
Twynholm Dumfries 106 D3
Twyning Glos 50 F3
Twyning Green Glos 50 F4
Twynllanan Carms 34 B1
Twynmynydd Carms 33 C7
Twywell Northants 53 B7
Ty-draw Conwy 83 F8
Ty-hen Carms 32 B4
Ty-hen Gwyn 70 D2
Ty-mawr Anglesey 82 C4
Ty Mawr Carms 46 E4
Ty Mawr Cwm Conwy 72 E3
Ty-nant Conwy 72 E3
Ty-nant Gwyn 59 B6
Ty-uchaf Powys 59 B7
Tyberton Hereford 49 F5
Tyburn W Mid 62 E5
Tycroes Carms 33 C7
Tycrwyn Powys 59 C8
Tydd Gote Lincs 66 C4
Tydd St Giles Cambs 66 C4
Tydd St Mary Lincs 66 C4
Tyddewi = St David's Pembs 44 C2
Tyddyn-mawr Gwyn 71 C6
Tye Green Essex 41 D7
Tye Green Essex 42 B3
Tye Green Essex 55 F6
Tyldesley Gtr Man 86 D4
Tyler Hill Kent 30 C5
Tylers Green Bucks 40 E2
Tylorstown Rhondda 34 E4
Tylwch Powys 59 F6
Tyn-y-celyn Wrex 73 F5
Tyn-y-coed Shrops 60 B2
Tyn-y-fedwen Powys 72 F5
Tyn-y-ffridd Powys 72 F5
Tyn-y-graig Powys 48 D2
Ty'n-y-groes Conwy 83 D7
Ty'n-y-maes Gwyn 83 E6
Tyn-y-pwll Anglesey 82 C4
Ty'n-yr-eithin Ceredig 47 C5
Tyncelyn Ceredig 46 C5
Tyndrum Stirling 131 F7
Tyne Tunnel T&W 111 C6
Tyneham Dorset 13 F6
Tynehead Midloth 121 D6
Tynemouth T&W 111 C6
Tynewydd Rhondda 34 E3
Tyninghame E Loth 122 B2
Tynron Dumfries 113 E8
Tynygongl Anglesey 82 C5
Tynygraig Ceredig 47 C5
Tŷ'r-felin-isaf Conwy 83 E8
Tyrie Aberds 153 B9
Tyringham M Keynes 53 E6
Tythecott Devon 9 C6
Tythegston Bridgend 21 B7
Tytherington Ches E 75 B6
Tytherington S Glos 36 F3
Tytherington Som 24 E2
Tytherington Wilts 24 E4
Tytherleigh Devon 11 D8
Tywardreath Corn 5 D5
Tywyn Conwy 83 D7
Tywyn Gwyn 58 D2

U

Uachdar W Isles 148 C2
Uags Highld 149 E12
Ubbeston Green Suff 57 B7
Ubley Bath 23 D7
Uckerby N Yorks 101 D7
Uckfield E Sus 17 B8
Uckington Glos 37 B6
Uddingston S Lanark 119 C6
Uddington S Lanark 119 F8
Udimore E Sus 19 D5
Udny Green Aberds 141 B7
Udny Station Aberds 141 B8
Udston S Lanark 119 D6
Udstonhead S Lanark 119 E7
Uffcott Wilts 25 B6
Uffculme Devon 11 C5
Uffington Lincs 65 D7
Uffington Oxon 38 F3
Uffington Shrops 60 C5
Ufford Pboro 65 D7
Ufford Suff 57 D6
Ufton Warks 51 C8
Ufton Nervet W Berks 26 C4
Ugadale Argyll 143 F8
Ugborough Devon 6 D4
Uggeshall Suff 69 F7
Ugglebarnby N Yorks 103 D6
Ughill S Yorks 88 E3
Ugley Essex 41 B8
Ugley Green Essex 41 B8
Ugthorpe N Yorks 103 C5
Uidh W Isles 148 J1
Uig Argyll 145 E10
Uig Highld 148 C6
Uig Highld 149 B8
Uigen W Isles 154 D5
Uigshader Highld 149 D9
Uisken Argyll 146 K6
Ulbster Highld 158 F5
Ulceby Lincs 79 B7
Ulceby N Lincs 90 C5
Ulceby Skitter N Lincs 90 C5
Ulcombe Kent 30 E2
Uldale Cumb 108 F2
Uley Glos 36 E4
Ulgham Northumb 117 E8
Ullapool Highld 150 B4
Ullenhall Warks 51 C6
Ullenwood Glos 37 C6
Ulleskelf N Yorks 95 E8
Ullesthorpe Leics 64 F2
Ulley S Yorks 89 F5
Ullingswick Hereford 49 E7
Ullinish Highld 149 E8
Ullock Cumb 98 B2
Ulnes Walton Lancs 86 C3
Ulpha Cumb 98 E3
Ulrome E Yorks 97 D7
Ulsta Shetland 160 E6
Ulva House Argyll 146 H7
Ulverston Cumb 92 B2
Ulwell Dorset 13 F8
Umberleigh Devon 9 B8
Unapool Highld 156 F5
Unasary W Isles 148 F2
Underbarrow Cumb 99 E6
Undercliffe W Yorks 94 F4
Underhoull Shetland 160 C7
Underriver Kent 29 D6
Underwood Notts 76 D4
Undy Mon 35 F8
Unifirth Shetland 160 H4
Union Cottage Aberds 141 E7
Union Mills IoM 84 E3
Union Street E Sus 18 B4
Unstone Derbys 76 B3
Unstone Green Derbys 76 B3
Unthank Cumb 108 F4
Unthank Cumb 109 E6
Unthank End Cumb 108 F4
Up Cerne Dorset 12 D4
Up Exe Devon 10 D4
Up Hatherley Glos 37 B6
Up Holland Lancs 86 D3
Up Marden W Sus 15 C8
Up Nately Hants 26 D4
Up Somborne Hants 25 F8
Up Sydling Dorset 12 D4
Upavon Wilts 25 D6
Upchurch Kent 30 C2
Upcott Hereford 48 D5
Upend Cambs 55 D7
Upgate Norf 68 C4
Uphall W Loth 120 B3
Uphall Station W Loth 120 B3
Upham Devon 10 D3
Upham Hants 15 B6
Uphampton Worcs 50 C3
Uphill N Som 22 D5
Uplawmoor E Renf 118 D4
Upleadon Glos 36 B4
Upleatham Redcar 102 C4
Uplees Kent 30 C3
Uploders Dorset 12 E3
Uplowman Devon 10 C5
Uplyme Devon 11 E8
Upminster London 42 F1
Upnor Medway 29 B8
Upottery Devon 11 D7
Upper Affcot Shrops 60 F4
Upper Ardchronie Highld 151 C9
Upper Arley Worcs 61 F7
Upper Arncott Oxon 39 C6
Upper Astrop Northants 52 F3
Upper Badcall Highld 156 E4
Upper Basildon W Berks 26 B3
Upper Beeding W Sus 17 C5
Upper Benefield Northants 65 F6
Upper Bighouse Highld 157 D11
Upper Boddington Northants 52 D2
Upper Borth Ceredig 58 F3
Upper Boyndlie Aberds 153 B9
Upper Brailes Warks 51 F8
Upper Breakish Highld 149 F11
Upper Breinton Hereford 49 E6
Upper Broadheath Worcs 50 D3
Upper Broughton Notts 64 B3
Upper Bucklebury W Berks 26 C3
Upper Burnhaugh Aberds 141 E7
Upper Caldecote C Beds 54 E2
Upper Catesby Northants 52 D3
Upper Chapel Powys 48 E2
Upper Church Village Rhondda 34 F4
Upper Chute Wilts 25 D7
Upper Clatford Hants 25 E8
Upper Clynnog Gwyn 71 C5
Upper Cumberworth W Yorks 88 D3
Upper Cwm-twrch Powys 34 C1
Upper Cwmbran Torf 35 E6
Upper Dallachy Moray 152 B3
Upper Dean Bedford 53 C8
Upper Denby W Yorks 88 D3
Upper Denton Cumb 109 C6
Upper Derraid Highld 151 H13
Upper Dicker E Sus 18 E2
Upper Dovercourt Essex 57 F6
Upper Druimfin Argyll 147 F8
Upper Dunsforth N Yorks 95 C7
Upper Eathie Highld 151 E10
Upper Elkstone Staffs 75 D7
Upper End Derbys 75 B7
Upper Farringdon Hants 26 F5
Upper Framilode Glos 36 C4
Upper Glenfintaig Highld 137 F5
Upper Gornal W Mid 62 E3
Upper Gravenhurst C Beds 54 F2
Upper Green Mon 35 C7
Upper Green W Berks 25 C8
Upper Grove Common Hereford 36 B2
Upper Hackney Derbys 76 C2
Upper Hale Sur 27 E6
Upper Halistra Highld 148 C7
Upper Halling Medway 29 C7
Upper Hambleton Rutland 65 D6
Upper Hardres Court Kent 31 D5
Upper Hartfield E Sus 29 F5
Upper Haugh S Yorks 88 E5
Upper Heath Shrops 61 F5
Upper Hellesdon Norf 68 C5
Upper Helmsley N Yorks 96 D2
Upper Hergest Hereford 48 D4
Upper Heyford Northants 52 D4
Upper Heyford Oxon 38 B4
Upper Hill Hereford 49 D6
Upper Hopton W Yorks 88 C2
Upper Horsebridge E Sus 18 D2
Upper Hulme Staffs 75 C7
Upper Inglesham Swindon 38 E2
Upper Inverbrough Highld 151 H11
Upper Killay Swansea 33 E6
Upper Knockando Moray 152 D1
Upper Lambourn W Berks 38 F3
Upper Leigh Staffs 75 F7
Upper Lenie Highld 137 B8
Upper Lochton Aberds 141 E5
Upper Longdon Staffs 62 C4
Upper Lybster Highld 158 G4
Upper Lydbrook Glos 36 C3
Upper Maes-coed Hereford 48 F5
Upper Midway Derbys 63 B6
Upper Milovaig Highld 148 D6
Upper Minety Wilts 37 E7
Upper Mitton Worcs 50 B3
Upper North Dean Bucks 39 E8
Upper Obney Perth 133 F7
Upper Ollach Highld 149 E10
Upper Padley Derbys 76 B2
Upper Pollicott Bucks 39 C7
Upper Poppleton York 95 D8
Upper Quinton Warks 51 E6
Upper Ratley Hants 14 B4
Upper Rissington Glos 38 C2
Upper Rochford Worcs 49 C8
Upper Sandaig Highld 149 G12
Upper Sanday Orkney 159 H6
Upper Sapey Hereford 49 C8
Upper Saxondale Notts 77 F6
Upper Seagry Wilts 37 F6
Upper Shelton C Beds 53 E7
Upper Sheringham Norf 81 C7
Upper Skelmorlie N Ayrs 118 C2
Upper Slaughter Glos 38 B1
Upper Soudley Glos 36 C3
Upper Stondon C Beds 54 F2
Upper Stowe Northants 52 D4
Upper Stratton Swindon 38 F1
Upper Street Hants 14 C2
Upper Street Norf 69 C6
Upper Street Norf 69 C6
Upper Street Suff 56 F5
Upper Strensham Worcs 50 F4
Upper Sundon C Beds 40 B3
Upper Swell Glos 38 B1
Upper Tean Staffs 75 F7
Upper Tillyrie Perth 128 D3
Upper Tooting London 28 B3
Upper Tote Highld 149 C10
Upper Town N Som 23 C7
Upper Treverward Shrops 48 B4
Upper Tysoe Warks 51 E8
Upper Upham Wilts 25 B7
Upper Wardington Oxon 52 E2
Upper Weald M Keynes 53 F5
Upper Weedon Northants 52 D4
Upper Wield Hants 26 F4
Upper Winchendon Bucks 39 C7
Upper Witton W Mid 62 E4
Upper Woodend Aberds 141 C5
Upper Woodford Wilts 25 F6
Upper Wootton Hants 26 D3
Upper Wyche Hereford 50 E2
Upperby Cumb 108 D4
Uppermill Gtr Man 87 D7
Uppersound Shetland 160 J6
Upperthong W Yorks 88 D2
Upperthorpe N Lincs 89 D8
Upperton W Sus 16 B3
Uppertown Derbys 76 C3
Uppertown Highld 158 C5
Uppertown Orkney 159 J5
Uppingham Rutland 65 E5
Uppington Shrops 61 D6
Upsall N Yorks 102 F2
Upshire Essex 41 D7
Upstreet Kent 31 C6
Upthorpe Suff 56 B3
Upton Cambs 54 B2
Upton Ches W 73 C8
Upton Corn 8 D4
Upton Dorset 12 F5
Upton Dorset 13 E7
Upton Hants 14 C4
Upton Hants 25 D8
Upton Leics 63 E7
Upton Lincs 90 F2
Upton Mers 85 F3
Upton Norf 69 C6
Upton Northants 52 C5
Upton Notts 77 B7
Upton Notts 77 D7
Upton Oxon 39 F5
Upton Pboro 65 D8
Upton Slough 27 B7
Upton Som 10 B4
Upton W Yorks 89 C5
Upton Bishop Hereford 36 B3
Upton Cheyney S Glos 23 C8
Upton Cressett Shrops 61 E6
Upton Cross Corn 5 B7
Upton Grey Hants 26 E4
Upton Hellions Devon 10 D3
Upton Lovell Wilts 24 E4
Upton Magna Shrops 61 C5
Upton Noble Som 24 F2
Upton Pyne Devon 10 E4
Upton Scudamore Wilts 24 E3
Upton St Leonard's Glos 37 C5
Upton Snodsbury Worcs 50 D4
Upton upon Severn Worcs 50 E3
Upton Warren Worcs 50 C4
Upwaltham W Sus 16 C3
Upware Cambs 55 B6
Upwell Norf 66 D4
Upwey Dorset 12 F4
Upwood Cambs 66 F2
Uradale Shetland 160 K6
Urafirth Shetland 160 F5
Urchfont Wilts 24 D5
Urdimarsh Hereford 49 E7
Ure Shetland 160 F4
Ure Bank N Yorks 95 B6
Urgha W Isles 154 H6
Urishay Common Hereford 48 F5
Urlay Nook Stockton 102 C1
Urmston Gtr Man 87 E5
Urpeth Durham 110 D5
Urquhart Highld 151 F8
Urquhart Moray 152 B2
Urra N Yorks 102 D3
Urray Highld 151 F8
Ushaw Moor Durham 110 E5
Usk = Brynbuga Mon 35 D7
Usselby Lincs 90 E4
Usworth T&W 111 D6
Utkinton Ches W 74 C2
Utley W Yorks 94 E3
Uton Devon 10 E3
Utterby Lincs 91 E7
Uttoxeter Staffs 75 F7
Uwchmynydd Gwyn 70 E2
Uxbridge London 40 F3
Uyeasound Shetland 160 C7
Uzmaston Pembs 44 D4

V

Valley Anglesey 82 D2
Valley Truckle Corn 8 F2
Valleyfield Dumfries 106 D3
Valsgarth Shetland 160 B8
Valtos Highld 149 B10
Van Powys 59 F6
Vange Essex 42 F3
Varteg Torf 35 D6
Vatten Highld 149 D7
Vaul Argyll 146 G3
Vaynor M Tydf 34 C4
Veensgarth Shetland 160 J6
Velindre Powys 48 F3
Vellow Som 22 F2
Veness Orkney 159 F6
Venn Green Devon 9 C5
Venn Ottery Devon 11 E5
Vennington Shrops 60 D3
Venny Tedburn Devon 10 E3
Ventnor IoW 15 G6
Vernham Dean Hants 25 D8
Vernham Street Hants 25 D8
Vernolds Common Shrops 60 F4
Verwood Dorset 13 D8
Veryan Corn 3 C8
Vicarage Devon 11 F7
Vickerstown Cumb 92 C1
Victoria Corn 4 C4
Victoria S Yorks 88 D2
Vidlin Shetland 160 G6
Viewpark N Lanark 119 C7
Vigo Village Kent 29 C7
Vinehall Street E Sus 18 C4
Vine's Cross E Sus 18 D2
Viney Hill Glos 36 D3
Virginia Water Sur 27 C8
Virginstow Devon 9 E5
Vobster Som 24 E2
Voe Shetland 160 E5
Voe Shetland 160 G6
Vowchurch Hereford 49 F5
Voxter Shetland 160 F5
Voy Orkney 159 G3

W

Wackerfield Durham 101 B6
Wacton Norf 68 E4
Wadbister Shetland 160 J6
Wadborough Worcs 50 E4
Waddesdon Bucks 39 C7
Waddingham Lincs 90 E3
Waddington Lancs 93 E7
Waddington Lincs 78 C2
Wadebridge Corn 4 B4
Wadeford Som 11 C8
Wadenhoe Northants 65 F7
Wadesmill Herts 41 C6
Wadhurst E Sus 18 B3
Wadshelf Derbys 76 B3
Wadsley S Yorks 88 E4
Wadsley Bridge S Yorks 88 E4
Wadworth S Yorks 89 E6
Waen Denb 72 C3
Waen Denb 72 C5
Waen Fach Powys 60 C2
Waen Goleugoed Denb 72 B4
Wag Highld 157 G13
Wainfleet All Saints Lincs 79 D7
Wainfleet Bank Lincs 79 D7
Wainfleet St Mary Lincs 79 D8
Wainfleet Tofts Lincs 79 D7
Wainhouse Corner Corn 8 E3
Wainscott Medway 29 B8
Wainstalls W Yorks 87 B8
Waitby Cumb 100 D2
Waithe Lincs 91 D6
Wake Lady Green N Yorks 102 E4
Wakefield W Yorks 88 B4
Wakerley Northants 65 E6
Wakes Colne Essex 42 B4
Walberswick Suff 57 B8
Walberton W Sus 16 D3
Walbottle T&W 110 C4
Walcot Lincs 78 F3
Walcot N Lincs 90 B2
Walcot Shrops 60 F3
Walcot Swindon 38 F1
Walcot Telford 61 C5
Walcot Green Norf 68 F4
Walcote Leics 64 F2
Walcote Warks 51 D6
Walcott Lincs 78 D4
Walcott Norf 69 A6
Walden N Yorks 101 F5
Walden Head N Yorks 100 F4
Walden Stubbs N Yorks 89 C6
Waldersey Cambs 66 D4
Walderslade Medway 29 C8
Walderton W Sus 15 C8
Walditch Dorset 12 E2
Waldley Derbys 75 F8
Waldridge Durham 111 D5
Waldringfield Suff 57 E6
Waldringfield Heath Suff 57 E6
Waldron E Sus 18 D2
Wales S Yorks 89 F5
Walesby Lincs 90 E5
Walesby Notts 77 B6
Walford Hereford 36 B2
Walford Hereford 49 B5
Walford Shrops 60 B4

Walford Heath Shrops 60 C4
Walgherton Ches E 74 E3
Walgrave Northants 53 B6
Walhampton Hants 14 E4
Walk Mill Lancs 93 F8
Walkden Gtr Man 86 D5
Walker T&W 111 C5
Walker Barn Ches E 75 B6
Walker Fold Lancs 93 E6
Walkerburn Borders 121 F6
Walkeringham Notts 89 E8
Walkerith Lincs 89 E8
Walkern Herts 41 B5
Walker's Green Hereford 49 E7
Walkerville N Yorks 101 E7
Walkford Dorset 14 E3
Walkhampton Devon 6 C3
Walkington E Yorks 97 F5
Walkley S Yorks 88 F4
Wall Northumb 110 C2
Wall Staffs 62 D5
Wall Bank Shrops 60 E5
Wall Heath W Mid 62 F2
Wall under Heywood Shrops 60 E5
Wallaceton Dumfries 113 F8
Wallacetown S Ayrs 112 B3
Wallacetown S Ayrs 112 D2
Wallands Park E Sus 17 C8
Wallasey Mers 85 E4
Wallcrouch E Sus 18 B3
Wallingford Oxon 39 F6
Wallington Hants 15 D6
Wallington Herts 54 F3
Wallington London 28 C3
Wallis Pembs 32 B1
Walliswood Sur 28 F2
Walls Shetland 160 J4
Wallsend T&W 111 C5
Wallston V Glam 22 B3
Wallyford E Loth 121 B6
Walmer Kent 31 D7
Walmer Bridge Lancs 86 B2
Walmersley Gtr Man 87 C6
Walmley W Mid 62 E5
Walpole Suff 57 B7
Walpole Cross Keys Norf 66 C5
Walpole Highway Norf 66 C5
Walpole Marsh Norf 66 C4
Walpole St Andrew Norf 66 C5
Walpole St Peter Norf 66 C5
Walsall W Mid 62 E4
Walsall Wood W Mid 62 D4
Walsden W Yorks 87 B7
Walsgrave on Sowe W Mid 63 F7
Walsham le Willows Suff 56 B3
Walshaw Gtr Man 87 C5
Walshford N Yorks 95 D7
Walsoken Cambs 66 C4
Walston S Lanark 120 E3
Walsworth Herts 54 F3
Walters Ash Bucks 39 E8
Walterston V Glam 22 B2
Walterstone Hereford 35 B7
Waltham Kent 30 E5
Waltham NE Lincs 91 D6
Waltham Abbey Essex 41 D6
Waltham Chase Hants 15 C6
Waltham Cross Herts 41 D6
Waltham on the Wolds Leics 64 B5
Waltham St Lawrence Windsor 27 B6
Walthamstow London 41 F6
Walton Cumb 108 C5
Walton Derbys 76 C3
Walton Leics 64 F2
Walton M Keynes 53 F6
Walton Mers 85 E4
Walton Pboro 65 D8
Walton Powys 48 D4
Walton Som 23 F6
Walton Staffs 75 F5
Walton Suff 57 F6
Walton Telford 61 C5
Walton W Yorks 88 C4
Walton W Yorks 95 E7
Walton Warks 51 D7
Walton Cardiff Glos 50 F4
Walton East Pembs 32 B1
Walton-in-Gordano N Som 23 B6
Walton-le-Dale Lancs 86 B3
Walton-on-Thames Sur 28 C2
Walton on the Hill Staffs 62 B3
Walton on the Hill Sur 28 D3
Walton-on-the-Naze Essex 43 B8
Walton on the Wolds Leics 64 C2
Walton-on-Trent Derbys 63 C6
Walton West Pembs 44 D3
Walwen Flint 73 B6
Walwick Northumb 110 B2
Walworth Darl 101 C7
Walworth Gate Darl 101 B7
Walwyn's Castle Pembs 44 D3
Wambrook Som 11 D7
Wanborough Sur 27 E7
Wanborough Swindon 38 F2
Wandsworth London 28 B3
Wangford Suff 57 B8
Wanlockhead Dumfries 113 C8
Wansford E Yorks 97 D6
Wansford Pboro 65 E7
Wanstead London 41 F7
Wanstrow Som 24 E2
Wanswell Glos 36 D3
Wantage Oxon 38 F3
Wapley S Glos 24 B2
Wappenbury Warks 51 C8
Wappenham Northants 52 E4
Warbleton E Sus 18 D3
Warblington Hants 15 D8
Warborough Oxon 39 E5
Warboys Cambs 66 F3
Warbreck Blackpool 92 F3
Warbstow Corn 8 E4
Warburton Gtr Man 86 F5
Warcop Cumb 100 C2
Ward End W Mid 62 F5
Ward Green Suff 56 C4
Warden Kent 30 B4
Warden Northumb 110 C2
Wardhill Orkney 159 F7
Wardington Oxon 52 E2
Wardlaw Borders 115 C5
Wardle Ches E 74 D3
Wardle Gtr Man 87 C7
Wardley Rutland 64 D5
Wardlow Derbys 75 B8
Wardy Hill Cambs 66 F4
Ware Herts 41 C6
Ware Kent 31 C6
Wareham Dorset 13 F7
Warehorne Kent 19 B6
Waren Mill Northumb 123 F7
Warenford Northumb 117 B7
Warenton Northumb 123 F7
Wareside Herts 41 C6
Waresley Cambs 54 D3
Waresley Worcs 50 B3
Warfield Brack 27 B6
Warfleet Devon 7 D6
Wargrave Wokingham 27 B5
Warham Norf 80 C5
Warhill Gtr Man 87 E7
Wark Northumb 109 B8
Wark Northumb 122 F4
Warkleigh Devon 9 B8
Warkton Northants 53 B6
Warkworth Northants 52 E2
Warkworth Northumb 117 D8
Warlaby N Yorks 101 E8
Warland W Yorks 87 B7
Warleggan Corn 5 C6
Warlingham Sur 28 D4
Warmfield W Yorks 88 B4
Warmingham Ches E 74 C4
Warmington Northants 65 E7
Warmington Warks 52 E2
Warminster Wilts 24 E3
Warmlake Kent 30 D2
Warmley S Glos 23 B8
Warmley Tower S Glos 23 B8
Warmonds Hill Northants 53 C7
Warmsworth S Yorks 89 D6
Warmwell Dorset 13 F5
Warndon Worcs 50 D3
Warnford Hants 15 B7
Warnham W Sus 28 F2
Warninglid W Sus 17 B6
Warren Ches E 75 B5
Warren Pembs 44 F4
Warren Heath Suff 57 E6
Warren Row Windsor 39 F8
Warren Street Kent 30 D3
Warrington M Keynes 53 D6
Warrington Warr 86 F4
Warsash Hants 15 D5
Warslow Staffs 75 D7
Warter E Yorks 96 D4
Warthermarske N Yorks 94 B5
Warthill N Yorks 96 D2
Wartling E Sus 18 E3
Wartnaby Leics 64 B4
Warton Lancs 86 B2
Warton Lancs 92 B4
Warton Northumb 117 D6
Warton Warks 63 D6
Warwick Warks 51 C7
Warwick Bridge Cumb 108 D4
Warwick on Eden Cumb 108 D4
Wasbister Orkney 159 E4
Wasdale Head Cumb 98 D3
Wash Common W Berks 26 C2
Washaway Corn 4 C5
Washbourne Devon 7 D5
Washfield Devon 10 C4
Washfold N Yorks 101 D5
Washford Som 22 E2
Washford Pyne Devon 10 C3
Washingborough Lincs 78 B3
Washington T&W 111 D6
Washington W Sus 16 C5
Wasing W Berks 26 C3
Waskerley Durham 110 E3
Wasperton Warks 51 D7
Wasps Nest Lincs 78 C3
Wass N Yorks 95 B8
Watchet Som 22 E2
Watchfield Oxon 38 E2
Watchfield Som 22 E5
Watchgate Cumb 99 E7
Watchhill Cumb 107 E8
Watcombe Torbay 7 C7
Watendlath Cumb 98 C4
Water Devon 10 F2
Water Lancs 87 B6
Water End E Yorks 96 F3
Water End Herts 40 C3
Water End Herts 41 D5
Water Newton Cambs 65 E8
Water Orton Warks 63 E5
Water Stratford Bucks 52 F4
Water Yeat Cumb 98 F4
Waterbeach Cambs 55 C5
Waterbeck Dumfries 108 B2
Waterden Norf 80 D4
Waterfall Staffs 75 D7
Waterfoot E Renf 119 D5
Waterfoot Lancs 87 B6
Waterford Hants 14 E4
Waterford Herts 41 C6
Waterhead Cumb 99 D5
Waterhead Dumfries 114 E4
Waterheads Borders 120 D5
Waterhouses Durham 110 E4
Waterhouses Staffs 75 D7
Wateringbury Kent 29 D7
Waterloo Gtr Man 87 D7
Waterloo Highld 149 F11
Waterloo Mers 85 E4
Waterloo N Lanark 119 D8
Waterloo Norf 68 C5
Waterloo Perth 133 F7
Waterloo Poole 13 E8
Waterloo Shrops 74 F2
Waterloo Port Gwyn 82 E4
Waterlooville Hants 15 D7
Watermeetings S Lanark 114 C2
Watermillock Cumb 99 B6
Waterperry Oxon 39 D6
Waterrow Som 11 B5
Water's Nook Gtr Man 86 D4
Waters Upton Telford 61 C6
Watersfield W Sus 16 C4
Waterside Aberds 141 B9
Waterside Blackburn 86 B5
Waterside Cumb 108 E2
Waterside E Ayrs 112 D4
Waterside E Ayrs 118 E4
Waterside E Dunb 119 B6
Waterside E Renf 118 D5
Waterstock Oxon 39 D6
Waterston Pembs 44 E4
Watford Herts 40 E4
Watford Northants 52 C4
Watford Gap Staffs 62 D5
Wath N Yorks 94 C4
Wath N Yorks 95 B6
Wath N Yorks 96 B2
Wath Brow Cumb 98 C2
Wath upon Dearne S Yorks 88 D5
Watlington Norf 67 C6
Watlington Oxon 39 E6
Watnall Notts 76 E5
Watten Highld 158 E4
Wattisfield Suff 56 B4
Wattisham Suff 56 D4
Wattlesborough Heath Shrops 60 C3
Watton E Yorks 97 D6
Watton Norf 68 D2
Watton at Stone Herts 41 C6
Wattston N Lanark 119 B7
Wattstown Rhondda 34 E4
Wauchan Highld 136 F2
Waulkmill Lodge Orkney 159 H4
Waun Powys 59 D5
Waun-y-clyn Carms 33 D5
Waunarlwydd Swansea 33 E7
Waunclunda Carms 47 F5
Waunfawr Gwyn 82 F5
Waungron Swansea 33 D6
Waunlwyd Bl Gwent 35 D5
Wavendon M Keynes 53 F7
Waverbridge Cumb 108 E2
Waverton Ches W 73 C8
Waverton Cumb 108 E2
Wavertree Mers 85 F4
Wawne E Yorks 97 F6
Waxham Norf 69 B7
Waxholme E Yorks 91 B7
Way Kent 31 C7
Way Village Devon 10 C3
Wayfield Medway 29 C8
Wayford Som 12 D2
Waymills Shrops 74 E2
Wayne Green Mon 35 C8
Wdig = Goodwick Pembs 44 B4
Weachyburn Aberds 153 C6
Weald Oxon 38 D3
Wealdstone London 40 F4
Weardley W Yorks 95 E5
Weare Som 23 D6
Weare Giffard Devon 9 B6
Wearhead Durham 109 F8
Weasdale Cumb 100 D1
Weasenham All Saints Norf 80 E4
Weasenham St Peter Norf 80 E4
Weatherhill Sur 28 E4
Weaverham Ches W 74 B3
Weaverthorpe N Yorks 97 B5
Webheath Worcs 50 C5
Wedderlairs Aberds 153 E8
Wedderlie Borders 122 D2
Weddington Warks 63 E7
Wedhampton Wilts 25 D5
Wedmore Som 23 E6
Wednesbury W Mid 62 E3
Wednesfield W Mid 62 D3
Weedon Bucks 39 C8
Weedon Bec Northants 52 D4
Weedon Lois Northants 52 E4
Weeford Staffs 62 D5
Week Devon 10 C2
Week St Mary Corn 8 E4
Weeke Hants 26 F2
Weekley Northants 65 F5
Weel E Yorks 97 F6
Weeley Essex 43 B7
Weeley Heath Essex 43 B7
Weem Perth 133 E5
Weeping Cross Staffs 62 B3
Weethley Gate Warks 51 D5
Weeting Norf 67 F7
Weeton E Yorks 91 B7
Weeton Lancs 92 F3
Weeton N Yorks 95 E5
Weetwood Hall Northumb 117 B6
Weir Lancs 87 B6
Weir Quay Devon 6 C2
Welborne Norf 68 D3
Welbourn Lincs 78 D2
Welburn N Yorks 96 C3
Welburn N Yorks 102 F4
Welbury N Yorks 102 D1
Welby Lincs 78 F2
Welches Dam Cambs 66 F4
Welcombe Devon 8 C4
Weld Bank Lancs 86 C3
Weldon Northumb 117 E7
Welford Northants 64 F3
Welford W Berks 26 B2
Welford-on-Avon Warks 51 D6
Welham Leics 64 E4
Welham Notts 89 F8
Welham Green Herts 41 D5
Well Hants 27 E5
Well Lincs 79 B7
Well N Yorks 101 F7
Well End Bucks 40 F1
Well Heads W Yorks 94 F3
Well Hill Kent 29 C5
Well Town Devon 10 D4
Welland Worcs 50 E2
Wellbank Angus 134 F4
Welldale Dumfries 107 C8
Wellesbourne Warks 51 D7
Welling London 29 B5
Wellingborough Northants 53 C6
Wellingham Norf 80 E4
Wellingore Lincs 78 D2
Wellington Cumb 98 D2
Wellington Hereford 49 E6
Wellington Som 11 B6
Wellington Telford 61 C6
Wellington Heath Hereford 50 E2
Wellington Hill W Yorks 95 F6
Wellow Bath 24 D2
Wellow IoW 14 F4
Wellow Notts 77 C6
Wellpond Green Herts 41 B7
Wells Som 23 E7
Wells Green Ches E 74 D3
Wells-Next-The-Sea Norf 80 C5
Wellsborough Leics 63 D7
Wellswood Torbay 7 C7
Wellwood Fife 128 F2
Welney Norf 66 E5
Welsh Bicknor Hereford 36 C2
Welsh End Shrops 74 F2
Welsh Frankton Shrops 73 F7
Welsh Hook Pembs 44 C4
Welsh Newton Hereford 36 C1
Welsh St Donats V Glam 22 B2
Welshampton Shrops 73 F8
Welshpool = Y Trallwng Powys 60 D2
Welton Cumb 108 E3
Welton E Yorks 90 B3
Welton Lincs 78 B3
Welton Northants 52 C3
Welton Hill Lincs 90 F4
Welton le Marsh Lincs 79 C7
Welton le Wold Lincs 91 F6
Welwick E Yorks 91 B7
Welwyn Herts 41 C5
Welwyn Garden City Herts 41 C5
Wem Shrops 60 B5
Wembdon Som 22 F4
Wembley London 40 F4
Wembury Devon 6 E3
Wembworthy Devon 9 D8
Wemyss Bay Inverclyd 118 C1
Wenallt Ceredig 47 B5
Wenallt Gwyn 72 E3
Wendens Ambo Essex 55 F6
Wendlebury Oxon 39 C5
Wendling Norf 68 C2
Wendover Bucks 40 D1
Wendron Corn 3 C5
Wendy Cambs 54 E4
Wenfordbridge Corn 5 B5
Wenhaston Suff 57 B8
Wennington Cambs 54 B3
Wennington Lancs 93 B6
Wennington London 41 F8
Wensley Derbys 76 C2
Wensley N Yorks 101 F5
Wentbridge W Yorks 89 C5
Wentnor Shrops 60 E3
Wentworth Cambs 55 B5
Wentworth S Yorks 88 E4
Wenvoe V Glam 22 B3
Weobley Hereford 49 D6
Weobley Marsh Hereford 49 D6
Wereham Norf 67 D6
Wergs W Mid 62 D2
Wern Powys 59 C6
Wern Powys 60 C2
Wernffrwd Swansea 33 E6
Wernyrheolydd Mon 35 C7
Werrington Corn 8 F5
Werrington Pboro 65 D8
Werrington Staffs 75 E6
Wervin Ches W 73 B8
Wesham Lancs 92 F4
Wessington Derbys 76 D3
West Acre Norf 67 C7
West Adderbury Oxon 52 F2
West Allerdean Northumb 123 E5
West Alvington Devon 6 E5
West Amesbury Wilts 25 E6
West Anstey Devon 10 B3
West Ashby Lincs 79 B5
West Ashling W Sus 16 D2
West Ashton Wilts 24 D3
West Auckland Durham 101 B6
West Ayton N Yorks 103 F7
West Bagborough Som 22 F3
West Barkwith Lincs 91 F5
West Barnby N Yorks 103 C6
West Barns E Loth 122 B2
West Barsham Norf 80 D5
West Bay Dorset 12 E2
West Beckham Norf 81 D7
West Bedfont Sur 27 B8
West Benhar N Lanark 119 C8
West Bergholt Essex 43 B5
West Bexington Dorset 12 F3
West Bilney Norf 67 C7
West Blatchington Brighton 17 D6
West Bowling W Yorks 94 F4
West Bradford Lancs 93 E7
West Bradley Som 23 F7
West Bretton W Yorks 88 C3
West Bridgford Notts 77 F5
West Bromwich W Mid 62 E4
West Buckland Devon 21 F5
West Buckland Som 11 B6
West Burrafirth Shetland 160 H4
West Burton N Yorks 101 F5
West Burton W Sus 16 C3
West Butterwick N Lincs 90 D2
West Byfleet Sur 27 C8
West Caister Norf 69 C8
West Calder W Loth 120 C3
West Camel Som 12 B3
West Challow Oxon 38 F3
West Chelborough Dorset 12 D3
West Chevington Northumb 117 E8
West Chiltington W Sus 16 C4
West Chiltington Common W Sus 16 C4
West Chinnock Som 12 C2
West Chisenbury Wilts 25 D6
West Clandon Sur 27 D8
West Cliffe Kent 31 E7
West Clyne Highld 157 J11
West Clyth Highld 158 G4
West Coker Som 12 C3
West Compton Dorset 12 E3
West Compton Som 23 E7
West Cowick E Yorks 89 B7
West Cranmore Som 23 E8
West Cross Swansea 33 F7
West Cullery Aberds 141 D6
West Curry Corn 8 E4
West Curthwaite Cumb 108 E3
West Darlochan Argyll 143 F7
West Dean W Sus 16 C2
West Dean Wilts 14 B3
West Deeping Lincs 65 D8
West Derby Mers 85 E4
West Dereham Norf 67 D6
West Didsbury Gtr Man 87 E6
West Ditchburn Northumb 117 B7
West Down Devon 20 E4
West Drayton London 27 B8
West Drayton Notts 77 B7
West Ella E Yorks 90 B4
West End Bedford 53 D7
West End E Yorks 96 F5
West End E Yorks 97 F7
West End Hants 15 C5
West End Lancs 86 B5
West End N Som 23 C6
West End N Yorks 94 D4
West End Norf 68 D2
West End Norf 69 C8
West End Oxon 38 D4
West End S Lanark 120 E2
West End S Yorks 89 D7
West End Suff 69 F7
West End Sur 27 C7
West End W Sus 17 C6
West End Wilts 13 B7
West End Wilts 24 B4
West End Green Hants 26 C4
West Farleigh Kent 29 D8
West Felton Shrops 60 B3
West Fenton E Loth 129 F6
West Ferry Dundee 134 F4
West Firle E Sus 17 D8
West Ginge Oxon 38 F4
West Grafton Wilts 25 C7
West Green Hants 26 D5
West Greenskares Aberds 153 B7
West Grimstead Wilts 14 B3
West Grinstead W Sus 17 B5
West Haddlesey N Yorks 89 B6
West Haddon Northants 52 B4
West Hagbourne Oxon 39 F5
West Hagley Worcs 62 F3
West Hall Cumb 109 C5
West Hallam Derbys 76 E4
West Halton N Lincs 90 B3
West Ham London 41 F7
West Handley Derbys 76 B3
West Hanney Oxon 38 E4
West Hanningfield Essex 42 E3
West Hardwick W Yorks 88 C5
West Harnham Wilts 14 B2
West Harptree Bath 23 D7
West Hatch Som 11 B7
West Head Norf 67 D5
West Heath Ches E 74 C5
West Heath Hants 26 D3
West Heath Hants 27 D6
West Helmsdale Highld 157 H13
West Hendred Oxon 38 F4
West Heslerton N Yorks 96 B5
West Hill Devon 11 E5
West Hill E Yorks 97 C7
West Hill N Som 23 B6
West Hoathly W Sus 28 F4
West Holme Dorset 13 F6
West Horndon Essex 42 F2
West Horrington Som 23 E7
West Horsley Sur 27 D8
West Horton Northumb 123 F6
West Hougham Kent 31 E6
West Houlland Shetland 160 H4
West-houses Derbys 76 D4
West Huntington York 96 D2
West Hythe Kent 19 B8
West Ilsley W Berks 38 F4
West Itchenor W Sus 15 D8
West Keal Lincs 79 C6
West Kennett Wilts 25 C6
West Kilbride N Ayrs 118 E2
West Kingsdown Kent 29 C6
West Kington Wilts 24 B3
West Kinharrachie Aberds 153 E9
West Kirby Mers 85 F3
West Knapton N Yorks 96 B4
West Knighton Dorset 12 F5
West Knoyle Wilts 24 F3
West Kyloe Northumb 123 E6
West Lambrook Som 12 C2
West Langdon Kent 31 E7
West Langwell Highld 157 J9
West Lavington W Sus 16 B2
West Lavington Wilts 24 D5
West Layton N Yorks 101 D6
West Lea Durham 111 E7
West Leake Notts 64 B2
West Learmouth Northumb 122 F4
West Leigh Devon 9 D8
West Lexham Norf 67 C8
West Lilling N Yorks 96 C2
West Linton Borders 120 D4
West Liss Hants 15 B8
West Littleton S Glos 24 B2
West Looe Corn 5 D7
West Luccombe Som 21 E7
West Lulworth Dorset 13 F6
West Lutton N Yorks 96 C5
West Lydford Som 23 F7
West Lyng Som 11 B8
West Lynn Norf 67 B6
West Malling Kent 29 D7
West Malvern Worcs 50 E2
West Marden W Sus 15 C8
West Marina E Sus 18 E4
West Markham Notts 77 B7
West Marsh NE Lincs 91 C6
West Marton N Yorks 93 D8
West Meon Hants 15 B7
West Mersea Essex 43 C6
West Milton Dorset 12 E3
West Minster Kent 30 B3
West Molesey Sur 28 C2
West Monkton Som 11 B7
West Moors Dorset 13 D8
West Morriston Borders 122 E2
West Muir Angus 135 C5
West Ness N Yorks 96 B2
West Newham Northumb 110 B3
West Newton E Yorks 97 F7
West Newton Norf 67 B6
West Norwood London 28 B4
West Ogwell Devon 7 B6
West Orchard Dorset 13 C6
West Overton Wilts 25 C6
West Park Hrtlpl 111 F7
West Parley Dorset 13 E8
West Peckham Kent 29 D7
West Pelton Durham 110 D5
West Pennard Som 23 F7
West Pentire Corn 4 C2
West Perry Cambs 54 C2
West Putford Devon 9 C5
West Quantoxhead Som 22 E3
West Rainton Durham 111 E6
West Rasen Lincs 90 F4
West Raynham Norf 80 E4
West Retford Notts 89 F7
West Rounton N Yorks 102 D2
West Row Suff 55 B7
West Rudham Norf 80 E4
West Runton Norf 81 C7
West Saltoun E Loth 121 C7
West Sandwick Shetland 160 E6
West Scrafton N Yorks 101 F5
West Sleekburn Northumb 117 F8
West Somerton Norf 69 C7
West Stafford Dorset 12 F5
West Stockwith Notts 89 E8
West Stoke W Sus 16 D2
West Stonesdale N Yorks 100 D3
West Stoughton Som 23 E6
West Stour Dorset 13 B5
West Stourmouth Kent 31 C6
West Stow Suff 56 B2
West Stowell Wilts 25 C6
West Strathan Highld 157 C8
West Stratton Hants 26 E3
West Street Kent 30 D3
West Tanfield N Yorks 95 B5
West Taphouse Corn 5 C6
West Tarbert Argyll 145 G7
West Thirston Northumb 117 E7
West Thorney W Sus 15 D8
West Thurrock Thurrock 29 B6
West Tilbury Thurrock 29 B7
West Tisted Hants 15 B7
West Tofts Norf 67 E8
West Tofts Perth 133 F8
West Torrington Lincs 90 F5
West Town Hants 15 E8
West Town N Som 23 C6
West Tytherley Hants 14 B3
West Tytherton Wilts 24 B4
West Walton Norf 66 C4
West Walton Highway Norf 66 C4
West Wellow Hants 14 C3
West Wemyss Fife 128 E5
West Wick N Som 23 C5
West Wickham Cambs 55 E7
West Wickham London 28 C4
West Williamston Pembs 32 D1
West Willoughby Lincs 78 E2
West Winch Norf 67 C6
West Winterslow Wilts 25 F7
West Wittering W Sus 15 E8
West Witton N Yorks 101 F5
West Woodburn Northumb 116 F4
West Woodhay W Berks 25 C8
West Woodlands Som 24 E2
West Worldham Hants 26 F5
West Worlington Devon 10 C2
West Worthing W Sus 16 D5
West Wratting Cambs 55 D7
West Wycombe Bucks 39 E8
West Wylam Northumb 110 C4
West Yell Shetland 160 E6
Westacott Devon 20 F4
Westbere Kent 31 C5
Westborough Lincs 77 E8
Westbourne Bmouth 13 E8
Westbourne Suff 56 E5
Westbourne W Sus 15 D8
Westbrook W Berks 26 B2
Westbury Bucks 52 F4
Westbury Shrops 60 D3
Westbury Wilts 24 D3
Westbury Leigh Wilts 24 D3
Westbury-on-Severn Glos 36 C4
Westbury on Trym Bristol 23 B7
Westbury-sub-Mendip Som 23 E7
Westby Lancs 92 F3
Westcliff-on-Sea Southend 42 F4
Westcombe Som 23 F8
Westcote Glos 38 B2
Westcott Bucks 39 C7
Westcott Devon 10 D5
Westcott Sur 28 E2
Westcott Barton Oxon 38 B4
Westdean E Sus 18 F2
Westdene Brighton 17 D6
Wester Aberchalder Highld 137 B8
Wester Balgedie Perth 128 D3
Wester Culbeuchly Aberds 153 B6
Wester Dechmont W Loth 120 C3
Wester Denoon Angus 134 E3
Wester Fintray Aberds 141 C7
Wester Gruinards Highld 151 B8
Wester Lealty Highld 151 D9
Wester Milton Highld 151 F12
Wester Newburn Fife 129 D6
Wester Quarff Shetland 160 K6
Wester Skeld Shetland 160 J4
Westerdale Highld 158 E3
Westerdale N Yorks 102 D4
Westerfield Shetland 160 H5
Westerfield Suff 57 E5
Westergate W Sus 16 D3
Westerham Kent 28 D5
Westerhope T&W 110 C4
Westerleigh S Glos 23 B9
Westerton Angus 135 D6
Westerton Durham 110 F5
Westerton W Sus 16 D2
Westerwick Shetland 160 J4
Westfield Cumb 98 B1
Westfield E Sus 18 D5
Westfield Hereford 50 E2
Westfield Highld 158 D2
Westfield N Lanark 119 B7
Westfield Norf 68 D2
Westfield W Loth 120 B2
Westfields Dorset 12 D5
Westfields of Rattray Perth 134 E1
Westgate Durham 110 F2
Westgate N Lincs 89 D8
Westgate Norf 80 C4
Westgate Norf 81 C5
Westgate on Sea Kent 31 B7
Westhall Aberds 141 B5
Westhall Suff 69 F7
Westham Dorset 12 G4
Westham E Sus 18 E3
Westham Som 23 E6
Westhampnett W Sus 16 D2
Westhay Som 23 E6
Westhead Lancs 86 D2
Westhide Hereford 49 E7
Westhill Aberds 141 D7
Westhill Highld 151 G10
Westhope Hereford 49 D6
Westhope Shrops 60 F4
Westhorpe Lincs 78 F5
Westhorpe Suff 56 C4
Westhoughton Gtr Man 86 D4
Westhouse N Yorks 93 B6
Westhumble Sur 28 D2
Westing Shetland 160 C7
Westlake Devon 6 D4
Westleigh Devon 9 B6
Westleigh Devon 11 C5
Westleigh Gtr Man 86 D4
Westleton Suff 57 C8
Westley Shrops 60 D3
Westley Suff 56 C2
Westley Waterless Cambs 55 D7
Westlington Bucks 39 C7
Westlinton Cumb 108 C3
Westmarsh Kent 31 C6
Westmeston E Sus 17 C7
Westmill Herts 41 B6
Westminster London 28 B4
Westmuir Angus 134 D3
Westness Orkney 159 F4
Westnewton Cumb 107 E8
Westnewton Northumb 122 F5
Westoe T&W 111 C6
Weston Bath 24 C2
Weston Ches E 74 D4
Weston Devon 11 F6
Weston Dorset 12 G4
Weston Halton 86 F3
Weston Hants 15 B8
Weston Herts 54 F3
Weston Lincs 66 B2
Weston N Yorks 94 E4
Weston Northants 52 E3
Weston Notts 77 C7
Weston Shrops 61 B5
Weston Shrops 61 E5
Weston Staffs 62 B3
Weston W Berks 25 B8
Weston Beggard Hereford 49 E7
Weston by Welland Northants 64 E4
Weston Colville Cambs 55 D7
Weston Coyney Stoke 75 E6
Weston Favell Northants 53 C5
Weston Green Cambs 55 D7
Weston Green Norf 68 C4
Weston Heath Shrops 61 C7
Weston Hills Lincs 66 B2
Weston-in-Gordano N Som 23 B6
Weston Jones Staffs 61 B7
Weston Longville Norf 68 C4
Weston Lullingfields Shrops 60 B4
Weston-on-the-Green Oxon 39 C5
Weston-on-Trent Derbys 63 B8
Weston Patrick Hants 26 E4
Weston Rhyn Shrops 73 F6
Weston-Sub-Edge Glos 51 E6
Weston-super-Mare N Som 22 C5
Weston Turville Bucks 40 C1
Weston under Lizard Staffs 62 C2
Weston under Penyard Hereford 36 B3
Weston under Wetherley Warks 51 C8
Weston Underwood Derbys 76 E2
Weston Underwood M Keynes 53 D6
Westonbirt Glos 37 F5
Westoncommon Shrops 60 B4
Westoning C Beds 53 F8
Westonzoyland Som 23 F5
Westow N Yorks 96 C3
Westport Argyll 143 F7
Westport Som 11 C8
Westrigg W Loth 120 C2
Westruther Borders 122 E2
Westry Cambs 66 E3
Westville Notts 76 E5
Westward Cumb 108 E2
Westward Ho! Devon 9 B6
Westwell Kent 30 E3
Westwell Oxon 38 D2
Westwell Leacon Kent 30 E3
Westwick Cambs 54 C5
Westwick Durham 101 C5
Westwick Norf 81 E8
Westwood Devon 10 E5
Westwood Wilts 24 D3
Westwoodside N Lincs 89 E8
Wetheral Cumb 108 D4
Wetherby W Yorks 95 E7
Wetherden Suff 56 C4
Wetheringsett Suff 56 C5
Wethersfield Essex 55 F8
Wethersta Shetland 160 G5
Wetherup Street Suff 56 C5
Wetley Rocks Staffs 75 E6
Wettenhall Ches E 74 C3
Wetton Staffs 75 D8
Wetwang E Yorks 96 D5
Wetwood Staffs 74 F4
Wexcombe Wilts 25 D7
Wexham Street Bucks 40 F2
Weybourne Norf 81 C7
Weybread Suff 68 F5
Weybridge Sur 27 C8
Weycroft Devon 11 E8
Weydale Highld 158 D3
Weyhill Hants 25 E8
Weymouth Dorset 12 G4
Whaddon Bucks 53 F6
Whaddon Cambs 54 E4
Whaddon Glos 37 C5
Whaddon Wilts 14 B2
Whale Cumb 99 B7
Whaley Derbys 76 B5
Whaley Bridge Derbys 87 F8
Whaley Thorns Derbys 76 B5
Whaligoe Highld 158 F5
Whalley Lancs 93 F7
Whalton Northumb 117 F7
Wham N Yorks 93 C7
Whaplode Lincs 66 B3
Whaplode Drove Lincs 66 C3
Whaplode St Catherine Lincs 66 B3
Wharfe N Yorks 93 C7
Wharles Lancs 92 F4
Wharncliffe Side S Yorks 88 E3
Wharram le Street N Yorks 96 C4
Wharton Ches W 74 C3
Wharton Green Ches W 74 C3
Whashton N Yorks 101 D6
Whatcombe Dorset 13 D6
Whatcote Warks 51 E8
Whatfield Suff 56 E4
Whatley Som 11 D8
Whatley Som 24 E2
Whatlington E Sus 18 D4
Whatstandwell Derbys 76 D3
Whatton Notts 77 F7
Whauphill Dumfries 105 E8
Whaw N Yorks 100 D4
Wheatacre Norf 69 E7
Wheatcroft Derbys 76 D3
Wheathampstead Herts 40 C4
Wheathill Shrops 61 F6
Wheatley Devon 10 E4
Wheatley Hants 27 E5
Wheatley Oxon 39 D5
Wheatley S Yorks 89 D6
Wheatley W Yorks 87 B8
Wheatley Hill Durham 111 F6
Wheaton Aston Staffs 62 C2
Wheddon Cross Som 21 F8
Wheedlemont Aberds 140 B3
Wheelerstreet Sur 27 E7
Wheelock Ches E 74 D4
Wheelock Heath Ches E 74 D4
Wheelton Lancs 86 B4
Wheen Angus 134 B3
Wheldrake York 96 E2
Whelford Glos 38 E1
Whelpley Hill Herts 40 D2
Whempstead Herts 41 B6
Whenby N Yorks 96 C2
Whepstead Suff 56 D2
Wherstead Suff 57 E5
Wherwell Hants 25 E8
Wheston Derbys 75 B8
Whetsted Kent 29 E7
Whetstone Leics 64 E2
Whicham Cumb 98 F3
Whichford Warks 51 F8
Whickham T&W 110 C5
Whiddon Down Devon 9 E8
Whigstreet Angus 134 E4
Whilton Northants 52 C4
Whim Farm Borders 120 D5
Whimble Devon 9 D5
Whimple Devon 10 E5
Whimpwell Green Norf 69 B6
Whinburgh Norf 68 D3
Whinnieliggate Dumfries 106 D4
Whinnyfold Aberds 153 E10
Whippingham IoW 15 E6
Whipsnade C Beds 40 C3
Whipton Devon 10 E4
Whirlow S Yorks 88 F4
Whisby Lincs 78 C2
Whissendine Rutland 64 C5
Whissonsett Norf 80 E5
Whistlefield Argyll 145 D10
Whistlefield Argyll 145 D11
Whistley Green Wokingham 27 B5
Whiston Mers 86 E2
Whiston Northants 53 C6
Whiston S Yorks 88 F5
Whiston Staffs 62 C2
Whiston Staffs 75 E7
Whitbeck Cumb 98 F3
Whitbourne Hereford 50 D2
Whitburn T&W 111 C7
Whitburn W Loth 120 C2
Whitburn Colliery T&W 111 C7
Whitby Ches W 73 B7
Whitby N Yorks 103 C6
Whitbyheath Ches W 73 B7
Whitchurch Bath 23 C8
Whitchurch Bucks 39 B7
Whitchurch Cardiff 35 F5
Whitchurch Devon 6 B2
Whitchurch Hants 26 E2
Whitchurch Hereford 36 C2
Whitchurch Oxon 26 B4
Whitchurch Pembs 44 C2
Whitchurch Shrops 74 E2
Whitchurch Canonicorum Dorset 11 E8
Whitchurch Hill Oxon 26 B4
Whitcombe Dorset 12 F5
Whitcott Keysett Shrops 60 F2
White Coppice Lancs 86 C4
White Lackington Dorset 12 E5
White Ladies Aston Worcs 50 D4
White Lund Lancs 92 C4
White Mill Carms 33 B5
White Ness Shetland 160 J5
White Notley Essex 42 C3
White Pit Lincs 79 B6
White Post Notts 77 D6
White Rocks Hereford 35 B8
White Roding Essex 42 C1
White Waltham Windsor 27 B6
Whiteacen Moray 152 D2
Whiteacre Heath Warks 63 E6
Whitebridge Highld 137 C7
Whitebrook Mon 36 D2
Whiteburn Borders 121 E8
Whitecairn Dumfries 105 D6
Whitecairns Aberds 141 C8
Whitecastle S Lanark 120 E3
Whitechapel Lancs 93 E5
Whitecleat Orkney 159 H6
Whitecraig E Loth 121 B6
Whitecroft Glos 36 D3
Whitecross Corn 4 B4
Whitecross Falk 120 B2
Whitecross Staffs 62 B2
Whiteface Highld 151 C10
Whitefarland N Ayrs 143 D9
Whitefaulds S Ayrs 112 D2
Whitefield Gtr Man 87 D6
Whitefield Perth 134 F1
Whiteford Aberds 141 B6
Whitegate Ches W 74 C3
Whitehall Blackburn 86 B4
Whitehall W Sus 16 B5
Whitehall Village Orkney 159 F7
Whitehaven Cumb 98 C1
Whitehill Hants 27 F5
Whitehills Aberds 153 B6
Whitehills S Lanark 119 D6
Whitehough Derbys 87 F8
Whitehouse Aberds 140 C5
Whitehouse Argyll 145 G7
Whiteinch Glasgow 118 C5
Whitekirk E Loth 129 F7
Whitelaw S Lanark 119 E6
Whiteleas T&W 111 C6
Whiteley Bank IoW 15 F6
Whiteley Green Ches E 75 B6
Whiteley Village Sur 27 C8
Whitemans Green W Sus 17 B7
Whitemire Moray 151 F12
Whitemoor Corn 4 D4
Whitemore Staffs 75 C5
Whitenap Hants 14 B4
Whiteoak Green Oxon 38 C3
Whiteparish Wilts 14 B3
Whiterashes Aberds 141 B7
Whiterow Highld 158 F5
Whiteshill Glos 37 D5
Whiteside Northumb 109 C7
Whiteside W Loth 120 C2
Whitesmith E Sus 18 D2
Whitestaunton Som 11 C7
Whitestone Devon 10 E3
Whitestone Devon 20 E3
Whitestone Warks 63 F7
Whitestones Aberds 153 C8
Whitestreet Green Suff 56 F3
Whitewall Corner N Yorks 96 B3
Whiteway Glos 37 C6
Whiteway Glos 37 E5
Whitewell Aberds 153 B9
Whitewell Lancs 93 E6
Whitewell Bottom Lancs 87 B6
Whiteworks Devon 6 B4
Whitfield Kent 31 E7
Whitfield Northants 52 F4
Whitfield Northumb 109 D7
Whitfield S Glos 36 E3
Whitford Devon 11 E7
Whitford Flint 72 B5
Whitgift E Yorks 90 B2
Whitgreave Staffs 62 B2
Whithorn Dumfries 105 E8
Whiting Bay N Ayrs 143 F11
Whitkirk W Yorks 95 F6
Whitland Carms 32 C2
Whitletts S Ayrs 112 B3
Whitley N Yorks 89 B6
Whitley Reading 26 B5
Whitley Wilts 24 C3
Whitley Bay T&W 111 B6
Whitley Chapel Northumb 110 D2
Whitley Lower W Yorks 88 C3
Whitley Row Kent 29 D5
Whitlock's End W Mid 51 B6
Whitminster Glos 36 D4
Whitmore Staffs 74 E5
Whitnage Devon 10 C5
Whitnash Warks 51 C8
Whitney-on-Wye Hereford 48 E4
Whitrigg Cumb 108 D2
Whitrigg Cumb 108 F2
Whitsbury Hants 14 C2
Whitsome Borders 122 D4
Whitson Newport 35 F7
Whitstable Kent 30 C5
Whitstone Corn 8 E4
Whittingham Northumb 117 C6
Whittingslow Shrops 60 F4
Whittington Glos 37 B7
Whittington Lancs 93 B6
Whittington Norf 67 E7
Whittington Shrops 73 F7
Whittington Staffs 62 F2
Whittington Staffs 63 D5
Whittington Worcs 50 D3
Whittle-le-Woods Lancs 86 B3
Whittlebury Northants 52 E4
Whittlesey Cambs 66 E2
Whittlesford Cambs 55 E5
Whittlestone Head Blackburn 86 C5
Whitton Borders 116 B3
Whitton N Lincs 90 B3
Whitton Northumb 117 D6
Whitton Powys 48 C4
Whitton Shrops 49 B7
Whitton Stockton 102 B1
Whitton Suff 56 E5
Whittonditch Wilts 25 B7
Whittonstall Northumb 110 D3
Whitway Hants 26 D2
Whitwell Derbys 76 B5
Whitwell Herts 40 B4
Whitwell IoW 15 G6
Whitwell N Yorks 101 E7

Whitwell Rutland 65 D6
Whitwell-on-the-Hill N Yorks 96 C3
Whitwell Street Norf 81 E7
Whitwick Leics 63 C8
Whitwood W Yorks 88 B5
Whitworth Lancs 87 C6
Whixall Shrops 74 F2
Whixley N Yorks 95 D7
Whoberley W Mid 51 B8
Whorlton Durham 101 C6
Whorlton N Yorks 102 D2
Whygate Northumb 109 B7
Whyle Hereford 49 C7
Whyteleafe Sur 28 D4
Wibdon Glos 36 E2
Wibsey W Yorks 88 A2
Wibtoft Leics 63 F8
Wichenford Worcs 50 C2
Wichling Kent 30 D3
Wick Bmouth 14 E2
Wick Devon 11 D6
Wick Highld 158 E5
Wick S Glos 24 B2
Wick Shetland 160 K6
Wick V Glam 21 B8
Wick W Sus 16 D4
Wick Wilts 14 B2
Wick Worcs 50 E4
Wick Hill Wokingham 27 C5
Wick St Lawrence N Som 23 C5
Wicken Cambs 55 B6
Wicken Northants 52 F5
Wicken Bonhunt Essex 55 F5
Wicken Green Village Norf 80 D4
Wickenby Lincs 90 F4
Wickersley S Yorks 89 E5
Wickford Essex 42 E3
Wickham Hants 15 C6
Wickham W Berks 25 B8
Wickham Bishops Essex 42 C4
Wickham Market Suff 57 D7
Wickham Skeith Suff 56 C4
Wickham St Paul Essex 56 F2
Wickham Street Suff 55 D8
Wickham Street Suff 56 C4
Wickhambreux Kent 31 D6
Wickhambrook Suff 55 D8
Wickhamford Worcs 51 E5
Wickhampton Norf 69 D7
Wicklewood Norf 68 D3
Wickmere Norf 81 D7
Wickwar S Glos 36 F4
Widdington Essex 55 F6
Widdrington Northumb 117 E8
Widdrington Station Northumb 117 E8
Wide Open T&W 110 B5
Widecombe in the Moor Devon 6 B5
Widegates Corn 5 D7
Widemouth Bay Corn 8 D4
Widewall Orkney 159 J5
Widford Essex 42 D2
Widford Herts 41 C7
Widham Wilts 37 F7
Widmer End Bucks 40 E1
Widmerpool Notts 64 B3
Widnes Halton 86 F3
Wigan Gtr Man 86 D3
Wiggaton Devon 11 E6
Wiggenhall St Germans Norf 67 C5
Wiggenhall St Mary Magdalen Norf 67 C5
Wiggenhall St Mary the Virgin Norf 67 C5
Wigginton Herts 40 C2
Wigginton Oxon 51 F8
Wigginton Staffs 63 D6
Wigginton York 95 D8
Wigglesworth N Yorks 93 D8
Wiggonby Cumb 108 D2
Wiggonholt W Sus 16 C4
Wighill N Yorks 95 E7
Wighton Norf 80 D5
Wigley Hants 14 C4
Wigmore Hereford 49 C6
Wigmore Medway 30 C2
Wigsley Notts 77 B8
Wigsthorpe Northants 65 F7
Wigston Leics 64 E3
Wigthorpe Notts 89 F6
Wigtoft Lincs 79 F5
Wigton Cumb 108 E2
Wigtown Dumfries 105 D8
Wigtwizzle S Yorks 88 E3
Wike W Yorks 95 E6
Wike Well End S Yorks 89 C7
Wilbarston Northants 64 F5
Wilberfoss E Yorks 96 D3
Wilberlee W Yorks 87 C8
Wilburton Cambs 55 B5
Wilby Norf 68 F3
Wilby Northants 53 C6
Wilby Suff 57 B6
Wilcot Wilts 25 C6
Wilcott Shrops 60 C3
Wilcrick Newport 35 F8
Wilday Green Derbys 76 B3
Wildboarclough Ches E 75 C6
Wilden Bedford 53 D8
Wilden Worcs 50 B3
Wildhern Hants 25 D8
Wildhill Herts 41 D5
Wildmoor Worcs 50 B4
Wildsworth Lincs 90 E2
Wilford Nottingham 77 F5
Wilkesley Ches E 74 E3
Wilkhaven Highld 151 C12
Wilkieston W Loth 120 C4
Willand Devon 10 C5
Willaston Ches E 74 D3
Willaston Ches W 73 B7
Willen M Keynes 53 E6
Willenhall W Mid 51 B8
Willenhall W Mid 62 E3
Willerby E Yorks 97 F6
Willerby N Yorks 97 B6
Willersey Glos 51 F6
Willersley Hereford 48 E5
Willesborough Kent 30 E4
Willesborough Lees Kent 30 E4
Willesden London 41 F5
Willett Som 22 F3
Willey Shrops 61 E6
Willey Warks 63 F8
Willey Green Sur 27 D7
Williamscot Oxon 52 E2
Willian Herts 54 F3
Willingale Essex 42 D1
Willingdon E Sus 18 E2
Willingham Cambs 54 B5
Willingham by Stow Lincs 90 F2
Willington Bedford 54 E2
Willington Derbys 63 B6
Willington Durham 110 F4
Willington T&W 111 C6
Willington Warks 51 F7
Willington Corner Ches W 74 C2
Willisham Tye Suff 56 D4
Willitoft E Yorks 96 F3
Williton Som 22 E2
Willoughbridge Staffs 74 E4
Willoughby Lincs 79 B7
Willoughby Warks 52 C3
Willoughby-on-the-Wolds Notts 64 B3
Willoughby Waterleys Leics 64 E2
Willoughton Lincs 90 E3
Willows Green Essex 42 C3
Willsbridge S Glos 23 B8
Willsworthy Devon 9 F7
Wilmcote Warks 51 D6
Wilmington Devon 11 E7
Wilmington E Sus 18 E2
Wilmington Kent 29 B6
Wilminstone Devon 6 B2
Wilmslow Ches E 87 F6
Wilnecote Staffs 63 D6
Wilpshire Lancs 93 F6
Wilsden W Yorks 94 F3
Wilsford Lincs 78 E3
Wilsford Wilts 25 D6
Wilsford Wilts 25 F6
Wilsill N Yorks 94 C4
Wilsley Pound Kent 18 B4
Wilsom Hants 26 F5
Wilson Leics 63 B8
Wilsontown S Lanark 120 D2
Wilstead Bedford 53 E8
Wilsthorpe Lincs 65 C7
Wilstone Herts 40 C2
Wilton Borders 115 C7
Wilton Cumb 98 C2
Wilton N Yorks 103 F6
Wilton Redcar 102 C3
Wilton Wilts 25 C7
Wilton Wilts 25 F5
Wimbish Essex 55 F6
Wimbish Green Essex 55 F7
Wimblebury Staffs 62 C4
Wimbledon London 28 B3
Wimblington Cambs 66 E4
Wimborne Minster Dorset 13 E8
Wimborne St Giles Dorset 13 C8
Wimbotsham Norf 67 D6
Wimpson Soton 14 C4
Wimpstone Warks 51 E7
Wincanton Som 12 B5
Wincham Ches W 74 B3
Winchburgh W Loth 120 B3
Winchcombe Glos 37 B7
Winchelsea E Sus 19 D6
Winchelsea Beach E Sus 19 D6
Winchester Hants 15 B5
Winchet Hill Kent 29 E8
Winchfield Hants 27 D5
Winchmore Hill Bucks 40 E2
Winchmore Hill London 41 E6
Wincle Ches E 75 C6
Wincobank S Yorks 88 E4
Windermere Cumb 99 E6
Winderton Warks 51 E8
Windhill Highld 151 G8
Windhouse Shetland 160 D6
Windlehurst Gtr Man 87 F7
Windlesham Sur 27 C7
Windley Derbys 76 E3
Windmill Hill E Sus 18 D3
Windmill Hill Som 11 C8
Windrush Glos 38 C1
Windsor N Lincs 89 C8
Windsor Windsor 27 B7
Windsoredge Glos 37 D5
Windygates Fife 128 D5
Windyknowe W Loth 120 C2
Windywalls Borders 122 F3
Wineham W Sus 17 B6
Winestead E Yorks 91 B6
Winewall Lancs 94 E2
Winfarthing Norf 68 F4
Winford IoW 15 F6
Winford N Som 23 C7
Winforton Hereford 48 E4
Winfrith Newburgh Dorset 13 F6
Wing Bucks 40 B1
Wing Rutland 65 D5
Wingate Durham 111 F7
Wingates Gtr Man 86 D4
Wingates Northumb 117 E7
Wingerworth Derbys 76 C3
Wingfield C Beds 40 B2
Wingfield Suff 57 B6
Wingfield Wilts 24 D3
Wingham Kent 31 D6
Wingmore Kent 31 E5
Wingrave Bucks 40 C1
Winkburn Notts 77 D7
Winkfield Brack 27 B7
Winkfield Row Brack 27 B6
Winkhill Staffs 75 D7
Winklebury Hants 26 D4
Winkleigh Devon 9 D8
Winksley N Yorks 95 B5
Winkton Dorset 14 E2
Winlaton T&W 110 C4
Winless Highld 158 E5
Winmarleigh Lancs 92 E4
Winnal Hereford 49 F6
Winnall Hants 15 B5
Winnersh Wokingham 27 B5
Winscales Cumb 98 B2
Winscombe N Som 23 D6
Winsford Ches W 74 C3
Winsford Som 21 F8
Winsham Som 11 D8
Winshill Staffs 63 B6
Winskill Cumb 109 F5
Winslade Hants 26 E4
Winsley Wilts 24 C3
Winslow Bucks 39 B7
Winson Glos 37 D7
Winson Green W Mid 62 F4
Winsor Hants 14 C4
Winster Cumb 99 E6
Winster Derbys 76 C2
Winston Durham 101 C6
Winston Suff 57 C5
Winston Green Suff 57 C5
Winstone Glos 37 D6
Winswell Devon 9 C6
Winter Gardens Essex 42 F3
Winterborne Clenston Dorset 13 D6
Winterborne Herringston Dorset 12 F4
Winterborne Houghton Dorset 13 D6
Winterborne Kingston Dorset 13 E6
Winterborne Monkton Dorset 12 F4
Winterborne Monkton Wilts 25 B6
Winterborne Stickland Dorset 13 D6
Winterborne Whitechurch Dorset 13 D6
Winterborne Zelston Dorset 13 E6
Winterbourne S Glos 36 F3
Winterbourne W Berks 26 B2
Winterbourne Abbas Dorset 12 E4
Winterbourne Bassett Wilts 25 B6
Winterbourne Dauntsey Wilts 25 F6
Winterbourne Down S Glos 23 B8
Winterbourne Earls Wilts 25 F6
Winterbourne Gunner Wilts 25 F6
Winterbourne Monkton Wilts 25 B6
Winterbourne Steepleton Dorset 12 F4
Winterbourne Stoke Wilts 25 E5
Winterburn N Yorks 94 D2
Winteringham N Lincs 90 B3
Winterley Ches E 74 D4
Wintersett W Yorks 88 C4
Wintershill Hants 15 C6
Winterton N Lincs 90 C3
Winterton-on-Sea Norf 69 C7
Winthorpe Lincs 79 C8
Winthorpe Notts 77 D8
Winton Bmouth 13 E8
Winton Cumb 100 C2
Winton N Yorks 102 E2
Wintringham N Yorks 96 B4
Winwick Cambs 65 F8
Winwick Northants 52 B4
Winwick Warr 86 E4
Wirksworth Derbys 76 D2
Wirksworth Moor Derbys 76 D3
Wirswall Ches E 74 E2
Wisbech Cambs 66 D4
Wisbech St Mary Cambs 66 D4
Wisborough Green W Sus 16 B4
Wiseton Notts 89 F8
Wishaw N Lanark 119 D7
Wishaw Warks 63 E5
Wisley Sur 27 D8
Wispington Lincs 78 B5
Wissenden Kent 30 E3
Wissett Suff 57 B7
Wistanstow Shrops 60 F4
Wistanswick Shrops 61 B6
Wistaston Ches E 74 D3
Wistaston Green Ches E 74 D3
Wiston Pembs 32 C1
Wiston S Lanark 120 F2
Wiston W Sus 16 C5
Wistow Cambs 66 F2
Wistow N Yorks 95 F8
Wiswell Lancs 93 F7
Witcham Cambs 66 F4
Witchampton Dorset 13 D7
Witchford Cambs 55 B6
Witham Essex 42 C4
Witham Friary Som 24 E2
Witham on the Hill Lincs 65 C7
Withcall Lincs 91 F6
Withdean Brighton 17 D7
Witherenden Hill E Sus 18 C3
Witheridge Devon 10 C3
Witherley Leics 63 E7
Withern Lincs 91 F8
Withernsea E Yorks 91 B7
Withernwick E Yorks 97 E7
Withersdale Street Suff 69 F5
Withersfield Suff 55 E7
Witherslack Cumb 99 F6
Withiel Corn 4 C4
Withiel Florey Som 21 F8
Withington Glos 37 C7
Withington Gtr Man 87 E6
Withington Hereford 49 E7
Withington Shrops 61 C5
Withington Staffs 75 F7
Withington Green Ches E 74 B5
Withleigh Devon 10 C4
Withnell Lancs 86 B4
Withybrook Warks 63 F8
Withycombe Som 22 E2
Withycombe Raleigh Devon 10 F5
Withyham E Sus 29 F5
Withypool Som 21 F7
Witley Sur 27 F7
Witnesham Suff 57 D5
Witney Oxon 38 C3
Wittering Pboro 65 D7
Wittersham Kent 19 C5
Witton Angus 135 B5
Witton Worcs 50 C3
Witton Bridge Norf 69 A6
Witton Gilbert Durham 110 E5
Witton-le-Wear Durham 110 F4
Witton Park Durham 110 F4
Wiveliscombe Som 11 B5
Wivelrod Hants 26 F4
Wivelsfield E Sus 17 B7
Wivelsfield Green E Sus 17 B7
Wivenhoe Essex 43 B6
Wivenhoe Cross Essex 43 B6
Wiveton Norf 81 C6
Wix Essex 43 B7
Wixford Warks 51 D5
Wixhill Shrops 61 B5
Wixoe Suff 55 E8
Woburn C Beds 53 F7
Woburn Sands M Keynes 53 F7
Wokefield Park W Berks 26 C4
Woking Sur 27 D8
Wokingham Wokingham 27 C6
Wolborough Devon 7 B6
Wold Newton E Yorks 97 B6
Wold Newton NE Lincs 91 E6
Woldingham Sur 28 D4
Wolfclyde S Lanark 120 F3
Wolferton Norf 67 B6
Wolfhill Perth 134 F1
Wolf's Castle Pembs 44 C4
Wolfsdale Pembs 44 C4
Woll Borders 115 B7
Wollaston Northants 53 C7
Wollaston Shrops 60 C3
Wollaton Nottingham 76 F5
Wollerton Shrops 74 F3
Wollescote W Mid 62 F3
Wolsingham Durham 110 F3
Wolstanton Staffs 75 E5
Wolston Warks 52 B2
Wolvercote Oxon 38 D4
Wolverhampton W Mid 62 E3
Wolverley Shrops 73 F8
Wolverley Worcs 50 B3
Wolverton Hants 26 D3
Wolverton M Keynes 53 E6
Wolverton Warks 51 C7
Wolverton Common Hants 26 D3
Wolvesnewton Mon 36 E1
Wolvey Warks 63 F8
Wolviston Stockton 102 B2
Wombleton N Yorks 102 F4
Wombourne Staffs 62 E2
Wombwell S Yorks 88 D4
Womenswold Kent 31 D6
Womersley N Yorks 89 C6
Wonastow Mon 36 C1
Wonersh Sur 27 E8
Wonson Devon 9 F8
Wonston Hants 26 F2
Wooburn Bucks 40 F2
Wooburn Green Bucks 40 F2
Wood Dalling Norf 81 E6
Wood End Herts 41 B6
Wood End Warks 51 B6
Wood End Warks 63 E6
Wood Enderby Lincs 79 C5
Wood Field Sur 28 D2
Wood Green London 41 E6
Wood Hayes W Mid 62 D3
Wood Lanes Ches E 87 F7
Wood Norton Norf 81 E6
Wood Street Norf 69 B6
Wood Street Sur 27 D7
Wood Walton Cambs 66 F2
Woodacott Devon 9 D5
Woodale N Yorks 94 B3
Woodbank Argyll 143 G7
Woodbastwick Norf 69 C6
Woodbeck Notts 77 B7
Woodborough Notts 77 E6
Woodborough Wilts 25 D6
Woodbridge Dorset 12 C5
Woodbridge Suff 57 E6
Woodbury Devon 10 F5
Woodbury Salterton Devon 10 F5
Woodchester Glos 37 D5
Woodchurch Kent 19 B6
Woodchurch Mers 85 F3
Woodcombe Som 21 E8
Woodcote Oxon 39 F6
Woodcott Hants 26 D2
Woodcroft Glos 36 E2
Woodcutts Dorset 13 C7
Woodditton Cambs 55 D7
Woodeaton Oxon 39 C5
Woodend Cumb 98 E3
Woodend Northants 52 E4
Woodend W Sus 16 D2
Woodend Green Northants 52 E4
Woodfalls Wilts 14 B2
Woodfield Oxon 39 B5
Woodfield S Ayrs 112 B3
Woodford Corn 8 C4
Woodford Devon 7 D5
Woodford Glos 36 E3
Woodford Gtr Man 87 F6
Woodford London 41 E7
Woodford Northants 53 B7
Woodford Bridge London 41 E7
Woodford Halse Northants 52 D3
Woodgate Norf 68 C3
Woodgate W Mid 62 F3
Woodgate W Sus 16 D3
Woodgate Worcs 50 C4
Woodgreen Hants 14 C2
Woodhall Herts 41 C5
Woodhall Invclyd 118 B3
Woodhall N Yorks 100 E4
Woodhall Spa Lincs 78 C4
Woodham Sur 27 C8
Woodham Ferrers Essex 42 E3
Woodham Mortimer Essex 42 D4
Woodham Walter Essex 42 D4
Woodhaven Fife 129 B6
Woodhead Aberds 153 E7
Woodhey Gtr Man 87 C5
Woodhill Shrops 61 F7
Woodhorn Northumb 117 F8
Woodhouse Leics 64 C2
Woodhouse N Lincs 89 D8
Woodhouse S Yorks 88 F5
Woodhouse W Yorks 88 B4
Woodhouse W Yorks 95 F5
Woodhouse Eaves Leics 64 C2
Woodhouse Park Gtr Man 87 F6
Woodhouselee Midloth 120 C5
Woodhouselees Dumfries 108 B3
Woodhouses Staffs 63 C5
Woodhurst Cambs 54 B4
Woodingdean Brighton 17 D7
Woodkirk W Yorks 88 B3
Woodland Devon 7 C5
Woodland Durham 101 B5
Woodlands Aberds 141 E6
Woodlands Dorset 13 D8
Woodlands Hants 14 C4
Woodlands Highld 151 E8
Woodlands N Yorks 95 D6
Woodlands S Yorks 89 D6
Woodlands Park Windsor 27 B6
Woodlands St Mary W Berks 25 B8
Woodlane Staffs 62 B5
Woodleigh Devon 6 E5
Woodlesford W Yorks 88 B4
Woodley Gtr Man 87 E7
Woodley Wokingham 27 B5
Woodmancote Glos 36 E4
Woodmancote Glos 37 B6
Woodmancote Glos 37 D7
Woodmancote W Sus 15 D8
Woodmancote W Sus 17 C6
Woodmancott Hants 26 E3
Woodmansey E Yorks 97 F6
Woodmansterne Sur 28 D3
Woodminton Wilts 13 B8
Woodnesborough Kent 31 D7
Woodnewton Northants 65 E7
Woodplumpton Lancs 92 F5
Woodrising Norf 68 D2
Wood's Green E Sus 18 B3
Woodseaves Shrops 74 F3
Woodseaves Staffs 61 B7
Woodsend Wilts 25 B7
Woodsetts S Yorks 89 F6
Woodsford Dorset 13 E5
Woodside Aberdeen 141 D8
Woodside Aberds 153 D10
Woodside Brack 27 B7
Woodside Fife 129 D6
Woodside Hants 14 E4
Woodside Herts 41 D5
Woodside Perth 134 F2
Woodside of Arbeadie Aberds 141 E6
Woodstock Oxon 38 C4
Woodstock Pembs 32 B1
Woodthorpe Derbys 76 B4
Woodthorpe Leics 64 C2
Woodthorpe Lincs 91 F8
Woodthorpe York 95 E8
Woodton Norf 69 E5
Woodtown Devon 9 B6
Woodtown Devon 9 B6
Woodvale Mers 85 C4
Woodville Derbys 63 C7
Woodyates Dorset 13 C8
Woofferton Shrops 49 C7
Wookey Som 23 E7
Wookey Hole Som 23 E7
Wool Dorset 13 F6
Woolacombe Devon 20 E3
Woolage Green Kent 31 E6
Woolaston Glos 36 E2
Woolavington Som 22 E5
Woolbeding W Sus 16 B2
Wooldale W Yorks 88 D2
Wooler Northumb 117 B5
Woolfardisworthy Devon 8 B5
Woolfardisworthy Devon 10 D3
Woolfords Cottages S Lanark 120 D3
Woolhampton W Berks 26 C3
Woolhope Hereford 49 F8
Woolhope Cockshoot Hereford 49 F8
Woolland Dorset 13 D5
Woollaton Devon 9 C6
Woolley Bath 24 C2
Woolley Cambs 54 B2
Woolley Corn 8 C4
Woolley Derbys 76 C3
Woolley W Yorks 88 C4
Woolmer Green Herts 41 C5
Woolmere Green Worcs 50 C4
Woolpit Suff 56 C3
Woolscott Warks 52 C2
Woolsington T&W 110 C4
Woolstanwood Ches E 74 D3
Woolstaston Shrops 60 E4
Woolsthorpe Lincs 65 B6
Woolsthorpe Lincs 77 F8
Woolston Devon 6 E5
Woolston Shrops 60 B3
Woolston Shrops 60 F4
Woolston Soton 14 C5
Woolston Warr 86 F4
Woolstone M Keynes 53 F6
Woolstone Oxon 38 F2
Woolton Mers 86 F2
Woolton Hill Hants 26 C2
Woolverstone Suff 57 F5
Woolverton Som 24 D2
Woolwich London 28 B5
Woolwich Ferry London 28 B5
Woonton Hereford 49 D5
Wooperton Northumb 117 B6
Woore Shrops 74 E4
Wootten Green Suff 57 B6
Wootton Bedford 53 E8
Wootton Hants 14 E3
Wootton Hereford 48 D5
Wootton Kent 31 E6
Wootton N Lincs 90 C4
Wootton Northants 53 D5
Wootton Oxon 38 C4
Wootton Oxon 38 D4
Wootton Shrops 49 B6
Wootton Shrops 60 B3
Wootton Staffs 62 B2
Wootton Staffs 75 E8
Wootton Bridge IoW 15 E6
Wootton Common IoW 15 E6
Wootton Courtenay Som 21 E8
Wootton Fitzpaine Dorset 11 E8
Wootton Rivers Wilts 25 C6
Wootton St Lawrence Hants 26 D3
Wootton Wawen Warks 51 C6
Worcester Worcs 50 D3
Worcester Park London 28 C3
Wordsley W Mid 62 F2
Worfield Shrops 61 E7
Work Orkney 159 G5
Workington Cumb 98 B1
Worksop Notts 77 B5
Worlaby N Lincs 90 C4
World's End W Berks 26 B2
Worle N Som 23 C5
Worleston Ches E 74 D3
Worlingham Suff 69 F7
Worlington Suff 55 B7
Worlingworth Suff 57 C6
Wormald Green N Yorks 95 C6
Wormbridge Hereford 49 F6
Wormegay Norf 67 C6
Wormelow Tump Hereford 49 F6
Wormhill Derbys 75 B8
Wormingford Essex 56 F3
Worminghall Bucks 39 D6
Wormington Glos 50 F5
Worminster Som 23 E7
Wormit Fife 129 B5
Wormleighton Warks 52 D2
Wormley Herts 41 D6
Wormley Sur 27 F7
Wormley West End Herts 41 D6
Wormshill Kent 30 D2
Wormsley Hereford 49 E6
Worplesdon Sur 27 D7
Worrall S Yorks 88 E4
Worsbrough S Yorks 88 D4
Worsbrough Common S Yorks 88 D4
Worsley Gtr Man 86 D5
Worstead Norf 69 B6
Worsthorne Lancs 93 F8
Worston Lancs 93 E7
Worswell Devon 6 E3
Worth Kent 31 D7
Worth W Sus 28 F4
Worth Matravers Dorset 13 G7
Wortham Suff 56 B4
Worthen Shrops 60 D3
Worthenbury Wrex 73 E8
Worthing Norf 68 C2
Worthing W Sus 16 D5
Worthington Leics 63 B8
Worting Hants 26 D4
Wortley S Yorks 88 E4
Wortley W Yorks 95 F5
Worton N Yorks 100 E4
Worton Wilts 24 D4
Wortwell Norf 69 F5
Wotherton Shrops 60 D2
Wotter Devon 6 C3
Wotton Sur 28 E2
Wotton-under-Edge Glos 36 E4
Wotton Underwood Bucks 39 C6
Woughton on the Green M Keynes 53 F6
Wouldham Kent 29 C8
Wrabness Essex 57 F5
Wrafton Devon 20 F3
Wragby Lincs 78 B4
Wragby W Yorks 88 C5
Wragholme Lincs 91 E7
Wramplingham Norf 68 D4
Wrangbrook W Yorks 89 C5
Wrangham Aberds 153 E6
Wrangle Lincs 79 D7
Wrangle Bank Lincs 79 D7
Wrangle Lowgate Lincs 79 D7
Wrangway Som 11 C6
Wrantage Som 11 B8
Wrawby N Lincs 90 D4
Wraxall Dorset 12 D3
Wraxall N Som 23 B6
Wraxall Som 23 F8
Wray Lancs 93 C6
Wraysbury Windsor 27 B8
Wrayton Lancs 93 B6
Wrea Green Lancs 92 F3
Wreay Cumb 99 B6
Wreay Cumb 108 E4
Wrecclesham Sur 27 E6
Wrecsam = Wrexham Wrex 73 D7
Wrekenton T&W 111 D5
Wrelton N Yorks 103 F5
Wrenbury Ches E 74 E2
Wrench Green N Yorks 103 F7
Wreningham Norf 68 E4
Wrentham Suff 69 F7
Wrenthorpe W Yorks 88 B4
Wrentnall Shrops 60 D4
Wressle E Yorks 96 F3
Wressle N Lincs 90 D3
Wrestlingworth C Beds 54 E3
Wretham Norf 68 F2
Wretton Norf 67 E6
Wrexham = Wrecsam Wrex 73 D7
Wrexham Industrial Estate Wrex 73 E7
Wribbenhall Worcs 50 B2
Wrightington Bar Lancs 86 C3
Wrinehill Staffs 74 E4
Wrington N Som 23 C6
Writhlington Bath 24 D2
Writtle Essex 42 D2
Wrockwardine Telford 61 C6
Wroot N Lincs 89 D8
Wrotham Kent 29 D7
Wrotham Heath Kent 29 D7
Wroughton Swindon 37 F8
Wroxall IoW 15 G6
Wroxall Warks 51 B7
Wroxeter Shrops 61 D5
Wroxham Norf 69 C6
Wroxton Oxon 52 E2
Wyaston Derbys 75 E8
Wyberton Lincs 79 E6
Wyboston Bedford 54 D2
Wybunbury Ches E 74 E4
Wych Cross E Sus 28 F5
Wychbold Worcs 50 C4
Wyck Hants 27 F5
Wyck Rissington Glos 38 B1
Wycoller Lancs 94 F2
Wycomb Leics 64 B4
Wycombe Marsh Bucks 40 E1
Wyddial Herts 54 F4
Wye Kent 30 E4
Wyesham Mon 36 C2
Wyfordby Leics 64 C4
Wyke Dorset 13 B5
Wyke Shrops 61 D6
Wyke Sur 27 D7
Wyke W Yorks 88 B2
Wyke Regis Dorset 12 G4
Wykeham N Yorks 96 B4
Wykeham N Yorks 103 F7
Wyken W Mid 63 F7
Wykey Shrops 60 B3
Wylam Northumb 110 C4
Wylde Green W Mid 62 E5
Wyllie Caerph 35 E5
Wylye Wilts 24 F5
Wymering Ptsmth 15 D7
Wymeswold Leics 64 B3
Wymington Bedford 53 C7
Wymondham Leics 65 C5
Wymondham Norf 68 D4
Wyndham Bridgend 34 E3
Wynford Eagle Dorset 12 E3
Wyng Orkney 159 J4
Wynyard Village Stockton 102 B2
Wyre Piddle Worcs 50 E4
Wysall Notts 64 B3
Wythall Worcs 51 B5
Wytham Oxon 38 D4
Wythburn Cumb 99 C5
Wythenshawe Gtr Man 87 F6
Wythop Mill Cumb 98 B3
Wyton Cambs 54 B3
Wyverstone Suff 56 C4
Wyverstone Street Suff 56 C4
Wyville Lincs 65 B5
Wyvis Lodge Highld 150 D7

Y

Y Bala = Bala Gwyn 72 F3
Y Barri = Barry V Glam 22 C3
Y Bont-Faen = Cowbridge V Glam 21 B8
Y Drenewydd = Newtown Powys 59 E8
Y Felinheli Gwyn 82 E5
Y Fenni = Abergavenny Mon 35 C6
Y Ffôr Gwyn 70 D4
Y Fflint = Flint Flint 73 B6
Y-Ffrith Denb 72 A4
Y Gelli Gandryll = Hay-on-Wye Powys 48 E4
Y Mwmbwls = The Mumbles Swansea 33 F7
Y Pîl = Pyle Bridgend 34 F2
Y Rhws = Rhoose V Glam 22 C2
Y Rhyl = Rhyl Denb 72 A4
Y Trallwng = Welshpool Powys 60 D2
Y Waun = Chirk Wrex 73 F6
Yaddlethorpe N Lincs 90 D2
Yafford IoW 14 F5
Yafforth N Yorks 101 E8
Yalding Kent 29 D7
Yanworth Glos 37 C7
Yapham E Yorks 96 D3
Yapton W Sus 16 D3
Yarburgh Lincs 91 E7
Yarcombe Devon 11 D7
Yard Som 22 F2
Yardley W Mid 62 F5
Yardley Gobion Northants 53 E5
Yardley Hastings Northants 53 D6
Yardro Powys 48 D4
Yarkhill Hereford 49 E8
Yarlet Staffs 62 B3
Yarlington Som 12 B4
Yarlside Cumb 92 C2
Yarm Stockton 102 C2
Yarmouth IoW 14 F4
Yarnbrook Wilts 24 D3
Yarnfield Staffs 75 F5
Yarnscombe Devon 9 B7
Yarnton Oxon 38 C4
Yarpole Hereford 49 C6
Yarrow Borders 115 B6
Yarrow Feus Borders 115 B6
Yarsop Hereford 49 E6
Yarwell Northants 65 E7
Yate S Glos 36 F4
Yateley Hants 27 C6
Yatesbury Wilts 25 B5
Yattendon W Berks 26 B3
Yatton Hereford 49 C6
Yatton N Som 23 C6
Yatton Keynell Wilts 24 B3
Yaverland IoW 15 F7
Yaxham Norf 68 C3
Yaxley Cambs 65 E8
Yaxley Suff 56 B5
Yazor Hereford 49 E6
Yeading London 40 F4
Yeadon W Yorks 94 E5
Yealand Conyers Lancs 92 B5
Yealand Redmayne Lancs 92 B5
Yealmpton Devon 6 D3
Yearby Redcar 102 B4
Yearsley N Yorks 95 B8
Yeaton Shrops 60 C4
Yeaveley Derbys 75 E8
Yedingham N Yorks 96 B4
Yeldon Bedford 53 C8
Yelford Oxon 38 D3
Yelland Devon 20 F3
Yelling Cambs 54 C3
Yelvertoft Northants 52 B3
Yelverton Devon 6 C3
Yelverton Norf 69 D5
Yenston Som 12 B5
Yeo Mill Devon 10 B3
Yeoford Devon 10 E2
Yeolmbridge Corn 8 F5
Yeovil Som 12 C3
Yeovil Marsh Som 12 C3
Yeovilton Som 12 B3
Yerbeston Pembs 32 D1
Yesnaby Orkney 159 G3
Yetlington Northumb 117 D6
Yetminster Dorset 12 C3
Yettington Devon 11 F5
Yetts o'Muckhart Clack 128 D2
Yieldshields S Lanark 119 D8
Yiewsley London 40 F3
Ynys-meudwy Neath 33 D8
Ynysboeth Rhondda 34 E4
Ynysddu Caerph 35 E5
Ynysgyfflog Gwyn 58 C3
Ynyshir Rhondda 34 E4
Ynyslas Ceredig 58 E3
Ynystawe Swansea 33 D7
Ynysybwl Rhondda 34 E4
Yockenthwaite N Yorks 94 B2
Yockleton Shrops 60 C3
Yokefleet E Yorks 90 B2
Yoker W Dunb 118 C5
Yonder Bognie Aberds 152 D5
York York 95 D8
York Town Sur 27 C6
Yorkletts Kent 30 C4
Yorkley Glos 36 D3
Yorton Shrops 60 B5
Youlgreave Derbys 76 C2
Youlstone Devon 8 C4
Youlthorpe E Yorks 96 D3
Youlton N Yorks 95 C7
Young Wood Lincs 78 B4
Young's End Essex 42 C3
Yoxall Staffs 62 C5
Yoxford Suff 57 C7
Yr Hôb = Hope Flint 73 D7
Yr Wyddgrug = Mold Flint 73 C6
Ysbyty-Cynfyn Ceredig 47 B6
Ysbyty Ifan Conwy 72 E2
Ysbyty Ystwyth Ceredig 47 B6
Ysceifiog Flint 73 B5
Yspitty Carms 33 E6
Ystalyfera Neath 34 D1
Ystrad Rhondda 34 E3
Ystrad Aeron Ceredig 46 D4
Ystrad-mynach Caerph 35 E5
Ystradfellte Powys 34 C3
Ystradffin Carms 47 E6
Ystradgynlais Powys 34 C1
Ystradmeurig Ceredig 47 C6
Ystradowen Carms 33 C8
Ystradowen V Glam 22 B2
Ystumtuen Ceredig 47 B6
Ythanbank Aberds 153 E9
Ythanwells Aberds 153 E6
Ythsie Aberds 153 E8

Z

Zeal Monachorum Devon 10 D2
Zeals Wilts 24 F2
Zelah Corn 4 D3
Zennor Corn 2 C3